DEVELOPMENTAL PSYCHOPATHOLOGY

DEVELOPMENTAL PSYCHOPATHOLOGY

SECOND EDITION

Volume Three: Risk, Disorder, and Adaptation

Editors

DANTE CICCHETTI

and

DONALD J. COHEN

WILEY

John Wiley & Sons, Inc.

Library of Congress Cataloging-in-Publication Data:

Developmental psychopathology / editors, Dante Cicchetti & Donald Cohen.—
2nd ed.
    p.   cm.
ISBN-13: 978-0-471-23736-5, ISBN-10: 0-471-23736-1 (v. 1 : cloth)
ISBN-13: 978-0-471-23737-2, ISBN-10: 0-471-23737-X (v. 2 : cloth)
ISBN-13: 978-0-471-23738-9, ISBN-10: 0-471-23738-8 (v. 3 : cloth)
ISBN-13: 978-0-471-23735-8, ISBN-10: 0-471-23735-3 (set)
[etc.]
  1. Mental illness—Etiology. 2. Developmental psychology. 3. Mental illness—Risk factors. 4. Adjustment (Psychology). I. Cicchetti, Dante. II. Cohen, Donald J.
  RC454.4.D483 2006
  616.89—dc22

Printed in the United States of America.

10 9 8 7 6 5 4 3 2 1

These volumes are dedicated to
Marianne Gerschel.

Contents

Preface to Developmental Psychopathology, *Second Edition*

It has been over a decade since the first two volumes of *Developmental Psychopathology* were published. These volumes were extremely well received: They have been highly cited in the literature and they have served as a valuable resource for researchers and practitioners alike. The expansion of the second edition of *Developmental Psychopathology* from two to three volumes speaks to the continued growth of the field, as well as to the ascendance of theory and research in the area of neuroscience informed by a developmental perspective.

There can be no doubt that the discipline of developmental psychopathology has grown significantly in a relatively short period of time. The more than 30 years that have elapsed since the initiation of the Schizophrenia high-risk projects (Garmezy & Streitman, 1974) have been marked by significant contributions to the field. Noteworthy among these are the publication of Achenbach's (1974) first text, Rutter and Garmezy's (1983) chapter in the *Handbook of Child Psychology,* and the continued growth of the journal *Development and Psychopathology,* including the Millennium Special Issue entitled *Reflecting on the Past and Planning for the Future of Developmental Psychopathology* (Cicchetti & Sroufe, 2000). A not insignificant contributor to this rapid growth can be found in the very definitional parameters of the discipline. Theorists and researchers in the field of developmental psychopathology use a lifespan framework to elucidate the many factors that can contribute to the development of mental disorders in individuals at high risk, as well as those operative in individuals who have already manifested psychological disturbances or who have averted such disorders despite their high risk status. In essence, a developmental psychopathology perspective provides a broad, integrative framework within which the contributions of diverse disciplines can be incorporated and enhanced (Cicchetti & Sroufe, 2000). Thus, rather than having to develop new theories and methods, those

working within a developmental psychopathology framework can build on and extend previously established traditions. The ability to incorporate knowledge from diverse disciplines and to encourage interdisciplinary research will expedite growth within the field of developmental psychopathology.

As with the previous edition, the current volumes were not organized exclusively around thematic psychiatric disorders. Rather, authors were encouraged to explore developmentally relevant theories, methods of assessment, and domains of functioning. Although many chapters do address specific psychiatric disorders, it is the processes that contribute to the emergence of psychopathology that are emphasized rather than the psychiatric disorders per se.

Volume I, *Theory and Method,* presents various approaches to understanding developmental influences on risk and maladaptation. As previously, the volume begins with an explication of the discipline of developmental psychopathology. Within this chapter, a number of significant advances within the field are noted, including the increased attention to processes and mechanisms, the use of multiple levels of analysis, the rise of developmental neuroscience, and the evolution of translational research paradigms. Chapters address a range of topics, including approaches to diagnoses of disorders, developmental epidemiology, diverse theoretical perspectives, various contextual issues, and new frontiers in statistical techniques for developmental phenomena. The volume concludes with a chapter on prevention and intervention.

Volume II, *Developmental Neuroscience,* was added to acknowledge the significant growth in this area since the publication of the first edition of this *Handbook.* Given the seminal historical role that neuroscience played in the emergence of developmental psychopathology (Cicchetti, 1990; Cicchetti & Posner, 2005), it is only fitting that developmental neuroscience has both informed and been informed by developmental psychopathology theorizing.

Neural plasticity, brain imaging, behavioral and molecular genetics, stress and neurobiology, immunology, and environmental influences on brain development are covered in this volume.

Volume III, *Risk, Disorder, and Adaptation* presents various perspectives on contributors to disorder. For example, chapters address the role of social support, family processes, and early experience on adaptation and maladaptation. Other chapters address specific disorders, including mental retardation, language disorders, Autism, disorders of attention, obsessive-compulsive disorders, Tourette's syndrome, social anxiety, Schizophrenia, antisocial disorders, substance abuse, and dissociative disorders. A number of chapters on resilience despite adversity also are included. The volume concludes with a chapter on stigma and mental illness.

All authors were asked to conclude their chapters with discussions of future research directions and needs. Thus, these volumes serve not only to highlight current knowledge in the field of developmental psychopathology, but also to suggest avenues to pursue for progress to continue. In particular, it is increasingly important to incorporate multiple-levels-of-analysis approaches when investigating maladaptation, psychopathology, and resilience (Cicchetti & Blender, 2004; Cicchetti & Dawson, 2002). The examination of multiple systems, domains, and ecological levels in the same individuals over developmental time will yield a more complete depiction of individual patterns of adaptation and maladapation. Moreover, such methods are likely to be extremely valuable in elucidating how interventions may affect brain-behavior relations (see, e.g., Caspi et al., 2002, 2003; Cicchetti & Posner, 2005; Fishbein, 2000; Goldapple et al., 2004; Kandel, 1979, 1998, 1999). Such endeavors could result in significant progress toward understanding psychopathology, highlighting efficacious interventions, and ultimately decreasing the burden of mental illness (Cicchetti & Toth, in press).

I now turn to more personal considerations. Although Donald Cohen is no longer with us, he worked closely with me as we developed our plans for the second edition of *Developmental Psychopathology*. Given our collaboration on the first edition of the volumes and our discussions leading up to the publication of these volumes, I thought it only fitting that he be listed as my coauthor. I believe in my heart that Donald would be pleased to have his name affiliated with these volumes and when I shared this plan with his wife, Phyllis, she gave her enthusiastic endorsement. However, I hasten to add that, unfortunately, Donald's illness and untimely death precluded his active involvement in editing the chapters in these volumes. Thus, despite our many

conversations as the plan for these volumes unfolded, I alone am responsible for the final editing of all chapters.

In closing, I want to dedicate these volumes to my dear friend, Marianne Gerschel. Marianne is a true visionary and she has contributed significantly to my work in the area of developmental psychopathology. Without her belief in the value of this field, my efforts and accomplishments would have been greatly compromised.

Finally, as I write this preface, I am ending a significant era in my life. After more than two decades as the director of Mt. Hope Family Center, I am leaving Rochester to accept a position at the Institute of Child Development, University of Minnesota. There I will be the director of an interdisciplinary center that will emphasize a multiple-levels-of-analysis approach to research and intervention in developmental psychopathology.

This transition is difficult, as Mt. Hope Family Center and my colleagues there have contributed greatly to the growth and development of the field of developmental psychopathology. It is reassuring to know that Mt. Hope Family Center will continue to build upon a solid foundation under the capable directorship of my long-time collaborator and friend, Sheree L. Toth. Although I welcome the new opportunities and challenges that await me, I cannot help being a bit sad to leave. My spirits are buoyed by the knowledge that my work at Mt. Hope Family Center will continue and by my excitement at returning to my roots at the Institute of Child Development where I will have both University and community support to use the field of developmental psychopathology to extend my vision for helping disenfranchised individuals and families throughout the nation and the world.

Dante Cicchetti, PhD

Rochester, NY
July 2005

REFERENCES

Achenbach, T. M. (1974). *Developmental psychopathology.* New York: Ronald Press.

Caspi, A., McClay, J., Moffitt, T., Mill, J., Martin, J., Craig, I. W., et al. (2002). Role of genotype in the cycle of violence in maltreated children. *Science, 297,* 851–854.

Caspi, A., Sugden, K., Moffitt, T. E., Taylor, A., Craig, I. W., Harrington, H. L., et al. (2003). Influence of life stress on depression: Moderation by a polymorphism in the 5-HTT gene. *Science, 301,* 386–389.

Cicchetti, D. (1990). A historical perspective on the discipline of developmental psychopathology. In J. Rolf, A. Masten, D. Cicchetti, K. Nuechterlein, & S. Weintraub (Eds.), *Risk and protective factors in the development of psychopathology* (pp. 2–28). New York: Cambridge University Press.

Cicchetti, D., & Blender, J. A. (2004). A multiple-levels-of-analysis approach to the study of developmental processes in maltreated children. *Proceedings of the National Academy of Sciences, 101*(50), 17325–17326.

Cicchetti, D., & Dawson, G. (Eds.). (2002). Multiple levels of analysis. *Development and Psychopathology, 14*(3), 417–666.

Cicchetti, D., & Posner, M. I. (Eds.). (2005). Integrating cognitive and affective neuroscience and developmental psychopathology. *Development and Psychopathology, 17*(3).

Cicchetti, D., & Sroufe, L. A. (Eds.). (2000). Reflecting on the past and planning for the future of developmental psychopathology. *Development and Psychopathology, 12*(3), 255–550.

Cicchetti, D., & Toth, S. L. (in press). A developmental psychopathology perspective on preventive interventions with high-risk children and families. In A. Renninger & I. Sigel (Eds.), *Handbook of child psychology (6th ed.)*. Hoboken, NJ: Wiley.

Fishbein, D. (2000). The importance of neurobiological research to the prevention of psychopathology. *Prevention Science, 1,* 89–106.

Garmezy, N., & Streitman, S. (1974). Children at risk: Conceptual models and research methods. *Schizophrenia Bulletin, 9,* 55–125.

Goldapple, K., Segal, Z., Garson, C., Lau, M., Bieling, P., Kennedy, S., et al. (2004). Modulation of cortical-limbic pathways in major depression. *Archives of General Psychiatry, 61*(1), 34–41.

Kandel, E. R. (1979). Psychotherapy and the single synapse. *New England Journal of Medicine, 301,* 1028–1037.

Kandel, E. R. (1998). A new intellectual framework for psychiatry. *American Journal of Psychiatry, 155,* 475–469.

Kandel, E. R. (1999). Biology and the future of psychoanalysis: A new intellectual framework for psychiatry revisited. *American Journal of Psychiatry, 156,* 505–524.

Rutter, M., & Garmezy, N. (1983). Developmental psychopathology. In E. M. Hetherington (Ed.), *Handbook of child psychology* (4th ed., Vol. 4, pp. 774–911). New York: Wiley.

Contributors

Carrie E. Bearden, PhD
University of California
Los Angeles, California

Jay Belsky, PhD
Birkbeck University of London
Institute for the Study of Children, Families, and
   Social Issues
London, England

April A. Benasich, PhD
Rutgers University
Newark, New Jersey

Jacob A. Burack, PhD
McGill University
Montreal, Quebec, Canada

Keith B. Burt, MA
University of Minnesota
Minneapolis, Minnesota

Tyrone D. Cannon, PhD
University of California
Los Angeles, California

Dante Cicchetti, PhD
Mt. Hope Family Center
University of Rochester
Rochester, New York
and
Institute of Child Development
University of Minnesota
Minneapolis, Minnesota

J. Douglas Coatsworth, PhD
Pennsylvania State University
University Park, Pennsylvania

E. Mark Cummings, PhD
University of Notre Dame
Notre Dame, Indiana

Patrick T. Davies, PhD
University of Rochester
Rochester, New York

Geraldine Dawson, PhD
University of Washington
Seattle, Washington

Thomas J. Dishion, PhD
University of Oregon
Eugene, Oregon

David W. Evans, PhD
Bucknell University
Lewisburg, Pennsylvania

Mary Fran Flood, PhD
University of Nebraska
Department of Psychology
Lincoln, Nebraska

Rebecca Goodvin, MA
Department of Psychology
University of Nebraska
Lincoln, Nebraska

Werner Greve, PhD
Criminological Research Insitute of Lower Saxony
Hannover, Germany

Sabine Heim, PhD
University of Konstanz
Konstanz, Germany

Stephen P. Hinshaw, PhD
University of California
Berkeley, California

Robert M. Hodapp, PhD
Vanderbilt University
Nashville, Tennessee

Cynthia Huang-Pollock, PhD
Penn State University
University Park, Pennsylvania

Sara R. Jaffee, PhD
University of Pennsylvania
Department of Psychology
Philadelphia, Pennsylvania

James F. Leckman, MD
Yale University School of Medicine
New Haven, Connecticut

Rachel L. Loewy, MA
University of California, Los Angeles
Los Angeles, California

Suniya S. Luthar, PhD
Teacher's College, Columbia University
New York, New York

Ann S. Masten, PhD
Institute of Child Development
University of Minnesota
Minneapolis, Minnesota

Linda C. Mayes, MD
Yale University School of Medicine
New Haven, Connecticut

Erin B. McClure, PhD
National Institute of Health
Mood and Anxiety Disorders Program
Bethesda, Maryland

Stephanie E. Meyer, PhD
University of California, Los Angeles
Los Angeles, California

Terrie E. Moffitt, PhD
Psychology Research Center
London, England

Tara A. Niendam, MA
University of California
Los Angeles, California

Joel T. Nigg, PhD
Michigan State University
East Lansing, Michigan

Thomas G. O'Connor, PhD
University of Rochester
Rochester, New York

Gerald R. Patterson, PhD
Oregon Social Learning Center
Eugene, Oregon

Bradley S. Peterson, MD
Columbia University College of Physicians and Surgeons
New York State Psychiatric Institute
New York, New York

Daniel S. Pine, MD
National Institute of Health
Mood and Anxiety Disorders Program
Bethesda, Maryland

Frank W. Putnam, MD
University of Cincinnati College of Medicine
Cincinnati Children's Hospital Medical Center
Cincinnati, Ohio

Alexandra L. Spessot, PhD
Columbia University College of Physicians and Surgeons
New York, New York

Ursula M. Staudinger, PhD
Dresden University of Technology
Dresden, Germany

Nancy E. Suchman, PhD
Yale University
New Haven, Connecticut

Ross A. Thompson, PhD
University of California
Department of Psychology
Davis, California

Karen Toth, MS
University of Washington
Seattle, Washington

Kristin Valentino, MA
University of Rochester
Rochester, New York

Robert A. Zucker, PhD
University of Michigan
Department of Psychiatry and
Addiction Reserch Center
Ann Arbor, Michigan

CHAPTER 1

Social Support and Developmental Psychopathology

ROSS A. THOMPSON, MARY FRAN FLOOD, and REBECCA GOODVIN

People commonly rely on the support of others in everyday circumstances. Friends and family offer emotional encouragement in times of stress. Coworkers and neighbors provide information and material assistance as it is needed. We turn to trusted friends and colleagues for helpful advice. Marital and romantic partners monitor the well-being of those they care for. Social support is among the most important features of the relationships that support healthy psychological functioning.

At times, social support is also offered in formal helping relationships. Physicians, religious advisors, social workers, and other professionals provide social support as part of their role responsibilities. Social support is a critical function of many approaches to psychological therapy, of course, whether the support is received from an individual mental health professional, a therapy group, or a special preschool, classroom, or adult education program designed to assist troubled individuals. In many respects, the efforts of formal helpers are meant to emulate the kinds of social support obtained from the most helpful individuals in natural support networks.

The relevance of social support to developmental psychopathology derives from its relationship to the etiology, maintenance, and treatment of childhood psychologi-

cal disorders. First, inadequate social support, often in the context of social isolation or dysfunctional social relationships, can contribute to the development of psychological problems in children. Children who face social adversity without the buffering assistance of supportive relationships are at a higher risk of developing clinical problems, especially if they encounter adversity in the home. This is why many preventive interventions for at-risk children and families emphasize strengthening formal and informal forms of social support, such as through home visitation programs. Second, for children with psychological disturbances, social support may help to diminish their problems, and lack of support can exacerbate their difficulties. Social support can assist in coping, increase children's social skills, and help them and their families access needed services. Conversely, many clinical conditions in childhood, including depression, conduct disorders, and child maltreatment, cause children to alienate or resist social support and to become further isolated within their families, peer groups, and communities. Enhancing existing avenues of social support and creating new ones thus becomes central to effective intervention. For this reason, most approaches to therapy for children enlist social support, whether in the context of group therapy, peer mentoring, parent education or parent support groups, social skills training, therapeutic preschool programs, mother-child psychotherapeutic intervention, or other avenues. Understanding the nature of social support and its relevance to psychological well-being and restoration improves understanding of the development and treatment of child clinical disorders.

Because social support is so often a part of everyday experience, it is easy to expect that social support can be straightforwardly provided to troubled children and families, and that there will be direct benefits from doing so. It is surprising, therefore, when socially isolated families actively resist efforts from supportive social networks, or home visitors quickly become exhausted by their efforts to provide assistance to at-risk families, or children in emotional turmoil continue to alienate those attempting to assist them. The same conditions that contribute to social isolation, in other words, make the enlistment of social support especially difficult. Social support is thus easy to conceptualize but difficult to implement in the lives of troubled children and their families. This has been the hard lesson of recent years of efforts to enlist social support into preventive and therapeutic efforts on behalf of children at risk. As a result, although clinicians and researchers remain convinced that social support is beneficial, they have become more aware that formal efforts to provide social support can be frustrated even when they are designed to emulate or build on the natural sources of support on which people commonly rely. Further, enlisting natural sources of support for therapeutic purposes can be challenging and, at times, problematic. Researchers and practitioners are only at the beginning of understanding and overcoming the obstacles that exist to providing social support as a component of preventive and treatment efforts.

Our goal is to profile the multifaceted ways that social support is relevant to developmental psychopathology. In the section that follows, we consider how to define social support and its functions in the lives of children and adults, drawing on the importance of social networks to developmental adaptation. Next we consider social support within the broader social context of development and psychopathology. This requires considering the independent and overlapping social networks of children and parents, developmental changes in support needs and capacities to elicit support, and the importance of peers and the community. We then examine social support in relation to psychopathology, discussing the role of support—or its absence—in the onset of clinical problems, their maintenance over time, and their remediation. Social support is relevant to etiological, maintenance, and treatment concerns in different and complex ways, in other words, and distinguishing among them emphasizes how social support and the absence of support has diverse applications to the problems of troubled children and families. In the next section, we try to understand the influences that can enhance or frustrate the efficacy of social support efforts, whether they occur in natural social networks or in formal interventions. These include clarity (or lack of it) concerning the intended goals of support, the needs of providers of support, and the complex reactions to receiving assistance from another. We also consider the cultural and community context of social support. From these considerations, we then proceed to profile the implications of these contingencies for interventions that have the goal of providing or enhancing social support, and consider the lessons learned for future efforts. We integrate these ideas in a concluding section in which we consider future directions for research and intervention.

WHAT IS SOCIAL SUPPORT? WHY IS IT IMPORTANT?

Because social support is such a familiar feature of everyday life, it is easy to assume that it is readily understood and that most people experience social support in comparable ways. Yet, a thoughtful analysis of what social support is and does reveals that it is both more multidimensional and more complexly offered and received than we often assume. Consider, for example, the following definition: "Social support consists of social relationships that provide (or can potentially provide) material and interpersonal resources that are of value to the recipient, such as counseling, access to information and services, sharing of tasks and responsibilities, and skill acquisition" (Thompson, 1995, p. 43). Embedded in this definition are several features of social support that underscore its complexity.

First, social support is given and received in the context of relationships, and relationships are psychologically complex (Badr, Acitelli, Duck, & Carl, 2001). Support may be obtained from relationships within natural social networks—such as with parents or offspring, extended kin, coworkers, teachers, peers, neighbors—or formal helping relationships, such as with a religious advisor, mentor, physician, mental health professional, social worker, or other professional.[1] The nature of the relationship deter-

---

[1] To be sure, social support usually but does not always occur in the context of relationships. For example, crisis hotline (and "warm-line") services can provide advice, support, and referrals for individuals who need immediate assistance, including children (see Peterson, 1990). For people who would otherwise resist the risks of discussing personal problems with a friend or counselor, the anonymous self-disclosure offered by services like these can be of benefit.

mines what kinds of support are possible and the limitations that may exist in receiving social support. On the broadest level, for example, some individuals are support generalists who provide many kinds of assistance, whereas others (especially people in formal helping relationships) are support specialists who have one particular form of social support to offer (Bogat, Caldwell, Rogosch, & Kriegler, 1985). The kind of assistance received from each person—and the circumstances in which one would seek their help—are likely to differ considerably.

The roles of relational partners also shape the support they can offer and limitations in that support. Extended family members, for example, can offer emotional guidance and understanding based on long-standing, close relationships. But the assistance of a relative may be colored by family traditions or a legacy of family conflict, and multigenerational assistance is often complicated by conflicting responsibilities to different generational networks (e.g., one's obligations to adult siblings may conflict with providing assistance to their offspring, especially when the latter are troubled by family problems). Neighbors can provide referrals to local help givers, material aid, emergency assistance, and respite child care. But in communities at risk, neighbors may experience the same economic and ecological problems as do the families who need their assistance, and neighbors may thus have little to offer because of their own needs. Neighbors may also be as concerned with distancing themselves from a family in turmoil as they are with providing aid. Peer friendships and group acceptance may buffer loneliness for a shy child and work in concert with other protective factors to prevent depression. But if the child's shyness leads to withdrawal that discourages age-mates from interacting with the child, the peer response may increase the child's vulnerability and enhance, rather than diminish, loneliness and vulnerability to depression.

The same "situation specificity" of relationships (Unger & Powell, 1980) is also true of formal support agents. A social worker may offer valuable assistance by connecting families to community resources and providing informal counseling. But an overwhelming caseload may diminish the caseworker's reliability or limit the other kinds of assistance that can be provided. A doctor or minister may be a source of professional guidance and can offer an expert and dispassionate perspective on family problems, but professional training and role definitions may shape the kind of support that is offered. Problems may be viewed through the prism of a professional's specialized expertise or background, for example, such that the kind of assistance that is offered (e.g., medication, counseling, referral) may or may not be what is really needed by the recipient. In other circumstances, the role responsibilities of professional helpers

may curb the involvement of other potential helpers. It is well-known, for example, that professionals who are legally mandated reporters of suspected child maltreatment are typically aware of many more child abuse cases than they formally report. This owes, in part, to the complications introduced into their professional relationships with families once a child abuse investigation has been inaugurated and the preference of many helping professionals to address family problems on their own (Zellman, 1990; Zellman & Anter, 1990). But their failure to enlist legal authorities means that additional sources of support are unavailable to families who might need them, and the clinician assumes a heavy burden of responsibility. Social support is thus mediated by the relationships through which it is offered and the other roles and responsibilities of those relationships.

Other features of relationships are also important to offering and receiving social support. In natural social networks, for example, assistance is usually provided in two-way relationships of mutual aid, where individuals can be providers as well as recipients of help. This helps to ensure feelings of mutual respect that contribute to relational satisfaction. When help giving is unidirectional, or when it occurs at considerable cost to the helper, it can make the recipient feel indebted and, as a consequence, inferior and vulnerable, and this can quickly undermine a helping relationship (Fisher, Nadler, & Witcher-Alagna, 1982; Shumaker & Brownell, 1984). When children are the recipients of social support from adults, the mutual obligations of help giving are less compelling because children are commonly recipients of one-way assistance. Nevertheless, their parents may feel indebted and vulnerable, especially if help giving is perceived as deriving from parental inadequacy. When children receive help from peers, mutuality may be especially important to the maintenance of the relationship and its positive influence. In formal helping relationships (such as with a counselor, therapist, or social worker), unidirectional assistance is part of the relationship and feelings of vulnerability are less likely. But formal relationships may be limited in the extent to which they influence the facets of a child's (or family's) private life in which assistance is truly needed. Thus, one of the significant challenges of offering social support in the context of relationships is understanding how support can be offered without the negative reactions that support can engender, especially when assistance is not bidirectional.

More generally, relationships are also complex constellations of mutual obligations that can offer support and affirmation but also create stress and difficulty, sometimes at the same time (Berscheid & Reis, 1998; W. A. Collins & Laursen, 1999). Belle's (1982) study of lower-income single mothers provocatively illustrates how their relationships with extended kin, neighbors, and boyfriends afforded support but at the same time the risks of rejection, criticism, privacy violations, and entrapping demands that relationships with family and romantic partners often entail. Likewise, although peer relationships can offer considerable social support to children, association with deviant peers, especially in adolescence, has been associated with antisocial behavior (Dishion, Andrews, & Crosby, 1995; Laird, Jordan, Dodge, Pettit, & Bates, 2001). The relationships affording the greatest support often entail a complex calculus of assistance and demand in which risks accompany receipt of support. Thus, it is not always wise to assume that integrating needy individuals, or isolated families, into broader social networks will necessarily increase social support or ameliorate psychopathological processes. Deriving social support from social networks depends on characteristics of needy recipients and of others with whom they have relationships.

A second feature of this definition of social support is that it is multifaceted. It includes emotional encouragement but can also incorporate access to information and services, counseling and guidance, material assistance, sharing of tasks and responsibilities, and skill acquisition. The importance of each of these facets of social supports depends on what is needed and is of value to the recipient. For adults under stress, for example, one of the most important benefits of supportive relationships is the sense that one is not alone and that others are emotionally "on your side" with compassionate encouragement. For others, however, assistance is best provided when people are also brokers of information or services, such as when friends and neighbors are consulted for childrearing advice, referrals to child care providers or counselors, or access to community agencies where further information or resources can be obtained. For individuals in economic difficulty, material assistance (such as lending money or a car) and services (such as respite child care) is an important form of social support. For others, help in acquiring vocational or personal skills (such as financial management skills) is especially valuable. For many people in difficulty, social support is received as counseling, advice, and guidance about troublesome issues, whether related to marital difficulty, parenting problems, or managing emotional stress. Even in children's peer relationships, social support is multifaceted. Parker and Asher (1993) found that the friendships of children who were highly accepted among their peers provided greater validation and caring, more help and guidance, greater conflict resolution, and more intimate exchange than friendships of children with lower peer acceptance. The friendships of children who were not well accepted were characterized by higher levels of conflict

and betrayal compared to the friendships of highly accepted children.

Of course, supportive relationships do not necessarily incorporate each of these facets of support, and, indeed, these features of support are not always complementary within relationships. Individuals who provide emotional encouragement to friends or neighbors may find it difficult, for example, to offer critical advice and still be perceived as supportive. This is the difficulty faced by those who urge family members or friends to reduce their smoking, drinking, or substance abuse as a way of improving family life or personal well-being. Their efforts to create more healthy practices in another may be perceived by the recipient as meddlesome and intrusive. In other circumstances, material assistance is deeply appreciated when it is freely offered, but if it becomes conditional on the recipient's compliance with behavioral expectations (which can occur in families, religious groups, and adolescent peer groups), it loses its emotionally supportive qualities. A young adult may appreciate the financial assistance that derives from moving back to the parent's home, for example, but the more limited freedom and parental monitoring that this entails may be experienced as demeaning and unsupportive.

When social support is viewed in the context of developmental psychopathology, there are additional potential facets of socially supportive relationships. Social support can be enlisted to monitor the well-being of at-risk children, such as when extended kin or a social worker regularly check in on a family member who is suspected of child neglect. In these instances, social support is enlisted for preventing harm. Social support can also be offered to improve parental conduct, such as through the guidance of a home visitor or the advice of a grandparent. By contrast with other forms of skill acquisition, its purpose is not only to enhance parental competency but also to indirectly benefit children by creating more positive, constructive parent-child relationships. Finally, social support can be enlisted for purposes of developmental remediation. As we shall explore further, supportive relationships contribute to psychological healing in children, whether via therapeutic child care programs that provide young children with secure attachments to caregivers, social skills training or peer mentors that help children experience more successful peer relationships, or individual therapy that focuses on the impact of problems on significant relationships. In these cases, supportive relationships are oriented toward treating troubled children and strengthening developing capacities that have been undermined by such problems as depression, conduct disorders, or parental abuse.

Taken together, these multifaceted qualities of social support have diverse applications to developmental psychopathology. Consider, for example, the challenges of preventing child maltreatment (Thompson, 1995). Families prone to child abuse are typically multiproblem families in economic difficulty, living in poor neighborhoods, and socially isolated from others in the community (Daro, 1988; Polansky, Chalmers, Buttenwieser, & Williams, 1981; Straus, Gelles, & Steinmetz, 1980). Child protection strategies often begin with integrating social support into family life, which can occur through a program of professional home visitation, efforts to strengthen neighborhood connections, enrolling parents in parenting classes, or through other community services. The general goals of such efforts are to reduce parenting stress through emotional support, strengthen parenting skills by providing developmental guidance and models of effective parenting practices, and monitor children's well-being through regular home visits or agency consultations. More ambitious efforts to prevent child maltreatment through social support sometimes include crisis counseling, material aid to families in economic distress, and programs to strengthen job skills or household competencies. When social support is enlisted to reduce abuse recidivism, interventions are typically more intensive, enduring, and focused than when social support strategies are part of a broader effort to prevent abuse in at-risk populations. The most intensive treatment programs, for example, can involve daily visits by a specially trained therapeutic social worker who works to reconstitute healthy family relationships (Thompson, 1995).

Social support alone is unlikely to be an effective answer to the complex problems faced by families at risk for child abuse or neglect or children facing the challenges of clinical disorders. But social support is probably an essential component of any multifaceted effort to prevent psychological difficulties in at-risk families and children or to provide therapeutic assistance when family problems have resulted in a troubled or harmed child. The challenge is to craft well-designed interventions that improve the support afforded by natural helpers and enlist the assistance of formal helpers, based on a careful assessment of the needs of the child or family at risk (Thompson & Ontai, 2000). Accomplishing this requires a thoughtful appreciation of the nature of social support, as well as the social context of development and psychopathology.

THE SOCIAL CONTEXT OF DEVELOPMENT AND PSYCHOPATHOLOGY

Whether the focus is on children's typical or atypical psychological growth, developmental psychopathologists are concerned with how early patterns of individual adaptation evolve into later adaptations as developmental transformations occur in thinking, behavior, and emotion (Cicchetti & Cohen, 1995; Dodge & Pettit, 2003; Sroufe & Rutter, 1984). Among the many influences on psychological growth, relationships are central to how children adapt to the opportunities and challenges of each period of life. Understanding the relevance of social support to developmental psychopathology thus requires appreciating the social context of development and psychopathology, as well as developmental changes in children's access to broadening networks of social support in their natural environments.

From the beginning of life, infants depend on the solicitude of others for protection, nurturance, and well-being. A well-functioning parent-child relationship provides a supportive context for development despite variations in external resources (such as the family's economic status) or internal characteristics (such as the child's temperament) because it can buffer the effects of disadvantage and provide significant psychological resources for healthy growth. Indeed, this relationship can be regarded as being socially supportive in all the facets just described (e.g., emotional encouragement, providing material and interpersonal resources, sharing activity, fostering skill acquisition), and this is why infants and young children rely so significantly on the assistance and nurturance of their caregivers. Early in infancy, for example, babies become quiet in anticipation of the mother's arrival when they are distressed (Lamb & Malkin, 1986), enlist the emotional information in the mother's face when encountering uncertain or perplexing situations (Baldwin & Moses, 1996), and turn to the caregiver for assistance when they are fearful or distressed.

Variations in the quality of parental nurture or sensitivity are important in young children's reliance on the support of their caregivers. An extensive literature on the security of attachment documents how young children develop secure relationships with caregivers who respond sensitively and appropriately to their signals and, conversely, develop insecure attachments when caregivers are inconsistently responsive (for reviews, see Cassidy & Shaver, 1999; Thompson, 1998). These variations in attachment security may be regarded as significant early differences in perceived support from caregivers on whom an infant must rely for emotional and physical well-being. These variations in security are apparent not only when young children are distressed but also in nonstressful circumstances, such as in the quality of emotional sharing between a toddler and an adult during play or social interaction. Differences in the security of attachment are, not surprisingly, developmentally significant. Attachment security is associated with many features of psychosocial growth, including the quality of children's relationships with other people, their capacities to interact sociably with unfamiliar adults, emotion understanding and emotion regulation, self-understanding, and even conscience development (see Thompson, 1999, for a review). These findings are consistent with the theoretical view that from the security of their relationships with caregivers, young children derive broader representations of relationships, themselves, and other people that guide their subsequent social encounters and their expectations for future relationships (Bretherton & Munholland, 1999; Thompson, 1998, 2000).

Moreover, the support entailed in a secure or insecure attachment foreshadows continuing support in later years as children encounter later developmental challenges. In one study, children's perceptions of emotional support from the mother at age 8 were predicted by the security of mother-child attachment at age 4 (Booth, Rubin, & Rose-Krasnor, 1998). Bost and her colleagues (1998) found that secure preschoolers had more extensive and supportive social networks and were also higher on sociometric assessments of peer competence (see Booth, Rubin, & Rose-Krasnor, 1998; DeMulder, Denham, Schmidt, & Mitchell, 2000, for similar results). Anan and Barnett (1999) also found, in a sample of lower-income African American 6½-year-olds, that secure attachment (assessed 2 years earlier) was associated with children's perceptions of greater social support, and social support mediated the association between secure attachment and lower scores on externalizing and internalizing problems. Viewed in the context of social support, therefore, young children derive foundational support from the parent-child relationship and are creating provisional representations from this relationship about the quality of support they can expect from others they encounter.

Responsive, warm parenting may thus be regarded as a protective factor in early psychological growth because of its positive psychological correlates and the confidence it inspires in parental responsiveness and because it creates more positive expectations of the support of others that may cause children to more competently elicit assistance when it is needed (Colman & Thompson, 2002). By contrast, parental harshness and unresponsiveness may be a risk factor for psychosocial problems, especially if parental behavior creates stress as well as being unsupportive. Consider, for example, the experience of young children living with a depressed parent (Cicchetti & Toth, 1998; Goodman & Gotlib, 1999; Zahn-Waxler & Kochanska, 1990). In these circumstances, children are emotionally attached to a mother who manifests a great deal of sad emotion, together with irritability, helplessness, and blame of others, including offspring. In the context of this emotional climate, moreover, depressed caregivers act in ways that enhance children's sense of guilt and responsibility for the adult's depression. Depressed parents have high expectations for the behavior of offspring, and thus they can also be demanding and critical, using love withdrawal and other techniques to enforce compliance with their demands. It is easy to see how children living with a depressed parent are themselves at risk for psychological problems (Cummings & Davies, 1994, 1996). Their vulnerability to a parent's depression begins as early as infancy (Zeanah, Boris, & Larrieu, 1997). Young children are especially prone to becoming enmeshed in the parent's affective difficulties because their emotional attachments to these caregivers, even if they are insecure, makes their emotional well-being contingent on that of their parents.

Parents are primary sources of social support for children or, in the words of Cauce, Reid, Landesman, and Gonzales (1990), "support generalists." Parents also mediate children's access to other sources of social support, both formal and informal (Cochran & Brassard, 1979; Parke & Bhavnagri, 1989). Most generally, parents' choices of housing, neighborhoods, and schools affect the range of children's options for forming social connections with others outside the family, and frequent residential mobility limits the breadth of a child's social network (Ladd, Hart, Wadsworth, & Golter, 1988). Children growing up in troubled schools or dangerous neighborhoods simply have fewer options for creating and maintaining supportive social relationships with peers and adults than do children living in more constructive settings. Parents also commonly arrange, facilitate, and monitor their children's contact with others as gatekeepers of children's access to them. Parents schedule activities, provide transportation, and supervise offspring during social and recreational activities with friends and neighbors, especially when children are young (Ladd & Le Sieur, 1995). O'Donnell and Steuve (1983) reported that lower-income and middle-class mothers differed significantly in the access they provided their school-age children to community activities, with middle-class mothers participating extensively with their offspring in these programs (often as volunteers and aides) and lower-income mothers declining to commit themselves in these ways and instead permitting their children greater unscheduled freedom for "just being with friends." As children become capable of bicycling, using public transportation, and later driving independently to their activities, parents still retain an important monitoring role. They do so less directly, such as by granting permission to participate in activities, providing funding, and consulting with offspring about their plans, but this supervision is developmentally appropriate by enlisting the adult's guidance in the increasingly independent social lives of their children. Parents also mediate children's contact with extended kin networks by facilitating opportunities to see grandparents and other extended family members or restricting access to them (Thompson, Scalora, Castrianno, & Limber, 1992).

In therapeutic contexts, of course, parents mediate children's access to clinical assistance not only by providing transportation but also by giving consent, paying for therapy, and supporting the clinician's efforts. When children are young, nearly all evidence-based treatments rely heavily on parental participation. Parental involvement is integral to therapies that decrease disruptive behavior problems, such as those experienced by children with Attention-Deficit/Hyperactivity Disorder (ADHD), Oppositional Defiant Disorder, or Conduct Disorder (e.g., Hembree-Kigin & McNeil, 1995; McMahon & Forehand, 2003; Webster-Stratton, 1998). Therapeutic interventions addressing internalizing disorders, such as anxiety (Kendall, Aschenbrand, & Hudson, 2003) or depression (Stark et al., 1996), require parental support to ensure that children complete therapeutic tasks in home, school, and neighborhood settings. This means that therapeutic assistance to children will be nearly impossible without the parent's cooperation (or tacit cooperation, in the case of adolescents). When children's difficulties arise from family problems or are maintained by family responses, parents may limit the effectiveness of treatment by denying that problems exist or resisting assistance. When parents experience their own mental health difficulties, obtaining therapeutic support for children can be challenging. This means that therapeutic efforts for children often require a two-generation approach in which the parent's needs receive attention as well as the child's, and this is especially true when social support is a central feature of the therapeutic effort.

The social networks of parents and offspring overlap in other ways. Parental networks have important consequences for children because they influence parents' well-being, offer opportunities to children for new experiences and relationships, and directly socialize parental behavior (Cochran, 1990; Cochran & Niego, 1995). Social support to parents has been found to improve parenting and, in doing so, to enhance many features of the psychological well-being of offspring, including attachment security, social competence, and emotional adjustment (see review by Thompson, 1995). Parents with many close friendships have offspring with better social skills and peer acceptance because, in part, of the peer relationships afforded by parents' social contacts (Parke, 2002; Parke et al., 2002). However, parental social networks can be sources of stress as well as support, and children's well-being can be undermined by the difficulties that parents experience in their relationships with coworkers, neighbors, or extended kin. Relatives can be critical and demanding as well as supportive, and coworkers can offer helpful advice but also heighten workplace strain. Thus, the nature of parents' social networks can have helpful or unhelpful implications for family functioning and children's well-being.

The shared social networks of parents and offspring, and their potentially helpful and hurtful consequences for psychological well-being, are also illustrated by the associations of socioeconomic status (SES) with social support. For many reasons related to the impact of financial and job stress, neighborhood disorganization and danger, and lack of community resources, the social networks of families in poverty are likely to be less supportive and, at times, more stressful than those of families living in economically more advantaged conditions (e.g., Belle, 1982; Ceballo & McLoyd, 2002). Socioeconomic stress and community problems can have direct impacts on children. Lynch and Cicchetti (2002) noted, for example, that children who reported that they had been exposed to high levels of community violence also reported feeling less secure with their mothers.

The stresses associated with socioeconomic difficulty can also moderate the influence of social support on parenting, but relevant studies offer contrary portrayals of how this occurs. In a study of low-SES African American women, for example, Ceballo and McLoyd (2002) found that for women in more difficult circumstances (i.e., poorer and more dangerous neighborhoods), the positive associations between emotional support and nurturant parenting decreased, as did relations between instrumental support and diminished reliance on punishment. In short, the positive connection between social support and constructive parenting was strained and attenuated in poorer, more dangerous neighborhoods even though social support needs were greater. However, studying a large, nationally representative sample, Hashima and Amato (1994) reported that the negative association between maternal perceptions of social support and reports of punitive behavior were strongest in lower-income families. In other words, social support appeared to have the greatest benefits for mothers when socioeconomic stresses were greatest. Although more research is needed to clarify these differences in conclusions, each study confirms that the stress-buffering effects of social support may vary according to income and neighborhood quality. This is important because children and parents share the economic conditions of the family, and thus the effects of income and neighborhood quality not only have direct effects on children (through the impact of neighborhood crime, poor schools, financial need, and related influences) but also indirect effects through the influence of stress and social support on parenting quality.

Research on the interaction of income with social support and stress is important also as a reminder that the social networks in which children and families live are not always potential sources of social support. At times, they are greater sources of stress and difficulty than of support. Indeed, one of the challenges of providing assistance to multiproblem families is that their living circumstances often do not provide avenues of informal social support because extended family members are in turmoil, neighbors and friends suffer from the same stress as do the targets of intervention, and communities are drained of potentially helpful social resources. This can make it difficult to find sources of support for needy families in difficult living conditions.

The intersection of parent and child social networks therefore has important implications for the association between developmental psychopathology and social support. When children's difficulties are associated with family problems, parents' social networks often do not provide meaningful support to the children. One of the characteristics of families at risk for child maltreatment is their social isolation, which significantly reduces potential sources of assistance for children (Limber & Hashima, 2002; Thompson, 1995). Within their more limited social networks, moreover, extended family and neighbors often fail to intervene when children are maltreated and may actually reinforce harsh parental attitudes and conduct that lead to abuse or neglect (Korbin, 1989, 1991). Thus, parents' social networks can exacerbate rather than help to remediate children's problems through their influences on parental conduct and family functioning. This is one reason child clinical problems must often be conceptualized as family problems when questions of etiology and treatment are concerned.

The overlap of social support networks for children and parents highlights the value of two-generation interventions for troubled children. Two-generation interventions are founded on the realization that treating a troubled child requires addressing the needs of the parent (and the family system) because a child's psychopathology and the remediation of clinical problems are typically associated with broader family difficulties and strengths. With respect to social support, two-generation interventions can include efforts to enlist the support of parents' social networks when network members can provide assistance—and reduce the influence of network associates when they contribute to children's difficulties—as a means of enlisting supportive assistance for the child. Two-generation interventions are the basis for many preventive and therapeutic programs for at-risk children, such as home visitation programs that are discussed subsequently in this chapter. The importance of thinking multigenerationally emphasizes how problems in developmental psychopathology must be addressed in ways that are distinct from conventional adult therapeutic approaches because of the reliance of children on their parents and families and the overlap of their social support networks.

With increasing age, children depend less exclusively on their parents for their emotional well-being, yet parents' continuing importance as social support agents should not be underestimated. In adolescence, for example, striving for autonomy and independence is not inconsistent with continuing needs for parental support (Allen & Land, 1999). Even as peers become more important consultants on issues like appearance, style, and taste, parents remain preferred advisors on core moral values, political and religious beliefs, and planning and achieving life goals (Coleman & Hendry, 1990). This suggests that in adolescence, parents and peers are each support agents with influence that differs in a domain-specific fashion, with young people relying on each in relation to specific issues and concerns. One of the important changes with increasing age, however, concerns children's attitudes toward help seeking. Seeking emotional reassurance or instrumental aid is natural and encouraged in young children, but adolescents are likely to resist help seeking if doing so is regarded as a threat to self-efficacy or perceived competence (Robinson & Garber, 1995). The combination of teenagers' reliance on their parents for support and the need to perceive themselves as self-reliant helps to account for the mixed signals that parents (and, to a lesser extent, peers) receive during this period of life and the ease with which adolescents' support needs within the family can be misunderstood.

With increasing age, children not only experience changes in their help-seeking attitudes but also achieve access to a greater variety of sources of social support outside the family. Infants and young children are influenced by the supportive or nonsupportive social environments of out-of-home care, of course, from an early age (Cochran & Brassard, 1979; Feiring & Lewis, 1988, 1989; Votruba-Drzal, Coley, & Chase-Lansdale, 2004). Child care experiences affect young children directly through the security of the relationships they develop with providers, the quality of the child care environment, and the developmental guidance providers offer. Child care affects young children indirectly as providers monitor the child's well-being, offer support and information to parents, and provide referrals (such as to mental health services or community agencies) from which children and parents can benefit (Thompson, Laible, & Robbennolt, 1997). In these ways, child care can be a significant source of social support early in life, contingent to a great extent on the quality of care. Entry into school further widens children's extrafamilial natural support networks through both curricular opportunities (such as relationships with teachers, counselors, and peers) and extracurricular activities (such as in sports, clubs, and service programs; Asp & Garbarino, 1983; Lynch & Cicchetti, 1997; Rose et al., 2003). Teachers can be especially important sources of social support because they, like child care providers, may be the first to identify problems that emerge in a child and can create a bridge between children and their parents with professionals who can offer assistance. Moreover, well-trained teachers can sensitively assess the constellation of difficulties a child exhibits by realizing, for example, that classroom behavior problems and emotional difficulties may be an indication of child maltreatment at home (Meehan, Hughes, & Cavell, 2003; Thompson & Wyatt, 1999). In adolescence, workplace and community associations further broaden potential sources of social support as young people achieve greater independence from family networks.

In all of these contexts, the emergence of extrafamilial sources of social support offers avenues of potential aid that are not entirely contingent on parental cooperation. Equally important, children and youth actively construct and maintain these networks. With increasing age, for example, they choose many of the activities in which they participate and the adults and peers with whom they affiliate. There are also significant developmental changes in the social skills that enable children to maintain affiliations that they experience as supportive. With increasing age, for example, children become more skilled at taking active initiative in maintaining the relationships that matter to them, and they develop the social skills required to make these relationships mutually rewarding. Furthermore, children of all ages are also active construers of the support likely to be provided by different partners in their social settings (Furman & Buhrmester, 1985, 1992; M. Reid, Landesman, Treder, & Jaccard, 1989). They readily distinguish the partners who are likely to offer aid and the situations in which these partners are likely to be most helpful, and this helps them to enlist assistance when it is needed.

The role of children as constructors, maintainers, and construers of their natural networks of social support is crucial to understanding the role of social support in developmental psychopathology. Children who experience psychological difficulty have considerable need for supportive relationships, but their clinical problems may also undermine the skills required to constructively maintain those associations. Indeed, children with conduct disorders, ADHD, and other clinical problems may, because of their behavioral difficulties, repel or drain potential support providers of helpful solicitude. Furthermore, children who are depressed, traumatized, or experience other affective disorders may have difficulty perceiving potential help providers as being genuinely supportive and, for this reason, may reject assistance that is offered. Thus, somewhat ironically, at the same time that they are in greatest need of natural sources of social support, children with clinical problems may be least capable of creating or maintaining the relationships that will provide them with aid or of perceiving assistance from the interpersonal sources from whom it may be most readily available. This constitutes a formidable challenge for those who seek to ally natural support networks in therapeutic efforts and is a challenge to formal helpers (e.g., counselors and therapists) who must also overcome these difficulties in their efforts to offer aid.

SOCIAL SUPPORT AND PSYCHOLOGICAL WELL-BEING

At its best, social support provides recipients with emotional understanding, instrumental aid, counseling and guidance, material resources, and/or referrals to other sources of assistance. Viewed in this light, there are at least two ways that social support mediates the impact of stress for individuals at risk (Barrera, 1986; Cohen & Wills, 1985; House, Umberson, & Landis, 1988; Vaux, 1988).

First, social support can be *stress-preventive*. Social support invests its recipients with the material and psychological resources that foster positive development and thus prevent many stresses from occurring. These resources include healthy practices (e.g., exercise, diet, socializing), self-esteem and a sense of belonging, social competencies and coping strategies, access to emergency aid, social monitoring, specific skills, and other benefits that arise from the examples, encouragement, and/or material aid of social partners. Having these resources reduces the likelihood that recipients will experience physical or psychological difficulty owing, for example, to poor health, social isolation or rejection, or hopelessness. The stress-preventive functions of social support are especially important to children who rely so significantly on others for their well-being; they highlight how the material and psychological resources of parents are instrumental to preventing many of the difficulties that their offspring might encounter. Parents who are warm and nurturant, support the positive self-esteem of offspring, encourage constructive social competencies, and foster academic success help to reduce stress in children by strengthening socioemotional competencies and self-confidence. Moreover, partly through parents' social networks, children have access to other support agents (e.g., teachers, extended family, neighbors, coaches, mentors, and peers) who also reduce stress by promoting skills and resiliency. In this respect, especially for children at risk, social support is one of the most important protective factors within the broader constellation of risks and vulnerabilities that children experience.

Second, when stress occurs, social support can be *stress-buffering*. In other words, the material and psychological resources available through supportive relationships diminishes the impact of stressful events by enhancing coping. Clinical studies have shown that social support is associated with a reduction of the effects of disease pathology and psychological distress on stressed individuals, contributing to less severe symptomatology, quicker recovery, enhanced coping, and diminished long-term sequelae (e.g., Cassel, 1974; Cobb, 1976; Cohen & Wills, 1985). This can occur by altering (e.g., by making more constructive or realistic) recipients' appraisals of stressful events, enhancing knowledge of coping strategies, providing useful information or instrumental aid, and supporting self-esteem and perceptions of self-efficacy. Social support as a stress buffer is important to children who lack the more sophisticated knowledge, appraisal skills, and coping capacities of adults and who are thus more vulnerable to the psychological challenges posed by negative life events. In this sense, it is even more important to children to have someone who is psychologically alongside them when encountering stressful events because of the assistance that an older individual can provide in effective coping.

There is recent evidence from molecular genetics research that social support can buffer the impact of stress and biological risk on children's vulnerability to psychopathology. A recent study by Kaufman and colleagues (2004) showed that among children with a history of maltreatment and with a genetic vulnerability to depression, those without social support had the highest depression ratings, whereas those with access to positive social supports exhibited only minimal increases in their depression scores. These findings illustrate the interaction of genes and environment in the development of vulnerability to psychopathology and the influence of social support as a potential moderator of the genetic vulnerability to clinical problems (see Cicchetti & Blender, 2004).

Quite often, the stress-preventive and stress-buffering functions of social support have simultaneously protective effects on psychological well-being. One important example is peer support in childhood. Developmental and clinical theorists, such as Sullivan (1953), have long emphasized how peer support shares the stress-preventive and stress-buffering characteristics of adult social support; this is reflected in current views of the association between peer relationships and developmental psychopathology. In their 1995 review, for example, Parker, Rubin, Price, and DeRosier described how children's and adolescents' friendships can contribute to enhancing self-esteem and positive self-evaluation, provide emotional security, offer a nonfamilial context for intimacy and affection, give informational and instrumental assistance, and provide companionship and stimulation. These benefits accrue through the influence of at least three features of peer relationships: peer acceptance (or popularity), number of reciprocal friendships, and friendship quality. Each of these features independently and collectively improves children's and adolescents' concurrent life satisfaction and feelings of self-worth (Parker & Asher, 1993). In these respects, then, peer relationships appear to have social support features similar to those noted earlier for adult relationships. Moreover, peer social support can have enduring influences. A longitudinal investigation of preadolescent friendship and adult adjustment found, for example, that peer group acceptance and friendships in the fifth and sixth grades were significantly predictive of adult life status, perceived competence, and psychopathology 12 years later. Peer group acceptance and friendship made unique contributions to psychological well-being: Having a reciprocal friendship in fifth or sixth grade showed a moderately strong association with general self-worth 12 years later, even when preadolescent levels of self-competence were controlled (Bagwell, Newcomb, & Bukowski, 1998).

In light of these influences of social support on stress, the absence or deterioration of social support can be associated with enhanced stress and poorer coping: Individuals who are isolated or rejected, or who experience the withdrawal of others' support, are more prone to difficulty. As we shall see in the section that follows, the absence of social support is, at times, implicated in the etiology of child psychopathology and the maintenance of children's problems over time. The enhancement of social support (especially the dimensions of support most relevant to a child's problems) is also associated with the remediation of symptomatology. Each of these processes underscores the stress-preventive and stress-buffering influences of natural sources of social support in everyday life.

The association between social support, stress, and psychological well-being is complicated, however, because enhanced stress can sometimes provoke the deterioration of social support for troubled individuals. Unfortunately, this is what often occurs when adults and children encounter difficulty. Although people often seek supportive partners when they are stressed, it is also true that stressors diminish social support as they cause individuals to withdraw from others because of their circumstances (e.g., job loss, divorce), their incapacity (e.g., hospitalization, emotional turmoil), or their humiliation and feelings of vulnerability arising from stressful events (Shinn, Lehman, & Wong, 1984; Vaux, 1988). Moreover, potential sources of support may withdraw from individuals under stress because the behavior of the recipient is disturbing (e.g., psychological disorders, domestic violence, sexual abuse of children), the problems of the recipient are emotionally challenging or overwhelming (e.g., terminal diagnosis; loss of a family member), or potential support providers are undermined by the same circumstances as the recipient (e.g., poverty, single parenting; Belle, 1982; Fischer, 1982; Wortman & Lehman, 1985). More generally, potential support providers may withdraw from troubled individuals because of the sheer emotional drain of providing one-way assistance to very needy individuals (Fisher et al., 1982; Shumaker & Brownell, 1984). The self-protective withdrawal of potential helpers derives from the difficulties of providing assistance to individuals who need so much. Stress may be associated with diminished (rather than enhanced) social support, therefore, because the circumstances associated with stress may cause potential recipients to be unable or unwilling to receive aid and potential help providers to withdraw. Children who have been abused may lose access to potential support agents, for example, because of their anguished withdrawal from social interaction with familiar people, a parent's efforts to isolate them from others, the deterioration of social relationships owing to the emotional impact of their abuse on social competence, or others' sense that something is very wrong with the family (Cicchetti & Bukowski, 1995; Ro-

gosch & Cicchetti, 1994; Salzinger, Feldman, Hammer, & Rosario, 1993). Emotional engagement itself can offer less positive support than might be expected. As the literature on expressed emotion suggests, high levels of emotional concern can too easily become intrusive or critical and thus damaging, especially when the emotional intensity interacts with an individual's temperamental or biological vulnerabilities (Brown, Birley, & Wing, 1972; Caspi et al., 2004; Hooley, Orley, & Teasdale, 1986; Miklowitz, Goldstein, Nuechterlein, Snyder, & Mintz, 1988; Rogosch, Cicchetti, & Toth, 2004). One study reported that toddlers' behavior problems were predicted by differences in the expressed emotion of mothers and fathers in families where maternal depression had characterized family life since the child's birth (Rogosch et al., 2004). Ironically, the individuals most in need of social support may find it least available within their natural social networks.

Childhood and adult depression also illustrates how social support may be least available to individuals who urgently need it, owing to the reactions of potential benefactors and recipients of support (see reviews by Cohen & Wills, 1985; Coyne & Downey, 1991; Robinson & Garber, 1995). The anhedonia of depressive symptomatology is typically accompanied by social withdrawal together with irritability and hostility, passivity, self-denigration, dependency, and a sense of helplessness and hopelessness. Not surprisingly, the demands these symptoms impose on close relationships can cause others to withdraw and avoid contact, which, in turn, confirms the depressed person's perceptions of being rejected by others and of relationships being unreliable (Coyne, Burchill, & Stiles, 1991; Coyne & Downey, 1991). Depression is thus associated with smaller social networks, fewer close relationships, and diminished perceptions of others' support by the depressed adult, and the same associations have been found for children and youth. DuBois, Felner, Brand, Adan, and Evans (1992), for example, found a negative association between social support and psychological distress 2 years later in young adolescents, with initial levels of distress as well as other sources of stress controlled. They also found evidence that distressed youth acted in ways that inadvertently reduced their access to social support and increased the stress of daily experiences.

In short, the association between social support and stress is complex. Support may be related to the prevention of stress, so that individuals in supportive networks encounter difficult circumstances less often than do those in small or disconnected networks. Support may also be a stress buffer such that heightened social support is associated with reduced levels of stress. However, although stress may lead to a mobilization of support networks and thus a reduction of stress, social support and stress may also be negatively associated because of the impact of stressful events on a person's access to and willingness to enlist supportive assistance. These complexities in the association between social support and stress suggest caution in studying the empirical relations between them and emphasize the importance of studying their relations over time in prospective longitudinal research designs.

Dimensions of Social Support and Psychological Well-Being

As a predictor of psychological functioning, social support can aid adaptive coping (Barrera, 1986; Robinson & Garber, 1995; Thompson, 1995). It is common to think of social support as a function of *social embeddedness,* which indexes the frequency of contact with social network members. Individuals who see others often, especially in large social networks, would be expected to derive many benefits from social contact, whereas social isolation would limit access to the personal and material resources that others can offer to assist in coping with difficulty. Consistent with this view, abusive and neglectful parents have been described as socially isolated and thus lacking the personal guidance, material aid, emotional support, and social monitoring that more typically occurs in well-integrated social networks (e.g., Daro, 1988; Polansky et al., 1981; Seagull, 1987). But social embeddedness is not, in itself, a strong index of the amount of social support that individuals expect, or receive, from their network associates (Barrera, 1986; Cohen & Wills, 1985). Social partners can be helpful or hurtful, and conflict often accompanies support in people's relationships with family members, neighbors, coworkers, and others in the social network. This means that straightforward efforts to increase the size of an individual's social network or enhance the frequency of social contact is unlikely to be an effective enlistment of social support on their behalf, even though this strategy has been common in the prevention of child maltreatment and other areas of developmental psychopathology. Instead, a deeper understanding of the amount or quality of support that is given and received, and the affective quality of social relationships within the network, is necessary.

Clinicians and researchers often focus on two other dimensions of social support: *enacted support* and *perceived support.* The first indexes the frequency of actual help giving in relationships, and the second assesses the individual's expectations of support from relational partners. Enacted support and perceived support are not, surprisingly, highly associated with each other, and this derives from their complex mutual association and the relation of each to the stressful circumstances in which social support is valuable (Barrera, 1986). People can have confidence in the assistance that is potentially available from others without actually utilizing their aid, which is one reason enacted support and perceived support are not necessarily strongly associated. In addition, social support can be given without the recipient's awareness (e.g., anonymous benefaction). Furthermore, many acts of social support are not perceived as being supportive by troubled recipients. Counseling that causes a person to critically reexamine aspects of his or her behavior, material aid that causes recipients to feel indebted or humiliated, and efforts to reduce another's drinking or other destructive habits may be motivated by genuine supportive concern but are likely to be regarded by recipients as painful, intrusive, or unnecessary.[2] This is important because it illustrates how recipient reactions to aid, and their effects on providers of social support, can complicate and sometimes undermine helpful assistance to needy individuals and families. It illustrates also how individuals may experience support without perceiving others as supportive or, conversely, may expect little support from network members who are actually striving to provide assistance. It all depends, in part, on individuals' expectations of social support.

Enacted support and perceived support may also be relevant to different features of coping with stress. If individuals are capable of mobilizing their social networks, enacted support may follow the onset of stressful or distressing circumstances, especially if potential helpers are available and willing to provide aid. Perceived support may, in turn, be especially important to subsequent coping, and to stress prevention, because of a sense that others are reliably "on your side." Each are likely to be predictive of

---

[2] Although it can be argued that genuinely supportive assistance will be offered in a manner that reduces negative reactions by recipients, it is nevertheless true that obtaining benefits from another—especially when it cannot be reciprocated, is undeserved, or derives from personal need—almost inevitably heightens feelings of indebtedness, failure, and vulnerability in recipients. As we discuss further, recognizing this not only helps to create more realistic expectations concerning the consequences of providing social support (such as in the context of a home visitation program), but also makes more comprehensible the apparently inexplicable rejection of further aid by the recipient that often occurs.

more successful adaptation in difficult circumstances,[3] although further research is needed to clarify the relations between enacted support, perceived support, and coping for children and adults.

Perceived support is the dimension of social support that is most strongly related to psychological well-being in adults and children (Barrera, 1986; Cohen & Wills, 1985; Jackson & Warren, 2000; Sarason, Shearon, Pierce, & Sarason, 1987). This is so because regardless of network size or social embeddedness, confidence in the availability and helpfulness of social partners is crucial to maintaining a sense that assistance is available and the hope that can ensue even in difficulty (this is, in a sense, what is meant by a secure attachment relationship early in life). Moreover, assessments of perceived support are inherently subjective of measures of social support, relying on how individuals appraise the reliability of their social networks, and thus measures of perceived support tap an important feature of emotional coping for individuals under stress. The significance of perceived support as a psychological resource for coping is important, moreover, for intervention strategies. It suggests that rather than seeking to engage troubled individuals in a broader social network or more frequent social interaction as a means of enhancing social support, it is sometimes more important to focus on the person's subjective experience of supportiveness from network associates, perhaps by carefully examining their expectations of support in relation to what they perceive to be provided by others around them.

There are developmental differences in perceived support from different network associates (Furman & Buhrmester, 1985, 1992; Levitt, Guacci-Franco, & Levitt, 1993; M. Reid et al., 1989). In self-report studies, adolescents report expecting less support from their parents than do younger children, and there are similar decreases in perceived support from other family members, such as siblings and grandparents. Expectations of support from peers in-

crease from childhood to early adolescence, but then stabilize or decline in later years. Teachers, by contrast, are rarely regarded as sources of social support. Individual differences in prior social experiences also contribute to differences in perceived support. In a study with African American 4½-year-olds, for example, Anan and Barnett (1999) reported that secure attachment predicted heightened perceived support in these preschoolers and that each variable predicted children's subsequent adjustment, with perceived support mediating the association between attachment and adjustment.

As these developmental and individual differences suggest, perceived support depends, in part, on one's expectations of support from different network associates. Thus, individual differences in perceived support derive, in part, from the quality of assistance that people expect from family members, neighbors, peers, coworkers, and others. There is considerable need for greater understanding of the factors contributing to individual differences in expectations of support because of its relevance to perceptions of support by troubled individuals. Besides the developmental differences noted earlier, for example, how do experiences of stress and the turmoil of psychopathology alter expectations of social support? Do the overwhelming emotional needs of depression and anxiety disorders heighten expectations of support or increase dissatisfaction with perceived support—or both (as studies reviewed earlier seem to suggest)? Or are individuals in turmoil grateful for whatever assistance they can find from their exhausted social networks, as is suggested by Belle's (1982) evocative study of socioeconomically distressed single mothers? Studying questions such as these is important to understanding the social support needs of at-risk children and adults.

As valuable as is perceived support, it is important to note that it does not encompass all of the important features of social support, especially those most relevant to assisting troubled individuals and families. This is because individuals may perceive support from network associates who are otherwise acting in a nonsupportive manner. This is tragically illustrated by Jill Korbin's (1989, 1991, 1995) interviews with mothers convicted of fatal child abuse. These mothers were surrounded by family, friends, and neighbors who were often painfully aware of the bruises, neglect, and other harms inflicted by the mothers on their offspring. But in their efforts to be emotionally supportive, these network associates failed to challenge abusive practices and instead overlooked signs of parental dysfunction, minimized the seriousness of abuse, and offered reassurance about the mothers' good intentions while providing noncritical emotional affirmation. In so doing, of course, they contributed

---

[3] The relationship between enacted support, perceived support, and coping is empirically complicated, moreover, by the fact that in correlational studies, (1) troubled individuals may be less capable of viewing others as sources of available support because of their emotional turmoil, (2) individuals in difficulty may be less able to mobilize supportive networks when they are needed, and (3) individuals who experience psychosocial well-being are more likely to be high in perceived support. For these reasons, process models of the relationship between stressful events and various kinds of social support, developed in the context of prospective longitudinal designs and using multiple measures of support (that include, but are not restricted to, subjective evaluations) are nec essary in future research.

little to curbing abusive practices or protecting the children, and were thus ineffective in preventing the death of these children. As Korbin (1991, p. 23) noted, "A high level of perceived support sustained, probably unintentionally, these women in their pattern of abusive behavior."

In short, the quantity of social relationships should not be mistaken for the quality of social support. People can be surrounded by a large network of social partners who offer little support or who are emotionally affirming while providing little other assistance to troubled individuals. This is one reason efforts to improve social support by increasing social network size or improving social embeddedness are unlikely to increase enacted or perceived support. In addition, a focus on perceived support highlights the importance of how children and adults with psychological disorders perceive—accurately or inaccurately—the supportiveness of their natural networks and the potential value of interventions that target these social perceptions.

Because social support is not the same thing as network size, it is noteworthy that in some cases, access to only one or a few confidants is sufficient to significantly aid coping under stress (Cohen & Wills, 1985; Gottlieb, 1985). With adults (Brown, 1987; Brown, Adler, & Bifulco, 1988) and children (Pellegrini et al., 1986), the absence of a confiding relationship has been found to significantly distinguish whether individuals under stress developed affective problems or not. For adults, supportive intimacy can be found with a romantic partner or spouse; in the study by Pelligrini and colleagues, it was the absence of a best friend that predicted risk for affective disorders in middle childhood. Taken together, these findings contribute to the conclusion that it is not number but quality of relationships that shapes perceptions of support and, in turn, the benefits of social support for coping with stress.

SOCIAL SUPPORT AND DEVELOPMENTAL PSYCHOPATHOLOGY

It is clear that social support is associated in complex ways with stress and coping. Support can be stress-preventive and it can be a stress buffer when difficulty ensues. Support can be mobilized when stress occurs, but stressful events can also reduce access to support networks and an individual's capacity to receive aid that is offered by others. The importance of perceived support adds further complexity to the association between social support and stress because of how stress can alter a person's awareness of supportive access to helpers.

It follows, therefore, that the association between social support and developmental psychopathology is also complex. In this section, we explore this complexity by distinguishing three phases in the course of psychological disorders. First, we consider how social support, especially its absence, is relevant to the initial development of psychological disorders. This is especially relevant to portrayals of social support as a preventive and buffering agent in stressful circumstances. Second, we examine the role of social support (and its absence) in the maintenance of psychopathology over time, underscoring the importance of social factors in the persistence of psychiatric symptomatology. Finally, we consider social support and the treatment of psychopathology and the alternative avenues that exist for enhancing support as a therapeutic aid.

Social Support and the Origins of Developmental Psychopathology

In light of the stress-preventive functions of social support, it is reasonable to expect that individuals who are socially isolated or are in social adversity in the context of stress would be at enhanced risk of psychological problems. Such people are, in a sense, denied the emotional, material, informational, and other kinds of assistance that companions can potentially provide. The important challenge is to understand the extent to which the lack of social support is crucial, independent of other risk factors, in contributing to risk for developmental psychopathology, and why.

The complexity of developmental processes, the diverse etiological contributions to clinical symptomatology, and the methodological challenges of research in developmental psychopathology together make it difficult to construct causal models linking social support to either healthy or unhealthy functioning. Current theoretical views posit complicated, reciprocal associations among biological, cognitive and emotional, and sociocultural processes that are mutually influential in a dynamic, nonlinear fashion to predict most developmental outcomes (see Cicchetti & Toth, 2003; Cicchetti, Toth, & Maughan, 2000; Dodge & Pettit, 2003; Sameroff & Chandler, 1975; Shonkoff & Phillips, 2000). In such models, both parent-child and peer relationships are typically regarded as primary social influences on development that have both direct and indirect effects on risk for psychopathology. Dodge and Pettit propose, for example, that parenting and peer experiences each mediate between biological predispositions or the sociocultural context and children's vulnerability to chronic antisocial conduct problems. A recent molecular genetics study by Kaufman and colleagues (2004) indicates that social support may moderate the effects of biological vulnerability and a history of maltreatment on children's proneness to depressive symptomatology. In short, social support is likely not only to have a direct relationship to the development of psychopathology but also to mediate the effects of other risk factors in complex ways.

The social isolation of families who have abused or neglected their offspring, or who are at significant risk of doing so, is the most extensively studied condition in which the absence of social support is believed to contribute to the development of psychopathology. In this case, children's risk of pathological development is mediated through their parents' social support. Many researchers have concluded that parents who abuse or neglect their offspring lack significant social connections to others in the extended family, neighborhood, and broader community and to social agencies that can provide assistance (e.g., Daro, 1988; Garbarino & Sherman, 1980a; Polansky et al., 1981; Seagull, 1987; Straus et al., 1980; see Thompson, 1995, for a review). As a consequence, their treatment of offspring is likely to remain undetected, there are few interpersonal resources to which parents can turn when they are stressed, and the ways that social connections with potential helpers can buffer the effects of stress, promote healthy behavior, and socialize positive parenting are less influential.

An extensive review of this research by Thompson (1995) yields a fairly complex picture of the association between social isolation and child maltreatment. Three conclusions from his review are important to this discussion of social support and developmental psychopathology. First, in most studies, the social isolation distinguishing abusive or high-risk parents consists of their smaller social networks or their more limited social contacts with network members (i.e., limited social embeddedness). Parents at risk of child abuse know fewer people and see them less often, compared to other parents in similar circumstances. But research findings are inconsistent about whether at-risk or abusive parents experience significant deficits in enacted support or perceived support from their network associates. A study by Lovell and Hawkins (1988) is typical, in which abusive mothers reported that very few of their network associates provided practical help with child care or parenting responsibilities, but mothers reported enjoying seeing nearly 80% of these companions very much and reported that they could "share their thoughts and feelings frequently" with nearly 50% of them. Like the fatally abusive mothers studied by Korbin (1989, 1991), perceived support from network associates was often satisfactory even though the social support mothers received did not significantly reduce abuse potential. Thus, on the most important dimension of social support for psychological well-being—perceived support—there are often negligible differences between maltreating parents and those who are nonabusive, even though the social networks of maltreating parents are smaller and less supportive in other ways.

Second, there are subgroups of maltreating parents who experience significant social isolation for specific reasons. Polansky and his colleagues (Polansky, Ammons, & Gaudin, 1985; Polansky et al., 1981; Polansky, Gaudin, Ammons, & David, 1985) have studied neglectful mothers who consistently reported feeling greater loneliness and lack of neighborhood support compared with socioeconomically comparable nonneglectful mothers. Polansky has described an "apathy-futility syndrome" consisting of a passive, withdrawn demeanor coupled with emotional "numbness," limited competence, distrust of others, retreat from social contact, and verbal "inaccessibility" to others that also makes them hard to reach socially (Gaudin & Polansky, 1986; Polansky & Gaudin, 1983). In Polansky's view, the social isolation of these mothers derives from their inability to develop and maintain supportive social ties owing to character disorders, deficient social skills, and difficulties in coping adaptively with life stress. In a sense, their neglect of offspring is part of a general syndrome associated with their broader neglect of social connections. By contrast, Garbarino has described a different kind of "social impoverishment" of families in neighborhoods that experience heightened rates of child maltreatment (Garbarino & Kostelny, 1992). By comparing neighborhoods with higher-than-expected child maltreatment rates (based on sociodemographic predictors) with neighborhoods with lower-than-expected maltreatment rates and using informants in each community, Garbarino has sought to characterize the neighborhood conditions associated with child abuse and neglect (Garbarino & Sherman, 1980a, 1980b). He found that mothers in higher-risk neighborhoods reported receiving less assistance from neighbors, finding fewer options for child care, and generally perceiving the neighborhood as a poorer place for raising children. On other assessments related to social support, such as perceptions of sources of potential assistance, the friendliness of neighborhoods, and recreational opportunities, however, mothers of higher-risk and lower-risk neighborhoods did not differ. By contrast with the characterological problems of the neglectful mothers studied by Polansky and his colleagues, therefore, the mothers of higher-risk neighborhoods studied by Garbarino lacked important features of social support owing to the diminished social resources of their neighborhoods and the diminished human capital of their communities.

Third, studies like these and others indicate that social isolation is not a homogeneous phenomenon, and consequently the reasons for social isolation are diverse in families at risk for child maltreatment (Thompson, 1995). For some, such as Polansky's neglectful mothers, isolation may derive from social marginality attributable to limited social and coping skills in the context of stressful life circumstances (see also Seagull, 1987). For others, such as Garbarino's higher-risk neighborhood residents, it arises from the impoverishment of social capital in difficult neighborhoods that may also be dangerous settings for children and that breed social insularity and distrust (see also Lynch & Cicchetti, 1998). For some, social isolation may be actively sought as a means of concealing abusive practices. For others, isolation may result from difficult circumstances that rob adults of the time or energy required to maintain social networks, or create feelings of humiliation and vulnerability and a desire to be left alone. And a significant proportion of high-risk families do not feel socially isolated at all, but are instead satisfied with their social interactions with a small network of close associates who provide emotional support but do not seem to constrain abusive or neglectful practices. "Social isolation," when it is apparent, can have diverse causes.

The multifaceted causes of social isolation in families at risk for child maltreatment is important for at least two reasons. First, these studies indicate that social insularity may be a significant factor in the origins of child maltreatment for some families, especially when the causes of social isolation derive from psychological problems in parents, difficult or dangerous neighborhood conditions, or active efforts to conceal abusive practices. In these circumstances, the absence of significant social connections increases risk for child maltreatment because there are few from outside the family who can provide emotional support or material aid or monitor parental conduct, especially in the context of life stress. However, it is unwarranted to inclusively generalize this portrayal of abusive families. For many other families, social isolation does not appear to be etiologically relevant because abusive practices occur in the context of active social networks from which parents derive emotional support. Social isolation is not necessarily implicated in child maltreatment—and perceived support is not necessarily a buffer against abusive parenting. Second, the multifaceted causes of social isolation are relevant to intervention. Strategies for enhancing social support for at-risk families who are socially isolated must also be multifaceted. They may require, for example, social skills training (Gaudin, Wodarski, Arkinson, & Avery, 1990–1991), improving recipient reactions to receiving assistance (Tracy, Whittaker, Boylan, Neitman, & Overstreet, 1995), incorporating new support agents into natural social networks, or other approaches depending on the causes of social insularity. As we discuss in a later section, when enlisting social support in clinical treatment, one size does *not* fit all.

Social support and social isolation are experienced not only by families, but within families as well. In particular, children may be deprived of social support in families characterized by marital conflict, domestic violence, parental affective disturbances, child maltreatment, or other problems. Extensive research literature documents the risks for the development of internalizing and externalizing problems for children growing up in disturbed family environments (Thompson & Calkins, 1996; Thompson, Flood, & Lundquist, 1995). Children in homes characterized by marital conflict, for example, seek to reestablish the emotional security they have lost by intervening in parental arguments, monitoring parental moods, and otherwise striving to manage their emotions in a conflicted home environment (Cummings & Davies, 1994, 1996; Davies & Forman, 2002; Grych & Fincham, 1990; Katz & Gottman, 1991). As a consequence, they show heightened sensitivity to distress and anger, tend to become overinvolved in their parents' emotional conflicts, have difficulty regulating the strong emotions that conflict arouses in them (in a manner resembling "emotional flooding"), and exhibit other indications of internalizing problems. The work of Shaw and his colleagues has shown how the early development of conduct problems in young children derives from the interaction of the child's temperamental vulnerability with maternal rejection and depression, parental conflict, and other indicators of family difficulty (Owens & Shaw, 2003; Shaw, Miles, Ingoldsby, & Nagin, 2003). Research on maternal depression shows, as earlier indicated, how the family environment presents children with overwhelming emotional demands deriving from the caregiver's sadness, irritability, helplessness, and guilt-inducing behavior, which contributes to children's enmeshment in the emotional problems of the adult and their own vulnerability to internalizing problems (Ashman & Dawson, 2002; Cummings & Davies, 1994, 1996; Zahn-Waxler & Kochanska, 1990).

These troubled family environments are deficient in much more than social support, of course. Children are also subjected to heightened parental negative affect, family conflict, and other challenges to their emotional well-being. The relevance of social support is highlighted, however, in interventions in which children are offered the assistance of adults outside the family to aid in their emotional coping (Sandler, Miller, Short, & Wolchick, 1989). In a study by Blanchard, Molloy, and Brown (1992; cited by Beeman, 2001), for example, children living in violent homes reported that the best support was from a caring adult located nearby with whom the child could talk about family conflict. Although considerably more research is needed to examine the effects of extrafamilial social support on children's coping with family problems, studies like these suggest that access to social support can help to buffer the effects of family difficulty.

As children mature, social support may be obtained from peer relationships as well as family networks, and, conversely, vulnerability to problems may be enhanced by peers as well as family members. Positive peer relationships are likely to be protective influences, therefore, in preventing and buffering stress, and peer rejection and relationships with deviant peers may contribute to the development of childhood and adolescent depression and conduct problems. Although peer experiences are more likely a mediator or moderator of other risk factors than a direct causal agent for most forms of childhood psychopathology, there is evidence that peer relationships can assume a significant role in their development. One large, prospective longitudinal study that followed more than 500 randomly selected children from preschool through early adulthood found that, as early as preschool, exposure to aggressive peers predicted later aggressive behavior (Sinclair, Pettit, Harris, Dodge, & Bates, 1994). In another longitudinal study, Gazelle and Ladd (2003) found that the combination of anxious solitude (an index of individual vulnerability) and peer exclusion predicted levels of depressive symptoms in a sample of 388 children studied from kindergarten to fourth grade. There is evidence for the stress-buffering effects of positive peer relationships as well. In the prospective longitudinal study by Dodge, Pettit, Bates, and their colleagues, peer acceptance moderated the effects of low SES, high family stress, single-parent status, and violent marital conflict on the development of externalizing behavior in early grade school (Criss, Pettit, Bates, Dodge, & Lapp, 2002). In the same study, peer acceptance and friendship overlapped in their moderation of the effects of harsh discipline on the same outcomes. These positive effects of peer relationships remained even when the researchers controlled for child temperament and social information-processing skills. Of course, the influence of peer relationships on risk for psychopathology is as complex as is the influence of parental social networks. Indeed, in some cases, the same friendships that protect children from internalizing problems, such as depression, may enhance antisocial behavior (Nangle, Erdley, Newman, Mason, & Carpenter, 2003).

Social Support and the Maintenance of Developmental Psychopathology

Psychological disorders have multifaceted origins, of course, arising from the interaction of biological vulnerability, ecological demands and stresses, cognitive constructions, and other influences. The absence of social support, especially in the context of conflict in close relationships, adds further risk to the development of internalizing and externalizing disorders, and the availability of social support can, in turn, help to buffer the onset of clinical symptomatology. Social support and its absence are relevant also to the persistence of symptomatology over time. In other words, once clinical problems have developed, their maintenance may be associated with continuing social adversity and social isolation. Several research fields suggest how this may be true.

Children with anxiety disorders are highly vigilant for and hyperresponsive to situations associated with fearful stimuli. They interpret everyday situations in ways that exaggerate potential threat, are acutely sensitive to their own visceral signs of fear arousal, and become preoccupied with their negative emotion (Vasey & Ollendick, 2000). Not surprisingly, they are challenging for caregivers to help, but research indicates that the efforts of parents to be supportive may exacerbate rather than remedy anxious symptomatology (Thompson, 2001; Vasey & Dadds, 2001). Many parents of anxious children respond sympathetically and protectively to the fear expressed by their offspring, assisting the child in avoiding the fear-provoking event but, as a consequence, offering few opportunities to master the anxiety (Dadds, Barrett, Rapee, & Ryan, 1996; Gerlsma, Emmelkamp, & Arrindell, 1990). This is more understandable in light of studies showing an intergenerational family history for anxiety disorders, suggesting that anxiety is learned in families as part of the shared environment and that parents may thus become anxious in situations in which their offspring are also fearful (Eley, 2001). Thus, a child who responds to an anticipated encounter with a fear-evoking event with screaming, tantrums, hiding, and aggressive resistance offers powerful incentives for adults to accede, and if the adult does so and the child subsequently calms down, each partner is negatively reinforced for behavior that helps to perpetuate anxious symptomatology

(Vasey & Ollendick, 2000). At the same time, parents may be worried about the effects of anxious pathology on the child's capacities to act in a socially and developmentally appropriate manner, and thus parental overprotectiveness may be coupled with criticism and rejection (Gerlsma et al., 1990).

Thus, childhood anxiety disorders are likely to be accompanied by troubled family relationships. They are troubled by aversive encounters focused on the child's efforts to avoid fear-provoking events that are inadvertently reinforced by parents' efforts to be supportive and helpful. They are troubled also by the parent's mixed response to the child's behavior—overprotective but also critical—that contributes to parent-child relationships of insecurity and uncertainty. It is important to note that parental behavior in these instances is well-intentioned: Adults are striving to provide social support, even though their efforts inadvertently reinforce anxious symptomatology in their children (Thompson, 2001). One reason for family difficulty is that the emotional support offered by parents does not contribute to alleviating anxious fear or symptomatology.

The development of antisocial behavior is another example of how family processes and child characteristics combine to create a social context that contributes to the maintenance of psychopathology. The well-known work on coercive family processes of Patterson and his colleagues (Patterson, 1982, 1986; J. B. Reid, Patterson, & Snyder, 2002) illustrates specific pathways by which parents may inadvertently foster difficult relationships between themselves and their children or adolescents. As Patterson has evocatively shown, antisocial behavior in children is maintained by parents through their responses to child misconduct. By initially resisting the bad behavior of offspring and then acceding when children escalate their aversive conduct, parents provide powerful negative reinforcement for bad behavior. Patterson's longitudinal studies have shown how such coercive interpersonal processes become generalized by children beyond the family and contribute to the development of antisocial behavior. Although parental practices within these families are not motivated by socially supportive intentions, this work illustrates the ways that aversive parent-child interactions contribute to the development and maintenance of psychopathological conduct through relational influences that victimize the entire family.

Another illustration of the influence of social support in the maintenance of clinical problems is the well-developed research literature linking peer relationship problems and childhood loneliness (see Asher, Parkhurst, Hymel, &

Williams, 1990, for a review). Several recent studies have explored the associations between peer relationships and depressive symptoms in children (e.g., Boivin, Hymel, & Bukowski, 1995; Boivin, Poulin, & Vitaro, 1994; Burks, Dodge, & Price, 1995; Nangle et al., 2003; Oldenburg & Kerns, 1997). Nangle and his colleagues, for example, found that a fully mediational model of the influence of peer relationships on children's loneliness and depression was warranted in their study of 193 third- through fourth-grade boys and girls. In this study, loneliness was the gateway through which peer relationships influenced the development of depression. However, friendships also buffered children from depressive symptomatology. The influence of popularity, or peer acceptance, was completely accounted for by the fact that peer acceptance temporally preceded friendship, suggesting that more popular children were likely to have both larger friendship networks and better relative quality of peer relationships. The researchers concluded that before adolescence, "the mutuality that is unique to friendships appears to be critical" (p. 552). Peer rejection is important not only to the development of depressive symptomatology but also to its maintenance over time, as children without friendships are likely to continue to feel lonely, self-deprecating, and isolated in their peer networks.

Social Support and the Treatment of Psychopathology

Social support is important to developmental psychopathology not only because of its contribution to understanding the etiology or maintenance of pathological symptomatology, but also because of its promise for pioneering avenues for therapeutic assistance. The core features of social support—counseling and guidance, emotional nurturance, information, skill acquisition, and sometimes material aid—are components of successful therapeutic efforts in all theoretical modalities. Whether in the context of individual therapy sessions, peer counseling, group therapy, parent education or parent support groups, therapeutic preschool programs, crisis counseling, or other therapeutic avenues, social support is an almost inescapable element of successful clinical intervention. Thus, understanding the nature of social support as well as obstacles to its efficacy in promoting psychological well-being and conditions that foster perceptions of support in troubled individuals are each important to successfully enlisting social support in therapeutic efforts. In addition, just as social support is incorporated into most forms of psychological treatment, it is also a central feature of prevention efforts to avert psychological problems or their recurrence. Social support is a contributor to long-term adaptive functioning as well as immediate assistance to individuals and families in need.

Despite its ubiquitous contribution to therapeutic endeavors, incorporating social support in prevention and intervention strategies presents significant challenges. The forms of social support that are most helpful to individuals experiencing psychological distress are not self-evident, and, as we have seen, not all social support efforts are effective in achieving therapeutic or preventive goals. These are crucial considerations because of the many ways that well-intentioned supportive efforts can be rendered ineffective in changing destructive behaviors, fostering psychological well-being, or accomplishing therapeutic goals. Earlier in this chapter, we considered examples of how the emotional support of family and friends did not prevent troubled mothers from committing fatal child abuse, and how parental efforts to respond sympathetically and protectively does not enable offspring with anxiety disorders to master their fears. To be effective, in other words, the purposes and functions of social support must be strategically considered within a broader array of therapeutic efforts, keeping in mind that social support should include not only emotional sustenance and counseling but also reeducation, behavioral change, and monitoring the well-being of those it is intended to assist. In the following section, we consider three distinct interventions that purposively incorporate aspects of social support to achieve particular treatment goals. First, we describe a treatment for depression that focuses almost exclusively on the social aspects of the disorder. Originally developed for adults, interpersonal psychotherapy has been adapted for adolescents because of the salience of relationships in adolescent development as well as the time-limited nature of this intervention (Mellin & Beamish, 2002; Mufson & Moreau, 1999). Next, we look at approaches that attempt to teach children to help each other in social situations as a means of enlisting social support from peers in developmental therapy. Finally, we briefly discuss a family support program that helps families whose children have Bipolar Disorder and that directly addresses a dimension of iatrogenic emotional engagement, expressed emotion (EE).

As we have noted, nearly all psychotherapy approaches rely on social support in the relationship between the therapist and the patient, and much of therapeutic content focuses on improving personal relationships. Interpersonal psychotherapy (IPT) is based on the premise that problems in relationships are important components of the maintenance of depressive symptoms. Interpersonal psychotherapy for adolescents (IPT-A) uses a three-phase, time-limited approach to help adolescents explore the impact of the interpersonal aspects of one or two problem areas on significant relationships (Mellin & Beamish, 2002; Mufson & Moreau, 1999; Mufson, Moreau, Weissman, & Klerman, 1993). Adolescents with Major Depressive Disorder or Dysthymia identify one or two problem areas from a group of five interpersonal concerns (i.e., grief, role disputes, role transitions, interpersonal deficits, or single-parent families). Specific strategies are recommended for each problem area to help adolescents express feelings, use the therapeutic relationship to increase awareness and understanding, and, ultimately, change their behavior in interpersonal situations. For example, the interpersonal deficits problem area identifies social isolation, unfulfilled social relationships, and chronic depression as targets for exploration of past relationships. In addition to exploring previous relationships and behavior patterns, the therapist provides support for the adolescent to change behavior in the interpersonal context. In a study of 71 Puerto Rican adolescents between the ages of 13 and 17 who were diagnosed with Major Depressive Disorder, Dysthymia, or both disorders, interpersonal psychotherapy and cognitive behavioral therapy were both more effective in reducing symptoms of depression when compared with a wait-list control group, and 82% of the IPT participants were able to function in an adequate range at posttreatment, as measured by scores on a depression inventory (Rossello & Bernal, 1999).

Another approach to enlisting social support to remediate clinical problems is to engage natural helpers. For children and adolescents, this usually means providing training and supervision to peers who are then expected to help classmates or friends with needs. The goals of such strategies may be to increase the total number of peers who interact with the target child or to teach the target child social skills that will help her or him to attract more friends. Enlisting healthy, socially skilled peers to help children or adolescents who have behavioral or emotional disorders or who are at risk for the development of such disorders has intuitive appeal because of the potential to address both of those goals. However, as we have learned throughout this discussion, what appears simple and straightforward is often deceptively so. Lewis and Lewis (1996) identified several concerns with involving peers in helping each other. Most notably, in programs without careful role definitions and professional supervision, young people who are motivated by a desire to help others may find themselves in situations that require significantly more training, expertise, and maturity than they have. Lewis and Lewis focused their analysis on risks to peer helpers in programs enlisting peer support for children at suicidal risk, and they reported findings from a descriptive study of Washington schools indicating that suicide rates were higher at schools where peer helpers were not supervised by professional counselors. As we note later with respect to home visitors, the potential advantages of enlisting natural supporters to aid troubled children or families must be balanced by their limitations in expertise and capability.

Behavioral theory suggests that designing interventions with carefully defined target behaviors and narrowly focused strategies is likely to avoid some of the ambiguity of more general supportive or mentoring approaches and provide more precise guidance about what works and what does not work. Consistent with this view, one group of researchers (Christopher, Hansen, & MacMillan, 1991; Guevremont, MacMillan, Shawchuck, & Hansen, 1989) trained 7- to 9-year-old children in specific social skills and rewarded them for playing with identified classmates. Same-sex peers were trained in initiating, responding to refusals, maintaining interactions, and responding to negative behavior. Each was then paired with a socially isolated, dysphoric child, and rewarded for playing with that child during one daily recess. The intervention resulted in an impressive increase in positive social interactions. The improvement in peer interactions for the target children occurred with both the designated helpers and also with other classmates, and the levels of positive interactions were comparable to those of social comparison children in the same setting. The treatment gains increased at a 4-month follow-up (Guevremont et al., 1989). In a similar study that targeted three socially isolated, dysphoric children, the researchers increased the training for peer helpers and achieved similarly promising results. Gains in positive interactions were maintained at the 4-month follow-up, and the positive effects generalized to situations when the intervention was not used. In addition, there was no evidence of negative impact of social support on the helpers (Christopher et al., 1991).

Interventions designed particularly for family members, especially parents, are often part of the therapeutic endeavor when children and adolescents experience psychopathology. Families are the primary source of support for children, and the quality and effectiveness of the support family members provide to children with clinical problems is crucial to the child's healthy adjustment. As we have seen, however, not all efforts to enhance social support are helpful; indeed, emotional support may not be effective in

remediating children's problems in some situations. In fact, the parent's emotional engagement may have negative effects in certain circumstances. For example, children's emotional or behavioral difficulties may lead to heightened criticism and hostility toward the child (Hooley & Richters, 1995). Expressed emotion (Hirshfeld, Biederman, Brody, Faraone, & Rosenbaum, 1997a) is an index of parental attitudes of criticism or emotional overinvolvement in the child's problems that has been studied as a contributor to the onset, maintenance, or relapse of a number of clinical problems, including Schizophrenia (Brown et al., 1972), depression (Hooley, Orley, & Teasdale, 1986), Bipolar Disorder (Miklowitz & Goldstein, 1997), behavioral inhibition (Hirshfeld et al., 1997a, 1997b), and Conduct Disorder (Calam, Bolton, & Roberts, 2002; Caspi et al., 2004; Rogosch et al., 2004). Family support or treatment components have been designed to include a specific focus on EE as a way of improving the quality of social support for young people with clinical problems. The RAINBOW treatment protocol, for example, is a child- and family-focused cognitive behavioral therapy for children with Bipolar Disorder that addresses the intense personal demands of raising a child with this disorder in an effort to decrease the potentially harmful effects of EE (Pavuluri et al., 2004). Elements of this program include encouraging family members to distinguish helpful from unhelpful reactions in their efforts to cope with a child who can be difficult to live with, helping parents model appropriate strategies for affect regulation, fostering shared effective problem-solving strategies in which parents and target children jointly participate, assisting children in their efforts to develop successful peer relationships, and identifying other sources of social support. Preliminary conclusions from a study of 34 families participating in this program indicated that symptom severity for children decreased significantly following therapy and parents reported strong satisfaction with the treatment, although there were no family-based measures of the emotional environment (Pavuluri et al., 2004).

Taken together, conclusions from these and other therapeutic interventions that explicitly attend to the social support needs of troubled children and families indicate that when carefully designed and thoughtfully implemented, social support can be an important contribution to therapeutic success. But because social support needs are multifaceted, one feature of the preventive or therapeutic enlistment of social support is that supportive interventions are multifaceted. They should include not only emotional aid and counseling but also information or educational guidance, help with everyday stresses and practical life skills (such as parenting), economic assistance or job training when it is warranted, and, when children are concerned, counseling and educational assistance. Although services must always be tailored to the needs of recipient families, a broad array of socially supportive interventions is most likely to address the salient needs of multiproblem individuals and families.

There are many examples of intervention programs with blended forms of social support. Gaudin's (Gaudin et al., 1990–1991) Social Network Intervention Project, for example, combines strategies to enhance informal social network support for families identified as neglectful with the assistance of regular volunteer aides, the enlistment of neighborhood helpers, and social skills training to enable family members to better create and maintain supportive relationships. Yoshikawa's (1994, p. 28) review of programs to prevent chronic juvenile delinquency concludes that "interventions combining comprehensive family support with early education may bring about long-term prevention through short-term protective effects on multiple risks." Programs like Childhaven combine quasi-therapeutic full-time day care services with practical parent education, casework support, parent support, family therapy groups, and social agency referrals for troubled families (Durkin, 1986; Miller & Whittaker, 1988). The Committee on Integrating the Science of Early Childhood Development of the National Academy of Sciences concluded an extensive review of the prevention research by finding:

> Model early childhood programs that deliver carefully designed interventions with well-defined objectives and that include well-designed evaluations have been shown to influence the developmental trajectories of children whose life course is threatened by socioeconomic disadvantage, family disruption, and diagnosed disabilities. Programs that combine child-focused educational activities with explicit attention to parent-child interaction patterns and relationship building appear to have the greatest impacts. In contrast, services that are based on generic family support, often without a clear delineation of intervention strategies matched directly to measurable objectives, and that are funded by more modest budgets, appear to be less effective. (Shonkoff & Phillips, 2000, p. 11)

To be sure, characterizing the variety of intervention strategies encompassed within these preventive efforts as consistently "socially supportive" threatens to overstretch the boundaries of the social support construct. But these reviews underscore that social support efforts must be multifaceted to effectively address the complex needs of troubled children and families, and that social support interventions must be undertaken in an individualized manner that is responsive to the specific needs of recipients and the specific goals of the intervention effort.

THE CONTINGENCIES OF SOCIAL SUPPORT EFFORTS

In a recent review article, Hogan, Linden, and Najarian (2002) asked, "Social support interventions: Do they work?" Their answer was that current research provides support for the general usefulness of social support interventions, but there is insufficient evidence to conclude which kinds of interventions work best for what problems. Likewise, Heller and Rook (2001) noted in their review of social support interventions that the effective ingredients of supportive interventions are still unknown. The problem in designing the most effective interventions to improve social support and increase healthy functioning in troubled individuals may be even broader. Robinson and Garber (1995) noted that there is currently no coherent theory of how social support should guide intervention efforts. Absent a well-developed and empirically based theoretical portrayal of social support, interventions are often guided by a general expectation that greater social support, usually indexed by increased social ties, is a good thing and will have broadly positive benefits. Unfortunately, this often means that social support interventions are vague and ill-defined and, without specific outcome expectations, sometimes fail to accomplish measurable improvement in the lives of their recipients.

In addition to problems in specifying the most effective ingredients of effective supportive interventions and identifying what interventions work best for what psychological problems (and for individuals of what ages), it is also important to understand the contingencies of social support efforts. In other words, what influences can enhance or hinder the efficacy of social support interventions? At times, thoughtfully designed social support efforts founder because of challenges concerning the needs of support providers, the complex recipient reactions to obtaining assistance from another, cultural factors associated with giving and receiving social support, and the goals of intervention. We consider these contingencies next.

Sources of Support and the Needs of Support Providers

Social support may be obtained from informal helpers (such as friends, neighbors, family members, coworkers, teachers, or classmates) or formal helpers (such as counselors or therapists, home visitors, social workers, or religious advisors). As earlier noted, each kind of support agent has particular strengths and weaknesses (Gottlieb, 1983, 2000). Relationships with natural social network members benefit recipients because of their convenience and mutuality. Each partner is likely to share congruent values and perspectives, and these relationships are influential because they are likely to be enduring and thus well-integrated into many aspects of the recipient's daily experiences (Cochran, Larner, Riley, Gunnarsson, & Henderson, 1990). But because natural helpers share the circumstances and values of recipients, they may also share their stresses and difficulties and may be less sensitive to, or unwilling to challenge, unhealthy or inappropriate conduct if it is typical for their reference group (such as harsh parenting or substance abuse). Formal helpers do not have these disadvantages because of their professional training, and their helping relationships with recipients are well-defined by their professional role responsibilities. But because they are less well integrated into the lives of recipient families, they may be unaware of many circumstances affecting their well-being. Formal helpers can also have difficulty engaging the consistent cooperation of their clients.

These distinctions between formal and informal sources of support are important for defining the capabilities and needs of support providers. Enlisting natural social networks into social support interventions can be valuable but is constrained by the limitations in expertise and skills of informal helpers. As illustrated earlier when describing efforts to enlist peers to support adolescents at risk of suicide, the ethical responsibility of program designers is to ensure that natural helpers like these are not put into situations that exceed their capabilities and skills, which can easily occur if they are striving to help others who have serious psychological problems (Lewis & Lewis, 1996). Likewise, volunteer home visitors have much to offer social support programs because they often share the backgrounds and orientations of recipient families, but most are inadequately prepared to address serious family problems arising from depression, domestic violence, or substance abuse, and they may have difficulty engaging challenging families or following a consistent curriculum (Margie & Phillips, 1999). Although informal helpers are convenient, inexpensive, and often highly motivated, it is unreasonable to expect that their efforts can accomplish as much as professionally trained formal helpers might achieve in similar circumstances, and it is ethically irresponsible to expect them to provide long-term help or to assist individuals with serious problems without training and support. In short, the source of social support enlisted into an intervention de-

fines, in part, the scope of results that might be reasonably expected from the effort.

The source of social support is an important consideration also because offering assistance to troubled individuals can be draining and demoralizing (A. H. Collins & Pancoast, 1976; Shumaker & Brownell, 1984). Recipients are needy but may also be demanding and critical for reasons described in the next section, and providing help in relationships of one-way assistance can be exhausting because support is not reciprocated. Moreover, the relationship between support providers and recipients can be difficult because each may have different goals, with recipients seeking noncritical emotional affirmation and providers also striving for changes in the recipient's behavior and attitudes. They may differ in their views of the recipient's problems and the best solutions to them. Crises may force support providers to focus on immediate needs (urged to do so by recipients) and neglect attention to long-term strategies for building healthy practices. For these reasons, it is common for providers and recipients each to feel frustrated by their relationship and sometimes to experience conflict. The professional training of formal helpers prepares them to cope with these challenges, but informal helpers may be surprised to discover how difficult it is to provide social support, especially if they began doing so with little training or guidance. It is common, therefore, that social support interventions enlisting natural helpers must address the frequent turnover and burnout of their staff, which is reduced but not eliminated when informal helpers are provided with appropriate training, guided supervision, frequent affirmation of the value and importance of what they are doing, and other forms of social support. In designing successful social support interventions involving natural support agents, in other words, it is as essential to train and support the helpers as it is to ensure that appropriate forms of social support are also offered to targeted recipients.

For this reason, integrating the efforts of formal helpers with those of informal helpers in recipients' natural social networks may offer the best opportunities for creating enduring preventive or therapeutic benefits (Froland, Pancoast, Chapman, & Kimboko, 1981; Miller & Whittaker, 1988). The teamwork of formal helpers with members of informal social networks can enable natural helpers to be supported in their efforts while ensuring the skill and expertise that formal helpers can provide. Their integrated efforts can occur in many ways. Formal and informal assistance is harmonized, for example, when a parent support group is organized around a local school or child care program, a perinatal home visitor encourages the company of extended kin during home visits, or a group therapy program for adolescents has connections to the school or to the peer group. The effective coordination of formal and informal support networks is not easy, however, because of the differences in background, values, goals, and definition of the problem that may provoke mutual distrust between formal and informal helpers. All too commonly, extended family members or neighbors reinforce a parent's skepticism of the potential helpfulness of a counselor or paraprofessional home visitor. Sometimes social workers undermine informal helpers by criticizing them or trying to assume their roles. But the integration of formal and informal helping is essential to promote the engagement of recipients in social support interventions and to provide a foundation for enduring assistance. Many well-meaning social support interventions fail because they do not sufficiently incorporate the natural helping networks of family members, resulting in assistance that is limited in time, scope, and impact.

Recipient Reactions to Assistance

Receiving assistance from another evokes surprisingly mixed reactions from most recipients. In addition to the feelings of pleasure and gratitude that helping naturally inspires, recipients may also experience various negative feelings (Fisher et al., 1982; Shumaker & Brownell, 1984). Receiving assistance can be humiliating and stigmatizing, especially when the need for assistance derives from inadequacies in the recipient (such as poor parenting, substance abuse, or inadequate personal or financial management) rather than from broader, impersonal circumstances (such as an economic recession or a natural disaster; Heller & Rook, 2001). Receiving help can also create feelings of failure, indebtedness, and inferiority, especially when assistance cannot be repaid, because of cultural norms of equity and reciprocity (Greenberg & Westcott, 1983). Moreover, if assistance cannot be reciprocated or compensated, the recipient may experience feelings of vulnerability or dependency because obtaining assistance from another violates norms of self-reliance and autonomy. There can also be sensitivity to privacy violations if helpers become intimately acquainted with aspects of the recipient's life that are not normally disclosed to others.

As a consequence of these reactions, recipients may rather paradoxically begin to resent the assistance they receive and the person providing it. This is especially likely when assistance is received from voluntary benefactors (whom one cannot reciprocate or otherwise compensate, enhancing the violation of equity and reciprocity norms) or strangers (with whom one does not share an ongoing rela-

tionship of mutual aid), and when the helper and the recipient are from similar backgrounds and circumstances (enhancing the inequity of the helping relationship). When recipients experience assistance as humiliating, demeaning, or intrusive, they are less likely to seek help in the future and are more likely to abridge or terminate a helping relationship if they are capable of doing so. This can explain why the recipients of assistance, to the surprise of their benefactors, may be ungrateful, fail to become engaged in the helping relationship, are often inexplicably absent from scheduled meetings, do not return phone calls, and progressively make the relationship unworkable or unsatisfying.

This analysis has surprising implications for providing social support to troubled individuals or families. It suggests that assistance is more easily accepted when recipients have opportunities to reciprocate or repay the aid they receive, perhaps in service to other individuals. It suggests that support is more readily received in circumstances that minimize the potential for humiliation or stigmatization, such as when support services are broadly available or universal (rather than specifically targeted to those in greatest need) and accessed in everyday settings (at home, for example, rather than at an agency office). This analysis suggests also that social support is more easily received when the recipient and the helper agree about the need for assistance and the reasons for the need. By contrast, assistance from another may be resented when the recipient perceives that it derives from unshared judgments of the recipient's inadequacy or incompetence. Provider efforts to preserve the dignity and the privacy of recipients are also important.

Other characteristics of the recipient can mediate the provision of social support. Because social support is given and received in relationships, many of the personal qualities necessary to creating and maintaining relationships are important also to the success of social support interventions (Cochran, 1990). When these capacities are deficient in troubled individuals owing to mental health or substance abuse problems, intellectual challenges, or the effects of stress itself, it can also complicate the receipt of social support (Heller & Swindle, 1983; Shinn et al., 1984). As earlier noted, for example, one portrayal of child neglect emphasizes the personal disorganization of neglectful parents, which becomes manifested as an inability to effectively organize home life, ensure children's physical well-being, and keep appointments with a help provider (Polansky et al., 1981; Seagull, 1987). These qualities, which are certainly not unique to child neglect, make it difficult for parents to create and maintain supportive helping relationships with other adults. For children and adults with emotional disorders, clinical symptomatology may undermine the willingness or ability to maintain formal or informal supportive relationships. Stress can cause individuals to feel overwhelmed by life difficulties and to lack the time, energy, or hope to seek support from others. This can be especially true when families at risk live in dangerous neighborhoods that undermine access to neighbors, extended family members, and formal help providers (Eckenrode, 1983; Eckenrode & Wethington, 1990).

Because social support is not passively received, these recipient characteristics can pose formidable barriers to interventions based on supportive social relationships. Indeed, one of the most intractable obstacles to the success of social support interventions is the limited engagement and participation of recipient families. This suggests that a careful analysis of recipient reactions to assistance is necessary. When resistance to obtaining assistance derives from feelings of indebtedness, humiliation, or dependency, the conditions of support can be altered to reduce these perceptions and enhance participation in supportive relationships. This can occur by involving recipients in activities that help others, or that assist the intervention program, or that mobilize the recipient's special skills or capabilities. When supportive relationships are undermined by characteristics of the recipient, these problems must often also be addressed in the context of the intervention, such as in a substance abuse treatment or a social skills training program. This is not an easy task, however, because the personal characteristics of recipients that undermine their acceptance of help are often deeply rooted.

Cultural and Contextual Considerations

Among the most important personal characteristics of the providers and recipients of social support is their cultural and ethnic identity (Tietjen, 1989; Vaux, 1985). Cultural norms affect many of the central influences on giving and receiving social support and its psychological effects, including understandings of relationships, the nature of informal social networks, reciprocity and equity expectations in giving and receiving help, values concerning the relation between the individual and the group, attitudes toward assistance from formal helpers (such as therapists), and how help itself is evaluated (Dilworth-Anderson & Marshal, 1996; Jacobson, 1987). An appreciation of cultural and contextual factors related to social support is essential for understanding its associations with psychological well-being and developmental psychopathology. Cultural understanding is also critical to designing interventions in which social support is offered in a culturally aware manner to ensure that potentially beneficial intervention strategies do not founder on delivery approaches that render them ineffective or even harmful.

A broad, well-known dimension by which concepts of the self in relation to others vary interculturally is that of individualism and collectivism (Triandis, 1989), or independence and interdependence (Markus & Kitayama, 1991). In cultures with an interdependent view of self, there is greater emphasis on connectedness with others and on deriving important features of identity and esteem from those associations; in cultures with a more independent view of self, there is a greater emphasis on the autonomy of personal thoughts and feelings, self-reliance, and privacy. These cultural views of the self are developed quite early and influence how children perceive themselves and their relationships from early childhood (e.g., Greenfield, Keller, Fuligni, & Maynard, 2003; Han, Leichtman, & Wang, 1998; Wang, 2004). By later childhood and adolescence, youth with backgrounds from interdependent cultures (such as Hispanic and Asian societies) acknowledge the expectation that they will assist and support family members more than do adolescents from European backgrounds (Fuligni & Pedersen, 2002; Fuligni, Tseng, & Lam, 1999). One study of Chinese American teenagers reported that such intergenerational expectations had neither positive nor negative consequences for psychological well-being (Fuligni, Yip, & Tseng, 2002). But the association between cultural values and social support is complex. A cultural emphasis on interdependence may facilitate help giving and help receiving through normative practices, but cultural values may make receiving help more difficult in many circumstances. One illustration is a study of older Japanese American adults living in New York City for whom norms of reciprocating support made receiving assistance difficult. Adults who held strong reciprocity norms and who received material support from their families were more depressed and were less satisfied with their lives than those who did not embrace strong reciprocity norms (Nemoto, 1998).

Cultural values and practices are related to a number of features of social networks and social support. Specifically, there is significant intercultural variability in the United States in (1) the nature and functioning of informal social networks, (2) the association between social support and psychological well-being, and (3) attitudes toward receiving assistance from formal helpers. Each of these sources of variability is relevant to designing culturally competent interventions involving social support and linking formal and informal sources of support to troubled children and their families.

Although the constituents of social networks are similar for families in different ethnic and cultural groups (e.g., including immediate and extended family, friends, neighbors, and the like), the relative importance of each of these network members for social support is likely to vary. MacPhee, Fritz, and Miller-Heyl (1996) compared lower-income Native American, Hispanic, and European American parents living in the United States on their self-reported sources of support. They found that Native Americans reported more interconnected social systems, more frequent contact with extended kin (but not friends), more members who knew one another, and greater closeness with members of their support networks. Hispanic parents reported having the largest social networks, and, although these networks were close-knit, Hispanics were in general most likely to rely primarily on kinship networks for emotional support. Although they reported the lowest proportion of network members who could offer emotional support, they also reported the highest proportion of network members who could provide instrumental support (e.g., material assistance). European American parents had more diffuse social networks but also reported having a higher proportion of members available for instrumental support. Unlike parents in the other two groups, they reported that friends were the primary providers of emotional support rather than family members. Children also exhibit intercultural variability in the network members on whom they rely for support. In a study of fourth and sixth graders, DeRosier and Kupersmidt (1991) reported that children from Costa Rica rated their parents as the most important providers of support, and children in the United States rated their best friend as the most important source. These intercultural differences are important for understanding the network members who are likely to provide the most helpful forms of informal social support to children and families in need, as well as the avenues by which such support can be offered. It is a much different task to enlist the assistance of other family members in close-knit extended kinships than to call on the help of friends or other extrafamilial associates to provide social support.

Understanding cultural variability in social networks is especially important when children are the targets of social support interventions. For example, it is not necessarily wise to assume that parents are young children's primary sources of social support or that parents are gatekeepers to other sources of support, contrary to the tenor of research findings reviewed earlier. Instead, for families from cultural minorities, a child's earliest sources of support may arise within the extended family or in broader "fictive kin" networks, which are common for Hispanic and African American youth (e.g., J. E. Rhodes, Ebert, & Fischer, 1992; Sanchez & Reyes, 1999). In African American families, for example, children and youth report receiving greater support from their extended families than do children from European families (Cauce, Felner, & Primavera, 1982; Dressler, 1985; Taylor, Casten, & Flickinger, 1993). Likewise, Hispanic values of familialism, involving strong feelings of support and reciprocity with family members, expand the social support networks of children to include adults beyond the immediate family unit (Sagobal, Marin, Otero-Sabogal, Van Oss Marin, & Perez-Stable, 1987). These conclusions are important not only for widening conceptions of the social networks of children and youth from culturally diverse families, but also for cautioning that problems in parent-child relationships, such as those arising from parental stress, substance abuse, or psychopathology, may not leave these children bereft of social support from other sources.

Likewise, parents may not act consistently as monitors, supervisors, and gatekeepers of children's access to other sources of social support. In recent immigrant families, for example, children and their parents may quickly differ in their familiarity with the environment, facility with the majority language, and access to social networks outside the family owing to different acculturation experiences at school and in the workplace. Although this may cause some parents to seek to restrict the access of children to extrafamilial social partners (Nanji, 1993), intergenerational differences in acculturative status mean that as children and youth become increasingly comfortable in the majority culture, parental restrictions are likely to become less effective and add stress to the parent-child relationship (Garcia Coll & Pachter, 2002). These influences may make it difficult for parents to function adequately as gatekeepers of children's access to extrafamilial sources of support.

Although social support comes from potentially diverse sources and is experienced in the context of cultural values, there is good evidence that social support contributes to psychological well-being for different cultural groups in the United States. Coatsworth and colleagues (2002) recently examined family, school, and friend support in relation to externalizing and internalizing behavior in Hispanic girls in middle school, and found that controlling for age, SES, and years in the United States, youth reports of greater perceived family support and teacher support (but not friend support) predicted fewer externalizing problems, and greater perceived family support and friend support (but not teacher support) predicted fewer internalizing problems. Support within the family was the strongest predictor of externalizing and internalizing symptomatology (Coatsworth et al., 2002). Likewise, in a short-term longitudinal study of African American male adolescents,

Zimmerman and colleagues (Zimmerman, Ramirez-Valles, Zapert, & Maton, 2000) found that although support from friends did not predict later outcomes, support from parents predicted diminished depression and anxiety. Rodriguez and colleagues examined perceptions of family and friend support in relation to stress and psychological adjustment in Hispanic college students (Rodriguez, Bingham Mira, Myers, Morris, & Cardoza, 2003). They found that higher support from family and friends predicted increased psychological well-being, although only friend support was a unique predictor of lower psychological distress.

However, cultural values may significantly mediate whether members of different ethnic and cultural minorities access formal—rather than informal—supports when facing psychological distress. This can occur for various reasons, including lack of awareness of formal services, distrust of providers (or providers who cannot speak their language), cultural beliefs that assistance from nonfamilial helpers is unnecessary or inappropriate, resistance to formal helpers from within the family or cultural group, or service delivery practices that are culturally uninformed. In the study of lower-income families described earlier, MacPhee and colleagues (1996) found that European American parents were significantly more likely to have sought professional therapy than were Native American or Hispanic parents, and they also tended more to seek professional help with parenting issues. Similar findings have been reported by Stevens (1988).

Findings such as these underscore the need for cultural awareness in designing interventions to enhance social support to children and families of culturally diverse groups. A culturally competent service delivery system will (1) identify groups that are underserved and seek to reduce cultural barriers that may interfere with service delivery by understanding their characteristics, resources, and needs; (2) orient program planning, staff training, and community involvement to ensure that the development, implementation, and evaluation of services are respectful of the values and practices of recipient families; (3) evaluate assessment and outcome procedures and instruments to ensure their appropriateness and validity for the children and families who are served; (4) build cross-cultural communication skills with program staff, including the appropriate use of interpreters and an ethnographic understanding of communication approaches within cultural groups; and (5) seek to develop an appreciation of cultural diversity as a facilitator rather than impediment to service delivery (Shonkoff & Phillips, 2000). These practices are especially important in services that seek to strengthen the benefits of social support interventions by linking formal support to informal support networks, especially in light of how "outside" helpers can be regarded with distrust or resentment by members of close-knit families or communities. In the end, cultural beliefs and practices are among the most significant personal characteristics mediating the needs of potential recipients and the providers of social support.

Clarity of Goals

Each of these contingencies in the efficacy of social support interventions underscores why clarity concerning the goals and purposes of intervention efforts is essential. Without clear goals, it is difficult to carefully design interventions that will accomplish specific goals for recipients that address their particular needs and living conditions and that result in measurable improvements (Gottlieb, 2000; Heller & Rook, 2001).

Achieving clarity in goals means answering a series of questions. First, in what ways do recipients lack social support that an intervention is expected to address? Answering this question requires a thoughtful understanding of potential recipients and their living circumstances and cultural background, including their personal needs and the resources as well as deficits that exist in their informal social networks and access to formal helpers. It is especially important to comprehend how stress is affecting potential recipients and their capacity to receive assistance from within or outside their natural social connections, and how shared stresses may affect the capacities of network associates to offer social support. Second, what are the specific goals that a social support intervention is meant to address? Multiple goals might be envisioned—providing emotional affirmation, offering instrumental or material aid, social support as a bridge to other forms of assistance, curbing inappropriate or dangerous conduct, preventing problematic behavior from occurring, promoting healing or developmental remediation, integrating formal with informal sources of support—but they should be related to the needs of recipients and identify outcome expectations that will enable an evaluation of the success of the effort. Third, who will offer support and how will they be identified, trained, and enabled to undertake this challenging task successfully? In what specific ways will they offer support, in what contexts, for how long and with what frequency and intensity, and in what social circumstances (e.g., working in teams or individually)? There are also trade-offs between the cost of an intervention and the training and professionalism of formal helpers, and the design of a social support intervention should approach these considerations thoughtfully, keeping in mind that volunteer helpers cannot be expected to undertake the challenges or provide the long-term assistance that professional helpers may be better prepared to provide.

Taken together, questions such as these that focus on the needs of potential recipients, the capabilities of support providers, and the purposes of intervention help to ensure that efforts involving social support are well-designed to address the ways that social support can support psychological well-being for specific families and individuals in need, and that the resources of support providers will be equal to addressing these challenges. Moreover, addressing such questions also identifies the specific outcomes that the social support intervention is intended to affect, making it easier to conduct later evaluations of intervention effectiveness that are carefully tailored to the goals of the program.

Implications

Because the availability of social support will not in itself ensure benefits to recipients, considering the contingencies of social support is essential to planning interventions that will have greatest beneficial impact (see Thompson, 1995). In general, social support efforts are likely to be most effective in the following circumstances:

- The contributions of formal helpers are integrated and coordinated with the efforts of informal helpers in natural social networks and the latter are provided affirmative support for their efforts.
- There are clear, well-defined goals in mobilizing social support that are based on a careful analysis of the needs of target individuals or families and their social networks, the specific purposes for intervention, and the capabilities of support providers, and that identify outcome expectations that can constitute the basis for subsequent evaluation studies.
- Program planners understand how stress may impact the capacity of recipients to receive assistance and the functioning of informal networks of social support.
- Cultural beliefs and practices receive careful consideration and interventions are designed to respond sensitively to cultural diversity.
- Social support interventions provide bridges to broader community resources or other resources that can offer recipients long-term assistance.
- Help providers are supported through continuing supervision, training, and other forms of assistance, especially if they are volunteers or paraprofessional helpers.

- There are efforts to improve recipient reactions to accepting aid, which may include reducing feelings of vulnerability, failure, or inferiority by providing opportunities to reciprocate aid, promoting recipients' voluntary participation in efforts to help other individuals, and developing an environment of mutual respect.
- The need for social support is normalized in the community, so that receiving assistance is not stigmatizing or humiliating.
- Social support interventions are coordinated with other services that address other needs of troubled individuals or families or help recipients to function more successfully in socially supportive relationships (such as through social skills or substance abuse programs).
- When children are the targets of intervention, considerable attention is devoted to the needs of their parents and families in the context of potential two-generation interventions and the impact of family processes on the child's capacity to benefit from social support efforts.

Although these conclusions may seem straightforward and intuitively sensible, there are many reasons that intervention practitioners ignore them (Gottlieb, 2000). One reason is that owing to resource limitations, program philosophy, or tradition, most agencies or programs have only a limited range of support services to offer needy recipients and are thus constrained in their capacity to tailor services to specific client needs (Thompson & Flood, 2002). Another reason is that a detailed needs assessment takes time and, in the absence of validated, readily implemented assessment tools, this process may be abridged or ignored in the rush to provide services. Finally, because the budgets of most intervention efforts are limited, providing support to helpers assumes a lower priority than providing direct services to clients, even though this often results in high turnover and burnout among staff, especially when they are volunteers or paraprofessionals. On the other hand, the same resource limitations make investment in well-trained or formal helpers an impossibility.

Nevertheless, the importance of these contingencies to program success is reflected in the costs of ignoring them when potentially helpful intervention approaches encounter difficulty. One illustration is home visitation. During the past several decades, home visitation has become the most enthusiastically supported and widely recognized approach to providing social support for needy families. The fundamental strategy uniting diverse home visitation programs is the delivery of information, guidance, and emotional support to family members in their homes, often in the context of two-generation efforts in which improving the well-being of the child is the basic goal. Doing so provides an avenue for offering diverse forms of social support, overcomes some of the barriers these families otherwise face when obtaining needed assistance (such as lack of transportation or health insurance) and establishes a relationship of trust with a home visitor who can provide individualized assistance and bridge connections to broader resources (Thompson, 1995; Wasik & Bryant, 2000). Home visitation has provided the foundation for a number of intervention efforts throughout the country, most notably the Healthy Families initiative, developed by the National Committee to Prevent Child Abuse, which has established a nationwide consortium of hundreds of home visitation programs throughout the country serving families at risk (Daro, 2000; Daro & Harding, 1999). A large number of home visitation programs are funded by direct legislative appropriation in many states, or by project grants from federal agencies, as central features of statewide efforts to strengthen child health and development, prevent child maltreatment, and improve parent-child relationships.

There have been a number of reviews and evaluations of home visitation initiatives (see, e.g., General Accounting Office [GAO], 1990; Olds & Kitzman, 1993), but the most recent and large-scale evaluation efforts have yielded the most startling conclusions. Based on sophisticated evaluation studies of six of the most well-known home visitation models that have been implemented nationally, Gomby, Culross, and Behrman (1999) concluded that program benefits were modest and inconsistent across program sites, benefits were enjoyed by only a subset of the families who participated in the program, and programs failed to accomplish most, if not all, of the goals of the home visitation effort. The recent results of a meta-analysis of 60 home visitation programs provided evidence that families in home visitation programs benefit from their participation, but these effects are modest and studies do not offer insight into what kinds of home visitation initiatives benefit what kind of participants. These reviewers concluded that "the utility of home visiting programs cannot be clearly stated" (Sweet & Appelbaum, 2004, p. 1448), and Gomby and colleagues recommended

> that any new expansion of home visiting programs be reassessed in light of the findings . . . [and] that existing programs focus on program improvement, that practitioners and policymakers recognize the inherent limitations in home visiting programs and embrace more modest expectations for their success, and that home visiting services are best funded as part of a broad set of services for families and young children. (p. 6)

Several problems of program implementation were identified by these reviewers and by other evaluations of family support programs emphasizing social support (e.g., Halpern, 2000; Larner, Halpern, & Harkavy, 1992) as helping to account for these discouraging conclusions. They include the inconsistent participation of recipients, the importance of supporting help providers, the need to develop community connections, and the problem of lack of clarity in program goals and expectations.

The failure to fully engage families in the program and the high attrition rates of participants have been identified as significant challenges for virtually all home visitation programs. According to Gomby and colleagues (1999), between 10% and 25% of families invited to participate in home visitation programs decline, and between 20% and 67% of the families who enroll fail to complete the program. Moreover, even when families enroll and remain in home visitation programs, they tend to receive only about half or fewer of the planned number of contacts with the home visitor. The reasons for problems in participant engagement are unclear but are likely related to residential relocation, busy or disorganized family schedules, and other typical characteristics of recipients. But lack of engagement may also be related to the mixed recipient reactions to obtaining assistance discussed earlier, especially if family members do not perceive that home visitation addresses their needs and concerns, or feel embarrassed, indebted, or vulnerable because of the services they receive (Margie & Phillips, 1999).

A second problem in successfully implementing home visitation programs is the lack of training, supervision, and support for home visitors, which contributes to the high turnover rates that are observed in most home visitation programs (GAO, 1990; Gomby et al., 1999). It is common for home visitors to report shorter visits than planned, broken appointments that are not rescheduled, and becoming preoccupied with immediate family crises rather than the delivery of intended education or guidance during home visits. Home visitors are further challenged when working with culturally or linguistically diverse families, at-risk populations, or parents who suffer from depression, domestic violence, or substance abuse (Margie & Phillips, 1999). Moreover, several studies have found that how the intended curriculum of a home visitation intervention is implemented varies significantly depending on the values and orientation of the home visitor (Baker, Piotrkowski, & Brooks-Gunn, 1999; Wagner & Clayton, 1999). At times, in other words, what actually occurs during home visitation may be much different from what program designers had intended. Furthermore, the high turnover of home visitors undermines the relationship between participants and the program, and this may be one contributor to the lack of family engagement. Turnover can be especially difficult for adults in the highest-risk families, who may have fewer alternative sources of support on which to rely and who often have histories of abandonment and relational dysfunction. These challenges to program implementation are directly related to the training, supervision, and support provided to home visitors, especially those who are volunteers or paraprofessionals. However, personnel, training, and supervision account for most of the costs of a home visitation program, and thus poorly or inconsistently funded programs are likely to scrimp on these essential features of service delivery.

Another challenge to effective program implementation is the failure of many home visitation programs to explicitly establish the development of community supports as a central goal for recipient families. This is unfortunate because, by contrast with the traditional social work model, the social support approach incorporated into home visitation recognizes that a home visitor cannot provide all that recipients need, and consequently one of the significant goals of intervention must be to help families forge associations within their communities to individuals and agencies that can offer longer-term support. Moreover, community connections and visibility can also enhance the positive regard for a home visitation program in the neighborhood, and this can contribute to improving family engagement and strengthening the connections between family members and community services.

Finally, the reviews by Gomby and colleagues (1999) and Sweet and Appelbaum (2004) each identified program goals as problematic because they were unclear, unduly ambitious, and/or were not carefully translated into intervention strategies. Gomby and colleagues emphasized, in particular, a renewed appreciation that home visitation programs must have modest expectations for what social support alone can accomplish for needy families. They suggest that home visitation efforts be combined with other services that can address other family needs. This is an additional reason for consolidating stronger connections between family members and community resources so that home visitors do not seek to do it all. Home visitation programs that focus on limited, clear, well-defined, and realistic objectives have the greatest chance of success by enabling program staff to sustain program focus and to use limited resources to achieve realistic expectations (GAO, 1990).

These concerns with the effective implementation of home visitation programs are familiar in light of the foregoing analysis of the contingencies of social support interventions. They do not indicate that efforts to improve social support in the lives of troubled children and their families are inappropriate or worthless. They do, however, suggest that it is crucial to move beyond a general expectation that providing social support in itself will yield many benefits to recipients. Programs must recognize that (1) social support is multifaceted; (2) potential recipients have diverse needs, expectations, and personal and cultural backgrounds; (3) their natural social networks have unique resources and difficulties; (4) their communities likewise have unique constellations of material and human capital; (5) support providers have needs for training and support that are central to an effective intervention; and (6) social support alone cannot address the complex needs of recipients. The importance of clear thinking concerning the purposes of social support interventions, how these objectives should be translated into program strategies, and how the outcomes of these efforts should be evaluated is warranted.

CONCLUSIONS AND FUTURE DIRECTIONS

One of the central conclusions from the research on social support and developmental psychopathology is how complicated the provision of social support in everyday circumstances is, yet how beneficial it is for psychological functioning. When people are surrounded by natural networks of family, friends, neighbors, coworkers, and others who offer emotional guidance and instrumental aid and monitor well-being, the odds in favor of psychological health and healing are meaningfully improved. However, another central conclusion of this research is how difficult it is to create the benefits of natural forms of social support in preventive or therapeutic interventions. This not only owes to the challenges of instituting formal helping relationships that can offer social support, but also because when natural social networks are not functioning supportively (because they are drained or stressed, for example), it is difficult to reconstitute them in healthy and helpful ways. Added to these challenges is the neediness of support recipients and how their personal and ecological characteristics can pose obstacles to the success of social support interventions. In short, the benefits of social support are easy to envision but difficult to implement. This poses a fundamental challenge for researchers, theorists, clinicians, and practitioners who, after the initial wave of enthusiasm for the preventive and therapeutic benefits of social support interventions 2 decades ago, must now confront the host of practical challenges to effectively implement social support in the lives of needy families. As the evaluation studies of home visitation interventions illustrate, however, there is cause for hope. From the varieties of programs that have documented measurable and predictable benefits for recipients—and from those that have failed to do so—there is now a wealth of good ideas for crafting more carefully conceived, thoughtfully designed social support interventions that have greater promise of success. It remains to be seen if the enthusiasm for the psychological benefits of social support interventions can be sustained in the current environment of conceptual rethinking, more careful and modest goal setting and, as always, limited budgets.

There are many ways an examination of social support and developmental psychopathology illustrates the principles of a developmental psychopathology perspective (Cicchetti & Cohen, 1995). Most fundamentally, there appears to be considerable consistency in the processes and outcomes of social support in diverse developing populations, both those that face atypical challenges and clinical difficulties and those that do not. Although at-risk children and families encounter unique problems in obtaining or receiving social support, and particular forms of support may be especially important to different recipient populations, the potential benefits of well-designed social support interventions are consistently clear in our review of diverse clinical and developmental literatures. The continuity in developmental processes between atypically and typically developing populations is, of course, a hallmark of the developmental psychopathology view and appears to be supported by the benefits that well-crafted social support interventions can offer needy individuals of all kinds. However, our review of research on social networks has shown that contrary to the simplified views of social support of several decades ago, there are both risk factors as well as protective factors in the everyday social relationships from which informal social support is constituted. Especially for troubled families and children, these relationships may be sources of stress and difficulty in neighborhoods that may be dangerous or deprived, and thus simply enfolding individuals into broader social networks will not ensure access to social support. Instead, thoughtfully designed social support interventions must carefully determine the resources as well as the liabilities that exist in natural social networks in order to evaluate whether these networks can be strengthened to increase support to target individuals, or whether new sources of social support must be identified. The need to consider both risk factors and protective factors as contributors to psychological health or dysfunction is an important feature of a developmental psychopathology analysis, as is the concept of multifinality, which is also illustrated in the social support research. Multifinality suggests that any component of a developmental system may function differently depending on the organization of the system in which it oper-

ates. In our review, we have indicated many instances in which social support can have benefits but also create liabilities for well-being depending on the form of social support and other features of the social ecology of the child and family. These include situations in which individuals offer emotional support but, in doing so, condone or excuse psychologically unhealthy practices (such as child maltreatment or pathological forms of child anxiety) and circumstances in which social support is offered at a price (of engaging in relationships that also cause stress) that significantly alters its benefits for the recipient. This affirms the conclusion that social support is not in itself a panacea, but its benefits avail only when it is thoughtfully incorporated into the lives of its recipients.

The research literature on social support is broad and expansive, yet there remain significant gaps in knowledge that future research must address, especially with respect to issues of developmental psychopathology. First, there is a critical need for better understanding of the social support *process,* especially when children and families are concerned. What are the specific ways that social support is given, experienced, and received in the everyday social relationships from which it is derived? What specific things do network associates do to make recipients feel supported? How is the process of social support experienced differently by young children, older children, and adolescents in relation to their relative understanding of the complexity of relationships and their own social support needs? In what ways is the experience of social support significantly altered by clinical psychopathology, whether children or parents are depressed, abusive (or abused), or troubled in other ways? In a similar fashion to an earlier generation of studies of the clinical process that helped to identify some of the important features of the therapeutic process related to clinical outcomes, understanding of social support would benefit from finer-grained investigations that examine the process of social support as it is experienced by helper and recipient (Barker & Pistrang, 2002). Such studies, which should include field studies as well as experimental probes, could meaningfully inform the design of social support interventions by promoting more effective intervention design and enabling better training of social support providers.

A related, and significant, concern for future research concerns determinants of the *perception* of social support. As we have noted, an individual's perception that social support is available and accessible is the most important dimension of social support predictive of psychological well-being, but it is not directly and strongly linked to enacted support (see also Hogan et al., 2002). This raises new questions concerning the other determinants of perceptions of social support and, more broadly, how individuals make judgments of social support. Lakey and his colleagues (e.g., Lakey & Lutz, 1996; G. L. Rhodes & Lakey, 1999) have argued that perceptions of social support derive from (1) personality characteristics of the recipient (e.g., a secure or insecure attachment history, interpretive biases, extraversion), (2) characteristics of the helper (e.g., personality factors such as empathy, enacted support), and, most important, (3) the interaction between helper and recipient (e.g., their similarity in background and outlook). This is a heuristically powerful analysis and invites both broader inquiry into the determinants of perceptions of social support and a thoroughgoing developmental analysis of these determinants (e.g., How do developmental changes in support needs, understanding of relationships, and other factors contribute to changing perceptions of social support with increasing age?). One important implication of research on this topic concerns intervention. If perceptions of social support are central to the preventive and therapeutic benefits of social support, then perhaps support interventions could be effectively oriented toward changing perceptions of social support in the minds of needy recipients. If needy individuals begin to perceive their existing social networks as offering greater opportunities for social support, is their own sense of well-being enhanced (even if there have been no significant changes in the behavior of network associates) and, more important, do they become more willing and capable of fostering social support on their own?

We also urge greater, and more systematic, examination of the nature and efficacy of interventions incorporating social support. As Barrera and Prelow (2000) have noted, there is very little research examining whether changes in social support are directly linked to changes in psychological well-being, despite a wealth of suggestive research findings. Moreover, there is relatively little inquiry into the long-term effects of social support interventions: Most evaluation studies examine immediate or short-term outcomes with little inquiry into enduring influences. Furthermore, much remains to be learned about the recipients of social support and, in particular, what kinds of families and children are likely to benefit most from social support interventions, and for whom such efforts are likely to prove ineffective. As the work of Polansky and his colleagues (1981) on neglectful families exemplifies, the research reviewed in this chapter shows that potential recipients differ significantly in their capacity to receive social support and to benefit from it, and further inquiry into individual and developmental differences will inform intervention design.

There is also considerable need for further study of developmental considerations related to giving and receiving social support within families. The intersection of the social networks of parents and offspring offers a start to understanding the direct and indirect avenues by which parents' experience of social support influences offspring, and the roles of parents as gatekeepers to children's access to social networks outside the home affirms the importance of two-generational thinking in providing social support to children. Beyond these, however, developmental inquiry into how children's social networks change with age, the manner in which these networks become increasingly self-regulated and independently accessed, how children's perceptions of social support and capacities to access support from others change with age, and related issues would contribute to a more fully developed understanding of social support in its normative and clinical dimensions.

Beyond these, there are a number of basic questions that continue to merit attention:

- How do natural networks of social support function in everyday life? How is their functioning affected by aspects of neighborhood and community life that may inhibit or encourage contact with others. How are they affected by cultural values?

- How do individuals experience support from informal and formal helpers in everyday life? How do they identify particular persons as sources of reliable assistance, and what are the characteristics of these people?

- How do stress, family turmoil, and the psychological problems of a family member affect social support processes within families? What causes some families to seek and gratefully accept assistance and other families to become withdrawn and isolated? What are the characteristics of potential help providers that may affect how families respond to offered aid?

Although inquiry into social support and its psychological benefits has been ongoing for several decades, this essential component of preventive and therapeutic success is current and vital. For children in psychological turmoil and families in distress, the work of developmental psychopathologists on social support remains essential.

REFERENCES

Allen, J. P., & Land, D. (1999). Attachment in adolescence. In J. Cassidy & P. R. Shaver (Eds.), *Handbook of attachment* (pp. 319–335). New York: Guilford Press.

Anan, R. M., & Barnett, D. (1999). Perceived social support mediates between prior attachment and subsequent adjustment: A study of urban African American children. *Developmental Psychology, 35,* 1210–1222.

Asher, S. R., Parkhurst, J. R., Hymel, S., & Williams, G. A. (1990). Peer rejection and loneliness in childhood. In S. R. Asher & J. D. Coie

(Eds.), *Peer rejection in childhood* (pp. 253–273). New York: Cambridge University Press.

Ashman, S. B., & Dawson, G. (2002). Maternal depression, infant psychobiological development, and risk for depression. In S. H. Goodman & I. H. Gotlib (Eds.), *Children of depressed parents* (pp. 37–58). Washington, DC: American Psychological Association.

Asp, E., & Garbarino, J. (1983). Social support networks and the schools. In J. Whittaker & J. Garbarino (Eds.), *Social support networks: Informal helping in the human services* (pp. 251–297). New York: Aldine.

Badr, H., Acitelli, L. K., Duck, S., & Carl, W. J. (2001). Weaving social support and relationships together. In B. R. Sarason & S. Duck (Eds.), *Personal relationships: Implications for clinical and community psychology* (pp. 1–14). Chichester, England: Wiley.

Bagwell, C. L., Newcomb, A. F., & Bukowski, W. M. (1998). Preadolescent friendship and peer rejection as predictors of adult adjustment. *Child Development, 69,* 140–153.

Baker, A. J. L., Piotrkowski, C. S., & Brooks-Gunn, J. (1999). The Home Instruction Program for Preschool Youngsters (HIPPY). *Future of Children, 9,* 116–133.

Baldwin, D. A., & Moses, L. J. (1996). The ontogeny of social information-processing. *Child Development, 67,* 1915–1939.

Barker, C., & Pistrang, N. (2002). Psychotherapy and social support: Integrating research on psychological helping. *Clinical Psychology Review, 22,* 361–379.

Barrera, M. (1986). Distinctions between social support concepts, measures, and models. *American Journal of Community Psychology, 14,* 413–445.

Barrera, M., & Prelow, H. (2000). Interventions to promote social support in children and adolescents. In D. Cicchetti, J. Rappaport, I. Sandler, & R. P. Weissberg (Eds.), *The promotion of wellness in children and adolescents* (pp. 309–339). Washington, DC: Child Welfare League of America Press.

Beeman, S. K. (2001). Critical issues in research on social networks and social supports of children exposed to domestic violence. In S. A. Graham-Berman & J. L. Edelson (Eds.), *Domestic violence in the lives of children* (pp. 219–234). Washington, DC: American Psychological Association.

Belle, D. (1982). Social ties and social support. In D. Belle (Ed.), *Lives in stress* (pp. 133–144). Beverly Hills, CA: Sage.

Berscheid, R., & Reis, H. (1998). Attraction and close relationships. In D. T. Gilbert, S. T. Fiske, & G. Lindzey (Eds.), *Handbook of social psychology* (4th ed., pp. 193–281). New York: McGraw-Hill.

Blanchard, A., Molloy, F., & Brown, L. (1992). *Western Australian children living with domestic violence: A study of the children's experiences and service provision.* Perth, Australia: Curtin University School of Social Work.

Bogat, G. A., Caldwell, R. A., Rogosch, F. A., & Kriegler, J. A. (1985). Differentiating specialists and generalists within college students' social support networks. *Journal of Youth and Adolescence, 14,* 23–35.

Boivin, M., Hymel, S., & Bukowski, W. M. (1995). The roles of social withdrawal, peer rejection, and victimization by peers in predicting loneliness and depression. *Development and Psychopathology, 7,* 765–785.

Boivin, M., Poulin, F., & Vitaro, F. (1994). Depressed mood and peer rejection in childhood. *Development and Psychopathology, 6,* 483–498.

Booth, C. L., Rubin, K. H., & Rose-Krasnor, L. (1998). Perceptions of emotional support from mother and friend in middle childhood: Links with social-emotional adaptation and preschool attachment security. *Child Development, 69,* 427–442.

Bost, K., Vaughn, B., Washington, W., Cielinski, K., & Bradbard, M. (1998). Social competence, social support, and attachment: Demarcation of construct domains, measurement, and paths of influence for preschool children attending Head Start. *Child Development, 69,* 192–218.

Bretherton, I., & Munholland, K. A. (1999). Internal working models in attachment relationships: A construct revisited. In J. Cassidy & P. R. Shaver (Eds.), *Handbook of attachment* (pp. 89–111). New York: Guilford Press.

Brown, G. W. (1987). Social factors and development and course of depressive disorders in women. *British Journal of Social Work, 17,* 615–634.

Brown, G. W., Adler, Z., & Bifulco, A. (1988). Life events, difficulties, and recovery from chronic depression. *British Journal of Psychiatry, 152,* 487–498.

Brown, G. W., Birley, J. L. T., & Wing, J. K. (1972). Influence of family life on the course of schizophrenic disorders: A replication. *British Journal of Psychiatry, 121,* 241–258.

Burks, V. S., Dodge, K. A., & Price, J. M. (1995). Models of internalizing outcomes of early rejection. *Development and Psychopathology, 7,* 683–695.

Calam, R., Bolton, C., & Roberts, J. (2002). Maternal expressed emotion, attributions and depression and entry into therapy for children with behaviour problems. *British Journal of Clinical Psychology, 41,* 213–216.

Caspi, A., Moffitt, T. E., Morgan, J., Rutter, M., Taylor, A., Arseneault, L., et al. (2004). Maternal expressed emotion predicts children's antisocial behavior problems: Using monozygotic-twin differences to identify environmental effects on behavioral development. *Developmental Psychology, 40,* 149–161.

Cassel, J. (1974). An epidemiological perspective on psychosocial factors in disease etiology. *American Journal of Public Health, 64,* 1040–1043.

Cassidy, J., & Shaver, P. (Eds.). (1999). *Handbook of attachment: Theory, research, and clinical applications.* New York: Guilford Press.

Cauce, A. M., Felner, R. D., & Primavera, J. (1982). Social support in high-risk adolescents: Structural components and adaptive impact. *American Journal of Community Psychology, 10,* 417–428.

Cauce, A. M., Reid, M., Landesman, S., & Gonzales, N. (1990). Social support in young children: Measurement, structure, and behavioral impact. In B. R. Sarason, I. G. Sarason, & G. R. Pierce (Eds.), *Social support: An interactional view* (pp. 64–94). New York: Wiley.

Ceballo, R., & McLoyd, V. (2002). Social support and parenting in poor, dangerous neighborhoods. *Child Development, 73,* 1310–1321.

Christopher, J. S., Hansen, D. J., & MacMillan, V. M. (1991). Effectiveness of a peer-helper intervention to increase children's social interactions: Generalization, maintenance, and social validity. *Behavior Modification, 15,* 22–50.

Cicchetti, D., & Blender, J. A. (2004). A multiple-levels-of-analysis approach to the study of developmental processes in maltreated children. *Proceedings of the National Academy of Sciences, 101,* 17325–17326.

Cicchetti, D., & Bukowski, W. M. (1995). Developmental processes in peer relations and psychopathology. *Development and Psychopathology, 7,* 587–589.

Cicchetti, D., & Cohen, D. J. (1995). Perspectives on developmental psychopathology. In D. Cicchetti & D. J. Cohen (Eds.), *Developmental psychopathology: Vol. 1. Theory and methods* (pp. 3–20). New York: Wiley.

Cicchetti, D., & Toth, S. L. (1998). The development of depression in children and adolescents. *American Psychologist, 53,* 221–241.

Cicchetti, D., & Toth, S. L. (2003). Child maltreatment: Past, present, and future perspectives. In R. P. Weissberg & H. J. Walberg (Eds.), *Long-term trends in the well-being of children and youth* (pp. 181–205). Washington, DC: Child Welfare League of America.

Cicchetti, D., Toth, S. L., & Maughan, A. (2000). An ecological-transactional model of child maltreatment. In A. J. Sameroff, M. Lewis, & S. Miller (Eds.), *Handbook of developmental psychopathology* (2nd ed., pp. 689–722). Dordrecht, The Netherlands: Kluwer Press.

Coatsworth, J. D., Pantin, H., McBride, C., Briones, F., Kurtines, W., & Szapocznik, J. (2002). Ecodevelopmental correlates of behavior problems in young Hispanic females. *Applied Developmental Science, 6,* 126–143.

Cobb, S. (1976). Social support as a moderator of life stress. *Psychosomatic Medicine, 38,* 300–314.

Cochran, M. (1990). Personal networks in the ecology of human development. In M. Cochran, M. Larner, D. Riley, L. Gunnarsson, & C. R. Henderson (Eds.), *Extending families: The social networks of parents and their children* (pp. 3–32). Cambridge, England: Cambridge University Press.

Cochran, M., & Brassard, J. A. (1979). Child development and personal social networks. *Child Development, 50,* 601–616.

Cochran, M., Larner, M., Riley, D., Gunnarsson, L., & Henderson, C. R. (Eds.). (1990). *Extending families: The social networks of parents and their children.* Cambridge, England: Cambridge University Press.

Cochran, M., & Niego, S. (1995). Parenting and social networks. In M. H. Bornstein (Ed.), *Handbook of parenting: Vol. 3. Status and social conditions of parenting* (pp. 393–418). Hillsdale, NJ: Erlbaum.

Cohen, S., & Wills, T. A. (1985). Stress, social support, and the buffering hypothesis. *Psychological Bulletin, 98,* 310–357.

Coleman, J. C., & Hendry, L. (1990). *The nature of adolescence* (2nd ed.). London: Routledge.

Collins, A. H., & Pancoast, D. L. (1976). *Natural helping networks: A strategy for prevention.* Washington, DC: National Association of Social Workers.

Collins, W. A., & Laursen, B. (Eds.). (1999). *Minnesota Symposia on Child Psychology: Vol. 30. Relationships as developmental contexts.* Mahwah, NJ: Erlbaum.

Colman, R., & Thompson, R. A. (2002). Attachment status, adaptive functioning, and problem-solving interaction styles in mother-child dyads. *Merrill-Palmer Quarterly, 48,* 337–359.

Coyne, J. C., Burchill, S. A. L., & Stiles, W. B. (1991). An interactional perspective on depression. In C. R. Snyder & D. O. Forsyth (Eds.), *Handbook of social and clinical psychology: The health perspective* (pp. 327–349). Elmsford, NY: Pergamon.

Coyne, J. C., & Downey, G. (1991). Social factors and psychopathology: Stress, social support, and coping processes. *Annual Review of Psychology, 42,* 401–425.

Criss, M. M., Petit, G. S., Bates, J. E., Dodge, K. A., & Lapp, A. L. (2002). Family adversity, positive peer relationships, and children's externalizing behavior: A longitudinal perspective on risk and resilience. *Child Development, 73,* 1220–1237.

Cummings, E. M., & Davies, P. (1994). Maternal depression and child development. *Journal of Child Psychology and Psychiatry, 35,* 73–112.

Cummings, E. M., & Davies, P. (1996). *Children and marital conflict: The impact of family dispute and resolution.* New York: Guilford Press.

Dadds, M. R., Barrett, P. M., Rapee, R. M., & Ryan, S. (1996). Family process and child psychopathology: An observational analysis of the FEAR effect. *Journal of Abnormal Child Psychology, 24,* 715–734.

Daro, D. (1988). *Confronting child abuse.* New York: Free Press.

Daro, D. (2000). Child abuse prevention: New directions and challenges. In D. J. Hansen (Ed.), *Nebraska Symposium on Motivation: Vol. 46. Motivation and child maltreatment* (pp. 161–219). Lincoln: University of Nebraska Press.

Daro, D., & Harding, K. A. (1999). Healthy Families America: Using research to enhance practice. *Future of Children, 9,* 152–176.

Davies, P. T., & Forman, E. M. (2002). Children's patterns of preserving emotional security in the interparental subsystem. *Child Development, 73,* 1880–1903.

DeMulder, E., Denham, S., Schmidt, M., & Mitchell, J. (2000). Q-sort assessment of attachment security during the preschool years: Links from home to school. *Developmental Psychology, 36,* 274–282.

DeRosier, M. F., & Kupersmidt, J. B. (1991). Costa Rican children's perceptions of their social networks. *Developmental Psychology, 27,* 656–662.

Dilworth-Anderson, P., & Marshal, S. (1996). Social support in its cultural context. In G. R. Pierce, B. R. Sarason, & I. G. Sarason (Eds.), *Handbook of social support and the family* (pp. 67–79). New York: Plenum Press.

Dishion, T. J., Andrews, D. E., & Crosby, L. (1995). Antisocial boys and their friends in early adolescence: Relationship characteristics, quality, and interactional process. *Child Development, 66,* 139–151.

Dodge, K. A., & Pettit, G. S. (2003). A biopsychosocial model of the development of chronic conduct problems in adolescence. *Developmental Psychology, 39,* 349–371.

Dressler, W. (1985). Extended family relationships, social support, and mental health in a southern Black community. *Journal of Health and Social Behavior, 26,* 39–48.

DuBois, D. L., Felner, R. D., Brand, S., Adan, A. M., & Evans, E. G. (1992). A prospective study of life stress, social support and adaptation in early adolescence. *Child Development, 63,* 542–557.

Durkin, R. (1986). The use of therapeutic day care to resolve the legal dilemma of protecting the rights of both children and parents in equivocal cases of abuse and neglect. *Child Care Quarterly, 15,* 138–140.

Eckenrode, J. (1983). The mobilization of social supports: Some individual constraints. *American Journal of Community Psychology, 11,* 509–528.

Eckenrode, J., & Wethington, E. (1990). The process and outcome of mobilizing social support. In S. Duck (Ed.), *Personal relationships and social support* (pp. 83–103). London: Sage.

Eley, T. C. (2001). Contributions of behavioral genetic research: Quantifying genetic, shared environmental and nonshared environmental influences. In M. W. Vasey & M. R. Dadds (Eds.), *The developmental psychopathology of anxiety* (pp. 45–59). London: Oxford University Press.

Feiring, C., & Lewis, M. (1988). The child's social network from three to six years: The effects of age, sex, and socioeconomic status. In S. Salzinger, J. Antrobux, & M. Hammer (Eds.), *Social networks of children, adolescents, and college students* (pp. 93–112). Hillsdale, NJ: Erlbaum.

Feiring, C., & Lewis, M. (1989). The social networks of girls and boys from early through middle childhood. In D. Belle (Ed.), *Children's social networks and social supports* (pp. 119–150). New York: Wiley.

Fischer, C. S. (1982). *To dwell among friends: Personal networks in town and city.* Chicago: University of Chicago Press.

Fisher, J. D., Nadler, A., & Witcher-Alagna, S. (1982). Recipient reactions to aid. *Psychological Bulletin, 91,* 27–54.

Froland, C., Pancoast, D. L., Chapman, N. J., & Kimboko, P. J. (1981). Linking formal and informal support systems. In B. H. Gottlieb (Ed.), *Social networks and social support* (pp. 259–275). Beverly Hills, CA: Sage.

Fuligni, A. J., & Pedersen, S. (2002). Family obligation and the transition to young adulthood. *Developmental Psychology, 38,* 856–868.

Fuligni, A. J., Tseng, V., & Lam, M. (1999). Attitudes toward family obligations among American adolescents with Asian, Latin American, and European backgrounds. *Child Development, 70,* 1030–1044.

Fuligni, A. J., Yip, T., & Tseng, V. (2002). The impact of family obligation on the daily activities and psychological well-being of Chinese American adolescents. *Child Development, 73,* 302–314.

Furman, W., & Buhrmester, D. (1985). Children's perceptions of the personal relationships in their social networks. *Developmental Psychology, 21,* 1016–1024.

Furman, W., & Buhrmester, D. (1992). Age and sex differences in perceptions of networks of personal relationships. *Child Development, 63,* 103–115.

Garbarino, J., & Kostelny, K. (1992). Child maltreatment as a community problem. *Child Abuse and Neglect, 16,* 455–464.

Garbarino, J., & Sherman, D. (1980a). High-risk neighborhoods and high-risk families: The human ecology of child maltreatment. *Child Development, 51,* 188–198.

Garbarino, J., & Sherman, D. (1980b). Identifying high-risk neighborhoods. In J. Garbarino & S. H. Stocking (Eds.), *Protecting children from abuse and neglect* (pp. 94–108). San Francisco: Jossey-Bass.

Garcia Coll, C., & Pachter, L. M. (2002). Ethnic and minority parenting. In M. H. Bornstein (Ed.), *Handbook of parenting: Vol. 4. Social conditions and applied parenting* (2nd ed., pp. 1–20). Mahwah, NJ: Erlbaum.

Gaudin, J. M., & Polansky, N. A. (1986). Social distancing of the neglectful family: Sex, race, and social class influences. *Child and Youth Services Review, 8,* 1–12.

Gaudin, J. M., Wodarski, J. S., Arkinson, M. K., & Avery, L. S. (1990–1991). Remedying child neglect: Effectiveness of social network interventions. *Journal of Applied Social Sciences, 15,* 97–123.

Gazelle, H., & Ladd, G. W. (2003). Anxious solitude and peer exclusion: A diathesis-stress model of internalizing trajectories in childhood. *Child Development, 74,* 257–278.

General Accounting Office. (1990). *Home visiting: A promising early intervention strategy for at-risk families* (GAO/HRD-90-83). Washington, DC: Government Printing Office.

Gerlsma, C., Emmelkamp, P. M. G., & Arrindell, W. A. (1990). Anxiety, depression, and perception of early parenting: A meta-analysis. *Clinical Psychology Review, 10,* 251–277.

Gomby, D. S., Culross, P. L., & Behrman, R. E. (1999). Home visiting: Recent program evaluations—Analysis and recommendations. *Future of Children, 9,* 4–26.

Goodman, S. H., & Gotlib, I. H. (1999). Risk for psychopathology in the children of depressed mothers: A developmental model for understanding mechanisms of transmission. *Psychological Review, 106,* 458–490.

Gottlieb, B. (1983). *Social support strategies.* Beverly Hills, CA: Sage.

Gottlieb, B. (1985). Theory into practice: Issues that surface in planning interventions which mobilize support. In I. G. Sarason & G. R. Sarason (Eds.), *Social support: Theory, research and applications* (pp. 417–437). The Hague, The Netherlands: Martinus Nijhoff.

Gottlieb, B. (2000). Selecting and planning support interventions. In S. Cohen, L. G. Underwood, & B. H. Gottlieb (Eds.), *Social support measurement and intervention* (pp. 195–220). New York: Oxford University Press.

Greenberg, M. S., & Westcott, D. R. (1983). Indebtedness as a mediator of reactions to aid. In J. D. Fisher, A. Nadler, & B. M. DePaulo (Eds.), *New directions in helping: Vol. 1. Recipient reactions to aid* (pp. 85–112). New York: Academic.

Greenfield, P. M., Keller, H., Fuligni, A., & Maynard, A. (2003). Cultural pathways through universal development. *Annual Review of Psychology, 54,* 461–490.

Grych, J. H., & Fincham, F. D. (1990). Marital conflict and children's adjustment: A cognitive-contextual framework. *Psychological Bulletin, 107,* 267–290.

Guevremont, D. C., MacMillan, V. M., Shawchuck, C. R., & Hansen, D. J. (1989). A peer-mediated intervention with clinic-referred socially isolated girls: Generalization, maintenance, and social validation. *Behavior Modification, 13,* 32–50.

Halpern, R. (2000). Early intervention for low income children and families. In J. P. Shonkoff & S. J. Meisels (Eds.), *Handbook of early childhood intervention* (2nd ed., pp. 361–386). New York: Cambridge University Press.

Han, J. J., Leichtman, M. D., & Wang, Q. (1998). Autobiographical memory in Korean, Chinese, and American children. *Developmental Psychology, 34,* 701–713.

Hashima, P. Y., & Amato, P. R. (1994). Poverty, social support, and parental behavior. *Child Development, 65,* 394–403.

Heller, K., & Rook, K. S. (2001). Distinguishing the theoretical functions of social ties: Implications for support interventions. In B. R. Sarason & S. Duck (Eds.), *Personal relationships: Implications for clinical and community psychology* (pp. 119–139). Chichester, England: Wiley.

Heller, K., & Swindle, R. W. (1983). Social networks, perceived social support, and coping with stress. In R. D. Felner, L. A. Jason, J. N. Moritsugu, & S. S. Farber (Eds.), *Preventive psychology: Theory, research, and practice* (pp. 87–103). New York: Pergamon Press.

Hembree-Kigin, T. L., & McNeil, C. B. (1995). *Parent-child interaction therapy.* New York: Plenum Press.

Hirshfeld, D. R., Biederman, J., Brody, L., Faraone, S. V., & Rosenbaum, J. F. (1997a). Associations between expressed emotion and child behavioral inhibition and psychopathology: A pilot study. *Journal of the American Academy of Child and Adolescent Psychiatry, 36,* 205–213.

Hirshfeld, D. R., Biederman, J., Brody, L., Faraone, S. V., & Rosenbaum, J. F. (1997b). Expressed emotion toward children with behavioral inhibition: Associations with maternal anxiety disorder. *Journal of the American Academy of Child and Adolescent Psychiatry, 36,* 910–917.

Hogan, B. E., Linden, W., & Najarian, B. (2002). Social support interventions: Do they work? *Clinical Psychology Review, 22,* 381–440.

Hooley, J. M., Orley, J., & Teasdale, J. D. (1986). Levels of expressed emotion and relapse in depressed patients. *British Journal of Psychiatry, 148,* 642–647.

Hooley, J. M., & Richters, J. E. (1995). Expressed emotion: A developmental perspective. In D. Cicchetti & S. Toth (Eds.), *Emotion, cognition, and representation* (pp. 133–166). Rochester, NY: University of Rochester Press.

House, J. H., Umberson, D., & Landis, K. R. (1988). Structures and processes of social support. In W. R. Scott & J. Blake (Eds.), *Annual review of sociology* (Vol. 14, pp. 293–318). Palo Alto, CA: Annual Reviews.

Jackson, Y., & Warren, J. S. (2000). Appraisal, social support, and life events: Predicting outcome behavior in school-age children. *Child Development, 71,* 1441–1457.

Jacobson, D. (1987). The cultural context of social support and social networks. *Medical Anthropology Quarterly, 1,* 42–67.

Katz, L. F., & Gottman, J. M. (1991). Marital discord and child outcomes: A social psychophysiological approach. In J. Garber & K. A. Dodge (Eds.), *The development of emotional regulation and dysregulation* (pp. 129–155). New York: Cambridge University Press.

Kaufman, J., Yang, B.-Z., Douglas-Palumberi, H., Houshyar, S., Lipschitz, D., Krystal, J. H., et al. (2004). Social supports and serotonin transporter gene moderate depression in maltreated children. *Proceedings of the National Academy of Sciences, 101,* 17316–17321.

Kendall, P. C., Aschenbrand, S. G., & Hudson, J. L. (2003). Child-focused treatment of anxiety. In A. E. Kazdin & J. R. Weisz (Eds.), *Evidence-based psychotherapies for children and adolescents* (pp. 81–100). New York: Guilford Press.

Korbin, J. E. (1989). Fatal maltreatment by mothers: A proposed framework. *Child Abuse and Neglect, 13,* 481–489.

Korbin, J. E. (1991, November). *Good mothers, babykillers, and fatal child abuse.* Paper presented to the annual meeting of the American Anthropological Association, Chicago.

Korbin, J. E. (1995). Social networks and family violence in cross-cultural perspective. In G. B. Melton (Ed.), *Nebraska Symposium on Motivation: Vol. 42. The individual, the family, and social good: Personal fulfillment in times of change* (pp. 107–134). Lincoln: University of Nebraska Press.

Ladd, G. W., Hart, C. H., Wadsworth, E. M., & Golter, B. S. (1988). Preschoolers' peer networks in nonschool settings: Relationship to family characteristics and school adjustment. In S. Salzinger, J. Antrobus, & M. Hammer (Eds.), *Social networks of children, adolescents, and college students* (pp. 61–92). Hillsdale, NJ: Erlbaum.

Ladd, G. W., & Le Sieur, K. D. (1995). Parents and children's peer relationships. In M. H. Bornstein (Ed.), *Handbook of parenting: Vol. 4. Applied and practical parenting* (pp. 377–409). Hillsdale, NJ: Erlbaum.

Laird, R. D., Jordan, K., Dodge, K. A., Pettit, G. S., & Bates, J. E. (2001). Peer rejection in childhood, involvement with antisocial peers in early adolescence, and the development of externalizing problems. *Development and Psychopathology, 13,* 337–354.

Lakey, B., & Lutz, C. J. (1996). Social support and preventive and therapeutic interventions. In G. R. Pierce, B. R. Sarason, & I. G. Sarason (Eds.), *Handbook of social support and the family* (pp. 435–465). New York: Plenum Press.

Lamb, M. E., & Malkin, C. M. (1986). The development of social expectations in distress-relief sequences: A longitudinal study. *International Journal of Behavioral Development, 9,* 355–367.

Larner, M., Halpern, R., & Harkavy, O. (Eds.). (1992). *Fair start for children: Lessons learned from seven demonstration projects.* New Haven, CT: Yale University Press.

Levitt, M. J., Guacci-Franco, N., & Levitt, J. L. (1993). Social network relationships as sources of maternal support and well-being. *Developmental Psychology, 22,* 310–316.

Lewis, M. W., & Lewis, A. C. (1996). Peer helping programs: Helper role, supervisor training, and suicidal behavior. *Journal of Counseling and Development, 74,* 307–314.

Limber, S. P., & Hashima, P. V. (2002). The social context: What comes naturally in child protection. In G. B. Melton, R. A. Thompson, & M. A. Small (Eds.), *Toward a child-centered, neighborhood-based child protection system: A report of the Consortium on Children, Families, and the Law* (pp. 41–66). Westport, CT: Praeger.

Lovell, M. L., & Hawkins, J. D. (1988). An evaluation of a group intervention to increase the personal social networks of abusive mothers. *Children and Youth Services Review, 10,* 175–188.

Lynch, M., & Cicchetti, D. (1997). Children's relationships with adults and peers: An examination of elementary and junior high school students. *Journal of School Psychology, 35,* 81–99.

Lynch, M., & Cicchetti, D. (1998). An ecological-transactional analysis of children and contexts: The longitudinal interplay among child maltreatment, community violence, and children's symptomatology. *Development and Psychopathology, 10,* 235–257.

Lynch, M., & Cicchetti, D. (2002). Links between community violence and the family system: Evidence from children's feelings of relatedness and perceptions of parent behavior. *Family Process, 41,* 519–532.

MacPhee, D., Fritz, J., & Miller-Heyl, J. (1996). Ethnic variations in personal social networks and parenting. *Child Development, 67,* 3278–3295.

Margie, N. G., & Phillips, D. (1999). *Revisiting home visiting: Summary of a workshop.* Washington, DC: National Academy of Sciences Press.

Markus, H. R., & Kitayama, S. (1991). Culture and the self: Implications for cognition, emotion, and motivation. *Psychological Review, 98,* 224–253.

McMahon, R. J., & Forehand, R. L. (2003). *Helping the noncompliant child: Family-based treatment for oppositional behavior* (2nd ed.). New York: Guilford Press.

Meehan, B. T., Hughes, J. N., & Cavell, T. A. (2003). Teacher-student relationships as compensatory resources for aggressive children. *Child Development, 74,* 1145–1157.

Mellin, E. A., & Beamish, P. M. (2002). Interpersonal theory and adolescents with depression: Clinical update. *Journal of Mental Health Counseling, 24,* 110–126.

Miklowitz, D. J., & Goldstein, M. J. (1997). *Bipolar disorder: A family-focused treatment approach.* New York: Guilford Press.

Miklowitz, D. J., Goldstein, M. J., Nuechterlein, K. H., Snyder, K. S., & Mintz, J. (1988). Family factors and the course of bipolar affective disorder. *Archives of General Psychiatry, 45,* 225–231.

Miller, J. L., & Whittaker, J. K. (1988). Social services and social support: Blended programs for families at risk for child maltreatment. *Child Welfare, 67,* 161–174.

Mufson, L., & Moreau, D. (1999). Interpersonal psychotherapy for depressed adolescents (IPT-A). In S. W. Russ & T. H. Ollendick (Eds.), *Handbook of psychotherapies with children and families* (pp. 239–253). New York: Kluwer Academic/Plenum Press.

Mufson, L., Moreau, D., Weissman, M. M., & Klerman, G. L. (1993). *Interpersonal psychotherapy for depressed adolescents.* New York: Guilford Press.

Nangle, D. W., Erdley, C. A., Newman, J. E., Mason, C. A., & Carpenter, E. M. (2003). Popularity, friendship quantity, and friendship quality: Interactive influences of children's loneliness and depression. *Journal of Clinical Child and Adolescent Psychology, 32,* 546–555.

Nanji, A. A. (1993). The Muslim family in North America: Continuity and change. In H. P. McAdoo (Ed.), *Family ethnicity: Strength in diversity* (pp. 229–244). Newbury Park, CA: Sage.

Nemoto, T. U. (1998). Subjective norms toward social support among Japanese American elderly in New York City: Why help does not always help. *Journal of Community Psychology, 26,* 293–316.

O'Donnell, L., & Steuve, A. (1983). Mothers as social agents: Structuring the community activities of school-age children. In H. Lopata & J. H. Pleck (Eds.), *Research on the interweave of social roles: Jobs and families: Vol. 3. Families and jobs* (pp. 113–129). Greenwich, CT: JAI Press.

Oldenburg, C. M., & Kerns, K. A. (1997). Associations between peer relationships and depressive symptoms: Testing moderator effects of gender and age. *Journal of Early Adolescence, 17,* 319–337.

Olds, D. L., & Kitzman, H. (1993). Review of research on home visiting for pregnant women and parents of young children. *Future of Children, 3,* 53–92.

Owens, E. B., & Shaw, D. S. (2003). Predicting growth curves of externalizing behavior across the preschool years. *Journal of Abnormal Child Psychology, 31,* 575–590.

Parke, R. D. (2002). Fathers' contributions to peer relationships. In C. Tamis-LeMonda & N. Cabrera (Eds.), *Handbook of father involvement* (pp. 141–167). Mahwah, NJ: Erlbaum.

Parke, R. D., & Bhavnagri, N. P. (1989). Parents as managers of children's peer relationships. In D. Belle (Ed.), *Children's social networks and social supports* (pp. 241–259). New York: Wiley.

Parke, R. D., Simpkins, S. D., McDowell, D. J., Kim, M., Killian, C., Dennis, J., et al. (2002). Relative contributions of families and peers to children's social development. In P. K. Smith & C. H. Hart (Eds.), *Blackwell handbook of childhood social development* (pp. 156–177). Oxford, England: Blackwell.

Parker, J. G., & Asher, S. R. (1993). Friendship and friendship quality in middle childhood: Links with peer group acceptance and feelings of loneliness and social dissatisfaction. *Developmental Psychology, 29,* 611–621.

Parker, J. G., Rubin, K. H., Price, J. M., & DeRosier, M. E. (1995). Peer relationships, child development, and adjustment: A developmental psychopathology perspective. In D. Cicchetti & D. J. Cohen (Eds.), *Developmental psychopathology* (Vol. 2, pp. 96–161). New York: Wiley.

Patterson, G. R. (1982). *Coercive family processes.* Eugene, OR: Castalia.

Patterson, G. R. (1986). Performance models for antisocial boys. *American Psychologist, 41,* 432–444.

Pavuluri, M. N., Graczyk, P. A., Henry, D. B., Carbray, J. A., Heidenreich, J., & Miklowitz, D. J. (2004). Child-focused cognitive-behavioral therapy for pediatric bipolar disorder: Development and preliminary results. *Journal of the American Academy of Child and Adolescent Psychiatry, 43,* 528–537.

Pellegrini, D., Kosisky, S., Nackman, D., Cytryn, L., McKnew, D. H., Gershon, E., et al. (1986). Personal and social resources in children of patience with bipolar affective disorder and children of normal control subjects. *American Journal of Psychiatry, 143,* 856–861.

Peterson, L. (1990). PhoneFriend: A developmental description of needs expressed by child callers to a community telephone support system for children. *Journal of Applied Developmental Psychology, 11,* 105–122.

Polansky, N. A., Ammons, P. W., & Gaudin, J. M. (1985). Loneliness and isolation in child neglect. *Social Casework, 66,* 38–47.

Polansky, N. A., Chalmers, M. A., Buttenwieser, E., & Williams, D. P. (1981). *Damaged parents: An anatomy of child neglect.* Chicago: University of Chicago Press.

Polansky, N. A., & Gaudin, J. M. (1983). Social distancing of the neglectful family. *Social Service Review, 57,* 196–208.

Polansky, N. A., Gaudin, J. M., Ammons, P. W., & David, K. B. (1985). The psychological ecology of the neglectful mother. *Child Abuse and Neglect, 9,* 265–275.

Reid, J. B., Patterson, G. R., & Snyder, J. (2002). *Antisocial behavior in children and adolescents: A developmental analysis and model for intervention.* Washington, DC: American Psychological Association.

Reid, M., Landesman, S., Treder, R., & Jaccard, J. (1989). My family and friends: Six- to twelve-year-old children's perceptions of social support. *Child Development, 60,* 896–910.

Rhodes, G. L., & Lakey, B. (1999). Social support and psychological disorder: Insights from social psychology. In R. M. Kowalsky & M. R. Leary (Eds.), *The social psychology of emotional and behavioral problems* (pp. 281–309). Washington, DC: American Psychological Association.

Rhodes, J. E., Elbert, L., & Fischer, K. (1992). Natural mentors: An overlooked resource in the social networks of young, African American mothers. *American Journal of Community Psychology, 20,* 445–461.

Robinson, N. S., & Garber, J. (1995). Social support and psychopathology across the life span. In D. Cicchetti & D. J. Cohen (Eds.), *Developmental psychopathology: Vol. 2. Risk, disorder, and adaptation* (pp. 162–209). New York: Wiley.

Rodriguez, N., Bingham Mira, C., Myers, H. F., Morris, J. K., & Cardoza, D. (2003). Family or friends: Who plays a greater supportive role for Latino college students? *Cultural Diversity and Ethnic Minority Psychology, 9,* 236–250.

Rogosch, F. A., & Cicchetti, D. (1994). Illustrating the interface of family and peer relations through the study of child maltreatment. *Social Development, 3,* 291–308.

Rogosch, F. A., Cicchetti, D., & Toth, S. L. (2004). Expressed emotion in multiple subsystems of the families of toddlers with depressed mothers. *Development and Psychopathology, 16,* 689–709.

Rose, R. J., Viken, R. J., Dick, D. M., Bates, J. E., Pulkkinen, L., & Kaprio, J. (2003). It *does* take a village: Nonfamilial environments and children's behavior. *Psychological Science, 14,* 273–277.

Rossello, J., & Bernal, G. (1999). The efficacy of cognitive-behavioral and interpersonal treatments for depression in Puerto Rican adolescents. *Journal of Consulting and Clinical Psychology, 67,* 734–745.

Sabogal, F., Marin, G., Otero-Sabogal, R., Van Oss Marin, B., & Perez-Stable, E. J. (1987). Hispanic familialism and acculturation: What changes and what doesn't? *Hispanic Journal of Behavioral Sciences, 9,* 397–412.

Salzinger, S., Feldman, R. S., Hammer, M., & Rosario, M. (1993). The effects of physical abuse on children's social relationships. *Child Development, 64,* 169–184.

Sameroff, A. J., & Chandler, M. J. (1975). Reproductive risk and the continuum of caretaking casualty. In F. D. Horowitz, M. Hetherington, S. Scarr-Salapatek, & G. Sigel (Eds.), *Review of child development research* (Vol. 4, pp. 187–244). Chicago: University of Chicago Press.

Sanchez, B., & Reyes, O. (1999). Descriptive profile of the mentorship relationships of Latino adolescents. *Journal of Community Psychology, 27,* 299–302.

Sandler, I., Miller, P., Short, J., & Wolchick, S. (1989). Social support as a protective factor for children in stress. In D. Belle (Ed.), *Children's social networks and social supports* (pp. 277–307). New York: Wiley.

Sarason, B. R., Shearon, E. N., Pierce, G. R., & Sarason, I. (1987). Interrelations of social support measures: Theoretical and practical implications. *Journal of Personality and Social Psychology, 50,* 845–855.

Seagull, E. A. W. (1987). Social support and child maltreatment: A review of the evidence. *Child Abuse and Neglect, 11,* 41–52.

Shaw, D. S., Miles, G., Ingoldsby, E. M., & Nagin, D. S. (2003). Trajectories leading to school-age conduct problems. *Developmental Psychology, 39,* 189–200.

Shinn, M., Lehmann, S., & Wong, N. W. (1984). Social interaction and social support. *Journal of Social Issues, 40,* 55–76.

Shonkoff, J. P., & Phillips, D. A. (Eds.). (2000). *From neurons to neighborhoods: The science of early childhood development. Report of the Committee on Integrating the Science of Early Childhood Development.* Washington, DC: National Academy Press.

Shumaker, S. A., & Brownell, A. (1984). Toward a theory of social support: Closing conceptual gaps. *Journal of Social Issues, 40,* 11–36.

Sinclair, J. J., Pettit, G. S., Harris, A. W., Dodge, K. A., & Bates, J. E. (1994). Encounters with aggressive peers in early childhood: Frequency, age differences, and correlates of risk for behaviour problems. *International Journal of Behavioural Development, 17,* 675–696.

Sroufe, L. A., & Rutter, M. (1984). The domain of developmental psychopathology. *Child Development, 55,* 17–29.

Stark, K. D., Napolitano, S., Swearer, S., Schmidt, K., Jaramilo, D., & Hoyle, J. (1996). Issues in the treatment of depressed children. *Applied and Preventive Psychology, 5,* 59–83.

Stevens, J. H., Jr. (1988). Social support, locus of control, and parenting in three low-income groups of mothers: Black teenagers, Black adults, and White adults. *Child Development, 59,* 635–642.

Straus, M. A., Gelles, R. J., & Steinmetz, S. (1980). *Behind closed doors: Violence in the American family.* Garden City, NY: Doubleday/Anchor.

Sullivan, H. S. (1953). *The interpersonal theory of psychiatry.* New York: Norton.

Sweet, M. A., & Appelbaum, M. I. (2004). Is home visiting an effective strategy? A meta-analytic review of home visiting programs for families with young children. *Child Development, 75,* 1435–1456.

Taylor, R. D., Casten, R., & Flickinger, S. M. (1993). Influence of kinship social support on the parenting experiences and psychosocial adjustment of African-American adolescents. *Developmental Psychology, 29,* 382–388.

Thompson, R. A. (1995). *Preventing child maltreatment through social support: A critical analysis.* Thousand Oaks, CA: Sage.

Thompson, R. A. (1998). Early sociopersonality development. In W. Damon (Series Ed.) & N. Eisenberg (Vol. Ed.), *Handbook of child psychology: Vol. 3. Social, emotional, and personality development* (5th ed., pp. 25–104). New York: Wiley.

Thompson, R. A. (1999). Early attachment and later development. In J. Cassidy & P. Shaver (Eds.), *Handbook of attachment* (pp. 265–286). New York: Guilford Press.

Thompson, R. A. (2000). The legacy of early attachments. *Child Development, 71,* 145–152.

Thompson, R. A. (2001). Childhood anxiety disorders from the perspective of emotion regulation and attachment. In M. W. Vasey & M. R. Dadds (Eds.), *The developmental psychopathology of anxiety* (pp. 160–182). London: Oxford University Press.

Thompson, R. A., & Calkins, S. (1996). The double-edged sword: Emotional regulation for children at risk. *Development and Psychopathology, 8,* 163–182.

Thompson, R. A., & Flood, M. F. (2002). Toward a child-oriented child protection system. In G. B. Melton, R. A. Thompson, & M. A. Small (Eds.), *Toward a child-centered, neighborhood-based child protection system: A report of the consortium on children, families, and the law* (pp. 155–194). Westport, CT: Praeger.

Thompson, R. A., Flood, M. F., & Lundquist, L. (1995). Emotion regulation and developmental psychopathology. In D. Cicchetti & S. Toth (Eds.), *Emotion, cognition, and representation* (pp. 261–299). Rochester, NY: University of Rochester Press.

Thompson, R. A., Laible, D. J., & Robbennolt, J. K. (1997). Child care and preventing child maltreatment. In S. Reifel (Series Ed.) & C. J. Dunst & M. Wolery (Vol. Eds.), *Advances in early education and day care: Vol. 9. Family policy and practice in early child care* (pp. 173–202). Greenwich, CT: JAI Press.

Thompson, R. A., & Ontai, L. (2000). Striving to do well what comes naturally: Social support, developmental psychopathology, and social policy. *Development and Psychopathology, 12,* 657–675.

Thompson, R. A., Scalora, M. J., Castrianno, L., & Limber, S. (1992). Grandparent visitation rights: Emergent psychological and psycholegal issues. In D. K. Kagehiro & W. S. Laufer (Eds.), *Handbook of psychology and law* (pp. 292–317). New York: Springer-Verlag.

Thompson, R. A., & Wyatt, J. M. (1999). Current research on child maltreatment: Implications for educators. *Educational Psychology Review, 11*(3), 173–201.

Tietjen, A. M. (1989). The ecology of children's social support networks. In D. Belle (Ed.), *Children's social networks and social support* (pp. 37–69). New York: Wiley.

Tracy, E. M., Whittaker, J. K., Boylan, F., Neitman, P., & Overstreet, E. (1995). Network interventions with high risk youth and families throughout the continuum of care. In I. Schwartz & P. AuClaire (Eds.), *Home-based services for troubled children* (pp. 122–167). Lincoln: University of Nebraska Press.

Triandis, H. C. (1989). The self and social behavior in differing cultural contexts. *Psychological Review, 96,* 506–520.

Unger, D. G., & Powell, D. R. (1980). Supporting families under stress: The role of social networks. *Family Relations, 29,* 566–574.

Vasey, M. W., & Dadds, M. R. (2001). An introduction to the developmental psychopathology of anxiety. In M. W. Vasey & M. R. Dadds (Eds.), *The developmental psychopathology of anxiety* (pp. 1–22). London: Oxford University Press.

Vasey, M. W., & Ollendick, T. H. (2000). Anxiety. In M. Lewis & A. Sameroff (Eds.), *Handbook of developmental psychopathology* (2nd ed., pp. 511–529). New York: Plenum Press.

Vaux, A. (1985). Variations in social support associated with gender, ethnicity, and age. *Journal of Social Issues, 41,* 89–110.

Vaux, A. (1988). *Social support: Theory, research, and intervention.* New York: Praeger.

Votruba-Drzal, E., Coley, R. L., & Chase-Lansdale, P. L. (2004). Child care and low-income children's development: Direct and moderated effects. *Child Development, 75,* 296–312.

Wagner, M. M., & Clayton, S. L. (1999). The Parents as Teachers Program: Results from two demonstrations. *Future of Children, 9,* 91–115.

Wang, Q. (2004). The emergence of cultural self-constructs: Autobiographical memory and self-description in European American and Chinese children. *Developmental Psychology, 40,* 3–15.

Wasik, B. H., & Bryant, D. M. (2000). *Home visiting* (2nd ed.). Newbury Park, CA: Sage.

Webster-Stratton, C. (1998). Preventing conduct problems in Head Start children: Strengthening parenting competencies. *Journal of Consulting and Clinical Psychology, 66,* 715–730.

Wortman, C. B., & Lehman, D. R. (1985). Reactions to victims of life crises: Support attempts that fail. In I. G. Sarason & B. R. Sarason (Eds.), *Social support: Theory, research, and applications* (pp. 463–489). Dordrecht, The Netherlands: Martinus Nihjoff.

Yoshikawa, H. (1994). Prevention as cumulative protection: Effects of early family support and education on chronic delinquency and its risks. *Psychological Bulletin, 115,* 28–54.

Zahn-Waxler, C., & Kochanska, G. (1990). The origins of guilt. In R. A. Thompson (Ed.), *Nebraska Symposium on Motivation: Vol. 36. Socioemotional development* (pp. 183–258). Lincoln: University of Nebraska Press.

Zeanah, C. H., Boris, N. W., & Larrieu, J. A. (1997). Infant development and developmental risk: A review of the past 10 years. *Journal of the American Academy of Child and Adolescent Psychiatry, 36,* 165–178.

Zellman, G. (1990). Child abuse reporting and failure to report among mandated reporters. *Journal of Interpersonal Violence, 5,* 1–11.

Zellman, G., & Anter, S. (1990). Mandated reporting and CPS: A study in frustration. *Public Welfare, 48,* 1–31.

Zimmerman, M. A., Ramirez-Valles, J., Zapert, M., & Maton, K. I. (2000). A longitudinal study of stress-buffering effects for urban African-American male adolescent problem behaviors and mental health. *Journal of Community Psychology, 28,* 17–33.

CHAPTER 2

The Multiple Determinants of Parenting

JAY BELSKY and SARA R. JAFFEE

By tradition, students of socialization have directed their primary energies toward understanding processes whereby parents' child-rearing strategies and behaviors shape and influence their offspring's development. It was possible 15 or so years ago, then, for Belsky and Vondra (1988, p. 153) to observe, on reviewing the literature on the determinants of parenting, that "whereas great effort has been expended studying the characteristics and consequences of parenting, much less attention has been devoted to studying why parents parent the way they do." Even though it remains the case that research on the sequelae of parenting outpaces that on the determinants of mothering and fathering, a great deal has changed over the past decade and a half with respect to empirical inquiry into "why parents parent the way they do." In large measure, this change was stimulated by Bronfenbrenner's (1979, 1986) writings on the ecology of human development, which did much to highlight the contextual embeddedness of child development. To under-

stand the development of children, Bronfenbrenner (1979) asserted, one needed to focus not only on the immediate environments—family, day care, and school—in which children spend so much of their waking day, but on the neighborhood, community, and broader societal context in which the child and family are embedded, including the workplace in which parents spend much of their time and the social supports available to them.

If one reflects on the empirical progress that has been made over the past 15 years, to say nothing about changes that have taken place in the way scholars conceptualize the determinants of parenting, then it becomes apparent very quickly that much has changed over the past half-century in thinking about the origins of individual differences in parenting. Such change is perhaps no better illustrated than by considering changing models of the etiology of child abuse and neglect. Child maltreatment, after all, can be regarded as a case of parenting gone awry or dysfunctional parenting, so it serves as a window through which to view changing notions of why parents parent the way they do. We begin this chapter, therefore, by outlining changing models of the causes of child abuse and, in so doing, underscore one of the core themes of developmental psychopathology, namely, the interrelation of normality and pathology (Cicchetti, 1984; Cicchetti & Cohen, 1995; Sroufe & Rutter, 1984). That is, by focusing on parental dysfunction, we presume that an understanding of its determinants can illuminate forces fostering more competent and growth-promoting parenting (Belsky & Vondra, 1988).

After considering changing conceptions of the causes of child maltreatment, we outline a model of the determinants of parenting that Belsky (1984) advanced almost 2 decades ago but that still serves to guide much research (e.g., van Bakel & Riksen-Walraven, 2002). Belsky's model will serve as the overarching framework guiding the review in the remainder of this chapter of relevant research that has (mostly) emerged since the model's original formulation. To further underscore the view that studies of the abnormal can illuminate understanding of the normal, and vice versa, the review focuses on work concerned with development and parenting within the normal range, as well as with psychopathology and disturbances in parenting.

Before proceeding to consider changing views of the etiology of child abuse and neglect and reviewing, using Belsky's (1984) conceptual framework, research on the determinants of parenting, it is necessary to consider an issue barely on the screen 2 decades ago, namely, the heritability of parenting. Such a focus is essential because virtually all of the evidence reviewed in the main body of this chapter fails to take into account the possibility that many findings presumed—and even interpreted (for heuristic purposes) in this chapter—to reflect environmental influences on parenting may actually be a function, at least in part, of genetic inheritance. It would be a serious error not to caution the reader about this severe limitation of most relevant research to ensure that all conclusions to be drawn in this chapter are tempered by appreciation of this core limit in the design and interpretation of so much research.

A CAUTION: THE HERITABILITY OF PARENTING

In addition to witnessing an outpouring of research on the determinants of parenting, the past 15 years have also witnessed an outpouring of research on the heritability of behavioral development. Included in this ever-expanding body of work has been research on parenting and the home environments that parents provide their offspring (McGuire, 2003). Much of this work has been viewed by those who conducted it as an antidote or corrective to that produced by many scholars interested in how parenting shapes psychological and behavioral development who do not entertain the possibility, or at least who do not design their research in light of the possibility, that the reason so much evidence connects parenting and child functioning is because genes passed on to children may shape both the parent's parenting and the child's development. Thus, associations linking parenting and child development may not document not environmental influences (i.e., parenting) on psychological and behavioral development, as so often presumed, but the influence on parents and their children of genes they share.

Several studies report genetic influence on individual differences in parenting (measured via self-report questionnaires; Plomin & Bergman, 1991; Spinath & O'Connor, 2003). In one, relying on retrospective child-rearing environments of adult twins who were reared apart, Hur and Bouchard (1995) found that genetic factors accounted for 44% of the variance in perceptions of support in the childhood family environment. In another study, of more than 700 sibling pairs 10 to 18 years of age, including identical or monozygotic (MZ) twins (sharing 100% genetic material), fraternal or dizygotic (DZ) twins (sharing 50%), full sibs (sharing 50%), half-sibs (sharing 25%), and stepsiblings (sharing 0%), Plomin, Reiss, Hetherington, and Howe (1994) documented significant genetic effects for 15 of 18 composite measures of the family environment (reported by parents and children), with average heritabilities of .27. More recently, Spinath and O'Connor reported genetic effects ranging from not different from zero (i.e., rejecting) to .73 (i.e., overprotective) in a sample of 300 German twin pairs who reported on their own parenting behavior. Clearly, when one looks across many related studies, findings are not entirely consistent (O'Connor, 2002), even when the same measure is used (Kendler, 1996; Losoya, Callor, Rowe, & Goldsmith, 1997; Perusse, Neale, Heath, & Eaves, 1994).

The first study to examine the heritability of parenting and the home environment was reported by Rowe (1981, 1983). Using the classical twin design, Rowe (1981) examined adolescent twins' ratings of parental warmth and control, finding that MZ twin pairs, who share 100% of their genes, were significantly more alike in how they perceived parental warmth than DZ twins, who share only 50% of their genes (like any two full siblings), indicating genetic influence, a finding that did not materialize with respect to parental control. Similar results emerged in Rowe's (1983) second study that focused on adolescent twins and nontwin siblings, with similarity in nontwin siblings being comparable to that of DZ twins and substantially less than that of MZ twins.

These early findings pertaining to the differential heritability of warmth and control dimensions of parenting were confirmed in a study of older Swedish twins who were asked about their family environment half a century earlier (Plomin, Pedersen, McClearn, Nesselroade, & Bergman, 1988) and in a study by Kendler (1996) of adult twins reporting on how they parented their (own) twins and their twin offspring reporting how they were parented. Plomin et al.'s (1994) aforementioned inquiry also found that parental control, as indexed by a parent report composite measure of monitoring, had the lowest heritability estimate of all 18 composites examined. Losoya and associates (1997), too, found greater evidence of heritability in the case of positive support/warmth (e.g., warm, encourage independence) than negative control (e.g., strictness, aggravation) in their investigation of the similarity of adult twins who were parents. In subsequent work, Perusse et al. (1994) studied a large sample of older twins who also reported on their previously experienced parenting practices; as in other studies, modest genetic effects emerged for the rearing dimensions of care and overprotection (i.e., warmth).

It is not always the case, however, that differential heritability for parental warmth and control emerge in genetically informed studies, as Baker and Daniels (1990) found significant genetic effects for both dimensions of parenting in a study of adult twins. Relatedly, Plomin, McClearn, Pedersen, Nesselroade, and Bergman (1989) detected significant heritability with respect to control in their investigation of the family environment of MZ and DZ twins who had been reared together or apart.

Evidence for genetic contribution to measures of parenting and the family environment is not limited to questionnaire assessments. Genetic effects have been found, for example, in sibling adoption studies comparing nonadoptive and adoptive siblings for videotape observations of mother-infant interaction (Dunn & Plomin, 1990) and mother-child-sibling interactions (Rende, Slomkowski, Stocker, Fulker, & Plomin, 1992). Genetic effects have also emerged in analyses of the widely used observation-interview instrument, Home Observation for Measurement of the Environment, also known as the HOME (Braungart, Plomin, & Fulker, 1992).

In sum, then, the reader should be cognizant of the fact that much of the correlational evidence to be considered linking various developmental and contextual factors with

parenting may reflect the impact of shared genes as much as true environmental influences.

HISTORICAL PERSPECTIVES: THE ETIOLOGY OF CHILD MALTREATMENT

By tradition, three general perspectives have been employed to account for the etiology of child maltreatment; these can be referred to as the psychiatric or psychological model, the sociological model, and the effect-of-the-child-on-the-caregiver model (Belsky, 1978; Parke & Collmer, 1975). By far, the account of child maltreatment most widely subscribed to by the lay public, at least traditionally, falls within the psychiatric model, which focuses exclusive attention on the individual maltreating parent. Essentially, the psychiatric model emphasizes the role that the parent plays, because it is the parent who is the direct perpetrator of mistreatment. Perhaps the most compelling evidence that implicated psychological factors in the etiology of child mistreatment, and thereby focused attention on the psychiatric/psychological makeup of the individual abuser, derived from reports linking parents' own (problematic) child-rearing histories with their subsequent (abusive) parenting (e.g., Altemeier, O'Connor, Vietze, Sandler, & Sherrod, 1982; Spinetta & Rigler, 1972).

Those whose view of the causes of child maltreatment emphasized the rearing histories and psychological character of abusive or neglectful parents were following a tradition established by students of Freud, who were among the first to formally advance ideas about why parents parent the way they do. These ideas grew out of their interest in the nature and structure of personality and the ways development could go astray in early childhood and result in psychopathology. Drawing from clinical experience, a central tenet of many of these theories was that the parent's personality determined the nature of parenting and the parent-child relationship and, in turn, child development. Attention was focused largely on pathological aspects of parental character and the ways these factors gave rise to child psychopathology. Anna Freud (1955/1970), for example, discussed mothers who rejected their children, sometimes due to psychosis but more often because of neurotic conflicts. She wrote, "The [mother's] behavior toward the child is understood best when viewed in terms of her own [intrapsychic] conflicts" (p. 382). Spitz (1970, p. 504), too, wrote about maternal rejection as well as permissive and hostile parenting behavior, arguing that "the mother's personality acts as the disease-provoking agent" in the parent-child relationship. Winnicott (1948/1975, p. 93) also emphasized problematic aspects of the parent's personality, asserting that "the child lives within the circle of the parent's personality and . . . this circle has pathological features." As Holden and Buck (2002) recently noted, the common theme among these psychoanalytic theorists was that if parents' emotional needs had not been met during the course of their own development, then these unresolved needs would be reflected in their (compromised) parenting behavior. Conversely, it was assumed that if parents had adaptive and flexible personalities, derived from emotionally supportive child-rearing histories, they would behave toward their children in growth-promoting ways.

A radical critique of the psychiatric model of child maltreatment was advanced by sociologists who contended that psychologists and psychiatrists placed too much—meaning virtually exclusive—emphasis on the attributes of the maltreating parents, failing to acknowledge the stressful conditions in which they lived (and parented) and, in consequence, essentially "blaming the victim" (Belsky, 1978). The psychiatric model, according to these sociological critics, failed to recognize and grant importance to the social conditions that create stresses that undermine family functioning, as well as the cultural values and practices that encourage societal violence in general and the corporal punishment of children in particular (Gelles, 1973, 1975; Gil, 1971; Light, 1973). Some of the most compelling evidence in support of this model derived from studies linking unemployment, labor market shrinkage, and social isolation with child abuse and/or neglect (Garbarino, 1976, 1977a; Gelles, 1975; Light, 1973).

According to sociological critics of the psychiatric model of child maltreatment, parents must be considered victims of these social forces. The basic premise of the sociological model of child abuse was that important societal characteristics foster child maltreatment. These include high levels of violence and its frequent usage as a strategy for settling human relations disputes, conceptions of children as the property of their parents, and the widespread embrace of such beliefs as "Spare the rod and spoil the child." Under such societal and cultural conditions, the fact that parent-child conflict eventuates in child abuse, especially when parents confront contextual stressors such as unemployment, social isolation, and marital distress, should not be surprising, according to the sociological model. In essence, the social and cultural soil is regarded as fertile when it comes to fostering the mistreatment of children.

Implicit in both the psychiatric and sociological models of child maltreatment was the assumption that parent-child relations are unidirectional, with only parents exercising influence in this subsystem of family relations. The effect-of-the-caregiver model challenged this basic assumption

and underscored the role that the child's own health and behavior played in determining the course of parent-child relations (Parke & Collmer, 1975). Evidence to suggest that children might be responsible for, or at least contribute to, the mistreatment they experience came from evidence indicating that one child within a family was often singled out for mistreatment (Kadushin & Martin, 1981). Also consistent with a child-effects point of view was evidence that prematurity and low birthweight characterized the perinatal histories of a disproportionate number of abused children (Fontana, 1971; Klein & Stern, 1971; Martin, Conway, Beezley, & Kempe, 1974) and that mistreated children exhibited deviations in social interactions and general functioning prior to their reported abuse (Starr, Dietrich, Fischhoff, Ceresnie, & Zweier, 1984).

Certainly by the mid-1970s, if not before, it had become apparent that a model narrow in scope, whether emphasizing the personality and developmental history of maltreating parents, the social stresses that abusive families experience and the social context in which they function, or the role that children play in eliciting their own mistreatment, must inevitably fail in its attempt to account for the multifaceted processes at work in child abuse (Parke & Collmer, 1975). In response to the widely recognized need to integrate these distinct approaches to the etiology of child maltreatment, Belsky (1980) offered an ecological synthesis of these clearly complementary approaches, using a modified version of Bronfenbrenner's (1979) ecological framework. More specifically, Belsky observed that

> while abusing parents enter the microsystem of the family with developmental histories that may predispose them to treat children in an abusive or neglectful manner (ontogenic development), stress-promoting forces both within the immediate family (the microsystem) and beyond it (the exosystem) increase the likelihood that parent-child conflict will occur. The fact that a parent's response to such conflict and stress takes the form of child maltreatment is seen to be a consequence of both the parent's own experience as a child (ontogenic development) and of the values and child-rearing practices that characterize the society or subculture in which the individual, family, and community are embedded (the macrosystem). (p. 33)

BELSKY'S (1984) SOCIAL-CONTEXTUAL MODEL OF THE DETERMINANTS OF PARENTING

When considered in their entirety, available theory and research on the etiology of child abuse and neglect drew attention to three general sources of influence on parental functioning: (1) the parents' ontogenic origins and personal psychological resources (psychiatric model/ontogenetic development), (2) the child's characteristics of individuality (effect-of-child-on-caregiver model/microsystem), and (3) contextual sources of stress and support (sociological model/exo- and macrosystems). Using this foundation, Belsky (1984) advanced, as part of a special issue of the journal *Child Development* focused on integrating the study of development and psychopathology (Cicchetti, 1984), a process model of the determinants of parenting to explain why parents perform well and poorly in the parental role, recognizing that insights into parenting in the normal range could derive from research and thinking about seriously problematic parenting (i.e., abuse and neglect). Belsky argued that parenting is directly influenced by forces emanating from within the individual parent (personality), from within the individual child (child characteristics), and from the broader social context in which the parent-child relationship is embedded, specifically, marital/partner relations, social networks, and occupational experiences of parents. Further, his process model presumed that parents' developmental histories, marital relations, social networks, and occupational experiences influenced their individual personalities and general psychological well-being and, thereby, parental functioning and, in turn, child development. He further theorized that the parent's psychological makeup, shaped in part by his or her developmental history, influenced marital relations, social network functioning, and experiences at work. As such, Belsky's model was based on the notion (1) that parenting is multiply determined, (2) but that characteristics of the parent, the child, and the social context are not equally influential in supporting or undermining growth-promoting parenting because (3) personality shapes parenting indirectly by first influencing the broader context in which parent-child relations exist (i.e., marital relations, social networks, occupational experiences), as well as directly.

Belsky's (1984) model of the determinants of parenting had much in common with thinking by Cicchetti (Cicchetti & Lynch, 1993; Cicchetti & Rizley, 1981; Cicchetti & Toth, 1998) about the etiology of child maltreatment. Both theoreticians assumed parenting to be determined by the relative balance of potentiating (i.e., risk) factors and compensating (i.e., protective) factors experienced by a given family. Problematic parenting, whether it took the form of child maltreatment or just harsh or inconsistent or neglectful or permissive parenting, was presumed to occur when risk factors, be they transient or enduring, outweighed any compensatory influences. Central to conceptual frameworks offered by both thinkers was the recognition of the multiple pathways by which individual (parental personality attributes or child characteristics), historical (parental developmental history), and social (marital quality, social support, occupational stress) factors and processes combine to shape parental functioning. These were not frameworks exclusively or even disproportionately emphasizing "main effects," then, as abusive or neglectful parenting—as well as competent, growth-promoting parenting—were regarded as resulting from the interaction between parental stresses and supports. At the same time, and as already noted, in Belsky's model in particular, all putative forces of influence were not regarded as equally powerful. Characteristics of parents themselves were considered of primary importance because they not only directly influenced parenting, but shaped the other forces also theorized to impact parenting. It is for this reason that attributes of parents are given disproportionate attention in this chapter, by including separate sections on parent's developmental history, parental psychopathology, and parental personality.

Having briefly reviewed the foundations of Belsky's (1984) model of the determinants of parenting in prior thinking about the etiology of child maltreatment, we turn now to examine research on the multiple determinants of parenting, beginning first with child characteristics, before moving on to consider characteristics of the parent and the social context. Given the tremendous growth of research in this general area of inquiry over the past 2 decades, we have decided not to cover all the domains of influence in Belsky's original model, choosing to emphasize those most directly reflective of the parent (developmental history, psychopathology, personality), the child, and the immediate family (i.e., the marriage). We thus do not address two other dimensions of Belsky's original model, namely, social support and occupational experiences. Instead, we examine a "forcefield" that was not even on the developmental horizon in 1984, but has come to be regarded as an important context of development beyond the immediate family and that shapes parenting, namely, the neighborhood, before drawing some general conclusions.

CHILD CHARACTERISTICS

Even though the child's role in shaping the parenting he or she receives has not always been appreciated, few students of parent-child relationships today fail to acknowledge the reciprocal nature of the relationship (Bell, 1968). Rothbart

(1989, p. 27) observed, for example, that "the infant's temperament regulates and is regulated by the actions of others from the earliest hours." This, of course, is a far cry from the perspective of social learning and psychoanalytic approaches to the study of parenting, which accorded the child a minor role in shaping the care received from parents. Temperament is the characteristic of children that has been examined most intensively in research on the determinants of parenting; it will thus be the exclusive focus of this section of the chapter.

Defining Temperament

Thomas, Chess, Birch, Hertzig, and Korn (1963) were perhaps the first to emphasize the role of individual differences in children when it came to understanding the ways parents treat their children. Intensive study of a small sample of middle-class Jewish families led them to propose a set of nine infant temperament categories (activity level, rhythmicity, approach versus withdrawal, adaptability, intensity, threshold, mood, distractability, and attention span) and identify types of infants, specifically "difficult" and "easy," based on the challenges they pose for their parents in taking care of them. Difficult infants scored high on negative mood and withdrawal, low in adaptability, high on intensity, and low on rhythmicity. Easy infants scored in reverse fashion on these select dimensions of temperament. Thomas et al. also emphasized the goodness of fit between characteristics of children and of parents when it came to understanding how parents responded to children's temperaments and the relation between temperament and future child functioning.

Although the notion of infant difficulty continues to influence the thinking of many developmentalists and clinicians, it remains the case that efforts to cluster children empirically based on Thomas et al.'s (1963) definition of difficultness have not met with great success (Bates, 1989). Moreover, extensive factor-analytic research on parent report measures of temperament indicates that fewer than the nine dimensions can be used to capture much of the individual variability in child behavior for purposes of studying parent-child relations (and many other topics; Rothbart & Mauro, 1990). Putnam, Sanson, and Rothbart (2002) draw attention to the following dimensions in infancy: fear, irritability/anger, positive affect, activity level, attentional persistence, and rhythmicity.

These same scholars highlight an emerging consensus with respect to temperament factors relevant for 3- to 8-year-old children, pointing to three broad dimensions (see also Rothbart, Ahadi, Hershey, & Fisher, 2001): surgency, defined in terms of approach, high-intensity pleasure, and activity level; negative affectivity, defined in terms of discomfort, fear, anger/frustration, sadness, and low soothability; and effortful control, defined in terms of inhibitory control, attentional focusing, low-intensity pleasure, and perceptual sensitivity. Especially interesting, perhaps, is that these three dimensions are very similar to three of the "Big Five" personality factors (see McCrae & Costa, 1987), with the negative affectivity dimension mapping onto the personality factor of neuroticism, the surgency dimension mapping onto the personality factor of extraversion, and the effortful control dimension mapping onto the personality factor control/constraint (Putnam et al., 2002).

Temperament and Parenting

When it comes to considering how temperament might affect parenting, hypotheses guiding research have been fairly general, and there has been no truly systematic effort to determine the differential influence of any of the sets of temperament dimensions just discussed. In terms of general predictions, it has been expected, for example, that children would be more likely to evoke warm and supportive care when they are easy to soothe, sociable, and adaptable. In contrast, the child who scores high on negative emotionality or is difficult would be expected to evoke less supportive and responsive care, and perhaps even elicit hostile, insensitive parenting, especially when parents confront additional stressors expected to undermine their parental competence. As it turns out, it is the potentially adverse effects of negative emotional characteristics that have received the most attention. The disproportionate interest that has been paid to difficult or negative infant and child characteristics no doubt stems from the prevailin hypothesis that it is hard-to-manage, negatively emotional, and demanding infants, toddlers, and children who are most likely to develop behavior problems, especially of the externalizing variety, in part because of the hostile-intrusive or even detached-uninvolved caregiving they evoke.

A number of investigations do provide evidence linking infant and child negativity/difficulty with less supportive, if not problematic, parenting (e.g., Hemphill & Sanson, 2000; Hinde, 1989; Linn & Horowitz, 1983). One of the more noteworthy studies was conducted by Van den Boom and Hoeksma (1994), who compared the mothering provided to highly irritable and nonirritable newborns across their first 6 months of life (see also Engfer, 1986). Over time, mothers of the irritable infants showed less visual and physical contact, less effective stimulation, less involvement, and less responsivity to positive signals from their infants. Such findings are consistent with, and reminiscent of, Maccoby, Snow, and Jacklin's (1984) discovery that mothers with more difficult boys became less involved in teaching activities with them across the period from 12 to 18 months of age. They are also in line with recent findings showing that 6-month-olds rated as more temperamentally difficult by their mother receive less affection from their father (Goldberg, Clarke-Stewart, Rice, & Dellis, 2002) and that 3- to 5-year-olds reported as being more (negatively) emotionally intense have a father who takes less responsibility for their care (McBride, Schoppe, & Rane, 2002).

In view of evidence that positive and negative emotionality are separable dimensions of temperament, even in infancy (Belsky, Hsieh, & Crnic, 1996), it is important to note that children who score high on positive affect and self-regulation experience more positively responsive parenting (e.g., Hinde, 1989; Kyrios & Prior, 1990). Fathers of more sociable preschool children, ones who score high on positive emotions, also are more involved with them than are fathers of children who score low on sociability, especially in the case of daughters (McBride et al., 2002).

The fact that most work on effects of child temperament on parenting, including all that just cited, is correlational in nature raises obvious interpretive problems. Instead of child negativity, for example, causally influencing parenting, it could be that the associations detected reflect the role of shared genes in shaping child temperament and parenting behavior. Pike, McGuire, Hetherington, Reiss, and Plomin (1996) were able to overcome this problem using a behavior-genetic-informed research design in their study of adolescents' families with identical and fraternal twins, full sibs, half-sibs, and stepsibs. Even after taking into consideration genetic effects, they found that more negative, irritable, or aggressive children were more likely to receive negative parenting than were other children.

Highlighting even more dramatically the causal role of the child in shaping parenting are the results of some creative experimental investigations. Brunk and Henggeler (1984), for example, trained 10-year-old child confederates to exhibit oppositional or socially withdrawn behavior while playing a board game with women who were mothers, including their own mother. The findings showed that mothers behaved quite differently in the new conditions (compared with pretraining). Using a somewhat different experimental strategy, Anderson, Lytton, and Romney (1986) observed mothers of normal and conduct-

disordered children interacting with their own child, someone else's normal child, and someone else's disordered child. The data revealed a substantial effect of deviant child behavior on maternal functioning. Barkley and Cunningham (1979) and Schachar, Taylor, Wieselberg, Thorley, and Rutter (1987) were able to demonstrate much the same thing by taking advantage of stimulant medication to alter child hyperactive behavior.

Despite the impression left by this rather brief summary of relevant research suggesting perhaps strong effects of temperament on parenting, beginning in the 1st year of life, it is critical to note that the overall corpus of relevant data is by no means consistent. Indeed, when Crockenberg (1986) reviewed 16 studies examining the proposition that infant negativity would be related to lower levels of maternal sensitivity almost 2 decades ago, she found that nine investigations yielded evidence consistent with the hypothesis, but that seven supported its converse, namely, that mothers of highly irritable infants are more positive and show more commitment when interacting with their babies! In the time since Crockenberg's review, inconsistent results have continued to be reported (Crockenberg & Leerkes, 2003a), with some showing that infant difficulty predicts less sensitive, supportive, and/or responsive mothering (R. Clark, Hyde, Essex, & Klein, 1997; Hagekull & Bohlin, 1986; Spangler, 1990), others showing that difficult infants experience more such parenting (Mangelsdorf, Gunnar, Kestenbaum, Lang, & Andreas, 1990; Seiffer, Schiller, Sameroff, Resnick, & Riordan, 1996; Washington, Minde, & Goldberg, 1986; Zahr, 1991), and still others failing to chronicle either positive or negative associations between measures of infant negativity and maternal behavior (P. R. Butcher, Kalverboer, Minderaa, Van Doormaal, & Ten Wolde, 1993; Fish & Stifter, 1993; Hagekull & Bohlin, 1986). These inconsistencies do not seem to be a simple function of variation in how temperament has been measured, how parenting has been assessed, or the age at which either have been evaluated (Crockenberg & Leerkes, 2003a; Pauli-Pott, Mertesacker, Bade, Bauer, & Beckmann, 2000).

Temperament in Context

Should this pattern of inconsistency lead to the conclusion that temperament does not affect parenting? Yes, perhaps, if only main effects of temperament are being entertained, but clearly otherwise if the effects of temperament are considered in the context of other factors that impinge on parenting. That is, seemingly inconsistent findings may reflect the fact that the impact that temperament has on parents varies as a function of other factors that shape parenting. A characteristic of the child that might have one consequence for parenting under one condition could have none—or even the opposite—under another (Crockenberg, 1986). Several strands of evidence suggest this to be the case. In what follows, we consider factors that Belsky (1984) included in his process model of the determinants of parenting.

We begin by considering interactions between one child characteristic, difficult temperament/negative affectivity, and another, child gender. Results from several investigations suggest that parents are more accepting of negative emotionality and difficulty in boys than in girls (Putnam et al., 2002). Consider in this regard B. Gordon's (1983) finding that whereas mothers gave more commands to 2- to 4-year-old daughters who were difficult, they directed more commands at sons who were easy (Rubin, Hastings, Stewart, Henderson, & Chen, 1997); discovery that greater emotion dysregulation predicted more warmth by mothers in the case of sons but not daughters; Rendina and Dickersheid's (1976) observation that fathers were more socially interactive with difficult sons and less interactive with difficult daughters; and Lamb, Frodi, Hwang, Forstromm, and Corry's (1982) fathering research showing men to be less involved with daughters who evinced high levels of negative affect and low levels of positive affect, but less involved with sons who manifested a more easy temperament.

As it turns out, it is not universally the case that the kind of gender-moderated findings just summarized emerge from investigations that look for them. In a study of infant irritability and mothering, Crockenberg (1986) found mothers to be less responsive to the crying of irritable boys than of girls. And in the aforementioned work by Maccoby et al. (1984), it was observed that resistant, hard-to-soothe girls evoked more maternal teaching effort than easy girls, with the reverse being true for boys. Exactly why such inconsistencies emerge in the literature remains unclear, but the possibility of random variation should be discounted. Nevertheless, the results, however inconsistent, highlight the need to consider child gender when examining effects of temperament on parenting behavior.

Characteristics of the parent may also interact with child temperament to predict child rearing. Teti and Gelfand (1991) argued, for example, that it was principally when maternal self-efficacy was low that their infants' fussy difficultness resulted in less warmth, engagement, and sensitivity. Not inconsistent with this view are results from Pauli-Pott et al.'s (2000) study of more than 100 Ger-

man mother-infant pairs, which revealed that high levels of infant negativity predicted less sensitive mother-infant interaction only when mothers showed high levels of depression. But it may not just be clinically relevant psychological states that interact with temperament in predicting parenting. L. A. Clark, Kochanska, and Ready (2000) found negative temperament to predict increased use of power assertion by mothers who scored high (but not low) in extraversion. And recent research by Crockenberg and Leerkes (2003b) and by Calkins and associates (cited in Crockenberg & Leerkes, 2003a) indicates that it may also be when mothers score low in self-efficacy that high levels of distress to limits on the part of infants is most likely to result in lower levels of sensitive/supportive care than would otherwise have been expected.

The broader social context in which parents care for their children may also need to be considered when it comes to understanding the effect of temperament on parenting. In this regard, social support was singled out by Crockenberg and McCluskey (1985) in their study of mother-infant interaction, on finding that neonatal irritability predicted less maternal sensitivity when infants were 1 year of age, but only when mothers reported that levels of social support were low. Also noteworthy are recent findings from work focused on more than one child in a family (Jenkins, Rasbash, & O'Connor, 2003). In this population-based investigation of Canadian 4- to 11-year-olds, greater child negativity predicted greater parental negativity, but it was also found that this child effect was amplified when families were economically disadvantaged. These results, consistent with some of the other findings reviewed, are in accord with the notion of cumulative risks, in that it is not so much a single risk factor, such as a difficult temperament, that may undermine parental competence and sensitivity, but rather the accumulation of risks (Belsky, 1984).

But context can operate in ways that are not easily assimilated into notions of cumulative risk. Consider in this regard the intriguing data from X. Chen et al. (1998), who found, as predicted, that whereas high levels of inhibition predicted less parental acceptance and encouragement of achievement and greater inclination to use punishment in a Canadian sample, this same child attribute predicted high maternal acceptance and encouragement of achievement and less rejection in a Chinese sample. In explanation of these results, the investigators noted that Chinese culture highly values inhibition and reticence, an orientation that is rather foreign to most North Americans, who place great store in being outgoing and sociable. In a sense, then,

Thomas et al.'s (1963) notion of goodness of fit would seem to account for the results under consideration, though the fit has more to do with culturally approved values of parents in the East and West than with particular characteristics of one parent versus another within the same culture.

PARENT'S DEVELOPMENTAL HISTORY

As noted earlier, the classic explanation of child maltreatment highlighted the adverse rearing experiences that abusive and neglectful parents themselves received while growing up in their family of origin. As such, this etiological perspective underscored the importance of parents' own developmental histories, especially their experiences being parented as children, when it comes to understanding why parents parent the way they do. In this section devoted to the role of developmental history, and most especially child-rearing history, in shaping parenting, we first consider evidence and arguments pertaining to child abuse and neglect per se before turning attention to parenting that is not so labeled, including harsh punishment in general and more positive aspects of parenting.

The Intergenerational Transmission of Child Maltreatment

During the 1970s, two of the clinicians at the forefront of inquiry into the etiology and sequelae of child maltreatment observed that "the most constant fact [concerning child abusers] is that parents themselves were nearly always abused or battered or neglected as children" (Fontana, 1973, p. 74) and that "we see an unbroken line in the repetition of parental abuse from childhood into the adult years" (Steele, 1976, p. 15). More than 30 years after these comments were made, there are few in the scientific community who would endorse them in their entirety (Belsky, 1993; Cicchetti & Toth, 1998; Oliver, 1993). Despite the abundance of evidence and reports linking the perpetration of child abuse and neglect with a childhood history of victimization (e.g., Altemeier, O'Connor, Vietze, Sandler, & Sherrod, 1984; Heyman & Slep, 2002; Whipple & Webster-Stratton, 1991), scholars have been all too aware for decades now of the inherent limitations of much of the available data (Belsky, 1980, 1993; Cicchetti & Rizley, 1981; Kaufman & Zigler, 1987; Widom, 1989). Most noteworthy, perhaps, have been the excessive reliance on retrospective reports, once perpetrators have been labeled as maltreaters; small clinical samples, all too often without adequate control groups; and data collectors not blind to parents' maltreatment status. A recent report addressing the specific issue of the validity of adult retrospective reports of adverse childhood experiences underscores concerns about evidence emanating from respondents' memories of their childhood. Hardt and Rutter's (2004) analysis of studies published between 1980 and 2001, in which there was a quantified assessment of the validity of retrospective recall of sexual abuse, physical abuse, physical/emotional neglect, or family discord, revealed that although retrospective reports of major adversities of an easily defined kind are not severely biased (e.g., parental death, father goes to war), the same cannot be said of reports pertaining to the quality of parenting experienced or of family relations more generally: "Little weight can be placed on the retrospective reports of details of early experiences or on reports of experiences that rely heavily on judgment or interpretation" (p. 260).

Despite the acknowledged limits of *much* of the relevant literature, it is noteworthy that a few well-designed, prospective studies clearly document a linkage between a *reported* history of childhood maltreatment and the *subsequent* perpetration of maltreatment (e.g., Egeland, Jacobvitz, & Papatola, 1987; Hunter & Kilstrom, 1979) and thereby underscore the significance of a parent's developmental history in shaping his or her parenting. One recent study, in fact, demonstrates that the more severe the physical abuse experienced (and reported by children), the more likely the next generation of children would report that they, too, had been subject to physically abusive parenting (Pears & Capaldi, 2001). More than a decade ago, the data were of sufficient quality that Belsky (1993) was led to question the much-cited conclusion of one set of distinguished scholars that "the time has come for the intergenerational myth to be placed aside" (Kaufman & Zigler, 1989, p. 135). Such questioning would seem especially appropriate because "countless studies" show that "antisocial behavior patterns are passed from one generation to the next at a rate well beyond chance," even after controls for confounding factors like family size, area of residence, and rates of criminal behavior have been implemented (Wahler & Dumas, 1986, p. 50).

Upon noting that among better-designed studies using standardized self-report measures (e.g., written questionnaires, structured interviews) and reasonably selected comparison groups consistent differences emerge in the developmental histories of index and control samples, Kaufman and Zigler (1987) estimated the actual rate of intergenerational transmission to be only 30% (plus or minus 5%), given a range in rates between 7% (Gil, 1971) and 70% (Egeland & Jacobvitz, 1984) chronicled in the literature. Thus, *only* about one-third of individuals who were abused or neglected will maltreat their own children. Such an estimate is not inconsistent with Oliver's (1993, p. 1315) subsequent conclusion that "one-third of child victims grow up to continue a pattern of seriously inept, neglectful, or abusive rearing as parents." Thus, although the intergenerational transmission of child maltreatment is by no means inevitable, the estimated rate still suggests that an adult's own child-rearing history may play a significant role in shaping his or her own parenting. Moreover, what remains most disconcerting about the Kaufman and Zigler (1987, 1989) analysis was the failure of these scholars to take into consideration the developmental status of the children under study (Belsky, 1993). For example, in discussing the results of Hunter and Kilstrom's (1979) prospective follow-up of at-risk and comparison mothers *1 year* after the birth of their child, Kaufman and Zigler (1989, p. 132) described a parent whose child had not been identified as maltreated as one "who broke the cycle of abuse." What they apparently failed to realize—or at least acknowledge—was that although only 19% of the at-risk parents in the Hunter and Kilstrom investigation maltreated the study child, those who were assumed to have broken the cycle had many more years to care for the study child, to say nothing of other children (including those not yet born).

There would seem to be other fundamental problems with conclusions based on the available data. Especially important are limitations in data that lead some to conclude that "the majority of abusive parents were not abused in their own childhoods" (Widom, 1989, p. 8). Although this may indeed turn out to be the case, it seems risky to embrace such a viewpoint without simultaneously acknowledging that retrospective reports of childhood experience can be inaccurate not only because of overreporting of maltreatment, but because of underreporting as well. As clinicians, attachment researchers, and cognitive scientists know, painful experiences in childhood are often excluded (unconsciously) from memory (Bowlby, 1980; G. Goodman, Emery, & Haugaard, 1998; Main, Kaplan, & Cassidy, 1985).

It thus remains all too conceivable that certain individuals who report no history of maltreatment simply cannot recollect their troubled childhood. In consequence, before any empirical estimates are taken at their face value, two things need to be acknowledged. The first is that a parent who has not mistreated a single 1-, 2-, or 3-year-old might still mistreat that child at an older age—or another child.

The second is that some parents with problematical developmental histories who contend they were not mistreated may not have access to the very memories required to respond accurately to the relevant inquiries. All this is not to argue that every mistreated child grows up to be a maltreating parent, or even that only individuals with histories of maltreatment will mistreat their own offspring (though this is a hypothesis that needs serious testing by means of skilled clinical interviews). As Kaufman and Zigler (1987, p. 190) themselves noted, even though "being maltreated puts one at risk for becoming abusive . . . the path between these points is far from direct or inevitable." What, though, determines whether or not a victim of maltreatment will grow up to become a perpetrator? To answer this question, it is useful to consider some of the possible psychological and behavioral mechanisms presumed to be responsible for transmission when it does occur.

Mechanisms of Transmission

Several mediating processes, none of which are mutually exclusive, may account for the intergenerational transmission of child maltreatment (Kaufman & Zigler, 1989; Simons, Whitbeck, Conger, & Chyi-In, 1991; van Ijzendoorn, 1992). The most obvious simply presumes that aggressive, antisocial behavior is learned in childhood and expressed in adulthood in the parenting role. Several types of learning can be distinguished, including modeling, direct reinforcement, and coercion training (in which escalating negative behavior is inadvertently rewarded when a parent gives up on trying to control a child who has responded adversely to the parent's own aversive behavior).

In addition to learning particular behaviors in childhood that are repeated in adulthood, intergenerational transmission may involve parents' philosophies of discipline. Thus, Simons et al. (1991) theorized and found in their study of the harsh parenting of early adolescents that a belief in the legitimacy of strict, physical discipline mediated (in part) the linkage between the experience of harsh discipline in childhood and its perpetration when an adult. Social-cognitions theorists emphasize the importance of ideas about parenting, especially attitudes and values toward the use of physical punishment (Deater-Deckard, Lansford, Dodge, Pettit, & Bates, 2003; Dodge, Bates, & Pettit, 1990), and point to a wealth of data showing that adults who have been spanked in childhood are more accepting of the use of corporal punishment (e.g., Bower-Russa, Knutson, & Winebarger, 2001; Deater-Deckard et al., 2003). Notable as well is evidence that by middle childhood, a link exists between past discipline experiences and current attitudes toward physical punishment (Holden & Zambarano, 1992), an association still in evidence to some degree during early adolescence (Deater-Deckard et al., 2003) and among college students (Bower & Knutson, 1996).

The effect of mistreatment in childhood may be more general than presumed by social learning theories focused on specific parenting behaviors or theories of social cognition emphasizing beliefs about discipline. In light of evidence that maltreated children have problems with emotion regulation, aggression, and empathy (for review, see Cicchetti & Lynch, 1993; Cicchetti & Toth, 1998), it seems plausible that abusive and neglectful childhoods may promote hostile personalities that become a proximate cause of maltreatment. Certainly, the data to be reviewed in the next two major sections of this chapter dealing with parental psychopathology and personality are not inconsistent with this mechanism of influence. Moreover, support for it emerged in the aforementioned study by Simons et al. (1991) after taking into consideration unmediated linkages between harsh parenting across generations as well as the mediating influence of parental disciplinary beliefs (see also Levendosky, Hutch-Bocks, Shapiro, & Semel, 2003). Several recent prospective studies document the role by "angry, aggressive behavior" (Conger, Nell, Kim, & Scaramella, 2003), "antisocial behavior" (Capaldi, Pears, Patterson, & Owen, 2003), and "adolescent delinquency" (Thornberry, Freeman-Gallant, Lizotte, Krohn, & Smith, 2003) in mediating the intergenerational transmission of parenting (Serbin & Karp, 2003). Notably, all of these investigations measured harsh parenting during adolescence, and then 5 to 10 years later measured the problematic parenting of the now grown-up adolescents who had young children. The fact that some of these investigations focused on mothers and fathers (Thornberry et al., 2003) or relied on observational assessments of parenting (in both generations; Capaldi et al., 2003; Conger et al., 2003) highlights the robust nature of the mediational effect under consideration. What these investigations could not determine, however, was the potential role that shared genes play in both the intergenerational continuity of parenting and the mediational effect of adolescent problem behavior (Serbin & Karp, 2003).

Not unrelated to the notion of general personality when it comes to conceptualizing the developmental process by which parenting is intergenerationally transmitted is the concept derived from attachment theory of an "internal working model." As van Ijzendoorn (1992, p. 79) observes, according to this perspective,

The parents' experiences with grandparental responsiveness, rejection, or ambivalence lead to an internal representation of the grandparent as (un-)responsive to the parental needs, and it is hypothesized that this internal representation will influence the degree of responsiveness the parents are able to show toward their children (Bowlby, 1988; Main et al., 1985). Parents who experienced a high degree of responsiveness in childhood are supposed to be more open to signals and needs of their infants than rejected or ambivalently treated parents, because the former parents are more able to take their children's perspective and to not feel threatened by signs of anxiety in their children. (Main et al., 1985)

In line with such theorizing, Crittenden (1985, p. 1301) noted, after observing various types of parents interacting with their young children, that

abusing parents behaved as though they perceived the world from an adversarial perspective, one that demanded that they establish control in order to satisfy wants that must be imposed on others in spite of objection. . . . Neglecting mothers behaved as though they did not believe that relationships could meet their needs or that they could effectively elicit a satisfying response; their model was one of emptiness and depression.

Subsequent work by Crittenden, Partridge, and Clausen (1991) further revealed that maltreating parents and their partners had rates of insecure working models of attachment (i.e., dismissing, preoccupied) in excess of 90%!

Breaking the Cycle: Lawful Discontinuity in Development

It is especially noteworthy that from the perspective of attachment theory, even though (some) intergenerational transmission of maltreatment is expected, it is by no means considered inevitable. Critical here is the theoretical proposition that child abuse and neglect will be intergenerationally transmitted when early negative experiences are not remembered or integrated into revised working models of relationships (Bowlby, 1980). Certainly consistent with this view are Main and Goldwyn's (1984) findings that women who remembered their mother as rejecting and their childhood as troubled but who had formed coherent accounts of them were *not* likely to reject their children. This contrasted markedly with the parental functioning of mothers who had yet to come to grips with their problematical childhoods.

That attachment theory provides a theoretical basis for the conditions under which, and the mechanisms by which, child maltreatment is not transmitted across generations represents one of its major strengths as a tool for understanding the determinants of parenting in general and the etiology of child maltreatment in particular. Especially intriguing, therefore, are the findings from several investigations that accord with theoretical tenets of attachment theory when it comes to accounting for "lawful discontinuity" in parenting across generations (Belsky & Pensky, 1988). In two separate, prospective studies of at-risk mothers followed from the postpartum period, it was found that parents with histories of maltreatment who did not maltreat their own children (during the study period) had more extensive social supports, had experienced a nonabusive and supportive close relationship with one parent while growing up, or were more openly angry and better able to give a detailed and coherent account of their earlier abuse than were repeaters (Egeland et al., 1987; Hunter & Kilstrom, 1979). Additionally, Egeland et al. found that involvement with a supportive spouse or boyfriend or a positive experience in therapy characterized the nonabusing parents with at-risk developmental histories. Such findings are consistent with Caliso and Milner's (1992) report showing that among mothers at risk for maltreating their offspring due to a history of abuse in their own childhood, those who did not abuse were involved in more satisfying interpersonal relationships than those who did. All these experiences are of the kind postulated by attachment theory to modify the internal working model, or representations and interpersonal expectations, of individuals with seriously troubled parent-child relationship histories and so enable them to care for their own offspring in a manner decidedly different from the way they themselves were cared for.

This interpretation also seems useful in understanding the results of an English study that did not focus on abuse and neglect per se but identified conditions that led some women with a problematic childhood (due to family conflict and institutional rearing) not to provide the low quality of care (hostility, rejection, spanking) that was generally characteristic of mothers with such histories. The women who broke the cycle in this instance tended to be married to supportive and nurturing men, thus suggesting that "the spouse's good qualities exerted a powerful ameliorating effect" on the parental functioning of women known to be at risk as a result of their developmental history (Quinton, Rutter, & Liddle, 1984, p. 115). Interestingly, in a study of teenage mothers with a history of parental rejection, Crockenberg (1987b) also found that support from a partner forecast less angry and punitive care toward a toddler than otherwise would have been expected. And, finally, Belsky, Pensky, and Youngblade

(1990) observed that the ameliorating influence of a positive partner relationship on negative parenting in the case of mothers with negative childhood experiences also was discernable in a nonrisk sample.

The common denominator in all of these inquiries seems to be emotionally supportive relationship experiences that function (apparently therapeutically) to modify, presumably, the feelings and expectations of these women. Whether these effects occur in the case of men remains unknown. Unknown, too, is the exact process—or processes—of influence. Is it the case, for example, that internal working models have actually been modified, as just theorized? Are actual parenting philosophies influenced? And what is the exact route by which parenting behavior is altered? Egeland et al.'s (1987) findings suggest that a conscious resolve not to repeat a history of abuse characterizes nonrepeaters, but under what conditions is such resolve sufficient? In any event, what these breaking-the-cycle investigations underscore is a core notion central to Belsky's (1984) determinants of the parenting model: that sources of risk can be buffered by sources of support. Or, to use Cicchetti's (Cicchetti & Rizley, 1981) terminology, protective factors can reduce the impact of risk factors. That is, it remains unlikely that any single factor will determine the course of a parent's child-rearing behavior, as parenting is multiply determined, with forces of influence that encourage growth-promoting parenting capable of off-setting the risks associated with forces that conspire against such child-rearing behavior.

Reflection on the breaking-the-cycle investigations and their findings also raises questions concerning which at-risk parents will be fortunate enough to experience "emotionally corrective" close relationships—either with a nonabusive parent, close friend, therapist, or spouse—and why. The work of Rutter and his colleagues (Quinton et al., 1984) suggests that self-efficacy-promoting experiences associated with schooling (academics, extracurricular activities) were important for determining which mothers-to-be married "better" men who would provide the emotional support that proved so beneficial to them. Thinking developmentally, though, we can still ask what led some girls to have more positive schooling experiences than others. Might it have been an early supportive relationship that led them to trust others or to develop interpersonal skills? Might physical attractiveness have had something to do with it? Two studies call attention to this latter possibility. In one, Elder, Van Nguyen, and Caspi (1985) found that hostile men who lost their jobs were less likely to treat their daughters harshly if the girls were attractive. In the other,

Belsky et al. (1990) found that the very women with negative histories who were in a happy marriage and were not negative to their 3-year-old were more physically attractive than women with equally negative histories who were negative toward their preschoolers and who were not in a happy marriage. Such findings raise the suspicion that the beneficial effect of a supportive mate in breaking the intergenerational transmission process may be driven, at least in part, by features of the woman herself.

This discussion is not meant to imply that physical attractiveness is *the* important factor when it comes to determining which women at risk for mistreating their children end up not doing so because they some how secure emotionally corrective relationship experiences. Rather, it is intended to highlight the fact that far more needs to be understood about who obtains the social-emotional support that seems so important, if not critical, for disrupting the intergenerational transmission process and about the exact processes through which the ameliorative effect is exerted. These comments notwithstanding, it is clear from these inquiries, even more so than from the difficult-to-interpret data about actual rates of intergenerational transmission, that even though a history of maltreatment is a risk factor of "considerable" (Kaufman & Zigler, 1989, p. 135) significance in the etiological equation, some—perhaps many, even most—parents do not repeat the cycle of maltreatment.

Parenting across Generations (in the "Normal" Range)

As some of the work cited in the preceding subsections indicates, not all research on the potential influence of child-rearing history on parenting has focused on child maltreatment per se (Serbin & Karp, 2003). Some of it has examined "harsh parenting," which, at the extreme, becomes very much like child abuse, even if it is not so labeled (e.g., Capaldi et al., 2003; Conger et al., 2003; Crockenberg, 1987a; Simons et al., 1991; Thornberry et al., 2003). But some of it focuses on more positive aspects of parenting (Z. Chen & Kaplan, 2001; Smith & Farrington, 2004). Like virtually all work on the intergenerational transmission of child maltreatment, much of this nonmaltreatment research relies on retrospective reports of the child rearing experienced by parents while growing up in their family of origin, or some variation on that theme; this state of affairs is changing, however, as children studied as adolescents are followed up as young adult parents (Capaldi et al., 2003; Z. Chen & Kaplan, 2001; Conger et al., 2003; Smith & Farrington, 2004; Thornberry et al., 2003). In some studies,

retrospective reports are provided by grandparents about the way they parented their now adult children (e.g., Wintre & Dhami, 2003) and in others by parents on the way they were reared as children or adolescents (e.g., Baydar, Reid, & Webster-Stratton, 2003; Bluestone & Tamis-LeMonda, 1999), sometimes assessed prior to the birth of a child (Crockenberg & Leerkes, 2003b; Feldman, Curran, Jacobvitz, Boyd-Soisson, & Jin, 2003). In some of the research on the intergenerational transmission of parenting, whether based on retrospective or prospective data, the parenting to be explained is observed (e.g., Baydar et al., 2003; Biringen, 1990; Capaldi et al., 2003; Conger et al., 2003; Meyers, 1999), whereas in other cases, it is reported by parents themselves (e.g., Z. Chen & Kaplan, 2001; Meyers, 1999; Thornberry et al., 2003) or by their children (e.g., Muller, Hunter, & Stollak, 1995).

Whereas most of the research that relies on retrospective assessments of parenting experienced while growing up (or provided by the grandparent when the parent in question was a child) employs brief and easy-to-complete, survey-research type instruments, this is not the case with one body of research that derives directly from mainstream attachment theory (rather than more general learning theories of the origins of parenting). When it comes to examining the intergenerational transmission of parenting (and a host of other developmental questions), many attachment researchers employ the Adult Attachment Interview (AAI). This clinical interview consists of 18 questions and is structured entirely around the topic of attachment, principally the individual's relationship to the mother and father during childhood (see Hesse, 1999). Interviewees are instructed to describe their relationships with their parents and to provide specific biographical episodes to substantiate global evaluations. Thus, individuals who report that their parent was very generous with them or highly affectionate toward them are asked to recall specific incidents of such behavior. Interviewees are asked directly about childhood experiences of rejection, being upset, ill, and hurt, as well as about loss, abuse, and separations. They are also asked to offer explanations for their parent's behavior and to describe their current relationships with their parents and the influence they consider their childhood experiences exerted on their development. The interview is designed to evoke not so much the adult's actual, veridical experiences in childhood but, rather, their reconstructions of the meaning and mental representations of early experiences.

The tape-recorded interview is transcribed by a typist, and, on the basis of the information obtained from the AAI, a specially trained evaluator rates the subject on a series of rating scales (e.g., role reversal: the extent to which the respondent parented the parent during childhood; idealization: the extent to which the respondent idealizes his or her parent; preoccupying anger: the extent to which the respondent is still very angry at the parent; inability to recall: the extent to which the respondent cannot remember events and experiences from childhood). These ratings, coupled with the evaluator's general sense of the entire transcript, especially how coherent (i.e., organized and integrated) it is, lead the evaluator to characterize the respondent's state of mind regarding attachment (i.e., internal working model) using a limited set of classification categories. Ultimately, the coding of AAI transcripts is based not on the participants' description of childhood experiences per se, but on the way these experiences and their effects on current functioning are reflected on and evaluated. It is significant that attachment classifications based on the AAI have been found to be independent of general intelligence and verbal ability (for review, see Hesse, 1999).

The *secure-autonomous* state of mind is reflected in an individual's inclination to value attachment relationships and regard attachment-related experiences as developmentally influential. In the course of the AAI, such persons appear self-reliant, objective and nondefensive. It is noteworthy that persons receiving this classification either convincingly describe a history of emotionally supportive relationship experiences or provide evidence that they have come to terms with a childhood lacking in them, thus permitting a balanced view of relationships.

Adults classified as *insecure-dismissing* have a tendency to deny negative experiences and emotions or to dismiss their developmental significance. These individuals can remember little and seem unable to reevoke the feelings associated with the experiences they do recall. Often, they offer an idealized picture of parent or parents but, in response to probes eliciting evidence to substantiate generalizations, may recall experiences quite inconsistent with their positive, global appraisals. For example, in response to a follow-up query from the interview asking for details about how a parent was generous, the respondent ends up talking about a parent's failure to attend his or her birthday party or his or her disappointment with a present received from a parent. Insecure-dismissing individuals present themselves as strong, independent people for whom closeness and attachment mean little. The defensive flavor of the detached pattern is reminiscent of the insecure-avoidant infant pattern.

Adults classified as *insecure-preoccupied* demonstrate a continuing involvement of preoccupation with their par-

ents. They appear confused, incoherent, and unobjective regarding relationships and their influences on them. Anger over the past and present seems not to be resolved but, instead, to be a major organizing theme of their current relationships with their parents. These individuals seem caught up in their early relationships, with little ability to move beyond them.

In the main, and rather consistently, research that relies on retrospective assessments of parenting reveals positive associations between parenting across generations (and so, too, do the more recent prospective studies; see later discussion): Supportive and/or authoritative parenting tends to predict supportive/authoritative parenting, whereas authoritarian and/or harsh parenting tends to predict authoritarian/harsh parenting. This pattern can be seen consistently in AAI-based research. Parents with secure attachments are more sensitive to their children than parents with dismissing or preoccupied attachment (Aviezer, Sagi, Joels, & Ziv, 1999; George & Solomon, 1996; Ward & Carlson, 1995). Some research has found that the caregiving of parents with secure attachment encouraged learning during teaching tasks (Crowell & Feldman, 1988; van Ijzendoorn, 1992) and that secure parents respond to their infants' affect in flexible ways (Haft & Slade, 1989). In contrast to mothers with secure attachments, those with dismissing attachments are less supportive and colder in interactions with their children (Crowell & Feldman, 1988, 1989). Preoccupied parents are found to be inconsistent in their parenting (Crowell & Feldman, 1988, 1989; Haft & Slade, 1989); they may alternate between secure-like parenting or controlling, confusing, and less sensitive parenting (van Ijzendoorn, 1995; Ward & Carlson, 1995). Some of the non-AAI work that is longitudinal in design also indicates, as noted already, that much, even if not all, of the intergenerational transmission of problematic parenting is mediated by problem behavior during adolescence (Capaldi et al., 2003; Conger et al., 2003; Serbin & Karp, 2003; Thornberry et al., 2003).

Whether assessed using brief survey questionnaires or the more lengthy and clinically sensitive AAI, studies of the intergenerational transmission of parenting based on retrospective reports produce associations of only modest size in parenting across generations, either because these are error-prone for reasons of memory distortion, as discussed earlier, or due to undetected—and unexamined—processes of lawful discontinuity. Recently, in fact, elements of the AAI have been called into question, basically because prospective data collected as part of a 20-year longitudinal study did not show that individuals classified on the AAI as secure but who reported—and supposedly overcame—problematic child-rearing histories (i.e., "earned secures") actually experienced more negative child-rearing experiences than agemates also classified secure but who did not report such adverse developmental experiences (Roisman, Padron, Sroufe, & Egeland, 2002). Ultimately, whatever the instrumentation, there will always be reasons to be cautious about embracing findings derived from retrospective reports of parenting. Fortunately, several interesting prospective studies can be singled out that actually include measurements of child rearing obtained during childhood/adolescence and of parenting secured during adulthood. As we will see, these studies, which yield results one can place more confidence in, generate findings not inconsistent with those emanating from most retrospective studies.

Elder and associates (1985) took advantage of the multigenerational Berkeley Growth Study to examine whether, and even how, the parenting that a parent experienced while growing up predicted the parenting that the parent provided as an adult. Of particular importance, although not all the data were prospective in the sense defined earlier, some data were. Longitudinal analysis revealed that growing up in a home in which parents' personalities could be described as unstable and in which parental care could be depicted as controlling, hostile, and lacking in affection led to the development of unstable personalities in these children as adults. Such psychological instability on the part of Berkeley parents, derived as it seemed to be from poor developmental experiences in the family of origin, itself proved predictive of tension in their own marriage. And marital tension, in the face of another generation of personal instability, contributed to extreme and arbitrary discipline for the third generation of Berkeley children. Moreover, exposure to such care resulted in the development of behavior problems in this third generation that proved predictive of undercontrolled behavior in adulthood. Thus, parenting difficulties, apparently originating from personality problems, seemed to leave a legacy of personal adjustment problems that were passed down through parenting from one generation to the next, testimony indeed for the role hypothesized for personality in Belsky's (1984) model (shaped in part by this work) in mediating between developmental history and parenting. Using a large sample of Iowa farm families experiencing financial stress due to poor macroeconomic conditions, Simons and associates (1991) report similar evidence showing, on the basis of retrospective reports of child-rearing history, that harsh parenting is intergenerationally transmitted via its impact on hostile personality. And, as already noted, three recent prospective studies that followed up adolescents when they were young parents provide additional supportive evidence of the mediational role of angry, aggressive, and antisocial personality characteristics and behavior in the intergenerational transmission of problematic parenting (Capaldi et al., 2003; Conger et al., 2003; Serbin & Karp, 2003; Thornberry et al., 2003).

But it looks like it is not just problematic parenting that can be expected to undermine the child's developmental competence which is passed on down the generations, but more growth-promoting parenting as well (Serbin & Karp, 2003). Z. Chen and Kaplan (2001) took advantage of a 2-decade longitudinal study and were able to link parenting measured during the childhoods of parents with the parenting they actually provided their own offspring. More specifically, children's reports of the parenting they received as seventh graders were used to predict the parenting they reported providing when in their mid- to late-30s to their own offspring. Structural equation modeling showed that higher levels of good parenting (e.g., parental acceptance, living in a happy home) experienced in childhood forecast the provision of higher levels of "constructive parenting," defined in terms of monitoring, communication, involvement in child's education, affection, and discipline (e.g., use of praise and reasoning). The fact that the linkage over time between parenting experienced in childhood and parenting provided in adulthood was only modest calls attention to the need to understand the developmental processes that break the cycle not only of child maltreatment or harsh parenting, but also of supportive parenting. After all, in the same way that it makes sense to ask under what conditions and through what mechanisms does problematic parenting in one generation not lead to problematic parenting in the next, one can wonder when and why supportive parenting in one generation does not promote similarly supportive parenting in the next. Fortunately, in the next few decades, any number of longitudinal studies initiated in the 1970s, 1980s, and 1990s should be in position, given ongoing follow-ups, to provide data on these and related topics concerning the role of child-rearing history in shaping parenting practices in adulthood.

PARENTAL PSYCHOPATHOLOGY

Most mental disorders show considerable continuity across generations. Whereas many disorders are heritable to some degree, genetic accounts do not fully explain why children whose parents have a history of psychiatric disorder are themselves at risk for psychopathology. In trying to understand how mental disorder is transmitted from one generation to the next, researchers have observed that psychiatric illness can adversely affect parent-child relations and that this may be one of the mechanisms by which risk for psychopathology is passed on from parent to child (S. H. Goodman & Gotlib, 1999). In this section, we consider how Major Depressive Disorder, alcohol abuse and dependence, Antisocial Personality Disorder, and Schizophrenia affect parents' attitudes about and interactions with their children. We restrict ourselves to these conditions, as these are the ones that have been most intensively (and productively) studied in terms of parenting. Reflecting the literature on parenting more generally (Tamis-LeMonda & Cabrera, 2002), the reviewed research focuses primarily on mothers (although the literature on parents with alcohol use disorders provides an exception; Connell & Goodman, 2002; McMahon & Rounsaville, 2002; Phares, 1992; Phares & Compas, 1992). For a more extensive review on parental psychopathology, see Zahn-Waxler, Duggal, and Gruber (2002).

Depression

Mood disorders include Major Depressive Disorder (MDD), Dysthymic Disorder, and Bipolar Disorder. Given the paucity of research on how Dysthymic and Bipolar Disorders affect parenting, the focus here is on parents with MDD. According to the *Diagnostic and Statistical Manual of Mental Disorders,* fourth edition (*DSM-IV*), the essential feature of a major depressive episode is a period of at least 2 weeks during which there is either depressed mood or the loss of interest or pleasure in nearly all activities. MDD is more common in women than in men. The lifetime risk for MDD in community samples ranges from 10% to 25% for women and from 5% to 12% for men (American Psychiatric Association, 2000).

Children whose parents are depressed are at risk for a range of adverse outcomes, including problems in self-regulation, peer relationships, and sleep regulation, attachment difficulties, behavioral and affective disorders, and academic difficulties (see reviews by Cummings & Davies, 1994; Downey & Coyne, 1990; Herring & Kaslow, 2002; Teti, Gelfand, & Pompa, 1990). Exposure to a depressed mother's negative cognitions, affect, and behavior is hypothesized to increase children's risk for problem behaviors (S. H. Goodman, Adamson, Riniti, & Cole, 1994).

Maternal Cognitions and Affective Style

Compared to well mothers, mothers with diagnoses of depression make more hostile and critical statements about their school-age children (Brennan, Hammen, Katz, & Le Brocque, 2002;[1] S. H. Goodman et al., 1994; Hamilton, Jones, & Hammen, 1993), although depressed and well mothers have been shown to be similar in the proportion of neutral or positive statements they make (S. H. Goodman et al., 1994). Depressed mothers are more likely than well mothers to attribute their young children's developmental outcomes to uncontrollable factors, such as genetic inheritance and biology, although they appear to be equally satisfied with their children's development (Kochanska, Radke-Yarrow, Kuczynski, & Friedman, 1987).

Parent-Child Interaction

Observational and self-report data suggest that maternal depression is associated with suboptimal parent-child interactions from infancy into adolescence. In infancy, depressed mothers tend to have difficulties responding contingently and sensitively to their infants, providing optimal levels of stimulation, or engaging their child's attention (Breznitz & Sherman, 1987; Carter, Garrity-Rokous, Chazan-Cohen, Little, & Briggs-Gowan, 2001; Jameson, Gelfand, Kulcsar, & Teti, 1997; Murray, Fiori-Cowley, Hooper, & Cooper, 1996; Stein et al., 1991). They show less positive and more negative affect when interacting with their infants (Campbell, Cohn, & Meyers, 1995; Cohn, Campbell, Matias, & Hopkins, 1990; Cohn, Matias, Tronick, Connell, & Lyons-Ruth, 1986; Dawson et al., 1999; Field, Healy, Goldstein, & Guthertz, 1990; Field et al., 1985, 1988; Teti et al., 1990), and they and their infants more frequently match each other's negative states while less frequently matching each other's positive affective states (Cohn et al., 1990; Field et al., 1990). When their children are toddlers or preschoolers, depressed mothers are, again, found to be more negative and/or less positive in interactions with their children (Kelley & Jennings, 2003; Lovejoy, 1991; Radke-Yarrow, Nottelmann, Belmont, & Welsh, 1993), and they engage in less effective control strategies (Kochanska, Kuczynski, Radke-Yarrow, & Welsh, 1987). To be noted is that not all research on mother-toddler interaction reveals such adverse effects of depression; and this is true even taking into account the type of depression and the mother's current depressive symptomatology (Frankel & Harmon, 1996). Depressed mothers continue to show more negative affect with school-age and adolescent children (D. Gordon et al., 1989; Hops

---

[1] In the Brennan et al. (2002) study, fathers diagnosed with depression were more likely than well fathers to make hostile and critical statements about their children.

et al., 1987; Nolen-Hoeksema, Wolfson, Mumme, & Guskin, 1995; Tarullo, DeMulder, Martinez, & Radke-Yarrow, 1994). Trained observers judge them as being less accepting and exercising more psychological control than other mothers (e.g., extent to which parent controls child by inducing guilt, instilling anxiety, or withdrawing love; Garber & Flynn, 2001). Compared to well mothers, mothers diagnosed with depression have been found to be less engaged with the school-age daughters (Tarullo et al., 1994).

These findings on parent-child interaction were summarized recently in a meta-analysis of 46 observational studies of maternal depression and parenting behavior (Lovejoy, Graczyk, O'Hare, & Neuman, 2000). Parenting behaviors were categorized as negative if they involved negative affect or hostile or coercive behavior, disengaged if mothers ignored or withdrew from their child, or positive if they involved pleasant, enthusiastic interactions with the child. Compared to nondepressed mothers, depressed mothers had more negative, disengaged, and less positive interactions with their children. The difference between the depressed and nondepressed mothers was moderate in size for negative behavior ($d = .40$, 95% CI = .31 to .49), smaller in size for disengaged behavior ($d = .29$, 95% CI = .17 to .41), and small for positive behavior ($d = .16$, 95% CI = .08 to .23). These effects were similar regardless of whether depression was measured as a disorder or on a symptom scale.

Fathers versus Mothers

Although the evidence is sparse, the research comparing parenting behavior among depressed mothers and fathers indicates that fathering is less affected than mothering by depression. For example, Jacob and Johnson (1997) reported that depression in mothers was more strongly associated with parent-child negativity during a problem-solving task than was depression in fathers. Similarly, Field, Hossain, and Malphurs (1999) found that depressed fathers had higher-quality interactions (e.g., were more active, positive, and facially expressive, and displayed more game playing and higher-quality vocalizations) with their 3- to 6-month-old infants than did depressed mothers. These findings are consistent with meta-analytic results showing that depression in mothers was more closely related to children's internalizing (but not externalizing) problems than depression in fathers (Connell & Goodman, 2002). To be noted, however, are findings from one study showing that in families in which the father was depressed, positive communications by one family member were less often met with positive responses by other family members than in households in which neither parent or only mother was depressed (Jacob & Johnson, 2001).

The Family System

There is some evidence that one parent's depression may affect children's interactions with the nondisordered parent. For example, Jacob and Johnson (1997) reported that in families where one parent was depressed, affective expression was dampened across the entire family, including the communications between the child and the nondepressed parent. Among families of depressed women, Hops and colleagues (1987) observed a cycle in which depressed mothers' dysphoric affect made their husbands and children less aggressive, but family members' caring and aggressive affect also worked to dampen depressed mothers' dysphoric affect.

Timing, Severity, and Chronicity of Depression

Evidence emerging from some investigations suggests that the timing, severity, or chronicity of a mother's depression better predicts the quality of parent-child interaction than diagnostic status per se (Campbell et al., 1995; D. Gordon et al., 1989; Kochanska & Kuczynski, 1991; Kochanska, Kuczynski, et al., 1987; Langrock, Compas, Keller, Merchant, & Copeland, 2002; Tarullo et al., 1994; Timko, Cronkite, Berg, & Moos, 2002). In fact, in the aforementioned meta-analysis (Lovejoy et al., 2000), whether mothers were currently depressed when they were observed interacting with their children proved to be a stronger predictor of negative parenting behavior than was a history of depression. Although deficits in parenting may not persist after the mother's depression has remitted, differences between the children of depressed and well mothers may still be detected (Billings & Moos, 1986), possibly as a result of difficulties in the parent-child relationship that arose when the mother was still depressed (Murray et al., 1999).

The Role of Social Stressors

Depressed parents experience a range of social stressors, including marital difficulties, financial problems, and low social support (Hammen, 2002). Social stressors have been shown to exacerbate (i.e., moderate) the effects of depression on parenting (Stein et al., 1991) as well as to mediate the effects of depression on parent-child interaction; that is, mothers diagnosed with depression experience more social stressors, which, in turn, are associated with suboptimal parenting practices (D. Gordon et al., 1989; Hamilton et al., 1993; Teti et al., 1990). Other research indicates, however, that even though mothers diagnosed with depression report elevated levels of life stressors, negative attitudes about their children, dissatisfaction with themselves as parents, and unhappiness, they cannot be distinguished from well mothers during interactions with their children (Frankel &

Harmon, 1996). This apparent inconsistency may be explained by the possibility that differences between depressed and well mothers emerge only when well mothers are free from significant social adversity (Murray et al., 1996).

The offspring of depressed parents are at risk for a range of problem behaviors and, in some cases, children's problem behaviors may themselves act as social stressors that elicit negative reactions from parents, particularly when parents are already vulnerable to depression. Feske and colleagues (2001) provided evidence consistent with this argument, as they found that mothers reported more stressful life events than nonmothers following the onset of a depressive episode because they experienced child-related stressors. Another study of affectively ill, medically ill, and control mothers found that not only did mothers' symptom severity and negativity increase the risk of children's problem behaviors and low self-esteem, but that children's problem behaviors and low self-esteem predicted mothers' symptom severity and negativity in a reciprocal fashion (Hammen, Burge, & Stansbury, 1990).

A Note on Bipolar Depression

Comparison of mothers diagnosed with Bipolar and Major (i.e., unipolar) Depression to well mothers indicates that the parenting of the former group appears more compromised than that of the latter (Radke-Yarrow, 1998). More specifically, mothers diagnosed with Bipolar Disorder tend to make more negative judgments about and show more overall negative affect with their young children (Inoff-Germain, Nottelmann, & Radke-Yarrow, 1992); display more sad and anxious affect with their young daughters (Radke-Yarrow et al., 1993); prove less successful in managing their toddlers' behavior, particularly when their symptomatology is severe (Kochanska, Kuczynski, et al., 1987); prove less successful in engaging their preadolescents' attention (Tarullo et al., 1994); and are more likely to attribute their children's behavioral development to uncontrollable life events (Kochanska, Radke-Yarrow, et al., 1987). However, mothers diagnosed with bipolar and unipolar depression cannot be distinguished in terms of the negative affect they show in interactions with their toddlers (Radke-Yarrow et al., 1993), nor do they differ in terms of the strategies they use to control their children's behavior (Kochanska, Kuczynski, et al., 1987).

Alcohol Use Disorders

At least two kinds of alcohol use disorders need to be distinguished, though they are not always in investigations of parenting. Alcohol dependence is characterized by compulsive drinking as well as tolerance to alcohol and symptoms of withdrawal following reduction of alcohol intake. Alcohol abuse is a maladaptive pattern of substance use manifested by recurrent and significant adverse consequences related to persistent alcohol use (American Psychiatric Association, 2000). Lifetime prevalence rates of alcohol dependence range from 8% to 14%, whereas prevalence rates of alcohol abuse have been estimated as 5% in community and national probability surveys (American Psychiatric Association, 2000). Alcohol abuse and dependence are more common in males than females (ratios as high as 5:1), although the sex ratio depends on the age group, with females starting to drink heavily later in life than males. The studies reviewed here typically include individuals who meet criteria for either alcohol dependence or abuse (or both).

Because of gender differences in the prevalence of alcohol use disorders, fathers rather than mothers tend to be the focus of studies on how alcohol use affects parenting, reversing the trend in the parenting literature more generally. Research on alcoholic fathers largely involves observations of families of alcoholics interacting in lab settings or in the home. These studies consistently find that when interacting with their children, alcoholic fathers tend to show higher levels of negativity (Ammerman, Loeber, Kolko, & Blackson, 1994; Moser & Jacob, 1997), lower levels of positivity and congeniality (Jacob, Krahn, & Leonard, 1991), lower levels of problem solving (Jacob et al., 1991) and ability to keep children on task (Whipple, Fitzgerald, & Zucker, 1995), less synchronicity (Whipple et al., 1995), and, with infants, less sensitivity and verbalization (Eiden, Chaves, & Leonard, 1999), thereby fostering insecure infant-father attachment bonds (Eiden, Edwards, & Leonard, 2002). Studies of children of alcoholics find that a family history of alcoholism is associated with a lack of emotional warmth in parents (Barnow, Schuckit, Lucht, John, & Freyberger, 2002), more parent-child conflict and physical and emotional abuse (Reich, Earls, & Powell, 1988), and lower levels of monitoring and disciplinary consistency (Chassin, Pillow, Curran, Molina, & Barrera, 1993), although such difference are not detected in each and every investigation (Callan & Jackson, 1986). The focus in this literature on maritally intact families of alcoholics obscures the fact that, as with antisocial behavior, many alcohol- and substance-abusing fathers are absent from the household in which their children grow up (McMahon et al., 2002).

Far more has been written about drug-abusing than alcohol-abusing mothers (Mayes, 1995). Nevertheless, the small research base suggests that alcoholism is more strongly linked to parenting problems among mothers than fathers. For example, Moser and Jacob (1997) observed parent-child interactions in families where only the mother, only the father, both parents, or neither parent was alcoholic. Alcoholic fathers were indistinguishable from control fathers unless both parents were alcoholics, in which case fathers had more negative and less positive interactions with their children relative to any other fathers. In contrast, mother-child interactions were characterized by high levels of negativity regardless of whether only the mother or both parents were alcoholics. Consistent with these findings are recent meta-analytic results showing that mothers' alcoholism and substance use disorders were more strongly linked to children's externalizing problems than were fathers' substance use disorders or alcoholism (Connell & Goodman, 2002).

As noted earlier in the case of depression, alcoholism in one parent has been associated with suboptimal parent-child interactions involving the nondisordered parent (Chassin et al., 1993; Haber, Leonard, & Rushe, 2000). However, the effects of one parent's drinking on the other's parenting behavior may depend on factors such as the quality of their relationship or the level of psychopathology in the other parent (Eiden & Leonard, 1996). Currently, there is very little evidence that a mother's behavior buffers her children from the effects of a father's alcoholism (Curran & Chassin, 1996).

Child Maltreatment

Several investigations reveal an association between parental alcohol abuse and child maltreatment (Widom & Hiller-Sturmhofel, 2001). A 1991 national survey found that 24% of substantiated reports of maltreatment involved a caretaker who abused alcohol (Magura & Laudet, 1996). The proportion of maltreating parents who abuse alcohol is even higher (31%) among families where maltreatment is deemed sufficiently serious to require the removal of the child into care (Murphy et al., 1991). The association between alcohol abuse and child maltreatment appears strongest when alcoholism is comorbid with other drug problems (Murphy et al., 1991). Moreover, although alcohol problems characterize a substantial proportion of parents who mistreat their children, there is little evidence that parents who abuse alcohol are at elevated risk of child maltreatment, with existing studies relying on retrospective reports of parental alcoholism and child abuse (Harter & Taylor, 2000; Miller, Maguin, & Downs, 1997).

Comorbidity and Causality

Alcohol disorder is highly comorbid with other mental disorders (Regier et al., 1990). Thus, when a parent is an alcoholic, it is not always clear whether suboptimal parenting is a function of alcoholism or comorbid psychopathology. Several researchers have attempted to delineate the unique effects of alcohol disorder on parenting practices (Chassin et al., 1993), but results have been inconsistent, with some reporting that high and low antisocial fathers could be distinguished in interactions with their wife and children (Haber et al., 2000) and others finding that antisocial behavior neither mediated nor moderated the effects of alcohol problems on parent-child interactions (Eiden et al., 1999; Moss, Lynch, Hardie, & Baron, 2002). However, Eiden and colleagues did find that alcoholic fathers interacted less sensitively with their infants because of their depressive symptomatology.

Given the reliance on correlational data in studies of alcohol use and parenting, most researchers have been unable to conclude that the effects of alcohol use on parenting are truly causal. Although the ethics of conducting experimental research on alcohol use and parenting have been questioned, some investigators have manipulated alcohol intoxication to illuminate its effects on parenting. Lang, Pelham, Atkeson, and Murphy (1999) developed an experimental paradigm in which sober parents and parents who were intoxicated as part of the experiment engaged in a problem-solving task with control children and with confederates who were trained to behave like children with Conduct Disorder or Attention-Deficit/Hyperactivity Disorder. Compared to parents who were sober, intoxicated parents were less attentive and engaged in more irrelevant talk while failing to sustain task-oriented work behaviors. Reflecting an inconsistent parenting style, they issued more commands while at the same time engaging in more indulgent behaviors. Moreover, intoxicated parents were less likely than sober parents to perceive the confederate's behavior as deviant. Lang and colleagues (1999) noted that attention and perception problems might mediate the association between parents' drinking and children's conduct problems. In a study in which alcoholic beverages were made available to participants, fathers (regardless of diagnostic status) were more negative during family problem-solving interactions if they were in the drink versus the no-drink condition (Jacob et al., 1991). Results of this work clearly suggest that although some of the impact of alcohol use disorder on mothering and fathering might be an artifact of other factors, this is unlikely to be the case entirely.

Antisocial Personality Disorder

According to *DSM-IV* (American Psychiatric Association, 2000), Antisocial Personality Disorder (ASPD) is characterized by a pervasive pattern of disregard for, and violation of, the rights of others that begins in childhood or early adolescence and continues into adulthood. ASPD is more common in men than women, with prevalence rates of about 3% among men and 1% among women in community samples (American Psychiatric Association, 2000). Given the dearth of research on diagnosed ASPD, this summary includes studies of parenting behavior and serious delinquency or criminality.

As with alcohol use disorder, research on parenting and ASPD focuses more heavily on fathers than mothers. Although young men who engage in high levels of antisocial behavior compose a small percentage of the population, they father a disproportionate number of children (Wei, Loeber, & Stouthamer-Loeber, 2002). Despite this, they are less likely than other fathers to see their children every day (because a considerable proportion are incarcerated), to be involved in their children's care, or to support their children financially (Jaffee, Moffitt, Caspi, & Taylor, 2003; Wei et al., 2002).

When fathers who have a history of antisocial behavior are involved with their children, the quality of their parenting may be compromised. Observing young fathers interacting with their toddlers during a puzzle-solving task, Fagot, Pears, Capaldi, Crosby, and Leve (1998) found that those who had a history of antisocial behavior more often told their children what to do (rather than offer strategies for solving the task) and provided them with more negative feedback compared to control fathers. Verlaan and Schwartzman (2002) reported that fathers who had a history of antisocial behavior reported using more hostile, rejecting behaviors with their sons, who, in turn, had more externalizing problems. Shears, Robinson, and Emde (2002) reported that in a sample of 87 low-income fathers, men with a history of antisocial behavior reported low ratings of themselves as fathers and were less involved with their children, although they did not report being less emotionally attached to their child.

Turning to the case of mothering and ASPD, the first thing to be noted is that girls who have a history of Conduct Disorder are disproportionately likely to become teen mothers (Bardone, Moffitt, Caspi, & Dickson, 1996; Jaffee, 2002; Kovacs, Krol, & Voti, 1994; Zoccolillo, Meyers, & Assister, 1997), and at least one study has shown that, among adolescent mothers, those who had more symptoms of antisocial behavior were less responsive with their infants, though not more controlling or less sensitive (Cassidy, Zoccolillo, & Hughes, 1996). These findings were echoed in study of 141 low-income women who were categorized into antisocial, clinical (e.g., depressed), or nonclinical groups based on their scores on the Antisocial Practices content scale of the Minnesota Multiphasic Personality Inventory 2 (J. N. Butcher, Dahlstrom, Graham,

Tellegen, & Kaemmer, 1989; see also Bosquet & Egeland, 2000). Observed during interactions with their 13- and 24-month-old infants, the clinical and nonclinical mothers were virtually indistinguishable. However, mothers in the antisocial group were less understanding of their children and more coercive, harsh, hostile, and abusive, although they did not differ from the nonantisocial groups in terms of more positive behaviors with their children.

A number of studies have shown that mothers who have a history of antisocial behavior are more likely to use ineffective disciplinary practices with their school-age children (Bank, Forgatch, Patterson, & Fetrow, 1993; Capaldi & Patterson, 1991; Simons, Beaman, Conger, & Chao, 1993a; Verlaan & Schwartzman, 2002). Simons and colleagues reported that individual characteristics of the mothers, such as their history of antisocial behavior, better accounted for variation in disciplinary effectiveness than did social stressors and supports (e.g., economic pressures, negative life events, and social supports). However, this study also showed that antisocial behavior and social stressors were closely related. For example, mothers who had a history of antisocial behavior reported more economic pressures and negative life events. They also reported more psychological distress, partly because of the negative life events they experienced. These factors, in turn, predicted ineffective discipline. Similarly, Capaldi and Patterson found that mothers who had a history of antisocial behavior were less skillful parents (which, in turn, was related to their boys' adjustment) and were also the parents whose relationships were the least stable.

Finally, a large research literature shows that parents who have a history of ASPD are at increased risk of abusing their children (Brown, Cohen, Johnson, & Salzinger, 1998; DeBellis et al., 2001; Dinwiddie & Bucholz, 1993; Moffitt, Caspi, Harrington, & Milne, 2002; Walsh, McMillan, & Jamieson, 2002). Moreover, mothers with a history of Conduct Disorder may be at increased risk of having their children removed into care (for review, see Pajer, 1998).

Schizophrenia

Schizophrenia is characterized by positive symptoms that reflect an excess or distortion of normal function (e.g., delusions, hallucinations, disorganized speech) and negative symptoms that include restrictions in the range and intensity of emotional expression, in the fluency and productivity of thought and speech, and in the initiation of goal-directed behavior (American Psychiatric Association, 2000). The lifetime prevalence of Schizophrenia is estimated at 0.5% to 1.0%. Schizophrenia is somewhat more common in men than women, although the sex ratio varies depending on diagnostic criteria and age of onset (Castle, 2000).

In clinic samples, the majority (59%) of women with nonaffective psychotic disorders are mothers (Hearle & McGrath, 2000). Although men with Schizophrenia are less likely than other men to have children (Jablensky, 1995), a study of psychiatric outpatients (most of whom had diagnoses of Schizophrenia) found that 51% had fathered children, although fewer than a third were being raised by their father and mother together (Coverdale, Schotte, Ruiz, Pharies, & Bayer, 1994). The lowered fertility rate coupled with the lack of paternal involvement among men with diagnoses of Schizophrenia may account for the dearth of evidence about their parenting practices.

As reviewed by Mowbray, Oyserman, Zemencuk, and Ross (1995), the majority of studies about parenting and Schizophrenia involve observations of mother-infant dyads admitted to psychiatric hospital mother-and-baby units (MBU). These inquiries involve small clinic samples, thus compromising the generalizability to the population of psychiatrically ill mothers; relatively short-term follow-ups of parents' behavior; and often lack nonpsychiatric control groups that would provide information about the degree to which the parenting of mothers diagnosed with Schizophrenia was impaired relative to that of well mothers. Nevertheless, clinic studies are generally consistent in showing that, compared to well mothers, mothers diagnosed with Schizophrenia are less sensitive and responsive with their infants and have difficulty matching their infants' affect or behavior (Cohler, Gallant, Grunebaum, Weiss, & Gamer, 1980; McNeil, Naslund, Persson-Blennow, & Kaij, 1985; Naslund, Persson-Blennow, & McNeil, 1985; Persson-Blennow, Naslund, & McNeil, 1984). In very rare cases, a parent who is experiencing a psychosis will threaten a child's life, but these instances of "terrorizing attacks" on children are uncommon (Anthony, 1986). One study found that the quality of parent-child interactions was related to changes in mothers' positive symptoms (e.g., thought disorder, paranoia) but not negative symptoms, possibly because negative symptoms showed relatively little improvement over the course of treatment. At discharge, mothers whose negative symptoms were more prominent were inattentive, unresponsive, understimulating, and disorganized in interactions with their infants (Snellen, Mack, & Trauer, 1999).

Results of at least three studies indicate that the quality of mother-child interactions is poorer among dyads where the mother has Schizophrenia compared to dyads where the mother is diagnosed with depressive disorder. Compared to mothers with depression, mothers diagnosed with Schizophrenia are less responsive and sensitive, more demanding and intrusive, less stimulating, more withdrawn, and provide a poorer quality physical environment (S. H. Goodman & Brumley, 1990; Hipwell & Kumar, 1996; Riordan, Appleby, & Faragher, 1999). In their observations of unipolar depressed, bipolar depressed, and schizophrenic mothers on an MBU, Hipwell and Kumar reported that, at discharge, over 75% of the mothers diagnosed with unipolar or bipolar depression had scores in the normal range on a mother-child interaction scale, whereas this was true of only 33% of the mothers diagnosed with Schizophrenia. Although the majority of mothers diagnosed with unipolar or bipolar depression were discharged home together with their child from the MBU with no recommended formal supervision, most mothers diagnosed with Schizophrenia were not so discharged.

As the Hipwell and Kumar (1996) research suggests, a major issue for mothers with Schizophrenia is the possibility that their children will be removed from their care. In a study of 58 mothers who had been hospitalized for severe mental illness (predominantly Schizophrenia), 68% had a child from whom they had been permanently separated by the time the child was 18 years of age (Dipple, Smith, Andrews, & Evans, 2002). In half the cases, separation occurred during the mother's first episode of illness and, following separation, 66% of the children had no further contact with their mother; 20% had only sporadic contact for the remainder of their childhood. Reasons for separation included concern by the authorities that the mother was providing inadequate care (physical and emotional abuse and neglect were common), a breakdown in the mother's relationship with the father, and a history of prolonged periods of hospitalization (Dipple et al., 2002).

Finally, some researchers have noted that poverty and lack of social supports often co-occur with severe mental illness, and they theorize that severe mental illness may affect parenting not only directly, but also indirectly, by increasing family stress and depleting family support systems (Oyserman, Bybee, Mowbray, & MacFarlane, 2002). In one of the few population studies of mothers with a serious mental illness (Schizophrenia, unipolar or bipolar depression), Oyserman and colleagues found that mothers whose first episode of disorder occurred at an early age had fewer social supports and were less involved in their children's schooling. Mothers whose current mental health and functioning was poor reported more social and material stressors, which were, in turn, associated with less positive parenting attitudes. Only the number of hospitalizations (per year of mental illness) had a direct effect on parenting: Mothers who reported more hospitalizations had more positive parenting attitudes, leading the authors to propose that hospitalization stabilized these mothers or increased the value they placed on motherhood. Consistent with these findings, Rogosch, Mowbray, and Bogat (1992) showed that among a sample of mothers diagnosed primarily with Schizophrenia, those who experienced more emotional support and had less frequent relapses reported more authoritative parenting attitudes.

Conclusion

Despite very different symptom presentations, there appears to be little specificity in the association between different mental disorders and parenting practices. High levels of comorbidity among disorders and the frequent co-occurrence of social stressors with psychiatric illness may account for the finding that most disorders are associated with a pattern of parenting characterized by less sensitive, less responsive, and contingent caregiving. Although some studies of psychiatric disorder and parenting practices report data from community samples, much of the research in this area still relies on clinic samples and samples of convenience, particularly the literature on parenting practices among parents diagnosed with alcoholism and Schizophrenia. Moreover, although a growing number of studies have shown that suboptimal parenting practices both mediate and moderate the association between parent and offspring psychopathology, more research is needed to explore bidirectional effects of parent and offspring disorder on parenting and to illuminate the circumstances under which parenting is not impaired. Finally, given the heritable nature of these disorders, genetically sensitive designs are needed to determine whether suboptimal parenting accounts for the association between parent and offspring psychopathology, even controlling for children's genetic risk for disorder.

PERSONALITY

Despite early interest by psychoanalytically oriented investigators in parental personality characteristics and their effects on parenting behavior, the study of these issues was interrupted by important shifts in the field of personality psychology during the 1970s and into the 1980s (for reviews, see Baumeister, 1999; Caspi, 1998; McAdams, 1997; Winter & Barenbaum, 1999). A major contribution to the reemergence of personality as an important area of inquiry came from the acknowledgment and embrace of the Big Five factor model of personality, which did much to organize a rather disparate area of inquiry. The Big Five factors—neuroticism, extraversion, openness to experience,

agreeableness, and conscientiousness—were identified first by Tupes and Christal (1961), who found through factor-analytic techniques that long lists of personality variables compiled by Cattell (1943, 1945) could be reduced to five broad-band personality factors. This five-factor structure has since been replicated in diverse samples and across numerous raters, such as self-reports, peers, and clinicians (John & Srivastava, 1999). In this chapter, we organize discussion of personality and parenting around these core dimensions of personality before proceeding in a final subsection to consider psychological mechanisms that may account for how personality comes to be related to parenting (see Belsky & Barends, 2002). Once again, it is important not to lose sight of the very real possibility that linkages detected to date between personality and parenting are genetically mediated. Having said that, attention should be directed to Spinath and O'Connor's (2003, p. 786) recently reported study of 300 pairs of adult twins (from Germany) showing that "the moderate phenotypic covariation between personality and parenting was attributed largely to nongenetic factors."

Neuroticism

Neuroticism reflects adjustment versus emotional instability, and measures of neuroticism identify individuals prone to psychological distress, unrealistic ideas, excessive cravings or urges, and maladaptive coping responses. A person scoring high on this trait worries a lot; is nervous; emotional, and insecure; and feels inadequate, whereas a person scoring low is calm, relaxed, unemotional, hardy, secure, and self-satisfied. Because factor-analytic studies indicate that indices of the negative emotions of anxiety, hostility, and depression all load on a single factor (Costa & McCrae, 1992), whether measured as states or traits, some prefer to use the term negative affectivity rather than neuroticism (Tellegen, Watson, & Clark, 1999; Watson & Clark, 1984).

The important point is less what this trait is called than what this trait reflects. And the fact that it reflects the proclivity or disposition to experience anxiety and hostility as well as depression raises important questions about the plethora of work carried out on depression and mothering in the field of developmental psychology over the past 2 decades. In point of fact, one is forced to wonder whether studies in which only depression is measured actually present evidence pertaining only to depression and mothering or, instead, negative affectivity more generally, including anxiety and hostility. Until these other negative emotion facets of neuroticism are examined in studies (of normal samples) that also include measures of depression (for a singular good example, see Leinonen, Solantaus, & Punamaki, 2003), it will be impossible to address this issue.

The fact that the empirical literature is the way it is means that much of the work to be considered in this section deals with depression. But because the effect of psychopathology on parenting has already been considered, we restrict ourselves here to research dealing with depression measured as a continuous variable in nonclinical samples. We begin with investigations focused on parents of infants and then proceed developmentally from that point forward. The reader will note a great deal of consistency between findings from studies reviewed previously dealing with clinical samples and the work considered here focused on nonclinical samples.

During the infancy period, maternal depression has been the facet of neuroticism that has received the most empirical attention. Although the evidence is not without some inconsistency, there is repeated indication, even in nonclinical samples, that when mothers experience more versus fewer symptoms of depression, they provide less sensitive care to their infants. This result emerged in the work of the NICHD Early Child Care Research Network (1999), in which depression was repeatedly measured in a sample of more than 1,000 mothers, as was maternal sensitivity, across the first 3 years of the child's life. Relatedly, Crockenberg (1987b) reported in a study of teenage mothers that those experiencing more psychological distress engaged in more simple custodial and unstimulating care of their infants than other mothers. And when Zaslow, Pedersen, Cain, Suwalsky, and Kramer (1985) examined relations between mothers' feeling "blue" on 8 or more days since the birth of their 4-month-old children and maternal behavior, they observed that increased depression predicted less smiling at, less speaking with, and less touching of the infant. In addition to undermining active involvement with the infant, negative affectivity may also promote negative and intrusive maternal behavior, as Diener and colleagues (Diener, Mangelsdorf, Contrerae, Hazelwood, & Rhodes, 1995; Goldstein, Diener, & Mangelsdorf, 1996) discovered on observing adolescent Latino mothers with their 3- to 24-month-olds.

During the preschool and middle childhood years, similar results were obtained. In one investigation of rural African American and European American families, for example, high levels of emotional distress (i.e., anxiety, depression, irritability) among mothers were related to low levels of positive parenting (e.g., hugs, praise) and high levels of negative parenting (e.g., threats, slaps, derogatory statements) and also strong endorsement of authoritarian child-rearing values during the course of structured parent-child interactions (Conger, McCarty, Yang, Lakey, & Kropp, 1984). In more recent research, Kanoy, Ulku-Steiner, Cox, and Burchinal (2003) found that higher levels of hostility, one facet of neuroticism, measured during pregnancy predicted high levels of physical punishment when children were 2 and 5 years of age in the case of both mothers and fathers. In other recent work, Kochanska, Aksan, and Nichols (2003) found that mothers scoring higher on neuroticism engaged in more power-assertive parenting when interacting with their 14- to 54-month-old children in a laboratory setting designed to evoked parental discipline. When Zelkowitz (1982) studied poor African American and European American mothers of 5- to 7-year-olds, she further observed that high levels of anxiety and depression predicted high expectations for immediate compliance on the part of the child, but inconsistency in following up such demands when the child did not comply. Furthermore, high levels of psychological distress were associated with more hostile and dominating behavior, less reliance on reasoning and loss of privileges when disciplining the child, and more intensive demands for the child's involvement in household maintenance (Longfellow, Zelkowitz, & Saunders, 1982).

During the teenage years, neuroticism or negative affectivity continues to be associated with problematic parenting. For example, Gondoli and Silverberg (1997) reported that mothers who experienced emotional distress (i.e., depression, anxiety, low self-efficacy) were less accepting of their teen's behavior during problem-solving discussions and were less supportive of the child's psychological autonomy than other mothers. In an analysis of almost 1,000 mothers and fathers of 10- to 17-year-olds interviewed as part of a national survey, Voydanoff and Donnelly (1988) found that feeling sad, blue, tense, tired, and overwhelmed was related to parents not participating in activities with their children, though such negative affectivity proved unrelated to parental monitoring. In a series of researches, Conger and associates (1992, 1993; Conger, Patterson, & Ge, 1995; Simons et al., 1993a) studied family interaction patterns in a large sample of Iowa farm families and discerned both direct and indirect effects of negative affectivity on maternal and paternal behavior. Not only did depression predict more harsh and inconsistent discipline on the part of both mothers and fathers (Conger et al., 1995; Simons, Beaman, Conger, & Chao, 1993b) and less nurturant behavior by both parents when interacting with sons (Conger et al., 1992), though not daughters (Conger et al., 1993), but in the case of both mothers and fathers with sons and daughters, elevated levels of depression predicted increased marital conflict and, thereby, lower levels of nurturant parenting (Conger et al., 1992, 1993). Such indirect pathways of influence of parents' general psychological functioning on their parenting are consistent with Belsky's (1984) process model of the determinants of parenting. Finally, Brody, Murry, Kim, and Brown (2002) have recently shown that higher levels of depression (in concert with lower levels of optimism and self-esteem) predict less involved/vigilant parenting and lower quality mother-teen discussions in their short-term longitudinal study of 150 African American families living in single-parent families in the rural South.

In sum, whether one considers research on infants, toddlers, preschoolers, school-age children, or adolescents, there is repeated indication that high levels of depression, even in nonclinical samples, and of other facets of neuroticism, including anxiety and irritability/hostility, are related to less competent parenting. This effect can take the form of less active and involved parenting, as well as more negative, intrusive, and overcontrolling parenting.

Extraversion

Extraversion reflects the quantity and intensity of interpersonal interaction, activity level, need for stimulation, and capacity for joy that characterize individuals. A person scoring high on extraversion is considered sociable, active, talkative, person-oriented, optimistic, fun-loving, and affectionate, whereas a low-scoring individual is reserved, sober, unexuberant, aloof, task-oriented, retiring, and quiet. One might anticipate, on the basis of this description, that extraverted individuals might function better as parents than less extraverted parents, if only because parenting is a social task involving another, though dependent, person. On the other hand, one might imagine that high levels of extraversion and especially of sociability might predispose one to be more interested in more social exchange than might be experienced by a parent, particularly one who remains home all day with children.

Although the database is by no means extensive, in general the evidence is supportive of the first prediction, namely, that of a positive association between extraversion and sensitive, responsive, emotionally engaged, and stimulating parenting. True virtually to the definition of extraversion, Levy-Shiff and Israelashvilli (1988) found that Israeli men scoring high on this construct manifested more positive affect and engaged in more toy play and teaching when interacting with their 9-month-olds in their homes than men scoring low on extraversion. Mangelsdorf and her colleagues (1990) detected similar personality-parenting associations when studying mothers of 9-month-olds. And

Belsky, Crnic, and Woodworth (1995) essentially replicated both sets of results during the course of naturalistic home observations with mothers, fathers, and their 15- and 21-month-old toddlers. These investigators reported that mothers and fathers alike who were more extraverted expressed more positive affect toward their children and were more sensitive and cognitively stimulating when observed at home late in the afternoon and early in the evening. Finally, in a study of mothers, fathers, and their children up to 8 years of age, more extraverted parents reported engaging in more positive supportive parenting, such as displaying positive affection and encouraging independence (Losoya et al., 1997). Apparently, the link between extraversion and positive parenting is not restricted to the infant-toddler period. To date, however, there are no studies linking this personality trait with parenting during the adolescent years.

Agreeableness

Agreeableness reflects one's interpersonal orientation along a continuum from compassion to antagonism in thoughts, feelings, and actions. A person scoring high on this trait is soft-hearted, good-natured, trusting, helpful, forgiving, gullible, and straightforward, whereas a person scoring low is cynical, rude, suspicious, uncooperative, vengeful, ruthless, irritable, and manipulative. Clearly, the basic prediction regarding parenting would be that more agreeable individuals would make better parents, at least from the child's perspective. As it turns out, only a handful of studies have examined the relation between this particular personality trait and parenting, three of which have just been mentioned and one of which failed to chronicle any linkage between agreeableness and parenting reported by a large sample of German parents (Spinath & O'Connor, 2003). In the aforementioned toddler work by Belsky et al. (1995), higher levels of agreeableness predicted greater maternal (but not paternal) positive affect and sensitivity and lower levels of negative affect and intrusive-overcontrolling behavior. In more recent research with toddlers and preschoolers, Kochanska et al. (2003) found that mothers scoring higher on agreeableness engaged in less power-assertive discipline when observed in a series of structured laboratory situations. Consistent with these findings, Losoya et al. (1997) found in their study of parents with children as old as 8 that agreeableness was positively associated with supportive parenting and negatively associated with negatively controlling parenting. Kochanska, Clark, and Goldman (1997) reported that lower levels of agreeableness were related to more power-assertive and less responsive parenting in their study of young children, although in other research by this team, only the agreeableness-responsiveness association was replicated (L. A. Clark et al., 2000). Clearly, the evidence just reviewed is rather consistent with the hypothesis originally advanced.

Openness to Experience

The person who is open to experience tends to enjoy new experiences, have broad interests, and be very imaginative; in contrast, a person scoring low on this trait is down-to-earth, practical, traditional, and pretty much set in his or her ways. Predictions from this trait to parenting are less straightforward than was the case with respect to the other Big Five traits considered to this point. Only three investigations have explored this topic, with one showing that Israeli fathers who were more open to experience engaged in more basic caregiving of their infants than fathers less open to experience (Levy-Shiff & Isarelashvilli, 1988), perhaps because the father role itself is a new experience worth exploring for these highly open men. The other study found that openness was positively related to positive parenting for mothers and fathers alike (Losoya et al., 1997). Finally, Spinath and O'Connor (2003, p. 803) found that German parents who were less open to experience engaged in more overprotective parenting, a result they explained by speculating that "individuals who are themselves not open to experiences" tend to "restrict the behaviors or intrude on the activities of their children."

Conscientiousness

Conscientiousness reflects the extent to which a person is well-organized and has high standards, always striving to achieve his or her goals. Thus, a person who scores low on conscientiousness is easygoing, not very well organized, tending toward carelessness, and preferring not to make plans. Once again, it is not exactly clear how this trait should relate to parental behavior, as it seems eminently possible that, however attractive high conscientious may appear, especially to an employer, it could prove too demanding to a child. At the same time, disorder and chaos, in contrast to organization, are typically not in children's best interests, so one could imagine low levels of conscientiousness also predicting parental behavior that might not be especially supportive of children's functioning. The study by Losoya et al. (1997) that examined this trait in relation to the child-rearing attitudes and practices of mothers and fathers with children under 8 years of age found conscientiousness to be positively related to supportive parenting

and negatively related to negative, controlling parenting. L. A. Clark and associates (2000) chronicled a similar relationship when looking at mothers of toddlers, finding that more conscientious mothers are more responsive and less power-assertive than less conscientious mothers. Although results of these two studies begin to suggest that conscientiousness and positive parenting go together, it should be noted that one German study failed to chronicle any significant linkage between this dimension of personality and four reliable, self-report measures of parenting (Spinath & O'Connor, 2003).

Processes Linking Personality and Parenting

This summary of research on personality and parenting makes it clear that if one had to choose a parent to provide care for oneself, one's development would likely benefit from choosing a parent who is low in neuroticism, high in extraversion and agreeableness, and perhaps high in openness to experience and conscientiousness. This is because these kinds of individuals have been repeatedly found to provide care that is more supportive, sensitive, responsive, and intellectually stimulating, almost irrespective of the child's age, though it must be acknowledged that, with the exception perhaps of recent work on negative affectivity (i.e., neuroticism), most research on the role of personality in shaping parenting has been carried out on parents of younger rather than older children. It is encouraging, nevertheless, that in the time since Belsky (1984) advanced his model of the determinants of parenting there is so much research to report on fathering.

It is one thing to observe, as we have, that a parent's personality is predictive of his or her parenting, and quite another to understand the mechanisms responsible for this relationship. Two possibilities that have received some limited attention in the literature deserve more attention in the future. The first involves attributions; the second, mood and emotion.

There is increasing appreciation in developmental research that attributions play an important role in close relationship processes, including in the parent-child relationship. More specifically, models of social cognition that have been advanced in the marital, developmental, and social psychology literatures (e.g., Bradbury & Fincham, 1990; Dix, Ruble, & Zamarano, 1989; Dodge, 1986) have been applied to the study of parenting (e.g., Bugental & Happaney, 2002; Bugental & Shennum, 1984). For example, it has been shown that parents who think their child is whining because he or she is tired are inclined to respond to the child in a manner quite different (i.e., sensitive) from when they believe the child is trying to manipulate them. Thus, Bugental and Shennum were able to show that mothers with more dysfunctional attributional styles responded to children in ways that maintained or enhanced the child's difficult behavior, a finding that was experimentally reproduced by Slep and O'Leary (1988) by manipulating parental attributions in a challenging situation. Relatedly, Johnston and Patenaude (1994) found that parents were more likely to regard oppositional-defiant child behavior as under the child's control than inattentive-overreactive behavior, and this accounted for why the former evoked more negative parental reactions than the latter.

The fact that such attributions predict much the same parenting behavior that personality characteristics predict raises the possibility that one means by which personality shapes parenting is via attributions. Is it the case, as seems likely, for example, that it is neurotic rather than agreeable parents who are most likely to attribute negative intent to their young children when they misbehave? And if so, does this dynamic account for why these personality traits predict parenting in the ways that they do?

Because attributions themselves are linked to emotion, it is reasonable to wonder further about the role that emotion plays in mediating the effect of personality on parenting. After all, in the aforementioned experimental study by Slep and O'Leary (1998), the manipulation of mothers' attributions affected the degree to which they felt angry with their children. Emotion, of course, is central to the personality traits of neuroticism, also labeled negative affectivity, and extraversion, sometimes referred to in terms of positive affectivity.

Two studies to date have examined the mediating role of emotion in accounting for personality-parenting relations. In a German investigation of almost 300 families with 8- to 14-year-old sons, Engfer and Schneewind (1982) showed, via path analysis, that maternal irritability and nervousness (i.e., neuroticism) promoted the harsh punishment of their children via mother's proneness to anger. Belsky et al. (1995) tested and found some support for an "affect-specific" process whereby personality affects mood and, thereby, parenting, in their home-observational study of families rearing 15- and 21-month old sons: Whereas extraversion with its emphasis on the experience of positive emotions predicted mothers' expressions of positive but not negative affect toward their toddlers, neuroticism with its emphasis on the experience of negative emotions predicted mothers' expressions of negative but not positive affect. In light of these results and those concerning attributions, it seems appropriate to encourage further work examining the mediating role of attributions and emo-

tion in accounting for some personality-parenting linkages, including the proposition that personality $\rightarrow$ emotion $\rightarrow$ attribution $\rightarrow$ parenting.

THE MARITAL/PARTNER RELATIONSHIP

A well-acknowledged fact, dating back as far as the 1930s, about the marital relationship and child psychopathology is that antisocial, aggressive, or otherwise problematical child behavior is found disproportionately in children growing up in families in which marital/partner relations are distressed and/or highly conflicted (Cummings & Davies, 2002; Emery, 1989; Fincham, 2003; Grych, 2002). Indeed, growing up in a high-conflict family or one in which discord and disharmony characterize the spousal relationship is known to be associated with externalizing disorders, including excessive aggression, unacceptable conduct, vandalism, noncompliance, and delinquency; dysfunctional social skills and relationships with peers and adults; as well as diminished academic performance, manifested by poor school grades and teachers' reports of problems in intellectual achievement and abilities (Cummings & Davies, 1994; Depner, Leino, & Chun, 1992; Reid & Crisafulli, 1990). In all likelihood, some of this association between troubled marital/partner relations and problematic child development is spurious, rather than causal, reflecting the correlated effects of heritable processes shared by parent(s) and child. Moreover, it is widely appreciated that some of the invariably causal contribution of marital distress to problematic child behavior is direct, emanating from children's exposure to conflict, especially unresolved, angry conflict (for review, see Cummings & Davies, 1994). Processes involving modeling and contagious emotion dysregulation have been posited to account for such direct effects of marriage on child functioning (Davies & Cummings, 1994; B. Wilson & Gottman, 2002). But it is also apparent that some of the association between distressed marriage and child dysfunction is mediated via parenting and parent-child relationship processes (Belsky, 1981, 1984; Elder, 1974; Engfer, 1988; Erel & Burman, 1995; Grych, 2002; Levendosky et al., 2003).

Belsky (1981) was among the first to draw attention to the need of developmentalists and clinicians to study marriage, parenting, and child development, pointing out that the scholarly investigation of these domains of inquiry was dispersed across distinctive and all too often unrelated literatures and even academic fields. Family sociologists, for example, paid a great deal of attention to marital quality, especially as it changed across the transition to parenthood and the life course more generally, but had little to say (at the time) about parenting and child development. Clinical psychologists, in contrast, focused on marital distress and child behavior problems but paid limited attention (at the time) to parenting. And developmental psychologists, who studied parenting and child development, usually within the normal range of functioning, treated the adults in the family (at the time) as if their only social roles were that of parent, basically ignoring the marital relationship. Over the past 2 decades, the study of family processes and child development have changed dramatically, so what once were disciplinarily isolated areas of inquiry have become much more interrelated.

One of the major forces of change in the study of child development in the family was the recognized need, back in the 1970s, to pay more attention to the role of the father. Belsky (1981) noted, for example, that once the father was added to the more traditional study of mother-child relationships, the complexity of the family changed, with a need to focus not only on an additional parent-child relationship, but on the relationship between parents—the marriage—and one that often existed prior to the arrival of children. Early students of the father-infant relationship emphasized the fact that the influence of the father on child functioning might be primarily indirect and mediated by the wife in her capacity as mother (e.g., Parke, 1978; Pedersen, Yarrow, Anderson, & Cain, 1978). When examined from the perspective of today, it is clear that a number of viewpoints highlight the role and nature of the marriage in shaping parenting and parent-child relationships (Grych, 2002). These will be discussed in turn before turning to consider empirical findings from the literature. All, it should be noted, are consistent with Belsky's (1981, 1984) claim that the marital relationship was the first-order support system for parents, especially mothers, and thus likely to impact parenting behavior.

Processes and Perspectives on the Marriage-Parenting Relationship

As Grych (2002) has pointed out, most (explicit or implicit) models of parenting presume some kind of affective spillover from the marriage to the parent-child relationship, though they differ in terms of the processes involved. In this section, we consider several alternative, but not mutually exclusive, models of influence.

Affective Spillover and Withdrawal

The notion that linkages exist between the quality of the marriage and in the nature and/or quality of parenting be-

cause emotions experienced in one relationship spill over and affect the other relationship is a guiding assumption in marriage-parenting research. From this perspective, anger and hostility that emerge from interactions and relations between husband and wife come to contaminate the way parents relate to their children. From a more encouraging standpoint, feelings of satisfaction, pleasure, and love emanating from the partner relationship help fuel positive and growth-promoting parenting practices.

A great deal of marriage-parenting research can be interpreted in terms of affective spillover, such as Goldberg et al.'s (2002) recent finding of a positive and significant association between self-reported marital adjustment and the expression of affection by fathers when interacting with their 6-month-olds. But it is rare for the measures of marriage and parenting to be affect-specific, as many focus on general marital quality or satisfaction (Grych, 2002). Easterbrooks and Emde (1988) provide a fortunate exception. In their study of the transition to parenthood, marital harmony, measured via observational assessments of spousal interaction, proved related to the affect-sharing, physical affection, and expression of approval that parents evinced while interacting with their infants.

Negative affective spillover also characterizes the marriage-parenting relationship. But feelings of negativity in the marriage may not always take an identical form in the parent-child relationship. In fact, rather than anger experienced in the marriage manifesting itself directly in the parent-child relationship, it may foster withdrawal. Parents who are distressed and overwhelmed by difficulties in their marriage may simply lack the emotional energy to engage their children. Osborne and Fincham (1996) noted that when this happens, lax or permissive parents can be experienced by their children as rejecting. Evidence indicates, interestingly, that greater interparental hostility is related to withdrawal in the parent-child relationship (Lindhal, Clements, & Markman, 1997; Lindahl & Malik, 1999) and that spouse's withdrawal during marital conflict is related to greater hostility and intrusiveness with children (Katz & Gottman, 1996; Lindahl & Malik, 1999).

Stress and Coping

Although, in theory at least, a marriage in contemporary culture is supposed to nurture and support the self, the sad fact of the matter is that all too often it is a source of stress that overwhelms the coping capacities of the adults involved (Belsky, 1984). Thus, parents who are busy dealing with a troubled marriage lack the energy and attention required to deal with children in sensitive, supportive ways. Of course, stress that overwhelms or even challenges coping capacities can evoke negative emotion, and so spillover processes and stress-coping ones can be difficult to distinguish when it comes to accounting for the impact of the marital relationship on parenting. Grych and Clark (1999) documented the undermining effects of marital stress in showing that when infants were 1 year of age and costs emanating from the marriage were high (e.g., fighting, being criticized) and rewards low (e.g., good communication, effective conflict resolution), fathers found it more difficult to balance parenting with other roles and responsibilities, felt less competent as a parent, and found interacting with the infant less rewarding.

But in addition to marriage serving as a source of stress, well-functioning marriages can function as a source of support. In a good marriage, the partner not only provides love, attention, and consideration, but is instrumentally helpful, too. Such activities and experiences can foster the very energy, attention, and motivation that is essential for the continual provision of growth-supporting parenting. Consider, in this regard, Cox, Owen, Lewis, and Henderson's (1989) findings showing that when marital partners experienced greater emotional closeness, as reflected in shared ideas and activities, expressed affection and appreciation, and mutual confiding, mothers evinced greater warmth and sensitivity when interacting with their infant daughters (but not sons) and fathers manifested more positive attitudes toward the infant and the parenting role (though no effect on fathering behavior was detected).

A supportive marriage can also serve to protect or buffer the parent-child relationship from stresses emanating from other sources (Belsky, 1984), whether it be the parent's experience at work, relations with friends and relatives, or even dealings with other children. When considered from this perspective, a well-functioning marriage can enable a parent who might otherwise prove to be less attentive, caring, and affectionate with his or her child to sustain such qualities in the face of challenges emanating from outside of the marital relationship. Some of the most compelling evidence for such an effect comes from Crockenberg and McClusky's (1986) research showing that the otherwise detectable and negative effect of the infant's difficult temperament on the quality of mothering received was not evident when high levels of spouse support were in evidence.

Family Systems Theory

Family systems theory is actually less a theory, at least as drawn on by empirically minded family researchers, than a philosophical perspective derived from Von Bertallanfy's (1950) writings about general systems theory by family therapists struggling to understand linkages between distressed marriages and disordered children (S. Minuchin, 1974). Central to the theory/perspective is the notion that the family system comprises hierarchically ordered power relations among its members (i.e., parents, children) and "boundaries" that shape the ways interactions among members of varying status (should) take place. Also important is the notion of bidirectional and even circular causal processes, rather than simple linear ones, and the prospect that as open systems, families are subject to influence—both supportive and undermining—of forces emanating from outside of the family (e.g., the workplace, the school, the neighborhood; Cox & Paley, 1997; P. Minuchin, 1985).

Students of family systems theory highlight two processes to account for why troubled marriages may undermine growth-promoting parenting (and the converse). Adult partners whose emotional needs go unmet, or are insufficiently met, in the spousal relation are hypothesized to compensate by seeking a more intimate relationship with their child, risking the development of an enmeshed or excessively close relationship that fails to provide sufficient autonomy, especially psychological autonomy, to the child. The prospect also arises that as a result of a problematic relationship between the child and one parent, the other parent endeavors to make up for this liability through excessive involvement with the child.

There are certainly data that are consistent with such thinking. Consider, in this regard, Belsky, Youngblade, Rovine, and Volling's (1991) finding from a study of more than 100 families raising toddlers that when an intrusive father-child relationship coincided with a deteriorating marital relationship, the mother-child relationship often appeared very positive, characterized by high (and perhaps too high) levels of positive and facilitative behavior directed by the mother to the child. Of course, rather than reflecting an effort by the mother to compensate for the problematic father-child relationship, such results might be a function of mother's attempt to compensate for a dissatisfying marriage, which itself undermined the father's sensitivity to the needs of the child (Grych, 2002). Such an interpretation would be in line with Engfer's (1988) finding that mothers reporting high levels of marital conflict when infants were 4 months of age, also reported greater emotional involvement and proved to be more protective of their children 14 months later than other mothers.

Family therapists working from a family systems framework have also emphasized boundary-violation processes such as triangulation, detouring, and scapegoating in an attempt to explain marriage-parenting relations (Grych, 2002). Triangulation refers to a cross-boundary process whereby husband-wife conflict is avoided by involving the child (S. Minuchin, 1974). When detouring or scapegoating characterizes this form of family dysfunction, the child becomes the focus of problems, particularly his or her supposedly troublesome behavior or illness, and difficulties in the marital/partner relationship itself are ignored. One anticipated consequence of such detouring is increased hostility toward and/or overinvolvement with the child. It may also be the case that a cross-generational coalition is established between one parent and the child that serves to position the other parent as an outsider. Such diverted emotional involvement with the child can be excessive, generating enmeshment, which can itself be an additional source of conflict between husband and wife, as one spouse finds the other spouse's level of involvement with the child beyond what might be regarded as normal or appropriate (see Margolin, Oliver, & Medina, 2001). Studying this process, Christensen and Margolin (1988) found that in troubled marriages, cross-generational coalitions were more evident and that conflict in the marriage was likely to contaminate the parent-child relationship. Kerig (1995) reported similar results in a study in which parents represented through hand-drawn and interlocking circles the nature of family relationships, finding that when cross-generational coalitions were pronounced, so was marital conflict. In a relevant longitudinal study, Lindahl et al. (1997) discovered that when fathers contributed more to the negative escalation of marital conflict, 5 years later they were more likely to involve (i.e., triangulate) their child in a family discussion task inappropriately.

Conclusion: Cause or Correlation?

Drawing formal lines between the models and mechanisms discussed linking marriage and parenting can be challenging, basically because there are not strict boundaries between the various perspectives considered. Parents who are stressed, for example, are likely to get angry, and such anger can contaminate the parent-child relationship. When this happens, is it a result of affective spillover, inability to cope in the face of stress, boundary violations, or some combination of the three? In point of fact, it may prove difficult to identify pure forms of these processes, as they are so often inextricably linked.

But a bigger cause for concern may be that even when (correlational) evidence emerges consistent with these models of marriage-to-parenting influence, such as that to be considered next, it may be inappropriate to draw strong causal inferences. This is because a "common factor" might be responsible for both the nature of the marital relationship and the parent-child one (Grych, 2002). As Belsky (1984) noted, the fact that the same psychological

agent—the spouse/parent—is involved in both the marriage and the parent-child relationship raises the prospect that a "third variable" reflecting enduring dispositional characteristics of the adult may account for the apparent effect of marriage on parenting. After all, it is not unlikely that an individual who had difficulty sustaining an emotionally supportive relationship with a partner may bring some of those same liabilities to his or her relationship with the child. It should not be forgotten that the husband and father are (often) one and the same person, as are the mother and wife.

Certainly consistent with this point of view is evidence from Engfer's (1988) aforementioned study showing that the personal psychological characteristics of neuroticism, depressiveness, and composure were associated with indices of both marriage and of parenting. Relatedly, Caspi and Elder's (1988) analysis of data from the Berkeley Growth Study indicated that adult personality drives both the marital and the parent-child relationship. The fact that most studies of marriage and parenting fail to appreciate, at least empirically, that the person filling the marital and parental roles are one and the same makes unclear the extent to which marriage is only correlated with parenting, as opposed to influencing it. Cox and associates (1989) have addressed this issue, finding evidence that even after taking into consideration parents' mental health, marital closeness predicted fathers' attitudes toward parenting and maternal sensitivity in interacting with daughters.

Empirical Findings Linking Marriage and Parenting

Although it was the case that the first work linking marriage and child development focused on children old enough to be diagnosed with behavior problems, most of the initial work examining marriage and parenting focused on the infant years. This is because it was developmental psychologists interested in the father-infant relationship who first recognized the failure of students of the family and of child development to simultaneously study marriage, parenting, and child development (Belsky, 1981). Thus, it remains the case that most of the relevant research, as even the earlier discussion suggests, has focused on infants. In recent years, however, this developmental base has broadened. In what follows, we review—illustratively rather than exhaustively—research documenting linkages between marriage and parenting as a function of the child's developmental status, considering first work on parent-infant relationships, then parent-child relationships, and finally parent-adolescent relationships. Thereafter, very recent work looking at what happens to parenting when the marital relationship turns violent is considered.

The Infant/Toddler Years

Sensitive-responsive parenting has been identified as promoting a secure infant-parent attachment, and cognitively stimulating interchanges between parent and infant/toddler have been identified as promoting early cognitive and language development. Thus, it is not surprising that these are the targets of parenting and of the parent-child relationships that investigators focused on during the child's first 2 to 3 years of life. Perhaps the earliest study was that reported by Pedersen (1975, 1982; Pedersen, Anderson, & Cain, 1977), now almost 3 decades old, showing that tension and conflict between husband and wife—as reported by fathers—predicted less observed maternal sensitivity and responsiveness when feeding the infant, whereas husband's esteem for the wife as a mother, reflecting direct emotional support, predicted greater maternal feeding competence.

As already noted, work by Cox and associates (1989), who measured marital closeness and intimacy by means of observational and self-report measures, demonstrated that such linkages between marriage and observed parent-infant interaction could not be fully explained by parental mental health, thereby suggesting a truly causal role for the marriage in shaping parenting. In a somewhat later study, Heinicke (1984) found that marital adjustment measured before the infant was even born predicted greater parental responsiveness to the child's needs (but not parental cognitive stimulation), not only when the child was 1 month of age, but 4 years later. In another study of the transition to parenthood, Cowan and Cowan (1992) observed that the more marital quality declined through the first 18 months postpartum, the more cold, competitive, and angry were marital interactions when children were 3.5 years of age; such patterning of marital conflict was itself related to lower expressions of warmth toward the child by mother and father, especially toward daughters. Notable is that in research on mothers rearing chronically undernourished infants in urban poverty in Chile, Valenzuela (1997) also found that martial satisfaction predicted greater maternal sensitivity.

In contrast to being sensitively responsive, parenting of an infant can be ill timed and intrusive. When Belsky and associates (1991) observed the fathering of men whose marriage had been repeatedly measured from the last trimester of pregnancy through 3 years postpartum, they found that men whose marriage decreased in love and whose feelings about their marital relationship increased in ambivalence more so than other men interacted with their

36-month-old children in a more affectively negative and overcontrolling-intrusive style than did other men (see also Cowan & Cowan, 1992). The fact that no similar relations emerged in the case of mothers in the Belsky et al. investigation, a result consistent with those from an earlier cross-sectional study of marriage and parenting (Belsky, 1979), seemed consistent with Belsky's conclusion that fathering may be more susceptible to marital influence than mothering, perhaps because fathering, especially during the infant years, is less scripted by social convention. Such differential results for mothers and fathers also emerged in Goldberg and Easterbrooks's (1984) study of toddlers, as they observed that greater marital quality predicted greater paternal though not maternal sensitivity (see also Volling & Belsky, 1991).

Before embracing the notion that fathering is more susceptible to marital influence than mothering, it is necessary to call attention to Erel and Burman's (1995) meta-analysis of 68 studies addressing the relationship between marriage and parenting. Despite repeated indications that marriage-parenting relations were stronger in the case of fathers than mothers, they failed to detect evidence that parent gender moderated the sizable and significant marriage-parenting relationship they detected across studies of children of all ages. What they were not in a position to determine, however, even given the seemingly large sample size they had to work with, was whether differential marriage-parenting relationships might obtain for mothers and fathers at some developmental periods rather than at others. Also of note is that when Krishnakumar and Buehler (2000) carried out their own meta-analysis of 39 studies a few years later, focused exclusively on interparental conflict (i.e., not marital satisfaction, cohesion), they detected a stronger marriage-parenting relationship in the case of fathers.

Not all relevant studies of marriage and parenting during the infancy period focus on parenting per se, as some research examines the quality of the parent-child relationship, usually by measuring the security of the infant-parent attachment relationship. This work also highlights positive associations between well- (or poorly) functioning marriages and well- (or poorly) functioning parent-child relationships. Indeed, three separate studies indicate that secure infant-parent attachment is related to higher marital quality, either measured contemporaneously (Goldberg & Easterbrooks, 1984), earlier in time (Howes & Markman, 1989), or repeatedly over time (Belsky & Isabella, 1988). Thus, for example, Howe and Markman observed that higher levels of marital satisfaction and communication quality and lower levels of interparental conflict were associated with secure rather than insecure attachments, and Isabella and Belsky (1985) found that deteriorating marital quality was related to insecure infant-mother (though not infant-father) attachment.

The Preschool and Childhood Years

Investigations linking marital relations and parenting during the preschool and middle childhood years are generally consistent with those just summarized that focus on parenting during the first 3 years of life. Two classic studies meriting attention are one by Bandura and Walters (1959) showing that mothers inclined to nag and scold their sons felt less warmth and affection toward their husband, and another by Sears, Maccoby, and Levin (1957) indicating that mothers' professed esteem for their husband is systematically related to the praise they direct at their preschool children. More recently, Katz and Gottman (1996) observed dyadic and triadic family interaction in households with 4- to 5-year-old children; they found that hostility in the marriage predicted father intrusiveness and reduced levels of father involvement. When fathers withdrew from marital conflict, mothers were found to be more intrusive and critical of their young children but less involved in interacting with them.

Lindahl and Malik (1999) also documented the relationship between troubled marriage and problematic fathering in their study of Latin American and European American families rearing 7- to 11-year-old boys. Fathers in couples showing destructive conflict styles during a marital interaction task (as opposed to harmonious or disengaged styles) evinced greater rejection and withdrawal when observed interacting with their sons, and this was especially so when marriages were otherwise characterized as highly distressed. In an earlier study, this one of parents of 4.5- to 6.5-year-olds, Stoneman, Brody, and Burke (1989) found that fathers who were in happier and less conflicted marriages proved more consistent in enforcing limits placed on child behavior, a pattern of parenting known to increase the likelihood of children's complying with parental directives. More recently, Harrist and Ainslie (1998) reported that marital conflict predicted lower-quality interactions between parents and their children. In the course of studying the determinants of sibling relations, two separate teams of investigators detected linkages between marriage and parenting. Erel, Margolin, and John (1998) found that, in families with 3- to 8-year-olds, negative marital relations forecast elevated levels of maternal power assertion; Stocker and Youngblade (1999) reported that marital conflict predicted maternal and paternal hostility toward 7- and 10-year-olds. When Katz and Woodin (2002) drew distinctions between couples rearing 4- to 5-year-olds on

the basis of communication during a high-conflict marital discussion task, they found that spouses who emphasized the negative when speaking to their partner and who were poor listeners were most likely to issue commands to their offspring during a family interaction assessment.

Although the general trend is for marital quality and parenting to be positively related, such that poorer-functioning marriages and parent-child relations go together, this is not always the case. In the research by Stoneman et al. (1989), for example, parents of boys in happier marriages were more likely than those in less happy marriages to rely on authoritarian discipline, and fathers who reported more conflict in their marriage were less likely to report relying on authoritarian disciplinary strategies than other fathers. Moreover, and consistent with family systems conceptions of boundary violations, Brody, Pillegrini, and Sigel (1986) reported in a study of parent-child interaction during book reading and teaching tasks that the more conflict mothers reported in their marriage, the more engaged they were while teaching their 5.5- to 7.5-year-old children, asking more questions, offering more information, and providing more positive feedback. Belsky et al. (1991) drew attention to this work on finding, in their own study of parenting 3-year-olds during a teaching task, that declines in marital satisfaction across the transition to parenthood were associated with positive and facilitative parenting.

Clearly, it would be a mistake to conclude that parenting is invariably more supportive, warmer, and less rejecting in the preschool and middle childhood years when parents are happier or more satisfied in their marriage. Nevertheless, this does appear to be the main trend in the evidence. The exceptions to the rule raise interesting questions about the conditions under which, to say nothing of the mechanisms by which, anticipated relationships between marriage and parenting are just the opposite of what was expected (at least by spillover and stress and coping perspectives).

The Adolescent Years

It is only relatively recently that the interrelationship of marriage and parenting during the adolescent years has attracted empirical attention. Major parenting issues during this developmental period follow on from those of the middle childhood years, having to do with the management of discipline and, especially, the child's emerging autonomy (in the face of dramatic biological and social changes). Thus, concern is not only for whether parents enact authoritative parenting practices characterized by high levels of warmth and control or authoritarian ones (low warmth, high control), but also whether they monitor their child's whereabouts. Parents who score low on control but high on warmth are often regarded as permissive, and those low in both warmth and control as neglectful.

Harold and Conger (1997; Harold, Fincham, Osborne, & Conger, 1997) examined the relationship between marital quality and parental rejection in a short-term longitudinal study of more than 400 seventh-grade children living in rural Iowa. Couples that evinced more hostility during the course of a husband-wife interaction episode (i.e., being critical, shouting, yelling, expressing anger) were, according to adolescent reports, more rejecting as parents 1 year later. These results were consistent with those obtained by Fauber, Forehand, Thomas, and Wierson (1990), who observed that higher levels of interparental conflict predicted greater maternal rejection and psychological control (but not lax control), as measured via videotaped interactions of mother and teen and teen reports of parenting, in their analysis of 46 maritally intact families rearing 11- to 15-year-olds. A much larger study based on a nationally representative survey of almost 1,000 families rearing 12- to 18-year-olds also reported marital conflict to predict greater use of harsh discipline by parents and, relatedly, more parent-adolescent conflict, findings generally consistent with, though somewhat stronger than, those emanating from similar analyses carried out on subsamples of families rearing 2- to 4-year-olds ($n = 623$) and 5- to 11-year-olds ($n = 974$; Buehler & Gerard, 2002). Of note, too, is that these relationships between marital conflict and ineffective parenting characterize both poor families and those who were not economically distressed.

Domestic Violence and Parenting

Although, as the preceding summary of research on marriage and parenting reveals, a good deal of attention has been devoted to investigating linkages between marital conflict and parenting, only recently have family researchers come to study parenting in the context of domestic violence. It can be argued that domestic violence should be distinguished from marital conflict rather than be judged as simply an extreme form of spousal discord (Jouriles, Norwood, McDonald, & Peters, 2001; Levendosky et al., 2003; Rossman, 1998). This is because of the traumatic impact of witnessing violence (e.g., Levendosky, Huth-Bocks, Semel, & Shapiro, 2002; Rossman, 1998), as well as the fact that whereas conflict is universal in marriage, at least to some degree, violence is not.

Violence between intimate partners, it turns out, is far more frequent than many would like to believe. Incident rates for violence from a romantic partner are approximately 16%, depending on whether only married or both married and dating couples are the focus of consideration (Morse, 1995; Straus & Gelles, 1986). Prevalence rates range from 9% to 66%, depending again on the definition of the partner (Brown et al., 1998). In their work relying on a National Institute of Justice database covering five major U.S. cities, Fantuzzo and associates (1991) found that children are disproportionately represented in households in which women are abused.

A multiplicity of studies now show that such exposure is detrimental to children's well-being. Young children (i.e., 3 to 5 years) have increased trauma and dissociative symptoms relative to children in nonviolent homes (Rossman, 1998), as well as lower self-esteem, lower levels of social functioning, and higher levels of depression and anxiety relative to children in nonviolent families (Fantuzzo et al., 1991; Hughes, 1988; Stagg, Wills, & Howell, 1989). The possibility that at least some of these correlates of exposure to domestic violence are mediated by parenting comes from two sets of work. The first, indirect evidence derives from studies linking domestic violence with parenting, showing that mothers who are victims of partner abuse provide less emotional support to their school-age children than counterparts who do not experience domestic violence, and this is so irrespective of whether mothering is measured via parent and child report (McCloskey, Figueredo, & Koss, 1995) or via observation of mother-child interaction (Levendosky & Graham-Berman, 2000). In this latter work, the investigators directly examined the role of parenting in mediating the effect of domestic violence on child functioning, showing, via (cross-sectional) path analysis, that domestic violence predicted less effective parenting and, thereby, elevated levels of problem behavior. Additionally, and also consistent with Belsky's (1984) model of the determinants of parenting, domestic violence affected parenting and thereby child aggression and disobedience by undermining maternal psychological well-being (i.e., depression, posttraumatic stress).

Conclusion

Whether one considers marital conflict, domestic violence, or other aspects of the marital relationship, including satisfaction, communication, or overall quality, or whether one considers parental sensitive responsiveness, warmth, control, harsh discipline, or a host of other features of parenting, linkages emerge between marriage and parenting. And as we have seen, this is so across the infant/toddler, preschool/middle childhood, and adolescent years. For the most part, though not exclusively, the evidence points to problematic marriages and problematic parenting co-occurring; the evidence for compensation in which parenting looks positive in response to troublesome marital processes is far more limited. Notable from the perspective of the child is that parental emotional unavailability (e.g., rejection, hostility, unresponsiveness), poor behavioral control (e.g., lax monitoring, inconsistent or harsh discipline), and psychological control (e.g., guilt induction, love withdrawal, dominating conversations) have been found to mediate, at least partially, the relationship between interparental conflict and other aspects of the marriage and child adjustment (e.g., Buehler & Gerard, 2002; Fauber et al., 1990; Harold et al., 1997), consistent with Belsky's (1981, 1984) formulations of the interrelationships of marriage, parenting, and child development (but see Frosch & Mangelsdorf, 2001, for an exception).

THE NEIGHBORHOOD

Research on neighborhood conditions and family functioning has been heavily influenced by urban sociological models of how neighborhoods and communities affect individual behavior (Coleman, 1988; Jencks & Mayer, 1990; Sampson, 1992; C. R. Shaw & McKay, 1942; W. J. Wilson, 1987, 1991) and by ecological models of human development in context (Belsky, 1984; Bronfenbrenner, 1979). Integrating these theoretical strands, developmentalists have explored how children's outcomes, including infant mortality, academic achievement, social competence, school dropout, teen childbearing, and delinquency, are influenced not only by the family context, but also by neighborhood structural characteristics (see Leventhal & Brooks-Gunn, 2000, 2003, for a review). Implicit in this research is the hypothesis that positive child outcomes depend on the skill with which parents buffer their children from the daily stresses of living in poor and dangerous neighborhoods (Furstenberg et al., 1993; Furstenberg, Cook, Eccles, Elder, & Sameroff, 1999; Garbarino & Kostelny, 1993). Yet, relatively few studies have explicitly modeled the degree to which parenting practices mediate or moderate the effects of neighborhood conditions on children's outcomes (Burton & Jarrett, 2000). In part, this reflects the focus of research on adolescents' as opposed to younger children's outcomes. Whereas most adolescents are regularly exposed to nonparental influences in school and the community, younger children are less likely to be exposed to neighborhood influences without their parents' knowledge (Klebanov, Brooks-Gunn, Chase-Lansdale, & Gordon, 1997). Thus, parents are likely to play a stronger

role in mediating the effects of neighborhood conditions on young children's development than they do for older children. In this section, we review the literature on how neighborhood conditions affect parenting behavior. That a disproportionate number of the studies reviewed in this section focus on how parenting is affected by living in poor and dangerous neighborhoods (as opposed to affluent neighborhoods) reflects the focus in this literature. A future direction for research may be to understand the ways affluent neighborhoods affect parenting. Conceptual and methodological limitations of this research are discussed at the end of the section.

Conceptions of How Neighborhoods Affect Parenting

W. J. Wilson (1987, 1991) has argued that living in neighborhoods characterized by high rates of unemployment, poverty, and single motherhood results in what he has termed "social isolation" from mainstream jobs and lifestyles. Social isolation can lead to family practices that do not foster the skills children need for success in school and work. Whereas parents in affluent neighborhoods emphasize the importance of daily routines, future goals, school and work skills, and parental self-efficacy, the efforts of poor families to foster these same skills are hindered by structural features of their communities that result in their isolation from formal and informal networks of support.

Consistent with Wilson's conceptualization of social isolation, Sampson and colleagues (Sampson, 1992; Sampson & Groves, 1989) contend that neighborhoods characterized by poverty, high residential turnover, and ethnic heterogeneity are vulnerable to social disorganization, meaning that these communities often fail to realize the common values of their residents or to maintain effective social controls over individual members. Families in socially disorganized communities lack social capital, a concept introduced by Coleman (1988) to refer to the network of relationships that allow individuals to achieve particular goals. Communities rich in social capital are characterized by an extensive set of obligations, expectations, and social networks that connect adults within the community and foster their ability to supervise and monitor children. Sampson and colleagues argue that socially disorganized neighborhoods promote an individualistic style of parenting in which families tend to isolate themselves and their children from the surrounding community and distrust local schools and services. In sum, families in poor communities often lack the formal and informal networks that provide them with material and social resources and that enable them to foster the skills their children need for educational and labor market success.

Neighborhoods and Parenting

Sampson's (1992; Sampson & Groves, 1989) theory of social disorganization is supported by ethnographic work conducted among Philadelphia neighborhoods. Furstenberg and associates (1993, 1999) found that poor, socially disorganized neighborhoods fostered a highly individualistic parenting style in which parents isolated themselves from neighbors, did not rely on neighborhood formal or informal institutions for help in raising their children, and spent enormous amounts of time personally monitoring, supervising, and controlling their children's behavior. In more cohesive neighborhoods, where parents and their friends and relatives had lived for several generations, parents perceived a neighborhood consensus about child-rearing values that made them more willing to entrust their children's care to formal and informal neighborhood networks. In these more cohesive neighborhoods, parents often took responsibility for supervising and monitoring children who were not their own. In contrast, what Furstenberg termed "super-motivated parenting" was required of parents in socially disorganized neighborhoods to protect their children from neighborhood dangers and to provide adequate opportunities (often located outside of their own neighborhoods) for their children (Furstenberg et al., 1993; Garbarino & Kostelny, 1993). Furstenberg noted that parents with ordinary levels of parental motivation would probably be able to create better opportunities for their children were they to live in neighborhoods that provided better resources and more support, a proposition to which we return in the section on experimental evaluations of neighborhood effects.

Qualitative studies of families in poor neighborhoods (Furstenberg et al., 1993, 1999; Jarrett, 1997) are consistent in showing that residence in poor, socially disorganized neighborhoods is associated with parenting practices that can be effective in the short term in promoting children's competencies and protecting children from undesirable influences. However, these family practices place an enormous burden on parents, whose often rational distrust of neighbors and community services leads them to isolate themselves and their families from potential sources of support. Moreover, by keeping children close to home, parents may unintentionally deprive them of opportunities for social interaction and physical exercise that may, ultimately, promote children's social mobility (Furstenberg et al., 1993; Garbarino & Kostelny, 1993).

Quantitative studies of how neighborhood conditions affect normative parenting behavior are scarce. However, the available data converge in showing that neighborhood characteristics such as poverty, joblessness, ethnic diversity, dissatisfaction with neighborhood conditions, and low affluence are associated with lower levels of parental warmth (Ceballo & McLoyd, 2002; Klebanov et al., 1997; Klebanov, Brooks-Gunn, & Duncan, 1994; Pinderhughes, Nix, Foster, Jones, & The Conduct Problems Prevention Group, 2001; Simons, Johnson, Conger, & Lorenz, 1997), more harsh and inconsistent discipline (Hill & Herman-Stahl, 2002; Pinderhughes et al., 2001; Simons et al., 1997), poorer physical home environments (Klebanov et al., 1994, 1997), and lower levels of cognitive stimulation (Klebanov et al., 1997), even controlling for family and individual characteristics that could have more proximal influences on parenting. It bears noting, however, that across these studies the same neighborhood characteristics are rarely associated with the same parenting outcomes. Moreover, the degree to which neighborhood conditions affect parenting behavior may depend on individual, family, or other contextual characteristics. For example, Klebanov and colleagues (1997) reported that neighborhood economic disadvantage had a stronger negative effect on parenting quality for low-income compared to high-income families. Relatedly, Ceballo and McLoyd found that the receipt of social support was more weakly associated with maternal nurturance and a lower reliance on punitiveness in neighborhoods characterized by violent crime and poverty than in lower-risk neighborhoods.

In contrast to the literature on normative parenting behaviors, the child maltreatment literature, influenced by Bronfenbrenner's (1979) work on the ecology of human development, has long recognized that neighborhood socioeconomic and demographic factors are strongly associated with rates of child maltreatment (Belsky, 1980, 1993; Garbarino, 1977b). Children who live in neighborhoods characterized by poverty, violence, unemployment, excessive numbers of children per adult resident, population turnover, and a concentration of female-headed households are at the greatest risk of maltreatment (Coulton, Korbin, Su, & Chow, 1995; Deccio, Horner, & Wilson, 1994; Drake & Pandey, 1996; Garbarino & Sherman, 1980; Korbin, Coulton, Chard, Platt-Houston, & Su, 1998; Lynch & Cicchetti, 1998; Steinberg, Catalano, & Dooley, 1981; Zuravin, 1989).

Garbarino and colleagues (Garbarino, 1977a; Garbarino & Crouter, 1978; Garbarino & Kostelny, 1992; Garbarino & Sherman, 1980) have argued that sociodemographically high-risk neighborhoods vary in the extent to which they are characterized by high rates of child maltreatment and neglect. Qualitative studies have shown that in poor neighborhoods where community leaders felt hopeful about their neighborhood's prospects, rates of maltreatment were lower than would be expected on the basis of the socioeconomic data alone (Garbarino & Kostelny, 1992). Apparently, social organization, especially the presence of supportive formal and informal networks, protected families from succumbing to neighborhood risk. However, other researchers have failed to replicate these findings. For example, Deccio and colleagues (1994) found no differences in perceived personal and parenting support among parents in neighborhoods that were demographically similar but differed in rates of child maltreatment. Still other researchers have questioned the direction of effects, noting that it is unclear whether abusive families lack social supports or simply fail to use them appropriately (Vondra, 1990). A number of researchers have shown that although abusive parents have extensive social networks, they are a drain on these networks and they discourage long-term relationships from forming (Crittenden, 1985; Vinson, Baldry, & Hargreaves, 1996; Vondra, 1990).

These failures to replicate and concerns about potential selection effects raise questions about the strength of the relationship between social support and child maltreatment (Seagull, 1987; Zuravin, 1989). Moreover, the child maltreatment literature has failed to show definitively that low social support and social disorganization are the mediating mechanisms by which neighborhood disadvantage results in child maltreatment. For example, using multilevel models, Coulton, Korbin, and Su (1999) found that structural characteristics of neighborhoods (e.g., impoverishment, child care burden) accounted for variation in child abuse potential beyond the effects of individual characteristics, but neighborhood *processes* (e.g., quality, facilities, disorder, lack of control of children) did not. In sum, research on neighborhood characteristics and child maltreatment has not advanced far beyond the state reported by Zuravin nearly 15 years ago in her review of the ecology of child maltreatment. That is, although researchers have demonstrated convincingly that rates of child maltreatment vary systematically with neighborhood conditions, more work is needed to specify potential confounding factors (e.g., selection and aggregation) and to identify the processes by which variations in neighborhood context are associated with variations in rates of maltreatment.

Some of the strongest evidence for the causal effects of neighborhoods on family functioning comes from experimental interventions in which families are offered the opportunity to relocate from low-income to higher-income neighborhoods. These programs are based on the premise that improving a person's residential location will increase his or her access to resources and opportunities (Del Conte & Kling, 2001). The Moving to Opportunities (MTO) program, sponsored by the U.S. Department of Housing and Urban Development, offered families living in federally subsidized housing in five cities the opportunity to move to better neighborhoods. A unique feature of MTO was that those who volunteered for the program were randomly assigned to treatment and control groups with different subsidies and services. Data from a follow-up survey at the New York City site (Leventhal & Brooks-Gunn, 2001), conducted 3 years after the program began, showed that mothers who had moved out of public housing had increased employment, were less reliant on welfare compared to control mothers, and were less likely to report symptoms of depression and anxiety. Most important for this chapter, these mothers were less harsh in their parenting, and their children's lives had become more structured.

Poor Mental Health as a Mediator of Neighborhood Effects on Parenting

The stress of living in poor and dangerous neighborhoods where parents are exposed to many uncontrollable life events may affect parenting by contributing to symptoms of depression and anxiety (Cutrona, Russell, Murry, Hessling, & Brown, 2000) which was shown to undermine growth-promoting parenting in preceding sections of this chapter. Several researchers have reported that individuals who live in more disadvantaged neighborhoods report more symptoms of depression or psychological distress (Cutrona et al., 2000; Hill et al., 2002; O'Brien, Hassinger, & Dershem, 1994; Ross, 2000), and the association with mental health problems appears to be stronger for neighborhood social disorder (i.e., chaotic, crime-ridden neighborhoods) than for neighborhood cohesion (i.e., the sense that community members have a common stake in the neighborhood). Moreover, high-quality neighborhoods have been shown to amplify the effects of individuals' positive characteristics, and poor-quality neighborhoods have been shown to amplify the effects of individuals' negative characteristics on their psychological functioning (Cutrona et al., 2000).

Several studies, controlling for a range of family and individual characteristics, have shown that parents who live in disadvantaged, chaotic, and unsafe neighborhoods use less effective parenting strategies (e.g., harsh, inconsistent discipline, low monitoring, low warmth) because they are more depressed (Hill et al., 2002; Simons et al., 1997). However, other work suggests that neighborhood effects on mental health and parenting may be principally a function of family income (Jones, Forehand, Brody, & Armistead, 2002). These findings are consistent with a large body of literature showing that mental health problems mediate the association between family-level disadvantage and parenting practices (see McLoyd, 1998, for a review).

Conceptual and Methodological Challenges to Neighborhood Research

A growing number of quantitative and qualitative studies, driven by a well-developed theoretical framework, have linked neighborhood characteristics with parenting practices, even controlling for individual and family conditions. Nevertheless, interpretation of neighborhood effects on parenting practices and children's outcomes is challenged by a host of conceptual and methodological problems (Duncan, Connell, & Klebanov, 1997; Duncan & Raudenbush, 2001; Ginther, Haveman, & Wolfe, 2000; Manski, 1993; Tienda, 1991). The *simultaneity problem* refers to the phenomenon whereby neighborhood conditions are not only causes of, but are simultaneously caused by, individual characteristics. For example, as described by Duncan and Raudenbush, Sampson, Raudenbush, and Earls (1997) have shown that a sense of collective efficacy among adults in a neighborhood deters youth problem behaviors. It is possible, however, that the sense of collective efficacy is derived, in part, by the low level of youth behavior problems in the community and that an increase in delinquency might undermine this sense of control. The *omitted-context-variables problem* refers to the possibility that models of neighborhood effects fail to estimate other important sources of contextual variation that are associated with the outcome in question. A related problem is the *endogenous membership problem,* which refers to the possibility that neighborhood conditions may simply reflect characteristics of the individuals who select themselves into those neighborhoods. For example, neighborhood poverty may be associated with suboptimal parenting practices because the parents who lack the wherewithal to escape poor and dangerous neighborhoods also lack the skills to provide competent parenting. The problem of modeling *the role of family demographic characteristics and processes* in neighborhood research refers to the need to move beyond tests of neighborhood conditions as direct effects on individual outcomes and to test whether neighborhood effects are mediated by or moderate other, more proximal processes. Finally, the problem of *obtaining sufficient variability in neighborhood contexts* refers to the need to measure a wide range of neighborhood contexts to move beyond simple assessments of a single "good" versus "bad" neighborhood dimension.

Essentially, these problems confound the estimation of neighborhood effects on parenting by potentially biasing the estimates, by creating problems of identification (e.g., when parenting outcomes are simultaneously caused by and causes of neighborhood conditions), and by producing statistically inefficient dependence across observations. As reviewed by Duncan and Raudenbush, these problems are not always intractable and can sometimes be adequately addressed in nonexperimental designs. They conclude, nevertheless, that experimental research on neighborhoods holds the most promise for accurately estimating neighborhood effects on parenting and children's outcomes.

Conclusion

There is ample theoretical reason to expect that neighborhood conditions should affect parenting, and the small empirical literature is generally consistent in demonstrating hypothesized effects. Nevertheless, the literature would benefit greatly from work that addresses the many conceptual and methodological problems that challenge this research. Better evidence for neighborhood effects on parenting and children's outcomes should come from experimental research on residential mobility, studies that use more sophisticated methods of analysis to deal with the methodological problems outlined here, and studies in which process variables are better measured and better conform to theory about how neighborhood conditions affect individual outcomes.

GENERAL CONCLUSION

As we have noted repeatedly throughout this chapter, it is difficult to conclude with any certainty that the factors considered in this review of research on the determinants of parenting truly operate in a classically causal fashion. With few exceptions, the research is based on correlational rather than experimental designs, so third-variable explanations often plague interpretation of results. Is it the case, for example, that personality causally contributes to parenting, or is any such association merely a function of common genes shaping personality and parenting? Relatedly, and illustratively, does marital quality or even neighborhood characteristics actually enhance or undermine parenting, or is it simply the case that certain kinds of people have certain kinds of marriages and/or select to live in particular kinds of neighborhoods, and that it is these selection processes that account for the associations detected in numerous studies between parenting and features of the marriage and the neighborhood? Such questions cannot be answered in the case of most research conducted or reported in this review, yet there is sufficiently tantalizing experimental evidence and work that endeavored to control for alternative explanations that we think it remains as a good working hypothesis that the factors considered in this analysis do actually contribute to parenting that either fosters or undermines the psychological and behavioral development of children. Nevertheless, the fact that the data are not more conclusive highlights one of major needs of future research.

As we enter the twenty-first century, some might thus conclude that it is a sorry state of affairs indeed that characterizes what we know—and do not know—about the determinants of parenting, given the major limitation just cited of much of the work that has been discussed in this chapter. But before we conclude that the determinants-of-parenting glass is half empty, it seems worth taking stock of how this arena of inquiry has advanced, perhaps supporting a claim that half full might be a better characterization. Consider in this regard that relative to when Belsky (1984) first proposed his model of the determinants of parenting and reviewed evidence on which it was based, great progress has been made in (1) including fathers in studies of parenting; (2) researching the parenting of children of school age and adolescents, not just infants and preschoolers; (3) considering the interactive role played by a variety of factors, so as to illuminate processes of amplification and buffering; (4) testing mediational processes linking determinants of parenting with child development outcomes or those linking one source of influence (e.g., marital quality) to another (e.g., psychological well-being) before being connected with parenting; and (5) conducting in some cases experimental research to illuminate causal processes and making efforts to discount alternative explanations by means of statistical control.

In light of all this progress that has been made, it remains as true today as it was 2 decades ago that parenting is multiply determined by forces that emanate from the child, the parent, and the social context; that these forces not only additively contribute to parenting, but interact to amplify and buffer the effects of one another; and that the factors often mediate one another so that parenting is likely to be influenced directly and/or indirectly by attributes of the child, the parent, and the social context (Belsky, 1984). It remains the case, as well, that these lessons, which originated in the study of the etiology of child maltreatment (Belsky & Vondra, 1988), clearly extend to parenting that is not disturbed (i.e., in the normal range of variation). As such, this entire body of work reminds us that if the goal is to enhance child development by enhancing parenting,

there are many handles for interventionists to grab on to and manipulate. Indeed, a fundamental take-home message for the applied developmentalist or clinician must be that efforts to enhance parenting and child development should be targeted to more than a single source of influence, as it is invariably the cumulative impact of the multiple sources of influence considered herein (and others: social support, occupational experiences) that determine the course of parenting, parent-child relations, and child development to a substantial degree.

REFERENCES

Altemeier, W., O'Connor, S., Vietze, P., Sandler, H., & Sherrod, K. (1982). Antecedents of child abuse. *Journal of Pediatrics, 100,* 823–829.

Altemeier, W., O'Connor, S., Vietze, P., Sandler, H., & Sherrod, K. (1984). Prediction of child abuse: A prospective study of feasibility. *Child Abuse and Neglect, 8,* 393–400.

American Psychiatric Association. (2000). *Diagnostic and statistical manual of mental disorders* (4th ed., text rev.). Washington, DC: Author.

Ammerman, R. T., Loeber, R., Kolko, D. J., & Blackson, T. C. (1994). Parental dissatisfaction with sons in substance abusing families: Relationship to child and parent dysfunction. *Journal of Child and Adolescent Substance Abuse, 3,* 23–37.

Anderson, K. E., Lytton, H., & Romney, D. M. (1986). Mothers' interactions with normal and conduct disordered boys: Who affects whom? *Developmental Psychology, 22,* 604–609.

Anthony, E. J. (1986). Terrorizing attacks on children by psychotic parents. *Journal of the American Academy of Child and Adolescent Psychiatry, 25,* 326–335.

Aviezer, O., Sagi, A., Joels, T., & Ziv, Y. (1999). Emotional availability and attachment representation in kibbutz infants and their mothers. *Developmental Psychology, 35,* 811–821.

Baker, L. A., & Daniels, D. (1990). Nonshared environmental influences and personality differences in adult twins. *Journal of Personality and Social Psychology, 58,* 103–110.

Bandura, A., & Walters, R. (1959). *Adolescent aggression.* New York: Ronald Press.

Bank, L., Forgatch, M. S., Patterson, G. R., & Fetrow, R. A. (1993). Parenting practices of single mothers: Mediators of negative contextual factors. *Journal of Marriage and the Family, 55,* 371–384.

Bardone, A. M., Moffitt, T. E., Caspi, A., & Dickson, N. (1996). Adult mental health and social outcomes of adolescent girls with depression and conduct disorder. *Development and Psychopathology, 8,* 811–829.

Barkley, R. A., & Cunningham, C. E. (1979). The effects of methylphenidate on the mother-child interactions of hyperactive children. *Archives of General Psychiatry, 36,* 201–208.

Barnow, S., Schuckit, M. A., Lucht, M., John, U., & Freyberger, H.-J. (2002). The importance of a positive family history of alcoholism, parental rejection and emotional warmth, behavioral problems and peer substance use for alcohol problems in teenagers: A path analysis. *Journal of Studies on Alcohol, 63,* 305–315.

Bates, J. E. (1989). Applications of temperament concepts. In G. A. Kohnstamm, J. E. Bates, & M. K. Rothbart (Eds.), *Temperament in childhood* (pp. 321–355). Chichester, England: Wiley.

Baumeister, R. F. (1999). On the interface between personality and social psychology. In L. A. Pervin & O. P. John (Eds.), *Handbook of per-*

sonality: Theory and research (2nd ed., pp. 367–378). New York: Guilford Press.

Baydar, N., Reid, M., & Webster-Stratton, C. (2003). The role of mental health factors and program engagement in the effectiveness of a preventive parenting program for Head Start mothers. *Child Development, 74,* 1433–1453.

Bell, R. Q. (1968). A reinterpretation of the direction of effects in studies of socialization. *Psychological Review, 75,* 81–89.

Belsky, J. (1978). Three theoretical models of child abuse: A critical review. *International Journal of Child Abuse and Neglect, 2,* 37–49.

Belsky, J. (1979). The interaction of parental and spousal behavior during infancy in traditional nuclear families: An exploratory analysis. *Journal of Marriage and the Family, 41,* 749–755.

Belsky, J. (1980). Child maltreatment: An ecological integration. *American Psychologist, 35,* 320–335.

Belsky, J. (1981). Early human experience: A family perspective. *Developmental Psychology, 17,* 3–23.

Belsky, J. (1984). The determinants of parenting: A process model. *Child Development, 55,* 83–96.

Belsky, J. (1993). Etiology of child maltreatment: A developmental-ecological analysis. *Psychological Bulletin, 114,* 413–434.

Belsky, J., & Barends, N. (2002). Personality and parenting. In M. Bornstein (Ed.), *Handbook of parenting: Vol. 3. Being and becoming a parent* (2nd ed., pp. 415–438). Mahwah, NJ: Erlbaum.

Belsky, J., Crnic, K., & Woodworth, S. (1995). Personality and parenting: Exploring the mediating role of transient mood and daily hassles. *Journal of Personality, 63,* 905–931.

Belsky, J., Hsieh, K., & Crnic, K. (1996). Infant positive and negative emotionality. *Developmental Psychology, 32,* 289–298.

Belsky, J., & Isabella, R. (1988). Maternal, infant and social-contextual determinants of infant-mother attachment. In J. Belsky & T. Nezworski (Eds.), *Clinical implications of attachment* (pp. 41–94). Hillsdale, NJ: Erlbaum.

Belsky, J., & Pensky, E. (1988). Developmental history, personality and family relationships: Toward an emergent family system. In R. Hinde & J. Stevenson-Hinde (Eds.), *Relationships within families* (pp. 193–217). Oxford: Clarendon Press.

Belsky, J., Pensky, E., & Youngblade, L. (1990). Childrearing history: Marital quality and maternal affect—Intergenerational transmission in a low-risk sample. *Development and Psychopathology, 1,* 291–304.

Belsky, J., & Vondra, J. (1988). Lessons from child abuse: The determinants of parenting. In D. Cicchetti & V. Carlson (Eds.), *Child maltreatment: Theory and research on the causes and consequences of child abuse and neglect* (pp. 153–202). New York: Cambridge University Press.

Belsky, J., Youngblade, L., Rovine, M., & Volling, B. (1991). Patterns of marital change and parent-child interaction. *Journal of Marriage and the Family, 53,* 487–498.

Billings, A. G., & Moos, R. H. (1986). Children of parents with unipolar depression: A controlled 1-year follow-up. *Journal of Abnormal Child Psychology, 14,* 149–166.

Biringen, Z. (1990). Direct observation of maternal sensitivity and dyadic interactions in the home. *Developmental Psychology, 26,* 278–284.

Bluestone, C., & Tamis-LeMonda, C. (1999). Correlates of parenting styles in predominantly working- and middle-class African American mothers. *Journal of Marriage and the Family, 61,* 881–893.

Bosquet, M., & Egeland, B. (2000). Predicting parenting behaviors from antisocial practices content scale scores of the MMPI-2 administered during pregnancy. *Journal of Personality Assessment, 74,* 146–162.

Bower, M., & Knutson, J. (1996). Attitudes toward physical discipline as a function of disciplinary history and self-labeling as physically abused. *Child Abuse and Neglect, 20,* 689–699.

Bower-Russa, M., Knutson, J., & Winebarger, A. (2001). Disciplinary history, adult disciplinary attitudes, and risk for abusive parenting. *Journal of Community Psychology, 29,* 219–240.

Bowlby, J. (1980). *Attachment and loss: Vol. 3. Loss.* New York: Basic Books.

Bowlby, J. (1988). *A secure base.* New York: Basic Books.

Bradbury, T., & Fincham, F. (1990). Attributions in marriage. *Psychological Bulletin, 107,* 3–33.

Braungart, J. M., Plomin, R., & Fulker, D. W. (1992). Genetic mediation of the home environment during infancy: A sibling adoption study of the home. *Developmental Psychology, 28,* 1048–1055.

Brennan, P. A., Hammen, C., Katz, A. R., & Le Brocque, R. M. (2002). Maternal depression, paternal psychopathology, and adolescent diagnostic outcomes. *Journal of Consulting and Clinical Psychology, 70,* 1075–1085.

Breznitz, Z., & Sherman, T. (1987). Speech patterning of natural discourse of well and depressed mothers and their young children. *Child Development, 58,* 395–400.

Brody, G., Murry, V., Kim, S., & Brown, A. (2002). Longitudinal pathways to competence and psychological adjustment among African American children living in rural single-parent households. *Child Development, 73,* 1505–1516.

Brody, G., Pillegrini, A. D., & Sigel, I. E. (1986). Marital quality and mother-child and father-child interactions with school-aged children. *Developmental Psychology, 22,* 291–296.

Bronfenbrenner, U. (1979). *The ecology of human development: Experiments by nature and design.* Cambridge, MA: Harvard University Press.

Bronfenbrenner, U. (1986). Ecology of the family as a context for human development: Research perspectives. *Developmental Psychology, 22,* 723–742.

Brown, J., Cohen, P., Johnson, J. G., & Salzinger, S. (1998). A longitudinal analysis of risk factors for child maltreatment: Findings of a 17-year prospective study of officially recorded and self-reported child abuse and neglect. *Child Abuse and Neglect, 22,* 1065–1078.

Brunk, M. A., & Henggeler, S. Q. (1984). Child influences on adult controls: An experimental investigation. *Developmental Psychology, 20,* 1074–1081.

Buehler, C., & Gerard, J. (2002). Marital conflict, ineffective parenting, and children's and adolescents' maladjustment. *Journal of Marriage and the Family, 64,* 78–92.

Bugental, D., & Happaney, K. (2002). Parental attributions. In M. Bornstein (Ed.), *Handbook of parenting: Vol. 3. Being and becoming a parent* (2nd ed., pp. 509–536). Mahwah, NJ: Erlbaum.

Bugental, D., & Shennum, W. (1984). Difficult children as elicitors and targets of adult communication patterns. *Monographs of the Society for Research in Child Development, 49*(1, Serial No. 205).

Burton, L. M., & Jarrett, R. L. (2000). In the mix, yet on the margins: The place of families in urban neighborhood and child development research. *Journal of Marriage and the Family, 62,* 1114–1135.

Butcher, J. N., Dahlstrom, W. G., Graham, J. R., Tellegen, A., & Kaemmer, B. (1989). *MMPI-2 (Minnesota Multiphasic Personality Inventory-2): Manual for administration and scoring.* Minneapolis: University of Minnesota Press.

Butcher, P. R., Kalverboer, F., Minderaa, R. B., Van Doormaal, F., & Ten Wolde, Y. (1993). Rigidity, sensitivity and quality of attachment: The role of maternal rigidity in the early socioemotional development of premature infants. *Acta Psychiatrica Scandinavica, 88,* 1–38.

Caliso, J., & Milner, J. (1992). Childhood history of abuse and child abuse screening. *Child Abuse and Neglect, 16,* 647–659.

Callan, V. J., & Jackson, D. (1986). Children of alcoholic fathers and recovered alcoholic fathers: Personal and family functioning. *Journal of Studies on Alcohol, 47,* 180–182.

Campbell, S. B., Cohn, J. F., & Meyers, T. (1995). Depression in first-time mothers: Mother-infant interaction and depression chronicity. *Developmental Psychology, 31,* 349–357.

Capaldi, D., & Patterson, G. R. (1991). Relation of parental transitions to boys' adjustment problems: I. A linear hypothesis. II. Mothers at risk for transitions and unskilled parenting. *Developmental Psychology, 27,* 489–504.

Capaldi, D., Pears, K., Patterson, G., & Owen, L. (2003). Continuity of parenting practices across generations in an at-risk sample: A prospective comparison of direct and mediated associations. *Journal of Abnormal Child Psychology, 31,* 127–142.

Carter, A. S., Garrity-Rokous, F. E., Chazan-Cohen, R., Little, C., & Briggs-Gowan, M. J. (2001). Maternal depression and comorbidity: Predicting early parenting, attachment security, and toddler social-emotional problems and competencies. *Journal of the American Academy of Child and Adolescent Psychiatry, 40,* 18–26.

Caspi, A. (1998). Personality development across the life course. In N. Eisenberg (Ed.), *Handbook of child psychology: Vol. 3. Social, emotional, and personality development* (5th ed., pp. 311–387). New York: Wiley.

Caspi, A., & Elder, G. H. (1988). Emergent family patterns: The intergenerational construction of problem behavior and relationships. In R. Hinde & J. Stevenson-Hinde (Eds.), *Relationships within families* (pp. 218–240). Oxford: Oxford University Press.

Cassidy, B., Zoccolillo, M., & Hughes, S. (1996). Psychopathology in adolescent mothers and its effects on mother-infant interactions: A pilot study. *Canadian Journal of Psychiatry, 41,* 379–384.

Castle, D. J. (2000). Women and Schizophrenia: An epidemiological perspective. In D. J. Castle, J. McGrath, & J. Kulkarni (Eds.), *Women and Schizophrenia* (pp. 19–33). Cambridge, England: Cambridge University Press.

Cattell, R. B. (1943). The description of personality: Basic traits resolved into clusters. *Journal of Abnormal and Social Psychology, 38,* 476–506.

Cattell, R. B. (1945). The principal trait clusters for describing personality. *Psychological Bulletin, 42,* 129–161.

Ceballo, R., & McLoyd, V. (2002). Social support and parenting in poor, dangerous neighborhoods. *Child Development, 73,* 1310–1321.

Chassin, L., Pillow, D. R., Curran, P. J., Molina, B. S. G., & Barrera, M., Jr. (1993). Relation of parental alcoholism to early adolescent substance use: A test of three mediating mechanisms. *Journal of Abnormal Psychology, 102,* 3–19.

Chen, X., Hastings, P. D., Rubin, K. H., Chen, H., Cen, G., & Stewart, S. L. (1998). Childrearing attitudes and behavioral inhibition in Chinese and Canadian toddlers: A cross-cultural study. *Developmental Psychology, 34,* 677–686.

Chen, Z., & Kaplan, H. (2001). The intergenerational transmission of constructive parenting. *Journal of Marriage and the Family, 63,* 17–31.

Christensen, A., & Margolin, G. (1988). Conflict and alliance in distressed and nondistressed families. In R. Hinde & J. Stevenson-Hinde (Eds.), *Relationships within families* (pp. 263–282). Oxford: Oxford University Press.

Cicchetti, D. (1984). The emergence of developmental psychopathology. *Child Development, 55,* 1–7.

Cicchetti, D., & Cohen, D. J. (1995). Perspectives on developmental psychopathology. In D. Cicchetti & D. J. Cohen (Eds.), *Developmental psychopathology* (pp. 3–20). New York: Wiley.

Cicchetti, D., & Lynch, M. (1993). Toward an ecological/transactional model of community violence and child maltreatment: Consequences for children's development. *Psychiatry, 56,* 96–118.

Cicchetti, D., & Rizley, R. (1981). Developmental perspectives on the etiology, intergenerational transmission and sequelae of child maltreatment. *New Directions for Child Development, 11,* 31–56.

Cicchetti, D., & Toth, S. (1998). Perspectives on research and practice in developmental psychopathology. In I. Sigel & K. A. Renninger (Eds.), *Handbook of child psychology: Vol. 4. Child psychology in practice* (5th ed., pp. 479–583). New York: Wiley.

Clark, L. A., Kochanska, G., & Ready, R. (2000). Mothers' personality and its interaction with child temperament as predictors of parenting behavior. *Journal of Personality and Social Psychology, 79,* 274–285.

Clark, R., Hyde, J. S., Essex, M. J., & Klein, M. H. (1997). Length of maternity leave and quality of mother-infant interactions. *Child Development, 68,* 364–383.

Cohler, B. J., Gallant, D. H., Grunebaum, H. U., Weiss, J. L., & Gamer, E. (1980). Child-care attitudes and development of young children of mentally ill and well mothers. *Psychological Reports, 46,* 31–46.

Cohn, J. F., Campbell, S. B., Matias, R., & Hopkins, J. (1990). Face-to-face interactions of postpartum depressed and nondepressed mother-infant pairs at 2 months. *Developmental Psychology, 26,* 15–23.

Cohn, J. F., Matias, R., Tronick, E. Z., Connell, D., & Lyons-Ruth, K. (1986). Face-to-face interactions of depressed mothers and their infants. In E. Z. Tronick & T. Field (Eds.), *Maternal depression and infant disturbance* (pp. 31–46). San Francisco: Jossey-Bass.

Coleman, J. (1988). Social capital in the creation of human capital. *American Journal of Sociology, 94,* 95–120.

Conger, R., Conger, K., Elder, G., Lorenz, F., Simons, R., & Whitbeck, L. (1992). A family process model of economic hardship and adjustment of early adolescent boys. *Child Development, 63,* 526–541.

Conger, R., Conger, K., Elder, G., Lorenz, F., Simons, R., & Whitbeck, L. (1993). Family economic stress and adjustment of early adolescent girls. *Developmental Psychology, 29,* 206–219.

Conger, R., McCarty, J., Yang, R., Lahey, B., & Kropp, J. (1984). Perception of child, childrearing values, and emotional distress as mediating links between environmental stressors and observed maternal behavior. *Child Development, 54,* 2234–2247.

Conger, R., Nell, T., Kim, K., & Scaramella, L. (2003). Angry and aggressive behaviour across three generations: A prospective, longitudinal study of parents and children. *Journal of Abnormal Child Psychology, 31,* 143–160.

Conger, R., Patterson, G., & Ge, X. (1995). It takes two to replicate: A mediational model for the impact of parents' stress on adolescent adjustment. *Child Development, 66,* 80–97.

Connell, A. M., & Goodman, S. H. (2002). The association between psychopathology in fathers versus mothers and children's internalizing and externalizing behavior problems: A meta-analysis. *Psychological Bulletin, 128,* 746–773.

Costa, P. T., & McCrae, R. R. (1992). *NEO PI-R professional manual.* Odessa, FL: Psychological Assessment Resources.

Coulton, C. J., Korbin, J. E., & Su, M. (1999). Neighborhoods and child maltreatment: A multi-level study. *Child Abuse and Neglect, 23,* 1019–1040.

Coulton, C. J., Korbin, J. E., Su, M., & Chow, J. (1995). Community level factors and child maltreatment rates. *Child Development, 66,* 1262–1276.

Coverdale, J. H., Schotte, D., Ruiz, P., Pharies, S., & Bayer, T. (1994). Family-planning needs of male chronic mental patients in the general-hospital psychiatry clinic. *General Hospital Psychiatry, 16,* 38–41.

Cowan, C. P., & Cowan, P. A. (1992). When partners become parents. New York: Basic Books.

Cox, M. J., Owen, M. T., Lewis, J. M., & Henderson, V. K. (1989). Marriage, adult adjustment, and early parenting. *Child Development, 60,* 1015–1024.

Cox, M. J., & Paley, B. (1997). Families as systems. *Annual Review of Psychology, 48,* 243–267.

Crittenden, P. M. (1985). Social networks, quality of child rearing, and child development. *Child Development, 56,* 1299–1313.

Crittenden, P., Partridge, M., & Clausen, A. (1991). Family patterns of relationship in normative and dysfunctional families. *Development and Psychopathology, 3,* 491–512.

Crockenberg, S. (1986). Are temperamental differences in babies associated with predictable differences in caregiving? In J. Lerner & R. Lerner (Eds.), *Temperament and interaction in infancy and childhood* (pp. 53–73). San Francisco: Jossey-Bass.

Crockenberg, S. (1987a). Predictors and correlates of anger toward and punitive control of toddlers by adolescent mothers. *Child Development, 58,* 964–975.

Crockenberg, S. (1987b). Support for adolescent mothers during the postnatal period. In C. Boukydis (Ed.), *Research on support for parents and infants in the postnatal period* (pp. 3–24). Norwood, NJ: Ablex.

Crockenberg, S., & Leerkes, S. (2003a). Infant negative emotionality, caregiving, and family relationships. In A. Booth & A. Crouter (Eds.), *Children's influence on family dynamics* (pp. 202–223). Mahwah, NJ: Erlbaum.

Crockenberg, S., & Leerkes, S. (2003b). Parental acceptance, postpartum depression and maternal sensitivity: Mediating and moderating processes. *Journal of Family Psychology, 17,* 80–93.

Crockenberg, S., & McCluskey, K. (1985, April). *Predicting infant attachment from early and current behavior of mothers and infants.* Paper presented at the meeting of the Society for Research in Child Development, Toronto.

Crockenberg, S., & McCluskey, K. (1986). Change in maternal behavior during the baby's first year of life. *Child Development, 57,* 746–753.

Crowell, J. A., & Feldman, S. S. (1988). Mothers' internal models of relationships and children's behavioural and developmental status: A study of mother-child interaction. *Child Development, 59,* 1273–1285.

Crowell, J. A., & Feldman, S. S. (1989). Assessment of mothers' working models of relationships: Some clinical implications. *Infant Mental Health Journal, 10,* 173–184.

Cummings, E. M., & Davies, P. (1994). *Children and marital conflict.* New York: Guilford Press.

Cummings, E. M., & Davies, P. (2002). Effects of marital conflict on children: Recent advances and emerging themes in process-oriented research. *Journal of Child Psychology and Psychiatry, 43,* 31–63.

Curran, P. J., & Chassin, L. (1996). A longitudinal study of parenting as a protective factor for children of alcoholics. *Journal of Studies on Alcohol, 57,* 305–313.

Cutrona, C. E., Russell, D. W., Murry, V., Hessling, R. M., & Brown, P. A. (2000). Direct and moderating effects of community context on the psychological well-being of African American women. *Journal of Personality and Social Psychology, 79,* 1088–1101.

Davies, P. Y., & Cummings, E. M. (1994). Marital conflict and child adjustment: An emotional security hypothesis. *Psychological Bulletin, 116,* 387–411.

Dawson, G., Frey, K., Panagiotides, H., Yamada, E., Hessl, D., & Osterling, J. (1999). Infants of depressed mothers exhibit atypical frontal electrical brain activity during interactions with mother and with a familiar nondepressed adult. *Child Development, 70,* 1058–1066.

Deater-Deckard, K., Lansford, J., Dodge, K., Pettit, G., & Bates, J. (2003). The development of attitudes about physical punishment. *Journal of Family Psychology, 17,* 351–360.

De Bellis, M. D., Broussard, E. R., Herring, D. J., Wexler, S., Moritz, G., & Benitez, J. G. (2001). Psychiatric co-morbidity in caregivers and children involved in maltreatment: A pilot research study with policy implications. *Child Abuse and Neglect, 25*(7), 923–944.

Deccio, G., Horner, W. C., & Wilson, D. (1994). High-risk neighborhoods and high-risk families: Replication research related to the human ecology of child maltreatment. *Journal of Social Service Research, 18,* 123–137.

Del Conte, A., & Kling, J. (2001). A synthesis of MTO research on self-sufficiency, safety and health, and behavior and delinquency. *Poverty Research News, 5,* 3–6.

Depner, C., Leino, E. V., & Chun, A. (1992). Interparental conflict and child adjustment: A decade review and meta-analysis. *Family and Conciliation Courts Review, 30,* 323–341.

Diener, M., Mangelsdorf, S., Contrerae, J., Hazelwood, L., & Rhodes, J. (1995, March). *Correlates of parenting competence among Latina adolescent mothers.* Paper presented at the meeting of the Society for Research in Child Development, Indianapolis, IN.

Dinwiddie, S. H., & Bucholz, K. K. (1993). Psychiatric diagnoses of self-reported child abusers. *Child Abuse and Neglect, 17,* 465–476.

Dipple, H., Smith, S., Andrews, H., & Evans, B. (2002). The experience of motherhood in women with severe and enduring mental illness. *Social Psychiatry and Psychiatric Epidemiology, 37,* 336–340.

Dix, T., Ruble, D., & Zambarano, R. (1989). Mothers' implicit theories of discipline. *Child Development, 60,* 1373–1391.

Dodge, K. (1986). A social information processing model of social competence in children. In M. Perlmutter (Ed.), *Minnesota Symposia on Child Psychology* (Vol. 18, pp. 77–125). Hillsdale, NJ: Erlbaum.

Dodge, K., Bates, J., & Pettit, G. (1990). Mechanisms in the cycle of violence. *Science, 250,* 1678–1683.

Downey, G., & Coyne, J. C. (1990). Children of depressed parents: A integrative review. *Psychological Bulletin, 108,* 50–76.

Drake, B., & Pandey, S. (1996). Understanding the relationship between neighborhood poverty and specific types of child maltreatment. *Child Abuse and Neglect, 20,* 1003–1018.

Duncan, G. J., Connell, J. P., & Klebanov, P. K. (1997). Conceptual and methodological issues in estimating causal effects of neighborhoods and family conditions on individual development. In J. Brooks-Gunn, G. J. Duncan, & J. L. Aber (Eds.), *Neighborhood poverty: Context and consequences for children* (pp. 219–250). New York: Russell Sage Foundation.

Duncan, G. J., & Raudenbush, S. W. (2001). Neighborhoods and adolescent development: How can we determine the links? In A. Booth & A. C. Crouter (Eds.), *Does it take a village? Community effects on children, adolescents, and families* (pp. 105–136). Mahwah, NJ: Erlbaum.

Dunn, J., & Plomin, R. (1990). *Separate lives: Why siblings are so different.* New York: Basic Books.

Easterbrooks, M., & Emde, R. (1988). Marital and parent-child relationships. In R. Hinde & J. Stevenson-Hinde (Eds.), *Relationships within families* (pp. 83–103). Oxford: Oxford University Press.

Egeland, B., & Jacobvitz, D. (March, 1984). *Intergenerational continuity in parental abuse: Causes and consequences.* Paper presented at the Conference on Biosocial Perspectives in Abuse and Neglect, York, ME.

Egeland, B., Jacobvitz, D., & Papatola, K. (1987). Intergenerational continuity of abuse. In R. Gelles & J. Lancaster (Eds.), *Child abuse and neglect: Biosocial dimensions* (pp. 255–276). New York: Aldine.

Eiden, R. D., Chaves, F., & Leonard, K. E. (1999). Parent-infant interactions among families with alcoholic fathers. *Development and Psychopathology, 11,* 745–762.

Eiden, R. D., Edwards, E., & Leonard, K. (2002). Mother-infant and father-infant attachment among alcoholic families. *Development and Psychopathology, 14,* 253–278.

Eiden, R. D., & Leonard, K. E. (1996). Paternal alcohol use and the mother-infant relationship. *Development and Psychopathology, 8,* 307–323.

Elder, G. H., Jr. (1974). *Children of the great depression.* Chicago: University of Chicago Press.

Elder, G., Van Nguyen, T., & Caspi, A. (1985). Linking family hardship to children's lives. *Child Development, 56,* 361–375.

Emery, R. E. (1989). Family violence. *American Psychologist, 44,* 321–328.

Engfer, A. (1986). Antecedents of perceived behavior problems in infancy. In G. Kohnstamm (Ed.), *Temperament discussed* (pp. 165–180). Lisse, The Netherlands: Swets and Zeitlinger.

Engfer, A. (1988). The interrelatedness of marriage and the mother-child relationship. In R. Hinde & J. Stevenson-Hinde (Eds.), *Relationships within families* (pp. 104–118). Oxford: Oxford University Press.

Engfer, A., & Schneewind, K. (1982). Causes and consequences of harsh parental punishment. *Child Abuse and Neglect, 6,* 129–139.

Erel, O., & Burman, B. (1995). Interrelatedness of marital relations and parent-child relations: A meta-analytic review. *Psychological Bulletin, 118,* 108–132.

Erel, O., Margolin, G., & John, R. (1998). Observed sibling interaction: Links with the marital and mother-child relationship. *Developmental Psychology, 34,* 288–298.

Fagot, B. I., Pears, K. C., Capaldi, D. M., Crosby, L., & Leve, C. S. (1998). Becoming an adolescent father: Precursors and parenting. *Developmental Psychology, 34,* 1209–1219.

Fantuzzo, J., DePaola, L., Lambert, L., Martino, T., Anderson, G., & Sutton, S. (1991). Effects of interparental violence on the psychological adjustment and competence of young children. *Journal of Clinical and Consulting Psychology, 59,* 258–265.

Fauber, R., Forehand, R., Thomas, A. M., & Wierson, M. (1990). A mediational model of the impact of marital conflict on adolescent adjustment in intact and divorced families: The role of disrupted parenting. *Child Development, 61,* 1112–1123.

Feldman, A., Curran, M., Jacobvitz, D., Boyd-Soisson, E., & Jin, M. (2003, April 26). *The intergenerational transmission of parent-child relationships: Links with children's peer relationships.* Paper presented at the biennial meetings of the Society for Research in Child Development, Tampa, FL.

Feske, U., Shear, M. K., Anderson, B., Cyranowski, J., Strassburger, M., Matty, M., et al. (2001). Comparison of severe life stress in depressed mothers and non-mothers: Do children matter? *Depression and Anxiety, 13,* 109–117.

Field, T., Healy, B., Goldstein, S., & Guthertz, M. (1990). Behavior state matching and synchrony in mother-infant interactions of nondepressed versus depressed dyads. *Developmental Psychology, 26,* 7–14.

Field, T., Healy, B., Goldstein, S., Perry, S., Bendall, D., Schanberg, S., et al. (1988). Infants of depressed mothers show "depressed" behavior even with nondepressed adults. *Child Development, 59,* 1569–1579.

Field, T., Hossain, Z., & Malphurs, J. (1999). "Depressed" fathers' interactions with their infants. *Infant Mental Health Journal, 20,* 322–332.

Field, T., Sandberg, D., Garcia, R., Vega-Lahr, N., Goldstein, S., & Guy, L. (1985). Prenatal problems, postpartum depression, and early mother-infant interactions. *Developmental Psychology, 12,* 1152–1156.

Fincham, F. (2003). Marital conflict: Correlates, structure, and context. *Current Directions in Psychological Science, 12,* 27.

Fish, M., & Stifter, C. A. (1993). Mother parity as a main and moderating influence on early mother-infant interaction. *Journal of Applied Developmental Psychology, 14,* 557–572.

Fontana, V. (1971). *The maltreated child.* Springfield, IL.: Thomas.

Fontana, V. (1973). The diagnosis of the maltreatment syndrome in children. *Pediatrics, 51,* 780–782.

Frankel, K. A., & Harmon, R. J. (1996). Depressed mothers: They don't always look as bad as they feel. *Journal of the American Academy of Child and Adolescent Psychiatry, 35,* 289–298.

Freud, A. (1970). The concept of the rejecting mother. In E. J. Anthony & T. Benedek (Eds.), *Parenthood: Its psychology and psychopathology* (pp. 376–386). Boston: Little, Brown. (Original work published 1955)

Frosch, C., & Mangelsdorf, S. (2001). Marital behavior, parenting behavior, and multiple reports of preschoolers' behavior problems: Mediation or moderation? *Developmental Psychology, 37,* 502–519.

Furstenberg, F., Belzer, A., Davis, C., Levine, J. A., Morrow, K., & Washington, M. (1993). How families manage risk and opportunity in dangerous neighborhoods. In W. J. Wilson (Ed.), *Sociology and the public agenda* (pp. 231–258). Newbury Park, CA: Sage.

Furstenberg, F., Cook, T. D., Eccles, J., Elder, G. H., Jr., & Sameroff, A. (1999). *Managing to make it: Urban families and adolescent success.* Chicago: University of Chicago Press.

Garbarino, J. (1976). A preliminary study of some ecological correlates of child abuse: The impact of socio-economic stress on mothers. *Child Development, 47,* 178–185.

Garbarino, J. (1977a). The human ecology of child maltreatment: A conceptual model for research. *Journal of Marriage and the Family, 39,* 721–735.

Garbarino, J. (1977b). The price of privacy in the social dynamics of child abuse. *Child Welfare, 56,* 565–575.

Garbarino, J., & Crouter, A. (1978). Defining the community context for parent-child relations: The correlates of child maltreatment. *Child Development, 49,* 604–616.

Garbarino, J., & Kostelny, K. (1992). Child maltreatment as a community problem. *Child Abuse and Neglect, 16,* 455–464.

Garbarino, J., & Kostelny, K. (1993). Neighborhood and community influences on parenting. In T. Luster (Ed.), *Parenting: An ecological perspective* (pp. 203–226). Hillsdale, NJ: Erlbaum.

Garbarino, J., & Sherman, D. (1980). High-risk neighborhoods and high-risk families: The human ecology of child maltreatment. *Child Development, 51,* 188–198.

Garber, J., & Flynn, C. (2001). Predictors of depressive cognitions in young adolescents. *Cognitive Therapy and Research, 25,* 353–376.

Gelles, R. (1973). Child abuse as psychopathology: A sociological critique and reformulation. *American Journal of Orthopsychiatry, 43,* 611–621.

Gelles, R. (1975). The social construction of child abuse. *American Journal of Psychiatry, 132,* 363–371.

George, C., & Solomon, J. (1996). Representational models of relationships: Links between caregiving and attachment. *Infant Mental Health Journal, 17,* 198–216.

Gil, D. (1971). Violence against children. *Journal of Marriage and the Family, 33,* 639.

Ginther, D., Haveman, R., & Wolfe, B. (2000). Neighborhood attributes as determinants of children's outcomes. *Journal of Human Resources, 34,* 603–641.

Goldberg, W., Clarke-Stewart, K. A., Rice, J., & Dellis, E. (2002). Emotional energy as an explanatory construct for fathers' engagement with their infants. *Parenting: Science and Practice, 2,* 379–408.

Goldberg, W., & Easterbrooks, A. (1984). Role of marital quality in toddler development. *Developmental Psychology, 20,* 504–514.

Goldstein, L., Diener, M., & Mangelsdorf, S. (1996). Maternal characteristics and social support across the transition to motherhood: Associations with maternal behavior. *Journal of Family Psychology, 10,* 60–71.

Gondoli, D., & Silverberg, S. (1997). Maternal emotional distress and diminished responsiveness. *Developmental Psychology, 33,* 861–868.

Goodman, G., Emery, R., & Haugaard, J. (1998). Developmental psychology and law: Divorce, child maltreatment, foster care, and adoption. In I. Sigel & K. A. Renninger (Eds.), *Handbook of child psychology: Vol. 4. Child psychology in practice* (5th ed., pp. 775–874). New York: Wiley.

Goodman, S. H., Adamson, L. B., Riniti, J., & Cole, S. (1994). Mothers' expressed attitudes: Associations with maternal depression and children's self-esteem and psychopathology. *Journal of the American Academy of Child and Adolescent Psychiatry, 33,* 1265–1274.

Goodman, S. H., & Brumley, H. E. (1990). Schizophrenic and depressed mothers: Relational deficits in parenting. *Developmental Psychology, 26,* 31–39.

Goodman, S. H., & Gotlib, I. H. (1999). Risk for psychopathology in the children of depressed mothers: A developmental model for understanding mechanisms of transmission. *Psychological Review, 106,* 458–490.

Gordon, B. (1983). Maternal perception of child temperament and observed mother-child interaction. *Child Psychiatry and Human Development, 13,* 153–167.

Gordon, D., Burge, D., Hammen, C., Adrian, C., Jaenicke, C., & Hiroto, D. (1989). Observations of interactions of depressed women with their children. *American Journal of Psychiatry, 146,* 50–55.

Grych, J. (2002). Marital relationships and parenting. In M. Bornstein (Ed.), *Handbook of parenting: Vol. 4. Social conditions and applied parenting* (2nd ed., pp. 203–225). Mahwah, NJ: Erlbaum.

Grych, J. H., & Clark, R. (1999). Maternal employment and development of the father-infant relationship in the first year. *Developmental Psychology, 35,* 893–903.

Haber, J. R., Leonard, K. E., & Rushe, R. (2000). Home interactions of high and low antisocial male alcoholics and their families. *Journal of Studies on Alcohol, 61,* 72.

Haft, W., & Slade, A. (1989). Affect attunement and maternal attachment: A pilot study. *Infant Mental Health, 10,* 157–172.

Hagekull, B., & Bohlin, G. (1986). Mother-infant interaction and perceived infant temperament. *International Journal of Behavioral Development, 9,* 297–313.

Hamilton, E. B., Jones, M., & Hammen, C. (1993). Maternal interaction style in affective disordered, physically ill, and normal women. *Family Process, 32,* 329–340.

Hammen, C. (2002). Context of stress in families of children with depressed parents. In S. H. Goodman & I. H. Gotlib (Eds.), *Children of depressed parents: Mechanisms of risk and implications for treatment* (pp. 175–199). Washington, DC: American Psychological Association.

Hammen, C., Burge, D., & Stansbury, K. (1990). Relationship of mother and child variables to child outcomes in a high-risk sample: A causal modeling analysis. *Developmental Psychology, 26,* 24–30.

Hardt, J., & Rutter, M. (2004). Validity of adult retrospective reports of adverse childhood experiences: Review of the evidence. *Journal of Child Psychology and Psychiatry, 45,* 260–273.

Harold, G. T., & Conger, R. D. (1997). Marital conflict and adolescent distress: The role of adolescent awareness. *Child Development, 68,* 333–350.

Harold, G. T., Fincham, F. D., Osborne, L. N., & Conger, R. D. (1997). Mom and Dad are at it again: Adolescent perceptions of marital conflict and adolescent psychological distress. *Developmental Psychology, 33,* 333–350.

Harrist, A. W., & Ainslie, R. C. (1998). Marital discord and child behavior problems: Parent-child relationship quality and child interpersonal awareness as mediators. *Journal of Family Issues, 19,* 140–163.

Harter, S. L., & Taylor, T. L. (2000). Parental alcoholism, child abuse, and adult adjustment. *Journal of Substance Abuse, 11,* 31–44.

Hearle, J., & McGrath, J. (2000). Motherhood and Schizophrenia. In D. J. Castle, J. McGrath, & J. Kulkarni (Eds.), *Women and Schizophrenia* (pp. 79–94). Cambridge, England: Cambridge University Press.

Heinicke, C. M. (1984). Impact of pre-birth parent personality and marital functioning on family development: A framework and suggestions for further study. *Developmental Psychology, 20,* 1044–1053.

Hemphill, S., & Sanson, A. (2000, July). *Relations between toddler and preschooler temperament and parenting style in an Australian sample.* Paper presented at the 16th biennial meetings of the International Society for the Study of Behavioral Development, Beijing, China.

Herring, M., & Kaslow, N. J. (2002). Depression and attachment in families: A child-focused perspective. *Family Process, 41,* 494–518.

Hesse, E. (1999). The adult attachment interview. In J. Cassidy & P. Shaver (Eds.), *Handbook of attachment: Theory, research and clinical applications* (pp. 395–433). New York: Guilford Press.

Heyman, R., & Slep, A. (2002). Do child abuse and interparental violence lead to adulthood family violence? *Journal of Marriage and the Family, 64,* 864–870.

Hill, N. E., & Herman-Stahl, M. A. (2002). Neighborhood safety and social involvement: Associations with parenting behaviors and depressive symptoms among African American and Euro-American mothers. *Journal of Family Psychology, 16,* 209–219.

Hinde, R. A. (1989). Temperament as an intervening variable. In G. A. Kohnstamm, J. E. Bates, & M. K. Rothbart (Eds.), *Temperament in childhood* (pp. 27–34). Chichester, England: Wiley.

Hipwell, A. E., & Kumar, R. (1996). Maternal psychopathology and prediction of outcome based on mother-infant interaction ratings (BMIS). *British Journal of Psychiatry, 169,* 655–661.

Holden, G., & Buck, M. (2002). Parental attitudes toward childrearing. In M. Bornstein (Ed.), *Handbook of parenting: Vol. 3. Being and becoming a parent* (pp. 537–562). Mahwah, NJ: Erlbaum.

Holden, G., & Zambarano, R. (1992). Passing the rod: Similarities between parents and their young children in orientation toward physical punishment. In I. Sigel, A. McGillicuddy-DeLisi, & J. Goodnow (Eds.), *Parental belief systems* (2nd ed., pp. 143–172). Hillsdale, NJ: Erlbaum.

Hops, H., Biglan, A., Sherman, L., Arthur, J., Friedman, L., & Osteen, V. (1987). Home observations of family interactions of depressed women. *Journal of Consulting and Clinical Psychology, 55,* 341–346.

Howes, P., & Markman, H. (1989). Marital quality and child functioning. *Child Development, 60,* 1044–1051.

Hughes, H. (1988). Psychological and behavioural correlates of family violence in child witnesses and victims. *American Journal of Orthopsychiatry, 58,* 77–90.

Hunter, R., & Kilstrom, N. (1979). Breaking the cycle in abusive families. *American Journal of Psychiatry, 136,* 1320–1322.

Hur, Y., & Bouchard, T. (1995). Genetic influences on the perceptions of childhood family environment: A reared apart twin study. *Child Development, 66,* 330–345.

Inoff-Germain, G., Nottelmann, E. D., & Radke-Yarrow, M. (1992). Evaluative communications between affectively ill and well mothers and their children. *Journal of Abnormal Child Psychology, 20,* 189–212.

Isabella, R., & Belsky, J. (1985). Marital change during the transition to parenthood and security of infant-parent attachment. *Journal of Family Issues, 6,* 505–522.

Jablensky, A. (1995). Schizophrenia: The epidemiological horizon. In S. R. Hirsch & D. R. Weinberger (Eds.), *Schizophrenia* (pp. 206–252). Oxford: Blackwell Science.

Jacob, T., & Johnson, S. L. (1997). Parent-child interaction among depressed fathers and mothers: Impact on child functioning. *Journal of Family Psychology, 11,* 391–409.

Jacob, T., & Johnson, S. L. (2001). Sequential interactions in the parent-child communications of depressed fathers and depressed mothers. *Journal of Family Psychology, 15,* 38–52.

Jacob, T., Krahn, G. L., & Leonard, K. (1991). Parent-child interactions in families with alcoholic fathers. *Journal of Consulting and Clinical Psychology, 59,* 176–181.

Jaffee, S. R. (2002). Pathways to adversity in young adulthood among early childbearers. *Journal of Family Psychology, 16,* 38–49.

Jaffee, S. R., Moffitt, T. E., Caspi, A., & Taylor, A. (2003). Life with (and without) father: The benefits of living with two biological parents depend on the father's antisocial behavior. *Child Development, 74,* 109–126.

Jameson, P. B., Gelfand, D. M., Kulcsar, E., & Teti, D. M. (1997). Mother-toddler interaction patterns associated with maternal depression. *Development and Psychopathology, 9,* 537–550.

Jarrett, R. L. (1997). Bringing families back in: Neighborhood effects on child development. In J. Brooks-Gunn, G. J. Duncan, & J. L. Aber (Eds.), *Neighborhood poverty: Policy implications in studying neighborhoods* (pp. 48–64). New York: Russell Sage Foundation.

Jencks, C., & Mayer, S. (1990). The social consequences of growing up in a poor neighborhood. In L. E. Lynn & M. F. H. McGeary (Eds.), *Inner-city poverty in the United States* (pp. 111–186). Washington, DC: National Academy Press.

Jenkins, J., Rasbash, J., & O'Connor, T. G. (2003). The role of the shared family context in differential parenting. *Developmental Psychology, 39,* 99–113.

John, O. P., & Srivastava, S. (1999). The Big Five trait taxonomy: History, measurement, and theoretical perspectives. In L. A. Pervin & O. P. John (Eds.), *Handbook of personality: Theory and research* (2nd ed., pp. 102–138). New York: Guilford Press.

Johnston, C., & Patenaude, R. (1994). Parent attributions for inattentive-overreactive and oppositional-defiant child behaviors. *Cognitive Therapy and Research, 18,* 261–275.

Jones, D. J., Forehand, R., Brody, G., & Armistead, L. (2002). Psychosocial adjustment of African American children in single-mother families: A test of three risk models. *Journal of Marriage and the Family, 64,* 105–115.

Jouriles, E., Norwood, W., McDonald, R., & Peters, B. (2001). Domestic violence and child adjustment. In J. Grych (Ed.), *Interparental conflict and child development* (pp. 315–336). New York: Cambridge University Press.

Kadushin, A., & Martin, J. (1981). *Child abuse: An interactional event.* New York: Columbia University Press.

Kanoy, K., Ulku-Steiner, B., Cox, M., & Burchinal, M. (2003). Marital relationship and individual psychological characteristics that predict physical punishment of children. *Journal of Family Psychology, 17,* 20–28.

Katz, L., & Gottman, J. M. (1996). Spillover effects of marital conflict: In search of parenting and coparenting mechanisms. In J. McHale & P. Cowan (Eds.), *Understanding how family-level dynamics affect children's development: Studies of two-parent families* (pp. 221–245). San Francisco: Jossey-Bass.

Katz, L., & Woodin, E. (2002). Hostility, hostile detachment, and conflict engagement in marriages: Effects on child and family functioning. *Child Development, 73,* 636–652.

Kaufman, J., & Zigler, E. (1987). Do abused children become abusive parents? *American Journal of Orthopsychiatry, 57,* 186–192.

Kaufman, J., & Zigler, E. (1989). The intergenerational transmission of child abuse. In D. Cicchetti & V. Carlson (Eds.), *Child maltreatment: Theory and research on the causes and consequences of child abuse and neglect* (pp. 129–150). New York: Cambridge University Press.

Kelley, S. A., & Jennings, K. D. (2003). Putting the pieces together: Maternal depression, maternal behavior, and toddler helplessness. *Infant Mental Health Journal, 24,* 74–90.

Kendler, K. (1996). Parenting: A genetic-epidemiological perspective. *American Journal of Psychiatry, 153,* 11–20.

Kerig, P. K. (1995). Triangles in the family circle: Effects of family structure on marriage, parenting, and child adjustment. *Journal of Family Psychology, 9,* 28–43.

Klebanov, P. K., Brooks-Gunn, J., Chase-Lansdale, P. L., & Gordon, R. A. (1997). Are neighborhood effects on young children mediated by features of the home environment? In J. Brooks-Gunn, G. J. Duncan, & J. L. Aber (Eds.), *Neighborhood poverty: Context and consequences for children* (pp. 119–145). New York: Russell Sage Foundation.

Klebanov, P. K., Brooks-Gunn, J., & Duncan, G. J. (1994). Does neighborhood and family poverty affect mothers' parenting, mental health, and social support? *Journal of Marriage and the Family, 56,* 441–455.

Klein, M., & Stern, L. (1971). Low birthweight and the battered child syndrome. *American Journal of Diseases of Childhood, 122,* 15–18.

Kochanska, G., Aksan, N., & Nichols, K. (2003). Maternal power assertion in disicipline and moral discourse contexts. *Developmental Psychology, 39,* 949–963.

Kochanska, G., Clark, L., & Goldman, M. (1997). Implications of mothers' personality for parenting and their young children's developmental outcomes. *Journal of Personality, 65,* 389–420.

Kochanska, G., & Kuczynski, L. (1991). Maternal autonomy granting: Predictors of normal and depressed mothers' compliance and noncompliance with the requests of five-year-olds. *Child Development, 62,* 1449–1459.

Kochanska, G., Kuczynski, L., Radke-Yarrow, M., & Welsh, J. D. (1987). Resolutions of control episodes between well and affectively ill mothers and their young children. *Journal of Abnormal Child Psychology, 15,* 441–456.

Kochanska, G., Radke-Yarrow, M., Kuczynski, L., & Friedman, S. L. (1987). Normal and affectively ill mothers' beliefs about their children. *American Journal of Orthopsychiatry, 57,* 345–350.

Korbin, J. E., Coulton, C. J., Chard, S., Platt-Houston, C., & Su, M. (1998). Impoverishment and child maltreatment in African American and European American neighborhoods. *Development and Psychopathology, 10,* 215–233.

Kovacs, M., Krol, R. S. M., & Voti, L. (1994). Early onset psychopathology and the risk for teenage pregnancy among clinically referred girls. *Journal of the American Academy of Child and Adolescent Psychiatry, 33,* 106–113.

Krishnakumar, A., & Buehler, C. (2000). Interparental conflict and parenting behaviors: A meta-analytic review. *Family Relations, 49,* 25–44.

Kyrios, M., & Prior, M. (1990). Temperament, stress and family factors in behavioural adjustment of 3–5-year-old children. *International Journal of Behavioral Development, 13,* 67–93.

Lamb, M. E., Frodi, M., Hwang, C., Forstromm, B., & Corry, T. (1982). Stability and change in parental attitudes following an infant's birth into traditional and non-traditional Swedish families. *Scandinavian Journal of Psychology, 23,* 53–62.

Lang, A. R., Pelham, W. E., Atkeson, B. M., & Murphy, D. A. (1999). Effects of alcohol intoxication on parenting behavior in interactions with child confederates exhibiting normal or deviant behaviors. *Journal of Abnormal Child Psychology, 27,* 177–189.

Langrock, A. M., Compas, B. E., Keller, G., Merchant, M. J., & Copeland, M. E. (2002). Coping with the stress of parental depression: Parents' reports of children's coping, emotional, and behavioral problems. *Journal of Clinical Child and Adolescent Psychology, 31,* 312–324.

Leinonen, J., Solantaus, T., & Punamaki, R. (2003). Parental mental health and children's adjustment: The quality of marital interaction and parenting as mediating factors. *Journal of Child Psychology and Psychiatry, 44,* 227–241.

Levendosky, A., & Graham-Berman, S. (2000). Behavioral observations of parenting in battered women. *Journal of Family Psychology, 14,* 80–94.

Levendosky, A., Huth-Bocks, A., Semel, M., & Shapiro, D. (2002). Trauma symptoms in preschool-age children exposed to domestic violence. *Journal of Interpersonal Violence, 17,* 150–164.

Levendosky, A., Huth-Bocks, A., Shapiro, D., & Semel, M. (2003). The impact of domestic violence on the maternal-child relationship and preschool-age children's functioning. *Journal of Family Psychology, 17,* 275–288.

Leventhal, T., & Brooks-Gunn, J. (2000). The neighborhoods they live in: The effects of neighborhood residence on child and adolescent outcomes. *Psychological Bulletin, 126,* 309–337.

Leventhal, T., & Brooks-Gunn, J. (2001). Moving to better neighborhoods improves health and family life among New York families. *Poverty Research News, 5,* 11–12.

Leventhal, T., & Brooks-Gunn, J. (2003). Children and youth in neighborhood contexts. *Current Directions in Psychological Science, 12,* 27–31.

Levy-Shiff, R., & Israelashvili, R. (1988). Antecedents of fathering. *Developmental Psychology, 24,* 434–441.

Light, R. (1973). Abused and neglected children in America: A study of alternative policies. *Harvard Educational Review, 43,* 556–598.

Lindahl, K. M., Clements, M., & Markman, H. (1997). Predicting marital and parent functioning in dyads and triads: A longitudinal investigation of marital processes. *Journal of Family Psychology, 11,* 139–151.

Lindahl, K. M., & Malik, N. M. (1999). Observations of marital conflict and power: Relations with parenting in the triad. *Journal of Marriage and the Family, 61,* 320–330.

Linn, P., & Horowitz, F. (1983). The relationship between infant individual differences and mother-infant interaction during the neonatal period. *Infant Behavior and Development, 6,* 415–427.

Longfellow, C., Zelkowitz, P., & Saunders, E. (1982). The quality of mother-child relationships. In D. Belle (Ed.), *Lives in stress* (pp. 163–176). Beverly Hills, CA: Sage.

Losoya, S., Callor, S., Rowe, D., & Goldsmith, H. (1997). Origins of familial similarity in parenting. *Developmental Psychology, 33,* 1012–1023.

Lovejoy, M. C. (1991). Maternal depression: Effects on social cognition and behavior in parent-child interactions. *Journal of Abnormal Child Psychology, 19,* 693–706.

Lovejoy, M. C., Graczyk, P. A., O'Hare, E., & Neuman, G. (2000). Maternal depression and parenting behavior: A meta-analytic review. *Clinical Psychology Review, 20,* 561–592.

Lynch, M., & Cicchetti, D. (1998). An ecological-transactional analysis of children and contexts: The longitudinal interplay among child maltreatment, community violence, and children's symptomatology. *Development and Psychopathology, 10,* 235–257.

Maccoby, E. E., Snow, M. E., & Jacklin, C. N. (1984). Children's dispositions and mother-child interaction at 12 and 18 months: A short-term longitudinal study. *Developmental Psychology, 20,* 459–472.

Magura, S., & Laudet, A. B. (1996). Parental substance abuse and child maltreatment: Review and implications for intervention. *Children and Youth Services Review, 18,* 193–220.

Main, M., & Goldwyn, R. (1984). Predicting rejection of her infant from mother's representation of her own experience: Implications for the abused-abusing intergenerational cycle. *Child Abuse and Neglect, 8,* 203–217.

Main, M., Kaplan, N., & Cassidy, J. (1985). Security in infancy, childhood and adulthood: A move to level of representation. In I. Bretherton & E. Waters (Eds.), Growing points in attachment theory and research. *Monographs for the Society for Research in Child Development, 50*(1–2, Serial No. 209), 66–104.

Mangelsdorf, S., Gunnar, M., Kestenbaum, R., Lang, S., & Andreas, D. (1990). Infant proneness-to-distress temperament, maternal personality, and mother-infant attachment: Associations and goodness of fit. *Child Development, 61,* 820–831.

Manski, C. F. (1993). Identification of endogenous social effects: The reflection problem. *Review of Economic Studies, 60,* 531–542.

Margolin, G., Oliver, P. H., & Medina, A. M. (2001). Conceptual issues in understanding the relation between interparental conflict and child adjustment. In J. Grych & F. Fincham (Eds.), *Interparental conflict and child development: Theory, research, and applications* (pp. 9–38). Cambridge, England: Cambridge University Press.

Martin, H., Conway, E., Beezley, P., & Kempe, H. C. (1974). The development of abused children, Part I: A review of the literature. *Advances in Pediatrics, 21,* 43.

Mayes, L. C. (1995). Substance abuse and parenting. In M. Borstein (Ed.), *Handbook of parenting: Applied and practical parenting* (pp. 101–125). Hillsdale, NJ: Erlbaum.

McBride, B., Schoppe, S., & Rane, T. (2002). Child characteristics, parenting stress, and parental involvement: Mothers and fathers. *Journal of Marriage and the Family, 64,* 998–1011.

McCloskey, L., Figueredo, A., & Koss, M. (1995). The effects of systemic family violence on children's mental health. *Child Development, 66,* 1239–1261.

McCrae, R. R., & Costa, P. T., Jr. (1987). Validation of the five-factor model of personality across instruments and observers. *Journal of Personality and Social Psychology, 52,* 81–90.

McGuire, S. (2003). The heritability of parenting. *Parenting, 3,* 73–94.

McLoyd, V. C. (1998). Socioeconomic disadvantage and child development. *American Psychologist, 53,* 185–204.

McMahon, T. J., & Rounsaville, B. J. (2002). Substance abuse and fathering: Adding Poppa to the research agenda. *Addiction, 97,* 1109–1115.

McNeil, T. F., Naslund, B., Persson-Blennow, I., & Kaij, L. (1985). Offspring of women with nonorganic psychosis: Mother-infant interaction at three-and-a-half and six months of age. *Acta Psychiatrica Scandinavica, 71,* 551–558.

Meyers, S. (1999). Mothering in context: Ecological determinants of parenting behavior. *Merrill-Palmer Quarterly, 45,* 332–357.

Miller, B. A., Maguin, E., & Downs, E. R. (1997). Alcohol, drugs, and violence in children's lives. In M. Galanter (Ed.), *Recent developments in alcoholism: Alcoholism and violence* (pp. 357–385). New York: Plenum Press.

Minuchin, P. (1985). Families and individual development: Provocations from the field of family therapy. *Child Development, 56,* 289–302.

Minuchin, S. (1974). *Families and family therapy.* Cambridge, MA: Harvard University Press.

Moffitt, T. E., Caspi, A., Harrington, H., & Milne, B. J. (2002). Males on the life-course-persistent and adolescence-limited antisocial pathways: Follow-up at age 26 years. *Development and Psychopathology, 14,* 179–207.

Morse, B. (1995). Beyond the Conflict Tactics Scale: Assessing gender differences in partner violence. *Violence and Victims, 10,* 251–273.

Moser, R. P., & Jacob, T. (1997). Parent-child interactions and child outcomes as related to gender of alcoholic parent. *Journal of Substance Abuse, 9,* 189–208.

Moss, H. B., Lynch, K. G., Hardie, T. L., & Baron, D. A. (2002). Family functioning and peer affiliation in children of fathers with antisocial personality disorder and substance dependence: Associations with problem behaviors. *American Journal of Psychiatry, 159,* 607–614.

Mowbray, C. T., Oyserman, D., Zemencuk, J. K., & Ross, S. R. (1995). Motherhood for women with serious mental illness: Pregnancy, childbirth, and the postpartum period. *American Journal of Orthopsychiatry, 65,* 21–38.

Muller, R., Hunter, J. E., & Stollak, G. (1995). The intergenerational transmission of corporal punishment. *Child Abuse and Neglect, 19,* 1323–1335.

Murphy, J. M., Jellinek, M., Quinn, D., Smith, G., Poitrast, F. G., & Goshko, M. (1991). Substance abuse and serious child mistreatment: Prevalence, risk, and outcome in a court sample. *Child Abuse and Neglect, 15,* 197–211.

Murray, L., Fiori-Cowley, A., Hooper, R., & Cooper, P. (1996). The impact of postnatal depression and associated adversity on early mother-infant interactions and later infant outcome. *Child Development, 67,* 2512–2526.

Murray, L., Sinclair, D., Cooper, P., Ducournau, P., Turner, P., & Stein, A. (1999). The socioemotional development of 5-year-old children of postnatally depressed mothers. *Journal of Child Psychology and Psychiatry, 40,* 1259–1271.

Naslund, B., Persson-Blennow, I., & McNeil, T. F. (1985). Offspring of women with nonorganic psychosis: Mother-infant interaction at 3 and 6 weeks of age. *Acta Psychiatrica Scandinavica, 71,* 441–450.

NICHD Early Child Care Research Network. (1999). Chronicity of maternal depressive symptoms, maternal sensitivity and child functioning at 36 months: Results from the NICHD Study of Early Child Care. *Developmental Psychology, 35,* 1297–1310.

Nolen-Hoeksema, S., Wolfson, A., Mumme, D., & Guskin, K. (1995). Helplessness in children of depressed and nondepressed mothers. *Developmental Psychology, 31,* 377–387.

O'Brien, D. J., Hassinger, E. W., & Dershem, L. (1994). Community attachment and depression among residents in two rural midwestern communities. *Rural Sociology, 59,* 255–265.

O'Connor, T. G. (2002). Annotation: The "effects" of parenting reconsidered: Findings, challenges, and applications. *Journal of Child Psychology and Psychiatry, 43,* 555–573.

Oliver, J. (1993). Intergenerational transmission of child abuse: Rates, research, and clinical implications. *American Journal of Psychiatry, 150,* 1315–1324.

Osborne, L., & Fincham, F. (1996). Marital conflict, parent-child relationships, and child adjustment. *Merrill-Palmer Quarterly, 42,* 48–65.

Oyserman, D., Bybee, D., Mowbray, C. T., & MacFarlane, P. (2002). Positive parenting among African American mothers with a serious mental illness. *Journal of Marriage and the Family, 64,* 65–77.

Pajer, K. A. (1998). What happens to "bad" girls? A review of the adult outcomes of antisocial adolescent girls. *American Journal of Psychiatry, 155,* 862–870.

Parke, R. (1978). Parent-infant interaction: Progress, paradigms and problems. In G. P. Sackett (Ed.), *Observing behavior: Vol. 1. Theory and applications in mental retardation* (pp. 133–155). Baltimore: University Park Press.

Parke, R., & Collmer, C. (1975). Child abuse: An interdisciplinary review. In E. M. Hetherington (Ed.), *Review of child development research* (Vol. 5, pp. 133–225). Chicago: University of Chicago Press.

Pauli-Pott, U., Mertesacker, B., Bade, U., Bauer, C., & Beckmann, D. (2000). Contexts of relations of infant negative emotionality to caregiver's reactivity/sensitivity. *Infant Behavior and Development, 23,* 23–39.

Pears, K., & Capaldi, D. (2001). Intergenerational transmission of abuse: A two-generational prospective study of an at-risk sample. *Child Abuse and Neglect, 25,* 1439–1461.

Pedersen, F. (1975, September). *Mother, father and infant as an interactive system.* Paper presented at the annual convention of the American Psychological Association, Chicago.

Pedersen, F. (1982). Mother, father and infant as an interactive system. In J. Belsky (Ed.), *In the beginning: Readings on infancy* (pp. 47–58). New York: Columbia University Press.

Pedersen, F., Anderson, B., & Cain, R. (1977, March). *An approach to understanding linkages between the parent-infant and spouse relationships.* Paper presented at the biennial meeting of the Society for Research in Child Development, New Orleans, LA.

Pedersen, F., Yarrow, L., Anderson, B., & Cain, R. (1978). Conceptualization of father influences in the infancy period. In M. Lewis & L. Rosenblum (Eds.), *The social network of the developing infant* (pp. 109–123). New York: Plenum Press.

Persson-Blennow, I., Naslund, B., & McNeil, T. F. (1984). Offspring of women with nonorganic psychosis: Mother-infant interaction at three days of age. *Acta Psychiatrica Scandinavica, 70,* 149–159.

Perusse, D., Neale, M., Heath, A., & Eaves, L. (1994). Human parental behavior: Evidence for genetic influence and potential implications for gene-culture transmission. *Behavior Genetics, 24,* 327–335.

Phares, V. (1992). Where's Poppa? The relative lack of attention to the role of fathers in child and adolescent psychopathology. *American Psychologist, 47,* 656–664.

Phares, V., & Compas, B. E. (1992). The role of fathers in child and adolescent psychopathology: Make room for Daddy. *Psychological Bulletin, 111,* 387–412.

Pike, A., McGuire, S., Hetherington, E., Reiss, D., & Plomin, R. (1996). Family enviornment and adolescent depressive symptoms and antisocial behavior: A multivariate genetic analysis. *Developmental Psychology, 32,* 590–603.

Pinderhughes, E. E., Nix, R., Foster, E. M., Jones, D., & The Conduct Problems Prevention Group. (2001). Parenting in context: Impact of neighborhood poverty, residential stability, public services, social networks, and danger on parental behavior. *Journal of Marriage and the Family, 63,* 941–953.

Plomin, R., & Bergman, C. S. (1991). Nature and nurture: Authors' response to commentaries. *Behavior and Brain Sciences, 14,* 414–424.

Plomin, R., McClearn, G. E., Pedersen, N. L., Nesselroade, J. R., & Bergman, C. S. (1989). Genetic influences on adults' ratings of their current family environment. *Journal of Marriage and the Family, 51,* 791–803.

Plomin, R., Pedersen, N. L., McClearn, G. E., Nesselroade, J. R., & Bergman, C. S. (1988). Genetic influences on childhood family environment perceived retrospectively from the last half of the life span. *Developmental Psychology, 24,* 738–745.

Plomin, R., Reiss, D., Hetherington, E., & Howe, G. (1994). Nature and nuture: Genetic contributions to measures of the family environment. *Developmental Psychology, 30,* 32–43.

Putnam, S., Sanson, A., & Rothbart, M. (2002). Child temperament and parenting. In M. Bornstein (Ed.), *Handbook of parenting: Vol. 1, Children and parenting* (2nd ed., pp. 255–277). Mahwah, NJ: Erlbaum.

Quinton, D., Rutter, M., & Liddle, C. (1984). Institutional rearing, parenting difficulties, and marital support. *Psychological Medicine, 14,* 107–124.

Radke-Yarrow, M. (1998). *Children of depressed mothers: From early childhood to maturity.* New York: Cambridge University Press.

Radke-Yarrow, M., Nottelmann, E., Belmont, B., & Welsh, J. D. (1993). Affective interactions of depressed and nondepressed mothers and their children. *Journal of Abnormal Child Psychology, 21,* 683–695.

Regier, D. A., Farmer, M. E., Rae, D. S., Locke, B. Z., Keith, S. J., Judd, L. L., et al. (1990). Comorbidity of mental disorders with alcohol and other drug abuse: Results from the Epidemiologic Catchment Area (ECA) Study. *Journal of the American Medical Association, 264,* 2511–2518.

Reich, W., Earls, F., & Powell, J. (1988). A comparison of the home and social environments of children of alcoholic and non-alcoholic parents. *British Journal of Addiction, 83,* 831–839.

Reid, W., & Crisafulli, A. (1990). Marital discord and child behavior problems: A meta-analysis. *Journal of Abnormal Child Psychology, 18,* 105–117.

Rende, R. D., Slomkowski, C. L., Stocker, C., Fulker, D. W., & Plomin, R. (1992). Genetic and environmental influences on maternal and sibling interaction in middle childhood: A sibling adoption study. *Developmental Psychology, 28,* 484–490.

Rendina, I., & Dickerscheid, J. D. (1976). Father involvement with firstborn infants. *Family Coordinator, 25,* 376–378.

Riordan, D., Appleby, L., & Faragher, B. (1999). Mother-infant interaction in post-partum women with Schizophrenia and affective disorders. *Psychological Medicine, 29,* 991–995.

Rogosch, F. A., Mowbray, C. T., & Bogat, G. A. (1992). Determinants of parenting attitudes in mothers with severe psychopathology. *Development and Psychopathology, 4,* 469–487.

Roisman, G., Padron, E., Sroufe, L. A., & Egeland, B. (2002). Earned-secure attachment status in retrospect and prospect. *Child Development, 73,* 1204–1219.

Ross, C. E. (2000). Neighborhood disadvantage and adult depression. *Journal of Health and Social Behavior, 41,* 177–187.

Rossman, B. (1998). Descartes's error and posttraumatic stress disorder. In G. Holden, R. Geffner, & E. Joriles (Eds.), *Children exposed to marital violence* (pp. 223–256). Washington, DC: American Psychological Association.

Rothbart, M. K. (1989). Temperament and development. In G. A. Kohnstamm, J. E. Bates, & M. K. Rothbart (Eds.), *Temperament in childhood* (pp. 187–247). Chichester, England: Wiley.

Rothbart, M. K., Ahadi, S. A., Hershey, K., & Fisher, P. (2001). Investigations of temperament at 3–7 years: The Children's Behavior Questionnaire. *Child Development, 72,* 1394–1408.

Rothbart, M. K., & Mauro, J. A. (1990). Questionnaire measures of infant temperament. In J. W. Fagen & J. Colombo (Eds.), *Individual differences in infancy: Reliability, stability and prediction* (pp. 411–429). Hillsdale, NJ: Erlbaum.

Rowe, D. C. (1981). Environmental and genetic influences on dimensions of perceived parenting: A twin study. *Developmental Psychology, 17,* 203–208.

Rowe, D. C. (1983). A biometrical analysis of perceptions of family environment: A study of twin and singleton siblings. *Child Development, 54,* 416–423.

Rubin, K. H., Hastings, P. D., Stewart, S. L., Henderson, H. A., & Chen, X. (1997). The consistency and concomitants of inhibition: Some of the children, all of the time. *Child Development, 68,* 467–483.

Sampson, R. J. (1992). Family management and child development: Insights from social disorganization theory. In J. McCord (Ed.), *Facts, frameworks, and forecasts: Advances in criminological theory* (pp. 63–93). New Brunswick, NJ: Transaction.

Sampson, R. J., & Groves, W. B. (1989). Community structure and crime: Testing social-disorganization theory. *American Journal of Sociology, 94,* 774–802.

Sampson, R. J., Raudenbush, S. W., & Earls, F. (1997). Neighborhoods and violent crime: A multilevel study of collective efficacy. *Science, 277,* 918–924.

Schachar, R., Taylor, E., Wieselberg, M. B., Thorley, G., & Rutter, M. (1987). Changes in family function and relationships in children who respond to methylphenidate. *Journal of the American Academy of Child and Adolescent Psychiatry, 26,* 728–732.

Seagull, E. A. W. (1987). Social support and child maltreatment: A review of the evidence. *Child Abuse and Neglect, 11,* 41–52.

Sears, R., Maccoby, E., & Levin, H. (1957). *Patterns of child rearing.* Evantson, IL: Row, Peterson.

Seifer, R., Schiller, M., Sameroff, A. J., Resnick, S., & Riordan, K. (1996). Attachment, maternal sensitivity, and infant temperament during the first year of life. *Developmental Psychology, 32,* 12–25.

Serbin, L., & Karp, J. (2003). Intergenerational studies of parenting and the transfer of risk from parent to child. *Current Directions in Psychological Science, 12,* 138–142.

Shaw, C. R., & McKay, H. D. (1942). *Juvenile delinquency and urban areas.* Chicago: University of Chicago Press.

Shears, J., Robinson, J., & Emde, R. N. (2002). Fathering relationships and their associations with juvenile delinquency. *Infant Mental Health Journal, 23,* 79–87.

Simons, R., Beaman, J., Conger, R. D., & Chao, W. (1993a). Childhood experience, conceptions of parenting, and attitudes of spouse as determinants of parental behavior. *Journal of Marriage and the Family, 55,* 91–106.

Simons, R., Beaman, J., Conger, R. D., & Chao, W. (1993b). Stress, support, and antisocial behavior trait as determinants of emotional well-being and parenting practices among single mothers. *Journal of Marriage and the Family, 55,* 385–398.

Simons, R. L., Johnson, C., Conger, R. D., & Lorenz, F. O. (1997). Linking community context to quality of parenting: A study of rural families. *Rural Sociology, 62,* 207–230.

Simons, R. L., Whitbeck, L. B., Conger, R. D., & Chyi-In, W. (1991). Intergenerational transmission of harsh parenting. *Developmental Psychology, 27,* 159–171.

Slep, A., & O'Leary, S. (1998). The effects of maternal attributions on parenting. *Journal of Family Psychology, 12,* 234–243.

Smith, C., & Farrington, D. (2004). Continuities in antisocial behaviour and parenting across three generations. *Journal of Child Psychology and Psychiatry, 45,* 230–247.

Snellen, M., Mack, K., & Trauer, T. (1999). Schizophrenia, mental state, and mother-infant interaction: Examining the relationship. *Australian and New Zealand Journal of Psychiatry, 33,* 902–911.

Spangler, G. (1990). Mother, child, and situational correlates of toddlers' social competence. *Infant Behavior and Development, 13,* 405–419.

Spinath, F., & O'Connor, T. (2003). A behavioural genetic study of the overlap between personality and parenting. *Journal of Personality, 71,* 785–808.

Spinetta, J., & Rigler, D. (1972). The child abusing parent: A psychological review. *Psychological Bulletin, 77,* 296–304.

Spitz, R. (1970). The effect of personality disturbance in the mother on the well-being of her infant. In E. J. Anthony & T. Benedek (Eds.), *Parenthood: Its psychology and psychopathology* (pp. 503–524). Boston: Little, Brown.

Sroufe, L. A., & Rutter, M. (1984). The domain of developmental psychopathology. *Child Development, 55,* 17–29.

Stagg, V., Wills, G., & Howell, M. (1989). Psychopathology in early childhood witnesses of family violence. *Topics in Early Childhood Special Education, 9,* 73–87.

Starr, R. H., Dietrich, K. N., Fischhoff, J., Ceresnie, S., & Zweier, D. (1984). The contribution of handicapping conditions to child abuse. *Topics in Early Childhood Special Education, 4,* 55–69.

Steele, B. (1976). Violence within the family. In C. H. Kempe & A. E. Helfer (Eds.), *Child abuse and neglect: The family and the community* (pp. 3–24). Cambridge, MA: Ballinger.

Stein, A., Gath, D. H., Bucher, J., Bond, A., Day, A., & Cooper, P. J. (1991). The relationship between post-natal depression and mother-child interaction. *British Journal of Psychiatry, 158,* 52.

Steinberg, L., Catalano, R., & Dooley, D. (1981). Economic antecedents of child abuse and neglect. *Child Development, 52,* 975–985.

Stocker, C., & Youngblade, L. (1999). Marital conflict and parental hostility: Links with children's sibling and peer relationships. *Journal of Family Psychology, 13,* 598–609.

Stoneman, Z., Brody, G. H., & Burke, M. (1989). Marital quality, depression, and inconsistent parenting: Relationship with observed mother-child conflict. *American Journal of Orthopsychiatry, 59,* 105–117.

Straus, M., & Gelles, R. (1986). Societal change and change in family violence from 1975–1985 as revealed in two national surveys. *Journal of Marriage and the Family, 48,* 465–479.

Tamis-LeMonda, C. S., & Cabrera, N. (2002). Multidisciplinary perspectives on father involvement: An introduction. In C. S. Tamis-LeMonda & N. Cabrera (Eds.), *Handbook of father involvement: Multidisciplinary perspectives* (pp. xi–xviii). Mahwah, NJ: Erlbaum.

Tarullo, L. B., DeMulder, E. K., Martinez, P. E., & Radke-Yarrow, M. (1994). Dialogues with preadolescents and adolescents: Mother-child interaction patterns in affectively ill and well dyads. *Journal of Abnormal Child Psychology, 22,* 33–51.

Tellegen, A., Watson, D., & Clark, L. (1999). On the dimensional and hierarchical structure of affect. *Psychological Science, 10,* 297–303.

Teti, D. M., & Gelfand, D. M. (1991). Behavioral competence among mothers of infants in the first year: The mediational role of maternal self-efficacy. *Child Development, 62,* 918–929.

Teti, D. M., Gelfand, D. M., & Pompa, J. (1990). Depressed mothers' behavioral competence with their infants: Demographic and psychosocial correlates. *Development and Psychopathology, 2,* 259–270.

Thomas, A., Chess, S., Birch, H. G., Hertzig, M. E., & Korn, S. (1963). *Behavioral individuality in early childhood.* New York: New York University Press.

Thornberry, T., Freeman-Gallant, A., Lizotte, A., Krohn, M., & Smith, C. (2003). Linked lives: The intergenerational transmission of antisocial behaviour. *Journal of Abnormal Child Psychology, 31,* 171–184.

Tienda, M. (1991). Poor people and poor places: Deciphering neighborhood effects on poverty outcomes. In J. Huber (Ed.), *Macro-micro linkages in sociology* (pp. 244–262). Newbury Park, CA: Sage.

Timko, C., Cronkite, R. C., Berg, E. A., & Moos, R. H. (2002). Children of parents with unipolar depression: A comparison of stably remitted, partially remitted, and nonremitted parents and nondepressed controls. *Child Psychiatry and Human Development, 32,* 165–185.

Tupes, E. C., & Christal, R. C. (1961). *Recurrent personality factors based on trait ratings* (Tech. rep.). Lackland Air Force Base, TX: U.S. Air Force.

Valenzuela, M. (1997). Maternal sensitivity in a developing society: The context of urban poverty and infant chronic undernutrition. *Developmental Psychology, 33,* 845–855.

Van Bakel, H., & Riksen-Walraven, J. (2002). Parenting and development of one-year-olds: Links with parental, contextual, and child characteristics. *Child Development, 73,* 256–273.

Van den Boom, D., & Hoeksma, J. (1994). The effect of infant irritability on mother-infant interaction: A growth curve analysis. *Developmental Psychology, 30,* 581–590.

van Ijzendoorn, M. H. (1992). Intergenerational transmission of parenting: A review of studies in nonclinical populations. *Developmental Review, 12,* 76–99.

van Ijzendoorn, M. H. (1995). Adult attachment representations, parental responsiveness, and infant attachment: A meta-analysis on the predictive validity of the Adult Attachment Interview. *Psychological Bulletin, 117,* 387–403.

Verlaan, P., & Schwartzman, A. E. (2002). Mother's and father's parental adjustment: Links to externalising behaviour problems in sons and daughters. *International Journal of Behavioral Development, 26,* 214–224.

Vinson, T., Baldry, E., & Hargreaves, J. (1996). Neighbourhoods, networks and child abuse. *British Journal of Social Work, 26,* 523–543.

Volling, B. L., & Belsky, J. (1991). Multiple determinants of father involvement during infancy in dual-earner and single-earner families. *Journal of Marriage and the Family, 59,* 461–474.

Von Bertallanfy, L. (1950). An outline of general systems theory. *British Journal of the Philosophy of Science, 1,* 134–165.

Vondra, J. (1990). The community context of child abuse and neglect. *Marriage and Family Review, 15,* 19–38.

Voydanoff, P., & Donnelly, B. (1988). Parents' risk and protective factors as predictors of parental well-being and behavior. *Journal of Marriage and the Family, 60,* 344–355.

Wahler, R. G., & Dumas, J. E. (1986). "A chip off the old block": Some interpersonal characteristics of coercive children across generations. In P. Strain, M. Guralnick, & H. Walkee (Eds.), *Children's social behavior: Development, assessment, and modification* (pp. 49–86). New York: Academic Press.

Walsh, C., McMillan, H., & Jamieson, E. (2002). The relationship between parental psychiatric disorder and child physical and sexual abuse: Findings from the Ontario Health Supplement. *Child Abuse and Neglect, 26,* 11–22.

Ward, M., & Carlson, E. (1995). Associations among adult attachment representations, maternal sensitivity, and infant-mother attachment in a sample of adolescent mothers. *Child Development, 66,* 69–79.

Washington, J., Minde, K., & Goldberg, S. (1986). Temperament in preterm infants: Style and stability. *Journal of the American Academy of Child Psychiatry, 25,* 493–502.

Watson, D., & Clark, L. (1984). Negative affectivity. *Psychological Bulletin, 95,* 465–490.

Wei, E. H., Loeber, R., & Stouthamer-Loeber, M. (2002). How many of the offspring born to teenage fathers are produced by repeat serious delinquents? *Criminal Behaviour and Mental Health, 12,* 83–92.

Whipple, E. E., Fitzgerald, H. E., & Zucker, R. A. (1995). Parent-child interactions in alcoholic and nonalcoholic families. *American Journal of Orthopsychiatry, 65,* 153–159.

Whipple, E. E., & Webster-Stratton, C. (1991). The role of parental stress in physically abusive families. *Child Abuse and Neglect, 15,* 279–291.

Widom, C. S. (1989). Does violence beget violence? A critical examination of the literature. *Psychological Bulletin, 106,* 3–28.

Widom, C. S., & Hiller-Sturmhofel, S. (2001). Alcohol abuse as a risk factor for and consequence of child abuse. *Alcohol Research and Health, 25,* 52–57.

Wilson, B., & Gottman, J. (2002). Marital conflict, repair, and parenting. In M. Bornstein (Ed.), *Handbook of parenting: Vol. 4. Social conditions and applied parenting* (2nd ed., pp. 227–258). Mahwah, NJ: Erlbaum.

Wilson, W. J. (1987). *The truly disadvantaged: The inner city, the underclass, and public policy.* Chicago: University of Chicago Press.

Wilson, W. J. (1991). Studying inner-city social dislocations: The challenge of public agenda research. *American Sociological Review, 56,* 1–14.

Winnicott, D. W. (1975). Reparation in respect of mothers' organized defense against depression. In D. W. Winnicott (Ed.), *Through paediatrics to psycho-analysis* (pp. 33–52). New York: Basic Books. (Original work published 1948)

Winter, D. G., & Barenbaum, N. B. (1999). History of modern personality theory and research. In L. A. Pervin & O. P. John (Eds.), *Handbook of personality: Theory and research* (2nd ed., pp. 3–30). New York: Guilford Press.

Wintre, M., & Dhami, N. (2003, April 26). *Parenting styles across generations as predictors of adolescents' psychological well being.* Poster presented at the biennial meetings of the Society for Research in Child Development, Tampa, FL.

Zahn-Waxler, C., Duggal, S., & Gruber, R. (2002). Parental psychopathology. In M. H. Bornstein (Ed.), *Handbook of parenting: Vol. 4. Social conditions and applied parenting* (2nd ed., pp. 295–327). Mahwah, NJ: Erlbaum.

Zahr, L. (1991). Correlates of mother-infant interaction in premature infants from low socio-economic backgrounds. *Pediatric Nursing, 17*(3), 259–264.

Zaslow, M., Pedersen, F., Cain, R., Suwalsky, J., & Kramer, E. (1985). Depressed mood in new fathers. *Genetic, Social, and General Psychology Monographs, 111,* 133–150.

Zelkowitz, P. (1982). Parenting philosophies and practices. In D. Belle (Ed.), *Lives in stress* (pp. 154–162). Beverly Hills, CA: Sage.

Zoccolillo, M., Meyers, J., & Assister, S. (1997). Conduct disorder, substance dependence, and adolescent motherhood. *American Journal of Orthopsychiatry, 67,* 152–157.

Zuravin, S. J. (1989). The ecology of child abuse and neglect: Review of the literature and presentation of data. *Violence and Victims, 4,* 101–120.

CHAPTER 3

Interparental Discord, Family Process, and Developmental Psychopathology

PATRICK T. DAVIES and E. MARK CUMMINGS

The effects of interparental discord on children's psychological adjustment has been a long-standing concern for scientists and practitioners across multiple disciplines in psychology, sociology, psychiatry, and epidemiology. The first generation of research on the interplay between interparental and child functioning was largely guided by two interlocking questions: Is the quality of the marital or interparental relationship associated with child psychological adjustment? And, if so, what is the nature of the risk in terms of its magnitude (i.e., effect size) and scope (i.e., applicability across domains of functioning) of effect? In addressing these questions, seminal studies in the 1930s and 1940s repeatedly documented links between marital discord and child psychological problems (e.g., Baruch & Wilcox, 1944; Towle, 1931).

Following a notable hiatus in research conducted on interparental and child functioning, researchers revisited and expanded on these research questions during the 1960s and 1970s. With marked rises in U.S. divorce rates during this period, a central objective was to unpack the multidimensional nature of marital dissolution by determining the relative risk posed by parent-child separation and interparental conflict to children's adjustment (Gregory, 1965; Hetherington, Cox, & Cox, 1976; Jacobson, 1978). By consistently supporting the hypothesis that interparental conflict was a stronger predictor of child psychological problems than parent-child separation per se, this body of work prompted a new sense of interest and urgency in studying the impact of interparental conflict

Preparation of this chapter was supported by the National Institute of Mental Health grants MH 57318 and MH 71256.

on children (Amato & Keith, 1991; Emery, 1982; Rutter, 1971). As Jaffe, Wolfe, and Wilson (1990, p. 33) aptly noted of the 1980s, "It was not until the past decade that family discord and spousal violence reached center stage as possible predeterminants of developmental psychopathology." During the 1980s, researchers specifically expanded research directions by systematically examining the generalizability or specificity of associations between different characteristics of interparental functioning and various dimensions of child functioning. These studies showed that interparental discord was associated with increased psychological difficulties across a wide developmental period encompassing infancy through young adulthood. Moreover, the vulnerability of children from high-conflict homes was demonstrated to be prevalent across a wide spectrum of functioning, as evidenced by elevated rates of social difficulties, behavioral problems, emotional symptoms, academic impairments, and psychophysiological reactivity.

Quantitative and qualitative reviews of this cumulative body of research have indicated that associations between interparental conflict and child maladjustment were generally small to medium in magnitude across a broad array of domains of psychological adjustment (Buehler, Anthony, Krishnakumar, & Stone, 1997; Grych & Fincham, 1990). In their qualitative review of the literature, Grych and Fincham reported that interparental conflict predicted between 4% and 20% of individual differences in children's functioning. In expanding on these conclusions, a meta-analysis evaluating the findings from a broader sampling of studies indicated that the effect size of the relationship between interparental conflict and child functioning was modest to moderate in magnitude (Buehler et al., 1997).

Guided by the consistency of the risk posed by marital conflict, many researchers have redirected their attention toward conducting a second generation of research. Rather than continuing to address the question of whether interparental difficulties are a risk factor for children, researchers over the past 2 decades have increasingly focused efforts on understanding how and why interparental discord is associated with child adjustment problems. Thus, a key component of this process-oriented research agenda is to identify the mechanisms and processes that explain or account for the vulnerability of children exposed to high levels of interparental discord. By the same token, the relatively modest magnitude of the developmental risk accompanying exposure to interparental discord also reflects that children exposed to similar levels of interparental stress evidence considerable variability in

their functioning. Consequently, another central component of the second generation of research is to identify the sources of heterogeneity in the outcomes of children. To address these process-oriented issues, scholarship in this second generation of research has evolved toward developing and testing more complex and sophisticated models of the interplay between interparental and child functioning (E. M. Cummings & Cummings, 1988; Fincham, 1994).

The overarching objective of this chapter is to illustrate how the principles, assumptions, and aims of developmental psychopathology can inform and advance current and future research directions in the interparental discord literature. To achieve this objective, the first part of the chapter provides a brief overview of a conceptual framework inspired by a developmental psychopathology perspective on interparental discord. In the second part, we review the large corpus of literature on the relationship between interparental and child functioning through the lens of our developmental psychopathology framework. Guided by the aims, principles, and concepts of developmental psychopathology, we specifically examine the developmental implications of interparental conflict in a larger biopsychosocial constellation of risk and protection. In the final part of the chapter, we address how the developmental psychopathology perspective may also serve as a heuristic for generating new conceptual and methodological directions in interparental discord research.

A DEVELOPMENTAL PSYCHOPATHOLOGY APPROACH TO UNDERSTANDING INTERPARENTAL DISCORD

The principles and aims of developmental psychopathology can provide valuable directions for developing, refining, and testing the interplay between interparental and child functioning. Transactional approaches to developmental psychopathology share the trademark assumption that child adaptation to adversity is an evolving product of a dynamic child in an ever-changing, multilayered ecological context. Understanding the nature of developmental trajectories of child adaptation requires an appreciation of the ongoing bidirectional exchanges of biopsychosocial resources and liabilities between the child and the multilevel, multivariate network of family and ecological factors. There is no simple one-to-one correspondence between a given risk factor such as interparental discord and a specific child outcome. Rather, consistent with the concept of developmental pluralism, individual differences in the interplay between the child and contextual characteristics conspire to engender multiple pathways toward normal and abnormal functioning. The mutually informative value of studying both normal and abnormal development necessitates a complementary focus on positive (e.g., protective) factors and outcomes (e.g., competence in the face of risk) and negative (e.g., risk and potentiating) factors and outcomes (e.g., psychopathology).

Two concepts have been enlisted from developmental systems theories to characterize the multiplicity of paths between risk factors and outcomes in developmental psychopathology (Cicchetti & Rogosch, 1996). First, the concept of *equifinality* specifically refers to the notion that a single outcome can be the result of multiple factors and processes. For example, children's success in sustaining competence in the face of interparental adversity may result from any number of child processes (e.g., ability to regulate emotion) or interpersonal conditions (e.g., supportive parent-child relationship). Second, *multifinality* reflects the notion that a diverse set of outcomes may result from a common factor or pathway. Thus, even children exposed to highly similar patterns of interparental discord are expected to evidence substantial variability in their outcomes by virtue of their different intrapersonal attributes, psychosocial resources, and multivariate constellations of risk. Consequently, there is a multitude of ways of developing along adaptive and maladaptive trajectories, as development may involve different starts and stops, directions toward competence and disorder as children get older. The developmental course of each child is to some degree unique due to the specific transactions between his or her prior and current experiences in family and ecological contexts and his or her own attributes, resources, and histories of adaptation. It follows that change in functioning can be lawfully predicted and explained at least in part by elucidating the nature of the interplay between the child and the environment. Although change is always to some extent possible, the concept of canalization specifies that the magnitude and quality of change is constrained by organizational adaptations resulting from past transactions between the child and contexts of development (Waddington, 1957). Thus, under the broad boundaries of developmental psychopathology, the rule of thumb is that "the longer an individual continues along a maladaptive ontogenetic pathway, the more difficult it is to reclaim a normal developmental trajectory" (Cicchetti & Cohen, 1995, p. 7). Likewise, individuals experiencing longer histories of adaptive pathways can withstand greater challenges to their psychological adjustment.

In applying this concept of development to the study of children exposed to interparental discord, Figure 3.1 is designed to provide a parsimonious illustration of the dynamic interplay between interparental relations and children's developmental outcomes in the broader organizational context of child attributes, family processes, and ecological characteristics. The model specifically proposes that interparental conflict increases child vulnerability to maladaptive trajectories through multiple mechanisms and pathways. Two specific classes of process models are especially useful tools for explicating the effects of these mechanisms. Mediational models, which constitute the first class of process models, are designed to determine *how* or *why* a particular factor, such as interparental conflict, poses a risk for child adjustment. Mediators are the *generative mechanisms* through which independent variables affect outcomes (Baron & Kenny, 1986; Holmbeck, 1997, 2002). Thus, in the parental conflict literature, a new generation of research has involved identifying the mechanisms and processes that explain how and why interparental conflict is associated with forms of child maladjustment. Analytically, identifying a mediator requires demonstrating that the focal process variable explains substantial amounts of variance in the link between interparental difficulties and child maladjustment.

Moderator models are the second class of process models that assist in the identification of diverse pathways and trajectories in associations between interparental relations and child adjustment. Moderator models specifically address the question of when a specific risk factor is most or least likely to be associated with a particular outcome. Thus, identifying whether the strength or direction of relations between an independent variable (e.g., interparental conflict) and a dependent variable (e.g., child functioning) varies at different levels of another variable is the principal aim of moderator models (Baron & Kenny, 1986; Holmbeck, 1997, 2002). Risk and protective frameworks of developmental psychopathology have distinguished between two specific types of moderators: protective factors and potentiating factors. Protective factors or buffers reflect factors that reduce or offset the risk associated with exposure to interparental discord. Conversely, potentiating factors are moderators that amplify the association between interparental conflict and child maladjustment.

Consistent with the mediator models, Path 1 in Figure 3.1 illustrates the assumption that the stressfulness of exposure to interparental difficulties directly sets in motion processes within children that ultimately increase their

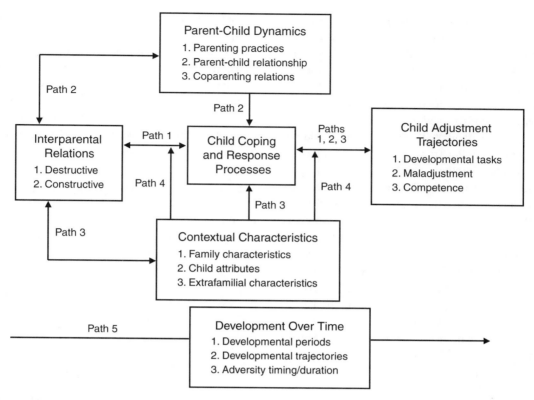

Figure 3.1   A model of the dynamic interplay between interparental relations and children's developmental outcomes in the broader organizational context of child attributes, family processes, and ecological characteristics.

risk for psychological problems. In the direct path component of our model, exposure to interparental discord is thought to undermine child mental health and welfare by engendering more maladaptive response patterns to interparental and family stress. Changes in children's response patterns to interparental and family stress are theorized to vary as a function of their exposure to specific dimensions of interparental conflict. Our model is therefore designed to highlight the utility of distinguishing between constructive and destructive characteristics of the conflict from the child's perspective. Specific experiential histories with these conflict characteristics are proposed to change children's reactivity to subsequent bouts of family and interparental stress across multiple levels and domains of child functioning, including emotional, cognitive, coping, and physiological responding.

Further illustrating the operation of mediational paths, Path 2 in our model postulates that part of the relationship between interparental conflict and child maladjustment is mediated by parent-child dynamics, including specific child-rearing practices, parent-child relationship features (e.g., attachment), and coparenting relationship qualities. In further broadening the scope of the model, an array of

broader contextual characteristics, including child, familial, and extrafamilial attributes, are theorized to alter both direct and indirect pathways involving interparental conflict and child maladaptation in several ways. For example, as illustrated by Path 3 in the model, contextual characteristics may mediate the vulnerability of children exposed to high levels of interparental discord. Likewise, guided by risk and protective models in developmental psychopathology, Path 4 illustrates that associations between interparental conflict and child maladaptation may be moderated by contextual characteristics. For example, interparental relations are considered to assume different meanings depending on the balance of resources and risk in the family and ecological setting.

Fully integrating interparental models of psychopathology in a developmental framework also necessitates consideration of other developmental issues. Accordingly, Path 5 in the model highlights the significance of developmental issues in the study of interparental functioning, with the core assumption being that the impact of interparental discord may vary depending on several developmental parameters. First, the magnitude and type of vulnerability of children may depend on the timing and duration of the conflict. For example, sensitive periods may be operating whereby environmental influences are particularly pronounced in specific developmental windows (e.g., Cicchetti, 1993). Likewise, in illustrating the significance of the duration of experiential histories of exposure to interparental process, the quality of subsequent change in child functioning may be constrained by prior organizational adaptations (Sroufe, Egeland, & Kreutzer, 1990; Waddington, 1957). Second, drawing from stage-salient models of developmental psychopathology, child adaptation to interparental conflict over time may be gauged by the ways children approach and resolve the unfolding series of developmental challenges that become particularly prominent during a given period of development (Cicchetti, 1993; Sroufe, 1979; Sroufe & Rutter, 1984). Third, from a developmental perspective, another important goal is to understand how the interplay among interparental conflict, contextual characteristics, and child response processes corresponds with children's developmental trajectories of psychopathology and resilience over time. Even though child maladaptive response patterns to family stress may mediate the risk of growing up in a discordant home, the concept of multifinality indicates that children who exhibit highly similar patterns of reactivity and coping may evidence different developmental trajectories. Therefore, a complete multivariate model of interparental conflict must incorporate developmental parameters of timing and duration of stressors, developmental periods, and developmental pathways.

DIRECT PATHWAYS AND PROCESSES IN MODELS OF INTERPARENTAL DISCORD

A primary aim of a process-oriented approach and, more broadly, developmental psychopathology, is to advance an understanding of the conceptual ordering of variables in direct paths between interparental conflict and the multiple levels of child functioning. A common strategy across different direct path models of interparental discord is to identify the specific processes and process relations in context that, over time, underlie what is classified diagnostically as normal development or psychopathology (see Path 1 in Figure 3.1). Originally distilled from models of developmental psychopathology (Cowan, Cowan, & Schulz, 1996), these theories draw distinctions among *risk factors, risk processes,* and *outcomes.* Risk factors in these models probabilistically increase child maladaptive outcomes. However, the operation of the risk is neither static nor instantaneous. Rather, repeated exposure to the risk factor results in the dynamic emergence of risk processes

characterized by regularity in child response patterns in specific contexts that, over time, intensify, broaden, and crystallize into symptomatology and psychopathology. Thus, the common aim across direct path models is to identify how interparental discord serves as a specific risk factor by engendering risk processes characterized by specific child response patterns that, in the long run, lay the foundation for negative outcomes (e.g., symptomatology, psychopathology, competence).

Direct Path Models of Interparental Discord

Despite adopting a common goal of distinguishing among risk factors, risk processes, and outcomes, various theories of interparental discord offer a diverse array of explanations for why interparental conflict is deleterious to child functioning. To illustrate the diversity in response processes addressed across theories, we provide a brief and selective review of the assumptions of some of the more established direct path models.

Social Learning Theory

Applications of social learning theory to the study of interparental discord have underscored how the child's responses are learned in the context of interparental interactions. Like the other direct path models, social learning theory hypothesizes that child exposure to interparental conflict tactics has direct effects on child functioning that cannot be accounted for by parenting or family processes. Observational learning or modeling is regarded as a primary process that organizes child responses (Bandura, 1973, 1983). In the context of interparental conflict, children are viewed as having opportunities to master new ways of engaging in aggressive behavior through vicariously observing adults engage in aggressive and hostile conflict tactics. Greater displays of hostility and aggression by children when exposed to interparental hostility are thought to emerge through multiple processes, including (1) precise imitation of specific hostile behaviors displayed by adults, (2) acquisition of generalized scripts or abstract rules for engaging in hostile behaviors, and (3) reduction of inhibitions about aggressing (Cox, Paley, & Harter, 2001; Emery, 1982; Margolin, Oliver, & Medina, 2001).

These main assumptions lead to a more precise articulation of the specific linkages among risk factors, risk processes, and outcomes. As illustrated in the first model in Figure 3.2, children are commonly hypothesized to display high levels of aggression and hostility with progressively greater exposure to bouts of interparental physical aggression, verbal hostility, and unvarnished anger dis-

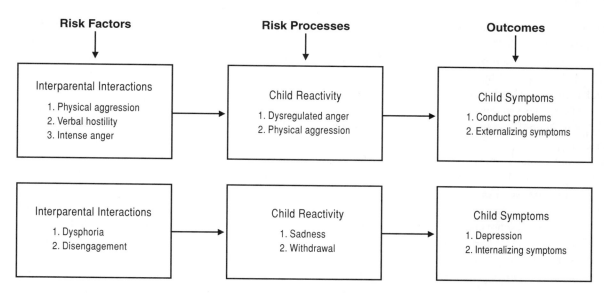

Figure 3.2 A social learning theory formulation of direct pathways and processes of interparental discord.

plays. In turn, these increasing tendencies to display aggression are proposed to intensify and broaden into conduct problems. Although the transmission of aggressive displays has received more attention in models of interparental discord, the potential value of social learning theory is not confined to explaining the operation of interparental discord in the genesis of conduct problems. For example, interparental discord can be expressed in multiple ways that include (but are not limited to) spousal disengagement and dysphoria. In illustrating this multiple pathways perspective, the second model in Figure 3.2 theorizes that interparental dysphoria or disengagement may specifically increase children's vulnerability to internalizing symptoms by fostering their vicarious displays of sadness and social withdrawal.

Emphasis on reinforcement contingencies in social learning theory has also generated hypotheses about additional developmental pathways to psychopathology. For example, in applying the negative reinforcement principles to the study of interparental conflict, Emery (1989) proposed a three-component model. First, interparental conflict is hypothesized to be an aversive event that produces distress in children. Second, children's dysregulated expressions of distress (e.g., aggression, temper tantrums) reduce their exposure to aversive interparental stimuli by distracting parents from engagement in ongoing conflicts. Third, misbehavior is more likely to be enacted by the child in subsequent conflicts because it reduces or eliminates the aversive stimulus (i.e., conflict). As this negative reinforcement process is repeated over time, children are proposed to show increasingly strong, persistent aversive

behaviors, which, in turn, pave the way for broader patterns of behavior problems.

Although social learning theory has been consistently invoked to explain associations between interparental conflict and child functioning (e.g., Crockenberg & Langrock, 2001a; Emery & O'Leary, 1982; Johnson & O'Leary, 1987), modeling explanations are typically provided post hoc. Studies have rarely been conducted for the explicit purpose of testing social learning processes, especially as they relate to proposed mediational pathways among risk factors (e.g., interparental aggression), risk processes (e.g., child aggressive reactions to conflict), and outcomes (e.g., child conduct problems). Thus, considerably more empirical precision is needed to sufficiently test hypotheses generated from social learning theory.

The Cognitive-Contextual Framework

Rooted in social-cognitive theories of interparental relations, the cognitive-contextual framework places particular emphasis on understanding how the cognitive dimensions of children's appraisals shape the impact of conflict on child adjustment (e.g., Grych & Fincham, 1990, 1993; Grych, Seid, & Fincham, 1992). Children are viewed as active agents who attempt to derive interpersonal meaning from the ways their parents manage conflict. However, in contrast to the primary focus of social learning theory on understanding the genesis of externalizing symptoms, the cognitive-contextual framework has been particularly useful in accounting for child vulnerability to internalizing symptoms. Two dimensions of child appraisals assume center stage in explaining why interparental conflict increases child vulnerability to psychopathology. In the first process pathway, exposure to high levels of parental conflict may pose a risk to children's adjustment by heightening their perceptions of threat posed by conflicts. Perceived threat is specifically characterized by children's analyses of the threat that conflicts pose to their welfare and ability to successfully cope with conflict. In the early stages of this unfolding series of processes, children are thought to become increasingly more prone to perceive parental conflicts as threatening with repeated exposure to angry, hostile, and unresolved disputes between parents. Increasing appraisals of threat, in turn, are thought to predispose children to experience anxiety, dysphoria, and helplessness and, as a result, increase their risk for developing internalizing symptoms (Grych, Fincham, Jouriles, & McDonald, 2000).

Child attributions regarding the cause of the conflict is the second set of mechanisms that are presumed to account for why interparental conflict directly affects children's functioning. A primary thesis is that children exposed to angry, hostile, and unresolved conflicts are likely to assume the role of parental peacekeeper, arbitrator, and confidante. However, the child's involvement in the conflict is not likely to play a significant role in resolving the complex adult problems or the accompanying emotional strife. Thus, as children increasingly bear the formidable responsibility of reducing interparental and family discord, they may be especially prone to blaming themselves for the maintenance or escalation of interparental difficulties. Increasing feelings of guilt, shame, helplessness, and poor self-worth, which are regarded as affective outgrowths of this appraisal process, are proposed to develop into broader patterns of internalizing symptoms.

Studies examining the roles of children's perceived threat and self-blame have provided some support for the proposed mediational pathways. Grych, Fincham, and colleagues (2000) have reported that perceived threat and self-blame were consistent mediators of the relationship between interparental conflict and child symptoms in both community and risk (i.e., battered women's shelters) families. In accordance with the emphasis on the genesis of internalizing symptoms, the mediational paths accounted for children's individual differences in internalizing symptoms but not externalizing symptoms. Similar patterns of findings regarding the mediational role of child perceived threat and self-blame have been reported in other studies (e.g., Dadds, Atkinson, Turner, Blums, & Lendich, 1999; Kerig, 1998). However, more recent longitudinal analyses conducted by Grych, Harold, and Miles (2003) have yielded a more complex pattern of findings (also see Davies, Harold, Goeke-Morey, & Cummings, 2002). Con-

sistent with earlier findings, interparental conflict was associated with subsequent increases in child appraisals of threat and self-blame across 1 year. Child threat appraisals, in turn, were consistent concurrent predictors of changes in child internalizing symptomatology. However, unlike earlier studies, perceived blame was actually a predictor of child externalizing symptoms. Moreover, because interparental conflict was negligibly associated with child psychological maladjustment, the findings failed to support a mediator model. Instead, the findings provided support for another type of indirect effect whereby child appraisals were intervening (rather than mediating) mechanisms linking interparental conflict and child maladjustment.

Although empirical work on the cognitive-contextual framework has been heavily rooted in elucidating the role of children's social-cognitive mechanisms, the theory conceptualizes appraisals as part of a more complex pattern of unfolding processes across multiple domains and levels of child functioning (Grych & Cardoza-Fernandes, 2001; Grych & Fincham, 1990). Histories of exposure to destructive interparental conflict are specifically theorized to engender a variety of appraisals that are not fully captured by a focus on perceived threat and self-blame (e.g., efficacy expectations, expectancies about the course of conflict). Constellations of appraisals, in turn, are thought to engender negative emotionality. In the final part of this response process, the reciprocal interplay between appraisals and emotional arousal is conceptualized as prompting children to reduce emotional arousal in the proximal stressful context through emotion-focused (e.g., avoidance) and problem-focused (e.g., intervention in conflict) coping. Given the paucity of research on other components of the cognitive-contextual framework, examining social-cognitive appraisals in this broader organization of response processes is an important direction for future research (Grych & Cardoza-Fernandes, 2001).

The Emotional Security Theory

A main assumption of the emotional security theory is that preserving a sense of security is an important goal that organizes children's emotional experiences (e.g., fear), action tendencies (e.g., withdrawal, intervention), and appraisals of self and interpersonal relationships (e.g., internal representations of threat to the self). Although the child evaluates interpersonal contexts in relation to multiple goals, the emotional security hypothesis postulates that protection, safety, and security are among the most salient and important in the hierarchy of human goals. Rather than postulating that preserving a sense of security is relevant only to the parent-child attachment, the emotional security theory hypothesizes that children also develop a sense of security in the context of the interparental relationship that is distinct in its substance, origins, and sequelae from attachment security. For example, children may evidence insecurity in the context of interparental relations but experience security in the mother-child or father-child attachment relationship.

Figure 3.3 illustrates the direct pathway prediction of the emotional security theory. The main thesis is that children's difficulties in preserving security in the interparental relationship partially mediates or explains the direct association between interparental conflict history and child vulnerability to adjustment problems. Path 1 illustrates the assumption that the threat associated with exposure to destructive interparental conflict is especially likely to sensitize children to concerns about the goal of preserving their security in subsequent contexts of interparental difficulties. Preserving emotional security, in turn, is conceptualized as a latent goal that regulates and is regulated by three observable classes of response processes: emotional reactivity, regulation of conflict exposure, and internal representations (see Path 2 in Figure 3.3). Thus, threats to the goal of security are posited to activate responding across the three classes of response processes, as reflected in greater emotional reactivity (i.e., proneness to prolonged and dysregulated experiences of fear, vigilance, and distress in the context of interparental problems), excessive regulation of conflict exposure (i.e., avoidance of and involvement in interparental problems),

and hostile internal representations of the consequences that interparental difficulties have for the welfare of the self and family (Davies & Cummings, 1994, 1998). Reflecting the bidirectional interplay between the goal and response processes, activation of three component processes is thought to serve the biological and evolutionary function of promoting the attainment of physical and psychological safety in the average expectable environment. Thus, emotional reactivity may be initially adaptive in emotionally tagging or highlighting the significance of potential threat present in high-conflict homes and in energizing children to quickly cope with impending adversity. Likewise, expending resources to intervene or avoid conflicts may be an effective way of preserving security by increasing the emotional or physical distance from threatening interparental events. Finally, child representations, which are geared toward processing the meaning of interparental conflict for family life, are thought to serve as radar systems for identifying interparental events that may proliferate to undermine the welfare of the self and family (Davies, Forman, Rasi, & Stevens, 2002; Davies, Harold, et al., 2002).

With repeated exposure to interparental conflict, a main premise is that the goal-corrected system of security becomes increasingly sensitized to subsequent conflict. Thus, experiential histories of interparental strife are specifically postulated to increase child insecurity, as manifested by high levels of emotional reactivity, regulation of conflict exposure, and hostile internal representations. Consistent

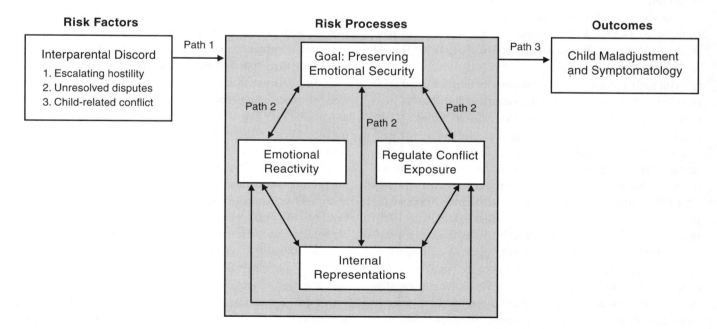

Figure 3.3   An emotional security formulation of the direct pathways and processes of interparental discord.

with these predictions, children exposed to high levels of interparental conflict exhibit high levels of emotional reactivity (e.g., fear, distress; Davies & Cummings, 1998; El-Sheikh, 1997; Garcia O'Hearn, Margolin, & John, 1997; Gordis, Margolin, & John, 1997), negative representations of interparental conflict (e.g., Davies & Cummings, 1998; Davies, Forman, et al., 2002; Davies, Harold, et al., 2002), and, at least in some cases, greater regulation of exposure to parental difficulties (e.g., Davies, Forman, et al., 2002; Garcia O'Hearn et al., 1997; Sandler, Tein, & West, 1994). In the second part of the mediational chain (see Path 3), the three classes of response processes in the emotional security system are hypothesized to increase child vulnerability to psychological symptoms. Although elevated concerns about security for children from high-conflict homes may hold adaptational value, the emotional security theory further postulates that these concerns may have maladaptive value for children's long-term functioning. For example, vigilance, distress, and preoccupation triggered by exposure to interparental difficulties are posited to lay the foundation for broader patterns of internalizing and externalizing symptoms. Likewise, prolonged operation of the emotional security system is theorized to require considerable expenditure of psychobiological resources thereby, depleting children of resources that are necessary to cope with and resolve other important developmental challenges and goals (Saarni, Mumme, & Campos, 1998; Thompson & Calkins, 1996). Consistent with these hypotheses, children's psychological symptoms have been predicted by their emotional reactivity, regulation of conflict exposure, and internal representations of marital relations (e.g., Davies & Cummings, 1998; Davies, Forman, et al., 2002; Davis, Hops, Alpert, & Sheeber, 1998; Harold & Conger, 1997).

Although identifying associations among interparental conflict history, child emotional security, and child adjustment is a prerequisite to testing mediational pathways, the final step requires demonstrating that emotional security accounts for a substantial portion of the variance in associations between interparental conflict history and child adjustment problems. The small corpus of studies directly addressing this association has yielded some support for this hypothesis. For example, Davies and Cummings (1998) reported that child emotional reactivity and negative representations in the context of parental conflict simulations partially accounted for the relationship between interparental conflict and child adjustment problems. In supporting the hypothesis that emotional insecurity is distinct from attachment security, emotional insecurity has also been shown to mediate the link between interparental con-

flict and child problems even after taking into account parenting and parent-child attachment security (Davies, Harold, et al., 2002).

Specific Emotions Theory

Congruent with emotional security theory, specific emotions theory is guided by the functionalist perspective and proposes that children's evaluations of and emotional reactivity to conflict, which are inextricably linked with goals, play a central role in explicating direct pathways between interparental conflict and child adjustment (Crockenberg & Langrock, 2001a, 2001b). However, whereas the emotional security hypothesis focuses specifically on the operation of security goals, specific emotions theory expands the conceptual boundaries in an attempt to incorporate multiple goals systems. Thus, according to specific emotions theory, children's appraisals and reactions develop in the context of any number of goals, both broad (e.g., security, affiliative) and specific (e.g., obtaining parental permission to engage in desirable activities; also see Jenkins, 2000, 2002). Children are specifically theorized to develop coherent ways of evaluating the meaning conflict has for the attainment of their goals from repeated experiences of interparental conflict events over time. In the unfolding series of processes, evaluations of the meaning of conflict in relation to specific goals result in specific emotional reactions. Consistent with the functionalist perspective (e.g., Saarni et al., 1998), child appraisals of the probability of successfully achieving or maintaining a valued goal in the context or aftermath of conflict organizes specific emotional experiences. Anger, with its function of marshaling psychological and biological resources to overcome obstacles and assert interpersonal dominance, is likely to develop when children evaluate a threatened or blocked goal as likely to be attainable. In contrast, sadness is associated with the conservation of intraorganismic resources and the elicitation of caregiving and support in interpersonal contexts. Accordingly, sadness is likely to emerge as a broader reaction pattern in contexts in which valued goals are repeatedly unattainable. Finally, fear and worry serve the function of energizing individuals to respond quickly to potential threat. Thus, contexts that pose a looming, but uncertain, threat to the preservation of goals are likely to trigger fear responses. Specific emotional responses to conflict, in turn, are thought to coalesce into broader patterns of adjustment and maladjustment. Proclivity to experience anger is hypothesized to trigger aggression and, in the process, portends subsequent externalizing symptoms, whereas withdrawal behaviors prompted by fearful responses are thought to engender broader patterns of internalizing symptoms.

Sadness is also proposed to increase child vulnerability to internalizing symptoms by fostering vegetative and withdrawal behaviors in the face of adversity. Finally, reflecting the interaction between specific emotional reactions to conflict, specific emotions theory suggests that angry responses that co-occur with fear are likely to inhibit aggressive responses and facilitate withdrawal behaviors and, more broadly, internalizing symptoms.

Given that specific emotions theory is in the early stages of development, tests of its derivative predictions have not been systematically undertaken (for exceptions, see Crockenberg & Forgays, 1996; Crockenberg & Langrock, 2001b). Incorporating the study of multiple goals and types of interplay between risk factors and processes is a strength of specific emotions theory. However, the accompanying limitation is that the broader explanatory scope of the model compromises its theoretical precision. Thus, further conceptual development and refinement will facilitate future empirical tests of the theory, particularly in more precisely articulating the interplay between interparental conflict histories and child appraisals and emotional reactivity.

For example, even though child appraisals and emotional reactivity were cast as mediators of interparental conflict in the initial theoretical exposition (Crockenberg & Langrock, 2001a), Crockenberg and Langrock (2001b) have subsequently proposed that identification of either a mediating or a moderating role of children's specific emotions would support a specific emotions theory. Likewise, broadening the explanatory power of the model by including multiple goal systems, each of which contains considerable complexity, also increases the challenge of precisely articulating how response processes (e.g., emotion reactivity, appraisals) function within the overall configuration of each goal system. From a developmental psychopathology perspective, it would also be useful to further articulate the pathways that link specific types of emotional reactions to the development of particular forms of psychological problems.

Summary

In summary, considerable progress has been made over the last 15 years in developing several theoretical accounts for why interparental conflict directly affects child functioning. These theoretical advances have specifically facilitated efforts to understand the multidimensional, dynamic function of risk factors and risk processes in direct path models.

In the next section, we expand on this theme by examining the value of specifying the nature of risk factors and processes in developmental psychopathology models of interparental conflict.

The Operation of Interparental Risk and Compensatory Factors in Direct Path Models

Despite the fact that interparental conflict is often treated as a homogeneous construct, interparental conflict, in fact, varies widely in impact and on multiple dimensions of behavioral and emotional expression. Thus, given the emphasis of the developmental psychopathology perspective on delineating the role of context, a fundamental goal is to differentiate the dynamic implications for child development of multiple and specific forms of marital conflict. At the same time, the principle of equifinality in developmental psychopathology underscores that multiple and alternative forms of expression of marital conflict can have similar implications from the perspective of the children (Davies, Myers, Cummings, & Heindel, 1999). For example, multiple behaviors may have similar meanings from the children's perspective as representations of constructive or destructive conflict. Thus, goals at this level of analysis should include both differentiating the effects of specific expressions of conflict and identifying higher-order categories or organizational meanings of conflict behaviors.

A developmental psychopathology perspective places particular emphasis on considering the normal and abnormal together (Sroufe, 1990). Interparental discord is related to risk for psychopathology in both parents and children (E. M. Cummings & Davies, 1994a; Du Rocher Schudlich, Papp, & Cummings, 2004). Thus, in principle, some forms of interparental conflict may serve as risk factors that probabilistically increase risk of psychopathology. However, failing to consider the operation of interparental conflict in normal family functioning runs the risk of overpathologizing conflict environments. Marital conflict is a normal characteristic of marital relationships that can be regarded as essential to the daily conduct of marital relations. Disagreements or expressions of negative emotions over everyday matters are common occurrences in marital and family life. Children not only may adapt to marital discord, but some forms of conflict expressions may broadly predict greater psychological adjustment regardless of whether individuals experience risk (E. M. Cummings, Davies, & Campbell, 2000). Thus, over time, marital conflict may contribute to normal and abnormal developmental trajectories in children, although risk associated with marital conflict is probabilistic rather than certain (Sroufe, 1997).

Strategies for Identifying Interparental Risk and Compensatory Factors

Recognizing that interparental conflict can serve as either a risk or a compensatory factor is an important first step in advancing tests of direct path models. However, a remaining challenge is to empirically test which conflict tactics serve as risk or compensatory factors. Supporting the assumption that methodological diversity is the key to substantive vigor in developmental psychopathology (E. M. Cummings et al., 2000), several complementary strategies have proven to be valuable in delineating the developmental implications of specific conflict tactics. One methodological strategy, which can be characterized as a categorical risk design, takes advantage of experiments of nature to more precisely isolate specific patterns of child exposure to interparental conflict tactics (Cicchetti, 2003). In these designs (e.g., Fantuzzo et al., 1991; O'Brien, Margolin, John, & Krueger, 1991), inclusion and exclusion criteria are developed and implemented to identify groups of children who differ in their exposure to specific conflict tactics but are highly similar in sociodemographic characteristics and other family experiences. For example, Fantuzzo and colleagues compared the psychological adjustment of children in four groups: (1) home residents exposed to verbal interparental aggression, (2) home residents exposed to both verbal and physical interparental aggression, (3) shelter residents exposed to verbal and physical interparental aggression, and (4) a control group of home residents exposed to negligible levels of interparental aggression. By carefully selecting naturally occurring groups of children who differ in their exposure to a well-defined set of family stressors, this design disentangled the specific risk posed by the form of aggression and residence (i.e., homelessness) to children's adjustment from a larger constellation of covarying demographic conditions. Even though the categorical risk design has proven to be an excellent strategy for increasing the specificity of conflict assessments, like other designs, it does have its share of limitations.

Classifying groups of children based on their exposure to specific types of conflict tactics in categorical risk designs often involves reducing rich, continuous assessments of conflict into a more simple categorical variable based on arbitrary cut points. Although this practice is an appropriate step in addressing some research questions, the trade-off is a substantial loss of information and statistical power. For example, implementing an arbitrary cutoff on a continuous measure of interparental conflict (e.g., verbal aggression) may yield a group of children who exhibit considerable heterogeneity in their exposure to the specific conflict tactic (e.g., moderate versus no exposure). Thus, categorical systems often fail to assess the full quantitative continuum of conflict risk (Seifer, 1995). Moreover, even if theory proposes qualitative shifts in the operation of a risk factor, specific categorical cut points may not correspond with the locus of the exponential change in the nature or magnitude of the conflict tactics.

To address these limitations, marital researchers complement clinical risk designs with retrospective field designs. The core objective of the continuous field design is to simultaneously examine the relative strength of continuous rather than arbitrary categorical assessments of conflict tactics predicting child functioning. For example, father-initiated violence in bouts of interparental conflict have been related to child behavior problems even after statistically controlling for general interparental discord (e.g., Fergusson & Horwood, 1998; McDonald, Jouriles, Norwood, Ware, & Ezell, 2000; Yates, Dodds, Sroufe, & Egeland, 2003). However, despite maximizing the use of rich data and statistical power, these designs rely heavily on the recall and report of interpartner conflict tactics and child functioning over relatively lengthy periods of time (e.g., months or years) by family members. Without the use of other approaches to complement this design, the validity of findings may be compromised by memory or response bias errors and inherent limitations of capturing precise (as opposed to global) dimensions of interparental and child functioning. Thus, retrospective field designs have been limited largely to the assessment of broad and easily discernable dimensions of child (e.g., conduct problems) and interparental (e.g., global indices of conflict frequency or violence) functioning (E. M. Cummings et al., 2000).

To address these methodological pitfalls, researchers have developed daily record or diary procedures (e.g., E. M. Cummings, Zahn-Waxler, & Radke-Yarrow, 1981, 1984; Garcia O'Hearn et al., 1997). Because diary records place less demand on memory and recall than questionnaires, these reports may provide more accurate assessments of specific interparental and child behaviors rather than global impressions. New methods of training mothers and fathers to complete home diaries and procedures for testing reliability and correspondence among parents as coders have yielded more psychometrically sound methods for recording interparental conflict events in the home (see E. M. Cummings, Goeke-Morey, & Dukewich, 2001; E. M. Cummings, Goeke-Morey, & Papp, 2003a). Moreover, daily records can now be completed in checklist rather than narrative format (e.g., E. M. Cummings, Goeke-Morey, & Papp, 2003b; Garcia O'Hearn et al., 1997), thereby decreasing demands on parents and increasing the accessibility of the methodology to a broader sampling of adults (e.g., adults with limited verbal skills). Thus, by providing assessments of specific spousal and child behaviors in the context of interparental conflict, daily record procedures have the potential to yield important findings on multiple pathways between interparental conflict tactics and child reactivity and coping. Corresponding progress has been made in examining how observer assessments of specific conflict tactics in interparental interactions in the laboratory are associated with particular dimensions of child functioning (e.g., Katz & Gottman, 1993; Katz & Woodin, 2002).

Another useful strategy for explicating the effects of specific conflict tactics on child risk processes consists of using laboratory simulations of interadult conflict. Precision and control afforded by analogue designs are especially useful in examining process associations between interparental conflict dimensions and child responses. For example, full experimental designs, which manipulate specific conflict tactics in the controlled setting of the laboratory and assess their effects on children, provides a useful way of disentangling interparental conflict tactics from the larger matrix of covarying family and interpersonal processes (E. M. Cummings & Davies, 1994a). As a result, more confident conclusions can be made about the direct effects of specific conflict tactics on child functioning (e.g., E. M. Cummings, Vogel, Cummings, & El-Sheikh, 1989; Davies, Myers, et al., 1999; El-Sheikh & Cheskes, 1995; Grych & Fincham, 1993). One ongoing research direction involves identifying higher-order categories or organizational meanings of conflict behaviors from the child's perspective. For example, Goeke-Morey, Cummings, Harold, and Shelton (2003) classified 11- and 12-year-old Welsh children's emotional responses to analogue presentations of marital conflict vignettes into destructive and constructive dimensions based on the balance and organization of children's positive and negative emotional reactivity to the vignettes. Analogue or experimental designs are also proving to be useful in testing the relative viability of predictions about the effects of specific conflict tactics derived from complementary theoretical frameworks. For example, Davies, Harold, and colleagues (2002) examined whether patterns of relationships between simulations of specific conflict tactics and children's negative affect were more consistent with predictions derived from the emotional security theory or social learning theory.

A common limitation of the experimental design is that ecological validity is compromised to maximize internal validity. However, quasi-experimental designs, which are characterized as hybrids of experimental and naturalistic designs, may provide a way of preserving some balance between internal and ecological validity. For example, several theories of interparental conflict (e.g., emotional security theory, cognitive-contextual framework) have postulated that histories of exposure to destructive interparental conflict sensitize children to subsequent conflict, as evidenced by heightened emotional distress, maladaptive coping, and negative appraisals and representations. Although field designs have demonstrated that children from high-conflict homes react more negatively to naturalistic conflicts in the home (e.g., Garcia O'Hearn et al., 1997), they cannot solely determine whether the negative emotional reactivity is due to the sensitizing effects of distal conflict histories or the proximal conflict context. Analogue studies, by contrast, can better isolate the effects of conflict history on children's subsequent responses to marital conflict. For example, in one analogue design (Davies, Myers, et al., 1999), children were randomly assigned to view videotapes of the same adult couple engaged in either four hostile, unresolved conflicts (i.e., destructive) or four mild, resolved conflicts (i.e., constructive) to simulate child exposure to conflict histories. Following this manipulation of conflict history, children were interviewed about their responses to a standard conflict between the same couple. Supporting the sensitization hypothesis, children who witnessed destructive conflict histories generally reported greater negative responding to the standard adult conflict than children exposed to constructive conflict histories. However, because they can ascertain only whether exposure to distal histories of adult conflict *can* cause sensitization in children, it is still unclear whether lengthier histories of conflict between actual parents actually cause sensitization (e.g., Davies, Myers, et al., 1999; El-Sheikh, Cummings, & Reiter, 1996). Thus, to preserve some degree of ecological validity, researchers have obtained reports of actual interparental conflict history from family members. In the same design, some level of experimental control and internal validity is achieved by assessing children's responses to standardized conflict simulations in the laboratory (e.g., Davies, Cummings, & Winter, 2004; El-Sheikh, 1997; Grych, 1998; O'Brien, Bahadur, Gee, Balto, & Erber, 1997).

Interparental Risk Factors in Direct Path Models

In direct path models, *risk* factors are defined as specific characteristics of interparental difficulties that probabilistically increase maladaptive patterns of child reactivity to interparental stress, which, in turn, ultimately amplify child risk for psychopathology. Distinctions are drawn between child reactivity and child psychopathology because, in a multiple-levels-of-analysis perspective, specific types of interparental risk may be associated with greater psychopathology without directly altering child response processes. For example, child maladjustment has been associated with specific types of interparental difficulties, including greater interspousal violence (Doumas, Margolin, & John, 1994; Fantuzzo et al., 1991; Jouriles, Murphy, & O'Leary, 1989), verbal aggression (Johnston, Gonzales, & Campbell, 1987), disengagement (Jenkins & Smith, 1991; Katz & Gottman, 1997; Katz & Woodin, 2002; Kerig, 1996), dysphoria (Du Rocher Schudlich & Cummings, 2003), and child-related conflict (Jouriles, Murphy, et al., 1991; Snyder, Klein, Gdowski, Faulstich, & LaCombe, 1988). Although these forms of interparental conflict are defined as general risk factors because they are associated with greater maladjustment, they are not regarded as specific risk factors in direct path models unless they increase risk for maladjustment by directly engendering maladaptive patterns of responding to interparental stress. Put another way, "specific" risk factors are defined as interparental conflict tactics that have a direct, deleterious impact on child functioning, whereas the term "general" risk factors is reserved for conflict tactics that influence child functioning indirectly through their associations with family functioning.

For some conflict tactics, studies demonstrate remarkable consistency in the classification of the same conflict tactics as serving as both a general and a specific risk factor. Thus, in addition to its role in the genesis of adjustment problems, exposure to interparental violence has also been associated with subsequent reaction patterns to conflict that are thought to lay the foundation for later psychological problems (Kitzmann, Gaylord, Holt, & Kenny, 2003). Specific reaction patterns that have been identified as candidates for mediating direct paths involving interparental violence include greater negative emotional reactivity, maladaptive coping responses, and hostile representations in the face of conflict (J. S. Cummings, Pellegrini, Notarius, & Cummings, 1989; Grych, 1998; Grych, Wachsmuth-Schlaefer, & Klockow, 2002; O'Brien & Bahadur, 1998).

For many other interparental risk factors, it is still too early to determine if they play a unique role in increasing vulnerability to child problems by directly altering children's adaptational capacities and patterns. For example, child-related disagreements are associated with adjustment problems even after statistically controlling for general interparental discord (e.g., Jouriles, Murphy, et al., 1991; Snyder et al., 1988). However, the sparse research addressing the specificity of associations between child exposure to child-related conflicts between parents and their maladaptive reaction patterns has yielded inconsistent findings

(e.g., Davies, Myers, & Cummings, 1996; Grych, 1998; Grych & Fincham, 1993). For example, a recent diary study indicated that children's increased aggression in response to conflicts about child-related themes in the home and conflicts about other personal, family themes had similar effects, so it is unclear that the child-related element of discussions was critical to elevated maladaptive responding (E. M. Cummings, Goeke-Morey, & Papp, 2004). Similarly, growing up in a home characterized by interparental hostile disengagement has been associated with more child psychological problems than exposure to interparental hostility alone (Katz & Woodin, 2002). However, little is known about whether disengagement between parents increases child vulnerability by taking a direct toll on children's coping and reaction patterns. Therefore, a plausible alternative hypothesis is that many of these conflict tactics may be associated with child problems through their association with family disturbances such as parenting difficulties, coparenting problems, or family-level adversity (Cox, Paley, Burchinal, & Payne, 1999; Katz & Woodin, 2002). Thus, identifying conflict tactics that operate as specific risk factors in direct path models will require more direct tests of mediational pathways between interparental conflict dimensions, children's reactivity to interparental conflict, and children's maladjustment.

Interparental Compensatory and Protective Factors in Direct Path Models

Conceptualizations of resilience and adjustment in developmental psychopathology can provide useful frameworks for more precisely clarifying how interparental conflict characteristics may operate to promote adjustment (Luthar, 1993; Luthar & Cicchetti, 2000; Luthar, Cicchetti, & Becker, 2000; Masten, Best, & Garmezy, 1990). Interpreted in these conceptualizations, constructive conflict behaviors can be usefully characterized as compensatory or protective factors in the development of psychopathology. Compensatory factors are defined as interparental conflict tactics that are broadly associated with heightened well-being in children, regardless of whether they face considerable adversity or risk, whereas protective factors are characterized by interparental conflict factors that reduce or offset risk in the face of substantial adversity.

Unfortunately, little is known about the dimensions of interparental conflict that may operate as protective or compensatory factors in children's development. Part of the knowledge gap can be attributed to the paucity of research on the constructive nature of conflict tactics. However, in issuing a call for more research in this area, we recommend that researchers use greater precision in identifying the multitude of roles that a given conflict tactic might assume as a constructive factor in the lives of children. For example, a series of analogue studies have indicated that children's distress and negative cognitions diminish significantly in response to adult conflict as the degree of interadult resolution and subsequent positivity increases (e.g., E. M. Cummings, Ballard, El-Sheikh, & Lake, 1991; Davies et al., 1996). Parent reports of conflict resolution in the home have also been consistently associated with lower levels of children's internalizing and externalizing symptoms (e.g., Kerig, 1996). An important next step is to ascertain whether these constructive parameters of the interparental conflict process actually serve as compensatory or protective factors.

Furthermore, given that child adjustment is conceptualized as entailing multiple layers and dimensions in developmental psychopathology, factors identified as promising candidates for compensatory or protective effects may operate differently across different levels or domains of functioning. Thus, it will be imperative to identify the scope of the compensatory or protective effects of constructive forms of conflict. Do these conflict characteristics have compensatory or protective effects that are broadly applicable to different domains and levels of child functioning? Or, alternatively, are the salubrious effects of the conflict dimensions limited to specific dimensions of child functioning? Addressing these questions will help to advance tests of direct path models by examining whether conflict resolution or other constructive conflict parameters are associated with lower levels of psychological symptoms by directly decreasing maladaptive coping patterns or amplifying adaptive coping patterns.

The Operation of Risk Processes in Direct Path Models

Consistent with the conceptualization of pluralism in etiological pathways of interparental conflict, our previous review and analysis of the direct path theories provides evidence for the notion that multiple child risk processes mediate exposure to interparental conflict. For example, children from high-conflict homes exhibit greater distress, fear, and vigilance in response to parental conflicts and conflict simulations (e.g., Davies & Cummings, 1998; Davies, Harold, et al., 2002; El-Sheikh, 1997; Garcia O'Hearn et al., 1997; Gordis et al., 1997). Dimensions of negative emotionality in response to conflict have been associated, in turn, with greater risk for psychological problems (e.g., Davies & Cummings, 1998; Davis et al., 1998). Similarly, child negative cognitions or appraisals of the

psychosocial consequences of interparental difficulties have been identified as mediators of interparental conflict in both concurrent and prospective models of child maladjustment (e.g., Grych, Fincham, et al., 2000; Grych et al., 2003). Other studies have also found that destructive interparental conflict is associated with specific types of coping and regulatory patterns characterized by greater avoidance and involvement in family stress (e.g., Davies, Forman, et al., 2002; Garcia O'Hearn et al., 1997; Sandler et al., 1994). In turn, some studies have identified associations between coping and regulatory patterns like avoidance and involvement in family difficulties and child psychological problems (e.g., Gordis et al., 1997).

Emphasis on distinguishing between adaptive and maladaptive functioning in developmental psychopathology raises a broader research question: Why would children from high-conflict homes exhibit high levels of negative affect, hostile cognitive appraisals and expectancies, and coping and regulatory difficulties? In other words, why would children become more rather than less sensitive to conflict with repeated exposure, especially given that high levels of reactivity to conflict are unpleasant and may jeopardize child functioning in the long run? According to the contextual and organizational principles of developmental psychopathology (E. M. Cummings et al., 2000), the adaptational function of risk processes may vary across different contexts. Thus, even though heightened emotional reactivity and negative appraisals may increase child risk for psychopathology in the long run, these risk processes may actually have adaptational value in the context of high-conflict homes. For example, theories guided by the functionalist perspective highlight the adaptive value of affect in facilitating the achievement of significant psychological goals (Crockenberg & Langrock, 2001a; Davies, Harold, et al., 2002; Saarni et al., 1998; Thompson & Calkins, 1996). Moreover, in accordance with transactional models of developmental psychopathology (Sameroff, 1995), the specific regulatory strategy adopted by children largely hinges on specific transactions and feedback loops between the children and familial contexts. The emotional security theory specifically maintains that only regulatory strategies that have successful track records of preserving security will be sustained in future contexts. For example, children facing severe family adversity (e.g., maltreatment, domestic violence) may be especially likely to mask their distress in response to interparental conflict as a way of reducing their salience as targets of hostility by distressed, violence-prone adults (Shipman, Zeman, Penza, & Champion, 2000). Likewise, in drawing on social learning theory, Emery (1989) postulated that feedback loops and transactions between the children and families culminate in higher levels of child involvement in interparental discord.

Diversity in the Operation of Risk Processes in Direct Path Models

Although a number of child responses have been identified as possible risk processes in direct path models of interparental conflict, different response processes do not necessarily carry the burden of interparental conflict in the same way. Accordingly, a key task is to further explicate the differential roles of specific response processes in the developmental psychopathology of angry home environments. For example, emotional distress and negative expectancies in the face of interparental difficulties have been shown to be robust mediators in associations between interparental conflict and child adjustment problems (Davies, Harold et al., 2002; Grych et al., 2003). In contrast, analyses of links between forms of interparental conflict, child regulatory or coping patterns (i.e., avoidance, involvement), and child maladjustment have yielded weak to modest support for mediational models (J. S. Cummings et al., 1989; Davies, Forman, et al., 2002; Jenkins, Smith, & Graham, 1989).

In further distinguishing among forms of child responding, researchers have suggested that the mixed support for the mediating role of involvement and avoidance may result from the failure to disaggregate the multidimensional nature of the constructs. For example, the emotional security theory postulates that the quality and substance of the regulatory strategy, rather than the mere presence, best captures emotional security and its long-term adaptational implications. Prolonged attempts to intervene that require considerable emotional and psychological investment or risk are theorized to reflect substantial difficulties restoring emotional security and lay the foundation for the development of psychopathology (Davies, 2002). Similarly, whereas brief and mild patterns of avoidance (e.g., distracting oneself through play) are postulated to reflect successful restoration of security, reflexive or dysregulated avoidance strategies (e.g., freezing, hastily fleeing the room) are predicted to signify considerable difficulties preserving security and may serve as precursors to later psychological problems. Similar progress has been made in identifying the specific roles of different types of child emotional reactions in models of interparental conflict (e.g., Crockenberg & Langrock, 2001a, 2001b; Davies, Harold, et al., 2002).

The paucity of empirical attention devoted to other indices of child reactivity has further contributed to the challenges of identifying variations in the mediational role of different risk processes. Progress in understanding the psychophysiological functioning of children from angry home environments has been particularly slow. However, emerging conceptual frameworks can provide useful conceptual guides in generating hypotheses. Reflecting a multilevel conceptualization of child functioning, useful distinctions have been drawn among different biological systems, including sympathetic-adrenomedullary (SAM) reactivity, hypothalamic-pituitary-adrenocortical (HPA) reactivity, and serotonergic functioning (see Repetti, Taylor, & Seeman, 2002). Building on the concept of allostatic load (e.g., McEwen, 1998; McEwen & Stellar, 1993), Repetti and colleagues specifically postulated that exposure to forms of family adversity lead to dysregulation in children's HPA, SAM, and serotonergic functioning over time that are manifested phenotypically in physical, neuropsychological, and psychological problems. Although noteworthy strides have been made in understanding linkages between forms of family adversity (e.g., maltreatment, attachment insecurity) and specific types of neurobiological dysregulation manifested in cardiovascular, brain electrical, and adrenocortical activity (Cicchetti, 2002; Repetti et al., 2002), the literature has lagged behind identifying the neurobiological and neuropsychological correlates of interparental conflict exposure. Moreover, the few studies addressing psychophysiological activity in models of interparental conflict, which have primarily focused on cardiovascular activity as a marker of SAM functioning, have yielded complex results (e.g., Ballard, Cummings, & Larkin, 1993; El-Sheikh, 1994; El-Sheikh, Harger, & Whitson, 2001; Katz & Gottman, 1997). For example, rather than serving as a mediator in associations between interparental conflict and child adjustment problems, as the allostatic load hypothesis predicts, some indices of cardiovascular activity (e.g., high basal vagal tone and vagal tone suppression) may act as moderators that protect or exacerbate the vulnerability of children exposed to high levels of conflict (see Katz & Gottman, 1997; El-Sheikh et al., 2001).

Although the operation of any given risk process has commonly been examined in isolation from the other risk processes, studies are beginning to make headway in understanding the relative role of multiple mechanisms in pathways between interparental conflict history and child adjustment problems. For example, tests of multiple appraisal processes in single statistical models designed to examine the cognitive-contextual framework indicated that the relative power of children's perceived threat and self-blame in models of interparental conflict varied depending on the type of psychological problem. Specifically, the findings indicated that perceived threat was a key mechanism linking interparental conflict to child internalizing symptoms, whereas interparental conflict was indirectly associated with child externalizing symptoms through its association with high levels of self-blame (Grych et al., 2003). Likewise, researchers are in the early stages of testing the relative empirical fit of theoretically guided models in relation to other plausible conceptual models. For example, in testing the relative roles of child processes derived from the emotional security and cognitive-contextual theories, Davies, Harold, and colleagues (2002) reported that emotional security and appraisals of threat and self-blame each played unique, mutually informative roles in understanding pathways between interparental conflict exposure and child adjustment problems.

The Interplay among Risk Processes in Direct Path Models

The most common approach to delineating pathways between interparental conflict, child response processes, and child adjustment has been to dissect and analyze each specific form of child reactivity to interparental conflict in isolation from the larger constellation of children's reaction patterns. However, this approach may not fully capture the function of child response processes in direct path models. According to the organizational perspective in developmental psychopathology (Cicchetti & Cohen, 1995), any single form of child responding gains meaning in the context of the larger organization of child responding across multiple domains and levels of functioning. Therefore, relying on methods of disaggregating and isolating the study of a single response pattern may obscure an accurate analysis of the meaning of any single response domain within the larger profile of children's behavioral, affective, cognitive, and physiological reactivity to conflict.

Two classes of analytic approaches have proven to be particularly valuable tools in empirically capturing higher-order patterns of child reactivity to conflict. Variable-based approaches, which examine variables and their interrelations as the main conceptual and analytic units, have been successfully used in explicating the interactive interplay between multiple response domains. For example, guided by gender socialization theory, Crockenberg and Langrock (2001b) proposed that girls' angry reactions to interparental conflict have different implications for their psychological adjustment depending on whether they experience co-occurring fear. Supporting this hypothesis, post hoc plotting of a significant interaction between anger and fear indicated that angry reactions to conflict were especially likely to predict girls' internalizing symptoms when

they also exhibited fear in response conflict. However, variable-based models do have their share of limitations, especially in the statistical constraints of obtaining a stable solution if the synergistic interplay among any more than two or three variables is examined.

To remedy this limitation, researchers are increasingly utilizing person-based approaches to capturing higher-order patterns of child responding. Because the person or child is the primary conceptual and analytic unit of analysis, the core objective of the person-based designs is to synthesize and integrate the study of child responding within the holistic organization of children's emotional, behavioral, cognitive, and physiological responses to interparental difficulties. The emotional security theory proposes that there is considerable heterogeneity across children in the strategies they use to attain and preserve a sense of security in interparental contexts. Thus, some children may express difficulties in attaining security by exhibiting overt distress and avoidance, whereas other children who are having difficulties preserving security may intervene in conflicts. Moreover, in the conceptualization of emotional security as a dynamic, nonlinear control system, the meaning of morphologically identical responses to conflict (e.g., low distress) cannot be deciphered unless they are examined in relation to the larger constellation of children's responses. For example, in the context of high levels of overt emotional reactivity and excessive regulation of conflict exposure, low levels of self-reported distress may reflect an insecure strategy of suppressing subjective threat. Alternatively, if low subjective distress occurs in the context of well-regulated concern and low levels of involvement and avoidance, it may be regarded as part of a secure pattern of coping with conflict.

One approach utilized by Cummings and colleagues is to classify children into different groups based on their holistic pattern of responding to interadult anger across multiple response domains, including social and emotional behavior, self-reported emotional and cognitive reactions, and physiological functioning (E. M. Cummings, 1987; El-Sheikh, Cummings, & Goetsch, 1989). This classification process yielded three distinct higher-order response patterns: (1) concerned children, who exhibited well-regulated bouts of distress and signs of empathy in response to anger; (2) ambivalent children, who experienced high levels of emotional arousal typified by high levels of positive and negative affect; and (3) unresponsive children, who reported feeling elevated anger despite showing no overt signs of negative affect. Whereas concerned patterns of responding have been hypothesized to evolve from warm, supportive family relationships and, in turn, set the stage for competent developmental trajectories, ambivalent or unresponsive profiles of responding were thought to result from exposure to chronic family adversity and increase child vulnerability to psychopathology. Partly supporting this hypothesis, Maughan and Cicchetti (2002) recently reported that the pathway between histories of maltreatment and child psychological symptoms was partially mediated by children's ambivalent response patterns to background anger.

In developing a pattern-based reformulation of the emotional security theory, Davies and Forman (2002) hypothesized that there were four primary styles of child emotional security in the context of parental conflict: secure, insecure-preoccupied, insecure-dismissing, and insecure-masking. *Secure* children, who were hypothesized to have confidence in their parents to manage disputes in a way that maintains family harmony, were postulated to exhibit well-regulated concern. The confidence of secure children was specifically theorized to evolve, in part, from witnessing well-managed parental disputes in the context of warm, cohesive interparental and family relationships and, in turn, set the stage for more healthy developmental outcomes. *Preoccupied* children were proposed to exhibit high levels of vigilance, anxiety, and involvement across behavioral and subjective indices of responding. This pattern, which was proposed to lay the foundation for negative self-perceptions and internalizing symptoms, was hypothesized to evolve from interparental and family processes that further draw children into interparental difficulties. *Dismissing* children, who were specifically posited to downplay the conscious experiences of threat in the interparental relationship, were hypothesized to exhibit high levels of overt distress but low levels of subjective distress and negative representations (also see Kobak, Cole, Ferenz-Gillies, Fleming, & Gamble, 1993). Downplaying the significance of interparental conflict was further hypothesized to develop in the context of disengaged interparental relations, and, in turn, breed greater externalizing symptoms. In drawing on adversity models in developmental psychopathology (e.g., Shipman et al., 2000), *masking* children were postulated to inhibit overt expressions of high levels of subjective distress in an effort to limit their salience as targets of angry, violent, or dysregulated adults. Although masking may be regarded as adaptive for children exposed to imminent threats to their welfare (e.g., interparental violence), this pattern was postulated to increase children's vulnerability to psychopathology in the long run. Initial empirical tests have provided some promising support for many of these predictions (see Davies & Forman, 2002, for more details).

INDIRECT PATHWAYS AND PROCESSES IN MODELS OF INTERPARENTAL DISCORD

Reflecting the multiplicity of pathways among risk factors, processes, and outcomes, Path 2 in Figure 3.1 on page 89 illustrates that interparental discord can increase child risk for maladaptive coping and, eventually, maladjustment indirectly through its association with disruptions in parent-child relationship dynamics. Although indirect effects models share the common assumption that family and contextual disturbances mediate the link between interparental conflict and child adjustment problems, models vary widely in the strength ascribed to the mediational pathways. Strong models of indirect paths, which make more assumptions about the power of contextual processes, postulate that parent-child relationship disturbances provide a complete explanation for why interparental discord is related to child adjustment (e.g., Erel, Margolin, & John, 1998; Fauber, Forehand, Thomas, & Wierson, 1990; Patterson, DeBaryshe, & Ramsey, 1989). Thus, according to these reductionist conceptualizations, interparental conflict is only indirectly associated with child psychopathology through its covariation with parent-child relationship processes. However, running counter to strong models, accumulating evidence supports the notion that interparental conflict is directly associated with children's reactivity to conflict and adjustment problems even in the context of parenting disturbances (e.g., Davies, Harold, et al., 2002; Emery, Fincham, & Cummings, 1992; Frosch & Mangelsdorf, 2001; Webster-Stratton & Hammond, 1999). Thus, at least at this early stage of research, weak models of indirect effects, which relax claims about the magnitude of indirect pathways, appear to provide a better representation of research findings. Weak versions of indirect path models specifically embrace the assumption of plurality and diversity in developmental pathways by postulating that parenting disturbances only partially explain the risk posed by interparental discord to child maladjustment. Consistent with Path 2 in Figure 3.1, the following discussion is organized around the specific operation of parent-child dynamics as mediators in relations between interparental difficulties and child maladaptive coping and psychopathology. Three properties of the parent-child subsystem have received the most conceptual attention in indirect models of interparental and child functioning: (1) parenting or child-rearing practices, (2) parent-child relationship quality, and (3) coparenting relations.

Parenting Practices

Predictions regarding the mediating role of parenting in models of interparental conflict have commonly been rooted in the integration of the spillover hypothesis (e.g., Erel & Burman, 1995; Floyd, Gilliom, & Costigan, 1998) and socialization models of parenting (Baumrind, 1971; Maccoby & Martin, 1983). In addressing the first link in the indirect path model of parenting, the spillover hypothesis specifically posits that parental anguish, indifference, and antipathy originally stemming from the unresolved spousal disputes is carried over into the parental interactions with children. Preoccupation, fatigue, and negative affect emanating from marital conflict is specifically thought to engender (1) poor behavioral management techniques reflected in lax monitoring and inconsistent or harsh discipline, (2) greater psychological control, characterized by efforts to control the child through manipulation and exploitation of the parent-child bond (e.g., love withdrawal, guilt induction), and (3) emotional unavailability, as evidenced by diminished responsiveness, sensitivity, and warmth. These specific types of parenting difficulties, in turn, are theorized to increase children's risk for psychopathology in socialization models of parenting.

Consistent empirical support for these indirect pathways is evident in the literature. Experimental, longitudinal, and sequential analyses have shown that disruptions in parenting increase over minutes, days, and months following interparental conflicts (e.g., Almeida, Wethington, & Chandler, 1999; Christensen & Margolin, 1988; Davies, Sturge-Apple, & Cummings, 2004; Jouriles & Farris, 1992; Kitzmann, 2000; Mahoney, Boggio, & Jouriles, 1996). Likewise, parental emotional unavailability, poor discipline and monitoring, and psychological control have been found to at least partially mediate the association between interparental conflict and child adjustment (e.g., Erel et al., 1998; Fauber et al., 1990; Gonzales, Pitts, Hill, & Roosa, 2000; Harold, Fincham, Osborne, & Conger, 1997; Webster-Stratton & Hammond, 1999).

Even in the face of ample empirical support for the mediational role of parenting, the nature of the interplay between marital conflict and parenting practices is not well understood. Little is known about whether the relative strength of indirect pathways varies across different parenting dimensions. It is plausible that some types of parenting practices may be particularly robust mediators of

marital conflict, whereas others may hold little or no power as explanatory processes. Supporting this possibility, the emphasis on affective processes in the spillover hypothesis and the emotional security theory suggests that parenting processes capturing emotional expressiveness in parenting are particularly potent mechanisms in indirect pathways of marital conflict (Davies & Cummings, 1994; Grych, 2002; Margolin et al., 2001).

Questions about how and why specific parenting practices exert their effects as mediators also remain largely unanswered. Developing a more formal and broader model that systematically integrates theories of parenting and marital conflict might provide a useful heuristic for advancing this next generation of research questions and hypotheses. In addressing the first link in the indirect path model of parenting, theoretical perspectives on marriage and parenting place differential emphasis on specific processes that accompany or result from interparental conflict and subsequently disrupt parenting (Sturge-Apple, Davies, & Cummings, in press). Although relationship perturbations, coping processes, negative affect, and personality attributes have been variously discussed as possible mechanisms, little attention has been devoted to developing precise conceptual and operational definitions of these hypotheses and simultaneously testing the relative merits of different mediating mechanisms (see Grych, 2002). Even testing processes within a specific conceptualization is likely to be challenging. For example, testing predictions derived from the spillover hypothesis will require increasingly complex perspectives on the affective processes by which interparental problems affect parenting. For example, the three-component affective model of parenting developed by Dix (1991) reveals that negative affect, in itself, may undermine parenting through multiple, distinct pathways, including (1) amplification of negative appraisals and attributions of child behavior, (2) constriction of attentional resources devoted to child-rearing activities, and (3) disruption of problem-solving abilities and facilitation of reflexive, dysregulated response patterns. By the same token, identifying the processes that account for why parenting problems in high-conflict homes increase child vulnerability to psychological difficulties would further the next generation of research. It is likely that exposure to various parenting difficulties may set in motion multiple processes within children (e.g., affective-motivational, social learning, social information processing) that ultimately serve as more proximal causes of their psychopathology (E. M. Cummings et al., 2000). Thus, evolving child response and coping patterns in parent-child and family contexts may help to explain why parenting processes mediate associations between marital conflict and child maladjustment (see the next section for a specific illustration).

At an even broader level, the joint influence of marital conflict and parenting practices may not only be manifested in patterns of mediation. Family systems theory underscores that properties of any family subsystem (e.g., parent-child subsystem) may regulate properties of another family subsystem (e.g., interparental subsystem) in nonlinear ways. For example, to maintain homeostasis in the face of growing perturbations in the interparental subsystem, some parents may successfully attempt to offset child vulnerability to interparental adversity by becoming more invested in supporting the child and managing their own behavior. Thus, it is possible that some parenting practices may actually protect or buffer children from the deleterious effects of interparental problems. Alternatively, some parents who are experiencing distress in their relationships with their partner may attempt to fulfill lingering intimacy needs in the parent-child relationship through triangulation processes (e.g., Cox et al., 2001; Grych, 2002). If this presupposition is correct, it is possible that overly involved or enmeshed parenting patterns may actually potentiate or amplify the psychological burdens that children must shoulder in high-conflict homes. Although these two conceptual explanations generate contradictory hypotheses, they share the assumption that parenting may actually serve as a moderator of interparental conflict in the prediction of child problems. However, parenting practices have generally been tested as mediators in models of interparental conflict, without consideration of alternative or competing family process models (e.g., moderator models). In the rare instances when both mediation and moderation are tested in the same study (e.g., Davies, Harold, et al., 2002; Frosch & Mangelsdorf, 2001), the findings do not uniformly support the viability of mediational paths of parenting over moderating role or parenting.

Parent-Child Relationship Quality

Associations between individual differences in exposure to interparental conflict and parenting practices and parent-child relationship processes further suggest that parent-child relationship dimensions may be vital to elucidating indirect path models. Attachment theory is a particularly promising conceptual tool in taking indirect path models one step further in the specification of family process. Central to attachment theory is the proposition that children's quality of attachment to caregivers mediates the link

between parental emotional availability (e.g., sensitivity, responsiveness) and the development of normal or psychopathological functioning (Ainsworth, Blehar, Waters, & Wall, 1978; Bowlby, 1969; Cicchetti, Cummings, Greenberg, & Marvin, 1990). Given that protection is a primary function of the attachment relationship, variations in the quality of attachment patterns are assumed to reflect individual differences in the ability of the children to use the caregiver as a haven of protection and safety (Cicchetti et al., 1990; Colin, 1996; Kobak, 1999). However, the substantive scope of attachment theory has, at least until recently, been largely confined to identifying specific parenting (e.g., responsiveness) and child (e.g., temperament) attributes in isolation from the broader family system (see Thompson, 1997).

To address this gap (Cowan, 1997), the emotional security theory has postulated two channels through which attachment patterns may mediate interparental conflict. Paths relevant to addressing these pathways are illustrated in Figure 3.4. First, as shown in Paths 2, 5, and 7 in Figure 3.4, parenting disruptions that accompany chronic interparental discord may increase child psychopathology by undermining children's confidence in parents as sources of protection and support. In support of part of this hypothesis (i.e., Paths 2 and 5), studies have demonstrated that parental emotional availability (e.g., sensitivity, support) partly mediates the link between marital conflict and child-parent attachment security (Frosch, Mangelsdorf, & McHale, 2000; Owen & Cox, 1997). In expanding on these findings, structural equation modeling revealed that the mediational role of parenting difficulties in associations

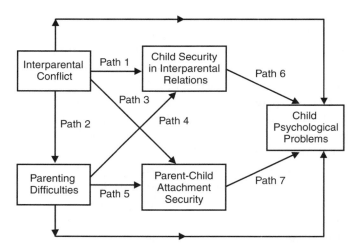

Figure 3.4 A conceptual model of the joint interplay between interparental conflict and parenting difficulties in predicting child security in family relationships and psychological adjustment.

between interparental conflict and early adolescent internalizing and externalizing symptoms was further mediated by children's doubts about the accessibility of their parents as support figures (Davies, Harold, et al., 2002).

Second, Paths 3 and 7 illustrate the hypothesis that exposure to interparental conflict may also be associated with child psychological problems by directly undermining child security in parent-child relationships. Witnessing frightening (e.g., violence, emotional volatility) and frightened (e.g., submissiveness, crying) parental behavior during interparental conflicts is specifically thought to compromise not only child security in the interparental relationship but also child confidence in parents as sources of protection and support (Owen & Cox, 1997). Consistent with this hypothesis, interparental conflict has been shown to predict insecure and disorganized parent-child attachment relations even after controlling for parental sensitivity and warmth (Frosch et al., 2000; Owen & Cox, 1997).

More research is needed to further elucidate associations between marital conflict and parent-child attachment. Given some null and inconsistent findings on the relationship between attachment and interparental conflict, it is possible that interparental discord predicts attachment difficulties only under certain contextual conditions (Belsky, 1999). For example, research by Das Eiden, Teti, and Corns (1995) indicates that the association between interparental discord and attachment difficulties specifically emerged when parents evidenced relational vulnerabilities (e.g., insecure adult attachment relations). Moreover, disentangling the constellation of relationships between specific interparental conflict behaviors and specific attachment patterns may also prove useful in future research. Specifically, forms of frightening and frightened spousal behaviors may have different implications for how children organize their attachment patterns. Frightened behavior manifested in submissiveness, crying, and fear may foster representations of the parent as incompetent and weak and, as a result, undermine child confidence in the parent as a source of protection and in the process lead to relatively coherent forms of insecure attachments (e.g., avoidance, resistance). Conversely, frightening parental behaviors characterized by aggression and coercion may not only undermine child confidence in parental support but also foster child representations of parents as sources of threat and alarm. As a result, these children may be at specific risk for developing disorganized attachments. In accordance with transactional conceptualizations of development, reciprocal feedback loops may exist between parent-child attachment patterns and interparental relations (Byng-Hall, 1999), with specific patterns of parent-child attachment

also regulating the quality of interparental interactions. For example, clinical observations suggest that dependency and distress underlying resistant attachment patterns serve a stabilizing function in some families by diverting attention away from serious interparental problems or fulfilling intimacy needs of parents in disengaged marriages (Byng-Hall, 1999; Marvin & Stewart, 1990).

The conceptual model in Figure 3.4 raises other key questions necessary to advance a comprehensive model of emotional security. Path 4 illustrates that poor parenting may, in itself, increase child insecurity in the context of interparental difficulties. Although comprehensive tests of this path await future research, findings from initial studies are intriguing (Davies & Forman, 2002). For example, Hennessy, Rabideau, Cicchetti, and Cummings (1994) reported that children with histories of physical abuse evidenced greater fear in response to simulated adult conflict than nonabused children (see Grych, 1998, for different results). Furthermore, Paths 6 and 7 raise questions about whether the magnitude of paths between emotional security and children's developmental paths vary as a function of the context of security (i.e., interparental versus parent-child) and the form of maladjustment (see Davies, Harold, et al., 2002).

Coparenting Relations

A common assumption of many theoretical frameworks is that discord between parents covaries with disruptions in the coparenting relationship or parental abilities to support each other and work together as a team in raising the children. For example, in the spillover hypothesis, the proliferation of distress from interparental discord is not necessarily limited to the parent-child subsystem abilities (e.g., Erel & Burman, 1995; Floyd et al., 1998). In fact, emotional difficulties with the spouse may be especially likely to be manifested in coparenting disruptions as attempts to undermine spousal authority in the family may be a powerful way to seek retribution for perceived emotional injustices stemming from the interparental relationship. Similarly, the principle of interdependency in family systems theory postulates that spousal discord reflects a larger constellation of transactional influences with coparenting disturbances, as perturbations in any one subsystem reverberate through other family relationships in a negative reciprocal cycle (e.g., Cox et al., 2001; P. Minuchin, 1985). Supporting these predictions, marital conflict has been associated with various disruptions in the ability of parents to jointly coordinate child-rearing activities, including disengagement, triangulation, hostility, and disparagement (e.g., Floyd & Zmich, 1991; Katz & Gottman, 1996; McHale et al., 2004; Sturge-Apple et al., in press). Coparenting disturbances, in turn, have been associated with a wide array of child psychological problems (Belsky, Putnam, & Crnic, 1996; Leary & Katz, 2004; McHale, Johnson, & Sinclair, 1999) even after statistically controlling for other family processes such as marital conflict and parenting practices (e.g., Jouriles, Murphy, et al., 1991; McHale & Rasmussen, 1998; Schoppe, Mangelsdorf, & Frosch, 2001).

Although these findings are consistent with indirect paths between marital conflict, coparenting relationships, and child functioning, direct, systematic tests of the mediational role of coparenting have yet to be undertaken. In the rare instances in which the predictive roles of coparenting and interparental difficulties have been examined simultaneously in models of child functioning (Jouriles, Murphy, et al., 1991; McHale & Rasmussen, 1998), statistical models have primarily been utilized to evaluate the unique, additive effects of the family predictors. Thus, advances in models of interparental conflict in the broader family system will require more direct tests of the mediational interplay between interparental conflict and coparenting dimensions in the prediction of child coping and functioning. Moreover, even if the mediational role of coparenting processes is demonstrated, it is also important to progressively broaden the study of these indirect pathways in the larger family system. For example, some findings indicate that the mediational role of coparenting processes may be magnified or diluted by various family and child characteristics (e.g., McHale et al., 2002; Schoppe et al., 2001). In drawing attention to another knowledge gap, Path 2 in Figure 3.1 illustrates the largely untested assumption that child response and coping processes may ultimately account for the mediating role of coparenting relations in associations between interparental conflict and child adjustment.

CONTEXTUAL RISK AND PROTECTIVE MODELS OF INTERPARENTAL DISCORD

Although there is ample empirical support for both direct and indirect path models of interparental conflict, the research also indicates that there is substantial heterogeneity in the magnitude of child coping and response processes and parent-child relationship dynamics as mediators of interparental conflict. Thus, a key question remains: Why is there considerable diversity in these mediational pathways? From a developmental psychopathology perspective, individual development is regarded as operating within open

systems characterized by an ongoing transactional interplay between an active changing organism in a dynamic changing context (Cicchetti, 1993; Davies & Cicchetti, 2004; Granic & Hollenstein, 2003). In applying this notion to work on interparental conflict, a derivative hypothesis is that individual differences in the strength of direct and indirect pathways will lawfully vary as a function of the broader multilevel matrix of contextual characteristics.

Open system conceptualizations in developmental psychopathology do pose a number of formidable challenges to understanding the role of contextual processes in mediational pathways across multiple domains and levels of analysis. First, there are important differences in the nature and properties of contextual risk factors. For example, in attempting to provide a parsimonious account of risk and protection across multiple topical areas in developmental psychopathology, Garmezy (1985) offered a tripartite framework consisting of (1) child dispositional attributes, including temperament, personality, and gender; (2) family characteristics, including family climate, parenting practices, and parent psychopathology; and (3) extrafamilial characteristics, including friendships, community, and cultural characteristics.

Second, in open systems conceptualizations, contextual characteristics can have different effects as architects of pathways between interparental and child functioning. Figure 3.5 provides a visual depiction of four of the more prominent roles of contextual factors in multivariate frameworks of interparental conflict. Models 1 and 2 in Figure 3.5 illustrate that mediational pathways may best capture the interplay between interparental conflict and a given contextual characteristic in the prediction of child maladaptation. Because it is often plausible to interchange interparental conflict and many contextual characteristics in conceptual roles as mediators of one another, precisely mapping the etiological pathways remains a critical challenge. Consistent with indirect path models, the first model proposes that child, family, and extrafamilial attributes may reduce the strength of direct and indirect pathways by partially mediating or accounting for the effects of interparental conflict. Thus, alternative contextual characteristics may also serve as mechanisms that help to explain why children exposed to destructive interparental conflict are at greater risk for developing psychopathology. In contrast, the second model postulates that contextual characteristics may influence child coping and adjustment indirectly through their associations with interparental conflict. Thus, mediational pathways may be reversed, so that interparental problems are more proximal mediators of contextual characteristics. However, identifying contextual characteristics as distal risk

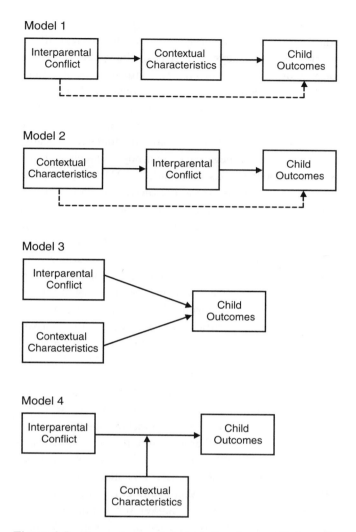

Figure 3.5 Conceptual models depicting the possible interplay between interparental conflict and contextual characteristics in the prediction of child maladaptation.

factors in a study of interparental conflict does not necessarily relegate it to a secondary conceptual status. Rather than falling into the reductionist trap of regarding "the smallest and most proximal event as the ultimate cause" (Emery et al., 1992, p. 910) of child psychopathology, distal effects of contextual characteristics are still regarded as playing an integral role in understanding the genesis of child psychopathology.

The final two models illustrate the possibility that mediational or causal chains may fail to adequately reflect the nature of the relationship between interparental conflict and a particular contextual characteristic in predicting child maladaptation. Even though the two factors may fail to explain one another's effects, the third model in Figure 3.5 indicates that interparental conflict and any given contextual risk can still operate as independent predictors

In accordance with this approach, some developmental psychopathology studies have aggregated multiple indices of risk into a single composite based on the tacit assumption that each risk factor contributes uniquely to predict child problems in an *additive effects* fashion (Luthar, 1993; Sameroff & Seifer, 1990). In contrast, the fourth model in Figure 3.5 highlights an alternative possibility that the interplay between interparental conflict and a given contextual characteristic may not necessarily be additive in nature. Potentiating and protective frameworks in developmental psychopathology specifically postulate that interparental conflict and contextual risk may interact in multiplicative or synergistic ways. By addressing questions of who is most and least at risk and when is the risk most or least pronounced, these frameworks have proven to be useful tools in identifying sources of variability in associations between interparental conflict and child functioning. Potentiating factors in these models are specifically conceptualized as amplifying or exponentially increasing the risk posed by interparental conflict. Conversely, protective factors serve to diminish or offset the deleterious effects of interparental conflict.

Third, contextual factors in open systems may vary in the locus of their effect in etiological pathways involving interparental conflict and child adjustment. Incorporating contextual characteristics into direct path models may advance an understanding of any link in the mediational chain, including links between interparental conflict and children's coping and response processes or children's coping and response processes and their developmental trajectories of adjustment. In a similar fashion, contextual factors may alter associations between interparental conflict and parent-child relationship dynamics, parent-child relationship dynamics and child adjustment trajectories, or both.

Given that contextual characteristics can vary in terms of form, function, and the locus of effect, we organize our following discussion around the theoretical value of distinguishing contextual attributes along these three dimensions. Consistent with the tripartite framework developed by Garmezy (1985), we selectively discuss how the three classes of contextual factors (i.e., child attributes, family characteristics, extrafamilial characteristics) may help to advance knowledge on direct and indirect path models of interparental conflict.

Child Dispositional Attributes

Although it is important to note that a variety of child attributes may figure prominently in the variability of children's adaptation to interparental conflict, we selectively focus on three primary dimensions for the sake of illustration: gender, age, and temperament.

Child Gender

In support of a "male vulnerability" model, many initial tests of the moderating effects of gender demonstrated that associations between marital conflict and child maladjustment were stronger for boys than girls (E. M. Cummings & Cummings, 1988). However, a rigorous analysis of more contemporary studies reveals that it is difficult to draw any clear-cut, simple conclusions regarding the role of gender. Many recent studies have produced complex and inconsistent results, with large sample studies and meta-analyses failing to find support for moderating effects (e.g., Buehler et al., 1997; Jouriles, Bourg, & Farris, 1991). Resolving this complexity may require greater sensitivity to the possibility that gender may operate in different ways across levels or domains of children's functioning. For example, the male vulnerability model may be applicable only in the prediction of specific forms of psychopathology (e.g., conduct problems). In expanding on this theme, it is also possible that girls and boys evidence comparable levels of distress that are manifested in different ways (Davies & Lindsay, 2001). Girls, in particular, may be especially likely to exhibit greater distress with corresponding increases in conflict hostility (E. M. Cummings et al., 1989; Davies, Myers, et al., 1999; Grych, 1998), especially when distress is reflected in subtle, covert channels (E. M. Cummings et al., 2000). Thus, researchers would do well to delineate gender-specific pathways in models that integrate the study of children's specific reactivity to conflict with indices of their global psychological adjustment (Davies & Lindsay, 2001).

Another key task facing researchers is to uncover the wide range of developmental and socialization pathways that lead to variability in outcomes experienced by boys and girls in high-conflict homes. For example, the relative susceptibility of boys and girls to marital conflict may vary across the developmental stages of the children (Hops, 1995). Boys' susceptibility to maladjustment, particularly in the form of externalizing symptoms, may be stronger in childhood than girls'. According to one biological explanation, boys may have weaker neuropsychological and psychobiological systems in early childhood that may serve to potentiate the stressful effects of interparental conflict (Emery, 1982). However, this explanation does not readily account for findings indicating that girls may evidence greater vulnerability to interparental discord than boys as children progress into adolescence (E. M. Cummings & Davies, 1994a; Davies & Windle, 1997; Hops, 1995; Pe-

tersen, 1988). According to the gender intensification hypothesis (Hill & Lynch, 1983), increasing physical differentiation between boys and girls during puberty sets in motion more pressure for girls to conform to conventional social roles of valuing close interpersonal and family relationships. In turn, this greater concern and preoccupation with maintaining harmonious family relations may increase girls' sensitivity to interparental conflict and cause them to react more negatively than boys (Davies & Lindsay, 2001, 2004; Davies & Windle, 1997). Alternatively, developmental models stress that the timing and nature of some developmental challenges may vary by gender. For example, girls not only perceive puberty as a more stressful event than boys do, but they are also more likely to experience the challenge of coping with other stressful events, such as the transition to the larger, more impersonal confines of secondary school systems (Windle, 1992). Thus, this dense temporal clustering of stressors may place undue burdens on coping abilities and resources and exacerbate the deleterious effects of interparental conflict for girls.

Age and Developmental Level

Although age is increasingly acknowledged as a potential moderator in models of interparental conflict (E. M. Cummings & Davies, 1994a; Grych & Fincham, 1990), it is difficult to decipher whether children in any specific age group or developmental period are, in any broad sense, more vulnerable to interparental conflict (Buehler et al., 1997).

Part of the challenge is that age in our process model is conceptualized as a general marker for a multiplicity of changes in biological and experiential processes. Accordingly, different domains of functioning change in different ways with age, with some changes resulting in greater risk for children and others resulting in less risk. For example, the vulnerability of preschool children to interparental conflict may be particularly pronounced by virtue of their dispositions to experience fear, self-blame, and threat in response to conflict (e.g., Covell & Abramovitch, 1987; E. M. Cummings et al., 1989; Davies, Myers, et al., 1999; Jouriles, Spiller, Stephens, McDonald, & Swank, 2000), low levels of perceived competence in coping (Cummings et al., 1991; Grych, 1998), and limited ability to enlist coping strategies to regulate affect (El-Sheikh & Cummings, 1995). Yet, relative to older children and adolescents, preschoolers' lower sensitivity to adult problems, briefer histories of exposure to interparental conflict, and weaker disposition to mediate conflicts may serve as protective factors that offset this risk.

Distinguishing among different forms of child maladjustment may also be critical in specifying the moderating role of age. Age-related vulnerability to marital conflict may be limited to specific forms of psychopathology rather than generalizable to multiple patterns of symptomatology. For example, whereas young children may largely express their distress in the form of externalizing difficulties in stressful interpersonal contexts (E. M. Cummings & Davies, 1994a), tendencies to exhibit internalizing symptoms and negative self-appraisals in response to stress increase with age (Jouriles et al., 2000). Thus, in the stressful context of repeated interparental conflict, younger children may be especially likely to express their distress in the form of externalizing symptoms, whereas older children may be increasingly prone to developing internalizing difficulties.

In the context of our process model, the moderating role of age may vary across different parts of the mediational pathways involving interparental conflict, children's response processes, and their developmental outcomes. For example, Davies, Myers, and colleagues (1999) found that late adolescents were significantly more likely to distinguish between destructive and constructive histories of interadult conflict in their appraisals of long-term relationship problems than were younger children. Likewise, Jouriles and colleagues (2000) reported that appraisal of self-blame was a more powerful predictor of child internalizing symptoms for 10- to 12-year-old children than for 8- to 9-year-old children. Thus, the key aim may involve not simply searching for age-specific vulnerabilities to interparental conflict, but rather explicating the specific locus of the moderating effects of age at different parts of the multichain process models of interparental conflict.

Temperament

Several conceptual frameworks have explicitly hypothesized that dimensions of temperament function as potentiating and protective factors in associations between interparental conflict and children's coping and adjustment (Davies & Cummings, 1994; Grych & Fincham, 1990). Initial empirical tests of this hypothesis have revealed that dimensions of difficult temperament appear to potentiate the risk interparental discord posed to adolescents' trajectories of psychological adjustment (Davies & Windle, 2001). However, beyond this single study, little is known about the nature of the multiplicative interplay between temperament and interparental conflict. Thus, examining the potential protective and potentiating effects of temperament and other behavioral and personality dispositions is an important research direction, especially in light of intriguing relations between children's behavioral difficulties and their adaptation to adult and marital dis-

cord (e.g., E. M. Cummings, Iannotti, & Zahn-Waxler, 1985; Davies & Windle, 2001).

As knowledge of these moderating effects accumulates, understanding why children with certain dispositions are more vulnerable to marital discord will also be a critical research direction. Conceptual frameworks that articulate the mechanisms that underlie the moderating effects of temperament may serve as valuable guides in this area of inquiry (Davies & Cummings, 1994; Grych & Fincham, 1990). For example, does heightened reactivity to negative events experienced by children with difficult temperaments increase their risk by magnifying their sensitization to conflict (Grych & Fincham, 1990)? Alternatively, do key features of difficult temperament (e.g., negative mood, high activity, poor attention) prompt children to rely on narrow, rigid, and maladaptive ways of coping with interparental conflict (Grych & Fincham, 1990)? Or, is it possible that transactional processes are operating whereby difficult temperaments tax the already fragile family relationships and, in turn, further fuel children's behavioral difficulties through exposure to greater family conflict (Davies & Cummings, 1994; Davies & Windle, 2001)?

Family Characteristics

A principle common to both family systems theory and the organizational perspective in developmental psychology is that functioning in any one domain is defined by and part of a broader constellation of functioning in the system as a whole. In the family system, organization, patterning, and regularity in the family as a whole regulates and is regulated by the interplay among interparental, parent-child, and coparenting subsystems (Cox & Paley, 1997; Mikulincer, Florian, Cowan, & Cowan, 2002; P. Minuchin, 1985; S. Minuchin, 1974). Consequently, interparental conflict styles can be usefully conceptualized as integral components of broader patterns of boundary maintenance (e.g., implicit rules for exchanging material and psychological resources across family subsystems), affective functioning, and relationship quality in the family, which, in turn, may further define how children adapt to interparental and family processes.

Advances in the study of family-level and triadic systems (e.g., conflict, instability, cohesion, expressiveness, support) are proving useful in integrating the examination of interparental conflict in a familywide model of functioning. For example, although McHale and Rasmussen (1998) did not explicitly examine whether observations of family-level perturbations mediated associations between interparental and intraparental distress and child functioning, family perturbations did uniquely predict child aggression 3 years later even after statistically controlling for intraparental and interparental functioning. As another example, Davies, Cummings, et al. (2004) used cluster-analytic methods to identify individual differences in the higher-order organization of family functioning based on the quality of relationships in the interparental, coparental, and parent-child subsystems. Consistent with previous work on family systems theory (Belsky, Rovine, & Fish, 1989; Cox & Paley, 1997; Kerig, 1995; Kretchmar & Jacobvitz, 2002; Marvin & Stewart, 1990), families fit into one of four profiles: (1) cohesive families, who maintained well-defined, flexible boundaries between subsystems that permitted access to relationship resources and support while also respecting autonomy; (2) enmeshed families, who experienced weak boundaries across family subsystems and, as a result, displayed high levels of conflict, hostility, and psychological control; (3) disengaged families, who experienced overly rigid, inflexible, and distant boundaries that are manifested in high levels of discord, hostility, and detachment across family subsystems; and (4) adequate families, who, despite some discord, generally exhibited healthy family functioning. Furthermore, in comparison to children in cohesive families, the results indicated that disengaged and enmeshed families exhibited greater signs of insecurity in the interparental relationship concurrently and internalizing and externalizing symptoms both concurrently and 1 year later (also see Belsky & Fearon, 2004; O'Connor, Hetherington, & Reiss, 1998). Although these studies lend support to the notion that interparental conflict may exert an impact on child mental health through its inextricable relationship with broader configurations of family functioning, direct tests of family configurations as intervening or mediating mechanisms in associations between interparental conflict and child maladjustment await further research.

Sibling Relations

Little is known about the joint influence of parental conflict and sibling relationship quality on children's adjustment, but the available evidence supports sibling relationships as also factoring in the effects of interparental conflict (Dunn & Davies, 2001). Contemporaneous and prospective relations between marital conflict and sibling conflict and poor relationship quality are reported (Brody, Stoneman, & McCoy, 1992; Stocker & Youngblade, 1999). Furthermore, research has begun to address the family (e.g., differential parental treatment, parental hostility) and child (e.g., self-blame) processes that may account for relationships among interparental conflict, compromised sibling relations, and child adjustment prob-

lems (McGuire, Dunn, & Plomin, 1995; Stocker & Youngblade, 1999).

Although the study of siblings constitutes an emerging area of study in the interparental conflict literature, the relatively scant literature from a process-oriented and appropriately familywide perspective on this topic offers little support for any reasonably comprehensive model for understanding siblings as an influence in the context of interparental discord. Addressing this gap, Dunn and Davies (2001) recently presented an initial conceptualization for indirect and direct pathways between interparental discord and quality of sibling relations. Building on the broader literature concerning direct and indirect pathways (E. M. Cummings & Davies, 2002), indirect pathways were hypothesized to reflect links between marital discord, the quality of both mothers' and fathers' relationships with children (e.g., negativity in parent-child relationships; more differential parent-child negativity), and quality of sibling relationships. Direct paths were also hypothesized, reflecting direct pathways between interparental hostility and children's negative relationships with their siblings (Dunn et al., 1998).

Consistent with potentiating and protective frameworks, other conceptualizations have cast sibling relationships as potential protective factors in high-conflict homes. Jenkins and colleagues (1989) reported that seeking contact with a sibling was a commonly used strategy for children coping with interparental conflict. E. M. Cummings and Smith (1993) demonstrated that positive affect increased among female siblings during exposure to adult conflict involving the mother. In directly testing sibling relations as a moderator, Jenkins and Smith (1990) reported that the association between interparental conflict and child symptoms was significantly weaker in magnitude for children with good sibling relations than for children with poor sibling relations. In fact, even the mere presence of a sibling may buffer children from the effects of family stress (Kempton, Armistead, Wierson, & Forehand, 1991; Sandler, 1980). By the same token, researchers must be careful not to simply assume that siblings will uniformly serve as buffers of interparental conflict. As a case in point, Nixon and Cummings (1999) found that children with disabled siblings reported greater distress, personal responsibility, and impulses to intervene in family conflicts than children without disabled siblings. Collectively, this body of research generates several important questions in advancing risk and potentiating models: Does being a recipient of protection and nurturance from a sibling largely explain why good sibling relations buffer children from interparental conflict? Do children incur benefits or, alternatively, psychological burdens from being the provider of safety and nurturance for a sibling?

Parent Psychological Symptoms

Parent psychological symptoms have also been implicated as central processes in indirect pathways of interparental discord. However, the nature of the interplay between parent psychological symptoms and interparental conflict has yet to be clearly elucidated. Supporting additive models, some studies have indicated that parental depressive symptoms and interparental discord are each independent predictors of child psychological maladjustment (Fendrich, Warner, & Weissman, 1990; Shaw & Emery, 1987). Conversely, some research and theory indicate that parent psychological symptoms may serve as distal risk factors that increase child vulnerability largely through their associations with family disturbances such as interparental conflict (E. M. Cummings & Davies, 1994b; Cummings, Keller, & Davies, in press). Still other work suggests that parent psychological symptoms are more proximal risk factors that mediate interparental conflict, at least under some conditions (Davies, Dumenci, & Windle, 1999; Downey & Coyne, 1990; Papp, Cummings, & Schermerhorn, 2004).

Variations in the conceptual ordering of marital conflict and parental psychological attributes across these studies may result from the specific expression of parental symptoms, marital conflict, and child psychopathology. For example, Downey and Coyne (1990) postulated that the specific mediational interplay between interparental conflict and parent depressive symptoms depends on the form of child maladjustment. Whereas parent depressive symptoms were specifically hypothesized to account for links between marital discord and child internalizing symptoms, marital discord was proposed to mediate the links between parent depressive symptoms and child externalizing symptoms. Supporting these hypotheses, maternal depressive symptomatology has been shown to mediate prospective associations between marital discord and adolescent depressive symptoms, and marital discord accounted for prospective associations between maternal depressive symptoms and adolescent delinquency (Davies, Dumenci, & Windle, 1999; also see Fendrich et al., 1990; Shaw & Emery, 1987).

Differences in how interparental conflict is expressed may also account for inconsistencies in mediational interplay involving parental adjustment problems and interparental conflict. In drawing on evidence that interparental dysphoria is a distinct dimension of conflict (Davis, Sheeber, Hops, & Tildesley, 2000), Du Rocher Schudlich and Cummings (2003) specifically examined constructive, destructive, and dysphoric marital conflict as mediators in links between parental depressive symptoms and child psychological symptoms. Whereas constructive and destructive conflict between parents failed to explain the risk posed by parental depressive symptoms, dysphoric marital conflict was a robust mediator in associations between parental depressive symptoms and child internalizing symptoms.

The nature of mediational pathways between marital conflict, parental attributes, and child problems may also depend on specific types of parental characteristics. On the one hand, some forms of parental psychopathology may assume a more distal role. For example, conceptual models have consistently cast interparental conflict as a central explanatory mechanism for why children exposed to parental drinking problems experience greater psychological problems (El-Sheikh & Cummings, 1997; Windle & Davies, 1999). In support of these models, empirical evidence has indicated that interparental conflict is a robust intervening mechanism linking parental problem drinking to child maladjustment (e.g., El-Sheikh & Flanagan, 2001; Keller, Cummings, & Davies, in press). On the other hand, other forms of psychopathology may assume more proximal roles as mediators of marital conflict (Emery, Waldron, Kitzmann, & Aaron, 1999). For example, in a study that examined broader constellations of parental psychological symptoms (e.g., anxiety, hostility, depressive symptoms), both maternal and paternal symptoms mediated associations between interparental discord and child maladjustment (Papp, Goeke-Morey, & Cummings, 2004). Although it is still premature to draw firm conclusions, one possibility is that the proximal risk posed by parental psychological distress in models of interparental discord may become amplified as children are exposed to progressively broader constellations of parental emotional difficulties.

It is also possible that children's stakes in interparental conflict differ depending on the specific adjustment patterns of the parents. For example, a recent study by Papp, Cummings, and Schermerhorn (2004) indicated that the multiplicative interaction between interparental discord and maternal psychological functioning (e.g., anxiety, depression) predicted child internalizing and externalizing symptoms above and beyond the sum of the risk factors considered singly. If specific forms of parental adjustment do prove to be consistent moderators of interparental conflict, an important next step is to more precisely identify the locus of the interaction in mediational pathways. For example, the emotional security theory specifically postulates that signs of adult psychological vulnerability, like parental symptoms, may potentiate or prime the impact that exposure to interparental conflict has on children's concerns about their security in the interparental relationship. Thus, parental depressive symptoms may amplify associations between interparental conflict and child psychopathology by more specifically catalyzing the threat that interparental conflict poses for child security. Another hypothesis derived from the emotional security theory is that insecure children may be especially vulnerable to developing psychopathology when they also have to cope with other sources of adversity in the family (e.g., parental psychological maladjustment; see Davies, Harold, et al., 2002).

Indirect pathways between interparental conflict, parenting practices, and child maladjustment may also vary as a function of parent depressive symptoms. Family systems theory specifically postulates that family perturbations, including parental maladjustment, may provoke subsequent reorganizations in family functioning and function as architects of interdependencies among interparental and parent-child subsystems (Grych, 2002). However, precisely how adult characteristics alter these pathways is not well understood. Guided by risk and potentiator models, it is plausible that difficulties regulating and containing negative spillover effects from interparental to parent-child subsystems are amplified for parents who are already experiencing psychosocial vulnerabilities. In support of this hypothesis, research has suggested that associations between interparental conflict and parenting difficulties or paternal hostility may be especially pronounced at high levels of maternal depressive symptoms (Davies, Sturge-Apple, et al., 2004) or paternal violent tendencies (Margolin, Gordis, & Oliver, 2004). Other models of developmental psychopathology caution against assuming that inherently negative characteristics necessarily have potentiating effects that are fixed across multiple contexts (E. M. Cummings et al., 2000; Toth & Cicchetti, 1996). Thus, under some contexts, the transmission of distress across interparental and parent-child subsystems may actually be diluted when parents evidence specific vulnerabilities (Davies, Sturge-Apple, et al., 2004).

Extrafamilial Characteristics

Larger ecological contexts in the form of culture, extended kin networks, neighborhood quality, school climate, exposure to media, and friendship and peer relations may alter the nature and magnitude of pathways between marital conflict and child adjustment. As Parke (1998, p. 4) noted, "The field of family psychology is increasingly recognized as contextualized and embedded in a set of complex extended family, neighborhood, institutional, and cultural

systems," and "one of the major challenges over the next decade is to better understand the interplay between family and other social systems." Although the ecological context consists of multiple possible levels of analysis (Bronfenbrenner, 1979), the scope of our review must, of necessity, be limited to illustrative contexts: peer, community, and cultural settings.

Peer Relations

Supporting a social ecological model, there is now a relatively substantial literature linking interparental difficulties to problematic peer relationships (e.g., Erel et al., 1998; Gottman & Katz, 1989; McHale et al., 1999; Stocker, Ahmed, & Stall, 1997; Stocker & Youngblade, 1999). Given these demonstrated links, the next step for a developmental psychopathological and process-oriented perspective is to identify the family (e.g., parent-child hostility) and intrachild (e.g., perceptions of marital conflict; emotional regulation) processes that mediate associations between marital conflict and children's peer relations (e.g., Parke et al., 2001; Stocker & Youngblade, 1999). In drawing on conceptualizations of internal working models (e.g., Bowlby, 1982), the emotional security theory considers child representations of family relationships to be key components of security that mediate relationships between marital conflict and child socioemotional functioning in multiple social contexts, including peer relationships (Davies, Harold, et al., 2002). Consistent with this hypothesis, Du Rocher Schudlich, Shamir, and Cummings (2004) reported that children's internal representations of negative mother-child and father-child relationships mediated links between destructive interparental conflict and their negative dispositions for hostile conflict behavior with peers.

Researchers are also facing the challenge of understanding the interplay between peer relations (i.e., exosystem) and marital conflict (i.e., microsystem) in the larger context of children's developmental outcomes over time. For example, interparental conflict may be a causal agent responsible for the early onset of some forms of maladjustment, whereas peer relations may play an increasingly important role in the developmental course of problems thereafter (Fincham, Grych, & Osborne, 1994). Moreover, complementary conceptualizations have stressed that peer and friendship quality may buffer children from the deleterious effects of interparental conflict (Wasserstein & LaGreca, 1996). In furthering a process-oriented approach, progress in this area will require specification of models that are sensitive to the multidimensional nature of peer relations and the various functions (e.g., mediator, moderator) they may assume in understanding direct and indirect path models of interparental conflict (Parke et al., 2001).

Community

As components of the exosystem in ecological-transactional frameworks of development (Bronfenbrenner, 1979; see also Cicchetti & Lynch, 1993; Lynch & Cicchetti, 2002), community factors (e.g., schools, neighborhood) constitute another important dimension for understanding the impact of interparental conflict on children. For example, Jenkins and Smith (1990) reported that community relations and activities such as positive recognition for school or extracurricular activities and the presence of close relations with extrafamilial adults (e.g., teachers) served as protective factors in associations between marital discord and child psychological symptoms. Although there has been very limited work on identifying the role that community factors play in models of interparental conflict, some promising research directions are evident. For example, one area of recent activity has been the examination of community violence as an ecological context for interparental conflict and violence. Community violence and aggression in the home have been linked to similar disturbances in coping and adjustment among children (Kitzmann et al., 2003; Lynch & Cicchetti, 2002; Margolin & Gordis, 2000). Given that community and family violence are theorized to be complexly interrelated in affecting children (Lynch & Cicchetti, 2002; Margolin & Gordis, 2000), future research is needed to understand the nature of the joint effects (e.g., additive, multiplicative, mediational) of community and marital disturbances on child development (e.g., Forehand & Jones, 2003).

Culture

Little is known about interrelations between marital conflict and children's coping and adjustment beyond White, middle-class U.S. or European samples (Depner, Leino, & Chun, 1992; Gonzalez et al., 2000; Parke & Buriel, 1998). Because the effects of interparental conflict on children have rarely been considered across diverse cultural or ethnic groups, questions remain regarding the cross-cultural applicability of relations between marital and child functioning. At one level, ethnicity has often been treated as a rough proxy for culture. Support for ethnic specificity in spillover of family stress is evidenced by stronger associations between family stress and family conflict in Caucasian families than in Hispanic families (Barrera, Li, & Chassin, 1995). On the other hand, tests of direct and indirect path models of interparental conflict are remarkably similar across studies that have independently utilized samples of predominantly Cau-

casian, middle-class samples and samples of multiethnic, low-income families (Fauber et al., 1990; Gonzalez et al., 2000; Grych, Fincham, et al., 2000; K. M. Lindahl & Malik, 1999; Tschann et al., 2002), thereby failing to support the hypothesis that ethnicity may protect children from the effects of marital conflict.

At another level, cross-cultural research may provide an especially revealing test of culture as a potentially powerful moderator of relations between marital conflict and children, given the likely amplified differences in ecological contexts (e.g., differences at the level of the macrosystem). For example, although parental and neighborhood processes are regarded as key factors contributing to relatively high rates of violence among Latin American children, adolescents, and young adults (Yunes & Zubarew, 2001), little research has been directed toward understanding marital and family processes in Spanish-speaking, Latin American families. In a rare study comparing responses of U.S. and Latin American children to marital conflict, E. M. Cummings, Wilson, and Shamir (2003) found considerable cross-cultural similarities in child adaptation to conflict, as evidenced by links between interparental conflict and child maladjustment and child reactivity to variations in marital conflict resolution. At the same time, culture moderated the amplitude of some relationships, with the pattern of findings suggesting that Chilean children were more sensitive to marital discord than U.S. children. Although these differences were small, one interpretation is that children's emotional security may be more closely tied to interparental discord in the collectivistic Chilean culture. Recent comparisons of responses of U.S. and Israeli kindergartners to analogue presentations of resolved and unresolved marital conflicts have also revealed many cross-cultural similarities in child reactions to marital conflict, especially in their sensitivity to escalating conflicts (Shamir, Cummings, Davies, & Goeke-Morey, in press). At the same time, the findings for resolved and unresolved conflicts supported the notion that U.S. children weight conflict resolution more heavily than Israeli children. Although further research is needed before drawing any conclusions, an intriguing interpretation is that variation in the geopolitical context accompanying the Israeli-Palestinian conflict may have contributed to these cultural differences.

DEVELOPMENT OVER TIME IN CONTEXTS OF INTERPARENTAL CONFLICT

Although models of direct and indirect pathways in the context of risk and protective factors underscore the dynamic nature of developmental processes, the value of developmental psychopathology cannot be fully realized without embedding the study of maladaptation within broader developmental windows than a single snapshot or narrow temporal clip. As illustrated in Path 5 of Figure 3.1, developmental models involve understanding the changing challenges and capacities of children in the context of shifting constellations of risk and protective factors over successive developmental periods.

The Timing and Duration of Adversity

Even though the majority of studies have tacitly treated interparental conflict as a static, stable trait, a developmental perspective considers risk factors, such as interparental conflict, as potentially dynamic processes (Fincham et al., 1994). In drawing attention to the temporal dimension of risk and protection, Cicchetti and colleagues distinguish between transient and enduring risk and protective factors in their developmental models (Cicchetti, 1989; Cicchetti & Toth, 1995). Whereas transient factors reflect relatively short-term, temporary states, enduring factors have relatively protracted life spans that can potentially last over periods of years. Because different couples face unique arrays of dispositions, challenges, and stressors, it is likely that there is considerable interfamilial variability in the enduring or transient nature of interparental conflict. Thus, drawing from literature on parental psychopathology (e.g., Seifer, 1995), one hypothesis is that the degree of risk posed by interparental conflict is a direct function of the chronicity of the parents' problems. At the same time, the enduring bouts of interparental discord may not be universally more powerful than transient bouts of conflict in predicting child problems, especially if transient conflicts are reflecting severe forms of destructive conflict (e.g., violence).

Variations in the developmental timing of the risk factor may also be associated with lawful differences in child adaptation and maladaptation. Thus, age differences in susceptibility to the effects of interparental conflict may reflect the operation of sensitive periods, a process in which specific environmental influences become particularly acute within certain windows of development. However, despite its conceptual appeal in developmental psychopathology, the concept of sensitive periods has rarely been implemented in the study of children's adaptation to interparental conflict. Thus, it can be hypothesized that the stress of living with chronic interparental conflict may more easily overwhelm adolescents, who, by virtue of their unique developmental status, experience (1) greater interpersonal sensitivity to family adversity, (2) a number

of challenging developmental tasks (e.g., autonomy from parents, establishment of romantic relationships, identity development), and (3) peak occurrence of stressful life events (Buchanan, Maccoby, & Dornbusch, 1991; Davies & Windle, 2001; Gelfand & Teti, 1990). Alternatively, it is plausible that the emerging dimensions of interpersonal understanding (e.g., concerns about safety and vulnerabilities of parents) in conjunction with relatively limited coping repertoires and support networks of young children may magnify the deleterious impact of interparental conflict (Cicchetti et al., 1990).

Developmental Periods

Building on the concept of sensitive periods, development can be further conceptualized as a series of developmental challenges that emerge as prominent at a given period and remain important throughout an individual's lifetime (Cicchetti, 1993). Because these developmental challenges constitute a period of normative transition for most, if not all, individuals and require significant reorganization in functioning, some level of change and discontinuity is expected by definition (Graber & Brooks-Gunn, 1996). At each developmental stage, individuals are faced with resolving a number of significant tasks across multiple domains of functioning. For illustrative purposes, Table 3.1 provides an overview of some developmental challenges from birth through adolescence (Cicchetti, 1991; Sroufe & Rutter, 1984). Given that these tasks are already challenging in themselves, their successful resolution may be particularly sensitive to the effects of risk and protective factors.

Integrating developmental challenges within risk models, Graber and Brooks-Gunn (1996) posited that transition-linked turning points, which are characterized by significant life events in the context of challenging periods of reorganization and transition, have a particularly enduring impact on subsequent development. Further applying these concepts to models of interparental conflict, the emotional security theory specifically postulates that prolonged concerns about emotional security in family relationships (e.g., interparental, parent-child) requires considerable expenditure of biopsychosocial resources necessary to regulate attention, affect, thought processes, and action tendencies. Diminished reserves of energy, in turn, are theorized to disrupt children's abilities to marshal physical and psychological resources necessary to successfully resolve stage-salient tasks. Thus, in this process, concerns about security are thought to broadly facilitate psychological maladaptation by disrupting children's abilities to meet developmental challenges (Davies & For-

TABLE 3.1 Developmental Challenges Faced by Children from Infancy through Adolescence

Developmental Period	Stage-Salient Challenges
Infancy	Modulation of arousal Physiological regulation Harmonious, synchronous interactions with caregivers Secure attachments with primary caregivers Interpersonal trust
Toddler	Awareness of self as distinct Exploration of social and object worlds Emotion regulation and management Awareness and responsivity to standards Mastery, persistence, and problem solving Autonomy Sociability Understanding of internal emotion states of others
Preschool	Flexible self-control Self-reliance Initiative Awareness of social roles Gender role development Establishing effective peer relations Empathy and prosocial behavior
Childhood	Social understanding (equity, fairness) Gender constancy Same-sex friendships Peer relations and reputation Sense of industry (competence) Social agency School adjustment Internalization of standards of conduct
Adolescence	Flexible perspective taking Abstract thinking Moral reasoning Reconciling ideal world with real world Loyal same-sex friendships Establishing romantic relationships Balancing emotional autonomy with relatedness to parents Identity development Interpersonal intimacy Sexuality Risk management (e.g., substance use, sexual promiscuity)

man, 2002; Davies, Harold, et al., 2002; Thompson & Calkins, 1996). In accordance with the orthogenetic principle (Cicchetti, 1993), the emotional security theory further postulates that interparental conflict may ultimately increase long-term patterns of maladaptation by disrupting children's abilities to resolve contemporaneous developmental challenges. Through the process of hierarchical motility, old psychological characteristics and structures, though not evidencing a one-to-one correspondence with new forms of functioning, are specifically carried over and incorporated into evolving new structures over time

(Cicchetti & Cohen, 1995). Consistent with this notion, early emerging difficulties with emotion regulation and working models of family relationships among toddlers from high-conflict homes may disrupt children's abilities to successfully resolve the task of developing peer relationships in childhood and romantic relationships in adolescence (Amato & Booth, 2001).

Developmental Trajectories

Conceptualizing development as guided by the transactions between a multifaceted, changing child and the multilayered, dynamic context, developmental psychopathology frameworks commonly assume that there are multiple, diverse developmental trajectories of child adjustment. Metaphors enlisted to represent the multiplicity of pathways in development commonly include a branching tree (Sroufe, 1997) and branching railroad tracks (Bowlby, 1973). Following the branching tree metaphor, normal development can be understood in terms of growth close to the trunk of the tree, whereas abnormal development is reflected in branches growing farther from the tree. Thus, disorder is defined by successive and changing patterns of deviation from normality resulting from the interplay between intra- and extraorganismic processes rather than something that solely resides as a static intrapersonal trait (Sroufe, 1990). Moreover, although it is more difficult to reclaim normal trajectories of development as individuals progressively continue along maladaptive pathways, change is always possible, and individuals may fluctuate between normal and abnormal development over time.

Accordingly, solely focusing on continuity of development limits the ability to identify dynamic changes in child functioning, whereas exclusively tracking discontinuity may underestimate continuities reflecting processes by which current functioning builds on past functioning. Moreover, there are multiple levels of continuity and discontinuity (see Caspi & Bem, 1990). For example, homotypic continuity reflects the expression of similar behaviors or attributes over time, whereas heterotypic continuity is characterized by coherence in underlying organization or meaning of behaviors over time. In reflecting another form of continuity, the operation of hierarchical motility in which processes of past organization are carried over into qualitatively new systems may serve to progressively limit possibilities for future change over time (i.e., canalization; Gottlieb, 1991; Waddington, 1957). Likewise, even broad concepts reflecting change and discontinuity indicate that there are many possible pathways to normal and abnormal development. As we noted earlier, multiple pathways may merge to lead to similar outcomes (i.e., equifinality), or similar pathways at one point in time may diverge into very different outcomes (i.e., multifinality).

However, the pathways model is relatively new and leaves many questions for future research on interparental discord and child development. At a minimum, prospective longitudinal research is essential to begin to identify pathways of development. For example, retrospective research designs readily overestimate causal relations between predictors and outcomes (Cowan et al., 1996). Longitudinal research designs based on multiple times of assessment are relatively rare in the study of relations between interparental discord and child development (Grych & Fincham, 2001). The identification of trajectories of development attributed to interparental discord is complicated by the fact that marital conflict is only one of the many possible risk or compensatory influences on children's development, as reflected by assumption of an ecological transactional framework (Cicchetti & Lynch, 1993).

FUTURE RESEARCH DIRECTIONS

Throughout our discussion of current theory and research, we have attempted to address specific substantive gaps in the literature and their implications for future research. However, it is also important to step back and contemplate broader thematic issues to formulate an integrative agenda for future research. Toward this goal, the remainder of this chapter is devoted to sketching some rough empirical blueprints for future research.

Multilevel, Multivariate Models of Interparental Conflict

The past decade has witnessed unprecedented progress in advancing more complex, multivariate models of interparental and child functioning that increasingly consider the interplay among multiple factors and interrelationships over time in identifying the causal processes that underlie child development (Davies, Harold, et al., 2002; Harold, Shelton, Goeke-Morey, & Cummings, 2004). The ultimate goal of the research program over the past decade has been to characterize how and why, and for whom and when, interparental conflict is associated with greater risk for psychological problems (E. M. Cummings & Davies, 2002). Although substantial progress has been made in empirically testing direct and indirect path models of inter-

parental conflict, the general failure to simultaneously examine these pathways raises important questions about how they might jointly operate in accounting for associations between interparental conflict and child maladjustment. Moreover, our integration of risk and protective frameworks within a broader ecological-transactional model generates unanswered inquiries about the nature of the interplay between interparental conflict and the multidimensional, multilayered constellation of contextual factors (e.g., familial, ecological, child). Thus, to advance a well-articulated account of pathways of interparental conflict in a biopsychosocial matrix, explicating the joint effects of interparental conflict and other contextual factors within mediator, moderator, and additive models will remain a central undertaking in future research (Baron & Kenny, 1986; Holmbeck, 1997, 2002).

In further broadening the scope of inquiry, greater conceptual and methodological sophistication will also be needed to fully capture the heterogeneity and diversity across individuals and development in the nature, operation, and sequence of processes underlying pathways between interparental conflict and child adjustment. On the one hand, moderator models provide a useful tool for identifying the intra- and extraorganismic characteristics that increase and decrease the vulnerability of children from high-conflict homes. Yet, at this relatively early stage of research, simply ending the inquiry at cataloguing the moderating effects of a particular attribute is conceptually unsatisfying without seeking to understand why individuals with certain characteristics or experiences evidence greater vulnerability. Addressing the question of why some individuals are more or less vulnerable to interparental conflict will require that moderator effects be followed up with specific applications of mediator models. For example, after identifying that adolescent girls exhibited significantly greater vulnerability to interparental conflict than their male counterparts, Davies and Lindsay (2004) sought to identify why adolescent gender moderated interparental conflict. Consistent with predictions derived from the gender intensification hypothesis (Davies & Lindsay, 2001; Hill & Lynch, 1983), the results indicated that girls' tendencies to experience greater levels of communion partially accounted for their greater vulnerability to interparental conflict. Such designs have the potential to provide broader conceptual and analytic blueprints for identifying the more proximal processes that explain why the impact of interparental conflict on children varies as a function of extrafamilial, familial, or other child attributes (also see Barrera et al., 1995).

On the other hand, the modest to moderate magnitude of mediational pathways in many family process models underscores the importance of identifying sources of individual differences in mediating processes. Thus, supplementing mediator tests with moderator analyses will likely prove useful in identifying the specific child, familial, and extrafamilial characteristics that may magnify or diminish the strength of mediational pathways (see Path 4 in Figure 3.1). For example, the emotional security theory postulates that the nature and strength of mediational pathways between interparental conflict, child emotional insecurity, and child maladjustment vary depending on the operation of processes in the larger family system (e.g., instability, cohesion, expressiveness). In supplementing tests of the mediation with moderator analyses at each link in the mediational chain, recent research supported these predictions by demonstrating that forms of family adversity were potentiating factors and forms of family harmony were protective factors in these mediational pathways (Davies, Harold, et al., 2002). Taken together, newly emerging research questions will challenge researchers to specify more complex blends of moderator and mediator models (Baron & Kenny, 1986; Kerig, 1998; Sturge-Apple et al., in press).

By the same token, these complex variable-based approaches often require extremely large sample sizes to obtain reliable estimates of parameters. Therefore, some of these statistical applications may not be feasible for researchers. Moreover, given that variable-based approaches are specifically designed to chart the average expectable relations between family processes and child adaptation, they run the risk of failing to sufficiently distinguish and capture the integrity and uniqueness of individual dimensions of family and child functioning. Because identifying individual differences in the organization of intraindividual and child functioning is a central aim in developmental psychopathology (Cicchetti & Rogosch, 1996; Richters, 1997), a complementary methodological direction is to expand and refine strategies for capturing the larger organization of child and family functioning at a pattern-based level. Specifically, future research may be able to fruitfully build on the foundational application of pattern-based measurement batteries (e.g., observational coding) and analytic models (e.g., latent class, cluster, or q-factor analyses) for identifying organizational patterns at the family level of functioning (e.g., Belsky & Fearon, 2004; Davies, Sturge-Apple, et al., 2004; P. K. Lindahl, 2001; O'Connor et al., 1998), child coping (E. M. Cummings, 1987; Davies & Forman, 2002; El-Sheikh et al., 1989), and child adjust-

ment (e.g., Grych, Jouriles, Swank, McDonald, & Norwood, 2000).

Protection, Resilience, and Competence

A trade-off of the predominant empirical focus of identifying the negative psychological sequelae of children from high-conflict homes has been the relative neglect of the study of children who manage to develop normally or even thrive in the face of interparental adversity (E. M. Cummings & Davies, 1994a). Thus, a broad recommendation for future research is to more fully complement the models of risk and vulnerability with the study of protection and resilience. Fully integrating the study of interparental conflict in frameworks of resilience and protection will hinge on corresponding challenges of precisely identifying incidences of resilience and the underlying factors and processes that account for child adaptation in high-conflict homes. In identifying resilient individuals, conceptualizations and assessments must be able to capture the dynamic nature of resilience, with particular recognition that some resilient children may experience bouts of considerable problems over time (Luthar & Cicchetti, 2000). Conclusions about resilience must also be sensitive to the multidimensional nature of resilience, as some children may demonstrate competence in some domains but psychopathology in other domains (Kaufman, Cook, Arny, Jones, & Pittinsky, 1994; Luthar, 1991).

After successfully meeting the challenge of identifying resilient individuals from high-conflict homes, the next step is to further delineate the protective factors and mechanisms that contribute to child competence despite exposure to destructive interparental conflict. Taxonomies that distinguish between various forms of protective effects are valuable tools in precisely characterizing how a given factor might contribute to adaptation (Luthar, 1993; Luthar & Cicchetti, 2000; Luthar et al., 2000). For example, an *ameliorative protective effect* diminishes, but does not completely offset, the potency of the vulnerability associated with interparental conflict. Conversely, a *neutralizing protective effect* is even more pronounced in the sense that marital conflict is benign at high levels of the protective factor. Thus, associations between interparental conflict and child psychological problems, which are robust at low levels of the protective factor, actually evidence a negligible relationship at high levels of the protective factor. Alternatively, *enhancing protective effects* occur when higher levels of interparental conflict are actually associated with less symptomatology (or better adjustment) despite having harmful effects at low levels of the protective factor.

Although the search for protective factors has proceeded as if the concept were synonymous with inherently positive characteristics, adverse or stressful factors can also have protective effects in models of interparental conflict. Challenge models, which follow the assumption that growth results from adversity, specify that stressful conditions, especially in small or moderate doses, may actually have "steeling effects" that serve to enhance coping and adjustment and inoculate individuals against subsequent psychological insult (Garmezy, Masten, & Tellegen, 1984; Rutter, 1987). By extension, exposure to destructive interparental conflict may trigger children to develop more effective skills for coping and adjusting to adversity if bouts of conflict are relatively infrequent. However, in spite of robust analogues in medicine (e.g., vaccines), little attention has been paid to this possibility in the interparental literature.

Specification of Process: Multiple Levels of Analysis

Although current conceptualizations and future theoretical refinements will continually challenge researchers to build on existing measures and analyses of children's emotional, social-cognitive, behavioral, and coping reactions to interparental conflict (Cummings et al., 2001), it is also important to note that several domains of risk processes are virtually unstudied. For example, very little is known about the physiological, neurobiological, and neuropsychological functioning of children from high-conflict homes (see "Diversity in the Operation of Risk Processes in Direct Path Models" section for more details). Corresponding gaps in knowledge also exist in the consideration of child functioning in the context of successive developmental or stage-salient tasks. Accordingly, a key challenge is to integrate these multiple systems of child functioning within theories and empirical tests of child coping and adjustment (e.g., El-Sheikh, 1994; El-Sheikh et al., 2001; Katz & Gottman, 1997). For example, in the emotional security theory (Davies, Harold, et al., 2002), managing concerns about emotional security requires considerable expenditure of biopsychosocial resources (e.g., attention, physiological resources, affect, thought processes, actions). Difficulties preserving security are theorized to alter and disrupt children's capacities to marshal physical and psychological resources and maintain homeostasis through efficient resource allocation. Thus, consistent with other models of family discord (e.g., Cicchetti & Rogosch, 2001a, 2001b), child concerns

about insecurity in homes marked by discord or violence are posited to be accompanied by irregularities in neurobiological and neuropsychological functioning and reactivity to subsequent stress. As part of this constellation of difficulties in resource regulation and allocation, children experiencing difficulties with insecurity may not have sufficient resources to successfully resolve significant developmental tasks and goals.

Future research will also need to develop strategies for simultaneously examining multiple levels of analysis in children's response processes. As we have seen, pattern-based approaches to studying children's higher-order patterns of coping and emotional security offer promise in understanding how child coping processes contribute to the development of psychopathology in high-conflict homes (E. M. Cummings, 1987; E. M. Cummings & Cummings, 1988; Davies & Forman, 2002; El-Sheikh et al., 1989; Maughan & Cicchetti, 2002). As the field advances, inclusion of multiple risk processes in models of interparental conflict will also permit tests of the relative viability of child coping and responses to interparental conflict derived from alternative theories. Over a decade ago, Fincham and colleagues (1994) cogently argued that testing process models in relation to alternative hypotheses derived from other conceptualizations provides significantly more conceptual yield than testing predictions in relation to the null hypothesis. Yet, despite this call, virtually no studies have simultaneously compared the efficacy of risk processes generated from different theories (Davies, Harold, et al., 2002). With the unprecedented theoretical advances in the area over the past decade, the urgency of testing the relative efficacy of different risk processes in future studies cannot be understated.

Interparental Conflict and Child Functioning in Abnormal Contexts

Guided by the assumption that little is known about risk in normal community families, Cowan and colleagues (1996, p. 31) aptly noted, "The frequency of distress in nonclinical families is (unfortunately) large enough to justify concerted attempts to apply risk paradigms to studies of normal family adaptation." Although this conclusion is applicable to many areas of developmental psychopathology, the opposite state of affairs actually exists in the interparental conflict literature. Rather than advancing developmental psychopathology models of interparental conflict through primary inclusion of high-risk samples, studies have overwhelmingly relied on community samples. Consequently, little is known about whether similar or different processes and pathways involving interparental and child problems that have been identified in community samples operate for families who are experiencing considerable adversity or vulnerability. For example, although children exposed to severe interparental violence are as much as 7 times more likely to exhibit significant psychological problems than are children in the general population, progress in identifying processes and pathways underlying the exposure to interparental violence has been slow. Because little is known about how and why interparental violence increases child vulnerability to psychopathology, future research would do well to identify the unfolding mediating mechanisms and the potentiating and protective conditions that shape the multiplicity of pathways underlying associations between interparental violence and child maladjustment (Kitzmann et al., 2003). In supporting a broader foray into high-risk processes, inclusion of parent and child psychological problems in models of interparental conflict does appear to alter some process relationships between interparental and child functioning (e.g., Davies & Windle, 2001; Emery et al., 1999; Papp, Cummings, et al., 2004). However, because these studies have predominantly examined individual differences in psychological adjustment indices in normal or well-functioning samples, how interparental conflict processes operate across a broad spectrum of risk and clinical disorder is still not known.

Transactional Relationships between Interparental and Child Functioning

Although developmental psychopathology strongly emphasizes the active role of the child in the dynamic transactional interplay between the child and interpersonal contexts (Zigler & Glick, 1986), unidirectional designs continue to be geared toward understanding the impact of interparental conflict on child functioning (E. M. Cummings & Schermerhorn, 2003). Child effects models are thus crucial for understanding the dynamics of family processes as influences on child development. Research has long demonstrated that children respond to marital conflict with apparently agentic behavior, that is, mediation or other attempts to reduce marital conflict (e.g., J. S. Cummings et al., 1989). Children's coping with marital conflict, including perceived control and effortful behavior toward regulating the conflict, has been advanced as possibly ameliorating the effects of marital conflict on children (Kerig, 1998, 2001; Rossman & Rosenberg, 1992).

However, due to the paucity of work on whether forms of child reactivity do more than help children feel more se-

cure about marital conflict, little is known about whether children's perceptions of agency or effortful behavior relate to changes in interparental conflict over time. To address this knowledge gap, Schermerhorn, Cummings, and Davies (in press) reported that interparental conflict was not only concurrently linked with children's perceived agency as predicted by the emotional security theory, but perceived agency also predicted declines in interparental conflict over 1 year (E. M. Cummings & Davies, 2002; Davies & Cummings, 1994).

In another study, bidirectional analyses between adolescent adjustment and marital discord revealed that adolescent symptomatology predicted reductions in interparental conflict over time, whereas interparental conflict was associated with subsequent increases in adolescent symptomatology (Schermerhorn, Goeke-Morey, Mitchell, & Cummings, 2004). Given these promising findings, systematically tracing transactions between children and interparental conflict is likely to be a central direction for future research.

Charting Developmental Pluralism in the Context of Interparental Conflict

The increasing use of longitudinal designs over time will permit greater flexibility in charting the nature, correlates, origins, and sequelae of individual differences in developmental pathways in models of interparental conflict. Although it is important not to understate the advantages of well-designed cross-sectional and short-term longitudinal studies for many important research questions (Rutter, 1994), these designs cannot readily examine a central aim of developmental psychopathology: identifying interindividual differences in developmental pathways over time. Rather, reliably charting individual differences in slope, starting points, and end points of children or family trajectories will require future longitudinal research to contain a minimum of three repeated measures of key constructs (Willett, Singer, & Martin, 1998). For example, using multiwave data in analytic techniques such as hierarchical linear modeling and latent growth models will specifically permit researchers to examine how interparental conflict processes factor into understanding the nature, origins, correlates, and sequelae of individual differences in child adjustment trajectories (e.g., E. M. Cummings et al., 2001; Windle, 2000). Moreover, even more recent analytic models no longer make the tacit assumption that individual differences in developmental pathways are continuously distributed around a single trajectory of functioning over time. Instead, such techniques as latent class growth analysis are specifically designed to parsimoniously identify the number and nature of distinct developmental trajectories of functioning and, as a result, permit analyses of the antecedents, correlates, and sequelae of these trajectories (Muthen & Muthen, 2000; Shaw, Gilliom, Ingoldsby, & Nagin, 2003). Thus, these analytic tools are likely to be particularly valuable in beginning to elucidate the interplay among interparental risk factors, risk processes, and multiple trajectories of child functioning.

Prevention and Public Policy Implications

The developmental psychopathology perspective, with its emphasis on relationships between pathways of development and adjustment, provides a clear conceptual rationale for advocating for prevention as an alternative to intervention for children's adjustment problems due to marital discord (Cicchetti & Cohen, 1995; E. M. Cummings et al., 2000). Also advocating for prevention approaches, problems of interparental discord are likely to be much more amenable to positive influence before the conflict process becomes escalated and highly negative (E. M. Cummings & Davies, 1994a). However, it is essential that optimal prevention efforts be closely informed by research, including the latest findings on marital conflict from the perspective of the children. Our literature review indicates that a relatively comprehensive process-oriented model for marital conflict and its effects on children and families, grounded in etiological theory, is available and merits careful consideration in formulating prevention and intervention directions. Although programs for enriching and enhancing marriages, especially premarital programs for new marriages, are widespread and have been proposed at least since the 1930s, there has been little inclusion of research-based conclusions or systematic and long-term evaluation of program effectiveness in most community-based programs.

The most extensively documented program for couples is the Prevention and Relationship Enhancement Program (Markman & Floyd, 1980), based on the notion that couples' deficits in communication and conflict resolution skills lead to marital distress (Markman, Jamieson, & Floyd, 1983). Although evidence for positive effects has accumulated (Markman, Renick, Floyd, Stanley, & Clements, 1993), support is not consistently found (van Widenfelt, Hosman, Schaap, & van der Staak, 1996), findings are relatively modest in long-term follow-ups, and implications for children are not evaluated. Other programs have addressed marital conflict issues in familywide psy-

choeducational programs (e.g., Positive Parenting Program; Sanders, Markie-Dadds, Tully, & Bor, 2000), but programs focusing on marital conflict and children have been minimally informed, at best, by the comprehensive model for processes and pathways associated with child maladjustment outlined in the present review. Programs have also been designed for interparental conflict and children, but primarily for children of divorce (Pedro-Carroll & Cowen, 1985; Shifflett & Cummings, 1999; Stolberg & Mahler, 1994), with rare exceptions (see Lindsay, Davies, & Pedro-Carroll, 2001). Finally, more rigorous tests of programs in this area are also needed, including random assignment to groups, treatment fidelity assessments, manualization of programs, adequate control groups, and long-term follow-ups concerning the effects on both parents and the children.

From a public policy perspective, translating research findings into viable prevention programs holds great promise in helping families and children. Efficacious prevention efforts have the potential to reach far more families than traditional clinical services in a more economically efficient manner. Moreover, given that it is more difficult for individuals to reclaim normal trajectories of development with longer histories of maladaptive experiences, prevention programs or, minimally, early intervention programs have greater potential to yield more positive outcomes than programs that target families with severe or chronic problems.

CONCLUSION

In conclusion, the emergence and growth of developmental psychopathology as a science over the past 2 decades has been accompanied by advances in the interparental conflict literature toward identifying the unfolding pathways between interparental characteristics, risk processes, and children's outcomes in the broader context of biopsychosocial factors. Developmental psychopathology, with its original armamentarium of concepts and principles (e.g., multiple pathways, risk and protective frameworks, multilevel processes), has been a central heuristic for a second generation of research designed to identify the moderating conditions and mediating mechanisms underlying the vulnerability of children from high-conflict homes (Margolin et al., 2001). Our attempt to further situate the study of interparental conflict within developmental psychopathology also illustrates the need for new research directions that examine interparental conflict within even more sophisticated multilevel, multivariate frameworks that capture the multiple pathways that evolve from the transactional interplay between interparental and child functioning. With the recent conceptual, methodological, and analytic advances noted throughout this chapter, it is hoped that a new generation of research will emerge that advances the integration of the interparental conflict literature in the discipline of developmental psychopathology.

REFERENCES

Ainsworth, M. D. S., Blehar, M. C., Waters, E., & Wall, S. (1978). *Patterns of attachment: A psychological study of the Strange Situation.* Hillsdale, NJ: Erlbaum.

Almeida, D. M., Wethington, E., & Chandler, A. L. (1999). Daily transmission of tensions between marital dyads and parent-child dyads. *Journal of Marriage and the Family, 61,* 49–61.

Amato, P. R., & Booth, A. (2001). The legacy of parents' marital discord: Consequences for children's marital quality. *Journal of Personality and Social Psychology, 81,* 627–638.

Amato, P. R., & Keith, B. (1991). Consequences of parental divorce for children's well-being: A meta-analysis. *Psychological Bulletin, 110,* 26–46.

Ballard, M. E., Cummings, E. M., & Larkin, K. (1993). Emotional and cardiovascular responses to adults' angry behavior and challenging tasks in children of hypertensive and normotensive parents. *Child Development, 64,* 500–515.

Bandura, A. (1973). *Aggression: A social learning analysis.* Englewood Cliffs, NJ: Prentice-Hall.

Bandura, A. (1983). Psychological mechanisms of aggression. In R. G. Geen & E. I. Donnerstein (Eds.), *Aggression: Theoretical and empirical reviews* (Vol. 1, pp. 1–40). New York: Academic Press.

Baron, R. M., & Kenny, D. A. (1986). The moderator-mediator variable distinction in social psychological research: Conceptual, strategic, and statistical considerations. *Journal of Personality and Social Psychology, 51,* 1173–1182.

Barrera, M., Li, S. A., & Chassin, L. (1995). Effects of parental alcoholism and life stress on Hispanic and non-Hispanic Caucasian adolescents: A prospective study. *American Journal of Community Psychology, 23,* 479–507.

Baruch, D. W., & Wilcox, J. A. (1944). A study of sex differences in preschool children's adjustment coexistent with interparental tensions. *Journal of Genetic Psychology, 64,* 281–303.

Baumrind, D. (1971). Current patterns of parental authority. *Developmental Psychology Monograph, 4*(1, Pt. 2), 1–103.

Belsky, J. (1999). Interactional and contextual determinants of attachment security. In J. Cassidy & P. R. Shaver (Eds.), *Handbook of attachment: Theory, research, and clinical applications* (pp. 249–264). New York: Guilford Press.

Belsky, J., & Fearon, R. M. P. (2004). Exploring marriage-parenting typologies: Their contextual antecedents and developmental sequelae. *Development and Psychopathology, 16,* 501–523.

Belsky, J., Putnam, S., & Crnic, K. (1996). Coparenting, parenting, and early emotional development. *New Directions for Child Development, 74,* 45–55.

Belsky, J., Rovine, K., & Fish, M. (1989). The developing family system. In M. Gunnar & E. Thelen (Eds.), *Minnesota Symposia on Child Psychology: Vol. 22. Systems and development* (pp. 119–166). Hillsdale, NJ: Erlbaum.

Bowlby, J. (1969). *Attachment and loss: Vol. 1. Attachment.* New York: Basic Books.

Bowlby, J. (1973). *Attachment and loss: Vol. 2. Separation.* New York: Basic Books.

Bowlby, J. (1982). Attachment and loss: Retrospect and prospect. *American Journal of Orthopsychiatry, 52,* 664–678.

Brody, G., Stoneman, Z., & McCoy, J. K. (1992). Associations of maternal and paternal direct and differential behavior with sibling relationships: Contemporaneous and longitudinal analyses. *Child Development, 63,* 82–92.

Bronfenbrenner, U. (1979). *The ecology of human development.* Cambridge, MA: Harvard University Press.

Buchanan, C. M., Maccoby, E. E., & Dornbusch, S. M. (1991). Caught between parents: Adolescents' experience in divorced homes. *Child Development, 62,* 1008–1029.

Buehler, C., Anthony, C., Krishnakumar, A., & Stone, G. (1997). Interparental conflict and youth problem behaviors: A meta-analysis. *Journal of Child and Family Studies, 6,* 223–247.

Byng-Hall, J. (1999). Family couple therapy: Toward greater security. In J. Cassidy & P. R. Shaver (Eds.), *Handbook of attachment: Theory, research, and clinical applications* (pp. 625–645). New York: Guilford Press.

Caspi, A., & Bem, D. J. (1990). Personality continuity and change across the life course. In L. A. Pervin (Ed.), *Handbook of personality: Theory and research* (pp. 549–575). New York: Guilford Press.

Christensen, A., & Margolin, G. (1988). Conflict and alliance in distressed and nondistressed families. In R. A. Hinde & J. Stevenson-Hinde (Eds.), *Relationships within families: Mutual influences* (pp. 263–282). New York: Oxford University Press.

Cicchetti, D. (1989). How research on child maltreatment has informed the study of child development: Perspectives from developmental psychopathology. In D. Cicchetti & V. Carlson (Eds.), *Child maltreatment: Theory and research on the causes and consequences of child abuse and neglect* (pp. 377–431). New York: Cambridge University Press.

Cicchetti, D. (1991). Fractures in the crystal: Developmental psychopathology and the emergence of self. *Developmental Review, 11,* 271–287.

Cicchetti, D. (1993). Developmental psychopathology: Reactions, reflections, projections. *Developmental Review, 13,* 471–502.

Cicchetti, D. (2002). The impact of social experience on neurobiological systems: Illustration from a constructivist view of child maltreatment. *Cognitive Development, 17,* 1407–1428.

Cicchetti, D. (2003). Editorial. Experiments of nature: Contributions to developmental theory. *Development and Psychopathology, 15,* 833–835.

Cicchetti, D., & Cohen, D. J. (1995). Perspectives on developmental psychopathology. In D. Cicchetti & D. J. Cohen (Eds.), *Developmental psychopathology: Vol. 1. Theory and methods* (pp. 3–20). New York: Wiley.

Cicchetti, D., Cummings, E. M., Greenberg, M. T., & Marvin, R. S. (1990). An organizational perspective on attachment beyond infancy. In M. T. Greenberg, D. Cicchetti, & E. M. Cummings (Eds.), *Attachment in the preschool years* (pp. 51–95). Chicago: University of Chicago Press.

Cicchetti, D., & Lynch, M. (1993). Toward an ecological/transactional model of community violence and child maltreatment: Consequences for children's development. *Psychiatry, 56,* 96–118.

Cicchetti, D., & Rogosch, F. A. (1996). Equifinality and multifinality in developmental psychopathology. *Development and Psychopathology, 8,* 597–600.

Cicchetti, D., & Rogosch, F. A. (2001a). Diverse patterns of neuroendocrine activity in maltreated children. *Development and Psychopathology, 13,* 677–694.

Cicchetti, D., & Rogosch, F. A. (2001b). The impact of child maltreatment and psychopathology upon neuroendocrine functioning. *Development and Psychopathology, 13,* 783–804.

Cicchetti, D., & Toth, S. L. (1995). A developmental psychopathology perspective on child abuse and neglect. *Journal of the American Academy of Child and Adolescent Psychiatry, 34,* 541–565.

Colin, V. L. (1996). *Human attachment.* New York: McGraw-Hill.

Covell, K., & Abramovitch, R. (1987). Understanding emotion in the family: Children's and parents' attributions of happiness, sadness, and anger. *Child Development, 58,* 985–991.

Cowan, P. A. (1997). Beyond meta-analysis: A plea for a family systems view of attachment. *Child Development, 68,* 601–603.

Cowan, P. A., Cowan, C. P., & Schulz, M. S. (1996). Thinking about risk and resilience in families. In E. M. Hetherington & E. A. Blechman (Eds.), *Stress, coping, and resiliency in children and families: Family research consortium—Advances in family research* (pp. 1–38). Hillsdale, NJ: Erlbaum.

Cox, M. J., & Paley, B. (1997). Families as systems. *Annual Review of Psychology, 48,* 243–267.

Cox, M. J., Paley, B., Bruchinal, M., & Payne, C. C. (1999). Marital perceptions and interactions across the transition to parenthood. *Journal of Marriage and Family, 61,* 611–625.

Cox, M. J., Paley, B., & Harter, K. (2001). Interparental conflict and parent-child relationships. In J. Grych & F. Fincham (Eds.), *Child development and interparental conflict* (pp. 249–272). New York: Cambridge University Press.

Crockenberg, S. B., & Forgays, D. (1996). The role of emotion in children's understanding and emotional reactions to marital conflict. *Merrill-Palmer Quarterly, 42,* 22–47.

Crockenberg, S. B., & Langrock, A. (2001a). The role of emotion and emotion regulation in children's responses to interparental conflict. In J. Grych & F. Fincham (Eds.), *Child development and interparental conflict* (pp. 129–156). New York: Cambridge University Press.

Crockenberg, S., & Langrock, A. (2001b). The role of specific emotions in children's responses to interparental conflict: A test of the model. *Journal of Family Psychology, 15,* 163–182.

Cummings, E. M. (1987). Coping with background anger in early childhood. *Child Development, 58,* 976–984.

Cummings, E. M., Ballard, M., El-Sheikh, M., & Lake, M. (1991). Resolution and children's responses to interadult anger. *Developmental Psychology, 27,* 462–470.

Cummings, E. M., & Cummings, J. S. (1988). A process-oriented approach to children's coping with adults' angry behavior. *Developmental Review, 3,* 296–321.

Cummings, E. M., & Davies, P. T. (1994a). *Children and marital conflict: The impact of family dispute and resolution.* New York: Guilford Press.

Cummings, E. M., & Davies, P. T. (1994b). Maternal depression and child development. *Journal of Child Psychology and Psychiatry, 35,* 73–112.

Cummings, E. M., & Davies, P. T. (2002). Effects of marital conflict on children: Recent advances and emerging themes in process-oriented research. *Journal of Child Psychology and Psychiatry, 43,* 31–63.

Cummings, E. M., Davies, P. T., & Campbell, S. B. (2000). *Developmental psychopathology and family process: Theory, research, and clinical implications.* New York: Guilford Press.

Cummings, E. M., Goeke-Morey, M. C., & Dukewich, T. L. (2001). The study of relations between marital conflict and child adjustment: Challenges and new directions for methodology. In J. H. Grych & F. D. Fincham (Eds.), *Child development and interparental conflict* (pp. 39–63). New York: Cambridge University Press.

Cummings, E. M., Goeke-Morey, M. C., & Papp, L. M. (2003a). A family-wide model for the role of emotion in family functioning. *Marriage and Family Review, 34,* 13–34.

Cummings, E. M., Goeke-Morey, M. C., & Papp, L. M. (2003b). Children's responses to everyday marital conflict tactics in the home. *Child Development, 74,* 1918–1929.

Cummings, E. M., Goeke-Morey, M. C., & Papp, L. M. (2004). Everyday marital conflict and child aggression. *Journal of Abnormal Child Psychology, 32,* 191–202.

Cummings, E. M., Iannotti, R. J., & Zahn-Waxler, C. (1985). The influence of conflict between adults on the emotions and aggression of young children. *Developmental Psychology, 21,* 495–507.

Cummings, E. M., Keller, P. S., & Davies, P. T. (in press). Towards a family process model of maternal and paternal depression: Exploring multiple relations with child and family functioning. *Journal of Child Psychology and Psychiatry.*

Cummings, E. M., & Schermerhorn, A. C. (2003). A developmental perspective on children as agents in the family. In L. Kuczynski (Ed.), *Handbook of dynamics of parent-child relations* (pp. 91–108). Thousand Oaks, CA: Sage.

Cummings, E. M., & Smith, D. (1993). The impact of anger between adults on siblings' emotions and social behavior. *Journal of Child Psychology and Psychiatry, 34,* 1425–1433.

Cummings, E. M., Vogel, D., Cummings, J. S., & El-Sheikh, M. (1989). Children's responses to different forms of expression of anger between adults. *Child Development, 60,* 1392–1404.

Cummings, E. M., Wilson, J., & Shamir, H. (2003). Reactions of Chilean and American children to marital discord. *International Journal of Behavioral Development, 27,* 437–444.

Cummings, E. M., Zahn-Waxler, C., & Radke-Yarrow, M. (1981). Young children's responses to expressions of anger and affection by others in the family. *Child Development, 52,* 1274–1282.

Cummings, E. M., Zahn-Waxler, C., & Radke-Yarrow, M. (1984). Developmental changes in children's reactions to anger in the home. *Journal of Child Psychology and Psychiatry, 25,* 63–74.

Cummings, J. S., Pellegrini, D., Notarius, C., & Cummings, E. M. (1989). Children's responses to angry adult behavior as a function of marital distress and history of interparental hostility. *Child Development, 60,* 1035–1043.

Dadds, M. R., Atkinson, E., Turner, C., Blums, G. J., & Lendich, B. (1999). Family conflict and child adjustment: Evidence for a cognitive-contextual model of intergenerational transmission. *Journal of Family Psychology, 13,* 194–208.

Das Eiden, R., Teti, D. M., & Corns, K. M. (1995). Maternal working models of attachment, marital adjustment, and the parent-child relationship. *Child Development, 66,* 1504–1518.

Davies, P. T. (2002). Conceptual links between Byng-Hall's theory of parentification and the emotional security hypothesis. *Family Process, 41,* 551–555.

Davies, P. T., & Cicchetti, D. (2004). Editorial: Toward an integration of family systems and developmental psychopathology approaches. *Development and Psychopathology, 16,* 477–481.

Davies, P. T., & Cummings, E. M. (1994). Marital conflict and child adjustment: An emotional security hypothesis. *Psychological Bulletin, 116,* 387–411.

Davies, P. T., & Cummings, E. M. (1998). Exploring children's emotional security as a mediator of the link between marital relations and child adjustment. *Child Development, 69*, 124–139.

Davies, P. T., Cummings, E. M., & Winter, M. A. (2004). Pathways between profiles of family functioning, child security in the interparental subsystem, and child psychological problems. *Development and Psychopathology, 16*, 525–550.

Davies, P. T., Dumenci, L., & Windle, M. (1999). The interplay between maternal depressive symptoms and marital distress in the prediction of adolescent adjustment. *Journal of Marriage and the Family, 61*, 238–254.

Davies, P. T., & Forman, E. M. (2002). Children's patterns of preserving emotional security in the interparental subsystem. *Child Development, 73*, 1880–1903.

Davies, P. T., Forman, E. M., Rasi, J. A., & Stevens, K. I. (2002). Assessing children's emotional security in the interparental subsystem: The Security in the Interparental Subsystem (SIS) Scales. *Child Development, 73*, 544–562.

Davies, P. T., Harold, G. T., Goeke-Morey, M., & Cummings, E. M. (2002). Children's emotional security and interparental conflict. *Monographs of the Society for Research in Child Development, 67*, 1–129.

Davies, P. T., & Lindsay, L. (2001). Does gender moderate the effects of conflict on children? In J. Grych & F. Fincham (Eds.), *Child development and interparental conflict* (pp. 64–97). New York: Cambridge University Press.

Davies, P. T., & Lindsay, L. (2004). Interparental conflict and adolescent adjustment: Why does gender moderate early adolescent vulnerability? *Journal of Family Psychology, 18*, 170–180.

Davies, P. T., Myers, R. L., & Cummings, E. M. (1996). Responses of children and adolescents to marital conflict scenarios as a function of the emotionality of conflict endings. *Merrill-Palmer Quarterly, 42*, 1–21.

Davies, P. T., Myers, R. L., Cummings, E. M., & Heindel, S. (1999). Adult conflict history and children's subsequent responses to conflict. *Journal of Family Psychology, 13*, 610–628.

Davies, P. T., Sturge-Apple, M. L., & Cummings, E. M. (2004). Interdependencies among interparental discord and parenting styles: The role of adult attributes and relationship characteristics. *Development and Psychopathology, 16*, 773–797.

Davies, P. T., & Windle, M. (1997). Gender-specific pathways between maternal depressive symptoms, family discord, and adolescent adjustment. *Developmental Psychology, 33*, 657–668.

Davies, P. T., & Windle, M. (2001). Interparental discord and adolescent adjustment trajectories: The potentiating and protective role of intrapersonal attributes. *Child Development, 72*, 1163–1178.

Davis, B., Hops, H., Alpert, A., & Sheeber, L. (1998). Child responses to parental conflict and their effect on adjustment: A study of triadic relations. *Journal of Family Psychology, 12*, 163–177.

Davis, B., Sheeber, L., Hops, H., & Tildesley, E. (2000). Adolescent responses to depressive parental behaviors in problem-solving interactions: Implications for depressive symptoms. *Journal of Abnormal Child Psychology, 28*, 451–465.

Depner, C. E., & Leino, E. V., & Chun, A. (1992). Interparental conflict and child adjustment: A decade review and meta-analysis. *Family and Conciliation Courts Review, 30*, 323–341.

Dix, T. (1991). The affective organization of parenting: Adaptive and maladaptive processes. *Psychological Bulletin, 110*, 3–25.

Doumas, D., Margolin, G., & John, R. S. (1994). The intergenerational transmission of aggression across three generations. *Journal of Family Violence, 9*, 157–175.

Downey, G., & Coyne, J. C. (1990). Children of depressed parents: An integrative review. *Psychological Bulletin, 108*, 50–76.

Dunn, J., & Davies, L. (2001). Sibling relationships and interparental conflict. In J. Grych & F. Fincham (Eds.), *Child development and interparental conflict* (pp. 273–290). New York: Cambridge University Press.

Dunn, J., Deater-Deckard, K., Pickering, K., O'Connor, T., Golding, J., & the ALSPAC Study Team. (1998). Children's adjustment and prosocial behavior in step-single and non-step family settings: Findings from a community study. *Journal of Child Psychology and Psychiatry, 39*, 1083–1095.

Du Rocher Schudlich, T. D., & Cummings, E. M. (2003). Parental dysphoria and children's internalizing symptoms: Marital conflict styles as mediators of risk. *Child Development, 74*, 1663–1681.

Du Rocher Schudlich, T. D., Papp, L. M., & Cummings, E. M. (2004). Relations of husbands' and wives' dysphoria to marital conflict resolution strategies. *Journal of Family Psychology, 18*, 171–183.

Du Rocher Schudlich, T. D., Shamir, H., & Cummings, E. M. (2004). Marital conflict: Children's representations of family relationships, and children's dispositions towards peer conflict strategies. *Social Development, 13*, 171–192.

El-Sheikh, M. (1994). Children's emotional and physiological responses to interadult angry behavior: The role of history of interparental hostility. *Journal of Abnormal Child Psychology, 22*, 661–678.

El-Sheikh, M. (1997). Children's response to adult-adult and mother-child arguments: The role of parental marital conflict and distress. *Journal of Family Psychology, 11*, 165–175.

El-Sheikh, M., & Cheskes, J. (1995). Background verbal and physical anger: A comparison of children's responses to adult-adult and adult-child arguments. *Child Development, 66*, 446–458.

El-Sheikh, M., & Cummings, E. M. (1995). Children's responses to angry adult behavior as a function of experimentally manipulated exposure to resolved and unresolved conflict. *Social Development, 4*, 75–91.

El-Sheikh, M., & Cummings, E. M. (1997). Marital conflict, emotional regulation, and the adjustment of children of alcoholics. In K. C. Barrett (Ed.), *New directions in child development: Emotion and communication* (pp. 25–44). San Francisco: Jossey-Bass.

El-Sheikh, M., Cummings, E. M., & Goetsch, V. (1989). Coping with adults' angry behavior: Behavioral, physiological, and self-reported responding in preschoolers. *Developmental Psychology, 25*, 490–498.

El-Sheikh, M., Cummings, E. M., & Reiter, S. (1996). Preschoolers' responses to interadult conflict: The role of experimentally manipulated exposure to resolved and unresolved arguments. *Journal of Abnormal Child Psychology, 24*, 655–679.

El-Sheikh, M., & Flanagan, E. (2001). Parental problem drinking and children's adjustment: Family conflict and parental depression as mediators and moderators of risk. *Journal of Abnormal Child Psychology, 29*, 417–432.

El-Sheikh, M., Harger, J., & Whitson, S. M. (2001). Exposure to interparental conflict and children's adjustment and physical health: The moderating role of vagal tone. *Child Development, 72*, 1617–1636.

Emery, R. E. (1982). Interparental conflict and the children of discord and divorce. *Psychological Bulletin, 92*, 310–330.

Emery, R. E. (1989). Family violence. *American Psychologist, 44*, 321–328.

Emery, R. E., Fincham, F. D., & Cummings, E. M. (1992). Parenting in context: Systemic thinking about parental conflict and its influence on children. *Journal of Consulting and Clinical Psychology, 60*, 909–912.

Emery, R. E., & O'Leary, K. D. (1982). Children's perceptions of marital discord and behavior problems of boys and girls. *Journal of Abnormal Child Psychology, 10*, 11–24.

Emery, R. E., Waldron, M., Kitzmann, K. M., & Aaron, J. (1999). Delinquent behavior, future divorce or nonmarital childbearing, and externalizing behavior among offspring: A 14-year prospective study. *Journal of Family Psychology, 13,* 568–579.

Erel, O., & Burman, B. (1995). Interrelatedness of marital relations and parent-child relations: A meta-analytic review. *Psychological Bulletin, 118,* 108–132.

Erel, O., Margolin, G., & John, R. S. (1998). Observed sibling interactions: Links with the marital and the mother-child relationship. *Developmental Psychology, 34,* 288–298.

Fantuzzo, J. W., DePaola, L. M., Lambert, L., Martino, T., Anderson, G., & Sutton, S. (1991). Effects of interparental violence on the psychological adjustment and competencies of young children. *Journal of Consulting and Clinical Psychology, 59,* 258–265.

Fauber, R. E., Forehand, R., Thomas, A. M., & Wierson, M. (1990). A mediational model of the impact of marital conflict on adolescent adjustment in intact and divorced families: The role of disrupted parenting. *Child Development, 61,* 1112–1123.

Fendrich, M., Warner, V., & Weissman, M. M. (1990). Family risk factors, parental depression, and psychopathology in offspring. *Developmental Psychology, 26,* 40–50.

Fergusson, D. M., & Horwood, L. J. (1998). Exposure to interparental violence in childhood and psychosocial adjustment in young adulthood. *Child Abuse and Neglect, 22,* 339–357.

Fincham, F. D. (1994). Understanding the association between marital conflict and child adjustment: An overview. *Journal of Family Psychology, 8,* 123–127.

Fincham, F. D., Grych, J. H., & Osborne, L. N. (1994). Does marital conflict cause child maladjustment? Directions and challenges for longitudinal research. *Journal of Family Psychology, 8,* 128–140.

Floyd, F., Gilliom, L. A., & Costigan, C. L. (1998). Marriage and the parenting alliance: Longitudinal prediction of change in parenting perceptions and behaviors. *Child Development, 69,* 1461–1479.

Floyd, F., & Zmich, D. E. (1991). Marriage and the parenting partnership: Perceptions and interactions of parents with mentally retarded and typically developing children. *Child Development, 62,* 1434–1448.

Forehand, R., & Jones, D. J. (2003). Neighborhood violence and coparent conflict: Interactive influence on child psychosocial adjustment. *Journal of Abnormal Child Psychology, 31,* 591–604.

Frosch, C. A., & Mangelsdorf, S. C. (2001). Marital behavior, parenting behavior, and multiple reports of preschoolers' behavior problems: Mediation or moderation? *Developmental Psychology, 37,* 502–519.

Frosch, C. A., Mangelsdorf, S. C., & McHale, J. L. (2000). Marital behavior and the security of the preschooler: Parent attachment relationships. *Journal of Family Psychology, 14,* 144–161.

Garcia O'Hearn, H., Margolin, G., & John, R. S. (1997). Mothers' and fathers' reports of children's reactions to naturalistic marital conflict. *Journal of the American Academy of Child and Adolescent Psychiatry, 36,* 1366–1373.

Garmezy, N. (1985). Stress-resistant children: The search for protective factors. *Journal of Child Psychology and Psychiatry Book* (Suppl. 4), 213–233. Oxford: Pergamon Press.

Garmezy, N., Masten, A. S., & Tellegen, A. (1984). The study of stress and competence in children: A building block for developmental psychopathology. *Child Development, 55,* 97–111.

Gelfand, D., & Teti, D. M. (1990). The effects of maternal depression on children. *Clinical Psychology Review, 10,* 329–353.

Goeke-Morey, M. C., Cummings, E. M., Harold, G. T., & Shelton, K. H. (2003). Categories and continua of destructive and constructive marital conflict tactics from the perspective of U.S. and Welsh children. *Journal of Family Psychology, 17,* 327–338.

Gonzales, N. A., Pitts, S. C., Hill, N. E., & Roosa, M. W. (2000). A mediational model of the impact of interparental conflict on child adjustment in a multiethnic, low-income sample. *Journal of Family Psychology, 14,* 365–379.

Gordis, E. B., Margolin, G., & John, R. (1997). Marital aggression, observed parental hostility, and child behavior during triadic family interaction. *Journal of Family Psychology, 11,* 76–89.

Gottlieb, G. (1991). Experiential canalization of behavioral development: Theory. *Developmental Psychology, 27,* 4–13.

Gottman, J. M., & Katz, L. F. (1989). Effects of marital discord on young children's peer interactions and health. *Developmental Psychology, 25,* 273–281.

Graber, J. A., & Brooks-Gunn, J. (1996). Transitions and turning points: Navigating the passage from childhood through adolescence. *Developmental Psychology, 32,* 768–776.

Granic, I., & Hollenstein, T. (2003). Dynamic systems methods for models of developmental psychopathology. *Development and Psychopathology, 15,* 641–669.

Gregory, I. (1965). Anterospective data following childhood loss of a parent. *Archives of General Psychiatry, 13,* 110–120.

Grych, J. H. (1998). Children's appraisals of interparental conflict: Situational and contextual influences. *Journal of Family Psychology, 12,* 437–453.

Grych, J. H. (2002). Marital relationships and parenting. In M. H. Bornstein (Ed.), *Handbook of parenting* (2nd ed., pp. 203–225). Mahwah, NJ: Erlbaum.

Grych, J. H., & Cardoza-Fernandes, S. (2001). Understanding the impact of interparental conflict on children: The role of social cognitive processes. In J. Grych & F. Fincham (Eds.), *Child development and interparental conflict* (pp. 157–187). New York: Cambridge University Press.

Grych, J. H., & Fincham, F. D. (1990). Marital conflict and children's adjustment: A cognitive-contextual framework. *Psychological Bulletin, 108,* 267–290.

Grych, J. H., & Fincham, F. D. (1993). Children's appraisals of marital conflict: Initial investigations of the cognitive-contextual framework. *Child Development, 64,* 215–230.

Grych, J. H., & Fincham, F. D. (2001). Interparental conflict and child adjustment: An overview. In J. H. Grych & F. D. Fincham (Eds.), *Interparental conflict and child development: Theory, research, and application* (pp. 1–6). New York: Cambridge University Press.

Grych, J. H., Fincham, F. D., Jouriles, E. N., & McDonald, R. (2000). Interparental conflict and child adjustment: Testing the mediational role of appraisals in the cognitive-contextual framework. *Child Development, 71,* 1648–1661.

Grych, J. H., Harold, G. T., & Miles, C. J. (2003). A prospective investigation of appraisals as mediators of the link between interparental conflict and child adjustment. *Child Development, 74,* 1176–1193.

Grych, J. H., Jouriles, E. N., Swank, P. R., McDonald, R., & Norwood, W. D. (2000). Patterns of adjustment among children of battered women. *Journal of Consulting and Clinical Psychology, 68,* 84–94.

Grych, J. H., Seid, M., & Fincham, F. D. (1992). Assessing marital conflict from the child's perspective. *Child Development, 63,* 558–572.

Grych, J. H., Wachsmuth-Schlaefer, T., & Klockow, L. L. (2002). Interparental aggression and young children's representations of family relationships. *Journal of Family Psychology, 16,* 259–272.

Harold, G. T., & Conger, R. D. (1997). Marital conflict and adolescent distress: The role of adolescent awareness. *Child Development, 68*, 330–350.

Harold, G. T., Fincham, F. D., Osborne, L. N., & Conger, R. D. (1997). Mom and Dad are at it again: Adolescent perceptions of marital conflict and adolescent psychological distress. *Developmental Psychology, 33*, 333–350.

Harold, G. T., Shelton, K. H., Goeke-Morey, M. C., & Cummings, E. M. (2004). Marital conflict and child adjustment: Prospective longitudinal tests of the mediating role of children's emotional security about family relationships. *Social Development, 13*, 350–376.

Hennessy, K. D., Rabideau, G. J., Cicchetti, D., & Cummings, E. M. (1994). Responses of physically abused children to different forms of interadult anger. *Child Development, 65*, 815–828.

Hetherington, E. M., Cox, M., & Cox, R. (1976). Divorced fathers. *Family Coordinator, 25*, 417–428.

Hill, J. P., & Lynch, M. E. (1983). The intensification of gender-related role expectations during early adolescence. In J. Brooks-Gunn & A. C. Petersen (Eds.), *Girls at puberty: Biological and psychosocial perspectives.* New York: Plenum Press.

Holmbeck, G. N. (1997). Toward terminology, conceptual, and statistical clarity in the study of mediators and moderators: Examples from the child clinical and pediatric psychology literatures. *Journal of Consulting and Clinical Psychology, 65*, 599–610.

Holmbeck, G. N. (2002). Post-hoc probing of significant moderational and mediational effects in studies of pediatric populations. *Journal of Pediatric Psychology, 27*, 87–96.

Hops, H. (1995). Age- and gender-specific effects of parental depression: A commentary. *Developmental Psychology, 31*, 428–431.

Jacobson, D. S. (1978). The impact of marital separation/divorce on children: II. Interparental hostility and child adjustment. *Journal of Divorce, 2*, 3–20.

Jaffe, P. G., Wolfe, D. A., & Wilson, S. K. (1990). *Children of battered women.* Newbury Park, CA: Sage.

Jenkins, J. M. (2000). Marital conflict and children's emotions: The development of an anger organization. *Journal of Marriage and the Family, 62*, 723–736.

Jenkins, J. M. (2002). Commentary: Mechanisms in the development of emotional regulation. *Monographs of the Society for Research in Child Development, 67*, 116–127.

Jenkins, J. M., & Smith, M. A. (1990). Factors protecting children living in disharmonious homes: Maternal reports. *Journal of the American Academy of Child and Adolescent Psychiatry, 29*, 60–69.

Jenkins, J. M., & Smith, M. A. (1991). Marital disharmony and children's behaviour problems: Aspects of poor marriage that affect children adversely. *Journal of Child Psychology and Psychiatry, 32*, 793–810.

Jenkins, J. M., Smith, M. A., & Graham, P. J. (1989). Coping with parental quarrels. *Journal of the American Academy of Child and Adolescent Psychiatry, 28*, 182–189.

Johnson, P. L., & O'Leary, K. D. (1987). Parental behavior patterns and conduct disorders in girls. *Journal of Abnormal Child Psychology, 15*, 573–581.

Johnston, J. R., Gonzalez, R., & Campbell, L. E. (1987). Ongoing postdivorce conflict and child disturbance. *Journal of Abnormal Child Psychology, 15*, 493–509.

Jouriles, E. N., Bourg, W. J., & Farris, A. M. (1991). Marital adjustment and child conduct problems: A comparison of the correlation across subsamples. *Journal of Consulting and Clinical Psychology, 59*, 354–357.

Jouriles, E. N., & Farris, A. M. (1992). Effects of marital conflict on subsequent parent-son interactions. *Behavior Therapy, 23*, 355–374.

Jouriles, E. N., Murphy, C., Farris, A. M., Smith, D. A., Richters, J. E., & Waters, E. (1991). Marital adjustment, childrearing disagreements, and child behavior problems: Increasing the specificity of the marital assessment. *Child Development, 62*, 1424–1433.

Jouriles, E. N., Murphy, C. M., & O'Leary, K. D. (1989). Interspousal aggression, marital discord, and child problems. *Journal of Consulting and Clinical Psychology, 57*, 453–455.

Jouriles, E. N., Spiller, L. C., Stephens, N., McDonald, R., & Swank, P. (2000). Variability in adjustment of children of battered women: The role of child appraisals of interparent conflict. *Cognitive Therapy and Research, 24*, 233–249.

Katz, L. F., & Gottman, J. M. (1993). Patterns of marital conflict predict children's internalizing and externalizing behaviors. *Developmental Psychology, 29*, 940–950.

Katz, L. F., & Gottman, J. M. (1996). Spillover effects of marital conflict: In search of parenting and coparenting mechanisms. *New Directions for Child Development, 74*, 57–76.

Katz, L. F., & Gottman, J. M. (1997). Buffering children from marital conflict and dissolution. *Journal of Clinical Child Psychology, 26*, 157–171.

Katz, L. F., & Woodin, E. M. (2002). Hostility, hostile detachment, and conflict engagement in marriages: Effects on child and family functioning. *Child Development, 73*, 636–651.

Kaufman, J., Cook, A., Arny, L., Jones, B., & Pittinsky, T. (1994). Problems defining resiliency: Illustrations from the study of maltreated children. *Development and Psychopathology, 6*, 215–229.

Keller, P. S., Cummings, E. M., & Davies, P. T. (in press). Family mediators of relations between parental problem drinking and child adjustment. *Journal of Child Psychology and Psychiatry.*

Kempton, T., Armistead, L., Wierson, M., & Forehand, R. (1991). Presence of a sibling as a potential buffer following parental divorce: An examination of young adolescents. *Journal of Clinical Child Psychology, 20*, 434–438.

Kerig, P. K. (1995). Triangles in the family circle: Effects of family structure on marriage, parenting, and child adjustment. *Journal of Family Psychology, 9*, 28–43.

Kerig, P. K. (1996). Assessing the links between interparental conflict and child adjustment: The Conflicts and Problem-Solving Scales. *Journal of Family Psychology, 10*, 454–473.

Kerig, P. K. (1998). Moderators and mediators of the effects of interparental conflict on children's adjustment. *Journal of Abnormal Child Psychology, 26*, 199–212.

Kerig, P. K. (2001). Children's coping with interparental conflict. In J. Grych & F. Fincham (Eds.), *Child development and interparental conflict* (pp. 213–248). New York: Cambridge University Press.

Kitzmann, K. M. (2000). Effect of marital conflict on subsequent triadic family interactions and parenting. *Developmental Psychology, 36*, 3–13.

Kitzmann, K. M., Gaylord, N. K., Holt, A. R., & Kenny, E. D. (2003). Child witnesses to domestic violence: A meta-analytic review. *Journal of Consulting and Clinical Psychology, 71*, 339–352.

Kobak, R. (1999). The emotional dynamics of disruptions in attachment relationships: Implications for theory, research, and clinical intervention. In J. Cassidy & P. R. Shaver (Eds.), *Handbook of attachment: Theory, research, and clinical applications* (pp. 21–43). New York: Guilford Press.

Kobak, R. R., Cole, H. E., Ferenz-Gillies, R., Fleming, W., & Gamble, W. (1993). Attachment and emotion regulation during mother-teen problem-solving: A control theory analysis. *Child Development, 64*, 231–245.

Kretchmar, M. D., & Jacobvitz, D. B. (2002). Observing mother-child relationships across generations: Boundary patterns, attachment, and the transmission of caregiving. *Family Process, 41,* 351–374.

Leary, A., & Katz, L. F. (2004). Coparenting, family-level processes, and peer outcomes: The moderating role of vagal tone. *Development and Psychopathology, 16,* 593–608.

Lindahl, K. M. (2001). Methodological issues in family observational research. In P. K. Kerig & K. M. Lindahl (Eds.), *Family observational coding systems: Resources for systemic research* (pp. 23–32). Mahwah, NJ: Erlbaum.

Lindahl, K. M., & Malik, N. M. (1999). Marital conflict, family processes, and boys' externalizing behavior in Hispanic American and European American families. *Journal of Clinical Child Psychology, 28,* 12–24.

Lindsay, L. L., Davies, P. T., & Pedro-Carroll, J. (2001, November). *The Family Conflict Intervention Program: A pilot of school-based groups for second and third grade children.* Paper presented at the annual conference of the National Council on Family Relations, Rochester, NY.

Luthar, S. S. (1991). Vulnerability and resilience: A study of high-risk adolescents. *Child Development, 62,* 600–616.

Luthar, S. S. (1993). Annotation: Methodological and conceptual issues in research on childhood resilience. *Journal of Child Psychology and Psychiatry, 34,* 441–453.

Luthar, S. S., & Cicchetti, D. (2000). The construct of resilience: Implications for interventions and social policies. *Development and Psychopathology, 12,* 857–885.

Luthar, S. S., Cicchetti, D., & Becker, B. (2000). The construct of resilience: A critical evaluation and guidelines for future work. *Child Development, 71,* 543–562.

Lynch, M., & Cicchetti, D. (2002). Links between community violence and the family system: Evidence from children's feelings of relatedness and perceptions of parent behavior. *Family Process, 41,* 519–532.

Maccoby, E. E., & Martin, J. (1983). Socialization in contexts of the family: Parent-child interaction. In E. M. Hetherington (Ed.), *Handbook of child psychology: Vol. 4. Socialization, personality, and social development* (4th ed., pp. 1–101). New York: Wiley.

Mahoney, A., Boggio, R., & Jouriles, E. (1996). Effects of verbal marital conflict on subsequent mother-son interactions in a child clinical sample. *Journal of Clinical Child Psychology, 25,* 262–271.

Margolin, G., & Gordis, E. B. (2000). The effects of family and community violence on children. *Annual Review of Psychology, 51,* 445–479.

Margolin, G., Gordis, E. B., & Oliver, P. (2004). Links between marital and parent-child interactions: Moderating role of husband-to-wife aggression. *Development and Psychopathology, 16,* 753–771.

Margolin, G., Oliver, P., & Medina, A. (2001). Conceptual issues in understanding the relation between interparental conflict and child adjustment: Integrating developmental psychopathology and risk/resilience perspectives. In J. Grych & F. Fincham (Eds.), *Child development and interparental conflict* (pp. 9–38). New York: Cambridge University Press.

Markman, H. J., & Floyd, F. (1980). Possibilities for the prevention of marital discord: A behavioral perspective. *American Journal of Family Therapy, 8,* 29–48.

Markman, H. J., Jamieson, K. J., & Floyd, F. J. (1983). The assessment and modification of premarital relationships: Preliminary findings on the etiology and prevention of marital and family distress. *Advances in Family Intervention, Assessment, and Theory, 3,* 41–90.

Markman, H. J., Renick, M. J., Floyd, F. J., Stanley, S. M., & Clements, M. (1993). Preventing marital distress through communication and conflict management training: A 4- and 5-year follow-up. *Journal of Consulting and Clinical Psychology, 61,* 70–77.

Marvin, R. S., & Stewart, R. B. (1990). A family systems framework for the study of attachment. In M. Greenberg, D. Cicchetti, & E. M. Cummings (Eds.), *Attachment in the preschool years: Theory, research, and intervention* (pp. 51–86). Chicago: University of Chicago Press.

Masten, A. S., Best, K. M., & Garmezy, N. (1990). Resilience and development: Contributions from the study of children who overcome adversity. *Development and Psychopathology, 2,* 425–444.

Maughan, A., & Cicchetti, D. (2002). Impact of child maltreatment and interadult violence on children's emotion regulation abilities and socioemotional adjustment. *Child Development, 73,* 1525–1542.

McDonald, R., Jouriles, E. N., Norwood, W., Ware, H. S., & Ezell, E. (2000). Husbands' marital violence and the adjustment problems of clinic-referred children. *Behavior Therapy, 31,* 649–665.

McEwen, B. S. (1998). Protective and damaging effects of stress mediators. *New England Journal of Medicine, 338,* 171–179.

McEwen, B. S., & Stellar, E. (1993). Stress and the individual: Mechanisms leading to disease. *Archives of Internal Medicine, 153,* 2093–2101.

McGuire, S., Dunn, J., & Plomin, R. (1995). Maternal differential treatment of siblings and children's behavioral problems: A longitudinal study. *Development and Psychopathology, 7,* 515–528.

McHale, J. P., Johnson, D., & Sinclair, R. (1999). Family dynamics, preschoolers' family representations, and preschool peer relationships. *Early Education and Development, 10,* 373–401.

McHale, J. P., Kazali, C., Rotman, T., Talbot, J., Carleton, M., & Lieberson, R. (2004). The transition to coparenthood: Parents' prebirth expectations and early coparental adjustment at 3 months post partum. *Development and Psychopathology, 16,* 711–733.

McHale, J. P., Khazan, I., Erera, P., Rotman, T., DeCourcey, W., & McConnell, M. (2002). Coparenting in diverse family systems. In M. H. Bornstein (Ed.), *Handbook of parenting: Vol. 3. Being and becoming a parent* (2nd ed., pp. 75–107). Mahwah, NJ: Erlbaum.

McHale, J. P., & Rasmussen, J. L. (1998). Coparental and family group-level dynamics during infancy: Early family precursors of child and family functioning during preschool. *Development and Psychopathology, 10,* 39–59.

Mikulincer, M., Florian, V., Cowan, P. A., & Cowan, C. P. (2002). Attachment security in couple relationships: A systemic model and its implications for family dynamics. *Family Process, 41,* 405–434.

Minuchin, P. (1985). Families and individual development: Provocations from the field of family therapy. *Child Development, 56,* 289–302.

Minuchin, S. (1974). *Families and family therapy.* Cambridge, MA: Harvard University Press.

Muthen, B., & Muthen, L. K. (2000). Integrating person-centered and variable-centered analyses: Growth mixture modeling with latent trajectory classes. *Alcoholism: Clinical and Experimental Research, 24,* 882–891.

Nixon, C. L., & Cummings, E. M (1999). Sibling disability and children's reactivity to conflicts involving family members. *Journal of Family Psychology, 13,* 274–285.

O'Brien, M., & Bahadur, M. A. (1998). Marital aggression, mother's problem-solving behavior with children, and children's emotional and behavioral problems. *Journal of Social and Clinical Psychology, 17,* 249–272.

O'Brien, M., Bahadur, M. A., Gee, C., Balto, K., & Erber, S. (1997). Child exposure to marital conflict and child coping responses as predictors of child adjustment. *Cognitive Therapy and Research, 21,* 39–59.

O'Brien, M., Margolin, G., John, R. S., & Krueger, L. (1991). Mothers' and sons' cognitive and emotional reactions to simulated marital and family conflict. *Journal of Consulting and Clinical Psychology, 59,* 692–703.

O'Connor, T. G., Hetherington, E. M., & Reiss, D. (1998). Family systems and adolescent development: Shared and nonshared risk and protective factors in nondivroced and remarried families. *Development and Psychopathology, 10,* 353–375.

Owen, M. T., & Cox, M. J. (1997). Marital conflict and the development of infant-parent attachment relationships. *Journal of Family Psychology, 11,* 152–164.

Papp, L. M., Cummings, E. M., & Schermerhorn, A. (2004). The impact of marital adjustment on mothers' and fathers' symptomatology: Implications for children's functioning. *Journal of Marriage and Family, 66,* 368–384.

Papp, L. M., Goeke-Morey, M. C., & Cummings, E. M. (2004). Mother' and fathers' psychological symptoms, marital relationships and children's psychological functioning. *Journal of Child and Family Studies, 13,* 469–482.

Parke, R. D. (1998). Editorial. *Journal of Family Psychology, 12,* 3–6.

Parke, R. D., & Buriel, R. (1998). Socialization in the family: Ethnic and ecological perspectives. In N. Eisenberg (Ed.), *Handbook of child psychology: Vol. 3. Social, emotional, and personality development* (5th ed., pp. 463–552). New York: Wiley.

Parke, R. D., Kim, M., Flyr, M., McDowell, D. J., Simkins, S. D., Killian, C. M., et al. (2001). Managing marital conflict: Links with sibling relationships. In J. Grych & F. Fincham (Eds.), *Child development and interparental conflict* (pp. 291–314). New York: Cambridge University Press.

Patterson, G. R., DeBaryshe, B., & Ramsey, E. (1989). A developmental perspective on antisocial behavior. *American Psychologist, 44,* 329–335.

Pedro-Carroll, J. L., & Cowen, E. L. (1985). The children of divorce intervention program: An investigation of the efficacy of a school-based prevention program. *Journal of Consulting and Clinical Psychology, 53,* 603–611.

Petersen, A. C. (1988). Adolescent development. *Annual Review of Psychology, 39,* 583–607.

Repetti, R. L., Taylor, S. E., & Seeman, T. E. (2002). Risky families: Families' social environments and the mental and physical health of offspring. *Psychological Bulletin, 128,* 330–366.

Richters, J. E. (1997). Toward a developmental perspective on conduct disorder. *Development and Psychopathology, 9,* 193–229.

Rossman, B. R., & Rosenberg, M. S. (1992). Family stress and functioning in children: The moderating effects of children's beliefs about their control over parental conflict. *Journal of Child Psychology and Psychiatry and Allied Disciplines, 33,* 699–715.

Rutter, M. (1971). Parent-child separation: Psychological effects on children. *Journal of Child Psychology and Psychiatry, 12,* 233–260.

Rutter, M. (1987). Psychosocial resilience and protective mechanisms. *American Journal of Orthopsychiatry, 57,* 316–331.

Rutter, M. (1994). Family discord and conduct disorder: Cause, consequence, or correlate? *Journal of Family Psychology, 8,* 170–186.

Saarni, C., Mumme, D. L., & Campos, J. J. (1998). Emotional development: Action, communication, and understanding. In N. Eisenberg (Ed.), *Handbook of child psychology: Vol. 3. Social, emotional, and personality development* (5th ed., pp. 237–309). New York: Wiley.

Sameroff, A. J. (1995). General systems theories and developmental psychopathology. In D. Cicchetti & D. J. Cohen (Eds.), *Developmental psychopathology: Vol. 1. Theory and methods* (pp. 659–695). New York: Wiley.

Sameroff, A. J., & Seifer, R. (1990). Early contributors to developmental risk. In J. Rolf, A. Masten, D. Cicchetti, K. Nuchterlein, & S. Weintraub (Eds.), *Risk and protective factors in the development of psychopathology* (pp. 52–66). New York: Cambridge University Press.

Sanders, M. R., Markie-Dadds, C., Tully, L. A., & Bor, W. (2000). The Triple P-Positive Parenting Program: A comparison of enhanced, standard, and self-directed behavioral family intervention for parents of children with early onset conduct problems. *Journal of Consulting and Clinical Psychology, 68,* 624–640.

Sandler, I. N. (1980). Social support resources, stress, and maladjustment of poor children. *American Journal of Community Psychology, 8,* 41–52.

Sandler, I. N., Tein, J. Y., & West, S. G. (1994). Coping, stress, and the psychological symptoms of children of divorce: A cross-sectional and longitudinal study. *Child Development, 65,* 1744–1763.

Schermerhorn, A. C., Cummings, E. M., & Davies, P. T. (in press). Children's perceived agency in the context of marital conflict: Relations with marital conflict over time. *Merrill-Palmer Quarterly.*

Schermerhorn, A. C., Goeke-Morey, M. C., Mitchell, P., & Cummings, E. M. (2004, March). *Children's agency in the context of interparental conflict during adolescence: A developmental perspective.* Paper presented at the conference of the Society for Research on Adolescence, Baltimore.

Schoppe, S. J., Mangelsdorf, S. C., & Frosch, C. (2001). Coparenting, family process, and family structure: Implications for preschoolers' externalizing behavior problems. *Journal of Family Psychology, 15,* 526–545.

Seifer, R. (1995). Perils and pitfalls of high-risk research. *Developmental Psychology, 31,* 420–424.

Shamir, H., Cummings, E. M., Davies, P. T., & Goeke-Morey, M. C. (in press). Children's reactions to marital conflict resolution in Israel and in the United States. *Parenting: Science and Practice.*

Shaw, D. S., & Emery, R. E. (1987). Parental conflict and other correlates of the adjustment of school-age children whose parents have separated. *Journal of Abnormal Child Psychology, 15,* 269–281.

Shaw, D. S., Gilliom, M., Ingoldsby, E. M., & Nagin, D. S. (2003). Trajectories leading to school-age conduct problems. *Developmental Psychology, 39,* 189–200.

Shifflett, K. S., & Cummings, E. M. (1999). A program for educating parents about the effects of divorce and conflict on children: An initial evaluation. *Family Relations, 48,* 79–89.

Shipman, K., Zeman, J., Penza, S., & Champion, K. (2000). Emotion management skills in sexually maltreated and nonmaltreated girls: A developmental psychopathology perspective. *Development and Psychopathology, 12,* 47–62.

Snyder, D. K., Klein, M. A., Gdowski, C. L., Faulstich, C., & LaCombe, J. (1988). Generalized dysfunction in clinic and nonclinic families: A comparative analysis. *Journal of Abnormal Child Psychology, 16,* 97–109.

Sroufe, L. A. (1979). The coherence of individual development: Early care, attachment, and subsequent developmental issues. *American Psychologist, 34,* 834–841.

Sroufe, L. A. (1990). Considering normal and abnormal together: The essence of developmental psychopathology. *Development and Psychopathology, 2,* 335–347.

Sroufe, L. A. (1997). Psychopathology as an outcome of development. *Development and Psychopathology, 9,* 251–268.

Sroufe, L. A., Egeland, B., & Kreutzer, T. (1990). The face of early experience following developmental change: Longitudinal approaches to individual adaptation in childhood. *Child Development, 61,* 1363–1373.

Sroufe, L. A., & Rutter, M. (1984). The domain of developmental psychopathology. *Child Development, 55,* 17–29.

Stocker, C., Ahmed, K., & Stall, M. (1997). Marital satisfaction and maternal emotional expressiveness: Links with children's sibling relationships. *Social Development, 6,* 373–385.

Stocker, C. M., & Youngblade, L. (1999). Marital conflict and parental hostility: Links with children's sibling and peer relationships. *Journal of Family Psychology, 13,* 598–609.

Stolberg, A. L., & Mahler, J. (1994). Enhancing treatment gains in a school-based intervention for children of divorce through skill training, parental involvement, and transfer procedures. *Journal of Consulting and Clinical Psychology, 62,* 147–156.

Sturge-Apple, M. L., Davies, P. T., & Cummings, E. M. (in press). Examining associations between marital hostility and withdrawal and mother's and father's emotional unavailability and inconsistent discipline. *Journal of Family Psychology.*

Thompson, R. A. (1997). Sensitivity and security: New questions to ponder. *Child Development, 68,* 595–597.

Thompson, R. A., & Calkins, S. D. (1996). The double-edged sword: Emotional regulation for children at risk. *Development and Psychopathology, 8,* 163–182.

Toth, S. L., & Cicchetti, D. (1996). The impact of relatedness with mother on school functioning in maltreated children. *Journal of School Psychology, 34,* 247–266.

Towle, C. (1931). The evaluation and management of marital status in foster homes. *American Journal of Orthopsychiatry, 1,* 271–284.

Tschann, J. M., Flores, E., Martin, B. V., Pasch, L. A., Baisch, E. M., & Wibbelsman, C. J. (2002). Interparental conflict and risk behaviors among Mexican American adolescents: A cognitive-emotional model. *Journal of Abnormal Child Psychology, 30,* 373–385.

van Widenfelt, B., Hosman, C., Schaap, C., & van der Staak, C. (1996). The prevention of relationship distress for couples at risk: A controlled evaluation with nine-month and two-year follow-ups. *Family Relations, 45,* 156–165.

Waddington, C. H. (1957). *The strategy of genes.* London: Allen & Unwin.

Wasserstein, S. B., & La Greca, A. M. (1996). Can peer support buffer against behavioral consequences of parental discord. *Journal of Clinical Child Psychology, 25,* 177–182.

Webster-Stratton, C., & Hammond, M. (1999). Marital conflict management skills, parenting style, and early-onset conduct problems: Processes and pathways. *Journal of Child Psychology and Psychiatry, 40,* 917–927.

Willett, J. B., Singer, J. D., & Martin, N. C. (1998). The design and analysis of longitudinal studies of development and psychopathology in context: Statistical models and methodological recommendations. *Development and Psychopathology, 10,* 395–426.

Windle, M. (1992). A longitudinal study of stress buffering for adolescent problem behaviors. *Developmental Psychology, 28,* 522–530.

Windle, M. (2000). A latent growth curve model of delinquent activity among adolescents. *Applied Developmental Science, 4,* 193–207.

Windle, M., & Davies, P. T. (1999). Developmental theory and research. In K. E. Leonard & H. T. Blane (Eds.), *Psychological theories of drinking and alcoholism* (pp. 164–202). New York: Guilford Press.

Yates, T. M., Dodds, M. F., Sroufe, L. A., & Egeland, B. (2003). Exposure to partner violence and child behavior problems: A prospective study controlling for child physical abuse and neglect, child cognitive ability, socioeconomic status, and life stress. *Development and Psychopathology, 15,* 199–218.

Yunes, J., & Zubarew, T. (2001). Homicide mortality in adolescents and young people: A challenge for the region of the Americas. In E. J. Bartell & A. O'Donnell (Eds.), *The child in Latin America: Health, development, and rights* (pp. 143–156). Notre Dame, IN: University of Notre Dame Press.

Zigler, E., & Glick, M. (1986). *A developmental approach to adult psychopathology.* New York: Wiley.

CHAPTER 4

An Ecological-Transactional Perspective on Child Maltreatment: Failure of the Average Expectable Environment and Its Influence on Child Development

DANTE CICCHETTI and KRISTIN VALENTINO

The notion of an average expectable environment for promoting normal development proposes that there are species-specific ranges of environmental conditions that elicit normative developmental processes (Hartman, 1958). Humans, like all other species, develop within a "normal range" when presented with such an average expectable environment (Dobzhansky, 1972; Gottesman,

1963). For infants, the expectable environment includes protective, nurturant caregivers and a larger social group to which the child will be socialized, whereas for older children, the normative environment includes a supportive family, a peer group, and continued opportunities for exploration and mastery of the environment. Variations within this range of environments afford opportunities for individuals to dynamically engage in the construction of their own experiences (Scarr & McCartney, 1983). When environments fall outside the expectable range, normal development is impeded.

Grants from the Office of Child Abuse and Neglect, the National Institute of Drug Abuse, the National Institute of Mental Health, and the Spunk Fund, Inc., supported our work on this chapter.

Elaborating on the role of the environment in the expression of genes, Scarr (1992, 1993) asserted that infants and children might be genetically preadapted to respond to a specific range of environmental experiences. Furthermore, Scarr added that individual developmental differences when in the context of the expectable environment are largely the result of genotypic differences. Thus, Scarr conceptualized the environment as providing a specific range of conditions that allow for the phenotypic expression of genes. Gottlieb (1991) has further contributed to our understanding of gene-environment interactions by pointing out that genetic activity does not act in isolation to produce either finished physical traits or complex individual personality characteristics. Instead, a systems view of development (Gottlieb, 1991, 1992) conceptualizes human development as hierarchically organized into multiple levels that have mutual influence on each other (Cicchetti & Cannon, 1999; Cicchetti & Lynch, 1995; Gottlieb, 1991, 1992; F. D. Horowitz, 1987). Bidirectional effects are expected to occur from the top down as well as from the bottom up among genetic activity, neural activity, behavior, and the environment (Cicchetti & Tucker, 1994). These bidirectional effects among levels of the system result in a probabilistic conceptualization of epigenetic development. Therefore, no single component of the system can "cause" development; rather, it is the mutual relationship among components of the developmental system that brings about development and phenotypic expression (Cicchetti & Cannon, 1999).

In the past decade, our understanding of the role of the environment and its interaction with genes has been further clarified, whereby reciprocal coactions between the environment and the individual have resulted in differential expression of genetic material (Cicchetti, 2002; Eisenberg, 1995; Kandel, 1998, 1999). Environmental conditions may interact with an individual's genetic makeup to alter processes such as the timing of the initiation of transcription and translation for a specific gene, the duration for which it does so, or whether the gene will ultimately be expressed. Thus, a new ecological level can be added to our systems model to acknowledge the distinction between genetic code and genetic expression, as well as how interactions with the environment at each level may contribute to our understanding of probabilistic epigenesis (Gottlieb, 1992).

So now we come to the question of what conditions fall within the range of the human average expectable environment to promote normal development and, alternatively, what happens to development when there are severe disturbances in such an environment. Consistent with a developmental psychopathology perspective, the examination of maladaptive and psychopathological development can elucidate the underlying mechanisms of normal development (Cicchetti, 1984, 1990a, 1990b, 1993; Rutter, 1986; Sroufe, 1990; Werner, 1948). In typical development, the component developmental systems may be so well integrated that it is difficult to determine how normal functioning is dependent on this integration (Cicchetti & Sroufe, 1976). From a systems perspective, the environment also exists as a component of the developmental system. Thus, when the conditions of an average expectable environment are available, the manner in which its components interact is also challenging to identify.

As proffered by Cicchetti (2003, p. 833), "When there is a clear perturbation or deficit in a component system, examination of how that atypicality relates to the organization of other component systems can reveal important information regarding the interdependence of components that are not apparent under normal conditions." Thus, "experiments of nature," such as being raised in a maltreating home, enable us to isolate components of the developmental system and elucidate the structural organization of the normal system. Through the examination of child maltreatment, which may represent the greatest failure of the environment to provide opportunities for normal development, we can begin to identify the range of conditions that encompass the average expectable environment. Moreover, we may come to an understanding of how serious deviations from this range may affect organism-environment coactions that play important roles in the emergence and timing of normal developmental change.

The goals of this chapter are to provide a review of child maltreatment, updating our chapter from the prior edition of these volumes (Cicchetti & Lynch, 1995). Although a thorough review of the literature is presented, the focus of this chapter is on the developments that have occurred in the field since 1995. Of particular salience is the growing contribution of neurobiological and genetic research to the study of child maltreatment, such that ontogenic development can be considered from both psychological and neurobiological perspectives. We then address how these recent advances may inform prevention and intervention efforts. Finally, we offer recommendations for future research and social policy initiatives.

EPIDEMIOLOGY

It is critically important to examine epidemiological estimates of child maltreatment, as the criteria used to define maltreatment affect the incidence and prevalence rates of child abuse and neglect, as well as the national services that are implemented to address this important societal issue. Since the passing of the Child Abuse Prevention and Treatment Act (CAPTA) in 1974, the National Center on Child Abuse and Neglect (NCCAN) was established as a federal research center aimed at understanding the causes and preventing the occurrence and negative consequences of child maltreatment. Since that time, National Incidence Studies (NIS) have been compiled by the NCCAN to provide a comprehensive source of information regarding the epidemiology of child abuse and neglect in the United States (U.S. Department of Human and Health Services [NIS-I], 1981; [NIS-II], 1988; [NIS-III], 1996). The 1988 amendments to the CAPTA directed the U.S. Department of Human and Health Services (USDHHS) to establish a national data collection and analysis program. Consequently, the National Child Abuse and Neglect Data System (NCANDS) has published the most recent national reports on child maltreatment. According to their report, an estimated 896,000 children in the United States were victims of child abuse or neglect in 2002, translating into a rate of victimization that equals 12.3 per 1,000 children in the national population (USDHHS, 2002).

Furthermore, an estimated 1,400 fatalities were reported in 2002, representing 1.98 children per 100,000 in the national population (USDHHS, 2002). Fatality, as defined by the NCANDS system, refers to the death of a child caused by an injury resulting from abuse or neglect, or where abuse or neglect were contributing factors. Additional studies, however, report that as many as 50% to 60% of deaths resulting from abuse or neglect are not reported (Crume, DiGuiseppi, Byers, Sirotnak, & Garret, 2002; Herman-Giddens et al., 1999), citing child neglect as the most underrecorded form of fatal maltreatment.

During 2002, 60.5% of documented child maltreatment victims experienced neglect, 18.6% were physically abused, 9.9% were sexually abused, and 6.5% were emotionally or psychologically maltreated. Furthermore, almost 20% were associated with "other" types of maltreatment based on specific state and law policies. Regarding the victims of abuse, children had the highest rates of victimization in the period from birth to 3 years, at 16 per 1,000 children, and girls were slightly more likely to be victims than boys. Among ethnic groups, American Indian and African American children had the highest rates of victimization (21.7 and 20.2 per 1,000 children, respectively), compared to the rate of victimization among European Americans (10.7 per 1,000 children). Reports on the perpetrators of maltreatment indicate that more than 80%

of perpetrators were parents; other relatives accounted for 7%, and unmarried partners of parents accounted for an additional 3% (USHDDS, 2002); women, mostly mothers, were a larger percentage of perpetrators (58%) than men (48%). Strikingly, children from single-parent families were at increased risk for abuse or neglect compared to children from two-parent homes (27.3 verses 15.5 per 1,000 children, respectively; USDHHS, 1996). Moreover, children from families whose incomes were less than $15,000 were 22 times more likely to experience some form of maltreatment than were children from families whose incomes exceeded $30,000 annually.

An estimated 2.6 million referrals of abuse or neglect, concerning nearly 4.5 million children, was received by Child Protective Services agencies in 2002. More than 66% of those referrals were accepted for investigation or assessment, and approximately 30% of the reports included at least one child who was found to be a victim of child abuse or neglect. Although 61% of the reports filed were found to be "unsubstantiated," evidence demonstrates that significant psychosocial maladjustment accompanies both unreported and unsubstantiated instances of child maltreatment (B. Drake, 1996). Given the heterogeneity contained among unsubstantiated reports of child maltreatment, caution should be taken against accepting the notion that unsubstantiated means that maltreatment did not occur (Barnett, Manly, & Cicchetti, 1993; Cicchetti & Toth, 2003; B. Drake, 1996).

In light of the alarming epidemiological rates of maltreatment, which likely underestimate the prevalence of child abuse and neglect in our country, one might wonder what social policy actions are being taken to address this serious national problem. On the national level, approximately 59% of victims and 31% of nonvictims received services as a result of investigation or assessment in 2002. Additionally, children who were prior victims of maltreatment were more than 80% more likely to receive services than first-time victims, as were children with multiple types of maltreatment in comparison to children with only one type of recorded maltreatment. To respond to the issue of receipt of services, the newly amended and reauthorized Child Abuse Prevention and Treatment Act, the Keeping Children and Families Safe Act of 2003 (PL 108-36), now requires states to refer abused and neglected young children to the Early Intervention Program (known as Part C of the Individuals with Disabilities Education Act; Dicker & Gordon, 2004). This revision was implemented to extend the act's original goal of child safety to focus on child well-being and permanency. The new referral requirement provides a rich entitlement for services for children under 3 years of age involved in substantiated cases of abuse or neglect and their families. Services include physical, occupational, and special therapies, psychological testing, special instruction, adaptive technology devices, nursing services, nutrition counseling, and transportation. Additional family support services include training, counseling, support groups, home visits, and special instruction to enhance child development. Practical challenges of initiating the referral, obtaining parental consent, and securing parental involvement to ensure the receipt of services must be met so that the potential of the CAPTA revision to increase the receipt of services to maltreated children is realized.

ISSUES OF DEFINITION

Despite widespread agreement that child maltreatment is a serious societal problem, placing children's welfare and normal development in jeopardy, there has been a long history of discordance among researchers, lawmakers, and clinicians on what constitutes maltreatment and how it should be defined (J. L. Aber & Zigler, 1981; Barnett et al., 1993; Besharov, 1981; Cicchetti & Manly, 2001; Cicchetti & Rizley, 1981; Emery, 1989; Juvenile Justice Standards Project, 1977). Contributing to the lack of consensus is a debate regarding whether it is realistic to expect professionals from various domains to agree on a single definitional approach given the widespread differences between fields in the purpose and utilization of such a definition. For example, the medical-diagnostic definition of maltreatment revolves around the individual abuser (J. L. Aber & Zigler, 1981) and focuses on overt signs of maltreatment. This approach tends to highlight physical abuse while minimizing psychological maltreatment. The legal definition focuses on demonstrable physical and emotional harm to children, particularly that which would be useful as evidence for prosecution (Juvenile Justice Standards Project, 1977). In contrast, parental acts and society's role in perpetuating maltreatment are important for the sociological definition, and evidence of environmental and familial contributors to the occurrence of maltreatment are necessary elements of the ecological approach (Cicchetti & Lynch, 1993; Cicchetti, Toth, & Maughan, 2000). Many researchers have asserted that the definition of maltreatment should focus on specific acts that endanger the child in some way (Barnett, Manly, & Cicchetti, 1991; Barnett et al., 1993; Cicchetti & Barnett, 1991b; Zuravin, 1991). This type of definition

would allow researchers to concentrate on the identifiable behaviors that compromise the child's maladaptive caretaking environment.

Even within the domain of research, however, a number of complexities contribute to the lack of consensus regarding the definition of maltreatment employed by various investigators, making comparability across studies difficult to achieve (Barnett et al., 1993). First, maltreatment is largely influenced by legal matters, as it is identified and defined by social service systems, rather than by researchers or mental health professionals. Furthermore, there is not a clear standard regarding the distinction between acceptable parental disciplinary practices and maltreatment (M. M. Black & Dubowitz, 1999; Cicchetti & Lynch, 1995); there is a lack of agreement on whether child maltreatment should be defined based on the actions of the perpetrator, the effects on the child, or a combination of the two (Barnett et al., 1991, 1993); and there is debate as to whether parental intent should be considered. These issues raise additional methodological concerns, as it is a greater challenge to measure parental intent than parental behavior. Moreover, linking maltreatment to child outcome leads to difficulty in separating child maltreatment from its subsequent sequelae (Barnett et al., 1991; Cicchetti & Manly, 2001; McGee & Wolfe, 1991).

Based on the wide range of challenges faced by maltreatment researchers, one clearly cannot expect all who study maltreatment to use the same methodology for operationalizing child abuse and neglect. However, all approaches must be derived from clear operational definitions of maltreatment such that replication may be possible across investigations (Cicchetti & Manly, 2001). Despite the challenges facing maltreatment researchers, four general categories of child maltreatment have been distinguished from one another and are widely accepted:

1. *Sexual abuse* refers to sexual contact or attempted sexual contact between a caregiver or other responsible adult and a child, for the purposes of the caregiver's sexual gratification or financial benefit.

2. *Physical abuse* refers to injuries that have been inflicted on a child by nonaccidental means.

3. *Neglect* refers to failure to provide minimum standards of care as well as adequate supervision.

4. *Emotional maltreatment* refers to persistent and extreme thwarting of a child's basic emotional needs.

Additionally, McGee and Wolfe (1991) offered a slightly different conceptualization for emotional maltreatment, which they called psychological maltreatment, which encompasses both psychologically abusive and psychologically neglectful experiences. Although each of these subtypes represent distinct deviations from the average expectable caregiving environment, it is well documented that they rarely occur in isolation from each other (Cicchetti & Manly, 2001). In actuality, the majority of maltreated children experience more than one subtype of maltreatment, presenting significant challenges for clinicians and researchers who strive to understand the unique effects of each type of maltreatment experience on development.

Responding to the need for a detailed classification system for maltreatment, Cicchetti and Barnett (1991b; see also Barnett et al., 1993) developed a multidimensional nosological system for categorizing children's maltreatment histories. In recognition of the need to include developmental considerations in assessing maltreatment, the Maltreatment Classification System (MCS; Barnett et al., 1993) not only provides operational definitions of maltreatment subtypes, with inclusion and exclusion criteria and exemplars of each of the five levels of severity for each subtype, but also includes measurement of the onset, frequency, and chronicity of each subtype, the developmental period(s) during which each subtype occurred, the severity of each subtype, and the perpetrator(s) of each subtype. This comprehensive assessment across and within dimensions of maltreatment has allowed for a more detailed understanding of the maladaptive developmental pathways associated with children's maltreatment experiences. For example, through the utilization of the MCS, the interaction between severity and frequency of maltreatment has emerged as a significant predictor of maladaptation (Manly, Cicchetti, & Barnett, 1994). Moreover, the chronicity of maltreatment has been identified as a robust dimension in predicting peer rejection and aggression (Bolger & Patterson, 2001; Bolger, Patterson, & Kupersmidt, 1998). The timing of maltreatment was noted as an important factor relating the impact of maltreatment on self-perceptions and relationships with peers (Bolger et al., 1998). Additionally, an investigation specifically examining the contributions of developmental timing and subtype to child adaptation highlighted the interaction of the severity of particular maltreatment subtypes with the developmental period during which the maltreatment began in differentially predicting internalizing and externalizing symptomatology (Manly, Kim, Rogosch, & Cicchetti, 2001). In particular, the impact of chronicity was underscored by noting that chronic maltreatment, especially with onset in the infancy-toddlerhood or preschool period, was linked with more maladaptive outcomes.

Apart from the significant advances in the classification of child maltreatment, further methodological challenges face researchers regarding the collection of information on which to base classification decisions. Of particular concern are the challenges associated with the identification and operationalization of child neglect. The "neglect of neglect" has been acknowledged in the literature for quite some time (Wolock & Horowitz, 1984), yet child neglect continues to be a relatively understudied aspect of maltreatment. Nonetheless, the experience of neglect should not be ignored as child neglect is consistently the most commonly reported form of child maltreatment in the United States (USDHHS, 2002), with consequences that can often be as severe as those associated with physical and sexual abuse (cf. Hildyard & Wolfe, 2002; Trickett & McBride-Chang, 1995). The pervasive nature of neglect, however, makes research on the effects of neglect, in isolation from other abuse experiences, particularly difficult. Unlike physical or sexual abuse, which often have overt physical consequences that are usually incident-specific and clearly identifiable, neglect is often a chronic experience that leaves little visible evidence and has an accumulating effect over time. Moreover, physical neglect, referring to the failure to adequately meet the physical needs of children, is closely related to poverty, so that it is increasingly hard to identify neglect over and above economic disadvantage.

An additional methodological concern relates to the strategy utilized to assess maltreatment. For example, self-report (by the perpetrator and/or victim) has frequently been used to ascertain the occurrence of maltreatment, as have observational paradigms and the use of official Child Protective Services reports (e.g., Dodge, Pettit, & Bates, 1997; Egeland & Sroufe, 1981; Manly et al., 1994). Each of these methods has a number of strengths and weaknesses that must be considered when offering interpretation of results based on such operational definitions. Furthermore, Newcomb and Locke (2001) assert that the methodologies of much of the existing research are marked by fundamental weaknesses, such as using case status alone to define subjects, adopting a dichotomous perspective of maltreatment without conceptualization on various dimensions and continua, and using operational definitions that fail to differentiate among maltreatment subtypes. Although the use of adult retrospective reports of maltreatment experienced as a child to identify and define maltreatment has received heavy criticism for its possible lack of validity (Widom, 1989), standardized assessments such as the Child Trauma Questionnaire have been developed as reliable and valid means for collecting retrospective data (Bernstein, Ahluvalia, Pogge, & Handelsman, 1997; Bernstein et al., 1994; Goodyear, Newcomb, & Allison, 2000; Rosen & Marton, 1998). Whenever possible, the research reviewed in this chapter focuses on that which has been the product of psychometrically accepted methodology.

Etiology of Maltreatment

Early views on the development of maltreatment emerged from a "main effects" perspective, in which it was believed that single risk factors such as poverty, parental psychopathology, or a personal history of maltreatment could alone provide an etiological account for the occurrence of child maltreatment (Cicchetti & Toth, 1995; Gelles, 1991). However, these unidimensional views on the etiology of child maltreatment soon gave way to more complex models, as it became clear that no single risk factor or set of risk factors would explain the development of maltreatment (Belsky, 1980; Cicchetti & Lynch, 1995; Cicchetti & Rizley, 1981). Emerging from the ecological-developmental theory set forth by Bronfenbrenner (1979), current theories acknowledge the contributions made by transacting factors operating at environmental, contextual, familial, and individual ecologies (Belsky, 1980, 1993; Cicchetti & Lynch, 1993; Cicchetti & Rizley, 1981; Garbarino, 1977; Parke & Collmer, 1975; Wolfe, 1991).

Applying Bronfenbrenner's (1979) theory of human development, the etiological model proposed by Belsky (1980) initiated dramatic changes in the conceptualization of child maltreatment, as it necessitated the consideration of the broader environment in which maltreatment occurs. According to Belsky, child maltreatment is a social-psychological phenomenon that cannot be understood in isolation from the community and the culture within which the family and the individual are embedded. As such, his model contains four levels of analysis: the *macrosystem,* including the cultural beliefs and values that contribute to and influence child maltreatment; the *exosystem,* including aspects of the community to contribute to the incidence of maltreatment; the *microsystem,* including factors within the family that contribute to the occurrence of maltreatment; and *ontogenic* development, including factors within the individual that are associated with being a perpetrator of maltreatment. Given that proximity to the individual increases with each subsequent level of the ecology (from the macrosystem to the ontogenic context), Belsky further highlighted that risk factors at ecological levels that are closer to the individual exert a more direct influence on an individual's development. Moreover, interactions exist between all levels of the ecology, contributing to and influencing the occurrence of child maltreatment.

Cicchetti and Rizley (1981), drawing on the work of Sameroff and Chandler (1975), introduced additional elements to the etiological model of maltreatment by proposing a transactional model. This model focused on the reciprocal interactions of the environment, the caregiver and the child, which together contribute to the outcomes of child development. An important distinction was made between two classes of risk factors: those that are potentiating, thereby increasing the risk for maltreatment, and those that are compensatory, which decrease the risk for maltreatment. Additionally, a temporal dimension was added to distinguish between risk factors that are transient versus those that are enduring. By combining these categorical and temporal dimensions of risk factors, Cicchetti and Rizley proposed four classes of determinants for the occurrence of child maltreatment: enduring vulnerability factors, transient challengers, enduring protective factors, and transient buffers. This model conceptualized the risk for child maltreatment as probabilistic, proposing that the likelihood of maltreatment occurring is determined by the balance among risk and protective factors and processes (Cicchetti & Carlson, 1989).

Integrating the etiological models of Belsky (1980) and of Cicchetti and Rizley (1981), Cicchetti and Lynch (1993) proposed the ecological-transactional model of child maltreatment. By incorporating the ideas of the average expectable environment and probabilistic epigenesis into a broad integrative framework, this model explains how processes at each level of ecology exert reciprocal influences on each other and shape the course of child development (Cicchetti & Lynch, 1993). As such, potentiating and compensatory risk factors associated with maltreatment are present at each level of the ecology and can influence processes in the surrounding environmental levels. These dynamic transactions, which operate both horizontally and vertically throughout the levels of ecology, determine the amount of risk for maltreatment that an individual faces at any given time (see Figure 4.1). The levels of ecology most proximal to the child have the most direct impact on child development relative to the more distally located macrosystem. Although characterized by an overall pattern in which risk factors outweigh protective factors, there are infinite permutations of these risk variables across and within each level of the ecology, providing multiple pathways to the occurrence of maltreatment.

Ultimately, it is the child's own ontogenic processes, as manifested by the particular developmental pathway that individuals engage in, that culminate in eventual adaptation

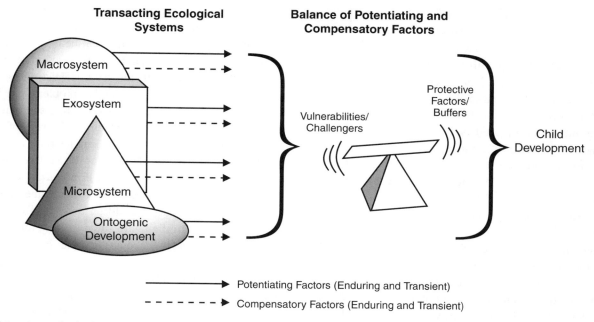

Transacting Ecological Systems

Balance of Potentiating and Compensatory Factors

Macrosystem

Exosystem

Microsystem

Ontogenic Development

Vulnerabilities/ Challengers

Protective Factors/ Buffers

Child Development

———————▶ Potentiating Factors (Enduring and Transient)

– – – – – – ▶ Compensatory Factors (Enduring and Transient)

Figure 4.1 An ecological-transactional model of child maltreatment.

or maladaptation. The challenges or supports presented to children by the family, community, and society contribute to these ontogenic processes; however, children also play an active role in their organismic development as they respond to these influences and engage in the resolution of stage-salient developmental issues. In the case of child maltreatment, one could imagine how an increased presence of enduring vulnerability factors and transient challenges associated with maltreatment at each level of ecology contributes to unsuccessful resolution of stage-salient developmental tasks, setting the child on a pathway to maladaptive developmental outcomes and psychopathology (Cicchetti, 1990). The ecological-transactional model may also aid in providing an account for resilient outcomes. The presence of enduring protective factors may approximate features of the average expectable environment, thus allowing some children to display successful adaptation in the face of maltreatment.

The ecological-transactional model of child maltreatment (Cicchetti & Lynch, 1993) has remained the predominant etiological model in the field, albeit with some modifications as we have come to a better understanding of ontogenic development in neurobiological as well as psychological realms. As in our chapter in the prior edition of these volumes, this model serves as a heuristic for reviewing the literature on the consequences of child maltreatment and for addressing our questions regarding the impact of the failure of the average expectable environment on development. In particular, attention is focused on the emer-

gence of genetic and neurobiological research in the ontogenic development of maltreated children.

MACROSYSTEM

The macrosystem is the most broad and distal ecological level, referring to the set of cultural values and beliefs that are reflected in the community services offered by a society and that infuse individual and family lifestyles (Cicchetti & Lynch, 1995). Among the cultural phenomena of American society, social acceptance of violent crime was one of the earliest values to be identified for its possible contribution to child maltreatment. In comparison to other Western nations, the United States is characterized by an exceptionally high level of violent crime (M. Aber & Rappaport, 1994; Christoffel, 1990; Fingerhut & Kleinman, 1990; Lykken, 1993). Although the national rate of violent crime has decreased over the past decade, violent crime victimization remains a serious part of American culture, particularly in low socioeconomic status, urban areas. Highlighting the pervasive exposure of young people to violence, Finkelhor, Ormrod, Turner, and Hamby (2005) conducted a comprehensive national survey of violence, crime, and victimization experiences in a nationally representative sample of children ages 2 to 17 years. One in 8 children in this sample reported experiencing a form of child maltreatment, and 1 in 3 had been a witness to violence or other form of indirect victimization. Only 29% reported no direct or indirect victimization (Finkelhor et al., 2005). Annual reports from the U.S. Department of Justice (2004) reveal that in 2003, U.S. residents age 12 or older experienced approximately 5.4 million crimes of violence. For every 1,000 persons age 12 or older, there occurred one rape or sexual assault, one assault with injury, and two robberies. Furthermore, about 1 in every 26 households in 2003 was either burglarized or had a member age 12 or older who was a victim of a violent crime committed by a stranger. Even more alarming, despite the drop in the national crime rate since 1993, juveniles have been consistently involved in 25% of serious violent victimizations annually over the past 25 years (U.S. Department of Justice, 2004).

Beyond attempts to identify specific cultural values such as the acceptance of violence that may characterize aspects of a generalized American culture, the application of culture to developmental psychopathology has shifted its focus toward identifying values within the multiple subcultures that constitute American society. The most recent approaches to cultural research are based on the premise that cultures that differ from the White, middle-class, mainstream cultural majority are legitimate adaptations to contextual demands and are valuable in their own right. This conceptualization thus moves away from deficit models, which had conceptualized these differences as deviation, maladaptation, or pathology that reflects deficits inherent in cultural values (Garica Coll, Akerman, & Cicchetti, 2000).

In addition to this new framework for approaching cultural influences, progress has been made in clarifying what is meant by the concept of culture. A plethora of definitions of culture have been offered, mainly focusing on the idea of culture as learned, as shared, and as the interpretive force that guides interactions among people (Korbin, 2002). Consistent with a developmental psychopathology perspective, these elaborations have noted that children are not passive recipients of socialization, but rather shape and reinterpret it. Each individual, therefore, experiences culture differently, as both interpretation and interaction are dynamic concepts. Previous to such elaborations, culture or ethnicity was traditionally identified and defined on the basis of phenotypic characteristics such as skin color. Some have argued that these groupings serve more as proxies of socioeconomic status (SES) than as meaningful cultural designations, asserting that lumping families and individuals under major demographic categories does not reflect culture, and may instead serve to mask rather than illuminate cultural differences (Abney, 1996; Fontes, 2001; Korbin, 1981, 1997, 2002).

In maltreatment research, culture has typically been treated as an independent variable to explain differences in incidence or prevalence of maltreatment; however, it has not often been partitioned from SES (Korbin, Coulton, Chard, Platt-Houston, & Su, 1998). Distinguishing between SES and culture is a complex problem that is difficult to resolve. Recent statistics regarding societal neglect report that after a decade of decline, the rate of children living in low-income families is on the rise, a trend that began in 2000. Today, 1 in 6 children live below the poverty line (Children's Defense Fund, 2004). Although the largest group of children in low-income families is White, Black and Latino children are significantly more likely to live in families with low incomes, and these minority groups largely account for the increase in low-income children (National Center for Children in Poverty, 2004). Thus, although it is important to distinguish poverty from culture when conducting cultural research, it seems that for some cultural groups, the presence of poverty is so pervasive that it becomes difficult to consider one in isolation from the other.

Among minority groups, there is disproportionate representation of child maltreatment reports (Holton, 1992); however, nothing in regard to cultural practices among minorities has been identified as contributing to child abuse and neglect (National Resource Council, 1993). As a consequence of reported rate differences, many studies have searched for cultural practices that are presumed to cause these rates, yet among them are few systematic investigations linking culture to maltreatment (for exceptions, see, e.g., Coohey, 2001; Dubanoski, 1981; Dubanoski & Snyder, 1980). NIS data have not reported any significant relationships between race, culture or ethnicity and the incidence of child maltreatment in any of their national investigations (USDHHS, 1981, 1988; Sedlack & Broadhurst, 1996).

In keeping with an ecological transactional view, an investigation of cultural influences on development should look to assess the vulnerability and protective factors associated with the culture of interest, such that cultural vulnerability factors would increase the risk for the occurrence of maltreatment, whereas protective factors might contribute to resilient functioning. For example, a study investigating the relationship between neighborhood structural factors and child maltreatment in African American and European American neighborhoods (Korbin et al., 1998) found that although there was a relationship between poverty and rates of reported child maltreatment, the strength of the relationship was weaker in predominantly African American neighborhoods as compared to predominantly European American neighborhoods. The relationship between poverty and maltreatment was experienced differently between the two neighborhoods, each of which was characterized by different cultural values. The results of this investigation suggest that the African American neighborhoods had a stronger social cohesiveness that reduced the risk for the incidence of child maltreatment for individuals living in those neighborhoods. This is consistent with other research finding strong kinship and friendship links in African American communities (e.g., Stack, 1974).

However, in considering the developmental sequelae of maltreatment, several studies suggest that minority children who have been abused are at increased risk for maladaptation (Cohen, Deblinger, Mannarino, & Arellana, 2001). For example, sexually abused African American and Latino children have demonstrated higher rates of behavioral problems, depressive symptoms, and emotional trauma in comparison to demographically matched European American children (Morrow & Sorrell, 1989; Russell, 1986; Sanders-Phillips, Moisan, Wadlington, Morgan, & English, 1995). Unfortunately, there is a paucity of research investigating specific vulnerability and protective factors within cultures in the United States. To date, only one investigation of maltreated children has evaluated specific predictors of functioning within a minority culture (Flores, Cicchetti, & Rogosch, 2005; see section on resilience for further discussion).

EXOSYSTEM

The exosystem represents the social structures that form the immediate context in which families and individuals function. These structures include systems such as neighborhoods and the interconnections among its elements, such as school, peer group, church, and workplace (Bronfenbrenner, 1977), as well as informal social networks and formal support groups. The exosystem additionally refers to the availability of services, the availability of employment, and the socioeconomic climate (Cicchetti & Lynch, 1995).

Poverty is among the most salient aspects of the exosystem that has been associated with child maltreatment (Ards, Chung, & Meyers, 1998; Berger, 2004; Brown, Cohen, Johnson, & Salzinger, 1998; Gil, 1970; Lindsey, 1994; Waldfogel, 1998). It has long been recognized that poverty conditions may put families at risk for maltreatment as it causes increased stress for the family (Edelman, 1987; Huston, 1991; McLoyd & Wilson, 1991; Waldfogel, 2000), and as such, it may be an indirect precipitating factor in the occurrence of maltreatment. Whether the relationship between poverty and maltreatment operates

through direct or indirect mechanisms, it is clear that there is a strong co-occurrence of poverty and violence (J. L. Aber, 1994), and a number of studies have reported that low SES is a risk factor for violent behavior against children (Gelles & Straus, 1988; Straus & Kaufman-Kantor, 1986; Wolfner & Gelles, 1993).

Illustrating how factors from the exosystem and microsystem interact with each other, studies have focused on the independent additive and interactive effects of low SES and maltreatment on children's development (J. L. Aber, Allen, Carlson, & Cicchetti, 1989; Kaufman & Cicchetti, 1989; Okun, Parker, & Levendosky, 1994; Trickett, Aber, Carlson, & Cicchetti, 1991; Vondra, Barnett, & Cicchetti, 1989) by looking at the relation between poverty and specific family or parenting characteristics. For example, an investigation conducted with a population of urban African American young adults found that lower family income and younger caregiver age were related to reports of caregiver's high use of negative strategies (Koening, Ialongo, Wagner, Poduska, & Kellam, 2002). These results suggest that the youngest and poorest caregivers use negative parenting strategies more frequently. Additionally, indicators of poverty such as perceived material hardship and infrequent employment, combined with parenting characteristics such as low parental warmth and use of physical discipline have been found to be predictive of child neglect (Slack, Holl, McDaniel, Yoo, & Bolger, 2004).

Specifically regarding unemployment, periods of high unemployment have been found to correlate with increases in the incidence of child abuse (Steinberg, Catalano, & Dooley, 1981). A number of studies have reported a link between unemployment and child maltreatment (Gelles & Hargreaves, 1981; Gil, 1970; Whipple & Webster-Stratton, 1991; Wolfner & Gelles, 1993). As with poverty, unemployment can be conceptualized as an exosystem factor that causes family stress and, perhaps through an indirect relationship, increases the likelihood for child maltreatment.

In the context of particular neighborhoods, the experience of community violence is another factor that has received particular attention with regard to its relation to child maltreatment (Cicchetti & Lynch, 1993, 1995; Lynch & Cicchetti, 1998; Martinez & Richters, 1993; Richters & Martinez, 1993), as high rates of community violence create stressful environments for family and individual functioning. For example, Lynch and Cicchetti conducted a 1-year longitudinal study of 7- to 12-year-old children to examine the mutual relationships among community violence, child maltreatment, and children's functioning over time. Rates of child maltreatment, particularly physical abuse, were related to levels of child-reported violence in the community. Community violence was also related to the rate of physical abuse and the severity of neglect. Together, child maltreatment and exposure to community violence were related to different aspects of children's functioning; specific effects were observed for neglect and sexual abuse and for witnessing and being victimized by violence in the community. Exposure to community violence was related to children's functioning over and above the effects of more proximal contextual features (maltreatment). Consistent with an ecological-transactional perspective, there was evidence that children and their contexts mutually influence each other over time. Even after controlling for the effects of maltreatment status and prior effects of exposure to community violence, children's externalizing behaviors at Time 1 significantly predicted increased victimization by and witnessing of violence in the community at Time 2. Thus, this investigation established a clear relationship between community violence and child maltreatment and, moreover, provided empirical support for the ecological-transactional model of development.

Finally, social isolation and perceived lack of social support are additional aspects of the exosystem that have been associated with child maltreatment (Crouch, Milner, & Thomsen, 2001; Egeland, Bosquet, & Chung, 2002; Runtz & Schallow, 1997). Early studies by Garbarino and colleagues (Garbarino & Crouter, 1978; Garbarino & Sherman, 1980) have revealed that child abuse rates are higher in neighborhoods with fewer social resources in comparison to equally socioeconomically disadvantaged neighborhoods where resources are more plentiful. This link between child maltreatment and limited access to social and economic resources has also been associated with neglecting families (Dubowitz, 1999). Moreover, in high-abuse neighborhoods, parents often do not use the resources that are available to them for preventive services or interventions, such that social isolation from neighborhood networks, support groups, and extended family is commonly associated with maltreatment (Garbarino, 1977, 1982; Hunter & Kilstrom, 1979; Kempe, 1973). Child rearing can be influenced by information from educational resources, media, and social networks (Belsky, 1984; Garbarino & Gilliam, 1980; Sigel, 1986); however, maltreating parents who are isolated may not be exposed to the information that can improve their child-rearing beliefs and practices (Trickett & Sussman, 1988). Thus, social isolation among maltreating families leaves these families without support or resources that could improve their parenting practices and may contribute to the perpetuation of maltreatment (Berger, 2004; Dubowitz, 1999).

MICROSYSTEM

Broadly defined, the microsystem consists of any environmental setting that contains the developing person, including the home, the school, and the workplace (Bronfenbrenner, 1977). According to Belsky (1980), however, the microsystem is more narrowly represented as the family environment and, by extension, includes family dynamics as well as the parents' developmental histories, psychological resources, and child-rearing styles. With regard to child maltreatment, the microsystem can be conceptualized as the immediate environment or context in which the maltreatment occurs. The microsystem of maltreated children is characterized by stressful, chaotic, and uncontrollable events (Cicchetti & Lynch, 1993; P. W. Howes & Cicchetti, 1993; P. W. Howes, Cicchetti, Toth, & Rogosch, 2000), largely resulting from the most salient aspect of this system: the experience of maltreatment itself. Thus, the features of the maltreatment experience, such as type, severity, chronicity, and timing of maltreatment, are all characteristics of the maltreating microsystem (Cicchetti & Barnett, 1991b). Moreover, these features can have significant independent and interactive effects on child development (Manly et al., 1994, 2001) and have been associated with increased risk for specific developmental outcomes. For example, using hierarchical regression analysis, Manly and colleagues (2001) analyzed the contributions of developmental timing, maltreatment subtype, and maltreatment severity on a wide range of measures used to assess children's adjustment. The results highlighted the role of severity of emotional maltreatment in the infancy-toddlerhood period and physical abuse during the preschool period in predicting externalizing behavior and aggression; severity of physical neglect, particularly during the preschool period, was associated with internalizing symptomatology and withdrawn behavior. Chronic maltreatment, especially with onset in infancy-toddlerhood or the preschool period, was linked with more maladaptive outcomes.

Intergenerational Transmission of Child Maltreatment

In considering what might contribute to the onset of a maltreating family environment, considerable attention has been paid to parents' developmental histories. Among normative samples, there is ample evidence supporting the intergenerational transmission of parenting styles (Jacobvitz, Morgan, Kretchmar, & Morgan, 1991; van Ijzendoorn, 1992). Research regarding the intergenerational transmission of maltreatment has consistently supported the notion that individuals with a history of maltreatment are more likely to maltreat their own children (Buchanan, 1996; Cicchetti & Aber, 1980; Conger, Burgess, & Barrett, 1979; Coohey & Braun, 1997; Egeland, 1988; Egeland, Jacobvitz, & Papatola, 1987; Egeland et al., 2002; Hunter & Kilstrom, 1979; Kaufman & Zigler, 1989; Widom, 1989). Offering theoretical explanations for these findings, some have asserted that the intergenerational transmission of abusive parenting behaviors may be a product of socialization and social learning (Feshbach, 1978; Herzberger, 1983). Others, however, argue that transmission occurs through the development of maladaptive representational models, which parents develop from their own early caregiving experiences. These experiences are then internalized and integrated into their self structures, organizing their subsequent parenting behaviors (Bowlby, 1980; Sroufe & Fleeson, 1986). Alternatively, Farrington, Jolliffe, Loeber, Stouthamer-Loeber, and Kalb (2001) suggest several additional pathways to the intergenerational transmission of violence, including the influence of genetics on temperament and personality.

Although empirical evidence is consistent in supporting the risk of continuity of maltreatment among those who endured childhood abuse experience themselves, there is a wide range of reported rates of its occurrence. For example, one prospective study that followed infants from birth through age 5 reported that 7.4% of parents with an abuse history maltreated their children (K. D. Browne & Herbert, 1997). In contrast, a retrospective study of the transmission of child sexual abuse reported that 33% of sexually abusive men and 50% of sexually abusive women experienced childhood sexual abuse (Collin-Vezina & Cyr, 2003). This discrepancy in reported rates has been associated with several methodological problems, including variation among studies in sample size, criteria for inclusion, and length of follow-up and whether a prospective or retrospective design was utilized (Egeland et al., 2002; Pears & Capaldi, 2002). Reliance on retrospective report in particular can often lead to overestimation (e.g., Hunter & Kilstrom, 1979). Therefore, it is difficult to estimate the rate of intergenerational transmission of maltreatment, especially when considering the complex interaction of risk, protective, and mediating factors that contribute to its emergence (Dixon, Browne, & Hamilton-Giachritsis, 2005; Egeland, 1988).

Several studies have focused on elucidating the mechanisms through which maltreatment is transmitted from one generation to the next by identifying specific protective and vulnerability factors (Bugental & Happaney, 2004;

Collin-Vezina & Cyr, 2003; Dixon, Browne, et al., 2005; Dunn et al., 2002; Leifer, Kilbane, & Kalick, 2004). For example, in a prospective investigation of families with newborns where at least one of the parents was physically and/or sexually abused as a child, 6.7% committed maltreatment by the time their child was 13 months old, in comparison to .4% of comparison families (Dixon, Browne, et al., 2005). Additionally, the presence of three significant risk factors provided partial mediation for the intergenerational transmission of child maltreatment: becoming a parent before age 21, residing with a violent adult, and having a history of mental illness and/or depression. This is consistent with other investigations that have suggested that poor maternal psychosocial functioning may promote escalation of risk across generations (Bifulco et al., 2002; Leifer et al., 2004).

In an extension of their investigation, Dixon, Browne, and colleagues (2005) found that the presence of poor parenting styles also mediated the intergenerational cycle of child maltreatment, although to a lesser degree than risk factors previously identified. Specifically, parents who had maltreatment histories had more negative attributions and unrealistic perceptions of their children and engaged their children in less positive interactions than parents who had not been maltreated as children. The presence of these poor parenting characteristics, when considered together with being a parent before the age of 21, having a history of mental illness, and/or living with a violent adult, provided a full mediation of the intergenerational cycle of maltreatment (Dixon, Hamilton-Giachritsis, & Browne, 2005).

In addition to research that has investigated the intergenerational transmission of maltreatment in a broad sense, a number of studies have focused specifically on the perpetuation of child sexual abuse. For example, one prospective study of sexually abused males revealed that particular experiences and patterns of childhood behavior are associated with victims becoming abusers later in life (Salter et al., 2003). Risk factors during childhood that predicted later offending included maternal neglect, lack of supervision, sexual abuse by a female, and frequent witnessing of serious intrafamilial violence. Additional investigations of the intergenerational transmission of child sexual abuse have identified severity of abuse, insecure attachment relationships with parental figures, and dissociative symptomatology following abuse as important distinguishing factors between those who break the cycle of abuse and those who perpetuate it (Collin-Vezina & Cyr, 2003). Together, these studies highlight the impact of risk factors occurring within multiple levels of the ecology in contributing to the risk for the intergenerational transmission of child maltreatment.

Consistent with the principle of multifinality (Cicchetti & Rogosch, 1996), not all children who are maltreated go on to become abusive parents. Attempting to understand the mechanisms by which the cycle of maltreatment may be broken, a number of prospective studies have noted protective factors among parents who were maltreated but do not maltreat their own children (Collins-Vezina & Cyr, 2003; Egeland, Jacobvitz, & Sroufe, 1988; Hunter & Kilstrom, 1979); these factors include current social support, particularly from a supportive spouse, the past experience of a positive relationship with an adult during childhood, having undergone therapy either during adolescence or adulthood, and the absence of dissociative symptomatology following a prior experience of abuse. In relation to the therapy experience, those who can reflect on their own experiences of abuse with appropriate anger and who can direct responsibility for its occurrence to the perpetrator, rather than to the self, are less likely to maltreat their own children.

According to Cicchetti and Lynch (1993), in the ecological-transactional model, the balance among risk and protective factors in one's environment determines the likelihood of maltreatment's occurrence and influences the course of subsequent adaptation or maladaptation. Therefore, the presence of enduring protective factors and transient buffers may promote adaptation, such as the ability to break the cycle of abuse. Relatedly, the presence of enduring vulnerability factors and transient challengers increases the potential of conditions that support maltreatment. Thus, potentiating factors that are present at more proximal levels of the ecology (such as the microsystem) might help explain the mechanisms through which maltreatment is transmitted from one generation to the next. Additionally, an imbalance between protective and vulnerability factors where potentiating processes are heavily favored in the midst of few positive buffers may provide an account for the development of new maltreatment behaviors in individuals who were not themselves maltreated.

Personal Resources of Maltreating Parents

The resources of parents in maltreating families also contribute to the construction of the microsystem. A number of studies have identified areas of functioning, both psychological and biological, in which maltreating parents have demonstrated deficits (see Azar, 2002, for review). For example, parents who become abusive have been described as less psychologically complex and personally integrated than parents who do not maltreat their children (Brunquell, Crichton, & Egeland, 1981). Parental psychopathology has been associated with an increased risk for maltreatment, specifically in regard to depression (Burke, 2003; Lahey, Conger, Atkeson, & Treiber, 1984; Sloan & Meier, 1983) and parental drug use (Ondersma, 2002; Windham et al., 2004; Wolfner & Gelles, 1993). Thus, the interaction of parental psychopathology with the experience of maltreatment poses a serious threat to normal child development (Walker, Downey, & Bergman, 1989).

Additionally, the ability to cope with stress has been well researched in relation to the risk for child maltreatment. Several studies have noted that maltreating parents lack impulse control, especially when aroused or stressed (Altemeier, O'Connor, Vietze, Sandler, & Sherrod, 1982; Brunquell et al., 1981), and suggest that perhaps they are biologically predisposed to overreact to stressful stimuli (McCanne & Milner, 1991; Milner, 2000). In light of the various macrosystem and exosystem challenges that face maltreating families, each of which contribute to the experience of stress, the failure to cope with stressful life events (Crittenden, 1985; Wolfe, 1985) does not bode well for maltreating individuals' ability to successfully handle the challenges associated with parenting (Cicchetti & Lynch, 1995).

FAMILY DYNAMICS/SYSTEMS

Maltreating families are commonly characterized by maladaptive and disruptive relationships. Moreover, anger and conflict are pervasive features of maltreating families (Trickett & Sussman, 1988), within which violent parents are likely to attack multiple family members. Several studies have supported the association between exposure to domestic violence and child maltreatment (Duncan, 1999; Edelson, 1999; Perry, Hodges, & Egan, 2001; Windham et al., 2004). Evidence regarding interparental aggression suggests that witnessing such conflict affects children's developing beliefs about close relationships and as such may contribute to later problems in social and emotional functioning (Grych, Wachsmuth-Schlaefer, & Klockow, 2002).

Whereas interpersonal conflict may be more characteristic of abusive families, social isolation may be more characteristic of neglecting families (Crittenden, 1985), limiting children's exposure to fewer nonparental models of emotional communication (Salzinger, Feldman, Hammer, & Rosario, 1993). In general, however, husbands and wives in maltreating families are less warm and supportive, less satisfied in their conjugal relationships, and more aggressive and violent than spousal partners in nonabusive families (P. W. Howes & Cicchetti, 1993; Margolin, 1998; A. Rosenbaum & O'Leary, 1981; Rosenberg, 1987; Straus, Gelles, & Steinmetz, 1980; Straus & Kaufman-Kantor, 1986).

A distinctive feature that has been noted in maltreating families is the chaotic and unstable nature of the family system, often characterized by a shifting constellation of adult and child figures moving into and out of the home (Polansky, Gaudin, & Kilpatrick, 1992). Recently, the application of a systems approach to understanding family interactions in maltreating families has received particular attention, as Davies and Cicchetti (2004) urge researchers toward better integration of developmental psychopathology and family systems constructs in guiding future research. Family systems theory (Minuchin, 1985) emphasizes the reciprocal relationships between various subsystems within the family (family dyads, triads, etc.). The principal goal in family systems research is to achieve a comprehensive rendering of the interplay among relationships and individuals in the whole family unit, with a specific focus on identifying relationship structures, interpersonal boundaries, power distributions, and communication patterns (Cox & Paley, 1997; Minuchin, 1985).

Most family systems research to date has focused on family conflict and marital conflict in relation to punishment of children and the development of aggression, and has not been conducted specifically with maltreating families. They are mentioned here, however, because understanding the emergence of patterns of physical conflict may provide information regarding the escalation of this conflict into child maltreatment. For example, one prospective study suggests that marital conflict and parental individual hostility has been associated with an increased risk for more frequent and severe physical punishment of children at ages 2 and 5 (Kanoy, Ulku-Steiner, Cox, & Burchinal, 2003). Additional work has linked parental physical aggression between partners (or in dyads where one is the aggressor and one is victim) to increased direct physical aggression toward their children (Mahoney, Donnelly, Boxer, & Lewis, 2003). Marital aggression was linked to externalizing problems among parents and children and also to children's internalizing problems. This provides support for the notion that individual parent and child characteristics as well as marital qualities must be examined in the context of the whole family over time to gain an understanding of the emergence of physical punishment patterns.

With respect to maltreating families, P. W. Howes et al. (2000) coded aspects of affective, organizational, and relational features in maltreating and nonmaltreating family units. Through this family systems analysis, some maltreating families could be reliably identified on the basis of systemic differences. Specifically, sexually abusive families had more difficulty regulating anger, evidenced more chaos and less role clarity, and relied less on adaptive-flexible relationship strategies than nonmaltreating families. Thus, P. W. Howes and colleagues posit that a pattern of disorganized roles and chaotic interactions, in combination with affect dysregulation and rigid relationship skills, are discriminating characteristics of sexually abusive family systems. This study highlights that a disorganized family structure may be as detrimental to children as the specific forms of abuse they suffer. The importance of family climate and structure, above and beyond individual maltreatment acts, has vast implications for the development of intervention and prevention policies, underscoring the need for interventions at the family level beyond those that are targeted solely at children (for further discussion, see later section on intervention and prevention).

Parenting Styles

Considering ecological proximity to the child, the actual parenting styles and attitudes that maltreating parents contribute to the family microsystem may have the most direct impact on their children's ontogenic development (Cicchetti & Lynch, 1993). In general, studies of parent-child interactions among maltreating families have revealed maladaptive and differential behaviors in maltreating families in comparison to nonmaltreating families. Maltreating parents are less satisfied with their children, perceive child rearing as more difficult and less enjoyable, use more controlling disciplinary techniques, do not encourage the development of autonomy in their children, and promote an isolated lifestyle for themselves and their children (Azar, 2002; Rogosch, Cicchetti, Shields, & Toth, 1995; Trickett et al., 1991; Trickett & Kuczynski, 1986; Trickett & Sussman, 1988). Specifically, abusive parents tend to show fewer physical and verbal behaviors to direct their children's attention (Alessandri, 1992; Bousha & Twentyman, 1984), have more unrealistic expectations of their child (Putallaz, Costanzo, Grimes, & Sherman, 1998), and attribute more negative intentions to their child's behavior in comparison to nonmaltreating parents (Dixon, Hamilton-Giachritsis, et al., 2005; Zeanah & Zeanah, 1989).

Abusive parents also show less positive affect and a low degree of reciprocity during dyadic interactions (Burgess & Conger, 1978; Lahey et al., 1984) and are less supportive, playful and responsive to their children (Burgess & Conger, 1978; Egeland, Breitenbucher, & Rosenberg, 1980; Kavanaugh, Youngblade, Reid, & Fagot, 1988; Reid,

Kavanaugh, & Baldwin, 1987; Trickett & Sussman, 1988; Twentyman & Plotkin, 1982). Even with infants, abusive mothers have been described as more controlling, interfering, and hostile (Crittenden, 1981, 1985). Moreover, abusive mothers consistently show higher rates of aversive behavior directed toward their children than do nonabusive mothers (Cerezo, 1997), with average rates as much as twice the rate of aversive behavior displayed by nonmaltreating mothers (Cerezo & D'Ocon, 1995). This is significant in light of the evidence that aversive behavior is more likely to be reciprocated, escalating into negative exchanges of longer duration than in nonabusive families (Loeber, Felton, & Reid, 1984). Regarding neglecting families, neglecting mothers tend to hold few expectations for their children, may be inconsistent in their response to them, and lack the ability to follow through with age-appropriate limits when upset (Crittenden, 1988).

Serious distortions in the parent-child relationship have often been noted in maltreating families, such that children are faced with the inappropriate expectation that the child should act as a caretaker for the parent (P. W. Howes & Cicchetti, 1993). Thus, children act as though they have traded roles with their caregiver (Dean, Malik, Richards, & Stringer, 1986), as the child appears to be the more nurturing and sensitive member of the dyad. Further support for the "parentification" phenomenon has been demonstrated through the analysis of narratives of maltreated preschoolers (Macfie et al., 1999). In this investigation, children completed story stems that introduced stressful family situations. Results indicated that maltreated children portrayed parents and children as responding to distress less often. Maltreated children portrayed themselves stepping into the story more often to relieve children's distress than did nonmaltreated preschoolers, thereby taking on the nurturing role. It seems that such role reversal may be indicative of a developing internal working model to give care rather than to receive it. (See later section on internal working models for further discussion of narrative representation among maltreated children.)

Finally, significant differences have emerged in terms of disciplinary practices of maltreating parents. Maltreating parents have been described as less verbal in approaching conflict resolution (Silber, 1990) and less successful at handling discipline confrontation (Rogosch, Cicchetti, Shields, et al., 1995). With regard to perceptual differences, abusive parents are more likely to view their children as aggressive, intentionally disobedient, and annoying, even when other observers fail to detect such differences (Dixon, Hamilton-Giachritsis, et al., 2005; Mash, John-ston, & Kovitz, 1983; Reid et al., 1987). Thus, differences in maltreating parents' perceptions and expectations of their children may contribute to the adoption of inappropriate disciplinary practices (Milner & Chilamkurti, 1991). For example, maltreating parents are more likely to use punishment, threats, coercion, and power assertion and less likely to use reasoning and affection in disciplining and controlling their children (Chilamkurti & Milner, 1993; Loeber et al., 1984; Oldershaw, Walters, & Hall, 1986; Trickett & Sussman, 1988). Furthermore, the disciplinary action chosen is less likely to be contingent on the type of behavior displayed by the child and may be age-inappropriate (Crittenden, 1981; Trickett & Kuczynski, 1986). Additionally, abusive parents are more intrusive, more inconsistent, and less flexible in their attempts to gain compliance from their children (Oldershaw et al., 1986), all of which are negatively associated with the development of internalization of parental ideals (Grusec & Goodnow, 1994). Thus, the negative discipline practices of maltreating parents may contribute to a cycle of escalating harsh parenting as children fail to internalize their parents' values and continue to behave in opposition to their parents' maladaptive expectations.

Some contend that rather than specific parental values, whole relationships are internalized and perpetuated by the individual, such that relationship history can influence children's attitudes, affects, and cognitions, organizing the self and shaping individual development (Sroufe & Fleeson, 1988). As a whole, maltreating families do not successfully resolve the salient issues of family development (Cicchetti & Howes, 1991); instead, maltreating parents do little to foster the success of their children as they face each stage-salient developmental challenge (cf. Cicchetti, 1989, 1990). Thus, maltreated children may be at a disadvantage to face subsequent challenges as the negative potentiating factors, which pervade their microsystem, may be internalized and carried throughout the life span.

PSYCHOLOGICAL ONTOGENIC DEVELOPMENT

The failure of the average expectable environment that is represented by child maltreatment culminates in its effects on children's ontogenic development. At the level of psychological ontogenic development, the negotiation of central tasks of each developmental period organizes one's developmental trajectory toward subsequent competence or incompetence (Cicchetti, 1989; Cicchetti & Lynch, 1995). An ecological-transactional perspective views child development as a progressive sequence of age- and stage-appropriate tasks in which successful resolution of tasks at each developmental level must be coordinated and integrated with the environment, as well as with subsequently emerging issues across the life span (Cicchetti & Lynch, 1993). These tasks include the development of emotion regulation, the formation of attachment relationships, the development of an autonomous self, symbolic development, moral development, the formation of peer relationships, adaptation to school, and personality organization. Thus, stage-salient tasks are hierarchically organized as each new task builds on and is influenced by the resolution of previous developmental tasks. Poor resolution of stage-salient issues may contribute to maladaptation over time as prior history influences the selection, engagement, and interpretation of subsequent experience; however, the current context is in constant transaction with environmental supports (Sroufe, Carlson, Levy, & Egeland, 1999). Thus, ontogenic development is a lifelong dynamic task, and consistent with Gottlieb's (1991, 1992) notions of probabilistic epigenesis, individuals are continually affected by new biological and psychological experiences, leaving developmental pathways susceptible to modification throughout the life span (Cicchetti & Lynch, 1995).

Emotion Regulation

Emotion regulation, conceptualized as the ability to modulate one's emotional arousal such that an optimal level of engagement with the environment is fostered, is a developmentally acquired process that emerges from increasing differentiation and hierarchical integration of biological and psychological systems (Cicchetti, 1993; Cicchetti, Ganiban, & Barnett, 1991; Cicchetti & Sroufe, 1978; Shields & Cicchetti, 1997). Emotion regulation evolves as a function of both intrinsic features and extrinsic socioemotional experiences within the context of early parent-child interactions (A. Maughan & Cicchetti, 2002; Thompson, 1990, 1994). At the biological level, important intraorganismic factors for the development of emotion regulation include organizational changes in central nervous system functioning, cerebral hemispheric lateralization, and the development of neurotransmitter systems (Cicchetti et al., 1991; Davidson, 1984; N. A. Fox & Davidson, 1984; Kelley & Stinus, 1984; Sperry, 1982; Tucker, 1981). Extraorganismically, children's emotional experiences, expressiveness, and arousal are influenced by care-

givers' response to and tolerance of affect. Parents' socialization of affective displays during early interpersonal exchanges serve as the model through which aspects of emotional regulation may be learned (Hesse & Cicchetti, 1982; Stern, 1985; Thompson, 1990).

Given the severe disturbances in the average expected environment provided by maltreating families, considerable evidence has mounted to demonstrate the detrimental effects of maltreatment on children's emotional development and regulation. Specifically, maltreated children have shown deviations in a number of processes that underlie the development of emotion regulation; these include emotion expression (e.g., Gaensbauer, 1982), recognition (e.g., Camras, Sacks-Alter, & Ribordy, 1996; Pollak, Cicchetti, Hornung, & Reed, 2000), understanding (e.g., Shipman, Zeman, Penza, & Champion, 2000), and communication (e.g., Beeghly & Cicchetti, 1994).

Emotion Expression

Divergence in maltreated children's emotional expression has been noted as early as 3 months of age, where severely physically abused infants have evinced increased rates of fearfulness, anger, and sadness during mother-infant interactions (Gaensbauer, Mrazek, & Harmon, 1981). The expression of fear and anger among physically abused infants at 3 months of age is a particularly salient finding considering that the normative ontogenic development of these affects does not typically occur until approximately 7 to 9 months of age (Sroufe, 1996). In contrast, neglected infants displayed an attenuated range of emotional expression and an increased duration of negative affect as compared to nonmaltreated infants (Gaensbauer et al., 1981).

To examine the affective input that maltreated children receive, Camras and colleagues (1988, 1990) conducted a series of investigations of maternal facial expressions. When asked to deliberately produce facial expressions, maltreating mothers' demonstrations of emotion faces were less easily identified by observers than were the expressions of nonmaltreating mothers (Camras et al., 1988). During mother-child interactions, maltreating mothers differed from nonmaltreating mothers with regard to the expression of sadness (Camras et al., 1990). Taken together, the emotion displays of abused and neglected infants highlights the centrality of interactions with caregivers in shaping the development of affect expression or differentiation. Moreover, maternal emotional expression ability contributes to their children's ability to recognize facial emotion (Camras et al., 1988). Thus, maltreated children are already at risk for differential emotion regulation developmental trajectories within the first 3 months of life.

Emotional Recognition

The ability to identify basic emotions from both facial and contextual cues is normatively mastered by the preschool years (Reichenbach & Masters, 1983; Walden & Field, 1982). Maltreated children, however, have demonstrated less accurate recognition of emotions than nonmaltreating children, above and beyond the effects of cognitive ability (Camras, Grow, & Ribordy, 1983; Camras et al., 1988; During & McMahon, 1991). Further investigation by Camras and colleagues (1990), however, has revealed that despite overall deficits in emotion recognition performance, analysis of maltreated children's processing errors suggested that maltreated children have a selective bias, or hypersensitivity, toward the detection of anger.

Developmentally, early limitations on the capacity for information processing require children to focus their attention on only the most salient aspects of the environment (Bjorklund, 1997); thus, children's emotional development is contingent on what is experienced. For physically abused children, displays of anger may be the greatest predictor of threat, often experienced as the most salient aspect of the environment. As such, Pollak et al. (2000) hypothesized that physically abused preschool children would demonstrate an increased sensitivity to anger-related cues perhaps also resulting in decreased attention to other emotional cues. The results of their study revealed that when physically abused children were exposed to a perceptual scaling task, they perceived angry faces as highly salient and more distinctive relative to other emotion categories (Pollak et al., 2000). Additionally, when asked to match facial expressions to an emotional situation, physically abused children showed a response bias for anger such that when they were uncertain which facial expression to choose, they showed a lower threshold for selecting anger. Moreover, physically abused children have displayed more broad perceptual category boundaries for perceiving anger than nonmaltreated children (Pollak & Kistler, 2002) and have required less visual information to detect the presence of angry facial expressions (Pollak & Sinha, 2002).

Consistent with behavioral findings, psychophysiological studies using event-related potentials (ERPs) have also provided support for the notion that physically abused children allocate more processing resources when attending to anger, but respond similarly to nonmaltreated children when attending to happy and fearful faces (Pollak, Cicchetti, Klorman, & Brumaghim, 1997; Pollak, Klorman,

Thatcher, & Cicchetti, 2001; Pollak & Tolley-Schell, 2003; see later section on cognitive brain event-related potentials). Thus, it seems that physically abused children do not have emotion recognition or affective information-processing deficits in a global sense; rather, differential processing of emotion appears to be specific to anger. It is certainly conceivable that an increased sensitivity to anger might be adaptive for physically abused children, as it would allow for hypervigilant detection of potential threats, but successful regulation includes the capacity for flexibility and control over attention. Pollak and Tolley-Schell posit that early experiences of abuse may alter the development of perceptual systems by decreasing the minimum amount of threat-related stimulation needed to engage focused attention on the threat-inducing stimuli; if physically abused children respond more quickly and/or strongly to signals of threat, then problems disengaging attention away from anger may emerge. Using a selective attention paradigm with an affective component, both physiological and behavioral measures were employed to assess children's orienting reaction and response time during valid trials, and children's disengagement reaction and response time during invalid trials (Pollak & Tolley-Schell, 2003). Psychophysiological data confirmed the hypothesis that physically abused children demonstrate a selective increase in ERP response (as measured by P3B) on invalid angry trials, providing evidence that increased attentional resources were required to disengage from previously cued angry faces only. Physically abused children also demonstrated faster reaction times in the valid angry condition, consistent with the notion that abused children orient rapidly to cues primed by anger. There were no differences, however, in physically abused children's psychophysiological responses or reaction times to happy trials, providing further support for a specific or differential deficit involving attentional processing of anger.

It is possible that the early expression of fear, anger, and sadness that emerges among physically abused infants within the first 3 months of life reflects deviations at the neural level, whereby fear-processing synapses are strengthened and/or positive affect-processing synapses are pruned, leading to later deviations in attentional control in response to anger-related cues. These emotion recognition and processing biases, which develop during the 1st year of life, could leave physically abused children vulnerable to unsuccessful resolution of stage-salient developmental tasks. For example, one possible pathway to maladaptation might include a predisposition for developing an atypical pattern of attachment, especially given that the development of disorganized attachment has been linked to early experiences of fear (Cicchetti & Lynch, 1993). At subsequent developmental levels, physically abused children might also be predisposed to manifest social information-processing deficits and difficulties with peer relationships. Social information biases that are prevalent among maltreated children's peer interactions indicate that maltreated children are more, rather than less, likely to respond to angry or aggressive emotional cues (Dodge, Pettit, & Bates, 1990; Dodge et al., 1997; Rieder & Cicchetti, 1989); thus, later social biases are consistent with early attentional biases in response to expressions of anger.

Emotional Behavioral Reactivity

Further evidence supports the persistence of emotion dysregulation into the preschool and school-age years, as demonstrated by studies of maltreated children's emotional behavioral reactivity to exposure to interadult anger (Cummings, Hennessy, Rabideau, & Cicchetti, 1994; Hennessy, Rabideau, Cicchetti, & Cummings, 1994; A. Maughan & Cicchetti, 2002). Specifically, physically abused school-age children display more fear in response to videotaped angry adult interactions as compared to nonabused comparison children who are matched on exposure to interpersonal aggression (Hennessey et al., 1994). Physically abused boys in particular show more aggression as well as more coping responses (i.e., intervening in the angry exchange or comforting mother) during exposure to live simulations of interadult anger (Cummings et al., 1994). Extending these findings, A. Maughan and Cicchetti applied a person-oriented approach to assess how different maltreatment experiences (physical abuse and neglect), in conjunction with a history of exposure to interadult violence, may impact children's emotion regulation abilities in response to live simulations of interadult anger directed toward their mother. Results indicated that maltreatment alone predicted children's complex patterns of emotion; neither interadult violence nor its interaction with maltreatment accounted for children's emotional response patterns to the interadult anger. Moreover, approximately 80% of the maltreated children evidenced dysregulated emotion patterns (undercontrolled/ambivalent or overcontrolled/unresponsive), in comparison to only 36% of the nonmaltreated children (A. Maughan & Cicchetti, 2002). Notably, the emotional response patterns of maltreated children provide support for Davies and Cummings's (1994) emotional security hypothesis that emotional security is largely determined by familial relations in the early care-giving environment. With regard to maltreated children, unpredictable and threatening interpersonal exchanges that occur during direct and indirect interactions with the caregiver often characterize their early environment, resulting in children's increased emotional insecurity. Without adequate emotional security, a child's self-regulatory abilities may be easily overwhelmed by environmental stressors, leading to the development of over- and underregulation (Cole, Michel, & Teti, 1994), as exemplified by the high rate of emotional dysregulation patterns found among maltreated children (A. Maughan & Cicchetti, 2002).

Maladaptive emotion regulation has additionally been observed among maltreated children during peer interactions. To investigate emotion regulation abilities among school-age children, Shields and Cicchetti (1997) developed an emotion regulation Q-sort to address the lack of available methods for the assessment of observed emotion regulation beyond early childhood. Both demonstrating convergent and divergent validity, the Emotion Regulation Q-sort was able to distinguish between maltreated and nonmaltreated children on the basis of whether their emotions were regulated or dysregulated. Through further applications of this methodology, Shields and Cicchetti (1998) demonstrated the relation of emotion dysregulation and attention to the development of reactive aggression among maltreated children. Specifically, maltreated children are more likely to show increased rates of aggression, as well as increased distractability, overactivity, and poor concentration (characteristic of children with deficits in attention modulation). Furthermore, attention deficits mediated the effects of maltreatment on emotional lability/negativity, inappropriate affect, and attenuated emotion regulation. Therefore, it seems that attention processes (which may have their roots in early anger recognition biases that develop during infancy) may interact with negative representations and maladaptive social information processing to foster emotional negativity and reactivity among maltreated children; this in turn seems to provoke reactive aggression, particularly among children with histories of physical abuse.

Additionally, evidence supports that emotional dysregulation may mediate the increased risk of bullying and victimization that has been noted among maltreated children (Shields & Cicchetti, 2001), highlighting how the internalization of salient aspects of the early caregiving relationship may have maladaptive implications among these children. As maltreated children are victimized by parents, they may develop a working model of relationships as dangerous and malevolent that incorporates the roles of both bully and victim. These cognitive-affective structures may then guide behaviors and peer interactions, promoting emotional constriction or atypical emotional responsiveness and coloring children's interpretations of the behavior of social partners.

FORMATION OF
ATTACHMENT RELATIONSHIPS

The formation of attachment relationships represents a major stage-salient developmental task for toddlers, beginning approximately at the end of the 1st year of life. While overt patterns of attachment emerge around 12 months of age, parent-child interactions throughout the 1st year create the context for early affect regulation experiences, physiological regulation, and biobehavioral patterns of response, all of which become the foundation from which the capacity for attachment emerges (Gunnar & Nelson, 1994; Hofer, 1987; Pipp & Harmon, 1987; Spangler & Grossman, 1993). Infants rely on their early experiences with their caregivers to derive a sense of security, and they use this relationship as a base from which to explore the environment (Sroufe, 1979). Thus, it is essential for the caregiver to be sensitive, responsive, and reliable, so that the child may use these regularities to develop internal models and create expectations for the future. The absence of contingent responsiveness on the part of parents can impede infants' ability to develop feelings of security in their primary attachment relationship (Sroufe & Waters, 1977).

Ultimately, successful resolution of this developmental task is for the child to be able to enter into a goal-corrected partnership where the caregiver and the child share internal states and goals (Bowlby, 1969/1982; Cicchetti, Cummings, Greenberg, & Marvin, 1990). The child forms representational models of the self, other, and self in relation to the other through negotiations and interactions within the primary caregiving relationship (Bowlby, 1969/1982). The mental representational models that emerge from interactions in the first attachment relationship organize children's affects, cognitions, and expectations about future interactions, thereby influencing all subsequent relationships (Cicchetti & Lynch, 1993; A. Nash & Hay, 1993; Sroufe, 1989; Sroufe, Carlson, & Shulman, 1993).

Studies of attachment among maltreated children, using the classic Strange Situation paradigm (Ainsworth & Wittig, 1969), have consistently found that maltreated children are more likely than nonmaltreated children to form insecure attachments with their caregivers (Cicchetti & Bar-

nett, 1991a; Crittenden, 1985; Egeland & Sroufe, 1981; Lamb, Gaensbauer, Malkin, & Schultz, 1985; Schneider-Rosen, Braunwald, Carlson, & Cicchetti, 1985). Utilizing the traditional classification scheme for attachment relationships, in which children may be classified as Type A, anxious avoidant; Type B, securely attached; or Type C, anxious resistant (Ainsworth, Blehar, Waters, & Wall, 1978), these early studies found that two-thirds of maltreated children displayed insecure attachment (Types A or C), whereas the reverse pattern was true in nonmaltreated children (Schneider-Rosen et al., 1985; Youngblade & Belsky, 1989).

The attachment behaviors of maltreated children, however, were frequently described as difficult to fit within this original attachment classification schema (e.g., Egeland & Sroufe, 1981); instead, maltreated children showed inconsistent or disorganized strategies for dealing with separations and reunions with their caregivers. Consequently, the observation of the attachment behaviors of maltreated children led to the identification of an additional pattern of attachment, named disorganized attachment, or Type D, by Main and Solomon (1990). Because inconsistent care is a hallmark of maltreating families, it is quite likely that parenting that is insensitively overstimulating (associated with avoidant attachment) and insensitively understimulating (associated with resistant attachment) may pervade parent-infant interactions in maltreating families (Belsky, Rovine, & Taylor, 1984; Crittenden, 1985; Lyons-Ruth, Connell, Zoll, & Stahl, 1987). The combination of these two contradictory caregiving styles could lead to the inconsistent behaviors that characterize Type D attachment (Cicchetti & Lynch, 1995). Beyond disorganization, infants with Type D attachment also often display bizarre behaviors in the presence of their caregiver, such as interrupted movements and expressions, apprehension, dazing, freezing, and stilling behaviors (see also Fraiberg, 1982).

Relatedly, Crittenden (1988) identified yet another atypical pattern of attachment through observation of maltreated children. This pattern, which she labeled avoidant-resistant or Type A-C attachment, describes a pattern encompassing displays of moderate to high levels of both avoidant and resistant attachment behaviors. There are theoretical distinctions between Main and Solomon's (1990) Type D attachment and Crittenden's (1988, 1992) Type A-C attachment; however, most researchers have come to consider the Type A-C pattern as a subset of behaviors within the range of Type D attachment patterns (Cicchetti, Toth, & Lynch, 1995). Regardless, there is consensus in the field that both Type A-C and Type D attachments represent atypical patterns of attachment that are distinct from secure and insecure patterns.

Apart from their association with maltreatment, atypical attachment patterns are also linked to having a caregiver with depression, substance abuse, or unresolved loss or trauma resulting from the parent's own childhood attachments (Ainsworth & Eichberg, 1991; Cicchetti et al., 1995; Lyons-Ruth, Repacholi, McLeod, & Silva, 1991; Main & Hesse, 1990; Teti, Gelfand, Messinger, & Isabella, 1995). Thus, converging evidence supports the role of experience in the development of disorganized patterns of attachment, which is not unique to the experience of maltreatment per se, but may emerge from the context of severely disturbed parenting.

Using revised attachment schemes to include the classification of atypical attachment in addition to traditional secure and insecure patterns, there is a huge preponderance of atypical or insecure attachment among maltreated children (Barnett, Manly, & Cicchetti, 1999; Carlson, Cicchetti, Barnett, & Braunwald, 1989; Crittenden, 1988; Lyons-Ruth, Connell, & Zoll, 1989; Lyons-Ruth et al., 1987). Many studies report attachment insecurity for maltreated children to be 80% to 90%. Specific to Type D attachment, apart from Type A or C insecure patterns, studies have reported that up to 80% of maltreated infants display disorganized patterns of attachment compared to rates of approximately 20% of Type D attachment among demographically comparable, low SES, nonmaltreated children (Carlson et al., 1989). A meta-analysis of disorganized attachment in early childhood reports about 15% Type D attachment in normative middle-class families; in other social contexts, such as the case of child maltreatment, rates are far higher (van Ijzendoorn, Schuengel, & Bakermans-Kranenburg, 1999).

Substantial stability in insecure patterns has also been noted among maltreated children, whereas those that display initial secure attachments tend to become insecure over time (Cicchetti & Barnett, 1991b; Schneider-Rosen et al., 1985). The opposite pattern tends to be true for nonmaltreated children such that secure attachment is stable, and children who are insecurely attached are likely to develop secure attachment (Lamb, Thompson, Garnder, & Charnov, 1985). Providing further support for the stability of insecure attachment across 12, 18, and 24 months, Barnett, Ganiban, and Cicchetti (1999) found support for a strong association between child maltreatment in infancy and the development of Type D attachment. Specifically, 66.7% of children were classified as Type D at both 12 and 18 months, with maltreated infants significantly more likely then nonmaltreated infants to be classified as Type D

at both ages (56% versus 19% for maltreated and comparison infants, respectively). Moreover, this pattern persisted at least through the toddler years, such that 81.3% of children classified as Type D at 18 months received the same classification at 24 months (Barnett et al., 1999). These findings suggest that Type D attachment is not transitory, reinforcing the notion that early attachment relationships organize future behavior. Additionally, this study extended our knowledge regarding the development of Type D attachment through the inclusion of measures of child temperament such as negative expressivity. Analyses revealed that Type D attachment is not a function of children's negative expressivity, indicating discriminant validity for the construct, nor is negative expressivity related to maltreatment, thus lending support to the notion that infant difficulty does not predispose one to maltreatment. Also, as rates of parenting problems increased in severity, atypical patterns of attachment increased and secure attachment patterns decreased, highlighting the influence of parenting behaviors on Type D attachment. Finally, attachment disorganization predicted the degree and direction of child vocal distress change such that the securely attached children decreased in vocal distress as they matured, but the Type D attached children increased in vocal distress between 12 and 18 months, suggesting that attachment disorganization may disrupt the development of emotional regulatory systems (Barnett et al., 1999).

Further research on the relationship between emotion and disorganized attachment has identified frightened and frightening behavior associated with the caregiver as central to the development of disorganized attachment. Once fear becomes connected to the caregiver, the child may become unable to rely on the attachment figure as a source of security or safety (Lyons-Ruth, Bronfman, & Parsons, 1999; Main & Hesse, 1990). The experience and expression of fear, which emerges early among many maltreated children, may impair children's ability to regulate and organize their affect during activation of their attachment system (Cicchetti & Lynch, 1993). Additional support for a link between disorganized attachment and the development of emotion regulation problems has been provided through physiological evidence. For example, children with Type D attachments have been found to display indices of physiological stress, such as increased heart rate and salivary cortisol responses, to the Strange Situation; infants with secure attachments do not display such stress responses (Hertsgaard, Gunnar, Erickson, & Nachmias, 1995; Spangler & Grossman, 1993). Similar patterns of physiological dysregulation have been associated with infants placed into foster care (Dozier, Levine, Stovall, & Eldreth, 2001).

Considering that all children who enter foster care have experienced severe disruptions in their relationships with primary caregivers, and that many have experienced maltreatment prior to their entrance into the foster care system, atypical patterns of glucocorticoid production among these youngsters underscores the relationship between attachment insecurity and emotion regulation difficulties.

The stability of early atypical attachment among maltreated children places them at extreme disadvantage to achieve adaptive outcomes in other domains of self- and interpersonal development (Cicchetti & Lynch, 1993). Consistent with the transactional nature of development, early attachment does not cause later maladaptation in a linear function; rather, prior history influences the subsequent selection, engagement, and interpretation of experience. Thus, early insecurity in attachment can be conceptualized as an "initiator of pathways probabilistically associated with later pathology" (Sroufe et al., 1999, p. 1). Among the developmental sequelae associated with insecure attachment are the presence of externalizing and internalizing symptomatology (Lyons-Ruth & Easterbrooks, 1995), problematic stress management, elevated risk for externalizing problem behavior, and the tendency to develop dissociative behavior later in life (Ogawa, Sroufe, Weinfield, Carlson, & Egeland, 1997; van Ijzendoorn et al., 1999). Additionally, maltreated children's representational models, which develop in the context of the attachment relationship, may moderate the effects of maltreatment on children's perceived competence and depressive symptomatology (Toth & Cicchetti, 1996). Furthermore, evidence supports that insecure patterns of attachment will persist into adulthood, contributing to difficulties with family relationships (Bartholemew, 1990; Crittenden, 1988; Crittenden & Ainsworth, 1989; Feldman & Downey, 1994; P. W. Howes & Cicchetti, 1993; Main & Goldwyn, 1984). For example, in examining results of the Adult Attachment Interview among maltreating parents, Crittenden, Partridge, and Claussen (1991) reported rates of either both dismissing, both preoccupied-engaged, or one of each within the maltreating couple that exceeded 90%. This was in stark contrast to demographically matched nonmaltreating couples where secure attachments from both partners were more likely. Among maltreating couples, however, unions between two securely attached individuals or between one secure and one insecure individual were nearly nonexistent, providing evidence for assortative mating that may perpetuate the intergenerational transmission of insecure attachment patterns as well as child maltreatment. From an ecological-transactional perspective, the primary attachment relationship remains a salient developmental

issue across the life span, as it lays the foundation for representational models and subsequently shapes an individual's selection, engagement, and interpretation of all future experiences, including the ability to successfully resolve ensuing developmental tasks.

DEVELOPMENT OF AN AUTONOMOUS SELF

The infant's concept of self is believed to emerge from early parent-child interactions within the context of the primary caregiving relationship (Bowlby, 1988; Bretherton & Waters, 1985; Emde, 1983; Mahler, Pine, & Bergman, 1975; Sroufe, 1989; Stern, 1989). Secure attachment to mother is associated with a number of adaptive self processes, including, for example, more complex self-knowledge (Pipp, Easterbrooks, & Harmon, 1992). Similarly, maltreated children who are able to develop secure attachments with their mother are less likely to display the self-concept deficits that are common among insecurely attached maltreated children (Beeghly & Cicchetti, 1994; Schneider-Rosen & Cicchetti, 1984; Toth & Cicchetti, 1996).

As development proceeds into toddlerhood, the stage-salient task shifts to the development of autonomous functioning, as the responsibility of self-management and the regulation of affect moves away from the context of the caregiver-infant relationship onto the toddler alone. Between 18 and 36 months, the autonomous self emerges as toddlers develop the ability for more differentiated and complex representations of the self in relation to others (Greenspan & Porges, 1984). The caregiver's sensitivity to and tolerance for the toddler's strivings for autonomy are necessary for successful resolution of this issue. Caregivers who feel rejected by their toddlers' new demands as they strive for autonomous functioning may inhibit the emergence of autonomy in their children if they are not supportive of this process or are unable to set age-appropriate limits (Cicchetti & Lynch, 1995). Moreover, extended periods of psychological unavailability from parents have been associated with expectations for the continued inaccessibility of the attachment figure and a view of the self as unlovable (Bowlby, 1973; Cummings & Cicchetti, 1990; Egeland & Sroufe, 1981). The child may then respond to novel situations and relationships in accord with the representational models that have emerged from this initial relationship experience and, furthermore, may actively select situations that are consistent with this relationship's goals (Sroufe, 1983).

The emergence of the development of self during early toddlerhood has traditionally been examined through investigations of visual self-recognition (M. Lewis & Brooks-Gunn, 1979). The capacity to recognize the rouge-marked self in the mirror emerges during the 2nd year of life and provides some insight into children's early self-concept. Although no differences have emerged in maltreated infants' ability for visual self-recognition as early as 18 months of age, evidence reveals that there are significant differences in their affective expressions upon viewing the self. Specifically, maltreated children are more likely to display neutral or negative affect in response to their rouge-marked self (Schneider-Rosen & Cicchetti, 1984, 1991) than are nonmaltreated children. Therefore, it seems that although maltreatment does not impede the cognitive maturation necessary for the development of self-recognition, there are observable affective differences in the self-representations of maltreated toddlers.

At 24 months of age, a tool-use paradigm has been used to measure children's emerging autonomy, independent exploration, and ability to cope with frustration (Egeland & Sroufe, 1981). During this problem-solving interaction, maltreated children become more angry, frustrated with the mother, and noncompliant than do nonmaltreated children of similar SES, thereby suggesting that maltreated children experience difficulty in developing an autonomous self.

Moving into late toddlerhood, the ability to talk about the self, label emotions, and discuss feelings of self and other emerges, allowing for observations of more overt expressions of self-representation. Self-other differentiation can be reflected in children's self-descriptions, use of personal pronouns, and active agency during symbolic play (Beeghly & Cicchetti, 1994; Kagan, 1981). During observations of mother-child play, delays in maltreated children's self systems have been noted through the analysis of verbal communicative abilities and internal state language. Specifically, maltreated children talk less about themselves and about their internal states than do nonmaltreated children, show less differentiation in their attributional focus, and are more context-bound in their use of internal state language (Beeghly & Cicchetti, 1994; Coster, Gersten, Beeghly, & Cicchetti, 1989). Among maltreated children, those with insecure attachments display the most compromised internal sate language (Beeghly & Cicchetti, 1994).

The dearth of negative internal state expression that has been noted among maltreated children is consistent with reports that maltreated children may inhibit negative affect, especially in the context of their relationship with their caregiver (Crittenden & DiLalla, 1988; Koenig, Cicchetti, & Rogosch, 2000; Lynch & Cicchetti, 1991). As sug-

gested by Cicchetti (1991), the suppression of negative emotions may reflect an adaptive process for children in the context of a maltreating environment. Through the modification of their behavior, maltreated children may mitigate their parents' responses to, as well as their own anxiety surrounding, particular uses of language (i.e., language that reflects negative emotion, references to the self and the self's desires) that have previously resulted in negative consequences. Outside of this context, however, the inability to acknowledge negative emotional states may impede maltreated children's ability to display empathy toward their peers and engage in successful social relationships (Main & George, 1985; Troy & Sroufe, 1987).

The investigation of the expression of self-conscious emotions has also been utilized as a way to assess self-representation among maltreated preschool children (Alessandri & Lewis, 1996). During problem-solving tasks between mother and child, significant differences emerged between maltreated and nonmaltreated children in the expression of both pride and shame. Maltreated girls were identified as at particular risk for negative self-conscious emotions, showing much less pride and more shame as compared to maltreated boys and nonmaltreated comparisons. There were also significant differences in the emotional responsivity of maltreating and nonmaltreating mothers in response to their children's successes and failures. Specifically, maltreating mothers provided more negative feedback and negative affective displays, especially toward their daughters, which likely impacts their children's expression of self-conscious emotion. The fact that maltreated girls showed fewer pride behaviors toward success and more shame toward failure is particularly noteworthy considering that the degree of affect children attribute to their performance abilities is an important contributor to their feelings of self-worth, competence, and motivation for school (J. L. Aber & Allen, 1987; Cassidy, 1988). Thus, the differences in maltreated children's expression of self-conscious emotion may represent precursory evidence for the development of low self-esteem and internalizing psychopathology.

Indeed, a number of investigations of self-esteem among maltreated children have been conducted, describing maltreated children as lower in ego control and self-esteem as early as the preschool years (Egeland, Sroufe, & Erickson, 1983) and revealing that maltreated school-age children report lower self-concepts than do nonmaltreated children (D. Allen & Tarnowski, 1989; Oates, Forrest, & Peacock, 1985). A closer developmental analysis of maltreated school-age children's self-concepts, however, supports a shift in self-esteem patterns across ages. Young maltreated children (ages 6 and 7) tend to demonstrate an inflated sense of self-competence and social self-efficacy, yet by ages 8 or 9 this overly positive sense of self is no longer present; instead, they perceive themselves as being less competent than do nonmaltreated children (Kim & Cicchetti, 2003; Vondra et al., 1989). Corroboration of children's self-evaluations with teachers' ratings reveals that children's perceptions may in fact become more accurate and realistic as they grow older and view themselves in a more negative light.

Therefore, it seems that the experience of the school environment may have multiple implications for maltreated children's sense of self and subsequent relationships. As noted previously, exposure to school may provide maltreated children with their first experience of nonthreatening relationships, thereby facilitating the development of more secure relatedness. During the young school-age period, maltreated children tend to develop inflated levels of perceived self-efficacy in peer interactions, which has been identified as a protective factor in the pathways to internalizing symptomatology (Kim & Cicchetti, 2003). However, it is possible that this exaggerated sense of self is reflective of deficits in social information processing. Maltreated children may misinterpret social cues in peer interactions and misunderstand their own role in peer conflict, resulting in an overly positive self-view (e.g., Crick & Dodge, 1996a, 1996b). These processing errors may decrease over time as children develop the capacity for social comparison and may gain a growing awareness of their social inefficacy (see later section on social information processing). Alternatively, young maltreated children's inflated self-concept may be related to immaturity in developing representational models that are derived from early attachment insecurity (Cassidy, 1988) or defensive processing, whereby maltreated children inhibit negative affect and exhibit false-positive affect (Beeghly & Cicchetti, 1994; Crittenden & DiLalla, 1988; Koenig et al., 2000). Such explanations are plausible considering that as maltreated children continue to mature in the context of peer relations, they begin to make more negative self-appraisals, which perhaps are more representative of their true models of the self (see section on peer relations for further discussion).

Clearly, maltreated children display a number of difficulties and maladaptive patterns in their struggle for autonomy and developing self. Their inability to discuss negative emotional states combined with their increasingly negative self-representations may exacerbate and contribute to their problems in self-other differentiation, as well as their ability for social information processing and the development of successful peer relationships.

Furthermore, child maltreatment experiences have been linked to pathology in self-definition and self-regulation (Fischer & Ayoub, 1994; Westen, 1994). Initial investigations of self system psychopathology focused on those who experienced the most extreme forms of maltreatment. For example, among girls who experienced chronic sexual abuse, a complex form of dissociation called "polarized affective splitting" has been noted (Calverley, Fischer, & Ayoub, 1994). More recent work, however, suggests that less heinous forms of maltreatment can lead to disruptions in self system processes and self-integration. The experience of traumatic abuse, beyond that specific to sexual abuse, can play a role in the etiology of dissociative disorders (Cole & Putnam, 1992). For example, using an observer report measure of dissociation for children, Putnam (1996) demonstrated that maltreated school-age children showed more dissociation than nonmaltreated children. To address questions regarding developmental pathways to dissociative symptomatology, a longitudinal prospective study of children at high risk for poor developmental outcomes was conducted with children between the toddler period and age 19 (Ogawa et al., 1997). The results of this study indicated that trauma, which was defined to include maltreatment, predicted levels of dissociation at all developmental periods. In particular, dissociation in the toddler-preschool period was predicted by physical abuse and neglect in infancy, and the severity and chronicity of trauma predicted future levels of dissociation.

Story stem narratives also have been used to determine the extent of dissociation in maltreated and nonmaltreated preschool-age children (Macfie, Cicchetti, & Toth, 2001b). In an initial investigation focusing on moral-conflictual themes in maltreated preschool children's narratives, maltreated children portrayed parents and children as responding less often, yet themselves as stepping into the story more often to relieve children's distress (Macfie et al., 1999). In a subsequent investigation, Macfie and colleagues (2001b) posited that dissociation might help to explain this finding that maltreated children were more likely to break the narrative frame to relieve children's distress themselves, suggesting that for maltreated children, the line between reality and fantasy is blurred in fearful situations. In an analysis of dissociative content in the narratives preschool children provided, maltreated children demonstrated more dissociation than nonmaltreated children, especially those who were physically abused and sexually abused. Additionally, different developmental trajectories for maltreated and nonmaltreated children were identified such that dissociation increased over time for the maltreated children, whereas such increases were not observed among the nonmaltreated children.

Another investigation extended findings on dissociation in maltreated children by analyzing subtype differences and also by incorporating measures of internalizing and externalizing symptomatology (Macfie, Cicchetti, & Toth, 2001a). Although clinical-range dissociation was associated with the experience of physical abuse only, children who experienced sexual abuse, physical abuse, or neglect each demonstrated more dissociation than the nonmaltreated group. Moreover, maltreatment severity, chronicity, multiple subtypes, and internalizing and externalizing symptomatology were each related to dissociation. Thus, it seems that the experience of maltreatment places children at considerable risk for dissociative symptomatology, highlighting the extreme extent to which maltreatment may disrupt one of the most central tendencies of ontogenic development: self system integration and development.

SYMBOLIC DEVELOPMENT

A critical cognitive achievement of toddlerhood is the development of representational thought using symbols (Piaget, 1962; Werner & Kaplan, 1963). This ability is expressed through language and play, where children can represent their growing awareness of self and other, in addition to practicing and cultivating behaviors that may become integrated into more complex behavioral sequences and problem-solving skills (Bruner, 1972; Cicchetti, 1990). Although the development of these symbolic capacities is largely a cognitive maturational process, representational thought does not emerge in isolation from socioemotional and environmental factors. In fact, as children develop the cognitive capacity for symbolic thought, ongoing relationships and experiences influence the organization and content of the representational models as they emerge. Representational models, and children's ability to manipulate them, may influence later cognitive processing abilities as well as social information-processing skills (Cicchetti & Lynch, 1995; Dodge et al., 1997).

Language

Although the capacity for language is highly canalized, a number of environmental factors are associated with the development of children's language competence, including socioeconomic status, maternal interactive behavior, and maternal psychosocial functioning (Eigsti & Cicchetti, 2004; Morisset, Barnard, Greenberg, Booth, & Spieker, 1990). Maltreatment, especially severe neglect, is related to linguistic delays affecting both receptive and expressive language (R. E. Allen & Oliver, 1982; Culp, Watkins, & Lawrence, 1991; L. Fox, Long, & Langlois, 1988). These language deficits are associated with caretaking environments where maltreating parents fail to provide adequate social language exchange and direct verbal teaching (Culp et al., 1991; Wasserman, Green, & Allen, 1983). Attachment security also plays a role in the development of communicative competence such that secure attachment may operate as a protective factor for language competence among maltreated children (Gersten, Coster, Schneider-Rosen, Carlson, & Cicchetti, 1986). However, the preponderance of atypical attachment security among maltreated children (Barnett et al., 1999) places them at significant risk for maladaptive language development.

In an analysis of communicative functioning, Coster and colleagues (1989) identified multiple signs of language impairment among maltreated children. For example, maltreated children demonstrated shorter mean length utterances and more limited expressive, but not receptive, language. Additionally, analysis of the pragmatic use of language suggested that maltreated toddlers, along with their mother, have developed an interaction style in which language predominantly functions as a medium to accomplish tasks rather than as a medium for social or affective exchanges. Considering the findings that maltreated children also produce less internal state speech (Beeghly & Cicchetti, 1994; Coster et al., 1989) and less contingent speech (Coster et al., 1989), the evidence converges to suggest that the development of language among maltreated children occurs to the neglect of its potential use as a medium for social or affective discourse. Maltreated children's deficits in the pragmatic use of language for social sharing may present further challenges in their ability to develop close relationships and feel a sense of belongingness in later peer group formations.

The vast majority of language studies with maltreated children have focused on the content rather than the form of language, or used qualitative rather than quantitative measures of communicative abilities. To address this gap in the literature, Eigsti and Cicchetti (2004) examined the syntactic complexity of language among mother-child dyads from maltreating and nonmaltreating families. Child maltreatment was associated with quantitative language delays both in vocabulary and production of syntactic structures. Maltreating mothers' utterances, however, were different in qualitative nature such that maltreating moms directed fewer utterances toward their children and produced fewer specific types of utterances (multiclause utterances and yes/no questions), consistent with previous work regarding maternal verbal attention-directing behaviors (Alessandri, 1992). Furthermore, maternal expansions and repetitions were related to child age among dyads from nonmaltreating families, but not from maltreating families. This suggests that the mothers from maltreating families were less responsive to child-specific factors as they failed to tailor the age-appropriateness of their verbal behaviors. Additionally, this investigation represents the first demonstration of child language delays and differences in maternal speech in a single maltreated sample.

Play

Play is one of the most significant tasks of child development as it requires the integration of cognitive, motivational, emotional, and social skills. Through play, children develop and practice the skills and strategies that can be later used in goal-directed activities (Weisler & McCall, 1976). Though the structure of play is cognitively based (Belsky & Most, 1981; Nicolich, 1977), the motivation behind play is affective in nature (Hesse & Cicchetti, 1982). Mastery motivation and other stylistic aspects of play such as engagement in play and quality of exploration have been associated with more mature forms of object play (Fein & Apfel, 1979). Higher cognitive levels of play are associated with self-control, low impulsivity, and low aggression (Singer, 1976). Furthermore, it has been demonstrated that play can be used as a window onto the social understanding of children, with the development of symbolic play in particular reflecting children's emerging conceptions of themselves and of others (Beeghly, Weiss-Perry, & Cicchetti, 1990; Bretherton, 1984; Cicchetti, 1990).

In an investigation of mother-child play and social competence among 12-month-old infants, Valentino, Cicchetti, Toth, and Rogosch (in press) noted that although no differences emerged in the average level or maximum level of play complexity achieved, differences in play style, as assessed though social interaction behaviors, were prominent between infants from maltreating and nonmaltreating families. Specifically, infants from abusing families exhibited more imitation during play than did the infants from nonmaltreating families. Infants from abusing families also engaged in less independent play than both the infants from neglecting families and the infants from nonmaltreating families. Additionally, mothers differed in their interactions during mother-child play such that mothers from abusing families demonstrated fewer attention-directing and limit-setting behaviors than did mothers from nonmaltreating families. Further analysis revealed that maternal attention-directing behaviors significantly predicted child play style behaviors but did not mediate the unique effects of maltreatment. Nonetheless, the differences in play style demonstrated by infants from abusing families represent the earliest indication of deviation in the development of sociocommunicative competence among maltreated children and suggests that these infants may already be at risk for atypical developmental pathways as young as 12 months of age (Valentino et al., in press).

Among preschool-age children, investigations of social play patterns have revealed that the play of maltreated children is both less cognitively mature and less socially mature than that of nonmaltreated children (Alessandri, 1991). Maltreated children spent less time engaged in play and more time in transition between play activities. Furthermore, most of their play was sensorimotor and functional, engaging in simple motoric activities and demonstrating greater touching of toys without any direct manipulations in both solitary and parallel social situations. In contrast, nonmaltreated children engaged in more cognitively mature and goal-oriented constructive play. The rates of dramatic play between maltreated and nonmaltreated children were comparable; however, the maltreated children demonstrated a restricted range of thematic content in their play. For example, maltreated children were much more imitative and likely to reenact everyday routines, and the nonmaltreated children were able to engage in more fantasy play; this is consistent with the differences noted among the play styles of infants from maltreating families during mother-child play at 12 months of age (Valentino et al., in press). Therefore, maltreatment does not seem to impede the cognitive maturation necessary for symbolic play. Rather, maltreatment's effects on play are manifest in the qualitative content of the play themes, a trend that is similar to differences noted among maltreated children's affective displays following self-recognition (Schneider-Rosen & Cicchetti, 1984, 1991).

In an additional investigation of maltreated preschool children's play behaviors, Alessandri (1992) demonstrated that differences in maltreated and nonmaltreated children's play are correlated with differences in mother-child interaction styles. Irrespective of maltreatment history, children who were exposed to low levels of maternal attention-directing behavior and to an aloof and critical mother were less likely to engage in higher forms of cognitive play, whereas those with mothers who focused their children's attention on objects and events and interacted in reciprocal manner were able to initiate, maintain, and engage in more complex forms of cognitive play. Mothers from maltreating families were more controlling and less involved with their children, used fewer physical and verbal strategies to direct their children's attention, and were more negative in comparison with nonmaltreating mothers. Taken together, these three studies elucidate the deleterious impact that behaviors associated with maltreating parents may have on the development of their children's play, especially with regard to the content and style of these play behaviors.

Representational Models

Mental representational models are believed to play a guiding role in the continuity of development. Emerging from early attachment relationships, which become internalized as the first representations of self and other, representational models foster the maintenance of developmental trajectories as they organize expectations and schemas for relationships (Bowlby, 1969/1982; Cicchetti & Toth, 1995; Lynch & Cicchetti, 1991; Sroufe, 1989). Among normative samples, the quality of children's attachment relationships to the primary caregiver is associated with the complexity of their knowledge of self and others (Pipp et al., 1992).

Self-other differentiation and understanding are necessary, however, before one can build representational models of the self and other. Investigations of false belief understanding suggest that the capacity for mentalizing, or theory of mind (ToM), an understanding that another can have a perspective that is different from one's own, is reflective of the ability to differentiate between the self and other as distinct entities with separate mental states. The capability of understanding that different people can have different perspectives about a single situation is an essential development in the ability to predict people's behavior across settings; thus, false belief understanding is often interpreted as an indication of a representational theory of mind (Perner, 1991). Though most commonly associated with the development of children with Autism, ToM deficits have also been observed among various other atypical populations, such as children with Down syndrome, children with mental retardation of undifferentiated etiology, and children with deafness (Cicchetti & Beeghly, 1990; Fowler, 1998; Pennington & Bennetto, 1998; C. C. Peterson & Siegal, 1995, 1999). In accord with the principle of equifinality (Cicchetti & Rogosch, 1996), C. C. Peterson and Siegal (2000) argue that there may be multiple pathways to the development of ToM deficits besides the innately damaged neurobiological module often proposed to explain the poor performance of children with Autism

on false belief tasks. Specifically, they assert that for other populations of children, there may be a critical threshold level of environmental input that must be reached to initiate the neurobiological processes necessary for the development of ToM. For example, among late-signing deaf children, a lack of conversational input during early development may account for later deficits in the development of ToM (C. C. Peterson & Siegal, 1999).

Given the clear deviations in the average expectable environment that characterize the early development of maltreated children, it is likely that maltreated children would also be at increased risk for ToM deficits. To investigate the impact of family contextual influences on ToM development, Cicchetti, Rogosch, Maughan, Toth, and Bruce (2003) investigated false belief understanding among low SES maltreated and nonmaltreated and middle SES nonmaltreated children. Among maltreated children, deficits in false belief understanding were noted such that the occurrence of maltreatment during the toddler period, and physical abuse in particular, was associated with delay in development of ToM (Cicchetti et al., 2003). These delays in the capacity for self-other differentiation may place maltreated children at increased risk for the development of maladaptive representational models.

Representational models are particularly important because once early attachment models are internalized, they may guide subsequent interpersonal relationships as event schemas (Bretherton, 1990). Therefore, internal representational models of early attachment relationships organize expectations about other potential social partners as well as the self in relation to them (Crittenden, 1990). Given the paucity of secure attachment organization among maltreated children, they may develop negative expectations of how others will behave and of how successful the self will be in relation to others (Bowlby, 1973, 1980; Bretherton, 1991; Cicchetti, 1991; Lynch & Cicchetti, 1991). Continuity in children's relationship patterns with parents, siblings, friends, and teachers are well documented; for example, children's attachment quality with their mother is related to quality of attachment with their father (N. A. Fox, Kimmerly, & Schafer, 1991), siblings (Teti & Ablard, 1989), preschool friends (Park & Waters, 1989), and teachers (C. Howes & Hamilton, 1992). Specific to maltreated children, quality of attachment to foster parents tends to be consistent with the attachment quality that would be expected toward the maltreating mother (C. Howes & Segal, 1993). Additionally, maltreated children's patterns of relatedness to their mother significantly impact their feelings of relatedness to others (Lynch & Cicchetti, 1991) and are concordant with their patterns of relatedness to teachers, peers, and best friends (Lynch & Cicchetti, 1992). These observed continuities in the quality and pattern of children's interactions across relationships lend support to the notion of enduring attachment organization, manifest in children's increasing use of organizing mental representations.

Direct research assessing maltreated and nonmaltreated children's representational models has flourished in the past decade. Initial research identifying differences between maltreated and nonmaltreated children's representational models emerged from the analysis of the complexity and organization of their person concepts, demonstrating that a child's pattern of relatedness to a particular person is significantly related to the descriptiveness, depth, evaluative consistency, and emotional tone of his or her open-ended description of that relationship figure (Cicchetti & Lynch, 1995). Further, children with optimal patterns of relatedness have relatively detailed conceptions of others that are associated with consistently positive affect, as opposed to the person concepts of children with nonoptimal patterns of relatedness (Cicchetti & Lynch, 1995).

Most recently, children's story stem narratives have been utilized as a medium for the assessment of representational models, beginning with a seminal paper by Toth, Cicchetti, Macfie, and Emde (1997). Analysis of the narratives of maltreated and nonmaltreated children revealed a complex pattern of distortions in the mental representations of maltreated children. Overall, the narratives of maltreated children contained more negative maternal representations and more negative self-representations than the narratives of the nonmaltreated children. Further examination of subtype differences revealed that physically abused children had the most negative maternal representations and more negative self-representations than the nonmaltreated children. Physically abused children had high levels of negative self-representations, and the neglected children emerged with low levels of positive representations compared to nonmaltreated children. This finding may be consistent with the lack of positive attention that characterizes neglected children's home environment, which may impede their overall development of self. Toth and colleagues conjectured that although physically abused children have experienced much negative parenting dysfunction, they may also have had periods when they were responded to positively (thus enabling positive self-representations). Sexually abused children manifested more positive self-representations than neglected children, which might be consistent with notions of a false self. This explanation seems plausible considering that their negative self-representations were comparable to the physically abused children's.

Extending their prior work to examine representations of caregiver and self over time, Toth, Cicchetti, Macfie, Maughan, and VanMeenen (2000) conducted a longitudinal investigation with maltreated and nonmaltreated preschoolers and found that maltreated children had more negative representations of parents and of self at the conclusion of the 1-year study period. Maltreated children also concurrently exhibited indices of negative and grandiose self-representations, which may be reflective of earlier attachment disorganization. Over time, maltreated preschool children displayed more grandiose self-representations, and nonmaltreated children displayed an opposite pattern. These findings are consistent with the exaggerated sense of self-competence and social self-efficacy that have been noted among young maltreated school-age children (Kim & Cicchetti, 2003; Vondra et al., 1989). By age 8 or 9, however, maltreated children's perceptions of self decrease such that they view themselves as less competent than nonmaltreated children; similarly, one might expect to see a comparable decline in maltreated children's self-representations as they progress into later childhood.

Derived from the early attachment relationship, children's mental representations of their caregivers should consolidate and generalize to form an organizing schema through which subsequent relationships may be interpreted. Therefore, in theory, children's mental representations of caregivers will influence their ability to engage in peer relationships. To assess the relationship between such mental representations and children's peer relationships, Shields, Ryan, and Cicchetti (2001) assessed maltreated and nonmaltreated children's narrative representations of caregivers and emotion regulation as predictors of later rejection by peers. Consistent with an organizational perspective of development, positive and coherent representations of caregivers were related to prosocial behavior and peer preference, whereas maladaptive representations were associated with emotion dysregulation, aggression, and peer rejection. Furthermore, mental representations mediated maltreatment's effects on peer rejection in part by undermining the ability for competent emotion regulation. Thus, mental representations of caregivers serve an important function in the development of peer relationships of at-risk children, in addition to the development of emotion regulation (see later sections on emotion regulation and peer relationships).

MORAL DEVELOPMENT

Alongside the development of representational models, an additional task of the preschool period is the development of self-regulatory mechanisms. Internalization of moral standards enables the child to shift from external to internal control. The facilitation of internalization in young children is largely reliant on the caregiver (Ryan, Deci, & Grolnick, 1995) and is fostered through autonomy-supportive parental behaviors such as conveying choice, acknowledging the child's feelings, and providing a meaningful rationale for limitations that are set (Deci, Egharri, Patrick, & Leone, 1994; Ryan et al., 1995).

In contrast to those behaviors that promote the development of internalization in children, maltreating mothers tend to rely more on punitive and power-assertive strategies and less on reasoning and positively oriented strategies to discipline their children than do nonmaltreating mothers (Oldershaw et al., 1986). Additionally, maltreating parents tend to have overly high expectations for their children, a low tolerance for misbehavior, and a greater expectancy for compliance than do nonmaltreating parents (Chilamkurti & Milner, 1993; Dixon, Hamilton-Giachritsis, et al., 2005; Reid et al., 1987). Considering the maladaptive discipline strategies parents employ when their children fail to meet their unrealistically high expectations, it follows that maltreated children are likely at risk for maladaptive moral development.

Initial efforts to assess the moral development of maltreated children focused on children's moral judgments and reasoning (Smetana, Kelley, & Twentyman, 1984; Smetana et al., 1998, 1999). Differences in moral maturity were not found between maltreated and nonmaltreated children; all children evaluated moral transgressions as very serious, punishable, and wrong in the absence of rules. Differences did emerge, however, in the children's affective responses to moral transgression as a function of maltreatment subtype and gender (Smetana et al., 1998). For example, physically abused male perpetrators reported more anger in actual situations than did females, and physically abused females reported more happiness in response to actual transgressions than did physically abused males; this latter finding is perhaps consistent with an emerging false self. In contrast, neglected children reported less sadness than nonmaltreated children when judging how hypothetical perpetrators would feel and more fear in response to the hypothetical instances of unfair resource distribution than did the physically abused or nonmaltreated children.

In an additional investigation, Smetana and colleagues (1999) assessed the effects of provocation on maltreated and nonmaltreated preschoolers' understanding of moral transgressions. Consistent with their prior study, no gender or maltreatment status differences in ratings of transgression severity and deserved punishment were found; instead,

differences emerging as a function of maltreatment subtype were noted among children's affective responses. Overall, evidence demonstrates that maltreated and nonmaltreated children may differ in the organization of their affective responses rather than in their moral evaluations. This profile of functioning is consistent with observations of maltreated children's visual self-recognition behaviors, in addition to the qualitative aspects of their symbolic play, such that maltreatment's effects are more salient in the affective realm (Alessandri, 1991; Schneider-Rosen & Cicchetti, 1984, 1991).

There are disadvantages, however, in the methodology employed in the aforementioned investigations, such that directly asking children for moral judgments may influence children to answer in a manner that is socially appropriate, potentially in contrast to what they actually may believe. To address these concerns, a structured narrative storytelling task was utilized to assess representations of moral-affiliative and conflictual themes among maltreated preschoolers (Toth, Cicchetti, Macfie, Rogosch, & Maughan, 2000) as narratives may be a more indirect method of assessment. Results indicated that the narratives of maltreated children contained more conflictual and fewer moral-affiliative themes than did the stories of the nonmaltreated children. Furthermore, conflictual representations partially mediated the relationship between maltreatment and later externalizing behavior problems, thus demonstrating the relationship between child maltreatment, children's organization of their life experiences, and their behavioral symptomatology.

Utilizing an alternative methodological strategy, the development of internalization in maltreated and nonmaltreated preschool children has been examined through the behavioral coding of child compliance/noncompliance behaviors during a mother-child interaction (Koenig, Cicchetti, & Rogosch, 2000). Results indicated that abused children exhibited less moral internalization than the nonmaltreated children. The neglected children did not significantly differ from the nonmaltreated children on their level of internalization; however, they displayed more negative affect. Moreover, the physically abused children engaged in a strategy of situational compliance, which is consistent with the compulsive compliant coping style that has been identified among maltreated toddlers (Crittenden & Di-Lalla, 1988) and involves the suppression of negative behaviors and immediate compliance with maternal demands. This behavioral pattern, in which children distort their own emotional responses, may contribute to a lack of need fulfillment, and has been associated with later difficulties in emotion regulation, the potential to develop a false self, and risk for psychopathology (Cicchetti, 1991; Crittenden & DiLalla, 1988; Ryan et al., 1995).

Additionally, an assessment of maternal behaviors revealed that maltreated and nonmaltreated groups differed in the techniques that best predicted child internalization. For the nonmaltreated dyads, a lower level of maternal joy predicted internalization; in contrast, among maltreating dyads, less maternal negative affect enhanced the child's ability to internalize the task. Further analysis revealed that child behaviors were more strongly predicted by maternal control strategies among maltreated children as compared to nonmaltreated children, supporting the notion that maltreated children are more reactive to maternal expression. Hypervigilance to affective expressions of others may serve an adaptive function for maltreated children so that they can detect potential signals of punishment or abuse (Pollak et al., 1997; Rieder & Cicchetti, 1989); however, it may occur at the expense of an awareness of one's own internal states, thereby hindering the development of internalization and other self-regulatory mechanisms.

Further deviations have been noted among 5-year-old maltreated children's moral development. Previous investigations with maltreated children focused on the behavioral indices of morality such as aggression and comforting responses to peers' distress. Koenig et al. (2004) expanded on the limited knowledge of moral development in physically abused, neglected, and nonmaltreated children by examining children's engagement in rule violations and by incorporating measures of "moral emotions" such as empathy and guilt. Findings revealed that different maltreatment experiences differentially impact moral development such that physically abused children engaged in more stealing behaviors and neglected children engaged in more cheating behavior and less rule-compatible behavior compared to nonmaltreated children. Moreover, maltreatment status differences interacted with gender on a number of moral paradigms, suggesting that the development of prosocial behaviors and moral emotions is more affected by maltreatment in girls than in boys. In particular, physically abused girls showed less guilt and fewer prosocial behaviors than neglected girls. Delays in internalization or underinternalization were associated with early physical abuse among girls; however, neglected girls were overinternalized (Koenig et al., 2004). Consequently, abused girls may be at risk for externalizing psychopathology and antisocial behavior, and neglected girls may be at risk for lower self-esteem and depression.

Overall, the extant research suggests that the experience of maltreatment exerts a deleterious impact on the development of self-regulatory mechanisms such as inter-

nalization. Future research should further examine specific vulnerability and protective factors; negative maternal affective expression, physical abuse, and female gender have each been associated with deviations in the development of moral internalization among maltreated children. Furthermore, maladaptive internalization may be associated with emotion regulation difficulties as well as later internalizing and externalizing symptomatology, each of which may have negative consequences for maltreated children's ability to resolve salient issues at the subsequent stages of development.

SOCIAL INFORMATION PROCESSING AND THE FORMATION OF PEER RELATIONSHIPS

As children proceed through development, they may rely on their representational models to aid processing of social information in addition to contextual and environmental inputs, which also influence the way children interpret their experiences. For example, among children developing in normative contexts, the presence of negative affective conditions is associated with more frequent information-processing errors (Bugental, Blue, Cortez, Fleck, & Rodriguez, 1992). Consistent with these findings, deficits in children's information processing are seen in association with harsh and maltreating parenting (Dodge et al., 1990). In particular, children who have been physically abused are less accurate in encoding social cues, they tend to generate a higher proportion of aggressive responses to problematic social situations, they view aggression more favorably, and they exhibit a hostile attribution bias (Dodge et al., 1997; Prince & Van Slyeke, 1991). Furthermore, maladaptive social information-processing patterns appear to mediate the relationship between the effects of harsh parenting on children's aggression (Weiss, Dodge, Bates, & Pettit, 1992).

Cognitive control functioning has been identified as one possible mechanism contributing to maltreated children's social information-processing deficits. Cognitive control refers to the capacity to maintain more differentiated, articulate perceptions of past and external stimuli and to detect nuances and differences in perceptual stimuli more accurately and readily (Rieder & Cicchetti, 1989; Rogosch, Cicchetti, & Aber, 1995). In particular, the cognitive control functioning of maltreated children is affected by the presence of aggressive stimuli such that maltreated children recall a greater number of distracting aggressive stimuli than do nonmaltreated children (Rieder & Cicchetti, 1989), and maltreated children readily assimilate these aggressive stimuli. These findings suggest that maltreated children's information processing differs from that of non-maltreated children by utilizing more negative affect information at the expense of less cognitive efficiency and impaired task performance. Moreover, these biases toward aggressive stimuli are consistent with the attentional biases maltreated children demonstrate in response to demonstrations of anger (Pine et al., 2005; Pollak et al., 1997, 2001; Pollak & Kistler, 2002; Pollak & Sinha, 2002; Pollak & Tolley-Schell, 2003).

Early deviations in cognitive and affective processing may adversely affect the development of peer relationships among maltreated children. Evidence supports that cognitive control functioning partially mediates both the influence of maltreatment on later dysregulated behavior in the peer setting and the effect of physical abuse on later rejection by peers (Rogosch, Cicchetti, & Aber, 1995). Specifically, maltreated children evidenced early deviations in their understanding of negative affect as well as immaturity in their cognitive controls. Moreover, maltreated children showed lower social effectiveness and higher levels of undercontrolled and aggressive behavior in school. Leveling/sharpening, one aspect of cognitive control, was identified as a salient contributor to later social effectiveness with peers, whereas negative affect understanding was more related to problems in behavior control and aggressiveness and to peer rejection among abused children. These findings are consistent with an organizational/transactional model whereby early parent-child relationships lead to poor organization of cognitive and affective processes, which in turn affects peer relationships and social dysfunction.

Because maltreated children's early histories are marred by negative and dysfunctional relationships, the opportunity to develop peer relationships and friendships may help to promote positive adaptation in maltreated children (Cicchetti, Lynch, Shonk, & Manly, 1992). Many important issues of children's social and emotional development are facilitated through relatedness with peers and exposure to an extended social network (Parker & Herrera, 1996). Thus, the development of peer relationships represents an important stage-salient task for school-age children.

Unfortunately, maltreated children approach engaging in peer interactions with the maladaptive representational models they have developed through their early caregiving experiences. As a result, maltreated children's relationships with their peers typically mirror their maladaptive representational models. In general, maltreated children interact less with their peers, exhibit more disturbed patterns of engagement when they do interact, and display fewer prosocial behaviors than nonmaltreated children

(Haskett & Kistner, 1991; Hoffman-Plotkin & Twentyman, 1984; Jacobson & Straker, 1982).

To empirically investigate whether representations of caregivers serve an important regulatory function in the peer relationships of at-risk children, Shields et al. (2001) assessed children's representation of mothers and fathers and emotion dysregulation as predictors of children's rejection by peers. In support of this organizational account for the difficulties noted in maltreated children's peer relationships, maltreated children's representations of caregivers were more negative/constricted and less positive/coherent than those of nonmaltreated children; such maladaptive representations were associated with emotion dysregulation, aggression, and peer rejection, whereas positive/coherent representations were related to prosocial behavior and peer preference. Thus, children's caregiver representations mediated maltreatment's effects on peer rejection in part by undermining emotion regulation.

Additional investigations have highlighted the role of severity, chronicity, and age of onset of maltreatment in the extent to which maltreated children display general maladjustment and incompetence with their peers (Bolger et al., 1998). Specifically, early onset of maltreatment has been associated with greater impairments in children's self-esteem. For emotionally maltreated children in particular, age at onset moderated the effect of emotional maltreatment on children's adjustment such that emotionally maltreated children were less likely to have a reciprocated best friend if their maltreatment began early in life. With regard to chronicity, Bolger and colleges revealed that children who experience chronic maltreatment were less well-liked by their peers. For example, maltreatment chronicity appeared to exacerbate the effect of abuse on the quality of physically abused children's friendships such that friendship quality declined as children's experiences of physical abuse increased in duration. In an additional prospective longitudinal investigation, Bolger and Patterson (2001) found further support for the notion that chronically maltreated children are likely to be rejected repeatedly across multiple years from childhood to early adolescence. Maltreatment chronicity was also associated with higher levels of aggressive behavior, which accounted in large part for the association between maltreatment and rejection by peers (Bolger & Patterson, 2001).

Maltreatment subtype has also been related to specific aspects of children's adjustment. For example, emotional maltreatment is related to difficulties in peer relationships but not to self-esteem, and the reverse pattern may be true for sexually abused children (Bolger & Patterson, 2001). Physically abused children are less popular with their peers, show less positive reciprocity in their interactions, and have social networks that are more insular and atypical with higher levels of negativity (Dodge, Pettit, & Bates, 1994; Haskett & Kistner, 1991; Salzinger et al., 1993). Even more alarming is evidence that rejection of maltreated children by peers may increase over time (Dodge et al., 1997).

Overall, two general developmental trajectories characterize maltreated children's peer relationships (Cicchetti et al., 1992; Cicchetti & Lynch, 1995; Mueller & Silverman, 1989). One pathway leads to the development of physical and verbal aggression in maltreated children's interactions with their peers, such that children who have been physically abused may be at heightened risk (Bolger & Patterson, 2001; George & Main, 1979; R. C. Herrenkohl & Herrenkohl, 1981; Hoffman-Plotkin & Twentyman, 1984; Kaufman & Cicchetti, 1989; Salzinger et al., 1993). Even as early as preschool age, abused children are more likely than are nonabused children to cause distress in their peers (Klimes-Dougan & Kistner, 1990). Moreover, maltreated children have been observed to respond with anger and aggression even to friendly and nonthreatening gestures from their peers (C. Howes & Eldredge, 1985).

The second developmental pathway leads to passive withdrawal as well as active avoidance behaviors that have been noted among maltreated children in the context of peer interactions; this may be especially prevalent among those who have been neglected (Dodge et al., 1994; George & Main, 1979; Hoffman-Plotkin & Twentyman, 1984; C. Howes & Espinosa, 1985; Jacobson & Straker, 1982). Withdrawn behavior is associated with poor peer outcomes; however, it may not account for the relationship between maltreatment and peer rejection (Bolger & Patterson, 2001). Rather, withdrawn behavior may be a function of maladaptive social expectations regarding peers (Salzinger, Feldman, Ng-Mak, Mojica, & Stockhammer, 2001), which has a more direct impact on children's peer relationships. Specifically, Salzinger and colleagues found that children's social expectations regarding peers mediated the relationship between abuse and children's positive social status; withdrawn behavior also mediated this relationship, but only as a function of social expectations.

In addition to these two generally diverging pathways, a subgroup of maltreated and nonmaltreated children has been identified who demonstrate both aggressive and withdrawn behaviors (Rogosch & Cicchetti, 1994). Concomitant heightened aggressiveness and social withdrawal may lead to increasing social isolation and peer rejection (Rubin, LeMare, & Lollis, 1990; Rubin & Lollis, 1988). Among maltreated children, those who evidence high aggression and high withdrawal demonstrate lower social effectiveness than is the case for nonmaltreated youngsters (Rogosch & Cicchetti, 1994). This unusual pattern of interaction with peers is consistent with the attachment history of maltreated children, which, characterized by disorganization, may be related to disorganized representational models and may result in disturbance in social encounters. By revealing indications of a predisposition to both "fight" and "flight" responses, maltreated children's interactions with peers lends support to the notion that these children have internalized both sides of their relationship with their caregiver (Troy & Sroufe, 1987). These findings are also consistent with the increased rates of bullying and victimization behaviors that have been noted among maltreated children (Shields & Cicchetti, 2001). Thus, maltreated children's representational models may have elements of both the victim and the victimizer, and these models may be enacted in their peer relationships.

Significant difficulties in cultivating and maintaining friendships have also been found among maltreated children (Parker & Herrera, 1996). Preadolescent and young adolescent physically abused children and their friends tend to display less intimacy in their interactions than do nonabused children and their friends. Friendships of physically abused children are more conflictual, especially during situations where emotion regulation skills are taxed, such as during competitive activities. However, evidence supports that if maltreated children can develop and maintain a close friendship, the presence of this relationship will be associated with improvement over time in self-esteem (Bolger et al., 1998).

Heightened aggressiveness, avoidance of and withdrawal from social interactions, and inappropriate responses to nonthreatening gestures render the development of effective relationships quite challenging for maltreated children. This maladaptive pattern of relationship histories represents yet another risk factor for negative developmental outcomes. For example, having poor peer relationships in childhood is associated with juvenile delinquency and other types of behavior disorders during adolescence (e.g., Cowen, Pederson, Babigian, Izzo, & Trost, 1973), as well as school dropout, criminality, delinquency, and psychological disturbance in adolescence and adulthood (Ollendick, Weist, Borden, & Greene, 1992; Parker & Asher, 1987; Rubin & Mills, 1988; Rubin & Ross, 1988). Each of the developmental pathways delineated may be associated with different maladaptive sequelae (Cicchetti et al., 1992). The aggression pathway may lead to the development of externalizing disorders as maltreated children's displays of hostility in relationships may lead to rejection by peer groups.

The experience of rejection may then turn children against the group and lead to the onset of externalizing problems. Providing support for this notion, a recent model of peer interactions proposed by Dodge et al. (2003) posits that initial processing biases and deficits lead to social rejection among children. The experience of social rejection (or lack of experience of positive peer relationships) then exacerbates processing biases and deficits that lead to aggressive behavior. The implications of this model are that social rejection by peers acts as a social stressor that increases the tendency to react aggressively among children who are so disposed, thus leading to a recursive model of antisocial development. Such a model is consistent with the chronic and repeated rejection by peers that has been noted among maltreated children (Bolger & Patterson, 2001).

In contrast, the withdrawn/avoidant pathway may lead to the development of internalizing problems. For example, children who react to the environment through withdrawal may also be viewed as deviant from age-appropriate norms, contributing to peer rejection. For these children, the experience of rejection may exacerbate social withdrawal and potentiate the development of internalizing problems.

ADAPTATION TO SCHOOL

Beginning in early childhood, the context of school is the major extrafamilial environment to which children are exposed. Beyond integration into peer groups, acceptable performance in the classroom and appropriate motivational orientations for achievement are important aspects of this stage-salient developmental task (Cicchetti & Lynch, 1995). Unsurprisingly, maltreated children appear to be at risk for unsuccessful resolution of these issues of development. Given evidence that children from high-risk samples with low socioeconomic backgrounds evidence a high percentage of difficulties at school (Egeland & Abery, 1991), maltreated children appear to be at heightened risk for maladjustment at school as a function of their socioeconomic status, apart from the effects of maltreatment. Compared to nonmaltreated children of similar socioeconomic backgrounds, however, maltreated children receive more discipline referrals and suspensions (Eckenrode & Laird, 1991; Eckenrode, Laird, & Doris, 1993) and are more dependent on their teachers (Egeland et al., 1983). Maltreated children perform worse on standardized tests, achieve lower grades, and are more likely to repeat a grade. Furthermore, they score lower on tests that assess cognitive maturity. However, it is unclear whether these difficul-

ties can be attributed to cognitive or motivational issues (Barahal, Waterman, & Martin, 1981).

With regard to motivation, J. L. Aber and Allen (1987) proposed that effectance motivation, which is the intrinsic desire to deal competently with one's environment, and successful relations with novel adults are important factors related to children's ability to adapt to their first major out-of-home environment. As such, they defined the concept of "secure readiness to learn" as characterized by high effectance motivation and low dependency, as a representation for the ability to establish secure relationships with adults while feeling free to explore and engage in the environment in ways that promote cognitive development. Maltreated children score lower on secure readiness to learn than do nonmaltreated children (J. L. Aber & Allen, 1987; J. L. Aber at al., 1989), which is consistent with what one might expect given the insecurity or atypicality that pervades maltreated children's attachment histories (Barnett et al., 1999).

To further assess the impact of relationships with caregivers on children's school functioning, Toth and Cicchetti (1996) examined the role of children's relationships with their mother in school adaptation. Nonmaltreated children who reported optimal/adequate relatedness to their mother (conceptually comparable to secure attachment) exhibited fewer school record risk factors as well as less externalizing symptomatology and more ego resilience than did maltreated children who reported nonoptimal patterns of relatedness. Thus, in the nonmaltreated group, optimal/adequate patterns of relatedness exerted a positive effect on multiple aspects of school functioning. However, in the maltreated group, optimal/adequate relatedness exerted a positive effect only on school records. Moreover, according to teacher-rated externalizing and social acceptance, maltreated children with nonoptimal patterns of relatedness evidenced more positive adaptation than maltreated children with optimal/adequate relatedness. Possible explanations for these findings include the potential role of defensive processing, in which child self-reported relatedness may be invalid such that insecurely attached children report being more secure, and the possible negative effect of having a positive relationship with a maltreating caregiver. Finally, the compulsive-compliant strategy that has been noted among maltreated children during interactions with their mother (Koenig et al., 2000) may be relevant here, such that the teacher's reports of compliant behavior may not be adequate to capture underlying maladaptation. The results highlight the complex role played by the child's representation of the primary caregiver in affecting school adaptation.

Nonetheless, maltreated children appear to display academic deficits, and a number of studies have suggested that the various subtypes of maltreatment may exert specific effects on children's academic competence. For example, several investigations have found that neglected children display the most severe academic deficits (Eckenrode et al., 1993; Wodarski, Kurtz, Gaudin, & Howing, 1990) in comparison to children who have experienced other maltreatment subtypes. In contrast, sexually abused children appear to be socially passive, excessively dependent on the teachers, and lacking autonomy in their school functioning (M. K. Erickson, Egeland, & Pianta, 1989). Additionally, studies specifically investigating the relation of sexual abuse to cognitive ability have found that sexually abused girls demonstrate poorer overall academic performance and receive more negative ratings of classroom social competence than do girls with no history of sexual abuse (Trickett, McBride-Chang & Putnam, 1994).

In assessments of social competence, teachers consistently perceive maltreated children as evidencing greater disturbance in social functioning than nonmaltreated children (Cicchetti & Rogosch, 1994). Specifically, maltreated children are rated as less socially competent and less accepted by their peers and display higher levels of behavioral disturbance, particularly involving externalizing behaviors. Classroom peers also distinguish maltreated children as more rejected or isolated by peer groups, with physically abused children showing the greatest differentiation from their nonmaltreated peers. Observations of maltreated children and their response to the task of school entry (M. K. Erickson et al., 1989) have revealed that aggressive, noncompliant, acting-out behaviors are common among physically abused children. In contrast, neglected children appeared uncooperative with teachers and insensitive and unempathic with peers. Clearly, these deviations in social functioning contribute to the maladaptive processes that characterize maltreated children's functioning in school. Research examining the mechanisms through which maltreatment may impact children's academic adjustment considered the contribution of deficits in multiple areas of functioning (Shonk & Cicchetti, 2001). Specifically, deficits in social competencies, academic engagement, ego resiliency, and ego control were hypothesized to negatively predict children's academic and behavioral adjustment. The results of this investigation highlighted the pathways through which maltreatment affects different domains of children's adjustment by revealing that whereas the effects of maltreatment on academic maladjustment are mediated by academic engagement, maltreatment's effects on behavior problems are fully mediated by social competencies and ego resiliency (Shonk & Cicchetti, 2001).

PERSONALITY ORGANIZATION

The extent of variation in personality characteristics and personality organization among maltreated children represents an area of investigation that has recently gained attention in the maltreatment literature. Given the vast array of developmental sequelae evidenced by maltreated children, this domain of development is likely to contribute to our understanding of differential vulnerability and resilience processes among maltreated youth (Rogosch & Cicchetti, 2004).

The application of temperament models has been prominent in characterizing individual differences among infants and young children (Rothbart, Posner, & Hershey, 1995). These models emphasized variation in behavioral characteristics that are presumed to be biologically based (Rothbart & Bates, 1998). As children proceed through development, the features of these temperamental systems are elaborated and consolidated into an individual's personality, as they are modified by environmental experiences (Kagan, 1994). Given the extreme failure of the average expectable environment that is associated with child maltreatment, one might expect maltreated children to manifest maladaptive personality organization.

To address the paucity of research on the personality development of maltreated children, Rogosch and Cicchetti (2004) utilized the five factor model (FFM) to study the emergent personality organization of maltreated children. The FFM approach is well established as a synthesizing descriptive system of personality that involves five primary personality dimensions: extraversion, agreeableness, conscientiousness, neuroticism, and openness to experience (McCrae & John, 1992). Research on children using the FFM has taken a personality-centered approach to identify individuals exhibiting patterns of organization among the FFM dimensions. For example, by applying a factor-analytic strategy, Robins, John, Caspi, Moffitt, and Stouthamer-Loeber (1996) identified three personality configurations emerging from the FFM which they named resilients, overcontrollers, and undercontrollers.

In their longitudinal assessment, Rogosch and Cicchetti (2004) examined the personality organization of 6-year-old maltreated and nonmaltreated children who were then followed up at 7, 8, and 9 years of age. Results indicated that the 6-year-old maltreated children exhibited lower agreeableness, conscientiousness, and openness to experience and higher neuroticism than nonmaltreated children. Using a similar analytic approach to that of Robins and colleagues, five personality clusters emerged: overcontroller, undercontroller, reserved, dysphoric, and gregarious. The gregarious and reserved clusters taken together closely resemble the resilient organization noted in previous studies (both are adaptive personality organizations). Maltreated children, however, were more frequently represented in the less adaptive personality clusters (overcontroller, undercontroller, and dysphoric). One particularly vulnerable profile, dysphoric, emerged predominantly among maltreated children who had been both abused and neglected; this organization, which represents a newly identified personality cluster, was characterized by low conscientiousness, agreeableness, and openness to experience, with high neuroticism. The dysphoric cluster was rarely observed among nonmaltreated children, which may explain why it had not previously been identified (D. Hart, Hofmann, Edelstein, & Keller, 1997; Robins et al., 1996).

Overall, maltreatment and personality clusters were related to individual differences that were perceived by peers. Furthermore, continuity and stability of children's personality organization and personality liabilities were found such that personality clusters at age 9 were maintained from age 6. Thus, there is substantial vulnerability in the personality features of maltreated children, highlighting the need for interventions to promote competence and prevent the consolidation of maladaptive personality organization.

MALADAPTATION: THE EMERGENCE OF BEHAVIOR PROBLEMS AND PSYCHOPATHOLOGY

In keeping with the dynamic systems concepts of equifinality and multifinality (Cicchetti & Rogosch, 1996), multiple pathways to adaptation and maladaptation, as well as varied developmental outcomes, are possible for maltreated children. The ecological conditions associated with maltreatment represent a severe deviation from the average expectable environment. Without adequate environmental supports, the probabilistic path of ontogenesis for maltreated children is characterized by an increased risk for unsuccessful resolution of many stage-salient issues of development. Failure at any stage-salient task increases the risk of unsuccessful resolution of subsequent developmental challenges. As reviewed, maltreated children are likely to exhibit atypicalities or deficits in neurobiological processes, physiological responsiveness, affect differentiation and regulation, attachment relationships, self-system processes, representational development, moral development, social information processing, peer relationships, adaptation to school, and personality organization. Furthermore, several continuities in maltreated children's patterns of maladaptation have become apparent; for example, disorganization in the early attachment relationship is reflected throughout subsequent stages of development, such as in children's aberrant representational models, parentified behaviors, bullying and victim internalizations, and concomitant aggression toward and withdrawal from peers. Other continuities include the apparent canalization of cognitive milestones in the face of maltreatment (e.g., the emergence of visual self-recognition, pretend play abilities), despite clear differences in affective displays accompanying such behaviors. Thus, maltreated children are at risk for developing a profile of relatively enduring vulnerability factors, placing them at high risk for future maladaptation (Cicchetti & Lynch, 1993).

Several long-term consequences to child maltreatment have been identified in adulthood (see Arnow, 2004, for review). However, the majority of research regarding the adverse outcomes of child maltreatment is limited by its reliance on retrospective reports (Brewin, Andrews, & Gotlib, 1993; A. V. Horowitz, Widom, McLaughlin, & White, 2001). For example, a retrospective study of homeless women found that childhood abuse has significant indirect effects on depression, chronic homelessness, and drug and alcohol problems, which are mediated through later physical abuse and self-esteem (J. A. Stein, Leslie, & Nyamathi, 2002). However, due to the use of retrospective methodology, it is difficult to determine causal links between abuse and later outcomes in adulthood. Given evidence that recollections of past abusive experiences may change over time in light of later events and changing definitions of abuse (Loftus, 1993), the reliability of findings of the long-term mental health effects of childhood abuse based on retrospective data has been subject to serious critique (Widom & Morris, 1997; Widom & Shepard, 1996). Furthermore, this technique is often applied to adult populations who have been identified as expressing a specific problem, thus bringing the generalizability of such findings into question.

Keeping in mind the limitations of retrospective analysis within specific pathological populations, the link between abuse and aggressive and violent behavior in adolescents and adults has been consistently documented in the literature. For example, higher rates of physical abuse are reported among adolescents who have specified problems with violence and aggression (D. O. Lewis, Mallouh, & Webb, 1989), among adults who are convicted of violent offenses or who are institutionalized and have violent tendencies (M. Rosenbaum & Bennett, 1986; Sack & Mason, 1980), and among adults who engage in partner violence (Ehrensaft et al., 2003), as well as among those who experience revictimization in adulthood (A. J. Lang, Stein, Kennedy, & Foy, 2004).

A history of physical abuse has also been linked to other forms of psychological disturbance. For example, depressed inpatients who had been physically abused have demonstrated higher levels of impulsivity, aggression, and lifetime suicide attempts in comparison to nonabused depressed inpatients (Brodsky et al., 2001). Children who have been physically abused are at risk for suicidal ideation (Finzi et al., 2001; Thompson et al., 2005), and this risk may extend into adulthood (Dube et al., 2001). Research on suicidality among maltreated children suggests that profound interpersonal difficulties during middle adolescence may mediate the associations between child maltreatment and suicide attempts during late adolescence and early adulthood (J. G. Johnson et al., 2002). Providing further support for the centrality of proximal stressors in predicting maltreated children's risk for suicide, a study with maltreated adolescents suggested that the link between maltreatment and suicidality could be largely accounted for by risk factors such as family functioning and parent or child psychopathology (Kaplan et al., 1999). Among younger maltreated children (age 8), witnessed violence and child maltreatment, as well as child psychological distress, substance use, and poor social problem solving, have each been associated with suicide. The effects of maltreatment and witnessed violence on suicidal ideation, however, were mediated by child functioning (Thompson et al., 2005). Consistent with an organizational developmental perspective, prior experiences of maltreatment leave children with fewer resources to master new developmental tasks and to protect themselves against subsequent challenges, thereby increasing their vulnerability for suicide in the face of proximal stress.

Although the aforementioned investigations have identified a number of maladaptive long-term sequelae of child maltreatment, studies that are prospective and longitudinal in design are much more informative with regard to identifying individual developmental pathways to adaptation or maladaptation. For example, a prospective longitudinal study by A. V. Horowitz and colleges (2001) indicated that

men and women who were physically abused and neglected as children had higher rates of Dysthymia and Antisocial Personality Disorder as adults than did matched controls. Women who had experienced abuse and neglect as children additionally endorsed more problems with alcohol abuse than did controls. Moreover, the abused and neglected groups reported not only more symptoms of psychopathology as adults, but also a greater number of lifetime stressors; these stressors accounted for much of the relationship between childhood abuse and adult mental health outcomes (A. V. Horowitz et al., 2001).

Among children, a longitudinal study conducted by Kim and Cicchetti (2004) demonstrated that maltreatment and mother-child relationship quality independently contributed to the development of children's internalizing and externalizing problems over time, both directly and indirectly through self-esteem and social competence. Specifically, maltreated children showed less socially adaptive behaviors with peers than the nonmaltreated children. Furthermore, maltreatment was related to internalizing and externalizing symptomatology, directly as well as indirectly through deficits in social competencies. Self-esteem mediated the impact of mother-child relationship quality on child adjustment outcomes for both maltreated and nonmaltreated children, such that secure attachment was negatively related to internalizing and externalizing at Time 2 (1 year later), via its influence on self-esteem at Time 1. Elevated internalizing and externalizing symptomatology is consistent with several additional studies showing that maltreated school-age children and adolescents manifest higher levels of depressed symptomatology, behavior problems at home and at school, and juvenile delinquency than do nonmaltreated children (Crittenden, Claussen, & Sugarman, 1994; Okun et al., 1994; Zingraff, Leiter, Myers, & Johnsen, 1993). Moreover, the maladaptive trajectories of maltreated children diverge from those of nonmaltreated children over time such that maltreated children's problems become more severe as children get older, especially in the domains of peer relationships and behavior problems such as aggression (Crittenden et al., 1994; Dodge et al., 1994).

Beyond general adjustment problems, maltreatment is associated with a higher prevalence of clinical-level psychiatric symptomatology and diagnoses than is observed among nonmaltreated children. For example, a significantly higher incidence of Attention-Deficit/Hyperactivity Disorder, Oppositional Defiant Disorder, and Posttraumatic Stress Disorder was found among maltreated children than nonmaltreated children, according to both the parent and child administrations of the Diagnostic Interview for Children and Adults (Famularo, Kinscherff, & Fenton, 1992). The child interviews revealed higher incidence of psychotic symptoms as well as personality and adjustment disorders, and the parent interviews indicated a greater incidence of conduct and mood disorders among maltreated children (Famularo et al., 1992). Physical and sexual abuse in particular have been related to a number of psychiatric disorders in childhood and adulthood, including panic disorders, anxiety disorders, depression, eating disorders, somatic complaints, dissociation and hysterical symptoms, sexual dysfunction, and Borderline Personality Disorder (A. Browne & Finklehor, 1986; Kessler, Davis, & Kendler, 1997; Merry & Andrews, 1994; Putnam, 2003; Weaver & Clum, 1993; Wolfe & Jaffe, 1991).

In general, research has largely focused on the role of maltreatment in the development of depression, Posttraumatic Stress Disorder, dissociative disorders, and personality disorders. Elevated rates of depressive symptomatology are consistently found among maltreated children in comparison to nonmaltreated children (Kim & Cicchetti, 2004; Sternberg et al., 1993; Toth & Cicchetti, 1996; Toth, Manly, & Cicchetti, 1992). Additionally, many maltreated children meet diagnostic criteria for Dysthymia (Kaufman, 1991). A variety of factors have been posited to mediate the impact of maltreatment on depression: subtype of maltreatment, children's patterns of relatedness to their mother, social support and stressful life events, attributional styles, social competence and self-esteem, and psychophysiology (Kaufman, 1991; Kim & Cicchetti, 2004; Koverla, Pound, Heger, & Lytle, 1993; Toth & Cicchetti, 1996; Toth et al., 1992; Toth, Maughan, Manly, Spagnola, & Cicchetti, 2002). For example, the relationship between cognitive style and subtype of maltreatment has been associated with the development of both nonendogenous depression and hopelessness depression in adulthood (Gibb, Wheeler, Alloy, & Abramson, 2001). Specifically, levels of child emotional maltreatment, but not physical or sexual abuse, have been related to levels of hopelessness and episodes of nonendogenous Major Depression and hopelessness depression. Evidence from this retrospective analysis supports that the presence of a negative cognitive style partially mediates the relationship between childhood emotional maltreatment and nonendogenous Major Depression and fully mediates the relation between emotional maltreatment and hopelessness depression (Gibb, Wheeler, et al., 2001). In an investigation of the relationship between child maltreatment, cognitive style, and depression, Toth, Cicchetti, and Kim (2002) concurrently assessed cognitive styles and

behavioral internalizing and externalizing symptomatology among maltreated and nonmaltreated school-age children. Children's attributional style emerged as a significant moderator of the relationship between maltreatment and externalizing symptoms, suggesting that attributional style may exert a protective effect against the negative consequences of maltreatment. Moreover, results indicated that children's perceptions of their mother functions as a mediator between maltreatment and the development of internalizing and externalizing symptomatology. Specifically, the findings support that maltreatment is related both directly and indirectly to behavioral maladjustment. The indirect pathway suggests that maltreatment contributes to children's forming less positive perceptions of their mother, which then exacerbates internalizing and externalizing psychopathology (Toth, Cicchetti, & Kim, 2002).

Alternatively, the experience of sexual abuse has been associated with an increased likelihood of impairments in a number of interrelated areas of development, including the development of self-esteem and self concepts; beliefs about personal power, control, and self-efficacy; the development of cognitive and social competencies; and emotional and behavioral self-regulation (Putnam & Trickett, 1993). A recent review of all published literature between 1989 and 2003 containing empirical data relevant to childhood sexual abuse found that depression in adulthood and sexualized behaviors in children are the best-documented outcomes of child sexual abuse (Putnam, 2003). For example, in a recent investigation among a sample of depressed women, those with and without a history of sexual abuse were comparable regarding the severity of depression; however, the women with child sexual abuse history were more likely to have attempted suicide and/or engaged in deliberate self-harm (Gladstone et al., 2004). Thus, depressed women with a history of sexual abuse may constitute a subgroup of patients who may require tailored interventions to battle depression recurrence and harmful and self-defeating coping strategies.

Kendler, Kuhn, and Prescott (2004) examined whether childhood sexual abuse (CSA) in women altered sensitivity in adulthood to the depressogenic effects of stressful life events (SLEs). Utilizing a population-based sample of 1,404 female adult twins, Kendler and colleagues found that previously assessed neuroticism and CSA and past-year SLEs predicted Major Depressive Disorder. Moreover, women with severe CSA had an increased risk for Major Depression and an increased sensitivity to the depressogenic effects of SLEs. These findings illustrate that early environmental risk factors, just as is the case with genetic factors, can produce long-term increases in the sensitivity of women to depressogenic life experiences.

Posttraumatic Stress Disorder (PTSD) develops in response to the occurrence of a major stressor and is characterized by frequent reexperiencing of the traumatic event through flashbacks, nightmares, or intrusive thoughts; a numbing of general responsiveness to current events; and persistent symptoms of increased arousal (American Psychiatric Association, 1987, 1994). The experience of childhood sexual abuse has been related to the development of immediate as well as long-term PTSD symptoms (Briere & Runtz, 1993; McLeer, Callaghan, Henry, & Wallen, 1994). Furthermore, children who have been sexually abused experience PTSD at rates higher than children who have experienced other subtypes of maltreatment (Deblinger, McLeer, Atkins, Ralphe, & Foa, 1989; Kendall-Tackett, Williams, & Finkehor, 1993; Kiser, Heston, Millsap, & Pruitt, 1991; Merry & Andrews, 1994).

Dissociation refers to a psychological phenomenon manifest by a disruption in the normally self-integrative processes of memory, identity, and consciousness (American Psychological Association, 1987, 1994). Dissociation states range on a continuum from normal minor occurrences of everyday life, such as daydreaming, to pathological manifestations such as that seen in Multiple Personality Disorder and fugue states (Fischer & Ayoub, 1994; Putnam & Trickett, 1993; Westen, 1994). Given the severe disruptions in self system development, including dissociative symptoms, that have been observed among maltreated children (Macfie et al., 2001a, 2001b), it follows that these children would be at risk for later emergence of dissociative psychopathology.

Sexual abuse in particular has been associated with dissociation, conceptualized clinically as a defensive process against overwhelming trauma (M. R. Nash, Hulsey, Sexton, Harralson, & Lambert, 1993). Higher rates of dissociation and splitting are seen among sexually abused children than in any other comparison group (Calverley et al., 1994; Kirby, Chi, & Dill, 1993; M. R. Nash et al., 1993). Further, there seems to be a unique relationship between sexual abuse and dissociation that is not present for physical abuse such that dissociation has been shown to have an important mediating role between sexual abuse and psychiatric disturbance (Kisiel & Lyons, 2001).

In a recent investigation, childhood interpersonal trauma as a whole was highly predictive of a diagnosis of Depersonalization Disorder and of scores denoting dissociation, pathological dissociation, and depersonalization (Simeon, Guralnik, Schmeidler, Sirof, & Knutelska, 2001). When an-

alyzing the effects of specific subtypes of trauma, emotional abuse alone emerged as the most significant predictor of both Depersonalization Disorder diagnosis and severity; it did not, however, predict general scores denoting dissociation. General dissociation scores were best predicted by the combined severity of emotional and sexual abuse. This suggests that a unique relationship may exist between emotional abuse and Depersonalization Disorder, whereas other subtypes or combinations of abuse may contribute to more severe dissociative symptoms.

Personality disorders are conceptualized as rather enduring, character-based patterns of pathology that emerge in adolescence or early adulthood. Etiological accounts often point to childhood experiences as central to the development of personality disorders (Battle et al., 2004; J. G. Johnson et al., 1999; Laporte & Guttman, 1996). Evidence supports that personality disorders are more prevalent among those who have a history of child abuse (Pribor & Dinwiddie, 1992; Silverman, Reinherz, & Giaconia, 1996), suggesting that child abuse and neglect may play a role in their etiology.

Of the personality disorders, Borderline Personality Disorder (BPD) has been best investigated with regard to adverse child experiences (for a full review, see Zanarini, 2000). In general, research with BPD patients indicates higher reporting of childhood abuse (Herman, Perry, & van der Kolk, 1989; Ogata et al., 1990; Soloff, Lynch, & Kelly, 2002; Zanarini, Gunderson, Marino, Schwartz, & Frenkenburg, 1989; Zanarini et al., 1997) and child neglect (J. G. Johnson et al., 2000; Zanarini et al., 1989, 1997) than among patients with other personality disorders (Zanarini et al., 1989) or other Axis I psychiatric disorders (Ogata et al., 1990); however, these reports should have been interpreted with caution given that they are retrospective in nature.

The impact of the subtypes of maltreatment on the development of BPD is somewhat less clear. Childhood sexual abuse has been identified as a factor that discriminated patients with BPD from those with other personality disorders (Weaver & Clum, 1993); however, it has been noted that when childhood sexual abuse history has been identified among BPD patients, multiple forms of abuse and neglect are additionally present (Ogata et al., 1990; Zanarini et al., 1997, 2000).

The majority of research on maltreatment and personality disorders has compared BPD with an "other personality disorder" category, with very limited research into specific disorders (for a review, see Battle et al., 2004). Although there seems to be some empirical support that in addition to BPD, other personality disorder groups report a high prevalence of childhood maltreatment histories (Gibb, Wheeler, et al., 2001), much of this evidence is again based on retrospective reports by psychiatric patients (B. Maughan & Rutter, 1997; Paris, 1997) and should be interpreted with caution (Widom & Morris, 1997; Widom & Shepard, 1996).

To address the limitation of retrospective data, a small body of longitudinal evidence is emerging in the field to support the hypothesis that childhood maltreatment increases risk for personality disorders in adulthood (R. E. Drake, Adler, & Vaillant, 1988; J. G. Johnson et al., 1999; Luntz & Widom, 1994). Such investigations have revealed that maltreatment is associated with the development of Antisocial Personality Disorder. Further, family instability and lack of parental affection and supervision during adolescence were associated with Dependent and Passive-Aggressive Personality Disorder among men. An additional community-based, longitudinal study showed that persons with documented child abuse were more than 4 times as likely as those who were not abused or neglected to be diagnosed with a personality disorder, after age, parental education, and parental psychiatric disorders were controlled statistically (J. G. Johnson et al., 1999). Specifically, physical abuse, sexual abuse, and neglect were each uniquely associated with elevated personality disorder symptom levels during early adulthood. Physical abuse was associated with Antisocial and Depressive Personality Disorder symptoms; sexual abuse was associated with elevated BPD symptoms; and neglect was associated with Antisocial, Avoidant, Borderline, Narcissistic, and Passive-Aggressive Personality Disorders. This investigation highlights the particular impact of neglect on personality disorder development (J. G. Johnson et al., 1999).

Finally, child maltreatment has been associated with maladaptive trajectories in the development of sexuality (i.e., Brown, Cohen, Chen, Smailes, & Johnson, 2004; Noll, Trickett, & Putnam, 2003). A recent prospective longitudinal study revealed that a history of two or more incidents of sexual abuse was associated with early puberty and early pregnancy, after gender, race, class, paternal absence, and mother's age at the birth of the study child were controlled statistically (Brown et al., 2004). In addition o heightened sexual activity and preoccupation, a subset of women with sexual abuse histories has been identified who exhibit sexual ambivalence or a heightened sexual preoccupation coupled with greater sexual aversion (Trickett & Putnam, 2003). In particular, pathological dissociation and biological father abuse may be associated with greater sexual aversion and sexual ambivalence. These investigations highlight the risk for premature sex-

ual behavior among maltreated adolescents; efforts to prevent teenage pregnancy should pay particular attention to sexually abused children as they enter puberty.

RESILIENT OUTCOMES

Consistent with a developmental psychopathology perspective, there is multifinality in developmental processes such that the manner in which the individual responds to and interacts with vulnerability and protective factors at each level of ecology allows for diversity of outcomes. Just as deviations from the average expectable environment potentiate some children toward the development of maladaptation, others evidence adaptation in the face of the same challenges. Thus, it is equally informative to understand the mechanisms that promote resilient functioning among maltreated children as it is to investigate developmental trajectories toward psychopathology (Masten, 1989). Maltreatment undisputedly represents an extremely adverse and stressful experience, yet not all maltreated children demonstrate maladaptive outcomes. Thus, the study of resilience among maltreated children seeks to understand the dynamic processes that influence how the various aspects of children's ecologies eventuate in multiplicity in child developmental outcome, adaptive or maladaptive.

Resilience has been conceptualized as the individual's capacity for adapting successfully and functioning competently, despite experiencing chronic stress or adversity following exposure to prolonged or severe trauma (Masten & Coatsworth, 1998). It is important that the construct of resilience be conceptualized as a dynamic process, not a static or trait-like condition (Cicchetti & Schneider-Rosen, 1986; Egeland, Carlson, & Sroufe, 1993; Luthar, Cicchetti, & Becker, 2000), so that resilience research may elucidate the mechanisms through which individuals are able to initiate or maintain their self-righting tendencies when confronted with adversity (cf. Cicchetti & Rizley, 1981; Waddington, 1957). Understanding resilience will contribute to our understanding of how ontogenic processes play a critical role in determining whether adaptation or maladaptation will manifest at each stage of development (Cicchetti & Tucker, 1994).

Initial resilience research sought to identify correlates of resilient outcomes in maltreated children; however, given the nature of resilience as a dynamic process, longitudinal research most adequately can address its development. Unfortunately, there are few longitudinal studies that track subsequent adaptive functioning among maltreated children. The extant longitudinal investigations of resilient functioning among young maltreated children through age

6 have highlighted both the dynamic nature of resilient processes and the poor developmental outcomes associated with maltreatment (Egeland & Farber, 1987; E. C. Herrenkohl, Herrenkohl, & Egolf, 1994). For example, Egeland and Farber found that not a single maltreated child included in their study consistently functioned competently across each age period assessed, in which competence was defined as successful resolution of a stage-salient issue at each level of development. Moreover, Herrenkohl, Herrenkohl, and Egolf found that fewer than 15% of children who had been maltreated prior to age 6 were identified as resilient, and when contacted in adolescence, nearly 50% of these previously resilient maltreated children were no longer demonstrating resilient functioning.

Among the protective factors that have been identified to promote resilient functioning are average or above-average intellectual performance, absence of physical abuse, the presence of at least one stable caregiver, and positive parental expectations regarding their children's academic performance (E. C. Herrenkohl et al., 1994; Masten et al., 1999). Highlighting the role of individual child characteristics in the development of adaptation, children's academic engagement, social competencies, and ego resiliency have all been positively associated with adaptation to school (Shonk & Cicchetti, 2001). Personality characteristics such as internal locus of control for good events and higher self-esteem are further examples of individual characteristics that serve a protective function for children, mitigating the risk for maladaptive outcomes (Moran & Eckenrode, 1992).

In perhaps the most comprehensive assessments of resilient functioning among maltreated school-age children, Cicchetti and Rogosch (1997) improved on their prior cross-sectional investigation of predictors and correlates of resilience (Cicchetti, Rogosch, Lynch, & Holt, 1993) by assessing the longitudinal adaptation of over 200 children over a 3-year period. For both studies, resilient adaptation among multiple areas of functioning was evaluated within a heterogeneous sample of economically disadvantaged maltreated children and nonmaltreated comparison children. In their earlier investigation, maltreated children evinced lower overall competence across multiple indices of functioning than the nonmaltreated children. Moreover, maltreated children were rated as more withdrawn, with significantly greater levels of internalizing symptomatology, more disruptive, and more aggressive. Nonetheless, ego resiliency, ego overcontrol, and self-esteem emerged as predictors of resilient adaptation for maltreated children. In contrast, only ego resiliency and positive self-esteem were associated with resilient functioning among nonmaltreated children (Cicchetti, Rogosch, et al., 1993).

Similarly, the longitudinal investigation revealed that a higher percentage of nonmaltreated children evidenced resilient functioning than did maltreated children; furthermore, a high percentage of maltreated children were functioning in the low-adaptive range (Cicchetti & Rogosch, 1997). Notably, different predictors of resilience emerged for the maltreated and nonmaltreated children such that for maltreated children, positive self-esteem, ego resilience, and ego overcontrol predicted resilient functioning, whereas relationship features were more influential for nonmaltreated children. These findings suggest that perhaps, in the face of unfulfilling relationships, the maltreated children who demonstrate resilient functioning have developed an adaptive coping mechanism toward less reliance on relatedness in their everyday functioning. Considering that personality resources and self-confidence were major predictors of resilient adaptation in maltreated children, Cicchetti and Rogosch posit that interventions that focus on the enhancement of self system processes such as autonomy, mastery, and self-determination may be effective (Ryan et al., 1995).

Highlighting additional pathways to resilient functioning, Flores et al. (2005) conducted a similar assessment of multiple domains of functioning with a sample of high-risk Latino maltreated and nonmaltreated children. Although prior research had identified predictors of resilient adaptation in maltreated children, there was a lack of knowledge regarding whether these same factors would be applicable to Latino children. Considering evidence that relationships are very highly valued in Latino cultures (Harrison, Wilson, Pine, Chan, & Buriel, 1990), Flores and colleagues sought to determine whether relationship features would serve as predictors of resilient adaptation for both maltreated and nonmaltreated Latino children. Consistent with prior investigations of resilience, which have been composed of mainly African American and Caucasian American children (Cicchetti & Rogosch, 1997; Cicchetti et al., 1993; McGloin & Widom, 2001), maltreated Latino children demonstrated a lower level of resilient functioning than did equally disadvantaged nonmaltreated Latino children. For both maltreated and nonmaltreated Latino children, higher ego resiliency and moderate ego overcontrol were associated with higher resilient functioning. Thus, in contrast to prior investigations (Cicchetti & Rogosch, 1997), the effects of ego resiliency and ego overcontrol did not differentially predict resilience for maltreated and nonmaltreated Latino children. In accord with previous findings, however, the predictive impact of relationship variables on resilience was more significant for nonmaltreated than maltreated Latino children (Flores et al.,

2005). These findings suggest that among Latino children, personal strengths such as ego resiliency and ego overcontrol may be more essential than relationship features in determining a pathway to resilient adaptation.

Taken together, it seems that self-reliance and self-confidence, in concert with interpersonal reserve, may bode well for the development of resilient adaptation in maltreated children. This is congruent with findings among highly stressed, disadvantaged youngsters, such that positive future expectations for the self are a predictor of resilient functioning (Wyman, Cowen, Work, & Kerley, 1993). Research on resilience attests to the critical role that children play in actively constructing their outcomes and in influencing their ultimate adaptation through mechanisms such as reliance on the self, confidence in the self, and interpersonal reserve.

Currently, the field of resilience is now headed toward an incorporation of neurobiological and physiological factors (Curtis & Cicchetti, 2003) in elucidating the biological mechanisms of ontogenic development and self-striving processes. According to a transactional-organizational perspective, which conceptualizes resilience as a dynamic process akin to all other developmental processes, resilience is influenced by neural and psychological self-organization as well as by transactions between the ecological context and the developing organism. Neural plasticity, in particular, may be well applied to the concept of resilience (Cicchetti, 2002, 2003; Curtis & Nelson, 2003), and may provide a neurobiological account for the ability of an individual to recover after exposure to trauma or adversity. Alternatively, it is possible that certain genetic predispositions may account for the variation of the extent to which individuals are impacted by environmental influences. Research from the fields of emotion regulation, psychophysiology, neuroendocrinology, and genetics are just beginning to elucidate how neurobiological and physiological mechanisms contribute to the self-striving tendencies of ontogenic development and through reciprocal interactions with varying levels of ecology exert an influence on developmental outcomes, both adaptive and maladaptive (Caspi et al., 2002; Cicchetti & Rogosch, 1997; Curtis & Cicchetti, 2003; McEwen, 1998).

NEUROBIOLOGICAL ONTOGENIC DEVELOPMENT AND GENE EXPRESSION: THE DEVELOPING BRAIN AS A SELF-ORGANIZING DYNAMIC SYSTEM

Scientific investigations on child maltreatment have focused predominantly on psychological processes and outcomes. In recent years, the examination of the neurobiological correlates and sequelae of child abuse and neglect have now begun to receive more attention from researchers. Such work holds great promise for elucidating the mechanisms underlying maladaptive development in maltreated children and for examining the impact that negative social experiences exert on brain structure and function, as well as on gene expression. As research on the effects of child maltreatment on neurobiological structure and function and on gene expression continues to burgeon, it is conceivable that the examination of the multifaceted neurobiological systems affected by child maltreatment, as well as the investigation of the impact that maltreatment experiences have on gene expression, will provide insight into some of the mediators and moderators linking child maltreatment with socioemotional and cognitive outcomes.

Although brain development is guided and controlled to some degree by genetic information, a not insignificant portion of postnatal brain structuration, neural patterning, and organization are thought to occur through interactions and transactions of the individual with the environment (J. Black, Jones, Nelson, & Greenough, 1998; M. H. Johnson, 1998). Thus, each individual may traverse a potentially unique and partly self-determined developmental pathway of brain building that we believe may have important consequences for the development of normal, abnormal, and resilient adaptation (J. Black et al., 1998; Cicchetti & Tucker, 1994; Curtis & Cicchetti, 2003).

In self-organizing brain development (Cicchetti & Tucker, 1994; Courchesne, Townsend, & Chase, 1995), some regions of the brain serve to stabilize and organize information for other areas, whereas other regions utilize experience to fine-tune their anatomy for optimal function. In this manner, individuals can use the interaction of genetic constraints and environmental information to self-organize their highly complex neural systems. Synaptogenesis appears to be generated in response to events that provide information to be encoded in the nervous system (Courchesne, Chisum, & Townsend, 1994). This experience-dependent synapse formation involves the brain's adaptation to information that is unique to the individual (Greenough, Black, & Wallace, 1987). Because all individuals encounter distinctive environments, each brain is modified in a singular fashion. Experience-dependent synaptogenesis is localized to the brain regions involved in processing information arising from the event experienced by the individual. Unlike the case with experience-expectant processes, experience-dependent processes do not take place within a stringent temporal interval because the timing or nature of experience that the individual engages or chooses cannot be entirely envisioned (Bruer, 1999). An important central mechanism for experience-dependent development is the formation of new neural connections, in contrast to the overproduction and pruning back of synapses often associated with experience-expectant processes (Greenough et al., 1987; Huttenlocher, 1994).

For example, children who develop in a resilient fashion despite having experienced significant adversity play an active role in constructing, seeking, and receiving the experiences that are developmentally appropriate for them (J. Black et al., 1998; Cicchetti & Tucker, 1994). Through utilizing experience-dependent processes, children who function resiliently likely modify and/or protect their brain anatomy to ensure an adaptive developmental outcome (Curtis & Cicchetti, 2003). At one level, different areas of the brain may attempt to compensate, and, at another, the organism may seek out new experiences in areas where it has strength (J. Black et al., 1998). Because experience-dependent plasticity is a central feature of the mammalian brain (M. Johnson, 1999), neither early brain anomalies nor aberrant experiences should be considered as determining the ultimate fate of the organism (Cicchetti & Tucker, 1994).

Furthermore, because the mechanisms of neural plasticity cause the brain's anatomical differentiation to be dependent on stimulation from the environment, it is now clear that the cytoarchitecture of the cerebral cortex is shaped by input from the social environment. Cortical development and organization should not be viewed as passive processes that depend exclusively on genetic and environmental input. Development, both psychological and biological, is more than nature-nurture interaction. Thus, corticogenesis should be conceived as processes of self-organization guided by self-regulatory mechanisms (Cicchetti & Tucker, 1994).

Children endowed with normal brains may encounter a number of experiences, including child maltreatment, extreme poverty, and community and domestic violence, that can not only exert a negative impact on brain structure, function, and organization, but also contribute to distorting these children's experiences of the world (Cicchetti, 2002; Pollak, Cicchetti, & Klorman, 1998). Perturbations that occur during brain development can potentiate a cascade of maturational and structural changes that eventuate in the neural system proceeding along a trajectory that deviates from that generally taken in normal neurobiological development (Courchesne et al., 1994; Nowakowski & Hayes, 1999). Early stresses, either physiological or emotional, may condition young neural networks to produce cascading

effects through later development, possibly constraining the child's flexibility to adapt to challenging situations with new strategies rather than with old conceptual and behavioral prototypes. Thus, early psychological trauma such as that experienced by maltreated children may eventuate not only in emotional sensitization (A. Maughan & Cicchetti, 2002), but also in pathological sensitization of neurophysiological reactivity (Cicchetti & Tucker, 1994; Pollak et al., 1998). Such early developmental abnormalities may lead to the development of aberrant neural circuitry and often compound themselves into relatively enduring forms of psychopathology (Cicchetti & Cannon, 1999; Nowakowski & Hayes, 1999).

Children may be especially vulnerable to the effects of pathological experiences during periods of rapid creation or modification of neuronal connections (J. Black et al., 1998). Pathological experience may become part of a vicious cycle, as the pathology induced in brain structure may distort the child's experience, with subsequent alterations in cognitive or social interactions causing additional pathological experience and added brain pathology (Cicchetti & Tucker, 1994; Pollak et al., 1998). Children who incorporate pathological experience during ongoing experience-expectant and experience-dependent processes may add neuropathological connections to their developing brains instead of functional neuronal connections (J. Black et al., 1998).

The Impact of Child Maltreatment on Neurobiological Processes

Adverse life experiences, exemplified by the experience of child maltreatment, are thought to affect neurobiological and psychological processes. Physiological and behavioral responses to maltreatment are expected to be interrelated and to contribute to children's making choices and responding to experiences in ways that generally produce pathological development. Because maltreated children experience the extremes of "caretaking casualty" (Sameroff & Chandler, 1975), they provide one of the clearest opportunities for scientists to discover the multiple ways in which social and psychological stressors can affect biological systems. Numerous interconnected neurobiological systems are affected by the various stressors associated with child maltreatment (Cicchetti, 2002; DeBellis, 2001). Moreover, each of these neurobiological systems influences and is influenced by multiple domains of psychological and biological development. Furthermore, in keeping with the principle of multifinality, the neurobiological development of maltreated children is not affected in the same way in all individuals. Not all maltreated children exhibit anomalies in their brain structure or functioning.

Neurobiological Structure: Neuroimaging

Magnetic resonance imaging (MRI) technology provides a noninvasive and safe methodology for examining brain morphology, physiology, and function in individuals who have experienced child maltreatment. Several MRI investigations have found reduced hippocampal volume in victims of psychological trauma with PTSD. Bremner, Krystal, Southwick, and Charney (1995) discovered that male combat veterans with PTSD evidenced decreased MRI-derived right-side hippocampal volume and that aspects of the memory deficits exhibited by the combat veterans with PTSD correlated with hippocampal volume. Gurvits and colleagues (1996) replicated the finding of reduced hippocampal volume in an MRI study of male combat veterans. In contrast to Bremner et al., Gurvits et al. found hippocampal reduction bilaterally. In a heterogeneous sample of men and women who experienced abuse in their childhood, Bremner et al. (1997) discovered a reduction in left-side hippocampal volume compared to nonabused comparisons. Relatedly, M. B. Stein, Yehuda, Koverola, and Hanna (1997) found that women who reported being sexually abused in childhood showed a reduced left-side hippocampal volume compared to nonsexually traumatized women. Vythilingam and colleagues (2002) conducted an MRI investigation of a group of adult females who had a current diagnosis of Major Depressive Disorder (MDD). Two-thirds of the women with MDD had a history of child physical or sexual abuse; the other depressed women had no abuse histories. The two groups of women with MDD were compared to a group of healthy women. Depressed women who had experienced abuse in their childhood have a significantly smaller hippocampal volume than the nonabused depressed women and the women in the healthy comparison group.

In a more recent investigation, Bremner and colleagues (2003) conducted an MRI and a positron emission tomography (PET) study with a group of women who experienced sexual abuse and PTSD in their childhood, another group of women who had experienced sexual abuse but who did not have PTSD, and a comparison group of women without sexual abuse or PTSD. Utilizing MRI, Bremner et al. found that women who had been sexually abused had significantly smaller hippocampi than either women who had been sexually abused without PTSD or women who were

without sexual abuse histories or PTSD. Additionally, the women with sexual abuse and PTSD showed a failure of left hippocampal activation during a verbal memory task that was measured by PET. This finding remained significant after adjusting for hippocampal atrophy.

In a functional magnetic resonance imaging (fMRI) study, Anderson, Teicher, Polcari, and Renshaw (2002) performed steady-state fMRI (T2 relaxometry) to assess resting blood flow in the cerebellar vermis. Adults who had been sexually abused in childhood manifested higher T2 relaxation times (T2-RT) than controls. Elevated T2-RT measures have been shown to be associated with decreased blood volume and neuronal activity. Anderson et al. interpreted the elevated T2-RT found in the cerebellar vermis of these adults who had experienced sexual abuse as indicative of a possible pathway from early abuse → functional deficits in the cerebellar vermis → reduced neuronal activity → decreased blood volume.

Over the course of the past decade, neuroimaging studies have been conducted with maltreated children and adolescents. DeBellis, Keshavan, and colleagues (1999) conducted an in-depth whole-brain volumetric analysis of a group of hospitalized maltreated children and adolescents with PTSD and a group of medically and psychiatrically well nonmaltreated comparison subjects. In keeping with the literature on child maltreatment, most of the participants had experienced multiple types of maltreatment. Moreover, in addition to PTSD, most of the children and adolescents who were maltreated had comorbid mental disorders. These included Major Depressive Disorder, Dysthymia, Oppositional Defiant Disorder, and Attention-Deficit/Hyperactivity Disorder. Of particular importance, given that the hippocampus is susceptible to the harmful effects of chronic alcohol abuse, substance and alcohol abuse were rare in the DeBellis, Keshavan, et al. study.

In contrast to the findings of the investigations of adults who had childhood histories of abuse reviewed above, DeBellis, Keshavan, et al. (1999) did not find a decrease in hippocampal volume in the group of maltreated children and adolescents with PTSD. Moreover, DeBellis, Hall, Boring, Frustaci, and Moritz (2001) examined hippocampal volumes longitudinally to determine if a history of childhood maltreatment and PTSD alter the growth of the hippocampus during puberty. DeBellis and colleagues (2001) utilized MRI to scan the brains of maltreated children with PTSD and healthy nonmaltreated comparison children matched on SES on two occasions, once when they were prepubertal and then again 2 to 3 years later during the later stages of puberty (i.e., Tanner Stages IV and V). MRI was used to measure the temporal lobes, amygdala, and hippocampal volumes of the two groups of children. There were no differences in temporal lobe, amygdala, or hippocampal volume between the group of maltreated children with PTSD and the matched group of nonmaltreated children, either at baseline or across longitudinal follow-up.

These apparent discrepant findings may be a function of the increase in volume that normatively occurs in neurobiological development during adolescence (Spear, 2000, 2003). Specifically, subcortical gray matter structures that include the hippocampus continue to develop, and these normative adolescent increases (i.e., the normal processes of brain development) may mask any effects that maltreatment and PTSD exert on the developing limbic system (e.g., amygdala, hippocampus). It is conceivable that the stress-induced hippocampal damage may not become apparent until postpubertal development has been initiated. Alternatively, because the maltreated children with PTSD in the DeBellis et al. (2001) sample were in ongoing individual or group treatment, it may be the case that these interventions may have eventuated in increases in hippocampal neurogenesis, thereby contributing to the lack of statistically significant differences.

After controlling for intracranial volume and SES, DeBellis and colleagues (DeBellis, Keshavan, et al., 1999) discovered a number of other MRI-based brain structural anomalies in their sample of maltreated children and adolescents with PTSD. These included smaller intracranial volumes, cerebral volumes, and midsagittal corpus callosum areas and larger lateral ventricles than in the group of nonmaltreated comparison children and adolescents. In addition, DeBellis, Keshavan, et al. found a positive correlation of intracranial volumes with age of onset of PTSD trauma and a negative correlation with the duration of maltreatment that led to a PTSD diagnosis, suggesting that there may be sensitive periods and dose effects for stress-related alterations in brain development. Furthermore, DeBellis, Keshavan, et al. interpret their finding that enlarged lateral ventricles in maltreated children and adolescents were correlated positively with the duration of the maltreatment experienced as suggesting that there may have been neuronal loss associated with severe stress (cf. Sapolsky, 1992).

In another investigation, DeBellis, Keshavan, Spencer, and Hall (2000) utilized magnetic resonance spectroscopy (MRS), a safe and novel neuroimaging methodology, to investigate the in vivo neurochemistry of neurobiological alterations in the brains of living children. DeBellis and colleagues used MRS to measure the relative concentration of N-acetyl aspartate (NAA) and creatine in the anterior cingulate cortex of a small group ($n = 11$) of maltreated children and adolescents who also had PTSD and a healthy nonmaltreated comparison group ($n = 11$) matched on SES. NAA is considered to be a marker of neural integrity; moreover, decreased concentrations of NAA are associated with increased metabolism and loss of neurons (Prichard, 1996). DeBellis et al. found that maltreated children and adolescents with PTSD had lower NAA-to-creatine ratios that are suggestive of neuronal loss in the anterior cingulate region of the medial prefrontal cortex compared to the nonmaltreated SES-matched comparisons. The reduction of NAA to creatine, in addition to DeBellis, Keshavan, et al.'s (1999) finding of enlargement in the lateral ventricles, buttress the hypothesis that maltreatment in childhood may alter the development of cortical neurons.

Teicher and colleagues (2004) investigated the corpus callosum in children who had been abused or neglected to ascertain whether there were structural abnormalities in its regional anatomy. The corpus callosum connects the left and right hemispheres and is the major myelinated tract in the brain. Regional corpus callosum area was measured by MRI in three groups of children: abused and neglected children, children admitted for psychiatric evaluation, and healthy controls. Teicher et al. found that the total area of the corpus callosum of the children who had experienced abuse and neglect was smaller than that of the children evaluated for psychiatric problems and the healthy controls. The latter two groups of children did not differ from each other. Child neglect was associated with a 15% to 18% reduction in corpus callosum regions; in contrast, reduced corpus callosum size in girls was most strongly associated with sexual abuse. These findings are congruent with our earlier assertion that negative early experiences can adversely affect neurobiological development.

In summary, the neuroimaging studies reviewed attest to the harmful impact that child maltreatment can exert on brain development and function. As important, not all maltreated children evidence the same neurobiological structural and functional anomalies. Moreover, some maltreated children appear to have normal neurobiological development and function despite experiencing great adversity. Many important questions remain to be answered (see conclusion and future directions section).

Neurobiological Functioning

Startle expression in humans and in laboratory animals is affected by emotional factors, a connection that may be grounded in the evolutionary value of startle for immediate protection. The disturbances of anxiety and traumatization that have been found in childhood maltreatment (Cicchetti & Lynch, 1995) and the sensitivity of the startle reflex to these conditions suggested the utility of examining startle patterns in maltreated children for developing objective physiological markers of the severity of traumatization. Accordingly, Klorman, Cicchetti, Thatcher, and Ison (2003) investigated acoustic startle in maltreated and nonmaltreated comparison children to a range of auditory intensities to describe any abnormalities in response magnitude, onset latency, and habituation. Additionally, startle differences among subtypes of maltreated children were examined.

The acoustic startle reflex is an obligatory response to a sudden and unexpected stimulus that is marked by the cessation of ongoing behaviors and by a particular series of protective behaviors (Davis, 1984). The eyeblink is the most sensitive and consistent startle response across individuals, and this is the response that is most often measured in studies of this reflex. The startle eyeblink in humans is measured by electromyographic activity detected by electrodes overlying the obicularis oculi muscle, located below each eye.

Klorman et al. (2003) examined acoustic startle to 24 randomly ordered 50-ms. binaural white noise burst probes of 70, 85, 100, and 115 dB while children were watching silent cartoons. The participants were maltreated and nonmaltreated children matched for age, sex, and socioeconomic status (see Klorman et al., 2003). Maltreated boys' startle blinks had smaller amplitude and slower onset latency and were less affected by increasing probe loudness than were those of comparison boys. Among maltreatment subtypes, this pattern was most salient for physically abused boys. Unfortunately, there were not enough physically abused girls to detect any potential differences from comparison children. The results for maltreated boys also are consistent with those of Ornitz and Pynoos (1989) for diminished startle responses among children with PTSD. These investigators suggested that startle diminution in traumatized children may reflect cortically mediated attentional dysfunction that affected brain stem mechanisms for startle responses. Thus, it is conceivable that the effects of social experiences, such as child abuse and neglect, on brain microstructure and biochemistry may be either pathological or adaptive.

The findings obtained with the physically abused boys are consistent with those of Cicchetti and Rogosch (2001a). These investigators found that physically abused children

displayed a suppression of cortisol and significantly less diurnal variation in hypothalamic-pituitary-adrenal (HPA) functioning than did other subtypes of maltreated children. Although startle responsiveness and cortisol regulation are linked to separate, but interconnected, neurobiological systems, in both investigations physically abused children exhibited diminished responsiveness. Physically abused children are often exposed to threat and danger, and their smaller responses to startle and their suppression of cortisol may reflect allostatic load, the cumulative long-term effect of physiologic responses to stress (Evans, 2004; McEwen, 2000, 2004; McEwen & Stellar, 1993). Repetitive social challenges in a child's environment, such as that engendered by child abuse and neglect, can cause disruptions in basic homeostatic and regulatory processes that are essential to the maintenance of optimal physical and mental health (Repetti, Taylor, & Seeman, 2002).

Neuroendocrine Functioning

Stress has been conceptualized as a perceived threat to an organism's homeostasis and as a situation that causes increases in autonomic nervous system activity or hormone secretion (Cicchetti & Walker, 2001). An overt insult or homeostatic mechanism initiates a stress response; however, as the term "perceived stress" connotes, psychological factors can initiate a stress response on their own. The confluence of a number of factors, including genetic makeup, prior experiences, and developmental history, either sensitize or protect the organism from subsequent stressful challenges (McEwen, 1998). In addition, more long-term stress responsiveness is characterized by interindividual variability and is related, in part, to experiential influences on gene expression (Meaney et al., 1996). In sum, then, there are multiple converging pathways—including not only the neural circuits that are activated by physical, psychological, and immunological stressors, but also the influence of genetics, early experience, and ongoing life events—that determine the neural response to different stressors (Sapolsky, 1994).

Stressful or threatening experiences such as child abuse and neglect create adaptational challenges, and the HPA axis is one of the physiological systems that has evolved in mammals to help direct and sustain cognitive, emotional, behavioral, and metabolic activity in response to threat. Basal activity of this neuroendocrine system follows a circadian rhythm, with high levels around the time of awakening, declining to low levels around the onset of sleep (Kirschbaum & Hellhammer, 1989). Basal levels of cortisol are necessary for normal brain growth and for the support of the metabolic activity necessary to sustain general functioning (McEwen, 1998).

Incidents of child maltreatment, such as sexual, physical, and emotional abuse, as well as neglect, may engender massive stress in vulnerable children. Acute threat and emotional distress, as is found in instances of child maltreatment, may activate the locus coeruleus, the major noradrenergic-containing nucleus in the brain, and the sympathetic nervous system (SNS), eventuating in the biological changes accompanying the "fight or flight" reaction. Stressful experiences such as child maltreatment may potentiate the increased production of corticotropin-releasing hormone (CRH) in the central amygdala and in the hypothalamus. CRH from the amygdala causes increased SNS activity, thereby promoting heightened behavioral and attentional arousal (Kaufman & Charney, 2001; Schulkin, McEwen, & Gold, 1994). CRH from the paraventricular nucleus of the hypothalamus, in concert with other hormones such as vasopressin, stimulate the production of adrenocorticotropic hormone (ACTH) in the anterior pituitary. The ACTH that is secreted into circulation selectively stimulates cells of the adrenal cortex to produce and release cortisol, a potent steroid hormone that impacts nearly all organs and tissues of the body (Lopez, Akil, & Watson, 1999; Vazquez, 1998). Cortisol, through negative feedback inhibition on the hypothalamus, pituitary, and additional brain structures, such as the hippocampus, suppresses the HPA axis, thereby bringing about restoration of basal levels of cortisol. Among its many influences, cortisol affects the central neural processes that are implicated in cognition, memory, and emotion.

The capacity to elevate cortisol in response to acute trauma is critical for survival. Brief elevations in corticosteroids following acute stressors appear to enhance the individual's ability to manage stressful experience competently, both physiologically and behaviorally. However, chronic hyperactivity of the HPA axis may eventuate in the accelerated loss or metabolism of hippocampal neurons, the inhibition of neurogenesis, lags in the development of myelination, abnormalities in synaptic pruning, and impaired affective and cognitive ability (Gould, Tanapat, McEwen, Flugge, & Fuchs, 1998; Sapolsky, 1992; Todd, Swarzenski, Rossi, & Visconti, 1995). Moreover, the elimination of glucocorticoids also can damage neurons (Gunnar & Vazquez, 2001; Heim, Ehlert, & Hellhammer, 2000). Specifically, there is a phenomenon known as hypocortisolism in which individuals who are experiencing chronic stressors such as ongoing maltreatment may manifest reduced adrenocortical secretion, reduced adrenocortical re-

activity, or enhanced negative feedback inhibition of the HPA axis (Gunnar & Vazquez, 2001; Heim et al., 2000). Consequently, it is in an organism's best interests to avoid both chronic glucocorticoid hypersecretion and hyposecretion (Sapolsky, 1996).

A number of investigations have been conducted that indicate atypical physiological processes in maltreated children. Noradrenergic, dopaminergic, serotonergic, and glucocorticoid systems, which are activated by stress, all are affected by child maltreatment (Kaufman & Charney, 2001). For example, abnormal noradrenergic activity, as evidenced by lower urinary norepinephrine (NE), has been found in children who have been abused and neglected (Rogeness, 1991). In addition, neglected children have been shown to have lower levels of dopamine (DA)-beta-hydroxylase (DBH), an enzyme involved in the synthesis of NE, than do abused children or normal controls (Rogeness & McClure, 1996). Neglected children also were found to have lower systolic and diastolic blood pressure, both of which are functions mediated by the NE system. These findings from Rogeness's laboratory suggest that the experience of child neglect modifies the genetic expression of DBH activity and the NE system.

Sexually abused girls have been shown to excrete significantly greater amounts of the DA metabolite homovanillic acid (DeBellis, Leffer, Trickett, & Putnam, 1994). Augmented mean morning serial plasma cortisol levels have been found in sexually abused girls, implicating altered glucocorticoid functioning in the HPA axis (Putnam, Trickett, Helmers, Dorn, & Everett, 1991). Relatedly, the attenuated plasma ACTH response to the ovine CRH stimulation test in sexually abused girls further suggests a dysregulatory disorder of the HPA axis, associated with hyporesponsiveness of the pituitary to exogenous CRH and normal overall cortisol secretion to CRH challenge (DeBellis et al., 1993). Sexually abused children with PTSD have been found to excrete significantly greater concentrations of baseline NE and DA in comparison to nonabused anxious and normal healthy controls (DeBellis, Baum, et al., 1999). These findings suggest that the combination of sexual abuse experiences and PTSD is associated with enduring alterations of biological stress systems.

In two separate studies, it has been found that maltreated school-age children with depressive disorder fail to manifest the expected diurnal decrease in cortisol secretion from morning to afternoon (J. Hart, Gunnar, & Cicchetti, 1996; Kaufman, 1991). In a subsequent investigation, it was shown that, when compared to depressed, abused, and normal nonmaltreated comparison children, maltreated prepubertal depressed children who were residing under conditions of chronic ongoing adversity displayed an increased human CRH-induced ACTH response but normal cortisol secretion. In contrast, depressed children with prior abuse histories but who were currently living in a stable environment did not differ in their HPA functioning from the depressed abused or the normal nonmaltreated comparison children (Kaufman et al., 1997). The finding that present microsystem supports can serve as a protective factor against HPA axis dysregulation highlights the malleability of the neuroendocrine system. DeBellis, Baum, et al. (1999) examined the relationship between psychiatric symptomatology and urinary free cortisol (UFC) and catecholamine (epinephrine [EPI], NE, and DA) excretion in prepubertal maltreated children with PTSD. Two groups of children served as the comparisons: nontraumatized children with Overanxious Disorder (OAD) and healthy nontraumatized children without any psychiatric disorder. DeBellis, Baum, and colleagues discovered that maltreated children with PTSD excreted significantly greater concentrations of urinary DA and NE over a 24-hour period than did the OAD and healthy comparison children. Moreover, maltreated children with PTSD excreted significantly greater concentrations of urinary EPI than did the children with OAD. Furthermore, childhood PTSD was related to greater comorbid psychopathology, including depressive and dissociative symptoms and increased incidents of lifetime suicide ideation and attempts. The findings of the DeBellis, Baum, et al. investigation provide further evidence that maltreatment experiences, in combination with PTSD, are associated with alterations in biological stress systems.

Cicchetti and Rogosch (2001a, 2001b) have conducted two investigations of cortisol regulation in school-age maltreated and nonmaltreated children. These studies were implemented in the context of a research summer day camp program. Because attendance at this summer camp was a novel experience, these youngsters did not know what to expect from the adult camp counselors (who were unfamiliar to the children). Moreover, children in the camp were unfamiliar with each other. Thus, the camp context constituted a social challenge for the children in attendance, making it a context appropriate to investigate the impact of stress on neuroendocrine function.

Saliva samples were collected twice daily through the week children participated in camp. One advantage of the naturalistic camp setting was that it permitted saliva to be collected from the children during uniform time periods (i.e., at 9 A.M., as soon as the children arrived at camp in a bus, and at 4 P.M., shortly before they were bused home at the end of the day). Cortisol assays were conducted

without awareness of the maltreatment status of participating children.

In the first investigation, Cicchetti and Rogosch (2001a) found substantial elevations in the morning cortisol levels of maltreated children who had been both sexually abused and physically abused, as well as neglected or emotionally maltreated. Additionally, many of the children in this multiple abuse group also exhibited elevated cortisol concentrations in both the morning and afternoon assayed saliva collections.

Unlike what was obtained in the multiple abuse group of children, a subgroup of youngsters who had experienced physical abuse evidenced a trend toward lower morning cortisol concentrations relative to the nonmaltreated children. Moreover, this physically abused subgroup of children displayed a significantly smaller decrease in cortisol levels from morning sample concentrations to afternoon sample concentrations. This pattern of cortisol production suggests relatively less diurnal variation for the physically abused group of children.

Finally, no differences in patterns of cortisol regulation were obtained between the neglected and the emotionally maltreated groups of children and the comparison group of nonmaltreated children.

The divergent patterns of cortisol regulation for the varying subgroup configurations of maltreated children suggest that it is highly unlikely that the brains of all children are uniformly affected by the experience of maltreatment. Not all maltreated children exhibited HPA axis functioning dysregulation. Only those maltreated children who experienced sexual and physical abuse in combination with neglect or emotional maltreatment displayed patterns akin to hypercortisolism. This group of children may be at extremely high risk for developing compromised neurobiological structure and function. Children in the physically abused subgroup manifested reduced adrenocortical reactivity, or enhanced negative feedback of the HPA axis, a pattern suggestive of hypocortisolism and that also may cause long-term neurobiological sequelae.

The children in the multiple abuse group had experienced chronic maltreatment across a range of developmental periods. This multifaceted assault on cognitive, social, emotional, and biological systems most likely contributes to these children's expectations of continued adversity. The pervasive negative experiences that these multiply abused children have encountered contribute significantly to these children's construction of their worlds as marked by fear and a hypersensitivity to future maltreatment.

In the second investigation, Cicchetti and Rogosch (2001b) examined the relations between neuroendocrine functioning and psychopathology in maltreated school-age children. The study also was implemented in a summer research day camp context. Once again, salivary samples were collected at the beginning and the end of the camp day. All samples were subsequently assayed for cortisol without knowledge of the children's maltreatment status.

Cicchetti and Rogosch (2001b) utilized the clinical cut points from the Teacher Report Form (TRF) and the Child Depression Inventory (CDI; Kovacs, 1985) to categorize maltreated and nonmaltreated children into clinical case groups. At the conclusion of the week, camp counselors completed the TRF and the children completed the CDI. Counselors were unaware of the children's maltreatment status. Children were identified as exhibiting clinical-level internalizing-only psychopathology if they had clinical-level scores on the TRF internalizing scale and/or the CDI and did not exhibit clinical-level problems on the TRF externalizing scale.

Maltreated children with clinical-level internalizing problems exhibited increased morning and across-the-day average levels of cortisol compared with the other groups of maltreated and nonmaltreated children (Cicchetti & Rogosch, 2001b). These results suggest that the presence of maltreatment moderated the impact of clinical-level internalizing problems. Furthermore, maltreated children with clinical-level internalizing problems displayed higher afternoon cortisol than did nonmaltreated children with clinical-level internalizing problems.

The increased levels of cortisol found in the maltreated children with clinical levels of internalizing problems differ from those typically obtained in samples of children and adolescents with MDD. The latter groups rarely exhibit the increase in cortisol that is characteristic of a regulatory dysfunction of the HPA axis (Dahl & Ryan, 1996). Consistent with the scientific literature on childhood depression, the nonmaltreated children with case-level internalizing problems in our study did not display increased levels of cortisol and an HPA axis dysregulation. Thus, it appears that the experience of maltreatment intensifies the usual effects of depressive disorder in childhood on neuroendocrine functioning. Accordingly, maltreated children with significant internalizing psychopathology may be at risk for developing the neurobiological anomalies associated with hypercortisolism.

Interestingly, the HPA axis abnormalities of maltreated children with clinical levels of internalizing problems bear striking similarity to those obtained with maltreated children with PTSD and MDD reported by DeBellis, Baum, and colleagues (1999) and with depressed adults who were sexually or physically abused during their childhood (Heim & Nemeroff, 2001; Heim, Newport, Bonsall, Miler, & Nemeroff, 2001; Lemieux & Coe, 1995).

Notably, not all maltreated children with clinical levels of internalizing psychopathology displayed the same pattern of cortisol regulation. This finding provides further evidence that maltreatment experiences do not uniformly affect neurobiological functioning in all children.

Finally, a number of retrospective investigations of neuroendocrine functioning in adults who had been exposed to maltreatment in childhood have been conducted. Although a detailed review of these studies is beyond the scope of this chapter, these studies cohere in concluding that maltreatment in childhood renders individuals more vulnerable to neuroendocrine dysregulation (assessed through urinary assessments of cortisol concentration and biological challenge tests) and psychopathology in adulthood (Heim et al., 2000, 2001, 2002; Lemieux & Coe, 1995; M. B. Stein et al., 1997; for a review, see Shea, Walsh, MacMillan, & Steiner, 2004).

Cognitive Brain Event-Related Potentials

Several experiments have examined maltreated children's processing of emotional information utilizing psychophysiological paradigms. This research has focused on elucidating the possible mechanisms through which the chronic stress experienced by children who have been maltreated could eventuate in problems in the processing of emotion (Pollak et al., 1998). As discussed earlier in this chapter, attachment systems have been theorized to be constructed to permit flexible responses to environmental circumstances, influence and be influenced by emotion regulatory abilities, and function through internal working models that children have of themselves and of their relationships with others (Bowlby, 1969/1982; Cassidy, 1994). In the experiments described next, the investigators strived to ascertain whether the activation of these representations may be reflected through physiological activity as well as behavior.

The event-related potential (ERP) is an index of central nervous system functioning thought to reflect the underlying neurological processing of discrete stimuli (Hillyard & Picton, 1987). ERPs represent scalp-derived changes in brain electrical activity over time, obtained by averaging time-locked segments of an electroencephalogram (EEG) that follow or precede the presentation of a stimulus. In this manner, ERPs allow for monitoring of neural activity associated with cognitive processing in real time (Donchin, Karis, Bashore, Coles, & Gratton, 1986).

One particular ERP component, the P300, is a positive wave that occurs approximately 300 to 600 ms after the presentation of a task-relevant stimulus and is maximal at the central-parietal scalp. The amplitude of the P300 varies as a function of task relevance and stimulus probability (R. Johnson, 1993) and has been utilized in conjunction with behavioral measures to classify specific cognitive operations such as the evaluation of stimulus significance. The P300 also may reflect processes involved in the updating of mental representations in working memory (Donchin et al., 1986). In general, such psychological processes serve to maintain accurate representations of one's environment by highlighting events that are significant.

Pollak and colleagues (1997, 2001) reasoned that the P300 component may be useful in illuminating the cognitive processes that accompany the encoding of salient emotional stimuli and highlight differences in such processes between maltreated and nonmaltreated children. The requirements of the task for both experiments were to recognize and respond to facial expressions of emotions. For all conditions, children were instructed to depress a hand-held button whenever they recognized the target facial expression. This emotional expression, the target, was only one of three emotions that were presented to the children (happy, angry, fearful). Across a variety of experimental conditions, children were required to attend to different facial expressions of emotion, and the probability of occurrence (rare or frequent) and task relevance (target or nontarget) were manipulated.

In the first experiment, Pollak and colleagues (1997) compared the ERPs of school-age maltreated and nonmaltreated children to a group of nonmaltreated children of comparable socioeconomic background and cognitive maturity. Children were instructed to respond to either a happy or an angry face. Because the amplitude of the ERP is influenced by the probability of occurrence of the stimuli, both happy and angry faces appeared infrequently (i.e., on 25% of the trials), whereas the nontarget neutral faces were displayed more frequently (i.e., on 50% of the trials). For both groups of children, there were few performance errors; thus, no distinctions could be made between emotion conditions (i.e., happy, angry, neutral) or between maltreated and nonmaltreated children with respect to accuracy or reaction time.

The ERPs of the nonmaltreated children were equivalent in both the happy and angry target conditions. The amplitude of the ERP was largest to the target stimuli, intermediate to the rare nontarget, and smallest to the frequent nontarget stimuli. In contrast, the ERPs of the maltreated children were larger in the angry than in the happy target conditions. The differential pattern of responding to emotion conditions suggests that, compared to nonmaltreated

children, different patterns of information processing were being evoked depending on the emotion to which the maltreated children were attending (Pollak et al., 1997).

Pollak and colleagues (1997) interpret these results as suggesting that angry and happy targets activated affective representations differentially for maltreated versus nonmaltreated children. They theorized that the ERP responses of the maltreated children reflected more efficient cognitive organization in the anger condition than in the happy condition. Such patterns of neurophysiological activation would be adaptive for coping with the stressful and threatening environments in which maltreated children reside (Cicchetti, 1991). However, biases toward negative affect or diminished responsiveness toward positive affect would place maltreated children at increased risk for encountering difficulties in their interactions with peers and adults (Dodge et al., 1997; Rieder & Cicchetti, 1989; Rogosch, Cicchetti, & Aber, 1995).

Emotion systems have been postulated to function as associative networks wherein input that matches significant mental representations activates memory systems (P. J. Lang, 1994). Pollak et al. (1997) conjectured, in this regard, that P300 amplitude may mark the match of facial stimuli with more complex affectively salient emotional memories. Theorists have invoked constructs such as schemas and working models to describe the mechanisms by which children integrate biologically relevant information with existing knowledge structures (Bowlby, 1969/1982; Cicchetti & Tucker, 1994). The findings of Pollak et al. provide corroborative empirical support for such hypothesized developmental processes.

Pollak and colleagues (2001) conducted a subsequent experiment in which they examined and compared the ERP responses of maltreated and nonmaltreated children to prototypic happy, angry, and fearful facial expressions. This investigation was conducted to determine the specificity of the relation between the ERP responses of the maltreated children and the nature of the eliciting stimuli. Specifically, Pollak and colleagues were interested in whether the ERPs of maltreated children generalized to positive versus negative emotional valence or were restricted to emotional displays of happiness versus anger. As we discussed earlier, negative emotions in addition to anger are frequently associated with maltreatment experiences. Thus, it is important to ascertain whether each discrete emotion may convey its own unique information and be processed in a distinct fashion.

Pollak et al. (2001) discovered that, as was the case in their earlier study, nonmaltreated children exhibited equivalent ERP amplitude responses to all of the target facial expressions of affect. However, the ERP amplitude responses of the maltreated children exceeded those of the nonmaltreated comparison children only in response to the angry target, but not to the fear or happy targets. These results suggest that there was specificity in maltreated children's differential processing of the emotional information. The fact that the maltreated children's greater P300 amplitude to angry facial expressions was obtained only when these stimuli served as targets in a task indicates that when maltreated children's attention is deployed to angry facial expressions, these youngsters are uniquely sensitive in detecting this emotion expression over others (for further corroboration of this interpretation, see Pollak & Kistler, 2002; Pollak & Sinha, 2002; Pollak & Tolley-Schell, 2003).

Taken together, these ERP experiments demonstrate that the socioemotional, cognitive, and behavioral difficulties observed in maltreated children affect multiple neurobiological systems. Specifically, the ERP findings suggest that the nature of the experiences that maltreated children encountered during their lives caused particular stimuli to become personally meaningful, based, in part, on the stored mental representations that have been associated with the stimulus over time. As such, prior experiences of maltreated children are reflected in these children's psychophysiological responses.

In an investigation that is congruent with this interpretation, Schiffer, Teicher, and Papanicolaou (1995) utilized auditory ERPs to examine laterality and hemisphere integration of memory in adults who reported having been maltreated during their childhood. These formerly maltreated adults all were currently well functioning and had no current Axis I mental disorder. A group of adults without a history of childhood trauma and no current Axis I disorder served as comparison individuals. All participants were asked to actively recall a neutral or work-related memory and were subsequently asked to recall a disturbing affective memory from childhood.

In individuals without a history of childhood traumatization, the left and right cerebral hemispheres both were equally involved in the recall of these memories. In contrast, adults who recollected having been maltreated in childhood revealed dramatic differences. Specifically, during recall of the neutral memory, adults with traumatization histories in childhood exhibited a marked suppression of the ERP over the left cerebral hemisphere, characteristic of increased processing in the left hemisphere. While recalling the disturbing memory, the adults who had experienced childhood trauma displayed a shift in laterality, with the ERP becoming suppressed over the right hemisphere, an index of enhanced activation in the right hemisphere.

In sum, it is highly plausible that the stresses associated with child abuse and neglect may enhance the memory of emotionally salient stimuli in the environment (Howe, Cicchetti, Toth, & Cerrito, 2004; Howe, Toth, & Cicchetti, Chapter 15, this *Handbook,* Volume 2). Relatedly, as discussed earlier in this chapter, maltreatment also appears to affect children's interpretation and comprehension of particular emotional displays (Pollak et al., 2000).

BEHAVIOR GENETIC AND MOLECULAR GENETIC STUDIES

Conventional behavior genetic approaches to psychopathology utilize "natural experiments" in genetically informative designs (e.g., twin studies) to demonstrate the multifactorial nature of genetic and nongenetic (i.e., shared and nonshared environment) factors in the development of mental disorders. These quantitative behavior genetic investigations have enhanced our understanding of the etiology of psychopathology through estimating the genetic and environmental variance components of a number of mental disorders at various points in the life span (Rende & Plomin, 1995). In recent years, the role of child maltreatment in the development of antisocial behavior has been investigated in twin study designs. Jaffee, Caspi, Moffitt, and Taylor (2004) utilized a classic twin study design to examine links between child maltreatment and children's antisocial behavior. Participants were sampled from the representative birth cohort Environmental Risk Longitudinal Twin Study, and investigation focused on detecting the ways genetic and environmental factors shape child development (Trouton, Spinath, & Plomin, 2002). The investigators found that physical abuse played a causal role in the development of antisocial behavior in childhood. Furthermore, genetic factors did not account for any significant variation between monozygotic (MZ) and dizygotic (DZ) twins' experience of physical abuse, thereby discounting the possibility that any heritable characteristics of the children from their parents provoked physical abuse (Jaffee et al., 2004).

In another investigation that utilized a sample from the representative birth cohort Environmental Risk Study, Jaffee and colleagues (Jaffee, Caspi, Moffitt, Polo-Tomas, et al., 2004) sought to ascertain whether the impact of physical abuse on risk for conduct problems was greater among twins who had high genetic risk for these problems. Children's genetic risk for developing conduct problems was computed as a function of their cotwin's Conduct Disorder status and the pair's zygosity (MZ or DZ). Jaffee, Caspi, Moffitt, Polo-Tomas, and colleagues discovered that the effect of physical abuse on Conduct Disorder was strongest for those children at highest genetic risk. Children who were physically abused who were at low genetic risk (i.e., DZ twins whose cotwin did not have Conduct Disorder) had a 2% probability of developing Conduct Disorder. In contrast, physically abused children at high genetic risk (i.e., MZ twins whose cotwin had Conduct Disorder) evidenced an increase of 24% in the likelihood of developing Conduct Disorder. Thus, the findings of Jaffee, Caspi, Moffitt, Polo-Tomas, et al. underscore that the prediction of psychopathology can achieve greater accuracy when both environmental pathogenic risk and genetic liability are simultaneously considered.

In recent years, a number of investigators have conducted molecular genetic studies of psychopathology with maltreated children. A major advantage of molecular genetic studies is that, in comparison to quantitative behavioral genetics approaches, they can elucidate specific genetic risk factors and the etiological mechanisms that link these risks with psychopathological and resilient outcomes (Cicchetti & Blender, 2004; Curtis & Cicchetti, 2003; Waldman, 2003). The confluence of several technological advances, including the ability to collect DNA using minimally invasive procedures (Freeman et al., 1997; Plomin & Crabb, 2000), more sophisticated genotyping methods (Craig & McClay, 2003; Watson & Akil, 1999), and the sequencing of the human genome (Venter et al., 2001), have enabled researchers to conduct investigations that only a decade earlier were possible only in our scientific imagination.

Caspi et al. (2002) examined how genetic factors contribute to why some maltreated children grow up to develop Antisocial Personality Disorder, whereas other maltreated children do not. In this longitudinal investigation of males who were studied from birth to adulthood, it was discovered that a functional polymorphism in the promoter of the gene encoding the neurotransmitter-metabolizing enzyme monoamine oxidase A (MAOA) moderated the effects of maltreatment. The MAOA gene is located on the X chromosome and encodes the MAOA enzyme, which metabolizes neurotransmitters such as norepinephrine, serotonin, and dopamine, rendering them inactive. The link between child maltreatment and antisocial behavior was far less pronounced among males with high MAOA than among those with low MAOA activity. Maltreatment groups did not differ on MAOA activity, suggesting that genotype did not influence exposure to maltreatment.

Of relevance to research on the biological contributors to resilience (cf. Charney, 2004; Curtis & Cicchetti, 2003), it is conceivable that the gene for high MAOA activity may confer a protective function against the development of Antisocial Personality Disorder in males who have been maltreated during their childhood. As described earlier in this chapter, maltreated children grow up in extremely stressful environments. The results of the Caspi et al. (2002) investigation suggest that a gene-by-environment (G×E) interaction helps to explain why some maltreated children, but not others, develop antisocial behavior via the effect that stressful experiences such as child maltreatment exert on neurotransmitter system development. Specifically, the probability that child maltreatment will eventuate in adult antisocial behavior is greatly increased among children whose MAOA is not sufficient to render inactive maltreatment-induced changes on neurotransmitter systems.

Foley et al. (2004) conducted an investigation with 514 male twins, ages 8 to 17 years, aimed at replicating the Caspi et al. (2002) study. The findings of this investigation replicated the major results of the Caspi et al. study. Specifically, low MAOA activity increased the risk for Conduct Disorder, but only in the presence of an adverse childhood environment, defined by interparental violence, parental neglect, and inconsistent discipline. Although there was a direct effect of familial adversity on risk for Conduct Disorder, there was not a main effect of MAOA genotype on developing Conduct Disorder. Once again, a G×E interaction is best supported by the results of this study. Furthermore, as with the Caspi et al. investigation, the predictive efficiency was vastly improved by including joint assessment of environmental risks and measured genes in the same study.

Caspi and colleagues (2003) conducted an investigation in which a functional polymorphism in the promoter region of the serotonin transporter (5-HTT) gene was shown to moderate the influence of stressful life events on depression. Specifically, individuals with one or two copies of the short (s) allele of the 5-HTT promoter polymorphism exhibited more depressive symptoms, depressive disorders, and suicidality than individuals homozygous for the long (l) allele when confronted with high stress. The s allele in the polymorphic region is associated with lower transcriptional efficiency of the promoter compared with the l allele (Lesch et al., 1996).

Additionally, Caspi and colleagues (2003) found that adult depression was predicted by the interaction between the s allele in the 5-HTT gene-linked polymorphic region and child maltreatment that occurred during the 1st decade of life. The G×E interaction revealed that child maltreatment predicted adult depressive disorder only among individuals carrying an s allele (i.e., s/s or s/l) but not among l/l homozygotes.

Kaufman and colleagues (2004) conducted a study similar to that of Caspi et al. (2003); however, they extended Caspi's previous experiment by studying children. The results of Kaufman et al. that, in children, the s allele in the 5-HTT gene-linked polymorphic region confers vulnerability to depression only in individuals with a history of significant life stress replicates the G×E result found in Caspi et al. with adults. Furthermore, the findings of Kaufman et al. demonstrate that social support in concert with this genetic factor additionally moderates the risk for depression in maltreated children. Specifically, maltreated children who were homozygous for the s allele and who had a dearth of positive social supports had depressive symptoms that were nearly twice as high as maltreated children with the s/s genotype and positive social supports. The latter group of maltreated children had levels of depressive symptoms that were comparable to those of nonmaltreated children in the comparison group with the same s/s genotype.

The risk for depression in maltreated children was moderated by the interplay of genetic and environmental factors. Thus, the negative developmental sequelae associated with child maltreatment are not inevitable. As discussed earlier in this chapter, there are many factors that contribute significantly to the ultimate developmental course embarked on by maltreated children. Of particular importance, the quality and availability of social supports were environmental factors that promoted resilience in maltreated children, even in the presence of a genotype that might otherwise be expected to confer vulnerability to psychiatric disorder.

INTERVENTION/PREVENTION

Despite the undisputed empirical evidence for the high risk of maladaptation as a developmental consequence of child maltreatment, there has been a paucity of theoretically informed intervention and prevention programs (Reppucci, Woolard, & Freid, 1999). Prevention efforts in the United States emanated from the areas of public health, epidemiology, and community psychology, initiated by the passage of the Child Abuse Treatment and Prevention Act in 1974. Early prevention efforts were largely geared toward increasing public awareness and acceptance of the problem of child abuse and neglect and involved tactics such as the use of public service announcements on television and radio (Daro & Donnelly, 2002) to disseminate information about child maltreatment. As a result of these efforts, public opinion surveys in the 1980s revealed that over 90% of the

public was aware of the problem of child maltreatment and could recognize that both societal and individual factors may contribute to its emergence (Daro & Gelles, 1992). Perhaps reflective of increased public knowledge about child maltreatment, concurrent epidemiological investigations revealed substantial increases in reports of suspected child maltreatment (McCurdy & Daro, 1994).

Although the efforts that were put forth were important from a public health perspective, little developmental influence was present in the conceptualization, implementation, or evaluation of these initiatives (Cicchetti & Toth, 1992; Toth, Maughan, et al., 2002). Early on, Zigler (1976) called for prevention efforts to consider the ecological context, predicting that single service models, which focused exclusively on the parent-child dyad, were overly simplistic and doomed to failure. Consequently, Zigler, among others, influenced the research field toward the adoption of more complex ecological transactional frameworks to guide both developmental theory and etiological theory on child maltreatment and, as an extension, called for such theory to inform intervention and prevention efforts (Belsky, 1980; Cicchetti & Lynch, 1995; Cicchetti & Rizley, 1981).

Intervention efforts have been slow, however, to incorporate theory-driven intervention and prevention programs, and even slower to apply an ecological-transactional model to such initiatives. Instead, the majority of studies that evaluated the effectiveness of prevention for maltreatment have focused on short-term behavioral strategies. Initial empirically tested prevention investigations were rooted in didactic instruction with parents, which have been shown to be rather ineffective (Daro, 1988), or home visitation programs, involving behavioral techniques such as modeling, practice, and feedback, to provide preliminary support to mother-child dyads during the 1st year of life (Kempe, 1976). For example, Olds and Henderson (1989) developed a home visitation prevention for mothers considered to be at risk for maltreating their infants. Young, single, low SES, pregnant women were assigned to one of two conditions: to receive home visits by nurses from pregnancy through the child's 2nd year or to receive comparison services. Results indicated a 50% reduction in child abuse and neglect among families in the treatment condition. In a 15-year longitudinal follow-up of this investigation (Olds et al., 1997), with nearly 80% of the women in their original study, women who had received the home visitation during pregnancy were less likely to be identified as perpetrators of child abuse or neglect or to be recipients of Aid to Families with Dependent Children than were women in the comparison group. Similar findings have been replicated by Kitzman et al. (1997).

Given these encouraging rates, the implementation of home visitation was expanded by the Healthy Families America (HFA) program, which sought to increase the availability of high-quality home visitation services and to create communitywide commitments to these services. Findings from this research initiative report that HFA programs may be successful in improving parent-child interactions but have more limited success in other areas, such as the prevention of child abuse and neglect. Moreover, HFA programs did not demonstrate significant improvements in children's development or social support (Daro & Harding, 1999), thus providing an impetus for researchers and practitioners to move beyond a narrow focus to consider the communitywide and national context.

Considering the impact of the family on both the onset of maltreatment as well as preventive efforts (Hays & Jones, 1994), recent prevention efforts have focused on the parents, seeking to provide social support and promote positive parenting (cf. Daro, 1990; Gaudin, Wodorski, Arkinson, & Avery, 1990; Olds, Henderson, Chamberlin, & Tatelbaum, 1986). For example, one recent randomized clinical trial was conducted to test the efficacy and sufficiency of parent-child interaction therapy in preventing re-reports of physical abuse among abusive parents (Chaffin et al., 2004). This investigation involved three intervention conditions: parent-child interaction therapy (PCIT), PCIT plus individualized enhanced services, and a community standard intervention. Based on social learning theory, the goal of using PCIT with abusive parents is to disrupt the escalating coercive cycles that are believed to characterize the maltreated children's family interactions (Patterson, 1976; Patterson & Reid, 1984; Patterson, Reid, & Dishion, 1992; Urquiza & McNeil, 1996). Results indicated that fewer parents in the PCIT groups had re-reports of abuse at follow-up (850 days) compared to the parents in the community standard condition; however, the additional services did not improve the efficacy of PCIT (Chaffin et al., 2004).

Alternatively, an investigation of a multilevel selected primary prevention of child maltreatment (L. Peterson, Tremblay, Ewigman, & Saldana, 2003) combined multiple perspectives on intervention techniques by including modeling, role-playing, Socratic dialogue, home practice, and home visits. Specifically, this intervention targeted improvements in parenting skills, developmentally appropriate interventions, developmentally appropriate beliefs, improving negative affect, acceptance of a responsible parent role, acceptance of a nurturing parent role, and self-efficacy. Successful intervention effects were noted at each level of the model, and effects remained at 1-year follow-up. Although a major strength of this intervention was its multimodal approach, it still targeted only a unidimensional aspect of child maltreatment by focusing on parental perceptions and behaviors.

In isolation, these treatments are likely to offer an incomplete solution to the problem of child maltreatment. Consistent with a developmental psychopathology perspective, unidimensional approaches to treatment are inadequate (Cicchetti & Toth, 2000; Toth & Cicchetti, 1993, 1999), whereas a comprehensive multidimensional approach to treatment would be better able to address the multiple domains in which maltreated children face vulnerability factors, placing them at increased risk for later maladaptation. The focus of interventions in child maltreatment, however, has largely been devoted to working with and addressing the problems of the maltreating parent to alleviate the risk for continued maltreatment, in isolation from other factors. The recurrence rates of child maltreatment provide the most solid support for the inadequacy of this approach, such that child welfare re-report rates of 40% or more within a few years are common. Notably, many of these re-reports are among physically abusive parents and are for recurrent physical abuse (DePanfilis & Zuravin, 1999; Way, Chung, Jonson-Reid, & Drake, 2001).

To begin to address the limitations of parent-focused treatments, interventions that are informed by developmental theory are being advocated for maltreated children (Cicchetti & Toth, 1993; Toth & Cicchetti, 1993; Toth, Maughan, et al., 2002). As theorized by this approach, clinicians may facilitate parents' understanding of their children's behavior by focusing attention on the manner in which children are negotiating stage-salient developmental issues. Thus, parenting interventions may be attuned to the resolution of these stage-salient developmental tasks.

With regard to the development of early attachment relationships, a number of attachment-informed interventions have been developed and hold promise for treatment in the area of abusive and neglectful parenting (M. F. Erickson, Korfmacher, & Egeland, 1992; Lieberman, Weston, & Pawl, 1991). Interventions that are informed by developmental theory often conceive of the mother-child attachment relationship as central to positive child outcomes (Fraiberg, Adelson, & Shapiro, 1975; Lieberman, 1991). In this infant-parent psychotherapy approach, mother and infant are seen together in sessions with a therapist, typically held in the client's home. A therapeutic relationship is formed, and through joint observation, the therapist tailors developmental guidance to the mother's level of functioning. Therapy includes exploration of the mother's own attachment organization and developmental experiences, in addition to her perceptions and reactions to her child, and the manner in which mother-child relate. Through reflection, redirection, and interpretation, the therapist strives to alter distortions in the mother-child relationship with the goal of changing internal representational models. A number of investigators have attempted to promote attachment security in samples of low-income mothers and their young children (see Lieberman & Zeanah, 1999, for review). Recognition of the importance of fostering maternal sensitivity and developmentally appropriate responsivity to children were central themes across all studies. Meta-analysis reveals, however, that the outcome data are inconsistent (van Ijzendoorn, Juffer, & Duyvesteyn, 1995), leaving questions about the efficacy of such intervention approaches.

Given the inconclusive evidence on the efficacy of interventions that are didactic versus dyadic, Cicchetti, Toth, and Rogosch (2005) conducted a randomized preventive intervention trial in which 12-month-old maltreated infants and their mothers were assigned to one of three intervention groups: (1) a psychoeducational home visitation (PHV) that focused on enhancing maternal knowledge of basic child development and improving parenting while reducing maternal stress and increasing maternal social supports; (2) an attachment theory-informed intervention, named infant-parent psychotherapy (IPP); and (3) the community standard (CS), which consisted of treatment typical of what was available in the community for maltreating families. Additionally, an equally socioeconomically disadvantaged nonmaltreated comparison (NC) group was matched to the three intervention groups. At baseline, infants from maltreating families exhibited a greater percentage of insecure attachment than did the infants from nonmaltreating families; the majority of the insecurity was classified as disorganized (Type D) attachment. Postintervention, approximately 1 year later, the infants from the PHV and IPP interventions both evidenced a significant change in their attachment security from baseline such that their attachment security no longer differed from the infants from nonmaltreating families. In contrast, the infants from the CS group demonstrated no improvement in their attachment security. These results have far-reaching implications as they demonstrate that disorganized attachment in maltreated infants can be modified through early intervention. Moreover, the equal effectiveness of the PHV and IPP interventions suggest that intervention efforts during infancy do not necessarily need to directly focus on attachment to improve this developmental domain.

Utilizing a similar treatment design, Toth, Maughan, et al. (2002) compared the relative efficacy of two interventions in altering maltreated preschool children's representational models. By incorporating a psychoeducational didactic treatment condition as well as a parent-child psychotherapy condition, this investigation was one of the first to allow for direct comparison between the effectiveness of these methods within a single design. Maltreating families were assigned to either preschooler-parent psychotherapy (PPP), psychoeducational home visit (PHV), or a CS condition, and an NC group served as an additional control condition. Children in PPP intervention evidenced more of a decline in maladaptive maternal representations over time, as assessed through story stem narratives, than did children in the PHV and CS conditions. In addition, PPP children displayed a greater decrease in negative self-representations than did children in the CS, PHV, and NC groups. Mother-child relationship expectations of PPP children became more positive over the course of intervention compared to NC and PHV. In contrast to interventions that target maltreated children in infancy (Cicchetti et al., 2005), the results of this study suggest that an attachment theory-informed model of intervention (PPP) is more effective at improving representations of the self and of caregivers than is a didactic model of intervention (PHV) directed at parenting skills. The major limitation of this study, however, was its exclusive focus on representations and not other outcomes such as parental knowledge about developmentally appropriate expectations, which may have had more substantial gains in the PHV group. Additional outcome measures would greatly inform our understanding of advantages and disadvantages of each approach to intervention.

Undoubtedly, more research is needed to further inform intervention and prevention efforts. As presented in the previous sections, maltreating parents exhibit a complex pattern of cognitive, affective, interpersonal, and behavioral processes that are in part derived from their own childhood relational experiences. Parental resources are further challenged by the influence of macrosystem factors as well as by poverty, community violence, and other aspects of the exosystem. For example, a recent study by Slack et al. (2004) revealed that indicators of poverty such as perceived material hardship and infrequent employment and parenting characteristics such as low parental warmth, use of physical discipline, and allowing children to engage in frequent television viewing are predictive of child neglect. Moreover, parenting characteristics did not mediate the relationship between perceived hardship and incidence of neglect. Thus, the implication for intervention and prevention is to address the material needs of families; given its link to child neglect over and above parenting characteristics, interventions that address only the parenting aspect of neglect may be ineffective.

Preventive programs in the community are also important for promoting competent parenting and reducing maltreatment. These programs typically strive to promote competence and sensitivity in parents and to improve their coping strategies with regard to stressful living conditions (Wolfe, 1993) by enhancing their social support system. For example, self-help groups, crisis intervention, and in-home services that are community agencies may reduce the incidence of problematic parenting and maltreatment, thereby reducing the need for more intensive intervention services when maltreatment does emerge (Wolfe & Wekerle, 1993).

Reduction in the rate of maltreatment has also been associated with participation in early school-based interventions, such as child-parent centers in the Chicago Longitudinal Study (Reynolds & Robertson, 2003). The child-parent centers provided child education and family support services in high-poverty areas. Participation in the program for 4 to 6 years was associated with significantly lower rates of maltreatment than participation in alternative kindergarten interventions.

Finally, knowledge gained from research on resilience among maltreated children is especially relevant to the development of intervention and prevention efforts (Luthar & Cicchetti, 2000). As resilience research identifies mechanisms that contribute to positive adaptation in the face of adversity, prevention and intervention programs may be tailored to capitalize on and enhance these processes in at-risk children. Consistent with an ecological-transactional model, these adaptive processes may derive from multiple levels of the ecology, including family, community, and cultural features, in addition to individual characteristics (Cicchetti & Rogosch, 2002). Moreover, Luthar and Cicchetti argue that because resilience is an ongoing dynamic process, preventions that are designed to promote resilience will likely be most effective as long-term programs that support children through successive periods of development.

Undeniably, there is a need for sufficient breadth in intervention and prevention programs that can address the complex developmental consequences of maltreated children as well as the parenting practices, relationship disturbances, and extensive needs of these families (Cicchetti & Toth, 1993, 2000; Olsen & Widom, 1993). The wide variety of techniques that have been applied to intervention efforts, ranging from nondirective play therapy to behavior modification, speaks to the multifinality of experience of maltreated children (Cicchetti & Rogosch, 1996) and to the notion that no one treatment paradigm will be equally appropriate for all maltreated children.

CONCLUSION AND FUTURE DIRECTIONS

In this chapter, we argued that the experience of child maltreatment, and the concomitant poor-quality parental care received by these children, exert a deleterious impact on psychological, genetic, and biological processes. Moreover, studies suggest that genetic and neurobiological factors may mediate or moderate the relationship between maltreatment and behavior.

A number of developmental processes have been postulated to exert an impact on the nature of brain-behavior relations: (1) aspects of the external environment that are atypical for most members of a species, (2) the specific type and amount of input received, and (3) the existence of biases for orienting toward particular classes of stimuli in the external environment (J. Black et al., 1998; Cicchetti, 2002; Dodge et al., 1997; R. Johnson, 1993).

In addition, the literature reviewed in this chapter has revealed that multiple psychological and neurobiological systems appear to be affected by the experience of child maltreatment. Clearly, multiple methods and approaches are necessary to explain the complex interplay between developing individuals and their maltreating environments. However, to date, most investigations of the neurobiological consequences of child abuse and neglect have examined one neural system. Similarly, many studies of the psychological sequelae of child maltreatment have focused on one domain. In the future, it will be essential to undertake investigations of maltreated children that examine multiple levels of psychological and neurobiological functioning and that employ multiple methods (cf. Cicchetti & Dawson, 2002).

The present maltreated versus comparison group differences approach needs to be augmented by an equal focus on individuals. Although groups of maltreated children differ from groups of nonmaltreated children on most of the psychological and neurobiological structures and functions investigated thus far, not all maltreated children are affected by their experiences in the same manner. Moreover, the neurobiological and psychological functioning of some maltreated children appears not to be negatively affected (Cicchetti & Rogosch, 2001a, 2001b), or it may be reflective of an enhanced neural plasticity in resilient individuals (Cicchetti & Rogosch, 1997; Curtis & Cicchetti, 2003). We do not know if the neurobiological structural and/or functional difficulties displayed by some maltreated children are permanent or irreversible, or, if reversible, when and to what degree. Additionally, we do not possess the knowledge regarding whether some to-be-identified neural systems may be more plastic than other neural systems that may be more refractory to change or have a more time-limited window when neural plasticity can occur. Thus, a person-oriented approach (Bergman & Magnusson, 1997; von Eye & Bergman, 2003), in which multiple neurobiological and psychological systems are studied within individuals over developmental time, should also be implemented in future research on the effects of maltreatment on biological, genetic, and psychological processes. In this manner, we can acquire vital information on how the neurobiological systems of maltreated children develop at different periods, as well as when such developing neural systems may be most vulnerable in different profiles of individuals who share similar aspects of neurobiological and psychological functioning and who may range from none or minimal damage to major neurobiological and psychological dysfunction.

Even in instances of long-term damage, the neurobiological and psychological consequences of maltreatment may not prove to be irreversible. Because postnatal brain structuration and neural patterning are thought to occur, in part, through interactions and transactions of the child with his or her environment, changes in the internal and external environment may lead to improvement in the ability of the individual to grapple with developmental challenges. Thus, although genetic and historical developmental factors canalize and constrain the adaptive process to some degree, it is conceivable that behavioral and neural plasticity are possible throughout the life course as a result of adaptive neural and psychological self-organization (Cicchetti, 2002; Cicchetti & Tucker, 1994; Curtis & Cicchetti, 2003). Additionally, pharmacological and behavioral/psychological interventions can be implemented to modify the structure and function of the brain and to ascertain how the structural and functional changes that are produced will change the ability of the brain to process the information it confronts during stressful situations. Successful interventions should alter behavior and physiology by producing changes in gene expression (transcription) that produce new structural and functional changes in the brain (Cicchetti & Blender, 2004; Kandel, 1999).

To achieve these goals, a number of additional advances in research on the neurobiological and psychological consequences of child maltreatment must be implemented in the future. First, sample sizes must increase in order for there to be sufficient statistical power to detect differences in multiple-level-of-analysis, multimethod, cross-sectional, and longitudinal investigations. Second, much of the scientific literature published to date on the neurobiology of child maltreatment has focused on hospitalized samples. Many of these maltreated individuals also have comorbid mental disorders and/or use or abuse substances and alcohol (cf. DeBellis, Keshavan, et al., 1999). Moreover, maltreated children in hospitalized samples also are receiving pharmacological and/or psychotherapeutic interventions. Although one can attempt to control for these factors statistically, their presence makes it difficult to disentangle the effects of maltreatment on brain structure and function from other competing conditions (e.g., mental illness, drug abuse, intervention) on the neurodevelopmental anomalies (or lack thereof) found in hospitalized maltreated children. It also will be essential for future research utilizing neuroimaging technologies to examine brain structure and function in community samples of maltreated children.

To comprehend neuropsychological development, it is essential to recognize that the brain is a mutable organ and that its structural organization reflects both what is important to the individual (i.e., the history of the organism) and what the individual is capable of at that particular time in development (Luu & Tucker, 1996). Thus, neuroscientists utilizing neuroimaging techniques to examine neurobiological structures in maltreated children must move beyond the descriptive anatomical level of structural MRI and begin to incorporate fMRI technology into their research armamentaria. Because the brain is a dynamic, self-organizing system that is mutable, future neuroimaging research should ascertain whether the brain structures and brain functioning of maltreated children designated as resilient through psychological criteria (see, e.g., Cicchetti & Rogosch, 1997) differ from those of nonresilient maltreated children. Increasingly, research on the correlates of and contributors to resilient functioning should incorporate multiple biological levels of analysis (e.g., HPA axis functioning, including stress-reactivity paradigms and diurnal regulation assessments; EEG coherence; EEG hemispheric activation asymmetries; acoustic and emotion-potentiated startle; ERPs); and neuroimaging methods, including MRI, MRS, diffusion tensor imaging, magnetoencephalography, and fMRI, and not merely focus on psychological processes (see Curtis & Cicchetti, 2003, for an elaboration).

Finally, because research with rodents and nonhuman primates has revealed that social experiences, such as maternal caregiving behaviors, maternal deprivation, and maternal separation, affect gene expression as well as brain structure and function (Kaufman & Charney, 2001; Levine, 1994; Meaney et al., 1996; Sanchez, Ladd, & Plotsky, 2001), it is quite likely that child maltreatment affects the expression of genes that impact brain structure and function as well as basic regulatory processes.

IMPLICATIONS FOR INTERVENTION

As knowledge on the psychological and biological sequelae of maltreatment, as well as their interrelation, continues to accrue, it is critically important to implement scientifically rigorous randomized clinical trial preventive interventions with maltreated children and their caregivers. The time has come to conduct interventions that not only assess behavioral changes but also ascertain whether neurobiological structures and functioning are modifiable or refractory to intervention. There is growing evidence that successful intervention modifies not only maladaptive behavior but also the cellular and physiological correlates of behavior (Cicchetti & Posner, 2005; Kandel, 1998, 1999). The fact that interventions are able to bring about beneficial effects beyond the early years of life suggests that there is a psychobiology and a neuropsychology of hope and optimism for maltreated children that can minimize or eradicate the adverse effects of their histories. Furthermore, just as knowledge of genetic predisposition to medical illness can result in the modification of behavior so as to minimize the expression of genes associated with medical illness, so, too, might knowledge of the effect of maltreatment on gene expression and a related genetic vulnerability to mental illness serve to help individuals alter their life course so as to inhibit the expression of genes that are associated with maladaptation and psychopathology. Moreover, it is conceivable that successful interventions may activate genes that protect maltreated individuals from pathological outcomes and promote resilient functioning.

Research that has found increased cortisol concentrations in children who have experienced multiple subtypes of maltreatment also underscores the critical need to provide intervention for these children given their risk for the emergence of impairments in cognitive, memory, and affective functioning (Cicchetti & Rogosch, 2001a; see also Sapolsky, 1992). Because of increasing economic pressures and resultant treatment availability to only the most impaired individuals, findings on HPA axis functioning in maltreated children could be used to help lobby for service availability. Increased cortisol levels in maltreated depressed children also indicates that interventions targeted at reducing depressive symptoms are especially important for children who have experienced abuse and neglect.

Work that suggests there may be neuronal loss in instances of prolonged maltreatment (DeBellis et al., 2000)

has both treatment and policy implications. Given the severe biological and psychological consequences of chronic maltreatment, there must be intensified efforts to either treat the maltreating family system effectively within a specified period of time, or to move toward placing the child in a safer environment.

The fact that child maltreatment exerts its influence on developmental processes at various levels of the ecology (Cicchetti & Lynch, 1993) highlights the importance of intervening in all components of the ecologies of children who have been abused and neglected. For example, because child maltreatment and community violence influence and transact with individual functioning to result in sustained adversity and disturbances in development (Lynch & Cicchetti, 1998), interventions must be directed at the contextual adversity that children from impoverished neighborhoods are likely to encounter. Ideally, the entire exosystem (e.g., schools, churches, neighborhood centers) should be marshaled to adequately deal with the pervasive influences that may compromise the development of maltreated children.

A crucial issue that can be informed by research on neuropsychological and psychophysiological functioning in maltreated children is determining whether the timing of interventions matters. A major implication of a dynamic developmental systems approach is that the implementation of intervention following the experience of trauma should ameliorate the intensity and severity of the response to the trauma, as well as the developmental course (Toth & Cicchetti, 1993, 1999). Such interventions that are closely timed to trauma, maladaptation, and disorder onset also should decrease the probability of developing, in a use-dependent fashion, sensitized neural systems that may cascade across development (Cicchetti, 2002). This is not to suggest that if intervention is *not* time-tied to the trauma, it will ultimately fail. Rather, one may need to ascertain alternative treatment methods that will address the sequelae of the maltreatment experience. Moreover, if a long-term course of trauma has occurred and a significant period of time has passed, it may be counterproductive to continue to revisit the trauma.

Although we possess more knowledge regarding the etiology and sequelae of child maltreatment than at any other point in history, it is crucial that researchers continue to design and conduct the scientific investigations that are necessary to provide definitive answers to the complex questions that remain concerning the effects of child maltreatment on psychological and neurobiological functioning and on gene expression. The knowledge gleaned from these studies will enable maltreated children to receive interventions that are based on sound scientific research. Furthermore, the translation of basic behavioral and neuroscience investigations into the development of preventive interventions will be inordinately helpful in reducing the burden of mental illness associated with this grave societal ill.

REFERENCES

Aber, J. L. (1994). Poverty, violence, and child development: Untangling family and community level effects. In C. A. Nelson (Ed.), *Minnesota Symposia on Child Psychology* (Vol. 27, pp. 229–272). Hillsdale, NJ: Erlbaum.

Aber, J. L., & Allen, J. P. (1987). The effects of maltreatment on young children's socioemotional development: An attachment theory perspective. *Developmental Psychology, 23,* 414–416.

Aber, J. L., Allen, J. P., Carlson, V., & Cicchetti, D. (1989). The effects of maltreatment on development during early childhood: Recent studies and their theoretical, clinical, and policy implications. In D. Cicchetti & V. Carlson (Eds.), *Child maltreatment: Theory and research on the causes and consequences of child abuse and neglect* (pp. 579–619). New York: Cambridge University Press.

Aber, J. L., & Zigler, E. (1981). Developmental considerations in the definition of child maltreatment. *New Directions for Child Development, 11,* 1–29.

Aber, M., & Rappaport, J. (1994). The violence of prediction: The uneasy relationship between social science and social policy. *Applied and Preventive Psychology, 3,* 43–54.

Abney, V. (1996). Cultural competency in the field of child maltreatment. In J. Briere, L. Berliner, J. Bulkley, C. Jenny, & T. Reid (Eds.), *The APSAC handbook on child maltreatment* (pp. 409–419). Thousand Oaks, CA: Sage.

Ainsworth, M. D. S., Blehar, M. C., Waters, E., & Wall, S. (1978). *Patterns of attachment: A psychological study of the Strange Situation.* Hillsdale, NJ: Erlbaum.

Ainsworth, M. D. S., & Eichberg, C. (1991). Effects on infant-mother attachment of mother's unresolved loss of an attachment figure, or other traumatic experience. In C. M. Parkes, J. Stevenson-Hinde, & P. Marris (Eds.), *Attachment across the life cycle* (pp. 160–183). New York: Routledge.

Ainsworth, M. D. S., & Wittig, B. A. (1969). Attachment and the exploratory behavior of one-year-olds in a Strange Situation. In B. M. Foss (Ed.), *Determinants of infant behavior* (Vol. 4, pp. 113–136). London: Methuen.

Alessandri, S. M. (1991). Play and social behavior in maltreated preschoolers. *Development and Psychopathology, 3,* 191–205.

Alessandri, S. M. (1992). Mother-child interactions correlates of maltreated and nonmaltreated children's play behavior. *Development and Psychopathology, 4,* 257–270.

Alessandri, S. M., & Lewis, M. (1996). Development of the self-conscious emotions in maltreated children. In M. Lewis & M. W. Sullivan (Eds.), *Emotional development in atypical children* (pp. 185–201). Hillsdale, NJ: Erlbaum.

Allen, D., & Tarnowski, K. (1989). Depressive characteristics of physically abused children. *Journal of Abnormal Child Psychology, 17,* 1–11.

Allen, R. E., & Oliver, J. N. (1982). The effects of child maltreatment on language development. *Child Abuse and Neglect, 6,* 299–305.

Altemeier, W. A., O'Connor, S., Vietze, P. M., Sandler, H. M., & Sherrod, L. R. (1982). Antecedents of child abuse. *Journal of Pediatrics, 100,* 823–829.

American Psychiatric Association. (1987). *Diagnostic and statistical manual of mental disorders* (3rd ed., rev.). Washington, DC: Author.

American Psychiatric Association. (1994). *Diagnostic and statistical manual of mental disorders* (4th ed.). Washington, DC: Author.

Anderson, C. M., Teicher, M. H., Polcari, A., & Renshaw, P. F. (2002). Abnormal T2 relaxation time in the cerebellar vermis of adults sexually abused in childhood: Potential role of the vermis in stress-enhanced risk for drug abuse. *Psychoneuroendocrinology, 27,* 231–244.

Ards, S., Chung, C., & Meyers, S. L. (1998). The effects of sample selection bias on racial differences in child abuse reporting. *Child Abuse and Neglect, 22*(2), 103–115.

Arnow, B. A. (2004). Relationships between childhood maltreatment, adult health and psychiatric outcome, and medical utilization. *Journal of Clinical Psychiatry, 65,* 10–15.

Azar, S. (2002). Parenting and child maltreatment. In M. H. Bornstein (Ed.), *Handbook of parenting: Vol. 4. Social conditions and applied parenting* (2nd ed., pp. 361–388). Mahwah, NJ: Erlbaum.

Barahal, R., Waterman, J., & Martin, H. (1981). The social-cognitive development of abused children. *Journal of Consulting and Clinical Psychology, 49,* 508–516.

Barnett, D., Ganiban, J., & Cicchetti, D. (1999). Maltreatment, negative expressivity, and the development of Type D attachments from 12- to 24-months of age. *Society for Research in Child Development Monograph, 64,* 97–118.

Barnett, D., Manly, J. T., & Cicchetti, D. (1991). Continuing toward an operational definition of psychological maltreatment. *Development and Psychopathology, 3,* 19–30.

Barnett, D., Manly, J. T., & Cicchetti, D. (1993). Defining child maltreatment: The interface between policy and research. In D. Cicchetti & S. L. Toth (Eds.), *Child abuse, child development, and social policy* (pp. 7–73). Norwood, NJ: Ablex.

Bartholomew, K. (1990). Avoidance of intimacy: An attachment perspective. *Journal of Social and Personal Relationships, 7,* 147–178.

Battle, C. L., Shea, M. T., Johnson, D. M., Yen, S., Zlotnick, C., Zanarini, M. C., et al. (2004). Childhood maltreatment associated with adult personality disorders: Findings from the Collaborative Longitudinal Personality Disorders Study. *Journal of Personality Disorders, 18*(2), 193–211.

Beeghly, M., & Cicchetti, D. (1994). Child maltreatment, attachment, and the self system: Emergence of an internal state lexicon in toddlers at high social risk. *Development and Psychopathology, 6,* 5–30.

Beeghly, M., Weiss-Perry, B., & Cicchetti, D. (1990). Beyond sensorimotor functioning: Early communicative and play development of children with Down syndrome. In D. Cicchetti & M. Beeghly (Eds.), *Children with Down syndrome: A developmental perspective* (pp. 329–368). New York: Cambridge University Press.

Belsky, J. (1980). Child maltreatment: An ecological integration. *American Psychologist, 35,* 320–335.

Belsky, J. (1984). The determinants of parenting: A process model. *Child Development, 55,* 83–96.

Belsky, J. (1993). Etiology of child maltreatment: A developmental-ecological analysis. *Psychological Bulletin, 114,* 413–434.

Belsky, J., & Most, R. (1981). From exploration to play: A cross-sectional study of infant free play behavior. *Developmental Psychology, 17,* 630–639.

Belsky, J., Rovine, M., & Taylor, D. G. (1984). The Pennsylvania Infant and Family Development Project: Pt. 3. The origins of individual differences in infant-mother attachment—Maternal and infant contributions. *Child Development, 55,* 718–728.

Berger, L. M. (2004). Income, family structure, and child maltreatment risk. *Children and Youth Services Review, 26,* 725–748.

Bergman, L. R., & Magnusson, D. (1997). A person-oriented approach in research on developmental psychopathology. *Development and Psychopathology, 9,* 291–319.

Bernstein, D. P., Ahluvalia, T., Pogge, D., & Handelsman, L. (1997). Validity of the Childhood Trauma Questionnaire in an adolescent psychiatric population. *Journal of the American Academy of Child and Adolescent Psychiatry, 36*(3), 340–348.

Bernstein, D. P., Fink, L., Handelsman, L., Foote, J., Lovejoy, M., Wenzel, K., et al. (1994). Initial reliability and validity of a new retrospective measure of child abuse and neglect. *American Journal of Psychiatry, 151,* 1132–1136.

Besharov, D. (1981). Toward better research on child abuse and neglect: Making definitional issues an explicit methodological concern. *Child Abuse and Neglect, 5,* 383–389.

Bifulco, A., Moran, P. M., Ball, C., Jacobs, C., Baines, R., Bunn, A., et al. (2002). Childhood adversity, parental vulnerability and disorder: Examining intergenerational transmission of risk. *Journal of Child Psychology and Psychiatry, 48,* 1075–1086.

Bjorkland, D. F. (1997). The role of immaturity in human development. *Psychological Bulletin, 122,* 153–169.

Black, J., Jones, T. A., Nelson, C. A., & Greenough, W. T. (1998). Neuronal plasticity and the developing brain. In N. E. Alessi, J. T. Coyle, S. I. Harrison, & S. Eth (Eds.), *Handbook of child and adolescent psychiatry* (pp. 31–53). New York: Wiley.

Black, M. M., & Dubowitz, H. (1999). Child neglect: Research recommendations and future directions. In H. Dubowitz (Ed.), *Neglected children: Research, practice and policy* (pp. 261–277). Thousand Oaks, CA: Sage.

Bolger, K. E., & Patterson, C. J. (2001). Pathways from child maltreatment to internalizing problems: Perceptions of control as mediators and moderators. *Development and Psychopathology, 13,* 913–940.

Bolger, K. E., Patterson, C. J., & Kupersmidt, J. B. (1998). Peer relationships and self esteem among children who have been maltreated. *Child Development, 69,* 1171–1197.

Bousha, D. M., & Twentyman, C. T. (1984). Mother-child interactional style in abuse, neglect, and control groups: Naturalistic observations in the home. *Journal of Abnormal Psychology, 93,* 106–114.

Bowlby, J. (1973). *Attachment and loss: Separation.* New York: Basic Books.

Bowlby, J. (1980). *Attachment and loss: Loss, sadness, and depression* (Vol. 3). New York: Basic Books.

Bowlby, J. (1982). *Attachment and loss* (Vol. 1). New York: Basic Books. (Original work published 1969)

Bowlby, J. (1988). *A secure base.* New York: Basic Books.

Bremner, J. D., Krystal, J. H., Southwick, S. M., & Charney, D. S. (1995). Functional neuroanatomical correlates of the effects of stress on memory. *Journal of Traumatic Stress, 8,* 527–553.

Bremner, J. D., Randall, P., Vermetten, E., Staib, L., Bronen, R. A., Mazure, C. J., et al. (1997). Magnetic resonance imaging–based measurement of hippocampal volume in posttraumatic stress disorder related to childhood physical and sexual abuse: A preliminary report. *Biological Psychiatry, 41,* 23–32.

Bremner, J. S., Vythilingam, M., Anderson, G., Vermetten, E., McClashan, T., Heniger, G., et al. (2003). Assessment of the hypothalamic-pituitary-adrenal axis over a 24-hour diurnal period and in response to neuroendocrine challenges in women with and without childhood sexual abuse and posttraumatic stress disorder. *Biological Psychiatry, 54*(7), 710–718.

Bretherton, I. (Ed.). (1984). *Symbolic play.* Orlando, FL: Academic Press.

Bretherton, I. (1990). Open communication and internal working models: Their role in the development of attachment relationships. In R. Thompson (Ed.), *Nebraska Symposium on Motivation: Vol. 36. Socioemotional development* (pp. 57–113). Lincoln: University of Nebraska Press.

Bretherton, I. (1991). Pouring new wine into old bottles: The social self as internal working model. In M. Gunnar & L. A. Sroufe (Eds.), *Minnesota Symposia on Child Development: Vol. 23. Self processes and development* (pp. 1–41). Hillsdale, NJ: Erlbaum.

Bretherton, I., & Waters, E. (Eds.). (1985). Growing points of attachment theory and research. *Monographs of the Society for Research in Child Development, 50*(209).

Brewin, C., Andrews, B., & Gotlib, I. H. (1993). Psychopathology and early experience: A reappraisal of retrospective reports. *Psychological Bulletin, 113,* 82–98.

Briere, J., & Runtz, M. (1993). Childhood sexual abuse: Long-term sequelae and implications for psychological assessment. *Journal of Interpersonal Violence, 8,* 312–330.

Brodsky, B. S., Oquendo, M., Ellis, S., Haas, G. L., Malone, K. M., & Mann, J. J. (2001). The relationship of childhood abuse to impulsivity and suicidal behavior in adults with major depression. *American Journal of Psychiatry, 158,* 1871–1877.

Bronfenbrenner, U. (1977). Toward the experimental ecology of human development. *American Psychologist, 32,* 513–531.

Bronfenbrenner, U. (1979). *The ecology of human development: Experiments by nature and design.* Cambridge, MA: Harvard University Press.

Brown, J., Cohen, P., Chen, H., Smailes, E. M., & Johnson, J. G. (2004). Sexual trajectories of abused and neglected youth. *Journal of Developmental and Behavioral Pediatrics, 25*(2), 77–82.

Brown, J., Cohen, P., Johnson, J. G., & Salzinger, S. (1998). A longitudinal analysis of risk factors for child maltreatment: Findings of a 17-year prospective study of officially recorded and self-reported child abuse and neglect. *Child Abuse and Neglect, 22*(11), 1078–1965.

Browne, A., & Finkelhor, D. (1986). Initial and long-term effects: A review of the research. In D. Finkelhor (Ed.), *A sourcebook on child sexual abuse* (pp. 143–179). Beverly Hills, CA: Sage.

Browne, K. D., & Herbert, M. (1997). *Preventing family violence.* Chichester, England: Wiley.

Bruer, J. (1999). *The myth of the first three years: A new understanding of early brain development and lifelong learning.* New York: Free Press.

Bruner, J. S. (1972). The nature and uses of immaturity. *American Psychologist, 27,* 287–708.

Brunquell, D., Crichton, L., & Egeland, B. (1981). Maternal personality and attitude in disturbances of child-rearing. *American Journal of Orthopsychiatry, 51,* 680–691.

Buchanan, A. (1996). *Cycles of child maltreatment.* Chichester, England: Wiley.

Bugental, D. B., Blue, J., Cortez, V., Fleck, K., & Rodriguez, A. (1992). Influences of witnessed affect on information processing in children. *Child Development, 63,* 774–786.

Bugental, D. B., & Happaney, K. (2004). Predicting infant maltreatment in low-income families: The interactive effects of maternal attributions and child status at birth. *Developmental Psychology, 40*(2), 234–243.

Burgess, R. L., & Conger, R. D. (1978). Family interaction in abusive, neglectful, and normal families. *Child Development, 49,* 1163–1173.

Burke, L. (2003). The impact of maternal depression on familial relationships. *International Review of Psychiatry, 15*(3), 243–255.

Calverley, R. M., Fischer, K. W., & Ayoub, C. (1994). Complex splitting of self representations in sexually abused adolescent girls. *Development and Psychopathology, 6,* 195–213.

Camras, L. A., Grow, G., & Ribordy, S. (1983). Recognition of emotion expressions by abused children. *Journal of Clinical Child Psychology, 12,* 325–328.

Camras, L. A., Ribordy, S., Hill, J., Martino, S., Sachs, V., Spaccarelli, S., et al. (1990). Maternal facial behavior and the recognition and production of emotional expression by maltreated and nonmaltreated children. *Developmental Psychology, 26*(2), 304–312.

Camras, L. A., Ribordy, S., Hill, J., Martino, S., Spaccarelli, S., & Stefani, R. (1988). Recognition and posing of emotional expressions by abused children and their mothers. *Developmental Psychology, 26,* 304–312.

Camras, L. A., Sachs-Alter, E., & Ribordy, S. (1996). Emotion understanding in maltreated children: Recognition of facial expressions and integration with other emotional cues. In M. Lewis & M. Sullivan (Eds.), *Emotional development in atypical children* (pp. 203–225). Hillsdale, NJ: Erlbaum.

Carlson, V., Cicchetti, D., Barnett, D., & Braunwald, K. (1989). Disorganized/disoriented attachment relationships in maltreated infants. *Developmental Psychology, 25,* 525–531.

Caspi, A., McClay, J., Moffitt, T., Mill, J., Martin, J., Craig, I. W., et al. (2002). Role of genotype in the cycle of violence in maltreated children. *Science, 297,* 851–854.

Caspi, A., Sugden, K., Moffitt, T. E., Taylor, A., Craig, I. W., Harrington, H. L., et al. (2003). Influence of life stress on depression: Moderation by a polymorphism in the 5-HTT gene. *Science, 301,* 386–389.

Cassidy, J. (1988). Child-mother attachment and the self in 6 year-olds. *Child Development, 59*(1), 121–134.

Cassidy, J. (1994). Emotion regulation: Influences of attachment relationships. *Monographs of the Society for Research in Child Development, 59,* 228–283.

Cerezo, M. A. (1997). Abusive family interaction: A review. *Aggression and Violent Behavior, 2,* 215–240.

Cerezo, M. A., & D'Ocon, A. (1995). Maternal inconsistent socialization: An interactional pattern with maltreated children. *Child Abuse Review, 4*(1), 14–31.

Chaffin, M., Silovsky, J. F., Funderbunk, B., Valle, L. A., Brestan, E., Balachova, T., et al. (2004). Parent-child interaction therapy with physically abusive parents: Efficacy for reducing future abuse reports. *Journal of Consulting and Clinical Psychology, 72,* 500–510.

Charney, D. (2004). Psychobiological mechanisms of resilience and vulnerability: Implications for successful adaptation to extreme stress. *American Journal of Psychiatry, 161,* 195–216.

Chilamkurti, C., & Milner, J. S. (1993). Perceptions and evaluations of child transgressions and disciplinary techniques in high- and low-risk mothers and their children. *Child Development, 64,* 1801–1814.

Children's Defense Fund. (2004). *The state of America's children, 2004.* Washington, DC: Author.

Christoffel, K. K. (1990). Violence, death, and injury in U.S. children and adolescents. *American Journal of Disease Control, 144,* 697–706.

Cicchetti, D. (1984). The emergence of developmental psychopathology. *Child Development, 55,* 1–7.

Cicchetti, D. (1989). How research on child maltreatment has informed the study of child development: Perspectives from developmental psychopathology. In D. Cicchetti & V. Carlson (Eds.), *Child maltreatment: Theory and research on the causes and consequences of child abuse and neglect* (pp. 377–431). New York: Cambridge University Press.

Cicchetti, D. (1990a). A historical perspective on the discipline of developmental psychopathology. In J. E. Rolf & A. S. Masten (Eds.), *Risk and protective factors in the development of psychopathology* (pp. 2–28). New York: Cambridge University Press.

Cicchetti, D. (1990b). The organization and coherence of socioemotional, cognitive, and representational development: Illustrations through a developmental psychopathology perspective on Down syndrome and child maltreatment. In R. Thompson (Ed.), *Nebraska Symposium on Motivation: Vol. 36. Socioemotional development* (pp. 259–366). Lincoln: University of Nebraska Press.

Cicchetti, D. (1991). Fractures in the crystal: Developmental psychopathology and the emergence of the self. *Developmental Review, 11,* 271–287.

Cicchetti, D. (1993). Developmental psychopathology: Reactions, reflections, projections. *Developmental Review, 13,* 471–502.

Cicchetti, D. (2002). How a child builds a brain: Insights from normality and psychopathology. In W. W. Hartup & R. A. Weinberg (Eds.), *Minnesota Symposia on Child Psychology: Vol. 32. Child psychology in retrospect and prospect* (pp. 23–71). Mahwah, NJ: Erlbaum.

Cicchetti, D. (2003). Experiments of nature: Contributions to developmental theory. *Development and Psychopathology, 15*(4), 833–1106.

Cicchetti, D., & Aber, J. L. (1980). Abused children–abusive parents: An overstated case? *Harvard Educational Review, 50,* 244–255.

Cicchetti, D., & Barnett, D. (1991a). Attachment organization in preschool-aged maltreated children. *Development and Psychopathology, 3,* 397–411.

Cicchetti, D., & Barnett, D. (1991b). Toward the development of a scientific nosology of child maltreatment. In W. Grove & D. Cicchetti (Eds.), *Thinking clearly about psychology: Essays in honor of Paul E. Meehl—Personality and psychopathology* (Vol. 2, pp. 346–377). Minneapolis: University of Minnesota Press.

Cicchetti, D., & Beeghly, M. (Eds.). (1990). *Children with Down syndrome: A developmental perspective.* New York: Cambridge University Press.

Cicchetti, D., & Blender, J. A. (2004). A multiple-levels-of-analysis approach to the study of developmental processes in maltreated children. *Proceedings of the National Academy of Sciences, 101*(50), 17325–17326.

Cicchetti, D., & Cannon, T. D. (1999). Neurodevelopmental processes in the ontogenesis and epigenesis of psychopathology. *Development and Psychopathology, 11,* 375–393.

Cicchetti, D., & Carlson, V. (Eds.). (1989). *Child maltreatment: Theory and research on the causes and consequences of child abuse and neglect.* New York: Cambridge University Press.

Cicchetti, D., Cummings, E. M., Greenberg, M. T., & Marvin, R. (1990). An organizational perspective on attachment beyond infancy: Implications for theory, measurement, and research. In M. T. Greenberg, D. Cicchetti, & E. M. Cummings (Eds.), *Attachment in the preschool years: Theory, research, and intervention* (pp. 3–49). Chicago: University of Chicago Press.

Cicchetti, D., & Dawson, G. (Eds.). (2002). Multiple levels of analysis [Special issue]. *Development and Psychopathology, 14*(3), 417–666.

Cicchetti, D., Ganiban, J., & Barnett, D. (1991). Contributions from the study of high risk populations to understanding the development of emotion regulation. In J. Garber & K. A. Dodge (Eds.), *The development of emotion regulation and dysregulation* (pp. 15–48). New York: Cambridge University Press.

Cicchetti, D., & Howes, P. W. (1991). Developmental psychopathology in the context of the family: Illustrations from the study of child maltreatment. *Canadian Journal of Behavioural Science, 23,* 257–281.

Cicchetti, D., & Lynch, M. (1993). Toward an ecological/transactional model of community violence and child maltreatment: Consequences for children's development. *Psychiatry, 56,* 96–118.

Cicchetti, D., & Lynch, M. (1995). Failures in the expectable environment and their impact on individual development: The case of child maltreatment. In D. Cicchetti & D. J. Cohen (Eds.), *Developmental psychology: Vol. 2. Risk, disorder, and adaptation* (pp. 32–71). New York: Wiley.

Cicchetti, D., Lynch, M., Shonk, S. M., & Manly, J. T. (1992). An organizational perspective on peer relations in maltreated children. In R. D. Parke & G. W. Ladd (Eds.), *Family-peer relationships: Modes of linkage* (pp. 345–383). Hillsdale, NJ: Erlbaum.

Cicchetti, D., & Manly, J. T. (Eds.). (2001). Operationalizing child maltreatment: Developmental processes and outcomes. *Development and Psychopathology, 13*(4), 755–1048.

Cicchetti, D., & Posner, M. I. (Eds.). (2005). Integrating cognitive and affective neuroscience and developmental psychopathology [Special issue]. *Development and Psychopathology, 17*(3).

Cicchetti, D., & Rizley, R. (1981). Developmental perspectives on the etiology, intergenerational transmission, and sequelae of child maltreatment. *New Directions for Child Development, 11,* 32–59.

Cicchetti, D., & Rogosch, F. A. (1994). The toll of child maltreatment on the developing child: Insights from developmental psychopathology. *Child and Adolescent Psychiatric Clinics of North America, 3,* 759–776.

Cicchetti, D., & Rogosch, F. A. (1996). Equifinality and multifinality in developmental psychopathology. *Development and Psychopathology, 8,* 597–600.

Cicchetti, D., & Rogosch, F. A. (1997). The role of self-organization in the promotion of resilience in maltreated children. *Development and Psychopathology, 9,* 799–817.

Cicchetti, D., & Rogosch, F. A. (2001a). Diverse patterns of neuroendocrine activity in maltreated children. *Development and Psychopathology, 13,* 677–694.

Cicchetti, D., & Rogosch, F. A. (2001b). The impact of child maltreatment and psychopathology upon neuroendocrine functioning. *Development and Psychopathology, 13,* 783–804.

Cicchetti, D., & Rogosch, F. A. (2002). A developmental psychopathology perspective on adolescence. *Journal of Consulting and Clinical Psychology, 70,* 6–20.

Cicchetti, D., Rogosch, F. A., Lynch, M., & Holt, K. (1993). Resilience in maltreated children: Processes leading to adaptive outcome. *Development and Psychopathology, 5,* 629–647.

Cicchetti, D., Rogosch, F. A., Maughan, A., Toth, S. L., & Bruce, J. (2003). False belief understanding in maltreated children. *Development and Psychopathology, 15,* 1067–1091.

Cicchetti, D., & Schneider-Rosen, K. (1986). An organizational approach to childhood depression. In M. Rutter, C. Izard, & P. Read (Eds.), *Depression in young people: Clinical and developmental perspectives* (pp. 71–134). New York: Guilford Press.

Cicchetti, D., & Sroufe, L. A. (1976). The relationship between affective and cognitive development in Down's syndrome infants. *Child Development, 47,* 920–929.

Cicchetti, D., & Sroufe, L. A. (1978). An organizational view of affect: Illustration from the study of Down's syndrome infants. In M. Lewis & L. Rosenblum (Eds.), *The development of affect* (pp. 309–350). New York: Plenum Press.

Cicchetti, D., & Toth, S. L. (1992). The role of developmental theory in prevention and intervention. *Development and Psychopathology, 4,* 489–493.

Cicchetti, D., & Toth, S. L. (Eds.). (1993). *Child abuse, child development, and social policy.* Norwood, NJ: Ablex.

Cicchetti, D., & Toth, S. L. (1995). A developmental psychopathology perspective on child abuse and neglect. *Journal of the American Academy of Child and Adolescent Psychiatry, 34,* 541–565.

Cicchetti, D., & Toth, S. L. (2000). Developmental processes in maltreated children. In D. J. Hansen (Ed.), *Motivation and child maltreatment* (pp. 85–160). Lincoln: University of Nebraska Press.

Cicchetti, D., & Toth, S. L. (2003). Child maltreatment: A research and policy agent for the dawn of the millennium. In R. P. Weissberg, L. H. Weiss, O. Reyes, & H. J. Walberg (Eds.), *Trends in the well-being of children and youth* (pp. 181–206). Washington, DC: CWLA Press.

Cicchetti, D., Toth, S. L., & Hennessy, K. D. (1993). Child maltreatment and school adaptation: Problems and promises. In D. Cicchetti & S. L. Toth (Eds.), *Child abuse, child development, and social policy* (pp. 301–330). Norwood, NJ: Ablex.

Cicchetti, D., Toth, S. L., & Lynch, M. (1995). Bowlby's dream comes full circle: The application of attachment theory to risk and psychopathology. *Advances in Clinical Child Psychology, 17,* 1–75.

Cicchetti, D., Toth, S. L., & Maughan, A. (2000). An ecological-transactional model of child maltreatment. In A. Sameroff, M. Lewis, & S. Miller (Eds.), *Handbook of developmental psychopathology* (2nd ed., pp. 689–722). New York: Kluwer Academic/Plenum Press.

Cicchetti, D., Toth, S. L., & Rogosch, F. A. (2005). *The efficacy of interventions for maltreated infants in fostering secure attachment.* Manuscript in preparation.

Cicchetti, D., & Tucker, D. (1994). Development and self-regulatory structures of the mind. *Development and Psychopathology, 6,* 533–549.

Cicchetti, D., & Walker, E. F. (Eds.). (2001). Stress and development: Biological and psychological consequences [Special issue]. *Development and Psychopathology, 13*(3), 413–753.

Cohen, J. A., Deblinger, E., Mannarino, A. P., & de Arellana, M. A. (2001). The importance of culture in treating abused and neglected children: An empirical review. *Child Maltreatment, 6,* 148–157.

Cole, P., & Putnam, F. (1992). Effect of incest on self and social functioning: A developmental psychopathology perspective. *Journal of Consulting and Clinical Psychology, 60,* 174–184.

Cole, P. M., Michel, M. K., & Teti, L. O. (1994). The development of emotion regulation and dysregulation: A clinical perspective. *Monographs of the Society for Research in Child Development, 59,* 73–100.

Collin-Vezina, D., & Cyr, M. (2003). Transmission of sexual violence: Description of the phenomenon and how to understand it. *Child Abuse and Neglect, 27*(5), 489–507.

Conger, R. D., Burgess, R. L., & Barrett, C. L. (1979). Child abuse related to life change and perceptions of illness: Some preliminary findings. *Family Coordinator, 28,* 73–78.

Coohey, C. (2001). The relationship between familism and child maltreatment. A multilevel analysis. *Child Abuse and Neglect, 23,* 1019–1024.

Coohey, C., & Braun, N. (1997). Toward an integrated framework for understanding child physical abuse. *Child Abuse and Neglect, 21,* 1081–1094.

Coster, W. J., Gersten, M. S., Beeghly, M., & Cicchetti, D. (1989). Communicative functioning in maltreated toddlers. *Developmental Psychology, 25,* 1020–1029.

Courchesne, E., Chisum, H., & Townsend, J. (1994). Neural activity-dependent brain changes in development: Implications for psychopathology. *Development and Psychopathology, 6,* 697–722.

Courchesne, E., Townsend, J., & Chase, C. (1995). Neurodevelopmental principles guide research on developmental psychopathologies. In D. Cicchetti & D. J. Cohen (Eds.), *Developmental psychopathology: Vol. 1. Theory and methods* (pp. 195–226). New York: Wiley.

Cowen, E., Pederson, A., Babigian, H., Izzo, L., & Trost, M. (1973). Long-term follow up of early detected vulnerable children. *Journal of Consulting and Clinical Psychology, 41,* 438–446.

Cox, M. J., & Paley, B. (1997). Families as systems. *Annual Review of Psychology, 48,* 243–267.

Craig, I. W., & McClay, J. (2003). The role of molecular genetics in the postgenomics era. In R. Plomin, J. C. Defries, I. W. Craig, & P. McGuffin (Eds.), *Behavioural genetics in the postgenomic era* (pp. 19–40). Washington, DC: American Psychological Association.

Crick, N. R., & Dodge, K. A. (1996a). A review and reformulation of social information processing mechanisms in children's social adjustment. *Psychological Bulletin, 115,* 74–101.

Crick, N. R., & Dodge, K. A. (1996b). Social information-processing mechanisms in reactive and proactive aggression. *Child Development, 67*(3), 993–1002.

Crittenden, P. M. (1981). Abusing, neglecting, problematic, and adequate dyads: Differentiation by patterns of interaction. *Merrill-Palmer Quarterly, 27,* 201–208.

Crittenden, P. M. (1985). Social networks, quality of child-rearing, and child development. *Child Development, 56*(5), 1299–1313.

Crittenden, P. M. (1988). Relationships at risk. In J. Belsky & T. Nezworski (Eds.), *Clinical implications of attachment theory* (pp. 136–174). Hillsdale, NJ: Erlbaum.

Crittenden, P. M. (1990). Internal representational models of attachment relationships. *Infant Mental Health Journal, 11,* 259–277.

Crittenden, P. M. (1992). Quality of attachment in the preschool years. *Development and Psychopathology, 4,* 209–241.

Crittenden, P. M., & Ainsworth, M. D. S. (1989). Child maltreatment and attachment theory. In D. Cicchetti & V. Carlson (Eds.), *Child maltreatment: Theory and research on the causes and consequences of child abuse and neglect* (pp. 432–463). New York: Cambridge University Press.

Crittenden, P. M., Claussen, A. H., & Sugarman, D. B. (1994). Physical and psychological maltreatment in middle childhood and adolescence. *Development and Psychopathology, 6,* 145–164.

Crittenden, P. M., & DiLalla, D. (1988). Compulsive compliance: The development of an inhibitory coping strategy in infancy. *Journal of Abnormal Child Psychology, 16,* 585–599.

Crittenden, P. M., Partridge, M. F., & Claussen, A. H. (1991). Family patterns of relationship in normative and dysfunctional families. *Development and Psychopathology, 3,* 491–512.

Crouch, J. L., Milner, J. S., & Thomsen, C. (2001). Childhood physical abuse, early social support, and risk for maltreatment: Current social support as a mediator of risk for child physical abuse. *Child Abuse and Neglect, 25*(1), 93–107.

Crume, T. L., DiGuiseppi, C., Byers, T., Sirotnak, A. P., & Garrett, C. J. (2002). Underascertainment of child maltreatment fatalities by death certificates, 1990–1998. *Pediatrics, 110*(2). (Article No. e18). Available from www.pediatrics.org/cgi/reprint/110/2/e18.pdf.

Culp, R. E., Watkins, R. V., & Lawrence, H. (1991). Maltreated children's language and speech development: Abused, neglected, and abused and neglected. *First Language, 11,* 377–389.

Cummings, E. M., & Cicchetti, D. (1990). Toward a transactional model of relations between attachment and depression. In M. T. Greenberg, D. Cicchetti, & E. M. Cummings (Eds.), *Attachment in the preschool years* (pp. 339–372). Chicago: University of Chicago Press.

Cummings, E. M., Hennessy, K. D., Rabideau, G. J., & Cicchetti, D. (1994). Responses of physically abused boys to interadult anger involving their mothers. *Development and Psychopathology, 6,* 31–41.

Curtis, W. J., & Cicchetti, D. (2003). Moving research on resilience into the twenty-first century: Theoretical and methodological considerations in examining the biological contributors to resilience. *Development and Psychopathology, 15,* 773–810.

Curtis, W. J., & Nelson, C. A. (2003). Toward building a better brain: Neurobehavioral outcomes, mechanisms, and processes of environmental enrichment. In S. Luthar (Ed.), *Resilience and vulnerability: Adaptation in the context of childhood adversities* (pp. 462–488). New York: Cambridge University Press.

Dahl, R., & Ryan, N. (1996). The psychobiology of adolescent depression. In D. Cicchetti & S. L. Toth (Eds.), *Rochester Symposium on Developmental Psychopathology: Adolescence—Opportunities and challenges* (Vol. 7, pp. 197–232). Rochester, NY: University of Rochester Press.

Daro, D. (1988). *Confronting child abuse: Research for effective program design.* New York: Free Press.

Daro, D. (1990). *Confronting child abuse: Research for effective program design.* New York: Free Press.

Daro, D., & Donnelly, A. C. (2002). Charting the waves of prevention: Two steps forward, one step back. *Child Abuse and Neglect, 26,* 731–742.

Daro, D., & Gelles, R. (1992). Public attitudes and behaviors with respect to child abuse prevention. *Journal of Interpersonal Violence, 7*(4), 517–531.

Daro, D., & Harding, K. A. (1999). Healthy Families America: Using research to enhance practice. *Future of Children, 9,* 152–176.

Davidson, R. J. (1984). Cerebral asymmetry and emotion. *Psychophysiology, 21,* 564.

Davies, P. T., & Cicchetti, D. (Eds.). (2004). Family systems and developmental psychopathology [Special issue]. *Development and Psychopathology, 16*(3).

Davies, P. T., & Cummings, E. M. (1994). Marital conflict and child adjustment: An emotional security hypothesis. *Psychological Bulletin, 116,* 387–411.

Davis, M. (1984). The mammalian startle response. In R. C. Eaton (Ed.), *Neural mechanisms of startle behavior* (pp. 287–351). New York: Plenum Press.

Dean, A., Malik, M., Richards, W., & Stringer, S. (1986). Effects of parental maltreatment on children's conceptions of interpersonal relationships. *Developmental Psychology, 22,* 617–626.

DeBellis, M. D. (2001). Developmental traumatology: The psychobiological development of maltreated children and its implications for research, treatment, and policy. *Development and Psychopathology, 13,* 539–564.

DeBellis, M. D., Baum, A. S., Birmaher, B., Keshavan, M. S., Eccard, C. H., Boring, A. M., et al. (1999). Developmental traumatology: Pt. I. Biological stress systems. *Biological Psychiatry, 45,* 1259–1270.

DeBellis, M. D., Chrousos, G., Dorn, L., Burke, L., Helmers, K., Kling, M., et al. (1993). Hypothalamic-pituitary-adrenal axis dysregulation in sexually abused girls. *Journal of Clinical Endocrinology and Metabolism, 77,* 1–7.

DeBellis, M. D., Hall, J., Boring, A. M., Frustaci, K., & Moritz, G. (2001). A pilot longitudinal study of hippocampal volumes in pediatric maltreatment related to posttraumatic stress disorder. *Society of Biological Psychiatry, 50,* 305–309.

DeBellis, M. D., Keshavan, M. S., Casey, B. J., Clark, D. B., Giedd, J., Boring, A. M., et al. (1999). Developmental traumatology: Biological stress systems and brain development in maltreated children with PTSD: Pt. II. The relationship between characteristics of trauma and psychiatric symptoms and adverse brain development in maltreated children and adolescents with PTSD. *Biological Psychiatry, 45,* 1271–1284.

DeBellis, M. D., Keshavan, M. S., Spencer, S., & Hall, J. (2000). N-acetylaspartate concentration in the anterior cingulate in maltreated children and adolescents with PTSD. *American Journal of Psychiatry, 33,* 320–327.

DeBellis, M. D., Leffer, L., Trickett, P. K., & Putnam, F. W. (1994). Urinary catecholamine excretion in sexually abused girls. *Journal of the American Academy of Child and Adolescent Psychiatry, 33,* 320–327.

Deblinger, E., McLeer, S. V., Atkins, M. S., Ralphe, D., & Foa, E. (1989). Post-traumatic stress in sexually abused, physically abused and nonabused children. *Child Abuse and Neglect, 13*(3), 403–408.

Deci, E. L., Egharri, H., Patrick, B. C., & Leone, D. R. (1994). Facilitating internalization: The self-determination theory perspective. *Journal of Personality, 62*(1), 119–142.

DePanfilis, D., & Zuravin, S. J. (1999). Predicting child maltreatment recurrences during treatment. *Child Abuse and Neglect, 23,* 729–744.

Dicker, S., & Gordon, E. (2004). Building bridges for babies in foster care: The Babies Can't Wait initiative. *Juvenile and Family Court Journal, 55*(2), 29–41.

Dixon, L., Browne, K., & Hamilton-Giachritsis, C. (2005). Risk factors of parents abused as children: A mediational analysis of the intergenerational continuity of child maltreatment: Pt. I. *Journal of Child Psychology and Psychiatry, 46*(1), 47–49.

Dixon, L., Hamilton-Giachritsis, C., & Browne, K. (2005). Attributions and behaviours of parents abused as children: A mediational analysis of the intergenerational continuity of child maltreatment: Pt. II. *Journal of Child Psychology and Psychiatry, 46*(1), 58–68.

Dobzhansky, T. (1972). Genetics and the diversity of behavior. *American Psychologist, 27*(6), 523–530.

Dodge, K. A., Lansford, J. E., Burks, V. S., Bates, J. E., Pettit, G. S., Fontaine, R., et al. (2003). Peer rejections and social information processing factors in development of aggressive behavior problems in children. *Child Development, 74*(2), 373–393.

Dodge, K. A., Pettit, G. S., & Bates, J. E. (1990). Mechanisms in the cycle of violence. *Science, 250,* 1678–1683.

Dodge, K. A., Pettit, G. S., & Bates, J. E. (1994). Effects of physical maltreatment on the development of peer relations. *Development and Psychopathology, 6,* 43–55.

Dodge, K. A., Pettit, G. S., & Bates, J. E. (1997). How the experience of early physical abuse leads children to become chronically aggressive. In D. Cicchetti & S. L. Toth (Eds.), *Rochester Symposium on Developmental Psychology: Vol. 8. Developmental perspectives on trauma—Theory, research, and intervention* (pp. 263–288). Rochester, NY: University of Rochester Press.

Donchin, E., Karis, D., Bashore, T. R., Coles, M. G. H., & Gratton, G. (1986). Cognitive psychophysiology and human information processing. In M. G. H. Coles, E. Donchin, & S. W. Porges (Eds.), *Psychophysiology* (pp. 244–267). New York: Guilford Press.

Dozier, M., Levine, S., Stovall, K., & Eldreth, D. (2001). *Atypical diurnal rhythms of cortisol production: Understanding foster children's neuroendocrine regulation.* Unpublished manuscript.

Drake, B. (1996). Unraveling "unsubstantiated." *Child Maltreatment, 1,* 262–271.

Drake, R. E., Adler, D. A., & Vaillant, G. E. (1988). Antecedents of personality disorders in a community sample of men. *Journal of Personality Disorders, 2*(1), 60–68.

Dubanoski, R. A. (1981). Child maltreatment in European- and Hawaiian-Americans. *Child Abuse and Neglect, 5,* 457–466.

Dubanoski, R. A., & Snyder, K. (1980). Patterns of child abuse and neglect in Japanese- and Samoan-Americans. *Child Abuse and Neglect, 4,* 217–225.

Dube, S. R., Anda, R. F., Felitti, V. J., Chapman, D. P., Williamson, D. F., & Giles, W. H. (2001). Childhood abuse, household dysfunction, and the risk of attempted suicide throughout the lifespan: Findings from the Adverse Child Experiences Study. *Journal of the American Medical Association, 286,* 3089–3096.

Dubowitz, H. (1999). The families of neglected children. In M. E. Lamb (Ed.), *Parenting and child development in nontraditional families* (pp. 327–345). Mahwah, NJ: Erlbaum.

Duncan, R. D. (1999). Peer and sibling aggression: An investigation of intra- and extrafamilial bullying. *Journal of Interpersonal Violence, 14,* 871–886.

Dunn, M. G., Tarter, R. E., Mezzich, A. C., Vanyukov, M., Kirisci, L., & Kirillova, G. (2002). Origins and consequences of child neglect in substance abuse families. *Clinical Psychology Review, 22*(7), 1063–1090.

During, S., & McMahon, R. (1991). Recognition of emotional facial expression by abusive mothers and their children. *Journal of Clinical Child Psychology, 20,* 132–139.

Eckenrode, J., & Laird, M. (1991, April). *Social adjustment of maltreated children in the school setting.* Paper presented at the biennial meeting of the Society for Research in Child Development, Seattle, WA.

Eckenrode, J., Laird, M., & Doris, J. (1993). School performance and disciplinary problems among abused and neglected children. *Developmental Psychology, 29,* 53–62.

Edelman, M. W. (1987). *Families in peril: An agenda for social change.* Cambridge, MA: Harvard University Press.

Edelson, J. L. (1999). The overlap between child maltreatment and woman battering. *Violence Against Women, 5*(2), 134–154.

Egeland, B. (1988). Breaking the cycle of abuse: Implications for prediction and intervention. In K. Browne, C. Davies, & P. Stratton (Eds.), *Early prediction and prevention of child abuse* (pp. 87–99). Chichester, England: Wiley.

Egeland, B., & Abery, B. (1991). A longitudinal study of high-risk children: Educational outcomes. *International Journal of Disability, Development, and Education, 38,* 271–287.

Egeland, B., Bosquet, M., & Chung, A. L. (2002). Continuities and discontinuities in the intergenerational transmission of child maltreatment: Implications for breaking the cycle of abuse. In K. Browne, H. Hanks, P. Stratton, & C. E. Hamilton (Eds.), *Early prediction and prevention of child abuse* (pp. 217–232). Chichester, England: Wiley.

Egeland, B., Breitenbucher, M., & Rosenberg, D. (1980). Prospective study of the significance of life stress in the etiology of child abuse. *Journal of Consulting and Clinical Psychology, 48,* 195–205.

Egeland, B., Carlson, E. A., & Sroufe, L. A. (1993). Resilience as process. *Development and Psychopathology, 5,* 517–528.

Egeland, B., & Farber, E. (1987). Invulnerability among abused and neglected children. In E. J. Anthony & B. J. Cohler (Eds.), *The invulnerable child* (pp. 253–288). New York: Guilford Press.

Egeland, B., Jacobvitz, D., & Papatola, K. (1987). Intergenerational continuity of abuse. In R. J. Gelles & J. B. Lancaster (Eds.), *Child abuse and neglect: Biosocial dimensions* (pp. 255–276). New York: Aldine.

Egeland, B., Jacobvitz, D., & Sroufe, L. A. (1988). Breaking the cycle of abuse. *Child Development, 59*(4), 1080–1088.

Egeland, B., & Sroufe, L. A. (1981). Developmental sequelae of maltreatment in infancy. *New Directions for Child Development, 11,* 77–92.

Egeland, B., Sroufe, L. A., & Erickson, M. F. (1983). Developmental consequence of different patterns of maltreatment. *Child Abuse and Neglect, 7,* 459–469.

Ehrensaft, M. K., Cohen, P., Brown, J., Smailes, E., Chen, H. N., & Johnson, J. G. (2003). Intergenerational transmission of partner violence: A 20-year prospective study. *Journal of Consulting and Clinical Psychology, 71,* 741–753.

Eigsti, I. M., & Cicchetti, D. (2004). The impact of child maltreatment on expressive syntax at 60 months. *Developmental Science, 7,* 88–102.

Eisenberg, L. (1995). The social construction of the human brain. *American Journal of Psychiatry, 152,* 1563–1575.

Emde, R. N. (1983). The pre-represenational self and its affective core. *Psychoanalytic Study of the Child, 38,* 165–192.

Emery, R. E. (1989). Family violence. *American Psychologist, 44,* 321–328.

Erickson, M. F., Korfmacher, J., & Egeland, B. (1992). Attachments past and present: Implications for therapeutic intervention with mother-infancy dyads. *Development and Psychopathology, 4,* 495–507.

Erickson, M. K., Egeland, B., & Pianta, R. (1989). The effects of maltreatment in the development of young children. In D. Cicchetti & V. Carlson (Eds.), *Child maltreatment: Theory and research on the causes and consequences of child abuse and neglect* (pp. 647–684). New York: Cambridge University Press.

Evans, G. W. (2004). The environment of childhood poverty. *American Psychologist, 59*(2), 77–92.

Famularo, R., Kinscherff, R., & Fenton, T. (1992). Psychiatric diagnoses of maltreated children: Preliminary findings. *Journal of the American Academy of Child and Adolescent Psychiatry, 31,* 863–867.

Farrington, D. P., Jolliffe, D., Loeber, R., Stouthamer-Loeber, M., & Kalb, L. M. (2001). The concentration of the offenders in families, and family criminality in the prediction of boys' delinquency. *Journal of Adolescence, 24,* 579–596.

Fein, G., & Apfel, N. (1979). The development of play: Style, structure, and situation. *Genetic Psychology Monographs, 99,* 231–250.

Feldman, S., & Downey, G. (1994). Rejection sensitivity as a mediator of the impact of childhood exposure to family violence in adult attachment behavior. *Development and Psychopathology, 6,* 231–247.

Feshbach, S. (1978). The development and regulation of aggression: Some research gaps and a proposed cognitive approach. In W. W. Hartup & J. DeWit (Eds.), *Origins of aggression* (pp. 163–187). New York: Mouton.

Fingerhut, L. A., & Kleinman, J. C. (1990). International and interstate comparisons of homicide among young males. *Journal of the American Medical Association, 263,* 3292–3295.

Finkelhor, D., Ormrod, R., Turner, H., & Hamby, S. L. (2005). The victimization of children and youth: A comprehensive, national survey. *Child Maltreatment, 10*(1), 5–25.

Finzi, R., Ram, A., Shnit, D., Har-Even, D., Tyano, S., & Weizman, A. (2001). Depressive symptoms and suicidality in physically abused children. *American Journal of Orthopsychiatry, 71,* 98–107.

Fischer, K. W., & Ayoub, C. (1994). Affective splitting and dissociation in normal and maltreated children: Developmental pathways for self in relationships. In D. Cicchetti & S. L. Toth (Eds.), *Rochester Symposium on Developmental Psychopathology: Vol. 5. Disorders and dysfunction of the self* (pp. 149–222). Rochester, NY: University of Rochester Press.

Flores, E., Cicchetti, D., & Rogosch, F. A. (2005). Predictors of resilience in maltreated and nonmaltreated Latino children. *Developmental Psychology, 41*(2), 428–442.

Foley, D. L., Eaves, L. J., Wormley, B., Silberg, J. L., Maes, H. H., Kuhn, J., et al. (2004). Childhood adversity, monoamine oxidase: A genotype, and risk for conduct disorder. *Archives of General Psychiatry, 61*(7), 738–744.

Fontes, L. (2001). Introduction: Those who do not look ahead, stay behind. *Child Maltreatment, 6,* 83–88.

Fowler, A. E. (1998). Language in mental retardation: Associations with and dissociations from general cognition. In J. A. Burack, R. M. Ho-dapp, & E. Zigler (Eds.), *Handbook of retardation and development* (pp. 290–333). Cambridge, MA: Cambridge University Press.

Fox, L., Long, S. H., & Langlois, A. (1988). Patterns of language comprehension deficit in abused and neglected children. *Journal of Speech and Hearing Disorders, 53*(3), 239–244.

Fox, N. A., & Davidson, R. J. (1984). Asymmetry in response to stranger and mother approach and separation in 10-month old infants. *Psychophysiology, 21*(5), 577.

Fox, N. A., Kimmerly, N. L., & Schaffer, W. D. (1991). Attachment to mother, attachment to father: A meta-analysis. *Child Development, 62*(1), 210–225.

Fraiberg, S. (1982). Pathological defenses in infancy. *Psychoanalytic Quarterly, 51,* 612–635.

Fraiberg, S., Adelson, E., & Shapiro, V. (1975). Ghosts in the nursery: A psychoanalytic approach to impaired infant-mother relationships. *Journal of the American Academy of Child Psychiatry, 14,* 387–421.

Freeman, B., Powell, J., Ball, D., Hill, L., Craig, I., & Plomin, R. (1997). DNA by mail: An inexpensive and noninvasive method for collecting DNA samples from widely dispersed populations. *Behavior Genetics, 127,* 251–257.

Gaensbauer, T. J. (1982). Regulation of emotional expression in infants from two contrasting caretaker environments. *Journal of Pediatric Psychology, 9,* 241–256.

Gaensbauer, T. J., Mrazek, D., & Harmon, R. (1981). Emotional expression in abused and/or neglected infants. In N. Frude (Ed.), *Psychological approaches to child abuse* (pp. 120–135). Totowa, NJ: Rowman & Littlefield.

Garbarino, J. (1977). The human ecology of child maltreatment: A conceptual model for research. *Journal of Marriage and the Family, 39,* 721–732.

Garbarino, J. (1982). *Children and families in the social environment.* Lexington, MA: Lexington Books.

Garbarino, J., & Crouter, A. Q. (1978). Defining the community context for parent-child relations: The correlates of child maltreatment. *Child Development, 49,* 604–616.

Garbarino, J., & Gilliam, G. (1980). *Understanding abusive families.* Lexington, MA: Lexington Books.

Garbarino, J., & Sherman, D. (1980). High-risk neighborhoods and high-risk families: The human ecology of child maltreatment. *Child Development, 51,* 188–198.

Garcia Coll, C., Akerman, A., & Cicchetti, D. (2000). Cultural influences on developmental processes and outcomes: Implications for the study of development and psychopathology. *Development and Psychopathology, 12,* 333–356.

Gaudin, J. M., Jr., Wodarski, J. S., Arkinson, M. K., & Avery, L. S. (1990). Remedying child neglect: Effectiveness of social network interventions. *Journal of Applied Social Sciences, 15,* 97–123.

Gelles, R. J. (1991). Physical violence, child abuse and child homicide: A continuum of violence or distinct behaviors? *Human Nature, 2,* 59–72.

Gelles, R. J., & Hargreaves, E. F. (1981). Maternal employment and violence toward children. *Journal of Family Issues, 2,* 509–530.

Gelles, R. J., & Straus, M. A. (1988). *Intimate violence.* New York: Simon & Schuster.

George, C., & Main, M. (1979). Social interactions of young abused children: Approach, avoidance and aggression. *Child Development, 50,* 306–318.

Gersten, M., Coster, W., Schneider-Rosen, K., Carlson, V., & Cicchetti, D. (1986). The socioemotional bases of communicative functioning: Quality of attachment, language development, and early maltreatment. In M. Lamb, A. L. Brown, & B. Rogoff (Eds.), *Advances in developmental psychology* (Vol. 4, pp. 105–151). Hillsdale, NJ: Erlbaum.

Gibb, B. E., Alloy, L. B., Abramson, L. Y., Rose, D. T., Whitehouse, W. G., Donovan, P., et al. (2001). History of childhood maltreatment, negative cognitive styles and episodes of depression in adulthood. *Cognitive Therapy and Research, 4,* 425–446.

Gibb, B. E., Wheeler, R., Alloy, L. B., & Abramson, L. Y. (2001). Emotional, physical, and sexual maltreatment in childhood versus adolescence and personality dysfunction in young adulthood. *Journal of Personality Disorders, 15*(6), 505–511.

Gil, D. B. (1970). *Violence against children: Physical child abuse in the United States.* Cambridge, MA: Harvard University Press.

Gladstone, G. L., Parker, G. B., Mitchell, P. B., Mahli, G. S., Wilhelm, K., & Austin, M. P. (2004). Implications of childhood trauma for depressed women: An analysis of pathways from childhood sexual abuse to deliberate self-harm and revictimization. *American Journal of Psychiatry, 161*(8), 1417–1425.

Goodyear, R. K., Newcomb, M. D., & Allison, R. D. (2000). Predictors of Latino men's paternity in teen pregnancy: Test of a mediational model of childhood experiences, gender role attitudes, and behaviors. *Journal of Counseling Psychology, 47,* 116–128.

Gottesman, I. I. (1963). Genetic aspects of intelligent behavior. In N. R. Ellis (Ed.), *Handbook of mental deficiency: Psychological theory and research* (pp. 253–296). New York: McGraw-Hill.

Gottlieb, G. (1991). Experiential canalization of behavioral development: Theory. *Developmental Psychology, 27,* 4–13.

Gottlieb, G. (1992). *Individual development and evolution: The genesis of novel behavior.* New York: Oxford University Press.

Gould, E., Tanapat, P., McEwen, B. S., Flugge, G., & Fuchs, E. (1998). Proliferation of granule cell precursors in the dentate gyrus of adult monkeys is diminished by stress. *Proceedings of the National Academy of Sciences, 95,* 3168–3171.

Greenough, W., Black, J., & Wallace, C. (1987). Experience and brain development. *Child Development, 58,* 539–559.

Greenspan, S. I., & Porges, S. W. (1984). Psychopathology in infancy and early childhood: Clinical perspectives on the organization of sensory and affective-thematic experience. *Child Development, 55,* 49–70.

Grusec, J. E., & Goodnow, J. J. (1994). Impact of parental discipline methods on the child's internalization of values: A reconceptualization of current points-of-view. *Developmental Psychology, 30*(1), 4–19.

Grych, J. H., Wachsmuth-Schlaefer, T., & Klockow, L. L. (2002). Interparental aggression and young children's representations of family relationships. *Journal of Family Psychology, 16,* 259–272.

Gunnar, M. R., & Nelson, C. A. (1994). Event-related potentials in year-old infants: Relations with emotionality and cortisol. *Child Development, 65,* 80–94.

Gunnar, M. R., & Vazquez, D. M. (2001). Low coritsol and a flattening of expected daytime rhythm: Potential indices of risk in human development. *Development and Psychopathology, 13,* 515–538.

Gurvits, T. V., Shenton, M. E., Hokama, H., Ohta, H., Lasko, N. B., Gilbertson, M. W., et al. (1996). Magnetic resonance imaging study of hippocampal volume in chronic, combat-related posttraumatic stress disorder. *Biological Psychiatry, 40,* 1091–1099.

Harrison, A. O., Wilson, M. N., Pine, C. J., Chan, E. Q., & Buriel, R. (1990). Family ecologies of ethnic minority children. *Child Development, 61,* 347–362.

Hart, D., Hofmann, V., Edelstein, W., & Keller, M. (1997). The relation of childhood personality types to adolescent behavior and development: A longitudinal study of Icelandic children. *Developmental Psychology, 33,* 195–205.

Hart, J., Gunnar, M., & Cicchetti, D. (1996). Altered neuroendocrine activity in maltreated children related to depression. *Development and Psychopathology, 8,* 201–214.

Hartmann, H. (1958). *Ego psychology and the problem of adaptation.* New York: International Universities Press.

Haskett, M. E., & Kistner, J. A. (1991). Social interactions and peer perceptions of young physically abused children. *Child Development, 62,* 979–990.

Hays, T., & Jones, L. (1994). Societal interventions to prevent child abuse and neglect. *Child Welfare, 73,* 370–403.

Heim, C., Ehlert, U., & Hellhammer, D. (2000). The potential role of hypocortisolism in the pathophysiology of stress-related bodily disorders. *Psychoneuroendocrinology, 25,* 1–35.

Heim, C., & Nemeroff, C. B. (2001). The role of childhood trauma in the neurobiology of mood and anxiety disorders: Preclinical and clinical studies. *Biological Psychiatry, 49,* 1023–1039.

Heim, C., Newport, D. J., Bonsall, R., Miler, A. H., & Nemeroff, C. B. (2001). Altered pituitary-adrenal axis responses to provocative challenge tests in adult survivors of childhood abuse. *American Journal of Psychiatry, 158,* 575–581.

Heim, C., Newport, D. J., Wagner, D., Wilcox, M. M., Miller, A. H., & Nemeroff, C. B. (2002). The role of early adverse experience and adulthood stress in the prediction of neuroendocrine stress reactivity in women: A multiple regression analysis. *Depression and Anxiety, 15*(3), 117–125.

Hennessy, K. D., Rabideau, G. J., Cicchetti, D., & Cummings, E. M. (1994). Responses of physically abused and nonabused children to different forms of interadult anger. *Child Development, 65,* 815–828.

Herman, J. L., Perry, J. C., & van der Kolk, B. A. (1989). Childhood trauma in borderline personality disorder. *American Journal of Psychiatry, 146,* 490–495.

Herman-Giddens, M. E., Brown, G., Verbiest, S., Carlson, P. J., Hooten, E. G., Howell, E., et al. (1999). Underascertainment of child abuse mortality in the United States. *Journal of the American Medical Association, 282*(5), 463–467.

Herrenkohl, E. C., Herrenkohl, R. C., & Egolf, M. (1994). Resilient early school-age children from maltreating homes: Outcomes in late adolescence. *American Journal of Orthopsychiatry, 64,* 301–309.

Herrenkohl, R. C., & Herrenkohl, E. C. (1981). Some antecedents and developmental consequences of child maltreatment. *New Directions for Child Development, 11,* 57–76.

Hertsgaard, L., Gunnar, M., Erickson, M. F., & Nachmias, M. (1995). Adrenocortical responses to the Strange Situation in infants with disorganized/disoriented attachment relationships. *Child Development, 66,* 1100–1106.

Herzberger, S. D. (1983). Social cognition and the transmission of abuse. In D. Finkelhor, R. Gelles, G. Hotaling, & M. Straus (Eds.), *The dark side of families: Current family violence research* (pp. 317–329). Beverly Hills, CA: Sage.

Hesse, P., & Cicchetti, D. (1982). Perspectives on an integrative theory of emotional development. *New Directions for Child Development, 16,* 3–48.

Hildyard, K. L., & Wolfe, D. A. (2002). Child neglect: Developmental issues and outcomes. *Child Abuse and Neglect, 26,* 679–695.

Hillyard, S. A., & Picton, T. W. (1987). Electrophysiology of cognition. In V. Mountcastle (Ed.), *Handbook of physiology: Higher functions of the brain* (Vol. 5, pp. 519–583). Bethesda, MD: American Physiological Society.

Hofer, M. A. (1987). Early social relationships: A psychobiologist's view. *Child Development, 58*(3), 633–647.

Hoffman-Plotkin, D., & Twentyman, C. T. (1984). A multimodel assessment of behavioral and cognitive deficits in abused and neglected preschoolers. *Child Development, 55,* 794–802.

Holton, J. (1992). African Americans' needs and participation in child maltreatment prevention services: Toward a community response to child abuse and neglect. *Urban Research Review, 14,* 1–6.

Horowitz, A. V., Widom, C. S., McLaughlin, J., & White, H. R. (2001). The impact of childhood abuse and neglect on adult mental health: A prospective study. *Journal of Health and Social Behavior, 42*(2), 184–201.

Horowitz, F. D. (1987). *Exploring developmental theories: Toward a structural/behavioral model of development.* Hillsdale, NJ: Erlbaum.

Howe, M. L., Cicchetti, D., Toth, S. L., & Cerrito, B. M. (2004). True and false memories in maltreated children. *Child Development, 75*(5), 1402–1417.

Howes, C., & Eldredge, R. (1985). Responses of abused, neglected, and non-maltreated children to the behaviors of their peers. *Journal of Applied Developmental Psychology, 6,* 261–270.

Howes, C., & Espinosa, M. P. (1985). The consequences of child abuse for the formation of relationships with peers. *International Journal of Child Abuse and Neglect, 9,* 397–404.

Howes, C., & Hamilton, C. E. (1992). Children's relationships with child care teachers: Stability and concordance with parental attachments. *Child Development, 63,* 867–878.

Howes, C., & Segal, J. (1993). Children's relationships with alternative caregivers: The special case of maltreated children removed from their homes. *Journal of Applied Developmental Psychology, 14,* 71–81.

Howes, P. W., & Cicchetti, D. (1993). A family/relational perspective on maltreating families: Parallel processes across systems and social policy implications. In D. Cicchetti & S. L. Toth (Eds.), *Child abuse, child development, and social policy* (pp. 249–300). Norwood, NJ: Ablex.

Howes, P. W., Cicchetti, D., Toth, S. L., & Rogosch, F. A. (2000). Affective, structural, and relational characteristics of maltreating families: A systems perspective. *Journal of Family Psychology, 14,* 95–110.

Hunter, R. S., & Kilstrom, N. (1979). Breaking the cycle of abusive families. *American Journal of Psychiatry, 136,* 1320–1322.

Huston, A. C. (1991). Children in poverty: Developmental and policy issues. In A. C. Huston (Ed.), *Children in poverty: Child development and public policy* (pp. 1–22). New York: Cambridge University Press.

Huttenlocher, P. R. (1994). Synaptogenesis, synapse elimination, and neural plasticity in human cerebral cortex. In C. A. Nelson (Ed.), *Minnesota Symposia on Child Psychology: Vol. 27. Threats to optimal development: Integrating biological, psychological, and social risk factors* (pp. 35–54). Hillsdale, NJ: Erlbaum.

Jacobson, R. S., & Straker, G. (1982). Peer group interaction of physically abused children. *International Journal of Child Abuse and Neglect, 6,* 321–327.

Jacobvitz, D. B., Morgan, E., Kretchmar, M. D., & Morgan, Y. (1991). The transmission of mother-child boundary disturbances across three generations. *Development and Psychopathology, 3,* 513–527.

Jaffee, S. R., Caspi, A., Moffitt, T. E., Polo-Tomas, M., Price, T. S., & Taylor, A. (2004). The limits of child effects: Evidence for genetically mediated child effects on corporal punishment but not on physical maltreatment. *Developmental Psychology, 40*(6), 1047–1058.

Jaffee, S. R., Caspi, A., Moffitt, T. E., & Taylor, A. (2004). Physical maltreatment victim to antisocial child: Evidence of an environmentally mediated process. *Journal of Abnormal Psychology, 113*(1), 44–55.

Johnson, J. G., Cohen, P., Brown, J., Smailes, E. M., & Bernstein, D. P. (1999). Childhood maltreatment increases risk for personality disorders during early adulthood. *Archives of General Psychiatry, 56,* 600–606.

Johnson, J. G., Cohen, P., Gould, M. S., Kasen, S., Brown, J., & Brook, J. S. (2002). Childhood adversities, interpersonal difficulties, and risk for suicide attempts during late adolescence and early adulthood. *Archives of General Psychiatry, 59,* 741–749.

Johnson, J. G., Smailes, E. M., Phil, M., Cohen, P., Brown, J., & Bernstein, D. P. (2000). Associations between four types of childhood neglect and personality disorder symptoms during adolescence and early adulthood: Findings from a community based longitudinal study. *Journal of Personality Disorders, 14,* 171–187.

Johnson, M. H. (1998). The neural basis of cognitive development. In D. Kuhn & R. Siegler (Eds.), *Handbook of child psychology: Vol. 2. Cognition, perception, and language* (pp. 1–49). New York: Wiley.

Johnson, M. H. (1999). Cortical plasticity in normal and abnormal cognitive development: Evidence and working hypotheses. *Development and Psychopathology, 11,* 419–438.

Johnson, R. (1993). On the neural generators of the P300 component of the event-related potential. *Psychophysiology, 30,* 90–97.

Juvenile Justice Standards Project. (1977). *Standards relating to child abuse and neglect.* Cambridge, MA: Ballinger.

Kagan, J. (1981). *The second year: The emergence of self-awareness.* Cambridge, MA: Harvard University Press.

Kagan, J. (1994). *Galen's prophecy: Temperament in human nature.* New York: Basic Books.

Kandel, E. R. (1998). A new intellectual framework for psychiatry. *American Journal of Psychiatry, 155,* 469–475.

Kandel, E. R. (1999). Biology and the future of psychoanalysis: A new intellectual framework for psychiatry revisited. *American Journal of Psychiatry, 156,* 505–524.

Kanoy, K., Ulku-Steiner, B., Cox, M., & Burchinal, M. (2003). Marital relationship and individual psychological characteristics that predict physical punishment of children. *Journal of Family Psychology, 17,* 20–28.

Kaplan, S. J., Pelcovitz, D., Salzinger, S., Mandel, F., Weiner, M., & LaBruna, V. (1999). Adolescent physical abuse and risk for suicidal behaviors. *Journal of Interpersonal Violence, 14,* 976–988.

Kaufman, J. (1991). Depressive disorders in maltreated children. *Journal of the American Academy of Child and Adolescent Psychiatry, 30,* 257–265.

Kaufman, J., Birmaher, B., Perel, J., Dahl, R. E., Moreci, P., Nelson, B., et al. (1997). The corticotropic-releasing hormone challenge in depressed abused, depressed nonabused, and normal control children. *Biological Psychiatry, 42,* 669–679.

Kaufman, J., & Charney, D. (2001). Effects of early stress on brain structure and function: Implications for understanding the relationship between child maltreatment and depression. *Development and Psychopathology, 13,* 451–471.

Kaufman, J., & Cicchetti, D. (1989). The effects of maltreatment on school-aged children's socioemotional development: Assessments in a day camp setting. *Developmental Psychology, 25,* 516–524.

Kaufman, J., Yang, B., Douglas-Palumberi, H., Houshyar, S., Lipschitz, D., Krystal, J., et al. (2004). Social supports and serotonin transporter gene moderate depression in maltreated children. *Proceedings of the National Academy of Sciences, USA, 101*(49), 17316–17321.

Kaufman, J., & Zigler, E. (1989). The intergenerational transmission of child abuse and the prospect of predicting future abusers. In D. Cicchetti & V. Carlson (Eds.), *Child maltreatment: Research and theory on consequences of child abuse and neglect* (pp. 129–150). New York: Cambridge University Press.

Kavanagh, K. A., Youngblade, L., Reid, J. B., & Fagot, B. I. (1988). Interactions between children and abusive versus control parents. *Journal of Clinical Child Psychology, 17,* 137–142.

Kelley, A. E., & Stinus, L. (1984). Neuroanatomical and neurochemical substrates of affective behavior. In N. A. Fox & R. J. Davidson (Eds.), *The psychobiology of affective development* (pp. 1–75). Hillsdale, NJ: Erlbaum.

Kempe, C. H. (1973). A practical approach to the protection of the abused child and rehabilitation of the abusing parent. *Pediatrics, 51,* 804–812.

Kempe, C. H. (1976). Predicting and preventing child abuse: Establishing children's rights by assuring access to health care through the health visitors concept. *Proceedings of the First National Conference on Child Abuse and Neglect, January 4–7, 1976* (pp. 67–75). Washington, DC: U.S. Department of Health, Education and Welfare.

Kendall-Tackett, K. A., Williams, L. M., & Finkelhor, D. (1993). Impact of sexual abuse on children: A review and synthesis of recent empirical studies. *Psychological Bulletin, 113,* 164–180.

Kendler, K. S., Kuhn, J. W., & Prescott, C. A. (2004). Childhood sexual abuse, stressful life events and risk for major depression in women. *Psychological Medicine, 34*(8), 1475–1482.

Kessler, R. C., Davis, C. G., & Kendler, K. S. (1997). Childhood adversity and adult psychiatric disorder in the U.S. National Comorbidity Survey. *Psychological Medicine, 27*(5), 1101–1119.

Kim, J., & Cicchetti, D. (2003). Social self-efficacy and behavior problems in maltreated and nonmaltreated children. *Journal of Clinical Child and Adolescent Psychology, 32*(1), 106–117.

Kim, J., &. Cicchetti, D. (2004). A process model of mother-child relatedness and psychological adjustment among maltreated and nonmaltreated children: The role of self-esteem and social competence. *Journal of Abnormal Child Psychology, 32,* 341–354.

Kirby, J. S., Chu, J. A., & Dill, D. L. (1993). Correlates of dissociative symptomatology in patients with physical and sexual abuse histories. *Comprehensive Psychiatry, 34*(4), 258–263.

Kirschbaum, C., & Hellhammer, D. H. (1989). Salivary cortisol in psychobiological research: An overview. *Neuropsychobiology, 22*(3), 150–169.

Kiser, L. J., Heston, J., Millsap, P. A., & Pruitt, D. B. (1991). Physical and sexual abuse in childhood: Relationship with post-traumatic stress disorder. *Journal of the American Academy of Child and Adolescent Psychiatry, 30,* 776–783.

Kisiel, C. L., & Lyons, J. S. (2001). Dissociation as a mediator of psychopathology among sexually abused children and adolescents. *American Journal of Psychiatry, 158,* 1034–1039.

Kitzman, H., Olds, D., Henderson, C., Hanks, C., Cole, R., Tatelbaum, R., et al. (1997). Effect of prenatal and infancy home visitation by nurses for pregnancy outcomes, childhood inquiries, and repeated childbearing: A randomized controlled trial. *Journal of the American Medical Association, 278,* 644–652.

Klimes-Dougan, B., & Kistner, J. A. (1990). Physically abused preschoolers' responses to peer distress. *Developmental Psychology, 26,* 599–602.

Klorman, R., Cicchetti, D., Thatcher, J. E., & Ison, J. R. (2003). Acoustic startle in maltreated children. *Journal of Abnormal Child Psychology, 31,* 359–370.

Koenig, A. L., Cicchetti, D., & Rogosch, F. A. (2000). Child compliance/noncompliance and maternal contributors to internalization in maltreating and nonmaltreating dyads. *Child Development, 71,* 1018–1032.

Koenig, A. L., Cicchetti, D., & Rogosch, F. A. (2004). Moral development: The association between maltreatment and young children's prosocial behaviors and moral transgressions. *Social Development, 13*(1), 87–106.

Koenig, A. L., Ialongo, N., Wagner, B. M., Poduska, J., & Kellam, S. (2002). Negative caregiver strategies and psychopathology in urban African-American young adults. *Child Abuse and Neglect, 26*(10), 1211–1233.

Korbin, J. E. (Ed.). (1981). *Child abuse and neglect: Cross cultural perspectives.* Berkeley: University of California Press.

Korbin, J. E. (1997). Culture and child maltreatment. In M. E. Helfer, R. Kempe, & R. Krugman (Eds.), *The battered child* (5th ed., pp. 29–48). Chicago: University of Chicago Press.

Korbin, J. E. (2002). Culture and child maltreatment: Cultural competence and beyond. *Child Abuse and Neglect, 26,* 637–644.

Korbin, J. E., Coulton, C. J., Chard, S., Platt-Houston, C., & Su, M. (1998). Impoverishment and child maltreatment in African American and European American neighborhoods. *Development and Psychopathology, 10,* 215–233.

Kovacs, M. (1985). The children's depression inventory. *Psychopharmacology Bulletin, 21,* 995–998.

Koverla, C., Pound, J., Heger, A., & Lytle, C. (1993). Relationship of child sexual abuse to depression. *Child Abuse and Neglect, 17,* 393–400.

Lahey, B. B., Conger, R. D., Atkeson, B. M., & Treiber, F. A. (1984). Parenting behavior and emotional status of physically abusive mothers. *Journal of Consulting and Clinical Psychology, 52,* 1062–1071.

Lamb, M., Gaensbauer, T. J., Malkin, C. M., & Schultz, L. A. (1985). The effects of child maltreatment on security of infant-adult attachment. *Infant Behavior and Development, 8,* 35–45.

Lamb, M., Thompson, R., Gardner, W., & Charnov, E. (1985). *Infant-mother attachment.* Hillsdale, NJ: Erlbaum.

Lang, A. J., Stein, M. B., Kennedy, C. M., & Foy, D. W. (2004). Adult psychopathology and intimate partner violence among survivors of childhood maltreatment. *Journal of Interpersonal Violence, 19*(10), 1102–1118.

Lang, P. J. (1994). The varieties of emotional experience: A meditation on James-Lange theory. *Psychological Review, 101,* 211–221.

Laporte, L., & Guttman, H. (1996). Traumatic childhood experiences as risk factors for borderline and other personality disorders. *Journal of Personality Disorders, 14,* 171–187.

Leifer, M., Kilbane, T., & Kalick, S. (2004). Vulnerability or resilience to intergenerational sexual abuse: The role of maternal factors. *Child Maltreatment, 9*(1), 78–91.

Lemieux, A. M., & Coe, C. L. (1995). Abuse-related posttraumatic stress disorder: Evidence for chronic neuroendocrine activation in women. *Psychosomatic Medicine, 57,* 110–115.

Lesch, K. P., Bengel, D., Heils, A., Sabol, S. A., Greenberg, B. S., Petir, S., et al. (1996). Association of anxiety-related traits with a polymorphism in the serotonin transporter gene regulatory region. *Science, 274*(5292), 1527–1531.

Levine, S. (1994). The ontogeny of the hypothalamic-pituitary-adrenal axis: The influence of maternal factors. *Annals of the New York Academy of Sciences, 746,* 275–288.

Lewis, D. O., Mallouh, C., & Webb, V. (1989). Child abuse, delinquency, and violent criminality. In D. Cicchetti & V. Carlson (Eds.), *Child maltreatment: Theory and research on the causes and consequences of child abuse and neglect* (pp. 707–721). New York: Cambridge University Press.

Lewis, M., & Brooks-Gunn, J. (1979). *Social cognition and the acquisition of self.* New York: Plenum Press.

Lieberman, A. F. (1991). Attachment theory and infant-parent psychotherapy: Some conceptual, clinical, and research considerations. In D. Cicchetti & S. L. Toth (Eds.), *Rochester Symposium on Developmental Psychopathology: Vol. 3. Models and integrations* (pp. 261–287). Rochester, NY: University of Rochester Press.

Lieberman, A. F., Weston, D., & Pawl, J. H. (1991). Preventive intervention and outcome with anxiously attached dyads. *Child Development, 62,* 199–209.

Lieberman, A. F., & Zeanah, C. H. (1999). Contributions of attachment theory to infant parent psychotherapy and other interventions with infants and young children. In J. Cassidy & P. R. Shaver (Eds.), *Handbook of attachment* (pp. 555–574). New York: Guilford Press.

Lindsey, D. (1994). *The welfare of children.* New York: Oxford University Press.

Loeber, R., Felton, D. K., & Reid, J. B. (1984). A social learning approach to the reduction of coercive processes in child abusive families: A molecular analysis. *Advances in Behaviour Research and Therapy, 6*(1), 29–45.

Loftus, E. F. (1993). The reality of repressed memories. *American Psychologist, 48*(5), 518–537.

Lopez, J. F., Akil, H., & Watson, S. J. (1999). Neural circuits mediating stress. *Biological Psychiatry, 46,* 1461–1471.

Luntz, B., & Widom, C. S. (1994). Antisocial personality disorder in abused and neglected children grown up. *American Journal of Psychiatry, 151,* 670–674.

Luthar, S. S., & Cicchetti, D. (2000). The construct of resilience: Implications for intervention and social policy. *Development and Psychopathology, 12,* 857–885.

Luthar, S. S., Cicchetti, D., & Becker, B. (2000). The construct of resilience: A critical evaluation and guidelines for future work. *Child Development, 71,* 543–562.

Luu, P., & Tucker, D. (1996). Self-regulation and cortical development: Implications for functional studies of the brain. In R. W. Thatcher, G. R. Lyon, J. Rumsey, & N. A. Krasnegor (Eds.), *Developmental neuroimaging: Mapping the development of brain behavior* (pp. 298–305). San Diego: Academic Press.

Lykken, D. T. (1993). Predicting violence in the violent society. *Applied and Preventive Psychology, 2,* 13–20.

Lynch, M., & Cicchetti, D. (1991). Patterns of relatedness in maltreated and nonmaltreated children: Connections among multiple representational models. *Development and Psychopathology, 3,* 207–226.

Lynch, M., & Cicchetti, D. (1992). Maltreated children's reports of relatedness to their teachers. *New Directions for Child Development, 57,* 81–107.

Lynch, M., & Cicchetti, D. (1998). An ecological-transactional analysis of children and contexts: The longitudinal interplay among child maltreatment, community violence, and children's symptomatology. *Development and Psychopathology, 10,* 235–257.

Lyons-Ruth, K., Bronfman, E., & Parsons, E. (1999). Maternal frightened, frightening, or atypical behavior and disorganized infant attachment patterns. *Monographs of the Society for Research in Child Development, 64*(3), 67–96.

Lyons-Ruth, K., Connell, D., & Zoll, D. (1989). Patterns of maternal behavior among infants at risk for abuse: Relations with infant attachment behavior and infant development at 12 months of age. In D. Cicchetti & V. Carlson (Eds.), *Child maltreatment: Theory and research on the causes and consequences of child abuse and neglect* (pp. 464–493). New York: Cambridge University Press.

Lyons-Ruth, K., Connell, D., Zoll, D., & Stahl, J. (1987). Infants at social risk: Relationships among infant maltreatment, maternal behavior, and infant attachment behavior. *Developmental Psychology, 23,* 223–232.

Lyons-Ruth, K., & Easterbrooks, M. A. (1995). Attachment relationships among children with aggressive behavior problems: The role of disorganized/controlling early attachment strategies. *Journal of Consulting and Clinical Psychology, 64,* 64–73.

Lyons-Ruth, K., Repacholi, B., McLeod, S., & Silva, E. (1991). Disorganized attachment behavior in infancy: Short-term stability, maternal and infant correlates, and risk-related subtypes. *Development and Psychopathology, 3,* 377–396.

Macfie, J., Cicchetti, D., & Toth, S. L. (2001a). The development of dissociation in maltreated preschool-aged children. *Development and Psychopathology, 13,* 233–254.

Macfie, J., Cicchetti, D., & Toth, S. L. (2001b). Dissociation in maltreated versus nonmaltreated preschool-aged children. *Child Abuse and Neglect, 25,* 1253–1267.

Macfie, J., Toth, S. L., Rogosch, F. A., Robinson, J., Emde, R. N., & Cicchetti, D. (1999). Effect of maltreatment on preschoolers' narrative representations of responses to relieve distress and of role reversal. *Developmental Psychology, 35,* 460–465.

Mahler, M., Pine, F., & Bergman, A. (1975). *The psychological birth of the human infant.* New York: Basic Books.

Mahoney, A., Donnelly, W. O., Boxer, P., & Lewis, T. (2003). Marital and severe parent-to-adolescent physical aggression in clinic-referred families: Mother and adolescent reports on co-occurrence and links to child behavior problems. *Journal of Family Psychology, 17,* 3–19.

Main, M., & George, C. (1985). Response of abused and disadvantaged toddlers to distress in agemates: A study in the day care setting. *Developmental Psychology, 21,* 407–412.

Main, M., & Goldwyn, R. (1984). Predicting rejecting of her infant from mother's representation of her own experience: Implications for the abused-abusing intergenerational cycle. *Child Abuse and Neglect, 8,* 203–217.

Main, M., & Hesse, P. (1990). Parents' unresolved traumatic experiences are related to infant disorganized attachment status: Is frightened and/or frightening parent behavior the linking mechanism? In M. Greenberg, D. Cicchetti, & E. M. Cummings (Eds.), *Attachment in the preschool years* (pp. 161–182). Chicago: University of Chicago Press.

Main, M., & Solomon, J. (1990). Procedures for identifying infants as disorganized/disoriented during the Ainsworth Strange Situation. In M. Greenberg, D. Cicchetti, & E. M. Cummings (Eds.), *Attachment in the preschool years* (pp. 121–160). Chicago: University of Chicago Press.

Manly, J. T., Cicchetti, D., & Barnett, D. (1994). The impact of subtype, frequency, chronicity, and severity of child maltreatment on social competence and behavior problems. *Development and Psychopathology, 6,* 121–143.

Manly, J. T., Kim, J. E., Rogosch, F. A., & Cicchetti, D. (2001). Dimensions of child maltreatment and children's adjustment: Contributions of developmental timing and subtype. *Development and Psychopathology, 13,* 759–782.

Margolin, G. (1998). Effects of domestic violence on children. In P. Trickett & C. J. Schellenbach (Eds.), *Violence against children in the family and the community* (pp. 57–101). Washington, DC: American Psychological Association.

Martinez, P., & Richters, J. E. (1993). The NIMH Community Violence Project: Pt. II. Children's distress symptoms associated with violence exposure. *Psychiatry, 56,* 22–35.

Mash, E. J., Johnston, C., & Kovitz, K. (1983). A comparison of the mother-child interactions of physically abused and non-abused children during play and task situations. *Journal of Clinical and Child Psychology, 12,* 337–346.

Masten, A. S. (1989). Resilience in development: Implications of the study of successful adaptation for developmental psychopathology. In D. Cicchetti (Ed.), *Rochester Symposium on Developmental Psychopathology: Vol. 1. The emergence of a discipline* (pp. 261–294). Hillsdale, NJ: Erlbaum.

Masten, A. S., & Coatsworth, J. D. (1998). The development of competence in favorable and unfavorable environments: Lessons from research on successful children. *American Psychologist, 53*(2), 205–220.

Masten, A. S., Hubbard, J. J., Gest, S. D., Tellegen, A., Garmezy, N., & Ramirez, M. (1999). Competence in the context of adversity: Pathways to resilience and maladaptation from childhood to late adolescence. *Development and Psychopathology, 11*(1), 143–169.

Maughan, A., & Cicchetti, D. (2002). The impact of child maltreatment and interadult violence on children's emotion regulation abilities. *Child Development, 73,* 1525–1542.

Maughan, B., & Rutter, M. (1997). Retrospective reporting of childhood adversity: Issues in assessing long-term recall. *Journal of Personality Disorders, 11,* 19–23.

McCanne, T. R., & Milner, J. S. (1991). Physiological reactivity of physically abusive and at-risk subjects to child-related stimuli. In J. S. Milner (Ed.), *Neuropsychology of aggression* (pp. 147–166). Boston: Kluwer Academic.

McCrae, R. R., & John, O. P. (1992). An introduction to the 5-factor model and its applications. *Journal of Personality, 60*(2), 175–215.

McCurdy, K., & Daro, D. (1994). Child maltreatment: A national study of reports and fatalities. *Journal of Interpersonal Violence, 9*(1), 75–94.

McEwen, B. S. (1998). Protective and damaging effects of stress mediators. *Seminars in Medicine of Beth Israel Deaconess Medical Center, 338,* 171–179.

McEwen, B. S. (2000). Allostasis and allostatic load: Implications for neuropsychopharmacology. *Neuropsychopharmacology, 22*(2), 108–124.

McEwen, B. S. (2004). Protection and damage from acute and chronic stress: Allostasis and allostatic overload and relevance to the pathophysiology of psychiatric disorders. *Annals of the New York Academy of Science, 1032,* 1–7.

McEwen, B. S., & Stellar, E. (1993). Stress and the individual mechanisms leading to disease. *Archives of Internal Medicine, 153,* 2093–2101.

McGee, R. A., & Wolfe, D. A. (1991). Between a rock and a hard place: Where do we go from here in defining psychological maltreatment? *Development and Psychopathology, 3,* 119–124.

McGloin, J. M., & Widom, C. S. (2001). Resilience among abused and neglected children grown up. *Development and Psychopathology, 13,* 1021–1038.

McLeer, S. V., Callaghan, M., Henry, D., & Wallen, J. (1994). Psychiatric disorders in sexually abused children. *Journal of the American Academy of Child and Adolescent Psychiatry, 33,* 313–319.

McLoyd, V. C., & Wilson, L. (1991). The strain of living poor: Parenting, social support, and child mental health. In A. C. Huston (Ed.), *Children in poverty: Child development and public policy* (pp. 105–135). New York: Cambridge University Press.

Meaney, M. J., Di Orio, J., Francis, D., Widdowson, J., LaBlante, P., Caldji, C., et al. (1996). Early environmental regulation of forebrain, glucocorticoid receptor gene expression: Implications for adrenocortical response to stress. *Developmental Neuroscience, 18,* 49–72.

Merry, S. N., & Andrews, L. K. (1994). Psychiatric status of sexually abused children 12 months after disclosure of abuse. *Journal of the American Academy of Child and Adolescent Psychiatry, 33,* 939–944.

Milner, J. S. (2000). Social information processing and child physical abuse: Theory and research. In D. J. Hansen (Ed.), *Nebraska Symposium on Motivation* (Vol. 45, pp. 39–84). Lincoln: University of Nebraska Press.

Milner, J. S., & Chilamkurti, C. (1991). Physical child abuse perpetrator characteristics: A review of the literature. *Journal of Interpersonal Violence, 6,* 345–366.

Minuchin, P. (1985). Families and individual development: Provocations from the field of family therapy. *Child Development, 56*(2), 289–302.

Moran, P. B., & Eckenrode, J. (1992). Protective personality characteristics among adolescent victims of maltreatment. *Child Abuse and Neglect, 16,* 743–754.

Morisset, C. E., Barnard, K. E., Greenberg, M. T., Booth, C. L., & Spieker, S. J. (1990). Environmental influences on early language development: The context of social risk. *Development and Psychopathology, 2,* 127–149.

Morrow, K. B., & Sorrell, G. T. (1989). Factors affecting self-esteem, depression, and negative behaviors in sexually abused female adolescents. *Journal of Marriage and the Family, 51,* 677–686.

Mueller, E., & Silverman, N. (1989). Peer relations in maltreated children. In D. Cicchetti & V. Carlson (Eds.), *Child maltreatment: Theory and research on the causes and consequences of child abuse and neglect* (pp. 529–578). New York: Cambridge University Press.

Nash, A., & Hay, D. F. (1993). Relationships in infancy as precursors of later relationships and psychopathology. In D. F. Hay & A. Angold (Eds.), *Precursors and causes in development and psychopathology* (pp. 199–232). New York: Wiley.

Nash, M. R., Hulsey, T. L., Sexton, M. C., Harralson, T. L., & Lambert, W. (1993). Long-term sequelae of childhood sexual abuse: Perceived family environment, psychopathology, and dissociation. *Journal of Consulting and Clinical Psychology, 61,* 276–283.

National Center for Children in Poverty. (2004). *Low-income children in the United States: 2004.* New York: Columbia University Mailman School of Public Health. Available from www.nccporg/pub-cpf04.html.

National Research Council. (1993). *Understanding child abuse and neglect.* Washington, DC: National Academy of Sciences.

Newcomb, M. D., & Locke, T. F. (2001). Intergenerational cycle of maltreatment: A popular concept obscured by methodological limitations. *Child Abuse and Neglect, 25*(9), 1219–1240.

Nicolich, L. (1977). Beyond sensorimotor intelligence: Assessment of symbolic maturity through analysis of pretend play. *Merrill-Palmer Quarterly, 23,* 89–99.

Noll, J. G., Trickett, P. K., & Putnam, F. W. (2003). A prospective investigation of the impact of childhood sexual abuse on the development of sexuality. *Journal of Consulting and Clinical Psychology, 17,* 575–586.

Nowakowski, R. S., & Hayes, N. L. (1999). CNS development: An overview. *Development and Psychopathology, 11,* 395–418.

Oates, R. K., Forrest, D., & Peacock, A. (1985). Self-esteem of abused children. *Child Abuse and Neglect, 9,* 159–163.

Ogata, S. N., Silk, K. R., Goodrich, S., Lohr, N. E., Westen, D., & Hill, E. M. (1990). Childhood sexual and physical abuse in adult patients with borderline personality disorder. *American Journal of Psychiatry, 147,* 1008–1013.

Ogawa, J. R., Sroufe, A., Weinfield, N. S., Carlson, E. A., & Egeland, B. (1997). Development and the fragmented self: Longitudinal study of dissociative symptomatology in a nonclinical sample. *Development and Psychopathology, 9,* 855–879.

Okun, A., Parker, J. G., & Levendosky, A. A. (1994). Distinct and interactive contributions of physical abuse, socioeconomic disadvantage, and negative life events to children's social, cognitive, and affective adjustment. *Development and Psychopathology, 6,* 77–98.

Oldershaw, L., Walters, G. C., & Hall, D. K. (1986). Control strategies and noncompliance in abuse mother-child dyads: An observational study. *Child Development, 57,* 722–732.

Olds, D. L., Eckenrode, J., Henderson, C. R., Jr., Kitzman, H., Powers, J., Cole, R., et al. (1997). Long term effects of home visitation on maternal life course and child abuse and neglect: Fifteen-year follow-up of a randomized trial. *Journal of the American Medical Association, 278,* 637–652.

Olds, D. L., & Henderson, C. (1989). The prevention of maltreatment. In D. Cicchetti & C. Carlson (Eds.), *Child maltreatment: Theory and research on the causes and consequences of child abuse and neglect* (pp. 722–763). New York: Cambridge University Press.

Olds, D., Henderson, C. R., Chamberlin, R., & Tatelbaum, R. (1986). Preventing child abuse and neglect: A randomized trial of nurse home visitation. *Pediatrics, 78*, 65–78.

Ollendick, T. H., Weist, M. D., Borden, M. C., & Greene, R. W. (1992). Sociometric status and academic, behavioral, and psychological adjustment: A 5-year longitudinal study. *Journal of Consulting and Clinical Psychology, 60*(1), 80–87.

Olsen, J. L., & Widom, C. S. (1993). Prevention of child abuse and neglect. *Applied and Preventive Psychology, 2*, 217–229.

Ondersma, S. J. (2002). Predictors of neglect within low-SES families: The importance of substance abuse. *American Journal of Orthopsychiatry, 72*(3), 383–391.

Ornitz, E. M., & Pynoos, R. S. (1989). Startle modulation in children with posttraumatic stress disorder. *American Journal of Psychiatry, 146*, 866–870.

Paris, J. (1997). Childhood trauma as an etiological factor in the personality disorders. *Journal of Personality Disorders, 11*(1), 34–49.

Park, K. A., & Waters, E. (1989). Security of attachment and preschool friendships. *Child Development, 60*(5), 1076–1081.

Parke, R. D., & Collmer, C. W. (1975). Child abuse: An interdisciplinary analysis. In E. M. Hetherington (Ed.), *Review of child development research* (Vol. 5, pp. 509–590). Chicago: University of Chicago Press.

Parker, J. G., & Asher, S. R. (1987). Peer acceptance and later personal adjustment: Are accepted children "at risk"? *Psychological Bulletin, 102*, 357–389.

Parker, J. G., & Herrera, C. (1996). Interpersonal processes in friendship: A comparison of maltreated and nonmaltreated children's experiences. *Developmental Psychology, 32*, 1025–1038.

Patterson, G. R. (1976). The aggressive child: Victim and architect of a coercive system. In E. J. Mash, L. A. Hamerlynck, & L. C. Handy (Eds.), *Behavior modification and families* (pp. 267–316). New York: Brunner/Mazel.

Patterson, G. R., & Reid, J. B. (1984). Social interaction processes within the family: The study of moment-to-moment transactions in which human social development is embedded. *Journal of Applied Developmental Psychology, 5*, 237–262.

Patterson, G. R., Reid, J. B., & Dishion, T. J. (1992). *Antisocial boys*. Eugene, OR: Castalia.

Pears, K. C., & Capaldi, D. M. (2002). Intergenerational transmission of abuse: A two-generational prospective study of an at-risk sample. *Child Abuse and Neglect, 25*, 1439–1462.

Pennington, B. F., & Bennetto, L. (1998). Toward a neuropsychology of mental retardation. In J. A. Burack, R. M. Hodapp, & E. Zigler (Eds.), *Handbook of retardation and development* (pp. 80–114). Cambridge, England: Cambridge University Press.

Perner, J. (1991). *Understanding the representational mind*. Cambridge, MA: MIT Press.

Perry, D. G., Hodges, E. V. E., & Egan, S. K. (2001). Determinants of chronic victimization by peers: A review and new model of family influence. In J. Juvonen & S. Graham (Eds.), *Peer harassment in school: The plight of the vulnerable and victimized* (pp. 73–104). New York: Guilford Press.

Peterson, C. C., & Siegal, M. (1995). Deafness, conversation, and theory of mind. *Journal of Child Psychology and Psychiatry and Allied Disciplines, 36*(3), 459–474.

Peterson, C. C., & Siegal, M. (1999). Representing inner worlds: Theory of mind in deaf, autistic, and normal hearing children. *Psychological Science, 10*, 126–129.

Peterson, C. C., & Siegal, M. (2000). Insights into theory of mind from deafness and Autism. *Mind and Language, 15*(1), 123–145.

Peterson, L., Tremblay, G., Ewigman, B., & Saldana, L. (2003). Multilevel selected primary prevention of child maltreatment. *Journal of Consulting and Clinical Psychology, 71*(3), 601–612.

Piaget, J. (1962). *Play, dreams, and imitation in childhood*. New York: Norton.

Pine, D. S., Mogg, K., Bradley, B. P., Montgomery, L., Monk, C. S., McClure, E., et al. (2005). Attention bias to threat in maltreated children: Implications for vulnerability to stress-related psychopathology. *American Journal of Psychiatry, 162*(2), 291–296.

Pipp, S., Easterbrooks, M. A., & Harmon, R. (1992). The relation between attachment and knowledge of self and mother in one-to-three-year-old infants. *Child Development, 63*, 738–750.

Pipp, S., & Harmon, R. J. (1987). Attachment as regulation: A commentary. *Child Development, 58*, 648–652.

Plomin, R., & Crabbe, J. (2000). DNA. *Psychological Bulletin, 126*(6), 806–828.

Polansky, N. A., Gaudin, J. M., & Kilpatrick, A. C. (1992). The Maternal Characteristics Scale: A cross validation. *Child Welfare, 71*(3), 271–280.

Pollak, S. D., Cicchetti, D., Hornung, K., & Reed, A. (2000). Recognizing emotion in faces: Developmental effects of child abuse and neglect. *Developmental Psychology, 36*, 679–688.

Pollak, S. D., Cicchetti, D., & Klorman, R. (1998). Stress, memory, and emotion: Developmental considerations from the study of child maltreatment. *Development and Psychopathology, 10*, 811–828.

Pollak, S. D., Cicchetti, D., Klorman, R., & Brumaghim, J. (1997). Cognitive brain event-related potentials and emotion processing in maltreated children. *Child Development, 68*, 773–787.

Pollak, S. D., & Kistler, D. (2002). Early experience alters categorical representations for facial expressions of emotion. *Proceedings of the National Academy of Sciences, USA, 99*, 9072–9076.

Pollak, S. D., Klorman, R., Thatcher, J. E., & Cicchetti, D. (2001). P3b reflects maltreated children's reactions to facial displays of emotion. *Psychophysiology, 38*, 267–274.

Pollak, S. D., & Sinha, P. (2002). Effects of early experience on children's recognition of facial displays of emotion. *Developmental Psychology, 38*, 784–791.

Pollak, S. D., & Tolley-Schell, S. A. (2003). Selective attention to facial emotion in physically abused children. *Journal of Abnormal Psychology, 112*(3), 323–338.

Pribor, E. F., & Dinwiddie, S. H. (1992). Psychiatric correlates of incest in childhood. *American Journal of Psychiatry, 149*, 52–56.

Prichard, J. W. (1996). MRS of the brain: Prospects for clinical application. In I. R. Young & H. C. Charles (Eds.), *MR spectroscopy: Clinical applications and techniques* (pp. 1–25). London: Livery House.

Prince, J. M., & Van Slyke, D. (1991, April). *Social information processing patterns and social adjustment of maltreated children*. Paper presented at the biennial meeting of the Society for Research in Child Development, Seattle, WA.

Putallaz, M., Costanzo, P. R., Grimes, C. L., & Sherman, D. M. (1998). Intergenerational continuities and their influences on children's social development. *Social Development, 7*(3), 389–427.

Putnam, F. W. (1996). Child development and dissociation. *Child and Adolescent Psychiatric Clinics of North America, 5*(2), 285–288.

Putnam, F. W. (2003). Ten-year research update review: Child sexual abuse. *Journal of the American Academy of Child and Adolescent Psychiatry, 42*(3), 269–273.

Putnam, F. W., & Trickett, P. K. (1993). Child sexual abuse: A model of chronic trauma. *Psychiatry, 56*, 82–95.

Putnam, F. W., Trickett, P. K., Helmers, K., Dorn, L., & Everett, B. (1991, May). *Cortisol abnormalities in sexually abused girls.* Paper presented at the 144th annual meeting of the American Psychiatric Association: New Orleans, LA.

Reichenbach, L., & Masters, J. C. (1983). Children's use of expressive and contextual cues in judgments of emotion. *Child Development, 54,* 993–1004.

Reid, J. B., Kavanaugh, K., & Baldwin, D. V. (1987). Abusive parents' perceptions of child problem behaviors: An example of parental bias. *Journal of Abnormal Child Psychology, 15,* 457–466.

Rende, R., & Plomin, R. (1995). Nature, nurture, and the development of psychopathology. In D. Cicchetti & D. Cohen (Eds.), *Developmental psychopathology: Vol. 1. Theory and methods* (pp. 291–314). New York: Wiley.

Repetti, R., Taylor, S., & Seeman, T. (2002). Risky families: Family social environments and the mental and physical health of offspring. *Psychological Bulletin, 128,* 330–366.

Reppucci, N. D., Woolard, J. L., & Fried, C. S. (1999). Social, community, and preventive interventions. *Annual Review of Psychology, 50,* 387–418.

Reynolds, A. J., & Robertson, D. L. (2003). School-based early intervention and later child maltreatment in the Chicago Longitudinal Study. *Child Development, 74*(1), 3–26.

Rieder, C., & Cicchetti, D. (1989). Organizational perspective on cognitive control functioning and cognitive-affective balance in maltreated children. *Developmental Psychology, 25,* 382–393.

Robins, R. W., John, O. P., Caspi, A., Moffitt, T. E., & Stouthamer-Loeber, M. (1996). Resilient, overcontrolled, and undercontrolled boys. *Journal of Personality and Social Psychology, 70,* 157–171.

Rogeness, G. A. (1991). Psychosocial factors and amine systems. *Psychiatry Research, 37*(2), 215–217.

Rogeness, G. A., & McClure, E. B. (1996). Development and neurotransmitter-environmental interactions. *Development and Psychopathology, 8*(1), 183–199.

Rogosch, F. A., & Cicchetti, D. (1994). Illustrating the interface of family and peer relations through the study of child maltreatment. *Social Development, 3,* 291–308.

Rogosch, F. A., & Cicchetti, D. (2004). Child maltreatment and emergent personality organization: Perspectives from the five-factor model. *Journal of Abnormal Child Psychology, 32*(2), 123–145.

Rogosch, F. A., Cicchetti, D., & Aber, J. L. (1995). The role of child maltreatment in early deviations in cognitive and affective processing abilities and later peer relationship problems. *Development and Psychopathology, 7,* 591–609.

Rogosch, F. A., Cicchetti, D., Shields, A., & Toth, S. L. (1995). Parenting dysfunction in child maltreatment. In M. Bornstein (Ed.), *Handbook of parenting* (pp. 127–159). Mahwah, NJ: Erlbaum.

Rosen, L. N., & Martin, L. (1998). Long-term effects of childhood maltreatment history on gender-related personality characteristics. *Child Abuse and Neglect, 22*(3), 197–211.

Rosenbaum, M., & Bennett, B. (1986). Homicide and depression. *American Journal of Psychiatry, 143,* 367–370.

Rosenbaum, A., & O'Leary, D. (1981). Marital violence: Characteristics of abusive couples. *Journal of Consulting and Clinical Psychology, 49,* 63–71.

Rosenberg, M. S. (1987). New directions for research on the psychological maltreatment of children. *American Psychologist, 42,* 166–171.

Rothbart, M. K., & Bates, J. E. (1998). Temperament. In W. Damon (Series Ed.) & N. Eisenberg (Vol. Ed.), *Handbook of child psychology: Vol. 3. Social, emotional, and personality development* (5th ed., pp. 105–176). New York: Wiley.

Rothbart, M. K., Posner, M. L., & Hershey, K. (1995). Temperament, attention and developmental psychopathology. In D. Cicchetti & D. J. Cohen (Eds.), *Developmental psychopathology: Vol. 1. Theory and method* (pp. 315–340). New York: Wiley.

Rubin, K. H., LeMare, L. J., & Lollis, S. (1990). Social withdrawal in childhood: Developmental pathways to peer rejection. In S. R. Asher & J. D. Coie (Eds.), *Peer rejection in childhood* (pp. 217–249). New York: Cambridge University Press.

Rubin, K. H., & Lollis, S. P. (1988). Beyond attachment: Possible origins and consequences of social withdrawal in childhood. In J. Belsky & T. Nezworski (Eds.), *Clinical implications of attachment* (pp. 219–252). Hillsdale, NJ: Erlbaum.

Rubin, K. H., & Mills, R. S. L. (1988). The many faces of isolation. *Journal of Consulting and Clinical Psychology, 6,* 916–924.

Rubin, K. H., & Ross, H. S. (1988). Toward the study of social competence, social status and social relations. In C. Howes (Ed.), *Peer interaction in younger children. Monographs of the Society for Research in Child Development, 53,* 79–87.

Runtz, M. G., & Schallow, J. R. (1997). Social support and coping strategies as mediators of adult adjustment following childhood maltreatment. *Child Abuse and Neglect, 21*(2), 211–226.

Russell, D. E. (1986). *The secret trauma: Incest in the lives of girls and women.* New York: Basic Books.

Rutter, M. (1986). Child psychiatry: The interface between clinical and developmental research. *Psychological Medicine, 16,* 151–160.

Ryan, R., Deci, E. L., & Grolnick, W. (1995). Autonomy, relatedness, and the self: The relation to development and psychopathology. In D. Cicchetti & D. Cohen (Eds.), *Developmental psychopathology: Vol. 1. Theory and methods* (pp. 618–655). New York: Wiley.

Sack, W. H., & Mason, R. (1980). Child abuse and conviction of sexual crimes: A preliminary finding. *Law and Human Behavior, 4,* 211–215.

Salter, D., McMillan, D., Richards, M., Talbot, T., Hodges, J., Bentovim, A., et al. (2003). Development of sexually abusive behavior in sexually abused victimized males: A longitudinal study. *Lancet, 361,* 471–476.

Salzinger, S., Feldman, R. S., Hammer, M., & Rosario, M. (1993). The effects of physical abuse on children's social relationships. *Child Development, 64,* 169–187.

Salzinger, S., Feldman, R. S., Ng-Mak, D. S., Mojica, E., & Stockhammer, T. F. (2001). The effect of physical abuse on children's social and affective status: A model of cognitive and behavioral processes explaining the association. *Development and Psychopathology, 13,* 805–825.

Sameroff, A. J., & Chandler, M. J. (1975). Reproductive risk and the continuum of caretaking casualty. In F. D. Horowitz (Ed.), *Review of child development research* (Vol. 4, pp. 187–244). Chicago: University of Chicago Press.

Sanchez, M. M., Ladd, C. O., & Plotsky, P. M. (2001). Early adverse experience as a developmental risk factor for later psychopathology: Evidence from rodent and primate models. *Development and Psychopathology, 13,* 419–450.

Sanders-Phillips, K., Moisan, P., Wadlington, S., Morgan, S., & English, K. (1995). Ethnic differences in psychological functioning among Black and Latino sexually abused girls. *Child Abuse and Neglect, 19,* 691–706.

Sapolsky, R. M. (1992). *Stress, the aging brain, and the mechanisms of neuron death.* Cambridge, MA: MIT Press.

Sapolsky, R. M. (1994). Individual differences and the stress response. *Seminars in the Neurosciences, 6,* 261–269.

Sapolsky, R. M. (1996). Stress, glucocorticoids, and damage to the NS: The current state of confusion. *Stress, 1,* 1–19.

Scarr, S. (1992). Developmental theories for the 1990s: Development and individual differences. *Child Development, 63,* 1–19.

Scarr, S. (1993). Biological and cultural diversity: The legacy of Darwin for development. *Child Development, 64,* 1333–1353.

Scarr, S., & McCartney, K. (1983). How people make their own environments: A theory of genotype-environment effects. *Child Development, 54,* 424–435.

Schiffer, F., Teicher, M. H., & Papanicolaou, A. C. (1995). Evoked potential evidence for right brain activity during recall of traumatic memories. *Journal of Neuropsychiatry and Clinical Neuroscience, 7,* 169–175.

Schneider-Rosen, K., Braunwald, K., Carlson, V., & Cicchetti, D. (1985). Current perspectives in attachment theory: Illustrations from the study of maltreated infants. *Monographs of the Society for Research in Child Development, 50,* 194–210.

Schneider-Rosen, K., & Cicchetti, D. (1984). The relationship between affect and cognition in maltreated infants: Quality of attachment and the development of visual self-recognition. *Child Development, 55,* 648–658.

Schneider-Rosen, K., & Cicchetti, D. (1991). Early self-knowledge and emotional development: Visual self-recognition and affective reactions to mirror self-image in maltreated and nonmaltreated toddlers. *Developmental Psychology, 27,* 481–488.

Schulkin, J., McEwen, B. S., & Gold, P. W. (1994). Allostasis, amygdala, and anticipatory angst. *Neuroscience and Biobehavioral Reviews, 18*(3), 385–396.

Sedlak, A. J., & Broadhurst, D. D. (1996). *The third national incidence study of child abuse and neglect.* Washington, DC: U.S. Department of Health and Human Services.

Shea, A., Walsh, C., MacMillan, H., & Steiner, M. (2004). Child maltreatment and HPA axis dysregulation: Relationship to major depressive disorder and post traumatic stress disorder in females. *Psychoneuroendocrinology, 30,* 162–178.

Shields, A., & Cicchetti, D. (1997). Emotion regulation among school-age children: The development and validation of a new criterion Q-sort scale. *Developmental Psychology, 33,* 906–916.

Shields, A., & Cicchetti, D. (1998). Reactive aggression among maltreated children: The contributions of attention and emotion dysregulation. *Journal of Clinical Child Psychology, 27,* 381–395.

Shields, A., & Cicchetti, D. (2001). Parental maltreatment and emotion dysregulation as risk factors for bullying and victimization in middle childhood. *Journal of Clinical Child Psychology, 30,* 349–363.

Shields, A., Ryan, R. M., & Cicchetti, D. (2001). Narrative representations of caregivers and emotion dysregulation as predictors of maltreated children's rejection by peers. *Developmental Psychology, 37,* 321–337.

Shipman, K., Zeman, J., Penza, S., & Champion, K. (2000). Emotion management skills in sexually maltreated and nonmaltreated girls: A developmental psychopathology perspective. *Development and Psychopathology, 12*(1), 47–62.

Shonk, S. M., & Cicchetti, D. (2001). Maltreatment, competency deficits, and risk for academic and behavioral maladjustment. *Developmental Psychology, 37,* 3–14.

Sigel, I. E. (1986). Reflections on the belief-behavior connection: Lessons learned from a research program on parental belief systems and teaching strategies. In R. D. Ashmore & D. M. Brodzinsky (Eds.), *Thinking about the family: Views of parents and children* (pp. 35–65). Hillsdale, NJ: Erlbaum.

Silber, S. (1990). Conflict negotiation in child abusing and nonabusing families. *Journal of Family Psychology, 3,* 368–384.

Silverman, A. B., Reinherz, H. Z., & Giaconia, R. M. (1996). The long-term sequelae of child and adolescent abuse: A longitudinal community study. *Child Abuse and Neglect, 20,* 709–723.

Simeon, D., Guralnik, O., Schmeidler, J., Sirof, B., & Knutelska, M. (2001). The role of childhood interpersonal trauma in depersonalization disorder. *American Journal of Psychiatry, 158,* 1027–1033.

Singer, J. L. (1976). Imaginative play and pretending in early childhood. In A. Davis (Ed.), *Child personality and psychopathology.* New York: Wiley.

Singer, J. L., & Singer, D. G. (1976). Imaginative play and pretending in early childhood: Some experimental approaches. In A. Davis (Ed.), *Child personality and psychopathology: Vol. 3. Current topics.* New York: Wiley.

Slack, K. S., Holl, J. L., McDaniel, M., Yoo, J., & Bolger, K. (2004). Understanding the risks of child neglect: An exploration of poverty and parenting characteristics. *Child Maltreatment, 9*(4), 395–408.

Sloan, M. P., & Meier, J. H. (1983). Typology for parents of abused children. *Child Abuse and Neglect, 7,* 443–450.

Smetana, J. G., Daddis, C., Toth, S. L., Cicchetti, D., Bruce, J., & Kane, P. (1999). Effects of provocation on maltreated and nonmaltreated preschoolers' understanding of moral transgressions. *Social Development, 8,* 335–348.

Smetana, J. G., Kelley, M., & Twentyman, C. T. (1984). Abused, neglected, and nonmaltreated children's conceptions of moral and social-conventional transgressions. *Child Development, 55,* 277–287.

Smetana, J. G., Toth, S. L., Cicchetti, D., Bruce, J., Kane, P., & Daddis, C. (1998). Maltreated and nonmaltreated preschoolers' conceptions of hypothetical and actual moral transgressions. *Developmental Psychology, 35,* 269–281.

Soloff, P. H., Lynch, K. G., & Kelly, T. M. (2002). Childhood abuse as a risk factor for suicidal behavior in borderline personality disorder. *Journal of Personality Disorders, 16,* 201–214.

Spangler, G., & Grossman, K. E. (1993). Biobehavioral organization in securely and insecurely attached infants. *Child Development, 64,* 1439–1450.

Spear, L. P. (2000). The adolescent brain and age-related behavioral manifestations. *Neuroscience and Behavioral Reviews, 24,* 417–463.

Spear, L. P. (2003). Neurodevelopment during adolescence. In D. Cicchetti & E. F. Walker (Eds.), *Neurodevelopmental mechanisms in psychopathology* (pp. 62–83). New York: Cambridge University Press.

Sperry, R. (1982). Some effects of disconnecting the cerebral hemispheres. *Science, 217,* 1223–1226.

Sroufe, L. A. (1979). The coherence of individual development: Early care, attachment, and subsequent developmental issues. *American Psychologist, 34,* 834–841.

Sroufe, L. A. (1983). Infant-caregiver attachment and patterns of adaptation in preschool: The roots of maladaptation and competence. In M. Perlmutter (Ed.), *Minnesota Symposia on Child Psychology* (Vol. 16, pp. 41–83). Hillsdale, NJ: Erlbaum.

Sroufe, L. A. (1989). Relationships, self, and individual adaptation. In A. J. Sameroff & R. N. Emde (Eds.), *Relationship disturbances in early childhood* (pp. 70–94). New York: Basic Books.

Sroufe, L. A. (1990). Considering normal and abnormal together: The essence of developmental psychopathology. *Development and Psychopathology, 2,* 335–347.

Sroufe, L. A. (1996). *Emotional development: The organization of emotional life in the early years.* New York: Cambridge University Press.

Sroufe, L. A., Carlson, E. A., Levy, A. K., & Egeland, B. (1999). Implications of attachment theory for developmental psychopathology. *Development and Psychopathology, 11,* 1–13.

Sroufe, L. A., Carlson, E., & Shulman, S. (1993). Individuals in relationships: Development from infancy through adolescence. In D. C. Funder, R. D. Parke, C. Tomlinson-Keasey, & K. Widaman (Eds.), *Studying lives through time* (pp. 315–342). Washington, DC: American Psychological Association.

Sroufe, L. A., & Fleeson, J. (1986). Attachment and the construction of relationships. In W. Hartup & Z. Rubin (Eds.), *Relationships and development* (pp. 51–76). Hillsdale, NJ: Erlbaum.

Sroufe, L. A., & Fleeson, J. (1988). The coherence of family relationships. In R. A. Hinde & J. Stevenson-Hinde (Eds.), *Relationships within families: Mutual influences* (pp. 27–47). Oxford, England: Oxford University Press.

Sroufe, L. A., & Waters, E. (1977). Attachment as an organizational construct. *Child Development, 48,* 1184–1199.

Stack, C. (1974). *All our kin: Strategies for survival in a Black community.* New York: Harper & Row.

Stein, J. A., Leslie, M. B., & Nyamathi, A. (2002). Relative contributions of parent substance use and childhood maltreatment to chronic homelessness, depression, and substance abuse problems among homeless women: Mediating roles of self esteem and abuse in adulthood. *Child Abuse and Neglect, 26,* 1011–1027.

Stein, M. B., Yehuda, R., Koverola, C., & Hanna, C. (1997). Enhanced dexamethasone suppression of plasma cortisol in adult women traumatized by childhood sexual abuse. *Biological Psychiatry, 42*(8), 680–686.

Steinberg, L., Catalano, R., & Dooley, D. (1981). Economic antecedents of child abuse and neglect. *Child Development, 52,* 975–985.

Stern, D. N. (1985). *The interpersonal world of the infant: A view from psychoanalysis and developmental psychology.* New York: Basic Books.

Stern, D. N. (1989). The representation of relational patterns: Some developmental considerations. In A. J. Sameroff & R. N. Emde (Eds.), *Relationship disturbances in early childhood* (pp. 52–89). New York: Basic Books.

Sternberg, K., Lamb, M., Greenbaum, C., Cicchetti, D., Dawud, S., Cortes, R., et al. (1993). Effects of domestic violence on children's behavior problems and depression. *Developmental Psychology, 29,* 44–52.

Straus, M. A., Gelles, R. J., & Steinmetz, S. K. (1980). *Behind closed doors: Violence in the American family.* New York: Anchor Press.

Straus, M. A., & Kaufman-Kantor, G. (1986). Stress and physical abuse. *Child Abuse and Neglect, 4,* 75–88.

Teicher, M. H., Dumont, N., Ito, Y., Vaituzis, A. C., Giedd, J., & Andersen, S. (2004). Childhood neglect is associated with reduced corpus callosum area. *Biological Psychiatry, 56,* 80–85.

Teti, D. M., & Ablard, K. E. (1989). Security of attachment and infant-sibling relationships: A laboratory study. *Child Development, 60*(6), 1519–1528.

Teti, D. M., Gelfand, D., Messinger, D., & Isabella, R. (1995). Maternal depression and the quality of early attachment: An examination of infants, preschoolers, and their mothers. *Developmental Psychology, 31,* 364–376.

Thompson, R. A. (1990). Emotions and self-regulation. In R. Thompson (Ed.), *Nebraska Symposium on Motivation: Vol. 36. Socioemotional development* (pp. 367–467). Lincoln: University of Nebraska Press.

Thompson, R. A. (1994). Emotion regulation: A theme in search of a definition. *Monographs of the Society for Research in Child Development, 59,* 25–52.

Thompson, R., Briggs, E., English, D. J., Dubowitz, H., Lee, L., Brody, K., et al. (2005). Suicidal ideation among 8-year olds who are maltreated and at risk: Findings from the LONGSCAN studies. *Child Maltreatment, 10*(1), 26–36.

Todd, R. D., Swarzenski, B., Rossi, P. G., & Visconti, P. (1995). Structural and functional development of the human brain. In D. Cicchetti & D. J. Cohen (Eds.), *Developmental psychopathology: Vol. 1. Theory and method* (pp. 161–194). New York: Wiley.

Toth, S. L., & Cicchetti, D. (1993). Child maltreatment: Where do we go from here in our treatment of victims? In D. Cicchetti & S. L. Toth (Eds.), *Child abuse, child development, and social policy* (pp. 399–438). Norwood, NJ: Ablex.

Toth, S. L., &. Cicchetti, D. (1996). Patterns of relatedness and depressive symptomatology in maltreated children. *Journal of Consulting and Clinical Psychology, 64,* 32–41.

Toth, S. L., & Cicchetti, D. (1999). Developmental psychopathology and child psychotherapy. In S. Russ & T. Ollendick (Eds.), *Handbook of psychotherapies with children and families* (pp. 15–44). New York: Plenum Press.

Toth, S. L., Cicchetti, D., & Kim, J. E. (2002). Relations among children's perceptions of maternal behavior, attributional styles, and behavioral symptomatology in maltreated children. *Journal of Abnormal Child Psychology, 30,* 478–501.

Toth, S. L., Cicchetti, D., Macfie, J., & Emde, R. N. (1997). Representations of self and other in the narratives of neglected, physically abused, and sexually abused preschoolers. *Development and Psychopathology, 9,* 781–796.

Toth, S. L., Cicchetti, D., Macfie, J., Maughan, A., & VanMeenen, K. (2000). Narrative representations of caregivers and self in maltreated preschoolers. *Attachment and Human Development, 2,* 271–305.

Toth, S. L., Cicchetti, D., Macfie, J., Rogosch, F. A., & Maughan, A. (2000). Narrative representations of moral-affiliative and conflictual themes and behavioral problems in maltreated preschoolers. *Journal of Clinical Child Psychology, 29,* 307–318.

Toth, S. L., Manly, J. T., & Cicchetti, D. (1992). Child maltreatment and vulnerability to depression. *Development and Psychopathology, 4,* 97–112.

Toth, S. L., Maughan, A., Manly, J. T., Spagnola, M., & Cicchetti, D. (2002). The relative efficacy of two interventions in altering maltreated preschool children's representational models: Implications for attachment theory. *Development and Psychopathology, 14,* 777–808.

Trickett, P. K., Aber, J. L., Carlson, V., & Cicchetti, D. (1991). The relationship of socioeconomic status to the etiology and developmental sequelae of physical child abuse. *Developmental Psychology, 27,* 148–158.

Trickett, P. K., & Kuczynski, L. (1986). Children's misbehaviors and parental discipline strategies in abusive and nonabusive families. *Developmental Psychology, 22,* 115–123.

Trickett, P. K., & McBride-Chang, C. (1995). The developmental impact of different types of child abuse and neglect. *Developmental Review, 15,* 311–337.

Trickett, P. K., McBride-Chang, C., & Putnam, F. (1994). The classroom performance and behavior of sexually abused females. *Development and Psychopathology, 6,* 183–194.

Trickett, P. K., & Sussman, E. J. (1988). Parental perceptions of child-rearing practices in physically abusive and nonabusive families. *Developmental Psychology, 24,* 270–276.

Trouton, A., Spinath, F. M., & Plomin, R. (2002). Twins Early Development Study (TEDS): A multivariate, longitudinal genetic investigation of language, cognition and behaviour problems in childhood. *Twin Research, 5,* 444–448.

Troy, M., & Sroufe, L. A. (1987). Victimization among preschoolers: The role of attachment relationship history. *Journal of the American Academy of Child and Adolescent Psychiatry, 26,* 166–172.

Tucker, D. M. (1981). Lateral brain function, emotion, and conceptualization. *Psychological Bulletin, 89,* 19–46.

Twentyman, C. T., & Plotkin, R. C. (1982). Unrealistic expectation of parents who maltreat their children: An educational deficit that pertains to child development. *Journal of Clinical Psychology, 38*(3), 497–503.

Urquiza, A. J., & McNeil, C. B. (1996). Parent-child interaction therapy: An intense dyadic intervention for physically abusive families. *Journal of the American Professional Society on the Abuse of Children, 1*(2), 134–144.

U.S. Department of Health and Human Services. (1981). *Study findings: National study of incidence and severity of child abuse and neglect* (DHDS No. 81-30325). Washington, DC: U.S. Government Printing Office.

U.S. Department of Health and Human Services. (1988). *Study findings: Study of national incidence and prevalence of child abuse and neglect* (DHDS No. 20-01099). Washington, DC: U.S. Government Printing Office.

U.S. Department of Health and Human Services. (1996). *The third national incidence study of child abuse and neglect*. Washington, DC: U.S. Government Printing Office.

U.S. Department of Health and Human Services, National Clearinghouse on Child Abuse and Neglect Information. (2002, April). *Children's Bureau, Administration on Children, Youth, and Families, National Child Abuse and Neglect Data System (NCANDS): Child maltreatment 2002: Summary of key findings*. Retrieved November 2004, from http://nccanch.acf.hhs.gov/pubs/factsheets/canstats.cfm.

U.S. Department of Justice. (2004). *National Crime Victimization Survey, 2003*. Retrieved December 2004, from http://www.ojp.usdoj.gov/bjs/cvict.htm.

Valentino, K., Cicchetti, D., Toth, S. L., & Rogosch, F. A. (in press). Mother-child play, social competence and the emerging self in infants from maltreating families. *Developmental Psychology*.

van Ijzendoorn, M. H. (1992). Intergenerational transmission of parenting: A review of studies in nonclinical populations. *Developmental Review, 12*, 76–99.

van Ijzendoorn, M. H., Juffer, F., & Duyvesteyn, M. G. C. (1995). Breaking the intergenerational cycle of insecure attachment: A review of the effects of attachment-based interventions on maternal sensitivity and infant security. *Journal of Child Psychology and Psychiatry, 36*, 225–248.

van Ijzendoorn, M. H., Schuengel, C., & Bakermans-Kranenburg, M. J. (1999). Disorganized attachment in early childhood: Meta-analyses of precursors, concomitants, and sequelae. *Development and Psychopathology, 11*, 225–249.

Vazquez, D. M. (1998). Stress and the developing limbic-hypothalamic-pituitary-adrenal axis. *Psychoneuroendocrinology, 23*, 663–700.

Venter, J. C., Adams, M. D., Myers, E. W., Li, P. W., Mural, R. J., Sutton, G. G., et al. (2001). The sequence of the human genome. *Science, 291*(5507), 1304–1351.

Vondra, J., Barnett, D., & Cicchetti, D. (1989). Perceived and actual competence among maltreated and comparison school children. *Development and Psychopathology, 1*, 237–255.

von Eye, A., & Bergman, L. R. (2003). Research strategies in developmental psychology: Dimensional identity and the person-oriented approach. *Development and Psychopathology, 15*, 553–580.

Vythilingam, M., Heim, C., Newport, J., Miller, A. H., Anderson, E., Bronen, R., et al. (2002). Childhood trauma associated with smaller hippocampal volume in women with major depression. *American Journal of Psychiatry, 159*(12), 2072–2080.

Waddington, C. H. (1957). *The strategy of genes*. London: Allen & Unwin.

Walden, T. A., & Field, T. M. (1982). Discrimination of facial expressions by preschool children. *Child Development, 53*, 1312–1319.

Waldfogel, J. (1998). *The future of child protection: How to break the cycle of abuse and neglect*. Cambridge, MA: Harvard University Press.

Waldfogel, J. (2000, September). *What we know and don't know about the state of child protective service system and the links between poverty and child maltreatment*. Remarks for Joint Center for Poverty Research Congressional Research Briefing on Child Welfare and Child Protection: Current Research and Policy Implications, Washington, DC.

Waldman, I. D. (2003). Prospects and problems in the search for genetic influences on neurodevelopment and psychopathology: Application to childhood disruptive disorders. In D. Cicchetti & E. Walker (Eds.), *Neurodevelopmental mechanisms in psychopathology* (pp. 257–292). New York: Cambridge University Press.

Walker, E., Downey, G., & Bergman, A. (1989). The effects of parental psychopathology and maltreatment on child behavior: A test of the diathesis-stress model. *Child Development, 60*, 15–24.

Wasserman, G., Green, A., & Allen, R. (1983). Going beyond abuse: Maladaptive patterns of interaction in abusing mother-infant pairs. *Journal of the American Academy of Child Psychiatry, 22*, 245–252.

Watson, S. J., & Akil, H. (1999). Gene chips and arrays revealed: A primer on their power and their uses. *Biological Psychiatry, 45*, 533–543.

Way, I., Chung, S., Jonson-Reid, M., & Drake, B. (2001). Maltreatment perpetrators: A 54 month analysis of recidivism. *Child Abuse and Neglect, 8*, 1093–1108.

Weaver, T., & Clum, G. (1993). Early family environments and traumatic experiences associated with borderline personality disorder. *Journal of Consulting and Clinical Psychology, 61*, 1068–1075.

Weisler, A., & McCall, R. (1976). Exploration and play. *American Psychologist, 31*, 492–508.

Weiss, B., Dodge, K. A., Bates, J. E., & Pettit, G. S. (1992). Some consequences of early harsh discipline: Child aggression and maladaptive social information processing style. *Child Development, 63*, 1321–1335.

Werner, H. (1948). *Comparative psychology of mental development*. New York: International Universities Press.

Werner, H., & Kaplan, B. (1963). *Symbol formation*. New York: Wiley.

Westen, D. (1994). The impact of sexual abuse on self structure. In D. Cicchetti & S. L. Toth (Eds.), *Rochester Symposium on Developmental Psychopathology* (Vol. 5, pp. 223–250). Rochester, NY: University of Rochester Press.

Whipple, E. E., & Webster-Stratton, C. (1991). The role of parental stress in physically abusive families. *Child Abuse and Neglect, 15*, 279–291.

Widom, C. S. (1989). The cycle of violence. *Science, 244*, 160–166.

Widom, C. S., & Morris, S. (1997). Accuracy of adult recollections of childhood victimization: Childhood sexual abuse. *Psychological Assessment, 9*(1), 34–46.

Widom, C. S., & Shepard, R. L. (1996). Accuracy of adult recollections of childhood victimizations: Pt. I. Childhood physical abuse. *Psychological Assessment, 8*, 412–421.

Windham, A. M., Rosenberg, L., Fuddy, L., McFarlane, E., Sia, C., & Duggan, A. K. (2004). Risk of mother-reported child abuse in the first 3 years of life. *Child Abuse and Neglect, 28*(6), 645–667.

Wodarski, J. S., Kurtz, P. D., Gaudin, J. M., & Howing, P. T. (1990). Maltreatment and the school-age child: Major academic, socioemotional and adaptive outcomes. *Social Work, 35*, 506–513.

Wolfe, D. A. (1985). Child-abusive parents: An empirical review and analysis. *Psychological Bulletin, 97*, 462–482.

Wolfe, D. A. (1991). *Preventing physical and emotional abuse of children*. New York: Guilford Press.

Wolfe, D. A. (1993). Prevention of child neglect: Emerging issues. *Criminal Justice and Behavior, 20*, 90–111.

Wolfe, D. A., & Jaffe, P. (1991). Child abuse and family violence as determinants of child psychopathology. *Canadian Journal of Behavioural Science, 23*, 282–299.

Wolfe, D. A., & McGee, R. (1991). Dimensions of child maltreatment and their relationship to adolescent adjustment. *Development and Psychopathology, 6,* 165–181.

Wolfe, D. A., & Wekerle, C. (1993). Treatment strategies for child physical abuse and neglect: A critical progress report. *Clinical Psychology Review, 13,* 501–540.

Wolfner, G. D., & Gelles, R. J. (1993). A profile of violence toward children: A national study. *Child Abuse and Neglect, 17,* 197–212.

Wolock, I., & Horowitz, B. (1984). Child maltreatment as a social problem: The neglect of neglect. *American Journal of Orthopsychiatry, 54,* 530–543.

Wyman, P. A., Cowen, E. L., Work, W. C., & Kerley, J. H. (1993). The role of children's future expectations in self-system functioning and adjustment to life stress: A prospective study of urban at-risk youth. *Development and Psychopathology, 5,* 649–661.

Youngblade, L. M., & Belsky, J. (1989). Child maltreatment, infant-parent attachment security, and dysfunctional peer relationships in toddlerhood. *Topics in Early Childhood Special Education, 9,* 1–15.

Zanarini, M. C. (2000). Childhood experiences associated with the development of borderline personality disorder. *Psychiatric Clinics of North America, 23,* 89–101.

Zanarini, M. C., Frankenburg, F. R., Reich, D. B., Marino, M. F., Lewis, R. E., Williams, A. A., et al. (2000). Biparental failure in the childhood experiences of borderline patients. *Journal of Personality Disorders, 14,* 264–273.

Zanarini, M. C., Gunderson, J. G., Marino, M. F., Schwartz, E. O., & Frenkenburg, F. R. (1989). Childhood experiences of borderline patients. *Comprehensive Psychiatry, 30,* 18–25.

Zanarini, M. C., Williams, A. A., Lewis, R. E., Reich, R. B., Vera, S. C., Marino, M. F., et al. (1997). Reported pathological childhood experiences associated with the development of personality disorder. *American Journal of Psychiatry, 154,* 1101, 1106.

Zeanah, C. H., & Zeanah, P. D. (1989). Intergenerational transmission of maltreatment: Insights from attachment theory and research. *Psychiatry: Interpersonal and Biological Processes, 52*(2), 177–196.

Zigler, E. (1976). Controlling child abuse in America: An effort doomed to failure. In W. A. Collins (Ed.), *Newsletter of the division on developmental psychology* (pp. 17–30). Washington, DC: American Psychological Association.

Zingraff, M. T., Leiter, J., Myers, K. A., & Johnsen, M. C. (1993). Child maltreatment and youthful problem behavior. *Criminology, 31*(2), 173–202.

Zuravin, S. J. (1991). Research definitions of child abuse and neglect: Current problems. In R. Starr & D. Wolfe (Eds.), *The effects of child abuse and neglect: Issues and research* (pp. 100–128). New York: Guilford Press.

CHAPTER 5

The Persisting Effects of Early Experiences on Psychological Development

THOMAS G. O'CONNOR

Questions about whether and by what mechanisms early exposures and experiences may have lasting effects on the organism are fundamental to the field of developmental psychopathology and constitute a substantial focus for research in the neuroscience fields. The history of this debate from the previous century through today illustrates how dramatically concepts concerning psychological development may be supplanted, updated, or reissued. Indeed, in the course of addressing this topic, a full range of opinion has been expressed, with extreme nativism on one hand and extreme environmentalism on the other.

Several themes are evident in contemporary research on the effects of early experience on later psychological development. The first is the amount of research dedicated to the issue. Recent interest is not so noteworthy in the animal research, which for decades has considered this question; rather, it is the attention directed toward this topic in

human research that is most notable. A second major theme is the weight placed on the possibility that there may be lasting effects of early experiences or exposures on psychological outcomes. That shift in emphasis reflects a growing trend toward translational research, greater sophistication in understanding the putative biological mechanisms that may be at work, and improved technology to detect potential effects. A third theme is the growing significance of the early experiences debate for policy and practice. That is seen in popular and academic books as well as in clinical settings, such as the adjustment of children who experienced early deprivation. These themes resurface throughout this chapter.

This chapter has several aims: (1) to examine key conceptual models that have been proposed to account for why, or why not, early experiences and exposure would have persisting effects on psychological development;

(2) to review some of the conceptual and methodological lessons that have been learned from existing studies of early experience; (3) to review several major lines of research that offer some of the strongest evidence of a persisting effect of early experience on psychological development; and (4) to evaluate what implications the study of early experience has for intervention and prevention. A concluding section considers some of the future directions for research in this area.

For the purposes of this chapter, "psychological development" is restricted to behavioral and other outcomes with a prominent cognitive-affective component; it is not meant to include all outcomes associated with brain processes. Thus, there are many lines of investigation that have a prominent place in research on early experience that are not covered (e.g., vision). Reference to these later outcomes and other health outcomes is considered only sporadically throughout the chapter.

CONCEPTUAL MODELS OF EARLY EXPERIENCE

Several conceptual models underlie research on early experiences. Three broad classes of models are considered here: sensitive period models, adaptive or programming models, and life course models. Inevitably, given space limitations and the broader aims of this chapter, it is necessary to simplify the definition and description of these models. These models are chosen as exemplars of developmental hypotheses about the role of early environmental experiences and exposures because they have generated and attracted considerable research in the animal and/or human literature, there are well-established paradigms to test their predictions, and there is ample available data to evaluate their claims.

Other models in the developmental neurosciences have been proposed but are not covered here. For example, the diathesis-stress model is not included because it is not inherently developmental; that is, in its basic form, the general diathesis-stress model is not fundamentally concerned with the proposition that some features of development may, per se, constitute a diathesis or that the effects of stress on a preexisting vulnerability are moderated by psychological or biological development. For somewhat parallel reasons, the experience-dependent model (Greenough, Black, & Wallace, 1987) is not included here insofar as it is primarily concerned with showing that there is a biological change following experience rather than how the developmental stage of the organism influences the type of envi-

ronmental input needed, the immediacy of the input, or the effects on subsequent development if inadequate environmental input is provided. Last, because the concern in this chapter is with hypotheses about if and how early experiences shape development, all the models covered here propose that environmental input is important in shaping individual differences and species-typical development. Extreme nativist models that presume that healthy maturation occurs without regard to environmental input or models that make no particular predictions about transactions between the organism and the environment are not covered in any detail. These latter models provide a sort of null hypothesis against which are set the sensitive period, programming, and life course models discussed in detail.

This review contrasts multiple models for understanding the effects of early experiences on psychological development according to four dimensions:

1. Individual differences versus species-typical development;
2. The nature of the environmental input, that is, how readily identified the input is and what magnitude of effect is presumed;
3. The putative role of psychological and/or biological mechanisms and the prominence of human versus animal studies; and
4. resilience and the likelihood of recovery following intervention. These dimensions were chosen because they describe an important element and implication of each model and provide a basis for distinguishing these models empirically. These four dimensions are not meant to completely characterize each model, but to provide a conceptual and methodological framework that will need to be kept open for revision.

Sensitive Period Models

Sensitive period models hypothesize that there is a period in the ontogeny of the organism in which environmental input is needed for normal development to proceed. A sensitive period may exist for each of several types of development within the same organism, from visual acuity to attachment; also, different species might be expected to show different sensitive periods—in terms of onset and length—for the same behavior. These latter two positions follow from the proposal that the sensitive period is determined by the active period of brain development linked with a particular behavioral or biological outcome.

How rigidly defined the period of sensitivity is remains uncertain, at least in most instances. Recent work in this area has, in fact, sought to extend the boundaries of the sensitive period, thereby rejecting the rigid boundaries governing sensitive periods that were often initially presumed. The net effect of these efforts has been to retain the sensitive period concept while also removing the condition that the sensitive period is necessarily rigidly defined.

Different terms have been used to express the hypothesis that there is a period in ontogeny at which certain environmental input is essential to ensure normal development; these terms include critical period (e.g., Bornstein, 1989), sensitive period, and experience-expectant (Greenough et al., 1987) models. There may be important differences among these terms, but they are considered in the same class of models here because they have been used interchangeably in the literature (particularly sensitive period and critical period), and, fundamentally, each sets up an expectation for the association between normal development and environmental experience.

Also, although sensitive periods are most frequently associated with early development, they may be found throughout the life course, such as a parent bonding with an offspring, as has been shown in the animal literature (Fleming, O'Day, & Kraemer, 1999).

There is growing evidence that sensitive or critical periods are under genetic control (Hensch, 2004). In one example (Huang et al., 1999), mice genetically manipulated to overexpress brain-derived neurotrophic factor (BDNF) showed accelerated development and early closure of the critical period in the visual cortex. These data suggest that genetically mediated processes regulate critical periods for species-typical development. A complementary proposal, that environmental exposure in a sensitive period in development may alter gene expression, has also been reported (Kinnunen, Koenig, & Bilbe, 2003). Thus, a picture is emerging of a dynamic interplay between environmental experience and genetics, and there is little doubt that this line of investigation will yield additional important insights into how sensitive periods are best conceptualized.

A final consideration for defining sensitive period models is their evolutionary basis. Most would assume that there is evolutionary significance to the existence of sensitive periods; for example, it might not be adaptive for the organism to be equally and endlessly mutable. In addition, as Berardi, Pizzorusso, and Maffei (2000) showed for the effects of monocular deprivation across several species, there is a very tight positive connection between the length of the critical period and the age span of the species. So, at least for visual acuity, the message is not that there is *not* a critical/sensitive period in humans as there is for animals, but rather that it is longer. Whether or not that lesson applies to other areas of development, such as attachment, remains to be seen and is considered later.

Individual Differences versus Species Typical Development

Sensitive period models are concerned with species-typical development, that is, the presence versus the absence of some essential behavior; the distinction in outcome is between normality and gross pathology that might seriously undermine species survival and adaptation. Thus, in research examples of sensitive periods, such as birdsong (Thorpe, 1963), vision (Hubel & Wiesel, 1970), imprinting, and social attachments (Harlow & Suomi, 1970; Insel, 1997), the animals that did not receive the normal or expected input were not merely disordered but showed fundamental deviations. Research of this sort, because of its emphasis on species-typical versus clearly aberrant development, is targeted to elucidate core principles about the organism; in contrast, there is much less (if any) interest in accounting for differences among individuals in behavior within the normal range.

Nature of the Environmental Input

Sensitive period models assume a major impact of the environment. The focus in research has tended to identify what dose of environmental input is required, what specific type of environmental input or experience is necessary for normal development to proceed, and when in development that input is most necessary. A major tactic in answering these questions is to expose animals to pathogenic environments (e.g., deprivation) rather than to gradients of environmental quality across the spectrum, although that is now changing somewhat. The tendency to study the effects of obviously pathogenic environments that manipulate dose, type, or timing of exposure may be partly explained by the early interest in assessing the extent to which putatively "instinctual behavior" required *any* environmental input. Consequently, a major aim in studying the organism's early experience was to identify the minimum threshold of environmental effect—the point at which the organism would acquire or develop species-typical behavior. The environmental dose of interest was the minimum necessary for the organism to develop apparently normally.

A second, related reason research adopting a sensitive period model focuses on the minimum threshold for normal development is that the outcomes of interest would be expected to be protected or canalized (Gottlieb, 1991). If that is the case, then it might follow that there may be comparatively modest demands on the environment for normal development to proceed. That is, if a particular function were so important to the normal development of the organism (e.g., reproductive fitness), then it might make little evolutionary sense for these outcomes to hinge on highly particular demands on the environment in terms of quality or quantity. Therefore, although sensitive period models place great importance on environmental input, they set a low demand threshold on what kind of input is needed or "good enough."

The Role of Psychological Mechanisms and the Prominence of Human versus Animal Studies

With few exceptions (e.g., vision and language; Itard, 1962; Johnson & Newport, 1989; Maurer, Lewis, Brent, & Levin, 1999), sensitive period models have not had a major influence on the study of human development. For those aspects of human research that have considered sensitive period models, the focus is on biological rather than psychological mechanisms. Claims that there may be a sensitive period for psychological (especially behavioral) outcomes are exceedingly rare and, to date, without solid foundation. Instead, studies testing sensitive period hypotheses are based almost exclusively on animal experimentation (e.g., Bornstein, 1989) and invoke a variety of alternative biological mechanisms.

Notwithstanding the lack of evidence for psychologically sensitive periods, there is ample evidence that biologically mediated sensitive periods exist for psychological or psychiatric phenotypes. For example, there is a link between exposure to rubella infection during the first trimester and an increased incidence of Autism Spectrum Disorders (Chess, 1977); also, nutritional deprivation in utero has been linked with major mental illness in adulthood (Brown, van Os, Driessens, Hoek, & Susser, 2000). These examples suggest that the search for sensitive periods for psychological development may benefit from adopting a broader biological model that may underlie psychological outcomes.

Likelihood of Recovery or Resilience

Just as there may be periods of ontogenetic vulnerability (Schneider, Roughton, Koehler, & Lubach, 1999), there may be periods of ontogenetic opportunity for intervention. That is, if a sensitive period for a particular outcome did exist, then interventions would need to be delivered during that sensitive period. Interventions delivered outside the sensitive period would have much less, if any, effect on the outcome of interest. Alternatively, a particular intervention might have a *different* effect depending on when in development it was delivered. Thus, the timing of the intervention is the key factor, according to a sensitive period

model. Also, according to a sensitive period model, the organism expects only "adequate" rather than "enriched" input for normal development to proceed. Enriched environments may have an effect if provided during a sensitive period, but are not portrayed as necessary for the acquisition of normal function. Indeed, given the lack of interest in individual differences, it is not surprising that little interest has been shown in resilient or supercompetent levels of functioning.

Lorenz's (1982) experiments on imprinting provide one of the better-known examples of how "treatment-resistant" an organism may be to interventions delivered after a sensitive period. He showed that those animals that imprinted (notably, on Lorenz himself) did not exhibit signs of subsequent imprinting on a member of the same species when it was introduced after the sensitive period; neither did the animals show any reduction in imprinting on Lorenz. Primate research also shows that timing of treatment is important and that degree of recovery is limited. For example, the effects of early deprivation on social behavior (e.g., Harlow & Harlow, 1969) are at best modestly remediable, with the likelihood of success depending on the timing of the intervention (Cameron, 2004; Martin, Spicer, Lewis, Gluck, & Cork, 1991; S. L. Ramey & Sackett, 2000). Other primate research demonstrates that the effects of early maternal deprivation persist into adulthood and are transmitted intergenerationally (although, interestingly, improvements in mothering were observed with second-born offspring without any intervention other than [poorly] mothering the first born; Ruppenthal, Arling, Harlow, Sackett, & Suomi, 1976). It is not known if there are comparable examples of treatment timing in humans. This possibility is gaining attention, particularly in the context of children who experienced severe and profound early deprivation.

Experience-Adaptive or Developmental Programming

There is now substantial evidence that the biology of the fetus and child adapts to its environment (Amiel-Tison et al., 2004a, 2004b; Bateson & Martin, 1999; Hales & Barker, 1992, 2001; Matthews, 2002). These adaptations are referred to as programming because they are thought to "set" the biological system of the organism in a manner that persists into adulthood. This adaptation occurs during a particular period in development, and in that way, the model has some similarities with the sensitive period models. However, programming models hypothesize a connection between the organism and its (early) experiences that differs from the connection in a sensitive period model.

Programming models predict variation among individuals within a species according to early exposure; therefore, individuals may vary from one another according to their early environmental experiences. In other words, the programming models attend not only to the nature of the organism (e.g., that the stress-response system is sensitive to experience in early development), but also to the variation in quality of early environmental experiences. Variation in early environmental exposure will determine an individual's "set point" and therefore influence how individuals might differ from one another in, for example, their response to a subsequent stress.

The notion that the fetus/infant *adapts* to the early environment is critical for what it says about organism-environment transactions (i.e., they are active from early in ontogeny) and for what it implies about an evolutionary influence (e.g., Crespi & Denver, 2005). The concept of adaptation reflects the view that this model is not so concerned with normal versus deviant development, but rather with the fit between the organism and its environment. So, for example, rather than view the programming of the hypothalamic-pituitary-adrenal (HPA) axis in the fetus or infant as a sign of vulnerability or pathology, it may be more appropriate to view the adaptation that is made as a signal of the organism's preparedness for its (later) environment. Thus, mothers who experience increased stress in pregnancy may be signaling to the offspring that a more responsive stress response may be adaptive for its particular environment. The possibility that there may be costs associated with certain kinds of adaptations is inherently context-dependent; that is, these adaptations can be judged only in relation to the organism's subsequent environment. This concern for the organism's environment later in development, after the "ontogenetic vulnerability," provides a further conceptual contrast between the sensitive period and programming models. Thus, adaptation or programming can be conceptually distinguished from sensitive period models—although the two may be difficult to distinguish empirically.

The concept of programming has been applied to several contexts. One widely replicated example is prenatal stress in animals. Many research teams have shown that exposing pregnant animals to uncontrollable mild stress programs the fetus's HPA axis to be stress-(over)responsive, and that this disposition is carried into adulthood and leads to a range of biobehavioral outcomes (Henry, Kabbaj, Simon, LeMoal, & Maccari, 1994). This exemplar of developmental programming is discussed in more detail later. Epidemiological investigations in humans suggest that there may be

fetal programming with respect to nutrition in pregnancy, fetal growth, and reduced glucose tolerance and cardiovascular fitness in adulthood (Barker, 1998; Erikkson et al., 1999; Hales & Barker, 1992, 2001; Lucas, 1998; Ravelli et al., 1998). That is, poor nutrition in fetal life leads to permanent alterations—adaptations—in the fetus and child; the thrifty phenotype that results may then be ill-prepared if the postnatal environment is not nutritionally poor.

Individual Differences versus Species Typical Development

Studies on developmental programming are typically concerned with differences in outcomes among a sample of individuals. Further, there is interest in linking differences among individual outcomes with variation in gradients of environmental exposure. That is shown in recent animal studies (Francis & Meaney, 2002) and human studies linking birthweight to adult risk for cardiovascular disease. Thus, in contrast to the sensitive period models, programming models tend to focus on variation within the normal and pathological range and not merely on species-atypical or grossly aberrant behaviors.

Nature of the Environmental Input

The programming model assumes a substantial role for the early environment on long-term development; indeed, it is the early environment that determines the set point for the organism—presumably within a range of species-bound set points. Thus, the impact of the early environment is substantial and lasting, and the timing of this input is essential. On the other hand, the identity of the particular environmental experience that programs the set point for the organism is not always precisely defined or determinate. So, for example, in the case of prenatal stress programming the fetal HPA axis, any of several types of environmental adversity that increase stress in the pregnant mother could serve the same programming effect.

The Role of Psychological Mechanisms and the Prominence of Human versus Animal Studies

Whereas research on sensitive periods is dominated by animal investigations, research on humans has played a key role in the popularization of the programming hypothesis. Nevertheless, the mechanism implied by the programming model is wholly biological. Several examples have been discussed involving a wide array of biological systems, such as the HPA axis, pancreatic function, and the cardiovascular system. There is no evidence yet of a psychological mechanism being programmed by early experience, although there have been few attempts at this sort of research. One of the few human studies to explicitly program effects for psychological outcomes (Rutter & O'Connor & the English and Romanian Adoptees Study Team, 2004) found evidence of persisting disturbances but no clear evidence of underlying psychological mediating factors (such as cognitive development). In fact, most psychological processes are described as open to change rather than set by early experience (Bowlby, 1988; Toth, Maughan, Manly, Spagnola, & Cicchetti, 2002).

Likelihood of Recovery or Resilience

The degree of recovery (or, more broadly, change of any sort) that can be expected following early programming is not yet clear. In the case of programming of the HPA axis, research findings lead to two important and complementary conclusions. The first is that the effects of prenatal stress are evident in adult offspring; the second is that the effect of prenatal stress may be eliminated by manipulating the early postnatal environment, through adoption or pharmacologically (Francis, Diorio, Liu, & Meaney, 1999; Ladd et al., 2000; Maccari et al., 1995). It can be asserted that an intervention delivered during the programming period would have a strong and persisting effect (e.g., to "reset" the set point). What has received far less attention is whether or not there is a point after which interventions would not effect change in the organism's set point. There is evidence that such a point does exist, such as the periadolescent period, but data are limited (Barbazanges et al., 1996; Darnaudery et al., 2004).

The implications of the programming hypothesis for interventions with humans are not known. To date, human investigations have simply demonstrated that such processes may exist. Whether or not response to intervention (e.g., for cardiovascular disease) differs according to the presence of a programming origin of the disease requires further research.

Life Course or Cumulative Effects Models

Life course developmental models propose that individual differences in psychological development arise from the individual's particular profile of risk and protective experiences as accumulated through development. The model is developmental because there is concern for when in development the individual was exposed to risk or protective factors and how they shape the trajectory or pathway that the individual follows. The metaphor of developmental pathways (Bowlby, 1988) is helpful in illustrating, first, that the link between early adversity and later outcome is probabilistic rather than deterministic and, second, that there is a developmental order or logic in connecting early experience through to later outcomes. Several implications follow from this, including the hypothesis that early experiences predict longer-term outcomes only insofar as the effects of the early risk exposure is reinforced or maintained by subsequent events. Early risk, in the absence of concurrent risk, would be expected to have little or no effect. Thus, in contrast to the previous two models, life span developmental models view the significance of early experience in terms of subsequent exposures and experiences. Life course models seek to explain and quantify what is carried forward in development. This perspective emphasizes that early experiences are not *directly* causally linked with long-term outcomes, but are instead mediated by the risk and protective factors that follow. To a considerable extent, life span developmental models are central to much of the research on risk and resilience in psychological development (A. M. Clarke & Clarke, 2000; Schaffer, 2000).

Normative and nonnormative transitions such as the transition to early adolescence and adjustment to parental divorce attract particular attention in life course models because these are points in the developmental pathway at which a turn for the better or for the worse might be most likely and most easily assessed. It is also noteworthy, for heuristic purposes, to place the developmental stage theories of Piaget, Freud (Anna and Sigmund), Erik Erikson, among others in this category of models. Stage theories are quintessentially developmental because they propose something specific about the organism at one stage in development that is distinct from another stage (e.g., the need to resolve autonomy conflicts) and further suggest that there is a carrying forward of the effects of successes and failures of resolving these developmental tasks into the next stage. So, for instance, as Sroufe (1996) proposed, an insecure attachment in infancy may be viewed as a risk *because* it increases the likelihood of failure at subsequent stage-salient tasks, such as emotion regulation and the formation of positive peer relationships.

Individual Differences versus Species-Typical Development

Life course developmental models seek to explain variation among individuals in the developmental pathways followed and how these different developmental pathways predict individual differences in adjustment. Thus, the focus is on variation within the normal-abnormal range. However, although the extremes on the continuum, such as serious psychopathology, are considered in research using this model, there is no presumption that the outcomes of interest are anything but species-typical behaviors. Moreover, for the most part, the kinds of environments under investigation are also within the normal range, although again, extremes of the continuum are considered, such as extreme poverty and parental maltreatment.

Nature of the Environmental Input

A focus in life span developmental research is to identify the kinds of risk experiences that are associated with individual differences in adjustment across the life span. A guiding hypothesis is that exposure to environmental risk is directly or indirectly linked with individual differences in adjustment. However, compared with previous models, life span developmental models assume a more complex, dynamic, and transactional connection between the organism and its environment. So, for example, if the goal is to predict depression in adulthood, life span developmental models would presume that any of a number of risks might play an important role, that no one risk experience is necessary or sufficient, and that, most likely, there is a complex of factors that, collectively and cumulatively (over time), predict adult depression. Related to this last point is the proposal that there is multifinality (exposure to a certain risk may lead to diverse outcomes among individuals) and equifinality (individuals may end up at the same [mal]adapted outcome by traversing different pathways or patterns of risk exposure; Cicchetti & Cohen, 1995). No such degree of flexibility between exposure and outcome is assumed in the sensitive period or programming models discussed earlier.

The Role of Psychological Mechanisms and the Prominence of Human versus Animal Studies

Whereas animal studies have been fundamental to testing sensitive period and programming hypotheses, animal studies are rarely designed to test life span developmental models. In other words, the favored model in research designs is different in animal and human research. There are a number of good and practical reasons for this. Nevertheless, an implication is that much of the research on early experience in animal studies may be difficult to translate to humans because research designs in the animal and human contexts make different presumptions about how early experience might confer risk for long-term development.

Life span models favor psychological mechanisms to explain links between early experience and longer-term outcomes, and due consideration is also made of the larger social and historical context (e.g., Schoon et al., 2002). Comparatively few examples exist to show that psychological mechanisms mediate connections between early experience and long-term outcome. This is not so much because there is no evidence for important psychological processes in the infant and child (Fonagy, Gergely, Jurist, & Target, 2002; Jaffee, Beebe, Feldstein, Crown, & Jasnow, 2001), but rather because there are not sufficient data to show that early experiences that led to certain psychological adaptations mediate long-term adjustment. Child-parent attachment may be one possibility (Waters, Merrick, Treboux, Crowell, & Albersheim, 2000), but available data do not demonstrate that it is attachment in infancy per se that predicts long-term adjustment. On the other hand, there is ample evidence starting from around midchildhood that comparatively stable and robust psychological mechanisms, such as attributional style and cognitive-behavioral style, may mediate long-term well-being. These characteristics are not readily recognizable in the infant or young child, however. Partly for this reason and based on their finding that behavioral continuity into adulthood was robust only from the early school years, Kagan and Moss (1962/1983) suggested that the early schools years may be a critical period of behavioral organization that may have lasting effects. Behavioral organization and psychological processes prior to middle school may have less persisting influence, although this question requires further direct and rigorous testing.

Likelihood of Recovery or Resilience

Life span developmental models are easily distinguished from the other models by emphasizing that there is substantial potential for recovery following early experiences or exposure to adversity. Indeed, the expectation from the risk/resilience literature, which is most amenable to the life course model, is that the individual is highly malleable, and there are comparatively few (if any) limits on whether an intervention may be applied to improve psychological well-being. In fact, the limits of resilience as it relates to when in development an intervention may be effective remain to be specified—because they are rarely made explicit. So, for example, major life events that occur later in development may be as important, and perhaps more important, as those in early life in shaping later adjustment. Empirical examples from naturalistic longitudinal studies that show dramatic change in life course pathways are provided by research on enrollment in the military (Elder, 1986) and marriage (Quinton & Rutter, 1988). Thus, life span developmental models (implicitly) propose that the timing of the intervention is not as important as the type or intensity of the intervention.

Discredited Models

Finally, it is worth noting some proposals about development and early experience that have been discredited. First among these is the idea that development can be "arrested" or "frozen," with the corollary that a goal of treatment is to "unfreeze" development. Currently, the application of this mistaken notion is seen in the case of children with an attachment disorder. It has been shown that children who experience extreme caregiving deprivation develop marked disturbances in attachment and social relations characterized by an apparent inability to develop selective or discriminating relationships with subsequent caregivers (see later discussion). Several authors (e.g., Howe & Fearnley, 1999; Keck & Kupecky, 1995) have proposed that because the children did not experience adequate early caregiving, including appropriate response to distress but also basic contact, features of the child's development were arrested or frozen. Radical forms of therapy, in which the child is forced into contact with a therapist, have been proposed as a solution. The holding that is incorporated into the treatment is thought to satisfy the needs of the older child-as-infant and "bring forward" the child's development into normality. Not surprisingly, that form of treatment has not been shown to be effective and may, in fact, exacerbate the child's disturbances. A problem here is that the concept of regression was taken literally to mean that the 8-year-old child is, in terms of attachment development, an infant and needs to be treated as such. Such a conceptualization of regression or developmental arrest is also out of step with contemporary psychoanalytic thinking (Eagle, 1984; Gedo, 1980), on which it was very loosely based. In fact, current psychoanalytic views of disturbance brought about by failure to resolve age-salient tasks (which may nevertheless differ according to schools of thought; e.g., Eagle, 1984) are more akin to standard models that guide developmental psychopathology research (Cicchetti & Cohen, 1995).

Summary

Evidence supporting the persisting effects of early experience was previously only robustly demonstrated in experimental animal studies. That is changing, as several lines of research demonstrate surprisingly strong and persisting effects of early experience in humans. Data of that sort have become available because of the opportunities afforded by "natural experiments" and the increasing technological sophistication available to study neuroscience phenomena. Recent reviews of ideas and data on early experience in animals and humans (Bruer, 1999; Cacioppo et al., 2002; A. M. Clarke & Clarke, 2000; Nelson & Luciana, 2001; Schaffer, 2000) suggest that no conceptual consensus has yet emerged and that there are important conceptual controversies that need clarification. It may be that each of the models just discussed have strengths and weaknesses in accounting for the accumulation of data on early experiences and long-term outcomes.

This section considered and contrasted several of the leading models of how, and if, early experience may have lasting psychological effects on the organism. This review was illustrative rather than exhaustive, both in terms of identifying models and articulating dimensions on which the models may be differentiated. Highlighting sources of conceptual and methodological leverage for testing these models is the focus of the next section.

CONCEPTUAL AND METHODOLOGICAL CONSIDERATIONS

This section examines the particular conceptual and methodological issues learned in the course of conducting research into the effects of early experiences, particularly with reference to applications in humans.

Design Strategies

Progress in understanding if and how early experiences may have persisting effects in humans is hampered by the fact that, in most circumstances, risk exposure is not precisely timed or restricted to a particular period in development. On the contrary, most environmental risks of conceptual or public health interest are continuous. Therefore, whether the risk is poverty, child maltreatment, or parental mental illness, children are exposed to persisting psychosocial risk, and so it is difficult to disentangle the effects of early experiences per se from the cumulative effects of continuous adversity. Complicating this situation further is the fact that the most important risks do not exist in isolation, and exposure to one kind of risk may increase the likelihood of exposure to additional and subsequent risks. For instance, poor parenting in infancy and early childhood is likely to be stable from childhood to adulthood, covary with social and economic risks (marital conflict, economic strain), and lead to poor peer relationships and exposure to deviant peers. Analytic strategies may be employed to account for these co-occurring risks, but demonstrating that there is an independent effect of one particular risk on outcome when others are covaried may not carry much weight if the nature of the risks is to covary in development. Thus, even in multivariate analyses, there may be dangers in drawing direct causal connections between any particular risk experienced at a particular point in development and psychological disturbance. Evidence of the complex interdependence of risks for compromised psychological development is one of the more important practical lessons from naturalistic studies of child development.

In contrast to naturalistic studies that dominate human research, animal studies make good use of experimental designs in which a particular early experience is randomly assigned to animals in different groups and the outcomes of the two groups are later compared. Experimental designs naturally afford greater security against undetected or unmeasured bias, although the generalizability and ecological validity of the findings may be threatened to the extent that excessive experimental control is introduced.

Experimentally introducing early stress in human studies in a way that resembles the experimental animal literature would not, of course, be ethical. However, "experiments in nature" (Bronfenbrenner, 1979) exist that might provide some leverage in testing hypotheses about early experiences in humans. Natural experiments are naturally arising conditions in which there is a possibility of separating otherwise confounded processes, or they provide opportunities to test developmental hypotheses that would not be possible because of ethical or practical reasons. Several natural experiments exist in the literature on early experiences, including studies of children who were rescued from institutional deprivation (Chisholm, 1998; Gunnar, Morison, Chisholm, & Schuder, 2001; O'Connor, Rutter, & the English and Romanian Adoptees Study Team, 2000), follow-up studies of adults whose mother experienced prenatal famine induced by war (Brown et al., 2000; Ravelli et al., 1998), and studies that examined the effects of specific stresses that were outside of the control of the subjects, such as an ice storm (Laplante et al., 2004) and an earthquake (Glynn, Wadhwa, Dunkel-Schletter, Chicz-Demet, & Sandman, 2001). Findings from these experiments in nature have provided critical data for documenting the persisting effects of early experiences in humans.

To the extent that "typical" experimental control is possible in human studies, it comes in the form of intervention or prevention trials. Many experimental intervention studies have targeted early experience, although comparatively few directly test the timing hypotheses that underlie the conceptual models reviewed earlier. Because of the importance of these studies they are considered separately in the final section.

Timing, Frequency, and Severity of Exposure and Ontogenetic Patterns

For most psychological outcomes of interest we do not have enough information to determine what the window of sensitivity is—if one exists at all. One strategy for identifying such periods is to base developmental investigation on what is known about the sharp periods of discontinuity in brain development. This has been shown most clearly in the area of cognitive development (Herschkowitz, Kagan, & Zilles, 1997; Huttenlocher, 1994); on the other hand, application to social outcomes is elusive. This is a strategy borrowed from the sensitive period model: Environmental input may be most important during periods of dramatic biological change, notably brain development. In other words, knowledge of ontogeny should shape the study of environmental experience and exposure.

Teicher et al.'s (2003; see also, Anderson, 2003) summary of the preclinical data suggested that there may be specific features of those brain regions that may be particularly vulnerable to early stressful experience. Characteristic features are thought to include a protracted postnatal development, including postnatal neurogenesis and a high density of glucocorticoid receptors. So, for example, research into the brain bases of persisting early effects might profitably target brain areas with these features. Additional strategic insight is being generated by genetic research on ontogenetic development. One recent example concerns the ontogeny of the glucocorticoid receptor gene and its expression in brain development (Speirs, Seckl, & Brown, 2004). Results from this type of investigation suggest which areas of the brain at which points in development may be most relevant to study the effects of early stress.

Translating ontogenetic findings into practical results will, by design, depend on the type of environmental experience and the mechanism involved. A strong example of an environmental effect (albeit in utero) being informed by ontogenetic development was reported by Hansen and colleagues (Hansen, Lou, & Olsen, 2000). They found that severe life events experienced in the first trimester of pregnancy increased the risk of congenital abnormalities in neural crest-derived organs in the fetus/child. The finding that the effect for this outcome was for the first trimester only is significant given that this is when gross organ formation would be most vulnerable. Somewhat comparable findings were reported by other investigators (e.g., Nimby, Lundberg, Sveger, & McNeil, 1999). On the other hand, research on prenatal stress/anxiety in relation to behavioral/emotional outcomes has produced inconsistencies as regards timing of stress in pregnancy. Thus, whereas some studies suggest that stress/anxiety in midpregnancy may be most predictive (Van den Bergh & Marcoen, 2004), others emphasize late pregnancy (O'Connor, Heron, Golding, Beveridge, & Glover, 2002). There may be methodological and practical reasons for these inconsistencies, such as the difficulty in timing anxiety or stress precisely; there may be biological explanations as well, as several kinds of effects on the developing brain at different points in development may yield similar-looking effects on, for example, attention and broad behavioral phenotypes. In any event, it is not clear how to reconcile these contrasting findings and synthesize them with experimental data suggesting that midgestation is the point after which the human fetus can mount its own (independent) stress response (Gitau, Fisk, Teixeira, Cameron, & Glover, 2001). In this case, knowledge of ontogenetic development is no guarantee that the nature of the environmental effect or the putative mechanism will be revealed.

Child-parent attachment is another area of study in which an ontogenetic model of the formation of discriminating attachments has been tested (Bowlby, 1982). Given the conceptual and empirical work in this area, it might be expected that the timing of the onset of caregiving deprivation may result in differential disturbances, and there is some evidence for this (Vorria, Rutter, Pickles, Wolkind, & Hobsbaum, 1998; Wolkind, 1974). For example, Wolkind found that disinhibition toward strangers was uniquely associated with *early* institutional care but not institutional care that occurred postinfancy, that is, past the point that the child formed a selective or discriminating attachment relationship with the caregiver. On the other hand, studies of child-parent attachment following early caregiving deprivation that started at or immediately following birth and continued into the early months and years of life find less distinct or qualitative differences in outcomes according to age at adoption (e.g., O'Connor et al., 2003). In fact, the finding that both early-placed children as well as later-placed children exhibit the same form of severe disturbance has raised some important ontogenetic and etiological questions.

There are different timing of measurement implications for testing life span models of early risk on later development. Specifically, each junction hypothesized along the risk trajectory (Quinton, Pickles, Maughan, & Rutter, 1993) requires assessment. Complementing the need to time assessments according to stage-salient issues and competencies is the view that the order of major life transitions (e.g., educational attainment, marriage, childbearing) should be considered. In support of this proposal are data suggesting that off-time transitions or transitions that do not follow a normative course may increase the risk for compromised long-term development (Rindfuss, Swicegood, & Rosenfeld, 1987). Whether it is the timing or the order of major events (or both), life course developmental models require a measurement-intensive approach to determine if the effects of early experience are mediated by later experience.

Questions about measurement intensity also arise in discussions of the so-called sleeper effect model, which is usually defined as the existence of a time lag between exposure to adversity and the detection of a putative effect. The possibility of sleeper effects has been raised in several developmental studies (e.g., Kagan & Moss, 1962/1983). Wallerstein (1985) proposed a similar process in suggesting that divorce in childhood may have not only immediate effects, but also effects at a later point in development, such as adolescence, when there is a rekindling of the early developmental struggle or vulnerability. The major problem with this model is largely one of measurement, as it can be supported only if it can be shown that there was no intervening effect mediating the link between exposure to early adversity and some later-detected outcome.

Individual Differences

The existence of individual differences in response to adverse environments, even gross deprivation, is often unaccounted for. This is so in the animal literature (S. L. Ramey & Sackett, 2000), notwithstanding the generally small samples included in research. Individual differences have proved to be substantial in studies following up children who experienced severe early deprivation. For example, despite more than 2 years in extreme institutional deprivation, children adopted following institutional deprivation had cognitive abilities ranging from severe delay to well above average by age 6 years of age (O'Connor et al., 2000), a pattern that continued in further follow-up assessments at age 11 years (O'Connor, 2003).

Human studies also show that there are differences among individuals in the kinds of disturbances that may result from early deprivation. Thus, whereas some children exhibit largely cognitive difficulties, others show primarily social deficits; a minority show a combination of deficits (Rutter, Kreppner, O'Connor, & the English and Romanian Adoptees [ERA] Study Team, 2001). In the ERA study, it could not be determined why institutional deprivation led to some children exhibiting quasi-autistic behavior but to others exhibiting inattention/overactivity or attachment disturbances. It cannot be ruled out that differences in the type of disturbance exhibited are accounted for by unmeasured differences in experiences in the institution or to unmeasured biological vulnerabilities that may or may not be partly genetic in nature. Modest differences among institutions in the level of deprivation did exist. This has been shown to account for only modest variation in cognitive ability at earlier assessments (Castle et al., 1999), but leaves unexplained most of the variability observed.

Further research into the sources of individual differences associated with early exposure to stress/adversity therefore needs to consider multiple outcomes to evaluate whether some children who seem resilient on some outcomes are nevertheless vulnerable on other indices of adjustment. Furthermore, subsequent research needs to account for the near certainty that there will be domain-specific patterns across outcomes; models developed to account for language acquisition may be irrelevant for understanding variation in, for example, attachment relationships.

Sex Differences

Sex differences in response to stress, sometimes compounded by age, are well documented and are observed at several levels of analysis, from stress reactivity (Gallucci et al., 1993; Kirschbaum, Wust, & Hallhammer, 1992), to response to early adversity and potentially genetically mediated responses (Barr, Newman, Schwandt, et al., 2004), to bona fide psychological disorder (Kessler, 2003). Indeed, human studies routinely consider and find evidence for sex differences in outcomes associated with risks such as parental divorce and remarriage (Hetherington, Bridges, & Insabella, 1998) trauma (Breslau, Peterson, Poisson, Schultz, & Lucia, 2004), and broader psychosocial risks (Werner, 1989). Given the robust sex differences across species on outcomes and mechanisms that are relevant to the development of psychopathology, it is no wonder that sex is a common moderator in studies of early experience.

Finding sex differences does not lead directly or necessarily to a mechanism. The reason is that sex (i.e., biologically based differences) and gender (i.e., socially based differences) are proxies for a range of hormonal, social, and cognitive differences that are often difficult to disentangle. Each of several aspects of sex or gender could underlie mean differences in rates of disturbance following exposure to early risk or more qualitative differences in the types of effects that are observed.

On the other hand, there are noteworthy failures to find sex differences in studies of early stress exposure. Studies of children adopted following institutional deprivation have found no or inconsistent sex differences, including on those outcomes for which there are strong sex differences, such as inattention and hyperactivity (Kreppner, O'Connor, Rutter, & the English and Romanian Adoptees Study Team et al., 2001). Indeed, in Kreppner et al.'s study, early institutional deprivation was associated with the absence of the expected sex difference. It seems unlikely that any sweeping proposal concerning sex differences in response to early stress exposure will fit the data. To the extent that sex differences are hypothesized, they need to be bound by age of assessment, outcome investigated, and proposed mechanism.

Animal and Human Models

A further obstacle to the synthesis of a model to account for early experience concerns generalizability across species. Berardi et al. (2000) and S. L. Ramey and Sackett (2000), among others, point out that demonstrations of sensitive periods are not as clear in primates as they are in birds and other species. S. L. Ramey and Sackett further note that differences between nonprimates and primates is clearly evident for socialization outcomes.

Several reasons exist for why there may not be generalizability across species. The task of translating findings from animal studies to the human context is complicated by several specific challenges, and these challenges may vary according to the risk being assessed. For example, in the particular area of prenatal stress, the threats to generalizability include (1) the varying maturity of the offspring at birth (e.g., between rats, sheep, and primates; Matthews, 2001); (2) the possible role of litter size on outcomes (Huot, Gonzalez, Ladd, Thrivikraman, & Plotsky, 2004); (3) the ease with which corticosterone crosses the placenta in the rodent compared with the protection provided against cortisol transfer in human and nonhuman primates associated with 11b-hydroxysteriod dehydrogenase (11b-HSD; Challis, Matthews, Van Meir, & Ramirez, 1995; Kajentie et al., 2003; Petraglia et al., 1990); (4) the differential distribution and likely differential functional significance of receptors involved in regulating stress in rodents and primates (Sanchez, Ladd, & Plotsky, 2001); and (5) differences in brain size at birth between monkeys and humans (60% of adult versus 24%, respectively; Coe et al., 2003), which confound comparisons between nonhuman primates and humans concerning the degree of resilience in brain development following early stress exposure.

Compounding these problems in generalizing across species are clear demonstrations of nongeneralizability within species. One such difference is found in attachment behavior in Old and New World monkeys (Suomi, 1999). But perhaps the most well-known example of this sort involves monogamous prairie voles and nonmonogamous montane voles whose behavioral differences in social and attachment behavior have been linked with differences in oxytocin and vasopressin receptor function in the brain (Insel, 1997; Young, Wang, & Insel, 1998).

Additionally, experimental animal research is based on precisely timed stressful manipulations that can be controlled in terms of duration, frequency, and intensity. Exposure to well-defined, precisely timed stressors is not representative of the kinds of even severe stresses that constitute the most significant risk phenotypes in humans. Accordingly, improving the applicability of animal findings to humans may depend on revising experimental paradigms to rely less on studies that induce extreme conditions such as deprivation and instead examine risks that are more obviously within the range of species-typical experiences. Several examples of this sort have been proposed. One paradigm used in several nonhuman primate studies is referred to as variable foraging demand (VFD; Rosenblum & Paully, 1984). In contrast to low foraging demand conditions, in which food is made available, and high foraging demand, in which the animal needs to search and dig for food, animals in the VFD condition do not have a predictable regimen. Several studies show that offspring of mothers in the VFD condition exhibit a range of behavioral problems that may be analogous to anxiety (Coplan et al., 1996); infants whose mothers were exposed to the VFD show a wide range of neurochemical abnormalities, including elevations in corticotropin-releasing factor, somatostatin, and metabolites of serotonin and dopamine (Coplan et al., 1998). Also in primates, Maestripieri (1999) has examined another naturally occurring adverse experience, maltreatment. The fact that this exists in nature and does not require experimental manipulation or contrived circumstances has presumed benefits for generalization, both for primates and potentially for humans. Similar efforts to examine the long-term effects of naturally occurring variation are also found in rat models (Caldji, Diorio, & Meaney, 2000). It will be important to establish if findings from these more naturalistic paradigms contrast with or confirm findings using less ecologically valid paradigms. Whether or not these efforts signal a move away from extreme experimental manipulations remains to be seen.

Candidate Mechanisms

A short list of candidate mechanisms emerged to account for the persisting effects of early experience and exposure on psychological development. In the areas of prenatal stress and caregiving deprivation there is considerable interest in an HPA-mediated mechanism (Gunnar, 2003). There are several reasons the study of early experience in humans, such as prenatal and early stresses, has focused on the HPA axis. These include the considerable animal data suggesting a programming mechanism, the documented role of HPA axis dysfunction in a range of psychological disturbances in children and adults, and emerging data from several laboratories that the effects of stress exposure can be seen in HPA axis activity. In addition, assessing HPA axis activity from salivary cortisol is comparatively easy and inexpensive. Accordingly, although basic questions remain about cortisol collection and analysis, it is one of the leading candidate mechanisms in human studies of early experience. Prospective longitudinal data on sufficiently large samples supporting the role of the HPA axis in mediating the persisting effect of early adverse exposure are still rare. However, several kinds of follow-back studies and other designs have been done (e.g., Heim et al., 2000), and this remains an active area of research.

More recent research considered genetic mechanisms, particularly those associated with neurotransmitters thought to underlie major mental illness. One study in mice (Ansorge, Zhou, Lira, Hen, & Gingrich, 2004) found that pharmacologically inhibiting serotonin transporter expression in early development with fluoxetine was associated with abnormal behavior that resembles animal models of anxiety and depression. The pharmacological intervention effect, which was found only in those animals that did not have the genetic variant of the serotonin transporter associated with reduced activity, demonstrated that altering serotonin expression for a restricted period in early development has long-term effects. The implications for use of selective serotonin reuptake inhibitors in pregnancy (for the fetus) and with young children are substantial and require follow up. Extant studies in humans are too limited in scope and length of follow-up to determine if a similar process may be operating.

Other research examined genetic moderation of the effects of early stress or deprivation. Barr, Newman, Lindell, and colleagues (2004) considered how the effects of deprivation on alcohol consumption in a nonhuman primate model would be moderated by genetic risk. They found that the effects of early deprivation were limited to those animals at genetic risk (in this case, also involving the serotonin transporter). Gene-environment interactions involving the serotonin transporter for aggressive outcomes have been reported in both nonhuman primates (Suomi, 2003) and humans (Caspi et al., 2002). In the Dunedin study reported by Caspi and colleagues, the environmental risk was maltreatment. Given the apparent consistency of the genetic moderation effect, whereby the environmental risk exposure is observed for those at genetic risk but not for those not at genetic risk, it might well be anticipated that future research into early experiences will include genetic factors as possible modifiers of effects.

The move toward multivariate models of candidate mechanisms, such as genotype-environment interactions, may prove more directly valuable to updating conceptual models and informing clinical and preclinical human studies because they more closely resemble the context in which human research is necessarily conducted, namely, a risk context in which there are multiple competing risks operating.

Summary

Recent reports illustrate several lines of evidence of increasing conceptual and methodological leverage for testing hypotheses concerning the persisting effects of early experiences on psychological outcomes, including diversity of research designs (especially those with ecological validity) and increasing sophistication in identifying and measuring potential mechanisms. Research into the effects of how early environments shape long-term psychological development has increased dramatically in recent years, and will likely continue, as the relevance of the animal data becomes greater and more widely appreciated and the technological sophistication for studying mechanisms in humans is advanced.

EMPIRICAL ILLUSTRATIONS

Two of the most widely used paradigms for studying the persisting effects of early experience in animals are prenatal stress and deprivation in the early postnatal period. Findings from experiments of this sort provide some of the most important and compelling findings to suggest that early experiences/exposures do have robust causal and lasting effects on cognitive, social, and behavioral development, as well as on a variety of other physical and health outcomes. Research using these paradigms is comparatively rare in humans. In the case of prenatal stress/anxiety, several human studies have emerged in recent years and, although these studies vary widely in terms of sample size, length of follow-up, and measurement strategy, they offer a reliable check on the relevance of the animal studies to humans. In the case of deprivation, there are obvious ethical reasons such research cannot be planned; however, the increase in international adoption, often involving children who experienced severe deprivation prior to placement, provides a natural experiment to examine if there are persisting effects of early adversity in the absence of current adversity. This section donates considerable attention to research using the prenatal stress and early deprivation paradigms because these are dominant paradigms in animal studies and because of the availability of human data.

Prenatal Stress/Anxiety and Fetal and Child Development

Over 60 years ago, Sontag (1941) suggested that a mother's psychological well-being in pregnancy was important for the healthy development of the fetus. That proposal was not based on available empirical data, but it did reflect a widespread belief found in many cultures dating back many centuries. It was not until many decades later that adequate empirical data were available in humans to evaluate Sontag's hypothesis.

A biological-conceptual model explaining why prenatal exposure to anxiety/stress might lead to lasting disturbances in offspring has been discussed by many authors (Glover & O'Connor, in press; Huizink, Mulder, & Buitlaar, 2004; Maccari et al., 2003; Matthews, 2002; Schneider & Moore, 2000; Wadhwa, Dunkel-Schetter, Chicz-DeMet, Porto, & Sandman, 1996; Weinstock, 2001). In brief, the model states that an increase in anxiety/stress in pregnancy accentuates activation of the maternal HPA axis, leading ultimately to a release of cortisol (corticosterone in rodents); furthermore, the maternal cortisol released is not fully metabolized by the placenta and crosses to the fetus, where it influences the developing fetal HPA axis and, more broadly, fetal brain development. There are many other important features of this model. One is that the placenta has a major but not yet fully understood role in this process. For example, the placenta acts as a protective barrier against the transfer of maternal cortisol to the fetus via the enzyme 11b-HSD. Significantly, however, although estimates vary about the extent to which maternal cortisol may be metabolized, available data indicate that there is significant maternal-fetal cortisol transfer, with a correlation in one study of $r = .58$ (Gitau, Cameron, Fisk, & Glover, 1998). There is also evidence for a substantial correlation between maternal and fetal plasma levels of corticotropin-releasing hormone (Gitau, Fisk, & Glover, 2004) and testosterone (Gitau, Adams, Fisk, & Glover, 2004); on the other hand, no evidence of maternal-fetal transfer was observed for noradrenaline (Giannakoulopoulos, Teixeira, Fisk, & Glover, 1999). These data suggest that there is maternal-fetal transfer, at least for several important substances, and therefore provide a useful basis for hypothesizing how maternal psychological states and their hormonal accompaniments may influence fetal and child development.

Another aspect of the model, yet to be adequately tested in humans, is that the developing fetal HPA axis is especially vulnerable to input during this period, although the boundaries that define this period of sensitivity are not certain and may include postnatal development. An additional component of the model is that this process operates in the context of the dramatic normative increase in maternal cortisol from mid- to late pregnancy, the causes and implications of which are not fully understood. Thus, elevated levels of glucocorticoids are regarded as a potential risk for child and obstetric outcomes, not least of which is premature birth (Wadhwa, Sandman, & Garite, 2001). However, even if there are adverse effects in some situations, it is equally clear that glucocorticoids serve important biological functions, such as preventing/reducing respiratory distress syndrome in children at risk of being born premature (e.g., MacArthur, Howie, Dezoete, & Elkins, 1981). The trick has been to find meaningful individual differences in maternal cortisol during pregnancy, a time of considerable normative increase, and relate this to fetal/child outcomes. That is the missing piece of the research puzzle, at least in humans.

As a result of this increased sensitivity or vulnerability to environmental input in early development, the HPA axis in the offspring may be set or programmed in early life. That, at least, is the conclusion of several authors based on the animal research reviewed next. Furthermore, an essential application of the model is that, because cortisol is involved in numerous biological systems, the effects of increased cortisol would have nonspecific effects on the offspring. These nonspecific effects arise from the putatively direct involvement of HPA axis activity in, for example, cognitive function (Lemaire, Koehl, LeMoal, & Abrous, 2000), stress response to threat (Griffin, Skinner, Salm, & Birkle, 2003; Ward, Johnson, Salm, & Birkle, 2000), and immune function (Coe, Kramer, Kirschbaum, Netter, & Fuchs, 2002; Coe & Lubach, 2001; Kay, Tarcic, Poltyrev, & Weinstock, 1998; Sobrian, Vaughn, Bloch, & Burton, 1992), as well as from the indirect involvement of the HPA system in the opioid and catecholamine systems (Insel, Kinsley, Mann, & Bridges, 1990; Peters, 1988).

Animal Findings

The model just described is based on, and is the basis for, extensive experimental animal research. Convergent findings from animal studies link stress experienced by the mother during pregnancy with impaired adjustment in the offspring. This is a remarkably robust finding that has been reported in many labs in several countries and dates back decades (Ader & Belfer, 1962; Thompson, 1957). Behavioral/emotional disturbances most likely to be affected include attentional problems, anxiety/withdrawal, motor impairments, sleep dysregulation, and increased behavioral response to stress (Alonso, Navarro, Santana, & Rodriguez, 1997; Lehmann, Stohr, & Feldon, 2000; Schneider, Coe, & Lubach, 1992; Williams, Hennessy, & Davis, 1995). As noted earlier, neurodevelopmental and biological levels of analysis provide an equally compelling set of adverse outcomes, with the primary disturbances being an enhanced physiological reactivity to stress paradigms, impairments in immune functioning, compromised neurogenesis particularly in the hippocampus, and poor cardiovascular outcomes, among others (Baum, Ortiz, & Quan, 2003; Biagini & Pich, 2002; A. S. Clarke, Wittwer, Abbott, & Schneider, 1994; Dodic, Abouantoun, O'Connor, Wintour, & Moritz, 2002; Edwards, Dortok, Tam, Won, & Burnham, 2002; Henry et al., 1994; Schneider et al., 1998; Szurman, Pliska, Pokorby, & Welzl, 2000).

Much of this work implicates changes in the HPA axis as one of several potential mechanisms mediating this link (Maccari et al., 2003; Schneider & Moore, 2000; Weinstock, 2001). This is supported by the finding that mimicking the physiological effects of stress by injection of adrenocorticotropin hormone (in nonstressed pregnant animals) has the same effect as exposing pregnant mothers to uncontrollable environmental stress (Schneider et al., 1992).

Collectively, evidence from experimental manipulations in these studies implies that prenatal stress *causes* adverse outcomes. Given the strength of these findings, it is surprising that large-scale systematic research in this area has been conducted only in the past 5 years.

Human Studies of Prenatal Stress/Anxiety

In humans, there is strong evidence that prenatal maternal anxiety/stress is associated with *fetal* behavior (DiPietro, Costigan, & Gurewitsch, 2003; DiPietro, Hilton, Hawkins, Costigan, & Pressman, 2002; Monk et al., 2000; Monk, Myers, Sloan, Ellman, & Fifer, 2003; Sandman et al., 2003). These studies show that, for example, fetal behavior (e.g., activity level) and heart rate are associated with maternal anxiety/stress, measured either as a state or trait characteristic or when induced experimentally. Specifically, DiPietro, Hodgson, Costigan, and Johnson (1996) reported that greater perceived stress in pregnant women was associated with reduced fetal heart rate variability; that may be significant insofar as heart rate variability may increase the likelihood for or be a marker of temperamental behavioral inhibition.

There is also extensive support for a link between prenatal maternal stress/anxiety and obstetric outcome (Copper et al., 1996; Hedegaard, Henriksen, Sabroe, & Secher, 1993; Wadhwa, Sandman, Porto, Dunkel-Schetter, & Garite, 1993), possibly via an HPA-mediated mechanism (Wadhwa, Porto, Garite, Chicz-DeMet, & Sandman, 1998). In the large ($N = 8,719$) Danish study reported by Hedegaard et al., maternal self-reported general distress at 30 weeks gestation predicted an increased risk of preterm delivery, defined as less than 37 weeks. A conclusion from these studies is that maternal life stress or anxiety is associated with a clinically significant reduction in birthweight and/or gestational age at delivery. What is not clear from these studies is whether the increased risk of poor obstetric outcome is associated with longer-term effects on the child.

Evidence supporting a direct link between prenatal maternal anxiety/stress and child development is limited but growing. Perhaps the earliest study to examine the issue in humans was reported by Stott (1973). In a sample of approximately 200 women, Stott found that maternal stresses reported during pregnancy predicted offspring poor health and behavioral development in early childhood. Other studies also addressed this issue, but suffered from one or other important methodological limitation, such as failure to distinguish pre- from postnatal stress or reliance on retrospective report. Nevertheless, some of the results deserve attention. For example, in a subsample of approximately 700 children in the Oregon Adolescent Development Project, Allen and colleagues (Allen, Lewinsohn, & Seeley, 1998) found an association (odds ratios of 2 or more) between retrospectively reported maternal emotional health and diagnosed anxiety, depression, disruptive behavior, and substance use disorder in the child at midadolescence; the link with disruptive behavior persisted after multiple covariates were included, such as numerous indicators of current risk.

Several prospective, longitudinal studies of prenatal maternal anxiety or stress that have been reported in recent years suggest (1) that there is a dose-response association between maternal prenatal distress and child outcomes; (2) that the effects pertain to behavioral/emotional development and problems, cognitive development, and neurological development; (3) and that the effects persist into childhood and perhaps early adolescence. To a considerable extent, then, these findings paint a surprisingly similar picture to the one drawn from animal findings.

Results from the Avon Longitudinal Study of Parents and Children (ALSPAC), a prospective longitudinal study of women living in southwest England, provide some of the strongest evidence to date that maternal prenatal stress/anxiety predicts behavioral/emotional problems in the child. Specifically, mothers who reported high levels of anxiety in late pregnancy had an approximately twofold increased risk of children with significantly elevated behavioral/emotional problems at 47 months, even after other prenatal, obstetric, and psychosocial risks and *postnatal* anxiety and depression were statistically accounted for (O'Connor et al., 2002). Follow-up of the children to 81 months indicated that the effect of prenatal anxiety not only remained significant, but was of comparable magnitude to what was found earlier (O'Connor, Heron, Golding, Glover, & the ALSPAC Study Team, 2003). More recent data, based on a subsample of approximately 70 children at age $10\frac{1}{2}$ years, indicated that prenatal maternal anxiety predicted children's diurnal salivary cortisol, with significant effects obtained from morning and afternoon levels (O'Connor et al., 2005). Data of this kind are needed to establish the HPA axis as a mediating mechanism in humans.

In their longitudinal study of 72 families in Belgium, Van den Bergh and Marcoen (2004) reported modest to moderate links between prenatal maternal anxiety assessed between 12 and 22 weeks gestation and cross-informant composite measures of attention and externalizing and self-reported anxiety in 8- to 9-year-old children; these effects were obtained after accounting for key covariates, such as smoking in pregnancy and socioeconomic status, and postnatal anxiety. Results from these studies have been replicated, to a surprising degree, in large-scale studies (e.g., Rodriguez & Bohlin, 2005). In younger children, several groups (Buitelaar, 2003; Huizink, de Medina, Mulder, Visser, & Buitelaar, 2002; Susman, Schmeelk, Ponirakis, & Gariepy, 2001) reported links between prenatal maternal anxiety and temperament in the child, thus carrying on the research predicting fetal behavior and likely anticipating the behavioral/emotional problem outcomes reported in the longer-term follow-up studies. Although the data so far reported suggest that prenatal maternal anxiety or stress is associated with a broad range of behavioral/emotional problems in children, there is a consistent tendency among studies to find that predictions of attentional problems are particularly strong. What that means is not yet clear, and there may be a number of explanations involving attention, memory, and other brain regions and systems. Longer-term follow-up periods into adolescence are necessary to ascertain if the effect carries over to bona fide depression, which is rare prior to adolescence but is the phenotype most closely linked with HPA axis dysregulation. In this regard, a recently reported finding from Murray and colleagues (Halligan, Herbert, Goodyer, & Murray, 2004) on their follow-up study of children of mothers who experienced postnatal depression may be significant. They found that 13-year-olds exposed to postnatal maternal depression exhibited elevated levels of morning cortisol, a pattern also found in depressed adolescents. The risk involved (at least) *post*natal depression, but the study is suggestive in showing that early experience may confer long-term risk by altering HPA axis functioning.

Complementing the data on behavioral/emotional outcomes are several studies that assess cognitive and language outcomes in children. A Montreal study found that prenatal maternal stress associated with a severe ice storm accounted for modest but significant variation in children's mental and language development scores in infancy (Laplante et al., 2004). Comparable associations, although based on different measures of stress/anxiety and outcome, were reported in other studies (Brouwers, van Baar, & Pop, 2001; Huizink et al., 2002). Field and colleagues (2003) found that maternal anxiety in pregnancy was associated with children's greater relative right frontal EEG activation and lower vagal tone; associations were also reported with sleep and scores on the Brazelton neonatal scale.

Still other research shows that an important aspect of neurodevelopment, atypical laterality, is linked with maternal prenatal anxiety. In the ALSPAC sample, Glover, O'Connor, Heron, and Golding (2004) reported that maternal prenatal anxiety at 18 weeks gestation was associated with a 23% increase in the child showing mixed handedness, independent of parental handedness and obstetric and other antenatal risks. Remarkably consistent with those findings were results reported by Obel, Hedegaard, Henriksen, Secher, and Olsen (2003) in a Danish study of 824 women who were assessed prospectively from pregnancy. Data from the Glover et al. and Obel et al. analyses are similar in several respects, including the prediction to mixed handedness (rather than, e.g., left handedness) and the link with anxiety rather than depression (despite different measures used in each study), although they differed on when in pregnancy anxiety was most strongly linked with outcome.

Multiple mechanisms may account for a link between maternal anxiety/stress in pregnancy and poorer obstetric and child behavioral and cognitive outcomes. Hypothesized mechanisms involving HPA axis activity are dominant, but alternative or complementary mechanisms may be at work.

Among the more likely candidates is testosterone. Experimental animal research demonstrates that fetal testosterone programs the male fetal brain for its masculine role (Goy & McEwen, 1980). Human data also suggest that testosterone exposure in utero may have lasting effects. So, for example, girls with congenital adrenal hyperplasia, who have a deficiency of cortisol but an excess of testosterone, exhibit a higher level of rough-and-tumble play, greater likelihood of choosing masculine toys in play (Berenbaum & Hines, 1992; Hines, Golombok, Rust, Johnston, & Golding, 2002), and altered laterality (Nass et al., 1987). It is interesting to note that treatment for congenital adrenal hyperplasia is prenatal dexamethasone, a glucocorticoid (Meyer-Bahlburg et al., 2004). Prenatal maternal stress, which may raise fetal cortisol level, may also cause an increase in testosterone level, a mechanism that may explain a link with several outcomes associated with prenatal stress, such as mixed handedness, Attention-Deficit/Hyperactivity Disorder, and learning disabilities. Still other mechanisms may be at play, including the opioid system (Insel, 1990). Furthermore, in a normal population Sjostrom, Valentin, Thelin, and Marsal (1997) found that in the third trimester, fetuses of women with high trait anxiety scores had reduced blood flow in the umbilical artery and in the fetal middle cerebral artery. Comparable findings were reported by Teixeira, Fisk, and Glover (1999). The implication of this research is that, although involvement of the HPA axis seems very likely, there are a range of alternative and complementary mechanisms that also require further study.

Early Maternal Deprivation and Subsequent Child Attachment and Social Relationships

Maternal or caregiving deprivation is the second paradigm to study early experiences and their persisting effects. As in the case of prenatal stress, much of the information derives from animal experiments, such as the work of Harlow and colleagues (1969, 1970), although in this case, the impetus for much of the animal work was the early clinical observations of humans by Bowlby (1951), Spitz (1946), and others.

Animal Studies

It has been appreciated in the animal research literature for many years that the quality of early caregiving has immediate and lasting effects on the offspring (Harlow & Suomi, 1970; S. L. Ramey & Sackett, 2000; Sackett, 1965; Suomi,

1999). Recent animal studies have made considerable progress in understanding the neurophysiological basis of these early experiences on brain development, including the possibility that these alterations may serve to transmit risk to subsequent generations (Caldji et al., 2000; Champagne & Meaney, 2001; Francis, Champagne, & Meaney, 2000; Kraemer & Clarke, 1996; Weaver et al., 2004).

The elegant work of Cameron (2004) shows a clear timing effect of caregiving deprivation. In her studies, rhesus monkeys were placed in a social group with other monkeys. Baby monkeys were then separated from their mother: One group experienced separation at 1 week, another group at 1 month, a third group at 3 months, and a final group experienced separation at 6 months of age. Monkeys were provided adequate nutrition and received adequate physical care, and so it could be inferred that subsequent group differences that were observed were due to the timing of maternal separation. Behavioral observations of the monkeys in the four distinct groups were recorded in several settings, and accounts were made of several types of behavior, including affective and affiliative behaviors and response to threat. Findings indicated that, across a range of behaviors and settings, consistent differences emerged, with monkeys who experienced early separation showing generally less competent, more distressed behavior. Biological differences were also observed that may underlie these behavioral differences, including neuronal development in the prefrontal cortex and gene expression in the amygdala.

Particularly interesting from Cameron's (2004) studies was the finding that monkeys separated at 1 week were different in kind from other monkeys, including those separated at 1 month. Whereas monkeys who experienced separation at 1 month showed modest behavioral abnormalities (e.g., excessive clinging) compared with the monkeys in the later-separated groups, monkeys experiencing separation at 1 week exhibited flagrantly more disturbed and abnormal behavior that was not observed in any other group. Monkeys separated at 1 week were especially distinguishable from monkeys in all other groups on several indicators, particularly involving seeking comfort. For example, only those monkeys who experienced maternal separation at 1 week showed little interest in seeking out others for comfort or protection. The meaning of and motivation for attachment and social behavior in these 1-week separated monkeys, when such opportunities were later observed, was clearly different from that in monkeys who experienced separation later in development. Arguably, these monkeys did not develop a selective attachment relationship with the mother, which is the foundation for attach-

ment. This is an intriguing explanation for the divergent behavioral effects because a strikingly similar pattern has been noted in a minority of children who experienced early severe and prolonged institutional deprivation and did not form early selective or discriminating attachments (O'Connor, Marvin, et al., 2003; Zeanah, Smyke, & Dumitrescu, 2002).

Human Studies

In addition to Bowlby (1982), one of the major contributors to research on the effects of early caregiving deprivation on psychological development is Rene Spitz (e.g., 1965), whose work is notable for its use of observational methods, interest in individual differences in normal and abnormal development, emphasis on experience over fantasy, and interest in stepping away from psychoanalytic structure and dynamics in the infant that were out of line with what is known about cognitive development (Peterfreund, 1978).

Among children whom he described as showing anaclitic depression, Spitz (1965) noted that all children affected (19 of 123 studied in the nursery setting) experienced a prolonged (defined as 3 months) separation from mother between the 6th and 8th month of life. He further noted that, when mothers were able to return to the children, most of the children recovered. Nevertheless, he wrote, "It is doubtful if the recovery is complete; I would assume that the disturbance will leave scars which will show in later years; conclusive evidence of this is still lacking" (p. 272). Spitz provided further follow-up data on the children and, from these data, concluded that reunion with the mother was associated with a substantial gain in developmental quotient points that were lost during the separation period; infants who experienced a separation lasting longer than 5 months did not show recovery in the follow-up period. Progress and disturbance were perhaps most easily quantified in terms of developmental quotient, but disturbance and recovery in emotional and social behavior were parallel.

The early human studies on the effects of deprivation by Spitz, Bowlby, and others suffered from methodological shortcomings of several types and were justifiably criticized (A. M. Clarke & Clarke, 2000; Rutter, 1981). Yet, several of the methodological limitations of these earlier studies have proved difficult to resolve (e.g., for ethical reasons). Nevertheless, early clinical investigators were sensitive to many of these limitations. So, for example, Spitz (1965) noted that the child's relationship with the mother prior to separation was a strong determinant of the child's adjustment to the separation.

More recent data from human studies have provided a second major wave of findings on the effects of caregiving deprivation, as several groups in the United States, Canada, the United Kingdom, Greece, and elsewhere have tracked the development of children who experienced early institutional deprivation. These studies provide the sort of natural experiment to examine the effects of early caregiving deprivation on children's development because exposure to deprivation was relatively precisely timed and restricted to the early months or years of life, after which the children were adopted into low- to normal-risk families. Thus, these studies are positioned to examine whether the effects of early deprivation persist in the absence of ongoing and concurrent deprivation. None of these studies is immune from methodological shortcomings, which is to say that whatever their benefits, natural experiments cannot provide the methodological control found in planned experimental studies.

Research on the effects of caregiving deprivation on attachment and social behavior includes studies of institutional settings that vary widely in terms of the degree and severity of deprivation; however, lack of opportunities to form selective or discriminating attachment relationships is a major commonality, and likely a causal factor (Bowlby, 1951; Chisholm, 1998; Freud & Burlingham, 1973; O'Connor et al., 2000; Provence & Lipton, 1962; Roy, Rutter, & Pickles, 2004; Spitz, 1965; Tizard & Rees, 1975; Vorria et al., 2003; Wolkind, 1974). There is remarkable consistency among studies in describing a behavioral disturbance that is referred to in the *Diagnostic and Statistical Manual of Mental Disorders,* fourth edition, as the inhibited form of a Reactive Attachment Disorder. Children exhibiting this disturbance show a marked indiscriminate social approach to strangers, an apparent willingness to wander off, and a failure to check back with caregivers in situations that would be expected to curtail exploration, increase wariness, and increase proximity to a caregiver. Questions remain about basic features of the phenotype, but at least in early childhood, there is growing evidence that this disturbance can be differentiated from forms of insecure attachment found in children who had the opportunity to form selective or discriminating attachments to caregivers, however insensitive those caregivers were (O'Connor, Marvin, et al., 2003).

Findings from the English and Romanian Adoptee Study has provided some of the strongest evidence to date that early institutional deprivation is associated with persisting disturbances in attachment and social relations in the absence of ongoing deprivation. That study followed up a sample of 165 children adopted into the United Kingdom after experiencing institutional deprivation that ranged from the first few months of life to 3½ years; these children were studied alongside 52 early-placed, within-U.K. adoptees who did not experience institutional deprivation. Children were extensively assessed at ages 4, 6, and 11 years (O'Connor et al., 2000; O'Connor, Marvin, et al., 2003; Rutter, O'Connor, & the English and Romanian Adoptee Study Team, 2004).

Several findings stand out from the longitudinal follow-up. First, at each assessment, the effect of duration of institutionalization was strongly associated with attachment disorder-related behavior in a dose-response manner. The absence of a threshold effect is an important observation insofar as it contrasts with the pattern from the animal data, including data for nonhuman primates. Second, early institutional deprivation predicted *persisting* deficits. For example, analyses of data collected at ages 4 and 6 years found considerable stability of individual differences ($r = .59$, $p < .001$) and no mean decrease in disturbances over time. This pattern of persisting problems is in contrast to other outcomes for which considerable improvement was observed in the same time period, notably quasi-autistic behavior (Rutter et al., 1999). Data on attachment relationships at age 11 years suggested a mixed picture of persistence and improvement (O'Connor, 2003). On the one hand, there was still a robust dose-response connection between duration of deprivation and disinhibited behavior at age 11 years. The magnitude of association between duration of deprivation and total score on the disinhibited attachment disorder behavior scale was nearly identical at ages 6 and 11 years ($r = .31$ and $r = .38$, respectively) for the 150 children on whom data were available. On the other hand, fewer children at age 11 years exhibited symptoms; for example, in those children adopted after 2 years of age, the rate of severe attachment disturbance decreased from 33% at age 6 years to 24% at age 11 years. Of particular importance, however, the overall decrease in symptoms was comparable across all children regardless of the age at entry into the United Kingdom. Thus, we can reject the possibility that the overall decrease in severe attachment disturbance in the Romanian sample was attributed to the children who were older at adoption (and who therefore had spent less time in a normal caregiving environment at the earlier assessment) "catching up" to the earlier placed children. Also, because the definition of attachment disorder symptoms was constructed for preschool-age children, it is possible that the disturbances seen at age 11 years did not carry the same meaning as at the earlier assessments (in fact, basic research is still needed to define the phenotype of attachment disorder past preschool age). If that is the case, some of the decrease found may reflect a decreased age sensitivity in defining the disturbance.

A second key finding was that there was substantial individual variation in attachment outcomes. Whereas some children showed severe impairment according to multiple indicators of attachment disturbance, other children showed no such disturbances and were classified as exhibiting a secure attachment according to the modified separation-reunion procedures (O'Connor, Marvin, et al., 2003). A comparable degree of variation was even observed among the sample of later-placed children who experienced at least 2 years and up to 3½ years of institutional deprivation. Indeed, it is striking how much variation there was given the duration and severity of deprivation.

A third finding of note was that individual differences in attachment outcomes and the degree of persistence were not apparently related to characteristics in the adoptive home environment (e.g., parent-child interaction quality observed in the home). The persistence of effect in a minority of children, despite many years in a low- to normal-risk family environment, is incompatible with the life span or cumulative effects hypotheses: In the absence of concurrent adversity, the effects of institutionalization on child-parent attachment disturbances persisted in a sizable minority of children.

The biological bases of these disturbances in attachment and social relationships have not yet been identified, but several candidates exist. Oxytocin is an obvious candidate because it has been linked in animal studies with parenting, affiliation, pair bonding, and other forms of social relationships (Carter, 1998; Fleming & Corter, 1988; Francis, Young, Meaney, & Insel, 2002; Insel, 2003; Lovic, Gonzalez, & Fleming, 2001). Progress in this area in humans may be limited, however, because the meaning of peripheral oxytocin (i.e., outside the central nervous system) is unknown and may not be closely connected with oxytocin in the brain. A second line of research might pick up on the observation that a minority of children who experience deprivation do not seem to find social relationships especially rewarding or pleasurable. That is, not only are there clear deficits in social connections, but there is an additional difficulty of these children not seeming to want to engage with others. That, at least, is a finding from clinical and anecdotal reports. Interestingly, a similar observation is made of monkeys who experienced early deprivation (Cameron, 2004). A search for reward systems in the brain might yield insights into the motivational aspects of attachment and how they may be undermined by early deprivation

(Insel, 2003). Involvement of dopaminergic pathways might be relevant here and might explain not only disturbances in attachment behavior, but also disturbances in attention that are commonly reported in children with attachment disorder behavior (O'Connor et al., 2000). A separate line of investigation, using a genetic knock-out mice model, has shown that animals lacking the μ-opioid receptors show deficits in several types of attachment behavior (Moles, Kieffer, & D'Amato, 2004). The authors suggested that their observations may provide a basis for severe attachment disturbances found in children with Autism or Reactive Attachment Disorder. By showing that severe disruption in the opioid system can result in severe attachment and social behavior abnormalities, these findings offer a further focus for biologically based human research.

In addition to these neurochemical alterations induced by early experiences, imaging studies are beginning to piece together how deprivation might affect brain development. Chugani and colleagues (2001) found reduced glucose metabolism in children adopted into the United States from institutions in Romania compared with adult and child epileptic comparisons. Several brain regions were affected, including orbital frontal cortex, prefrontal cortex, and medial temporal structures that include the amygdala and hippocampus. The findings are of interest because they support previous animal work and are consistent with prior neuropsychological research on brain regions involved in social and cognitive deficits. Lesion studies in animals have also shown that damage to the hippocampal formation is associated with a range of behavioral disturbances, such as stereotypies and reductions in social interactions (Bachevalier, Alvarado, & Malkova, 1999). More imaging studies are needed to support these findings on the structural and functional consequences on the brain of early deprivation; this area will likely gain greater attention in the near future. The implication from these studies is that a multitude of biological mechanisms may be at play and may interact with one another in producing vulnerability.

Given the complex nature of the behavioral effects that have been reported in most studies, it is probably unrealistic to expect to find disturbance in a single brain region to account for these observations.

Additional Illustrations

The focus on prenatal maternal stress/anxiety and caregiving deprivation is not meant to imply that these are the only paradigms considered in research testing early effects hypotheses. Many other examples of environmental experience have been studied, and, indeed, not all have concluded that early experience is in some way essential. For example, Klaus and Kennell's (1976) hypothesis of a sensitive period after birth during which the mother needs to bond with the child to ensure healthy normal development was ultimately rejected, notwithstanding the animal data that continue to show evidence for this effect.

Another example of environmental adversity that is being increasingly incorporated into research to assess the persisting effects of the early environment is maltreatment (Nemeroff, 2004). It is now established that child maltreatment is associated with a range of adverse biobehavioral outcomes via a number of mediating mechanisms (Cicchetti, 2004). Several studies have sought to examine if these adverse outcomes can be linked specifically to early maltreatment (e.g., Bolger & Patterson, 2001). In general, available data do not allow firm conclusions to be drawn about the effects of early maltreatment per se because of the continuity in adverse caregiving environments experienced by children who experience early maltreatment. On the other hand, data from cross-sectional, prospective, and follow-back studies all suggest that there is at least correlational evidence that early maltreatment is linked with a number of early-appearing psychological vulnerabilities, including perception, decoding and response to facial expression of emotion (Pollak & Kistler, 2002; Pollak, Klorman, Thatcher, & Cicchetti, 2001), neurohormonal changes (Cicchetti & Rogosch, 2001; Teicher et al., 2003), stress reactivity (Heim et al., 2000), structural changes in the brain (Teicher et al., 2003), and many behavioral disturbances (Kim & Cicchetti, 2004; Rogosch & Cicchetti, 2004; Toth, Cicchetti, Macfie, Maughan, & VanMeenen, 2000). These findings provide compelling evidence of the types of effects associated with maltreatment and identify plausible mechanisms that might mediate long-term links between early maltreatment and long-term outcomes. If there are lasting biobehavioral effects of maltreatment on health and disease, the high prevalence of maltreatment means that this particular risk carries very substantial implications for public health.

Summary

Available data from human studies of prenatal maternal stress and postnatal deprivation are consistent with some of the key findings from animal studies in many ways. Most important, there is now evidence for lasting effects of these two types of early experiences. However, whereas sensitive period and programming models can readily account for the animal data, these models are less able to account for the extant human data. That is seen in the case of the severe attachment disturbances associated with institutional deprivation. Findings from these studies challenge the existing models of early experience, as none is able to handle the combination of wide individual differences, a dose-response pattern of association, and, in only a minority of cases, persisting disturbance in the absence of contemporaneous risk. Thus, simple versions of many models of early experience can be rejected. Developing alternative models to explain how and under what circumstances early experiences may have lasting effects may benefit from considering studies that make greater use of experimental designs, notably the prevention and intervention research reviewed in the next section.

IMPLICATIONS FOR PREVENTION AND INTERVENTION

This section examines how findings from prevention and intervention studies can contribute to the debate on the persisting effects of early experiences. Several themes are emphasized. First, although many prevention and intervention studies are predicated on the view that early experiences can have persisting effects, few are specifically designed to test this premise. A second theme is that prevention and intervention studies can provide particularly strong leverage in resolving questions of early experience because of the experimental control they afford. The third theme is that public and policy debates in this area are well under way, and there are examples of good but also bad clinical practice linked to notions of how early experiences shape psychological development.

Targets of Treatment and Expected Gains

Developmental frameworks for preventive interventions now in place (Coie et al., 1993; Conduct Problems Prevention Research Group, 1992, 2002; Hinshaw, 2002; Reiss & Price, 1996) emphasize child development and the developmental challenges facing the child. Almost without exception, existing frameworks adopt a life span perspective on how early experiences—whether it is adversity or treatment—shape long-term development. Within this perspective, the question of whether or not the individual returns to normal development following intervention is attributable to receiving an adequate and sufficiently targeted dose of intervention for the range of problems exhibited, and not because the intervention was provided "too late" in development. To the extent that timing is important, it is not because of assumptions of sensitive periods. Rather, interventions applied earlier in development may be more effective because it is easier to bring back to a "normal" developmental trajectory an individual who has only recently strayed onto a deviant course. Later interventions can be just as effective as early ones, but need to be far more extensive than earlier interventions and, at the extreme, might involve inpatient care. In other words, age of the child predicts the intensity of the intervention rather than possible intervention effectiveness (Cowen & Durlak, 2000; Olds, 2002; C. T. Ramey & Ramey, 1998).

The notion that an intervention may be especially effective in preventing disturbance if it is delivered at a sensitive period has been rejected in some quarters; in others, it is held up as a distinct possibility. This debate has not advanced, however, because there remain questions about the meaning of timing, as implied earlier, and there are considerable practical difficulties of delivering "comparable" interventions to children of very different ages. In the area of parent-child relationship quality, for example, effective interventions exist for children of all ages, from infants to adolescents. However, the kinds of interventions developed for these different age groups take different forms and are typically based on different theoretical models. Whereas parent-child interventions for infants and toddlers tend to adopt an attachment theory focus, interventions for school-age and older children tend to adopt a social learning theory model. Thus, at present, it is difficult to see how timing could be injected into a study design, at least in the area of parent-child relationship and child adjustment, one of the most active areas of intervention research: Timing would be confounded with treatment type.

Intervention timing is thought to be important in a variety of other contexts, including those involving psychological mechanisms. In the area of cognitive-behavioral therapy for children, there is some evidence that older children respond more positively and that this may be accounted for by the greater sophistication to access cognitive processes that mediate treatment (Durlak, Fuhrman, & Lampman, 1991). Another example concerns intervention for substance use, for which there is a suggestion that programs are most effective if delivered prior to the initiation of or experimentation with substance use; interventions delivered after that period may be ineffective (Dishion, Kavanagh, Schneiger, Nelson, & Kaufman, 2002). Thus, in this case, timing may need to be defined in terms of stage of disturbance or exposure level or opportunities.

Research on mood disorders suggests that timing of the disorder may be important for intervention and recovery. For example, several studies show that first episodes of de-pressive illness may be linked with psychosocial factors, but subsequent episodes are more autonomous from psychosocial risk, and that may be increasingly so with repeated episodes (Post, 1992). The implication is that the initial episode may make the individual more vulnerable to subsequent episodes because of neurobiological changes brought on by the illness (Post, Weiss, & Leverich, 1994; see also, Clarke & O'Callaghan, 2003). If that is so, the treatment implication is that the earlier treatment is administered, the less likely the individual will be neurobiologically sensitized and vulnerable to recurrent episodes. In this case, timing is not tied to development, but to the presumed progression of the disease and its effect on the brain.

As some of these examples illustrate, the suggestion that timing is important is not the same as suggesting that early intervention is essential. Adolescence is characterized by considerable biological changes, such as neuronal overproduction to alterations in neurotransmitter levels and genetic expression. This has led several researchers to question whether the periadolescent period might constitute an opportune time to intervene to reduce previously induced biological vulnerabilities. Evidence of success has been shown in a rat model, in which adolescent-onset treatment was effective for reducing the social behavioral effects of prenatal maternal stress (Morley-Fletcher, Rea, Maccari, & Laviola, 2003). At a minimum, these data suggest that the window of opportunity to alter biological mechanisms may extend beyond early developmental periods, or that windows of opportunity reopen (possibly involving different mechanisms from those involved at earlier developmental stages). What is not clear is if that window of opportunity is continuously open or, like brain development, shows marked discontinuity in development. Further research along these lines will likely yield important clinical insights and basic information on the malleability of central mechanisms involved in mediating the effects of early stress exposure.

Finally, there is growing evidence of a connection between the mechanism thought to account for persisting effects and the focus of (biologically based) treatments. Because HPA axis disregulation is an established risk for and correlate of psychiatric disturbance, and because conventional pharmacological agents are also known to affect HPA axis functioning, it is currently a focus for treatment (Arborelius, Owens, Plotsky, & Nemeroff, 1999; Kaufman, Plotsky, Nemeroff, & Charney, 2000). If treatments of this sort prove effective, then the benefits can be measured in terms of greater clinical options and in terms of scientific evidence of the correctability of HPA axis disregulation—

an issue about which there is little available information in humans. Treatment failures would also offer important lessons. Thus, resistance of the HPA axis to pharmacological intervention in adulthood might signal a degree of programmability that may match what has been found in the animal literature.

Model, Illustrative, and Sample Intervention Programs

As noted, very few examples of a timing effect on intervention are available. Nevertheless, examples do exist of early interventions having robust and lasting effects, with most focusing on some aspect of academic success/school readiness (Barnett, 1995; Campbell & Ramey, 1994; Reynolds, 1994; Reynolds & Robertson, 2003). One such example is the Abecedarian Project, a longitudinal study of the effectiveness of an intervention with high-risk children who were randomly assigned to treatment or control conditions (Campbell, Pungello, Johnson, Burchinal, & Ramey, 2002; Campbell & Ramey, 1994). Three treatment groups were compared with the control group. One group of children were given the intervention from infancy through 3 years of schooling; a second group received the preschool treatment only; a third group received only the school-based treatment. Each group consisted of approximately 25 children. Findings at age 12 years (Campbell & Ramey, 1994) indicated that the children who received the continuous intervention from infancy scored highest on intellectual and achievement tests; children who received only the preschool intervention performed lower, and lower still were children who received the intervention only from school-age. Each of these intervention groups performed better than the control children, but all groups performed worse than a nonrisk comparison sample. Interestingly, what was important for predicting age 12 outcomes was whether or not the child received the intervention in the preschool period. A further follow-up at age 21 years revealed that the early intervention continued to have long-term effects on cognitive and academic outcomes. However, the role of early experience in this study remains unproven because the children who received the early intervention received more years of intervention than those who received the intervention starting in school.

Reports of findings from the Chicago Child-Parent Center (CPC; Reynolds, Temple, Robertson, & Mann, 2001) program are important for additional reasons. The CPC provided comprehensive educational, family, and health services to children living in 25 sites in Chicago character-

ized by dense areas of poverty. Long-term follow-up analyses of the children in the study contrasted those in the index group of 989 children who received preschool and school-age services with a comparison group of 550 children who received alternative early intervention programs (these comparison children were entitled to services given their level of poverty, and so no child could be refused treatment). The CPC has advantages of an effectiveness rather than efficacy design, but also has some attendant methodological disadvantages, such as a comparison group that received uncertain treatment and variation in the amount and duration of treatment in the index group.

Analyses of outcomes at ages 18 to 20 indicate that children in the CPC preschool program had higher rates of high school completion by age 20 than comparison children (49.7% versus 38.5%) and a lower rate of school dropout than comparison children (46.7% versus 55%). Program effects were also detected in official arrest data; for example, 16.9% of children in the CPC program were arrested by age 18, compared with 25.1% in the comparison group. Program effects also carried over to need for remedial services; for example, 14.4% of the index children required special education placement, compared with 24.6% in the comparison group. These findings attest to significant and clinically meaningful differences and the persistence of effect into late adolescence/early adulthood despite the program's officially terminating in third grade.

One other feature of the study is that not all children received the intervention from preschool through school-age. Therefore, as with the Abecedarian Project, it is possible to contrast the outcomes of children who received early intervention only—in the CPC case, through preschool—with children who received more protracted intervention—in the CPC case, into third grade. It may not be possible to make any strong deductions from these comparisons because the opportunity to compare these subgroups of children arose serendipitously rather than through design. Nevertheless, the results are of interest. In particular, findings showed that school-age participation was not associated with a significant gain over the preschool intervention for the educational attainment or delinquency outcomes, but did confer additional benefit for the use of school remedial services. Specifically, participation in the school program (for at least 1 additional year) predicted modestly lower rates of special education, grade retention, and years of special education services compared with children whose receipt of the intervention stopped after preschool (Reynolds et al., 2001). That finding suggests that we might expect some but not other outcomes to show an effect in direct proportion to the length of intervention, whereas other outcomes may show effects particular to early intervention per se. What cannot be easily predicted from existing data from the CPC or any other study is which outcomes might benefit from ongoing, cumulative impact and which outcomes seem more sensitive to early intervention effects.

Another model program of early intervention comes from the well-known work of Olds, Kitzman, and colleagues (Kitzman et al., 1997; Olds et al., 1997, 2004). Their nurse home visiting program, now replicated in diverse urban, rural, and minority samples, has shown that interventions starting in pregnancy have effects that may last into adulthood and affect a range of outcomes that were not initially targeted. That means that the cost-effectiveness is substantial (as well as complex to calculate) and that program effects probably come about via broad-ranging and interconnected psychosocial processes.

These studies may not have been designed to demonstrate that it is early experience per se that matters, but they do demonstrate the positive cumulative or even multiplicative effects of influencing the developmental trajectory at an early age.

An additional set of intervention studies deserving attention targets children who experienced extreme deprivation. Zeanah and colleagues (2002) reported that improving the child : staff ratio and increasing consistency of staff led to sizable decreases in severely disturbed or disordered attachment behavior associated with institutional rearing. This is one of the few instances of how an enriched environment, or, more accurately, a reduced deprivation environment, can lead to positive improvements in humans (A. D. B. Clarke, Clarke, & Reiman, 1958; S. L. Ramey & Sackett, 2000; see also, Duyme, Dumaret, & Tomkiewicz, 1999). Given the unfortunate and inevitable commonplace nature of institutions to care for children because of war and parental death by AIDS and other factors, further research of this type is needed to show how institutional care may be organized to reduce the likelihood of those disturbances most closely linked with institutional rearing.

Studies that follow children who were adopted following institutional rearing provide an important and complex footnote to the findings on intervention. Although none of these studies was designed as an experimental intervention, each examines the effect of probably the most extreme type of intervention: adoption. For some outcomes, notably physical development, catch-up may be swift, dramatic, and, in many cases, essentially complete. However, these same longitudinal follow-up studies also show limited evidence for complete catch-up in other areas, most notably social outcomes. In the specific case of attachment, for example (O'Connor et al., 2000), the amount of improvement observed in children following adoption was modest or even undetectable between 4 and 6 years, and what positive change that was observed could not be explained by the later-placed children catching up to their earlier-placed peers' level of functioning.

Not all early interventions are effective, or may be effective only for subsamples of those individuals treated. For example, the 8-year follow-up of a large sample of children who received an early intervention to compensate for low birthweight found no lasting overall effects. Intervention effects were detected, but only in the heavier low birthweight premature children (McCarton et al., 1997). That may well have been expected and may have a compelling biosocial explanation. Findings from the Infant Health and Development Project noted earlier illustrate that intervention studies may need to target vulnerable individuals, even in already carefully targeted samples. In other words, as our models of biopsychosocial risk become more sophisticated, so, too, must our expectations of for whom interventions would be most effective.

Finally, it is worth noting that there are many naturally occurring examples of interventions that can test timing effects. The most common is age at starting school and, more broadly, the recognition that schooling per se (i.e., without any form of additional enrichment) is a type of intervention that has beneficial effects (Gorman & Pollitt, 1996).

Results from many projects, including the ones already reviewed, demonstrate that early intervention projects can alter life course trajectories and that the gains in important public health outcomes may more than offset costs of service delivery. On the other hand, many of these same studies show that the outcomes of the treated group are still poor relative to those in the nonrisk comparison group, indicating that even the most effective preventive interventions delivered early in development may not eliminate the effects of the preexisting risk.

Public and Policy Debating Points

Several books (e.g., Bruer, 1999) have taken on the question of whether the 1st months or years of life represent a critical or sensitive period in human development, with the corollary that it is essential that interventions are delivered during this period if the effects of early adversity are to be eliminated and optimal development is to be achieved. A key thesis of Bruer's book is that the case for early intervention has not yet been proven, and that the neuroscientific evidence collated to support such claims is preliminary or, in some cases, overextended. That view has generated controversy but is consistent with the available evidence. His thesis was premised on the fact that there are comparatively few interventions that are designed to test the early (versus later) experience hypothesis. This is not to say that we do not have evidence that early interventions are not effective or do not have lasting effect. As described above, there are many such demonstrations. Instead, the point is that most of the interventions showing substantial clinical effect cannot rule out the hypothesis that similar interventions delivered later in development would not have comparable effects. That is an issue that may not be at the forefront of social policy (offered an option of a proven intervention, most clinicians and policymakers would be happy to advocate for it, whether or not it supports a particular early experience hypothesis), but it is an important scientific issue that has gone underresearched.

Whatever the state of the debate of the role of early experiences, there is general recognition that, ultimately, understanding the effects of early experience on later development is not a purely scientific matter, but one with public health implications (e.g., Dawson, Ashman, & Carver, 2000). There are, in fact, many examples in clinical practice that are based on judgments about the effects of early experience and the mechanisms by which early adversity has persisting effect, including bad practice. It is worth describing one example to illustrate that there are important costs associated with wrong theory and distorted notions of early experience.

As discussed earlier, there is considerable evidence in humans that early caregiving deprivation is associated with severe and persisting disturbances in attachment and social relations in a minority of children. Parents' concerns about these children, many of whom were adopted from overseas institutions, were often met with uncertain and inadequate responses from child mental health professionals. Many parents then turned to alternative treatments that were aggressively promoted for children with a real or suspected Reactive Attachment Disorder. The treatment promoted for these children in select circles is broadly referred to as holding therapy. This treatment approach is based on "rage reduction" techniques, which presumed that the disordered child put up defenses against the outside world because of past experiences of trauma. There was the further proposal that radical forms of intervention were necessary to "break through" the child's defenses to access the child's hurt/trauma. Once accessed, that early trauma could then be resolved and normal development would proceed. These interventions also borrowed and distorted features of attachment theory to justify the holding treatments. So, for

example, it was proposed that the child's lack of sensitive care and touch in infancy could be redressed by intensive holding in childhood; some practitioners even coerced holding to stimulate the regression to infancy that was thought to be necessary for successful treatment. Underlying this treatment were proposals that the effect of early caregiving deprivation could be permanent, had a presumed (but not confirmed) neuroscientific foundation, and required radical intensive intervention to resume normal development.

It is hardly surprising that there is no evidence that these methods are effective in treating attachment problems; that could have been predicted from their mistaken conceptual foundation. Nevertheless, these treatments continue to be aggressively promoted on the Internet and elsewhere. This is despite the fact that several professional organizations have made statements exposing the coercive form of holding therapy as dangerous and the existence of legislation specifically prohibiting coercive forms of holding therapy in several states. The case of holding therapy for attachment disorder is perhaps the most striking example of how misapplication and misunderstanding of theory and research on early experience have had dangerous consequences for children and their families.

One likely reason this form of inadequate and dangerous treatment has persisted is the slow and muted style in which evidence-based clinical investigators have engaged in the debate on this treatment. Fortunately, that is now changing, but evidence-based practitioners have an uphill battle to inform the public and correct widely dispersed mistaken notions concerning early experience and psychological development.

Summary

A thesis of this chapter is that intervention studies will likely play an important role in differentiating alternative hypotheses concerning the role of early experience on long-term adjustment. This view derives, in large part, from the difficulty of naturalistic studies to disentangle early effects from cumulative or concurrent experiences. However, such studies are rare, and what little data do exist are insufficient to test alternative predictions concerning the mechanisms by which early experiences confer risk for long-term adaptation. To date, the role of timing of the intervention as a predictor of program success is less certain because there are very few interventions comparing the effectiveness of interventions delivered early versus later in development.

CONCLUSIONS AND FUTURE DIRECTIONS

This concluding section focuses on some of the promising future directions for research on early experiences. This discussion is organized by three overarching themes: the notion and strategy of translational research, individual differences, and the use of research designs and paradigms.

Translational Research

The concept of translational research is now firmly rooted as a mission or a strategy for research. It is a concept that needs some unpacking. Several kinds of translations are implied by the term, including preclinical to clinical research and the move from basic biological processes to behavioral phenotypes that attract clinical attention. Regardless of which sort of translation is implied, however, the underlying general notion is that there is substantial basic knowledge that, for one reason or another, has not yet filtered into practice, whether the level of practice is the individual clinician or a community-level initiative.

Future research on the role of early experiences needs to heed this call to translational research. That can be interpreted and accomplished in a number of ways. One is by focusing on the concept of timing in development. Basic research findings from animal experiments have made a strong case for timing, based on a growing database of ontogenetic periods and processes. On the other hand, this information has not been widely incorporated into human research using observational or intervention designs. That may reflect the only recent shift in considering the hypothesis that there may be persisting effects of early experience or genuine difficulties in mapping the boundaries of potentially sensitive or vulnerable periods in human development. Nevertheless, research of this sort may yield valuable basic and applied information. Intervention studies are now moving to a point of asking for whom interventions are effective. A somewhat parallel question can be added to that list: Intervention studies are now justified in asking when in development the intervention is likely to have the strongest effect.

A second form of translation needing additional attention is that linking brain, biology, and behavior. One of the potentially more promising avenues for this sort of integrative research is to incorporate biological mechanisms within experimental intervention designs. The benefits of such a study are clear enough: We need to understand not only that the intervention effects a behavioral change, but also what the underlying and sustaining mechanisms are.

The early intervention/prevention studies may be especially well suited to this sort of translational research. To date, many of these studies do not include measures of brain development, but they do point to a pattern of behavioral development and change whose biological basis may be very amenable to current assessment techniques (Bachevalier et al., 1999; Goldman-Rakic, Isseroff, Schwartz, & Bugbee, 1983). The conceptual case for multivariate, multilevel, biopsychosocial models of applied research is compelling. Promoting further progress in this area is not merely a matter of a conceptual imperative, however, but will require additional training and, likely, creative funding mechanisms.

Individual Differences

One of the most striking observations from human research that has followed children who experienced severe early adversity is the wide array of individual differences in long-term adjustment. There are numerous examples for each of many major serious risk factors. Findings of children who experienced early institutional deprivation are perhaps most telling about the importance of individual differences. These children have experienced arguably the most severe form of adversity—far in excess of high-risk samples in most studies—and for a prolonged period of time. In the course of their deprivation experience, the children completely missed out on sensitive parenting and attachment experiences, affect attunement, opportunities for emotion regulation, cognitive stimulation such as scaffolding, and many other psychological processes that have been linked with healthy development in diverse samples of children. Yet, although there are clear difficulties in the long-term social and cognitive development of *some* children, many children have shown remarkable resilience and appear to be functioning well within normal limits; other children are thriving. Given that at least some of these studies used systematic ascertainment and stratified sampling strategies, we can rule out the possibility that there is a major selection bias in those who participate in this sort of research (in any event, the degree of individual differences is substantial regardless of how the sample was obtained). Arguably, then, one of the most important lessons from contemporary studies of children adopted from institutions is that individual differences are retained under even the most severe forms of environmental deprivation. It is interesting that there is not such an obviously wide degree of individual differences and outcome diversity in the animal research.

What are the implications of the strength of individual differences for future research? Two are suggested. One is that research hypotheses need to be tailored more to individual differences and the certainty of outcome diversity, whether the exposure is adversity or, just as important, intervention. Predicting an overall group change is obviously important in showing that an intervention may have import value in serving a wide and diverse community. Alernatively, variation within the group that received the intervention is likely to be as large and as important as the variation between the treated and nontreated groups. Accounting for this within-group variation is important both for refining the interventions and for informing developmental theory.

The second implication is that individual differences are a natural conceptual framework for incorporating and integrating research on genetics, early life experiences, and life course experiences in predicting well-being. Inevitably, however, there are statistical power considerations that will limit how broad the research models can be, and that may prove especially problematic for specific risks (be they genetic or environmental) that are expected to have important but small effect sizes.

Research Paradigms

The third area of future study concerns the paradigms used in animal and human research, particularly their compatibility and ecological validity. The basic underlying question here is one of generalizability: Can findings from one type of study of early adversity project general lessons for early experience, or are the implications likely to be limited in scope and the type of outcome assessed? This has emerged as an important recent issue in the animal research, as several studies have begun to document that specific stresses (auditory versus shock, for instance) may have differential effects. That may not be wholly surprising, but it does raise questions about how specific the fit is between risk exposure and outcome.

The degree of generalizability of findings across diverse risk exposures in humans also requires additional research attention. The study of children adopted from institutions again provides a useful illustration. Studies of formerly institutionalized children show perhaps better than any other study that there is tremendous resilience in human development and that the limits of this resilience are limited. Once we move beyond that broad fact to consider more specific outcomes and mechanisms, however, the issue of generalizability emerges. On the one hand, the kinds of behavioral

and emotional disturbances found in formerly institutionalized children differ from those in "ordinary" high-risk settings, notably the sort of Reactive Attachment Disorder-like behaviors. Even where similar problems emerge (e.g., inattention/hyperactivity), they may take on a slightly different form and/or have different sets of co-occurring problems from what is typically found. Collectively, these findings suggest that the differences between formerly institutionalized and ordinary high-risk samples may be different not only in degree, but also in kind. Does the latter finding imply different brain regions? Perhaps not, but these findings do underscore the need for a firmer biological basis of how early adverse experiences get translated in brain processes, and how these processes are then carried forward to continue to shape development.

In addition to strengthening the biological background to research paradigms, a key implication is that future efforts to assess the role of early experiences need to emphasize comparative approaches, comparing across species and across research paradigms within species.

Given the central significance of understanding the effects of early experience on the development of psychopathology, it is surprising that comparatively few studies are designed to assess this issue directly. The difficulty in addressing this issue is not simply a matter of conducting long-term longitudinal studies, but rather in providing the kind of data that would differentiate alternative models of early experience that now guide animal and human studies.

Extant human databases from naturalistic and intervention studies may be adequate for guiding major clinical and policy decisions, but they are inadequate for resolving core debates concerning the long-term effects of early experiences and the mechanisms that underlie these effects. This important limitation of existing research has kindled controversy and will continue to spur further creative and rigorous research efforts.

REFERENCES

Ader, R., & Belfer, M. (1962). Prenatal maternal anxiety and offspring emotionality in the rat. *Physiological Reports, 10,* 711–718.

Allen, N. B., Lewinsohn, P. M., & Seeley, J. R. (1998). Prenatal and perinatal influences on risk for psychopathology in childhood and adolescence. *Development and Psychopathology, 10,* 513–529.

Alonso, S. J., Navarro, E., Santana, C., & Rodriguez, M. (1997). Motor lateralization, behavioral despair and dopaminergic brain asymmetry after prenatal stress. *Pharmacology, Biochemistry and Behavior, 58,* 443–448.

Amiel-Tison, C., Cabrol, D., Denver, R., Jarreau, P. H., Papiernik, E., & Piazza, P. V. (2004a). Fetal adaptation to stress. Part I: Acceleration of fetal maturation and earlier birth triggered by placental insufficiency in humans. *Early Human Development, 78,* 15–27.

Amiel-Tison, C., Cabrol, D., Denver, R., Jarreau, P. H., Papiernik, E., & Piazza, P. V. (2004b). Fetal adaptation to stress: Part II. Evolutionary aspects; stress-induced hippocampal damage; long-term effects on behavior; consequences on adult health. *Early Human Development, 78,* 81–94.

Anderson, S. L. (2003). Trajectories of brain development: Point of vulnerability or window of opportunity? *Neuroscience and Biobehavior Reviews, 27,* 3–18.

Ansorge, M. S., Zhou, M., Lira, A., Hen, R., & Gingrich, J. A. (2004). Early-life blockade of the 5-HT transporter alters emotional behavior in adult mice. *Science, 306,* 879–881.

Arborelius, L., Owens, M. J., Plotsky, P. M., & Nemeroff, C. B. (1999). The role of corticotropin-releasing factor in depression and anxiety disorders. *Journal of Endocrinology, 160,* 1–12.

Bachevalier, J., Alvarado, M. C., & Malkova, L. (1999). Memory and socioemotional behavior in monkeys after hippocampal damage incurred in infancy or in adulthood. *Biological Psychiatry, 46,* 329–339.

Barbazanges, A., Vallee, M., Mayo, W., Day, J., Simon, H., Le Moal, M., et al. (1996). Early and later adoptions have different long-term effects on male rat offspring. *Journal of Neuroscience, 16,* 7783–7790.

Barker, D. J. (1998). In utero programming of chronic disease. *Clinical Science, 95,* 115–128.

Barnett, W. S. (1995). Long-term effects of early childhood programs on cognitive and school outcomes. *Future of Children, 5,* 25–50.

Barr, C. S., Newman, T. K., Lindell, S., Shannon, C., Champoux, M., Lesch, K. P., et al. (2004). Interaction between serotonin transporter gene variation and rearing condition in alcohol preference and consumption in female primates. *Archives of General Psychiatry, 61,* 1146–1152.

Barr, C. S., Newman, T. K., Schwandt, M., Shannon, C., Dvoskin, R. L., Lindell, S. G., et al. (2004). Sexual dichotomy of an interaction between early adversity and the serotonin transporter gene promoter variant in rhesus macaques. *Proceedings of the National Academy of Sciences, USA, 101,* 12358–12363.

Bateson, P., & Martin, P. (1999). *Design for a life: How behaviour develops.* London: Jonathan Cape.

Baum, M., Ortiz, L., & Quan, A. (2003). Fetal origins of cardiovascular disease. *Current Opinion in Pediatrics, 15,* 166–170.

Berardi, N., Pizzorusso, T., & Maffei, L. (2000). Critical periods during sensory development. *Current Opinion in Neurobiology, 10,* 138–145.

Berenbaum, S. A., Hines, M. (1992). Early androgens are related to childhood sex-typed toy preferences. *Psychological Science, 3,* 203–206.

Biagini, G., & Pich, E. M. (2002). Coticosterone administration to rat pups, but not maternal separation, affects sexual maturation and glucocorticoid receptor immunoreactivity in the testis. *Pharmacology, Biochemistry and Behavior, 73,* 95–103.

Bolger, K. E., & Patterson, C. J. (2001). Developmental pathways from child maltreatment to peer rejection. *Child Development, 72,* 549–568.

Bornstein, M. H. (1989). Sensitive periods in development: Structural characteristics and causal interpretations. *Psychological Bulletin, 105,* 179–197.

Bowlby, J. (1951). *Maternal care and mental health.* Geneva, Switzerland: World Health Organization.

Bowlby, J. (1982). *Attachment and loss: Attachment* (2nd ed.). New York: Basic Books.

Bowlby, J. (1988). Developmental psychiatry comes of age. *American Journal of Psychiatry, 145,* 1–10.

Breslau, N., Peterson, E. L., Poisson, L. M., Schultz, L. R., & Lucia, V. C. (2004). Estimating post-traumatic stress disorder in the community: Lifetime perspective and the impact of typical traumatic events. *Psychological Medicine, 34,* 889–898.

Bronfenbrenner, U. (1979). *The ecology of human development: Experiments by nature and design.* Cambridge, MA: Harvard University Press.

Brouwers, E. P. M., van Baar, A. L., & Pop, V. J. M. (2001). Maternal anxiety during pregnancy and subsequent infant development. *Infant Behavior and Development, 24,* 95–106.

Brown, A. S., van Os, J., Driessens, C., Hoek, H. W., & Susser, E. S. (2000). Further evidence of relation between prenatal famine and major affective disorder. *American Journal of Psychiatry, 157,* 190–195.

Bruer, J. T. (1999). *The myth of the first three years.* New York: Free Press.

Buitelaar, J. K. (2003). Stress during pregnancy is associated with developmental outcome in infancy. *Journal of Child Psychology and Psychiatry, 44,* 810–818.

Cacioppo, J. T., Bernstein, G. G., Adolphs, R., Carter, C. S., Davidson, R. J., McClintock, M. K., et al. (Eds.). (2002). *Foundations of social neuroscience.* Cambridge, MA: MIT Press.

Caldji, C., Diorio, J., Meaney, M. J. (2000). Variations in maternal care in infancy regulate the development of stress reactivity. *Biological Psychiatry, 48,* 1164–1174.

Cameron, J. L. (2004, June 21–22). *The use of animal models for mechanistic and developmental studies.* Paper presented at the NIMH Workshop on the Prevention of Depression in Children and Adolescents, Rockville, MD.

Campbell, F. A., Pungello, E. P., Johnson, S. M., Burchinal, M., & Ramey, C. T. (2001). The development of cognitive and academic abilities: Growth curves from an early childhood educational experiment. *Developmental Psychology, 37,* 231–242.

Campbell, F. A., & Ramey, C. T. (1994). Effects of early intervention on intellectual and academic achievement: A follow-up study of children in low income families. *Child Development, 65,* 684–698.

Carter, C. S. (1998). Neuroendocrine perspectives on social attachment and love. *Psychoneuroendocrinology, 23,* 779–818.

Caspi, A., McClay, J., Moffitt, T. E., Mill, J., Martin, J., Craig, I. W., et al. (2002). Role of genotype in the cycle of violence in maltreated children. *Science, 297,* 851–854.

Castle, J., Groothues, C., Bredenkamp, D., Beckett, C., O'Connor, T. G., & Rutter, M. (1999). Effects of qualities of institutional care on cognitive attainment. *American Journal of Orthopsychiatry, 69,* 424–437.

Challis, J. R., Matthews, S. G., Van Meir, C., & Ramirez, M. M. (1995). Current topic: The placental corticotrophin-releasing hormone–adrenocorticotrophin axis. *Placenta, 16,* 481–502.

Champagne, F., & Meaney, M. J. (2001). Like mother, like daughter: Evidence for non-genomic transmission of parental behavior and stress responsivity. *Progress in Brain Research, 133,* 287–302.

Chess, S. (1977). Follow-up report on Autism in congenital rubella. *Journal of Autism and Childhood Schizophrenia, 7,* 69–81.

Chisholm, K. (1998), A three year follow-up of attachment and indiscriminate friendliness in children adopted from Romanian orphanages. *Child Development, 69,* 1092–1106.

Chugani, H. T., Behen, M. E., Muzik, O., Juhasz, C., Nagy, F., & Chugani, D. C. (2001). Local brain functional activity following early deprivation: A study of postinstitutionalized Romanian orphans. *NeuroImage, 14,* 1290–1301.

Cicchetti, D. (2004). An odyssey of discovery: Lessons learned through three decades of research on child maltreatment. *American Psychologist, 59,* 731–741.

Cicchetti, D., & Cohen, D. J. (1995). Perspectives in developmental psychopathology. In D. Cicchetti & D. J. Cohen (Eds.), *Developmental psychopathology* (Vol. 1, pp. 2–20). New York: Wiley.

Cicchetti, D., & Rogosch, F. A. (2001). The impact of child maltreatment and psychopathology on neuroendocrine functioning. *Development and Psychopathology, 13*, 783–804.

Clarke, A. D. B., Clarke, A. M., & Reiman, S. (1958). Cognitive and social changes in the feebleminded: Three further studies. *British Journal of Psychology, 49*, 144–157.

Clarke, A. M., & Clarke, A. D. B. (2000). *Early experience and the life path.* London: Jessica Kingsley.

Clarke, A. S., Wittwer, D. J., Abbott, D. H., & Schneider, M. L. (1994). Long-term effects of prenatal stress on HPA reactivity in juvenile rhesus monkeys. *Developmental Psychobiology, 27*, 257–269.

Clarke, M., & O'Callaghan, E. (2003). Is earlier better? At the beginning of Schizophrenia: Timing and opportunities for early intervention. *Psychiatric Clinics of North America, 26*, 65–83.

Coe, C. L., Kramer, M., Czeh, B., Gould, E., Reeves, A. J., Kirschbaum, C., et al. (2003). Prenatal stress diminishes neurogenesis in the dentate gyrus of juvenile rhesus monkeys. *Biological Psychiatry, 54*, 1025–1034.

Coe, C. L., Kramer, M., Kirschbaum, C., Netter, P., & Fuchs, E. (2002). Prenatal stress diminishes the cytokine response of leukocytes to endotoxin stimulation in juvenile rhesus monkeys. *Journal of Clinical Endocrinology and Metabolism, 87*, 675–681.

Coe, C., & Lubach, G. R. (2001). Prenatal influences on neuroimmune set points in infancy. *Annals of the New York Academy of Science*, 468–477.

Coie, J. D., Watt, N. F., West, S. G., Hawkins, J. D., Asarnow, J. R., Markman, J. H., et al. (1993). The science of prevention: A conceptual model and some directions for a national research program. *American Psychologist, 48*, 1013–1022.

Conduct Problems Prevention Research Group. (1992). A developmental and clinical model for the prevention of conduct disorder: The Fast Track program. *Development and Psychopathology, 4*, 509–527.

Conduct Problems Prevention Research Group. (2002). The implementation of the Fast Track program: An example of a large-scale prevention science efficacy trial. *Journal of Abnormal Child Psychology, 30*, 1–17.

Coplan, J. D., Andrews, M. W., Rosenblum, L. A., Owens, M. J., Friedman, S., Gorman, J. M., et al. (1996). Persistent elevations of cerebrospinal fluid concentrations of corticotropin-releasing factor in adult nonhuman primates exposed to early-life stressors: Implications for the pathophysiology of mood and anxiety disorders. *Proceedings of the National Academy of Sciences, 93*, 1619–1623.

Coplan, J. D., Trost, R. C., Owens, M. J., Cooper, T. B., Gorman, J. M., Nemeroff, C. B., et al. (1998). Cerebrospinal fluid concentrations of somatostatin and biogenic amines in grown primates reared by mothers exposed to manipulated foraging conditions. *Archives of General Psychiatry, 55*, 473–477.

Copper, R. L., Goldenberg, R. L., Das, A., Elder, N., Swain, M., Norman, G., et al. (1996). The preterm prediction study: Maternal stress is associated with spontaneous preterm birth at less than thirty-five weeks' gestation. *American Journal of Obstetrics and Gynecology, 175*, 1286–1292.

Cowen, E. L., & Durlak, J. A. (2000). Social policy and prevention in mental health. *Development and Psychopathology, 12*, 815–834.

Crespi, E. J., & Denver, R. J. (2005). Ancient origins of human developmental plasticity. *American Journal of Human Biology, 17*, 44–54.

Darnaudery, M., Koehl, M., Barbazanges, A., Cabib, S., Le, M. M., & Maccari, S. (2004). Early and later adoptions differently modify mother-pup interactions. *Behavioral Neuroscience, 118*, 590–596.

Dawson, G., Ashman, S. B., & Carver, L. J. (2000). The role of early experience in shaping behavioral and brain development and its implications for social policy. *Development and Psychopathology, 12*, 695–712.

DiPietro, J. A., Costigan, K. A., & Gurewitsch, E. D. (2003). Fetal response to induced maternal stress. *Early Human Development, 74*, 125–138.

DiPietro, J. A., Hilton, S. C., Hawkins, M., Costigan, K. A., & Pressman, E. K. (2002). Maternal stress and affect influence fetal neurobehavioral development. *Developmental Psychology, 38*, 659–668.

DiPietro, J. A., Hodgson, D. M., Costigan, K. A., & Johnson, T. R. (1996). Fetal antecedents of infant temperament. *Child Development, 67*, 2568–2583.

Dishion, T. J., Kavanagh, K., Schneiger, A., Nelson, S., & Kaufman, N. K. (2002). Preventing early adolescent substance use: A family-centered strategy for the public middle school. *Prevention Science, 3*, 191–201.

Dodic, M., Abouantoun, T., O'Connor, A., Wintour, E. M., & Moritz, K. M. (2002). Programming effects of short prenatal exposure to dexamethasone in sheep. *Hypertension, 40*, 729–734.

Durlak, J. A., Fuhrman, T., & Lampman, C. (1991). Effectiveness of cognitive-behavioral therapy for maladapting children: A meta-analysis. *Psychological Bulletin, 110*, 204–214.

Duyme, M., Dumaret, A. C., & Tomkiewicz, T. C. (1999). How can we boost IQs of "dull children"? A late adoption study. *Proceedings of the National Academy of Sciences, 96*, 8790–8794.

Eagle, M. N. (1984). *Recent developments in psychoanalysis: A critical evaluation.* New York: McGraw-Hill.

Edwards, H. E., Dortok, D., Tam, J., Won, D., & Burnham, W. M. (2002). Prenatal stress alters seizure thresholds and the development of kindled seizures in infant and adult rats. *Hormones and Behavior, 42*, 437–447.

Elder, G. H. (1986). Military time and turning points in men's lives. *Developmental Psychology, 22*, 233–245.

Erikkson, J. G., Forsen, T., Tuomilehto, J., Winter, P. D., Osmond, C., & Barker, D. J. (1999). Catch-up growth in childhood and death from coronary heart disease: Longitudinal study. *British Medical Journal, 318*, 427–431.

Field, T., Diego, M., Hernandez-Reif, M., Schanberg, S., Kuhn, C., Yando, R., et al. (2003). Pregnancy anxiety and comorbid depression and anger: Effects on the fetus and neonate. *Depression and Anxiety, 17*, 140–151.

Fleming, A. S., & Corter, C. (1988). Factors influencing maternal responsiveness in humans: Usefulness of an animal model. *Psychoneuroendocrinology, 13*, 189–212.

Fleming, A. S., O'Day, D. H., & Kraemer, G. W. (1999). Neurobiology of mother-infant interactions: Experience and central nervous system plasticity across development and generations. *Neuroscience and Biobehavioral Reviews, 23*, 673–685.

Fonagy, P., Gergely, G., Jurist, E. L., & Target, M. (2002). *Affect regulation, mentalization, and the development of the self.* New York: Other Press.

Francis, D., Champagne, F. C., & Meaney, M. J. (2000). Variations in maternal behaviour are associated with differences in oxytocin receptor levels in the rat. *Journal of Neuroendocrinology, 12*, 1145–1148.

Francis, D., Diorio, J., Liu, D., & Meaney, M. J. (1999). Nongenomic transmission across generations of maternal behavior and stress response in the rat. *Science, 286*, 1155–1158.

Francis, D., & Meaney, M. J. (2002). Maternal care and the development of stress responses. In J. T. Cacioppo, G. G. Bernstein, R. Adolphs, C. S. Carter, R. J. Davidson, M. K. McClintock, et al. (Eds.), *Foundations of social neuroscience* (pp. 763–773). Cambridge, MA: MIT Press.

Francis, D., Young, L. J., Meaney, M. J., & Insel, T. R. (2002). Naturally occurring differences in maternal care are associated with the expression of oxytocin and vasopressin (V1a) receptors: Gender differences. *Journal of Neuroendocrinology, 14*, 349–353.

Freud, A., & Burlingham, D. (1973). *The writings of Anna Freud: Vol. III. Infants without families 1939–1945.* New York: International Universities Press.

Gallucci, W. T., Baum, A., Laue, L., Rabin, D. S., Chrousos, G. P., Gold, P. W., et al. (1993). Sex differences in sensitivity of the hypothalamic pituitary adrenal axis. *Health Psychology, 12,* 420–425.

Gedo, J. E. (1980). Reflections on some current controversies in psychoanalysis. *Journal of the American Psychoanalytic Association, 28,* 363–383.

Giannakoulopoulos, X., Teixeira, J., Fisk, N., & Glover, V. (1999). Human fetal and maternal noradrenaline responses to invasive procedures. *Pediatric Research, 45*(4, Pt. 1), 494–499.

Gitau, R., Adams, D., Fisk, N. M., & Glover, V. (2005). Fetal plasma testosterone correlates positively with cortisol. Archives of the Diseases of Childhood 2004. *Archives of Disease in Childhood Fetal and Neonatal Edition, 90,* F166–F169.

Gitau, R., Cameron, A., Fisk, N. M., & Glover, V. (1998). Fetal exposure to maternal cortisol. *Lancet, 352,* 707–708.

Gitau, R., Fisk, N. M., & Glover, V. (2004). Human fetal and maternal corticotrophin releasing hormone responses to acute stress. *Archives of Disease of Child Fetal and Neonatal Medicine, 89,* F29–F32.

Gitau, R., Fisk, N., Teixeira, J., Cameron, A., & Glover, V. (2001). Fetal HPA stress responses to invasive procedures are independent of maternal responses. *Journal of Clinical Endocrinology and Metabolism, 86,* 104–109.

Glover, V., & O'Connor, T. G. (in press). Antenatal programming of child behaviour and neurodevelopment: Links with maternal stress and anxiety. In D. Hodgson & C. Coe (Eds.), *Perinatal programming: Early life determinants of adult health and disease.* London: Taylor & Francis Medical Books.

Glover, V., O'Connor, T. G., Heron, J., & Golding, J. (2004). Antenatal maternal anxiety is linked with atypical handedness in the child. *Early Human Development, 79,* 107–118.

Glynn, L. M., Wadhwa, P. D., Dunkel-Schletter, C., Chicz-Demet, A., & Sandman, C. A. (2001). When stress happens matters: Effects of earthquake timing on stress responsivity in pregnancy. *American Journal of Obstetrics and Gynecology, 184,* 637–642.

Goldman-Rakic, P. S., Isseroff, A., Schwartz, L., & Bugbee, N. M. (1983). The neurobiology of cognitive development. In P. Mussen (Ed.), *Handbook of cognitive development* (Vol. 2, pp. 282–344). New York: Wiley.

Gorman, K. S., & Pollitt, E. (1996). Does schooling buffer the effects of early risk? *Child Development, 67,* 314–326.

Gottlieb, G. (1991). Experiential canalization of behavioral development: Theory. *Developmental Psychology, 27,* 4–13.

Goy, R. W., & McEwen, B. S. (1980). *Sexual differentiation of the brain.* Cambridge, MA: MIT Press.

Greenough, W. T., Black, J. E., & Wallace, C. S. (1987). Experience and brain development. *Child Development, 58,* 539–559.

Griffin, W. C., Skinner, H. D., Salm, A. K., & Birkle, D. L. (2003). Mild prenatal stress in rats is associated with enhanced conditioned fear. *Hormones and Behavior, 79,* 209–225.

Gunnar, M. R. (2003). Integrating neuroscience and psychological approaches in the study of early experiences. *Annals of the New York Academy of Sciences, 1008,* 238–247.

Gunnar, M. R., Morison, S. J., Chisholm, K., & Schuder, M. (2001). Salivary cortisol levels in children adopted from Romanian orphanages. *Development and Psychopathology, 13,* 611–628.

Hales, C. N., & Barker, D. J. (1992). Type 2 (non-insulin-dependent) diabetes mellitus: The thrifty phenotype hypothesis. *Diabetologia, 35,* 595–601.

Hales, C. N., & Barker, D. J. (2001). The thrifty phenotype hypothesis. *British Medical Bulletin, 60,* 5–20.

Halligan, S. L., Herbert, J., Goodyer, I. M., & Murray, L. (2004). Exposure to postnatal depression predicts elevated cortisol in adolescent offspring. *Biological Psychiatry, 55,* 376–381.

Hansen, D., Lou, H. C., & Olsen, J. (2000). Serious life events and congenital malformations: A national study with complete follow-up. *Lancet, 356,* 875–880.

Harlow, H. F., & Harlow, M. K. (1969). Effects of various mother-infant relationships on rhesus monkey behaviors. In B. M. Foss (Ed.), *Determinants of infant behavior* (Vol. 4, pp. 15–36). London: Methuen.

Harlow, H., & Suomi, S. (1970). The nature of love—simplified. *American Psychologist, 25,* 161–168.

Hedegaard, M., Henriksen, T. B., Sabroe, S., & Secher, N. J. (1993). Psychological distress in pregnancy and preterm delivery. *British Medical Journal, 307,* 234–239.

Heim, C., Newport, D. J., Heit, S., Graham, Y. P., Wilcox, M., Bonsall, R., et al. (2000). Pituitary-adrenal and autonomic responses to stress in women after sexual and physical abuse in childhood. *Journal of the American Medical Association, 284,* 592–597.

Henry, C., Kabbaj, M., Simon, H., LeMoal, M., & Maccari, S. (1994). Prenatal stress increases the hypothalamic-pituitary-adrenal axis response in young and adult rats. *Journal of Neuroendocrinology, 6,* 341–345.

Hensch, T. K. (2004). Critical period regulation. *Annual Review of Neuroscience, 27,* 549–579.

Herschkowitz, N., Kagan, J., & Zilles, K. (1997). Neurobiological bases of behavioral development in the first year. *Neuropediatrics, 28,* 296–306.

Hetherington, E. M., Bridges, M., & Insabella, G. M. (1998). What matters? What does not? Five perspectives on the association between marital transitions and children's adjustment. *American Psychologist, 53,* 167–184.

Hines, M., Golombok, S., Rust, J., Johnston, K. J., & Golding, J. (2002). Testosterone during pregnancy and gender role behavior of preschool children: A longitudinal, population study. *Child Development, 73,* 1678–1687.

Hinshaw, S. P. (2002). Intervention research, theoretical mechanisms, and causal processes related to externalizing behavior patterns. *Development and Psychopathology, 14,* 789–818.

Howe, D., & Fearnley, S. (1999). Disorders of attachment and attachment therapy. *Adoption and Fostering, 23,* 19–30.

Huang, Z. J., Kirkwood, A., Pizzorusso, T., Porciatti, V., Morales, B., Bear, M. F., et al. (1999). BDNF regulates the maturation of inhibition and the critical period of plasticity in mouse visual cortex. *Cell, 98,* 739–755.

Hubel, D. H., & Wiesel, T. N. (1970). The period of susceptibility to the physiological effects of unilateral eye closure in kittens. *Journal of Physiology, 206,* 419–436.

Huizink, A. C., Medina, P. G. R., Mulder, E. J. H., Visser, G. H. A., & Buitelaar, J. K. (2002). Psychological measures of prenatal stress as predictors of infant temperament. *Journal of the American Academy of Child and Adolescent Psychiatry, 41,* 1078–1085.

Huizink, A. C., Mulder, E. J. H., & Buitlaar, J. K. (2004). Prenatal stress and risk for psychopathology: Specific effects of induction of general susceptibility. *Psychological Bulletin, 130,* 115–142.

Huot, R. L., Gonzalez, M. E., Ladd, C. O., Thrivikraman, K. V., & Plotsky, P. M. (2004). Foster litters prevent hypothalamic-pituitary-adrenal axis sensitization mediated by neonatal maternal separation. *Psychoneuroimmunology, 29,* 279–289.

Huttenlocher, P. R. (1994). Synaptogenesis, synapse elimination, and neural plasticity in human cerebral cortex. In C. A. Nelson (Ed.), *Minnesota Symposia on Child Psychology: Vol. 27. Threats to optimal development: Integrating biological, psychological, and social risk factors* (pp. 35–54). Hillsdale, NJ: Erlbaum.

Insel, T. R. (1990). Prenatal stress has long term effects on brain opiate receptors. *Brain Research, 511,* 93–97.

Insel, T. R. (1997). A neurobiological basis of social attachment. *American Journal of Psychiatry, 154,* 726–735.

Insel, T. R. (2003). Is social attachment an addictive disorder? *Physiology and Behavior, 79,* 351–357.

Insel, T. R., Kinsley, C. H., Mann, P. E., & Bridges, R. S. (1990). Prenatal stress has long-term effects on brain opiate receptors. *Brain Research, 511,* 93–97.

Itard, J. M. G. (1962). *The wild boy of Aveyron* (G. Humphrey & M. Humphrey, Trans.). New York: Appleton Century Crofts.

Jaffee, J., Beebe, B., Feldstein, S., Crown, C. L., & Jasnow, M. D. (2001). Rhythms of dialogue in infancy. *Monographs of the Society for Research on Child Development, 66*(2, Serial No. 265).

Johnson, J. S., & Newport, E. L. (1989). Critical period effects in second language learning: The influence of maturational state on the acquisition of English as a second language. *Cognitive Psychology, 21,* 60–99.

Kagan, J., & Moss, H. A. (1983). *Birth to maturity.* New York: Wiley. (Original work published 1962)

Kajentie, E., Dunkel, L., Turpeinen, U., Stenman, U.-H., Wood, P. J., Nuutila, M., et al. (2003). Placental 11b-hydroxysteroid dehydrogenase-2 and fetal cortisol/cortisone shuttle in small preterm infants. *Journal of Endocrinology and Metabolism, 88,* 493–500.

Kaufman, J., Plotsky, P. M., Nemeroff, C. B., & Charney, D. S. (2000). Effects of early adverse experiences on brain structure and function: Clinical implications. *Biological Psychiatry, 48,* 778–790.

Kay, G., Tarcic, N., Poltyrev, T., & Weinstock, M. (1998). Prenatal stress depresses immune function in rats. *Physiology and Behavior, 63,* 397–402.

Keck, G. C., & Kupecky, R. (1995). *Adopting the hurt child.* Colorado Springs, CO: Pinon Press.

Kessler, R. C. (2003). Epidemiology of women and depression. *Journal of Affective Disorders, 74,* 5–13.

Kim, J., & Cicchetti, D. (2004). A longitudinal study of child maltreatment, mother-child relationship quality and maladjustment: The role of self-esteem and social competence. *Journal of Abnormal Child Psychology, 32,* 341–354.

Kinnunen, A. K., Koenig, J. I., & Bilbe, G. (2003). Repeated variable prenatal stress alters pre- and postsynaptic gene expression in the rat frontal lobe. *Journal of Neurochemistry, 86,* 736–748.

Kirschbaum, C., Wust, S., & Hallhammer, D. H. (1992). Consistent sex differences in cortisol responses to psychological stress. *Psychosomatic Medicine,* 648–657.

Kitzman, H., Olds, D. L., Henderson, C. R., Jr., Hanks, C., Cole, R., Tatelbaum, R., et al. (1997). Effect of prenatal and infancy home visitation by nurses on pregnancy outcomes, childhood injuries, and repeated childbearing: A randomized controlled trial. *Journal of the American Medical Association, 278,* 644–652.

Klaus, M. H., & Kennell, J. H. (1976). *Maternal-infant bonding.* St. Louis: Mosby.

Kraemer, G. W., & Clarke, A. S. (1996). Social attachment, brain function, and aggression. *Annals of the New York Academy of Sciences, 794,* 121–135.

Kreppner, J. M., O'Connor, T. G., Rutter, M., & the English and Romanian Adoptees Study Team. (2001). Can inattention/hyperactivity be a deprivation disorder? *Journal of Abnormal Child Psychology, 29,* 513–528.

Ladd, C. O., Huot, R. L., Thrivikraman, K. V., Nemeroff, C. B., Meaney, M. J., & Plotsky, P. M. (2000). Long-term behavioral and endocrine adaptations to adverse early experience. *Progress in Brain Research, 122,* 81–103.

Laplante, D. P., Barr, R. G., Brunet, A., Galbaud du Fort, G., Meaney, M. L., Saucier, J. F., et al. (2004). Stress during pregnancy affects general intellectual and language functioning in human toddlers. *Pediatric Research, 56,* 400–410.

Lehmann, J., Stohr, T., & Feldon, J. (2000). Long-term effects of prenatal stress experience and postnatal maternal separation on emotionality and attentional processes. *Behavior and Brain Research, 107,* 133–144.

Lemaire, V., Koehl, M., LeMoal, M., & Abrous, D. N. (2000). Prenatal stress produces learning deficits associated with an inhibition of neurogenesis in the hippocampus. *Proceedings of the National Academy of Science, USA, 97,* 11032–11037.

Lorenz, K. (1982). *The foundations of ethology.* New York: Springer-Verlag.

Lovic, V., Gonzalez, A., & Fleming, A. S. (2001). Maternally separated rats show deficits in maternal care in adulthood. *Developmental Psychobiology, 39,* 19–33.

Lucas, A. (1998). Programming by early nutrition: An experimental approach. *Journal of Nutrition, 128,* S401–S406.

MacArthur, B. A., Howie, R. N., Dezoete, J. A., & Elkins, J. (1981). Cognitive and psychosocial development of 4-year-old children whose mothers were treated antenatally with betamethasone. *Pediatrics, 68,* 638–643.

Maccari, S., Darnaudery, M., Morley-Fletcher, S., Zuena, A. R., Cinque, C., & Van Reeth, O. (2003). Prenatal stress and long-term consequences: Implications of glucocorticoid hormones. *Neuroscience and Biobehavioral Reviews, 27,* 119–127.

Maccari, S., Piazza, P. V., Kabbaj, M., Barbazanges, A., Simon, H., & Le Moal, M. (1995). Adoption reverses the long-term impairment in glucocorticoid feedback induced by prenatal stress. *Journal of Neuroscience, 15,* 110–116.

Maestripieri, D. (1999). The biology of human parenting: Insights from nonhuman primates. *Neuroscience and Biobehavioral Reviews, 23,* 411–422.

Martin, J. L., Spicer, D. M., Lewis, M. H., Gluck, J. P., & Cork, L. C. (1991). Social deprivation in rhesus monkeys alters the chemoarchitecture of the brain: Pt. I. Subcortical regions. *Journal of Neuroscience, 11,* 3344–3358.

Matthews, S. G. (2001). Antenatal glucocorticoids and programming of the developing CNS. *Pediatric Research, 47,* 291–300.

Matthews, S. G. (2002). Early programming of the hypothalamic-pituitary-adrenal axis. *Trends in Endocrinology and Metabolism, 13,* 373–380.

Maurer, D., Lewis, T. L., Brent, H. P., & Levin, A. V. (1999). Rapid improvement in the acuity of infants after visual input. *Science, 286,* 108–110.

McCarton, C. M., Brooks-Gunn, J., Wallace, I. F., Bauer, C. R., Bennett, F. C., Bernbaum, J. C., et al. (1997). Results at age 8 years of early intervention for low-birth-weight premature infants: The Infant Health and Development Program. *Journal of the American Medical Association, 277,* 126–132.

Meyer-Bahlburg, H. F. L., Dolezal, C., Baker, S. W., Carlson, A. D., Obeid, J. S., & New, M. I. (2004). Cognitive and motor development of children with and without congenital adrenal hyperplasia after early-prenatal dexamethasone. *Journal of Clinical Endocrinology and Metabolism, 89,* 610–614.

Moles, A., Kieffer, B. L., & D'Amato, F. R. (2004). Deficit in attachment behavior in mice lacking the μ-opioid receptor gene. *Science, 304,* 1983–1986.

Monk, C., Fifer, W. P., Myers, M. M., Sloan, R. P., Trien, L., & Hurtado, A. (2000). Maternal stress responses and anxiety during pregnancy: Effects on fetal heart rate. *Developmental Psychobiology, 36,* 67–77.

Monk, C., Myers, M. M., Sloan, R. P., Ellman, L. M., & Fifer, W. P. (2003). Effects of women's stress-elicited physiological activity and chronic anxiety on fetal heart rate. *Journal of Developmental and Behavioral Pediatrics, 24,* 32–38.

Morley-Fletcher, S., Rea, M., Maccari, S., & Laviola, G. (2003). Environmental enrichment during adolescence reverses the effects of prenatal stress on play behaviour and HPA axis reactivity in rats. *European Journal of Neuroscience, 18,* 3367–3374.

Nass, R., Baker, S., Speiser, P., Virdis, R., Balsamo, A., Cacciari, E., et al. (1987). Hormones and handedness: Left-hand bias in female congenital adrenal hyperplasia patients. *Neurology, 37,* 711–715.

Nelson, C. A., & Luciana, M. (Eds.). (2001). *Handbook of Developmental Cognitive Neuroscience.* Cambridge, MA: MIT Press.

Nemeroff, C. B. (2004). Neurobiological consequences of childhood trauma. *Journal of Clinical Psychiatry, 65*(Suppl. 1), 18–28.

Nimby, G. T., Lundberg, L., Sveger, T., & McNeil, T. F. (1999). Maternal distress and congenital malformations: Do mothers of malformed fetuses have more problems? *Journal of Psychiatric Research, 33,* 291–301.

Obel, C., Hedegaard, M., Henriksen, T. B., Secher, N. J., & Olsen, J. (2003). Psychological factors in pregnancy and mixed-handedness in the offspring. *Developmental Medicine and Child Neurology, 45,* 557–561.

O'Connor, T. G. (2003, April 27). *Developmental programming effects of psychological outcomes: 11-year follow-up of children adopted from institutions in Romania.* Presentation at SRCD biennial conference, Tampa, FL.

O'Connor, T. G., Ben-Shlomo, Y., Heron, J., Golding, J., Adams, D., & Glover, V. (2005). Prenatal anxiety predicts individual differences in cortisol in pre-adolescent children. *Biological Psychiatry, 58,* 211–217.

O'Connor, T. G., Heron, J., Golding, J., Beveridge, M., & Glover, V. (2002). Maternal antenatal anxiety and children's behavioural/emotional problems at 4 years. *British Journal of Psychiatry, 180,* 502–508.

O'Connor, T. G., Heron, J., Golding, J., Glover, V., & the ALSPAC Study Team. (2003). Maternal antenatal anxiety and behavioural/emotional problems in children: A test of a programming hypothesis. *Journal of Child Psychology and Psychiatry, 44,* 1025–1036.

O'Connor, T. G., Marvin, R. S., Rutter, M., Olrick, J., Britner, P. A., & the English and Romanian Adoptees Study Team. (2003). Child-parent attachment following early institutional deprivation. *Development and Psychopathology, 15,* 19–38.

O'Connor, T. G., Rutter, M., & the English and Romanian Adoptees Study Team. (2000). Attachment disorder behavior following early severe deprivation: Extension and longitudinal follow-up. *Journal of the American Academy of Child and Adolescent Psychiatry, 39,* 703–712.

Olds, D. L. (2002). Prenatal and infancy home visiting by nurses: From randomized controlled trials to community replication. *Prevention Science, 3,* 153–172.

Olds, D. L., Eckenrode, J., Henderson, C. R., Jr., Kitzman, H., Powers, J., Cole, R., et al. (1997). Long-term effects of home visitation on maternal life course and child abuse and neglect: Fifteen-year follow-up of a randomized trial. *Journal of the American Medical Association, 278,* 637–643.

Olds, D. L., Kitzman, H., Cole, R., Robinson, J., Sidora, K., Luckey, D. W., et al. (2004). Effects of nurse home-visiting on maternal life course and child development: Age 6 follow-up results of a randomized trial. *Pediatrics, 114,* 1550–1559.

Peterfreund, E. (1978). Some critical comments on psychoanalytic conceptions of infancy: International. *Journal of Psychoanalysis, 59,* 427–441.

Peters, D. A. V. (1988). Both prenatal and postnatal factors contribute to the effects of maternal stress on offspring behavior and central 5-hydroxytryptamine receptors in the rat. *Pharmacology, Biochemistry and Behavior, 30,* 669–673.

Petraglia, F., Volpe, A., Genazzani, A. R., Rivier, J., Sawchenko, P. E., & Vale, W. (1990). Neuroendocrinology of the human placenta. *Frontiers in Neuroendocrinology, 11,* 6–37.

Pollak, S. D., & Kistler, D. J. (2002). Early experience is associated with the development of categorical representations for facial expressions of emotion. *Proceedings of the National Academy of Sciences, USA, 99,* 9072–9076.

Pollak, S. D., Klorman, R., Thatcher, J. E., & Cicchetti, D. (2001). P3b reflects maltreated children's reactions to facial displays of emotion. *Psychophysiology, 38,* 267–274.

Post, R. M. (1992). Transduction of psychosocial stress into the neurobiology of recurrent affective disorder. *American Journal of Psychiatry, 149,* 999–1010.

Post, R. M., Weiss, S. R. B., & Leverich, G. S. (1994). Recurrent affective disorder: Roots in developmental neurobiology and illness progression based on changes in gene expression. *Development and Psychopathology, 6,* 781–813.

Provence, S., & Lipton, R. C. (1962). *Infants reared in institutions.* New York: International Universities Press.

Quinton, D., Pickles, A., Maughan, B., & Rutter, M. (1993). Partners, peers, and pathways: Assortative mating and continuities in conduct disorder. *Development and Psychopathology, 5,* 763–783.

Quinton, D., & Rutter, M. (1988). *Parenting breakdown: The making and breaking of inter-generational links.* Aldershot, England: Avebury.

Ramey, C. T., & Ramey, S. L. (1998). Early intervention and early experience. *American Psychologist, 53,* 109–120.

Ramey, S. L., & Sackett, G. P. (2000). The early caregiving environment: Expanding views on nonparental care and cumulative life experiences. In A. J. Sameroff, M. Lewis, & S. M. Miller (Eds.), *Handbook of developmental psychopathology* (2nd ed., pp. 365–380). New York: Kluwer Academic/Plenum Press.

Ravelli, A. C., van der Meulen, J. H., Michels, R. P., Osmond, C., Barker, D. J., Hales, C. N., et al. (1998). Glucose tolerance in adults after prenatal exposure to famine. *Lancet, 351,* 173–177.

Reiss, D., & Price, R. H. (1996). National research agenda for prevention research: The National Institute of Mental Health report. *American Psychologist, 51,* 1109–1115.

Reynolds, A. J. (1994). Effects of a preschool plus follow-on intervention for preschool children at risk. *Developmental Psychology, 30,* 787–804.

Reynolds, A. J., & Robertson, D. L. (2003). School-based early intervention and later child maltreatment in the Chicago Longitudinal Study. *Child Development, 74,* 3–26.

Reynolds, A. J., Temple, J. A., Robertson, D. L., & Mann, E. A. (2001). Long-term effects of an early childhood intervention on educational achievement and juvenile arrest: A 15-year follow-up of low-income children in public schools. *Journal of the American Medical Association, 285,* 2339–2346.

Rindfuss, R. R., Swicegood, C. G., & Rosenfeld, R. A. (1987). Disorder in the life course: How common and does it matter? *American Sociological Review, 52,* 785–801.

Rodriguez, A., & Bohlin, G. (2005). Are maternal smoking and stress during pregnancy related to ADHD symptoms in children? *Journal of Child Psychology and Psychiatry, 46,* 246–254.

Rogosch, F. A., & Cicchetti, D. (2004). Child maltreatment and emergent personality organization: Perspectives from the five-factor model. *Journal of Abnormal Child Psychology, 32,* 123–145.

Rosenblum, L. A., & Paully, G. S. (1984). The effects of varying environmental demands on maternal and infant behavior. *Child Development, 55,* 305–314.

Roy, P., Rutter, M., & Pickles, A. (2004). Institutional care: Associations between overactivity and lack of selectivity in social relationships. *Journal of Child Psychology and Psychiatry, 45,* 866–873.

Ruppenthal, G. C., Arling, G. L., Harlow, H. F., Sackett, G. P., & Suomi, S. J. (1976). A 10-year perspective on motherless-mother monkey behavior. *Journal of Abnormal Psychology, 88,* 341–349.

Rutter, M. (1981). *Maternal deprivation reassessed* (2nd ed.). Hammondsworth, England: Penguin Classics.

Rutter, M., Anderson-Wood, L., Beckett, C., Bredenkamp, D., Castle, J., Groothues, C., et al. (1999). Quasi-autistic patterns following severe early global privation. *Journal of Child Psychology and Psychiatry, 40,* 537–549.

Rutter, M., Kreppner, J., O'Connor, T. G., & the English and Romanian Adoptees Study Team. (2001). Specificity and heterogeneity in children's responses to profound deprivation. *British Journal of Psychiatry, 179,* 97–103.

Rutter, M., O'Connor, T. G., & the English and Romanian Adoptees Study Team. (2004). Are there biological programming effects for psychological development? Findings from a study of Romanian adoptees. *Developmental Psychology, 40,* 81–94.

Sackett, G. P. (1965). Effects of rearing conditions upon the behavior of rhesus monkeys (Macaca mulatta). *Child Development, 36,* 855–868.

Sanchez, M. M., Ladd, C. O., & Plotsky, P. M. (2001). Early adverse experience as a developmental risk factor for later psychopathology: Evidence from rodent and primate models. *Development and Psychopathology, 13,* 419–449.

Sandman, C. A., Glynn, L., Wadhwa, P. D., Chicz-DeMet, A., Porto, M., & Garite, T. (2003). Maternal hypothalamic-pituitary-adrenal disregulation during the third trimester influences human fetal responses. *Developmental Neuroscience, 25,* 41–49.

Schaffer, H. R. (2000). The early experience assumption: Past, present, and future. *International Journal of Behavioral Development, 24,* 5–14.

Schneider, M. L., Clarke, A. S., Kraemer, G. W., Roughton, E. C., Lubach, G. R., Rimm-Kaufman, S., et al. (1998). Prenatal stress alters brain biogenic amine levels in primates. *Development and Psychopathology, 10,* 427–440.

Schneider, M. L., Coe, C. L., & Lubach, G. L. (1992). Endocrine activation mimics the adverse effects of prenatal stress on the neuromotor development of the infant primate. *Developmental Psychobiology, 25,* 427–439.

Schneider, M. L., & Moore, C. F. (2000). Effect of prenatal stress on development: A nonhuman primate model. In C. Nelson (Ed.), *Minnesota Symposia on Child Psychology* (pp. 201–243). Hillsdale, NJ: Erlbaum.

Schneider, M. L., Roughton, E. C., Koehler, A. J., & Lubach, G. R. (1999). Growth and development following prenatal stress exposure in primates: An examination of ontogenetic vulnerability. *Child Development, 70,* 263–274.

Schoon, I., Bynner, J., Joshi, H., Parsons, S., Wiggins, R. D., & Sacker, A. (2002). The influence of context, timing, and duration of risk experiences for the passage from childhood to midadulthood. *Child Development, 73,* 1486–1504.

Sjostrom, K., Valentin, L., Thelin, T., & Marsal, K. (1997). Maternal anxiety in late pregnancy and fetal hemodynamics. *European Journal of Obstetrics and Gynecology: Reproductive Biology, 74*(2), 149–155.

Sobrian, S. K., Vaughn, V. T., Bloch, E. F., & Burton, L. E. (1992). Influence of prenatal maternal stress on the immunocompetence of the offspring. *Pharmacology, Biochemistry and Behavior, 43,* 537–547.

Sontag, L. W. (1941). The significance of fetal environmental differences. *American Journal of Obstetrics and Gynecology, 42,* 996–1003.

Speirs, H. J., Seckl, J. R., & Brown, R. W. (2004). Ontogeny of glucocorticoid receptor and 11beta-hydroxysteroid dehydrogenase type-1 gene expression identifies potential critical periods of glucocorticoid susceptibility during development. *Journal of Endocrinology, 181,* 105–116.

Spitz, R. A. (1946). Anaclitic depression: An inquiry into the genesis of psychiatric conditions in early childhood. *Psychoanalytic Study of the Child, 1,* 53–74.

Spitz, R. A. (1965). *The first year of life.* New York: International Universities Press.

Sroufe, L. A. (1996). *Emotional development.* New York: Cambridge University Press.

Stott, D. H. (1973). Follow-up study from birth of the effects of prenatal stresses. *Developmental Medicine and Child Neurology, 15,* 770–787.

Suomi, S. J. (1999). Attachment in rhesus monkeys. In J. Cassidy & P. Shaver (Eds.), *Handbook of attachment* (pp. 181–197). New York: Guilford Press.

Suomi, S. J. (2003). Gene-environment interactions and the neurobiology of social conflict. *Annals of the New York Academy of Science, 1008,* 132–139.

Susman, E. J., Schmeelk, K. H., Ponirakis, A., & Gariepy, J. L. (2001). Maternal prenatal, postpartum, and concurrent stressors and temperament in 3-year-old children: A person and variable analysis. *Development and Psychopathology, 13,* 629–654.

Szurman, T., Pliska, V., Pokorby, J., & Welzl, H. (2000). Prenatal stress in rats: Effects on plasma corticosterone, hippocampal glucocorticoids receptors, and maze performance. *Physiology and Behavior, 71,* 353–362.

Teicher, M. H., Andersen, S. L., Polcari, A., Anderson, C. M., Navalta, C. P., & Kim, D. M. (2003). The neurobiological consequences of early stress and childhood maltreatment. *Neuroscience and Biobehavioral Reviews, 27,* 33–44.

Teixeira, J. M., Fisk, N. M., & Glover, V. (1999). Association between maternal anxiety in pregnancy and increased uterine artery resistance index: Cohort based study. *British Medical Journal, 318,* 153–157.

Thompson, W. R. (1957). Influence of prenatal maternal anxiety on emotionality in young rats. *Science, 125,* 698.

Thorpe, W. H. (1963). *Learning and instinct in animals* (2nd ed.). Cambridge, MA: Harvard University Press.

Tizard, B., & Rees, J. (1975). The effect of early institutional rearing on the behavioural problems and affectional relationships of four-year-old children. *Journal of Child Psychology and Psychiatry, 16,* 61–73.

Toth, S. L., Cicchetti, D., Macfie, J., Maughan, A., & VanMeenen, K. (2000). Narrative representations of caregivers and self in maltreated pre-schoolers. *Attachment and Human Development, 2,* 271–305.

Toth, S. L., Maughan, A., Manly, J. T., Spagnola, M., & Cicchetti, D. (2002). The relative efficacy of two interventions in altering maltreated preschool children's representational models: Implications for attachment theory. *Development and Psychopathology, 14,* 877–908.

Van den Bergh, B. R., & Marcoen, A. (2004). High antenatal maternal anxiety is related to ADHD symptoms, externalizing problems, and anxiety in 8- and 9-year-olds. *Child Development, 75,* 1085–1097.

Vorria, P., Papaligoura, Z., Dunn, J., van Ijzendoorn, M. H., Steele, H., Kontopoulou, A., et al. (2003). Early experiences and attachment relationships of Greek infants raised in residential group care. *Journal of Child Psychology and Psychiatry, 44,* 1208–1220.

Vorria, P., Rutter, M., Pickles, A., Wolkind, S., & Hobsbaum, A. (1998). A comparative study of Greek children in long-term residential group care and in two-parent families: Pt. I. Social, emotional, and behavioural differences. *Journal of Child Psychology and Psychiatry, 39,* 225–236.

Wadhwa, P. D., Dunkel-Schetter, C., Chicz-DeMet, A., Porto, M., & Sandman, C. A. (1996). Prenatal psychosocial factors and the neuroendocrine axis in human pregnancy. *Psychosomatic Medicine, 58,* 432–446.

Wadhwa, P. D., Porto, M., Garite, T. J., Chicz-DeMet, A., & Sandman, C. A. (1998). Maternal corticotropin-releasing hormone levels in the early third trimester predict length of gestation in human pregnancy. *American Journal of Obstetrics and Gynecology, 179,* 1079–1085.

Wadhwa, P. D., Sandman, C. A., & Garite, T. J. (2001). The neurobiology of stress in human pregnancy: Implications for prematurity and development of the fetal central nervous system. *Progress in Brain Research, 133,* 131–142.

Wadhwa, P. D., Sandman, C. A., Porto, M., Dunkel-Schetter, C., & Garite, T. J. (1993). The association between prenatal stress and infant birth weight and gestational age at birth: A prospective investigation. *American Journal of Obstetrics and Gynecology, 169,* 858–865.

Wallerstein, J. S. (1985). Children of divorce: Preliminary report of a ten-year follow-up of older children and adolescents. *Journal of the American Academy of Child Psychiatry, 24,* 545–553.

Ward, H. E., Johnson, E. A., Salm, A., & Birkle, D. L. (2000). Effects of prenatal stress on defensive withdrawal behavior and corticotropin releasing factor systems in rat brain. *Physiology and Behavior, 70,* 359–366.

Waters, E., Merrick, S., Treboux, D., Crowell, J., & Albersheim, L. (2000). Attachment security in infancy and early adulthood: A twenty-year longitudinal study. *Child Development, 71,* 684–689.

Weaver, I. C., Cervoni, N., Champagne, F. A., D'Alessio, A. C., Sharma, S., Seckl, J. R., et al. (2004). Epigenetic programming by maternal behavior. *Nature Neuroscience, 7,* 847–854.

Weinstock, M. (2001). Alterations induced by gestational stress in brain morphology and behaviour of the offspring. *Progress in Neurobiology, 65,* 427–451.

Werner, E. E. (1989). High-risk children in young adulthood: A longitudinal study from birth to 32 years. *American Journal of Orthopsychiatry, 59,* 72–81.

Williams, M. T., Hennessy, M. B., & Davis, H. N. (1995). CRF administered to pregnant rats alters offspring behavior and morphology. *Pharmacology, Biochemistry and Behavior, 52,* 161–167.

Wolkind, S. N. (1974). The components of "affectionless psychopathy" in institutionalized children. *Journal of Child Psychology and Psychiatry, 15,* 215–220.

Young, L. J., Wang, Z., & Insel, T. R. (1998). Neuroendocrine bases of monogamy. *Trends in Neuroscience, 21,* 71–75.

Zeanah, C. H., Smyke, A. T., & Dumitrescu, A. (2002). Attachment disturbances in young children: Pt. II. Indiscriminate behavior and institutional care. *Journal of the American Academy of Child and Adolescent Psychiatry, 41,* 983–989.

CHAPTER 6

Developmental Approaches to Children with Mental Retardation: A Second Generation?

ROBERT M. HODAPP and JACOB A. BURACK

Fields, like children, develop at uneven rates. For any individual child, some time periods feature only slow and steady development, whereas other periods show rapid, almost overwhelming, advances. Such rapid advances best characterize the past 10 to 15 years of research in mental retardation. During this period, totally new topics appeared and researchers endeavored to tie historically prominent areas to new issues and concerns. Overall, the period from about 1990 can be characterized as a time of renewed interest, excitement, and rapid scientific advance.

One way to appreciate these advances is to compare the current chapter to the mental retardation chapter in *Developmental Psychopathology*'s first edition, published in 1995. In that first chapter, Hodapp and Zigler (1995) described the history of developmentally oriented work in mental retardation; the two-group approach; similar sequences, structures, rates, and transitions; and personality-motivational variables, mother-child interaction, and families. Although we revisit several of these topics in this chapter, virtually every topic features new findings that

changed the way we had previously thought. Indeed, the amount of new work in each area is staggering.

But even more remarkable is what was not included in that earlier chapter: issues that were either never or only slightly discussed in the early to mid-1990s. These many topics pertain to research groups in mental retardation research, the age groups studied, and the family and other contexts in which these individuals develop. In terms of populations, the 1995 chapter included only short discussions of the effects of genetic etiology on children's development because the many findings concerning Down syndrome, Prader-Willi syndrome, Williams syndrome, and other genetic disorders were still mostly on the horizon. Even more fundamentally, how one should consider different research groups, how one should compare or contrast such groups, how behavioral profiles change with age (and why) were all unknown and, for the most part, not yet even actively discussed. Similarly unknown were ties of behavioral profiles to specific brain structures, development, and functioning.

Beyond development of children themselves, a decade ago we as a field were also much less clear about a host of issues relating to the contexts of development. For example, researchers have only recently examined how behaviors commonly seen in a particular genetic disorder might indirectly affect parents, siblings, teachers, friends, and others in the child's surrounding environment. So, too, has the entire issue of life span developmental approaches become prominent in developmentally oriented mental retardation studies during the past few years (e.g., Heller, 2004). Such work, though it has a long way to go, now encompasses both the life span development of persons with mental retardation themselves and of their families, a notion almost totally unexplored a decade or two ago.

Finally, we must appreciate that all of these advances have occurred against a background of both scientific and societal changes. Scientifically, advances in genetics have allowed for the discovery and specification of many genetic disorders. To give a few examples, Ewart et al. (1993) discovered in the early 1990s that a microdeletion on chromosome 7 was the cause of Williams syndrome; and in 2004, M. G. Butler, Bittel, Kibiryeva, Talebizadeh, and Thompson found that there are two behaviorally distinct deletion forms of Prader-Willi syndrome. In the same way, the technological advances behind structural and functional brain imaging have only recently come online, allowing for the specification of brain areas responsible for particular high-level behaviors.

Changes in society also constitute an important backdrop. Consider the entire topic of life span development. Until the past few decades, individuals with such genetic disorders as Prader-Willi syndrome or Down syndrome did not live into middle age or old age. Today they do. It has become imperative to determine how these individuals function throughout the adult years, and how certain disorders (e.g., Down syndrome) relate to other aging-related diseases (Alzheimer's). Moreover, such changes will intensify in the future. At present, 526,000 individuals 60 years and older with disabilities live in the United States; that number is expected to triple—to 1.5 million—by the year 2030 (National Center for Family Support, 2000). Advances in developmental approaches to mental retardation cannot be considered apart from changes in other scientific areas and in society at large.

In the early years of the twenty-first century, then, examining developmental approaches to mental retardation involves more than updating per se. We seem on the cusp of a new, even revolutionary, era, a time in which a developmental psychopathological view toward mental retardation seems more important and timely than ever.

To provide a flavor of the newest perspectives and advances in this area, we begin with a short description of the role of mental retardation from the perspective of developmental psychopathology before providing a brief summary of historical forays into this area. We then devote a section to the population itself, beginning with Zigler's (1967, 1969) two-group approach and then describing children with various genetic etiologies. Throughout these discussions, we also tackle the question of behavioral phenotypes and briefly hint at several methodological issues. We update several aspects of organismic development, particularly sequences and cross-domain relations. We then provide more extensive discussions of families, parents, siblings, and other contextual issues before concluding this chapter with a section discussing directions for the decades to come.

TIES OF MENTAL RETARDATION TO DEVELOPMENTAL PSYCHOPATHOLOGY

In the field of developmental psychopathology, mental retardation is unique. On one hand, mental retardation is essentially defined by a single developmental criterion: a significant delay in general cognitive development (along with adaptive impairments that generally accompany such cognitive deficits). Paradoxically, 1,000 different disorders can cause mental retardation.

To some extent, mental retardation is not a tangible disorder, like Autism or Obsessive-Compulsive Disorder, but a designation based on the construct of intelligence. Although failure at school, in the home, or in everyday life generally brings a child to the attention of professionals (MacMillan, Gresham, Siperstein, & Bocian, 1996), the formal diagnosis of mental retardation is made using performance on behavioral tasks to infer underlying levels of reasoning processes. In addition, deficits in intelligence, at least during the childhood years, are defined by discrepancies between the child's rate of intellectual development compared to typical, nonretarded children. Indeed, prior to the mid-1970s, IQ was defined in terms of developmental rates, as indicated by the historical formula "MA (mental age) divided by CA (chronological age) multiplied by 100."

Two other issues pertaining to mental retardation are noteworthy. First, the pattern of IQ subtest scores is irrelevant to the mental retardation diagnosis. As long as the final score falls below the IQ cutoff, the child or adult is considered to have mental retardation. Despite advances in understanding the genetic contributions to intellectual development (Iarocci, in press; Spinath, Harlaar, Ronald, &

Plomin, 2004), mental retardation reflects an arbitrarily chosen cutoff score of a gross behavioral measure of intellectual processes.

Second, the precise IQ cutoff has changed over time. Although an IQ of 70 or below has usually constituted the IQ cutoff, such has not always been the case. In Heber's (1961) manual of the American Association on Mental Deficiency (now American Association on Mental Retardation, the field's main professional group), an IQ cutoff of 85 and below was proposed. Later, Grossman (1973) moved the cutoff to IQ 70 or below. In 1992, the American Association on Mental Retardation (AAMR; 1992) proposed a cutoff of IQ 70 or 75 and below, before the IQ 70 and below cutoff was reestablished in the AAMR's 2002 manual.

Ironically, this single, arbitrarily designated measure of cognitive delay can arise from more than 1,000 different etiologies. These etiologies represent a smorgasbord of genetic, chromosomal, viral, and other physiological disorders. In addition, the developmental differences among these various disorders extend well beyond the degree of delay to unique cognitive-developmental characteristics that are sometimes so pervasive that they are clearly identifiable even when considering individual differences within a group (Burack, 1990; Burack, Hodapp, & Zigler, 1988, 1990; Dykens, Hodapp, & Finucane, 2000). Rates and trajectories of development, as well as profiles of relative strengths and weaknesses, are all highlighted in the more precise differentiation of various etiological groups.

Etiological differences also allow for unique insights into general developmental theory (for earlier reviews, see Cicchetti & Pogge-Hesse, 1982; Hodapp & Burack, 1990). To borrow a phrase from Urie Bronfenbrenner (1979), by studying different etiological groups, we begin to examine "experiments of nature." Such experiments of nature allow us to identify aspects of development that are universal, that occur in spite of vast differences across etiological groups, as opposed to aspects that might differ in different groups. Investigations of such issues are enhanced by researchers' ability to uniquely observe development in slow motion, thereby observing specific aspects of development that might not be observable when development progresses at a typical rate (Wagner, Ganiban, & Cicchetti, 1990).

Finally, behavioral differences across different etiological groups also relate to the very meaning of the term "development." In addition to sequences, stages, and other within-the-child developments, the reactions and behaviors of others to the developing child are part of developmental analyses. Just as the wider field of developmental psychology now includes more contextual and outside-of-the-child ideas within developmental frameworks, so, too, can contextual factors be included in developmental approaches applied to different etiologies.

We now turn to a brief historical background, highlighting questions of both what development is and how one should classify children with mental retardation.

HISTORICAL BACKGROUND

In addition to paying respect to the developmental forerunners of today's mental retardation field, this brief historical survey highlights the long-running tensions surrounding the contents of developmental approaches, the nature of the population to which these approaches are or should be applied, and the interplay between the two. As we hope to demonstrate, some of developmental psychology's most distinguished early theorists sensed these tensions and provided the groundwork for today's more detailed, more sophisticated analyses.

Heinz Werner

The first major early developmentalist to consider children with mental retardation is Heinz Werner. Although today Werner has been forgotten by many, he is historically best known for his grand theory of development. This theory is embodied in his orthogenetic principle, the view that development "proceeds from a state of relative globality and lack of differentiation to a state of differentiation, articulation, and hierarchic integration" (Werner, 1957, p. 126). This overarching theoretical principle was to be applied to such seemingly different phenomena as children, dream states, psychopathology, primitive societies, and "microgenesis" (or development "in the moment"), all issues studied by Werner and his students at Clark University.

Before his more well-known Clark University days, however, Werner worked from 1937 to 1943 as a research psychologist at the MacGregor Laboratories of the Wayne County Training School outside of Detroit. There, along with his colleague Alfred Strauss, Werner published approximately 30 studies on children with mental retardation (Witkin, 1964).

Several themes characterize this work. First, Werner (1937) originated the distinction between "process and achievement," the idea that the child's underlying mental processes were not necessarily equivalent to the child's achievement, or behavior. This realization amply demonstrated itself in children with mental retardation. In one study, children were asked to put together a multipiece puzzle. Werner and Strauss (1939, p. 39) noted that, in contrast to nonretarded children, the children with mental retardation "merely put the parts together quite mechanically, taking care only that the edges of the different pieces agreed perfectly with one another." By adopting this strategy, children with mental retardation could sometimes perform selected behaviors as well as their nonretarded peers.

Yet, in terms of the processes themselves, Werner (1957) generally viewed children with mental retardation as less developed, showing less "differentiation and hierarchic integration" than same-aged nonretarded children. In conceptualizing these children as developing normally but at slower rates than nonretarded children, Werner was the first major Western developmental theorist to apply theories of normal, nonretarded development to children with mental retardation.

Werner's contributions also included the distinction between organic and familial mental retardation. Specifically, Werner (1941) felt that only those children showing no specific cause of their retardation—those who were "endogenous" in their mental retardation—necessarily showed "normal" (albeit slower) developments. Other children were not considered to follow the usual developmental progressions, specifically those whose mental retardation was due to such external or "exogenous" causes as Down syndrome, anoxia at birth, or other organic etiologies.

Jean Piaget and Barbel Inhelder

Although Heinz Werner may have initiated the idea of a general developmental approach, Jean Piaget allowed for the approach's elaboration. Beginning in the 1920s, Piaget proposed a series of hierarchically organized stages with numerous specific, detailed sequences by which development occurred. Developmentally oriented researchers could then determine whether these sequences also held for children with mental retardation. In subsequent studies, Piagetian sequences were examined in children with mental retardation during the 1930s (Lane & Kinder, 1939), 1940s (Prothro, 1943), and 1950s (Woodward, 1959, 1963).

Most important, though, was the work of Piaget's colleague Barbel Inhelder. In her studies of children with mental retardation of various etiologies, Inhelder (1943/1968) noted both similarities and differences between these children and children without mental retardation. Like nonretarded children, children with mental retardation also appeared to develop along similar sequences in various Piagetian domains. Yet, in other ways, children with mental retardation differed markedly from

those without. Inhelder pointed to regressions, incomplete developments, and oscillations in children's responses between higher- and lower-level answers. She thus highlighted that children with mental retardation show more fits and starts, more tentative, more fragile development than do nonretarded children.

Lev Vygotsky

If Werner began and Piaget-Inhelder made specific the developmental analyses of children with mental retardation, Lev Vygotsky previews analyses that have yet to be done. Like Werner, Vygotsky worked with children with disabilities early in his career, from about 1924 to 1930 (van der Veer & Valsiner, 1991). His disability work centered on three major ideas: developmental analyses, mediation, and sociogenesis (Wertsch, 1985).

Like Werner and Piaget, Vygotsky was a "big picture" developmentalist who focused on many aspects of development. He was therefore acutely interested in how development occurs in children with disabilities. His focus was on how the child's entire personality structure is reorganized in relation to a particular disability (Reiber & Carton, 1993). Vygotsky's writings presaged ideas of compensation that permeate the wider field of developmental psychopathology.

A centerpiece of such developmental analyses involves mediation. Vygotsky conceptualized mediation in two ways: the adult mediating the child's development and the child mediating his or her own development. In the first, more social sense, mediation involves mother-child interactions and other individual or societal contacts that aid the developing child. Concerning children with disabilities, Vygotsky was particularly interested in how special education should be performed and whether these children should be in contact primarily with others like themselves or with the wider society. His goal, always, was for children with disabilities to become fully functioning, fully contributing members of their society. In contrast to Werner and Piaget, then, Vygotsky's mediational views contributed to current debates concerning integration, normalization, and how best to educate children with disabilities (Hodapp, 1998).

The third major theme in Vygotsky's work involved sociogenesis, or the idea that higher developments occur as a result of interactions with adults. Such views led to Vygotsky's (1978) zone of proximal development, probably his best-known idea among most Western psychologists. Even early on, Vygotsky applied this zone to children with mental retardation (van der Veer & Valsiner, 1991). His idea was to use the width of the zone—the time between the child's successful behaviors with and without adult help—to predict future development in individual children with mental retardation. To Vygotsky, two children with mental retardation can have identical levels of current functioning (i.e., mental ages) but very different prognoses. If, with adult help, one child is able to perform higher-level behaviors than the other, that first child has a wider zone and therefore a better prognosis.

Overview

In considering the work of Werner, Piaget, and Vygotsky, several issues deserve mention. First, in comparing Vygotsky to Werner and Piaget, one sees an early instance of the debate about the meaning of the term development. Is development related to children alone, or do developmental analyses also include the child's larger environment or child-environment interactions? For the most part, Werner and Piaget focused on the child as their object of development (although Werner, 1926/1948, did address the "Umwelt," or larger environment of different organisms). Through Vygotsky's emphasis on sociogenesis, his interest in child-environment interactions, and his desire to understand how children thrived in society in spite of their disabilities, he would be considered the more context-oriented developmentalist.

A second issue pertains to the use of children with mental retardation as natural experiments (for a recent discussion, see Cicchetti, 2003). Just as researchers today examine children with mental retardation to determine the connections and disconnections among levels of various domains, so did Werner, Piaget, and Vygotsky examine mental retardation with an eye toward applying and testing their theories. Hence Piaget's (1943/1968, p. 10) exclamation, "We must admit that we did not suspect that this [Piagetian] method would become central in her [Inhelder's] everyday practice."

Third, the three developmentalists differ as to whether the cause of mental retardation is relevant to developmental analyses. Neither Vygotsky nor Piaget-Inhelder mention the child's etiology in their writings on the development of children with mental retardation. In contrast, Werner (1941, p. 253) distinguished between endogenous and exogenous mental retardation, noting that "the assumption seems justified that deficiencies of this sort [i.e., exogenous, organic causes] must impede the learning processes in a way peculiar to the type of mental deficiency." Al-

though he never became more explicit, Werner presaged Zigler's two-group approach to mental retardation, which in more recent years has evolved into studies examining developmental differences in children with different genetic (and nongenetic) causes for their mental retardation.

DEVELOPMENT IN CHILDREN WITH MENTAL RETARDATION: DOES ETIOLOGY MATTER?

The question of who constitutes the subject group has long pervaded behavioral research in mental retardation. This issue continues to this day, has important developmental repercussions, and constitutes an area of enormous progress over the past 10 to 15 years.

Historically within the field of mental retardation behavioral research, most researchers have had little interest in how children come to have mental retardation. Mental retardation per se was thought to be prima facie evidence of some type of "brain impairment," and little else mattered. Over the decades, then, one notes numerous statements, often from the major researchers on behavior in individuals with mental retardation, that etiology does not matter (see Burack, Evans, Klaiman, & Iarocci, 2001). In contrast is attention to Zigler's two groups of persons with mental retardation and then, later, to different specific etiological groups.

Zigler's Two-Group Approach

In contrast to those who argued that the cause or etiology of the child's mental retardation is irrelevant, Zigler (1967, 1969) proposed his two-group approach to mental retardation: one group that does not show clear organic cause and another that does.

Specifically, proponents of the two-group approach hold that the first group consists of persons who show no identifiable cause for their mental retardation. Such individuals are generally more mildly impaired and tend to blend in with other, nonretarded persons. Probable causes range from polygenic inheritance to environmental deprivation (or overstimulation); different persons may have different polygenic or environmental causes, or there may be an interplay between the two. In Zigler's (1967, 1969) original formulations, he conceptualized this group as constituting the lower tail of the normal or Gaussian distribution of intelligence. This type of mental retardation has been referred to as familial, cultural familial, or sociocultural familial; nonorganic, nonspecific, or undifferentiated; and mental retardation due to environmental deprivation. This list highlights the discrepant beliefs about the causes of mental retardation in these individuals.

In contrast to those with cultural-familial mental retardation, other individuals show one or more organic causes for their mental retardation. Such causes include hundreds of separate organic insults. These insults can occur prenatally, perinatally, or postnatally. Prenatal causes include all of the 1,000+ genetic mental retardation disorders, Fetal Alcohol Syndrome (FAS), Fetal Alcohol Exposure (FAE), rubella, as well as all accidents in utero. Perinatal causes include prematurity, anoxia at birth, and other birth-related complications. Postnatal causes range from sickness (e.g., meningitis) to head trauma. In addition, those with organic mental retardation are more likely to show greater degrees of intellectual impairments; in most surveys, as IQ levels decrease, increasingly higher percentages of persons show an identifiable organic cause (Stromme & Hagberg, 2000).

Although various researchers (including Werner) had noted the existence of two groups of persons with mental retardation, Zigler was the first to make clear behavioral distinctions. In terms of behavioral development, children with cultural-familial—but not necessarily with organic—mental retardation were predicted to show both sequences and structures similar to those shown by typically developing children. Thus, the so-called similar-sequence hypothesis predicted that children with (cultural-familial) mental retardation should, like typically developing children, proceed in order through Piagetian or other normative stages of development. For the most part, this similar-sequence hypothesis has held true, even with children with various organic forms of mental retardation (e.g., Weisz & Zigler, 1979).

The second prediction, the similar-structure hypothesis, concerned the structure of cognitive-linguistic abilities from one domain to another. Specifically, Zigler held that cultural-familial mental retardation was not caused by any defect or deficit related to a single area of functioning. Instead, children with cultural-familial mental retardation were predicted to show a more generalized delay, affecting all areas of development to similar degrees, as evidenced by even or flat developmental profiles at the child's mental-age level. Much contradictory evidence exists concerning the similar-structure hypothesis, some even for children with cultural-familial mental retardation (e.g., Mundy & Kasari, 1990; Weiss, Weisz, & Bromfield, 1986; Weisz, 1990).

What about children with organic mental retardation? Here Zigler hedged his bets, believing that children with organic mental retardation might not follow universal sequences (similar-sequence hypothesis) or show flat or even developmental profiles (similar-structure hypothesis). To quote Zigler (1969):

> If the etiology of the phenotypic intelligence (as measured by an IQ) of two groups differs, *it is far from logical* to assert that the course of development is the same, or that even similar contents in their behaviors are mediated by exactly the same cognitive processes. (p. 533; italics added)

Viewed from the early twenty-first century, one could criticize several aspects of this two-group approach. First, the approach lumps into a single organic group individuals with many different types of mental retardation. In Zigler's defense, his *Science* article appeared in 1967, just 8 years after Lejeune, Gautier, and Turpin (1959) discovered that Down syndrome was caused in most cases by a third chromosome 21. Genetic knowledge and technology were relatively undeveloped, and the identification of most genetic disorders was decades away.

By the late 1980s, however, Zigler and his colleagues were beginning to question the utility of classifying so many separate etiologies into a single organic group. Noting different IQ trajectories in children with Down syndrome, cerebral palsy, and boys with Fragile X syndrome, Burack, Hodapp, and Zigler (1988, 1990) suggested differentiating the organic category. Not only was the organic group composed of children with many separate etiologies, but these etiologies might also lead to different, etiology-related behaviors.

Genetic Etiology and Behavioral Phenotypes

Among the most important recent advances is the focus on behavior in specific etiologies of mental retardation. By examining individuals with over 1,000 different genetic mental retardation syndromes, one can see diverse strengths-weaknesses and connections-disconnections across domains of development. One can also begin to tie together genetic anomalies, brain functioning, and behavior, the gene-brain-behavior relationships that have been the focus of research on many different conditions. Beyond the individuals themselves, one sees examples of different reactions by mothers, fathers, siblings, teachers, and others in the child's environment. Finally, by separately examining functioning in different genetic disorders, one can envision more targeted behavioral, educational, pharmacological, and other interventions.

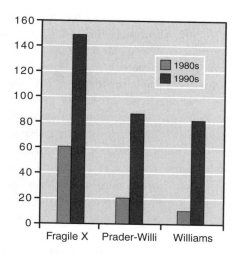

Figure 6.1 Behavioral research articles, 1980s versus 1990s. *Source:* From "Genetic and Behavioural Aspects: Application to Maladaptive Behaviour and Cognition" (pp. 13–48), by R. M. Hodapp and E. M. Dykens, in *Intellectual Disabilities: Genetics, Behavioural, and Inclusion,* J. A. Rondal, R. M. Hodapp, S. Soreci, E. M. Dykens, & L. Nota (Eds.), 2004, London: Whurr.

But before describing these many advances, it is instructive to document the move toward etiology-related studies. Consider the percentage of articles examining etiology from 1975 to 1980, 1985 to 1990, and 1995 to 2000 in the *American Journal on Mental Retardation,* the main research journal of behavioral work in mental retardation. Even taking a less stringent definition of etiology—any study examining as one of its research groups any organic condition—one sees remarkable change in even the past 20 years. In the late 1970s, 9% of research articles included one or more organic groups (mainly Down syndrome or phenylketonuria). By the late 1980s, this percentage had doubled to 17%, before almost doubling again, to 32%, by the late 1990s (Hodapp, 2004a).

Looked at another way, one could also examine studies on different genetic disorders over time. This time comparing the 1980s to the 1990s, large increases again occur in the number of behavioral research articles on such disorders as Williams, Prader-Willi, Rett, 5p– (Cri-du-chat), and Smith-Magenis syndromes (Figure 6.1, from Hodapp & Dykens, 2004). Examining both organicity in general and individual genetic disorders more specifically, behavioral research has proliferated on genetic mental retardation syndromes during the past 10 to 15 years (Dykens & Hodapp, 2001).

Definition of Behavioral Phenotypes

Given that behavioral research has exploded, how do genetic disorders affect those who have them? We here enter into the entire question of behavioral phenotypes, a term first used by William Nyhan (1972) over 3 decades ago, but whose definition remains contested to this day.

In its most basic meaning, the term behavioral phenotype highlights the outcomes or phenotypes—in this case, concerning behavior—that result from a particular genotype. Beyond this statement, however, researchers vary. One definition, provided by Flint and Yule (1994, p. 666), states that "a behavioral phenotype should consist of a distinct behavior that occurs in almost every case of a genetic or chromosomal disorder, and rarely (if at all) in other conditions." This definition thus reserves the term for behaviors that are distinctive, occur commonly among individuals with a genetic syndrome ("in almost every case"), and are unique to a single syndrome ("rarely . . . in other conditions").

We propose a less stringent definition, but one that may ultimately prove to be more useful for both research and intervention. According to Dykens (1995, p. 523), a behavioral phenotype involves "the heightened probability or likelihood that people with a given syndrome will exhibit certain behavioral and developmental sequelae relative to those without the syndrome." This second, more probabilistic definition highlights four basic facts:

1. *Many, but not all, individuals with a given syndrome will show the syndrome's "characteristic" behaviors.* A more probabilistic definition acknowledges the large amount of variance within specific etiologies. Indeed, rarely are etiology-related behaviors found in every person with a particular syndrome. Consider the case of Down syndrome. Even compared to their overall mental ages, children and adults with Down syndrome generally show deficits in linguistic grammar (Chapman & Hesketh, 2000: Fowler, 1990) and often show receptive language abilities in advance of expressive abilities (Miller, 1992, 1999). In addition, approximately 95% of mothers of children with Down syndrome report that others have difficulty understanding their child's articulation of words and phrases (Kumin, 1994).

Despite such commonly observed deficits, not every person with Down syndrome shows particular difficulties with grammar, articulation, or expressive language. Rondal (1995) recently reported on the case of Françoise, a 32-year-old woman whose IQ is 64. Although Françoise has trisomy 21, she nevertheless utters long and complex sentences. Rondal reports her saying (translated), "And that does not surprise me because dogs are always too warm when they go outside" ("Et ça m'étonné pas parce que les chiens ont toujours trop chaud quand ils vont à la port");

p. 117). Thus, although grammatical, articulatory, and expressive language problems may be common in Down syndrome, not every person with the syndrome shows such behavioral characteristics.

2. *Some etiology-related behaviors will be unique to a single syndrome, whereas others are common to two or more syndromes.* The second corollary of a more probabilistic definition considers whether an etiology-related distinctive behavior must occur "rarely (if at all) in other conditions." Recent research strongly implies that etiology-related behaviors are often not unique to a single syndrome.

In fact, connections between genetic syndromes and specific outcomes appear to be of at least two types. The first involves connections that truly are unique, that appear in one and only one genetic syndrome. The second involves connections that are "partially specific" (Hodapp, 1997), in that a few syndromes show a particular behavior that is not generally found in others with intellectual disabilities.

In the first, unique pattern, a genetic syndrome results in a behavioral outcome that is not seen in other genetic disorders. At present, the following behaviors seem unique to one and only one syndrome:

- Extreme hyperphagia (overeating; Dykens, 1999) in Prader-Willi syndrome
- The "cat-cry" (Gersh et al., 1995) in 5p– syndrome
- Extreme self-mutilation (Anderson & Ernst, 1994) in Lesch-Nyhan syndrome
- Stereotypic hand washing or hand-wringing (Van Acker, 1991) in Rett syndrome
- Body self-hugging (Finucane, Konar, Haas-Givler, Kurtz, & Scott, 1994) and putting objects into bodily orifices (Greenburg et al., 1996) in Smith-Magenis syndrome

Obviously, given such a short list, there are probably only a few instances in which a genetic disorder is unique in its behavioral effects. Flint and Yule (1994, p. 667) also noted this peculiarity, nominating as unique (in their term, as examples of a behavioral phenotype) only the self-mutilating behaviors in Lesch-Nyhan syndrome, overeating and abnormal food seeking in Prader-Willi syndrome, and the hand-wringing in Rett syndrome. Although Flint and Yule also propose a few other examples in which a behavior might be unique to one syndrome, such 1:1 relationships are relatively rare.

In contrast, many more instances seem to exist in which partial specificity is at work. To give but a few examples, a particular advantage in simultaneous (i.e., holistic, Gestalt-like) processing compared to sequential (step-by-step) pro-

cessing has now been found in boys with Fragile X syndrome (Burack et al., 1999; Dykens, Hodapp, & Leckman, 1987; Kemper, Hagerman, & Altshul-Stark, 1988) and in children with Prader-Willi syndrome (Dykens, Hodapp, Walsh, & Nash, 1992). Similarly, compared to groups with intellectual disabilities in general, hyperactivity is more frequently found in children with 5p– syndrome (Dykens & Clarke, 1997) and in boys with Fragile X syndrome (Baumgardner, Reiss, Freund, & Abrams, 1995). In both instances, a pattern of strengths and weaknesses or a particular type of maladaptive behavior-psychopathology is found in a few genetic disorders to much greater degree (or in higher percentages of individuals) than is commonly noted among others with mental retardation.

Finally, partially specific behavioral effects seem more in line with many areas of genetics, child psychiatry, and psychiatry. Across these different disciplines, researchers are now discussing the many pathways, both genetic and environmental, by which one comes to have one or another psychiatric disorder. In the terminology of developmental psychopathology, such partially specific pathways involve *equifinality,* the idea that, "in an open system, . . . the same end state may be reached from a variety of different initial conditions and through different processes" (Cicchetti & Rogosch, 1996, p. 597). The clinical geneticist John Opitz (1985, p. 9) put it well when he noted, "The causes are many, but the common developmental pathways are few."

3. *Etiology-related behaviors occur across many behavioral domains.* Behavioral phenotypes can be found in many different domains. Although much work has centered on maladaptive behaviors common to children with Prader-Willi, Williams, velocardiofacial, and other syndromes (Dykens et al., 2000), many other areas of functioning also show etiology-related behaviors. Thus, in growing numbers of detailed studies of the language of children with Williams syndrome, psycholinguists are gaining insights into whether language is indeed a "modular" system (Fodor, 1983). Such studies compare or correlate levels of functioning across different linguistic and nonlinguistic domains (e.g., Mervis, Morris, Bertrand, & Robinson, 1999). Similarly, various studies have focused on issues pertaining to visuospatial skills in children with Williams syndrome (Bellugi, Mills, Jernigan, Hickok, & Galaburda, 1999), jigsaw-puzzle playing in Prader-Willi syndrome (Dykens, 2002), and music in children with Williams syndrome (Lenhoff, 1998). The point is that behavioral phenotypes need not be limited to psychopathology or to any single domain of functioning. Moreover, at times, what is of interest is not a single behavior per se, but a pattern of strengths and weaknesses, connected or disconnected behaviors, or other patterns seen

in one or a few syndromes more often than in others with intellectual disabilities.

4. *A genetic disorder predisposes children to display a particular behavior or set of behaviors, which in turn elicit predictable reactions from others.* Although one generally thinks of behavior as the final outcome of genetic disorders, in many ways the child's behavior constitutes a midpoint in ongoing interactions and transactions with others.

In ongoing work, we have distinguished between direct effects and indirect effects of genetic mental retardation disorders (Hodapp, 1997; Ly & Hodapp, in press). Direct effects relate to the child's behaviors; genetic disorders predispose children and adults who have them to show specific, etiology-related patterns of strengths and weaknesses, developmental trajectories, and specific maladaptive behaviors and personalities. Indirect behaviors, in contrast, involve the effects that such behavioral characteristics have on others (Hodapp, 1999). To complicate matters, parental, sibling, teacher, and peer reactions and behaviors (indirect effects) can then feed back onto children themselves, helping to reinforce, extinguish, or modify the original behavior.

In recent years, we have been impressed by both the nature and complexity of such indirect effects. As we demonstrate later, children with different genetic disorders elicit behaviors from surrounding individuals partly based on their own etiology-related behaviors, and partly based on the meaning of their specific syndrome to parents and families. In addition, the child's behavior may not be the sole personal characteristic that elicits reactions and behaviors from others, and parental behaviors may operate differently in different contexts, tasks, and situations. We have barely begun to understand how, when, and why children with different genetic syndromes affect people in their surrounding environments.

ORGANISMIC ISSUES

Given the shift from examining "children with mental retardation" to examining "children with a specific syndrome," all discussions of organismic, and even of contextual, development must now occur on three distinct levels. One thus asks whether patterns of development seen in typically developing children are also seen in children with mental retardation more generally, in children with organic versus cultural-familial mental retardation, and in children with different genetic (or other organic) syndromes. We use this three-level approach to highlight issues concerning developmental sequences and cross-domain relations, the two main organismic issues. As noted subsequently, new

findings are changing the ways that these two venerable developmental topics are being conceptualized.

Similar Sequences

As briefly noted earlier, Zigler's (1967, 1969) developmental approach to mental retardation began with two hypotheses. With regard to the similar-sequence hypothesis, Zigler (1967) hypothesized that children with (cultural-familial) mental retardation would develop in the usual or normative sequences of development. Generally, the idea of similar sequences involves a clear, specifiable order to developmental attainments, measures of sequential development over time or cross-sectionally, and sequential development within a single domain. We first discuss these several subparts.

Clear, Specifiable Order to Developmental Attainments

By necessity, sequences must be clear and specifiable. The theorist must state what, exactly, is the behavior of interest, explaining what does and does not qualify for the child to be considered to have attained a specific stage or substage. In the object permanence subdomain of Piagetian sensorimotor stages, for example, behaviors specifically involve the child uncovering an object under 1 versus 3 cloths, first with visible and then with invisible displacement, and specifications as to how often such behaviors must occur (e.g., 1 out of 2 trials; Dunst, 1980; Uzgiris & Hunt, 1975).

In the same way, the sequence or ordering itself must be specified. The child in the earliest step or substep will be able to recognize an entire object from seeing only a part of that object. In contrast, at a higher level, the child will retrieve a partially hidden object, then a totally hidden object, then an object hidden under more than one screen, and finally an object hidden invisibly (within the experimenter's hand) under one of the three screens. In short, the progression from Step 1 to Step 2 to Step 3 to Step 4 is clear and testable.

Over Time or Cross-Sectional Indicators

Strictly speaking, sequences only appear over time. To continue with the object permanence example, a typically developing child of 4 months would be expected to identify a bottle in which the nipple was turned away, but to be able to perform no other tasks. A few weeks or months later, the child would be able to perform the easier task, but now might also be able to retrieve an object hidden under one cloth. Later still, the two easier tasks would be performed, but the child would also be able to retrieve an object hidden under three cloths, with invisible displacements.

Though normative developmental sequences are best examined longitudinally, attempts have been made to examine sequences cross-sectionally. Such tests can be performed in several ways. One test involves order-of-difficulty examinations (Weisz, Yeates, & Zigler, 1982). Consider three groups of typically developing children, ages 8 months, 12 months, and 16 months. According to Piaget's theory, most 8-month-olds should be able to retrieve an object that was partially hidden, fewer would find an object hidden under a single screen, and almost none would be able to find an object hidden under three screens. Among the 12-month-olds, all should be able to find partially hidden objects, most should be able to retrieve an object under a single screen, and a few might even be able to solve the 3-screen task. Finally, 16-month-olds should all be able to solve the first two problems, and most should be able to retrieve an object hidden under three screens.

In addition to using three groups to demonstrate sequential development, similar findings can be noted using diverse groups of children at different ages. Here one relies on Guttman scaling (Green, 1956; Guttman, 1950), along with recent modifications and extensions (e.g., Rasch modeling; see Dawson, 2002, for a reanalysis of Kohlberg's moral reasoning tasks). The idea, now applied to each single child, is that, if three different tasks occur in a set sequence, and if lower-order tasks do not drop out when higher-level tasks come in, then the child should show sequential ordering of difficulty. Thus, if tasks occur in a 1, 2, 3 order, then a child might pass item 1 but not 2 and 3, or pass 1 and 2 but not 3, or pass or fail all three items. Rarely, if ever, should a child pass item 2 but fail item 1, or pass 3 and fail either item 1 or item 2.

Within a Single Domain

A final issue, that sequences occur within a specific domain or even subdomain, is not so often noted. To Piaget, cognition during infancy can be divided into such subdomains as object permanence, causality, symbolic play, means-ends relations, and vocal and gestural imitation. Later sensorimotor scales were used to examine sequential development within each of these different subdomains separately.

But what constitutes a single subdomain of intellectual functioning is not so obvious. Simply stated, it is not always clear which particular behaviors constitute an underlying "skills family." For example, most early language researchers would consider early hand gestures, such as pointing or showing, as evidence of the same early communicative skills that will later result in spoken language. Other domains of cognition or language may also exist.

Similar Sequence Findings

This background into sequential development helps frame the similar-sequence findings. Until recently, the findings related to the similar-sequence hypothesis appeared clearcut. Looking at most domains and subdomains, children with mental retardation follow, in order, the usual or normative sequences of development (Weisz & Zigler, 1979). Moving to the two groups of children with organic and cultural-familial mental retardation, this statement still mostly holds. One possible exception might involve children with severe seizure disorders, but here difficulties arise in relation to what constitutes a valid test of these children's abilities. Children with mental retardation may also become less systematic or differently sequential when tasks are more social, or occur later in development, as opposed to these children's usual invariant sequential developments on earlier and less social tasks (Hodapp, 1990).

But the issue becomes more interesting when one considers specific etiological groups. Children with Down syndrome, the most studied group, usually follow the hypothesized normative sequences (Cicchetti & Beeghly, 1990; Dunst, 1990), but other differences may arise. Specifically, Dunst (1990) and Wishart and Duffy (1990) noted an increased "fragility" of development among children with Down syndrome, such that a "2 steps forward, 1 step backward" pattern seems more likely to hold. Some even question whether the fragility of development in Down syndrome extends beyond greater numbers of regressions per se, as children do not always show patterns of failing the highest stage earlier achieved (Morss, 1983).

But the most intriguing findings concern the early communicative development of children with Williams syndrome. In most typically developing children, gestural communication, what Bates, Camaioni, and Volterra (1975) call "proto-declaratives" and "proto-imperatives," occur prior to verbal expression of words per se. But Mervis, Robinson, Rowe, Becerra, and Klein-Tasman (2003) reported that this sequence of pointing before speaking was not found in 9 of 10 children with Williams syndrome. On average, these 9 children with Williams syndrome produced referential object labels ("ball") 6 months before beginning to comprehend or produce referential pointing gestures. Although this finding makes sense given the intellectual profiles shown by most children with William syndrome (discussed later), such findings nevertheless have many theoretical and practical implications.

Cross-Domain Relations

The second of Zigler's developmental predictions concerned the structuring of development from one domain to another. According to the similar-structure hypothesis, when matched on overall mental age to nonretarded children, children with mental retardation should perform similarly on a specific cognitive or linguistic task. For example, groups matched on overall mental age (i.e., MA matches) should perform similarly on linguistic, attentional, or other cognitive-linguistic tasks. In essence, there should be no outstanding strengths or weaknesses in the intellectual abilities of children with mental retardation; these children should be developing at a slower rate than nonretarded children, but their developmental profiles should be flat or even.

Historically, the similar-structure hypothesis has two sources, one explicit and one implicit. Explicitly, Zigler was arguing against those who theorized many defects in mental retardation. He argued that, if children with cultural-familial retardation did not have any single defect causing their mental retardation, then they should show MA-level performances on Zeaman and House's attentional, Luria's language mediational, or Ellis's stimulus trace tasks. Zigler has long been criticized for arguing that "no differences" findings support the similar-structure position (Spitz, 1983); technically, when two groups do not differ statistically, one can state only that they do not differ, not that their performances are necessarily the same (see also Weisz et al., 1982). Such studies do imply, however, that no single skill appears as a deficit below the child's overall level of mental age. By inference, no single deficit seems to be causing the child's mental retardation. Such reasoning led to Zigler's adherence of MA matches in retarded-nonretarded comparisons of intellectual or linguistic functioning.

Implicitly, Zigler was also influenced by Piaget's horizontal stage notion of development. If children with cultural-familial mental retardation develop like nonretarded children, then they, too, should show identical or near-identical level functioning across various cognitive tasks, as Piaget proposed (Kessen, 1962). Although such views of Piagetian structures have since been criticized (Fodor, 1983; Gardner, 1983), Zigler implicitly followed the idea of horizontally organized developments in his theorizing about children with cultural-familial mental retardation.

Findings

Findings seem fairly clear for the similar-structure hypothesis. The similar-structure hypothesis holds up reasonably well for children with cultural-familial mental retardation, although even here children display performance that is below overall MA levels on some information-processing tasks (Weiss et al., 1986). Less clear is why such lower-than-expected functioning occurs. Some researchers have postulated that children with cultural-familial mental retardation really do have a deficit in their information-processing abilities (Mundy & Kasari, 1990); conversely, any seeming deficit may be due more to the boring, repetitive nature of many information-processing tasks (Weisz, 1990) or other motivational factors such as outerdirectedness (Bybee & Zigler, 1998). In contrast, all would agree that children with organic mental retardation show performance on several cognitive-linguistic tasks that falls below their overall mental ages.

Again, the most discrepant findings relate to specific genetic mental retardation disorders. Over the past 10 to 15 years, a variety of etiology-related strengths-weaknesses have been noted in different genetic mental retardation disorders. Some of these findings concern different aspects of intellectual functioning. Findings of this sort include the simultaneous-over-sequential processing results for boys with Fragile X syndrome and for individuals of both genders with Prader-Willi syndrome. Other strengths-weaknesses relate across tests, for example, the many findings of language-over-visuospatial abilities among children with Williams syndrome (Mervis et al., 1999). See Table 6.1 for a description of several of the more striking cognitive-linguistic strengths and weaknesses in several etiological groups.

Remaining Issues

Recent etiologically related findings of strengths and weakness are intriguing for a variety of reasons. To families and teachers of children with different syndromes, these profiles of development may lead to more targeted programs of intervention (Hodapp & Fidler, 1999). But etiology-related profiles also relate to critical developmental questions, a few of which we describe next.

What Are the Connections (or Disconnections) across Various Domains of Functioning? Here, the recent (and many ongoing) studies of children with Williams syndrome are most instructive. Particularly in earlier studies, language functioning was thought to be modular in Williams syndrome. Modularity, in Fodor's (1983) sense, refers to an encapsulated system that develops with little or no contact with other elements of the child's development (see also Gardner's, 1983, multiple intelligences). Given the high-level language abilities of some children with

TABLE 6.1   Prominent Genetic Forms of Mental Retardation

Disorder	Genetics	Prevalence	Prominent Behavioral Features
Down syndrome	95% involve trisomy 21	1–1.5/1,000 live births	Moderate MR; social strengths; weaknesses in grammar and speech; relative strengths in auditory versus visual short-term memory
Prader-Willi syndrome	66% involve deletions on chromosome 15, now known to be of two types; remainder involve maternal disomy	1/15,000 live births	Mild MR; proneness to obesity, food foraging, and preoccupations; stubbornness and obsessive-compulsive behaviors; visuospatial strengths (especially in jigsaw puzzles)
Williams syndrome	Microdeletion on chromosome 7	1/20,000 live births	Mild MR; high levels of sociability; relatively strong language skills and weak visuospatial skills; hyperacusis; high levels of fearfulness and anxiety

Williams syndrome, a strong case for modularity of language seemed to have been made.

In recent years, however, the picture has changed markedly. The main issue here concerns strengths and weaknesses, which obviously occur, and the degree to which a "strong area" is connected to a "weak area." If modularity truly holds, few connections should obtain; if the areas are linked, then we have evidence of specific strengths and weaknesses, but not of modularity per se. This latter conclusion seems most likely. Unlike what would be predicted from a modular perspective, Mervis et al. (1999) found strong correlations (from .47 to .64) between various measures of short-term memory and grammatical levels. Although language is relatively strong and visuospatial skills weak in children with Williams syndrome, these children's language is also not totally modular. In line with typically developing children, language in children with Williams syndrome connects to other areas of these children's cognition.

How and Why Do Various Strengths and Weaknesses Develop?   A second issue concerns the development of these various strengths and weaknesses over time. Obviously, etiology-related strengths and weaknesses do not appear fully formed at birth; no child with Williams syndrome has perfect language at birth, no child with any other syndrome shows such pronounced patterns of strengths and weaknesses, fully formed, at birth. But how such strengths and weaknesses appear has only begun to be examined. During the past few years, several researchers have examined cognitive-linguistic profiles over time in children with several different etiologies of mental retardation. Most studies have been cross-sectional, although a few recent studies have examined evolving profiles as the child develops.

Across several etiological groups, with increasing chronological age the children's strengths develop more

quickly than do their weaknesses. In Down syndrome, the pattern of visual-over-auditory short-term memory becomes more pronounced during the late teen years (Hodapp & Ricci, 2002), and, among boys with Fragile X syndrome, the advantage of simultaneous-over-sequential processing also becomes more pronounced as these children get older (Hodapp, Dykens, Ort, Zelinsky, & Leckman, 1991). In the sole longitudinal study, Jarrold, Baddeley, Hewes, and Phillips (2001) examined children with Williams syndrome to determine the development of vocabulary (a relative strength in this syndrome) versus visuospatial skills (a relative weakness). Examining 15 children and adolescents on six occasions over a 4-year period, Jarrold et al. found that vocabulary levels developed much more quickly over time than did visuospatial skills. Such divergent trajectories allow already existing relative strengths to become gradually stronger and relative weaknesses gradually weaker as these children get older.

Although no good explanations exist as to why strengths become stronger and weaknesses weaker over time, one possibility involves an interplay between etiology-related propensities and subsequent experiences. One measure of experience involves the child's everyday, leisure-time activities, that is, those behaviors that children (or their parents) choose to perform every day. In one study, Rosner, Hodapp, Fidler, Sagun, and Dykens (2004) examined the everyday leisure activities of three groups of children: those with Williams syndrome, with Prader-Willi syndrome, and with Down syndrome. Using parent reports of leisure-time behavior from Achenbach's (1991) Child Behavior Checklist, behaviors were grouped into those involving music, reading, visual-motor activities, athletics, pretend play, and focused interests.

The findings mostly reflect etiology-related strengths and weaknesses. In line with their excellent skills in jigsaw puzzles, 50% of children with Prader-Willi syndrome played with jigsaw puzzles, whereas only 9% and 2%, respectively, of persons with Down syndrome and Williams syndrome engaged in this activity. Conversely, in line with their visuospatial weaknesses, children with Williams syndrome did not engage in visuospatial activities. In the overall category of visual-motor activities, only 31% of those with Williams syndrome participated in any visual-motor activities, compared to 76% and 60% of persons with Prader-Willi and Down syndromes, respectively. Specific behaviors like arts-and-crafts activities were listed for 35% of the group with Down syndrome and for 30% of individuals with Prader-Willi syndrome, but for only 7% of those with Williams syndrome. Persons with Williams syndrome (or their parents) seem to avoid activities that these children may find difficult to perform.

Our suspicion is that genetic etiologies predispose children to particular cognitive-linguistic profiles, but that these profiles then become more pronounced due to the child's ongoing experiences. For most syndromes, the degree of difference between levels of strong versus weak areas is probably relatively small during the early years. As children more often perform activities in strong areas and avoid activities in weaker areas, however, increasing discrepancies arise. A snowball effect may thus result from the interplay of the child's etiology-related propensities and the child's ongoing transactions with the environment. Such views also seem consonant with the late-appearing gestures (as opposed to verbal labels) in the early communication of children with Williams syndrome (Mervis et al., 2003).

This perspective also seems in line with the notion that behavioral phenotypes are best conceptualized within a dynamic, developmental framework. To quote Karmiloff-Smith and Thomas (2003, p. 980), "More complex cognitive structure = less complex structure × process of development." In essence, then, Williams syndrome, like all genetic disorders, simply sets the stage for later interactions-transactions with the environment over time. But exactly how such interplays proceed—and their effects on the child's developing brain—must remain open at present.

What Is the Relationship between Similar Sequences and Cross-Domain Profiles? When describing the similar-sequence hypothesis, we noted that sequences were generally considered within single domains or subdomains. Thus, one examined sequences within object permanence or among early communicative development. The idea of strong and weak areas did not enter in.

Given recent findings, however, it becomes necessary to link sequences and cross-domain relations. Consider the finding that children with Williams syndrome do not show the sequence of communicative gestures before verbal words. Examined only as an example of the similar-sequence hypothesis (without reference to the usual Williams syndrome profile of cognitive-linguistic strengths and weaknesses), one simply reports an example of nonnormative sequences. By joining both sequences and cross-domain profiles, however, one sees the influence of etiology-related strengths-weaknesses even on sequences within a single domain or subdomain. In this case, children with Williams syndrome show particular difficulties on many visual-spatial tasks. Even in infancy, then, they seem to have difficulty in gestures, even those (such as pointing and showing) that relate to early communication. For our purposes, it now seems necessary to link sequences, which have always been considered within a single domain, and cross-domain relations. The two seem related, and it is likely that, once one knows the specific strengths and weaknesses demonstrated by several different etiological groups, one might almost be able to predict examples in which most children with a particular syndrome might be likely *not* to show the usual or normative sequences of development.

Summary

Although questions of sequences and cross-domain organization pervade developmental work over many decades, our understandings of these issues have advanced greatly over the past decade. Even until the year 2000, the similar-sequence finding held for most conditions and developmental sequences. Only recently have several nonnormative sequences been noted, complicating the idea that development in children with mental retardation is merely slowed compared to typically developing children. Similarly, with respect to cross-domain relations, recent findings highlight which particular domains within which particular etiologies are relative strengths or weaknesses. Even more recent work begins to document that etiology-related strengths and weaknesses become more pronounced with age and, in a preliminary way, explains why such intensifications of cognitive-intellectual profiles might occur.

Finally, sequences and structures need to be examined within a single conceptual framework. Though their connections might seem obvious, similar-sequence and similar-structure studies have, until now, generally proceeded in isolation one from another. But if indeed nonnormative sequences most often occur within weak areas of functioning, we begin to see how the two interrelate. Remaining to be examined are the implications of this basic interrelationship for interventions and for better understandings of cross-domain relations and sequential developments. Given the new studies of behavioral development in many different etiological groups, we are only now truly understanding sequences and structures.

CONTEXTUAL DEVELOPMENT

Compared to sequences and structures of children's own development, the contexts in which children with mental retardation develop have been studied for a much shorter time. This relatively short research history reflects relations between developmental psychology proper and developmental approaches to mental retardation.

To provide a brief history, Zigler (1967, 1969) formalized the developmental approach to mental retardation in the late 1960s. With Weisz in the 1970s and with Cicchetti, Beeghly, Pogge-Hesse, Hodapp, and Burack from the 1980s on, that approach was tested, applied to new (mostly organic) populations, and updated. The updates from the 1980s informed traditional issues of sequences and structures but also capitalized on newer work in the wider field of developmental psychology. Bell's (1968) work on interactionism and mother-child interactions, Sameroff and Chandler's (1975) transactional model, and Bronfenbrenner's (1979) ecology of childhood all began to be included in developmental approaches, in preliminary form during the 1980s (Zigler & Hodapp, 1986), with more elaboration during the 1990s (Burack, Hodapp, & Zigler, 1998; Hodapp, 1998; Hodapp & Zigler, 1995).

Four Preliminary Issues

Other background issues go beyond the history of developmental approaches to mental retardation per se. Before discussing mother-child interactions and families of children with disabilities, we first note four preliminary issues that frame such topics.

Subject Groups

Just as in studies of children themselves, studies of parents and families must be evaluated based on who is being studied. Does a particular study examine parents or families of children with disabilities, of children with mental retardation, or of children with a particular syndrome? As before, many more studies exist concerning either parents-families of children with disabilities or with mental retardation in general; fewer focus on children with a specific genetic

syndrome (usually Down syndrome) or psychiatric disorder (usually Autism).

But as we are increasingly appreciating, differences may arise depending on which parents or families one examines. Parents and families overall react differently to children with one versus another genetic mental retardation syndrome. Such reactions relate to the child's personality and maladaptive behavior or, in certain circumstances, to the child's actual or perceived cognitive-linguistic strengths and weaknesses. Further complications may also relate to the child's age and the parents' knowledge of etiology-related behaviors. Different findings may occur when one is examining parents or families of children with mental retardation compared to parents-families of children with one or another particular genetic syndrome (Seltzer, Abbeduto, Krauss, Greenberg, & Swe, 2004).

Same but Different Sets of Parental-Familial Needs

Parents and families of children with disabilities have some needs in common and some that differ from those of parents-families of typically developing children. On one hand, the needs of the two groups are similar. Both sets of parents need to provide for and socialize their children, promote their children's development, and launch their adolescents into (hopefully successful) adult lives. At the same time, these families face reactions and needs that are specific to parents and families of children with disabilities. In contrast to parents of typically developing children, parents of children with disabilities need to learn about the many support services available in their community; about the many legal rights, hearings, and appeals that surround educational and other services; and about detailed aspects of the services themselves, the individualized family service plans (IFSPs) during preschool, individualized educational plans (IEPs) during school years, and individualized transition plans (ITPs) during the transition from adolescence to adulthood.

Parents of children with specific genetic syndromes have other, more specialized needs. These needs relate to learning about their child's specific condition, about which professionals, centers, schools, group homes, or respite care settings might be most helpful, and about parent groups specific to their child's disability. Parent needs therefore exist on three levels: as parents of any child, as parents of a child with disabilities, and as parents of a child with a specific disability condition.

Cutting across these differing needs are both formal (professional) and informal (nonprofessional) support systems. To most family researchers, support can be divided into three types (e.g., Kazak, 1987). First, *emotional support* helps parents and other family members come to terms with the strong emotional reactions that accompany raising a child with disabilities. Second, *informational support* involves gaining knowledge about the child, the child's condition, necessary services, and treatment options available in one's own local community. Third, *tangible support* concerns money, interventions, and the performance of such day-to-day tasks as providing babysitting or respite care or driving the child to out-of-home-based therapy. Each type of support is important, and each is probably needed by most parents some of the time.

Changing Perspectives toward Families in the Disabilities Field

In developmental psychology, studies are relatively new of families, mother-child interaction, and the larger ecology of childhood. Depending on the specific topic, such studies date to the early to late 1970s. In contrast, families of children with disabilities have been examined for over 100 years (Blacher & Baker, 2002), with more sustained research attention over the past 40. But even from about 1960 on, such history has changed dramatically.

Most early studies considered only the negative consequences that may arise from parenting a child with disabilities. Using Freud's (1917/1957) model of mourning in response to losses of any kind, Solnit and Stark (1961) described what they called "maternal mourning." On the birth of a child with disabilities, mothers mourn, as in a death, the loss of the idealized, perfect child. Mothers were thought to experience grieving that was characterized by a specific, stage-like process (see Blacher, 1984). Following Solnit and Stark, family studies of the 1960s and 1970s then focused on depression, neuroticism, role tensions, and other adverse psychological effects. Some researchers examined depression in mothers (Cummings, Bayley, & Rie, 1966; Friedrich & Friedrich, 1981) and in fathers (Cummings, 1976). Others studied siblings, noting that the oldest nondisabled daughters may be most at risk for psychological problems due to increased household or child care responsibilities (Lobato, 1983). The general conclusion was that bad things happen to families of children with disabilities.

Beginning in the early 1980s, researchers began to adopt a more balanced view of these families. In 1983, Crnic, Friedrich, and Greenberg proposed that, instead of necessarily negative or pathological outcomes, the outcomes arising from parenting a child with disabilities might better be construed in terms of stress and coping. In stress-and-coping models, the child with disabilities is considered an increased stressor on the family, but one that different parents and families handle differently. Parenting the child with disabilities thus became akin to handling any stressor, such as coping with the illness of a parent or child, or losing a job, or moving. Like reactions to all stressors, parents and families can react either positively or negatively.

This shift from negative-pathological to stress-and-coping models had several effects on subsequent research. The main effect was a more positive view. Parents and families of children with disabilities were no longer thought to always be negatively affected, although they could be. Instead, researchers began to search for risk and protective factors within children, parents, and families (Hodapp, 2002).

Secular Changes toward Children with Disabilities and Their Families

At the same time as disability professionals changed their conceptualizations of these parents and families, parallel changes occurred in society at large (Glidden, 2002). Consider where and how children with disabilities live. In the mid- to late 1960s, many more persons, including children, resided in large, often impersonal institutions. In 1967, almost 200,000 Americans lived in institutions, including 91,000 children. By 1997, that number had fallen to 56,161, including fewer than 3,000 children (Anderson, Lakin, Mangan, & Prouty, 1998; Lakin, Prouty, Braddock, & Anderson, 1997). Of those children who remained at home during the 1960s and early 1970s, access to formal education varied widely, depending mainly on the generosity of their particular town or state. Only in 1974, with the passage of the federal Education for All Handicapped Children Act (PL 94-142), were U.S. states and towns required to provide a "free, appropriate public education" to all students, including those with disabilities (see Hallahan & Kauffman, 2002).

Over these past few decades, services have also extended beyond simply schooling. Across the United States, states now provide early intervention services during the 0- to 3-year period. Later, after the school-age years, transition and adult services help young adults with disabilities to work and live as independently as possible (Wehman, 2001). Services for individuals and their families are thus lifelong, and one must consider the interplay between children-parents-families and the service-delivery system from a life span perspective.

Beyond the presence of services themselves, one must consider how such services are conceptualized. Partly due to the change from pathological to stress-and-coping models, service delivery is now considered in terms of supporting families. Instead of being conceptualized as patients who need to be cured, today's parents, siblings, and families are conceptualized as consumers of services who require different sets of long- or short-term support to cope more effectively. This "support revolution" has changed the nature of services and how such services are understood by families and professionals (Hallahan & Kauffman, 2002).

Mother-Child Interactions

These four issues, then, frame our examinations of contextual issues related to children with disabilities. As in our discussions of organismic developmental topics, we again highlight two issues: mother-child interactions and family coping. Here again we focus on more general findings relating to parents-families of children with disabilities as well as on newer work examining both interactions and family reactions concerning children with different genetic disorders.

Studies of Mothers and Children with Mental Retardation

Owing much to Bell's (1968) interactionism, in the early 1970s researchers began to examine mother-child interactions when children had mental retardation. The initial question was one of "same or different": Were mothers' behaviors toward their child with mental retardation the same as or different from maternal behaviors to typically developing children?

Such differences were found in most early studies. Buium, Rynders, and Turnure (1974) and Marshall, Hegrenes, and Goldstein (1973) found that mothers of children with Down syndrome provided less complex verbal input and were more controlling in their interactive style than were mothers of same-age nonretarded children. Although these authors noted only that the two groups of mothers differed in their behaviors, later workers citing these studies referred to the "verbal deprivation" (Mahoney, 1975) encountered by children with mental retardation.

But not all studies found such differences in maternal input. Rondal (1977) and Buckhalt, Rutherford, and Goldberg (1978) observed that mothers of children with mental retardation behaved similarly to mothers of nonretarded children. Rondal noted that, when children with Down syndrome and nonretarded children were matched on the child's mean length of utterance (MLU), "None of the comparisons of mothers' speech to normal and to Down

Syndrome children led to differences that were significant or close to significant" (p. 242) between the two groups. Additionally, both groups of mothers adjusted their language upward (e.g., longer MLUs) as the children's language level increased. Rondal concluded, "The maternal linguistic environment of DS children between MLU 1 and 3 is an appropriate one" (p. 242).

In reconciling such divergent findings, most differences across studies seem to be due to methodological differences. In general, when children with mental retardation were matched to nonretarded children on chronological age (CA), mothers of children with mental retardation interacted differently. But children with mental retardation are, by definition, functioning at levels below nonretarded agemates; CA matching may thus be inappropriate. A more appropriate strategy might be to match mother-child dyads on the child's mental age (MA) or the child's level of language (MLU).

An additional issue concerns the focus of the interaction. Although mothers of children with mental retardation are equivalent to mothers of typically developing, MA- (or MLU-) matched children on their levels of linguistic input, such is usually not the case when maternal style is examined. Compared to mothers of typically developing children, mothers of children with mental retardation are often found to be more didactic, directive, and intrusive (Marfo, 1990). Such stylistic differences between mothers of children with and without mental retardation are seen on a number of levels. Tannock (1988) found that, compared to mothers of nonretarded children, mothers of children with Down syndrome took interactive turns that were longer and more frequent; in addition, these mothers more often "clashed," or spoke at the same time as their children (also Vietze, Abernathy, Ashe, & Faulstich, 1978). These mothers also switched the topic of conversation more often, and less often silently responded to the child's utterance.

Although this stylistic difference has since been noted in many studies, why mothers in the two groups differ remains unclear. The most common explanation is that mothers of children with mental retardation inject their parenting concerns into the interactive session. Greater numbers of mothers of children with mental retardation consider interactions as "teaching sessions," as moments not to be squandered in the nonstop effort to intervene effectively (Cardoso-Martins & Mervis, 1984; Jones, 1980). In contrast, mothers of typically developing children display fewer fears and concerns; they may simply desire to play—in a more spontaneous, less directive manner—with their typically developing children.

Studies of Mothers and Children with Specific Genetic Etiologies

Over the past decade, studies began to examine mother-child interactions when children have different genetic etiologies. Following from the indirect effects model described earlier (Hodapp, 1999), the question concerns how different genetic disorders lead to different child behaviors, which in turn lead to different maternal reactions.

To date, two sets of studies show such etiology-related differences in maternal behaviors. The first concerns children with Down syndrome and so-called dependency cues. To simplify somewhat, compared to children with mental retardation overall, children with Down syndrome have long been considered to have upbeat, sociable personalities (Carr, 1995; Hornby, 1995) and to show lesser amounts of maladaptive behavior-psychopathology (Dykens & Kasari, 1997; Meyers & Pueschel, 1991). But these children may also have other characteristics that lead others to want to nurture them. Compared to typical children of the same chronological age, children with Down syndrome generally display more infantile, "babylike" faces (Allanson, O'Hara, Farkas, & Nair, 1993). As Zebrowitz (1997) showed, adults perceive babyfaced (as opposed to more "adult-faced") individuals as more sociable, warmer, dependent, naïve, and compliant. In one study in which naïve adults rated children's faces, adults perceived children with Down syndrome (compared to children with other types of mental retardation) as more dependent, babylike, and warmer (Fidler & Hodapp, 1999).

In further work, Fidler (2003) examined the nature of maternal vocalizations—so-called motherese—provided to children with Down syndrome. As one might expect when interacting with more immature, dependent-looking children, mothers gave more high-pitched and variably pitched intonation patterns in interactions with their children with Down syndrome than to children with mixed mental retardation of similar mental ages. Although it remains unclear what exactly mothers were reacting to (the child's personality, lack of psychopathology, or facial appearance), mothers of children with Down syndrome nevertheless showed differences in their interactive behaviors compared to mothers of children with other types of mental retardation.

A second set of studies relates to mothers' reactions to their child's cognitive strengths and weaknesses. In one study, Ly and Hodapp (in press) examined child effects on parents' behaviors in parent-child dyads of children with Prader-Willi syndrome versus with Williams syndrome. These two groups were chosen due to the fact that children with Prader-Willi syndrome are, on average, particularly proficient in jigsaw puzzles (Dykens, 2002). In contrast, children with Williams syndrome are generally deficient in a wide variety of visual-spatial skills (including jigsaw puzzles). In a short parent-child interaction, Ly and Hodapp measured parents' amount of helping and reinforcement behaviors in response to interacting with their child to complete a jigsaw puzzle task. From attribution theory (Graham, 1991), parents of children with Williams syndrome (versus with Prader-Willi syndrome) were hypothesized to provide more help and reinforcement during the jigsaw puzzle interaction task.

Compared to parents of children with Prader-Willi syndrome, parents of children with Williams syndrome provided more helping and more reinforcement behaviors. Within the 5-minute interaction session, parents of children with Williams syndrome helped their child 49 times, compared to slightly fewer than 24 times for the Prader-Willi parents. Similarly, parents of children with Williams syndrome reinforced their children over twice as often as did parents of children with Prader-Willi syndrome (means = 14.14 and 5.75, respectively). Further analyses showed that both the child's level of puzzle abilities and the specific etiology (and, presumably, the mother's sense of what her child with Williams or Prader-Willi syndrome "should do") both contributed to these between-group differences in maternal interactive behaviors.

These findings indicate that different genetic mental retardation syndromes may have indirect effects on parents. If parents of children with Down syndrome react to their child's more pleasant personality, lack of maladaptive behavior, and babylike facial appearance, and those of children with Prader-Willi and Williams syndromes react to high versus low puzzle abilities (respectively), then different genetic disorders may indirectly affect surrounding adults.

Families

More than most areas of mental retardation work, family research has been affected by changing perspectives over the past 20 years. In contrast to the more negative, pathological view held by professionals a few decades ago, researchers now conceptualize families of children with mental retardation more from stress-and-coping perspectives. This change has led to new theoretical models, studies of families of children with specific etiologies, and approaches in how research is performed.

Theoretical Models

The shift from negative-pathological to stress-and-coping perspectives has spurred new models that emphasize heterogeneity from one family to another. Consider the so-called Double ABCX model (Minnes, 1988; adapted from McCubbin & Patterson's, 1983, ABCX model). According to the Double ABCX model, the effects of the "crisis" of having a child with retardation (X in the model) is due to specific characteristics of the child (the "stressor event," or A), mediated by the family's internal and external resources (B) and by the family's perceptions of the child (C). But because children with mental retardation and their effects on families change over time, the term "Double" has been applied to the original ABCX model. The Double emphasizes that characteristics of the child change as the child gets older, the family's internal and external resources may change, and changes may occur in the family's perceptions of the child.

Although overly broad, the Double ABCX framework has nevertheless served researchers well. In its most general sense, the model helps explain both negative and positive consequences of rearing a child with mental retardation (Minnes, 1988). For all families, children who display fewer emotional problems and require less physical caretaking may help parents and families to adjust more positively. In the same way, families with few internal or external resources are more likely to be negatively affected by the child with retardation; families with more resources should do better.

Two elements of the model have been particularly informative. The first pertains to parents' internal and external resources, the B term of the Double ABCX model. Parents who take a more active, problem-solving approach to rearing their child with disabilities experience less depression than "emotion-based" copers (i.e., those who either dwell on or, conversely, deny all emotions; Essex, Seltzer, & Krauss, 1999; Seltzer, Greenberg, & Krauss, 1995; Turnbull et al., 1993). Similarly, parents with larger, more effective support systems do better. To take the most obvious examples, mothers in good versus bad marriages cope better, as do parents in two-parent versus one-parent families, and those at higher socioeconomic levels (see Shapiro, Blacher, & Lopez, 1998, for a review).

Second, children's own characteristics (A of the Double ABCX model) may elicit better or worse coping from their families. Children who are more dependent on their parents, as well as those showing a lack of social responsiveness, unusual caregiving demands, or aggressiveness, are most problematic for parents (Beckman, 1983; Frey, Greenberg, & Fewell, 1989; Minnes, 1988). Moreover, the direction of effects likely runs from child behavior to parent reaction. Keogh, Garnier, Bernheimer, and Gallimore (2000) examined families when the children with disabilities were 3, 7, and 11 years old. Using path analyses, they showed that the child's higher levels of behavior problems, greater degrees of cognitive impairment, and lower levels of personal-social competence affected parent and family adaptation. In contrast, parental changes and adaptations of the family routine usually did not influence later child behaviors.

Etiology-Related Studies

Similar to research on parent-child interactions, family work focusing on different genetic syndromes is relatively new. The single exception is Down syndrome, a group of families that have been examined over many years. To date, many findings of etiology-related family work reinforce earlier work that examined families of children with mixed or heterogeneous forms of mental retardation. But, as we illustrate, the potential of examining families of children with specific genetic disorders goes beyond mere replication.

So far, several studies have examined the stress levels of children with different genetic forms of mental retardation. Some studies have examined a single etiological group, and others have compared two or more groups. As when families of children with mixed or heterogeneous mental retardation have been examined, these studies find that children with different genetic etiologies also cause greater levels of parental stress when children show higher levels of maladaptive behaviors (Hodapp, Dykens, & Masino, 1997; Hodapp, Wijma, & Masino, 1997).

But beyond this connection between the child's maladaptive behavior and parental stress, other, more intriguing effects of etiology have also been noted. Consider the so-called Down syndrome advantage (Seltzer & Ryff, 1994). Parents of children with Down syndrome generally report less stress compared to parents of children with Autism or with other types of mental retardation. Comparing to same-age children with Autism, Holroyd and MacArthur (1976) found that parents of children with Down syndrome reported less stress overall, and Kasari and Sigman (1997) found that parents of children with Down syndrome versus with Autism reported less child-related stress. Sanders and Morgan (1997) found that both mothers and fathers of children with Down syndrome versus with Autism experienced similar levels of parental pessimism but fewer parent and family problems.

Other studies compared stress levels in parents of children with Down syndrome to levels in parents of children and adults with other types of mental retardation. Fidler, Hodapp, and Dykens (2000) found that parents of 3- to 10-year-old children with Down syndrome reported less stress relative to parents of children with Williams syndrome or

Smith-Magenis syndrome. In a study comparing mothers of children with heterogeneous causes of mental retardation, mothers of children with Down syndrome reported lower total child-related stress levels (Hodapp, Ricci, Ly, & Fidler, 2003). This Down syndrome advantage was also present when Seltzer, Krauss, and Tsunematsu (1993) compared parenting stress in mothers of 35-year-old adults with Down syndrome to stress in mothers of adults with other forms of mental retardation.

Although a few studies do not find advantages for families of children with Down syndrome versus with other disabilities (e.g., Cahill & Glidden, 1996; Hanson & Hanline, 1990), the large majority do. However, this advantage is not seen when comparisons are made to parents of children with same-age, typically developing children (Roach, Orsmond, & Barratt, 1999; Scott, Atkinson, Minton, & Bowman, 1997). Furthermore, many studies find that, apart from overall stress levels, parents report their children with Down syndrome as being especially reinforcing to them (Hodapp, Ly, Fidler, & Ricci, 2001). Although by no means problem free, parents and families of children with Down syndrome do seem to be advantaged compared to families of children with mental retardation overall.

What accounts for this potential Down syndrome advantage? Two explanations seem possible. First, parents and families may benefit from aspects of Down syndrome that are apart from the child's behavior per se. Down syndrome is a relatively common disorder known to laypeople and professionals alike and has many active parent groups. Parents are also more likely to be older and to have parented other children. Such factors might be considered variables that are associated with the syndrome itself. Second, on average, children with Down syndrome may differ from others with mental retardation. As we noted earlier, children with Down syndrome are generally considered to have upbeat personalities, sociable natures, and a relative lack of psychopathology. Although associated and child-related explanations are both possible—and the two are not mutually exclusive—the behaviors of children with Down syndrome probably at least partially account for parent and family reactions.

In thinking about this issue, we are also struck by the ways behaviors of children with different genetic syndromes might serve as stand-ins or proxies for certain behaviors (Hodapp, 2004b). These behaviors then elicit reactions from others. To take some examples, children with Down syndrome might be considered to have upbeat, sociable personalities and a relative lack of psychopathology; those with Prader-Willi syndrome show hyperphagia, obsessions and compulsions, and temper tantrums (Dykens,

1999); those with Williams syndrome seem friendly, even overly friendly, and anxious (Dykens, 2003). Similarly, many genetic syndromes show patterns of cognitive-linguistic strengths and weaknesses, which—as in the Williams syndrome versus Prader-Willi syndrome jigsaw-puzzle study—may elicit differential emotional and behavioral reactions from others. The task now is to identify which etiology-related behaviors, in which contexts, and for which people (parents, siblings, teachers), elicit which specific reactions from others.

Mix of Studies

Given the earlier, dominant view that parents and families coped poorly and that child characteristics were unimportant, most early family research adopted a group-difference perspective. Thus, most researchers of the 1960s and 1970s compared parents of children with disabilities to parents of same-age children without disabilities. In many ways, within-group variability became an "error" that detracted from finding group differences showing how poorly these families were actually coping.

Although there continues to be a need to document whether families of children with disabilities cope the same as, better, or worse than families of same-age typically developing children, these between-group studies are now being supplemented with many within-group studies (Hodapp, 2002). Such within-group studies are consistent with the change to a stress-and-coping perspective. If parents and families differ widely in how they cope, which factors might predispose certain parents to cope well and others poorly? The identification of such factors—in children, parents, and families as a whole—has now become a major focus of disability family research. Such within-group work also has both scientific and practical consequences. By identifying protective or risk variables in children, parents, and families, family researchers begin to understand the mechanisms by which better or worse adaptation comes about. We can now go beyond judgments of better or worse to understand why, exactly, some families cope well and others poorly.

Identifying mechanisms, in turn, allows us to know with whom, when, and how to intervene. If, for example, mothers who approach problems in a less active way are most at risk, interventions can be tailored to help these particular women. Parents or families also may be more adversely affected at certain times. In Down syndrome, for example, many hospitalizations, mostly for heart and respiratory problems, occur during the preschool years. For families of these children, but maybe not for other families, the preschool period may prove especially stressful. Finally, if we can understand which parents, siblings, and families are most at risk, when they most likely face such risks, and the reasons such risks occur we may be able to better devise the contents and approaches of intervention. Linking stress-and-coping models with etiology-related approaches makes possible the eventual answers to these questions.

REMAINING ISSUES

Although developmentally oriented work has progressed greatly over the past 10 to 15 years, much remains to be done. Indeed, some of the field's basic issues remain unresolved. In an effort to facilitate developmentally oriented work in future years, then, we end this chapter by discussing five issues that are essential to continued progress.

Control-Contrast Groups

The control-contrast group issue continues to be problematic in studies of children with mental retardation and their families. Historically, this question revolved around the use of chronological age versus mental age comparison groups and was also tied to the issue of whether children with mental retardation develop differently from or slower than typically developing children. But as these issues have become more complicated in recent times, we first describe historical issues, then more recent concerns. Particularly when dealing with more recent concerns, we detail the many ways that control and contrast groups have been used in research examining children with different genetic syndromes of mental retardation.

Historical Background

Over the past 40 years, a long-standing controversy has related to two types of comparisons to typically developing children. One group, referred to by the term "defect theorists," asserted that etiology does not matter, that all children with mental retardation suffer from organic defects. These researchers generally compared children with mental retardation to typically developing children of the same chronological age.

An entire research tradition has shown that, relative to typically developing children, numerous aspects of cognition and language are deficient in children with mental retardation. Different researchers emphasized different core defects, including cognitive rigidity (Kounin, 1941; Lewin, 1936), memory processes (Ellis, 1963), discrimination learning (Zeaman & House, 1963), and attention-retention capabilities (Fisher & Zeaman, 1973; for a review, see Burack, 1990).

In all of these studies, children with mental retardation were matched to children of the same chronological age. But, as developmentalists repeatedly noted, mental retardation is, by definition, marked by slower rates of development (Burack, Evans, Klaiman, & Iarocci, 2001). On almost every measure, then, children with mental retardation will show lower levels of cognitive functioning than CA-matched typically developing children. As Cicchetti and Pogge-Hesse (1982) noted, children with mental retardation function below children of the same chronological age in most areas of cognition, but *the important and challenging research questions concern the developmental processes*" (p. 279; italics in original). Such processes can only be determined using MA-matched typically developing controls, thereby showing which areas are more or less affected.

To give one example, Iarocci and Burack (1998) reevaluated the literature on attention deficits among persons with mental retardation. They concluded that attention deficits were much more likely to be found when matching between the groups of participants with and without mental retardation was based on CA rather than MA. Furthermore, even the few examples of deficits in studies with MA matching were not particularly strong methodologically, as confounding factors of organic etiology and institutionalization were not considered (Burack et al., 2001).

As we note in our discussions about control-contrast groups in etiology-based studies, the techniques for matching by developmental level continue to be discussed and developed (Mervis & Robinson, 1999; Sigman & Ruskin, 1999). Among others, Loveland and Kelley (1986) and Burack, Iarocci, Flanagan, and Bowler (2004) highlight the need to further fine-tune matching developmental level so that the matching is not by general developmental level but is linked to the specific task.

For certain issues, it may even be possible to forgo matching altogether. For example, Jarrold and Brock (2004), after criticizing most matching strategies because of unclear relationships between background matching measures and performance on the experimental task, advocate regression techniques. These techniques seem particularly useful for charting developmental change. Like all sophisticated statistical analyses, however, such techniques require sufficient numbers of participants and time points in order that change over time can be charted most effectively.

Contrast Groups in Etiology-Based Research on Children

As etiology-based developmental research has proliferated over the past decade, researchers have needed to choose ap-

TABLE 6.2 Strengths and Weaknesses of Some Common Etiology-Based Research Approaches

Control Group	Characteristics	Strengths-Weaknesses
Strategies to Determine Whether a Specific Disorder Has Strengths-Weaknesses		
1. None	Performance "against self"	Shows etiology strength.
2. Typical	Equated on MA Equated on CA	Shows relative strength (versus MA) or intact functioning (versus CA); unclear if profile is unique, partially shared, or similar to all persons with mental retardation (MR).
Strategies to Determine Whether Behavioral Characteristics Differ from Others with Intellectual Disabilities		
3. Mixed ID	Mixed causes of MR	Shows that etiology strength-weakness is not due to MR. Weaknesses = hard to find; control group changes across studies; mixed ≠ nonspecific.
4. Down	DS	Shows behavior not due to any syndrome, but DS has its own behavioral syndrome characteristics (may lead to inaccurate conclusions if DS = "all MR").
Strategies to Further Delineate Etiology-Specific Behaviors		
5. Same-but-different MR	Etiology similar in behavior to group	Highlights fine-grained differences in behavior if two or more etiologies have similar behaviors to make contrast meaningful.
6. Special	Group with special behavior	Shows ways that etiology is similar to or different from group with special problem or profile (but without MR).

Adapted from "Strengthening Behavioral Research on Genetic Mental Retardation Disorders," by R. M. Hodapp and E. M. Dykens, 2001, *American Journal on Mental Retardation, 106*, pp. 4–15.

propriate control-contrast groups (some might prefer the term "comparison group" to "control group," as no experimental manipulation is being performed; Burack et al., 2004). In Table 6.2, we present three broad research questions (comprising six research strategies) that have been commonly used in etiology-based behavioral research (from Hodapp & Dykens, 2001).

Do Children Show an Etiology-Related Profile?
Given the interest in relative strengths and weaknesses in different etiological groups, a first strategy is to have *no control or contrast group*. To determine whether children with Williams syndrome show strengths in language versus visuospatial processing, Bellugi et al. (1999) compared each child's functioning on a language domain to that same child's performance on another domain. Children thus become their own controls, as their functioning levels in one domain are compared to more general, overall functioning levels.

Although widely used, this self-as-control technique has several limitations. Technically, one can compare the person's performance only on one versus another domain on the same test. Different tests are standardized on different samples, and intelligence test scores tend to increase from decade to decade (Flynn, 1999). One should therefore compare different domains only of the same test. In addition, such domains as theory of mind, mother-child interaction, and family functioning have few well-normed, reliable, or valid psychometric instruments.

A second technique also attempts to answer the relative strength or weakness question. Here, the researcher compares persons with mental retardation to *typically developing children of the same mental age*. Depending on the question of interest, the process might be thought of as comparing the child with mental retardation to typical children of similar functioning levels (Burack et al., 2004). To determine areas of adaptive strength or weakness, one might compare children with Down syndrome to typically developing children using the Vineland Adaptive Behavior Scales; to determine whether aspects of language are relative strengths, one might match on the child's MLU to examine aspects of pragmatics or semantics. In each case, the researcher compares children with a particular genetic syndrome to typically developing children of similar age-equivalent performance.

But, at times, CA-matches may be informative. Specifically, only by comparing to typically developing children of similar chronological age can one determine if certain groups are "spared" in their functioning in a behavioral domain. A good example involves Williams syndrome, earlier thought to be spared in certain areas of language. Although sparing now seems unlikely for groups (as opposed to for a few individuals) with Williams syndrome (Karmiloff-Smith, 1997; Mervis et al., 1999), the test for spared functioning involves comparing to typically developing age-mates either explicitly (using a typical CA-matched group) or implicitly (using standard scores from a standardization sample). Researchers do need to be aware, however, that similar functioning between CA-matched groups has not occurred due to the use of tasks that are not sufficiently sensitive or developmentally appropriate to detect group differences (Burack, 1997; Burack et al., 2001).

Are Such Profiles Seen in Children with Mental Retardation More Generally? This second general research question also features two often used techniques. In the first, researchers compare persons with a particular mental retardation syndrome to a *mixed or nonspecific group* who are equated on both mental age and chronological age. If behavioral phenotypes do indeed involve "the heightened probability or likelihood that people with a given syndrome will exhibit certain behavioral and developmental sequelae relative to those without the syndrome" (Dykens, 1995, p. 523), such a mixed or heterogeneous group best approximates those without the syndrome.

As before, several issues arise. The first concerns the proper mixture of the mixed group, and how to ensure that one's sample does indeed approximate the larger population with mental retardation. Unfortunately, in contrast to our knowledge about many psychiatric disorders, the field of mental retardation has performed few such epidemiological studies. An additional issue concerns heterogeneity. Because children in this group possess a wide variety of conditions (and no clear conditions at all), this group may, in theory, be more heterogeneous in its functioning than groups from a single etiological group. Still, this heterogeneous group does constitute the best approximation to those without the genetic disorder of interest. Different researchers disagree as to the appropriateness of using or not using a mixed or heterogeneous group with mental retardation as the contrast group in studies of etiology-related functioning (for alternative viewpoints, see Burack, 1997; Hodapp & Dykens, 2001).

A second technique in this class compares one etiological group with *children with Down syndrome.* Although groups with Down syndrome are often used as a control group with mental retardation, we consider this strategy to be inappropriate. As a group, persons with Down syndrome show relative weaknesses in various aspects in language, and they may have particular personalities and a general lack of psychopathology. Especially when examining etiology-related profiles in these areas, then, comparing a group with the etiology of interest to children with Down syndrome as the control group seems ill advised.

Still, there may be certain instances in which children with Down syndrome constitute an informative contrast group. Consider, for example, the issue of modularity and the finding that auditory short-term memory levels are generally tied to levels of grammar in children with

Williams syndrome (Mervis et al., 1999). If indeed children with Down syndrome also show such cross-domain connections, more evidence has been amassed for a universal connection across these two domains (i.e., the same connection has occurred in two separate syndromes). Thus, although the use of children with Down syndrome as a stand-in for all children with mental retardation, though widely done, seems ill advised, there may be occasions in which children with Down syndrome may constitute an informative contrast group.

How Do Children in a Specific Etiological Group Compare to Nonretarded Persons with Similar Conditions or Behaviors? This final approach compares persons who have a genetic syndrome to "specialized" nonretarded persons in an area of interest. Here again, the general approach can be seen through the use of two specific research techniques. In the first, persons with a particular syndrome are compared to *nonretarded persons with a diagnosed psychiatric disorder.* Dykens, Leckman, and Cassidy (1996) compared persons with Prader-Willi syndrome to nonretarded outpatients with Obsessive-Compulsive Disorder. With very few exceptions, the two groups were very similar in their mean number and severity of compulsions and in percentages within each group displaying most behaviors (e.g., cleaning, ordering/arranging, repeating rituals).

A specialized-group strategy can also be shown in a second technique, this one comparing to *nonretarded persons who show particular cognitive-linguistic profiles.* How, for example, might children with Prader-Willi syndrome, who show simultaneous-over-sequential processing abilities, compare to nonretarded persons who similarly show such simultaneous processing advantages? How do children with Prader-Willi syndrome compare to typically developing children who are "good puzzlers"? Are the two groups approaching problems in the same way? This strategy probably best approaches Cicchetti and Pogge-Hesse's (1982) call for research that examines developmental processes in children with mental retardation. Although using specialized nonretarded groups risks producing no-difference findings, we still consider this approach informative and, at present, underutilized.

Contrast Groups in Research on Mother-Child Interaction and Families

The issue of control-contrast groups becomes even more complicated when one thinks about parent-child interactions and families. In the field of mother-child interactions, early studies examined parental (mainly maternal)

behaviors to children of the same chronological age as typically developing children. Beginning with Rondal (1977), groups came to be equated more on age-equivalent scores, and either mental-age or language-age comparisons have predominated over the past few decades.

As we gain in our knowledge of children with different types of mental retardation, such issues become more complicated. Consider the finding that children with Williams syndrome show relative strengths in language (compared to mental age), or that children with Prader-Willi syndrome show excellent performance, even above typical children of identical chronological age, on jigsaw puzzles (Dykens, 2002). What is the appropriate maternal input relative to these tasks?

One suggestion is that children with different genetic mental retardation syndromes might be used as proxies for particular emotional-behavioral problems, personalities, or skill levels on specific tasks (Hodapp, 2004b). In such analyses, one might use children with Prader-Willi syndrome versus with Williams syndrome as good versus poor jigsaw puzzlers, respectively. Other syndromes might also be used as proxies for one or another etiology-related behavior. The question then becomes whether parents or others react similarly or differently to nonretarded children who have similar high or low skills on a specific task. Throughout these parent-child interactions, however, some variant of MA or level-of-functioning comparisons seems best.

But different issues arise when discussing control-contrast groups involving families. In fact, most studies compare families of children with mental retardation to families of typically developing children of the same chronological, not mental, age. The reasoning here involves family life cycles (Carter & McGoldrick, 1988). Consider the case of a child who is 13 years old but functioning at the 5-year level (i.e., MA = 5 years). Which aspect of the child—the child's chronological age or mental age—is most salient to families? Under family life span theory, having lived for 13 years with a child with mental retardation may be the most important issue for parental stress levels and family coping styles.

We are left, then, in a strange place. For most issues of the child's own development, MA comparisons, or comparisons related to some other level-of-functioning measure, seem preferable most of the time. The few exceptions concern instances of possibly spared development, when it will be useful to add comparisons to same-age, typically developing children. Similarly, MA or other level-of-functioning comparisons seem best when one is examining maternal behaviors in mother-child interactions. In contrast, due to issues involving family life cycles, CA comparisons might be best when considering families of children with mental retardation.

Within-Group Heterogeneity

Some of the most exciting phenotypic studies currently examine individuals with the same etiology, but who differ in one or more aspects of behavior. Although the reasons for within-group heterogeneity are not always known, a few factors are beginning to be examined.

Within-Syndrome Genetic Variants

The first factor involves slight genetic variations within a particular genetic syndrome (for a review, see Einfeld, 2004). To give a few examples, in Prader-Willi syndrome, a distinction exists between individuals who have a deletion on chromosome 15 contributed from the father (i.e., paternal deletion) versus those who have two chromosome 15s from the mother (i.e., uniparental maternal disomy, or UPD). Individuals with UPD more often suffer from psychotic disorders that first appear in early adulthood (Clarke et al., 1998; Vogels et al., 2004). But behavior in Prader-Willi syndrome may also be differentially affected by the child's type of deletion. M. G. Butler et al. (2004) noted that deleted individuals have one of two distinct types of deletions. In Type I deletion, individuals have a larger deletion than in Type II deletions. Individuals with Type I deletions show lower adaptive behavior scores and several specific obsessive-compulsive behaviors. Although preliminary, such within-syndrome genetic differences seem an important avenue of research in coming years.

Non-Etiology-Related Background Genetics

A genetic disorder—be it a trisomy 21 (Down syndrome) or a deletion on chromosome 15 (Prader-Willi syndrome)—affects only a single chromosome or part of a chromosome. All other chromosomes are left unaffected. Background genetics involves the idea that, in addition to one's genetic disorder, these other chromosomes contain genetic predispositions that are at work in every individual.

In studies from several different laboratories, researchers are using background genetics to examine proneness to different behaviors and treatments. For example, May, Potts, Phillips, Blakely, and Kennedy (2005) examined the effects of two different genetic variants, which had earlier been shown to predispose nonretarded individuals to increased aggression. Their findings suggest that, in persons with mental retardation as well, those who have one versus another genetic variant also have aggression-related effects. Similarly, Roof, Shelton, Wilkinson, Kim, and Dykens (2005) examined genes involved in psychotropic drug metabolism in individuals with Prader-Willi syndrome. In both cases, researchers are going from genetic, clinical-genetic, or pharmacogenetic findings earlier shown to operate in typical, nonretarded persons and applying these findings to persons with mental retardation. Such studies highlight the idea that individuals with genetic disorders are more than their genetic disorders per se.

Developmental Change and Its Effects

In discussing sequences and cross-domain relations, we noted that, in many syndromes, strengths become stronger and weaknesses weaker as children get older. In the Jarrold et al. (2001) study, for example, adolescents and young adults with Williams syndrome advanced at faster rates in measures of linguistic versus visuospatial processing. Why such findings occur remains mostly unresolved. Although sheer amount of experience in different types of task is one possibility (Rosner et al., 2004), no studies have yet looked in depth at the interplay between the environment and the child's development at various age spans.

An additional issue involves concomitant brain changes. So far, only a few studies have even tied etiology-related cognitive-linguistic profiles to brain-related tasks. For example, following from hypotheses developed by Nadel (1996, 1999) about hippocampal deficits in children with Down syndrome, Pennington, Moon, Edgin, Stedron, and Nadel (2003) compared these children to MA-matched typically developing children on two sets of tasks. The first set related to functioning of the prefrontal cortex, which involves holding information in active or working memory. The second set examined hippocampal functioning, which relates to the storage of episodic information into long-term memory. As predicted, children with Down syndrome performed more poorly than MA matches on tasks involving the hippocampus and equivalently on tasks relating to the prefrontal cortex.

Although the Pennington et al. (2003) study is noteworthy as one of the first brain-related examinations of children with any specific etiology, other, related questions remain unanswered for children with all genetic etiologies. How, for example, does using "strong skills" over time (and not using one's "weak skills") change brain circuitry? Do compensations occur, and how well can children who compensate perform a host of different types of tasks? In no genetic disorders have researchers yet tied together—over time—experience, behavior, and brain functioning.

Need for Greater Amount of Basic Information

Compared to our knowledge about most other diagnostic categories covered in the *Diagnostic and Statistical Manual of Mental Disorders* and the *International Classification of Diseases,* our knowledge about mental retardation remains woefully lacking. We do not know, for example, how many persons with mental retardation there are, or what percentages have Down syndrome or any other genetic (or other) condition. Granted, some issues are difficult due to basic disagreements about definition of the group itself. Recall our earlier discussion about changing mental retardation IQ cutoffs, which by definition affect prevalence rates.

But beyond definition and prevalence, we continue to lack basic information about a wide range of issues. For example, we know little about the health status of children with many different disorders, even those in whom health-related problems seem reasonably common. Consider the health issues in Down syndrome, in which heart problems and surgeries to repair such problems often occur in the 1st year of life. How often do such hospitalizations and surgeries occur? How might these and other health issues affect these children's development or their family's functioning? Although some larger-scale, epidemiological studies of health-related issues are beginning to appear on certain syndromes (e.g., J. V. Butler et al.'s, 2002, work on Prader-Willi syndrome), the mental retardation field remains only vaguely knowledgeable about health-related issues in many different groups.

Other topics are also generally unresearched. Consider the entire issue of gender differences. Although a common issue in developmental psychology proper and a major factor in clinical depression and dysthymia, the topic remains almost completely unstudied in groups with mental retardation. Hodapp and Dykens (2005) recently surveyed the reporting of gender and analysis of gender differences in the *American Journal on Mental Retardation* and the *Journal of Intellectual Disability Research,* the two main journals of mental retardation behavioral research. They found that, in these two journals, only about a quarter of research articles both listed the number of participants of each sex and analyzed for sex differences. Given the inattention to such basic child characteristics, we remain unsure of how gender identity develops. Similarly, in typically developing samples, girls and women seem about twice as likely as boys and men to become clinically depressed sometime during their lives (Wolk & Weissman, 1995), and sex differences in prevalence rates of female (as opposed to male) depressive symptoms (not associated with full-blown depression) begin in the 10- to 15-year period (Garber, Keiley, & Martin, 2002). We do not know whether rates of depression or depressive symptomatology also show strong gender changes when children have mental retardation (or different types of mental retardation).

Consider as well the entire issue of child abuse. For many years, child abuse professionals suspected that children with mental retardation were more likely to be abused (Westcott & Jones, 1999). But only in the past few years have such differential rates been documented in a strong, epidemiologically based study that joined records from schools, child protective services, criminal justice, and hospitals-clinics. Once such records were joined, Sullivan and Knutson (2000) were able to document that children with mental retardation are approximately 4 times more likely than nondisabled children to be abused. Now that we have the basic numbers, countless additional questions arise concerning when and what types of abuse occur, and why these children suffer abuse so often.

What Do Others React To?

In considering the high rates of child abuse of children with mental retardation, we return, from a slightly different angle, to the entire problem of what parents or others react to in the child with mental retardation. This simple-seeming problem actually has several subproblems buried within.

Do Others React to Behavior Alone?

Following Bell (1968) in a theoretical sense and Rondal (1977) in terms of input language, our original thinking focused on behavior. That is, in children with mental retardation or with particular syndromes, parents will react to the behavior that they experience from their children. Our initial ideas also focused on a single, salient behavior from children with one or another genetic mental retardation syndrome (Hodapp, 1999). More recently, we have come to question which of many etiology-related behaviors might matter, to whom, and under which circumstances (Hodapp & Ly, 2005).

But behavior may be one among several of the child's personal characteristics to which parents respond. Consider the babyface studies discussed earlier. In both cases, unfamiliar adults (Fidler & Hodapp, 1999) and mothers (Fidler, 2003) were responding to the more immature, "babylike" faces of children with Down syndrome. We have recently been intrigued by the impact of child hospitalization and health problems on parental and familial reactions. In short, we suspect that the child's behavior is not the sole personal characteristic to which parents and others respond.

Do Others' Reactions to Identical Behaviors Differ Based on the Child's Specific Syndrome?

In several studies, the child's etiological group may moderate parental reactions to the child's behavior (or other personal characteristic). Specifically, parents react to the

child's behavior, but mainly in the context of what parents know or perceive of their child's syndrome. In one study, for example, Ly and Hodapp (2002) asked parents of children with Down syndrome versus with other forms of mental retardation to make causal attributions in response to hypothetical vignettes in which their child performed each of two common, noncompliant behaviors. Parents of children considered more sociable and outgoing attributed their child's noncompliant behaviors to normative concerns ("My child is acting like other children his or her age"). But such connections between child personality and normalizing behaviors were found only in the Down syndrome group. Thus, among parents of children with Down syndrome, those who saw their child as more sociable also more highly rated normalizing as the reason for their child's noncompliance. But among parents of children with mixed forms of mental retardation, no such connections existed between child personality and parental ratings of normalizing attributions.

Such findings suggest a complex interplay between the child's behavior, on one hand, and parental knowledge or perceptions of etiology-related behavior, on the other. In the case of Down syndrome, the degree to which parents felt that their child possesses a "Down syndrome personality" elicited greater degrees of parental normalizing attributions. In contrast, no such connections between perceived child personality and parental normalizing attributions occurred for parents of children with mental retardation in general. There seems, then, to be a complex interaction between the behaviors themselves and what mothers know about their child's type of mental retardation.

What Do Parents Know?

If parental perceptions and knowledge of their child's etiology are so important, what do parents know? Although a major area in parenting studies of typically developing children (Goodnow, 2002; Okagaki & Divecha, 1993), parental perceptions and attributions are relatively unexplored among parents of children with disabilities (Ly & Kazemi, 2005). In a few syndromes, however, we do have some sense of what parents know about their child's etiology. For example, Fidler, Hodapp, and Dykens (2002) asked parents of children with Prader-Willi syndrome, Down syndrome, and Williams syndrome about several education-related aspects of their child's behavioral characteristics and school accommodations. Whereas parents of children with Down syndrome were aware of their child's cognitive-linguistic strengths (e.g., visual short-term memory) and weaknesses (e.g., expressive language), parents in the two other groups knew much less. Parents of children with Prader-Willi syndrome knew of their child's extreme overeating and tantrums, but were less aware of their child's strong visuospatial abilities. Similarly, parents of children with Williams syndrome were aware of their children's many fears and anxieties (Dykens, 2003), but less aware of these children's propensity to have relatively strong linguistic skills and weak visuospatial skills.

Though suggestive, these findings leave unanswered countless other questions. Where do mothers receive their information, and when do they receive it? How might such information be related to parental access to and abilities in searching the Internet, or to a parent's degree of involvement with an etiology-related parent group? How do schools and other service systems relate to parents who present etiology-based information, particularly given the general disregard of etiology-related information that has historically characterized the field of special education (see Hodapp & Fidler, 1999, for a review)? To these questions, we remain woefully uninformed.

CONCLUSIONS AND FUTURE DIRECTIONS

Fields, like children, develop at different rates at different times. As we have shown, work on both organismic and contextual developmental issues has increased rapidly over the past decade. Many of the most exciting studies involved children with genetic mental retardation syndromes or the etiology-related reactions to these children by parents, siblings, and others. Considered overall, the past 10 to 15 years have constituted an exciting, even exhilarating, time for developmental studies of children with mental retardation and their families.

And yet, for all of the information learned during the past decade, we remain uninformed about many issues. Many of these unknown areas relate to questions of control-contrast groups, within-syndrome heterogeneity, developmental change, basic health information, and child-parent and child-family relations. But moving beyond these specific content areas, we also see two major needs for the future.

Need for Between-Level Syntheses

The first, more scientific need concerns examining how different levels of analyses relate to one another. Like all systems theorists, developmentalists conceptualize the child in relation to within-child systems (e.g., brain) and such out-of-child systems as the family (Sameroff, 1995). The question of how development occurs can therefore be asked on multiple levels simultaneously, and changes in one level often relate to changes at other levels.

For mental retardation, one can look in both directions: within and outside of children themselves. How, for example, do changes in etiology-related strengths and weaknesses over time—in, for example, children with Williams syndrome or with Down syndrome—relate to changes in brain structures or function? How do children's behaviors affect others in their surrounding environments? Do changes in others' behaviors reflect back on children themselves?

Although currently unknown, such linkage issues seem especially timely given the history of the mental retardation field, particularly the rise of etiology-related studies over the past decade. As Hodapp (2004a) noted, research on behavioral phenotypes can be characterized as having its own Wernerian developmental pattern. Within this perspective, the years up to and through the 1980s could essentially be considered the prehistory of etiology-based studies, with little information and more global and undifferentiated senses of organicity and etiology. In contrast, the 1990s featured an explosion of information about children with many different disorders. For at least Fragile X, Prader-Willi, Williams, and a few other syndromes, researchers determined basic cognitive, linguistic, and adaptive profiles, as well as the nature and course of etiology-related maladaptive behaviors. For the most part, however, such bits of information were unconnected, leaving knowledge that is, in Werner's terms, "differentiated but unintegrated."

Now, as we enter the early years of the new century, we are ready to put together the various levels. We are poised to examine children's development itself, in terms of both sequences and cross-domain relations, as well as to examine how that development relates to levels within and without. The search for gene-brain-behavior connections, the use of various syndromes as models for biobehavioral syntheses, the connections of child behaviors to parental reactions and behaviors—all constitute the coming together of levels of the system.

Again, such multilevel approaches fit well within the larger field of developmental psychopathology. Indeed, in summarizing the history of advances in the field of developmental psychopathology, Cicchetti and Dawson (2002, p. 418) noted:

> Most of what is known about the causes, correlates, course, and consequences of psychopathology was gleaned from investigations that focused on relatively narrow domains of variables. Yet it is apparent from the questions addressed by developmental psychopathologists that progress toward process-level understanding of mental disorder will require research designs and strategies that call for the simultaneous

assessment of multiple domains of variables both within and outside of the developing person.

So, too, with our understanding of individuals with mental retardation. Whereas more narrowly tailored, single-discipline analyses have characterized most studies until now, more collaborative, multidisciplinary studies and findings will likely pave the way for tomorrow's advances.

Need for Greater Attention to Etiology-Based Interventions

An additional issue concerns intervention. Since Cicchetti's (1984) earliest writings, developmental psychopathology has been a hybrid field, one in which proponents are simultaneously interested in both basic and applied issues. To some researchers, Williams syndrome is a genetic etiology that tells us much about whether (or not) humans show linguistic modularity; to others, the syndrome is one showing particularly high rates of anxiety and fears that may require clinical interventions (Dykens, 2003). Both are true; both simply reflect different sides of the single coin of developmental psychopathology.

Given these interests in using basic information to help us develop more precise, targeted interventions, we again see the importance of etiology-based research. Once one knows that children with Williams syndrome, in general, show relatively strong linguistic and weak visuospatial skills, one can begin to consider tailoring intervention programs. Once one knows about the relative strengths seen in most children with each of several genetic disorders, one can begin to know how to intervene.

The task now is to take our knowledge of etiology-related profiles and determine if intervention strategies can either play to strengths or ameliorate weaknesses. From one direction, for several etiological groups we may currently have enough preliminary information to directly test hypothesized underlying functional deficits. If language is strong and visuospatial abilities weak in Williams syndrome, or if visual-spatial (particularly jigsaw puzzle) abilities are strong in Prader-Willi syndrome, we may be ready to develop new and more effective ways to intervene.

From the opposite perspective, several subdomains of functioning now have sufficient normative information that etiology-related abilities can be directly examined for a complex behavior's component skills. Consider reading. For many years, Buckley and her colleagues (Buckley & Bird, 2002; Byrne, Buckley, MacDonald, & Bird, 1995) argued that children with Down syndrome should be taught to read. Given these children's relative strengths (i.e., above overall MA levels) in visual short-term memory and

weaknesses in grammar, expressive language, and articulation, readind might even be considered an entryway into language for these children.

Although such arguments may seem reasonable, only recently have researchers directly examined children with Down syndrome using fine-grained reading tests. In three studies, Snowling, Hulme, and Mercer (2002) compared typical children to children with Down syndrome on segmentation, nursery rhyme knowledge, rhyme detection, and phoneme detection. They also examined letter names and sounds, print in the daily environment, single-word reading, and nonword reading. As might be expected, children with Down syndrome with good, as opposed to poor, phonological skills were better readers, but letter-sound knowledge was not a concurrent predictor of reading performance. Further, children with Down syndrome performed significantly worse than control children on rhyme judgment.

Compared to typical children, then, children with Down syndrome may follow a qualitatively different path as they develop reading and phonological skills. These children may be reading without the full understanding of all aspects of phonemic awareness. To some extent, children with Down syndrome use grapheme-phoneme strategies but are also accessing other strategies (such as whole-word recognition). Such detailed knowledge about etiology-related profiles could only be attained through more detailed, fine-grained tasks that tap specific subskills involved in reading. The task now is to use that information to develop more effective reading instructions for these (and other) children.

We end this chapter with many more questions than answers, with a bucketful of important, unanswered questions that remain to be tackled. At the same time as we are humbled by just how much information remains to be discovered, we are also heartened by the progress that has already been made. Indeed, comparing developmentally oriented knowledge in mental retardation to only 10 or 15 years ago, progress is staggering. Like a child's development, our trajectory is clearly upward, rapidly so over the past decade. Our hope—and expectation—is that upcoming decades will continue to feature the same, seemingly exponential advances in our understanding of children with mental retardation and their families.

REFERENCES

Achenbach, T. M. (1991). *Manual for the Child Behavior Checklist/4–18 and 1991 profile.* Burlington: University of Vermont, Department of Psychiatry.

Allanson, J. E., O'Hara, P., Farkas, G., & Nair, R. C. (1993). Anthropometric craniofacial pattern profiles in Down syndrome. *American Journal of Medical Genetics, 47,* 748–752.

American Association on Mental Retardation. (1992). *Mental retardation: Definition, classification, and systems of supports* (9th ed.). Washington, DC: Author.

American Association on Mental Retardation. (2002). *Mental retardation: Definition, classification, and systems of supports* (10th ed.). Washington, DC: Author.

Anderson, L., & Ernst, M. (1994). Self-injury in Lesch-Nyhan disease. *Journal of Autism and Developmental Disorders, 24,* 67–81.

Anderson, L., Lakin, K. C., Mangan, T. W., & Prouty, R. W. (1998). State institutions: Thirty years of depopulation and closure. *Mental Retardation, 36,* 431–443.

Bates, E., Camaioni, L., & Volterra, V. (1975). The acquisition of performatives prior to speech. *Merrill-Palmer Quarterly, 21,* 205–226.

Baumgardner, T. L., Reiss, A. L., Freund, L. S., & Abrams, M. T. (1995). Specification of the neurobehavioral phenotype in males with Fragile X syndrome. *Pediatrics, 95,* 744–752.

Beckman, P. (1983). Influence of selected child characteristics on stress in families of handicapped children. *American Journal of Mental Deficiency, 88,* 150–156.

Bell, R. Q. (1968). A reinterpretation of direction of effects in studies of socialization. *Psychological Review, 75,* 81–95.

Bellugi, U., Mills, D., Jernigan, T., Hickok, G., & Galaburda, A. (1999). Linking cognition, brain structure, and brain function in Williams syndrome. In H. Tager-Flusberg (Ed.), *Neurodevelopmental disorders* (pp. 111–136). Cambridge, MA: MIT Press.

Blacher, J. (1984). Sequential stages of parental adjustment to the birth of the child with handicaps: Fact or artifact? *Mental Retardation, 22,* 55–68.

Blacher, J., & Baker, B. (Eds.). (2002). *Best of AAMR: Families and mental retardation. A collection of notable AAMR journal articles across the 20th century.* Washington, DC: American Association on Mental Retardation.

Bronfenbrenner, U. (1979). *The ecology of human development.* Cambridge, MA: Harvard University Press.

Buckhalt, J. A., Rutherford, R., & Goldberg, K. (1978). Verbal and nonverbal interactions of mothers with their Down syndrome and nonretarded infants. *American Journal of Mental Deficiency, 82,* 337–343.

Buckley, S., & Bird, G. (2002). Cognitive development and education: Perspectives on Down syndrome from a twenty-year research programme. In M. Cuskally, A. Jobling, & S. Buckley (Eds.), *Down syndrome across the life-span* (pp. 66–80). London: Whurr Publishers.

Buium, N., Rynders, J., & Turnure, J. (1974). Early maternal linguistic environment of normal and Down syndrome language learning children. *American Journal of Mental Deficiency, 79,* 52–58.

Burack, J. A. (1990). Differentiating mental retardation: The two-group approach and beyond. In R. M. Hodapp, J. A. Burack, & E. Zigler (Eds.), *Issues in the developmental approach to mental retardation* (pp. 27–48). New York: Cambridge University Press.

Burack, J. A. (1997). The study of atypical and typical populations in developmental psychopathology: The quest for a common science. In S. S. Luthar, J. A. Burack, D. Cicchetti, & J. R. Weisz (Eds.), *Developmental psychopathology: Perspectives on adjustment, risk and disorder* (pp. 139–165). New York: Cambridge University Press.

Burack, J. A., Evans, D. W., Klaiman, C., & Iarocci, G. (2001). The mysterious myth of attention deficits and other defect stories: Contemporary issues in the developmental approach to mental retardation. *International Review of Research in Mental Retardation, 24,* 299–320.

Burack, J. A., Hodapp, R. M., & Zigler, E. (1988). Issues in the classification of mental retardation: Differentiating among organic etiologies. *Journal of Child Psychology and Psychiatry, 29,* 765–779.

Burack, J. A., Hodapp, R. M., & Zigler, E. (1990). Technical note: Toward a more precise understanding of mental retardation. *Journal of Child Psychology and Psychiatry, 31,* 471–475.

Burack, J. A., Hodapp, R. M., & Zigler, E. (Eds.). (1998). *Handbook of mental retardation and development.* Cambridge, England: Cambridge University Press.

Burack, J. A., Iarocci, G., Flanagan, T. D., & Bowler, D. M. (2004). On mosaics and melting pots: Conceptual considerations of comparison and matching strategies. *Journal of Autism and Developmental Disorders, 34,* 65–73.

Burack, J. A., Shulman, C., Katzir, E., Schaap, T., Brennan, J., Iarocci, G., et al. (1999). Cognitive and behavioral development of males with Fragile X and Down syndrome. *International Journal of Behavioral Development, 23,* 519–531.

Butler, J. V., Whittington, J. E., Holland, A. J., Boer, H., Clarke, D. J., & Webb, T. (2002). Prevalence of, and risk factors for, physical ill-health in people with Prader-Willi syndrome: A population-based study. *Developmental Medicine and Child Neurology, 44,* 248–255.

Butler, M. G., Bittel, D. C., Kibiryeva, N., Talebizadeh, Z., & Thompson, T. (2004). Behavioral differences among subjects with Prader-Willi syndrome and type I or type II deletion and maternal disomy. *Pediatrics, 113,* 565–573.

Bybee, J. A., & Zigler, E. (1998). Outerdirectedness in individuals with and without mental retardation: A review. In J. A. Burack, R. M. Hodapp, & E. Zigler (Eds.), *Handbook of mental retardation and development* (pp. 434–461). Cambridge, England: Cambridge University Press.

Byrne, A., Buckley, S., MacDonald, J., & Bird, G. (1995). Investigating the literacy, language, and memory skills of children with Down's syndrome. *Down's Syndrome: Research and Practice, 3,* 53–58.

Cahill, B. M., & Glidden, L. M. (1996). Influence of child diagnosis on family and parent functioning: Down syndrome versus other disabilities. *American Journal on Mental Retardation, 101,* 149–160.

Cardoso-Martins, C., & Mervis, C. (1984). Maternal speech to prelinguistic children with Down syndrome. *American Journal of Mental Deficiency, 89,* 451–458.

Carr, J. (1995). *Down's syndrome: Children growing up.* Cambridge, England: Cambridge University Press.

Carter, B., & McGoldrick, M. (1988). *The changing family life cycle: A framework for family therapy* (2nd ed.). New York: Gardner Press.

Chapman, R. S., & Hesketh, L. J. (2000). Behavioral phenotype of individuals with Down syndrome. *Mental Retardation and Developmental Disabilities Research Reviews, 6,* 84–95.

Cicchetti, D. (1984). The emergence of developmental psychopathology. *Child Development, 55,* 1–7.

Cicchetti, D. (2003). Experiments of nature: Contributions to developmental theory. *Development and Psychopathology, 15,* 833–835.

Cicchetti, D., & Beeghly, M. (Eds.). (1990). *Children with Down syndrome: A developmental perspective.* New York: Cambridge University Press.

Cicchetti, D., & Dawson, G. (2002). Multiple levels of analysis. *Development and Psychopathology, 14,* 417–420.

Cicchetti, D., & Pogge-Hesse, P. (1982). Possible contributions of the study of organically retarded persons to developmental theory. In E. Zigler & D. Balla (Eds.), *Mental retardation: The developmental-difference controversy* (pp. 277–318). Hillsdale, NJ: Erlbaum.

Cicchetti, D., & Rogosch, F. A. (1996). Equifinality and multifinality in developmental psychopathology. *Development and Psychopathology, 8,* 597–600.

Clarke, D. J., Boer, H., Webb, T., Scott, P., Frazer, S., Vogels, A., et al. (1998). Prader-Willi syndrome and psychotic symptoms: I. Case descriptions and genetic studies. *Journal of Intellectual Disability Research, 42,* 440–450.

Crnic, K., Friedrich, W., & Greenberg, M. (1983). Adaptation of families with mentally handicapped children: A model of stress, coping, and family ecology. *American Journal of Mental Deficiency, 88,* 125–138.

Cummings, S. (1976). The impact of the child's deficiency on the father: A study of fathers of mentally retarded and chronically ill children. *American Journal of Orthopsychiatry, 46,* 246–255.

Cummings, S., Bayley, H., & Rie, H. (1966). Effects of the child's deficiency on the mother: A study of mentally retarded, chronically ill, and neurotic children. *American Journal of Orthopsychiatry, 36,* 595–608.

Dawson, T. L. (2002). New tools, new insights: Kohlberg's moral judgment stages revisited. *International Journal of Behavioral Development, 26,* 154–166.

Dunst, C. J. (1980). *A clinical and educational model for use with the Uzgiris-Hunt Scales for Infant Development.* Baltimore: University Park Press.

Dunst, C. J. (1988). Stage transitioning in the sensorimotor development of Down's syndrome infants. *Journal of Mental Deficiency Research, 32,* 405–410.

Dunst, C. J. (1990). Sensorimotor development of infants with Down syndrome. In D. Cicchetti & M. Beeghly (Eds.), *Children with Down syndrome: A developmental perspective* (pp. 180–230). Cambridge, England: Cambridge University Press.

Dykens, E. M. (1995). Measuring behavioral phenotypes: Provocations from the "new genetics." *American Journal on Mental Retardation, 99,* 522–532.

Dykens, E. M. (1999). Prader-Willi syndrome. In H. Tager-Flusberg (Ed.), *Neurodevelopmental disorders* (pp. 137–154). Cambridge, MA: MIT Press.

Dykens, E. M. (2002). Are jigsaw puzzles "spared" in persons with Prader-Willi syndrome? *Journal of Child Psychology and Psychiatry, 43,* 343–352.

Dykens, E. M. (2003). Anxiety, fears, and phobias in persons with Williams syndrome. *Developmental Neuropsychology, 23,* 291–316.

Dykens, E. M., & Clarke, D. J. (1997). Correlates of maladaptive behavior in individuals with 5p– (Cri du chat) syndrome. *Developmental Medicine and Child Neurology, 39,* 752–756.

Dykens, E. M., & Hodapp, R. M. (2001). Research in mental retardation: Toward an etiologic approach. *Journal of Child Psychology and Psychiatry, 42,* 49–71.

Dykens, E. M., Hodapp, R. M., & Finucane, B. M. (2000). *Genetics and mental retardation syndromes: A new look at behavior and interventions.* Baltimore: Paul H. Brookes.

Dykens, E. M., Hodapp, R. M., & Leckman, J. F. (1987). Strengths and weaknesses in intellectual functioning of males with Fragile X syndrome. *American Journal of Mental Deficiency, 92,* 234–236.

Dykens, E. M., Hodapp, R. M., Walsh, K. K., & Nash, L. (1992). Profiles, correlates, and trajectories of intelligence in Prader-Willi syndrome. *Journal of the American Academy of Child and Adolescent Psychiatry, 31,* 1125–1130.

Dykens, E. M., & Kasari, C. (1997). Maladaptive behavior in children with Prader-Willi syndrome, Down syndrome, and non-specific mental retardation. *American Journal on Mental Retardation, 102,* 228–237.

Dykens, E. M., Leckman, J. F., & Cassidy, S. (1996). Obsessions and compulsions in persons with Prader-Willi syndrome: A case-controlled study. *Journal of Child Psychology and Psychiatry, 37,* 995–1002.

Einfeld, S. L. (2004). Behaviour phenotypes of genetic disorders. *Current Opinion in Psychiatry, 17,* 343–349.

Ellis, N. R. (1963). The stimulus trace and behavioral inadequacy. In N. R. Ellis (Ed.), *Handbook of mental deficiency, psychological theory and research* (pp. 134–158). New York: McGraw-Hill.

Essex, E. L., Seltzer, M. M., & Krauss, M. W. (1999). Differences in coping effectiveness and well-being among aging mothers and fathers of adults with mental retardation. *American Journal on Mental Retardation, 104,* 454–563.

Ewart, A. K., Morris, C. A., Atkinson, D., Jin, W., Sternes, K., Spallone, P., et al. (1993). Hemizygosity at the elastin locus in a developmental disorder, Williams syndrome. *Nature Genetics, 5,* 11–16.

Fidler, D. J. (2003). Parental vocalizations and perceived immaturity in Down syndrome. *American Journal on Mental Retardation, 108,* 425–434.

Fidler, D. J., & Hodapp, R. M. (1999). Craniofacial maturity and perceived personality in children with Down syndrome. *American Journal on Mental Retardation, 104,* 410–421.

Fidler, D. J., Hodapp, R. M., & Dykens, E. M. (2000). Stress in families of young children with Down syndrome, Williams syndrome, and Smith-Magenis syndrome. *Early Education and Development, 11,* 395–406.

Fidler, D. J., Hodapp, R. M., & Dykens, E. M. (2002). Educational experiences of children with Down syndrome, Prader-Willi syndrome, and Williams syndrome. *Journal of Special Education, 36,* 80–88.

Finucane, B. M., Konar, D., Haas-Givler, B., Kurtz, M. D., & Scott, C. I. (1994). The spasmodic upper-body squeeze: A characteristic behavior in Smith-Magenis syndrome. *Developmental Medicine and Child Neurology, 36,* 78–83.

Fisher, M. A., & Zeaman, D. (1973). An attention-retention theory of retarded discrimination learning. *International Review of Research in Mental Retardation, 6,* 169–256.

Flynn, J. R. (1999). IQ gains over time: Toward finding the causes. In U. Neisser (Ed.), *The rising curve: Long-term gains in IQ and related measures* (pp. 25–66). Washington, DC: American Psychological Association.

Flint, J., & Yule, W. (1994). Behavioural phenotypes. In M. Rutter, E. Taylor, & L. Hersov (Eds.), *Child and adolescent psychiatry: Modern approaches* (3rd ed., pp. 666–687). London: Blackwell Scientific.

Fodor, J. (1983). *Modularity of mind: An essay on faculty psychology.* Cambridge, MA: MIT Press.

Fowler, A. (1990). The development of language structure in children with Down syndrome. In D. Cicchetti & M. Beeghly (Eds.), *Children with Down syndrome: A developmental approach* (pp. 302–328). Cambridge, England: Cambridge University Press.

Freud, S. (1957). Mourning and melancholia. In J. Rickman (Ed.), *A general selection from the works of Sigmund Freud* (pp. 124–140). Garden City, NY: Doubleday. (Original work published 1917)

Frey, K., Greenberg, M., & Fewell, R. (1989). Stress and coping among parents of handicapped children: A multidimensional perspective. *American Journal on Mental Retardation, 94,* 240–249.

Friedrich, W. L., & Friedrich, W. N. (1981). Psychosocial assets of parents of handicapped and nonhandicapped children. *American Journal of Mental Deficiency, 85,* 551–553.

Garber, J., Keiley, M. K., & Martin, N. C. (2002). Developmental trajectories of adolescents' depressive symptoms: Predictors of change. *Journal of Consulting and Clinical Psychology, 70,* 79–95.

Gardner, H. (1983). *Frames of mind: The theory of multiple intelligences.* New York: Basic Books.

Gersh, M., Goodart, S. A., Pasztor, L. M., Harris, D. J., Weiss, L., & Overhauser, J. (1995). Evidence for a distinct region causing a cat-like cry in patients with 5p– deletions. *American Journal of Human Genetics, 56,* 1404–1410.

Glidden, L. M. (2002). Parenting children with developmental disabilities: A ladder of influence. In J. L. Borkowski, S. L. Ramey, & M. Bristol-Powers (Eds.), *Parenting and the child's world: Influences on academic, intellectual, and socio-emotional development* (pp. 329–344). Mahwah, NJ: Erlbaum.

Goodnow, J. J. (2002). Parents' knowledge and expectations: Using what we know. In M. Bornstein (Ed.), *Handbook of parenting: Vol. 3. Being and becoming a parent* (2nd ed., pp. 439–460). Mahwah, NJ: Erlbaum.

Graham, S. (1991). A review of attribution theory in achievement contexts. *Educational Psychology Review, 3*, 5–39.

Green, B. (1956). A method of scalogram analysis using summary statistics. *Psychometrika, 21*, 79–88.

Greenberg, F., Lewis, R. A., Potocki, L., Glaze, D., Parke, J., Killian, J., et al. (1996). Multidisciplinary clinical study of Smith-Magenis syndrome (deletion 17 p. 11.2). *American Journal of Medical Genetics, 62*, 247–254.

Grossman, H. (1973). *Manual on terminology and classification in mental retardation* (Special Publications Series No. 2). Washington, DC: American Association on Mental Deficiency.

Guttman, L. (1950). The basis of scalogram analysis. In S. A. Stouffer et al. (Eds.), *Measurement and prediction* (Vol. 4). Princeton, NJ: Princeton University Press.

Hallahan, D. P., & Kauffman, J. M. (2002). *Exceptional children: Introduction to special education* (9th ed.). Boston: Allyn & Bacon.

Hanson, M., & Hanline, M. F. (1990). Parenting a child with a disability: A longitudinal study of parental stress and adaptation. *Journal of Early Intervention, 14*, 234–248.

Heber, R. (1961). Modifications in the manual on terminology and classification in mental retardation. *American Journal of Mental Deficiency, 65*, 499–500.

Heller, T. (Ed.). (2004). Special issue on aging: Family and service system supports. *American Journal on Mental Retardation, 109*(5), 349–443.

Hodapp, R. M. (1990). One road or many? Issues in the similar sequence hypothesis. In R. M. Hodapp, J. A. Burack, & E. Zigler (Eds.), *Issues in the developmental approach to mental retardation* (pp. 49–70). Cambridge, England: Cambridge University Press.

Hodapp, R. M. (1997). Direct and indirect behavioral effects of different genetic disorders of mental retardation. *American Journal on Mental Retardation, 102*, 67–79.

Hodapp, R. M. (1998). *Development and disabilities: Intellectual, sensory, and motor impairments.* Cambridge, England: Cambridge University Press.

Hodapp, R. M. (1999). Indirect effects of genetic mental retardation disorders: Theoretical and methodological issues. *International Review of Research in Mental Retardation, 22*, 27–50.

Hodapp, R. M. (2002). Parenting children with mental retardation. In M. Bornstein (Ed.), *Handbook of parenting: Vol. 1. How children influence parents* (2nd ed., pp. 355–381). Hillsdale, NJ: Erlbaum.

Hodapp, R. M. (2004a). Behavioral phenotypes: Going beyond the two-group approach. *International Review of Research in Mental Retardation, 29*, 1–30.

Hodapp, R. M. (2004b). Studying interactions, reactions, and perceptions: Can genetic disorders serve as behavioral proxies? *Journal of Autism and Developmental Disorders, 34*, 29–34.

Hodapp, R. M., & Burack, J. A. (1990). What mental retardation tells us about typical development: The examples of sequences, rates, and cross-domain relations. *Developmental Psychopathology, 2*, 213–225.

Hodapp, R. M., & Dykens, E. M. (2001). Strengthening behavioral research on genetic mental retardation disorders. *American Journal on Mental Retardation, 106*, 4–15.

Hodapp, R. M., & Dykens, E. M. (2004). Genetic and behavioural aspects: Application to maladaptive behaviour and cognition. In J. A. Rondal, R. M. Hodapp, S. Soreci, E. M. Dykens, & A. Nota (Eds.), *Genetic, behavioural, and inclusion aspects of intellectual disabilities* (pp. 13–48). London: Whurr.

Hodapp, R. M., & Dykens, E. M. (2005). Problems of girls and young women with mental retardation (intellectual disabilities). In D. Bell-Dolan, S. Foster, & E. Mash (Eds.), *Handbook of behavioral and emotional disorders in girls* (pp. 239–262). New York: Kluwer Academic/Plenum Press.

Hodapp, R. M., Dykens, E. M., & Masino, L. L. (1997). Families of children with Prader-Willi syndrome: Stress-support and relations to child characteristics. *Journal of Autism and Developmental Disorders, 27*, 11–24.

Hodapp, R. M., Dykens, E. M., Ort, S. I., Zelinsky, D. G., & Leckman, J. F. (1991). Changing patterns of intellectual strengths and weaknesses in males with Fragile X syndrome. *Journal of Autism and Developmental Disorders, 21*, 503–516.

Hodapp, R. M., & Fidler, D. J. (1999). Special education and genetics: Connections for the 21st century. *Journal of Special Education, 33*, 130–137.

Hodapp, R. M., & Ly, T. M. (2005). Parenting children with developmental disabilities. In T. Luster & L. Okagaki (Eds.), *Parenting: An ecological perspective* (2nd ed., pp. 177–201). Mahwah, NJ: Erlbaum.

Hodapp, R. M., Ly, T. M., Fidler, D. J., & Ricci, L. A. (2001). Less stress, more rewarding: Parenting children with Down syndrome. *Parenting: Science and Practice, 1*, 317–337.

Hodapp, R. M., & Ricci, L. A. (2002). Behavioural phenotypes and educational practice: The unrealized connection. In G. O'Brien (Eds.), *Behavioural phenotypes in clinical practice* (pp. 137–151). London: Mac Keith Press.

Hodapp, R. M., Ricci, L. A., Ly, T. M., & Fidler, D. J. (2003). The effects of the child with Down syndrome on maternal stress. *British Journal of Developmental Psychology, 21*, 137–151.

Hodapp, R. M., Wijma, C. A., & Masino, L. L. (1997). Families of children with 5p– (Cri du chat) syndrome: Familial stress and sibling reactions. *Developmental Medicine and Child Neurology, 39*, 757–761.

Hodapp, R. M., & Zigler, E. (1995). Past, present, and future issues in the developmental approach to mental retardation and developmental disabilities. In D. Cicchetti & D. Cohen (Eds.), *Manual of developmental psychopathology: Vol. 2. Risk, disorder, and adaptation* (pp. 299–331). New York: Wiley.

Holroyd, J., & MacArthur, D. (1976). Mental retardation and stress on parents: A contrast between Down's syndrome and childhood Autism. *American Journal on Mental Deficiency, 80*, 431–436.

Hornby, G. (1995). Fathers' views of the effects on their families of children with Down syndrome. *Journal of Child and Family Studies, 4*, 103–117.

Iarocci, G. (in press). Updating the two-group approach: I. Children with familial mental retardation. In R. M. Hodapp, J. A. Burack, & E. Zigler (Eds.), *Developmental approaches to mental retardation: A look to the future.* Cambridge, England: Cambridge University Press.

Iarocci, G., & Burack, J. A. (1998). Understanding the development of attention in persons with mental retardation: Challenging the myths. In J. A. Burack, R. M. Hodapp, & E. Zigler (Eds.), *Handbook of mental retardation and development* (pp. 349–381). Cambridge, England: Cambridge University Press.

Inhelder, B. (1968). *The diagnosis of reasoning in the mentally retarded* (W. B. Stephens et al., Trans.). New York: John Day Company. (Original work published 1943)

Jarrold, C., Baddeley, A. D., Hewes, A. K., & Phillips, C. (2001). A longitudinal assessment of diverging verbal and non-verbal abilities in the Williams syndrome phenotype. *Cortex, 37,* 423–431.

Jarrold, C., & Brock, J. (2004). To match or not to match? Methodological issues in Autism-related research. *Journal of Autism and Developmental Disorders, 34,* 81–86.

Jones, O. (1980). Prelinguistic communication skills in Down's syndrome and normal infants. In T. Field, S. Goldberg, D. Stern, & A. Sostek (Eds.), *High-risk infants and children: Adult and peer interaction* (pp. 205–225). New York: Academic Press.

Karmiloff-Smith, A. (1997). Crucial differences between developmental cognitive neuroscience and adult neuropsychology. *Developmental Neuropsychology, 13,* 513–524.

Karmiloff-Smith, A., & Thomas, M. (2003). What can developmental disorders tell us about neurocomputational constraints that shape development? The case of Williams syndrome. *Development and Psychopathology, 15,* 969–990.

Kasari, C., & Sigman, M. (1997). Linking parental perceptions to interactions in young children with Autism. *Journal of Autism and Developmental Disorders, 27,* 39–57.

Kazak, A. (1987). Families with disabled children: Stress and social networks in three samples. *Journal of Abnormal Child Psychology, 15,* 137–146.

Kemper, M. B., Hagerman, R. J., & Altshul-Stark, D. (1988). Cognitive profiles of boys with Fragile X syndrome. *American Journal of Medical Genetics, 30,* 191–200.

Keogh, B. K., Garnier, H. E., Bernheimer, L. P., & Gallimore, R. (2000). Models of child-family interactions for children with developmental delays: Child-driven or transactional? *American Journal on Mental Retardation, 105,* 32–46.

Kessen, W. (1962). Stage and structure in the study of children. In W. Kessen & C. Kuhlman (Eds.), Thought in the young child. *Monographs of the Society for Research in Child Development, 27,* 444–449.

Kounin, J. (1941). Experimental studies of rigidity: II. The explanatory power of the concept of rigidity as applied to retarded persons. *Character and Personality, 9,* 273–282.

Kumin, L. (1994). Intelligibility of speech in children with Down syndrome in natural settings: Parents' perspectives. *Perceptual and Motor Skills, 78,* 307–313.

Lakin, C., Prouty, B., Braddock, D., & Anderson, L. (1997). State institution populations: Smaller, older, more impaired. *Mental Retardation, 35,* 231–232.

Lane, E. B., & Kinder, E. F. (1939). Relativism in the thinking of subnormal subjects as measured by certain of Piaget's tests. *Journal of Genetic Psychology, 54,* 107–118.

Lejeune, J., Gautier, M., & Turpin, R. (1959). Etudes des chromosomes somatique de neuf enfants mongoliens. *Comptes Rendus de l'Academie les Sciences, 48,* 1721–1722.

Lenhoff, H. M. (1998). Insights into the musical potential of cognitively impaired people diagnosed with Williams syndrome. *Music Therapy, 16,* 33–36.

Lewin, K. (1936). *A dynamic theory of personality.* New York: McGraw-Hill.

Lobato, D. (1983). Siblings of handicapped children: A review. *Journal of Autism and Developmental Disorders, 13,* 347–364.

Loveland, K. A., & Kelley, M. L. (1988). Development of adaptive behavior in adolescents and young adults with Autism and Down syndrome. *American Journal on Mental Retardation, 93,* 84–92.

Ly, T. M., & Hodapp, R. M. (2002). Maternal attribution of child noncompliance in children with mental retardation: Down syndrome versus other etiologies. *Journal of Developmental and Behavioral Pediatrics, 23,* 322–329.

Ly, T. M., & Hodapp, R. M. (in press). Children with Prader-Willi syndrome vs. Williams syndrome: Parents' attributional cues on a jigsaw puzzle task. *Journal of Intellectual Disability Research.*

Ly, T. M., & Kazemi, E. (2005). *Parents' attributions of children with disabilities: A review within achievement context.* Submitted for publication.

MacMillan, D. L., Gresham, F. M., Siperstein, G. N., & Bocian, K. M. (1996). The labyrinth of IDEA: School decisions on referred students with subaverage general intelligence. *American Journal on Mental Retardation, 101,* 161–174.

Mahoney, G. (1975). Ethological approach to delayed language acquisition. *American Journal of Mental Deficiency, 80,* 139–148.

Marfo, K. (1990). Maternal directiveness in interactions with mentally handicapped children: An analytical commentary. *Journal of Child Psychology and Psychiatry, 31,* 531–549.

Marshall, N., Hegrenes, J., & Goldstein, S. (1973). Verbal interactions: Mothers and their retarded children versus mothers and their nonretarded children. *American Journal of Mental Deficiency, 77,* 415–419.

May, M. E., Potts, T., Phillips, J. A., Blakely, R. D., & Kennedy, C. H. (2005). *A functional polymorphism in the monoamine oxidase A promoter gene predicts aggressive behavior in developmental disabilities.* Manuscript submitted for publication.

McCubbin, H., & Patterson, J. (1983). Family transitions: Adaptations to stress. In H. McCubbin & C. Figley (Eds.), *Stress and the family: Vol. 1. Coping with normative transitions* (pp. 5–25). New York: Brunner/Mazel.

Mervis, C. B., Morris, C. A., Bertrand, J., & Robinson, B. F. (1999). Williams syndrome: Findings from an integrated program of research. In H. Tager-Flusberg (Ed.), *Neurodevelopmental disorders* (pp. 65–110). Cambridge, MA: MIT Press.

Mervis, C. B., & Robinson, B. F. (1999). Methodological issues in cross-syndrome comparisons: Matching procedures, sensitivity, and specificity. *Monographs of the Society for Research in Child Development, 64,* 115–130.

Mervis, C. B., Robinson, B. F., Rowe, M. L., Becerra, A. M., & Klein-Tasman, B. P. (2003). Language abilities of individuals with Williams syndrome. *International Review of Research in Mental Retardation, 27,* 35–81.

Meyers, B. A., & Pueschel, S. M. (1991). Psychiatric disorders in persons with Down syndrome. *Journal of Nervous and Mental Diseases, 179,* 609–613.

Miller, J. (1992). Lexical development in young children with Down syndrome. In R. Chapman (Ed.), *Processes in language acquisition and disorders* (pp. 202–216). St. Louis, MO: Mosby.

Miller, J. (1999). Profiles of language development in children with Down syndrome. In J. F. Miller, M. Leddy, & L. A. Leavitt (Eds.), *Improving the communication of people with Down syndrome* (pp. 11–39). Baltimore: Paul H. Brookes.

Minnes, P. (1988). Family stress associated with a developmentally handicapped child. *International Review of Research on Mental Retardation, 15,* 195–226.

Morss, J. R. (1983). Cognitive development in the Down's syndrome infant: Slow or different? *British Journal of Educational Psychology, 53,* 40–47.

Mundy, P., & Kasari, C. (1990). The similar structure hypothesis and differential rate of development in mental retardation. In R. M. Hodapp, J. A. Burack, & E. Zigler (Eds.), *Issues in the developmental approach to mental retardation* (pp. 71–92). New York: Cambridge University Press.

Nadel, L. (1996). Learning, memory, and neural functioning in Down's syndrome. In J. A. Rondal, J. Perera, L. Nadel, & A. Comblain (Eds.), *Down's syndrome: Psychological, psychobiological, and soci-educational perspectives* (pp. 21–42). London: Whurr.

Nadel, L. (1999). Learning and memory in Down syndrome. In J. A. Rondal, J. Perera, & L. Nadel (Eds.), *Down syndrome: A review of current knowledge* (pp. 133–142). London: Whurr.

National Center for Family Support. (2000, Winter). Aging family caregivers: Needs and policy concerns. *Family support policy brief No. 3.* National Center for Family Support at HSRI. Available at http://www.familysupprt-HSRI.org.

Nyhan, W. (1972). Behavioral phenotypes of organic genetic disease: Presidential address to the Society of Pediatric Research, May 1, 1971. *Pediatric Research, 6,* 1–9.

Okagaki, L., & Divecha, D. J. (1993). Development of parental beliefs. In T. Luster & L. Okagaki (Eds.), *Parenting: An ecological perspective* (pp. 35–67). Hillsdale, NJ: Erlbaum.

Opitz, J. M. (1985). Editorial comment: The developmental field concept. *American Journal of Medical Genetics, 21,* 1–11.

Pennington, B. F., Moon, J., Edgin, J., Stedron, J., & Nadel, L. (2003). The neuropsychology of DS: Evidence for hippocampal dysfunction. *Child Development, 74,* 75–93.

Piaget, J. (1968). Preface to the first edition. In B. Inhelder (Ed.), *The diagnosis of reasoning in the mentally retarded.* New York: John Day. (Original work published 1943)

Prothro, E. T. (1943). Egocentricity and abstraction in children and in adult aments *American Journal of Psychology, 56,* 66–77.

Rieber, R. W., & Carton, A. S. (Eds.). (1993). *The fundamentals of defectology: Vol. 2. The collected works of L. S. Vygotsky* (J. Knox & C. B. Stephens, Trans.). New York: Plenum Press.

Roach, M. A., Orsmond, G. I., & Barratt, M. S. (1999). Mothers and fathers of children with Down syndrome: Parental stress and involvement in childcare. *American Journal on Mental Retardation, 104,* 422–436.

Rondal, J. (1977). Maternal speech in normal and Down's syndrome children. In P. Mittler (Ed.), *Research to practice in mental retardation: Vol. 3. Education and training* (pp. 239–243). Baltimore: University Park Press.

Rondal, J. (1995). *Exceptional language development in Down syndrome.* New York: Cambridge University Press.

Roof, E., Shelton, R., Wilkinson, G., Kim, R., & Dykens, E. M. (2005, March). *Psychotropic medications and pharmacogenetics in Prader-Willi syndrome.* Presentation to the 38th annual Gatlinburg Conference on Research and Theory in Intellectual and Developmental Disabilities, Annapolis, MD.

Rosner, B. A., Hodapp, R. M., Fidler, D. J., Sagun, J. N., & Dykens, E. M. (2004). Social competence in persons with Prader-Willi, Williams, and Down syndromes. *Journal of Applied Research in Intellectual Disabilities, 17,* 209–217.

Sameroff, A. J. (1995). General systems theories and developmental psychopathology. In D. Cicchetti & D. Cohen (Eds.), *Manual of developmental psychopathology: Vol. 2. Risk, disorder, and adaptation* (pp. 659–695). New York: Wiley.

Sameroff, A. J., & Chandler, M. (1975). Reproductive risk and the continuum of caretaker casualty. In F. D. Horowitz, M. Hetherington, S. Scarr-Salapatek, & G. Siegel (Eds.), *Review of child development research* (Vol. 4, pp. 187–244). Chicago: University of Chicago Press.

Sanders, J. L., & Morgan, S. B. (1997). Family stress and adjustment as perceived by parents of children with Autism or Down syndrome: Implications for intervention. *Child and Family Behavior Therapy, 19,* 15–32.

Scott, B. S., Atkinson, L., Minton, H. L., & Bowman, T. (1997). Psychological distress of parents of infants with Down syndrome. *American Journal on Mental Retardation, 102,* 161–171.

Seltzer, M. M., Abbeduto, L., Krauss, M. W., Greenberg, J., & Swe, A. (2004). Comparison groups in Autism family research: Down syndrome, Fragile X syndrome, and Schizophrenia. *Journal of Autism and Developmental Disorders, 34,* 41–48.

Seltzer, M. M., Greenberg, J. S., & Krauss, M. W. (1995). A comparison of coping strategies of aging mothers of adults with mental retardation. *Psychology and Aging, 10,* 64–75.

Seltzer, M. M., Krauss, M. W., & Tsunematsu, N. (1993). Adults with Down syndrome and their aging mothers: Diagnostic group differences. *American Journal on Mental Retardation, 97,* 496–508.

Seltzer, M. M., & Ryff, C. (1994). Parenting across the lifespan: The normative and nonnormative cases. *Life-Span Development and Behavior, 12,* 1–40.

Shapiro, J., Blacher, J., & Lopez, S. R. (1998). Maternal reactions to children with mental retardation. In J. A. Burack, R. M. Hodapp, & E. Zigler (Eds.), *Handbook of mental retardation and development* (pp. 606–636). Cambridge, England: Cambridge University Press.

Sigman, M., & Ruskin, E. (1999). Continuity and change in the social competence of children with Autism, Down syndrome, and developmental delays. *Monographs of the Society for Research in Child Development, 64,* 1–114.

Snowling, M. J., Hulme, C., & Mercer, R. C. (2002). A deficit in rime awareness in children with Down syndrome. *Reading and Writing: An Interdisciplinary Journal, 15,* 471–495.

Solnit, A., & Stark, M. (1961). Mourning and the birth of a defective child. *Psychoanalytic Study of the Child, 16,* 523–537.

Spinath, F. M., Harlaar, N., Ronald, A., & Plomin, R. (2004). Substantial genetic influence on mild mental impairment in early childhood. *American Journal on Mental Retardation, 109,* 34–43.

Spitz, H. (1983). Critique of the developmental position in mental retardation research. *Journal of Special Education, 17,* 261–294.

Stromme, P., & Hagberg, G. (2000). Aetiology in severe and mild mental retardation: A population-based study of Norwegian children. *Developmental Medicine and Child Neurology, 42,* 76–86.

Sullivan, P. M., & Knutson, J. F. (2000). Maltreatment and disabilities: A population-based epidemiological study. *Child Abuse and Neglect, 24,* 1257–1273.

Tannock, R. (1988). Mothers' directiveness in their interactions with children with and without Down syndrome. *American Journal on Mental Retardation, 93,* 154–165.

Turnbull, A. P., Patterson, J. M., Behr, S. K., Murphy, D. L., Marquis, J. G., & Blue-Banning, M. J. (Eds.). (1993). *Cognitive coping, families, and disability.* Baltimore: Paul H. Brookes.

Uzgiris, I., & Hunt, J. McV. (1975). *Assessment in infancy: Ordinal Scales of Infant Psychological Development.* Urbana: University of Illinois Press.

Van Acker, R. (1991). Rett Syndrome: A review of current knowledge. *Journal of Autism and Developmental Disorders, 21,* 381–406.

van der Veer, R., & Valsiner, J. (1991). *Understanding Vygotsky: A quest for synthesis*. Oxford: Blackwell.

Vietze, P., Abernathy, S., Ashe, M., & Faulstich, G. (1978). Contingency interaction between mothers and their developmentally delayed infants. In G. P. Sackett (Ed.), *Observing behavior* (Vol. 1, pp. 115–132). Baltimore: University Park Press.

Vogels, A., De Hert, M., Descheemaeker, M. J., Govers, V., Devriendt, K., Legius, E., et al. (2004). Psychotic disorders in Prader-Willi syndrome. *American Journal of Medical Genetics, 127A,* 238–243.

Vygotsky, L. S. (1978). *Mind in society*. Cambridge, MA: Harvard University Press.

Wagner, S., Ganiban, J. M., & Cicchetti, D. (1990). Attention, memory, and perception in infants with Down syndrome: A review and commentary. In D. Cicchetti & M. Beeghly (Eds.), *Children with Down syndrome: A developmental perspective* (pp. 147–179). Cambridge, England: Cambridge University Press.

Wehman, P. (2001). *Life beyond the classroom: Transition strategies for young people with disabilities* (3rd ed.). Baltimore: Paul H. Brookes.

Weiss, B., Weisz, J. R., & Bromfield, R. (1986). Performance of retarded and nonretarded persons on information-processing tasks: Further tests of the similar-structure hypothesis. *Psychological Bulletin, 100,* 157–175.

Weisz, J. R. (1990). Cultural-familial mental retardation: A developmental perspective on cognitive performance and "helpless" behavior. In R. M. Hodapp, J. A. Burack, & E. Zigler (Eds.), *Issues in the developmental approach to mental retardation* (pp. 137–168). Cambridge, England: Cambridge University Press.

Weisz, J. R., Yeates, O., & Zigler, E. (1982). Piagetian evidence and the developmental-difference controversy. In E. Zigler & D. Balla (Eds.), *Mental retardation: The developmental-difference controversy* (pp. 213–276). Hillsdale, NJ: Erlbaum.

Weisz, J. R., & Zigler, E. (1979). Cognitive development in retarded and nonretarded persons: Piagetian tests of the similar sequence hypothesis. *Psychological Bulletin, 86,* 831–851.

Werner, H. (1937). Process and achievement: A basic problem of education and developmental psychology. *Harvard Educational Review, 7,* 353–368.

Werner, H. (1941). Psychological processes investigating deficiencies in learning. *American Journal of Mental Deficiency, 46,* 233–235.

Werner, H. (1948). *Comparative psychology of mental development* (Rev. ed.). New York: International Universities Press. (Original work published 1926)

Werner, H. (1957). The concept of development from a comparative and organismic point of view. In D. Harris (Ed.), *The concept of development* (pp. 125–148). Minneapolis: University of Minnesota Press.

Werner, H., & Strauss, A. (1939). Problems and methods of functional analysis in mentally deficient children. *Journal of Abnormal and Social Psychology, 34,* 37–62.

Wertsch, J. V. (1985). *Vygotsky and the social formation of mind*. Cambridge, MA: Harvard University Press.

Westcott, H. L., & Jones, D. P. H. (1999). The abuse of disabled children. *Journal of Child Psychology and Psychiatry, 40,* 497–506.

Wishart, J. G., & Duffy, L. (1990). Instability of performance of cognitive tests in infants and young children with Down's syndrome. *British Journal of Educational Psychology, 60,* 10–22.

Witkin, H. (1964). Heinz Werner: 1890–1964. *Child Development, 30,* 307–328.

Wolk, S. I., & Weissman, M. M. (1995). Women and depression: An update. In J. Oldham & M. Riba (Eds.), *American Psychiatric Press review of psychiatry* (Vol. 14, pp. 227–259). Washington, DC: American Psychiatric Press.

Woodward, M. (1959). The behavior of idiots interpreted by Piaget's theory of sensorimotor development. *British Journal of Educational Psychology, 29,* 60–71.

Woodward, M. (1963). The application of Piaget's theory of research in mental deficiency. In N. R. Ellis (Ed.), *Handbook of mental deficiency* (pp. 297–324). New York: McGraw-Hill.

Zeaman, D., & House, B. (1963). The role of attention in retardate discriminant learning. In N. R. Ellis (Ed.), *Handbook of mental deficiency, psychological theory and research* (pp. 159–223). New York: McGraw-Hill.

Zebrowitz, L. A. (1997). *Reading faces: Window to the soul?* Boulder, CO: Westview Press.

Zigler, E. (1967). Familial mental retardation: A continuing dilemma. *Science, 155,* 292–298.

Zigler, E. (1969). Developmental versus difference theories of retardation and the problem of motivation. *American Journal of Mental Deficiency, 73,* 536–556.

Zigler, E., & Hodapp, R. M. (1986). *Understanding mental retardation*. Cambridge, England: Cambridge University Press.

CHAPTER 7

Developmental Disorders of Language

SABINE HEIM and APRIL A. BENASICH

A major principle of developmental psychopathology pertains to the reciprocal interplay between normality and pathology. At this juncture, adaptive and maladaptive processes encounter a multiple-levels-of-analysis perspective from molecular to sociocultural systems (Cicchetti & Dawson, 2002). Research in the field of developmental language disorders has a long history, being intimately intertwined with the exploration of normal language acquisition. Accounts describing normative language development are often mutually exclusive and still a matter of intense debate. Even after many years of study, the fundamental mechanisms and neural substrate that mediate language acquisition are not fully delineated. Thus, typical and atypical language trajectories as well as their interface characterize an enduring research interest and illustrate the strength of a developmental psychopathology approach (Cicchetti & Toth, 1992).

Work was supported by grants from NICHD (RO1-HD29419) to AAB and the German Research Council to SH (HE3500/1), a Rutgers University Board of Trustees Excellence in Research Award to AAB, with additional support from the Elizabeth H. Solomon Center for Neurodevelopmental Research. We thank Dr. Andreas Keil for helpful comments on this chapter.

Disorders of language rank among the most prevalent of developmental disabilities. It is estimated that roughly 20% of preschool- and school-age children suffer from deficits in oral and/or written language (Beitchman, Nair, Clegg, Patel, et al., 1986; S. E. Shaywitz & Shaywitz, 2001). Disturbances in language development may be associated with sensory impairments (e.g., hearing loss, blindness) or neurological disease (e.g., acquired aphasia, epilepsy). They may be part of several syndromes related to mental retardation, such as Down syndrome or Fetal Alcohol syndrome. Language problems may also accompany pervasive developmental disorders, such as Rett's syndrome or Autism Spectrum Disorders. Anomalies in language skills characterize one crucial aspect of the autistic triad (impairments in communication, social interaction, and behavior repertoire) and represent an important feature of the syndrome as a whole.

A subset of children demonstrate significant limitations in oral language ability despite absence of the aforementioned causes, a condition often termed *specific language impairment*. More than 50% of children having specific language impairment continue on to develop dyslexia, encompassing difficulties in the literacy domain (e.g., Stark et al., 1984; Tomblin, Zhang, Buckwalter, & Catts, 2000). Conversely, many dyslexic individuals show deficits in parameters of oral language (e.g., Byrne, 1981; Joanisse, Manis, Keating, & Seidenberg, 2000). Longitudinal studies as well as family genetic studies demonstrate considerable overlap in etiology and co-occurrence between specific oral language disorders and reading problems, such as dyslexia (Catts, 1993; Flax et al., 2003; Rissman, Curtiss, & Tallal, 1990; see L. B. Leonard, 1998; Snow, Burns, & Griffin, 1998). To highlight the continuity between language and reading/spelling difficulties, Tallal coined the term *language learning impairment* (Tallal, Allard, Miller, & Curtiss, 1997). Epidemiological research also indicates that language-learning impaired individuals are vulnerable to psychosocial problems as well as deficits in regulation of affect and behavior (e.g., Beitchman et al., 2001; Benasich, Curtiss, & Tallal, 1993; Gadeyne, Ghesquière, & Onghena, 2004).

This chapter focuses on specific language impairment and developmental dyslexia from a converging methodological/developmental perspective under the rhetoric of language learning impairment. We propose a multilevel approach, which aims to integrate molecular, cellular, macroscopic, and behavioral evidence. Current etiological models from psychological and biological domains are addressed. Prospective studies beginning early in the life span and studies targeting remedial intervention complete the picture. The chapter concludes with recommendations and future directions regarding basic research as well as remedial work in developmental language disorders.

A HISTORICAL PERSPECTIVE ON DEVELOPMENTAL LANGUAGE DISORDERS

The study of individuals with developmental language disorders dates back to the nineteenth century. It was in 1822 when Franz Joseph Gall, the originator of what was later termed *phrenology,* published descriptions of children who had remarkable difficulties in oral language but did not show characteristics of other known syndromes. More than 50 years later, the first cases with unexpected disturbances in literacy skills were reported and considered a member of the family of aphasias. The early publications on language deficits entailed a series of case studies that continued to the 1st decades of the twentieth century. The incipient reports were written mainly from a medical perspective and not seen as pertinent for educational purposes; subsequent work accentuated the need for implementing therapies. Up to the 1990s, several different diagnostic classifications were suggested to describe these language disabilities of

unknown origin. In what follows, we provide a brief historical survey of the study of specific language impairment and developmental dyslexia.

Research on Language Learning Impairments: The Origins

Research on language-based learning impairments has its roots in the study of language disturbances that typically result from a single lesion to the left cerebral hemisphere. These medical conditions are known as the aphasias. As early as 1822, French-German anatomist and physiologist Gall described a patient who could not voluntarily repeat spoken words. Gall linked this impairment to trauma of the left brain. However, it was not until the seminal studies of neurologists Pierre Paul Broca (1861) and Carl Wernicke (1874) that localization of language functions received particular interest. In his native France, Broca reported a case of speech loss due to a lesion in the posterior part of the second and third frontal convolution. This left hemisphere area was then designated "Broca's area." In Germany, Wernicke discovered that damage to the first temporal gyrus on the left might induce deficits in language comprehension and literacy skills. This particular region has become known as "Wernicke's area."

In 1872, Sir William Henry Broadbent, a physician from Yorkshire, reported cases of "loss of speech and writing." The medical history of an intelligent adult male who suffered from right hemiplegia reads as follows:

> It was impossible to understand him when he attempted a phrase, or when he tried to say anything to which I had no clue. He laboured through the title page of a book given him to read, but, without looking at the book, only one or two words would have been recognised. A peculiarity of his attempts to read or speak was his persevering effort to master a word, syllable by syllable, by trying on and on again. (pp. 161–162)

Inspired by the Zeitgeist, the German physician Adolf Kussmaul became involved in the study of acquired language disorders and introduced the concepts of "word deafness" and "word blindness." His terminology reflected the observation that reading problems could occur as an isolated condition:

> In medical literature we find cases recorded as aphasia which should not properly be designated by this name, since the patients were still able to express their thoughts by speech and writing. They had not lost the power either of speaking or of writing; they were no longer able, however, although the hearing was perfect, to understand the words which they heard,

or, although the sight was perfect, to read the written words which they saw. This morbid inability we will style, in order to have the shortest possible names at our disposition, word-deafness and word-blindness [*surditas et caecitas verbalis*]. (Kussmaul, 1877, p. 770, cited in Hallahan & Mercer, 2002)

A Brief History of Specific Language Impairment

The literature of the late nineteenth century provides several case histories of children showing impairments in expressive language. English and French authors usually published their brief descriptions under the umbrella of "congenital aphasia" or "aphasie congénitale," a phrase coined by deaf instructor Léon Vaïsse in 1866. Broadbent (1872) presented a then detailed report on an 11-year-old boy, including observations on general intelligence, speech, and literacy. Typical remarks were:

> He plays with other children. . . . He can find his way about the streets. . . . Can be sent errands with a note, . . . will see that he has the proper change if told beforehand how much it should be. . . . He clearly understands everything that is said to him, but cannot utter a single connected sentence, and has never talked. To most questions he answers by a sound which may be represented by "keegurkruger," whether the required answer be long or short. He says "no" distinctly, "yes" indistinctly, that is, without the y or s; helping out the meaning by an affirmative nod. . . . He wrote his name pretty well, and copied several words from a printed card in written characters, but could not write yes or no when told to do so; could not write the name of the street in which he lived. Did not understand on this or any occasion the simplest *written* request. (pp. 156–157)

The German literature of the late nineteenth century used the designation *Hörstummheit* (hearing mutism or audimutism) to describe children suffering from congenital aphasia. This term was introduced in 1886 by one of the Sprachärzte (literally, "speech doctors"), Raphael Coën, who resided in Austrian Vienna. The speech doctors devoted their work to the diagnosis and treatment of communication disorders. Based on clinical observations, they presented extensive reports of children with severe limitations in language output, proposed etiological models, and designed therapy programs for the condition under consideration (see Weiner, 1986, for a stimulating review).

In 1886, citing Kussmaul's transcoding diagram of speech processing, Coën inferred that the impediment must be functional in nature. Accordingly, the brain of the affected child was thought to be equipped with a normally

functioning "sensory center for acoustic word images (sound images)." The pathway between this center and the "center for conceptions" ("ideational center") was believed to be intact. Hence, the audimute child should be capable of perceiving, storing, and understanding spoken words. However, in this view, he or she either could not utilize the connection between the sound image center and the "motor center for the coordination of the sound movements into spoken words," or the motor center for speech itself was only partially operative. Consequently, the child was thought to be mute or near mute, a condition resembling that of Broca aphasia.

Coën suggested that the functional disturbance was hereditary, but might also be related to psychological factors and trauma. Guided by his theoretical assumptions as well as observations on normal child development, he devised a therapy that encompassed both intensive "bodily gymnastic" and "mental gymnastic" (1886, 1888) methods. The former building block included exercises for general functioning. The mental gymnastic component aimed at (1) assembling visual images, word sounds, and semantics in the sensory and ideational centers; (2) training of sensorimotor pathways and the motor coordination center by using written sound symbols; and (3) implementing elementary instructions in reading, writing, and arithmetic. Adding to these building blocks, three speech doctors from Berlin, Leopold Treitel (1893), Hermann Gutzmann (1896), and Albert Liebmann (1898), highlighted the importance of attention and memory as mediating factors in therapy.

Liebmann's exceptional commitment to the education of practicing physicians motivated him to offer a refinement of the syndrome. In the style of acquired aphasia terminology, he proposed three subtypes of hearing mutism (1898): One, the motor type, concerned children who were near or actually mute, or else uttered only unintelligible sounds due to a malformation of the speech organs. A second form, the sensorimotor, was said to involve children who succeeded only in comprehending single words. The third or sensory type was characterized by a lack of language comprehension. In the literature in English of the early twentieth century, reports on the last subtype were published under the notion of "congenital word deafness" (McCall, 1911) or "congenital auditory imperception" (Worster-Drought & Allen, 1929).

Whereas early research on developmental language disorders focused on cases with profound limitations in expressive language, subsequent studies also included children whose abilities extended to multiword utterances. This led to a growing interest in grammatical and syntactic structures of disturbed language (e.g., Menyuk, 1964; Morley, Court, Miller, & Garside, 1955). As the twentieth century progressed, systematic use was made of intelligence measures, such as the Binet and Simon test. Despite this progress in methodology, validity of the studies was limited in a variety of ways: Often, sample size did not exceed two cases, an adequate control group was missing, language data were frequently based on an insufficient number of utterances, and information on experimental context was rarely given (L. B. Leonard, 1979).

Paralleling methodological and conceptual developments, terminology underwent several changes. In the 1950s, efforts in distinguishing deficits of production from those involving both comprehension and production resulted in the terms *expressive developmental aphasia* and *receptive-expressive developmental aphasia*. Stimulating contemporary theories and presaging a still ongoing debate (see section on Psychological Models), Benton (1964, p. 51) then suggested that the latter condition might be based on a "higher-level auditory perceptual deficit":

> This is, of course, not the same as saying that they are "partially" deaf. It is not so much a question of elevation of auditory thresholds (it is evident that many of these children show no such elevation) but of deficits in the orientational, discriminative and integrative aspects of auditory cognition.

The term *dysphasia* appeared in the 1960s and became the most frequent term in use (*developmental dysphasia*) about 2 decades later (classically, the prefix "a-" indicates absence, whereas "dys-" denotes difficulties). However, both terms did not prevail. Many other phrases were created to describe the syndrome, such as "deviant language" (L. B. Leonard, 1972), "delayed language" (Weiner, 1974), "developmental language disorder" (Aram & Nation, 1975), "specific language impairment" (Fey & Leonard, 1983), and "language/learning impairment" (Tallal, Ross, & Curtiss, 1989b). "Specific language impairment" has proved to be the most widely adopted notion in the current Anglo-American literature (L. B. Leonard, 1998). Because of the relationship between oral language disability and subsequent problems in literacy skills, several contemporary researchers also preferred the term *language learning impairment* (Tallal & Benasich, 2002). Its raison d'être also manifests in partially overlapping etiological theories proposed for developmental dyslexia (see the following paragraph).

A Brief History of Developmental Dyslexia

As early as 1887, German ophthalmologist Rudolf Berlin characterized a group of patients who experienced severe reading difficulties following cerebral disease. He classified them as having "dyslexia" but regarded the disorder as a manifestation of aphasia. Subsequently, Joseph Déjérine (1892), a Swiss-born neurologist, linked discrete reading disability ("pure word blindness") to a disconnection of the left angular gyrus from the right visual cortex. It was only a couple of years later when English school physician Pringle Morgan (1896, p. 1378) published an article describing for the first time a "congenital" form of reading disorder:

> Percy F. . . . aged 14 . . . has always been a bright and intelligent boy, quick at games, and in no way inferior to others of his age. His great difficulty has been—and is now—his inability to learn to read. This inability is so remarkable, and so pronounced, that I have no doubt it is due to some congenital defect. He has been at school or under tutors since he was 7 years old, and the greatest efforts have been made to teach him to read, but, in spite of this laborious and persistent training, he can only with difficulty spell out words of one syllable. . . . His visual memory for words is defective or absent; which is equivalent to saying that he is what Kussmaul has termed *word blind* (*caecitas syllabaris et verbalis*).

Morgan assumed that Percy's disorder was caused by a defective development of the left angular gyrus, which is consistent with Déjérine's tenet.

The term *congenital word blindness* was adopted and used by James Hinshelwood, a Scottish eye surgeon, in his classic 1917 monograph. His account of the rhetoric or synonym *congenital dyslexia* referred to

> children with otherwise normal and undamaged brains characterised by a difficulty in learning to read so great that it is manifestly due to a pathological condition, and where the attempts to teach the child by the ordinary methods have completely failed. (p. 40)

Hinshelwood noted that the condition might be hereditary and that it was more common in males than it was in females. He postulated poor visual memory for words and letters as the primary disability. Because the symptoms paralleled those in adults with acquired reading deficits, he believed that the congenital form was caused by faulty development of the angular gyrus of the dominant hemisphere (see Morgan, 1896). Hinshelwood emphasized the need to observe a strict nomenclature to avoid confusion between children with the "pure type of congenital word-blindness" and "generalized cerebral defects." He was also convinced that the pure type is susceptible to remedial strategies based on multisensory training.

The earliest theoretical account incorporating biological, psychological, and behavioral information on developmental dyslexia was made by American neuropathologist Samuel Torrey Orton (1925, 1937). Orton observed a striking tendency in reading-disabled children to twist the order of letters in words while reading or spelling, which led him to introduce the term *strephosymbolia* (literally, twisted symbols). Because letter reversals were "not an outstanding feature" (1937, p. 93) of the condition, he also recommended the notion of "specific reading disability." Orton favored the concept of "developmental" over "congenital," as the former was thought to highlight both hereditary and environmental factors. Agreeing with Morgan and Hinshelwood regarding the absence of intellectual impediment in specific reading disability, he made extensive use of the Stanford-Binet Intelligence Scale in understanding literacy.

In terms of etiology, Orton did not agree with the angular gyrus hypothesis suggested earlier. Among other reasons, he noticed the lack of neuroanatomical evidence and argued that the complex cognitive processes of literacy cannot be linked to a single brain structure. Alternatively, he proposed that the syndrome could be due to a developmental delay of the language-specific left hemisphere resulting in mixed or incomplete cerebral dominance. This theory was based on observations of high incidence of atypical handedness and eyedness among reading-disabled individuals and their relatives. A high number of reversal errors in reading and spelling were taken as further support.

A considerable portion of Orton's work was devoted to treatment of specific reading disability. He was confident that many of the affected individuals could improve their reading difficulties by training strategies that exploited auditory and kinesthetic senses, which did not seem to be impaired. Specifically, he advocated teaching the phonic equivalents for every letter of the alphabet and then working on the blending of the letter sounds. Tactile tracing of letters while sounding them out were assumed to support the learning process. This multisensory approach (see Hinshelwood, 1917) was elaborated on later by Anna Gillingham and Bessie Stillman (1936). Today, these practices are established as the Orton-Gillingham method, a phonics-based training using visual, auditory, and kinesthetic modalities for reading and spelling.

Neither word blindness nor strephosymbolia has become an accepted term in the dyslexia literature, however, primarily because of their focus on isolated, nonspecific fea-

tures of the disorder. Although Orton's view of cerebral dominance did not meet unanimous agreement, his theoretical accounts had a sustained influence on the study and treatment of developmental dyslexia. The foundation of the International Dyslexia Association, originally named the Orton Dyslexia Society, has reflected Orton's impact on the field.

Many approaches that followed this pioneering work are closely aligned with contemporary research and are discussed in more detail in the section titled "Etiology and Mechanisms." Up to the 1970s, visual deficits were assumed to be at the core of children's difficulty with written language. The influential studies of Isabelle Liberman and others (Fischer, Liberman, & Shankweiler, 1978; I. Y. Liberman, Shankweiler, Orlando, Harris, & Berti, 1971; see Vellutino, 1979) initiated a rethinking toward the idea that dyslexia is based on phonological deficits within the language processing system. However, in the past 3 decades the hypothesis that dyslexia is associated with impaired perceptual processes has been reconsidered. Several theories have been developed on the basis of auditory (Tallal, 1980) and visual (Lovegrove, Martin, & Slaghuis, 1986) deficits, cerebellar dysfunctions (Nicolson, Fawcett, & Dean, 2001), and general sensorimotor impairments (Stein, 2001). Extensive studies on neuroanatomical as well as neurophysiological correlates of dyslexia have been conducted since Norman Geschwind (1962; Geschwind & Levitsky, 1968) published his seminal work on cerebral asymmetry in the 1960s. Concerning the early observation that dyslexia tends to run in families, innovative methods to study the genetics of the disorder have led to novel theoretical accounts (see Grigorenko, 2001; Pennington, 1995; Schulte-Körne, 2001). Psychological as well as neurobiological approaches have inspired the development of tailored interventions (see Habib, 2003), which in turn have influenced current theorizing.

LANGUAGE LEARNING IMPAIRMENTS

The maxim of a developmental psychopathology perspective—the interplay between typical and atypical development—constitutes an important element in the study of language learning impairments. As outlined earlier, the issue of definition and phenomenology has been related to progress made in research addressing topics of etiology, therapy, and epidemiology. Conversely, diagnostic criteria have had a major impact on data collection and interpretation. This section thus introduces contemporary concepts of language learning impairments, followed by a comprehensive discussion of biological and psychological theoretical models of the disorder. Reviewing this literature, we focus on essential components of language and language learning, namely, basic sensory processing and phonology.

Definition: Specific Language Impairment

Children usually acquire language rapidly and with little apparent effort. Parents report that children understand words from about 8 months and start to produce words around their first birthday (Fenson et al., 1994). By the age of 2 to 3 years, most toddlers are speaking in short sentences that incorporate many aspects of the syntactic structures present in adult grammar (Bates, O'Connell, & Shore, 1987). Some children show slow progress during this early phase but catch up with the peer group at around 3 years. They are what have been called "late bloomers." Other children's language difficulties persist, leaving them at a disadvantage when formal education begins. When the language delay is significant and is not due to other clinical conditions, these children receive the diagnosis specific language impairment (SLI).

Most researchers and practitioners employ standardized language tests for assessing receptive and/or expressive language delay. Although there is variation across investigations and clinical settings, the delay required for this diagnosis is at least 1 standard deviation below the mean of normal (Tallal & Benasich, 2002). The *Diagnostic and Statistical Manual of Mental Disorders,* fourth edition (*DSM-IV;* American Psychiatric Association, 1994) distinguishes between two categories of Developmental Language Disorder or SLI: Expressive Language Disorder affects language production, whereas Mixed Receptive-Expressive Language Disorder includes both language comprehension and production deficits. A similar distinction is made by the *International Classification of Diseases 10* (*ICD-10;* World Health Organization, 1992). Here, the mixed type is labeled Receptive Language Disorder. Comprehension and/or production problems may manifest within one or more of the components of language, including phonology (organization of speech sounds), lexicon (word meaning), morphology (word formation), syntax (phrase and sentence formation), and pragmatics (interactive conversational skills). For instance, typical phonological problems observed in the speech of children and even adults with SLI are consonant cluster reduction (e.g., snow [no]) or final consonant deletion (e.g., boat [bo]; L. B. Leonard, 1998).

In particular, young children often meet criteria for Phonological/Specific Speech Articulation Disorder (*DSM-IV, ICD-10*), which refers to the difficulty in clearly and correctly producing one or more of the sounds in speech. The manifold language deficits present in SLI hence point to a heterogeneous group of children.

SLI is primarily a diagnosis made by the exclusion of other causes for delayed or deviant language. Mental impairment, hearing or other sensory deficits, neurological disease (e.g., seizure disorders, cerebral palsy, brain lesions), abnormalities of oral structure, Autism Spectrum Disorders, and lack of adequate opportunity are the most widely accepted exclusionary criteria (American Psychiatric Association, 1994; L. B. Leonard, 1998). At least three of these criteria, however, have limitations. First, exclusion of mental impairment is largely based on a nonverbal intelligence measure. A generally applied cutoff for diagnosing SLI rather than mental impairment is a nonverbal intelligence quotient (IQ) of 85. Some children with language problems, however, score in the borderline range (70 to 84) on a performance test; such values are considered too low for SLI but too high for a diagnosis of mental retardation. But even assessment of nonverbal IQ may be directly affected by language deficit as test instructions are usually verbal. Further, intellectual capacity appears to decrement somewhat with age in children diagnosed with SLI, probably due to the close link between general cognition and language abilities (Benasich et al., 1993). The more abstract abilities tested under the label of nonverbal IQ are less tightly linked with oral language abilities. However, differences in the amount of information received in the environment as a function of effortful interaction with adults as well as peers has a cumulative effect on the child's knowledge base. Other investigators stipulate a discrepancy of at least 1 standard deviation between nonverbal intelligence and verbal abilities to place a child in the SLI category with reasonable certainty. However, little difference has been observed in the profiles of SLI children with or without a significant discrepancy score (Tallal & Benasich, 2002).

Second, hearing problems may be the result of otitis media (middle ear infection) with effusion (fluid accumulation). During their preschool years, many children experience several episodes of ear infection without developing disturbances in language. Consequently, it is neither necessary nor sufficient to cause SLI, which led some authors to disregard otitis media with effusion as a straightforward exclusionary criterion (Rapin, Allen, & Dunn, 1992). Other researchers lowered the criterion to "no recent episodes"

(L. B. Leonard, 1998). Even in normal preschoolers, however, fluid in the middle ear can persist for many months. Diagnosis of SLI should therefore take into account the biographical and environmental context together with specific conditions, such as otitis media with effusion (Roberts, Burchinal, & Zeisel, 2002).

Third, conventionally SLI and Autism are regarded as distinct developmental disorders. Recently, this view has been challenged for several reasons (see Bishop, 2003): (1) SLI tends to cluster in families of individuals with Autism (Rapin, 1996a); (2) children with Autism display mixed receptive-expressive language dysfunctions similar to those seen in SLI (Kjelgaard & Tager-Flusberg, 2001; Rapin, 1996b); (3) enlargement of cerebral white matter and atypical cortical asymmetry have been found in both disorders (Herbert et al., 2004, 2005); and (4) some children exhibit characteristics intermediate between Autism and SLI (Bishop & Norbury, 2002). It has thus been suggested that both disorders are on a continuous spectrum rather than being discrete conditions (Herbert et al., 2004; Karmiloff-Smith, 1998). Alternatively, Bishop (2003) proposes regarding Autism as a form of SLI ("SLI plus"), in which a broader range of impairment is evident.

The exclusion of various disabling factors in the diagnosis of SLI does not rule out co-occurrence of other problems and clinical disorders. Children with SLI frequently show clumsiness or slow motor responses typical of younger children (e.g., American Psychiatric Association, 1994; Bishop, 1990; Bishop & Edmundson, 1987b; Stark & Tallal, 1988; Tallal, Dukette, & Curtiss, 1989). Enuresis (childhood incontinence), Attention-Deficit/Hyperactivity Disorder, and emotional problems such as anxiety and depression as well as social withdrawal are also not uncommon in SLI (e.g., American Psychiatric Association, 1994; Beitchman, Nair, Clegg, Ferguson, et al., 1986; Benasich et al., 1993). Yet, little is known about how these disturbances are related to SLI, or the neural mechanisms mediating the comorbidity.

Longitudinal research studying children with SLI either retrospectively or prospectively from the preschool years converge to demonstrate that oral language deficits often persist, usually in subtle form, into later childhood, adolescence, and, in several cases, adulthood (e.g., Aram, Ekelman, & Nation, 1984; Beitchman, Wilson, Brownlie, Walters, & Lancee, 1996; Bishop & Edmundson, 1987a; Stark et al., 1984; Tallal, Curtiss, & Kaplan, 1988; Tomblin, Freese, & Records, 1992). In a large-scale prospective study, Tallal et al. assessed 101 children with SLI annually for 5 years, beginning at age 4. The majority of children were receiving speech therapy and/or spe-

cial educational services in school. Although symptoms ameliorated across time, children with SLI were consistently outperformed by their nonimpaired peers across the entire set of spoken language tests. Throughout the study, the oral language profile of the affected group was reminiscent of that seen in normal developers 1 to 2 years younger.

In this vein, longitudinal studies on SLI frequently report a high incidence of poor academic achievement. Reading and spelling deficits pertinent to dyslexia are estimated to occur in 25% to 90% of classroom children with a preschool history of SLI (e.g., Bishop & Adams, 1990; Catts, 1993; Stark et al., 1984; Tomblin et al., 2000). Differences in definition of oral and written language disorders, age of initial diagnosis, length of follow-up, and sample recruitment may well account for the variation in figures. Recently, it was shown that the rate of literacy problems in SLI increased between the ages of 8 and 15 years; for reading accuracy, the increment was 37% across the 8-year interval, with a starting value of 6% (Snowling, Bishop, & Stothard, 2000). A study by Tomblin et al. suggests that the risk for reading disability is greater than the risk for behavioral problems among second graders with a preschool history of SLI. Moreover, the occurrence of behavioral disorders, such as attention deficits and externalizing problems, in SLI seems to be mediated by reading performance. What has not been well understood is the specific neurocognitive profile underlying the interaction of oral and written language difficulties. This issue is addressed when we turn to etiological models.

Definition: Developmental Dyslexia

Although symptoms of dyslexia may be present as early as preschool age, affected children are not diagnosed until they have tried and failed to learn to read. Especially in children demonstrating above-average intellectual ability, the disorder may not be manifest before the fourth grade, or even later (*DSM-IV*). According to the *ICD-10* manual, Specific Reading Disorder denotes problems in learning to read, spell, and write despite adequate intellectual capacity, educational resources, and social background. At the same time, sensory acuity deficits, neurological pathology, and psychiatric disease are absent. In the *DSM-IV*, dyslexia is coded as Reading Disorder, similarly emphasizing poor reading skills by the exclusion of extraneous factors.

Core symptoms in reading and spelling encompass omissions (e.g., "ply" instead of "play"), substitutions (e.g., "hand" for "finger"), inversions (e.g., "aks" instead of "ask"), or additions (e.g., "to" and "of") of words or fragments of words. Decoding is frequently slow. Passage reading is associated with problems that dyslexic children have keeping their place in lines of text, as are errors in comprehension. At the beginning of first grade, there may be weakness in learning the alphabet, naming letters, producing rhymes, and categorizing speech sounds. In secondary school and adulthood, deficits in spelling often are more salient than reading problems (*ICD-10*). Generally, frequency and type of errors in literacy components vary as a function of skills learned and the difficulty of the task (Grissemann, 1972).

Preceding and accompanying poor literacy skills, the disorder often manifests in various sensorimotor and cognitive dysfunctions, including problems in fine motor coordination (e.g., tying shoelaces), clumsiness, poor visual discrimination, weakness in auditory segmenting, limitations in working memory, linguistic disturbances (e.g., misarticulation of sounds, deficits in language comprehension and/or production), or a combination of these (*DSM-IV, ICD-10*). It is not uncommon for dyslexia to accompany psychosocial problems and clinically relevant conditions. As described in *DSM-IV* and *ICD-10,* dyslexic children may suffer from demoralization, low self-esteem, and deficient social skills. Problems in school adjustment or even an increased risk for dropping out of formal schooling have been reported. Adult dyslexics may have significant problems in occupational functioning and social adjustment. The disorder is also often related to a higher rate of Attention-Deficit/Hyperactivity Disorder, conduct problems, and emotional disturbances. A longitudinal study by Fergusson and Lynskey (1997) demonstrates that the co-occurrence of conduct problems and reading difficulties arise because reading-delayed children are characterized by disadvantageous features that were already present at preschool age. A person's general intellectual ability, amount of support received, and socioeconomic status have been suggested as factors influencing the course of dyslexia (Naylor, Felton, & Wood, 1990). Nevertheless, research has shown that problems of the dyslexic population may persist into adulthood (Boetsch, Green, & Pennington, 1996; Maughan, 1995; Undheim, 2003).

Standard definitions of dyslexia imply impairment in special achievement (*DSM-IV, ICD-10*). To be diagnosed as dyslexic, a child's reading and spelling skills should significantly fall below the performance expected given his or her age, intelligence, and educational level. In the *ICD-10* research criteria, a discrepancy of at least 2 standard deviations between achievement and both age norm and general IQ is recommended. However, it is commonly intelligence

that has received the most attention in diagnostics and research. Because a 2 standard deviation achievement-IQ discrepancy would exclude a large percentage of dyslexic individuals, in many studies, the criterion has been lowered to 1 to 1.5 standard deviations (see Schulte-Körne, Deimel, & Remschmidt, 2001, for discussion).

Over the past decade, the definition and use of the term *dyslexia* has been controversial as several researchers have argued that the conventional discrepancy model is empirically unfounded and theoretically inadequate (e.g., Aaron, 1997; Fletcher et al., 1998; Gustafson & Samuelsson, 1999; Stanovich, 1996). For instance, the relationship between intelligence and reading has proved ambiguous in that only 16% to 25% of the variance in decoding can be accounted for by IQ (Aaron, 1997; Gustafson & Samuelsson, 1999). Reading disability may have a detrimental effect on IQ test performance, as poor readers spend less time in reading activities and therefore often exhibit limited knowledge and a decline in language skills (Aaron, 1997). More globally, verbal IQ may decrease as a consequence of dysfunctional and effortful reading, a phenomenon known as the "Matthew effect" (Stanovich, 1986). Also, no difference in reading-related tasks has been observed between reading-impaired children showing high or low IQ, which indicates that they might similarly benefit from intervention techniques (Gustafson & Samuelsson, 1999; Stanovich, 1996).

The functional significance of the discrepancy definition is that children with an IQ in the borderline (70 to 84) range who cannot learn reading and writing are not considered dyslexic. They are sometimes labeled "backward readers" (Rutter & Yule, 1975), "garden-variety poor readers" (Stanovich, 1991), or "low achievers" (Fletcher et al., 1994). In most countries, these children are not eligible for special educational services because their failure to initiate reading and spelling is accounted for by their general pattern of performance.

To summarize, both dyslexia and SLI may reflect a heterogeneous group of disorders. After reaching school age, children with SLI are at risk for learning problems similar to those seen in dyslexics; conversely, children with developmental dyslexia typically have been found to be deficient in some linguistic tasks (e.g., Aram et al., 1984; Bishop & Adams, 1990; Catts, 1993; Flax et al., 2003; Scarborough, 1990; Tallal et al., 1988; Tomblin et al., 2000). On the basis of such performance profiles, it has been proposed that dyslexia, at least for some dyslexics, may be a less severe form of SLI (Kamhi & Catts, 1986). Although there is supporting evidence from behavioral as well as neurobiological studies (see section on Etiology and Mechanisms), this assumption is still a matter of intense debate (L. B. Leonard,

1998; Snowling et al., 2000). Nevertheless, the striking convergence between the characteristics of developmental dyslexia and SLI has given rise to the classification language learning impairment (LLI; Tallal, 2004).

Prevalence Estimates: Specific Language Impairment

Epidemiological work indicates that nearly 20% of preschool- and school-age children have some form of language deficit. The majority of childhood language problems are related to other primary conditions, such as hearing loss, mental retardation, or neurological disease (Beitchman, Nair, Clegg, Patel, et al., 1986). In a large-scale project including more than 7,000 children, Tomblin et al. (1997) observed that 7.4% of 5- to 6-year-olds experienced significant delays in language of unknown origin. This is a higher prevalence rate of SLI than previously expected. Interestingly, more than 70% of these children met the research criteria for SLI (inter alia language skills at least 1.25 standard deviations below population average) but have never been diagnosed based on reports of parents, physicians, or teachers. In line with those figures, the *DSM-IV* manual provides estimates of 3% to 5% for children having Expressive Language Disorder and 3% for children suffering from both receptive and expressive deficits.

A number of studies have shown that SLI occurs across generations. The affectance rate in families with a history of SLI is roughly 20% to 40% (e.g., Flax et al., 2003; Lahey & Edwards, 1995; Neils & Aram, 1986; Tallal et al., 2001; Tallal, Ross, & Curtiss, 1989a; Tomblin, 1989). Using direct testing methods, Tallal et al. (2001) found that 30% of the children diagnosed with SLI (ages 4 to 14 years) had affected primary relatives (parents and siblings), compared to 7% of the control children. In a similar vein, Flax et al. report elevated rates of both SLI and reading impairment in immediate and extended family members (viz., 25% and 23%, respectively), with a high degree of co-occurrence of the disorders (46%) in affected individuals.

SLI is more prominent in males than in females; the ratio is approximately 2:1 to 3:1 (e.g., Bishop, 1997; Flax et al., 2003; R. B. Johnston, Stark, Mellits, & Tallal, 1981; Tallal et al., 1989b; Tomblin, 1997; Tomblin & Buckwalter, 1994). This imbalance has also been observed in a prospective family study by Choudhury and Benasich (2003). Here, 41% of boys as compared to 16% of girls born into families with a history of SLI were affected. On the other hand, Rice, Haney, and Wexler (1998) did not find gender differences in families of language-impaired individuals. An issue raised in this regard is the ascertainment bias, with more boys than girls receiving a diagnosis given the higher incidence of attention and behavioral problems in boys (Benasich et al., 1993).

Prevalence Estimates: Developmental Dyslexia

Dyslexia is the most common learning disability, affecting around 3% to 10% of Western populations (e.g., American Psychiatric Association, 1994; Esser & Schmidt, 1994; Miles, 2004; Rutter, Tizard, Yule, Graham, & Whitmore, 1976; S. E. Shaywitz, Shaywitz, Fletcher, & Escobar, 1990). Figures as high as 17% have been reported among regular classroom children in North America (S. E. Shaywitz & Shaywitz, 2001). In Asian countries, dyslexia rates are estimated at 1% to 5% (Leong, Nitta, & Yamada, 2003; Tarnopol & Tarnopol, 1981). However, it may well be the case that this is an underestimate of actual prevalence due to low ascertainment (Leong et al., 2003; Leong & Tan, 2002). Variations in prevalence levels are thought to arise from several factors involving language characteristics, cultural expectations, investment in literacy education, diagnostic assessment, variants of dyslexia (milder versus severe cases), and sample size (Lovett, 1992; Miles, 2004). For instance, alphabetic languages vary in degrees of phonic regularity. English consists of 40 speech sounds or phonemes, which can be spelled in 1,120 different ways. In contrast, Italian speakers need to map only 25 phonemes to 33 letter combinations or graphemes (Helmuth, 2001). Whereas the English orthography demands a great deal of the learning individual, an Italian child with dyslexia may master the more regular phoneme-grapheme correspondences in his or her language (albeit memorization of the correspondence rules may be prolonged, as decoding speed is commonly reduced). Likewise, written Japanese provides highly consistent (Kana) syllabograms, and its nonalphabetic (Kanji) ideograms offer possibilities for whole-unit responses (H. W. Stevenson et al., 1982).

Substantial evidence continues to accrue that dyslexia aggregates in families (see Grigorenko, 2001). Pennington (1995) reviewed four family studies, finding that recurrence rates for siblings and parents ranged from 39% to 43% and 27% to 49%, respectively. An extended comparison across eight studies, in which parents of dyslexic children were examined, showed a median incidence rate of 46% among fathers and 33% among mothers (Scarborough, 1998). Posterior probability estimates indicate that the median increase in risk to a child having a dyslexic parent is about 8 times the population probability of 5% (Gilger, Pennington, & DeFries, 1991). A similar magnitude has been observed in a longitudinal study from before kindergarten to the end of second grade (Pennington & Lefly, 2001). Here, 34% of the children from families with a history of reading disabilities compared to 6% from control families developed dyslexia.

A core topic in dyslexia is the notion that male children are affected more frequently than females. Although several epidemiological studies have found dyslexia to be about 2 to 4 times more common in boys than in girls (Finucci & Childs, 1981; Flannery, Liederman, Daly, & Schultz, 2000; C. Lewis, Hitch, & Walker, 1994; Rutter & Yule, 1975), others have demonstrated a more balanced gender ratio (Flynn & Rahbar, 1994; S. E. Shaywitz et al., 1990; Wadsworth, DeFries, Stevenson, Gilger, & Pennington, 1992). This difference has been attributed to referral bias (i.e., problems in boys being more salient than in girls), but recent work based on large samples (Rutter et al., 2004) comes to the conclusion that reading disabilities are clearly more prominent in boys than in girls.

ETIOLOGY AND MECHANISMS

Over the past 2 decades, evidence supporting a continuum between oral and written language impairments has continued to mount. These investigations showed that children classified as SLI and those having a diagnosis of dyslexia manifest a variety of sensory and motor problems as well as linguistic deficits, particularly in the area of phonology and grammatical morphology (see Bishop & Snowling, 2004; L. B. Leonard, 1998). Whether these commonalities derive from speech-specific mechanisms or more basic processing deficits is currently the center of theoretical debate. Added to this picture are neurobiological models involving studies on the neuropathology of LLI as well as animal research. Evidence pointing to family aggregation of both disorders has led to a body of heritability research, including pedigree, twin, and gene linkage investigations.

Psychological Models

Considerable attention has been focused on trying to understand the neurocognitive determinants of LLI, using models derived from the cognitive neurosciences to inform developmental psychopathology in terms of etiology. Given the lack of homogeneity among children showing delayed oral and written language development, it is unlikely that a single etiology will be found. Several theories of the etiology of SLI and dyslexia have been put forward in the literature,

but no consensus for the cause of both disorders is agreed on. We limit our review to hypotheses pertaining to processing deficits in specific mechanisms, particularly phonological and basic sensory skills. For a survey of accounts on disturbances in nonphonological parameters of language, such as grammatical knowledge, the reader is referred to L. B. Leonard (1998) and Bishop and Snowling (2004).

Phonological Processing Deficit

Impaired phonological processing has been frequently put forward as a core deficit in developmental dyslexia (Goswami, 2000; Snowling, 2001; Wagner & Torgesen, 1987). Phonological processing refers to "the use of phonological information (i.e., the sounds of one's language) in processing written and oral language" (Wagner & Torgesen, 1987, p. 192) and encompasses at least three components: phonological or phonemic awareness, phonological retrieval, and phonological short-term memory.

Phonological awareness is defined as "conscious access to the phonemic level of the speech stream and some ability to cognitively manipulate representations at this level" (Stanovich, 1986, p. 362). Research on typical language acquisition has demonstrated that very young children use holistic representations of words. As they grow older, children begin to segment sounds in words, namely, syllables (gar-den) and onset rhymes (br-ush, s-eet). The ultimate representation at the level of the individual phoneme is believed to depend on being taught an alphabetic script. Such children would be aware that, for example, *cat* and *act* are composed of the same phonological elements (Boucher, 1994; Jusczyk, 1993; Metsala & Walley, 1998). This pattern of development has been found to occur across languages (Goswami, 2000).

Phonological awareness tasks involve counting, deleting, and substituting phonemes within words, reversing the order of phonemes within words, blending phonemes presented in isolation to form a word, and segmenting words into phonemes. Other tasks are concerned with awareness of broader sound structures; these encompass rhyming skills, counting or deleting syllables within words, and segmenting words into intrasyllabic units (Rack, 1994; Wagner & Torgesen, 1987). The former skills have been referred to as phonological awareness in the narrow sense, the latter as phonological awareness in the broad sense (Skowronek & Marx, 1989).

In their classic study, Bradley and Bryant (1978) presented 10-year-old dyslexic children with rhyme and alliteration tasks. The children were required to indicate which was the odd one in a sequence of four spoken words (e.g., *weed peel need deed* or *nod red fed bed* or *sun see sock rag*).

Dyslexic children performed less well than younger reading-level-matched controls. This suggests that poor rhyme and word-onset awareness may have a role in their reading impairment. Further evidence was reported by Rack (1985), who found that dyslexic children have difficulty in simple rhyme judgments.

A large body of work shows that children with dyslexia are impaired on a variety of phonological awareness skills in the narrow sense (e.g., Bruck, 1992; Fawcett & Nicolson, 1995; Joanisse et al., 2000; Olson, Wise, Conners, & Rack, 1990; Swan & Goswami, 1997). The dyslexic children were not only outperformed by their age-matched controls, but were worse when compared with younger reading-level-matched normal developers. Thus, performance on these phonological awareness tasks was not simply a function of reading level.

In a similar vein, poor awareness for various linguistic units has repeatedly been documented in SLI (e.g., Bird, Bishop, & Freeman, 1995; Joffe, 1998; Leitão, Hogben, & Fletcher, 1997; Snowling et al., 2000). Also, deficits in phonological awareness have been found to be related to reading impairment in a variety of these investigations.

There is substantial evidence demonstrating that preschool phonological awareness predicts later reading achievement across alphabetic writing systems (e.g., Bradley & Bryant, 1983, 1985; Lundberg, Olofsson, & Wall, 1980; Marx, Jansen, Mannhaupt, & Skowronek, 1993; Wagner, Torgesen, & Rashotte, 1994). For instance, Bradley and Bryant conducted a 4-year longitudinal study providing data from 368 children ages 4 to 5 years at initial screening. Phonological awareness was measured using the rhyme-oddity task (see earlier); the 4-year-olds listened to series of three words, the 5-year-olds to series of four. Results indicate a significant relationship between preliterate children's awareness of rhyme and word onsets and subsequent performance on reading and spelling tests. When age at initial testing and general cognitive ability were controlled, rhyming and alliteration skills explained 4% to 10% of the variance in reading and 6% to 8% of the variance in spelling. This seemed to be specific, as rhyme-oddity detection accounted for less of the variance (1% to 4%) in later math ability.

In a quantitative meta-analysis of controlled U.S. studies, Bus and van IJzendoorn (1999) showed that training of phonological awareness reliably improves children's phonological and reading skills. The combined effect sizes for phonemic awareness and reading were 0.73 ($n = 739$) and 0.70 ($n = 745$), respectively. As noted by the authors, approximately 500 studies with null results would be required

to turn this finding into nonsignificance. Thus, phonological awareness should be considered an important condition for early reading.

Phonological retrieval denotes the ability to access the lexicon by utilizing sound-based representations. It seems to be especially important at early stages of reading acquisition and even useful in the sophisticated reader for less familiar or unknown words (Wagner & Torgesen, 1987). Phonological retrieval is typically assessed through measures of naming accuracy and speed. The classic rapid automatized naming (RAN) task entails the naming of familiar items under timed conditions. Denckla and Rudel (1976) found dyslexic children to perform more slowly on series of objects, colors, digits, and letters compared to both age controls and nondyslexic learning-disabled individuals. Subsequent RAN studies confirm that dyslexic children exhibit deficiencies in naming speed (Bowers & Swanson, 1991; Goswami et al., 2002; Lovett, 1987; Semrud-Clikeman, Guy, Griffin, & Hynd, 2000; Wolf, Bally, & Morris, 1986). Several researchers observed prominent differences for reading-age-matched comparisons (Ackerman & Dykman, 1993; Wimmer, 1993; Wolf, 1991; Wolf & Segal, 1999). RAN tasks have also been shown to distinguish SLI children from normal developers (Catts, 1993; Katz, Curtiss, & Tallal, 1992; Leitão et al., 1997). Katz et al., for instance, reported RAN speed to be significantly associated with reading abilities in both language-impaired and control subjects. Moreover, both groups demonstrated an increase in naming speed between the ages of 4 and 8 years. A similar result was obtained in reading-disabled children, suggesting that processes tapped by RAN tasks become more automatized with maturation (Watson & Willows, 1995; Wolf et al., 1986).

Various studies concede the predictive value of preschool RAN performance for early reading achievement (e.g., Catts, 1993; Wolf et al., 1986). The findings by Wolf et al. indicate that the relationship of speeded naming to reading is mediated by the subject's age and stimulus type. Whereas nongraphological RAN symbols (i.e., objects and colors) lost their predictive power at the time children entered elementary grades, naming rate for graphological symbols (i.e., letters and digits) continued to predict word reading scores.

Some authors have suggested that deficits in RAN speed are not inherently phonologic, but rather reflect a general impairment in automatizing low-level subprocesses involved in reading (Wolf, 1991; Wolf & Bowers, 1999; Wolf et al., 2002). Wolf and Bowers propose that problems in phonological awareness and RAN are separable sources of reading impairment. This so-called double-deficit hypothesis predicts three categories of reading-disabled individuals: the phonological-deficit reader, who encounters poor phonological awareness skills with otherwise intact naming speed; the rate-deficit reader, exhibiting the precisely reversed profile; and the double-deficit reader, showing a deficiency in either process. Phonological-deficit readers are specifically impaired in word-identification accuracy, rate-deficit readers tend to be slower in word decoding, and double-deficit readers exhibit a general dysfunction on all decoding measures. Although this literature is not conclusive, both dimensions appear relatively independent and additive (Compton, DeFries, & Olson, 2001; Wolf et al., 2002). Supportive evidence emerges from studies examining naming speed and phonological awareness in regular orthographies, such as Dutch (van den Bos, 1998) and German (Wimmer, 1993). For instance, Wimmer found that German fourth graders with dyslexia were at the same level as reading-level-matched second graders on phonological awareness tasks. In contrast, dyslexic subjects showed slower RAN performance than the younger controls. A similar pattern held true for word and pseudoword reading: Dyslexic children displayed high decoding accuracy, although they experienced marked speed decrements. This finding is striking with respect to pseudowords, that is, arbitrary letter strings that can be pronounced as if they are real words. Pseudoword decoding indicates to what extent a child has mastered grapheme-phoneme mapping, a task that English dyslexic children find very difficult (see Rack, Snowling, & Olson, 1992).

Phonological short-term memory can be conceived as forming sound-based representations of written symbols being sustained for a period of time. Efficient phonetic recoding appears to be an important tool for the novice reader. Unlike the able reader, the beginner devotes the maximum amount of cognitive resources possible to the process of blending phonemes to generate words (Wagner & Torgesen, 1987). Serial recall of diverse speech materials, digit and word span, and verbal repetition of words, pseudowords, or sentences exemplify measures of phonological short-term memory (Rack, 1994; Wagner & Torgesen, 1987). Early studies have shown that elementary school children with difficulty in word recognition tended to make more errors in serial-recall tasks, including spoken letter names (Shankweiler, Liberman, Mark, Fowler, & Fischer, 1979), consonant-vowel syllables (Brady, Mann, & Schmidt, 1987), and words (Brady, Shankweiler, & Mann, 1983; Mann, Liberman, & Shankweiler, 1980), as compared to their normal-reading peers. Poor readers were also

distinguished from good readers regarding their memory for printed letter strings (Shankweiler et al., 1979). In addition, poor readers were found to show a reduced or even absent phonological similarity effect (i.e., superior recall performance for phonemically dissimilar versus rhyming items) that is evident in normal individuals even at early reading stages (e.g., Brady et al., 1983; Mann et al., 1980; Shankweiler et al., 1979). These findings suggest that poor readers do not rely on codes in phonological short-term memory. However, it was subsequently demonstrated that poor readers show a phonological similarity effect comparable to normal controls when they (1) were presented with list lengths adjusted to their memory spans (Hall, Wilson, Humphreys, Tinzmann, & Bowyer, 1983; Holligan & Johnston, 1988), (2) were comparable or equated on memory span (Irausquin &. de Gelder, 1997; R. S. Johnston, Rugg, & Scott, 1987), or (3) were matched on reading level (Holligan & Johnston, 1988; R. S. Johnston et al., 1987). This indicates that poor readers use phonetic recoding in short-term memory, but less efficiently, and hence have more limited capacity to remember linguistic material.

A wealth of studies has used pseudoword repetition to investigate phonological memory in developmental language disorders. Limitations in pseudoword repetition have frequently been shown in both SLI (e.g., Bishop, North, & Donlan, 1996; Botting & Conti-Ramsden, 2001; J. Edwards & Lahey, 1998; Gathercole & Baddeley, 1990; Montgomery, 1995; Snowling et al., 2000) and dyslexia (e.g., Kamhi & Catts, 1986; Snowling, 1981; Snowling, Goulandris, Bowlby, & Howell, 1986; van Daal & van der Leij, 1999). For instance, Snowling and colleagues (Snowling, 1981; Snowling et al., 1986) found dyslexic individuals performing worse than reading-level-matched controls. As for SLI, Kamhi, Catts, Mauer, Apel, and Gentry (1988) reported specific decrements in performance as a function of the number of syllables contained in pseudowords. From a theoretical perspective, Gathercole and Baddeley (1993) conjectured as to the role of phonological memory as a common factor affecting acquisition of vocabulary and grammar. Moreover, ability on pseudoword repetition predicts literacy achievement later in life.

In summary, there is substantial evidence that particular children with dyslexia, but also children having SLI, are affected by phonological processing deficits. Recently, a more general picture has emerged, viewing phonological deficits in the context of other variables. First, phonological skills often remain deficient into adulthood and even exist in individuals whose early language problems have resolved (e.g., Bishop et al., 1996; Bruck, 1992; Elbro,

Nielsen, & Petersen, 1994; Gallagher, Laxon, Armstrong, & Frith, 1996; Pennington, Van Orden, Smith, Green, & Haith, 1990). Second, the relationship between phonological skills and literacy appears to be reciprocal in nature. Wagner et al. (1994) assessed indices of phonological processing and reading-related knowledge from kindergarten through second grade. Although there were considerable influences of phonological abilities on word decoding, letter-name knowledge exerted a moderate effect on phonological skills. Third, the underlying mechanism of phonological impairments is still unclear. An integrating account derived from developmental theories of spoken word recognition maintains that language difficulties arise from poorly specified phonological representations (Goswami, 2000; Snowling, 2001). However, its causal primacy is under debate as well. Contrary to the proponents of the phonological deficit hypothesis, others hold the opinion that such problems are secondary to a more fundamental auditory processing deficit (Farmer & Klein, 1995; Tallal, 2004). This approach is discussed next.

Auditory Rate Processing Deficit

Research on auditory processing in language-based learning disorders has been particularly influenced by the work of Tallal and colleagues. Their model emphasizes the role of timing in the auditory system. The rate of information processing is considered essential for encoding brief and rapidly changing or rapidly occurring successive events (Tallal, 1984). Originally, Tallal's research focused on children with SLI. However, it was the striking similarity between SLI and dyslexia that led her to assume that the auditory deficit may be causally related to both conditions. Hence, low temporal sensitivity in the auditory system is assumed to be associated with difficulties in forming segmental phonological representations (Tallal, 2004).

Tallal and Piercy (1973a, 1973b, 1974, 1975) reported data from SLI children ranging from 7 to 9 years and age-matched normal developers. In the first study, Tallal and Piercy (1973a) used two different complex tones having a duration of 75 ms. The children learned to associate each specific isolated tone with a specific response panel. Subsequently, sequences of two tones (high-high, high-low, low-high, or low-low) were presented, and the child was asked to push the respective panels in the correct order. The SLI children performed above chance level when the tones were separated by an interstimulus interval (ISI) exceeding 300 ms, but their performance deteriorated when shorter ISIs were used. The controls maintained high-level performance at shorter ISIs and scored at above-chance levels with ISIs as brief as 8 ms. A similar pattern of

results was demonstrated when the child was asked to indicate whether two tones in a series were the same or different. This suggests that the sequencing difficulty experienced by the children with SLI was secondary to their impairment in discriminating rapidly occurring tones.

In a second study, Tallal and Piercy (1973b) manipulated the tone duration in addition to the ISI. When the tone duration was 250 ms, the SLI children repeated the two-element patterns as accurately as the control children throughout ISIs (8 to 428 ms). When the tone duration was 175 ms, the SLI children were outscored by the controls at short ISIs of 15 ms or less. Tones of 125 ms or 75 ms differentiated the two groups even for ISIs as long as 150 ms. Thus, the total duration of the stimulus pattern appeared to be critical to the SLI children's performance. Tallal and Piercy concluded that children with SLI exhibit a deficit in perceiving auditory events, which occur on a time scale of 10s of milliseconds. These temporal characteristics led the researchers to focus on the phonemic level of speech. Consonant and vowel phonemes are perceived by different temporally coded acoustic cues (e.g., A. M. Liberman, Cooper, Shankweiler, & Studdert-Kennedy, 1967). The acoustic cue for vowels is the relation among the frequencies (called formants), remaining uniform throughout the stimulus duration. Stop consonants,[1] in contrast, are characterized by brief transitional periods during which the frequencies of the formants change very rapidly over time. Figure 7.1 illustrates the acoustic spectra of sounds that are perceived as the vowel phonemes /a/ and /ae/ (Figure 7.1 left) and the stop consonant-vowel syllables /ba/ and /da/ (Figure 7.1 right). The formant frequencies of the two vowels are stationary and differ from each other by a constant amount throughout their entire 150-ms duration. The two syllables share identical stationary formants of the vowel /a/ for most of the 240 ms and differ only in the initial portion, during which the frequencies change within some 40 ms. Consequently, the perception of a difference between stop-consonant syllables crucially depends on the accurate analysis of the very brief formant transitions.

Given the phonemes' temporal characteristics, Tallal and Piercy (1974) hypothesized that children with SLI would be (1) unimpaired in distinguishing the vowel phonemes /E/ and /ae/ of 250 ms, and (2) impaired in distinguishing the stop consonant-vowel syllables /ba/ and

---

[1] Stop consonants or plosives are produced by closing the vocal tract. Most languages have six stop consonants in common: b, d, g, p, t, k. The first three stops are voiced (i.e., they cause vibration of the vocal cords), the second three are unvoiced (i.e., vocal cords are not vibrating; e.g., A. M. Liberman et al., 1967).

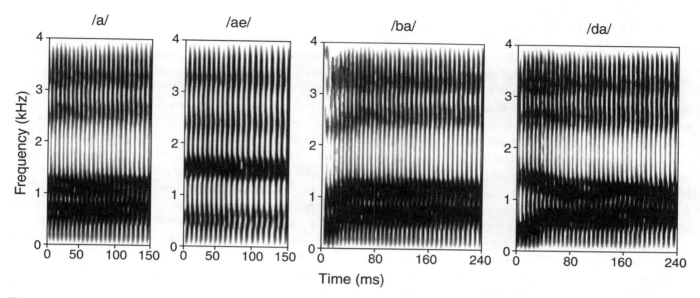

Figure 7.1   Sound spectrograms of vowels /a/ and /ae/ (left) and stop consonant-vowel syllables /ba/ and /da/ (right). Component frequencies (in kHz) are represented on the ordinate, and time (in ms) is shown on the abscissa. Intensity is coded by the darkness of the traces (see text for details).

/da/. The latter have a total duration of 250 ms and a formant transition period of 43 ms. Tallal and Piercy observed no differences between SLI and control groups in sequencing the two vowels. In contrast, each control child succeeded in distinguishing /ba/ and /da/, but only 2 out of 12 SLI children could discriminate and sequence the syllables correctly.

In a study concluding this series, Tallal and Piercy (1975) examined whether SLI children's poor performance on tests with stop-consonant syllables was due to an inability to utilize brief cues within phonemes or was due to impairment in processing transitional speech elements. Children were presented with two pairs of synthesized speech stimuli: (1) the vowel-vowel pairs /EI/ and /aeI/, in which the first (stationary) vowel was 43 ms in duration, followed by the second vowel (207 ms duration); and (2) the consonant-vowel pairs /ba/ and /da/, in which the initial transitional period was extended from 43 ms to 95 ms and the duration of the stationary vowel was reduced to 155 ms. The SLI children displayed problems with the temporally reduced vowel-vowel syllables, but performed as accurately as the age controls did on the temporally extended stop-consonant pairs. This lends support to the notion that the brevity of the contrastive information represents a core variable in SLI children's sound difficulties. Remedial implications are discussed later.

Using an expanded set of synthesized syllables, Tallal and Stark (1981) added evidence that vowel and consonant confusions could not solely be attributed to the duration of acoustic cues. Instead, problems appear to be greatest when brief stimuli are followed by rapid successive information.

The question arises as to the relevance of the auditory rate processes for perception of more complex speech stimuli. Tallal, Stark, Kallman, and Mellits (1980b) administered a perceptual-constancy task,[2] which required the child to push one panel for stimuli comprising the phoneme /b/ (/ba/, /be/, /bi/), and another panel for stimuli comprising /d/ (/de/, /dae/, /di/). Forty-one percent of the SLI children versus 63% of the controls managed the task. Those who succeeded participated in another task (Tallal, Stark, Kallman, & Mellits, 1980a) in which bisyllabic words were approximated by presenting the syllables adjacent in time (e.g., /dae/ 50-ms interval /di/, for *daddy*). Again, children with SLI had greater difficulty in sequencing the syllables than did the controls. The authors concluded that the added linguistic redundancy of the stimulus material was not sufficient to counteract the auditory processing deficit observed in children with SLI.

Phonetic analyses of language output data from SLI children versus age controls have shown a remarkable similarity

---

[2] In speech, perceptual constancy refers to the ability to detect acoustic information that remains constant over changes in phonetic context, characteristics of the speaker (e.g., gender), and speaking rate (A. M. Liberman et al., 1967; Strange, Jenkins, & Johnson, 1983). Perceptual constancy for the phonemes /b/ and /d/ occurring in various vowel environments (i.e., phonetic context) was assessed in the Tallal et al. (1980b) study.

between profiles of auditory processing constraints and speech production problems (Stark & Tallal, 1979). Production errors specifically occurred in voicing (e.g., voiceless [p] for voiced /b/ in word/syllable final position), followed by errors in place of articulation (e.g., alveolar [d] for velar /g/ in word/syllable initials). Parallels have also been drawn between rate processing in other sensory modalities (visual, tactile, and cross-modally) and data from motor tasks. Stark and Tallal (1988) reported that children with SLI were impaired in their ability to discriminate, sequence, or remember any brief stimulus (verbal or nonverbal) that was followed rapidly by another event, regardless of the modality of presentation. A similar performance profile was observed for the production of rapid, sequential oral or manual movements, regardless of whether the stimuli were verbal or nonverbal. Thus, rate processing deficits may not be specific to the auditory modality. Moreover, Tallal, Stark, and Mellits (1985) demonstrated the role of timing well beyond the domain of low-level speech processing. The degree of poor temporal integration in the auditory system was significantly correlated with the degree of language comprehension deficits.

In summary, many children with SLI have difficulty with tasks involving rapid auditory processing, though at least some of these children exhibit impaired frequency discrimination abilities as well (Stark & Heinz, 1996; Tallal & Stark, 1981). Furthermore, some children with SLI have been reported to be impaired in sequencing more slowly presented sounds (Bishop, Bishop, et al., 1999; Tallal, Stark, Kallman, & Mellits, 1981), possibly pointing to a more general auditory deficit. There is also empirical evidence that temporal constraints are present in other sensory modalities as well as motor systems (Katz et al., 1992; Stark & Tallal, 1988). This may have significant implications for theories on neurocognitive mechanisms underlying speech in humans.

The same series of auditory tasks as used in the Tallal and Piercy (1973b, 1974) studies was administered to children diagnosed with dyslexia. Tallal (1980) observed that 10-year-old dyslexics performed as well as younger normal developers when the tones were presented slowly (428 ms ISI), but did less well when the presentation rate was increased (ISIs declining from 305 to 8 ms). Their errors in auditory rate processing were found to correlate significantly with errors in tests of spelling ($r = .67$), word discrimination ($r = .64$), word knowledge ($r = .64$), and pseudoword reading ($r = .81$). The last correlation is of particular importance as it supports an association between auditory rate processing and phonological decoding (i.e.,

the use of grapheme-phoneme conversion rules). Tallal concluded that the auditory dysfunction might disrupt the ability to learn to use phonetic codes adequately.

Reed (1989) confirmed and extended the findings of Tallal (1980) in dyslexic second- and third graders versus age-matched controls. Sequencing performance at varying ISIs was assessed using pairs of vowels and stop consonant-vowel syllables with a duration of 250 ms as well as pairs of complex tones with a duration of 75 ms. Dyslexics' performance decreased as a function of ISI length (declining from 400 to 10 ms) for tones and consonant syllables. As predicted, they performed within the normal range when vowels were used. The difficulty with brief and rapidly changing cues and mastery with long-duration stimuli were also observed in tasks simulating natural speech conditions: Performance was poor when they were asked to match pictures with auditory words differing in their initial stop consonant, but they had no unusual problems in sequencing long vowels embedded in white noise. Reed also examined whether rate processing deficits and phonological impairments are characteristic of the same individuals with dyslexia. Children participated in a categorical perception task, which entailed a nine-item continuum varying from /ba/ at one end point to /da/ at the other end point. Dyslexics were impaired in discriminating syllable pairs that cross the phonetic boundary. Additionally, they were less consistent than normal readers in identifying syllables near the /ba/-/da/ boundary. Thus, dyslexic children exhibited less sharply defined categorical borders. The perceptual difficulty with brief and rapidly changing cues might contribute to inadequately defined sound representations and hence interfere with the processing of phonological information.

This work indicates that auditory rate dysfunction is present in children with dyslexia, as it might be co-occurring with a phonological deficit. However, Tallal (1980) observed that performance in pseudoword reading and auditory rate processing varied considerably within the dyslexic group. Fifty-five percent of the dyslexics scored within normal limits when presented with rapid successive tones, and 45% showed a similar, albeit less impaired, pattern of performance as that found in SLI children (Tallal & Piercy, 1973b). Tallal inferred two subgroups of dyslexia: one group with concomitant oral language delay, who exhibit both deficits in temporal processing and "phonics skills," and another group with normal language skills showing none of these deficits. In line with this notion, Tallal and Stark (1982) reported that dyslexic children without oral language delay differed from normal readers neither in sequencing rapid tones nor in their knowledge of word parts, which is a measure of phonics skills. However, to completely support Tallal's subgroup hypothesis, dyslexic children having normal oral language should be compared with both normally developing peers and dyslexics suffering from concomitant oral language weakness. This study was carried out by Heath, Hogben, and Clark (1999), whose findings provide no direct evidence for the subgroup's profile proposed by Tallal.

Dyslexia has also been associated with a cross-modal rate processing deficit (see Farmer & Klein, 1995). The empirical evidence for the co-occurrence of visual and auditory impairments is not conclusive, however. For instance, Van Ingelghem et al. (2001) reported that 7 out of 10 dyslexic children had higher thresholds than normal readers both for auditory and visual gap detection. In contrast, Heim, Freeman, Eulitz, and Elbert (2001) found high-level visual performance in a small group of dyslexic children showing impaired discrimination of rapidly changing stop consonant-vowel syllables. The conflicting results could either be sample related and/or task related (V. T. Edwards et al., 2004; Fitch & Tallal, 2003). Another possibility is that the findings are moderated as a function of age, with visual deficits disappearing through development in certain individuals with LLI (Di Lollo, Hanson, & McIntyre, 1983; Tallal et al., 1981). To test this hypothesis, Heim, Keil, and Ruf (2005) compared two age groups on tasks measuring auditory and visual rate processing. Auditory performance was assessed by means of a syllable-discrimination task; visual performance was indexed by judgments of temporal order of lightness changes. Dyslexic children exhibited higher visual thresholds than the controls did. This was in contrast to what was observed in older participants. Both young (11-year-old) dyslexics and older (13-year-old) controls demonstrated no relationship between auditory accuracy and visual thresholds. In contrast, significant relationships were found in the young control and older dyslexic group. The findings suggest the co-occurrence of visual and auditory impairments in young children with dyslexia. Visual processing deficits, however, seem to recover across development. Hence, young dyslexic children may have deficits in both modalities, but older dyslexics may not show co-occurrence of visual and auditory impairments.

If deficient auditory rate processing can be considered a primary symptom of the lifelong condition, then distinctive features should also be detected in adults with dyslexia. For instance, Hari and Kiesilä (1996) employed trains of binaural clicks (four left-ear clicks followed by four right-ear clicks), which produce an illusory perception of saltatory sound movement (from left to right) at short ISIs. In controls, this movement illusion disappeared at ISIs exceeding 90 to 120 ms. In dyslexics, who as a group were inferior to the controls on different measures of phonological processing, the illusion persisted up to ISIs of 250 to 500 ms. "Dyslexic adults thus seem to have a deficit in the processing of rapid sound sequences, which is also manifested in significant delays in their conscious auditory percepts" (p. 138).

Focusing on the Gestalt aspects of sound processing, Helenius, Uutela, and Hari (1999) studied auditory stream segregation[3] in adults. Controls segregated a single sequence of alternating high- and low-pitched tones into two separate (one high and one low) streams at stimulus-onset asynchronies (SOA) of 130 ms and less, and dyslexics showed this same segregation effect already at SOAs around 210 ms. This was discussed as evidence for a prolonged auditory integration window in dyslexic individuals. Stream segregation correlated significantly with naming speed in dyslexics, indicating that slow access of phonological information is related to abnormal processing of rapid tone sequences.

Taken together, these auditory problems may be present and associated with phonological deficits in a significant proportion of dyslexic individuals. Findings provided by the adult literature on auditory perception seem to be less conflicting than those in the child population. An influence of experimental methods cannot be ruled out, however. Tasks administered to adults are often more challenging than those presented to children. The assumption that a rate processing deficit is causally related to phonological impairments in LLI has not received unequivocal support (Bishop, Bishop, et al., 1999; Marshall, Snowling, & Bailey, 2001). It remains to be seen whether the auditory dysfunction predicts phonological deficits or even LLI, or whether the perceptual problems are instead associated symptoms that are milder and less consistent in occurrence (Studdert-Kennedy & Mody, 1995; but see Denenberg, 1999, 2001). Prospective longitudinal studies including children who are at high familial risk for LLI may represent one avenue for revealing its causal relevance. This new line of evidence is introduced later in the chapter.

According to a recent version of the rate processing hypothesis, the deficit is not limited to the auditory modality.

---

[3] Rapid alternation of high and low tone sequences leads to the perception of two separate streams, that is, a high- and a low-pitched stream.

Similar constraints in coping with brief and rapidly occurring events have also been reported for other sensory and motor modalities in SLI and dyslexia. A multimodal or "pansensory" (Tallal, Miller, & Fitch, 1993, p. 27) rate processing dysfunction, although controversial, is assumed to have a particularly severe impact on the development of spoken and written language (Tallal, 1984; Tallal et al., 1993). Temporal sensitivity in the visual domain has also been investigated in the context of the magnocellular deficit hypothesis for dyslexia. This hypothesis is considered next.

Magnocellular Deficit

In the 1980s, Lovegrove and collaborators capitalized on the observation that poor readers may have visual problems, which could not solely be attributed to poor phonological awareness. Their experimental work has led to novel approaches stimulating research on visual processing in dyslexia (e.g., Lovegrove et al., 1982, 1986; Martin & Lovegrove, 1984, 1987, 1988; Slaghuis & Lovegrove, 1984, 1985, 1986). Lovegrove's experiments were designed to test for visible persistence[4] and contrast sensitivity differences between normal and dyslexic readers using grating stimuli. Findings indicate that children with dyslexia display longer-lasting visible persistence at low spatial frequencies (i.e., coarse gratings) and less sensitivity to gratings, particularly at low spatial frequencies, low contrasts, low luminances, and high temporal frequencies (i.e., fast-flickering gratings). Dyslexics often showed shorter visible persistence and slightly elevated contrast sensitivity at higher spatial frequencies than controls did (Lovegrove et al., 1982, 1986; Martin & Lovegrove, 1984, 1987, 1988; Slaghuis & Lovegrove, 1984, 1985, 1986). Problems in visual processing were observed in approximately 75% of a dyslexic group (Lovegrove et al., 1986; Slaghuis & Lovegrove, 1985). These digressions are present before children commence reading practice (Lovegrove

---

[4] "Visible persistence is defined as any continued visible response occurring after stimulus offset that is phenomenally indistinguishable from that occurring during the actual presence of the stimulus" (Lovegrove et al., 1982, p. 309). Duration of visible persistence has been typically assessed by displaying spatial frequency gratings sequentially in time (e.g., Slaghuis & Lovegrove, 1985). For example, participants are required to report detection of a blank field between the grating stimuli. Failure to detect the blank field indicates that the image of the first stimulus was still apparent at the onset of the second. Thus, the duration of the interstimulus interval at which the blank field becomes detectable can be regarded as a measure of the duration of visible persistence.

et al., 1986) and continue into adulthood (Slaghuis, Twell, & Kingston, 1996).

Psychophysical studies of various laboratories have confirmed Lovegrove's findings (e.g., Borsting et al., 1996; Felmingham & Jakobson, 1995). Evidence is also provided by electrophysiological studies demonstrating that brain responses in dyslexic individuals were reduced or delayed for stimuli with low spatial and high temporal frequencies (e.g., Kubová, Kuba, Peregrin, & Nováková, 1995; Lehmkuhle, Garzia, Turner, Hash, & Baro, 1993; Livingstone, Rosen, Drislane, & Galaburda, 1991).

Lovegrove and colleagues discussed these results in terms of transient and sustained channels of the visual system. The transient system responds rapidly to low spatial and high temporal frequencies, low contrasts, and low luminances. The sustained system responds more slowly to medium and high spatial frequencies, low temporal frequencies, medium and high contrasts, and color differences (Maunsell & Van Essen, 1983; Merigan & Maunsell, 1993; Shapley, 1990). Transient visual processing is mainly mediated by large magnocells that constitute the magnocellular pathway between retina and cortex. Sustained processing, in turn, depends on the sensitivity of the smaller parvocells constituting the retinocortical parvocellular pathway (Merigan & Maunsell, 1993; Milner & Goodale, 1995). On the basis of primate and human visual studies, Breitmeyer and Ganz (1976) suggested that with each saccadic eye movement, transient/magnocellular channels normally inhibit sustained/parvocellular channels. As a consequence, the eidetic image of the previous fixation does not persist and does not mask the subsequent fixation. In dyslexic children, high persistence would cause masking and, ultimately, visual confusion during reading. Lovegrove et al. (1986) therefore proposed that the visual deficit in dyslexia reflects a failure of the transient system on sustained inhibition. A number of research groups, however, have found the magnocellular/transient system to be suppressed during saccades rather than the parvocellular/sustained system (Burr, Holt, Johnstone, & Ross, 1982; Burr, Morrone, & Ross, 1994).

Alternatively, Vidyasagar (2004) proposed that reading can be viewed as a serial search process. He draws from recent findings in monkeys and humans, pointing to an interaction of the dorsal and ventral stream of visual cortical information processing. In this model, the dorsal stream is dominated by magnocellular input controlling information flow into the ventral stream, which predominantly processes parvocellular input. In dyslexia, a deficit of the magnocellular/dorsal stream or a dysfunction at the level of interaction between the two pathways may affect the spatiotemporal gating functions, which are necessary for reading. Such models will make significant progress when additional findings on neurocognitive mechanisms of visual processing emerge.

Several psychophysical and electrophysiological studies failed to confirm that reduced contrast sensitivity is associated with dyslexia (Gross-Glenn et al., 1995; Hayduk, Bruck, & Cavanagh, 1996; Johannes, Kussmaul, Münte, & Mangun, 1996; Victor, Conte, Burton, & Nass, 1993; Walther-Müller, 1995). Two factors are discussed in this context: (1) Only a subgroup of the dyslexic population exhibits abnormal visual magnocellular function, and (2) spatiotemporal contrast sensitivity tasks may not be sensitive enough for stimulating the magnocellular retinocortical stream. Experiments in monkey visual cortex indicate that motion stimuli are most selective for the magnocellular system (Newsome & Paré, 1988). Indeed, individuals with dyslexia were less sensitive than controls to moving stimuli both in psychophysical (Cornelissen, Richardson, Mason, Fowler, & Stein, 1995; Everatt, Bradshaw, & Hibbard, 1999; Slaghuis & Ryan, 1999; Talcott, Hansen, Assoku, & Stein, 2000; Witton et al., 1998) and brain-imaging (Demb, Boynton, & Heeger, 1997, 1998; Eden et al., 1996) paradigms. Furthermore, performance in pseudoword reading, which is a measure of phonological skills, was found to be correlated with the sensitivity of detecting visual coherent motion in both dyslexic and normally literate adults (Witton et al., 1998). In contrast, Cornelissen, Hansen, Hutton, Evangelinou, and Stein (1998) reported that children's letter errors were best explained by independent contributions from motion detection and phonological awareness. Similar evidence comes from a study of Talcott, Witton, et al. (2000) involving an unselected sample of 10-year-old children. After controlling for effects of intelligence and reading, measures of auditory and visual sensitivity were found to explain independent variance in phonological awareness (manipulating phonemes in spoken words) and orthographic ability (discriminating written real words from pseudohomophones; e.g., *rain* versus *rane*), respectively. Thus, auditory and visual magnocellular function may separately affect the ability to extract phonological and orthographic information during reading.

Unlike grating contrast-sensitivity measurements, which were dominated by the retinothalamic pathway, motion detection critically involves more central functions of the magnocellular system (Stein, Talcott, & Walsh, 2000). Central functions are assumed to be closer to cognitive skills required for reading. Alternative mechanisms have been put forward, by which a magnocellular/transient-system deficit could cause visual confusion during reading at higher levels of processing (Stein & Walsh, 1997). For instance, attentional deficits or destabilized binocular fixation may represent indices of such putative central dysfunction (Stein & Fowler, 1981, 1993; Stein, Richardson, & Fowler, 2000).

A recent unifying hypothesis maintains that the magnocellular dysfunction is not restricted to the visual pathways, but is generalized to all sensory modalities (auditory, visual, and tactile) as well as motor systems controlling fine-grained movements. The general deficit may lead to a variety of sensorimotor symptoms and, consequently, phonological impairments, depending on the most affected system (Stein, 2001). It is posited to evolve early in development of genetically predisposed individuals. The premise is that magnocells constitute a unique population arising from a separate developmental lineage with common surface antigens, heavy myelination, and rapid membrane dynamics, all of which contribute to their exquisite temporal resolution. However, these common characteristics may also render them, as a class, more vulnerable to immunological attack. Evidence for such pathophysiological mechanisms is suggested from genetic as well as neurobiological research in both dyslexia and SLI (see the following sections).

Neurobiological Approaches

SLI and dyslexia have long been assumed to have a neurodevelopmental origin. During the past decades there has been a growing interest in the neurobiological correlates of both conditions. In what follows, relevant findings from postmortem, neuroimaging, and electrophysiological studies are reviewed. Related animal data conclude the section on neurobiological approaches.

Postmortem Studies

Galaburda and colleagues have conducted a series of postmortem studies of diagnosed cases of dyslexia (Galaburda, Sherman, Rosen, Aboitiz, & Geschwind, 1985; Humphreys, Kaufmann, & Galaburda, 1990; Jenner, Rosen, & Galaburda, 1999), providing evidence of small areas of cortical dysgenesis. This includes small nests of abnormally placed neurons called ectopias and focally distorted cortical lamination or dysplasia. The dysgenesis varied in number and location from brain to brain and tended to involve the language-related perisylvian cortex. The observed dysgenesis might reflect neuronal migration errors that may have occurred during fetal development.

The planum temporale in the left hemisphere has for long been suggested to be an important index of left hemispheric language lateralization. It is a triangular landmark situated on the supratemporal surface just posterior to the first Heschl's gyrus, inside the Sylvian fissure (see Figure 7.2). The left planum coincides with part of Wernicke's speech comprehension area (Galaburda, 1993; Shapleske, Rossell, Woodruff, & David, 1999). Postmortem observations of 200 adult brains (Geschwind & Levitsky, 1968; Wada, Clarke, & Hamm, 1975) revealed a dissymetrically larger left planum temporale in 73.5% of the brains, whereas 10.5% showed a rightward asymmetry and 16% a symmetrically sized organization. Corresponding figures reported on 307 ordinary fetal or neonatal specimens were 55%, 16%, and 29% (Chi, Dooling, & Gilles, 1977; Wada et al., 1975). Galaburda et al. (1985) and Humphreys et al. (1990) found symmetrically sized planum temporale in the dyslexic brains due to an enlarged right hemisphere planum.

Another set of postmortem examinations was performed on thalamic structures, that is, the lateral geniculate nucleus (LGN) of the visual pathway and the medial geniculate nucleus (MGN) of the auditory pathway. The magnocellular layers of the LGN were found to be more disorganized in dyslexic than in normal brains (Galaburda & Livingstone, 1993; Livingstone et al., 1991). Furthermore, dyslexic brains' magnocell bodies were 27% smaller and appeared more variable in size and shape. No differences were seen in the parvocellular lamination or the parvocell size of the LGN. In the same autopsy specimens, Galaburda, Menard, and Rosen (1994) reported smaller MGN neurons on the left side for the dyslexic brains specifically. These also exhibited a relative excess of small neurons and a relative paucity of large neurons on the left side as compared to control brains. The structural deviances found in the LGN of dyslexic brains may reflect slowness in the early segments of magnocellular channels, whereas the MGN differences may be related to auditory rate processing dysfunctions described in language-impaired children (Galaburda, Schrott, Sherman, Rosen, & Denenberg, 1996).

Galaburda's group has presented autopsy data on nine brains of individuals (six males and three females) with a history of dyslexia. Three of the male and one of the female patients were reported to have histories of delayed language acquisition (Galaburda et al., 1985; Humphreys et al., 1990). All dyslexic brains have displayed evidence of symmetric plana temporali (Galaburda, 1988, 1989; Humphreys et al., 1990). Neuronal ectopias and architectonic dysplasias were observed in all male cases and two of the females (Galaburda, 1993). Other cerebrocortical deviances in dyslexic autopsy specimens such as microgyria and cortical scars were less uniform than the pattern of dysgenesis (Galaburda, 1993). Overall, dyslexic female brains showed fewer and differently located microcortical malformations when compared to male brains (Humphreys et al., 1990). Histological differences in thalamic structures are limited to reports on five dyslexic brains versus five (Livingstone et al., 1991) or seven (Galaburda et al., 1994) control brains. Galaburda (1988, 1989, 1993; Galaburda et al., 1996) has hypothesized that dyslexia arises as a consequence of anomalous neural development, possibly resulting from brain injury during the prenatal period.

To complete the picture, two postmortem findings in SLI children should be briefly mentioned here. Landau, Goldstein, and Kleffner (1960) observed bilateral perisylvian cystic lesions with surrounding dysplasia and a severe retrograde degeneration in the MGN of a male brain. In a female autopsy specimen, Cohen, Campbell, and Yaghmai (1989) found a dysplastic microgyrus in the left insular cortex and decreased asymmetry of the plana temporali.

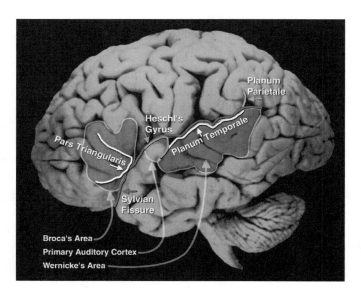

Figure 7.2 Approximate location of perisylvian areas of the left hemisphere. Note that anatomical structure varies among individual brains. Adapted from *MRI Measurements of Broca's Area Predict Naming Speed,* by C. M. Leonard, et al., 2003, Proceedings of the Bangor Dyslexia Conference, available from http://www.dyslexia.bangor.ac.uk/conferences.html. Brain image from the Brain Biodiversity Bank of the National Museum of Health and Medicine, The Michigan State University, and the University of Wisconsin supported by the U.S. National Science Foundation, http://www.brainmuseum.org, http://www.brains.rad.msu.edu. Reprinted with permission.

Despite the robustness of most of the findings provided by Galaburda and collaborators, there are methodological issues complicating the interpretation of the results. For instance, many subjects with dyslexia had a history of comorbid disorders or prior head injuries (Galaburda et al., 1985; Humphreys et al., 1990), which would have prevented their participation in neuroimaging studies. Another concern may be seen in storage duration of postmortem brains. It is conceivable that the brains of dyslexic subjects have been stored for a longer period of time than those of the control subjects, putting them at higher risk of cell shrinkage. Also, the number of autopsy specimens examined so far is small. In postmortem studies, reliable identification of microanatomical deviances in general and the boundaries of the planum temporale in particular have often proved to be difficult (Kirch & Weinberger, 1986; Shapleske et al., 1999).

Structural Neuroimaging Studies

The irregularity with respect to the planum temporale has also been observed in vivo neuroimaging studies of perisylvian language regions. Authors employing magnetic resonance imaging (MRI) reported unusual asymmetry (i.e., Right hemisphere = Left hemisphere or right hemisphere > Left hemisphere) of the planum temporale in individuals with SLI (Gauger, Lombardino, & Leonard, 1997) or dyslexia (Flowers, 1993; Hynd, Semrud-Clikeman, Lorys, Novey, & Eliopulos, 1990; Larsen, Høien, Lundberg, & Ødegaard, 1990). Larsen et al. found that 13 out of 19 dyslexic adolescents displayed symmetric plana as compared to only 5 out of 17 normal readers. All dyslexics exhibiting phonological problems showed absence of typical leftward asymmetry. This led the authors to propose that symmetrical plana temporali might be a possible neurobiological substrate for phonological processing impairment in dyslexia.

Measurements of the greater perisylvian region in the vicinity of the planum temporale have also yielded deviations in both SLI and dyslexia (see Figure 7.2). Plante, Swisher, Vance, and Rapcsak (1991) evaluated MRI scans of the broader perisylvian-language area in 16 boys with and without SLI. Seventy-five percent of the SLI children did not show the usual leftward asymmetry, and 25% of the controls showed atypical perisylvian configuration. Deviant asymmetry patterns were also observed more frequently in first-degree relatives of children with SLI, supporting the notion of a biological predisposition (Plante, 1991).

In SLI, Gauger et al. (1997) demonstrated greater rightward asymmetry of planum+, which includes both planum

temporale and planum parietale (i.e., the posterior, vertical part of the planum). Heiervang et al. (2000) found no changes in the lateralization of the planum+ in boys with dyslexia. Analyzing the planum parietale, they found that dyslexics were less likely to show the expected rightward asymmetry than controls.

Regarding anterior portions of the perisylvian region, SLI children showed a tendency toward atypical right-greater-than-left asymmetry of the pars triangularis, which coincides with parts of Broca's speech production area (Gauger et al., 1997). De Fosse et al. (2004) replicated observations of reversed asymmetry in anterior language cortex in boys with SLI. In a similar vein, adult male dyslexics demonstrated stronger right-hemisphere preponderance for Broca's region (Robichon, Levrier, Farnarier, & Habib, 2000).

The issue of perisylvian asymmetries is not conclusive, however. There have been other contradictory observations reported in both SLI and dyslexia. Some investigators have challenged the view of altered planum temporale asymmetry (Best & Demb, 1999; Heiervang et al., 2000; C. M. Leonard et al., 1993; Preis, Jäncke, Schittler, Huang, & Steinmetz, 1998; Robichon et al., 2000; Rumsey, Donohue, et al., 1997; Schultz et al., 1994). For instance, C. M. Leonard et al. found an exaggerated leftward asymmetry in the planum temporale in a group of compensated dyslexics compared to unaffected relatives and controls. Best and Demb observed similar asymmetries in planum temporale lateralization; however, this lateralization was reduced when the sulcul tissue was excluded from analysis. Criticism has also arisen with respect to planum parietale asymmetries (Gauger et al., 1997; C. M. Leonard et al., 1993; Preis et al., 1998; Rumsey, Donohue, et al., 1997). Eckert et al. (2003) have suggested a different anatomical basis in pars triangularis and the cerebellum. They found that measures of the right cerebellar anterior lobe and the left and right pars triangularis correctly classified a majority of the subjects (72% dyslexics and 88% controls). Several factors may contribute to these inconsistencies. For instance, variations in measurement techniques (such as defining the anatomical boundaries) as well as methodological and design flaws (such as small sample sizes, differences in diagnostic standards, and comorbidity) have been proposed (Heim & Keil, 2004).

As a promising new variable, parameters of white matter morphometry have been studied. Examining the microstructure of temporoparietal areas using diffusion tensor imaging, Klingberg et al. (2000) observed reduced integrity of white matter tied to the left hemisphere as a function of reading test performance. In a study by Herbert et al. (2004), radiate white matter volume of SLI children was enlarged compared to controls. These findings have been interpreted as evidence for a general deficit in cerebral connectivity as an etiological factor contributing to developmental language disorders.

One suggestion proposed to explain the observed reduction in cerebral asymmetry in LLI is that it might be the result of anomalous interhemispheric pathways coursing through the corpus callosum to the perisylvian-language regions (Filipek, 1995). Based on animal models, Galaburda's group (Galaburda, Rosen, & Sherman, 1990; Rosen, Sherman, & Galaburda, 1989) has hypothesized that more symmetric brains have a stronger interhemispheric connectivity, which may be reflected by a larger size of the corpus callosum and vice versa. To date, there are only a few studies using MRI that compare the size of the corpus callosum in individuals with dyslexia and nondyslexic controls (Duara et al., 1991; Hynd et al., 1995; Larsen, Høien, & Ødegaard, 1992; Robichon & Habib, 1998; Rumsey et al., 1996; von Plessen et al., 2002). Results of these are not convergent. Some found an increase in the size of the corpus callosum in dyslexic individuals, especially in the posterior splenium (Duara et al., 1991; Rumsey et al., 1996) and its rostrally adjacent segment, the isthmus (Robichon & Habib, 1998; Rumsey et al., 1996), but others did not report this difference (Hynd et al., 1995; Larsen et al., 1992; von Plessen et al., 2002).

Mixed results characterize the literature on SLI as well. Gauger et al. (1997) measured normal total callosum size in children with SLI, although they tended to be less likely to show typical asymmetry patterns in perisylvian-language regions. Njiokiktjien, deSonneville, and Vaal (1994) found the corpus callosum to be larger in an LLI group exhibiting both familial SLI and dyslexia compared with nonfamilial cases. No differences for absolute corpus callosum size and its subareas were observed by Preis, Steinmetz, Knorr, and Jäncke (2000).

It is apparent that no consistent structural correlates have been associated with SLI or dyslexia using MRI techniques. Several factors possibly accounting for the inconsistent findings have been outlined earlier. Because the relationship of neurostructural deviances and behavior remains elusive, more insights can be expected from functional brain-imaging methods.

Functional Neuroimaging Studies

Regarding SLI, functional neuroimaging studies mainly presented single photon emission computer tomography (SPECT) data (Chiron et al., 1999; Denays et al., 1989; Tzourio, Heim, Zilbovicius, Gerard, & Mazoyer, 1994).

Their findings favor the hypothesis of deviant language lateralization in children with SLI. For instance, Denays et al. observed hypoperfusion in the inferior frontal convolution of the left hemisphere, encompassing Broca's area, in children with expressive impairments. In children having both production and comprehension deficits, hypoperfusion was evident in the left temporoparietal region as well as in the upper and middle areas of the right frontal cortex. Although Chiron et al. found similar hypoactivity in Broca's area of the expressive type, functional brain-imaging studies in SLI are sparse and need further corroboration.

The neuroimaging literature on dyslexia offers a number of functional investigations, using positron emission tomography (PET) or functional magnetic resonance imaging (fMRI). These techniques provide higher spatial resolution than SPECT. Most of the studies were conducted in adult individuals and primarily targeted mechanisms hypothesized to be compromised in dyslexia: phonological processing, auditory rate processing, and visual motion perception (magnocellular dysfunction).

Brain Activation during Phonological Tasks.   Rumsey et al. (1992) were one of the first teams to perform PET scans on dyslexic adults. Male subjects participated in two tasks: a phonological awareness task, in which they were asked to press a button when two spoken words rhymed with each other, and a nonverbal task, in which they were required to push a button whenever a simple target tone in a sequence of others was detected. In controls, activation of left temporoparietal regions (angular/supramarginal gyrus) was specifically related to rhyme judgments. Dyslexics showed reduced blood flow in the left temporoparietal cortex during rhyming, but did not differ from controls in this area during rest or tone detection. The pattern of results was assumed to indicate a left temporoparietal dysfunction associated with phonological task demands in dyslexia.

S. E. Shaywitz et al. (1998) investigated dyslexic adults with fMRI using a set of hierarchically organized visual tasks intended to progressively increase demands on phonological analysis. The tasks required same-different judgments concerning line orientation (e.g., [\\V]-[\\V]), letter case (e.g., [bbBb]-[bbBb]), single-letter rhyme (e.g., [T]-[V]), pseudoword rhyme (e.g., [leat]-[jete]), and semantic category (e.g., [corn]-[rice]). On tasks making explicit demands on phonological processing (e.g., pseudoword rhyming), dyslexic adults in contrast to unimpaired readers showed a relative underengagement of left posterior regions (Wernicke's area, the angular gyrus, and striate cortex) coupled with a disproportionately elevated response in a left anterior region (inferior frontal gyrus). This has been suggested to be a reflection of functional disruption in the posterior cortical systems engaged in phonological decoding and a compensatory reliance on Broca's area.

Similar brain imaging results using visual presentation of various phonological tasks have been reported by other researchers (Brunswick, McCrory, Price, Frith, & Frith, 1999; Paulesu et al., 1996; Rumsey, Nace, et al., 1997). These studies indicate that adults with dyslexia show typical or enhanced activity in left hemisphere frontal regions, but reduced or absent activity in left posterior areas. In contrast, McCrory, Frith, Brunswick, and Price (2000) observed right hemisphere differences during auditory verbal repetition. Dyslexic men demonstrated less hemodynamic activation than normal readers in the right superior temporal and right postcentral gyri. The mixed results seem to imply that the neural manifestation of phonological disruption in dyslexia is perhaps task specific. In fact, a current PET study by McCrory, Mechelli, Frith, and Price (2005) showed diminished metabolism in a left occipitotemporal area during word reading and picture naming.

Based on findings in adults, it is not possible to determine whether the digressions from typical cerebral response patterns in dyslexia reflect a fundamental deficit of phonological processing or are a compensation for poor reading in adulthood. There is hence growing interest in examining children and adolescents using fMRI. Temple et al. (2001) recorded data for 11-year-old dyslexic and normal-reading children during tasks of rhyming and matching visually presented letter pairs (e.g., *Do T and D rhyme?* and *Are P and P the same?* respectively). During (phonological) letter rhyming, activity in left frontal-lobe regions was evident in both groups, whereas activity in the left temporoparietal cortex was observed only in controls. During (orthographic) letter matching, normal readers demonstrated activity throughout the extrastriate visual cortex, whereas dyslexic readers showed reduced extrastriate responses. Thus, altered temporoparietal activation probed by rhyme letters in dyslexic children parallels prior findings in dyslexic adults, indicating a core phonological deficit. Moreover, childhood dyslexia may be characterized by impaired extrastriate activity thought to be important for orthographic processing.

In a study by Georgiewa et al. (1999), 14-year-old dyslexics showed reduced activation in Broca's area and in the left inferior temporal lobe during tasks that invoke substantial grapheme-phoneme conversions and phonological awareness. Neither the dyslexic nor the control group displayed temporoparietal activity, however. This finding is in contrast to what has been observed in younger children

(Temple et al., 2001) as well as in adult samples (see earlier remarks). The differences could be task related (covert behavioral response in the Georgiewa study versus overt response in the other studies), which has also been suggested by a more recent fMRI experiment of Georgiewa et al. (2002).

Studying a large sample of 144 individuals (7 to 18 years), B. A. Shaywitz et al. (2002) reported that dyslexic readers exhibited lesser activation than unimpaired readers in posterior brain regions (including parietotemporal sites and sites in the occipitotemporal area) and in the inferior frontal gyri during tasks relying on phonology. The reduced activity in anterior regions contrasted their earlier findings in adults (S. E. Shaywitz et al., 1998). However, a positive correlation between chronological age and bilateral activation in the inferior frontal gyri of dyslexic individuals led these researchers to suggest that frontal sites become increasingly incorporated with age in compensating for the posterior regions. Even though the notion of compensation is promising (S. E. Shaywitz et al., 2003), the influence of chronological age as an important factor needs to be examined in greater detail.

Brain Activation in Auditory Rate Processing. Although many imaging studies have explored the phonological hypothesis, only a few studies investigating the neural correlates of auditory rate processing in dyslexia have been carried out until recently. Using fMRI, Temple et al. (2000) employed nonspeech analogues of consonant-vowel-consonant stimuli with either brief (rapid) or temporally extended (slow) acoustic transitions differing in pitch in an active paradigm. Adult participants had to identify the higher pitched sound. Unimpaired readers displayed increased activity in the left prefrontal cortex in response to rapid relative to slow transitions, but dyslexic readers showed no differential activity. Further, magnitude of the differential response was inversely correlated with performance in rapid auditory processing, as measured by threshold needed for sequencing three 20-ms tones presented at different rates. Following these results, Temple and collaborators point to the possible role of left prefrontal regions as mediating rapid auditory processing.

Comparable evidence was obtained by Ruff, Cardebat, Marie, and Démonet (2002) using naturally spoken speech stimuli. Functional MRI scans of adult dyslexics and controls were compared during passive discrimination of syllable pairs selected from a /ma/-/na/ continuum. Speech rate was either normal or slowed down. Only in controls was discrimination of normally paced syllables associated with activation in a frontal-parietal network (Broca's area and left supramarginal gyrus). The frontal component was less responsive to slowed speech in controls but predominantly activated in dyslexics. No modulation by speech rate was found in the parietal component, which has been considered pivotal for phoneme representations (Démonet, Fiez, Paulesu, Petersen, & Zatorre, 1996). The authors suggested that enhanced activation of Broca's area might reflect a neural correlate of improved performance on temporally extended syllables reported in children with SLI. Further, the left supramarginal gyrus was assumed to be compromised by a more severe deficit than speech rate dysfunction.

In a sample of healthy adults, Zaehle, Wüstenberg, Meyer, and Jäncke (2004) demonstrated shared neural networks (viz., posterior perisylvian regions) for both verbal and nonverbal tasks. Such work needs to be conducted in both children and adults with LLI.

Brain Activation during Visual Motion Perception. Several fMRI investigations provided evidence for a selective deficit in the magnocellular system in adults with dyslexia (e.g., Demb et al., 1997, 1998; Eden et al., 1996). Eden et al. measured cerebral activation while participants passively viewed either a coherently moving dot stimulus (magnocellular stimulus) or a stationary pattern (parvocellular stimulus). Moving stimuli were expected to elicit strong responses in area V5 (MT) that is located in an extrastriate region at the junction of the occipital and temporal lobes (Zeki, 1993). In unimpaired readers, the magnocellular stimulus activated V5/MT bilaterally, but it failed to activate this area in dyslexic readers. Parvocellular stimulus did not elicit any differences between the two groups.

Demb et al. (1997, 1998) examined brain signals in response to low-luminance moving gratings (magnocellular stimuli) as opposed to control stimuli "designed to stimulate multiple pathways" (1997, p. 13363). Dyslexic individuals showed reduced activity relative to controls both in primary visual cortex (V1) and several extrastriate regions (inter alia MT+) in response to moving gratings of various contrasts. Participants exhibiting stronger V1 and MT+ activity demonstrated better speed discrimination performance and tended to be faster readers.

Discrepancies in results might be attributable to differences in sample selection, stimuli, or procedures used for localizing visual brain areas. Whereas the phonological hypothesis of dyslexia has received valuable support from recent PET and fMRI research, hemodynamic studies on both visual magnocellular and auditory rate processing are limited, specifically in child populations.

Electrophysiological Studies

Functional MRI and PET provide excellent spatial resolution in examining brain processes believed to be compromised in LLI, and electroencephalography (EEG) and magnetoencephalography (MEG) allow us to investigate temporal processes in greater detail (see Figures 7.3a and 7.3b). Event-related potentials (ERPs)[5] of the EEG are increasingly used in developmental and clinical research as they are noninvasive (like fMRI) and do not require overt responses by an individual (see Cheour, Leppänen, & Kraus, 2000; Leppänen & Lyytinen, 1997; Molfese et al., 2002; Nelson & Monk, 2001; Rockstroh et al., 1999). Their magnetic counterparts, termed *event-related fields* (ERFs), can be analyzed using methods increasing spatial resolution and estimating underlying sources. Therefore, MEG has the added advantage of high spatial resolution as compared to EEG and, in some instances, PET (Elbert, 1998).

Electroencephalography/Event-Related   Potentials. Visual ERPs have been frequently used to examine putative deficits in the magnocellular pathways in dyslexia. This work has demonstrated that dyslexics' ERP components were reduced or delayed for visual stimuli with low spatial and high temporal frequencies (e.g., Kubová et al., 1995; Lehmkuhle et al., 1993; Livingstone et al., 1991). Most recently, tasks involving moving stimuli, which are particularly sensitive to magnocellular deficits, have yielded supportive evidence in children (Scheuerpflug et al., 2004; Schulte-Körne, Bartling, Deimel, & Remschmidt, 2004).

A promising parameter suitable to investigate auditory processing in both normal samples and clinical conditions happens to be mismatch negativity (MMN). The mismatch response is elicited by a so-called passive oddball paradigm, in which infrequent acoustic (deviant) stimuli are interspersed in a series of frequently presented (standard) stimuli. The MMN likely reflects temporofrontal neural activity and usually peaks between 100 and 250 ms after stimulus onset. It is assumed to index a preattentive neuronal change-detection mechanism (Näätänen, 2001).

Mismatch studies using stop consonant-vowel syllables showed attenuated response in dyslexic and learning-impaired individuals compared to controls (Bradlow et al., 1999; Kraus et al., 1996; Schulte-Körne, Deimel, Bartling, & Remschmidt, 1998, 2001). Kujala et al. (2000) addressed

---

[5] Event-related potentials are characterized by precise time locking to a sensory stimulus (e.g., luminance change, tone, or mechanical tap) or internal event (e.g., preparation for a target stimulus). They can be detected by averaging single-trial responses.

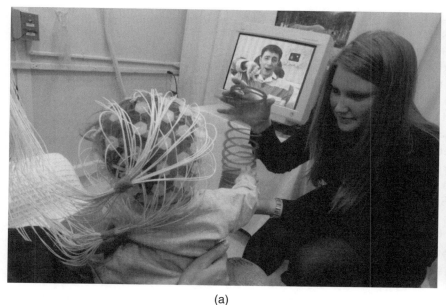
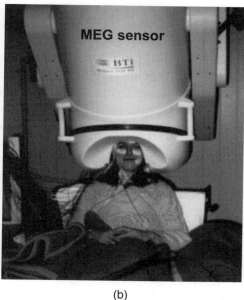

(a)   (b)

Figure 7.3   (a) An EEG/ERP testing session showing a 9-month-old child seated on her mother's lap and being entertained by an experimenter during a passive auditory oddball paradigm. ERPs are recorded from 62 scalp sites (64 in adults) using the Geodesic Sensor Net (Electrical Geodesics, Inc., Eugene, Oregon). (b) An adult subject in a MEG laboratory. Pictured is a whole-head neuromagnetometer (MAGNES 2500, 4D Neuroimaging, San Diego, CA) inside a magnetically shielded chamber. The device houses 148 detection coils (magnetometers), forming a helmet-like array. It is sensitive to changes in magnetocortical activity, having temporal resolution in the range of milliseconds.

the issue of whether this mitigated mismatch response is due to a phonological processing deficit or a more general auditory impairment. They used two sets of stimuli, which were presented to adult dyslexics and normal readers: The test stimuli consisted of four 500-Hz tones with silent intertone intervals of either 200, 150, and 50 ms (standard pattern) or 200, 50, and 150 ms (deviant pattern); the control stimuli comprised 500-Hz tone pairs separated by either 150 ms (standard pair) or 50 ms (deviant pair). No group differences were found in the MMN amplitude to the temporal change in the control condition. In the test condition, for normal readers biphasic MMNs were elicited, but dyslexic readers showed only the second MMN. The biphasic MMN reflected a response to the two deviations in the test stimuli: a quick tone following the second sound, and a delayed tone following the third sound. The auditory system of the dyslexics seems to discriminate only the second deviation. Behavioral discrimination performance paralleled the mismatch findings. Kujala and collaborators inferred that dyslexic individuals have problems in processing auditory temporal information only when presented in a complex context, as in the case of the linguistic domain (i.e., phonemes in words), not otherwise. This study is one of the most informative concerning the two competing hypotheses. However, we need further work to clarify the relation between auditory rate processing and phonological skills, as other studies using simple nonverbal stimuli often showed normal MMN to duration changes in both SLI and dyslexia (Baldeweg, Richardson, Watkins, Foale, & Gruzelier, 1999; Korpilahti & Lang, 1994).

Magnetoencephalography/Event-Related Fields. Most MEG studies in dyslexia have been concerned with magnetic source imaging[6] during performance of various reading tasks (Helenius, Salmelin, Service, & Connolly, 1999; Helenius, Tarkiainen, Cornelissen, Hansen, & Salmelin, 1999; Salmelin, Service, Kiesilä, Uutela, & Salonen, 1996; Simos, Breier, Fletcher, Bergman, & Papanicolaou, 2000; Simos, Breier, Fletcher, Foorman, et al., 2000). Overall, these studies support the findings of hemodynamic deviances in language-related brain sites in dyslexia (see section on Functional Neuroimaging Studies). For instance, Salmelin et al. found that print processing was associated with enhanced source activity in the inferior temporo-occipital border of the left hemisphere at about 180 ms following

---

[6] Neuronal source activity within a defined time window of ERFs is estimated and projected onto structural brain images.

stimulus onset in controls but not in dyslexic adults. Also, between 200 and 400 ms, controls showed activation in the left temporal region and dyslexic participants showed activation of the left inferior frontal cortex (approximately in Broca's area). This pattern may reflect posterior cortical anomaly and compensatory reliance on frontal lobe systems, which has been related to the phonological deficit discussed earlier. Differences in source activity in posterior brain sites have been detected in children with dyslexia during engagement in printed pseudoword rhyme-matching and word-recognition tasks (Simos, Breier, Fletcher, Bergman, et al., 2000; Simos, Breier, Fletcher, Foorman, et al., 2000). Dyslexics displayed reduced activity in the left temporoparietal cortex following stimulus onset, coupled with a high density of source clusters in homologous right hemisphere regions as compared to normal developers.

Some recent MEG experiments in the auditory domain have examined early sensory components elicited by tones or speech sounds (e.g., Helenius, Salmelin, Richardson, Leinonen, & Lyytinen, 2002; Helenius, Salmelin, Service, et al., 2002; Nagarajan et al., 1999). In the context of the auditory rate processing hypothesis, Nagarajan et al. compared adult poor readers and controls on tone-sequence perception. Sequences of two brief sinusoidal tones differing in pitch were presented at each of three different ISIs, and participants were asked to press the appropriate buttons to indicate the correct order. Early ERF amplitudes (around 100 ms) for the second stimulus of a sequence were smaller in poor readers than in controls for ISIs of 100 or 200 ms, but not for the long ISI of 500 ms. This neuronal deviance was corroborated by a similar performance profile on tasks measuring perceptual interference between rapidly successive stimuli.

In the very same latency range, Heim, Eulitz, and Elbert (2003a, 2003b) reported asymmetrical localization of ERFs elicited by stop consonant-vowel syllables in controls. This asymmetry reflected a more anterior localization in the right hemisphere than in the left and was not present in dyslexic children or in dyslexic adults. Whereas there was no group difference in the left, dyslexics' sources in the right hemisphere were located posterior to those of controls. Right hemisphere anomaly also characterizes later time segments (150 to 300 ms) of the cortical response to syllables in language-impaired children (Heim, Eulitz, Keil, Rockstroh, & Elbert, 2003). These findings may reflect atypical organization of the primary auditory cortex and adjacent areas, in particular the planum temporale. As a consequence, other (right posterior) perisylvian

regions may become involved in auditory processing. Substituted regions, however, may not perform the task as efficiently as a normally developed planum temporale would.

Given the inconsistencies with functional neuroimaging studies, it is legitimate to ask whether SLI and dyslexia are necessarily limited to one or the other hemisphere. Various deficits making up the complex disorders might be associated with different neural bases. A complete picture, therefore, should include both high temporal and spatial resolution data as provided by a combined approach of electrocortical parameters and imaging techniques and, most important, theory-driven behavioral tasks (Heim & Keil, 2004).

Animal Studies

Given the neuroanatomic variance seen in the postmortem and neuroimaging studies described, it is posited that brain abnormalities hypothesized to be associated with LLI may occur quite early in life. As SLI may involve basic acoustic abilities that support language but are not speech specific, it is possible to examine such processes in an animal model (Clark, Rosen, Tallal, & Fitch, 2000; Fitch, Tallal, Brown, Galaburda, & Rosen, 1994). Studies of animals with induced cortical neuromigrational or genetic anomalies designed to mimic those found in LLI provide a converging framework to examine the existence of a common neurobiological mechanism, which acts developmentally to disrupt sensory processing systems (Fitch & Tallal, 2003). Research using animal models has improved our understanding of the ontogeny of these anomalies. Results obtained to date suggest that focal cellular anomalies such as ectopias and microgyria arise as a consequence of interference with critical periods of neuromigration, possibly resulting from focal ischemic damage (e.g., Dvořák, Feit, & Jurankova, 1978; Humphreys, Rosen, Press, Sherman, & Galaburda, 1991; Rosen, Sherman, Richman, Stone, & Galaburda, 1992; see Fitch & Tallal, 2003), originating in the prenatal period.

Studies using an animal model of induced neocortical microgyric lesions revealed that rats tested in a behavioral paradigm, similar to the infant tasks used by Benasich and colleagues (see section on Prospective Studies in Infants and Kindergartners), showed significant deficits in rapid auditory processing (Fitch et al., 1994). Such findings suggest that a common mechanism underlies specialization for rate processing in both humans and animals (Fitch & Tallal, 2003). Furthermore, these animals show anomalies in the thalamic medial geniculate nucleus or MGN (Herman, Galaburda, Fitch, Carter, & Rosen, 1997). Event-related responses recorded from either surface electrodes or implanted electrodes (placed in the primary auditory cortex and in MGN) in mice with ectopias also document altered rapid auditory processing (Frenkel, Sherman, Bashan, Galaburda, & LoTurco, 2000). A strong and specific relation was shown between alterations in auditory ERPs and number of ectopias.

Several studies shed further light on the consequences of microgyric lesions in this animal model in the developing rat (Friedman, Peiffer, Clark, Benasich, & Fitch, 2004; Peiffer, Friedman, Rosen, & Fitch, 2004; Peiffer, Rosen, & Fitch, 2002). Specifically, it was demonstrated that developmental shifts in gap detection abilities are observable across early development, and that improvements in auditory acuity due to repeated testing can be observed even at the youngest ages (Friedman et al., 2004). In another study, juvenile rats with bilateral microgyria, but not their adult counterparts, exhibited impaired detection of short-duration silent gaps in white noise when compared to age-matched sham littermates (Peiffer et al., 2004). In adult rats, more temporally demanding acoustic discrimination tasks were required to elicit the deleterious effects of microgyria. These findings converge on data from humans with impairments in rapid auditory processing. In infancy and early childhood, an initial difficulty in gap detection is seen. Adults with a history of SLI or dyslexia may not show this deficit (McAnally & Stein, 1996; Protopapas, Ahissar, & Merzenich, 1997), nor is it consistent in older children (Bishop, Carlyon, Deeks, & Bishop, 1999). However, more demanding acoustic tasks (rapid, sequential, and brief stimuli) continue to elicit higher thresholds in dyslexic adults (e.g., Hari & Kiesilä, 1996).

Another current study indicates that the consequences of bilateral microgyria lesions (e.g., reorganization, alterations in thalamic morphology, and rapid auditory processing deficits) are surprisingly robust and do not appear to be ameliorated by passive acoustic stimulation across development (Peiffer et al., 2002).

Thus, the converging research cited here suggests that morphological abnormalities observed in the cortex and thalamic nuclei in both human and animal subjects may well play a part in inefficient rapid auditory processing (Herman et al., 1997; Jernigan, Hesselink, Sowell, & Tallal, 1991; Tallal, Jernigan, & Trauner, 1994). Further, there are clear differences elicited in the rat and mouse models as a function of age and perhaps environment, as has been proposed in humans (see Bishop & Snowling, 2004). Results of this kind support the utility of animal models in elucidating the potential mechanisms underlying finely

tuned auditory resolution, including the study of developmental changes in the auditory system (Fitch et al., 1994; see Fitch, Read, & Benasich, 2001).

Genetic Approaches

Over the past decades, evidence was collected in support of the hypothesis that SLI and dyslexia, or at least some subtypes of these conditions, may be hereditary. Initial reports of family aggregation derived from individual family case histories, and case-control family studies followed. Other research focused on examining the concordance of oral and written language impairments in twins as a means of looking at the rate of heritability. Findings of both family aggregation and twin studies have stimulated the quest for genes involved in the transmission of LLI.

Family Aggregation Studies

Both SLI and dyslexia cluster in families and in many cases co-occur in the same individuals (see section on Prevalence Estimates). Case studies capitalizing on family histories of language-impaired children showed that 24% to 63% of the children had at least one affected relative (Byrne, Willerman, & Ashmore, 1974; Gopnik & Crago, 1991; Hurst, Baraitser, Auger, Graham, & Norell, 1990; Ingram, 1959; Luchsinger, 1970; Robinson, 1987). The wide range in frequency rates might be due to differences in diagnostic standards and subject characteristics. Plante, Shenkman, and Clark (1996) compared direct testing versus questionnaire data in groups of parents of children with SLI and adult controls. Questionnaire results indicated that 38% of the parents having an affected child exhibited prior impairments in oral and/or written language skills. None of the controls reported such history. Corresponding SLI figures based on test battery scores were 63% and 17%. Gopnik and Crago tested 20 (out of 36) members of a three-generation family and found only seven to fall in the normal range of language development. Some of the affected members, however, would not be considered SLI by conventional diagnostic standards (see section on Definition: Specific Language Impairment). The phenotype or behavioral profile was quite broad, including virtually every aspect of language. Also, mental impairments, a history of psychiatric problems, or oral-motor dysfunctions have been documented (Gopnik, 1994; Vargha-Khadem, Watkins, Alcock, Fletcher, & Passingham, 1995).

Several investigations determined the prevalence of speech and language problems in the family members of individuals with SLI as compared to data from relatives of controls with no speech or language disorder history. In many of these case-control studies, the affected individual (proband) was clinically identified, and information about the family was collected by questionnaires (Bishop & Edmundson, 1986; Neils & Aram, 1986; Rice et al., 1998; Tomblin, 1989). Overall, a robust effect of familiality was suggested. Rates of impairments in families of SLI probands ranged from approximately 20% to 25% versus 3% to 7% in control families. Higher percentages were seen when researchers used a broader phenotype that encompassed language and learning problems (Tallal et al., 1989a; van der Lely & Stollwerck, 1996). Here, the incidence of SLI was on the order of 40% to 80% in proband families and 20% to 30% in control families.

More recently, Tallal et al. (2001) used direct testing in a case-control family design and found the rate of SLI for the first-degree relatives of probands (30%) to be significantly higher than for control families (7%). Affectance rates for fathers and mothers were approximately equal, whereas brothers showed about 3 times higher incidence than sisters did. In proband families, SLI occurred in 13% of offspring (excluding the proband) with neither parent affected, 40% of offspring with one parent affected, and 71% of offspring with both parents having SLI.

Evidence of familial aggregation in dyslexia has been reported in very early case studies. For instance, Stephenson (1907) described a three-generation family history of dyslexia affecting six individuals. In a classic study based on interview data from more than 100 families, Hallgren (1950) estimated the risk for first-degree relatives to be 41%. Similar estimates have been obtained by researchers using direct testing, with familial recurrence rates for siblings and parents ranging from 39% to 43% and 27% to 49%, respectively (Finucci, Guthrie, Childs, Abbey, & Childs, 1976; Gilger et al., 1991; Vogler, DeFries, & Decker, 1985). The Colorado Longitudinal Family Reading Study tested reading and cognitive abilities in 125 reading-disabled proband families and 125 matched controls. Manifold deficits were found in primary relatives of probands, providing indirect evidence for the familial nature of the disorder (DeFries, Singer, Foch, & Lewitter, 1978). Although the phenotype of dyslexia varied considerably across these investigations, recurrence rates demonstrate striking similarity. Further, siblings appear to be at greater risk for reading and spelling impairments when at least one parent is diagnosed (Gilger, Hanebuth, Smith, & Pennington, 1996; Wolff & Melngailis, 1994).

Taken together, there is a high probability for family members to have some type of SLI or dyslexia when one other member is affected. Communalities of the two disorders in terms of psychological and neurobiological variables raise the question of etiological interrelationships. This issue has been addressed by a very recent case-control family study, using a battery of language, reading, and auditory rate processing tests (Flax et al., 2003). Approximately two-thirds of the SLI probands also met diagnostic criteria for reading disability. The occurrence rates of SLI (25%) and reading disability (23%) in their immediate and extended relatives were significantly elevated compared to rates for controls. Of particular importance, a high co-occurrence (46%) of the two conditions was also manifest in the same sample of relatives. Consistent with epidemiological research, gender differences were observed in proband families for both conditions. Specifically, male family members outbalanced females by a factor of 2.

Family aggregation studies provide information about the extent to which SLI and dyslexia run down generations. Because family members share environmental factors as well as genes, this approach cannot be used to assess the heritability of any given disorder. Twin studies offer one possibility to answer research questions related to the genetic transmission in a natural environment.

Twin Studies

Twin studies take advantage of the fact that monozygotic (MZ) twins are genetically identical, whereas dizygotic (DZ) twins share on average 50% of their genes. Consequently, MZ twins should be concordant for inherited traits roughly twice as often as DZ twins. In this vein, Tomblin and Buckwalter (1994) examined 82 pairs of twins that included at least one child having SLI (proband). Based on direct testing, concordance rate of SLI was 80% for MZ and 38% for DZ twins. Similar rates have been reported by B. A. Lewis and Thomson (1992) in twins suffering from a variety of speech, language, and learning difficulties. Here, concordance rates amounted to 86% and 48%, respectively. In addition, Bishop (1992) demonstrated an interesting interplay between environment and genetic endowment, both differentially contributing to past and present language ability. Work from the same laboratory (Bishop, North, & Donlan, 1995) showed higher concordance for males than females, exemplifying the often reported gender ratio for SLI.

Concordance rate differences have also been demonstrated for dyslexia. Zerbin-Rüdin (1967) reviewed 51 cases, of whom at least one twin within a pair suffered from reading problems. Level of concordance was nearly 100% for MZ and 35% for DZ pairs. Recruiting 62 pairs from a mother-of-twins club, Bakwin (1973) reported rates of 84% and 20% for MZ and DZ twins, respectively. Subsequent research demonstrated a somewhat lower but still significant concordance ratio (68% for MZ twins versus 38% for DZ twins), possibly as a result of avoiding methodological shortcomings pertaining to sample recruitment and diagnostic standards (see DeFries & Alarcón, 1996).

Other behavior genetic studies make use of correlational and multiple regression analyses to assess heritability of language/literacy ability in the normal and deficient range. Such methods are based on the assumption that oral and written language skills represent continuous traits being normally distributed in the population. Heritability in the normal range is evident when correlations between probands' and co-twins' test scores are significantly higher for MZ compared to DZ pairs. When probands are ascertained by extreme low test scores, co-twins' scores on the same test will regress toward the performance mean of an unselected population. To the degree that the disability is heritable, there should be greater regression in DZ co-twin scores. If heritability estimates for LLI twins exceed those for normal samples, this indicates that certain genes contribute to the linguistic variance observed among affected individuals, but not to the variance in the general population (DeFries & Fulker, 1985; LaBuda, DeFries, & Fulker, 1986).

In a current project, Viding et al. (2004) assessed the heritability of SLI in a large community sample ($n = 972$ pairs) of 4-year-old twins. Regression analyses indicated that language disability as indexed by a composite score is being substantially influenced by genes. Group heritability showed an increasing trend from 38% to 76% as a function of severity of impairment. Although more boys than girls were found to be impaired, no differences emerged in terms of genetic and environmental contributions.

Moderate but significant heritability has also been demonstrated for the normal range of language ability at 4 years, which has amounted to 39% (Colledge et al., 2002). More than 50% of the genetic influence on language performance was found to overlap with genetic influence on nonverbal cognitive skills. This overlap may be even more pronounced at later stages of development (see the discussion on interrelations between verbal and nonverbal abilities in the sections on "Definition").

The two studies in preschoolers suggest similar heritability estimates for milder language disability (38%) and language ability in the normal range (39%). When the most severe cases are considered, heritability for language disability exceeds the value for normal language ability by approximately a factor of 2. This raises the possibility that genes may be more important in causing severe language impairment than milder variants of the condition. It is also conceivable that additional genes contribute to the phenotype of language disability, but not to the variance in normal language skills.

A study by Bishop, Bishop, et al. (1999) focused on heritability estimates of phonological and auditory processing skills in children with SLI and normal developers. Correlations between proband and co-twin on auditory scores were equally high for MZ and DZ pairs, suggesting an interpretation in terms of shared environment rather than genes. Nonsignificant results of extreme score analyses were asserted as further evidence for this view. In contrast, substantial heritability was demonstrated for phonological skills in the normal as well as deficient range. Following these and additional findings, Bishop, Carlyon, and collaborators (1999) propose that auditory deficits are neither necessary nor sufficient for causing SLI, but nevertheless can affect severity of impairment in genetically predisposed individuals.

Within the scope of the Colorado Twin Reading Study, DeFries, Fulker, and LaBuda (1987) performed regression analyses on literacy skills in a sample of 64 MZ and 55 DZ pairs (8 to 18 years). Group heritability for a composite score indicated that about 30% of the cognitive profile in dyslexia is attributable to heritable factors. This value increased to nearly 60% when a larger sample of 223 MZ and 169 DZ twins was examined (Wadsworth, Olson, Pennington, & DeFries, 2000). Alarcón and DeFries (1997) extended their analyses to a normal group of Colorado twins and likewise found substantial genetic influence (66%) on literacy scores.[7]

Somewhat different findings emerged from the London Twin Study involving 13-year-old children (J. Stevenson, 1991; J. Stevenson, Graham, Fredman, & McLoughlin, 1987). Deficits in spelling appeared to be significantly heritable, whereas reading performance was best explained by shared environment. Considerable variations in reading instructions among the U.K. children have been put forth as one possibility to explain the disparity (Bishop, 2001).

Several twin studies provide evidence that some components of reading and spelling performance are under strong genetic influence (see Grigorenko, 2001; Schulte-Körne, 2001). The Colorado Study (Olson, Wise, Conners, Rack, & Fulker, 1989) reported heritability (about 46%) for a

---

[7] In a proband group, heritability for the very same measure was 82%.

phonological decoding measure with a strong genetic contribution to reading performance on the order of 90%. Orthographic skills were not heritable, however. Research including a larger sample showed that 56% of orthographic ability in the lower range could be accounted for by genes (Olson, Forsberg, & Wise, 1994). Data on phonological awareness scores add similar evidence. More recently, high heritability scores have been obtained for rapid automatized naming (58% to 65%). Its relationship with reading measures suggested that reading deficits covary genetically with impaired rapid naming (Davis et al., 2001).

Olson and Datta (2002) explored the association of reading skills and visual processing across the full range of reading ability. Generally, children with better word-reading performance tended to display higher visual contrast sensitivity. Proband-co-twin correlations of test scores indicated significant genetic influence on individual differences in reading, but not in contrast sensitivity. The authors claim that the modest shared variance between these measures should be attributed to environmental factors.

Bishop and colleagues (Bishop, 2001; Bishop, Adams, & Norbury, 2004) addressed the issue of a common basis of SLI and dyslexia. Heritability of reading disability was strikingly high in children having difficulty in repeating pseudowords, whereas those with intact pseudoword repetition performance did not show impact of genes. Thus, genetic factors are specifically relevant when literacy problems are severe and/or accompanied by oral language impairment.

In summary, the genetic basis of at least some proportion of LLI has been repeatedly demonstrated. A word of caution is in order, however. First, the mechanism of genetic transmission remains to be elucidated, as there is evidence for both major locus and polygenic inheritance (see L. B. Leonard, 1998; Pennington, 1995; Schulte-Körne, 2001). Second, estimates of genetic variance still face a substantial number of methodological issues. For instance, less stringent criteria in selection of research participants tend to lower heritability estimates. Whereas environmental factors may be of particular importance for milder language and literacy impairments (see earlier discussion), subtype classification may promote more homogeneous results in behavioral genetic studies (e.g., Castles, Datta, Gayán, & Olson, 1999).

Molecular-Genetic Studies

In both SLI and dyslexia, several methods have been pursued to identify genes predisposing to disorder. Linkage analysis (indirect DNA analysis) aims at locating a disease gene with respect to its chromosomal region. There are regions of human DNA, so-called polymorphic markers, that vary substantially across individuals but do not affect the phenotype. The familial transmission of the marker allele is compared with the transmission of the trait phenotype. Their genetic loci are considered to be linked when they are inherited more frequently than expected by chance. This linkage does narrow down the search to genes that are close to the marker on the chromosome (see Pennington, 2001).

For linkage studies, either multiple family members from large pedigrees or a number of nuclear families (or sibling pairs) need to be compiled, based on an affected proband. As far as SLI is concerned, several genetic loci have been identified. The SLI Consortium (2002) found linkage sites on the long arms (q) of chromosomes 16 and 19 when the phenotype trait was defined by impaired phonological memory or poor expressive language, respectively. Bartlett et al. (2002) reported evidence for linkage between a region on chromosome 13q and susceptibility for SLI by use of an LLI phenotype.

The majority of families segregating SLI show complex patterns of inheritance. The KE family, a three-generation pedigree, represents one exception in that approximately half the members encounter severe disturbances in speech and language. All affected individuals, but none of the unaffected, carry a defective gene (FOXP2) located on chromosome 7q. This suggests an autosomal-dominant transmission of a monogenic trait (Fisher, Vargha-Khadem, Watkins, Monaco, & Pembrey, 1998). To date, there is no evidence that language-impaired individuals unrelated to the KE family exhibit such mutation (Meaburn, Dale, Craig, & Plomin, 2002; Newbury et al., 2002). Recently, O'Brien, Zhang, Nishimura, Tomblin, and Murray (2003) documented significant associations of two loci in the vicinity of FOXP2 and a language-impaired phenotype.

Gene linkage investigations in dyslexia posit loci on chromosomes 1 to 3, 6, 15, and 18 (see Fisher & DeFries, 2002; Grigorenko, 2001; Schulte-Körne, 2001). As one of the first teams in the field, Smith, Kimberling, Pennington, and Lubs (1983) observed linkage between the centromeric region of chromosome 15 and reading disability in families with apparent autosomal dominant transmission. Addition of more multiplex families provided evidence for the genetic heterogeneity of the disorder (Smith, Kimberling, & Pennington, 1991): Linkages were spread to a more distal region on 15q as well as on a site of the short arm (p) of chromosome 6. Significant localizations on the long arm of chromosome 15 have also been reported by other researchers (e.g., Grigorenko et al., 1997; Schulte-Körne, Grimm, et al., 1998). Close to these regions, Taipale et al. (2003) uncovered a candidate gene for developmental dyslexia.

One of the most consistent findings provides linkage of dyslexia-related phenotypes to loci on chromosome 6p, especially in the vicinity of the human leukocyte antigen (HLA) region (Cardon et al., 1994; Fisher et al., 1999; Gayán et al., 1999; Grigorenko et al., 1997; Smith et al., 1991). HLA belongs to the major histocompatibility complex, a cluster of genes essential to the immune system. Several autoimmune disorders (such as Type 1 diabetes and rheumatoid arthritis) have been localized to HLA. An association between autoimmune disease and dyslexia was originally proposed by Geschwind and Behan (1982). Some researchers detected unusual serum antibodies in mothers of dyslexic children (Behan, Behan, & Geschwind, 1985; Vincent et al., 2002), but reports of comorbidity in probands with dyslexia and their immediate relatives for autoimmune disorders remain controversial (e.g., Gilger et al., 1998; Hugdahl, Synnevag, & Satz, 1990). Nevertheless, Stein (2001) suggested a possible neural-immune interaction in that the development of surface antigens common to magnocells is probably regulated by major histocompatibility complex molecules. Maternal prenatal mechanisms might modify the offspring's immunological profile (Gilger et al., 1998), contributing to deficient development of magnocells. In line with this notion, Benasich (2002) found that infants with a positive family history of autoimmune disorders performed less well on rapid auditory processing and language tests than controls did. Conversely, families with a positive history for SLI tended to exhibit elevated rates of autoimmune disorders (Choudhury & Benasich, 2003). Thus far, however, SLI has not been linked to chromosome 6.

The current studies suggest a potential genetic component underlying at least a subset of individuals with LLI. There is no evidence for overlap between the gene linkages found in SLI and dyslexia. Consistency of the molecular genetic data is moderated by a variety of variables, including phenotype definition, sample size, and statistical methods used. Traditional linkage mapping is based on univariate analyses performed on several measures (e.g., phonological decoding, rapid automatized naming) constituting the phenotype. Usually, statistical adjustments are made for multiple tests. Marlow et al. (2003) demonstrated that the power to detect significant linkage increased when multivariate analysis was run. Therefore, one cannot infer that SLI and dyslexia are mediated by separate genetic mechanisms. None of the linkage results can be considered definite and detection of additional gene loci associated with oral and written language disturbances will likely emerge.

PROSPECTIVE STUDIES IN INFANTS AND KINDERGARTNERS

Substantial evidence continues to accrue that both SLI and dyslexia tend to occur across generations (see section on Genetic Approaches). Therefore, it is possible to study children who are at genetic risk as a function of family history for LLI even at a very early stage in their development. Prospective approaches using behavioral paradigms and electrocortical parameters may shed light on long-standing questions regarding etiology, developmental course, and pattern of deficits seen in these conditions. Moreover, interactive processes essential to normal and atypical language development may be delineated.

Specific Language Impairment

Given the extraordinary ability of very young infants to discriminate both speech and nonspeech acoustic input, differences in rapid auditory processing (RAP) thresholds should be detectable very early in infancy and could serve as a predictor of later language competence (Benasich & Read, 1999; Benasich & Tallal, 1996).

In infancy, RAP abilities are assessed in several different ways, including operantly conditioned head-turn procedures (Benasich & Tallal, 1996; Richardson, Leppänen, Leiwo, & Lyytinen, 2003; Trehub & Henderson, 1996), auditory-visual habituation and recognition memory tasks (AVH/RM; Benasich & Tallal, 1996), and EEG/ERPs (e.g., Benasich, Thomas, Choudhury, & Leppänen, 2002; Leppänen et al., 2002). Each paradigm capitalizes on systematic variations of the temporal properties inherit in the acoustic signal. In the head-turn procedure, an infant's orienting response to a target auditory signal is visually reinforced until a contingency develops and the child is able to reliably discriminate between target and nontarget sounds (see Figure 7.4). This task requires an infant to focus on the relevant auditory signal, learn the contingency, and sustain attention to the relevant auditory signal throughout the test session. AVH/RM paradigms are based on the well-known propensity of infants to differentially prefer novel as compared to familiar stimuli. Infants are first habituated to a complex auditory-visual stimulus, and auditory discrimination is assessed by the introduction of a novel auditory stimulus while keeping the visual component constant. A recovery of attention to the new auditory stimulus is taken as an indicator of auditory perceptual discrimination and recognition memory.

In a series of studies, Benasich and colleagues (Benasich & Tallal, 1996, 2002; Benasich et al., 2002; Choudhury &

Panel A   Panel B

Figure 7.4 Photographs of a 9-month-old infant attending to the experimenter performing a puppet show across the table from her (Panel A) and then correctly responding to a target sound (Panel B) in the test phase of a go/no go operant conditioning head-turn paradigm. Correct head-turns are contingently reinforced by activation of an electronic toy.

Benasich, 2003; Spitz, Tallal, Flax, & Benasich, 1997) examined two groups of infants: normal controls with no known family history of SLI (FH−) and infants born into families with a positive history of SLI (FH+). Group and individual differences in RAP abilities were examined using converging paradigms. In the initial study, infants were trained in a two-alternative forced choice procedure to discriminate two tone sequences that differed in pitch (100 and 100 Hz, or 100 and 300 Hz) with 75-ms duration tones and 500-ms intertone intervals (Benasich & Tallal, 1996). Once the tone-pair/direction contingency was acquired, the interval between the tones was dropped to 300 ms and then gradually decreased until the infant could no longer discriminate between the two tone sequences (the infant's RAP threshold). Infants first tested at 7.5 months of age were prospectively followed through 36 months (Benasich & Tallal, 2002; Benasich et al., 2002). At the initial visit, significant differences in RAP thresholds were ob-

served in FH+ infants as compared to FH− infants, with about 50% of the FH+ infants showing elevated thresholds (Benasich & Tallal, 1996).

Follow-up of this sample revealed that RAP performance in infancy was the best predictor of expressive and receptive language at 12, 16, and 24 months (Benasich & Tallal, 2002). Infant RAP threshold and being male together predicted 39% to 41% of the variance in 36-month language outcome. Discriminate function analyses permitted accurate classification to language-impaired versus nonimpaired groups at 36 months (using a criterion for impaired of at least 1 standard deviation below the mean of Stanford-Binet language subtests). Interestingly, no predictive relations were seen to nonverbal abilities such as motor or spatial skills.

These findings have been replicated in additional samples (see Benasich & Leevers, 2003). Detailed analysis of the data suggests that linguistic outcomes are related to early RAP thresholds in both normally developing infants and infants at high familial risk for SLI.

Recently, Benasich's team (Benasich et al., 2005) showed that 6-month-old FH+ and FH– infants also differ in patterns of brain activation to virtually the same sounds presented in the behavioral RAP tasks. Moreover, amplitude and latency of a negative ERP component were reported to be inversely associated with expressive and receptive language abilities at 24 months of age. In a similar vein, Friedrich, Weber, and Friederici (2004) reported a delayed mismatch-like response to stop consonant-vowel syllables in German 2-month-old infants born into families with a history of SLI. Follow-up of these children as they begin to enter school is critically important.

The idea that individual variability in infant sensory processing is predictive of later language abilities fits well with findings from several other studies. For example, Trehub and Henderson's (1996) retrospective study revealed that children who performed above the median on auditory gap detection tasks in infancy had larger productive vocabularies, used longer, more complex sentences, and produced more irregular words at 16 to 29 months as compared with those who had scored below the median. In an ERP study conducted within 36 hours after birth, Molfese and Molfese (1985, 1997) reported that specific brain response patterns elicited by consonant-vowel syllables allow children to be sorted as to whether their verbal IQ is above or below the norm at 5 years of age.

It seems likely that early deficits in lower-level processing skills have their effect quite early on in development, when acoustic and phonological maps are being constructed (Benasich & Read, 1999). Slower, more effortful processing of acoustic information may contribute to an inability to extract the acoustic key features of a language and to map its unique phoneme distribution into the auditory cortex.

Developmental Dyslexia

The original and pioneering study in this area was done by Scarborough (1990, 1991), who followed a sample of 32 children, born into families with a history of dyslexia, from age 30 months through 8 years. At the end of grade 2, 65% of the at-risk children could be classified as reading disabled. Retrospective analyses of early language skills revealed that already at 30 months of age, those children who later became dyslexic produced shorter and less complex utterances as well as more errors in pronunciation. Tests of

receptive and expressive language at 36 and 42 months showed poorly developed vocabulary skills and continuing syntactic weakness. At age 60 months, these children were impaired in terms of letter-sound knowledge, object naming, and rhyming. They also had lower productive vocabularies, but the syntactic deficits reported for the younger age appeared reduced. The changing patterns of deficit reported were not observed in children from dyslexic families who became normal readers. Thus, dyslexics' deficits in early linguistic skills may not be exclusively phonological in nature and may manifest differently as a function of age.

Converging evidence is provided by other research teams. For instance, Lefly and Pennington (1996) followed 73 children at high risk for dyslexia and 57 low-risk controls from before entry to kindergarten through just before the start of first grade. In kindergarten, high-risk children were impaired in areas of letter knowledge, initial consonant detection, rhyme oddity, and rapid naming. Imminent to first grade, the two groups differed in terms of phonological awareness skills. Follow-up at the end of second grade revealed that 34% of the high-risk children had been diagnosed as reading disabled, compared with 6% of the controls (Pennington & Lefly, 2001). Even more striking was the finding that at-risk children, who were well within the normal reading range at the end of second grade, scored lower than controls on most measures of reading and spelling. However, children who went on to be dyslexic showed a broader phonological deficit encompassing both implicit (phonological retrieval and short-term memory) and explicit (phonological awareness) skills. Letter-name knowledge at age 5 continued to be a moderately good predictor of reading disability (Pennington & Lefly, 2001). In a similar vein, Elbro, Borstrøm, and Petersen (1998) reported that Danish kindergartners with a history of parental dyslexia exhibited deficits on tests of morpheme deletion and articulation, but only those who later became dyslexic demonstrated collateral impairments in letter naming and a variety of phonological skills.

More recently, Gallagher, Frith, and Snowling (2000) documented literacy outcomes in children having a first-degree dyslexic relative and controls from nondyslexic families. When first seen at 45 months of age, at-risk children already showed signs of slower language development. At 6 years of age, 57% of the at-risk group was delayed in literacy development compared to 12% of the controls. Letter knowledge at 45 months was the strongest predictor of literacy level at age 6 years. A follow-up of this sample to age 8 years strongly suggests that children born into dyslexic families have an increased risk of literacy problems even when classified as normal readers (Snowling, Gallagher, & Frith, 2003).

Following these findings, several researchers hold the view that dyslexia reflects a multifactorial trait consistent with the interaction of multiple genes and environmental factors, resulting in continuous phenotype variations (e.g., Pennington & Lefly, 2001; Snowling et al., 2003). "Arguably, when the level of risk reaches a certain threshold, the classic dyslexia profile emerges, but there are varying degrees of subclinical impairment, particularly in dyslexic families" (Snowling et al., 2003, p. 359).

Examination of developmental trajectories of prelinguistic infants differing as a function of familial risk for dyslexia is the focus of the collaborative Jyväskylä Longitudinal Study (see Lyytinen et al., 2004). Approximately 200 Finnish at-risk children and controls have been followed from birth through school age by using both behavioral and ERP paradigms. At the neural level, the earliest group differences have already been observed within a few days of birth: Whereas in controls, ERP responses to stop-consonant syllables were most evident over the left hemisphere, at-risk newborns showed greater activity over right temporal and parietal areas (Guttorm, Leppänen, Richardson, & Lyytinen, 2001; Guttorm, Leppänen, Tolvanen, & Lyytinen, 2003). The disparity was even more prominent when rate of stimulus presentation was slowed down (Leppänen, Pihko, Eklund, & Lyytinen, 1999).

Leppänen et al. (2002) further evaluated ERP components in 6-month-olds. Here, infants with a positive family history were found to exhibit less differential response to consonant-duration changes. Using a behavioral paradigm, Richardson and colleagues (Richardson, 1998; Richardson et al., 2003) demonstrated that at-risk infants of this age group required longer consonant duration to categorize speech sounds than controls did. This same divergence was observed in their dyslexic parents.

Maximal sentence length at age 2 years turned out to be the earliest language measure that differentiated the two groups. From age 3.5 years, at-risk children exhibited less well-developed phonological and naming skills and continued to be delayed when entering school and moving through the early grades. These early deficits were predictive of language and reading outcomes at school age (Lyytinen et al., 2001, 2004).

Overall, the earliest measures that highlight group differences are basic indices of speech processing in infancy. Significant predictive associations from infancy to school age have also emerged when early reading scores were used as dependent variables. Of particular interest is the finding that predictive relationships exist across the entire sample,

albeit higher in the at-risk group given its larger variance in predictor and dependent variables (Lyytinen et al., 2004).

As detailed here, a very large literature has accrued in the area of LLI and many studies have been conducted in older children already diagnosed with the disorder. Longitudinal studies have shown that more than 50% of children who meet diagnostic criteria for SLI subsequently or concurrently also meet the criteria for dyslexia, and many, but by no means all, dyslexic individuals show oral language deficits. Prospective studies extend research demonstrating differences between LLI and normal individuals to at-risk infants as a function of family history of language-based learning disorders. Such data indicate that identification and remediation must begin in the 1st years of life to prevent early impairments from exerting negative cascading effects on language, academic, and social skills.

REMEDIAL INTERVENTION

Research in animals and humans has demonstrated that central nervous system mechanisms can be modified by experience (see Buonomano & Merzenich, 1998; Elbert, Heim, & Rockstroh, 2001). As a consequence, neural plasticity has become an important research topic and theoretical framework for contemporary developmental psychopathology. For instance, animals raised in enriched environments or trained on motor tasks show relative increases of brain volume and number of synapses (Nelson, 1999). Experience-related changes in the sensory cortex are posited to occur as a consequence of heavy training schedules realized in behaviorally relevant settings (Elbert & Heim, 2001; Elbert et al., 2001). A promising approach to understand the neural underpinnings in SLI and dyslexia would thus be to assess the effect of training on affected individuals beyond the behavioral level. In fact, there has been a spurt in literature monitoring neurophysiological correlates of various intervention techniques.

As one point of departure, Merzenich and Tallal (Merzenich et al., 1996; Tallal et al., 1996) implemented a hierarchy of computer-based audiovisual training exercises aiming to ameliorate auditory rate processing and, ultimately, language skills. Considering both the mechanisms of neural plasticity and the finding of deficient processing of rapidly successive sounds, they submitted children with LLI to a daily training extended over 4 weeks. Rapid transitional speech and nonspeech stimuli were initially disambiguated by prolonging them in time and/or amplifying them. As training progressed and the children demonstrated success, the modified acoustic stimuli were presented at rates that became closer and closer to those that occur in natural speech. Exercises resulted not only in improvements of auditory rate skills, but also in performance gains on phonological and language tests. Habib et al. (1999) found comparable evidence in children with dyslexia.

The effect of training on the brain processes underlying these changes was examined by Temple et al. (2003) using fMRI. They documented significant improvements in dyslexic children's oral language and reading performance following training. At the neural level, intervention effects were observed in brain regions typically associated with phonological processing (left temporoparietal cortex and left inferior frontal gyrus) as well as right hemisphere frontal and temporal regions and anterior cingulate gyrus.

Another potential method to parameterize the cortical effects of behavioral plasticity is the electrocortical mismatch response. Kujala et al. (2001) found enhanced MMN and faster reaction time to sound sequences following audiovisual training without linguistic material in a group of dyslexic children. Because these changes were accompanied by improvements in reading skills, the authors suggest that the disorder is at least partially based on a general auditory deficit.

In an intervention study with SLI children, Heim, Eulitz, Keil, et al. (2003) examined the magnetic counterpart of the MMN, the so-called mismatch field (MMF) evoked by stop consonant-vowel syllables. Children participated in multimodal training that included syllabic speaking, writing, and reading. The training of reading and writing followed a syllabic principle developed by Buschmann (Hofmann, 1998). Writing training had three major characteristics: First, the child said a word while writing it down (coarticulation); second, coarticulation was performed on a syllable-by-syllable basis (syllabic speaking); and third, before the child had learned coarticulation, he or she practiced syllabic speaking with flourishes of the writing arm while stepping sideways in the writing direction (flourishing exercise). Reading training was similar. Syllabic speaking was the same as during writing training, but the children coarticulated while drawing small inverted arches under the syllables. Improvements on various measures of literacy skills were found. Moreover, the syllabic training seemed to normalize neural response to phoneme processing: Before training, the SLI children displayed a stronger mismatch response in the right hemisphere than in the left, whereas their left hemispheric MMF was similar to that observed in controls. After training, groups did not differ in the magnitude of the right hemispheric MMF, leading to a comparable left-lateralized mismatch activity pattern.

Simos et al. (2002) used magnetic source imaging during a pseudoword reading task in children with dyslexia. They found a similar increase in the right hemisphere prior to intervention. Following training emphasizing phonology, there was a significant enhancement in the left superior temporal gyrus, although the peak activation was still delayed compared to the control children.

The MEG findings (Heim, Eulitz, Keil, et al., 2003; Simos et al., 2002) are in contrast to what has been observed using fMRI (Temple et al., 2003) with respect to the role of the right hemisphere during remediation. The inconsistencies could be modality related or task related. Another possibility is that there might be multiple subtypes of LLI with different underlying neuronal profiles: Heim, Eulitz, and Elbert (2002) contrasted the neuronal responses between two subgroups of dyslexic individuals. Group 1 displayed improved discrimination on temporally extended stop-consonant pairs, whereas group 2 did not show any difference. In terms of the neurophysiological correlates, only group 1 exhibited a right hemispheric MMF enhancement to prolonged syllables.

This brief survey indicates that remedial training in LLI can impact not only psychological and behavioral processes, but also neurophysiological parameters of cortical organization. Future studies need to address issues emanating from different subtypes of LLI, different modalities, different training methods, different tasks tapping various aspects of language/literacy skills, and also whether the resulting neural plasticity is a transient or permanent phenomenon. Nevertheless, findings on basic research represent an important avenue for the development and implementation of preventive interventions, which in turn may fertilize current theorizing.

FUTURE DIRECTIONS AND RECOMMENDATIONS

Despite almost 2 centuries of intense study and debate, there is surprisingly much that remains unspecified regarding the etiology, developmental trajectory, and mutability of childhood language disorders. Although substantial achievements in diagnostics, epidemiology, and remedial intervention of LLI have emerged in the face of technical advances in the behavioral and molecular neurosciences, considerable theoretical dissent still exists. An enduring question is whether phonological deficits observed in LLI are specific to linguistic systems or derive from constraints in basic mechanisms, encompassing attention, perception, memory, and/or motor processes. The research reviewed in this chapter clearly indicates that both SLI and dyslexia reflect a heterogeneous group of disorders. Although the two conditions differ in several ways, there are also striking communalities in terms of behavior, epidemiology, heritability, functional neuroanatomy, and developmental precursors. However, the specific neurocognitive profile underlying the genesis and putative interaction of oral and written language difficulties is not as yet well understood. Thomas and Karmiloff-Smith (2002) recently claimed that the developmental process is pivotal for explaining the "end-state impairments" seen in such conditions. Similarly, Johnson (1997) put forth an interactive specialization approach, in which the process of organization of the interactions between brain areas across development is stressed. Cicchetti and Toth (1992) argued that developmental models are necessary to inform prevention and intervention efforts. Conversely, prevention and intervention trials in childhood disorders can contribute to our understanding of normal and abnormal developmental theory (Cicchetti & Hinshaw, 2002). Adopting a developmental psychopathology approach based on a multiple-levels-of-analysis perspective, we offer the following recommendations for future research:

1. Several studies failed to replicate the finding of an auditory rate processing deficit observed in SLI and dyslexia (see McArthur & Bishop, 2001). Negative results may arise from the use of less strict diagnostic standards (e.g., inclusion of children who scored only slightly below the norm in reading ability), advent of inappropriate tasks (e.g., very easy tasks produce ceiling effects), and the possibility that not all language/literacy impairments evolve from an auditory rate dysfunction (Fitch & Tallal, 2003). Recent work, however, suggests that subjects' age and maturation moderate auditory skills in LLI (Bishop & McArthur, 2004; Hautus, Setchell, Waldie, & Kirk, 2003; Wright & Zecker, 2004). Benasich and colleagues (Benasich & Tallal, 2002; Benasich et al., 2002, 2005) documented that rapid auditory processing abilities in infants differed as a function of family history for SLI and were predictive of later language outcome. This has been demonstrated by using behavioral as well as electrocortical parameters. Bishop and McArthur reported divergence of ERP and behavioral data in older individuals. Adolescents with SLI performed as well as controls in an auditory backward-masking task, yet all of the SLI participants showed aberrant ERP responses to the same stimuli presented in the behavioral paradigm. This may point to the possibility that older subjects have developed compensatory neural implementation to cope with behavioral deficits, and perhaps language/literacy skills. The use of convergent methodologies is hence highly recommended to detect (even subtle) sensory deficits and monitor developmental/maturational characteristics.

2. Continued research on basic deficits across modalities (auditory, visual, tactile, and motor) within the same LLI samples is required to evaluate the viability of a panmodality model (Stein, 2001; Tallal et al., 1993). Within this framework, several aspects should be addressed: (1) the impact of task difficulty or complexity, (2) the notion that a deficit in one or more modalities represents a subgroup-specific phenomenon, and (3) whether the putative cross-modal phenotype varies as a function of age.

3. The major competing hypotheses (phonological, auditory rate, and magnocellular deficit) for LLI should be studied in multiple case designs across different age groups to clarify outstanding issues regarding associative and causal relationships between the deficits (see also Ramus et al., 2003). Theory-driven behavioral tasks as well as exploitation of high-temporal and high-spatial resolution technologies (e.g., EEG and fMRI, respectively) may provide a complete picture.

4. Various techniques, such as EEG, MEG, fMRI, and PET, have been used to investigate the functional neuroanatomy of LLI. The findings, however, are not consistent in that many studies have observed a divergence from normal patterns related to the left hemisphere (e.g., Brunswick et al., 1999; S. E. Shaywitz et al., 1998; Temple et al., 2000), whereas others have reported a deviance related to the right hemisphere (e.g., Heim, Eulitz, & Elbert, 2003a, 2003b; Heim, Eulitz, Keil, et al., 2003; McCrory et al., 2000). As discussed earlier, the disparity might occur for a number of reasons, including the heterogeneity of disorders, task differences (e.g., reading versus auditory verbal repetition), and kind of measurement technique used (e.g., high-temporal MEG or high-spatial fMRI). It is conceivable that different subtypes of both SLI and dyslexia are associated with different neural substrates. Also, symptom diversity of the complex conditions may be reflected in a variety of neural bases. Systematic investigation of the aforementioned variables is therefore required to clarify these possibilities.

5. Another issue that needs to be examined carefully is whether the observed deviations in functional neuroanatomy vary in lower levels (phoneme or syllable) and higher (word or sentence) stages of linguistic processing (Hellige, 1993). There has been a burst of new

findings in the auditory literature indicating hemispheric differences with regard to rapid versus slower temporal processing (e.g., Poeppel et al., 2004; Zatorre & Belin, 2001). Poeppel and collaborators documented that auditory word/pseudoword judgments, categorical perception of consonant-vowel syllables, and direction discrimination of frequency-modulated tones differentially engage left and right auditory cortex. Such results suggest differential lateralization of phonetic versus prosodic processing for speech on the basis of differing spectral properties of the auditory input. However, neither the lateralization of phonemes (e.g., Tervaniemi et al., 2000) nor that of prosody (e.g., Baum & Dwivedi, 2003) has been completely understood yet. These issues might have implications in the understanding of the neural bases of LLI. One of the latest hypotheses proposed by Goswami et al. (2002) suggests that dyslexic children might in fact be impaired in rhythm detection, and this process of rhythm detection operates at a syllabic level. Further work is needed to understand the neural implications of this hypothesis.

6. Neurophysiological studies in child samples are necessary to investigate whether deviations from typical brain responses reflect a fundamental deficit or compensation for poor language and literacy skills in adulthood. There are a limited number of fMRI investigations exploring phonological and orthographic skills in dyslexic children, but auditory and visual rate processing needs to be examined in greater detail. As far as SLI is concerned, hemodynamic and electrophysiological studies are particularly scarce.

7. Another promising way to address the causality-compensatory issue is to assess the effect of training on neural processes. One goal that needs to be pursued for the advancement of both SLI and dyslexia research is to design clearly delimited intervention paradigms that tap specific deficits of the conditions or use the currently available techniques and clarify the effect of their specific components.

8. Early brain injury in rodents has been found to result in behavioral and morphological changes that vary as a function of age and experience and may produce altered psychophysical thresholds comparable to those observed in individuals with dyslexia and SLI (see section on Animal Studies). These variables have also been proposed to moderate basic sensory processing in humans (see Bishop & Snowling, 2004). Animal models are hence crucial for elucidating the potential substrates and mechanisms underlying acoustic processes in the course of development.

9. Prospective longitudinal studies beginning in early infancy are still few in number. Continued research in this area is needed to advance our understanding of developmental trajectories characterizing normal and atypical language. Here the use of different methodologies, such as theory-driven behavioral tasks, neurophysiological techniques, and molecular genetic approaches seems indispensable. For instance, ERP measurements can already be conducted in neonates and thus provide insights in early sensory processing. Data derived from at-risk infants compared to infants with a negative family history for LLI give us perhaps the most compelling evidence of the developmental impact of early sensory processing skills on language development and disorders under consideration.

10. Family-risk studies in dyslexia suggest that well-developed language skills help children to compensate for reading and spelling problems (Pennington & Lefly, 2001; Snowling et al., 2003). Literacy assessment should therefore always be accompanied by oral-language testing. Moreover, training of language skills needs to be considered an important building block of reading and spelling intervention programs.

11. There is a high risk of LLI in children whose immediate relatives themselves experienced language and/or literacy impairments (see section on Prospective Studies in Infants and Kindergartners). During early infancy, critical foundations of phonemic perception and later language are laid down. The potential for altering later outcome may be maximally effective during this early period. Development of age-appropriate training strategies based on prospective longitudinal research will be of great importance.

12. So far, linkage mapping and related analysis methods have revealed no overlap in gene loci for SLI and dyslexia (see section on Molecular-Genetic Studies). As outlined earlier in this chapter, statistical pitfalls (i.e., use of univariate testing) may have influenced such results. Further molecular-genetic investigations adopting a multivariate-analysis approach (Marlow et al., 2003) may open a new avenue to explore similarities or dissimilarities in SLI and dyslexia genotypes (see also Bishop & Snowling, 2004).

The overview presented here underscores the complexity of developmental language disorders and the critical importance of adopting a convergent methodological/developmental perspective. We have attempted to present an integrated view of molecular, cellular, macroscopic, and behavioral evidence gleaned across disciplines that contribute to our current understanding of language disorders. It seems quite likely not only that the precursors of LLI can be seen very early in the 1st year of life, but also that language deficits persist, usually in subtle form, into later childhood, adolescence, and conceivably into adulthood. Therefore, the impact of developmental disorders of language on society is substantive. LLI has been shown to lead to reading and other academic achievement problems, an increased incidence of social and emotional problems, higher adjudication rates, and school dropout (see Snow et al., 1998; Tallal, 2004; Tallal & Benasich, 2002). The broad recommendations we delineate here represent an attempt to summarize the critical directions for basic research in this burgeoning field. With the advent of more sophisticated neuroimaging procedures and increasing use of converging methodologies and multiple levels of analysis, the opportunity for narrowing down the candidate causal mechanisms for such disorders is within our grasp. Future research may well lead to a better understanding of the neurobiological origins of language-based learning disabilities and the development of effective intervention techniques.

REFERENCES

Aaron, P. G. (1997). A component-based approach to the diagnosis and treatment of reading disabilities. In B. Ericson & J. Rönnberg (Eds.), *Reading disability and its treatment* (EMIR Report No. 2, pp. 37–66). Norrköping, Sweden: Eve Malmquist Institute for Reading, Linköping University.

Ackerman, P. T., & Dykman, R. A. (1993). Phonological processes, confrontational naming, and immediate memory in dyslexia. *Journal of Learning Disabilities, 26,* 597–609.

Alarcón, M., & DeFries, J. C. (1997). Reading performance and general cognitive ability in twins with reading difficulties and control pairs. *Personality and Individual Differences, 22,* 793–803.

American Psychiatric Association. (1994). *Diagnostic and statistical manual of mental disorders* (4th ed.). Washington, DC.

Aram, D. M., Ekelman, B. L., & Nation, J. E. (1984). Preschoolers with language disorders: 10 years later. *Journal of Speech and Hearing Research, 27,* 232–244.

Aram, D. M., & Nation, J. E. (1975). Patterns of language behavior in children with developmental language disorders. *Journal of Speech and Hearing Research, 18,* 229–241.

Bakwin, H. (1973). Reading disability in twins. *Developmental Medicine and Child Neurology, 15,* 184–187.

Baldeweg, T., Richardson, A., Watkins, S., Foale, C., & Gruzelier, J. (1999). Impaired auditory frequency discrimination in dyslexia detected with mismatch evoked potentials. *Annals of Neurology, 45,* 495–503.

Bartlett, C. W., Flax, J. F., Logue, M. W., Vieland, V. J., Bassett, A. S., Tallal, P., et al. (2002). A major susceptibility locus for specific language impairment is located on 13q21. *American Journal of Human Genetics, 71,* 45–55.

Bates, E., O'Connell, B., & Shore, C. (1987). Language and communication in infancy. In J. D. Osofsky (Ed.), *Handbook of infant development* (pp. 149–203). New York: Wiley.

Baum, S. R., & Dwivedi, V. D. (2003). Sensitivity to prosodic structure in left- and right-hemisphere-damaged individuals. *Brain and Language, 87,* 278–289.

Behan, W. M., Behan, P. O., & Geschwind, N. (1985). Anti-Ro antibody in mothers of dyslexic children. *Developmental Medicine and Child Neurology, 27,* 538–540.

Beitchman, J. H., Nair, R., Clegg, M., Ferguson, B., & Patel, P. G. (1986). Prevalence of psychiatric disorders in children with speech and language disorders. *Journal of the American Academy of Child Psychiatry, 25,* 528–535.

Beitchman, J. H., Nair, R., Clegg, M., Patel, P. G., Ferguson, B., Pressman, E., et al. (1986). Prevalence of speech and language disorders in 5-year-old kindergarten children in the Ottawa-Carleton region. *Journal of Speech and Hearing Disorders, 51,* 98–110. (Erratum published in 1987, *Journal of Speech and Hearing Disorders, 52,* 94)

Beitchman, J. H., Wilson, B., Brownlie, E. B., Walters, H., & Lancee, W. (1996). Long-term consistency in speech/language profiles: I. Developmental and academic outcomes. *Journal of the American Academy of Child and Adolescent Psychiatry, 35,* 804–814.

Beitchman, J. H., Wilson, B., Johnson, C. J., Atkinson, L., Young, A., Adlaf, E., et al. (2001). Fourteen-year follow-up of speech/language-impaired and control children: Psychiatric outcome. *Journal of the American Academy of Child and Adolescent Psychiatry, 40,* 75–82.

Benasich, A. A. (2002). Impaired processing of brief, rapidly presented auditory cues in infants with a family history of autoimmune disorder. *Developmental Neuropsychology, 22,* 351–372.

Benasich, A. A., Choudhury, N., Friedman, J. T., Realpe-Bonilla, T., Chojnowska, C., & Gou, Z. (2005). *The infant as a prelinguistic model for language learning impairments: Predicting from event-related potentials to behavior.* Neuropsychologia, in press.

Benasich, A. A., Curtiss, S., & Tallal, P. (1993). Language, learning, and behavioral disturbances in childhood: A longitudinal perspective. *Journal of the American Academy of Child and Adolescent Psychiatry, 32,* 585–594.

Benasich, A. A., & Leevers, H. J. (2003). Processing of rapidly presented auditory cues in infancy: Implications for later language development. In H. Hayne & J. Fagan (Eds.), *Progress in infancy research* (Vol. 3, pp. 245–288). Mahwah, NJ: Erlbaum.

Benasich, A. A., & Read, H. L. (1999). Representation: Picture or process? In I. E. Sigel (Ed.), *Development of mental representation: Theories and applications* (pp. 33–60). Mahwah, NJ: Erlbaum.

Benasich, A. A., & Tallal, P. (1996). Auditory temporal processing thresholds, habituation, and recognition memory over the 1st year. *Infant Behavior and Development, 19,* 339–357.

Benasich, A. A., & Tallal, P. (2002). Infant discrimination of rapid auditory cues predicts later language impairment. *Behavioral Brain Research, 136,* 31–49.

Benasich, A. A., Thomas, J. J., Choudhury, N., & Leppänen, P. H. (2002). The importance of rapid auditory processing abilities to early language development: Evidence from converging methodologies. *Developmental Psychobiology, 40,* 278–292.

Benton, A. L. (1964). Developmental aphasia and brain damage. *Cortex, 1,* 40–52.

Berlin, R. (1887). *Eine besondere Art der Wortblindheit (Dyslexie).* Wiesbaden, Germany: Bergmann.

Best, M., & Demb, J. B. (1999). Normal planum temporale asymmetry in dyslexics with a magnocellular pathway deficit. *Neuroreport, 10,* 607–612.

Bird, J., Bishop, D. V., & Freeman, N. H. (1995). Phonological awareness and literacy development in children with expressive phonological impairments. *Journal of Speech and Hearing Research, 38,* 446–462.

Bishop, D. V. (1990). Handedness, clumsiness and developmental language disorders. *Neuropsychologia, 28,* 681–690.

Bishop, D. V. (1992). The biological basis of specific language impairment. In P. Fletcher & D. Hall (Eds.), *Specific speech and language disorders in children* (pp. 2–17). London: Whurr.

Bishop, D. V. (1997). Pre- and perinatal hazards and family background in children with specific language impairments: A study of twins. *Brain and Language, 56,* 1–26.

Bishop, D. V. (2001). Genetic influences on language impairment and literacy problems in children: Same or different? *Journal of Child Psychology and Psychiatry, 42,* 189–198.

Bishop, D. V. (2003). Autism and specific language impairment: Categorical distinction or continuum? In G. Bock & J. Goode (Eds.) *Novartis Foundation Symposium* (pp. 213–234, 281–288). Chichester, England: Wiley.

Bishop, D. V., & Adams, C. (1990). A prospective study of the relationship between specific language impairment, phonological disorders and reading retardation. *Journal of Child Psychology and Psychiatry, 31,* 1027–1050.

Bishop, D. V., Adams, C. V., & Norbury, C. F. (2004). Using nonword repetition to distinguish genetic and environmental influences on early literacy development: A study of 6-year-old twins. *American Journal of Medical Genetics, 129B,* 94–96.

Bishop, D. V., Bishop, S. J., Bright, P., James, C., Delaney, T., & Tallal, P. (1999). Different origin of auditory and phonological processing problems in children with language impairment: Evidence from a twin study. *Journal of Speech, Language, and Hearing Research, 42,* 155–168.

Bishop, D. V., Carlyon, R. P., Deeks, J. M., & Bishop, S. J. (1999). Auditory temporal processing impairment: Neither necessary nor sufficient for causing language impairment in children. *Journal of Speech, Language, and Hearing Research, 42,* 1295–1310.

Bishop, D. V., & Edmundson, A. (1986). Is otitis media a major cause of specific developmental language disorders? *British Journal of Disorders of Communication, 21,* 321–338.

Bishop, D. V., & Edmundson, A. (1987a). Language-impaired 4-year-olds: Distinguishing transient from persistent impairment. *Journal of Speech and Hearing Disorders, 52,* 156–173.

Bishop, D. V., & Edmundson, A. (1987b). Specific language impairment is a maturational lag: Evidence from longitudinal data on language and motor development. *Developmental Medicine and Child Neurology, 29,* 442–459.

Bishop, D. V., & McArthur, G. M. (2004). Immature cortical responses to auditory stimuli in specific language impairment: Evidence from ERPs to rapid tone sequences. *Developmental Science, 7,* F11–F18.

Bishop, D. V., & Norbury, C. F. (2002). Exploring the borderlands of autistic disorder and specific language impairment: A study using standardised diagnostic instruments. *Journal of Child Psychology and Psychiatry, 43,* 917–929.

Bishop, D. V., North, T., & Donlan, C. (1995). Genetic basis of specific language impairment: Evidence from a twin study. *Developmental Medicine and Child Neurology, 37,* 56–71.

Bishop, D. V., North, T., & Donlan, C. (1996). Nonword repetition as a behavioural marker for inherited language impairment: Evidence from a twin study. *Journal of Child Psychology and Psychiatry, 37,* 391–403.

Bishop, D. V., & Snowling, M. J. (2004). Developmental dyslexia and specific language impairment: Same or different? *Psychological Bulletin, 130,* 858–886.

Boetsch, E. A., Green, P. A., & Pennington, B. F. (1996). Psychosocial correlates of dyslexia across the life span. *Development and Psychopathology, 8,* 539–562.

Borsting, E., Ridder, W. H., III, Dudeck, K., Kelley, C., Matsui, L., & Motoyama, J. (1996). The presence of a magnocellular defect depends on the type of dyslexia. *Vision Research, 36,* 1047–1053.

Botting, N., & Conti-Ramsden, G. (2001). Non-word repetition and language development in children with specific language impairment (SLI). *International Journal of Language and Communication Disorders, 36,* 421–432.

Boucher, V. J. (1994). Alphabet-related biases in psycholinguistic enquiries: Considerations for direct theories of speech production and perception. *Journal of Phonetics, 22,* 1–18.

Bowers, P. G., & Swanson, L. B. (1991). Naming speed deficits in reading disability: Multiple measures of a singular process. *Journal of Experimental Child Psychology, 51,* 195–219.

Bradley, L., & Bryant, P. E. (1978). Difficulties in auditory organisation as a possible cause of reading backwardness. *Nature, 271,* 746–747.

Bradley, L., & Bryant, P. E. (1983). Categorizing sounds and learning to read: A causal connection. *Nature, 301,* 419–421.

Bradley, L., & Bryant, P. (1985). *Rhyme and reason in reading and spelling.* Ann Arbor: University of Michigan Press.

Bradlow, A. R., Kraus, N., Nicol, T. G., McGee, T. J., Cunningham, J., Zecker, S. G., et al. (1999). Effects of lengthened formant transition duration on discrimination and neural representation of synthetic CV syllables by normal and learning-disabled children. *Journal of the Acoustical Society of America, 106,* 2086–2096.

Brady, S., Mann, V., & Schmidt, R. (1987). Errors in short-term memory for good and poor readers. *Memory and Cognition, 15,* 444–453.

Brady, S., Shankweiler, D., & Mann, V. (1983). Speech perception and memory coding in relation to reading ability. *Journal of Experimental Child Psychology, 35,* 345–367.

Breitmeyer, B. G., & Ganz, L. (1976). Implications of sustained and transient channels for theories of visual pattern masking, saccadic suppression, and information processing. *Psychological Review, 83,* 1–36.

Broadbent, W. H. (1872). On the cerebral mechanism of speech and thought. *Medico-Chirurgical Transactions, 55,* 145–194.

Broca, P. P. (1861). Remarques sur le siége de la faculté du langage articulé, suivies d'une observation d'aphémie (perte de la parole) [Remarks by the faculty of articulated language following an observation of aphemia (loss of speech)]. *Bulletin de la Société Anatomique de Paris, 6*(Sér. 2), 330–357. Bruck, M. (1992). Persistence of dyslexics' phonological awareness deficits. *Developmental Psychology, 28,* 874–886.

Brunswick, N., McCrory, E., Price, C. J., Frith, C. D., & Frith, U. (1999). Explicit and implicit processing of words and pseudowords by adult developmental dyslexics: A search for Wernicke's Wortschatz? *Brain, 122,* 1901–1917.

Buonomano, D. V., & Merzenich, M. M. (1998). Cortical plasticity: From synapses to maps. *Annual Review of Neuroscience, 21,* 149–186.

Burr, D. C., Holt, J., Johnstone, J. R., & Ross, J. (1982). Selective depression of motion sensitivity during saccades. *Journal of Physiology, 333,* 1–15.

Burr, D. C., Morrone, M. C., & Ross, J. (1994). Selective suppression of the magnocellular visual pathway during saccadic eye movements. *Nature, 371,* 511–513.

Bus, A. G., & van IJzendoorn, M. H. (1999). Phonological awareness and early reading: A meta-analysis of experimental training studies. *Journal of Educational Psychology, 91,* 403–414.

Byrne, B. M. (1981). Deficient syntactic control in poor readers: Is a weak phonetic memory code responsible? *Applied Psycholinguistics, 2,* 201–212.

Byrne, B. M., Willerman, L., & Ashmore, L. L. (1974). Severe and moderate language impairment: Evidence for distinctive etiologies. *Behavior Genetics, 4,* 331–345.

Cardon, L. R., Smith, S. D., Fulker, D. W., Kimberling, W. J., Pennington, B. F., & DeFries, J. C. (1994). Quantitative trait locus for reading disability on chromosome 6. *Science, 266,* 276–279. (Erratum published in 1995, *Science, 268,* 1553)

Castles, A., Datta, H., Gayán, J., & Olson, R. K. (1999). Varieties of developmental reading disorder: Genetic and environmental influences. *Journal of Experimental Child Psychology, 72,* 73–94.

Catts, H. W. (1993). The relationship between speech-language impairments and reading disabilities. *Journal of Speech and Hearing Research, 36,* 948–958.

Cheour, M., Leppänen, P. H., & Kraus, N. (2000). Mismatch negativity (MMN) as a tool for investigating auditory discrimination and sensory memory in infants and children. *Clinical Neurophysiology, 111,* 4–16.

Chi, J. G., Dooling, E. C., & Gilles, F. H. (1977). Left-right asymmetries of the temporal speech areas of the human fetus. *Archives of Neurology, 34,* 346–348.

Chiron, C., Pinton, F., Masure, M. C., Duvelleroy-Hommet, C., Leon, F., & Billard, C. (1999). Hemispheric specialization using SPECT and stimulation tasks in children with dysphasia and dystrophia. *Developmental Medicine and Child Neurology, 41,* 512–520.

Choudhury, N., & Benasich, A. A. (2003). A family aggregation study: The influence of family history and other risk factors on language development. *Journal of Speech, Language and Hearing Research, 46,* 261–272.

Cicchetti, D., & Dawson, G. (2002). Editorial: Multiple levels of analysis. *Development and Psychopathology, 14,* 417–420.

Cicchetti, D., & Hinshaw, S. P. (2002). Editorial: Prevention and intervention science: Contributions to developmental theory. *Development and Psychopathology, 14,* 667–671.

Cicchetti, D., & Toth, S. L. (1992). Editorial: The role of developmental theory in prevention and intervention. *Development and Psychopathology, 4,* 489–493.

Clark, M. G., Rosen, G. D., Tallal, P., & Fitch, R. H. (2000). Impaired processing of complex auditory stimuli in rats with induced cerebrocortical microgyria: An animal model of developmental language disabilities. *Journal of Cognitive Neuroscience, 12,* 828–839.

Coën, R. (1886). *Pathologie und Therapie der Sprachanomalien.* Wien, Austria: Urban & Schwarzenberg.

Coën, R. (1888). Die Hörstummheit und ihre Behandlung. *Wiener Klinik, 7,* 201–230.

Cohen, M., Campbell, R., & Yaghmai, F. (1989). Neuropathological abnormalities in developmental dysphasia. *Annals of Neurology, 25,* 567–570.

Colledge, E., Bishop, D. V., Koeppen-Schomerus, G., Price, T. S., Happé, F. G., Eley, T. C., et al. (2002). The structure of language abilities at 4 years: A twin study. *Developmental Psychology, 38,* 749–757.

Compton, D. L., DeFries, J. C., & Olson, R. K. (2001). Are RAN- and phonological awareness-deficits additive in children with reading disabilities? *Dyslexia, 7,* 125–149.

Cornelissen, P., Hansen, P. C., Hutton, J. L., Evangelinou, V., & Stein, J. F. (1998). Magnocellular visual function and children's single word reading. *Vision Research, 38,* 471–482.

Cornelissen, P., Richardson, A., Mason, A., Fowler, S., & Stein, J. (1995). Contrast sensitivity and coherent motion detection measured at photopic luminance levels in dyslexics and controls. *Vision Research, 35,* 1483–1494.

Davis, C. J., Gayán, J., Knopik, V. S., Smith, S. D., Cardon, L. R., Pennington, B. F., et al. (2001). Etiology of reading difficulties and rapid naming: The Colorado Twin Study of Reading Disability. *Behavior Genetics, 31,* 625–635.

De Fosse, L., Hodge, S. M., Makris, N., Kennedy, D. N., Caviness, V. S., Jr., McGrath, L., et al. (2004). Language-association cortex asymmetry in Autism and specific language impairment. *Annals of Neurology, 56,* 757–766.

DeFries, J. C., & Alarcón, M. (1996). Genetics of specific reading disability. *Mental Retardation and Developmental Disabilities Research Reviews, 2,* 39–47.

DeFries, J. C., & Fulker, D. W. (1985). Multiple regression analysis of twin data. *Behavior Genetics, 15,* 467–473.

DeFries, J., C., Fulker, D. W., & LaBuda, M. C. (1987). Evidence for a genetic aetiology in reading disability of twins. *Nature, 329,* 537–539.

DeFries, J. C., Singer, S. M., Foch, T. T., & Lewitter, F. I. (1978). Familial nature of reading disability. *British Journal of Psychiatry, 132,* 361–367.

Déjérine, J. (1892). Contribution à l'étude anatomo-pathologique et clinique des différentes variétés de cécité verbale. *Mémoires de la Société de Biologie, 4*(Sér. 9), 61–90.

Demb, J. B., Boynton, G. M., & Heeger, D. J. (1997). Brain activity in visual cortex predicts individual differences in reading performance. *Proceedings of the National Academy of Sciences, USA, 94,* 13363–13366.

Demb, J. B., Boynton, G. M., & Heeger, D. J. (1998). Functional magnetic resonance imaging of early visual pathways in dyslexia. *Journal of Neuroscience, 18,* 6939–6951.

Démonet, J. F., Fiez, J. A., Paulesu, E., Petersen, S. E., & Zatorre, R. J. (1996). PET studies of phonological processing: A critical reply to Poeppel. *Brain and Language, 55,* 352–379.

Denays, R., Tondeur, M., Foulon, M., Verstraeten, F., Ham, H., Piepsz, A., et al. (1989). Regional brain blood flow in congenital dysphasia: Studies with technetium-99m HM-PAO SPECT. *Journal of Nuclear Medicine, 30,* 1825–1829.

Denckla, M. B., & Rudel, R. G. (1976). Rapid "automatized" naming (R.A.N.): Dyslexia differentiated from other learning disabilities. *Neuropsychologia, 14,* 471–479.

Denenberg, V. H. (1999). A critique of Mody, Studdert-Kennedy, and Brady's "Speech perception deficits in poor readers: Auditory processing or phonological coding?" *Journal of Learning Disabilities, 32,* 379–383.

Denenberg, V. H. (2001). More power to them: Statistically, that is: A commentary on Studdert-Kennedy, Mody and Brady's criticism of a critique. *Journal of Learning Disabilities, 34,* 299–303.

Di Lollo, V., Hanson, D., & McIntyre, J. S. (1983). Initial stages of visual information processing in dyslexia. *Journal of Experimental Psychology/Human Perception and Performance, 9,* 923–935.

Duara, R., Kushch, A., Gross-Glenn, K., Barker, W. W., Jallad, B., Pascal, S., et al. (1991). Neuroanatomic differences between dyslexic and normal readers on magnetic resonance imaging scans. *Archives of Neurology, 48,* 410–416.

Dvorák, K., Feit, J., & Jurankova, Z. (1978). Experimentally induced focal microgyria and status verrucosus deformis in rats: Pathogenesis and interrelation—Histological and autoradiographical study. *Acta Neuropathologica (Berlin), 44,* 121–129.

Eckert, M. A., Leonard, C. M., Richards, T. L., Aylward, E. H., Thomson, J., & Berninger, V. W. (2003). Anatomical correlates of dyslexia: Frontal and cerebellar findings. *Brain, 126,* 482–494.

Eden, G. F., VanMeter, J. W., Rumsey, J. M., Maisog, J. M., Woods, R. P., & Zeffiro, T. A. (1996). Abnormal processing of visual motion in dyslexia revealed by functional brain imaging. *Nature, 382,* 66–69.

Edwards, J., & Lahey, M. (1998). Nonword repetitions of children with specific language impairment: Exploration of some explanations for their inaccuracies. *Applied Psycholinguistics, 19,* 279–309.

Edwards, V. T., Giaschi, D. E., Dougherty, R. F., Edgell, D., Bjornson, B. H., Lyons, C., et al. (2004). Psychophysical indexes of temporal processing abnormalities in children with developmental dyslexia. *Developmental Neuropsychology, 25,* 321–354.

Elbert, T. (1998). Neuromagnetism. In W. Andrä & H. Nowak (Eds.), *Magnetism in medicine* (pp. 190–262). New York: Wiley.

Elbert, T., & Heim, S. (2001). Cortical reorganization: A light and a dark side. *Nature, 411,* 139.

Elbert, T., Heim, S., & Rockstroh, B. (2001). Neural plasticity and development. In C. A. Nelson & M. Luciana (Eds.), *Handbook of developmental cognitive neuroscience* (pp. 191–202). Cambridge, MA: MIT Press.

Elbro, C., Borstrøm, I., & Petersen, D. K. (1998). Predicting dyslexia from kindergarten: The importance of distinctness of phonological representations of lexical items. *Reading Research Quarterly, 33,* 36–60.

Elbro, C., Nielsen, I., & Petersen, D. K. (1994). Dyslexia in adults: Evidence for deficits in non-word reading and in the phonological representation of lexical items. *Annals of Dyslexia, 44,* 205–226.

Esser, G., & Schmidt, M. H. (1994). Children with specific reading retardation: Early determinants and long-term outcome. *Acta Paedopsychiatrica, 56,* 229–237.

Everatt, J., Bradshaw, M. F., & Hibbard, P. B. (1999). Visual processing and dyslexia. *Perception, 28,* 243–254.

Farmer, M. E., & Klein, R. M. (1995). The evidence for a temporal processing deficit linked to dyslexia: A review. *Psychonomic Bulletin and Review, 2,* 460–493.

Fawcett, A. J., & Nicolson, R. I. (1995). Persistence of phonological awareness deficits in older children with dyslexia. *Reading and Writing, 7,* 361–376.

Felmingham, K. L., & Jakobson, L. S. (1995). Visual and visuomotor performance in dyslexic children. *Experimental Brain Research, 106,* 467–474.

Fenson, L., Dale, P. S., Reznick, J. S., Bates, E., Thal, D. J., & Pethick, S. J. (1994). Variability in early communicative development. *Monographs of the Society for Research in Child Development, 59,* 1–173.

Fergusson, D. M., & Lynskey, M. T. (1997). Early reading difficulties and later conduct problems. *Journal of Child Psychology and Psychiatry, 38,* 899–907.

Fey, M., & Leonard, L. B. (1983). Pragmatic skills of children with specific language impairment. In T. Gallagher & C. Prutting (Eds.), *Pragmatic assessment and intervention issues in language* (pp. 65–82). San Diego: College-Hill Press.

Filipek, P. A. (1995). Neurobiologic correlates of developmental dyslexia: How do dyslexics' brains differ from those of normal readers? *Journal of Child Neurology, 10*(Suppl. 1), 62–69.

Finucci, J. M., & Childs, B. (1981). Are there really more dyslexic boys than girls? In A. Ansara, N. Geschwind, A. M. Galaburda, M. Albert, & N. Gartrell (Eds.), *Sex differences in dyslexia* (pp. 1–9). Towson, MD: Orton Dyslexia Society.

Finucci, J. M., Guthrie, J. T., Childs, A. L., Abbey, H., & Childs, B. (1976). The genetics of specific reading disability. *Annals of Human Genetics, 40,* 1–23.

Fischer, F. W., Liberman, I. Y., & Shankweiler, D. (1978). Reading reversals and developmental dyslexia: A further study. *Cortex, 14,* 496–510.

Fisher, S. E., & DeFries, J. C. (2002). Developmental dyslexia: Genetic dissection of a complex cognitive trait. *Nature Reviews, Neuroscience, 3,* 767–780.

Fisher, S. E., Marlow, A. J., Lamb, J., Maestrini, E., Williams, D. F., Richardson, A. J., et al. (1999). A quantitative-trait locus on chromosome 6p influences different aspects of developmental dyslexia. *American Journal of Human Genetics, 64,* 146–156.

Fisher, S. E., Vargha-Khadem, F., Watkins, K. E., Monaco, A. P., & Pembrey, M. E. (1998). Localisation of a gene implicated in a severe speech and language disorder. *Nature Genetics, 18,* 168–170. (Erratum published in 1998, *Nature Genetics, 18,* 298)

Fitch, R. H., Read, H. L., & Benasich, A. A. (2001). Neurophysiology of speech perception in normal and impaired systems. In A. F. Jahn & J. Santos-Sacchi (Eds.), *Physiology of the ear* (2nd ed., pp. 651–672). San Diego: Singular Publishing Group.

Fitch, R. H., & Tallal, P. (2003). Neural mechanisms of language-based learning impairments: Insights from human populations and animal models. *Behavioral and Cognitive Neuroscience Reviews, 2,* 155–178.

Fitch, R. H., Tallal, P., Brown, C. P., Galaburda, A. M., & Rosen, G. D. (1994). Induced microgyria and auditory temporal processing in rats: A model for language impairment? *Cerebral Cortex, 4,* 260–270.

Flannery, K. A., Liederman, J., Daly, L., & Schultz, J. (2000). Male prevalence for reading disability is found in a large sample of Black and White children free from ascertainment bias. *Journal of the International Neuropsychological Society, 6,* 433–442.

Flax, J. F., Realpe-Bonilla, T., Hirsch, L. S., Brzustowicz, L. M., Bartlett, C. W., & Tallal, P. (2003). Specific language impairment in families: Evidence for co-occurrence with reading impairments. *Journal of Speech, Language, and Hearing Research, 46,* 530–543.

Fletcher, J. M., Francis, D. J., Shaywitz, S. E., Lyon, G. R., Foorman, B. R., Stuebing, K. K., et al. (1998). Intelligent testing and the discrepancy model for children with learning disabilities. *Learning Disabilities Research and Practice, 13,* 186–203.

Fletcher, J. M., Shaywitz, S. E., Shankweiler, D. P., Katz, L., Liberman, I. Y., Stuebing, K. K., et al. (1994). Cognitive profiles of reading disability: Comparisons of discrepancy and low achievement definitions. *Journal of Educational Psychology, 86,* 6–23.

Flowers, D. L. (1993). Brain basis for dyslexia: A summary of work in progress. *Journal of Learning Disabilities, 26,* 575–582.

Flynn, J. M., & Rahbar, M. H. (1994). Prevalence of reading failure in boys compared with girls. *Psychology in the Schools, 31,* 66–71.

Frenkel, M., Sherman, G. F., Bashan, K. A., Galaburda, A. M., & LoTurco, J. J. (2000). Neocortical ectopias are associated with attenuated neurophysiological responses to rapidly changing auditory stimuli. *Neuroreport, 11,* 575–579.

Friedman, J. T., Peiffer, A. M., Clark, M. G., Benasich, A. A., & Fitch, R. H. (2004). Age and experience-related improvements in gap detection in the rat. *Brain Research/Developmental Brain Research, 152,* 83–91.

Friedrich, M., Weber, C., & Friederici, A. D. (2004). Electrophysiological evidence for delayed mismatch response in infants at-risk for specific language impairment. *Psychophysiology, 41,* 772–782.

Gadeyne, E., Ghesquière, P., & Onghena, P. (2004). Psychosocial functioning of young children with learning problems. *Journal of Child Psychology and Psychiatry, 45,* 510–521.

Galaburda, A. M. (1988). The pathogenesis of childhood dyslexia. In F. Plum (Ed.), *Language, communication, and the brain* (pp. 127–138). New York: Raven Press.

Galaburda, A. M. (1989). Ordinary and extraordinary brain development: Anatomical variation in developmental dyslexia. *Annals of Dyslexia, 39,* 67–80.

Galaburda, A. M. (1993). Neuroanatomic basis of developmental dyslexia. *Neurologic Clinics, 11,* 161–173.

Galaburda, A. M., & Livingstone, M. (1993). Evidence for a magnocellular defect in developmental dyslexia. *Annals of the New York Academy of Sciences, 682,* 70–82.

Galaburda, A. M., Menard, M. T., & Rosen, G. D. (1994). Evidence for aberrant auditory anatomy in developmental dyslexia. *Proceedings of the National Academy of Sciences, USA, 91,* 8010–8013.

Galaburda, A. M., Rosen, G. D., & Sherman, G. F. (1990). Individual variability in cortical organization: Its relationship to brain laterality and implications to function. *Neuropsychologia, 28,* 529–546.

Galaburda, A. M., Schrott, L. M., Sherman, G. F., Rosen, G. D., & Denenberg, V. H. (1996). Animal models of developmental dyslexia. In C. H. Chase, G. D. Rosen, & G. F. Sherman (Eds.), *Developmental dyslexia: Neural, cognitive, and genetic mechanisms* (pp. 3–14). Baltimore: York Press.

Galaburda, A. M., Sherman, G. F., Rosen, G. D., Aboitiz, F., & Geschwind, N. (1985). Developmental dyslexia: Four consecutive patients with cortical anomalies. *Annals of Neurology, 18,* 222–233.

Gall, F. J. (1822). *Sur les fonctions du cerveau et sur celles de chacune de ses parties, avec des observations sur la possibilité de reconnoitre les instincts, les penchans, les talens, ou les dispositions morales et intellectuelles des hommes et des animaux, par la configuration de leur cerveau et de leur tête* [On the functions of the brain and of each of its parts: With observations on the possibility of determining the instincts, propensities, and talents, or the moral and intellectual dispositions of men and animals, by the configuration of the brain and head]. Paris: Ballière.

Gallagher, A. M., Frith, U., & Snowling, M. J. (2000). Precursors of literacy delay among children at genetic risk of dyslexia. *Journal of Child Psychology and Psychiatry, 41,* 203–213.

Gallagher, A. M., Laxon, V., Armstrong, E., & Frith, U. (1996). Phonological difficulties in high-functioning dyslexics. *Reading and Writing, 8,* 499–509.

Gathercole, S. E., & Baddeley, A. D. (1990). Phonological memory deficits in language disordered children: Is there a causal connection? *Journal of Memory and Language, 29,* 336–360.

Gathercole, S. E., & Baddeley, A. D. (1993). Phonological working memory: A critical building block for reading development and vocabulary acquisition? *European Journal of Psychology of Education, 8,* 259–272.

Gauger, L. M., Lombardino, L. J., & Leonard, C. M. (1997). Brain morphology in children with specific language impairment. *Journal of Speech, Language, and Hearing Research, 40,* 1272–1284.

Gayán, J., Smith, S. D., Cherny, S. S., Cardon, L. R., Fulker, D. W., Brower, A. M., et al. (1999). Quantitative-trait locus for specific language and reading deficits on chromosome 6p. *American Journal of Human Genetics, 64,* 157–164.

Georgiewa, P., Rzanny, R., Gaser, C., Gerhard, U. J., Vieweg, U., Freesmeyer, D., et al. (2002). Phonological processing in dyslexic children: A study combining functional imaging and event related potentials. *Neuroscience Letters, 318,* 5–8.

Georgiewa, P., Rzanny, R., Hopf, J. M., Knab, R., Glauche, V., Kaiser, W. A., et al. (1999). fMRI during word processing in dyslexic and normal reading children. *Neuroreport, 10,* 3459–3465.

Geschwind, N. (1962). The anatomy of acquired disorders of reading. In J. Money (Ed.), *Reading disability, progress and research needs in dyslexia* (pp. 115–129). Baltimore: Johns Hopkins University Press.

Geschwind, N., & Behan, P. (1982). Left handedness: Association with immune disease, migraine, and developmental learning disorder. *Proceedings of the National Academy of Sciences, USA, 79,* 5097–5100.

Geschwind, N., & Levitsky, W. (1968). Human brain: Left-right asymmetries in temporal speech region. *Science, 161,* 186–187.

Gilger, J. W., Hanebuth, E., Smith, S. D., & Pennington, B. F. (1996). Differential risk for developmental reading disorders in the offspring of compensated versus noncompensated parents. *Reading and Writing, 8,* 407–417.

Gilger, J. W., Pennington, B. F., & DeFries, J. C. (1991). Risk for reading disability as a function of parental history in three family studies. *Reading and Writing, 3,* 205–217.

Gilger, J. W., Pennington, B. F., Harbeck, R. J., DeFries, J. C., Kotzin, B., Green, P., et al. (1998). A twin and family study of the association between immune system dysfunction and dyslexia using blood serum immunoassay and survey data. *Brain and Cognition, 36,* 310–333.

Gillingham, A., & Stillman, B. W. (1936). *Remedial work for reading, spelling, and penmanship* (Rev., enlarged ed.). Long Island City, NY: Sackett & Wilhelms.

Gopnik, M. (1994). The family. *McGill Working Papers in Linguistics, 10,* 1–4.

Gopnik, M., & Crago, M. B. (1991). Familial aggregation of a developmental language disorder. *Cognition, 39,* 1–50.

Goswami, U. (2000). Phonological representations, reading development and dyslexia: Towards a cross-linguistic theoretical framework. *Dyslexia, 6,* 133–151.

Goswami, U., Thomson, J., Richardson, U., Stainthorp, R., Hughes, D., Rosen, S., et al. (2002). Amplitude envelope onsets and developmental dyslexia: A new hypothesis. *Proceedings of the National Academy of Sciences, USA, 99,* 10911–10916.

Grigorenko, E. L. (2001). Developmental dyslexia: An update on genes, brains, and environments. *Journal of Child Psychology and Psychiatry, 42,* 91–125.

Grigorenko, E. L., Wood, F. B., Meyer, M. S., Hart, L. A., Speed, W. C., Shuster, A., et al. (1997). Susceptibility loci for distinct components of developmental dyslexia on chromosomes 6 and 15. *American Journal of Human Genetics, 60,* 27–39.

Grissemann, H. (1972). *Die Legasthenie als Deutungsschwäche* (2nd ed.). Bern, Switzerland: Huber.

Gross-Glenn, K., Skottun, B. C., Glenn, W., Kushch, A., Lingua, R., Dunbar, M., et al. (1995). Contrast sensitivity in dyslexia. *Visual Neuroscience, 12,* 153–163.

Gustafson, S., & Samuelsson, S. (1999). Intelligence and dyslexia: Implications for diagnosis and intervention. *Scandinavian Journal of Psychology, 40,* 127–134.

Guttorm, T. K., Leppänen, P. H., Richardson, U., & Lyytinen, H. (2001). Event-related potentials and consonant differentiation in newborns with familial risk for dyslexia. *Journal of Learning Disabilities, 34,* 534–544.

Guttorm, T. K., Leppänen, P. H., Tolvanen, A., & Lyytinen, H. (2003). Event-related potentials in newborns with and without familial risk for dyslexia: Principal component analysis reveals differences between the groups. *Journal of Neural Transmission, 110,* 1059–1074.

Gutzmann, H. (1896). Über Hemmungen der Sprachentwicklung. *Verhandlungen der Gesellschaft für Kinderheilkunde, 12,* 186–195.

Habib, M. (2003). Rewiring the dyslexic brain. *Trends in Cognitive Sciences, 7,* 330–333.

Habib, M., Espesser, R., Rey, V., Giraud, K., Bruas, P., & Gres, C. (1999). Training dyslexics with acoustically modified speech: Evidence of improved phonological performance. *Brain and Cognition, 40,* 143–146.

Hall, J. W., Wilson, K. P., Humphreys, M. S., Tinzmann, M. B., & Bowyer, P. M. (1983). Phonemic-similarity effects in good vs. poor readers. *Memory and Cognition, 11,* 520–527.

Hallahan, D. P., & Mercer, C. D. (2002). *Learning disabilities: Historical perspectives.* National Research Center on Learning Disabilities. Available from http://www.nrcld.org/html/info.html.

Hallgren, B. (1950). Specific dyslexia ("congenital word-blindness"): A clinical and genetic study. *Acta Psychiatrica et Neurologica* (Suppl. 65), 1–287.

Hari, R., & Kiesilä, P. (1996). Deficit of temporal auditory processing in dyslexic adults. *Neuroscience Letters, 205,* 138–140.

Hautus, M. J., Setchell, G. J., Waldie, K. E., & Kirk, I. J. (2003). Age-related improvements in auditory temporal resolution in reading-impaired children. *Dyslexia, 9,* 37–45.

Hayduk, S., Bruck, M., & Cavanagh, P. (1996). Low-level visual processing skills of adults and children with dyslexia. *Cognitive Neuropsychology, 13,* 975–1015.

Heath, S. M., Hogben, J. H., & Clark, C. D. (1999). Auditory temporal processing in disabled readers with and without oral language delay. *Journal of Child Psychology and Psychiatry, 40,* 637–647.

Heiervang, E., Hugdahl, K., Steinmetz, H., Smievoll, A. I., Stevenson, J., Lund, A., et al. (2000). Planum temporale, planum parietale and dichotic listening in dyslexia. *Neuropsychologia, 38,* 1704–1713.

Heim, S., Eulitz, C., & Elbert, T. (2002). Psychophysiological differentiation of language dysfunction in dyslexia. *Psychophysiology, 39*(Suppl. 1), 41.

Heim, S., Eulitz, C., & Elbert, T. (2003a). Altered hemispheric asymmetry of auditory N100m in adults with developmental dyslexia. *Neuroreport, 14,* 501–504.

Heim, S., Eulitz, C., & Elbert, T. (2003b). Altered hemispheric asymmetry of auditory P100m in dyslexia. *European Journal of Neuroscience, 17,* 1715–1722.

Heim, S., Eulitz, C., Keil, A., Rockstroh, B., & Elbert, T. (2003). Interventionseffekte auf phonologische Verarbeitung und kortikale Organisation bei Kindern mit spezifischer Sprachbeeinträchtigung. In G. Schiepek (Ed.), *Neurobiologie der Psychotherapie* (pp. 273–292). Stuttgart, Germany: Schattauer.

Heim, S., Freeman, R. B., Jr, Eulitz, C., & Elbert, T. (2001). Auditory temporal processing deficit in dyslexia is associated with enhanced sensitivity in the visual modality. *Neuroreport, 12,* 507–510.

Heim, S., & Keil, A. (2004). Large-scale neural correlates of developmental dyslexia. *European Child and Adolescent Psychiatry, 13,* 125–140.

Heim, S., Keil, A., & Ruf, M. (2005). *Cross-modal temporal dysfunction in children with dyslexia: Is age a mediating factor?* Manuscript submitted for publication.

Helenius, P., Salmelin, R., Richardson, U., Leinonen, S., & Lyytinen, H. (2002). Abnormal auditory cortical activation in dyslexia 100 msec after speech onset. *Journal of Cognitive Neuroscience, 14,* 603–617.

Helenius, P., Salmelin, R., Service, E., & Connolly, J. F. (1999). Semantic cortical activation in dyslexic readers. *Journal of Cognitive Neuroscience, 11,* 535–550.

Helenius, P., Salmelin, R., Service, E., Connolly, J. F., Leinonen, S., & Lyytinen, H. (2002). Cortical activation during spoken-word segmentation in nonreading-impaired and dyslexic adults. *Journal of Neuroscience, 22,* 2936–2944.

Helenius, P., Tarkiainen, A., Cornelissen, P., Hansen, P. C., & Salmelin, R. (1999). Dissociation of normal feature analysis and deficient processing of letter-strings in dyslexic adults. *Cerebral Cortex, 9,* 476–483.

Helenius, P., Uutela, K., & Hari, R. (1999). Auditory stream segregation in dyslexic adults. *Brain, 122,* 907–913.

Hellige, J. (1993). *Hemispheric asymmetry: What's right and what's left?* Cambridge, MA: Harvard University Press.

Helmuth, L. (2001). Neuroscience: Dyslexia—Same brains, different languages. *Science, 291,* 2064–2065.

Herbert, M. R., Ziegler, D. A., Deutsch, C. K., O'Brien, L. M., Kennedy, D. N., Filipek, P. A., et al. (2005). Brain asymmetries in Autism and developmental language disorder: A nested whole-brain analysis. *Brain, 128,* 213–226.

Herbert, M. R., Ziegler, D. A., Makris, N., Filipek, P. A., Kemper, T. L., Normandin, J. J., et al. (2004). Localization of white matter volume increase in Autism and developmental language disorder. *Annals of Neurology, 55,* 530–540.

Herman, A. E., Galaburda, A. M., Fitch, R. H., Carter, A. R., & Rosen, G. D. (1997). Cerebral microgyria, thalamic cell size and auditory temporal processing in male and female rats. *Cerebral Cortex, 7,* 453–464.

Hinshelwood, J. (1917). *Congenital word-blindness.* London: Lewis.

Hofmann, B. (1998). *Lese-Rechtschreibschwäche—Legasthenie.* München, Germany: Oldenbourg.

Holligan, C., & Johnston, R. S. (1988). The use of phonological information by good and poor readers in memory and reading tasks. *Memory and Cognition, 16,* 522–532.

Hugdahl, K., Synnevag, B., & Satz, P. (1990). Immune and autoimmune diseases in dyslexic children. *Neuropsychologia, 28,* 673–679. (Erratum published in 1991, *Neuropsychologia, 29,* 211)

Humphreys, P., Kaufmann, W. E., & Galaburda, A. M. (1990). Developmental dyslexia in women: Neuropathological findings in three patients. *Annals of Neurology, 28,* 727–738.

Humphreys, P., Rosen, G. D., Press, D. M., Sherman, G. F., & Galaburda, A. M. (1991). Freezing lesions of the developing rat brain: A model for cerebrocortical microgyria. *Journal of Neuropathology and Experimental Neurology, 50,* 145–160.

Hurst, J. A., Baraitser, M., Auger, E., Graham, F., & Norell, S. (1990). An extended family with a dominantly inherited speech disorder. *Developmental Medicine and Child Neurology, 32,* 352–355.

Hynd, G. W., Hall, J., Novey, E. S., Eliopulos, D., Black, K., Gonzalez, J. J., et al. (1995). Dyslexia and corpus callosum morphology. *Archives of Neurology, 52,* 32–38.

Hynd, G. W., Semrud-Clikeman, M., Lorys, A. R., Novey, E. S., & Eliopulos, D. (1990). Brain morphology in developmental dyslexia and attention deficit disorder/hyperactivity. *Archives of Neurology, 47,* 919–926.

Ingram, T. T. (1959). Specific developmental disorders of speech in childhood. *Brain, 82,* 450–467.

Irausquin, R. S., & de Gelder, B. (1997). Serial recall of poor readers in two presentation modalities: Combined effects of phonological similarity and word length. *Journal of Experimental Child Psychology, 65,* 342–369.

Jenner, A. R., Rosen, G. D., & Galaburda, A. M. (1999). Neuronal asymmetries in primary visual cortex of dyslexic and nondyslexic brains. *Annals of Neurology, 46,* 189–196.

Jernigan, T. L., Hesselink, J. R., Sowell, E., & Tallal, P. A. (1991). Cerebral structure on magnetic resonance imaging in language- and learning-impaired children. *Archives of Neurology, 48,* 539–545.

Joanisse, M. F., Manis, F. R., Keating, P., & Seidenberg, M. S. (2000). Language deficits in dyslexic children: Speech perception, phonology, and morphology. *Journal of Experimental Child Psychology, 77,* 30–60.

Joffe, V. L. (1998). Rhyming and related skills in children with specific language impairment. *Cahiers de Psychologie Cognitive/Current Psychology of Cognition, 17,* 479–512.

Johannes, S., Kussmaul, C. L., Münte, T. F., & Mangun, G. R. (1996). Developmental dyslexia: Passive visual stimulation provides no evidence for a magnocellular processing defect. *Neuropsychologia, 34,* 1123–1127.

Johnson, M. H. (1997). *Developmental cognitive neuroscience: An introduction.* Oxford: Blackwell.

Johnston, R. B., Stark, R. E., Mellits, E. D., & Tallal, P. (1981). Neurological status of language-impaired and normal children. *Annals of Neurology, 10,* 159–163.

Johnston, R. S., Rugg, M. D., & Scott, T. (1987). Phonological similarity effects, memory span and developmental reading disorders: The nature of the relationship. *British Journal of Psychology, 78,* 205–211.

Jusczyk, P. W. (1993). From general to language-specific capacities: The WRAPSA model of how speech perception develops. *Journal of Phonetics, 21,* 3–28.

Kamhi, A. G., & Catts, H. W. (1986). Toward an understanding of developmental language and reading disorders. *Journal of Speech and Hearing Disorders, 51,* 337–347.

Kamhi, A. G., Catts, H. W., Mauer, D., Apel, K., & Gentry, B. F. (1988). Phonological and spatial processing abilities in language- and reading-impaired children. *Journal of Speech and Hearing Disorders, 53,* 316–327.

Karmiloff-Smith, A. (1998). Development itself is the key to understanding developmental disorders. *Trends in Cognitive Sciences, 2,* 389–398.

Katz, W. F., Curtiss, S., & Tallal, P. (1992). Rapid automatized naming and gesture by normal and language-impaired children. *Brain and Language, 43,* 623–641.

Kirch, D. G., & Weinberger, D. R. (1986). Anatomical neuropathology in Schizophrenia: Post-mortem findings. In H. A. Nasrallah (Ed.), *Handbook of Schizophrenia* (pp. 325–348). Amsterdam: Elsevier.

Kjelgaard, M. M., & Tager-Flusberg, H. (2001). An investigation of language impairment in Autism: Implications for genetic subgroups. *Language and Cognitive Processes in Developmental Disorders, 16,* 287–308.

Klingberg, T., Hedehus, M., Temple, E., Salz, T., Gabrieli, J. D., Moseley, M. E., et al. (2000). Microstructure of temporo-parietal white matter as a basis for reading ability: Evidence from diffusion tensor magnetic resonance imaging. *Neuron, 25,* 493–500.

Korpilahti, P., & Lang, H. A. (1994). Auditory ERP components and mismatch negativity in dysphasic children. *Electroencephalography and Clinical Neurophysiology, 91,* 256–264.

Kraus, N., McGee, T. J., Carrell, T. D., Zecker, S. G., Nicol, T. G., & Koch, D. B. (1996). Auditory neurophysiologic responses and discrimination deficits in children with learning problems. *Science, 273,* 971–973.

Kubová, Z., Kuba, M., Peregrin, J., & Nováková, V. (1995). Visual evoked potential evidence for magnocellular system deficit in dyslexia. *Physiological Research, 44,* 87–89.

Kujala, T., Karma, K., Cluhleponiene, R., Belitz, S., Turkkila, P., Tervaniemi, M., et al. (2001). Plastic neural changes and reading improvement caused by audiovisual training in reading-impaired children. *Proceedings of the National Academy of Sciences, USA, 98,* 10509–10514.

Kujala, T., Myllyviita, K., Tervaniemi, M., Alho, K., Kallio, J., & Näätänen, R. (2000). Basic auditory dysfunction in dyslexia as demonstrated by brain activity measurements. *Psychophysiology, 37,* 262–266.

LaBuda, M. C., DeFries, J. C., & Fulker, D. W. (1986). Multiple regression analysis of twin data obtained from selected samples. *Genetic Epidemiology, 3,* 425–433.

Lahey, M., & Edwards, J. (1995). Specific language impairment: Preliminary investigation of factors associated with family history and with patterns of language performance. *Journal of Speech and Hearing Research, 38,* 643–657.

Landau, W. M., Goldstein, R., & Kleffner, F. R. (1960). Congenital aphasia: A clinicopathologic study. *Neurology, 10,* 915–921.

Larsen, J. P., Høien, T., Lundberg, I., & Ødegaard, H. (1990). MRI evaluation of the size and symmetry of the planum temporale in adolescents with developmental dyslexia. *Brain and Language, 39,* 289–301.

Larsen, J. P., Høien, T., & Ødegaard, H. (1992). Magnetic resonance imaging of the corpus callosum in developmental dyslexia. *Cognitive Neuropsychology, 9,* 123–134.

Lefly, D. L., & Pennington, B. F. (1996). Longitudinal study of children at high family risk for dyslexia: The first two years. In M. L. Rice (Ed.), *Toward a genetics of language* (pp. 49–75). Hillsdale, NJ: Erlbaum.

Lehmkuhle, S., Garzia, R. P., Turner, L., Hash, T., & Baro, J. A. (1993). A defective visual pathway in children with reading disability. *New England Journal of Medicine, 328,* 989–996.

Leitão, S., Hogben, J., & Fletcher, J. (1997). Phonological processing skills in speech and language impaired children. *European Journal of Disorders of Communication, 32,* 91–111.

Leonard, C. M., Eckert, M. A., Lombardino, L. J., Eden, G., Berninger, V., & Richards, T. (2003). *MRI measurements of Broca's area predict naming speed.* Proceedings of the Bangor Dyslexia Conference. Available from http://www.dyslexia.bangor.ac.uk/conferences.html.

Leonard, C. M., Voeller, K. K., Lombardino, L. J., Morris, M. K., Hynd, G. W., Alexander, A. W., et al. (1993). Anomalous cerebral structure in dyslexia revealed with magnetic resonance imaging. *Archives of Neurology, 50,* 461–469.

Leonard, L. B. (1972). What is deviant language? *Journal of Speech and Hearing Disorders, 37,* 427–446.

Leonard, L. B. (1979). Language impairment in children. *Merrill-Palmer Quarterly, 25,* 205–232.

Leonard, L. B. (1998). *Children with specific language impairment.* Cambridge, MA: MIT Press.

Leong, C. K., Nitta, N., & Yamada, J. (2003). Phonological analysis abilities of Chinese and Japanese children learning to read. In R. M. Joshi, C. K. Leong, & B. L. Kaczmarek (Eds.), *Literacy acquisition: The role of phonology, morphology and orthography* (pp. 25–48). Amsterdam: IOS Press.

Leong, C. K., & Tan, L. H. (2002). Phonological processing in learning to read Chinese: In search of a framework. In E. Hjelmquist & C. von Euler (Eds.), *Dyslexia and literacy: A tribute to Ingvar Lundberg* (pp. 126–150). London: Whurr.

Leppänen, P. H., & Lyytinen, H. (1997). Auditory event-related potentials in the study of developmental language-related disorders. *Audiology and Neuro-Otology, 2,* 308–340.

Leppänen, P. H., Pihko, E., Eklund, K. M., & Lyytinen, H. (1999). Cortical responses of infants with and without a genetic risk for dyslexia: II. Group effects. *Neuroreport, 10,* 969–973.

Leppänen, P. H., Richardson, U., Pihko, E., Eklund, K. M., Guttorm, T. K., Aro, M., et al. (2002). Brain responses to changes in speech sound durations differ between infants with and without familial risk for dyslexia. *Developmental Neuropsychology, 22,* 407–422.

Lewis, B. A., & Thompson, L. A. (1992). A study of developmental speech and language disorders in twins. *Journal of Speech and Hearing Research, 35,* 1086–1094.

Lewis, C., Hitch, G. J., & Walker, P. (1994). The prevalence of specific arithmetic difficulties and specific reading difficulties in 9- to 10-year-old boys and girls. *Journal of Child Psychology and Psychiatry, 35,* 283–292.

Liberman, A. M., Cooper, F. S., Shankweiler, D. P., & Studdert-Kennedy, M. (1967). Perception of the speech code. *Psychological Review, 74,* 431–461.

Liberman, I. Y., Shankweiler, D., Orlando, C., Harris, K. S., & Berti, F. B. (1971). Letter confusions and reversals of sequence in the beginning reader: Implications for Orton's theory of developmental dyslexia. *Cortex, 7,* 127–142.

Liebmann, A. (1898). *Vorlesungen über Sprachstörungen, 3, Hörstummheit.* Berlin, Germany: Coblentz.

Livingstone, M. S., Rosen, G. D., Drislane, F. W., & Galaburda, A. M. (1991). Physiological and anatomical evidence for a magnocellular defect in developmental dyslexia. *Proceedings of the National Acad-*

emy of Sciences, USA, 88, 7943–7947. (Erratum published in 1993, Proceedings of the National Academy of Sciences, USA, 90, 2556)

Lovegrove, W., Martin, F., Bowling, A., Blackwood, M., Badcock, D., & Paxton, S. (1982). Contrast sensitivity functions and specific reading disability. Neuropsychologia, 20, 309–315.

Lovegrove, W., Martin, F., & Slaghuis, W. (1986). A theoretical and experimental case for a visual deficit in specific reading disability. Cognitive Neuropsychology, 3, 225–267.

Lovett, M. W. (1987). A developmental approach to reading disability: Accuracy and speed criteria of normal and deficient reading skill. Child Development, 58, 234–260.

Lovett, M. W. (1992). Developmental dyslexia. In S. J. Segalowitz & I. Rapin (Eds.), Handbook of neuropsychology (Vol. 7, pp. 163–185). New York: Elsevier.

Luchsinger, R. (1970). Inheritance of speech deficits. Folia Phoniatrica, 22, 216–230.

Lundberg, I., Olofsson, A., & Wall, S. (1980). Reading and spelling skills in the first school years predicted from phonemic awareness skills in kindergarten. Scandinavian Journal of Psychology, 21, 159–173.

Lyytinen, H., Ahonen, T., Eklund, K., Guttorm, T., Kulju, P., Laakso, M. L., et al. (2004). Early development of children at familial risk for dyslexia: Follow-up from birth to school age. Dyslexia, 10, 146–178.

Lyytinen, H., Ahonen, T., Eklund, K., Guttorm, T. K., Laakso, M. L., Leinonen, S., et al. (2001). Developmental pathways of children with and without familial risk for dyslexia during the first years of life. Developmental Neuropsychology, 20, 535–554.

Mann, V. A., Liberman, I. Y., & Shankweiler, D. (1980). Children's memory for sentences and word strings in relation to reading ability. Memory and Cognition, 8, 329–335.

Marlow, A. J., Fisher, S. E., Francks, C., MacPhie, I. L., Cherny, S. S., Richardson, A. J., et al. (2003). Use of multivariate linkage analysis for dissection of a complex cognitive trait. American Journal of Human Genetics, 72, 561–570.

Marshall, C. M., Snowling, M. J., & Bailey, P. J. (2001). Rapid auditory processing and phonological ability in normal readers and readers with dyslexia. Journal of Speech, Language, and Hearing Research, 44, 925–940.

Martin, F., & Lovegrove, W. (1984). The effects of field size and luminance on contrast sensitivity differences between specifically reading disabled and normal children. Neuropsychologia, 22, 73–77.

Martin, F., & Lovegrove, W. (1987). Flicker contrast sensitivity in normal and specifically disabled readers. Perception, 16, 215–221.

Martin, F., & Lovegrove, W. J. (1988). Uniform-field flicker masking in control and specifically-disabled readers. Perception, 17, 203–214.

Marx, H., Jansen, H., Mannhaupt, G., & Skowronek, H. (1993). Prediction of difficulties in reading and spelling on the basis of the Bielefeld Screening. In H. Grimm & H. Skowronek (Eds.), Language acquisition problems and reading disorders: Aspects of diagnosis and intervention (pp. 219–241). Berlin, Germany: de Gruyter.

Maughan, B. (1995). Annotation: Long-term outcomes of developmental reading problems. Journal of Child Psychology and Psychiatry, 36, 357–371.

Maunsell, J. H., & Van Essen, D. C. (1983). Functional properties of neurons in middle temporal visual area of the macaque monkey: I. Selectivity for stimulus direction, speed, and orientation. Journal of Neurophysiology, 49, 1127–1147.

McAnally, K. I., & Stein, J. F. (1996). Auditory temporal coding in dyslexia. Proceedings of the Royal Society of London. Series B, Biological Sciences, 263, 961–965.

McArthur, G. M., & Bishop, D. V. (2001). Auditory perceptual processing in people with reading and oral language impairments: Current issues and recommendations. Dyslexia, 7, 150–170.

McCall, E. (1911). Two cases of congenital aphasia in children. British Medical Journal, 2628, 1105.

McCrory, E., Frith, U., Brunswick, N., & Price, C. (2000). Abnormal functional activation during a simple word repetition task: A PET study of adult dyslexics. Journal of Cognitive Neuroscience, 12, 753–762.

McCrory, E. J., Mechelli, A., Frith, U., & Price, C. J. (2005). More than words: A common neural basis for reading and naming deficits in developmental dyslexia? Brain, 128, 261–267.

Meaburn, E., Dale, P. S., Craig, I. W., & Plomin, R. (2002). Language-impaired children: No sign of the FOXP2 mutation. Neuroreport, 13, 1075–1077.

Menyuk, P. (1964). Comparison of grammar of children with functionally deviant and normal speech. Journal of Speech and Hearing Research, 7, 109–121.

Merigan, W. H., & Maunsell, J. H. (1993). How parallel are the primate visual pathways? Annual Review of Neuroscience, 16, 369–402.

Merzenich, M. M., Jenkins, W. M., Johnston, P., Schreiner, C., Miller, S. L., & Tallal, P. (1996). Temporal processing deficits of language-learning impaired children ameliorated by training. Science, 271, 77–81.

Metsala, J. L., & Walley, A. C. (1998). Spoken vocabulary growth and the segmental restructuring of lexical representations: Precursors to phonemic awareness and early reading ability. In J. L. Metsala & L. C. Ehri (Eds.), Word recognition in beginning literacy (pp. 89–120). Mahwah, NJ: Erlbaum.

Miles, T. R. (2004). Some problems in determining the prevalence of dyslexia. Electronic Journal of Research in Educational Psychology, 2, 5–12.

Milner, A. D., & Goodale, M. A. (1995). The visual brain in action. Oxford: Oxford University Press.

Molfese, D. L., & Molfese, V. J. (1985). Electrophysiological indices of auditory discrimination in newborn infants: The bases for predicting later language development? Infant Behavior and Development, 8, 197–211.

Molfese, D. L., & Molfese, V. J. (1997). Discrimination of language skills at five years of age using event-related potentials recorded at birth. Developmental Neuropsychology, 13, 135–156.

Molfese, D. L., Molfese, V. J., Key, S., Modglin, A., Kelley, S., & Terrell, S. (2002). Reading and cognitive abilities: Longitudinal studies of brain and behavior changes in young children. Annals of Dyslexia, 52, 99–119.

Montgomery, J. W. (1995). Examination of phonological working memory in specifically language-impaired children. Applied Psycholinguistics, 16, 355–378.

Morgan, W. P. (1896). A case of congenital word blindness. British Medical Journal, 1871, 1378.

Morley, M., Court, D., Miller, H., & Garside, R. F. (1955). Delayed speech and developmental aphasia. British Medical Journal, 4937, 463–467.

Näätänen, R. (2001). The perception of speech sounds by the human brain as reflected by the mismatch negativity (MMN) and its magnetic equivalent (MMNm). Psychophysiology, 38, 1–21.

Nagarajan, S., Mahncke, H., Salz, T., Tallal, P., Roberts, T., & Merzenich, M. M. (1999). Cortical auditory signal processing in poor readers. Proceedings of the National Academy of Sciences, USA, 96, 6483–6488.

Naylor, C. E., Felton, R. H., & Wood, F. B. (1990). Adult outcome in developmental dyslexia. In G. Th. Pavlidis (Ed.), Perspectives on dyslexia (Vol. 2, pp. 215–229). Chichester, England: Wiley.

Neils, J., & Aram, D. M. (1986). Family history of children with developmental language disorders. Perceptual and Motor Skills, 63, 655–658.

Nelson, C. A. (1999). Neural plasticity and human development. Current Directions in Psychological Science, 8, 42–45.

Nelson, C. A., & Monk, C. S. (2001). The use of event-related potentials in the study of cognitive development. In C. A. Nelson & M. Luciana (Eds.), *Handbook of developmental cognitive neuroscience* (pp. 125–136). Cambridge, MA: MIT Press.

Newbury, D. F., Bonora, E., Lamb, J. A., Fisher, S. E., Lai, C. S., Baird, G., et al. (2002). FOXP2 is not a major susceptibility gene for Autism or specific language impairment. *American Journal of Human Genetics, 70*, 1318–1327.

Newsome, W. T., & Paré, E. B. (1988). A selective impairment of motion perception following lesions of the middle temporal visual area (MT). *Journal of Neuroscience, 8*, 2201–2211.

Nicolson, R. I., Fawcett, A. J., & Dean, P. (2001). Developmental dyslexia: The cerebellar deficit hypothesis. *Trends in Neurosciences, 24*, 508–511.

Njiokiktjien, C., deSonneville, L., & Vaal, J. (1994). Callosal size in children with learning disabilities. *Behavioural Brain Research, 64*, 213–218.

O'Brien, E. K., Zhang, X., Nishimura, C., Tomblin, J. B., & Murray, J. C. (2003). Association of specific language impairment (SLI) to the region of 7q31. *American Journal of Human Genetics, 72*, 1536–1543.

Olson, R., & Datta, H. (2002). Visual-temporal processing in reading-disabled and normal twins. *Reading and Writing, 15*, 127–149.

Olson, R. K., Forsberg, H., & Wise, B. (1994). Genes, environment, and the development of orthographic skills. In V. W. Berninger (Ed.), *The varieties of orthographic knowledge 1: Theoretical and developmental issues* (pp. 27–71). Dordrecht, The Netherlands: Kluwer Press.

Olson, R. K., Wise, B., Conners, F. A., & Rack, J. P. (1990). Organization, heritability, and remediation of component word recognition and language skills in disabled readers. In T. H. Carr & B. A. Levy (Eds.), *Reading and its development: Component skills approaches* (pp. 261–322). San Diego: Academic Press.

Olson, R. K., Wise, B., Conners, F., Rack, J., & Fulker, D. (1989). Specific deficits in component reading and language skills: Genetic and environmental influences. *Journal of Learning Disabilities, 22*, 339–348.

Orton, S. T. (1925). "Word-blindness" in school children. *Archives of Neurology and Psychiatry, 14*, 581–615.

Orton, S. T. (1937). *Reading, writing, and speech problems in children.* New York: Norton.

Paulesu, E., Frith, U., Snowling, M., Gallagher, A., Morton, J., Frackowiak, R. S., et al. (1996). Is developmental dyslexia a disconnection syndrome? Evidence from PET scanning. *Brain, 119*, 143–157.

Peiffer, A. M., Friedman, J. T., Rosen, G. D., & Fitch, R. H. (2004). Impaired gap detection in juvenile microgyric rats. *Brain Research/Developmental Brain Research, 152*, 93–98.

Peiffer, A. M., Rosen, G. D., & Fitch, R. H. (2002). Rapid auditory processing and MGN morphology in microgyric rats reared in varied acoustic environments. *Brain Research/Developmental Brain Research, 138*, 187–193.

Pennington, B. F. (1995). Genetics of learning disabilities. *Journal of Child Neurology, 10*(Suppl. 1), 69–77.

Pennington, B. F. (2001). Genetic methods. In C. A. Nelson & M. Luciana (Eds.), *Handbook of developmental cognitive neuroscience* (pp. 149–158). Cambridge, MA: MIT Press.

Pennington, B. F., & Lefly, D. L. (2001). Early reading development in children at family risk for dyslexia. *Child Development, 72*, 816–833.

Pennington, B. F., Van Orden, G. C., Smith, S. D., Green, P. A., & Haith, M. M. (1990). Phonological processing skills and deficits in adult dyslexics. *Child Development, 61*, 1753–1778.

Plante, E. (1991). MRI findings in the parents and siblings of specifically language-impaired boys. *Brain and Language, 41*, 67–80.

Plante, E., Shenkman, K., & Clark, M. M. (1996). Classification of adults for family studies of developmental language disorders. *Journal of Speech and Hearing Research, 39*, 661–667.

Plante, E., Swisher, L., Vance, R., & Rapcsak, S. (1991). MRI findings in boys with specific language impairment. *Brain and Language, 41*, 52–66.

Poeppel, D., Guillemin, A., Thompson, J., Fritz, J., Bavelier, D., & Braun, A. R. (2004). Auditory lexical decision, categorical perception, and FM direction discrimination differentially engage left and right auditory cortex. *Neuropsychologia, 42*, 183–200.

Preis, S., Jäncke L., Schittler, P., Huang, Y., & Steinmetz, H. (1998). Normal intrasylvian anatomical asymmetry in children with developmental language disorder. *Neuropsychologia, 36*, 849–855.

Preis, S., Steinmetz, H., Knorr, U., & Jäncke, L. (2000). Corpus callosum size in children with developmental language disorder. *Brain Research/Cognitive Brain Research, 10*, 37–44.

Protopapas, A., Ahissar, M., & Merzenich, M. M. (1997). Auditory processing is related to reading ability. *Journal of the Acoustical Society of America, 102*, 3188.

Rack, J. P. (1985). Orthographic and phonetic coding in developmental dyslexia. *British Journal of Psychology, 76*, 325–340.

Rack, J. P. (1994). Dyslexia: The phonological deficit hypothesis. In A. Fawcett & R. Nicolson (Eds.), *Dyslexia in children: Multidisciplinary perspectives* (pp. 5–37). New York: Harvester Wheatsheaf.

Rack, J. P., Snowling, M. J., & Olson, R. K. (1992). The nonword reading deficit in developmental dyslexia: A review. *Reading Research Quarterly, 27*, 28–53.

Ramus, F., Rosen, S., Dakin, S. C., Day, B. L., Castellote, J. M., White, S., et al. (2003). Theories of developmental dyslexia: Insights from a multiple case study of dyslexic adults. *Brain, 126*, 841–865.

Rapin, I. C. (1996a). Historical data. In I. C. Rapin & L. Wing (Eds.), *Preschool children with inadequate communication: Developmental language disorder, Autism, low IQ* (pp. 58–97). London: Mac Keith Press.

Rapin, I. C. (1996b). Practitioner review: Developmental language disorders: A clinical update. *Journal of Child Psychology and Psychiatry, 37*, 643–655.

Rapin, I. C., Allen, D. A., & Dunn, M. A. (1992). Developmental language disorders. In S. J. Segalowitz & I. C. Rapin (Eds.), *Handbook of neuropsychology* (Vol. 7, pp. 111–137). New York: Elsevier.

Reed, M. A. (1989). Speech perception and the discrimination of brief auditory cues in reading disabled children. *Journal of Experimental Child Psychology, 48*, 270–292.

Rice, M. L., Haney, K. R., & Wexler, K. (1998). Family histories of children with SLI who show extended optional infinitives. *Journal of Speech, Language, and Hearing Research, 41*, 419–432.

Richardson, U. (1998). *Familial dyslexia and sound duration in the quantity distinctions of Finnish infants and adults.* Unpublished doctoral dissertation, Studia Philologica Jyväskyläensia, University of Jyväskylä, Finland.

Richardson, U., Leppänen, P. H., Leiwo, M., & Lyytinen, H. (2003). Speech perception of infants with high familial risk for dyslexia differ at the age of 6 months. *Developmental Neuropsychology, 23*, 385–397.

Rissman, M., Curtiss, S., & Tallal, P. (1990). School placement outcomes of young language impaired children. *Journal of Speech-Language Pathology and Audiology, 14*, 49–58.

Roberts, J. E., Burchinal, M. R., & Zeisel, S. A. (2002). Otitis media in early childhood in relation to children's school-age language and academic skills. *Pediatrics, 110*, 696–706.

Robichon, F., & Habib, M. (1998). Abnormal callosal morphology in male adult dyslexics: Relationships to handedness and phonological abilities. *Brain and Language, 62*, 127–146.

Robichon, F., Levrier, O., Farnarier, P., & Habib, M. (2000). Developmental dyslexia: Atypical cortical asymmetries and functional significance. *European Journal of Neurology, 7*, 35–46.

Robinson, R. J. (1987). The causes of language disorder: Introduction and overview. In J. A. Martin, P. Fletcher, P. Grunwell, & D. Hall (Eds.), *Proceedings of the First International Symposium on Specific Speech and Language Disorders in Children* (pp. 1–19). London: Association for All Speech Impaired Children.

Rockstroh, B., Cohen, R., Hauk, O., Dobel, C., Berg, P., Horvat, J., et al. (1999). Topography of the post-imperative negative variation in schizophrenic patients and controls obtained from high-resolution ERP maps. *Electroencephalography and Clinical Neurophysiology* (Suppl., 49), 210–214.

Rosen, G. D., Sherman, G. F., & Galaburda, A. M. (1989). Interhemispheric connections differ between symmetrical and asymmetrical brain regions. *Neuroscience, 33,* 525–533.

Rosen, G. D., Sherman, G. F., Richman, J. M., Stone, L. V., & Galaburda, A. M. (1992). Induction of molecular layer ectopias by puncture wounds in newborn rats and mice. *Brain Research/Developmental Brain Research, 67,* 285–291.

Ruff, S., Cardebat, D., Marie, N., & Démonet, J. F. (2002). Enhanced response of the left frontal cortex to slowed down speech in dyslexia: An fMRI study. *Neuroreport, 13,* 1285–1289.

Rumsey, J. M., Andreason, P., Zametkin, A. J., Aquino, T., King, A. C., Hamburger, S. D., et al. (1992). Failure to activate the left temporoparietal cortex in dyslexia: An oxygen 15 positron emission tomographic study. *Archives of Neurology, 49,* 527–534. (Erratum published in 1994, *Archives of Neurology, 51,* 243)

Rumsey, J. M., Casanova, M., Mannheim, G. B., Patronas, N., DeVaughn, N., Hamburger, S. D., et al. (1996). Corpus callosum morphology, as measured with MRI, in dyslexic men. *Biological Psychiatry, 39,* 769–775.

Rumsey, J. M., Donohue, B. C., Brady, D. R., Nace, K., Giedd, J. N., & Andreason, P. (1997). A magnetic resonance imaging study of planum temporale asymmetry in men with developmental dyslexia. *Archives of Neurology, 54,* 1481–1489.

Rumsey, J. M., Nace, K., Donohue, B., Wise, D., Maisog, J. M., & Andreason, P. (1997). A positron emission tomographic study of impaired word recognition and phonological processing in dyslexic men. *Archives of Neurology, 54,* 562–573.

Rutter, M., Caspi, A., Fergusson, D., Horwood, L. J., Goodman, R., Maughan, B., et al. (2004). Sex differences in developmental reading disability: New findings from 4 epidemiological studies. *Journal of the American Medical Association, 291,* 2007–2012.

Rutter, M., Tizard, J., Yule, W., Graham, P., & Whitmore, K. (1976). Research report: Isle of Wight Studies, 1964–1974. *Psychological Medicine, 6,* 313–332.

Rutter, M., & Yule, W. (1975). The concept of specific reading retardation. *Journal of Child Psychology and Psychiatry, 16,* 181–197.

Salmelin, R., Service, E., Kiesilä, P., Uutela, K., & Salonen, O. (1996). Impaired visual word processing in dyslexia revealed with magnetoencephalography. *Annals of Neurology, 40,* 157–162.

Scarborough, H. S. (1990). Very early language deficits in dyslexic children. *Child Development, 61,* 1728–1743.

Scarborough, H. S. (1991). Early syntactic development of dyslexic children. *Annals of Dyslexia, 41,* 207–220.

Scarborough, H. S. (1998). Early identification of children at risk for reading disabilities. In B. K. Shapiro, P. J. Accardo, & A. J. Capute (Eds.), *Specific reading disability: A view of the spectrum* (pp. 75–119). Timonium, MD: York Press.

Scheuerpflug, P., Plume, E., Vetter, V., Schulte-Körne, G., Deimel, W., Bartling, J., et al. (2004). Visual information processing in dyslexic children. *Clinical Neurophysiology, 115,* 90–96.

Schulte-Körne, G. (2001). Annotation: Genetics of reading and spelling disorder. *Journal of Child Psychology and Psychiatry, 42,* 985–997.

Schulte-Körne, G., Bartling, J., Deimel, W., & Remschmidt, H. (2004). Visual evoked potential elicited by coherently moving dots in dyslexic children. *Neuroscience Letters, 357,* 207–210.

Schulte-Körne, G., Deimel, W., Bartling, J., & Remschmidt, H. (1998). Auditory processing and dyslexia: Evidence for a specific speech processing deficit. *Neuroreport, 9,* 337–340.

Schulte-Körne, G., Deimel, W., Bartling, J., & Remschmidt, H. (2001). Speech perception deficit in dyslexic adults as measured by mismatch negativity (MMN). *International Journal of Psychophysiology, 40,* 77–87.

Schulte-Körne, G., Deimel, W., & Remschmidt, H. (2001). Zur Diagnostik der Lese-Rechtschreibstörung. *Zeitschrift für Kinder und Jugendpsychiatrie und Psychotherapie, 29,* 113–116.

Schulte-Körne, G., Grimm, T., Nöthen, M. M., Müller-Myhsok, B., Cichon, S., Vogt, I. R., et al. (1998). Evidence for linkage of spelling disability to chromosome 15. *American Journal of Human Genetics, 63,* 279–282.

Schultz, R. T., Cho, N. K., Staib, L. H., Kier, L. E., Fletcher, J. M., Shaywitz, S. E., et al. (1994). Brain morphology in normal and dyslexic children: The influence of sex and age. *Annals of Neurology, 35,* 732–742.

Semrud-Clikeman, M., Guy, K., Griffin, J. D., & Hynd, G. W. (2000). Rapid naming deficits in children and adolescents with reading disabilities and attention deficit hyperactivity disorder. *Brain and Language, 74,* 70–83.

Shankweiler, D., Liberman, I. Y., Mark, L. S., Fowler, C. A., & Fischer, F. W. (1979). The speech code and learning to read. *Journal of Experimental Psychology: Human Learning and Memory, 5,* 531–545.

Shapleske, J., Rossell, S. L., Woodruff, P. W., & David, A. S. (1999). The planum temporale: A systematic, quantitative review of its structural, functional and clinical significance. *Brain Research/Brain Research Reviews, 29,* 26–49.

Shapley, R. (1990). Visual sensitivity and parallel retinocortical channels. *Annual Review of Psychology, 41,* 635–658.

Shaywitz, B. A., Shaywitz, S. E., Pugh, K. R., Mencl, W. E., Fulbright, R. K., Skudlarski, P., et al. (2002). Disruption of posterior brain systems for reading in children with developmental dyslexia. *Biological Psychiatry, 52,* 101–110.

Shaywitz, S. E., & Shaywitz, B. A. (2001). The neurobiology of reading and dyslexia. *Focus on Basics: Connecting Research and Practice, 5,* A. Available from http://ncsall.gse.harvard.edu/fob.

Shaywitz, S. E., Shaywitz, B. A., Fletcher, J. M., & Escobar, M. D. (1990). Prevalence of reading disability in boys and girls: Results of the Connecticut Longitudinal Study. *Journal of the American Medical Association, 264,* 998–1002.

Shaywitz, S. E., Shaywitz, B. A., Fulbright, R. K., Skudlarski, P., Mencl, W. E., Constable, R. T., et al. (2003). Neural systems for compensation and persistence: Young adult outcome of childhood reading disability. *Biological Psychiatry, 54,* 25–33.

Shaywitz, S. E., Shaywitz, B. A., Pugh, K. R., Fulbright, R. K., Constable, R. T., Mencl, W. E., et al. (1998). Functional disruption in the organization of the brain for reading in dyslexia. *Proceedings of the National Academy of Sciences, USA, 95,* 2636–2641.

Simos, P. G., Breier, J. I., Fletcher, J. M., Bergman, E., & Papanicolaou, A. C. (2000). Cerebral mechanisms involved in word reading in dyslexic children: A magnetic source imaging approach. *Cerebral Cortex, 10,* 809–816.

Simos, P. G., Breier, J. I., Fletcher, J. M., Foorman, B. R., Bergman, E., Fishbeck, K., et al. (2000). Brain activation profiles in dyslexic children during non-word reading: A magnetic source imaging study. *Neuroscience Letters, 290,* 61–65.

Simos, P. G., Fletcher, J. M., Bergman, E., Breier, J. I., Foorman, B. R., Castillo, E. M., et al. (2002). Dyslexia-specific brain activation profile becomes normal following successful remedial training. *Neurology, 58,* 1203–1213.

Skowronek, H., & Marx, H. (1989). The Bielefeld Longitudinal Study on early identification of risks in learning to read and write: Theoretical background and first results. In M. Brambring, F. Lösel, & H. Skowronek (Eds.), *Children at risk: Assessment, longitudinal research, and intervention* (pp. 268–294). Oxford: de Gruyter.

Slaghuis, W. L., & Lovegrove, W. J. (1984). Flicker masking of spatial-frequency-dependent visible persistence and specific reading disability. *Perception, 13,* 527–534.

Slaghuis, W. L., & Lovegrove, W. J. (1985). Spatial-frequency-dependent visible persistence and specific reading disability. *Brain and Cognition, 4,* 219–240.

Slaghuis, W. L., & Lovegrove, W. J. (1986). The critical duration in spatial-frequency-dependent visible persistence and specific reading disability. *Bulletin of the Psychonomic Society, 24,* 416–418.

Slaghuis, W. L., & Ryan, J. F. (1999). Spatio-temporal contrast sensitivity, coherent motion, and visible persistence in developmental dyslexia. *Vision Research, 39,* 651–668.

Slaghuis, W. L., Twell, A. J., & Kingston, K. R. (1996). Visual and language processing disorders are concurrent in dyslexia and continue into adulthood. *Cortex, 32,* 413–438.

SLI Consortium. (2002). A genomewide scan identifies two novel loci involved in specific language impairment (SLI). *American Journal of Human Genetics, 70,* 384–398.

Smith, S. D., Kimberling, W. J., & Pennington, B. F. (1991). Screening for multiple genes influencing dyslexia. *Reading and Writing, 3,* 285–298.

Smith, S. D., Kimberling, W. J., Pennington, B. F., & Lubs, H. A. (1983). Specific reading disability: Identification of an inherited form through linkage analysis. *Science, 219,* 1345–1347.

Snow, C. E., Burns, M. S., & Griffin, P. (1998). *Preventing reading difficulties in young children.* Washington, DC: National Academy Press.

Snowling, M. J. (1981). Phonemic deficits in developmental dyslexia. *Psychological Research, 43,* 219–234.

Snowling, M. J. (2001). From language to reading and dyslexia. *Dyslexia, 7,* 37–46.

Snowling, M., Bishop, D. V., & Stothard, S. E. (2000). Is preschool language impairment a risk factor for dyslexia in adolescence? *Journal of Child Psychology and Psychiatry, 41,* 587–600.

Snowling, M., Gallagher, A., & Frith, U. (2003). Family risk of dyslexia is continuous: Individual differences in the precursors of reading skill. *Child Development, 74,* 358–373.

Snowling, M., Goulandris, N., Bowlby, M., & Howell, P. (1986). Segmentation and speech perception in relation to reading skill: A developmental analysis. *Journal of Experimental Child Psychology, 41,* 489–507.

Spitz, R. V., Tallal, P., Flax, J., & Benasich, A. A. (1997). Look who's talking: A prospective study of familial transmission of language impairments. *Journal of Speech, Language, and Hearing Research, 40,* 990–1001.

Stanovich, K. E. (1986). Matthew effects in reading: Some consequences of individual differences in the acquisition of literacy. *Reading Research Quarterly, 21,* 360–406.

Stanovich, K. E. (1991). Discrepancy definitions of reading disability: Has intelligence led us astray? *Reading Research Quarterly, 26,* 7–29.

Stanovich, K. E. (1996). Toward a more inclusive definition of dyslexia. *Dyslexia, 2,* 154–166.

Stark, R. E., Bernstein, L. E., Condino, R., Bender, M., Tallal, P., & Catts, H. (1984). Four-year follow-up study of language impaired children. *Annals of Dyslexia, 34,* 49–68.

Stark, R. E., & Heinz, J. M. (1996). Vowel perception in children with and without language impairment. *Journal of Speech and Hearing Research, 39,* 860–869.

Stark, R. E., & Tallal, P. (1979). Analysis of stop consonant production errors in developmentally dysphasic children. *Journal of the Acoustical Society of America, 66,* 1703–1712.

Stark, R. E., & Tallal, P. (1988). *Language, speech, and reading disorders in children: Neuropsychological studies.* Boston: Little, Brown.

Stein, J. F. (2001). The neurobiology of reading difficulties. In M. Wolf (Ed.), *Dyslexia, fluency, and the brain* (pp. 3–23). Timonium, MD: York Press.

Stein, J. F., & Fowler, M. S. (1981). Visual dyslexia. *Trends in Neurosciences, 4,* 77–80.

Stein, J. F., & Fowler, M. S. (1993). Unstable binocular control in dyslexic children. *Journal of Research in Reading, 16,* 30–45.

Stein, J. F., Richardson, A. J., & Fowler, M. S. (2000). Monocular occlusion can improve binocular control and reading in dyslexics. *Brain, 123,* 164–170.

Stein, J. F., Talcott, J., & Walsh, V. V. (2000). Controversy about the visual magnocellular deficit in developmental dyslexics. *Trends in Cognitive Sciences, 4,* 209–211.

Stein, J. F., & Walsh, V. (1997). To see but not to read: The magnocellular theory of dyslexia. *Trends in Neurosciences, 20,* 147–152.

Stephenson, S. (1907). Six cases of congenital word-blindness affecting three generations of one family. *Ophthalmoscope, 5,* 482–484.

Stevenson, H. W., Stigler, J. W., Lucker, G. W., Lee, S., Hsu, C., & Kitamura, S. (1982). Reading disabilities: The case of Chinese, Japanese, and English. *Child Development, 53,* 1164–1181.

Stevenson, J. (1991). Which aspects of processing text mediate genetic effects? *Reading and Writing, 3,* 249–269.

Stevenson, J., Graham, P., Fredman, G., & McLoughlin, V. (1987). A twin study of genetic influences on reading and spelling ability and disability. *Journal of Child Psychology and Psychiatry, 28,* 229–247.

Strange, W., Jenkins, J. J., & Johnson, T. L. (1983). Dynamic specification of coarticulated vowels. *Journal of the Acoustical Society of America, 74,* 695–705.

Studdert-Kennedy, M., & Mody, M. (1995). Auditory temporal perception deficits in the reading-impaired: A critical review of the evidence. *Psychonomic Bulletin and Review, 2,* 508–514.

Swan, D., & Goswami, U. (1997). Phonological awareness deficits in developmental dyslexia and the phonological representations hypothesis. *Journal of Experimental Child Psychology, 66,* 18–41.

Taipale, M., Kaminen, N., Nopola-Hemmi, J., Haltia, T., Myllyluoma, B., Lyytinen, H., et al. (2003). A candidate gene for developmental dyslexia encodes a nuclear tetratricopeptide repeat domain protein dynamically regulated in brain. *Proceedings of the National Academy of Sciences, USA, 100,* 11553–11558.

Talcott, J. B., Hansen, P. C., Assoku, E. L., & Stein, J. F. (2000). Visual motion sensitivity in dyslexia: Evidence for temporal and energy integration deficits. *Neuropsychologia, 38,* 935–943.

Talcott, J. B., Witton, C., McLean, M. F., Hansen, P. C., Rees, A., Green, G. G., et al. (2000). Dynamic sensory sensitivity and children's word decoding skills. *Proceedings of the National Academy of Sciences, USA, 97,* 2952–2957.

Tallal, P. (1980). Auditory temporal perception, phonics, and reading disabilities in children. *Brain and Language, 9,* 182–198.

Tallal, P. (1984). Temporal or phonetic processing deficit in dyslexia? That is the question. *Applied Psycholinguistics, 5,* 167–169.

Tallal, P. (2004). Improving language and literacy is a matter of time. *Nature Reviews Neuroscience, 5,* 721–728.

Tallal, P., Allard, L., Miller, S., & Curtiss, S. (1997). Academic outcomes of language impaired children. In C. Hulme & M. Snowling. (Eds.), *Dyslexia: Biology, cognition and intervention* (pp. 167–181). London: Whurr.

Tallal, P., & Benasich, A. A. (2002). Developmental language learning impairments. *Development and Psychopathology, 14,* 559–579.

Tallal, P., Curtiss, S., & Kaplan, R. (1988). The San Diego Longitudinal Study: Evaluating the outcomes of preschool impairment in language development. In S. E. Gerber & G. T. Mencher (Eds.), *International perspectives on communication disorders* (pp. 86–126). Washington, DC: Gallaudet University Press.

Tallal, P., Dukette, D., & Curtiss, S. (1989). Behavioral/emotional profiles of preschool language-impaired children. *Development and Psychopathology, 1,* 51–67.

Tallal, P., Hirsch, L. S., Realpe-Bonilla T., Miller S., Brzustowicz, L. M., Bartlett C., et al. (2001). Familial aggregation in specific language impairment. *Journal of Speech, Language, and Hearing Research, 44,* 1172–1182.

Tallal, P., Jernigan, T., & Trauner, D. (1994). Developmental bilateral damage to the head of the caudate nuclei: Implications for speech-language pathology. *Journal of Medical Speech and Language Pathology, 2,* 23–28.

Tallal, P., Miller, S. L., Bedi, G., Byma, G., Wang, X., Nagarajan, S. S., et al. (1996). Language comprehension in language-learning impaired children improved with acoustically modified speech. *Science, 271,* 81–84.

Tallal, P., Miller, S., & Fitch, R. H. (1993). Neurobiological basis of speech: A case for the preeminence of temporal processing. *Annals of the New York Academy of Sciences, 682,* 27–47.

Tallal, P., & Piercy, M. (1973a). Defects of non-verbal auditory perception in children with developmental aphasia. *Nature, 241,* 468–469.

Tallal, P., & Piercy, M. (1973b). Developmental aphasia: Impaired rate of non-verbal processing as a function of sensory modality. *Neuropsychologia, 11,* 389–398.

Tallal, P., & Piercy, M. (1974). Developmental aphasia: Rate of auditory processing and selective impairment of consonant perception. *Neuropsychologia, 12,* 83–93.

Tallal, P., & Piercy, M. (1975). Developmental aphasia: The perception of brief vowels and extended stop consonants. *Neuropsychologia, 13,* 69–74.

Tallal, P., Ross, R., & Curtiss, S. (1989a). Familial aggregation in specific language impairment. *Journal of Speech and Hearing Disorders, 54,* 167–173.

Tallal, P., Ross, R., & Curtiss, S. (1989b). Unexpected sex-ratios in families of language/learning-impaired children. *Neuropsychologia, 27,* 987–998.

Tallal, P., & Stark, R. E. (1981). Speech acoustic-cue discrimination abilities of normally developing and language-impaired children. *Journal of the Acoustical Society of America, 69,* 568–574.

Tallal, P., & Stark, R. E. (1982). Perceptual/motor profiles of reading impaired children with or without concomitant oral language deficits. *Annals of Dyslexia, 32,* 163–176.

Tallal, P., Stark, R. E., Kallman, C., & Mellits, D. (1980a). Developmental dysphasia: Relation between acoustic processing deficits and verbal processing. *Neuropsychologia, 18,* 273–284.

Tallal, P., Stark, R. E., Kallman, C., & Mellits, D. (1980b). Perceptual constancy for phonemic categories: A developmental study with normal and language impaired children. *Applied Psycholinguistics, 1,* 49–64.

Tallal, P., Stark, R. E., Kallman, C., & Mellits, D. (1981). A reexamination of some nonverbal perceptual abilities of language-impaired and normal children as a function of age and sensory modality. *Journal of Speech and Hearing Research, 24,* 351–357.

Tallal, P., Stark, R. E., & Mellits, D. (1985). The relationship between auditory temporal analysis and receptive language development: Evidence from studies of developmental language disorder. *Neuropsychologia, 23,* 527–534.

Tarnopol, L., & Tarnopol, M. (1981). *Comparative reading and learning difficulties.* Lexington, MA: Lexington Books.

Temple, E., Deutsch, G. K., Poldrack, R. A., Miller, S. L., Tallal, P., Merzenich, M. M., et al. (2003). Neural deficits in children with dyslexia ameliorated by behavioral remediation: Evidence from functional MRI. *Proceedings of the National Academy of Sciences, USA, 100,* 2860–2865.

Temple, E., Poldrack, R. A., Protopapas, A., Nagarajan, S., Salz, T., Tallal, P., et al. (2000). Disruption of the neural response to rapid acoustic stimuli in dyslexia: Evidence from functional MRI. *Proceedings of the National Academy of Sciences, USA, 97,* 13907–13912.

Temple, E., Poldrack, R. A., Salidis, J., Deutsch, G. K., Tallal, P., Merzenich, M. M., et al. (2001). Disrupted neural responses to phonological and orthographic processing in dyslexic children: An fMRI study. *Neuroreport, 12,* 299–307.

Tervaniemi, M., Medvedev, S. V., Alho, K., Pakhomov, S. V., Roudas, M. S., van Zuijen, T. L., et al. (2000). Lateralized automatic auditory processing of phonetic versus musical information: A PET study. *Human Brain Mapping, 10,* 74–79.

Thomas, M., & Karmiloff-Smith, A. (2002). Are developmental disorders like cases of adult brain damage? Implications from connectionist modelling. *Behavioral and Brain Science, 25,* 727–787.

Tomblin, J. B. (1989). Familial concentration of developmental language impairment. *Journal of Speech and Hearing Disorders, 54,* 287–295.

Tomblin, J. B. (1997). Epidemiology of specific language impairment. In M. Gopnik (Ed.), *The inheritance and innateness of grammars* (pp. 91–109). New York: Oxford University Press.

Tomblin, J. B., & Buckwalter, P. R. (1994). Studies of genetics of specific language impairment. In R. V. Watkins & M. L. Rice (Eds.), *Specific language impairments in children* (Vol. 4, pp. 17–34). Baltimore: Paul H. Brookes.

Tomblin, J. B., Freese, P. R., & Records, N. L. (1992). Diagnosing specific language impairment in adults for the purpose of pedigree analysis. *Journal of Speech and Hearing Research, 35,* 832–843.

Tomblin, J. B., Records, N. L., Buckwalter, P., Zhang, X., Smith, E., & O'Brien, M. (1997). Prevalence of specific language impairment in kindergarten children. *Journal of Speech, Language, and Hearing Research, 40,* 1245–1260.

Tomblin, J. B., Zhang, X., Buckwalter, P., & Catts, H. (2000). The association of reading disability, behavioral disorders, and language impairment among second-grade children. *Journal of Child Psychology and Psychiatry, 41,* 473–482.

Trehub, S. E., & Henderson, J. L. (1996). Temporal resolution in infancy and subsequent language development. *Journal of Speech and Hearing Research, 39,* 1315–1320.

Treitel, L. (1893). Über Aphasie im Kindesalter. *Sammlung Klinischer Vorträge, 64,* 629–654.

Tzourio, N., Heim, A., Zilbovicius, M., Gerard, C., & Mazoyer, B. M. (1994). Abnormal regional CBF response in left hemisphere of dysphasic children during a language task. *Pediatric Neurology, 10,* 20–26.

Undheim, A. M. (2003). Dyslexia and psychosocial factors: A follow-up study of young Norwegian adults with a history of dyslexia in childhood. *Nordic Journal of Psychiatry, 57,* 221–226.

Vaïsse, L. (1866). Des sourds-muets et de certains cas d'aphasie congénitale. *Bulletin de la Société d'Anthropologie de Paris, 1*(Sér 2), 146–150.

van Daal, V., & van der Leij, A. (1999). Developmental dyslexia: Related to specific or general deficits? *Annals of Dyslexia, 49,* 71–104.

van den Bos, K. (1998). IQ, phonological awareness and continuous-naming speed related to Dutch children's poor decoding performance on two word identification tests. *Dyslexia, 4,* 73–89.

van der Lely, H. K., & Stollwerck, L. (1996). A grammatical specific language impairment in children: An autosomal dominant inheritance? *Brain and Language, 52,* 484–504.

Van Ingelghem, M., van Wieringen, A., Wouters, J., Vandenbussche, E., Onghena, P., & Ghesquière, P. (2001). Psychophysical evidence for a general temporal processing deficit in children with dyslexia. *Neuroreport, 12,* 3603–3607.

Vargha-Khadem, F., Watkins, K., Alcock, K., Fletcher, P., & Passingham, R. (1995). Praxic and nonverbal cognitive deficits in a large family with genetically transmitted speech and language disorder. *Proceedings of the National Academy of Sciences, USA, 92,* 930–933.

Vellutino, F. R. (1979). *Dyslexia: Theory and research.* Cambridge, MA: MIT Press.

Victor, J. D., Conte, M. M., Burton, L., & Nass, R. D. (1993). Visual evoked potentials in dyslexics and normals: Failure to find a difference in transient or steady-state responses. *Visual Neuroscience, 10,* 939–946.

Viding, E., Spinath, F. M., Price, T. S., Bishop, D. V., Dale, P. S., & Plomin, R. (2004). Genetic and environmental influence on language impairment in 4-year-old same-sex and opposite-sex twins. *Journal of Child Psychology and Psychiatry, 45,* 315–325.

Vidyasagar, T. R. (2004). Neural underpinnings of dyslexia as a disorder of visuo-spatial attention. *Clinical and Experimental Optometry, 87,* 4–10.

Vincent, A., Deacon, R., Dalton, P., Salmond, C., Blamire, A. M., Pendlebury, S., et al. (2002). Maternal antibody-mediated dyslexia? Evidence for a pathogenic serum factor in a mother of two dyslexic children shown by transfer to mice using behavioural studies and magnetic resonance spectroscopy. *Journal of Neuroimmunology, 130,* 243–247.

Vogler, G. P., DeFries, J. C., & Decker, S. N. (1985). Family history as an indicator of risk for reading disability. *Journal of Learning Disabilities, 18,* 419–421.

von Plessen, K., Lundervold, A., Duta, N., Heiervang, E., Klauschen, F., Smievoll, A. I., et al. (2002). Less developed corpus callosum in dyslexic subjects: A structural MRI study. *Neuropsychologia, 40,* 1035–1044.

Wada, J. A., Clarke, R., & Hamm, A. (1975). Cerebral hemispheric asymmetry in humans: Cortical speech zones in 100 adults and 100 infant brains. *Archives of Neurology, 32,* 239–246.

Wadsworth, S. J., DeFries, J. C., Stevenson, J., Gilger, J. W., & Pennington, B. F. (1992). Gender ratios among reading-disabled children and their siblings as a function of parental impairment. *Journal of Child Psychology and Psychiatry, 33,* 1229–1239.

Wadsworth, S. J., Olson, R. K., Pennington, B. F., & DeFries, J. C. (2000). Differential genetic etiology of reading disability as a function of IQ. *Journal of Learning Disabilities, 33,* 192–199.

Wagner, R. K., & Torgesen, J. K. (1987). The nature of phonological processing and its causal role in the acquisition of reading skills. *Psychological Bulletin, 101,* 192–212.

Wagner, R. K., Torgesen, J. K., & Rashotte, C. A. (1994). Development of reading-related phonological processing abilities: New evidence of bidirectional causality from a latent variable longitudinal study. *Developmental Psychology, 30,* 73–87.

Walther-Müller, P. U. (1995). Is there a deficit of early vision in dyslexia? *Perception, 24,* 919–936.

Watson, C., & Willows, D. M. (1995). Information-processing patterns in specific reading disability. *Journal of Learning Disabilities, 28,* 216–231.

Weiner, P. S. (1974). A language-delayed child at adolescence. *Journal of Speech and Hearing Disorders, 39,* 202–212.

Weiner, P. S. (1986). The study of childhood language disorders: Nineteenth century perspectives. *Journal of Communication Disorders, 19,* 1–47.

Wernicke, C. (1874). *Der aphasische Symptomencomplex: Eine psychologische Studie auf anatomischer Basis* [The aphasia symptomcomplex: A psychological study on an anatomic basis]. Breslau, Germany: Cohn & Weigert.

Wimmer, H. (1993). Characteristics of developmental dyslexia in a regular writing system. *Applied Psycholinguistics, 14,* 1–33.

Witton, C., Talcott, J. B., Hansen, P. C., Richardson, A. J., Griffiths, T. D., Rees, A., et al. (1998). Sensitivity to dynamic auditory and visual stimuli predicts nonword reading ability in both dyslexic and normal readers. *Current Biology, 8,* 791–797.

Wolf, M. (1991). Naming speed and reading: The contribution of the cognitive neurosciences. *Reading Research Quarterly, 26,* 123–141.

Wolf, M., Bally, H., & Morris, R. (1986). Automaticity, retrieval processes, and reading: A longitudinal study in average and impaired readers. *Child Development, 57,* 988–1000.

Wolf, M., & Bowers, P. G. (1999). The double-deficit hypothesis for the developmental dyslexias. *Journal of Educational Psychology, 91,* 415–438.

Wolf, M., Goldberg O'Rourke, A., Gidney, C., Lovett, M., Cirino, P., & Morris, R. (2002). The second deficit: An investigation of the independence of phonological and naming-speed deficits in developmental dyslexia. *Reading and Writing, 15,* 43–72.

Wolf, M., & Segal, D. (1999). Retrieval rate, accuracy and vocabulary elaboration (RAVE) in reading-impaired children: A pilot intervention programme. *Dyslexia, 5,* 1–27.

Wolff, P. H., & Melngailis, I. (1994). Family patterns of developmental dyslexia: Clinical findings. *American Journal of Medical Genetics, 54,* 122–131.

World Health Organization. (1992). *The ICD-10 classification of mental and behavioural disorders.* Geneva, Switzerland: Author.

Worster-Drought, C., & Allen, I. M. (1929). Congenital auditory imperception (congenital word-deafness): With report of a case. *Journal of Neurology and Psychopathology, 9,* 193–208.

Wright, B. A., & Zecker, S. G. (2004). Learning problems, delayed development, and puberty. *Proceedings of the National Academy of Sciences, USA, 101,* 9942–9946.

Zaehle, T., Wüstenberg, T., Meyer, M., & Jäncke, L. (2004). Evidence for rapid auditory perception as the foundation of speech processing: A sparse temporal sampling fMRI study. *European Journal of Neuroscience, 20,* 2447–2456.

Zatorre, R. J., & Belin, P. (2001). Spectral and temporal processing in human auditory cortex. *Cerebral Cortex, 11,* 946–953.

Zeki, S. (1993). *A vision of the brain.* Boston: Blackwell Scientific.

Zerbin-Rüdin, E. (1967). Kongenitale Wortblindheit oder spezifische Dyslexie (Congenital word-blindness). *Bulletin of the Orton Society, 17,* 47–54.

CHAPTER 8

Autism Spectrum Disorders

GERALDINE DAWSON and KAREN TOTH

Autism Spectrum Disorder is the term that is currently used to describe the broad range of pervasive developmental disorders. These disorders include Autistic Disorder, Asperger's Disorder (also referred to as Asperger's syndrome), Rett's Disorder, Childhood Disintegrative Disor-

der, and Pervasive Developmental Disorder Not Otherwise Specified (PDD-NOS).

The Autism spectrum disorders involve impairments in reciprocal social interaction and communication and the presence of restricted, stereotyped, and repetitive interests and behaviors. Of these three symptom domains, impairments in social interaction are considered a primary feature of these disorders. These impairments include a lack of social and emotional reciprocity; atypical nonverbal behaviors such as atypical eye-to-eye gaze, facial expressions, body postures, and gestures to regulate social interaction;

The writing of this chapter was supported by the National Institute of Child Health and Human Development and the National Institute on Deafness and Communication Disorders (U19HD35465) and the National Institute of Mental Health (U54MH066399).

lack of interest and/or difficulty relating to others, particularly peers; and a failure to share enjoyment and interests with others. A great deal of heterogeneity exists among the Autism spectrum disorders in terms of the number and severity of symptoms across the three domains (social, communication, and stereotyped/restricted interests and behaviors) and in cognitive and adaptive functioning. Further, within each diagnostic category, impairments differ across individuals and, for any given individual, symptoms may change across the life span.

DIAGNOSIS, COURSE, AND PROGNOSIS

The *Diagnostic and Statistical Manual of Mental Disorders,* fourth edition (*DSM-IV;* American Psychiatric Association, 1994) and the *International Classification of Diseases,* 10th edition (*ICD-10;* World Health Organization, 1992) are two widely used systems for diagnosing Autism spectrum disorders. The specific criteria for each of the Autism spectrum disorders are described next.

Autistic Disorder

The diagnostic criteria for Autistic Disorder include at least six symptoms across three domains of functioning, with at least two symptoms in the area of social interaction, one in communication, and one in restricted interests and behaviors. Delays or abnormal functioning in at least one area—social interaction, language, symbolic or imaginative play—must be present before 3 years of age, and symptoms cannot be better accounted for by Rett's Disorder or Childhood Disintegrative Disorder (see following discussion). Individuals with Autism vary widely in symptom expression, cognitive level, and adaptive abilities. For a more detailed discussion, see the section on Symptom Presentation later in this chapter.

Asperger's Disorder

The characteristics that define Asperger's Disorder include intact formal language skills (e.g., vocabulary, grammar), with impairments in the social use of language and in nonverbal expression, social awkwardness, and idiosyncratic and consuming interests (Volkmar & Klin, 2001). Although motor clumsiness is not a defining feature of Asperger's Disorder, it is often observed (Volkmar & Klin, 2001). The *DSM-IV* diagnostic criteria for Asperger's Disorder include at least two symptoms in the domain of social interaction and one symptom in the domain

of restricted interests and behaviors. Further, individuals with Asperger's Disorder do not demonstrate clinically significant delays in general cognitive ability, self-help skills, and adaptive development. Differentiating Asperger's Disorder and high-functioning Autism is often difficult to do clinically, and the empirical validity of such a distinction has not yet been unequivocally established (Ozonoff & Griffith, 2000; Volkmar & Klin, 2001).

Asperger's Disorder was included as a separate diagnostic category only in the more recent revisions of the *DSM-IV* and *ICD-10* classification systems, and epidemiologic data on this subtype of Autism Spectrum Disorder are scarce. The first systematic epidemiologic study of Asperger's Disorder was conducted in Sweden and yielded a prevalence rate of 28.5 per 10,000 (Ehlers & Gillberg, 1993). In a review of epidemiologic surveys, Fombonne and Tidmarsh (2003) concluded that the number of children with Autism was 5 times that of children with Asperger's Disorder, on average, suggesting that the prevalence of Asperger's is approximately 2 per 10,000. The authors note that future studies should focus on slightly older children (ages 8 to 12 years) as Asperger's Disorder is often diagnosed much later than Autism.

Rett's Disorder

Rett's Disorder occurs in 1 in 10,000 to 15,000 individuals, has been reported only in females, and involves a progressive deterioration of functioning between 6 and 18 months of age. Children with Rett's Disorder follow an apparently normal prenatal and perinatal period of development, with typical, early psychomotor development and normal head circumference at birth. This period of fairly typical development is followed by a gradual loss of speech and purposeful hand use and the development of microcephaly, seizures, autistic features, difficulties in coordinating gait or trunk movements, and stereotypic hand movements. Interest in social engagement diminishes in the first few years following onset, but may reemerge later. Individuals with Rett's Disorder have severe impairment in language development, severe psychomotor retardation, and severe to profound mental retardation. It was discovered that some cases of Rett's Disorder are caused by mutations in the gene (MECP2) encoding X-linked methyl-CpG-binding protein 2 (Amir et al., 1999).

Childhood Disintegrative Disorder

Childhood Disintegrative Disorder (CDD), also termed Heller's syndrome, is characterized by a marked regression in several areas of functioning following typical development in the first 2 years of life. Regression can occur any time after the first 2 years and before age 10, but onset typically occurs before 4 years of age. This regression typically includes a loss of previously acquired skills in at least two of the following areas: expressive or receptive language, social abilities or adaptive behavior, bowel or bladder control, play, and motor skills. Individuals with this disorder also demonstrate impairments in two of the three domains that characterize Autism: social interaction, communication, and restricted, repetitive behavior.

Approximately 1 in 3 to 5 children with Autism are also reported to show a regression in language and social skills following a period of ostensibly typical development, but this regression generally occurs prior to 24 months of age. These children are classified as having Autism rather than Childhood Disintegrative Disorder. For a more detailed discussion of developmental course in Autism, see later discussion.

CDD is very rare and much less common than Autistic Disorder (*DSM-IV;* American Psychiatric Association, 1994).

Pervasive Developmental Disorder Not Otherwise Specified

A diagnosis of PDD-NOS is given when there exist clinically significant impairments in social interaction and/or communication, or restricted interests and behaviors are present, but criteria for a specific Autism Spectrum Disorder are not met. This usually occurs in cases where symptoms are present but are too few in number to meet criteria for a specific diagnosis. Similar to the other diagnostic categories, a diagnosis of PDD-NOS includes individuals of varying symptom severity, cognitive ability, and level of adaptive skills.

Differential Diagnosis and Comorbidity

Accurate diagnosis is critical for obtaining proper treatment and the best possible outcome. Therefore, it is important to understand how Autism spectrum disorders differ from other commonly diagnosed disorders of childhood and which conditions are comorbid with Autism.

Differentiating among the Autism Spectrum Disorders

Although the *DSM-IV* defines Autistic Disorder, Asperger's Disorder, and PDD-NOSpecified as separate disorders, children often receive different diagnoses within the Autism spectrum depending on the clinician and diagnostic instrument used to make the diagnosis. Although this can be confusing to parents and, in some cases, can impact

a family's eligibility for federal- and state-mandated intervention services, treatment recommendations are essentially the same across the spectrum (see section on interventions later in this chapter).

Mental Retardation

Estimates of the percentage of individuals with Autism who also have mental retardation range from 75% to 89% (Filipek et al., 1999; Fombonne, 1999; Steffenburg & Gillberg, 1986) to 40% to 71% (Baird et al., 2000; Chakrabarti & Fombonne, 2001). More recent (lower) estimates may reflect an increase in diagnoses of higher-functioning individuals and/or effective early intervention.

Although approximately 75% of children with Autism also have mental retardation, the two disorders can be distinguished based on differences in a number of areas. Studies that have compared children with Autism to children with mental retardation of similar intellectual ability have shown that children with Autism often exhibit an uneven cognitive profile that is different from children with mental retardation. This pattern consists of higher scores on measures of visual-spatial skills and auditory rote memory and lower scores on verbal comprehension (Happe, 1994; Lockyer & Rutter, 1970). In addition, a number of studies have identified differences between children with Autism and children with mental retardation in nonverbal communication skills, motor imitation, social cognition, play, and emotion recognition and expression (see Symptom Presentation section later in this chapter). Similarities include simple motor stereotypes, including self-injurious behaviors, which appear to be a function of mental age rather than diagnosis (G. Dawson, Meltzoff, Osterling, & Rinaldi, 1998; Wing, 1978).

Due to the high comorbidity of Autism and mental retardation, the individual's developmental level and a thorough knowledge of typical developmental milestones is critical to making an accurate diagnosis.

Specific Language Impairment

All children with Autism have deficits in the communicative use of language (Lord & Paul, 1997; Tager-Flusberg, 1999; Wilkinson, 1998), and most have impairments as well in the formal aspects of language, such as vocabulary, complex syntax, and morphology, similar to those shown by children with specific language impairment (SLI)[1] (Bartak, Rutter, & Cox, 1975; Bishop, North, & Donlan, 1996;

---

[1] SLI is a developmental language disorder that refers to below-average performance on standardized language tests in the absence of other disorders, such as mental retardation or hearing loss.

Dollaghan & Campbell, 1998; Gathercole & Baddeley, 1990; Tager-Flusberg & Cooper, 1999). Thus, Autism and SLI appear to be distinct disorders but highly comorbid. Research has compared the language profiles of children with Autism to those of children with SLI and found striking similarities. Children with Autism (ages 4 to 14 years) were given a language battery to assess phonological, lexical, and higher-order semantic and grammatical language skills (Kjelgaard & Tager-Flusberg, 2001). The sample was then divided into three groups based on their overall scores on the battery: normal, borderline, and impaired language. Children with impaired language demonstrated language profiles that were very similar to those previously observed in children with SLI, including better vocabulary relative to higher-order language abilities, poor performance on phonological processing (nonword repetition test), and difficulties in marking tense. This same group of researchers then examined the brain structure of children with Autism using magnetic resonance imaging (MRI), focusing specifically on the language regions of the cortex. Similar to children with SLI, the children with Autism showed larger right cortical regions relative to left regions, unlike controls, who showed larger left regions. These authors conclude that there is a subtype of children with Autism with the same neurocognitive phenotype as children with SLI. Genetic studies provide further clues to a shared genetic basis of these two disorders (see section on Etiology).

Nonverbal Learning Disability

Nonverbal learning disability (NLD) is characterized by lower nonverbal skills (i.e., visual-spatial, mathematics, handwriting) relative to verbal skills. Children with NLD also tend to be clumsy and exhibit social difficulties. Many children with Asperger's Disorder and some children with high-functioning Autism also meet criteria for NLD and may benefit from special educational services aimed at improving math and motor skills (Ozonoff, Dawson, & McPartland, 2002).

Tic Disorders

Many individuals with Autism exhibit stereotypic movements or vocalizations that are considered to be volitional and do not cause distress to the individual. Tics, however, refer to sudden, rapid, recurrent, stereotypical movements or vocalizations that cause marked distress to the individual and are generally believed to be involuntary. A study of 447 individuals with Autism spectrum disorders reported the presence of tics in more than 30% of the sample, with 4.3% meeting criteria for a specific tic disorder, Tourette's syndrome (Baron-Cohen, Scahill, Izaguirre, Hornsey, &

Robertson, 1999). An additional 2.2% were diagnosed with probable Tourette's syndrome, yielding a combined rate of 6.5%, which is greater than the general population risk. These results suggest an increased risk for tic disorders in individuals with Autism, although larger-scale epidemiological studies are needed.

Attention-Deficit/Hyperactivity Disorder

One of the most common initial misdiagnoses, particularly for children with high-functioning Autism and Asperger's Disorder, is Attention-Deficit/Hyperactivity Disorder (ADHD; Ozonoff et al., 2002). Children with ADHD show difficulties sustaining attention and organizing tasks, are easily distracted, often do not seem to listen when spoken to, exhibit an excessive activity level, interrupt others, and talk excessively. Many children with Autism and Asperger's Disorder exhibit these same symptoms, but for very different reasons. For instance, due to the significant social and executive function deficits in Autism, these children may not seem to be listening when spoken to and may interrupt others, talk excessively, and show difficulty in organizing tasks and following through on assignments. Key distinguishing features of Asperger's Disorder are profound difficulties in social interaction and the presence of preoccupations and restricted range of interests.

Obsessive-Compulsive Disorder

Children with Autism often exhibit an insistence on routines and rituals and a high need for order, which may be confused with Obsessive-Compulsive Disorder (OCD; Ozonoff et al., 2002). Most children with OCD experience their behavior as intrusive and odd and wish that they could stop performing the behaviors. They also experience anxiety that is alleviated by engaging in the behaviors. In contrast, children with Autism have little insight into the nature of their repetitive and ritualistic behaviors, do not realize that the behaviors may be considered odd, and do not try to stop engaging in them. In addition, the need for routine and order in Autism is only one in a constellation of symptoms that characterize the disorder. In some cases, an individual may suffer from both Autism and OCD. Comorbid diagnosis of Autism Spectrum Disorder and OCD ranges from 1.5% to 29% (Lainhart, 1999). In such cases, treatment should address both disorders.

Other Anxiety Disorders

Symptoms of anxiety are frequently observed in children across the Autism spectrum, making it difficult to determine whether these symptoms represent a truly separate disorder. Nevertheless, Lainhart (1999) estimated a 7% to

84% comorbid rate of anxiety disorders in individuals with Autism, with Generalized Anxiety Disorder, agoraphobia, separation anxiety, and simple phobia being the most common. Symptoms of anxiety can often be ameliorated by medication and/or appropriate behavioral interventions (see section on interventions later in this chapter).

Depression

Depression is commonly comorbid with Autism, occurring at rates ranging from 4% to 58% (Lainhart, 1999). Although symptoms of depression occur most frequently in adolescents and adults with Asperger's Disorder or PDD-NOS, they can occur in children (Ghaziuddin & Greden, 1998; Wozniak et al., 1997). Primary symptoms are not always related to mood and may include increased agitation, aggression, self-injurious behavior, increased engagement in compulsive and repetitive behaviors, social withdrawal, changes in sleep and appetite, and general deterioration in functioning (Howlin, 1997; Lainhart & Folstein, 1994). Major Depression in individuals with Autism is often ameliorated by antidepressant therapy (Lainhart & Folstein, 1994).

Seizure Disorders

Individuals with Autism are at increased risk for developing seizure disorders, with prevalence rates ranging from 5% to 39% (Ballaban-Gil & Tuchman, 2000; Tidmarsh & Volkmar, 2003) and age of onset either before 3 years of age or, more frequently, during puberty (11 to 14 years; Gillberg & Steffenburg, 1987; Goode, Rutter, & Howlin, 1994; Rutter, 1970; Volkmar & Nelson, 1990). Seizure disorders are more common in very low-functioning individuals (i.e., IQ of less than 50) and in females (Rutter, 1984; Volkmar & Nelson, 1990). In addition, epileptiform abnormalities without evidence of clinical seizures are also common (one study reported 21% of 392 children) in Autism (Tuchman & Rapin, 1997).

Early Identification

Some parents of children with Autism report being concerned about their child's development since birth, and, by 18 months, most parents raise concerns with their primary health care provider (Howlin & Asgharian, 1999; Rogers, 2001; Siegel, Pilner, Eschler, & Elliot, 1988). However, the age at which a diagnosis is confirmed tends to be much older. In a survey of 770 parents of children with Autism and Asperger's Disorder, the *average* age at which a formal diagnosis was confirmed was 5.5 years for Autism and 11 years for Asperger's Disorder (Howlin & Asgharian, 1999). Refining methods of early identification and diagnosis allows for early intervention and better outcomes for young children with these disorders.

Reliability and Stability of Early Diagnosis

Research indicates that symptoms of Autism are often present during infancy and that Autism spectrum disorders can be detected as early as 18 months of age and reliably diagnosed by 20 to 24 months (Baron-Cohen et al., 1996; Rogers, 2001). Further, there is now evidence that a diagnosis of Autism at age 2 remains stable over time. For instance, Lord (1995) found that 14 of 16 children receiving a clinical diagnosis of Autism at age 2 received an independent clinical diagnosis of Autism at age 3. Baron-Cohen et al. reported that 10 out of 10 children diagnosed with Autism at 18 to 20 months retained the diagnosis at 3.5 years. W. L. Stone et al. (1999) showed that 96% of the children in their study retained a diagnosis of Autism or PDD-NOS from age 2 to 3. Others have shown that diagnosis of Autism spectrum disorders in children under 3 years of age is reliable across clinicians, although less so when distinguishing Autism from PDD-NOS (W. L. Stone et al., 1999; Volkmar, Szatmari, & Sparrow, 1993).

Early Symptoms

Previous studies have identified a number of characteristics that distinguish preschool and early elementary school-age children with Autism from those with developmental delay. These include impairments in joint attention, imitation, symbolic play, and responses to emotion (e.g., Charman & Baron-Cohen, 1997; Charman et al., 1998; G. Dawson, Meltzoff, Osterling, & Rinaldi, 1998; G. Dawson, Meltzoff, Osterling, Rinaldi, & Brown, 1998; Mundy, Sigman, Ungerer, & Sherman, 1986; W. L. Stone, Ousley, & Littleford, 1997; W. L. Stone et al., 1999). Relatively few controlled studies, however, have examined how children with Autism below age 3 differ from children with related disabilities, such as developmental delays, and most of these have relied on observations made from home videotapes (e.g., Baranek, 1999; Osterling, Dawson, & Munson, 2002). Charman et al. (1998) found that 20-month-olds with Autism were more impaired in joint attention, responses to another's distress, pretend play, and imitation, compared to those with language delay. Other studies found that 24-month-olds with Autism performed fewer joint attention gestures, including pointing and showing, and had more impaired language and imitation skills than typically developing and language impaired children (Lord & Paul, 1997; W. L. Stone et al., 1997).

Retrospective studies of home videotapes have been an especially fruitful area of research. Using this method, investigators have been able to observe the early social, language, motor, and play behaviors of infants who later receive a diagnosis on the Autism spectrum and to examine developmental differences between infants with Autism and typically developing infants (Mars, Mauk, & Dowrick, 1998; Osterling & Dawson, 1994) and infants with mental retardation (Baranek, 1999; Osterling & Dawson, 1999). In one such study, Osterling and Dawson (1994) examined videotapes of 1st birthday parties and demonstrated that 1-year-olds later diagnosed with Autism could be distinguished from 1-year-old typically developing infants. How often a child looked at the face of another person (gaze) correctly classified the greatest number of children (77%). When gaze was combined with the behaviors of showing, pointing, and orienting to name (i.e., social orienting), 91% of the infants with typical development and with Autism were correctly classified. These results were replicated by Mars et al., who used blind scoring to evaluate home videotapes of 1st birthday parties of 25 infants later diagnosed with Autism and 25 typically developing infants. Again, the variable "looks at faces" was found to be a powerful discriminator between the two groups, as well as joint attention (e.g., pointing) behaviors.

A subsequent home videotape study compared 1-year-olds later diagnosed with an Autism Spectrum Disorder (ASD) with 1-year-olds later diagnosed with mental retardation and 1-year-olds with typical development. This study showed that 1-year-olds with ASD could be distinguished not only from typical 1-year-olds, but also from 1-year-olds with mental retardation (Osterling et al., 2002). This is important due to the high comorbidity of Autism and mental retardation. In this study, the infants with ASD were less likely to look at others and to orient to their name than were infants with mental retardation. Joint attention behaviors, however, did not distinguish between ASD and developmental delay at 1 year of age, suggesting that other behaviors related to attending to people and other's speech might be important in distinguishing ASD from developmental delay at very young ages. In yet another home videotape study, a failure to orient to name was the best discriminator between 8- to 10-month-olds with ASD versus typical development (Werner, Dawson, Osterling, & Dinno, 2000). Again, joint attention did not distinguish the two groups at this young age.

Screening Instruments

A number of promising early screening methods have been developed to detect symptoms of Autism in infants and toddlers, including the Checklist for Autism in Toddlers (CHAT; Baron-Cohen, Allen, & Gillberg, 1992), the Modified Checklist for Autism in Toddlers (M-CHAT; Robins, Fein, Barton, & Green, 2001), the Pervasive Developmental Disorders Screening Tests (PDDST; Siegel & Hayer, 1999), and the Screening Tool for Autism in Two Year Olds (STAT; W. L. Stone, Coonrod, & Ousley, 2000). However, none of these instruments are currently in widespread use. The CHAT, a parent report and behavioral observation measure, has been shown to have high specificity (98%) but low sensitivity (38%), suggesting that it is not adequate for screening in public health settings (Baird et al., 2000). More promising results have been shown for the M-CHAT, a parent report measure, with a specificity of 95% and a sensitivity of 97% (Robins et al., 2001). The PDDST differs from the CHAT and the M-CHAT in that it offers different versions for primary care clinics, developmental clinics, and Autism specialty clinics. The primary care version yielded a sensitivity of 85% and specificity of 71% (Siegel & Hayer, 1999). The STAT is still under development but has been shown to discriminate well between children with Autism and other developmental disorders in a small sample of 2-year-olds (W. L. Stone et al., 2000).

It is likely that screening methods currently under development will continue to need refinement. This refinement will depend on research aimed at identifying early emerging behaviors that can distinguish very young children with Autism from those with related disabilities, such as developmental delay. Behaviors such as joint attention, gestures, verbal language, and pretend play may have limited utility in distinguishing infants and toddlers with Autism from those with developmental delay as these behaviors are not normally present until 1 to 2 years of age; 18- to 24-month-old toddlers with significant developmental delay would not be expected to show these behaviors.

Developmental Course

There are generally two patterns of symptom development in Autism. The most common course involves the emergence of symptoms in the 1st year of life. In roughly a third of cases, however, there is a regression in skills following a period of fairly typical development.

Early Onset

Symptoms of Autism typically emerge early, within the first 12 months of life. This pattern of symptom development is referred to as early-onset Autism. Both parent report (Lord, 1995) and home videotape studies (Baranek, 1999; Osterling & Dawson, 1994; Werner et al., 2000;

Werner, Dawson, & Munson, 2001) have confirmed that for many children with Autism, symptoms may emerge as early as 8 months of age.

Regression

Symptoms of Autism may also appear after a period of fairly typical development, with a regression or loss of previously acquired skills generally occurring prior to 24 months of age. This pattern of symptom emergence in Autism has been estimated to occur in 20% to 47% of cases (e.g., Davidovitch, Glick, Holtzman, Tirosh, & Safir, 2000; Kurita, 1985; Lord, 1995; B. A. Taylor et al., 2002), with typical age of onset ranging from 16 months (B. J. Williams & Ozonoff, 2001) to 24 months (Davidovitch et al., 2000). Primarily, there is a loss of language skills, although losses can occur in social interest and responsiveness, nonverbal communication, cognitive ability, and self-help/adaptive behavior. Osterling and Dawson (1999) examined home videotapes of children with reported regression and found that, indeed, these children displayed typical social and communication behaviors at 1 year of age. However, using retrospective parent report, two other studies have shown that approximately 50% of the children who were reported to have lost skills after 1 year of age actually showed a delay in skills prior to the reported regression (Werner et al., 2001; B. J. Williams & Ozonoff, 2001). Werner and colleagues found that children with versus without a history of early regression did not differ in language, cognitive, or symptom outcome at age 3 to 4 years (Werner, Dawson, Munson, & Osterling, in press).

Autism across the Life Span

Although Autism is considered to be a lifelong disorder, the specific constellation of symptoms and the severity of those symptoms tend to fluctuate across development (Lord, 1997). One study reported improvements from age 5 in social and communication skills and in repetitive behaviors in a sample of 38 adolescents and young adults, with 13% of the sample no longer meeting criteria for Autism (Piven, Harper, Palmer, & Arndt, 1996).

With such changing patterns and severity of symptoms, both current and historical reports of symptoms are often required to make an accurate diagnosis and for inclusion in genetic studies of Autism. The Autism Diagnostic Interview-Revised (Le Couteur, Lord, & Rutter, 2003; Lord, Rutter, & Le Couteur, 1994) is a standardized, semistructured parent interview that provides both a current and a lifetime diagnosis for individuals with a mental age of 18 months or

greater. However, it relies on retrospective parent report and should therefore be combined with other sources of information, such as behavioral observation, in making a diagnosis. One such behavioral measure that is widely used is the Autism Diagnostic Observation Schedule (ADOS; Lord et al., 2000; Lord, Rutter, DiLavore, & Risi, 1999; Lord, Rutter, Goode, & Heemsbergen, 1989), designed to assess individuals at varying stages of development and language level, from nonverbal children to high-functioning adults (there are four modules in all). The ADOS is a standardized, semistructured play interaction that provides opportunities for reciprocal social interaction, communication, and imaginative play and can be used across a wide range of chronological and mental ages (normative data exist for ages ranging from 15 months to 40 years).

Prognosis

Although the diagnosis of Autism tends to be quite stable into adolescence and adulthood, outcome is more varied. For as many as 75% of individuals with Autism, outcome tends to be poor. However, fair to good outcomes (i.e., adequate functioning in social, work, and school domains) are observed in at least 25% of individuals (Gillberg & Steffenburg, 1987; Nordin & Gillberg, 1998; Sigman & Norman, 1999). A more recent study that followed children with Autism from age 2 to age 9 found that as many as 40% obtained good outcomes based on language and cognitive scores (W. L. Stone, Turner, Pozdol, & Smoski, 2003). Although outcome is typically best for individuals with normal to near-normal intelligence, it is still lower than expected based on general intellectual ability. For instance, many individuals with Autism who have normal intelligence nevertheless require supervised living arrangements, are employed in low-level jobs, and do not develop friendships or marry (Tsatsanis, 2003). Compared to earlier studies (i.e., prior to 1980), however, there is evidence of better outcome in Autism in more recent years (Howlin & Goode, 1998). Improved outcome is likely related to availability of early and appropriate interventions.

Predictors of Outcome

Identifying specific factors that predict outcome in Autism is of critical importance for both researchers and clinicians and can lead to improved, targeted early interventions. IQ above 50 and language (specifically, meaningful speech by 5 to 6 years of age) remain the strongest predictors of positive outcomes for these children (Bartak & Rutter, 1976; Gillberg, 1991; Gillberg & Steffenburg, 1987; Lincoln, Courchesne, Kilman, Elmasian, & Allen,

1988; Lockyer & Rutter, 1970). Early language ability has been shown to predict both academic achievement and social competence (Howlin, Mawhood, & Rutter, 2000; Venter, Lord, & Schopler, 1992). In addition, a number of studies have indicated that early, intensive behavioral intervention is associated with higher IQ scores, a greater likelihood of developing language, and an increased chance of being placed in a regular education classroom (G. Dawson & Osterling, 1997; Lord & Schopler, 1989; Lovaas, 1987; McEachin, Smith, & Lovaas, 1993; Sigman & Ruskin, 1999).

Other predictors of language and social outcome include total speech and language therapy received, early expressive language ability, imitation and joint attention abilities, social interaction and shared affect, toy play, and age of diagnosis, with earlier diagnoses relating to poorer outcomes (Rogers & Hepburn, 2003; W. L. Stone et al., 2003; Toth, Dawson, Munson, Estes, & Abbott, 2003). Of particular importance, gains in verbal IQ have been observed in children with Autism beyond the preschool years (Lord, DiLavore, Shulman, Risi, & Pickles, 2003; Nordin & Gillberg, 1998; W. L. Stone et al., 2003).

EPIDEMIOLOGY

Autism was once believed to be a rare disorder, occurring at a rate of 4 to 5 in 10,000. In recent years, however, reported cases of Autism have increased significantly, leading to both public and scientific debate as to whether these estimates reflect a true increase in the number of children with this disorder, or increased awareness and detection along with a broadening definition of Autism.

Prevalence

The prevalence of Autism spectrum disorders has increased significantly in the past few decades. A large epidemiological study conducted by the Centers for Disease Control (CDC) found a prevalence rate of 34 per 10,000 among 3- to 10-year-old children in metropolitan Atlanta (Yeargin-Allsopp et al., 2003). One of the strengths of this study was sample size: 987 confirmed cases, compared to many previous studies with a median sample size of 50 (Fombonne, 2003). However, this rate of 34 per 10,000 is likely to be an underestimate. Higher-functioning individuals may have been missed, and younger children may not have been identified. Fombonne suggests that the rate reported for 5- to 8-year-olds in the CDC study—of 41 to 45 in 10,000—may be more accurate and is similar to other

surveys that report a prevalence rate of 60 per 10,000 (Baird et al., 2000; Bertrand et al., 2001; Chakrabarti & Fombonne, 2001; Fombonne, 2003). There has been public debate about a possible epidemic of Autism as rates are 3 to 4 times higher than in the 1970s. However, this apparent rise in rates may be, in part, the result of a broadening definition of Autism, particularly at the less severe end of the spectrum; methodological differences in surveys of prevalence, particularly in methods for case finding (e.g., relying on single versus multiple sources for case identification); and an increasing use of the diagnosis of Autism so that families can take advantage of federally mandated early intervention programs (Fombonne, 2003).

Gender

Autism affects males at rates 3 to 4 times higher than females (Fombonne, 1999; Volkmar et al., 1993; Yeargin-Allsopp et al., 2003). However, when females are affected, they more often fall in the severe mental retardation range (IQ < 35) and exhibit more severe symptomatology than males with the disorder (Volkmar et al., 1993). Further, the recurrence risk rate for siblings of females with Autism is twice that of siblings of males with Autism (Jorde et al., 1990).

Socioeconomic Status and Culture

Autism affects individuals at all socioeconomic levels (Fombonne, 1999, 2003; Steffenburg & Gillberg, 1986; Wing & Gould, 1979) and in all parts of the world, including Canada (Bryson, Clark, & Smith, 1988), England (Chakrabarti & Fombonne, 2001; Wing & Gould, 1979), France (Cialdella & Mamelle, 1989; Fombonne, Bolton, Prior, Jordan, & Rutter, 1997), Sweden (Steffenburg & Gillberg, 1986), Norway (Sponheim & Skjeldal, 1998), Iceland (Magnusson & Saemundsen, 2001), Japan (Honda, Shimizu, Misumi, Nimi, & Ohashi, 1996; Sugiyama & Abe, 1989), Hong Kong (Chung, Luk, & Lee, 1990), Russia (Lebedinskaya & Nikolskaya, 1993), and Croatia (Bujas-Petkovic, 1993).

SYMPTOM PRESENTATION

Symptoms of Autism include impairments in the broad domains of social interaction, play, language and communication, and a restrictive range of interests and activities.

Specific symptoms in each of these broader domains are described next.

Impairments in Social Interaction

Although symptom presentation varies widely across individuals and across the life span, impairments in social attention are a primary early feature of the disorder. It has been hypothesized that a lack of normal attention to social stimuli, such as faces, voices, and emotional expressions, deprives the child with Autism of social information input during the 1st years of life, disrupting normal brain and behavioral development as well as subsequent social development (Mundy & Neal, 2001). Such impairments in social attention, particularly joint attention skills, are believed to also impede the development of language (Bono, Daley, & Sigman, 2003; Carpenter, Nagell, & Tomasello, 1998; G. Dawson, Toth, et al., 2004; Mundy, Sigman, & Kasari, 1990; Rogers & Hepburn, 2003; Sigman & Ruskin, 1999; Tomasello & Farrar, 1986).

One theory that has been proposed to explain the social attention impairments in Autism is that these impairments are the result of an underlying impairment in social motivation, or a failure to find social stimuli inherently rewarding (G. Dawson, Toth, et al., 2004; G. Dawson, Webb, et al., 2002; Mundy & Neal, 2001). According to this view, the preferential attention to social stimuli (faces, emotional expressions, voices) that is typically present very early in life is most often accompanied by affective sharing between infant and caregiver. This mutual exchange of positive affect during episodes involving eye contact is inherently rewarding to the typically developing toddler and serves to motivate the child to notice and attend to social and affective cues. It is hypothesized that the child with Autism fails to find eye-to-eye gaze inherently rewarding and is therefore less motivated and less likely to attend to social stimuli, make meaning out of others' emotional expressions, and participate in early social exchanges. As a result, the child with Autism has fewer opportunities to engage in acts that allow for the acquisition and development of social communication and language skills.

Social Orienting Impairments

Perhaps the first social attention impairment in Autism is a lack of normal "social orienting," namely, the tendency to spontaneously orient to naturally occurring social stimuli in one's environment (G. Dawson, Meltzoff, Osterling, Rinaldi, & Brown, 1998). In typical development, infants devote particular attention to social stimuli, including faces, voices, and other aspects of human beings (Rochat & Striano, 1999). Indeed, by 6 months of age, typically developing infants will actively orient (i.e., turn head and/or eyes) to novel stimuli, particularly social stimuli (e.g., being called by name; Trevarthen, 1979). Children with Autism, however, exhibit early impairments in social orienting. Home videotape studies of infants later diagnosed with Autism (Osterling & Dawson, 1994; Osterling et al., 2002; Werner et al., 2000) revealed social attention impairments, including a failure to look at others and orient to their name in 12-month-olds, and a failure to orient to name in 8- to 10-month-old infants. In two experimental studies of preschool children with Autism and mental age-matched children with developmental delay, children with Autism more frequently failed to orient to both social and nonsocial stimuli, but the impairment was more severe for social stimuli (G. Dawson, Meltzoff, & Osterling, 1995; G. Dawson, Toth, et al., 2004).

Joint Attention

Joint attention behaviors include sharing attention to an object or event (e.g., through the use of alternating eye gaze), following the attention of another (e.g., following a gaze or point), and directing attention (e.g., showing and pointing to objects/events). Some infants display some aspects of joint attention (e.g., matching direction of mother's gaze to a visible target) as early as 6 months of age (Morales, Mundy, & Rojas, 1998), and most infants display all of these skills by 12 months of age (Carpenter et al., 1998; Leekam & Moore, 2001). Research has established joint attention ability as a core social-communication impairment in children with Autism, present by 1 year of age and incorporated into the diagnostic criteria for the disorder (Mundy et al., 1986; *DSM-IV*, American Psychiatric Association, 1994). Impairments in joint attention skills have been found to distinguish preschool-age children with Autism from those with typical and delayed development (Bacon, Fein, Morris, Waterhouse, & Allen, 1998; Charman et al., 1998; G. Dawson, Meltzoff, Osterling, & Rinaldi, 1998; G. Dawson, Munson, et al., 2002; Mundy et al., 1986). Additionally, impairments in protodeclarative joint attention behaviors (e.g., pointing to show, sharing) seem to be more severe than impairments in protoimperative joint attention behaviors (e.g., pointing to make a request) in children with Autism (Mundy et al., 1986, 1990; Sigman, Mundy, Sherman, & Ungerer, 1986). Joint attention ability is predictive of both concurrent language ability and future gains in expressive language skills for children with Autism (Mundy et al., 1990; Mundy, Sigman, Ungerer, & Sherman,

1987; Sigman & Ruskin, 1999; Toth et al., 2003). Taken together, these findings suggest that joint attention ability is a pivotal skill in Autism as it appears to lay a foundation for the development of more complex abilities, such as pretend play, language, and theory of mind (Charman, 1997, 2003; Mundy & Crowson, 1997; Sigman, 1997).

Face Recognition

At birth, typically developing infants display a visual preference for the sounds, movements, and features of the human face (Goren, Sarty, & Wu, 1975; Maurer & Salapatek, 1976; Morton & Johnson, 1991). Very early in life, infants are not only able to recognize their mother's face (Bushnell, Sai, & Mullin, 1989), but they can also discriminate some facial expressions (Nelson, 1993). Children with Autism, however, do not show this same preference for and fascination with faces. Osterling and Dawson (1994) found in a study of home videotapes that a failure to look at others' faces best discriminated 12-month-olds with Autism from 12-month-old typically developing infants.

Face matching and face recognition impairments have been found across a number of studies in both children and adults with Autism (Boucher & Lewis, 1992; Boucher, Lewis, & Collis, 1998; Cipolotti, Robinson, Blair, & Frith, 1999; Hauck, Fein, Maltby, Waterhouse, & Feinstein, 1998; Jambaque, Mottron, Ponsot, & Chiron, 1998; Klin et al., 1999; Ozonoff, Pennington, & Rogers, 1990; Tantam, Monaghan, Nicholson, & Stirling, 1989; Teunisse & DeGelder, 1994). Using electrophysiological measures, G. Dawson and colleagues (G. Dawson, Carver, et al., 2002; McPartland, Dawson, Carver, & Panagiotides, 2001a, 2001b) showed that 3- to 4-year-old children with Autism failed to show a differential brain electrical response to mother's versus stranger's face, as did children with delayed and typical development. Interestingly, however, the children with Autism did show greater event-related potential (ERP) responses to the familiar versus unfamiliar object, similar to the pattern of responses shown by chronological age-matched typical children. This finding suggests that, in children with Autism, the recognition memory impairment is specific to faces and that this impairment is present by at least 3 years of age.

Other studies have shown that individuals with Autism process faces differently from controls (Celani, Battacchi, & Arcidiacono, 1999; Davies, Bishop, Manstead, & Tantam, 1994). For example, whereas typically developing individuals tend to focus on the eyes when processing faces, individuals with Autism often focus on the mouth (Klin, Jones, Schultz, Volkmar, & Cohen, 2002; Klin et al., 1999; Langdell, 1978). Additionally, individuals with Autism do

not show the typical difficulty in processing inverted as opposed to upright faces (Hobson, Ouston, & Lee, 1988; Langdell, 1978; McPartland et al., 2001a, 2001b). In a recent ERP study, high-functioning adolescents and adults with Autism were shown to exhibit longer latencies of the N170 (face-specific) ERP component as compared to IQ-matched adolescents and adults. In addition to overall slower processing of face stimuli, the individuals with Autism showed similar ERP patterns in response to upright versus inverted faces and did not show the right-lateralized ERP that is found in typical individuals (McPartland et al., 2001a, 2001b).

Functional magnetic resonance imaging (fMRI) techniques have also been used to study face processing in Autism. Schultz et al. (2000) found that when individuals with Autism were shown pictures of faces, they showed less activation in the fusiform gyrus, a specialized region of the brain devoted to face processing, than in the inferior temporal gyri, a region of the brain that is typically used to process objects. Future research is needed to explore the connection between abnormalities in face processing and other social attention impairments in Autism.

Emotion Recognition and Expression

In typical development, infants are able to recognize and express emotions at a very young age. At 6 months of age, infants respond differentially to happy versus sad expressions (Cohn, Campbell, Matias, & Hopkins, 1990; Termine & Izard, 1988). At 12 months, infants are able to modulate their own behavior in response to the emotions expressed by their mother, approaching an object when mother displays a joyful expression but not when she displays a fearful expression (Klinnert, Campos, Sorce, Emde, & Svejda, 1983). By the end of the 2nd year of life, children are beginning to talk about emotions and can label simple emotions, such as happy, mad, and sad (Bretherton & Beeghly, 1982; Smiley & Huttenlocher, 1989). Children with Autism, however, generally do not exhibit this typical pattern of emotional development. A number of studies have shown that children with Autism are impaired on tasks requiring recognition and matching of emotional faces and responding to the emotional displays of others (Bormann-Kischkel, Vilsmeier, & Baude, 1995; Celani et al., 1999; G. Dawson, Meltzoff, Osterling, & Rinaldi, 1998; G. Dawson, Toth, et al., 2004; Hobson, Ouston, & Lee, 1989; Loveland et al., 1997; Sigman, Kasari, Kwon, & Yirmiya, 1992; Sigman, Ungerer, Mundy, & Sherman, 1987). Baron-Cohen, Spitz, and Cross (1993) reported that children with Autism are able to recognize simple emotions, such as happy and sad, which are typically caused by situations, but show greater difficulty than controls in recognizing surprise, which is typically caused by beliefs. Others, however, have shown that emotion recognition impairments may not be specific to Autism, but related rather to verbal memory and performance IQ (Buitelaar, van der Wees, Swaab-Barneveld, & van der Gaag, 1999). In a study of children and adolescents ages 8 to 18, no differences were found between children with Autism and age- and verbal IQ-matched ADHD controls on emotion matching and emotion recognition tasks (Buitelaar et al., 1999).

In one of the earliest studies of emotional expression in Autism, children with Autism were found to exhibit significantly more negative emotions as well as incongruous blends of emotion as compared to typical controls (Yirmiya, Kasari, Sigman, & Mundy, 1989). Further, children with Autism failed to show positive affect even in situations where positive affect is typically displayed, such as in joint attention interactions (Kasari, Sigman, Mundy, & Yirmiya, 1990). Dawson, Hill, Spencer, Galpert, and Watson (1990) examined mother-child interactions and found that children with Autism smiled as frequently as receptive language age-matched typically developing children, but were less likely to combine smiles with eye contact or to smile reciprocally. These authors proposed that children with Autism may have a specific impairment in their ability to engage in affective sharing experiences. When talking about emotion, children with Autism required more time and more prompts, and their responses were more scripted, as compared to age-matched typically developing controls (Capps, Yirmiya, & Sigman, 1992). Finally, although individuals with Autism are able to spontaneously display facial expressions, Loveland et al. (1994) reported that they showed a particular difficulty producing affective expressions upon request without a model.

Many studies that have assessed emotion perception in children with Autism have required language, making results difficult to interpret. G. Dawson and colleagues (G. Dawson, Webb, Carver, Panagiotides, & McPartland, 2004) used ERPs to determine whether 3- to 4-year-old children with Autism Spectrum Disorder exhibited differential brain responses to a fear versus a neutral facial expression, present in typical development by 7 months of age. It was found that children with ASD did not show the typical difference in amplitude of an early ERP component to the fear versus neutral face, indicating early differences in neural processing of emotion in Autism.

Imitation

Meltzoff and Moore (1977) demonstrated that newborns are able to imitate facial expressions, which suggests that this is an innate ability. Children with Autism, however, show impairments in both immediate and deferred motor imitation (G. Dawson, Meltzoff, Osterling, & Rinaldi, 1998; Sigman & Ungerer, 1984; W. L. Stone et al., 1997). Of particular importance, imitation skills in children with Autism have been shown to predict later social and language learning (Charman et al., 2000, 2003; W. L. Stone et al., 1997; W. L. Stone & Yoder, 2001). In one study, body imitation was found to predict expressive language ability, whereas object imitation predicted play skills (W. L. Stone et al., 1997). Additionally, it has been theorized that a failure to engage in social imitative play may interfere with the development of joint attention, social reciprocity, and later theory of mind abilities (G. Dawson, 1991; Meltzoff & Gopnick, 1993; Rogers & Pennington, 1991).

Theory of Mind

The ability to infer mental states, including intentions, memories, and beliefs, and to then use this information to understand and predict the behavior of others is "one of the quintessential abilities that makes us human" (Baron-Cohen, 2000, p. 3; see also Whiten, 1993). This ability is referred to as "theory of mind" and typically develops between 3 and 5 years of age (Flavell, 1999; Wellman, 1993; Wellman, Cross, & Watson, 2001). Children with Autism, however, show impairments on standard theory of mind tasks, such as false-belief tasks that require the child to infer what another person will think or do (Baron-Cohen, 2000; Baron-Cohen, Leslie, & Frith, 1985; Peterson, 2002). In one study, children were required to attribute beliefs to a puppet that differed from their own (Baron-Cohen et al., 1985). Only 20% of the children with Autism were able to do so, compared to 86% of children with Down syndrome and typical development. Interestingly, preschool-age children with Autism have been shown to outperform typically developing preschoolers on a particular form of theory of mind task, the false-drawing task (Peterson, 2002). In this task, children with Autism were asked to draw a red apple with a green pen. When they were finished, a green apple was placed next to the red apple and the children were then told that another child would be coming in the room and asked which apple was drawn. The children with Autism were then asked the false-belief test question, "What will he say?" One possible explanation for this superior understanding of false belief in a drawing context is that children with Autism may be able to gain early insight into mental states in relation to familiar and nonverbal activities such as drawing, even when fully developed theory of mind is absent (Peterson, 2002). Some have argued that theory of mind development in

Autism is not only delayed but is qualitatively different from the typical pattern of development. For instance, in a study of children with PDD-NOS who were given a story-book theory of mind task, the children with PDD-NOS showed specific difficulties in understanding and predicting others' emotions but were able to predict actions from beliefs and desires (Serra, Loth, van Geert, Hurkens, & Minderaa, 2002). Zelazo, Jacques, Burack, and Frye (2002) examined rule-based reasoning in conjunction with theory of mind tasks in older children and adolescents with Autism and found that, for severely impaired individuals, theory of mind performance was unrelated to rule use. However, in less severely impaired individuals, the correlation between theory of mind and rule use was high. These findings suggest that poor performance on theory of mind tasks may be related to a general difficulty in using rules to integrate two incompatible perspectives. Some researchers have proposed that theory of mind deficits are primary in Autism and at the root of the difficulties observed in social interaction and communication (Baron-Cohen et al., 1985); others argue that theory of mind abilities hinge on earlier developing social communication skills, such as joint attention (Mundy & Sigman, 1989).

Play and Language

Impairments in symbolic play, language, and communication skills are present at an early age in individuals with Autism.

Symbolic Play

Representational, or symbolic, play typically emerges between 14 and 22 months of age and includes using an object to represent another object (e.g., a block to represent a car), using absent objects as if they were present (e.g., food that does not exist), or animating objects (e.g., pretending that stuffed animals can talk; Leslie, 1987). In children with Autism, symbolic play is often absent at 18 months of age (Baron-Cohen et al., 1996) or is delayed relative to mental age-matched developmentally delayed and typical children (Charman et al., 1998; G. Dawson, Meltzoff, Osterling, & Rinaldi, 1998; Mundy et al., 1987; Wing & Gould, 1979). For those children with Autism who do acquire symbolic play skills, their level of symbolic play often remains below that of their language abilities (Amato, Barrow, & Domingo, 1999; Ungerer, 1989; Wing, 1978) and is often less diverse and elaborate compared to that of developmentally delayed and typical children (Ungerer & Sigman, 1981). Further, symbolic play has been associated with both concurrent language and later social ability in young

children with Autism (Sigman & Ruskin, 1999). There exists some controversy as to the cause of this impairment; some believe that it results from impairments in joint attention and understanding others, whereas others believe it hinges on deficits in symbolic thinking and executive functioning (Charman, 1997).

Language Ability

The acquisition and development of language in Autism is often delayed and/or deviant, with approximately 30% of individuals never acquiring spoken language (Bryson, 1996; Lord & Paul, 1997). This is hardly surprising given that individuals with Autism often show early impairments in symbolic play, imitation, and joint attention, which have been shown to predict language ability. In addition to delays in language acquisition, persons with Autism often exhibit atypical speech patterns, including immediate or delayed echolalia (i.e., verbatim repetition of words or phrases), unusual prosody (e.g., atypical intonation, rhythm, stress, and volume), and pronoun reversal (e.g., "*you* want a drink" instead of "*I* want a drink"), which can persist into adulthood (Cantwell, Baker, Rutter, & Mawhood, 1989; Kanner, 1943; Lee, Hobson, & Chiat, 1994).

Moreover, individuals with Autism exhibit impairments in both the pragmatic and the semantic aspects of language (Kjelgaard & Tager-Flusberg, 2001; Lord & Paul, 1997; Tager-Flusberg, 1993, 1999, 2001). Pragmatic impairments include difficulty maintaining an appropriate level of detail (e.g., often providing excessive or irrelevant details), speaking in a pedantic manner, and difficulties in reciprocity, characterized by a failure to respond to questions and comments initiated by the other person, a tendency to monopolize the conversation (generally associated with perseveration on favorite topics), and difficulties staying on topic (i.e., often inserting random and tangential comments; Capps, Kehres, & Sigman, 1998; Eales, 1993; Tager-Flusberg, 1999, 2001). Some (Eales, 1993; Tager-Flusberg, 1993, 1996) have argued that these pragmatic impairments, as well as abnormal pronoun use, are related to deficits in perspective taking (i.e., understanding another person's intentions).

Children with Autism also show impairments in how effectively they use language. In studies comparing children with Autism to children with Down syndrome matched on age and expressive language ability, children with Autism showed less variety in their use of nouns, verbs, and adjectives and used language less often to provide or elicit information (Howlin, 1984; Tager-Flusberg, 1993, 1999). Further, Kjelgaard and Tager-Flusberg (2001) found that children with Autism who had impaired language demonstrated better vocabulary relative to higher-order language abilities, with poor performance on phonological processing and difficulties in marking tense, similar to children with specific language impairment. Finally, in their comprehension of language, children with Autism often rely on syntax as opposed to semantic content when deciphering the meaning of a sentence (Paul, Fischer, & Cohen, 1988) and often interpret what is said to them in a concrete and literal manner (e.g., "It's raining cats and dogs").

For a discussion of overlap between language impairment in Autism and specific language impairment, see the earlier section on Diagnosis.

Restricted, Repetitive Interests and Behaviors

The third symptom domain in Autism is a restricted range of behaviors, activities, and interests. Such behaviors include repetitive, stereotypic motor movements, including hand flapping, finger flicking, and complex whole-body movements, such as toe-walking and spinning, as well as persistent preoccupation with parts of objects or repetitive and nonfunctional use of objects (e.g., spinning wheels, lining things up; Campbell et al., 1990; Turner, 1999; Wing, 1988; Wing & Gould, 1979). More elaborate and complex ritualistic interests and behaviors can include precise arrangement of objects; insistence on a particular sequence of actions (i.e., compulsions); adherence to sameness in terms of routine, structure, and ordering of physical space; and intense and focused preoccupations relating to particular topics and typically involving memorization of facts (e.g., movies, camera models). Preoccupations with specific topics are often seen in high-functioning individuals (Campbell et al., 1990; Turner, 1999; Wing, 1988; Wing & Gould, 1979).

Studies that have attempted to identify the earliest emerging impairments in Autism (i.e., within the first 12 months of life) have not shown stereotypic motor movements or intense interests to be commonly present at that early age (Baron-Cohen et al., 1996; Osterling & Dawson, 1994; Robins et al., 2001). Further, young, typically developing children and children with other developmental disabilities, including mental retardation and Obsessive-Compulsive Disorder, often exhibit distress due to changes in routine and a preference for sameness (Evans et al., 1997). However, what may be specific to Autism is the number and severity of these symptoms (Charman & Swettenham, 2001).

Other Related Behaviors

The following behaviors are also common in Autism, although the number and severity of these symptoms varies across individuals.

Sensory Issues

Persons with Autism often seek sensory stimulation or have heightened negative responses to sensory stimuli. For instance, children with Autism may exhibit strong negative reactions to sounds that would not affect most individuals, such as the vacuum cleaner or noises at a distance. They may also exhibit a hypersensitivity to touch, including the feel of tags in clothing or a light embrace, while at the same time appearing insensitive to pain or showing a preference for deep pressure (e.g., tight hugs). Other children may repetitively seek out certain textures (e.g., hair, metal), touch objects to their tongue, or peer at objects out of the corner of their eyes. These sensory issues can be mild or can take up a large amount of time, interfering with family activities and/or the child's social functioning. Ornitz (1989) has argued that an impairment in the ability to modulate sensory information can lead to both under- and over-reactivity to sensory stimuli.

Attention Impairments and Hyperactivity

Estimates of overactivity and/or attentional problems in Autism range from 21% to 72% (Lainhart, 1999). Children with Autism often lack attention to people and to activities that others want them to focus on, but then show overly focused attention on objects or other nonsocial stimuli. Hyperactivity in Autism appears to decrease with age but can persist into adulthood in some individuals (Kobayashi & Murata, 1998). Certain medications may improve attention and decrease hyperactivity in some children, but more controlled studies are needed (McDougle, 1998).

Self-Injurious Behaviors

Self-injurious behaviors include biting, scratching, head banging, and hair pulling and are often an expression of frustration (Donnellan, Mirenda, Mesaros, & Fassbender, 1984; Lainhart, 1999). In a recent study of 222 children with Autism under age 7, 50% demonstrated self-injurious behaviors, with as many as 15% showing severe behaviors (Baghdadli, Pascal, Grisi, & Aussilloux, 2003). Risk factors for self-injurious behaviors include lower chronological age, more severe symptoms of Autism, and more severe delays in daily living skills (Baghdadli et al., 2003). Others have argued that these behaviors are related to level of cognitive functioning (J. Dawson, Matson, & Cherry, 1998).

Sleep and Eating Problems

Rates of sleep disturbances in Autism have been estimated to range from 11% to 65% (Chung et al., 1990; Rutter & Lockyer, 1967; Taira, Takase, & Sasaki, 1998), with average age of onset being 2 years, 3 months (Taira et al., 1998). The most common problems are difficulty falling asleep, frequent awakening, and waking early in the morning (Taira et al., 1998). Approximately 20% of adults with Autism also exhibit sleep problems (Kobayashi & Murata, 1998). However, sleep difficulties in children with Autism appear to occur at rates similar to those found in children with other psychiatric disorders (Rutter & Lockyer, 1967) and are thus not unique to Autism.

There are frequent clinical reports of restricted eating and unusual food preferences in Autism. For instance, some individuals with Autism will eat only a few foods or will eat only foods of a certain texture, color, or taste. Others exhibit rigidity at meal times, such as insisting on eating only certain brands of foods or using only certain utensils. Although eating problems can persist into adulthood, they do tend to improve as children grow older (Rutter, 1970).

ETIOLOGY

Over the past 25 years, considerable evidence has accumulated implicating genetic factors in Autism. Environmental factors and gene-environment interactions likely also contribute to the development of this disorder.

Environmental Risk Factors

Understanding environmental influences in Autism is important for several reasons. First, a better understanding of environmental factors that contribute to the disorder could help to confirm or refute reports of geographic clusters of Autism and an overall increase in rates of Autism. Second, environmental influences may help to shed light on the neurobiology of Autism. Finally, environmental factors would help to account for the high degree of heterogeneity observed in the disorder (Rodier & Hyman, 1998).

An increased rate of Autism has been reported in children who were exposed to rubella infection in the first trimester (Chess, 1977). It is likely that exposure to infectious diseases such as rubella during prenatal development may increase the risk of Autism by adding to other etiological factors, such as genetic predisposition (Rodier & Hyman, 1998). Many studies have investigated whether general suboptimal conditions (complications) during pregnancy, delivery, or infancy may contribute to Autism. No single factor has emerged consistently, and individual adverse events appear to have minimal impact (Bolton et al., 1994, 1997; Bryson et al., 1988; Gillberg & Gillberg, 1983; Levy, Zoltak, & Saelens, 1988; Lord, Mulloy, Wendelboe, & Schopler, 1991). In studies of individuals with high-functioning Autism, only one factor, a gestation period of more than 42 weeks, was found to be associated with the disorder (Lord et al., 1991). Piven et al. (1993) found that first- or fourth-born children had Autism more often than their siblings. Others have found no differences on pre- and perinatal optimality measures when comparing the births of children with Autism to those of typically developing children (Cryan, Byrne, O'Donovan, & O'Callaghan, 1996). Bolton and colleagues (1997) have concluded that optimality factors are not likely to play a direct role in Autism. Such factors are more likely related to extant fetal abnormalities, genetic factors (Bolton et al., 1994, 1997), or possibly to teratologic factors (Rodier & Hyman, 1998). Teratogenic exposure to thalidomide has been associated with Autism (Miller & Strömland, 1993). These researchers found that 5 of 15 thalidomide cases that had exposure between the 20th and 24th days of gestation had Autism, a rate of 33% during this critical period in prenatal development. Prenatal exposure to valproic acid (Moore et al., 2000; J. Williams, Whiten, Suddendorf, & Perrett, 2001) and cocaine (Davis et al., 1992) may also increase the risk of Autism.

In the late 1990s, it was proposed that a new variant of Autism caused by immunization with the combined measles, mumps, and rubella vaccine was responsible for the increase in rates of the disorder (Wakefield, 1999; Wakefield et al., 1998). These claims were made based on a sample size of 12 children with Pervasive Developmental Disorder who were referred for the evaluation of gastrointestinal diseases associated with developmental regression. A number of epidemiological studies since then have failed to confirm an association between the MMR vaccine and Autism (for reviews, see Dales, Hammer, & Smith, 2001; Farrington, Miller, & Taylor, 2001; Fombonne & Chakrabarti, 2001; Kaye, del Mar Melero-Montes, & Jick, 2001; E. N. Taylor et al., 1999; Wilson, Mills, Ross, McGowan, & Jadad, 2003). In addition, Andrews et al. (2002) have found that parents of children with Autism with regression, who were diagnosed after the publicity alleging the link between the MMR vaccine and Autism, tended to recall onset shortly after the vaccine more often than parents of similar children who were diagnosed prior to the publicity. Thimerosal, a preservative containing ethyl mercury that is added to many vaccines, has also come under scrutiny. In 1999, the FDA determined that infants receiving multiple vaccines might be exposed to greater levels of mercury than is recommended. Although a recent review found no evidence of harm from thimerosal in vaccines (Ball, Ball, & Pratt, 2001), thimerosal-free vaccines are now available for all routine childhood immunizations (Kimmel, 2002). Several studies are currently under way examining the effects of thimerosal on childhood disorders.

Genetic Risk Factors

Next, we review what is known about genetic factors in Autism.

Single Gene Disorders

Five to 10% of Autism cases are due to an identifiable medical disorder with a known inheritance pattern, including Fragile X syndrome, untreated phenylketonuria (PKU), tuberous sclerosis, and neurofibromatosis (Szatmari, Jones, Zwaigenbaum, & MacLean, 1998). Fragile X syndrome in particular accounts for about 8% of cases of Autism (Smalley, Asarnow, & Spence, 1988).

Twin and Family Studies

A number of twin studies have provided evidence of a strong genetic component to Autism (Bailey, Le Couteur, Gottesman, & Bolton, 1995; Folstein & Rutter, 1977; Le Couteur, Bailey, & Rutter, 1989; Ritvo, Freeman, Mason-Brothers, Mo, & Ritvo, 1985; Steffenburg et al., 1989). These studies have shown a higher concordance rate for Autism in monozygotic (MZ), or identical, twin pairs than in dizygotic (DZ), or fraternal, twins. In their seminal study, Folstein and Rutter reported that 36% of MZ twins were concordant for Autism, as compared to 0% of DZ twins. When they included related social or cognitive impairments, such as reading disability, language delay, articulation disorder, and mental handicap, 82% of the MZ twins and 10% of the DZ twins were concordant for Autism. A more recent study found that 60% of MZ twins were concordant for the full syndrome of Autism, and more than 90% were concordant when related social and cognitive impairments were included (Bailey et al., 1995). Heritability estimates are quite high, ranging from 91% to 93% (Bailey et al., 1995).

Family studies have provided further evidence of the heritability of Autism. The likelihood of having a second child with Autism has been estimated at 4.5% (Jorde et al., 1990, 1991), which is 45 to 90 times greater than the population risk (Cook, 1998). Further, the recurrence risk rate for siblings of females with Autism is twice that of siblings of males with Autism (Jorde et al., 1990). Recurrence risk rates following the birth of a second child with Autism range from 16% to 35% (Szatmari et al., 1998). Autism rates in second- (0.18%) and third- (0.12%) degree relatives are much lower (Szatmari et al., 1998). This sharp decrease in risk rates from first- to second- and third-degree relatives indicates that Autism is most likely the result of multiple gene (5 to 10 or more) interactions (Jorde et al., 1990; Pickles et al., 1995; Risch et al., 1999).

Broader Autism Phenotype

A broader Autism phenotype, or "lesser variant" of Autism, is defined as having one or more difficulties in social functioning, communication, cognition, and interests/behaviors (Baron-Cohen & Hammer, 1997). Broader phenotype studies have been on the rise in recent years and have examined characteristics of first-, second-, and third-degree relatives of individuals with Autism. As many as 10% to 25% of siblings who do not meet criteria for Autism demonstrate broader phenotype impairments, including learning difficulties, language and communication deficits, and social impairments (Bolton et al., 1994; Bolton & Rutter, 1990). A more recent study reported that 12% of siblings and 10% of parents exhibited broader phenotype characteristics (Starr et al., 2001).

Parents of children with Autism were 3 times as likely as parents of children with Down syndrome to have had definite or probable language problems in childhood, including articulation deficits, trouble learning to read, or trouble with spelling, and showed a significant split between verbal and performance IQ scores relative to controls (Folstein et al., 1999). A study of personality traits in first-degree relatives found that relatives of individuals with Autism were more anxious, impulsive, aloof, shy, sensitive, irritable, and eccentric than relatives of individuals with Down syndrome (Murphy et al., 2000). In this same study, three factors were derived for the Autism group: withdrawn, difficult, and tense. The authors concluded that the withdrawn and difficult factors appeared to reflect social functioning impairments, whereas the tense factor appeared to be related to the burden of raising a child with Autism. In multiplex families (i.e., those with two or more children with Autism), parents of children with high rates of repetitive behaviors showed significantly more obsessive-compulsive traits and were more likely to have Obsessive-Compulsive

Disorder than parents of children with low repetitive behavior scores (Hollander, King, Delaney, Smith, & Silverman, 2003). Still other studies have reported increased rates of pragmatic language impairments (Landa et al., 1992) and executive function deficits (e.g., set shifting and planning; Hughes, Plumet, & Leboyer, 1999) and difficulties in reading comprehension and rapid automatized naming (Piven & Palmer, 1997) in family members.

In second- and third-degree relatives, Szatmari et al. (2000) found that 10% demonstrated communication impairments, 7% exhibited repetitive activities, 14% showed social impairments, 23% met criteria for the "broad" definition of the lesser variant, and 7% met criteria for the "narrow" definition of the lesser variant, as defined by Bolton et al. (1994).

Like Autism, broader phenotype characteristics are much more common in males than females, although this is less true of the mildest cases, and are usually evident in early childhood (Bailey, Phillips, & Rutter, 1996). However, unlike Autism, individuals with broader phenotype characteristics are generally of normal intelligence, and no association with epilepsy has been found (Bailey et al., 1996). Some researchers have proposed that the broader phenotype is simply a lower dose of the genetic predisposition to Autism, whereas others argue a "two-hit" mechanism. In this view, one set of factors predisposes the individual to the broader phenotype, and a separate set of factors is involved in the development of Autism (Bailey et al., 1996). In any case, these findings in the broader phenotype literature suggest that incorporating quantitative measures of autistic traits that may be expressed to a lesser degree in relatives may be useful in studies of the genetic basis of Autism.

Sibling Linkage and Quantitative Trait Locus Analyses

Sibling linkage studies use highly variable polymorphisms spaced evenly throughout the genome to identify chromosome regions that are shared among siblings with Autism. Thus far, findings from Autism linkage studies have been inconsistent. Possible susceptibility regions include chromosomes 1p, 2q, 7q, 13q, 16p, and 19q (Alarcon, Cantor, Liu, & Gilliam, 2002; Ashley-Koch et al., 1999; Bailey et al., 1998; Barrett et al., 1999; Bradford et al., 2001; Buxbaum et al., 2001; International Molecular Genetic Study of Autism Consortium, 1998, 2001; Liu, 2001; Philippe et al., 1999; Risch et al., 1999). Only regions 2q and 7q have been implicated in more than one study, with chromosome 7 appearing the most promising (Ashley-Koch et al., 1999; Barrett et al., 1999; Collaborative Linkage Study of Autism, 2001). Chromosome 7 has been linked

both to Autism and to language disorders, such as specific language impairment (Folstein & Mankoski, 2000; Warburton et al., 2000). In addition, the 7q31 region contains other genes of interest, including the serotonin receptor gene and the reelin gene (see section on Candidate Gene Studies).

Quantitative trait loci (QTL) refer to genetic loci that modify the expression of a phenotypic trait in a continuous rather than categorical way. In a study of multiplex families that included parent and proband language phenotypes, Bradford et al. (2001) found that the highest signals, on chromosome 7q and 13q, were primarily accounted for by families in which both probands exhibited language delay. Similarly, a nonparametric multipoint linkage analysis of 152 families from the Autism Genetic Resource Exchange that included QTL from the Autism Diagnostic Interview ("age at first word," "age at first phrase," and a composite of "repetitive and stereotyped behavior") revealed the most robust QTL results for "age at first word" on chromosome 7q (Alarcon et al., 2002).

Autism and Specific Language Impairment

Both Autism and SLI are highly heritable, complex genetic disorders (Santangelo & Folstein, 1999; Tallal & Benasich, 2002; Tomblin & Zhang, 1999) that involve several genes. In addition, family studies have distinguished a broader phenotype. In family members of persons with Autism, elevated rates of language-related impairments have been found, including language delay and language-related learning deficits (Bolton et al., 1994; Fombonne et al., 1997; Piven & Palmer, 1997). Among siblings of persons with SLI, there is an elevated risk of Autism (Tomblin, Hafeman, & O'Brien, 2003). In addition, genetic studies have reported linkage to the same region on chromosome 7 for both disorders (Fisher, Vargha-Khadem, Watkins, Monaco, & Pembrey, 1998; International Molecular Genetic Study of Autism Consortium, 1998). Therefore, it is possible that families with SLI and Autism share some of the same genetic and phenotypic characteristics. Future research that targets the subgroup of children with Autism who exhibit those aspects of language impairment that are also characteristic of SLI may be useful in defining the genetic phenotype of Autism.

Candidate Gene Studies

Numerous candidate gene studies in Autism have been conducted, with little success thus far. Here, a few of such studies are reviewed.

Increased blood and urinary serotonin levels and the positive effect of selective serotonin reuptake inhibitors (SSRIs) on some symptoms of Autism (see Intervention section later in this chapter) led to studies of genes involved in the serotonin system. Although initial studies implicated the serotonin transporter gene (Cook et al., 1997), later studies did not confirm a link (Klauck, Poustka, Benner, Lesch, & Poustka, 1997; Maestrini et al., 1999; Persico et al., 2000; Zhong et al., 1999).

Rodier, Ingram, Tisdale, Nelson, and Romano (1996) conducted an autopsy study to examine the motor nuclei in the brain stem of an individual with Autism. They found shortening of the brain stem between the trapezoid body and the inferior olive, and near-complete absence of the facial nucleus and superior olive, abnormalities similar to those reported in HoxA-1 gene knock-out mice. The HoxA and HoxD genes have also been shown to influence differentiation of the fingers and toes. One trait, the relative length of the second and fourth digits, has been found to correlate with Autism (Manning, Callow, & Bundred, 2003). These findings suggest that the Hox genes may be implicated in Autism. However, other studies have reported conflicted findings regarding an association between the HoxA-1 gene and Autism (B. Devlin et al., 2002; Gallagher, Hawi, Kearney, Fitzgerald, & Gill, 2004; Ingram et al., 2000; Li et al., 2002).

Reelin is an important secretory glycoprotein that regulates normal layering of the brain, normal cell signaling, correct axonal growth, synaptic plasticity, and programmed cell death (Adams & Cory, 1998; Fatemi, Stary, Halt, & Realmuto, 2001; Ogawa et al., 1995). Fatemi and colleagues found a decrease in the level of reelin in the autistic cerebellum, which may be responsible for some of the cognitive deficits in Autism. In another study by these same researchers (Fatemi, Stary, & Egan, 2002), a reelin 410 deficiency was observed in autistic twins and their first-degree relatives (mothers, fathers, and typically developing siblings). A genetic study of affected sib pairs did not provide support for the reelin gene as a susceptibility gene in Autism, but a family-based association study using data from the Autism Diagnostic Interview-Revised found that children with at least one large reelin gene allele (> 11 repeats) tended to have earlier onset of phrase speech (Zhang et al., 2002). Therefore, the reelin gene may play a role in the etiology of some cases of Autism. However, it should be noted that reelin has also been implicated in Schizophrenia (Fatemi, Earle, & McMenomy, 2000; Guidotti et al., 2000; Impagnatiello et al., 1998), Bipolar Disorder (Fatemi et al., 2000; Guidotti et al., 2000), Major Depression (Fatemi et al., 2000), and possibly Schizoaffective Disorder (Fatemi, Stary, & Egan, 2002). Furthermore, a more recent study found no evidence for a link between reelin and Autism (G. Devlin et al., 2004).

Future Directions

Over the past 25 years, we have achieved a deeper understanding of the genetic and environmental risk factors involved in the development of Autism. Regarding the study of genetic factors in particular, we now know that Autism cannot be attributed to a single gene, but rather, to multiple gene interactions. Each gene acts as a risk factor for an element of this complex disorder, with the greatest risk resulting from a large number of genes acting in concert. Recent research also suggests that Autism susceptibility genes may produce effects on a phenotypic continuum. Given this possibility, future research will incorporate the use of dimensional measures—behavioral and/or biological—of core Autism traits to aid in the identification of the specific genes involved in this disorder.

BRAIN FUNCTIONING AND DEVELOPMENT IN AUTISM

It is believed that the brain regions affected in Autism are disrupted early in development, very likely during the prenatal period. Brain regions hypothesized to be affected include the cerebellum, temporal lobe areas (e.g., medial temporal lobe, fusiform gyrus, superior temporal sulcus), the prefrontal cortex (both ventromedial and dorsolateral prefrontal cortex and Broca's area), and the inferior parietal cortex (Bachevelier, 1994; Baron-Cohen et al., 2000; Bauman & Kemper, 1994; Courchesne, 1989; G. Dawson, Webb, et al., 2002).

Enlarged Cerebral Volume

Increased cerebral volume is one of the earliest abnormalities in brain development apparent in children with Autism (Bailey et al., 1998; Piven, Harper, et al., 1995, 1996; Sparks et al., 2002). In a recent study by Courchesne and colleagues (Courchesne, Carper, & Akshoomoff, 2003), it was found that head circumference at birth in infants later diagnosed with Autism Spectrum Disorder was significantly smaller than that found in typically developing infants; however, between 1 to 2 months of age and 6 to 14 months of age, there was an abnormally accelerated rate of growth in head circumference in infants with ASD, more so for those with Autistic Disorder as compared to PDD-NOS. These results suggest that increased brain volume may be an early indicator of Autism, preceding the behavioral onset of the disorder (Courchesne et al., 2003). Further, Aylward, Minshew, Field, Sparks, and Singh (2002) found that children with Autism age 12 years and younger had significantly larger brain volumes than controls; however, brain volumes for individuals with Autism over 12 years of age did not differ from controls, suggesting that there is a slight decrease in brain volume beginning in adolescence in children with Autism at the same time that typically developing children are experiencing a slight increase in volume. Although other studies have also shown brain enlargement in younger children with Autism, but not in older children or adults with Autism (Akshoomoff, Pierce, & Courchesne, 2002; Courchesne, Bartholomeusz, Karns, & Townsend, in press; Courchesne et al., 2001), brain enlargement has also been observed in older individuals with Autism through postmortem and imaging studies; thus, within individuals, the course of brain development may vary (Bailey et al., 1998; Bauman & Kemper, 1985; Courchesne, Muller, & Saitoh, 1999; Lainhart et al., 1997; Piven, Harper, et al., 1995; Piven et al., 1996).

Cerebellum

Neuropathological studies have found reduced numbers of Purkinje or granule cells in the cerebellum (Bailey et al., 1998; Bauman & Kemper, 1994; Raymond, Bauman, & Kemper, 1996). Courchesne (1989) has argued that loss of Purkinje cells may disrupt normal cerebellar functioning necessary for rapid shifts of attention, motor behaviors, and associative learning, and may lead to excitatory interference to brain stem and thalamic systems, which mediate attention and arousal. Early impairments in the cerebellum may also affect later development of limbic regions (Courchesne, Chisum, & Townsend, 1994).

Medial Temporal Lobe

Based on MRI of 3- to 4-year-old children with Autism Spectrum Disorder compared to those with developmental delay or typical development, Sparks et al. (2002) reported that amygdala enlargement exceeded that of overall increased cerebral volume and was related to more severe joint attention and face recognition impairments (Howard et al., 2000; Sparks et al., 2002). Right amygdala enlargement was found to predict a slower rate of growth in social and language skills between ages 3 to 4 years and 6 to 7 years for children with Autistic Disorder (Munson et al., 2004). Taken together, these findings suggest that early increased amygdala volume may be a marker of severity of Autism impairment.

Autopsy studies have revealed abnormalities of the medial temporal lobe (MTL), including the amygdala, hippocampus, and surrounding regions (Bauman & Kemper, 1994). Young children with Autism perform poorly on MTL tasks, including visual recognition memory (paired comparison, delayed nonmatched to sample) and deferred imitation tasks (G. Dawson, Meltzoff, Osterling, & Rinaldi, 1998; G. Dawson, Munson, et al., 2002). It has been hypothesized that Autism might involve an impairment in other aspects of hippocampal functioning as well, such as feature binding (i.e., binding of items or events into a cohesive memory), context memory, and source memory (G. Dawson, Webb, et al., 2002). Such memory functions are important in representing social events (see H. Cohen et al., 1999; N. Cohen & Eichenbaum, 1993). An impairment in feature binding, that is, a failure to integrate information into a meaningful whole (Mottron, Belleville, & Menard, 1999; Shah & Frith, 1993), has also been demonstrated in parents of children with Autism (Happe, Briskman, & Frith, 2001) and may explain the difficulties in face processing found in Autism.

A number of studies have shown that the MTL is involved in social perception (Bachevalier, 2000; Baron-Cohen et al., 2000; G. Dawson, 1996), including recognition of faces and facial expressions (Aggleton, 1992; Jacobson, 1986; Nelson & deHaan, 1996), forming associations between stimuli and reward value (Baxter & Murray, 2000; Gaffan, 1992; Malkova, Gaffan, & Murray, 1997), recognizing the affective significance of stimuli (LeDoux, 1987), perceiving body movements, such as gaze direction (Brothers, Ring, & Kling, 1990), and certain cognitive abilities that may be important for social perception and imitation (Murray & Mishkin, 1985).

In a study by G. Dawson and colleagues (G. Dawson, Meltzoff, Osterling, & Rinaldi, 1998), MTL and prefrontal function in school-age children with Autism was assessed by using the delayed nonmatch to sample (DNMS) and delayed response tasks, respectively. They found that children with Autism were impaired on the DNMS task and the delayed response task compared to mental age-matched children with developmental delays and typical development. Severity of Autism symptoms correlated strongly with DNMS performance, but not with performance on the delayed response task. To extend this study, a more comprehensive set of neuropsychological tasks was administered to a younger and larger sample of children with Autism (G. Dawson, Munson, et al., 2002). The test battery included three tasks measuring dorsolateral prefrontal function and three tasks assessing MTL and/or MTL-ventromedial prefrontal function. Interest in ventromedial prefrontal function was based on findings that patients with ventromedial prefrontal lesions also exhibited deficits in social cognition and theory of mind (Cicerone & Tanenbaum, 1997; Damasio, Tranel, & Damasio, 1990; V. E. Stone, Baron-Cohen, & Knight, 1998). Furthermore, fMRI studies have shown ventromedial prefrontal activation during theory of mind and social attribution tasks (Fletcher et al., 1995; Happe et al., 1996; Schultz, Romanski, & Tsatsanis, 2002).

G. Dawson, Munson, et al. (2002) examined the relationship between performance on the neuropsychological tasks and a core Autism symptom, joint attention. Results showed that the children with Autism were significantly impaired in joint attention ability compared to controls and that performance on the MTL-ventromedial prefrontal tasks was more strongly related to joint attention ability than performance on the dorsolateral prefrontal tasks. These findings suggest that core Autism symptoms, such as joint attention ability, may be related to dysfunction of the MTL-ventromedial prefrontal circuit.

A number of investigators have suggested that the severity or extent of MTL dysfunction varies across individuals with Autism and may account for the variability in functioning (Bachevalier, 1994; Barth, Fein, & Waterhouse, 1995; G. Dawson, 1996; Waterhouse, Fein, & Modahl, 1996). This idea is based on the work of Bachevalier, who found that monkeys with both hippocampal and amygdala lesions exhibited more severe memory and social impairments than monkeys with amygdala lesions alone. In individuals with Autism, memory impairments related to MTL function were found only in lower-functioning individuals (Ameli, Courchesne, Lincoln, Kaufman, & Grillon, 1988; Barth et al., 1995; Boucher, 1981; Boucher & Warrington, 1976; Rumsey & Hamburger, 1988). G. Dawson and colleagues (G. Dawson, Meltzoff, Osterling, & Rinaldi, 1998) found that children with Autism who performed fewer immediate and deferred imitative acts (hippocampal system) also required more trials to reach criterion on the DNMS, an MTL task, and exhibited more severe symptoms of Autism, such as greater joint attention impairments.

A variation on this hypothesis posits that individuals with less severe symptoms are impaired in the temporal-parietal association regions and the parietal cortex but have little or no MTL dysfunction, whereas individuals with more severe symptoms have significant MTL dysfunction that then leads to prefrontal impairments (Waterhouse et al., 1996). In this view, prefrontal impairments are the downstream consequence of faulty MTL function-

ing. In support of this hypothesis, studies with monkeys have shown that early MTL damage disrupts prefrontal cortex development (Bertolino et al., 1997; Chlan-Fourney, Webster, Felleman, & Bachevalier, 2000; Saunders, Kolachana, Bachevalier, & Weinberger, 1998). In studies of very young children with Autism (age 3 to 4), no differences in prefrontal performance were found relative to mental age-matched controls (G. Dawson, Munson, et al., 2002; Griffith, Pennington, Wehner, & Rogers, 1999). However, older elementary school-age children with Autism have demonstrated prefrontal (executive function) deficits compared to controls (G. Dawson, Meltzoff, Osterling, & Rinaldi, 1998; McEvoy, Rogers, & Pennington, 1993; Pennington & Ozonoff, 1996). These results are not surprising given that executive function ability is just emerging during the preschool period (Diamond & Goldman-Rakic, 1989). Longitudinal studies of executive function in younger, and also in more severely affected, individuals with Autism are needed to better understand the course of prefrontal dysfunction in Autism.

Abnormalities in Brain Regions Involved in Face Processing

Studies have shown that individuals with Autism are impaired in their ability to recognize and match faces (Boucher & Lewis, 1992; Boucher et al., 1998; Cipolotti et al., 1999; Hauck et al., 1998; Jambaque et al., 1998; Klin et al., 1999; Ozonoff et al., 1990; Tantam et al., 1989; Teunisse & DeGelder, 1994) and use atypical strategies for processing faces (Hobson et al., 1988; Joseph, 2001; Klin et al., 2002; Langdell, 1978). For typical individuals, the most salient parts of the face are, in order of importance, eyes, mouth, and nose (Shepherd, 1981). Individuals with Autism, however, spend more time looking at the lower half of the face rather than the eyes and are better at matching faces when matching is based on the lower half of the face as opposed to the upper face or eyes (Joseph, 2001; Langdell, 1978). Further, Klin and colleagues (2002) used eye-tracking technology to demonstrate that when viewing emotional and dramatic scenes from a movie, adults with Autism spent more time looking at mouths, bodies, and objects than eyes.

Functional MRI studies in Autism show no activation of the fusiform gyrus, a brain area specialized for face processing (Pierce, Muller, Ampbrose, Allen, & Courchesne, 2001; Schultz et al., 2000), and increased activation in the frontotemporal regions, but not the amygdala, when making inferences from the eyes (Baron-Cohen, Scahill, et al.,

1999). Electrophysiological studies also have demonstrated face processing abnormalities. As mentioned in the section on Symptom Presentation, G. Dawson and colleagues (G. Dawson, Carver, et al., 2002) found that 3- to 4-year-old children with Autism failed to show differential ERPs to faces, whereas they showed normal ERPs to objects. A study of ERPs in adolescents and adults with Autism demonstrated that these individuals have slower processing of faces, fail to show a processing speed advantage for faces relative to nonface stimuli, and have atypical lateralization of ERPs to faces (McPartland et al., 2001a, 2001b).

It is possible that abnormal face processing in Autism is related to an innate abnormality in face processing regions, such as the fusiform face area and superior temporal sulcus. This would result in impairments in early stage face processing (faulty "starter set" for encoding). Alternatively, face processing impairments might be secondary to an impairment in social motivation/sensitivity to social reward. Specifically, an impairment in social motivation might result in reduced attention to faces and facial expressions. This might further lead to a failure to develop expertise in face processing (Carver & Dawson, 2002; G. Dawson, Ashman, & Carver, 2000; Dawson & Zanolli, 2003; Grelotti, Gauthier, & Schultz, 2002; Mundy & Neal, 2001). If the latter explanation is correct, then early intervention might be expected to have a significant impact on face processing development. Early intervention approaches often focus on rewarding children for looking at others and making eye contact (G. Dawson & Zanolli, 2003). Current studies are examining the impact of such early interventions on the development of face processing in children with Autism.

Brain Regions Involved in Motor Imitation

Motor imitation impairments are well documented in Autism (G. Dawson & Adams, 1984; G. Dawson & Lewy, 1989; DeMyer et al., 1972; Meltzoff & Gopnik, 1993; Rogers, 1999; Rogers & Pennington, 1991; I. M. Smith & Bryson, 1994; J. Williams et al., 2001) and may be a precursor to the development of theory of mind (Meltzoff & Gopnik, 1993). A number of brain regions are involved in imitation. For example, patients with left frontal lesions display dyspraxia (Goldenberg, 1995; Goldenberg & Hagman, 1997; Merians et al., 1997); the left hemisphere is activated during imitation of hand and facial movements (G. Dawson, Warrenburg, & Fuller, 1985), and, in animals, cells in the superior temporal sulcus code the movements of the face, limbs, and whole body (Oram & Perrett, 1994;

Perrett et al., 1984, 1985, 1989). In the prefrontal cortex in monkeys, "mirror neurons" fire when a monkey performs or views another monkey performing certain actions (Gallese, Fadiga, Fogassi, & Rizzolatti, 1996; Rizzolatti, Fadiga, Matelli, et al., 1996). Other brain areas that are important in motor imitation include the parietal and prefrontal regions (premotor cortex and Broca's area; Grafton, Arbib, Fadiga, & Rizzolatti, 1996; Rizzolatti, Fadiga, Gallese, & Fogassi, 1996) and the superior temporal gyrus (Decety, Chaminade, Grezes, & Meltzoff, 2002). Thus far, few, if any, functional brain imaging studies have examined patterns of brain activation during imitation in Autism; this is an area ripe for study.

Brain Regions Involved in Language

As described in the sections on Diagnosis and Etiology, some have argued that there is overlap between Autism and specific language impairment, with a subgroup of individuals with Autism showing the characteristic profile of SLI (Kjelgaard & Tager-Flusberg, 2001; Tager-Flusberg, 2003, in press; Tager-Flusberg & Joseph, 2003). MRI findings have shown that this subgroup of children with Autism has the same neurocognitive phenotype as children with SLI. Other studies of SLI have reported volumetric and asymmetry differences in the planum temporale and parietal and frontal cortex, as well as alterations in the magnocellular neurons in the lateral geniculate nucleus and medial geniculate nucleus (see Tallal & Benasich, 2002). Positron emission tomography (PET) studies of phonological processing have most consistently activated Broca's area (Demonet et al., 1992; Paulescu, Frith, & Frackowiak, 1993; Zatorre, Evans, Meyer, & Gjedde, 1992), the secondary auditory cortex (Demonet et al., 1992; Paulescu et al., 1993; Sergent, Zuck, Levesque, & MacDonald, 1992), and the supramarginal gyrus (Paulescu et al., 1993; Petersen, Fox, Posner, Mintun, & Raichle, 1989; Zatorre et al., 1992).

A phonological processing impairment in 3- to 4-year-old children with Autism was found in a study of speech processing using an electrophysiological mismatch negativity (MMN) paradigm (Coffey-Corina & Kuhl, 2001). In this study, the children watched a video of their choice while passively listening to two different speech sounds: One syllable, /wa/, was presented on 85% of the trials (standard), and a different syllable, /ba/, was presented on the remaining 15% of trials (deviant). Results indicated that whereas typically developing children showed a significant difference between standards and deviants, children with Autism showed no significant difference for the two types of speech stimuli. Therefore, in some children with Autism, basic auditory-linguistic processing may be fundamentally different.

Summary

In summary, Autism involves dysfunction of multiple brain regions. Our understanding of the neural bases of Autism has increased as a result of both structural and functional brain imaging studies, many of which have only recently included younger children. Additional research, particularly longitudinal studies of brain function in individuals with Autism, is needed to better understand the complex course of brain development and function in this disorder.

NEUROCHEMICAL FINDINGS AND PHARMACOLOGICAL INTERVENTIONS

Findings from a number of studies suggest that neurochemical factors play a major role in Autism (Tsai, 1999). Studies that have examined neurotransmitters in individuals with Autism are reviewed next.

Serotonin

Serotonin is a neurotransmitter that affects a range of behaviors and processes, including sleep, appetite, learning, memory, pain and sensory perception, motor function, and early brain development and plasticity (Azmitia & Whitaker-Azmitia, 1997; Lauder, 1993; Volkmar & Anderson, 1989). Hyperserotonemia (i.e., having peripheral serotonin levels in the upper 5% of the normal distribution) has been consistently reported in about one-third of persons with Autism, with mean levels ranging from 17% 128% higher than controls (G. M. Anderson et al., 1987; G. M. Anderson, Horne, Chatterjee, & Cohen, 1990; G. M. Anderson & Hoshino, 1987; Cook et al., 1993; Herault et al., 1996; Piven et al., 1991). Using PET technology, researchers have been able to examine serotonin more directly. For instance, in a study of seven boys with Autism, a pattern of increased synthesis of serotonin in the contralateral dentate nucleus of the cerebellum and decreased synthesis of serotonin in the thalamus and frontal cortex was observed (Chugani et al., 1997). Interestingly, elevated levels of serotonin have also been observed in roughly 50% of mothers and fathers and in 87% of siblings of persons with Autism (Leboyer et al., 1999).

Dopamine

Most studies of dopamine in Autism have focused on homovanillic acid (HVA), the main metabolite of dopamine. Although results have not been consistent, some studies have found elevated HVA levels in children with Autism (Gillberg & Svennerholm, 1987). In another study, elevated HVA levels were found in more severely impaired children, especially those with more severe stereotypic and repetitive motor behaviors (Narayan, Srinath, Anderson, & Meundi, 1993). Dopamine agonists, such as stimulants, have been shown to increase stereotypies, aggression, and hyperactivity in children with Autism (Young, Kavanagh, Anderson, Shaywitz, & Cohen, 1982), which suggests that the dopamine system is involved in this disorder.

Epinephrine and Norepinephrine

Epinephrine and norepinephrine impact memory, attention, arousal, movement, anxiety, and respiratory and cardiac function (Volkmar & Anderson, 1989). Researchers have investigated the idea that increased levels of norepinephrine (a neurotransmitter and hormone) may influence symptoms of arousal and anxiety in individuals with Autism. A number of studies have found no differences between Autism subjects and controls in cerebral spinal fluid, plasma, and urinary excretion of norepinephrine's principal metabolite, 3-methoxy-4-hydroxyphenyleneglycol, or in urinary excretion rates of epinephrine, norepinephrine, and vanillylmandelic acid (Gillberg, Svennerholm, & Hamilton-Hellberg, 1983; Minderaa, Anderson, Volkmar, Akkerhuis, & Cohen, 1994; Young et al., 1982). In one study, however, both epinephrine and norepinephrine were significantly lower in the Autism group than in controls (Launay et al., 1987).

Endogenous Opioids

Endogenous opioid peptides, or endorphins, have been linked to social behaviors, emotion, motor activity, and pain perception (Panksepp & Sahley, 1987). Some researchers have suggested that elevated opioids may play a role in the self-injurious behaviors and cognitive and socioemotional deficits observed in Autism (Panksepp, 1979; Panksepp & Sahley, 1987). Thus far, however, results have been inconsistent, with some reporting increased levels of opioids (Tordjman et al., 1997) and others reporting decreased levels of endorphins in Autism (Leboyer et al., 1994; Sandman, Barron, Chicz-DeMet, & DeMet, 1990).

Pharmacological Treatments

Most of the pharmacological studies to date have been open trial (rather than controlled) studies with very small sample sizes. Nevertheless, a number of drugs have been shown to be promising in ameliorating certain symptoms of Autism. Most of these drugs target related symptoms, such as hyperactivity and self-injurious behavior, but some (e.g., SSRIs) have recently been shown to improve core social symptoms of Autism.

Serotonergic Drugs

Two groups of medications that influence the serotonin system—antidepressants and antianxiety drugs—have been studied in Autism.

SSRIs and Other Antidepressants. Medications that influence serotonin include clomipramine, fluoxetine (Prozac), fluvoxamine, and sertraline. Extant evidence suggests that these drugs may reduce hyperactivity in children with Autism (Gordon, Rapoport, Hamburger, State, & Mannheim, 1992; Gordon, State, Nelson, Hamburger, & Rapoport, 1993) and improve obsessive-compulsive symptoms, social withdrawal, reciprocal social interaction, motor stereotypies, aggression, and self-injurious behaviors (Gordon et al., 1993; Harvey & Cooray, 1995; Hellings, Kelley, Gabrielli, Kilgore, & Shah, 1996; McDougle, Price, & Goodman, 1990; Potenza & McDougle, 1997; Steingard, Zimnitzky, DeMaso, Bauman, & Bucci, 1997). However, use of these drugs can lead to serious cardiovascular side effects and lowered seizure thresholds and should therefore be prescribed with caution.

Antianxiety Drugs. In two studies of buspirone, reductions in hyperactivity were noted (McCormick, 1997; Realmuto, August, & Garfinkel, 1989). More research needs to be done on the efficacy of antianxiety drugs in treating symptoms of Autism.

Dopaminergic Drugs

Antipsychotics, including haloperidol, risperidone, and clozapine, have all been shown to produce at least moderate reductions in symptoms of hyperactivity, but effects are less clear on symptoms of impulsivity and inattention (L. T. Anderson & Campbell, 1989; L. T. Anderson et al., 1984; Campbell et al., 1978; Fisman & Steele, 1996; Horrigan & Barnhill, 1997; Joshi, Capozzoli, & Coyle, 1988; Malek-Ahmadi & Simonds, 1998; McDougle et al., 1997; Nicolson, Awad, & Sloman, 1998; Perry, Pataki, Munoz-Silva, Armenteros, & Silva, 1997; Potenza, Holmes, Kanes,

& McDougle, 1999; Zuddas, Ledda, Fratta, Muglia, & Cianchetti, 1996). Risperidone and clozapine are both dopamine and serotonin receptor antagonists.

Epinephrine- and Norepinephrine-Related Drugs

Clonidine is an adrenergic receptor agonist that decreases norepinephrine neurotransmission (Tsai, 1999). There is modest evidence that clonidine may reduce symptoms of hyperactivity in children with Autism (Frankhauser, Karumanchi, German, Yates, & Karumanchi, 1992; Jaselskis, Cook, Fletcher, & Leventhal, 1992). The use of clonidine for managing hyperactivity and sleep problems in children with Autism has escalated in recent years, although the empirical data supporting its efficacy are scanty. Desipramine is a selective norepinephrine uptake inhibitor that has been shown to reduce hyperactivity in children with Autism (Gordon et al., 1992).

Psychostimulants

Again, very few studies have been done to assess the effects of psychostimulants, such as Ritalin and d-amphetamine. However, initial results suggest that these drugs may be helpful in improving attention and social responsiveness (Vitriol & Farber, 1981), irritability (Quintana et al., 1995), and hyperactivity (Geller, Guttmacher, & Bleeg, 1981; Handen, Johnson, & Lubetsky, 2000). Other studies have shown deleterious effects following the use of stimulants in patients with pervasive developmental disorders, including overactivity and stereotypical behavior (Schmidt, 1982), fearfulness, separation anxiety, and increased hyperactivity (Realmuto et al., 1989), and agitation, aggression, and motor and phonic tics (Volkmar, Hoder, & Cohen, 1985).

Opiate Agonists

Naltrexone has been shown to reduce hyperactivity in individuals with Autism (Campbell et al., 1993; Campbell, Overall, Small, & Sokol, 1989; Kolmen, Feldman, Handen, & Janosky, 1995, 1997; Willemsen-Swinkels, Buitelaar, Nijhof, & Van Engeland, 1995; Willemsen-Swinkels, Buitelaar, & Van Engeland, 1996). Opiate blockers may also reduce self-injurious behaviors (Werry & Aman, 1999).

Vitamin and Diet Therapies

It should be noted that rigorous empirical studies of the efficacy of vitamin and dietary treatments for Autism are lacking. Nevertheless, there has been some evidence for metabolic abnormalities, including high or low excretion of uric acid (Coleman & Gillberg, 1993; Lis, McLaughlin, Lis, & Stubbs, 1976), high excretion of hippuric acid (Lis et al., 1976), low urinary tyrosine (Visconti et al., 1994), and excretion of peptides (Kniusberg, Wiig, Lind, Nogland, & Reichelt, 1990; Reichelt, Kniusberg, Nodland, & Lind, 1994), related to gut symptomatology (i.e., "leaky gut") in some individuals with Autism. A few studies have examined vitamin and dietary therapies to address metabolic abnormalities. For instance, pyridoxine (vitamin B$_6$) has been reported to improve social behavior and language, increase interest in the environment, and reduce aggression in subjects with Autism (Coleman, 1989; Kleijnen & Knipschild, 1991; Lelord, Barthelemy, & Martineau, 1988). Folic acid has been reported to decrease hyperactivity and increase attention and social behavior in subjects with Autism with Fragile X syndrome (Coleman, 1989). The diet most often associated with the treatment of Autism is the low-casein and/or low-gluten diet (Kniusberg et al., 1990). This diet is purported to improve symptoms of Autism by removing proteins that produce toxic peptides. A diet low in casein and gluten was reported to increase social interaction, improve language, and increase interest in the environment after 1 year (Kniusberg et al., 1990). More research on dietary intervention is clearly needed.

PSYCHOSOCIAL INTERVENTIONS

A number of psychosocial treatments are available for individuals with Autism. These treatments target skill domains that are typically impaired in Autism, including social, cognitive, language, and behavioral functioning. Regardless of the treatment approach, it is important that intervention begin at an early age for the best prognosis.

Early Intervention

Early social and language input is critical for normal brain and behavioral development (Mundy & Neal, 2001; Rogers, 1998). If Autism can be identified early and intervention can begin during the first few sensitive years of life, there is the greatest potential for having a significant impact on the developing nervous system and improved social and behavioral outcomes for children with Autism (G. Dawson, Ashman, et al., 2000; Rogers, 1998).

Several studies suggest that early intervention can result in dramatic improvements in some children with Autism (Birnbrauer & Leach, 1993; G. Dawson & Osterling, 1997; Fenske, Zalenski, Krants, & McClannahand, 1985; Harris, Handleman, Gordon, Kristoff, & Fuentes, 1991; Lovaas, 1987; McEachin et al., 1993; Rogers, 1998; Sheinkopf &

Siegel, 1998). As summarized by G. Dawson and Osterling, Green, Brennan, and Fein (2002), Rogers, and the National Research Council (2001), although intervention approaches have varied across different outcome studies, most have several features in common:

1. A focus on the curriculum domains of attention, imitation, language, toy play, and social interaction;
2. Programs that incorporate developmental sequence;
3. Teaching strategies that offer a high level of support for the child, many of which rely on principles of applied behavioral analysis (see later discussion);
4. Specific strategies focused on reducing interfering /problem behaviors;
5. A high level of involvement of parents;
6. Careful transitioning from one-to-one teaching to small groups;
7. Highly trained staff;
8. High levels of supervision of therapists;
9. Intensive intervention consisting of about 25 hours a week of structured intervention lasting for at least 2 years; and
10. Onset of intervention by 2 to 4 years.

When these features are present, results have been impressive for a subgroup of children, including robust gains in IQ, language, and educational placement (G. Dawson & Osterling, 1997; Rogers, 1998). There is evidence that very early intervention, by 2 to 3 years of age, results in more positive outcomes than intervention that begins later (Simeonsson, Olley, & Rosenthal, 1987).

There is some debate as to the optimal number of hours of early intervention. Lovaas's (1987) original study advocated 40 hours per week of one-on-one behavioral intervention during the preschool period. The National Research Council (2001) currently recommends at least 25 hours of structured intervention for children with Autism, with a strong emphasis on one-on-one intervention, which can include specialized education, speech and language therapy, occupational therapy, applied behavioral analysis, and other services that promote the child's communication and social development.

To date, most studies on the effectiveness of early intervention have had significant methodological limitations (for reviews, see G. Dawson & Osterling, 1997; Rogers, 1998; T. Smith, 1999). Lovaas's (1987) original study showing positive effects of early intervention, although important and provocative, had methodological limitations with respect to choice of outcome measures, selection bias, and representativeness of sample (Gresham & MacMillan, 1998). In a randomized study, T. Smith,

Groen, and Wynn (2000) compared a group of 15 children receiving "intensive intervention" consisting of an average of 24 hours of early intervention weekly (with reduction in hours after year 1) to a group of 13 children whose parents were taught to use early intervention techniques for 5 hours per week over a 3- to 9-month period, with consultation every 3 months thereafter. Children began treatment at about age 3 and were seen at follow-up at about age 7 to 8. At follow-up, the intensive treatment group had a statistically significant advantage over the parent training group in IQ, visual-spatial skills, and language development, but not adaptive behavior. Within the intensively treated group, children with a diagnosis of PDD-NOS obtained higher outcome scores than those with a diagnosis of Autism, although these differences were not statistically significant. In both groups, large individual differences in response were apparent. In the intensive treatment group, a standard deviation of 24 IQ points was found at outcome. Some children in the intensive treatment group obtained high achievement on language tests, but others remained nonverbal and severely cognitively impaired.

Given the tremendously high cost and burden of early intervention for parents and society, it is important that the efficacy of early intervention be examined more thoroughly. Moreover, additional research is needed to determine how best to transfer the university-based treatment model to community school settings, which have fewer resources available (Gresham & MacMillan, 1998). In the next sections, early intervention approaches on which data have been published are discussed.

Applied Behavior Analysis

Applied behavior analysis (ABA) refers to a set of principles, including operant learning, that are applied in an individualized, one-on-one setting to promote communication, social, adaptive, and academic functioning. ABA, specifically a traditional approach called discrete trial teaching, was first applied to children with Autism in the 1960s by \Ivar Lovaas at UCLA. Since that time, the techniques used in the ABA approach to treating children with Autism have become much more varied, with discrete trial teaching being only one of many effective ABA strategies.

In general, ABA involves the functional analysis of the child's behavior and motivation. It involves clearly defined and observable goals based on the child's abilities and challenges and regular (i.e., daily or weekly) collection of data to assess progress. These techniques are often used in home programs to supplement educational services received in the community, and a number of preschool intervention programs have modified these techniques for use in the classroom (S. R. Anderson, Campbell, & Cannon, 1994; Handleman & Harris, 1994; McClannahan & Krantz, 1994; Strain & Cordisco, 1994).

Naturalistic Interventions Incorporating Applied Behavior Analysis Principles

In recent years, more naturalistic ABA strategies have included incidental teaching (Hart & Risley, 1980; McGee, Daly, Izeman, Mann, & Risley, 1991), natural language paradigm or pivotal response training (an approach that focuses on pivotal behaviors, such as motivation and attention; R. L. Koegel & Koegel, 1995; R. L. Koegel, O'Dell, & Koegel, 1987; Laski, Charlop, & Schreibman, 1988; Schreibman & Koegel, 1996), milieu teaching (Kaiser & Hester, 1996), and the Denver model (Rogers, 1998; Rogers & Lewis, 1989). These approaches emphasize naturally occurring teaching opportunities and consequences that encourage child motivation and initiation of learning. Some approaches emphasize affective engagement and social relatedness (Rogers & Lewis, 1989).

Studies have shown that naturalistic approaches can result in more generalized responding, increased spontaneity, and improved efficiency in teaching acquisition and generalization simultaneously (Schreibman, 1997; Schreibman & Koegel, 1996). Further, these approaches have been shown to be associated with more positive affect and fewer disruptive behaviors than more traditional ABA teaching approaches (R. L. Koegel & Egel, 1979; Schreibman, Kaneko, & Koegel, 1991). These approaches are currently being used in the Walden Program at Emory University (McGee, Daly, & Jacobs, 1994), the Learning Experiences, an Alternative Program (Strain, Kohler, & Goldstein, 1996), and the Denver treatment model developed by Sally Rogers (Rogers & Lewis, 1989).

Treatment and Education of Autistic and Related Communication-Handicapped Children

The Treatment and Education of Autistic and Related Communication-Handicapped Children (TEACCH) program was developed in the 1960s by Eric Schopler and colleagues (Schopler, Mesibov, Shigley, & Bashford, 1984). This approach emphasizes visual structure and environmental modifications and supports to promote independence and maximize generalization of skills. The TEACCH program uses the visual, mechanical, and rote memory strengths of many children with Autism to bootstrap less developed language, imitation, cognitive, and social skills. For example, the classroom is structured to provide children with predictability and to ease transitions from one activity to the next. Visual formats, such as picture schedules to outline tasks and show what is expected and what comes next, are emphasized, as they are easily understood and lessen anxiety, frustration, and tantrums. Such work systems are especially useful for promoting attention, independent functioning, and successful completion of tasks. Other intervention programs borrow from this approach, for example, by employing visual cues and environmental supports to increase comprehension, facilitate the exchange of information, and decrease problem behaviors (Dalrymple, 1995). In practice, many TEACCH strategies are incorporated into both traditional and naturalistic ABA programs.

Language and Communication Interventions

Improved language interventions that include motivational techniques, such as following the child's lead, emphasizing the child's motivation to respond, and providing frequent opportunities for expressive language in natural settings, have been shown to have a significant impact on the verbal communication skills of children with Autism. As many as 85% to 90% of children who began such interventions before the age of 5 learned to use verbal communication as a primary mode of communication (L. K. Koegel & Koegel, 1995; McGee et al., 1994). For children who were initially nonverbal, these interventions yielded greater increases in immediate and deferred verbal imitation, word production, and spontaneous utterances as compared to more structured approaches (e.g., discrete trial training; R. L. Koegel et al., 1987). For verbal children with delayed language, greater improvements in verbal attempts, word approximations, word production, and word combinations were found compared to discrete trial training formats (R. L. Koegel, Koegel, & Surratt, 1992). Effective procedures are currently available for teaching children with Autism to use language functions such as asking questions and other verbal initiations, which are necessary for social competence (Hung, 1977; L. K. Koegel, Camarata, Valdez-Menchaca, & Koegel, 1998; L. K. Koegel, Koegel, Shoshan, & McNerney, 1999; B. A. Taylor & Harris, 1995; Warren, Baxter, Anderson, Marshall, & Baer, 1981).

Augmentative and alternative communicative (AAC) systems are also available for nonverbal children with Autism, although problems with failure to generalize and use these systems spontaneously have been noted by some (Mirenda & Mathy-Laikko, 1989; Schlosser, Belfiore, Nigam, Blischak, & Hetzroni, 1997; Stiebel, 1999; Storey & Provost, 1996). Such systems include sign language, photographs, picture exchange systems, communication books, and computer systems, among others.

Interventions Targeting Social Behavior

A number of interventions have been shown to facilitate social interactions among children with Autism of all ages. Play-based interventions were shown to enhance the social interactions of preschool-age children with Autism with parents and other adults (G. Dawson & Galpert, 1990; Krantz & McClannahan, 1998; Rogers, Herbison, Lewis, Pantone, & Reis, 1986; Stahmer, 1995). To increase peer interactions, typically developing peer models are taught to initiate play with perseverance (Lord, 1984; Strain et al., 1996). This approach has been shown to increase the social interactions of young children with Autism, and both generalization and maintenance of effects were demonstrated (Goldstein, Kaczmarek, Pennington, & Shafer, 1992; Hoyson, Jamieson, & Strain, 1984; Odom et al., 1999; Odom & Strain, 1986; Strain, Kerr, & Ragland, 1979; Strain, Shores, & Timm, 1977). However, increases have not always generalized to untrained peers (Lord, 1984).

For school-age children and adolescents with Autism, a number of techniques have been shown to increase social interactions, including pivotal response training to teach sociodramatic role play (Thorp, Stahmer, & Schreibman, 1995), video modeling (Charlop & Milstein, 1989), direct instruction (Coe, Matson, Fee, Manikam, & Linarello, 1990), social stories (Gray & Garand, 1993), peer-mediated approaches (Lord, 1984; Lord & Magill-Evans, 1995; Shafer, Egel, & Neef, 1984; Strain et al., 1979), social skills groups (Kamps, Leonard, Vernon, Dugan, & Delquadri, 1992; Ozonoff & Miller, 1995), and visual cuing (Krantz & McClannahan, 1993, 1998).

Special Education Services

There are a number of classroom options for children with Autism, ranging from fully self-contained special education classrooms to inclusion in regular education classrooms with modifications. Federal legislation requires that schools provide fair and unbiased evaluations to determine eligibility for special services. These special services, including accommodations and objectives, form the basis of an individualized education program. However, a diagnosis of an Autism Spectrum Disorder does not always guarantee eligibility for special education services. In these cases, parents can rely on Section 504 of the Federal Rehabilitation Act of 1973, which provides for appropriate public education for all people with disabilities, with "disabilities" broadly defined. Under Section 504, educational accommodations and modifications can be stipulated to help children with Autism succeed in school. Such accommodations include posted classroom schedules, written instructions, a special work area or divider to remove distractions, allocation of additional time to complete assignments, permission to take exams in an alternative format or to have extra time, behavior modification plans (which may involve token or other systems to reinforce appropriate behavior), handwriting alternatives (e.g., tape-recorded lectures and notes), and special help with transitions (Ozonoff et al., 2002).

Occupational Therapy, Sensory Integration Therapy, and Auditory Integration Therapy

Very few controlled studies have been conducted to examine the efficacy of occupational therapy, sensory integration therapy, and auditory integration therapy in addressing sensory and fine and gross motor impairments in Autism. Occupational therapy is a common component of intervention programs for young children with Autism and is designed to promote skill development in the context of play and adaptive behavior. Sensory integration therapy (Ayres, 1972, 1979) emphasizes the relation between sensory experiences and behavior. Strategies include the use of vestibular, proprioceptive, and somatosensory activities, such as swinging and deep pressure, to promote functional and adaptive responses to sensory stimuli. Although sensory and motor impairments are common among children with Autism, these interventions have not been well validated empirically (G. Dawson & Watling, 2000).

Adults with Autism

State government agencies that provide services to people with disabilities may provide some funding to families for vocational training and assisted or semi-independent residential living programs.

Vocational Skills Training and Employment Options

Research has shown that training in vocational and adaptive living skills is best achieved in a naturalistic setting (Schopler & Mesibov, 1983). Further, persons with Autism perform best in occupational settings that provide continued support and in vocations that involve their particular interests as well as concrete and linear processes (Mathews, 1996; Sugiyama & Takahasi, 1996). The main agency that provides vocational assistance to individuals with disabilities is the Rehabilitation Services Administration, which has chapters in each state. Employment options include sheltered employment at a job site operated by the local vocational training agency, with jobs such as mail processing, woodworking, and product assembly; secure employment, similar to sheltered employment with the exception that the

adult with Autism is provided training in improving job skills and behavior, which allows for the possibility of eventually working in a more competitive and independent workplace; supported employment, working alongside adults without disabilities but with the support and supervision of a job coach (i.e., a professional or volunteer employed by the employment training agency, not the employer); and competitive employment, completely independent work requiring a mastery of both job skills and behavior (Holmes, 2000).

Residential Living Programs

In the past, the only choices of living options for adults with Autism were to keep these individuals at home with their parents or place them in a segregated institution. In more recent years, there has been a movement toward community integration, although not every area of the country offers all of the following options: independent living in a house or apartment with support services provided by agencies and families to assist with complex issues such as money management; supervised group living, usually in a residential setting with trained staff; adult foster care, wherein families receive government money to open their home to adults with disabilities; skill development homes, similar to adult foster care homes with the exception that these families are trained to work with individuals with Autism; and state-operated or privately run institutions (Autism Society of America, 2001).

Independent Living

With effective intervention and social support, many adults with Autism are able to lead independent, or semi-independent, lives that are productive and satisfying. The special strengths often associated with Autism, such as strong rote memory and excellent visualization skills, as well as artistic and musical capabilities, have allowed many persons with Autism to work productively. Social skills training and adult support groups have helped such individuals develop meaningful relationships, including friendships and marriage.

CONCLUSION

This is an exciting period in research and clinical practice aimed at helping individuals with Autism spectrum disorders, as increasingly more research is being conducted that will improve our understanding of the cause, nature, course, and treatment of these disorders. As children are recognized at earlier ages and high-quality early behavioral interventions are more readily provided, the long-term prognosis for individuals with Autism is improving, with a substantial subgroup attaining college-level education, satisfying relationships, and independent lives.

Progress in understanding the cause, nature, and treatment of Autism will depend on an integration of scientific approaches from genetics, cognitive neuroscience, and psychology (developmental and clinical). This is a fundamental premise of the discipline of developmental psychopathology (Cicchetti, 1984, 1990, 1993). The rapidly emerging fields of the neuroscience of emotion and social behavior will inform our understanding of Autism, just as studies of Autism are informing those same fields. New findings and approaches to studying gene-environment relations and genetic regulation of brain development and plasticity surely will inform our understanding of Autism and help elucidate the effects of early intervention on brain development and behavior in Autism. Studies of the impact of early interventions on brain and behavioral functioning in young children with Autism will allow us to learn about the development and plasticity of neural systems mediating face processing, imitation, and language, among others. The genetics of Autism will allow us to understand the genetic bases of social and language abilities and help explain normal variability in the phenotypic expression of these abilities.

Discovery of Autism susceptibility genes will likely have a significant impact on how we understand the behavioral phenotype of Autism, its subtypes, early detection, and how to improve clinical intervention. For example, as genes are discovered and animal models are developed, we will begin to understand how early signs of Autism are manifest and develop and how altered experience related to brain dysfunction affects the development of later brain structures and function. We very likely will be able to identify infants at risk for Autism based on the presence of Autism susceptibility genes. This will lead to methods of very early intervention. As many symptoms associated with the Autism syndrome might be caused by the downstream consequences of an early altered trajectory of brain and behavioral development, very early intervention might potentially have a tremendous impact on outcome for many children. As such, we can hope that eventually, some cases of Autism might be preventable.

REFERENCES

Adams, J. M., & Cory, S. (1998). The Bcl-2 protein family: Arbiters of cell survival. *Science, 281,* 1322–1326.

Aggleton, J. (1992). The functional effects of amygdala lesions in humans: A comparison with findings from monkeys. In J. P. Aggleton (Ed.), *The amygdala: Neurobiological aspects of emotion, memory, and mental dysfunction* (pp. 485–503). New York: Wiley-Liss.

Akshoomoff, N., Pierce, K., & Courchesne, E. (2002). The neurobiological basis of Autism from a developmental perspective. *Development and Psychopathology, 14,* 613–634.

Alarcon, M., Cantor, R. M., Liu, J., & Gilliam, T. C. (2002). The Autism Genetic Resource Exchange Consortium, Geschwind, DH: Evidence for a language quantitative trait locus on chromosome 7q in multiplex families. *American Journal of Human Genetics, 70,* 60–71.

Amato, J., Barrow, M., & Domingo, R. (1999). Symbolic play behavior in very young verbal and nonverbal children with Autism. *Infant-Toddler Intervention, 9,* 185–194.

Ameli, R., Courchesne, E., Lincoln, A., Kaufman, A. S., & Grillon, C. (1988). Visual memory processes in high-functioning individuals with Autism. *Journal of Autism and Developmental Disorders, 18,* 601–615.

American Psychiatric Association. (1994). *Diagnostic and statistical manual of mental disorders* (4th ed.). Washington, DC: Author.

Amir, R. E., Van den Veyver, I. B., Wan, M., Tran, C. Q., Francke, U., & Zoghbi, H. Y. (1999). Rett syndrome is caused by mutations in X-linked MECP2, encoding methyl-CpG-binding protein 2. *Nature Genetics, 23,* 185–188.

Anderson, G. M., Freedman, D. X., Cohen, D. J., Volkmar, F. R., Hoder, W. L., McPhedran, P., et al. (1987). Whole blood serotonin in autistic and normal subjects. *Journal of Child Psychology and Psychiatry, 28,* 885–900.

Anderson, G. M., Horne, W. C., Chatterjee, D., & Cohen, D. J. (1990). The hyperserotonemia of Autism. *Annals of the New York Academy of Sciences, 600,* 331–342.

Anderson, G. M., & Hoshino, Y. (1987). Neurochemical studies of Autism. In D. J. Cohen & A. Donnellan (Eds.), *Handbook of Autism and pervasive developmental disorders* (pp. 164–191). New York: Wiley.

Anderson, L. T., & Campbell, M. (1989). The effects of haloperidol on discrimination learning and behavioral symptoms in autistic children. *Journal of Autism and Developmental Disorders, 19,* 227–239.

Anderson, L. T., Campbell, M., Grega, D. M., Perry, R., Small, A. M., & Green, W. H. (1984). Haloperidol in the treatment of infantile Autism: Effects on learning and behavioral symptoms. *American Journal of Psychiatry, 141,* 1195–1202.

Anderson, S. R., Campbell, S., & Cannon, B. O. (1994). The May Center for early childhood education. In S. Harris & J. Handleman (Eds.), *Preschool education program for children with Autism* (pp. 15–36). Austin, TX: ProEd.

Andrews, N., Miller, E., Taylor, B., Lingam, R., Simmons, A., Stowe, J., et al. (2002). Recall bias, MMR, and Autism. *Archives of Disease in Childhood, 87,* 493–494.

Ashley-Koch, A., Wolpert, C. M., Menold, M. M., Zaeem, L., Basu, S., Donnelly, S. L., et al. (1999). Genetic studies of autistic disorder and chromosome 7. *Genomics, 61,* 227–236.

Autism Society of America. (2001). A place to call home: Residential living options for adults with Autism. *Advocate, first edition* (pp. 24–27, 34).

Aylward, E. H., Minshew, N. J., Field, K., Sparks, B. F., & Singh, N. (2002). Effects of age on brain volume and head circumference in Autism. *Neurology, 59,* 175–183.

Ayres, A. J. (1972). *Sensory integration and learning disorders.* Los Angeles: Western Psychological Services.

Ayres, A. J. (1979). *Sensory integration and the child.* Los Angeles: Western Psychological Services.

Azmitia, E., & Whitaker-Azmitia, P. (1997). Development and adult plasticity of serotonergic neurons and their target cells. In H. Baumbgartener & M. Goethert (Eds.), *Serotonergic neurons and 5-HT receptors in the central nervous system* (pp. 1–39). New York: Springer.

Bachevalier, J. (1994). Medial temporal lobe structures and Autism: A review of clinical and experimental findings. *Neuropsychologia, 32,* 627–648.

Bachevalier, J. (2000). The amygdala, social behavior, and Autism. In J. P. Aggleton (Ed.), *The amygdala: A functional analysis* (2nd ed., pp. 509–554). New York: Oxford University Press.

Bacon, A. L., Fein, D., Morris, R., Waterhouse, L., & Allen, D. (1998). The responses of autistic children to the distress of others. *Journal of Autism and Developmental Disorders, 28,* 129–142.

Baghdadli, A., Pascal, C., Grisi, S., & Aussilloux, C. (2003). Risk factors for self-injurious behaviours among 222 young children with autistic disorders. *Journal of Intellectual Disabilities Research, 47,* 622–627.

Bailey, A., LeCouteur, A., Gottesman, I., & Bolton, P. (1995). Autism as a strongly genetic disorder: Evidence from a British twin study. *Psychological Medicine, 25,* 63–77.

Bailey, A., Luthert, P., Dean, A., Harding, B., Janota, I., Montgomery, M., et al. (1998). A clinicopathological study of Autism. *Brain, 121,* 889–905.

Bailey, A., Phillips, W., & Rutter, M. (1996). Autism: Towards an integration of clinical, genetic, neuropsychological, and neurobiological perspectives. *Journal of Child Psychology and Psychiatry, 37,* 89–126.

Baird, G., Charman, T., Baron-Cohen, S., Cox, A., Swettenham, J., Wheelwright, S., et al. (2000). A screening instrument for Autism at 18 months of age: A 6-year follow-up study. *Journal of the American Academy of Child and Adolescent Psychiatry, 39,* 694–702.

Ball, L. K., Ball, R., & Pratt, R. D. (2001). An assessment of thimerosal use in childhood vaccines. *Pediatrics, 107,* 1147–1154.

Ballaban-Gil, K., & Tuchman, R. (2000). Epilepsy and epileptiform EEG: Association with Autism and language disorders. *Mental Retardation and Developmental Disabilities Research Reviews, 6,* 300–308.

Baranek, G. T. (1999). Autism during infancy: A retrospective video analysis of sensory-motor and social behaviors at 9–12 months of age. *Journal of Autism and Developmental Disorders, 29,* 213–224.

Baron-Cohen, S. (2000). Theory of mind and Autism: A fifteen year review. In S. Baron-Cohen, H. Tager-Flusberg, & D. Cohen (Eds.), Understanding other minds: Perspectives from developmental cognitive neuroscience (2nd ed.). Oxford: Oxford University Press.

Baron-Cohen, S., Allen, J., & Gillberg, C. (1992). Can Autism be detected at 18 months? The needle, the haystack, and the CHAT. *British Journal of Psychiatry, 161,* 839–843.

Baron-Cohen, S., Cox, A., Baird, G., Swettenham, J., Nightingale, N., Morgan, K., et al. (1996). Psychological markers in the detection of Autism in infancy in a large population. *British Journal of Psychiatry, 168,* 158–163.

Baron-Cohen, S., & Hammer, J. (1997). Parents of children with Asperger syndrome: What is the cognitive phenotype? *Journal of Cognitive Neuroscience, 9,* 548–554.

Baron-Cohen, S., Leslie, A. M., & Frith, U. (1985). Does the autistic child have a "theory of mind"? *Cognition, 21,* 37–46.

Baron-Cohen, S., Ring, H. A., Bullmore, E. T., Wheelwright, S., Ashwin, C., & Williams, S. C. R. (2000). The amygdala theory of Autism. *Neuroscience and Biobehavioral Reviews, 24*(3), 355–364.

Baron-Cohen, S., Ring, H. A., Wheelwright, S., Bullmore, E., Brammer, M., Simmons, A., et al. (1999). Social intelligence in the normal and autistic brain: An fMRI study. *European Journal of Neuroscience, 11,* 1891–1898.

Baron-Cohen, S., Scahill, V. L., Izaguirre, J., Hornsey, H., & Robertson, M. M. (1999). The prevalence of Gilles de le Tourette syndrome in children and adolescents with Autism: A large scale study. *Psychological Medicine, 29,* 1151–1159.

Baron-Cohen, S., Spitz, A., & Cross, P. (1993). Do children with Autism recognize surprise? A research note. *Cognition and Emotion, 7,* 507–516.

Barrett, S., Beck, J., Bernier, R., Bisson, E., Braun, T., Casavant, T., et al. (1999). An autosomal genomic screen for Autism. *American Journal of Medical Genetics, 88,* 609–615.

Bartak, L., & Rutter, M. (1976). Differences between mentally retarded and normally intelligent autistic children. *Journal of Autism and Childhood Schizophrenia, 6,* 109–120.

Bartak, L., Rutter, M. L., & Cox, A. (1975). A comparative study of infantile Autism and specific developmental language disorder: I. The children. *British Journal of Psychiatry, 126,* 127–145.

Barth, C., Fein, D., & Waterhouse, L. (1995). Delayed match-to-sample performance in autistic children. *Developmental Neuropsychology, 11,* 53–69.

Bauman, M., & Kemper, T. (1985). Histoanatomic observations of the brain in early infantile Autism. *Neurology, 35,* 866–874.

Bauman, M., & Kemper, T. (1994). Neuroanatomic observations of the brain in Autism. In M. L. Bauman & T. L. Kemper (Eds.), *The neurology of Autism* (pp. 119–145). Baltimore: Johns Hopkins University Press.

Baxter, M. G., & Murray, E. A. (2000). Reinterpreting the behavioral effects of amygdala lesions in non-human primates. In J. P. Aggleton (Ed.), *The amygdala: A functional analysis* (2nd ed., pp. 545–568). New York: Oxford University Press.

Bertolino, A., Saunders, R. C., Mattay, V. S., Bachevalier, J., Frank, J. A., & Weinberger, D. R. (1997). Altered development of prefrontal neurons in rhesus monkeys with neonatal mesial temporo-limbic lesions: A proton magnetic resonance spectroscopic imaging study. *Cerebral Cortex, 7,* 740–748.

Bertrand, J., Mars, A., Boyle, C., Bove, F., Yeargin-Allsopp, M., & Decoufle, P. (2001). Prevalence of Autism in a United States population: The Brick Township, New Jersey, investigation. *Pediatrics, 108,* 1155–1161.

Birnbrauer, J. S., & Leach, D. J. (1993). The Murdoch Early Intervention Program after 2 years. *Behaviour Change, 10*(2), 63–74.

Bishop, D., North, T., & Donlan, C. (1996). Nonword repetition as a behavioral marker for inherited language impairment: Evidence from a twin study. *Journal of Child Psychology and Psychiatry, 36,* 1–13.

Bolton, P., MacDonald, H., Pickles, A., Rios, P., Goode, S., Crowson, M., et al. (1994). A case control family history study of Autism. *Journal of Child Psychology and Psychiatry and Allied Disciplines, 35,* 877–900.

Bolton, P., Murphy, M., Macdonald, H., Whitlock, B., Pickles, A., & Rutter, M. (1997). Obstetric complications in Autism: Consequences or causes of the condition? *Journal of the American Academy of Child and Adolescent Psychiatry, 36,* 272–281.

Bolton, P., & Rutter, M. (1990). Genetic influences in Autism. *International Review of Psychiatry, 2,* 67–70.

Bono, M. A., Daley, T. C., & Sigman, M. D. (2003, April). *Relations among joint attention, amount of intervention and language gain in early Autism.* Paper presented at the biennial meeting of the Society for Research in Child Development, Tampa, FL.

Bormann-Kischkel, C., Vilsmeier, M., & Baude, B. (1995). The development of emotional concepts in Autism. *Journal of Child Psychology and Psychiatry, 36,* 1245–1259.

Boucher, J. (1981). Immediate free recall in early childhood Autism: Another point of behavioral similarity with amnesic syndrome. *British Journal of Psychology, 72,* 211–215.

Boucher, J., & Lewis, V. (1992). Unfamiliar face recognition in relatively able autistic children. *Journal of Child Psychology and Psychiatry, 33,* 843–859.

Boucher, J., Lewis, V., & Collis, G. (1998). Familiar face and voice matching and recognition in children with Autism. *Journal of Child Psychology and Psychiatry, 39,* 171–181.

Boucher, J., & Warrington, E. K. (1976). Memory deficits in early infantile Autism: Some similarities to the amnesic syndrome. *British Journal of Psychology, 67,* 73–87.

Bradford, Y., Haines, J., Hutcheson, H., Gardiner, M., Braun, T., Sheffield, V., et al. (2001). Incorporating language phenotypes strengthens evidence of linkage to Autism. *American Journal of Medical Genetics, 105,* 539–547.

Bretherton, I., & Beeghly, M. (1982). Talking about internal states: The acquisition of an explicit theory of mind. *Developmental Psychology, 18,* 906–921.

Brothers, L. A., Ring, B. D., & Kling, A. S. (1990). Response of temporal lobe neurons to social stimuli in Maraca arctoides. *Society of Neuroscience Abstract, 16,* 184.

Bryson, S. E. (1996). Brief report: Epidemiology of Autism. *Journal of Autism and Developmental Disorders, 26,* 165–168.

Bryson, S. E., Clark, B. S., & Smith, I. M. (1988). First report of a Canadian epidemiological study of autistic syndromes. *Journal of Child Psychology and Psychiatry, 29,* 433–445.

Buitelaar, J. K., van der Wees, M., Swaab-Barneveld, H., & van der Gaag, R. J. (1999). Verbal memory and performance IQ predict theory of mind and emotion recognition ability in children with autistic spectrum disorders and psychiatric control children. *Journal of Child Psychology and Psychiatry, 40,* 869–881.

Bujas-Petkovic, Z. (1993). The three-dimensional modeling ability of a boy with Autism [Letter to the editor]. *Journal of Autism and Developmental Disorders, 23,* 569–571.

Bushnell, I. W. R., Sai, F., & Mullin, J. T. (1989). Neonatal recognition of the mother's face. *British Journal of Developmental Psychology, 7,* 3–15.

Buxbaum, J. D., Silverman, J. M., Smith, C. J., Kilifarski, M., Reichert, J., Hollander, E., et al. (2001). Evidence for a susceptibility gene for Autism on chromosome 2 and for genetic heterogeneity. *American Journal of Human Genetics, 68,* 1514–1520.

Campbell, M., Anderson, L. T., Meier, M., Cohen, I. L., Small, A. M., Samit, C., et al. (1978). A comparison of haloperidol and behavior therapy and their interaction in autistic children. *Journal of the American Academy of Child Psychiatry, 17,* 640–655.

Campbell, M., Anderson, L. T., Small, A. M., Adams, P., Gonzalez, N. M., & Ernst, M. (1993). Naltrexone in autistic children: Behavioral symptoms and attentional learning. *Journal of the American Academy of Child and Adolescent Psychiatry, 32,* 1283–1291.

Campbell, M., Locascio, J., Choroco, M., Spencer, E. K., Malone, R. P., Kafantaris, V., et al. (1990). Stereotypes and tardive dyskinesia: Abnormal movements in autistic children. *Psychopharmacology Bulletin, 26*(2), 260–266.

Campbell, M., Overall, J. E., Small, A. M., & Sokol, M. S. (1989). Naltrexone in autistic children: An acute open dose range tolerance trial. *Journal of the American Academy of Child and Adolescent Psychiatry, 28,* 200–206.

Cantwell, D. P., Baker, L., Rutter, M., & Mawhood, L. (1989). Infantile Autism and developmental receptive dysphasia: A comparative follow-up into middle childhood. *Journal of Autism and Developmental Disorders, 19,* 19–31.

Capps, L., Kehres, J., & Sigman, M. (1998). Conversational abilities among children with Autism and children with developmental delays. *Autism, 2,* 325–344.

Capps, L., Yirmiya, N., & Sigman, M. (1992). Understanding of simple and complex emotions in non-retarded children with Autism. *Journal of Child Psychology and Psychiatry and Allied Disciplines, 33,* 1169–1182.

Carpenter, M., Nagell, K., & Tomasello, M. (1998). Social cognition, joint attention, and communicative competence from 9 to 15 months of age. *Monographs of the Society for Research in Child Development, 63*(4, Serial No. 176).

Carver, L., & Dawson, G. (2002). Evidence for an early impairment in neural systems for face recognition in Autism. *Molecular Psychiatry, 7*(Suppl. 2), 18–20.

Celani, G., Battacchi, M. W., & Arcidiacono, L. (1999). The understanding of the emotional meaning of facial expressions in people with Autism. *Journal of Autism and Developmental Disorders, 29,* 57–66.

Chakrabarti, S., & Fombonne, E. (2001). Pervasive developmental disorders in preschool children. *Journal of the American Medical Association, 285,* 3093–3099.

Charlop, M. H., & Milstein, J. P. (1989). Teaching autistic children conversational speech using video modeling. *Journal of Applied Behavior Analysis, 22,* 275–285.

Charman, T. (1997). The relationship between joint attention and pretend play in Autism. *Development and Psychopathology, 9,* 1–16.

Charman, T. (2003). Why is joint attention a pivotal skill in Autism? *Philosophical Transcripts of the Royal Society of London: Series B. Biological Sciences, 358,* 315–324.

Charman, T., & Baron-Cohen, S. (1997). Brief report: Prompted pretend play in Autism. *Journal of Autism and Developmental Disorders, 27,* 325–332.

Charman, T., Baron-Cohen, S., Swettenham, J., Baird, G., Cox, A., & Drew, A. (2000). Testing joint attention, imitation, and play as infancy precursors to language and theory of mind. *Cognitive Development, 15,* 481–498.

Charman, T., Baron-Cohen, S., Swettenham, J., Baird, G., Drew, A., & Cox, A. (2003). Predicting language outcome in infants with Autism and pervasive developmental disorder. *International Journal of Language and Communication Disorders, 38,* 265–285.

Charman, T., & Swettenham, J. (2001). Repetitive behaviors and social-communicative impairments in Autism: Implications for developmental theory and diagnosis. In J. A. Burack, T. Charman, N. Yirmiya, & P. R. Zelazo (Eds.), *The development of Autism: Perspectives from theory and research* (pp. 325–345). Mahwah, NJ: Erlbaum.

Charman, T., Swettenham, J., Baron-Cohen, S., Cox, A., Baird, G., & Drew, A. (1998). An experimental investigation of social-cognitive abilities in infants with Autism: Clinical implications. *Infant Mental Health Journal, 19,* 260–275.

Chess, S. (1977). Follow-up report on Autism in congenital rubella. *Journal of Autism and Childhood Schizophrenia, 7,* 69–81.

Chlan-Fourney, J., Webster, M. G., Felleman, D. J., & Bachevalier, J. (2000). Neonatal medial temporal lobe lesions alter the distribution of tyrosine hydroxylase immunoreactive varicosities in the macaque prefrontal cortex. *Society for Neuroscience Abstract, 26,* 609.

Chugani, D. C., Muzik, O., Rothermel, R., Behen, M., Chakraborty, P., Mangner, T., et al. (1997). Altered serotonin synthesis in the dentatothalamocortical pathway in autistic boys. *Annals of Neurology, 42,* 666–669.

Chung, S. Y., Luk, S. L., & Lee, P. W. H. (1990). A follow-up study of infantile Autism in Hong Kong. *Journal of Autism and Developmental Disorders, 20,* 221–232.

Cialdella, P., & Mamelle, N. (1989). An epidemiological study of infantile Autism in a French department (Rhone): A research note. *Journal of Child Psychology and Psychiatry, 30,* 165–175.

Cicchetti, D. (1984). The emergence of developmental psychopathology. *Child Development, 55,* 1–7.

Cicchetti, D. (1990). A historical perspective on the discipline of developmental psychopathology. In J. Rott, A. S. Masten, D. Cicchetti, &

K. H. Nuechterlein (Eds.), *Risk and protective factors in the development of psychopathology* (pp. 2–28). New York: Cambridge University Press.

Cicchetti, D. (1993). Developmental psychopathology: Reactions, reflections, projections. *Developmental Review, 13,* 471–502.

Cicerone, K. D., & Tanenbaum, L. N. (1997). Disturbance of social cognition after traumatic orbitofrontal brain injury. *Archives of Clinical Neuropsychology, 12*(2), 173–188.

Cipolotti, L., Robinson, G., Blair, J., & Frith, U. (1999). Fractionation of visual memory: Evidence from a case with multiple neurodevelopmental impairments. *Neuropsychologica, 37,* 455–465.

Coe, D., Matson, J., Fee, V., Manikam, R., & Linarello, C. (1990). Training nonverbal and verbal play skills to mentally retarded and autistic children. *Journal of Autism and Developmental Disorders, 20,* 177–187.

Coffey-Corina, S., & Kuhl, P. K. (2001, November). *Mismatch negativity using speech stimuli in 3–5 year old children with Autism and typically developing children.* Paper presented at the International Meeting for Autism Research, San Diego, CA.

Cohen, H., Ryan, J., Hunt, C., Romine, L., Wszalek, T., & Nash, C. (1999). Hippocampal system and declarative (relational) memory: Summarizing the data from functional neuroimaging studies. *Hippocampus, 9,* 83–98.

Cohen, N., & Eichenbaum, H. (1993). *Memory, amnesia, and the hippocampal system.* Cambridge, MA: MIT Press.

Cohn, J. F., Campbell, S. B., Matias, R., & Hopkins, J. (1990). Face-to-face interactions of postpartum depressed and nondepressed mother-infant pairs at 2 months. *Developmental Psychology, 26,* 15–23.

Coleman, M. (1989). Autism: Nondrug biological treatments. In C. Gillberg (Ed.), *Diagnosis and treatment of Autism* (pp. 219–235). New York: Plenum Press.

Coleman, M., & Gillberg, C. (1993). *Biology of the autistic syndromes.* London: MacKeith.

Collaborative Linkage Study of Autism. (2001). An autosomal genomic screen for Autism. *American Journal of Medical Genetics, 105,* 609–615.

Cook, E. H. (1998). Genetics of Autism. *Mental Retardation and Developmental Disabilities Research Reviews, 4,* 113–120.

Cook, E. H., Arora, R. C., Anderson, G. M., Berry-Kravis, E. M., Yan, S. Y., Yeoh, H. C., et al. (1993). Platelet serotonin studies in hyperserotonemic relatives of children with autistic disorder. *Life Science, 52,* 2005–2015.

Cook, E. H., Courchesne, R., Lord, C., Cox, N. J., Yan, S., Lincoln, A., et al. (1997). Evidence of linkage between the serotonin transporter and autistic disorder. *Molecular Psychiatry, 2,* 247–250.

Courchesne, E. (1989). Neuroanatomical systems involved in infantile Autism: The implications of cerebellar abnormalities. In G. Dawson (Ed.), *Autism: Nature, diagnosis, and treatment* (pp. 234–289). New York: Guilford Press.

Courchesne, E., Bartholomeusz, H., Karns, C., & Townsend, J. (in press). MRI and head circumference evidence of abnormal brain enlargement in young but not adult autistic patients. *Biological Psychiatry.*

Courchesne, E., Carper, R., & Akshoomoff, N. (2003). Evidence of brain overgrowth in the first year of life in Autism. *Journal of the American Medical Association, 290,* 337–344.

Courchesne, E., Chisum, H., & Townsend, J. (1994). Neural activity-dependent brain changes in development: Implications for psychopathology. *Development and Psychopathology, 6,* 697–722.

Courchesne, E., Karns, C. M., Davis, H. R., Ziccardi, R., Carper, R. A., Tigue, Z. D., et al. (2001). Unusual brain growth patterns in early life in patients with autistic disorder: An MRI study. *Neurology, 57,* 245–254.

Courchesne, E., Muller, R. A., & Saitoh, O. (1999). Brain weight in Autism: Normal in the majority of cases, megalencephalic in rare cases. *Neurology, 52,* 1057–1059.

Cryan, E., Byrne, M., O'Donovan, A., & O'Callaghan, E. (1996). Brief report: A case-control study of obstetric complications and later autistic disorder. *Journal of Autism and Developmental Disorders, 26,* 453–460.

Dales, L., Hammer, S. J., & Smith, N. J. (2001). Time trends in Autism and in MMR immunization coverage in California. *Journal of the American Medical Association, 285,* 1183–1185.

Dalrymple, N. (1995). Environmental supports to develop flexibility and independence. In K. Quill (Ed.), *Teaching children with Autism* (pp. 166–200). New York: Delmar.

Damasio, A. R., Tranel, D., & Damasio, H. (1990). Individuals with sociopathic behavior caused by frontal damage fail to respond autonomically to social stimuli. *Behavioural Brain-Research, 41,* 81–94.

Davidovitch, M., Glick, L., Holtzman, G., Tirosh, E., & Safir, M. P. (2000). Developmental regression in Autism: Maternal perception. *Journal of Autism and Developmental Disorders, 30,* 113–119.

Davies, S., Bishop, D., Manstead, A. S. R., & Tantam, D. (1994). Face perception in children with Autism and Asperger's syndrome. *Journal of Child Psychology and Psychiatry, 35,* 1033–1057.

Davis, E., Fennoy, I., Laraque, D., Kanem, N., Brown, G., & Mitchell, J. (1992). Autism and developmental abnormalities in children with perinatal cocaine exposure. *Journal of the National Medical Association, 84,* 315–319.

Dawson, G. (1991). A psychobiological perspective on the early socioemotional development of children with Autism. In D. Cicchetti & S. Toth (Eds.), *Developmental psychopathology* (Vol. 3, pp. 207–234). Hillsdale, NJ: Erlbaum.

Dawson, G. (1996). Brief report: Neuropsychology of Autism: A report on the state of the science. *Journal of Autism and Developmental Disorders, 26,* 179–184.

Dawson, G., & Adams, A. (1984). Imitation and social responsiveness in autistic children. *Journal of Abnormal Child Psychology, 12,* 209–225.

Dawson, G., Ashman, S. B., & Carver, L. J. (2000). The role of early experience in shaping behavioral and brain development and its implications for social policy. *Development and Psychopathology, 12,* 695–712.

Dawson, G., Carver, L., Meltzoff, A., Panagiotides, H., McPartland, J., & Webb, S. (2002). Neural correlates of face and object recognition in young children with Autism spectrum disorder, developmental delay, and typical development. *Child Development, 73,* 700–717.

Dawson, G., & Galpert, L. (1990). Mother's use of imitative play for facilitating social responsiveness and toy play in young autistic children. *Development and Psychopathology, 2,* 151–162.

Dawson, G., Hill, D., Spencer, A., Galpert, L., & Watson, L. (1990). Affective exchanges between young autistic children and their mothers. *Journal of Abnormal Child Psychology, 18,* 335–345.

Dawson, G., & Lewy, A. (1989). Arousal, attention, and the socioemotional impairments of individuals with Autism. In G. Dawson (Ed.), *Autism: Nature, diagnosis, and treatment* (pp. 49–74). New York: Guilford Press.

Dawson, G., Meltzoff, A. N., & Osterling, J. (1995, March). *Autistic children fail to orient to naturally occurring social stimuli.* Poster session presented at the biennial meeting of the Society for Research in Child Development, Indianapolis, IN.

Dawson, G., Meltzoff, A. N., Osterling J., & Rinaldi, J. (1998). Neuropsychological correlates of early symptoms of Autism. *Child Development, 69,* 1276–1285.

Dawson, G., Meltzoff, A. N., Osterling, J., Rinaldi, J., & Brown, E. (1998). Children with Autism fail to orient to naturally occurring social stimuli. *Journal of Autism and Developmental Disorders, 28,* 479–485.

Dawson, G., Munson, J., Estes, A., Osterling, J., McPartland, J., Toth, K., et al. (2002). Neurocognitive function and joint attention ability in young children with Autism spectrum disorder versus developmental delay. *Child Development, 73*, 345–358.

Dawson, G., & Osterling, J. (1997). Early intervention in Autism. In M. Guralnick (Ed.), *The effectiveness of early intervention* (pp. 307–326). Baltimore: Paul H. Brookes.

Dawson, G., Toth, K., Abbott, R., Osterling, J., Munson, J., Estes, A., et al. (2004). Social attention impairments in young children with Autism: Social orienting, joint attention, and attention to distress. *Developmental Psychology, 40*, 271–283.

Dawson, G., Warrenburg, S., & Fuller, P. (1985). Left hemisphere specialization for facial and manual imitation in children and adults. *Psychophysiology, 22*, 237–243.

Dawson, G., & Watling, R. (2000). Interventions to facilitate auditory, visual, and motor integration in Autism: A review of the evidence. *Journal of Autism and Developmental Disorders, 30*, 415–421.

Dawson, G., Webb, S., Carver, L., Panagiotides, H., & McPartland, J. (2004). Young children with Autism show atypical brain responses to fearful versus neutral facial expressions of emotion. *Developmental Science, 7*, 340–359.

Dawson, G., Webb, S., Schellenberg, G. D., Dager, S., Friedman, S., Aylward, E., et al. (2002). Defining the broader phenotype of Autism: Genetic, brain, and behavioral perspectives. *Development and Psychopathology, 14*, 581–611.

Dawson, G., & Zanolli, K. (2003). Early intervention and brain plasticity in Autism. In M. Rutter (Ed.), *Autism: Neural bases and treatment possibilities* (pp. 266–297). London: Novartis.

Dawson, J., Matson, J., & Cherry, K. (1998). An analysis of maladaptive behaviors in persons with Autism, PDD-NOS, and mental retardation. *Research in Developmental Disabilities, 19*, 439–448.

Decety, J., Chaminade, T., Grezes, J., & Meltzoff, A. N. (2002). A PET exploration of the neural mechanisms involved in reciprocal imitation. *Neuroimage, 15*, 265–272.

Demonet, J. F., Chollet, F., Ramsay, S., Cardebat, D., Nespoulous, J. L., Wise, R., et al. (1992). The anatomy of phonological and semantic processing in normal subjects. *Brain, 115*, 1753–1768.

DeMyer, M. K., Alpern, G., Barton, S., DeMyer, W. E., Churchill, D. W., Hingtgen, N. J., et al. (1972). Imitation in autistic, early schizophrenic, and nonpsychotic subnormal children. *Journal of Autism and Childhood Schizophrenia, 2*, 264–287.

Devlin, B., Bennett, P., Cook, E. H., Jr., Dawson, G., Gonen, D., Grigorenko, E. L., et al. (2002). No evidence for linkage of liability to Autism to HOXA1 in a sample from the CPEA network. *American Journal of Medical Genetics, 114*(6), 667–672.

Devlin, G., Bennett, P., Dawson, G., Figlewicz, D. A., Grigorenko, E. L., McMahon, W., et al. (2004). Alleles of a reelin CGG repeat do not convey liability to Autism in a sample from the CPEA network. *American Journal of Medical Genetics, 126B*, 46–50.

Diamond, A., & Goldman-Rakic, P. S. (1989). Comparison of human infants and rhesus monkeys on Piaget's AB task: Evidence for dependence on dorsolateral prefrontal cortex. *Experimental Brain Research, 74*, 24–40.

Dollaghan, C., & Campbell, T. (1998). Nonword repetition and child language impairment. *Journal of Speech, Language, and Hearing Research, 41*, 1136–1146.

Donnellan, A. M., Mirenda, P. L., Mesaros, R. A., & Fassbender, L. L. (1984). Analyzing the communicative functions of aberrant behavior. *Journal of the Association for Persons with Severe Handicaps, 9*, 201–212.

Eales, M. J. (1993). Pragmatic impairments in adults with childhood diagnoses of Autism or developmental receptive language disorder. *Journal of Autism and Developmental Disorders, 23*, 593–617.

Ehlers, S., & Gillberg, C. (1993). The epidemiology of Asperger syndrome: A total population study. *Journal of Child Psychology and Psychiatry and Allied Disciplines, 34*, 1327–1350.

Evans, D., Leckman, J., Carter, A., Reznick, S., Henshaw, D., King, R., et al. (1997). Ritual, habit, and perfectionism: The prevalence and development of compulsive-like behavior in normal young children. *Child Development, 68*, 58–68.

Farrington, C. P., Miller, E., & Taylor, B. (2001). MMR and Autism: Further evidence against a causal association. *Vaccine, 19*, 3632–3635.

Fatemi, S. H., Earle, J. A., & McMenomy, T. (2000). Reduction in reelin immunoreactivity in hippocampus of subjects with Schizophrenia, bipolar disorder and major depression. *Molecular Psychiatry, 5*, 654–663.

Fatemi, S. H., Stary, J. M., & Egan, E. A. (2002). Reduced blood levels of reelin as a vulnerability factor in pathophysiology of autistic disorder. *Cellular and Molecular Neurobiology, 22*, 139–152.

Fatemi, S. H., Stary, J. M., Halt, A., & Realmuto, G. (2001). Dysregulation of reelin and Bcl-2 in autistic cerebellum. *Journal of Autism and Developmental Disorders, 31*, 529–535.

Fenske, E. C., Zalenski, S., Krants, P. J., & McClannahand, L. E. (1985). Age at intervention and treatment outcome for autistic children in a comprehensive intervention program. *Analysis and Intervention in Developmental Disabilities, 5*, 49–58.

Filipek, P. A., Accardo, P. J., Baranek, G. T., Cook, E. H., Dawson, G., Gordon, B., et al. (1999). The screening and diagnosis of autistic spectrum disorders. *Journal of Autism and Developmental Disorders, 29*, 439–484.

Fisher, S. E., Vargha-Khadem, F., Watkins, K. E., Monaco, A. P., & Pembrey, M. E. (1998). Localisation of a gene implicated in a severe speech and language disorder. *Nature Genetics, 18*, 168–170.

Fisman, S., & Steele, M. (1996). Use of risperidone in pervasive developmental disorders: A case series. *Journal of Child and Adolescent Psychopharmacology, 6*, 177–190.

Flavell, J. H. (1999). Cognitive development: Children's knowledge about the mind. *Annual Review of Psychology, 50*, 21–45.

Fletcher, P. S., Happe, F., Frith, U., Baker, S. C., Dolan, R. J., Frackowiak, R. S., et al. (1995). Other minds in the brain: A functional imaging study of "theory of mind" in story comprehension. *Cognition, 57*, 109–128.

Folstein, S. E., & Mankoski, R. E. (2000). Chromosome 7q: Where Autism meets language disorder? *American Journal of Human Genetics, 67*, 278–281.

Folstein, S. E., & Rutter, M. (1977). Infantile Autism: A genetic study of 21 twin pairs. *Journal of Child Psychology and Psychiatry, 18*, 297–321.

Folstein, S. E., Santangelo, S. L., Gilman, S. E., Piven, J., Landa, R., Lainhart, J., et al. (1999). Predictors of cognitive test patterns in Autism families. *Journal of Child Psychology and Psychiatry, 40*, 1117–1128.

Fombonne, E. (1999). The epidemiology of Autism: A review. *Psychological Medicine, 29*, 769–786.

Fombonne, E. (2003). Epidemiology of pervasive developmental disorders. *Trends in Evidence-Based Neuropsychiatry, 5*(1), 29–36.

Fombonne, E., Bolton, P., Prior, J., Jordan, H., & Rutter, M. (1997). A family study of Autism: Cognitive patterns and levels in parents and siblings. *Journal of Child Psychology and Psychiatry and Allied Disciplines, 38*, 667–683.

Fombonne, E., & Chakrabarti, S. (2001). No evidence for a new variant of measles-mumps-rubella-induced Autism. *Pediatrics, 108*, E58.

Fombonne, E., & Tidmarsh, L. (2003). Epidemiologic data on Asperger disorder. *Child and Adolescent Psychiatric Clinics of North America, 12*, 15–21.

Frankhauser, M. P., Karumanchi, V. C., German, M. L., Yates, A., & Karumanchi, S. D. (1992). A double-blind, placebo-controlled study of the efficacy of transdermal clonidine in Autism. *Journal of Clinical Psychiatry, 53*, 77–82.

Gaffan, D. (1992). Amygdala and the memory of reward. In J. O. Aggleton (Ed.), *The amygdala: Neurobiological aspects of emotion, memory, and dysfunction* (pp. 471–485). New York: Wiley-Liss.

Gallagher, L., Hawi, Z., Kearney, G., Fitzgerald, M., & Gill, M. (2004). No association between allelic variants of HOXA1/HOXB1 and Autism. *American Journal of Medical Genetics Neuropsychiatric Genetics: Part B. Neuropsychiatric Genetics—The Official Publication of the International Society of Psychiatric Genetics, 124*, 64–67.

Gallese, V., Fadiga, L., Fogassi, L., & Rizzolatti, G. (1996). Action recognition in the premotor cortex. *Brain, 119*, 593–609.

Gathercole, S., & Baddeley, A. (1990). Phonological memory deficits in language disordered children: Is there a causal connection? *Journal of Memory and Language, 29*, 336–360.

Geller, B., Guttmacher, L. B., & Bleeg, M. (1981). Coexistence of childhood onset pervasive developmental disorder and attention deficit disorder with hyperactivity. *American Journal of Psychiatry, 138*, 388–389.

Ghaziuddin, M., & Greden, J. (1998). Depression in children with Autism/pervasive developmental disorders: A case control family history study. *Journal of Autism and Developmental Disorders, 28*, 111–115.

Gillberg, C. (1991). Outcome in Autism and autistic-like conditions. *Journal of the American Academy of Child and Adolescent Psychiatry, 30*, 375–382.

Gillberg, C., & Gillberg, I. C. (1983). Infantile Autism: A total population study of reduced optimality in the pre-, peri-, and neonatal period. *Journal of Autism and Developmental Disorders, 13*, 153–166.

Gillberg, C., & Steffenburg, S. (1987). Outcome and prognostic factors in infantile Autism and similar conditions: A population-based study of 46 cases followed through puberty. *Journal of Autism and Developmental Disorders, 17*, 273–287.

Gillberg, C., & Svennerholm, L. (1987). CSF monoamines in autistic syndromes and other pervasive developmental disorders of early childhood. *British Journal of Psychiatry, 151*, 89–94.

Gillberg, C., Svennerholm, L., & Hamilton-Hellberg, C. (1983). Childhood psychosis and monoamine metabolites in spinal fluid. *Journal of Autism and Developmental Disorders, 13*, 383–396.

Goldenberg, G. (1995). Imitating gestures and manipulating a manikin: The representatioin on the human body in ideomotor apraxia. *Neuropsychologia, 33*, 63–72.

Goldenberg, G., & Hagman, S. (1997). The meaning of meaningless gestures: A study of visuo-imitative apraxia. *Neuropsychologia, 5*, 333–341.

Goldstein, H., Kaczmarek, L., Pennington, R., & Shafer, K. (1992). Peer-mediated intervention: Attending to, commenting on, and acknowledging the behavior of preschoolers with Autism. *Journal of Applied Behavior Analysis, 25*, 289–305.

Goode, S., Rutter, M., & Howlin, P. (1994). *A twenty-year follow-up of children with Autism.* Paper presented at the 13th biennial meeting of ISSBD, Amsterdam, The Netherlands.

Gordon, C. T., Rapoport, J. L., Hamburger, S. D., State, R. C., & Mannheim, G. B. (1992). Differential response of seven subjects with autistic disorder to clomipramine and desipramine. *American Journal of Psychiatry, 149*, 363–366.

Gordon, C. T., State, R., Nelson, J., Hamburger, S., & Rapoport, J. (1993). A double blind comparison of clomipramine, desipramine, and placebo in the treatment of autistic disorder. *Archives of General Psychiatry, 50*(6), 441–447.

Goren, C., Sarty, M., & Wu, P. (1975). Visual following and pattern discrimination of face like stimuli by newborn infants. *Pediatrics, 56*, 544–549.

Grafton, S. T., Arbib, M. A., Fadiga, L., & Rizzolatti, G. (1996). Localization of grasp representations in human by PET. *Experimental Brain Research, 112*, 103–111.

Gray, C., & Garand, J. (1993). Social stories: Improving responses of students with Autism with accurate social information. *Focus on Autistic Behavior, 8*, 1–10.

Green, G., Brennan, L. C., & Fein, D. (2002). Intensive behavioral treatment for a toddler at high risk for Autism. *Behavior Modification, 26*, 69–102.

Grelotti, D. J., Gauthier, I., & Schultz, R. T. (2002). Social interest and the development of cortical face specialization: What Autism teaches us about face processing. *Developmental Psychobiology, 40*, 213–225.

Gresham, F. M., & MacMillan, D. L. (1998). Early intervention project: Can its claims be substantiated and its effects replicated? *Journal of Autism and Developmental Disorders, 28*(1), 5–13.

Griffith, E. M., Pennington, B. F., Wehner, E. A., & Rogers, S. J. (1999). Executive function in young children with Autism. *Child Development, 70*, 817–832.

Guidotti, A., Auta, J., Davis, J., Dwivedi, Y., Grayson, D., Impagnatiello, F., et al. (2000). Decrease in reelin and glutamic acid decarboxylase 67 (GAD67) expression in Schizophrenia and bipolar disorder: A postmortem brain study. *Archives of General Psychiatry, 57*, 1061–1069.

Handen, B. I., Johnson, C. R., & Lubetsky, M. (2000). Efficacy of methylphenidate among children with Autism and symptoms of ADHD. *Journal of Autism and Developmental Disorders, 30*, 245–255.

Handleman, J., & Harris, S. (1994). The Douglass Developmental Disabilities Center. In S. Harris & J. Handleman (Eds.), *Preschool education programs for children with Autism* (pp. 71–86). Austin, TX: ProEd.

Happe, F. (1994). Wechsler IQ profile and theory of mind in Autism: A research note. *Journal of Child Psychology and Psychiatry and Allied Disciplines, 35*, 1461–1471.

Happe, F., Briskman, J., & Frith, U. (2001). Exploring the cognitive phenotype of Autism: Weak "central coherence" in parents and siblings of children with Autism: I. Experimental tests. *Journal of Child Psychology and Psychiatry, 42*, 299–308.

Happe, F., Ehlers, S., Fletcher, P., Frith, U., Johansson, J., Gillberg, C., et al. (1996). Theory of mind in the brain: Evidence from a PET scan study of Asperger syndrome. *NeuroReport, 8*, 197–201.

Harris, S., Handleman, J., Gordon, R., Kristoff, B., & Fuentes, F. (1991). Changes in cognitive and language functioning of preschool children with Autism. *Journal of Autism and Developmental Disorders, 21*(3), 281–290.

Hart, B., & Risley, T. R. (1980). In vivo language intervention: Unanticipated general effects. *Journal of Applied Behavior Analysis, 13*, 407–432.

Harvey, R. J., & Cooray, S. E. (1995). The effective treatment of severe repetitive behaviour with fluvoxamine in a 20 year old autistic female. *International Clinical Psychopharmacology, 10*, 201–203.

Hauck, M., Fein, D., Maltby, N., Waterhouse, L., & Feinstein, C. (1998). Memory for faces in children with Autism. *Child Neuropsychology, 4*, 187–198.

Hellings, J. A., Kelley, L. A., Gabrielli, W. F., Kilgore, E., & Shah, P. (1996). Sertraline response in adults with mental retardation and autistic disorder. *Journal of Clinical Psychiatry, 57*, 333–336.

Herault, J., Petit, E., Martineau, J., Cherpi, C., Perrot, A., Barthelemy, C., et al. (1996). Serotonin and Autism: Biochemical and molecular biology features. *Psychiatry Research, 65*, 33–43.

Hobson, R. P., Ouston, J., & Lee, A. (1988). Emotion recognition in Autism: Coordinating faces and voices. *Psychological Medicine, 18,* 911–923.

Hobson, R. P., Ouston, J., & Lee, A. (1989). Naming emotion in faces and voices: Abilities and disabilities in Autism and mental retardation. *British Journal of Developmental Psychology, 7,* 237–250.

Hollander, E., King, A., Delaney, K., Smith, C. J., & Silverman, J. M. (2003). Obsessive-compulsive behaviors in parents of multiplex Autism families. *Psychiatry Research, 117,* 11–16.

Holmes, D. L. (2000). The years ahead: Adults with Autism. In M. D. Powers (Ed.), *Children with Autism: A parents' guide* (pp. 279–302). Bethesda, MD: Woodbine House.

Honda, W., Shimizu, Y., Misumi, K., Nimi, M., & Ohashi, Y. (1996). Cumulative incidence and prevalence of childhood Autism in children in Japan. *British Journal of Psychiatry, 169,* 228–235.

Horrigan, J. P., & Barnhill, L. J. (1997). Risperidone and explosive aggressive Autism. *Journal of Autism and Developmental Disorders, 27,* 313–323.

Howard, M. A., Cowell, P. E., Boucher, J., Broks, P., Mayes, A., Farrant A., et al. (2000). Convergent neuroanatomical and behavioral evidence of an amygdala hypothesis of Autism. *Brain Imaging, 11,* 2931–2935.

Howlin, P. (1984). The acquisition of grammatical morphemes in autistic children: A critique and replication of the findings of Bartolucci, Pierce, and Streiner, 1980. *Journal of Autism and Developmental Disorders, 14,* 127–136.

Howlin, P. (1997). Prognosis in Autism: Do specialist treatments affect long-term outcome? *European Child and Adolescent Psychiatry, 6,* 55–72.

Howlin, P., & Asgharian, A. (1999). The diagnosis of Autism and Asperger syndrome: Findings from a survey of 770 families. *Developmental Medicine and Child Neurology, 41,* 834–839.

Howlin, P., & Goode, S. (1998). Outcome in adult life for people with Autism and Asperger's syndrome. In F. R. Volkmar (Ed.), *Autism and pervasive developmental disorders* (pp. 209–241). Cambridge, England: Cambridge University Press.

Howlin, P., Mawhood, L., & Rutter, M. (2000). Autism and developmental receptive language disorder: A follow-up comparison in early adult life: Pt. II. Social, behavioral, and psychiatric outcomes. *Journal of Child Psychology and Psychiatry, 41,* 561–578.

Hoyson, M., Jamieson, B., & Strain, P. S. (1984). Individualized group instruction of normally developing and autistic-like children: The LEAP curriculum model. *Journal of the Division of Early Childhood, 8,* 157–172.

Hughes, C., Plumet, M., & Leboyer, M. (1999). Towards a cognitive phenotype for Autism: Increased prevalence of executive dysfunction and superior spatial span amongst siblings of children with Autism. *Journal of Child Psychology and Psychiatry, 40,* 705–718.

Hung, D. W. (1977). Generalization of "curiosity" questioning behavior in autistic children. *Journal of Behavior Therapy and Experimental Psychiatry, 8,* 237–245.

Impagnatiello, F., Guidotti, A., Pesold, C., Dwivedi, Y., Caruncho, H., Pisu, M. G., et al. (1998). A decrease of reelin expression as a putative vulnerability factor in Schizophrenia. *Proceedings of the National Academy of Sciences, USA, 95,* 15718–15723.

Ingram, J. L., Stodgell, C. J., Hyman, S. L., Figlewicz, D. A., Weitkamp, L. R., & Rodier, P. M. (2000). Discovery of allelic variants of HOXA1 and HOXB1: Genetic susceptibility in autistic spectrum disorders. *Teratology, 62,* 393–405.

International Molecular Genetic Study of Autism Consortium. (1998). A full genome screen for Autism with evidence for linkage to a region on chromosome 7q. *Human Molecular Genetics, 7,* 571–578.

International Molecular Genetic Study of Autism Consortium. (2001). A genomewide screen for Autism: Strong evidence for linkage to

chromosomes 2q, 7q, and 16p. *American Journal of Human Genetics, 69,* 570–581.

Jacobson, R. (1986). Case report: Disorders of facial recognition, social behavior and affect after combined bilateral amygdalotomy and subcaudate tractotomy: A clinical and experimental study. *Psychological Medicine, 16,* 439–450.

Jambaque, I., Mottron, L., Ponsot, G., & Chiron, C. (1998). Autism and visual agnosia in a child with right occipital lobectomy. *Journal of Neurology, Neurosurgery, and Psychiatry, 65,* 555–560.

Jaselskis, C. A., Cook, E. H., Fletcher, K. E., & Leventhal, B. L. (1992). Clonidine treatment of hyperactive and impulsive children with autistic disorder. *Journal of Clinical Psychopharmacology, 12,* 322–327.

Jorde, L. B., Hasstedt, S., Ritvo, E., Mason-Brothers, A., Freeman, B., Pingree, C., et al. (1991). Complex segregation analysis of Autism. *American Journal of Human Genetics, 49,* 932–938.

Jorde, L. B., Mason-Brothers, A., Waldmann, R., Ritvo, E. R., Freeman, B. J., Pingree, C., et al. (1990). The UCLA–University of Utah epidemiologic survey of Autism: Genealogical analysis of familial aggregation. *American Journal of Medical Genetics, 36,* 85–88.

Joseph, R. M. (2001, April). *Face recognition processes in typically developing children and children with Autism.* Poster session presented at the biannual meeting of the Society for Research in Child Development, Minneapolis, MN.

Joshi, P. T., Capozzoli, J. A., & Coyle, J. T. (1988). Low-dose neuroleptic therapy for children with childhood-onset pervasive developmental disorder. *American Journal of Psychiatry, 145,* 335–338.

Kaiser, A. P., & Hester, P. P. (1996). How everyday environments support children's communication. In L. K. Koegel, R. L. Koegel, & G. Dunlap (Eds.), *Positive behavioral support: Including people with difficult behavior in the community* (pp. 145–162). Baltimore: Paul H. Brookes.

Kamps, D. M., Leonard, B. R., Vernon, S., Dugan, E. P., & Delquadri, J. C. (1992). Teaching social skills to students with Autism to increase peer interactions in an integrated first-grade classroom. *Journal of Applied Behavior Analysis, 25,* 281–288.

Kanner, L. (1943). Autistic disturbances of affective contact. *Nervous Child, 2,* 217–250.

Kasari, C., Sigman, M., Mundy, P., & Yirmiya, N. (1990). Affective sharing in the context of joint attention interactions of normal, autistic, and mentally retarded children. *Journal of Autism and Developmental Disorders, 20,* 87–100.

Kaye, J. A., del Mar Melero-Montes, M., & Jick, H. (2001). Mumps, measles, and rubella vaccine and the incidence of Autism recorded by general practitioners: A time trend analysis. *British Medical Journal, 322,* 460–463.

Kimmel, S. R. (2002). Vaccine adverse events: Separating myth from reality. *American Family Physician, 66,* 2113–2120.

Kjelgaard, M. M., & Tager-Flusberg, H. (2001). An investigation of language impairment in Autism: Implications for genetic subgroups. *Language and Cognitive Processes, 16,* 287–308.

Klauck, S. M., Poustka, F., Benner, A., Lesch, K. P., & Poustka, A. (1997). Serotonin transporter (5-HTT) gene variants associated with Autism? *Human Molecular Genetics, 6,* 2233–2238.

Kleijnen, J., & Knipschild, P. (1991). Niacin and vitamin B6 in mental functioning: A review of controlled trials in humans. *Biological Psychiatry, 29,* 931–941.

Klin, A., Jones, W., Schultz, R., Volkmar, F., & Cohen, D. (2002). Visual fixation patterns during viewing of naturalistic social situations as predictors of social competence in individuals with Autism. *Archives of General Psychiatry, 59,* 809–816.

Klin, A., Sparrow, S. S., de Bildt, A., Cicchetti, D. V., Cohen, D. J., & Volkmar, F. R. (1999). A normed study of face recognition in Autism and related disorders. *Journal of Autism and Developmental Disorders, 29,* 499–508.

Klinnert, M. D., Campos, J. J., Sorce, J. F., Emde, R. N., & Svejda, M. (1983). Emotions as behavior regulators: Social referencing in infancy. In R. Plutchik & H. Kellerman (Eds.), *Emotion: Theory, research and experience* (Vol. 2, pp. 57–86). New York: Academic Press.

Kniusberg, A. M., Wiig, K., Lind, G., Nogland, M., & Reichelt, K. L. (1990). Dietary intervention in autistic syndromes. *Developmental Brain Dysfunction, 3,* 315–327.

Kobayashi, R., & Murata, T. (1998). Behavioral characteristics of 187 young adults with Autism. *Psychiatry and Clinical Neuroscience, 52,* 383–390.

Koegel, L. K., Camarata, S., Valdez-Menchaca, M. C., & Koegel, R. L. (1998). Setting generalization of question-asking by children with Autism. *American Journal on Mental Retardation, 102,* 346–357.

Koegel, L. K., & Koegel, R. L. (1995). Motivating communication in children with Autism. In E. Schopler & G. Mesibov (Eds.), *Learning and cognition in Autism* (pp. 73–87). New York: Plenum Press.

Koegel, L. K., Koegel, R. L., Shoshan, Y., & McNerney, E. (1999). Pivotal response intervention: Pt. II. Preliminary long-term outcome data. *Journal of the Association for Persons with Severe Handicaps, 24,* 186–198.

Koegel, R. L., & Egel, A. L. (1979). Motivating autistic children. *Journal of Abnormal Psychology, 88,* 418–426.

Koegel, R. L., & Koegel, L. K. (1995). *Teaching children with Autism.* Baltimore: Paul H. Brookes.

Koegel, R. L., Koegel, L. K., & Surratt, A. V. (1992). Language intervention and disruptive behavior in preschool children with Autism. *Journal of Autism and Developmental Disorders, 22,* 141–153.

Koegel, R. L., O'Dell, M. C., & Koegel, L. K. (1987). A natural language paradigm for teaching nonverbal autistic children. *Journal of Autism and Developmental Disorders, 17,* 187–199.

Kolmen, B. K., Feldman, H. M., Handen, B. L., & Janosky, J. E. (1995). Naltrexone in young autistic children: Double-blind, placebo-controlled crossover study. *Journal of the American Academy of Child and Adolescent Psychiatry, 34,* 223–231.

Kolmen, B. K., Feldman, H. M., Handen, B. L., & Janosky, J. E. (1997). Naltrexone in young autistic children: Replication study and learning measures. *Journal of the American Academy of Child and Adolescent Psychiatry, 36,* 1570–1578.

Krantz, P. J., & McClannahan, L. E. (1993). Teaching children with Autism to initiate to peers: Effects of a script-fading procedure. *Journal of Applied Behavior Analysis, 26,* 121–132.

Krantz, P. J., & McClannahan, L. E. (1998). Social interaction skills for children with Autism: A script-fading procedure for beginning readers. *Journal of Applied Behavior Analysis, 31,* 191–202.

Kurita, H. (1985). Infantile Autism with speech loss before the age of thirty months. *Journal of the American Academy of Child Psychiatry, 24,* 191–196.

Lainhart, J. E. (1999). Psychiatric problems in individuals with Autism, their parents and siblings. *International Review of Psychiatry, 11,* 278–298.

Lainhart, J. E., & Folstein, S. (1994). Affective disorders in people with Autism: A review of published cases. *Journal of Autism and Developmental Disorders, 24,* 587–601.

Lainhart, J. E., Piven, J., Wzorek, M., Landa, R., Santangelo, S. L., Coon, H., et al. (1997). Macrocephaly in children and adults with Autism. *Journal of the American Academy of Child and Adolescent Psychiatry, 36,* 282–290.

Landa, R., Piven, J., Wzorek, M. M., Gayle, J. O., Chase, G. A., & Folstein, S. E. (1992). Social language use in parents of autistic individuals. *Psychological Medicine, 22,* 245–254.

Langdell, T. (1978). Recognition of faces: An approach to the study of Autism. *Journal of Child Psychology and Psychiatry, 19,* 255–268.

Laski, K. E., Charlop, M. H., & Schreibman, L. (1988). Training parents to use the natural language paradigm to increase their autistic children's speech. *Journal of Applied Behavior Analysis, 21,* 391–400.

Lauder, J. (1993). Neurotransmitters as growth regulatory signals: Role of receptors and second messengers. *Trends in Neuroscience, 16,* 233–240.

Launay, J. M., Bursztejn, C., Ferrari, P., Dreux, C., Braconnier, A., Zarifian, E., et al. (1987). Catecholamine metabolism in infantile Autism: A controlled study of 22 autistic children. *Journal of Autism and Developmental Disorders, 17,* 333–347.

Lebedinskaya, K. S., & Nikolskaya, O. S. (1993). Brief report: Analysis of Autism and its treatment in modern Russian defectology. *Journal of Autism and Developmental Disorders, 23,* 675–679.

Leboyer, M., Bouvard, M. P., Recasens, C., Philippe, A., Guilloud-Bataille, M., Bondoux, D., et al. (1994). Differences between plasma N- and C-terminally directed beta-endorphin immunoreactivity in infantile Autism. *American Journal of Psychiatry, 151,* 1797–1801.

Leboyer, M., Phillipp, A., Bouvard, M., Guilloud-Bataille, M., Bondoux, D., Tabuteau, F., et al. (1999). Whole blood serotonin and plasma beta-endorphins in autistic probands and their first-degree relatives. *Biological Psychiatry, 45,* 158–163.

Le Couteur, A., Bailey, A., & Rutter, M. (1989, August). *Epidemiologically based twin study of Autism.* Paper presented at the First World Congress on Psychiatric Genetics, Cambridge.

Le Couteur, A., Lord, C., & Rutter, M. (2003). *Autism Diagnostic Interview-Revised.* Los Angeles: Western Psychological Services.

LeDoux, J. E. (1987). Emotion. In V. B. Mountcastle, F. Plum, & S. R. Geiger (Eds.), *Handbook of physiology* (Vol. 5, Sec. 1, pp. 419–459). Bethesda, MD: American Physiological Society.

Lee, A., Hobson, R. P., & Chiat, S. (1994). I, you, me, and Autism: An experimental study. *Journal of Autism and Developmental Disorders, 24,* 155–176.

Leekam, S., & Moore, C. (2001). The development of attention and joint attention in children with Autism. In J. A. Burack, T. Charman, N. Yirmiya, & P. R. Zelazo (Eds.), *The development of Autism: Perspectives from theory and research* (pp. 105–129). Mahwah, NJ: Erlbaum.

Lelord, G., Barthelemy, C., & Martineau, N. (1988). Clinical and biological effects of vitamin B6 plus magnesium in autistic subjects. In J. Laklam & R. Reynolds (Eds.), *Vitamin B6 responsive disorders in humans* (pp. 329–356). New York: Wiley-Liss.

Leslie, A. M. (1987). Pretence and representation: The origins of "theory of mind." *Psychological Review, 94,* 412–426.

Levy, S., Zoltak, B., & Saelens, T. (1988). A comparison of obstetrical records of autistic and nonautistic referrals for psychoeducational evaluations. *Journal of Autism and Developmental Disorders, 18,* 573–581.

Li, J., Tabor, H. K., Nguyen, L., Gleason, C., Lotspeich, L. J., Spiker, D., et al. (2002). Lack of association between HOXA1 and HOXB1 gene variants and Autism in 110 multiplex families. *American Journal of Medical Genetics: Part B. Neuropsychiatric Genetics—The Official Publication of the International Society of Psychiatric Genetics, 114,* 24–30.

Lincoln, A. J., Courchesne, E., Kilman, B. A., Elmasian, R., & Allen, M. (1988). A study of intellectual abilities in high-functioning people with Autism. *Journal of Autism and Developmental Disorders, 18,* 505–524.

Lis, A. W., McLaughlin, R. K., Lis, E. W., & Stubbs, E. G. (1976). Profiles of ultraviolet absorbing components of urine from autistic children, as obtained by high-resolution ion-exchange chromatography. *Clinical Chemistry, 22,* 1528–1532.

Liu, A. (2001). Genomewide screen for Autism susceptibility loci. *American Journal of Human Genetics, 69,* 327.

Lockyer, L., & Rutter, M. (1970). A five to fifteen year follow-up study of infantile psychosis, IV. Patterns of cognitive ability. *British Journal of Social and Clinical Psychology, 9,* 1952–1963.

Lord, C. (1984). The development of peer relations in children with Autism. In F. J. Morrison, C. Lord, & D. P. Keating (Eds.), *Applied developmental psychology* (Vol. 1, pp. 165–230). New York: Academic Press.

Lord, C. (1995). Follow-up of two-year-olds referred for possible Autism. *Journal of Child Psychology and Psychiatry and Allied Disciplines, 36,* 1365–1382.

Lord, C. (1997). Diagnostic instruments in Autism spectrum disorders. In D. J. Cohen & F. R. Volkmar (Eds.), *Handbook of Autism and pervasive developmental disorders* (2nd ed., pp. 460–483). New York: Wiley.

Lord, C., DiLavore, P., Shulman, C., Risi, S., & Pickles, A. (2003, April). *Autism from two to nine years.* Paper presented at the biennial meeting of the Society for Research in Child Development, Tampa, FL.

Lord, C., & Magill-Evans, J. (1995). Peer interactions of autistic children and adolescents. *Development and Psychopathology, 7,* 611–626.

Lord, C., Mulloy, C., Wendelboe, M., & Schopler, E. (1991). Pre- and perinatal factors in high-functioning females and males with Autism. *Journal of Autism and Developmental Disorders, 21,* 197–209.

Lord, C., & Paul, R. (1997). Language and communication in Autism. In D. J. Cohen & F. R. Volkmar (Eds.), *Handbook of Autism and pervasive developmental disorders* (2nd ed., pp. 195–225). New York: Wiley.

Lord, C., Risi, S., Lambrecht, L., Cook, E. H., Leventhal, B. L., DiLavore, P. C., et al. (2000). The Autism Diagnostic Observation Schedule: Generic—A standard measure of social and communication deficits associated with the spectrum of Autism. *Journal of Autism and Developmental Disorders, 30,* 205–223.

Lord, C., Rutter, M., DiLavore, P., & Risi, S. (1999). *Autism Diagnostic Observation Schedule.* Los Angeles: Western Psychological Services.

Lord, C., Rutter, M. L., Goode, S., & Heemsbergen, J. (1989). Autism Diagnostic Observation Schedule: A standardized observation of communicative and social behavior. *Journal of Autism and Developmental Disorders, 19,* 185–212.

Lord, C., Rutter, M., & Le Couteur, A. (1994). Autism Diagnostic Interview-Revised: A revised version of a diagnostic interview for caregivers of individuals with possible pervasive developmental disorders. *Journal of Autism and Developmental Disorders, 24,* 659–685.

Lord, C., & Schopler, E. (1989). The role of age at assessment, developmental level, and test in the stability of intelligence scores in young autistic children. *Journal of Autism and Developmental Disorders, 19,* 483–499.

Lovaas, O. I. (1987). Behavioral treatment and normal educational and intellectual functioning in young autistic children. *Journal of Consulting and Clinical Psychology, 55,* 3–9.

Loveland, K. A., Tunali-Kotoski, B., Chen, Y. R., Ortegon, J., Pearson, D. A., Brelsford, K. A., et al. (1997). Emotion recognition in Autism: Verbal and nonverbal information. *Development and Psychopathology, 9,* 579–593.

Loveland, K. A., Tunali-Kotoski, B., Pearson, D. A., Brelsford, K. A., Ortegon, J., & Chen, R. (1994). Imitation and expression of facial affect in Autism. *Development and Psychopathology, 6,* 433–444.

Maestrini, E., Lai, C., Marlow, A., Matthews, N., Wallace, S., Bailey, A., et al. (1999). Serotonin transporter (5-HTT) and gamma-aminobutyric acid receptor subunit beta3 (GABRB3) gene polymorphisms are not associated with Autism in the IMGSA families: The International Molecular Genetic Study of Autism Consortium. *American Journal of Medical Genetics, 88,* 492–496.

Magnusson, P., & Saemundsen, E. (2001). Prevalence of Autism in Iceland. *Journal of Autism and Developmental Disorders, 31,* 153–163.

Malek-Ahmadi, P., & Simonds, J. F. (1998). Olanzapine for autistic disorder with hyperactivity. *Journal of the American Academy of Child and Adolescent Psychiatry, 37,* 902.

Malkova, L., Gaffan, D., & Murray, E. A. (1997). Excitotoxic lesions of the amygdala fail to produce impairment in visual learning for auditory secondary reinforcement but interfere with reinforcer devaluation effects in rhesus monkey. *Journal of Neuroscience, 17,* 6011–6020.

Manning, J. T., Callow, M., & Bundred, P. E. (2003). Finger and toe ratios in humans and mice: Implications for the aetiology of diseases influenced by HOX genes. *Medical Hypotheses, 60,* 340–343.

Mars, A. E., Mauk, J. E., & Dowrick, P. W. (1998). Symptoms of pervasive developmental disorders as observed in prediagnostic home videos of infants and toddlers. *Journal of Pediatrics, 132,* 1–5.

Mathews, A. (1996). Employment training and the development of a support model within employment for adults who experience Asperger's syndrome and Autism: The Gloucestershire group homes model. In H. Morgan (Ed.), *Adults with Autism: A guide to theory and practice* (pp. 163–184). Cambridge, England: Cambridge University Press.

Maurer, D., & Salapatek, P. (1976). Developmental changes in the scanning of faces by young children. *Child Development, 47,* 523–527.

McClannahan, L., & Krantz, P. (1994). The Princeton Child Development Institute. In S. Harris & J. Handleman (Eds.), *Preschool education programs for children with Autism* (pp. 107–126). Austin, TX: ProEd.

McCormick, L. H. (1997). Treatment with buspirone in a patient with Autism. *Archives of Family Medicine, 6,* 368–370.

McDougle, C. J. (1998). Psychopharmacology. In F. R. Volkamr (Ed.), *Autism and pervasive developmental disorders* (pp. 169–192). Cambridge, England: Cambridge University Press.

McDougle, C. J., Holmes, J. P., Bronson, M. R., Anderson, G. M., Volkmar, F. R., Price, L. H., et al. (1997). Risperidone treatment of children and adolescents with pervasive developmental disorders: A prospective open-label study. *Journal of the American Academy of Child and Adolescent Psychiatry, 36,* 685–693.

McDougle, C. J., Price, L. H., & Goodman, W. K. (1990). Fluvoxamine treatment of coincident autistic disorder and obsessive compulsive disorder: A case report. *Journal of Autism and Developmental Disorders, 20,* 537–543.

McEachin, J. J., Smith, T., & Lovaas, O. I. (1993). Long-term outcome for children with Autism who received early intensive behavioral treatment. *American Journal on Mental Retardation, 97,* 359–372.

McEvoy, R. E., Rogers, S. J., & Pennington, B. F. (1993). Executive function and social communication deficits in young autistic children. *Journal of Child Psychology and Psychiatry, 34,* 563–578.

McGee, G. G., Daly, T., Izeman, S. G., Mann, L., & Risley, T. R. (1991). Use of classroom materials to promote preschool engagement. *Teaching Exceptional Children, 23,* 44–47.

McGee, G. G., Daly, T., & Jacobs, H. A. (1994). The Walden preschool. In S. Harris & J. Handleman (Eds.), *Preschool education programs for children with Autism* (pp. 127–152). Austin, TX: ProEd.

McPartland, J., Dawson, G., Carver, L., & Panagiotides, H. (2001a, April). *Neural correlates of face perception in Autism.* Poster session presented at the biennial meeting of the Society for Research in Child Development, Minneapolis, MN.

McPartland, J., Dawson, G., Carver, L., & Panagiotides, H. (2001b, November). *Neural correlates of face perception in individuals with Autism spectrum disorder.* Poster session presented at the International Meeting for Autism Research, San Diego, CA.

Meltzoff, A. N., & Gopnick, A. (1993). The role of imitation in understanding persons and developing a theory of mind. In S. Baron-Cohen, H. Tager-Flusberg, & D. J. Cohen (Eds.), *Understanding other minds: Perspectives from Autism* (pp. 335–366). Oxford: Oxford University Press.

Meltzoff, A. N., & Moore, M. (1977). Imitation of facial and manual gestures by human neonates. *Science, 198,* 75–78.

Merians, A. S., Clark, M., Poizner, H., Macauley, G., Gonzalez-Rothi, L. J., & Heilman, K. (1997). Visual-imitative dissociation apraxia. *Neuropsychologia, 35,* 1483–1490.

Miller, M. T., & Strömland, K. (1993). Thalidomide embryopathy: An insight into Autism? *Teratology, 47,* 387–388.

Minderaa, R. B., Anderson, G. M., Volkmar, F. R., Akkerhuis, G. W., & Cohen, D. J. (1994). Noradrenergic and adrenergic functioning in Autism. *Biological Psychiatry, 36,* 237–241.

Mirenda, P., & Mathy-Laikko, P. (1989). Augmentative and alternative communication applications for persons with severe congenital communication disorders: An introduction. *Augmentative and Alternative Communication, 5,* 3–13.

Moore, S. J., Turnpenny, P., Quinn, A., Glover, S., Lloyd, D. J., Montgomery, T., et al. (2000). A clinical study of 57 children with fetal anticonvulsant syndromes. *Journal of Medical Genetics, 37,* 489–497.

Morales, M., Mundy, P., & Rojas, J. (1998). Brief report: Following the direction of gaze and language development in 6-month-olds. *Infant Behavior and Development, 21,* 373–377.

Morton, J., & Johnson, M. H. (1991). CONSPEC and CONLERN: A two-process theory of infant face recognition. *Psychological Review, 2,* 164–181.

Mottron, L., Belleville, S., & Menard, E. (1999). Local bias in autistic subjects as evidenced by graphic tasks: Perceptual hierarchization or working memory deficit? *Journal of Child Psychology and Psychiatry and Allied Disciplines, 40,* 743–755.

Mundy, P., & Crowson, M. (1997). Joint attention and early social communication: Implications for research on intervention with Autism. *Journal of Autism and Developmental Disorders, 27,* 653–675.

Mundy, P., & Neal, A. R. (2001). Neural plasticity, joint attention and a transactional social-orienting model of Autism. In L. M. Glidden (Ed.), *International review of research in mental retardation: Autism* (Vol. 23, pp. 139–168). San Diego: Academic Press.

Mundy, P., & Sigman, M. (1989). The theoretical implications of joint-attention deficits in Autism. *Development and Psychopathology, 1,* 173–183.

Mundy, P., Sigman, M., & Kasari, C. (1990). A longitudinal study of joint attention and language development in autistic children. *Journal of Autism and Developmental Disorders, 20,* 115–128.

Mundy, P., Sigman, M., Ungerer, J., & Sherman, T. (1986). Defining the social deficits of Autism: The contribution of nonverbal communication measures. *Journal of Child Psychology and Psychiatry, 27,* 657–669.

Mundy, P., Sigman, M., Ungerer, J., & Sherman, T. (1987). Nonverbal communication and play correlates of language development in autistic children. *Journal of Autism and Developmental Disorders, 17,* 349–364.

Munson, J., Dager, S., Friedman, S., Shaw, D., Sparks, S., Artru, A., et al. (2004, May). *Amygdala size as an early biological index of symptom severity and course in Autism.* Poster presented at the annual meeting of the NIH Collaborative Program of Excellence, Besthesda, MD.

Murphy, M., Bolton, P., Pickles, A., Fombonne, E., Piven, J., & Rutter, M. (2000). Personality traits of the relatives of autistic probands. *Psychological Medicine, 30,* 1411–1424.

Murray, E. A., & Mishkin, M. (1985). Amygdalectomy impairs cross-modal association in monkeys. *Science, 228,* 604–606.

Narayan, M., Srinath, S., Anderson, G. M., & Meundi, D. B. (1993). Cerebrospinal fluid levels of homovanillic acid and 5-hydroxyindoleacetic acid in Autism. *Biological Psychiatry, 33,* 630–635.

National Research Council, Committee on Educational Interventions for Children with Autism, National Academy of Sciences. (2001). *Educating children with Autism.* Washington, DC: National Academy Press.

Nelson, C. A. (1993). The recognition of facial expressions in infancy: Behavioral and electrophysiological correlates. In B. de Boysson-Bardies, S. de Schonen, P. Jusczyk, P. MacNeilage, & J. Morton (Eds.), *Developmental neurocognition: Speech and face processing in the first year of life* (pp. 187–193). Hingham, MA: Kluwer Academic Press.

Nelson, C. A., & deHaan, M. (1996). A neurobiological approach to the recognition of facial expressions in infancy. In J. A. Russell (Ed.), *The psychology of facial expression* (pp. 176–204). Cambridge, MA: Cambridge University Press.

Nicolson, R., Awad, G., & Sloman, L. (1998). An open trial of risperidone in young autistic children. *Journal of the American Academy of Child and Adolescent Psychiatry, 37,* 372–376.

Nordin, V., & Gillberg, C. (1998). The long-term course of autistic disorders: Update on follow-up studies. *Acta Psychiatrica Scandinavia, 97,* 99–108.

Odom, S. L., McConnell, S. R., McEvoy, M. A., Peterson, C., Ostrosky, M., Chandler, L. K., et al. (1999). Relative effects of interventions for supporting the social competence of young children with disabilities. *Topics in Early Childhood Special Education, 19,* 75–92.

Odom, S. L., & Strain, P. S. (1986). A comparison of peer-initiation and teacher-antecedent interventions for promoting reciprocal social interaction of autistic preschoolers. *Journal of Applied Behavior Analysis, 19,* 59–71.

Ogawa, M., Miyata, T., Nakajima, K., Yagyu, K., Seike, M., Ikenaka, K., et al. (1995). The reeler gene-associated antigen on Cajal-Retzius neurons is a crucial molecule for laminar organization of cortical neurons. *Neuron, 14,* 899–912.

Oram, M. W., & Perrett, D. I. (1994). Responses of anterior superior temporal polysensory (STP) neurons to "biological motion" stimuli. *Journal of Cognitive Neuroscience, 6,* 99–116.

Ornitz, E. M. (1989). Autism at the interface between sensory and information processing. In G. Dawson (Ed.), *Autism: Nature, diagnosis, and treatment* (pp. 174–207). New York: Guilford Press.

Osterling, J., & Dawson, G. (1994). Early recognition of children with Autism: A study of first birthday home videotapes. *Journal of Autism and Developmental Disorders, 24,* 247–257.

Osterling, J., & Dawson, G. (1999, April). *Early recognition of infants with Autism versus mental retardation.* Poster session presented at the biennial meeting of the Society for Research in Child Development, Albuquerque, NM.

Osterling, J. A., Dawson, G., & Munson, J. A. (2002). Early recognition of 1-year-old infants with Autism spectrum disorder versus mental retardation. *Development and Psychopathology, 14,* 239–251.

Ozonoff, S., Dawson, G., & McPartland, J. (2002). *A parent's guide to Asperger syndrome and high-functioning Autism: How to meet the challenges and help your child thrive.* New York: Guilford Press.

Ozonoff, S., & Griffith, E. M. (2000). Neuropsychological function and the external validity of Asperger syndrome. In A. Klin, F. R. Volkmar, & S. S. Sparrow (Eds.), *Asperger syndrome* (pp. 72–96). New York: Guilford Press.

Ozonoff, S., & Miller, J. N. (1995). Teaching theory of mind: A new approach to social skills training for individuals with Autism. *Journal of Autism and Developmental Disorders, 25,* 415–433.

Ozonoff, S., Pennington, B. F., & Rogers, S. J. (1990). Are there emotion perception deficits in young autistic children? *Journal of Child Psychology and Psychiatry and Allied Disciplines, 31,* 343–361.

Panksepp, J. (1979). A neurochemical theory of Autism. *Trends in Neuroscience, 2,* 174–177.

Panksepp, J., & Sahley, T. L. (1987). Possible brain opioid involvement in disrupted social intent and language development of Autism. In E. Schopler & G. B. Mesibov (Eds.), *Neurobiological issues in Autism* (pp. 357–372). New York: Plenum Press.

Paul, R., Fischer, M. L., & Cohen, D. J. (1988). Brief report: Sentence comprehension strategies in children with Autism and specific language disorders. *Journal of Autism and Developmental Disorders, 18,* 669–677.

Paulescu, R., Frith, C. D., & Frackowiak, R. S. J. (1993). The neural correlates of the verbal components of working memory. *Nature, 362,* 342–345.

Pennington, B., & Ozonoff, S. (1996). Executive functions and developmental psychopathology. *Journal of Child Psychology and Psychiatry, 36,* 459–474.

Perrett, D. I., Harries, M. H., Bevan, R., Thomas, S., Benson, P. J., Mistlin, A. J., et al. (1989). Frameworks of analysis for the neural representation of animate objects and actions. *Journal of Experimental Biology, 146,* 683–694.

Perrett, D. I., Smith, P. A., Mistlin, A. J., Chitty, A., Head, A., Potter, D., et al. (1985). Visual analysis of body movements by neurons in the temporal cortex of the macaque monkey: A preliminary report. *Behavioral Brain Research, 16,* 153–170.

Perrett, D. I., Smith, P. A., Potter, D. D., Mistlin, A. J., Head, A. S., Milner, A. D., et al. (1984). Neurons responsive to faces in the temporal cortex: Studies of functional organization, sensitivity to identity and relation to perception. *Human Neurobiology, 3,* 197–208.

Perry, R., Pataki, C., Munoz-Silva, D. M., Armenteros, J., & Silva, R. R. (1997). Risperidone in children and adolescents with pervasive developmental disorder: Pilot trial and follow-up. *Journal of Child and Adolescent Psychopharmacology, 7,* 167–179.

Persico, A. M., Militerni, R., Bravaccio, C., Schneider, C., Melmed, R., Conciatori, M., et al. (2000). Lack of association between serotonin transporter gene promoter variants and autistic disorder in two ethnically distinct samples. *American Journal of Medical Genetics (Neuropsychiatric Genetics), 96,* 123–127.

Petersen, S. E., Fox, P. T., Posner, M. I., Mintun, M., & Raichle, M. E. (1989). Positron emission tomographic studies of the processing of single words. *Journal of Cognitive Neuroscience, 1,* 153–170.

Peterson, C. (2002). Drawing insight from pictures: The development of concepts of false drawing and false belief in children with deafness, normal hearing, and Autism. *Child Development, 73,* 1442–1459.

Philippe, A., Martinez, M., Guilloudbataille, M., Gillberg, C., Rastam, M., Sponheim, E., et al. (1999). Genome-wide scan for Autism susceptibility genes. *Human Molecular Genetics, 8,* 805–812.

Pickles, A., Bolton, P., Macdonald, H., Bailey, A., Le Couteur, A., Sim, L., et al. (1995). Latent class analysis of recurrence risks for complex phenotypes with selection and measurement error: A twin and family history study of Autism. *American Journal of Human Genetics, 57,* 717–726.

Pierce, K., Muller, R., Ampbrose, J., Allen, G., & Courchesne, E. (2001). Face processing occurs outside the fusiform "face area" in Autism: Evidence from functional MRI. *Brain, 124,* 2059–2073.

Piven, J., Arndt, S., Bailey, J., & Andreasen, N. (1996). Regional brain enlargement in Autism: A magnetic resonance imaging study. *Journal of the American Academy of Child and Adolescent Psychiatry, 35,* 530–536.

Piven, J., Arndt, S., Bailey, J., Havercamp, S., Andreasen, N. C., & Palmer, P. (1995). An MRI study of brain size in Autism. *American Journal of Psychiatry, 152,* 1145–1149.

Piven, J., Harper, J., Palmer, P., & Arndt, S. (1996). Course of behavioral change in Autism: A retrospective study of high-IQ adolescents and adults. *Journal of the American Academy of Child and Adolescent Psychiatry, 35,* 523–529.

Piven, J., & Palmer, P. (1997). Cognitive deficits in parents from multiple-incidence Autism families. *Journal of Child Psychology and Psychiatry and Allied Disciplines, 38,* 1011–102I.

Piven, J., Simon, J., Chase, G. A., Wzorek, M., Landa, R., Gayle, J., et al. (1993). The etiology of Autism, pre-, peri- and neonatal factors. *Journal of the American Academy of Child and Adolescent Psychiatry, 32,* 1256–1263.

Piven, J., Tsai, G. C., Nehme, E., Coyle, J. T., Chase, G. A., & Folstein, S. (1991). Platelet serotonin, a possible marker for familial Autism. *Journal of Autism and Developmental Disorders, 21,* 51–59.

Potenza, M. N., Holmes, J. P., Kanes, S. J., & McDougle, C. J. (1999). Olanzapine treatment of children, adolescents and adults with pervasive developmental disorders: An open-label pilot study. *Journal of Clinical Psychopharmacology, 19,* 37–44.

Potenza, M. N., & McDougle, C. J. (1997). The role of serotonin in Autism-spectrum disorders. *CNS Spectrums, 2,* 25–42.

Quintana, H., Birmaher, B., Stedge, D., Lennon, S., Freed, J., Bridge, J., et al. (1995). Use of methylphenidate in the treatment of children with autistic disorder. *Journal of Autism and Developmental Disorders, 25,* 283–294.

Raymond, G. V., Bauman, M. L., & Kemper, T. L. (1996). Hippocampus in Autism: A Golgi analysis. *Acta Neuropathologica, 9,* 117–119.

Realmuto, G., August, G., & Garfinkel, B. (1989). Clinical effect of buspirone in autistic children. *Journal of Clinical Psychopharmacology, 9,* 122–125.

Reichelt, K. L., Kniusberg, A. M., Nodland, M., & Lind, G. (1994). Nature and consequences of hyperpeptiduria and bovine casomorphins found in autistic syndromes. *Developmental Brain Dysfunction, 7,* 71–85.

Risch, N., Spiker, D., Lotspeich, L., Nouri, N., Hinds, D., Hallmayer, J., et al. (1999). A genomic screen of Autism: Evidence for a multilocus etiology. *American Journal of Genetics, 65,* 493–507.

Ritvo, E. R., Freeman, B. J., Mason-Brothers, A., Mo, A., & Ritvo, A. M. (1985). Concordance for the syndrome of Autism in 40 pairs of affected twins. *American Journal of Psychiatry, 142,* 74–77.

Rizzolatti G., Fadiga, L., Gallese, V., & Fogassi, L. (1996). Premotor cortex and the recognition of motor actions. *Brain Research. Cognitive Brain Research, 3*(2), 131–141.

Rizzolatti, G., Fadiga, L., Matelli, M., Bettinardi, V., Paulesu, E., Perani, D., et al. (1996). Localization of grasp representation in human by PET. *Experimental Brain Research, 11,* 246–252.

Robins, D. L., Fein, D., Barton, M. L., & Green, J. A. (2001). The modified checklist for Autism in toddlers: An initial study investigating the early detection of Autism and pervasive developmental disorders. *Journal of Autism and Developmental Disorders, 31,* 131–144.

Rochat P., & Striano, T. (1999). Social-cognitive development in the first year. In P. Rochat (Ed.), *Early social cognition: Understanding others in the first months of life* (pp. 3–34). Mahwah, NJ: Erlbuam.

Rodier, P. M., & Hyman, S. L. (1998). Early environmental factors in Autism. *Mental Retardation and Developmental Disabilities Research Reviews, 4,* 121–128.

Rodier, P. M., Ingram, J. L., Tisdale, B., Nelson, S., & Romano, J. (1996). Embryological origin for Autism: Developmental anomalies of the cranial nerve motor nuclei. *Journal of Comparative Neurology, 370,* 247–261.

Rogers, S. J. (1998). Empirically supported comprehensive treatments for young children with Autism. *Journal of Clinical Child Psychology, 27,* 168–179.

Rogers, S. J. (1999). An examination of the imitation deficit in Autism. In J. Nadel & G. Butterworth (Eds.), *Imitation in infancy* (pp. 254–283). Cambridge, England: Cambridge University Press.

Rogers, S. J. (2001). Diagnosis of Autism before the age of 3. In L. M. Glidden (Ed.), *International review of research in mental retardation: Autism* (Vol. 23, pp. 1–31). San Diego: Academic Press.

Rogers, S. J., & Hepburn, S. L. (2003, April). *Individual variability and predictors of preschool language outcomes in Autism.* Paper presented at the biennial meeting of the Society for Research in Child Development, Tampa, FL.

Rogers, S. J., Herbison, J., Lewis, H., Pantone, J., & Reis, K. (1986). An approach for enhancing the symbolic, communicative, and interpersonal functioning of young children with Autism and severe emotional handicaps. *Journal of the Division of Early Childhood, 10,* 135–148.

Rogers, S. J., & Lewis, H. (1989). An effective day treatment model for young children with pervasive developmental disorders. *Journal of the American Academy of Child and Adolescent Psychiatry, 28,* 207–214.

Rogers, S. J., & Pennington, B. (1991). A theoretical approach to the deficits in infantile Autism. *Development and Psychopathology, 3,* 137–162.

Rumsey, J. M., & Hamburger, S. D. (1988). Neuropsychological findings in high-functioning men with infantile Autism, residual state. *Journal of Clinical and Experimental Neuropsychology, 10,* 201–221.

Rutter, M. (1970). Autistic children: Infancy to adulthood. *Seminars in Psychiatry, 2,* 435–450.

Rutter, M. (1984). Autistic children growing up. *Developmental Medicine and Child Neurology, 26,* 122–129.

Rutter, M., & Lockyer, L. (1967). A five to fifteen year follow-up study of infantile psychosis: I. Description of sample. *British Journal of Psychiatry, 113,* 1169–1182.

Sandman, C. A., Barron, J. L., Chicz-DeMet, A., & DeMet, E. M. (1990). Plasma b-endorphin levels in patients with self-injurious behavior and stereotypy. *American Journal on Mental Retardation, 95,* 84–92.

Santangelo, S. L., & Folstein, S. E. (1999). Autism: A genetic perspective. In H. Tager-Flusberg (Ed.), *Neurodevelopmental disorders* (pp. 431–447). Cambridge, MA: MIT Press.

Saunders, R. C., Kolachana, B. S., Bachevalier, J., & Weinberger, D. R. (1998). Neonatal lesions of the medial temporal lobe disrupt prefrontal cortical regulation of striatal dopamine. *Nature, 393,* 169–171.

Schlosser, R. W., Belfiore, P. J., Nigam, R., Blischak, D., & Hetzroni, O. (1997). The effects of speech output technology in the learning of graphic symbols. *Journal of Applied Behavior Analysis, 30,* 537–549.

Schmidt, K. (1982). The effect of stimulant medication in childhood-onset pervasive developmental disorder: A case report. *Journal of Developmental and Behavioral Pediatrics, 3,* 244–246.

Schopler, E., & Mesibov, G. B. (Eds.). (1983). *Autism in adolescents and adults.* New York: Plenum Press.

Schopler, E., Mesibov, G. B., Shigley, H., & Bashford, A. (1984). Helping autistic children through their parents: The TEACCH model. In E. Schopler & G. B. Mesibov (Eds.), *The effects of Autism on the family* (pp. 65–81). New York: Plenum Press.

Schreibman, L. (1997). Theoretical perspectives on behavioral intervention for individuals with Autism. In D. J. Cohen & F. R. Volkmar (Eds.), *Handbook of Autism and pervasive developmental disorders* (2nd ed., pp. 920–933). New York: Wiley.

Schreibman, L., Kaneko, W. M., & Koegel, R. L. (1991). Positive affect of parents of autistic children: A comparison across two teaching techniques. *Behavior Therapy, 22,* 479–490.

Schreibman, L., & Koegel, R. L. (1996). Fostering self-management: Parent-delivered pivotal response training for children with autistic disorder. In E. D. Hibbs & P. S. Jensen (Eds.), *Psychosocial treatment for child and adolescent disorders: Empirically based strategies for clinical practice* (pp. 525–552). Washington, DC: American Psychological Association.

Schultz, R. T., Gauthier, I., Klin, A., Fulbright, R. K., Anderson, A. W., Volkmar, F., et al. (2000). Abnormal ventral temporal cortical activity during face discrimination among individuals with Autism and Asperger syndrome. *Archives of General Psychiatry, 57,* 331–340.

Schultz, R. T., Romanski, L. M., & Tsatsanis, K. (2002). Neurofunctional models of autistic disorder and Asperger syndrome: Clues from neu-

roimaging. In A. Klin, F. R. Volkmar, & S. S. Sparrow (Eds.), *Asperger syndrome* (pp. 172–209). New York: Guilford Press.

Sergent, J., Zuck, E., Levesque, M., & MacDonald, B. (1992). Positron emission tomography study of letter and object processing: Empirical findings and methodological considerations. *Cerebral Cortex, 2,* 68–80.

Serra, M., Loth, F. L., van Geert, P. L. C., Hurkens, E., & Minderaa, R. B. (2002). Theory of mind in children with "lesser variants" of Autism: A longitudinal study. *Journal of Child Psychology and Psychiatry and Allied Disciplines, 43,* 885–900.

Shafer, M. S., Egel, A. L., & Neef, N. A. (1984). Training mildly handicapped peers to facilitate changes in the social interaction skills of autistic children. *Journal of Applied Behavior Analysis, 17,* 461–476.

Shah, A., & Frith, U. (1993). Why do autistic individuals show superior performance on the block design task? *Journal of Child Psychology and Psychiatry, 34,* 1351–1364.

Sheinkopf, S., & Siegel, B. (1998). Home based behavioral treatment of young children with Autism. *Journal of Autism and Developmental Disorders, 28,* 15–23.

Shepherd, J. (1981). Social factors in face recognition. In G. Davies, H. Ellis, & J. Shepherd (Eds.), *Perceiving and remembering faces* (pp. 55–79). New York: Academic Press.

Siegel, B., & Hayer, C. (1999, April). *Detection of Autism in the 2nd and 3rd year: The Pervasive Developmental Disorders Screening Test (PDDST).* Paper presented at the meeting of the Society for Research in Child Development, Albuquerque, NM.

Siegel, B., Pliner, C., Eschler, J., & Elliot, G. R. (1988). How children with Autism are diagnosed: Difficulties in identification of children with multiple developmental delays. *Developmental and Behavioral Pediatrics, 9,* 199–204.

Sigman, M. (1997). The Emmanuel Miller memorial lecture 1997: Change and continuity in the development of children with Autism. *Journal of Child Psychology and Psychiatry, 39,* 817–827.

Sigman, M., Kasari, C., Kwon, J., & Yirmiya, N. (1992). Responses to the negative emotions of others by autistic, mentally retarded, and normal children. *Child Development, 63,* 796–807.

Sigman, M., Mundy, P., Sherman, T., & Ungerer, J. (1986). Social interactions of autistic, mentally retarded and normal children and their caregivers. *Journal of Child Psychology and Psychiatry and Allied Disciplines, 27,* 647–656.

Sigman, M., & Norman, K. (1999). Continuity and change in the development of children with Autism. In S. Broman & J. Fletcher (Eds.), *The changing nervous system: Neurobehavioral consequences of early brain disorders* (pp. 274–291). New York: Oxford University Press.

Sigman, M., & Ruskin, E. (1999). Continuity and change in the social competence of children with Autism, Down syndrome, and developmental delays. *Monographs of the Society for Research in Child Development, 64*(1, Serial No. 256).

Sigman, M., & Ungerer, J. (1984). Cognitive and language skills in autistic, mentally retarded, and normal children. *Developmental Psychology, 20,* 293–302.

Sigman, M., Ungerer, J. A., Mundy, P., & Sherman, T. (1987). Cognition in autistic children. In D. J. Cohen, A. M. Donnellan, & P. Rhea (Eds.), *Handbook of Autism and pervasive developmental disorders* (pp. 103–120). New York: Wiley.

Simeonsson, R. J., Olley, J. G., & Rosenthal, S. L. (1987). Early intervention for children with Autism. In M. J. Guralnick & F. C. Bennet (Eds.), *The effectiveness of early intervention for at-risk and handicapped children* (pp. 275–296). New York: Academic Press.

Smalley, S. L., Asarnow, R. F., & Spence, A. (1988). Autism and genetics: A decade of research. *Archives of General Psychiatry, 45,* 953–961.

Smiley, P., & Huttenlocher, J. (1989). Young children's acquisition of emotion concepts. In C. Saarni & P. L. Harris (Eds.), *Children's un-*

derstanding of emotion: Cambridge studies in social and emotional development (pp. 27–49). New York: Cambridge University Press.

Smith, I. M., & Bryson, S. E. (1994). Imitation and action in Autism: A critical review. *Psychology Bulletin, 116,* 259–273.

Smith, T. (1999). Outcome of early intervention for children with Autism. *Clinical Psychology: Science and Practice, 6,* 33–49.

Smith, T., Groen, A. D., & Wynn, J. W. (2000). Randomized trial of intensive early intervention for children with pervasive developmental disorder. *American Journal on Mental Retardation, 105*(4), 269–285.

Sparks, B. F., Friedman, S. D., Shaw, D. W., Aylward, E. H., Echelard, D., Artru, A. A., et al. (2002). Brain structural abnormalities in young children with Autism spectrum disorder. *Neurology, 59,* 184–192.

Sponheim, E., & Skjeldal, O. (1998). Autism and related disorders: Epidemiological findings in a Norwegian study using ICD-10 diagnostic criteria. *Journal of Autism and Developmental Disorders, 28,* 217–227.

Stahmer, A. C. (1995). Teaching symbolic play skills to children with Autism using pivotal response training. *Journal of Autism and Developmental Disorders, 25,* 123–142.

Starr, E., Berument, S. K., Pickles, A., Tomlins, M., Bailey, A., Papanikolaou, K., et al. (2001). A family genetic study of Autism associated with profound mental retardation. *Journal of Autism and Developmental Disorders, 31,* 89–96.

Steffenburg, S., & Gillberg, C. (1986). Autism and autistic-like conditions in Swedish rural and urban areas: A population study. *British Journal of Psychiatry, 149,* 81–87.

Steffenburg, S., Gillberg, C., Hellgren, L., Andersson, L., Gillberg, I. C., Jakobsson, G., et al. (1989). A twin study of Autism in Denmark, Finland, Iceland, Norway, and Sweden. *Journal of Child Psychology and Psychiatry, 30,* 405–416.

Steingard, R. J., Zimnitzky, B., DeMaso, D. R., Bauman, M. L., & Bucci, J. P. (1997). Sertraline treatment of transition-associated anxiety and agitation in children with autistic disorder. *Journal of Child and Adolescent Psychopharmacology, 7,* 9–15.

Stiebel, D. (1999). Promoting augmentative communication during daily routines: A parent problem-solving intervention. *Journal of Positive Behavior Interventions, 1,* 159–169.

Stone, V. E., Baron-Cohen, S., & Knight, R. T. (1998). Frontal lobe contributions to theory of mind. *Journal of Cognitive Neuroscience, 10,* 640–656.

Stone, W. L., Coonrod, E. E., & Ousley, O. Y. (2000). Brief report: Screening tool for Autism in two-year-olds (STAT): Development and preliminary data. *Journal of Autism and Developmental Disorders, 30,* 607–612.

Stone, W. L., Lee, E. B., Ashford, L., Brissie, J., Hepburn, S. L., Coonrod, E. E., et al. (1999). Can Autism be diagnosed accurately in children under 3 years? *Journal of Child Psychology and Psychiatry and Allied Disciplines, 40,* 219–226.

Stone, W. L., Ousley, O. Y., & Littleford, C. D. (1997). Motor imitation in young children with Autism: What's the object? *Journal of Abnormal Child Psychology, 25,* 475–485.

Stone, W. L., Turner, L. M., Pozdol, S. L., & Smoski, M. J. (2003, April). *Changes in diagnostic and developmental features from age 2 to age 9 in children with ASD.* Paper presented at the biennial meeting of the Society for Research in Child Development, Tampa, FL.

Stone, W. L., & Yoder, P. J. (2001). Predicting spoken language level in children with Autism spectrum disorders. *Autism, 5,* 341–361.

Storey, K., & Provost, O. (1996). The effect of communication skills instruction on the integration of workers with severe disabilities in supported employment settings. *Education and Training in Mental Retardation and Developmental Disabilities, 31,* 123–141.

Strain, P. S., & Cordisco, L. K. (1994). LEAP preschool. In S. Harris & J. Handleman (Eds.), *Preschool education programs for children with Autism* (pp. 225–244). Austin, TX: ProEd.

Strain, P. S., Kerr, M. M., & Ragland, E. U. (1979). Effects of peer-mediated social initiations and prompting/reinforcement procedures on the social behavior of autistic children. *Journal of Autism and Developmental Disorders, 9,* 41–54.

Strain, P. S., Kohler, F. W., & Goldstein, H. (1996). Learning experiences—An alternative program: Peer-mediated interventions for young children with Autism. In E. D. Hibbs & P. S. Jensen (Eds.), *Psychosocial treatments for child and adolescent disorders: Empirically based strategies for clinical practice* (pp. 573–587). Washington, DC: American Psychological Association.

Strain, P. S., Shores, R. E., & Timm, M. A. (1977). Effects of peer social initiations on the behavior of withdrawn preschool children. *Journal of Applied Behavior Analysis, 10,* 289–298.

Sugiyama, T., & Abe, T. (1989). The prevalence of Autism in Nagoya, Japan: A total population study. *Journal of Autism and Developmental Disorders, 19,* 87–96.

Sugiyama, T., & Takahasi, O. (1996). Employment of autistics. *Japanese Journal of Child and Adolescent Psychiatry, 37*(1), 19–25.

Szatmari, P., Jones, M. B., Zwaigenbaum, L., & MacLean, J. E. (1998). Genetics of Autism: Overview and new directions. *Journal of Autism and Developmental Disorders, 28,* 351–368.

Szatmari, P., MacLean, J. E., Jones, M. B., Bryson, S. E., Zwaigenbaum, L., Bartolucci, G., et al. (2000). The familial aggregation of the lesser variant in biological and nonbiological relatives of PDD probands: A family history study. *Journal of Child Psychology and Psychiatry, 41,* 579–586.

Tager-Flusberg, H. (1993). What language reveals about the understanding of minds in children with Autism. In S. Baron-Cohen, H. Tager-Flusberg, & D. J. Cohen (Eds.), *Understanding other minds: Perspectives from Autism* (pp. 138–157). Oxford: Oxford University Press.

Tager-Flusberg, H. (1996). Brief report: Current theory and research on language and communication in Autism. *Journal of Autism and Developmental Disorders, 26,* 169–172.

Tager-Flusberg, H. (1999). A psychological approach to understanding the social and language impairments in Autism. *International Review of Psychiatry, 11,* 325–334.

Tager-Flusberg, H. (2001). Understanding the language and communicative impairments in Autism. *International Review of Research in Mental Retardation, 23,* 185–205.

Tager-Flusberg, H. (2003). Language impairments in children with complex neurodevelopmental disorders: The case of Autism. In Y. Levy & J. Schaeffer (Eds.), *Language competence across populations: Toward a definition of specific language impairment* (pp. 297–321). Mahwah, NJ: Erlbaum.

Tager-Flusberg, H. (in press). Do Autism and specific language impairment represent overlapping language disorders? In M. L. Rice & S. Warren (Eds.), *Developmental language disorders: From phenotypes to etiologies.* Mahwah, NJ: Erlbaum.

Tager-Flusberg, H., & Cooper, J. (1999). Present and future possibilities for defining a phenotype for specific language impairment. *Journal of Speech, Language, and Hearing Research, 42,* 1001–1004.

Tager-Flusberg, H., & Joseph, R. M. (2003). Identifying neurocognitive phenotypes in Autism. *Philosophical Transactions of the Royal Society: Biological Sciences, 358,* 303–314.

Taira, M., Takase, M., & Sasaki, H. (1998). Development and sleep: Sleep disorder in children with Autism. *Psychiatry and Clinical Neuroscience, 52,* 182–183.

Tallal, P., & Benasich, A. A. (2002). Developmental language learning impairments. *Development and Psychopathology, 14,* 559–579.

Tantam, D., Monaghan, L., Nicholson, J., & Stirling, J. (1989). Autistic children's ability to interpret faces: A research note. *Journal of Child Psychology and Psychiatry, 30,* 623–630.

Taylor, B. A., & Harris, S. L. (1995). Teaching children with Autism to seek information: Acquisition of novel information and generalization of responding. *Journal of Applied Behavior Analysis, 28,* 3–14.

Taylor, B. A., Miller, E., Lingam, R., Andrews, N., Simmons, A., & Stowe, J. (2002). Measles, mumps, and rubella vaccination and bowel problems or developmental regression in children with Autism: Population study. *British Medical Journal, 324,* 393–396.

Taylor, E. N., Miller, E., Farrington, C. P., Petropoulos, M. C., Favot-Mayoud, I., Li, J., et al. (1999). Autism and measles, mumps, and rubella vaccine: No epidemiological evidence for a causal association. *Lancet, 353,* 2026–2029.

Termine, N. T., & Izard, C. E. (1988). Infants' responses to their mothers' expressions of joy and sadness. *Developmental Psychology, 24,* 223–229.

Teunisse, J., & DeGelder, B. (1994). Do autistics have a generalized face processing deficit? *International Journal of Neuroscience, 77,* 1–10.

Thorp, D. M., Stahmer, A. C., & Schreibman, L. (1995). Effects of sociodramatic play training on children with Autism. *Journal of Autism and Developmental Disorders, 25,* 265–282.

Tidmarsh, L., & Volkmar, F. R. (2003). Diagnosis and epidemiology of Autism spectrum disorders. *Canadian Journal of Psychiatry, 48,* 517–525.

Tomasello, M., & Farrar, M. J. (1986). Joint attention and early language. *Child Development, 57,* 1454–1463.

Tomblin, J. B., Hafeman, L. L., & O'Brien, M. (2003). Autism and Autism risk in siblings of children with specific language impairment. *International Journal of Language and Communication Disorders, 38,* 235–250.

Tomblin, J. B., & Zhang, X. (1999). Language patterns and etiology in children with specific language impairment. In H. Tager-Flusberg (Ed.), *Neurodevelopmental disorders* (pp. 361–382). Cambridge, MA: MIT Press/Bradford Books.

Tordjman, S., Anderson, G., McBride, A., Hertzig, M. E., Snow, M. E., Hall, L. M., et al. (1997). Plasma b-endorphin, adrenocorticotropic hormone, and cortisol in Autism. *Journal of Child Psychology and Psychiatry, 38,* 705–715.

Toth, K., Dawson, G., Munson, J., Estes, A., & Abbott, R. (2003, April). *Role of joint attention, social interaction, and play in language and social growth in young children with Autism.* Paper presented at the biennial meeting of the Society for Research in Child Development, Tampa, FL.

Trevarthen, C. (1979). Communication and cooperation in early infancy: A description of primary intersubjectivity. In M. Bullowa (Ed.), *Before speech: The beginning of interpersonal communication* (pp. 321–347). Cambridge, England: Cambridge University Press.

Tsai, L. Y. (1999). Psychopharmacology in Autism. *Psychosomatic Medicine, 61,* 651–665.

Tsatsanis, K. D. (2003). Outcome research in Asperger syndrome and Autism. *Child and Adolescent Psychiatric Clinics of North America, 12,* 47–63.

Tuchman, R. F., & Rapin, I. (1997). Regression in pervasive developmental disorders: Seizures and epileptiform electroencephalogram correlates. *Pediatrics, 99,* 560–566.

Turner, M. (1999). Annotation: Repetitive behavior in Autism: A review of psychological research. *Journal of Child Psychology and Psychiatry, 40,* 839–849.

Ungerer, J. (1989). The early development of autistic children: Implications for defining primary deficits. In G. Dawson (Ed.), *Autism: Nature, diagnosis, and treatment* (pp. 75–91). New York: Guilford Press.

Ungerer, J., & Sigman, M. (1981). Symbolic play and language comprehension in autistic children. *Journal of the American Academy of Child Psychiatry, 20,* 318–337.

Venter, A., Lord, C., & Schopler, E. (1992). A follow-up study of high-functioning autistic children. *Journal of Child Psychology and Psychiatry, 33,* 489–507.

Visconti, P., Piazzi, S., Posar, A., Santi, A., Pipitone, E., & Rossi, P. G. (1994). Amino acids and infantile Autism. *Developmental Brain Dysfunction, 7,* 86–92.

Vitriol, C., & Farber, B. (1981). Stimulant medication in certain childhood disorders. *American Journal of Psychiatry, 138,* 1517–1518.

Volkmar, F., & Anderson, G. (1989). Neurochemical perspectives on infantile Autism. In G. Dawson (Ed.), *Autism: Nature, diagnosis, and treatment* (pp. 208–224). New York: Guilford Press.

Volkmar, F., Hoder, E. L., & Cohen, D. J. (1985). Compliance, "negativism," and the effects of treatment structure in Autism: A naturalistic, behavioral study. *Journal of Child Psychology and Psychiatry, 26,* 865–877.

Volkmar, F., & Klin, A. (2001). Asperger's disorder and higher functioning Autism: Same or different? In L. M. Glidden (Ed.), *International review of research in mental retardation: Autism* (Vol. 23, pp. 83–110). San Diego: Academic Press.

Volkmar, F., & Nelson, I. (1990). Seizure disorders in Autism. *Journal of the American Academy of Child and Adolescent Psychiatry, 29,* 127–129.

Volkmar, F., Szatmari, P., & Sparrow, S. S. (1993). Sex differences in pervasive developmental disorders. *Journal of Autism and Developmental Disorders, 23,* 579–59I.

Wakefield, A. J. (1999). MMR vaccination and Autism. *Lancet, 354,* 949–950.

Wakefield, A. J., Murch, S. H., Anthony, A., Linnell, J., Casson, D. M., Malik, M., et al. (1998). Ileal-lymphoid-nodular hyperplasia, non-specific colitis, and pervasive developmental disorder in children. *Lancet, 351,* 637–641.

Warburton, P., Baird, G., Chen, W., Morris, K., Jacobs, B. W., Hodgson, S., et al. (2000). Support for linkage of Autism and specific language impairment to 7q3 from two chromosome rearrangements involving band 7q31. *American Journal of Medical Genetics, 96,* 228–234.

Warren, S. F., Baxter, D. K., Anderson, S. R., Marshall, A., & Baer, D. M. (1981). Generalization of question-asking by severely retarded individuals. *Journal of the Association for Persons with Severe Handicaps, 6,* 15–22.

Waterhouse, L., Fein, D., & Modahl, C. (1996). Neurofunctional mechanisms in Autism. *Psychological Review, 103,* 457–489.

Wellman, H. M. (1993). Early understanding of mind: The normal case. In S. Baron-Cohen, H. Tager-Flusberg, & D. J. Cohen (Eds.), *Understanding other minds: Perspectives from Autism* (pp. 10–39). Oxford: Oxford University Press.

Wellman, H. M., Cross, D., & Watson, J. (2001). Meta-analysis of theory-of-mind development: The truth about false belief. *Child Development, 72,* 655–684.

Werner, E., Dawson, G., & Munson, J. A. (2001, April). *Regression in Autism: A description and validation of the phenomenon using a parent report and home video tapes.* Poster session presented at the biennial meeting of the Society for Research in Child Development, Minneapolis, MN.

Werner, E., Dawson, G., Munson, J. A., & Osterling, J. (in press). Variations in early course of development in Autism and its relation with behavioral outcome at 3–4 years of age. *Journal of Autism and Developmental Disorders.*

Werner, E., Dawson, G., Osterling, J. A., & Dinno, N. (2000). Brief report: Recognition of Autism spectrum disorder before one year of age: A retrospective study based on home videotapes. *Journal of Autism and Developmental Disorders, 30,* 157–162.

Werry, J. S., & Aman, M. G. (1999). Anxiolytics, sedatives, and miscellaneous drugs. In J. S. Werry & M. G. Aman (Eds.), *Practitioner's guide to psychoactive drugs for children and adolescents* (2nd ed., pp. 433–469). New York: Plenum Medical Book.

Whiten, A. (1993). Evolving a theory of mind: The nature of non-verbal mentalism in other primates. In S. Baron-Cohen, H. Tager-Flusberg, & D. J. Cohen (Eds.), Understanding other minds: Perspectives from Autism (pp. 367–396). Oxford: Oxford University Press.

Wilkinson, K. M. (1998). Profiles of language and communication skills in Autism. *Mental Retardation and Developmental Disabilities Research Reviews, 4,* 73–79.

Willemsen-Swinkels, S. H., Buitelaar, J. K., Nijhof, G. J., & Van Engeland, H. (1995). Placebo-controlled acute dosage naltrexone study in young autistic children. *Psychiatry Research, 58,* 203–215.

Willemsen-Swinkels, S. H., Buitelaar, J. K., & Van Engeland, H. (1996). The effect of chronic naltrexone treatment in young autistic children: A double-blind placebo-controlled crossover study. *Biological Psychiatry, 39,* 1023–1031.

Williams, B. J., & Ozonoff, S. (2001, April). *Parental report of the early development of autistic children who experience a regression.* Poster session presented at the biennial meeting of the Society for Research in Child Development, Minneapolis, MN.

Williams, J., Whiten, A., Suddendorf, W., & Perrett, D. (2001). Imitation, mirror neurons and Autism. *Neuroscience and Biobehavioral Reviews, 25,* 287–295.

Wilson, K., Mills, E., Ross, C., McGowan, J., & Jadad, A. (2003). Association of autistic spectrum disorder and the measles, mumps, and rubella vaccine: A systematic review of current epidemiological evidence. *Archives of Pediatrics and Adolescent Medicine, 157,* 628–634.

Wing, L. (1978). Social, behavioral, and cognitive characteristics: An epidemiological approach. In M. Rutter & E. Schopler (Eds.), *Autism: A reappraisal of concepts and treatment* (pp. 27–46). New York, Plenum Press.

Wing, L. (1988). The continuum of autistic characteristics. In E. Schopler & G. Mesibov (Eds.), *Diagnosis and assessment in Autism* (pp. 91–110). New York: Plenum Press.

Wing, L., & Gould, J. (1979). Severe impairments of social interaction and associated abnormalities in children: Epidemiology and classification. *Journal of Autism and Developmental Disorders, 9,* 11–29.

World Health Organization. (1992). *International classification of diseases* (10th ed.). Geneva, Switzerland: Author.

Wozniak, J., Biederman, J., Faraone, S. V., Frazier, J., Kim, J., Millstein, R., et al. (1997). Mania in children with pervasive developmental disorder revisited. *Journal of the American Academy of Child and Adolescent Psychiatry, 36,* 1552–1559.

Yeargin-Allsopp, M., Rice, C., Karapurkan, T., Doernberg, N., Boyle, C., & Murphy, C. (2003). Prevalence of Autism in a U.S. metropolitan area. *Journal of the American Medical Association, 289,* 49–55.

Yirmiya, N., Kasari, C., Sigman, M., & Mundy, P. (1989). Facial expressions of affect in autistic, mentally retarded and normal children. *Journal of Child Psychology and Psychiatry and Allied Disciplines, 30,* 725–735.

Young, J. G., Kavanagh, M. E., Anderson, G. M., Shaywitz, B. A., & Cohen, D. J. (1982). Clinical neurochemistry of Autism and associated disorders. *Journal of Autism and Developmental Disorders, 12,* 147–165.

Zatorre, R., Evans, A., Meyer, E., & Gjedde, A. (1992). Lateralization of phonetic and pitch discrimination in speech processing. *Science, 256,* 846–849.

Zelazo, P. D., Jacques, S., Burack, J. A., & Frye, D. (2002). The relation between theory of mind and rule use: Evidence from persons with Autism-spectrum disorders. *Infant and Child Development, 11,* 171–195.

Zhang, H., Liu, X., Zhang, C., Mundo, E., Macciardi, F., Grayson, D. R., et al. (2002). Reelin gene alleles and susceptibility to Autism spectrum disorders. *Molecular Psychiatry, 7,* 1012–1017.

Zhong, N., Ye, L., Ju, W., Brown, W. T., Tsiouris, J., & Cohen, I. (1999). 5-HTTLPR variants not associated with autistic spectrum disorders. *Neurogenetics, 2,* 129–131.

Zuddas, A., Ledda, M. G., Fratta, A., Muglia, P., & Cianchetti, C. (1996). Clinical effects of clozapine on autistic disorder. *American Journal of Psychiatry, 153,* 738.

CHAPTER 9

Disorders of Attention and Impulse Regulation

JOEL T. NIGG, STEPHEN P. HINSHAW, and CYNTHIA HUANG-POLLOCK

Few child difficulties generate as much controversy and concern in our society as problems with attention and impulse control. Much of this discussion centers on the clinical syndrome of Attention-Deficit/Hyperactivity Disorder (ADHD; American Psychiatric Association, 1994). Dramatically rising rates of medication treatments for children, particularly stimulants (Rappley, Gardiner, Jetton, & Houang, 1995; Robison, Sclar, Skaer, & Galin, 1999; Safer & Zito, 1999), have drawn the attention of social critics and clinical scientists alike (Brown, 2003). Sociologists point

out that medicalization of behavior occurs when a problem falls under the purview of the medical profession; for example, American society has seen the medicalization of pregnancy and birth, drinking problems, and other processes and conditions (Barsky & Borus, 1995; Conrad, 1992). The medicalization of attentional problems and hyperactivity, as well as disruptive behavior more generally, has spurred controversy over the validity of ADHD as a psychiatric disorder (Searight & Mcclaren, 1998) and sparked concern that rising medication rates may indicate an important shortage of other needed psychological or educational interventions for children (Safer & Krager, 1992) or that social control is being served rather than mental health (Menzies, 1997). The concerns and criticisms attending ADHD have become so vehement, and so misguided at many levels, that a group of clinical and developmental scientists recently issued a consensus statement asserting the validity of the clinical syndrome of ADHD (Barkley, 2002) and experts continue to restate the elements of support for its validity (Faraone, 2005).

Along with the running public controversy, research on ADHD has also witnessed advances in the past decade. Particularly notable has been the development of more detailed neuropsychological theories that attempt to integrate the various cognitive findings regarding children with ADHD (Barkley, 1997, 2006; Nigg, 2001, 2006; Sagvolden, Johansen, Aase, & Russell, 2005; Sergeant, Oosterlaan, & van der Meere, 1999). These models emphasize the regulatory functions involved in executive control, regulation of arousal, and related processes that we discuss in this chapter. At the same time, theories that integrate the role of socialization processes along with neuropsychology in the *development* of these problem behaviors have been in shorter supply (Campbell, 2002; Johnston & Mash, 2001; Olson, 2002).

In light of widespread interest in it, we devote considerable space in this chapter to the ADHD syndrome, its likely causal mechanisms, its heterogeneity and subtypes, the boundaries of its validity as a disease construct, and its place in a developmental psychopathology framework. Because so much ongoing controversy and recent theorizing concerns the status of within-child developmental mechanisms, we emphasize internal neural and psychological control systems and their development. We also highlight the often overlooked role of the child's interpersonal network, plus wider societal contextual factors, which have key roles to play in the development and display of self-regulatory functions. First, the attainment of self regulation in the preschool years is inherently an interpersonal process influenced by both child temperament and parent responsivity (Greenberg, Kusche, & Speltz, 1991; Stoolmiller, 2001). Second, family processes may be a primary mediator for the expression, over time, of the genetic mechanisms reflected in the apparently high heritability of these behavior problems. Third, at a broader level, societal concerns over the inattentive and disruptive behaviors of children have attained salience largely through the advent of compulsory education in our relatively recent historical past. Indeed, school- and community-related pressures for earlier and earlier academic competence in

recent years may well be influencing the development of attention processes across all children, as well as rates of referral for these problems in society.

We highlight at the outset that genetic and other child-specific mechanisms that influence *individual differences* in the expression of given traits or conditions (e.g., ADHD) are not commensurate with societal factors that shape the *overall levels* of such traits or conditions (see Rutter & Silberg, 2002; Nigg, 2006). For instance, individual differences in height are generally highly heritable, but the secular trends over the past century regarding substantially increased stature in the population at large (in developed nations) are the result of dietary and other environmental factors. Thus, we cannot ignore the rapid changes in society and in socialization influences on children as contributory factors to children's attentional and regulatory processes in general. Indeed, needed data on recent secular influences on ADHD-related problems are in short supply. Overall, we consider the notions of attention, impulse control, and self-regulation from the viewpoint of both normal and disordered developmental processes, because only through such a systematic developmental psychopathology perspective can an integrative account of this controversial area be promoted.

Before addressing ADHD per se, we note that problems with inattention and impulsivity cut across a range of psychiatric and clinical conditions. With regard to inattention, for example, Mirsky and Duncan (2001) listed some 17 conditions associated with disordered attention, including Schizophrenia, Autism, Fetal Alcohol Syndrome, closed-head injury, and narcolepsy. To their illustrative list could be added other medical conditions plus anxiety disorders, depression, and Obsessive-Compulsive Disorder from the psychopathology domain. Crucially, however, the term "attention" connotes multiple functions; not all such functions are equally affected across these various conditions. Thus, behavioral problems that appear as "inattention" may or may not be related to dysfunction in attentional mechanisms defined more formally. A range of causal mechanisms within the child could, in fact, be related to inattentive and otherwise dysregulated *behavior*.

Likewise, impulse control is multiply defined (see Nigg, 2000) and appears in one form or another in a range of conditions, of which ADHD may be the most prominent but is hardly the sole exemplar. Antisocial behaviors (including conduct problems and psychopathy), eating disorders, personality disorders (notably Borderline Personality Disorder and Antisocial Personality Disorder), substance abuse disorders, tic disorders, Obsessive-Compulsive Disorder, and Bipolar Disorder are only some of the psychopathologies readily associated with serious maldevelopment of impulse control (Coles, 1997). Further, an entire section of the fourth edition of the *Diagnostic and Statistical Manual of Mental Disorders* (*DSM-IV*) is devoted to "impulse control disorders," including kleptomania, intermittent explosive disorder, pyromania, pathological gambling, and trichotillomania (see Hucker, 1997, for further discussion). Many of these are syndromes primarily observed in adulthood, and their relation to childhood impulsivity is largely unstudied; yet there clearly is no one-to-one correspondence between the topic of disorders of attention and impulse control and the clinical syndrome of ADHD. Finally, as all of this implies, many different mechanisms have been suggested as causal within children with ADHD, not to mention related impulsive behavioral difficulties (Barkley, 1997; Berger & Posner, 2000; Casey, Tottenham, & Fossella, 2002; Castellanos & Tannock, 2002; Douglas, 1972, 1999; Newman & Wallace, 1993; Nigg, 2001, 2006; Nigg, Swanson, & Hinshaw, 1997; Sagvolden et al., 2005; Satterfield & Dawson, 1971; Sergeant, Oosterlaan, & van der Meere, 1999; Zentall & Zentall, 1983). We address many of the still viable hypotheses for ADHD in our coverage of the most studied mechanisms herein, as we also note intriguing new directions in the field for which data are still emerging. The extent to which the mechanisms we discuss may pertain to the full range of other impulse-related disorders remains a topic for another day.

We begin with a brief historical account of the clinical syndrome of ADHD and a description of its key features. Next, we consider in some detail the formal constructs of attention and impulse control, providing definitions of each as well as evidence for developmental patterns related to their display throughout childhood. Space does not allow us to catalogue the particular attention or impulse disturbances associated with every potentially relevant condition suggested earlier. Instead, we outline the core components of the development of attention and impulse control, pointing out particular implications for ADHD and emphasizing progress in the past 10 years, since the first edition of this volume. Developmental changes are notable throughout the life span, including young adulthood (Nigg, Stavro, et al., 2005) and old age (Hasher & Zacks, 1988; Zacks & Hasher, 1994), and we highlight very briefly the burgeoning research literature on ADHD in adults. Then, in keeping with the developmental psychopathology perspective of multiple levels of analysis (see Cicchetti & Dawson, 2002), we outline a multilevel, developmental perspective on ADHD and its variants during childhood, adolescence, and early adulthood. Our overall goal is to point out major pathways related to ADHD in an attempt to move the field toward a more developmentally informed understanding of psychopathologies of attention and impulse control. We close with a comment on multiple developmental pathways and our view of key issues for the field in the coming decade.

ATTENTION-DEFICIT/HYPERACTIVITY DISORDER: HISTORICAL VIEWS AND RECENT NOSOLOGICAL ISSUES

The changes in conceptual definition of and treatment rates for ADHD over the years are one contributor to controversy about its status and meaning. It therefore is important to briefly review key historical changes in its conception and in rates of treatment. For additional historical review, see Barkley (2006).

Brief History

Well before current conceptual models began to be developed, educators and clinicians began to notice clinical-level manifestations of inattention, impulsivity, and dysregulated behavior in school-age children. Still (1902) presented a clinical description of so-called moral deficits in children, referring to problems of attention and deportment that were not clearly associated with mental subnormality. Thus, compulsory education was apparently leaving in its wake a subset of children who had salient difficulties in behavioral and emotional regulation or in the basics of reading and writing (with the latter eventually termed *learning disabilities*).

Following the worldwide influenza epidemic during and after World War I, some children developed encephalitis, and it was noted that many survivors of this infection developed significant problems in attentional deployment, regulation of impulses, and general behavioral control. Though a notable example of fallacious reasoning from consequent to presumed cause, this set of symptoms—whether or not triggered by encephalitis—became known as a "minimal brain damage" syndrome, a term later softened to "minimal brain dysfunction," or MBD (e.g., Strauss & Lehtinen, 1947). By the 1960s, the boundaries of MBD had been stretched to include scores of symptoms, spanning nearly all of child psychopathology and learning problems (Clements & Peters, 1962; Wender, 1971). This historical category of pathology thus suffered from two key shortcomings: a vastly overinclusive list of constituent symptoms and a presumed (though unproven) neural etiology.

Others were calling for narrower and more descriptive appellations. Laufer and Denhoff (1957) described a "hyperkinetic disorder of childhood," focusing more specifically on dysregulated motor behavior. The second edition of the *DSM* (American Psychiatric Association, 1968) adopted this narrower conception and nomenclature. An empirical tradition was also expanding, in which adult informant ratings of child behavior problems were subjected to factor analyses in an attempt to discern identifiable, empirically supported syndromes of psychopathology (e.g., Quay, 1972). Factors labeled "hyperactivity" and "immaturity" began to appear in such dimensionalized accounts of child problem behavior.

Based largely on the research of Douglas and colleagues (e.g., Douglas, 1972), in the 1970s and 1980s researchers in North America began to reconceptualize the core deficit of children considered "hyperkinetic" as related to dysregulated attention and impulse control rather than motor overactivity per se. By the time of *DSM-III* (American Psychiatric Association, 1980), the condition had been renamed "attention deficit disorder," which was posited to consist of a subtype without hyperactivity and a second subtype with hyperactivity. The empirical tradition continued, with efforts to develop empirically based taxonomies of children that included dimensions related to hyperactivity and inattention (Achenbach, 1991; Achenbach & Edelbrock, 1978, 1983). By this time, research on children with clinically significant attentional and impulse control problems had begun to proliferate at an exponential rate. Further, stimulant medication treatments, which had originated decades earlier with the pioneering work of Bradley (1937), were generating controversy (Sroufe & Stewart, 1973), a theme that was to continue into the 1980s, 1990s, and beyond (Jacobvitz, Sroufe, Stewart, & Leffert, 1990; Safer & Krager, 1992).

Renamed Attention-Deficit/Hyperactivity Disorder, or ADHD, in *DSM-III-R* and *DSM-IV* (American Psychiatric Association, 1987, 1994, 2000), the condition's core subtypes were expanded in the fourth edition to three: a Predominantly Inattentive type (similar to the *DSM-III* notion of attention deficit disorder without hyperactivity), a Predominantly Hyperactive-Impulsive type (unprecedented in previous nomenclatures), and a Combined type in which both symptom clusters were clinically salient.

By the 1990s, research on ADHD constituted a growth industry (e.g., Quay & Hogan, 1999). Legislative changes in the early 1990s yielded the inclusion of ADHD as a potential trigger for special education services in public schools, a factor that undoubtedly increased its salience to many families and clinicians. Prescription rates for stimulants, as for other psychotropic medications used with youth, had doubled in the United States in the 1980s, with even more rapid rises in the 1990s (Safer & Zito, 1999;

Zito et al., 2003). Meanwhile, major clinical trials had evidenced the efficacy of stimulant pharmacologic treatment for ADHD, if implemented carefully and with thorough monitoring, with combined medication-behavioral treatments yielding the highest likelihood of clinically meaningful improvement (Conners et al., 2001; MTA Cooperative Group, 1999). Finally, prospective longitudinal investigations were showing that ADHD was a condition likely to persist into adolescence in a majority of cases and to continue to yield impairment into adulthood in a substantial percentage (Mannuzza & Klein, 2000). Those findings led to the blossoming of research on ADHD in adults and the gradual recognition of the unique developmental issues facing the field in establishing validity of the construct in that age range, reflecting recognition of a research and clinical domain that was quietly under way for 3 decades (Wood, Reimherr, Wender, & Johnson, 1976). Thus, today ADHD is no longer considered a condition restricted to childhood or even adolescence, as growing interest in adults with this disorder characterizes today's clinical and research landscape.

Features and Issues

Table 9.1 lists the *DSM-IV* features of ADHD, the *International Classification of Diseases* (*ICD-10;* World Health Organization, 1972) symptoms of hyperkinetic disorder (HKD), and the current diagnostic algorithms in use to define this disorder. Although the symptom lists are similar, several distinctions can be seen between ADHD and HKD, reflecting ongoing differences in how this syndrome is defined in Europe and the United States. It is unclear to what extent major findings apply equally to HKD and the more broadly defined ADHD. We nonetheless use the term ADHD to cover both constructs and to cover studies in which ADHD was defined by extreme rating scale scores. Like most psychiatric/developmental disorders of childhood onset, ADHD shows a male preponderance, on the order of 3:1 in community samples (Wolraich, Hannah, Baumgaertel, & Feurer, 1998). Among many possible salient issues and questions, we highlight several core issues for this construct.

First, note from Table 9.1 that the diagnosis of ADHD requires not only above-threshold numbers of symptoms but also (1) the early onset of these symptoms, (2) their developmental extremity (a key point, given that problems of inattention and impulsivity are ubiquitous in young children), (3) their cross-situational display (i.e., at home, at school, and often in the peer group or work setting), and (4) the requirement that they yield functional impairment.

TABLE 9.1   Diagnostic Criteria for ADHD in *DSM-IV* and Hyperkinetic Disorder in *ICD-10*

1. Fails to give close attention to details or makes careless mistakes in schoolwork, work, or other daily activities.
2. Has difficulty sustaining attention on tasks or play activities.
3. Does not seem to listen when spoken to directly.
4. Does not follow through on instructions and fails to finish schoolwork, chores, or duties in the workplace (not due to oppositional behavior or failure to understand instructions).
5. Has difficulty organizing tasks and activities (*ICD-10:* "Is often impaired in organizing tasks").
6. Avoids, dislikes, or is reluctant to engage in tasks that require sustained mental effort such as schoolwork or homework.
7. Loses things necessary for tasks or activities (e.g., toys, school assignments, pencils, books, or tools).
8. Is easily distracted by extraneous stimuli (*ICD-10:* "by external stimuli").
9. Is forgetful in daily activities (*ICD-10:* "in the course of daily activities").
10. Fidgets with hands or feet or squirms in seat (*ICD-10:* "on seat").
11. Leaves seat in classroom or in other situations in which remaining seated is expected.
12. Runs about or climbs excessively in situations in which it is inappropriate (in adolescents or adults, may be limited to subjective feelings of restlessness).
13. Has difficulty playing or engaging in leisure activities quietly (*ICD-10:* "Is often unduly noisy in playing or has difficulty in engaging quietly in leisure activities").
14. Is "on the go" or often acts as if "driven by a motor" (*ICD-10:* "Exhibits a persistent pattern of excessive motor activity that is not substantially modified by social context or demands").
15. Talks excessively (*ICD-10:* "without appropriate response to social constraints").
16. Blurts out answers before the questions have been completed.
17. Has difficulty awaiting turn (*ICD-10:* "Fails to wait in lines or await turns in games or group situations").

18. Interrupts or intrudes on others (e.g., butts into conversations or games).

Each behavior must occur "often" and must persist for at least 6 months to a degree that is maladaptive and inconsistent with developmental level.

Subtypes

DSM-IV ADHD-C: 6 items from 1–9, plus 6 items from 10–18.

DSM-IV ADHD-PI: 6 items from 1–9.

DSM-IV ADHD-HI: 6 items from 10–18.

ICD-10 Hyperkinetic Disorder: 6 items from 1–9, plus 3 items from 10–14, plus 1 item from 16–18.

DSM-IV specifies a diagnosis of "in partial remission" for adolescents or adults who formerly met full criteria but now have some symptoms without meeting full criteria.

Comorbidity

ICD-10: Specifies "do not diagnose" if child meets criteria for Pervasive Developmental Disorder, manic episode, depressive episode, or anxiety disorders. Specifies that Conduct Disorder excludes HDK diagnosis.

DSM-IV: Specifies that symptoms should not be "better accounted for" by another mental disorder.

Additional Criteria

Onset: Symptoms that caused impairment had to be present before 7 years of age (*DSM-IV*), or "onset of the disorder" is no later than age 7 (*ICD-10*).

Pervasiveness: Impairment must be present (*DSM-IV*) or criteria must be met (*ICD-10*) in two or more settings.

Impairment: There must be clear evidence of clinically significant impairment in functioning (*DSM-IV*); impairment or distress (*ICD-10*).

Source: Adapted from *Diagnostic and Statistical Manual of Mental Disorders,* fourth edition, by the American Psychiatric Association, 1994, Washington, DC: Author; and *The ICD-10 Classification of Mental and Behavioral Disorders: Clinical Descriptions and Diagnostic Guidelines,* by the World Health Organization, 1992, Geneva, Switzerland: Author.

These guidelines have strong empirical support. Failure to assess impairment, in particular, likely inflates prevalence estimates (Gordon et al., 2005) and inclusion of parent and teacher standardized ratings greatly enhances assessment validity (Pelham, Fabiano, & Massetti, 2005). Thus, accurate assessment requires, at a minimum, the taking of a careful history; reports from multiple adult informants with well-normed rating instruments; differential diagnostic procedures to distinguish ADHD from either normal developmental variation or a host of medical and psychiatric conditions that feature inattention and impulse control problems in their presentation; and, when possible, direct observation of the child in family and school contexts. Careful consideration of functional adjustment in multiple domains can further assist with treatment tailoring (Pelham et al., 2005). Indeed, much of the controversy surrounding ADHD relates to the unfortunate tendency—

fueled by inadequate funding of thorough evaluations—for clinicians to make a diagnosis based on extremely short periods of assessment utilizing nonstandard and subjective diagnostic procedures.

Second, is the clinical syndrome of ADHD a distinct category or taxon, or do the constituent symptoms conform more closely to a dimension of behavioral dysregulation? A formal taxometric analysis (Waller & Meehl, 1998) is lacking. In the meantime, most relevant research converges on the conclusion that ADHD is better viewed as a dimension than as a distinct category, even at the level of underlying genetic risk for the condition (Levy, Hay, McStephen, Wood, & Waldman, 1997; Levy, McStephen, & Hay, 2001; Willcutt, Pennington, & DeFries, 2000). Yet, as with other dimensional entities (e.g., hypertension, depression), this likelihood does not negate the clinical importance of identifying and treating ADHD as a clinical syndrome. Indeed, the *DSM-IV* conception of ADHD identifies children with functional impairments in key areas of developmental relevance, such as peer rejection, academic underachievement, family dysfunction, lowered independence, and high risk for accidental injury (Hinshaw, 2002b). Such impairments are evident as early as the preschool years (Lahey et al., 1998). ADHD is also a risk factor for problems later in development: It fuels an early start of aggressive behavior in some cases, which is predictive of delinquency, and it is also associated with school dropout, problems in social competence, and underemployment by adolescence and adulthood (Johnston, 2002).

Third, what is the status of the current subtyping scheme for ADHD as represented in *DSM-IV*? At a *dimensional* level, numerous investigations have confirmed a two-factor structure underlying the constituent symptomatology, corresponding to inattentive-disorganized and hyperactive-impulsive symptom domains. Both areas can be reliably measured by parent and teacher rating scale instruments. They show divergent validity, with inattentive behaviors uniquely associated with academic problems and hyperactive/impulsive behaviors aggregating with disruptive tendencies in school and home settings (Lahey & Willcutt, 2002). Thus, the underlying dimensions of ADHD show considerable psychometric viability. On the other hand, despite contentions that the purely Inattentive type of ADHD is qualitatively distinct from the Combined and Hyperactive-Impulsive (HI) variants (Milich, Balentine, & Lynam, 2001), empirical data are far from conclusive in this regard (Hinshaw, 2001; Lahey, 2001). In fact, with respect to neuropsychological processes, the Inattentive and Combined types often reveal more similarities than differences (Chhabildas, Pennington, & Willcutt, 2001; Hinshaw, Carte, Sami, Treuting, & Zupan, 2002; Nigg, Blaskey, Huang-Pollock, & Rappley, 2002), although they may be distinguishable on key measures such as response suppression (Nigg, Blaskey, Huang-Pollock, & Rappley, 2002). Family studies asking whether ADHD subtypes "breed true" have been mixed; a recent meta-analysis suggests that reliable familial separation of the Combined and Inattentive types exists, but only to a small extent, perhaps due to heterogeneity in both groups (Stawicki, Nigg, & von Eye, in press). Meantime, innovative behavioral genetic analyses suggest that the HI type is, unlike the others, not heritable (Willcutt et al., 2000); its validity in school-age children may be in question. Last but not least, the stability of subtype classification over time remains unclear (Lahey et al., in press). Alternative subtype schemes may enable clearer genetic effects (Neu-

man et al., 1999). In all, the subtyping scheme for ADHD mandates further scrutiny.

Fourth, although ADHD does not disappear with puberty, as was formerly contended, the cessation of formal schooling and the development of coping mechanisms may assist many adults in making important adaptations to this condition. Indeed, long-term outcomes for children with ADHD are highly variable (Barkley, 2006; Mannuzza & Klein, 2000). Along developmental lines, we note that the hyperactive-impulsive symptom cluster is likely to be particularly salient during the preschool and grade school years but fades in frequency and intensity by adolescence. On the other hand, the inattentive symptom cluster, which becomes recognizable with the advent of formal schooling, is more stable throughout adolescence (Hart, Lahey, Loeber, Applegate, & Frick, 1995). Thus, the HI subtype of ADHD, evident during preschool years, may give way to the Combined type once formal schooling begins (Lahey et al., in press). Furthermore, symptoms of overtly hyperactive behavior may give way to subtler forms of impulsivity once childhood is left behind, so that the inattentive problems may become most salient for late adolescents and adults. Finally, heterotypic continuity is not well addressed in the diagnostic system: Behaviors that describe ADHD in children may not be the best descriptors of the problems that impair affected individuals as adolescents or adults. Formal criteria to reflect any such developmental changes are completely lacking in the *DSM-IV* and *ICD-10*. However, research efforts are under way to fill this gap (Achenbach, 1991; Conners, 1997).

Although space permits only a limited comment on the rich topic of ADHD in adulthood, we highlight that when ADHD is identified in adults, the two largest and most definitive studies to date demonstrate similar magnitudes of neuropsychological impairment in executive functioning as that seen in children with the condition (Murphy, Barkley, & Bush, 2001; Nigg, Stavro, et al., 2005). These data strongly suggest that neuropsychological difficulties are not simply part of a developmental delay, but are a persistent feature of the syndrome when it persists into adulthood. Moreover, new impairments unique to adults must be considered, notably the potential for driving accidents and driving-related problems and problems in maintaining steady employment and intimate relationships (Barkley, 2004). A final complexity unique to the condition in adults concerns the potential for misdiagnosis in relation to Axis II psychopathology, or, in other words, the possibility that ADHD may develop into an enduring maladaptive personality style or trait by adulthood. This question has been scarcely studied. Initial data from the Michigan State study indicate that ADHD is associated with elevated risk of several personality disorders in both the impulsive cluster (Borderline, Histrionic, and Antisocial Personality Disorders) and the anxious cluster (Avoidant Personality Disorder), but that these co-occurring disorders do not account for either the impairments experienced by these adults or for their neuropsychological deficits (T. Miller, Nigg, & Stavro, 2005). We address additional developmental trends again subsequently.

Fifth, ADHD is highly likely to exist in concert with other, presumably independent psychiatric conditions. Thus, substantial rates of overlap exist with disruptive disorders (Oppositional Defiant Disorder and Conduct Disorder), anxiety disorders, and learning disorders (Angold, Costello, & Erkanli, 1999). Such comorbidity is a huge and fascinating topic in its own right (see Caron & Rutter, 1991; Jensen, Martin, & Cantwell, 1997). The presence of ADHD in conjunction with additional childhood conditions presents major issues with respect to its heterogeneity. Indeed, some have contended that when ADHD co-occurs with clinically significant aggression or with major internalizing (anxious, depressed) features, it constitutes a substantially different condition than when it exists alone (e.g., Jensen et al., 2001). Indeed, unlike the *DSM,* the *ICD-10* diagnostic criteria explicitly recognize such comorbid forms as separable diagnostic categories (e.g., hyperkinetic conduct disturbance; see Table 9.1).

Moreover, virtually all neuropsychological findings pertaining to ADHD (e.g., executive function, arousal, reward abnormalities) can also be observed to at least some degree in children with other conditions, including, notably, other externalizing disorders such as Conduct Disorder, illustrating the nonspecificity of most such effects (Sergeant, Geurts, & Oosterlaan, 2002). Only a very few studies have controlled for possible ADHD symptoms in children with Oppositional Defiant or Conduct Disorder, or controlled for oppositional or conduct symptoms in children with ADHD, in order to begin to tease this out. Those few studies generally suggest that neuropsychological weaknesses hold for ADHD even when other symptoms are covaried (Chhabildas et al., 2001; Hinshaw et al., 2002; Klorman et al., 1999; Nigg, 1999; Nigg, Hinshaw, Carte, & Treuting, 1998). Yet the converse—that is, neuropsychological weaknesses in Conduct Disorder or aggression when ADHD is covaried—has also been reported (Seguin, Boulerice, Harden, Tremblay, & Pihl, 1999; Seguin, Nagin, Assaad, & Tremblay, 2004). Whereas specificity is not a necessary requirement for causality in multifactorial disorders such as ADHD (Garber & Hollon, 1991) and although effect sizes

on key neuropsychological probes are typically larger in relation to ADHD than other conditions (Oosterlaan, Logan, & Sergeant, 1998; Pennington & Ozonoff, 1996), this state of affairs exemplifies that the current nosology is descriptive and not etiologically anchored. We do not report on this general nonspecificity in each subsequent section, but we note here its overarching importance as a context for theorizing.

Sixth, as for a brief highlighting of risk and etiologic factors, a spate of behavioral genetic investigations in the past 15 years has provided evidence that the heritability of ADHD symptoms as well as of the syndrome is moderate to strong (see Levy, McStephen, & Hay, 2001; Swanson & Castellanos, 2002). We highlight, in passing, that the high end of some of these heritability estimates (.8 and above) emanate from investigations in which parents, who typically provide information on the twins' zygosity, are also the source of the behavioral ratings of the children. These estimates are likely inflated by rater contrast effects (Eaves et al., 2000). When teacher data constitute the dependent variable, estimates of heritability are lower, albeit still substantial. Molecular genetic evidence is still being accumulated; many candidate genes with replicated effects in ADHD are related to dopamine neurotransmission (Faraone et al., 2005; Kirley et al., 2002), although these individual genes contribute only a small fraction of the genetic variance, suggesting that many genes are likely involved. Genes affecting other neural systems, notably noradrenergic receptors, are undoubtedly implicated as well (Biederman & Spencer, 1999; Comings et al., 2000; Faraone et al., 2005; Park et al., 2005). Other biological risk factors include, in some cases, prenatal and perinatal problems, such as low birthweight and maternal tobacco or alcohol use during pregnancy (e.g., Botting, Powls, Cooke, & Marlow, 1997; Taylor, 1999), postnatal lead exposure (Canfield, Gendle, & Cory-Slechta, 2004), and potentially other widespread environmental toxins and contaminants (Koger, Schettler, & Weiss, 2005; Nigg, 2006; Rice, 2000). Several neuroimaging studies now confirm that groups of children with ADHD have smaller neural structures in key regions of the prefrontal cortex, basal ganglia, and cerebellum (Swanson & Castellanos, 2002). These dysplasias appear early in development, prior to treatment, and are apparently nonprogressive (Castellanos et al., 2002), although longitudinal studies remain vanishingly rare.

Only a handful of investigations implicate faulty parental discipline styles as causal risk factors for ADHD (E. A. Carlson, Jacobvitz, & Sroufe, 1995). In fact, the typical assumption is that disrupted parenting and discordant parent-child interactions result from, rather than cause, temperamentally mediated child noncompliance and impulsivity. We point out, however, that problematic parent-child relationships may well be significant maintaining and exacerbating factors related to ADHD, yielding reciprocal, transactional chains of influence in conjunction with the child's core symptomatology (Hinshaw, 1999; Johnston & Mash, 2001). To foreshadow one of our themes, developmental paths to clinically significant inattention and impulse control problems are highly likely to involve both equifinality, meaning that several causal routes are contributory to ADHD, and multifinality, whereby early risks for ADHD may yield substantially divergent outcomes contingent on socialization and contextual processes (Cicchetti & Rogosch, 1996; Hinshaw, 1999).

With all that said, perhaps the most pressing issue at present concerns resolution of *within-child* causal mechanisms that contribute to ADHD's multifactorial expression as a behavioral syndrome. Thus, from here on, we are concerned less with the syndromal definition of ADHD and more with within-child mechanisms that may be related to development of behavior problems related to inattention and impulse dyscontrol (including their expression as the clinical syndrome of ADHD). Given the evidence for the heterogeneity of ADHD at multiple levels, such as symptomatology and subtypes, comorbidity, etiologic and risk factors, and developmental course, we therefore now explicitly take up the topic of more formally defined attention and regulation mechanisms as a means of clarifying and specifying the origins of such heterogeneity. Appreciation of attentional and regulatory processes at specific levels of understanding may help in the quest for understanding the highly variable behavioral manifestations of disorders of "attention" such as ADHD. In fact, because they are candidates for specifying within-child causal mechanisms in ADHD, understanding these specific attention and impulse control mechanisms may be essential to putting to rest debates about whether ADHD is a valid disorder (Wakefield, 1992). Thus, we move now to an analysis of psychological, behavioral, and neural systems underlying the development of these problems.

ATTENTION AND IMPULSE CONTROL IN DEVELOPMENT: OVERVIEW OF PSYCHOLOGICAL, BEHAVIORAL, AND NEURAL SYSTEMS

The development of attention and of impulse control are closely related. Both can be influenced, for example, by sensory reflex response, although we emphasize those effects primarily in our discussion of attention. Another,

more salient arena of their conceptual integration is in affect and motivation: Both attention and impulse can be redirected by strong anxiety due to a potential threat or strong excitement due to potential reward. This reactive regulation of attention and impulse control can be observed as early as late infancy (Rothbart & Ahadi, 1994). Another obvious area of their intersection is in the widely discussed domain of executive functions, which develop somewhat later than reactive effects and the precursors of which begin to influence children's attention and behavior by the toddler years in the form of effortful redirection of attention (Rothbart & Bates, 1998). Likewise, both attention and impulse control are moderated by the child's *energetic state,* that is, the level of arousal or tendency to arousability. Thus, from early infancy on, developing attention mechanisms assist with self-regulation and impulse control (including emotion regulation, behavioral control, and cognitive control). Likewise, the neural systems that support certain attentional skills are closely related to those that support control of motor responses, or impulses (Calkins & Fox, 2002). Finally, the development of these neural and behavioral systems is in constant interplay with the child's interpersonal world (e.g., parenting attunement, verbalization of affect; Greenberg et al., 1991).

Despite their close connections, however, for expository purposes the elements of attention and impulse control can be understood as partially distinct. They do not always operate in perfect tandem; they may develop at different rates and they can be measured in distinct ways. We therefore adopt a taxonomic approach to the various functional domains at hand. Skipping sensory or motor reflexive responses for now, and saving discussion of arousal until our coverage of attention proper, our plan is next to provide a description of reactive (motivated) processes and an introduction to strategic control via the integrative, widely discussed, and much critiqued concept of *executive functioning.* With that background, we then proceed to a developmental conceptual framework for attention functions and then impulse control functions. We subsequently highlight the main findings relevant to ADHD in both the attention and impulse control domains.

Reactive or Motivational Processes in Attention and Impulse Control

In contradistinction to the deliberate or strategic allocation of attention (or control of impulse), reactive processes involve emotional and affective states. Thus, when she notices something anxiety-provoking, a child may direct her attention to the concerning event or person (Gray, 1982;

Gray & McNaughton, 1996; Kagan, Reznick, & Snidman, 1987). Likewise, anxiety or excitement can narrow the focus of attention (Derryberry & Tucker, 1994). Thus, even though attention is usually viewed as a cognitive process, it is just as often (if not always, to some degree) motivated by incentive concerns. These same incentives can also influence impulse control, leading either to a very strong impulse to action (e.g., excitement from an imminent reward) or to inhibiting some or all behavior (e.g., confrontation with an anxiety-provoking or unfamiliar situation). Such motivated responses are often relatively spontaneous, and they are relatively more automatic than the more deliberate responding characteristic of effortful control.

Neurally, these reactive or affectively guided responses and shifts of attention and impulse are influenced by limbic networks, including the hippocampal formation and the amygdaloid complex (Gray, 1982; Kagan & Snidman, 2004). We already noted that these reactive processes come online and influence attention and impulse control earlier in development than do effortful types of processes (Rothbart & Ahadi, 1994). In considering both attention and impulse control, then, we consider how the role of affective and motivated responding can contribute to understanding ADHD. However, reactive processes interact with effortful processes in guiding moment-to-moment attention and impulse control by the early preschool years onward.

Executive Functions and Cognitive Control in Both Attention and Impulse Control

Another intersection of attention and impulse control is that both are related to the important but ill-defined domain of *executive function* (EF). It is widely agreed both that executive functioning is central to understanding attention and impulse control and that it is an underspecified construct (Pennington & Ozonoff, 1996; Zelazo, Muller, Frye, & Marcovitch, 2003). In a neuropsychological framework, EF refers to strategic or relatively deliberate regulation of response to context and maintenance of behavior in relation to goals (Pennington & Ozonoff, 1996). In the cognitive neuroscience field, this term is being supplanted by the term "cognitive control," which refers to such operations as control of interfering information and suppression of reflexive responding (Casey et al., 2002). We take note of insights from that work but retain the older term EF here due to its continued widespread use in the clinical and developmental literatures. Several initial explanatory points about EF are in order.

First, although a common factor may underlie many executive tasks, EF cannot be readily analyzed only at the global level. Instead, it generally must be viewed through the lens of component operations, which themselves are insufficiently specified. These components presumably work together to create the potential for strategic—or what we experience as deliberate—control of attention and impulse. Yet, agreement is not at hand as to the correct subdividing of the multidimensional EF domain (Barkley, 1997; Lyon & Krasnegor, 1996; Monsell & Driver, 1998). That literature is beyond the scope of our discussion, but we emphasize that subdividing is helpful in specifying mechanisms of ADHD. Numerous studies indicate that EF measures tap partially dissociable functions (Friedman & Miyake, 2004; Mirsky & Duncan, 2001; Miyake, Friedman, Emerson, Witzki, & Howerter, 2000). For example, one dimension involves working memory, selective attention, control of interfering information, and set shifting (Dempster, 1993; Engle, 2002; Mirsky & Duncan, 2001). We discuss those abilities in our coverage of attention later. Another dimension entails the ability to inhibit competing information and/or suppress a response, perhaps aided by a primary goal set (Friedman & Miyake, 2004; Logan & Cowan, 1984; Nigg, 2000; Pennington, 1997), although whether the actual operative mechanism is in various measurement paradigms is an inhibitory one remains unclear for many tasks. Such deliberate *response suppression* figures prominently in our subsequent coverage of impulse control. Numerous other functions have been attributed to the executive domain, underscoring the various conceptions of this construct. For example, in his influential theory of ADHD, Barkley (1997, 2006) offers very broad constructs that entail nearly all of self-regulation, including response inhibition, working memory, regulation of arousal-affect-motivation, internalization of speech, and reconstitution. Pennington and Ozonoff (1996) suggest set shifting, working memory, planning, behavioral inhibition, and interference control as among the key functions. Fuster (1997), as we noted, emphasizes temporal organization of behavior. That perspective has heavily influenced psychopathology research, as illustrated by theorists recent emphasis on temporal information processing in ADHD (Barkley, 1997; Castellanos & Tannock, 2002).

Second, tractable models of EF are emerging (Lyon & Krasnegor, 1996; Posner & DiGirolamo, 1998), with a developmental focus (Diamond, Prevor, Callender, & Druin, 1997; Zelazo et al., 2003) and anchored in the neural sciences, where the term *cognitive control* (Monsell & Driver, 1998) has gained ascendancy as noted. These neural models all emphasize anterior networks in the brain and associated cortical-subcortical neural circuits (Casey et al., 2002). For example, with regard to attention, Posner and

DiGirolamo describe a control module that involves the anterior cingulate (a region of the frontal cortex) during active suppression of a competing response (e.g., the Stroop task) but not during automatic or rote responding (also see Norman & Shallice, 1986). Parenthetically, it is unclear whether the anterior cingulate is involved in monitoring response consequences (whether the consequence was expected or unexpected; Ito, Stuphorn, Brown, & Schall, 2003) or detecting response conflict (Botvinick, Braver, Barch, Carter, & Cohen, 2001). Either way, it anchors a network relevant to the development of attention and thus potentially to ADHD.

With regard to impulse control, similar frontal-subcortical neural circuits are implicated in suppressing responses (Casey et al., 2002). For example, suppressing inappropriate motor response during complex behavior appears to involve the dorsolateral prefrontal cortex, at least in young children (Diamond et al., 1997), as well as the orbitoprefrontal cortex (Aron, Fletcher, Bullmore, Sahakian, & Robbins, 2003; Posner & DiGirolamo, 1998) and the subcortical connections to each. Indeed, the subcortical and striatal structures to which these prefrontal regions are connected may be crucial in the actual suppression of a response (Kimberg & Farah, 1998) at least in certain contexts (Nigg & Casey, in press). A recent process conception of EF emphasizes deliberate problem-solving steps, such as representing and manipulating the problem in working memory (planning), carrying out an intended action rather than a competing action, and detecting mismatch to expected results or success (Zelazo et al., 2003). Those functions likewise have clear relevance to attention and impulse control.

Third, we stress that our division into attention and impulse control functions is heuristic, yet to some degree untenable. In moment-to-moment behavior, these functions are virtually inseparable. Likewise, the neural systems we describe are closely related. As a result, Posner and Rothbart (2000) argue that the anterior neural system associated with executive functions is involved in the strategic control of both attention and motor response. Psychometrically, recent data in adults also support the idea that certain functions, such as protecting attention from interference and suppressing a response conflict, are closely related (Friedman & Miyake, 2004), whereas other functions, such as set shifting, can be distinguished from these (Miyake et al., 2000).

Fourth, relevant to our developmental interest, these models all describe abilities that emerge and develop rapidly in the preschool period, continue to mature through middle childhood and adolescence, peak in early adulthood, and are among the first abilities to wane with the passing of middle age. This trajectory may be related to the late maturation of the frontal cortex: Neural development of these frontal networks (especially via synaptic pruning; Casey, Durston, & Fossella, 2001) appears to continue even into early adulthood (Benes, 2001), and it is generally believed that the last abilities to mature are the first to decay with late age-related decline in cognitive efficiency (Plude, Enns, & Brodeur, 1994). With regard to early development, strategic control of impulse is related in part to the *effortful control* construct in temperament theory (the ability to delay or interrupt task-inappropriate behavior; Rothbart & Bates, 1998). Therefore, early precursors of EF, in the form of effortful control, can be observed in the toddler years well before most cognitive EF probes can be employed or true complex behavioral sequencing is possible. Effortful control shows longitudinal stability, with high scores for this ability associated with development of adaptive behaviors (Kochanska, Murray, & Coy, 1997; Kochanska, Murray, & Harlan, 2000). Excessively *high* control is associated with internalizing problems. Important for our purposes, *low* levels of this potential precursor of later executive control are associated with externalizing behavior problems over the preschool years (Murray & Kochanska, 2002). In all, it is important to recognize that the EF capacities are expected to mature slowly in conjunction with the maturation of frontal cortical neural structures through adolescence and beyond. Their development in childhood is therefore a key area for understanding how psychopathologies of attention and impulse control emerge. Moreover, their relatively late maturation may illuminate ADHD's changing presentation in adolescence/adulthood.

Fifth, on the basis of the temperament literature, examining the development of these within-child functions enables us to consider the role of *scaffolding* by caregivers in the early rearing environment as well as the role of *stress* and *learning* in the development and maintenance of problems in attention and impulse control. Therefore, after we consider executive control of attention and impulses, we look more closely at socialization. In fact, a key theme of this chapter is that exclusively biological views of temperament and executive functions, without due consideration of social factors and of interactions and transactions between within-child factors and environmental influences, are destined to be inadequate to the task of understanding the development of problematic attention, impulse control, and self-regulation. Having given reactive and executive processes initial definition, we now proceed to a more extensive conceptual framework for attention and impulse control per se.

Attention: Conceptual Framework

Attention usually refers to the facilitated processing of one source of information over another, although broad usages of the term can include capacity pool (Engle, 2002) as well as response readiness, arousal, and regulation (Taylor, 1995) and other abilities (Mirsky & Duncan, 2001). With regard to mechanisms, as outlined by Yantis (1998), attentional selection can be based on spatial location (Erikson & Hoffman, 1972), object features (Triesman & Gelade, 1980; Wolf, 1998), and timing (Shapiro & Raymond, 1994), movement, or other object characteristics (Kahneman & Henik, 1981). Attentional selection is influenced by multiple component functions, including bottom-up stimulus-driven processes that are relatively automatic and relatively early developing, and top-down goal-driven processes that are strategic, relatively deliberate, related to the concept of executive control, and later developing. These two types of processes interact continuously, each placing constraints on the other (Schneider & Shiffrin, 1977). Researchers attempt to isolate these two influences in varying ways. At the same time, as noted earlier, often overlooked in the purely cognitive approaches to attention is the role of affective motivation in attentional allocation (Pennington, 2002).

The complexity of the cognitive component of attention alone has led to a massive literature. We cannot do justice to the many approaches available (Theuwes, Atchley, & Kramer, 1998; Triesman & Gelade, 1980; Yantis, 1998; see Monsell & Driver, 1998). Instead, we comment illustratively on key approaches that have influenced research on the psychopathology of attention in ADHD in recent years. The framework we adopt posits three basic functional distributed neural networks (Posner & Peterson, 1990), implementing in turn (1) reflexive and (2) strategic attention as well as (3) general alertness. In noting different models of attention, we reference them to these three basic networks. Table 9.2 schematizes the networks in relation to basic operations. As it indicates, within this general framework, we

can begin by thinking of visual *orienting* (facilitation of processing at specific locations in space) as well as object *selection* (filtering of information once a location is attended), both of which are supported by neural attention systems located in the posterior (relatively automatized operations) as well as anterior (relatively deliberate operations) anatomical regions of the brain.

Posterior Attention System

With regard to spatial orienting, we note that location holds a special place in the success of attention (at least visually) because in many respects, attention must be directed to a specific location for other processing to occur there (see Yantis, 1998, for discussion). Visual orienting has therefore been of particular interest in the study of ADHD (Huang-Pollock & Nigg, 2003). It refers simply to the location in space at which processing is facilitated. Reflexive orienting (e.g., to a sudden onset of light) is guided by a posterior neural network that includes the parietal cortex as well as subcortical and thalamic structures, known collectively as the posterior attention system. However, once we are oriented to a location in space, we still have a limited capacity to process the available information. Thus, we must further select those objects at a given location to which we will attend. When there is too much information for deliberate or cognitive processing to handle, selection of objects occurs relatively early in the stream of information processing, in an automatic bottom-up manner (Lavie, 1995; Table 9.2). Selection in this case is based on surface or perceptual features such as movement, color, or line orientation, as noted above (Triesman & Gelade, 1980). Neurally, this "early selection" is also related to a posterior cortical-subcortical network. Thus, for heuristic purposes, we group (1) automatic spatial *orienting* and (2) early (perceptual) *selection* together, as two related domains of the posterior attention network.

Anterior Attention System

Visual orienting and object selection both can also occur in a top-down strategic manner. In that instance, they share the qualities of requiring mental resources, being fairly responsive to deliberate and strategic considerations, and being associated in neuroimaging studies with the anterior neural networks that include the anterior cingulate cortex (Posner & Peterson, 1990). We thus group strategic orienting and selection together in Table 9.2 as probes of an anterior attention system. They may be thought of as components of executive function that are specifically attentional. Strategic orienting occurs in response to a sign,

TABLE 9.2   Three Attentional Brain Networks and Suggested Operations Derived from Different Attention Models

Neural System	Functional Cognitive Mechanisms
Posterior Attention System	Reflexive orienting Early or perceptual selection
Anterior Attention System	Strategic orienting Late or cognitive selection Conflict detection
Vigilance System	Alerting Sustained attention

such as an arrow pointing to a target. Strategic object selection occurs late in the stream of information processing (called "late selection"), where it is based on cognitive meaning and the strategic importance of the material (one classic example is a Stroop task). Late selection can be thought of as an executive function in that it is deliberate, requires resources, and is supported by the anterior neural networks noted earlier, in parallel with strategic orienting (Table 9.2). Note that further suggestions for fractionating the executive domain of attention are extensive and include sub-elements such as working memory capacity, cognitive interference control, and set shifting (Mirsky & Duncan, 2001; Table 9.2).

Conceptualized this way, orienting and selection are both guided by relatively automatic or reflexive processes, as well as by relatively strategic or deliberate processes. Developmentally, posterior and anterior processes reveal distinct trajectories in infancy and childhood, as well as late adulthood. Posner and Rothbart (2000) point out that in early infancy, reflexive orienting to cues guides attention, even before reactive (affective) responding and well before deliberate directing of attention can be observed (the latter emerges during the toddler years). Likewise, Huang-Pollock, Carr, and Nigg (2002) compared children in second through sixth grades on a computerized selection task to show that late selection was progressively more mature in the older groups. Even sixth graders were still well below adult level capabilities, although they were notably better than fourth graders. In contrast, early perceptual selection was essentially fully mature, at adult levels, even in the second graders (Huang-Pollock et al., 2002). These types of data are all consistent with the proposition that relatively automatic attentional processes develop earlier and complete their development at a much younger age than do anterior or cognitively demanding attentional processes, exemplifying the idea that neural development proceeds along a posterior-to-anterior gradient. This pattern also is consistent with the frontal cortical neural networks' gradual maturation throughout adolescence, with mylenation and synaptic pruning ongoing through early adulthood (Benes, 2001).

Vigilance and Alerting

Moderating the posterior and anterior attention systems are state regulation functions referred to by Posner and Peterson (1990) as a *vigilance* system (see Table 9.2). This system is responsible for arousal/alerting and vigilance/sustained attention. Alerting, which refers to the ability to respond appropriately and efficiently to phasic stimuli, is related to the older concept of *arousal,* which also referred to degree of alertness (Mirsky & Duncan, 2001). The nuances of arousal, alerting, and the associated term *activation* (which pertains to readiness for motor response) are discussed later. For now, we refer to alerting or arousal interchangeably. However, distinct from those, this system is also responsible for maintaining task focus over time, called *vigilance* (Posner & Peterson, 1990) or *sustained attention;* (Mirsky & Duncan, 2001). Debate continues as to whether alerting/arousal and vigilance/sustained attention constitute not just distinct operations, but distinct neural networks (Parasuraman, Warm, & See, 1998). For simplicity, we group arousal/alerting and vigilance/sustained attention together as two major operations of a vigilance system (following Posner & Peterson, 1990). Also for simplicity, we refer to arousal as a single process when summarizing the ADHD literature, although it is probably not unitary either (Derryberry & Rothbart, 1988).

Developmentally, arousal is an important characteristic even in infants and is considered perhaps the earliest hallmark of self-regulation (Olson, 2002). Crucially, regulation of arousal from very early in life is heavily dependent on caregiver responsiveness. For example, a large body of literature notes the difficulty in arousal regulation experienced by children with insecure attachments to their parents when in stressful situations, and some evidence suggests that this relation is not merely "temperament driven" but is at least in part a reflection of the quality of the parent-child interaction (Olson, 2002; Schore, 1994). Similarly, early sleep regulation is partly temperamental and partly related to parental monitoring (Dahl, 1996; Peirano, Algarin, & Uauy, 2003). Whether these different examples of arousal are all addressing the same underlying processes is an open question. We conceive of the vigilance system and arousal as crucial in early development but as continuing to mature throughout childhood and adolescence. They moderate other attention and impulse control operations.

Conclusion: Three Core Attention Networks and Their Subfunctions

Because the important distinction between automatic and deliberate attention suggests differential activation of posterior versus anterior attention networks, we can group selection and orienting operations into (1) multiple, early developing, relatively automatic processes of the posterior attention system and (2) multiple, later developing, relatively deliberate operations of the anterior neural network related to executive functioning, selective attention, and working memory. The third moderating system, the vigilance network, is distinct from both of these and includes multiple operations as well, including arousal (phasic) and sustained attention. Overlooking many other models of attention in the interest of space, we can illustrate what is known about the psychopathology of ADHD in terms of these three basic networks governing attention, and their subfunctions. In relation to ADHD, we thus first discuss the early maturing, relatively automatic processes of (1a) reflexive visual-spatial orienting and (1b) early (perceptual) object selection. We second consider the later maturing processes related to executive functioning or "controlled processing" (Monsell & Driver, 1998), which include (2a) strategic or deliberate visual-spatial orienting, (2b) late (cognitive) object selection, and (2c) operations of working memory, as well as supplemental information on the concept of (2d) "set-shift." Third, we take up the moderating or "state regulation" capacities of (3a) alerting/arousal and (3b) vigilance, ending with consideration of the related concept of *activation*. Before we take up the ADHD findings, however, we more formally conceptualize impulse control.

Impulse Control: Conceptual Framework

Impulse control can also be thought of as being regulated by multiple, interrelated behavioral and neural systems in the child, in addition to the interpersonal and incentive context in which the child is acting. Within the child, we can simplify the descriptive options for a moment by considering a deceptively simple question: How does a behavior (e.g., an impulse, or a response that was about to be carried out) get stopped, interrupted, suppressed, or inhibited? Developmental studies suggest that either (1) more than one process is involved in controlling impulses in this way, or (2) an underlying control mechanism becomes able to interrupt different kinds of behavior at different points in development. For example, Dempster (1993) noted that the ability of children to suppress or inhibit motor movements develops earlier than the ability to suppress or inhibit word meanings in language use, although whether this is due to the differential rates at which motor and language skills develop or to distinct control operations coming online remains uncertain.

Consider further that impulses can arise in at least two basic ways: via an immediate incentive (reaction) that invites approach or a long-term goal that comprises a series of "next steps" (strategic planning). Correspondingly, impulses to action (motor or vocal response) are *controlled* by two distinct higher-order neural networks or mechanisms (Nigg, 2001; Rothbart & Bates, 1998). First is the re-

active or motivated suppression of response, which is relatively spontaneous (Gray & McNaughton, 1996; Kagan, 1997). A simple illustration involves stopping what one is doing due to anxiety about a new person or a new event that appears. For example, a child may stop playing if an unfamiliar child walks into the room because of mild anxiety about the unknown that this child represents. This process operates in response to the elicitation of anxiety or fear (immediate, short term, and relatively automatic), related to cues for uncertainty or for imminent punishment. When serving to interrupt a behavior, it can be termed *reactive* response suppression (or reactive behavioral inhibition; this has also been called by us "motivational inhibition"; see Nigg, 2000). Note that whereas extreme fear may lead to a freeze response (suppression of all behavior), when anxiety is operative, this same process also redirects attention, including both spatial orienting and filtering or object processing. This redirection exemplifies the close relation of attention and impulse control in moment-to-moment behavior. Along with anxiety, strength of incentive *approach* (excitement to a reward cue) also influences impulsivity. In other words, the stronger the original approach tendency, the more difficult it is for anxiety to interrupt it. Thus, impulse control also can fail because such approach processes are dysfunctionally strong. The *relative* strength of approach and behavioral inhibition processes has thus been proposed as further etiology of impulsivity (Newman & Wallace, 1993).

The second general control process is characterized by the involvement of strategic (i.e., deliberate, long-term) responses to events and their relation to long-term goals, closely connected to the now familiar construct of executive functions. This type of control can thus be termed *executive* or deliberate response suppression (referred to as executive inhibition in Nigg, 2000). It refers to the deliberate suppression of a response in order to achieve a later, internally represented goal (e.g., not scratching a mosquito bite so that it will heal faster; managing not to interrupt a long-winded colleague so as to fulfill a personal resolution to be more patient). Neurally, the specific suppression of a motor response for strategic reasons (a hallmark of cognitive control) is related to a subset of the associated frontal networks, namely, a neural loop that includes the prefrontal cortex (in particular, orbitoprefrontal and right inferior frontal, especially inferior frontal gyrus; Aron, Fletcher, Bullmore, Sahakian, & Robbins, 2003), basal ganglia (especially the caudate), and thalamus (Alexander, Crutcher, & DeLong, 1991; Middleton & Strick, 2002). It is modulated by frontal-cerebellar loops throughout development (Diamond, 2000; Middleton & Strick, 2001).

The reactive and executive processes likely are dialetically related developmentally and in action selection, and both are closely involved in all aspects of behavioral regulation. These two processes thus likely modulate each other and can override each other in particular contexts (Nigg, 2001). For example, to achieve an important goal, one might overcome fear of a possible punishment (a new professor anxious about speaking in front of colleagues does so anyway in order to explain his work). At the same time, anxiety might interrupt deliberate processes (the new professor forgets his next point due to the intrusion of a worry about how the talk is going).

As was the case for attention, our heuristic two-process model of impulse control is in some respects too general, in that these two core processes are each amenable to further differentiation. For instance, in the reactive domain, Asendorpf (1990) followed preschool children for several years. Two kinds of *reactive* behavioral inhibition were coded. The first was inhibition when meeting new children, or inhibition to social novelty, which *weakened* with development over the preschool period. In other words, children were less fearful when meeting new children as they matured during preschool. The second type of inhibition was stopping a behavior based on a learned negative association, or inhibition in response to punishment cues. It *strengthened* as the children developed: Children were more effective at stopping behavior contingent on a warning of punishment as they matured. This study suggests that two kinds of reactive behavioral inhibition, meeting strange peers versus responding to learned punishment cues, may be related to distinct developmental mechanisms that follow different behavioral trajectories during the preschool period. Failure of either process to develop within an acceptable range might lead to later problems with impulse control.

Furthermore, the preceding discussion of reactive control emphasized anxiety response and alluded only briefly to fear. An extreme fear or "panic" response is widely considered to dissociable from anxiety (Depue & Lenzenweger, 2005; Gray & McNaughton, 1996). This fear/panic or fight-flight system can lead to the "freeze" response and then to vigorous action. Gray's (1971) initial suggestions about the role of the fight-flight system in disinhibitory psychopathology were long overlooked but have recently been revived (Beauchaine, Katkin, Strassberg, & Snarr, 2001). In all, reactive behavioral suppression is not strictly unitary, even though we generally treat it as such for simplicity.

Similarly, in the domain of strategic control, the degree of fractionation of functions remains in debate. For example, (1) stopping a primary, intended response on the basis of new information, (2) suppressing a competing and never intended response, or (3) inhibiting a reflex response may be construed as distinct or similar, depending on the conceptual framework (see Barkley, 1997; Friedman & Miyake, 2004; Miyake et al., 2000; Nigg, 2000). We note, however, that the temporal relations of cognitive and motor functions suggest some differentiation. For example, holding a goal in working memory may be distinct from carrying out a goal-directed behavior or resisting interference from a competing, tempting response (Zelazo et al., 2003).

As implied in the preceding, it is important to recognize that reactivity can change with developmental context and experience. For example, some children who are behaviorally inhibited in preschool (i.e., highly reactive or anxious in novel situations) do not show this behavior pattern in elementary school, whereas other children show stability in this trait (Kagan, 1997; Kagan & Snidman, 2004). The socialization context may prove crucial for helping some children to overcome their proclivity for anxious inhibition (Kagan, 2003). Furthermore, and unsurprisingly, executive control continues to develop from preschool to childhood and then into adolescence and on into adulthood. In particular, the ability to strategically control an impulse undergoes consolidation from the preschool to early school years (Carver, Livesey, & Charles, 2001), and then continues to steadily improve into middle to late adolescence (Bedard et al., 2002; Williams, Ponesse, Schachar, Logan, & Tannock, 1999). Such developmental trends are consistent with the continued maturation of frontal-subcortical neural networks during development, maturation that does not terminate even with the end of adolescence.

As a final caution, we note that other processes are involved in behavioral control as well. For one thing, children with behavioral problems, such as those diagnosable with ADHD, often think up rather unexpected impulses that might not occur to the average child; this phenomenon may have to do with an unusual learning history or motivational structure that is outside of our framework here. In addition, central and peripheral motor systems in the child may have experienced delays in development, compounding efforts at motor impulse control (Piek et al., 2004). Finally, as we highlight later, language development plays an important part in impulse control during development. Nonetheless, for the most part, when we discuss impulse control we focus on two related processes: reactive and strategic interruption of a potential response.

Final Overview Comment

As a final note on this preliminary conceptual section, many other models and conceptions could be discussed in an encyclopedic review of self-regulation, attention, or impulse control, including several that have been influential in the psychopathology literature, such as "hot and cool" delay of gratification (Metcalfe & Mischel, 1999), ego control (Block & Block, 1980), activation and effort (Pribram & McGuinness, 1975), extraversion (Eysenck & Eysenck, 1985), behavioral inhibition (Quay, 1988), regulation (Calkins & Fox, 2002; Kopp, 1982), response regulation (MacCoon, Wallace, & Newman, 2004; Newman & Wallace, 1993), and key socialization models (Greenberg, Speltz, DeKlyne, & Jones, 2001; Kopp, 1982). Rather than survey all of these or their many overlaps with our perspective (for additional review, see Douglas, 1999; Nigg, 2000; Rothbart & Bates, 1998; Sergeant, Oosterlaan, & van der Meere, 1999), we emphasize the basic two-factor heuristic just presented that partially integrates temperament with models from cognitive science.

With these qualifications in mind, we consider the functional component systems that can be roughly assigned to distinct distributed neural networks. We consider these networks first from the perspective of attention and then with regard to impulse control. Whereas we initially isolate these functions for expository purposes, the relationship among the regulatory domains will be important when we subsequently consider developmental pathways.

ATTENTION AND PSYCHOPATHOLOGY IN RELATION TO ATTENTION-DEFICIT/HYPERACTIVITY DISORDER

We now consider whether attention may be a core mechanism that is impaired, in some way, in children or adults with what are termed attentional disorders. To do so, we view attention from several angles, working through the posterior network, anterior network, and alerting/vigilance.

Early Developing Processes: Posterior Attention Network and Attention-Deficit/Hyperactivity Disorder

We noted that the posterior attention network subserves easily studied visual functions, including reflexive orienting and perceptual selection. Because ADHD, at least in the Combined subtype form (ADHD-C), is often associated with problems in executive functioning (e.g., Barkley, 1997), we might expect that ADHD-C would *not* be associated with posterior attentional problems. Most evidence over the past 10 years has confirmed this guess. With regard to orienting, we recently reviewed all published data

on visual-spatial orienting that relied on the widely used, computerized orienting task, finding no consistent meta-analytic evidence for such a problem in children with ADHD-C, across 14 studies in the past decade and a half (Huang-Pollock & Nigg, 2003). Intriguing, isolated findings of posterior shift (not to be confused with executive set shifting, later) or disengage problems simply could not be replicated.

With regard to selection, historically the data have argued against a perceptual selection problem in ADHD-C (Berman, Douglas, & Barr, 1999; McIntyre, Blackwell, & Denton, 1978; Sergeant & van der Meere, 1988; Sharma, Halperin, Newcorn, & Wolf, 1991). Many such investigations, however, lacked systematic control of perceptual load in addition to other limitations (see critique by Douglas, 1999). The issue of load in particular was a potentially important gap in light of subsequent theories of load and selection (Lavie, 1995). Yet, a recent investigation controlled perceptual load more systematically using these newer paradigms, again with no evidence of perceptual selection problems in ADHD-C (Huang-Pollock, Nigg, & Carr, 2005).

In the face of growing consensus that the posterior attention network functions are not primarily involved in ADHD-C, theorists have suggested that the posterior attention network may be a mechanism in children with ADHD Inattentive type (ADHD-I; Goodyear & Hynd, 1992; Milich et al., 2001). Very few data address this possibility formally. However, the few data on automatic visual-spatial orienting in ADHD-I do not support deficits in this domain (Huang-Pollock & Nigg, 2003), casting doubt on the potential for that particular probe of a posterior attention system. Similar results emerged in a study that varied perceptual load to isolate early selection (Huang-Pollock et al., 2005). Yet, studies are so few that the status of posterior attention network abilities in ADHD-I remains uncertain.

At the same time, there has been substantial concern in the nosology literature that the ADHD-I type may not be well-specified. In particular, it may be that items tapping sluggish cognitive tempo (a tendency of a child to be "spacy," underactive rather than overactive, and have low energy) are important to recognize when defining a subgroup with purely inattentive forms of ADHD (C. Carlson & Mann, 2002; McBurnett, Pfiffner, & Frick, 2001). Indeed, in *DSM-IV*, the inattentive type includes, by definition, children who are overactive (but just below the threshold for ADHD-C) plus children who are clearly underactive. The latter group may be those most affected by a posterior attention system dysfunction (see Milich et al.,

2001). Huang-Pollock et al. (2005) reported some intriguing possible support for this idea in their investigation of perceptual load, but the sample was small. More study of this idea is likely to be one element of future work in the field.

Notably, in contrast to the hypothesis that ADHD-I may be related to underfocused selection in the posterior system, it has also been suggested that automatic overselection ("overfocused" attention) may be a mechanism involved in psychopathy (Hiatt, Schmitt, & Newman, 2004; MacCoon, Wallace, & Newman, 2004; Newman & Wallace, 1993). In view of the possibility that a subgroup of children with severe hyperactivity, impulsivity, and aggression may be at risk for future psychopathy (Lynam, 1998), further study of this possibility will be of interest.

Summary

Various probes of the posterior attention system, such as automatic visual-spatial orienting and early perceptual object selection, suggest that this system is not promising as a locus of core dysfunction in ADHD-C. However, a subset of children with ADHD-I may have problems in that domain; data are too sparse to draw conclusions at this point. Key limitations in this work to date include insufficient empirical study of ADHD-I and limited consideration of motivation as a contributor to automatic attention allocation. Future work that probes such reactive processes (e.g., through priming designs) will be of interest, as will future work on the inattentive subtype. Other models not discussed here may also be important, such as Newman and colleagues' (e.g., MacCoon et al., 2004) discussion of the role played in self-regulation by the ability to detect warning cues.

Later Developing Processes: Anterior Attention Network and Attention-Deficit/Hyperactivity Disorder

We now move to perhaps the most heavily studied domain of attention in ADHD, that of executive attention related to the anterior attention network. It has been often theorized as centrally involved with ADHD-C. Several abilities are included, depending on which model of executive control one prefers. Drawing upon the aforementioned cognitive models as well as related neuropsychological models (e.g., Mirsky & Duncan, 2001; Pennington & Ozonoff, 1996), we organize our remarks in relation to a set of four basic abilities: (1) late selective attention or interference control, (2) strategic attentional orienting, (3) set shifting, and (4) working memory (and its components, including short term memory).

Late Selective Attention/Interference Control

Late selection, or interference control, figures prominently in many theories of ADHD (Barkley, 1997; Berger & Posner, 2000). The most classic test of anterior attentional selection, or interference control, is the Stroop task (MacLeod, 1991). One must name the ink color of color-words (e.g., the word "red" printed in green ink); reading the word is more automatic than naming the color, so interference results. Both qualitative (Nigg, 2001) and quantitative (Homack & Riccio, 2004; Van Mourik, Oosterlaan, & Sergeant, 2005) reviews have concluded that Stroop interference is at most minimally impaired in ADHD-C in childhood. However, the null findings may be related to methodological limitations. Most saliently, studies relying on the paper-and-pencil version of the Stroop task, and thus utilizing a single "total items within 45 seconds" score timed with a stopwatch, have not yielded evidence for large problems in interference control on the part of participants with ADHD, apart from the slow naming speeds characteristic of this disorder (reviewed in detail by Nigg, 2001). Yet, investigations using computerized interference control tasks, which enable calculation of reaction time for each item and then averaging all of these individual item reaction times, have had more success (Carter, Krener, Chaderjian, Northcutt, & Wolfe, 1995; Jonkman et al., 1999), though not unequivocally (Huang-Pollock et al., 2005). Overall, then, interference control has yet to be clearly confirmed as a replicable dysfunction in ADHD-C.

This ability is also factored in psychometric studies with other neuropsychological tests, such as the Trailmaking test (Mirsky & Duncan, 2001), which requires rapidly tracing a line between alternating letters and numbers (e.g., 1-a-2-b-3-c). Although such a grouping may be debatable (Pennington & Ozonoff, 1996, group Trailmaking under "set shifting," next section), the Trailmaking test shows modest ADHD-related deficits (e.g., Nigg, Blaskey, Huang-Pollock, & Rappley, 2002) with meta-analytic effect size estimated at $d = .55$ across 14 investigations (Willcutt, Doyle, Nigg, Faraone, & Pennington, 2005). Yet its demand for ongoing motor control and set shifting call into question the Trailmaking test's purity as evidence of an attention problem per se.

Set Shifting

Although not featured in most cognitive neuroscience models, set shifting is regularly implicated in many neuropsychological tasks. Aside from the Trailmaking test as a possible measure, one classic neuropsychological measure of this concept is the perseveration errors score on the Wisconsin Card Sort Test (WCST; Mirsky & Duncan, 2001; Miyake et al., 2000). The WCST requires children to adopt a response set (e.g., match cards by color) and then to switch to a different response set (e.g., match cards by shape). Perseverating on the initial response set is viewed as a weakness in set shifting. This measure likewise shows only modest effects in ADHD: As recently reported, the meta-analytic effect size across 24 studies of ADHD was $d = .46$, with the majority of individual investigations failing to find a significant effect (Willcutt et al., 2005). The largest WCST studies accordingly provide mixed results (Houghton et al., 1999; Klorman et al., 1999; Pineda, Ardelli, & Rosselli, 1999; Willcutt et al., 2001). However, as a measure of set shifting, the WCST is limited by a reliance on errors rather than reaction times (error scores are notoriously problematic in terms of psychometric properties; see M. B. Miller, Chapman, Chapman, & Collins, 1995) and lacks the precision of millisecond reaction time probes. Alternative error measures of set shifting ability may show an ADHD-related deficit (Koschack, Kunert, Derichs, Weniger, & Irle, 2003) but face the same psychometric limitations. Therefore, recent studies have borrowed task-switching designs from cognitive psychology that rely on reaction time measures. Although varying in detail, these designs all induce a response set and then measure reaction times when the primary response set must be changed; they can monitor dual-task performance (performance cost of doing two things at once) or switching costs (see Pashler, 1998). Application of these more refined paradigms to ADHD has barely begun. Initial studies provide some evidence of rapid, controlled shifting deficits (Cepeda, Cepeda, & Kramer, 2000; Hollingsworth, McAuliffe, & Knowlton, 2001; Oosterlaan & Sergeant, 1998b; Perchet et al., 2001; Schachar, Tannock, Marriott, & Logan, 1995), but studies to date are too few and varying in method to allow firm conclusions about the magnitude of the effect.

Working Memory

Working memory is a vast topic in itself, yet it is clearly related to attention because it is also described as a limited-capacity system with two basic elements. The first element, commonly referred to as the "central executive" (Baddeley & Hitch, 1994) or "working memory capacity," is viewed as a domain general ability that essentially taps the same construct as the anterior attention network discussed earlier (Engle, 2001, 2002). It involves the ability to protect and manipulate information in mind, and likely depends in part on dorsolateral-prefrontal cortex (Kane &

Engle, 2002). The second element entails domain-specific, short-term memory modules for temporarily holding information. The most common division of these is into the visual sketch pad (visual working memory) and the phonological loop (speech-based information or verbal working memory; Baddeley & Hitch, 1994). At least 20 experimental studies have looked at working memory and related abilities (short term memory, planning) in ADHD in recent years. These are most interpretable if sorted into verbal versus spatial domains.

In the verbal domain, Tannock, Ickowicz, and Schachar (1995) noted ADHD-related deficits on a serial addition task, which were improved by medication only for those children with low comorbid anxiety. Others also found that children with ADHD (usually ADHD-C) performed worse than controls on verbal working memory tasks (McInerney & Kerns, 2003; Stevens, Quittner, Zuckerman, & Moore, 2002). Such effects, however, may depend on the particular measure used and do not appear to be robust to covarying the influence of comorbid symptoms (McInnes, Humphries, Hogg-Johnson, & Tannock, 2003; Sonuga-Barke, Dalen, Daley, & Remington, 2002). In their meta-analysis of digit span backward and sentence span tasks, Willcutt et al. (2005) reported a composite effect size of $d = .55$ across 11 studies; similar results were reported by Martinussen, Hayden, Hogg-Johnson, and Tannock (2005). Notably, Martinussen et al. observed a similar effect size for short term memory (e.g., digit span forward) and working memory (e.g., digit span backwards). In all, verbal working memory deficits in ADHD appear to be modest in magnitude.

Measures of visual-spatial working memory show more dependable ADHD-related effects. This appears on three kinds of tasks: (1) planning tasks (such as Tower of Hanoi), (2) traditional working memory tasks such as spatial span backwards, and (3) short-term memory tasks (e.g., spatial span forwards). In planning tasks (e.g., Tower of Hanoi or Tower of London, in which the child must rearrange discs or balls on wooden pegs by mentally looking ahead at the necessary moves; Klorman et al., 1999; Nigg, Blaskey, Huang-Pollock, & Rappley, 2002) or the self-ordered pointing task (Shue & Douglas, 1992), meta-analytic effect sizes are robust, with $d = .69$ for 6 studies using the Tower of Hanoi (but only $d = .51$ for 6 studies with the Tower of London; Willcutt et al., 2005). However, these tasks appear to involve reasoning as well as working memory. In the second type of task (working memory), Martinussen et al. (2005) found $d > 1.0$ in a meta-analysis of 7 studies of spatial span backwards or similar tasks. Third are short-term memory tasks that tap storage capacity but not executive control or protection, using tasks such as the spatial span of apprehension (Karatekin & Asarnow, 1998; McInnes et al., 2003) or the CANTAB spatial working memory task (Barnett et al., 2001). These types of measures yielded a composite effect size of $d = .85$ across 9 studies (Martinussen et al., 2005). Thus, whereas ADHD clearly involves some type of difficulty in spatial short term or working memory, it is unclear to what extent difficulties in visual working memory are due to difficulties with the protection of working memory (interference control, or anterior attention) versus the functioning of the spatial working memory scratch pad per se (see Martinussen et al., 2005). The picture is compounded by evidence that visual working and short term memory tasks both may tend to entail executive control, and more so than do auditory tasks (Miyake, Friedman, Rettinger, Shah, & Hegarty, 2001). For now, it may be most parsimonious to view the ADHD difficulty in these studies in terms of the executive control of attention (protecting working memory; or in other words, the working memory "central executive"), but more differentiated work will be of interest. The large effect sizes apparent in these initial studies are provocative, and their magnitude after more studies have been completed will be of interest.

Summary

Evidence for a modest anterior attention dysfunction in ADHD exists from a wide range of neuropsychological investigations, although it is unclear that such deficits are as robust or large as might be needed for a convincing core deficit in ADHD. In particular, effect sizes on widely studied clinical neuropsychological measures, such as the Wisconsin Card Sort and the Stroop test, are of small to at most medium magnitude. However, aspects of working memory or short term memory appear to be more clearly involved, at least in the spatial domain. Newer, more refined measures of cognitive selection and working memory that capitalize on reliable reaction time measures or that emphasize components of working memory (e.g., visual working memory) may clarify matters in coming years.

Moderating Processes: The Vigilance Attention Network and Attention-Deficit/Hyperactivity Disorder

Recall that the vigilance system (Posner & Peterson, 1990) is responsible for establishing and maintaining an alert state ("ready for anything"). Lapses in this attention function are apparent to anyone who is tired or sleepy; they are also salient in such medical conditions as epilepsy and narcolepsy (Mirsky & Duncan, 2001). Vigilance depends on a

network of neural structures that include the noradrenergic system originating in the locus coeruleus, the cholinergic system of the basal forebrain, the intralaminar thalamic nuclei, the right prefrontal cortex (Parasuraman et al., 1998; Posner & Peterson, 1990; Rothbart, Derryberry, & Posner, 1994), and possibly the ascending reticular activating system (Mirsky & Duncan, 2001; the latter is related to wakefulness). We noted two distinct functions: phasic *alerting* to a stimulus (Berger & Posner, 2000; called "arousal" by Pribram & McGuinness, 1975, and "stabilize" by Mirsky & Duncan, 2001), followed by tonic sustaining of attention to the stimulus, called *vigilance* (Posner & Peterson, 1990) or "sustained" attention (Mirksy & Duncan, 2001). Grouping these functions together is conceptually helpful (Posner & Peterson, 1990), although their degree of neuroscientific linkage remains unclear (see Mirsky & Duncan, 2001; Parasuraman et al., 1998).

A complication for readers of the ADHD literature is that the concept of tonic vigilance is related in some models to still another concept, that of "activation" (Pribram & McGuinness, 1975), a term itself often used in differing ways in the ADHD literature and in the developmental and temperament literature. The lack of isomorphism in handling "activation" across theories is related to distinct historical streams of thought (Strelau, 1994). One stream, exemplified by Gray (1982), arose from research on temperament and learning theory reaching back through the work of Eysenck to Pavlov's early conceptions of learning, in which activation was closely related to reward responding. The second stream, exemplified by Posner and Peterson (1990) and Pribram and McGuinness (1975), arose from the cognitive sciences and information-processing approaches, which de-emphasized incentive response and emphasized global response readiness and attention. Table 9.3 summarizes the scientific traditions that distinguish arousal from activation in these two different ways. As a result, one current thread of theorizing about ADHD draws on temperament and learning theory (and, more recently, associated animal models of ADHD), thus emphasizing reward response (e.g., Sagvolden et al., 1998, 2005). Another thread of ADHD theorizing draws on cognitive and information-processing theory and emphasizes impaired demand-response preparation generally (e.g., Sergeant et al., 1999).

We distinguish these two meanings of activation because they sometimes make different predictions (e.g., regarding importance of reward) and have distinct theorized neural concomitants. Thus, the reward-based activation concept is related to dopaminergic reward pathways, whereas the vigilance system under discussion in this section is related to noradrenergic projections. We therefore

TABLE 9.3 Parallel Yet Distinct Historical Conceptions of State Regulation by Arousal and Activation

	Arousal/Alerting Marker		Activation/Approach/Vigilance Marker	
	Neural	Response	Neural	Response
Temperament Theories of Arousal-Activation				
1. Eysenck (1967)	RAS	Extraversion	Autonomic response	Neuroticism
2. Gray (1971)	RAS	After incentive cue increase next response intensity	Ascending DA fibers to basal ganglia, limbic, and prefrontal (mesolimbic DA)	Motor response to reward cue
Information Processing Theories				
1. Pribram and McGuinness (1975)	RAS, amgydala hypothalamus	Time-locked, phasic responding, heart rate deceleration, *CPT d'*	Basal ganglia striatum	Tonic physiological change; in vigilance tasks, *CPT beta*
2. Tucker and Williamson (1984)	Right lateral NA neurons	For any stimulus input, enhance signal; noise detection	Left lateralized DA projections	Preparation for motor response
3. Posner and Petersen (1990)	Right latera NA neuronsl frontal/parietal	Phasic alerting to new signal	Right alerting network	Tonic vigilance to ongoing signal; sustained RT rate over time

Notes: DA = Dopaminergic brain projections; NA = Noradrenergic brain projections; RAS = Brain stem to cortex ascending reticular activating system and associated corticoreticular neural loop. D-prime and beta refer to parameters on the continuous performance test, which is a laboratory cognitive task.

consider activation in two different ways. First, we consider it as a demand-response function along with our consideration of the vigilance system in the present section, as Activation. We do so even though, as noted in Table 9.3, the neural instantiation of this response-readiness type of activation has been disputed and may not be in the same neural system as vigilance or sustained attention as we have described it. Second, we consider responsiviness to reward incentive cues in a later section, under the rubric of reactive or motivational response.

Collectively, these functions are sometimes referred to as *state regulation* rather than attention functions (Sergeant et al., 1999). Here, we adopt the framework of Posner and Peterson (1990; Table 9.3), while highlighting key divergences related to other perspectives. Our main theme is that the data on these two broad types of functions—alerting and sustained attention—are distinct in relation to ADHD.

Alerting

Alerting refers to initial response to a stimulus. It involves the ability to prepare for what is about to happen. It is relevant the instant a warning is received, or when there is a need to be ready to respond without warning. An example might be waiting during a short-answer test for the next question from the teacher, or waiting in a track meet for the starting gun to sound. It is closely related to the older concept of cortical *arousal,* and for our purposes those two terms can be put together. We view arousal as a right brain lateralized process of activation by noradrenergic neurons. It responds to stimulus input and prepares to take advantage of new information by enhancing the signal: noise ratio for novelty detection (Posner & Peterson, 1990). Recent theories and data have used the term "alerting" to refer to specific deficits related to ADHD (Berger & Posner, 2000), whereas classic theories of ADHD emphasize a deficit in cortical "arousal" (Satterfield, Cantwell, & Satterfield, 1974; Zentall & Zentall, 1983) or, concomitantly, disruption in ascending noradrenergic neural systems that facilitate signal: noise detection (McCracken, 1991).

Alerting can be assessed in several different ways, most of them relating to reaction time or physiological response in the first seconds after encountering a stimulus of some kind. Thus, with regard to reaction time and errors, an effective alerting system prepares for a rapid, accurate response. As a result, when alerting is impaired, we predict that children will make slow, inaccurate responses when fast responses are required, in the same way that a tired driver has slower reaction times to a sudden traffic stop. Thus, in the laboratory, a deficit in alerting (or phasic arousal) is usually marked by poor performance (slow, variable response times) either on a series of single abrupt-onset trials (e.g., detect the light the moment it appears and touch the key as quickly as possible) or poor performance from the very beginning of a reaction time task. At the same time, when waiting or reflection is required, someone who is not alert or who has low cortical arousal would be expected to have difficulty waiting, because such waiting and reflecting requires appropriate arousal; in that context, our tired friend would respond too hastily.

Therefore, two different kinds of performance problem are consistent with an alerting deficit: slow and variable responses to fast tasks, and hasty, inaccurate responses to slow-careful tasks. Both kinds of response patterns are typical in impulsive children and children with ADHD. Failures in this system therefore could account for inability to regulate behavior or attention effectively in ADHD. (Note that *excess* arousal would lead to a classic impulsive style of hasty, inaccurate responding, but not slow, variable responses on fast reaction time tasks; therefore, the predominant view regarding ADHD is that it involves low rather than high arousal. Other forms of impulsivity may be precipitated by high arousal.)

The evidence for slow and variable responses, and poor responses from the very beginning of reaction time tasks, comes from several reviews and meta-analyses. This pattern was evident in a detailed review of the early literature (Sergeant & Scholten, 1985), a meta-analysis of this function in 8 studies using the stop task (Oosterlaan, Logan, et al., 1998), and recent, large-sample studies (Swanson et al., 2000). However, a review of orienting studies did not observe a dependable slow and variable response pattern across all studies, even though most studies did observe that effect (Huang-Pollock & Nigg, 2003). Leth-Steensen, Elbaz, and Douglas (2000) also reported a sophisticated analysis of variable response profiles in ADHD, emphasizing that children with ADHD make an excess of very slow responses, consistent with variable attention or low arousal.

Other evidence is also consistent with this idea. For example, the continuous performance task (CPT) d′ parameter, a signal-detection measure reflecting sensitivity to the difference between a target and a nontarget (Lachman, Lachman, & Butterfield, 1979), shows an aggregate ADHD-related deficit in meta-analytic reports (Losier, McGrath, & Klein, 1996). This finding can be interpreted as evidence of an arousal or alertness dysfunction. Further, EEG slow wave findings and early evoked response potential (ERP) tend to be consistent with an arousal dysfunction. Among the first efforts to use contemporary definitions of ADHD and viable EEG methods was conducted by Satterfield and colleagues (Satterfield et al., 1974; Satterfield & Dawson, 1971). Recent electrophysiological work has often, though not unequivocally, been supportive (Brandeis et al., 1998; Monastra et al., 1999; Silberstein et al., 1998). A salient finding entails an excess ratio of theta:beta activity, or excess relative slow wave activity, in ADHD (for a review of EEG, see Barry, Clarke, & Johnstone, 2003a; for ERP, Barry, Clarke, & John-

stone, 2003b). Barry et al. (2003a, 2003b) concluded that the EEG and ERP evidence both are consistent with central nervous system (CNS) hypoarousal in a percentage of children with ADHD-C as well as ADHD-I.

Caveats to this argument were pointed out by van der Meere and colleagues (Sergeant et al., 1999; van der Meere, 2002), who argued that most studies (e.g., with the CPT) failed to consider event rate and that (1) failure to find sustained attention deficits on fast-event rate CPT tasks contradicts an arousal dysfunction hypothesis and (2) many of the performance data may in fact reflect a problem in activation (see later discussion). Moreover, strategy effects (e.g., speed-for-accuracy trade-off) were often overlooked. Nonetheless, some of the evidence just reviewed is most parsimoniously viewed as indicative of arousal or alertness problems, at least in ADHD-C.

Vigilance or Sustained Attention

Broadly speaking, sustained attention refers to maintaining focus on a task over time and is thus related to the concept of activation, which refers to the ability to prepare ongoing responses in the late stages of behavioral control and organization. When referred to as "sustained attention" (Mirsky & Duncan, 2001), this ability is among the most common ideas of an ADHD core deficit, albeit one not readily supported by available evidence. In the cognitive psychology literature, it means the ability to maintain a state of alertness and wakefulness during "prolonged mental activity" (Weinberg & Harper, 1993). This notion can clearly include the child's paying attention throughout a class at school or staying focused during a sports event waiting for the cue to action. For everyone, performance shows a decrement (slower and more variable responses, more errors) as the minutes and hours go by (Parasuraman et al., 1998). ADHD-related deficits in sustained attention should result in an *excess* decline over time versus controls, yielding a group-by-time interaction.

Yet, even though children with ADHD appear to lose interest in tasks quickly, it turns out that they typically do *not* show a decline in accuracy (or in speed) over time on laboratory tasks (Sergeant et al., 1999; Sergeant & Sholten, 1985; Sergeant & van der Meere, 1990). Although reliant on interpreting null interaction findings in often small-sample studies (see Douglas, 1999), the likelihood of a true sustained attention deficit in this syndrome has been judged doubtful by most commentators in the field. Data are less plentiful for ADHD-I and ADHD-H. In the case of ADHD-C, instead of a decrement over time, these children seem to show performance deficits from the very beginning of a task or response (Sergeant &

van der Meere, 1990). This pattern suggests a problem in *alerting* or arousal, as described in the prior paragraphs, but not *sustained attention* per se. However, this finding may depend on the event rate; some data indicate that at slow event rates, a sustained attention deficit is observed (van der Meere, 2002), pointing again to the issue of weak *activation*. We now turn to this topic and consider evidence for it more directly.

Activation

Tucker and Williamson (1984) recast the time-on-task domain as *activation* (Table 9.3), dramatically shifting the conceptual emphasis to output preparation during each discrete response, rather than merely global time-on-task attentional ability (Sergeant et al., 1999). This conception affords a broader consideration of relevant evidence, now with an emphasis on motor preparation rather than attention. Indeed, left-lateralized dopamine systems are emphasized, rather than the right-lateralized system that is thought to support arousal and vigilance per se, so that some view it as an executive function (Berger & Posner, 2000). Regardless, when activation is viewed in this way, evidence is more supportive of an ADHD-related deficit. As noted earlier, Dutch scientists using time-on-task and event rate data reported that children with ADHD show normalized performance at medium event rates but weaknesses at slow and fast event rates on CPT (van der Meere, Shalev, Borger, & Gross-Tsur, 1995) and go/no go tasks (Borger & van der Meere, 2000; van der Meere & Stermerdink, 1999), leading these investigators to favor an underactivation explanation of ADHD cognitive and performance deficits (Sergeant et al., 1999; van der Meere, 2002). In other words, varying the rate at which a computer presents stimuli can moderate and nearly normalize response accuracy for children with ADHD. Further evidence for a deficit in activation or the related concept of effort comes from the difficulty children with ADHD have in producing rapid motor responses over time (Carte, Nigg, & Hinshaw, 1996). In addition, some physiological data, in particular heart rate data, appear to be supportive (van der Meere, 2002).

Caveats to this argument entail failure of some activation predictions to materialize. For example, deficits on the CPT beta parameter (an index of response bias, that is, risky versus conservative) have not been confirmed in meta-analyses (Losier et al., 1996), raising problems for an activation account. On balance, however, an activation dysfunction in ADHD remains an important possibility, with intriguing evidence of context-dependent functional deficits in children with ADHD.

Summary

The vigilance network and associated state regulation functions are extremely important for understanding ADHD. In particular, substantial evidence supports an underarousal or alerting dysfunction in ADHD, particularly ADHD-C. Contrary to popular lore, evidence fails to consistently support a sustained attention or vigilance problem in ADHD, but that conclusion depends on interpreting null findings, which are vulnerable to low statistical power, and apparently on event rate. Effects of event rate on children with ADHD suggest that a modified activation (motor preparation) account is promising. Most such research has focused on ADHD-C; the performance of other ADHD subtypes remains underinvestigated.

Attention and Attention-Deficit/Hyperactivity Disorder: Interim Conclusions

Clearly, the turning of the field to attention as a potential core deficit in ADHD in the 1970s, including renaming of the syndrome to emphasize deficits in attention, has yielded a number of important discoveries. Perhaps most surprising has been the difficulty of establishing what seems, at first glance, the most obvious candidate for an ADHD deficit, namely, a problem in sustained attention. In fact, children with ADHD appear to be less task-ready and more inattentive during all phases of task presentation, even beginning stages. As important (if less surprising) is that attentional processes associated with the early maturing posterior attention network, such as reflexive orienting and perceptual selection, are also generally spared in ADHD, at least in the visual modality and at least in children with ADHD-C. Thus, two kinds of attention—sustained attention and automatic orienting—are apparently intact in most children diagnosed with ADHD-C. Whereas the later maturing *executive* or anterior attention domain is widely viewed as important in ADHD, establishing clear and well-defined dysfunctions in executive *attention* has been elusive because of wide variations in measurement approaches and inconsistent results from traditional neuropsychological measures, resulting in small to moderate effect sizes in meta-analyses.

The safest conclusion about executive attention may be that it is a domain of only modest deficit in ADHD-C, perhaps representing a secondary rather than primary etiological dysfunction. On the other hand, arousal and related operations of the moderating noradrenergic vigilance network offer a promising candidate for a core within-child causal mechanism. Further specification and study of the idea of activation—as distinct from sustained attention and more closely related to dopamine systems and to output or motor responding—may be fruitful and could lead to a better integration of the arousal and attention findings. Closer scrutiny of children with ADHD-I, especially those with sluggish cognitive tempo, is a key future direction for this arena of study. Finally, the intersection of motivation with arousal and executive attention findings is poorly understood in the case of ADHD. We consider motivational effects more closely in our next section.

IMPULSE CONTROL AND PSYCHOPATHOLOGY IN RELATION TO ATTENTION-DEFICIT/ HYPERACTIVITY DISORDER

As highlighted earlier, impulse control can be viewed in terms of two broad functions: reactive (motivational) and executive control. We first consider reactive control, because it is the earlier developing of these two broad mechanisms. Reactive response to incentive cues—that is, possible punishment or possible reward—comes online in late infancy (Rothbart & Ahadi, 1994). We note both reactive *suppression* of response and reward or *approach* responding as potentially important. After that, we revisit the executive domain, this time emphasizing impulse control rather than attention. Deliberate control of response begins to emerge in precursive form in the toddler years, and we highlight several kinds of evidence about those processes in ADHD throughout development. We briefly note alternative approaches to understanding the impulse control problems in children with ADHD, including motor timing and the fight-flight system.

Early Developing, Reactive Mechanisms: I. Response Inhibition and Attention-Deficit/Hyperactivity Disorder

Reactive or motivational suppression of behavior occurs in response to anxiety or fear (with variation in this suppression across anxiety and fear). Overresponding by this system can lead to internalizing and anxiety disorders (and perhaps anxious-impulsive behavior). Our main concern, however, is whether the reactive system underresponds in impulse-control disorders like ADHD, thus failing to adequately interrupt inappropriate behavior and redirect attention. This *reactive inhibitory* function depends on both the integrity of the behavioral-interruption process, which we discuss in this subsection, and the intensity of the affective states that compete with it, including excitement (positive

approach) and anger, discussed in the next subsection. Two theoretical traditions inform the temperament concept of reactive control.

In the first, Kagan and colleagues (Kagan, 1997; Kagan, Reznick, & Snidman, 1987; Kagan & Snidman, 2004) propose a temperament that is inhibited versus one that is uninhibited. Children with inhibited temperament suppressed impulses in the presence of novel social encounters (typically, novel peers) while experiencing high internal arousal. This program of research links such behavioral suppression to greater autonomic arousal and perhaps to greater limbic activation (Kagan, 1997). Over the course of development, some children with inhibited temperament develop anxiety-related difficulties (Biederman et al., 2001; Kagan, Snidman, Zentner, & Peterson, 1999), whereas those with extremes of uninhibited temperament are at risk for externalizing behavior problems (impulse control problems). As noted earlier, however, these paths are far from invariant. A notable percentage of children with inhibited temperament can move out of their classification during preschool and early childhood. Thus, this type of impulse control is detectable early on as a temperamental characteristic but may change notably with developmental context during childhood.

In the second line of thinking, Gray (1982) refers to a similar type of behavioral inhibition but with greater emphasis on the appearance of a signal for danger or punishment, though he includes the unexpected as well. An example of a cue for punishment might be when a bullying child refrains from further provocation on hearing his victim's big brother approaching, instead listening for the threat. An important point here is that when reactive suppression of impulses occurs, behavior does not stop entirely. Instead, the *current* behavior is interrupted, and *attention* is reactively and automatically redirected to the threat stimulus (Gray & McNaughton, 1996). Anxiety is the hallmark psychological concomitant of activation in this system (Gray, 1982), so that dysfunction involves low anxiety and failure to learn or adequately respond to punishment cues. Debate remains vigorous as to the critical role of response to the unexpected versus response to potential danger (Kagan & Snidman, 2004), and subsequent theories have modified Gray's model in important ways (Depue & Lenzenweger, 2005). Work on ADHD, however, has relied heavily on Gray.

Thus, following directly from Gray's thinking, theorists asked 2 decades ago whether ADHD was associated with failure to respond to punishment cues (Quay, 1988, 1997). However, most data were unconvincing (Daugherty & Quay, 1991; Milich, Hartung, Martin, & Haigler, 1994). In fact, a central confound to this hypothesis concerns the relatively numerous subset of cases (as many as a third of children with ADHD) with a comorbid anxiety disorder. By definition, they should have an *over*responsive reactive inhibition system. In contrast, the subset of ADHD children with low anxiety and perhaps with comorbid Conduct Disorder appears most likely to fail to respond to punishment cues (see Nigg, 2003). Perhaps as a result of failure to systematically consider these crucial comorbid conditions, experimental studies that manipulate punishment cues and examine children's response times and error rates have yielded, at best, inconsistent results for ADHD (Iaboni, Douglas, & Baker, 1995; O'Brian & Frick, 1996; O'Brian, Frick, & Lyman, 1994; Pliszka, Hatch, Borcherding, & Rogeness, 1993).

A mixed picture also emerges from physiological studies, which examine skin conductance and heart rate under varying incentive conditions, making use of sophisticated theories of central-to-peripheral nerve system responding (Fowles, 1980). Although some studies show an ADHD effect (e.g., Iaboni, Douglas, & Ditto, 1997), failure to control for associated antisocial behaviors or comorbid disruptive behavior disorders remains a limitation and results are inconsistent. Pliszka, Borcherding, Spratley, Leon, and Irick (1997) failed to substantiate an ADHD-related reactive inhibition response. However, Beauchaine et al. (2001) had more positive results using a similar approach, and O'Connell, Bellgrove, Dockree, and Robertson (2004) found abnormal skin conductance in response to errors in ADHD subjects.

Further physiological studies therefore will be of interest in the coming decade. In particular, further incorporation of specific cardiac measures such as heart rate deceleration and vagal tone may be promising to asses this aspect of functioning in ADHD. For example, Calkins and Fox (2002) reviewed a body of research indicating that poor behavioral regulation is indexed by these physiological measures. Relevant studies of children with ADHD are few.

As a final note, we point out that an alternative mechanism of behavioral inhibition would be via the fight-flight response—the fear response, as distinct from an anxiety response (Depue & Lenzenweger, 2005; Gray, 1982). This response would be expected to cause a freeze response to fear or imminent danger (suppression of all behavior) but also to trigger excessive, situationally inappropriate anger and aggressive behavior when dysfunctional (Gray, 1991). Beauchaine (2001) has theorized that this system may play a role in ADHD, and initial physiological data are intriguing (Beauchaine et al., 2001).

Summary

Overall, reactive behavioral inhibition is an important function but so far does not emerge as a likely core domain of deficit in most cases of ADHD apart from those children with early-onset, comorbid Conduct Disorder. However, research in this area remains in the early stages, with only a handful of relevant physiological studies to date and virtually no early observational or other studies of temperamental reactivity per se in children with ADHD, either cross-sectional or longitudinal.

Early Developing, Reactive Mechanisms: II. Reward Response and Attention-Deficit/Hyperactivity Disorder

We noted that reactive processes also include approach processes and that impulse control is also affected by the strength of affective states, such as excited approach to reward and angry response to frustration. In the case of ADHD, theorists have been especially interested in the possibility that impulse control can fail because such *approach* processes (excitement to a reward cue) are either over- or underresponsive to context.

The neural locus of this system is also of interest because it corresponds to neuroimaging findings in ADHD, with an important role for ascending dopaminergic fibers in the brain's appetitive system, known as the mesolimbic dopamine system (Depue & Collins, 1999; Gray, 1971, 1982). These fibers proceed from the substantia nigra and ventral tegmentum to the basal ganglia (especially the caudate nucleus), limbic system, lateral hypothalamus, and prefrontal cortex, thus touching several structures implicated in ADHD and overlapping with the dopaminergic projections thought to modulate executive behavioral control. Note that a related motivational concept, that of *effort,* is discussed in alternative theoretical traditions (Sergeant et al., 1999). We include effort in our broad concept of motivational approach, following Scheres, Oosterlaan, and Sergeant (2001) and Sergeant (2005).

Historically, there was initial interest in the hypothesis of an *over*responsive approach system in ADHD while also considering the possibility of underresponsivity (Gorenstein & Newman, 1980; Gray, 1991; Haenlein & Caul, 1987; Newman & Wallace, 1993). Experimentally, we would expect that an *overactive* reward system would lead children with ADHD to overrespond in the presence of reward cues, but not when reward cues are absent. It has been difficult, however, to isolate such a context-specific effect in ADHD (Iaboni et al., 1995; Oosterlaan & Sergeant, 1998a) raising an important obstacle for a straightforward excess-reward-response model. Clarifying this picture, other behavioral findings suggest that ADHD children are overresponsive to recent or immediate reward but underresponsive to more time-distal contingencies (Douglas, 1988; Tripp & Alsop, 1999). Failure to consider temporal properties of the reward could account for the inconsistent results in a number of studies.

As a result, in the past decade, theorists emphasized the temporal properties of the reward as key to understanding impulsivity and ADHD. Children with ADHD are hypothesized to be underresponsive to delayed rewards but normally or even excessively responsive to immediate incentives. This pattern is described as a steepened "delay-reward gradient" because a graph of strength of response by time to reward shows a much steeper curve for ADHD than normal. In other words, the drop-off in performance for individuals with ADHD when rewards are delayed is precipitous (an effect demonstrable in certain animal models of ADHD; Sagvolden et al., 2005). In short, under this hypothesis, abnormal relative weighting of delayed and immediate incentives leads to impulsive behavior. Sagvolden and colleagues, in a well-focused theory derived from animal models, hypothesized that extinction following learning should be impaired if there is a reward dysfunction, because new learning will fail to replace the prior overlearned behavior, an effect seen in their animal model (the spontaneously hypertensive rat).

Their preliminary studies of children appear supportive (Johansen, Aase, Meyer, & Sagvolden, 2002), although more replications are needed and data across a wide range of studies are inconsistent with regard to reinforcement responding in ADHD (Luman et al., 2005). Boosting this theory has been recognition that difficulty tolerating delay may be related to reward dysfunction. Sonuga-Barke and colleagues (2002) found that children with ADHD consistently chose immediate small rewards over delayed larger rewards—although they attributed this to strategic avoidance of delay rather than sensitivity to reward itself. In any event, this tendency is as strong as dysfunctional executive inhibition as a correlate of ADHD symptoms (Nigg, Willcutt, et al., 2005; Solanto et al., 2001).

Summary

In summary, a steepened delay-reward gradient (dramatic drop in performance as rewards become more delayed) appears to be one element in the development of ADHD, particularly its hyperactive-impulsive symptoms, that deserves

close scrutiny. Early development of this process during the infancy and toddler years could shed valuable light on the viability of this view as explanatory for some children with problems in impulse control. It represents an area in which an explicitly developmental focus—from very early childhood through middle childhood and beyond—will be essential for future progress.

Later Developing Deliberate or Executive Control of Impulse and Attention-Deficit/Hyperactivity Disorder

With regard to impulse control, executive processes have among their functions that of suppressing task or goal-irrelevant motor responses. This type of impulse-control process is deliberate or effortful and can occur without substantial fear or anxiety motivating it. It involves a distributed neural system that is conceptually and anatomically closely related to the anterior attention system we featured earlier, including the inferior frontal gyrus and a structure in the subcortical basal ganglia called the caudate (Aron et al., 2003).

Convergence of approaches in describing the executive control system is apparent, given that deliberate or effortful control of responding is emphasized in theories of both early cognitive development (Zelazo et al., 2003) and early social-emotional development (Murray & Kochanska, 2002). However, these approaches have not yet been fully applied to the development of risk for ADHD. For example, surprisingly little research has considered *temperament* antecedents such as effortful control or personality outcomes such as Conscientiousness and Constraint in relation to ADHD (Nigg, Goldsmith, & Sachek, 2004; Olson, 2002; Sanson, Smart, Prior, & Oberklaid, 1993).

Yet, the few studies to do so are quite consistent in suggesting that a broadly defined deliberate control domain (usually studied as Conscientiousness in adults, or as Effortful Control in children) is associated with ADHD symptoms in preschool children (Goldsmith, Lemery, & Essex, 2004), school-age children (Martel & Nigg, 2005), and adults (Nigg, Blaskey, Huang-Pollock, & John, 2002; Nigg, John, et al., 2002). However, unsurprisingly for such a broad, higher-order construct, those findings are nonspecific. That is, many childhood psychopathologies are related to effortful control. However, initial efforts to parse specificity and comorbidity have been promising as well. For example, we showed that Big Five conscientiousness was related to symptoms of inattention-disorganization even with antisocial behaviors partialled; the converse was not true (Nigg, Blaskey, Huang-Pollock, & John, 2002). Using partial correlations to isolate effects, we also found that in children, effortful control was related to inattention-disorganization, whereas, other traits were related to other disruptive behaviors (Martel & Nigg, 2005). It will be important for future research to consider the key subcomponents of effortful control (Murray & Kochanska, 2002) and of conscientiousness/constraint. In the meantime, of considerable interest are more fractionated measures of strategic impulse control in the laboratory.

Some two dozen different measurement tasks have been claimed to measure behavioral inhibition of the strategic or executive variety (see Nigg, 2000, 2001). However, only a handful come close to isolating the ability to suppress a response, as distinct from attention, working memory, and the like—and even those do not succeed entirely. Perhaps the most theoretically pure measure of the ability to stop an impulse for strategic (rather than affective) reasons is the stop task (Logan, 1994). This task uses varied timing of warnings to evaluate how much time individuals need to interrupt a response they were about to make. Although the task has some psychometric problems (e.g., the variance in stop signal reaction time is unknown), it has performed well in simulation studies (Band, van der Molen, & Logan, 2003). Some 27 studies have used this measure with ADHD and they generally identify a moderate-size weakness in the time needed to stop a response, on the order of $d = .61$ versus normal controls, with over 80% of these studies finding a group effect (Nigg, 1999; Schachar & Logan, 1990; Schachar, Mota, Logan, Tannock, & Klim, 2000; for reviews, see Nigg, 2001; Oosterlaan, Logan, et al., 1998; Willcutt et al., 2005). Thus, this measure of response inhibition is among the most well established correlates of ADHD in the field.

Other measures, such as the oculomotor antisaccade task (Castellanos et al., 2000; Nigg, Butler, Huang-Pollock, & Henderson, 2002) and the go/no go task (Trommer, Hoeppner, & Zecker, 1991; Yong et al., 2000) are also widely viewed as operational measures of strategic response suppression. Such measures also generally show a deficit in children with ADHD versus normal controls, although nonreplications can be noted (see Nigg, 2001, for detailed review). The ability to strategically interrupt or prevent a response may be more strongly associated with behavioral symptoms of inattention than of hyperactivity-impulsivity (Castellanos & Tannock, 2002), converging with personality data, in which trait conscientiousness, the personality proxy for effortful control, was related most clearly to inattention symptoms (Nigg, John, et al., 2002).

Consistent with that picture, in their large study of adults with ADHD, Nigg, Stavro, et al. (2005) used composite measures of inattention-disorganization and hyperactivity-impulsivity (each taken from the subject and two other reporters who completed clinical structured interviews about the subject, validated with a confirmatory factor model fitting analysis) to statistically predict a composite executive function latent variable (based on 5 tasks and also validated with a latent variable confirmatory factor analysis); only inattention symptoms were uniquely related to the executive control score. However, in a logistic regression analysis to predict ADHD subtype with both a composite executive function score and a composite output speed score (as a crude indicator of state regulation or activation), ADHD-C was predicted by executive function weakness but not slow response speed, whereas ADHD-"other" (a compendium of less severe groups, including inattentive, residual, and hyperactive types) was predicted by slow response speed. Thus, partial progress is at hand with regard to specificity of executive deficits to symptom domains by adulthood, but translating this into actual subgroups of individuals with ADHD is as yet incomplete. More work is needed to verify this picture in children, for whom this structure may be less stable.

Impulse Control: Interim Conclusions and Additional Considerations

It is important to recognize that other potential mechanisms in impulse control (and inattention) have received scant discussion here. For example, we noted that the fight-flight response is beginning to receive study. Likewise, because of strong neuroimaging findings of cerebellum abnormality in ADHD (Geidd, Blumenthal, Molloy, & Castellanos, 2001), a long-standing interest in time perception and timing in impulsive adults (see Parker & Bagby, 1997, for a review of early studies) is rapidly expanding into a new body of literature on children as well as adults with ADHD (Barkley, Murphy, & Bush, 2001; Ben-Pazi, Gross-Tsur, Bergmann, & Shalev, et al., 2003; Brown & Vickers, 2004; Sonuga-Barke, Saxton, & Hall, 1998; Toplak, Rucklidge, Hetherington, John, & Tannock, 2003) and may eventually prove quite central to a complete picture of the disorder. Likewise, we have bypassed the literature on serotonergic functioning, a major topic in the literature on impulsive aggression (Coscina, 1997). Finally, the role of language functioning in self-regulation represents a notable omission in our coverage to this point. We say more about it subsequently.

Nonetheless, much has been learned in the past decade as the field has focused heavily on impulse control via inhibition models of ADHD. Three salient if preliminary conclusions can be noted. First, reactive or anxiety-based response suppression (behavioral inhibition) does not appear to be central to ADHD, apart from its linkage to early-onset Conduct Disorder. Second, abnormal reward response, particularly related to temporal properties of reward, shows promise as a potential contributing causal mechanism in at least some cases of ADHD and to the hyperactive-impulsive behavioral symptom domain. Third, measures of strategic or executive response suppression show consistent and moderate-size effects in children with ADHD, albeit clearest and most well-replicated in only a few measurement paradigms (e.g., stop signal task) that still receive some debate as to their properties. These response suppression measures may be related to symptoms of inattention-disorganization as much or more so than to symptoms of hyperactivity-impulsivity. Other executive functions, including control of working memory, also appear to be involved. In all, reward functioning and executive control, perhaps in the form of response suppression, emerge as potential core causal mechanisms in ADHD. Notably, it remains unclear whether difficulty in one of these domains explains the others. For example, increasing reward salience may normalize problems in "stop inhibition" related to ADHD (Konrad, Gauggel, Manz, & Scholl, 2000; Oosterlaan & Sergeant, 1998a; Scheres et al., 2001; Slusarek, Velling, Bunk, & Eggers, 2001), or such "stop inhibition" problems may relate to a failure to alert quickly to the warning cue (Brandeis et al., 1998), but designs to evaluate the contribution of executive dysfunction to motivation or alerting problems are lacking. In all, sorely needed are additional integrative studies that consider multiple neurocognitive domains in the same sample.

As a result, leading theories of ADHD differ in the primacy placed on key processes, with some placing executive functions as the driver of ADHD difficulties (Barkley, 1997; Schachar, Tannock, & Logan, 1993), and others placing reactive or state regulation (arousal, activation, or motivation) processes as the driver of the problems (Sagvolden et al., 2005; Sergeant et al., 1999; Zentall & Zentall, 1983). However, all tend to incorporate to at least some degree executive control, arousal and/or activation, and motivation or reward response. What remains is clarification, both dynamically (i.e., in online behavior response) and developmentally, of how breakdowns in one process may lead to breakdowns in the others, in an effort to clarify whether one process is the predominant driver of

these multiple process dysfunctions in the majority of children with ADHD.

TOWARD A DEVELOPMENTAL, MULTILEVEL PERSPECTIVE ON CONTROL OF ATTENTION AND IMPULSE IN ATTENTION-DEFICIT/ HYPERACTIVITY DISORDER

Thus far, although we have pointed out the developmental trajectories of key mechanisms implicated in ADHD, we still have treated mechanisms of attention and impulse control in relatively individualistic and static fashion, primarily by considering psychological processes *within the child.* As we noted early on, however, the developmental progression of these within-child processes is highly related to socialization contexts: early parent-family interactions and later peer and school environments. Although this point is well recognized, it is not often reflected in empirical reports. We therefore move to a developmental perspective that enables us to take a multilevel view of the regulation problems under consideration, in keeping with the multilevel approach advocated in developmental psychopathology (Cicchetti & Dawson, 2002). To do so, we emphasize a temperament-based perspective, which enables us to capture in a single framework effortful control, affect/motivation, and arousal, while we also consider a key cognitive domain not yet discussed, language development.

Regarding the last item, we note the following. Language plays an important role in self-regulation as one mechanism by which control is exerted (e.g., by internalized speech; Berk, 1986). It is a key mechanism mediating the socialization of self-control via parental verbalization of affect states and other behavioral expectations (Greenberg et al., 1991). The importance of language in self-regulation for ADHD was a fundamental insight in the influential developmental theory offered by Barkley (1997). However, in our account, we emphasize the putative mutual influence between language and executive function development, which we argue likely parallels the interactive relationship between reactive and executive control processes. The scaffolding of these interrelated control processes in early development can help us understand how disorders of attention and impulse regulation emerge.

As these interrelated, within-child regulatory processes proceed across development, they are collectively entwined in yet another mutual-influence relationship: their interface with the socialization environment. The key consideration in that regard concerns recent clarification that neural development is plastic to experience (Huttenlocher, 2002) and that experiences support both cognitive and language development (Hollich, Hirsh-Pasek, & Golinkoff, 2000; Posner & Rothbart, 2000). At the same time, just as child social and cognitive development is said to depend on "good enough" caregiving, the socialization process also depends on "good enough" development of executive, reactive, arousal regulation, and language mechanisms in the child. Attention and language are the most obvious points of interface between caregivers or peers and a child's internal self-control abilities. Over time, the *internalization* of those socialization mechanisms (e.g., in the formation of conscience) is an important yet poorly understood element of the development of self-control. Let us unpack these multiple developmental components in a bit more detail.

Regulatory and Reactive Processes in Development of Self-Control, Revisited

The early development of self-control capacities has been provocative from the viewpoint of considering precursors to attention and impulse control problems. Rothbart and Ahadi (1994) outlined a developmental sequence based on their work with infants, which is similar to several other conceptions in the literature (Block & Block, 1980; Eisenberg et al., 1997; Kochanska et al., 1997; Murray & Kochanska, 2002) and informs our illustration in Table 9.4. This outline is, of course, closely related to our framework of reactive and strategic or executive impulse control mechanisms, a framework that also draws on their work. Using this perspective, we can readily extend our discussion, at a conceptual level, to early precursors (see Sanson et al., 1993).

Early on, infants allocate their attention (and their motor responses) simply on the basis of stimulus response and reflex response, which are largely midbrain-mediated processes that correspond to the reflexive attentional mechanisms discussed earlier. However, by later in infancy, sometime in the 1st year of life, children begin to respond to cues for incentives by directing their attention and making motor responses such as approaching a potential reward or withdrawing from a potentially distressing signal (Rothbart & Ahadi, 1994). These latter responses correspond to the *reactive* allocation of attention and control of behavior that we discussed earlier. By the beginning of the toddler period, roughly about the age of 14 months, infants can be observed to deliberately turn their attention away from upsetting material, exemplifying a precursor to deliberate regulation of behavior and affect by executive control. As discussed much earlier, this process illustrates the concept of effortful control, which (along with the term "regulation") has emerged in the temperament literature to describe the earliest manifestations of deliberate attention allocation by infants and then toddlers and preschoolers (Rothbart & Bates, 1998).

Effortful control develops rapidly in the toddler years. By about 30 months of age, children can begin to inhibit stimulus-driven motor response (Diamond et al., 1997; Posner & Rothbart, 2000) and thus begin to be evaluated using some of the laboratory measures of attention and impulse control that we reviewed earlier in relation to ADHD findings. For example, by this age, they can engage in interference control, go/no go, and stopping tasks (Diamond et al., 1997). Diamond and colleagues documented a steady development in the ability to inhibit competing, stimulus-driven motor responses by ages 3, 4, and 5 years (see also

TABLE 9.4   Schematic of the Developmental Timing of Different Behavioral Systems Involved in Impulse Control and Attention Regulation

Process	First Emerges in Development	Later Development
1. Reactive approach and inhibition	Infancy (middle of 1st year)	Canalizes or changes with experience in early to middle childhood
2. Effortful/executive control of impulse and attention (anterior attention system)	Toddler (years 1–2) → onward	Matures throughout childhood and adolescence
3. Language	Toddler (years 1–2) → onward	Matures in childhood with growing skill through middle adulthood
4. Posterior attention system	Infancy (1st year)	Matures by early to middle childhood
5. Vigilance/arousal	Infancy (early in 1st year)	Temperament trait responsive to context and caregiving
6. Socialization	Infancy (attachment/attunement)	Internalization of conscience, peer relations in childhood/adolescence

Note: Based in part on "Temperament and the Development of Personality," by M. K. Rothbart and S. A. Ahadi, 1994, *Journal of Abnormal Psychology, 103,* pp. 55–66. Adapted from "On Inhibition/Disinhibition in Developmental Psychopathology: Views from Cognitive and Personality Psychology and a Working Inhibition Taxonomy," by J. T. Nigg, 2000, *Psychological Bulletin, 126,* pp. 200–246.

Zelazo et al., 2003). However, Diamond et al. observed subtle difficulties in children with early treated phenylketonuria (PKU). PKU is of interest because this metabolic disease interferes with development of the prefrontal cortex. These results therefore are of note because, unlike frank PKU, which causes mental retardation, the early treated children (i.e., those whose diets are phenylalanine-free) display generally normal-range cognitive development yet often have remaining subtle delays in development of the dopamine-rich neural pathways in the dorsolateral prefrontal cortex that are important to later executive functioning (Diamond et al., 1997). Such early treated PKU cases therefore may serve as one model for the subtle neural injury that may cause executive dysfunction in early development in cases of ADHD.

Effortful control in the form of strategic attentional and impulse control continues to develop throughout childhood, yielding steady progress in the ability to ignore competing stimulus-driven responses over the second- to sixth-grade years (Huang-Pollock, Carr, & Nigg, 2002) and the ability to inhibit primary responses over the period from about ages 5 to 7 and beyond (Carver et al., 2001). The ability to suppress responses continues to develop through adolescence (Bedard et al., 2002), presumably aided by ongoing myelination and pruning of frontal cortical neural networks in conjunction with socialization and learning experiences (Benes, 2001). Table 9.4 summarizes this basic developmental sequence in early childhood. Note that these are the same abilities that we reported earlier are assessed as key weaknesses in children with ADHD, suggesting that children with ADHD are in part characterized by difficulties in this developmental progression.

A further clue with regard to potential pathways to ADHD comes from the insight that reactive and effortful processes likely support and modulate each other in early development (Rothbart & Ahadi, 1994) as well as subsequently. Thus, each process depends on the support of the other for optimal development and for optimal self-regulation (Derryberry & Rothbart, 1997; Derryberry & Tucker, 1994; Rothbart & Bates, 1998). If reactive processes are atypical (e.g., very strong approach tendency), then this imbalance may disrupt development of executive functioning by exceeding the "expectable local environment" for those functions. The reverse can also happen, in that weak executive functioning may result in failure of reactive processes to consolidate.

In turn, as the child matures in the social context, the strength of this two-process self-regulation system is likely to influence the child's capacities to be normally socialized by average expectable parenting and peer environments

(Cicchetti & Lynch, 1995) and achieve adequate socialization adaptively in adverse or suboptimal caregiving environments. The import here is that if a child has very strong reactive processes (e.g., extremely strong negative affect), these may interfere with development of effortful control, in turn further weakening ability to regulate the reactive affects. Conversely, weak effortful control as an early temperamental characteristic could lead to difficulty with affect regulation as part of a two-way mutual influence process. This formulation may help to explain why executive and affective difficulties so often co-occur in children with disruptive behavior problems and ADHD. It also raises the possibility, as yet virtually untested, that certain types of early rearing environments or certain types of traumatic experience may predispose individuals to attentional and inhibitory dysregulation even in the absence of temperamental vulnerability (Kreppner et al., 2001).

At the same time, the arousal and alerting processes we described earlier, which are potentially crucial in ADHD, interact with the effortful and reactive processes under consideration in this discussion. Strong reactive responses (e.g., intense anxiety, excitement, or anger) influence arousal levels (Gray, 1982, 1991), with a cascade of associated physiological responses. If the arousal response is dysfunctional, this will also lead to difficulty in modulating reactive response. Moreover, executive control contributes to regulation of arousal, and optimal arousal is likely necessary for effective effortful control (Barkley, 1997; Rothbart et al., 1994).

Therefore, as we consider the development of attention, arousal regulation, reactive processes such as reward responsivity, and executive or effortful control, we can see that in the case of ADHD, there is potential for linking the various laboratory findings with early temperament models. These may be integrated in developmental analyses that identify temperaments at risk if not in infancy (where it is limited by the fact that very early temperament measures typically do not show reliable cross-time stability coefficients) then perhaps in the toddler years, and then measure this risk with laboratory measures in the middle childhood years, as they are consolidating. Thus, the field has the potential, at present, to begin to map early risk pathways toward childhood ADHD if temperamental precursors can be identified and show some stability in instances in which ADHD emerges. In other words, those early risk pathways may be mediated by early temperamental risks, which then mature into primary difficulties in some combination of arousal, approach, and executive impulse control abilities. Crucially, all of these systems are bound to be responsive to socialization contexts and experiences. We return to these ideas shortly after considering language functions.

Language and Regulatory Processes in Development of Self-Control

We alluded to the need to consider language development to understand self-regulation. The importance of verbal processes such as internalized speech for the development of self-regulation (i.e., executive control) has been well described (Barkley, 1997; Berk, 1986). Yet a mutual influence process is also potentially salient here, although it remains speculative. That is, toddlers typically transition from babbling to interpersonal word usage at about 10 to 14 months of age (Woodward & Markman, 1998). Language development then proceeds rapidly during the 2nd through 4th years of life. Of particular importance, this timing converges with the coming online of deliberate control mechanisms described earlier. This is probably no coincidence, as language learning is highly likely to be facilitated by attentional control (the youngster's ability to attend to caregivers when language or vocabulary teaching is going on; R. Brand & D. Baldwin, personal communication, August, 2005; Hollich et al., 2000). In short, children learn what they attend to. Because attentional control may be unduly influenced by reactive as well as arousal processes in a child with delayed development of effortful control, language learning may be delayed or altered by these attentional determinants during the toddler years in some children. For example, to enable language to advance rapidly, the child must be able to look away from stimulus-driven attentional targets and toward strategic targets cued by caregivers (Bloom & Tinker, 2001). In all, verbal facility, vocabulary, and general language effectiveness may be supported by the involvement of emerging effortful control of attention in the 2nd through 4th years of life.

Such advances in language are then theorized to support further strengthening of executive control in a bootstrapping manner, for example, via internalized speech and self-talk (Barkley, 1997). Verbal learning problems are a frequently identified correlate of antisocial development (T. E. Moffitt, 1993). However, verbal learning and language problems are not typically emphasized in the etiology of ADHD, even though they are frequent correlates (Barkley, 1997; Tannock & Schachar, 1996) and may well deserve more scrutiny (Tannock & Schachar, 1996). Indeed, Baker and Cantwell (1992) found that a high percentage of children with ADHD during the grade school years had histories of language problems earlier in development (i.e., during the preschool period). Although some of these

problems may have been subtle (e.g., mild dysarticulation), others involved more fundamental receptive or expressive language problems. Note that the mechanism of risk for ADHD could be direct in such instances: Poor language development may delay the ability to regulate behavior via self-talk strategies. It may also be indirect, in that caregivers may become frustrated while interacting with children who do not readily comprehend what is asked of them or who are not themselves easy to understand. Hence, socialization mechanisms may well be an indirect pathway through which developmental language problems contribute to the genesis of ADHD.

In summary, several core processes operate synergistically in early development to provide the child with adequate self-control: reactive processes (including behavioral inhibition and approach directly influencing arousal regulation), effortful control or executive functions, and language. In turn, these within-child self-control processes interact dynamically with socialization in infancy, preschool, and the school-age years. Figure 9.1 illustrates schematically several of the self-regulation mechanisms

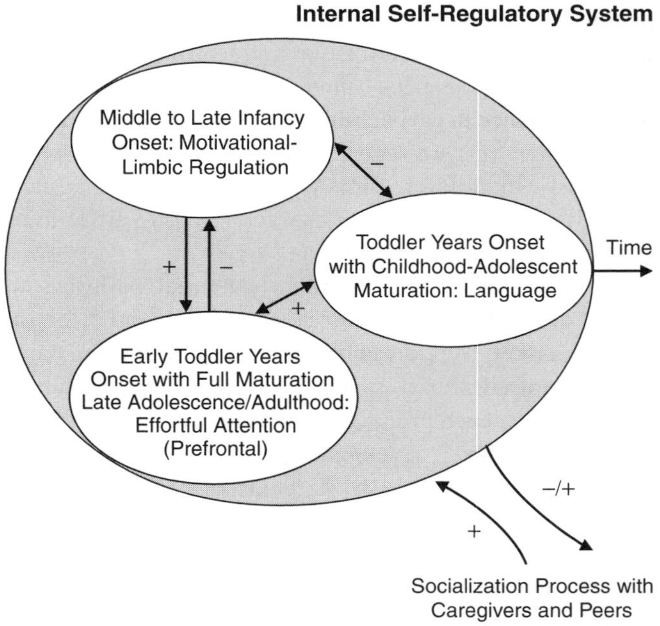

Figure 9.1 Schematic illustration of the within-child processes related to self-regulation and their collective interrelation with socialization effects. Adapted from "An Early Onset Model of the Role of Executive Functions and Intelligence in Conduct Disorder/Delinquency" (pp. 227–253), by J. T. Nigg & C. L. Huang-Pollock, 2003, in *The Causes of Conduct Disorder and Serious Juvenile Delinquency,* B. B. Lahey, T. Moffitt, & A. Caspi (Eds.), New York: Guilford Press.

we have discussed, indicating their interrelations and developmental phasing.

Interpersonal and Socialization Influences in the Development of Self-Control

The child's developmental status with regard to self-control interacts with socialization in a bidirectional and even transactional manner. Thus, children's reactive, control, and language processes depend for their development on adequate social interactions. We note again, in this regard, the notion of the "average expectable environment" necessary for the child's genotype to be expressed and his or her temperament to emerge adaptively (Cicchetti & Lynch, 1995). At the same time, the child's own abilities influence his or her preparedness to internalize social norms (e.g., internalized self-control, later conscience) and, at the same time, provide interpersonal stimuli that shape the responses of interaction partners (parents, peers). In other words, the child's proclivities and tendencies in the domains of attentional control and impulse regulation both shape and are shaped by the interpersonal context in which he or she develops. Thus, we view gene-environment correlations and gene-environment interactions as essential factors related to the development of attention and impulse control (Rutter & Silberg, 2002). Note that the developmental processes we outline here are also relevant to impulsivity as expressed in antisocial behavior (Nigg & Huang-Pollock, 2003, provide a similar analysis, e.g., in relation to antisocial development, which is closely related to ADHD; see Hinshaw, 1987; Hinshaw & Lee, 2003). We point out, however, that different elements and processes in the self-control system may contribute to different manifestations of externalizing psychopathology (Nigg, 2003), allowing some clear distinctions to be made despite the overlap of attention and impulse control problems with antisocial behaviors (see Waschbusch, 2002).

Again, child characteristics can interfere with socialization and make it more difficult for the child to be taught social rules (Johnston & Mash, 2001). This difficulty can lead, for example, to breakdowns in the normal development of conscience (Kochanska et al., 1997), particularly if the rearing environment is not well attuned to the child's needs (Greenberg et al., 1991). Also possible, but less well supported empirically, is that subtle or greater failures in normal socialization (short of frank trauma), such as parental psychopathology, preoccupation, impulsivity, or conflict, may directly impede the child's development of internalized self-regulation (Johnston & Mash, 2001). A

recursive loop then can develop in which the child inadvertently contributes to negative socialization experiences (Hughes, White, Sharpen, & Dunn, 2000) and vice versa. The preschool years are an especially critical time for these socialization dynamics, as language, deliberate effortful control, and affect regulation develop rapidly via interpersonal relations with caregivers. Various kinds of family stressors therefore may be related to inattention and impulse-related ADHD symptoms, perhaps because they disrupt the ability of caregivers to participate fully in this developmental dialectic. In turn, various characteristics of caregivers—including emotional dysregulation, disorganization, anger, and hostile interchanges with partners—can influence children's attention and behavior through genetic mediation of both parental and child characteristics (note, in this regard, the moderate to strong heritability of ADHD-related symptoms), through direct socialization influences, and through temperamental elicitation of particular caregiver responses. In short, an array of direct genetic linkages, direct psychosocial influences, and correlated genetic/biological and psychosocial risks are all likely to play a role in the transactional patterns that develop (Hinshaw, 1999, 2002a).

At times, this disruption may be driven by the difficulty of the child's behavior, limitations of the child's effortful control of attention, or intensity of child's affective reactions. The last would represent cases in which the child's characteristics (which, as we have just noted, are likely to be genetically influenced) lead to later ADHD, through both the continuity of the underlying temperamental characteristics and the mediating and accentuating mechanisms of disrupted parent responses (Rutter & Silberg, 2002; Scarr & McCartney, 1983). In other instances, as suggested earlier, it may be that marked disruptions in rearing environments are the key causal variable. Most likely is the possibility of transactional, reciprocally deterministic pathways.

At this point, we briefly review what *is* known about how socialization influences the development of ADHD as well as the types of aggressive and disruptive behavior that frequently accompany this condition. First of all, we highlight that most commentators contend that parenting and socialization are largely unrelated to the early display of disrupted attentional processes and impulse control problems (e.g., Barkley, 1998; Hinshaw, 1994) because of at least two factors: (1) As was discussed earlier, the symptoms of ADHD show strong levels of heritability throughout development (Hay, Bennett, McStephen, Rooney, & Levy, 2004), along with almost zero levels of shared environmental contributions; (2) there is no evidence for any association between disruptions in attachment status and subsequent ADHD patterns in the child (Hinshaw, 1999). On the other hand, insecure attachment between caregiver and child is a common correlate of frankly aggressive behavior in children, providing at least preliminary evidence for the contention that early problems in bonding between children and parents are related far more specifically to disruptive and antisocial behavior than to attention and impulse control problems per se (Greenberg et al., 2001).

Second, however, isolated reports indicate a potential linkage between early disruptions in parent-child relationships and later ADHD. One group (E. A. Carlson et al., 1995; Jacobvitz & Sroufe, 1989) provided evidence that, in a low-socioeconomic sample, early maternal misattunement to the child's cues predicts ADHD-related symptomatology several years later. A related study suggested that hostility between family members in the toddler years predicted ADHD symptoms in grade school in a small sample of non-diagnosed children, although toddler levels of behavior problems were not controlled (Jacobvitz, Hazen, Curran, & Hitchens, 2004). Perhaps consistent with those findings, Jester et al. (2005) followed a large sample of at-risk children from preschool to adolescence, examining the family and parenting predictors of four trajectories of development of attention problems (by the Child Behavior Checklist and Teacher Report Form attention problems scale, which includes hyperactivity items) and aggression. Lower emotional support and lower intellectual stimulation by the parents in early childhood predicted membership in the most problematic inattention trajectory, even when the trajectory for aggression was held constant. Conversely, conflict and lack of cohesiveness in the family environment predicted membership in a worse developmental trajectory of aggressive behavior with inattention/hyperactivity trajectories held constant. Those findings provide some of the first evidence for the potential specific contribution of distinct parenting or home experiences to ADHD spectrum and aggressive behaviors. Despite these intriguing reports, however, in the absence of a genetically informative design, it is unknown whether these instances of possible psychosocial mediation are, in fact, related more specifically to shared genetic characteristics between mother and offspring. Although Jester et al. did covary parental ADHD status with no change in results, most family studies failed to control parent ADHD. Thus, nearly all research on socialization influences across developmental psychopathology suffers from the key problem that genetic and psychosocial mediation of parenting or family life are confounded when biological parents and children are investigated (Rutter, Pickles, Murray, & Eaves, 2001). The types of adoption or twin de-

signs designed to isolate the separate and interactive contributions of genes and environmental/socialization influences as related to the development of attention and impulse dyscontrol have simply not been performed.

Third, the predominant perspective over the past 25 years or so has been that associations between negative parenting or disrupted socialization on the one hand, and ADHD symptomatology on the other are the product of child effects on caregivers, rather than the predominant view during the middle of the twentieth century that socialization was clearly the causal route for nearly all child behavioral disturbance (see Bell, 1968). The classic investigation of Barkley and Cunningham (1979) was paradigmatic in this regard: When hyperactive children were switched from placebo to medicated status, the negative/controlling maternal behaviors observed during objectively coded interactions were dramatically reduced. (Note, however, that positive parenting behaviors did not yield such a clear, reciprocal increase as a function of child medication status.) Such work has prompted the predominant view that parenting styles are a reaction to, rather than a contributor to, ADHD-related noncompliance and oppositionality.

Fourth, however, such studies of the acute effects of stimulant medication in yielding reciprocal reductions of parental negativity do not speak to the longer-term, interactive influences between temperament and socialization in shaping ADHD-related symptomatology. That is, there may be a history of negative interaction patterns—spurred initially by parental difficulties in reacting to difficult temperamental styles in the child—that propel intensification of attentional and impulse control problems. Along this line, we highlight at the outset that clear experimental evidence exists regarding the decisive role of negative parenting practices in shaping and maintaining aggressive and externalizing behavior patterns in children (G. R. Patterson, Reid, & Dishion, 1998; Snyder, Reid, & Patterson, 2003). In other words, interventions designed to test parent management programs aimed toward reduction of aggressive behavior indicate that the interventions are effective and improvements in parental discipline practices mediate such outcomes. Furthermore, as noted, severe disruptions in early caregiving may have specific effects on attentional and impulse control (Kreppner et al., 2001).

With regard to research evidence for the influence of parenting factors on ADHD and associated symptomatology, cross-sectional research utilizing ample statistical controls has demonstrated that, among boys with ADHD age 6 to 12 years, maternal negativity predicts rates of stealing and noncompliance even when the child's negative and noncompliant behavior with the mother is partialled

(Anderson, Hinshaw, & Simmel, 1994), and authoritative parenting beliefs (emphasizing warmth, clear limit setting, and a push toward autonomy) predict social competence for these boys (but not comparison boys), even with control of the child's behavior patterns in the peer group (Hinshaw, Zupan, Simmel, Nigg, & Melnick, 1997). Thus, parenting appears to make an independent contribution to antisocial behavior patterns and peer relationships in boys with ADHD, albeit not to the symptoms of the disorder per se.

Furthermore, longitudinal research demonstrates that parenting style and parenting practices predict the maintenance of ADHD-related symptomatology across the preschool years into middle childhood (Campbell, 2002), even with initial rates of hyperactivity and impulsivity controlled. As for experimental evidence, Hinshaw et al. (2000) examined the effects of self-reported parenting practices on child outcome in the context of a large, randomized clinical trial for children with ADHD that featured the treatments of stimulant medication, intensive behavior therapy, and the combination of the two (MTA Cooperative Group, 1999). The crucial finding was that, as hypothesized, reductions in negative/ineffective discipline practices mediated large increases in teacher-reported social skills and were associated with the full normalization of teacher-reported disruptive behavior across the 14-month period of active intervention. That is, children receiving the multimodal treatment featuring carefully monitored medication plus consistent behavior management training whose parents reported the strongest improvements in their negative/ineffective discipline were those whose school behavior had normalized across the treatment period. Thus, even for a condition as heritable as ADHD, changes in parental discipline style during middle childhood are associated with, and explain statistically, school-based improvements in social skills and disruptive behavior.

Still unknown are the following: At the level of specifically and formally defined attentional and impulse control mechanisms, how do parenting and other forms of socialization interact with child temperament and the within-child mechanisms discussed earlier to shape the development of self-control? Do wider community and systems influences, perhaps even including the extreme societal press for earlier and earlier display of academic excellence and the barrage of media influences via television and computers, propel the enhancement (or, in some cases, the diminution) of attentional mechanisms in the developing child? How salient are sex differences (see Blachman & Hinshaw, 2002; Gaub & Carlson, 1997; A. Moffitt, Caspi, Rutter, & Silva, 2001; Nigg, Blaskey, Huang-Pollock, & Rappley, 2002) and cultural/ethnic differences (Mueller et al., 1995) in this re-

gard? Unfortunately, hardly any sound data exist with regard to these putative triggers and moderator mechanisms. We do note, however, that ADHD is not a phenomenon solely displayed in the United States or even Western nations; its manifestations and impairments appear to be cross-cultural, at least to some extent (Barkley, 2006; Hinshaw & Park, 1999). Sorely needed are ambitious research programs that include genetically informative designs, which can tease apart genetic and environmental (and interactive) influences on the development of attention and impulse control; longitudinal follows-up of children in such investigations; and prevention and intervention studies designed to help address putative risk and causal mechanisms (Hinshaw, 2002a).

Summary

We highlighted that the development of self-control is dynamic within the child: Reactive, executive, and language processes mutually influence one another to enable the regulation of attention, arousal, and impulse control. In turn, the child's capabilities influence the socialization environment and vice versa. Interactive and transactional processes (still poorly understood) are thus likely to be the rule rather than the exception for the development of attention and impulse dysregulation. In all, considerable etiological heterogeneity is likely in the pathways to problematic inattention and impulse control. In other words, it is quite possible for some children to exhibit poor self-control due largely or exclusively to contextual problems; for others to exhibit similar problems due to within-child weaknesses in self-control via reactive, executive, or other intraindividual processes; and for many (if not most) to reveal a complex blending of these causal paths.

HETEROGENEITY AND MULTIPLE DEVELOPMENTAL PATHWAYS

Following our last point, most reviewers of the ADHD literature now explicitly note that multiple causal pathways are highly likely to be involved in the development of the many children identified as having ADHD, exemplifying equifinality and, more often, multifinality in system process (Cicchetti & Rogosch, 1996). Yet, as we consider how to construct even better theories of ADHD for the twenty-first century, one of the most striking limitations in theories of this condition until the past decade was that they often did not formally address the likelihood of such multiple causal pathways, or etiological heterogeneity (Taylor,

1999). Heterogeneity is obvious at the clinical level. Children with impulse control or attention problems vary widely with regard to the associated behavioral and emotional problems they display. Recall, for instance, the high rates of various clinical comorbidities associated with ADHD, with some children exhibiting comorbid anxiety, others antisocial behavior and conduct problems, others learning disabilities, and some showing problems in all such domains.

The importance of heterogeneity is also evident from examining the distributional properties of test scores in mechanism-based studies of clinical samples. The typical overlap of, for example, executive functioning scores between ADHD and control children is on the order of 50% or less (Nigg, Willcutt, Doyle, & Sonuga-Barke, 2005; Swanson et al., 2000). As a result, sensitivity and specificity of cognitive measures to ADHD remains notoriously poor (Fischer, Newby, & Gordon, 1995; Grodzinsky & Barkley, 1999). Although this overlap may indicate variation in two homogeneous populations, the point that half of children with ADHD have normal-range results on any particular cognitive, neural, or physiological measure (including neuroimaging measures) could also suggest that some proportion of children diagnosed with ADHD in terms of the current behaviorally based criteria do not have an internal dysfunction that would be associated with a formally defined disorder (Wakefield, 1992). Such neuropsychological or genetic heterogeneity almost surely exists *within* the present *DSM-IV* subtypes. Thus, based on their findings of neuropsychological weakness in one group and dopamine gene dysfunction in another group, Swanson et al. suggested that one group of children with ADHD has a genetically influenced temperamental disposition, and the other has neuropsychological deficits with a different etiology, perhaps as a function of perinatal neural injury or other genes. Additionally, Nigg, Blaskey, Stawicki, and Sachek (2004) divided children with ADHD into "normal" and "impaired" (defined as worse than the 90th percentile) on a series of executive function tasks. They observed that relatives of the EF-impaired children had weaker neuropsychological performance than relatives of the non-EF-impaired ADHD children. Furthermore, relatives of non-EF-impaired ADHD children performed similarly to relatives of non-ADHD control children. Those data provide some initial support for the validity of a subgroup of children with ADHD who have executive function weaknesses. Biederman et al. (2004) conducted a similar analysis looking at academic impairment and noted that children with ADHD with poor executive functioning had more impairment than other children with ADHD. In line with these types of data,

Sonuga-Barke (2002) suggested that two developmental pathways may be disturbed, one driven by within-child neuropsychological difficulties with executive functioning, the other by a mismatch between temperament and socialization, leading to a resultant breakdown in reward regulation and motivation.

Heterogeneity is also apparent within the ADHD-I type. Recent work suggests the potential importance of differentiating children with sluggish, hypoactive style from those with normal or above-normal activity level (C. Carlson & Mann, 2002; McBurnett et al., 2001). EEG studies have begun to examine individual differences in children with ADHD using cluster analytic and related techniques. At least some concluded that ADHD-C is, in fact, heterogeneous, including a group with a high theta-beta ratio, interpreted as CNS *hypo*arousal, and a smaller group with excess beta activity, interpreted as CNS *hyper*arousal (Chabot & Serfontein, 1996; Clarke, Barry, McCarthy, & Selikowitz, 2001a, 2001b). Again, such evidence suggests strongly that children within a given *DSM-IV* subtype are not etiologically homogeneous.

Aside from the possibility that different causal mechanisms may lead to the same ADHD phenotype—exemplifying equifinality but therefore complicating etiological research as well as the quest for definitions of which children are most appropriately viewed as displaying a true clinical disorder—another multiple-pathway possibility exists. That is, the multiple co-occurring problems in ADHD (e.g., language problems, motor control problems) could reflect multiple causal processes rather than one core process operating *within* each child. For example, Sagvolden and colleagues (2005) suggest that disruption in dopaminergic systems leads to (1) breakdown in basic reward response in one dopamine pathway, the mesolimbic pathway, resulting in impulsivity, and (2) breakdown in a basic motor control pathway, the nigrostriatal pathway, leading to hyperactivity. Beauchaine (2001) advises consideration of motivational plus autonomic systems in concert. As noted earlier, Nigg, Stavro, et al. (2005) reported that executive function weakness was associated with inattention-disorganization, and response speed with hyperactivity-impulsivity.

These types of models are an important step forward in theoretical perspectives. However, they do not explicitly address the questions of when and how during development the particular functional breakdowns may occur, or how they are maintained over time in some cases and improve in other cases. Therefore, a next step in such models is to suggest alternative *developmental* sequences, timing, or influences with respect to multiple pathways. To illustrate, we can again borrow from the dialectic logic described earlier, which draws on the work of Rothbart and colleagues (Rothbart & Ahadi, 1994; Rothbart & Bates, 1998). If we draw out the implications of that model for ADHD and its co-morbid expressions, we can suggest alternative routes with diverse "primary dysfunctions" (see Nigg, Goldsmith, et al., 2004).

For example, considering again Table 9.4 and Figure 9.1, we speculate that ADHD could develop in some children due to a breakdown in early effortful control processes, perhaps related to early abnormalities of neural development or, alternatively, to temperament or temperament-socialization dynamics beginning in the toddler years. Still lacking is specification of the precise types of socialization influences that are crucial—although harsh, emotionally dysregulated, and inconsistent parenting would be a prime suspect. Other children may develop ADHD symptoms as a result of excessive or unusual reactive processes (e.g., strong approach tendencies), perhaps evident as early as infancy but also dependent on breakdowns or at least suboptimal socialization and attunement by caregivers. Some may have very strong inborn traits that overwhelm socialization efforts, whereas others may reflect difficulty adapting to insufficient or unresponsive social contexts. In any case, it is doubtful that all children with ADHD will exhibit, executive function problems, reinforcement-response problems, or any other single neuro-cognitive dysfunction. Rather, such claims will be applicable only to an as yet unspecified subset of children to whom the diagnostic label is currently assigned.

Speculations and even data exist on complex, across-time relationships that may be pertinent to such contentions. For example, G. E. Patterson, diGormo, and Knutson (2001) contend that ADHD is a precursor to antisocial behavior in a pertinent subset of children, consistent with the relative rarity of finding clinical levels of conduct problems and antisocial behavior in children who are not impulsive and hyperactive. Of course, heterogeneity exists in the developmental trajectories leading to antisocial outcomes, in that one route appears to be a lifelong path beginning with temperamental problems, early manifestations of ADHD and verbal processing deficits, and increasingly conflictual family interactions, whereas another, less pathological trajectory begins during adolescence without the same psychopathological precursors in childhood (T. E. Moffitt, 1993). As highlighted earlier, clearly needed are the kinds of research designs that can incorporate the potential for uncovering disparate developmental trajectories, that feature measurement of basic attention and impulse-related processes as well as behavioral indicators of dysfunction, and that pay careful attention to socialization influences as

well. In all, more formal definitions of multiple pathways to ADHD and its subtypes are needed to guide the next generation of etiological research.

FUTURE DIRECTIONS AND CONCLUSIONS

As should be apparent from this review, no single mechanism or perspective will be sufficient to explain the phenomenon of disorders of attention and self-regulation in children. We have highlighted that along with a handful of key cognitive functions (executive control of attention and response suppression, reward response, and state regulation implicating arousal or activation functions), socialization contexts are important mediators of problem development. We have also called for deeper analysis and theorizing of developmental processes (rather than static "dysfunctional mechanisms") in children with these disorders. Finally, we have emphasized the importance of more formal consideration of heterogeneity in empirical and theoretical efforts. Before we conclude, we note several key questions confronting the field at this juncture. Progress in the coming decade may well depend on the answers to these questions. We largely bypass the important domains of continued work on behavioral and molecular genetics, neuroimaging, and pharmacology related to ADHD (see Levy & Hay, 2001; Solanto, Arnsten, & Castellanos, 2001; Swanson & Castellanos, 2002), because those domains are currently well recognized as important in the field. Instead, we highlight issues that may be less well appreciated at present.

First, as we intimated, progress is likely to be limited until more explicit parsing of heterogeneity in neuropsychological, genetic, and other etiological approaches is accomplished. Until then, small effect sizes and inconsistent replication (often using underpowered samples) are likely to sow confusion among scientists and foster continued disputes about ADHD as a disorder. Molecular genetic approaches may be of help here (Swanson et al., 2000), but they will not be sufficient by themselves. Absolutely required are more sophisticated statistical efforts to uncover subgroups related to cognitive profiles in the effort to evaluate whether children with normal versus extreme cognitive dysfunctions (e.g., in executive control of response, arousal, reward response, or related domains) can be reliably and stably distinguished over time. Currently, such children are lumped together in most cross-sectional studies; indeed, the degree to which they can be distinguished post hoc is unexamined. At a more general level, this point underscores the contention that the current subtyping scheme related to

ADHD is highly descriptive and almost certainly quite pre-liminary—a warning against premature reification of the ex-isting construct.

Second, longitudinal investigations of toddlers and preschoolers may be quite productive in better identifying sequences of developmental breakdown of competing inter-nal regulation systems. That is, investigators need to begin their longitudinal studies earlier in life than they typically do (for a parallel argument related to the need for studies of antisocial behavior to begin in infancy or even prenatally, see Tremblay, 2000). For example, do we observe that chil-dren with early effortful control weaknesses are protected from ADHD if they have strong language learning and lan-guage socialization? Is it the case that children with poor reward response are protected in the face of executive function strengths? Or is it generally true that a breakdown in one system is enough to pull a child away from adaptive development? Furthermore, can strong family ties or clear, consistent discipline patterns serve to buffer deficits in these areas?

Third, it is essential that we better clarify the contextual moderators of expression of problems in children with ADHD (Johnston & Mash, 2001). Generally, it is observed that extreme scores on neuropsychological tasks are ob-served in very few well-adapted children but in about half of poorly adjusted children with attention deficits and im-pulsivity. What are the contextual and family correlates of those few poor scores in the well-adjusted children, and of those many normal scores in the poorly adjusted children? More generally, multilevel studies that consider simultane-ously family context and neuropsychological (and/or ge-netic) correlates are sorely needed. Single-level-of-analysis investigations are still typical and can still inform the field, yet the coming decade should witness greater re-liance on investigations that can parse the inherent com-plexity of disorders of attention and impulse control.

Fourth, whereas much research has emphasized the im-portant domain of *mechanisms,* we have insufficient under-standing of *etiology,* especially concerning factors that may influence a whole population (rather than factors that con-tribute to individual differences; Nigg, 2006). Indeed, it is not even clear whether we are currently experiencing a sec-ular trend of increasing child ADHD problems (see Achen-bach, Dumenci, & Rescorla, 2002; Achenbach & Howell, 1993), and more data are needed to clarify matters. If there is such a trend, what accounts for such effects? Potential specific etiologies have not gone far beyond perinatal prob-lems, common teratogens such as smoking and alcohol use, the recognition that increased survival of children born at low birthweight may contribute to a subset of cases (Bres-

lau & Chilcoat, 2000), and the most obvious postnatal toxic exposures (i.e., extensive lead poisoning; Barkley, 2002). Deeper questioning of such etiological risks is warranted. For example, as we speculated earlier, media influences on early neural development remain poorly understood in light of the now intensive exposure of many American young-sters to video and electronic games at very early ages (An-derson & Bushman, 2001). With regard to neurotoxins, low-level ("acceptable") lead exposures are increasingly being questioned and may remain a contributing problem on a larger scale than previously thought (Bernard, 2003; Canfield et al., 2003). As another example, the influence on behavior of other and more pervasive environmental neuro-toxins than lead, notably polychlorinated biphenyls and re-lated compounds that likely affect dopamine systems, is virtually unstudied despite concerning initial findings about the effects of ubiquitous, background-level exposures in both humans (Jacobson & Jacobson, 1996; Korrick, 2001) and animals (Holena, Nafstad, Skaare, & Sagvolden, 1998; Rice, 1999). It is noteworthy that Rice (see also Rice & Hayward, 1997) exposed infant monkeys to low levels of PCBs comparable to background exposures undergone by the average American child. In adolescence, those monkeys had greater impairments in working memory than monkeys receiving no PCB exposure. Thus, more scrutiny of the role of these contaminants in human attention problems is war-ranted. Finally, and perhaps more speculatively, after ini-tial excessive claims about food additives and then sugar were largely disproven (Conners, 1980; Milich, Wolraich, & Lindgren, 1986), more recent suggestions for ubiquitous dietary effects may still warrant investigation (Richardson & Ross, 2000). Animal models as well as human epidemio-logical and experimental studies will be clarifying in all these domains.

Most important, however, is greater attention to the po-tential for gene-by-environment interplay, in which these ecological or environmental risks may have small "main ef-fects" but large effects on segments of the population (i.e., those with a particular genotype; see Rutter & Silberg, 2002 for general overview; see Nigg, 2005 for an overview in relation to ADHD, and Nigg, 2006 for detailed discus-sion in relation to ADHD). Such interplay is now replicated in relation to antisocial behavior (see incisive discussion by Moffitt, 2005). Identification of the relevant environmental triggers for a particular disorder is key to this strategy. For ADHD, those just mentioned here appear worthy of study in conjunction with molecular genetic designs.

Finally, it needs to be acknowledged bluntly that the field has a woefully inadequate understanding of cultural variation in the mechanisms of attention and impulse control problems (Hinshaw & Park, 1999). How universal are the mechanisms cited herein? How is their expression different in different ethnic groups in the United States, as well as in different nations and subcultures? In the United States, for example, there is little work investigating the determinants or expression of ADHD in African American or Latino populations or on developmental processes particular to those groups, despite isolated reports that ethnicity and culture can sharply affect behavioral ratings and other evaluations of children (e.g., Mueller et al., 1995). Furthermore, far more is known about ADHD in boys than in girls (Gaub & Carlson, 1997), despite a growing database on female manifestations of this condition (e.g., Hinshaw, 2002c; Hinshaw et al., 2002; Levy, Hay, Bennet, & McStephen, 2005).

The long-term goal of prevention and amelioration of these disruptive problems in children's development, in a manner that enhances child competence and not merely social control, will depend on cogent answers to these overarching questions. Arguably, the field is well on its way. It is characterized at present by a high degree of optimism related to ongoing insights from molecular genetics and neuroimaging. Those insights will continue to be essential for a complete picture of the phenomenon. Moreover, as we identify neuropsychological problems in a subset of children, the validity of ADHD and its status as a formal disease entity will be greatly enhanced (Barkley, 2002). We expect that the definition of ADHD will continue to evolve and sharpen along the way as well.

Nonetheless, multilevel integration will be vital for the field to reach a more powerful level of understanding. The past decade has seen remarkable developments in the sophistication of mechanism-based theories of ADHD (e.g., Barkley, 1997; Douglas, 1999; Sagvolden et al., 2005; Sergeant et al., 1999). The challenge for the next decade (indeed, decades) is to continue to articulate multipathway models (see Berger & Posner, 2002; Nigg, 2006; Nigg, Goldsmith, et al., 2004; Sagvolden et al., 2005; Sonuga-Barke, 2005) and conceptualizations that integrate multiple levels of analysis, including genetic, neuropsychological, and contextual factors. The latter have scarcely emerged; indeed, such studies are daunting in terms of conceptual complexity as well as methodological difficulty and cost. One partial solution may be to embed experimental substudies into randomly selected (or intentionally enriched) subsamples of large, population-based investigations. Another partial solution is to use molecular genetic designs to examine environmental effects in relation to genotype. In the end, the conceptual challenges, clinical realities, and developmental conundrums posed by children with disorders of impulse and attention make the kinds of multilevel efforts we advocate here extremely worthwhile.

REFERENCES

Achenbach, T. M. (1991). *Manual for the Young Adult Self Report and Young Adult Behavior Checklist.* Burlington: University of Vermont Psychiatry.

Achenbach, T. M., Dumenci, L., & Rescorla, L. A. (2002). Is American student behavior getting worse? Teacher ratings over an 18-year period. *School Psychology Review, 31,* 428–442.

Achenbach, T. M., & Edelbrock, C. S. (1978). The classification of child psychopathology: A review and analysis of empirical efforts. *Psychological Bulletin, 85,* 1275–1301.

Achenbach, T. M., & Edelbrock, C. S. (1983). *Manual for the Child Behavior Profile and Child Behavior Checklist.* Burlington, VT: Author.

Achenbach, T. M., & Howell, C. T. (1993). Are American children's problems getting worse? A 13-year comparison. *Journal of the American Academy of Child and Adolescent Psychiatry, 32,* 1145–1154.

Alexander, G. E., Crutcher, M. D., & DeLong, M. R. (1991). Basal ganglia thalamocortical circuits: Parallel substrates for motor, oculomotor, prefrontal and limbic functions. *Progress in Brain Research, 85,* 119–145.

American Psychiatric Association. (1968). *Diagnostic and statistical manual of mental disorder* (2nd ed.). Washington, DC: Author.

American Psychiatric Association. (1980). *Diagnostic and statistical manual of mental disorders* (3rd ed.). Washington, DC: Author.

American Psychiatric Association. (1987). *Diagnostic and statistical manual of mental disorders* (3rd ed., rev.). Washington, DC: Author.

American Psychiatric Association. (1994). *Diagnostic and statistical manual of mental disorders* (4th ed.). Washington, DC: Author.

American Psychiatric Association. (2000). *Diagnostic and statistical manual of mental disorders* (4th ed., text rev.). Washington, DC: Author.

Anderson, C. A., & Bushman, B. J. (2001). Effects of violent video games on aggressive behavior, aggressive cognition, aggressive affect, physiological arousal, and prosocial behavior: A meta-analytic review of the scientific literature. *Pyschological Science, 12,* 353–359.

Anderson, C. A., Hinshaw, S. P., & Simmel, C. (1994). Mother-child interactions in ADHD and comparison boys: Relationships to overt and covert externalizing behaviors. *Journal of Abnormal Child Psychology, 22,* 247–265.

Angold, A., Costello, E. J., & Erkanli, A. (1999). Comorbidity. *Journal of Child Psychology and Psychiatry, 40,* 57–87.

Aron, A. R., Fletcher, P. C., Bullmore, E. T., Sahakian, B. J., & Robbins, T. W. (2003). Stop signal inhibition disrupted by damage to right inferior frontal gyrus in humans. *Nature Neuroscience, 6,* 115–116.

Asendorpf, J. B. (1990). Development of inhibition during childhood: Evidence for situational specificity and a two-factor model. *Developmental Psychology, 26,* 721–730.

Baddeley, A. D., & Hitch, G. J. (1994). Developments in the concept of working memory. *Neuropsychology, 8,* 485–493.

Baker, L., & Cantwell, D. P. (1992). Attention deficit disorder and speech/language problems. *Comprehensive Mental Health Care, 2,* 3–16.

Band, G. P. H., van der Molen, M. W., & Logan, G. D. (2003). Horse-race model simulations of the stop-signal procedure. *Acta Psychologica, 112,* 105–142.

Barkley, R. A. (1997). Behavioral inhibition, sustained attention, and executive function: Constructing a unified theory of ADHD. *Psychological Bulletin, 121,* 65–94.

Barkley, R. A. (2006). *Attention deficit hyperactivity disorder* (3rd ed.). New York: Guilford Press.

Barkley, R. A. (2002). International consensus statement on ADHD. *Clinical Child and Family Psychology Review, 5,* 89–111.

Barkley, R. A. (2004). Driving impairments in teens and adults with attention-deficit/hyperactivity disorder. *Psychiatric Clinics of North America, 27*(2), 233–260.

Barkley, R. A., & Cunningham, C. (1979). The effects of methylphenidate on the mother-child interactions of hyperactive children. *Archives of General Psychiatry, 36,* 201–208.

Barnett, R., Maruff, P., Vance, A., Luk, E. S. L., Costin, J., Wood, C., et al. (2001). Abnormal executive function in attention deficit hyperactivity disorder: The effect of stimulant medication and age on spatial working memory. *Psychological Medicine, 31,* 1107–1115.

Barry, R. J., Clarke, A. R., & Johnstone, S. J. (2003a). A review of electrophysiology in attention-deficit/hyperactivity disorder: I. Qualitative and quantitative electroencephalography. *Clinical Neurophysiology, 114,* 171–183.

Barry, R. J., Clarke, A. R., & Johnstone, S. J. (2003b). A review of electrophysiology in attention-deficit/hyperactivity disorder: II. Event-related potentials. *Clinical Neurophysiology, 114,* 184–198.

Barsky, A. J., & Borus, J. F. (1995). Somaticization and medicalization in the era of managed care. *Journal of the American Medical Association, 274,* 1931–1934.

Beauchaine, T. P. (2001). Vagal tone, development, and Gray's motivational theory: Toward an integrated model of autonomic nervous system functioning in psychopathology. *Development and Psychopathology, 13,* 183–214.

Beauchaine, T. P., Katkin, E. S., Strassberg, Z., & Snarr, J. (2001). Disinhibitory psychopathology in male adolescents: Discriminating conduct disorder from attention-deficit/hyperactivity disorder through concurrent assessment of multiple autonomic states. *Journal of Abnormal Psychology, 110,* 610–624.

Bedard, A. C., Nichols, S., Barbosa, J. A., Schachar, R., Logan, G. D., & Tannock, R. (2002). The development of selective inhibitory control across the life span. *Developmental Neuropsychology, 21,* 93–111.

Bell, R. Q. (1968). A reinterpretation of the direction of effects in studies of socialization. *Psychological Review, 75,* 81–95.

Benes, F. M. (2001). The development of prefrontal cortex: The maturation of neurotransmitter systems and their interactions. In C. A. Nelson & M. Luciana (Eds.), *Handbook of developmental cognitive neuroscience* (pp. 79–92). Cambridge, MA: MIT Press.

Ben-Pazi, H., Gross-Tsur, V., Bergman, H., & Shalev, R. S. (2003). Abnormal rhythmic motor response in children with attention-deficit-hyperactivity disorder. *Developmental Medicine and Child Neurology, 45,* 743–745.

Berger, A., & Posner, M. I. (2000). Pathologies of brain attentional networks. *Neuroscience and Biobehavioral Reviews, 24,* 3–5.

Berk, L. E. (1986). Relationship of elementary school children's private speech to behavioral accompaniment to task, attention, and task performance. *Developmental Psychology, 22,* 671–680.

Berman, T., Douglas, V., & Barr, R. (1999). Effects of methylphenidate on complex cognitive processing in attention-deficit hyperactivity disorder. *Journal of Abnormal Psychology, 108,* 90–105.

Bernard, S. M. (2003). Should the Centers for Disease Control and Prevention's childhood lead poisoning intervention level be lowered? *American Journal of Public Health, 93,* 1253–1260.

Biederman, J., Hirshfeld-Becker, D. R., Rosenbaum, J. F., Herot, C., Friedman, D., Snidman, N., et al. (2001). Further evidence of association between behavioral inhibition and social anxiety in children. *American Journal of Psychiatry, 158,* 1673–1679.

Biederman, J., Monuteaux, M. C., Doyle, A. E., Seidman, L. J., Wilens, T. E., Ferrero, F., et al. (2004). Impact of executive function deficits and attention-deficit/hyperactivity disorder (ADHD) on academic outcomes in children. *Journal of Consulting and Clinical Psychology, 72,* 757–766.

Biederman, J., & Spencer, T. (1999). Attention-deficit/hyperactivity disorder (ADHD) as a noradrenergic disorder. *Biological Psychiatry, 46,* 1234–1242.

Blachman, D. R., & Hinshaw, S. P. (2002). Patterns of friendship among girls with and without attention-deficit/hyperactivity disorder. *Journal of Abnormal Child Psychology, 30,* 625–640.

Block, J. H., & Block, J. (1980). The role of ego-control and ego-resiliency in the organization of behavior. In W. A. Collins (Ed.), *Minnesota Symposia on Child Psychology: Vol. 13. Development of cognition, affect, and social relations* (pp. 39–100). Hillsdale, NJ: Erlbaum.

Bloom, L., & Tinker, E. (2001). The intentionality model of language acquisition. *Monographs of the Society for Research in Child Development, 66*(4), 1–89.

Borger, N., & van der Meere, J. (2000). Motor control and state regulation in children with ADHD: A cardiac response study. *Biological Psychology, 51,* 247–267.

Botting, N., Powls, A., Cooke, R. W. I., & Marlow, N. (1997). Attention deficit hyperactivity disorders and other psychiatric outcomes in very low birth weight children at 12 years. *Journal of Child Psychology and Psychiatry, 38,* 931–941.

Botvinick, M., Braver, T. S., Barch, D. M., Carter, C. S., & Cohen, J. D. (2001). Conflict monitoring and cognitive control. *Psychological Review, 108,* 624–652.

Bradley, C. (1937). The behavior of children receiving benzedrine. *American Journal of Psychiatry, 94,* 577–585.

Brandeis, D., van Leeuwen, T. H., Rubia, K., Vitacco, D., Steger, J., Pascual-Marqui, R. D., et al. (1998). Neuroelectric mapping reveals precursor of stop failures in children with attention deficits. *Behavioral Brain Research, 94,* 111–125.

Breslau, N., & Chilcoat, H. D. (2000). Psychiatric sequalae of low birthweight at 11 years of age. *Biological Psychiatry, 47,* 1005–1011.

Brown, K. (2003, July 11). New attention to ADHD genes. *Science, 30,* 160–161.

Brown, L. N., & Vickers, J. N. (2004). Temporal judgments, hemispheric equivalence, and interhemispheric transfer in adolescents with attention deficit hyperactivity disorder. *Experimental Brain Research, 154,* 76–84.

Calkins, S. D., & Fox, N. A. (2002). Self-regulatory processes in early personality development: A multilevel approach to the study of childhood social withdrawal and aggression. *Development and Psychopathology, 14,* 477–498.

Campbell, S. B. (2002). *Behavior problems in preschool children* (2nd ed.). New York: Guilford Press.

Canfield, R. L., Gendle, M. H., & Cory-Slechta, D. A. (2004). Impaired neuropsychological functioning in lead exposed children. *Developmental Neuropsychology, 26,* 513–540.

Canfield, R. L., Henderson, D. R., Cory-Slechta, D. A., Cox, C., Jusko, T. A., & Lanphear, B. P. (2003). Intellectual impairment in children with blood lead concentrations below 10 microg per deciliter. *New England Journal of Medicine, 348*(16), 1517–1526.

Carlson, C., & Mann, M. (2002). Sluggish cognitive tempo predicts a different pattern of impairment in the attention deficit hyperactivity disorder, predominantly inattentive type. *Journal of Clinical Child and Adolescent Psychology, 31,* 123–129.

Carlson, E. A., Jacobvitz, D., & Sroufe, L. A. (1995). A developmental investigation of inattentiveness and hyperactivity. *Child Development, 66,* 37–54.

Caron, C., & Rutter, M. (1991). Comorbidity in child psychopathology: Concepts, issues and research strategies. *Journal of Child Psychology and Psychiatry, 32,* 1063–1080.

Carte, E. C., Nigg, J. T., & Hinshaw, S. P. (1996). Neuropsychological functioning, motor speed, and language processing in boys with and without ADHD. *Journal of Abnormal Child Psychology, 24,* 481–498.

Carter, C. S., Krener, P., Chaderjian, M., Northcutt, C., & Wolfe, V. (1995). Abnormal processing of irrelevant information in attention deficit hyperactivity disorder. *Psychiatry Research, 56,* 59–70.

Carver, A. C., Livesey, D. J., & Charles, M. (2001). Further manipulation of the stop-signal task: Developmental changes in the ability to inhibit responding with longer stop-signal delays. *International Journal of Neuroscience, 111,* 39–53.

Casey, B. J., Durston, S., & Fossella, J. A. (2001). Evidence for a mechanistic model of cognitive control. *Clinical Neuroscience Research, 1,* 267–282.

Casey, B. J., Tottenham, N., & Fossella, J. (2002). Clinical, imaging, lesion, and genetic approaches toward a model of cognitive control. *Developmental Psychobiology, 40,* 237–254.

Castellanos, F. X., Lee, P. P., Sharp, W., Jeffries, N. O., Greenstein, D. K., Clasen, L. S., et al. (2002). Developmental trajectories of brain volume abnormalities in children and adolescents with attention-deficit/hyperactivity disorder. *Journal of the American Medical Association, 288*(14), 1740–1748.

Castellanos, F. X., Marvasti, F. F., Ducharme, J. L., Walter, J. M., Israel, M. E., Krain, A., et al. (2000). Executive function oculomotor tasks in girls with ADHD. *Journal of the American Academy of Child and Adolescent Psychiatry, 39,* 644–650.

Castellanos, F. X., & Tannock, R. (2002). Neuroscience of attention-deficit/hyperactivity disorder: The search for endophenotypes. *Nature Reviews Neuroscience, 3,* 617–628.

Cepeda, N. J., Cepeda, M. L., & Kramer, A. F. (2000). Task switching and attention deficit hyperactivity disorder. *Journal of Abnormal Child Psychology, 28,* 213–226.

Chabot, R. J., & Serfontein, G. (1996). Quantitative electroencephalographic profiles of children with attention deficit disorder. *Biological Psychiatry, 40,* 951–963.

Chhabildas, N., Pennington, B. F., & Willcutt, E. G. (2001). A comparison of the neuropsychological profiles of the DSM-IV subtypes of ADHD. *Journal of Abnormal Child Psychology, 29,* 529–540.

Cicchetti, D., & Dawson, G. (2002). Multiple levels of analysis. *Development and Psychopathology, 14,* 417–420.

Cicchetti, D., & Lynch, M. (1995). Failures in the expectable environment and their impact on individual development: The case of child maltreatment. In D. Cicchetti & D. J. Cohen (Eds.), *Developmental psychopathology: Vol. 2. Risk, disorder, and adaptation* (pp. 32–71). New York: Wiley.

Cicchetti, D., & Rogosch, F. A. (1996). Equifinality and multifinality in developmental psychopathology. *Development and Psychopathology, 8,* 597–600.

Clarke, A., Barry, R., McCarthy, R., & Selikowitz, M. (2001a). EEG-defined subtypes of children with attention-deficit/hyperactivity disorder. *Clinical Neurophysiology, 112,* 2098–2105.

Clarke, A., Barry, R., McCarthy, R., & Selikowitz, M. (2001b). Excess beta in children with attention-deficit/hyperactivity disorder: An atypical electrophysiological group. *Psychiatry Research, 103,* 205–218.

Clements, S. D., & Peters, J. E. (1962). Minimal brain dysfunction in the school-age child: Diagnosis and treatment. *Archives of General Psychiatry, 6,* 185–197.

Coles, E. M. (1997). Impulsivity in major mental and personality disorders. In C. D. Webster & M. A. Jackson (Eds.), *Impulsivity: Theory, assessment, and treatment* (pp. 195–211). New York: Guilford Press.

Comings, D. E., Gade-Andavolu, R., Gonzalez, N., Wu, S., Muhleman, D., Blake, H., et al. (2000). Comparison of the role of dopamine, serotonin, and noradrenaline genes in ADHD, ODD and Conduct Disorder: Multivariate regression analysis of 20 genes. *Clinical Genetics, 57,* 178–196.

Conners, C. K. (1980). *Food additives and hyperactive children.* New York: Plenum Press.

Conners, C. K. (1997). *Conners Adult Rating Scales: Technical manual* (Rev.). Toronto: Multi-Health Systems.

Conners, C. K., Epstein, J. N., March, J. S., Angold, A., Wells, K. C., Klaric, J., et al. (2001). Multimodal treatment of ADHD in the MTA: An alternative outcome analysis. *Journal of the American Academy of Child and Adolescent Psychiatry, 40,* 159–167.

Conrad, P. (1992). Medicalization and social control. *Annual Review of Sociology, 18,* 209–232.

Coscina, D. V. (1997). The biopsychology of impulsivity: Focus on brain serotonin. In C. D. Webster & M. A. Jackson (Eds.), *Impulsivity: Theory, assessment, and treatment* (pp. 95–115). New York: Guilford Press.

Dahl, R. E. (1996). The regulation of sleep and arousal: Development and psychopathology. *Development and Psychopathology, 8,* 3–28.

Daugherty, T. K., & Quay, H. C. (1991). Response perseveration and delayed responding in childhood behavior disorders. *Journal of Child Psychology and Psychiatry and Allied Professions, 32,* 453–461.

Dempster, F. N. (1993). Resistence to interference: Developmental changes in a basic processing mechanism. In M. L. Howe & R. Pasnak (Eds.), *Emerging themes in cognitive development: Vol. 1. Foundations* (pp. 3–27). New York: Springer-Verlag.

Depue, R. A., & Collins, P. F. (1999). Neurobiology of the structure of personality: Dopamine, facilitation of incentive motivation, and extraversion. *Behavioral and Brain Sciences, 22,* 491–569.

Depue, R. A., & Lenzenweger, M. F. (2005). A neurobehavioral dimensional model of personality disturbance. In M. F. Lenzenweger & J. F. Clarkin (Eds.), *Major theories of personality disorder, second edition* (pp. 391–453). New York: Guilford Press.

Derryberry, D., & Rothbart, M. K. (1988). Arousal, affect, and attention as components of temperament. *Journal of Personality and Social Psychology, 55,* 958–966.

Derryberry, D., & Rothbart, M. K. (1997). Reactive and effortful processes in the organization of temperament. *Development and Psychopathology, 9,* 633–652.

Derryberry, D., & Tucker, D. M. (1994). Motivating the focus of attention. In P. Niedenthal & S. Kiayama (Eds.), *The heart's eye: Emotional influences on perception and attention* (pp. 167–196). San Diego: Academic Press.

Diamond, A. (2000). Close interrelation of motor development and cognitive development and of the cerebellum and prefrontal cortex. *Child Development, 71,* 44–56.

Diamond, A., Prevor, M. B., Callender, G., & Druin, D. P. (1997). Prefrontal cortex cognitive deficits in children treated early and continuously for PKU. *Monographs of the Society for Research in Child Development, 62*(4), 1–205.

Douglas, V. I. (1972). Stop, look, and listen: The problem of sustained attention and impulse control in hyperactive and normal children. *Canadian Journal of Behavioral Science, 4,* 259–282.

Douglas, V. I. (1988). Cognitive deficits in children with attention deficit disorder with hyperactivity. In L. M. Bloomingdale & J. Sergeant (Eds.), *Attention deficit disorder: Criteria, cognition, intervention* (pp. 65–81). New York: Pergamon Press.

Douglas, V. I. (1999). Cognitive control processes in ADHD. In H. C. Quay & A. E. Hogan (Eds.), *Handbook of disruptive behavior disorders* (pp. 105–138). New York: Kluwer/Plenum Press.

Eaves, L., Rutter, M., Silberg, J. L., Shillady, L., Maes, H., & Pickles, A. (2000). Genetic and environmental causes of covariation in interview assessments of disruptive behavior in child and adolescent twins. *Behavior Genetics, 30,* 321–334.

Eisenberg, N., Guthrie, I. K., Fabes, R. A., Reiser, M., Murphy, B. C., Holgren, R., et al. (1997). The relations of regulation and emotionality to resiliency and competent social functioning in elementary school children. *Child Development, 68,* 295–311.

Engle, R. W. (2001). What is working memory capacity? In H. L. Roediger, J. S. Nairne, I. Neath, & A. M. Suprenant (Eds.), *The nature of remembering: Essays in honor of Robert G. Crowder* (pp. 297–314). Washington, DC: American Psychological Association.

Engle, R. W. (2002). Working memory capacity as executive attention. *Current Directions in Psychological Science, 11*(1), 19–23.

Erikson, C. W., & Hoffman, J. E. (1972). Temporal and spatial characteristics of selective encoding from visual displays. *Perception and Psychophysics, 12,* 201–204.

Eysenck, H. J. (1967). *The biological basis of personality.* Springfield, IL: Charles C. Thomas.

Eysenck, H. J., & Eysenck, M. W. (1985). *Personality and individual differences.* New York: Plenum Press.

Faraone, S. V. (2002). The scientific foundation for understanding attention-deficit/hyperactivity disorder as a valid psychiatric disorder. *European Journal of Child and Adolescent Psychiatry, 14,* 1–10.

Faraone, S. V., Perlis, R. H., Doyle, A. E., Smoller, J. W., Goralnick, J. J., Holmgren, M. A., et al. (2005). Molecular genetics of attention-deficit hyperactivity disorder. *Biological Psychiatry, 57,* 1313–1323.

Fischer, M., Newby, R. F., & Gordon, M. (1995). Who are the false negatives on continuous performance tests? *Journal of Clinical Child Psychology, 24,* 427–433.

Fowles, D. C. (1980). The three-arousal model: Implications of Gray's two-factor learning theory for heart rate, electrodermal activity, and psychopathy. *Psychophysiology, 17,* 84–104.

Friedman, N. P., & Miyake, A. M. (2004). The relations among inhibition and interference control functions: A latent variable analysis. *Journal of Experimental Psychology: General, 133,* 101–135.

Fuster, J. M. (1997). *The prefrontal cortex: Anatomy, physiology and neuropsychology of the frontal lobe* (3rd ed.). New York: Raven.

Garber, J., & Hollon, S. D. (1991). What can specificity designs say about causality in psycyhopathology research? *Psychological Bulletin, 110,* 129–136.

Gaub, M., & Carlson, C. L. (1997). Gender differences in ADHD: A meta-analysis and critical review. *Journal of the American Academy of Child and Adolescent Psychiatry, 36,* 1036–1045.

Geidd, J. N., Blumenthal, J., Molloy, E., & Castellanos, F. X. (2001). Brain imaging of attention deficit/hyperactivity disorder. *Annals of the New York Academy of Sciences, 931,* 33–49.

Goldsmith, H. H., Lemery, K. S., & Essex, M. J. (2004). Roles for temperament in the liability to psychopathology in childhood. In L. DiLalla (Ed.), *Behavior genetic principles: Development, personality, and psychopathology* (pp. 19–39). Washington, DC: American Psychological Association.

Goodyear, P., & Hynd, G. W. (1992). Attention-deficit disorder with (ADD/H) and without (ADD/WO) hyperactivity: Behavioral and neuropsychological differentiation. *Journal of Clinical Child Psychology, 21,* 273–305.

Gordon, M., Antshel, K., Faraone, S., Barkley, R. A., Lewandowsky, L., Hudziak, J., et al. (2005). Symptoms versus impairment: The case for respecting DSM-IV's Criterion D. *The ADHD Report, 13*(4), 1–9.

Gorenstein, E. E., & Newman, J. P. (1980). Disinhibitory psychopathology: A new perspective and a model for research. *Psychological Review, 87,* 301–315.

Gray, J. A. (1971). *The psychobiology of fear and stress.* Cambridge, England: Cambridge University Press.

Gray, J. A. (1982). *The neuropsychology of anxiety: An enquiry into the functions of the septo-hippocampal system.* New York: Oxford University Press.

Gray, J. A. (1991). Neural systems, emotion, and personality. In J. Madden (Ed.), *Neurobiology of learning, emotion, and affect* (pp. 273–306). New York: Raven Press.

Gray, J. A., & McNaughton, N. (1996). The neuropsychology of anxiety: Reprise. In R. Zinbarg, R. J. McNally, D. H. Barlow, B. F. Chorpita, & J. Turovsky (Eds.), *Nebraska Symposium on Motivation: Vol. 43. Perspectives on anxiety, panic, and fear* (pp. 61–134). Lincoln: University of Nebraska Press.

Greenberg, M. T., Kusche, C. A., & Speltz, M. (1991). Emotional regulation, self-control, and psychopathology: The role of relationships in early childhood. In D. Cicchetti & S. L. Toth (Eds.), *Rochester Symposium on Development and Psychopathology: Vol. 2. Internalizing and externalizing expressions of dysfunction* (pp. v, 312). Hillsdale, NJ: Erlbaum.

Greenberg, M. T., Speltz, M. L., DeKlyne, M., & Jones, K. (2001). Correlates of clinic referral for early conduct problems: Variable- and person-oriented approaches. *Development and Psychopathology, 13,* 255–276.

Grodzinsky, G. M., & Barkley, R. A. (1999). Predictive power of frontal lobe tests in the diagnosis of attention-deficit hyperactivity disorder. *Clinical Neuropsychologist, 13,* 12–21.

Haenlein, M., & Caul, W. F. (1987). Attention deficit disorder with hyperactivity: A specific hypothesis of reward dysfunction. *Journal of the American Academy of Child and Adolescent Psychiatry, 26,* 356–362.

Hart, E. L., Lahey, B. B., Loeber, R., Applegate, B., & Frick, P. J. (1995). Developmental changes in attention-deficit hyperactivity disorder in boys: A four year longitudinal study. *Journal of Abnormal Child Psychology, 23,* 729–750.

Hasher, L., & Zacks, R. T. (1988). Working memory, comprehension, and aging: A review and a new view. *Psychology of Learning and Motivation, 22,* 193–225.

Hay, D. A., Bennett, K. S., McStephen, M., Rooney, R., & Levy, F. (2004). Attention deficit-hyperactivity disorder in twins: A developmental genetic analysis. *Australian Journal of Psychology, 56,* 99–107.

Hiatt, K. D., Schmitt, W. A., & Newman, J. P. (2004). Stroop tasks reveal abnormal selective attention among psychopathic offenders. *Neuropsychology, 18,* 50–59.

Hinshaw, S. P. (1987). On the distinction between attentional deficits/hyperactivity and conduct problems/aggression in child psychopathology. *Psychological Bulletin, 101,* 443–463.

Hinshaw, S. P. (1994). *Attention deficits and hyperactivity in children.* Thousand Oaks, CA: Sage.

Hinshaw, S. P. (1999). Psychosocial intervention for childhood ADHD: Etiologic and developmental themes, comorbidity, and integration with pharmacotherapy. In D. Cicchetti & S. L. Toth (Eds.), *Rochester Symposium on Developmental Psychopathology: Vol. 9. Developmental approaches to prevention and intervention* (pp. 221–270). Rochester, NY: University of Rochester Press.

Hinshaw, S. P. (2001). Is the inattentive type of ADHD a separate disorder? *Clinical Psychology: Science and Practice, 8,* 498–501.

Hinshaw, S. P. (2002a). Intervention research, theoretical mechanisms, and causal processes related to externalizing behavior patterns. *Development and Psychopathology, 14,* 789–818.

Hinshaw, S. P. (2002b). Is ADHD an impairing condition in childhood and adolescence? In P. S. Jensen & J. R. Cooper (Eds.), *Attention-deficit hyperactivity disorder: State of the science, best practices* (pp. 5.1 to 5.21). Kingston, NJ: Civic Research Institute.

Hinshaw, S. P. (2002c). Preadolescent girls with attention-deficit/hyperactivity disorder: I. Background characteristics, comorbidity, cognitive and social functioning, and parenting practices. *Journal of Consulting and Clinical Psychology, 70,* 1086–1098.

Hinshaw, S. P., Carte, E. T., Sami, N., Treuting, J. J., & Zupan, B. A. (2002). Preadolescent girls with attention-deficit/hyperactivity disorder: II. Neuropsychological performance in relation to subtypes and individual classification. *Journal of Consulting and Clinical Psychology, 70,* 1099–1111.

Hinshaw, S. P., & Lee, S. S. (2003). Oppositional defiant and conduct disorder. In E. J. Mash & R. A. Barkley (Eds.), *Child psychopathology* (2nd ed., pp. 144–198). New York: Guilford Press.

Hinshaw, S. P., Owens, E. B., Wells, K. C., Kraemer, H. C., Abikoff, H. B., Arnold, L. E., et al. (2000). Family processes and treatment outcome in the MTA: Negative/ineffective parenting practices in relation to multimodal treatment. *Journal of Abnormal Child Psychology, 28,* 555–568.

Hinshaw, S. P., & Park, T. (1999). Research issues and problems: Toward a more definitive science of disruptive behavior disorders. In H. C. Quay & A. E. Hogan (Eds.), *Handbook of disruptive behavior disorders* (pp. 593–620). New York: Plenum Press.

Hinshaw, S. P., Zupan, B. A., Simmel, C., Nigg, J. T., & Melnick, S. M. (1997). Peer status in boys with and without attention-deficit hyperactivity disorder: Predictions from overt and covert antisocial behavior, social isolation, and authoritative parenting beliefs. *Child Development, 64,* 880–896.

Holena, E., Nafstad, I., Skaare, J. U., & Sagvolden, T. (1998). Behavioral hyperactivity in rats following postnatal exposure to sub-toxic doses of polychlorinated biphenyl cogeners 153 and 126. *Behavioral Brain Research, 94,* 213–224.

Hollich, G. J., Hirsh-Pasek, K., & Golinkoff, R. M. (2000). Breaking the language barrier: An emergenist coalition model for the origins of word learning. *Monographs of the Society for Research in Child Development, 65*(3), 1–135.

Hollingsworth, D. E., McAuliffe, S. P., & Knowlton, B. J. (2001). Temporal allocation of visual attention in adult attention deficit hyperactivity disorder. *Journal of Cognitive Neuroscience, 13,* 298–305.

Homack, S., & Riccio, C. A. (2004). A meta-analysis of the sensitivity and specificity of the Stroop Color and Word Test with children. *Archives of Clinical Neuropsychology, 19,* 725–743.

Houghton, S., Douglas, G., West, J., Whiting, K., Wall, M., Langsford, S., et al. (1999). Differential patterns of executive function in children with attention-deficit hyperactivity disorder according to gender and subtype. *Journal of Child Neurology, 14,* 801–805.

Huang-Pollock, C. L., Carr, T. H., & Nigg, J. T. (2002). Development of selective attention: Perceptual load influences early versus late attentional selection in children and adults. *Developmental Psychology, 38,* 363–375.

Huang-Pollock, C. L., & Nigg, J. T. (2003). Searching for the attention deficit in attention deficit hyperactivity disorder: The case of visuospatial orienting. *Clinical Psychology Review, 23,* 801–830.

Huang-Pollock, C. L., Nigg, J. T., & Carr, T. H. (2005). Selective attention in ADHD using a perceptual load paradigm. *Journal of Child Psychology and Psychiatry.*

Hucker, S. J. (1997). Impulsivity in DSM-IV impulse-control disorders. In C. D. Webster & M. A. Jackson (Eds.), *Impulsivity: Theory, assessment, and treatment* (pp. 212–232). New York: Guilford Press.

Hughes, C., White, A., Sharpen, J., & Dunn, J. (2000). Antisocial, angry, and unsympathetic: "Hard to manage" preschoolers' peer problems and possible cognitive influences. *Journal of Child Psychology and Psychiatry, 41,* 169–179.

Huttenlocher, P. R. (2002). *Neural plasticity: The effects of environment on the development of the cerebral cortex.* Cambridge, MA: Harvard University Press.

Iaboni, F., Douglas, V. I., & Baker, A. G. (1995). Effects of reward and response costs on inhibition in ADHD children. *Journal of Abnormal Psychology, 104,* 232–240.

Iaboni, F., Douglas, V. I., & Ditto, B. (1997). Psychophysiological response of ADHD children to reward and extinction. *Psychophysiology, 34,* 116–123.

Ito, S., Stuphorn, V., Brown, J. W., & Schall, J. D. (2003). Performance monitoring by the anterior cingulated cortex during saccade countermanding. *Science, 302*(3), 120–122.

Jacobson, J. L., & Jacobson, S. W. (1996). Intellectual impairment in children exposed to polychlorinated biphenyls in utero. *New England Journal of Medicine, 335,* 783–789.

Jacobvitz, D., Hazen, N., Curran, M., & Hitchens, K. (2004). Observations of early triadic family interactions: Boundary disturbances in the family predict symptoms of depression, anxiety, and attention-deficit/hyperactivity disorder in middle childhood. *Development and Psychopathology, 16,* 577–592.

Jacobvitz, D., & Sroufe, L. A. (1989). The early caregiver-child relationship and attention deficit disorder with hyperactivity: A prospective study. *Child Development, 58,* 1496–1504.

Jacobvitz, D., Sroufe, L. A., Stewart, M., & Leffert, N. (1990). Treatment of attentional and hyperactive problems in children with sympathomimetic drugs: A follow up review. *Journal of the American Academy of Child and Adolescent Psychiatry, 29,* 677–688.

Jensen, P. S., Hinshaw, S. P., Kraemer, H. C., Lenora, N., Newcorn, J. H., Abikoff, H. B., et al. (2001). ADHD comorbidity findings from the MTA study: Comparing comorbid subgroups. *Journal of the American Academy of Child and Adolescent Psychiatry, 40,* 147–158.

Jensen, P. S., Martin, D., & Cantwell, D. (1997). Comorbidity in ADHD: Implications for research, practice, and DSM-IV. *Journal of the American Academy of Child and Adolescent Psychiatry, 36,* 1065–1079.

Jester, J. M., Nigg, J. T., Adams, K., Fitzgerald, H. E., Puttler, L. I., Wong, M. M., et al. (in press). Inattention/hyperactivity and aggression from early childhood to adolescence: Heterogeneity of trajectories and differential influence of family environment characteristics. *Development and Psychopathology.*

Johansen, E. B., Aase, H., Meyer, A., & Sagvolden, T. (2002). Attention deficit/hyperactivity disorder behavior explained by dysfunctional reinforcement and extinction processes. *Behavioral Brain Research, 130,* 37–45.

Johnston, C. (2002). Impact of attention deficit hyperactivity disorder on social and vocational functioning in adults. In P. S. Jensen & J. R. Cooper (Eds.), *Attention deficit hyperactivity disorder: Sate of the science, best practices* (pp. 6-1–6-21). Kingston, NJ: Civic Research Institute.

Johnston, C., & Mash, E. J. (2001). Families of children with attention-deficit/hyperactivity disorder: Review and recommendations for future research. *Clinical Child and Family Psychology Review, 4*(3), 183–207.

Jonkman, L., Kemmer, C., Verbaten, M., van Engeland, H., Kenemans, J., Camfferman, G., et al. (1999). Perceptual and response interference in children with attention-deficit hyperactivity disorder and the effects of methylphenidate. *Psychophysiology, 36,* 419–429.

Kagan, J. (1997). Temperament and the reactions to the unfamiliar. *Child Development, 68,* 139–143.

Kagan, J. (2003). Behavioral inhibition as a temperamental category. In R. J. Davidson, K. R. Scherer, & H. H. Goldsmith (Eds.), *Handbook of affective sciences* (pp. 320–331). New York: Oxford University Press.

Kagan, J., Reznick, J. S., & Snidman, N. (1987). The physiology and psychology of behavioral inhibition in children. *Child Development, 58,* 1459–1473.

Kagan, J., & Snidman, N. (2004). *The long shadow of temperament.* Cambridge, MA: Harvard University Press.

Kagan, J., Snidman, N., Zentner, M., & Peterson, E. (1999). Infant temperament and anxious symptoms in school age children. *Development and Psychopathology, 11,* 209–224.

Kahneman, D., & Henik, A. (1981). Perceptual organization and attention. In K. Kubovy & J. R. Pomerantz (Eds.), *Perceptual organization* (pp. 181–211). Hillsdale, NJ: Erlbaum.

Kane, M. J., & Engle, R. W. (2002). The role of prefrontal cortex in working memory capacity, executive attention, and general fluid intelligence: An individual differences perspective. *Psychonomic Bulletin & Review, 9,* 637–671.

Karatekin, C., & Asarnow, R. F. (1998). Working memory in childhood-onset Schizophrenia and attention-deficit/hyperactivity disorder. *Psychiatry Research, 80,* 165–176.

Kimberg, D. Y., & Farah, M. J. (1998). Is there an inhibitory module in the prefrontal cortex? Working memory and the mechanisms underlying cognitive control. In S. Monsell & J. Driver (Eds.), *Control of cognitive processes: Attention and performance* (Vol. 18, pp. 740–751). Cambridge, MA: MIT Press.

Kirley, A., Hawi, Z., Daly, G., McCarron, M., Mullins, C., Millar, N., et al. (2002). Dopaminergic system genes in ADHD: Toward a biological hypothesis. *Neuropsychopharmacology, 27,* 607–619.

Klorman, R., Hazel-Fernandez, L. A., Shaywitz, S. E., Fletcher, J. M., Marchione, K. E., Holahan, J. M., et al. (1999). Executive functioning deficits in attention-deficit/hyperactivity disorder are independent of oppositional defiant or reading disorder. *Journal of the American Academy of Child and Adolescent Psychiatry, 38,* 1148–1155.

Kochanska, G., Murray, K., & Coy, K. C. (1997). Inhibitory control as a contributor to conscience in childhood: From toddler to early school age. *Child Development, 68,* 263–277.

Kochanska, G., Murray, K., & Harlan, E. T. (2000). Effortful control in early childhood: Continuity and change, antecedents, and implications for social development. *Developmental Psychology, 36,* 220–232.

Koger, S. M., Schettler, T., & Weiss, B. (2005). Environmental toxicants and developmental disabilities. *American Psychologist, 60,* 243–255.

Konrad, K., Gauggel, S., Manz, A., & Scholl, M. (2000). Lack of inhibition: A motivational deficit in children with attention deficit/hyperactivity disorder and children with traumatic brain injury. *Child Neuropsychology, 6,* 286–296.

Kopp, C. B. (1982). Antecedents of self-regulation: A developmental perspective. *Developmental Psychology, 18,* 199–214.

Korrick, S. A. (2001). Polychlorinated biphenyls (PCBs) and neurodevelopment in general population studies. In L. W. Robertson & L. G. Hansen (Eds.), *PCBs: Recent advances in environmental toxicology and health effects* (pp. 143–154). Lexington: University Press of Kentucky.

Koschack, J., Kunert, H. J., Derichs, G., Weniger, G., & Irle, E. (2003). Impaired and enhanced attentional function in children with attention deficit/hyperactivity disorder. *Psychological Medicine, 33,* 481–489.

Kreppner, J. M., O'Connor, T. G., Rutter, M., Beckett, C., Castle, J., Croft, C., et al. (2001). Can inattention/overactivity be an institutional deprivation syndrome? *Journal of Abnormal Child Psychology, 29,* 513–528.

Lachman, R., Lachman, J. L., & Butterfield, E. C. (1979). *Cognitive psychology and information processing: An introduction.* Hillsdale, NJ: Erlbaum.

Lahey, B. B. (2001). Should the combined and predominantly inattentive types of ADHD be considered distinct and unrelated disorders? Not now, at least. *Clinical Psychology: Science and Practice, 8,* 494–497.

Lahey, B. B., Pelham, W. E., Loney, J., Lee, S. S., & Willcutt, E. (in press). Instability of the DSM-IV subtypes of ADHD from preschool through elementary school. *Archives of General Psychiatry.*

Lahey, B. B., Pelham, W. E., Stein, M. A., Loney, J., Trapani, C., Nugent, K., et al. (1998). Validity of DSM-IV attention-deficit/hyperactivity disorder for younger children. *Journal of the American Academy of Child and Adolescent Psychiatry, 37,* 695–702.

Lahey, B. B., & Willcutt, E. G. (2002). Validity of the diagnosis and dimensions of attention deficit hyperactivity disorder. In P. S. Jensen & J. R. Cooper (Eds.), *Attention deficit hyperactivity disorder: Sate of the science, best practices* (pp. 1-1–1-23). Kingston, NJ: Civic Research Institute.

Laufer, M. W., & Denhoff, E. (1957). Hyperkinetic behavior syndrome in children. *Journal of Pediatrics, 50,* 463–473.

Lavie, N. (1995). Perceptual load as a necessary condition for selective attention. *Journal of Experimental Psychology, 21,* 451–468.

Leth-Steensen, C., Elbaz, Z., & Douglas, V. (2000). Mean response times, variability, and skew in the responding of ADHD children: A response time distributional approach. *Acta Psychologica, 104,* 167–190.

Levy, F., & Hay, D. A. (2001). *Attention, genes, and ADHD.* Philadelphia: Brunner-Routledge.

Levy, F., Hay, D. A., Bennett, K. S., & McStephen, M. (2005). Gender differences in ADHD subtype comorbidity. *Journal of the American Academy of Child and Adolescent Psychiatry, 44,* 368–376.

Levy, F., Hay, D. A., McStephen, M., Wood, C., & Waldman, I. I. (1997). Attention-deficit hyperactivity disorder: A category or a continuum? Genetic analysis of a large-scale twin study. *Journal of the American Academy of Child and Adolescent Psychiatry, 36,* 737–744.

Levy, F., McStephen, M., & Hay, D. A. (2001). The diagnostic genetics of ADHD symptoms and subtypes. In F. Levy & D. A. Hay (Eds.), *Attention, genes, and ADHD* (pp. 35–57). Philadelphia: Taylor & Francis.

Logan, G. D. (1994). A user's guide to the stop signal paradigm. In D. Dagenbach & T. Carr (Eds.), *Inhibition in language, memory, and attention* (pp. 189–239). San Diego: Academic Press.

Logan, G. D., & Cowan, W. B. (1984). On the ability to inhibit thought and action: A theory of an act of control. *Psychological Review, 91,* 295–327.

Losier, B. J., McGrath, P. J., & Klein, R. M. (1996). Error patterns on the continuous performance test in non-medicated and medicated samples of children with and without ADHD: A meta-analytic review. *Journal of Child Psychology and Psychiatry, 37,* 971–988.

Luman, M., Oosterlaan, J., & Sergeant, J. A. (2005). The impact of reinforcement contingencies on AD/HD: A review and theoretical appraisal. *Clinical Psychology Review, 25,* 183–213.

Lynam, D. R. (1998). Early identification of the fledgling psychopath: Locating the psychopathic child in the current nomenclature. *Journal of Abnormal Psychology, 107,* 566–575.

Lyon, G. R., & Krasnegor, N. A. (1996). *Attention, memory and executive function.* Baltimore: Paul H. Brookes.

MacCoon, D. G., Wallace, J. F., & Newman, J. P. (2004). Self-regulation: Context-appropriate balanced attention. In K. D. Vohs & R. F. Baumeister (Eds.), *Handbook of self-regulation: Research, theory, and applications* (pp. 422–444). New York: Guilford Press.

MacLeod, C. M. (1991). Fifty years of the Stroop effect: An integrative review and reinterpretation of effects. *Psychological Bulletin, 114,* 376–390.

Mannuzza, S., & Klein, R. G. (2000). Long-term prognosis in attention-deficit/hyperactivity disorder. *Child and Adolescent Psychiatric Clinics of North America, 9,* 711–726.

Martel, M., & Nigg, J. T. (2005). *Temperamental regulation, control, and resiliency in relation to ADHD symptoms in children.* Manuscript under review.

Martinussen, R., Hayden, J., Hogg-Johnson, S., & Tannock, R. (in press). A meta-analysis of working memory impairments in children with attention deficit hyperactivity disorder. *Journal of the American Academy of Child and Adolescent Psychiatry.*

McBurnett, K., Pfiffner, L. J., & Frick, P. J. (2001). Symptom properties as a function of ADHD type: An argument for the continued study of sluggish cognitive tempo. *Journal of Abnormal Child Psychology, 29,* 207–213.

McCracken, J. T. (1991). A two-part model of stimulant action on attention-deficit hyperactivity disorder in children. *Journal of Neuropsychiatry and Clinical Neurosciences, 3,* 201–209.

McInerney, R. J., & Kerns, K. A. (2003). Time reproduction in children with ADHD: Motivation matters. *Child Neuropsychology, 9,* 91–108.

McInness, A., Humphries, T., Hogg-Johnson, S., & Tannock, R. (2003). Listening comprehension and working memory are impaired in attention-deficit hyperactivity disorder irrespective of language impairments. *Journal of Abnormal Child Psychology, 31,* 427–444.

McIntyre, C., Blackwell, S., & Denton, C. (1978). Effect of noise distractibility on the spans of apprehension of hyperactive boys. *Journal of Abnormal Psychology, 6,* 483–492.

Menzies, R. (1997). A sociological perspective on impulsivity: Some cautionary comments on the genesis of a clinical construct. In C. D. Webster & M. A. Jackson (Eds.), *Impulsivity: Theory, assessment, and treatment* (pp. 42–62). New York: Guilford Press.

Metcalfe, J., & Mischel, W. (1999). A hot/cool-system analysis of delay of gratification: Dynamics of willpower. *Psychological Review, 106,* 3–19.

Middleton, F. A., & Strick, P. L. (2001). Cerebellar projections to the prefrontal cortex of the primate. *Journal of Neuroscience, 2,* 700–712.

Middleton, F. A., & Strick, P. L. (2002). Basal-ganglia "projections" to the prefrontal cortex of the primate. *Cerebral Cortex, 9,* 926–935.

Milich, R., Balentine, A., & Lynam, D. (2001). ADHD combined type and ADHD predominantly inattentive type are distinct and unrelated disorders. *Clinical Psychology Science and Practice, 8,* 463–488.

Milich, R., Hartung, C. M., Martin, C. A., & Haigler, E. D. (1994). Behavioral disinhibition and underlying processes in adolescents with disruptive behavior disorders. In D. K. Routh (Ed.), *Disruptive behavior disorders in childhood* (pp. 109–138). New York: Plenum Press.

Milich, R., Wolraich, M., & Lindgren, S. (1986). Sugar and hyperactivity: A critical review of empirical findings. *Clinical Psychology Review, 6,* 493–513.

Miller, M. B., Chapman, J. P., Chapman, L. J., & Collins, J. (1995). Task difficulty and cognitive deficits in Schizophrenia. *Journal of Abnormal Psychology, 104,* 251–258.

Miller, T., Nigg, J. T., & Stavro, G. (April, 2005). *Axis I and Axis II comorbidity in ADHD in adolescence and early adulthood.* Paper presented at the annual meeting of the Society for Research in Child Development, Atlanta, GA.

Mirsky, A. F., & Duncan, C. C. (2001). A nosology of disorders of attention. *Annals of the New York Academy of Sciences, 931,* 17–32.

Miyake, A. F., Friedman, N. P., Emerson, M. J., Witzki, A. H., & Howerter, A. (2000). The unity and diversity of executive functions and their contributions to complex "frontal lobe" tasks: A latent variable analysis. *Cognitive Psychology, 41,* 49–100.

Miyake, A., Friedman, N. P., Rettinger, D. A., Shah, P., & Hegarty, M. (2001). How are visuospatial working memory, executive functioning, and spatial abilities related? A latent-variable analysis. *Journal of Experimental Psychology: General, 130,* 621–640.

Moffitt, A., Caspi, M., Rutter, M., & Silva, P. (2001). *Sex differences in antisocial behaviour.* Cambridge, England: Cambridge University Press.

Moffitt, T. E. (1993). Adolescence-limited and life-course-persistent antisocial behavior: A developmental taxonomy. *Psychological Review, 100,* 674–701.

Moffiit, T. E. (2005). The new look of behavioral genetics in developmental psychopathology: Gene-environment interplay in antisocial behaviors. *Psychological Bulletin, 131,* 533–554.

Monastra, V. J., Lubar, J. F., Linden, M., VanDeusen, P., Green, G., Wing, W., et al. (1999). Assessing attention deficit hyperactivity disorder via qauntitative electroencephalography: An initial validation study. *Neuropsychology, 13,* 424–433.

Monsell, S., & Driver, J. (1998). Banishing the control homunculus. In S. Monsell & J. Driver (Eds.), *Control of cognitive processes: Attention and performance* (Vol. 18, pp. 4–32). Cambridge, MA: MIT Press.

MTA Cooperative Group. (1999). Moderators and mediators of treatment response for children with ADHD: The MTA study. *Archives of General Psychiatry, 56,* 1088–1096.

Mueller, C. W., Mann, E. M., Thanapum, S., Humris, E., Ikeda, Y., Takahashi, A., et al. (1995). Teachers' ratings of disruptive behavior in five countries. *Journal of Clinical Child Psychology, 24,* 434–442.

Murphy, K., Barkley, R. A., & Bush, T. (2001). Executive functions in young adults with attention deficit hyperactivity disorder. *Neuropsychology, 15,* 211–220.

Murray, K. T., & Kochanska, G. (2002). Effortful control: Factor structure and relation to externalizing and internalizing behaviors. *Journal of Abnormal Child Psychology, 30,* 503–514.

Neuman, R. J., Todd, R. D., Heath, A. C., Reich, W., Hudziak, J. J., Bucholz, K. K., et al. (1999). Evaluation of ADHD typology in three contrasting samples: A latent class approach. *Journal of the American Academy of Child and Adolescent Psychiatry, 38,* 25–33.

Newman, J. P., & Wallace, J. F. (1993). Diverse pathways to deficient self-regulation: Implications for disinhibitory psychopathology in children. *Clinical Psychology Review, 13,* 690–720.

Nigg, J. T. (1999). The ADHD response inhibition deficit as measured by the stop task: Replication with DSM-IV combined type, extension, and qualification. *Journal of Abnormal Child Psychology, 27,* 391–400.

Nigg, J. T. (2000). On inhibition/disinhibition in developmental psychopathology: Views from cognitive and personality psychology and a working inhibition taxonomy. *Psychological Bulletin, 126,* 200–246.

Nigg, J. T. (2001). Is ADHD an inhibitory disorder? *Psychological Bulletin, 127,* 571–598.

Nigg, J. T. (2003). Response inhibition and disruptive behaviors: Toward a multi-process conception of etiological heterogeneity for ADHD combined type and conduct disorder early onset type. In J. King, C. A. Ferris, & I. I. Lederhendler (Eds.), *Annals of the New York Academy of Sciences: Vol. 1008. Roots of mental illness in children* (pp. 170–182). New York: New York Academy of Sciences.

Nigg, J. T. (2005). What role do environmental contaminants play in the etiology of ADHD? *The ADHD Report, 13*(2), 6–7, 12–16.

Nigg, J. T. (2006). *ADHD: What science can tell us about causes and mechanisms.* New York: Guilford Press.

Nigg, J. T., Blaskey, L. B., Huang-Pollock, C., & John, O. P. (2002). ADHD and personality traits: Is ADHD an extreme personality trait? *ADHD Report, 10*(1), 6–11.

Nigg, J. T., Blaskey, L. B., Huang-Pollock, C., & Rappley, M. D. (2002). Neuropsychological executive functions and ADHD DSM-IV subtypes. *Journal of the American Academy of Child and Adolescent Psychiatry, 41,* 59–66.

Nigg, J. T., Blaskey, L. B., Stawicki, J., & Sachek, J. (2004). Evaluating the endophenotype model of ADHD neuropsychological deficit: Results for parents and siblings of children with DSM-IV ADHD combined and inattentive subtypes. *Journal of Abnormal Psychology, 113,* 614–625.

Nigg, J. T., Butler, K. M., Huang-Pollock, C. L., & Henderson, J. M. (2002). Inhibitory processes in adults with persistent childhood onset ADHD. *Journal of Consulting and Clinical Psychology, 70,* 153–157.

Nigg, J. T., & Casey, B. J. (in press). An integrative theory of attention-deficit/hyperactivity disorder based on the cognitive and affective neurosciences. *Development and Psychopathology.*

Nigg, J. T., Goldsmith, H. H., & Sachek, J. (2004). Temperament and attention-deficit/hyperactivity disorder: The development of a multiple pathway model. *Journal of Clinical Child and Adolescent Psychology, 33,* 42–53.

Nigg, J. T., Hinshaw, S. P., Carte, E. T., & Treuting, J. (1998). Neuropsychological correlates of antisocial behavior and comorbid disruptive behavior disorders in children with ADHD. *Journal of Abnormal Psychology, 107,* 468–480.

Nigg, J. T., & Huang-Pollock, C. L. (2003). An early onset model of the role of executive functions and intelligence in conduct disorder/delinquency. In B. B. Lahey, T. Moffitt, & A. Caspi (Eds.), *The causes of conduct disorder and serious juvenile delinquency* (pp. 227–253). New York: Guilford Press.

Nigg, J. T., John, O. J., Blaskey, L., Huang-Pollock, C., Willcutt, E., Hinshaw, S. H., et al. (2002). Big Five dimensions and ADHD symptoms: Links between personality traits and clinical symptoms. *Journal of Personality and Social Psychology, 83,* 451–469.

Nigg, J. T., Stavro, G., Ettenhofer, M., Hambrick, D., Miller, T., & Henderson, J. M. (2005). Executive functions and ADHD in adults: Evidence for selective effects on ADHD symptom domains. *Journal of Abnormal Psychology, 114.*

Nigg, J. T., Swanson, J., & Hinshaw, S. P. (1997). Covert visual attention in boys with attention deficit hyperactivity disorder: Lateral effects, methylphenidate response, and results for parents. *Neuropsychologia, 35,* 165–176.

Nigg, J. T., Willcutt, E., Doyle, A. E., & Sonuga-Barke, J. S. (2005). Causal heterogeneity in ADHD: Do we need a neuropsychologically impaired subtype? *Biological Psychiatry, 57,* 1224–1230.

Norman, D. A., & Shallice, T. (1986). Attention to action: Willed and automatic control of behavior. In R. J. Davidson, G. E. Schwartz, & D. Shapiro (Eds.), *Consciousness and self regulation* (pp. 1–18). New York: Plenum Press.

O'Brian, B. S., & Frick, P. J. (1996). Reward dominance: Associations with anxiety, conduct problems, and psychopathology in children. *Journal of Abnormal Child Psychology, 24,* 223–240.

O'Brian, B. S., Frick, P. J., & Lyman, R. D. (1994). Reward dominance among children with disruptive behavior disorders. *Journal of Psychopathology and Behavioral Assessment, 16,* 131–145.

O'Connell, R. G., Bellgrove, M. A., Dockree, P. M., & Robertson, I. H. (2004). Reduced electrodermal response to errors predicts poor sustained attention performance in attention deficit hyperactivity disorder. *NeuroReport, 15,* 2535–2538.

Olson, S. (2002). Developmental perspectives. In S. Sandberg (Ed.), *Hyperactivity and attention disorders of childhood* (2nd ed., pp. 242–289). Cambridge, England: Cambridge University Press.

Oosterlaan, J., Logan, G. D., & Sergeant, J. A. (1998). Response inhibition in AD/HD, CD, comorbid AD/HD+CD, anxious, and control children: A meta-analysis of studies with the stop task. *Journal of Child Psychology and Psychiatry, 39,* 411–425.

Oosterlaan, J., & Sergeant, J. A. (1998a). Effects of reward and response cost on response inhibition in AD/HD, disruptive, anxious, and normal children. *Journal of Abnormal Child Psychology, 26,* 161–174.

Oosterlaan, J., & Sergeant, J. A. (1998b). Response inhibition and response re-engagement in attention-deficit/hyperactivity disorder, disruptive, anxious and normal children. *Behavioral Brain Research, 94,* 33–43.

Parasuraman, R., Warm, J. S., & See, J. E. (1998). Brain systems of vigilance. In R. Parasuraman (Ed.), *The attentive brain* (pp. 221–256). Cambridge, MA: MIT Press.

Park, L., Nigg, J. T., Waldman, I., Nummy, K. A., Huang-Pollock, C., Rappley, M., et al. (2005). Association and linkage of a-2A adrenergic receptor gene polymorphisms with childhood ADHD. *Molecular Psychiatry, 10,* 572–580.

Parker, J. D. A., & Bagby, R. M. (1997). Impulsivity in adults: A critical review of measurement approaches. In C. D. Webster & M. A. Jackson (Eds.), *Impulsivity: Theory, assessment, and treatment* (pp. 142–157). New York: Guilford Press.

Pashler, H. (1998). Task switching and multi-task performance. In S. Monsell & J. Driver (Eds.), *Control of cognitive processes: Attention and performance* (Vol. 18, pp. 277–307). Cambridge, MA: MIT Press.

Patterson, G. E., diGormo, D. S., & Knutson, N. (2001). Hyperactivity and antisocial behavior: Comorbid or two points in the same process? *Development and Psychopathology, 12,* 91–106.

Patterson, G. R., Reid, J. B., & Dishion, T. J. (1998). Antisocial boys. In J. M. Jenkins, K. Oatley, & N. L. Stein (Eds.), *Human emotions: A reader* (pp. 330–336). Malden, MA: Blackwell.

Peirano, P., Algarin, C., & Uauy, R. (2003). Sleep-wake states and their regulatory mechanisms throughout early human development. *Journal of Pediatrics, 143*(Suppl. 2), S70–S79.

Pelham, W. E., Jr, Fabiano, G. A., & Massetti, G. M. (2005). Evidence-based assessment of attention deficit hyperactivity disorder in children and adolescents. *Journal of Clinical Child and Adolescent Psychology, 34,* 449–476.

Pennington, B. F. (1997). Dimensions of executive functions in normal and abnormal development. In N. A. Krasnegor, G. R. Lyon, & P. S. Goldman-Rakic (Eds.), *Development of the prefrontal cortex: Evolution, neurobiology, and behavior* (pp. 265–281). Baltimore: Paul H. Brookes.

Pennington, B. F. (2002). *The development of psychopathology.* New York: Guilford Press.

Pennington, B. F., & Ozonoff, S. (1996). Executive functions and developmental psychopathology. *Journal of Child Psychology and Psychiatry, 37,* 51–87.

Perchet, C., Revol, O., Fourneret, P., Mauguiere, F., & Garcia-Larrea, L. (2001). Attention shifts and anticipatory mechanics in hyperactive children: An ERP study using the Posner paradigm. *Biological Psychiatry, 50,* 44–57.

Piek, J. P., Dyck, M. J., Nieman, A., Anderson, M., Hay, D., Smith, L. M., et al. (2004). The relationship between motor coordination, executive functioning and attention in school aged children. *Archives of Clinical Neuropsychology, 19,* 1063–1076.

Pineda, D., Ardila, A., & Rosselli, M. (1999). Neuropsychological and behavioral assessment of ADHD in seven- to twelve-year-old children: A discriminant analysis. *Journal of Learning Disabilities, 32,* 159–173.

Pliszka, S. R., Borcherding, S. H., Spratley, K., Leon, S., & Irick, S. (1997). Measuring inhibitory control in children. *Journal of Developmental Pediatrics, 18,* 254–259.

Pliszka, S. R., Hatch, J. P., Borcherding, S. H., & Rogeness, G. A. (1993). Classical conditioning in children with attention deficit hyperactivity disorder (ADHD) and anxiety disorders: A test of Quay's model. *Journal of Abnormal Child Psychology, 21,* 411–423.

Plude, D., Enns, J., & Brodeur, D. (1994). The development of selective attention: A life-span overview. *Acta Psychologica, 86,* 227–272.

Posner, M. I., & DiGirolamo, G. J. (1998). Executive attention: Conflict, target detection, and cognitive control. In R. Parasuraman (Ed.), *The attentive brain* (pp. 401–423). Cambridge, MA: MIT Press.

Posner, M. I., & Petersen, S. (1990). The attention system of the human brain. *Annual Review of Neuroscience, 13,* 25–42.

Posner, M. I., & Rothbart, M. K. (2000). Developing mechanisms of self-regulation. *Development and Psychopathology, 12,* 427–441.

Pribram, K. H., & McGuinness, D. (1975). Arousal, activation, and effort in the control of attention. *Psychological Review, 82,* 116–149.

Quay, H. C. (1972). Patterns of aggression, withdrawal, and immaturity. In H. C. Quay & J. S. Werry (Eds.), *Psychopathological disorders of childhood* (pp. 1–29). New York: Wiley.

Quay, H. C. (1988). Attention-deficit disorder and the behavioral inhibition system: The relevance of the neuropsychological theory of Jeffrey A. Gray. In L. M. Bloomingdale & J. Sergeant (Eds.), *Attention-deficit disorder: Criteria, cognition, intervention* (pp. 117–126). New York: Pergamon Press.

Quay, H. C. (1997). Inhibition and attention deficit hyperactivity disorder. *Journal of Abnormal Child Psychology, 25,* 7–13.

Quay, H. C., & Hogan, A. E. (Eds.). (1999). *Handbook of disruptive behavior disorders.* New York: Kluwer Academic/Plenum Press.

Rappley, M. D., Gardiner, J. C., Jetton, J. R., & Houang, R. T. (1995). The use of methylphenidate in Michigan. *Archives of Pediatrics and Adolescent Medicine, 149,* 675–679.

Rice, D. C. (1999). Behavioral impairment produced by low-level postnatal PCB exposure in monkeys. *Environmental Research, 80*(Suppl. 2, Pt. 2), S113–S121.

Rice, D. C. (2000). Parallels between attention deficit hyperactivity disorder and behavioral deficits produced by neurotoxic exposure in monkeys. *Environmental Health Perspectives, 108*(Suppl. 3), 405–408.

Rice, D. C., & Haward, S. (1997). Effects of postnatal exposure to a PCB mixture in monkeys on nonspatial discrimination reversal and delayed alternation performance. *Neurotoxicology, 18,* 479–494.

Richardson, A. J., & Ross, M. A. (2000). Fatty acid metabolism in neurodevelopmental disorder: A new perspective on associations between attention-deficit/hyperactivity disorder, dyslexia, dyspraxia and the autistic spectrum. *Prostoglandins, Leukotrienes and Essential Fatty Acids, 63,* 1–9.

Robison, L. M., Sclar, D. A., Skaer, T. L., & Galin, R. S. (1999). National trends in the prevalence of attention-deficit/hyperactivity disorder and the prescribing of methylphenidate among school age children: 1990–1995. *Clinical Pediatrics, 38,* 209–217.

Rothbart, M. K., & Ahadi, S. A. (1994). Temperament and the development of personality. *Journal of Abnormal Psychology, 103,* 55–66.

Rothbart, M. K., & Bates, J. E. (1998). Temperament. In W. Damon (Series Ed.) & N. Eisenberg (Vol. Ed.), *Handbook of child psychology: Vol. 3. Social, emotional, and personality development* (pp. 105–176). New York: Wiley.

Rothbart, M. K., Derryberry, D., & Posner, M. I. (1994). A psychobiological approach to the development of temperament. In J. E. Bates & T. D. Wachs (Eds.), *Temperament: Individual differences at the interface of biology and behavior* (pp. 83–116). Washington, DC: American Psychological Association.

Rutter, M., Pickles, A., Murray, R., & Eaves, L. (2001). Testing hypotheses on specific environmental causal effects on behavior. *Psychological Bulletin, 127,* 291–324.

Rutter, M., & Silberg, J. (2002). Gene-environment interplay in relation to emotional and behavioral disturbance. *Annual Review of Psychology, 53,* 463–490.

Safer, D. J., & Krager, J. M. (1992). Effect of a media blitz and a threatened lawsuit on stimulant treatment. *Journal of the American Medical Association, 268,* 1004–1007.

Safer, D. J., & Zito, J. M. (1999). Psychotropic medication for ADHD. *Mental Retardation and Developmental Disabilities Research Reviews, 5,* 237–242.

Sagvolden, T., Aase, H., Zeiner, P., & Berger, D. F. (1998). Altered reinforcement mechanisms in attention deficit/hyperactivity disorder. *Behavioral Brain Research, 94,* 61–71.

Sagvolden, T., Johansen, E. B., Aase, H., & Russell, V. A. (2005). A dynamic developmental theory of attention-deficit/hyperactivity disorder (ADHD) predominantly hyperactive/impulsive and combined subtypes. *Behavioral and Brain Sciences, 28*(3), 397–419.

Sanson, A., Smart, D., Prior, M., & Oberklaid, F. (1993). Precursors of hyperactivity and aggression. *Journal of the American Academy of Child and Adolescent Psychiatry, 32,* 1207–1216.

Satterfield, J. H., Cantwell, D. P., & Satterfield, B. T. (1974). Pathophysiology of the hyperactive child syndrome. *Archives of General Psychiatry, 31,* 839–844.

Satterfield, J. H., & Dawson, M. E. (1971). Electrodermal correlates of hyperactivity in children. *Psychophysiology, 8,* 191–197.

Scarr, S., & McCartney, K. (1983). How people make their own environments: A theory of genotype > environment effects. *Child Development, 54,* 424–435.

Schachar, R., & Logan, G. D. (1990). Impulsivity and inhibitory control in normal development and childhood psychopathology. *Developmental Psychology, 26,* 710–720.

Schachar, R., Mota, V. L., Logan, G. D., Tannock, R., & Klim, P. (2000). Confirmation of an inhibitory control deficit in attention-deficit/hyperactivity disorder. *Journal of Abnormal Child Psychology, 28,* 227–235.

Schachar, R., Tannock, R., & Logan, G. (1993). Inhibitory control, impulsiveness, and attention deficit hyperactivity disorder. *Clinical Psychology Review, 13,* 721–739.

Schachar, R., Tannock, R., Marriott, M., & Logan, G. (1995). Deficient inhibitory control in attention deficit hyperactivity disorder. *Journal of Abnormal Child Psychology, 23,* 411–437.

Scheres, A., Oosterlaan, J., & Sergeant, J. A. (2001). Response inhibition in children with DSM-IV subtypes of AD/HD and related disruptive disorders: The role of reward. *Child Neuropsychology, 7,* 172–189.

Schettler, T. (2001). Toxic threats to neurological development of children. *Environmental Health Perspectives, 109*(Suppl. 6), 813–816.

Schneider, W., & Shiffrin, R. M. (1977). Controlled and automatic human information processing: I. Detection, search, and attention. *Psychological Review, 84,* 1–66.

Schore, A. (1994). *Affect regulation and the origin of the self: The neurobiology of emotional development.* Hillsdale, NJ: Erlbaum.

Searight, H. R., & McLaren, A. L. (1998). Attention-deficit hyperactivity disorder: The medicalization of misbehavior. *Journal of Clinical Psychology in Medical Settings, 5,* 467–495.

Seguin, J. R., Boulerice, B., Harden, P. W., Tremblay, R. E., & Pihl, R. O. (1999). Executive functions and physical aggression after controlling for attention deficit hyperactivity disorder, general memory, and IQ. *Journal of Child Psychology and Psychiatry, 40,* 1197–1208.

Seguin, J. R., Nagin, D., Assaad, J. M., & Tremblay, R. E. (2004). Cognitive-neuropsychological function in chronic physical aggression and hyperactivity. *Journal of Abnormal Psychology, 113,* 603–613.

Sergeant, J. A. (2005). The cognitive energetic model and ADHD. *Biological Psychiatry.*

Sergeant, J. A., Geurts, H., & Oosterlaan, J. (2002). How specific is a deficit of executive functioning for attention-deficit/hyperactivity disorder? *Behavioral Brain Research, 130,* 3–28.

Sergeant, J. A., Oosterlaan, J., & van der Meere, J. (1999). Information processing and energetic factors in attention-deficit/hyperactivity disorder. In H. C. Quay & A. E. Hogan (Eds.), *Handbook of disruptive behavior disorders* (pp. 75–104). New York: Kluwer Academic/ Plenum Press.

Sergeant, J. A., & Scholten, C. A. (1985). On data limitations in hyperactivity. *Journal of Child Psychology and Psychiatry, 26,* 111–124.

Sergeant, J. A., & van der Meere, J. J. (1988). What happens after a hyperactive child commits an error? *Psychological Research, 24,* 157–164.

Sergeant, J. A., & van der Meere, J. J. (1990). Additive factor methodology applied to psychopathology with special reference to hyperactivity. *Acta Psychologica, 74,* 277–295.

Shapiro, K. L., & Raymond, J. E. (1994). Temporal allocation of visual attention: Inhibition or interference? In D. Dagenbach & T. H. Carr (Eds.), *Inhibitory processes in attention, memory, and language* (pp. 151–188). New York: Academic Press.

Sharma, V., Halperin, J., Newcorn, J., & Wolf, L. (1991). The dimension of focused attention: Relationship to behavior and cognitive functioning in children. *Perceptual and Motor Skills, 72,* 787–793.

Shue, K. L., & Douglas, V. I. (1992). Attention deficit hyperactivity disorder and the frontal lobe syndrome. *Brain and Cognition, 20,* 104–124.

Silberstein, R. B., Farrow, M., Levy, F., Pipingas, A., Hay, D. A., & Jarman, F. C. (1998). Functional brain electrical activity mapping in boys with attention-deficit/hyperactivity disorder. *Archives of General Psychiatry, 55,* 1105–1112.

Slusarek, M., Velling, S., Bunk, D., & Eggers, C. (2001). Motivational effects on inhibitory control in children with ADHD. *Journal of the American Academy of Child and Adolescent Psychiatry, 40,* 355–363.

Snyder, J., Reid, J., & Patterson, G. (2003). A social learning model of child and adolescent antisocial behavior. In B. B. Lahey, T. Moffitt, & A. Caspi (Eds.), *The causes of conduct disorder and serious juvenile delinquency* (pp. 27–48). New York: Guilford Press.

Solanto, M. V., Abikoff, H., Sonuga-Barke, E., Schachar, R., Logan, G. D., Wigal, T., et al. (2001). The ecological validity of delay aversion and response inhibition as measures of impulsivity in AD/HD: A supplement to the NIMH Multimodal Treatment Study of AD/HD. *Journal of Abnormal Child Psychology, 29,* 215–228.

Solanto, M. V., Arnsten, A. F. T., & Castellanos, F. X. (2001). *Stimulant drugs and ADHD: Basic and clinical neuroscience.* New York: Oxford University Press.

Sonuga-Barke, E. J. S. (2002). Psychological heterogeneity in AD/HD: A dual pathway model of behaviour and cognition. *Behavioural Brain Research, 130,* 29–36.

Sonuga-Barke, E. J. (2005). Causal models of attention-deficit/hyperactivity disorder: From common simple deficits to multiple developmental pathways. *Biological Psychiatry, 57,* 1231–1238.

Sonuga-Barke, E. J. S., Dalen, L., Daley, D., & Remington, B. (2002). Are planning, working memory, and inhibition associated with individual differences in preschool ADHD symptoms? *Developmental Neuropsychology, 21,* 255–272.

Sonuga-Barke, E. J. S., Saxton, T., & Hall, M. (1998). The role of interval underestimation in hyperactive children's failure to suppress responses over time. *Behavioral Brain Research, 94,* 45–50.

Sroufe, L. A., & Stewart, M. A. (1973). Treating problem children with stimulant drugs. *New England Journal of Medicine, 289*(8), 407–413.

Stawick, J. A., Nigg, J. T., & von Eye, A. (in press). Familial aggregation data on the relation of ADHD Combined and Inattentive subtypes: New data and meta-analysis. *Journal of Child Psychology and Psychiatry.*

Stevens, J., Quittner, A., Zuckerman, J., & Moore, S. (2002). Behavioral inhibition, self-regulation of motivation, and working memory in children with attention-deficit hyperactivity disorder. *Developmental Neuropsychology, 21,* 117–139.

Still, G. (1902). Some abnormal psychical conditions in children. *Lancet, 1,* 1008–1012.

Stoolmiller, M. (2001). Synergistic interaction of child manageability problems and parent-discipline tactics in predicting future growth in externalizing behavior in boys. *Developmental Psychology, 37,* 814–825.

Strauss, A. A., & Lehtinen, L. E. (1947). *Psychopathology and education of the brain-injured child.* New York: Grune & Stratton.

Strelau, J. (1994). The concepts of arousal and arousability as used in temperament studies. In J. E. Bates & T. D. Wachs (Eds.), *Temperament: Individual differences at the interface of biology and behavior* (pp. 117–141). Washington, DC: American Psychological Association.

Swanson, J. M., & Castellanos, F. X. (2002). Biological bases of ADHD: Neuroanatomy, genetics, and pathophysiology. In P. S. Jensen & J. R. Cooper (Eds.), *Attention-deficit hyperactivity disorder: State of the science, best practices* (pp. 7-1–7-20). Kingston, NJ: Civic Research Institute.

Swanson, J. M., Oosterlaan, J., Murias, M., Shuck, S., Flodman, P., Spence, A., et al. (2000). Attention deficit/hyperactivity disorder in children with a 7-repeat allele of the dopamine receptor D4 gene have extreme behavior but normal performance on critical neuropsychological tests of attention. *Proceedings of the National Academy of Sciences, USA, 97,* 4754–4759.

Tannock, R., Ickowicz, A., & Schachar, R. (1995). Differential effects of methylphenidate on working memory in ADHD children with and without comorbid anxiety. *Journal of the American Academy of Child and Adolescent Psychiatry, 34,* 886–896.

Tannock, R., & Schachar, R. (1996). Executive dysfunction as an underlying mechanism of behavior and language problems in attention deficit hyperactivity disorder. In J. H. Beitchman, N. J. Cohen, M. M. Konstantareas, & R. Tannock (Eds.), *Language, learning, and behavior disorders* (pp. 128–155). Cambridge, England: Cambridge University Press.

Taylor, E. (1995). Dysfunctions of attention. In D. Cicchetti & D. J. Cohen (Eds.), *Developmental psychopathology: Vol. 2. Risk, disorder, and adaptation* (pp. 243–273). New York: Wiley.

Taylor, E. (1999). Developmental neuropsychopathology of attention deficit and impulsiveness. *Development and Psychopathology, 11,* 607–628.

Theuwes, J., Atchley, P., & Kramer, A. F. (1998). On the time course of top-down and bottom-up control of visual attention. In S. Monsell & J. Driver (Eds.), *Control of cognitive processes* (pp. 105–124). Cambridge, MA: MIT Press.

Toplak, M. E., Rucklidge, J. J., Hetherington, R., John, S. C. F., & Tannock, R. (2003). Time perception deficits in attention-deficit/hyperactivity disorder and comorbid reading difficulties in child and adolescent samples. *Journal of Child Psychology and Psychiatry, 44,* 1–16.

Tremblay, R. E. (2000). The development of aggressive behaviour during childhood: What have we learned in the last century? *International Journal of Behavioral Development, 24,* 129–141.

Triesman, A., & Gelade, G. (1980). A feature integration theory of attention. *Cognitive Psychology, 12,* 97–136.

Tripp, G., & Alsop, B. (1999). Sensitivity to reward frequency in boys with attention deficit hyperactivity disorder. *Journal of Clinical Child Psychology, 28,* 366–375.

Trommer, B. L., Hoeppner, J. B., & Zecker, S. G. (1991). The go-no go test in attention deficit disorder is sensitive to methylphenidate. *Journal of Child Neurology, 6,* S128–S131.

Tucker, D. M., & Williamson, P. A. (1984). Asymmetric neural control systems in human self-regulation. *Psychological Review, 91,* 185–215.

van der Meere, J. J. (2002). The role of attention. In S. Sandberg (Ed.), *Hyperactivity and attention disorders of childhood* (2nd ed., pp. 162–213). Cambridge, England: Cambridge University Press.

van der Meere, J. J., Shalev, R. S., Borger, N., & Gross-Tsur, V. (1995). Sustained attention, activation, and MPH in ADHD. *Journal of Child Psychology and Psychiatry, 36,* 697–703.

van der Meere, J. J., & Stermerdink, N. (1999). The development of state regulation in normal children: An indirect comparison with children with ADHD. *Developmental Neuropsychology, 16,* 213–225.

Van Mourik, R., Oosterlaan, J., & Sergeant, J. A. (2005). The Stroop revisited: A meta-analysis of interference control in AD/HD. *Journal of Child Psychology and Psychiatry, 46,* 150–165.

Wakefield, J. C. (1992). The concept of mental disorder: On the boundary between biological facts and social values. *American Psychologist, 47,* 373–388.

Waller, N. G., & Meehl, P. E. (1998). *Multivariate taxometric procedures: Distinguishing types from continua—Advanced quantitative techniques in the social sciences* (Vol. 9). Thousand Oaks, CA: Sage.

Waschbusch, D. A. (2002). A meta-analytic examination of comorbid hyperactive-impulsive-attention problems and conduct problems. *Psychological Bulletin, 18,* 118–150.

Weinberg, W. A., & Harper, C .R. (1993). Vigilance and its disorders. *Neurologic Clinics, 11,* 59–78.

Wender, P. H. (1971). *Minimal brain dysfunction in children.* New York: Wiley.

Willcutt, E. G., Doyle, A. E., Nigg, J. T., Faraone, S. V., & Pennington, B. F. (2005). Validity of the executive function theory of ADHD: Meta-analytic review. *Biological Psychiatry.*

Willcutt, E. G., Pennington, B. F., Boada, R., Ogline, J. S., Tunick, R. A., Chhabildas, N. A., et al. (2001). A comparison of the cognitive deficits in reading disability and attention-deficit/hyperactivity disorder. *Journal of Abnormal Psychology, 110,* 157–172.

Willcutt, E. G., Pennington, B. F., & DeFries, J. C. (2000). Etiology of inattention and hyperactivity/impulsivity in a community sample of twins with learning difficulties. *Journal of Abnormal Psychology, 28,* 149–159.

Williams, B. R., Ponesse, J. S., Schachar, R. J., Logan, G. D., & Tannock, R. (1999). Development of inhibitory control across the life-span. *Developmental Psychology, 35,* 205–213.

Wolf, J. M. (1998). Visual search. In H. Pashler (Ed.), *Attention* (pp. 13–73). London: Psychology Press.

Wolraich, M. L., Hannah, J. N., Baumgaertel, A., & Feurer, I. D. (1998). Examination of DSM-IV criteria for attention-deficit/hyperactivity disorder in a county-wide sample. *Developmental and Behavioral Pediatrics, 19,* 162–168.

Wood, D. R., Reimherr, F. W., Wender, P. H., & Johnson, G. E. (1976). Diagnosis and treatment of minimal brain dysfunction in adults. *Archives of General Psychiatry, 3,* 1453–1460.

Woodward, A., & Markman, E. (1998). Early word learning. In W. Damon (Series Ed.) & D. Kuhn & R. Siegler (Vol. Eds.), *Handbook of child psychology: Vol. 2. Cognition, perception, and language* (pp. 371–420). New York: Wiley.

World Health Organization. (1992). *The ICD-10 classification of mental and behavioral disorders: Clinical descriptions and diagnostic guidelines.* Geneva, Switzerland: Author.

Yantis, S. (1998). Goal-directed and stimulus-driven determinants of attentional control. In S. Monsell & J. Driver (Eds.), *Control of cognitive processes: Attention and performance* (Vol. 18, pp. 73–103). Cambridge, MA: MIT Press.

Yong, L. G., Robaey, P., Karayanidis, F., Bourassa, M., Pelletier, G., & Geoffroy, G. (2000). ERPs and behavioral inhibition in a go/no-go task in children with attention-deficit hyperactivity disorder. *Brain and Cognition, 43,* 215–220.

Zacks, R. T., & Hasher, L. (1994). Directed ignoring: Inhibitory regulation of working memory. In D. Dagenbach & T. H. Carr (Eds.), *Inhibitory processes in attention, memory, and language* (pp. 241–264). New York: Academic Press.

Zelazo, P. D., Muller, U., Frye, D., & Marcovitch, S. (2003). The development of executive function: Cognitive complexity and control-Revised. *Monographs of the Society for Research in Child Development, 68*(3), 93–119.

Zentall, S., & Zentall, T. (1983). Optimal stimulation: A model of disordered activity and performance in normal and deviant children. *Psychological Bulletin, 94,* 446–471.

Zito, J. M., Safer, D. J., DosReis, S., Gardner, J. F., Magder, L., Soeken, K., et al. (2003). Psychotropic practice patterns for youth: A 10-year perspective. *Archives of Pediatric and Adolescent Medicine, 157,* 17–25.

CHAPTER 10

Origins of Obsessive-Compulsive Disorder: Developmental and Evolutionary Perspectives

DAVID W. EVANS and JAMES F. LECKMAN

In this chapter, we consider Obsessive-Compulsive Disorder (OCD) from developmental and evolutionary perspectives. We begin with a definition of obsessions and compulsions and a description of this diagnostic category. We then examine several normal epochs of develop-

This work was supported in part by NIH grants MH44843, MH49351, HD03008, RR00125, and RR06022 (General Clinical Research Centers) and grants from the Institute for Research on Unlimited Love. Portions of this chapter have appeared in earlier publications, including Leckman and Mayes (1998, 1999); Leckman et al. (1999); A. Carter, Leckman, and Pauls (1995); Evans (2000); Evans et al. (2004; especially the section on neural circuitry); and Schultz et al. (1999).

ment that are characterized by obsessive-compulsive behaviors that resemble those encountered in OCD. Next, we take a closer look at the phenomenology and natural history of OCD before reviewing the available genetic, epigenetic, neuropsychological, neurochemical, neuroendocrine, and neuroimaging data that bear on OCD and related normal phenotypes. We then detail a number of theoretical models of pathogenesis and the treatments they have engendered. Finally, we offer an integrative model that emphasizes evolutionary and developmental perspectives and describe its potential utility in providing a coherent, multidisciplinary framework for future work in this area.

DEFINITIONS AND CLINICAL DESCRIPTIONS

In the following section we define obsessions and compulsions, and we describe the clinical presentations associated with each construct. In so doing, we hope to emphasize the broad range of behaviors associated with both obsessions and compulsions.

Obsessional Thoughts

Obsessions are intrusive thoughts, impulses, or images that are troubling and persistent and that may dominate the mental life of the individual afflicted (American Psychiatric Association, 2000). Patients often view these preoccupations as being senseless and bizarre. Obsessions are typically regarded as being ego dystonic, in that they are distressing and contrary to the individual's view of himself or herself. For example, a patient may have intrusive thoughts of having been responsible for harm befalling a close family member, or fear that a loved one will be harmed because of some inadvertent act. Similarly, a new parent may suddenly experience an urge to harm or even kill her precious infant, or a pious individual may be plagued by the obsessive urge to desecrate a holy statue. Typically, the individual is aware that he or she will not act on these troubling impulses, but that does little to diminish the distress that the thoughts engender. Another relatively common obsession involves excessive worries about germs or contracting a fatal disease. Some individuals with OCD are painfully preoccupied with the idea that they may have left a stove on or a door unlocked. Still other obsessions focus on a need for symmetry or exactness or concerns about not discarding things that most people would regard as useless.

Although many of us may have experienced similar thoughts, we are generally able to dismiss them. For individuals with OCD, however, their intrusive thoughts, once initiated, are tenacious and nearly impossible to dismiss. Even in the face of evidence to the contrary, the individual with OCD is often unable to interrupt the flow of these disturbing images and thoughts.

Compulsions

Compulsions include a broad array of repetitive behaviors that a person feels driven to perform, often according to a strict set of rules that must be rigidly applied. The range of compulsions is vast and may include repetitive and excessive hand washing, checking behaviors (checking doors, stoves, or whether a parent is okay), elaborate routines or rituals surrounding bedtime (dressing or undressing in a certain order or manner, such as left side of the body first) or mealtime (eating foods in a certain order, or avoiding foods of a particular color or texture), or bizarre routines involving movements such as touching or tapping upon crossing a threshold, or "evening-up" behaviors. Some individuals with OCD have strong preferences for symmetry, balance, or wholeness that "requires" that they arrange particular objects in a certain order. Still other compulsions may include repeatedly asking questions or seeking reassurance, or mental rituals such as repeating certain words or phrases to oneself, or needing to repeatedly count to a particular number.

Whereas some compulsions involve elaborate and observable routines or rituals, others are more covert and internal, though even some elaborate rituals may be performed only in private and remain unknown to others. The perceived senselessness of compulsions may bring about psychological distress, yet it is also the case that compulsions may bring temporary relief from anxiety. That is, hand washing temporarily relieves the anxiety from contamination obsessions. This temporary anxiety reduction that results from engaging in a compulsion may have (negative) reinforcing properties that perpetuate the symptom expression in OCD. Similar to avoidance behavior and escape seen in simple phobias, the anxiety reduction served by compulsions may strengthen the stimulus-response connection between obsessions and compulsions. Finally, woven into many compulsions is the "just right" criterion: The individual may engage repeatedly in a ritual or routine or other compulsion until some subjective criterion is reached, so that it feels "just right." Often, however, this sense of the world being just right is short-lived, and the thoughts and behaviors begin all over again.

In many instances, certain obsessions are concomitant with particular compulsions. Germ obsessions commonly accompany hand washing. Particular doubting obsessions are associated with checking compulsions (worry about the stove being left on typically is coupled with checking the stove). The degree to which this obsession-compulsion pairing seems logical to an outside observer varies considerably. One can understand, for example, why someone who fears germs might feel the compulsion to wash. Similarly, it makes some sense for someone concerned that a stove was left on to check the stove. Though clearly in excess (hand washing may occur to the point where the individual's hands are bleeding and he or she is confined to his or her home for fear of contracting disease), there is a certain logic that ties together the obsession and the compulsion.

By contrast, other compulsions in response to obsessions may seem to be less "logically" connected for most observers. Take, for example, the individual who is plagued with obsessions that his or her parents are going to die in a car crash and who attempts to ward off this imagined event by retracing steps when crossing a threshold. In this case, the connection between the obsession and the compulsion seems more tenuous, as it requires a considerable leap of logic and seems to invoke a greater degree of magical thinking to link the psychological event and the physical behavior. Such magical thinking is present in other disorders as well (e.g., schizotypal personality). The potential difference between the former "logical" obsessive-compulsive behaviors and the latter "magical" obsessive-compulsive behaviors has received virtually no empirical attention but may speak to specific OCD subtypes. We return to this topic in our discussion of normative compulsive-like behaviors in young children. First, we address the clinical entity of OCD.

Obsessive-Compulsive Disorder

OCD is an Axis I disorder in the class of anxiety disorders and is defined by the presence of obsessions and/or compulsions to the point where they interfere significantly with an individual's daily adaptive, social, or occupational functioning (*Diagnostic and Statistical Manual of Mental Disorders,* fourth edition [*DSM-IV*]; American Psychiatric Association, 2000). The symptoms are viewed as inappropriate and excessive and are of sufficient frequency, intensity, or duration to cause significant subjective distress. The thoughts, impulses, worries, or anxieties that constitute the obsessional thoughts are not generally reactions to real-life situations, or, if they are in reaction to genuine threats, they are grossly excessive relative to the threat. Unlike symptoms associated with thought disorders such as Schizophrenia, the thought disturbances associated with OCD are perceived by the individual as products of his or her own mind (not thought insertion, as with Schizophrenia). Diagnostic criteria also prescribe that significant resistance must exist; that is, in realizing the senselessness of the thoughts or behaviors associated with OCD, the individual makes significant efforts to resist the thoughts and/or behaviors, which are generally unsuccessful.

Constructs such as psychological resistance, subjective distress, and ego dystonia exemplify the psychological turmoil associated with obsessions and compulsions. These constructs require a certain degree of self-understanding, self-perception, and abstract thinking. It is questionable, therefore, whether young children can fully experience resistance and ego dystonia. Because of

this, the insight-related *DSM* criteria (recognition of the excessiveness, ego dystonia) are waived in the current version of the manual (*DSM-IV-TR,* American Psychiatric Association, 2000). Similarly, some debate has surrounded whether children with Autism experience obsessions and compulsions as, presumably, children with Autism are incapable of the metacognitive ability to reflect on their own mental states (Baron-Cohen, 1988). This issue is not fully resolved and has important implications for the definitions of obsessions and compulsions and for the diagnosis of OCD in young children and children with cognitive disabilities.

Table 10.1 represents the *DSM-IV-TR* criteria for OCD. Under these guidelines, an individual must exhibit either obsessions or compulsions that are time-consuming (more than 1 hour per day) or interfere with the person's normal routine or adaptive functioning. The *DSM-IV-TR* criteria also specify that if the object of certain obsessive, intrusive thoughts is better accounted for by another disorder, then a diagnosis of OCD should not be made. In the case of obsessive thoughts about body image or about foods seen in some eating disorders, an eating disorder or body dysmorphic disorder might be the preferred diagnosis. Similarly, the obsessional state of an individual who is addicted to and preoccupied with alcohol or another drug of abuse would likely be regarded as symptomatic of substance abuse, not OCD.

OCD shares a relatively high comorbidity rate with a great number of other psychiatric conditions, including anxiety disorders, Panic Disorder, simple phobias, mood disorders, and tic disorders. Estimates of OCD comorbidity with other anxiety disorders range from 25% to 75% (Flament et al., 1988; Francis & Gragg, 1996). As many as 83% of patients with OCD report panic attacks (Barlow, DiNardo, Vermilyea, Vermilyea, & Blanchard, 1986). Separation Anxiety Disorder is much more common in older children and adolescents with OCD compared to adults (A. Carter, Pauls, & Leckman, 1996). Mood disorders are found in approximately 25% to 35% of children and adolescents with OCD (Flament et al., 1988, 1990; Last, Perrin, Hersen, & Kazdin, 1992), and some 65% of individuals with OCD also meet diagnostic criteria for depression (Pauls, Leckman, & Cohen, 1994). Tourette's syndrome is diagnosed in approximately 15% of OCD probands (A. H. Zohar et al., 1992). Conversely, among Tic Disorder probands, OCD is diagnosed in 50% to 70% of cases (Apter et al., 1993; Frances & Gragg, 1996); interestingly, first-degree relatives of patients with OCD are significantly more likely to have a Tic Disorder compared to the general population (Rosario-Campos, in press).

TABLE 10.1 *DSM-IV-TR* Diagnostic Criteria for Obsessive-Compulsive Disorder

A. Either obsessions or compulsions:

Obsessions as defined by (1), (2), (3), and (4):

(1) recurrent and persistent thoughts, impulses, or images that are experienced , at some time during the disturbance, as intrusive and inappropriate and that cause major anxiety or distress

(2) the thoughts, impulses, or images are not simply excessive worries about real-life problems

(3) the person attempts to ignore or suppress such thoughts, impulses, or images or to neutralize them with some other thought or action

(4) the person recognized that the obsessional thoughts, impulses, or images are a product of his or her own mind (not imposed from without as in thought insertion)

Compulsions as defined by (1) and (2):

(1) repetitive behaviors (e.g., handwashing, ordering, checking) or mental acts (e.g. praying, counting, repeating words silently) that the person feels driven to perform in response to an obsession, or according to rules that must be applied rigidly

(2) the behaviors or mental acts are aimed at preventing or reducing distress or preventing some dreaded event or situation; however, these behaviors or mental acts either are not connected in a realistic way with what they are designed to neutralize or are clearly excessive

B. At some point during the course of the disorder, the person has recognized that the obsessions or compulsions are excessive or unreasonable. **Note: This does not apply to children.**

C. The obsessions or compulsions cause marked distress, are time-consuming (take more than 1 hour a day), or significantly interfere with the person's normal routines, occupational (or academic) functioning, or usual social activities or relationships.

D. If another Axis I disorder is present, the content of the obsessions or compulsions is not restricted to it (e.g., preoccupation with food in the presence of an Eating Disorder; hair-pulling in the presence of Trichotillomania; concern with appearance in the presence of Body Dysmorphic Disorder; preoccupation with drugs in the presence of a Substance Use Disorder; preoccupation with sexual urges or fantasies in the presence of a Paraphilia; or guilty ruminations in the presence of Major Depressive Disorder).

E. The disturbance is not due to the direct physiological effects of a substance (e.g., a drug of abuse, a medication) or a general medical condition.

Specify if:

With Poor Insight: If, for most of the time during the current episode, the person does not recognize that the obsessions and compulsions are excessive or unreasonable.

Reprinted with permission from the *Diagnostic and Statistical Manual of Mental Disorders,* Copyright 2000. American Psychiatric Association.

Obsessive-Compulsive Personality Disorder

Although Obsessive Compulsive Personality Disorder (OCPD) shares the words "obsessive" and "compulsive" with OCD, the clinical manifestations of these disorders are quite different. OCPD is characterized by "a preoccupation with orderliness, perfectionism and mental and interpersonal control, at the expense of flexibility, openness and efficiency" (American Psychiatric Association, 1994,

p. 672). To receive a diagnosis of OCPD, the *DSM-IV* criteria require that at least four of the following are present: (1) preoccupations with details, rules, lists, order, organization, or schedules to the extent that "the major point of the activity is lost"; (2) perfectionism that interferes with task completion; (3) excessive devotion to work and productivity to the exclusion of leisure activities and relationships; (4) being overly conscientious, scrupulous, and inflexible about matters of morality, ethics, or values; (5) an inability to discard worn-out or worthless objects even when they have no sentimental value; (6) a reluctance to delegate responsibility unless others agree to submit to his or her way of doing things; (7) a miserly spending style toward both self and others; and (8) being overly rigid and stubborn.

In contrast to OCD, in OCPD, the individual does not consciously experience ego dystonicity, a lack of control, or resistance to his or her symptoms. Indeed, there is minimal overlap in the current diagnostic features of OCPD and OCD. Consequently, it is usually easy to distinguish between them. Hoarding behaviors are the only *DSM-IV* criteria for OCPD that may overlap directly with OCD. The diagnoses of OCD and OCPD are not mutually exclusive.

DEVELOPMENTAL TRAJECTORIES OF NORMAL OBSESSIVE-COMPULSIVE BEHAVIORS

Consideration of continuities and discontinuities between normality and psychopathology is a hallmark of developmental psychopathology (Cicchetti, 1993; Cicchetti & Cohen, 1995a; Zigler & Glick, 1986). In this section, we examine a range of normal mental states and behaviors that may inform our efforts to understand OCD. We are intrigued by the possibility that in certain contexts, behaviors that strongly resemble obsessions and compulsions may reflect normative developmental trajectories, serving adaptive functions and stemming from well-conserved vestiges of our phylogenetic roots.

Childhood Rituals

Beginning around the 2nd year of life, most children develop a variety of rituals, habits, routines, and preferences, some of which resemble the behaviors associated with OCD (Evans et al., 1997; Leonard, Goldberger, Rapoport, Cheslow, & Swedo, 1990). The idea that compulsive ritualistic behaviors may be normative in young children is not a new idea. Gesell and his colleagues (Ames, Ilg, & Frances, 1976; Gesell, 1928; Gesell, Ames, & Ilg, 1974) were among the first to recognize that young children, particularly those around the age of 2½, begin to establish rigid routines that Gesell termed the "ritualisms of the ritualist" (Gesell et al., 1974). Rather than addressing emotional needs, Gesell believed children engage in rituals to master the tasks of a specific developmental epoch characterized by gaining mastery in matters of feeding, toileting, and dressing, among others. Such tasks are facilitated by adherence to rules, and behavioral routines reflect mastery motivation. Developing behavioral routines and habits requires establishing mental representation of behavioral sequences and cognitive schema for the way things "should be" (see also Kagan, 1981). When such expectations are violated, as occurs with interruptions in daily routines or habits, changes in the physical environment or alterations of familiar objects, significant distress may result. In addition to Gesell's description of children's elaborate bedtime rituals and the need for sameness, his descriptions of normative ritualistic behaviors include references to "just right" phenomena, as well as preoccupations with balance, symmetry, and wholeness.

To Freud (1919), the rituals of young children were associated with efforts to control, organize, delay, and resist unconscious sexual impulses directed at their caregivers, which in turn are driven by the child's wish to be the exclusive focus of the parents' love and attention. Even normative rituals and compulsions stem from unconscious urges and efforts to reduce anxiety.

Winnicott (1958b) described "transitional objects" and transitional behaviors (e.g., routines and habits) as vehicles by which young children can sustain an emotional contiguity with their primary caregivers. Habits such as the use of and attachment to treasured objects like teddy bears and security blankets reflect the child's focus on particular objects, and presumably these represent a kind of transfer of parental attachment. That these security blankets and other objects gain particular importance at times of stress is telling in terms of their role in emotion regulation (Passman, 1976, 1977, 1987). Of bedtime routines, Winnicott noted that children engage parents in elaborate rituals, weaving the parents into "a transitional web," and thus these typical rituals serve to soften the loss of the parent as sleep and separation approach.

Erikson (1968) posited a developmental model of ritualization whereby infancy was characterized by "mutuality of recognition": a daily bonding ceremonial engaged in by infants and their primary caregivers that gives rise to self-awareness and awareness of self as distinct from other. An infant "signaling" that he or she is awake elicits in the parent a repertoire of emotive, verbal, and manipulative behaviors (Erikson, 1968), such as looking, feeling, and sniffing

as the parent searches for further signals that communicate the subjective state of the infant. The infant reinforces these behaviors by his or her responses. Though Erikson described such behaviors as highly ritualized, they are also individualized and attuned to each dyad. Erikson was clear in his beliefs that such interpersonal rituals in infancy are similar to religious rituals, in that both kinds of rituals involve an affirmation of self and belonging. These parent-child ritualizations "bestow convincing simplicity on dangerously complex behaviors" (p. 205). Rituals, then, simplify and clarify actions to make unambiguous the behaviors and goals in situations in which ambiguity would bring about disorganization and problematic outcomes in terms of the developing self and self-other relationships. To Erikson, rituals are vital to our interpersonal interaction and serve to establish both a sense of self and a sense of self in relation to others.

Though Piaget did not refer specifically to rituals or compulsions per se, his description of the development of cognitive operations certainly shed light on them. Piaget (1962) stressed the role of repetitive movements or circular motor reactions in early development as the child hones innate reflexes into more voluntary actions that aid in the manipulation of and adaptation to the environment. By the end of the sensorimotor period, however, children are able to engage in representational thought, whereby their understanding of the physical world is no longer gleaned through trial and error but by cognitive representations for specific sequences of actions to achieve a goal.

In deferred imitation, children are able to enact a relatively complex sequence of behaviors that they have previously observed. Memory for actions involves encoding a sequence of behaviors culminating in a behavioral totality. So, too, is this the case with sociodramatic play; roles are prescribed, and violations of social roles in play (or in real life) are not easily permitted. Classification and seriation—two hallmarks of the late preoperational and early concrete operational periods—exemplify the child's abilities to focus on and organize objects according to certain criteria or logical rules. In the preoperational period, children's understanding of classification and group membership is limited to a single feature. Only later does the child develop the concept that a single object may simultaneously embody multiple features, and depending on the rule of classification, an object may be classified in any number of groups.

A defining feature of compulsivity is the inappropriate perseveration of behavioral patterns. In his well-known experiments demonstrating the development of object permanence, Piaget (1962) noted that young children make perseverative errors—the A-NOT-B error. That is, they continue to search for an object in a location where it was previously hidden (A), even when they have witnessed the object's being moved to another location (B; Diamond, 1988; Diamond & Taylor, 1996). Prior motor activities are repeated even when the child has been exposed to information indicating that the previous action will be inadequate to retrieve the hidden object. More recently, Zelazo and Reznick (1991; Zelazo & Jacques, 1996) noted that preschoolers will perseverate on a sorting task when the sorting rule is switched (say, from color to shape), despite the fact that when asked, they can recall the new sorting rule. Thus, activities that constitute core aspects of compulsivity—sorting, classifying, and arranging objects, and perseveration of previously learned behaviors beyond their adaptive utility—are paramount in the cognitive development of the young child.

Perhaps more clearly than any other scholar of development, Werner (1948, 1957; see Evans, 2000, for a review) devised a comparative and organismic theory that affords a developmental analysis of both typical and atypical development, including rituals and compulsions. Werner explored the processes of mental development in terms of the nature of the organism-environment relationship across a variety of contexts, including childhood, certain cultural practices, and in psychopathology. His belief was that the basic mental and relational patterns of these three apparently disparate contexts could be construed as fundamentally (though not entirely) similar.

Werner recognized that young children often engage in ritualistic, compulsive behavior. To Werner, both normative and pathological rituals reflected a syncretic interaction style—a relative lack of differentiation between the organism and its environment. Put another way, rituals signify a magical connectedness between organism and environment and between thoughts and actions, where "motor and affective elements are intimately merged in the perception of things" (1948, p. 337).

Werner saw rituals as a kind of tool that, in conjunction with magical beliefs, melds the organism and the environment in a complex of causal relations between the ceremonial act and some desired outcome. He viewed magic and ritual as "indissoluble totalities, unitary acts which either fulfill themselves according to an all-or-nothing reaction, or are completely abortive" (1948, p. 344). Cultural rituals, children's rituals, and pathological compulsive rituals involve completion or totality, whereby "any disruption of the form, any failure in the performance—a stumbling, stuttering or even a pause—often occasions a magical inadequacy and inefficacy, since the very magical significance

of the whole event is vital only within an unbroken totality" (1948, p. 344).

Rituals and associated magical beliefs were, to Werner, typical of a level of organism-environment interactions that he defined as perceptual, such that the organism's relation to the environment is relatively fused and undifferentiated. These syncretic modes of interaction may emerge under any number of conditions and are seen as key elements for some of the richest of human experience, such as the basis of emotion and art. Werner differentiated cultural rituals from children's rituals, defining cultural rituals as a "rounded, organized way of life," (1948, p. 357) whereas children's rituals "can only occupy an isolated position" (1948, p. 357). With this distinction he placed children's rituals in closer proximity to pathological ones, in that, as we will see, the "organization" that is seen in childhood and pathological rituals is not well integrated into their entire repertoire of behavior. Childhood and pathological rituals are, by definition, circumscribed and limited to a particular sphere of life. Werner described the child's world as marked by "unbreakable organization, which occasions and demands rigidity of behavior" (1948, p. 358). These ceremonies invoke all-or-nothing thinking, where the ritual is either carried out properly or not at all.

> We all know that during infancy children want to eat and be dressed in some particular habitual fashion. In agreement with this attitude are those ceremonial rules and ritualistic practices of the child. . . . These rituals may be so set that any neglect or alteration is felt to be a symbol of disruption of a state of affairs in which "something is wrong." . . . We are unable to state definitively just how and when the . . . all or nothing reaction evolves into the formal ceremonial, that is, when it becomes real magical behavior. (1948, p. 359)

According to Werner's (1948) analysis, many of the rituals engaged in by children are in response to some fear or anxiety about the external world or the unknown aspects of sleep, dreams, and the supernatural aspects of the night, such as ghosts and the mystery of the dark. The creation of these rituals, beginning as simple rules come to serve a symbolic meaning that protects the child during sleep (Werner, 1948) and also reflects the child's desire to be protected by rules. In this sense, children's bedtime ceremonies resemble the kinds of compulsive rituals that are seen in Obsessive-Compulsive Disorder: They ward off dreaded events, ensure safety, or, more generally, serve to reduce anxiety states.

Despite numerous references to normative compulsive behavior in young children, the similarities and differences between normative and pathological compulsive behaviors have been all but absent from the empirical literature. Such analyses may offer insights into the adaptive origins of pathological obsessive-compulsive behaviors, as well as possibly uncovering developmental themes that underlie OCD. Identifying differences in the nature of early developmental rituals in children with and without OCD has obvious practical implications in terms of the early identification and treatment of OCD.

In recent years, Leonard and colleagues (Leonard et al., 1990) explored whether early developmental rituals can distinguish children who later developed OCD from those who did not. These retrospective parental reports suggested that the early developmental rituals in children might have practical implications in terms of the early identification of OCD. The reports suggested that the early developmental rituals of OCD probands and controls were similar when excluding those behaviors that were clearly symptomatic. That is, aside from behaviors such as repetitive hand washing, an act that was clearly thought to be diagnostically significant, the two groups of children did not differ from each other as to their habits and rituals.

Over the past decade, we and others have explored the normative variants of compulsive behavior in young children, including its natural history, and associations with cognitive development, adaptive behavior, and maladaptive behavior. The first of these studies involved a population-based survey of roughly 1,500 parents with children between 8 and 72 months living in the greater New Haven, Connecticut, area (Evans et al., 1997). An inventory was constructed (the Childhood Routines Inventory, or CRI) that reflected symptoms of Obsessive-Compulsive Disorder but that were cast in a normative framework.

The CRI contains 19 items that fall into two principal components. The first component is composed of items reflecting the repetitive behaviors on the CRI, such as "repeats certain actions over and over," "prefers the same household schedule or routine," and "engages in the same play over and over." The second component includes items that refer to what we call "just right" behaviors: sensory-perceptual phenomena that often involve arranging or rearranging, lining up objects in straight lines or symmetrical patterns, or behaviors woven into a ritual, such that certain behaviors must be repeated until they feel "just right." "Just right" behaviors also include a heightened sensitivity to slight imperfections in toys or clothes (Evans, Gray, & Leckman, 1999; Evans et al., 1997) and attention to details such as subtle changes in the environment.

In our initial study (Evans et al., 1997), parents indicated on the CRI whether their children engaged in each behavior using a 5-point Likert scale. Figure 10.1 includes

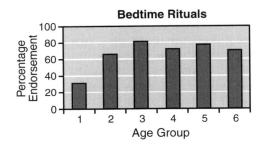
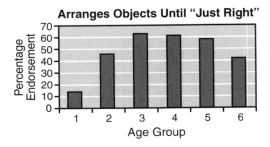

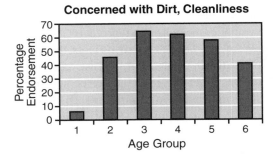

Figure 10.1 Histograms displaying percentage of children engaging in four of the behaviors assessed by the Childhood Routines Inventory.

the rates of endorsement of selected items on the CRI. The results confirmed our hypothesis that compulsive behaviors on the CRI are prevalent during childhood, especially during the 2nd, 3rd, and 4th years of life (Evans et al., 1997). Specifically, 65% of the 1-year-olds in our sample were said to have engaged in bedtime rituals, whereas 80% of 2-year-olds were reported to engage in elaborate bedtime rituals. The prevalence rates for bedtime rituals remain in the 70% range for 3-, 4-, and 5-year-old children as well (Evans et al., 1997).

Over half of the 2-year-olds in our sample were reported to be "very aware" of minute details, such as imperfections in toys and clothes. Forty-one percent of children under the age of 1 year and 36% of children age 5 were described this way. Seventy-seven percent of parents of 2-year-olds endorsed the item "Is your child a perfectionist?" compared with 29% of children less than 1 year of age and 50% of children age 5 years. Parents of 2-year-olds were also nearly twice as likely to endorse the item "Is very concerned with dirt, cleanliness or neatness" than were parents of 5-year-olds and almost 7 times more likely than parents of children less than age 1. Whereas almost 50% of the 2-year-olds were reported to "insist that certain belongings go in their place," only 28% of 5-years-olds were reported to do this. Finally, 63% of 2-year-olds were reported to arrange objects until they are "just right" compared to 4% of children >1 year and 41% of 5-year-olds. The findings are also consistent with work by Kagan (1981), who reports that by age 2, children develop standards for the way objects "should be" such that they may become upset when presented with "imperfect" objects, such as a doll with a missing arm (Evans et al., 1999).

Similar results were reported in a smaller sample of 228 Israeli children age 20 to 59 months (A. H. Zohar & Felz, 2001). In terms of the onset of particular compulsive-like behaviors, the following behaviors were the first to emerge: attached to one favorite object (mean onset 13.85 months); preferred the same household schedule or routine every day (15.43 months); had persistent habits (15.80 months); and strong preferences for certain foods (17.14 months). Later emerging compulsive-like behaviors included the following: acted out the same thing over and over in play (24.14 months); collected/stored objects (25.29 months); seemed very aware of/sensitive to how clothes feel (25.92); and has strong preferences for wearing certain articles of clothing (25.92). The Israeli sample studied by A. H. Zohar and Felz displayed similar sequences in terms of the emergence of items on the CRI (the age of onset for the CRI items = 84 months for the two samples). A. H. Zohar and Felz report a mean difference of 3 months in terms of the onset of the U.S. and Israeli samples, however (Israeli means >3 months of U.S. mean ages of onset).

These data suggest that compulsive-like behaviors are a relatively common aspect of normal child development. Ritualistic and repetitive behavior as well as sensory-perceptual, or "just right" phenomena are highly prevalent among children and appear to be most prevalent between the ages of 2 and 4 years. The exact reasons for the emergence of these behaviors are not known, but it seems reasonable to assume—and some data support—that a variety of neurobiological, cognitive, emotional, and social factors contribute to the development of normative compulsive-like behaviors.

Given the assumption that some compulsivity and obsessionality represents a variant of normative—even adaptive—evolutionarily conserved tendencies in humans and other species, we should see some adaptive correlates of these rituals in young children. A subset ($n = 880$) of our original sample (Evans et al., 1997) was administered the CRI and also a brief version of the Vineland Adaptive Behavior Scales (VABS) assessing children's adaptive behaviors in the areas of socialization and daily living skills. One might hypothesize that during the period of development when children are particularly prone to engage in compulsive-like behaviors (especially 2 to 3 years of age), these behaviors may serve some adaptive emotional and practical functions. Indeed, it seems to be the case that at ages 2 and 3, children's compulsive-like behaviors were moderately associated with adaptive behaviors, whereas the associations between compulsive-like behaviors and adaptive behaviors were not significant for children at age 4, and for 5-year-olds correlation coefficients between compulsive-like behaviors and adaptive behaviors were in a negative direction.

As noted earlier in this chapter, some obsessive-compulsive behaviors invoke a certain amount of magical belief such that thoughts and behaviors are relatively fused and undifferentiated. Many obsessive-compulsive symptoms seem to infer causal links between thoughts and behaviors. In two separate studies, researchers noted that the typical compulsions of young children are associated with children's magical beliefs. In one study (Evans, Milanak, Medeiros, & Ross, 2002), children's beliefs in the power of wishing and their beliefs in magic were positively associated with compulsive-like rituals and habits. Bolton and colleagues (Bolton, Dearsley, Madronal-Luque, & Baron-Cohen, 2002) also noted that compulsive behaviors are related to magical thinking in children ranging in age from 5 to 17 years.

Some evidence suggests that even in young children, normative compulsivity may be related to emotional development (Evans et al., 1999; A. H. Zohar & Felz, 2001). For children less than 4 years of age, repetitive behaviors were significantly and positively related to overall fear and to fear of strangers (Evans et al., 1999). Bedtime fears (fear of the dark, of monsters) were related to hoarding objects; fear of death was significantly associated with strong attachment to a specific object; and fear of animals was related to bedtime rituals.

For children older than age 4, a greater number of correlations emerged. Most notably, overall scores on the rituals inventory were related to bedtime fears. "Just right" behaviors were related to fears of contamination and fear of separation; fear of death was positively related to "repeats actions over and over" and "arranges objects" until they are "just right" (Evans et al., 1999).

These findings echo the theorizing of Winnicott, Erikson, and Werner that children's rituals are associated with anxiety states brought on by the many fears and uncertainties that are common in childhood and that they bear some relationship to the presence of attachment figures as a source of security and syncretic wholeness. These findings also emphasize the range of ritual behaviors and the emerging need young children have to compare elements of the outside world with existing mental representations, as discussed by Gessell and Piaget, so that important aspects of the world are "just right." These findings suggest that the rituals and compulsions that emerge in normal ontogeny not only are similar to pathological rituals and compulsions, but they may also serve similar functions and represent common fundamental mental processes.

Obsessional Thoughts and Compulsive Behaviors among Older Children and Adolescents

Given the cognitive processing that is involved in obsessional thoughts, it is not surprising that more is known about the development of rituals and compulsions in childhood. Nevertheless, several population-based studies have been completed in children ranging in age from 8 to 17 years (Berg, Whitaker, Davies, Flament, & Rapoport, 1988; A. H. Zohar & Bruno, 1997). A. H. Zohar and Bruno studied one of the youngest cohorts in a large community sample of children in Israel. Children were in grades 4, 6, and 8 ($N = 1,083$) and ranged in age from 8 to 14 years. Among the fourth-grade students, five items from a questionnaire of the Maudsley Obsessive-Compulsive Inventory concerning cleanliness, checking, and guilt about lying were endorsed by more than 50% of the children. Although the level of obsessional thought and compulsive behaviors was significantly lower in the eighth grade than in the sixth and fourth, there was an elevation of children with very high levels in the eighth grade.

A second study employed a survey of the Leyton Obsessional Inventory-Child Version with more than 5,000 non-referred adolescents (Berg et al., 1988). As in the study of younger children, a sizable proportion of the population studied (>46% of the sample) endorsed one or more obsessive-compulsive symptoms. The items most frequently endorsed were "thinking repetitive thoughts and words," "hating dirt and dirty things," "worrying about being clean enough," and being "fussy" about keeping one's hands clean. The adolescent girls in this sample endorsed a greater number of obsessional items and had significantly higher interference scores compared to their male counterparts. In this sample, the responses did not differ significantly by the age of the adolescent.

Adult Obsessions and Compulsions

Three independent studies have found that approximately 90% of the normal population report intrusive thoughts whose content is similar, if not identical, to obsessions (Freeston, Ladouceur, Thibodeau, & Gagnon, 1991; Rachman & de Silva, 1978; Salkovskis & Harrison, 1984). In addition to content, the obsessive thoughts reported among normal adults appear to be similar to the obsessions reported among clinical populations in terms of the increased distress associated with the inability to dismiss the thoughts (Rachman & de Silva, 1978; Salkovskis & Harrison, 1984). However, compared with clinical cases of OCD, the obsessions of nonclinical subjects tend to be less frequent, briefer in duration, and more easily dismissed.

Obsessive-Compulsive Features of Early Parenting

There are times in life when adults appear to be more vulnerable to obsessive-compulsive thoughts and behaviors. One of the most distinctive periods surrounds the birth of a child. Winnicott (1958a) described an altered mental state that he termed "primary maternal preoccupation" that characterizes the first weeks of a mother's relationship with her infant. Suggesting that such a state of preoccupation or a state of "heightened sensitivity" develops toward the end of pregnancy and lasts for the first few postnatal weeks, he likened it to a withdrawn or dissociated state that, in the absence of pregnancy and a newborn, would resemble a mental illness of acute onset. In this period, mothers are deeply focused on the infant to the apparent conscious exclusion of all else, and this preoccupation permits them to anticipate the infant's needs, learn his or her unique signals, and over time to develop a sense of the infant as an individual. Winnicott emphasizes the crucial importance of such a stage for the infant's self-development and the developmental consequences for infants when mothers are unable to tolerate such a level of intense preoccupation. Central to our discussion is the described phenomenology of a heightened state of maternal preoccupation centered around the late third trimester and 1st postnatal weeks that usually wanes by the 2nd or 3rd month postpartum as the infant is more socially differentiated.

In a prospective longitudinal study of 82 parents, we have documented the course of early preoccupations and found that they peak around the time of delivery (Leckman et al., 1999). Although fathers and mothers displayed a similar time course, the degree of preoccupation was significantly less for the fathers in our study. For example, at 2 weeks after delivery, mothers of normal infants, on average, report spending nearly 14 hours per day focused exclusively on the infant, whereas fathers report spending approximately half that amount of time. Although the thematic content of these preoccupations includes thoughts of reciprocity and unity with the infant and thoughts about the "perfect" appearance of the infant, anxious intrusive worries concerning the parents' adequacy as parents and the infant's safety and well-being also were commonplace. Virtually all of the parents (>95%) reported recurrent worries about the well-being of their child. More than 80% of the mothers and 70% of the fathers were concerned about the possibility of something bad happening to their baby, including worries about the child's health, development, and appearance. Several parents explicitly mentioned sudden infant death syndrome as the reason they needed to check their infant. The spontaneous narratives recorded at the interview included frequent concerns about the baby falling or being dropped or thrown. One mother described worries about traveling in the car with her infant son and possibly having an accident due to her negligence. Another mother dreamed that her baby had "cuts around her eyes because Mom hadn't cut her baby's finger nails and she had scratched herself." Several parents reported worries about pets or other animals injuring the infant because of some negligence on their part. Consistent with our expectation, a number of parents said such things as, "I tell myself it is ridiculous to think about this, the likelihood is so remote."

Thirty-two percent of the parents (9 mothers and 10 fathers) reported that they had had abhorrent thoughts of harming the infant during the weeks after the birth. A few parents linked their thoughts to the child's demands for attention, such as "When my baby is crying at 2 A.M., I can understand why parents hurt their children." Another father wondered out loud "Am I capable of child molesta-

tion?" However, most of the images focused on acts of negligence, "accidentally dropping the baby or making a mistake by being inattentive." Indeed, one insightful mother initially mentioned that she thought of only other parents harming their babies, but then said, "I guess we are frightened of our aggressive impulses and displace them onto others." In most instances, these were fleeting or momentary thoughts, but seven parents described these thoughts as occurring "occasionally." At 2 weeks after birth, only a small minority of parents report that these unpleasant thoughts are a definite source of interference (10% of both mothers and fathers) or that they caused moderate or severe emotional distress (15% of mothers and 5% of fathers). In response to these anxious or unpleasant thoughts, 59% of the mothers and 42% of the fathers reported that they performed various actions. In this subset of parents, their actions included checking on the baby (60%), talking to others (54%), or making an effort to distract themselves (9%).

Virtually all of the parents (>90%) reported checking on their babies, usually in response to some signal from the infant. However, more than 75% of the parents also described the need to check even though they knew that everything was okay. At this time, nine mothers (22%) and seven fathers (17%) reported that they checked in this compulsive fashion "frequently" or "very frequently." However, only 27% of the mothers and 20% of the fathers recall telling themselves that such compulsive checking was unnecessary or silly. A majority of parents (83% of mothers and 68% of fathers) stated that they would be "moderately" or "severely" distressed if they were prevented from checking on their child.

In this study, we found that 95% of the mothers and 80% of the fathers had such recurrent, anxious intrusive thoughts in the weeks preceding birth. In the weeks following delivery, this percentage declined only slightly to 80% and 73% for mothers and fathers, respectively. At 3 months postpartum, these figures were unchanged. Other investigators have reported similar findings of increased worries that, in particular, may stress relations between the parents as the time for delivery approaches (Cowan & Cowan, 1992). After delivery and on returning home, most frequently cited were concerns about feeding the baby, about the baby's crying, reflecting on the responsibility of caring for the baby, and thoughts about the baby's physical well-being. Conditions such as these are more commonly reported among parents of very sick preterm infants (Goldberg & DiVitto, 1995), infants with serious congenital disorders or malformations, or infants with serious birth complications (Hodapp, 1995).

Even before the child is born parents preoccupy themselves with creating a safe and secure environment for the infant. Major cleaning and renovation projects are commonplace as the human form of nest building unfolds. Uppermost among parental concerns are the safety of their child and their unimpeded access to the child. Safety issues include the cleanliness of the infant's immediate environment. After birth, this same sense of heightened responsibility will compel parents to check on the baby frequently, even when they know the baby is fine. This heightened sense of responsibility and vigilance concerning possible threats to the child's well-being remains a part of parenthood well into the 1st decade and beyond and is a central element of parenthood. For example, as the child matures and becomes more mobile, parents need to child-proof their home to prevent the child's finding toxic chemicals or being at risk for falling down stairs.

EPIDEMIOLOGY AND NATURAL HISTORY OF OBSESSIVE-COMPULSIVE DISORDER

OCD is among the most common psychiatric disorders, with lifetime prevalence estimates as high as 3% and 1-year prevalence rates ranging from 0.5% to 2.1%. These numbers are comparable for both adult and childhood/adolescent OCD (American Psychiatric Association, 2000; Karno, Golding, Sorenson, & Burnam, 1988; Rasmussen & Eisen, 1998; Valleni-Basile et al., 1994; A. H. Zohar, 2001). Modal age of onset is between 6 and 15 years of age for males and 20 and 29 years of age for females (American Psychiatric Association, 2000; Rasmussen & Eisen, 1998).

The natural course of early-onset OCD is variable and often difficult to predict (Flament et al., 1988, 1990; Leonard et al., 1993; Wewetzer et al., 2001). Fluctuations in symptom severity are commonplace and make predictions concerning short-term outcomes unreliable (Lin et al., 2002; A. H. Zohar, 1999). Viewed prospectively, the boundary of the diagnosis of OCD is not always easy to establish, as a significant proportion of childhood-onset OCD cases ascertained at one time point will be judged to be subthreshold at a later time point and vice versa (Berg et al., 1988; Peterson, Pine, Cohen, & Brook, 2001; A. H. Zohar, 2001). Of note is the fact that in several studies of children with OCD, the mean age at onset of compulsions is earlier than the onset of obsessions (Geller et al., 1998; Rapoport, 1989) and differs from the usual pattern seen in individuals with an adult onset. Some investigators have also found that the early-onset individuals are more burdened by compulsions (Rosario-Campos et al., 2001).

A second peak of OCD onset is associated with puberty and the years following. In general, the course of adult OCD shows a range of outcomes: (1) chronic unremitting; (2) phasic, with periods of complete remission; and (3) episodic, with incomplete remission that allows some degree of normal functioning (Goodwin, Guze, & Robins, 1969; Skoog & Skoog, 1999). Studies vary considerably regarding the proportion of patients in each category, but there are at least 10% who exhibit an unremitting course.

The development of efficacious pharmacological and behavioral treatments has led to a significant improvement in outcomes over the past 2 decades. However, once present, a vulnerability to disabling obsessions and compulsions is often a lifelong challenge.

OBSESSIVE-COMPULSIVE SPECTRUM DISORDERS

In recent years, there has been a growing popularity of the concept of a spectrum of disorders related to OCD (Hollander, 1993; Rasmussen, 1994). Although there has been some debate about the breadth of membership and the criteria used for inclusion, certain disorders, including chronic tic disorders, Body Dysmorphic Disorder, eating disorders, and Trichotillomania, are routinely considered to be part of this spectrum (Jenike & Wilhelm, 1998).

Initially, the grounds for grouping these disorders rested on clinical impressions of phenotypic similarities such as a failure to inhibit repetitive behaviors and a subjective urge or compulsive need to engage in these maladaptive behaviors (Hollander, 1993; Rasmussen, 1994). Consequently, support linking this spectrum of disorders to OCD has accumulated from a variety of sources. These include epidemiological studies (Cohen et al., 1995; K. A. Phillips, Gunderson, Mallya, McElroy, & Carter, 1998), family genetic studies that have evaluated the recurrence risk in first-degree family members (Bienvenu et al., 2000; Lenane et al., 1992; Pauls, Alsobrook, Goodman, Rasmussen, & Leckman, 1995; K. A. Phillips et al., 1998), neurobiological and neuroimaging studies (O'Sullivan et al., 1997; Peterson, Staib, et al., 2001; Stein, 2000), and studies of treatment response (Goodman, Ward, Kablinger, & Murphy, 1997; Hollander, 1998; K. A. Phillips, 1996; Ravindran, Lapierre, & Anisman, 1999). These data are far from uniform, and a much stronger case can be made for some disorders, such as chronic tic disorders, compared to others. However, this growing body of data is sufficiently compelling that some investigators have hypothesized that some members of this spectrum may be best understood as variant phenotypes of a common obsessive-compulsive genetic diathesis (Billett, Richter, & Kennedy, 1998; Pauls et al., 1995; Swedo & Leonard, 1992). Alternatively, Yaryura-Tobias and colleagues (2000) have proposed that these disorders might be better classified simply as variants of OCD. This spectrum concept and the accumulating data point to the inherent limitations of current nosological classification schemes and the need for new approaches to gain deeper insights into the genetic and neurobiological origins of these disorders.

EFFORTS TO REFINE BEHAVIORAL PHENOTYPES: SYMPTOM DIMENSIONS VERSUS DISCRETE SUBTYPES

The *DSM-IV* regards OCD as a unitary nosological entity. This parsimony has a certain aesthetic and practical appeal, but it may be misleading. Given the heterogeneity of the clinical picture, course of illness, response to treatment, and emerging neurobiological and genetic findings, investigators have used a variety of approaches to refine this complex set of phenotypes. In this section, we consider these efforts.

Obsessive-Compulsive Symptom Dimensions

The symptoms used to define OCD are diverse. Two individuals with OCD may have totally different and nonoverlapping symptom patterns (Rasmussen & Eisen, 1998). Studies of psychopathology, genetics, neurobiology, and treatment outcomes have frequently and usefully simplified this complex array in several ways, one of which is the use of global severity rating scales such as the Yale-Brown Obsessive Compulsive Scale (Goodman, Price, Rasmussen, Mazure, Delgado, et al., 1989; Goodman, Price, Rasmussen, Mazure, Fleischmann, et al., 1989).

Historically, attempts to classify OCD patients based on their clinical phenotype have met with limited success. Early descriptive efforts yielded a rough topology but lacked a sound empirical basis (Janet & Raymond, 1903/1976; Lewis, 1936). Other difficulties have included the use of symptom inventories that are biased toward specific symptoms such as checking or cleaning or that omit key symptoms such as hoarding, obsessions concerning symmetry or exactness, ordering and arranging obsessions and compulsions, and religious obsessions (Hodgson & Rachman, 1977; Minichiello, Baer, Jenike, & Holland, 1990). As pointed out by Baer (1993) and colleagues, such

biases inherently limit the value of these reports. More problematic was the use of composite severity ratings based on all of the patient's obsessions and compulsions (Fals-Stewart, 1992; Kim, Dysken, Pheley, & Hoover, 1994; McKay, Danyko, Neziroglu, & Yaryura-Tobias, 1995). The use of such composite severity ratings assumes the unity of the OCD construct and loses the rich diversity of symptomatology. Still other studies relied solely on inventories of current symptoms (Baer, 1993; Fals-Stewart, 1992). This approach fails to take into account the changing constellation of symptoms that can be observed over time. Finally, many of these studies have relied on data from a relatively small number of subjects that yield unstable estimates from factor analyses.

Keeping in mind these limitations, earlier studies have consistently paired washing and cleaning compulsions with contamination obsessions. Similarly, aggressive, sexual, and religious obsessions tend to co-occur. Obsessions of symmetry and exactness were found to accompany repeating rituals, counting compulsions, and ordering/arranging compulsions. Similarly, hoarding compulsions often co-occur with hoarding and saving obsessions.

Based on these earlier studies, a series of factor-analytic studies involving more than 2,000 OCD patients have identified at least four obsessive-compulsive symptom dimensions (Baer, 1993; Cavallini, Di Bella, Siliprandi, Malchiodi, & Bellodi, 2002; Leckman et al., 1997; Leckman et al., 2003; Leckman, Zhang, Alsobrook, & Pauls, 2001; Mataix-Cols, Rauch, Manzo, Jenike, & Baer, 1999; Mataix-Cols, Rosario-Campos, & Leckman, 2005; Summerfeldt, Richter, Antony, & Swinson, 1999). One dimension is characterized by aggressive, sexual, and religious obsessions and checking compulsions. A second factor is characterized by obsessions of symmetry and exactness and ordering and arranging compulsions. A third factor includes contamination obsessions and cleaning/washing compulsions, and the fourth factor includes hoarding obsessions and compulsions. In some studies, hoarding symptoms are included with obsessions of symmetry and exactness and ordering and arranging compulsions (Baer, 1993); in other studies, aggressive obsessions and checking behaviors are separate from sexual and religious obsessions (Mataix-Cols, Rauch, et al., 1999).

Preliminary data supporting the validity of these dimensions come from longitudinal studies (Mataix-Cols, Rauch, et al., 2002) in which the strongest predictor of the presence of a particular symptom dimension was having had that symptom dimension in the past. These data suggest that the nature of the obsessive-compulsive symptoms are relatively stable across time, with waxing and waning of symptoms rarely involving shifts between dimensions. Longer follow-up studies involving larger samples are needed to better understand the fluctuations of OCD symptoms across time.

As discussed earlier, recent data provide evidence for the orderly emergence of similar compulsive traits in normally developing children (Evans et al., 1997; A. H. Zohar & Felz, 2001). Many of the rituals and compulsions of childhood appear to be aligned with obsessions of symmetry and exactness and compulsions involving ordering and arranging. However, elements of each of the factors can be traced to early childhood, including worries about attachment figures and an increased concern about dirt and germs. Similarly, the heightened sensitivity to threat that is seen in new parents can contain preoccupations and behaviors that are congruent with each of these dimensions.

As reviewed in later sections of this chapter, preliminary data supporting the validity of these dimensions come from genetic studies (Leckman et al., 2003; Rosario-Campos et al., 2005; Zhang et al., 2002), functional brain imaging studies (Mataix-Cols et al., 2003, 2004; M. L. Phillips et al., 2000; Rauch et al., 1998), and treatment studies (Black et al., 1998; Mataix-Cols, Marks, Greist, Kobak, & Baer, 2002).

Discrete Subtypes

Investigators have argued that there are some distinctive forms of OCD that are best regarded as discrete subtypes, each with its own natural history, genetic vulnerabilities, neurobiology, and treatment response. Some of the most compelling data concern tic-related OCD, early-onset OCD, and hoarding as discrete subtypes.

Tic-Related Obsessive-Compulsive Disorder

The obsessions and compulsions found in individuals with Tourette's syndrome and other chronic tic disorders cover a broad range in terms of content, intensity, persistence, impairment, degree of perceived ego syntonicity, and relationship to the individual's tic symptoms. A growing number of studies examining symptom type, natural history, sex ratio, family genetic data, neurobiological correlates, and treatment response lend increasing support to the hypothesis that tic-related OCD constitutes a distinctive subtype. Compared to OCD in individuals without a history of tics, this subtype appears to be characterized by an earlier age of onset and a greater proportion of males (King, Leckman, Scahill, & Cohen, 1998; Leckman, Walker, Goodman, Pauls, & Cohen, 1994). They also have a more frequent family history of chronic tics (Grados et al., 2001; Pauls et al., 1995), a worse long-term prognosis (Wewetzer et al.,

2001), higher afternoon plasma prolactin levels and more normal cerebrospinal fluid oxytocin levels (Leckman, Goodman, et al., 1994a, 1994b), and a poorer therapeutic response to monotherapy with serotonin reuptake inhibitors, albeit with marked improvement with the addition of a neuroleptic (McDougle et al., 1993, 1994).

Early-Onset Obsessive-Compulsive Disorder

Most studies have found that early-onset OCD (onset under the age of 12 years), when compared to adult onset, is typically characterized by significantly higher frequencies of tic-like compulsions, sensory phenomena preceding repetitive behaviors, higher probability of comorbid tic disorders or Tourette's disorder, higher rates of OCD and tics among first-degree relatives (Nestadt et al., 2000; Pauls et al., 1995; Rosario-Campos et al., in press), and a poorer short-term treatment response to antiobsessional agents (Rosario-Campos et al., 2001).

Hoarding

Hoarding occurs relatively frequently in OCD, and there is evidence that patients with hoarding symptoms have more severe OCD and are less responsive to treatment (Black et al., 1998; Mataix-Cols, Baer, Rauch, & Jenike, 2000). Hoarders frequently exhibit obsessions of symmetry, as well as counting and ordering compulsions (Samuels et al., 2002). Hoarders also exhibit a high rate of obsessive-compulsive spectrum conditions, including social phobia, personality disorders, and pathological grooming behaviors (skin picking, nail biting, and Trichotillomania). Hoarding and tics are also more frequent in first-degree relatives of hoarding than nonhoarding OCD patients. Genetic linkage data (Samuels et al., 2002; Zhang et al., 2002) and neuroimaging studies support the utility of seeing hoarding as a distinctive subtype of OCD (Mataix-Cols et al., 2004; Saxena et al., 2004).

NEUROPSYCHOLOGY

Recent neuropsychological evidence suggests that patients with OCD perform poorly on some executive function (EF) tasks, which typically involve recruitment of the frontal cortices. Executive functions include goal-directed behavior, sustained attention, working memory, maintaining a cognitive set, and cognitive set shifting, as well as motor inhibition and response suppression (Evans, Lewis, & Iobst, 2004; Schultz, Evans, & Wolff, 1999).

Some evidence suggests that patients with OCD may perform significantly worse on tasks of set shifting (e.g., the Wisconsin Card Sort Task [WCST]) relative to normal controls as well as compared to other psychiatric groups (Head, Bolton, & Hymas, 1989; Hollander & Wong, 1995; Hymas, Lees, Bolton, Epps, & Head, 1991; Lucey et al., 1997). For example, OCD subjects make significantly more perseverative errors on the WCST than normal controls (Lucey et al., 1997). In particular, reports of obsessions are linearly related to WCST errors. Still more specifically, OCD patients who exhibit obsessional slowness perform worse on cognitive set-shifting tasks relative to OCD patients not exhibiting obsessional slowness (Gehring, Himle, & Nisenson, 2000). In addition to perseverative errors on the WCST, patients with OCD tend to have longer response latencies on EF tasks (Gehring et al., 2000). Greater response latency may indicate that subjects spend more time generating alternative responses. Patients with OCD may also be more likely to check or doubt their responses on such tasks and to experience greater error detection, which may slow response rates. Longer response latencies observed with OCD patients appear to be limited to these EF tasks and do not generalize to other, non-EF tasks (Behar et al., 1984), as behavioral responses on other tasks can be performed at normal speeds. It seems that only those behaviors that involve linking and sequencing behaviors are slowed in patients with OCD (Galderisi, Mucci, Catapano, D'Amato, & Maj, 1995; Sawle, Hymas, Lees, & Frackowiak, 1991; Schultz et al., 1999). Even within the normal range along the obsessive-compulsive spectrum, obsessive-compulsive behaviors are associated with poorer set-shifting abilities (A.H. Zohar, LaBuda, & Moschel-Ravid, 1995). In a typical sample, scores on the checking factor of the Maudsley Obsessive-Compulsive Inventory are related to perseverative errors and reaction time, though the amount of shared variance is modest. Nonclinical subjects whose self-reported obsessive-compulsive behaviors fall 1 standard deviation above the mean performed poorly on the Tower of Hanoi (TOH; a measure of planning ability), relative to subjects whose self-reports fall 1 standard deviation below the mean on the Maudsley Inventory (Mataix-Cols, Junque, et al., 1999). Both checking behaviors and total score on the Inventory are correlated to number of moves and time to complete the TOH. These findings argue for a continuum approach to OCD, such that similar cognitive deficits associated with OCD may play a role in subclinical obsessions and compulsions (Evans et al., 2004; Schultz et al., 1999).

Still, some question whether set-shifting deficits are peculiar to OCD. In studies employing strict matching strategies (i.e., age, sex, education level, and IQ) between OCD patients and comparison groups, previously observed differences on set-shifting tasks disappear (Abbruzzese, Ferri, & Scarone, 1995). Others (e.g., Cox, 1997; Grau, 1991) argue that IQ is a better predictor of performance on the WCST than are the symptoms associated with OCD, suggesting that set-shifting deficits in OCD may have been overestimated in the past (Schultz et al., 1999).

Although the role of set shifting in OCD remains somewhat unclear, findings linking motor inhibition/response suppression and obsessive-compulsive behaviors are more consistent. In a study of children and adolescents with OCD, symptom severity correlated positively with response suppression errors (Cox, Fedio, & Rapoport, 1989; Rosenberg, Dick, O'Hearn, & Sweeney, 1997). Relative to controls, patients with OCD demonstrate poor performance on an oculomotor suppression (antisaccade) task (Rosenberg, Averbach, et al., 1997). These findings are consistent with previous work (Tien, Pearlson, Machlin, Bylsma, & Hoehn-Saric, 1992) noting greater error rate on a goal-guided antisaccade task. The task requires that subjects move their eyes away from, rather than toward, a novel stimulus (Schultz et al., 1999). Several other studies reports similar deficits in patients with OCD on tasks of object alternation, but not on set-shifting tasks. Object alternation tasks require that subjects give a certain response for one stimulus, but not for another, followed by reversal of the response rule (Cavedini, Ferri, Sarcone, & Bellodi, 1998; Gross-Isseroff et al., 1996). Not only do these studies report group differences between OCD and non-OCD subjects, but they also report linear associations between symptom severity and perseverative errors of commission on response suppression/object alternation tasks (Gross-Isseroff et al., 1996), again supporting a spectrum approach to obsessive-compulsive symptoms and associated neuropsychological performance. In sum, research examining EF and obsessive-compulsive symptoms indicates impairment of response suppression and motor inhibition abilities in subjects exhibiting obsessive-compulsive behaviors. The findings are somewhat less consistent on set-shifting tasks. For each of these EF tasks, evidence points to longer response latencies with increasing obsessive-compulsive symptom expression.

To return briefly to the normative development of compulsivity and perseverative behaviors mentioned earlier in this chapter, our recent findings echo some of these interesting associations linking compulsive behaviors and neuropsychological performance (Pietrefesa & Evans, in press). Response inhibition and set-shifting abilities, in addition to their association with OCD, undergo important developments during childhood, particularly during the preschool and early school-age years, and presumably as a function of frontal lobe maturation (Evans et al., 2004; Zelazo & Jacques, 1996). In children less than 6 years of age, errors of commission on a go/no go task (the continuous performance task), as well as errors on a Stroop-like task, were positively related to compulsive-like behaviors, whereas for children over the age of 6 years, errors of commission were negatively associated with compulsive behaviors (Pietrefesa & Evans, in press). Response inhibition and compulsivity, which appear to be linked in OCD, are also linked in normative development. At a certain point in normative development, however, the neurobiological structures controlling response inhibition (see later discussion) begin to do their job to effectively organize and regulate behavior (Pietrefesa & Evans, in press), whereas earlier in development (and in OCD), impulsivity and compulsivity may be more closely related, reflecting the dysregulation of associated neurobiological structures and functions. These findings are preliminary, however, and require further study.

GENETIC FACTORS

Recent advances in molecular genetics have greatly increased the capacity to localize disease genes on the human genome. These methods are now being applied to complex disorders, including OCD (Hanna et al., 2002; Willour et al., 2004). One of the major difficulties in the application of these approaches is the likely etiologic heterogeneity of OCD and related phenotypes. Heterogeneity reduces the power of gene-localization methods, such as linkage analysis (Alcais & Abel, 1999; Gu, Province, Todorov, & Rao, 1998; Zhang & Risch, 1996). Etiologic heterogeneity may be reflected in phenotypic variability. Thus, it would be highly desirable to dissect the syndrome, at the level of the phenotype, into valid quantitative heritable components.

As reviewed earlier, recent factor analyses have consistently identified several symptom dimensions (Mataix-Cols et al., 2005), two of which are associated with increased familial risk for OCD: aggressive, sexual, and religious obsessions and checking compulsions and symmetry and ordering obsessions and compulsions (Alsobrook, Leckman, Goodman, Rasmussen, & Pauls, 1999; Leckman et al., 2003). Both of these symptom dimensions are also frequently seen in association with Tourette's syndrome (TS).

Using data collected by the Tourette Syndrome Association International Consortium for Genetics (TSAICG) Affected Sibling Pair Study, Leckman et al. (2003) selected all available affected TS pairs and their parents for which

these obsessive-compulsive symptom dimensions (factor scores) could be generated using the four-factor algorithm first presented by Leckman et al. (1997). Remarkably, over 50% of the siblings with TS were found to have comorbid OCD, and greater than 30% of mothers and 10% of fathers also had a diagnosis of OCD. The factor scores for aggressive, sexual, and religious obsessions and checking compulsions and symmetry and ordering obsessions and compulsions scores were significantly correlated in sibling pairs concordant for TS. In addition, the mother-child correlations, but not father-child correlations, were also significant for these two factors. Based on the results of the complex segregation analyses, significant evidence for genetic transmission was obtained for all factors.

More recently, a genome scan of the hoarding dimension was completed using the same TSAICG data set (Zhang et al., 2002). The analyses were conducted for hoarding as both a dichotomous trait and a quantitative trait. Not all sib pairs in the sample were concordant for hoarding. Standard linkage analyses were performed using GENEHUNTER and Haseman-Elston methods. In addition, novel analyses with a recursive-partitioning technique were employed. Significant allele sharing was observed for both the dichotomous and the quantitative hoarding phenotypes for markers at 4q34, 5q35.2, and 17q25. The 4q site is in proximity to D4S1625, which was identified by the TSAICG as a region linked to the TS phenotype. A recursive-partitioning analytic technique also examined multiple markers simultaneously. Results suggest joint effects of specific loci on 5q and 4q.

In sum, the use of quantitative traits that are familial may provide a powerful way to detect the genetic susceptibility loci that contribute to OCD presentations (Alcais & Abel, 1999; Elston, Buxbaum, Jacobs, & Olson, 2000; Leckman et al., 2001; Zhang & Risch, 1996). Thus far, this approach has provided especially promising leads with regard to the hoarding phenotype. Next steps include, first, the use of these symptom dimensions in large multigenerational families to refine the initial genetic linkage results for the hoarding phenotype. Obviously, if specific loci are identified, this will provide compelling evidence for the validity of this multidimensional approach to OCD. Second, genome scans need to be conducted using the remaining obsessive-compulsive symptom dimensions. Families segregating for TS or early-onset OCD may be especially valuable in this enterprise. Given the high mother-child correlations in the Leckman et al. (2003) study, it may also be valuable to examine the linkage results for alleles that are identical by descent from the mother. Third, twin and cross-fostering studies are needed to further evaluate the heritability of these symptom dimensions within the general population. Finally, future genetic studies will need to examine the relationship between these dimensions and other closely related phenotypes, including various eating disorders (Halmi et al., 2003) and Body Dysmorphic Disorder.

Epigenetic Risk and Protective Factors

Pregnancy and the immediate postpartum period is a time of increased risk for the onset of OCD, with rates among women varying from 11% to 47% (Buttolph, Peets, & Holland, 1998; Ingram, 1961; Lo, 1967; Neziroglu, Anemone, & Yaryura-Tobias, 1992; Pollitt, 1957). Most of these cases begin during late pregnancy or a few days to 2 weeks after delivery. Other frequently reported precipitants include a recent move, sexual or marital problems, and the illness or death of a near relative (Ingram, 1961; Lo, 1967; Pollitt, 1957).

NEUROBIOLOGY

Multiple converging lines of evidence indicate that specific neural circuits and neurotransmitter and neuromodulatory systems play a crucial role in the expression of obsessive-compulsive symptoms. After examining the available evidence, we consider the role these circuits and systems may play in the development of normal forms of obsessive-compulsive behavior and raise the question whether OCD is best viewed as a single disorder or as a complex set of vulnerabilities that in one way or another relate to our appraisals of the environment with regard to its safety.

Neural Circuits

Neuroimaging studies have implicated a variety of neural structures, particularly frontal-striatal circuits, in the neurobiology of OCD (Baxter et al., 1992; Insel, 1992; Rauch et al., 1994; Rauch, Savage, Alpert, Dougherty, et al., 1997). Several regions of the prefrontal cortex are presumably involved in executive functions and are implicated in the pathobiology of OCD. Specifically, OCD patients typically show hyperactivity of the lateral orbital frontal cortex (OFC), caudate nucleus, and anterior cingulated cortex (ACC), all three of which are thought to work together to inhibit or terminate inappropriate responses and to select and monitor preferred behavioral sequences. The OFC in particular appears to have a specific role in decision making based on emotional cues (Anderson, Bechara, Damasio,

Tranel, & Damasio, 1999; Bechara, Damasio, Damasio, & Anderson, 1994; Rolls, 2000). Positron emission tomography (PET) studies indicate increased glucose metabolism in the OFC, caudate, ACC, and thalamus (Baxter, 1990; Baxter et al., 1992; Baxter et al., 1987; Nordahl et al., 1989; Rauch et al., 1994; Rauch, Savage, Alpert, Fischman, & Jenike, 1997; Schwartz, Stoessel, Baxter, Martin, & Phelps, 1996). In dense-array event-related potential (ERP) research, OCD patients demonstrate an exaggerated error-monitoring component localized to the region of the ACC (Gehring et al., 2000; see Evans et al., 2004, for a review). In PET studies, symptom provocation in OCD is associated with increases in blood flow to the OFC and caudate (McGuire et al., 1994; Rauch et al., 1994), and functional magnetic resonance imaging (fMRI) work has noted increased activation of the medial OFC, ACC, and caudate as well as the insular cortex and amygdala (Breiter & Rauch, 1996; Breiter et al., 1996).

Successful intervention seems to reduce these activation patterns. Baxter and colleagues (1992; see also Schwartz et al., 1996) observed reductions in glucose metabolization in the OFC and caudate nucleus in OCD patients following a 10-week trial of both pharmacological and cognitive-behavioral therapy. Saxena et al. (2002) found symptom reduction induced by pharmacological therapy to correspond with reduced metabolism in the right lateral-anterior OFC as well as the right caudate nucleus. Thus, not only are the symptoms of OCD associated with orbitostriatal hyperactivation, but perhaps more remarkably, these studies suggest that the causal relation between brain and behavior associated with OCD may be bidirectional (Evans et al., 2004). These brain-behavior relations are thought to characterize children and adolescents as well as adults (Bradshaw & Sheppard, 2000; Santosh, 2000).

The OFC is involved in a broad range of intersecting functions, including cognitive, emotional, and behavioral regulation (Evans et al., 2004). These functions include evaluation of the motivational significance of stimuli, learning appropriate responses to rewarding and aversive stimuli, and adaptive switching of behavioral responses, as well as processing and regulating emotional states (Bechara, Damasio, & Damasio, 2000; Davidson & Irwin, 1999; Rolls, 2000). The OFC also is responsible for its own kind of working memory, including representations of the significance of stimuli and of one's own emotional states. The OFC includes several distinct regions, each unique in its anatomy, connectivity, and cell structure. These regions may be divided into medial and lateral areas. The medial region is involved in reward and incentive motivation and stimulus-response learning; it is more directly connected to paralimbic and limbic structures involved in emotion regulation (e.g., insular cortex, amygdala, hypothalamus; Evans et al., 2004). The lateral region of the OFC is implicated in behavioral inhibition, response suppression, selection of one response over others (e.g., Bokura, Yamaguchi, & Kobayashi, 2001; Bradshaw & Sheppard, 2000), and the reappraisal (or effortful regulation) of emotional significance (Ochsner, Bunge, Gross, & Gabrieli, 2002). This region is more richly connected to higher neocortical systems, particularly the dorsal lateral prefrontal cortex.

Both the medial and lateral OFC systems are connected to the basal ganglia, including the striatum. The medial OFC is strongly connected to the ventral tegmental area and nucleus accumbens, with which it participates in a circuit controlling basic incentive motivation (Depue & Collins, 1999). The lateral OFC is connected to the caudate nucleus, with which it participates in the coordination of motor activity. Both orbital-striatal streams project to the thalamus, from where they return to frontal and motor cortical systems, comprising feedback circuits that modulate motivation and action. Finally, regions of the OFC are connected to the ACC, another frontal system involved in executive functions. The ACC is involved in overriding prepotent response patterns, self-monitoring and error detection, and selection among competing responses (Botvinick, Nystrom, Fissell, Carter, & Cohen, 1999; C. S. Carter et al., 2000), functions that overlap with the lateral OFC.

As noted earlier, several OCD symptom dimensions have been identified. Despite this phenotypic heterogeneity, only one neuroimaging study thus far has examined the neural correlates of specific OCD symptom factors (Rauch et al., 1998). This study found that a factor comprising aggressive, religious, and sexual obsessions and checking compulsions correlated significantly with blood flow in the striatum bilaterally, whereas a factor of contamination obsessions and cleaning or washing compulsions correlated with blood flow in bilateral ACC, left OFC, and other cortical areas. Symmetry-related and order-related OCD symptoms had a trend toward negative correlation with blood flow in the right striatum. More recently, Mataix-Cols et al. (2004) found a distinct pattern of activation associated with several of the symptom dimensions. Patients viewed in the MRI machine alternating blocks of emotional (washing-related, checking-related, or hoarding-related) and neutral pictures while listening to scenarios related to the content of each picture type. Specifically, OCD patients demonstrated significantly greater activation than controls in bilateral ventromedial prefrontal regions and right caudate nucleus in response to washing stimuli; putamen/globus pallidus, thalamus, and dorsal cortical areas in

response to aggressive/checking stimuli; and left precentral gyrus and right orbitofrontal cortex in response to hoarding stimuli. Although these are preliminary results, they raise the question of whether the heterogeneity in the findings of previous functional imaging studies of OCD could be partially accounted for by phenotypic variations among their subject pools.

Neurotransmitters and Neuromodulators

In addition to imaging studies, pharmacological and neurobiological studies have implicated several central neurotransmitter systems in the pathophysiology of OCD and related conditions. The strongest pharmacological evidence concerns the serotonergic system and the well-established efficacy of potent serotonin reuptake inhibitors in the treatment of OCD (cf. Goodman, Price, Rasmussen, Delgado, et al., 1989; J. Zohar & Insel, 1987). However, other systems also have been implicated. Specifically, central dopaminergic and opioid systems seem to be important in the expression of some forms of OCD (Goodman et al., 1990; Hanna, McCracken, & Cantwell, 1991; Insel & Pickar, 1983; McDougle et al., 1993, 1994; Senjo, 1989). Several studies have implicated two closely related neuropeptides, arginine vasopressin (AVP), and oxytocin (OT), in the pathobiology of some forms of OCD (Altemus et al., 1992; Annsseau et al., 1987; de Boer & Westenberg, 1992; Leckman et al., 1994b; Swedo et al., 1992). Both AVP and OT have been implicated in the manifestation of memory, grooming, sexual, and aggressive behaviors (Leckman, Goodman, et al., 1994b).

OT has been called the "amnesic" neuropeptide because of its action to attenuate memory consolidation and retrieval. This property has led some clinical investigators to administer OT to OCD patients in the hope that it would help to extinguish compulsions. The results of these trials are mixed, with some patients showing slight worsening of obsessive-compulsive symptoms (Leckman, Goodman, et al., 1994b). Animal data suggest that the OT effects on memory are bimodal and site-dependent. Whereas low doses attenuate memory, moderate doses can actually improve memory. Grooming behavior can be elicited pharmacologically with the administration of either AVP or OT. Administered OT shows a clear dose-response relationship: Increased doses lead to more frequent grooming behavior. The pattern of OT-related grooming involves autogrooming of the head and anogenital regions in many species. Given the close association of animal models of grooming behaviors and human compulsions (e.g., hand washing), AVP and OT continue to be of interest as potential mediators of obsessive and compulsive behaviors. Some of the most compelling data in animals concern the role of OT and AVP in parental and affiliative behaviors (Insel & Young, 2001).

The past decade has seen the emergence of a substantial literature indicating that a variety of neuropeptides are also intimately involved in the regulation of these processes (C. S. Carter, DeVries, & Taymans, 1997; Insel & Harbaugh, 1989; Leckman & Herman, 2002; Numan, 1994). For example, in the case of maternal behavior, several studies have reported that OT given centrally (but not peripherally) to virgin female rats induces full maternal behavior within minutes (Pedersen & Prange, 1979). In contrast, blocking central OT pathways using centrally administered antagonists, antisera, or lesions blocks the onset of maternal behavior (Fahrbach, Morrell, & Pfaff, 1985; Insel & Harbaugh, 1989; Pedersen, Caldwell, Johnson, Fort, & Prange, 1985). One key feature of these studies is that OT antagonists do not appear to disrupt maternal behavior per se, as the same intervention following parturition when maternal behavior is already established is without effect.

Neurobiological Perspectives on the Development of Normal Obsessive-Compulsive Behaviors

The existence of structural and functional differences, specific pharmacological responses in humans exhibiting clinically significant manifestations of obsessions and compulsions, and neurobiological findings consistent with animal models of obsessive-compulsive behaviors suggest that these biological mechanisms might play a role in the development of normal obsessions and compulsions. To date, however, little is known about the specific neurobiological mechanisms involved in the emergence of ritualistic behavior and obsessional thought. Indeed, it has only been in the past several years that investigators have begun to examine normal subjects in response to stimuli that are known to provoke OC symptoms in vulnerable individuals. For example, Mataix-Cols and colleagues (2003) imaged 10 normal controls while viewing alternating blocks of emotional (normally aversive, washing-relevant, checking-relevant, or hoarding-relevant pictures) and neutral pictures and imagining brief scenarios related to the content of each picture. They found that the normally aversive images activated regions previously identified during symptom provocation in OCD patients (OFC, lateral frontal cortex, ACC, temporal cortex, basal ganglia, thalamus, amygdala, insula), and distinct patterns of neural response were identified that were associated with the anxiety related to each symptom dimension. In another study, Lor-

berbaum and colleagues (2002) examined the areas of brain activation in new mothers after listening to infant cries. They found activation in the ACC, the right OFC, the medial thalamic nuclei, the bilateral mesial prefrontal cortex, and the hypothalamus and central gray extending to the ventral tegmental area and ventral striatal/basal forebrain regions in the vicinity of the nucleus accumbens and the bed of the stria terminalis.

Although there is considerable disagreement about the specific brain regions that may be involved in OCD and/or nonpathological forms of obsessions and compulsions, frontal lobe, limbic cortices, basal ganglia systems, midbrain, and hypothalamic sites are likely to be involved. Advances in the neurobiology of OCD and other perseverative behavior disorders may shed light on the maturational changes that give rise to repetitive behaviors, intrusive thoughts, and circumscribed interest patterns that are common in the behavioral repertoire of typically developing young children. Studies of normal individuals during specific developmental epochs may be particularly revealing. The model of overactive interrelated threat-detection circuits appears to be heuristically promising across the course of development.

ETIOLOGICAL PERSPECTIVES AND APPROACHES TO TREATMENT

A remarkable diversity of causes has been identified as contributing to the development of OCD, ranging from demonic possession to diversions of psychic energy to unconscious psychological conflicts to dysfunctional habits and faulty appraisals of normally occurring thoughts to neurochemical hypotheses to discrete brain injuries and post-infectious autoimmune responses. Although we remain largely ignorant of the actual causes of this disease, many of these theories have led to specific treatments, some with clear efficacy. In this section, we briefly examine these etiological perspectives as they relate to the phenomenology, natural history, and especially the treatment of OCD. This compilation will also set the stage for an integrative hypothesis offered at a later point in this chapter.

Descriptive Psychiatry and the Origins of Behavior Therapy

Berrios (1996) has nicely reviewed the historical origins of OCD as a nosological category. Focusing mostly on French and German sources in the nineteenth century, he has documented how OCD was successively explained as a disorder of volition, intellect, and emotions. Janet (Janet & Raymond, 1903/1976; Pitman, 1987b) is often credited with providing the first definitive account of OCD. Although this point is in dispute (Berrios, 1996), Janet did provide one of the first descriptions of what is now termed exposure therapy, including the name itself, as quoted by Baer and Minichiello (1998):

> The guide, the therapist, will specify to the patient the action as precisely as possible. He will analyze it into its elements if it should be necessary to give the patient's mind an immediate and proximate aim. By continually repeating the order to perform the action, that is, exposure, he will help the patient greatly by words of encouragement at every sign of success, however insignificant, for encouragement will make the patient realize these little successes and will stimulate him with the hopes aroused by glimpses of greater successes in the future.

Janet's account is of particular interest as it emphasizes the need for the patient to be fully in the present moment and to perform "real actions" involving considerable effort—hallmarks of most cognitive-behavioral interventions in OCD. It is also striking that Janet described OCD as the result of "psychasthenia," a condition that grew out of a state of "incompleteness" (*inachèvement*). Although the actual meaning of these words may be obscure, the fact that he saw this state as leading to a range of conditions, in addition to OCD, including tic disorders and other diagnoses, shows his appreciation for what is now called the obsessive-compulsive spectrum disorders (Hollander, 1993). Janet's call to "give the patient's mind an immediate and proximate aim" resonates with the capacity of the individual to experience a reappraisal of the emotional significance of specific environmental cues via mechanisms active in the OFC and its connections with reward pathways originating in the midbrain.

Unconscious Conflict, the Vicissitudes of Development, and Psychoanalysis

Freud, working in the same era as Janet, came to view OCD as arising from unconscious psychological conflicts, associated with aggressive and sexual urges to hurt, soil, and control that were capable of generating tremendous anxiety. In his famous description of the Rat Man, Freud (1909/1966) described a range of characteristic mental operations, including denial, reaction formation, isolation, magical thinking, doubting, intellectualization, and undoing that he believed served as defenses against the intrusion of these urges into conscious awareness. This theory served

as one of the foundation stones of psychoanalysis, an intensive form of therapy aimed at gaining a deeper understanding of an individual's unconscious drives and defensive maneuvers. Although there is no controlled evidence to suggest that traditional psychodynamic psychotherapy or psychoanalysis is effective in treating the symptoms of OCD, this form of therapy was the standard for several decades, before being replaced over the past 20 years by cognitive-behavioral interventions and pharmacotherapy (Marks, 1987). It also is of interest that Freud's theory was one in which development played a crucial role. Indeed, he saw the overt or concealed tendencies toward cruelty and anal eroticism as reflecting a fixation on or a regression to an earlier stage of mental development. It is perhaps no accident that the normal developmental period that corresponds to toilet training is contemporaneous with the emergence of rituals, habits, and perfectionism in normal young children (Evans et al., 1997).

Learning Theory and Behavior Therapy

The learning theory that has received the most attention in OCD is Mowrer's (1960) two-stage learning theory, which states that anxiety is classically conditioned to a specific environmental event (stage 1, classical conditioning). The individual then uses compulsive or ritualistic behavior to lessen the anxiety. If the compulsion succeeds in reducing anxiety, then behavior is reinforced, making it more likely that the compulsion will be repeated when the anxiety recurs (stage 2, operant conditioning). It is thought that because the individual does not remain in contact with the eliciting stimulus for a sufficient time for the conditioned anxiety to habituate, obsessions persist. This, combined with the anxiety reduction associated with the performance of the compulsions, produces a cycle that is difficult to break.

V. Meyer, Levy, and Schnurer (1974) were among the first to use a technique called exposure and response prevention to successfully treat 15 patients with OCD. A group at the Maudsley Hospital in London that included Rachman, Hodgson, Marks, and Mawson provided evidence from the first controlled trials that systematic exposure to feared stimuli associated with the decision not to perform the compulsion (response prevention; Marks et al., 1988; Rachman & Hodgson, 1980) provided positive results. These initial positive results have been extended and refined over the past 2 decades by several research groups in the United States and Europe (Emmelkamp, 1982; Foa & Goldstein, 1978). Meta-analyses of this technique have confirmed the short- and longer-term efficacy of this technique (Christensen, Hadzi-Pavlovic, Andrews, & Matrick, 1987; van Balkom et al., 1994).

Rachman and Hodgson (1980) also have tested aspects of this two-stage theory. As predicted, exposure to the stimulus results in an increase in both subjective and physiological indices of anxiety. They also documented that when patients were allowed to engage in their compulsive behaviors, there were measurable reductions in their level of anxiety. These findings, however, appear to be limited to OCD patients with contamination worries and washing and cleaning compulsions. Among OCD patients with checking compulsions, the level of anxiety reduction following checking rituals was less noticeable. Indeed, in 7 of 36 trials, the patients reported an increase in anxiety. These findings are consistent with the view that OCD is not a homogeneous condition. They also raise the question of whether this diversity is best accounted for by identifying discrete subgroups of OCD patients or by using the dimensional approach to obsessive-compulsive symptoms outlined earlier.

Cognitive Theories and Treatments of Obsessive-Compulsive Disorder

Cognitive models of OCD have emphasized problems with threat appraisal and cognitive processing. In the area of thought appraisal, an exaggerated sense of responsibility has attracted the most interest. For example, Salkovskis (1985) has argued that the intrusive thoughts and images characteristic of OCD are nearly universal cognitive events. According to this theory, what distinguishes individuals with OCD is their appraisal of these thoughts rather than their occurrence. Indeed, three independent studies have found that approximately 90% of the normal population report intrusive thoughts whose content is similar, if not identical, to obsessions (Freeston et al., 1991; Rachman & de Silva, 1978; Salkovskis & Harrison, 1984). Other cognitive domains that may contain faulty appraisals include threat estimation, a need for perfectionism, overvaluing of thoughts, a need to control all aspects of one's life, and doubting the veracity of one's sensory experience (Obsessive-Compulsive Cognitions Working Group, 1997). Controlled clinical trials of cognitive therapy for OCD show promise and indicate that cognitive therapy and exposure and response prevention are likely to have similar effects over comparable time periods (Cottraux et al., 2001; van Oppen et al., 1995). Of interest in these comparative trails, exposure and response prevention was found to influence in a positive direction several cognitive indices in these clinical trials, including some having to do with

faulty appraisals of inferiority, guilt, and responsibility (Cottraux et al., 2001).

A second cognitive approach to OCD posits the deficits in basic processes of decision making, attention, and memory. These theories have provided a fertile field for empirical study, but the results thus far are in large part preliminary and have not yielded distinctive approaches to treatment (Steketee, Frost, Rheaume, & Wilheim, 1998).

Taken together, these cognitive deficits and distortions complement and extend the range of obsessive-compulsive symptomatology such that any comprehensive model should take into account the presence of such faulty appraisals, indecisiveness, and loss of confidence in memory or dissatisfaction that is commonplace among OCD patients. They also reinforce the point that through effortful reappraisals of the emotional significance of specific environmental cues, individuals are able to alter their brain activity patterns, as reflected in a decrease in activity of the OFC and its connections following successful cognitive therapies (Schwartz & Begley, 2002).

Medical and Neurobiological Etiologies and Neurosurgical Treatments

As summarized by Jenike (1998), a number of case reports describe the development of obsessive-compulsive symptoms following head trauma, brain tumors, and drug abuse; however, in most of these cases, it is difficult to implicate a particular circuit or brain region. In a second review, Peterson, Bronen, and Duncan (1996) reported three additional cases in which the patient's obsessive-compulsive symptoms showed a worsening during a period of tumor progression. Based on the localization of the lesions, the authors concluded that the limbic system, including the hypothalamus, ACC, and the caudate nucleus, were potentially involved in the neurobiology of OCD. Additional information comes from the work of Laplane and colleagues (1989), who studied eight patients with brain damage due to anoxic or toxic insults and who shared the combination of bilateral basal ganglia lesions and a frontal lobe-like syndrome. Each of the patients showed stereotyped activities with obsessive-compulsive behavior. The bilateral lesions appeared to be confined to the striatum and the globus pallidus. In addition, PET in seven patients revealed hypometabolism of the prefrontal cortex relative to other parts of the brain. Although this is a fascinating series, most of these patients also demonstrated a form of psychic inertia manifested by a loss of drive and a loss of goal-directed behavior, features not commonly associated with OCD. It is worth noting that the co-occurrence of tic symptoms and stereotypic behavior was not an uncommon clinical feature in many of the case reports cited in this section.

There also is a strong association between OCD and a diverse array of infectious, metabolic, and neuropsychiatric disorders, including von Economo's encephalitis (Claude, Bourk, & Lamache, 1927), diabetes insipidus (Barton, 1965), Huntington's disease (Miguel, Rauch, & Jenike, 1997), Tourette's syndrome (Pauls & Leckman, 1986), Sydenham's chorea (Swedo et al., 1989), and pediatric autoimmune neuropsychiatric disorders associated with streptococcal infections (Swedo et al., 1998). Generally speaking, these reports provide further support for OCD being a disease involving the basal ganglia and limbic forebrain as well as hypothalamic and hippocampal regions.

A variety of neurosurgical techniques including the OFC, as in subcaudate tractotomy (Knight, 1972), internal capsule (A. Meyer & Beck, 1954), thalamus, and ACC (Jenike et al., 1991), have been used to treat refractory OCD cases with largely favorable results. These findings lend support to the notion of an OCD-relevant neuronal circuitry extending over all of these structures. Capsulotomy, in particular, is designed to interrupt reciprocal thalamocortical projections contained in the internal capsule and to interfere with a postulated overactivation of the OFC (as reviewed earlier). Of interest, deep brain stimulation using quadripolar electrodes implanted bilaterally in the anterior limbs of the internal capsules has been successfully applied in patients with treatment-refractory OCD (Cosyns, Gabriels, & Nuttin, 2003). Acute deep brain stimulation is reported to result in an immediate improvement of speech, mood, eye contact, and motor function, and chronic deep brain stimulation is reported to improve obsessional and compulsive symptomatology in a majority of patients.

Animal Models

A number of animal models of OCD have been proposed, mostly based on early ethologists' conceptualization of "fixed-action patterns," behaviors necessary for survival that are encoded in the brain as motor (emotive and cognitive) programs that are activated by specific environmental cues, and the concept of "displacement" (out-of-context actions that occur when motivated behaviors cannot be executed; Dodman, 1998). Observed in a wide array of species, the most common classes of displacement activities involve fixed-action patterns associated with grooming, feeding, cleaning, and nest building. These displacement activities

often arise when an animal is faced with a conflict between aggression and escape motivations. Pitman (1991) noted the similarity between the ethologists' observations of displacement activities and Janet and Raymond's (1903/1976) characterization of forced agitations in humans as well as the central role Freud (1909) assigned to conflict in the emergence of obsessive-compulsive symptoms.

These displacement activities have been proposed as an animal model for studying OCD (Dodman, 1998). For example, Greer and Capecchi (2002) have reported that mice with disruptions of a homeodomain-containing gene, Hoxb8, show pathological grooming leading to hair removal and lesions. Of interest, these mice excessively groom normal cage mates.

There is considerable comparability between the content of human compulsions and the fixed-action patterns observed across species (e.g., grooming, washing, hoarding, ensuring safety). By their very nature, fixed-action patterns are invariant sequences of behaviors that are both biologically conserved and cued by environmental stimuli. Presumably, such behaviors serve adaptive functions, and for many such behaviors it is easy to comprehend how this may be so. Grooming and washing, for example, have obvious adaptive value in warding off disease and infection, as well as serving potentially adaptive social significance, particularly among nonhuman primates. Hoarding behaviors, too, are not uncommon, and repetitive movements suggestive of vigilance in the process of protecting offspring, for example, are other examples of adaptive repetitive behaviors that may provide keys for understanding pathological repetitive behaviors and associated thoughts.

In addition, the universality of symptoms observed in OCD across cultures and time suggests that compulsive behaviors may represent response tendencies selected through evolution, which become activated out of context in OCD. Although it is important to recognize differences between proximate and ultimate levels of analysis in considering behavioral data, it is also tempting to entertain the possibility that many obsessive-compulsive behaviors represent a kind of run-away selection, such that certain obsessive-compulsive behaviors reflect themes of evolutionary significance. It is possible, for example, that humans are equipped with a biological propensity to engage in certain kinds of repetitive behaviors that represent our phylogenetic legacy, ensuring our biological fitness. There are instances, however, when such behaviors become exaggerated and are performed to excess and in the absence of "appropriate" social or environmental cues, thereby ceasing their adaptive role.

INTEGRATIVE MODEL: THE MELDING OF DEVELOPMENTAL AND EVOLUTIONARY PERSPECTIVES

The full range of obsessive-compulsive symptoms can be normal and adaptive at given points during development. There is a preset neurobiology and presumably a preset group of genes that contribute to these conserved behaviors and preoccupations. Pathological forms of OCD arise when these normal and adaptive systems become dysregulated due to genetic vulnerability, adverse environmental change during the course of development (maladaptive learning leading to brain changes), or brain injury. Viewed in this light, the diverse behaviors and mental states encountered in OCD are not in themselves pathological. It is only by their distress, persistence, and tendency to occupy time to the exclusion of more normal activities that they become pathological.

Evolutionary Perspective on Developmental Psychopathology

Before reviewing the data that support this point of view, an examination of our theoretical model is in order. The principal goal of an evolutionary perspective on psychopathology is to provide a coherent framework from which to view patterns of maladaptive behavior that are persistent in human populations (Leckman & Mayes, 1998). In such an evolutionary framework, the issue of persistence appears to be paradoxical given the editing power of natural selection. Darwin's (1859/1993) principle of natural selection posits (1) the existence of variation among individuals, (2) differential reproductive success for those individuals who exhibit traits that are useful in "the struggle for life," and (3) differential inheritance of those factors that gave rise to the favorable traits. Why, then, would particular variations persist that place individuals at a reproductive disadvantage in the struggle for life? From our perspective, the answer to this question is that the improbable cascade of evolutionary events that has led to the emergence of our species and our particular set of conserved behavioral and mental capacities also has left us vulnerable to certain forms of psychopathology. By "conserved behavioral and mental capacities," we refer simply to those more or less species-typical potentialities of our species. With regard to OCD, we focus primarily on a limited set of these behaviors (and associated mental states) that include the existence of endogenous brain-based alarm systems that are activated by perceived external threats such as separation from an attachment figure (Table 10.2). Intrinsic to this point of view is the understanding that natural selection is largely powerless to edit out many of these vulnerabilities.

TABLE 10.2   Threat Domains, Conserved Behaviors, and Developmental Epochs Associated with Heightened Sensitivity

Threat Domain	Focus of Concern	Mental State	Behavioral Response	Developmental Epochs
Aggressive	Well-being of self and close family members	Intrusive images or thoughts that contain feared outcomes of separation or loss; among older children and adults, a heightened sense of responsibility	Physical proximity; checking to ensure safety; avoidance of danger	Early childhood: formation of attachment to caregivers; early family life: pregnancy, delivery and care of young children; threats to family members due to injury or other external threats
Physical security	Immediate home environment	Heightened attention to the placement of specific objects in the environment	Checking to ensure that things look "just right" and are in their expected place	Early childhood: initial period of exploration of the home environment by infants and toddlers; early family life: pregnancy, delivery and early childhood; threats to family members due to injury or other external threats
Environmental cleanliness	Personal hygiene; hygiene of family members; cleanliness of the home	Preoccupation with intrusive images or thoughts that contain feared outcomes of being dirty or causing others to be ill; among older children and adults, a heightened sense of responsibility	Washing; checking to ensure cleanliness; avoidance of shared or disgusting items	Early childhood: initial period of selection of items of food and drink by toddlers; early family life: pregnancy, delivery and care of young children; threats to family members due to injury or other external threats
Privation	Essential resources	Preoccupation with intrusive images or thoughts that contain feared outcomes of privation; a heightened sense of responsibility	Collecting items; checking to ensure the sufficient supplies are available	Latency: initial period of collecting; early family life: pregnancy, delivery and care of young children

Our body plans, nervous systems, behavioral repertoires, and mental states are highly constrained. Simply put, the elimination of our vulnerability to certain psychopathological states would interfere with species-specific behaviors and mental states that are essential for the survival and reproductive success of our species.

A Model of the Dynamic Interplay of Threat and Attachment and the Vulnerability to Develop Obsessive-Compulsive Disorder

Here we emphasize the dynamic interplay between threat and attachment. During the evolution of our species, it is likely that unless our forebears were acutely attuned to potential external threats posed by other humans, by predators, by the external manifestations of microbial disease, or by periods of privation due to drought, natural disasters, or internecine conflict, our species would not have survived. Likewise, unless there was a determined effort to nurture and ensure the survival of our family members, most especially our offspring, our species would have died off long ago.

We hypothesize that at the level of genes and neurobiology, there will be a clear linkage between our endogenous alarm systems and our capacity to form attachments and that it is this larger system that is dysregulated in OCD. At the level of overt behavior, we posit that the normal rituals of early childhood reflect the earliest maturation of our capacity to judge and respond to external threats and that this period coincides with the phase in our development when normal children begin to explore more actively their rapidly expanding physical and social world. Although most of our knowledge about the ontogeny of attachment behavior is based on studies conducted during the first 18 months of life, a few naturalistic studies (Blurton-Jones, 1972; Konner, 1976) and a number of laboratory-based studies (Main & Cassidy, 1988; Marvin, 1977; Marvin & Greenberg, 1982) document the normative course of attachment behavior during the toddler and preschool years. Two-year-olds, as they move away from their attachment figures, tend to maintain as much (or more) proximity to their mother as do 1-year-olds (Marvin & Britner, 1999). Toddlers tend actively to monitor not only the mother's movements but also her attention, so that when she is not attending to him or her, the child often does something with the apparent goal of regaining her attention (Schaffer & Emerson, 1964). Subsequently, things change so that most 3- and 4-year-olds, if left to wait with a friendly adult, are able to wait for the attachment figure's return before executing attachment behavior (Marvin, 1977). In tra-

ditional cultures, children maintain very close physical ties with their mother until sometime between 3 and 4 years of age (Konner, 1976). This behavioral transition coincides with the emergence of a child's heightened sensitivity to change in the external world, to performance of rituals to maintain sameness, and to alarm reactions/anxiety when changes in the environment do occur (Evans et al., 1997).

Similarly, parental behavior is a highly conserved set of behavioral capacities that are crucial for reproductive success. As reviewed earlier, in humans this period is associated with intense parental preoccupations (Leckman & Mayes, 1999; Leckman et al., 1999; Winnicott, 1958a). The content of these preoccupations includes intrusive worries concerning the parents' adequacy as parents and the infant's safety and well-being. These thoughts and the harm-avoidant behavior they engender resemble those encountered in OCD. Nursing and feeding are the parental behaviors that are perhaps most associated with a new infant. Women describe breast-feeding as a uniquely close, very physical, at times sensual experience and one that creates a particular unity between the mother and her infant. Cleaning, grooming, and dressing behaviors also carry a special valence inasmuch as they permit closeness between parent and infant and are times for close inspection of the details of the infant's body and appearance. Viewed from an evolutionary perspective, it seems nearly self-evident that the behavioral repertoires associated with early parenting skills would be subject to intense selective pressure (Bretherton, 1987; Hinde, 1974; Hofer, 1995; Stevenson-Hinde, 1994). For one's genes to self-replicate, sexual intimacy must occur and the progeny of such unions must survive. Pregnancy and the early years of an infant's life are fraught with mortal dangers. Indeed, it has only been during the past century that, in Europe, infant mortality rates have fallen from over 100/1,000 live births in 1900 to about 10/1,000 in 1984 (Corsini & Viazzo, 1997). Little wonder, then, that a specific state of heightened sensitivity on the part of new parents would be evolutionarily conserved.

THE MODEL'S HEURISTIC VALUE AND FUTURE DIRECTIONS

The conceptual framework underlying emerging models of brain evolution and normal development provides a powerful framework for understanding aspects of disease pathogenesis. This framework is consistent with the pioneering efforts of investigators such as Darwin (1872), Baldwin (1902), Bowlby (1969, 1973), Waddington (1977), Ekman (1980), and Fiske and Haslam (1997), who have applied evolutionary and developmental principles to the study of normal variation and/or psychopathology. This model's appeal is that it provides a multidisciplinary framework to view a range of pathological behaviors and related normal behaviors—from genes and environmental stressors to theories concerning the active ingredients in cognitive therapies and the neurobiological substrates they effect. For example, theorists in the area of thought appraisal have identified an exaggerated sense of responsibility as being at the root of OCD; our model links this theory with a rational basis for this exaggerated sense of responsibility in that it is akin to the heightened sense of responsibility that new parents experience with the birth of their children and specifies the neurobiological substrates involved. The natural history of OCD, with the high rate of onset or exacerbation of symptoms associated with the illness or death of near family members, the occurrence of sexual problems and/or marital difficulties, and during late pregnancy and the early postpartum period, also provides circumstantial evidence of a link between OCD and these naturally occurring periods of heightened sensitivity to threat.

Although progress has been slow, due in part to the scope and complexity of the emerging scientific knowledge base, incremental progress can be anticipated that should enrich and refine our emerging models of disease pathogenesis. Future progress is likely to follow in the wake of powerful and promising technologies in genetics, neurodevelopment, neuroimaging, and information processing. Some genes are likely to count more than others (Leckman & Herman, 2002). There may be particular alleles acting alone or together that are lethal for the normal emergence of species-typical behavioral patterns (as may occur in some forms of Autism). In the short term on the genetics front, studies using techniques that have been successfully applied in other complex diseases, such as diabetes, are under way (Botstein & Risch, 2003). It is reasonable to expect the eventual identification of loci and alleles of major and minor effect for OCD. Characterization of the vulnerability alleles should permit the development of animal models using transgenic and gene knock-out techniques (Tecott, 2003). Transgenic studies in which human genes are placed in other genomes (such as Drosophila or mice) may be quite revealing. Among other possibilities, they may permit the testing of the effectiveness of novel pharmaceutical agents as well as a deeper understanding of how the expression of these particular alleles constrain the developing nervous system. However, species differences and ethical constraints place a natural limit on the testability of evolutionary and developmental explanations of human psychopathology. Also, the ability to genotype accurately

individual patients with regard to known vulnerability alleles may lead to more accurate clinical predictions of course, outcome, and treatment response. Similarly, the results of neuropsychological, neuroimaging, and other biological studies may become more interpretable by classifying patients according to their respective genotypes. We would also predict that prospective longitudinal brain imaging studies of individuals in the midst of normal periods of development that are associated with heightened threat sensitivities will resemble patients with OCD both in terms of their phenomenology and the neurobiological circuits activated.

Future progress may also depend on the refinement of psychopathological phenotypes. It may well be that decomposing more complex syndromes such as OCD into a small number of component dimensions is a useful strategy. Consequently, the development of a dimensional rating scale for measuring OCD symptom severity across the various domains should provide a more accurate appraisal of patients' long-term course and response to treatment (Rosario-Campos et al., in press). Alternatively, other measurable neurophysiological, biochemical, endocrinological, neuroanatomical, cognitive, or neuropsychological components of OCD dimensions may also serve as useful endophenotypes that exist along the pathway between genetic susceptibility and distal clinical phenotypes (Gottesman & Gould, 2003).

For developmental neurobiologists, the identification of specific epigenetic risk factors should open fields of inquiry concerning the mechanisms responsible for observed effects and how they vary according to the timing and degree of exposure. Again, linking such studies with knowledge of relevant genotypes may be particularly useful in clarifying the nature of the resulting biological constraints on brain development through the use of animal models (Tecott, 2003).

Given the ethical limitations associated with the study of human brain development, many experimental studies cannot be performed. Future simulation studies of neural networks increasingly configured to resemble ensembles of neurons in the central nervous system have promise, particularly when investigators begin to vary connections and configuration of units to reflect changes consistent with those observed in patient groups (Jones, Cho, Nystrom, Cohen, & Braver, 2002). Alternatively, the development of scanning procedures that allow for the performance of experiments in which participants interact with each other while fMRI is acquired in synchrony may permit a more complete exploration of the neural substrates of obsessive-compulsive phenomena in patients and controls.

Clinical Implications

The present conceptualization of neurodevelopment and the factors that selectively influence its course has important implications for the prevention, treatment, and care of individuals with OCD. This conceptualization emphasizes the environment as a crucial factor in designing treatment interventions. Identifying features in the home and educational environments that will allow children to feel secure in their attachment to caregivers and confident in the safety of their home environment should continue to be a major priority for research. However, advances in our understanding of those components of the environment that are most crucial for sustaining successful adaptations will doubtless refine these interventions. Analysis of obsessive-compulsive symptoms across a variety of attachment types in children raised in threatening (i.e., maltreating) environments may provide useful avenues for understanding the role of the environment in the onset and development of repetitive behaviors, such as those associated with OCD.

Finally, aspects of this approach may permit a deeper empathetic understanding of individuals with OCD. Specifically, if some forms of OCD bear some relationship to the mental states associated with highly conserved behavioral repertoires typically encountered in expectant parents (intrusive worries about some misfortune befalling the fetus or infant), it should be easier for clinicians to have a deeper emotional empathy for the anguish the patient experiences as they can relate the patient's symptoms to emotional experiences in their own lives (Leckman & Mayes, 1999). Although these models can be accused of being reductionistic, mindless approaches that neglect the inner worlds of children, some of the emerging models of mental development are compatible with the rich, dynamic complexity of intrapsychic states that we encounter in ourselves and in the consulting room.

REFERENCES

Abbruzzese, M. B., Ferri, S., & Carcone, S. (1995). Wisconsin Card Sorting Test performance in obsessive-compulsive disorder: No evidence for involvement of dorsolateral prefrontal cortex. *Psychiatry Research, 58,* 37–43.

Alcais, A., & Abel, L. (1999). Maximum-likelihood-binomial method for genetic model-free linkage analysis of quantitative traits in sibships. *Genetic Epidemiology, 17,* 102–117.

Alsobrook, J. P., II, Leckman, J. F., Goodman, W. K., Rasmussen, S. A., & Pauls, D. L. (1999). Segregation analysis of obsessive-compulsive disorder using symptom-based factor scores. *American Journal of Medical Genetics, Neuropsychiatric Genetics, 88,* 669–675.

Altemus, M., Pigott, T., Kalogeras, K. T., Demitrack, M., Dubbert, B., Murphy, D. L., et al. (1992). Abnormalities in the regulation of vasopressin and corticotrophin releasing factor secretion in obsessive-compulsive disorder. *Archives of General Psychiatry, 49,* 9–20.

American Psychiatric Association. (1994). *Diagnostic and statistical manual of mental disorders* (4th ed.). Washington, DC: Author.

American Psychiatric Association. (2000). *Diagnostic and statistical manual of mental disorders* (4th ed., text rev.). Washington, DC: Author.

Anderson, S. W., Bechara, A., Damasio, H., Tranel, D., & Damasio, A. R. (1999). Impairment of social and moral behaviour related to early damage in human prefrontal cortex. *Nature Neuroscience, 2,* 1032–1037.

Ansseau, M., Legros, J. J., Mormont, C., Cerfontaine, J., Papart, P., Genen, V., et al. (1987). Intranasal oxytocin in obsessive-compulsive disorder. *Psychoneuroendocrinology, 1,* 231–236.

Apter, A., Pauls, D., Bleich, A., Zohar, A. H., Kron, S., Ratzoni, G., et al. (1993). An epidemiologic study of Gilles de la Tourette's syndrome in Israel. *Archives of General Psychiatry, 50*(9), 734–738.

Baer, L. (1993). Factor analysis of symptom subtypes of obsessive-compulsive disorder and their relation to personality and tics. *Journal of Clinical Psychiatry, 55*(Suppl. 3), 18–23.

Baer, L. (1994). Factor analysis of symptom subtypes of obsessive-compulsive disorder and their relation to personality and tic disorders. *Journal of Clinical Psychiatry, 55,* 18–23.

Baer, L., & Minichiello, W. E. (1998). Behavior therapy for obsessive-compulsive disorder. In M. A. Jenike, L. Baer, & W. E. Minichiello (Eds.), *Obsessive-compulsive disorders: Practical management* (pp. 337–367). St. Louis, MO: Mosby.

Baldwin, J. W. (1902). *Development and evolution.* New York: Macmillan.

Barlow, D., DiNardo, P. A., Vermilyea, B., Vermilyea, J., & Blanchard, E. B. (1986). Co-morbidity and depression among the anxiety disorders: Issues in diagnosis and classification. *Journal of Nervous and Mental Diseases, 174,* 63–72.

Baron-Cohen, S. (1988). Do children with Autism have obsessions and compulsions? *British Journal of Clinical Psychology, 28,* 193–200.

Barton, R. (1965). Diabetes insipidus and obsessional neurosis: A syndrome. *Lancet, 1*(7377), 133–135.

Baxter, L. R. (1990). Brain imaging as a tool in establishing a theory of brain pathology in obsessive-compulsive disorder. *Journal of Clinical Psychiatry, 51,* 22–25.

Baxter, L. R., Jr., Phelps, M. E., Mazziotta, J. C., Guze, B. H., Schwartz, J. M., & Selin, C. E. (1987). Local cerebral glucose metabolic rates in obsessive-compulsive disorder. A comparison with rates in unipolar depression and in normal controls. *Archives of General Psychiatry, 44,* 211–218.

Baxter, L. R., Schwartz, J. M., Bergman, K. S., Szuba, M. P., Guze, B. H., Mazziotta, J. C., et al. (1992). Caudate glucose metabolic rate changes with both drug and behavior therapy for obsessive-compulsive disorder. *Archives of General Psychiatry, 49,* 681–689.

Bechara, A., Damasio, H., & Damasio, A. R. (2000). Emotion, decision making and the orbitofrontal cortex. *Cerebral Cortex, 10*(3), 295–307.

Bechara, A., Damasio, A. R., Damasio, H., & Anderson, S. W. (1994). Insensitivity to future consequences following damage to human prefrontal cortex. *Cognition, 50,* 7–15.

Behar, D., Rapoport, J. L., Berg, C., Denckla, M. B., Mann, L., Cox, C., et al. (1984). Computerized tomography and neuropsychological test measures in children with obsessive-compulsive disorder. *American Journal of Psychiatry, 141,* 363.

Berg, C. A., Whitaker, A., Davies, M., Flament, M. F., & Rapoport, J. L. (1988). The survey form of the Leyton Obsessional Inventory–Child Version: Norms from an epidemiological study. *Journal of the American Academy of Child and Adolescent Psychiatry, 28,* 528–533.

Berrios, G. E. (1996). *The history of mental symptoms: Descriptive psychopathology since the nineteenth century.* Cambridge, UK: Cambridge University Press.

Bienvenu, O. J., Samuels, J. F., Riddle, M. A., Hoehn-Saric, R., Liang, K., Cullen, B. A., et al. (2000). The relationship of obsessive-compulsive disorder to possible spectrum disorders: Results from a family study. *Biological Psychiatry, 48,* 287–293.

Billett, E. A., Richter, M. A., & Kennedy, J. L. (1998). Genetics of obsessive-compulsive disorder. In R. P. Swinson, M. M. Anthony, S. Rachman, & M. A. Richter (Eds.), *Obsessive-compulsive disorder: Theory, research, and treatment* (pp. 181–206). New York: Guilford Press.

Black, D. W., Monahan, P., Gable, J., Blum, N., Clancy, G., & Baker, P. (1998). Hoarding and treatment response in 38 nondepressed subjects with obsessive-compulsive disorder. *Journal of Clinical Psychiatry, 59,* 420–425.

Blurton-Jones, N. (1972). *Ethological studies of child behavior.* New York: Cambridge University Press.

Bokura, H., Yamaguchi, S., & Kobayashi, S. (2001). Electrophysiological correlates for response inhibition in a go/no go task. *Clinical Neurophysiology, 112*(12), 2224–2232.

Bolton, D., Dearsley, P., Madronal-Luque, R., & Baron-Cohen, S. (2002). Magical thinking in childhood and adolescence: Development and relation to obsessive compulsion. *British Journal of Developmental Psychology, 20*(4), 479–494.

Botstein, D., & Risch, N. (2003). Discovering genotypes underlying human phenotypes: Past successes for Mendelian disease, future approaches for complex disease. *Nature Genetics, 33*(Suppl.), 228–237.

Botvinick, M., Nystrom, L. E., Fissell, K., Carter, C. S., & Cohen, J. D. (1999). Conflict monitoring versus selection-for-action in anterior cingulate cortex. *Nature, 402*(6758), 179–181.

Bowlby, J. (1969). *Attachment and loss: Vol. 1. Attachment.* New York: Basic Books.

Bowlby, J. (1973). *Attachment and loss: Vol. 2. Separation, anxiety and anger.* New York: Basic Books.

Bradshaw, J. L., & Sheppard, D. M. (2000). The neurodevelopmental frontostriatal disorders: Evolutionary adaptiveness and anomalous lateralization. *Brain and Language, 73*(2), 297–320.

Breiter, H. C., & Rauch, S. L. (1996). Functional MRI and the study of OCD: From symptom provocation to cognitive-behavioral probes of cortico-striatal systems and the amygdala. *Neuroimage, 4*(Suppl. 3, Pt. 3), S127–S138.

Breiter, H. C., Rauch, S. L., Kwong, K. K., Baker, J. R., Weisskoff, R. M., Kennedy, D. N., et al. (1996). Functional magnetic resonance imaging of symptom provocation in obsessive-compulsive disorder. *Archives of General Psychiatry, 53*(7), 595–606.

Bretherton, I. (1987). New perspectives on attachment relations: Security, communication, and internal working models. In J. D. Osofsky (Ed.), *Handbook of infant development* (pp. 1061–1100). New York: Wiley.

Buttolph, M. L., Peets, K. E., & Holland, A. D. (1998). Obsessive-compulsive symptoms and medication treatment in pregnancy. In M. A. Jenike, L. Baer, & W. E. Minichiello (Eds.), *Obsessive-compulsive disorders: Practical management* (pp. 84–96). St. Louis, MO: Mosby.

Carter, A., Pauls, D., & Leckman, J. F. (1996). The developmental of obsessionality: Continuities and discontinuities. In D. Cicchetti & D. Cohen (Eds.), *The handbook of developmental psychopathology: Vol. 2. Risk, disorder and adaptation* (pp. 9609–9632). New York: Wiley.

Carter, A., Pauls, D., Leckman, J. F., & Cohen, D. J. (1994). A prospective longitudinal study of Gilles de la Tourette's syndrome. *Journal of the American Academy of Child and Adolescent Psychiatry, 33*(3), 377–385.

Carter, C. S. (1992). Oxytocin and sexual behavior. *Neuroscience and Biobehavioral Review, 16,* 131–144.

Carter, C. S., DeVries, A. C., & Taymans, S. E. (1997). Peptides, steroids, and pair bonding. *Annals of the New York Academy of Sciences, 807,* 260–272.

Carter, C. S., Macdonald, A. M., Botvinick, M., Ross, L. L., Stenger, V. A., Noll, D., et al. (2000). Parsing executive processes: Strategic vs. evaluative functions of the anterior cingulate cortex. *Proceedings of the National Academy of Sciences, USA, 97*(4), 1944–1948.

Cavallini, M. C., Di Bella, D., Siliprandi, F., Malchiodi, F., & Bellodi, L. (2002). Exploratory factor analysis of obsessive-compulsive patients and association with 5-HTTLPR polymorphism. *American Journal of Medical Genetics, Neuropsychiatric Genetics, 114*(3), 347–353.

Cavedini, P., Ferri, S., Sarcone, S., & Bellodi, L. (1998). Frontal lobes dysfunction in obsessive-compulsive disorder and major depression: A clinical-neuropsychological study. *Psychiatric Research, 78,* 21.

Christensen, K. J., Hadzi-Pavlovic, D., Andrews, G., & Matrick, R. P. (1987). Behavior therapy and tricyclic medication in the treatment of obsessive-compulsive disorder: A quantitative review. *Journal of Consulting and Clinical Psychology, 55,* 701–711.

Cicchetti, D. (1993). Developmental psychopathology: Reactions, reflections, and projections. *Developmental Review, 13,* 471–502.

Cicchetti, D., & Cohen, D. (Eds.). (1995a). *Developmental psychopathology: Vol. 1. Theory and methods.* New York: Wiley.

Cicchetti, D., & Cohen, D. (Eds.). (1995b). *Developmental psychopathology: Vol. 2. Risk, disorder, and adaptation.* New York: Wiley.

Claude, H., Bourk, H., & Lamache, A. (1927). Obsessive-impulsions consecutives à l'encéphalite épidémique. *Encéphale, 22,* 716–722.

Cohen, L. J., Stein, D. J., Simeon, D., Spadaccini, E., Rosen, J., Aronowitz, B., et al. (1995). Clinical profile, comorbidity, and treatment history in 123 hair pullers: A survey study. *Journal of Clinical Psychiatry, 56,* 319–326.

Corsini, C. A., & Viazzo, P. (1997). *The decline of infant and child mortality: The European experience, 1750–1990.* The Hague, The Netherlands: Kluwer Law International.

Cosyns, P., Gabriels, L., & Nuttin, B. (2003). Deep brain stimulation in treatment refractory obsessive compulsive disorder. *Verh K Acad Geneeskd Belg, 65*(6), 385–399.

Cottraux, J., Note, I., Yao, S. N., Lafont, S., Note, B., Mollard, E., et al. (2001). A randomized controlled trial of cognitive therapy versus intensive behavior therapy in obsessive-compulsive disorder. *Psychotherapy and Psychosomatics, 70*(6), 288–297.

Cowan, C. P., & Cowan, P. A. (1992). *When partners become parents.* New York: Basic Books.

Cox, C. S. (1997). Neuropsychological abnormalities in obsessive-compulsive disorder and their assessments. *International Review of Psychiatry, 9,* 45–59.

Cox, C. S., Fedio, P., & Rapoport, J. L. (1989). Neuropsychological testing of obsessive-compulsive adolescents. In J. L. Rapoport (Ed.), *Obsessive-compulsive disorder in children and adolescents* (pp. 73–85). Washington, DC: American Psychiatric Press.

Darwin, C. (1872). *The expression of emotions in man and animals.* London: Murray.

Darwin, C. (1993). *The origin of species.* New York: Modern Library. (Original work published 1859)

Davidson, R. J., & Irwin, W. (1999). The functional neuroanatomy of emotion and affective style. *Trends in Cognitive Science, 3*(1), 11–21.

de Boer, J. A., & Westenberg, H. G. M. (1992). Oxytocin in obsessive-compulsive disorder. *Peptides, 13,* 1083–1085.

Depue, R. A., & Collins, P. F. (1999). Neurobiology of the structure of personality: Dopamine, facilitation of incentive motivation, and extraversion. *Behavioral and Brain Sciences, 22*(3), 491–569.

Diamond, A. (1988). Abilities and neural mechanisms underlying AB performance. *Child-Development, 59*(2), 523–527.

Diamond, A., & Taylor, C. (1996). Development of an aspect of executive control: Development of the abilities to remember what I said and to "Do as I say, not as I do." *Developmental Psychobiology, 29*(4), 315–334.

Dodman, N. H. (1998). Veterinary models of obsessive-compulsive disorder. In M. A. Jenike, L. Baer, & W. E. Minichiello (Eds.), *Obsessive-compulsive disorders: Practical management* (pp. 318–334). St. Louis, MO: Mosby.

Ekman, P. E. (1980). *The face of man.* New York: Garland STPM Press.

Elston, R. C., Buxbaum, S., Jacobs, K. B., & Olson, J. M. (2000). Haseman and Elston revisited. *Genetic Epidemiology, 19,* 1–17.

Emmelkamp, P. M. G. (1982). *Phobic and obsessive-compulsive disorders: Theory research, and practice.* New York: Plenum Press.

Erikson, E. H. (1968). *Identity: Youth and crisis.* London: Faber & Faber.

Evans, D. W. (2000). Rituals and other syncretic tools: Insights from Werner's comparative psychology. *Journal of Adult Development, 7,* 49–61.

Evans, D. W., Gray, F. L., & Leckman, J. F. (1999). Rituals, fears and phobias: Insights from development, psychopathology and neurobiology. *Child Psychiatry and Human Development, 29,* 261–276.

Evans, D. W., Leckman, J. F., Carter, A., Reznick, J. S., Henshaw, D., King, R. A., et al. (1997). Ritual, habit and perfectionism: The prevalence and development of compulsive-like behaviors in normal young children. *Child Development, 68,* 58–68.

Evans, D. W., Lewis, M. D., & Iobst, E. (2004). The role of the orbitofrontal cortex in normally developing compulsive-like behaviors and obsessive-compulsive disorder. *Brain and Cognition, 55,* 220–234.

Evans, D. W., Milanak, M., Medeiros, B., & Ross, J. (2002). Magical beliefs and rituals in young children. *Child Psychiatry and Human Development, 33,* 43–58.

Fahrbach, S. E., Morrell, J. I., & Pfaff, D. W. (1985). Possible role for endogenous oxytocin in estrogen-facilitated maternal behavior in rats. *Neuroendocrinology, 40*(6), 526–532.

Fals-Stewart, W. (1992). A dimensional analysis of the Yale-Brown Obsessive Compulsive Scale. *Psychological Reports, 70,* 238–240.

Fiske, A. P., & Haslam, N. (1997). Is obsessive-compulsive disorder a pathology of the human disposition to perform socially meaningful rituals? Evidence of similar content. *Journal of Nervous and Mental Diseases, 185*(4), 211–222.

Flament, M. F., Koby, E., Rapoport, J. L., Berg, C. J., Zahn, T., Cox, C., et al. (1990). Childhood obsessive-compulsive disorder: A prospective follow-up study. *Journal of Child Psychology and Psychiatry, 31,* 363–380.

Flament, M. F., Whitaker, A., Rapoport, J. L., Davies, M., Zarembabere, C., Kalikow, K., et al. (1988). Obsessive compulsive disorder in adolescence: An epidemiologic study. *Journal of the American Academy of Child and Adolescent Psychiatry, 27,* 764–771.

Foa, E. B., & Goldstein, A. (1978). Continuous exposure and complete response prevention in the treatment of obsessive-compulsive neurosis. *Behavioral Research and Therapy, 9,* 821–829.

Francis, G., & Gragg, R. T. (1996). Childhood obsessive compulsive disorder. In A. Kazdin (Ed.), *Developmental clinical psychology and psychiatry* (p. 35). Thousand Oaks, CA: Sage.

Freeston, M. H., Ladouceur, R., Thibodeau, N., & Gagnon, F. (1991). Cognitive intrusions in a non-clinical population: Pt. I. Response style, subjective experience, and appraisal. *Behavioral Research and Therapy, 29,* 233–248.

Freud, S. (1919). *The problem of anxiety.* New York: Norton.

Freud, S. (1966). Notes upon the case of obsessional neurosis. In J. Stratchey (Ed.), *Standard edition of the complete psychological works*

of Sigmund Freud, 12, 311–26. London: Hogarth Press. (Original work published 1909)

Galderisi, S., Mucci, A., Catapano, F., D'Amato, A. C., & Maj, M. (1995). Neuropsychological slowness in obsessive-compulsive patients: Is it confined to tests involving the fronto-subcortical systems? *British Journal of Psychiatry, 167,* 394–398.

Gehring, W. J., Himle, J., & Nisenson, L. G. (2000). Action monitoring dysfunction in obsessive-compulsive disorder. *Psychological Science, 11,* 1–6.

Geller, D., Biederman, J., Jones, J., Park, K., Schwartz, S., Shapiro, S., et al. (1998). Is juvenile obsessive-compulsive disorder a developmental subtype of the disorder? A review of the pediatric literature. *Journal of the American Academy of Child and Adolescent Psychiatry, 37,* 420–427.

Gesell, A. (1928). *Infancy and human growth.* New York: Macmillan.

Gesell, A., Ames, L. B., & Ilg, F. L. (1974). *Infant and the child in the culture today.* New York: Harper & Row.

Goldberg, S., & DiVitto, B. (1995). Parenting children born preterm. In M. Bornstein (Ed.), *Handbook of parenting* (Vol. 1, pp. 209–231). Mahwah, NJ: Erlbaum.

Goodman, W. K., McDougle, C. J., Price, L. H., Riddle, M. A., Pauls, D. L., & Leckman, J. F. (1990). Beyond the serotonin hypothesis: A role for dopamine in some forms of obsessive compulsive disorder? *Journal of Clinical Psychiatry, 51,* 36–43.

Goodman, W. K., Price, L. H., Rasmussen, S. A., Delgado, P. L., Heninger, G. R., & Charney, D. S. (1989). Efficacy of fluvoxamine in obsessive-compulsive disorder: A double-blind comparison with placebo. *Archives of General Psychiatry, 46,* 36–44.

Goodman, W. K., Price, L. H., Rasmussen, S. A., Mazure, C., Delgado, P., Heninger, G. R., et al. (1989). The Yale-Brown Obsessive Compulsive Scale: Pt. II. Validity. *Archives of General Psychiatry, 46,* 1012–1016.

Goodman, W. K., Price, L. H., Rasmussen, S. A., Mazure, C., Fleischmann, R. L., Hill, C. L., et al. (1989). The Yale-Brown Obsessive Compulsive Scale: Pt. I. Development, use and reliability. *Archives of General Psychiatry, 46,* 1006–1011.

Goodman, W. K., Ward, H., Kablinger, A., & Murphy, T. (1997). Fluvoxamine in the treatment of obsessive-compulsive disorder and related conditions. *Journal of Clinical Psychiatry, 58,* 32–49.

Goodwin, D. W., Guze, S. B., & Robins, E. (1969). Follow-up studies in obsessional neuroses. *Archives of General Psychiatry, 20,* 182–187.

Gottesman, I. I., & Gould, T. D. (2003). The endophenotype concept in psychiatry: Etymology and strategic intentions. *American Journal of Psychiatry, 160*(4), 636–645.

Grados, M. A., Riddle, M. A., Samuels, J. F., Liang, K. Y., Hoehn-Saric, R., Bienvenu, O. J., et al. (2001). The familial phenotype of obsessive-compulsive disorder in relation to tic disorders: The Hopkins OCD family study. *Biological Psychiatry, 50*(8), 559–565.

Grau, A. (1991). Estudio neuropsicologico sle trastorno obsesivo-compulsivo. (Primera parte). *Revista de Psiquiatria de la facultdad se Medicina de Barcelona, 18,* 11–22.

Greer, J. M., & Capecchi, M. R. (2002). Hoxb8 is required for normal grooming behavior in mice. *Neuron, 33,* 23–34.

Gross-Isseroff, R., Sasson, Y., Voet, H., Hendler, T., Luca-Haimovici, K., Kandel-Sussman, H., et al. (1996). Alternation learning in obsessive-compulsive disorder. *Biological Psychiatry, 39*(8), 733–738.

Gu, C., Province, M., Todorov, A., & Rao, D. C. (1998). Meta-analysis methodology for combining non-parametric sibpair linkage results: Genetic homogeneity and identical markers. *Genetic Epidemiology, 15,* 609–626.

Halmi, K. A., Sunday, S. R., Klump, K., Strober, M., Leckman, J. F., Fichter, M., et al. (2003). Obsessions and compulsions in anorexia nervosa subtypes. *International Eating Disorders Journal, 33*(3), 308–319.

Hanna, G. L., McCracken, J. T., & Cantwell, D. P. (1991). Prolactin in childhood obsessive-compulsive disorder: Clinical correlates and response to clomipramine. *Journal of the American Academy of Child and Adolescent Psychiatry, 30,* 173–178.

Hanna, G. L., Veenstra-VanderWeele, J., Cox, N. J., Boehnke, M., Himle, J. A., Curtis, G. C., et al. (2002, July). Genome-wide linkage analysis of families with obsessive-compulsive disorder ascertained through pediatric probands. *American Journal of Medical Genetics, 114*(5), 541–552.

Head, D., Bolton, D., & Hymas, N. (1989). Deficit in cognitive shifting ability and obsessive-compulsive disorder. *Biological Psychiatry, 25,* 929–937.

Hinde, R. A. (1974). *Biological bases of human social behavior.* New York: McGraw-Hill.

Hodapp, R. M. (1995). Parenting children with Down syndrome and other types of mental retardation. In M. Bornstein (Ed.), *Handbook of parenting* (Vol. 1, pp. 233–253). Mahwah, NJ: Erlbaum.

Hodgson, R. J., & Rachman, S. (1977). Obsessional-compulsive complaints. *Behavioral Research and Therapy, 15* 389–395.

Hofer, M. A. (1995). An evolutionary perspective on anxiety. In R. A. Glick & S. Roose (Eds.), *Anxiety as symptom and signal* (pp. 17–38). Hillsdale, NJ: Analytic Press.

Hollander, E. (1993). Obsessive-compulsive spectrum disorders: An overview. *Psychiatric Annals, 23,* 355–358.

Hollander, E. (1998). Treatment of obsessive-compulsive spectrum disorders with SSRIs. *British Journal of Psychiatry, 173*(Suppl. 35), 7–12.

Hollander, E., & Wong, C. M. (1995). Obsessive-compulsive spectrum disorders. *Journal of Clinical Psychiatry, 56*(Suppl. 4), 3–6.

Hymas, N., Lees, A., Bolton, D., Epps, K., & Head, D. (1991). The neurology of obsessional slowness. *Brain, 114,* 2203–2233.

Ingram, I. M. (1961). Obsessional illness in mental hospital patients. *Journal of Mental Science, 107,* 380–402.

Insel, T. R. (1992). Toward a neuroanatomy of obsessive-compulsive disorder. *Archives of General Psychiatry, 49,* 739–744.

Insel, T. R., & Harbaugh, C. R. (1989). Lesions of the hypothalamus paraventicular nucleus disrupt the initiation of maternal behavior. *Physiology and Behavior, 45,* 1033–1041.

Insel, T. R., & Pickar, D. (1983). Naloxone administration in obsessive-compulsive disorder: Report of two cases. *American Journal of Psychiatry, 140,* 1219–1220.

Insel, T. R., & Young, L. J. (2001). The neurobiology of attachment. *Nature Reviews Neuroscience, 2*(2), 129–136.

Janet, P., & Raymond, F. (1976). *Les obsessions et la psychastenie* (Vol. I). New York: Arno Press. (Original work published in 1903)

Jenike, M. A. (1998). Theories of etiology. In M. A. Jenike, L. Baer, & W. E. Minichiello (Eds.), *Obsessive-compulsive disorders: Practical management* (pp. 203–221). St. Louis, MO: Mosby.

Jenike, M. A., Baer, L., Ballantine, T., Martuza, R. L., Tynes, S., Giriunas, I., et al. (1991). Cingulotomy for refractory obsessive-compulsive disorder. A long-term follow-up of 33 patients. *Archives of General Psychiatry, 48*(6), 548–555.

Jenike, M. A., & Wilhelm, S. (1998). Illnesses related to obsessive-compulsive disorder. In M. A. Jenike, L. Baer, & W. E. Minichiello (Eds.), *Obsessive-compulsive disorders: Practical management* (pp. 121–142). St. Louis, MO: Mosby.

Jones, A., Cho, R., Nystrom, L., Cohen, J., & Braver, T. (2002). A computational model of anterior cingulate function in speeded response tasks: Effects of frequency, sequence, and conflict. *Cognitive Affective and Behavioral Neuroscience, 2*(4), 300–317.

Kagan, J. (1981). *The second year: The emergence of self-awareness.* Cambridge, MA: Harvard University Press.

Karno, M., Golding, J. M., Sorenson, S. B., & Burnam, M. A. (1988). The epidemiology of obsessive-compulsive disorder in five U.S. communities. *Archives of General Psychiatry, 45,* 1094–1099.

Kim, S. W., Dysken, M. W., Pheley, A. M., & Hoover, K. M. (1994). The Yale-Brown Obsessive-Compulsive Scale: Measures of internal consistency. *Psychiatry Research, 51,* 203–211.

King, R. A., Leckman, J. F., Scahill, L. D., & Cohen, D. J. (1998). Obsessive-compulsive disorder, anxiety, and depression. In J. F. Leckman & D. J. Cohen (Eds.), *Tourette's syndrome—Tics, obsessions, compulsions: Developmental psychopathology and clinical care* (pp. 43–62). New York: Wiley.

Knight, C. C. (1972). Bifrontal stereotaxic tractotomy in the substantia innominata: An experience of 450 cases. In E. Hitchcock, L. Laitinen, & K. Vaernet (Eds.), *Psychosurgery* (pp. 267–277). Springfield, IL: Charles C. Thomas.

Konner, M. (1976). Maternal care, infant behavior and development among the !Kung. In R. Lee & I. DeVore (Eds.), *Kalahari hunter gathers: Studies of the !Kung San and their neighbors* (pp. 377–394). Cambridge, MA: Harvard University Press.

Laplane, D., Levasseur, M., Pillon, B., Dubois, B., Baulac, M., Mazoyer, B., et al. (1989). Obsessive-compulsive and other behavioural changes with bilateral basal ganglia lesions. A neuropsychological, magnetic resonance imaging and positron tomography study. *Brain, 112,* 699–725.

Last, C. G., Perrin, S., Hersen, M., & Kazdin, A. E. (1992). A prospective study of childhood anxiety disorders. *Journal of the American Academy of Child and Adolescent Psychiatry, 35*(11), 1502–1510.

Leckman, J. F., Goodman, W. K., North, W. G., Chappell, P. B., Price, L. H., Pauls, D. L., et al. (1994a). Elevated levels of CSF oxytocin in obsessive compulsive disorder: Comparison with Tourette's syndrome and healthy controls. *Archives of General Psychiatry, 51,* 782–792.

Leckman, J. F., Goodman, W. K., North, W. G., Chappell, P. B., Price, L. H., Pauls, D. L., et al. (1994b). The role of oxytocin in obsessive-compulsive disorder and related normal behavior. *Psychoneuroendocrinology, 9,* 723–749.

Leckman, J. F., Grice, D. E., Barr, L. C., deVries, A. L. C., Martin, C., Cohen, D. J., et al. (1995). Tic-related vs. non-tic related obsessive compulsive disorder. *Anxiety, 1,* 208–215.

Leckman, J. F., Grice, D. E., Boardman, J., Zhang, H., Vitale, A., Bondi, C., et al. (1997). Symptoms of obsessive-compulsive disorder. *American Journal of Psychiatry, 154,* 911–917.

Leckman, J. F., & Herman, A. (2002). Maternal behavior and developmental psychopathology. *Biological Psychiatry, 51*(1), 27–43.

Leckman, J. F., & Mayes, L. C. (1998). Understanding developmental psychopathology: How useful are evolutionary accounts? *Journal of the American Academy of Child and Adolescent Psychiatry, 37*(10), 1011–1021.

Leckman, J. F., & Mayes, L. C. (1999). Preoccupations and behaviors associated with romantic and parental love: The origin of obsessive-compulsive disorder? *Child and Adolescent Psychiatric Clinics of North America, 8,* 635–665.

Leckman, J. F., Mayes, L. C., Feldman, R., Evans, D., King, R. A., & Cohen, D. J. (1999). Early parental preoccupations and behaviors and their possible relationship to the symptoms of obsessive-compulsive disorder. *Acta Psychiatrica Scandinavica, 100*(Suppl. 396), 1–26.

Leckman, J. F., Pauls, D. L., Zhang, H., Rosario-Campos, M. C., Katsovich, L., Kidd, K. K., et al. (2003). Obsessive-compulsive symptom dimensions in affected sibling pairs diagnosed with Gilles de la Tourette syndrome. *American Journal of Medical Genetics, 116,* 60–68.

Leckman, J. F., Zhang, H., Alsobrook, J. P., & Pauls, D. L. (2001). Symptom dimensions in obsessive-compulsive disorder: Toward quantitative phenotypes. *American Journal of Medical Genetics, 105*(1), 28–30.

Lenane, M. C., Swedo, S. E., Rapoport, J. L., Leonard, H., Sceery, W., & Guroff, J. J. (1992). Rates of obsessive-compulsive disorder in the first-degree relatives of patients with trichotillomania. *Journal of Child Psychology and Psychiatry, 33,* 925–933.

Leonard, H. L., Goldberger, E. L., Rapoport, J. L., Cheslow, B. S., & Swedo, S. (1990). Childhood rituals: Normal development or obsessive-compulsive symptoms? *Journal of the American Academy of Child and Adolescent Psychiatry, 29,* 17–23.

Leonard, H. L., Swedo, S. E., Lenane, M. C., Rettew, D. C., Hamburger, S. D., Bartko, J. J., et al. (1993). A 2- to 7-year follow-up study of 54 obsessive-compulsive children and adolescents. *Archives of General Psychiatry, 50*(6), 429–439.

Lewis, A. J. (1936). Problems of obsessional illness. *Proceedings of the Royal Society of Medicine, 29,* 325–336.

Lin, H. Q., Yeh, C. B., Peterson, B. S., Scahill, L., Grantz, H., Findley, D., et al. (2002). Assessment of symptom exacerbations in a longitudinal study of children with Tourette syndrome or obsessive-compulsive disorder. *Journal of the American Academy of Child and Adolescent Psychiatry, 41,* 1070–1077.

Lo, W. H. (1967). A follow-up study of obsessional neurotics in Hong Kong Chinese. *British Journal of Psychiatry, 113,* 823.

Lorberbaum, J. P., Newman, J. D., Horwitz, A. R., Dubno, J. R., Lydiard, R. B., Hamner, M. B., et al. (2002). A potential role for thalamocingulate circuitry in human maternal behavior. *Biological Psychiatry, 51*(6), 431–445.

Lucey, L. V., Burness, C. E., Costa, D. C., Gacinovic, S., Pilowsky, L. S., Ell, P. J., et al. (1997). Wisconsin Card Sort Task (WCST) errors and cerebral blood flow in obsessive-compulsive disorder (OCD). *British Journal of Medical Psychology, 70,* 403–411.

Main, M., & Cassidy, J. (1988). Categories of response to reunion with the parent at age six. *Developmental Psychology, 24,* 415–426.

Marks, I. M. (1987). *Fears, phobias and rituals.* New York: Oxford University Press.

Marks, I. M., Lelliott, P., Basoglu, M., Noshirvani, H., Montero, W., & Kasvikis, Y. (1988). Clomipramine, self-exposure and therapist aided exposure in obsessive-compulsive ritualisers. *British Journal of Psychiatry, 152,* 522–534.

Marvin, R. S. (1977). An ethological-cognitive model for the attenuation of mother-child attachment behavior. In T. M. Alloway, L. L. Krames, & P. Pliner (Eds.), *Advances in the study of communication and affect: Vol. 3. Attachment behavior* (pp. 25–60). New York: Plenum Press.

Marvin, R. S., & Britner, P. A. (1999). Normative development: The ontogeny of attachment. In J. Cassidy & P. R. Shaver (Eds.), *Handbook of attachment* (pp. 44–67). New York: Guilford Press.

Marvin, R. S., & Greenberg, M. T. (1982). Preschoolers' changing conceptions of their mothers: A social-cognitive study of mother-infant attachment. In D. Forbes & M. T. Greenberg (Eds.), *New directions in child development: No. 18. Children's planning strategies* (pp. 47–60). San Francisco: Jossey-Bass.

Mataix-Cols, D., Baer, L., Rauch, S. L., & Jenike, M. A. (2000). Relation of factor-analyzed symptom dimensions of obsessive-compulsive disorder to personality disorders. *Acta Psychiatrica Scandinavica, 102,* 199–202.

Mataix-Cols, D., Cullen, S., Lange, K., Zelaya, F., Andrew, C., Amaro, E., et al. (2003). Neural correlates of anxiety associated with obsessive-compulsive symptom dimensions in normal volunteers. *Biological Psychiatry, 53,* 482–493.

Mataix-Cols, D., Junque, C., Sanchez-Turet, M., Vallejo, J., Verger, K., & Barrios, M. (1999). Neuropsychological functioning in a subclinical obsessive-compulsive sample. *Biological Psychiatry, 45*(7), 898–904.

Mataix-Cols, D., Marks, I. M., Greist, J. H., Kobak, K. A., & Baer, L. (2002). Obsessive-compulsive symptom dimensions as predictors of compliance with and response to behaviour therapy: Results from a controlled trial. *Psychotherapy and Psychosomatics, 71*(5), 255–262.

Mataix-Cols, D., Rauch, S. L., Baer, L., Eisen, J. L., Shera, D. M., Goodman, W. K., et al. (2002). Symptom stability in adult obsessive-compulsive disorder: Data from a naturalistic two-year follow-up study. *American Journal of Psychiatry, 159,* 263–268.

Mataix-Cols, D., Rauch, S. L., Manzo, P. A., Jenike, M. A., & Baer, L. (1999). Use of factor-analyzed symptom dimensions to predict outcome with serotonin reuptake inhibitors and placebo in the treatment of obsessive-compulsive disorder. *American Journal of Psychiatry, 156*(9), 1409–1416.

Mataix-Cols, D., Rosario-Campos, M. C., & Leckman, J. F. (2005). A multidimensional model of obsessive-compulsive disorder. *American Journal of Psychiatry, 162,* 228–238.

Mataix-Cols, D., Wooderson, S., Lawrence, N., Brammer, M. J., Speckens, A., & Phillips, M. L. (2004, June). Distinct neural correlates of washing, checking, and hoarding symptom dimensions in obsessive-compulsive disorder. *Archives of General Psychiatry, 61*(6), 564–576.

McDougle, C. J., Goodman, W. K., Leckman, J. F., Barr, L. C., Heninger, G. R., & Price, L. H. (1993). The efficacy of fluvoxamine in obsessive-compulsive disorder: Effects of comorbid chronic tic disorder. *Journal of Clinical Psychopharmacology, 13,* 354–358.

McDougle, C. J., Goodman, W. K., Leckman, J. F., Lee, N. C., Heninger, G. R., & Price, L. H. (1994). Haloperidol addition in fluvoxamine-refractory obsessive-compulsive disorder: A double blind, placebo-controlled study in patients with and without tics. *Archives of General Psychiatry, 51,* 302–308.

McGuire, P. K., Bench, C. J., Frith, C. D., Marks, I. M., Frackowiak, R. S., & Dolan, R. J. (1994). Functional anatomy of obsessive-compulsive phenomena. *British Journal of Psychiatry, 164*(4), 459–468.

McKay, D., Danyko, S., Neziroglu, F., & Yaryura-Tobias, J. A. (1995). Factor structure of the Yale-Brown Obsessive-Compulsive Scale: A dimensional measure. *Behavioral Research and Therapy, 33,* 865–869.

Meyer, A., & Beck, E. (1954). *Prefrontal leucotomy and related operations.* London: Oliver & Boyd.

Meyer, V., Levy, R., & Schnurer, A. (1974). The behavioral treatment of obsessive-compulsive disorders. In H. R. Beech (Ed.), *Obsessional states.* London: Methuen.

Miguel, E. C., Rauch, S. L., & Jenike, M. A. (1997). Obsessive-compulsive disorder. *Psychiatric Clinics of North America, 20,* 863–883.

Minichiello, W. E., Baer, L., Jenike, M. A., & Holland, A. (1990). Age of onset of major subtypes of obsessive-compulsive disorder. *Journal of Anxiety Disorders, 4,* 147–150.

Mowrer, O. H. (1960). *Learning theory and behavior.* New York: Wiley.

Nemiah, I. (1985). Obsessive-compulsive neurosis. In A. Freedman, H. Kaplan, & B. Sadock (Eds.), *A comprehensive textbook of psychiatry* (pp. 1241–1255). Baltimore: Williams & Wilkins.

Nestadt, G., Samuels, J., Riddle, M., Bienvenu, O. J., III, Liang, K. Y., LaBuda, M., et al. (2000). A family study of obsessive-compulsive disorder. *Archives of General Psychiatry, 57*(4), 358–363.

Neziroglu, F., Anemone, R., & Yaryura-Tobias, J. A. (1992). Onset of obsessive-compulsive disorder in pregnancy. *American Journal of Psychiatry, 149,* 947–950.

Nordahl, T. E., Benkelfat, C., Semple, W., Gross, M., King, A. C., & Cohen, R. M. (1989). Cerebral glucose metabolic rates in obsessive-compulsive disorder. *Neuropsychopharmacology, 2,* 23–28.

Numan, M. (1994). Maternal behavior. In E. Knobil & J. D. Neill (Eds.), *The physiology of reproduction* (2nd ed.). New York: Raven Press.

Obsessive Compulsive Cognitions Working Group. (1997). Cognitive assessment of obsessive-compulsive disorder. *Behavior Research and Therapy, 35,* 667–681.

Ochsner, K. N., Bunge, S. A., Gross, J. J., & Gabrieli, J. D. (2002). Rethinking feelings: An fMRI study of the cognitive regulation of emotion. *Journal of Cognitive Neuroscience, 14*(8), 1215–1229.

O'Sullivan, R. L., Rauch, S. L., Breiter, H. C., Grachev, I. D., Baer, L., Kennedy, D. N., et al. (1997). Reduced basal ganglia volumes in trichotillomania measured via morphometric magnetic resonance imaging. *Biological Psychiatry, 42,* 39–45.

Passman, R. H. (1976). Arousal-reducing properties of attachment objects: Testing the function limits of security blanket relative to the mother. *Developmental Psychology, 12,* 421–436.

Passman, R. H. (1977). Providing attachment objects to facilitate learning and reduce stress: Effects of mother and security blanket. *Developmental Psychology, 13,* 25–28.

Passman, R. H. (1987). Attachment objects: Are children with security blankets insecure? *Journal of Consulting and Clinical Psychology, 55,* 825–830.

Pauls, D. L., Alsobrook, J. P., II, Goodman, W. K., Rasmussen, S., & Leckman, J. F. (1995). A family study of obsessive-compulsive disorder. *American Journal of Psychiatry, 152,* 76–84.

Pauls, D. L., & Leckman, J. F. (1986). The inheritance of Gilles de la Tourette syndrome and associated behaviors: Evidence for autosomal dominant transmission. *New England Journal of Medicine, 315,* 993–997.

Pauls, D. L., Leckman, J. F., & Cohen, D. J. (1994). Evidence against a genetic relationship between the Gilles de la Tourette syndrome and anxiety, depression, panic and phobic disorders. *British Journal of Psychiatry, 164,* 215–221.

Pedersen, C. A., Caldwell, J. D., Johnson, M. F., Fort, S. A., & Prange, A. J., Jr. (1985). Oxytocin antiserum delays onset of ovarian steroid-induced maternal behavior. *Neuropeptides, 6*(2), 175–182.

Pedersen, C. A., & Prange, A. J., Jr. (1979). Induction of maternal behavior in virgin rats after intracerebroventricular administration of oxytocin. *Proceedings of the National Academy of Sciences, USA, 76,* 6661–6665.

Peterson, B. S., Bronen, R. A., & Duncan, C. C. (1996). Three cases of symptom change in Tourette's syndrome and obsessive-compulsive disorder associated with paediatric cerebral malignancies. *Journal of Neurology, Neurosurgery, and Psychiatry, 61*(5), 497–505.

Peterson, B. S., Pine, D. S., Cohen, P., & Brook, J. S. (2001). Prospective, longitudinal study of tic, obsessive-compulsive, and attention-deficit/hyperactivity disorders in an epidemiological sample. *Journal of the American Academy of Child and Adolescent Psychiatry, 40,* 685–695.

Phillips, K. A. (1996). Pharmacologic treatment of body dysmorphic disorder. *Pharmacological Bulletin, 32,* 597–605.

Phillips, K. A., Gunderson, C. G., Mallya, G., McElroy, S. L., & Carter, W. (1998). A comparison study of body dysmorphic disorder and obsessive-compulsive disorder. *Journal of Clinical Psychiatry, 59,* 568–575.

Phillips, M. L., Marks, I. M., Senior, C., Lythgoe, D., O'Dwyer, A. M., Meehan, O., et al. (2000). A differential neural response in obsessive-compulsive patients with washing compared with checking symptoms to disgust. *Psychological Medicine, 30,* 1037–1050.

Piaget, J. (1962). *Play, dreams and imitation in childhood.* New York: Norton.

Pietrefesa, A., & Evans, D. W. (in press). Children's rituals and executive function: Insights from the neurobiology of obsessive-compulsive disorder. *Brain and Cognition.*

Pitman, R. K. (1987). Pierre Janet on obsessive-compulsive disorder (1903): Review and commentary. *Archives of General Psychiatry, 44,* 226–232.

Pitman, R. K. (1989). Animal models of compulsive behavior. *Biological Psychiatry, 26,* 189–198.

Pitman, R. K. (1991). Historical considerations. In J. Zohar, T. Insel, & S. Rasmussen (Eds.), *The psychobiology of obsessive-compulsive disorder* (pp. 1–12). New York: Springer.

Pollitt, J. (1957). Natural history of obsessional states. *British Medical Journal, 26,* 194.

Rachman, S. J., & de Silva, P. (1978). Abnormal and normal obsessions. *Behavior Research and Therapy, 16,* 233–248.

Rachman, S. J., & Hodgson, R. J. (1980). *Obsessions and compulsions.* Englewood Cliffs, NJ: Prentice-Hall.

Rapoport, J. L. (1989). Summary. In J. L. Rapoport (Ed.), *Obsessive-compulsive disorder in children and adolescents* (pp. 347–350). Washington, DC: American Psychiatric Press.

Rasmussen, S. A. (1994). Obsessive-compulsive spectrum disorders. *Journal of Clinical Psychiatry, 55,* 89–91.

Rasmussen, S. A., & Eisen, J. L. (1991). Phenomenology of OCD: Clinical subtypes, heterogeneity and coexistence. In J. Zohar, T. Insel, & S. Rasmussen (Eds.), *The psychobiology of obsessive-compulsive disorder* (pp. 13–43). New York: Springer.

Rasmussen, S. A., & Eisen, J. L. (1998). Clinical and epidemiological features of obsessive-compulsive disorder. In M. A. Jenike, L. Baer, & W. E. Minichiello (Eds.), *Obsessive-compulsive disorders: Practical management* (pp. 12–43). St. Louis, MO: Mosby.

Rasmussen, S. A., & Tsuang, M. T. (1984). The epidemiology of obsessive-compulsive disorder. *Journal of Clinical Psychiatry, 45,* 450–457.

Rauch, S. L., Dougherty, D. D., Shin, L. M., Alpert, N. M., Manzo, P., Leahy, L., et al. (1998). Neural correlates of factor-analyzed OCD symptom dimensions: A PET study. *CNS Spectrums, 3,* 37–43.

Rauch, S. L., Jenike, M. A., Alpert, N. M., Baer, L., Breiter, H. C., Savage, C. R., et al. (1994). Regional cerebral blood flow measured during symptom provocation in obsessive-compulsive disorder using oxygen 15-labeled carbon dioxide and positron emission tomography. *Archives of General Psychiatry, 51,* 62–70.

Rauch, S. L., Savage, C. R., Alpert, N. M., Dougherty, D., Kendrick, A., Curran, T., et al. (1997). Probing striatal function on obsessive-compulsive disorder: A PET study of implicit sequence learning. *Journal of Neuropsychiatry and Clinical Neuroscience, 9,* 568–573.

Rauch, S. L., Savage, C. R., Alpert, N. M., Fischman, A. J., & Jenike, M. A. (1997). The functional neuroanatomy of anxiety: A study of three disorders using positron emission tomography and symptom provocation. *Biological Psychiatry, 42*(6), 446–452.

Ravindran, A. V., Lapierre, Y. D., & Anisman, H. (1999). Obsessive-compulsive spectrum disorders: Effective treatment with paroxetine. *Canadian Journal of Psychiatry, 44,* 805–807.

Rolls, E. T. (2000). The orbitofrontal cortex and reward. *Cerebral Cortex, 10,* 284–294.

Rosario-Campos, M. C., Leckman, J. F., Curi, M., Quantrano, S., Katsovich, L., Miguel, E. C., et al. (2005). A family study of early-onset obsessive-compulsive disorder. *American Journal of Medical Genetics (Neuropsychiatric Genet).*

Rosario-Campos, M. C., Leckman, J. F., Mercadante, M. T., Shavitt, R. G., Prado, H. S., Sada, P., et al. (2001). Adults with early-onset obsessive-compulsive disorder. *American Journal of Psychiatry, 158*(11), 1899–1903.

Rosario-Campos, M. C., Miguel, E. C., Quantrano, S., Chacon, P., Ferrao, Y., Findley, D., et al. (in press). *The Dimensional Yale-Brown Obsessive Compulsive Scale (DY-BOCS): An instrument for assessing obsessive-compulsive symptom dimensions.* Manuscript in preparation.

Rosenberg, D. R., Averbach, D. H., O'Hearn, K. M., Seymour, A. B., Birmaher, B., & Sweeney, J. A. (1997). Oculomotor response inhibition abnormalities in pediatric obsessive-compulsive disorder. *Archives of General Psychiatry, 54,* 824.

Rosenberg, D. R., Dick, E. L., O'Hearn, K. M., & Sweeney, J. A. (1997). Response inhibition deficits in obsessive-compulsive disorder: An indicator of dysfunction in fronto-striatal circuits. *Journal of Psychiatric Neuroscience, 22,* 29–38.

Salkovskis, P. M. (1985). Obsessive-compulsive problems: A cognitive-behavioural analysis. *Behavioral Research and Therapy, 23,* 571–583.

Salkovskis, P. M., & Harrison, J. (1984). Abnormal and normal obsessions: A replication. *Behavioral Research and Therapy, 22,* 549–552.

Samuels, J., Bienvenu, O. J., III, Riddle, M. A., Cullen, B. A., Grados, M. A., Liang, K. Y., et al. (2002). Hoarding in obsessive compulsive disorder: Results from a case-control study. *Behavioral Research and Therapy, 40,* 517–528.

Santosh, P. J. (2000). Neuroimaging in child and adolescent psychiatric disorders. *Archives of the Diseases of Children, 82*(5), 412–419.

Sawle, G. V., Hymas, N. F., Lees, A. J., & Frackowiak, R. S. (1991). Obsessional slowness: Functional studies with positron emission tomography. *Brain, 114,* 2191–2202.

Saxena, S., Brody, A. L., Ho, M. L., Alborzian, S., Maidment, K. M., Zohrabi, N., et al. (2002). Differential cerebral metabolic changes with paroxetine treatment of obsessive-compulsive disorder vs. major depression. *Archives of General Psychiatry, 59*(3), 250–261.

Saxena, S., Brody, A. L., Maidment, K. M., Smith, E. C., Zohrabi, N., Katz, E., et al. (2004, June). Cerebral glucose metabolism in obsessive-compulsive hoarding. *American Journal of Psychiatry, 61*(6), 1038–1048.

Schaffer, H. R., & Emerson, P. E. (1964). The development of social attachments in infancy. *Monographs for the Society for Research on Child Development, 29*(3, Serial No. 94).

Schultz, R. T., Evans, D. W., & Wolfe, M. (1999). Neuropsychological models of childhood obsessive-compulsive disorder. *Child and Adolescent Psychiatric Clinics of North America, 8,* 513–531.

Schwartz, J. M., & Begley, S. (2002). *The mind and the brain: Neuroplasticity and the power of mental force.* New York: Regan Books.

Schwartz, J. M., Stoessel, P. W., Baxter, L. R., Jr., Martin, K. M., & Phelps, M. E. (1996). Systematic changes in cerebral glucose metabolic rate after successful behavior modification treatment of obsessive-compulsive disorder. *Archives of General Psychiatry, 53,* 109–113.

Senjo, M. (1989). Obsessive-compulsive disorder in people that abuse codeine. *Acta Psychiatrcia Scandinavica, 79,* 619–620.

Skoog, G., & Skoog, I. (1999). A 40-year follow-up of patients with obsessive-compulsive disorder. *Archives of General Psychiatry, 56,* 121–127.

Stein, D. J. (2000). Neurobiology of obsessive-compulsive spectrum disorders. *Biological Psychiatry, 47,* 296–304.

Steketee, G. S., Frost, R. O., Rheaume, J., & Wilheim, S. (1998). Cognitive theory and treatment of obsessive-compulsive disorder. In M. A. Jenike, L. Baer, & W. E. Minichiello (Eds.), *Obsessive-compulsive disorders: Practical management* (pp. 368–400). St. Louis, MO: Mosby.

Stevenson-Hinde, J. (1994). An ethological perspective. *Psychological Inquiry, 5,* 62–65.

Summerfeldt, L. J., Richter, M. A., Antony, M. M., & Swinson, R. P. (1999). Symptom structure in obsessive-compulsive disorder: A confirmatory factor-analytic study. *Behavioral Research and Therapy, 37,* 297–311.

Swedo, S. E., & Leonard, H. (1992). Trichotillomania: An obsessive compulsive spectrum disorder? *Psychiatric Clinics of North America, 15,* 777–790.

Swedo, S. E., Leonard, H. L., Garvey, M., Mittleman, B., Allen, A. J., Perlmutter, S., et al. (1998). Pediatric autoimmune neuropsychiatric disorders associated with streptococcal infections: Clinical description of the first 50 cases. *American Journal of Psychiatry, 155*(2), 264–271.

Swedo, S. E., Leonard, H. L., Kruesi, M. J. P., Rettew, D. C., Listwak, S. J., Berrettini, W., et al. (1992). Cerebrospinal fluid neurochemistry in children and adolescents with obsessive-compulsive disorder. *Archives of General Psychiatry, 49,* 29–36.

Swedo, S. E., Rapoport, J. L., Cheslow, D. L., Leonard, H. L., Ayoub, E. M., Hosier, D. M., et al. (1989). High prevalence of obsessive-compulsive symptoms in patients with Sydenham's chorea. *American Journal of Psychiatry, 146*(2), 246–249.

Tecott, L. (2003). The genes and brains of mice and men. *American Journal of Psychiatry, 160*(4), 646–656.

Tien, A. Y., Pearlson, G. D., Machlin, S. R., Bylsma, F. W., & Hoehn-Saric, R. (1992). Oculomotor performance in obsessive-compulsive disorder. *American Journal of Psychiatry, 149,* 641–646.

Valleni-Basile, L. A., Garrison, C. Z., Waller, J. L., Addy, C. L., McKeown, R. E., Jackson, K. L., et al. (1994). Frequency of obsessive-compulsive disorder in a community sample of young adolescents. *Journal of the American Academy of Child and Adolescent Psychiatry, 33*(6), 782–791.

van Balkom, A. J., van Oppen, P., Vermeulen, A. W. A., van Dyck, R., Nauta, M. C. E., & Vorst, H. C. M. (1994). A meta-analysis on the treatment of obsessive-compulsive disorder: A comparison of antidepressants, behavior therapy and cognitive therapy. *Clinical Psychological Reviews, 14,* 359–381.

van Oppen, P., De Haan, E., van Balkom, A. J., Spinhoven, P., Hoogduin, K., & van Dyck, R. (1995). Cognitive therapy and exposure in vivo in the treatment of obsessive-compulsive disorder. *Behavioral Research and Therapy, 33,* 379–390.

Waddington, C. H. (1977). *Tools for thought.* New York: Basic Books.

Werner, H. (1948). *The comparative psychology of mental development.* New York: International Universities Press.

Werner, H. (1957). The concept of development from a comparative and organismic point of view. In D. B. Harris (Ed.), *The concept of development* (pp. 125–146). Minneapolis: University of Minnesota Press.

Wewetzer, C., Jans, T., Muller, B., Neudorfl, A., Bucherl, U., Remschmidt, H., et al. (2001). Long-term outcome and prognosis of obsessive-compulsive disorder with onset in childhood or adolescence. *European Child and Adolescent Psychiatry, 10*(1), 37–46.

Willour, V. L., Yao Shugart, Y., Samuels, J., Grados, M., Cullen, B., Bienvenu, O. J., III, et al. (2004). Replication study supports evidence for linkage to 9p24 in obsessive-compulsive disorder. *American Journal of Human Genetics, 75*(3), 508–513.

Winnicott, D. W. (1958a). Primary maternal preoccupation. In *Collected papers: Through paediatrics to psycho-analysis* (pp. 300–305). New York: Basic Books. (Original work published 1956)

Winnicott, D. W. (1958b). Transitional objects and transitional phenomena. In *Collected papers: Through paediatrics to psycho-analysis* (pp. 229–242). New York: Basic Books. (Original work published 1951)

Yaryura-Tobias, J. A., Grunes, M. S., Todaro, J., McKay, D., Neziroglu, F. A., & Stockman, R. (2000). Nosological insertion of Axis I disorders in the etiology of obsessive-compulsive disorder. *Journal of Anxiety Disorders, 14,* 19–30.

Zelazo, P., & Jacques, S. (1996). Children's rule use: Representation, reflection and cognitive control. In R. Vasta (Ed.), *Annals of child development* (Vol. 12, pp. 119–126). London: Jessica Kingsley Press.

Zelazo, P. D., & Reznick, J. S. (1991). Age-related asynchrony of knowledge and action. *Child Development, 62*(4), 719–735.

Zhang, H., Leckman, J. F., Tsai, C. P., Kidd, K. K., Rosario Campos, M. C., & Tourette Syndrome Association International Consortium for Genetics. (2002). Genome wide scan of hoarding in sibling pairs both diagnosed with Gilles de la Tourette syndrome. *American Journal of Human Genetics, 70*(4), 896–904.

Zhang, H., & Risch, N. (1996). Mapping quantitative-trait loci in humans by use of extreme concordant sib pairs: Selected sampling by parental phenotypes. *American Journal of Human Genetics, 59,* 951–957.

Zigler, E., & Glick, M. (1986). *A developmental approach to adult psychopathology.* New York: Wiley.

Zohar, A. H. (1999). The epidemiology of obsessive-compulsive disorder in children and adolescents. *Child and Adolescent Psychiatric Clinics of North America, 8,* 445–460.

Zohar, A. H., & Bruno, R. (1997). Normative and pathological obsessive-compulsive behavior and ideation in childhood: A question of timing. *Journal of Child Psychology and Psychiatry and Allied Disciplines, 38*(8), 993–999.

Zohar, A. H., & Felz, L. (2001). Ritualistic behavior in young children. *Journal of Abnormal Child Psychology, 29*(2), 121–128.

Zohar, A. H., LaBuda, M., & Moschel-Ravid, O. (1995). Obsessive-compulsive behaviors and cognitive functioning: A study of compulsivity, frame-shifting and Type A activity patterns in a normal population. *Neuropsychiatry, Neuropsychology and Behavioral Neurology, 8,* 163–167.

Zohar, A. H., Ratzoni, G., Pauls, D. L., Apter, A., Dycian, A., Binder, M., et al. (1992). An epidemiological study of obsessive-compulsive disorder and related disorders in Israeli adolescents. *Journal of the American Academy of Child and Adolescent Psychiatry, 31*(6), 1057–1061.

Zohar, J., & Insel, T. R. (1987). Obsessive-compulsive disorder: Psychobiological approaches to diagnosis, treatment, and pathophysiology. *Biological Psychiatry, 2,* 667–687.

CHAPTER 11

Tourette's Syndrome: A Multifactorial, Developmental Psychopathology

ALEXANDRA L. SPESSOT and BRADLEY S. PETERSON

Tourette's syndrome (TS) is defined by the presence of chronic motor and phonic tics that wax and wane in frequency, forcefulness and complexity. These tics typically begin in early childhood, continue throughout childhood and adolescence, and attenuate substantially by early adulthood. Various cognitive, behavioral, and emotional disturbances tend to co-occur with TS, including Obsessive-Compulsive Disorder (OCD) and Attention-Deficit/Hyperactivity Dis-

This work was supported in part by NIMH grants MH01232, MH59139, and MH068318, the Thomas D. Klingenstein and Nancy D. Perlman Family Fund, and the Suzanne Crosby Murphy Endowment at Columbia University. We are grateful to James Leckman and Donald Cohen for their intellectual contributions and friendship over many years that helped to inform the content of this manuscript.

order (ADHD; D. J. Cohen, Friedhoff, Leckman, & Chase, 1992; D. J. Cohen & Leckman, 1994).

TS was first reported in the 1880s by neurologist Georges Gilles de la Tourette (1885), who described several cases of "a disorder of the nervous system characterized by motor incoordination accompanied by echolalia and coprolalia." In the decades immediately following its initial description, TS was thought by neurologists and psychiatrists to be a variant of hysteria or chorea, rather than a distinct entity (Brissaud, 1896; Kushner, 2000). In the mid-1900s, the syndrome was understood in terms of psychoanalytic theories of character, obsessive-compulsive neurosis, and narcissism (Mahler, Luke, & Daltroff, 1945). After haloperidol was shown to be effective in reducing tic symptoms in the 1960s, TS was regarded largely as a disorder of neurochemical regulation (A. K. Shapiro, Shapiro, Young, & Feinberg, 1988a). In the late 1980s and 1990s, attention turned to defining the range of phenotypic expression of TS, as well as to identifying the underlying genetic vulnerability to the disorder (Eapen, Pauls, & Robertson, 1993; Pauls & Leckman, 1986; van de Wetering & Heutink, 1993).

Studies attempting to locate the putative TS vulnerability genes have been largely unsuccessful, however, suggesting that the disorder may not be caused simply by a single genetic anomaly that is present only in those who overtly manifest tic behaviors. Instead, genetic vulnerability to tics may be present in a relatively large percentage of the population but expressed in only a minority of those who carry it. In this model of the pathogenesis of TS, the expression and severity of tic behaviors in those who carry the genetic diathesis are mediated by a number of environmental determinants that act together during critical periods of development to activate tic symptoms (Cohen, 1991; Leckman & Peterson, 1993). Each environmental determinant alone is neither necessary nor sufficient to cause tics, but together, in varying combinations, these determinants contribute to a wide variety of clinical presentations within a spectrum of tic disorders and other semi-involuntary behaviors. Tic symptoms, for example, can lie anywhere on a spectrum of frequency and forcefulness, and the presence of a small number of infrequent, minimally forceful tics probably represents a variant of normal behavior. This conceptualization of TS as a disorder caused by multiple genetic and environmental risk factors, the combination and timing of which determine where on a spectrum of clinical presentations a particular person's symptoms lie, is likely applicable to a wide range of complex neuropsychiatric disorders (Cicchetti & Rogosch, 1996; Kopnisky, Cowan, & Hyman, 2002).

The current model for the pathogenesis of TS has been derived using multiple levels of analysis (Cicchetti & Dawson, 2002), including clinical observations, phenomenological studies, family genetic investigations, and developmental and clinical neurosciences (Cohen & Leckman, 1994; Leckman & Peterson, 1993). Examining TS from these varied perspectives leads not only to a greater appreciation of this particular disorder, but also to a fuller understanding of normal human developmental processes. Because the most important factors affecting human development are necessarily ubiquitous and therefore hard to detect, those factors can be more easily recognized when they are studied in the presence of anomalous central nervous system (CNS) development (Cicchetti, 1984, 1990a, 1990b, 1993, 2003). Indeed, studies of the spectrum of tic disorders have taught us much about the importance of varying genetic vulnerabilities, life experiences, and compensatory processes to the normal development of the CNS. Understanding that multiple environmental factors can contribute to the expression of genetic vulnerabilities will continue to shed light on the response of the CNS to constitutional and environmental stress and will ultimately lead to a fuller appreciation of the mechanisms that compensate for these stressors throughout development.

PHENOMENOLOGY AND NATURAL HISTORY

Understanding the natural history and phenomenology of TS is important in effectively educating, counseling, and treating persons with TS and their families. Furthermore, knowledge of the clinical presentation and phenomenology of TS is crucial for the development of clinically relevant research and appropriate diagnostic instruments. Grasping the full range of phenotypic expression of TS allows for an appreciation of its continuities with normal development and of the ways disordered development can result in functional disability.

Phenomenology

Tics are sudden, repetitive, stereotyped movements or phonic productions that, to varying degrees, mimic normal behaviors. Motor and phonic tics are characterized as either simple or complex. Simple tics are brief, usually lasting less than 1 second, and appear purposeless. Complex tics last longer and usually appear more purposeful. Examples of motor tics include eye blinks, head jerks, shoulder shrugs, and facial grimaces. Phonic tics vary from sniffing, throat clearing, or coughing, to complex speech fragments, including syllables, words, and entire phrases. In extreme cases, patients with TS may exhibit coprophenomena, including the utterance of obscenities and profanities (coprolalia) and, more rarely, the performance of obscene gestures (copropraxia). Although relatively uncommon, coprophenomena are among the most socially disabling symptoms of TS (C. Singer, 1997).

The clinical presentation of tic disorders is highly variable across individuals, such that individuals with completely different, nonoverlapping profiles of tic symptoms can fulfill the same diagnostic criteria for TS. Despite this variability, tic symptoms have been reported to cluster together into one of at least four major groups that may be inherited independently: purely motor and phonic tic symptoms; compulsive behaviors (e.g., touching others or objects); aggressive behaviors (e.g., kicking, temper tantrums); and tapping and absence of grunting (Alsobrook & Pauls, 2002). The group of aggressive tic behaviors tends to co-occur with ADHD. The simple motor and phonic tic grouping tends to occur more in males than in females. Compulsive phenomena are seen in individuals with an earlier onset of tics and in those who have family members with either ADHD or OCD.

Individual tics can occur either alone or together with other tics in what appears to be an orchestrated pattern. In the short term, tics seem to occur in bouts or bursts, and in the long term, they typically wax and wane in frequency, forcefulness, and complexity. The patterning of tics over time, though difficult to predict, is not random (Leckman, King, & Cohen, 1999). Three tic states exist: a baseline state, consisting of tics of intermediate duration and frequency; a bursting state, consisting of short-duration, high-frequency tics; and a state of relative quiescence, consisting of tics of longer duration and frequency. The baseline intermediate state sustains itself but is vulnerable to interruptions by abrupt switches between bursting and quiescence. This pattern of switching between the extreme states of tic frequency continues until the individual is able to return to baseline once again. The factors that cause the fall from baseline and allow the return to it are currently unknown (Peterson & Leckman, 1998). Although not yet supported by empirical studies, this pattern of bursting and quiescent behavior, which has been observed over minutes to hours, could give rise to the long-term waxing and waning of tics, observed over days to weeks and even months, which has been noted in clinical observation.

A child may not be aware of his or her tics initially but will usually become cognizant of them over months or years. Most adolescents and adults are aware of a "premonitory urge" preceding most, but not necessarily all, tics. A "premonitory urge" is characterized by a sense of increasing tension or discomfort that is relieved temporarily by movement of the muscle groups that produce the tic (Kwak, Dat Vuong, & Jankovic, 2003; Leckman, Walker, & Cohen, 1993; Scahill, Leckman, & Marek, 1995). When these urges can be localized to a specific part of the body, they are identified most often in the shoulder girdle, throat, hands, midline of the stomach, or front of the thighs and feet (Leckman et al., 1993). Although performing a tic may relieve the premonitory urge in the short-term, the individual soon feels a mounting, renewed tension that prompts repetition of the tic. The frequent repetition of this cycle of tension and relief may lead to paroxysms of tics that are both physically and emotionally exhausting.

Individuals with TS are highly attuned to sensory changes within themselves and in their external environments (A. J. Cohen & Leckman, 1992; Leckman et al.,

1999). As was first documented by Gilles de la Tourette (1885), the tics of some individuals may involve copying the behavior (echopraxia) and speech (echolalia) of others and of themselves (palilalia). Some individuals may also experience a premonitory urge as arising in other people or in objects; these extracorporeal "phantom" tics are typically associated with the need to touch the person or object in a particular way (Bliss, 1980; Karp & Hallett, 1996).

Continuity of Tic Phenomenology with Normal Behaviors

Many normal people execute spontaneous movements that resemble motor tics. These movements may involve any part of the body, and they may or may not be associated with a conscious urge to move (Keller & Heckhausen, 1990). Such movements often are noted only through active introspection and conscious attempts to inhibit them.

The continuity between normal motor behaviors and motor tic behaviors is well illustrated by the example of eye blinking. Like tics, blinks can be suppressed voluntarily only for a short time. The urge to blink that results from the voluntary suppression of blinking is typically reported by persons with TS to be similar in quality to the urge to tic.

Simple motor tics often involve the orbital musculature (Nomoto & Machiyama, 1990), and these eye-blinking tics are often the first tic behaviors to appear in a child with TS (A. K. Shapiro et al., 1988b). An abnormal blink reflex has been reported in individuals with TS (Raffaele et al., 2004), and one study found an increased frequency of normal blinking in persons with TS compared to control subjects (Tulen et al., 1999). The frequency of eye blinking has also been associated with the overall number and severity of tics in TS (Karson, Kaufmann, Shapiro, & Shapiro, 1985). These studies support the idea that dopaminergic activity, which modulates central nervous system tonus in normal blinking (Karson, 1983; Kleven & Koek, 1996), may also play a part in tic pathogenesis.

Normal children may exhibit "nervous habits," such as thumb sucking and nail biting, or stereotyped motor behaviors, such as body rocking, that can resemble tics. These behaviors are often semicompulsory, in that children may experience an urge to perform the movements and may resist stopping them. A study of nervous habits and stereotypies in children ages 3 to 6 (Foster, 1998) found these behaviors to be quite common in this age group, with parents reporting thumb sucking and nail biting in 25% and 23% of children, respectively. Their high prevalence rates in children of this age group suggests that these movements may be part of the normal behavioral repertoires of small children and raise the question of whether they may even serve some kind of adaptive function in motor development.

Stereotyped movements of childhood may persist into adulthood in some individuals. One study found stereotypic behaviors to be common in a college population and showed a positive correlation between the number of stereotypic behaviors and obsessive-compulsive symptoms, perfectionism, and impulsion-aggression (Niehaus, Emsley, Brink, & Stein, 2000). A subset of the individuals with persistent stereotypies experience these behaviors as disruptive to activities of daily living, thereby meeting the criteria for Stereotypic Movement Disorder (SMD) outlined in the *Diagnostic and Statistic Manual of Mental Disorders,* fourth edition (*DSM-IV*). There exists some poorly controlled data suggesting comorbidity of SMD with anxiety and affective disorders (Castellanos, Ritchie, Marsh, & Rapoport, 1996).

The diagnosis of SMD can be difficult to make, as stereotyped movements may closely resemble the tics of TS or the compulsions of OCD. When distinguishing among the three disorders, it is helpful to consider the entire history of the individual, with special attention to any previous history of tics or true obsessions and compulsions. When these symptoms are absent from a patient's history, SMD is the likely diagnosis of exclusion.

The stereotyped movements that tend to most resemble the tics of TS are transient and chronic motor tics. Whether these tic disorders are etiologically related to TS remains controversial, although studies suggest that TS, Transient Tic Disorder, and Chronic Tic Disorder are part of the same disease entity, with TS being the more severe form of the disorder (Golden, 1978; Kurlan, Behr, Medved, & Como, 1988; Spencer, Biederman, Harding, Wilens, & Faraone, 1995). Phenomenologically, transient and chronic tics are similar to, if not indistinguishable from, the tics of TS (Nomoto & Machiyama, 1990), and these less severe tic disorders are present in 5 to 20 percent of the general population (Achenbach & Edelbrock, 1978; Khalifa & von Knorring, 2003; Lapouse & Monk, 1964; Nomoto & Machiyama, 1990; Rutter & Hemming, 1970; Rutter et al., 1974). Transient and chronic tics appear in early childhood, like those of TS, likely as a result of maturational changes in the normal central nervous system. Unlike the tics in TS, however, transient tics by definition disappear within months of their occurrence, suggesting that the normal central nervous system may undergo plastic changes to attenuate tics that may be impaired or absent in TS (Peterson, Leckman, & Cohen, 1995).

Assessing Tic Severity

The most commonly used clinical rating instrument for the severity of tics measures the number, frequency, intensity, and complexity of tics, as well as the degree to which tics interfere with motor or speech acts (Leckman et al., 1989). Other instruments for rating the severity of tics have examined how apparent an individual's tics are to others, and the extent to which others view the individual's behavior or appearance bizarre (A. K. Shapiro et al., 1988b). Videotaped counts of tics have also been used to supplement clinical ratings in medication trials and challenge studies (Chappell et al., 1992; Chappell, McSwiggan-Hardin, et al., 1994; Leckman et al., 1991; Lombroso, Mack, Scahill, King, & Leckman, 1991; E. Shapiro et al., 1989).

Commonly Co-occurring Conditions: Attention-Deficit/Hyperactivity Disorder and Obsessive-Compulsive Disorder

Children with TS frequently experience behavioral problems before the onset of tics. About 40% to 50% of children who present clinically with tics already have a history of being overly active, inattentive, and impulsive (D. J. Cohen et al., 1992; Comings & Comings, 1987a). Approximately 60% of the children who present clinically with such problems have difficulties severe enough to satisfy criteria for ADHD. One study of adults with tics and ADHD showed that the onset of tics was, on average, 6 years later than the onset of ADHD symptoms (Spencer et al., 2001).

ADHD is a heterogeneous clinical syndrome characterized by inattention or distractibility, motor hyperactivity, and impulsivity. Children with ADHD tend to perform poorly on tasks requiring sustained attention, motor inhibition, organization, planning, and complex, multisequence problem solving (Barkley, Grodzinsky, & DuPaul, 1992; Geurts, Verte, Oosterlaan, Roeyers, & Sergeant, 2004; Rucklidge & Tannock, 2002). ADHD often co-occurs with or predicts strongly the future development of Oppositional Defiant Disorder, conduct disorders, affective and anxiety disorders, substance use, and aggressive behaviors (Biederman, Newcorn, & Sprich, 1991; Biederman et al., 1995; Peterson, Pine, Cohen, & Brook, 2001; Pliszka, 2000, 2003; Scahill et al., 1999).

The causal relationship underlying this common clinical association of TS with ADHD has been studied extensively but remains unclear. Some family studies have hypothesized that TS and ADHD are variant expressions of the same genetic diathesis, with both conditions resulting from disturbances in a shared neural substrate, such as dysfunction of the basal ganglia (Comings & Comings, 1984; Pauls, Leckman, & Cohen, 1993). If tics and ADHD do in fact share the same neural substrate and if dysfunction of this substrate does contribute to their co-occurrence, then the severity of the symptoms of TS and ADHD might be expected to correlate positively with one another, a possibility that has received support from some (Randolph, Hyde, Gold, Goldberg, & Weinberger, 1993) but not all studies. One recent study, for example, found no significant difference in tic severity between children with TS alone and those with TS and ADHD (Sukhodolsky et al., 2003).

Other family studies suggest that some children with TS may inherit their tic disorder and ADHD independently from one another (Pauls, Hurst, et al., 1986; Pauls et al., 1993). These findings suggest that the observed clinical association between TS and ADHD is the likely result of referral bias (Berkson, 1946). Children with ADHD exhibit behavioral problems that prompt parents to seek clinical attention. During that evaluation, these children with ADHD may be more often diagnosed with TS than children with tics alone simply because they are more likely to be brought to a clinic. Alternatively, some children with TS may exhibit ADHD-like symptoms that are not a result of a genetic relationship between the two disorders, but that are in some way a direct consequence of having tics. For example, tics or the need to suppress them might interfere with a child's attentional capacities in the classroom and contribute to the identification and clinical labeling of the child as having ADHD.

Whatever the reason for the common clinical co-occurrence of TS and ADHD, numerous studies have documented clearly and convincingly that ADHD symptoms constitute the main source of cognitive, behavioral, and emotional impairment in children and adults who have TS. Studies of cognitive function in TS suggest that the deficits in visuomotor skills and the impairment in executive functions found in TS may be attributable to co-occurring ADHD (Channon, Pratt, & Robertson, 2003; Harris et al., 1995; Silverstein, Como, Palumbo, West, & Osborn, 1995; Yeates & Bornstein, 1994). One recent behavioral study showed that children with both TS and ADHD, when compared with children with TS alone and with normal controls, had more disruptive behavior, greater functional impairment, and higher levels of family dysfunction (Sukhodolsky et al., 2003). The group with both TS and ADHD did not differ from the ADHD-only group, however, suggesting that the risk for problem behaviors in children with TS derives largely from the presence of ADHD, and not from the tic disorder. Other studies using peer, parent,

and self-evaluations found that children with TS and ADHD tend to be less popular than their peers, exhibiting externalizing behavior problems such as aggression, internalizing behavior problems such as social withdrawal, and poor social adaptation (Bawden, Stokes, Camfield, Camfield, & Salisbury, 1998; Carter et al., 2000; Spencer et al., 1998; Stokes, Bawden, Camfield, Backman, & Dooley, 1991). Children with TS alone, in contrast, appear to exhibit internalizing behavior problems only. All of these studies highlight the potential risks posed by co-occurring ADHD to the neuropsychological profile, behavioral patterns, and emotional stability of children with TS. Early diagnosis of ADHD in children with TS, combined with appropriate educational and psychosocial intervention, may improve developmental outcome in these children (Carter et al., 2000).

Over 40% of clinically referred adult TS patients meet formal criteria for OCD (King, Leckman, Scahill, & Cohen, 1999). OCD is an anxiety spectrum disorder defined by persistent, recurring thoughts, ideas, or images (obsessions) that are perceived as intrusive and distressing. These are usually accompanied by intentional repetitive behaviors (compulsions) that relieve the subjective distress associated with the obsession. OCD symptoms tend to cluster into at least four major groups, which have been identified in factor analyses of OCD (Baer, 1994; Cavallini, Di Bella, Siliprandi, Malchiodi, & Bellodi, 2002; Leckman et al., 1997; Leckman, Zhang, Alsobrook, & Pauls, 2001; Mataix-Cols, Rauch, Manzo, Jenike, & Baer, 1999; Summerfeldt, Richter, Antony, & Swinson, 1999). One of these groups includes aggressive, religious, and sexual obsessions, as well as checking compulsions. Another group comprises obsessions and compulsions that pertain primarily to symmetry and ordering. A third group includes contamination obsessions and cleaning or washing compulsions, and a fourth group includes obsessions and compulsions related to hoarding (Leckman et al., 2003).

Family studies have shown repeatedly that OCD is present in the families of individuals with tic disorders more often than it is present in control families, whether or not the individual with tics has co-occurring OCD (Eapen et al., 1993; Pauls, Leckman, Towbin, Zahner, & Cohen, 1986; Pauls, Raymond, Stevenson, & Leckman, 1991). Conversely, tics are present in the family members of individuals with OCD more often than they are present in control families, whether or not the individual with OCD has a co-occurring tic disorder (Leonard et al., 1992; Pauls, Alsobrook, Goodman, Rasmussen, & Leckman, 1995). This co-occurrence of tic disorders and OCD in families suggests that tics and obsessive-compulsive behaviors represent variable expressions of the same underlying genetic vulnerability. The probable genetic relationship between TS and OCD in turn suggests that although their phenotypes seem to differ significantly, these phenotypes may be more closely related than they appear to be on the surface. The symptoms of TS and OCD, for example, may lie on a spectrum of semicompulsory behaviors (Jaisoorya, Reddy, & Srinath, 2003; Richter, Summerfeldt, Antony, & Swinson, 2003). Urges to carry out these behaviors mount until they become irresistible, at which point, executing the behaviors brings relief. In this model, symptoms with little or no ideational component may belong to the simple tics of TS at one end of the spectrum, whereas symptoms with a prominent ideational component may belong to OCD on the other end of the spectrum. Complex tics may lie somewhere between these two extremes (Peterson & Thomas, 2000).

The forms of OCD that are related to tic symptoms differ qualitatively from the forms of OCD without a personal or family history of tics. Tic-related OCD, compared with the non-tic-related form of OCD, has an earlier age of onset (in childhood or adolescence rather than in adulthood; George, Trimble, Ring, Sallee, & Robertson, 1993; Holzer et al., 1994; Leckman, Grice, et al., 1994; Leckman, Walker, Goodman, Pauls, & Cohen, 1994), a male preponderance (George et al., 1993; Holzer et al., 1994; Leckman, Grice, et al., 1994; Leckman, Walker, et al., 1994), a weaker response to standard antiobsessional medications (Ackerman, Greenland, Bystritsky, Morgenstern, & Katz, 1994; Ravizza, Barzega, Bellino, Bogetto, & Maina, 1995), fewer washing-, cleaning-, and hoarding-related symptoms (Leckman et al., 2003), and a greater likelihood of first-degree family members having a tic disorder (Leonard et al., 1992; Pauls et al., 1995; Riddle et al., 1990). Preliminary findings from one study of clinically referred adults suggest that tic-related OCD may confer a greater degree of clinical morbidity than either TS or OCD alone. Those with TS and OCD had higher rates of anxiety, mood disorders, disruptive behavior, substance use, and OCD spectrum disorders than did adult subjects with TS or OCD alone (Coffey et al., 1998). Whether these findings from a clinically referred sample of adults generalize to the larger population of individuals who have a lifetime with TS, however, is unclear.

Putative Causal Links of Tourette's Syndrome with Attention-Deficit/Hyperactivity Disorder and Obsessive-Compulsive Disorder

The observed co-occurrence of tic disorders, OCD, and ADHD in clinical samples has led to speculation that these conditions may share a common etiology. Family studies of clinic patients provide fairly strong evidence that TS and OCD are variable expressions of the same genetic diathesis. The link between these two disorders and ADHD has not been well established in family studies, though some investigators still consider ADHD an additional variable manifestation of putative TS vulnerability genes.

The co-occurrence of TS, OCD, and ADHD in families does not necessarily prove that these disorders are etiologically related, because various biases may affect familial aggregation (Peterson, Leckman, & Cohen, 1995; Shapiro & Shapiro, 1992). Family members, for example, may share certain environmental factors that could predispose them to particular symptoms of TS, OCD, and ADHD, which might then produce an apparent association between the disorders even if the disorders are not actually related. Alternatively, characteristics of parents may affect their tolerance of psychopathology in their children, which might increase the representation of certain families in clinical samples. For example, parents with OCD may be more likely to notice and report tics in their children, thus increasing representation of families with both TS and OCD in clinical populations and in the studies that use clinical samples.

If tics, OCD, and ADHD are in fact intrinsically related, then they should co-occur in the general population without clinical referral bias. Cross-sectional epidemiological studies may not capture a true association, however, because of the differing natural history and course of each disorder. Prospective, longitudinal studies of epidemiological samples would provide the best evidence for or against an etiologic relationship.

One prospective longitudinal study of an epidemiological sample (Peterson, Pine, et al., 2001) has shed some light on the natural history of TS, ADHD, and OCD and the associations among the three conditions throughout childhood and into early adulthood. In this study, tics and OCD were significantly associated with one another, as were OCD and ADHD, during late adolescence and early adulthood. Tics in childhood or early adolescence were predictive of OCD symptoms later in adolescence or in early adulthood. Conversely, OCD in late adolescence was predictive of tics in adulthood. ADHD in early adolescence was only weakly predictive of tics in late adolescence but was more strongly predictive of OCD in adulthood. OCD in late adolescence was predictive of ADHD in adulthood. The strongest associations in these analyses were those of tics with OCD and OCD with ADHD. There were no significant associations between tics and ADHD at any time point.

These findings are consistent with the family genetic studies that suggest an etiologic association between tic disorders and OCD. The common co-occurrence of tics and ADHD that has been observed in referred samples was not found in this epidemiological sample, suggesting that the co-occurrence in clinical populations may be due partly to the complex interactions across development between various psychopathological risk factors, including OCD, other anxiety disorders, mood disorders, and conduct disturbances (Peterson, Pine, et al., 2001). Perhaps most interesting are the independent associations between OCD and TS and between OCD and ADHD. This finding suggests that OCD rather than TS may be the "parent" disorder, and tics and ADHD may represent variable manifestations of an OCD genetic diathesis.

Natural History

TS typically begins in early childhood, with one or several simple tics that are often regarded by parents and teachers as benign habits or odd mannerisms. Tics steadily increase in number, frequency, forcefulness, and complexity, reaching a peak in severity at around age 10 or 11. They then tend to decline gradually in severity throughout adolescence (Pappert, Goetz, Louis, Blasucci, & Leurgans, 2003); in fact, by 18 years of age, about 90% of individuals with TS will experience a substantial reduction in tic symptoms, and over 40% will be free of symptoms (Bloch et al., 2004; Burd et al., 2001; Leckman et al., 1998). Superimposed on this rise, plateau, and decline in the severity of tics through childhood and adolescence is an unpredictable waxing and waning in severity over minutes, hours, days, and weeks.

Onset

The mean age of onset of motor tics in TS and other tic disorders is between 5 and 6 years of age (Leckman et al., 1998), although tics may appear as early as 1 year of age or as late as adolescence (Burd & Kerbeshian, 1987). Late-onset tics in the absence of a family history of tic disorders necessitate a thorough workup for other primary causes. Most commonly, the onset of TS is gradual, with one or several transient episodes of seemingly benign childhood tics or mannerisms. These episodes are then followed by periods of more persistent and severe motor and phonic tics.

The first tics to appear are typically transient, simple motor tics of the face, most commonly eye blinking tics (Bruun, 1988). These initial tics are subsequently replaced by, or sometimes joined by, more persistent, forceful, and complex movements. Motor tics typically progress in a gen-eral cephalocaudal direction, most commonly affecting other head and neck structures, and less frequently affecting the upper and lower extremities. Phonic tics usually appear several years following the onset of motor tics (Leckman et al., 1999), and follow a similar progression from transient, simple sounds to longer-lasting, increasingly exaggerated and complex words and phrases. Each individual has his or her own unique repertoire of motor and phonic tics, the overall severity of which waxes and wanes in cycles lasting days, weeks, or months. The factors that affect these cycles are as yet poorly defined, although exacerbations of tics have been noted in the context of major losses or other stressors.

Early Intramorbid Course

The progressive worsening of tics in young children typically culminates in a period of peak severity at around age 10, although this period of worst-ever severity can occur as early as 7 and as late as 15 years of age (Leckman et al., 1998). During this period many children become increasingly aware of their tics and begin reporting premonitory urges (Bliss, 1980; A. J. Cohen & Leckman, 1992; Kurlan, Lichter, & Hewitt, 1989; Leckman et al., 1993). About 30% to 60% of older children and early adolescents with TS will also begin to experience obsessional thoughts and engage in compulsive rituals (Leckman, Walker, et al., 1994). Compulsive behaviors commonly appear first, and may often resemble complex motor tics. These compulsions initially are typically not associated with obsessional thoughts (Swedo, Rapoport, Leonard, Lenane, & Cheslow, 1989), although some individuals may express a need for things to feel or look "just right" (Leckman et al., 1993).

Tics and associated behavioral problems may interfere with normal social development in childhood and early adolescence. Schoolchildren with TS are often mocked and socially isolated as a result of their tics, and these children tend to view themselves as less attractive than their peers (Carter, Pauls, Leckman, & Cohen, 1994). Children with TS are in fact usually viewed by classmates and teachers as less popular, more withdrawn, and more aggressive (Stokes et al., 1991) than their peers.

Postpubertal Intramorbid Course

A minority of adolescents may experience a worsening of complex tics, along with an increase in anxiety symptoms, mood disturbances, and aggression toward self and others. Most adolescents with TS, however, experience greater self-awareness of their tics, and an increased capacity for self-regulatory control over unwanted behaviors. Up to

90% of late adolescents experience some degree of attenuation of their tic symptoms. Despite this reduction in tic symptoms, however, many adolescents continue to experience the impaired social development and decreased emotional well-being associated with having suffered tics (Bruun, 1988). Adolescents may also experience continuing morbidity related to OCD, ADHD, or other disturbances that may co-occur with TS.

Adolescents with TS often encounter emotional difficulty during the psychological phase of separation and individuation, as they require but resent the continuing involvement of parents around their tics and related symptoms. Any physical stigma can have profound, adverse psychological effects during adolescence, a time of heightened interest in and awareness of one's body. Thus, the highly visible, audible, and tangible bodily manifestations of TS—the unusual movements, strange utterances, occasionally obscene behaviors, and aggression—can impair the formation and solidification of self-image and identity during adolescence (Peterson, Leckman, & Cohen, 1995). Socialization can continue to suffer (Dykens et al., 1990) regardless of the severity of tic symptoms (Stokes et al., 1991), as many adolescents with TS continue to be perceived by their peers as immature, withdrawn, and aggressive.

Adult Outcomes

The severity of tics typically stabilizes by the early 20s (Bruun, 1988; Erenberg, Cruse, & Rothner, 1987). In rare circumstances, individuals with TS may experience exacerbations of tic symptoms later on in adulthood (Nee, Polinsky, & Ebert, 1982). The severity of tics during childhood and adolescence seems to predict only weakly the severity of tics in adulthood (Bloch et al., 2004), although older adolescents who present with severe tic symptoms may hold a relatively poor prognosis (Leckman et al., 1998).

Most individuals with TS experience an attenuation of their symptoms during adulthood; however, some may continue to have tics and associated learning and behavioral problems. Two studies (Erenberg et al., 1987; Goetz, Tanner, Stebbins, Leipzig, & Carr, 1992) have reported that tics and related symptoms remain in the majority of individuals with TS, but these studies must be interpreted with caution because of a poor response rate on patient surveys (only about 60% identified eligible subjects participated in the interviews) and absence of characterization of nonrespondents. One recent but unreplicated study using objective measures of tic symptoms found that 90% of a sample of adults who had been clinic patients as children still had tics, although the tics had improved substantially since childhood (Pappert et al., 2003).

Difficulties Predicting Outcome

Predicting the longitudinal course of TS for a specific individual is not yet possible, although general predictions can be made using the known natural history of the disorder. Tic symptoms that begin early in childhood can be expected to peak in severity sometime in late childhood or pre-adolescence. For most individuals, tics will gradually improve through late adolescence and early adulthood, with a substantial reduction in the number and severity of symptoms (Bloch et al., 2004; Burd et al., 2001; Leckman et al., 1998; Pappert et al., 2003).

EPIDEMIOLOGY

Epidemiological studies have sought to estimate the prevalence and distribution of TS and related tic disorders in the general population. TS and other tic disorders have been documented across all races, ethnic groups, and socioeconomic classes. Transient simple motor and phonic tics are quite common, occurring in 4% to 24% of school-age children (Jankovic, 1997; Khalifa & von Knorring, 2003; Kurlan et al., 2001; A. K. Shapiro et al., 1988b; H. S. Singer & Walkup, 1991; Snider et al., 2002). Chronic tic disorders are much less common, occurring in 1% to 2% of the general population (H. S. Singer & Walkup, 1991). TS is the least common tic disorder, with an estimated prevalence of 0.03% to 0.6% of the population. Tic disorders are found predominantly in males, with a male-to-female ratio ranging from 1.6:1 to 9:1 (Apter et al., 1993; Burd, Kerbeshian, Wikenheiser, & Fisher, 1986; Caine et al., 1988; Comings, Himes, & Comings, 1990; Khalifa & von Knorring, 2003).

The wide range of prevalence estimates reflects various methodological difficulties in conducting epidemiological studies of tic disorders (Peterson, Leckman, & Cohen, 1995). First, samples for these studies have been ascertained from different populations, including patients in mental health clinics, community surveys using self-reports or physician reporting, and recruits in obligatory military service. Ascertainment from mental health clinics has yielded prevalence estimates an order of magnitude larger than the estimates found in ascertainments from community surveys. Second, the ages of sample populations have varied widely across studies. Studies of children tend to produce higher prevalence estimates compared with studies of adolescents and adults, likely because the typical attenuation in the severity of tic symptoms during adolescence reduces the number of positive identifications in temporal cross-section. Third, studies have used different diagnostic instruments to identify individuals with tic disorders. Studies that rely on self-reports and parental questionnaires for identification of tic behaviors probably underestimate the prevalence of TS because children or their parents tend to underreport symptoms, especially mild ones. Studies that rely on identification from clinical samples overestimate rates of TS and co-occurring illnesses because individuals with more severe tics and more co-occurring conditions are more likely to seek clinical attention (Berkson, 1946).

One of the most methodologically sophisticated epidemiological studies of TS to date (Apter et al., 1993) used a three-stage procedure to diagnose affected 16- and 17-year-old recruits in the Israeli army. These recruits constitute the vast majority of the Israeli population in that age group. TS was diagnosed in 0.043%, with a male-to-female ratio of 1.6:1. The strengths of this study include the direct assessment of tics by an expert clinician in the final stage of ascertainment, the large sample size (>28,000 recruits), and the sampling of virtually the entire population of the country in that age range. The study probably underestimated the lifetime prevalence of TS in that population, however, because the sample consisted only of adolescents, whose tics likely had already improved by that age. Furthermore, young people in Israel generally take pride in their military service and may underreport medical conditions that may adversely affect their possible placement in the more desirable branches of service. Finally, although the study sample did represent the majority of Israelis in the 16- to 17-year-old age group, a minority population of religious women who do not serve in the military was systematically excluded.

A recent epidemiological study of TS examined all 4,479 schoolchildren ages 7 to 15 living in a small Swedish town (Khalifa & von Knorring, 2003). A three-stage procedure was used to identify those with tic disorders. In the first stage, parents completed a screening questionnaire about their child's symptoms. In the second stage, positive respondents from the first stage were interviewed to confirm or refute the diagnosis. In the third stage, children who were confirmed in the second stage as having tics were examined by a trained clinician. A tic disorder was diagnosed in 6.6% of the population, and boys were affected 1.6 times more often than were girls. The prevalence of TS was 0.6%, with a male-to-female ratio of 9:1. Both the prevalence estimate and the male-to-female ratio of TS in this study were considerably higher than those reported in the Israeli army study, probably because the Swedish sample studied the full age range during which TS symptoms emerge, peak, and subside. The higher propor-

tion of boys with TS compared with those who have any tic disorder may suggest that boys are more likely to have a tic disorder that is chronic and that involves both movements and vocalizations.

In light of the limitations of cross-sectional studies and the uncertainties that they confer on lifetime prevalence estimates for tic disorders, prospective, longitudinal studies of representative, community samples are needed to provide more accurate estimates of tic disorders over a lifetime. One study followed 976 children residing in upstate New York for 15 years (Peterson, Pine, et al., 2001). The lifetime prevalence of TS was approximately 0.4%, a value within the range of those reported in previous studies (Costello et al., 1996; Nomoto & Machiyama, 1990; Verhulst, van der Ende, Ferdinand, & Kasius, 1997). More prospective, longitudinal studies of samples representative of the general population are needed to clarify further the prevalence of TS, other tic disorders, and associated conditions.

HEREDITY AND GENETIC VULNERABILITY

In his original reports, Gilles de la Tourette hypothesized a role for hereditary factors in the etiology of TS; for the next century, however, the genetics of TS were largely ignored. The past few decades have seen a renewed and intense interest in the multigenerational transmission of tic disorders (Kidd, Prusoff, & Cohen, 1980). Evidence for a strong genetic role in the expression of TS symptoms has come from twin and family studies, the results of which have prompted association and genetic linkage studies seeking to identify the gene or group of genes involved in TS.

Twin Studies

Studies of twins have suggested that genetic factors are important in the transmission and expression of TS and related disorders. Monozygotic twin pairs have been found to be highly concordant for TS (50% to 90%) and for other tic disorders (77% to 100%; Hyde, Aaronson, Randolph, Rickler, & Weinberger, 1992; Price, Kidd, Cohen, Pauls, & Leckman, 1985; Walkup et al., 1988). Although sample sizes of dizygotic twins have generally been smaller that those of monozygotic twins, the concordance rates for TS (8%) and other tic disorders (23%) in dizygotic twins are much lower than the rates in monozygotic twins. This difference in concordance between monozygotic and dizygotic twins strongly implicates genetic factors in the etiology of TS.

Family Studies

Numerous studies of large numbers of families have been completed in recent years: five in American or European families (Eapen et al., 1993; Hebebrand, Klug, et al., 1997; Pauls et al., 1991; van de Wetering & Heutink, 1993; Walkup et al., 1996) and one in Japanese families (Kano, Ohta, Nagai, Pauls, & Leckman, 2001). All of these studies used direct, structured interviews of probands with TS to obtain information regarding tics and co-occurring disorders. First-degree relatives of probands were also interviewed whenever possible, and best-estimate diagnostic procedures were used to make a consensus diagnosis in these family members.

These studies all report a significantly higher frequency of tic disorders in first-degree relatives of TS probands compared to rates in control samples or in the general population. In the studies using American and European samples, the prevalence of TS among first-degree family members ranged from 10% to 15%, and the prevalence of other tic disorders ranged from 15% to 20%. The first-degree relatives of the Japanese probands, compared to the American and European samples, had significantly lower rates of TS (2%) and other tic disorders (12%). These data, if replicated, may suggest a different etiology of tic disorders in the Japanese population compared to Western populations (Pauls, 2003).

Mode of Genetic Transmission

Segregation analyses seek to identify the pattern of transmission of a disorder within families. The majority of segregation analyses of TS families suggest that major genes play an important role in the expression of tic disorders. Several studies have reported autosomal dominant transmission of the TS genetic diathesis (Eapen et al., 1993; Pauls & Leckman, 1986; van de Wetering & Heutink, 1993), whereas others have proposed a semidominant pattern of inheritance with greater penetrance in affected homozygotes than heterozygotes (Hasstedt, Leppert, Filloux, van de Wetering, & McMahon, 1995; Pauls et al., 1991; Walkup et al., 1996). One study also suggested multifactorial (polygenic) inheritance of TS (Walkup et al., 1996).

Some studies have raised the possibility of a more complex pattern of inheritance for tic disorders. The phenomenon of imprinting, for example, has been implicated as a complicating factor in the genetics of TS. One study (Lichter, Jackson, & Schachter, 1995) examined the TS phenotype of subjects with clear matrilineal and patrilineal inheritance of the syndrome. Subjects with matrilineal in-

heritance of TS tended to exhibit complex motor tics and ritualistic behaviors more frequently than those subjects with patrilineal inheritance. Subjects with patrilineal inheritance had more frequent phonic tics, an earlier onset of phonic tics relative to motor tics, and more prominent ADHD symptoms, including motor restlessness. Although these findings have yet to be replicated, this study illustrates the increasing complexity of the genetics of TS as this field of inquiry evolves. The mechanisms underlying the inheritance of TS are likely to be multifaceted, involving a number of different vulnerability genes.

Searching for Vulnerability Genes

Association and genetic linkage are the two major types of study design that have been used in the search for the TS vulnerability genes. In genetic association studies, a sample of individuals affected with a disease is compared with a sample of unaffected individuals, and the frequency with which certain alleles are present in each of these groups is tested for correlation with the disease. The major advantage of these studies is that a specific mode of inheritance does not need to be assumed in the analysis. The major disadvantage to association studies is their susceptibility to false-positive results, which can be minimized in part by matching the race and ethnicity of all subjects as closely as possible (Gelernter, Pauls, Leckman, Kidd, & Kurlan, 1994; Pauls & Tourette Syndrome Association International Consortium on Genetics, 2001). If precisely matching the control and patient populations on relevant demographic characteristics proves too costly or difficult, investigators may use the haplotype relative risk method (Falk & Rubinstein, 1987; Terwilliger & Ott, 1992) or the related transmission disequilibrium test (Spielman & Ewens, 1996) to study gene-disease associations. Rather than drawing affected and unaffected samples from the general population, these methods examine the DNA of affected probands and their parents. The proband's two alleles constitute the "affected" group, and the alleles that were not transmitted from the parents to the proband form the "unaffected" group. Because both parents donate alleles equally to the affected and unaffected groups, the groups are matched perfectly for race and ethnicity (Pauls, 2003).

The principle of genetic linkage states that genes located close to one another on a chromosome tend to be transmitted together during meiosis, the process of cell division by which germ cells are produced. In genetic linkage studies, members of families are examined to determine whether DNA marker regions that have known chromosomal locations cosegregate with a disease within the family. If a particular marker is found in family members affected with a disease but not in unaffected members, then that marker is assumed to be sufficiently close to the disease allele such that the marker and the disease are inherited together (Pauls & Tourette Syndrome Association International Consortium on Genetics, 2001). If linkage is demonstrated, the identified area on the chromosome is probed further to locate more precisely the region of interest and, ideally, to identify the specific gene that confers vulnerability to the disease.

Most genetic linkage analyses have studied large, multigenerational families. Although these families do provide a valuable sample of affected and unaffected members, the statistical methods used in these studies require specification of a particular mode of inheritance. In diseases for which the mode of inheritance is unclear or heterogeneous, as is likely the case with TS, misspecification of inheritance parameters can lead to inaccurate or invalid results. Alternatively, many investigators now commonly compare the number of alleles at a given locus that are shared by two affected siblings (sib pairs; Kruglyak & Lander, 1995). Although sib-pair studies are statistically less powerful than are traditional linkage studies, they do not require specifications about the pattern of inheritance of a disease, making them effective tools for the study of diseases whose precise modes of inheritance are unknown. Sibling-pair studies can provide important preliminary information that can be used to direct more statistically powerful approaches (Pauls & Tourette Syndrome Association International Consortium on Genetics, 2001).

Findings

In light of the generally positive response of people with tics to neuroleptic medications, TS has long been suspected to involve central dopaminergic pathways. Because of this hypothesized etiological connection, the various dopamine receptor genes have, to date, been the most frequently targeted genes for directed analyses in association studies. Association has been excluded between TS and the dopamine receptors DRD1 (Chou et al., 2004; Gelernter et al., 1993; Thompson, Comings, Feder, George, & O'Dowd, 1998), DRD3 (Devor, Dill-Devor, & Magee, 1998; Diaz-Anzaldua et al., 2004; Hebebrand et al., 1993), and DRD5 (Barr, Wigg, Zovko, Sandor, & Tsui, 1997). One study reported an association between TS and DRD2 (Comings et al., 1991), but others have failed to detect such an association (Devor et al., 1990; Diaz-Anzaldua et al., 2004; Gelernter et al., 1990; Nothen et al., 1994). Two studies have detected a possible association between

TS and the DRD4*7 allele of the DRD4 dopamine receptor (Diaz-Anzaldua et al., 2004; Grice et al., 1996), but other studies have failed to replicate these findings (Barr, Wigg, Zovko, Sandor, & Tsui, 1996; Hebebrand, Nothen, et al., 1997). Studies attempting to associate TS with the dopamine transporter gene (SLC6A3) have also been unsuccessful (Diaz-Anzaldua et al., 2004; Gelernter, Vandenberg, et al., 1995; Vandenberg et al., 2000). One recent study (Diaz-Anzaldua et al., 2004) detected a possible association between TS and the monoamine oxidase-A (MAO-A) gene in a French Canadian founder population, but these results have not been replicated to date.

A number of other candidate genes have been excluded to date, including the 5HT7 serotonin receptor gene (Gelernter, Rao, et al., 1995), the 5HT1A serotonin receptor gene (Brett, Curtis, Robertson, & Gurling, 1995), the alpha-1 subunit of the glycine receptor gene (Brett, Curtis, Robertson, & Gurling, 1997), the adrenergic receptor genes ADRA1C and ADRA2A (Xu et al., 2003), and the Rett syndrome (MeCP2) gene (Rosa, Jankovic, & Ashizawa, 2003). In light of recent theories concerning a possible autoimmune etiology of TS, one study examined the HLA-DRB alleles in 83 unrelated family trios but failed to detect any association between this locus and a diagnosis of TS (Schoenian et al., 2003).

Chromosomal translocations have been detected in some individuals with TS, and several studies have examined possible associations between TS and these disrupted chromosomal regions. Two studies, for example, have reported an apparent association between TS and a translocation between chromosomes 7 and 18 (Boghosian-Sell, Comings, & Overhauser, 1996; Comings et al., 1986). A study examining chromosomes 7 and 18 in 15 multigenerational Dutch families failed to replicate these findings (Heutink et al., 1990). Translocations in persons with TS have also been identified between chromosomes 3 and 8 (Brett, Curtis, Robertson, Dahlitz, & Gurling, 1996) and between chromosomes 1 and 8 (Matsumoto et al., 2000), but on closer examination these translocations were not shown to be significant in the etiology of tic disorders.

A recent study has renewed interest in chromosome 18 as a possible site for the TS vulnerability genes. An inversion between chromosomes 18 and 22 was described in a young boy with chronic tics and OCD, and characterization of the disrupted interval identified two structurally normal transcripts (State et al., 2003). However, further analysis of the region and its products revealed significantly delayed replication timing of the inverted chromosome compared to control subjects. In other words, the inversion produced normal transcripts and proteins, but the rate of transcription of the abnormal chromosome was slowed. The results of this study have yet to be replicated, but the findings suggest that chromosome 18 warrants further investigation in the search for the genes responsible for TS.

Early genetic linkage analyses assumed that TS is a homogeneous condition, that it is genetically related to chronic tic disorders, and that it is transmitted in an autosomal dominant pattern. Over thirty multigenerational families have been studied to date, and more than 95% of the genome has been excluded from linkage under these assumptions (Heutink et al., 1995; Pakstis et al., 1991; Pauls et al., 1990). Given these resoundingly negative findings, the Tourette Syndrome Association International Consortium for Genetics (TSAICG; 1999) conducted a sib-pair study consisting of 76 families and 110 sibling pairs. Although no results reached statistical significance, two major regions of interest were identified with MLS scores of greater than 2.0, one on chromosome 4 and the other on chromosome 8.

Other linkage studies have identified various chromosomal regions of preliminary interest. One genome scan of a sample of South African Afrikaners with TS found evidence for linkage on chromosomes 2, 8, and 11 (Simonic, Gericke, Ott, & Weber, 1998; Simonic et al., 2001). Another study of several multigenerational families with TS detected evidence for linkage on chromosomes 5 and 19 (Barr et al., 1999). Notably, the region identified on chromosome 19 in this study also showed moderate evidence for linkage in the TSAICG sib-pair study. A study of a large French Canadian family with TS (Merette et al., 2000) identified a region of interest on chromosome 11, in the same region of this chromosome that was implicated in the South African study. A recent study of two large independent pedigrees with TS (Paschou et al., 2004) detected evidence for linkage on chromosome 17, in regions of the chromosome that were also implicated in a study of a large pedigree from Utah (Leppert et al., 1996) and in a study of sib-pairs with TS who were concordant for the obsessive-compulsive phenotype of hoarding (Zhang et al., 2002).

Though identification of a putative TS gene or group of genes would undoubtedly advance the research of tic disorders, it would be only a small step toward elucidating the neurobiology of TS. The pathways leading from the vulnerability genes to disordered protein production, abnormal cellular functioning, and the disordered structure and functioning of neural systems that give rise to tic-related behaviors will still need to be defined. Knowledge of the genetic basis of TS will not easily or immediately answer the most pressing clinical questions concerning TS, including what factors contribute to exacerbations and remissions of tic symptoms, what coping strategies are determined by an individual's response to tic symptoms, and what determinants affect the natural history and long-term prognosis for any given individual. Answers to such questions can be gleaned through a combination of genetic, epigenetic, molecular biological, and neuroimaging studies.

ENVIRONMENTAL DETERMINANTS

The expression and severity of tics in an individual are determined not only by an underlying genetic susceptibility to tic disorders, but also by numerous non-genetic determinants in the individual's environment before, during, and after birth. Some possible non-genetic determinants that have been studied to date include prenatal and postnatal exposure to excess androgens, previous infection with Group A Beta Hemolytic Streptococcus, adverse perinatal events, exposure to stimulant medications, comorbid psychiatric conditions, and stressful life events. Although these determinants have been reported to affect the development and severity of tics and related behaviors, their precise contributions to the TS phenotype remain unclear. Further research is needed to identify additional environmental determinants, and to elucidate the influence of each individual determinant on the pathophysiology of tic behaviors.

Sex Hormones

Tic disorders tend to occur predominantly in males, suggesting that sex-specific determinants may either predispose males to developing tic behaviors or protect females from developing them. Clinical observations support a role for sex steroid hormones in modulating the severity of tics (G. M. Alexander & Peterson, 2004). First, tics typically peak in severity shortly before or during puberty, a time when gonadal androgen production increases significantly in both males and females. Second, some women experience more severe tics during the estrogenic phase of their menstrual cycle (Kompoliti, Goetz, Leurgans, Raman, & Comella, 2001; Schwabe & Konkol, 1992). Third, administration of androgens to adults has been reported to worsen tics (Leckman & Scahill, 1990), whereas blockade of androgen receptors has been shown to attenuate them (Peterson et al., 1994; Peterson, Zhang, Anderson, & Leckman, 1998).

Previous studies involving manipulations of androgen levels in adults have supported a role for postnatal sex hormones in the pathophysiology of tics. A recent study, however, suggested that an altered androgen-dependent differentiation of the brain during prenatal development may also play an important part in determining the severity of tics in later life. In this study (G. M. Alexander & Peterson, 2004), the cognitive functioning and sex-specific behaviors of a large sample of children and adults with TS were compared with those of a group of matched control subjects. The study found that females with TS were more gender-dysphoric, preferred more "masculine" styles of play, and showed a more "masculine" pattern of performance on two sex-typed spatial tasks than did female controls. Furthermore, males with TS showed more "masculine" play preferences than did male controls, the magnitude of which was associated positively with the severity of tics. These findings resemble those reported previously in children with confirmed pathological elevations in prenatal androgen levels. This hypothesized androgenization before birth presumably affects organizational processes in the genome and in brain architecture that are activated by either normal or elevated circulating hormone levels during late childhood and adolescence in individuals who develop tics (Peterson et al., 1992; Peterson, Zhang, et al., 1998).

In light of the evidence suggesting a role for sex steroids in the pathophysiology of TS, imaging studies have sought to identify disturbances in sexual differentiation of the brain that might contribute to the expression and severity of tics. One study of regional brain and ventricular volumes in TS (Peterson, Staib, et al., 2001), for example, reported that the normal differences between males and females in volume of the parieto-occipital cortices were decreased in persons with TS. Whereas this region was larger in female controls than in male controls, its size in females with TS was similar to that of male controls and of males with TS. Because smaller volumes of the parieto-occipital cortex were associated with severity of tic symptoms in this study, a profile more like males in this area of the brain could possibly render females with TS vulnerable to more severe tics. Recent unpublished neuroimaging data also suggest that parietal and limbic regions in females with TS are morphologically similar to those of normal males (B. S. Peterson, personal communication to A. Spessot, January 5, 2004). This similarity suggests that more "male"-typed brain structures may predispose females to tic behaviors.

Pediatric Autoimmune Neuropsychiatric Disorders Associated with Streptococcus

Pharyngeal infection with group A Beta hemolytic streptococcus (GABHS) may produce an autoimmune response that, if it occurs in the CNS, can cause a range of fluctuating neuropsychiatric symptoms, including tics, obsessions, compulsions, hyperactivity, and distractibility, and that are collectively subsumed under the acronym PANDAS (Pediatric Autoimmune Neuropsychiatric Disorders Associated with Streptococcus; A. J. Allen, Leonard, & Swedo, 1995; Swedo et al., 1997, 1998). The symptoms of PANDAS are generally indistinguishable from those of TS, OCD, and ADHD, suggesting that these latter conditions may in some instances share an autoimmune etiology. Several preliminary clinical studies have supported this possibility by reporting a temporal relationship between GABHS infection and the onset of tic and OCD symptoms in some individuals, as well as improvement in some cases in response to immune-suppressing therapies (Kiessling, Marcotte, & Culpepper, 1993; Kondo & Kabasawa, 1978; Matarazzo, 1992).

Several immunological studies support the nosological construct of PANDAS and also suggest an autoimmune etiology for wild-type TS and OCD. First, elevated levels of antibodies have been detected against basal ganglia structures, both in living children with TS following GABHS infection and in postmortem samples from patients with TS (Kiessling, Marcotte, & Culpepper, 1993; Kiessling et al., 1994; Morshed et al., 2001; H. S. Singer et al., 1998). Furthermore, serum IgG from persons with TS, when infused into rodents, has been reported to produce stereotyped motor movements and vocalizations (J. J. Hallett, Harling-Berg, Knopf, Stopa, & Kiessling, 2000). Lastly, PANDAS patients as well as patients with wild-type TS and OCD may be more likely than controls to express D8/17, a putative B-cell marker for rheumatic fever and other autoimmune sequelae of infection with GABHS (T. K. Murphy et al., 1997; Swedo et al., 1997). Some recent literature disputes these immunological findings. One study, for example, found little to no difference in the levels of anti-basal ganglia antibodies in children with PANDAS compared with controls (H. S. Singer et al., 2004).

Despite this modest preliminary evidence suggesting the existence of a subtype of TS that has an autoimmune etiology, little evidence exists to suggest that TS and related disorders are a direct consequence of GABHS infection. The onset of tics and GABHS infection, for example, are likely to occur in close temporal proximity simply by chance. Because many children are unaffected carriers of GABHS, and because the onset of tic and OCD symptoms in children is often acute, it would not be uncommon to find children with acute tic or OCD symptoms who are GABHS-positive via throat culture or serum antibody testing (Bodner & Peterson, 2003). As a common and stressful illness in children, GABHS pharyngitis may precede tic exacerbations owing simply to the stress sensitivity of tic symptoms (Chappell, Riddle, et al., 1994; Kurlan, 2001).

Elevated levels of antineuronal antibodies have not been found consistently in TS patients, nor have they been absent consistently in normal control subjects. Thus, antineuronal antibody studies in TS (Kiessling et al., 1993; H. S. Singer et al., 1998; Trifiletti, 1998; Trifiletti, Altemus, Packard, Bandele, & Zabriskie, 1998) have not yet proven that antibodies are directed against brain tissue in persons with TS more than in control subjects. Furthermore, even if those antibodies are ultimately deemed elevated in persons with TS, that association may be caused by some underlying, as yet unknown, process, such as a disruption of the blood-brain barrier that could increase antibody levels nonspecifically in the CNS (Bodner & Peterson, 2003). Double-blind, controlled, longitudinal studies are needed to clarify the associations, if any, between GABHS pharyngitis, antineuronal antibodies, and the onset or exacerbation of tic symptoms.

Perinatal Events

Various environmental factors affecting mothers and their fetuses during the perinatal period may influence the expression and severity of TS and co-occurring disorders. One early study, for example, reported that birth complications were more common in children with TS than in controls (Pasamanick & Kawi, 1956). A more recent twin study identified low birthweight as a risk factor predisposing children to tics of greater severity than those occurring in children of normal birthweight (Leckman et al., 1987). Another study (Leckman et al., 1990) found a significantly higher rate of obstetrical complications in mothers of individuals with TS than in the general population. Severe maternal nausea and vomiting in the first trimester, for example, accounted for 50% of the variance in the severity of tics in children. Severity of maternal life stress during pregnancy was also associated with the severity of tics and with the level of overall psychosocial functioning in children with TS. Perinatal events that have been associated with an increased risk of developing co-occurring OCD in persons who have TS include delivery by forceps and prenatal exposure to tobacco, alcohol, or caffeine (Santangelo et al., 1994).

The reported associations of obstetrical complications with the subsequent development of TS or of more severe illness do not prove that the obstetrical complications cause or worsen the severity of TS. Although these complications may injure the CNS and thus contribute to the development of tics, an alternative interpretation of the data is also plausible, in that the genetic diathesis to TS may interfere with prenatal development in some unknown way and thereby induce or increase the risk for perinatal complications (Walkup, 2001).

Exposure to Stimulants

Some studies have suggested that exposure to the stimulant medications used to treat symptoms of ADHD may also exacerbate tic symptoms (Klein & Bessler, 1992; Mesulam, 1986). Recent long-term studies, however, show no clear or consistent effect of stimulant medications on severity of tics in most children with tic disorders and co-occurring ADHD (Gadow, Sverd, Sprafkin, Nolan, & Ezor, 1995; Gadow, Sverd, Sprafkin, Nolan, & Grossman, 1999; Tourette's Syndrome Study Group, 2002; Wilens et al., 2003). One well-designed, randomized controlled trial suggested that stimulants improve not only ADHD symptoms, but also the symptoms of TS (Kurlan & Tourette's Syndrome Study Group, 2000). Despite this encouraging data from controlled trials, extensive clinical experience and single case studies suggest that an ill-defined subgroup of patients with tics and ADHD that is not captured in group statistics may indeed experience a dramatic worsening of tics in response to use of stimulant medications (Peterson & Cohen, 1998; Walkup, 2001). Children with TS who are being treated with stimulants for co-occurring ADHD should therefore be monitored closely for changes in tic severity.

Life Events and Co-occurring Psychiatric Conditions

Persons with TS appear to be more vulnerable to the adverse effects of stressors in daily life, and they often experience worsening of tic symptoms during times of duress (Chappell, Riddle, et al., 1994; Walkup, 2001). Whether co-occurring psychiatric disorders affect tic severity is unclear. Clinical experience suggests, however, that the treatment of mood and anxiety disorders in persons with TS can often improve dramatically the severity of tics, presumably by reducing the overall emotional burden and psychosocial stress associated with those illnesses.

NEUROBIOLOGICAL SUBSTRATE

The symptoms of TS are thought to arise from anatomical and functional disturbances in cortico-striatal-thalamo-cortical (CSTC) circuits (G. E. Alexander & DeLong, 1985; Baldwin, Frost, & Wood, 1954; Graybiel & Canales,

2001; Kelley, Lang, & Gauthier, 1988; Maclean & Delgado, 1953; Mink, 2001). These circuits contain numerous partially overlapping but largely parallel pathways that direct information from nearly all regions of the cerebral cortex to the basal ganglia and thalamus, and then back again to specific cortical regions (G. E. Alexander, DeLong, & Strick, 1986). The cortical portions of CSTC circuits presumably contribute to self-regulation of behaviors, including the regulation of tic behaviors, by modulating activity in the basal ganglia and thalamus, which in turn modulate activity in the cortex (Goldman-Rakic, 1987; Leung, Skudlarski, Gatenby, Peterson, & Gore, 2000; Peterson et al., 2002). Although the number of pathways remains controversial (G. E. Alexander, Crutcher, & DeLong, 1990; Goldman-Rakic & Selemon, 1990; Parent & Hazrati, 1995), current consensus holds that CSTC circuitry has at least four anatomically and functionally distinct components: those initiating from and projecting back to the sensorimotor cortex, the orbitofrontal cortex (OFC), the limbic and associated anterior cingulate cortices, and the association cortices. Converging evidence from many investigational modalities suggests that motor portions of CSTC circuits are primarily involved in the pathophysiology of tics, OFC portions of the circuits are involved in OCD, and association portions of the circuits are involved in ADHD.

Anatomical Basis

The components of CSTC circuits have long been implicated in the pathophysiology of tic disorders. Electrical or chemical stimulation of the basal ganglia has been shown to produce movements in animals and humans that resemble tics (G. E. Alexander & DeLong, 1985; Baldwin et al., 1954; Kelley et al., 1988; Maclean & Delgado, 1953). Lesions such as tumors in the ventral nuclei of the thalamus have been shown to worsen tic symptoms (Peterson, Bronen, & Duncan, 1996), and surgical lesions in the ventral, medial, and intralaminar nuclei of the thalamus have been shown to attenuate tics (Korzen, Pushkov, Kharitonov, & Shustin, 1991; Rauch, Baer, Cosgrove, & Jenike, 1995). Electrical stimulation of the ventral intermediate and ventral oralis posterior nuclei of the thalamus during surgery has also been reported to produce sensations similar to the premonitory urges that are experienced by many persons with TS prior to performing tics (Tasker & Dostrovsky, 1993). Similarly, electrical stimulation of the supplementary motor area can produce urges to move in normal people that may be similar to premonitory urges (Fried et al., 1991; Lim et al., 1994).

Though studies using methods such as electrical stimulation have implicated indirectly the roles of CSTC components in producing tics, only recently have neuroimaging technologies demonstrated directly the involvement of these components in the pathophysiology of TS. By providing a window into the structure and function of the brain *in vivo*, neuroimaging technologies have revolutionized the study of TS, offering new clues about the brain structures that are inherently dysfunctional in the disorder, as well as about the mechanisms used to compensate for and suppress tic symptoms. The main imaging modalities used to study TS are magnetic resonance imaging (MRI), positron emission tomography (PET), and single photon emission computed tomography (SPECT). The latter two techniques, which require exposure to radiation, are not used in children for ethical reasons. Most imaging studies of TS populations, therefore, have used anatomical and functional MRI to image the brains of children.

The first functional MRI (fMRI) study of TS (Peterson, Skudlarski, et al., 1998) sought to define the contributions of individual components of CSTC circuits to the voluntary suppression of tics. In this study, adult subjects with TS were asked to alternate between 40 second epochs of being allowed to tic freely and 40 second epochs of suppressing their tics. The images obtained while tics were being suppressed were compared with those obtained when subjects were allowed to tic spontaneously, and the magnitudes of signal change in the images were then correlated with various measures of tic severity. Signal intensity increased significantly in the prefrontal cortex and in the caudate nucleus during epochs of tic suppression, whereas signal intensity decreased significantly in the putamen, globus pallidus, and thalamus during these periods. The increased frontal activity detected during tic suppression was associated with the increased caudate activity, a finding that is consistent with the known excitatory projections from the frontal cortex to the caudate nucleus. Increased caudate activity was in turn associated with greater decreases in activity of the putamen, globus pallidus, and thalamus, a finding that is consistent with the known inhibitory projections between the caudate and these other subcortical structures. The magnitude of the increase in activity of the prefrontal cortex did not correlate significantly with the severity of tics, whereas the magnitudes of the decreases in activity of the caudate and other subcortical nuclei were inversely correlated with severity of tic symptoms outside of the MRI scanner. Given the known flow of information between the cortical and subcortical components of CSTC circuits, the correlations between tic severity and subcortical activity were interpreted as downstream effects of correlations established upon entry into subcortical portions of the circuit, specifically in the projections into or out of the caudate nucleus. The greater the malfunction of these projections into or out of the caudate, the more severe the individual's tic symptoms were likely to be outside of the scanner.

This implication that the caudate nucleus is the origin of functional disturbances in CSTC circuitry is consistent with a recent anatomical MRI study of basal ganglia volumes in a sample of children and adults with TS compared with a sample of matched control subjects (Peterson et al., 2003). Smaller basal ganglia volumes were detected in both children and adults with TS compared with controls, and further analyses revealed that these volume abnormalities were specific to the caudate nucleus. Adults with TS were found to have smaller basal ganglia volumes than children with TS, reflecting smaller volumes of the putamen and globus pallidus in adults but not in children with TS. Basal ganglia volumes were not significantly associated with the severity of tics.

These anatomical findings shed some light on the role of the basal ganglia in the pathophysiology of TS. First, the significantly smaller caudate nuclei in both children and adults with TS suggested that hypoplasia of this structure might represent a morphological abnormality inherent to TS. Second, the decreased volumes of the putamen and globus pallidus that were observed in adults but not in children with TS, by definition, were not generalizable to the larger population of individuals with TS, as most persons with TS experience a substantial reduction in tic symptoms in adolescence and early adulthood. Thus, the decreased metabolism and blood flow in the putamen and globus pallidus of adults with TS (Braun et al., 1993; Hall, Costa, & Shields, 1990; Klieger, Fett, Dimitsopulos, & Karlan, 1997; Moriarty et al., 1995; Riddle, Rasmusson, Woods, & Hoffer, 1992) reported in PET and SPECT studies likely reflect the generally smaller volumes of these structures in adults with TS. The PET and SPECT findings are therefore probably not generalizable to populations of children with TS, in whom volumes of these structures are normal (Spessot, Plessen, & Peterson, 2004).

While anatomical and functional MRI studies have implicated the caudate nucleus as the site of a morphologic trait abnormality in TS, these studies have also suggested that the cortical components of CSTC circuits are involved in the expression and regulation of tic symptoms in those with a diathesis to tics. The first study measuring the volumes of cortical regions in individuals with TS compared a sample of children and adults with TS to a sample of matched control subjects (Peterson, Staib, et al., 2001). Overall cortical volumes in the TS group were larger than those in the control group, reflecting primarily the presence of larger dorsal prefrontal volumes in both males and females with TS. Within the TS group, however, the larger dorsal prefrontal volumes were observed in children, but smaller volumes were detected in adults. Moreover, larger volumes of the orbitofrontal and parieto-occipital regions were significantly associated with decreased severity of tics. These inverse correlations of prefrontal volumes with severity of tics suggest that the larger cortical volumes in children with TS may represent an adaptive or compensatory process that helps to attenuate tics. This latter possibility is supported by the findings of the fMRI study of voluntary tic suppression described earlier, in which broad regions within the prefrontal cortices activated strongly during tic suppression. As children with TS meet an ever-increasing need to suppress tics in academic and social situations, their prefrontal regions would presumably be activated frequently and repeatedly, thereby inducing plastic hypertrophy of these areas. This activity-dependent hypertrophy of prefrontal regions would in turn help to decrease the severity of tic symptoms by increasing inhibitory reserve and improving the child's capacity to self-regulate tic behaviors. This interpretation of the role of the prefrontal cortex in mediating expression and severity of tics is consistent with the known role of this region in mediating tasks that require decisions of whether, when, and how to act across a time delay. An intact ability to make such decisions is needed for behavioral inhibition, working memory, and go/no go tasks (Fuster, 1989). The prefrontal cortex probably inhibits the behavioral response to the somatosensory urge to tic; it probably also determines when to release tic behaviors from voluntary suppression. Dysfunction of prefrontal regions in TS thus likely impairs an individual's capacity to inhibit tic symptoms.

An impaired ability to generate activity-dependent hypertrophy in prefrontal regions in response to a continuous need to inhibit tics should theoretically result in more severe tic symptoms. Indeed, a failure to generate this plastic response likely explains the finding of smaller prefrontal volumes in adults with TS compared to children with TS. Although tics typically improve substantially by early adulthood, the adults who participated in the previously described imaging studies had persistent, severe tics. These adults therefore represented a unique minority in the general population of individuals with a lifetime history of TS: those whose symptoms do not attenuate during adolescence.

The smaller prefrontal volumes in adults with TS probably represent a failure to induce the plastic hypertrophy of these regions in response to tics that would help to suppress them. In the absence of this compensatory plastic response, more severe tic symptoms would likely persist through adolescence and adulthood (Spessot et al., 2004).

The smaller volumes of prefrontal cortices detected in adults with TS thus likely reflect an ascertainment bias in which adults with persistent tic symptoms were recruited for the study. The significantly different findings in adults and children with TS that follow from this ascertainment bias emphasize the need to exercise caution when conducting and interpreting studies of adults with TS. They also emphasize the inherent difficulties in making inferences about the developmental trajectories and longitudinal course of TS from cross-sectional studies alone (Gerard & Peterson, 2003; Kraemer, Yesavage, Taylor, & Kupfer, 2000; Peterson, 2003).

Their shortcomings notwithstanding, MRI studies of TS thus far suggest that disturbances in the anatomy and function of the caudate nucleus may render an individual vulnerable to tics, and impaired neural regulatory systems based in the prefrontal cortex may unmask this vulnerability to tics in individuals with TS. Additional unpublished longitudinal data suggest further that caudate nucleus volumes in childhood are predictive of the persistence and severity of tics in late adolescence and early adulthood (B. S. Peterson, personal communication to A. Spessot, January 5, 2004). This finding is consistent with the hypothesis that a smaller caudate nucleus represents a trait morphological abnormality in TS that is present across all stages of the disorder. Measures of prefrontal volumes and activity within the basal ganglia during the suppression of tics correlate with the severity of tics at the time of scanning, whereas prefrontal volumes measured in childhood do not appear to predict the severity of tics in adulthood. Childhood measures of prefrontal volume, therefore, appear to be more important determinants of the severity of tics in the short term, around the time of scanning. Although prefrontal cortex volumes do not predict the severity of tics in adulthood, those who fail to generate a compensatory hypertrophic plastic response in this region seem to suffer severe tic symptoms that persist throughout adulthood.

Other brain structures have been studied in TS that are not themselves components of CSTC circuits but that are intimately related to the components of these circuits. The corpus callosum (CC), for example, has been examined in individuals with TS because it is believed to inhibit activity in prefrontal cortices through its major white matter pathways that connect the prefrontal cortices across the cerebral midline (Carr & Sesack, 1998). One study examining CC size in children and adults with TS compared to control subjects (Plessen et al., 2004) reported that subjects with TS had significantly smaller CC sizes than controls. CC size also correlated positively with current and worst-ever severity of tics, suggesting that smaller CCs in subjects with TS may be associated with fewer tic symptoms. Having a small CC could therefore represent a compensatory plastic response to the presence of tics, similar to a large prefrontal cortex in a child with TS. CC size correlated inversely with prefrontal cortex volumes in both the TS and control groups, although the magnitudes of these inverse correlations were significantly greater in the TS group. These results suggest that smaller CCs may contribute to or influence the growth of prefrontal cortices in all individuals, but that the normal influence of the CC on prefrontal development may be exaggerated in individuals with TS. This exaggeration presumably represents an adaptive or compensatory process in the brains of individuals with TS, given that smaller CCs and larger prefrontal cortices appear to result in less severe tic symptoms. In other words, a developmental process that happens normally in the CC may be altered and used to serve adaptive purposes in those with TS. The plastic process that produces a smaller CC may also result in a reduction of excitatory input from the CC to the GABAergic interneurons in the prefrontal cortex, thus helping to reduce inhibition of prefrontal self-regulatory control in persons with TS (Carr & Sesack, 1998; Kimura & Baughman, 1997; Krnjevic, Randic, & Straughan, 1966). This decreased inhibition of prefrontal self-regulatory functions, in turn, would facilitate the control of tic symptoms by the prefrontal cortices.

Neurotransmitters

The clinical efficacy of neuroleptic medications in the treatment of tics suggests that the midbrain dopaminergic pathways to the basal ganglia may be dysfunctional in persons with TS (Peterson & Cohen, 1998). Studies measuring levels of dopamine metabolites in cerebrospinal fluid (CSF), postmortem brain tissue, and urine of individuals with TS, however, have yielded either inconsistent results or no evidence of group differences (Anderson, Leckman, & Cohen, 1999). Ligand studies of the dopamine D2 receptor (Brooks, Turjanski, Sawle, Playford, & Lees, 1992; H. S. Singer et al., 1992; Turjanski et al., 1994; Wolf et al., 1996; Wong et al., 1997), the dopamine transporter (Albin et al., 2003; Malison et al., 1995; Meyer et al., 1999; Stamenkovic et al., 2001), and the dopamine decarboxylase system (Ernst et al., 1999) have also produced inconsistent findings, with the few positive findings generally failing to replicate (Peterson & Thomas, 2000). These results suggest that the central synthesis and metabolism of dopamine in individuals with TS does not differ dramatically from dopamine synthesis and metabolism in healthy individuals and that perhaps dopamine systems in TS are not significantly altered.

The noradrenergic system is a major modulator of the acute response to stress in normal individuals; its dysfunction has been implicated in TS owing to the sensitivity of tic symptoms to stress (Chappell, Riddle, et al., 1994) and to the successful treatment of tics in some patients with the alpha-2 receptor agonist clonidine (Leckman et al., 1991). One study comparing levels of norepinephrine and its metabolite, 3-methoxy-4-hydroxyphenylglycol (MHPG) in the CSF of individuals with TS versus healthy controls found comparable MHPG levels in the two groups but nearly twice as much norepinephrine in the TS group compared to controls (Leckman et al., 1995). Given the shorter half-life of norepinephrine compared to MHPG, these results suggest that the basal stress response in TS is normal but that some individuals with TS may exhibit an exaggerated response to acute stress.

The well-established genetic relationship between TS and OCD suggests that a dysfunctional serotonergic system, which is believed to subserve symptoms of OCD, could also be responsible for tic symptoms. Studies of the serotonin metabolite 5-hydroxyindoleacetic acid (5-HIAA) in CSF have yielded mixed results, with one of the largest studies to date showing similar levels of 5-HIAA in the CSF of persons with TS, those with OCD, and normal controls (Leckman et al., 1995). Although preliminary studies of the postmortem brain tissue of a small sample of persons with TS have reported decreased serotonin, 5-HIAA, and the serotonin precursor tryptophan in most all cortical and subcortical regions (Anderson et al., 1992a, 1992b), these findings require replication.

In addition to the dopaminergic, noradrenergic, and serotonergic systems, other neurotransmitters that have been investigated in TS include gamma aminobutyric acid (GABA), glutamate, acetylcholine, and the endogenous opioids. Although some promising leads have been reported for all of these neurotransmitter systems, most of these studies in persons with TS have been largely equivocal. The absence of robust evidence that would identify a single pathological neurotransmitter suggests that subtle imbalances may exist among several or many transmitter systems in this condition. The involvement of several neurotransmitters is possible simply because many neurotransmitter systems function together to produce the complex thoughts and behaviors associated with TS. Alternatively, a malfunction at the cellular level, including disordered second-messenger systems, abnormal proteins for vesicle release, or disturbances in the synaptic membrane, could affect the neurons of a wide variety of neurotransmitter systems and contribute to the subtle and varied disturbances in neurotransmitter levels reported in persons with TS (H. S. Singer & Wendlandt, 2001).

ELECTROPHYSIOLOGY: ELECTROENCEPHALOGRAMS AND STARTLE PARADIGMS

Early electroencephalogram (EEG) studies suggested the presence of nonspecific sharp waves and diffuse slowing in medicated individuals with TS (Bergen, Tanner, & Wilson, 1982; Krumholz, Singer, Niedermeyer, Burnite, & Harris, 1983; Volkmar et al., 1984). Other studies, however, have not detected significant differences in the EEGs of unmedicated persons with TS compared to those of normal controls (Neufeld, Berger, Chapman, & Korczyn, 1990; van Woerkom, Fortgens, van de Wetering, & Martens, 1988). Quantitative analyses of EEGs, in which the relative power contributions of each of the EEG frequency bands in specific electrode positions are compared between subjects with TS and normal controls, have similarly detected no significant abnormalities in electrical activity in the brains of persons with TS (Drake, Hietter, Bogner, & Andrews, 1992; Neufeld et al., 1990). Studies of brain stem auditory and visual evoked responses have also been equivocal (Syrigou-Papavasiliou, Verma, & LeWitt, 1988). Abnormal EEG findings in patients with TS, therefore, are thought simply to represent the effects of medication used to control tic symptoms.

One study of monozygotic twins with TS detected greater abnormalities on EEG in the twin with lower birthweight, who also typically suffered more severe tic symptoms (Hyde, Emsellem, Randolph, Rickler, & Weinberger, 1994). These findings are consistent with the hypothesis that the severity of tics may be influenced by nongenetic determinants (in this case, birthweight) that are mediated by or correlated with abnormal patterns of EEG activity (M. Hallett, 2001).

Studies attempting to classify tics as voluntary or involuntary have examined the bereitschaftpotential, a deflection in the baseline of the EEG that precedes a self-paced, voluntary movement and that is thought to represent cortical preparation for movement (Jahanshai et al., 1995). Studies of the bereitschaftpotential are technically challenging to perform and have yielded inconclusive results concerning the voluntary nature of tics. One study of six patients was unable to document the presence of a bereitschaftpotential preceding tics (Obeso, Rothwell, & Marsden, 1981), another purported to show it in two out of five subjects (Karp, Porter, Toro, & Hallett, 1996), and yet another reported it in three TS subjects (Duggal & Nizamie, 2002). Discrepancies in the findings of these studies may be attributed to differences in the tics that were studied and to differences in patient characteristics. For example, all three patients in the third study reported premonitory urges, but these urges were not assessed in the first and largest study. Perhaps tics preceded by an urge are experienced as voluntary and have a bereitschaftpotential, and those not preceded by an urge could be experienced as involuntary and may not have an associated bereitschaftpotential as an indicator of preparation for movement.

The startle reflex is an abrupt involuntary contraction of the facial or skeletal muscles in response to a sudden sensory stimulus. An enhanced startle reflex was a feature of TS observed by Gilles de la Tourette (1885) in his original descriptions of tic disorders. More than a century later, however, studies examining the startle reflex in TS patients have produced conflicting results. In one descriptive study, 3 of 53 individuals with TS were reported to respond to an intense auditory stimulus by a blink and subsequently by a whole-body jerk that closely resembled a tic (Lees, Robertson, Trimble, & Murray, 1984). A quantitative study comparing the acoustic startle response in a small sample of persons with TS versus normal controls reported that two of the subjects with TS failed to habituate to the auditory stimulus with time, suggesting the presence of a clinically asymptomatic but exaggerated startle in some individuals with TS (Stell, Thickbroom, & Mastaglia, 1995). Another study, in contrast, showed that children with TS had startle reflexes that were similar in magnitude and habituation to those of controls. However, the automatic attenuation of the startle response immediately following a weak stimulus ("prepulse inhibition") was significantly impaired in these children (Swerdlow et al., 2001). These results stand in contrast to those of another study, which found no differences between subjects with TS and controls in various components of the startle response, including onset latency, amplitude, first peak latency, and habituation of the startle (Sachdev, Chee, & Aniss, 1997). Taken together, these studies suggest that the startle reflex may be abnormal in some individuals with TS but that this abnormality is relatively uncommon, often inconsequential, and possibly not more prevalent than in healthy controls.

SLEEP DISTURBANCES AND TOURETTE'S SYNDROME

Sleep disturbances, including sleep walking, sleep talking, night terrors, nightmares, difficulties falling asleep, and difficulties staying asleep, have been reported frequently in persons with TS (R. P. Allen, Singer, Brown, & Salam, 1992; Barabas & Matthews, 1985; Barabas, Matthews, & Ferrari, 1984b; Comings & Comings, 1987b; Erenberg, 1985). These sleep disturbances may be associated with more severe tic symptoms (Cohrs et al., 2001; Comings & Comings, 1987b). A number of studies have suggested that sleep disturbances in TS may be more strongly associated with co-occurring ADHD than with TS itself (R. P. Allen et al., 1992; Comings & Comings, 1987b).

Polysomnography and videotape monitoring have been used to examine sleep disturbances objectively in persons with TS, but the results of these studies have been inconsistent, probably because of small sample sizes and differing subject ages across studies (Kostanecka-Endress et al., 2003; Rothenberger et al., 2001). One recent polysomnographic study (Kostanecka-Endress et al., 2003) compared a clinical sample of TS children without ADHD to a sample of closely matched controls and found that children with TS, even in the absence of ADHD, experience a poorer quality of sleep, with particular difficulties in initiating and maintaining sleep. Further research is needed to clarify the contributions of co-occurring ADHD to sleep disturbances in persons with TS. The finding of more frequent sleep disturbances in persons with TS alone suggests that in some individuals TS is accompanied by disturbances in arousal, which is presumably mediated by the reticular activating system (Barabas, Matthews, & Ferrari, 1984a).

Polysomnographic studies of both children and adults have also detected the presence of tics during sleep in up to 80% of persons with TS (Cohrs et al., 2001; Glaze, Frost, & Jankovic, 1983; Jankovic & Rohaidy, 1987; Rothenberger et al., 2001; Silvestri et al., 1995). Although the tics that appear during sleep are similar in quality to those that appear during wakefulness, they are typically less frequent and less forceful during sleep (Cohrs et al., 2001; Fish et al., 1991). The presence of tics during sleep is evidence for the claim that tics are largely involuntary and originate in subcortical brain regions.

NEUROPSYCHOLOGY

Many children with TS have specific cognitive and learning deficits that can contribute to poor academic performance and delayed psychosocial development. Early intervention for these children might improve their academic achievement and, in doing so, enhance their self-esteem and increase their productivity.

Early neuropsychological studies of TS were limited by small sample sizes and various other methodological difficulties. Perhaps most importantly, the majority of these studies did not account for the presence of co-occurring ADHD or OCD, each of which may carry its own profile of disturbances in neuropsychological functioning that may or may not overlap with the deficits in TS. Most recent neuropsychological studies characterize more precisely the cognitive functions of persons with TS by controlling for these co-occurring disorders.

General intellectual ability, as measured by intelligence quotient (IQ) testing, does not appear to differ in persons with TS compared with the general population (Apter et al., 1993; Bornstein, 1991). Some studies have suggested that persons with TS have lower Performance IQ (PIQ) scores than Verbal IQ (VIQ) scores, which would indicate that persons with TS experience a relative difficulty with tasks that involve visuomotor speed, visual-perceptual function, and visuomotor integration (Incagnoli & Kane, 1981; A. K. Shapiro, Shapiro, Young, & Feinberg, 1988a). Other studies, however, have attributed the discrepancy between PIQ and VIQ in persons with TS to the presence of co-occurring ADHD (Bornstein, 1990). Therefore, although it is widely accepted that those with TS tend to encounter some difficulty with nonverbal tasks, further studies are needed to clarify the contribution of ADHD to these difficulties (Como, 2001).

Approximately 22% of individuals with TS suffer from learning disabilities (Abwender et al., 1996; Erenberg, Cruse, & Rothner, 1986; Schuerholz, Baumgardner, Singer, Reiss, & Denckla, 1996), a prevalence similar to that of 15% to 20% reported in the general population (Berger, Yule, & Rutter, 1975; Pennington, 1991). The most common learning disabilities in TS may be in math and written language (Schuerholz et al., 1996), whereas reading disabilities predominate in the general population (Pennington, 1991). Co-occurring ADHD in children with TS has been reported to confer up to a fourfold greater risk for academic problems than TS in the absence of ADHD (Abwender et al., 1996; Erenberg et al., 1986; Schuerholz et al., 1996).

Other neuropsychological studies have sought to identify specific cognitive deficits in TS, focusing on tasks thought to be subserved by the basal ganglia. One of the most consistently observed cognitive deficits in TS is the impaired integration of visual and motor processes, as is needed, for example, in copying simple and complex geometric designs (Brookshire, Butler, Ewing-Cobbs, & Fletcher, 1994; Ferrari, Matthews, & Barabas, 1984; Hagin, Beecher, Pagano, & Kreeger, 1982; Harris et al., 1995; Incagnoli & Kane, 1981; Lucas, Kauffman, & Morris, 1967; Randolph et al., 1993; Schultz, Carter, Gladstone, et al., 1998; A. K. Shapiro et al., 1988a; E. Shapiro, Shapiro, & Clarkin, 1974; Sutherland, Kolb, Schoel, Whishaw, & Davies, 1982). Similar deficits in visuomotor processing have been reported in children with ADHD, however, and most studies of individuals with TS have failed to control for co-occurring ADHD (Schultz, Carter, Scahill, & Leckman, 1998). Deficits in fine motor skills have also been reported in TS patients (Bornstein, 1990, 1991; Yeates & Bornstein, 1994), particularly when the required task depends on visual perceptual skills, as with pegboard tests. A deficit in fine motor skill may also affect one's ability to copy geometric designs effectively. Thus, the presence of deficits in fine motor skills in persons with TS may contribute to an overestimation of weaknesses in visuomotor skills because the copying tasks used to measure visuomotor performance usually require adequate fine motor skills.

In addition to impairments in visuomotor and fine motor skills, individuals with TS may have difficulty with *executive functioning* (EF), a term comprising a number of cognitive and behavioral constructs that include mental tracking, sustained attention, working memory, planning and organization, goal-directedness, cognitive flexibility during problem solving, impulse control, and self-regulation (Como, 2001). Frontostriatal circuits are thought to subserve performance on EF tasks, and thus the documented abnormalities in frontostriatal circuits in persons with TS are consistent with reported disturbances in executive functions in this same population. Studies of EF in TS have yielded inconsistent results, however, probably caused by the use of differing measures of EF across studies. Perhaps the most consistently reported EF deficit in studies of TS has been delayed reaction times in a number of testing paradigms, including the continuous performance test. Children with TS tend to perform more slowly than controls during these tests, suggesting that they may have difficulty with sustaining attention during the task (Como & Kurlan, 1991; Harris et al., 1995; Shucard, Benedict, Tekok-Kilic, & Lichter, 1997).

Variability in EF findings in persons with TS may also be explained by the presence or absence of co-occurring ADHD or OCD. Both ADHD (Barkley, 1997; Barkley, Edwards, Laneri, Fletcher, & Metevia, 2001; K. R. Murphy, Barkley, & Bush, 2001) and OCD (Head, Bolton, & Hymas,

1989; Hollander & Wong, 1996; Roth, Baribeau, Milovan, & O'Connor, 2004; Spitznagel & Suhr, 2002) alone have been associated independently with impairment in EF. One recent study of EF examined a group of children and adolescents ages 9 to 18 with TS alone, another group with TS and ADHD, and a third group with TS and OCD (Channon et al., 2003). Subjects with TS alone were impaired on only one EF measure that involved sentence completion. Subjects with TS plus ADHD, however, were impaired on three EF measures that involved sentence completion and multitasking. Subjects with TS and OCD did not differ from controls on any EF measure. These findings support further the putative role of co-occurring ADHD in the development of neuropsychological deficits in TS.

Two recent studies (Keri, Szlobodnyik, Benedek, Janka, & Gadoros, 2002; Marsh et al., 2004) have suggested that children and adults with TS have difficulties with the implicit or "unconscious" learning of skills, motor sequences, and habits, also known as *habit learning.* Studies have shown that this form of learning is mediated by CSTC circuits, particularly the dorsal striatum, in contrast to the explicit, "conscious" learning of motor behaviors and factual knowledge, termed *declarative learning,* which is subserved by structures in the mesial-temporal lobe and diencephalon (Knowlton, Mangels, & Squire, 1996; Packard & Knowlton, 2002; Squire & Kandel, 1999; Squire & Zola, 1996). In both studies, the subjects with TS who had more severe tics also displayed greater habit-learning impairment. This correlation of habit learning with the severity of tic symptoms suggests that tics may be a consequence of the degree to which striatal learning systems are dysfunctional, a possibility that is consistent with the role of the caudate nucleus in habit learning and its anatomical and functional disturbances in persons with TS. Thus, deficits in habit learning conceivably could either cause tics or influence their severity (Marsh et al., 2004).

PEER RELATIONSHIPS AND ADAPTIVE FUNCTIONING

The social, emotional, and behavioral problems that occur in TS may be just as, if not more, disruptive in day-to-day functioning as the motor and phonic tics that define the disorder. Studies have shown consistently that children with TS are at risk for social and emotional difficulties, although whether these problems are affected by the severity of tics is unclear (Bawden et al., 1998; Nolan, Sverd, Gadow, Sprafkin, & Ezor, 1996; Rosenberg, Brown, & Singer, 1995). In one study, children with TS were rated by their peers as more withdrawn and less popular than their classmates, and they were rated by their teachers as more withdrawn and more aggressive than their peers (Stokes et al., 1991). Social difficulties in children with TS have also been reported frequently by parents (Dykens et al., 1990).

Some studies have suggested that children with TS and ADHD may have less favorable social-emotional profiles than children with TS alone. Studies using peer, parent, and self-evaluations have reported that children with TS and co-occurring ADHD tend to exhibit externalizing behavior problems such as aggression, internalizing behavior problems such as social withdrawal, and poor social adaptation. Children with TS alone, in contrast, appear to exhibit internalizing behavior problems without the additional difficulties found with co-occurring ADHD (Bawden et al., 1998; Carter et al., 2000; Spencer et al., 1998). The social withdrawal observed in children with TS alone may be a consequence of peer teasing and psychosocial stress associated with uncontrollable motor and phonic tics (Carter et al., 2000).

The families of persons with TS appear to be at risk for poor psychosocial functioning (Hubka, Fulton, Shady, Champion, & Wand, 1988; Matthews, Eustace, Grad, Pelcovitz, & Olson, 1985; Robertson, 1989). Psychosocial stress in family members can in turn increase stress in the child with TS, and stress often increases the severity of tics and other problem behaviors. Conversely, management of stress in family members can help children with TS cope with their own experience of stress. One study found, for example, that children with TS who perceived their parent's behavior as positive had more positive self-regard and less anxiety than did children with TS who had more negative perceptions of parental behavior (Edell & Motta, 1989). A follow-up study reported a significant positive association between the self-regard of children with TS and the self-regard of their mothers (Edell-Fisher & Motta, 1990).

Most reports of peer relations and adaptive functioning in persons with TS have studied clinically referred samples, thus limiting the generalizability of the findings to nonclinical populations. Nevertheless, the studies have emphasized the need for psychosocial interventions for children with TS, such as training in social skills and peer education programs in the schools that aim to reduce the stigma associated with tic disorders (Bawden et al., 1998; Carter et al., 2000). These studies have also emphasized the risks that co-occurring ADHD poses for the emotional life of children who have tics. The early diagnosis of ADHD, combined with appropriate psychosocial, educational, and treatment interventions, might reduce this emotional burden and improve the longer-term psychosocial outcomes for these children (Carter et al., 2000). Recent findings also suggest that helping parents to respond more constructively to stress may substantially benefit the emotional life of their child with tics.

TOURETTE'S SYNDROME: A MULTISTRIKE ETIOLOGY

The current conceptualization of TS is of a syndrome that develops under certain environmental circumstances in individuals who carry a specific genetic diathesis. The tic symptoms that develop may be of little or no consequence, or they may be severe enough to cause significant impairment in activities of daily life. Various conditions have been reported to co-occur with tics, such as OCD, ADHD, learning difficulties, aggressive behaviors, and sleep disturbances. These conditions, when present, appear to contribute more to functional impairment than do the tics themselves. Although some or all of the conditions that co-occur with TS may be genetically related to TS, their frequent association with TS might also be the result of a clinical ascertainment bias within individuals with TS and their families. The extent of this bias likely will be greater with co-occurring illnesses that presumably share the same neurobiological substrate with TS, such as OCD. Ascertainment bias will also be greater in families with psychopathologies that render them more intolerant of behaviors related to TS. The clinical presentation of children with TS is thus highly individualized and contextualized by myriad physiological, psychological, and social determinants.

Genetic Vulnerability

Twin and family studies suggest that genetic factors are important in determining the phenotypic expression of TS. These studies also suggest, however, that carrying the genetic diathesis to TS is neither necessary nor sufficient for producing tics or related symptoms. Carrying the putative TS genes is not necessary for producing tics because, although rare, sporadic cases of TS have been reported that presumably represent either new genetic mutations or phenocopies of TS. Carrying the TS genes is not always sufficient for producing tics because carriers do not always express the genes. As studies of monozygotic twins have shown, concordance rates for TS are high, but they are not 100%. Furthermore, the tic symptoms of monozygotic twins often differ significantly in quality and severity, sug-

gesting that environmental factors also play a role in determining the presence and severity of tics.

Because carrying the putative TS genes is neither necessary nor sufficient for producing tics and related behaviors, the concept of genetic *vulnerability* is most appropriately applied to TS. This vulnerability confers to persons carrying the genes a diathesis to tic, OCD, and likely other groups of symptoms that have yet to be identified. In most genetically vulnerable people these symptoms will be mild, if present at all. In many cases, however, various environmental determinants in combination will play a crucial role in determining an individual's clinical presentation within the spectrum of tic disorders and other semi-voluntary behaviors.

Genetic studies attempting to identify the putative TS genes have been largely unsuccessful. The search for these genes has been complicated by the wide range of phenotypic expression of the genes in quality and severity, be it expression as uncontrollable movements, as obsessions and compulsions, or as mild symptoms that are continuous with normal behavioral repertoires. When considered along with the difficulty that has been encountered in locating the putative TS genes, the continuity of tics with normal behaviors supports the possibility that these genes may not usually be expressed pathologically and that they might be present more frequently in the population than was thought previously.

Environmental Determinants

Although genetic factors are important for establishing a diathesis to TS and related disorders, environmental determinants appear to play an equally central role in determining who manifests the underlying vulnerability and the degree to which that vulnerability is expressed. These environmental determinants need to be identified before we can appreciate fully the range of phenotypic expression of the TS genes.

At present, we can only speculate about the precise contributions of individual environmental determinants to the expression of the TS phenotype. Neuroimaging studies suggest, for example, that disturbances in the structure and functioning of prefrontal cortices and other brain regions, such as the corpus callosum, may result in the inability to suppress tic behaviors. This type of disturbance might result from a failure of the prefrontal cortex to develop and organize itself properly during early childhood. It might also result from a failure of the prefrontal cortex to remodel itself in later childhood or adolescence in response to the continuous need to suppress tics in an increasingly diverse set of circumstances. Failure to establish these compensatory responses is thought to unmask the genetic vulnerability to develop tic-related symptoms.

Compelling evidence exists suggesting that neuroendocrine factors are among the most important environmental determinants of tic expression and severity. These neuroendocrine determinants may include increased levels of sex steroids or an enhanced responsiveness of end-organs to normal levels of circulating hormones or to normal variations in the levels of these hormones. They may also include the organizational effects of sex steroid hormones on the brain during the prenatal period, which act to sensitize the brain to the activational effects of steroid hormones later in life. These neuroendocrine influences appear to predominantly confer additional risk of developing TS to females with a genetic diathesis to the disorder. By masculinizing their brain structure and function, neuroendocrine determinants increase the probability that genetically vulnerable girls will develop a neuropsychiatric disorder that typically affects boys.

Additional nongenetic determinants have been reported to increase a genetically susceptible individual's risk for developing TS, including prior infection with GABHS, perinatal complications, and stimulant medications. Psychosocial stressors appear to affect tic symptom severity in the short term, although consequences in the long term are less clear.

This model of the pathophysiology of TS comprises multiple genetic and nongenetic "strikes," each of which confers risk but none of which is sufficient for developing TS. This model is useful not only for understanding the complexities of TS, but it is probably also applicable generally to most complex neuropsychiatric disorders (Cicchetti & Rogosch, 1996). The combination of and interactions between specific risk factors and protective factors likely determine the pattern of expression, the severity, and the natural history of a neuropsychiatric disorder. Genetic and environmental influences interact in complex ways on many levels to produce a given disorder in a particular individual. This interaction is further contextualized by the individual's biologically and environmentally determined capacities to adapt and self-regulate behavior. The final individual represents a composite of his or her genetic and environmental strengths and vulnerabilities, which have been shaped and remodeled by life experiences to determine the overall set of symptoms and adaptive capacities that will be carried throughout life.

FUTURE DIRECTIONS

A thorough understanding of TS and related tic disorders requires the recognition of a specific genetic vulnerability that, under specific environmental circumstances, may develop into a group of symptoms that includes not only tics, but also a broad array of other behavioral and emotional disturbances. Future research will aim to understand better the full range of expression of tic disorders, especially milder phenotypic variants that typically present with subtler disturbances of movement and behavior. Research will also focus on defining the genetic diathesis to tic disorders and on uncovering further the range of environmental factors that contribute to the development of these disorders. The goal of research, ultimately, is to inform preventive measures and therapeutic interventions that will influence positively the physical and emotional well-being of children, adolescents, and adults who suffer from tics and co-occurring disorders.

Among the most important sources of information about the phenomenology and natural history of tic disorders are epidemiological samples that are followed prospectively and longitudinally. By eliminating the ascertainment bias inherent in studies that use clinical samples, and by studying the same groups of individuals over an extensive period of time, prospective longitudinal studies of epidemiological samples will provide researchers with more accurate data regarding the progression of tic disorders during childhood and their gradual abatement in most people during adolescence. Longitudinal assessments will also allow for analysis of the cross-sectional and prospective associations between tic disorders and the conditions that co-occur with them. The most prominent of these conditions are OCD and ADHD, but disorders of learning, anxiety, mood, and sleep may also be present; with further study, these may become additional defining features of tic disorders. Clarification of these sometimes subtle, co-occurring conditions will be valuable, in that they are often more disruptive to the lives of individuals with tic disorders than are the tics themselves. Information obtained from prospective longitudinal studies will prove useful to those studying the developmental psychopathology of tic disorders, to those developing models for prevention of these disorders, and to those investigating modalities for treatment of the disorders. The success or failure of these measures for prevention and treatment will, in turn, help to shape further our theories regarding the etiology and pathophysiology of tics and co-occurring disturbances.

Future research will need to assess the many possible environmental factors that may influence the development and severity of tics and associated behavioral and emotional problems. Studies thus far have suggested, for example, that adverse events during the perinatal period, including maternal toxic exposures, obstetric complications, and low birth weight, may affect the development of tic disorders. The precise contributions of these events, however, to the pathophysiology of tic behaviors have yet to be elucidated. Similarly, though substantial evidence suggests that sex hormones in both the pre- and postnatal periods may predispose certain individuals to developing more severe tics, the mechanism by which hormones achieve this effect is still unknown. Again, prospective longitudinal neuroimaging studies of epidemiological samples would help to characterize further the changes in brain morphology that are driven by sex hormones and how the brains of individuals with tics may differ from normal brains with respect to sexual differentiation. Another important area that warrants further research is the possibility of an autoimmune, postinfectious etiology of tic disorders and co-occurring conditions, particularly OCD. The evidence thus far has been mixed; double-blind, controlled, longitudinal studies are still needed to clarify any relationship between infection with group A beta hemolytic streptococcus and the development or exacerbation of tics or obsessive-compulsive symptoms.

Numerous efforts to date have been aimed at identifying the genes that, in the presence of specific environmental determinants, produce symptoms of tic disorders. Results of the studies have been largely inconclusive, however, so future genetic studies will aim to replicate the relatively meager existing linkage and association data. Identification of the putative TS genes and the products of these genes will contribute to our knowledge of the neurobiochemical pathways involved in producing the TS phenotype. In the long term, this knowledge of the pathophysiology of tics will inform both measures to prevent the development of tic behaviors and measures to treat tics when they do present.

Novel strategies will be employed to identify genes associated with TS, including high-resolution, high throughput, cytogenetics techniques in individuals with TS associated with physical stigma of a clearly genetic etiology (State et al., 2003). These techniques will also be applied to the study of high-density families, including rare consanguineous pedigrees. Although such techniques are likely to identify genes that account for a small percentage of tic disorders in the general population, the approaches may help to identify underlying molecular and cellular pathways, presumably in frontostriatal systems, that produce tic disorders. Similar approaches have proved fruitful in the identification of genes and molecular pathways involved in other complex disorders, including Alzheimer's (Song & Jung, 2004; Wilquet & De Strooper, 2004) and Parkinson's (Selkoe, 2004) diseases and systemic hypertension (Lifton, Wilson, Choate, & Geller, 2002). Use of

dimensional variables derived from cognitive neuroscience studies such as quantitative trait loci (Almasy & Blangero, 1998; Amos, 1994) in genetic linkage studies will also be important directions for future research of the genetic bases of tic disorders. Similar approaches have made major advances in defining genes involved in the various components of reading pathways in persons with reading disability (Grigorenko et al., 1997; Grigorenko, Wood, Meyer, & Pauls, 2000). Combining brain imaging measures with genetic studies will help to define neurobiological subtypes of tic disorders and the influence of individual genes on specific neural pathways involved in the genesis of tic and compensatory circuits.

Neuroimaging studies of children and adults with tic disorders, particularly those using anatomical and functional MRI, have already contributed significantly to our understanding of the brain pathways that appear to malfunction in individuals with tic disorders. Specifically, the caudate nucleus has been identified as the likely location of the trait morphological abnormality in tic disorders. The frontal lobe, on the other hand, appears to be a site where the morphological changes visible on MRI represent compensatory mechanisms for tics. Differences in various other areas in the brain have also been detected in individuals with tics compared to normal subjects. The interpretation of these findings has proven difficult, however, as it is nearly impossible to distinguish whether these differences represent causes, consequences, or epiphenomena of tic disorders. Prospective, longitudinal studies of populations at risk for developing tic disorders, such as young siblings or children of individuals with tics, will be valuable for separating trait morphological differences from compensatory responses and incidental findings. Even more useful might be prospective longitudinal neuroimaging of an epidemiological sample, so that differences in brain structure between normal individuals and those who will develop tics might be captured as early as the perinatal period.

Also important in future imaging studies will be the acquisition of data from multiple imaging modalities within the same individuals. Studies will increasingly need to acquire, for example, imaging data on brain structure using anatomical MRI, function using fMRI and perfusion imaging, anatomical connectivity using diffusion tensor imaging (DTI), and brain metabolism and neurotransmitter status using magnetic resonance spectroscopy (MRS), PET, and SPECT. The power of collecting these data within the same individuals will be to correlate measures of caudate hypoplasia and frontal hypertrophy (using anatomical MRI), for instance, with measures of neuronal density (using MRS) and neurotransmitter levels (using MRS and

PET) in those regions and the axonal connectivity (using DTI) between them. These within-subject analyses will help to explain the neural systems involved in tic disorders across multiple levels of brain organization. Finally, improved postmortem studies that are under way will help to define the molecular and cellular pathways that link the vulnerability genes for tics with their manifestations in altered brain structure and function.

REFERENCES

Abwender, D. A., Como, P. G., Kurlan, R., Parry, K., Fett, K. A., Cui, L., et al. (1996). School problems in Tourette's syndrome. *Archives of Neurology, 53,* 509–511.

Achenbach, T. M., & Edelbrock, C. S. (1978). The classification of child psychopathology: A review and analysis of empirical efforts. *Psychological Bulletin, 85,* 1275–1301.

Ackerman, D. L., Greenland, S., Bystritsky, A., Morgenstern, H., & Katz, R. J. (1994). Predictors of treatment response in obsessive-compulsive disorder: Multivariate analyses from a multicenter trial of clomipramine. *Journal of Clinical Psychopharmacology, 14,* 247–254.

Albin, R. L., Koeppe, R. A., Bohnen, N. I., Nichols, T. E., Meyer, P., Wernette, K., et al. (2003). Increased ventral striatal monoaminergic innervation in Tourette syndrome. *Neurology, 61,* 310–315.

Alexander, G. E., Crutcher, M., & DeLong, M. (1990). Basal ganglia-thalamocortical circuits: Parallel substrates for motor, oculomotor, "prefrontal," and "limbic" functions. *Progress in Brain Research, 85,* 119–146.

Alexander, G. E., & DeLong, M. R. (1985). Microstimulation of the primate neostriatum: II. Somatotopic organization of striatal microexcitable zones and their relation to neuronal response properties. *Journal of Neurophysiology, 53,* 1417–1430.

Alexander, G. E., DeLong, M. R., & Strick, P. L. (1986). Parallel organization of functionally segregated circuits linking basal ganglia and cortex. *Annual Review of Neuroscience, 9,* 357–381.

Alexander, G. M., & Peterson, B. S. (2004). Testing the prenatal hormone hypothesis of tic-related disorders: Gender identity and gender role behavior. *Development and Psychopathology, 16,* 407–420.

Allen, A. J., Leonard, H. L., & Swedo, S. E. (1995). Case study: A new infection-triggered, autoimmune subtype of pediatric OCD and Tourette's syndrome. *Journal of the American Academy of Child and Adolescent Psychiatry, 34,* 307–311.

Allen, R. P., Singer, H. S., Brown, J. E., & Salam, M. M. (1992). Sleep disorders in Tourette syndrome: A primary or unrelated problem? *Pediatric Neurology, 8,* 275–280.

Almasy, L., & Blangero, J. (1998). Multipoint quantitative-trait linkage analysis in general pedigrees. *American Journal of Human Genetics, 62,* 1198–1211.

Alsobrook, J. P., II, & Pauls, D. L. (2002). A factor analysis of tic symptoms in Gilles de la Tourette's syndrome. *American Journal of Psychiatry, 159,* 291–296.

Amos, C. I. (1994). Robust variance-components approach for assessing genetic linkage in pedigrees. *American Journal of Human Genetics, 54,* 535–543.

Anderson, G. M., Leckman, J. F., & Cohen, D. J. (1999). Neurochemical and neuropeptide systems. In J. F. Leckman & D. J. Cohen (Eds.), *Tourette's syndrome—Tics, obsessions, compulsions: Developmental psychopathology and clinical care* (pp. 261–280). New York: Wiley.

Anderson, G. M., Pollak, E. S., Chatterjee, D., Leckman, J. F., Riddle, M. A., & Cohen, D. J. (1992a). Brain monoamines and amino acids in Gilles de la Tourette's syndrome: A preliminary study of subcortical regions. *Archives of General Psychiatry, 49,* 584–586.

Anderson, G. M., Pollak, E. S., Chatterjee, D., Leckman, J. F., Riddle, M. A., & Cohen, D. J. (1992b). Postmortem analysis of subcortical monoamines and amino acids in Tourette syndrome. *Advances in Neurology, 58,* 123–133.

Apter, A., Pauls, D. L., Bleich, A., Zohar, A. H., Kron, S., Ratzoni, G., et al. (1993). An epidemiologic study of Gilles de la Tourette's syndrome in Israel. *Archives of General Psychiatry, 50,* 734–738.

Baer, L. (1994). Factor analysis of symptom subtypes of obsessive compulsive disorder and their relation to personality and tic disorders. *Journal of Clinical Psychiatry, 55,* 18–23.

Baldwin, M., Frost, L. L., & Wood, C. D. (1954). Investigation of the primate amygdala: Movements of the face and jaws. *Neurology, 4,* 596–598.

Barabas, G., & Matthews, W. S. (1985). Homogeneous clinical subgroups in children with Tourette syndrome. *Pediatrics, 75,* 73–75.

Barabas, G., Matthews, W. S., & Ferrari, M. (1984a). Disorders of arousal in Gilles de la Tourette's syndrome. *Neurology, 34,* 815–817.

Barabas, G., Matthews, W. S., & Ferrari, M. (1984b). Somnambulism in children with Tourette syndrome. *Developmental Medicine and Child Neurology, 26,* 457–460.

Barkley, R. A. (1997). Attention-deficit/hyperactivity disorder, self-regulation, and time: Toward a more comprehensive theory. *Journal of Developmental and Behavioral Pediatrics, 18,* 271–279.

Barkley, R. A., Edwards, G., Laneri, M., Fletcher, K., & Metevia, L. (2001). Executive functioning, temporal discounting, and sense of time in adolescents with attention deficit hyperactivity disorder (ADHD) and oppositional defiant disorder (ODD). *Journal of Abnormal Child Psychology, 29,* 541–556.

Barkley, R. A., Grodzinsky, G., & DuPaul, G. J. (1992). Frontal lobe functions in attention deficit disorder with and without hyperactivity: A review and research report. *Journal of Abnormal Child Psychology, 20,* 163–188.

Barr, C. L., Wigg, K. G., Pakstis, A. J., Kurlan, R., Pauls, D., Kidd, K. K., et al. (1999). Genome scan for linkage to Gilles de la Tourette syndrome. *American Journal of Medical Genetics, 88,* 437–445.

Barr, C. L., Wigg, K. G., Zovko, E., Sandor, P., & Tsui, L. C. (1996). No evidence for a major gene effect of the dopamine D4 receptor gene in the susceptibility to Gilles de la Tourette syndrome in five Canadian families. *American Journal of Medical Genetics, 67,* 301–305.

Barr, C. L., Wigg, K. G., Zovko, E., Sandor, P., & Tsui, L. C. (1997). Linkage study of the dopamine D5 receptor gene and Gilles de la Tourette syndrome. *American Journal of Medical Genetics, 74,* 58–61.

Bawden, H. N., Stokes, A., Camfield, C. S., Camfield, P. R., & Salisbury, S. (1998). Peer relationship problems in children with Tourette's disorder or diabetes mellitus. *Journal of Child Psychology and Psychiatry and Allied Disciplines, 39,* 663–668.

Bergen, D., Tanner, C. M., & Wilson, R. (1982). The electroencephalogram in Tourette syndrome. *Annals of Neurology, 11,* 382–385.

Berger, M., Yule, W., & Rutter, M. (1975). Attainment and adjustment in two geographical areas: I. The prevalence of specific learning disabilities. *British Journal of Psychiatry, 126,* 510–526.

Berkson, J. B. (1946). Limitations of the application of fourfold table analysis to hospital data. *Biometrics, 2,* 47–51.

Biederman, J., Newcorn, J., & Sprich, S. (1991). Comorbidity of attention deficit hyperactivity disorder with conduct, depressive, anxiety, and other disorders. *American Journal of Psychiatry, 148,* 564–577.

Biederman, J., Wilens, T., Mick, E., Milberger, S., Spencer, T. J., & Faraone, S. V. (1995). Psychoactive substance use disorders in adults with attention deficit hyperactivity disorder (ADHD): Effects of ADHD and psychiatric comorbidity. *American Journal of Psychiatry, 152,* 1652–1658.

Bliss, J. (1980). Sensory experiences of Gilles de la Tourette syndrome. *Archives of General Psychiatry, 37,* 1343–1347.

Bloch, M. H., Peterson, B. S., Scahill, L., Otka, J., Katsovich, L., & Leckman, J. F. (2004). *Clinical predictors of future tic and OCD severity in children with Tourette syndrome.* Manuscript submitted for publication.

Bodner, S. M., & Peterson, B. S. (2003). Pediatric autoimmune neuropsychiatric disorders associated with streptococcus: The PANDAS syndrome in children and adults. *Directions in Psychiatry, 23,* 235–251.

Boghosian-Sell, L., Comings, D. E., & Overhauser, J. (1996). Tourette syndrome in a pedigree with a 7;18 translocation: Identification of a YAC spanning the translocation breakpoint at 18q22.3. *American Journal of Human Genetics, 59,* 999–1005.

Bornstein, R. A. (1990). Neuropsychological performance in children with Tourette's syndrome. *Psychiatry Research, 33,* 73–81.

Bornstein, R. A. (1991). Neuropsychological correlates of obsessive characteristics in Tourette syndrome. *Journal of Neuropsychiatry and Clinical Neurosciences, 3,* 157–162.

Braun, A. R., Stoetter, B., Randolph, C., Hsiao, J. K., Vladar, K., Gernert, J., et al. (1993). The functional neuroanatomy of Tourette's syndrome: An FDG-PET study: Pt. I. Regional changes in cerebral glucose metabolism differentiating patients and controls. *Neuropsychopharmacology, 9,* 277–291.

Brett, P. M., Curtis, D., Robertson, M. M., Dahlitz, M., & Gurling, H. M. (1996). Linkage analysis and exclusion of regions of chromosomes 3 and 8 in Gilles de la Tourette syndrome following the identification of a balanced reciprocal translocation 46 XY, t(3:8)(p21.3 q24.1) in a case of Tourette syndrome. *Psychiatric Genetics, 6,* 99–105.

Brett, P. M., Curtis, D., Robertson, M. M., & Gurling, H. M. (1995). Exclusion of the 5-HT1A serotonin neuroreceptor and tryptophan oxygenase genes in a large British kindred multiply affected with Tourette's syndrome, chronic motor tics, and obsessive-compulsive behavior. *American Journal of Psychiatry, 152,* 437–440.

Brett, P. M., Curtis, D., Robertson, M. M., & Gurling, H. M. (1997). Neuroreceptor subunit genes and the genetic susceptibility to Gilles de la Tourette syndrome. *Biological Psychiatry, 42,* 941–947.

Brissaud, É. (1896). La chorée variable des dégenerés. *Revue Neurologique, 4,* 417–431.

Brooks, D. J., Turjanski, N., Sawle, G. V., Playford, E. D., & Lees, A. J. (1992). PET studies on the integrity of the pre and postsynaptic dopaminergic system in Tourette syndrome. *Advances in Neurology, 58,* 227–231.

Brookshire, B. L., Butler, I. J., Ewing-Cobbs, L., & Fletcher, J. M. (1994). Neuropsychological characteristics of children with Tourette syndrome: Evidence for a nonverbal learning disability? *Journal of Clinical and Experimental Neuropsychology, 16,* 289–302.

Bruun, R. D. (1988). The natural history of Tourette's syndrome. In D. J. Cohen, R. D. Bruun, & J. F. Leckman (Eds.), *Tourette's syndrome and tic disorders: Clinical understanding and treatment* (pp. 21–39). New York: Wiley.

Burd, L., & Kerbeshian, P. J. (1987). Onset of Gilles de la Tourette's syndrome before 1 year of age. *American Journal of Psychiatry, 144,* 1066–1067.

Burd, L., Kerbeshian, P. J., Barth, A., Klug, M. G., Avery, P. K., & Benz, B. (2001). Long-term follow-up of an epidemiologically defined cohort of patients with Tourette syndrome. *Journal of Child Neurology, 16,* 431–437.

Burd, L., Kerbeshian, P. J., Wikenheiser, M., & Fisher, W. (1986). A prevalence study of Gilles de la Tourette syndrome in North Dakota school-age children. *Journal of the American Academy of Child Psychiatry, 25,* 552–553.

Caine, E. D., McBride, M. C., Chiverton, P., Bamford, K. A., Rediess, S., & Shiao, J. (1988). Tourette's syndrome in Monroe County school children. *Neurology, 38,* 472–475.

Carr, D. B., & Sesack, S. R. (1998). Callosal terminals in the rat prefrontal cortex: Synaptic targets and association with GABA-immunoreactive structures. *Synapse, 29,* 193–205.

Carter, A. S., O'Donnell, D. A., Schultz, R. T., Scahill, L., Leckman, J. F., & Pauls, D. L. (2000). Social and emotional adjustment in children affected with Gilles de la Tourette's syndrome: Associations with ADHD and family functioning. *Journal of Child Psychology and Psychiatry and Allied Disciplines, 41,* 215–223.

Carter, A. S., Pauls, D. L., Leckman, J. F., & Cohen, D. J. (1994). A prospective longitudinal study of Gilles de la Tourette's syndrome. *Journal of the American Academy of Child and Adolescent Psychiatry, 33,* 377–385.

Castellanos, F. X., Ritchie, G. F., Marsh, W. L., & Rapoport, J. L. (1996). DSM-IV stereotypic movement disorder: Persistence of stereotypies of infancy in intellectually normal adolescents and adults. *Journal of Clinical Psychiatry, 57,* 116–122.

Cavallini, M. C., Di Bella, D., Siliprandi, F., Malchiodi, F., & Bellodi, L. (2002). Exploratory factor analysis of obsessive-compulsive patients and association with 5-HTTLPR polymorphism. *American Journal of Medical Genetics, 114,* 347–353.

Channon, S., Pratt, P., & Robertson, M. M. (2003). Executive function, memory, and learning in Tourette's syndrome. *Neuropsychology, 17,* 247–254.

Chappell, P. B., Leckman, J. F., Riddle, M. A., Anderson, G. M., Listwack, S. J., Ort, S. I., et al. (1992). Neuroendocrine and behavioral effects of naloxone in Tourette syndrome. *Advances in Neurology, 58,* 253–262.

Chappell, P. B., McSwiggan-Hardin, M. T., Scahill, L., Rubenstein, M., Walker, D. E., & Cohen, D. J. (1994). Videotape tic counts in the assessment of Tourette's syndrome: Stability, reliability, and validity. *Journal of the American Academy of Child and Adolescent Psychiatry, 33,* 386–393.

Chappell, P. B., Riddle, M., Anderson, G., Scahill, L., Hardin, M., Walker, D., et al. (1994). Enhanced stress responsivity of Tourette syndrome patients undergoing lumbar puncture. *Biological Psychiatry, 36,* 35–43.

Chou, I. C., Tsai, C. H., Lee, C. C., Kuo, H. T., Hsu, Y. A., Li, C. I., et al. (2004). Association analysis between Tourette's syndrome and dopamine D1 receptor gene in Taiwanese children. *Psychiatric Genetics, 14,* 219–221.

Cicchetti, D. (1984). The emergence of developmental psychopathology. *Child Development, 55,* 1–7.

Cicchetti, D. (1990a). A historical perspective on the discipline of developmental psychopathology. In J. Rolf, A. Masten, D. Cicchetti, K. Nuechterlein, & S. Weintraub (Eds.), *Risk and protective factors in the development of psychopathology* (pp. 2–28). New York: Cambridge University Press.

Cicchetti, D. (1990b). Perspectives on the interface between normal and atypical development. *Development and Psychopathology, 2,* 329–333.

Cicchetti, D. (1993). Developmental psychopathology: Reactions, reflections, projections. *Developmental Review, 13,* 471–502.

Cicchetti, D. (2003). Experiments of nature: Contributions to developmental theory. *Development and Psychopathology, 15,* 833–835.

Cicchetti, D., & Dawson, G. (2002). Multiple levels of analysis. *Development and Psychopathology, 14,* 417–420.

Cicchetti, D., & Rogosch, F. A. (1996). Equifinality and multifinality in developmental psychopathology. *Development and Psychopathology, 8,* 597–600.

Coffey, B. J., Miguel, E. C., Biederman, J., Baer, L., Rauch, S. L., O'Sullivan, R. L., et al. (1998). Tourette's disorder with and without obsessive-compulsive disorder in adults: Are they different? *Journal of Nervous and Mental Diseases, 186,* 201–206.

Cohen, A. J., & Leckman, J. F. (1992). Sensory phenomena associated with Gilles de la Tourette's syndrome. *Journal of Clinical Psychiatry, 53,* 319–323.

Cohen, D. J. (1991). Tourette's syndrome: A model disorder for integrating psychoanalytic and biological perspectives. *International Review of Psychoanalysis, 18,* 195–209.

Cohen, D. J., Friedhoff, A. J., Leckman, J. F., & Chase, T. N. (1992). Tourette syndrome: Extending basic research to clinical care. *Advances in Neurology, 58,* 341–362.

Cohrs, S., Rasch, T., Altmeyer, S., Kinkelbur, J., Kostanecka, T., Rothenberger, A., et al. (2001). Decreased sleep quality and increased sleep related movements in patients with Tourette's syndrome. *Journal of Neurology, Neurosurgery, and Psychiatry, 70,* 192–197.

Comings, D. E., & Comings, B. G. (1984). Tourette's syndrome and attention deficit disorder with hyperactivity: Are they genetically related? *Journal of the American Academy of Child Psychiatry, 23,* 138–146.

Comings, D. E., & Comings, B. G. (1987a). A controlled study of Tourette syndrome: Pt. I. Attention-deficit disorder, learning disorders, and school problems. *American Journal of Human Genetics, 41,* 701–741.

Comings, D. E., & Comings, B. G. (1987b). A controlled study of Tourette syndrome: Pt. VI. Early development, sleep problems, allergies, and handedness. *American Journal of Human Genetics, 41,* 822–838.

Comings, D. E., Comings, B. G., Dietz, G., Muhleman, D., Okada, T. A., Sarinana, F., et al. (1986). Evidence the Tourette syndrome gene is at 18q22.1. In F. Vogel & K. Sperling (Eds.), *Human Genetics: Proceedings of the VIIth International Congress of Human Genetics Abstract Part II* (p. 620). Berlin: Springer.

Comings, D. E., Comings, B. G., Muhleman, D., Dietz, G., Shahbahrami, B., Tast, D., et al. (1991). The dopamine D2 receptor locus as a modifying gene in neuropsychiatric disorders. *Journal of the American Medical Association, 266,* 1793–1800.

Comings, D. E., Himes, J. A., & Comings, B. G. (1990). An epidemiologic study of Tourette's syndrome in a single school district. *Journal of Clinical Psychiatry, 51,* 463–469.

Como, P. G. (2001). Neuropsychological function in Tourette syndrome. *Advances in Neurology, 85,* 103–111.

Como, P. G., & Kurlan, R. (1991). An open-label trial of fluoxetine for obsessive-compulsive disorder in Gilles de la Tourette's syndrome. *Neurology, 41,* 872–874.

Costello, E. J., Angold, A., Burns, B. J., Stangl, D. K., Tweed, D. L., Erkanli, A., et al. (1996). The Great Smoky Mountains study of youth: Goals, design, methods, and the prevalence of DSM-III-R disorders. *Archives of General Psychiatry, 53,* 1129–1136.

Devor, E. J., Dill-Devor, R. M., & Magee, H. J. (1998). The Bal I and Msp I polymorphisms in the dopamine D3 receptor gene display: Linkage disequilibrium with each other but no association with Tourette syndrome. *Psychiatric Genetics, 8,* 49–52.

Devor, E. J., Grandy, D. K., Civelli, O., Litt, M., Burgess, A. K., Isenberg, K. E., et al. (1990). Genetic linkage is excluded for the D2-dopamine receptor lambda HD2G1 and flanking loci on chromosome 11q22-q23 in Tourette syndrome. *Human Heredity, 40,* 105–108.

Diaz-Anzaldua, A., Joober, R., Riviere, J. B., Dion, Y., Lesperance, P., Richer, F., et al. (2004). Tourette syndrome and dopaminergic genes: a family-based association study in the French Canadian founder population. *Molecular Psychiatry, 9,* 272–277.

Drake, M. E., Jr., Hietter, S. A., Bogner, J. E., & Andrews, J. M. (1992). Cassette EEG sleep recordings in Gilles de la Tourette syndrome. *Clinical Electroencephalography, 23,* 142–146.

Duggal, H. S., & Nizamie, S. H. (2002). Bereitschaftspotential in tic disorders: A preliminary observation. *Neurology India, 50,* 487–489.

Dykens, E., Leckman, J., Riddle, M., Hardin, M., Schwartz, S., & Cohen, D. (1990). Intellectual, academic, and adaptive functioning of Tourette syndrome children with and without attention deficit disorder. *Journal of Abnormal Child Psychology, 18,* 607–615.

Eapen, V., Pauls, D. L., & Robertson, M. M. (1993). Evidence for autosomal dominant transmission in Tourette's syndrome: United Kingdom cohort study. *British Journal of Psychiatry, 162,* 593–596.

Edell, B. H., & Motta, R. W. (1989). The emotional adjustment of children with Tourette's syndrome. *Journal of Psychology, 123,* 51–57.

Edell-Fisher, B. H., & Motta, R. W. (1990). Tourette syndrome: Relation to children's and parents' self-concepts. *Psychological Reports, 66,* 539–545.

Erenberg, G. (1985). Sleep disorders in Gilles de la Tourette's syndrome. *Neurology, 35,* 1397.

Erenberg, G., Cruse, R. P., & Rothner, A. D. (1986). Tourette syndrome: An analysis of 200 pediatric and adolescent cases. *Cleveland Clinic Quarterly, 53,* 127–131.

Erenberg, G., Cruse, R. P., & Rothner, A. D. (1987). The natural history of Tourette syndrome: A follow-up study. *Annals of Neurology, 22,* 383–385.

Ernst, M., Zametkin, A. J., Jons, P. H., Matochik, J. A., Pascualvaca, D., & Cohen, R. M. (1999). High presynaptic dopaminergic activity in children with Tourette's disorder. *Journal of the American Academy of Child and Adolescent Psychiatry, 38,* 86–94.

Falk, C., & Rubinstein, P. (1987). An easy reliable way to construct a proper control sample for risk calculations. *Annals of Human Genetics, 51,* 227–233.

Ferrari, M., Matthews, W. S., & Barabas, G. (1984). Children with Tourette syndrome: Results of psychological tests given prior to drug treatment. *Journal of Developmental and Behavioral Pediatrics, 5,* 116–119.

Fish, D. R., Sawyers, D., Allen, P. J., Blackie, J. D., Lees, A. J., & Marsden, C. D. (1991). The effect of sleep on the dyskinetic movements of Parkinson's disease, Gilles de la Tourette syndrome, Huntington's disease, and torsion dystonia. *Archives of Neurology, 48,* 210–214.

Foster, L. G. (1998). Nervous habits and stereotyped behaviors in preschool children. *Journal of the American Academy of Child and Adolescent Psychiatry, 37,* 711–717.

Fried, I., Katz, A., McCarthy, G., Sass, K., Spencer, S., & Spencer, D. (1991). Functional organization of human supplementary motor cortex studies by electrical stimulation. *Journal of Neuroscience, 11,* 3656–3666.

Fuster, J. M. (1989). *The prefrontal cortex: Anatomy, physiology, and neuropsychology of the frontal lobe.* New York: Raven Press.

Gadow, K. D., Sverd, J., Sprafkin, J., Nolan, E. E., & Ezor, S. M. (1995). Efficacy of methylphenidate for ADHD in children with tic disorder. *Archives of General Psychiatry, 52,* 444–455.

Gadow, K. D., Sverd, J., Sprafkin, J., Nolan, E. E., & Grossman, S. (1999). Long-term methylphenidate therapy in children with comorbid attention-deficit hyperactivity disorder and chronic multiple tic disorder. *Archives of General Psychiatry, 56,* 330–336.

Gelernter, J., Kennedy, J. L., Grandy, D. K., Zhou, Q. Y., Civelli, O., Pauls, D. L., et al. (1993). Exclusion of close linkage of Tourette's syndrome to D1 dopamine receptor. *American Journal of Psychiatry, 150,* 449–453.

Gelernter, J., Pakstis, A. J., Pauls, D. L., Kurlan, R., Gancher, S. T., Civelli, O., et al. (1990). Gilles de la Tourette syndrome is not linked to D2-dopamine receptor. *Archives of General Psychiatry, 47,* 1073–1077.

Gelernter, J., Pauls, D. L., Leckman, J., Kidd, K. K., & Kurlan, R. (1994). D2 dopamine receptor alleles do not influence severity of Tourette's syndrome: Results from four large kindreds. *Archives of Neurology, 51,* 397–400.

Gelernter, J., Rao, P. A., Pauls, D. L., Hamblin, M. W., Sibley, D. R., & Kidd, K. K. (1995). Assignment of the 5HT7 receptor gene (HTR7) to chromosome 10q and exclusion of genetic linkage with Tourette syndrome. *Genomics, 26,* 207–209.

Gelernter, J., Vandenbergh, D., Kruger, S. D., Pauls, D. L., Kurlan, R., Pakstis, A. J., et al. (1995). The dopamine transporter protein gene (SLC6A3): Primary linkage mapping and linkage studies in Tourette syndrome. *Genomics, 30,* 459–463.

George, M. S., Trimble, M. R., Ring, H. A., Sallee, F. R., & Robertson, M. M. (1993). Obsessions in obsessive-compulsive disorder with and without Gilles de la Tourette's syndrome. *American Journal of Psychiatry, 150,* 93–97.

Gerard, E., & Peterson, B. S. (2003). Developmental processes and brain imaging studies in Tourette syndrome. *Journal of Psychosomatic Research, 55,* 13–22.

Geurts, H. M., Verte, S., Oosterlaan, J., Roeyers, H., & Sergeant, J. A. (2004). How specific are executive functioning deficits in attention deficit hyperactivity disorder and Autism? *Journal of Child Psychology and Psychiatry and Allied Disciplines, 45,* 836–854.

Glaze, D. G., Frost, J. D., Jr., & Jankovic, J. (1983). Sleep in Gilles de la Tourette's syndrome: Disorder of arousal. *Neurology, 33,* 586–592.

Goetz, C. G., Tanner, C. M., Stebbins, G. T., Leipzig, G., & Carr, W. C. (1992). Adult tics in Gilles de la Tourette's syndrome: Description and risk factors. *Neurology, 42,* 784–788.

Golden, G. S. (1978). Tics and Tourette's: A continuum of symptoms? *Annals of Neurology, 4,* 145–148.

Goldman-Rakic, P. (1987). Circuitry of primate prefrontal cortex and regulation of behavior by representational memory. In V. Mountcastle, F. Plum, & S. Geiger (Eds.), *Handbook of physiology: The nervous system* (pp. 373–416). Bethesda, MD: American Physiological Society.

Goldman-Rakic, P., & Selemon, L. (1990). New frontiers in basal ganglia research. *Trends in Neurosciences, 13,* 241–243.

Graybiel, A. M., & Canales, J. J. (2001). The neurobiology of repetitive behaviors: Clues to the neurobiology of Tourette syndrome. *Advances in Neurology, 85,* 123–131.

Grice, D. E., Leckman, J. F., Pauls, D. L., Kurlan, R., Kidd, K. K., Pakstis, A. J., et al. (1996). Linkage disequilibrium between an allele at the dopamine D4 receptor locus and Tourette syndrome, by the transmission-disequilibrium test. *American Journal of Human Genetics, 59,* 644–652.

Grigorenko, E. L., Wood, F. B., Meyer, M. S., Hart, L. A., Speed, W. C., Shuster, A., et al. (1997). Susceptibility loci for distinct components of developmental dyslexia on chromosomes 6 and 15. *American Journal of Human Genetics, 60,* 27–39.

Grigorenko, E. L., Wood, F. B., Meyer, M. S., & Pauls, D. L. (2000). Chromosome 6p influences on different dyslexia-related cognitive processes: Further confirmation. *American Journal of Human Genetics, 66,* 715–723.

Hagin, R. A., Beecher, R., Pagano, G., & Kreeger, H. (1982). Effects of Tourette syndrome on learning. *Advances in Neurology, 35,* 323–328.

Hall, M., Costa, D., & Shields, J. (1990). Brain perfusion patterns with Tc-99m-HMPAO/SPECT in patients with Gilles de la Tourette syndrome. *European Journal of Nuclear Medicine, 16,* WP18.

Hallett, J. J., Harling-Berg, C. J., Knopf, P. M., Stopa, E. G., & Kiessling, L. S. (2000). Anti-striatal antibodies in Tourette syndrome cause neuronal dysfunction. *Journal of Neuroimmunology, 111,* 195–202.

Hallett, M. (2001). Neurophysiology of tics. *Advances in Neurology, 85,* 237–244.

Harris, E. L., Schuerholz, L. J., Singer, H. S., Reader, M. J., Brown, J. E., Cox, C., et al. (1995). Executive function in children with Tourette syndrome and/or attention deficit hyperactivity disorder. *Journal of the International Neuropsychological Society, 1,* 511–516.

Hasstedt, S. J., Leppert, M., Filloux, F., van de Wetering, B. J., & McMahon, W. M. (1995). Intermediate inheritance of Tourette syndrome, assuming assortative mating. *American Journal of Human Genetics, 57,* 682–689.

Head, D., Bolton, D., & Hymas, N. (1989). Deficit in cognitive shifting ability with obsessive-compulsive disorder. *Biological Psychiatry, 25,* 929–937.

Hebebrand, J., Klug, B., Fimmers, R., Seuchter, S. A., Wettke-Schafer, R., Deget, F., et al. (1997). Rates for tic disorders and obsessive compulsive symptomatology in families of children and adolescents with Gilles de la Tourette syndrome. *Journal of Psychiatric Research, 31,* 519–530.

Hebebrand, J., Nothen, M. M., Lehmkuhl, G., Poustka, F., Schmidt, M., Propping, P., et al. (1993). Tourette's syndrome and homozygosity for the dopamine D3 receptor gene: German Tourette's Syndrome Collaborative Research Group. *Lancet, 341,* 1483–1484.

Hebebrand, J., Nothen, M. M., Ziegler, A., Klug, B., Neidt, H., Eggermann, K., et al. (1997). Nonreplication of linkage disequilibrium between the dopamine D4 receptor locus and Tourette syndrome. *American Journal of Human Genetics, 61,* 238–239.

Heutink, P., van de Wetering, B. J., Breedveld, G. J., Weber, J., Sandkuyl, L. A., Devor, E. J., et al. (1990). No evidence for genetic linkage of Gilles de la Tourette syndrome on chromosomes 7 and 18. *Journal of Medical Genetics, 27,* 433–436.

Heutink, P., van de Wetering, B. J., Pakstis, A. J., Kurlan, R., Sandor, P., Oostra, B. A., et al. (1995). Linkage studies on Gilles de la Tourette syndrome: What is the strategy of choice? *American Journal of Human Genetics, 57,* 465–473.

Hollander, E., & Wong, C. M. (1996). The relationship between executive impairment and serotonergic sensitivity in obsessive-compulsive disorder. *Neuropsychiatry, Neuropsychology, and Behavioral Neurology, 9,* 230–233.

Holzer, J. C., Goodman, W. K., McDougle, C. J., Baer, L., Boyarsky, B. K., Leckman, J. F., et al. (1994). Obsessive-compulsive disorder with and without a chronic tic disorder: A comparison of symptoms in 70 patients. *British Journal of Psychiatry, 164,* 469–473.

Hubka, G. B., Fulton, W. A., Shady, G. A., Champion, L. M., & Wand, R. (1988). Tourette syndrome: Impact on Canadian family functioning. *Neuroscience and Biobehavioral Reviews, 12,* 259–261.

Hyde, T. M., Aaronson, B. A., Randolph, C., Rickler, K. C., & Weinberger, D. R. (1992). Relationship of birth weight to the phenotypic expression of Gilles de la Tourette's syndrome in monozygotic twins. *Neurology, 42,* 652–658.

Hyde, T. M., Emsellem, H. A., Randolph, C., Rickler, K. C., & Weinberger, D. R. (1994). Electroencephalographic abnormalities in monozygotic twins with Tourette's syndrome. *British Journal of Psychiatry, 164,* 811–817.

Incagnoli, T., & Kane, R. (1981). Neuropsychological functioning in Gilles de la Tourette's syndrome. *Journal of Clinical Neuropsychology, 3,* 165–169.

Jahanshai, M., Jenkins, I. H., Brown, R. G., Marsden, C. D., Passingham, R. E., & Brooks, D. J. (1995). Self-initiated versus externally triggered movements. *Brain, 118,* 913–933.

Jaisoorya, T. S., Reddy, Y. C., & Srinath, S. (2003). The relationship of obsessive-compulsive disorder to putative spectrum disorders: Results from an Indian study. *Comprehensive Psychiatry, 44,* 317–323.

Jankovic, J. (1997). Tourette syndrome: Phenomenology and classification of tics. *Neurologic Clinics, 15,* 267–275.

Jankovic, J., & Rohaidy, H. (1987). Motor, behavioral and pharmacologic findings in Tourette's syndrome. *Canadian Journal of Neurological Sciences, 14,* 541–546.

Kano, Y., Ohta, M., Nagai, Y., Pauls, D. L., & Leckman, J. F. (2001). A family study of Tourette syndrome in Japan. *American Journal of Medical Genetics, 105,* 414–421.

Karp, B. I., & Hallett, M. (1996). Extracorporeal "phantom" tics in Tourette's syndrome. *Neurology, 46,* 38–40.

Karp, B. I., Porter, S., Toro, C., & Hallett, M. (1996). Simple motor tics may be preceded by a premotor potential. *Journal of Neurology, Neurosurgery, and Psychiatry, 61,* 103–106.

Karson, C. N. (1983). Spontaneous eye-blink rates and dopaminergic systems. *Brain, 106,* 643–653.

Karson, C. N., Kaufmann, C. A., Shapiro, A. K., & Shapiro, E. (1985). Eye-blink rate in Tourette's syndrome. *Journal of Nervous and Mental Diseases, 173,* 566–569.

Keller, I., & Heckhausen, H. (1990). Readiness potentials preceding spontaneous motor acts: Voluntary vs. involuntary control. *Electroencephalography and Clinical Neurophysiology, 76,* 351–361.

Kelley, A. E., Lang, C. G., & Gauthier, A. M. (1988). Induction of oral stereotypy following amphetamine microinjection into a discrete subregion of the striatum. *Psychopharmacology, 95,* 556–559.

Keri, S., Szlobodnyik, C., Benedek, G., Janka, Z., & Gadoros, J. (2002). Probabilistic classification learning in Tourette syndrome. *Neuropsychologia, 40,* 1356–1362.

Khalifa, N., & von Knorring, A. L. (2003). Prevalence of tic disorders and Tourette syndrome in a Swedish school population. *Developmental Medicine and Child Neurology, 45,* 315–319.

Kidd, K. K., Prusoff, B. A., & Cohen, D. J. (1980). Familial pattern of Gilles de la Tourette syndrome. *Archives of General Psychiatry, 37,* 1336–1339.

Kiessling, L. S., Marcotte, A. C., & Culpepper, L. (1993). Antineuronal antibodies in movement disorders. *Pediatrics, 92,* 39–43.

Kiessling, L. S., Marcotte, A. C., & Culpepper, L. (1994). Antineuronal antibodies: Tics and obsessive-compulsive symptoms. *Journal of Developmental and Behavioral Pediatrics, 15,* 421–425.

Kimura, F., & Baughman, R. W. (1997). GABAergic transcallosal neurons in developing rat neocortex. *European Journal of Neuroscience, 9,* 1137–1143.

King, R. A., Leckman, J. F., Scahill, L., & Cohen, D. J. (1999). Obsessive-compulsive disorder, anxiety, and depression. In J. F. Leckman & D. J. Cohen (Eds.), *Tourette's syndrome—Tics, obsessions, compulsions: Developmental psychopathology and clinical care* (pp. 43–62). New York: Wiley.

Klein, R., & Bessler, A. (1992). Stimulant side effects in children. In J. Lieberman (Ed.), *Adverse effects of psychotropic drugs* (pp. 470–496). New York: Guilford Press.

Kleven, M. S., & Koek, W. (1996). Differential effects of direct and indirect dopamine agonists on eye blink rate in cynomolgus monkeys. *Journal of Pharmacology and Experimental Therapeutics, 279,* 1211–1219.

Klieger, P. S., Fett, K. A., Dimitsopulos, T., & Karlan, R. (1997). Asymmetry of basal ganglia perfusion in Tourette's syndrome shown by technetium-99m-HMPAO SPECT. *Journal of Nuclear Medicine, 38,* 188–191.

Knowlton, B. J., Mangels, J. A., & Squire, L. R. (1996). A neostriatal habit learning system in humans. *Science, 273,* 1399–1402.

Kompoliti, K., Goetz, C. G., Leurgans, S., Raman, R., & Comella, C. L. (2001). Estrogen, progesterone, and tic severity in women with Gilles de la Tourette syndrome. *Neurology, 57,* 1519.

Kondo, K., & Kabasawa, T. (1978). Improvement in Gilles de la Tourette syndrome after corticosteroid therapy. *Annals of Neurology, 4,* 387.

Kopnisky, K. L., Cowan, W. M., & Hyman, S. E. (2002). Levels of analysis in psychiatric research. *Development and Psychopathology, 14,* 437–461.

Korzen, A. V., Pushkov, V. V., Kharitonov, R. A., & Shustin, V. A. (1991). Stereotaxic thalamotomy in the combined treatment of Gilles de la Tourette's disease. *Zhurnal Nevropatologii i Psikhiatrii Imeni S. S. Korsakova, 91*(3) 100–101.

Kostanecka-Endress, T., Banaschewski, T., Kinkelbur, J., Wullner, I., Lichtblau, S., Cohrs, S., et al. (2003). Disturbed sleep in children with Tourette syndrome: A polysomnographic study. *Journal of Psychosomatic Research, 55,* 23–29.

Kraemer, H. C., Yesavage, J. A., Taylor, J. L., & Kupfer, D. (2000). How can we learn about developmental processes from cross-sectional studies, or can we? *American Journal of Psychiatry, 157,* 163–171.

Krnjevic, K., Randic, M., & Straughan, D. W. (1966). Nature of a cortical inhibitory process. *Journal of Physiology (London), 184,* 49–77.

Kruglyak, L., & Lander, E. S. (1995). Complete multipoint sib-pair analysis of qualitative and quantitative traits. *American Journal of Human Genetics, 57,* 439–454.

Krumholz, A., Singer, H. S., Niedermeyer, E., Burnite, R., & Harris, K. (1983). Electrophysiological studies in Tourette's syndrome. *Annals of Neurology, 14,* 638–641.

Kurlan, R. (2001). Could Tourette syndrome be a neurologic manifestation of rheumatic fever? *Advances in Neurology, 85,* 307–310.

Kurlan, R., Behr, J., Medved, L., & Como, P. (1988). Transient tic disorder and the spectrum of Tourette's syndrome. *Archives of Neurology, 45,* 1200–1201.

Kurlan, R., Dermott, M. C., Deely, C., Como, P. G., Brower, B. S., Eapen, S., et al. (2001). Prevalence of tics in school children and association with placement in special education. *Neurology, 57,* 1383–1388.

Kurlan, R., Lichter, D., & Hewitt, D. (1989). Sensory tics in Tourette's syndrome. *Neurology, 39,* 731–734.

Kurlan, R., & Tourette's Syndrome Study Group. (2000). Treatment of attention-deficit-hyperactivity disorder in children with Tourette's syndrome (TACT trial). *Annals of Neurology, 48,* 953.

Kushner, H. I. (2000). A brief history of Tourette syndrome. *Revista Brasiliera de Psiquiatria, 22,* 76–79.

Kwak, C., Dat Vuong, K., & Jankovic, J. (2003). Premonitory sensory phenomenon in Tourette's syndrome. *Movement Disorders, 18,* 1530–1533.

Lapouse, R., & Monk, M. A. (1964). Behavior deviations in a representative sample of children: Variation between sex, age, race, social class, and family size. *American Journal of Orthopsychiatry, 34,* 436–446.

Leckman, J. F., Dolnansky, E. S., Hardin, M. T., Clubb, M., Walkup, J. T., Stevenson, J., et al. (1990). Perinatal factors in the expression of Tourette's syndrome: An exploratory study. *Journal of the American Academy of Child and Adolescent Psychiatry, 29,* 220–226.

Leckman, J. F., Goodman, W. K., Anderson, G. M., Riddle, M. A., Chappell, P. B., McSwiggan-Hardin, M. T., et al. (1995). Cerebrospinal fluid biogenic amines in obsessive compulsive disorder, Tourette's syndrome, and healthy controls. *Neuropsychopharmacology, 12,* 73–86.

Leckman, J. F., Grice, D. E., Barr, L. C., de Vries, A. L., Martin, C., Cohen, D. J., et al. (1994). Tic-related vs. non-tic-related obsessive compulsive disorder. *Anxiety, 1,* 208–215.

Leckman, J. F., Grice, D. E., Boardman, J., Zhang, H., Vitale, A., Bondi, C., et al. (1997). Symptoms of obsessive-compulsive disorder. *American Journal of Psychiatry, 154,* 911–917.

Leckman, J. F., Hardin, M. T., Riddle, M. A., Stevenson, J., Ort, S. I., & Cohen, D. J. (1991). Clonidine treatment of Gilles de la Tourette's syndrome. *Archives of General Psychiatry, 48,* 324–328.

Leckman, J. F., King, R. A., & Cohen, D. J. (1999). Tics and tic disorders. In J. F. Leckman & D. J. Cohen (Eds.), *Tourette's syndrome—Tics, obsessions, compulsions: Developmental psychopathology and clinical care* (pp. 23–42). New York: Wiley.

Leckman, J. F., Pauls, D. L., Zhang, H., Rosario-Campos, M. C., Katsovich, L., Kidd, K. K., et al. (2003). Obsessive-compulsive symptom dimensions in affected sibling pairs diagnosed with Gilles de la Tourette syndrome. *American Journal of Medical Genetics, 116B,* 60–68.

Leckman, J. F., & Peterson, B. S. (1993). The pathogenesis of Tourette's syndrome: Epigenetic factors active in early CNS development. *Biological Psychiatry, 34,* 425–427.

Leckman, J. F., Price, R. A., Walkup, J. T., Ort, S., Pauls, D. L., & Cohen, D. J. (1987). Nongenetic factors in Gilles de la Tourette's syndrome. *Archives of General Psychiatry, 44,* 100.

Leckman, J. F., Riddle, M. A., Hardin, M. T., Ort, S. I., Swartz, K. L., Stevenson, J., et al. (1989). The Yale Global Tic Severity Scale: Initial testing of a clinician-rated scale of tic severity. *Journal of the American Academy of Child and Adolescent Psychiatry, 28,* 566–573.

Leckman, J. F., & Scahill, L. (1990). Possible exacerbation of tics by androgenic steroids. *New England Journal of Medicine, 322,* 1674.

Leckman, J. F., Walker, D. E., & Cohen, D. J. (1993). Premonitory urges in Tourette's syndrome. *American Journal of Psychiatry, 150,* 98–102.

Leckman, J. F., Walker, D. E., Goodman, W. K., Pauls, D. L., & Cohen, D. J. (1994). "Just right" perceptions associated with compulsive behavior in Tourette's syndrome. *American Journal of Psychiatry, 151,* 675–680.

Leckman, J. F., Zhang, H., Alsobrook, J. P., & Pauls, D. L. (2001). Symptom dimensions in obsessive-compulsive disorder: Toward quantitative phenotypes. *American Journal of Medical Genetics, 105,* 28–30.

Leckman, J. F., Zhang, H., Vitale, A., Lahnin, F., Lynch, K., Bondi, C., et al. (1998). Course of tic severity in Tourette syndrome: The first two decades. *Pediatrics, 102,* 14–19.

Lees, A. J., Robertson, M., Trimble, M. R., & Murray, N. M. (1984). A clinical study of Gilles de la Tourette syndrome in the United Kingdom. *Journal of Neurology, Neurosurgery, and Psychiatry, 47,* 1–8.

Leonard, H. L., Lenane, M. C., Swedo, S. E., Rettew, D. C., Gershon, E. S., & Rapoport, J. L. (1992). Tics and Tourette's disorder: A 2- to 7-year follow-up of 54 obsessive-compulsive children. *American Journal of Psychiatry, 149,* 1244–1251.

Leppert, M., Peiffer, A., Snyder, B., van de Wetering, B. J. M., Filloux, F., Coon, H., et al. (1996). Two loci of interest in a family with Tourette syndrome. *American Journal of Human Genetics, Suppl. 59,* A225.

Leung, H. C., Skudlarski, P., Gatenby, J. C., Peterson, B. S., & Gore, J. C. (2000). An event-related functional MRI study of the Stroop color word interference task. *Cerebral Cortex, 10,* 552–560.

Lichter, D. G., Jackson, L. A., & Schachter, M. (1995). Clinical evidence of genomic imprinting in Tourette's syndrome. *Neurology, 45,* 924–928.

Lifton, R. P., Wilson, F. H., Choate, K. A., & Geller, D. S. (2002). Salt and blood pressure: New insight from human genetic studies. *Cold Spring Harbor Symposium on Quantitative Biology, 67,* 445–450.

Lim, S. H., Dinner, D. S., Pillay, P. K., Luders, H., Morris, H. H., Klem, G., et al. (1994). Functional anatomy of the human supplementary sensorimotor area: Results of extraoperative electrical stimulation. *Electroencephalography and Clinical Neurophysiology, 91,* 179–193.

Lombroso, P. J., Mack, G., Scahill, L., King, R. A., & Leckman, J. F. (1991). Exacerbation of Gilles de la Tourette's syndrome associated with thermal stress: A family study. *Neurology, 41,* 1984–1987.

Lucas, A. R., Kauffman, P. E., & Morris, E. M. (1967). Gilles de la Tourette's disease: A clinical study of fifteen cases. *Journal of the American Academy of Child Psychiatry, 6,* 700–722.

Maclean, P. D., & Delgado, J. M. R. (1953). Electrical and chemical stimulation of frontotemporal portion of limbic system in the waking animal. *Electroencephalography and Clinical Neurophysiology, 5,* 91–100.

Mahler, S. M., Luke, J. A., & Daltroff, W. (1945). Clinical and follow-up study of the tic syndrome in children. *American Journal of Orthopsychiatry, 15,* 631–647.

Malison, R. T., McDougle, C. J., van Dyck, C. H., Scahill, L., Baldwin, R. M., Seibyl, J. P., et al. (1995). [123I]beta-CIT SPECT imaging of striatal dopamine transporter binding in Tourette's disorder. *American Journal of Psychiatry, 152,* 1359–1361.

Marsh, R., Alexander, G. M., Packard, M. G., Zhu, H., Winegard, J. C., Quackenbush, G., et al. (2004). Habit learning in Tourette syndrome: A translational neuroscience approach to a developmental psychopathology. *Archives of General Psychiatry, 61,* 1259–1268.

Mataix-Cols, D., Rauch, S. L., Manzo, P. A., Jenike, M. A., & Baer, L. (1999). Use of factor-analyzed symptom dimensions to predict outcome with serotonin reuptake inhibitors and placebo in the treatment of obsessive-compulsive disorder. *American Journal of Psychiatry, 156,* 1409–1416.

Matarazzo, E. B. (1992). Tourette's syndrome treated with ACTH and prednisone: A report of two cases. *Journal of Child and Adolescent Psychopharmacology, 2,* 215–226.

Matsumoto, N., David, D. E., Johnson, E. W., Konecki, D., Burmester, J. K., Ledbetter, D. H., et al. (2000). Breakpoint sequences of an 1;8 translocation in a family with Gilles de la Tourette syndrome. *European Journal of Human Genetics, 8,* 875–883.

Matthews, M., Eustace, C., Grad, G., Pelcovitz, D., & Olson, M. (1985). A family systems perspective on Tourette's syndrome. *International Journal of Family Psychiatry, 6,* 53–66.

Merette, C., Brassard, A., Potvin, A., Bouvier, H., Rousseau, F., Emond, C., et al. (2000). Significant linkage for Tourette syndrome in a large French Canadian family. *American Journal of Human Genetics, 67,* 1008–1013.

Mesulam, M. M. (1986). Cocaine and Tourette's syndrome. *New England Journal of Medicine, 315,* 398.

Meyer, P., Bohnen, N. I., Minoshima, S., Koeppe, R. A., Wernette, K., Kilbourn, M. R., et al. (1999). Striatal presynaptic monoaminergic vesicles are not increased in Tourette's syndrome. *Neurology, 53,* 371–374.

Mink, J. W. (2001). Neurobiology of basal ganglia circuits in Tourette syndrome: Faulty inhibition of unwanted motor patterns? *Advances in Neurology, 85,* 113–122.

Moriarty, J., Costa, D. C., Schmitz, B., Trimble, M. R., Ell, P. J., & Robertson, M. M. (1995). Brain perfusion abnormalities in Gilles de la Tourette's syndrome. *British Journal of Psychiatry, 167,* 249–254.

Morshed, S. A., Parveen, S., Leckman, J. F., Mercadante, M. T., Bittencourt Kiss, M. H., et al. (2001). Antibodies against neural, nuclear, cytoskeletal, and streptococcal epitopes in children and adults with Tourette's syndrome, Sydenham's chorea, and autoimmune disorders. *Biological Psychiatry, 50,* 566–577. (Erratum published in December 15, 2001, *Biological Psychiatry, 50*(12), following p. 1009)

Murphy, K. R., Barkley, R. A., & Bush, T. (2001). Executive functioning and olfactory identification in young adults with attention deficit-hyperactivity disorder. *Neuropsychology, 15,* 211–220.

Murphy, T. K., Goodman, W. K., Fudge, M. W., Williams, R. C., Jr., Ayoub, E. M., Dalal, M., et al. (1997). B lymphocyte antigen D8/17: A peripheral marker for childhood-onset obsessive-compulsive disorder and Tourette's syndrome? *American Journal of Psychiatry, 154,* 402–407.

Nee, L. E., Polinsky, R. J., & Ebert, M. H. (1982). Tourette syndrome: Clinical and family studies. *Advances in Neurology, 35,* 291–295.

Neufeld, M. Y., Berger, Y., Chapman, J., & Korczyn, A. D. (1990). Routine and quantitative EEG analysis in Gilles de la Tourette's syndrome. *Neurology, 40,* 1837–1839.

Niehaus, D. J., Emsley, R. A., Brink, P., & Stein, D. J. (2000). Stereotypies: Prevalence and association with compulsive and impulsive symptoms in college students. *Psychopathology, 33,* 31–35.

Nolan, E. E., Sverd, J., Gadow, K. D., Sprafkin, J., & Ezor, S. N. (1996). Associated psychopathology in children with both ADHD and chronic tic disorder. *Journal of the American Academy of Child and Adolescent Psychiatry, 35,* 1622–1630.

Nomoto, F., & Machiyama, Y. (1990). An epidemiological study of tics. *Japanese Journal of Psychiatry and Neurology, 44,* 649–655.

Nothen, M. M., Hebebrand, J., Knapp, M., Hebebrand, K., Camps, A., von Gontard, A., et al. (1994). Association analysis of the dopamine D2 receptor gene in Tourette's syndrome using the haplotype relative risk method. *American Journal of Medical Genetics, 54,* 249–252.

Obeso, J. A., Rothwell, J. C., & Marsden, C. D. (1981). Simple tics in Gilles de la Tourette's syndrome are not prefaced by a normal premovement EEG potential. *Journal of Neurology, Neurosurgery, and Psychiatry, 44,* 735–738.

Packard, M. G., & Knowlton, B. J. (2002). Learning and memory functions of the basal ganglia. *Annual Review of Neuroscience, 25,* 563–593.

Pakstis, A. J., Heutink, P., Pauls, D. L., Kurlan, R., van de Wetering, B. J., Leckman, J. F., et al. (1991). Progress in the search for genetic linkage with Tourette syndrome: An exclusion map covering more than 50% of the autosomal genome. *American Journal of Human Genetics, 48,* 281–294.

Pappert, E. J., Goetz, C. G., Louis, E. D., Blasucci, L., & Leurgans, S. (2003). Objective assessments of longitudinal outcome in Gilles de la Tourette's syndrome. *Neurology, 61,* 936–940.

Parent, A., & Hazrati, L. (1995). Functional anatomy of the basal ganglia: Pt. I. The cortico-basal ganglia-thalamo-cortical loop. *Brain Research Reviews, 20,* 91–127.

Pasamanick, B., & Kawi, A. (1956). A study of the association of prenatal and perinatal factors in the development of tics in children. *Journal of Pediatrics, 48,* 596–602.

Paschou, P., Feng, Y., Pakstis, A. J., Speed, W. C., DeMille, M. M., Kidd, J. R., et al. (2004). Indications of linkage and association of Gilles de la Tourette syndrome in two independent family samples: 17q25 is a putative susceptibility region. *American Journal of Human Genetics, 75,* 545–560.

Pauls, D. L. (2003). An update on the genetics of Gilles de la Tourette syndrome. *Journal of Psychosomatic Research, 55,* 7–12.

Pauls, D. L., Alsobrook, J. P., II, Goodman, W., Rasmussen, S., & Leckman, J. F. (1995). A family study of obsessive-compulsive disorder. *American Journal of Psychiatry, 152,* 76–84.

Pauls, D. L., Hurst, C. R., Kruger, S. D., Leckman, J. F., Kidd, K. K., & Cohen, D. J. (1986). Gilles de la Tourette's syndrome and attention deficit disorder with hyperactivity: Evidence against a genetic relationship. *Archives of General Psychiatry, 43,* 1177–1179.

Pauls, D. L., & Leckman, J. F. (1986). The inheritance of Gilles de la Tourette's syndrome and associated behaviors: Evidence for autosomal dominant transmission. *New England Journal of Medicine, 315,* 993–997.

Pauls, D. L., Leckman, J. F., & Cohen, D. J. (1993). Familial relationship between Gilles de la Tourette's syndrome, attention deficit disorder, learning disabilities, speech disorders, and stuttering. *Journal of the American Academy of Child and Adolescent Psychiatry, 32,* 1044–1050.

Pauls, D. L., Leckman, J. F., Towbin, K. E., Zahner, G. E., & Cohen, D. J. (1986). A possible genetic relationship exists between Tourette's syndrome and obsessive-compulsive disorder. *Psychopharmacology Bulletin, 22,* 730–733.

Pauls, D. L., Pakstis, A. J., Kurlan, R., Kidd, K. K., Leckman, J. F., Cohen, D. J., et al. (1990). Segregation and linkage analyses of Tourette's syndrome and related disorders. *Journal of the American Academy of Child and Adolescent Psychiatry, 29,* 195–203.

Pauls, D. L., Raymond, C. L., Stevenson, J. M., & Leckman, J. F. (1991). A family study of Gilles de la Tourette syndrome. *American Journal of Human Genetics, 48,* 154–163.

Pauls, D. L., & Tourette Syndrome Association International Consortium on Genetics. (2001). Update on the genetics of Tourette syndrome. *Advances in Neurology, 85,* 281–293.

Pennington, B. F. (1991). *Diagnosing learning disorders.* New York: Guilford Press.

Peterson, B. S. (2003). Conceptual, methodological, and statistical challenges in brain imaging studies of developmentally based psychopathologies. *Developmental Psychopathology, 15,* 811–832.

Peterson, B. S., Bronen, R. A., & Duncan, C. C. (1996). Three cases of symptom change in Tourette's syndrome and obsessive-compulsive disorder associated with paediatric cerebral malignancies. *Journal of Neurology, Neurosurgery, and Psychiatry, 61,* 497–505.

Peterson, B. S., & Cohen, D. J. (1998). The treatment of Tourette's syndrome: Multimodal, developmental intervention. *Journal of Clinical Psychiatry, 59,* 62–72.

Peterson, B. S., Kane, M. J., Alexander, G. M., Lacadie, C., Skudlarski, P., Leung, H. C., et al. (2002). An event-related functional MRI study comparing interference effects in the Simon and Stroop tasks. *Cognitive Brain Research, 13,* 427–440.

Peterson, B. S., & Leckman, J. F. (1998). The temporal dynamics of tics in Gilles de la Tourette syndrome. *Biological Psychiatry, 44,* 1337–1348.

Peterson, B. S., Leckman, J. F., & Cohen, D. J. (1995). Tourette's Syndrome: A genetically predisposed and an environmentally specified developmental psychopathology. In D. Cicchetti & D. J. Cohen (Eds.), *Developmental Psychopathology* (pp. 213–242). New York: Wiley.

Peterson, B. S., Leckman, J. F., Scahill, L., Naftolin, F., Keefe, D., Charest, N. J., et al. (1992). Steroid hormones and CNS sexual dimorphisms modulate symptom expression in Tourette's syndrome. *Psychoneuroendocrinology, 17,* 553–563.

Peterson, B. S., Leckman, J. F., Scahill, L., Naftolin, F., Keefe, D., Charest, N. J., et al. (1994). Steroid hormones and Tourette's syndrome: Early experience with antiandrogen therapy. *Journal of Clinical Psychopharmacology, 14,* 131–135.

Peterson, B. S., Pine, D. S., Cohen, P., & Brook, J. S. (2001). Prospective, longitudinal study of tic, obsessive-compulsive, and attention-deficit/hyperactivity disorders in an epidemiological sample. *Journal of the American Academy of Child and Adolescent Psychiatry, 40,* 685–695.

Peterson, B. S., Skudlarski, P., Anderson, A. W., Zhang, H., Gatenby, J. C., Lacadie, C. M., et al. (1998). A functional magnetic resonance imaging study of tic suppression in Tourette syndrome. *Archives of General Psychiatry, 55,* 326–333.

Peterson, B. S., Staib, L., Scahill, L., Zhang, H., Anderson, C., Leckman, J. F., et al. (2001). Regional brain and ventricular volumes in Tourette syndrome. *Archives of General Psychiatry, 58,* 427–440.

Peterson, B. S., & Thomas, P. (2000). Functional brain imaging in Tourette's syndrome: What are we really imaging? In M. Ernst & J. Rumsey (Eds.), *Functional neuroimaging in child psychiatry* (pp. 242–265). Cambridge, UK: Cambridge University Press.

Peterson, B. S., Thomas, P., Kane, M. J., Scahill, L., Zhang, H., Bronen, R., et al. (2003). Basal ganglia volumes in patients with Gilles de la Tourette syndrome. *Archives of General Psychiatry, 60,* 415–424.

Peterson, B. S., Zhang, H., Anderson, G. M., & Leckman, J. F. (1998). A double-blind, placebo-controlled, crossover trial of an antiandrogen in the treatment of Tourette's syndrome. *Journal of Clinical Psychopharmacology, 18,* 324–331.

Plessen, K. J., Wentzel-Larsen, T., Hugdahl, K., Feineigle, P., Klein, J., Staib, L. H., et al. (2004). Altered interhemispheric connectivity in individuals with Tourette syndrome. *American Journal of Psychiatry, 161,* 2028–2037.

Pliszka, S. R. (2000). Patterns of psychiatric comorbidity with attention-deficit/hyperactivity disorder. *Child and Adolescent Psychiatric Clinics of North America, 9,* 525–540.

Pliszka, S. R. (2003). Psychiatric comorbidities in children with attention deficit hyperactivity disorder: Implications for management. *Paediatric Drugs, 5,* 741–750.

Price, R. A., Kidd, K. K., Cohen, D. J., Pauls, D. L., & Leckman, J. F. (1985). A twin study of Tourette syndrome. *Archives of General Psychiatry, 42,* 815–820.

Raffaele, R., Vecchio, I., Alvano, A., Proto, G., Nicoletti, G., & Rampello, L. (2004). Blink reflex abnormalities in Tourette syndrome. *Clinical Neurophysiology, 115,* 320–324.

Randolph, C., Hyde, T. M., Gold, J. M., Goldberg, T. E., & Weinberger, D. R. (1993). Tourette's syndrome in monozygotic twins: Relationship of tic severity to neuropsychological function. *Archives of Neurology, 50,* 725–728.

Rauch, S. L., Baer, L., Cosgrove, G. R., & Jenike, M. A. (1995). Neurosurgical treatment of Tourette's syndrome: A critical review. *Comprehensive Psychiatry, 36,* 141–156.

Ravizza, L., Barzega, G., Bellino, S., Bogetto, F., & Maina, G. (1995). Predictors of drug treatment response in obsessive-compulsive disorder. *Journal of Clinical Psychiatry, 56,* 368–373.

Richter, M. A., Summerfeldt, L. J., Antony, M. M., & Swinson, R. P. (2003). Obsessive-compulsive spectrum conditions in obsessive-compulsive disorder and other anxiety disorders. *Depression and Anxiety, 18,* 118–127.

Riddle, M. A., Rasmusson, A. M., Woods, S. W., & Hoffer, P. B. (1992). SPECT imaging of cerebral blood flow in Tourette syndrome. *Advances in Neurology, 58,* 207–211.

Riddle, M. A., Scahill, L., King, R., Hardin, M. T., Towbin, K. E., Ort, S. I., et al. (1990). Obsessive compulsive disorder in children and adolescents: Phenomenology and family history. *Journal of the American Academy of Child and Adolescent Psychiatry, 29,* 766–772.

Robertson, M. M. (1989). The Gilles de la Tourette syndrome: The current status. *British Journal of Psychiatry, 154,* 147–169.

Rosa, A. L., Jankovic, J., & Ashizawa, T. (2003). Screening for mutations in the MECP2 (Rett syndrome) gene in Gilles de la Tourette syndrome. *Archives of Neurology, 60,* 502–503.

Rosenberg, L. A., Brown, J., & Singer, H. S. (1995). Behavioral problems and severity of tics. *Journal of Clinical Psychology, 51,* 760–767.

Roth, R. M., Baribeau, J., Milovan, D. L., & O'Connor, K. (2004). Speed and accuracy on tests of executive function in obsessive-compulsive disorder. *Brain and Cognition, 54,* 263–265.

Rothenberger, A., Kostanecka, T., Kinkelbur, J., Cohrs, S., Woerner, W., & Hajak, G. (2001). Sleep and Tourette syndrome. *Advances in Neurology, 85,* 245–259.

Rucklidge, J. J., & Tannock, R. (2002). Neuropsychological profiles of adolescents with ADHD: Effects of reading difficulties and gender. *Journal of Child Psychology and Psychiatry and Allied Disciplines, 43,* 988.

Rutter, M., & Hemming, M. (1970). Individual items of deviant behavior: Their prevalence and clinical significance. In M. Rutter, J. Tizard, & K. Whitmore (Eds.), *Education, health and behavior* (pp. 202–232). London: Longman, Brown, Green, and Longmans.

Rutter, M., Yule, W., Berger, M., Yule, B., Morton, J., & Bagley, C. (1974). Children of West Indian immigrants: I. Rates of behavioral deviance and psychiatric disorder. *Journal of Child Psychology and Psychiatry, 15,* 241–262.

Sachdev, P. S., Chee, K. Y., & Aniss, A. M. (1997). The audiogenic startle reflex in Tourette's syndrome. *Biological Psychiatry, 41,* 796–803.

Santangelo, S. L., Pauls, D. L., Goldstein, J. M., Faraone, S. V., Tsuang, M. T., & Leckman, J. F. (1994). Tourette's syndrome: What are the influences of gender and comorbid obsessive-compulsive disorder? *Journal of the American Academy of Child and Adolescent Psychiatry, 33,* 795–804.

Scahill, L. D., Leckman, J. F., & Marek, K. L. (1995). Sensory phenomena in Tourette's syndrome. *Advances in Neurology, 65,* 273–280.

Scahill, L. D., Schwab-Stone, M., Merikangas, K. R., Leckman, J. F., Zhang, H., & Kasl, S. (1999). Psychosocial and clinical correlates of ADHD in a community sample of school-age children. *Journal of the American Academy of Child and Adolescent Psychiatry, 38,* 976–984.

Schoenian, S., Konig, I., Oertel, W., Remschmidt, H., Ziegler, A., Hebebrand, J., et al. (2003). HLA-DRB genotyping in Gilles de la Tourette patients and their parents. *American Journal of Medical Genetics, 119B,* 60–64.

Schuerholz, L. J., Baumgardner, T. L., Singer, H. S., Reiss, A. L., & Denckla, M. B. (1996). Neuropsychological status of children with Tourette's syndrome with and without attention deficit hyperactivity disorder. *Neurology, 46,* 958–965.

Schultz, R. T., Carter, A. S., Gladstone, M., Scahill, L., Leckman, J. F., Peterson, B. S., et al. (1998). Visual-motor integration functioning in children with Tourette syndrome. *Neuropsychology, 12,* 134–145.

Schultz, R. T., Carter, A. S., Scahill, L., & Leckman, J. F. (1998). Neuropsychological findings. In J. F. Leckman & D. J. Cohen (Eds.), *Tourette's syndrome—Tics, obsessions, compulsions: Developmental psychopathology and clinical care* (pp. 80–103). New York: Wiley.

Schwabe, M. J., & Konkol, R. J. (1992). Menstrual cycle-related fluctuations of tics in Tourette syndrome. *Pediatric Neurology, 8,* 43–46.

Selkoe, D. J. (2004). Cell biology of protein misfolding: The examples of Alzheimer's and Parkinson's diseases. *Nature Cell Biology, 6,* 1054–1061.

Shapiro, A. K., & Shapiro, E. S. (1992). Evaluation of the reported association of obsessive-compulsive symptoms or disorder with Tourette's disorder. *Comprehensive Psychiatry, 33,* 152–165.

Shapiro, A. K., Shapiro, E. S., Young, J. G., & Feinberg, T. E. (1988a). *Gilles de la Tourette's syndrome* (2nd ed.). New York: Raven Press.

Shapiro, A. K., Shapiro, E. S., Young, J. G., & Feinberg, T. E. (1988b). Signs, symptoms, and clinical course. In A. K. Shapiro, E. S. Shapiro, J. G. Young, & T. E. Feinberg (Eds.), *Gilles de la Tourette syndrome* (pp. 127–193). New York: Raven Press.

Shapiro, E., Shapiro, A. K., & Clarkin, J. (1974). Clinical psychological testing in Tourette's syndrome. *Journal of Personality Assessment, 38,* 464–478.

Shapiro, E., Shapiro, A. K., Fulop, G., Hubbard, M., Mandeli, J., Nordlie, J., et al. (1989). Controlled study of haloperidol, pimozide and placebo for the treatment of Gilles de la Tourette's syndrome. *Archives of General Psychiatry, 46,* 722–730.

Shucard, D. W., Benedict, R. H., Tekok-Kilic, A., & Lichter, D. G. (1997). Slowed reaction time during a continuous performance test in children with Tourette's syndrome. *Neuropsychology, 11,* 147–155.

Silverstein, M. S., Como, P. G., Palumbo, D. R., West, L. L., & Osborn, L. M. (1995). Multiple sources of attentional dysfunction in adults with Tourette's syndrome: Comparison with attention deficit-hyperactivity disorder. *Neuropsychology, 2,* 157–164.

Silvestri, R., Raffaele, M., De Domenico, P., Tisano, A., Mento, G., Casella, C., et al. (1995). Sleep features in Tourette's syndrome, neuroacanthocytosis and Huntington's chorea. *Neurophysiologie Clinique, 25,* 66–77.

Simonic, I., Gericke, G. S., Ott, J., & Weber, J. L. (1998). Identification of genetic markers associated with Gilles de la Tourette syndrome in an Afrikaner population. *American Journal of Human Genetics, 63,* 839–846.

Simonic, I., Nyholt, D. R., Gericke, G. S., Gordon, D., Matsumoto, N., Ledbetter, D. H., et al. (2001). Further evidence for linkage of Gilles de la Tourette syndrome (GTS) susceptibility loci on chromosomes 2p11, 8q22 and 11q23-24 in South African Afrikaners. *American Journal of Medical Genetics, 105,* 163–167.

Singer, C. (1997). Tourette syndrome: Coprolalia and other coprophenomena. *Neurologic Clinics, 15,* 299–308.

Singer, H. S., Giuliano, J. D., Hansen, B. H., Hallett, J. J., Laurino, J. P., Benson, M., et al. (1998). Antibodies against human putamen in children with Tourette syndrome. *Neurology, 50,* 1618–1624.

Singer, H. S., Loiselle, C. R., Lee, O., Minzer, K., Swedo, S., & Grus, F. H. (2004). Anti-basal ganglia antibodies in PANDAS. *Movement Disorders, 19,* 406–415.

Singer, H. S., & Walkup, J. T. (1991). Tourette syndrome and other tic disorders: Diagnosis, pathophysiology, and treatment. *Medicine, 70,* 15–32.

Singer, H. S., & Wendlandt, J. T. (2001). Neurochemistry and synaptic neurotransmission in Tourette syndrome. *Advances in Neurology, 85,* 163–178.

Singer, H. S., Wong, D. F., Brown, J. E., Brandt, J., Krafft, L., Shaya, E., et al. (1992). Positron emission tomography evaluation of dopamine D-2 receptors in adults with Tourette syndrome. *Advances in Neurology, 58,* 233–239.

Snider, L. A., Seligman, L. D., Ketchen, B. R., Levitt, S. J., Bates, L. R., Garvey, M. A., et al. (2002). Tics and problem behaviors in schoolchildren: Prevalence, characterization, and associations. *Pediatrics, 110,* 331–336.

Song, S., & Jung, Y. K. (2004). Alzheimer's disease meets the ubiquitin-proteasome system. *Trends in Molecular Medicine, 10,* 565–570.

Spencer, T. J., Biederman, J., Faraone, S., Mick, E., Coffey, B., Geller, D., et al. (2001). Impact of tic disorders on ADHD outcome across the life cycle: Findings from a large group of adults with and without ADHD. *American Journal of Psychiatry, 158,* 611–617.

Spencer, T. J., Biederman, J., Harding, M., O'Donnell, D., Wilens, T., Faraone, S., et al. (1998). Disentangling the overlap between Tourette's disorder and ADHD. *Journal of Child Psychology and Psychiatry and Allied Disciplines, 39,* 1037–1044.

Spencer, T. J., Biederman, J., Harding, M., Wilens, T., & Faraone, S. (1995). The relationship between tic disorders and Tourette's syndrome revisited. *Journal of the American Academy of Child and Adolescent Psychiatry, 34,* 1133–1139.

Spessot, A. L., Plessen, K. J., & Peterson, B. S. (2004). Neuroimaging of developmental psychopathologies: The importance of self-regulatory and neuroplastic processes in adolescence. *Annals of the New York Academy of Sciences, 1021,* 86–104.

Spielman, R., & Ewens, W. (1996). The TDT and other family-based tests for linkage disequilibrium and association. *American Journal of Human Genetics, 59,* 983–989.

Spitznagel, M. B., & Suhr, J. A. (2002). Executive function deficits associated with symptoms of schizotypy and obsessive-compulsive disorder. *Psychiatry Research, 110,* 151–163.

Squire, L. R., & Kandel, E. R. (1999). *Memory: From Mind to Molecules.* New York: Scientific American Library.

Squire, L. R., & Zola, S. M. (1996). Structure and function of declarative and nondeclarative memory systems. *Proceedings of the National Academy of Sciences, USA, 93,* 13515–13522.

Stamenkovic, M., Schindler, S. D., Asenbaum, S., Neumeister, A., Willeit, M., Willinger, U., et al. (2001). No change in striatal dopamine re-uptake site density in psychotropic drug naive and in currently treated Tourette's disorder patients: A [(123)I]-beta-CIT SPECT study. *European Neuropsychopharmacology, 11,* 69–74.

State, M. W., Greally, J. M., Cuker, A., Bowers, P. N., Henegariu, O., Morgan, T. M., et al. (2003). Epigenetic abnormalities associated with a chromosome 18(q21-q22) inversion and a Gilles de la Tourette syndrome phenotype. *Proceedings of the National Academy of Sciences, USA, 100,* 4684–4689.

Stell, R., Thickbroom, G. W., & Mastaglia, F. L. (1995). The audiogenic startle response in Tourette's syndrome. *Movement Disorders, 10,* 723–730.

Stokes, A., Bawden, H. N., Camfield, P. R., Backman, J. E., & Dooley, J. M. (1991). Peer problems in Tourette's disorder. *Pediatrics, 87,* 936–942.

Sukhodolsky, D. G., Scahill, L., Zhang, H., Peterson, B. S., King, R. A., Lombroso, P. J., et al. (2003). Disruptive behavior in children with Tourette's syndrome: Association with ADHD comorbidity, tic severity, and functional impairment. *Journal of the American Academy of Child and Adolescent Psychiatry, 42,* 98–105.

Summerfeldt, L. J., Richter, M. A., Antony, M. M., & Swinson, R. P. (1999). Symptom structure in obsessive-compulsive disorder: A confirmatory factor-analytic study. *Behaviour Research and Therapy, 37,* 297–311.

Sutherland, R. J., Kolb, B., Schoel, W. M., Whishaw, I. Q., & Davies, D. (1982). Neuropsychological assessment of children and adults with Tourette syndrome: A comparison with learning disabilities and Schizophrenia. *Advances in Neurology, 35,* 311–322.

Swedo, S. E., Leonard, H. L., Garvey, M., Mittleman, B., Allen, A. J., Perlmutter, S., et al. (1998). Pediatric autoimmune neuropsychiatric disorders associated with streptococcal infections: Clinical description of the first 50 cases. *American Journal of Psychiatry, 155,* 264–271.

Swedo, S. E., Leonard, H. L., Mittleman, B. B., Allen, A. J., Rapoport, J. L., Dow, S. P., et al. (1997). Identification of children with pediatric autoimmune neuropsychiatric disorders associated with streptococcal infections by a marker associated with rheumatic fever. *American Journal of Psychiatry, 154,* 110–112.

Swedo, S. E., Rapoport, J. L., Leonard, H., Lenane, M., & Cheslow, D. (1989). Obsessive-compulsive disorder in children and adolescents: Clinical phenomenology of 70 consecutive cases. *Archives of General Psychiatry, 46,* 335–341.

Swerdlow, N. R., Karban, B., Ploum, Y., Sharp, R., Geyer, M. A., & Eastvold, A. (2001). Tactile prepuff inhibition of startle in children with Tourette's syndrome: In search of an "fMRI-friendly" startle paradigm. *Biological Psychiatry, 50,* 578–585.

Syrigou-Papavasiliou, A., Verma, N. P., & LeWitt, P. A. (1988). Sensory evoked responses in Tourette syndrome. *Clinical Electroencephalography, 19,* 108–110.

Tasker, R. R., & Dostrovsky, J. O. (1993). What goes on in the motor thalamus? *Stereotactic and Functional Neurosurgery, 60,* 121–126.

Terwilliger, J. D., & Ott, J. (1992). A haplotype-based "haplotype relative risk" approach to detecting allelic associations. *Human Heredity, 42,* 337–346.

Thompson, M., Comings, D. E., Feder, L., George, S. R., & O'Dowd, B. F. (1998). Mutation screening of the dopamine D1 receptor gene in Tourette's syndrome and alcohol dependent patients. *American Journal of Medical Genetics, 81,* 241–244.

Tourette, G. (1885). Etude sur une affection nerveuse caracterisée par de l'incoordination motrice accompagnée d'echolalie et de copralalie. *Archives of Neurology, Paris, 9,* 19–42, 158–200.

Tourette Syndrome Association International Consortium for Genetics. (1999). A complete genome screen in sib pairs affected by Gilles de la Tourette syndrome: The Tourette Syndrome Association International Consortium for Genetics. *American Journal of Human Genetics, 65,* 1428–1436.

Tourette's Syndrome Study Group. (2002). Treatment of ADHD in children with tics: A randomized controlled trial. *Neurology, 58,* 527–536.

Trifiletti, R. R. (1998). TS83: Candidate target brain autoantigen in Tourette syndrome and OCD. *Annals of Neurology, 44,* 561.

Trifiletti, R. R., Altemus, M., Packard, A. M., Bandele, A. N., & Zabriskie, J. B. (1998). Changes in antineuronal antibodies following conventional and immunosuppressive therapy for Tourette's syndrome and obsessive-compulsive disorder. *Annals of Neurology, 44,* 561.

Tulen, J. H., Azzolini, M., de Vries, J. A., Groeneveld, W. H., Passchier, J., & van De Wetering, B. J. (1999). Quantitative study of spontaneous eye blinks and eye tics in Gilles de la Tourette's syndrome. *Journal of Neurology, Neurosurgery, and Psychiatry, 67,* 800–802.

Turjanski, N., Sawle, G. V., Playford, E. D., Weeks, R., Lammerstma, A. A., Lees, A. J., et al. (1994). PET studies of the presynaptic and postsynaptic dopaminergic system in Tourette's syndrome. *Journal of Neurology, Neurosurgery, and Psychiatry, 57,* 688–692.

Vandenbergh, D. J., Thompson, M. D., Cook, E. H., Bendahhou, E., Nguyen, T., Krasowski, M. D., et al. (2000). Human dopamine transporter gene: Coding region conservation among normal, Tourette's disorder, alcohol dependence and attention-deficit hyperactivity disorder populations. *Molecular Psychiatry, 5,* 283–292.

van de Wetering, B. J., & Heutink, P. (1993). The genetics of the Gilles de la Tourette syndrome: A review. *Journal of Laboratory and Clinical Medicine, 121,* 638–645.

van Woerkom, T. C., Fortgens, C., van de Wetering, B. J., & Martens, C. M. (1988). Contingent negative variation in adults with Gilles de la Tourette syndrome. *Journal of Neurology, Neurosurgery, and Psychiatry, 51,* 630–634.

Verhulst, F. C., van der Ende, J., Ferdinand, R. F., & Kasius, M. C. (1997). The prevalence of DSM-III-R diagnoses in a national sample of Dutch adolescents. *Archives of General Psychiatry, 54,* 329–336.

Volkmar, F. R., Leckman, J. F., Detlor, J., Harcherik, D. F., Prichard, J. W., Shaywitz, B. A., et al. (1984). EEG abnormalities in Tourette's syndrome. *Journal of the American Academy of Child Psychiatry, 23,* 352–353.

Walkup, J. T. (2001). Epigenetic and environmental risk factors in Tourette syndrome. *Advances in Neurology, 85,* 273–279.

Walkup, J. T., LaBuda, M. C., Singer, H. S., Brown, J., Riddle, M. A., & Hurko, O. (1996). Family study and segregation analysis of Tourette syndrome: Evidence for a mixed model of inheritance. *American Journal of Human Genetics, 59,* 684–693.

Walkup, J. T., Leckman, J. F., Price, R. A., Hardin, M., Ort, S. I., & Cohen, D. J. (1988). The relationship between obsessive-compulsive disorder and Tourette's syndrome: A twin study. *Psychopharmacology Bulletin, 24,* 375–379.

Wilens, T., Pelham, W., Stein, M., Conners, C. K., Abikoff, H., Atkins, M., et al. (2003). ADHD treatment with once-daily OROS methylphenidate: Interim 12-month results from a long-term open-label study. *Journal of the American Academy of Child and Adolescent Psychiatry, 42,* 424–433.

Wilquet, V., & De Strooper, B. (2004). Amyloid-beta precursor protein processing in neurodegeneration. *Current Opinion in Neurobiology, 14,* 582–588.

Wolf, S. S., Jones, D. W., Knable, M. B., Gorey, J. G., Lee, K. S., Hyde, T. M., et al. (1996). Tourette syndrome: Prediction of phenotypic variation in monozygotic twins by caudate nucleus D2 receptor binding. *Science, 273,* 1225–1227.

Wong, D. F., Singer, H. S., Brandt, J., Shaya, E., Chen, C., Brown, J., et al. (1997). D2-like dopamine receptor density in Tourette syndrome measured by PET. *Journal of Nuclear Medicine, 38,* 1243–1247.

Xu, C., Ozbay, F., Wigg, K., Shulman, R., Tahir, E., Yazgan, Y., et al. (2003). Evaluation of the genes for the adrenergic receptors alpha 2A and alpha 1C and Gilles de la Tourette syndrome. *American Journal of Medical Genetics, 119B,* 54–59.

Yeates, K. O., & Bornstein, R. A. (1994). Attention deficit disorder and neuropsychological functioning in children with Tourette's syndrome. *Neuropsychology, 8,* 65–74.

Zhang, H., Leckman, J. F., Pauls, D. L., Tsai, C. P., Kidd, K. K., Campos, M. R., et al. (2002). Genomewide scan of hoarding in sib pairs in which both sibs have Gilles de la Tourette syndrome. *American Journal of Human Genetics, 70,* 896–904.

CHAPTER 12

Social Anxiety and Emotion Regulation: A Model for Developmental Psychopathology Perspectives on Anxiety Disorders

ERIN B. MCCLURE and DANIEL S. PINE

Anxiety disorders, though widely prevalent throughout development, have been relatively understudied until the past few decades. Although they are commonly perceived as less severe than other forms of psychopathology, recent research has shown that anxiety disorders are associated with a variety of adverse outcomes, including school dropout, development of other psychiatric disorders such as Major Depression, and suicide (Katzelnick et al., 2001; Pine, Cohen, Gurley, Brook, & Ma, 1998; Stein & Kean, 2000). Recent research demonstrates that the majority of adults who suffer from a mood or anxiety disorder will have developed the initial signs of their illness during childhood or adolescence, manifest as an anxiety disorder (Costello et al., 2002; Pine, Cohen, Cohen, & Brook, 1999; Pine, Cohen, & Brook, 2001; Pine et al., 1998). Anxiety disorders also exact a large financial toll on society; they are associated with sharply elevated medical costs and uti-

lization rates (Hunkeler, Spector, Fireman, Rice, & Weisner, 2003; Martin & Leslie, 2003), as well as decreased productivity at work (Dewa & Lin, 2000; Kessler & Frank, 1997). Finally, anxiety disorders are severely distressing and impairing for children (R. G. Klein & Pine, 2002; Langley, Bergman, McCracken, & Piacentini, 2004). Understanding how anxiety disorders emerge and evolve across the course of development, as well as how these disorders relate to normal manifestations of anxiety, is thus of critical importance.

For the current review of the literature on childhood anxiety disorders, we draw from a developmental psychopathology perspective that emphasizes several core tenets (Cicchetti & Cohen, 1995). Central among these is the assumption that multiple factors interact in a dynamic, transactional fashion to affect how a disorder emerges. Not only may a given etiological factor produce any of several different effects depending on the system or context in which it operates (principle of multifinality), but a wide range of factors may lead to similar outcomes (principle of equifinality). Thus, the appearance of an anxiety disorder at a given point in development depends on the evolving inter-

Section on Development and Affective Neuroscience, Mood and Anxiety Disorders Program, National Institute of Mental Health, National Institutes of Health, Department of Health and Human Services.

play among vulnerabilities and protective factors for a particular child.

The developmental psychopathology perspective also assumes that normal and deviant development must be studied in concert. This assumption is predicated on the idea that an accurate understanding of dysfunction necessitates a comparable understanding of normal or successfully adaptive developmental paths. Anxiety, for instance, is an integral part of human existence throughout the life span; only under some circumstances does it manifest in a dysfunctional way. It is therefore critical to describe normative experiences of anxiety if pathological manifestations are to be identified and studied.

An additional core tenet of the developmental psychopathology perspective informing this chapter is that the role of development must be considered in the emergence of a disorder. Symptoms vary in their meaning and import at different points in development. Fear of separation from a parent, for instance, is normative in a toddler but potentially pathological in an older child.

This review of recent perspectives on childhood anxiety disorders is divided into three sections. First, we define relevant terms and review available literature on classification of childhood anxiety disorders. Specifically, we examine data regarding commonalities and differences among the anxiety disorders as they present in juveniles and in adults. In the second section, we review in more detail the data on one childhood anxiety disorder: Social Phobia or Social Anxiety Disorder. Available data on longitudinal outcome, family history, and treatment suggest clear distinctions among the anxiety disorders, with Social Anxiety Disorder, Posttraumatic Stress Disorder (PTSD), and Obsessive-Compulsive Disorder (OCD) showing discrete profiles. Full examination of each of these disorders, however, is beyond the scope of this chapter. We focus specifically on Social Anxiety Disorder due to the fact that research on this disorder has increased recently from clinical psychopathology, cognitive neuroscience, and developmental psychology perspectives. Social Anxiety Disorder therefore provides an excellent model for integrating these viewpoints, especially insofar as they have each grappled with the constructs of emotion and emotion regulation. Third, we summarize recent advances in basic neuroscience that relate to Social Anxiety Disorder and emotion regulation. Much like research in developmental psychology and psychopathology, these advances in neuroscience suggest that fear states might be best conceptualized as a family of distinct but related entities. Evidence regarding both shared and discrete aspects of various fear states is reviewed.

DEFINITION OF TERMS

Our aim is to integrate recent insights from several related but diverse fields, including developmental psychology, psychiatry, cognitive neuroscience, and epidemiology, under the rubric of developmental psychopathology. Such an integrative effort is destined to fail before it begins unless a common terminology is established that bridges all of the disciplines of interest. Hence, we begin by clarifying terms. We recognize that building a common lexicon requires simplifying key concepts in ways that may obscure nuances recognized in one field or another. However, in the interest of uniting multiple disciplines, we consider it more important to establish a common core language than to elucidate subtle differences.

We use the term *emotion* to refer to a brain state associated with a reward or a punishment. Changes in such brain states necessarily are reflected both in measures of neurophysiology and in measures of information processing; they can be, but do not have to be, reflected in measures of subjectively reported experience. As a result, we use *emotion* to apply to reward- or punishment-linked brain states and associated patterns of physiological response or information processing. We do not use the term to describe subjective experience. The term *reward* refers to any stimulus that an animal or a human will extend effort to procure, whereas the term *punishment* refers to any stimulus that an animal or human will extend effort to avoid (Rolls, 1999).

Consistent with Damasio (2001; Damasio et al., 2000), we use the terms *feeling* and *emotion* to refer to different constructs. We restrict our use *feeling* to the subjectively experienced, reliably describable state associated with the occurrence of an emotion. Changes in feelings represent core aspects of psychiatric disorders as they are currently conceptualized in the standard nosology of the *Diagnostic and Statistical Manual of Mental Disorders* (*DSM*). Many diagnostic criteria rest on subjectively reported changes in emotional states or behaviors; very few rely on objective measures of behavior; none rely on direct measures of changes in brain states.

This focus on feelings in current understandings of most psychiatric diagnoses makes it difficult to conduct translational work that integrates research across human and nonhuman species in an effort to better understand mental disorders. In particular, subjectively experienced states are central to our definition of feeling. Yet, the degree to which various nonhuman organisms experience feelings is unclear, even though there is striking continuity among many mammalian species in terms of experienced emotion (Davis & Whalen, 2001; LeDoux, 1994, 1998, 2000).

Therefore, truly translational studies must grapple with the interface between feelings and emotions, an interface that remains imprecisely specified across species.

In addition to distinguishing between emotions and feelings, we consider fear and anxiety to represent different constructs. The term *fear* refers to both the emotion and the feeling state that humans experience when they directly encounter stimuli that they perceive as threatening or as capable of producing harm and that elicit avoidance. Like fear, the term *anxiety* applies to both an emotion and a feeling state experienced by humans. The two constructs involve similar changes in behavior, cognition, and physiology but unlike fear, anxiety occurs in the absence of overt threat or punishment. As defined, anxiety does not necessarily connote a pathological state. We discuss the distinction between *normal* and *pathological* anxiety states when we review childhood anxiety disorders and their classification.

The current chapter discusses anxiety in the context of research on emotion regulation, a construct that requires precise and careful definition. The term *emotion regulation* has been used to describe diverse clinical and psychological phenomena. Consistent with Thompson (1994, pp. 27–28), we adopt a narrow definition, restricting our use of the term to describe "processes responsible for monitoring, evaluating, and modifying emotional reactions . . . to accomplish one's goals." Given our emphasis on the distinction between emotions and feelings, perhaps a parallel focus on feeling regulation is warranted. For the sake of simplicity, our use of *emotion regulation* encompasses both processes that regulate emotions and processes that regulate feelings, as the two are inextricably linked.

When applied to research on anxiety, this narrow definition of emotion regulation inherently encompasses two related constructs. The first consists of the stimuli and circumstances that can elicit fear and/or anxiety. The second consists of the behavioral, cognitive, and neural processes that are engaged in the service of monitoring, evaluating, and modifying the emotional reaction of fear or anxiety that a stimulus elicits. In many areas of developmental psychopathology, mental disorders have been conceptualized as disorders of emotion regulation. Using our definitions, this view would suggest that pathology lies less in the circumstances that elicit emotion or the magnitude of an initial emotional reaction and more in the degree to which processes can be engaged to regulate this reaction once it emerges.

Davidson (1998) provides a complementary view to this perspective on emotion regulation with a model that emphasizes "affective chronometry," or the temporal dynamics involved in the processing of emotionally evocative stimuli. In particular, he distinguishes between processes engaged as an affective reaction rises to its peak and processes engaged as the reaction subsides. According to this perspective, it may be arbitrary to make conceptual distinctions between emotional reactions and emotional regulation. Instead, these two constructs may represent temporally distinct phases in an individual's response to an emotional stimulus. Different forms of pathology, Davidson suggests, may thus relate to different patterns of disruption in the temporal sequence of emotional responding. Whereas some disorders may relate to perturbations that occur early in the course of a response, others may relate to perturbations that are evident later, during the processing of emotional stimuli.

Different theoretical perspectives provide various hypotheses linking abnormalities in either emotional reactions or emotion regulation, as they are measured in the laboratory, to developmental psychopathologies. As of this writing, these remain novel, but largely untested, hypotheses. This caveat applies, in particular, to current research on anxiety disorders.

CLASSIFICATION OF CHILDHOOD ANXIETY DISORDERS

The fourth edition of the *DSM* (*DSM-IV*; American Psychiatric Association, 1994) recognizes nine distinct anxiety disorders: Separation Anxiety Disorder (SAD), Social Phobia, Generalized Anxiety Disorder (GAD), Specific Phobia, PTSD, Acute Stress Disorder, Panic Disorder, and OCD. These anxiety disorders, with the exception of SAD, are all diagnosed using similar criteria for children, adolescents, and adults. By definition, SAD must begin before adulthood according to *DSM-IV*. In addition, fewer symptoms must be evident in juveniles than in adults to meet criteria for GAD. The strong parallels in diagnostic criteria for individuals at different developmental stages in *DSM-IV* represent a change from earlier versions of the *DSM*. This change reflects the *DSM-IV* nosological convention of using identical diagnostic criteria across development unless there are strong data that support using an alternative scheme.

For each of the nine anxiety disorders, as with virtually all other mental conditions in *DSM-IV*, individuals must exhibit a specific set of symptoms and show signs of either impairment or "significant distress." The latter requirement has been called the "impairment/distress" criterion. Beginning with revisions in *DSM-III* in 1980 (American Psychiatric Association, 1980), recent conceptualizations of mental illnesses have increasingly emphasized such impairment or distress criteria to differentiate normal fluctuations in psychiatric symptoms from categorically distinct disorders. At the conceptual level, the impairment/distress criteria facilitate relatively clear distinctions between normal and abnormal levels of symptomatology. However, in practice, it is easier to distinguish normal from abnormal levels of symptoms in some conditions than in others. For example, some conditions, such as pervasive developmental disorders and psychosis, typically present with intense or severe symptoms, such as frank delusions, that are rarely seen as normal in any context. Such conditions are also usually associated with marked impairment. Distinguishing these conditions from normality is therefore relatively easy. In contrast, distinguishing normal but slightly elevated levels of anxiety from an anxiety disorder can be difficult, particularly in the absence of specific functional impairment criteria (Beidel, Silverman, & Hammond-Laurence, 1996). This difficulty is compounded by the fact that diagnostic decisions in anxiety disorders must often be made against the background of normative developmental changes in behavior. For example, marked distress associated with separation from a parent might be considered normal in a preschooler but abnormal in a child only a few years older. The developmental psychopathology perspective's emphasis on considering normal and deviant processes in conjunction is thus particularly appropriate to the study of anxiety disorders.

The subtlety of the distress/impairment threshold for anxiety disorders complicates not only the identification of pathology in individuals, but also the determination of population-level prevalence rates. Studies that set different impairment thresholds tend to find dramatically different prevalence rates for anxiety disorders. In contrast, the threshold for impairment has a much smaller influence on rates for other psychiatric conditions, such as depression and Conduct Disorder (Costello, Mustillo, Erkanli, Keeler, & Angold, 2003; Shaffer et al., 1996).

The challenges associated with differentiating normal from abnormal anxiety illustrate a basic problem with current methods for diagnosing mental disorders. Namely, identification and categorization of most psychopathology depends exclusively on clinical evaluation. Alternative, more objective approaches, such as assessments of physiology, genetics, or brain function, are used only for the diagnosis of mental disorders that result from underlying nonpsychiatric medical illnesses. In light of this limited method of diagnosis, current definitions of most mental disorders must be regarded as preliminary. As knowledge of pathophysiology advances, the criteria we use to distinguish health from disease and normal from abnormal anxiety may change. Moreover, some psychiatric conditions, including certain anxiety disorders, may eventually be recognized as extremes on continua with normality, just as some forms of hypertension are thought to represent the extreme end of the blood pressure continuum. In contrast, other psychiatric conditions such as the psychoses, may come to be recognized as categorically distinct from normality, just as a fractured bone differs categorically from a healthy bone.

The nine anxiety disorders in *DSM-IV* are broadly related, in that anxiety symptoms of some sort constitute their central features. However, they do not form a neatly unified group. In general, five sets of standards have been used to distinguish among the anxiety disorders, although relatively few data are available that use these criteria to validate specific anxiety disorders in children and adolescents. First, *DSM-IV* defines these conditions as distinct by setting forth different sets of diagnostic criteria for each disorder. These criterion sets identify symptoms that most frequently cluster in patients with one or another condition. Second, the specific longitudinal trajectory and associated pattern of comorbidity for each anxiety disorder mark the individual conditions as distinct. Third, studies delineate unique patterns of aggregation within families for different anxiety disorders and associated conditions. Fourth, distinct anxiety disorders have been associated with specific risk factors or perturbations in biological systems reflective of underlying pathophysiology. Finally, for some adult anxiety disorders, treatment studies identify unique response patterns to psychotherapeutic or psychopharmacologic interventions. Table 12.1 summarizes some of the key factors from this perspective that distinguish among the anxiety disorders.

Within the pediatric anxiety disorders, probably the strongest evidence for specificity derives from studies of OCD, which is characterized by recurrent, time-consuming, and impairing compulsions and/or obsessions. With respect to longitudinal trajectory and associated comorbidity, OCD exhibits relatively strong cross-sectional and longitudinal associations with disorders of impulse control, including tic disorders and Attention-Deficit/Hyperactivity Disorder (ADHD; Grados et al., 2001; Peterson, Pine, Cohen, & Brook, 2001). Similarly, OCD that occurs early in development predicts an increased risk for OCD either later in adolescence or during adulthood (Peterson et al., 2001). Family-genetic studies show similar patterns of co-aggregation, with associations among OCD, tics, and ADHD emerging frequently within families (Pauls, Also-brook, Goodman, Rasmussen, & Leckman, 1995; Pauls,

TABLE 12.1   Distinctions among the Anxiety Disorders

	OCD[a]	PTSD[b]	Social Anxiety Disorder	Separation Anxiety Disorder/(Panic)	GAD[c]
Symptoms	Obsessions and/or compulsions	Reexperiencing, arousal, and avoidance associated with trauma	Anxiety in social or performance situations	Anxiety regarding separation from attachment figures	Persistent anxiety and worry across multiple areas
Course/ comorbidity	Associated with ADHD[d] and tic disorders	Associated with a wide range of disorders (MDD,[e] disruptive behavior disorders, etc.)	Relatively restricted comorbidity and risk profile	Associated with Panic Disorder	Associated with MDD[e] and a range of anxiety disorders
Familiality	Associated with ADHDd and tic disorders	Associated with a wide range of disorders (MDD,[e] disruptive behavior disorders, etc.)	Relatively restricted comorbidity and risk profile	Associated with Panic Disorder and MDD[e]	Associated with MDD[e]
Biology	Basal ganglia dysfunction	HPA[f] axis dysfunction	Possible amygdala dysfunction in the context of socially threatening stimuli	Respiratory dysfunction	?
Treatment	SSRI[g]	SSRI[g]	MAOI,[h] SSRI[g]	TCA,[i] SSRI,[g] MAOI[h]	TCA,[i] SSRI,[g] MAOI[h]

Notes: [a]Obsessive-Compulsive Disorder, [b]Posttraumatic Stress Disorder, [c]Generalized Anxiety Disorder, [d]Attention-Deficit/Hyperactivity Disorder, [e]Major Depressive Disorder, [f]hypothalamic-pituitary-adrenal, [g]selective serotonin reuptake inhibitor, [h]monamine oxidase inhibitor, [i]tricyclic antidepressant.

Leckman, Towbin, Zahner, & Cohen, 1986; Peterson et al., 2001). Such patterns of comorbidity are thought to reflect dysfunction in a common neural circuit encompassing the prefrontal cortex, striatum, and thalamus, forming so-called cortico-striato-thalamo-cortical (CSTC) loops. In some cases, the associations among OCD, tics, and ADHD have been related to streptococcal infection (Swedo et al., 1998), which is thought to disrupt functional aspects of CSTC circuitry. In general, these findings on comorbidity patterns, familial aggregation, and pathophysiology are specific to OCD and related conditions, distinguishing them from other anxiety disorders.

Although the evidence of specificity is not as strong as in OCD, relatively consistent findings also differentiate PTSD and Acute Stress Disorder (ASD) from other anxiety disorders. First, both conditions are unique in the *DSM,* in that a specific causal factor, in the form of a frightening event or stressor, is explicitly tied to the onset of both disorders. The pattern of associated symptoms and comorbidities is also distinctive in PTSD, in that they are highly influenced by the context of the stressor. For example, PTSD can develop following an isolated traumatic event that occurs against a background of relatively low stress, or it may develop following a prolonged period of multiple stressors and traumas. Not only are these conditions associated with high levels of anxiety, arousal, and avoidance, but they also typically involve reexperiencing and dissociation symptoms that are not associated with other anxiety disorders. This has led to some debate as to whether the

conditions might be better conceptualized as dissociative disorders, mood disorders, or in their own category as stress-related disorders (Brett, 1997; G. M. Sullivan & Gorman, 2002).

Patterns of comorbidity also tend to differ between traumatized children, who often exhibit signs of dysfunction in multiple domains, and children with other anxiety disorders, whose dysfunction is relatively circumscribed. Not only do traumatized children show symptoms of PTSD or ASD, but they also frequently exhibit symptoms of *DSM-IV* behavior disorders and mood disorders (Ackerman, Newton, McPherson, Jones, & Dykman, 1998).

Relatively few studies examine longitudinal outcomes or familial aggregation in childhood PTSD. Nevertheless, some data do demonstrate associations between PTSD in children and signs of stress-related psychopathology in their parents (Yehuda, Halligan, & Bierer, 2001; Yehuda, Halligan, & Grossman, 2001). Similarly, relatively few studies differentiate aspects of risk or pathophysiology associated with PTSD from those found in other anxiety states that arise following trauma. Nevertheless, particularly in adults, evidence suggests that PTSD is characterized by a specific pattern of dysfunction in the hypothalamic-pituitary-adrenal axis and associated neural structures, including the hippocampus and amygdala (Bremner, Narayan, et al., 1999; Bremner, Staib, et al., 1999; Yehuda, 2001, 2002). In general, data distinguishing childhood PTSD from other childhood conditions have been weaker than those in adult PTSD, though some findings are consistent in children and adults (Pine, 2003). Finally, optimal psychotherapeutic treatment of PTSD also differs from that for other anxiety disorders, in that it often involves a heavy focus on traumatic events (J. A. Cohen, 2003).

Investigators have adopted conflicting conceptualizations of SAD during the past few decades. For many years, this condition has been viewed as strongly related to Panic Disorder. Panic Disorder is characterized by sudden, unexpected paroxysms of extreme anxiety or terror. Although panic attacks can occur at any point during the life span, the onset of spontaneous, recurrent panic attacks rarely occurs before adolescence. In severe cases, the disorder typically follows a developmental course in which isolated, spontaneous panic attacks begin during adolescence and are followed later in life by multiple, recurrent panic attacks that meet criteria for Panic Disorder (R. G. Klein & Pine, 2002; Pine, 1999; Pine et al., 1998). Agoraphobia, or anxiety about being in places or circumstances from which escape would be difficult or embarrassing in the case of a panic attack, is a common ensuing complication. The conceptualization of SAD as related to Panic Disorder derives largely from clinical data in adults with Panic Disorder, who report high rates of SAD during childhood (Bandelow et al., 2001; Silove et al., 1995). Such data are vulnerable to various types of biases, including referral biases and retrospective distortions. In general, data from family and longitudinal studies provide some support for the view that SAD relates to Panic Disorder; however, the data are not especially compelling (R. G. Klein & Pine, 2002; Pine, 1999; Pine et al., 1998). Much more supportive findings have emerged, however, in studies of respiratory function, where both panic attacks and SAD have been linked to similar perturbations in respiration (Goodwin & Pine, 2002; Johnson et al., 2000; Pine, Klein, et al., 2000). An alternative conceptualization of SAD identifies the disorder as a nonspecific response to various forms of distress. Consistent with this perspective, high rates of SAD are found in offspring of parents with Major Depression (Biederman, Faraone, et al., 2001), in individuals who have experienced traumatic stress (Goenjian et al., 1995; Pine & Cohen, 2002), and even in the context of streptococcal infection (Swedo et al., 1998).

Finally, Generalized Anxiety Disorder is characterized by a recurrent pattern of worries and anxiety about a range of topics. Although comorbidity is high for all pediatric anxiety disorders, GAD virtually always presents with another concurrent anxiety disorder (R. G. Klein & Pine, 2002; Research Unit on Pediatric Psychopharmacology [RUPP], 2001). This has led to considerable debate about

the validity of the diagnosis, with some contending that GAD represents a complicating factor in other anxiety disorders rather than an independent disorder (R. G. Klein & Pine, 2002).

The diagnosis of GAD changed with the revision to *DSM-IV*. Prior to this revision, children who presented with a pattern of recurrent worries were diagnosed with Overanxious Disorder and adults with similar symptoms were diagnosed with GAD. However, with the publication of *DSM-IV,* the GAD diagnosis subsumed Overanxious Disorder so that age could be eliminated as a defining diagnostic criterion (Shaffer, 1996). Some debate continues concerning the advisability of this change, reflecting the fact that relatively weak data are available to support either position. Perhaps the way GAD differs most from other anxiety disorders is in the strength of its relationship with Major Depressive Disorder (MDD). Most anxiety disorders, including OCD, PTSD, and Panic Disorder, show strong associations with MDD. However, in children as well as adults, GAD is particularly tightly linked with MDD. Evidence for this close relationship emerges both in family genetic research (Breslau, Davis, & Prabucki, 1987; Kendler, 2001; Silberg, Rutter, & Eaves, 2001) and in longitudinal studies (Pine et al., 1998).

Taken together, evidence identifying unique patterns of symptoms and familial aggregation patterns, as well as markers of neurophysiological dysfunction, supports the view that anxiety disorders can be defined as a family of related but distinct conditions. However, for some disorders, the evidence of commonalities is almost as strong as the evidence of specificity. For example, common to virtually all of the anxiety disorders is a persistent tendency to experience any of a wide range of anxious symptoms, which can be somatic (e.g., racing heart, sweating, nausea, trembling), cognitive (e.g., worry, fear), or behavioral (e.g., avoidance, tearfulness). These symptoms may occur discretely or in clusters; when four or more somatic or cognitive symptoms suddenly co-occur and rapidly peak in the context of intense fear, they constitute a panic attack. As noted earlier, in individuals with Panic Disorder, panic attacks occur spontaneously and without apparent provocation, sometimes leading to agoraphobia, or a fear of experiencing panic symptoms or attacks in a public setting. However, individuals with other anxiety disorders also experience panic attacks, which are cued by specific feared stressors. For example, individuals with Social Anxiety Disorder may experience panic when confronted with particular social cues. Children with SAD may experience panic when leaving for school in the morning. Worry also represents a core feature of most anxiety states. In GAD, worry and excessive anxiety develop about a variety of events or circumstances. Objects of worry may also be circumscribed objects or situations, as in Specific Phobia, SAD, or Social Phobia. Symptom patterns vary relatively little across the phobias and GAD; consequently, these disorders are differentiated primarily on the basis of the environmental cues that precipitate anxious reactions.

The present chapter focuses on one type of anxiety disorder, Social Phobia, which has also been termed Social Anxiety Disorder. The recent shift from the term Social Phobia to the term Social Anxiety Disorder is based on evidence that Social Anxiety Disorder differs dramatically from specific phobias in several ways. These differences are apparent on measures of impairment, treatment-seeking behavior, longitudinal outcome, and familial aggregation (Fyer, 1998; Fyer, Mannuzza, Chapman, Martin, & Klein, 1995; Pine et al., 1998). Unlike the various forms of Specific Phobia, which are each associated with low rates of impairment and high rates of familial aggregation, Social Anxiety Disorder is associated with relatively high rates of impairment (Fyer, 1998). Moreover, familial aggregation data suggest that Social Anxiety Disorder should not be considered a subcategory of the larger family of phobias (Fyer et al., 1995).

In individuals with Social Anxiety Disorder, anticipation of embarrassment in social or performance situations is the primary trigger for anxiety symptoms. *DSM-IV* recognizes two forms of Social Anxiety Disorder: One form is narrow and specific and is characterized by an isolated fear of public speaking; the other is more generalized and is characterized by high levels of anxiety in a range of social situations. Virtually all studies examining commonalities and differences between the specific and generalized forms of Social Anxiety Disorder have focused on adults (Fyer, 1993; Kendler, 2001; Mannuzza et al., 1995; Schneier, Spitzer, Gibbon, Fyer, & Liebowitz, 1991). This body of research provides emergent support for *DSM-IV*'s assertion that the two types of Social Anxiety Disorder are distinct. Specifically, the generalized type of Social Anxiety Disorder is associated with more impairment and more extensive comorbidity than is the specific type (R. G. Klein & Pine, 2002; Schneier et al., 1991). This pattern of findings has led to a greater focus in therapeutic and developmental studies on the generalized type.

Prior to *DSM-IV*, children with severe avoidance of social situations could be diagnosed with Avoidant Disorder of Childhood instead of Social Phobia. In the revisions leading to the publication of *DSM-IV*, Social Anxiety Disorder subsumed Avoidant Disorder of Childhood, just as GAD subsumed Overanxious Disorder of Childhood. This change

reflected the fact that the distinction between Avoidant Disorder and Social Phobia appeared relatively arbitrary in clinical practice and epidemiological settings. Not only did this change eliminate age as a diagnostic criterion, but it also decreased redundancy among diagnoses, given that Avoidant Disorder appeared to be a rare condition that overlapped considerably with Social Anxiety Disorder.

Selective mutism, a condition characterized by a consistent failure to speak in social situations, also shows some overlap with Social Anxiety Disorder. Although anxiety symptoms are not among the diagnostic criteria for selective mutism, a large proportion of children with selective mutism endorse marked social anxiety (Bergman, Piacentini, & McCracken, 2002), and a substantial number also meet criteria for Social Anxiety Disorder (R. G. Klein & Pine, 2002). Though some controversy remains, current consensus suggests that at least some subgroups of children with selective mutism are likely to suffer from a condition with a strong pathophysiologic resemblance to Social Anxiety Disorder (R. G. Klein & Pine, 2002).

In general, data differentiating Social Anxiety Disorder from other anxiety disorders and related conditions are relatively strong. We review these data in detail. Briefly stated, however, the available evidence suggests that the disorder can be differentiated from other anxiety states on the basis of symptoms, longitudinal outcome, familial aggregation, and pathophysiology. In fact, the data on specificity in childhood Social Anxiety Disorder are as strong as or stronger than those for any other anxiety disorder except OCD. A focus on Social Anxiety Disorder is also warranted in light of recent findings in developmental psychology and cognitive neuroscience research. These findings provide novel insights concerning behavioral, cognitive, and neural aspects of social relationships, particularly where such relationships involve perturbations in emotion. This natural intersection offers an unusual opportunity to bridge recent research on clinical psychopathology, which focuses on social anxiety per se, and recent research on broader aspects of social relationships and emotion regulation.

HISTORICAL PERSPECTIVE

If the published record is an accurate indication, anxiety among children and adolescents has been of limited interest to clinicians and researchers throughout much of history. In their carefully researched historical overview of youth anxiety, Treffers and Silverman (2001) found few published references to anxiety in children before the early nineteenth century. Indeed, between the fourth century B.C., when Hippocrates (460–370 B.C./1886) cited "fears" as one of the illnesses of infants, and the past 200 years, the literature on youth anxiety is remarkably sparse.

When pediatric anxiety was addressed in early medical writings, specific fears and nightmares were frequently the focus. Several medieval and Renaissance medical pamphlets suggested cures for these problems, which were thought to stem from imbalanced humors or digestive upsets. The English physician Robert Pemell (1653/2000), for instance, recommended keeping the child on a "moderate diet" and administering laxatives to "take away the corrupt humours in the stomach." Others, such as Marcin of Urzedow, a Polish herbalist, suggested dill as an effective treatment for nightmares (Knab, 1995).

Historical considerations of anxiety in children, as well as in adults, reflect the tension inherent in current conceptualizations between a focus on specific anxiety symptoms and broad categories of anxiety states. Writings over the past centuries recognize anxiety surrounding social interactions as one specific form of anxiety state. Darwin (1998), for example, noted cross-species parallels in the manifestations of anxiety when encountering threatening conspecifics. Nevertheless, the degree to which such anxiety has been considered distinct from other fears remains unclear. Social anxiety per se received little attention in medieval medical treatises, although Treffers and Silverman (2001) mention a notable exception in which the Italian doctor Girolamo Mercuriale cited fear as a contributing factor to children's stammering in his tract "De Morbis Puerorum." Social anxiety, like separation anxiety, was instead more commonly discussed in educational materials. Some of the earliest specific references to childhood anxiety about social interaction, for example, appeared in advice and etiquette manuals or "books of nurture" during the Middle Ages, which contained instructive aphorisms and verses on a wide range of problems, including timidity or shyness and school refusal (Wardle, 1991).

By the mid-nineteenth century, discussions of social anxiety began to appear in the medical literature (Pelissolo & Lepine, 1995), with an initial focus on phobic fears of blushing, or erythrophobia. Although these reports typically centered on adult patients, it was not unusual for their symptoms to date back to adolescence. In one of the earliest case studies, the German physician Johann Ludwig Casper (1846) described a 21-year-old medical student who had suffered from a severe fear of blushing since the age of 13. Tormented by this phobia, which left him unable to bear even the company of his best friend, he became increasingly depressed and ultimately committed suicide.

Pitres and Régis (1897) described two adult brothers whose fears of blushing could be traced back to puberty.

A number of comparable cases were reported around the turn of the twentieth century, and increasingly, they were grouped with cases of more broadly conceptualized social anxiety (Pitres & Régis, 1897). In his taxonomy of phobias, Pierre Janet (1903, p. 210) classified erythrophobia among the "phobies sociales" or "phobies de la société," a specialized type of situational phobia that also included such diverse and specific problems as phobias about marriage, teaching schoolchildren, and supervising a domestic staff. The French psychiatrist Paul Hartenberg (1901, p. 201) similarly grouped erythrophobia with "maladies de la timidité," or disorders of shyness. For Hartenberg, such disorders stemmed from a combination of fear, particularly fear of humiliation or of being perceived as inferior, and shame. As Fairbrother (2002) has noted, Hartenberg's conceptualization of socially oriented anxiety was remarkably similar to the *DSM-IV* definition of Social Phobia, particularly in its emphasis on fear of negative evaluation as a cardinal symptom. Hartenberg was also one of the few clinicians of his time to discuss social anxiety as a problem that affected children as well as adults. However, he believed that until puberty, children were unlikely to perceive their shyness or timidity as a problem that needed to be addressed.

Although the phenomenology of Social Phobia was well-documented during the late nineteenth century, clinicians struggled to understand the disorder's etiology. In Casper's (1846, p. 286) case study, for instance, he expressed bafflement about what had caused his patient's distress, musing at one point about whether it could have been a "punishment from God" or a "consequence of original sin." Patients themselves attributed their social anxieties to a variety of causes during the second half of the century. In his list of patients' explanations for their social fears, Hartenberg (1901, pp. 134–135) included "anemia," "lack of air," "my state of nervous weakness," "modesty," "fear of ridicule," "my detestable education," "lack of money," and "awkwardness."

As case observations accumulated, clinicians began to piece together more plausible hypotheses about etiology, and by the turn of the century, ascendant theories closely resembled those that are currently favored. Several clinicians, including Hartenberg (1901) and the Swiss psychologist Edouard Claparède (1902), noted that multiple members of the same family often exhibited problems with social anxiety. As a consequence, these clinicians agreed that the disorder must have a hereditary component. Additionally, Hartenberg implicated environmental factors in the disorder, listing a variety of situations and social stimuli that tend to elicit anxiety from those who are genetically vulnerable.

There was little consensus at the turn of the twentieth century regarding optimal treatments for pathological social anxiety. Adult case reports described a number of treatments that practitioners implemented with varying degrees of success. These therapies included hypnosis, psychotherapy, opium, bromides, and, for erythrophobia, bleeding with leeches (Pitres & Régis, 1897). For children, Hartenberg (1901) presciently suggested using strategies that closely resembled graduated exposure to decrease fears of speaking in class or social interaction. He also advocated structuring children's experiences at school in ways that would prevent social anxiety. By helping children to be less emotional, strengthening their self-confidence, and habituating them to interactions with strangers, schools played an important role in steering children from future nervous problems.

As the twentieth century progressed, psychodynamic and strict behaviorist theories of anxiety became prominent. Although they varied considerably in their interpretations of maladaptive or neurotic anxiety, the psychodynamic theorists were loosely united by two beliefs about the construct. First, there was consensus that it stemmed from unconscious, internal conflicts related to early patterns of interaction between an individual and his or her parents, especially the mother (see May, 1950, for a review). Harry Stack Sullivan (1953), the most interpersonally oriented of the psychodynamic theorists, went so far as to assert that all anxiety arose from early apprehension about disapproval from significant others. Second, the vulnerability to experience neurotic anxiety was thought to be inherited. In contrast, behaviorists such as John Broadus Watson (1929) held that maladaptive emotional reactions such as anxiety constituted patterns of behavior that stemmed largely from conditioning experiences. According to Watson, negative or aversive conditioning events were especially likely to lead to maladaptive behavior if they occurred in infancy or childhood, because habits were typically acquired and modified during those periods.

Given the primacy of psychodynamic theory in medical circles during much of the early twentieth century, it is not surprising that social anxiety in youth was again addressed largely in educational contexts (e.g., Dealy, 1923; Goodenough, 1929; Uger, 1938). Teachers and parents were encouraged to help shy or timid children become more outgoing and confident, and, in a few cases, psychotherapeutic approaches were applied to increase such children's comfort in social interactions (e.g., Solomon & Axelrod, 1944).

Although research interest in adult social anxiety increased steadily during the last half of the twentieth century (e.g., Cheek & Buss, 1981; D. Watson & Friend, 1969), it was not until the 1980s that social anxiety among children and adolescents became a prominent focus of study (Pine, 1999). Indeed, as recently as 1966, the typical age of onset for Social Phobia was thought to be 19 years (Marks & Gelder, 1966), thus, largely precluding the need to examine the disorder in younger individuals.

Research that accumulated in the second half of the twentieth century led to a gradual erosion of the view that social anxiety or fear of conspecifics could be lumped together with the larger family of neurotic states or fears associated either with internal conflicts or with exposures to conditioning experiences. Increasingly, specific anxiety states were recognized as distinct conditions. Current conceptualizations of anxiety disorders were largely shaped by three major sets of research findings from the last half of the twentieth century. One of these sets of findings emerged largely from research in adults, a second from research in children and adolescents, the third from research in the neurosciences. We briefly review findings in clinical research that stimulated this changing perspective; findings in basic research are reviewed in a later section of the chapter.

Late twentieth-century developments in adult clinical psychopharmacology greatly influenced modern conceptualizations of anxiety disorders in general and Social Anxiety Disorder in particular. One of the most important advances derived from D. F. Klein's (1964) observation that adults with spontaneous panic attacks showed a distinctive clinical response to the tricyclic antidepressant (TCA) imipramine. This finding led him to suggest that unique responses to specific pharmacological agents may characterize specific anxiety states. Although specifics of Klein's initial argument are still debated, his broader position on the utility of so-called "pharmacological dissection" is widely accepted.

Large-scale pharmacological studies during the 1990s have provided further support for the view that anxiety states are a family of distinct but related conditions. Probably the strongest evidence of specificity comes from recent clinical pharmacology research on adult Social Anxiety Disorder and OCD. Social Anxiety Disorder, in particular, is characterized by a positive response to monoamine oxidase inhibitors (MAOIs) and selective serotonin reuptake inhibitors (SSRIs), but not to TCAs (Blanco et al., 2003; R. G. Klein & Pine, 2002; Liebowitz et al., 1988). Similarly, OCD is characterized by a pattern of response to serotonergic agents such as SSRIs and clomipramine, but not to nonserotonergic TCAs or MAOIs

(R. G. Klein & Pine, 2002; Pine, 2002b; Riddle et al., 2001). Other anxiety states, such as Panic Disorder and GAD, tend to respond to all three classes of medication (R. G. Klein & Pine, 2002). These relatively robust and consistent pharmacological findings in adults have led to parallel genetics and pathophysiology research on the differences, as well as the commonalities, among the anxiety disorders. Only recently have clinical trials begun to examine specificity of pharmacological effects in children (RUPP, 2001). To date, findings do not parallel those from adult studies, in that specific response patterns have not clearly been delineated for specific subtypes of childhood anxiety disorders.

Whereas adult psychopharmacological studies have yielded substantive evidence regarding specificity of anxiety states, developmental research from an epidemiological perspective has shed light on patterns of heterogeneity in outcome among anxiety states. Since LaPouse and Monk's (1964) classic study of behavior problems in children, a series of community-based epidemiological studies has documented alarmingly high rates of anxiety symptoms among children and adolescents (e.g., P. Cohen et al., 1993; Costello et al., 2003; Pine et al., 1998). Through the first half of the twentieth century, these symptoms were considered normal manifestations of behavior that waxed and waned across development. However, refinements in the standardized assessment of childhood psychopathology facilitated relatively large longitudinal studies that followed youth into adulthood. Such longitudinal studies found that even mild anxiety symptoms in young children and adolescents robustly predicted the onset of later, relatively serious clinical disorders, including MDD, Social Anxiety Disorder, OCD, and Panic Disorder (Costello et al., 2002; Peterson et al., 2001; Pine, Cohen, et al., 2001; Pine et al., 1998). However, although most adults with mood and anxiety disorders had experienced childhood anxiety, the majority of anxious children did not go on to develop adult disorders (Costello et al., 2002; Pine et al., 1998). This observation led to an increasing research emphasis on identifying factors that distinguished between mildly anxious children who would go on to develop serious mental disorders as adults and those who would experience only transient problems.

SOCIAL ANXIETY

In the following sections we provide an overview of social anxiety, both its normal and pathological manifestations, across development. In our examination of normative social anxiety, we focus on its evolution during several developmental stages, as well as on adaptive approaches to managing social fears and concerns. We then shift our focus to more impairing levels of social anxiety and describe both the phenomenology of Social Anxiety Disorder and potential mechanisms underlying its development.

Normal Social Anxiety across Development

With the emerging emphasis on specificity in anxiety states, a focus on developmental changes in individual symptoms and symptom patterns has followed. This has stimulated a series of studies specifically on changes in social anxiety across development. By adulthood, a large proportion of people acknowledge having experienced at least transient social anxiety on occasion, predominantly regarding public speaking or performing in front of others (B. J. Cox, McWilliams, Clara, & Stein, 2003; Kessler, Stein, & Berglund, 1998). In a large telephone survey, 61% of randomly selected adult participants reported experiencing high levels of anxiety in at least one type of social situation (Stein, Walker, & Forde, 1994). The most commonly feared situation was public speaking, which 55% of the respondents endorsed as anxiety provoking. This type of fear appears to emerge early; 50% of surveyed individuals who endorsed anxiety about public speaking dated its onset to early adolescence, and 90% reported that it had emerged before they reached adulthood (Stein, Walker, & Forde, 1996). A variety of other social situations also frequently elicit anxiety. Speaking to small groups of familiar people was anxiety provoking for a quarter of the participants in Stein and colleagues' (1994) study, and large numbers of participants endorsed anxiety when dealing with people in authority (23.3%), attending social gatherings (14.5%), and interacting with new people (13.7%).

A relatively small number of adults experience social fears that are severe or chronic enough to meet criteria for Social Phobia. Among adult participants in the National Comorbidity Survey, 38.6% endorsed marked social fears of any type, but only approximately 33% of this group met criteria for lifetime history of Social Phobia (Kessler et al., 1998). Similarly, in a study comparing shy and nonshy college students, the disorder was significantly more common among shy individuals (18% affected) than among those who were not shy (3% affected) but was relatively uncommon in either group (Heiser, Turner, & Beidel, 2003).

Among youth, patterns of normal-range anxiety evolve across development. In general, anxiety and fearfulness are common among children. Among 4- to 12-year-olds, 67% report currently experiencing worries, and 75.8% report current fears (Muris, Merckelbach, Gadet, & Moulaert, 2000). Over time, these symptoms appeared to decline markedly, and other research has indicated that decreases in normal anxiety and fear continue into adolescence (Gullone, King, & Ollendick, 2001; Ollendick, King, & Frary, 1989). Anxiety specifically about social situations, however, shows a different pattern of development. As the following sections outline, interpersonally oriented anxiety shifts in focus from concerns about separation to concerns about evaluation as children pass from infancy through childhood and into adolescence.

Infancy and Early Childhood

Among infants and very young children, social anxiety, particularly fear of negative evaluation, is rarely reported or observed. Instead, during this developmental period, anxiety about separation is the predominant type of interpersonal concern. Studies examining the trajectory of separation anxiety among children demonstrate that it emerges around 6 to 8 months of age, peaks at around 15 months, and decreases over time (e.g., Kagan, Kearsley, & Zelazo, 1978). F. N. Cox and Campbell (1968), for instance, placed children between 13 and 47 months in a playroom for 12 minutes, during 4 of which their mother was absent from the room. The 13- to 15-month-old children showed significantly greater decreases in play, speech, and movement after their mother left the room than did older children, which suggested that the effects of separation were greatest in the youngest children. In a replication and extension of this study, Gershaw and Schwarz (1971) found not only that 15- to 29-month-old boys showed decreased play behavior relative to 31- to 42-month-old boys during maternal separation, but also that they cried and watched the door more while their mother was absent. Concerns about separation appear to persist into middle childhood, but with progressively decreasing frequency and intensity. For example, whereas 4- to 6-year-olds in one study reported separation from their parents as the topic that caused them the most worry, older children were much less likely to identify separation as a prominent source of concern (Muris et al., 2000). In fact, developmental stage represents one of the main factors that distinguish "normal" separation anxiety from pathological separation anxiety, or Separation Anxiety Disorder. This condition is typically characterized as an extreme form of normal separation anxiety that persists into the latency or early adolescent years, when normal separation anxiety is expected to wane.

It is not entirely clear when other types of socially oriented fear and anxiety, including fear of negative evalua-tion, initially emerge. Studies of normal variations in temperament indicate that some children may be vulnerable to these and other fears from a very early age. In a classic series of studies, Kagan and colleagues found marked individual differences in patterns of response to both social and nonsocial novelty in a large sample of children followed longitudinally from early infancy to adulthood (Kagan, 1997). At 4 months of age, approximately 20% of the sample showed marked signs of distress when presented with novel stimuli; of these children, approximately a fifth went on to show both consistently high levels of fear as toddlers and a timid pattern of interaction as preschoolers. Among these children, whom Kagan termed "behaviorally inhibited," rates of Social Phobia at age 11 years were elevated relative to rates among uninhibited peers (Kagan, Reznick, & Snidman, 1988). This basic pattern of findings has been replicated in other laboratories (Fox, Henderson, Rubin, Calkins, & Schmidt, 2001). Clearly, at least some inhibited children show a heightened vulnerability to social fears; however, it remains unclear whether such concerns emerge earlier in these children than in other subsets of youth.

Studies on the development of embarrassment among toddlers and preschoolers in general suggest that social fears are preceded developmentally by a sort of bashfulness in the face of scrutiny or attention and by the emergence of shame. In an observational study of preschoolers, Lewis and colleagues (Lewis, Stanger, Sullivan, & Barone, 1991) described the behavior of 22-month-old and 35-month-old children in a variety of situations designed to elicit embarrassment. Of the 22-month-olds, 52% showed behavioral signs of embarrassment, such as smiling while averting their gaze and touching their face or body when they were pointed to, asked unexpectedly to dance, or complimented. Such behaviors were even more common among the 35-month-old children, 83% of whom acted in an embarrassed manner.

Because this type of embarrassment reflects "exposure of the self when the individual is the object of attention from others" rather than negative evaluation in performance situations, Lewis and Ramsay (2002, p. 1034) refer to it as "exposure embarrassment." "Evaluation embarrassment," which is evident in the context of perceived failure or negative feedback, appears to emerge later in development, around the age of 3 years (Lewis, Alessandri, & Sullivan, 1992), and to be associated with elevated cortisol (Lewis & Ramsay, 2002). This developmental progression is thought to reflect changes during early childhood in self-awareness and in capacity to evaluate one's performance against external standards (e.g., Lewis & Ramsay, 2002;

Stipek, Gralinski, & Kopp, 1990). Further, although very young children appear capable of experiencing both types of embarrassment, some evidence suggests that explicit awareness of the two distinct constructs emerges even later in development (Crozier & Burnham, 1990).

In studies that have presented young children with hypothetical scenarios about potentially embarrassing situations, other developmental trends have been evident. For example, when 5-year-old and 8-year-old children were read vignettes in which a person's actions were greeted with either a supportive or a derisive response and then asked how they would feel if they had been the person in the vignette, their responses varied with age (Bennett, 1989; Bennett & Gillingham, 1991). Whereas all children reported that they would have felt embarrassed in the face of derision, only the older children said that they would have been embarrassed when others expressed support. The authors postulate that this difference in pattern of response reflects cognitive differences between the preschoolers and the older children, such that the younger children were less aware that some situations could be intrinsically embarrassing, regardless of others' reactions. Findings from another study suggest that 5-year-old children are also less likely than 8- or 11-year-old children to feel embarrassment when someone else, with whom they are associated, publicly violates a rule (Bennett, Yuill, Banerjee, & Thomson, 1998).

It appears clear that very young children experience emotional responses to situations that involve potential negative evaluation, even though their responses differ in several ways from those of older children. Little research, however, has examined preschoolers' capacity and proclivity to anticipate or worry about negative feedback from others. Results from the few studies of normative worry among preschoolers suggest that such concerns may be present at a fairly young age, even if children do not articulate them. When 5- to 6-year-old children were interviewed directly, they reported few evaluative worries relative to older children (Vasey, Crnic, & Carter, 1994). When preschoolers' parents were asked about their children's worries, however, they reported that their 3- to 5-year-old children frequently worried about meeting new people or entering groups of children (Spence, Rapee, McDonald, & Ingram, 2001). Parents of 4- and 5-year-old participants also reported that their children commonly feared talking in front of a group, and 5-year-olds, according to their parents, worried about appearing stupid in front of others.

Regardless of the source of their social inhibition, however, a subset of preschoolers are readily identifiable by observers as excessively shy. A study of 4-year-olds found that these highly shy children, relative to peers who show average or low levels of shyness, are prone to experience negative moods, pervasive worries and fears, and poor adjustment (Stevenson-Hinde & Glover, 1996). Further, both tendencies toward shy behavior and their associated problems appear to persist in these children. When Stevenson-Hinde and colleagues (Fordham & Stevenson-Hinde, 1999) reexamined their longitudinally followed sample at the ages of roughly 8 to 10 years, they found shy behavior to be highly consistent over time. Additionally, shy behavior and social adjustment difficulties, including perceived poorer friendship quality, trait anxiety, and lower ratings of global self-worth, were significantly related, particularly in the older children in the sample.

Middle Childhood and Adolescence

During later childhood and adolescence, socially oriented concerns increase (Westenberg, Drewes, Goedhart, Siebelink, & Treffers, 2004). In their interview study of children's fears between 4 and 12 years, Muris and colleagues (2000) found that whereas fears regarding some topics, including animals and safety, were prevalent across the entire age span, worries about evaluation were more evident in older children. Similarly, in a study of normal children's worries between second and sixth grades, concerns about performance in school (e.g., getting good grades, being called on in class) were among the most common, along with worries about health and personal safety (Silverman, La Greca, & Wasserstein, 1995). Of the more common worries reported across 14 categories, 22% pertained to interpersonally relevant issues such as peer rejection, neglect, or scapegoating; personal appearance; or concern about others' feelings. When performance-related concerns, which often also involve social-evaluative components, were included, 40% of the worries could be classified as interpersonally related.

Among healthy adolescents, social-evaluative concerns are widely prevalent; some evidence suggests that this is particularly true for girls. West and Sweeting (2003) interviewed two cohorts of 15-year-olds about their worries and found that for girls, the most consistently prevalent worries were about school performance (40.1% and 45.6%) and weight (29% and 38.3%), whereas for boys, the most prevalent concerns were school performance (39.1% and 35.6%) and unemployment (35.6% and 25%). Anxiety about dating also appears to be common among adolescents, particularly those in their middle teens, and to be distinguishable from more global social anxiety (Glickman & La Greca, 2004).

Similar patterns of worry were evident in a sample of 6- to 16-year-old youth diagnosed with anxiety disorders

(Weems, Silverman, & La Greca, 2000). Like the children in Silverman and colleagues' (1995) community sample, these children and adolescents were most likely to worry about safety and school performance. These children differed from participants in Silverman and coworkers' study primarily in the intensity of their worries rather than the content or frequency of worry. Interestingly, the clinical sample in this study reported fewer worries on average than did high anxious children in the community sample.

Most studies of worries among children and adolescents have used self-report measures or interviews to gather data. Although these approaches have clear advantages, particularly in light of evidence that parents and teachers tend to underestimate internalizing symptoms among youth (R. G. Klein & Pine, 2002), they also have some limitations. As Gullone (1999) has pointed out, the marked variability among youth of different ages, their reporting biases, their awareness of their own internal states, and their verbal and cognitive skills must be taken into account when interpreting findings based on child and adolescent self-report.

Social Anxiety and Coping Skills

Although social-evaluative concerns are common among school-age children and adolescents, youth vary in the degree to which they cope successfully with these concerns. A large body of literature indicates that instrumental, problem-focused coping techniques that involve voluntary shifts of attention away from negative feelings are particularly effective for managing worry and emotional discomfort (Clark, Beck, & Stewart, 1990; R. G. Klein & Pine, 2002; MacLeod, Rutherford, Campbell, Ebsworthy, & Holker, 2002). Individuals with high levels of social fears or shyness are less likely than peers to use such coping methods (Glyshaw, Cohen, & Towbes, 1989; Mellings & Alden, 2000), instead relying on avoidance, rumination, and other strategies that do little to alleviate their discomfort (Garnefski, Legerstee, Kraaij, Van Den Kommer, & Teerds, 2002; Hymel, Woody, & Bowker, 1993).

The ability to shift attention away from negative internal states may be especially critical to the management and prevention of social anxiety. Ruminative or emotion-focused coping strategies, for example, which involve sustained focus on internal discomfort, have been shown to relate to elevated levels of anxiety (Blankstein, Flett, & Watson, 1992; Rose, 2002). The direction of the association with coping style is unclear, but some evidence suggests that skill at such voluntary redirection of attention from threat cues to neutral cues may modulate the effects of anxiety on coping (Derryberry & Reed, 2002). Addi-

tionally, the tendency to internalize and focus attention on negative emotions during preschool has been shown to predict shy behavior 4 to 6 years later (Eisenberg, Shepard, Fabes, Murphy, & Guthrie, 1998). These findings suggest that poor attentional control during negative emotional states may amplify later anxiety and anxious behavior. We discuss the role of such cognitive skills in the development and maintenance of social anxiety in more detail in the section on anxiety and neuroscience.

Clinical-Range Social Anxiety: Social Phobia

Although the experience of transient social anxiety is normative, symptoms are persistent and impairing for a subset of the population. In the following section we describe clinically significant manifestations of social anxiety and factors that may contribute to their emergence.

Clinical Presentation

As noted earlier, the diagnosis of Social Anxiety Disorder or Social Phobia is based on the presence of fear or anxiety about situations in which an individual may be scrutinized. These situations may be social, as in parties or school gatherings, or they may be academic or work related. In both the generalized form of Social Anxiety Disorder, where most social situations are feared, and in the specific form, which consists of an isolated fear of public speaking, anxiety must be of sufficient severity to cause extreme distress or impairment. The broad definition of Social Anxiety Disorder has changed relatively little since the publication of *DSM-III* in 1980, but there has been increasing recognition in recent years of the need to integrate data on distress and impairment into assessments of social anxiety symptoms. Such a shift of emphasis to impairment is likely to influence the threshold differentiating clinical and subclinical manifestations of social anxiety.

Rates of Social Phobia appear to increase as children, particularly girls, pass through adolescence and into adulthood (Costello et al., 2003; McGee, Feehan, Williams, & Anderson, 1992; Pine et al., 1998; Wittchen, Stein, & Kessler, 1999). In the Great Smoky Mountain Study sample, 3-month prevalence rates rose from 0.3% in 9- to 11-year-old children to 1.1% when these youth reached 15 years of age (Costello et al., 2003). This change was largely driven by increased prevalence of the disorder among girls. Pine and colleagues (1998) also found marked gender difference in the prevalence of Social Phobia across development. For girls in this study, 12-month prevalence rates remained relatively stable, ranging from 10.1% when the sample was 9 to 18 years old to 12.5% 2 years subsequently and 9.5% after an additional 7 years. For boys, in contrast, rates declined over time from 6.7% and 6.8% at the first two time points to 1.7% at the most recent one. The nearly 10-fold difference in rates of Social Anxiety Disorder between these two longitudinal epidemiological studies is highly notable. This variation may reflect differences in sampling procedures or demographics across the two samples. However, differences in assessment and categorization are also likely to contribute heavily to the disparate findings across studies. To meet criteria for a diagnosis in Costello and colleagues' study, participants were required to demonstrate more evidence of clinically significant distress or impairment than were participants in Pine and coworkers' research.

Consistent across both studies, however, are findings that rates of Social Anxiety Disorder increase across development in females, but not in males (see Figure 12.1). Further, developmental gender differences in prevalence are comparable for normal social fears and frank Social Anxiety Disorder. Both phenomena appear to peak in adolescence, particularly among girls. From adolescence onward, gender differences in prevalence remain largely constant.

Although anxiety disorders and symptoms often have been considered transient or minimally impairing conditions, longitudinal research in children and adolescents suggests otherwise. In a large study of 9- to 16-year-olds, presence of an anxiety disorder was associated with a nearly threefold increase in risk for future dysfunction, particularly in terms of family relationships. These rates were comparable to those for other disorders, particularly depression, which is often considered more impairing than anxiety (Ezpeleta, Keeler, Erkanli, Costello, & Angold, 2001). Elevated risk for other problems, such as school dropout, is also associated with the presence of an anxiety disorder during adolescence (Vander Stoep, Weiss, McKnight, Beresford, & Cohen, 2002). Among anxious youth, other types of psychopathology are common, both concurrently and later in development. In a community sample of adolescents who kept electronic diaries over a 4-day period, for example, those who reported moderate to high levels of anxiety symptoms also more frequently reported feeling sad, angry, stressed, and hassled than did low-anxiety peers (Henker, Whalen, Jamner, & Delfino, 2002).

Relatively few studies have examined outcomes of childhood anxiety disorders, let alone outcomes that are specific to a particular diagnosis, such as Social Anxiety Disorder. Of the existing findings regarding outcome, some of the most reliable come from prospective community-based studies, which are free of the referral and recall biases that limit conclusions from studies using other designs. Using a community-based sample, Pine and colleagues (1998) prospectively examined relationships between adolescent and adult anxiety disorders and noted a relatively specific association between Social Anxiety Disorder diagnoses in adolescence and in adulthood. Adult Social Anxiety Disorder, however, also related to other childhood anxiety disorders, including childhood Overanxious Disorder/Generalized Anxiety Disorder. Similarly, Pine Cohen, Cohen, and Brook (2000) noted a highly specific relationship between Social Anxiety Disorder and Conduct Disorder. Unlike other anxiety disorders, Social Anxiety Disorder predicted a relatively benign course for subsequent Conduct Disorder. Such longitudinal associations are consistent with data on psychopathy, which is characterized both by low levels of anxiety and by chronic, recurrent behavior problems (Blair, 2003). Research on adult psychopathy and Social Anxiety Disorder, as reviewed later in the chapter, implicates dysfunction in a common underlying neural circuit that encompasses the amygdala and ventral prefrontal cortex.

Relatively little community-based longitudinal research has examined outcome in children or adolescents with specific anxiety disorders; a notable exception is Pine et al.'s (1998) study. The few such available studies that have specifically focused on Social Anxiety Disorder have found that it predicts a broader array of conditions than did Pine and colleagues. For example, Stein and coworkers

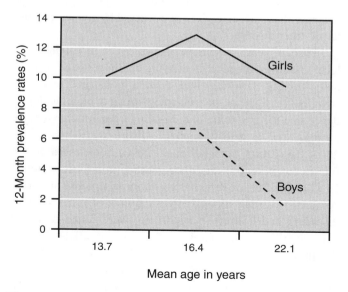

Figure 12.1 Gender differences in rates of social phobia in a longitudinally studied sample at three time points. Graph based on data from "The Risk for Early-Adulthood Anxiety and Depressive Disorders in Adolescents with Anxiety and Depressive Disorders" by D. S. Pine, P. Cohen, D. Gurley, J. S. Brook, and Y. Ma, 1998, *Archives of General Psychiatry, 55*(1), pp. 56–64.

(2001) found that Social Anxiety Disorder related to both mood and anxiety disorders in a sample of adolescents and adults followed longitudinally. However, associations with mood disorder were stronger in the older participants in this study than in the younger participants. Further, with respect to clinical samples, Last, Hansen, and Franco (1997) reported generally positive outcomes for Social Anxiety Disorder and for other pediatric anxiety disorders. More recently, follow-up research on youth treated with cognitive-behavioral therapy for anxiety disorders suggests that treatment enhances the likelihood of enduring positive sequelae (Kendall, Safford, Flannery-Schroeder, & Webb, 2004).

Few family genetic studies have explicitly examined associations between Social Anxiety Disorder in parents and their children. However, a relatively large series of studies document comparable relationships among family members. For example, Social Anxiety Disorder in an adult proband confers a strong and specific risk for the disorder in first-degree relatives when comorbidity is properly controlled (Fyer, Mannuzza, Chapman, Liebowitz, & Klein, 1993; Fyer et al., 1995). Studies focused on children also note associations between parent and offspring anxiety disorders (e.g., Mancini, van Ameringen, Szatmari, Fugere, & Boyle, 1996; Unnewehr, Schneider, Florin, & Margraf, 1998). Further, one study explicitly linked Social Anxiety Disorder in a parent to shyness in the children (Cooper & Eke, 1999). No specific associations between parent and child Social Anxiety Disorder per se, however, have been demonstrated.

Pathways to Social Phobia: Risk and Protective Factors

The developmental psychopathology perspective emphasizes that multiple pathways can lead to the onset of psychopathology and that a wide variety of factors can confer risk or protection. With regard to Social Anxiety Disorder, previous reviews have outlined numerous factors hypothesized to contribute to risk (Hudson & Rapee, 2000; Ollendick & Hirshfeld-Becker, 2002; Vasey & Dadds, 2001). We examine several of these, including genetics, temperament, parenting, conditioning events, and, in the final section of the chapter, neurocognitive factors.

Genetic Factors

As the family studies described earlier suggest, Social Anxiety Disorder appears to aggregate within families. Using twin designs, several behavioral genetic studies have examined the relative contributions of hereditary and environmental factors to this tendency for the disorder to be familial. For example, results from studies examining a large population-based sample of adult female twins indicate a significant, albeit modest, genetic component, with heritability estimates of 30% to 50% (Kendler, Karkowski, & Prescott, 1999; Kendler, Neale, Kessler, Heath, & Eaves, 1992). Findings from a subsequent study of adult male twins from the same sample yielded a comparable heritability estimate of 31% for the disorder and associated irrational social fears. Of note, similar, relatively modest degrees of heritability are found for most anxiety disorders, including Panic Disorder and Generalized Anxiety Disorder.

Although these studies suggest that genetic factors play similar roles in the onset of social anxiety for males and females, gender differences in the prevalence of the disorder, particularly during adolescence, have led to questions about the impact of gender on risk. The one twin study to date that has directly compared genetic and environmental risk across males and females found evidence consistent with gender differences in patterns of liability (Kendler, Jacobson, Myers, & Prescott, 2002). According to this study, whereas twin resemblances among females were predominantly due to family environment, resemblances in males largely reflected genetic factors. The authors caution, however, that the strong effect of family environment seen in females is inconsistent with their previous findings and note that such effects have occurred by chance in studies of other disorders.

In recent years, researchers have begun to conduct molecular studies aimed at identifying candidate genes for Social Anxiety Disorder and related constructs such as shyness. In light of pharmacological and biological evidence that the serotonin and dopaminergic systems may be dysregulated in Social Anxiety Disorder (Blanco et al., 2003; Pine, 2001; Schneier et al., 2000), some research has focused on potential candidate genes within these systems. In a study of clinic-referred children, symptoms of Social Anxiety Disorder, along with symptoms of other anxiety disorders and Tourette's syndrome, were found to relate significantly to the number of 10-repeat alleles of the dopamine transporter gene (DAT1; Rowe et al., 1998). In contrast, Stein, Chartier, Kozak, King, and Kennedy (1998) found no evidence of linkage for either the serotonin transporter gene (SLC6A4) or the serotonin type 2A receptor gene ($5HT_{2A}R$) in a sample of 17 probands with generalized Social Anxiety Disorder and their family members. However, as the authors note, linkage analysis may not be an optimal approach for studying complex psychiatric disorders. Instead, genomic association studies, which can detect relatively weak effects, may be necessary to shed light on the genetic basis of Social Anxiety Disorder (Stein et al., 1998).

Studies focused on broader behavioral styles that may relate to Social Anxiety Disorder, such as behavioral inhibition (BI) and shyness, have yielded modest associations with potentially relevant genetic polymorphisms. Results from a family-based association study of BI indicated a small but significant association between BI and the glutamic acid decarboxylase gene (65 kDA isoform; Smoller et al., 2001). This gene, which is involved in the synthesis of the neurotransmitter GABA, was targeted because it had previously been implicated in mouse models of BI. Additionally, in a sample of second graders, Arbelle and colleagues (2003) found a small but statistically significant association between shyness and the long form of the serotonin transporter promoter region 44 base pair deletion/insertion polymorphism (5-HTTLPR; Arbelle et al., 2003).

It appears clear that genetic factors play a role in the development of Social Anxiety Disorder. Much remains to be learned, however, about the specific genes involved and the ways their expression varies as a function of environmental factors and developmental stage. Large-scale genetic association studies and translational approaches, such as knock-out studies that manipulate the expression of specific genes in rodents, are among the promising methods for addressing such questions.

Temperamental Factors

Certain temperamental variations may constitute risk factors for the later development of Social Anxiety Disorder. As we noted earlier, some evidence suggests that behavioral inhibition to the unfamiliar may relate to later social anxiety. In relatively small, intensively studied samples, several studies have shown associations between BI and Social Anxiety Disorder in both affected children and their family members, particularly if the BI remains stable throughout early childhood (Biederman, Hirshfeld-Becker et al., 2001; Hirshfeld et al., 1992; Rosenbaum et al., 1991; Schwartz, Snidman, & Kagan, 1999). Other research, however, has found such associations to be small when examined in a larger, less precisely selected sample of children studied with a less intensive temperament assessment battery (Prior, Smart, Sanson, & Oberklaid, 2000).

Some physiological evidence indicates parallels between children with BI and individuals with social-evaluative fears or Social Anxiety Disorder. Correlations between BI and a variety of physiological variables, including heart rate, morning salivary cortisol, and activation of neural structures thought to mediate withdrawal or avoidance resemble those found in youth and adults with social-evaluative fears or Social Anxiety Disorder (Beidel, 1988; Davidson, 1994; Heimberg, Hope, Dodge, & Becker, 1990; Kagan et al., 1988). Additionally, findings from one functional magnetic resonance imaging (fMRI) study suggest that high BI in infancy modestly predicts adult amygdala response to novel social cues (Schwartz, Wright, Shin, Kagan, & Rauch, 2003). Such a response is consistent with findings among adults with Social Anxiety Disorder of amplified amygdala activity in the presence of novel facial cues, particularly those that signal potential threats (Birbaumer et al., 1998; Stein, Goldin, Sareen, Zorrilla, & Brown, 2002).

Some controversy remains regarding associations between BI and anxiety disorders. In a critical review of the literature, Turner, Beidel, and Wolff (1996) pointed out two central limitations. First, studies vary widely in the stringency with which they identify BI. Whereas some BI samples were selected on the basis of consistently inhibited behaviors across multiple tasks, others were identified on the basis of parent report alone. These differences in the ways that participants were classified make it difficult to compare results across studies. Second, studies do not always provide data regarding the psychiatric histories of participants' parents. In the absence of such data, it is not possible to differentiate the effects of BI and the effects of a family history of anxiety disorders.

Other researchers have raised questions about the degree to which BI relates to the emergence of social-evaluative concerns. Asendorpf (1990, 1993) argued that temperamental inhibition is associated with wariness of unfamiliar people, but not with social-evaluative concerns and associated patterns of behavior. Instead, he contended that the quality of children's relationships with peers predicts the degree to which they exhibit social inhibition and evaluative fears, particularly in familiar settings such as the classroom. Although there is some evidence in support of this distinction in healthy children (Eisenberg et al., 1998), its relevance to youth with Social Anxiety Disorder remains unclear.

Parental Influences

Parenting behavior has long been considered a potential mechanism underlying the development of anxiety in children. According to a model that Craske (1999) has proposed, parenting can contribute to anxiety in several ways.

First, certain broad, pervasive styles of parenting may facilitate the development of general anxiety in children. Parents whose styles tend to be critical or controlling, for example, might create a home environment that is conducive to anxiety in their offspring. Second, specific parenting behaviors, such as expression of apprehension when the child engages in a potentially risky activity, may encourage the development of anxiety in specific contexts or around specific topics. Most research on anxiety and parenting behavior has targeted general rather than specific forms of anxiety; very few studies have concentrated on how parenting may figure in the development of social anxiety per se.

A considerable body of research has examined associations between general parenting styles and the development of child anxiety, with a particular focus on control, warmth, and acceptance. In a recent critical review of this literature, little evidence emerged that these broad parental styles relate meaningfully to child anxiety (Wood, McLeod, Sigman, Hwang, & Chu, 2003). The authors note, however, that most studies were limited by their use of nonrepresentative samples and global self-report measures of parenting style. Additionally, as Rapee (1997) pointed out, a number of studies relied on participants' recollections of their parents' child-rearing practices, yielding data that may have been affected by reporting or recall biases.

A much smaller body of work has focused on observed parenting behaviors in the context of specific family interactions. In their review of these studies, Wood and colleagues (2003) found some support for a concurrent association between maternal criticism and child anxiety. A similar relationship between maternal acceptance and child anxiety also emerged in some cross-sectional studies; however, consistent with McClure, Brennan, Hammen, and Le Brocque's (2001) findings regarding general parenting styles in a longitudinally followed sample, this relationship may have been driven by maternal anxiety. Whether specific parenting behaviors mediate the relationship between parent and child anxiety is unclear; findings from one recent observational study, however, suggest that any such mediation may be minimal (Turner, Beidel, Roberson-Nay, & Tervo, 2003). In this study, which compared anxiety disordered and nonanxious parents' behaviors as they observed their children engaging in mildly risky play activities, few between-group differences emerged.

Conditioning Events

Theorists from behavioral perspectives have hypothesized that learning experiences may play a role in the onset of youth fears and anxieties. Rachman (1977) proposed that

three types of learning or conditioning events contribute to the development of anxiety. The first type, direct conditioning, involves in vivo exposure to an aversive stimulus (e.g., the child is mocked while presenting a book report to classmates). The second type, vicarious conditioning, involves observation of another individual's fearful behavior around an aversive stimulus (e.g., the child observes an older sibling's fear before presenting a book report). The final type, instruction/information, involves hearing from others that stimuli are fear inducing (e.g., the child hears stories from peers about bad experiences during the presentation of book reports).

In general, findings are mixed regarding these three pathways to the onset of fears and anxieties. King, Gullone, and Ollendick (1998) summarized research findings from studies that examined the role of learning in the acquisition of a variety of specific phobias and found that results varied markedly. Whereas most participants in some studies cited conditioning events as precipitants of a phobia, most participants in others reported having "always been afraid" of the phobic stimulus. Most of the studies reviewed were limited by their use of retrospective parent or child reports and the absence of meaningful comparison participants; consequently, it is difficult to draw conclusions from this literature.

More recent studies have used prospective designs to measure the effects of different types of conditioning on the development of fears or anxieties. In one of the few studies to focus on the role of learning in the development of social fears, Field, Hamilton, Knowles, and Plews (2003) measured 10- to 13-year-old children's attitudes toward three types of potentially frightening social situations (public speaking, eating in public, meeting new children) both before and after the presentation of either positive, neutral, or negative information about each situation. Results provided some support for Rachman's (1977) theory, but demonstrated that the effects of information on fear varied according to whether a peer or a teacher provided the information. Further work using prospective designs and in vivo encounters with conditioned stimuli is needed before the roles of different learning types in the onset of anxiety are fully understood.

Summary Regarding Risk

Consistent with the developmental psychopathology assumption of multideterminism (Cicchetti & Cohen, 1995), a wide range of factors clearly interact to influence the onset of anxiety in general and social anxiety in particular. Biologically based factors, such as genetic predisposition and temperament, appear particularly important for further study, especially in light of the neuroscience findings presented in the last section of this chapter. Nonetheless, given that social anxiety, like other types of anxiety, is likely multiply determined, it will be important for future research to examine the many potential risk factors, both those that are primarily biological and those that are primarily environmental, in concert. Consideration of the context in which anxiety symptoms and disorders develop will also be critical in light of evidence that different types of life events and experiences relate differently to the onset of different types of psychopathology (Tiet et al., 2001).

ANXIETY FROM A NEUROSCIENCE PERSPECTIVE

Research reviewed in the preceding sections of this chapter on clinical, developmental, and familial aspects of anxiety raises three essential questions for which current data provide few answers. First, it is not clear where the boundary lies between developmentally appropriate adolescent increases in social anxiety and clinical manifestations of an anxiety disorder, such as Social Anxiety Disorder. Both typical and pathological social anxiety become increasingly common as youth enter adolescence, and it is difficult to distinguish cases that are normal from those that are potentially problematic. Second, it remains unclear how to identify those youth affected by an anxiety disorder who will go on to develop chronic problems with anxiety and mood disorders. Although anxiety disorders represent the most common class of psychiatric disorder in children, with Social Anxiety Disorder particularly prevalent during adolescence, only a minority of affected youth will suffer significant long-term clinical effects. It is important that this minority be identified prospectively because, as its members mature, they will go on to account for a large proportion of adults with mood and anxiety disorders. Third, it remains unclear how to differentiate at-risk adolescents who are particularly vulnerable to developing anxiety disorders from those who are likely to be resilient. Despite the strong associations between various risk factors, particularly parental psychopathology, and childhood anxiety disorders, a sizable proportion of youth exposed to such risk factors will not develop clinical disorders.

There is no shortage of clinical research that has attempted to answer these three basic questions. Nevertheless, answers have not readily been forthcoming (Pine, 2002a, 2003; Pine & Charney, 2002). One alternative means of pursuing answers to these clinical questions involves embracing recent insights from neuroscience re-

search. Ultimately, variations in many domains of human experience, including anxiety, are reflected in functional aspects of neurophysiology. As a result, knowledge about how neurophysiology relates to anxiety may provide clinicians with novel tools for identifying children who are particularly at risk or resilient. Such advances in knowledge are unlikely to occur soon because it is difficult to translate research on neurophysiology into clinical insights. Basic and clinical studies have traditionally targeted different levels of inquiry, with basic science focusing on general aspects of behavior and its development, and clinical research focusing on between-group differences in behavioral patterns and developmental trajectories. Research on anxiety provides an excellent starting point for integrating basic and clinical studies. Already, considerable neuroscience research has examined the role of neural circuits in anxiety-related behaviors. In the current section, we review insights from this research that may ultimately provide a basis for breakthroughs in clinical investigations.

Fear Conditioning

In the late 1970s, research in the neurosciences shifted away from a relatively restricted focus on basic aspects of perception and motor control. Following the work of Davis (Davis & Whalen, 2001), LeDoux (2000), and others, investigators began to trace neural circuits that were engaged when animals experienced emotions or changes in brain states associated with reward and punishment. Much of this work initially concentrated on fear, as punishing stimuli produce robust changes in behavior, information processing, and physiology that are markedly similar across a range of mammalian species. In particular, neuroscientists developed a keen interest in the process of fear conditioning.

In the standard fear conditioning experiment, as shown in Figure 12.2, a neutral conditioned stimulus (CS+), such as a tone or a light, is paired with an aversive unconditioned stimulus (UCS), such as a shock or an aversive air puff. Following a series of such pairings, presentation of the CS+ begins to elicit behaviors, information-processing patterns, and physiological responses that were formerly associated with presentation of the UCS. Over the past 30 years, the neural circuitry engaged by this process has been precisely delineated in rodents, nonhuman primates, and, more recently, humans. Current understanding of this "fear circuit" extends to the genetic level, with recent findings identifying specific genes that are activated in isolated sets of neurons (Fanselow & LeDoux, 1999; Killcross, Robbins, & Everitt, 1997; LeDoux, 2000). Information concerning

Training

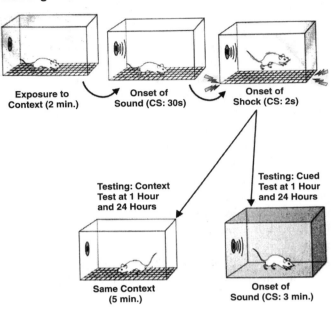

Figure 12.2 Fear conditioning experiment. After the animal is familiarized with the experiment context, a tone, which serves as the neutral conditioned stimulus (CS+), is paired with a foot shock, which acts as an aversive unconditioned stimulus (UCS). Following a series of such pairings, presentation of the CS+ alone elicits a fear response that was formerly associated with presentation of the UCS. *Source:* From *Memory: From Mind to Molecules* by Larry R. Squire and Eric R. Kandel. Copyright © 1999 by Scientific American Library. Reprinted by permission of Henry Holt and Company, LLC.

perceptual aspects of the CS+ is processed in two neural pathways. One of these extends from peripheral perceptual organs (e.g., the ears or eyes) to the thalamus, a relay station for information processed in sensory modalities. From the thalamus, projections arise that directly innervate the amygdala, a collection of nuclei located in the anterior medial temporal lobe of mammals. The other pathway extends from the thalamus to posterior portions of the cerebral cortex that are devoted to processing perceptual aspects of stimuli encountered in the environment. These cortical neurons form a complex web of interconnected synapses that ultimately innervate the amygdala after information passes to relatively anterior portions of the posterior hemisphere (LeDoux, 2000).

Fear conditioning research has led to a detailed understanding of functional aspects of the amygdala in rodents and nonhuman primates (Davidson et al., 2002; Davis & Whalen, 2001; LeDoux, 1998, 2000). Conditioning or emotional learning occurs as a consequence of changes in gene expression in amygdala neurons. These gene-level changes

in turn lead to conditioning-linked alterations in behavior, information processing, and physiology (Meaney, 2001a). The precise roles that specific amygdala nuclei play in fear conditioning are the topic of some controversy. In one account (LeDoux, 2000), perceptual information is channeled through the basolateral nucleus, where long-term potentiation facilitates new learning. Information then progresses through the central nucleus, which has widespread connections with brain structures involved in behavioral, cognitive, and physiologic regulation. As it disseminates via these connections, broad changes in physiology, information processing, and behavior occur. In other accounts (Everitt et al., 1999; Everitt & Robbins, 2000; Killcross et al., 1997; Robbins & Everitt, 2002), pathways restricted to the basolateral nucleus mediate some forms of conditioning. Despite this uncertainty about which amygdala nuclei participate in specific types of emotional learning, there is broad agreement that cortical-amygdala circuitry plays a critical role in the processes, particularly in the context of fear conditioning. Although the same circuitry figures in other types of emotional learning besides fear conditioning, detailed discussion of these learning types is beyond the scope of the current chapter.

Insights into neural aspects of fear conditioning have generated great interest among clinically oriented investigators. Using neuroimaging and brain lesion techniques, these investigators have demonstrated that the circuit operating during fear conditioning in human adults parallels that found in rodents and nonhuman primates (Buchel & Dolan, 2000). This circuit encompasses the human thalamus, posterior neocortex, and amygdala. More recently, studies using adaptations of the fear conditioning experiment that are appropriate for children and adolescents have extended knowledge about developmental aspects of emotional learning and its neural basis (Grillon, Dierker, & Merikangas, 1998; Merikangas, Avenevoli, Dierker, & Grillon, 1999; Monk, Grillon, et al., 2003; Pine, Fyer, et al., 2001).

It initially appeared that neuroscience research on fear conditioning would provide an avenue for extending insights from behavioral research on emotional learning in anxiety disorders. In particular, patients with anxiety disorders were hypothesized to exhibit enhanced fear conditioning relative to healthy individuals (Gorman, Kent, Sullivan, & Coplan, 2000). Such findings would have created an arena where clinical and neuroscience research converged naturally, permitting translational research focused explicitly on elucidating anxiety at a neural level. Demonstrating such between-group differences in fear conditioning, however, has proved difficult. Indeed, some evidence has even emerged to suggest that anxiety disorders are associated with *deficits* in fear learning in the context of fear conditioning paradigms (Grillon, 2002).

Translational Research and Anxiety: Going beyond Fear Conditioning

The exchange between basic and clinical researchers regarding fear conditioning has provided an exciting model for further translational research endeavors. Based on this body of research, basic researchers have begun to examine processes beyond fear conditioning with the aim of understanding how these processes may inform clinical studies. Some of this research focuses on processes that conform to our narrow definition of emotion regulation. Research on extinction provides a particularly compelling example.

Following the instantiation of fear through conditioning, the response to a CS+ can be changed or eliminated through a process known as "extinction." Extinction, which involves repeated presentation of the CS+ in the absence of the UCS, maps neatly onto our concept of emotion regulation. The animal's initial response to the newly conditioned CS, for instance, parallels the "emotional reaction" in Thompson's (1994) definition of emotional regulation. Then, during the process of extinction, the animal regulates its response in a manner resembling the monitoring, evaluating, and modifying that forms the substance of emotion regulation.

Conceptualizations of the extinction process have changed based on findings in neuroscience over the past decade. Formerly, models of extinction emphasized a process of "forgetting," in which an organism no longer recalled the salience of the CS+, as a predictor of shock once the CS+ had been extinguished (Bouton, 2002). However, recent data suggest that extinction is a far more active process that occurs when new learning overlays the results of conditioning (Bouton, 2002; Bouton, Mineka, & Barlow, 2001). Some have suggested that extinction "contextualizes" knowledge of the CS+-UCS relationship (Bouton et al., 2001). In a sense, extinction involves learning that a CS+ predicts a UCS in some contexts but not in others.

At a neural level, this process engages a broader circuit than the one linked to fear conditioning. This circuit encompasses the amygdala, ventral and medial aspects of the prefrontal cortex (PFC), and the hippocampus (Bouton, 2002; Davis & Whalen, 2001; Grillon, 2002; LeDoux, 2000; Milad & Quirk, 2002; Quirk, 2002; Quirk & Gehlert, 2003) and likely includes structures that are critical to aspects of human fear-related behaviors and psychiatric symptoms (see Figure 12.3). Consistent with this possibility, clinical re-

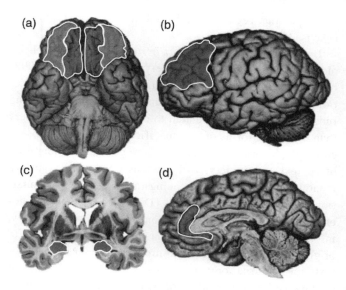

Figure 12.3 Neural structures thought to participate in regulation of fear and other emotions. (a) Orbitofrontal cortex highlighted in light gray, ventromedial prefrontal cortex highlighted in dark gray. (b) Dorsolateral prefrontal cortex. (c) Amygdala. (d) Anterior cingulate cortex. *Source:* From "Dysfunction in the Neural Circuitry of Emotion Regulation: A Possible Prelude to Violence," by R. J. Davidson, K. M. Putnam, and C. L. Larson, 2000, *Science, 289,* 591–594. From *Structure of the Human Brain: A Photographic Atla*s 3/1 by S. J. DeArmond, M. M. Fusco, and M. M. Dewey. Copyright 1974, 1976, 1989 by Oxford University Press, Inc. Used by permission of Oxford University Press.

searchers have been more successful in demonstrating that extinction processes differ across healthy and anxious individuals than they have in demonstrating comparable between-group differences in fear acquisition (Grillon, 2002). Such clinical advances have even led to the piloting of novel potential anxiolytic pharmacological compounds, such as D-cycloserine, that are known to facilitate extinction in rodents (Grillon, 2002).

Contextual stimuli have been found to play a role in extinction in rodents (Bouton, 2002); consequently, research has begun to examine the relevance of context for fear learning across species. During the classic fear conditioning experiment, rodents not only develop a fear response to the CS+, but they also, through a process known as "conditioning to context," develop a new reaction to the context in which the CS+-UCS relationship has been embedded (Davis, 1998). Thus, when placed in the cage used for the fear conditioning experiment, even in the absence of the CS+ or UCS, the rodent shows changes in behavior, physiology, and information processing (see Figure 12.2, testing in context). Like extinction, context conditioning is thought to involve neural circuits that extend beyond the amygdala, encompassing regions implicated in emotion regulation (Davis, 1998).

Based on neurochemical data in rodents and psychophysiology data in humans with anxiety disorders, Davis (1998) has suggested that context conditioning, much like extinction, engages neural structures and information-processing functions more closely related to clinical anxiety disorders than do simple forms of cue-specific fear conditioning. Accordingly, he has embarked on a more general consideration of context and anxiety, with a focus on contexts that are innately perceived as threatening in the absence of conditioning or learning experiences (Davis, 1998). This consideration has involved research on changes in physiology, information processing, and behavior in rodents exposed to brightly lit open fields, which are innately dangerous contexts for nocturnal organisms. In a small, parallel series of studies, he has also studied responses in humans placed in dark rooms, which are innately dangerous contexts for diurnal organisms (Grillon et al., 1999).

Just as neuroscientists have begun to focus on innately dangerous contexts, researchers in other fields are examining a variety of inherently dangerous or fear-inducing stimuli. Interest in such stimuli is long-standing; many investigators have noted cross-species similarities in the behavioral, information-processing, and physiological changes that mammals undergo in response to dangerous or punishing stimuli (Darwin, 1998; Davis & Whalen, 2001; Rolls, 1999).

Among the numerous inherently dangerous stimuli available for study, threatening displays by conspecifics have aroused particular interest. Facial displays of emotion, particularly of anger, constitute principal signals of threat for humans and other highly social primates (Darwin, 1998; Haxby, Hoffman, & Gobbini, 2002). They are therefore optimal stimuli for research aimed at understanding social anxiety and Social Anxiety Disorder, both of which revolve around fear of interpersonal threat.

One important question that facial stimuli are useful for addressing is whether individuals with Social Anxiety Disorder respond differently than do nonanxious individuals when they view angry faces. For instance, an enhanced initial attention-orienting reaction to angry faces or a bias in the threshold for considering faces to be angry might characterize Social Anxiety Disorder. Either of these differences would represent anxiety-associated dysfunction in what Thompson (1994) terms emotional reactions. As we review later, studies in adults indicate that those with Social Anxiety Disorder differ from nonanxious peers in their attentional orienting to angry faces. It is also possible that initial reactions to angry faces or other social threat cues

are normal in Social Anxiety Disorder, and instead, the condition is characterized by abnormalities in the evaluation, monitoring, and modification of responses to such cues. Differences of this sort would represent dysfunction in emotion regulation.

It is important to note that the demonstration of any differences in socially anxious individuals' experience or regulation of emotional responses or the neural concomitants of these processes in no way suggests that they are static or primarily congenital in origin. Recent research documents the malleability of face emotion-processing skills. For example, these studies suggest that experiences during childhood, such as abuse and neglect, can alter an individual's threshold for detecting anger in a face (Pollak, 2003; Pollak, Klorman, Thatcher, & Cicchetti, 2001; Pollak & Sinha, 2002). Psychopathological states may similarly affect perception of threat cues; some evidence suggests that particular mood and anxiety disorders are associated with distinctive abnormalities in facial threat processing (McClure, Pope, Hoberman, Pine, & Leibenluft, 2003). For clinically oriented investigators with an interest in anxiety, an important task is to relate such differences in information processing both to functional aspects of neural circuits and to specific subtypes of anxiety, such as social anxiety. One approach to this task is to focus on Social Anxiety Disorder as it is currently conceptualized in *DSM-IV*. An alternative approach might focus on particular subtypes of the disorder that exhibit unique patterns of aggregation within families, comorbidity, or persistence over time.

The latter approach is consistent with evidence that biological substrates of different types of fear state vary considerably at fundamental levels. Recent advances in neuroscience have allowed investigators to conduct increasingly molecular studies of neural processing, thus, extending knowledge about brain circuits and even particular neurons that are engaged in highly specific anxious or fearful states. Thus, even though neurochemical and neurophysiological studies demonstrate clear differences in circuitry involved in learned and innate fears, molecular genetic evidence suggests that neither of these types of fear constitutes a monolithic category. Using genetic manipulation strategies, researchers have developed knock-out mice, which lack functional activity in genes that are central to the experience of highly specific types of fear. A manipulation that interferes with separation fears, for example, may not interfere with fear of inherently dangerous contexts. The effect that a manipulation has on a particular fear or anxiety depends not only on the gene that is targeted, but also on the organism's developmental stage at the time of the manipulation. For example, inactivation of the gene for the 5HT1a receptor in the mouse produces an increase in anxious behavior only when inactivation occurs early in life. Moreover, reactivation of this gene during adulthood has no effect on this type of behavior (Gross et al., 2002). Data from highly molecular neuroscience research thus dovetail nicely with behavioral findings in rodents and nonhuman primates to indicate that fear states in animals are heterogeneous. This parallels clinical findings in humans suggesting that clinical anxiety disorders are best conceptualized as related but distinct.

Anxiety and Information Processing

Alterations in information processing are consistently observed following presentation of both conditioned fear stimuli and inherently fear-provoking stimuli. In particular, fear-provoking stimuli reliably affect two cognitive processes: attention and memory. Recent studies in neuroscience demonstrate how the neural circuit depicted in Figure 12.3 participates in these processes when fear or anxiety has been evoked.

Attention

Because organisms possess limited capacity to process the many stimuli that they confront in the environment, they engage the cognitive and neural processes that constitute *attention* to help prioritize these stimuli. In particular, rodents, nonhuman primates, and humans selectively attend to stimuli that possess either punishing or rewarding properties. The neural circuitry devoted to the prioritization of perceptual information has been precisely elucidated in rodents and nonhuman primates (Davis & Whalen, 2001). This circuitry encompasses many of the key brain structures involved in fear conditioning, including the amygdala, posterior association cortex, and PFC. In particular, medial regions of the PFC, such as the anterior cingulate gyrus, play a central role in interactions between attention and emotional salience (Miller & Cohen, 2001). Many theories attempt to differentiate the stimuli, contexts, and other circumstances that engage distinct aspects of this circuit (Damasio et al., 2000; Davis & Whalen, 2001; Kalin, Shelton, Davidson, & Kelley, 2001; LeDoux, 2000). However, considerable disagreement persists on this issue.

Research in humans using "attention interference" tasks such as the emotional Stroop has demonstrated that anxiety-provoking stimuli affect attention. Attention interference tasks require study participants simultaneously to process nonemotional features of a stimulus (e.g., the color of ink in which a word is printed) and to ignore emotional aspects of the stimulus (e.g., the word's emotionally laden meaning). People tend to find it more difficult to ignore emotional aspects of stimuli that convey threat (e.g., the word "death"), which slows their color-naming performance (Williams, Mathews, & MacLeod, 1996). This tendency, which is greater in individuals with anxiety disorders and possibly those at risk for anxiety disorders, is presumably mediated by stimulus effects on attention allocation.

Effects of anxiety on attention have also been demonstrated in studies using visual search and attention orientation tasks. Visual search tasks involve locating nonemotional stimuli that are embedded in a field of emotionally evocative stimuli. Studies using these tasks have found that the presence of salient, emotional stimuli influence the speed at which a nonemotional target can be detected (Davis & Whalen, 2001; Hadwin et al., 2003; Mogg & Bradley, 1998). Studies using attention orientation tasks, which involve the processing of nonemotional stimuli that are either spatially or temporally contiguous to emotional stimuli, have yielded similar results (Mogg & Bradley, 1998, 2002). Much like attention interference, these effects have been shown to differ between individuals with and without anxiety disorders, including Social Anxiety Disorder (Mogg & Bradley, 2002; Mogg, Philippot, & Bradley, 2004). Additionally, when stimuli are presented briefly (33 msec or shorter exposure) and masked so that they cannot be consciously perceived, biases in attention orientation remain apparent, particularly in individuals with anxiety disorders (Mogg & Bradley, 1999; Mogg, Bradley, & Williams, 1995). This may reflect desynchrony between cortical and subcortical pathways involved in interactions between anxiety and attention, or it may reflect specific perturbations in the subcortical path extending directly from the thalamus to the amygdala (LeDoux, 1998).

One of the major controversies concerning the relationship between attention and anxiety relates to the direction of the association. Many theories suggest that underlying abnormalities in attention regulation predispose individuals toward anxious behavior and frank anxiety disorders (Clark et al., 1990; MacLeod et al., 2002; Mogg & Bradley, 2002). If confirmed, this hypothesis suggests a means for distinguishing among subgroups of children with anxiety disorders and identifying those subgroups at highest risk for anxiety. For example, among offspring of adults with an anxiety disorder, those who show particular orienting reactions to anxiety-provoking stimuli may be at heightened risk for developing a clinical disorder in the future. Although this hypothesis is plausible and enjoys some support (MacLeod et al., 2002; Merikangas et al., 1999), it is equally conceivable that increases or decreases in anxiety might influence attention. Fear conditioning experiments demonstrate such an effect. Moreover, children who undergo traumatic experiences, whether they endorse anxiety symptoms or not, also demonstrate abnormalities in attention orienting to threat stimuli (Dalgleish, Moradi, Taghavi, Neshat-Doost, & Yule, 2001). If this hypothesis were confirmed, it would suggest that abnormalities in attention bias are epiphenomena rather than risk or causal factors associated with later development of anxiety. Experimental studies in humans are just beginning to explore these alternative explanations for the consistent association between anxiety and attention abnormalities. Interestingly, the bulk of evidence to date suggests that abnormalities in attention for threat may represent risk factors for anxiety.

Memory

Both observational and experimental studies of humans have demonstrated that emotionally salient stimuli are easier to encode and recall than are neutral stimuli (Lang, Bradley, & Cuthbert, 1998; LeDoux & Muller, 1997; Phelps & Anderson, 1997). Recall of these two stimulus types also appears to involve different neurochemical systems. It remains unclear if these effects are driven primarily by differences in stimulus valence or in the degree to which different stimuli induce arousal. Some evidence suggests that negatively valenced stimuli, which can induce anxiety, are more easily encoded than positively valenced stimuli (Lang et al., 1998). However, it is difficult to equate positive and negative stimuli on arousal, and these findings may have emerged because the negative stimuli were more arousing than were the positive stimuli. The neural circuitry involved in the prioritization of stimuli for encoding in memory has been precisely delineated, and convergent findings across rodents, nonhuman primates, and humans indicate that the amygdala plays a central role in this process (Lang et al., 1998; Phelps & Anderson, 1997). However, in marked contrast to findings with regard to attention and anxiety, it has been difficult to demonstrate consistent relationships between clinical measures of anxiety and memory for negatively valenced stimuli (McNally, 1997). Some studies clearly document a memory advantage for negative stimuli in individuals with specific anxiety disorders, and other studies have found abnormalities in memory for face emotions in adults with Social Anxiety Disorder (Foa, Gilboa-Schechtman, Amir, & Freshman, 2000; Lundh & Ost, 1996; McNally, 1997). Most of these findings, however, have not been well replicated, and other data indicate that emotional memory perturbations are more closely associated with MDD than

with anxiety disorders (Blaney, 1986; McNally, 1997). In light of the well-documented influence of attention on memory, the failure to find a consistent memory advantage for threatening information in anxious individuals, who show enhanced attention for threatening information, is perplexing.

INFORMATION PROCESSING, SOCIAL ANXIETY DISORDER, AND COGNITIVE NEUROSCIENCE

The consistency and strength of associations between anxiety and information processing in rodents, nonhuman primates, and humans provide an excellent avenue for translational research that integrates basic and clinical approaches. Not only have behavioral effects been consistently observed in experimental paradigms relevant to anxiety, but the neural structures involved in these effects (see Figure 12.3) have also been identified in multiple laboratories using a variety of techniques. In addition, extensive rodent studies and emerging studies of nonhuman primates document developmental changes in functional aspects of this circuit that are relevant to anxiety (Coplan et al., 2001; Meaney, 2001b).

These bodies of research, in concert with findings of associations between human information processing and both the risk for and the presence of anxiety disorders, provide a solid foundation for the generation of precise hypotheses about the roles of specific neural structures in anxious behavior. With recent advances in fMRI, it has become possible to test such hypotheses, not only in human adults, but also in children and adolescents. Using fMRI, researchers derive an index of changes in blood flow that occur while study participants perform specific cognitive tasks. Differences in the magnetic susceptibility properties of oxygenated and deoxygenated hemoglobin provide the brain with its own endogenous contrast agent, such that increases in the flow of oxygenated blood to particular brain regions are reflected in patterns of activation in fMRI scans.

Although fMRI provides unusual opportunities to implement developmentally oriented translational studies, such research remains difficult to conduct. One major problem arises because neuroscience studies of human fear and anxiety have traditionally used a range of aversive stimuli, including electric shocks, noxious smells, grotesque pictures, verbal prompts, and pharmacological compounds. Many of these stimuli are too aversive to use with children. Others, such as abstract verbal representations of fearful events, may not evoke emotion as reliably in children as they do in adults. Photographs of emotionally expressive facial displays have emerged as adequately evocative stimuli that are well suited for developmental research on emotion and information processing.

The use of facial emotion displays in such research followed observations that facial displays could induce emotion in observers across developmental stages, cultures, and species (Darwin, 1998; Nelson et al., 2002). Photographs of such displays have served as stimuli in numerous cognitive studies of healthy adults and children (Haxby et al., 2002; Monk, McClure, et al., 2003) that have demonstrated reliable interactions between emotion and information processing. Findings indicate, for example, that angry faces can engage attention and can interfere with performance on nonemotional tasks (Mogg & Bradley, 2002). Moreover, angry faces have been shown to be more memorable than other expressions under some circumstances (Lundh & Ost, 1996). These effects likely reflect influences of angry faces on the engagement of specific brain regions, such as the PFC, and associated aspects of information processing. Functional MRI studies document reliable activations of ventral and medial PFC regions by angry facial displays as well as activation of the amygdala during viewing of fearful faces, which may convey cues of indirect threat (Haxby et al., 2002).

Although these recent successes in neuroimaging have generated considerable enthusiasm, they are still far removed from the advances that they may eventually facilitate in the study and treatment of anxiety disorders. Ongoing research in other types of adult psychopathology provides some guideposts that translational research on anxiety disorders might follow to comprehensively capitalize on the strengths of fMRI techniques. Studies of Schizophrenia and Alzheimer's disease, for example, provide specific examples of one potentially fruitful path for fMRI research on pediatric anxiety, particularly pediatric Social Anxiety Disorder.

Neuroimaging research on both Schizophrenia and Alzheimer's disease has its foundation in studies of psychiatrically healthy individuals. In the case of Alzheimer's disease, research on healthy adults led to two important findings. First, it demonstrated that relevant cognitive paradigms could capture subtle memory abnormalities that occur early in the course of Alzheimer's disease (Bookheimer et al., 2000). Second, it showed that these paradigms reliably engaged regions of the brain, such as the hippocampus, that research in rodents and nonhuman primates had previously implicated in mnemonic functions. In the case of Schizophrenia, initial studies established cognitive paradigms sensitive to abnormalities in

working memory that are associated with both the disease and the underlying risk for the disease (Marenco & Weinberger, 2000). Subsequently, fMRI studies mapped the brain circuit encompassing dorsal components of the PFC that become engaged during working memory tasks (Callicott & Weinberger, 1999).

Such findings permitted the conduct of highly focused fMRI studies on patients that implemented cognitive tasks carefully chosen to target predicted deficits. This approach is potentially problematic, because differences in brain activation between patients and controls may result from one group's failure to properly perform the requisite cognitive operations, rather than from an underlying brain abnormality. To solve this problem, studies in both patient groups used tasks that included behavioral measures on which subjects' performance strategies could be explicitly monitored. Additionally, by using event-related and parametric fMRI research designs, researchers were able to assess brain activation during cognitive tasks relative to each subject's level of performance.

Functional MRI research on Schizophrenia and Alzheimer's disease has demonstrated abnormalities in brain activation during normal performance on tasks where patients and comparison subjects usually differ. For each disorder, such findings have led to hypotheses implicating inefficient engagement of particular brain regions in the genesis of psychopathology (Bookheimer et al., 2000; Callicott & Weinberger, 1999). These hypotheses have shaped recent ideas about risk, methods for early identification, and the role of genetics for both conditions. To successfully extend insights from clinical and cognitive studies in pediatric anxiety, similar groundwork must be laid in developmentally oriented fMRI studies.

Functional MRI studies in healthy adults initially demonstrated reliable activation in anxiety-relevant structures using face emotion-viewing paradigms (Haxby et al., 2002). These findings led to research using comparable paradigms in psychiatric populations. In these studies, adults with Social Anxiety Disorder, MDD, and PTSD each have been shown to exhibit abnormal activation in the amygdala during the viewing of face emotions (Rauch et al., 2000; Sheline et al., 2001). Moreover, such abnormalities have been linked to potential genetic susceptibility markers for each condition (Hariri et al., 2002).

The success of adult fMRI studies set the stage for extensions to studies of development and developmental psychopathology. Although such work is still in its infancy, initial studies have yielded evidence of some parallels in patterns of activation to threat cues between children and adults. Children with anxiety disorders, for example, like adults with Social Anxiety Disorder, show evidence of enhanced amygdala activation during the viewing of some emotional facial displays (Thomas et al., 2001). However, some differences also have emerged between children and adults on these tasks. For example, one of the more consistent findings in adults is reliable amygdala activation during the viewing of fearful faces (Haxby et al., 2002). This finding has not been consistently replicated in children. In fact, some studies suggest that children show greater activation to neutral than to fearful faces (Thomas et al., 2001).

Recent developmentally oriented studies of face-emotion processing have also been limited by their lack of emphasis on behavioral data. Most studies either have used passive viewing tasks, which require no behavioral response, or have relied on relatively easy behavioral tasks, such as gender discrimination, where no developmental differences in associated cognitive processes are anticipated. These approaches deviate from the path outlined earlier for studies of Schizophrenia or Alzheimer's disease, which emphasized acquisition of fMRI data during the performance of a cognitive task expected to differentiate between groups.

Recent experimental psychology research lays the groundwork for informative fMRI studies in research on adolescent development and Social Anxiety Disorder. We provide two examples relevant to research on emotion reactions and emotional regulation. First, attention-orienting tasks, which measure an emotional reaction in the absence of subsequent implicit or explicit efforts at regulation, show promise for use in studies of Social Anxiety Disorder and development. Studies using such tasks have shown that angry faces reliably capture attention when they are presented in the context of nonemotional faces (Mogg & Bradley, 1998). This effect is thought to occur because angry faces more readily engage the amygdala and key components of the PFC, including the ventral or orbital frontal cortex and the medial or cingulate aspect of the PFC, than do other emotional faces (Haxby et al., 2002). Behaviorally, individuals with Social Anxiety Disorder, as well as those with other anxiety disorders, have been shown to exhibit behavioral differences on attention-orienting tasks (Mogg & Bradley, 2002). These behavioral group differences are also hypothesized to result from anxiety-associated decreases in the threshold for engaging the amygdala and ventral and medial PFC during tasks designed to elicit orienting to emotionally salient cues (Pine, 2001). Thus, tests of attention orienting, which have been shown to effectively capture one type of emotional reaction and activity within its associated neural circuitry, pro-

vide a measure of emotional reaction that is appropriate for studies of developmental psychopathology.

Second, other cognitive tasks that use face emotions as stimuli hold promise for use in developmental studies mapping neural circuits associated with anxiety and emotion regulation. These tasks require effortfully controlled attentional focus on nonemotional cues under conditions in which distracting, emotionally salient stimuli are present. Such tasks are clinically relevant because negative emotional displays from others are difficult for individuals with Social Anxiety Disorder to screen out, even when their attention is directed to performance of another task. This type of cognitive dysfunction is central to the genesis or maintenance of Social Anxiety Disorder. Indeed, most effective therapies for the disorder target problems with directing attention under states of high arousal, a basic emotion regulatory capacity. Tasks requiring attentional focus on nonemotional cues in the presence of emotional distracters are also developmentally relevant, because enhanced ability to control the direction of attention under states of high arousal represents one of the more robust changes associated with successful maturation from latency into adolescence and adulthood (Mischel, Shoda, & Rodriguez, 1989).

We have developed a cognitive paradigm that requires research participants to alternately direct their attention to their own emotional reaction to facial expressions and to either emotional or nonemotional features of faces that do not relate to their internal emotional responses. In healthy adults, such manipulations of attention during the viewing of evocative photographs have been shown to differentially engage the ventral and medial PFC (Monk, McClure, et al., 2003). Some controversy persists about whether the amygdala is also differentially engaged during such manipulations, with some studies indicating that it is and other studies suggesting that this structure becomes reliably engaged under both attention states (Dolan, 2002; Pessoa, McKenna, Gutierrez, & Ungerleider, 2002). In adolescents, however, these brain regions show differential modulation across types of emotional stimuli but not across attention states. These developmental differences are consistent with the idea that adults can modulate activity in relevant brain structures based on attentional demands, whereas such modulation in adolescents, whose neural structures are still immature, is driven by emotional content.

In light of findings from experimental studies, it appears likely that Social Anxiety Disorder is also associated with differential engagement of the amygdala and ventral and medial PFC during emotion response tasks such as attention orienting and emotion regulation tasks. Just as neuroimaging findings have laid important foundations for our understanding of Schizophrenia and Alzheimer's disease, the successful demonstration of differential neural engagement patterns in social anxiety could have considerable implications for future studies on underlying risk for and prevention of the disorder.

CONCLUSIONS AND RECOMMENDATIONS FOR FUTURE WORK

In this chapter, we reviewed the literature on childhood anxiety disorders with a specific focus on Social Anxiety Disorder, which provides a model for integrating research from clinical psychopathology, developmental psychology, and cognitive neuroscience. Research on anxiety disorders from each of these perspectives has burgeoned in recent years, and the confluence of findings across fields holds promise for elucidating new prevention and treatment approaches for this type of psychopathology. The findings we reviewed form several themes that suggest directions for future study.

First, relative to other disorders, such as depression, anxiety disorders and their manifestations across development are broadly understudied. This reflects, in part, the historical belief that anxiety disorders constitute "mild" psychopathology. In light of recent evidence that childhood anxiety predicts a variety of negative outcomes, including the later development of Major Depressive Disorder (Pine et al., 1998), however, it has become clear that understanding anxiety disorders is critically important. In particular, research from a developmental psychopathology perspective would be useful for clarifying boundaries between normal and abnormal anxiety, for describing the paths that lead from early anxiety to either positive or negative outcomes, and for further explicating factors that confer risk for or protection against the development of pathological anxiety.

More specifically, recent research in developmental psychopathology suggests the need to consider alternative classification schemes for anxiety given advances in both basic and clinical neuroscience. This research shows that anxiety disorders are likely to represent the end result of a complex interplay among many risk factors operating across increasingly complex levels. For example, some risk factors may involve specific genetically based perturbations. These risk factors, in turn, may exert their effects through interactions either with other genes or with environmental factors. At a higher level, such effects are likely to shape underlying brain systems and their associated in-

formation-processing functions. Finally, whether or not perturbations in brain systems and associated information-processing functions ultimately manifest as clinical syndromes may depend on broader contextual influences on the developing organism. Given the complexity of these issues, our understanding of classification may change as our understanding of mechanisms advances. For example, children currently classified in the same broad category may ultimately be differentially categorized as we understand divergent mechanistic pathways to similarly appearing clinical syndromes. Conversely, children currently classified in distinct categories may ultimately be combined as we understand how core pathways can produce various clinical syndromes.

Ultimately, such efforts will require research on mechanisms through which risk factors influence phenotypic expression. Surprisingly, little is known about how various risk factors influence patterns of adaptation in developing individuals. In particular, offspring of adults with Social Anxiety Disorder, as well as other types of psychopathology, are at elevated risk for developing anxiety of their own. How the presence of this heightened risk, regardless of whether it eventually manifests as a disorder, influences children's and adolescents' negotiation and mastery of salient developmental tasks is poorly understood and worthy of research attention. For example, do youth at high risk for social anxiety by virtue of parental psychopathology differ from peers at lower risk in their patterns of attachment, peer relations, or conceptions of self? Further, are such differences evident in individuals who prove resilient to anxiety despite their high-risk status?

Additionally, much existing research has focused on individual risk factors in isolation. Integrative studies that approach risk from multiple perspectives simultaneously would provide a more accurate picture of the complex interplay among genetics, neurobiology, family environment, peer relations, and other influences. Recently, studies combining genetic approaches with neuroimaging techniques have begun to emerge in the literature, offering one example of how such integrative research might manifest.

Second, research in clinical psychopathology strongly suggests that the anxiety disorders constitute a set of related but distinct pathologies. Although, in general terms, all of these disorders involve perturbation in the capacity to regulate anxious states, it appears likely that specific pathophysiologic profiles are associated with the particular patterns of maladaptation that characterize individual disorders. Additionally, data from the developmental psychology literature underscore the fact that anxious states are pervasive and common across the life span. Consequently, the line between normal and abnormal anxiety is difficult to identify, particularly at the level of behavior, where a normal, transient anxiety state can closely resemble states that occur in the context of an enduring disorder. Further complicating the distinction of typical from pathological anxiety is the variability across developmental stages in the manifestations of anxiety that are considered normal. It is therefore important that studies be conducted that further illuminate the distinctive pathophysiology of each anxiety disorder across development, with an eye to identifying markers of risk and optimal pathways for treatment. Such efforts will require a bridging of perspectives from clinical and basic sciences.

For example, conceptualizations of clinical characteristics may advance if they describe behaviors in a fashion that is amenable to research in experimental psychology and neuroscience. This will require a more precise specification of behavior than currently available in the clinical literature. Current clinical conceptualizations describe relatively broad perturbations in cognition, such as enhanced vigilance in anxiety. To facilitate integration with psychology and neuroscience, future conceptualizations will need to describe in more detail the precise circumstances under which attention is perturbed in the anxiety disorders.

Finally, researchers in other clinical areas, such as Schizophrenia and Alzheimer's disease, have begun to develop paradigms that elegantly bridge the gap between basic science and clinical utility. Anxiety disorders are primed for similar translational work that capitalizes on converging findings across multiple diverse areas of research. In particular, fMRI studies provide a promising avenue for integrating the provocative data that have emerged recently from work on fear conditioning and extinction across different species, threat cue processing in humans, and genetics. These disparate areas of study each provide important information regarding the processes involved in emotion regulation that, taken together, could eventually revolutionize the treatment of anxiety.

REFERENCES

Ackerman, P. T., Newton, J. E., McPherson, W. B., Jones, J. G., & Dykman, R. A. (1998). Prevalence of post traumatic stress disorder and other psychiatric diagnoses in three groups of abused children (sexual, physical, and both). *Child Abuse and Neglect, 22*(8), 759–774.

American Psychiatric Association. (1980). *Diagnostic and Statistical Manual of Mental Disorders* (3rd ed.). Washington, DC: Author.

Arbelle, S., Benjamin, J., Golin, M., Kremer, I., Belmaker, R. H., & Ebstein, R. P. (2003). Relation of shyness in grade school children to the genotype for the long form of the serotonin transporter promoter region polymorphism. *American Journal of Psychiatry, 160,* 671–676.

Asendorpf, J. B. (1990). Development of inhibition during childhood: Evidence for situational specificity and a two-factor model. *Developmental Psychology, 26,* 721–730.

Asendorpf, J. B. (1993). Beyond temperament. In K. H. Rubin & J. B. Asendorpf (Eds.), *Social withdrawal, inhibition, and shyness in childhood* (pp. 265–289). Hillsdale, NJ: Erlbaum.

Bandelow, B., Alvarez Tichauer, G., Spath, C., Broocks, A., Hajak, G., Bleich, S., et al. (2001). Separation anxiety and actual separation experiences during childhood in patients with panic disorder. *Canadian Journal of Psychiatry, 46*(10), 948–952.

Beidel, D. C. (1988). Psychophysiological assessment of anxious emotional states in children. *Journal of Abnormal Psychology, 97,* 80–82.

Beidel, D. C., Silverman, W. K., & Hammond-Laurence, K. (1996). Overanxious disorder: Subsyndromal state or specific disorder? A comparison of clinic and community samples. *Journal of Clinical Child Psychology, 25,* 25–32.

Bennett, M. (1989). Children's self-attribution of embarrassment. *British Journal of Developmental Psychology, 7,* 207–217.

Bennett, M., & Gillingham, K. (1991). The role of self-focused attention in children's attributions of social emotions to the self. *Journal of Genetic Psychology, 152,* 303–309.

Bennett, M., Yuill, N., Banerjee, R., & Thomson, S. (1998). Children's understanding of extended identity. *Developmental Psychology, 34,* 322–331.

Bergman, R. L., Piacentini, J., & McCracken, J. T. (2002). Prevalence and description of selective mutism in a school-based sample. *Journal of the American Academy of Child and Adolescent Psychiatry, 41*(8), 938–946.

Biederman, J., Faraone, S. V., Hirshfeld-Becker, D. R., Friedman, D., Robin, J. A., & Rosenbaum, J. F. (2001). Patterns of psychopathology and dysfunction in high-risk children of parents with panic disorder and major depression. *American Journal of Psychiatry, 158*(1), 49–57.

Biederman, J., Hirshfeld-Becker, D. R., Rosenbaum, J. F., Herot, C., Friedman, D., Snidman, N., et al. (2001). Further evidence of association between behavioral inhibition and social anxiety in children. *American Journal of Psychiatry, 158,* 1673–1679.

Birbaumer, N., Grodd, W., Diedrich, O., Klose, U., Erb, M., Lotze, M., et al. (1998). FMRI reveals amygdala activation to human faces in social phobics. *NeuroReport, 9,* 1223–1226.

Blair, R. J. R. (2003). Neurobiological basis of psychopathy. *British Journal of Psychiatry, 182,* 5–7.

Blanco, C., Schneier, F. R., Schmidt, A., Blanco-Jerez, C. R., Marshall, R. D., Sanchez-Lacay, A., et al. (2003). Pharmacological treatment of social anxiety disorder: A meta-analysis. *Depression and Anxiety, 18*(1), 29–40.

Blaney, P. H. (1986). Affect and memory: A review. *Psychological Bulletin, 99,* 229–246.

Blankstein, K. R., Flett, G. L., & Watson, M. S. (1992). Coping and academic problem-solving ability in test anxiety. *Journal of Clinical Psychology, 48,* 37–46.

Bookheimer, S. Y., Strojwas, M. H., Cohen, M. S., Saunders, A. M., Pericak-Vance, M. A., Mazziotta, J. C., et al. (2000). Patterns of brain activation in people at risk for Alzheimer's disease. *New England Journal of Medicine, 343,* 450–456.

Bouton, M. E. (2002). Context, ambiguity, and unlearning: Sources of relapse after behavioral extinction. *Biological Psychiatry, 52*(10), 976–986.

Bouton, M. E., Mineka, S., & Barlow, D. H. (2001). A modern learning theory perspective on the etiology of panic disorder. *Psychological Review, 108*(1), 4–32.

Bremner, J. D., Narayan, M., Staib, L. H., Southwick, S. M., McGlashan, T., & Charney, D. S. (1999). Neural correlates of memories of childhood sexual abuse in women with and without posttraumatic stress disorder. *American Journal of Psychiatry, 156*(11), 1787–1795.

Bremner, J. D., Staib, L. H., Kaloupek, D., Southwick, S. M., Soufer, R., & Charney, D. S. (1999). Neural correlates of exposure to traumatic pictures and sound in Vietnam combat veterans with and without posttraumatic stress disorder: A positron emission tomography study. *Biological Psychiatry, 45*(7), 806–816.

Breslau, N., Davis, G. C., & Prabucki, K. (1987). Searching for evidence on the validity of generalized anxiety disorder: Psychopathology in children of anxious mothers. *Psychiatry Research, 20*(4), 285–297.

Brett, E. A. (1997). The classification of posttraumatic stress disorder. In B. A. van der Kolk, A. C. McFarlane, & L. Weisaeth (Eds.), *Traumatic stress: The effects of overwhelming experience on mind, body, and society* (pp. 117–128). New York: Guilford Press.

Buchel, C., & Dolan, R. J. (2000). Classical fear conditioning in functional neuroimaging. *Current Opinions in Neurobiology, 10*, 219–223.

Callicott, J. H., & Weinberger, D. R. (1999). Neuropsychiatric dynamics: The study of mental illness using functional magnetic resonance imaging. *European Journal of Radiology, 30*, 95–104.

Casper, J. L. (1846). Biographie d'une idée fixe (Lalanne, Trans. into French 1902). *Archives de Neurologie, 13*, 270–287.

Cheek, J. M., & Buss, A. H. (1981). Shyness and sociability. *Journal of Personality and Social Psychology, 41*, 330–339.

Cicchetti, D., & Cohen, D. J. (1995). Perspectives on developmental psychopathology. In D. Cicchetti & D. J. Cohen (Eds.), *Developmental psychopathology: Vol. 1. Theory and methods* (pp. 3–20). New York: Wiley.

Claparède, E. (1902). L'Obsession de la rougeur: A propos d'un cas d'éreutophobie. *Archives de Psychologie de la Suisse Romande, 2*, 307–334.

Clark, D. A., Beck, A. T., & Stewart, B. (1990). Cognitive specificity and positive-negative affectivity: Complementary or contradictory views on anxiety and depression? *Journal of Abnormal Psychology, 99*, 148–155.

Cohen, J. A. (2003). Treating acute posttraumatic reactions in children and adolescents. *Biological Psychiatry, 53*(9), 827–833.

Cohen, P., Cohen, J., Kasen, S., Velez, C. N., Hartmark, C., Johnson, J., et al. (1993). An epidemiological study of disorders in late childhood and adolescence: Pt. I. Age- and gender-specific prevalence. *Journal of Child Psychology and Psychiatry, 34*(6), 851–867.

Cooper, P. J., & Eke, M. (1999). Childhood shyness and maternal social phobia: A community study. *British Journal of Psychiatry, 174*, 439–443.

Coplan, J. D., Smith, E. L., Altemus, M., Scharf, B. A., Owens, M. J., Nemeroff, C. B., et al. (2001). Variable foraging demand rearing: Sustained elevations in cisternal cerebrospinal fluid corticotropin-releasing factor concentrations in adult primates. *Biological Psychiatry, 50*, 200–204.

Costello, E. J., Mustillo, S., Erkanli, A., Keeler, G., & Angold, A. (2003). Prevalence and development of psychiatric disorders in childhood and adolescence. *Archives of General Psychiatry, 60*(8), 837–844.

Costello, E. J., Pine, D. S., Hammen, C., March, J. S., Plotsky, P. M., Weissman, M. M., et al. (2002). Development and natural history of mood disorders. *Biological Psychiatry, 52*(6), 529–542.

Cox, B. J., McWilliams, L. A., Clara, I. P., & Stein, M. B. (2003). The structure of feared situations in a nationally representative sample. *Journal of Anxiety Disorders, 17*, 89–101.

Cox, F. N., & Campbell, D. (1968). Young children in a new situation with and without their mothers. *Child Development, 39*, 123–131.

Craske, M. G. (1999). *Anxiety disorders: Psychological approaches to theory and treatment.* Boulder, CO: Westview Press.

Crozier, W. R., & Burnham, M. (1990). Age-related differences in children's understanding of shyness. *British Journal of Developmental Psychology, 8*, 179–185.

Dalgleish, T., Moradi, A. R., Taghavi, M. R., Neshat-Doost, H. T., & Yule, W. (2001). An experimental investigation of hypervigilance for threat in children and adolescents with post-traumatic stress disorder. *Psychological Medicine, 31*(3), 541–547.

Damasio, A. R. (2001). Fundamental feelings. *Nature, 413*(6858), 781.

Damasio, A. R., Grabowski, T. J., Bechara, A., Damasio, H., Ponto, L. L., Parvizi, J., et al. (2000). Subcortical and cortical brain activity during the feeling of self-generated emotions. *Nature Neuroscience, 3*(10), 1049–1056.

Darwin, C. (1998). *The expression of the emotions in man and animals* (3rd ed.). New York: Oxford University Press.

Davidson, R. J. (1994). Asymmetric brain function, affective style, and psychopathology: The role of early experience and plasticity. *Development and Psychopathology, 6*, 741–758.

Davidson, R. J. (1998). Affective style and affective disorders: Perspectives from affective neuroscience. *Cognition and Emotion, 12*(3), 307–330.

Davidson, R. J., Lewis, D. A., Alloy, L. B., Amaral, D. G., Bush, G., Cohen, J. D., et al. (2002). Neural and behavioral substrates of mood and mood regulation. *Biological Psychiatry, 52*, 478–502.

Davis, M. (1998). Are different parts of the extended amygdala involved in fear versus anxiety? *Biological Psychiatry, 44*, 1239–1247.

Davis, M., & Whalen, P. J. (2001). The amygdala: Vigilance and emotion. *Molecular Psychiatry, 6*, 13–34.

Dealy, C. E. (1923). Problem children in the early school grades. *Journal of Abnormal Psychology and Social Psychology, 18*, 125–136.

Derryberry, D., & Reed, M. A. (2002). Anxiety-related attentional biases and their regulation by attentional control. *Journal of Abnormal Psychology, 111*(2), 225–236.

Dewa, C. S., & Lin, E. (2000). Chronic physical illness, psychiatric disorder and disability in the workplace. *Social Science and Medicine, 51*(1), 41–50.

Dolan, R. J. (2002). Emotion, cognition, and behavior. *Science, 298*, 1191–1194.

Eisenberg, N., Shepard, S. A., Fabes, R. A., Murphy, B. C., & Guthrie, I. K. (1998). Shyness and children's emotionality, regulation, and coping: Contemporaneous, longitudinal, and across-context relations. *Child Development, 69*, 767–790.

Everitt, B. J., Parkinson, J. A., Olmstead, M. C., Arroyo, M., Robledo, P., & Robbins, T. W. (1999). Associative processes in addiction and reward: The role of amygdala-ventral striatal subsystems. *Annals of the New York Academy of Sciences, 877*, 412–438.

Everitt, B. J., & Robbins, T. W. (2000). Second-order schedules of drug reinforcement in rats and monkeys: Measurement of reinforcing efficacy and drug-seeking behaviour. *Psychopharmacology, 153*(1), 17–30.

Ezpeleta, L., Keeler, G., Erkanli, E., Costello, E. J., & Angold, A. (2001). Epidemiology of psychiatric disability in childhood and adolescence. *Journal of Child Psychology, Psychiatry, and Allied Disciplines, 42*, 901–914.

Fairbrother, N. (2002). The treatment of social phobia: 100 years ago. *Behaviour Research and Therapy, 40*, 1291–1304.

Fanselow, M. S., & LeDoux, J. E. (1999). Why we think plasticity underlying Pavlovian fear conditioning occurs in the basolateral amygdala. *Neuron, 23*, 229–232.

Field, A. P., Hamilton, S. J., Knowles, K. A., & Plews, E. L. (2003). Fear information and social phobic beliefs in children: A prospective paradigm and preliminary results. *Behaviour Research and Therapy, 41,* 113–123.

Foa, E. B., Gilboa-Schechtman, E., Amir, N., & Freshman, M. (2000). Memory bias in generalized social phobia: Remembering negative emotional expressions. *Journal of Anxiety Disorders, 14,* 501–519.

Fordham, K., & Stevenson-Hinde, J. (1999). Shyness, friendship quality, and adjustment during middle childhood. *Journal of Child Psychology and Psychiatry, 40*(5), 757–768.

Fox, N. A., Henderson, H. A., Rubin, K. H., Calkins, S. D., & Schmidt, L. A. (2001). Continuity and discontinuity of behavioral inhibition and exuberance: Psychophysiological and behavioral influences across the first four years of life. *Child Development, 72,* 1–21.

Fyer, A. J. (1993). Heritability of social anxiety: A brief review. *Journal of Clinical Psychiatry, 54*(Suppl.), 10–12.

Fyer, A. J. (1998). Current approaches to etiology and pathophysiology of specific phobia. *Biological Psychiatry, 44*(12), 1295–1304.

Fyer, A. J., Mannuzza, S., Chapman, T. F., Liebowitz, M. R., & Klein, D. F. (1993). A direct interview family study of social phobia. *Archives of General Psychiatry, 50,* 286–293.

Fyer, A. J., Mannuzza, S., Chapman, T. F., Martin, L. Y., & Klein, D. F. (1995). Specificity in familial aggregation of phobic disorders. *Archives of General Psychiatry, 52*(7), 564–573.

Garnefski, N., Legerstee, J., Kraaij, V. V., Van Den Kommer, T., & Teerds, J. (2002). Cognitive coping strategies and symptoms of depression and anxiety: A comparison between adolescents and adults. *Journal of Adolescence, 25,* 603–611.

Gershaw, N. J., & Schwarz, J. C. (1971). The effects of a familiar toy and mother's presence on exploratory and attachment behaviors in young children. *Child Development, 42,* 1662–1666.

Glickman, A. R., & La Greca, A. M. (2004). The dating anxiety scale for adolescents: Scale development and associations with adolescent functioning. *Journal of Clinical Child and Adolescent Psychology, 33*(3), 566–578.

Glyshaw, K., Cohen, L. H., & Towbes, L. C. (1989). Coping strategies and psychological distress: Prospective analyses of early and middle adolescents. *American Journal of Community Psychology, 17,* 607–623.

Goenjian, A. K., Pynoos, R. S., Steinberg, A. M., Najarian, L. M., Asarnow, J. R., Karayan, I., et al. (1995). Psychiatric comorbidity in children after the 1988 earthquake in Armenia. *Journal of the American Academy of Child and Adolescent Psychiatry, 34*(9), 1174–1184.

Goodenough, F. L. (1929). The emotional behavior of young children during mental tests. *Journal of Juvenile Research, 13,* 204–219.

Goodwin, R. D., & Pine, D. S. (2002). Respiratory disease and panic attacks among adults in the United States. *Chest, 122*(2), 645–650.

Gorman, J. M., Kent, J. M., Sullivan, G. M., & Coplan, J. D. (2000). Neuroanatomical hypothesis of panic disorder, revised. *American Journal of Psychiatry, 157*(4), 493–505.

Grados, M. A., Riddle, M. A., Samuels, J. F., Liang, K. Y., Hoehn-Saric, R., Bienvenu, O. J., et al. (2001). The familial phenotype of obsessive-compulsive disorder in relation to tic disorders: The Hopkins OCD family study. *Biological Psychiatry, 50*(8), 559–565.

Grillon, C. (2002). Associative learning deficits increase symptoms of anxiety in humans. *Biological Psychiatry, 51*(11), 851–858.

Grillon, C., Dierker, L., & Merikangas, K. R. (1998). Fear-potentiated startle in adolescent offspring of parents with anxiety disorders. *Biological Psychiatry, 44*(10), 990–997.

Grillon, C., Merikangas, K. R., Dierker, L., Snidman, N., Arriaga, R. I., Kagan, J., et al. (1999). Startle potentiation by threat of aversive stimuli and darkness in adolescents: A multi-site study. *International Journal of Psychophysiology, 32*(1), 63–73.

Gross, C., Zhuang, X., Stark, K., Ramboz, S., Oosting, R., Kirby, L., et al. (2002). Serotonin1A receptor acts during development to establish normal anxiety-like behaviour in the adult. *Nature, 416*(6879), 396–400.

Gullone, E. (1999). The assessment of normal fear in children and adolescents. *Clinical Child and Family Psychological Review, 2*(2), 91–106.

Gullone, E., King, N. J., & Ollendick, T. H. (2001). Self-reported anxiety in children and adolescents: A three-year follow-up study. *Journal of Genetic Psychology, 162*(1), 5–19.

Hadwin, J. A., Donnelly, N., French, C. C., Richards, A., Watts, A., & Daley, D. (2003). The influence of children's self-report trait anxiety and depression on visual search for emotional faces. *Journal of Child Psychology and Psychiatry, 44*(3), 432–444.

Hariri, A. R., Mattay, V. S., Tessitore, A., Kolachana, B., Fera, F., Goldman, D., et al. (2002). Serotonin transporter genetic variation and the response of the human amygdala. *Science, 297*(5580), 400–403.

Hartenberg, P. (1901). *Les timides et la timidité.* Paris: Felix Alcan.

Haxby, J. V., Hoffman, E. A., & Gobbini, M. I. (2002). Human neural systems for face recognition and social communication. *Biological Psychiatry, 51*(1), 59–67.

Heimberg, R. G., Hope, D. A., Dodge, C. S., & Becker, R. E. (1990). DSM-III-R subtypes of social phobia: Comparison of generalized social phobics and public speaking phobics. *Journal of Nervous and Mental Diseases, 178*(3), 172–179.

Heiser, N. A., Turner, S. M., & Beidel, D. C. (2003). Shyness: Relationship to social phobia and other psychiatric disorders. *Behaviour Research and Therapy, 41,* 209–221.

Henker, B., Whalen, C. K., Jamner, L. D., & Delfino, R. J. (2002). Anxiety, affect, and activity in teenagers: Monitoring daily life with electronic diaries. *Journal of the American Academy of Child and Adolescent Psychiatry, 41,* 660–670.

Hippocrates. (1886). *The genuine works of Hippocrates* (F. Adams, Trans.). New York: Wood & Company. (Original work published 460–370 B.C.)

Hirshfeld, D. R., Rosenbaum, J. F., Biederman, J., Bolduc, E. A., Faraone, S. V., Snidman, N., et al. (1992). Stable behavioral inhibition and its association with anxiety disorder. *Journal of the American Academy of Child and Adolescent Psychiatry, 31,* 103–111.

Hudson, J. L., & Rapee, R. M. (2000). The origins of social phobia. *Behavior Modification, 24,* 102–129.

Hunkeler, E. M., Spector, W. D., Fireman, B., Rice, D. P., & Weisner, C. (2003). Psychiatric symptoms, impaired function, and medical care costs in an HMO setting. *General Hospital Psychiatry, 25*(3), 178–184.

Hymel, S., Woody, E., & Bowker, A. (1993). Social withdrawal in childhood: Considering the child's perspective. In K. H. Rubin & J. B. Asendorp (Eds.), *Social withdrawal, inhibition, and shyness in childhood* (pp. 237–262). Hillsdale, NJ: Erlbaum.

Janet, P. (1903). *Les obsessions et la psychasthénie* (Vol. 1). Paris: Felix Alcan.

Johnson, J. G., Cohen, P., Pine, D. S., Klein, D. F., Kasen, S., & Brook, J. S. (2000). Association between cigarette smoking and anxiety disorders during adolescence and early adulthood. *Journal of the American Medical Association, 284*(18), 2348–2351.

Kagan, J. (1997). Temperament and the reactions to unfamiliarity. *Child Development, 68,* 139–143.

Kagan, J., Kearsley, R. B., & Zelazo, P. R. (1978). *Infancy: Its place in human development.* Cambridge, MA: Harvard University Press.

Kagan, J., Reznick, J. S., & Snidman, N. (1988). Biological bases of childhood shyness. *Science, 240,* 167–171.

Kalin, N. H., Shelton, S. E., Davidson, R. J., & Kelley, A. E. (2001). The primate amygdala mediates acute fear but not the behavioral and physiological components of anxious temperament. *Journal of Neuroscience, 21,* 2067–2074.

Katzelnick, D. J., Kobak, K. A., DeLeire, T., Henk, H. J., Greist, J. H., Davidson, J. R., et al. (2001). Impact of generalized social anxiety disorder in managed care. *American Journal of Psychiatry, 158*(12), 1999–2007.

Kendall, P. C., Safford, S., Flannery-Schroeder, E., & Webb, A. (2004). Child anxiety treatment: Outcomes in adolescence and impact on substance use and depression at 7.4-year follow-up. *Journal of Consulting and Clinical Psychology, 72*(2), 276–287.

Kendler, K. S. (2001). Twin studies of psychiatric illness: An update. *Archives of General Psychiatry, 58*(11), 1005–1014.

Kendler, K. S., Jacobson, K. C., Myers, J., & Prescott, C. A. (2002). Sex differences in genetic and environmental risk factors for irrational fears and phobias. *Psychological Medicine, 32,* 209–217.

Kendler, K. S., Karkowski, L. M., & Prescott, C. A. (1999). Fears and phobias: Reliability and heritability. *Psychological Medicine, 29,* 539–553.

Kendler, K. S., Neale, M. C., Kessler, R. C., Heath, A. C., & Eaves, L. J. (1992). The genetic epidemiology of phobias in women: The inter-relationship of agoraphobia, social phobia, situational phobia and simple phobia. *Archives of General Psychiatry, 49,* 273–281.

Kessler, R. C., & Frank, R. G. (1997). The impact of psychiatric disorders on work loss days. *Psychological Medicine, 27*(4), 861–873.

Kessler, R. C., Stein, M. B., & Berglund, P. (1998). Social phobia subtypes in the National Comorbidity Survey. *American Journal of Psychiatry, 155,* 613–619.

Killcross, S., Robbins, T. W., & Everitt, B. J. (1997). Different types of fear-conditioned behaviour mediated by separate nuclei within amygdala. *Nature, 388,* 377–380.

King, N. J., Gullone, E., & Ollendick, T. H. (1998). Etiology of childhood phobias: Current status of Rachman's three pathways theory. *Behaviour Research and Therapy, 36,* 297–309.

Klein, D. F. (1964). Delineation of two drug responsive anxiety syndromes. *Psychopharmacologia, 5,* 397–408.

Klein, R. G., & Pine, D. S. (2002). Anxiety disorders. In M. Rutter, E. Taylor, & L. Hersov (Eds.), *Child and adolescent psychiatry: Modern approaches* (4th ed., pp. 486–509). London: Blackwell.

Knab, S. H. (1995). *Polish herbs, flowers, and folk medicine.* New York: Hippocrene Books.

Lang, P. J., Bradley, M. M., & Cuthbert, B. N. (1998). Emotion, motivation, and anxiety: Brain mechanisms and psychophysiology. *Biological Psychiatry, 44,* 1248–1263.

Langley, A. K., Bergman, R. L., McCracken, J., & Piacentini, J. C. (2004). Impairment in childhood anxiety disorders: Preliminary examination of the Child Anxiety Impact Scale–parent version. *Journal of Child and Adolescent Psychopharmacology, 14*(1), 105–114.

LaPouse, R., & Monk, M. A. (1964). Behavior deviations in a representative sample of children: Variation by sex, age, race, social class, and family size. *American Journal of Orthopsychiatry, 34,* 436–446.

Last, C. G., Hansen, C., & Franco, N. (1997). Anxious children in adulthood: A prospective study of adjustment. *Journal of the American Academy of Child and Adolescent Psychiatry, 36,* 645–652.

LeDoux, J. E. (1994). Emotion, memory and the brain. *Scientific American, 270,* 50–57.

LeDoux, J. E. (1998). Fear and the brain: Where have we been, and where are we going? *Biological Psychiatry, 44,* 1229–1238.

LeDoux, J. E. (2000). Emotion circuits in the brain. *Annual Review of Neuroscience, 23,* 155–184.

LeDoux, J. E., & Muller, J. (1997). Emotional memory and psychopathology. *Philosophical Transactions of the Royal Society of London: Series B, 352,* 1719–1726.

Lewis, M., Alessandri, S. M., & Sullivan, M. W. (1992). Differences in shame and pride as a function of children's gender and task difficulty. *Child Development, 63,* 630–638.

Lewis, M., & Ramsay, D. (2002). Cortisol response to embarrassment and shame. *Child Development, 73,* 1034–1045.

Lewis, M., Stanger, C., Sullivan, M. W., & Barone, P. (1991). Changes in embarrassment as a function of age, sex and situation. *British Journal of Developmental Psychology, 9,* 485–492.

Liebowitz, M. R., Gorman, J. M., Fyer, A. J., Campeas, R., Levin, A. P., Sandberg, D., et al. (1988). Pharmacotherapy of social phobia: An interim report of a placebo-controlled comparison of phenelzine and atenolol. *Journal of Clinical Psychiatry, 49*(7), 252–257.

Lundh, L. G., & Ost, L. G. (1996). Recognition bias for critical faces in social phobics. *Behaviour Research and Therapy, 34,* 787–794.

MacLeod, C., Rutherford, E., Campbell, L., Ebsworthy, G., & Holker, L. (2002). Selective attention and emotional vulnerability: Assessing the causal basis of their association through the experimental manipulation of attentional bias. *Journal of Abnormal Psychology, 111,* 107–123.

Mancini, C., van Ameringen, M., Szatmari, P., Fugere, C., & Boyle, M. (1996). A high-risk pilot study of the children of adults with social phobia. *Journal of the American Academy of Child and Adolescent Psychiatry, 35*(11), 1511–1517.

Mannuzza, S., Schneier, F. R., Chapman, T. F., Liebowitz, M. R., Klein, D. F., & Fyer, A. J. (1995). Generalized social phobia: Reliability and validity. *Archives of General Psychiatry, 52*(3), 230–237.

Marenco, S., & Weinberger, D. R. (2000). The neurodevelopmental hypothesis of Schizophrenia: Following a trail of evidence from cradle to grave. *Development and Psychopathology, 12,* 501–527.

Marks, I. M., & Gelder, M. G. (1966). Different ages of onset in various phobias. *American Journal of Psychiatry, 123,* 218–221.

Martin, A., & Leslie, D. (2003). Psychiatric inpatient, outpatient, and medication utilization and costs among privately insured youths, 1997–2000. *American Journal of Psychiatry, 160*(4), 757–764.

May, R. (1950). *The meaning of anxiety.* New York: Ronald Press.

McClure, E. B., Brennan, P. A., Hammen, C., & Le Brocque, R. M. (2001). Parental anxiety disorders, child anxiety disorders, and the perceived parent-child relationship in an Australian high-risk sample. *Journal of Abnormal Child Psychology, 21,* 1–10.

McClure, E. B., Pope, K., Hoberman, A. J., Pine, D. S., & Leibenluft, E. (2003). Facial expression recognition in adolescents with mood and anxiety disorders. *American Journal of Psychiatry, 160*(6), 1172–1174.

McGee, R., Feehan, M., Williams, S., & Anderson, J. (1992). DSM-III disorders from age 11 to age 15. *Journal of the American Academy of Child and Adolescent Psychiatry, 31,* 50–59.

McNally, R. J. (1997). Memory and anxiety disorders. *Philosophical Transactions of the Royal Society of London: Series B, 352,* 1755–1759.

Meaney, M. J. (2001a). Maternal care, gene expression, and the transmission of individual differences in stress reactivity across generations. *Annual Review of Neuroscience, 24,* 1161–1192.

Meaney, M. J. (2001b). Nature, nurture, and the disunity of knowledge. *Annals of the New York Academy of Sciences, 935,* 50–61.

Mellings, T. M. B., & Alden, L. E. (2000). Cognitive processes in social anxiety: The effects of self-focus, rumination and anticipatory processing. *Behaviour Research and Therapy, 38,* 243–257.

Merikangas, K. R., Avenevoli, S., Dierker, L., & Grillon, C. (1999). Vulnerability factors among children at risk for anxiety disorders. *Biological Psychiatry, 46*(11), 1523–1535.

Milad, M. R., & Quirk, G. J. (2002). Neurons in medial prefrontal cortex signal memory for fear extinction. *Nature, 420*(6911), 70–74.

Miller, E. K., & Cohen, J. D. (2001). An integrative theory of prefrontal cortex function. *Annual Review of Neuroscience, 24,* 167–202.

Mischel, W., Shoda, Y., & Rodriguez, M. I. (1989). Delay of gratification in children. *Science, 244,* 933–938.

Mogg, K., & Bradley, B. P. (1998). A cognitive-motivational analysis of anxiety. *Behaviour Research and Therapy, 36*(9), 809–848.

Mogg, K., & Bradley, B. P. (1999). Some methodological issues in assessing attentional biases for threatening faces in anxiety: A replication study using a modified version of the probe detection task. *Behaviour Research and Therapy, 37*(6), 595–604.

Mogg, K., & Bradley, B. P. (2002). Selective orienting of attention to masked threat faces in social anxiety. *Behaviour Research and Therapy, 40*(12), 1403–1414.

Mogg, K., Bradley, B. P., & Williams, R. (1995). Attentional bias in anxiety and depression: The role of awareness. *British Journal of Clinical Psychology, 34*(Pt. 1), 17–36.

Mogg, K., Philippot, P., & Bradley, B. P. (2004). Selective attention to angry faces in clinical social phobia. *Journal of Abnormal Psychology, 113*(1), 160–165.

Monk, C. S., Grillon, C., Baas, J. M., McClure, E. B., Nelson, E. E., Zarahn, E., et al. (2003). A neuroimaging method for the study of threat in adolescents. *Developmental Psychobiology, 43*(4), 359–366.

Monk, C. S., McClure, E. B., Nelson, E. E., Zarahn, E., Bilder, R. M., Leibenluft, E., et al. (2003). Adolescent immaturity in attention-related brain engagement to emotional facial expressions. *Neuroimage, 20*(1), 420–428.

Muris, P., Merckelbach, H., Gadet, B., & Moulaert, V. (2000). Fears, worries, and scary dreams in 4- to 12-year-old children: Their content, developmental pattern, and origins. *Journal of Clinical Child Psychology, 29,* 43–52.

Nelson, C. A., Bloom, F. E., Cameron, J. L., Amaral, D., Dahl, R. E., & Pine, D. (2002). An integrative, multidisciplinary approach to the study of brain-behavior relations in the context of typical and atypical development. *Developmental Psychopathology, 14*(3), 499–520.

Ollendick, T. H., & Hirshfeld-Becker, D. R. (2002). The developmental psychopathology of social anxiety disorder. *Biological Psychiatry, 51,* 44–58.

Ollendick, T. H., King, N. J., & Frary, R. B. (1989). Fears in children and adolescents: Reliability and generalizability across gender, age, and nationality. *Behaviour Research and Therapy, 27,* 19–26.

Pauls, D. L., Alsobrook, J. P., II, Goodman, W., Rasmussen, S., & Leckman, J. F. (1995). A family study of obsessive-compulsive disorder. *American Journal of Psychiatry, 152*(1), 76–84.

Pauls, D. L., Leckman, J. F., Towbin, K. E., Zahner, G. E., & Cohen, D. J. (1986). A possible genetic relationship exists between Tourette's syndrome and obsessive-compulsive disorder. *Psychopharmacological Bulletin, 22*(3), 730–733.

Pelissolo, A., & Lepine, J. P. (1995). Social phobia: Historical and conceptual perspectives [Article in French]. *Encephale, 21,* 15–24.

Pemell, R. (2000). *De morbis puerorum, or, a treatise of the diseases of children.* Retrieved September 10, 2004, from http://www.neonatology.org/classics/pemell.html#Chap11. (Original work published 1653)

Pessoa, L., McKenna, M., Gutierrez, E., & Ungerleider, L. G. (2002). Neural processing of emotional faces requires attention. *Proceedings of the National Academy of Sciences, 99*(17), 11458–11463.

Peterson, B. S., Pine, D. S., Cohen, P., & Brook, J. S. (2001). Prospective, longitudinal study of tic, obsessive-compulsive, and attention-deficit/hyperactivity disorders in an epidemiological sample. *Journal of the American Academy of Child and Adolescent Psychiatry, 40*(6), 685–695.

Phelps, E. A., & Anderson, A. K. (1997). Emotional memory: What does the amygdala do? *Current Biology, 7,* R311–R314.

Pine, D. S. (1999). Pathophysiology of childhood anxiety disorders. *Biological Psychiatry, 46*(11), 1555–1566.

Pine, D. S. (2001). Affective neuroscience and the development of social anxiety disorder. *Psychiatric Clinics of North America, 24*(4), 689–705.

Pine, D. S. (2002a). Brain development and the onset of mood disorders. *Seminars in Clinical Neuropsychiatry, 7*(4), 223–233.

Pine, D. S. (2002b). Treating children and adolescents with selective serotonin reuptake inhibitors: How long is appropriate? *Journal of Child and Adolescent Psychopharmacology, 12*(3), 189–203.

Pine, D. S. (2003). Developmental psychobiology and response to threats: Relevance to trauma in children and adolescents. *Biological Psychiatry, 53,* 796–808.

Pine, D. S., & Charney, D. S. (2002). Children, stress, and sensitization: An integration of basic and clinical research on emotion? *Biological Psychiatry, 52,* 773.

Pine, D. S., Cohen, E., Cohen, P., & Brook, J. (1999). Adolescent depressive symptoms as predictors of adult depression: Moodiness or mood disorder? *American Journal of Psychiatry, 156*(1), 133–135.

Pine, D. S., Cohen, E., Cohen, P., & Brook, J. S. (2000). Social phobia and the persistence of conduct problems. *Journal of Child Psychology and Psychiatry, 41*(5), 657–665.

Pine, D. S., & Cohen, J. A. (2002). Trauma in children and adolescents: Risk and treatment of psychiatric sequelae. *Biological Psychiatry, 51*(7), 519–531.

Pine, D. S., Cohen, P., & Brook, J. (2001). Adolescent fears as predictors of depression. *Biological Psychiatry, 50*(9), 721–724.

Pine, D. S., Cohen, P., Gurley, D., Brook, J., & Ma, Y. (1998). The risk for early-adulthood anxiety and depressive disorders in adolescents with anxiety and depressive disorders. *Archives of General Psychiatry, 55*(1), 56–64.

Pine, D. S., Fyer, A., Grun, J., Phelps, E. A., Szeszko, P. R., Koda, V., et al. (2001). Methods for developmental studies of fear conditioning circuitry. *Biological Psychiatry, 50*(3), 225–228.

Pine, D. S., Klein, R. G., Coplan, J. D., Papp, L. A., Hoven, C. W., Martinez, J., et al. (2000). Differential carbon dioxide sensitivity in childhood anxiety disorders and nonill comparison group. *Archives of General Psychiatry, 57*(10), 960–967.

Pitres, A., & Régis, E. (1897). Obsession de la rougeur (ereuthophobia). *Archives de Neurologie, 3,* 1–26.

Pollak, S. D. (2003). Experience-dependent affective learning and risk for psychopathology in children. *Annals of the New York Academy of Sciences, 1008,* 102–111.

Pollak, S. D., Klorman, R., Thatcher, J. E., & Cicchetti, D. (2001). P3b reflects maltreated children's reactions to facial displays of emotion. *Psychophysiology, 38*(2), 267–274.

Pollak, S. D., & Sinha, P. (2002). Effects of early experience on children's recognition of facial displays of emotion. *Developmental Psychology, 38*(5), 784–791.

Prior, M., Smart, D., Sanson, A., & Oberklaid, F. (2000). Does shy-inhibited temperament in childhood lead to anxiety problems in adolescence? *Journal of the American Academy of Child and Adolescent Psychiatry, 39,* 461–468.

Quirk, G. J. (2002). Memory for extinction of conditioned fear is long-lasting and persists following spontaneous recovery. *Learning and Memory, 9*(6), 402–407.

Quirk, G. J., & Gehlert, D. R. (2003). Inhibition of the amygdala: Key to pathological states? *Annals of the New York Academy of Sciences, 985,* 263–272.

Rachman, S. (1977). The conditioning theory of fear acquisition: A critical examination. *Behaviour Research and Therapy, 15,* 375–387.

Rapee, R. M. (1997). Potential role of childrearing practices in the development of anxiety and depression. *Clinical Psychology Review, 17,* 47–67.

Rauch, S. L., Whalen, P. J., Shin, L. M., McInerney, S. C., Macklin, M. L., Lasko, N. B., et al. (2000). Exaggerated amygdala response to masked facial stimuli in posttraumatic stress disorder: A functional MRI study. *Biological Psychiatry, 47,* 769–776.

Research Unit on Pediatric Psychopharmacology. (2001). Fluvoxamine for the treatment of anxiety disorders in children and adolescents: The Research Unit on Pediatric Psychopharmacology Anxiety Study Group. *New England Journal of Medicine, 344*(17), 1279–1285.

Riddle, M. A., Reeve, E. A., Yaryura-Tobias, J. A., Yang, H. M., Claghorn, J. L., Gaffney, G., et al. (2001). Fluvoxamine for children and adolescents with obsessive-compulsive disorder: A randomized, controlled, multicenter trial. *Journal of the American Academy of Child and Adolescent Psychiatry, 40*(2), 222–229.

Robbins, T. W., & Everitt, B. J. (2002). Limbic-striatal memory systems and drug addiction. *Neurobiology of Learning and Memory, 78*(3), 625–636.

Rolls, E. T. (1999). *The brain and emotion.* Oxford: Oxford University Press.

Rose, A. J. (2002). Co-rumination in the friendships of girls and boys. *Child Development, 73,* 1830–1843.

Rosenbaum, J. F., Biederman, J., Hirshfeld, D. R., Bolduc, E. A., Faraone, S. V., Kagan, J., et al. (1991). Further evidence of an association between behavioral inhibition and anxiety disorders: Results from a family study of children from a non-clinical sample. *Journal of Psychiatric Research, 25,* 49–65.

Rowe, D. C., Stever, C., Gard, J. M., Cleveland, H. H., Sanders, M. L., Abramowitz, A., et al. (1998). The relation of the dopamine transporter gene (DAT1) to symptoms of internalizing disorders in children. *Behavior Genetics, 28,* 215–225.

Schneier, F. R., Liebowitz, M. R., Abi-Dargham, A., Zea-Ponce, Y., Lin, S. H., & Laruelle, M. (2000). Low dopamine D(2) receptor binding potential in social phobia. *American Journal of Psychiatry, 157*(3), 457–459.

Schneier, F. R., Spitzer, R. L., Gibbon, M., Fyer, A. J., & Liebowitz, M. R. (1991). The relationship of social phobia subtypes and avoidant personality disorder. *Comprehensive Psychiatry, 32*(6), 496–502.

Schwartz, C. E., Snidman, N., & Kagan, J. (1999). Adolescent social anxiety as an outcome of inhibited temperament in childhood. *Journal of the American Academy of Child and Adolescent Psychiatry, 38,* 1008–1015.

Schwartz, C. E., Wright, C. I., Shin, L. M., Kagan, J., & Rauch, S. L. (2003). Inhibited and uninhibited infants grown up: Adult amygdalar response to novelty. *Science, 300,* 1952–1953.

Shaffer, D. (1996). A participant's observations: Preparing DSM-IV. *Canadian Journal of Psychiatry, 41*(6), 325–329.

Shaffer, D., Fisher, P., Dulcan, M. K., Davies, M., Piacentini, J., Schwab-Stone, M. E., et al. (1996). The NIMH Diagnostic Interview Schedule for Children Version 2.3 (DISC-2.3): Description, acceptability, prevalence rates, and performance in the MECA Study—Methods for the epidemiology of child and adolescent mental disorders study. *Journal of the American Academy of Child and Adolescent Psychiatry, 35*(7), 865–877.

Sheline, Y. I., Barch, D. M., Donnelly, J. M., Ollinger, J. M., Snyder, A. Z., & Mintun, M. A. (2001). Increased amygdala response to masked emotional faces in depressed subjects resolves with antidepressant treatment: An fMRI study. *Biological Psychiatry, 50,* 651–658.

Silberg, J. L., Rutter, M., & Eaves, L. (2001). Genetic and environmental influences on the temporal association between earlier anxiety and later depression in girls. *Biological Psychiatry, 49*(12), 1040–1049.

Silove, D., Harris, M., Morgan, A., Boyce, P., Manicavasagar, V., Hadzi-Pavlovic, D., et al. (1995). Is early separation anxiety a specific precursor of panic disorder-agoraphobia? A community study. *Psychological Medicine, 25*(2), 405–411.

Silverman, W. K., La Greca, A. M., & Wasserstein, S. (1995). What do children worry about? Worries and their relation to anxiety. *Child Development, 66*(3), 671–686.

Smoller, J. W., Rosenbaum, J. F., Biederman, J., Susswein, L. S., Kennedy, J., Kagan, J., et al. (2001). Genetic association analysis of behavioral inhibition using candidate loci from mouse models. *American Journal of Medical Genetics, 105,* 226–235.

Solomon, J. C., & Axelrod, P. L. (1944). Group psychotherapy for withdrawn adolescents. *American Journal of Diseases of Children, 68,* 86–101.

Spence, S. H., Rapee, R., McDonald, C., & Ingram, M. (2001). The structure of anxiety symptoms among preschoolers. *Behaviour Research and Therapy, 39,* 1293–1316.

Squire, L. R., & Kandel, E. R. (1999). *Memory: From mind to molecules.* New York: Scientific American Library.

Stein, M. B., Chartier, M. J., Kozak, M. V., King, N., & Kennedy, J. L. (1998). Genetic linkage to the serotonin transporter protein and 5HT2A receptor genes excluded in generalized social phobia. *Psychiatry Research, 81,* 283–291.

Stein, M. B., Fuetsch, M., Muller, N., Hofler, M., Lieb, R., & Wittchen, H. U. (2001). Social anxiety disorder and the risk of depression: A prospective community study of adolescents and young adults. *Archives of General Psychiatry, 58,* 251–256.

Stein, M. B., Goldin, P. R., Sareen, J., Zorrilla, L. T. E., & Brown, G. G. (2002). Increased amygdala activation to angry and contemptuous faces in generalized social phobia. *Archives of General Psychiatry, 59*(11), 1027–1034.

Stein, M. B., & Kean, Y. M. (2000). Disability and quality of life in social phobia: Epidemiologic findings. *American Journal of Psychiatry, 157*(10), 1606–1613.

Stein, M. B., Walker, J. R., & Forde, D. R. (1994). Setting diagnostic thresholds for social phobia: Considerations from a community survey of social anxiety. *American Journal of Psychiatry, 151,* 408–412.

Stein, M. B., Walker, J. R., & Forde, D. R. (1996). Public-speaking fears in a community sample: Prevalence, impact on functioning, and diagnostic classification. *Archives of General Psychiatry, 53,* 169–174.

Stevenson-Hinde, J., & Glover, A. (1996). Shy girls and boys: A new look. *Journal of Child Psychology and Psychiatry, 37*(2), 181–187.

Stipek, D. J., Gralinski, J. H., & Kopp, C. B. (1990). Self-concept development in the toddler years. *Developmental Psychology, 26,* 972–977.

Sullivan, G. M., & Gorman, J. M. (2002). Finding a home for post-traumatic stress disorder in biological psychiatry: Is it a disorder of anxiety, mood, stress, or memory? *Psychiatric Clinics of North America, 25*(2), ix, 463–468.

Sullivan, H. S. (1953). *The interpersonal theory of psychiatry.* New York: Norton.

Swedo, S. E., Leonard, H. L., Garvey, M., Mittleman, B., Allen, A. J., Perlmutter, S., et al. (1998). Pediatric autoimmune neuropsychiatric disorders associated with streptococcal infections: Clinical description of the first 50 cases. *American Journal of Psychiatry, 155*(2), 264–271.

Thomas, K. M., Drevets, W. C., Dahl, R. E., Ryan, N. D., Birmaher, B., Eccard, C. H., et al. (2001). Amygdala response to fearful faces in anxious and depressed children. *Archives of General Psychiatry, 58*(11), 1057–1063.

Thompson, R. A. (1994). Emotion regulation: A theme in search of a definition. *Monographs of the Society for Research in Child Development, 59,* 25–52.

Tiet, Q. Q., Bird, H. R., Hoven, C. W., Moore, R., Wu, P., Wicks, J., et al. (2001). Relationship between specific adverse life events and psychiatric disorders. *Journal of Abnormal Child Psychology, 29,* 153–164.

Treffers, P. D. A., & Silverman, W. K. (2001). Anxiety and its disorders in children and adolescents before the twentieth century. In W. K. Silverman & P. D. A. Treffers (Eds.), *Anxiety disorders in children and adolescents: Research, assessment, and intervention* (pp. 1–22). Cambridge, England: Cambridge University Press.

Turner, S. M., Beidel, D. C., Roberson-Nay, R., & Tervo, K. (2003). Parenting behaviors in parents with anxiety disorders. *Behaviour Research and Therapy, 41,* 541–554.

Turner, S. M., Beidel, D. C., & Wolff, P. L. (1996). Is behavioral inhibition related to the anxiety disorders? *Clinical Psychology Review, 16,* 157–172.

Uger, C. (1938). The relationship of teachers' attitudes to children's problem behavior. *School and Society, 47,* 246–248.

Unnewehr, S., Schneider, S., Florin, I., & Margraf, J. (1998). Psychopathology in children of patients with panic disorder or animal phobia. *Psychopathology, 31*(2), 69–84.

Vander Stoep, A., Weiss, N. S., McKnight, B., Beresford, S. A. A., & Cohen, P. (2002). Which measure of adolescent psychiatric disorder—diagnosis, number of symptoms, or adaptive functioning—best predicts adverse young adult outcomes? *Journal of Epidemiology and Community Health, 56,* 56–65.

Vasey, M. W., Crnic, K. A., & Carter, W. G. (1994). Worry in childhood: A developmental perspective. *Cognitive Therapy and Research, 18,* 529–549.

Vasey, M. W., & Dadds, M. R. (2001). An introduction to the developmental psychopathology of anxiety. In M. W. Vasey & M. R. Dadds (Eds.), *The developmental psychopathology of anxiety* (pp. 3–26). New York: Oxford University Press.

Wardle, C. J. (1991). Historical influences on services for children and adolescents before 1900. In G. E. Berrios & H. Freeman (Eds.), *150 years of British psychiatry, 1841–1991* (pp. 279–293). London: Gaskell.

Watson, D., & Friend, R. (1969). Measurement of social-evaluative anxiety. *Journal of Consulting and Clinical Psychology, 33,* 448–457.

Watson, J. B. (1929). *Psychology from the standpoint of a behaviorist.* Philadelphia: Lippincott.

Weems, C. F., Silverman, W. K., & La Greca, A. M. (2000). What do youth referred for anxiety problems worry about? Worry and its relation to anxiety and anxiety disorders in children and adolescents. *Journal of Abnormal Child Psychology, 28*(1), 63–72.

West, P., & Sweeting, H. (2003). Fifteen, female and stressed: Changing patterns of psychological distress over time. *Journal of Child Psychology and Psychiatry, 44,* 399–411.

Westenberg, P. M., Drewes, M. J., Goedhart, A. W., Siebelink, B. M., & Treffers, P. D. A. (2004). A developmental analysis of self-reported fears in late childhood through mid-adolescence: Social-evaluative fears on the rise? *Journal of Child Psychology and Psychiatry, 45*(3), 481–495.

Williams, J. M., Mathews, A., & MacLeod, C. (1996). The emotional Stroop task and psychopathology. *Psychological Bulletin, 120*(1), 3–24.

Wittchen, H. U., Stein, M. B., & Kessler, R. C. (1999). Social fears and social phobia in a community sample of adolescents and young adults: Prevalence, risk factors and co-morbidity. *Psychological Medicine, 29,* 309–323.

Wood, J. J., McLeod, B. D., Sigman, M., Hwang, W., & Chu, B. C. (2003). Parenting and childhood anxiety: Theory, empirical findings, and future directions. *Journal of Child Psychology and Psychiatry, 44,* 134–151.

Yehuda, R. (2001). Biology of posttraumatic stress disorder. *Journal of Clinical Psychiatry, 62*(Suppl. 17), 41–46.

Yehuda, R. (2002). Post-traumatic stress disorder. *New England Journal of Medicine, 346*(2), 108–114.

Yehuda, R., Halligan, S. L., & Bierer, L. M. (2001). Relationship of parental trauma exposure and PTSD to PTSD, depressive and anxiety disorders in offspring. *Journal of Psychiatry Research, 35*(5), 261–270.

Yehuda, R., Halligan, S. L., & Grossman, R. (2001). Childhood trauma and risk for PTSD: Relationship to intergenerational effects of trauma, parental PTSD, and cortisol excretion. *Development and Psychopathology, 13,* 733–753.

CHAPTER 13

The Development and Ecology of Antisocial Behavior in Children and Adolescents

THOMAS J. DISHION and GERALD R. PATTERSON

Antisocial behavior is disruptive to the individual, to family and friends, and to the community at large. It is for this reason that adults attempt to reduce antisocial behavior in efforts to socialize children. When such efforts fail, parents and caregivers often seek help, such as in mental health clinics. It is estimated that 50% to 75% of all referrals focus on behavior problems in children (Kazdin, 1987, 1993).

Among all the child adjustment problems, the literature on the study of child and adolescent antisocial behavior is the most abundant and historically rich (see Costello & Angold, 2000). Initially, thinking about the origins and solutions to antisocial behavior in children and adults was largely philosophical and speculative. Plato's *The Republic* (Hamilton & Cairns, 1973), written c. 360 B.C., provides a detailed sociopolitical system for promoting the character of youth so as to minimize behaviors thought to detract from a harmonious state and promote behaviors conducive to community living.

A critical piece to the philosophical puzzle is whether antisocial tendencies are innate or are acquired through the vagaries of social living and misguided socialization efforts. Hobbes, in *Leviathan* (Rogers & Schulman, 1651/2003), assumes that antisocial tendencies are innate, and consequently, prosocial behavior conducive to group living required careful training and socialization. In contrast, in his

treatise on *Emile,* Rousseau (Friedlander, 1762/2004) proposed that children by nature are prosocial but misguided efforts by adults transform goodness into antisocial behavior. The implication is that if children were raised in a natural, benevolent state, many problem behaviors would be minimized or eliminated. John Locke (Anstey, 2003) proposed a position that could be seen as neutral to these two perspectives, assuming that children were a tabula rasa with respect to good and evil and that all behaviors were simply outcomes of experience and learning. This has often been associated with learning theory accounts of individual differences. A fourth perspective, attributable to Darwin (1991), is that individuals actively learn behaviors that promote survival of the individual and the species. Thus, individuals come to social living with a propensity to learn some behaviors over others, based on biologically based biases in learning. The key is that behaviors are more easily learned when they function to increase the survival of the individual and genetically related kin. As we shall see, the fourth perspective is a compelling philosophical framework for thinking about the development and ecology of antisocial behavior.

Not until recently have the tools and strategies of science been applied to understanding human behavior in general and antisocial behavior in particular. There is a clear sense that empirical formulations of antisocial behavior are progressing in respect to replication as well as validation in the context of intervention (Dishion & Patterson, 1999). However, in considering the impressions of the earliest professionals charged with the responsibility of managing antisocial children, one wonders just how much progress has been made. For example, consider the following statement by Adams (Carpenter, 1970, p. 15), who was responsible for managing antisocial youth in a reformatory school in nineteenth-century England:

> Sergeant Adams states before the Select Committee of the Lords, that of the 100 prisoners whom he has to try every fortnight, from 16 to 40 are boys; some even of the age of 7; a few of 8, and a great number of 9 and upwards; of these children the offenses are, for the most part, of a pilfering description, to which the young children are tempted by older persons. "A large portion of these poor children," says Mr. Adam, "are wholly and entirely without friends and relations of any kind; others have profligate parents who neglect them; and almost all are quite uninstructed in religious, moral and social duties. I should say the evil is far more deeply seated than in the natural disposition of the children themselves. I do not think they are naturally worse than other children themselves; but that these offenses spring from the want of proper moral and religious education and in the want of proper friends to attend to them."

From Sergeant Adams' perspective, many antisocial youth are early starters, often male, have poor peer relations, and come from families that could be described as disrupted parenting. Sergeant Adams would minimize the contribution of genetic factors in favor of environmental effects.

The early work on antisocial behavior was largely concerned with managing children who broke the law and required remedial, or at least custodial, intervention. In the twentieth century, however, psychologists entered the intellectual landscape. Healy (1926) published the first psychologically oriented treatise theorizing on the etiology and treatment of antisocial behavior. His thinking, heavily influenced by the psychodynamic theory of that time, emphasized internal, intraindividual factors in the etiology of crime, especially lack of cognitive abilities (i.e., "dull thinking"), and secondarily, problematic parenting. Even though he notes that peers are most often a proximal factor in the commission of antisocial acts (nearly every case reviewed!), in his mind, peers were unlikely to be a significant etiological factor. His thinking was that failure to care about mores and to inhibit antisocial behaviors was an intrapersonal characteristic that could only be solved by treating the individual. Despite this individual orientation, Healy was also an empirical pragmatist. Ten years later, he

published quasi-experimental findings on outcomes associated with two different correctional practices in Chicago and Boston, noting that about 61% of the males and 46% of the females would eventually recidivate (Healy & Bronner, 1936). Rates of recidivism, he noted, vary as a function of the correctional strategy used. In Chicago, where institutionalism was the dominant strategy, failure rates reached 70%, whereas in Boston, where foster care was the pervasive practice, recidivism was only 27%. These writers, aware of the limitations of quasi-experimental strategies, tentatively suggested that institutionalization may not be the ideal solution for diverting lives of crime for antisocial youth. This suggestion has gone largely unheeded, despite the results of later studies using random assignment (Chamberlain & Reid, 1998; Eddy & Chamberlain, 2000).

The continued application of psychodynamically oriented treatments for antisocial children and adolescents generally did not produce satisfactory results. Influential practitioners and theorists such as Redl and Wineman (1951, 1952) reported dramatic failures in their efforts to treat antisocial youth. These failures were followed by extensive reformulations of psychoanalytic theory and the introduction of the attachment construct and ethological theory (Bowlby, 1969). The pessimism was supported by empirical findings: Nothing was effective when working with antisocial children (Levitt, 1957, 1971).

The *internal trait* model was the overarching paradigm that integrated these theories and interventions designed by psychologists and criminologists. From this perspective, the traits are intraindividual dynamics whose prime characteristics are stability and continuity of behavior. Indeed, the stability and continuity of antisocial behavior was such that the use of the term *trait* was empirically justified (Loeber & Dishion, 1983; Olweus, 1979). A trait model (Goldberg, 1994), however, contained no information about mechanisms of change. The trait models are indeed empirically based but fall short of identifying mechanisms that account for stability and, more important, provide no guidance as to how to prevent or reduce antisocial behavior in children and adolescents. Not until the 1970s and 1980s was it understood that there is an important link between understanding a development process and selecting the appropriate prevention and treatment.

Considerable progress has been made during the past 20 years in providing an empirical account for antisocial behavior in children and adolescents. These studies represent a fusion of the seminal works by Lee Robins (1966) and other sociologists (see review by Loeber & Dishion, 1983), the life course perspective of Glen Elder (1985), measurement theorists (Campbell & Fiske, 1959; Cronbach &

Meehl, 1955), and the careful observation research of criminologists (e.g., McCord, McCord, & Howard, 1963) and developmental (e.g., Dawe, 1934) and clinical psychologists (e.g., Patterson, Littman, & Bricker, 1967; Raush, 1965). These investigators brought forth a strong focus on measurement, longitudinal designs, and a consistent pattern of findings of environmental correlates and predictors of antisocial behavior. More recently, investigators have moved to what we refer to as a *process account* of antisocial behavior, which provides an analysis of the etiological dynamics of growth and desistance over time. In this way, the new wave of studies in the past 2 decades represents a strategy of linking longitudinal research with intervention studies, where developmental processes are targeted in the efforts to reduce problem behavior, but also to test hypotheses regarding the mechanism of change.

At this juncture, we are able to provide a stronger proposal for the etiology of antisocial behavior in children and adolescents, compared with our previous review (Dishion, French, & Patterson, 1995). In some ways, the picture has simplified, especially with respect to what we know about the nature and timing of major environmental effects, biological underpinnings, and dynamic and functional processes as they unfold over time. To begin, however, it is necessary to consider what we now know about the developmental variation and changing form of antisocial behavior from early childhood to late adolescence.

DEVELOPMENTAL PATTERNS

All forms of *antisocial behavior* share a common characteristic: They are experienced as aversive, disruptive, or unpleasant by those who are victims or those who are close to the youth. During adolescence, new behaviors are added, such as drug use and sexual activity. These behaviors are often thought of as "victimless." Adolescent substance use and precocious sexual behavior are known to lead to problematic adult adjustment and also to be a source of conflict between adults and youth. To address this heterogeneity, the more general term of *problem behavior* is used. Figure 13.1 provides an overview of the kinds of behaviors that are experienced as aversive by victims or deemed problematic by adults from early childhood to late adolescence. The perspective of the current *Diagnostic and Statistical Manual of Mental Disorders* (*DSM*) is reflected in Figure 13.1 as well.

Several investigators recognized distinct types of antisocial behavior and conduct problem children (e.g., Jesness, 1977; Patterson, 1982; Quay, 1993). Our first efforts to observe antisocial children and their families suggested that

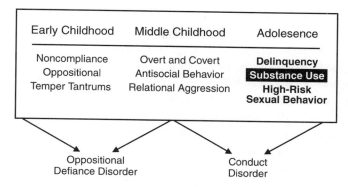

Figure 13.1 The labeling of problem behavior through childhood to adolescence.

interactions observed in the homes of youngsters referred primarily for aggression were fundamentally different from those referred for stealing (Patterson, 1982). The differences were detectable in the observed behavior of both the child and the parents. Considering findings such as these as well as a meta-analysis of child referral problems, Loeber and Schmaling (1985) introduced the terms *overt* and *covert* antisocial behavior, a taxonomy that has stimulated a great deal of research over the past 2 decades (e.g., Hinshaw & Anderson, 1996; Hinshaw, Lahey, & Hart, 1993; Liau, Barriga, & Gibbs, 1998).

If we take a psychometric approach to conceptualizing antisocial behavior, we might consider covert and overt antisocial behavior as different behaviors within an overall trait for being antisocial (see Dishion, French, et al., 1995; Patterson, Reid, & Dishion, 1992). This would be consistent with problem behavior theory (Jessor & Jessor, 1977) in which adolescent problem behaviors are considered to be one overall syndrome. The findings from the Oregon Youth Study provided support for such a perspective. Using structural equation modeling, we found a correlation of 1.0 between the two constructs (Patterson, Reid, et al., 1992). Obviously, boys who engage in high rates of overt antisocial behavior also engage in high rates of covert antisocial behavior. The correlation speaks to the fact that by early adolescence, both forms belong to the same general class of behaviors.

Within the class of aggression, distinctions can also be made. The most critical appears to be that between *reactive* and *proactive* aggression in children (Dodge & Coie, 1987). Again, reactive and proactive types of aggression are highly intercorrelated (Dodge & Coie, 1987; Poulin & Boivin, 2000b). A developmental analysis of proactive and reactive aggression suggests unique antecedent conditions, sequelae, and functional mechanisms (Crick & Dodge, 1996; Poulin &

Boivin, 2000a; Price & Dodge, 1989; Pulkkinen, 1996; Vitaro, Brendgen, & Tremblay, 2002).

More recently, the concept of relational aggression has been put forward, fitting best within the realm of covert antisocial behavior (Cairns & Cairns, 1994; Crick, 1996; Crick & Bigbee, 1998; Crick et al., 1997; Grotpeter & Crick, 1996; Underwood, 2003). Relational aggression is directed to peers and involves behaviors such as spreading rumors, ostracizing, and purposely manipulating relationships to the detriment and pain of a recipient.

As can be seen in Figure 13.1, the developmental sequence from overt to covert behaviors can be mapped onto the *DSM-IV* nomenclature of Oppositional Defiant Disorder and Conduct Disorder. However, relational aggression, to date, has no clear home in this or the *International Classification of Diseases* diagnostic system.

In contrast to our earlier review (Dishion, French, et al., 1995), we see the value in making distinctions between highly correlated but topographically unique forms of child and adolescent problem behavior. As a heuristic model, in this review, we group reactive forms of aggression and antisocial behavior as overt and antisocial behaviors that often involve peer coordination and avoidance of adult detection as covert. As we shall see, the critical issue is the developmental and relationship context in which these behaviors emerge. Studies show that overt and covert forms of behavior come into play at very different developmental stages and are controlled by very different functional mechanisms and social agents. Building a model of child antisocial behavior requires an intimate knowledge of these unique developmental patterns.

Overt Antisocial Behavior

During the first 2 years of life, it is not unusual for children to be oppositional and difficult to control at times. Tremblay (2000) has argued that if 2-year-olds were physically as large as adults they would be dangerous, as they do hit and become quite angry. By middle childhood, the range of child behavior, the places in which they occur, and their form and function become more complex.

Given that children begin to engage in aggression and oppositional behavior as toddlers, maternal reports would seem relevant to understanding early developmental trajectories. Systematic study of maternal reports in a large Canadian cohort, in fact, reveals a clear decrease in these behaviors from ages 2 to 11 (Tremblay, Masse, Pagani, & Vitaro, 1996; see Figure 13.2). The findings are consistent with those from mothers' longitudinal ratings of overt antisocial behaviors cited earlier. Longitudinal studies by

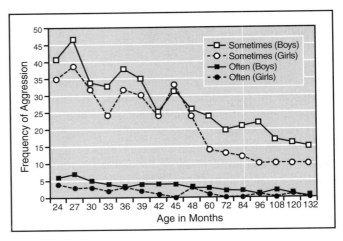

Figure 13.2 Decreases in aggression in early childhood. Adapted from Tremblay et al., 1996.

Cairns, Cairns, Neckerman, Gest, and Gariepy (1988) found a similar decrease in physical aggression between ages 10 and 18 years, based both on teacher ratings and self-report data. Tremblay et al. (1999) also found a decrease in teacher reports of physical aggression for boys from 6 to 15 years of age. The large-scale Dutch longitudinal study of maternal ratings of children ages 5 through 18 years showed negative slopes for both boys and girls on aggressive behavior (Stanger, Achenbach, & Verhulst, 1997).

Of particular interest in the work of Tremblay and his colleagues is the finding that during the elementary grades, there are few if any new cases of physical aggression added to the cases identified by grade 1 (e.g., a low false-negative error; Nagin & Tremblay, 1999). The findings were essentially replicated in the longitudinal study of at-risk boys from grades 1 through 5 (Patterson & DeGarmo, 1997). Only 1.5% of the boys in the normal range at grade 1 had moved to a clinical range for overt antisocial behavior by grade 5. Again, this suggests a very low false-negative error in predicting later adjustment. Evidently, the most severe problems associated with overt antisocial behavior are in place before grade 1, and few new cases are added after that. The fact that there are few new cases added suggests that the preschool, familial training phase is critical in understanding the emergence of aggression in young children.

There is a strong negative slope describing the relation between the age of the child and the frequency of reported overt forms of antisocial behavior. This relation holds across teacher, parent, and observers as assessment agents. The consistency of the developmental findings demands an explanation. Why is there a drop?

We hypothesize that as children age, adults become increasingly vigilant and attentive to all forms of overt antisocial behavior and effectively reduce such behavior through punishment or by reinforcing prosocial alternatives to aggression (asking, waiting, sharing, turn taking, etc.). The term reactive aggression also provides a clue. Children who initially engage in aggression are essentially reactively coercive, using such tactics as crying, whining, hitting, and persistence to reduce adult socialization efforts or aversive intrusions by peers. Fortunately, over time and through socialization, children become more regulated and planful in their response to their social environment. They become less reactive to aversive experiences, and if they do not, they pay the consequences of poor peer relations and social rejection (Coie & Kupersmidt, 1983; Dodge, 1983; Poulin & Boivin, 2000a).

The picture is more complex, however. As children desist in some forms of antisocial behavior, they pick up new behaviors. For example, proactive aggression emerges in middle childhood (Poulin & Boivin, 2000b), which appears be a consequence of involvement with other, aggressive peers. Snyder (Snyder, Reid, & Patterson, 2003) hypothesized that the effect of these changes in adult and peer contingency might drive aggression "underground." Some children may simply learn to avoid detection and, in so doing, also avoid the negative consequences supplied by adults. In this sense, they become more regulated but also, unfortunately, more deviant as well. The child simply shifts to more covert forms.

Covert Antisocial Behavior

As defined earlier, covert antisocial behavior includes aggressive acts that seem designed to avoid detection. For example, proactive and relational aggression can be seen as a covert form of antisocial behavior. As such, forms of covert antisocial behavior are detectible in middle childhood (age 6 years), increasing slowly during late childhood, then accelerating at early adolescence. Of particular relevance for socialization theory is the fact that throughout the developmental course, growth in overt and covert behaviors have diametrically opposite slopes. After the age of 2 years, the slope for overt forms is essentially negative through adult years. Developmentally, covert behavior begins with a neutral slope and then shifts dramatically to positive during early adolescence. An analysis of maternal ratings of boys' covert antisocial behavior is summarized in Figure 13.3. Based on data from a large prevention sample ($N = 204$), the ratings covered the interval from grades 1 through 5 (males; Patterson & Yoerger, 1997). Similarly, the longitudinal analyses of maternal ratings for grades 1 through 5 showed a nonsignificant positive slope (Patterson & Yoerger, 2002).

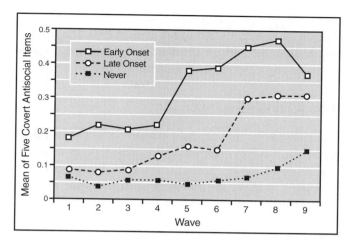

Figure 13.3 Changes in covert antisocial behavior for three groups of LIFT buys. Adapted from Patterson and Yoeger, 2002.

It becomes difficult, therefore, to really know whether there is an overall decrease in aggression from age 2 years through adolescence. It is conceivable that as overt forms decrease, adding the growth in covert behavior would generate a total output score that is closer to a zero slope. Maternal ratings from a large prevention trial sample offer some support for the idea that total output may remain stable from one grade to the next for grades 1 through 5 (Patterson & Yoerger, 2002).

It would be expected that measures of overt antisocial behavior during childhood would provide low-level but significant predictions of adolescent and adult crime. For example, in a systematic analysis of six longitudinal data sets, overt forms of antisocial behavior predicted both adolescent physical aggression and covert antisocial behavior (Broidy et al., 2003). It is noteworthy that female adolescent antisocial behavior is not predicted by early overt antisocial behaviors in these six longitudinal data sets.

This raises the question as to the most significant predictors for adolescent and adult crime. For example, it could be that the more severe forms of antisocial behaviors were the best predictors. We were pleased to find that such weighting schemes were not necessary. In fact, the total frequency of relatively trivial forms of antisocial behavior is strongly correlated with more severe forms of delinquent behavior. For example, in the Oregon Youth Study (OYS) by Capaldi and Patterson (1996), the frequency of self-reported trivial crimes correlated .63 with the frequency of self-reported severe crimes. Also, youth who commit more frequent crimes are at significantly greater risk to commit violent crimes. For example, if the adolescent had been arrested three or more times, the likelihood was .47 that he would commit a violent crime. The comparable figure for Farrington's (1991) London cohort was .49. Frequency, of course, suggests versatility (Loeber, 1991; Loeber, Green, Keenan, & Lahey, 1995; Loeber et al., 1993). Initially, we had thought that perhaps the more severe forms of overt or covert behavior would serve as better predictors.

Delinquent Behavior

Delinquent behaviors are an important subset of antisocial (overt and covert) behavior. What makes them unique is that society considers them to be illegal. What makes this complex is that the definition of what is illegal can, and does, change over time. Many delinquent behaviors also have a victim. Examples include robbery, theft, burglary, and vandalism. Other behaviors are statutory, such as substance use and sexual precocity. Here, victim's status is unclear, but technically, our definition of antisocial behavior requires a victim. Thus, substance use is included in this review only as it relates to the etiology and course of antisocial behavior. It is clear that there are youth who engage in these behaviors but who are not involved in antisocial behavior (Dishion & Loeber, 1985; Loeber, 1988), and peer and family dynamics reflect this difference (Dishion & Loeber, 1985), in that youth who use substances and are not antisocial are generally exposed to less risk within the family and peer domains.

If one focuses narrowly on illegal, criminal, or delinquent behavior, it is clear that there are enormous differences in the age at which individuals first engage in these behaviors. There are 7-year-olds who are arrested; others are arrested in adolescence (Moffitt, 1993; Patterson, Crosby, & Vuchinich, 1992; Robins, 1966). Generally, there is positive growth in criminal behavior during adolescence (Achenbach & Edelbrock, 1979), which peaks somewhere between 16 and 18, depending on the context and behaviors included in the study. Following the peak is a relatively rapid decrease in illegal behavior, forming a negative quadratic function. This is often referred to as the age-crime curve (Gottfredson & Hirschi, 1990). One of the most interesting findings from the OYS sample was the data showing that 18% of youth arrested as adults had no prior history of arrests; some of the males waited until adult status to commit their first crime (Patterson & Yoerger, 2002).

The developmental trends in criminal behavior among youth and young adults are likely to be obscured by trends in *learning to avoid detection*. By definition, teachers and parents probably have only a limited awareness of the frequency of covert acts. For example, early-onset boys in the OYS show the expected decrease in police arrests starting at around age 17 years. During that same interval, however,

the early-onset boys self-reported a fourfold increase in index crimes (Patterson & Yoerger, 1993). According to the *learning to avoid detection* hypothesis, this may simply reflect the fact that after several arrests, the boys improved their skills in learning to escape police detection. Farrington, Jolliffe, Hawkins, Catalano, Hill et al. (2000) found that the probability of being referred to juvenile court actually decreased as a function of frequency of self-reported crimes. Again, this suggests to the present writers that the more prolific offenders had learned to avoid detection.

Criminology's study of specialization would be one well-known alternative to the frequency hypothesis. Are there numerous paths to each specialized crime (e.g., safe-cracking, mugging, arson)? Farrington's (1991) analysis of the London cohort study found no tendency for males in the sample to specialize in property or person crimes.

We hypothesized that understanding the overt-to-covert sequence is absolutely essential in planning prevention studies. We also hypothesized that measures of the overt-covert sequence should provide a useful basis for predicting later juvenile and adult crime. If the model includes only measures of overt antisocial behavior, the prediction model will be weakened. It is also assumed that a model based only on measures of covert antisocial behavior assessed during adolescence will be very effective in predicting adolescent offending but weak when predicting adult crime. The reason for this is that both the early- and late-onset boys are heavily involved with deviant peers, as shown in Patterson and Yoerger (1993, 2002). The OYS data show that most of the late-onset boys score high on covert scores but as adults become desistors (Patterson & Yoerger, 1997). When predicting adult crimes, the most effective prediction model would include the sequence of first overt and then covert (Broidy et al., 2003; Patterson & Yoerger, 1997, 1999).

Trajectories that are high on both overt and covert forms would also be characterized by high overall frequencies. Both sets of information would predict early onset for delinquency. Loeber (1991; Loeber et al., 1993, 1995) showed that indeed it is the case that simply combining overt and covert generates significant predictions. As yet, no one has compared the relative efficiency of using childhood frequency measures of overt and covert, adolescent measures of covert, and various sequential patterns.

Age of onset for delinquent behavior occupies a salient place in the traditional literature of criminology. Robins (1966) noted that boys arrested at a young age had more serious outcomes than those arrested in later adolescent years. Several decades of studies firmly establish the correlation between early onset and total frequency of later arrests (Loeber & Farrington, 2000; Patterson, 1996; Patterson, DeBaryshe, & Ramsey, 1989; Patterson & Yoerger, 1997). It is, therefore, not surprising that the earlier the onset, the greater the risk for chronic arrests. For example, in a study of the OYS, Patterson and Yoerger (1993) found a correlation of .93 between the age of onset of first arrest and the likelihood of a fourth arrest. Given early onset (arrest before age 14 years), the likelihood of three or more juvenile offenses was .76 (Patterson, Forgatch, Yoerger, & Stoolmiller, 1998).

Several writers have emphasized the utility of differentiating between early- and late-onset delinquents (Moffitt, 1993; Patterson et al., 1989; Robins, 1966). In the OYS studies, about half of the police arrests involve early offenders and half involve late offenders. In the Dunedin studies, about 10% of the sample were defined as early onset (life-course-persistent) and 25% as late onset (adolescent-limited). The prevalence rates for the Oregon sample were 26% and 29% for early and late, respectively. The differences in prevalence for the early starters reflect the fact that the Oregon sample consisted of at-risk families living in high-crime areas, whereas the Dunedin studies were based on carefully drawn birth cohorts. Although the Oregon and New Zealand studies agree on the importance of differentiating the two paths, they are in almost complete disagreement as to the mechanisms that produce these outcomes. The causal mechanism models are reviewed in a later section.

It is now understood that the commission of antisocial acts usually precedes the commission of delinquent acts by several years. For example, data from three samples showed that 10% to 25% of the sample self-reported serious and violent behavior by age 10 years (Loeber & Farrington, 2000). Data from the OYS were used to test the hypothesis that boys from disadvantaged families and inept discipline practices would be among the first to be arrested (Patterson, Crosby, et al., 1992). Both variables made significant contributions to early arrest. It was assumed that a composite (overt plus covert) measure of antisocial behavior assessed at age 10 years would be the major predictor. In effect, the contribution of inept discipline to age of first arrest would be mediated by the antisocial variable. In the event history analyses, as predicted, when the trait score was introduced into the regression analyses, the relative contributions of discipline and socioeconomic status became nonsignificant. The highly significant contribution of the antisocial trait score showed that the more antisocial the boy, the earlier his first arrest.

In that study, the findings from the distribution of hazard rates carry a particularly interesting piece of informa-

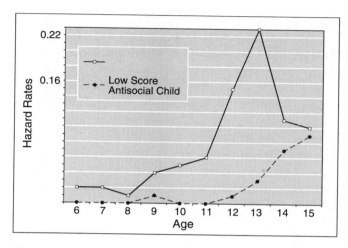

Figure 13.4 Distribution of hazard rates for high- and low-antisocial boys.

tion. The hazard rate describes the percentage of boys' first arrest at a particular point in time. Figure 13.4 compares the distribution of hazard rates for boys scoring above the median on the antisocial composite with those scoring below the mean for the antisocial trait. It can be seen that at age 10, about 5% to 6% of the boys were involved in their first arrest. The peak risk for this group occurred at age 13, when 23% of those not previously arrested were arrested.

Of particular interest is the distribution of hazard rates for boys below the mean for antisocial behavior (i.e., late-onset boys). At ages 14 and 15, there was a steady increase in risk for first arrest. These findings describe the trajectories for the late-starter group. In the Oregon model, the late-starter group tends to be less antisocial as children and are at increasing risk for a first arrest after the age of 15.

Moffitt, Caspi, Harrington, and Milne (2002) followed up the Dunedin sample through age 26 to demonstrate that, as adults, the early-onset group was more at risk for substance use, mental and personality problems, financial and work problems, and violent crime. The late-onset group also tended to be at elevated risk for most of these problems, but at less extreme levels. Moffitt et al. assume that the late-onset group is very near to normal levels in terms of childhood risk variables: "However, because their predelinquent development was normal and healthy, most young people who become AL (adolescent limited, late onset) are able to desist from crime when they age into real adult roles" (p. 280).

We hypothesize that developmental and relationship dynamics account for the differences in adult outcomes observed between early- and late-starting delinquent adolescents. In fact, we see the distinction between the two groups as one of gradations and the groups unlikely to be unique taxonomic groups. For example, DiLalla and Gottesman (1989) compared persistent and transitory offenders and found that the latter were better adjusted than persistent offenders. However, it was also the case that the transitory offenders were less well adjusted than were the nonoffenders. Findings from the OYS were consistent with the hypothesis that the late-onset group was less deviant than the early-onset group but more deviant than nonoffenders.

In our previous review, we introduced the "marginal deviation hypothesis," which was essentially a statement of equifinality, especially for late-onset delinquent behavior (Dishion, French, et al., 1995). Simply put, a variety of social and biological circumstances (e.g., temperament, academic problems, divorce, stepparenting) can be linked to engagement in peer groups that support growth in specific forms of problem behavior. Indeed, for this group, having positive peer relationships may be part of the problem. Indeed, a composite rating (peers, teachers, parents) showed that the late-onset group had better relationships with peers than did the early-onset group. As noted in a later section, the evidence suggests that early onset is correlated with more pervasive family dysfunction, and late onset and persistence among early starters is explained by the emergence of peer dynamics in adolescence (Patterson & Yoerger, 1997, 2002). Despite the diverse etiological circumstances of each developmental pattern, it is reasonable to conclude that late-onset delinquents are anything but normal; their problems are simply less severe. This may in part be a function of positive aspects of their socialization, in particular the development of a modicum of self-regulation and control, which enables the eventual formation of positive work and relationship skills.

Although the topic of causal mechanisms is discussed in a later section, it should be noted here that the critical variable determining membership in early, late, or nonoffending trajectories is a time-dependent measure of involvement with deviant peers, as shown in the studies by Patterson and Yoerger (1997, 2002). Several studies now show that bursts in involvement in deviant peers is associated with increases in substance use (Dishion & Medici Skaggs, 2000) and delinquent behavior (Elliott & Menard, 1996; Patterson & Yoerger, 2002). Although many theorists emphasize the role of peers (e.g., Elliott, Huizinga, & Ageton, 1985; Moffitt, 1993; D. W. Osgood, Wilson, O'Malley, Bachman, & Johnson, 1996; Warr, 1993), we specifically target the social interaction dynamics and behavior contingencies as critical for understanding the emergence and progression of antisocial behavior in adolescence (Dishion, Spracklen, Andrews, & Patterson, 1996). The added emphasis on rela-

tionship dynamics, we hope, is useful for the design and execution of interventions that reduce antisocial behavior.

Trajectories

The analysis of developmental patterns was often described as an analysis of "pathways" (e.g., Loeber, 1988). The idea is that there are unique events that unfold in an orderly sequence that lead to a final developmental outcome. This appealing metaphor was just that until recently, when the advances in quantitative methods allowed for estimation of person-centered longitudinal patterns that are now referred to as *trajectories* (Muthén & Muthén, 2000; Muthén & Shedden, 1999; Nagin, 1999).

These quantitative innovations have led to several interesting trajectory studies, confirming the points made earlier. For example, Shaw, Gillom, Ingoldsby, and Nagin (2003) identified longitudinal trajectories of aggressive behavior that were highly predictive of school-age conduct problems. The work by Lacourse, Nagin, Tremblay, Vitaro, and Claes (2003) examines developmental trajectories leading to delinquency and violence in adolescence. Most analyses of developmental trajectories produce a high stable group and a consistently prosocial group. The remaining groups vary with respect to developmental patterns. For example, the study by Wiesner and Capaldi (2003) produced six different trajectories with the sample of 204 OYS males. These elegant statistical models will certainly become the wave of the future. As is typical, new quantitative models provide a basis for seeing new complexities in establishing trajectories that may depend on measurement issues, sample size, the kinds of causal predictors entered into the analysis, and the developmental period under consideration. A simple case in point is that arrest, self-report, teacher report, and parent report data may provide unique perspectives on the number and shape of developmental trajectories in antisocial behavior, as found in the study by Cairns and colleagues (Cairns, Cairns, Neckerman, & Gariepy, 1989). Moreover, the trajectories for male and female youth may be distinct, as indicated by less of a connection between overt antisocial behavior and the later emergence of covert behavior problems in girls (Moffitt, Caspi, Rutter, & Silva, 2001).

An often neglected issue in studying trajectories is the explanation of persistence and desistance. In Loeber's (1982) reanalysis of conviction data, both suggest that the actual shape of the trajectory curves vary as a function of age of onset. For example, in examining data sets based on official records, Patterson and Yoerger (1993) found that boys who begin their arrest career by ages 10 through 12 years had a unique shape to their trajectory. The curve was initially flat or even positive and then dropped steadily to young adult years. However, the boys first arrested at ages 14 to 18 years started somewhat lower and showed an immediate precipitous drop at young adult years (Patterson & Yoerger, 1993).

Desistance is particularly interesting. An analysis of the OYS longitudinal data set showed that at grade 4, 49 boys scored at the 75th percentile on a composite measure of overt antisocial behavior. Of these, 22 failed to become involved in growth for covert behavior over the ensuing 8 years (Patterson & Yoerger, 1999). From our perspective, this failure implies that they were not involved in deviancy training provided by deviant peers (Patterson, Dishion, & Yoerger, 2000), or that they actively avoided deviant peers and their influences to persist on a normative trajectory (T. Gardner & Dishion, 2005). This third group is of real interest because it directly addresses a comment made by Robins (1966) and frequently cited by trait theorists to the effect that most (about half) antisocial children do not grow up to be antisocial adults. In the OYS study, this group represented 44% of the subset of overt antisocial boys. Moffitt et al.'s (2002) careful analyses of the adult follow-up data for the Dunedin study showed very similar findings. They found that about 8% of their male cohort (10% for OYS) were members of a subset who showed high levels of antisocial involvement during childhood but only low to moderate participation during adolescence. Moffitt and her colleagues labeled them "the recovery group," implying a shift away from the antisocial trajectory. However, from the perspective of the Oregon model, this subset failed to move on and receive advanced training from deviant peers. In the Oregon model, we assumed that these individuals are anything but recovered: They remain antisocial but are limited to overt forms of expression. The fact that they did not participate in activities with their deviant peers suggests either poor peer relationships or active efforts on the part of the child and family to avoid deviant contexts.

Moffitt et al.'s (2002) analyses of this third group found that, as adults, they were suffering from internalizing forms of psychopathology, none had married, many had difficulty in making friends, and many were isolates. According to Moffitt et al., 28% of this third group as adults had court records. This was compared to 8% of the Oregon marginal-isolate group. We hypothesized that this third group would make a substantial contribution in accounting for individuals identified by Robins (1966) as antisocial

children who failed to continue on to become adult criminals. As noted earlier, the 22 members of this third trajectory represented 45% of our sample that had been identified as severely antisocial children.

We suggest that there are three pathways necessary to understand delinquent behavior. Each of them has a very different childhood history. The early-onset delinquent was trained by family members to engage in high rates of overt antisocial behavior and lacks a wide array of social skills. He then moved on to be trained by deviant peers in covert skills. He was arrested before the age of 14 years. The likelihood of adult arrest (from 18 through age 23 years) was .65. The second path began in childhood, with average to low levels of overt antisocial behavior and a relatively marginal level of social skills. As a late-onset group, they become involved with deviant peers in midadolescence. There is the expected increase in covert forms. Most of them desist offending. The third group (marginal-isolate), demonstrate only overt antisocial behavior, predicting juvenile and adult noninvolvement in delinquency.

Loeber and his colleagues (Loeber & Farrington, 2000) have also developed a model that describes three paths to delinquent outcomes. Their overt path is thought to begin in childhood with the advent of minor bullying and aggression. The assumption is that over time, the individual progresses to more extreme behaviors such as fighting and then later strong-arm attacks. The second path, covert antisocial behavior, may also begin in childhood, when it might include relatively minor forms such as lying, truancy, stealing in the home, and vandalism. However, younger performers may also engage in fire setting and shoplifting. In adolescence, the more extreme forms may include substance abuse and health-risking sexual behavior and burglary. The third path, authority conflict, begins with noncompliance and defiance, escalating to running away and truancy. Being on this path increases the risk of also moving along the other paths. The average age for involvement in serious delinquency was found to be 11.9 years. Initiation and maintenance on any or all of the paths are thought to be determined by a combination of 41 risk variables described by Loeber and Farrington.

Whether one takes a simple frequency approach to studying antisocial behavior in children and adolescents or focuses on sequential progressions based on developmental data, it is helpful to consider the ecology within which the behavior emerges and grows. Investigators have found repeatedly that entering in predictors can be useful for improving the understanding of developmental processes and for making critical distinctions in the forms of antisocial behavior. For example, Poulin and Boivin (2000a) found that proactive aggression was predicted by deviant peer involvement, whereas reactive aggression in middle childhood was not. Moreover, Patterson (1993) found that coercive discipline and associated family management practices accounted for the initial and chronic levels of problem behavior, and peer deviance accounted for growth in problem behavior, mostly in adolescence. An empirical account of antisocial behavior must address the fact that it changes form with development. Furthermore, the mechanisms that produce the changes vary from one form to the other, as do the agents and settings in which the changes occur. In a very real sense, this developmental model shows heterotypic continuity (Cicchetti, 1990). We propose that a functional perspective on social behavior and socialization provides an account of the timing and developmental variation observed in various forms of overt and covert behaviors. For this reason, we review literature about the onset, duration, and course of antisocial behavior as a critical foundation for explanation and, more important, intervention.

THE ECOLOGY

As the science of development and psychopathology matures, one sees clearly the need for integration of various levels of analysis, from biological influences, to microsocial analyses of relationship dynamics, to the study of context, including neighborhoods, schools, and communities. An ecological framework is helpful for organizing these levels of analysis (Bronfenbrenner, 1979, 1989).

The basic tenet of an ecological framework is that adaptation is functional. Our emphasis on social interaction patterns narrows the search to focus on functional dynamics in close relationships that elicit and/or maintain antisocial behavior in children and adolescents. We see the antisocial pattern as functional on at least three time scales. First, the overt antisocial behaviors we described earlier are functional at the microsocial level, in that they effectively control behavior. There seem to be two different mechanisms associated with producing immediate short-term control over the behavior of the other person. The first one identified in our observation studies followed an "escape-conditioning sequence": During a conflict bout, the child's persistent or escalating aversive reactions are followed by the other person terminating the bout; for example, the child wins. The other mechanism, and one we frequently encounter in our videotapes of Nor-

wegian families, fits an "avoidance-conditioning model." If a child's demands are not met, the child will punish the parents by having a temper tantrum; the parents avoid the temper tantrums by immediately complying with all child demands. Yelling, screaming, profanity, hitting, slander, and psychological assault become tools of microsocial coercive interactions. They are learned implicitly, forming the grammar of family life.

At a longer time scale, but still microsocial, is the role of deviance in forming the glue of friendships. Friendships are unique in the preponderance of positive behaviors. Indeed, when deviance is functional for keeping a relationship together, it remains a primary "shopping" strategy (Patterson, Reid, et al., 1992). Thus, the time scale is both seconds (probably at the very beginning of new friendships) to months and years (Dishion & Owen, 2002). We call this a "deviant friendship process," or deviancy training for short. The functional time scale may be extended somewhat further as we speculate about the probable function of the deviant peer group in promoting sexual relationships and contexts for early selection of sexual partners (Capaldi & Crosby, 1997; Dishion, Poulin, & Medici Skaggs, 2000; French & Dishion, 2003).

A key assumption of a functional emphasis on social interaction is that thoughts and feelings about relationships may or may not accurately reflect the actual relationship dynamics as revealed through observation analysis (Patterson & Reid, 1984; Patterson, Reid, et al., 1992). Parents referred to clinical settings with a problem child rarely identify their own reaction patterns as part of the problem. Youth are often unaware that their friends are moving them toward behaviors and decisions that will certainly undermine their health and development. Individuals feel their way through the social world, "choosing" responses that avoid or result in punishment. In this sense, consistent with several developmental theorists, relationships define the proximal environment in which change and development transpire (Bronfenbrenner, 1989; Hinde, 1989; Patterson, 1982).

As we shall see, the evidence is compelling that relationship dynamics are part of the problem, but more important, they are critical to the solution in child and adolescent antisocial behavior. Understanding the family and peer relationship dynamics is fundamental to understanding why some interventions intended to reduce antisocial behavior work and others do not (Dishion & Stormshak, in press).

There is a compelling sense, however, in which individuals shape their own futures. An individual can become aware of problematic relationships and dynamics and work to change or avoid those dynamics or reduce their influence. Individuals clearly shape, manipulate, select, and plan their own futures and avoid pitfalls and take advantage of opportunities to realize goals. This ability to regulate oneself in the social world would seem to increase with age. The ability to do so would be considered a resiliency factor, and the opposite, the inability to resist pressures for deviance and/or addiction, a vulnerability.

Our group has had some difficulty in measuring a construct that reflects individual-level resilience that is not empirically redundant to the antisocial construct. For example, when we formed a multiagent and multimethod construct of competence, we found it correlated −.85 with a similarly formed composite measure of antisocial behavior (Patterson, Reid, et al., 1992). We concluded that the global ratings we used to define children's competence and antisocial behavior were simply positive and negative items on a single "good/bad" dimension. Psychometrically, there is a strong tendency for rating individuals, to reduce one's judgments to the least common denominator, which is simply whether the person is liked or disliked (i.e., good or bad; C. E. Osgood, 1962). This fundamental tendency in rater bias is what underlies the validity problem known as monomethod bias (Cook & Campbell, 1979). Another, less technical term for this is what we refer to as the "glop" problem (Bank, Dishion, Skinner, & Patterson, 1990).

The best strategy for avoiding glop is to become more focused and microsocial when measuring a construct (Fiske, 1986, 1987). In the past decade, progress has been made in linking genetic, brain, and behavioral dimensions to define competence as a process of self-regulation (see Rothbart & Posner, Chapter 11, this *Handbook*, Volume 2). In this chapter, we integrate this emerging literature to discuss the possible role of self-regulation in the development of antisocial behavior. Consistent with a social interaction perspective, we assume that self-regulation is highly embedded in relationship dynamics, consisting of a set of behaviors such as turn taking and listening to others. At another level (and temporal scale), it involves following through on tasks, avoiding situations where the temptation to engage in deviant behavior would be too great, controlling how one thinks and feels about things, and planning ahead. These self-regulatory skills are also those often emphasized in effective interventions for reducing antisocial behavior in children (Dishion & Kavanagh, 2003; Dishion & Stormshak, in press; Kazdin, Siegel, & Bass, 1992; Lochman, Barry, & Pardini, 2003; Lochman & Wells, 1996). Self-regulation, therefore, is the most promising candidate for linking individual characteristics to the ecology in a way that will be helpful in understanding the development of antisocial behavior.

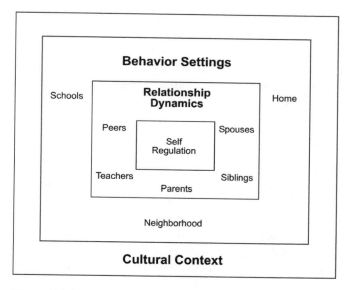

Figure 13.5 The ecology of antisocial behavior.

As shown in Figure 13.5, we invoke three broad domains of constructs to explain the age of onset and severity of antisocial behavior:

1. Relationship dynamics focuses primarily on interactions with parents, siblings, and peers as the proximal training ground for the learning and maintenance of antisocial behavior from childhood through adulthood. Such dynamics are studied by conducting microsocial analyses of interactive dynamics and contingencies, cognition and emotion.

2. Behavior setting stimuli describe the characteristics of contexts to the structuring of relationships that influence problem behavior. Because peer interactions are so important in the development of antisocial behavior, we focus our attention on the public school setting and the formation of peer interactions in children and adolescents.

3. Self-regulation describes the individual's ability to become self-directed with respect to managing daily, weekly, and monthly routines, regulating emotions, keeping in check dysfunctional thinking, and selecting environments conducive to goal-directed behavior.

In addition to these three domains, Figure 13.5 adds the cultural and community context as a conditional variable when considering the viability of an explanatory model. In the past 10 years, a variety of studies have shown variations in dynamics associated with the etiology of antisocial behavior as a function of culture and ethnicity. We address these issues as they pertain to each of the domains reviewed next.

As mentioned, we propose a single model for the development of antisocial behavior that has the potential to be a general application and is relevant to the systematic effort to treat and prevent problem behavior in children and adolescents. We begin with a detailed discussion of relationship dynamics.

Relationship Dynamics

Regardless of theoretical perspective, it is generally agreed that in childhood and adolescent relationships with parents, siblings, peers, and teachers are the basic social ecologies within which antisocial behavior is displayed, practiced, learned, accelerated, or suppressed. During late adolescence and early adulthood, romantic relationships transform into long-term commitments and families; peers become coworkers; authority figures gradually change from teachers to supervisors.

The contribution of parents and peers to the development and course of antisocial behavior can be seen as a layered process that begins in infancy and proceeds through adolescence (see Figure 13.6). From a social interactional perspective (Reid, Patterson, & Snyder, 2002), child socialization is an effortful process that requires adult attention, effort, and skills in managing the minutiae of daily parent-child interaction, as well as the proactive structuring of children's development trajectories. The layers of influence in the socialization process can be seen as hierarchical integration.

The earliest relationship is that of the caregiver and child. Both behaviorists and attachment theorists agree in emphasizing the key role played by the variable *caregiver responsivity* (Patterson & Fisher, 2002). As measured by Martin (1981) and Maccoby (1992) and replicated by Shaw

and Winslow (1997), the variable emphasizes maternal sensitivity and warmth in reacting to infant behavior. What gradually emerges are two general dimensions that describe the parenting domain. One dimension can be characterized as affective in that it emphasizes warmth and relational characteristics. The other dimension can be characterized as contingent/noncontingent; for example, the warm relational parent who is also noncontingent (permissive) is likely to produce an aggressive child, as shown by Baumrind (1971). The coercion model emphasizes the noncontingent parent with only weak relational ties to the child.

Caregiver skills in behavior management (i.e., social and material contingencies) build on the caregiver relationship. Attachment is viewed as a necessary, but not sufficient, precondition for socialization to occur. The child must learn to adapt to the intricate network of implicit and explicit rules that govern behavior and that vary as a function of age and gender.

Figure 13.6 shows that parent relationships influence, and, in turn are altered by, parent-guided socialization. For example, obvious failures to socialize the child are received by the parent as negative feedback and alter several components of the parent-child relationship. A study of the OYS sample showed that school failure was highly correlated with measures of maternal rejection (Patterson, 1986). In turn, both of these areas of activity are bidirectionally related to what transpires in interactions with peers. The sections that follow trace out the details of this interconnected aspect of the socialization process as they unfold over the time course between early childhood and late adolescence.

Parenting Practices

The interest in the relationship between parenting and the development of antisocial behavior cuts across disciplines. In longitudinal studies seeking to predict male adolescent antisocial behavior, parenting practices were among the most powerful predictors (Loeber & Dishion, 1983). Although the general relationship is well established, there is variability from study to study in the magnitude of predictive validity, primarily because of differences in the measurement procedures used to define parenting. Use of parents' recall or reconstruction of their parenting behavior tends to produce lower predictability (Brook, Whiteman, Gordon, & Cohen, 1986; Patterson & Bank, 1986). Children's reports of parenting practices lead to somewhat higher predictive validity (e.g., Nye, 1958; Slocum & Stone, 1965). Outside sources for information about par-

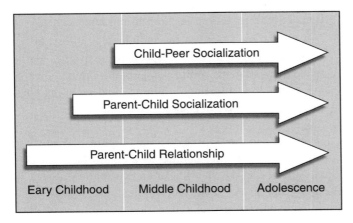

Figure 13.6 Relationship dynamics from early childhood to adolescence.

enting, whether from official records of parent criminality, home visitor ratings, or direct observations, consistently produce the highest level of predictive validity for current and future antisocial behavior.

Patterson's (1982) coercion model focused specifically on the contributions of parent-child interactions to child antisocial behavior. This social interaction model implies an emphasis on parent-child exchanges as the proximal cause of antisocial behavior throughout the life span. Even in this early model, parental cognitions were thought to play a significant role. For example, it was hypothesized that during conflict episodes, both parent negative attributions and anger contributed to the likelihood of escalation. A series of laboratory studies showed that parents of aggressive children tended to be overly inclusive in their definitions of deviant child behavior (Patterson, Reid, et al., 1992). Child behaviors classified by trained observers as within normal range were classified as deviant by parents of problem children. It was assumed that these laboratory measures of parent negative attributions could serve as predictors for disruptions in parental discipline practices.

In keeping with this prediction, Nix et al. (1999) found a low-level path coefficient showing covariation between maternal negative attributions to (teacher- and peer-defined) school aggression constructs. However, as shown in Figure 13.7, the path from parent attributions to school aggression was mediated by parent discipline practices. Snyder, Cramer, Afrank, and Patterson (2005) replicated this mediational model. Social cognitions play a powerful role in disrupting parental discipline practices. However, it is the disciplinary exchanges themselves that function as a di-

rect effects model for overt forms of child aggression. In a later section, we examine findings that show an even more dramatic role for maternal social cognitions in understanding future growth in aggression.

To date, the chief focus of the coercion model has been on the process by which the child learns antisocial behavior within parent-child and sibling-child exchanges. The concept of negative reinforcement is the key to understanding the interaction patterns we see occurring between parents and antisocial children, even in the toddler and preschool years. Such interactions occur at some level in all families from time to time. A high rate of coercive exchanges, however, is hypothesized to train children to use a wide range of coercive behaviors in their effort to shape their social environment.

An important corollary of a coercive parent-child relationship is the concomitant reduction in the adult's attention to the child's development of self-regulation, critical to a variety of prosocial skills (Eisenberg & Fabes, 1998). Again, we do not know which comes first: Does the coercive child behavior cause the shutdown in skill development? Or is it the reduced level of positive parent involvement that sets the stage for the development of coercion? The result is clear and dramatic: It produces long-term outcomes such as failure to acquire homework skills, failure to care for or understand others' thoughts and feelings (empathy), and failure to engage in organized games or group activities. In this fashion, the problem child is doubly handicapped.

Coercion is not only about aggression; it also accounts for general tendencies to avoid and, eventually, conceal and manipulate. The child learns to avoid parent demands through a process of negative reinforcement. Repeated over thousands of trials, the child learns to use coercive behaviors to gain control over a disrupted, chaotic, or unpleasant family environment. In these families, aversive events occur as often as one event every 3 minutes. A conflict bout occurs about once every 16 minutes. Given intensive practice, these coercive patterns become overlearned and automatic. This is contrary to the position taken by Bandura (1989, p. 88) in his influential statement, "Because outcomes effect behavior largely through the mediation of thought, consequences alone often produce little change in behavior." Alternatively, the present writers assume that coercive contingencies operate without conscious, cognitive control. In point of fact, the Nix et al. (1999), Snyder, Cramer, et al. (2005), and Snyder, Schrepferman, et al. (2005) studies show that the impact of cognitions on behavior is mediated by contingencies rather than the other way

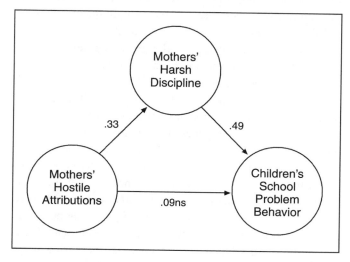

Figure 13.7 Maternal hostile attributions in the coercion cycle. Adapted from Nix et. al. 1999.

around. One of the major goals in interventions targeting parenting practices is to help the parent become aware of these automatic patterns and to bring them under more cognitive control (Forgatch & Patterson, 1989).

In the absence of countervailing forces, children may increase the frequency of coercive behaviors, and this, in turn, predicts their moving toward the more severe forms for their age group (e.g., to temper tantrums and physical attacks). As suggested, the coercion process is often not recognized by the participants. Family explanations evolve that suggest that if the child is stubborn (like his or her father?), the marriage is bad, work is interfering, or the school is unfair. We have often found that parent reports about what they are doing yield low predictive validities (Capaldi & Patterson, 1989). The development of observational methodology to record objectively the moment-by-moment interchanges between parents and their children has been critical in evaluating the coercion model. In the OYS, Patterson, Reid, et al. (1992) compared behavior observations and parent interview measures of discipline practices. They found that the correlations between these were low (correlations in the .2 to .3 range), barely satisfying the minimal requirements of convergent validity in construct validation.

The careful longitudinal studies by Shaw and his colleagues (2003) trace out the details for the continuity between toddler and middle childhood status. Toddlers who are low in self-regulation (for their age) and mothers who are depressed are most at risk for engaging in an extended version of the coercion process, accounting for the majority of the children entering elementary school with behavior problems (Shaw et al., 2003). Left on their own, these parents are least likely to improve their parenting practices to the normal range during their child's adolescent. Patterson and colleagues (Patterson & Dishion, 1985; Patterson & Stouthamer-Loeber, 1984) found an association between inept parent discipline practices, parent monitoring, and child antisocial behavior in midadolescence. Thus, cumulative continuity (Caspi, Bem, & Elder, 1989) takes its toll by rendering a very antisocial and violence-prone adolescent (Capaldi & Patterson, 1991; Lykken, 1993).

The issue of whether coercion applies across cultural and ethnic groups is a bit more complex. It certainly is true that parenting practices covary with problem behavior for children across ethnic groups (Catalano et al., 1992; Deater-Deckard & Dodge, 1997; Dishion & Bullock, 2001; Mason, Cauce, Gonzales, & Hiraga, 1996; Steinberg, Dornbusch, & Brown, 1992). There are important differences, however, in the precise form that the coercion process may take across cultural groups. For example, in the recent work by Deater-Deckard and Dodge, reports of

physical spanking were correlated with lower rates of problem behavior among European American children but not with African American youth. We used direct observations to compare high-risk and successful early adolescents in the context of their family (Dishion & Bullock, 2001). When we looked at direct observations of specific parenting practices, such as limit setting and relationship quality, there were anomalies in the findings. For example, relationship quality was quite high in the observations of high-risk African American boys with their parent(s), whereas it was less so for successful African American youth and their parents. Moreover, limit-setting practices were rated as lower for successful African American youth, compared to high-risk African American youth. When using an aggregate family management score based on the 45 minutes of direct observation, we found that the ethnic differences dissolved, and only the differences between high-risk and successful remained. These findings underscore the assertion that to measure parenting well, it is important to consider the pattern of contingencies surrounding the performance of positive, neutral, and negative behavior, and that even global ratings of direct observations are vulnerable to biases and obfuscation (Yasui, Dishion, & Dorham, in press). A final point is that interventions that target family management work equally well for all ethnic groups (Connell, Dishion, & Deater-Deckard, in press; Dishion, Nelson, & Kavanagh, 2003; Gross et al., 2003; Henggeler, Schoenwald, Borduin, Rowland, & Cunningham, 1998).

As children move into adolescence, monitoring becomes an increasingly important aspect of parenting. Patterson and Dishion (1985) found a strong correlation between parent monitoring practices, adolescent delinquent behavior, and deviant peer associations. Inadequate parent monitoring seems to be important in the emergence and maintenance of antisocial behavior in children from middle childhood through adolescence.

Rowe (1994) and Harris (1998) reviewed the findings from twin and adoption studies designed to test for the relative contributions of genes and environments to phenotypic behaviors such as aggression. They concluded that there was no support for the contribution of shared environments to the development of any phenotypic behavior, including children's aggression. They also concluded there was no evidence for the contribution of parenting practices to child aggression. If anything, the evidence indicated that it was the child's behavior that governed parenting practices. There are at least three well-known flaws in the behavior genetics approach that would normally give pause to anyone making such strong claims. The flaws were reviewed in detail by Bronfenbrenner and Ceci (1994) and Collins, Everitt, Robbins, Roberts, and Wilkinson (2000). The most salient problems are these:

1. The range is restricted, as shown by Stoolmiller (1998) and by Turkheimer (1991). This is a problem for both adoption and twin designs. Both strategies employ truncated environments, and as a result, the chances of finding environmental effects are severely curtailed.

2. It is the twin design studies that fail to find any effects for shared environments or for parenting practices. There are now three major studies that show that identical twins share an environment that significantly increases their similarity (Carey, 1992; Rose & Kaprio, 1987; Tambs, Harris, & Magnus, 1995). This means that the heritability equation 2 (monozygotic-dizygotic) is confounded.

3. The estimate of heritability varies widely as a function of method of measurement. After reviewing 24 studies, Miles and Carey (1997) concluded that the most salient finding was that estimates of heritability varied as a function of method of measurement. Estimates based on parent ratings tended to show high values for heritability, whereas those based on observation data were very low. These conclusions were supported by two more recent studies by Leve, Winebarger, Fagot, Reid, and Goldsmith (1998) and Deater-Deckard (2000).

In reacting to the Rowe-Harris claims, developmental psychologists such as Collins et al. (2000) took the position that the strongest test of the parenting practices model would be an experiment in which families were randomly assigned to experimental and comparison groups. The experimental group would receive parent management training and the comparison group would not. The design would require data showing significant improvements in parenting skills for families in the experimental group, but not in the comparison group. Furthermore, the data must show improvements in child outcomes for the experimental group but not for the comparison group. Finally, the magnitude of change in parenting must covary with the magnitude of change in child outcomes.

The study by Dishion and Kavanagh (2003) was one of the first to fulfill the demands for an effective experiment. They randomly assigned parents of 150 problematic early adolescents (males and females) to the Adolescent Transitions Program (ATP) or to a nontreatment control group. ATP consisted of three versions of intervention: parent-focused training, teen-focused training, and a joint focus on parent and teen. Involvement in ATP was associated with

reductions in parent-child observed negative engagement, which, in turn, were reliability correlated with reductions in teacher ratings of antisocial behavior in school. More recently, Dishion, Bullock, and Granic (2002) found that random assignment to family-centered interventions reduced deviant peer involvement and adolescent substance use (Dishion, Kavanagh, Schneiger, Nelson, & Kaufman, 2002). An analysis of direct observation of parent monitoring practices revealed that changes in parent monitoring where associated with changes in deviant peer involvement and substance use.

The most careful mediation analyses to date are those conducted and reported by Forgatch and colleagues studying children undergoing divorce. The researchers documented that random assignment to parenting interventions showed significant increases in effective discipline and monitoring and in measures of positive parenting, and produced parent-child coercion, which, in turn, was associated with reductions in child antisocial behavior (Martinez & Forgatch, 2001). These changes were associated further with significant improvements in child antisocial behavior, delinquency, and school achievement (Forgatch & De-Garmo, 1999, 2002). It is important to note that the evaluation of these intervention studies carefully selected independent and objective indices of behavior (not parents' report) to minimize the Hawthorn effect on global ratings of functioning.

Attachment and Positive Parenting

As noted earlier, there are impressive areas of agreement between attachment and coercion theories (Patterson & Fisher, 2002). Both theories agree on the fundamental importance of parental responsiveness as being a necessary condition for socialization. Both theories define parental responsiveness as the contingent actions of the parent in reacting to the child. Both the attachment theorists (Van den Boom, 1994) and the behavioral approaches (Martin, 1981; Shaw & Winslow, 1997) predict the association between noncontingent parenting and infant distress. Both would see the impact of contextual factors, such as maternal depression, leading to negative child outcomes as mediated by disruptions in parental responsiveness.

As pointed out in Patterson and Fisher (2002), the two theories differ dramatically in their explanations of the means by which parental responsiveness produces child outcomes. In the behavioral view, the contingent reactions shape both the child outcomes and parent behavior. Some of the literature relevant to this assumption is reviewed in a later section. Attachment theorists (Ainsworth, 1989;

Ainsworth & Bowlby, 1991; Rutter, 1995) take the position that the impact of parental responsiveness on child outcome is entirely mediated by mechanisms such as infant level of attachment, the child's internalization of parental values and standards, and the child's attributions. The brief review by Fagot and Kavanagh (1991) suggested only limited predictability from attachment classification to child adjustment for males but not for females and for at-risk families, rather than for normal families. It can be said that in terms of variance accounted for, attachment theory makes only a limited contribution.

Although both theories agree in their emphasis on the importance of parental positivity on child outcomes, the empirical findings testing these assumptions pose an interesting problem for both theories. When we constructed multimethod, multiagent indicators for a range of child deviant and prosocial behaviors, our correlational models showed a very interesting pattern of findings (Patterson, Reid, et al., 1992, see Table 5.7). As expected, when examining antisocial outcomes, the measures of disrupted parenting (monitor and discipline) accounted, on average, for about 16% of the variance, and measures of positive parenting accounted, on average, for about 3%. We had expected that models built to account for prosocial outcomes such as achievement, self-esteem, and peer relationships would show the reverse pattern. Our best attempts to specify parent involvement, parent support, and dyadic problem solving produced significant correlations with child achievement, but on average, they accounted for only about 3% of the variance. The results were disappointing and lead us to believe that perhaps we did not focus enough on specifying the measurement models for positive parenting.

We were surprised to find that the measures of disrupted monitoring and discipline seemed to predict both negative and prosocial outcomes. They accounted for about 3 times as much variance as did measures of positive parenting! The findings suggest the interesting possibility that when the coercion process is well under way, one of the most important concomitants is a shutdown of all prosocial support mechanisms. If the family is extremely coercive, it is known that there is little reinforcement or support for prosocial activities. The amount of support for prosocial behavior is entirely a function of the level of pathology. If this is true, then an experiment should show that reducing coercion levels would be accompanied but a sudden increase in the relative contribution of parent support, parent involvement, and problem solving.

Some recent findings from prevention studies are of particular interest because they seem to support such an idea.

The data from a randomized prevention trial showed that growth in parent positivity (support, involvement, problem solving) played a dominant role in bringing about change in child compliance behaviors (Martinez & Forgatch, 2001). The path coefficient from growth in positive parenting to changes in child compliance was −.54. The comparable path for improvements in discipline and growth in compliance was also significant, but a much lower .19. A single study is hardly creditable, but the findings set the question in proper perspective. What does positive parenting contribute to the process of change?

F. E. M. Gardner (1989) made significant progress on this scientific issue. She asserts that it is necessary not only to look at the immediate reaction of compliance or noncompliance, but also to consider the outcome of the conflict minutes afterward. Using this approach, she found that mothers of conduct problem children were 8 times more likely to relinquish demands than mothers of normal children. Also, mothers of nonproblem children handled 43% of the conflict episodes inconsistently, compared with 5% of mothers of normal children.

Another criticism by F. E. M. Gardner (in press) of the coercion model is that it is too clinically oriented and does not fully consider the causal impact of positive features of the family environment. In coercion theory, it is the use of aversive exchanges, rather than positive exchanges that disrupts child development. In her observation, the more entrenched the parents become in the coercion process, the further they shrink from relationship skills that they would enjoy under more favorable circumstances.

F. E. M. Gardner (in press) went on to isolate deficits in positive interactions that characterize families with antisocial children. She found that proactive parenting, in particular, differentiated parent-child interactions of conduct problem and normal children. This parenting skill involves a combination of structuring situations to avoid misbehavior, engaging the child in positive, joint activities, and using verbal prompts that elicit positive behavior in children. Although these positive practices may be disrupted because of the coercion process, the lack of proactive parenting may have a unique effect on multiple aspects of child social development not predicted by coercive interactions.

Patterson (1986) tested a structural equation model that demonstrated a strong correlation between harsh, abrasive, and inconsistent parent discipline and child antisocial behavior. This model was replicated across the two cohorts of the OYS with a single-parent sample and a clinical sample (Forgatch, 1991). The longitudinal studies by Shaw and colleagues (1998) demonstrated that these processes are in place at a very early age. Their models combine both a contingency and an attachment view and use it to account for the emergence of behavior problems in early childhood. To measure the attachment relationship, however, they did not use the Strange Situation task, but innovated a process measure. They employed an innovative highchair task pioneered by Martin (1981) to measure parents' responsiveness to the child. Shaw and colleagues found that the lack of parent responsiveness in infancy combined to account for variation in antisocial behavior.

These variables interact to account for the very early emergence of behavior problems (Shaw, Keenan, & Vondra, 1994). The study showed that child noncompliance and mother's nonresponsiveness combined to predict overall levels of aggression by age 24 months. Moreover, at 24 months, an aggression-by-maternal-nonresponsiveness interaction term predicted overall levels of aggression by age 36 months. As the longitudinal study proceeded, rejecting parenting was added to the prediction equation. Rejecting parenting at 24 months predicted the highest rates of aggressive behavior by age 4 (Shaw et al., 1998). Levels of marital conflict were also highly correlated with rejecting parenting (Shaw, Winslow, & Flanagan, 1999), which combined to account for behavior problems by age 5. Ingoldsby, Shaw, and Garcia (2001) followed the sample into school, finding that the pervasiveness of family conflict predicted aggression with peers at school. Most recently, using a trajectory analysis approach to analyze their longitudinal data, Shaw and colleagues (2003) found that children with low levels of self-regulation (in this case, inhibitory control), who also had depressed mothers, were most likely to be aggressive as toddlers and to continue on the antisocial trajectory to the second grade of elementary school.

Most investigators working in this area feel that the parenting model can be strengthened. For example, F. E. M. Gardner's work suggests the importance of identifying proactive parenting skills, and Shaw's work reveals the unique role of parents' responsiveness in toddlerhood to socialization.

The groundbreaking studies by Nix et al. (1999) and Snyder, Cramer, et al. (2005) dramatically expand the model by integrating parenting variables with measures of parental attribution. In this area, there are also studies by Stoolmiller and Snyder (2004) that stitch together models for emotion with models for parenting. There is one more dimension to this struggle that should be noted: A study by Forgatch, Patterson, and Ray (1996) showed that the parenting models that adequately described individual differences in aggression did not fit when applied to growth data

for aggression. Patterson (1993) also found that the model that explained intercept values for antisocial behavior did not fit in models for growth in antisocial behavior. Different models were also required for intercept and growth models of delinquency.

It seems, then, that we may require one parenting model to explain individual differences in aggression but a quite different one for modeling growth in antisocial behavior. In keeping with this distinction, Snyder, Cramer, et al. (2005) found that discipline practices did not contribute to measures of growth assessed at home or school. However, a product term (discipline) by mother (negative attribution) was a significant predictor for growth in both settings.

In summary, there is little doubt that parenting practices are highly correlated with child antisocial behavior. It is also the case that improvements in parenting practices during well-designed intervention studies produce decreases in a child's antisocial behavior. The strength of these findings and the fact that they are replicated means that we can now set about the task of improving the models.

Siblings

It has been said that siblings are no more alike than two people chosen at random (Plomin & Daniels, 1987). It turns out that method variance again distorts our view of the contribution of siblings (Hoffman, 1991); that is, the lack of similarity among siblings ($r = .16$) found across samples may be an artifact of data based on personality inventories. Research employing alternative assessment methods, including direct observation, paints a different picture of similarity between siblings on several indices of adaptation in the home and school settings in the middle childhood years. It turns out that when effective measures are employed across siblings, there is a robust correlation for aggression.

Studies that attempt to disentangle the influence of different family agents on the socialization of the child and the development of antisocial behavior are just beginning. Considerable evidence suggests that the influence of siblings is significant. One recalls the finding, first reported by West and Farrington (1973), that 5% of the families accounted for 50% of the crimes in an urban London sample. This finding implied that siblings share a common trait for antisocial behavior. We suspect that siblings are fellow travelers on the path to antisocial behavior (Patterson, 1986).

Clinical experience tells us that children referred for conduct problems often differ little from their nonreferred siblings. In their home, siblings' rates of aversive behavior frequently are comparable to that of the target child. Patterson (1986) reported a correlation of .61 among brothers referred for conduct problems who were observed in the home. Patterson, Dishion, and Bank (1984) found a correlation of .43 among boys and their siblings as observed in the home. Patterson (1984) proposed that siblings, as well as other family members, shared a mutual trait toward aggressiveness. The thought is that the coercion process, as previously discussed, is elicited by inept parenting practices (Patterson, 1982; Patterson, Reid, et al., 1992) and has an impact on all members of a family system.

Strong support for the parenting hypothesis was provided in an intervention study reported by Arnold, Levine, and Patterson (1975). In a reanalysis of clinical cases seen for child aggressive behavior, they found that all siblings decreased observed aversive behavior following parent training, even though only the problem child was targeted for treatment. However, the high correlations between siblings on observed aggressive behavior are confounded because siblings are most often interacting with each other when observed in the home. The finding also needs to be replicated with a randomly assigned experimental control group.

There is some evidence for sibling similarity outside the home. For example, the work of Lewin, Hops, Davis, and Dishion (1993) showed convergence among siblings on such measures as negative peer nominations ($r = .65$), teacher ratings on aggression ($r = .48$), and observed positive peer behavior in the classroom ($r = .47$). The correlation among siblings in teachers' reactions to each child in separate classrooms was surprising. Behavior observations in the classroom revealed a correlation of .72 ($p < .001$) in observed teacher disapproval. Note that these were independent observations of each of the siblings in separate classrooms with different teachers.

A simple generalization model cannot account for siblings' similarity in the school setting. Although siblings' behavior in school is intercorrelated, as is siblings' behavior in the home, two studies showed that there is not a high correlation between children's aversive exchanges with their siblings and their peer acceptance of antisocial behavior in school (Abramovitch, Carter, Pepler, & Stanhope, 1986; Dishion, 1987). Bank and Burraston (2001) also showed that sibling conflicts in the home were a poor predictor for deviant peer contacts in the school.

Aside from the contribution of siblings to the coercion process, there is recent evidence that siblings may function to facilitate antisocial behavior by two mechanisms: first, by reinforcing deviant talk and behavior in families, and second, by forming coalitions that undermine parents' ability to socialize young adolescents. The process has

been referred to as *sibling collusion* (Bullock & Dishion, 2002). In this study, observers coded videotapes of family interactions of high-risk and normative young adolescents for sibling collusion. We found that sibling collusion was highly correlated with young adolescent problem behavior, as defined by teachers and self-reported, and that this effect held when controlling for involvement with deviant peers. Incidentally, sibling collusion was also highly correlated with the young adolescents' involvement with deviant peers, suggesting yet a third function of siblings, in that older siblings may in fact provide a bridge to the deviant peer group.

In a second study, Stormshak, Comeau, and Shepard (2004) examined the role of sibling "deviancy training" as measured by direct observations without the parents present. Using latent growth modeling, they found that direct observations of sibling deviancy training and their own problem behavior were strongly associated with growth in adolescent problem behavior, even when controlling for the behavior of peers. Of course, in many ways, the contribution of siblings is difficult to study in isolation from peers, as sibling relationships are often embedded within peer networks, especially in adolescence.

More recently, Bullock, Bank, and Burraston (2002) examined the prognostic value of sibling conflict to adult continuance in antisocial behavior. These investigators examined collected expressed emotion indices of sibling negative affectivity and conflict. Compared to earlier measures of home observations of sibling conflict, coded expressed emotion from 5 minutes of audiotaped speech samples predicted long-term patterns in antisocial behavior over and above direct observations of coercive sibling interactions. These data point to the potential importance of the expressed emotion methodology for studying relationship processes and indicate the potential long-term and unique influence of siblings to antisocial behavior.

Peers

It has become increasingly clear that most covert forms of antisocial behavior (proactive aggression, relational aggression, stealing, etc.) are embedded within peer and friendship relationships. In contrast to our previous review, we posit peers as a major proximal cause of antisocial behavior, beginning in early childhood and accelerating in influence during early adolescence.

We see this as being accomplished in three major ways: (1) Antisocial behavior interferes with positive peer relations, depriving children of the positive benefits of peer learning and confining them within the social niches of marginal adjustment; (2) children may act as models and a source of reinforcement for antisocial behavior; and (3) as children develop friendship networks, support for antisocial behavior is established by providing both reinforcement and opportunity for such behavior. We address each of these issues in turn.

Entry to school may be the first occasion during which the child is exposed to significant numbers of nonrelated age mates (French, 1987) and, as such, provides the conditions for establishing the peer culture. Patterson et al. (1967) have shown that one of the consequences of exposure to other children is an increase in aggression. Their microanalysis of preschool children's interactions revealed that peers provide very rich schedules of positive reinforcement for coercive behavior, with 80% of coercive behavior producing successful outcomes. Instigators and victims are not random: Certain children provide reinforcement for aggression, with the consequence being an increase in the victimization of these children (Olweus, 1979). Snyder, West, Stockemer, Givens, and Almquist-Parks (1996) found that, in Head Start preschools, peer choice and reinforcement were salient predictors of early aggression. Affiliative structures and coalitions seem fundamental to the human condition even in early childhood and are germane to the development of antisocial behavior (Strayer & Santos, 1996). A recent study by Snyder, Schrepferman, et al. (2005), and colleagues revealed that as early as the 1st year of elementary school, peer interactions (i.e., deviancy training; see later discussion) could be identified among children and their classmates that predict escalations in antisocial behavior during the 1st and 2nd years of school. Kellam, Ling, Merisca, Brown, and Ialongo (1998) also find that the level of aggression in children's 1st-year classroom predicts long-term patterns of problem behavior. These reinforced patterns of aggression are common and continue into at least early adolescence. We see the early school maladaptation leading to marginal school adjustment, which amplifies deviant peer affiliation networks, which, in turn, provide a proximal context for the refinement and growth in new forms of problem behavior.

The impact of peers on antisocial behavior is also seen in the work of Dodge, Price, Coie, and Christopoulos (1990). Using data from a series of playgroup sessions involving previously unacquainted peers, they found that 50% of the aggression observed in these play sessions was accounted for by a mere 20% of the dyads. As might be expected, these dyads consisted primarily of members identified by their aggressiveness. This research is complemented by a paper presented by Cillessen (1989), in which

it was found that triads of low-status first-grade children were the most highly aggressive; mixed dyads (low and high status) produced considerably lower levels of aggressive behaviors. Thus, the antisocial traits of individuals merge to create a dyadic tendency to engage in antisocial behavior. When both members are antisocial, an amplification of maladaptive characteristics is likely. These data also raise the issue of deviant peer influences as early as middle childhood.

Much of the research on the role of peers in middle childhood antisocial behavior focuses on children's acceptance within the peer group, or sociometric status. Antisocial behavior has emerged as the most consistent correlate of social rejection in children (e.g., Coie & Dodge, 1988; French & Waas, 1987). Aggression is not, however, consistently associated with peer disapproval. Fighting back from a provoked attack may be positively associated with social status (Olweus, 1979), whereas unprovoked attacks seem to be a pathogenic sign of a general antisocial trait. Furthermore, antisocial behavior appears to account for only about 50% of peer rejection in boys (French, 1988) and somewhat less in girls (French, 1990).

The clearest evidence of the impact of aggression comes from observations of playgroups comprising previously unacquainted members. Coie and Kupersmidt (1983) formed playgroups consisting of four boys who differed in status. Rejected boys exhibited more physical and verbal aggression than other group members. Similar findings were obtained by Dodge (1983) in a study of unacquainted groups comprising eight boys unselected by status. Boys who eventually were rejected by their companions exhibited more physical aggression, inappropriate play, and hostile verbalization than other group members. In comparing the role of overt aggression and relational aggression to peer rejection, Crick (1996) found that overt aggression was most correlated with peer dislike.

It is not always true that antisocial behavior is associated with peer dislike. Stormshak et al. (1999) examined the covariation across classrooms between peer social preference and behavior problems. Apparently, some classrooms are settings for peer contagion, as in these, behavior problems lead to positive peer relationships.

The child's movement out of middle childhood into adolescence is marked by increased involvement with peers and affiliations with larger social groups. Much of the research on the contribution of peers to the development of antisocial behavior has focused on the impact of social groups. These are larger than friendship dyads and can be categorized as cliques or crowds (Brown, 1989). Cliques generally consist of fewer than 10 members who frequently interact with each other. In contrast, crowds are defined on the basis of reputation, and members may or may not interact with each other.

There is evidence that children who are rejected by their peers (a significant percentage of whom exhibit antisocial behavior) begin to associate together during the elementary school years. These children are more likely to interact with younger peers, other rejected children, and individuals with whom they are not friends (Ladd, 1983). These groups become increasingly solidified during early adolescence. Contributing to the formation of these groups is the adolescent quest for autonomy and vulnerability to peer pressure (Steinberg & Silverberg, 1986). An additional factor is the normative transition from the small elementary school environment to the larger, more impersonal middle and high school settings, where there are large numbers of age mates with whom to associate and considerable freedom from adult scrutiny.

Dishion, Patterson, Stoolmiller, and Skinner (1991) found that low parent monitoring, poor academic skills, and peer rejection in middle childhood accounted for associations with deviant peers by early adolescence, even after controlling for prior levels of antisocial behavior. Although the deviant peer construct was stronger at a later age, there was indication that deviant peers were identifiable in the elementary school setting, as reported by children, teachers, and parents (Dishion, 1990). There was respectable stability in involvement with antisocial peers from ages 9 to 10 and 11 to 12, reflected in a standardized beta of .26 ($p < .01$) when controlling for family, school, and the child's behavior at age 9 to 10. Cairns, Cairns, Neckerman, Gest, and Gariepy (1988) found that aggressive children in middle school tended to associate more as a function of mutual attraction than of peer rejection. In addition, Cairns, Cadwallader, and Neckerman (1997) reviewed literature suggesting that adolescent members of gangs are a cast of the formerly ostracized and alienated. We recently established that peer rejection in the 1st year of middle school was a unique predictor of gang affiliation by the end of middle school, controlling for earlier measures of antisocial behavior (Dishion, Nelson, & Yasui, in press). One interpretation of peer aggregation is that children actively select environments that fit their genotype, and that these environments serve as nonshared environmental influences on child and adolescent problem behavior (Harris, 1995; Rowe, Woulbroun, & Gulley, 1994).

A study by Bullock, Deater-Deckard, and Leve (in press) was one of the few behavior genetic studies on deviant peer affiliation conducted using a multiagent and multimethod assessment. This study used a twin study (Leve et al., 1998) to determine heritability of deviant peer affiliation. Multiple ratings of deviant peer affiliation were obtained for monozygotic and dizygotic twins, including direct observations of friendship interactions and two independent teacher ratings (teachers rated siblings and peers independently). The portion of variance attributable to genotype and shared and nonshared environments varied dramatically by assessment method (one measure of teacher ratings yielding the highest heritability). Consistent with previous analyses of this sample, direct observations produce zero heritability coefficients and high shared environmental coefficients. The studies from this sample are critical for our understanding of the methodological barriers to disentangling, unambiguously, nature from nurture on many indices of social development, including deviant peer affiliation.

Association with deviant peers is the strongest predictor of escalating adolescent problem behavior. The large-scale, longitudinal study using a national probability sample reported by Elliott et al. (1985) focused on the role of deviant peers in the etiology of adolescent delinquent behavior. They found that self-reported involvement in a deviant peer group accounted for substantial variance in subsequent levels of self-reported delinquency in middle and late adolescence, even after accounting for previous levels of delinquency. This held for males and females and generalized from minor delinquency to more serious index offenses and serious substance use.

Even more compelling is the work by Thornberry and Krohn (1997) on the influence of gangs on problem behavior. One would think that gangs were simply another form of deviant peer group influence. The important work of Thornberry and Krohn shows that gangs actually contribute to increases in delinquency, after controlling for deviant peer affiliation. Although deviant peer behavior and gang membership are highly correlated, the latter provides independent prediction of problem behavior. This suggests that formation of strong group ties with a verbal label amplifies the influence of deviant peers on behavior. This emerging area of research is very important and, we hope, will lead to further clarity about the possible mechanisms. Kiesner and colleagues (Kiesner, Dishion, & Poulin, 2001) found that identification with a deviant peer group increased the level of influence on future behavior. We discuss later in the chapter the complementary hypothesis that the social interactions within a gang, replete with mutual identification, account for the influence of gangs on problem behavior.

Not only do adolescents who engage in antisocial behavior tend to associate with other antisocial adolescents, but these groups often commit criminal acts. Aultman (1980) carefully reviewed juvenile records in Maryland and found that 63% of all recorded offenses were committed in the company of two or three peers. Group involvement tended to vary with the type of offense, with 68% of property offenses and 43% of violent offenses committed by groups. Girls were also likely to commit offenses in the company of others, with 57% of their offenses committed in groups. In an analysis of self-reported delinquent acts, Gold (1970) estimated that 75% of all delinquent acts were committed in the company of friends.

The correlations between deviant peer involvement and antisocial behavior were quite high ($r = .40$ to $.59$) and held when both constructs were measured using multiple methods of measurement for both constructs (Patterson & Dishion, 1985). The relation held when the antisocial trait scores were correlated, based on independent reports, for two boys who were friends. For example, Dishion, Andrews, and Crosby (1995) found a correlation of .42 ($n = 181$) between the OYS boy's antisocial behavior and that of his best friend. The correlation between the boy's substance use was even higher ($r = .52$; Dishion et al., 1995), supportive of the finding reported by Kandel (1986) that attitudes toward substance use tend to be a salient sorter of friendship cliques in early adolescence.

To study the friendship interactions associated with antisocial behavior, OYS boys 13 to 14 years old were asked to bring in their closest friend to complete a 25-minute videotaped problem-solving discussion. Dishion, Andrews, and Crosby (1995) found a tendency for the friendships of antisocial boys to be abrasive, less stable, and less satisfying to the boys themselves. As would be expected from coercion theory, the antisocial boys tended to be bossy with their friends, were involved in negative reciprocal cycles, and developed relationships that tended to end in disharmony within a year.

Since our last writing, we have conducted several studies identifying the mutual influence processes in adolescent friendships that are associated with escalations in substance use (Dishion, Capaldi, Spracklen, & Li, 1995), self-reported delinquency (Dishion et al., 1996), and adolescent violence (Dishion, Eddy, Haas, Li, & Spracklen, 1997). When the videotapes were recoded using a system that captures a process we refer to as deviancy training, the predictive validity of those friendship interactions increased considerably. The process involves a statistically reliable contingency between deviant talk and laughter, analyzed at the level of the dyad. In each of the studies that follow, 25 to 30 minutes of videotape coded for deviancy training was associated with increases in problem behavior, controlling for past behavior. The findings were extended to understanding problem behavior in adolescent girls (Dishion, 2000). Patterson et al. (2000) found that de-

viant friendship process predicted multiple forms of adult antisocial behavior (arrests, unsafe sexual practices, and substance abuse), controlling for deviant peer association.

As one might suspect, the causal linkage between deviancy training and problem behavior is bidirectional. Dishion and Owen (2002) followed the OYS boys from age 10 through age 24. They found that, as hypothesized, deviant friendship process at age 14 predicted multiple forms of substance use at age 16 years. However, substance use at age 16 invariably predicted selecting deviant friendship process at age 18. Thus, substance use reduced the stability of deviancy training from ages 14 to 18 ($r = .53$, for a 30-minute sample of behavior). We concluded that substance use could also serve as a process for connecting youth to friendship networks and cliques that encourage deviancy training.

Several models have been applied to the direct observation data that assess deviancy training in adolescent friendships. The most exciting to date is the application of a dynamic systems framework to understanding peer influence. In a study conducted by Granic and Dishion (2003), we found that the tendency for some adolescents to engage in deviant talk could be conceptualized as an attractor. In this analysis, it was found that some dyads' deviant talk episodes tended to get longer in duration over the course of the 30-minute observation session. The slope score describing this growth in duration was actually predictive of future adolescent problem behavior, controlling for prior behavior.

One of the advantages of a dynamic systems framework is the use of state-space grids to capture the entire social interaction matrix of a relationship (Lewis, 2000). As shown in Figure 13.8, a state-space grid provides a visual inspection tool for identifying multiple dimensions of relationship dynamics, including attractors, phase transitions, flexibility, rigidity, and the like. We have applied information theory, in general, and the entropy index, in particular, to describe the level of organization in a sequential relationship interaction (Krippendorf, 1986). Low entropy suggests a highly organized interaction process, in that two individuals are moving together in synchrony. High entropy reflects a state of complexity and randomness. In classic thermodynamics, high levels of organization in movement require more energy than randomness. Thus, in general, if relationships are like matter in the universe, there is a tendency toward randomness without effort and attention from the interacting partners. As can be seen in Figure 13.8, both antisocial and normal dyads have low and high entropy scores. In fact, level of entropy was uncorrelated with concurrent problem behavior (Dishion, Nelson, Winter, & Bullock, 2004).

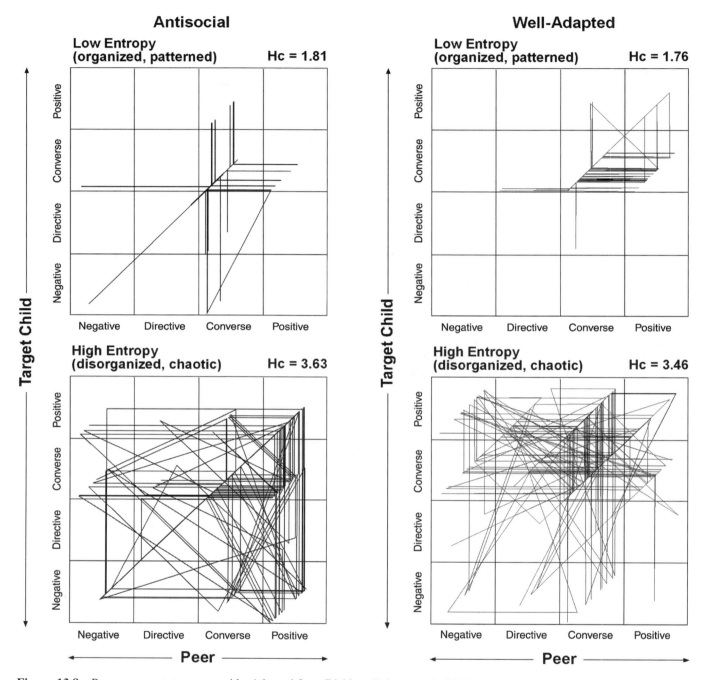

Figure 13.8 Peer process state space grids. Adapted from Dishion, Nelson, et al., 2004.

When following the OYS boys to age 26 and predicting their adult substance use and antisocial behavior, we found that boys with high levels of deviancy training and low entropy scores at age 14 were the most likely to engage in these multiple forms of problem behavior in adulthood. The interaction between the deviancy training and entropy scores was so dramatic that it appeared that the adolescents who organize their relationships around deviance are the most at risk for long-term adjustment process. This is an important finding as it suggests that deviance is an active, constructive process for some individuals, not just a form of arrested socialization.

We recently took the entropy analysis one step further. As mentioned previously, we have had some trouble in trying to measure a construct of competence and social skill that was empirically nonredundant to antisocial behavior.

Dishion and Piehler (2005) recently observed a group of friendship interactions of three groups of adolescents: early-starting persistent, late-starting, and successful youth. In addition to coding deviancy training, as defined earlier, a measure of dyadic mutuality was used as a macro rating of each interaction episode. Mutuality was defined as listening, turn taking, lack of self-centeredness, empathy, and shared understanding. As suspected, as a group, early-starting persistent youth were generally lower on mutuality and highest on deviant talk compared to late-starting and successful youth. Moreover, females were much higher on mutuality than males. What is interesting, however, is that there was an interaction between friendship mutuality and the youths' deviance in predicting problem behavior. Like the entropy finding, youth who were both more mutual and deviant were the most likely to be arrested.

Dyadic mutuality is assumed to be a partial reflection of the youth's ability to self-regulate, with respect to selecting friends with similar values and being able to be skillful in relationship interactions. However, as we see, if a youngster is deviant, this trait may not bode well for his or her long-term outcomes. The measurement of regulation is quite complex and requires adding specific responses to social interactions at its core.

Sophistication in measurement, analytic models, or longitudinal data does not ignore experimentation in establishing causal influence (Cook & Campbell, 1979). One would think that if peers are powerful in their influence on problem behavior, they could potentially be used therapeutically in promoting self-regulation or prosocial behavior. It is interesting, in fact, that despite the widespread aggregation of high-risk youth into programs, interventions, and settings for delivery of therapeutic, educational, and remedial interventions, there are very few studies that show these programs are effective.

In fact, we found that aggregating high-risk young adolescents into cognitive-behavioral interventions to promote prosocial self-regulation actually increased problem behavior. In a randomized trial involving assignment to parent and peer interventions, we found that youth assigned to peer interventions show short-term (Dishion & Andrews, 1995) and long-term increases in self-reported smoking and teacher ratings of problem behavior (Poulin, Dishion, & Burraston, 2001). Negative effects for peer aggregation were indeed attributable to informal interactions among youth in the groups (before and after the session) that were coded as deviancy training (Poulin, Dishion, & Burraston, 2001). Had our study been the only one that documented iatrogenic effects for peer aggregation, we might have accepted these data as anomalous. However, in collaboration

with our colleague, Joan McCord, we also found that the 30-year iatrogenic effects of the Cambridge Sommerville Youth Study were, indeed, attributable to the young adolescent boys being sent to summer camps. The odds were 10 to 1 that if a high-risk boy was sent to a summer camp on two consecutive occasions, he was likely to have a 30-year negative outcome compared to his randomly assigned control (Dishion, McCord, & Poulin, 1999).

A repeating theme in this chapter, and in developmental psychopathology in general, is the synergistic relationship between intervention research and developmental research. The random assignment studies showing negative peer effects suggest that peer dynamics are indeed powerfully causal (at least bidirectional causation) with respect to problem behavior in early adolescence. There is a need for a broader ecological view on peer influence, one that incorporates parent and peer influence simultaneously.

Parent-Peer Mesosystem

The challenge to developmental theorists and researchers is to think systemically about the joint influence of multiple relationship contexts on social behavior. Most of the work in this area has considered the joint influence of parents and peers. It is often said that parental influences diminish during adolescence, whereas peer influences increase. Early in the study of antisocial behavior, Robins (1966) found that macro characteristics of children's peer groups, parent characteristics, and school performance, in combination, accounted for a substantial number of subsequent antisocial adolescents. For this reason, it is surprising that more data addressing the joint influence of parents and peers at different developmental stages are not available. Parent-peer models hold the most promise for guiding comprehensive intervention strategies that prevent or reduce antisocial behavior prior to adulthood.

Bronfenbrenner (1979, 1989) refers to such models as *mesosystem* models. A true mesosystem model not only incorporates the additive univariate effects into a multivariate model, thereby explaining variance in antisocial behavior, but it also assesses the interaction between the microsystems. The research reviewed in this section assesses the joint influence of parents and peers on antisocial behavior, as well as the impact of parent and peer systems on each other. Studies that incorporate these developmental questions are also included here.

Based on data collected from families and peer groups in the 1950s and 1960s, Elder (1980) found that adolescents coming from less nurturing, less positive, and less involved parent-child relationships were more likely to become invested in a deviant peer group and to respond to the deviant group norms with like behaviors. Conversely, children who had close and positive relationships with their parents tended to select values congruent with their parents', which were often prosocial and conventional. These findings suggest that a shift may occur in adolescence, when it becomes ever more critical for parents to maintain and enhance their relationship and involvement with adolescents. Kerr and Stattin (2000) point out that, inadvertently, parents' intrusive efforts to monitor can actually undermine adolescents' willingness to self-disclose. Dishion and McMahon (1998) make a similar point, positing that parent monitoring is based on positive family relationships. Invariably, adolescents involved in problem behavior are less open about their activities than adolescents with nothing to hide, and to this extent, the exchange of information necessary for monitoring is bidirectional.

As children move toward adolescence and spend more time outside direct adult scrutiny, parental monitoring becomes an increasingly important predictor of delinquent behavior. Stoolmiller (1990) referred to this preadolescent behavior as *child wandering,* and this can be added to the list of problematic behaviors exhibited by the persistently antisocial child. Dishion et al. (2000) proposed a premature autonomy mesosystem model, which integrates an evolutionary perspective with learning theory. Adolescence is a time of rapid biosocial change, and these biological changes affect the salience and energy of peer relationships (Spear, 2000). As several ethologists have discussed, adolescence is a developmental period when peer coalitions are critical for facilitating reproduction and survival (Sameroff & Suomi, 1996). Thus, we speculated that deviant peer affiliations were an adaptation of marginalized young adolescents.

We tested the premature autonomy model with a sample of high-risk young adolescent males and females, finding that school maladaptation (peer rejection, behavior problems), poor parent monitoring, and puberty predicted deviant peer affiliation. Deviant peer affiliation and puberty were the strongest predictors of early-onset sexual intercourse and number of partners with whom the adolescents had sex at ages 15 to 16 (Dishion et al., 2000). These findings build on the groundbreaking research of Magnusson, Stattin, and Allen (1985) showing the provocative effect of early female maturation on affiliation with older deviant males. We propose that the same effect is likely to apply to males of marginal social status.

As noted earlier, mediation models seemed appropriate when considering the contribution of parent attributions in parenting models. However, nonlinear moderator models seemed more appropriate when considering growth in antisocial behavior. The distinction also seems particularly appropriate when considering the roles of deviant peers in the socialization process. Latent growth modeling applies structural equation modeling to the analysis of longitudinal data, providing the capability to model both intercept and slope. Patterson (1993) tested a model that accounted for both aspects of child antisocial behavior as measured from fourth to eighth grade. In this model, the boy's relative ranking (i.e., intercept) over the 4-year interval was associated with parenting practices in the fourth grade, as defined by discipline (home observations) and monitoring. Linear growth in antisocial behavior, however, was independently accounted for by two factors: the child's increase in unsupervised wandering and his association with deviant peers. This model is particularly helpful because it points to the synergistic influences of parents and peers on antisocial behavior. Parenting practices account for the boy's antisocial trait, and deviant peers account for the boy's learning new and creative forms of antisocial behavior. The model provides an intuitively appealing picture of the joint influences of parents and peers in the maintenance and course of antisocial behavior in adolescents.

Parent involvement with continuous conflict seems to take its toll, as shown by the longitudinal analyses of the OYS parents (Dishion, Nelson, & Bullock, 2004). The data were collected every other year, consisting of directly observed parents and boys solving problems on videotape. Global ratings were made on the parents' use of family management skills from ages 9 to 18. We compared changes in observed family management for boys defined as early starters and those who were never involved in antisocial behavior. As can be seen in Figure 13.9, there was a slow but significant deteriorating in the practices of parents of antisocial boys. Forgatch and DeGarmo (2002) showed a similar decrease in effective parenting over a 3-year interval for an untreated comparison group of recently divorced mothers.

Next, we examined the joint influence of parent disengagement and observed deviancy training with friends on young adult antisocial behavior (Dishion, Nelson, & Bullock, 2004). As expected, the intercept of family management and deviant friendship process was correlated ($r = -.42$), and the intercept on both constructs negatively predicted growth. It was interesting that the intercept on deviant friendship process predicted parents' disengagement from monitoring, but not the reverse. This finding is consistent with our current emphasis on the critical role of peers in adolescent development. It may actually be that coalitions with deviant peers attenuate family ties, as well

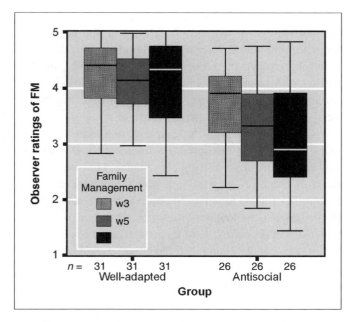

Figure 13.9 Observed family management in adolescence for low- and high-risk youth.

as provide a proximal context for escalations in problem behavior. Indeed, when we entered the family management slope score with the deviant friendship process intercept score in a hierarchical regression, we found an interaction between the two constructs in predicting adult antisocial behavior. Boys whose parents disengaged and who selected deviant friends were those who were highly antisocial at age 26.

These findings provide the basis for considering hypotheses regarding the social origins of the early- and late-starter developmental trajectories. It may be that children who start early are essentially adapting to coercive, chaotic parenting practices. In this sense, negative reinforcement may be an operational mechanism. For those who start late, positive reinforcement by peers may be the operating mechanism whereby problem behavior becomes a means to establish connectedness to a peer group.

It seems that early- and late-onset delinquents may come from two different worlds. Even the contingencies (positive reinforcement versus negative reinforcement) that maintain the antisocial behavior are different. In a discriminant function analysis, the variables that differentiated early-onset arrest from late-onset were poor discipline, unemployed parents, frequent transitions, and antisocial parent behavior (Patterson & Yoerger, 2002). In young adulthood, those same variables differentiated among those who would remain or drop out of adult crime. As we discovered recently, the linkage between parents' antisocial behavior and the so-

cial processes leading to the youth's antisocial behavior may be what distinguishes the early- from late-onset trajectory. In our analysis, we found that the father's antisocial tendency was the best predictor of the youth's future involvement in deviancy training 5 years later (Dishion, Bullock, & Owen, in press). This further supports the need to consider functional dynamics at different time scales. Some youth may be primed to find and interact with a deviant peer group early on, which results in the early display of the more serious conduct problem systems and the amplification of coercive dynamics at home, until, of course, the parent gives up. Thus, the nature of the world the child lives in makes a difference at both the micro and the macro levels.

Summary

Evidence was reviewed that provides support for the hypothesis that socialization exchanges within relationships are both a cause and an outcome of antisocial behavior. Over the past 25 years, considerable progress has been made in understanding the impact of parenting practices, both in longitudinal research and in the context of longitudinal field experiments. Parenting clearly makes a difference. However, it is unrealistic to consider either parenting or peer influences in isolation. A mesosystem model that incorporates both parenting practices and peer influences helps to explain the persistence and continuance of antisocial behavior into adulthood. We need more studies that demonstrate how it is that these two systems influence each other. Peer management and structuring practices may be one of the central roles of parents in effecting long-term adjustment in their children.

Behavior Settings

In much of the research on antisocial behavior, the impact of relationships is assessed as if it occurs in a vacuum. The ecological model alerts us to the importance of the context in which these relationships are embedded. Following Glen Elder's (Elder & Caspi, 1988; Elder, van Nguyen, & Caspi, 1985) persuasive lead, we conceptualize the impact of contextual variables, such as divorce, poverty, and neighborhood, on child outcomes to be mediated by the impact on parenting practices. Elder and his colleagues demonstrated that prolonged exposure to such major stressors as the economic depression of the 1930s did, indeed, lead to negative child outcomes. The effect was mediated by the presence of an irritable father and disrupted paternal discipline practices.

Extensive use was made of Elder's mediated model when studying the impact of various contexts on child outcomes in the OYS. The findings consistently support the model. For example, divorce is associated with negative child outcomes only for those mothers whose parenting practices are disrupted (Forgatch & DeGarmo, 2002). The findings are reviewed in Patterson, Reid, et al. (1992) and Capaldi, DeGarmo, Patterson, and Forgatch (2002).

The problem of studying contextual factors that contribute to individual-level psychopathology is not new. As in the study of peer influence, the issue becomes one of contrasting selection with influence. Families often select settings, and therefore, setting factors may simply reflect vulnerability associated with maladaptation. Parenting occurs in homes, which are in neighborhoods. Peer interactions take place in neighborhoods, in schools, at the bus stop, on the street, in shopping malls, in organized activities, and in families.

There are two new developments in research neighborhood effects. In this research, it is clear that neighborhood context contributes to the early onset of antisocial behavior (Ingoldsby & Shaw, 2002). The relationship tends to be mediated by parenting practices as much as the correlation between stress, poverty, and the development of antisocial behavior (Conger, Patterson, & Ge, 1995; Conger et al., 2002; McLoyd, 1990; McLoyd & Steinberg, 1998; Patterson, 1985; Sampson & Laub, 1994).

We know that deviancy in school is related to deviancy in the home. It is also clear that children who are deviant in both settings have a poorer prognosis. In several early studies, we found that maladaptation at home and school was a particularly poor sign for children and adolescents. For example, Dishion and Loeber (1985) found that boys who were physically aggressive at home and school showed high levels of risk on mother-son coercion, deviant peer association, and maternal rejection. More recently, young adolescents identified as *externalizing* and *internalizing* at home and school were found to be at extreme risk for substance abuse, arrests, and high-risk sexual behavior 2 to 3 years later in middle adolescence (Dishion, 2000).

By and large, the correlation in antisocial behavior across the two settings is not high. There are only a few studies that have collected careful observation data in both the home and the school setting. In an analysis of consistency in coercive interaction patterns, as observed in the playground and the laboratory setting with parents, we found a coefficient of .19 (Dishion, Duncan, Eddy, Fagot, & Fetrow, 1994), statistically reliable but unimpressive. In the Wichita study, Snyder et al. (2003) observed parent-child interactions in a standardized series of laboratory settings and sampled playground interactions with peers. Teacher ratings of aggression defined the classroom setting. A parent-child interaction composite correlated .25 with playground interactions with peers and .46 with teacher ratings of classroom behavior. The findings are in agreement with the conventional wisdom that trait behaviors generalize modestly across settings.

As discussed later in the chapter, some individuals are more sensitive to disrupted environments and therefore may show more cross-setting consistency. For example, in a study of home observation and school behavior problems, Stoolmiller (2001) found an interaction between the child's temperament (i.e., low inhibitory control) and parenting interactions in predicting long-term patterns of antisocial behavior at school. Using retrospective parent reports of child's poor self-regulation and direct observations of parent discipline, he found that inclusion of the interaction term between the two constructs accounted for growth in teacher-reported behavior problems at school from ages 9 to 14. This is a critical analysis for two reasons. First, the settings are relatively independent (home and school), and second, the model accounted for 38% of the variation in nonoverlapping constructs. The findings are quite consistent with those reported by two other investigative teams (Bates, Pettit, & Dodge, 1995; Shaw et al., 2003).

The contribution of schools to the etiology and course of antisocial behavior is likely to be much more complex than can be captured in a cross-setting consistency coefficient. To understand the contribution of schools to antisocial behavior, it is critical to examine academic failure, peer rejection, and the formation of peer groups (Patterson, Reid, et al., 1992). Our initial studies showed that most children who showed high rates of antisocial problems in the home tended to be academically below standard (Patterson, 1982). The analyses of data from the OYS showed a path coefficient of −.57 between a latent construct for antisocial behavior and the construct for school achievement (Patterson, Reid, et al., 1992). The Forgatch and DeGarmo (2002) review of findings from the Oregon Divorce Studies replicate this correlation between poor academic achievement and children's antisocial behavior.

As discussed earlier, there is more support than not for the idea that failure in academics and peer rejection contribute to the coalescence of deviant peer cliques over and above what would be predicted by the attraction of children who share antisocial behavior. We have referred to this process as the *confluence hypothesis* (Dishion, Patterson, & Griesler, 1994). However, the contribution of schools to the development and course of antisocial behavior may be most pronounced in early adolescents, with the advent of the middle school environment. We were able to predict the early formation of gangs in a multiethnic public school by academic failure and peer rejection (Dishion, Nelson, et al., in press). More recently, we examined the confluence hypothesis in eight middle schools in a suburban setting, with mostly European American early adolescents. Building off the work of recent studies (e.g., Laird, Jordan, Dodge, Pettit, & Bates, 2001; Rodkin, Farmer, Pearl, & Van Acker, 2000), we used both liking and rejection nominations to predict the formation of deviant peer cliques. We found that a multiplicative term of liking and rejection defined the likelihood that a young adolescent was to be submerged in a deviant peer clique in the next 2 years of middle school. As expected, growth in involvement in deviant peer cliques was associated with growth in problem behavior, using constructs that were defined by independent methods (Dishion, Light, & Yasui, 2004 paper presentation at ISSBD). Finally, there was significant variability by schools in peer rejection, deviant clique formation, and problem behavior; the three experiences were clearly concordant.

These are promising beginnings. But it is obvious that some pieces of the puzzle are missing. If schools contribute to the development and course of antisocial behavior, then it would be expected that effective school-based interventions and prevention strategies would have a profound impact. If such were the case, this would have a profound impact on public policy. The work by Kellam and colleagues (Ialongo, Poduska, Werthhamer, & Kellam, 2001) does suggest that interventions targeting the school environment do have long-term effects on the development and course of problem behavior. Recent progress in the development of school interventions that promote a more organized approach to managing student behavior is particularly compelling in this regard (Crone & Horner, 2003; Sugai, Horner, & Sprague, 1999). However, these schoolwide intervention strategies have yet to be tested in a randomized trial that includes data collected in both home and school. If school aggression is eliminated, as was the case for the LIFT study (Stoolmiller, Eddy, & Reid, 2000), what are the effects on aggression observed in the home? If levels of aggression occurring in the home are dramatically reduced, what is the impact on the school behaviors? At what point in development can such effects be expected? These are the three big next-generation questions that must be answered if we are to continue in our efforts to build a theory.

Self-Regulation

As we discussed, there is a paradox inherent in the research linking self-regulation with antisocial development. On the one hand, as hypothesized by Moffitt (1993), early-starting youth are less organized, regulated, and mutual in their social interactions with friends (Dishion, Nelson, Winter, et al., 2004; Dishion, Nelson, et al., in press). However, it is the youth who are both *antisocial* and *self-regulated* that are the most prone to continuing their deviance into adulthood. An untested assumption is that youth who become more polished and refined in manipulation are also more successful in avoiding detection for increasingly more serious crimes (burglary, robbery, drug sales). This would be a major wrinkle in the early-starting persistent hypothesis, but is quite consistent with an ecological view of adaptation (e.g., Bronfenbrenner, 1989; Hinde, 1989). Soldiers who survive the vicissitudes of war become better at killing; youth who survive the antisocial lifestyle get better at being deviant. The dynamic of self-regulated deviance certainly needs further exploration, but the idea that youth become more calloused and manipulative fits some of the literature relevant to adult psychopaths (Hare, Forth, & Strachan, 1992; Newman, Widom, & Nathan, 1985; Raine, 1993, 2002).

The majority of the literature on self-regulation, however, emphasizes individuals' ability to inhibit or avoid committing antisocial acts. To this extent, the construct itself may be vulnerable to the empirical quagmire described earlier, with global ratings of competence highly (negatively) correlated with global ratings of antisocial behavior.

There are several lines of research suggesting that measures of self-regulation are *not* redundant to the antisocial construct. Several investigators have empirically linked the concepts of resiliency, self-regulation, and problem behavior (Lengua & Sandler, 1996; Masten, Best, & Garmezy, 1990; Masten & Coatsworth, 1998; Miller & Brown, 1991; Wills & Dishion, 2004; Windle, 1990). A critical feature of resiliency at the individual level appears to be the capacity to engage in planful, goal-directed action, which includes selection of friends and partners conducive to one's goals (Haggerty, Sherrod, Garmezy, & Rutter, 1994; Rutter, 1989).

The notion of self-regulation is conceptually linked to the construct of temperament. Two decades of programmatic research on child temperament consistently reveal attentive control and inhibitory control as central to adjustment in socialization (Kohnstamm, Bates, & Rothbart, 1989). The capacity for self-control of behavior, cognition, and emotion falls under the rubric of executive attention (Rothbart, Ellis, & Posner, 2004). Recent neural imaging studies (e.g., Sowell & Jernigan, 1998) provide evidence of substantial adolescent and postadolescent brain development in frontal areas thought to serve executive functions such as attentive control. These executive functions are largely located in the prefrontal cortex and, more specifically, the anterior cingulate cortex (ACC; Frith & Frith, 2001).

Linking neural imaging studies to pragmatic measures that assess individual differences and attentive control has been a recent goal. Posner and colleagues (Fan, McCandliss, Sommer, Raz, & Posner, 2002) developed a task under conditions of neural imaging that linked alerting, orienting, and executive attention to activity in the ACC as revealed in functional magnetic resonance imaging. The basic strategy in the attention network task (i.e., ANT) is to use perceptual conflict (i.e., Stroop) to engage various aspects of attention. The variation in reaction time is considered to be a useful index of attentive regulation, such as the ability to alert, orient to new stimuli, and deal with distractive stimuli.

From a developmental perspective, it makes sense that the form of self-regulation would vary from early childhood through young adulthood. For example, in the work by Kochanska (1993, 2002; Kochanska, Murray, Jacques, Koenig, & Vandegeest, 1996), inhibitory control is a key component of self-regulation in early childhood. However, as children adapt to new contexts such as the public school setting, other facets of self-regulation are likely to become critical. For example, as the demands increase for children to complete tasks with multiple steps, such as chores and homework, it is critical that behavior activation becomes a key component of self-regulation. In adolescence, with the introduction of free time and autonomy, it becomes critical for young people to resist temptation and stay the course on long-term objectives related to academic achievement and/or skill development. Finally, in young adulthood, a key component of self-regulation is the selection and identification of social and economic contexts that fit well with one's social, motor, and intellectual abilities.

The work on self-regulation and problem behavior is limited to understanding the development and course of adolescent drug use. In this work, the construct of self-control has been invoked as an individual characteristic that reduces the likelihood of developing a drug and alcohol problem once exposed (Miller & Brown, 1991; Wills & Dishion, 2004). In understanding substance use, self-regulation is seen as a moderator variable, explaining those youth who do not develop serious drug and alcohol problems given exposure by peers and spouses.

As discussed earlier, a process model for the development of antisocial behavior should describe the mechanism accounting for the normative decreases in overt antisocial behavior, the age-crime curve, desistence from antisocial

behavior in late adolescence, and the fact that many youth exposed to deviant peer influences (i.e., growing up in the same neighborhoods and schools) are unaffected. In fact, if one looks at the data in even the highest risk settings, it is clear that 40% to 50% do not develop any signs of problem behavior; they are the zeros in our skewed distributions of problem behavior. Statistical innovations that allow for the formation of developmental trajectories (e.g., Muthén & Shedden, 1999; Nagin & Tremblay, 1999) always yield a large low-risk group (e.g., Connell et al., in press).

If self-regulation is a construct of empirical utility for explaining the development of antisocial behavior, then it should account for unique (nonredundant) variance, or at least function as a moderator variable. That is, self-regulation may explain why some children do *not* become antisocial given exposure to the right environmental conditions.

The literature establishing interaction effects on any dimension of child self-regulation and problematic environments is underdeveloped at this stage. If one focuses on the genetic underpinnings of self-regulation, there is some evidence supporting complex interaction between pervasive environmental experience and biological predisposition (see Caspi et al., 2002; Cloninger & Gottesman, 1987; Deater-Deckard, in press; Leve et al., 1998; Maccoby, 2000; Neiderhiser, Reiss, & Hetherington, 1996; Rhee & Waldman, 2002; Taylor, Iacono, & McGue, 2000). Perhaps most noteworthy in these studies is work reported by Caspi et al. showing an interaction among genetic vulnerability, abusive parenting environments in childhood, and propensity to violence in adulthood. However, the amount of variation accounted for by the interaction term is limited. This elaborate and innovative study requires further replication and extension.

Moderation Hypothesis

In our recent research on understanding and preventing adolescent problem behavior, we assessed self-regulation among adolescents at ages 15 to 17 years. We used two strategies for the assessment of self-regulation. The first was the Rothbart (Rothbart et al., 2004) measure of temperament extended into adolescence. This measure includes two scales assessing effortful attention control, otherwise referred to as attention control. The items on these scales are not simply the reverse of antisocial behavior, including behaviors specific to the ability to attend, persist in tasks, and regulate oneself in the context of competing demands. In addition, we assessed the youth's ability to alert, orient, and exercise executive control in the context of a computerized attention task referred to as the ANT. To consider the role of self-regulation in the development of problem behavior, we formulated three developmental groups based on longitudinal data from six yearly assessments. Both male and female adolescents following early- ($n = 39$) and late-starting ($n = 38$) and successful ($n = 37$) pathways were selected for the study.

The assessment of temperament included youth and parent report. The effortful attention control factor comprises the following subfactors: activation control, attention, and inhibitory control. The ANT assessment involves a flanker conflict paradigm that includes a central target arrow flanked on either side by arrows pointing in either the same (congruent) or the opposite (incongruent) direction of the target arrow. Incongruent trials generally produce longer reaction times than congruent trials, because the presence of incongruent flanker arrows causes a degree of attention conflict. The task allows calculation of individual difference scores in attention control. The score is computed via subtraction of congruent flanker trial reaction times from incongruent flanker reaction trials.

Unexpectedly, we found no covariation between the youth's performance on the ANT conflict task with either child or parent report of self-regulation. However, self-regulation was correlated moderately between parent and child report ($r = .34$). Therefore, we included only parent and child report of attention control as a measure of the youth's ability to self-regulate.

Figure 13.10 provides an overview of the findings. As can be seen, there is an orderly progression from less to more self-regulation when considering early starters, late starters, and successful students, respectively. Also of interest is the normality of the distribution across the two samples. The child report shows less variation than the parent report; however, both show increasing self-regulation associated with the developmental onset of antisocial behavior and the probable prognosis (Moffitt, 1993; Patterson & Yoerger, 1993).

If self-regulation is a resiliency factor, then youth who are highly self-regulated are likely to be less influenced by deviant peers. A general construct for the youth's antisocial behavior was formulated on self-reported delinquency and antisocial behavior and substance use. As revealed in a hierarchical linear regression, both self-regulation and deviant peer involvement significantly predicted antisocial behavior in middle adolescence. It is relevant that self-regulation added to the prediction accounting for 43% of the variation in antisocial behavior (total $R2 = .43$ with both predictors). In a second step, the interaction between self-regulation and deviant peer involvement was entered into the equation. A significant interaction was found between self-regulation and deviant

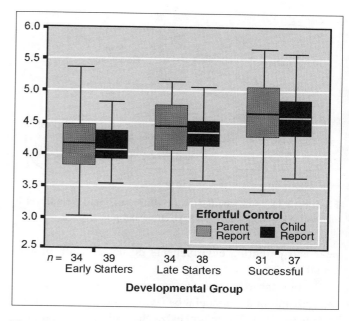

Figure 13.10 Toward a single model for the development of antisocial behavior.

peer involvement. Plotting of the interaction term revealed a tendency for youth who were high in self-regulation to be less affected by the influence of deviant peers on antisocial behavior. In contrast, for youth low in self-regulation, the level of antisocial behavior varied quite dramatically as a function of their deviant peer involvement (T. Gardner & Dishion, 2005).

These data show some support for the construct of self-regulation as a resiliency factor in the development of antisocial behavior. Significant methodological problems require attention, however, before the research can be considered conclusive. First, the lack of correlation between the attention measure of self-regulation and both parent and adolescent reports of attention control requires some explanation. One likely explanation is that early in development, children's ability to control attention in a laboratory setting may, in fact, predict parent ratings of self-regulation. By adolescence, self-regulation may become more domain-specific. For example, the ability to regulate oneself in detailed, tedious tasks may be highly influenced by the content and practice with similar tasks (e.g., videogames, writing, math). Second, we used the ANT measure of attention control in the home and the research center, using a variety of computers. The context of the task may require more control to accurately assess individual differences in attention control. Third, a more rigorous test of the resiliency hypothesis is to show longitudinal, interaction effects. That is, youth with higher levels of self-regulation who were also exposed to pathogenic

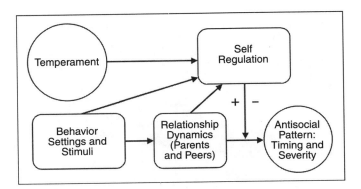

Figure 13.11   Self regulation by timing of the development of antisocial behavior in Project Alliance sample.

peer and parenting environments do not escalate in antisocial behavior.

Despite these barriers, we propose a hypothesis linking self-regulation to antisocial behavior, which is summarized in Figure 13.11. We hypothesize that self-regulation *moderates* the relationship between relationship dynamics, such as coercive family interaction or peer deviancy training, and the timing and severity of child and adolescent antisocial behavior. Because the parenting environment of the early-starting group is disrupted, these youngsters are less able to navigate their own future. Late starters, however, benefit from early family management and therefore have higher levels of self-regulation. Consistent with recent work in neuroscience, we see self-regulation as linked to growth of attention networks that empower behavior inhibition and that early childhood is an important time for the development of this ability (Rothbart & Posner, Chapter 11, this *Handbook,* Volume 2).

Particularly important for further investigation are the family management underpinnings of self-regulation in children. One can see that setting limits and behavior management of children require the child's exercise of behavior inhibition and therefore growth in self-regulation. This hypothesis requires more attention, in particular, in the context of intervention trials that address family management. Do improvements in family management in early childhood, a time critical for the development of self-regulation, have long-term effects on adolescent problem behavior? The work by Olds and colleagues (1997) suggests it does. More to the point, do interventions that specifically target self-regulation in children have independent effects on the prevention of antisocial behavior, as suggested by the work of Lochman and Kazdin (e.g., Kazdin et al., 1992; Lochman & Wells, 1996)?

If these research hurdles are surpassed, the mechanisms linking socialization processes and the acquisition of rule-

governed behavior need explication. In the learning theory literature, Hayes and colleagues (Hayes, Gifford, & Ruckstuhl, 1996; Hayes & Hayes, 1992; Hayes, Hayes, Sato, & Ono, 1994) provide the most comprehensive account of the role of language in human learning. The ability to follow rules is built on the acquisition of a linguistic frame that presumes "it's worth it to be prosocial." The framework is theoretically rich but has yet to be linked to observations of family living and individual differences in child and adolescent self-regulation and engagement in antisocial behavior.

SUMMARY AND IMPLICATIONS

Over the past 10 years, enormous progress has been made in understanding the development of antisocial behavior. Figure 13.12 is a summary of empirical linkages that have been established, as well as those that, at this writing, are tentative and require further testing. Four points are emphasized in this summary:

1. Although antisocial behavior is a robust, psychometrically sound construct, it is useful to understand developmental process and gender differences to consider specific forms of antisocial behavior, including distinctions between overt (physical and verbal aggression, reactive aggression) and covert (proactive aggression, relational aggression, stealing, etc.).

2. Parent-child interaction and management dynamics play a significant role in establishing the child's trajectory into antisocial behavior in early and middle childhood as well as adolescence, and intervention research reveals that targeting parenting practices produces reductions in child and adolescent risk.

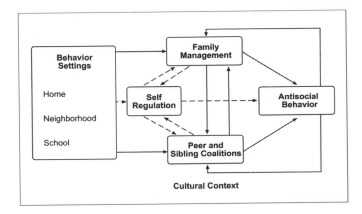

Figure 13.12   Empirical summary for the development and ecology of antisocial behavior.

3. Peer influences are now a dominant theme in the etiology of antisocial behavior, beginning in early childhood and increasing during adolescence. Intervention research, inadvertently, underscores the power of peer contagion in amplifying adolescent problem behavior.

4. Neuroscience and developmental research are converging at understanding the basic brain-behavior linkages that explain the emergence and growth of executive control and, ultimately, self-regulation. Future research in this area might lead to a theory of normative socialization, resilience, and differential prognosis associated with age of onset of antisocial behavior and, perhaps, other forms of psychopathology.

In Figure 13.12, the solid arrows represent hypotheses that are supported by previous longitudinal and intervention research, and the dotted lines are hypotheses that require further testing and development. In contrast to 10 years ago, the field has extended research to children of different cultural and racial groups. At some point, isolating the mechanisms that explain contextual differences in child and adolescent problem behavior remains a scientific need. Similarly, process-oriented research that considers the interplay between biology and family and peer dynamics, especially around developmental transitions such as adolescence, is still needed.

At this stage, we assert that enough is known to fill in a rough sketch of the antisocial developmental process, especially for understanding boys who exhibit a persistent life course pattern. The development of more serious and chronic antisocial behavior seems to follow a stage-like progression, consistent with notions of hierarchical integration. In the coercion model, the practice of aversive pain control in the family undermines relationships and entrains response patterns that facilitate the emergence of antisocial behavior in other settings, such as schools (with teachers and peers). Eventually, the antisocial behavior is less reactive, and children develop peer groups that encourage problem behavior and even plan and collude to commit antisocial acts. As shown in the classic analyses by Jones, Reid, and Patterson (1975), deviant children are, indeed, less responsive to setting differences. They react coercively over time and across settings.

This style of interacting with peers becomes automatic and highly stable across adolescence, providing a basis for ongoing shopping for relationships and settings that support previously established behaviors and patterns. If unabated, parents eventually give up and peers take over, accounting for the persistence of adolescent problem behaviors into adulthood. Those who start early, then, ac-

tively construct social experiences that minimize their pain and maximize their gain. In the short run, such social optimization functions well. Unfortunately, in the long run, the antisocial pattern undermines the maturation into adult roles and the formation of new families. Selection of an antisocial spouse could permanently cement the developing adult in a life of maladaptation through criminal behavior, incarceration, and ever more coercive family relationships (Quinton, Pickles, Maughan, & Rutter, 1993; Woodward, Fergusson, & Horwood, 2002).

One of the barriers the present authors continually confront is how to integrate positive aspects of development with our understanding of the biological and environmental influences in antisocial development. We project that the next 10 years will be marked by progress on this issue. In particular, we consider a convergence of findings on understanding young children's development of emotional regulation, attentional control, tendency to comply with adult requests, and prosocial behavior. Eisenberg and Fabes (1998) provide a comprehensive review of this rapidly growing literature.

The promise of the developmental psychopathology perspective is to continue to focus on the intervention implications of etiologic research (Cicchetti & Toth, 1992). An explicit strategy for the programmatic integration of etiologic research and intervention trials has been proposed (Patterson, Reid, et al., 1992). We can suggest alternative intervention strategies to reduce or prevent antisocial behavior (Dishion & Stormshak, in press). The key idea, however, is not only to get intervention effects (i.e., reductions in antisocial behavior), but to document how the intervention effects are achieved—that is, to understand the process of change (Dodge, 1993). Such an approach makes developmental psychopathology a dynamic science and, as applied to the understanding and prevention of child and adolescent antisocial behavior, worthy of further pursuit.

REFERENCES

Abramovitch, P., Carter, C., Pepler, D. J., & Stanhope, L. (1986). Sibling and peer interaction: A final follow-up and a comparison. *Child Development, 57*, 217–229.

Achenbach, T. M., & Edelbrock, C. S. (1979). *Child Behavior Checklist*. Bethesda, MD: National Institute of Mental Health.

Ainsworth, M. S. (1989). Attachments beyond infancy. *American Psychologist, 44*(4), 709–716.

Ainsworth, M. S., & Bowlby, J. (1991). An ethological approach to personality development. *American Psychologist, 46*(4), 333–341.

Anstey, P. (2003). *The Philosophy of John Locke: New Perspectives*. New York: Routledge Publishing.

Arnold, J. E., Levine, A. G., & Patterson, G. R. (1975). Changes in sibling behavior following family intervention. *Journal of Consulting and Clinical Psychology, 43,* 683–688.

Aultman, M. (1980). Group involvement in delinquent acts: A study of offense types and male-female participation. *Criminal Justice and Behavior, 7*(2), 185–192.

Bandura, A. (1989). Social cognitive theory. In R. Vasta (Ed.), *Annals of child development: Vol. 6. Six theories of child development: Revised formulations and current issues* (pp. 1–60). London: JAI.

Bank, L., & Burraston, B. (2001). Abusive home environments as predictors of poor adjustment during adolescence and early adulthood. *Journal of Community Psychology, 29*(3), 195–217.

Bank, L., Dishion, T. J., Skinner, M., & Patterson, G. R. (1990). Method variance in structural equation modeling: Living with "glop." In G. R. Patterson (Ed.), *Depression and aggression in family interaction* (pp. 247–279). Hillsdale, NJ: Erlbaum.

Bates, S. E., Pettit, G. S., & Dodge, K. A. (1995). Family and child factors in stability and change in children's aggressiveness in elementary school. In J. McCord (Ed.), *Coercion and punishment in long-term perspective* (pp. 124–138). New York: Basic Books.

Baumrind, D. (1971). Harmonious parents and their preschool children. *Developmental Psychology, 4,* 99–102.

Bowlby, J. (1969). Disruption of affectional bonds and its effects on behavior. *Canada's Mental Health Supplement, 59,* 12.

Broidy, L. M., Tremblay, R. E., Brame, B., Fergusson, D., Horwood, J. L., Laird, R. D., et al. (2003). Developmental trajectories of childhood disruptive behaviors and adolescent delinquency: A six-site, cross-national study. *Developmental Psychology, 39,* 222–245.

Bronfenbrenner, U. (1979). *The ecology of human development: Experiments by nature and by design.* Cambridge, MA: Harvard University Press.

Bronfenbrenner, U. (1989). Ecological systems theory. In R. Vasta (Ed.), *Annals of child development: Vol. 6. Six theories of child development-Revised formulations and current issues* (pp. 187–249). London: JAI.

Bronfenbrenner, U., & Ceci, S. J. (1994). Nature-nurture reconceptualized in developmental perspective: A bioecological model. *Psychological Review, 101,* 568–586.

Brook, J. S., Whiteman, M., Gordan, A. S., & Cohen, P. (1986). Some models and mechanisms for explaining the impact of maternal and adolescent characteristics on adolescent stage of drug use. *Developmental Psychology, 22,* 460–467.

Brown, B. B. (1989). The role of the peer group in adolescents' adjustment to secondary school. In T. J. Berndt & L. W. Ladd (Eds.), *Peer relationships in child development* (pp. 174–215). New York: Wiley.

Bullock, B. M., Bank, L., & Burraston, B. (2002). Adult sibling expressed emotion and fellow sibling deviance: A new piece of the family process puzzle. *Journal of Family Psychology, 16*(3), 307–317.

Bullock, B. M., Deater-Deckard, K., & Leve, L. D. (in press). Deviant peer affiliation and problem behavior: A test of genetic and environmental influences *Journal of Abnormal Child Psychology.*

Bullock, B. M., & Dishion, T. J. (2002). Sibling collusion and problem behavior in early adolescence: Toward a process model for family mutuality. *Journal of Abnormal Child Psychology, 30*(2), 143–153.

Cairns, R. B., Cadwallader, D. E., & Neckerman, H. (1997). Groups to gangs: Developmental and criminological perspectives and relevance to prevention. In D. M. Stoff, J. Breiling, & J. Maser (Eds.), *Handbook of antisocial behavior* (pp. 194–205). New York: Wiley.

Cairns, R. B., & Cairns, B. D. (1994). *Lifelines and risks: Pathways of youth in our time.* New York: Cambridge University Press.

Cairns, R. B., Cairns, B. D., Neckerman, H. J., & Gariepy, J. L. (1989). Growth and aggression: 1. Childhood to early adolescence. *Developmental Psychology, 25,* 1–30.

Cairns, R. B., Cairns, B. D., Neckerman, H. J., Gest, S. D., & Gariepy, J. (1988). Social networks and aggressive behavior: Peer support or peer rejection. *Developmental Psychology, 24,* 815–823.

Campbell, D. T., & Fiske, D. W. (1959). Convergent and discriminant validation by the multitrait and multimethod matrix. *Psychological Bulletin, 56*(2), 81–105.

Capaldi, D. M., & Crosby, L. (1997). Observed and reported psychological and physical aggression in young, at-risk couples. *Social Development, 6*(2), 184–206.

Capaldi, D. M., DeGarmo, D., Patterson, G. R., & Forgatch, M. (2002). Contextual risk across the early life span and association with antisocial behavior. In J. B. Reid, G. R. Patterson, & J. J. Synder (Eds.), *Antisocial behavior in children and adolescents: A developmental analysis and model for intervention* (pp. 123–145). Washington, DC: American Psychological Association.

Capaldi, D. M., & Patterson, G. R. (1989). *Psychometric properties of fourteen latent constructs from the Oregon Youth Study.* New York: Springer.

Capaldi, D. M., & Patterson, G. R. (1991). The relation of parental transitions to boys' adjustment problems: I. A test of linear hypothesis. II. Mothers at risk for transitions and unskilled parenting. *Development and Psychopathology, 3,* 277–300.

Capaldi, D. M., & Patterson, G. R. (1996). Can violent offenders be distinguished from frequent offenders: Prediction from childhood to adolescence. *Journal of Research in Crime and Delinquency, 33,* 206–231.

Carey, G. (1992). Twin imitation for antisocial behavior: Implications for genetic and family environment research. *Journal of Abnormal Psychology, 101*(1), 18–25.

Carpenter, M. (1970). *Reformatory schools for children of the perishing and dangerous classes and for juvenile offenders.* Montclair, NJ: Patterson Smith.

Caspi, A., Bem, D. J., & Elder, G., Jr. (1989). Continuities and consequences of interactional styles across the life course. *Journal of Personality, 57*(2), 375–406.

Caspi, A., McClay, J., Moffitt, T. E., Mill, J., Martin, J., Craig, I. W., et al. (2002). Role of genotype in the cycle of violence in maltreated children. Science, 298, 851–854.

Catalano, R. F., Morrison, D. M., Wells, E. A., Gilmore, M. R., Irritani, B., & Hawkins, J. D. (1992). Ethnic differences and family factors related to early drug initiation. *Journal of Studies on Alcohol, 53,* 208–217.

Chamberlain, P., & Reid, J. (1998). Comparison of two community alternatives to incarceration for chronic juvenile offenders. *Journal of Consulting and Clinical Psychology, 6,* 624–633.

Cicchetti, D. (1990). Perspectives on the interface between normal and atypical development. *Development and Psychopathology, 2,* 329–333.

Cicchetti, D., & Toth, S. L. (1992). The role of developmental theory in prevention and intervention. *Development and Psychopathology, 4,* 489–493.

Cillessen, T. (1989, April). *Aggression and liking in same-status versus different-status groups.* Paper presented at the meeting of the Society for Research in Child Development, Kansas City, MO.

Cloninger, C. R., & Gottesman, I. I. (1987). Genetic and environmental factors in antisocial behavior disorders. In S. A. Mednick, T. E. Moffitt, & S. A. Stack (Eds.), *The causes of crime: New biological approaches* (pp. 92–109). New York: Cambridge University Press.

Coie, J. D., & Dodge, K. A. (1988). Multiple sources of data on social behavior and social status in the school: A cross-age comparison. *Child Development, 59,* 815–829.

Coie, J. D., & Kupersmidt, J. B. (1983). A behavioral analysis of emerging social status in boys' groups. *Child Development, 54,* 1400–1416.

Collins, P., Everitt, B. J., Robbins, T. W., Roberts, A. C., & Wilkinson, L. S. (2000). The effect of dopamine depletion from the caudate nucleus of the common marmoset (Callithrix jacchus) on tests of prefrontal cognitive function. *Journal of Behavioral Neuroscience, 114*(1), 3–17.

Conger, R. D., Patterson, G. R., & Ge, X. (1995). It takes two to replicate: A mediational model for the impact of parents' stress on adolescent adjustment. *Child Development, 66,* 80–97.

Conger, R., Wallace, L. E., Sun, Y., Simons, R. L., McLoyd, V. C., & Brody, G. H. (2002). Economic pressure in African American families: A replication and extension of the family stress model. *Developmental Psychology, 38*(2), 179–193.

Connell, A. M., Dishion, T. J., & Deater-Deckard, K. (in press). *A mixture model analysis of early adolescent drug use: Linking peer, family, and intervention effects with developmental trajectories.* Unpublished manuscript, 2005 draft.

Cook, T. D., & Campbell, D. T. (1979). *Quasi-experimentation design and analysis issues for field settings.* Boston: Houghton Mifflin.

Costello, E. J., & Angold, A. (2000). Bad behavior: An historical perspective on disorders of conduct. In J. Hill & B. Maughan (Eds.), *Conduct disorders in childhood and adolescence* (pp. 1–31). Cambridge, England: Cambridge University Press.

Crick, N. R. (1996). The role of overt aggression, relational aggression, and prosocial behavior and the prediction of children's future social adjustment. *Child Development, 67,* 2317–2327.

Crick, N. R., & Bigbee, M. A. (1998). Relational and overt forms of peer victimization: A multi-informant approach. *Journal of Consulting and Clinical Psychology, 66,* 337–347.

Crick, N. R., & Dodge, K. A. (1996). Social information-processing mechanisms in reactive and proactive aggression. Child Development, 67, 993–1002.

Crick, N. R., Wellman, N. E., Casas, J. F., O'Brien, K. M., Nelson, D. A., Grotpeter, J. K., et al. (1997). Childhood aggression and gender: A new look at an old problem. In D. Bernstein (Ed.), *Symposium on motivation* (Vol. 45).

Cronbach, L. J., & Meehl, P. E. (1955). Construct validity in psychological tests. *Psychological Bulletin, 52,* 281–302.

Crone, D. A., & Horner, R. H. (2003). *Building positive behavior support systems in schools: Functional behavioral assessment.* New York: Guilford Press.

Dawe, H. C. (1934). An analysis of two hundred quarrels of preschool children. *Child Development, 5,* 139–157.

Deater-Deckard, K. (2000). Parenting and child behavioral adjustment in early childhood: A quantitative genetic approach to studying family processes and child development. *Child Development, 71,* 468–484.

Deater-Deckard, K. (in press). A genetic analysis of extremes in externalizing behaviors and negative family environments. In S. Petrill, R. Plomin, J. C. DeFries, & J. Hewitt (Eds.), *Nature and nurture in the transition to early adolescence.* Oxford: Oxford University Press.

Deater-Deckard, K., & Dodge, K. A. (1997). Externalizing behavior problems and discipline revisited: Nonlinear effects in variation by culture, context, and gender. *Psychological Inquiry, 8,* 161–175.

DiLalla, L. R., & Gottesman, I. I. (1989, April). *Early predictors of delinquency and adult criminality.* Paper presented at the Society for Research in Child Development, Kansas City, MO.

Dishion, T. J. (1987). *A developmental model for peer relations: Middle childhood correlates and one-year sequelae.* Unpublished doctoral dissertation, University of Oregon, Eugene.

Dishion, T. J. (1990). Peer context of troublesome behavior in children and adolescents. In P. Leone (Ed.), *Understanding troubled and troublesome youth* (pp. 128–153). Beverly Hills, CA: Sage.

Dishion, T. J. (2000). Cross-setting consistency in early adolescent psychopathology: Deviant friendships and problem behavior sequelae. *Journal of Personality, 68*(6), 1109–1126.

Dishion, T. J., & Andrews, D. (1995). Preventing escalations in problem behaviors with high-risk young adolescents: Immediate and 1-year outcomes. *Journal of Consulting and Clinical Psychology, 63,* 538–548.

Dishion, T. J., Andrews, D. W., & Crosby, L. (1995). Antisocial boys and their friends in early adolescence: Relationship characteristics, quality, and interactional process. *Child Development, 66,* 139–151.

Dishion, T. J., & Bullock, B. M. (2001). Parenting and adolescent problem behavior: An ecological analysis of the nurturance hypothesis. In J. G. Borkowski, S. L. Ramey, & M. Bristol-Power (Eds.), *Parenting and the child's world: Influences on academic, intellectual, and social-emotional development* (pp. 231–249). Mahwah, NJ: Erlbaum.

Dishion, T. J., Bullock, B. M., & Granic, I. (2002). Pragmatism in modeling peer influence: Dynamics, outcomes, and change processes. *Development and Psychopathology, 14,* 969–981.

Dishion, T. J., Bullock, B. M., & Owen, L. (in press). Deviant norms in families: Constructing a process bridge to peer culture. *European Journal of Developmental Psychology.*

Dishion, T. J., Capaldi, D., Spracklen, K. M., & Li, F. (1995). Peer ecology of male adolescent drug use. *Development and Psychopathology, 7,* 803–824.

Dishion, T. J., Duncan, T. E., Eddy, J. M., Fagot, B. I., & Fetrow, R. (1994). The world of parents and peers: Coercive exchanges and children's social adaptation. *Social Development, 3,* 255–268.

Dishion, T. J., Eddy, J. M., Haas, E., Li, F., & Spracklen, K. (1997). Friendships and violent behavior during adolescence. *Social Development, 6,* 207–223.

Dishion, T. J., French, D., & Patterson, G. R. (1995). The development and ecology of antisocial behavior. In D. Cicchetti & D. Cohen (Eds.), *Manual of developmental psychopathology: Risk, disorder, and adaptation* (Vol. 2, pp. 421–471). New York: Wiley.

Dishion, T. J., & Kavanagh, K. (2003). *Intervening in adolescent problem behavior: A family-centered approach.* New York: Guilford Press.

Dishion, T. J., Kavanagh, K., Schneiger, A., Nelson, S. E., & Kaufman, N. (2002). Preventing early adolescent substance use: A family-centered strategy for the public middle-school ecology. In R. L. Spoth, K. Kavanagh, & T. J. Dishion (Eds.), *Universal family-centered prevention strategies: Current findings and critical issues for public health impact* [Special issue]. *Prevention Science, 3,* 191–201.

Dishion, T. J., Light, J., Yasui, M., & Stormshak, E. A. (2005). *A network analysis of the confluence hypothesis in early adolescence.* Manuscript in preparation. Child and Family Center, Eugene, OR.

Dishion, T. J., & Loeber, R. (1985). Adolescent marijuana and alcohol use: The role of parents and peers revisited. *American Journal of Drug and Alcohol Abuse, 11,* 11–25.

Dishion, T. J., McCord, J., & Poulin, F. (1999). When interventions harm: Peer groups and problem behavior. *American Psychologist, 54*(9), 755–764.

Dishion, T. J., & McMahon, R. J. (1998). Parental monitoring and the prevention of child and adolescent problem behavior: A conceptual and empirical formulation. *Clinical Child and Family Psychology Review, 1,* 61–75.

Dishion, T. J., & Medici Skaggs, N. (2000). An ecological analysis of monthly "bursts" in early adolescent substance use. *Applied Developmental Science, 4,* 89–97.

Dishion, T. J., Nelson, S. E., & Bullock, B. M. (2004). Premature adolescent autonomy: Parent disengagement and deviant peer process in the amplification of problem behaviour. *Journal of Adolescence, 27*(5), 515–530.

Dishion, T. J., Nelson, S. E., & Kavanagh, K. (2003). The family check-up for high-risk adolescents: Preventing early-onset substance use by parent monitoring. In J. E. Lochman & R. Salekin (Eds.), *Behavior oriented interventions for children with aggressive behavior and/or conduct problems* [Special issue]. *Behavior Therapy, 34,* 553–571.

Dishion, T. J., Nelson, S. E., Winter, C. E., & Bullock, B. M. (2004). Adolescent friendship as a dynamic system: Entropy and deviance in the etiology and course of male antisocial behavior. *Journal of Abnormal Child Psychology, 32*(6), 651–663.

Dishion, T. J., Nelson, S. E., & Yasui, M. (in press). The development and ecology of early adolescent gang involvement: A longitudinal analysis of school-based predictors. *Journal of Clinical Child and Adolescent Psychology.*

Dishion, T. J., & Owen, L. D. (2002). A longitudinal analysis of friendships and substance use: Bidirectional influence from adolescence to adulthood. *Developmental Psychology, 28*(4), 480–491.

Dishion, T. J., & Patterson, G. R. (1999). Model-building in development psychopathology: A pragmatic approach to understanding and intervention. *Journal of Clinical Child Psychology, 28,* 502–512.

Dishion, T. J., Patterson, G. R., & Griesler, P. C. (1994). Peer adaptation in the development of antisocial behavior: A confluence model. In L. R. Huesmann (Ed.), *Aggressive behavior: Current perspectives* (pp. 61–95). New York: Plenum Press.

Dishion, T. J., Patterson, G. R., Stoolmiller, M., & Skinner, M. S. (1991). Family, school, and behavioral antecedents to early adolescent involvement with antisocial peers. *Developmental Psychology, 27,* 172–180.

Dishion, T. J., & Piehler, T. (2005). *Peer dynamics in the development and change of child and adolescent problem behavior.* Manuscript in preparation. University of Oregon, Eugene, OR.

Dishion, T. J., Poulin, F., & Burraston, B. (2001). Peer group dynamics associated with iatrogenic effects in group interventions with high-risk young adolescents. In C. Erdley & D. W. Nangle (Eds.), *Damon's new directions in child development: The role of friendship in psychological adjustment* (pp. 79–92). San Francisco: Jossey-Bass.

Dishion, T. J., Poulin, F., & Medici Skaggs, N. (2000). The ecology of premature adolescent autonomy: Biological and social influences. In K. A. Kerns, S. M. Contreras, & A. M. Neal-Barnett (Eds.), *Explaining associations between family and peer relationships* (pp. 27–45). Westport, CT: Praeger.

Dishion, T. J., Spracklen, K. M., Andrews, D. W., & Patterson, G. R. (1996). Deviancy training in male adolescent friendships. *Behavior Therapy, 27,* 373–390.

Dishion, T. J., & Stormshak, E. A. (in press). *An ecological approach to child clinical and counseling psychology.* Washington, DC: American Psychological Association Books.

Dodge, K. A. (1983). Behavioral antecedents: A peer social status. *Child Development, 54,* 1386–1399.

Dodge, K. A. (1993). The future of research and the treatment of conduct disorder. *Development and Psychopathology, 5,* 311–319.

Dodge, K. A., & Coie, J. D. (1987). Social information-processing factors in reactive and proactive aggression in children's peer groups. *Journal of Personality and Social Psychology, 53,* 1146–1158.

Dodge, K. A., Price, J. M., Coie, J., & Christopoulos, D. (1990). On the development of aggressive dyadic relationships in boys' peer groups. *Human Development, 33,* 260–270.

Eddy, J. M., & Chamberlain, P. (2000). Family management and deviant peer association as mediators of the impact of treatment condition on youth antisocial behavior. *Journal of Consulting and Clinical Psychology, 68,* 857–863.

Eisenberg, N., & Fabes, R. A. (1998). Prosocial development. In W. Damon & N. Eisenberg (Eds.), *Handbook of child psychology: Vol. 3. Social, emotional, and personality development* (pp. 701–779). New York: Wiley.

Elder, G. H., Jr. (1980). *Family structure and socialization.* New York: Arno Press.

Elder, G. H., Jr. (1985). Perspectives on the life course. In G. H. Elder Jr. (Ed.), *Life course dynamics* (pp. 23–49). Ithaca, NY: Cornell University Press.

Elder, G. H., & Caspi, A. (1988). Economic stress in lives: Developmental perspectives. *Journal of Social Issues, 44*(4), 25–45.

Elder, G. H., van Nguyen, T., & Caspi, A. (1985). Linking family hardship to children's lives. *Child Development, 56*(2), 361–375.

Elliott, D. S., Huizinga, D., & Ageton, S. (1985). *Explaining delinquency and drug use.* Beverly Hills, CA: Sage.

Elliott, D. S., & Menard, S. (1996). Delinquent friends and delinquent behavior: Temporal and developmental patterns. In J. D. Hawkins (Ed.), *Delinquency and crime: Current theories—Cambridge criminology series* (pp. 28–67). New York: Cambridge University Press.

Fagot, B. I., & Kavanagh, K. (1991). *Using play as a diagnostic tool with physically abusive parents and their children.* New York: Wiley.

Fan, J., McCandliss, B. D., Sommer, T., Raz, A., & Posner, M. I. (2002). Testing the efficiency and independence of attentional networks. *Journal of Cognitive Neuroscience, 14*(3), 340–347.

Farrington, D. P. (1991). Childhood aggression and adults' violence: Early precursors and later-life outcomes. In D. J. Pepler & K. H. Rubin (Eds.), *The development and treatment of childhood aggression* (pp. 5–29). Hillsdale, NJ: Erlbaum.

Farrington, D. P., Jolliffe, D., Hawkins, J. D., Catalano, R. F., Hill, K. G., & Kosterman, R. (2000, June). *Comparing delinquency careers in court records and self-reports.* Seattle, WA.

Fiske, D. W. (1986). Specificity of method and knowledge in social science. In D. W. Fiske & R. A. Shweder (Eds.), *Metatheory in social science: Pluralisms and subjectivities* (pp. 61–82). Chicago: University of Chicago Press.

Fiske, D. W. (1987). Construct invalidity comes from method effects. *Educational and Psychological Measurement, 47,* 285–307.

Forgatch, M. S. (1991). The clinical science vortex: Developing a theory for antisocial behavior. In D. J. Pepler & K. H. Rubin (Eds.), *The development and treatment of childhood aggression* (pp. 291–315). Hillsdale, NJ: Erlbaum.

Forgatch, M. S., & DeGarmo, D. S. (1999). Parenting through change: An effective prevention program for single mothers. *Journal of Consulting and Clinical Psychology, 67,* 711–724.

Forgatch, M. S., & DeGarmo, D. (2002). Extending and testing the social interaction learning model with divorce samples. In J. B. Reid, G. R. Patterson & J. J. Synder (Eds.), *Antisocial behavior in children and adolescents: A developmental analysis and model for intervention* (pp. 235–256). Washington, DC: American Psychological Association.

Forgatch, M. S., & Patterson, G. R. (1989). *Parents and adolescents.* Eugene, OR: Castalia.

Forgatch, M. S., Patterson, G. R., & Ray, J. A. (1996). Divorce and boys' adjustment problems: Two paths with a single model. In E. M. Hetherington & E. A. Blechman (Eds.), *Stress, coping, and resiliency in children and families: Family research consortium—Advances in family research* (pp. 67–105). Hillsdale, NJ: Erlbaum.

French, D. C. (1987). Children's social interaction with older, younger, and same-age peers. *Journal of Social and Personal Relationships, 4*(1), 63–86.

French, D. C. (1988). Heterogeneity of peer-rejected boys: Aggressive and nonagressive subtypes. *Child Development, 59,* 882–886.

French, D. C. (1990). Heterogeneity of peer rejected girls. *Child Development, 61,* 2028–2031.

French, D. C., & Dishion, T. J. (2003). Predictors of early initiation of sexual intercourse among high-risk adolescents. *Journal of Early Adolescence, 23*(3), 295–315.

French, D. C., & Waas, G. A. (1987). Social-cognitive and behavioral characteristics of peer-rejected boys. *Professional School Psychology, 2,* 103–112.

Friedlander, E. (2004). *J. J. Rousseau: An afterlife of words.* Cambridge, MA: Harvard University Press. (Original work published 1762)

Frith, U., & Frith, C. (2001). The biological basis of social interaction. *Current Directions in Psychological Science, 10*(5), 151–155.

Gardner, F. E. M. (1989). Inconsistent parenting: Is there evidence for a link with children's conduct problems? *Journal of Abnormal Child Psychology, 17,* 223–233.

Gardner, F. E. M. (in press). Proactive parenting processes as predictors of the early development of children's conduct problems: Innovative approaches to examining social processes in the development of antisocial behavior [Special issue]. *Social Development.*

Gardner, T., & Dishion, T. J. (2005). *Effortful attention control as a moderator for adolescent deviant peer influence.* Manuscript submitted for publication.

Gold, M. (1970). *Delinquent behavior in an American city.* San Francisco: Brooks & Coleman.

Goldberg, L. R. (1994). How not to whip a straw dog. *Psychological Inquiry, 5,* 128–130.

Gottfredson, M. R., & Hirschi, T. (1990). *A general theory of crime.* Stanford, CA: Stanford University Press.

Granic, I., & Dishion, T. J. (2003). Deviant talk in adolescent friendships: A step toward measuring a pathogenic attractor process. *Social Development, 12,* 314–334.

Gross, D., Fogg, L., Webster-Stratton, C., Garvey, C., Julion, W., & Grady, J. (2003). Parent training of toddlers in day care in low-income urban communities. *Journal of Consulting and Clinical Psychology, 71*(2), 261–278.

Grotpeter, J. K., & Crick, N. R. (1996). Relational aggression, overt aggression, and friendship. *Child Development, 67,* 2328–2338.

Haggerty, R. J., Sherrod, L. R., Garmezy, N., & Rutter, M. (1994). *Stress, risk, and resilience in children and adolescents.* Cambridge, UK: Cambridge University Press.

Hamilton, E., & Cairns, H. (1973). *Plato: Collected dialogues.* Princeton: Princeton University Press.

Hare, R. D., Forth, A. E., & Strachan, K. E. (1992). Psychopathy and crime across the life span. In R. D. Peters, R. J. McMahon, & V. L. Quinsey (Eds.), *Aggression and violence throughout the life span* (pp. 285–300). Newbury Park, CA: Sage.

Harris, J. R. (1995). Where is the child's environment? A group socialization theory of development. *Psychological Review, 102,* 458–489.

Harris, J. R. (1998). *The nurture assumption.* New York: Free Press.

Hayes, S. C., Gifford, E., & Ruckstuhl, L. E. (1996). Relational frame theory and a behavioral approach to executive function. In R. Lyon (Ed.), *Attention, memory, and executive function* (pp. 279–305). Baltimore: Paul H. Brookes.

Hayes, S. C., & Hayes, L. J. (Eds.). (1992). *Understanding verbal relations.* Reno, NV: Context.

Hayes, S. C., Hayes, L. J., Sato, M., & Ono, K. (1994). *Behavior analysis of language and cognition.* Reno, NV: Context.

Healy, W. (1926). Preventing delinquency among children. *Proceedings and Addresses of the National Educational Association, 64,* 113–118.

Healy, W., & Bronner, A. F. (1936). *New light on delinquency and its treatment.* New Haven, CT: Yale University Press.

Henggeler, S. W., Schoenwald, S. K., Borduin, C. M., Rowland, M. D., & Cunningham, P. B. (1998). *Multisystemic treatment of antisocial behavior in children and adolescents.* New York: Guilford Press.

Hinde, R. A. (1989). Ethological and relationship approaches. In R. Vasta (Ed.), *Annals of child development: Vol. 6. Six theories of child development-Revised formulations and current issues* (pp. 251–285). Hillsdale, NJ: Erlbaum.

Hinshaw, S. P., & Anderson, C. A. (1996). Conduct and oppositional defiant disorders. In E. J. Mash & R. A. Barkley (Eds.), *Child psychopathology* (pp. 113–149). New York: Guilford Press.

Hinshaw, S. P., Lahey, B. B., & Hart, E. L. (1993). Issues of taxonomy and comorbidity in the development of conduct disorder. *Development and Psychopathology, 5*(1/2), 31–49.

Hoffman, L. W. (1991). The influence of family environment on personality: Accounting for sibling differences. *Psychological Bulletin, 110,* 187–203.

Ialongo, N., Poduska, J., Werthhamer, L., & Kellam, S. (2001). The distal impact of two first-grade preventive interventions on conduct problems and disorder in early adolescence. *Journal of Emotional and Behavioral Disorders, 9,* 146–160.

Ingoldsby, E., & Shaw, D. S. (2002). Neighborhood contextual factors and the onset and progression of early-starting antisocial pathways. *Clinical Child and Family Psychology Review, 5*(1), 21–55.

Ingoldsby, E., Shaw, D. S., & Garcia, M. M. (2001). Intrafamily conflict in relation to boy's adjustment at school. *Development and Psychopathology, 13,* 35–52.

Jesness, C. F. (1977). When is a delinquent a delinquent? A reply to Shark and Handal. *Journal of Consulting and Clinical Psychology, 45*(4), 696–697.

Jessor, R., & Jessor, S. L. (1977). *Problem behavior and psychosocial development.* New York: Academic.

Jones, R. R., Reid, J. B., & Patterson, G. R. (1975). Naturalistic observations in clinical assessment. In P. McReynolds (Ed.), *Advances in psychological assessment* (pp. 42–95). San Francisco: Jossey-Bass.

Kandel, D. B. (1986). Process of peer influence on adolescence. In R. K. Silbereisen (Ed.), *Development as action in context* (pp. 33–52). Berlin, Germany: Springer-Verlag.

Kazdin, A. E. (1987). Treatment of antisocial behavior in children: Current status and future directions. *Psychological Bulletin, 102,* 187–203.

Kazdin, A. E. (1993). Treatment of conduct disorder: Progress and directions in psychotherapy research. *Development and Psychopathology, 5,* 277–310.

Kazdin, A. E., Siegel, T. C., & Bass, D. (1992). Cognitive problem solving skills training and parent management training in the treatment of antisocial behavior in children. *Journal of Consulting and Clinical Psychology, 60,* 733–747.

Kellam, S., Ling, X., Merisca, R., Brown, H., & Ialongo, N. (1998). The effect of the level of aggression in the first grade classroom on the course of malleability of aggressive behavior into the middle school. *Development and Psychopathology, 10*(2), 165–185.

Kerr, M., & Stattin, H. (2000). What parents know, how they know it, and several forms of adolescent adjustment: Further support for a reinterpretation of monitoring. *Developmental Psychology, 36,* 366–380.

Kiesner, J., Dishion, T. J., & Poulin, F. (2001). A reinforcement model of conduct problems in children and adolescents: Advances in theory and intervention. In I. M. Goodyear, J. Hill, & B. Maughan (Eds.), *Cambridge child and adolescent psychiatry: Conduct disorders in childhood and adolescence* (pp. 264–291). Cambridge, England: Cambridge University Press.

Kochanska, G. (1993). Toward a synthesis of parental socialization and child temperament in early development of conscience. *Child Development, 64,* 325–347.

Kochanska, G. (2002). Committed compliance, moral self, and internalization: A mediational model. *Developmental Psychology, 38,* 339–351.

Kochanska, G., Murray, K., Jacques, T. Y., Koenig, A. L., & Vandegeest, K. A. (1996). Inhibitory control in young children and its role in emerging internalization. *Child Development, 67,* 490–507.

Kohnstamm, G. A., Bates, J. E., & Rothbart, M. K. (Eds.). (1989). *Temperament in childhood.* Chichester, UK: Wiley.

Krippendorf, K. (1986). *Information theory: Structural models for qualitative data.* Newbury Park, CA: Sage.

Lacourse, E., Nagin, D., Tremblay, R. E., Vitaro, F., & Claes, M. (2003). Developmental trajectories of boys' delinquent group membership and facilitation of violent behaviors during adolescence. *Development and Psychopathology, 15,* 183–197.

Ladd, G. W. (1983). Social networks of popular, average, and rejected children in school settings. *Merrill-Palmer Quarterly, 29,* 283–307.

Laird, R. D., Jordan, K. Y., Dodge, K. A., Pettit, G., & Bates, J. E. (2001). Peer rejection in childhood, involvement with antisocial peers in early adolescence, and the development of externalizing behavior problems. *Development and Psychopathology, 13,* 337–354.

Lengua, L. J., & Sandler, I. N. (1996). Self-regulation as a moderator of the relation between coping and symptomatology in children of divorce. *Journal of Abnormal Child Psychology, 24*(6), 681–701.

Leve, L. D., Winebarger, A. A., Fagot, B. I., Reid, J. B., & Goldsmith, H. H. (1998). Environmental and genetic variance in children's observed and reported maladaptive behavior. *Child Development, 69,* 1286–1298.

Levitt, E. E. (1957). The results of psychotherapy with children: An evaluation. *Journal of Consulting and Clinical Psychology, 21,* 189–197.

Levitt, E. E. (1971). Research on psychotherapy with children. In A. E. Bergin & S. L. Garfield (Eds.), *Handbook of psychotherapy and behavior change* (pp. 474–494). New York: Wiley.

Lewin, L. N., Hops, H., Davis, B., & Dishion, T. J. (1993). Multimethod comparison of similarity in school adjustment of siblings and unrelated children. *Developmental Psychology, 29,* 963–969.

Lewis, M. D. (2000). The promise of dynamic systems approaches for an integrated account of human development. *Child Development, 71,* 36–43.

Liau, A. K., Barriga, A., & Gibbs, J. (1998). Relations between self-serving cognitive distortions and overt vs. covert antisocial behavior in adolescents. *Aggressive Behavior, 24,* 335–346.

Lochman, J. E., Barry, T. D., & Pardini, D. A. (2003). Anger control training for aggressive youth. In A. E. Kazdin & J. R. Weisz (Eds.), *Evidence-based psychotherapies for children and adolescents* (pp. 263–281). New York: Guilford Press.

Lochman, J. E., & Wells, K. C. (1996). A social-cognitive intervention with aggressive children: Prevention effects and contextual implementation issues. In R. D. Peters & R. J. McMahon (Eds.), *Preventing childhood disorders, substance abuse, and delinquency* (pp. 111–143). Thousand Oaks, CA: Sage.

Loeber, R. (1982). The stability of antisocial and delinquent child behavior: A review. *Child Development, 53,* 1431–1446.

Loeber, R. (1988). Natural histories of conduct problems, delinquency, and associated substance use: Evidence for developmental progressions. In B. B. Lahey & A. E. Kazdin (Eds.), *Advances in clinical child psychology* (pp. 73–124). New York: Plenum Press.

Loeber, R. (1991). Antisocial behavior: More enduring than changeable? *Journal of the American Academy of Child and Adolescent Psychiatry, 30*(3), 393–397.

Loeber, R., & Dishion, T. (1983). Early predictors of male delinquency: A review. *Psychological Bulletin, 94,* 68–99.

Loeber, R., & Farrington, D. P. (2000). Young children who commit crime: Epidemiology, developmental origins, risk factors, early interventions, and policy implications. *Development and Psychopathology, 12,* 737–762.

Loeber, R., Green, S. M., Keenan, K., & Lahey, B. B. (1995). Which boys will fare worse? Early predictors of the onset of conduct disorder in a six-year longitudinal study. *Journal of the American Academy of Child and Adolescent Psychiatry, 34,* 499–509.

Loeber, R., & Schmaling, K. B. (1985). Empirical evidence for overt and covert patterns of antisocial conduct problems: A meta-analysis. *Journal of Abnormal Child Psychology, 13,* 337–352.

Loeber, R., Wung, P., Keenan, K., Giroux, B., Stouthamer-Loeber, M., van Kammen, W. B., et al. (1993). Developmental pathways in disruptive child behavior. *Development and Psychopathology, 5,* 103–133.

Lykken, D. T. (1993). Predicting violence in a violent society. *Applied and Preventative Psychology, 2,* 13–20.

Maccoby, E. E. (1992). The role of parents in the socialization of children: An historical overview. *Developmental Psychology, 28,* 1006–1017.

Maccoby, E. E. (2000). Parenting and its effects on children: On reading and misreading behavior genetics. *Annual Review of Psychology, 51,* 1–27.

Magnusson, D., Stattin, H., & Allen, D. L. (1985). Biological maturation and social development: A longitudinal study of some adjustment processes from mid-adolescence to adulthood. *Journal of Youth and Adolescence, 14*(4), 267–283.

Martin, J. A. (1981). A longitudinal study of the consequences of early mother-infant interaction: A microanalytic approach. *Monographs of the Society for Research in Child Development, 46*(3), 59.

Martinez, C. R., Jr., & Forgatch, M. S. (2001). Preventing problems with boys' noncompliance: Effects of a parent training intervention for divorcing mothers. *Journal of Consulting and Clinical Psychology, 69,* 416–428.

Mason, C. A., Cauce, A. M., Gonzales, N., & Hiraga, Y. (1996). Neither too sweet nor too sour: Problem peers, maternal control, and problem behavior in African American adolescents. *Child Development, 67,* 2115–2130.

Masten, A. S., Best, K. M., & Garmezy, N. (1990). Resilience and development: Contributions from the study of children who overcome adversity. *Development and Psychopathology, 2*(4), 425–444.

Masten, A. S., & Coatsworth, J. D. (1998). The development of competence in favorable and unfavorable environments. *American Psychologist, 53*(2), 205–220.

Mayr, E. (1991). *Charles Darwin and the genesis of modern evolutionary thought.* Cambridge, MA: Harvard University Press.

McCord, J., McCord, W., & Howard, A. (1963). Family interaction as antecedent to the direction of male aggressiveness. *Journal of Abnormal and Social Psychology, 66*(3), 239–242.

McLoyd, V. C. (1990). The impact of economic hardship on Black families and children: Psychological distress, parenting, and socioemotional development. *Child Development, 61,* 311–346.

McLoyd, V. C., & Steinberg, L. (Eds.). (1998). *Studying minority adolescents: Conceptual, methodological and theoretical issues.* Mahwah, NJ: Erlbaum.

Miles, D. R., & Carey, G. (1997). Genetic and environmental architecture on human aggression. *Journal of Personality and Social Psychology, 72*(1), 207–217.

Miller, W. R., & Brown, J. M. (1991). Self-regulation as a conceptual basis for the prevention and treatment of addictive behaviours. In N. Heather, W. R. Miller, & J. Greeley (Eds.), *Self-control and the addictive behaviours* (pp. 3–82). Sydney, Australia: Maxwell Macmillan.

Moffitt, T. E. (1993). Adolescence-limited and life-course-persistent antisocial behavior: A developmental taxonomy. *Psychological Review, 100,* 674–701.

Moffitt, T. E., Caspi, A., Harrington, H., & Milne, B. J. (2002). Males on the life-course persistent and adolescence-limited antisocial pathways: Follow-up at age 26. *Development and Psychopathology, 14,* 179–207.

Moffitt, T. E., Caspi, A., Rutter, M., & Silva, P. A. (2001). *Sex differences in antisocial behavior: Conduct disorder, delinquency, and violence in the Dunedin longitudinal study.* Cambridge, England: Cambridge University Press.

Muthén, B. O., & Muthén, L. K. (2000). Integrating person-centered and variable-centered analysis: Growth mixture modeling with latent trajectory classes. *Alcoholism: Clinical and Experimental Research, 24,* 882–891.

Muthén, B. O., & Shedden, K. (1999). Finite mixture modeling with mixture outcomes using the EM algorithm. *Biometrics, 55,* 463–469.

Nagin, D. S. (1999). Analyzing developmental trajectories: A semi-parametric, group-based approach. *Psychological Methods, 4*(2), 139–157.

Nagin, D. S., & Tremblay, R. E. (1999). Trajectories of boys' physical aggression, opposition, and hyperactivity on the path to physically violent and nonviolent juvenile delinquency. *Child Development, 70,* 1181–1196.

Neiderhiser, J. M., Reiss, D., & Hetherington, E. M. (1996). Genetically informative designs for distinguishing developmental pathways during adolescence: Responsible and antisocial behavior. *Development and Psychopathology, 8*(4), 779–791.

Newman, J. P., Widom, C. S., & Nathan, S. (1985). Passive avoidance in syndromes of disinhibition: Psychopathy in extroversion. *Journal of Personality and Social Psychology, 48,* 1316–1327.

Nix, R. L., Pinderhughes, E. E., Dodge, K. A., Bates, J. E., Pettit, G. S., & McFadyen-Ketchum, S. A. (1999). The relation between mothers' hostile attribution tendencies and children's externalizing behavior problems: The mediating role of mothers' harsh discipline practices. *Child Development, 70,* 896–909.

Nye, F. I. (1958). *Family relationships and delinquent behavior.* New York: Wiley.

Olds, D. L., Eckenrode, J., Henderson, C. R., Kitzman, H., Powers, J., Cole, R., et al. (1997). Long-term effects of home visitation on maternal life course and child abuse and neglect. *Journal of the American Medical Association, 278,* 637–643.

Olweus, D. (1979). Stability of aggressive reaction patterns in males: A review. *Psychological Bulletin, 86,* 852–875.

Osgood, C. E. (1962). Studies on the generality of affective meaning systems. *American Psychologist, 17,* 10–28.

Osgood, D. W., Wilson, J. K., O'Malley, P. M., Bachman, J. G., & Johnston, L. D. (1996). Routine activities and individual deviant behavior. *American Sociological Review, 61,* 635–655.

Patterson, G. R. (1982). *A social learning approach: Vol. 3. Coercive family process.* Eugene, OR: Castalia.

Patterson, G. R. (1984). Siblings: Fellow travelers in coercive family process. *Advances in the Study of Aggression, 1,* 173–213.

Patterson, G. R. (1985). Beyond technology: The next stage in developing an empirical base for training. In L. L. Abate (Ed.), *Handbook of family psychology and therapy* (pp. 1344–1379). Homewood, IL: Dorsey.

Patterson, G. R. (1986). The contribution of siblings to training for fighting: A microsocial analysis. In D. Olweus, J. Block, & M. Radke-Yarrow (Eds.), *Development of antisocial and prosocial behavior: Research, theories and issues* (pp. 263–284). New York: Academic Press.

Patterson, G. R. (1993). Orderly change in a stable world: The antisocial trait as a chimera. *Journal of Consulting and Clinical Psychology, 61,* 911–919.

Patterson, G. R. (1996). Some characteristics of a developmental theory for early onset delinquency. In M. F. Lenzenweger & J. J. Haugaard (Eds.), *Frontiers of developmental psychopathology* (pp. 81–124). New York: Oxford University Press.

Patterson, G. R., & Bank, L. (1986). Bootstrapping your way in the nomological thicket. *Behavioral Assessment, 8,* 49–73.

Patterson, G. R., Crosby, L., & Vuchinich, S. (1992). Predicting risk for early police arrest. *Journal of Quantitative Criminology, 8,* 333–355.

Patterson, G. R., DeBaryshe, B. D., & Ramsey, E. (1989). A developmental perspective on antisocial behavior. *American Psychologist, 44,* 329–335.

Patterson, G. R., & DeGarmo, D. S. (1997, November). *In search of growth in antisocial behavior: Prelude to early-onset delinquency.* Paper presented at the American Society of Criminology, San Diego.

Patterson, G. R., & Dishion, T. J. (1985). Contributions of families and peers to delinquency. *Criminology, 23,* 63–79.

Patterson, G. R., Dishion, T. J., & Bank, L. (1984). Family interaction: A process model of deviancy training. *Aggressive Behavior, 10,* 253–267.

Patterson, G. R., Dishion, T. J., & Yoerger, K. (2000). Adolescent growth in new forms of problem behavior: Macro- and micro-peer dynamics. *Prevention Science, 1,* 3–13.

Patterson, G. R., & Fisher, P. A. (2002). Recent developments in our understanding of parenting: Bidirectional effects, causal models, and the search for parsimony. In M. H. Bornstein (Ed.), *Handbook of parenting: Vol. 5. Practical issues in parenting* (2nd ed., pp. 59–88). Mahwah, NJ: Erlbaum.

Patterson, G. R., Forgatch, M. S., Yoerger, K., & Stoolmiller, M. (1998). Variables that initiate and maintain an early-onset trajectory for juvenile offending. *Development and Psychopathology, 10,* 541–547.

Patterson, G. R., Littman, R. A., & Bricker, W. (1967). Assertive behavior in children: A step towards a theory of aggression. *Monographs of the Society for Research in Child Development, 32*(5), 1–43.

Patterson, G. R., & Reid, J. B. (1984). Social interactional processes within the family: The study of moment-by-moment family transactions in which human development is embedded. *Journal of Applied Developmental Psychology, 5,* 237–262.

Patterson, G. R., Reid, J. B., & Dishion, T. J. (1992). *A social interactional approach: Vol. 4. Antisocial boys.* Eugene, OR: Castalia.

Patterson, G. R., & Stouthamer-Loeber, M. (1984). The correlation of family management practices and delinquency. *Child Development, 55,* 1299–1307.

Patterson, G. R., & Yoerger, K. (1993, October). *Differentiating outcomes and histories for early and late onset arrests.* Paper presented at the American Society of Criminology, Phoenix, AZ.

Patterson, G. R., & Yoerger, K. (1997). A developmental model for late-onset delinquency. In D. W. Osgood (Ed.), *Nebraska Symposium on Motivation: Vol. 44. Motivation and delinquency* (pp. 119–177). Lincoln: University of Nebraska Press.

Patterson, G. R., & Yoerger, K. (1999). Intraindividual growth in covert antisocial behavior: A necessary precursor to chronic and adult arrests? *Criminal Behaviour and Mental Health, 9,* 86–100.

Patterson, G. R., & Yoerger, K. (2002). A developmental model for early- and late-onset delinquency. In J. B. Reid, G. R. Patterson, & J. Snyder (Eds.), *Antisocial behavior in children and adolescents: A developmental analysis and model for intervention* (pp. 147–172). Washington, DC: American Psychological Association.

Plomin, R., & Daniels, D. (1987). Why are children in the same families so different from one another? *Behavioral and Brain Sciences, 10,* 1–60.

Poulin, F., & Boivin, M. (2000a). The formation and development of friendship in childhood: The role of proactive and reactive aggression. *Developmental Psychology, 36,* 233–240.

Poulin, F., & Boivin, M. (2000b). Proactive and reactive aggression: Evidence of a two-factor model. *Psychological Assessment, 12,* 115–122. Poulin, F., Dishion, T. J., & Burraston, B. (2001). 3-year iatrogenic effects associated with aggregating high-risk adolescents in cognitive-behavioral preventive interventions. *Applied Development Science, 5*(4), 214–224.

Price, J. M., & Dodge, K. A. (1989). Reactive and proactive aggression in childhood: Relations to peer status and social context dimensions. *Journal of Abnormal Child Psychology, 17,* 455–471.

Pulkkinen, L. (1996). Proactive and reactive aggression in early adolescence as precursors to anti- and prosocial behavior in young adults. *Aggressive Behavior, 22,* 241–257.

Quay, H. C. (1993). The psychobiology of undersocialized aggressive conduct disorder: A theoretical perspective. *Development and Psychopathology, 5,* 165–180.

Quinton, D., Pickles, A., Maughan, B., & Rutter, M. (1993). Partners, peers and pathways: Assortative pairing and continuities in conduct disorder. *Developmental Psychology, 5,* 763–783.

Raine, A. (1993). *The psychopathology of crime: Criminal behavior as a clinical disorder.* San Diego: Academic Press.

Raine, A. (2002). Biosocial studies of antisocial and violent behavior in children and adults: A review. *Journal of Abnormal Child Psychology, 30,* 311–326.

Raush, H. L. (1965). Interaction sequences. *Journal of Personality and Social Psychology, 2,* 487–499.

Redl, F., & Wineman, D. (1951). *Children who hate: The disorganization and breakdown of behavior controls.* Glencoe, IL: Free Press.

Redl, F., & Wineman, D. (1952). *Controls from within: Techniques for the treatment of the aggressive child.* Glencoe, IL: Free Press.

Reid, J. B., Patterson, G. R., & Snyder, J. J. (2002). Antisocial behavior in children and adolescents: A developmental analysis and model for intervention. Washington, DC: American Psychological Association.

Rhee, S. H., & Waldman, I. D. (2002). Genetic and environmental influences on antisocial behavior: A meta-analysis of twin and adoption studies. *Psychological Bulletin, 128,* 490–529.

Robins, L. N. (1966). *Deviant children grown up: A sociological and psychiatric study of sociopathic personality.* Baltimore: Williams & Wilkins.

Rodkin, P. C., Farmer, T. W., Pearl, R., & Van Acker, R. (2000). Heterogeneity of popular boys: Antisocial and prosocial configurations. *Developmental Psychology, 36,* 14–24.

Rogers, G., & Schulman, K. (2003). Leviathan/Thomas Hobbes: A critical edition. Bristol: Thoemmes Continuum. (Original work published 1651)

Rose, R. J., & Kaprio, J. (1987). Shared experience and similarity of personality: Positive data from Finnish and American twins. *Behavioral and Brain Sciences, 10*(1), 35–36.

Rothbart, M. K., Ellis, L. K., & Posner, M. I. (2004). Temperament and self-regulation. In R. F. Baumeister & K. D. Vohs (Eds.), *Handbook of self-regulation: Research, theory, and applications* (pp. 357–370). New York: Guilford Press.

Rowe, D. C. (1994). *The limits of family influence.* New York: Guilford Press.

Rowe, D. C., Woulbroun, E. G., & Gulley, B. L. (1994). Peers and friends as nonshared environmental influences. In E. M. Hetherington, D. Reis, & R. Plomin (Eds.), *Separate social worlds of siblings* (pp. 159–173). Hillsdale, NJ: Erlbaum.

Rutter, M. (1989). Pathways from childhood to adult life. *Journal of Child Psychology and Psychiatry, 30,* 23–51.

Rutter, M. (1995). Clinical implications of attachment concepts: Retrospect and prospect. *Journal of Child Psychology and Psychiatry and Allied Disciplines, 36*(4), 549–571.

Sameroff, A. J., & Suomi, S. J. (1996). Primates and persons: A comparative developmental understanding of social organization. In R. B. Cairns & G. H. Elder Jr. (Eds.), *Developmental science: Cambridge studies in social and emotional development* (pp. 97–120). New York: Cambridge University Press.

Sampson, R. J., & Laub, J. H. (1994). Urban poverty and the family context of delinquency: A new look at structure and process in a classic study. *Child Development, 65,* 523–540.

Shaw, D. S., Gilliom, M., Ingoldsby, E. M., & Nagin, D. (2003). Trajectories leading to school-age conduct problems. *Developmental Psychology, 39,* 189–200.

Shaw, D. S., Keenan, K., & Vondra, J. I. (1994). Developmental precursors of externalizing behavior: Ages 1 to 3. *Developmental Psychology, 30,* 355–364.

Shaw, D. S., & Winslow, E. B. (1997). Precursors and correlates of antisocial behavior from infancy to preschool. In D. M. Stoff, J. Breiling, & J. D. Maser (Eds.), *Handbook of antisocial behavior* (pp. 148–158). New York: Wiley.

Shaw, D. S., Winslow, E. B., & Flanagan, C. (1999). A prospective study of the effects of marital status and family relations on young children's adjustment among African American and European American families. *Child Development, 70,* 742–755.

Shaw, D. S., Winslow, E. B., Owens, E. B., Vondra, J. I., Cohn, J. E., & Bell, R. Q. (1998). The development of early externalizing problems among children from low-income families: A transformational perspective. *Journal of Abnormal Child Psychology, 26,* 95–107.

Slocum, W. I., & Stone, C. I. (1965). Family culture patterns and delinquent-type behavior. *Marriage and Family Living, 25,* 202–208.

Snyder, J. J., Cramer, A., Afrank, J., & Patterson, G. R. (2005). The contributions of ineffective discipline and parental hostile attributions of child misbehavior to the development of conduct problems at home and school. *Developmental Psychology, 41,* 30–41.

Snyder, J. J., Reid, J. B., & Patterson, G. R. (2003). A social learning model of child and adolescent antisocial behavior. In B. B. Lahey, T. E. Moffitt, & A. Caspi (Eds.), *The causes of conduct disorder and juvenile delinquency* (pp. 27–48). New York: Guilford Press.

Snyder, J. J., Schrepferman, L., Oeser, J., Patterson, G., Stoolmiller, M., Johnson, K., et al. (2005). Deviancy training and affiliation with deviant peers in young children: Occurrence and contributions to early-onset conduct problems. *Development and Psychopathology, 17,* 397–413.

Snyder, J. J., West, L., Stockemer, V., Givens, S., & Almquist-Parks, L. (1996). A social learning model of peer choice in the natural environment. *Journal of Applied Developmental Psychology, 17,* 215–237.

Sowell, E. R., & Jernigan, T. L. (1998). Further MRI evidence of late brain maturation: Limbic volume increases and changing asymmetries during childhood and adolescence. *Developmental Neuropsychology, 14*(4), 599–617.

Spear, L. P. (2000). Neurobehavioral changes in adolescence. *Current Directions in Psychological Science, 9*(4), 111–114.

Stanger, C., Achenbach, T. M., & Verhulst, F. C. (1997). Accelerated longitudinal comparisons of aggressive versus delinquent syndromes. *Development and Psychopathology, 9,* 43–58.

Steinberg, L., Dornbusch, S. M., & Brown, B. B. (1992). Ethnic differences in adolescent achievement: An ecological perspective. *American Psychologist, 47,* 723–729.

Steinberg, L., & Silverberg, S. B. (1986). The vicissitudes of autonomy in early adolescence. *Child Development, 57,* 841–851.

Stoolmiller, M. S. (1990). *Parent supervision, child unsupervised wandering, and child antisocial behavior: A latent growth curve analysis.* Unpublished doctoral dissertation, University of Oregon, Eugene.

Stoolmiller, M. S. (1998). Correcting estimates of shared environmental variance for range restriction in adoption studies using a truncated multivariate normal model. *Behavior Genetics, 28*(6), 429–441.

Stoolmiller, M. S. (2001). Synergistic interaction of child manageability problems and parent-discipline tactics in predicting future growth in externalizing behavior for boys. *Developmental Psychology, 37,* 814–825.

Stoolmiller, M., Eddy, J. M., & Reid, J. B. (2000). Detecting and describing preventive intervention effects in a universal school-based randomized trial targeting delinquent and violent behavior. *Journal of Consulting and Clinical Psychology, 68,* 1–11.

Stoolmiller, M., & Snyder, J. (2004). A multilevel analysis of parental discipline and child antisocial behavior. *Behavior Therapy, 35*(2), 365–402.

Stormshak, E. A., Bierman, K. L., Bruschi, C., Dodge, K. A., Coie, J. D., & the Conduct Problems Prevention Research Group. (1999). The relation between behavior problems and peer preference in different classroom contexts. *Child Development, 70,* 169–182.

Stormshak, E. A., Comeau, C. A., & Shepard, S. A. (2004). The relative contributions of sibling deviance and peer deviance in the prediction of substance use across middle childhood. *Journal of Abnormal Child Psychology, 32,* 635–649.

Strayer, F. F., & Santos, A. J. (1996). Affiliative structures in preschool peer groups. *Social Development, 5,* 117–130.

Sugai, G., Horner, R. H., & Sprague, J. R. (1999). Functional-assessment-based behavior support planning: Research to practice to research. *Behavior Disorders, 24,* 253–257.

Tambs, K., Harris, J. R., & Magnus, P. (1995). Sex-specific causal factors and effects of common environment for symptoms of anxiety and depression in twins. *Behavior Genetics, 25*(1), 33–44.

Taylor, J., Iacono, W. G., & McGue, M. (2000). Evidence for a genetic etiology of early-onset delinquency. *Journal of Abnormal Psychology, 109,* 634–643.

Thornberry, T., & Krohn, M. D. (1997). Peers, drug use, and delinquency. In D. M. Stoff, J. Breiling, & J. Maser (Eds.), *Handbook of antisocial behavior* (pp. 218–234). New York: Wiley.

Tremblay, R. E. (2000). The development of aggressive behaviour during childhood: What have we learned in the past century? *International Journal of Behavioral Development, 24,* 129–141.

Tremblay, R. E., Japel, C., Perusse, D., Boivin, M., Zoccolillo, M., Montplaisir, J., et al. (1999). The search for the age of "onset" of physical aggression: Rousseau and Bandura revisited. *Criminal Behaviour and Mental Health, 9,* 8–23.

Tremblay, R. E., Masse, L. C., Pagani, L., & Vitaro, F. (1996). From childhood physical aggression to adolescent maladjustment: The Montreal prevention experiment. In R. D. Peters & R. J. McMahon (Eds.), *Preventing childhood disorders, substance abuse, and delinquency: Vol. 3. Banff international behavioral science series* (pp. 268–298). Thousand Oaks, CA: Sage.

Turkheimer, E. (1991). Individual and group differences in adoption studies of IQ. *Psychological Bulletin, 110*(3), 392–405.

Underwood, M. K. (2003). *Social aggression among girls.* New York: Guilford Press.

van den Boom, D. C. (1994). The influence of temperament and mothering on attachment and exploration: An experimental manipulation of sensitive responsiveness among lower-class mothers with irritable infants. *Child Development, 65*(5), 1457–1477.

Vitaro, F., Brendgen, M., & Tremblay, R. E. (2002). Reactively and proactively aggressive children: Antecedent and subsequent characteristics. *Journal of Child Psychology and Psychiatry, 43,* 495–505.

Warr, M. (1993). Age, peers, and delinquency. *Criminology, 31,* 17–40.

West, D. J., & Farrington, D. P. (1973). *Who becomes delinquent?* New York: Crane, Russak.

Wiesner, M., & Capaldi, D. M. (2003). Relations of childhood and adolescent factors to offending trajectories of young men. *Journal of Research in Crime and Delinquency, 40*(3), 231–262.

Wills, T. A., & Dishion, T. J. (2004). Temperament and adolescent substance use: A transactional analysis of emerging self-control. In P. Frick & W. Silverman (Eds.), *Temperament and childhood psychopathology* [Special issue]. *Journal of Clinical Child and Adolescent Psychology, 33*(1), 69–81.

Windle, M. (1990). A longitudinal study of antisocial behaviors in early adolescence as predictors of late adolescence substance use: Gender and ethnic group differences. *Journal of Abnormal Psychology, 99,* 86–91.

Woodward, L. J., Fergusson, D. M., & Horwood, L. J. (2002). Deviant partner involvement and offending risk in early adulthood. *Journal of Child Psychology and Psychiatry and Allied Disciplines, 43*(2), 177–190.

Yasui, M., Dishion, T. J., & Dorham, C. L. (in press). Ethnic identity and psychological adjustment: Comparing validities for European American and African American adolescents. *Journal of Adolescent Research.*

CHAPTER 14

The Neurodevelopmental Model of Schizophrenia: Updated

CARRIE E. BEARDEN, STEPHANIE E. MEYER, RACHEL L. LOEWY, TARA A. NIENDAM, and TYRONE D. CANNON

Schizophrenia is a severe mental illness afflicting about 1% of the population (T. D. Cannon, 1996). Its characteristic symptoms include hallucinations, delusions, disorganized speech and thought, and abnormalities in emotional expression and motivation (American Psychiatric Association, 1994). Throughout most of the twentieth century, our understanding of the origins and developmental course of this disorder was substantially influenced by Emil Kraepelin (1918), who proposed that Schizophrenia is a deteriorating brain disorder similar in natural history to Alzheimer's disease, but with onset in early adult life. Although Kraepelin himself speculated that some cases were likely due to early insults that caused cerebral maldevelopment, this view of Schizophrenia as a neurodegenerative disorder persisted.

Over the past 25 years, there has been a major shift toward a neurodevelopmental model of Schizophrenia which posits that the neural underpinnings of the disorder arise primarily during early central nervous system development (see left section of Figure 14.1; T. D. Cannon, 1997; Wein-

berger, 1987). Support for this theoretical viewpoint comes from several lines of evidence. Numerous prospective studies have revealed associations between prenatal and perinatal complications and elevated risk for Schizophrenia, thus implicating adverse events during early life as contributing to the development of the disorder. Additionally, a large body of evidence documents the presence of subtle deficits in cognition and behavior during childhood among individuals who ultimately develop Schizophrenia as adults, suggesting that signs of brain compromise are present long before illness onset (Bearden et al., 2000; T. D. Cannon, Rosso, et al., 2000; Rosso, Bearden, et al., 2000). Moreover, postmortem neuropathology studies have in general failed to detect evidence of a dementia-like degenerative process in Schizophrenia (Arnold & Trojanowski, 1996); rather, the reductions in cortical gray matter volume in these patients appear to be accounted for largely by reductions in the degree of dendritic arborization and density of synaptic contacts on pyramidal neurons (i.e., reductions in neuropil volume; Glantz & Lewis, 2000; Selemon &

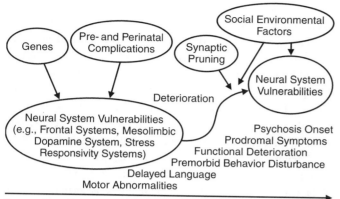

Figure 14.1 Theoretical framework illustrating early and late neurodevelopmental influences in the etiology and pathogenesis of Schizophrenia.

Goldman-Rakic, 1999), findings that suggest involvement of cellular plasticity mechanisms rather than neuronal degeneration per se.

Nevertheless, the notion that the risk factors for Schizophrenia emerge exclusively during prenatal and perinatal brain development begs the question of why formal diagnostic symptoms and signs of the disorder do not typically manifest until late adolescence and early adulthood. Indeed, there is a remarkable consistency in age-at-onset distributions for Schizophrenia from around the world, implicating the late adolescent/early adult period as the peak period of risk for onset (Jablensky et al., 1992). Adolescence also represents a period of active brain development, during which increases in neuronal efficiency are accompanied by a reduction (i.e., pruning) of excess synapses and by myelination of axonal connections in regions critical for higher-order cognition, particularly the prefrontal cortex (Huttenlocher, 1979). Together, these considerations have led several theorists to suggest that processes associated with adolescent brain development may play a role in the pathogenesis of Schizophrenia (see right section of Figure 14.1; Feinberg, 1990; Hoffman & McGlashan, 1997). Interestingly, some structural magnetic resonance imaging (MRI) studies have observed progressive gray matter reductions in first-episode patients with Schizophrenia, with a leveling off after the first few years of active illness (Gur et al., 1998; Thompson et al., 2001). Although the sources of this progression remain controversial, given that most of the first-episode patients who have been scanned in these studies are in the adolescent to early adult period, it is possible that this progression reflects a process associated with the mechanisms underlying synaptic pruning. Such

processes may be overly aggressive in individuals predisposed to developing Schizophrenia (e.g., due to a Schizophrenia-related defect in synaptic plasticity mechanisms), or these processes may be normal but interact with previously existing compromises of brain structure in winnowing neuronal connectivity to below some hypothetically critical threshold. To evaluate these theoretical notions in samples in which adolescent brain developmental processes can be disambiguated from the influences of medication and active psychosis, a new research paradigm has recently been developed, ascertaining individuals who are initially showing symptoms consistent with a high risk for imminent onset of psychosis (i.e., prodromal patients) and following them over time to characterize the course of neurobiological change among those who develop full-blown psychosis and to elucidate predictors of this outcome (T. D. Cannon et al., 2003; Yung & McGorry, 1996).

This chapter reviews and evaluates evidence bearing on the questions of whether and how both early (i.e., pre- and perinatal) and late (i.e., adolescent) neurodevelopmental influences may be involved in the etiology and pathogenesis of Schizophrenia. We first describe briefly the various neural disturbances that have been detected in Schizophrenia, followed by an analysis of studies investigating the roles of genetic and nongenetic factors in these brain abnormalities. These studies provide a useful framework for hypothesis generation concerning the timing of onset and course of brain abnormalities in Schizophrenia, as certain of these brain abnormalities appear to be reflective of an inherited vulnerability state and are thus likely to emerge prior to illness onset and to be fairly stable after their initial appearance, whereas other abnormalities are unique to (or more severe in) individuals who manifest the illness phenotype and may thus first appear or significantly worsen as one moves beyond an inherited vulnerability state to a fully symptomatic psychotic state. We then turn to a review and analysis of the various literatures bearing more directly on the question of the timing of onset and course of brain abnormalities in Schizophrenia. The principal conclusions that can be reached from this review are that (1) the case for involvement of early neurodevelopmental influences in the etiology and pathogenesis of Schizophrenia is consistent and compelling, including evidence from human epidemiological studies, prospective studies of birth cohorts and samples at risk, postmortem neuropathology studies, and experimental studies using animal models; and (2) the case for involvement of later neurodevelopmental processes is still largely circumstantial, but at minimum such processes appear likely to influence the timing of onset of diagnostic symptoms and signs. We conclude this chapter with an updated version of the neurodevelopmental hypothesis of Schizophrenia, specifying a number of ways in which particular sets of early and late influences might interact in determining the timing of onset and course of the disorder.

NATURE AND SOURCES OF BRAIN ABNORMALITIES IN SCHIZOPHRENIA

In the past 2½ decades, significant progress has been made in the characterization of brain abnormalities in Schizophrenia and in elucidating the contributions of genetic and nongenetic influences to these abnormalities. Disturbances in prefrontal and temporolimbic systems and their interconnections are particularly prominent in this disorder (J. D. Cohen & Servan-Schreiber, 1992; Grace, Moore, & O'Donnell, 1998; Gray, Feldon, Rawlins, & Hemsley, 1991). In neuropsychological studies, where patients with Schizophrenia have been found to show performance deficits on nearly all measures of functioning, working memory, attention, abstraction, episodic learning and memory, and language functions appear to be more severely affected (T. D. Cannon, Huttunen, et al., 2000; Saykin, Shtasel, Gur, & Kester, 1994). These findings have been corroborated by evidence of abnormal physiologic activity (i.e., altered blood flow) in prefrontal and temporal lobe regions in patients with Schizophrenia during performance of tests assessing these domains of functioning (e.g., Berman, Torrey, Daniel, & Weinberger, 1992; Callicott et al., 1998; Yurgelun-Todd et al., 1996). At the structural-anatomical level, patients with Schizophrenia show a variety of volumetric changes throughout the brain, including reduced cortical, hippocampal, and thalamic volumes and increased sulcal and ventricular volumes (Pfefferbaum & Marsh, 1995). Some neuroimaging work indicates a relatively greater degree of reduction in frontal and temporal cortical volumes compared with posterior cortical volumes (T. D. Cannon, van Erp, et al., 1998).

Based on postmortem evidence of decreased thickness of the prefrontal cortex without a reduction in the number of cell bodies (Selemon, Rajkowska, & Goldman-Rakic, 1995; Selemon, Rajkowska, & Goldman-Rakic, 1998), it has been suggested that a reduction of interneuronal neuropil underlies in vivo MRI findings of cortical gray matter reduction in Schizophrenia (Selemon & Goldman-Rakic, 1999), a prediction that has been confirmed by observations of reduced dendritic spine density on prefrontal cortical pyramidal neurons (Glantz & Lewis, 2000). This pattern implies a disruption in cellular plasticity mecha-

nisms rather than neuronal degeneration per se, an interpretation that is also supported by lack of gliosis, or the scarring associated with degeneration of cortical neurons, in the brains of patients with Schizophrenia, a pattern that would be expected to result from an active neurodegenerative process (Bogerts et al., 1993; Casanova & Kleinman, 1990). This interpretation is also supported by findings of cellular positioning abnormalities that are consistent with disturbances of neuronal migration during gestation (Akbarian, Bunney, et al., 1993; Akbarian, Vinuela, et al., 1993; Arnold, Hyman, Van Hoesen, & Damasio, 1991; T. D. Cannon & Mednick, 1993; Jakob & Beckmann, 1986; Kovelman & Scheibel, 1984; Weintraub, 1987). Although these latter findings clearly imply that risk factors for Schizophrenia are operative in utero, it is not yet known whether the cellular positioning abnormalities play a role in the pathophysiology of Schizophrenia or whether they are related to the gross morphological findings such as gray matter reduction.

Liability-Related versus Disease-Specific Brain Abnormalities

A question of major importance is whether some of the brain abnormalities associated with Schizophrenia are shared by the nonpsychotic first-degree relatives of these patients. Such a pattern could occur given the complexity of the inheritance of the disorder, in which multiple genes of small effect and a nontrivial environmental component aggregate to increase risk for phenotypic expression (T. D. Cannon, Kaprio, Lonnqvist, Huttunen, & Koskenvuo, 1998). That is, many first-degree relatives of Schizophrenia patients would be expected to carry one or more genes in a predisposing configuration but remain clinically unaffected.

There are now several studies demonstrating that unaffected biological relatives of patients with Schizophrenia display qualitatively similar, but quantitatively milder, neuropsychological impairments when compared with normal controls, even after accounting for substance abuse and other psychiatric diagnoses (T. D. Cannon, Huttunen, et al., 2000; Faraone et al., 1999; Park, Holzman, & Goldman-Rakic, 1995). Such findings support the view that these deficits are reflective of a diathesis for Schizophrenia, rather than resulting from the disease process or pharmacological intervention. T. D. Cannon et al. (1994) found that patients with Schizophrenia and their unaffected siblings showed similar patterns of deficit with regard to verbal memory, abstraction, attention, and language functions. Similarly, Toulopoulo, Rabe-Hesketh, King, Murray, and Morris (2003) showed that healthy relatives of patients with Schizophrenia exhibited deficits on verbal memory tasks, and Staal et al. (2000) reported frontal lobe impairment among unaffected siblings of patients with Schizophrenia. Other studies have reported attentional impairments among parents of patients with Schizophrenia (Michie et al., 2000).

Widespread neuropsychological deficits appear to be more severe among patients and relatives in multiply affected families. In the UCLA Family Study, normal control participants from the community with a family history of Schizophrenia had significantly poorer general intelligence, expressive and receptive vocabulary abilities, poorer visual-motor coordination, and slower motor speed than community controls without such a family loading (Asarnow et al., 2002). Additionally, Faraone et al. (2000) found that relatives from multiplex families (as defined by two or more first-degree relatives with Schizophrenia) had significantly lower scores on measures of estimated intelligence and verbal and visual recall than relatives from simplex families. Such findings support the hypothesis that impaired information processing aggregates among family members of patients with Schizophrenia and may serve as an indicator of genetic vulnerability to the disorder.

Findings of neuroanatomic abnormalities among unaffected relatives of patients with Schizophrenia may also be reflective of underlying genetic influences. Evidence from structural MRI studies of healthy relatives of patients with Schizophrenia have revealed global volumetric deficits (T. D. Cannon, van Erp, et al., 1998) and ventricular enlargement (Reveley, Reveley, Clifford, & Murray, 1982), as well as more specific structural anomalies. In a study involving a Helsinki birth cohort, significant reductions in frontal and temporal gray matter volumes and significant increases in the corresponding cerebrospinal fluid (CSF) regions were observed in both patients and their full siblings. In contrast, ventricular CSF volume increases and white matter reduction were apparent only among probands as compared to their siblings and unrelated controls (T. D. Cannon, Kaprio, et al., 1998). Reduced gray matter volume has been found among unaffected relatives outside the period of risk (Seidman et al., 1997, 1999; Suddath, Christison, Torrey, Casanova, & Weinberger, 1990), indicating that these gray matter reductions may be a stable vulnerability factor in relatives of Schizophrenia patients. Additionally, Seidman et al. (2002) found that relatives of patients with Schizophrenia, particularly those from multiplex families, had significantly smaller left hippocampal volumes as compared to matched controls. In these families, hippocampal volumes did not differ between patients with Schizophrenia and their nonpsychotic relatives.

In a recent functional MRI (fMRI) study, an N-back working memory task was employed to assess working memory-related cortical physiology in unaffected siblings of patients with Schizophrenia (Callicott et al., 2003). In this study, siblings showed an exaggerated physiological response in the right dorsolateral prefrontal cortex that appeared qualitatively similar to that seen in earlier fMRI studies of patients with Schizophrenia, indicating a primary physiological abnormality in prefrontal circuitry in individuals at elevated genetic risk for Schizophrenia without manifest cognitive abnormality. In addition, abnormal activation patterns in prefrontal and parietal regions during spatial working memory task performance have been reported in children of Schizophrenia patients (Keshavan et al., 2002).

Neurocognitive and neuroimaging studies of twins discordant for Schizophrenia allow for the separation of genetic and nongenetic contributions to the brain abnormalities associated with the illness. Because healthy monozygotic (MZ) and dizygotic (DZ) cotwins of patients with Schizophrenia differ by a ratio of 2:1 with regard to genetic liability for the disease, it is possible to test whether degree of cognitive or neuroanatomical deficit increases with genetic proximity to a proband. Further, because discordant MZ cotwins are 100% genetically identical, any abnormalities that are unique to or more severe in the affected compared with unaffected cotwins must be nongenetic in origin (M. Cannon, Jones, & Murray, 2002). A study of an epidemiologically ascertained sample of Finnish twins revealed that impaired performance on tests of spatial working memory and structural abnormalities in prefrontal brain regions varied in a dose-dependent fashion with degree of genetic loading for Schizophrenia. Specifically, MZ unaffected cotwins were significantly more impaired than DZ unaffected cotwins, who in turn were significantly impaired compared to control subjects (M. Cannon et al., 2002; T. D. Cannon, Huttunen, et al., 2000; Glahn et al., 2002). In contrast, deficits in long-term memory and anatomical changes in the hippocampus and adjacent temporal cortex were specifically more pronounced in patients compared with their own healthy MZ cotwins, indicating that nongenetic, disease-related factors must be involved in these abnormalities (T. D. Cannon, Huttunen, et al., 2000).

Given the substantial body of evidence indicating impairments in brain structure and function in relatives of patients with Schizophrenia, it should be possible to identify specific genes that underlie these disturbances. As one example, T. D. Cannon et al. (in press) examined a series of haplotype blocks of single nucleotide polymorphic (SNP) markers from a segment of chromosome 1q42 spanning the Disrupted-In-Schizophrenia-1 (DISC1) and Translin-Associated Factor-X (TRAX) genes, using samples of Finnish twin pairs concordant and discordant for Schizophrenia and healthy control twins. Recessive transmission of a common 3-SNP haplotype incorporating markers near a translocation breakpoint of DISC1 and dominant transmission of a rare 4-SNP haplotype incorporating markers from both the DISC1 and TRAX genes were significantly more common among individuals with Schizophrenia. These haplotypes were also associated with several quantitative endophenotypic traits previously observed to covary with Schizophrenia and genetic liability to Schizophrenia, including impairments in short- and long-term memory functioning and reduced gray matter density in the prefrontal cortex, as demonstrated using a population-based brain atlas methodology. Thus, specific alleles of the DISC1 and TRAX genes on 1q42 appear to contribute to genetic risk for Schizophrenia through disruptive effects on the structure and function of the prefrontal cortex and other brain regions, effects that are consistent with their production of proteins that play roles in neurite outgrowth, neuronal migration, synaptogenesis, and glutamatergic neurotransmission.

In the remaining sections, we evaluate the various lines of evidence bearing on the question of the sources, timing of onset, and course of brain abnormalities in Schizophrenia, dividing our consideration of these studies into those that implicate early developmental processes and those that suggest involvement of later developmental processes. Based on the foregoing, in general, one would expect that deficits associated with an inherited diathesis to Schizophrenia, such as structural and functional abnormalities of the prefrontal cortex, would be present before onset of illness and thus may be related to causal risk factors arising from early in life, whereas deficits that are more severe in the affected compared with unaffected MZ cotwins, such as structural and functional abnormalities of the medial temporal lobe, may be influenced by both early risk factors and those occurring more proximally to onset of formal diagnostic symptoms and signs.

THE CASE FOR INVOLVEMENT OF EARLY NEURODEVELOPMENTAL PROCESSES IN SCHIZOPHRENIA

There is now an accumulation of evidence that subtle indicators of disturbance are present long before illness onset in individuals who ultimately develop Schizophrenia. Here

we review these various lines of evidence; specifically, we examine the role of prenatal and perinatal complications in Schizophrenia, and evidence from high-risk studies examining early neurodevelopmental deviance in genetically vulnerable individuals.

The Role of Prenatal and Perinatal Complications in the Development of Schizophrenia

Of all early environmental factors proposed to play a role in the etiology of Schizophrenia, prenatal and perinatal complications, particularly those associated with fetal hypoxia, appear to be most robustly associated with increased risk for the disorder. Fetal hypoxia appears as a risk factor in a larger proportion of the cases (30% to 40%) than all forms of pregnancy complications (including viral exposure) and signs of fetal maldevelopment (T. D. Cannon, 1997). Complications associated with fetal hypoxia are also of interest because fetal oxygen deprivation represents a plausible mechanism for explaining much of the structural pathology of the brain detected in neuroimaging studies of adult patients with Schizophrenia (T. D. Cannon, 1997). For example, in an MRI study of a Helsinki birth cohort, we found that a history of fetal hypoxia was associated with significant decreases in gray matter density in both prefrontal and temporal lobe regions among patients with Schizophrenia and their healthy siblings, but not in controls at low genetic risk for the disorder, and more so in the patients than in their siblings (T. D. Cannon, van Erp, & Glahn, 2002). This pattern appears to be consistent with a genotype-environment interaction, in which hypoxia-related obstetric complications represent random environmental events, which may add to or multiply the risk for phenotypic expression of Schizophrenia when they occur in a genetically vulnerable individual.

The hippocampus in particular is acutely vulnerable to hypoxic-ischemic damage (Vargha-Khadem et al., 1997; Zola & Squire, 2001). One twin study showed that, among MZ twins discordant for Schizophrenia, relatively small hippocampi in the ill twin were significantly related to labor-delivery complications and to prolonged labor, both risk factors associated with fetal oxygen deprivation (McNeil, Cantor-Graae, & Weinberger, 2000). Van Erp et al. (2002) found that Schizophrenia probands who experienced fetal hypoxia have smaller hippocampal volumes than those who did not, a difference not noted among unaffected siblings and healthy comparison subjects. Moreover, hippocampal volume differences occurred in a stepwise fashion with each increase in genetic load for Schizophrenia, suggesting that, in patients with Schizophrenia spectrum disorders, hippocampal volume is influenced in part by Schizophrenia susceptibility genes, as well as an interaction of these genes with fetal hypoxia.

At the cellular level, the neural sequelae of hypoxia vary in severity from alterations in neurite outgrowth to neuronal cell death (Nyakas, Buwalda, & Luiten, 1996). In the former case, immature neurons may survive the hypoxic insult but still have a compromised elaboration of synaptic interconnections (Nyakas et al., 1996). More recent evidence from animal studies indicates that sublethal hypoxia results in global dysynchrony in brain maturation programs due to profound loss of coordinate regulation of neuronal gene transcription (Curristin et al., 2002). In a mouse model, chronic sublethal hypoxia resulted in alteration of 38% of genes subserving synaptic function, maturation, and neural transmission. Genes involved in myelination, glial maturation, and cytoskeletal organization were also affected, leading to retardation of synapse formation and reduction of cytoskeletal systems needed to form neuritic processes and synaptic structures. In addition, fetal hypoxia leads to up-regulation of stress and hypoxia response pathways, which may further retard neuronal maturation. Intriguing findings come from a rat model of Schizophrenia, in which direct lesions of the hippocampus early in life were found to produce deficits in prepulse inhibition, enhanced sensitivity to stress, and differential response to amphetamine, all of which do not become apparent until the postpubertal period (Lipska & Weinberger, 2002). Further, these investigators found that even transient inactivation of the ventral hippocampus during a critical period of development may be sufficient to disrupt normal maturation of the prefrontal cortex and trigger behavioral changes comparable to those observed in animals with permanent excitotoxic hippocampal lesions (Lipska & Weinberger, 2002).

Evidence for Cognitive, Motor, and Behavioral Impairment in Infancy and Childhood

Central to the neurodevelopmental hypothesis of Schizophrenia (Weinberger, 1987) is the identification of developmental anomalies preceding overt clinical symptoms of the disorder (M. Cannon et al., 2002; Weinberger, 1987). Retrospective studies, as well as high-risk studies of the offspring of parents with Schizophrenia, have consistently demonstrated the existence of cognitive impairment and behavioral and neurobiologic abnormalities long before the onset of Schizophrenia. Such studies offer substantial evidence that such early events may be less quiescent and more function-

ally apparent than was previously believed. Although the majority of patients with Schizophrenia show no signs of outright psychotic symptomatology until adolescence or early adulthood, there is substantial evidence that the pathologic processes that predispose to the disorder are evident earlier in life in more subtle forms.

In the domain of cognitive development, one meta-analysis of the high-risk literature (Aylward, Walker, & Bettes, 1984) revealed that preschizophrenic children showed deficits on standard IQ tests in comparison with matched groups of peers or siblings who did not develop psychiatric illness. Moreover, such deficits were shown to predict an early-onset form of Schizophrenia with poor prognostic features. Similarly, longitudinal high-risk studies have consistently found children of parents with Schizophrenia to perform more poorly on neuropsychological tests than children of parents with no history of psychiatric illness (Asarnow & MacCrimmon, 1978; Bergman & Walker, 1995; Fish, 1987; Goodman, 1987; Hallett, Quinn, & Hewitt, 1986; Landau, Harth, Othnay, & Sharfhertz, 1972; Lifshitz, Kugelmass, & Karov, 1985; Marcus, Hans, Auerbach, & Auerbach, 1993; Mednick & Schulsinger, 1964; Sameroff, Seifer, Zax, & Barocas, 1987; Schreiber, Stolz-Born, Kornhuber, & Born, 1992; Sohlberg, 1985; Weintraub, 1987). Such studies have shown that children with an elevated risk for Schizophrenia exhibit deficits in attention (Erlenmeyer-Kimling & Cornblatt, 1978; Weintraub, 1987), language (Gruzelier, Mednick, & Schulsinger, 1979; Hallett et al., 1986; Harvey, Winters, Weintraub, & Neale, 1981), learning and memory (Driscoll, 1984; Klein & Salzman, 1984; Rutschmann, Cornblatt, & Erlenmeyer-Kimling, 1980), and other information-processing domains (Erlenmeyer-Kimling & Cornblatt, 1987).

Early receptive (M. Cannon et al., 2002) and expressive (Bearden et al., 2000) language abnormalities are a robust finding among retrospective studies of individuals with Schizophrenia. Premorbid impairments of language production and comprehension are particularly striking in childhood-onset Schizophrenia (Hollis, 1995; Nicolson et al., 2000), suggesting that there may be a specific link between very early onset cases and impairment in the processes underlying language development. This notion is supported by a follow-back study of patients with childhood-onset Schizophrenia (Asarnow, 1999) showing that nearly 80% of the sample exhibited gross deficits in early language development. However, at follow-up during late childhood, these children performed within the expected range on multiple tests of language function, indicating that these skills are delayed but are not static neuropsychological deficits.

In contrast, attentional deficits may represent a trait marker of vulnerability to Schizophrenia. The New York High Risk Project has followed children at risk for Schizophrenia and affective disorder (by virtue of having an affected parent) for over 30 years with neurocognitive, behavioral, and clinical measures. In this study, impairments in attention and short-term memory were detectable by a mean age of 9 in children at high risk for Schizophrenia, a time when subjects were free of any overt behavioral signs of illness (e.g., Cornblatt, Lenzenweger, Dworkin, & Erlenmeyer-Kimling, 1992; Erlenmeyer-Kimling & Cornblatt, 1978, 1987). Subjects who later developed a Schizophrenia spectrum disorder consistently displayed a lower performance level on the continuous performance test (CPT), a measure of sustained and selective attention, relative to subjects in all comparison groups (unaffected children of parents with Schizophrenia, children of parents with affective disorder, and normal comparison subjects), and the magnitude of this deficit remained constant across development. Further, a measure of cognitive performance deviance at age 9 (composed largely of CPT performance measures) had high specificity and moderate sensitivity for predicting relatively serious behavioral disturbances (including social impairment and problems at school and at home) emerging in high-risk subjects during mid-adolescence (Cornblatt & Erlenmeyer-Kimling, 1985). These findings suggest that these early attentional deficits are associated with later emerging social difficulties in genetically at-risk individuals (Cornblatt et al., 1992).

Although high-risk studies have been instrumental in revealing a relationship between genetic liability to Schizophrenia and early forms of impairment, such findings may not be generalizable, given that only 5% to 10% of patients with Schizophrenia have a parent with Schizophrenia. Further, because offspring in most high-risk samples have not passed through the period of elevated risk for onset of Schizophrenia, and those that have include only a small number of participants who ultimately develop the disorder, there are limited data on the degree to which early deficits predict adult Schizophrenia in such samples. Thus, population-based cohorts are necessary to determine which precursors, or combination thereof, represent true risk factors for Schizophrenia. Using data from the 1946 British birth cohort, Jones, Rodgers, Murray, and Marmot (1994) found that individuals who were later diagnosed with Schizophrenia had lower educational test scores at ages 8, 11, and 15 than nonpsychiatric controls from the same cohort. Additionally, there was a linear trend of increased risk for Schizophrenia across decreasing levels of cognitive performance, which became stronger with age. In

a study of male conscripts from the 1969 to 1970 Swedish army cohort, David, Malmberg, Brandt, Allebeck, and Lewis (1997) demonstrated a similar linear relationship between IQ at age 18 and subsequent development of Schizophrenia, such that the risk for Schizophrenia increased as IQ decreased across the range of cognitive ability. In a Philadelphia birth cohort of approximately 10,000 subjects, T. D. Cannon, Huttunen, et al. (2000) found significant cognitive impairment in school-age individuals who later developed Schizophrenia. Moreover, there were significant linear trends in the distribution of IQ scores, indicating that preschizophrenic individuals were significantly over-represented in the lowest quintile of cognitive performance and increasingly under-represented among the upper quintiles.

There remains some question as to the developmental course of such early cognitive impairments in preschizophrenic individuals. Russell, Munro, Jones, Hemsley, and Murray (1997) examined change in IQ among individuals who presented to Maudsley Hospital as children and subsequently developed Schizophrenia as adults. Although the mean Full-Scale IQ (FSIQ) in this group was over 1 standard deviation below the scores of the general population, there was no evidence of a decline from child to adult IQ. The authors concluded that the deficit in intellectual function observed in Schizophrenia may be present in childhood and remain stable throughout this developmental period. In contrast to the findings of Russell et al., a study of Israeli military draftees found that draftees who eventually developed Schizophrenia showed a measurable decline in cognitive performance that began about 2 years prior to illness onset, concomitant with impaired social functioning that became progressively worse during the course of late adolescence (Davidson et al., 1999). Consistent with this finding, adolescent and young adult participants in the Edinburgh High Risk Study exhibited significantly lower premorbid IQ, as assessed by the National Adult Reading Test, and lower FSIQ on the Weschler Adult Intelligence Scale at baseline when compared to controls (Byrne, Hodges, Grant, Owens, & Johnstone, 1999). At 2-year follow-up, those high-risk participants who had experienced an increase in psychotic symptoms exhibited an apparent decline in IQ and memory (Cosway et al., 2000), suggesting that onset of psychosis may coincide with a decline in cognitive function.

There is considerable variation in the kind of early behavioral problems displayed by individuals who ultimately develop Schizophrenia. Retrospective and prospective cohort studies have consistently documented the existence of abnormalities in premorbid social development in preschizophrenic individuals, ranging from solitary play preference at age 4 to social anxiety, withdrawal, and acting-out behavior in adolescence (Jones et al., 1994). Preschizophrenic children are more likely than comparison children to be described by their teachers as "introverted," "disagreeable" and "emotionally unstable" (Watt, 1978). Studies of childhood films have additionally revealed affective abnormalities in preschizophrenic children, with increases in negative facial expression as early as age 1 (Walker, Grimes, Davis, & Smith, 1993), suggesting that vulnerability to Schizophrenia may be associated more generally with "difficult" infant temperament (Walker, Lewine, & Neumann, 1996). In a prospective longitudinal study of a Philadelphia birth cohort, social maladjustment at age 7 was a significant predictor of adult Schizophrenia (Bearden et al., 2000). Rates of deviant behaviors (e.g., echolalia, meaningless laughter, and stereotyped behaviors) at ages 4 and 7 were significantly elevated in both preschizophrenic children and their unaffected siblings, suggesting that such problems may indicate genotypic susceptibility to the disorder and/or shared early environmental influences.

Interestingly, there is some evidence that childhood behavior problems among patients with Schizophrenia may provide clues regarding their ultimate illness presentation. For example, in the Copenhagen High-Risk Study, Cannon, Mednick, Parnas, et al. (1993) found different patterns of premorbid behavior among patients with predominantly negative or predominantly positive symptom Schizophrenia. Specifically, positive symptoms (i.e., hallucinations, delusions, thought disorder) were correlated with premorbid conduct disorder and acting-out behavior, and those patients with predominantly negative symptoms (i.e., apathy, anhedonia, social withdrawal) had more severe premorbid social maladjustment than those without such symptoms. Other studies have similarly documented poorer premorbid functioning and insidious onset with a predominantly negative symptom picture, providing support for the positive-negative symptom distinction in terms of natural history (McGlashan & Fenton, 1992; Pogue-Geile & Harrow, 1984).

Neurologic and motor abnormalities have also been identified in children vulnerable to Schizophrenia (Marcus, Auerbach, Wilkinson, & Burack, 1981; Mednick & Schulsinger, 1964). Fish (1977) found evidence of early neurological disturbance and delays in gross motor skills and visual-motor development in infant children of mothers with Schizophrenia. These infants tended to show unusually quiet behavior, including hypotonia, absence of crying, and underactivity. In a follow-up study, significant correlations were reported between the severity of neu-

rointegrative deficit and adult psychiatric status (Fish, 1987). Similarly, longitudinal follow-up of infants studied as part of the Jerusalem Infant Development Study revealed that the neurobehavioral deficits displayed in infancy by offspring of schizophrenic parents persisted over time, and the children who had developed Schizophrenia spectrum diagnoses by adolescence demonstrated poor neurobehavioral functioning across the developmental periods studied (Hans et al., 1999). A study of home movies obtained from families in which one child later developed Schizophrenia indicated that preschizophrenic children had significantly more neuromotor abnormalities and less developed motor skills than both their healthy siblings and individuals who later developed affective disorder (Walker, Savoie, & Davis, 1994). These findings have been confirmed in general population studies. In a Finnish birth cohort, early achievement of developmental milestones reduced the risk for psychotic disorder, whereas delayed milestones were predictive of psychosis (Isohanni et al., 2001). Additionally, two British cohort studies found that preschizophrenic children were retarded in their attainment of gross motor milestones during the first 2 years of life and were impaired on tests of motor coordination at 7 years of age (Crow, Done, & Sacker, 1995; Jones et al., 1994). Further, delayed motor development during infancy and impaired motor coordination during childhood have consistently discriminated between individuals at high and low genetic risk for Schizophrenia, indicating that early motor deviance may be a marker of genetic liability (Egan et al., 2001). Consistent with this interpretation, in the Philadelphia cohort of the National Collaborative Perinatal Project (NCPP), Rosso, Bearden, et al. (2000) found that deviance on motor coordination measures at age 7 was associated with both adult Schizophrenia and unaffected sibling status, suggesting that a cofamilial (and perhaps genetic) factor underlies motor coordination deficits in Schizophrenia. In addition, adolescents with schizotypal personality disorder have been reported to have elevated rates of involuntary movements of the head, trunk, and upper limbs as compared to nonill comparison subjects and adolescents with other personality disorders, further supporting the notion that certain motor abnormalities may reflect a genetic vulnerability to the disorder (Walker, Diforio, & Baum, 1999).

Several high-risk studies have found that the presence of multiple premorbid indicators, across domains of functioning, are associated with an elevated risk for Schizophrenia over and above single risk factors (Fish, 1987; Goodman, 1987; Marcus, Hans, Mednick, Schulsinger, & Michelsen, 1985). Consistent with this literature, findings from the

Philadelphia cohort of the NCPP showed that preschizophrenic children were more likely to exhibit multiple signs of impairment. This finding became increasingly pronounced over the course of development (T. D. Cannon, Rosso, Bearden, Sanchez, & Hadley, 1999). Evidence from the Dunedin, New Zealand, Health and Development Study further supports these findings, showing that persistent, multidimensional impairment in early childhood predicts psychotic symptoms in childhood and adulthood (M. Cannon et al., 2002). Whereas emotional problems and interpersonal difficulties were present in children who later developed psychotic, mood, or anxiety disorders, significant impairments in neuromotor, receptive language, and cognitive development were present only among children later diagnosed with schizophreniform disorder. This study also provides some of the first evidence of continuity of psychotic symptoms over the life span: Self-reported delusional beliefs and hallucinatory experiences at age 11 predicted a 16-fold increase in risk for schizophreniform disorder (but not mood disorder) at age 26 (Poulton et al., 2000). Such investigations are critical for the delineation of compelling risk factors that may increase positive predictive value in the identification of young people at risk for Schizophrenia.

Interestingly, there is emerging evidence suggesting that functional impairment during adolescence may have more predictive value in the identification of young people at high risk for Schizophrenia than that attained in studies of childhood functioning (Davidson et al., 1999). Because of this, epidemiologic studies of Schizophrenia risk have begun to move forward in the ontology of the illness, progressing from stages that clearly precede clinical signs of the disorder to those more proximal to the onset of psychosis (Cornblatt, Lencz, & Obuchowski, 2002).

THE CASE FOR INVOLVEMENT OF LATER NEURODEVELOPMENTAL PROCESSES IN SCHIZOPHRENIA

By definition, a substantial decline in role functioning and a severe disruption in integrated cognitive and emotional processing occurs around the time of onset of Schizophrenia during late adolescence and early adulthood. In view of this pattern, it is tempting to postulate that there are brain changes in addition to those instantiated through early neurodevelopmental influences that occur proximally to the onset of psychosis, thus acting as triggers for this functional

decline and psychotic symptom expression (see right section of Figure 14.1). As noted previously, the most well-established disease-related deficits in Schizophrenia involve frontal and temporal lobe structures, abnormalities of which have been linked to the occurrence of hypoxia-associated birth complications among individuals with Schizophrenia. Nevertheless, as we shall see, the hippocampus and surrounding temporal cortex are also among the regions that have been shown in some studies to deteriorate in the early course of Schizophrenia (Giedd et al., 1999). The question then becomes, if these disease-related deficits are present to some degree from early in life, what mechanisms cause them to further deteriorate in adolescence/early adulthood, and are these mechanisms primary or secondary to the emergence of psychosis?

Anatomical Changes in First-Episode Schizophrenia

Longitudinal prospective studies of patients during their first episode of psychosis can deepen our understanding of late processes underlying onset of Schizophrenia, as these patients have had minimal exposure to potential confounding factors, such as pharmacological agents and chronicity (Bagary et al., 2003). Moreover, there is evidence that structural brain changes associated with Schizophrenia are at their peak intensity during the initial stage of illness (Gur et al., 1998; Kasai et al., 2003). Several lines of evidence suggest that developmental anomalies associated with Schizophrenia may vary depending on the developmental stage of the individual at illness onset (Brewer et al., 2003; Mathalon, Rapoport, Davis, & Krystal, 2003; Mehler & Warnke, 2002). The National Institute of Mental Health (NIMH) study of childhood-onset Schizophrenia has been instrumental in shedding light on the ways in which age of onset may interact with normative developmental processes during early disease progression. Thompson et al. (2001) analyzed repeated high-resolution MRI brain scans of adolescent patients with childhood-onset Schizophrenia. The authors discovered a dynamic pattern of gray matter loss that began in the parietal region and progressed forward to the temporal and frontal cortices. The final pattern of loss was consistent with cross-sectional studies of adults with Schizophrenia, showing a relatively greater degree of reduction in frontal and temporal cortical volumes. Further reports from the NIMH study have revealed deviant patterns of development in the corpus callosum and the cerebellum among patients with childhood-onset Schizophrenia (Keller, Castellanos, et al.,

2003; Keller, Jeffries, et al., 2003). Notably, there appears to be diagnostic specificity to this pattern of progressive gray matter loss: For children and adolescents with transient psychotic symptoms that did not meet criteria for Schizophrenia, gray matter reduction over time did not differ from that observed in healthy comparison subjects (Gogtay et al., 2003). These patients provide a valuable comparison group to the childhood-onset Schizophrenia patients because they had a similar level of cognitive functioning and had received a similar course of treatment with antipsychotic medication, indicating that these brain changes are intrinsic to the illness and do not result from medication exposure. In addition, the unaffected siblings of these childhood-onset Schizophrenia patients were found to have smaller total brain volume and reduced total, frontal, and parietal gray matter volume as compared to healthy controls (Gogtay et al., 2003). When divided into younger and older age groups, the younger siblings (under 18 years old) had smaller parietal gray matter volumes than matched controls, and older siblings showed trends toward smaller total cerebral volume and smaller frontal gray matter volume. Although a longitudinal study is required to confirm the significance of this finding, it suggests that healthy siblings of childhood-onset Schizophrenia patients share neuroanatomic abnormalities that may follow a similar pattern of developmental progression.

Findings from longitudinal prospective studies of adult first-episode patients have been mixed. Some studies have revealed broad changes in whole-brain volume but no detectable progression in specific regions, such as the temporal or frontal lobe structures (Cahn et al., 2002; DeLisi et al., 1997; Pantelis, Yucel, Wood, McGorry, & Velakoulis, 2003). Other studies of adults have revealed patterns of change similar to those seen in patients with childhood-onset Schizophrenia but of a much smaller magnitude (Gur et al., 1998). One study of adolescents and adults with recent-onset Schizophrenia, which utilized high-resolution scanning and differentiated gray and white matter, showed progressive decreases in gray matter volume in the left superior temporal gyrus during the 1st year and a half following initial hospitalization, followed by a leveling off of cortical deterioration (Kasai et al., 2003). To better understand age-related differences in brain development, future studies should differentiate between patterns of change in adolescents and adults. The only longitudinal imaging study that has specifically focused on patients with adolescent-onset Schizophrenia failed to show a pattern of progressive reduction in gray matter volume (James, Javaloyes, James, & Smith, 2002), except in the posterior inferior vermis

among male participants (James, James, Smith, & Javaloyes, 2004). The authors speculated that their negative findings may have reflected a leveling off of gray matter loss in late adolescence, as was found in the NIMH study (Sporn et al., 2003). However, it is notable that this study included a very small patient sample ($n = 16$). Thus, replication is warranted to determine if the degree of progressive gray matter loss found in the NIMH study is specific to childhood-onset Schizophrenia, or if similar patterns will be seen among adolescent-onset patients as they go through the same period of development.

Several studies have begun to explore the association between structural brain changes and clinical presentation during the first 2 years of illness. Gur et al. (1998) found that reductions in frontal and temporal lobe volume were associated with less improvement in negative symptoms and hallucinations in first-episode adult patients, as well as greater improvement with regard to delusions, when controlling for medication dose and compliance. Similar results have been reported by Sporn and colleagues (2003) and DeLisi, Sakuma, Ge, and Kushner (1998). In discussing these findings, investigators have proposed that this inverse relationship may be reflective of a process by which diseased tissue is removed through "compensatory pruning" (Gur et al., 1998; Sporn et al., 2003). In other words, it may be that the brain's normative process of synaptic elimination results in the removal of deviant neural connections, thus leading to clinical improvement.

Recently, there has been a debate in the literature regarding the value of longitudinal MRI studies for understanding the developmental neurobiology of Schizophrenia (Mathalon et al., 2003; Weinberger & McClure, 2002). Weinberger and McClure have challenged the validity of such studies for several reasons. First, they argue that the rates of neurodegeneration that have been reported in the literature seem unreasonably high, such that "by the time a patient with Schizophrenia reached age 60, there would be little brain left" (p. 556). Mathalon et al. counter this argument by citing evidence that rates of decline in gray matter level off with age, thus preserving significant brain tissue. Weinberger and McClure also note that variation in measurement and analysis techniques within and across studies makes it difficult to interpret findings. In response, Mathalon et al. point out that "the general convergence of recent findings despite these myriad sources of variance supports the likelihood that progressive morphometric changes in Schizophrenia do occur" (p. 846). These authors concede that longitudinal MRI studies cannot illuminate the mechanisms underlying progressive structural change, but they emphasize the importance of these findings in moving the field beyond a strict "early influences" neurodevelopmental model.

Neuropsychological Changes in First-Episode Schizophrenia

Neuropsychological studies have similarly revealed that age of onset is a source of heterogeneity among patients with first-episode psychosis. Specifically, findings generally suggest that earlier onset yields more significant impairment across domains of cognitive functioning (Basso, Nasrallah, Olson, & Bornstein, 1997; Collinson et al., 2003). For example, Basso et al. compared adolescent-onset and adult-onset patients with chronic Schizophrenia and showed that patients with adolescent onset performed significantly less well than did patients with adult-onset Schizophrenia, particularly on memory and executive function tasks. Pantelis and colleagues (Pantelis, Velakoulis, et al., 2003) hypothesized that brain functions that typically develop during the peak period of risk will be most impaired among patients with Schizophrenia. For example, this group of investigators showed that working memory, a skill that develops throughout adolescence and peaks at age 20 (Pantelis, Velakoulis, et al., 2003), was more compromised among individuals in their sample of adolescents and young adults with Schizophrenia than was set shifting, a cognitive function that purportedly emerges earlier in development.

Studies exploring the longitudinal course of cognitive functioning during the initial stages of Schizophrenia may provide clues to the pathophysiology of the disorder. Such investigations have revealed that, in general, adults with first-episode Schizophrenia are impaired across broad domains of cognitive functioning but do not exhibit significant deterioration in abilities during the initial stages of illness. On the other hand, some cognitive abilities appear to show moderate improvement during this same period (DeLisi et al., 1995; Gold, Arndt, Nopoulos, O'Leary, & Andreasen, 1999; Heydebrand et al., 2003; Hoff et al., 1999), possibly as a result of treatment with antipsychotic medication and/or acute symptom remission. The one longitudinal study of cognitive function in first-episode adolescent patients used a cross-sectional design comparing recent-onset and chronic adolescent patients (Kravariti, Morris, Rabe-Hesketh, Murray, & Frangou, 2003). Results showed that patients at all stages of illness exhibited deficits in broad domains of cognitive functioning, but there was no evidence that chronic patients were more impaired than those with recent onset. These findings suggest

a lack of progressive deterioration in cognitive function over the course of illness.

Investigations of the relation between cognitive functioning and clinical features during the initial stage of Schizophrenia have shown that improvement with regard to negative symptoms is associated with enhanced performance on tests of memory, verbal fluency, psychomotor speed, and executive function (Heydebrand et al., 2003), as well as Performance IQ (PIQ) and FSIQ (Gold et al., 1999).

Magnetic Resonance Spectroscopy Studies

Although direct measures of abnormal neuronal growth and degeneration processes are difficult to quantify in vivo, nuclear magnetic resonance spectroscopy (MRS) offers a method of assessing brain phospholipid and energy metabolism that corresponds to developmental neuronal changes. This methodology allows a noninvasive investigation of human brain development and is well suited to identifying abnormalities in synaptic pruning that may occur in adolescence (Pettegrew, Klunk, Panchalingam, McClure, & Stanley, 2000). Two MRS techniques that are currently utilized in Schizophrenia research are phosphorus magnetic resonance spectroscopy (^{31}P-MRS) and proton magnetic resonance spectroscopy (^{1}H-MRS). In vivo ^{31}P-MRS examines indirect indicators of cell membrane synthesis and degradation in addition to measures of energy metabolism (Ross & Michaelis, 1994). ^{31}P-MRS studies have identified alterations of membrane phospholipid metabolites in the frontal cortex of first-episode, neuroleptic-naïve Schizophrenia subjects, as compared to matched controls (Keshavan, Pettegrew, Panchalingam, & Kaplan, 1991; Pettegrew, Keshavan, Panchalingam, & Strychor, 1991; Williamson, Pelz, Merskey, & Morrison, 1991), suggesting decreased synthesis and increased breakdown of membrane phospholipids in recent-onset Schizophrenia patients. This pattern resembles an exaggerated form of the changes observed in normal aging (Pettegrew & Minshew, 1992). Such findings may reflect an increase in membrane phospholipid turnover, perhaps because of an accelerated synaptic pruning process during late childhood and early adolescence (Keshavan et al., 2003). Keshavan et al. (1991) also found this pattern in one case prior to onset, suggesting that this process may be causally related to the onset of the disorder.

To further address this neurodevelopmental perspective, Stanley et al. (1995) used ^{31}P-MRS to examine the dorsolateral prefrontal cortex (DLPFC) in 11 drug-naïve, 8 newly diagnosed and medicated, and 10 medicated and chronic patients with Schizophrenia. Results showed decreased phospholipid synthesis in all three groups, which implies lower levels of cell membrane synthesis at all stages of the disorder. Additionally, there was an increased level of phospholipid breakdown in the drug-naïve group, suggesting that earlier stages of Schizophrenia may be characterized by increased breakdown of cell membranes. At the level of structural neuroanatomy, these metabolic changes may correspond to increased gray matter volume loss in the early stages of illness. Abnormalities in phospholipid metabolism have also been observed in the DLPFC of high-risk adolescents (Keshavan, Stanley, Montrose, Minshew, & Pettegrew, 2003; Klemm et al., 2001; Rzanny et al., 2003). Such findings of aberrant phospholipid metabolism suggest a pattern of increased membrane turnover at illness onset with a continued pattern of membrane abnormalities throughout the course of the disorder (Berger et al., 2002).

^{1}H-MRS also provides indirect measures of metabolites related to neuronal and glial energy metabolism as well as phopholipid metabolism (Ross & Michaelis, 1994). Of the metabolites examined in ^{1}H-MRS, N-Acetylaspartate (NAA) is primarily seen as a marker of neuronal integrity (Keshavan, Stanley, & Pettegrew, 2000) that can be used to identify neurons and their dendritic and axonal extensions and is mostly concentrated in pyramidal neurons. NAA increases during the course of normal development until the adolescent period, when there is a decrease associated with pruning of superfluous neuronal connections. This is less drastic than the sharp decrease in NAA that is seen in neurodegenerative diseases (Moore, Slovis, & Chugani, 1998). Choline includes metabolites that are involved in the synthesis of myelin and cell membrane metabolism (Ross & Michaelis, 1994), and creatine (Cr) is defined as a general marker of energy metabolism (Passe, Charles, Rajagopalan, & Krishnan, 1995). The observation of decreased levels of NAA or a decreased NAA:Cr ratio is believed to indicate some form of neuronal loss, such as synaptic pruning or neuronal dysfunction, whereas increased levels of choline or an increased choline:Cr ratio signals deafferentiation (Ross & Michaelis, 1994). Glutamine is primarily found in glial cells; decreased levels of this metabolite are thought to represent neuronal loss, dysfunction, or deafferentiation (Ross & Michaelis, 1994).

Studies of ^{1}H-MRS in Schizophrenia have consistently reported reduced NAA levels in the hippocampus, mesial temporal lobe, and frontal lobe, including the DLPFC, in both adult- (Bertolino & Weinberger, 1999; Steel et al., 2001) and child-onset schizophrenic patients (Bertolino et al., 1998). Significant reductions in NAA:Cr ratios have been found in these regions in both chronic Schizophrenia patients (Bertolino et al., 1996; Yamasue et al., 2002; Yurgelun-Todd et al., 1996) and neuroleptic-naïve first-

episode patients (Cecil et al., 1998), as well as children with Schizophrenia spectrum disorders (Brooks et al., 1998). Supporting the idea that NAA:Cr ratio may mark genetic vulnerability to Schizophrenia, Callicott et al. (1998) showed a decreased NAA:Cr ratio in the hippocampi of both schizophrenic patients and their unaffected siblings when compared to healthy controls. Moreover, Keshavan and colleagues (1997) found that offspring of parents with Schizophrenia showed a reduced NAA:choline ratio in the anterior cingulate region when compared to healthy controls. Recent studies of neuroleptic-naïve patients with Schizophrenia (Bartha et al., 1997; Theberge et al., 2002) and offspring of parents with Schizophrenia (Tibbo, Hanstock, Valiakalayil, & Allen, 2004) have also revealed increased glutamate/glutamine levels in the medial frontal cortex, anterior cingulate, and thalamus, signaling possible dysfunction of glutamate in the pathogenesis of Schizophrenia.

Thus, although these studies demonstrate that altered NAA levels in frontal and temporal regions are associated with risk for Schizophrenia, it is not yet clear how anomalies in brain metabolites highlighted by MRS techniques correspond to brain volumetric changes and abnormalities of cellular migration in Schizophrenia. Some researchers have suggested that findings of decreased frontal NAA ratios may be related to effects of long-term antipsychotic treatment (Bustillo et al., 2001, 2002). Future refinements in MRS methodology offer the promise of more detailed exploration of neurogenesis and the processes of myelination, synaptic pruning, and gliosis.

The Schizophrenia Prodrome

With the shift in focus from a neurodevelopmental model of Schizophrenia to increasing interest in more proximal developmental risk factors, a new research strategy has emerged. Building on traditional high-risk approaches, the so-called ultra-high-risk (UHR) paradigm (Yung & McGorry, 1996; Yung et al., 1998) goes beyond indicators of genetic vulnerability to focus on clinical features that are believed to reflect heightened vulnerability for psychosis. A central goal in UHR research is to prospectively follow a well-characterized group of putatively prodromal individuals through the period of conversion to gain a deeper understanding of the progression of clinical, biological, and neurocognitive changes that characterize the onset of psychosis (T. D. Cannon et al., 2003; Meyer et al., 2005). Such studies may enhance our understanding of the pathophysiology of psychotic illness and allow for the discrimination of the Schizophrenia prodrome from that of other conditions (e.g., affective psychosis), thus informing early treatment strategies (Phillips, Yung, Yuen, Pantelis, & McGorry, 2002). Finally, results of UHR research may aid in identifying late risk factors for the transition into psychosis, as well as protective factors or interventions that may alleviate, delay, or possibly prevent the onset of psychotic illness (T. D. Cannon et al., 2003; Yung et al., 2003).

Developmentally, the prodrome can be viewed as the transition between the premorbid and psychotic stages of illness (Cornblatt et al., 2002; Yung & McGorry, 1996). The first signal of deterioration occurs within 3 to 5 years of onset and consists of a constellation of gradually developing, low-grade psychiatric symptoms and signs, including reduced concentration (attention), decreased drive and motivation (anergia), depressed mood, sleep disturbance, anxiety, social withdrawal, suspiciousness, deterioration in role functioning, and irritability. Because these symptoms and signs are nonspecific—they also appear in primary affective and anxiety states—we refer to this initial period as the "predifferentiation" phase. The predifferentiation phase is typically followed, within about 1 year of onset, by the emergence of subpsychotic disturbances of thought and perception, including paranoid ideation, ideas of reference, unusual beliefs/magical thinking, perceptual disturbances (e.g., depersonalization, derealization), changes in thought and speech patterns, and atypical behavior and/or appearance. As these features represent attenuated forms of the cardinal symptoms and signs of psychosis, we refer to this period as the "differentiation" phase. The differentiation phase is often followed, within a few months of onset, by the emergence of transient psychotic symptoms, including hallucinations, delusions, and/or disorganized speech, which subside spontaneously within a period of a few hours to several days. We refer to this period of brief intermittent psychotic symptoms as the "micropsychotic" phase. The micropsychotic phase is considered to have evolved into full-blown Schizophrenia when prodromal behavioral features have been present continuously for at least 6 months and psychotic symptoms have persisted continuously for at least 1 month (American Psychiatric Association, 1994).

Over the past decade, investigators have identified three putatively prodromal syndromes that map onto the developmental sequence described. Criteria for these syndromes currently focus on three groups of individuals: (1) those who are experiencing attenuated positive psychotic symptoms that have emerged or worsened in the past year, (2) those who describe brief and intermittent periods of frank psychotic symptoms with recent onset, and (3) those with familial risk for a psychotic disorder and who have experi-

enced a significant decline in functioning in the past year. Operational definitions for these syndromes differ slightly across research programs. Table 14.1 presents the most widely used criteria for diagnosing the three prodromal states: the Criteria of Prodromal Syndromes (COPS; T. J. Miller et al., 2003) and the Comprehensive Assessment of At-Risk Mental States (CAARMS; Yung et al., 2003).

Although attempts to define the prodrome prospectively in clinical samples are relatively recent, initial evidence indicates that 22% to 54% of treatment-seeking individuals ascertained in a putatively prodromal state will convert to full-blown psychotic disorder within 2 years (McGlashan, Miller, & Woods, 2001; McGorry, Yung, & Phillips, 2003; Yung & McGorry, 1996; Yung et al., 1998). Thus, these studies offer the unique opportunity to identify behavioral and neurobiological markers most predictive of Schizophrenia outcome and, by extension, to develop interventions that may be implemented prior to onset of the full-blown disorder.

Results thus far have identified several baseline clinical variables that appear to be predictive of conversion to psychosis over and above prodromal criteria alone. Specifically, findings from the Melbourne Prodromal Study (Yung et al., 2003) suggest that poor functioning, as indicated by the following, was predictive of conversion to psychosis in their prodromal sample: a global assessment of functioning (GAF) score less than 51; prolonged duration of untreated prodromal symptoms (>900 days); high overall level of psychopathology, as measured by a total score on the Brief Psychiatric Rating Scale (BPRS) greater than 15; subthreshold psychotic symptoms, as measured by a BPRS psychotic subscale score greater than 2; depression, as measured by a Hamilton score greater than 18; and clinically significant avolition and anxiety. Strikingly, 87% of those participants who had four or more of these risk factors converted to psychosis within 6 months after study entry.

Investigators have also begun to explore neuropsychological and structural brain changes associated with conversion to psychosis. Early results from the Melbourne UHR study suggest that none of the neuropsychological variables that were assessed at baseline successfully distinguished between those UHR patients who converted to psychosis and those who did not (Wood et al., 2003). Investigators from this study examined tasks of spatial working memory and delayed matching-to-sample in 38 young people at ultra high-risk of developing psychosis (of whom nine later became psychotic), as compared to 49 healthy controls. Performance on both tasks was significantly poorer in the UHR group overall. Those who later became psychotic generally performed more poorly than

TABLE 14.1   Criteria for the Three Prodromal Syndromes as Defined by the Criteria of Prodromal Syndromes (COPS) and the Comprehensive Assessment of At-Risk Mental States (CAARMS)

		Criteria of Prodromal Syndromes (COPS; T. Miller et al., 2003)	Comprehensive Assessment of At-Risk Mental States (CAARMS; Yung et al., 2003)
Group 1	Attenuated Positive Symptom Syndrome	At least one of the following five scales is scored within the attenuated range: 1. Unusual thought content/delusional ideas. 2. Suspiciousness/persecutory ideas. 3. Grandiosity. 4. Perceptual abnormalities/hallucinations. 5. Disorganized communication. Symptoms began within the past year or have intensified within the past year. Symptoms have occurred at least once per week for the past month.	At least one of the following symptoms is scored within the attenuated range and held with a reasonable degree of conviction, as defined by a score of 2 on the Comprehensive Assessment of Symptoms and History (CASH; Andreasen et al., 1992): 1. Ideas of reference. 2. Odd beliefs or magical thinking. 3. Perceptual disturbance. 4. Paranoid ideation. 5. Off thinking and speech. 6. Odd behavior and appearance. Symptoms have been present for at least 1 week and no longer than 5 years. Symptoms occur at least several times per week.
Group 2	Brief Intermittent Psychotic Symptoms Syndrome (SIPS) OR Brief Limited Intermittent Psychotic Symptoms (CAARMS)	One or more of the above five scales is scored within the psychotic range. Symptoms began in the past 3 months. Symptoms presently occur for at least several minutes per day at least once per month.	Transient positive psychotic symptoms last less than a week. Symptoms resolve spontaneously. Onset is within the past year.
Group 3	Genetic Risk and Deterioration Syndrome (SIPS) OR Trait and State Risk Factors (CAARMS)	Participant has a first-degree relative with a history of any psychotic disorder. OR Participant meets criteria for Schizotypal Personality Disorder. Participant has experienced a 30% drop in global assessment of functioning (GAF) from premorbid level. Change in GAF has lasted for at least a month.	Participant has a first-degree relative with a psychotic disorder or Schizotypal Personality Disorder. OR Participant meets criteria for Schizotypal Personality Disorder. Participant has experienced a 30-point drop in GAF from premorbid level. Change in mental status or functioning has lasted for at least a month. Onset is within the past year.

those who did not, but this difference did not reach statistical significance. A significant correlation between spatial working memory errors and negative symptoms was seen in the later-psychotic group only, suggesting that this may be a useful predictive factor to examine in future studies. Additionally, in a larger group of UHR participants, these investigators found significantly impaired olfactory identification ability in those who later developed a Schizophrenia spectrum disorder, but not in any other group, suggesting that impaired olfactory identification may be a premorbid marker of transition to Schizophrenia (Brewer et al., 2003). Replication is warranted to determine whether this finding may be generalizable to other prodromal samples.

With regard to structural anatomic risk factors, Pantelis and colleagues (Pantelis, Velakoulis, et al., 2003) reported striking baseline differences in regional gray matter volume between those participants who subsequently developed a psychotic illness and those who did not. Specifically, those who developed psychosis had less gray matter in the right medial temporal, lateral temporal, and inferior frontal cortex, and in the cingulate cortex bilaterally. Longitudinal follow-up indicated that individuals who developed psychosis showed a postmorbid reduction in gray matter in the left parahippocampal, fusiform, orbitofrontal and cerebellar cortices, and the cingulate gyri, whereas longitudinal changes were restricted to the cerebellum in those who did not become psychotic. Interestingly, contrary to expectation, *larger* left hippocampal volume at intake was associated with the subsequent development of acute psychosis, rather than smaller volumes (Phillips, Velakoulis, et al., 2002). These results appear to be at odds with the genetic high-risk studies described earlier and highlight the importance of different ascertainment strategies in terms of defining risk, as well as the need for more longitudinal research on prodromal subjects who are both genetically at risk for psychosis and exhibiting early symptoms.

The Role of Stressful Life Events and Their Neurobiological Effects

We have described the role of prenatal stress as an early occurring factor and now turn our attention to the potential moderating role of psychosocial stress as a late factor in adolescence and adulthood (see right section of Figure 14.1). Diathesis-stress models of Schizophrenia suggest that environmental stress may interact with genetic vulnerability in triggering the onset of psychotic symptoms and exacerbating symptoms during the course of the disorder. A 1985 review of the behavioral literature regarding the role of psychosocial stress in Schizophrenia concluded that evidence for a causal role was weak, though some findings pointed to a potential role of stress in activating symptoms in previously diagnosed psychotic patients (Tennant, 1985). Additional research since that time has continued to support these conclusions, with the addition of a more complex understanding of the neurobiological effects of stress on the central nervous system.

Several studies have examined the temporal relationship between stressful life events and symptom severity, pointing to a role for environmental stressors in psychotic symptom exacerbation and relapse. In a landmark study, retrospective assessments indicated that independent life events (those life events judged *not* to be due to the mental illness) were more likely to occur in the 3 weeks prior to onset of a psychotic episode in Schizophrenia patients than in a similar period of time for nonpsychiatric control participants (Brown & Birley, 1968). This sample included first-episode and more chronic patients, all of whom had a rapid increase in symptoms prior to episode onset. The authors calculated that onset was "brought forward" by 10 weeks, on average, for these patients, thus providing the first evidence for the "triggering hypothesis" (Birley & Brown, 1970; Brown & Birley, 1968). This theory proposes that an underlying biological vulnerability causes psychosis, and environmental stress may trigger the precise timing of onset. In an early study by Leff, Hirsch, Gaind, Rohde, and Stevens (1973), in the 5 weeks preceding psychotic relapse, patients with Schizophrenia maintained on antipsychotic medications were more likely to experience an independent life event (89% of patients) than both well patients taking antipsychotic medications (27%) and well or relapsed pa-

tients taking a placebo (38% and 31%, respectively). However, other studies failed to replicate the increase in independent events prior to episode onset (Jacobs & Myers, 1976), and the theory cannot be said to generalize to patients with a gradual onset of psychotic symptoms.

In a review of the behavioral literature on stress and Schizophrenia, Norman and Malla (1993) examined 23 studies that retrospectively assessed life events prior to psychotic onset or relapse (only three assessed first-episode patients) and reported that 77% of the studies showed significant evidence that higher stress levels were associated with more severe symptoms in schizophrenic samples. Thirty-six percent of the comparisons between Schizophrenia patients and nonpsychiatric controls showed higher rates of independent events in the lives of patients, and none of the studies that compared Schizophrenia patients to control subjects with other psychiatric disorders showed higher rates of life events for the Schizophrenia patients compared to patients with other psychiatric disorders (Norman & Malla, 1993). Although the measurement of independent events attempts to control for the effect of illness in creating life stress, the direction of causality is not yet clear: Life events could exacerbate symptoms, and increased symptoms could increase the level of stressful events in a patient's life. Additionally, psychosocial stress may not have a unique effect on psychotic symptoms, as life events have also been linked to an increase in mood symptoms in patients with Schizophrenia (Ventura, Nuechterlein, Subotnik, Hardesty, & Mintz, 2000) and patients with purely affective disorders (Brown & Harris, 1978). Life stress is thought to exacerbate psychiatric symptoms across a variety of mental disorders and may also exacerbate immune system functioning and the symptoms of physical illness in diseases such as diabetes, cardiovascular disease, and cancers (S. Cohen & Herbert, 1996; Spiegel & Kato, 1996; Strike & Steptoe, 2004).

High-risk paradigms are just beginning to examine the link between stress and symptoms. Among genetically high-risk participants who did not qualify for a psychotic disorder diagnosis, the number of lifetime major life events were related to psychotic symptom severity (P. Miller et al., 2001). However, these subjects have not yet been followed through the period of risk for conversion to psychosis. No prospective studies of stressful life events prior to illness onset have been completed, although they are the best test of the stress-vulnerability hypothesis because they reduce recall bias. Corcoran and colleagues (2003) proposed a model for examining the effects of stress on symptom onset for clinically at-risk (prodromal) groups, in which both life events and neurobiological assays can be used to measure stress and patients' stress response. This design would allow researchers to directly examine potential candidate biological mechanisms that may link stress to symptoms.

A hypothetical neurochemical mechanism linking the stress system to symptoms of Schizophrenia is altered activity of the hypothalamic-pituitary-adrenal (HPA) axis. The cascade of hormones in response to stress proceeds through the HPA pathway as cells in the periventricular nucleus of the hypothalamus secrete corticotropin-releasing hormone, which increases adrenocorticotropic hormone secretion by the pituitary gland, which stimulates the adrenal gland to release glucocorticoids, which then feed back via glucocorticoid receptors in the hippocampus to dampen the system once the stressor has passed (Figure 14.2).

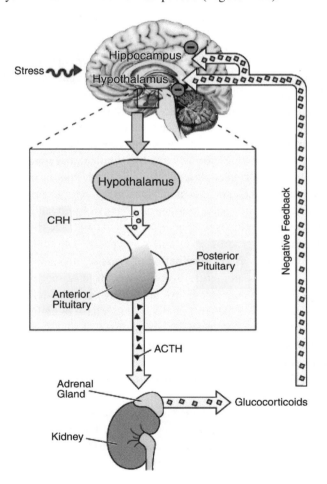

Figure 14.2 The hypothalamic-pituitary-adrenal (HPA) axis. The HPA axis activates in response to stress and is inhibited via a negative feedback loop. Reproduced with permission from Sinauer Associates. Rosenzweig et al., 1999, *Biological Psychology, 3rd ed.*

Elevated levels of cortisol may exacerbate symptoms through a neurotoxic effect on the hippocampus (McEwen & Seeman, 1999) and by ultimately increasing dopaminergic activity in the prefrontal cortex (Walker & Diforio, 1997). In animal models, prolonged stress has been shown to result in a dysregulated negative feedback circuit, whereby damaged hippocampi fail to correctly modulate HPA axis activity (Sapolsky, Uno, Rebert, & Finch, 1990). On the basis of animal models, some have argued that stress also increases glutamate in both the prefrontal cortex (PFC) and the hippocampus, which can result in altered dopamine levels (Moghaddam, 2002). The increase in PFC glutamate, as opposed to the hippocampus, does not appear to be dependent on glucocorticoids, and therefore may represent a second pathway that is activated as part of the brain's "fast response" to stress, which occurs prior to and during the stress response via the HPA axis (Lowy, Gault, & Yamamoto, 1993; Moghaddam, Bolinao, Stein-Behrens, & Sapolsky, 1994). Although a review of basic research on stress in animal models as related to Schizophrenia is outside the scope of this chapter (see Corcoran et al., 2003, for a review), this type of research has vastly increased our understanding of the body's complex stress response and its effects on the mind and brain.

Studies of patients with Schizophrenia have primarily utilized cortisol assays to assess HPA axis integrity. Walder, Walker, and Lewine (2000) reported that salivary cortisol levels were related to symptom severity in a sample of patients with Schizophrenia, as well as performance on neuropsychological tasks in a combined sample of patients with Schizophrenia, affective disorder, or no history of psychiatric illness. Kaneda, Fujii, and Ohmori (2002) found that patients with Schizophrenia showed heightened baseline plasma corticotropin (ACTH) levels, in addition to elevated cortisol levels in response to physical stressors in a research setting (Jansen, Gispen-de Wied, & Kahn, 2000). In contrast, other studies have shown that patients with Schizophrenia show a dampened cortisol response to psychosocial stress such as public speaking (Jansen et al., 1998, 2000). Differences in findings across studies may reflect variation in research procedures such as the collection of assays (plasma versus salivary cortisol) and the timing of tests, as circadian rhythms greatly affect stress hormone levels (Kirschbaum & Hellhammer, 1989).

Although no studies of HPA axis functioning in the premorbid or prodromal periods of Schizophrenia have been published to date, one study has focused on adolescents with schizotypal personality disorder (SPD). Individuals diagnosed with SPD are at higher risk for developing Axis I psychotic disorders and may possess a similar genetic vulnerability to Schizophrenia (Fenton & McGlashan, 1989; Siever, Kalus, & Keefe, 1993). Adolescents with SPD were found to have higher levels of salivary cortisol than adolescents with other personality disorders and normal controls, especially at the first sample of the day (Weinstein, Diforio, Schiffman, Walker, & Bonsall, 1999). In a longitudinal follow-up, cortisol levels at baseline and follow-up assessments were correlated with schizotypal symptoms at the second assessment, pointing to a potential relationship between HPA axis functioning and the development of psychiatric symptoms in psychosis, although this study has not yet followed the participants through the complete period of risk for onset of psychotic disorders (Walker, Walder, & Reynolds, 2001). Longitudinal studies can also help to determine the long-term effects of chronic stress on HPA axis functioning in Schizophrenia.

Genetic and Hormonal Regulation of Synaptic Pruning

In addition to the role of hormones in mediating stress response, hormones are likely to play a key role in adolescent brain maturation (Walker & Bollini, 2002). Gonadal and adrenal hormones have been shown to affect structural development, as well as immediate functional properties, of the brain. Some of the behavioral influences exerted by these hormones are short-term "nongenomic" effects, mediated by receptors on the surface of neurons; steroid hormones also affect later gene expression via intracellular hormonal receptors in neurons (McEwen, 1994; Watson & Gametchu, 1999). Animal research has demonstrated that hormones can trigger gene expression relevant to postpubertal neuromaturational processes (Ojeda & Ma, 1999). For example, estrogen-induced cyclic synaptogenesis has been observed in the adult rat hippocampus (McEwen, 1994). These genomic effects of hormones involve changes in the expression of messenger RNA that codes for specific proteins that, in turn, play a role in receptor density, reuptake, and neurotransmitter synthesis. These proteins can also trigger the expression of genes that impact neuronal survival (govern maturational processes such as proliferation and elimination of neurons). Thus, structural plasticity is an important aspect of steroid hormone action in the developing nervous system (McEwen, 1994). The role of genomic hormonal effects in triggering onset of Schizophrenia is purely speculative, but some investigators have hypothesized that hormonal changes during adolescence, especially of the reproductive steroids, may trigger the expression of faulty genes, possibly affecting

synaptic pruning and/or myelination (Amateau & McCarthy, 2002). This is supported by observations that age-related gray matter volume reductions during adolescence in healthy males might be steeper than those of healthy females (DeBellis et al., 2001). One mechanism by which rising hormone levels in adolescence may trigger expression of a latent genetic predisposition to Schizophrenia is through dysregulation of the HPA axis. It is also possible that early hippocampal insult (i.e., due to prenatal complications) may increase the likelihood that a latent genetic predisposition to Schizophrenia will be expressed in adolescence (Walker & Bollini, 2002). Thus, early environmental insult may alter gonadal hormone expression; alternatively, effects of hormones may alter the nature of the early insult (Andersen, 2003).

Interactions between Early and Late Risk Factors

Theories regarding the development of psychotic symptomatology in the adolescent period must also account for findings of early childhood abnormalities in patients with Schizophrenia (Walker & Bollini, 2002). Keshavan and colleagues (Keshavan, 1999; Keshavan & Hogarty, 1999) have proposed that Schizophrenia arises from both an early brain abnormality and late maturational processes of brain development interacting with adverse biochemical and psychosocial factors during adolescence and early adulthood. That is, prenatal and/or early postnatal factors (genetic or environmental) produce anomalous neural connectivity, resulting in premorbid impairment. Subsequently, during adolescence, the onset of prodromal or fully psychotic symptoms may result from excessive elimination of synapses and, secondarily, phasic dopaminergic overactivity. Because normal ingrowth of dopamine fibers occurs during the late adolescent period (Benes, 1997), other investigators have hypothesized that developmental changes in dopamine levels may drive the onset of positive symptoms of Schizophrenia at that time, thereby moderating the expression of congenital neuropathology in vulnerable individuals (Walker et al., 1994; Weinberger, 1995).

Such a progressive developmental pathophysiology of the illness during adolescence (Woods, Grafton, Holmes, Cherry, & Mazziotta, 1998) may result from several factors working singly or in combination. First, genetic factors may predispose to an excess synaptic elimination, increased neuronal apoptosis (i.e., programmed cell death), decreased cell somal size, or a combination of these processes during adolescence. Such changes might result from altered expression of genes that are critical for neurodevelopmental processes (Nawa, Takahashi, & Patterson, 2000; Olney & Farber, 1995) or altered dynamics of dopaminergic and GABAergic neurotransmitter systems (Costa et al., 2001). Second, hormonal changes, especially of the reproductive steroids, could modulate brain maturational processes such as synaptic pruning and/or myelination (Amateau & McCarthy, 2002). Third, psychosocial environmental factors might play a significant role. It is known that environmental enrichment leads to increased spine density and dendritic arborization (Globus, Rosenzweig, Bennett, & Diamond, 1973). Likewise, environmental impoverishment or stress could conceivably lead to the opposite, that is, an increased fall-out of synapses and/or neurons (Teicher, Andersen, Polcari, Anderson, & Navalta, 2002) and decreased neuronal viability (DeBellis et al., 2001).

Findings linking gray matter reductions and other gross morphological changes in Schizophrenia to fetal hypoxia (T. D. Cannon, van Erp, Rosso, et al., 2002) suggest a specific mechanism by which such early influences interact with later maturational changes in influencing the timing of onset of the disorder. Of particular importance, fetal hypoxia is consistently associated with earlier onset forms of the disorder (Bearden et al., 2000; Rosso, Cannon, et al., 2000; Verdoux et al., 1997), suggesting that the presence of this risk factor may in some manner predispose to an earlier age at onset. The neural sequelae of hypoxia vary in severity from alterations in neurite outgrowth to neuronal cell death (Nyakas et al., 1996). In the former case, immature neurons may survive the hypoxic insult but still have a compromised elaboration of synaptic interconnections (Nyakas et al., 1996). Studies in fetal sheep have shown that hypoxia secondary to chronic placental insufficiency is associated with reduced cortical thickness and increased cortical neuronal density, without any observable neuronal loss (Rees et al., 1998). The pattern of morphologic changes associated with hypoxia in studies of Schizophrenia is thus compatible with an animal model of chronic fetal hypoxia and with the observed cellular pathology in schizophrenic patients. In this context, processes associated with cortical synaptic pruning during late adolescence and early adulthood (Feinberg, 1982; Keshavan, Anderson, & Pettegrew, 1994) might interact with the earlier hypoxia-related effects in lowering interneuronal connectivity to below a threshold critical for integrated cognitive activity, leading to further behavioral deterioration at that time.

Thus, current models offer promising hypotheses regarding mechanisms by which processes associated with postpubertal brain development might interact with earlier compromises of the brain in predisposing to Schizophrenia. Nevertheless, theories as to why adolescence represents a time of increased risk for Schizophrenia onset remain speculative. It may be that heterogeneity in the course and outcome of Schizophrenia is a function of the interaction of early brain pathology with normal or abnormal developmental factors occurring throughout life, up until the time when the illness commences (Pantelis, Yucel, et al., 2003). The role of later environmental stressors, and how they may impact an already vulnerable individual, warrants further investigation in naturalistic human studies and via experimental animal models.

SUMMARY AND CONCLUSIONS

According to the original neurodevelopmental hypothesis of Schizophrenia, the disorder results from a set of basic biological errors that occur early in life and lead to a combination of structural, functional, and/or biochemical anomalies in the developing brain (T. D. Cannon & Mednick, 1993). This model of Schizophrenia has been highly influential and has moved the field substantially forward by focusing attention on early developmental deviation in individuals who develop the illness in adulthood. Specifically, in the area of epidemiology, this model has led to the investigation of early signs of functional compromise in individuals destined to develop Schizophrenia in adulthood, and the interaction of specific obstetric complications with genetic factors in the etiology of psychotic illness. Convergent evidence from neuropathological investigations indicates patterns of neuronal displacement consistent with a neurodevelopmental origin.

However, a major limitation of this model is that it does not account for the delay in onset of the disorder. Why does full-blown Schizophrenia typically manifest during the late adolescent/early adult period? Taken together with recent evidence of neuroanatomic change during the early phase of illness, it seems likely that additional factors active during this period play a role in the disease process.

Recent advances in our understanding of processes that occur proximal to illness onset call for an update to the neurodevelopmental model. It is important to keep in mind that progressive anatomic changes do not preclude the existence of a neurodevelopmental insult in Schizophrenia, as an inherited neurodevelopmental abnormality may also have progressive features (Mathalon et al., 2003). Here we have outlined a model in which some neurocognitive and neuroanatomic abnormalities reflect genetic trait markers, others are environmentally mediated, and the development of frank psychosis may involve a third, partially overlapping series of structural and functional changes. Theorists have focused on two sources of influence that might account for neuronal disruption proximal to the time of onset of illness: pruning-related plasticity processes that occur as a normative aspect of brain development during adolescence, and stress-related and other hormonal changes that may have neurotoxic effects in pathways implicated in the pathophysiology of Schizophrenia. In regard to the former, certain Schizophrenia-related factors may disrupt the regulation of regressive brain maturational events at this time. Such a model is supported by evidence of a Schizophrenia-promoting variant in a plasticity-related gene (DISC1) associated with prefrontal cortical gray matter reduction. However, it is also possible that there is nothing intrinsically wrong with these later maturational brain processes in individuals predisposed to Schizophrenia, but these processes nevertheless participate in determining the timing of onset of functional deterioration and psychotic symptom formation by reducing the reserve of interneuronal connectivity to below some hypothetically critical threshold (Hoffman & McGlashan, 1997).

Clearly, the question of whether brain abnormalities in Schizophrenia are static or dynamic is one that is critical for future research to resolve. If the primary pathologic condition in Schizophrenia indeed reflects anomalous processes that occur early in development (e.g., Murray & Lewis, 1987; Weinberger, 1987), it has yet to be resolved whether such an abnormality signifies a failure of normal development due to a fixed early insult, a failure in an ongoing maturational process such as synaptic pruning, a degenerative process from a stage achieved through normal development, or some combination of these factors (T. D. Cannon et al., 2003). A deeper understanding of normal neurodevelopmental events is clearly critical for elucidating the potentially abnormal pathophysiological processes at work in Schizophrenia.

Increasingly sophisticated methodologies such as high-resolution MRI and MRS currently offer researchers the possibility of investigating these neurobiological processes. However, it is not yet known whether such brain metabolic alterations are causally relevant to onset or merely epiphenomena of other neurodevelopmental processes at work. In this regard, the functional significance of volumetric reduction noted in longitudinal MRI studies is a paramount question. As such changes do not appear to be accompanied by neurodegenerative processes at the cellular level, it is possible they may reflect short-term physiological variability or plasticity that does not signify ongoing deterioration.

A second, related issue is the differentiation of risk factors that are causal and could thus represent potentially important therapeutic targets, as compared to markers of vulnerability that may identify those at greatest risk but do not necessarily or directly impact the later course of illness. The identification of causal risk factors, such as particular neurocognitive deficits or brain abnormalities, has obvious implications both for research and for the development of new treatments that may improve the quality of life for individuals suffering from the disorder and is thus a primary goal of current clinical high-risk research.

From a developmental perspective, the unfolding of the clinical disorder is a long-term process, involving multiple developmental phases, different types of risk factors, and the understanding that psychosis is in no way an inevitable outcome (Cornblatt et al., 2002). A better understanding of the developmental trajectory of neurobiological processes in Schizophrenia will inform early intervention strategies as to the most vulnerable brain functions and/or structures, as well as the stages of the illness most amenable to treatment (Pantelis, Yucel, et al., 2003). Such intervention strategies offer promise that the functional deterioration related to onset of the clinical disorder may be delayed, attenuated, or ultimately prevented altogether.

FUTURE DIRECTIONS

There are several critical avenues for future research, which are currently in the early stages, but show great promise for both advancing our understanding of the pathophysiology of Schizophrenia, and improving outcomes for individuals who suffer from the illness. These include: (1) advances in early identification and intervention for at-risk individuals, (2) identification of neural endophenotypes, which are likely to be closer to the underlying genetic etiology of the disease, and (3) utilizing these more discrete, quantifiable definitions of pathological phenotypes in order to improve treatment and interventions for Schizophrenia.

Advances in Early Intervention

It is clear from the literature summarized here that the first few years of psychosis represent a critical period in that many patients show substantial cognitive and social deterioration, which has extremely detrimental effects on long-term success in functioning independently (Hafner & Nowotny, 1995; Yung & McGorry, 1996). Nevertheless, because current mental health care practices are largely reactive rather than proactive in nature, and because the public is poorly educated about the nature and early signs of mental illness, there is often a substantial delay before young people with onset of psychotic symptoms are evaluated and treated psychiatrically (Johnstone, Crow, Johnson, & MacMillan, 1986; Loebel et al., 1992). Antipsychotic drug therapy is effective in producing partial symptom relief in many patients, but it is not curative (Glick, Suppes, DeBattista, Hu, & Marder, 2001; Marder, 1996). Findings indicating poorer treatment response and functional impairment given longer duration of untreated psychosis (e.g., Crow, MacMillan, Johnson, & Johnstone, 1986; Loebel et al., 1992) argue for a new approach to ascertain at-risk individuals before the onset of Schizophrenia and to provide interventions designed to stave off illness progression and to improve functioning and long-term outcome.

A better understanding of the neurodevelopmental trajectory in high-risk individuals who develop Schizophrenia, as compared to those who do not, will advance our knowledge regarding aspects of brain structure and function that may improve the prediction of onset of Schizophrenia over and above that associated with behavioral prodromal features and family history. Such studies will also elucidate the temporal and spatial pattern of neural and behavioral changes associated with the emergence of prodromal and psychotic symptoms. This information, in turn, will provide important evidence validating the early prodromal phases as critical periods for testing the effectiveness of primary preventive intervention programs and may suggest strategies for the development of novel preventive treatments that can correct or compensate for the specific neurodevelopmental and psychological changes associated with the formation of psychotic symptoms during late adolescence and early adulthood.

A major impediment that has particularly hindered the success of many such investigations to date is that of sample ascertainment. The low incidence of Schizophrenia and the lack of early, specific signs of vulnerability renders the identification of those who are most at risk extraordinarily difficult. As such, it is a significant challenge to amass samples that are sufficiently powered to address questions of interest with regard to neurobiological, genetic, and psychosocial risk factors that distinguish individuals who develop Schizophrenia from those who develop other psychotic disorders from those whose symptoms remain stable or improve (e.g., Heinssen, Cuthbert, Breiling, Colpe, & Dolan-Sewell, 2003). Such difficulties have led to the development of large-scale collaborative efforts in which data are pooled across multiple sites to allow researchers to better delineate risk factors for psychosis, as such efforts will substantially increase the power for hypothesis testing

available to any one site alone. Pooling of databases across international sites will allow investigators to answer questions of fundamental importance regarding early detection, prediction, and prevention, which could not otherwise be resolved within a reasonable time frame.

Identification of Neural Endophenotypes

Given recent dramatic advances in molecular genetics, there has been a major shift in the focus of psychiatric genetic investigations from investigating patterns of familial transmission to localizing genes underlying mental disorders using genetic linkage and association strategies (Merikangas & Risch, 2003). Although early successes of linkage studies of Mendelian diseases (see Risch, 2000, for a review) engendered optimism that this approach would also be successful for complex psychiatric disorders such as Schizophrenia, efforts to date have proved largely unsuccessful (Glazier, Nadeau, & Aitman, 2002). Progress on this front has been hindered by complex patterns of inheritance, as well as diagnostic heterogeneity and imprecision (Freimer & Sabatti, 2003). Conventional diagnostic phenotypes are marked by such heterogeneity and overlap that genomic analyses using current syndrome definitions are questionable. As discussed in this chapter, the development of endophenotypes—phenotypic traits or markers proposed to represent more direct expressions of underlying genes—may yield far more informative results than studies of aggregate psychiatric phenotypes (Gottesman & Gould, 2003). As such, an endophenotype-based approach is likely to aid in unraveling the complexity of transmission of complex mental disorders such as Schizophrenia.

With revisions to our current diagnostic classification system (*Diagnostic and Statistical Manual of Mental Disorders,* fifth edition; American Psychiatric Association, 2000) under way, it is critical that scientific evidence be better utilized in its development (Kupfer, First, & Regier, 2002). Several investigators in the field have highlighted the need to increasingly strive for classification that more closely represents expression of underlying biologic systems (Merikangas & Risch, 2003). For example, although Schizophrenia and bipolar disorder have traditionally been viewed as distinct disorders, recent work has revealed substantial familial coaggregation and overlap in the genomic regions showing linkage and association with these two disorders (Badner & Gershon, 2002; Berrettini, 2003; Murray et al., 2004). Elucidating the specific genetic and neural mechanisms influencing susceptibility to and expression of these illnesses, and explaining the nature of the overlap between them, is critical to understanding the necessary and sufficient conditions for overt psychosis and to the identification of underlying genes. As the accumulation of genomic and gene expression knowledge accelerates, the ability to use more refined neural endophenotypes will be crucial to the success of these investigations.

Improving Treatment and Interventions for Schizophrenia: Using a Phenomics Approach

The generation of more discrete, quantifiable definitions of pathological phenotypes not only will inform investigations of genetic etiology, but is also likely to aid in the development of rational pharmacotherapies for Schizophrenia. Despite major advances in neuroscience, drug discovery, and pharmacogenomics, the treatments currently available for Schizophrenia have only limited effectiveness. Existing diagnoses rely on symptoms far removed from drug targets, such that the discovery of new treatments is almost always serendipitous. Defining new phenotypes of the disorder at a neural-systems level, with links to drug mechanisms-of-action and patterns of gene expression, could yield dramatic advances in neuropsychiatric therapeutics, such as those that have resulted from the identification of neuropathological and neurochemical targets in Parkinson's disease (DeKosky & Marek, 2003; Samii, Nutt, & Ransom, 2004).

A variety of approaches, ranging from interview-based assessments and neurocognitive testing to functional neuroimaging and even measurements of gene expression have generated a diversity of candidate phenotypes for research. A focus on endophenotypes examined through a multidisciplinary approach that capitalizes on convergent technologies, from molecular to behavioral, is likely to accelerate the discovery of new treatments.

In particular, cognitive abnormalities, known to be a core feature of Schizophrenia, offer quantitative phenotypes for genomic studies and clinical trials and provide clear bridges to connect to informative neural systems models. Cognitive constructs are highly quantitative, enabling phenotypic assessments to be conducted with the high throughput necessary for adequately powered genomic association studies and multicenter clinical trials.

Phenomics is an innovative new direction in the field, in which a multidisciplinary approach is utilized to examine candidate disease phenotypes that can be measured not only across syndromes but across species, and may be used in validity testing at multiple physiological levels, including the neural systems and cellular and molecular levels. This approach may open innovative prospects for both pathophysiological modeling and drug discovery. Combining information across multiple levels of phenotypic expression, with modeling of the neural systems that support these functions, can advance definitions of phenotypes that can prompt various new research threads and raises the promise of novel and even genomically targeted therapeutic approaches. This is a time in which the field may very well be on the verge of multiple breakthroughs with regard to our understanding of Schizophrenia; further focus on enhancing methods for the study of new phenotypes is likely to be vital for accelerating the pace of discovery.

REFERENCES

Akbarian, S., Bunney, W. E., Jr., Potkin, S. G., Wigal, S. B., Hagman, J. O., Sandman, C. A., et al. (1993). Altered distribution of nicotinamide-adenine dinucleotide phosphate-diaphorase cells in frontal lobe of schizophrenics implies disturbances of cortical development. *Archives of General Psychiatry, 50*(3), 169–177.

Akbarian, S., Vinuela, A., Kim, J. J., Potkin, S. G., Bunney, W. E., Jr., & Jones, E. G. (1993). Distorted distribution of nicotinamide-adenine dinucleotide phosphate-diaphorase neurons in temporal lobe of schizophrenics implies anomalous cortical development. *Archives of General Psychiatry, 50*(3), 178–187.

Amateau, S. K., & McCarthy, M. M. (2002). A novel mechanism of dendritic spine plasticity involving estradiol induction of prostaglandin-E2. *Journal of Neuroscience, 22*(19), 8586–8596.

American Psychiatric Association. (2000). *Diagnostic and statistical manual of mental disorders* (4th ed., text rev.). Washington, DC: Author.

Andersen, S. L. (2003). Trajectories of brain development: Point of vulnerability or window of opportunity? *Neuroscience and Biobehavioral Reviews, 27*(1/2), 3–18.

Andreasen, N. C., Flaum, M., & Arndt, S. (1992). The Comprehensive Assessment of Symptoms and History (CASH). (1992). An instrument for assessing diagnosis and psychopathology. *Archives of General Psychiatry, 49*(8), 615–623.

Arnold, S. E., Hyman, B. T., Van Hoesen, G. W., & Damasio, A. R. (1991). Some cytoarchitectural abnormalities of the entorhinal cortex in Schizophrenia. *Archives of General Psychiatry, 48*(7), 625–632.

Arnold, S. E., & Trojanowski, J. Q. (1996). Recent advances in defining the neuropathology of Schizophrenia. *Acta Neuropathologica, 92*(3), 217–231.

Asarnow, R. F. (1999). Neurocognitive impairments in Schizophrenia: A piece of the epigenetic puzzle. *European Child and Adolescent Psychiatry, 8*(Suppl. 1), 15–18.

Asarnow, R. F., & MacCrimmon, D. J. (1978). Residual performance deficit in clinically remitted schizophrenics: A marker of Schizophrenia? *Journal of Abnormal Psychology, 87*(6), 597–608.

Asarnow, R. F., Nuechterlein, K. H., Subotnik, K. L., Fogelson, D. L., Torquato, R. D., Payne, D. L., et al. (2002). Neurocognitive impairments in nonpsychotic parents of children with Schizophrenia and attention-deficit/hyperactivity disorder: The University of California, Los Angeles family study. *Archives of General Psychiatry, 59*(11), 1053–1060.

Aylward, E., Walker, E., & Bettes, B. (1984). Intelligence in Schizophrenia: Meta-analysis of the research. *Schizophrenia Bulletin, 10*(3), 430–459.

Badner, J., & Gershon, E. (2002). Meta-analysis of whole-genome linkage scans of bipolar disorder and Schizophrenia. *Molecular Psychiatry, 7,* 405–411.

Bagary, M. S., Symms, M. R., Barker, G. J., Mutsatsa, S. H., Joyce, E. M., & Ron, M. A. (2003). Gray and white matter brain abnormalities in first-episode Schizophrenia inferred from magnetization transfer imaging. *Archives of General Psychiatry, 60,* 779–788.

Bartha, R., Williamson, P. C., Drost, D. J., Malla, A., Carr, T. J., Cortese, L., et al. (1997). Measurement of glutamate and glutamine in the medial prefrontal cortex of never-treated schizophrenic patients and healthy controls by proton magnetic resonance spectroscopy. *Archives of General Psychiatry, 54*(10), 959–965.

Basso, M. R., Nasrallah, H. A., Olson, S. C., & Bornstein, R. A. (1997). Cognitive deficits distinguish patients with adolescent- and adult-onset Schizophrenia. *Neuropsychiatry, Neuropsychology, and Behavioral Neurology, 10*(2), 107–112.

Bearden, C. E., Rosso, I. M., Hollister, J. M., Sanchez, L. E., Hadley, T., & Cannon, T. D. (2000). A prospective cohort study of childhood behavioral deviance and language abnormalities as predictors of adult Schizophrenia. *Schizophrenia Bulletin, 26*(2), 395–410.

Benes, F. M. (1997). The role of stress and dopamine-GABA interactions in the vulnerability for Schizophrenia. *Journal of Psychiatric Research, 31*(2), 257–275.

Berger, G. E., Wood, S. J., Pantelis, C., Velakoulis, D., Wellard, R. M., & McGorry, P. D. (2002). Implications of lipid biology for the pathogenesis of Schizophrenia. *Australian and New Zealand Journal of Psychiatry, 36*(3), 355–366.

Bergman, A. J., & Walker, E. (1995). The relationship between cognitive functions and behavioral deviance in children at risk for psychopathology. *Journal of Child Psychology and Psychiatry, 36*(2), 265–278.

Berman, K. F., Torrey, E. F., Daniel, D. G., & Weinberger, D. R. (1992). Regional cerebral blood flow in monozygotic twins discordant and concordant for Schizophrenia. *Archives of General Psychiatry, 49*(12), 927–934.

Berrettini, W. (2003). Evidence for shared susceptibility in bipolar disorder and Schizophrenia. *American Journal of Medical Genetics, 123C,* 59–64.

Bertolino, A., Callicott, J. H., Elman, I., Mattay, V. S., Tedeschi, G., Frank, J. A., et al. (1998). Regionally specific neuronal pathology in untreated patients with Schizophrenia: A proton magnetic resonance spectroscopic imaging study. *Biological Psychiatry, 43*(9), 641–648.

Bertolino, A., Nawroz, S., Mattay, V. S., Barnett, A. S., Duyn, J. H., Moonen, C. T., et al. (1996). Regionally specific pattern of neurochemical pathology in Schizophrenia as assessed by multislice proton magnetic resonance spectroscopic imaging. *American Journal of Psychiatry, 153*(12), 1554–1563.

Bertolino, A., & Weinberger, D. R. (1999). Proton magnetic resonance spectroscopy in Schizophrenia. *European Journal of Radiology, 30*(2), 132–141.

Birley, J. L., & Brown, G. W. (1970). Crises and life changes preceding the onset or relapse of acute Schizophrenia: Clinical aspects. *British Journal of Psychiatry, 116*(532), 327–333.

Bogerts, B., Lieberman, J. A., Ashtari, M., Bilder, R. M., Degreef, G., Lerner, G., et al. (1993). Hippocampus-amygdala volumes and psychopathology in chronic Schizophrenia. *Biological Psychiatry, 33*(4), 236–246.

Brewer, W., Wood, S., McGorry, P. D., Francey, S., Phillips, L., Yung, A. R., et al. (2003). Impairment of olfactory identification ability in individuals at ultra-high risk for psychosis who later develop Schizophrenia. *American Journal of Psychiatry, 160*(10), 1790–1794.

Brooks, W. M., Hodde-Vargas, J., Vargas, L. A., Yeo, R. A., Ford, C. C., & Hendren, R. L. (1998). Frontal lobe of children with Schizophrenia spectrum disorders: A proton magnetic resonance spectroscopic study. *Biological Psychiatry, 43*(4), 263–269.

Brown, G. W., & Birley, J. L. (1968). Crises and life changes and the onset of Schizophrenia. *Journal of Health and Social Behavior, 9*(3), 203–214.

Brown, G. W., & Harris, T. (1978). Social origins of depression: A reply. *Psychological Medicine, 8*(4), 577–588.

Bustillo, J. R., Lauriello, J., Rowland, L. M., Jung, R. E., Petropoulos, H., Hart, B. L., et al. (2001). Effects of chronic haloperidol and clozapine treatments on frontal and caudate neurochemistry in Schizophrenia. *Psychiatry Research, 107*(3), 135–149.

Bustillo, J. R., Lauriello, J., Rowland, L. M., Thomson, L. M., Petropoulos, H., Hammond, R., et al. (2002). Longitudinal follow-up of neurochemical changes during the first year of antipsychotic treatment in Schizophrenia patients with minimal previous medication exposure. *Schizophrenia Research, 58*(2/3), 313–321.

Byrne, M., Hodges, A., Grant, E., Owens, D. C., & Johnstone, E. C. (1999). Neuropsychological assessment of young people at high genetic risk for developing Schizophrenia compared with controls: Preliminary findings of the Edinburgh High Risk Study (EHRS). *Psychological Medicine, 29*(5), 1161–1173.

Cahn, W., Hulshoff Pol, H. E., Lems, E. B. T. E., van Haren, N. E. M., Schnack, H. G., van der Linden, J. A., et al. (2002). Brain volume changes in first-episode Schizophrenia. *Archives of General Psychiatry, 59,* 1002–1010.

Callicott, J. H., Egan, M. F., Bertolino, A., Mattay, V. S., Langheim, F. J., Frank, J. A., et al. (1998). Hippocampal N-acetyl aspartate in unaffected siblings of patients with Schizophrenia: A possible intermediate neurobiological phenotype. *Biological Psychiatry, 44*(10), 941–950.

Callicott, J. H., Egan, M. F., Mattay, V. S., Bertolino, A., Bone, A. D., Verchinksi, B., et al. (2003). Abnormal fMRI response of the dorsolateral prefrontal cortex in cognitively intact siblings of patients with Schizophrenia. *American Journal of Psychiatry, 160*(4), 709–719.

Cannon, M., Jones, P. B., & Murray, R. M. (2002). Obstetric complications and Schizophrenia: Historical and meta-analytic review. *American Journal of Psychiatry, 159*(7), 1080–1092.

Cannon, T. D. (1996). Abnormalities of brain structure and function in Schizophrenia: Implications for aetiology in pathophysiology. *Annals of Medicine, 28*(6), 533–539.

Cannon, T. D. (1997). On the nature and mechanisms of obstetric influences in Schizophrenia: A review and synthesis of epidemiologic studies. *International Review of Psychiatry, 9*(4), 387–397.

Cannon, T. D., Hennah, W., van Erp, T. G. M., Thompson, P., Lonnqvist, J., Huttunen, M. O., et al. (in press). DISC1/TRAX haplotypes associate with Schizophrenia, reduced prefrontal gray matter, and impaired working memory. *Archives of General Psychiatry.*

Cannon, T. D., Huttunen, M. O., Lonnqvist, J., Tuulio-Henriksson, A., Pirkola, T., Glahn, D., et al. (2000). The inheritance of neuropsychological dysfunction in twins discordant for Schizophrenia. *American Journal of Human Genetics, 67*(2), 369–382.

Cannon, T. D., Kaprio, J., Lonnqvist, J., Huttunen, M., & Koeskenvuo, M. (1998). The genetic epidemiology of Schizophrenia in a Finnish twin cohort: A population-based modeling study. *Archives of General Psychiatry, 55*(1), 67–74.

Cannon, T. D., & Mednick, S. A. (1993). The Schizophrenia high-risk project in Copenhagen: Three decades of progress. *Acta Psychiatrica Scandinavica, 370,* 33–47.

Cannon, T. D., Mednick, S. A., Parnas, J., Schulsinger, F., Præstholm, J., & Vestergaard, Å. (1993). Developmental brain abnormalities in the offspring of schizophrenic mothers: Vol. 1. Contributions of genetic and perinatal factors. *Archives of General Psychiatry, 50,* 551–564.

Cannon, T. D., Rosso, I. M., Bearden, C. E., Sanchez, L. E., & Hadley, T. (1999). A prospective cohort study of neurodevelopmental processes in the genesis and epigenesis of Schizophrenia. *Development and Psychopathology, 11*(3), 467–485.

Cannon, T. D., Rosso, I. M., Hollister, J. H., Bearden, C. E., Sanchez, L. E., & Hadley, T. (2000). A prospective cohort study of genetic and perinatal influences in the etiology of Schizophrenia. *Schizophrenia Bulletin, 26*(2), 351–366.

Cannon, T. D., van Erp, T. G., Bearden, C. E., Loewy, R., Thompson, P., Toga, A. W., et al. (2003). Early and late neurodevelopmental influences in the prodrome to Schizophrenia: Contributions of genes, environment, and their interactions. *Schizophrenia Bulletin, 29*(4), 653–669.

Cannon, T. D., van Erp, T. G., & Glahn, D. C. (2002). Elucidating continuities and discontinuities between schizotypy and Schizophrenia in the nervous system. *Schizophrenia Research, 54*(1/2), 151–156.

Cannon, T. D., van Erp, T. G., Huttunen, M., Lonnqvist, J., Salonen, O., Valanne, L., et al. (1998). Regional gray matter, white matter, and cerebrospinal fluid distributions in schizophrenic patients, their siblings, and controls. *Archives of General Psychiatry, 55*(12), 1084–1091.

Cannon, T. D., van Erp, T. G., Rosso, I. M., Huttunen, M., Lonnqvist, J., Pirkola, T., et al. (2002). Fetal hypoxia and structural brain abnormalities in schizophrenic patients, their siblings, and controls. *Archives of General Psychiatry, 59*(1), 35–41.

Cannon, T. D., Zorrilla, L. E., Shtasel, D., Gur, R. E., Gur, R. C., Marco, E. J., et al. (1994). Neuropsychological functioning in siblings discordant for Schizophrenia and healthy volunteers. *Archives of General Psychiatry, 51*(8), 651–661.

Casanova, M. F., & Kleinman, J. E. (1990). The neuropathology of Schizophrenia: A critical assessment of research methodologies. *Biological Psychiatry, 27*(3), 353–362.

Cecil, K. M., Hills, E. C., Sandel, M. E., Smith, D. H., McIntosh, T. K., Mannon, L. J., et al. (1998). Proton magnetic resonance spectroscopy for detection of axonal injury in the splenium of the corpus callosum of brain-injured patients. *Journal of Neurosurgery, 88*(5), 795–801.

Cohen, J. D., & Servan-Schreiber, D. (1992). Context, cortex, and dopamine: A connectionist approach to behavior and biology in Schizophrenia. *Psychological Review, 99*(1), 45–77.

Cohen, S., & Herbert, T. B. (1996). Health psychology: Psychological factors and physical disease from the perspective of human psychoneuroimmunology. *Annual Review of Psychology, 47,* 113–142.

Collinson, S. L., Mackay, C. E., James, A. C., Quested, D. J., Phillips, T., Roberts, N., et al. (2003). Brain volume, asymmetry and intellectual impairment in relation to sex in early-onset Schizophrenia. *British Journal of Psychiatry, 183,* 114–120.

Corcoran, C., Walker, E., Huot, R., Mittal, V., Tessner, K., Kestler, L., et al. (2003). The stress cascade and Schizophrenia: Etiology and onset. *Schizophrenia Bulletin, 29*(4), 671–692.

Cornblatt, B. A., & Erlenmeyer-Kimling, L. (1985). Global attentional deviance as a marker of risk for Schizophrenia: Specificity and predictive validity. *Journal of Abnormal Psychology, 94*(4), 470–486.

Cornblatt, B. A., Lencz, T., & Obuchowski, M. (2002). The Schizophrenia prodrome: Treatment and high-risk perspectives. *Schizophrenia Research, 54*(1/2), 177–186.

Cornblatt, B. A., Lenzenweger, M. F., Dworkin, R. H., & Erlenmeyer-Kimling, L. (1992). Childhood attentional dysfunctions predict social deficits in unaffected adults at risk for Schizophrenia. *British Journal of Psychiatry, 163*(18), 59–64.

Costa, E., Davis, J., Grayson, D. R., Guidotti, A., Pappas, G. D., & Pesold, C. (2001). Dendritic spine hypoplasticity and downregulation of reelin and GABAergic tone in Schizophrenia vulnerability. *Neurobiology of Disease, 8*(5), 723–742.

Cosway, R., Byrne, M., Clafferty, R., Hodges, A., Grant, E., Abukmeil, S. S., et al. (2000). Neuropsychological change in young people at high risk for Schizophrenia: Results from the first two neuropsychological assessments of the Edinburgh High Risk Study. *Psychological Medicine, 30*(5), 1111–1121.

Crow, T. J., Done, D. J., & Sacker, A. (1995). Childhood precursors of psychosis as clues to its evolutionary origins. *European Archives of Psychiatry and Clinical Neuroscience, 245*(2), 61–69.

Crow, T. J., MacMillan, J., Johnson, A., & Johnstone, E. (1986). A randomised controlled trial of prophylactic neuroleptic treatment. *British Journal of Psychiatry, 148,* 120–127.

Curristin, S. M., Cao, A., Stewart, W. B., Zhang, H., Madri, J. A., Morrow, J. S., et al. (2002). Disrupted synaptic development in the hypoxic newborn brain. *Proceeds of the National Academy of Science, USA, 99*(24), 15729–15734.

David, A. S., Malmberg, A., Brandt, L., Allebeck, P., & Lewis, G. (1997). IQ and risk for Schizophrenia: A population-based cohort study. *Psychological Medicine, 27*(6), 1311–1323.

Davidson, M., Reichenberg, A., Rabinowitz, J., Weiser, M., Kaplan, Z., & Mark, M. (1999). Behavioral and intellectual markers for Schizophrenia in apparently healthy male adolescents. *American Journal of Psychiatry, 156*(9), 1328–1335.

De Bellis, M. D., Keshavan, M. S., Beers, S. R., Hall, J., Frustaci, K., Masalehdan, A., et al. (2001). Sex differences in brain maturation during childhood and adolescence. *Cerebral Cortex, 11*(6), 552–557.

DeKosky, S. T., & Marek, K. (2003). Looking backward to move forward: Early detection of neurodegenerative disorders. *Science, 302*(5646), 830–834.

DeLisi, L. E., Sakuma, M., Ge, S., & Kushner, M. (1998). Association of brain structural change with the heterogeneous course of Schizophrenia from early childhood through five years subsequent to a first hospitalization. *Psychiatry Research, 84*(2/3), 75–88.

DeLisi, L. E., Sakuma, M., Tew, W., Kushner, M., Hoff, A. L., & Grimson, R. (1997). Schizophrenia as a chronic active brain process: A study of progressive brain structural change subsequent to the onset of Schizophrenia. *Psychiatry Research: Neuroimaging Section, 74,* 129–140.

DeLisi, L. E., Tew, W., Xie, S., Hoff, A. L., Sakuma, M., Kushner, M., et al. (1995). A prospective follow-up study of brain morphology and cognition in first-episode schizophrenic patients: Preliminary findings. *Biological Psychiatry, 38*(6), 349–360.

Driscoll, R. M. (1984). Intentional and incidental learning in children vulnerable to psychopathology. In N. F. Watt, E. J. Anthony, L. C. Wynne, & J. E. Roif (Eds.), *Children at risk for Schizophrenia: A longitudinal perspective* (pp. 320–326). New York: Cambridge University Press.

Egan, M. F., Hyde, T. M., Bonomo, J. B., Mattay, V. S., Bigelow, L. B., Goldberg, T. E., et al. (2001). Relative risk of neurological signs in siblings of patients with Schizophrenia. *American Journal of Psychiatry, 158*(11), 1827–1834.

Erlenmeyer-Kimling, L., & Cornblatt, B. (1978). Attentional measures in a study of children at high-risk for Schizophrenia. *Journal of Psychiatric Research, 14*(1/4), 93–98.

Erlenmeyer-Kimling, L., & Cornblatt, B. (1987). High-risk research in Schizophrenia: A summary of what has been learned. *Journal of Psychiatric Research, 21*(4), 401–411.

Faraone, S. V., Seidman, L. J., Kremen, W. S., Toomey, R., Pepple, J. R., & Tsuang, M. T. (1999). Neuropsychological functioning among the nonpsychotic relatives of schizophrenic patients: A 4-year follow-up study. *Journal of Abnormal Psychology, 108*(1), 176–181.

Faraone, S. V., Seidman, L. J., Kremen, W. S., Toomey, R., Pepple, J. R., & Tsuang, M. T. (2000). Neuropsychologic functioning among the nonpsychotic relatives of schizophrenic patients: The effect of genetic loading. *Biological Psychiatry, 48*(2), 120–126.

Feinberg, I. (1982). Schizophrenia: Caused by a fault in programmed synaptic elimination during adolescence? *Journal of Psychiatric Research, 17*(4), 319–334.

Feinberg, I. (1990). Cortical pruning and the development of Schizophrenia. *Schizophrenia Bulletin, 16*(4), 567–570.

Fenton, W. S., & McGlashan, T. H. (1989). Risk of Schizophrenia in character disordered patients. *American Journal of Psychiatry, 146*(10), 1280–1284.

Fish, B. (1977). Neurobiologic antecedents of Schizophrenia in children: Evidence for an inherited, congenital neurointegrative defect. *Archives of General Psychiatry, 34*(11), 1297–1313.

Fish, B. (1987). Infant predictors of the longitudinal course of schizophrenic development. *Schizophrenia Bulletin, 13*(3), 395–409.

Freimer, N., & Sabatti, C. (2003). The human phenome project. *Nature Genetics, 34*(1), 15–21.

Giedd, J. N., Jeffries, N. O., Blumenthal, J., Castellanos, F. X., Vaituzis, A. C., Fernandez, T., et al. (1999). Childhood-onset Schizophrenia: Progressive brain changes during adolescence. *Biological Psychiatry, 46*(7), 892–898.

Glahn, D. C., Kim, J., Cohen, M. S., Poutanen, V. P., Therman, S., Bava, S., et al. (2002). Maintenance and manipulation in spatial working memory: Dissociations in the prefrontal cortex. *Neuroimage, 17*(1), 201–213.

Glantz, L. A., & Lewis, D. A. (2000). Decreased dendritic spine density on prefrontal cortical pyramidal neurons in Schizophrenia. *Archives of General Psychiatry, 57*(1), 65–73.

Glazier, A., Nadeau, J., & Aitman, T. (2002). Finding genes that underlie complex traits. *Science, 298*, 2345–2349.

Glick, I., Suppes, T., DeBattista, C., Hu, R., & Marder, S. (2001). Psychopharmacologic treatment strategies for depression, bipolar disorder, and Schizophrenia. *Annals of Internal Medicine, 134*(1), 47–60.

Globus, A., Rosenzweig, M. R., Bennett, E. L., & Diamond, M. C. (1973). Effects of differential experience on dendritic spine counts in rat cerebral cortex. *Journal of Comparative and Physiological Psychology, 82*(2), 175–181.

Gogtay, N., Sporn, A., Clasen, L. S., Greenstein, D., Giedd, J. N., Lenane, M., et al. (2003). Structural brain MRI abnormalities in healthy siblings of patients with childhood-onset Schizophrenia. *American Journal of Psychiatry, 160*(3), 569–571.

Gold, S., Arndt, S., Nopoulos, P., O'Leary, D. S., & Andreasen, N. C. (1999). Longitudinal study of cognitive function in first-episode and recent-onset Schizophrenia. *American Journal of Psychiatry, 156*(9), 1342–1348.

Goodman, S. H. (1987). Emory University project on children of disturbed parents. *Schizophrenia Bulletin, 13*(3), 411–423.

Gottesman, I. I., & Gould, T. D. (2003). The endophenotype concept in psychiatry: Etymology and strategic intentions. *American Journal of Psychiatry, 160*, 636–645.

Grace, A. A., Moore, H., & O'Donnell, P. (1998). The modulation of corticoaccumbens transmission by limbic afferents and dopamine: A model for the pathophysiology of Schizophrenia. *Advances in Pharmacology, 42*, 721–724.

Gray, J. A., Feldon, J., Rawlins, J. N., & Hemsley, D. R. (1991). The neuropsychology of Schizophrenia. *Behavioral and Brain Sciences, 14*(1), 1–84.

Gruzelier, J., Mednick, S. A., & Schulsinger, F. (1979). Lateralized impairment in the WISC profile of children at risk for psychopathology. In J. Gruzelier & P. Flor-Henry (Eds.), *Hemisphere asymmetries of function in psychopathology* (Vol. 3, pp. 105–109). New York: Elsevier.

Gur, R. E., Cowell, P., Turetsky, B. I., Gallacher, F., Cannon, T., Bilker, W., et al. (1998). A follow-up magnetic resonance imaging study of Schizophrenia: Relationship of neuroanatomical changes to clinical and neurobehavioral measures. *Archives of General Psychiatry, 55*(2), 145–152.

Hafner, H., & Nowotny, B. (1995). Epidemiology of early-onset Schizophrenia. *European Archives of Psychiatry and Clinical Neuroscience, 245*(2), 80–92.

Hallett, S., Quinn, D., & Hewitt, J. (1986). Defective interhemispheric integration and anomalous language lateralization in children at risk for Schizophrenia. *Journal of Nervous and Mental Diseases, 174*, 418–427.

Hans, S. L., Marcus, J., Nuechterlein, K. H., Asarnow, R. F., Styr, B., & Auerbach, J. G. (1999). Neurobehavioral deficits at adolescence in children at risk for Schizophrenia: The Jerusalem Infant Development Study. *Archives of General Psychiatry, 56*(8), 741–748.

Harvey, P., Winters, K., Weintraub, S., & Neale, J. M. (1981). Distractibility in children vulnerable to psychopathology. *Journal of Abnormal Psychology, 90*(4), 298–304.

Heinssen, R. K., Cuthbert, B. N., Breiling, J., Colpe, L. J., & Dolan-Sewell, R. (2003). Overcoming barriers to research in early serious mental illness: Issues for future collaboration. *Schizophrenia Bulletin, 29*(4), 737–745.

Heydebrand, G., Weiser, M., Rabinowitz, J., Hoff, A. L., DeLisi, L., & Csernansky, J. G. (2004). Correlates of cognitive deficits in first episode Schizophrenia. *Schizophrenia Research, 68*(1), 1–9.

Hoff, A. L., Sakuma, M., Wieneke, M., Horon, R., Kushner, M., & DeLisi, L. E. (1999). Longitudinal neuropsychological follow-up study of patients with first-episode Schizophrenia. *American Journal of Psychiatry, 156*(9), 1336–1341.

Hoffman, R. E., & McGlashan, T. H. (1997). Synaptic elimination, neurodevelopment, and the mechanism of hallucinated "voices" in Schizophrenia. *American Journal of Psychiatry, 154*(12), 1683–1689.

Hollis, C. (1995). Child and adolescent (juvenile onset) Schizophrenia: A case control study of premorbid developmental impairments. *British Journal of Psychiatry, 166*(4), 489–495.

Huttenlocher, P. R. (1979). Synaptic density in human frontal cortex: Developmental changes and effects of aging. *Brain Research, 163*(2), 195–205.

Isohanni, M., Jones, P. B., Moilanen, K., Rantakallio, P., Veijola, J., Oja, H., et al. (2001). Early developmental milestones in adult Schizophrenia and other psychoses: A 31-year follow-up of the northern Finland 1966 birth cohort. *Schizophrenia Research, 52*(1/2), 1–19.

Jablensky, A., Sartorius, N., Ernberg, G., Anker, M., Korten, A., Cooper, J. E., et al. (1992). Schizophrenia: Manifestations, incidence and course in different cultures—A World Health Organization ten-country study. *Psychological Medicine, 20*, 1–97.

Jacobs, S., & Myers, J. (1976). Recent life events and acute schizophrenic psychosis: A controlled study. *Journal of Nervous and Mental Diseases, 162*(2), 75–87.

Jakob, H., & Beckmann, H. (1986). Prenatal developmental disturbances in the limbic allocortex in schizophrenics. *Journal of Neural Transmission, 65*(3/4), 303–326.

James, A. C. D., James, S., Smith, D. M., & Javaloyes, A. (2004). Cerebellar, prefrontal cortex, and thalamic volumes over two time points in adolescent-onset Schizophrenia. *American Journal of Psychiatry, 161*(6), 1023–1029.

James, A. C. D., Javaloyes, A., James, S., & Smith, D. M. (2002). Evidence for non-progressive changes in adolescent-onset Schizophrenia. *British Journal of Psychiatry, 180,* 339–344.

Jansen, L. M., Gispen-de Wied, C. C., Gademan, P. J., De Jonge, R. C., van der Linden, J. A., & Kahn, R. S. (1998). Blunted cortisol response to a psychosocial stressor in Schizophrenia. *Schizophrenia Research, 33*(1/2), 87–94.

Jansen, L. M., Gispen-de Wied, C. C., & Kahn, R. S. (2000). Selective impairments in the stress response in schizophrenic patients. *Psychopharmacology, 149*(3), 319–325.

Johnstone, E., Crow, T., Johnson, A., & MacMillan, J. (1986). The Northwick Park study of first episodes of Schizophrenia: Pt. I. Presentation of the illness and problems relating to admission. *British Journal of Psychiatry, 148,* 115–120.

Jones, P., Rodgers, B., Murray, R., & Marmot, M. (1994). Child development risk factors for adult Schizophrenia in the British 1946 birth cohort. *Lancet, 344*(8934), 1398–1402.

Kaneda, Y., Fujii, A., & Ohmori, T. (2002). The hypothalamic-pituitary-adrenal axis in chronic schizophrenic patients long-term treated with neuroleptics. *Progress in Neuro-Psychopharmacology and Biological Psychiatry, 26*(5), 935–938.

Kasai, K., Shenton, M. E., Salisbury, D. F., Hirayasu, Y., Lee, C. U., Ciszewski, A. A., et al. (2003). Progressive decrease of left superior temporal gyrus gray matter volume in patients with first-episode Schizophrenia. *American Journal of Psychiatry, 160*(1), 156–164.

Keller, A., Castellanos, F. X., Vaituzis, A. C., Jeffries, N. O., Giedd, J. N., & Rapoport, J. L. (2003). Progressive loss of cerebellar volume in childhood-onset Schizophrenia. *American Journal of Psychiatry, 160*(1), 128–133.

Keller, A., Jeffries, N. O., Blumenthal, J., Clasen, L. S., Liu, H., Giedd, J. N., et al. (2003). Corpus callosum development in childhood-onset Schizophrenia. *Schizophrenia Research, 62,* 105–114.

Keshavan, M. S. (1999). Development, disease and degeneration in Schizophrenia: A unitary pathophysiological model. *Journal of Psychiatric Research, 33*(6), 513–521.

Keshavan, M. S., Anderson, S., & Pettegrew, J. W. (1994). Is Schizophrenia due to excessive synaptic pruning in the prefrontal cortex? The Feinberg hypothesis revisited. *Journal of Psychiatric Research, 28*(3), 239–265.

Keshavan, M. S., Diwadkar, V. A., Spencer, S. M., Harenski, K. A., Luna, B., & Sweeney, J. A. (2002). A preliminary functional magnetic resonance imaging study in offspring of schizophrenic parents. *Progress in Neuro-Psychopharmacology and Biological Psychiatry, 26*(6), 1143–1149.

Keshavan, M. S., & Hogarty, G. E. (1999). Brain maturational processes and delayed onset in Schizophrenia. *Development and Psychopathology, 11*(3), 525–543.

Keshavan, M. S., Montrose, D. M., Pierri, J. N., Dick, E. L., Rosenberg, D., Talagala, L., et al. (1997). Magnetic resonance imaging and spectroscopy in offspring at risk for Schizophrenia: Preliminary studies. *Progress in Neuro-Psychopharmacology and Biological Psychiatry, 21*(8), 1285–1295.

Keshavan, M. S., Pettegrew, J. W., Panchalingam, K. S., & Kaplan, D. (1991). Phosphorus 31 magnetic resonance spectroscopy detects altered brain metabolism before onset of Schizophrenia. *Archives of General Psychiatry, 48*(12), 1112–1113.

Keshavan, M. S., Stanley, J. A., Montrose, D. M., Minshew, N. J., & Pettegrew, J. W. (2003). Prefrontal membrane phospholipid metabolism of child and adolescent offspring at risk for Schizophrenia or schizoaffective disorder: An in vivo 31P MRS study. *Molecular Psychiatry, 8*(3), 251, 316–323.

Keshavan, M. S., Stanley, J. A., & Pettegrew, J. W. (2000). Magnetic resonance spectroscopy in Schizophrenia: Methodological issues and findings: Pt. II. *Biological Psychiatry, 48*(5), 369–380.

Kirschbaum, C., & Hellhammer, D. H. (1989). Salivary cortisol in psychobiological research: An overview. *Neuropsychobiology, 22*(3), 150–169.

Klein, E. H., & Salzman, L. F. (1984). Response contingent learning in children at risk. In N. F. Watt, E. J. Anthony, L. C. Wynne, & J. E. Rolf (Eds.), *Children at risk for Schizophrenia: A longitudinal perspective* (pp. 371–375). New York: Cambridge University Press.

Klemm, S., Rzanny, R., Riehemann, S., Volz, H. P., Schmidt, B., Gerhard, U. J., et al. (2001). Cerebral phosphate metabolism in first-degree relatives of patients with Schizophrenia. *American Journal of Psychiatry, 6,* 958–960.

Kovelman, J. A., & Scheibel, A. B. (1984). A neurohistological correlate of Schizophrenia. *Biological Psychiatry, 19*(12), 1601–1621.

Kraepelin, E. (1918). *Clinical psychiatry: A text-book for students and physicians* (A. R. Diefendorf, Trans.). New York: Macmillan.

Kravariti, E., Morris, R. G., Rabe-Hesketh, S., Murray, R. M., & Frangou, S. (2003). The Maudsley early onset Schizophrenia study: Cognitive function in adolescents with recent onset Schizophrenia. *Schizophrenia Research, 61,* 137–148.

Kupfer, D., First, M., & Regier, D. (2002). *A research agenda for DSM-V.* Washington, DC: American Psychological Association.

Landau, R., Harth, P., Othnay, N., & Sharfhertz, C. (1972). The influence of psychotic parents on their children's development. *American Journal of Psychiatry, 129*(1), 38–43.

Leff, J. P., Hirsch, S. R., Gaind, R., Rohde, P. D., & Stevens, B. C. (1973). Life events and maintenance therapy in schizophrenic relapse. *British Journal of Psychiatry, 123,* 659–660.

Lifshitz, M., Kugelmass, S., & Karov, M. (1985). Perceptual-motor and memory performance of high-risk children. *Schizophrenia Bulletin, 11*(1), 74–84.

Lipska, B. K., & Weinberger, D. R. (2002). A neurodevelopmental model of Schizophrenia: Neonatal disconnection of the hippocampus. *Neurotoxicity Research, 4*(5/6), 469–475.

Loebel, A., Lieberman, J., Alvir, J., Mayerhoff, D., Geisler, S., & Szymanski, S. (1992). Duration of psychosis and outcome in first-episode Schizophrenia. *American Journal of Psychiatry, 149*(9), 1183–1188.

Lowy, M. T., Gault, L., & Yamamoto, B. K. (1993). Adrenalectomy attenuates stress-induced elevations in extracellular glutamate concentrations in the hippocampus. *Journal of Neurochemistry, 61*(5), 1957–1960.

Marcus, J., Auerbach, J., Wilkinson, L., & Burack, C. M. (1981). Infants at risk for Schizophrenia: The Jerusalem Infant Development Study. *Archives of General Psychiatry, 38*(6), 703–713.

Marcus, J., Hans, S. L., Auerbach, J. G., & Auerbach, A. G. (1993). Children at risk for Schizophrenia: The Jerusalem Infant Development Study: II. Neurobehavioral deficits at school age. *Archives of General Psychiatry, 50*(10), 797–809.

Marcus, J., Hans, S. L., Mednick, S. A., Schulsinger, F., & Michelsen, N. (1985). Neurological dysfunctioning in offspring of schizophrenics in Israel and Denmark: A replication analysis. *Archives of General Psychiatry, 42*(8), 753–761.

Marder, S. (1996). Pharmacological treatment strategies in acute Schizophrenia. *International Clinical Psychopharmacology, 11*(Suppl. 2), 29–34.

Mathalon, D. H., Rapoport, J. L., Davis, K. L., & Krystal, J. H. (2003). Neurotoxicity, neuroplasticity, and magnetic resonance imaging morphometry. *Archives of General Psychiatry, 60,* 846–848.

McEwen, B. S. (1994). Corticosteroids and hippocampal plasticity. *Annals of the New York Academy of Sciences, 746,* 134–142.

McEwen, B. S., & Seeman, T. (1999). Protective and damaging effects of mediators of stress: Elaborating and testing the concepts of allostasis and allostatic load. *Annals of the New York Academy of Sciences, 896,* 30–47.

McGlashan, T. H., & Fenton, W. S. (1992). The positive-negative distinction in Schizophrenia: Review of natural history validators. *Archives of General Psychiatry, 49*(1), 63–72.

McGlashan, T. H., Miller, T. J., & Woods, S. W. (2001). Pre-onset detection and intervention research in Schizophrenia psychoses: Current estimates of benefit and risk. *Schizophrenia Bulletin, 27*(4), 563–570.

McGorry, P. D., Yung, A. R., & Phillips, L. J. (2003). The "close-in" or ultra high-risk model: A safe and effective strategy for research and clinical intervention in prepsychotic mental disorder. *Schizophrenia Bulletin, 29*(4), 771–790.

McNeil, T. F., Cantor-Graae, E., & Weinberger, D. R. (2000). Relationship of obstetric complications and differences in size of brain structures in monozygotic twin pairs discordant for Schizophrenia. *American Journal of Psychiatry, 157*(2), 203–212.

Mednick, S. A., & Schulsinger, F. (1964). A pre-schizophrenic sample. *Acta Psychiatrica Scandinavica, 40*(Suppl.), 135.

Mehler, C., & Warnke, A. (2002). Structural brain abnormalities specific to childhood-onset Schizophrenia identified by neuroimaging techniques. *Journal of Neural Transmission, 109,* 219–234.

Merikangas, K., & Risch, N. (2003). Will the genomics revolution revolutionize psychiatry? *American Journal of Psychiatry, 160*(4), 625–635.

Meyer, S. E., Bearden, C. E., Lux, S. R., Gordon, J. L., Johnson, J. K., O'Brien, M. P., et al. (2005). The psychosis prodrome in adolescent patients viewed through the lens of DSM-IV. *Journal of Child and Adolescent Psychopharmacology, 15*(3), 434–451.

Michie, P. T., Kent, A., Stienstra, R., Castine, R., Johnston, J., Dedman, K., et al. (2000). Phenotypic markers as risk factors in Schizophrenia: Neurocognitive functions. *Australian and New Zealand Journal of Psychiatry, 34*(Suppl.), S74–S85.

Miller, P., Lawrie, S. M., Hodges, A., Clafferty, R., Cosway, R., & Johnstone, E. C. (2001). Genetic liability, illicit drug use, life stress and psychotic symptoms: Preliminary findings from the Edinburgh study of people at high risk for Schizophrenia. *Social Psychiatry and Psychiatric Epidemiology, 36*(7), 338–342.

Miller, T. J., McGlashan, T. H., Rosen, J. L., Cadenhead, K., Ventura, J., McFarlane, W., et al. (2003). Prodromal assessment with the Structured Interview for Prodromal Syndromes and the Scale of Prodromal Symptoms: Predictive validity, interrater reliability, and training to reliability. *Schizophrenia Bulletin, 29*(4), 703–715.

Moghaddam, B. (2002). Stress activation of glutamate neurotransmission in the prefrontal cortex: Implications for dopamine-associated psychiatric disorders. *Biological Psychiatry, 51*(10), 775–787.

Moghaddam, B., Bolinao, M. L., Stein-Behrens, B., & Sapolsky, R. (1994). Glucocorticoids mediate the stress-induced extracellular accumulation of glutamate. *Brain Research, 655*(1/2), 251–254.

Moore, G. J., Slovis, T. L., & Chugani, H. T. (1998). Proton magnetic resonance spectroscopy in children with Sturge-Weber syndrome. *Journal of Child Neurology, 13*(7), 332–335.

Murray, R. M., & Lewis, S. W. (1987). Is Schizophrenia a neurodevelopmental disorder? *British Medical Journal, 295*(6600), 681–682.

Murray, R. M., Sham, P., Van Os, J., Zanelli, J., Cannon, M., & McDonald, C. (2004). A developmental model for similarities and dissimilarities between Schizophrenia and bipolar disorder. *Schizophrenia Research, 71,* 405–416.

Nawa, H., Takahashi, M., & Patterson, P. H. (2000). Cytokine and growth factor involvement in Schizophrenia: Support for the developmental model. *Molecular Psychiatry, 5*(6), 594–603.

Nicolson, R., Lenane, M., Singaracharlu, S., Malaspina, D., Giedd, J. N., Hamburger, S. D., et al. (2000). Premorbid speech and language impairments in childhood-onset Schizophrenia: Association with risk factors. *American Journal of Psychiatry, 157*(5), 794–800.

Norman, R. M., & Malla, A. K. (1993). Stressful life events and Schizophrenia: I. A review of the research. *British Journal of Psychiatry, 162,* 161–166.

Nyakas, C., Buwalda, B., & Luiten, P. G. (1996). Hypoxia and brain development. *Progress in Neurobiology, 49*(1), 1–51.

Ojeda, S. R., & Ma, Y. J. (1999). Glial-neuronal interactions in the neuroendocrine control of mammalian puberty: Facilitatory effects of gonadal steroids. *Journal of Neurobiology, 40*(4), 528–540.

Olney, J. W., & Farber, N. B. (1995). Glutamate receptor dysfunction and Schizophrenia. *Archives of General Psychiatry, 52*(12), 998–1007.

Pantelis, C., Velakoulis, D., McGorry, P. D., Wood, S. J., Suckling, J., Phillips, L. J., et al. (2003). Neuroanatomical abnormalities before and after onset of psychosis: A cross-sectional and longitudinal MRI comparison. *Lancet, 361,* 281–288.

Pantelis, C., Yucel, M., Wood, S. J., McGorry, P. D., & Velakoulis, D. (2003). Early and late neurodevelopmental disturbances in Schizophrenia and their functional consequences. *Australian and New Zealand Journal of Psychiatry, 37*(4), 399–406.

Park, S., Holzman, P. S., & Goldman-Rakic, P. S. (1995). Spatial working memory deficits in the relatives of schizophrenic patients. *Archives of General Psychiatry, 52*(10), 821–828.

Passe, T. J., Charles, H. C., Rajagopalan, P., & Krishnan, K. R. (1995). Nuclear magnetic resonance spectroscopy: A review of neuropsychiatric applications. *Progress in Neuro-Psychopharmacology and Biological Psychiatry, 19*(4), 541–563.

Pettegrew, J. W., Keshavan, M. S., Panchalingam, K., & Strychor, S. (1991). Alterations in brain high-energy phosphate and membrane phospholipid metabolism in first-episode, drug-naive schizophrenics: A pilot study of the dorsal prefrontal cortex by in vivo phosphorus 31 nuclear magnetic resonance spectroscopy. *Archives of General Psychiatry, 48*(6), 563–568.

Pettegrew, J. W., Klunk, W. E., Panchalingam, K., McClure, R. J., & Stanley, J. A. (2000). Molecular insights into neurodevelopmental and neurodegenerative diseases. *Brain Research Bulletin, 53*(4), 455–469.

Pettegrew, J. W., & Minshew, N. J. (1992). Molecular insights into Schizophrenia. *Journal of Neural Transmission, 36,* 23–40.

Pfefferbaum, A., & Marsh, L. (1995). Structural brain imaging in Schizophrenia. *Clinical Neuroscience, 3*(2), 105–111.

Phillips, L. J., Velakoulis, D., Pantelis, C., Wood, S., Yuen, H. P., Yung, A. R., et al. (2002). Non-reduction in hippocampal volume is associated with higher risk of psychosis. *Schizophrenia Research, 58*(2/3), 145–158.

Phillips, L. J., Yung, A. R., Yuen, H. P., Pantelis, C., & McGorry, P. D. (2002). Prediction and prevention of transition to psychosis in young people at incipient risk for Schizophrenia. *American Journal of Medical Genetics, 114*(8), 929–937.

Pogue-Geile, M. F., & Harrow, M. (1984). Negative and positive symptoms in Schizophrenia and depression: A followup. *Schizophrenia Bulletin, 10*(3), 371–387.

Poulton, R., Caspi, A., Moffitt, T. E., Cannon, M., Murray, R., & Harrington, H. (2000). Children's self-reported psychotic symptoms and adult schizophreniform disorder: A 15-year longitudinal study. *Archives of General Psychiatry, 57*(11), 1053–1058.

Rees, S., Mallard, C., Breen, S., Stringer, M., Cock, M., & Harding, R. (1998). Fetal brain injury following prolonged hypoxemia and placental insufficiency: A review. *Comprehensive Biochemical Physiological and Molecular Integrated Physiology, 119*(3), 653–660.

Reveley, A. M., Reveley, M. A., Clifford, C. A., & Murray, R. M. (1982). Cerebral ventricular size in twins discordant for Schizophrenia. *Lancet, 1*(8271), 540–541.

Risch, N. (2000). Searching for genetic determinants in the new millennium. *Nature, 405*, 847–856.

Rosenzweig, M. R., Leiman, A. L., & Breedlove, S. M. (2002). *Biological psychology* (3rd ed.). Sunderland, MA: Sinauer.

Ross, B., & Michaelis, T. (1994). Clinical applications of magnetic resonance spectroscopy. *Magnetic Resonance Quarterly, 10*(4), 191–247.

Rosso, I. M., Bearden, C. E., Hollister, J. M., Gasperoni, T. L., Sanchez, L. E., Hadley, T., et al. (2000). Childhood neuromotor dysfunction in Schizophrenia patients and their unaffected siblings: A prospective cohort study. *Schizophrenia Bulletin, 26*(2), 367–378.

Rosso, I. M., Cannon, T. D., Huttunen, T., Huttunen, M. O., Lonnqvist, J., & Gasperoni, T. L. (2000). Obstetric risk factors for early-onset Schizophrenia in a Finnish birth cohort. *American Journal of Psychiatry, 157*(5), 801–807.

Russell, A. J., Munro, J. C., Jones, P. B., Hemsley, D. R., & Murray, R. M. (1997). Schizophrenia and the myth of intellectual decline. *American Journal of Psychiatry, 154*(5), 635–639.

Rutschmann, J., Cornblatt, B., & Erlenmeyer-Kimling, L. (1980). Auditory recognition memory in adolescents at risk for Schizophrenia: Report on a verbal continuous recognition task. *Psychiatry Research, 3*(2), 151–161.

Rzanny, R., Klemm, S., Reichenbach, J. R., Pfleiderer, S. O., Schmidt, B., Volz, H. P., et al. (2003). 31P-MR spectroscopy in children and adolescents with a familial risk of Schizophrenia. *European Radiology, 13*(4), 763–770.

Sameroff, A., Seifer, R., Zax, M., & Barocas, R. (1987). Early indicators of developmental risk: Rochester Longitudinal Study. *Schizophrenia Bulletin, 13*(3), 383–394.

Samii, A., Nutt, J. G., & Ransom, B. R. (2004). Parkinson's disease. *Lancet, 363*(9423), 1783–1793.

Sapolsky, R. M., Uno, H., Rebert, C. S., & Finch, C. E. (1990). Hippocampal damage associated with prolonged glucocorticoid exposure in primates. *Journal of Neuroscience, 10*(9), 2897–2902.

Saykin, A. J., Shtasel, D. L., Gur, R. E., & Kester, D. B. (1994). Neuropsychological deficits in neuroleptic naive patients with first-episode Schizophrenia. *Archives of General Psychiatry, 51*(2), 124–131.

Schreiber, H., Stolz-Born, G., Kornhuber, H. H., & Born, J. (1992). Event-related potential correlates of impaired selective attention in children at high risk for Schizophrenia. *Biological Psychiatry, 32*(8), 634–651.

Seidman, L. J., Faraone, S. V., Goldstein, J. M., Goodman, J. M., Kremen, W. S., Matsuda, G., et al. (1997). Reduced subcortical brain volumes in nonpsychotic siblings of schizophrenic patients: A pilot magnetic resonance imaging study. *American Journal of Medical Genetics, 74*(5), 507–514.

Seidman, L. J., Faraone, S. V., Goldstein, J. M., Goodman, J. M., Kremen, W. S., Toomey, R., et al. (1999). Thalamic and amygdala-hippocampal volume reductions in first-degree relatives of patients with Schizophrenia: An MRI-based morphometric analysis. *Biological Psychiatry, 46*(7), 941–954.

Seidman, L. J., Faraone, S. V., Goldstein, J. M., Kremen, W. S., Horton, N. J., Makris, N., et al. (2002). Left hippocampal volume as a vulnerability indicator for Schizophrenia: A magnetic resonance imaging morphometric study of nonpsychotic first-degree relatives. *Archives of General Psychiatry, 59*(9), 839–849.

Selemon, L. D., & Goldman-Rakic, P. S. (1999). The reduced neuropil hypothesis: A circuit based model of Schizophrenia. *Biological Psychiatry, 45*(1), 17–25.

Selemon, L. D., Rajkowska, G., & Goldman-Rakic, P. S. (1995). Abnormally high neuronal density in the schizophrenic cortex: A morphometric analysis of prefrontal area 9 and occipital area 17. *Archives of General Psychiatry, 52*(10), 805–818.

Selemon, L. D., Rajkowska, G., & Goldman-Rakic, P. S. (1998). Elevated neuronal density in prefrontal area 46 in brains from schizophrenic patients: Application of a three-dimensional, stereologic counting method. *Journal of Comparative Neurology, 392*(3), 402–412.

Siever, L. J., Kalus, O. F., & Keefe, R. S. (1993). The boundaries of Schizophrenia. *Psychiatric Clinics of North America, 16*(2), 217–244.

Sohlberg, S. C. (1985). Personality and neuropsychological performance of high-risk children. *Schizophrenia Bulletin, 11*(1), 48–60.

Spiegel, D., & Kato, P. M. (1996). Psychosocial influences on cancer incidence and progression. *Harvard Review of Psychiatry, 4*(1), 10–26.

Sporn, A. L., Greenstein, D. K., Gogtay, N., Jeffries, N. O., Lenane, M., Gochman, P., et al. (2003). Progressive brain volume loss during adolescence in childhood-onset Schizophrenia. *American Journal of Psychiatry, 160*, 2181–2189.

Staal, W. G., Hulshoff Pol, H. E., Schnack, H. G., Hoogendoorn, M. L., Jellema, K., & Kahn, R. S. (2000). Structural brain abnormalities in patients with Schizophrenia and their healthy siblings. *American Journal of Psychiatry, 157*(3), 416–421.

Stanley, J. A., Williamson, P. C., Drost, D. J., Carr, T. J., Rylett, R. J., Malla, A., et al. (1995). An in vivo study of the prefrontal cortex of schizophrenic patients at different stages of illness via phosphorus magnetic resonance spectroscopy. *Archives of General Psychiatry, 52*(5), 399–406.

Steel, R. M., Bastin, M. E., McConnell, S., Marshall, I., Cunningham-Owens, D. G., Lawrie, S. M., et al. (2001). Diffusion tensor imaging (DTI) and proton magnetic resonance spectroscopy (1H MRS) in schizophrenic subjects and normal controls. *Psychiatry Research, 106*(3), 161–170.

Strike, P. C., & Steptoe, A. (2004). Psychosocial factors in the development of coronary artery disease. *Progress in Cardiovascular Diseases, 46*(4), 337–347.

Suddath, R. L., Christison, G. W., Torrey, E. F., Casanova, M. F., & Weinberger, D. R. (1990). Anatomical abnormalities in the brains of monozygotic twins discordant for Schizophrenia. *New England Journal of Medicine, 322*(12), 789–794.

Teicher, M. H., Andersen, S. L., Polcari, A., Anderson, C. M., & Navalta, C. P. (2002). Developmental neurobiology of childhood stress and trauma. *Psychiatric Clinics of North America, 25*(2), vii–viii, 397–426.

Tennant, C. C. (1985). Stress and Schizophrenia: A review. *Integrative Psychiatry, 3*(4), 248–255.

Theberge, J., Bartha, R., Drost, D. J., Menon, R. S., Malla, A., Takhar, J., et al. (2002). Glutamate and glutamine measured with 4.0 T proton MRS in never-treated patients with Schizophrenia and healthy volunteers. *American Journal of Psychiatry, 159*(11), 1944–1946.

Thompson, P. M., Vidal, C., Giedd, J. N., Gochman, P., Blumenthal, J., Nicolson, R., et al. (2001). Mapping adolescent brain change reveals dynamic wave of accelerated gray matter loss in very early-onset Schizophrenia. *Proceeds of the National Academy of Science, USA, 98*(20), 11650–11655.

Tibbo, P., Hanstock, C., Valiakalayil, A., & Allen, P. (2004). 3-T proton MRS investigation of glutamate and glutamine in adolescents at high genetic risk for Schizophrenia. *American Journal of Psychiatry, 161*(6), 1116–1118.

Toulopoulou, T., Rabe-Hesketh, S., King, H., Murray, R. M., & Morris, R. G. (2003). Episodic memory in schizophrenic patients and their relatives. *Schizophrenia Research, 63*(3), 261–271.

Van Erp, T. G., Saleh, P. A., Rosso, I. M., Huttunen, M., Lonnqvist, J., Pirkola, T., et al. (2002). Contributions of genetic risk and fetal hypoxia to hippocampal volume in patients with Schizophrenia or schizoaffective disorder, their unaffected siblings, and healthy unrelated volunteers. *American Journal of Psychiatry, 159*(9), 1514–1520.

Vargha-Khadem, F., Gadian, D. G., Watkins, K. E., Connelly, A., Van Paesschen, W., & Mishkin, M. (1997). Differential effects of early hippocampal pathology on episodic and semantic memory. *Science, 277*(5324), 376–380. (See comments, erratum published in August 22, 1997, *Science, 277*(5329), 1117.

Ventura, J., Nuechterlein, K. H., Subotnik, K. L., Hardesty, J. P., & Mintz, J. (2000). Life events can trigger depressive exacerbation in the early course of Schizophrenia. *Journal of Abnormal Psychology, 109*(1), 139–144.

Verdoux, H., Geddes, J. R., Takei, N., Lawrie, S. M., Bovet, P., Eagles, J. M., et al. (1997). Obstetric complications and age at onset in Schizophrenia: An international collaborative meta-analysis of individual patient data. *American Journal of Psychiatry, 154*(9), 1220–1227.

Walder, D. J., Walker, E. F., & Lewine, R. J. (2000). Cognitive functioning, cortisol release, and symptom severity in patients with Schizophrenia. *Biological Psychiatry, 48*(12), 1121–1132.

Walker, E. F., & Bollini, A. M. (2002). Pubertal neurodevelopment and the emergence of psychotic symptoms. *Schizophrenia Research, 54*(1/2), 17–23.

Walker, E. F., & Diforio, D. (1997). Schizophrenia: A neural diathesis-stress model. *Psychological Review, 104*(4), 667–685.

Walker, E. F., Diforio, D., & Baum, K. (1999). Developmental neuropathology and the precursors of Schizophrenia. *Acta Psychiatrica Scandinavica, 395*, 12–19.

Walker, E. F., Grimes, K. E., Davis, D. M., & Smith, A. J. (1993). Childhood precursors of Schizophrenia: Facial expressions of emotion. *American Journal of Psychiatry, 150*(11), 1654–1660.

Walker, E. F., Lewine, R. R., & Neumann, C. (1996). Childhood behavioral characteristics and adult brain morphology in Schizophrenia. *Schizophrenia Research, 22*(2), 93–101.

Walker, E. F., Savoie, T., & Davis, D. (1994). Neuromotor precursors of Schizophrenia. *Schizophrenia Bulletin, 20*(3), 441–451.

Walker, E. F., Walder, D. J., & Reynolds, F. (2001). Developmental changes in cortisol secretion in normal and at-risk youth. *Development and Psychopathology, 13*(3), 721–732.

Watson, C. S., & Gametchu, B. (1999). Membrane-initiated steroid actions and the proteins that mediate them. *Proceedings of the Society for Experimental Biology and Medicine, 220*(1), 9–19.

Watt, N. F. (1978). Patterns of childhood social development in adult schizophrenics. *Archives of General Psychiatry, 35*(2), 160–165.

Weinberger, D. R. (1987). Implications of normal brain development for the pathogenesis of Schizophrenia. *Archives of General Psychiatry, 44*, 660–669.

Weinberger, D. R. (1995). From neuropathology to neurodevelopment. *Lancet, 346*(8974), 552–557.

Weinberger, D. R., & McClure, R. K. (2002). Neurotoxicity, neuroplasticity, and magnetic resonance imaging morphometry: What is happening in the schizophrenic brain? *Archives of General Psychiatry, 59*(6), 553–558.

Weinstein, D. D., Diforio, D., Schiffman, J., Walker, E., & Bonsall, R. (1999). Minor physical anomalies, dermatoglyphic asymmetries, and cortisol levels in adolescents with schizotypal personality disorder. *American Journal of Psychiatry, 156*(4), 617–623.

Weintraub, S. (1987). Risk factors in Schizophrenia: The Stony Brook High-Risk Project. *Schizophrenia Bulletin, 13*(3), 439–450.

Williamson, P., Pelz, D., Merskey, H., & Morrison, S. (1991). Correlation of negative symptoms in Schizophrenia with frontal lobe parameters on magnetic resonance imaging. *British Journal of Psychiatry, 159*, 130–134.

Wood, S. J., Pantelis, C., Proffitt, T., Phillips, L. J., Stuart, G. W., Buchanan, J. A., et al. (2003). Spatial working memory ability is a marker of risk-for-psychosis. *Psychological Medicine, 33*, 1239–1247.

Woods, R. P., Grafton, S. T., Holmes, C. J., Cherry, S. R., & Mazziotta, J. C. (1998). Automated image registration: I. General methods and intrasubject, intramodality validation. *Journal of Computer Assisted Tomography, 22*(1), 139–152.

Yamasue, H., Fukui, T., Fukuda, R., Yamada, H., Yamasaki, S., Kuroki, N., et al. (2002). 1H-MR spectroscopy and gray matter volume of the anterior cingulate cortex in Schizophrenia. *NeuroReport, 13*(16), 2133–2137.

Yung, A. R., & McGorry, P. D. (1996). The prodromal phase of first-episode psychosis: Past and current conceptualizations. *Schizophrenia Bulletin, 26*, 353–370.

Yung, A. R., Phillips, L. J., McGorry, P. D., McFarlane, C. A., Francey, S., Harrigan, S., et al. (1998). Prediction of psychosis: A step towards indicated prevention of Schizophrenia. *British Journal of Psychiatry, 172*, 14–20.

Yung, A. R., Phillips, L. J., Yuen, H. P., Francey, S. M., McFarlane, C. A., Hallgren, M., et al. (2003). Psychosis prediction: 12-month follow up of a high-risk ("prodromal") group. *Schizophrenia Research, 60*(1), 21–32.

Yurgelun-Todd, D. A., Waternaux, C. M., Cohen, B. M., Gruber, S. A., English, C. D., & Renshaw, P. F. (1996). Functional magnetic resonance imaging of schizophrenic patients and comparison subjects during word production. *American Journal of Psychiatry, 153*(2), 200–205.

Zola, S. M., & Squire, L. R. (2001). Relationship between magnitude of damage to the hippocampus and impaired recognition memory in monkeys. *Hippocampus, 11*(2), 92–98.

CHAPTER 15

Life-Course-Persistent versus Adolescence-Limited Antisocial Behavior

TERRIE E. MOFFITT

This chapter reviews 10 years of research into a developmental taxonomy of antisocial behavior that proposed two primary hypothetical prototypes: life-course-persistent versus adolescence-limited offenders. The taxonomic theory was fully articulated for the first time in a chapter written for the first edition of *Developmental Psychopathology* (Caspi & Moffitt, 1995). Therefore, it is particularly appropriate to review for the second edition the research published since then. According to the taxonomic theory, life-course-persistent offenders' antisocial behavior has its origins in neurodevelopmental processes; it begins in childhood and continues persistently thereafter. In contrast, adolescence-limited offenders' antisocial behavior has its origins in social processes; it begins in adolescence and desists in young adulthood. According to the theory, life-

Preparation of this chapter was supported by grants from the U.S. National Institute of Mental Health (MH45070 and MH4941) and the British Medical Research Council (G9806489 and G0100527). Terrie Moffitt is a Royal Society-Wolfson Merit Award Holder. This chapter is an update of an earlier, shorter chapter published in *The Causes of Conduct Disorder and Serious Juvenile Delinquency,* by B. Lahey, T. E. Moffitt, and A. Caspi, 2003, New York: Guilford Press.

course-persistent antisocial individuals are few, persistent, and pathological. Adolescence-limited antisocial individuals are common, relatively transient, and near normative (Moffitt, 1990, 1993, 1994, 1997, 2003).

Discussions in the literature have pointed out that if the taxonomic theory is proven accurate, it could usefully improve classification of subject groups for research (Nagin, Farrington, & Moffitt, 1995; Silverthorn & Frick, 1999; Zucker, Ellis, Fitzgerald, Bingham, & Sanford, 1996), focus research into antisocial personality and violence toward the most promising causal variables (Brezina, 2000; Lahey, Waldman, & McBurnett, 1999; Laucht, 2001; Osgood, 1998), and guide the timing and strategies of interventions for delinquent types (Howell & Hawkins, 1998; Scott & Grisso, 1997; Vermeiren, 2002). Several writers have extracted implications for intervention from the taxonomy. Howell and Hawkins observed that preventing life-course-persistent versus adolescence-limited antisocial behavior requires interventions that differ in both timing and target. Preventing life-course-persistent lifestyles requires early childhood interventions in the family. In contrast, adolescence-limited offending ought to be prevented by treating adolescents individually to counteract peer influence (instead of in groups that facilitate deviant peer influence; Dishion, McCord, & Poulin, 1999). Scott and Grisso argued compellingly that the juvenile justice system should identify adolescence-limited delinquents and give them room to reform. Surveys of juvenile court judges and forensic psychologists reveal that the offender characteristics they rely on to recommend a juvenile for transfer to adult court match the characteristics that distinguish life-course-persistent delinquents (Slaekin, Yff, Neumann, Leistico, & Zalot, 2002). In contrast, Scott and Grisso argue that sending life-course-persistent delinquents to adult court is inappropriate because the cognitive deficits typical of these delinquents render them unlikely to meet legal criteria for competency to stand trial.

The taxonomy of childhood- versus adolescent-onset antisocial behavior has been codified in the fourth edition of the *Diagnostic and Statistical Manual of Mental Disorders* (American Psychiatric Association, 1994), presented in many abnormal psychology and criminology textbooks, and invoked in the National Institute of Mental Health (2000) fact sheet *Child and Adolescent Violence Research,* the U.S. Surgeon General's (2001) report *Youth Violence,* the World Health Organization's (2002) *World Report on Violence and Health,* and the National Institutes of Health's (2004) *State-of-the-Science Consensus Statement on Preventing Violence.* But is it valid?

The reader is referred to two prior publications that articulate the main hypotheses derived from this taxonomic theory. The first article published that proposed the two prototypes and their different etiologies ended with a section headed "Strategies for Research," which described predictions about epidemiology, age, social class, risk correlates, offense types, desistance from crime, abstainers from crime, and the longitudinal stability of antisocial behavior (Moffitt, 1993, pp. 694–696). The article specified which findings would disconfirm the theory. A version published elsewhere specified disconfirmable hypotheses about sex and race (Moffitt, 1994). When these hypotheses from the taxonomy were put forward 10 years ago, none of them had been tested, but since then several have been tested by us and by others. This chapter reviews the results of that research, as of summer 2004, and points out where more research is needed.

A BRIEF INTRODUCTION TO THE TWO PROTOTYPES

In a nutshell, we suggested that life-course-persistent antisocial behavior originates early in life, when the difficult behavior of a high-risk young child is exacerbated by a high-risk social environment. According to the theory, the child's risk emerges from inherited or acquired neuropsychological variation, initially manifested as subtle cognitive deficits, difficult temperament, or hyperactivity. The environment's risk comprises factors such as inadequate parenting, disrupted family bonds, and poverty. The environmental risk domain expands beyond the family as the child ages, to include poor relations with people such as peers and teachers. Opportunities to learn prosocial skills are lost. Over the first 2 decades of development, transactions between the individual and the environment gradually construct a disordered personality with hallmark features of physical aggression and antisocial behavior persisting to midlife. The theory predicts that antisocial behavior will infiltrate multiple adult life domains: illegal activities, problems with employment, and victimization of intimate partners and children. This infiltration diminishes the possibility of reform.

In contrast, we suggested that adolescence-limited antisocial behavior emerges alongside puberty, when otherwise ordinary healthy youngsters experience psychological discomfort during the relatively role-less years between their biological maturation and their access to mature privileges and responsibilities, a period we called the "maturity gap." They experience dissatisfaction with their dependent status as a child and impatience for what they anticipate are the privileges and rights of adulthood. While young people are in this gap, it is virtually normative for them to find the delinquent style appealing and to mimic it as a way to demonstrate autonomy from parents, win affiliation with peers, and hasten social maturation. However, because their predelinquent development was normal, most adolescence-limited delinquents are able to desist from crime when they age into real adult roles, returning gradually to a more conventional lifestyle. This recovery may be delayed if the antisocial activities of adolescence-limited delinquents attract factors we called "snares," such as a criminal record, incarceration, addiction, or truncated education without credentials. Such snares can compromise the ability to make a successful transition to adulthood.

The literature contains other theoretical statements about early- versus late-onset antisocial behavior, but our theory differed in three ways. First, it offered not only an account of onset processes but also included an explanation of the developmental processes leading to the maintenance of and desistance from antisocial behavior. Second, whereas other theories emphasize inept parenting as the primary cause initiating life-course-persistent antisocial behavior, this theory argued that children's own characteristics are a primary force in the transactions between child and environment. Third, whereas other theories emphasize poor parental supervision and monitoring as the primary cause of adolescence-limited delinquent behavior, this theory argued that adolescent-limited delinquency emerges from the age-appropriate developmental process of building autonomy, in which young people move away from childhood parent-child relationships and toward mature peer-to-peer relationships.

THE HYPOTHESIS THAT LIFE-COURSE-PERSISTENT ANTISOCIAL DEVELOPMENT EMERGES FROM EARLY NEURODEVELOPMENTAL AND FAMILY ADVERSITY RISK FACTORS

The original hypothesis about childhood risk specified that predictors of life-course-persistent antisocial behavior should include "health, gender, temperament, cognitive abilities, school achievement, personality traits, mental disorders (e.g., hyperactivity), family attachment bonds, child-rearing practices, parent and sibling deviance, and socioeconomic status, but not age" (Moffitt, 1993, p. 695).

Our own tests of this hypothesis have been carried out in the Dunedin Multidisciplinary Health and Development Study, a 32-year longitudinal study of a birth cohort of 1,000 New Zealanders. A full description of the Dunedin Study and the New Zealand research setting can be found in Moffitt, Caspi, Rutter, and Silva (2001). These tests have examined childhood predictors measured between ages 3 and 13, operationalizing the two prototypes of antisocial behavior using both categorical and continuous statistical approaches. These studies showed that the life-course-persistent path was differentially predicted by individual risk characteristics, including undercontrolled temperament measured by observers at age 3, neurological abnormalities and delayed motor development at age 3, low intellectual ability, reading difficulties, poor scores on neuropsychological tests of memory, hyperactivity, and slow heart rate (Jeglum-Bartusch, Lynam, Moffitt, & Silva, 1997; Moffitt, 1990; Moffitt & Caspi, 2001; Moffitt, Lynam, & Silva, 1994). The life-course-persistent path was also differentially predicted by parenting risk factors, including teenage single parent, mother with poor mental health, and mother who was observed to be harsh or neglectful, as well as by experiences of harsh and inconsistent discipline, much family conflict, many changes of primary caretaker, low family socioeconomic status (SES), and rejection by peers in school. In contrast, study members on the adolescence-limited path, despite being involved in teen delinquency to the same extent as their counterparts on the life-course-persistent path, tended to have backgrounds that were normative, or sometimes even better than the average Dunedin child's (Moffitt & Caspi, 2001). A replication of this pattern of differential findings was reported by a study of 800 children followed from birth to age 15 years (Brennan, Hall, Bor, Najman, & Williams, 2003). An early-onset persistent antisocial group, an adolescent-onset antisocial group, and a nonantisocial group were identified. Measured biological risks (e.g., neuropsychological test deficits at age 15) and childhood social risks (e.g., harsh discipline, maternal hostility), and an interaction between these two risks predicted membership in the early-onset persistent group, but membership in the adolescent-onset group was unrelated to childhood social risks or biological risks.

The Dunedin findings about differential neurodevelopmental and family risk correlates for childhood-onset versus adolescent-onset offenders are generally in keeping with findings reported from other samples in Australia, Canada, England, Mauritius, New Zealand, Norway, Russia, Sweden, and several states in the United States. These studies operationalized the types using a variety of conceptual approaches, many different measures of antisocial behaviors, and very different statistical methods (Aguilar, Sroufe, Egeland, & Carlson, 2000; Arseneault, Tremblay, Boulerice, & Saucier, 2002; Brennan et al., 2003; Chung, Hill, Hawkins, Gilchrist, & Nagin, 2002; Dean, Brame, & Piquero, 1996; Donnellan, Ge, & Wenk, 2000; Fergusson,

Horwood, & Nagin, 2000; Kjelsberg, 1999; Kratzer & Hodgins, 1999; Lahey et al., 1998; Magnusson, af Klintberg, & Stattin, 1994; Maughan, Pickles, Rowe, Costello, & Angold, 2001; Mazerolle, Brame, Paternoster, Piquero, & Dean, 2000; McCabe, Hough, Wood, & Yeh, 2001; Nagin et al., 1995; Nagin & Tremblay, 1999, 2001b; Patterson, Forgatch, Yoerger, & Stoolmiller, 1998; Piquero, 2001; Piquero & Brezina, 2001; Raine et al., 2005; Raine, Yaralian, Reynolds, Venables, & Mednick, 2002; Roeder, Lynch, & Nagin, 1999; Ruchkin, Koposov, Vermeiren, & Schwab-Stone, 2003; Tibbetts & Piquero, 1999; Tolan & Thomas, 1995; Wiesner & Capaldi, 2003). Each of these studies added support for the taxonomy's construct validity by reporting differential correlates for early-onset/persistent antisocial behavior versus later-onset/temporary antisocial behavior. However, at least one research team found mixed evidence for the taxonomy (cf. Brame, Bushway, & Paternoster, 1999, versus Paternoster & Brame, 1997).

Other studies, although not necessarily presented as a formal test of the two types, have reported findings consonant with our predictions about the types' differential childhood risks. For example, children's hyperactivity interacts with poor parenting skills to predict antisocial behavior that has an early onset and escalates to delinquency (Patterson, DeGarmo, & Knutson, 2000), an interaction that fits the hypothesized origins of the life-course-persistent path. Other studies have reported that measures reflecting infant nervous system maldevelopment interact with poor parenting and social adversity to predict aggression that is chronic from childhood to adolescence (Arseneault et al., 2002). Measures indexing infant nervous system maldevelopment and social adversity also interact to predict early-onset violent crime (Raine, Brennan, & Mednick, 1994; Raine, Brennan, Mednick, & Mednick, 1996) but do not predict nonviolent crime (Arseneault, Tremblay, Boulerice, Seguin, & Saucier, 2000; Raine, Brennan, & Mednick, 1997). Two additional findings are consistent with our prediction that infant nervous system maldevelopment contributes to long-term life-course-persistent antisocial outcomes. First, prenatal malnutrition has been found to predict adult Antisocial Personality Disorder (Neugebauer, Hoek, & Susser, 1999). Second, adults with Antisocial Personality Disorder exhibit two nervous system abnormalities attributable to disruption of brain development in early life: enlargement of the corpus callosum, assessed by structural magnetic resonance imaging, and abnormal corpus callosum connective function, assessed by divided visual field tests (Raine et al., 2003).

Our differential risk prediction encountered a particular challenge from a longitudinal study of a low-SES Minneapolis sample (Aguilar et al., 2000). This research team observed that differences between their childhood-onset and adolescent-onset groups were not significant for neurocognitive and temperament measures taken prior to age 3, although they found that significant differences did emerge later in childhood. The authors inferred that childhood psychosocial adversity is sufficient to account for the origins of life-course-persistent antisocial behavior, which is similar to Patterson and Yoerger's (1997) thesis that unskilled parenting is sufficient to account for the early-onset antisocial type. Such exclusive socialization hypotheses are probably not defensible in view of emerging evidence that the life-course-persistent pattern of antisocial behavior appears to have substantial heritable liability (DiLalla & Gottesman, 1989; Eley, Lichtenstein, & Moffitt, 2003; Taylor, Iacono, & McGue, 2000), a finding we revisit later in this chapter. The lack of significant early childhood differences in the Minneapolis study may have arisen from methodological features of the study, including the unrepresentative and homogeneous nature of the sample (all high-risk, low-SES families) and irregular sex composition of the groups (more females than males were antisocial), or weak psychometric qualities of the infant measures (unknown predictive validity). Infant measures are known for their poor predictive validity (McCall & Carriger, 1993), and thus it is possible that the failure of the infant measures to predict the life-course-persistent path is part of such measures' more general failure to predict outcomes.

One study has reported that difficult temperament assessed at age 5 months distinguished a group of children who showed a trajectory of high rates of physical aggression, as compared to cohort peers, across ages 17, 30, and 42 months (Tremblay et al., 2004). However, until this cohort of 572 infants is followed beyond age 3.5 years into adolescence, we cannot be confident that they represent youngsters on the life-course-persistent pathway. Other studies have reported a significant relation between life-course-persistent-type offending and problems known to be associated with neurocognitive and temperamental difficulties in infancy: perinatal complications, minor physical anomalies, and low birthweight (Arseneault et al., 2000, 2002; Kratzer & Hodgins, 1999; Raine et al., 1994; Tibbetts & Piquero, 1999). These studies illustrate desirable features for testing neurodevelopmental risks from the beginning of infancy for persistent antisocial behavior: large samples, representative samples, infant measures with proven predictive validity, and attention to interactions between neurodevelopmental and social adversity (Cicchetti & Walker, 2003).

What Research Is Needed?

Research already documents that life-course-persistent antisocial behavior has the predicted neurodevelopmental correlates in the perinatal and middle childhood periods, but the Aguilar et al. (2000) study remains the only one that has reported objective measures of infants' temperament and neurocognitive status prior to age 3 years, and it did not find the associations predicted by the theory. This study constitutes an important challenge that must be taken seriously, particularly as Brennan et al. (2003) also found no significant connection between temperament or vocabulary assessed in early life and early-onset persistent aggression. Clearly, more research is needed to fill in the critical gap between birth and age 3 years. This might be accomplished by following up the antisocial outcomes of infants tested with newer neurocognitive measures having documented predictive validity, such as the infant attention-habituation paradigm (Sigman, Cohen, & Beckwith, 1997).

Another feature of life-course-persistent theory that needs testing is the argument that antisocial behavior becomes persistent because a child's early difficult behavior provokes harsh treatment or rejection from parents, teachers, and peers, which in turn promotes more difficult child behavior. Adoption and twin studies have documented an initial "child effect"; that is, children carrying a genetic liability to antisocial behavior provoke harsh responses from their parents (Ge et al., 1996; Jaffee, Caspi, Moffitt, Polo-Tomas, et al., 2004; O'Connor, Deater-Deckard, Fulker, Rutter, & Plomin, 1998; Riggins-Caspers, Cadoret, Knutson, & Langbehn, 2003). Such genetically informative studies should be followed up to ascertain whether this process, beginning with a child effect, ultimately leads to antisocial behavior that persists long term.

THE HYPOTHESIS THAT GENETIC ETIOLOGICAL PROCESSES CONTRIBUTE MORE TO LIFE-COURSE-PERSISTENT THAN ADOLESCENCE-LIMITED ANTISOCIAL DEVELOPMENT

Journalists have drawn the public's attention to families that appear to contain far more than their share of criminal family members for several generations (Butterfield, 1996, 2002). This concentration of crime in families has been confirmed by studies of large populations of families. In general, fewer than 10% of the families in any community account for more than half of criminal offenses (Farrington, Barnes, & Lambert, 1996; Farrington, Jolliffe, Loeber, Stouthamer-Loeber, & Kalb, 2001; Rowe & Farrington, 1997). Moreover, research has shown that parental crime and parental psychopathology are more strongly associated with early-onset antisocial behavior than late-onset antisocial behavior among offspring (Moffitt & Caspi, 2001; Raine et al., 2005; Taylor et al., 2000). These findings seem to implicate a genetic influence on life-course-persistent antisocial behavior, but they could also be explained by social transmission of antisocial behavior within families. Therefore, we next review studies using genetically sensitive research designs to glean insights about life-course-persistent antisocial behavior. If genetic etiological processes contribute more to life-course-persistent than to adolescence-limited antisocial development, we would expect to find that estimates of genetic influence are larger for antisocial behaviors committed by young children and adults than for antisocial behaviors committed by adolescents.

DiLalla and Gottesman (1989) first observed that adult crime seemed to be more heritable than adolescent juvenile delinquency. Our 1993 paper (Moffitt, 1993, p. 694) agreed with these authors that if the life-course-persistent type's causal factors are partly inherited, and if most antisocial adults are life-course-persistent but most antisocial adolescents are not, then this could account for the observed greater genetic influence on individual differences in adult than adolescent samples. As it turns out, the lack of heritability among juveniles in the DiLalla and Gottesman review probably resulted from low power and insensitive measurement; in 1989, the entire literature of behavior genetic studies of juvenile delinquency consisted of fewer than 200 twin pairs, and the measure of antisocial behavior was conviction, a rare outcome for juveniles. Since then, a large number of better-designed behavioral genetic studies have proven that juvenile antisocial behavior is at least somewhat heritable. However, among these, four groups of studies provide circumstantial evidence that life-course-persistent antisocial behavior does have stronger heritable origins than adolescence-limited antisocial behavior.

The first group comprises four studies of large representative samples of very young twins. Because life-course-persistent antisocial behavior begins early in life, if it is genetically influenced we would expect high heritability coefficients from studies of very young children. Dionne, Tremblay, Boivin, Laplante, and Perusse (2003) report 58% heritability for aggression among Canadian 19-month-olds. Van den Oord, Verhulst, and Boomsma (1996) report 69%

heritability for aggression among Dutch 3-year-olds. In a different Dutch cohort, van der Valk, Verhulst, Stroet, and Boomsma (1998) report 50% heritability for externalizing behaviors among 2- to 3-year-old boys and 75% for girls. Arseneault et al. (2003) report heritabilities of 61%, 69%, and 76% among British 5-year-olds for ratings of antisocial behaviors made by observers, mothers, and teachers, respectively. These high estimates for very young twins are in contrast to the lower estimate of 41% heritability from a meta-analysis of older samples (Rhee & Waldman, 2002).

A second group of studies has identified the two subtypes on the basis of the heterogeneity in the phenotype, often using the Aggression and Delinquency narrow-band scales from the Child Behavior Checklist (CBCL; Achenbach, 1985). The Aggression scale is thought to be associated with the life-course-persistent prototype because it measures antisocial personality and physical violence and its scores are stable across development, whereas the Delinquency scale is associated with the adolescence-limited prototype because it measures rule breaking and its mean scores rise steeply during adolescence (Stanger, Achenbach, & Verhulst, 1997). In fact, both life-course-persistent and adolescence-limited young people engage in the behaviors on the Delinquency scale, but adolescence-limited young people are relatively more numerous, and if they have less genetic risk, then we would expect the Delinquency scale to yield lower heritability estimates than the Aggression scale. Twin and adoption studies of these scales report higher heritability for Aggression (around 60%) than Delinquency (around 30% to 40%), but the shared environment is significant only for the Delinquency scale (also around 30% to 40%; e.g., Deater-Deckard & Plomin, 1999; Edelbrock, Rende, Plomin, & Thompson, 1995; Eley, Lichtenstein, & Stevenson, 1999; but see Schmitz, Fulker, & Mrazek, 1995). The approach of contrasting two phenotypes within antisocial behavior was also taken by Viding and colleagues (Viding, Blair, Moffitt, & Plomin, 2005), who reported that genes influenced 81% of the variation in antisocial behavior among callous-unemotional children, but only 30% of variation among the other study children, who engaged in ordinary antisocial behaviors. A different approach to contrasting two heterogeneous phenotypes was followed by Arseneault et al. (2003), who found that antisocial behavior that was pervasive across settings was more heritable than antisocial behavior that was situational; heritability was 82% if a child's antisocial behavior was agreed on by four different reporters across settings at home and at school, but lower (28% to 51%) for antisocial behavior limited to one setting or one reporter.

A third group of studies has defined life-course-persistent antisocial behavior in terms of preadolescent onset, contrasting it against antisocial behavior that begins during the adolescent period. One study found early onset to be strongly familial and substantially heritable, in contrast to adolescent onset which was less familial and largely influenced by environment (Taylor et al., 2000). In a Swedish twin study, 5-year continuity from childhood to adolescence in the CBCL Aggression scale was largely mediated by genetic influences, whereas continuity in the Delinquency scale was mediated both by the shared environment and genetic influences (Eley et al., 2003).

A fourth group of studies has taken a developmental approach to the other end of the life span, defining life-course-persistent antisocial behavior in terms of presence in adolescence combined with subsequent persistence to adulthood Antisocial Personality Disorder. Two studies demonstrated that such persistent antisocial behavior was significantly more heritable than that limited to adolescence (Jacobson, Neale, Prescott, & Kendler, 2003; Lyons et al., 1995). These longitudinal studies are supported by a meta-analysis containing adolescent and adult samples assessed with similar measures of aggression, in which adult samples generated significantly higher heritability estimates, on average, than adolescent samples (Miles & Carey, 1997). Rhee and Waldman's (2002) meta-analysis did not find higher heritability for adults than adolescents, because in the pool of studies they examined, age was wholly confounded with reporting source; adolescent studies used rating scales, and adult studies used official crime records.

Taken together, the four groups of existing studies suggest that the pattern of antisocial behavior that (1) begins early in life, (2) is pervasive across settings, (3) is characterized by aggressive personality traits, (4) includes physical aggression, and (5) persists into adulthood is associated with relatively more genetic influence than is the pattern of later-onset, situational, transient delinquency. *What does this high heritability estimate mean?* It does not mean that environmental experiences have a negligible effect on life-course-persistent antisocial development. To the contrary, a heritability estimate, as calculated, reflects the additive effects of specific genes on a phenotype, but it also includes two types of interplay between genes and environments. Correlations between genes and environments (GrE) increase the heritability estimate if genes lead study members to encounter environments that in turn exacerbate the phenotype. Interactions between genes and environments (GxE) increase the heritability estimate when genes condition the effects of environments on the phenotype by influencing study members' vulnerability or resistance to risky environments. When estimates of heritability are very large, this encourages researchers to look for GxE and GrE effects on that phenotype. Following from our taxonomic theory of life-course-persistent antisocial behavior, the genetic component of variation in antisocial behavior measured in early childhood ought to comprise not only the direct effects of genes, but also the effects of correlations between vulnerability genes and risky environments, and interactions between them as well.

Studies have documented the existence of correlations between children's genetic predisposition toward antisocial behavior and their rearing environments, or GrE. Specifically, three adoption studies and one twin study have now shown that children with a genetic liability for antisocial behavior tend to evoke harsher discipline from their parents than do children lacking this liability (Ge et al., 1996; Jaffee, Caspi, Moffitt, Polo-Tomas, et al., 2004; O'Connor et al., 1998; Riggins-Caspers et al., 2003). However, to our knowledge, no research has examined whether this evocative child effect in turn *exacerbates* levels of the children's antisocial behavior when they are followed over time. Evidence of exacerbation is necessary to answer whether gene-environment correlations increase estimates of heritability for antisocial behavior over and above any direct effects of genes.

There is somewhat better evidence that interactions between genetic and environmental risk, or GxE, contribute to the heritability of life-course-persistent antisocial behavior. We tested GxE in two studies of one of the strongest risk factors for persistent antisocial behavior: child maltreatment. The first study used data from our Environmental-risk Longitudinal Twin Study (called E-risk) to test whether the effect of maltreatment on risk for antisocial behavior was strongest among 5-year-olds who were at high genetic risk for it. The E-risk Study follows a representative 1994 to 1995 cohort of 1,116 British twin pairs and their families (Moffitt & the E-Risk Study Team, 2002). Each child's genetic risk for conduct problems was estimated as a function of his or her cotwin's Conduct Disorder status and the pair's zygosity. For example, a child whose monozygotic (MZ) twin already had Conduct Disorder was deemed at highest genetic risk, whereas a child whose dizygotic (DZ) twin had Conduct Disorder was at lower genetic risk, and a child whose MZ twin was free from conduct problems was at the lowest genetic risk of all. Results showed that the effects of maltreatment were most detrimental for the children at high genetic risk. The experience of maltreatment was associated with an increase of

2% in the probability of a Conduct Disorder diagnosis among young children at low genetic risk for Conduct Disorder but an increase of 24% among children at high genetic risk (Jaffee et al., 2005).

Our second study used data from the male members of the Dunedin cohort to test whether this general GxE effect could be specified for a particular candidate gene. We used Dunedin men's DNA to genotype a polymorphism in the gene encoding the neurotransmitter-metabolizing enzyme monoamine oxidase A (MAOA). We selected this gene because it was known to be functional in the brain and it had earlier been related to aggression in mice and in a human family pedigree. MAOA genotype moderated the effect of maltreatment (Caspi et al., 2002). Of the severely maltreated children with a genotype conferring low levels of MAOA expression, 85% developed one or more antisocial outcomes, as measured at different stages in the life course (e.g., a childhood diagnosis of Conduct Disorder up to age 15, conviction for violent crimes between ages 17 and 26, antisocial personality traits at age 26, and diagnosed Antisocial Personality Disorder at age 26). In contrast, despite being maltreated, children with a genotype conferring high levels of MAOA expression were less likely to develop antisocial problems. Although individuals having the combination of low-activity MAOA genotype and maltreatment were only 12% of the birth cohort, they accounted for 44% of the cohort's convictions for violent crimes. This finding has been replicated and extended in the Virginia Study of Adolescent Twin Development. This study was able to control for the parents' antisocial histories to rule out the possibility that a family liability toward aggression jointly influenced parents' maltreating behavior and children's antisocial outcome (Foley et al., 2004). Together, the E-risk, Dunedin, and Virginia studies of GxE illustrate how the high heritability of the life-course-persistent form of antisocial behavior is played out in the transactions between a genetically vulnerable child and high-risk environment that were specified in the theory of life-course-persistent antisocial development.

What Research Is Needed?

It would be useful to ascertain the genetic and environmental architecture of individual differences in trajectories of antisocial behavior over time. Such trajectories could be derived in longitudinal studies of twins by applying semiparametric mixture modeling tools to repeated measures of antisocial behavior (for explanations of these models, see Nagin et al., 1995; Nagin & Tremblay, 2001a; Roeder et al., 1999). The theory would predict stronger monozygotic twin similarity for membership in a childhood-onset, life-course-persistent trajectory, but less twin similarity for membership in an adolescent-onset trajectory. Because no twin studies to our knowledge have yet followed a sample of twins from childhood to adulthood while measuring antisocial behavior, a study of twin similarity in developmental trajectories of antisocial behavior is yet in the future. However, genetically informative studies could examine as proxies the elements of crime careers that characterize the life-course-persistent type: early onset of antisocial acts, recidivistic physical aggression, and psychopathic personality traits. One study has attempted this approach and reported that genetic influence is very strong among children who exhibit a callous, unemotional personality style by age 7 years (Viding et al., 2005).

IS A THIRD GROUP NEEDED? CHILDHOOD-LIMITED AGGRESSIVE CHILDREN MAY BECOME LOW-LEVEL CHRONIC CRIMINAL OFFENDERS WITH PERSONALITY DISORDERS

The original theoretical taxonomy asserted that two prototypes, life-course-persistent and adolescence-limited offenders, account for the preponderance of the population's antisocial behavior and thus warrant the lion's share of attention by theory and research. However, our analyses revealed a small group of Dunedin study males who had exhibited extreme, pervasive, and persistent antisocial behavior problems during childhood, but who surprisingly engaged in only low to moderate delinquency during adolescence from age 15 to 18, not extreme enough to meet criteria for membership in the life-course-persistent group (Moffitt, Caspi, Dickson, Silva, & Stanton, 1996). Like the life-course-persistent offenders, they had extremely undercontrolled temperaments as 3-year-olds (Moffitt et al., 1996), and in childhood they, too, suffered family adversity and parental psychopathology and had low intelligence (unpublished analyses). The existence of a small group of boys who exhibit serious aggression in childhood but are not notably delinquent in adolescence has been replicated in the Pittsburgh Youth Survey, where they were called "childhood-limited" antisocial children (Raine et al., 2005). In the Pittsburgh cohort, too, these boys had many risk factors, including family adversity, parental psychopathology, and severe neuropsychological deficits.

This group was a surprise to the theory, because the theory argued that an early-onset chain of cumulative interactions between aggressive children and high-risk environments will perpetuate disordered behavior. On that basis, we had predicted that "false positive subjects, who meet criteria for a stable and pervasive antisocial childhood history and yet recover (eschew delinquency) after puberty, should be extremely rare" (Moffitt, 1993, p. 694). When we discovered this group, we optimistically labeled it the "recovery group" (Moffitt et al., 1996). Many researchers, we among them, hoped that this group would allow us to identify protective factors that can be harnessed to prevent childhood aggression from persisting and becoming more severe. However, our study of this group has revealed no protective factors.

Researchers testing for the presence of the life-course-persistent and adolescence-limited types have since uncovered a third type that replicates across longitudinal studies, first identified in trajectory analyses of a British cohort (Nagin et al., 1995). This third group of offenders have been labeled "low-level chronics" because they have been found to offend persistently but at a low rate from childhood to adolescence (Fergusson et al., 2000) or from adolescence to adulthood (D'Unger, Land, McCall, & Nagin, 1998; Nagin et al., 1995). Persuaded by these findings, we followed up the so-called recovery group in the Dunedin cohort at age 26 to see if they might fit the low-level chronic pattern as adults. We found that recovery was clearly a misnomer, as their modal offending pattern over time fit a pattern referred to by criminologists as "intermittency," in which some offenders are not convicted for a period but then reappear in the courts (Laub & Sampson, 2001). This Dunedin group's long-term offending pattern closely resembles that of the low-level chronic offender.

Anticipating true recoveries from serious childhood Conduct Disorder to be extremely rare, the taxonomic theory had argued that teens who engage in less delinquency than predicted on the basis of their childhood conduct problems might have off-putting personal characteristics that excluded them from the social peer groups in which most delinquency happens. Consistent with this prediction, a group in the Oregon Youth Study, who showed high levels of antisocial behavior at age 12 that decreased thereafter, scored low as adolescents on a measure of involvement with pro-delinquency peers (Wiesner & Capaldi, 2003). In the Dunedin cohort followed up to age 26, the members of this low-level chronic group, unlike other cohort men, were often social isolates; their informants reported that they had difficulty making friends, none had married, few held jobs, and many had diagnoses of Agoraphobia and/or Social Phobia. Almost all social phobics meet criteria for

Avoidant, Dependent, and/or Schizotypal Personality Disorder (Alnaes & Torgersen, 1988), and we speculate that men in this group may suffer from these isolating personality disorders. As many as one-third of this group had diagnosable depression, their personality profile showed elevated neuroticism, and their informants rated them as the most depressed, anxious men in the cohort. This pattern, in which formerly antisocial boys develop into depressed, anxious, socially isolated men, resembles closely a finding from a British longitudinal study of males followed from ages 8 to 32. In that study, too, at-risk antisocial boys who became adult "false positives" (committing fewer crimes than predicted) had few or no friends, held low-paid jobs, lived in dirty home conditions, and had been described in case records as withdrawn, highly strung, obsessional, nervous, or timid (Farrington, Gallagher, Morley, St. Ledger, & West, 1988).

Robins (1966) is often quoted as having said that half of conduct problem boys do not grow up to have antisocial personalities. Such quotations are intended to imply that early conduct problems are fully malleable and need not be a cause for pessimism. However, less often quoted is Robins's observation that conduct problem boys who do not develop antisocial personalities generally suffer other forms of maladjustment as adults. This is an assertion of "multifinality" in the poor outcomes of at-risk children (Cicchetti & Cohen, 1995). In the Dunedin birth cohort, 87 boys had childhood conduct problems (i.e., 47 in the life-course-persistent group and 40 in the so-called recovery group). Of these 87 males, only 15% ($n = 13$) seemed to have truly recovered as adults, escaping all adjustment problems measured in the study at age 26. Taken together, findings from Dunedin and the studies by Farrington and Robins are consistent with our taxonomic theory's original assertion that childhood-onset antisocial behavior is *virtually always* a prognosticator of poor adult adjustment.

What Research Is Needed?

Several studies have detected an unexpected group, variously labeled "recoveries," "childhood-limited," or "low-level chronic offenders," depending on how long the cohort was followed. However, few studies have been able to shed any light on their personal characteristics. The characteristics revealed so far are suggestive of Avoidant, Dependent, Schizotypal Personality Disorders and/or low intelligence, but these outcomes have not been directly measured in adulthood. It is important to know if this group has adult psychopathology to test the theory's assertion that serious childhood-onset antisocial behavior reliably predicts long-term maladjustment.

IS A FOURTH GROUP NEEDED? ADULT-ONSET ANTISOCIAL BEHAVIOR

On the basis of examining official data sources, some investigators have suggested that significant numbers of offenders first begin to offend as adults (Eggleston & Laub, 2002; Farrington, Ohlin, & Wilson, 1986). This would appear to challenge our developmental taxonomy's assertion that two groups, life-course-persistent and adolescence-limited, suffice to account for the majority of antisocial participation across the life course. However, the observation that many antisocial individuals are adult-onset offenders appears to be largely an artifact of official measurement. Estimates of the age at which antisocial behavior begins depend on the source of the data. For example, in the Dunedin study, only 4% of boys had been convicted in court by age 15 years, but 15% had been arrested by police by age 15, and 80% had self-reported the onset of illegal behaviors by age 15 (Moffitt et al., 2001, chap. 7). This suggests that official data lag behind the true age of onset by a few years. Similar findings have emerged from other studies in other countries. For example, a Canadian survey showed that self-reported onset antedated conviction by about 3.5 years (Loeber & LeBlanc, 1990), and a U.S. survey showed that self-reported onset of "serious" delinquency antedated the first court contact by 2.5 years and onset of "moderate" delinquency antedated the first court contact by 5 years (U.S. Office of Juvenile Justice and Delinquency Prevention, 1998). In the Seattle Social Development cohort, the self-reported onset of crime antedated the first court referral by 2.4 years, and the study estimated that the average offender committed 26 crimes before his official crime record began (Farrington et al., 2003). These comparisons of data sources suggest that investigations relying on official data will ascertain age of onset approximately 3 to 5 years after it has happened. A 3-to 5-year lag is relevant because most studies have defined adult-onset offenders as those whose official crime record began at or after age 18 years (Eggleston & Laub, 2002).

It also is useful to note that whereas the 18th birthday may have marked adulthood for young people born before 1960, the 18th birthday falls only midway between puberty and adulthood for contemporary generations. This shift emerged because contemporary generations are experiencing a more protracted adolescence, lasting until the mid-

20s (Arnett, 2000) or even into the early 30s for the cohort born after 1970 (Ferri, Bynner, & Wadsworth, 2003; Furstenberg, Cook, Sampson, & Slap, 2002). Although adult-onset crime begins at age 18 in legal terms, in developmental terms for contemporary cohort samples, it begins sometime after age 25.

In contrast to studies using official crime records, self-report cohort studies show that fewer than 4% of males commit their first criminal offense after age 17 (Elliott, Huizinga, & Menard, 1989). Self-report studies of American and European cohorts agree (Junger-Tas, Terlouw, & Klein, 1994). By age 18, virtually all of the Dunedin study members had already engaged in some form of illegal behavior at some time, according to their self-reports (Moffitt et al., 2001). Only 9% of Dunedin males and 14% of females remained naïve to all delinquency by age 18, and only 3% of males and 5% of females first offended as an adult, between ages 18 and 21. These findings carry an important lesson for methodology in developmental research into antisocial behavior. "Adult-onset" offenders cannot be defined for study with any certainty unless self-reported data are available to rule out juvenile onset prior to participants' first official contact with the judicial system. When self-report data are consulted, they reveal that onset of antisocial behavior after adolescence is extremely rare. This conclusion extends to serious and violent offending (Elliott, 1994).

One way to ascertain whether adult-onset offenders constitute a significant group for study is to apply semiparametric modeling techniques (Nagin, 1999; Nagin & Tremblay, 2001a; Roeder et al., 1999) to identify trajectories within a population-representative cohort of individuals whose behavior has been followed into adulthood. Three studies have done so. The Dunedin study identified no adult-onset trajectory in self-reports of delinquency from ages 7 to 26 years (see Figure 15.1). The Oregon Youth Study identified no adult-onset trajectory in self-reports of offending from ages 12 to 24 years (Wiesner & Capaldi, 2003). The Cambridge Longitudinal Study identified no adult-onset trajectory in official crime records followed to age 32 for a cohort born in the 1950s (Nagin et al., 1995).

The original theoretical taxonomy asserted that two prototypes, life-course-persistent and adolescence-limited offenders, can account for the preponderance of the population's antisocial behavior. After more than 10 years of research, this assertion appears to be correct. Some studies of the taxonomy have reported an adult-onset group (e.g., Kratzer & Hodgins, 1999). However, these studies used official crime data, and thus most of their adult-onset offend-

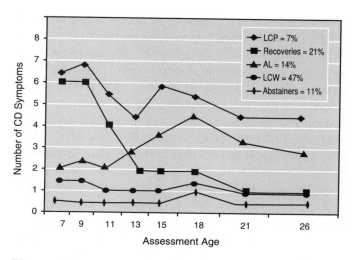

Figure 15.1 Twenty-year trajectories of conduct disorder symptoms among 525 Kunedin males.

ers would probably be revealed as adolescent-onset if self-report data were available. These so-called adult-onset offenders can probably be accommodated by the adolescence-limited theory because when studied, the alleged adult-onset group has not differed from ordinary adolescent offenders (Eggleston & Laub, 2002). Moreover, like adolescence-limited offenders, adult-onset offenders' crime careers tend to be brief and not serious (Farrington et al., 1986). In our view, the existence of individuals whose official crime record begins after age 18 does not constitute a threat to the taxonomy.

THE HYPOTHESIS THAT ADOLESCENCE-LIMITED ANTISOCIAL BEHAVIOR IS INFLUENCED BY THE MATURITY GAP AND BY SOCIAL MIMICRY OF ANTISOCIAL MODELS

The original theory asserted that

> individual differences should play little or no role in the prediction of short-term adolescent offending careers. Instead, the strongest predictors of adolescence-limited offending should be peer delinquency, attitudes toward adolescence and adulthood reflecting the maturity gap [such as a desire for autonomy], cultural and historical contexts influencing adolescence, and age. (Moffitt, 1993, p. 695)

Most research on the taxonomy to date has focused on testing hypotheses about the etiology of life-course-persistent offenders. Unfortunately, adolescence-limited offenders have been relegated to the status of a contrast group, and the original hypotheses about the distinct etiology of adolescent-onset offending have not captured the research imagination. This is unfortunate because adolescent-onset offenders are quite common (one quarter of both males and females as defined in the Dunedin cohort) and their antisocial activities are not benign. They are found among adjudicated delinquents as well as in the general population (Scholte, 1999). Moreover, even if adolescence-limited individuals commit fewer violent offenses than life-course-persistent individuals, the size of the adolescence-limited group is much larger than the size of the life-course-persistent group, and as a result the adolescence-limited group can be expected to account for an important share of a society's serious and violent offenses. In Dunedin, life-course-persistent men (10% of the cohort) accounted for 53% of the cohort's 554 self-reported violent offenses at age 26, but adolescence-limited men (26% of the cohort) accounted for 29% of the cohort's violent offenses, a nontrivial amount of violence (Moffitt, Caspi, Harrington, & Milne, 2002).

Do adolescents find the maturity gap psychologically aversive, and does this motivate their newfound interest in delinquency? Aguilar et al. (2000) discovered that adolescent-onset delinquents experienced elevated internalizing symptoms and perceptions of stress at age 16, which may be consistent with the taxonomy's assertion that these adolescents experience psychological discomfort during the maturity gap. The theory suggested that this discomfort motivated adolescents to engage in antisocial behavior to seem older. In a study of the Gluecks' sample, adolescents' concerns about appearing immature increased their likelihood of delinquency (Zebrowitz, Andreoletti, Collins, Lee, & Blumenthal, 1998). One interesting ethnographic study has made use of the maturity gap to explain *kortteliralli,* the street-racing alcohol youth culture of Finland (Vaaranen, 2001). The Victoria Adolescence Project studied 452 adolescents and their parents to examine how young people negotiate the maturity gap (Galambos, Barker, & Tilton-Weaver, 2003). This study identified a group of 25% of adolescents who exhibited a cluster of characteristics they called "pseudo-maturity." These adolescents, relative to their age cohort, were characterized by more advanced biological pubertal status, older subjective age ("I feel a lot older than my age"), elevated perceptions of self-reliance, more wishes to emulate older brothers (but not sisters), more older friends, a greater desire to be older ("I would like to look a lot older than my age"), more involvement in pop culture, and less involvement in school but more involvement with peers. This cluster was not associated with SES level. The study concluded that for a large proportion

of teens, pubertal maturation brings about a poor fit between their developmental stage and their social environment: "They are caught in the maturity gap" (Galambos et al., 2003, p. 262). Parent and self-reports confirmed that this pseudo-mature group of teenagers engaged in elevated rates of problem behaviors, as expected by the theory of adolescence-limited delinquency.

Do adolescence-limited teenagers want to be more like life-course-persistent offenders? The theory of adolescence-limited delinquency borrowed the concept of "social mimicry" from the field of ethology to explain how adolescents might mimic the antisocial behavior of life-course-persistent antisocial boys in their midst in an effort to attain the mature status embodied in the antisocial lifestyle. New developmental research has shown that when ordinary young people age into adolescence, they begin to admire good students less and to admire aggressive, antisocial peers more (Bukowski, Sippola, & Newcomb, 2000; Luthar & McMahon, 1996; Rodkin, Farmer, Pearl, & Van Acker, 2000). One sociometric study that followed 905 children from age 10 to 14 reported that the association between physical aggression and being disliked by peers dissolved during this age period; as they grew older, the teenagers came to perceive their aggressive age-mates as having higher social status and more influence (Cillessen & Mayeux, 2004). Moreover, during adolescence, young people who place a high value on conforming to adults' rules become unpopular with their peers (Allen, Weissberg, & Hawkins, 1989).

Our Dunedin studies documented that an increase in young teens' awareness of peers' delinquency antedates and predicts onset of their own later delinquency (Caspi, Lynam, Moffitt, & Silva, 1993). We also showed that the adolescence-limited path is more strongly associated with delinquent peers, as compared to the life-course-persistent path (Jeglum-Bartusch et al., 1997; Moffitt & Caspi, 2001). However, one study that traced peer affiliation trajectories concluded that peers were as influential for childhood-onset persistent offenders as for adolescent-onset offenders (LaCourse, Nagin, Tremblay, Vitaro, & Claes, 2003). In contrast, others have shown that delinquent peer influences directly promote increases in delinquency, specifically among young males whose antisocial behavior begins in adolescence (Simons, Wu, Conger, & Lorenz, 1994; Vitaro, Tremblay, Kerr, Pagani, & Bukowski, 1997). In contrast, these same studies suggest that among males whose antisocial behavior begins in childhood, the direction of influence runs the other way; the child's own early antisocial behavior promotes increases at adolescence in the number of delinquent peers who selectively affiliate with him. This is consistent with our life-course-persistent theory's assertion that during adolescence, life-course-persistent antisocial boys become "magnets" for peers who wish to learn delinquency.

The most direct test of the adolescence-limited etiological hypothesis was carried out in the Youth in Transition Survey of 2,000 males (Piquero & Brezina, 2001). This study was introduced to the literature with lyrics from a song entitled "Eighteen" by rocker Alice Cooper that express the ennui of the maturity gap: "I'm in the middle without any plans, I'm a boy and I'm a man." The study tested the hypothesis that desires for autonomy promoted adolescent-onset offending. It found that, as predicted, the offenses committed by adolescence-limited delinquents were primarily rebellious (not physically aggressive) and that this rebellious offending was accounted for by the interaction between maturational timing and aspects of peer activities that were related to personal autonomy. However, one measure of youth autonomy in this study did not predict offending.

It is important to acknowledge that alternative accounts of late-onset delinquency have been put forward. In particular, Patterson and Yoerger (1997) outlined a learning model in which decreases in parents' monitoring and supervision when their children enter adolescence cause adolescents to begin offending. We had argued that although parents' monitoring and supervision were certainly negatively correlated with adolescent-onset delinquency, the direction of cause and effect was unclear, and our adolescence-limited theory would say that this correlation arises because teens' desires to gain autonomy via delinquency motivate them to evade their parents' supervision (Moffitt, 1993, p. 693). A longitudinal study of 1,000 Swedish 14-year-olds and their parents suggested that our interpretation is correct (Kerr & Stattin, 2000). Adolescents actively controlled their parents' access to information about their activities, and teens who took part in deviant behavior limited their parents' capacity to monitor them. The study showed that parents' efforts to supervise and monitor were not very effective in controlling their teenagers' activities, and could even backfire if teens felt controlled.

What Research Is Needed?

Clearly, there is not very much research testing whether measures of the maturity gap and social mimicry can account for adolescence-limited delinquency, so any new studies with this aim would add to our understanding. Agnew (2003) offers a cogent breakdown of maturity gap elements

that can be tested. Short-term longitudinal studies of young teens might ask if a developmental increase in attitudes rejecting childhood and favoring autonomy is correlated with a growing interest in and approval of illicit activities. Moreover, there is the curious fact that life-course-persistent antisocial individuals are rejected by peers in childhood but later become more popular with peers in adolescence. The theory of social mimicry predicted this shift in popularity, but more longitudinal research following individuals' changes in social standing is needed to understand it fully. Finally, we should consult historical and anthropological work to ascertain if historical periods and cultures characterized by a clearly demarcated transition from childhood dependency to adulthood rights and responsibilities are also characterized by relatively low levels of delinquency and adolescent rebelliousness.

THE HYPOTHESIS THAT ABSTAINERS FROM DELINQUENCY ARE RARE INDIVIDUALS WHO ARE EXCLUDED FROM NORMATIVE PEER GROUP ACTIVITIES IN ADOLESCENCE

If, as the theory says, adolescence-limited delinquency is normative adaptational social behavior, then the existence of teens who abstain from delinquency requires an explanation. In other words, if ordinary teens take up delinquent behavior, then teens who eschew delinquency must be extraordinary in some way. The original theory speculated that teens committing no antisocial behavior would be rare and that they must have either structural barriers that prevent them from learning about delinquency, no maturity gap because of early access to adult roles, or personal characteristics unappealing to other teens that cause them to be excluded from teen social group activities (Moffitt, 1993, pp. 689, 695). As noted earlier, research has shown that during adolescence, young people who place a high value on conforming to adults' rules become unpopular with their peers (Allen et al., 1989).

We have studied male abstainers in the Dunedin cohort. Consistent with the rarity prediction, the Dunedin cohort contained only a very small group of males who avoided virtually any antisocial behavior during childhood and adolescence; abstainers were fewer than 10% of the cohort (Moffitt et al., 1996). The very small size of this group has been confirmed in other samples. Only 13% of 17-year-olds in the National Longitudinal Survey of Youth replied that they had never done any of the survey's 13 offense items (Piquero, Brezina, & Turner, in press). Two longitudinal cohort studies used a theory-free method to characterize heterogeneous trajectories within repeated measures of aggressive behavior: Nagin and Tremblay (1999) detected an abstainer trajectory from childhood to adolescence containing very few males, and Wiesner and Capaldi (2003) detected an abstainer trajectory from adolescence to adulthood containing even fewer males (5%).

The small group of Dunedin abstainers described themselves at age 18 on personality measures as extremely overcontrolled, fearful, interpersonally timid, and socially inept, and they were latecomers to sexual relationships (i.e., virgins at age 18). Dunedin abstainers fit the profile that Shedler and Block (1990) reported for youth who abstained from drug experimentation in a historical period when it was normative: overcontrolled, not curious, not active, not open to experience, socially isolated, and lacking social skills. Dunedin abstainers were unusually good students, fitting the profile of the compliant good student who, during adolescence, can become unpopular with peers (Allen et al., 1989; Bukowski et al., 2000). Other studies have suggested that abstention from delinquency and substance use during adolescence is associated with feeling socially isolated from peers (Dunford & Elliott, 1984), having few friends (Farrington & West, 1993), or being a loner (Tolone & Tieman, 1990). Such findings prompted Shedler and Block (1990, p. 627) to comment that abstention is "less the result of moral fiber or successful prevention programs than the result of relative alienation from peers and a characterological overcontrol of needs and impulses."

Dunedin's age-26 follow-up data confirmed that the teenage abstainers did not become so-called adult-onset offenders (Moffitt, Caspi, et al., 2002). Although their teenage years had been socially awkward for them, their style became more successful in adulthood. As adults they retained their self-constrained personality, had virtually no crime or mental disorder, were likely to have settled into marriage, were delaying children (a desirable strategy for a generation needing prolonged education to succeed), were likely to be college-educated, held high-status jobs, and expressed optimism about their own future.

Another study of abstainers from delinquency was conducted using 1,600 17-year-olds from the 1997 National Longitudinal Survey of Youth (Piquero, Brezina, et al., in press). Consistent with theoretical prediction, relative to participants in delinquency the abstainers were few in number, more closely monitored by their parents, more attached to teachers, and less physically mature, reported less autonomy, dated less, and were less involved with friends who drank, smoked, tried drugs, and cut classes. However, an unexpected new finding was that abstainers were not wholly friendless; rather, they reported that they had prosocial peers who "go to church regularly," "plan to go to college," and "participate in volunteer work." This study also attempted to test the theory's prediction that abstainers have personalities that make them unattractive to peers, using an item called "sadness/depression" intended to assess a morose, uncheerful style unlikely to appeal to peers. However, the study found that sadness/depression was correlated with delinquent participation, not abstention. This test was ambiguous because the depression item probably did not measure the overcontrolled, incurious, timid, socially inept personality style thought to preclude delinquency. Thus, this study provided some modest support for the taxonomy's view of abstainers as a minority that exists outside the social scene that creates opportunities for delinquency among the teen majority. Moreover, the study suggested the provocative new finding that abstainers do have friends, who are prosocial like themselves.

What Research Is Needed?

To our knowledge, our finding that abstainers are social introverts as teens remains to be confirmed or discounted by another study directly designed to test this hypothesis. Adolescent sociometric studies might ask if delinquent abstention is indeed correlated with unpopularity and social isolation. Further study of abstainers is critical for testing the hypothesis that adolescence-limited offenders' delinquency is normative adaptational behavior by ordinary young people.

THE HYPOTHESIS THAT LIFE-COURSE-PERSISTENT AND ADOLESCENCE-LIMITED DELINQUENTS DEVELOP DIFFERENT PERSONALITY STRUCTURES

The original theory hypothesized the following about the development of life-course-persistent offenders:

> Over the years, an antisocial personality is slowly and insidiously constructed, and accumulating consequences of the youngster's personality problems prune away options for change. . . . A person-environment interaction process is needed to account for emerging antisocial behavior, but after some age, will the "person" main effect alone predict adult outcome? (Moffitt, 1993, p. 684)

Our Dunedin studies of adolescents' personality characteristics measured at age 18 showed that the life-course-persistent path was differentially associated with weak bonds to family and with the psychopathic personality traits of alienation, callousness, and impulsivity. In contrast, the adolescence-limited path at age 18 was differentially associated with a tendency to endorse unconventional values and with a personality trait called "social potency" (Moffitt et al., 1996). We assessed personality traits 10 years later at age 26, this time using not only self-reports but reports from informants who knew the Dunedin study members well (Moffitt, Caspi, et al., 2002). The self- and informant-reports concurred that the life-course-persistent men had more negative emotionality (were more stress-reactive, alienated, and aggressive) and they were less agreeable (had less social closeness, were more callous) compared to adolescence-limited men. Life-course-persistent men were no longer particularly impulsive at age 26, but the adolescence-limited men were still somewhat elevated on this scale at age 26. It appears from these repeated Dunedin assessments that the life-course-persistent pathway leads to a disordered antisocial personality structure resembling the psychopath: aggressive, alienated, and callous. Adolescence-limited men, in contrast, are unconventional, valuing spontaneity and excitement.

In another study, 4,000 California Youth Authority (CYA) inmates were given the California Personality Inventory (Gough, 1987) in the 1960s and then followed up into the 1980s (Donnellan, Ge, & Wenk, 2002). Taxonomy comparison groups were defined as early starters versus later starters, and as chronic adult arrestees versus those arrested less often. The early-starter, chronic arrestees could be discriminated by extreme personality scale scores, in particular low communality, little concern with impression, irresponsibility, low control of emotions, low achievement motivation, low socialization, low tolerance (hostile, distrustful), and low well-being. Early starters also scored higher than late starters on the Schizophrenia and Hypomania scales of the Minnesota Multiphasic Personality Inventory (Dahlstrom, Welsh, & Dahlstrom, 1972), two scales that measure a tendency to think in a confused and suspicious way (Ge, Donnellan, & Wenk, 2003). Using different instruments and different informants, these CYS findings echo our Dunedin findings, in which life-course-persistent offenders were disagreeable and high on negative emotionality.

What Research Is Needed?

To our knowledge, the personality correlates of the taxonomy have been examined in only two samples (Dunedin and CYA), so the finding of differential personality structures remains to be verified by wider replication. Moreover, the unanticipated Dunedin finding that many adolescence-limited offenders are unconventional excitement-seekers raises the question of whether this approach-oriented personality style is present prospectively before they take up delinquency and is an individual-difference risk factor for adolescent onset. If so, that was not anticipated by the theory. Childhood temperament studies that have measured the approach style might follow up their participants to ask if approach predicts adolescent-onset delinquency. Longitudinal research is also needed to determine if and when the antisocial personality style becomes set, that is, able to predict adult antisocial outcomes alone, without any further environmental input.

THE HYPOTHESIS THAT LIFE-COURSE-PERSISTENT DEVELOPMENT IS DIFFERENTIALLY ASSOCIATED IN ADULTHOOD WITH SERIOUS OFFENDING AND VIOLENCE

The original theory predicted that life-course-persistent offenders, as compared to adolescence-limited offenders, would engage in a wider variety of offense types, including "more of the victim-oriented offenses, such as violence and fraud" (Moffitt, 1993, p. 695).

By the time the Dunedin cohort reached age 18, we reported that the life-course-persistent pathway was differentially associated with conviction for violent crimes (Jeglum-Bartusch et al., 1997; Moffitt et al., 1996), and the adolescence-limited pathway was differentially associated with nonviolent delinquent offenses (Jeglum-Bartusch et al., 1997). These Dunedin findings are buttressed by reports from other samples that physical aggression usually begins in childhood and seldom begins in adolescence (e.g., Brame, Nagin, & Tremblay, 2001). Moreover, we had shown that preadolescent antisocial behavior that was accompanied by neuropsychological deficits predicted greater persistence of crime and more violence up to age 18 (Moffitt et al., 1994).

Our follow-up at age 26 confirmed that life-course-persistent men as a group particularly differed from adolescence-limited men in the realm of violence, including violence against the women and children in their homes. This finding was corroborated with large effect sizes by data from multiple independent sources, including self-reports, informant reports, and official court conviction records (Moffitt, Caspi, et al., 2002). In a comparison of specific offenses, life-course-persistent men tended to specialize in serious offenses (carrying a hidden weapon, assault, robbery, violating court orders), whereas adolescence-limited men specialized in nonserious offenses (theft less than $5, public drunkenness, giving false information on application forms, pirating computer software). Life-course-persistent men accounted for 5 times their share of the cohort's violent convictions. Thus, although they were a small group (10% of males), they accounted for 43% of the cohort's officially sanctioned violent crime.

Domestic violence against women and children at home was specifically predicted to be an outcome of the life-course-persistent group (Moffitt, 1993). At the age-26 Dunedin follow-up, this group's scores were elevated on self-reported and official conviction measures of abuse toward women, both physical abuse (e.g., beating her up, throwing her bodily) and controlling abuse (e.g., stalking her, restricting her access to her friends and family). Because the Dunedin cohort has been interviewed repeatedly about illicit behaviors for many years, study members now trust the study's guarantee of confidentiality and can be asked questions about hitting children, with the expectation of valid responses. Life-course-persistent men were the most likely to report that they had hit a child out of anger, not in the course of normal discipline. Our finding that life-course-persistent offenders perpetrated more domestic violence was supported by the Christchurch study's finding that young adults with childhood-onset antisocial behavior engaged in significantly more violence against partners than did those with adolescent-onset behavior (Woodward, Fergusson, & Horwood, 2002). Similarly, a study of New York parolees reported that those defined as life-course-persistent based on a childhood-onset offense record engaged in twice as much domestic violence as parolees with an adolescent-onset offense record (Mazerolle & Maahs, 2002).

In general, a large empirical literature shows that the strongest long-term predictors of violence are the same predictors implicated by our theory of life-course-persistent offending: early-onset antisocial behavior, neurodevelopmental risk factors, and family risk factors (for a review, see Farrington, 1998). Moreover, research comparing violent crime versus general nonviolent delinquency has shown that violence is differentially predicted by birth complications (Raine et al., 1997), minor physical anomalies (Arseneault et al., 2000), difficult temperament (Henry, Caspi, Moffitt, & Silva, 1996), and cognitive deficits (Piquero, 2001), each of which is a hypothetical risk for life-course-persistent development (for a review, see Raine, 2002). The Christchurch study reported that people with serious childhood-onset conduct problems, compared to children without conduct problems, engaged

in 10 times more violent crime by age 25 (Fergusson, Horwood, & Ridder, 2005). The Patterns of Care Study of 1,715 service users ages 6 to 17 years compared childhood-onset versus adolescent-onset Conduct Disorder cases and reported that the childhood-onset group committed significantly more bullying but not more of the other physically aggressive Conduct Disorder symptoms (McCabe et al., 2001). However, this study did not have an adult follow-up. Lahey and colleagues (1998) reported more physical aggression associated with adolescent-onset than with childhood-onset Conduct Disorder.

What Research Is Needed?

The literature makes it clear that neurodevelopmental and family risks predict violence when it is measured on a continuum, but only a few studies have compared the adult violent outcomes of *groups* defined on the basis of early versus late antisocial onset. In addition, research is needed to clarify why life-course-persistent offenders are more violent. Our theory implies that verbal cognitive deficits may limit their options for handling conflict (a neuropsychological explanation), that they may have learned in their family that violence is an effective way to manage conflict (a social-cognition explanation), and that broken attachment bonds lead to alienation from their potential victims (an attachment explanation; Moffitt, 1994; Moffitt & Caspi, 1995). All of these explanations specify early childhood as a critical period influencing adult violence. But which, if any, of these explanatory processes are correct? Research using designs that control for genetic transmission of a predisposition to aggression in families has now documented that experiences in the family do promote childhood-onset aggression through processes that are environmentally mediated. Environmental effects on children's aggression have now been documented for exposure to parents' domestic violence (Jaffee, Moffitt, Caspi, Taylor, & Arseneault, 2002), being reared by an antisocial father (Jaffee, Moffitt, Caspi, & Taylor, 2003), being reared by a depressed mother (Kim-Cohen, Moffitt, Taylor, Pawlby, & Caspi, 2005), being a recipient of maternal hostility (Caspi et al., 2004), and being a victim of child maltreatment (Jaffee, Caspi, Moffitt, & Taylor, 2004). These studies controlled for familial liability to psychopathology, suggesting that the risk factors influence children through environmental experience. This information gives fresh impetus for research to uncover how these experiences are mediated via the child's thoughts and emotions to produce persistent aggression. Research is needed on mediating developmental processes, because findings will point to targets for intervention.

THE HYPOTHESIS THAT CHILDHOOD-ONSET ANTISOCIAL BEHAVIOR WILL PERSIST INTO MIDDLE ADULTHOOD, WHEREAS ADOLESCENT-ONSET ANTISOCIAL BEHAVIOR WILL DESIST IN YOUNG ADULTHOOD

Inherent in the name "life-course-persistent" is the assertion that the antisocial activities of these individuals will persist across the life course. Though the rest of the population may decrease its antisocial participation as it ages, the life-course-persistent individuals should remain at the top of the heap on antisocial behaviors. Thus, the taxonomy accepts that antisocial participation declines markedly in midlife; nonetheless, it expects rank-order stability, particularly on age-relevant measures of antisocial activity. To test the differential desistance prediction, it is necessary to follow a cohort's antisocial behavior from childhood to adulthood, but only a few studies have done this.

We followed up the Dunedin cohort at age 26 (Moffitt, Caspi, et al., 2002) to test hypotheses critical to this part of the theory: Childhood-onset antisocial behavior, but not adolescent-onset antisocial behavior, should be associated in adulthood with antisocial personality and continued serious antisocial behavior that expands into maladjustment in work life and victimization of partners and children (Moffitt, 1993, p. 695). Followed to age 26, the adolescent-onset delinquents at 26 were still engaging in elevated levels of property offending and they had financial problems, but they did not show a pattern of serious offending. Interestingly, the adolescent-onset delinquents self-reported problems with mental health and substance dependence, but these difficulties were not corroborated by informants who knew them well. Consistent with the taxonomy's predictions, the childhood-onset delinquents at age 26 were the most elevated on psychopathic personality traits, mental health problems, substance dependence, numbers of children sired, financial problems, work problems, domestic abuse of women and children, and drug-related and violent crimes.

In a study of 4,000 CYA inmates followed into their 30s, significantly more early starters than later starters continued offending past age 21, past age 25, and past age 31. Moreover, early onset and low cognitive ability significantly predicted which inmates continued to offend past age 31 (Ge, Donnellan, & Wenk, 2001). A different study of CYA offenders looked in depth at predictors of criminal career duration among 377 parolees released on average at age 24 and followed for 12 years (Piquero, Brame, & Lynam, 2004). This study found that criminal career dura-

tion was predicted by low tested cognitive abilities and by the interaction between childhood poverty status and cognitive ability. Similarly, a large Swedish study reported less crime in adulthood among offenders who possessed positive personal characteristics resembling the characteristics of Dunedin adolescence-limited offenders (Stattin, Romelsjo, & Stenbacka, 1997).

These findings were obtained using groups of adolescence-limited and life-course-persistent males defined by applying commonsense clinical cutoffs (e.g., Moffitt et al., 1996). However, in the past decade, new analytic methods have become available for ascertaining whether distinctive trajectories exist within a population of individuals whose behavior has been measured repeatedly during development (Nagin, 1999; Nagin & Tremblay, 2001a; Roeder et al., 1996). These new semiparametric methods offer several advantages over the clinical cutoffs approach. First, the methods are agnostic with respect to taxonomic theories, and thus results are relatively free from investigator bias. Second, the methods can search a longitudinal data set to ask whether there is indeed more than one developmental trajectory in it, as a taxonomy implies. Third, they can ascertain the relative goodness of fit of competing models having 1, 2, 3, 4, or more trajectories to ascertain whether the taxonomic theory has specified the right number of developmental subtypes in the population. Fourth, they generate output from the best-fitting model that reveals whether its trajectories rise and fall at ages specified by the theory. Fifth, they generate output about which study participants belong to which trajectory, making it possible to ascertain whether each trajectory group approximates its population prevalence as specified by the theory. It is important to keep in mind that what researchers put into the method determines what they can get out, and therefore testing the taxonomy of life-course-persistent and adolescence-limited antisocial behavior calls for representative samples, repeated measures taken at informative ages from childhood to adulthood, and measures of antisocial behavior that capture its heterotypic continuity across developmental periods. In these respects, the Dunedin data set, although not perfect, was pretty good fodder for the semiparametric method.

We applied this method to counts of Conduct Disorder symptoms assessed (via self-, mother-, and teacher-reports) for 525 male study members at ages 7, 9, 11, 13, 15, 18, 21, and 26 years. Conduct Disorder symptoms are fighting, bullying, lying, stealing, cruelty to people or animals, vandalism, and disobeying rules; three such symptoms earn a formal diagnosis. The model that best fit the Dunedin data detected the following groups (see Figure 15.1). A life-course-persistent group, 7% of the cohort, had a fairly stable high trajectory, exhibiting between 4 and 7 antisocial symptoms at every age from 7 to 26 years. This group had more symptoms than any of the other groups at every age. A group whose trajectory resembled an adolescence-limited pattern began with 2 symptoms at age 7 but increased to a peak of 4.5 symptoms at age 18, and then decreased on a slight downward trajectory to 3.5 symptoms at age 26. A recovery group, 21% of the cohort (similar to the childhood-limited or low-level chronic groups described in an earlier section of this chapter), began with 6 symptoms at age 7 but decreased steadily with age and had only 1 symptom by ages 21 and 26. An abstainer group, 11%, had less than 1 symptom on average at every age. Two further trajectory groups were identified. The first of these took an adolescence-limited shape, but at a low level, and the second took a recovery shape, but also at a low level. For illustrative purposes, in Figure 15.1 these two groups were collapsed into a consistently low group, 47% of the cohort, which had 1 to 2 symptoms on average at each age. Thus, the best-fitting model bore a not unreasonable resemblance to the taxonomy. Differential outcomes for the trajectory groups mirrored the outcomes for the clinically defined Dunedin groups (Moffitt, Caspi, et al., 2002). Males on the adolescence-limited trajectory were still engaging in property offending and substance abuse but not serious offending at age 26. Males on the life-course-persistent trajectory were the most elevated at age 26 on mental health problems and substance dependence, numbers of children sired, financial and work problems, domestic abuse of women and children, and drug-related and violent crimes.

Other cohort studies have applied trajectory analysis to repeated measures of antisocial behavior from childhood to adulthood. A British longitudinal study followed official crime records for a 1950s birth cohort of 400 men to age 32 and detected chronic and adolescence-limited trajectories that showed the expected differential desistance (Nagin et al., 1995). Unexpectedly, offenders defined as adolescence-limited had desisted from criminal offending according to their official police records, but according to their self-reports they continued into their 30s to drink heavily and get into fights. The South Holland epidemiological study followed 2,000 Dutch children from age 4 to 30 years (Bongers, Koot, van der Ende, Donker, & Verhulst, in press). This study reported two trajectories of young people with high levels of externalizing problems, as assessed by the CBCL (Achenbach, 1985). One trajectory was normative and distinguished by increasing truancy and alcohol and drug use, but did not markedly increase the risk of adult offending. The other trajectory was characterized by increasing oppositional behavior and hot temper and was associated with elevated risk of serious and violent adult offending. Low trajectories were also detected.

The Rutgers Health and Human Development Project followed its longitudinal sample into adulthood and reported a test of the taxonomy using nonparametric mixture modeling to detect trajectory groups (H. R. White, Bates, & Buyske, 2001). However, White et al.'s figure 1, showing delinquency trajectories for the resulting groups, suggests that the group labeled "persistent" in this study was in reality adolescence-limited, because this group's trajectory showed very low levels of offending at ages 12 and 28 but a very pronounced adolescent offending peak at age 18. This sample may not have contained life-course-persistent members, because it was recruited via random telephone dialing with an initial 17% rate of refusal to the phone call and afterward a 52% completion rate for enrollment in data collection. Families with life-course-persistent risk characteristics are known to be difficult to engage as research participants (Farrington, Gallagher, Morley, St. Ledger, & West, 1990), and therefore they were probably among those who did not take part in the Rutgers study. Given the strong possibility that groups were mislabeled in this study, it is unclear what to make of it vis-à-vis the taxonomy.

The Oregon Youth Study applied trajectory analysis to 200 males followed from age 12 to 24 (Wiesner & Capaldi, 2003). In addition to the abstainer trajectory and the decreasing trajectory discussed in earlier sections of this chapter, the analysis also yielded a group whose antisocial behavior was chronically at the cohort's highest level (life-course-persistent?) and a group whose antisocial behavior increased somewhat from age 12 to a peak at 19, and then decreased from age 20 to 24 (adolescence-limited?). It is not clear that Wiesner and Capaldi would agree with our characterization of their groups; indeed, they used different labels for them. In any case, although these two groups seemed fairly similar in late adolescence, they diverged at the study's age 23 to 26 outcome point, with the chronic group showing much higher levels of alcohol use, drug use, and depression symptoms, as well as more adult antisocial behavior (Wiesner, Kim, & Capaldi, in press).

One clear shortcoming of the available longitudinal data that have been used to test for the presence of life-course-persistent versus adolescence-limited subtypes is that the data are "right-hand censored"; in other words, study participants have generally been followed only until their 20s or 30s. What is needed is a cohort that represents the general population and that has been followed through the age period of risk for most criminal offending, up to midlife.

Such a cohort does not yet exist. However, in the absence of the ideal representative cohort, there is one important study that warrants our focus. Sampson and Laub (2003) reported a follow-up of half of the Gluecks' sample, those who were adolescent inmates in Massachusetts in the 1940s. The authors constructed a unique database of official criminal records for almost 500 men, covering the period from age 7 years to the end of each offender's life, up to age 70 years. The study was noteworthy for collecting nationwide FBI records and for attending to artifacts in crime records arising from periods of incarceration or the offender's premature death. The authors' analyses were motivated by their skepticism about the idea of prospectively predicting a group of offenders who will account for a disproportionate amount of society's serious crime. Sampson and Laub reported two findings from the study that they believed challenge this idea. First, they found that almost all of the men in the Gluecks' sample desisted from criminal offending sooner or later. Second, they found heterogeneity in adulthood crime career patterns within the sample of adolescent inmates, and they found that this heterogeneity was not explained by measures of childhood risk. Because the Sampson and Laub publication was represented as a challenge to the life-course-persistent taxonomy, we must take a closer look at whether or not these two findings discredit the taxonomy. In so doing, it is useful to consider the nature of the sample studied by Sampson and Laub. According to the taxonomy, virtually all of the men studied would have been regarded as candidates for the life-course-persistent subtype. They had been incarcerated as young adolescents in reform schools, a status reserved at that time for a very small fraction of a state's youth, those having established already by adolescence the most serious, persistent records of deviance that could not be controlled by parents or schools. It is well documented that as a group, the boys had backgrounds of marked family adversity, social disadvantage, and childhood antisocial conduct. Sampson and Laub note details about the sample that fit the life-course-persistent pattern, such as low mean IQ and mean first arrest at 11.9 years. Thus, this sample born in 1924 to 1932 probably comprised, relative to the much larger population of Boston males their age, a small subgroup who had started on the life-course-persistent pathway.

Sampson and Laub's (2003, p. 577) first finding was that the men in the Gluecks' sample desisted from criminal offending sooner or later: "Aging out of crime appears to reflect a general process." Unfortunately, Sampson and Laub misrepresented the taxonomy's prediction; they set up a straw prediction to test that life-course-persistent offenders should carry on committing crimes at the same high rate from adolescence through old age and to their death. Clearly, this was never implied by the taxonomy, because it acknowledged the populationwide process of aging out of crime and explained that the term life-course-persistent antisocial behavior did not require crime in old age, but referred to the persistence of antisocial personality characteristics or antisocial behaviors within the family (Moffitt, 1993, p. 680). The taxonomy's actual prediction was that delinquents like the Gluecks' would continue offending well beyond the age when most young men in their cohort population desisted. The study followed only reform school boys, and thus it could not provide comparative data on crime careers for Boston men born 1924 to 1932, but it is known that desistance from delinquency in young adulthood was the norm for this cohort, which came of age in the postwar era of near full employment. In contrast to that norm, 84% of the study men were arrested between ages 17 and 24, 44% were arrested in their 40s, 23% were arrested in their 50s, and 12% were arrested in their 60s. The reform school sample's mean crime career length was 25.6 years. It seems reasonable to believe that such remarkable statistics do not also describe the rest of the male population of Boston. Thus, the study's results seem reasonably consistent with the taxonomy's prediction that boys who begin life on the life-course-persistent pathway will have unusually extended offending careers, thereby accounting for more than their share of the crime rate.

Sampson and Laub's (2003) second finding was of heterogeneity in adulthood crime career patterns within the Gluecks' sample. Again, the alternative hypothesis seems to be a straw man. The alternative would be that males who spent their youth and early adulthood on the life-course-persistent pathway can show no variation in subsequent offending during midlife and aging over a span of many years. Such uniformity is implausible, and the taxonomic theory did not make such a prediction. Within the Gluecks' sample, six trajectories emerged from a semiparametric group-based modeling analysis. Thus, the men, all of whom began on the life-course-persistent pathway, varied subsequently in their age at desistance from crime and in their rate of offending up to the point of their desistance. Of particular importance, child and family characteristics did not discriminate among these six trajectories. On the one hand, this failure of discrimination is not surprising given that the cohort members' childhood backgrounds were almost uniformly high-risk. On the other hand, this finding suggests that to the extent that different crime careers emerge during midlife within a group of life-course-persistent men, concurrent life experiences must account for the divergence. This would constitute an interesting extension to the taxonomic theory on a topic it did not originally address: heterogeneity within life-course-persistent delinquents in the ways they age out of crime.

This study by Sampson and Laub (2003) was well executed and well intentioned. The authors were concerned about practitioners who have reified the life-course-persistent idea, treating it as if it describes a group having hard boundaries, made up of individual children who are easy to identify in early childhood and who deserve radical interventions to avert their inevitable destiny as predatory criminals. The authors' concern is well placed, and their efforts to dissuade such reification are laudable. To their credit, the authors point out that "the current bandwagon . . . is not consistent with the logic of Moffitt's actual argument" (p. 576). Nonetheless, to make their points, the authors inadvertently had to misrepresent the original taxonomy as having made predictions that it did not make. Here we set the record straight. Life-course-persistent delinquents do not have to be arrested for illegal crimes steadily up to age 70, but they do have to maintain a constellation of antisocial attitudes, values, and proclivities that affect their behavior toward others. Life-course-persistent delinquents do not have to live exactly the same crime trajectory as they age out of crime; it is interesting to learn how their lives diverge. Laub and Sampson (2003) are leading the way in researching these questions using qualitative as well as quantitative methods.

What Research Is Needed?

Overall, our theory's prediction that childhood-onset antisocial behavior persists longer into adulthood than adolescent-onset delinquency seems to be on fairly solid empirical footing. It has been known for decades that early onset of offending predicts a longer duration of crime career, and this association was recently affirmed by two careful reviews (Gendreau, Little, & Goggin, 1996; Krohn, Thornberry, Rivera, & LeBlanc, 2001). Nonetheless, the adolescence-limited groups in the Dunedin cohort and other cohorts continued to experience some adjustment problems as adults, and we need research to understand what accounts for this. The original taxonomy put forward the hypothesis that we should expect some adolescence-limited delinquents to recover to good adult adjustment later than others, and that this age variation might be explained by snares such as a conviction record that harms job prospects (Moffitt, 1993, p. 691). The idea is that engaging in even limited delinquency as a young person can diminish the probability of subsequent good outcomes, par-

ticularly if one is caught and sanctioned. Also important is the information emerging from the work of Laub and Sampson (2003) pointing to marked heterogeneity within the life-course-persistent group in middle and late life, suggesting that research into midlife turning-point experiences is needed. Overall, longitudinal studies are needed that follow the life-course-persistent, low-level chronic, abstainer, and adolescence-limited groups to reveal the very long-term implications of their experiences in the first 2 decades of life.

GENDER: THE HYPOTHESIS THAT MOST FEMALE ANTISOCIAL BEHAVIOR IS THE ADOLESCENCE-LIMITED TYPE

The original statement of the taxonomy asserted that the theory describes the behavior of females as well as it describes the behavior of males. The full text of the theory that included predictions about females was published as a book chapter that is not widely available (Moffitt, 1994). Therefore, we quote the original statement, written in January 1991:

> The crime rate for females is lower than for males. In this developmental taxonomy, much of the gender difference in crime is attributed to sex differences in the risk factors for life-course persistent antisocial behavior. Little girls are less likely than little boys to encounter all of the putative initial links in the causal chain for life-course persistent antisocial development. Research has shown that girls have lower rates than boys of symptoms of nervous system dysfunction, difficult temperament, late verbal and motor milestones, hyperactivity, learning disabilities, reading failure, and childhood conduct problems. . . . Most girls lack the personal diathesis elements of the evocative, reactive, and proactive person/environment interactions that initiate and maintain life-course persistent antisocial behavior.
>
> Adolescence-limited delinquency, on the other hand, is open to girls as well as to boys. According to the theory advanced here, girls, like boys, should begin delinquency soon after puberty, to the extent that they (1) have access to antisocial models, and (2) perceive the consequences of delinquency as reinforcing. . . . However, exclusion from gender-segregated male antisocial groups may cut off opportunities for girls to learn delinquent behaviors. . . . Girls are physically more vulnerable than boys to risk of personal victimization (e.g., pregnancy, or injury from dating violence) if they affiliate with life-course persistent antisocial males. Thus, lack of access to antisocial models and perceptions of serious personal risk may dampen the vigor of girls'

delinquent involvement somewhat. Nonetheless, girls should engage in adolescence-limited delinquency in significant numbers. (pp. 39–40)

The original theory thus proposed that (1) fewer females than males would become delinquent (and conduct disordered) overall and that (2) among delinquents, the percentage who are life-course-persistent would be larger for males than females. Following from this, (3) the majority of delinquent females will be of the adolescence-limited type, and (4) their delinquency will have the same causes as adolescence-limited males' delinquency.

These predictions were borne out in the Dunedin cohort (Moffitt & Caspi, 2001; Moffitt et al., 2001). As predicted, the male:female difference was very large for the life-course-persistent form of antisocial behavior (10:1) but negligible for the adolescence-limited form (1.5:1). Childhood-onset females had high-risk neurodevelopmental and family backgrounds, but adolescent-onset females did not, which documented that females and males on the same trajectories share the same risk factors. We have described the elements of the adolescence-limited causal pathway among Dunedin females, showing that each girl's delinquency onset is linked to the timing of her own puberty (Moffitt et al., 2001), that delinquent peers are a necessary condition for onset of delinquency among adolescent girls (Caspi et al., 1993; Caspi & Moffitt, 1991), and that an intimate relationship with an offender promotes girls' antisocial behaviors (Moffitt et al., 2001).

Few empirical tests of this taxonomy have compared how females and males fit the two developmental trajectories, but it appears that our findings about Dunedin females are broadly consistent with these previous studies. Fergusson and colleagues (2000, 2002), studying the Christchurch sample ($n = 1,000$), found that a single model described male and female trajectories of antisocial behavior, and the male to female ratio was 4:1 for early-onset, versus only 2:1 for late-onset subjects. Kratzer and Hodgins (1999), studying a Swedish cohort ($n = 13,000$), found similar childhood risk factors for males and females in the life-course-persistent group, and the male to female ratio was 15:1 for early-onset, versus only 4:1 for late-onset subjects. Mazerolle et al. (2000), studying a Philadelphia cohort ($n = 3,655$), reported that early onset signaled persistent and diverse offending for males and females alike. A longitudinal study of 820 girls analyzed with a semiparametric mixture model found a stable, highly antisocial group, but this group contained only 1.4% of the girls (Cote, Zoccolillo, Tremblay, Nagin, & Vitaro, 2001).

All studies concur that females are seldom childhood-onset- or life-course-persistent-type (the exception is Aguilar et al., 2000, whose early-onset group had as many girls as boys).

The application of our developmental taxonomy to females was questioned by Silverthorn and Frick (1999), who put forward a contrasting, female-specific theory. They suggested that despite the fact that girls' onset of antisocial behavior is delayed until adolescence, this adolescent-onset pathway in girls is not analogous to the adolescence-limited pathway in boys. Instead, this theory argued, all delinquent girls have the same high-risk causal backgrounds as life-course-persistent males. To evaluate this alternative hypothesis, we conducted analyses in the Dunedin study (Moffitt et al., 1996) using self-reports, mothers' reports, and teachers' reports of antisocial behavior to define girls on the adolescence-limited and life-course-persistent paths. This study resulted in two findings: First, the vast majority of female delinquents fit the adolescence-limited, late-starter pattern; second, the childhood backgrounds of these females who exhibited adolescent-onset antisocial behavior were like the backgrounds of adolescence-limited delinquent boys, normative and not pathological. The proposal from Silverthorne and Frick has also been tested in the African American Philadelphia cohort of the National Collaborative Perinatal Project (N. A. White & Piquero, in press), using official crime records to define adolescence-limited and life-course-persistent offenders. This study, too, reported that most female offenders followed the adolescence-limited pattern, and that female and male adolescence-limited offenders scored similarly, and better than life-course-persistent offenders, on measures of family and individual risk such as childhood cognitive ability. Similar conclusions were reached in the Patterns of Care Study of 300 children receiving services for Conduct Disorder (McCabe, Rodgers, Yeh, & Hough, 2004). Because the African American cohort and the Patterns of Care sample were selected for high-risk status, childhood-onset girls were found at higher prevalence than in the Dunedin cohort, which represents the general population.

These accumulating findings suggest that the two theories of the origins of life-course-persistent and adolescence-limited offending describe the developmental course of antisocial behavior across the sexes and irrespective of sex. Because few females have the risk factors for life-course-persistent development, this theory explains the wide sex difference in serious, persistent antisocial behavior. Because the risk factors for adolescence-limited offending are equal-opportunity, this theory explains the sex similarity for nonserious, transient delinquency during the teenage years (Moffitt et al., 2001).

What Research Is Needed?

The dearth of gender comparisons originates from a pragmatic circumstance. An ideal test of this theory requires a large representative (nonclinical, nonadjudicated) sample followed longitudinally from childhood to adulthood with repeated measures of antisocial behavior. To date, few such studies have included females. It would be useful to have a large sample including both life-course-persistent and adolescence-limited girls in sufficient numbers to test all components of our theory. The new longitudinal study of Pittsburgh girls may help in this regard (Hipwell et al., 2002).

RACE: THE HYPOTHESIS THAT BOTH LIFE-COURSE-PERSISTENT AND ADOLESCENCE-LIMITED DEVELOPMENTAL PROCESSES ARE EXACERBATED BY SOCIETAL RACE PREJUDICE

The original statement of the taxonomy asserted that the theory applies to ethnic minority populations as well as to Whites. The discussion of race was published in a book that is not easy to obtain (Moffitt, 1994). Therefore, we paraphrase the original statement:

> In the United States, the crime rate for black Americans is higher than the crime rate for whites. The race difference may be accounted for by a relatively higher prevalence of both life-course persistent and adolescence-limited subtypes among contemporary African Americans. Life-course persistent antisocials might be anticipated at elevated rates among black Americans because the putative root causes of this type are elevated by institutionalised prejudice and by poverty. Among poor black families, prenatal care is less available, infant nutrition is poorer, and the incidence of exposure to toxic and infectious agents is greater, placing infants at risk for the nervous system problems that research has shown to interfere with prosocial child development. To the extent that family bonds have been loosened and poor black parents are under stress . . . and to the extent that poor black children attend disadvantaged schools . . . for poor black children the snowball of cumulative continuity may begin rolling earlier, and it may roll faster downhill. In addition, adolescence-limited crime is probably elevated among black youths as compared to white youths in contemporary America. If racially segregated communities provide greater exposure to life-course persistent role models, then circumstances are ripe for black

teens with no prior behavior problems to mimic delinquent ways in a search for status and respect. Moreover, black young people spend more years in the maturity gap, on average, than whites because ascendancy to valued adult roles and privileges comes later, if at all. Legitimate desirable jobs are closed to many young black men; they do not often shift from having "little to lose" to having a "stake in conformity" overnight by leaving schooling and entering a good job. Indeed, the biological maturity gap is perhaps best seen as an instigator of adolescent-onset delinquency for black youths, with an economic maturity gap maintaining offending into adulthood. (p. 39)

Thus, the taxonomy expected that both life-course-persistent and adolescence-limited causal processes should work the same way in African American and White American groups, but any excess of offending among poor African American youth could be attributed to an excess of the risk factors for both delinquent subtypes. Our research with the Pittsburgh Youth Survey has documented that childhood risk factors associated with life-course-persistent offending (low IQ and impulsive undercontrol) are related to early-onset, frequent delinquent offending and physical aggression among Black and White males alike (Caspi et al., 1994; Lynam et al., 2000; Lynam, Moffitt, & Stouthamer-Loeber, 1993). However, these studies have not specifically divided Pittsburgh delinquents into childhood-versus adolescent-onset comparison groups (because the cohort of the Pittsburgh study having IQ and personality data was not followed beyond age 13).

We know of only a few studies that have directly compared life-course-persistent versus adolescence-limited offender patterns across races, and they seem to offer opposing findings. Donnellan et al. (2000) designated the taxonomy groups in 2,000 young adult CYA inmates. On a comprehensive set of measures of cognitive ability, life-course-persistent offenders scored below adolescence-limited offenders. However, this predicted finding of differential cognitive risk applied to adjudicated Whites and Hispanics but not to adjudicated African Americans. The opposite pattern of race differences emerged from a different study of 377 CYA offenders released on average at age 24 and followed for 12 years (Piquero et al., 2004). This study found that African American parolees had worse childhood poverty and lower cognitive test scores than White parolees, the interaction between poverty and low cognitive ability predicted longer criminal career duration, and this prediction was stronger among African American than White parolees.

A study of the Baltimore sample of the National Collaborative Perinatal Project was able to test for race differences in the etiological process hypothesized to underlie life-course-persistent antisocial behavior (Piquero, Moffitt, & Lawton, in press). Results showed that several variables helped to explain differences between Whites and Blacks in the level of chronic offending. However, although Black participants had higher mean levels of risk factors than Whites, the developmental processes predicting chronic offending were the same across groups defined by race. Specifically, low birthweight in combination with adverse familial environments predicted chronic offending from adolescence to age 33 among Whites and African Americans alike, although the effect size reached statistical significance among only African Americans, a pattern opposite that reported by Donnellan et al. (2000). Most, but not all, of these studies of African American cohorts fit our theory's notion that causal developmental processes are the same across racial groups, but that African Americans end up with higher levels of crime because they begin the processes with higher levels of risk factors.

One further set of studies is relevant. A study of the Philadelphia sample of the National Collaborative Perinatal Project, which includes only African American families, showed that childhood measures of school discipline problems and low tested IQ predicted a more serious offending career (Piquero & Chung, 2001). In this same Philadelphia African American cohort, low scores on an achievement test of cognitive ability predicted early onset and subsequent persistence of offending (McGloin & Pratt, 2003), and neuropsychological test scores at ages 7 to 8 years and 13 to 14 years predicted patterns of life-course-persistent offending to age 39 (Piquero & White, 2003). In the Providence sample of the National Collaborative Perinatal Project, Piquero and Buka (2002) found the expected higher prevalence of offenders among African Americans compared to Whites. However, crime career patterns such as the concentration of crimes in a few offenders and the significant prediction of adult crime from chronic juvenile delinquency, applied equally well to both races. It has been shown that earlier onset of delinquent offending among African American males predicts a more serious crime career (Piquero & Chung, 2001) and a longer duration of crime career (Piquero et al., 2004), which suggests that the life-course-persistent pattern applies to Black samples as well as White samples.

What Research Is Needed?

The theory asserted that life-course-persistent and adolescence-limited processes should apply to both Whites and ethnic minorities (neurodevelopmental and family risks should predict the earlier onset, greater seriousness, and longer duration of antisocial behavior across racial groups, and the maturity gap and peer influences should predict late onset across racial groups). Together, these causal processes should be able to account for the elevated prevalence of delinquency among ethnic minorities because minority group members experience higher levels of both sets of risk factors. Rowe, Vazsonyi, and Flannery (1994) provide an explanation of how to test this.

Most of the studies of African Americans cited here used cohorts defined in the period between 1955 and 1980. Of course, only cohorts defined some time ago can yield information about the duration and seriousness of crime careers followed into the 3rd decade of life, but research on more contemporary cohorts is also needed.

There is one caveat: If the maturity gap lasts longer for African American young men than for Whites, this would make it difficult to distinguish the life-course-persistent from adolescence-limited groups in Black samples on the basis of chronic offending into adulthood. Therefore, researchers examining contemporary cohorts of ethnic minorities should operationalize the life-course-persistent and adolescence-limited groups using other distinguishing features, such as early childhood onset of conduct problems, antisocial personality traits, or recidivistic youth violence.

RESEARCH NEEDED ON OTHER HYPOTHESES

Before 1993, virtually no research compared delinquent subtypes defined on a developmental basis, but now this research strategy has become almost commonplace. Many research teams have assessed representative samples with prospective measures of antisocial behavior from childhood to adulthood, and this has enabled comparisons based on age of onset and persistence. Now that the requisite databases are available, other hypotheses derived from the original taxonomic theory need to be tested.

First, we suggested that childhood measures of antisocial behavior in longitudinal studies should be more highly correlated with adult measures than with adolescent measures of antisocial behavior (Moffitt, 1993, p. 695). This hypothesis derived from the taxonomy's assertion that the people participating in antisocial behavior in childhood and adulthood are the same people, but they are joined in adolescence by other people whose reasons for participation are different. If childhood measures did correlate with adult measures better than with adolescent measures, it would be a surprising violation of the so-called longitudinal law that measures taken closer together in time are more strongly correlated than measures taken further apart in time. In the Dunedin study, we asked how closely age-3 undercontrolled temperament was associated with later antisocial diagnostic outcomes (controlling for sex). Age-3 undercontrol was a significant predictor of adult diagnoses 2 decades later: OR = 3.1 (CI = 1.3 –7.5) for age-26 Antisocial Personality Disorder and OR = 4.1 (CI: 2.0 to 8.4) for age-21 Conduct Disorder. However, the associations between age-3 temperament and adolescent diagnoses were not significant: OR = 1.7 (CI = 0.9 to 3.4) for age 15 Conduct Disorder and OR = 1.8 (CI = 0.9 to 3.8) for age 18 Conduct Disorder. The South Holland epidemiological study reported a similar finding: Antisocial behaviors assessed at ages 6 to 11 years predicted antisocial behaviors at ages 12 to 17 years only weakly (OR = 2.5), but predicted antisocial behavior at ages 20 to 25 years strongly (OR = 6.7; Donker, Smeenk, van der Laan, & Verhulst, 2003). More such tests of the hypothesis that childhood antisocial behavior predicts adult outcome better than adolescent outcome are needed.

Second, we speculated that adolescence-limited offenders must rely on peer support for crime, but life-course-persistent offenders should be willing to offend alone (although in adolescence, they serve as magnets for less expert offenders; Moffitt, 1993, p. 688). To our knowledge, this hypothesis has not been systematically examined.

Third, we suggested that snares (such as a criminal record, incarceration, addiction, and truncated education without credentials) should explain variation in the age at desistance from crime during the adult age period, particularly among adolescence-limited offenders (Moffitt, 1993, p. 691). One study reported that alcohol and cannabis dependence can ensnare young people in an antisocial lifestyle; most individuals' personal curve of antisocial participation from age 18 to 26 generally grows downward, but a spell of substance dependence temporarily deflects this curve upward (Hussong, Curran, Moffitt, Caspi, & Carrig, 2004). More such tests of the hypothesis that snares mediate continuing offending are needed.

Fourth, we asserted that the two groups would react differently to turning-point opportunities: Life-course-persistent offenders would selectively get undesirable partners and jobs and would in turn expand their repertoire into domestic abuse and workplace crime, whereas adolescence-limited offenders would get good partners and jobs and would in turn desist from crime (Moffitt, 1993, p. 695). One study showed that the potential turning point of school grade retention could prompt antisocial behavior among ordinary boys, but in contrast, retention had little effect on boys who had been on a chronic life-course-persistent tra-

jectory since childhood; the authors speculated that the chronic boys' antisocial behavior was already so ingrained that it was difficult to influence for good or for bad (Nagin, Pagani, Tremblay, & Vitaro, 2003). More such tests of the hypothesis that antisocial history moderates turning points are needed.

Fifth, we put forward a new prediction here, that the life-course-persistent antisocial individual will be at high risk in midlife for poor physical health, cardiovascular disease, and early disease morbidity and mortality (Moffitt, 2001). We based this prediction on our observation that life-course-persistent antisocial behavior is associated in adolescence with factors that are known to predict disease morbidity in midlife (Gallo & Matthews, 1999; McEwen, 2002; Repetti, Taylor, & Seeman, 2002). Such risk factors include health risk behaviors (e.g., heavy smoking, unprotected sex), high levels of stress (e.g., conflictual relationships, family dissolution, financial insecurity), and personality traits associated with physiological vulnerability (e.g., hostility, stress-reactivity, alienation). Our preliminary analyses of health indicators collected when the Dunedin study members were 26 years old has revealed that, compared to the adolescence-limited men, the life-course-persistent antisocial men already had somewhat lower high-density lipoprotein and significantly poorer tested cardiorespiratory aerobic fitness (Moffitt et al., 2005). Follow-up assessments of longitudinal studies of antisocial development should measure more physical health outcomes.

CONCLUSIONS

After 10 years of research, what can be stated with some certainty is that the hypothesized life-course-persistent antisocial individual exists, at least during the first 3 decades of life. Consensus about this group has emerged from all studies that have applied trajectory-detection analyses to a representative cohort sample having longitudinal repeated measures of antisocial behavior. Tremblay et al. (2004) detected a "high physical aggression" group constituting 14% of Canadian children followed from age 17 to 42 months. Broidy et al. (2003) detected a "chronic aggressive" group constituting 3% to 11% of children followed from age 6 to 13 years in six different cohorts from three countries. Maughan et al. (2001) detected a "stable high aggressive" group constituting 12% of North Carolina youth followed from ages 9 to 16 years. Brame et al. (2001) detected a "high chronic aggressive" group constituting 3% of Canadian youth followed from ages 6 to 17 years.

Raine et al. (2005) detected a "life-course persistent path" group that constituted 13% of Pittsburgh youth followed from ages 7 to 17 years. Fergusson et al. (2000) detected a "chronic offender" group constituting 6% of Christchurch youth followed from ages 12 to 18 years. Chung et al. (2002) detected a "chronic offender" group constituting 7% of Seattle youth followed from ages 13 to 21 years. Wiesner and Capaldi (2003) detected a "chronic high-level" group constituting 16% of Oregon youth followed from ages 12 to 24 years. Moffitt et al. (this chapter) detected a "high-persistent" group that constituted 7% of Dunedin young people followed from ages 7 to 26 years. Nagin et al. (1995) detected a "high-level chronic" group that constituted 12% of London males followed from ages 10 to 32 years. So far as we know, no research team that has looked for a persistent antisocial group has failed to find it.

A number of other postulates from the taxonomy have received modest or mixed empirical support, but overall they appear to be supported:

- Life-course-persistent antisocial behavior emerges from early neurodevelopmental and family adversity risk factors, but adolescence-limited delinquency does not.
- Genetic etiological processes contribute more to life-course-persistent than adolescence-limited antisocial development.
- Childhood-limited aggressive children, if followed to adulthood, become low-level chronic criminal offenders with personality disorders.
- Abstainers from delinquency are rare individuals who become unpopular with teen peers.
- Life-course-persistent and adolescence-limited delinquents develop different personality structures by adulthood.
- Life-course-persistent development is differentially associated with serious offending and violence in adulthood.
- Life-course-persistent antisocial development is almost exclusively male, whereas most female antisocial behavior is of the adolescence-limited type.

Some findings have received beginning support, but more research is needed:

- Adolescence-limited antisocial behavior is influenced by the maturity gap between childhood and adulthood and by social mimicry of antisocial role models.
- Childhood-onset antisocial behavior persists at least into middle adulthood, whereas adolescent-onset antisocial behavior desists in young adulthood.

Some predictions from the taxonomy have not been tested sufficiently:

- Life-course-persistent antisocial individuals will be at high risk in midlife for poor physical health, cardiovascular disease, and early disease morbidity and mortality.
- Adolescence-limited offenders must rely on peer support for crime, but life-course-persistent offenders should be willing to offend alone (although in adolescence, they serve as magnets for less expert offenders).
- Snares (such as a criminal record, incarceration, addiction, and truncated education without credentials) should explain variation in the age at desistence from crime during the adult age period, particularly among adolescence-limited offenders.
- The two groups should react differently to turning-point opportunities: Adolescence-limited offenders should get good partners and jobs that help them to desist from crime, whereas life-course-persistent offenders should selectively get undesirable partners and jobs and in turn expand their repertoire into domestic abuse and workplace crime.

It is pleasing that the taxonomy has generated interest and research. Some findings have been faithful to the hypotheses originally formulated. Other findings have pointed to important revisions needed to improve the fit between the taxonomy and nature, and some findings raise serious challenges to aspects of the taxonomy. All three kinds of findings are much appreciated. Obviously, there is still a lot of work to do.

REFERENCES

Achenbach, T. M. (1985). *Assessment and taxonomy of child and adolescent psychopathology.* Newbury Park, CA: Sage.

Agnew, R. (2003). An integrated theory of the adolescent peak in offending. *Youth and Society, 34,* 263–299.

Aguilar, B., Sroufe, L. A., Egeland, B., & Carlson, E. (2000). Distinguishing the early-onset-persistent and adolescent-onset antisocial behavior types: From birth to 16 years. *Development and Psychopathology, 12,* 109–132.

Allen, J. P., Weissberg, R. P., & Hawkins, J. A. (1989). The relation between values and social competence in early adolescence. *Developmental Psychology, 25,* 458–464.

Alnaes, R., & Torgersen, S. (1988). The relationship between DSM-III symptom disorders (Axis I) and personality disorders (Axis II) in an outpatient population. *Acta Psychiatrica Scandinavica, 78,* 485–492.

American Psychiatric Association. (1994). *Diagnostic and statistical manual of mental disorders* (4th ed.). Washington, DC: Author.

Arnett, J. J. (2000). Emerging adulthood: A theory of development from the late teens through the twenties. *American Psychologist, 55,* 469–480.

Arseneault, L., Moffitt, T. E., Caspi, A., Taylor, A., Rijsdijk, F., Jaffee, S., et al. (2003). Strong genetic effects on cross-situational antisocial behavior among 5-year-old children, according to mothers, teachers, examiner-observers, and twins' self-reports. *Journal of Child Psychology and Psychiatry, 44,* 832–848.

Arseneault, L., Tremblay, R. E., Boulerice, B., & Saucier, J.-F. (2002). Obstetric complications and adolescent violent behaviors: Testing two developmental pathways. *Child Development, 73,* 496–508.

Arseneault, L., Tremblay, R. E., Boulerice, B., Seguin, J. R., & Saucier, J.-F. (2000). Minor physical anomalies and family adversity as risk factors for adolescent violent delinquency. *American Journal of Psychiatry, 157,* 917–923.

Bongers, I. L., Koot, H. M., van der Ende, J., Donker, A., & Verhulst, F. C. (in press). Predicting delinquency in young adulthood from developmental pathways of externalizing behavior. *Journal of Abnormal Psychology.*

Brame, R., Bushway, S., & Paternoster, R. (1999). On the use of panel research designs and random effects models to investigate static and dynamic theories of criminal offending. *Criminology, 37,* 599–642.

Brame, R., Nagin, D. S., & Tremblay, R. E. (2001). Developmental trajectories of physical aggression from school entry to late adolescence. *Journal of Child Psychology and Psychiatry, 42,* 503–512.

Brennan, P. A., Hall, J., Bor, W., Najman, J. M., & Williams, G. (2003). Integrating biological and social processes in relation to early-onset persistent aggression in boys and girls. *Developmental Psychology, 39,* 309–323.

Brezina, T. (2000). Delinquent problem-solving: An interpretive framework for criminological theory and research. *Journal of Research in Crime and Delinquency, 37,* 3–30.

Broidy, L., Broidy, L. M., Nagin, D. S., Tremblay, R. E., Brame, R. E., Dodge, B. et al. (2003). Developmental trajectories of childhood disruptive behaviour disorders and adolescent delinquency: A six-sample replication. *Developmental Psychology, 39,* 222–245.

Bukowski, W. M., Sippola, L. K., & Newcomb, A. F. (2000). Variations in patterns of attraction to same- and other-sex peers during early adolescence. *Developmental Psychology, 36,* 147–154.

Butterfield, F. (1996). *All God's children: The Bosket family and the American tradition of violence.* New York: Avon.

Butterfield, F. (2002, August 21). Father steals best: Crime in an American family. *New York Times.* Available from http://www.nytimes.com/2002/08/21/national/21FAMI.html.

Caspi, A., Lynam, D., Moffitt, T. E., & Silva, P. A. (1993). Unraveling girls' delinquency: Biological, dispositional, and contextual contributions to adolescent misbehavior. *Developmental Psychology, 29,* 19–30.

Caspi, A., McClay, J., Moffitt, T. E., Mill, J., Martin, J., Craig, I., et al. (2002). Evidence that the cycle of violence in maltreated children depends on genotype. *Science, 297,* 851–854.

Caspi, A., & Moffitt, T. E. (1991). Individual differences are accentuated during periods of social change: The sample case of girls at puberty. *Journal of Personality and Social Psychology, 61,* 157–168.

Caspi, A., & Moffitt, T. E. (1995). The continuity of maladaptive behavior: From description to explanation in the study of antisocial behavior. In D. Cicchetti & D. Cohen (Eds.), *Developmental psychopathology* (Vol. 2, pp. 472–511). New York: Wiley.

Caspi, A., Moffitt, T. E., Morgan, J., Rutter, M., Taylor, A., Arseneault, L., et al. (2004). Maternal expressed emotion predicts children's antisocial behavior problems: Using MZ-twin differences to identify environmental effects on behavioral development. *Developmental Psychology, 40,* 149–161.

Caspi, A., Moffitt, T. E., Silva, P. A., Stouthamer-Loeber, M., Schmutte, P., & Krueger, R. (1994). Are some people crime-prone? Replications

of the personality-crime relation across nation, gender, race, and method. *Criminology, 32,* 301–333.

Chung, I., Hill, L. D., Hawkins, J. D., Gilchrist, K. G., & Nagin, D. (2002). Childhood predictors of offense trajectories. *Journal of Research in Crime and Delinquency, 39,* 60–90.

Cicchetti, D., & Cohen, D. J. (1995). Perspectives on developmental psychopathology. In D. Cicchetti & D. Cohen (Eds.), *Developmental psychopathology* (Vol. 1, pp. 3–20). New York: Wiley.

Cicchetti, D., & Walker, E. R. (2003). *Neurodevelopmental mechanisms in psychopathology.* New York: Cambridge University Press.

Cillessen, A. H. N., & Mayeux, L. (2004). From censure to reinforcement: Developmental changes in the association between aggression and social status. *Child Development, 75,* 147–163.

Cote, S., Zoccolillo, M., Tremblay, R. E., Nagin, D., & Vitaro, F. (2001). Predicting girls' conduct disorder in adolescence from childhood trajectories of disruptive behaviors. *Journal of the American Academy of Child and Adolescent Psychiatry, 40,* 678–684.

Dahlstrom, W. G., Welsh, G. S., & Dahlstrom, L. E. (1972). *An MMPI handbook.* Minneapolis: University of Minnesota Press.

Dean, C. W., Brame, R., & Piquero, A. R. (1996). Criminal propensities, discrete groups of offenders, and persistence in crime. *Criminology, 34,* 547–574.

Deater-Deckard, K., & Plomin, R. (1999). An adoption study of the etiology of teacher and parent reports of externalising behavior problems in middle childhood. *Child Development, 70,* 144–154.

DiLalla, L. F., & Gottesman, I. I. (1989). Heterogeneity of causes for delinquency and criminality: Lifespan perspectives. *Development and Psychopathology, 1,* 339–349.

Dionne, G., Tremblay, R., Boivin, M., Laplante, D., & Perusse, D. (2003). Physical aggression and expressive vocabulary in 19-month-old twins. *Developmental Psychology, 39,* 261–273.

Dishion, T. J., McCord, J., & Poulin, F. (1999). Iatrogenic effects in interventions that aggregate high-risk youth. *American Psychologist, 54,* 1–10.

Donker, A. G., Smeenk, W. H., van der Laan, P. H., & Verhulst, F. C. (2003). Individual stability of antisocial behavior from childhood to adulthood: Testing the stability postulate of Moffitt's developmental theory. *Criminology, 41,* 593–610.

Donnellan, M. B., Ge, X., & Wenk, E. (2000). Cognitive abilities in adolescence-limited and life-course-persistent criminal offenders. *Journal of Abnormal Psychology, 109,* 396–402.

Donnellan, M. B., Ge, X., & Wenk, E. (2002). Personality characteristics of juvenile offenders: Differences in the CPI by age at first arrest and frequency of offending. *Personality and Individual Differences, 33,* 727–740.

Dunford, F. W., & Elliott, D. S. (1984). Identifying career offenders using self-reported data. *Journal of Research in Crime and Delinquency, 21,* 57–86.

D'Unger, A. V., Land, K. C., McCall, P. L., & Nagin, D. S. (1998). How many latent classes of delinquent/criminal careers? *American Journal of Sociology, 103,* 1593–1630.

Edelbrock, C., Rende, R., Plomin, R., & Thompson, L. A. (1995). A twin study of competence and problem behavior in childhood and early adolescence. *Journal of Child Psychology and Psychiatry, 36,* 775–785.

Eggleston, E. P., & Laub, J. H. (2002). The onset of adult offending: A neglected dimension of the criminal career. *Journal of Criminal Justice, 30,* 603–622.

Eley, T. C., Lichtenstein, P., & Moffitt, T. E. (2003). A longitudinal analysis of the etiology of aggressive and non-aggressive antisocial behaviour. *Development and Psychopathology, 15,* 155–168.

Eley, T. C., Lichtenstein, P., & Stevenson, J. (1999). Sex differences in the etiology of aggressive and non-aggressive antisocial behavior: Results from two twin studies. *Child Development, 70,* 155–168.

Elliott, D. S. (1994). Serious violent offenders: Onset, developmental course, and termination. *Criminology, 32,* 1021.

Elliott, D. S., Huizinga, D., & Menard, S. (1989). *Multiple problem youth: Delinquency, substance use, and mental health problems.* New York: Springer-Verlag.

Farrington, D. P. (1998). Predictors, causes, and correlates of male youth violence. *Crime and Justice: A Review of Research, 24,* 421–476.

Farrington, D. P., Barnes, G. C., & Lambert, S. (1996). The concentration of offending in families. *Legal and Criminological Psychology, 1,* 47–63.

Farrington, D. P., Gallagher, B., Morley, L., St. Ledger, R. J., & West, D. (1988). Are there any successful men from criminogenic backgrounds? *Psychiatry, 51,* 116–130.

Farrington, D. P., Gallagher, B., Morley, L., St. Ledger, R. J., & West, D. (1990). Minimizing attrition in longitudinal research. In L. R. Bergman & D. Magnusson (Eds.), *Data quality in longitudinal research* (pp. 122–147). New York: Cambridge University Press.

Farrington, D. P., Jolliffe, D., Hawkins, J. D., Catalano, R. F., Hill, K. G., & Kosterman, R. (2003). Comparing delinquency careers in court records and self-reports. *Criminology, 41,* 933–958.

Farrington, D. P., Jolliffe, D., Loeber, R., Stouthamer-Loeber, M., & Kalb, L. (2001). The concentration of offenders in families, and family criminality in the prediction of boys' delinquency. *Journal of Adolescence, 24,* 579–596.

Farrington, D. P., Ohlin, L., & Wilson, J. Q. (1986). *Understanding and controlling crime.* New York: Springer-Verlag.

Farrington, D. P., & West, D. J. (1993). Criminal, penal and life histories of chronic offenders. *Criminal Behaviour and Mental Health, 3,* 492–523.

Fergusson, D. M., & Horwood, L. J. (2002). Male and female offending trajectories. *Development and Psychopathology, 14,* 159–177.

Fergusson, D. M., Horwood, L. J., & Nagin, D. S. (2000). Offending trajectories in a New Zealand birth cohort. *Criminology, 38,* 525–552.

Fergusson, D. M., Horwood, L. J., & Ridder, E. M. (2005). Show me the child at seven: The consequences of conduct problems in childhood for psychosocial functioning in adulthood. *Journal of Child Psychology and Psychiatry, 46*(8), 837–849.

Ferri, E., Bynner, J., & Wadsworth, M. (2003). *Changing Britain, changing lives: Three generations at the turn of the century.* London: University of London, Institute of Education.

Foley, D., Wormley, B., Silberg, J., Maes, H., Hewitt, J., Eaves, L., et al. (2004). Childhood adversity, MAOA genotype, and risk for conduct disorder. *Archives of General Psychiatry, 61,* 738–744.

Furstenberg, F. F., Jr., Cook, T. D., Sampson, R., & Slap, G. (Eds.). (2002). *Early adulthood in cross-national perspective.* London: Sage.

Galambos, N. L., Barker, E. T., & Tilton-Weaver, L. C. (2003). Who gets caught in the maturity gap? A study of pseudomature, immature, and mature adolescents. *International Journal of Behavioral Development, 27,* 253–263.

Gallo, L. C., & Matthews, K. A. (1999). Do negative emotions mediate the association between socioeconomic status and health? *Annals of the New York Academy of Sciences, 896,* 226–300.

Ge, X., Conger, R. D., Cadoret, R. J., Neiderhauser, J. M., Yates, W., Troughton, E., et al. (1996). The developmental interface between nature and nurture: A mutual influence model of child antisocial behavior and parent behaviors. *Developmental Psychology, 32,* 574–589.

Ge, X., Donnellan, M. B., & Wenk, E. (2001). The development of persistent criminal offending in males. *Criminal Justice and Behavior, 28,* 731–755.

Ge, X., Donnellan, M. B., & Wenk, E. (2003). Early starters: Patterns of recidivism and personality differences. *Journal of the American Academy of Psychiatry and the Law, 31,* 68–77.

Gendreau, P., Little, T., & Goggin, C. (1996). A meta-analysis of the predictors of adult offender recidivism: What works! *Criminology, 34,* 575–607.

Gough, H. (1987). *California Psychological Inventory administrator's guide.* Palo Alto, CA: Consulting Psychologists Press.

Henry, B., Caspi, A., Moffitt, T. E., & Silva, P. A. (1996). Temperamental and familial predictors of violent and non-violent criminal convictions: From age 3 to age 18. *Developmental Psychology, 32,* 614–623.

Hipwell, A., Loeber, R., Stouthamer-Loeber, M., Keenan, K., White, H. R., & Kroneman, L. (2002). Characteristics of girls with early onset disruptive and antisocial behaviour. *Criminal Behaviour and Mental Health, 12,* 99–118.

Howell, J. C., & Hawkins, J. D. (1998). Prevention of youth violence. *Crime and Justice: A Review of Research, 24,* 263–316.

Hussong, A. M., Curran, P. J., Moffitt, T. E., Caspi, A., & Carrig, M. K. (2004). Substance abuse ensnares young adults in trajectories of antisocial behavior. *Development and Psychopathology, 16,* 1029–1046.

Jacobson, K. C., Neale, M. C., Prescott, C. A., & Kendler, K. S. (2003, June). *Behavioural genetic confirmation of a life-course perspective on antisocial behavior.* Presentation at the annual meeting of the Behaviour Genetics Association, Cambridge, England.

Jaffee, S. R., Caspi, A., Moffitt, T. E., Dodge, K., Rutter, M., Taylor, A., et al. (2005). Nature × nurture: Genetic vulnerabilities interact with physical maltreatment to promote conduct problems. *Development and Psychopathology, 17,* 67–84.

Jaffee, S. R., Caspi, A., Moffitt, T. E., Polo-Tomas, M., Price, T., & Taylor, A. (2004). The limits of child effects: Evidence for genetically mediated child effects on corporal punishment, but on physical maltreatment. *Developmental Psychology, 40,* 1047–1058.

Jaffee, S. R., Caspi, A., Moffitt, T. E., & Taylor, A. (2004). Physical maltreatment victim to antisocial child: Evidence of an environmentally mediated process. *Journal of Abnormal Psychology, 113,* 44–55.

Jaffee, S. R., Moffitt, T. E., Caspi, A., & Taylor, A. (2003). Life with (or without) father: The benefits of living with two biological parents depend on the father's antisocial behavior. *Child Development, 74,* 109–126.

Jaffee, S. R., Moffitt, T. E., Caspi, A., Taylor, A., & Arseneault, L. (2002). The influence of adult domestic violence on children's internalizing and externalizing problems: An environmentally-informative twin study. *Journal of the American Academy of Child and Adolescent Psychiatry, 41,* 1095–1103.

Jeglum-Bartusch, D., Lynam, D., Moffitt, T. E., & Silva, P. A. (1997). Is age important? Testing general versus developmental theories of antisocial behavior. *Criminology, 35,* 13–47.

Junger-Tas, J., Terlouw, G., & Klein, M. (1994). *Delinquent behaviour among young people in the Western world.* Amsterdam: Kugler Publications.

Kerr, M., & Stattin, H. (2000). What parents know, how they know it, and several forms of adolescent adjustment: Further support for reinterpretation of monitoring. *Developmental Psychology, 36,* 366–380.

Kim-Cohen, J., Moffitt, T. E., Taylor, A., Pawlby, S., & Caspi, A. (2005). Maternal depression and child antisocial behavior: Nature and nurture effects. *Archives of General Psychiatry, 62,* 173–181.

Kjelsberg, E. (1999). Adolescent-limited versus life-course persistent criminal behaviour in adolescent psychiatric inpatients. *European Child and Adolescent Psychiatry, 8,* 276–282.

Kratzer, L., & Hodgins, S. (1999). A typology of offenders: A test of Moffitt's theory among males and females from childhood to age 30. *Criminal Behaviour and Mental Health, 9,* 57–73.

Krohn, M. D., Thornberry, T. P., Rivera, C., & LeBlanc, M. (2001). Later delinquency careers of very young offenders. In R. Loeber & D. P. Farrington (Eds.), *Child delinquents* (pp. 67–94). Thousand Oaks, CA: Sage.

LaCourse, E., Nagin, D., Tremblay, R. E., Vitaro, F., & Claes, M. (2003). Developmental trajectories of boys' delinquent group membership and facilitation of violent behaviors during adolescence. *Development and Psychopathology, 15,* 183–197.

Lahey, B. B., Loeber, R., Quay, H. C., Applegate, B., Shaffer, D., Waldman, I., et al. (1998). Validity of DSM-IV subtypes of conduct disorder based on age of onset. *Journal of the American Academy of Child and Adolescent Psychiatry, 37,* 435–442.

Lahey, B., Moffitt, T. E., & Caspi, A. (Eds.). (2003). *The causes of conduct disorder and serious juvenile delinquency.* New York: Guilford Press.

Lahey, B. B., Waldman, I. D., & McBurnett, K. (1999). The development of antisocial behavior: An integrative causal model. *Journal of Child Psychology and Psychiatry, 40,* 669–682.

Laub, J. H., & Sampson, R. J. (2001). Understanding desistance from crime. *Crime and Justice: A Review of Research, 28,* 1–69.

Laub, J. H., & Sampson, R. J. (2003). *Shared beginnings, divergent lives: Delinquent boys to age 70.* Cambridge, MA: Harvard University Press.

Laucht, M. (2001). Antisoziales Verhalten im jugendalter: Entstehungsbedingungen und Verlaufsformen. *Zeitschrift fur Kinder-Jugendpsychiatry, 29,* 297–311.

Loeber, R., & LeBlanc, M. (1990). Toward a developmental criminology. *Crime and Justice: A Review of Research, 7,* 29–149.

Luthar, S. S., & McMahon, T. J. (1996). Peer reputation among inner-city adolescents: Structure and correlates. *Journal of Research on Adolescence, 6,* 581–603.

Lynam, D. R., Caspi, A., Moffitt, T. E., Wikström, P. O., Loeber, R., & Novak, S. P. (2000). The interaction between impulsivity and neighborhood context on offending: The effects of impulsivity are stronger in poorer neighborhoods. *Journal of Abnormal Psychology, 109,* 563–574.

Lynam, D. R., Moffitt, T. E., & Stouthamer-Loeber, M. (1993). Explaining the relation between IQ and delinquency: Class, race, test motivation, school failure, or self-control? *Journal of Abnormal Psychology, 102,* 187–196.

Lyons, M. J., True, W. R., Eisen, S. A., Goldberg, J., Meyer, J. M., Faraone, S. V., et al. (1995). Differential heritability of adult and juvenile antisocial traits. *Archives of General Psychiatry, 53,* 906–915.

Magnusson, D., af Klintberg, B., & Stattin, H. (1994). Juvenile and persistent offenders: Behavioral and physiological characteristics. In R. D. Kettelinus & M. Lamb (Eds.), *Adolescent problem behaviors* (pp. 81–91). Hillsdale, NJ: Erlbaum.

Maughan, B., Pickles, A., Rowe, R., Costello, E. J., & Angold, A. (2001). Developmental trajectories of aggressive and non-aggressive conduct problems. *Journal of Quantitative Criminology, 16,* 199–222.

Mazerolle, P., Brame, R., Paternoster, R., Piquero, A., & Dean, C. (2000). Onset age, persistence, and offending versatility: Comparisons across gender. *Criminology, 38,* 1143–1172.

Mazerolle, P., & Maahs, J. (2002). *Developmental theory and battering incidents: Examining the relationship between discrete offender groups and intimate partner violence.* Final report submitted to the U.S. National Institute of Justice, U.S. Department of Justice.

McCabe, K. M., Hough, R., Wood, P. A., & Yeh, M. (2001). Childhood and adolescent onset conduct disorder: A test of the developmental taxonomy. *Journal of Abnormal Child Psychology, 29,* 305–316.

McCabe, K. M., Rodgers, C., Yeh, M., & Hough, R. (2004). Gender differences in childhood onset conduct disorder. *Development and Psychopathology, 16,* 1–14.

McCall, R. B., & Carriger, M. S. (1993). A meta-analysis of infant habituation and recognition memory performance as predictors of later IQ. *Child Development, 64,* 57–79.

McEwen, B. (2002). *The end of stress as we know it.* Washington, DC: Joseph Henry Press.

McGloin, J. M., & Pratt, T. C. (2003). Cognitive ability and delinquent behavior among inner-city youth: A life-course analysis of main, mediating, and interaction effects. *International Journal of Offender Therapy and Comparative Criminology, 47,* 253–271.

Miles, D. R., & Carey, G. (1997). Genetic and environmental architecture of human aggression. *Journal of Personality and Social Psychology, 72,* 207–217.

Moffitt, T. E. (1990). Juvenile delinquency and attention-deficit disorder: Developmental trajectories from age three to fifteen. *Child Development, 61,* 893–910.

Moffitt, T. E. (1993). "Life-course-persistent" and "adolescence-limited" antisocial behavior: A developmental taxonomy. *Psychological Review, 100,* 674–701.

Moffitt, T. E. (1994). Natural histories of delinquency. In E. Weitekamp & H. J. Kerner (Eds.), *Cross-national longitudinal research on human development and criminal behavior* (pp. 3–61). Dordrecht, The Netherlands: Kluwer Academic Press.

Moffitt, T. E. (1997). Adolescence-limited and life-course-persistent offending: A complementary pair of developmental theories. In T. Thornberry (Ed.), *Advances in criminological theory: Developmental theories of crime and delinquency* (pp. 11–54). London: Transaction Press.

Moffitt, T. E. (2001). *Life-course persistent antisocial behavior: A proposal to the U.K. Medical Research Council.* London: Institute of Psychiatry.

Moffitt, T. E. (2003). Life-course persistent and adolescence-limited antisocial behaviour: A 10-year research review and a research agenda. In B. Lahey, T. E. Moffitt, & A. Caspi (Eds.), *The causes of conduct disorder and serious juvenile delinquency* (pp. 49–75). New York: Guilford Press.

Moffitt, T. E., Arseneault, L., Taylor, A., Nagin, D., Milne, B., & Harrington, H. (2005). *Life-course persistent and adolescence-limited antisocial trajectories detected in a 26-year longitudinal study using theory-agnostic semiparametric modelling.* Manuscript in preparation. Available from T.moffitt@iop.kcl.ac.uk.

Moffitt, T. E., & Caspi, A. (2001). Childhood predictors differentiate life-course persistent and adolescence-limited pathways, among males and females. *Development and Psychopathology, 13,* 355–375.

Moffitt, T. E., Caspi, A., Dickson, N., Silva, P. A., & Stanton, W. (1996). Childhood-onset versus adolescent-onset antisocial conduct in males: Natural history from age 3 to 18. *Development and Psychopathology, 8,* 399–424.

Moffitt, T. E., Caspi, A., Harrington, H., & Milne, B. (2002). Males on the life-course persistent and adolescence-limited antisocial pathways: Follow-up at age 26. *Development and Psychopathology, 14,* 179–206.

Moffitt, T. E., Caspi, A., Rutter, M., & Silva, P. A. (2001). *Sex differences in antisocial behaviour: Conduct disorder, delinquency, and violence in the Dunedin longitudinal study.* Cambridge, England: Cambridge University Press.

Moffitt, T. E., & the E-Risk Study Team (39 authors). (2002). Teen-aged mothers in contemporary Britain. *Journal of Child Psychology and Psychiatry, 43,* 727–742.

Moffitt, T. E., Lynam, D., & Silva, P. A. (1994). Neuropsychological tests predict persistent male delinquency. *Criminology, 32,* 101–124.

Nagin, D. S. (1999). Analyzing developmental trajectories: Semi-parametric, group-based approach. *Psychological Methods, 4,* 139–177.

Nagin, D. S., Farrington, D. P., & Moffitt, T. E. (1995). Life-course trajectories of different types of offenders. *Criminology, 33,* 111–139.

Nagin, D. S., Pagani, L., Tremblay, R. E., & Vitaro, F. (2003). Life course turning points: The effect of grade retention on physical aggression. *Development and Psychopathology, 15,* 343–361.

Nagin, D. S., & Tremblay, R. E. (1999). Trajectories of boys' physical aggression, opposition, and hyperactivity on the path to physically violent and non-violent juvenile delinquency. *Child Development, 70,* 1181–1196.

Nagin, D. S., & Tremblay, R. E. (2001a). Analyzing developmental trajectories of distinct but related behaviors: A group-based method. *Psychological Medicine, 6,* 18–34.

Nagin, D. S., & Tremblay, R. E. (2001b). Parental and early childhood predictors of persistent physical aggression in boys from kindergarten to high school. *Archives of General Psychiatry, 58,* 389–394.

National Institute of Mental Health. (2000). *Child and adolescence violence research* (NIH Publication No. 00-4706). Bethesda, MD: Author.

National Institutes of Health. (2004). *State-of-the-science consensus statement on preventing violence and related health-risking social behaviors in adolescents.* Bethesda, MD: Author. Available from http://consensus.nih.gov.

Neugebauer, R., Hoek, H. W., & Susser, E. (1999). Prenatal exposure to wartime famine and development of antisocial personality disorder in early adulthood. *Journal of the American Medical Association, 282,* 455–462.

O'Connor, T. G., Deater-Deckard, K., Fulker, D., Rutter, M., & Plomin, R. (1998). Genotype-environment correlations in later childhood and early adolescence: Antisocial behavioral problems and coercive parenting. *Developmental Psychology, 34,* 970–981.

Osgood, D. W. (1998). Interdisciplinary integration: Building criminology by stealing from our friends. *Criminologist, 23,* 1–4.

Paternoster, R., & Brame, R. (1997). Multiple routes to delinquency? A test of developmental and general theories of crime. *Criminology, 35,* 49–84.

Patterson, G. R., DeGarmo, D. S., & Knutson, N. (2000). Hyperactive and antisocial behaviors: Comorbid or two points in the same process? *Development and Psychopathology, 12,* 91–106.

Patterson, G. R., Forgatch, M. S., Yoerger, K. L., & Stoolmiller, M. (1998). Variables that initiate and maintain an early onset trajectory for juvenile offending. *Development and Psychopathology, 10,* 531–548.

Patterson, G. R., & Yoerger, K. L. (1997). A developmental model for later-onset delinquency. In R. Deinstbeir & D. W. Osgood (Eds.), *Motivation and delinquency* (pp. 119–177). Lincoln: University of Nebraska Press.

Piquero, A. R. (2001). Testing Moffitt's neuropsychological variation hypothesis for the prediction of life-course persistent offending. *Psychology, Crime and Law, 7,* 193–216.

Piquero, A. R., Brame, R., & Lynam, D. (2004). Studying the factors related to career length. *Crime and Delinquency, 50,* 412–435.

Piquero, A. R., & Brezina, T. (2001). Testing Moffitt's account of adolescence-limited delinquency. *Criminology, 39,* 353–370.

Piquero, A. R., Brezina, T., & Turner, M. G. (in press). Testing Moffitt's theory of delinquency abstinence. *Journal of Research in Crime and Delinquency.*

Piquero, A. R., & Buka, S. (2002). Linking juvenile and adult patterns of criminal activity in the Providence cohort of the National Collaborative Perinatal Project. *Journal of Criminal Justice, 30,* 259–272.

Piquero, A. R., & Chung, H. L. (2001). On the relationships between gender, early onset, and the seriousness of offending. *Journal of Criminal Justice, 29,* 189–206.

Piquero, A. R., Moffitt, T. E., & Lawton, B. (in press). Race and crime: The contribution of individual, familial, and neighborhood level risk factors to life-course-persistent offending. In D. Hawkins & K. Kempf-Leonard (Eds.), *Race, crime, and the juvenile justice system.* Chicago: University of Chicago Press.

Piquero, A. R., & White, N. (2003). On the relationship between cognitive abilities and life-course persistent offending among a sample of African-Americans: A longitudinal test of Moffitt's hypothesis. *Journal of Criminal Justice, 31,* 399–409.

Raine, A. (2002). Annotation: The role of prefrontal deficits, low autonomic arousal, and early health factors in the development of antisocial and aggressive behaviour in children. *Journal of Child Psychology and Psychiatry, 43,* 417–434.

Raine, A., Brennan, P., & Mednick, S. A. (1994). Birth complications combined with early maternal rejection at age 1 year predispose to violent crime at age 18 years. *Archives of General Psychiatry, 51,* 984–988.

Raine, A., Brennan, P., & Mednick, S. A. (1997). Interaction between birth complications and early maternal rejection in predisposing individuals to adult violence: Specificity to serious, early-onset violence. *American Journal of Psychiatry, 154,* 1265–1271.

Raine, A., Brennan, P., Mednick, B., & Mednick, S. A. (1996). High rates of violence, crime, academic problems, and behavioral problems in males with both early neuromotor deficits and unstable family environments. *Archives of General Psychiatry, 53,* 544–549.

Raine, A., Lencz, T., Taylor, K., Hellige, J. B., Bihrle, S., Lacasse, L., et al. (2003). Corpus callosum abnormalities in psychopathic antisocial individuals. *Archives of General Psychiatry, 60,* 1134–1142.

Raine, A., Moffitt, T. E., Caspi, A., Loeber, R., Stouthamer-Loeber, M., & Lynam, D. (2005). Neurocognitive and psychosocial deficits in life-course persistent offenders. *Journal of Abnormal Psychology, 114,* 38–49.

Raine, A., Yaralian, P. S., Reynolds, C., Venables, P. H., & Mednick, S. A. (2002). Spatial but not verbal cognitive deficits at age 3 years in persistently antisocial individuals. *Development and Psychopathology, 14,* 25–44.

Repetti, R. L., Taylor, S. E., & Seeman, T. E. (2002). Risky families: Family social environments and the mental and physical health of offspring. *Psychological Bulletin, 128,* 330–366.

Rhee, S. J., & Waldman, I. D. (2002). Genetic and environmental influences on antisocial behavior: A meta-analysis. *Psychological Bulletin, 128,* 490–529.

Riggins-Caspers, K. M., Cadoret, R. J., Knutson, J. F., & Langbehn, D. (2003). Biology-environment interaction and evocative biology-environment correlation: Contributions of harsh discipline and parental psychopathology to problem adolescent behaviors. *Behavior Genetics, 33,* 205–220.

Robins, L. N. (1966). *Deviant children grown up.* Baltimore: Williams & Wilkins.

Rodkin, P. C., Farmer, T. W., Pearl, R., & Van Acker, R. (2000). Heterogeneity of popular boys: Antisocial and prosocial configurations. *Developmental Psychology, 36,* 14–24.

Roeder, K., Lynch, K. G., & Nagin, D. S. (1999). Modeling uncertainty in latent class membership: A case study in criminology. *Journal of the American Statistical Association, 94,* 766–776.

Rowe, D. C., & Farrington, D. P. (1997). The familial transmission of criminal convictions. *Criminology, 35,* 177–201.

Rowe, D. C., Vazsonyi, A. T., & Flannery, D. J. (1994). No more than skin deep: Ethnic and racial similarity in developmental process. *Psychological Review, 101,* 396–413.

Ruchkin, V., Koposov, R., Vermeiren, R., & Schwab-Stone, M. (2003). Psychopathology and the age of onset of conduct problems in juvenile delinquents. *Journal of Clinical Psychiatry, 64,* 913–920.

Sampson, R. J., & Laub, J. H. (2003). Life-course desisters? Trajectories of crime among delinquent boys followed to age 70. *Criminology, 41,* 555–592.

Schmitz, S., Fulker, D. W., & Mrazek, D. A. (1995). Problem behavior in early and middle childhood: An initial behavior genetic analysis. *Journal of Child Psychology and Psychiatry, 36,* 1443–1458.

Scholte, E. M. (1999). Factors predicting continued violence into adulthood. *Journal of Adolescence, 22,* 3–20.

Scott, E. S., & Grisso, T. (1997). The evolution of adolescence: A developmental perspective on juvenile justice reform. *Journal of Criminal Law and Criminology, 88,* 137–189.

Shedler, J., & Block, J. (1990). Adolescent drug use and psychological health. *American Psychologist, 45,* 612–630.

Sigman, M., Cohen, S. E., & Beckwith, L. (1997). Why does infant attention predict adolescent intelligence? *Infant Behavior and Development, 20,* 133–140.

Silverthorn, P., & Frick, P. J. (1999). Developmental pathways to antisocial behavior: The delayed-onset pathway in girls. *Development and Psychopathology, 11,* 101–126.

Simons, R. L., Wu, C. I., Conger, R., & Lorenz, F. O. (1994). Two routes to delinquency: Differences between early and late starters in the impact of parenting and deviant peers. *Criminology, 32,* 247–275.

Slaekin, R. T., Yff, R. M., Neumann, C. S., Leistico, A. R., & Zalot, A. A. (2002). Juvenile transfer to adult courts: A look at the prototypes of dangerousness, sophistication-maturity, and amenability to treatment through a legal lens. *Psychology, Public Policy and Law, 8,* 373–410.

Stanger, C., Achenbach, T., & Verhulst, F. C. (1997). Accelerated longitudinal comparisons of aggressive versus delinquent syndromes. *Development and Psychopathology, 9,* 43–58.

Stattin, H., Romelsjo, A., & Stenbacka, M. (1997). Personal resources as modifiers of the risk for future criminality. *British Journal of Criminology, 37,* 198–223.

Taylor, J., Iacono, W. G., & McGue, M. (2000). Evidence for a genetic etiology for early-onset delinquency. *Journal of Abnormal Psychology, 109,* 634–643.

Tibbetts, S., & Piquero, A. (1999). The influence of gender, low birth weight and disadvantaged environment on predicting early onset of offending: A test of Moffitt's interactional hypothesis. *Criminology, 37,* 843–878.

Tolan, P. H., & Thomas, P. (1995). The implications of age of onset for delinquency risk: Pt. II. Longitudinal data. *Journal of Abnormal Child Psychology, 23,* 157–181.

Tolone, W. L., & Tieman, C. R. (1990). Drugs, delinquency, and "nerds": Are loners deviant? *Journal of Drug Education, 20,* 153–162.

Tremblay, R. E., Nagin, D. S., Seguin, J. R., Zoccolillo, M., Zelazo, P. D., Boivin, M., et al. (2004). Physical aggression during early childhood: Trajectories and predictors. *Pediatrics, 114,* E43–E50.

U.S. Office of Juvenile Justice and Delinquency Prevention. (1998). *Serious and violent juvenile offenders.* Washington, DC: U.S. Department of Justice.

U.S. Surgeon General. (2001). *Youth violence: A report of the surgeon general.* Available from http://www.surgeongeneral.gov/library /youthviolence.

Vaaranen, H. (2001). The blue-collar boys at leisure: An ethnography on cruising club boys' drinking, driving, and passing time in cars in Helsinki. *Mannsforsking, 1,* 48–57.

van den Oord, E. J. C. G., Verhulst, F. C., & Boomsma, D. I. (1996). A genetic study of maternal and paternal ratings of problem behaviors in 3-year-old twins. *Journal of Abnormal Psychology, 105,* 349–357.

van der Valk, J. C., Verhulst, F. C., Stroet, T. M., & Boomsma, D. I. (1998). Quantitive genetic analysis of internalising and externalising problems in a large sample of 3-year-old twins. *Twin Research, 1,* 25–33.

Vermeiren, R. (2002). Psychopathology and delinquency in adolescents: A descriptive and developmental perspective. *Clinical Psychology Review, 583,* 1–42.

Viding, E., Blair, J. R., Moffitt, T. E., & Plomin, R. (2005). Psychopathic syndrome indexes strong genetic risk for antisocial behaviour in 7-year-olds. *Journal of Child Psychology and Psychiatry, 46,* 592–597.

Vitaro, F., Tremblay, R. E., Kerr, M., Pagani, L., & Bukowski, W. M. (1997). Disruptiveness, friends' characteristics, and delinquency in early adolescence: A test of two competing models of development. *Child Development, 68,* 676–689.

White, H. R., Bates, M. E., & Buyske, S. (2001). Adolescence-limited versus persistent delinquency: Extending Moffitt's hypothesis into adulthood. *Journal of Abnormal Psychology, 110,* 600–609.

White, N. A., & Piquero, A. R. (in press). A preliminary empirical test of Silverthorn and Frick's delayed-onset pathway in girls using an urban, African-American, U.S.-based sample. *Criminal Behaviour and Mental Health.*

Wiesner, M., & Capaldi, D. M. (2003). Relations of childhood and adolescent factors to offending trajectories of young men. *Journal of Research in Crime and Delinquency, 40,* 231–262.

Wiesner, M., Kim, H. K., & Capaldi, D. (in press). *Developmental trajectories of offending: Validation and prediction to young adult alcohol use, drug use, and depressive symptoms.*

Woodward, L. J., Fergusson, D. M., & Horwood, L. J. (2002). Romantic relationships of young people with early and late onset antisocial behavior problems. *Journal of Abnormal Child Psychology, 30,* 231–243.

World Health Organization. (2002). *World report on violence and health.* Geneva, Switzerland: Author.

Zebrowitz, L. A., Andreoletti, C., Collins, M., Lee, S. H., & Blumenthal, J. (1998). Bright, bad, babyfaced boys: Appearance stereotypes do not always yield self-fulfilling prophecy effects. *Journal of Personality and Social Psychology, 75,* 1300–1320.

Zucker, R. A., Ellis, D. A., Fitzgerald, H. E., Bingham, C. R., & Sanford, K. (1996). Other evidence for at least two alcoholisms: II. Life-course variation in antisociality and heterogeneity of alcoholic outcome. *Development and Psychopathology, 8,* 831–848.

CHAPTER 16

Developmental Pathways to Substance Abuse

LINDA C. MAYES and NANCY E. SUCHMAN

Accidents, suicides, and homicides account for more than 80% of deaths in adolescence, and of these, at least half of the deaths involve drugs and alcohol (Soderstrom & Dearing-Stuck, 1993). Two-thirds of adolescents in juvenile detention facilities and nearly half of those in day and residential state programs have problems with substance abuse (Greenbaum, Prange, Friedman, & Silver, 1991), suggesting that substance abuse is at least a central, if not a primary, factor in problem behavior in adolescence. At the same time, the use of illicit drugs, especially during early adolescence, may interfere with normative cognitive, social, and emotional development, which in turn may place youths at risk for school problems and problematic peer relationships (Costello, Erkanli, & Federman, 1999; Kandel et al., 1999; Rao et al., 1999; Stacy & Newcomb, 1999; Wilens et al., 1999). Early illicit drug abuse has been linked with problem behaviors such as early sexual activity, truancy, violence, and access to weapons (Amaro,

Zuckerman, & Cabral, 1989; Brookoff, O'Brien, Cook, Thompson, & Williams, 1997). These behaviors may lead to sexually transmitted diseases and human immunodeficiency virus (HIV) infection, pregnancy, school failure, injury and accidents, homicides, and suicides (Hicks, Bemis, Bemis, & Imai, 1993).

Recent data suggest that nearly half of adolescents have tried an illicit drug at least once by the end of the 12th grade and that over three-quarters have used alcohol (Johnston, O'Malley, & Buchannan, 2001). Thus, adolescence is a critical developmental period for initiation into licit and illicit drug use and, for some individuals, the beginning of their trajectory toward substance dependence and abuse. Key questions are these: What factors predict those adolescents who will shift from licit to illicit drug use? What predicts the transition from use to dependence and abuse? What are the morbidities associated with both substance use and abuse that also impact a young person's developmental trajectory at this critical developmental period?

In this chapter, we discuss the magnitude of the problem of substance use and abuse in adolescence, risk factors for initiating substance use, including comorbid conditions, and similarly those factors that are either risky or protective for a trajectory to substance abuse. We also suggest two complementary models for these trajectories, one that

This work was supported by NIDA grants RO1-DA-06025 (LCM) and KO2-DA00222 (LCM), R01-DA-17294 (NES), K23-DA14606 (NES), and NICHD P01-HD03008. Additionally, the work was supported in part by the Yale Children's Clinical Research Center grant MO1-RR06022, General Clinical Research Centers Program, National Center for Research Resources, NIH.

emphasizes the pathway to use and abuse and a second that illustrates the factors leading to a transition from abuse to dependence. We conclude with a summary of possible future directions to elucidate further adolescent trajectories to substance use and dependence.

MAGNITUDE OF THE PROBLEM

Since 1975, nationwide data have been systematically collected about drug use among high school seniors (Johnston, O'Malley, & Bachman, 2001). In 1991, the annual survey was expanded to include data from 8th- and 10th graders. In 2002, more than 43,000 students in these grades in 394 schools nationwide were surveyed about lifetime, past year, past month, and daily use of drugs, alcohol, cigarettes, and smokeless tobacco. Over the 28 years that these data have been systematically collected, there have been notable fluctuations in the rates of use of licit and illicit drugs among American teenagers. For example, in 1996, use of illicit drugs among children 12 to 17 years of age had doubled from those rates reported in 1992 and was at levels comparable to those reported in the late 1970s and early 1980s, when marijuana use was reported to be as high as 1 in 2 high school students. But beginning in 1997, rates of illicit drug use among adolescents once again began to decline, and 2002 marked the 6th year in a row that illicit drug use among 8th, 10th, and 12th graders remained stable or decreased.

However, although rates of use of illicit drugs (i.e., heroin, cocaine, marijuana), alcohol, and tobacco are presently declining among adolescents, the amount of use continues to be significant. For example, in 2002 among those students surveyed, 26.7% of high school seniors, 17.7% of 10th graders, and 10.7% of 8th graders reported use of cigarettes or smokeless tobacco in the previous month; 9.1% of seniors, 4.4% of 10th graders, and 2.1% of 8th graders admitted to at least a half pack of daily use in that same period. Past month marijuana use among 12th, 10th, and 8th graders in 2002 was reported as 21.5%, 17.8%, and 8.3%, respectively. Nearly half of high school seniors (48.6%) reported using alcohol in the past 30 days; rates for 10th- and 8th graders were 35.4% and 19.6%, respectively. When any illicit drug use was examined, 25.4% of seniors, 20.4% of 10th graders, and 10.4% of 8th graders reported use at least once in the previous month. Although these prevalence rates have decreased since 1997, each is still in the same order of magnitude in that 6-year time period. Thus, illicit drug use, as well as alcohol and tobacco use, remain prevalent health problems among American adolescents. It has also been commonly reported

in studies of teenage substance abuse that specific substances are rarely used exclusively but that polydrug use is quite common (Clayton & Ritter, 1985). In the more recent phases of the Monitoring the Future Study, systematic data were collected regarding adolescents' perceptions of the perceived risks of drug use and the availability of drugs. For many illicit drugs, adolescents' perceived risk of drug use decreased between 2001 and 2003, suggesting that 8th- to 12th graders are less cautious about illicit drug use.

Gender and ethnic differences among adolescent drug users are also notable in the yearly survey data (Johnston, O'Malley, & Bachman, 2003; Wallace et al., 2003). Over the years covered by the survey, the gender gap in use of illicit drugs, alcohol, and/or tobacco has remained largely unchanged. Males have higher rates of illicit drug use, particularly higher rates of frequent use, and higher rates of marijuana and alcohol use. However, girls are as likely as boys to report being daily smokers. These gender differences tend to appear more as children get older. Ethnic differences in drug use, for boys as well as girls, are much wider than are gender differences. Contrary to popular assumption, African American boys and girls tend to have substantially lower rates of illicit and licit drug use than Whites. Cigarette use is especially lower for African Americans. Native American teenagers are most likely to smoke daily and African Americans least likely. Similar patterns are found for heavy alcohol use (five or more drinks in a row within the past 2 weeks) and for marijuana, though African American boys are much more likely to use marijuana compared to African American girls. Hispanics have rates of use that fall between White and African American youths, though usually closer to the rates for Whites than for Blacks. Hispanics do have the highest reported rates of use for some drugs in 12th grade—crack, heroin with a needle, and ice—and their level of heroin, cocaine, methamphetamine, and steroid use is roughly equivalent to that of Whites. But in 8th grade, Hispanics tend to use the most of any class of drugs. One possible reason for this change in Hispanic drug use between the 8th and 12th grade may be because of the higher rates of school dropout of Hispanic youth. Thus, more of those Hispanic adolescents who are drug using or drug-prone leave school before the 12th grade compared to White and African American children.

Differences in overall illicit drug use associated with population density are not very large or consistent over the years of the survey (Johnston et al., 2003). Drug use is a widespread phenomenon among American youth from both urban and rural settings. In surveys from recent years, the use of a number of licit and illicit drugs has actually declined in some urban areas relative to nonurban areas; in contrast to popular belief, crack cocaine and heroin use among adolescents or adults is not concentrated in urban areas. Similarly contrary to commonly held assumptions is the finding that for many drugs, differences in use by socioeconomic class are very small; in general, trends for patterns of use have been similar across social classes. Patterns of distribution and availability of drugs surely influence differences by socioeconomic class. For example, in the early 1980s, cocaine use was more prevalent among higher socioeconomic classes, but with the appearance of crack, a cheaper form of cocaine, that difference disappeared by the mid- to late 1980s. Cigarette smoking has shown a similar homogenization across socioeconomic classes as students from poorer families have stopped smoking or not begun use in recent years with the increasing overall negative publicity associated with tobacco use. Nonetheless, even with these shifts, there still remains a slightly greater use of tobacco among students from poorer, less educated families.

Early use of some drugs may predict later involvement in illicit drug use (Lynskey, Coffey, Degenhardt, Carlin, & Patton, 2003; Wagner & Anthony, 2001; Wilcox, Wagner, & Anthony, 2002). The so-called gateway theory of adolescent drug use suggests that drugs such as tobacco and alcohol are entry-level drugs for later use of marijuana and other illegal drugs such as cocaine and hallucinogens. Similarly, marijuana is regarded by several as the gateway drug for illicit drug use (Fergusson & Horwood, 2000; Yamaguchi & Kandel, 1984). Drugs such as tobacco, alcohol, and marijuana may serve as gateways to other drug use because they provide opportunities for users to obtain other drugs; perhaps some users actively seek out these opportunities, whereas others are more passive recipients of drug exposure opportunities (Wagner & Anthony, 2002).

Using annual survey data from the 1991 through 1994 National Household Survey on Drug Abuse, investigators analyzed the responses of 26,015 individuals ages 12 to 18 regarding marijuana use and the responses of 44,624 individuals ages 12 to 25 who answered questions regarding cocaine use (Wilcox et al., 2002). Alcohol and tobacco users were more likely than nonusers to try marijuana when the opportunity arose. About 75% of alcohol or tobacco users reported an opportunity to try marijuana by age 18, and more than 85% of them made the transition to marijuana use. Conversely, only 25% of nonsmokers and nondrinkers were given an opportunity to try marijuana by the same age, and of these, fewer than 25% began smoking marijuana within 6 years after they were first given the opportunity. Overall, alcohol or tobacco users were 7 times more likely to start using marijuana than individuals who had used neither alcohol nor tobacco. Previous marijuana use was also associated with the opportunity to try cocaine and the likelihood of an adolescent's starting to use cocaine once given the opportunity. Among the youth who were given the chance to try cocaine, those who were already using marijuana were 15 times more likely to use cocaine than those who did not use marijuana. About 50% of marijuana users tried cocaine within 2 years of their first opportunity to do so. However, among young people who never used marijuana, fewer than 10% initiated cocaine use. Although males are more likely than females to have opportunities to use drugs at any age, both are equally likely to make a transition into drug use once an opportunity to try a drug has occurred.

Early drug use not only affords adolescents more exposure to other drugs, but the early user is more likely to take advantage of these opportunities to try other drugs. And among those users, a proportion will go on to drug dependence. For example, data from the National Comorbidity Study conducted between 1990 and 1992 with detailed interviews with more than 8,000 women and men ages 15 to 54 showed that first use of marijuana occurs on average at age 18, and on average, 9% of users will become dependent on the drug, most likely before age 25 (Anthony, Warner, & Kessler, 1994). For cocaine, first use is most likely around age 20, and progression to dependence is more rapid; the peak incidence of transition to dependence occurs between ages 23 and 25 for on average 21% of individuals who have used cocaine at least once. Not only is early use of alcohol or tobacco associated with more opportunities for trying marijuana or cocaine, but early use of these drugs may set in motion a pathway to early illicit drug dependence for a significant proportion of adolescents and young adults (Anthony et al., 1994). And once an adolescent develops a substance abuse problem, he or she is also very likely to suffer other medical and mental health problems. Data from the Drug Abuse Treatment Outcome Study for Adolescents, a multisite longitudinal study of adolescents in residential, outpatient, and inpatient treatment, reported that 64% of the sample had at least one comorbid mental disorder, most often Conduct Disorder. Adolescents who had accompanying mental health problems also had more problems with family, school, and criminal involvement (Grella, Hser, Joshi, & Rounds-Bryant, 2001). Jainchill and colleagues (Jainchill, De Leon, & Yagelka, 1997) report high rates of psychiatric comorbid conditions in a sample of 829 adolescents entering residential placements; more than 90% of the sample had a psychiatric diagnosis other than their substance use disorder (primarily Conduct Disorder and Oppositional Defiant Disorder).

It is important to note one potential flaw in the yearly survey data from the National Institute on Drug Abuse (NIDA) sponsored Monitoring the Future Study (Johnston, O'Malley, & Bachman, 2001). This study is based solely on students in middle and high school. Many severely substance abusing adolescents may already have dropped out of high school sometime between the 8th and 12th grade, as was suggested for the apparent decline in Hispanic drug use by late high school. These more severely drug-using adolescents are then not included in the survey data, with the result that the problem is underestimated and prevalence estimates from the survey population data may not be adequately reflective of more clinical populations that present for treatment and/or other health or psychosocial difficulties in their late teens and early 20s.

Despite this caveat, the survey data do describe several important trends. These data, accumulated from many years, suggest that licit and illicit drug use begins in early adolescence for a significant number of children even though the rates are apparently slowly declining. Children are susceptible across socioeconomic class, gender, cities and community size, and population density. Those who begin early tend to continue, and the rate of beginning use increases through high school. Those adolescents who are already using licit drugs by the time they graduate high school are more likely to continue their drug use, to begin illicit drug use, and to become involved in other problem behaviors. The factors explaining these trajectories are multivariate and interactive. Key to understanding the developmental trajectory of substance use is identifying which factors tip the balance between use and dependence, with the attendant social, physical, and psychiatric comorbidity associated with drug addiction. We turn now to the various risk factors that appear to increase an adolescent's likelihood of beginning and sustaining drug use and the factors that contribute to the development of drug dependence among a proportion of drug users.

RISK FACTORS

Risk factors are those conditions that are associated with a greater likelihood of negative outcomes, such as substance use and abuse. Recent perspectives conceptualize substance abuse as a developmental disorder with genetic, neurobiological, and environmental determinants (Riggs & Whitmore, 1999). Many factors contribute to the risk for developing substance abuse or dependence. Newcomb (1995, 1997) descriptively divides risk factors for sub-

stance abuse into four domains: cultural and societal, interpersonal, psychobehavioral, and biogenetic. (In this taxonomy, psychiatric comorbidity is included under psychobehavioral risks.) In a more functional taxonomy, Pandina (1996) suggests that risk factors for substance abuse may be grouped into three categories: markers or surface indicators, modifiers that either increase or decrease the relative risks, and mediators or causal mechanisms. Cicchetti and Rogosch (1999) divide markers into those that are fixed, such as gender or a perinatal event such as prematurity, and those that are variable, such as the availability of drugs or use among peers. However classified, clearly, no one risk factor is causal and no one factor is completely protective. Generally, the more risk factors one has, the greater the risk of developing the disorder, or more specifically, the greater the risk of substance abuse and possibly dependence. And different combinations of risk factors lead to different potentials for negative outcomes based on the strength and nature of the individual factors. Multiple individual and experiential conditions combine to form multiple pathways or trajectories to substance use and abuse (Fergusson, 1998). At the same time, some factors may cushion the impact of a risk factor and may modify the severity of or prevent a negative outcome. Indeed, a number of investigators have begun to study the interaction between risk and protective factors on the trajectory toward substance abuse (Newcomb, 1995; Pandina, Johnson, & Labouvie, 1992).

Specific risk factors have greater impact at certain developmental stages compared to others (Newcomb, 1995). For example, using Newcomb's (1995, 1997) descriptive categories, societal and cultural risk factors such as drug availability and societal norms favorable to drug use have an impact throughout all developmental stages, but interpersonal factors, including parental care, family disruption, and peer relations, may be developmentally most critical for children and adolescents. Biogenetic risk factors, including psychophysiological vulnerability to drug effects, may be most critical in the transition from drug use to drug dependence. We first discuss these risk factors in these descriptive groupings and then provide a more functional analysis of those that serve as fixed or variable markers, those that appear most often to serve as moderators, and those that may serve a mediating role.

Societal and Cultural Factors

Cultural and societal factors include living in a community where one can procure drugs with ease and where laws and norms more readily permit or do not strongly discourage a drug culture (Newcomb, 1995). For the United States, the National Household Survey on Drug Abuse (P. B. Johnson & Richter, 2002; U.S. Department of Health and Human Services, 1999) reported that over 50% of teenagers between the ages of 12 and 17 believed marijuana to be easily obtainable, and 35% had been offered the drug. When marijuana was easy to obtain, the percentage of White adolescents who had used the drug within the past 12 months was 26%; however, only 2% used the drug when they found it hard to obtain. Availability issues may also be impacted by living in a poorly organized and highly dense neighborhood in which there are more concentrated rates of criminal activity and drugs are a central part of the neighborhood economy. Although, as already cited, minority ethnic status and poverty are not necessarily more often associated with beginning substance use, these same factors moderate individual adolescents' trajectory toward dependence after they have initiated use (Fergusson, 1998; Hawkins, Catalano, & Miller, 1992; Riggs & Whitmore, 1999).

Interpersonal Factors

Interpersonal factors include those that describe parental behavior with the child, parental psychopathology (which in turn influences parental behavior), parental attitudes toward substance abuse, family dynamics, and the presence of abuse. For older children, peer relationships become as influential as parents and families in exposing children to opportunities for drug use. Among the parental factors implicated to increase the risk of adolescent substance use are how strongly parents believe drugs are harmful and how much parents actively monitor their children and/or are involved in their children's activities (Chilcoat & Anthony, 1996; Duncan, Biglan, & Ary, 1998; J. L. Johnson & Leff, 1999; Molina, Chassin, & Curran, 1994). Parents who have lower academic aspirations or, more generally, convey less of a sense of optimism and a future for their children may also increase the risk for their children's entry into early substance use and/or into less socially integrated peer groups that are more likely to use drugs (Brook, Linkoff, & Whiteman, 1980). Family abuse, including domestic violence, family disruption, negative communication patterns, and lack of anger control, are also often reported as characteristics of the families of substance-using adolescents and young adults (Baumrind, 1983; Reilly, 1979). These latter family characteristics appear to increase the risk of substance use in the child whether or not the parents are actively using drugs (Bennett & Kempfer, 1994).

How much parents attend to their younger children's activities, their friends, and specifically their opportunities for substance use has a strong impact on preadolescents' beginning drug use. Rates of illicit drug use such as cocaine or marijuana are higher among middle school children who report less parental concern and involvement in their lives (Chilcoat & Anthony, 1996). Parental use of licit drugs such as tobacco or alcohol models an acceptance of drug use that increases the likelihood of young children trying these drugs. Not only are their children more likely to try tobacco or alcohol, but the impact of perceived parental acceptance increases the likelihood of continued use (Jackson, Henriksen, Dickinson, Messer, & Robertson, 1998).

A range of peer factors have been cited as putting a child at risk for substance use, including affiliation with a deviant and substance-abusing peer group and affiliation with peers who have low adherence to conventional societal norms (Fergusson, 1998; Hawkins et al., 1992; O'Donnell, Schwab-Stone, & Muyeed, 2002; Riggs & Whitmore, 1999). Peer influence has been consistently regarded as the strongest predictor for substance use among adolescents (Oxford, Harachi, Catalano, & Abbott, 2000). Peer attitudes about the use of substances predict the initiation of alcohol and other substance use (Bauman & Ennett, 1994). Indeed, by adolescence, peer attachments may be stronger than family attachments in predicting susceptibility to substance use (Brook et al., 1980). O'Donnell and colleagues evaluated the extent to which family, school, and peer support factors contributed to two different dimensions: (1) mental health problems such as depression, anxiety, and somatization, and (2) conduct problems such as drug abuse, delinquency, and school misconduct, in children with various levels of community violence exposure. The participants in this study were divided into three groups: a victim group, a witness group, and a no-exposure group. Among all three groups, peers served as a negative influence on resilience in terms of substance abuse and school misconduct, particularly for the victim group.

Friedman and Glassman (2000) found that association with a delinquent peer group was the strongest predictor for later substance use in childhood and adolescence. The percentage of children who tried marijuana rose sharply for those whose friends would not be upset at all if they tried marijuana versus those who would be upset (i.e., 44% versus 2%). In turn, children who experience school failure and emotional distress may be more prone to affiliate with deviant peers, thus increasing their risk of future substance use (Ingram & Price, 2001). The low adherence to societal norms is illustrated in early sexual involvement by males, which predicted drug use (Newcomb, 1995). In addition, a negative social environment, including peer rejection, may increase an adolescent's sense of isolation and risk of future substance use (Hawkins et al., 1992). Peer influence also plays a role in predicting relapse after substance abuse treatment. For example, one study showed that 90% of the adolescents who had a relapse attributed their returning to drugs to peer pressure (Brown, 1993).

Psychobehavioral Factors

These factors include children's age, degree of academic success or failure, motivation for learning, the presence of early and persistent behavioral problems, and poor impulse control or inability to delay gratification. Children who begin drinking at an early age (11 or 12 years) are much more likely to develop a substance abuse disorder in their teens or early adulthood compared even with those who delay their use of alcohol until later in high school. Those who begin drinking at age 19 or 20 years have much lower rates of later substance use (<2%; DeWitt, Adlaf, Offord, & Ogborne, 2000). The progression to substance abuse disorders appears more related to the age of initiation and the frequency rather than the duration of use (DeWitt et al., 2000; Kandel et al., 1999). Those individuals with early-onset use have a shorter time from first use to dependence than do groups with later use and adult-onset addictive disorders (Clark, Kirisci, & Tarter, 1998). Beginning alcohol use at an early age is also associated with a greater likelihood to use other substances, including illicit drugs. Adults who began their alcohol use in adolescence have higher lifetime rates of marijuana and other illicit drug use and higher rates of depression and disruptive behavior problems (Clark et al., 1998).

The school environment is an important context in which risk factors may be identified. Level of academic success and behavior in the school setting can be powerful predictors of later substance use. Educational factors that have been shown to be associated with substance use include low IQ, poor academic achievement, specific learning disabilities, disruptive behavior/conduct problems and truancy, and poor social skills (Fergusson, 1998; Scheier, Botvin, Diaz, & Griffin, 1999; Stacy, Newcomb, & Bentler, 1993). School failure has been shown to increase the likelihood that a child will use drugs, with some reports indicating failure at the elementary school level and others pinpointing academic difficulties in later grades (Hawkins et al., 1992; Haynes, Troutman, & Nwachuku, 1998). Similarly, a low degree of commitment to school has been linked to an adolescent's greater likelihood of beginning

drug use (Hawkins et al., 1992). Wallace and Muroff (2002) found that African American children are more exposed to contextual risk factors, such as economic deprivation and academic failure, and White children are more exposed to individual and interpersonal risk factors, such as sensation seeking and peer use. Both factors may contribute to the adolescent's beginning drug use, but the trajectories may be different for children from different ethnic groups.

Other psychological characteristics may influence which adolescents continue their substance use and develop dependence disorders as young adults and which do not. Indeed, although early use is a strong predictor for continued and more severe use, there are nonetheless adolescents who begin their use early and who do not go on to develop substance abuse disorders (Hasin, Grant, & Endicott, 1990). Longitudinal studies of, for example, early alcohol use suggest that young adults who continue to be problem drinkers are more likely to have been rebellious, nonconformist, deviant, or isolated during high school (Newcomb, 1997). Temperament dimensions have been related to substance use in early adolescence and to addiction and behavior problems by early adulthood (Caspi, Henry, McGee, Moffitt, & Silva, 1995; Masse & Tremblay, 1997; Pulkkimen & Pirkanen, 1994; Wills, DuHummel, & Vaccaro, 1995). Individual traits such as sensation seeking, low harm avoidance, poor impulse control, and negative emotionality are personality factors associated with later substance use (Colder & Chassin, 1997; Hawkins et al., 1992; Wills, Sandy, Shinar, & Yaeger, 1999). Kubicka and colleagues (Kubicka, Matejcek, Dytrych, & Roth, 2001) found that novelty seeking and low harm avoidance characteristics predicted substance use in 15-year-olds. They also found a possible link between childhood extraversion and later alcohol use and smoking. In a study of 508 adolescents, personality-related risk factors for substance abuse were associated with using substances for coping and conformity (Comeau, Stewart, & Loba, 2001). Admitting that affective states may have a general role in substance abuse, Wills et al. hypothesized that high levels of positive affect might reduce substance use and operate as a buffering agent. They conducted a longitudinal study in which they followed 1,699 students from 7th to 10th grade for 4 years. The results showed that positive and negative affect showed independent contributions to substance use: Negative affect was related to increased substance use, and positive affect was inversely related to change in substance use. The relationship between internalizing disorders, their temperamental substrates, and risk for substance use is an important line of study (Price

& Lento, 2001), especially in the consideration of those factors that reduce the risk between exposure to opportunities for drug use and substance abuse.

Psychiatric Comorbidity

Psychiatric disorders influence substance use and abuse throughout life, and there is a considerable literature on psychiatric comorbidity. Rates of mood and disruptive disorders are higher in adolescents with substance abuse problems than in those without. Rates of comorbidity of substance abuse with other psychiatric disorders are the same in adolescents as in adults, except for Disruptive and Antisocial Personality Disorders, higher rates for which are found in adults. Adolescents who relapse after drug treatment programs are also more likely to have comorbid psychiatric disorders (Kaminer & Burleson, 1999).

Among populations of adolescents referred for substance abuse treatment, Conduct Disorder, Major Depression, and Attention Deficit Disorder are the most common concomitants of substance dependence (Jaycox, Morral, & Juvonen, 2003). In young women, depression is more often the usual comorbid disorder (Whitmore et al., 1997); also commonly associated with substance abuse disorder in women in Posttraumatic Stress Disorder, usually with depression (Clark et al., 1997). Studies examining the predictors of comorbid substance abuse in depressed adolescents referred for treatment document longer depression episodes, more conduct problems and general psychosocial impairment and isolation, and more school and/or work problems (King et al., 1996).

Depression

Depression occurs in approximately 20% of adolescents (Lewinsohn, Hops, Roberts, Seeley, & Andrews, 1993) and substance use disorders in 25% of depressed adolescents (Fleming & Offord, 1990). Risk factors common to both depression and substance use in adolescents include poor coping skills, interpersonal conflict with parents, poor academic achievement, and low academic motivation (Lewinsohn, Gotlib, & Seeley, 1995). Therefore, those children and adolescents experiencing depression, attentional problems, or Conduct Disorder have an elevated risk for substance abuse (Deykin, Buka, & Zeena, 1992).

The combination of depression and substance abuse is particularly problematic in young girls. Usually, Major Depression is associated with a more severe level of substance dependence. Conversely, depression in adolescence also raises the risk of more severe substance use and a rapid entry into dependence (Riggs, Baker, Mikulich, Young, & Crowley, 1995). In a study comparing depressed adolescents without prior substance abuse histories to nondepressed controls, the rate of substance use was high in both groups but higher in the depressed group (34.6% in the depressed group and 24.1% in the controls). Depressed girls who were abusing drugs were more psychosocially impaired, had more anxiety traits, and had dysregulated circadian fluctuations in cortisol compared to depressed girls who were not abusing drugs. Also, those girls who were both depressed and substance abusing had an earlier onset of their substance use compared to nondepressed girls who were using drugs (Rao et al., 1999). Each of these associations suggests that depression in adolescents, particularly in girls, marks a high-risk time for their beginning substance use and a critical point for intervention focused as much on the risk of drug use as on their depression.

For boys, depression also plays a significant role but with a slightly different profile marked by more difficulties with conduct and attentional problems. Depressed boys who are also abusing substances are more likely to have Posttraumatic Stress Disorder, anxiety disorders, and Attention-Deficit/Hyperactivity Disorder (ADHD; Riggs et al., 1995). Conduct Disorder and depression increase the risk of an earlier onset of substance dependence. But is the comorbidity between Conduct Disorder and substance abuse more a reflection of the impact of a number of illicit drugs on behavior? In other words, what is the risk to develop Conduct Disorder independent of substance dependence? Although this has not been studied directly, one study examined the relationship between adolescent-onset Bipolar Disorder and substance abuse and found that adolescents with Bipolar Disorder had over 8 times greater risk to develop substance dependence compared to those with child-onset Bipolar Disorder. Conduct Disorder did not account for this elevated risk, suggesting that substance dependence and conduct problems are not entirely overlapping (Wilens et al., 1999; see also next paragraphs).

The risk of suicide is elevated among adolescents and young adults who are substance abusers. For example, postmortem case reviews of adolescents who committed suicide have found that 70% were drug and alcohol users (Shafii et al., 1988). Among adolescents who actually commit suicide, a much greater proportion were using alcohol at the time of their death (Brent et al., 1993). Multiple risks involving substance use appear to converge for suicide victims. These include active substance dependence with Major Depression, a family history of depression and substance use, and the ready availability of firearms in the home (Brent, Perper, & Allman, 1987; Bukstein et al.,

1993). Indeed, White boys who are intoxicated are much more likely to commit suicide using a firearm if one is readily available (Kaminer, 1992). Persistently high levels of problem drinking and/or other substance use and depressive symptoms are also associated with high levels of suicidal thoughts and attempts, and the longer the duration of suicidal thoughts along with substance dependence, the higher the likelihood of suicide (Deykin & Baka, 1994).

Conduct Disorder

The presence of Conduct Disorder before the development of substance abuse seems to carry a poorer prognosis for the adolescent than for those who develop their conduct problems concomitant with their substance abuse (Myers, Stewart, & Brown, 1998). Conduct problems comorbid with attentional regulatory difficulties also presage a higher risk for involvement with drugs. Adolescents with ADHD and Conduct Disorder are at a higher risk of developing substance abuse problems than those with ADHD alone (Wilens, Biederman, & Spencer, 1996). A prospective study longitudinally followed for 8 years children with ADHD and children with ADHD plus Conduct Disorder. Those with both ADHD and Conduct Disorder used as much as 5 times more alcohol and cigarettes than those with ADHD alone (Barkley, Fischer, Edelbrock, & Smallish, 1990). Another study examined 626 pairs of 17-year-old twins. Once again, ADHD alone did not increase the risk for substance abuse unless there were also concomitant conduct problems (Disney, Elkins, McGue, & Iacono, 1997).

There are apparent differences in the presentations of girls and boys who have conduct problems along with their substance dependence. Boys are more likely to have aggressive symptoms, including stealing, destruction of property, cruelty to animals, fighting with weapons, and criminal activity such as breaking and entering. The severity of the aggression and the presence of ADHD and depression predict an earlier and more severe onset of substance dependence in boys; in girls, only Major Depression seems to predict earlier and more severe substance abuse (Riggs et al., 1995). Girls with conduct problems and substance abuse are more likely to have a diagnosis of nicotine dependence, to start drinking at a later age and to have more running away behavior compared to boys, and to be involved in less criminal or aggressive activity (Mezzich et al., 1994).

Later-onset conduct problems (in late adolescence) not associated with ADHD are also associated with increased risk for substance dependence. Grillo and colleagues (Grillo et al., 1996) suggest that later-onset conduct problems are a form of personality dysfunction and are more

likely to be accompanied by substance abuse than are early-onset ADHD and conduct problems, which may reflect neurobehavioral difficulties secondary to ADHD. Another insight into this distinction comes from studies with juvenile offenders (Randall, Henggeler, Pickrel, & Brondino, 1999). Substance-abusing juvenile offenders with externalizing disorders and high rates of antisocial behavior had a much worse trajectory as studied for 16 months than those juvenile offenders who were only substance abusing or those who also had internalizing disorders. It may be that internalizing symptoms such as anxiety buffer the more deleterious and destructive effects of conduct problems comorbid with substance abuse.

Anxiety Disorders

Children who suffer from anxiety with or without antisocial personality characteristics coupled with chronically stressful living environments may have greater risk for later substance use (Newcomb, 1995). Like other disorders already mentioned, it appears that the onset of anxiety disorders usually precedes the onset of substance use and abuse, a finding that has been replicated across cultures (Merikangas et al., 1998). The most common type of anxiety disorder that is apparently associated with substance abuse is Posttraumatic Stress Disorder (Clark et al., 1995), especially for children who have grown up exposed to chronic stress and parental abuse and/or neglect.

Another form of anxiety that may play a role in the development of substance dependence is Social Phobia. In a study of 1,035 adolescents 13 to 17 years of age, Social Phobia was highly comorbid with depression and substance abuse (Essau, Conradt, & Peterman, 1999). Another study showed that Social Phobia and Agoraphobia seemed to precede the onset of alcohol abuse, whereas more generalized anxiety or panic disorders did not (Kushner, Sher, & Erickson, 1999). Other long-term studies have shown that anxiety manifest as shyness coupled with aggressiveness in adolescents were strong predictors over 2 decades later of cocaine abuse in adults (Swan, 1995).

Methodological Caveats

Each of these associations raises another question regarding comorbidity of depression, Conduct Disorder, anxiety, or other disorders with substance abuse problems: Do these comorbid disorders usually precede the development of substance abuse problems, or are they more likely to follow the initiation of heavy drug use? Costello and colleagues (1999) showed that ADHD, Conduct Disorder, Oppositional Defiant Disorder, and anxiety disorders seemed to occur long before the onset of actual substance dependence (though not as clearly before the initiation of substance use). However, depressive symptoms seemed to occur at least 1 year after the onset of alcohol abuse but 2 years before the onset of smoking. In the case of both depression and disruptive disorders, the rates and age of onset of substance dependence were significantly higher and earlier than in youths without comorbid mood or conduct problems. A study examining hospitalized adolescent substance abusers showed that for at least half, their Dysthymia had preceded the development of their substance dependence (Hovens, Cantwell, & Kiriakos, 1994). A study of adolescents with Dysthymia and problem behavior showed that moderate to heavy alcohol consumption appeared to follow the earlier psychiatric and behavioral history (King, Naylor, Hill, Shaina, & Gredena, 1993).

A second major methodological issue plaguing each of these studies is that the majority of the work on comorbidity and substance abuse utilizes clinically referred samples, that is, adolescents who are sufficiently ill to be referred for treatment by physicians, family, child welfare, or the legal system. Thus, the clinical correlates, the comorbid disorders, may actually be correlates of the referral population regardless of whether or not the comorbid disorders appear before or after the substance abuse (Angold, Costello, & Erkanli, 1999). Longitudinal methods of large population-based samples such as those accomplished by Newcomb and colleagues (Newcomb, 1995, 1997; Newcomb & Bentler, 1988b) are the best solution to this problem, but there are very few of these studies in the literature.

A third methodological issue is the overlapping symptoms among the various diagnostic categories. Poor impulse control may be a feature of ADHD, conduct problems, and substance dependence. Dysphoria may be a result of chronic drug use. Indeed, even some of the stimulants such as cocaine are associated with profound lows following the highs, especially after chronic use. Thus, some of the symptoms characteristic of certain comorbid disorders may be both exacerbated by substance use and mimicked by the effects of the drugs.

Each of these methodological issues illustrates the complexity of this area of work in adolescent substance abuse and the need for research designs that creatively attempt to tease apart overlapping symptoms and disorders.

Biological and Genetic Factors

A considerable literature has developed about the generational transmission of substance abuse, particularly alcoholism. In a large epidemiological survey, 8,865 secondary school students were asked about their own and their parents' use of drugs and alcohol (Smart & Fejer, 1972). For all 12 drugs (including alcohol) that students were asked about, there was high agreement between students' and parents' use of drugs, and the specific drug was often concordant. The strongest relationship in parent-child use was maternal and children's use of tranquilizers. Annis (1974) studied 539 adolescents and their families and found a significant relationship between parents' and adolescents' use of alcohol, with similar patterns of use grouping within mother-daughter and father-son pairs. In a study using child and separate mother and father interviews (Fawzy, Coombs, & Gerber, 1983), teenagers were significantly more likely to use drugs or alcohol if their parents were users or if the teenager perceived the parent to be a user. For example, of the parents reported by the teenager to be a marijuana user, 81% of fathers and 78% of mothers had substance-abusing adolescents. Similarly, if parents reported themselves to have at least one drink of beer or wine per day, 72% of fathers and 77% of mothers were likely to have a substance-abusing teenage.

Each of these studies raises the question of how drug use is transmitted across generations and what are the genetic as well as environmental contributions to the notable concordance in parental and child drug use (Deren, 1986). More recent findings suggest that the multigenerational transmission patterns of substance abuse may be mediated by gender. Among families of addicts, higher rates of alcoholism have been found in fathers as compared with mothers; conversely, higher rates of affective disorders are found in mothers (Mirin, Weiss, Griffin, & Michael, 1991). In a sample of adolescents in treatment, the extent of drug use by the child related to the extent of alcohol use by the father but related more strongly to the use of drugs, not alcohol, by the mother (Friedman & Utada, 1992).

Until recently, few studies have moved beyond the correlational design to examine other factors, such as socioeconomic status and parental psychological and psychiatric characteristics, that may contribute to the parental substance abuse and compound the genetic risk for the children. For example, among substance abusers' parents and siblings, there is a high rate of psychiatric disorders such as depression and Antisocial Personality Disorder that are also comorbid with substance abuse (Mirin et al., 1991; Rounsaville et al., 1991). In a study of 492 parents and 673 siblings of cocaine abusers and 400 parents and 476 siblings of opiate abusers (Luthar, Merikangas, & Rounsaville, 1993), several variables, including gender and psychiatric status of the parent, ethnicity, and type of drug abused, seemed to mediate the relationship between parental and child drug use. Maternal depression was associated with both depression and drug use in the adult offspring. Similarly, paternal alcoholism was significantly associated with alcoholism or drug abuse in adult offspring, but only for African American and not Caucasian families.

It may be that genes play a role in an individual's individual susceptibility to dependence once a person begins to experiment with drugs, usually during adolescence or young adulthood. In other words, the inherited vulnerability may be a psychophysiological susceptibility to the addictive effects of drugs (McGue, Elkins, & Iacono, 2000; Newcomb, 1995). Indeed, in contrast to the gateway model mentioned earlier that suggests certain drugs such as marijuana serve as a gateway or stepping stone to greater illicit drug use (Fergusson & Horwood, 2000; Yamaguchi & Kandel, 1984), there is an emerging literature suggesting that marijuana and other illicit drug use is moderately heritable (Morral, McCaffrey, & Paddock, 2002). Twin studies have estimated that 30% to 60% of the variance in marijuana use in adolescence (Kendler, Karkowski, Neale, & Prescott, 2000; Kendler et al., 2002; Kendler & Prescott, 1998a; Lynskey et al., 2002) and 45% to 62% of the variance in marijuana dependence can be attributed to heritable factors (Kendler & Prescott, 1998a, 1998b; Lynskey et al., 2002). Similar estimates are made for the heritability of other illicit drug use and drug dependence (True et al., 1999; Tsuang et al., 1998).

In the mature brain exposed repeatedly to cocaine (and other drugs of abuse), neuronal functions gradually change (e.g., tolerance), and these changes may endure even after cessation of drug use. Such delayed, gradually developing, and persistent changes in function suggest that a candidate mechanism for addictive phenomena may be long-term changes in neuronal gene expression (Nestler, Bergson, Gultart, & Hope, 1993). In the mature brain, genes regulate the synthesis of neuropeptides, monoamines, their receptors, second messengers, and more. (Second messenger systems are those chemical events within a cell that are generated in response to the binding of a hormone or neurotransmitter to their receptor on the surface of the cell. The second messengers, including G proteins, then trigger a series of molecular interactions that alter the physiologic state of the cell.)

The expression of specific genes in the central nervous system appears regulated by a class of DNA-binding proteins termed transcription factors. These transcription factors bind to the regulatory regions of certain genes and affect the rate at which these genes are transcribed (and thus the synthesis of the relevant synaptic components). These transcription factors, called as a group "immediate

early genes" (IEGs; Sheng & Greenberg, 1990), appear rapidly (within minutes) in response to neuronal stimulation. The messenger RNAs (mRNAs) transcribed from IEGs often have a very short half-life; that is, the induction of these genes is short-lived. For example, the IEG c-Fos can be undetectable within a half-hour of stimulus induction (Sheng & Greenberg, 1990). For the induction of c-Fos, c-Jun, and Zif268 in response to novel stimulation, mRNA transcription occurs within 5 minutes, with peak steady-state levels of mRNA at 30 to 45 minutes and peak protein synthesis within 2 hours of stimulation (Kosofsky & Hyman, 1993). IEGs may activate or repress the rate at which other genes are transcribed, though the mechanism for this regulation of transcription rate is not yet clear (Plashne & Gann, 1990). The transient nature of the mRNA from induction of IEGs suggests a complicated stimulus-dependent mechanism for regulating such events as the synthesis of receptors and transporters. The IEG response can also be used as a marker of neuronal activation (Sheng & Greenberg, 1990).

Drugs of abuse affect the expression of IEGs in the mature and the developing animal, and the effect is apparent during and after treatment. This relationship may be one mechanism to explain how substances of abuse alter genetic programs in the different phases of neural ontogeny in both early development and during puberty, as with the vulnerable adolescent. That is, drug-induced alterations in IEG expression can modify neural gene expression during development and thereby alter, perhaps permanently, cellular identity and the neuronal repertoire (Kosofsky & Hyman, 1993). In the adult animal, exposure to cocaine enhances the expression of several IEGs, including c-Fos and Zif268, as well as genes encoding for neuropeptides such as substance P and dynorphin involved in the predominantly striatonigral dopaminergic pathways (Steiner & Gerfen, 1993, 1995) that are critical to reward pathways in the brain. Similar induction of these same IEGs is seen with agents that stimulate the dopamine D_1 system (Robertson, Vincent, & Fibiger, 1992). The cocaine-related induction can be blocked with D_1 antagonists (Steiner & Gerfen, 1995) and does not occur in a D_1-deficient mouse (Drago, Gerfen, Westphal, & Steiner, 1996; Moratella, Xu, Tonegawa, & Graybiel, 1996). Similarly, with chronic exposure, there may be long-term perturbations in IEG expression. For example, during withdrawal from cocaine treatment, adult rats showed reduction in c-Fos expression for several days (Ennulat, Babb, & Cohen, 1994).

Thus, it may be that social circumstances facilitate opportunities for initial experimentation with illicit drugs but that genetic factors play a significant role in how individuals move beyond that initial experimentation. Those who have a greater genetic predisposition to become dependent or substance abusing may be more susceptible to the effects of, for example, alcohol on gene expression, a model developed in detail by Nestler and colleagues (Nestler, Bergson, Gultart, & Hope, 1993; Nestler, Gao, & Tamminga, 1997; Nestler, Hope, & Widnell, 1993). In this model, continued exposure of specific subcortical regions of the brain (e.g., ventral tegmentum and nucleus accumbens) permanently changes second messenger systems within the cell, which in turn influences the function of immediate early genes and salience reward mechanisms central to the response to the drug.

Polymorphisms of the dopamine D_2 receptor (D_2(A1) allele) have been associated with addictive behaviors, substance abuse generally, and cocaine and/or alcohol abuse specifically (Berrettini & Persico, 1996; Comings et al., 1991; Compton, Anglin, Khalsa-Denison, & Paredes, 1996; George, Cheng, Nguyen, Israel, & O'Dowd, 1993; Goldman, Urbanek, Guenther, Robin, & Long, 1997; Noble, 1993; Noble et al., 1993; Smith et al., 1992; Uhl, Persisco, & Smith, 1992). Similarly, polymorphisms of the dopamine transporter gene have been associated with cocaine-induced paranoia in Caucasian substance abusers (Gelernter, Kranzler, Satel, & Rao, 1994). The functional significance of these polymorphisms is not known, and many studies suggesting a genetic hypothesis for substance abuse are flawed by heterogeneous samples. It is highly unlikely that substance abuse is a monogenic disorder; it is more likely that these particular (and/or other) alleles may work in concert with other genes and environmental contexts to convey increased risk for substance abuse in a *certain proportion* of substance users. This possibly increased genetic risk is particularly relevant to the offspring of those affected and addicted individuals, for they may convey the same genetic risk (and susceptibility to addiction) to their children. Moreover, a possible association of dopamine system alleles with susceptibility to the pathogenic effects of stress and to disordered attention and anxiety regulation (Comings, Muhleman, & Gysin, 1996; Gill, Daly, Heron, Hawi, & Fitzgerald, 1997; Rowe et al., 1998) suggests that this profile of behaviors, seen more often among the offspring of cocaine-addicted individuals, may *for some* reflect a genetically based functional alteration or susceptibility in the dopamine system apart from or in addition to the effects of prenatal substance exposure. Though to date not studied in longitudinally maintained samples, it may also be that this same genetic vulnerability conveys a similar risk for addiction to these children as they reach adolescence. For example, adoption studies show an increased risk of alcoholism and other drug abuse in adopted children whose biological parents were alcoholic whereas alcohol use by the adoptive parents did not increase the risk of alcoholism in the adoptive children if all other risk conditions did not prevail (Cadoret, Troughton, O'Gorman, & Heywood, 1986; Cloninger, Bohman, Sigvardisson, & von Knorring, 1985; Goodwin et al., 1974).

Thus, greater genetic susceptibility may be a strong predictor of risk for substance abuse compared to the impact of adoptive parents who use substances. At the same time, both genetic and environmental conditions may be important in the initiation of substance use; that is, environmental conditions and availability may contribute to an adolescent's initial experimentation with drugs, and progression to abuse and dependence may be mediated more by genetic factors. Studies of marijuana and cocaine use and the progression to dependence on either drug have been conducted in studies of monozygotic and dizygotic twins (Kendler & Prescott, 1998a, 1998b; Schukit, 1999) and have demonstrated that for both drugs, an adolescent's initial risk of using was related to both genetic and experiential factors, but the likelihood of an individual going on to abuse and dependence seemed more genetically conveyed.

Impact of Adolescent Substance Use

What are the consequences of adolescent drug use on other aspects of adult functioning? It is commonly assumed that adolescent drug use compromises most aspects of an individual's interpersonal, academic, and work life, but there are few longitudinal studies following an adolescent into young adulthood. Newcomb and Bentler (1988a, 1988b) followed 654 individuals who provided complete data at three testings over a period of 8 years, from early adolescence to young adulthood. Various types of teenage drug use, with the exception of alcohol use, but particularly cigarettes and hard drug use, had a range of negative consequences in young adulthood. These negative effects included problems with psychosomatic symptoms, dysphoric emotional functioning, impaired romantic attachments, and trouble with parents and family. Teenage drug use also increases job instability in young adults. Of particular importance, there is no single targeted area of impact of teenage drug use; rather, drug use impedes a range of important domains central to an adolescent's adaptive transition to mature adulthood. These observed effects are not the result of experimental or infrequent drug use, but of relatively heavy use during early and late adolescence. Heavy use, abuse, or misuse of substances in adolescence and not the occasional social use at a party or among friends is associated with the overall serious impairments in later adult adjustment.

Marijuana has been particularly well studied for the impact on adolescents' educational performance and attainment (Lynskey & Hall, 2000). Increasing and sustained marijuana use is associated with poorer school performance, more negative attitudes toward school, and early school dropout (Ellickson, Collins, & Bell, 1999; Fergusson & Horwood, 1997; Fergusson, Horwood, & Swain-Campbell, 2002; Fergusson, Lynskey, & Horwood, 1996). Further, early cannabis use is associated with decreased college participation (Krohn, Lizotte, & Perez, 1997; Tanner, Davies, & O'Grady, 1999) and hence, fewer employment opportunities and less earning capacity. Additionally, long-term marijuana use produces subtle and selective impairments of cognitive functioning, which, although not usually severe deficits, nonetheless may impact an individual's job and educational adjustment (Solowij, 1999). Of particular importance, prospective studies (Lynskey, Coffey, Degenhardt, Carlin, & Patton, 2003) suggest that early, rather than later, use is associated with more problematic behaviors and complications, including continued substance abuse, risky sexual behavior, and criminal activity (Brook et al., 1998; Fergusson & Horwood, 1997). Although it is possible that a number of factors, including genetic factors (Plomin & Craig, 1997), may potentially contribute to these relationships (see later discussion), twin studies (Lynskey, Heath, et al., 2003) suggest that early use is associated for many youths with the adoption of an unconventional, more isolated lifestyle with easier access to drugs and for which early school dropout is one indicator.

PROTECTIVE FACTORS

Protective factors are conditions that can have their own independent effects on a given outcome and, at the same time, can moderate the relationship between risk factors and negative outcomes (Luthar & Zigler, 1991; Rutter, 1987). In the past decade, investigators have focused on the possibility that a number of protective factors may mitigate the impact of risk factors on the trajectory to substance use and abuse in adolescence (Hawkins et al., 1992; Wills, Vaccaro, & McNamara, 1992). Jessor and colleagues (Jessor, Van Den Bos, Vanderryn, Costa, & Turbin, 1995) studied students in grades 7 through 9 at four time points with repeated assessments of six measures of risk and seven measures of protection. The latter included attitudes toward school, health, behavioral deviance, and relationships with adults, as well as perceived level of control, selection

of friends as models of conventional or acceptable behavior, and participation in prosocial activities such as volunteering, school clubs, and activities with family. Across gender and ethnicity, students higher in protective factors (e.g., those endorsing more positive attitudes, greater perceived level of control, seeking friends as models of acceptable behavior, and engaged in more prosocial activities) had a much reduced risk of later problem behaviors, including substance use. Also, these protective factors moderated or reduced the relationship between those risk factors that were present to later substance use.

Level of self-control or regulatory abilities may be most central to the other aspects of protectiveness, including selection of friends and adaptive attitudes. Wills, Gibbons, Gerard, and Brody (2000) tested predictions from a self-regulation model of factors relevant for early onset of substance use with African American children. It was found that temperament characteristics were related to indices of behavioral self-control, and self-control indices were related to variables that either deterred or promoted substance use. In other words, protective processes reflected good self-control and involvement in school that in turn were mediated by temperamental characteristics such as good task attentional orientation and positive emotionality. Vulnerability processes were expressed through poor self-control and risk taking that also originated in temperamental dimensions of activity level and negative emotionality.

Coping abilities have been studied as protective or buffering factors against early substance use. A longitudinal study of children from seventh to ninth grade examined rates of alcohol, tobacco, and marijuana use and also styles of coping (Wills, Sandy, Yaeger, Cleary, & Shinar, 2001). Adaptive styles of coping were those that involved a child's active problem solving versus disengaged styles, including anger and avoidance. Those adolescents who typically used more active, problem-solving styles of coping were less likely to initiate substance use or to have peers that were involved with early substance use, whereas more disengaged styles were associated with higher rates of initiating substance use and of associating with substance-using peers. The impact of either style was greater when the adolescent had experienced significant life stressors; that is, more active styles buffered the relationship between life stressors and initiating substance use. It may be that those children with more active styles of problem solving are also more likely to gather information and consider alternative plans before acting, a form of self-control (Wills et al., 2001) that buffers the individual against the opportunities for experimenting with illicit drugs or using drugs as a means of coping during stressful times.

MODELS FOR A DEVELOPMENTAL TRAJECTORY TO SUBSTANCE USE AND SUBSTANCE DEPENDENCE

Returning to the distinctions among variables that serve as markers (fixed or variable), moderators, and mediators, the various risks and protective factors previously discussed may be placed in models for the initiation of substance use and for the trajectory from substance use to dependence. There is considerable work yet to be done to fully explicate these models.

The Model for Initiation of Substance Use

Considering first the initiation of substance use (Figure 16.1), it is likely, as discussed earlier, that genetic factors mediate an individual's initiation into substance use. One set of pathways by which genetic factors mediate the initiation of substance use involves the genetic basis for emotional regulation and self-control. These abilities influence individual development of emotional and behavioral capacities (e.g., on-task behavior, positive emotionality, and active problem solving) in early years that, in turn, mediate individual adaptation to the school environ-

ment (e.g., positive attitude toward school, good social skills) and, ultimately, successful school performance. Likewise, genetic influences on capacities for emotional regulation and self-control may be negative, mediating subsequent problems with emotional negativity and impulsive or risk-taking behavior. These less adaptive characteristics, in turn, may mediate the child's negative response to the school environment (e.g., a lower degree of commitment to school, disruptive behavior, conduct problems, poor social skills, and poor academic achievement) and, ultimately, failure at school.

As a child enters adolescence, his or her prior experience in the school setting may mediate peer choices at just the time when the peer group's influence on substance use initiation may be strongest. Children who have good emotional regulatory capacities and have experienced school success may be more likely to affiliate with prosocial peer groups that adhere to conventional societal norms and object to drug use. They may also be more likely to receive peer acceptance and support. Membership in a prosocial peer group may also further moderate the child's attitudes about school, drug use, social conventions, and social expectations. Likewise, if a child has had problems with emotional distress and impulsive behavior in early years and has not adapted well to the school environment, cumulative

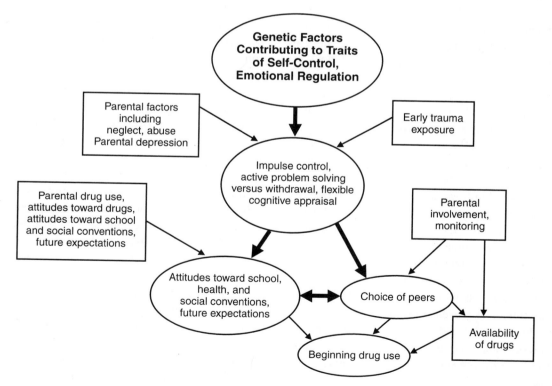

Figure 16.1   Model for initiation of substance use in adolescence.

risk may mediate his or her affiliation with a deviant or delinquent peer group that does not adhere to conventional societal norms, accepts drug use and early sexual involvement, engages in disruptive or delinquent behavior, and/or pressures its members to continue drug use. Membership in a deviant peer group may further moderate the child's attitudes about school, drug use, social conventions, and social expectations, further altering the trajectory toward initiation and experimentation. Alternatively, a child who has had any number of negative responses to school during early years may simply be rejected by adolescent peers, becoming socially isolated and alighting on a different but equally adverse trajectory toward initiating substance use.

The possible protective function of the child's capacity for emotional regulation and self-control (or the risk function of the inverse) must be considered in the context of family and cultural factors. First, genetic factors notwithstanding, some family factors, including early histories of abuse and neglect or exposure to trauma and violence, appear to directly alter individual emotional and stress regulatory capacities early in development, thus striking another pathway to substance use. Second, family acceptance of drug use (expressed in attitudes and/or drug use behavior) may lessen the perceived negative consequences of initial experimentation or use. Third, parental attitudes (e.g., academic aspirations and level of optimism about their children's future) and parenting behavior (e.g., levels of involvement and monitoring), particularly during early childhood, may alter the trajectory of the child's response to school during early years and the trajectory of peer involvement later during adolescence.

Societal acceptance of drug use, the legality versus illegality of a specific drug, or the presence of local neighborhood drug economies may also shift individual trajectories toward or away from initial experimentation and use at any time during childhood and adolescent years. For example, before the considerable health hazards of tobacco were well understood, smoking was an accepted, even positive mode of social interaction and friendship. In this kind of setting, initial use is more likely and also less negatively perceived, possibly even among adolescents whose individual trajectories otherwise confer more protection and less risk. The legal status of a drug removes the necessary involvement of criminal behavior as a deterrent to initiation or experimentation. The presence of an active drug-based economy in a local neighborhood setting not only conveys acceptance of substance use but also provides additional reinforcement for involvement in criminal activities that sustain the economy when buying and selling of drugs is

perceived as a faster means of gaining access to resources and social status.

The Model for Continued Substance Use and Dependence

The model for continued substance use and dependence also has a genetic component that mediates the trajectory for some, though not all, individuals (Figure 16.2). Indeed, problem use, abuse, and dependence may be more heritable and less influenced by environment than the initiation or use of substances, including alcohol and tobacco as well as illicit drugs (Kendler et al., 2000; Kendler & Prescott, 1998a, 1998b; McGue et al., 2000; True et al., 1997; Van Den Bres, Johnson, Neale, & Pickens, 1998). Other genes contributing to vulnerability for depression, anxiety, and/or Posttraumatic Stress Disorder may also play a role in an individual's move from early substance use to ongoing use and dependence.

Mood and disruptive behavior disorders appear to play a central moderating role in shifting individual trajectories from substance use to abuse and/or dependence. Multiple pathways, depending on the nature of disorder, appear to shift trajectories from use to abuse and dependence. For example, internalizing disorders, particularly depression and Posttraumatic Stress Disorder, may be an extension of emotional dysregulation that accelerates an individual from use to abuse and dependence. Alternatively, Conduct Disorder may be an extension of problems with behavioral control that also tip the scales toward dependence. However, the currently entangled etiologies of comorbid psychiatric disorders and substance dependence, as evidenced by their overlapping antecedents (e.g., family conflict and school failure) and patterns of mutual influence (e.g., drug use exacerbating mood, which, in turn, extends drug use), have so far made it difficult to discern empirically or clinically their mechanisms of interaction.

Individual gender specifically appears to moderate the ways psychiatric comorbidity moderates substance abuse and dependence. For example, for girls, depression is the most likely psychiatric moderator of substance abuse severity, whereas for boys, conduct disorders and attentional problems are more likely to influence this pathway.

Sociocultural factors (e.g., ethnicity) may also moderate the ways psychiatric comorbidity moderates substance abuse and dependence. In terms of ethnicity, being White appears to confer vulnerability for substance dependence when individual and interpersonal risk factors are present, whereas being African American appears to confer risk

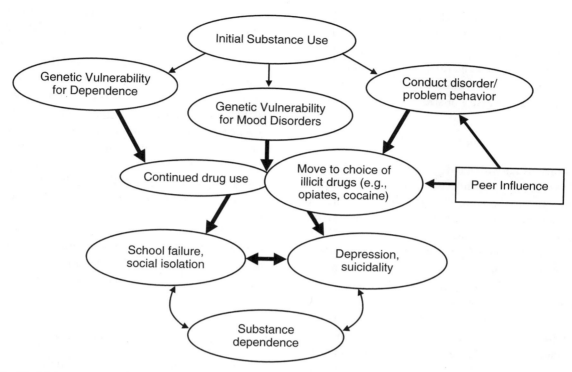

Figure 16.2   Model for progression to continued substance use and dependence.

when exposure to economic deprivation and academic failure are present.

Another prominent factor in determining pathways from substance use to abuse and dependence is the age of initial substance use. Initiation of use before 12 years of age increases the likelihood of dependence, suggesting that understanding the occurrence of risk in early years is going to be critical for understanding pathways to dependence.

The impact of ongoing substance use and abuse on social adjustment, peer relations, and work and school security also creates a cyclical effect by which substance abuse feeds continued dysphoria and a spiraling downward of an individual's environmental stability. For example, recent treatment approaches to substance dependence emphasize dramatic changes in an individual's social environment so as to diminish contacts with both stimuli that may accentuate drug craving and also provide opportunities for social contacts that are not connected with a drug-using world (Higgins, Heil, & Lussier, 2004; Thompson, 2003).

FUTURE DIRECTIONS

Considerable work has yet to be done to explicate fully the pathways to substance use and dependence proposed in

these models. Of particular importance, most of what is currently known about adolescent substance use and dependence is based on findings that have demonstrated correlation but not necessarily causation.

Mechanisms of Risk

The models presented here are best considered heuristic springboards rather than definitive maps. As Cicchetti and Cohen (1995) have suggested, distinguishing between factors that mark an event from those that play a causal role is a critical task to understanding how risk and protective factors work together to influence outcomes. Perhaps the greatest task now faced by developmental and addiction researchers is to move from identifying correlates to understanding their respective roles in causal risk mechanisms.

Future research will need to establish which among the currently known correlates operate in causal ways to generate substance use and abuse outcomes and how these risk mechanisms function and interact. Consider, for example, the respective functions of emotional regulation, coping style, and family dynamics in substance use. In the presence of adverse family dynamics, the capacity for emotional regulation may be a necessary causal factor promoting active problem solving, which, in turn, moderates the influence of adverse family dynamics on an individual's substance use trajectory. In a more favorable family context, the capacity for emotional regulation and coping may be less critical. In other words, it may be that emotional regulation and coping style are important causal factors only when an individual faces environmental adversity or stress.

Equifinality and Multifinality

Model limitations notwithstanding, given the multitude of factors at varying levels of influence that have been identified as correlates in these early stages of investigation, the search for any one variable or pathway as *the* precursor to drug experimentation or abuse is not likely to be fruitful. Rather, the examination of patterns of developmental trajectories involving cumulative factors holds more promise for accurately mapping this complex phenomenon. Given the many potential trajectories to drug use initiation, the concepts of equifinality and multifinality (Cicchetti & Cohen, 1995) are particularly relevant to research and intervention development that aim to understand and alter adverse trajectories toward adolescent substance abuse and dependence.

Applying the concept of *equifinality* to the study of substance use initiation allows for the assumption that many divergent pathways can and will lead to the same outcome. For example, pathways to drug abuse and dependence for boys and girls appear to be carved through different risk mechanisms. For girls, internalizing disorders (e.g., depression) appear to shift trajectories toward prolonged use and dependence, whereas for boys, trajectories appear to shift in the presence of externalizing disorders. Similarly, pathways to substance abuse and dependence are influenced not only by membership in a socially deviant peer group but by social withdrawal and alienation from peers. Other examples of equifinality have yet to be examined. For example, in communities where teen idolization of drug- and crime-involved celebrities is considered socially deviant, pathways to drug abuse and dependence may occur only through membership in a disenfranchised peer group. In other communities, where teen idolization of drug- and crime-involved celebrities is considered more mainstream, pathways to drug abuse and dependence may more likely occur through membership in popular peer groups. Likewise, the increasing prevalence of substance abuse among adolescents in affluent communities suggests that alternative trajectories to substance abuse in the context of economic privilege also exist.

Applying the concept of *multifinality* to the study of initiation allows for the assumption that individual starting points that may confer risk (e.g., genetic disposition toward poor self-regulation, parental acceptance of drug use) may or may not lead to drug use initiation, depending on the presence or absence of other intervening risk and protective factors. For example, as stated earlier, a temperamental predisposition to emotional dysregulation may confer risk only when specific constellations of environmental risk factors are present. In a context of frequent parental involvement and close monitoring, where optimism about the future and intolerance toward drug use are clearly expressed, a child with poor emotional regulation or self-control may remain on a trajectory toward relatively little experimentation. Alternatively, a child with good emotional regulation attending school in a neighborhood supported by a drug economy may easily become involved in peer networks where experimentation with substances is a social norm. In each case, the more commonly expected trajectory shifts based on the presence or absence of other specific risk mechanisms.

Implications for Intervention Research

Developmental interventions for children, adolescents, and parents can, at the same time, contribute to and benefit from the investigation of mechanisms by which substance use transitions to abuse and dependence. For instance, research that expands on developmental models of substance abuse by identifying key sources of influence over time (e.g., parents during early childhood and peers during adolescence) can help inform the timing and targeted population for specific intervention strategies. Longitudinal investigations in which individual trajectories of psychopathology and substance use are tracked over time may help determine which combinations of psychopharmacological and psychosocial interventions are likely to be most effective. Understanding the mechanisms by which problems in emotional regulatory capacities trigger substance use experimentation (e.g., the moderating role of the stressful environment) can help specify which populations of children at risk would benefit most from early childhood parenting interventions.

Carefully designed intervention research involving comparison groups, particularly in early phases when individual risk factors are targeted, can help clarify the mechanisms by which these targeted factors influence substance use. For example, the potentially causal role of self-regulation in substance use can be clarified by tracking substance use trajectories of children whose self-regulation improves in response to an early parenting intervention and comparing them with children whose parents were assigned to the control group. In other words, hypothesized causal mechanisms of risk targeted in carefully designed intervention research (i.e., research in which integrity and intensity of intervention are monitored and a well-conceived control group is used in a randomized trial) can be tested by determining if improvement in the targeted risk factor favorably alters individual trajectories toward problematic substance use.

SUMMARY

Although prevalence estimates have been relatively stable in the past decade, a significant percentage of adolescents initiate licit and illicit drug use during their high school years. Genetic factors strongly contribute to the likelihood that an adolescent's early experimentation with drugs will progress to regular use and/or dependence, but in addition, peer group, availability of drugs, and community acceptance are important contributions. Adolescents who begin their drug use early are at much greater risk for continued use and dependence as well as for the associated comorbidities of school dropout, social isolation, and involvement in criminal activity. Protective factors include perception of a high level of self-control and of stable, caring peers and adults. Models describing the trajectory from early to regular use and dependence are necessarily multivariate and causally interactive, with no one factor being singularly predictive for the likelihood or severity of later dependence. Research that (1) examines multiple pathways to substance use and dependence, (2) identifies protective factors that can alter adverse trajectories, and (3) tests hypothetical causal mechanisms of risk is likely to be the most fruitful. Investigations involving intervention development can be particularly useful in the confirmation of causal mechanisms.

REFERENCES

Amaro, H., Zuckerman, B., & Cabral, H. (1989). Drug use among adolescent mothers: Profile of risk. *Pediatrics, 84*(1), 144–151.

Angold, A., Costello, J., & Erkanli, A. (1999). Comorbidity. *Journal of Child Psychology and Psychiatry, 40*, 57–87.

Annis, H. M. (1974). Patterns of intra-familial drug use. *British Journal of Addictions, 69*, 361–369.

Anthony, J. C., Warner, L. A., & Kessler, R. C. (1994). Comparative epidemiology of dependence on tobacco, alcohol, controlled substances, and inhalants: Basic findings from the National Comorbidity Survey. *Experimental and Clinical Psychopharmacology, 2*, 224–268.

Barkley, R. A., Fischer, M., Edelbrock, C. S., & Smallish, L. (1990). Research criteria: I. An 8 year old prospective study. *Journal of the American Academy of Child and Adolescent Psychiatry, 29*, 546–557.

Bauman, K. E., & Ennett, S. (1994). Peer influence on adolescent drug use. *American Psychologist, 49*, 820–822.

Baumrind, D. (1983). Familial antecedents of adolescent drug use: A developmental perspective. In C. L. Jones & R. J. Battjes (Eds.), *Etiology of drug abuse: Implications and prevention, 56*(13–44). Washington, DC: National Institute on Drug Abuse.

Bennett, E. M., & Kempfer, K. J. (1994). Is abuse during childhood a risk factor for developing substance abuse problems as an adult? *Journal of Developmental and Behavioral Pediatrics, 15*, 426–429.

Berrettini, W., & Persico, A. (1996). Dopamine D2 receptor gene polymorphisms and vulnerability to substance abuse. *Biological Psychiatry, 40*, 144–147.

Brent, D. A., Perper, J. A., & Allman, C. J. (1987). Alcohol, firearms, and suicide among youth. *Journal of the American Medical Association, 257*, 3369–3372.

Brent, D. A., Perper, J. A., Moritz, G., Allman, C., Friend, A., Roth, C., et al. (1993). Psychiatric risk factors for adolescent suicide: A case control study. *Journal of the American Academy of Child and Adolescent Psychiatry, 32*, 521–529.

Brook, J. S., Brook, D., DeLa Rosa, M. M., Duque, L., Rodriquez, E., Montoya, I., et al. (1998). Pathways to marijuana use among adolescents: Cultural, ecological, family, peer, and personality influences. *Journal of the American Academy of Child and Adolescent Psychiatry, 37*, 759–766.

Brook, J. S., Linkoff, I. F., & Whiteman, M. (1980). Initiation into adolescent marijuana use. *Journal of General Psychiatry, 137*, 133–142.

Brookoff, D., O'Brien, K., Cook, C. S., Thompson, T. D., & Williams, C. (1997). Characteristics of participants in domestic violence. *Journal of the American Medical Association, 277*, 1369–1373.

Brown, S. A. (1993). Recovery patterns in adolescent substance abusers. In J. S. Baer, G. A. Marlatt, & R. J. McMahon (Eds.), *Addictive behavior across the life-span: Prevention, treatment, and policy issues* (pp. 61–163). Beverly Hills, CA: Sage.

Bukstein, O. G., Brent, D. A., Perpe, J. A., Moritz, G., Baugher, M., Schweers, J., et al. (1993). Risk factors for completed suicide among adolescents with a lifetime history of substance abuse: A case control study. *Acta Psychiatrica Scandinavica, 88*, 403–408.

Cadoret, R. J., Troughton, E., O'Gorman, T. W., & Heywood, E. (1986). An adoption study of genetic and environmental factors in drug use. *Archives of General Psychiatry, 43*, 1131–1136.

Caspi, A., Henry, B., McGee, R. O., Moffitt, T. E., & Silva, P. A. (1995). Temperamental origins of child and adolescent behavior problems: From age three to age fifteen. *Child Development, 66*, 55–68.

Chilcoat, H. D., & Anthony, J. C. (1996). Impact of parent monitoring on initiation of drug use through later childhood. *Journal of the American Academy of Child and Adolescent Psychiatry, 35*, 91–100.

Cicchetti, D., & Cohen, D. J. (1995). *Developmental psychopathology: Vol. 1. Theory and methods.* New York: Wiley.

Cicchetti, D., & Rogosch, F. A. (1999). Psychopathology as a risk for adolescent substance use disorders: A developmental psychopathology paper. *Journal of Clinical Child Psychology, 28*, 355–365.

Clark, D. B., Bukstein, O. G., Smith, M. G., Kaczynski, N. A., Mezzich, A. C., & Donovan, J. E. (1995). Identifying anxiety disorders in adolescents, hospitalized for alcohol abuse or dependence. *Psychiatric Services, 46*, 618–620.

Clark, D. B., Kirisci, L., & Tarter, R. E. (1998). Adolescent versus adult onset and the development of substance use disorders in males. *Drug and Alcohol Dependence, 49*, 115–121.

Clark, D. B., Pollock, N., Bukstein, O. G., Mezzich, A. C., Bromberger, J. T., & Donovan, J. E. (1997). Gender and comorbid psychopathology in adolescents with alcohol dependence. *Journal of the American Academy of Child and Adolescent Psychiatry, 36*, 1195–1203.

Clayton, R. R., & Ritter, C. (1985). The epidemiology of alcohol and drug abuse among adolescents. *Advances in Alcohol and Substance Abuse, 4,* 69–97.

Cloninger, C. R., Bohman, M. C., Sigvardisson, S., & von Knorring, A. L. (1985). Psychopathology in adopted out children of alcoholics: The Stockholm Adoption Study. *Recent Developments in Alcoholism, 3,* 37–50.

Colder, C., & Chassin, L. (1997). Affectivity and impulsivity: Temperamental risk for adolescent alcohol involvement. *Psychology of Addictive Behaviors, 11,* 83–87.

Comeau, N., Stewart, S. H., & Loba, P. (2001). The relations of trait anxiety, anxiety sensitivity, and sensation seeking to adolescents' motivations for alcohol, cigarette, and marijuana use. *Addictive Behaviors, 26,* 803–825.

Comings, D. E., Comings, B. G., Muhleman, D., Dietz, G., Shahbahrami, B., Tast, D., et al. (1991). The dopamine D2 receptor locus as a modifying gene in neuropsychiatric disorders. *Journal of the American Medical Association, 266,* 1793–1800.

Comings, D. E., Muhleman, D., & Gysin, R. (1996). Dopamine receptor (DRD2) gene and susceptibility to posttraumatic stress disorder: A study and replication. *Biological Psychiatry, 40,* 368–372.

Compton, P. A., Anglin, M. D., Khalsa-Denison, E., & Paredes, A. (1996). The D2 dopamine receptor gene, addiction, and personality: Clinical correlates in cocaine abusers. *Biological Psychiatry, 39,* 302–304.

Costello, E. J., Erkanli, A., & Federman, E. (1999). Development of psychiatric comorbidity with substance abuse in adolescents: Effect of timing and sex. *Journal of Clinical Child Psychology, 28,* 298–311.

Deren, S. (1986). Children of substance abusers: A review of the literature. *Journal of Substance Abuse Treatment, 3,* 7–94.

DeWit, D. J., Adlaf, E. M., Offord, D. R., & Ogborne, A. C. (2000). Age of first alcohol use: A risk factor for the development of alcohol disorders. *American Journal of Psychiatry, 157,* M745–M750.

Deykin, E. Y., & Baka, S. L. (1994). Suicidal ideation and attempts among chemically dependent adolescents. *American Journal of Public Health 84,* 634–639.

Deykin, E. Y., Buka, S., & Zeena, T. (1992). Depressive illness among chemically dependent adolescents. *American Journal of Psychiatry, 149,* 1341–1347.

Disney, E. R., Elkins, I. J., McGue, M., & Iacono, W. G. (1997). Effects of ADHD, conduct disorder, and gender on substance abuse in adolescents. *American Journal of Psychobiology, 156,* 1515–1521.

Drago, J., Gerfen, C. R., Westphal, H., & Steiner, H. (1996). D1 dopamine receptor-deficient mouse: Cocaine-induced regulation of immediate-early gene and substance P expression in the striatum. *Neuroscience, 74,* 813–823.

Duncan, T. E., Biglan, A., & Ary, D. V. (1998). Contributions of the social context to the development of adolescent substance use: A multivariate latent growth modeling approach. *Drug and Alcohol Dependence, 50,* 57–71.

Ellickson, P. L., Collins, R. I., & Bell, R. M. (1999). Adolescent use of illicit drugs other than marijuana: How important is social bonding and for which ethnic groups? *Substance Use and Misuse, 34,* 317–346.

Ennulat, D. J., Babb, S. M., & Cohen, B. M. (1994). Persistent reduction of immediate early gene mRNA in rat forebrain following single or multiple doses of cocaine. *Brain Research, 26,* 106–112.

Essau, C. A., Conradt, J., & Peterman, F. (1999). Frequency and co-morbidity of social fears in adolescents. *Behavior Research and Therapy, 37,* 831–843.

Fawzy, F., Coombs, R., & Gerber, B. (1983). Generational continuity in the use of substances: The impact of parental substance use on adolescent substance use. *Addictive Behaviors, 8,* 109–114.

Fergusson, D. M. (1998). The stability and change in externalizing behaviours. *European Archives of Psychiatry and Clinical Neuroscience, 248,* 4–13.

Fergusson, D. M., & Horwood, I. J. (1997). Early onset cannabis use and psychosocial adjustment in young adults. *Addiction, 92,* 279–296.

Fergusson, D. M., & Horwood, I. J. (2000). Does cannabis use encourage other forms of illicit drug use? *Addiction, 95,* 505–520.

Fergusson, D. M., Horwood, I. J., & Swain-Campbell, N. (2002). Cannabis use and psychosocial adjustment in adolescence and young adulthood. *Addiction, 97,* 1123–1135.

Fergusson, D. M., Lynskey, M., & Horwood, I. J. (1996). The short-term consequences of early cannabis use. *Journal of Abnormal Psychology, 24,* 499–512.

Fleming, J. E., & Offord, D. R. (1990). Epidemiology of childhood depressive disorders. *Journal of the American Academy Child Adolescent Psychiatry, 29,* 571–580.

Friedman, A. S., & Glassman, K. (2000). Family risk factors versus peer risk factors for drug abuse: A longitudinal study of an African American urban community sample. *Journal of Substance Abuse Treatment, 18,* 267–275.

Friedman, A. S., & Utada, A. (1992). The family environments of adolescent drug abusers. *Family Dynamics of Addiction Quarterly, 2,* 32–45.

Gelernter, J., Kranzler, H. R., Satel, S. L., & Rao, P. A. (1994). Genetic association between dopamine transporter protein alleles and cocaine-induced paranoia. *Neuropsychopharmacology, 11*(3), 195–200.

George, S., Cheng, R., Nguyen, T., Israel, Y., & O'Dowd, B. (1993). Polymorphisms of the D4 dopamine receptor alleles in chronic alcoholism. *Biochemical and Biophysical Research Communications, 196,* 1107–1114.

Gill, M., Daly, G., Heron, S., Hawi, Z., & Fitzgerald, M. (1997). Confirmation of association between attention deficit hyperactivity disorder and a dopamine transporter polymorphism. *Molecular Psychiatry, 2*(4), 311–313.

Goldman, D., Urbanek, M., Guenther, D., Robin, R., & Long, J. C. (1997). Linkage and association of a functional DRD2 variant and DRD2 markers to alcoholism, substance abuse, and Schizophrenia in southwestern American Indians. *American Journal of Medical Genetics, 74,* 386–394.

Goodwin, D. W., Schlusinger, F., Moller, W., Hermansen, L., Winokur, G., & Guze, S. (1974). Drinking problems in adopted and non-adopted sons of alcoholics. *Archives of General Psychiatry, 31,* 164–169.

Greenbaum, P. E., Prange, M. E., Friedman, R. M., & Silver, S. E. (1991). Substance abuse prevalence and comorbidity with other psychiatric disorders among adolescents with severe emotional disturbances. *Journal of the American Academy of Child and Adolescent Psychiatry, 30,* 575–583.

Grella, C., Hser, Y., Joshi, V., & Rounds-Bryant, J. (2001). Drug treatment outcomes for adolescents with comorbid mental and substance use disorders. *Journal of Nervous and Mental Diseases, 189,* 384–392.

Grillo, C., Becker, D., Fehon, D., Walker, M. L., Edell, W. S., & McGlashan, T. H. (1996). Coexisting conduct and substance use disorders in adolescent patients. *American Journal of Psychiatry, 153,* 914–920.

Hasin, P. S., Grant, B. F., & Endicott, J. (1990). The natural history of alcohol abuse: Implications for definitions of alcohol use disorders. *American Journal of Psychiatry, 147,* 1537–1541.

Hawkins, J. D., Catalano, R. F., & Miller, J. Y. (1992). Risk and protective factors for alcohol and other drug problems in adolescence and early adulthood: Implications for substance abuse prevention. *Psychological Bulletin, 112,* 64–105.

Haynes, N. M., Troutman, M. R., & Nwachuku, U. (1998). School factors in substance abuse prevention among young male African Americans. *Journal of Educational and Psychological Consultation, 9,* 143–154.

Hicks, R. D., Bemis, B. G., Bemis, B. W., & Imai, W. K. A. M. (1993). Psychiatric, developmental, and adolescent medicine issues in adolescent substance use and abuse. *Adolescent Medicine, 4,* 453–468.

Higgins, S. T., Heil, S. H., & Lussier, J. P. (2004). Clinical implications of reinforcement as a determinant of substance use disorders. *Annual Review of Psychology, 55,* 431–461.

Hovens, J. G., Cantwell, D. P., & Kiriakos, R. (1994). Psychiatric comorbidity in hospitalized adolescent substance abusers. *Journal of the American Academy of Child and Adolescent Psychiatry, 33,* 476–483.

Ingram, R. E., & Price, J. M. (2001). *Vulnerability to psychopathology: Risk across the lifespan.* New York: Guilford Press.

Jackson, C., Henriksen, L., Dickinson, D., Messer, L., & Robertson, S. B. (1998). A longitudinal study predicting patterns of cigarette smoking in late childhood. *Health Education Behavior, 25,* 436–477.

Jainchill, N., De Leon, G., & Yagelka, J. (1997). Ethnic differences in psychiatric disorders among adolescent substance abusers in treatment. *Journal of Psychopathology and Behavioral Assessment, 19,* 133–148.

Jaycox, L. H., Morral, A. R., & Juvonen, J. (2003). Mental health and medical problems and service use among adolescent substance users. *Journal of the American Academy of Child and Adolescent Psychiatry, 42,* 701–709.

Jessor, R., Van Den Bos, J., Vanderryn, J., Costa, F. M., & Turbin, M. S. (1995). Protective factors in adolescent problem behavior: Moderator effects and developmental change. *Developmental Psychology, 31,* 923–933.

Johnson, J. L., & Leff, M. (1999). Children of substance abusers: Overview of research findings. *Pediatrics, 103,* 1085–1099.

Johnson, P. B., & Richter, L. (2002). The relationship between smoking, drinking, and adolescents' self-perceived health and frequency of hospitalization: Analyses from the 1997 National Household Survey on Drug Abuse. *Journal of Adolescent Health, 30*(3), 175–183.

Johnston, L. D., O'Malley, P. M., & Bachman, J. G. (2001). *Monitoring the Future national results on adolescent drug use: Overview of key findings, 2000.* Bethesda, MD: National Institute on Drug Abuse.

Johnston, L. D., O'Malley, P. M., & Bachman, J. G. (2003). *Monitoring the Future national results on adolescent drug use: Overview of key findings, 2002.* Bethesda, MD: National Institute on Drug Abuse.

Kaminer, Y. (1992). Clinical implications of the relationship between ADHD and psychoactive substance use disorders. *American Journal of Addictions, 1,* 257–264.

Kaminer, Y., & Burleson, J. (1999). Psychotherapies for adolescent substance abusers: 15 month follow-up of a pilot study. *American Journal of Addictions, 8,* 114–119.

Kandel, D. B., Johnson, J., Bird, H., Weissman, M. M., Goodman, S. H., Lahey, B. B., et al. (1999). Psychiatric co-morbidity among adolescents with substance use disorders: Findings from the MECA study. *Journal of the American Academy of Child and Adolescent Psychiatry, 138,* 693–699.

Kendler, K. S., Karkowski, I. M., Neale, M. C., & Prescott, C. A. (2000). Illicit psychoactive substance use, heavy use, abuse and dependence in a U.S. population-based sample of male twins. *Archives of General Psychiatry, 57,* 261–269.

Kendler, K. S., Neale, M. C., Thornton, I. M., Aggen, S. H., Gilman, S. E., & Kessler, R. C. (2002). Cannabis use in a U.S. national sample of twin and sibling pairs. *Psychological Medicine, 32,* 551–554.

Kendler, K. S., & Prescott, C. A. (1998a). Genetic and environmental risk factors for cannabis use, abuse, dependence: A study of female twins. *American Journal of Psychiatry, 155,* 1016–1022.

Kendler, K. S., & Prescott, C. A. (1998b). Cocaine use, abuse and dependence in a population-based sample of female twins. *British Journal of Psychiatry, 173,* 345–350.

King, C., Ghaziuddin, N., McGovern, L., Brand, E., Hill, E., & Naylor, M. (1996). Predictors of comorbid alcohol and substance abuse. *Journal of the American Academy of Child and Adolescent Psychiatry, 35,* 743–751.

King, C., Naylor, M., Hill, E., Shaina, B., & Gredena, J. F. (1993). Dysthymia characteristics of heavy alcohol use in depressed adolescents. *Biological Psychiatry, 33,* 210–212.

Kosofsky, B. E., & Hyman, S. E. (1993). The ontogeny of immediate early gene response to cocaine: A molecular analysis of the effects of cocaine on developing rat brain. *NIDA Research Monographs, 125,* 161–171.

Krohn, M., Lizotte, A., & Perez, C. (1997). The interrelationship between substance use and precocious transitions to adult statuses. *Journal of Health and Social Behavior, 38,* 87–103.

Kubicka, L., Matejcek, Z., Dytrych, Z., & Roth, Z. (2001). IQ and personality traits assessed in childhood as predictors of drinking and smoking behavior in middle-aged adults: A 24-year follow up study. *Addiction, 96,* 1615–1628.

Kushner, M. G., Sher, K. J., & Erickson, D. J. (1999). Prospective analysis of the relation between DSM-III anxiety disorders and alcohol use disorders. *American Journal of Psychiatry, 156,* 723–732.

Lewinsohn, P. M., Gotlib, I. H., & Seeley, J. R. (1995). Specificity of psychosocial risk factors for depression and substance abuse in older adolescents. *Journal of the American Academy of Child and Adolescent Psychiatry, 34,* 1221–1229.

Lewinsohn, P. M., Hops, H., Roberts, R. E., Seeley, J. R., & Andrews, J. A. (1993). Adolescent psychopathology. *Journal of Abnormal Psychology, 102,* 133–144.

Luthar, S., Merikangas, K. R., & Rounsaville, B. J. (1993). Parental psychopathology and disorders in offspring. *Journal of Nervous and Mental Disorders, 181,* 351–357.

Luthar, S. S., & Zigler, E. (1991). Vulnerability and competence: A view of research on resilience in childhood. *American Journal of Orthopsychiatry, 61,* 6–22.

Lynskey, M., Coffey, C., Degenhardt, L., Carlin, J. B., & Patton, G. (2003). A longitudinal study of the effects of adolescent cannabis use on high school completion. *Addiction, 98,* 685–692.

Lynskey, M., & Hall, W. (2000). The effects of adolescent cannabis use on educational attainment: A review. *Addiction, 95,* 1621–1630.

Lynskey, M., Heath, A. C., Bucholz, K., Slutske, W. S., Madden, P. A. F., Nelson, E. C., et al. (2003). Escalation of drug use in early onset cannabis users vs. co-twin controls. *Journal of the American Medical Association, 289,* 427–433.

Lynskey, M., Heath, A. C., Nelson, E. C., Bucholz, K., Madden, P. A. F., Slutske, W. S., et al. (2002). Genetic and environmental contributions to cannabis dependence in a national twin sample. *Psychological Medicine, 32,* 195–207.

Masse, L. C., & Tremblay, R. E. (1997). Behavior of boys in kindergarten and the onset of substance use during adolescence. *Archives of General Psychiatry, 54,* 62–68.

McGue, M., Elkins, I., & Iacono, W. G. (2000). Genetic and environmental influences on adolescent substance use and abuse. *American Journal of Medical Genetics, 96,* 671–677.

Merikangas, K., Mehta, R. L., Molnar, B. E., Walters, E. E., Swendsen, J. D., Auilar-Gaziola, S., et al. (1998). Comorbidity of substance use disorders with mood and anxiety disorders: Results of international consortium in psychiatric epidemiology. *Addictive Behaviors, 23,* 893–907.

Mezzich, A. C., Moss, H., Tarter, R. E., Wolfenstein, M., Hsieh, Y., & Mauss, R. (1994). Gender differences in the pattern and progression of substance use in conduct disordered adolescents. *American Journal on Addictions, 3,* 289–295.

Mirin, S. M., Weiss, R. D., Griffin, M. L., & Michael, J. L. (1991). Psychopathology in drug abusers and their families. *Comprehensive Psychiatry, 32,* 36–51.

Molina, B. S. B., Chassin, L., & Curran, P. J. (1994). A comparison of mechanisms underlying substance use for early adolescent children of alcoholics and controls. *Journal of the Study of Alcoholism, 55,* 269–275.

Moratella, R., Xu, M., Tonegawa, S., & Graybiel, A. M. (1996). Cellular responses to psychomotor stimulant and neuroleptic drugs are abnormal in mice lacking the D1 receptor. *Proceedings of the National Academy of Sciences, 93,* 14928–14933.

Morral, A. R., McCaffrey, D. F., & Paddock, S. M. (2002). Reassessing the marijuana gateway effect. *Addiction, 97,* 1493–1504.

Myers, M. G., Stewart, D. G., & Brown, S. A. (1998). Progression of conduct disorder to antisocial personality disorder following treatment for adolescent substance abuse. *American Journal of Psychiatry, 155,* 479–485.

Nestler, E. J., Bergson, C. M., Gultart, X., & Hope, B. T. (1993). Regulation of neural gene expression in opiate and cocaine addiction. *NIDA Research Monograph, 125,* 92–116.

Nestler, E. J., Gao, X. M., & Tamminga, C. A. (1997). Molecular biology: Pt. V. Immediate early genes. *American Journal of Psychiatry, 15,* 312.

Nestler, E. J., Hope, B. T., & Widnell, K. L. (1993). Drug addiction: A model for the molecular basis of neural plasticity. *Neuron, 11,* 995–1006.

Newcomb, M. D. (1995). Identifying high-risk youth: Prevalence and patterns of adolescent drug abuse. In E. Rahdert & D. Czechowicz (Eds.), *Adolescent drug abuse: Clinical assessment and therapeutic interventions* (Vol. 156, pp. 7–38). Washington, DC: NIDA Research Monographs.

Newcomb, M. D. (1997). Psychosocial predictors and consequences of drug use: A developmental perspective within a prospective study. *Journal of Addictive Diseases, 16,* 51–89.

Newcomb, M. D., & Bentler, E. M. (1988a). *Consequences of teenage drug use: Impact on the lives of young adults.* Beverly Hills, CA: Sage.

Newcomb, M. D., & Bentler, E. M. (1988b). Impact of adolescent drug use and social support on problems of young adults: A longitudinal study. *Journal of Abnormal Psychology, 97,* 64–75.

Noble, E. P. (1993). The D2 dopamine receptor gene: A review of association studies in alcoholism. *Behavioral Genetics, 23,* 119–129.

Noble, E. P., Blum, K., Khalsa, M. E., Ritchie, T., Montgomery, A., Wood, R. C., et al. (1993). Allelic association of the D2 dopamine receptor gene with cocaine dependence. *Drug and Alcohol Dependence, 33,* 271–285.

O'Donnell, D. A., Schwab-Stone, M. E., & Muyeed, A. Z. (2002). Multidimensional resilience in urban children exposed to community violence. *Child Development, 73,* 1265–1282.

Oxford, M. L., Harachi, T. W., Catalano, R. F., & Abbott, R. D. (2000). Preadolescent predictors of substance initiation: A test of both the direct and mediated effect of family social control factors on deviant peer associations and substance initiation. *American Journal of Drug and Alcohol Abuse, 27,* 599–616.

Pandina, R. (1996). Risk and protective factors in adolescent drug use: Putting them to work for prevention. *National Conference on Abuse Prevention Research: Presentations, Papers, and Recommendations,*

Plenary Session #2 (Publication No. 98-4293). Bethesda, Maryland, National Institute on Drug Abuse.

Pandina, R. J., Johnson, V., & Labouvie, E. W. (1992). Affectivity: A central mechanism in the development of drug dependence. In M. Glantz & R. Pickens (Eds.), *Vulnerability to drug abuse* (pp. 179–209). Washington, DC: American Psychological Association.

Plashne, M., & Gann, A. F. (1990). Activators and targets. *Nature, 346,* 329–331.

Plomin, R., & Craig, I. (1997). Human behavioural genetics of cognitive abilities and disabilities. *Bioessays, 19,* 1117–1124.

Price, J. E., & Lento, J. (2001). The nature of child and adolescent vulnerability: History and definitions. In R. E. Ingram & J. E. Price (Eds.), *Vulnerability to psychopathology: Risk across the lifespan* (pp. 20–38). New York: Guilford Press.

Pulkkimen, L., & Pirkanen, T. (1994). A prospective study of the precursors to problem drinking in young adulthood. *Journal of Studies on Alcohol, 55,* 578–587.

Randall, J., Henggeler, S. W., Pickrel, S. G., & Brondino, M. J. (1999). Psychiatric comorbidity and the 16 month trajectory of substance abusing and substance dependent juvenile offenders. *Journal of the American Academy of Child and Adolescent Psychiatry, 38,* 1118–1124.

Rao, U., Ryan, N., Dahl, D. E., Birmaher, B., Rao, R., Williamson, D. E., et al. (1999). Factors associated with the development of substance use disorders in depressed adolescents. *Journal of the American Academy of Child and Adolescent Psychiatry, 38,* 1109–1117.

Reilly, P. M. (1979). Family factors in the etiology and treatment of youthful drug abuse. *Family Therapy, 11,* 149–171.

Riggs, P. D., Baker, S., Mikulich, S. K., Young, S. E., & Crowley, T. J. (1995). Depression in substance-dependent delinquents. *Journal of the American Academy of Child and Adolescent Psychiatry, 34,* 764–771.

Riggs, P. D. G., & Whitmore, E. A. (1999). Substance use disorders and disruptive behavior disorders. In R. L. Hendren (Ed.), *Disruptive behavior disorders in children and adolescents: Review of psychiatry series* (pp. 133–173). Washington, DC: American Psychiatric Association.

Robertson, G. S., Vincent, S. R., & Fibiger, H. C. (1992). D1 and D2 dopamine receptors differentially regulate c-Fos expression in striatonigral and striatopallidal neurons. *Neuroscience, 49,* 285–296.

Rounsaville, B. J., Kosten, T. R., Weissman, M. M., Prusoff, B. A., Pauls, D., Foley, S., et al. (1991). Psychiatric disorders in the relatives of probands with opiate addicts. *Archives of General Psychiatry, 48,* 33–42.

Rowe, D. C., Stever, C., Gard, J. M., Cleveland, H. H., Sanders, M. L., Abramowitz, A., et al. (1998). The relation of the dopamine transporter gene (DAT1) to symptoms of internalizing disorders in children. *Behavior Genetics, 28,* 215–225.

Rutter, M. (1987). Psychosocial resilience and protective mechanisms. *American Journal of Orthopsychiatry, 57,* 316–331.

Scheier, L. M., Botvin, C. J., Diaz, T., & Griffin, K. W. (1999). Social skills, competence, and drug refusal efficacy as predictors of adolescent alcohol use. *Journal of Drug Education, 29,* 251–278.

Schukit, M. A. (1999). A 10 year study of sons of alcoholics: Preliminary results. *Alcohol* (Suppl. 1), 147–149.

Shafii, M., Steltz-Linarsky, J., Derrick, A. M., Beckner, C., & Whittinghill, J. R. (1988). Comorbidity of mental disorders in the post mortem diagnosis of completed suicides in children and adolescents. *Journal of Affective Disorders, 15,* 227–233.

Sheng, M., & Greenberg, M. E. (1990). The regulation and function of c-Fos and other immediate early genes in the nervous system. *Neuron, 4,* 477–485.

Smart, R. G., & Fejer, D. (1972). Drug use among adolescents and their parents: Closing the generation gap in mood modification. *Journal of Abnormal Child Psychology, 79,* 153–160.

Smith, S. S., O'Hara, B. F., Persico, A. M., Gorelick, D. A., Newlin, D. B., Vlahov, D., et al. (1992). Genetic vulnerability to drug abuse: The D2 dopamine receptor Taq I B1 restriction length polymorphism appears more frequently in polysubstance abusers. *Archives of General Psychiatry, 49,* 723–727.

Soderstrom, C. A., & Dearing-Stuck, B. A. (1993). Substance misuse and trauma: Clinical issues and injury prevention. *Adolescent Medicine, 4,* 423–438.

Solowij, N. (1999). Long-term effects of cannabis on the central nervous system. In H. Kalant, W. Corrigall, & W. Hall (Eds.), *The health effects of cannabis* (pp. 195–266). Toronto: Centre for Addiction and Mental Health.

Stacy, A. W., & Newcomb, M. D. (1999). Adolescent drug use and adult drug problems in women: Direct, interactive, and mediational effects. *Experimental and Clinical Psychopharmacology, 7,* 160–173.

Stacy, A. W., Newcomb, M. D., & Bentler, P. M. (1993). Cognitive motivations and sensation seeking as long-term predictors of drinking problems. *Journal of Social and Clinical Psychology, 12,* 1–24.

Steiner, H., & Gerfen, C. R. (1993). Cocaine-induced c-Fos messenger RNA is inversely related to dynorphin expression in striatum. *Journal of Neuroscience, 13,* 5066–5081.

Steiner, H., & Gerfen, C. R. (1995). Dynorphin opioid inhibition of cocaine-induced, D1 dopamine receptor-mediated immediate-early gene expression in the striatum. *Journal of Comparative Neurology, 353,* 200–212.

Swan, N. (1995). Early childhood behavior and temperament predict later substance abuse. *NIDA Notes, 10,* 1–6.

Tanner, J., Davies, S., & O'Grady, B. (1999). Whatever happened to yesterday's rebels? Longitudinal effects of youth delinquency on education and employment. *Social Problems, 46,* 250–274.

Thompson, V. K. (2003). A community reinforcement approach to addiction treatment. *International Journal of Social Psychiatry, 49,* 312.

True, W. R., Heath, A. C., Scherrer, J. F., Waterman, B., Goldberg, J., Lin, N., et al. (1997). Genetic and environmental contributions to smoking. *Addiction, 92,* 1277–1287.

True, W. R., Xian, H., Scherrer, J. F., Madden, P. A. F., Bucholz, K., Heath, A. C., et al. (1999). Common genetic vulnerability for nicotine and alcohol dependence in men. *Archives of General Psychiatry, 56,* 655–661.

Tsuang, M. T., Lyons, M. J., Meyer, J. M., Doyle, T., Eisen, S. A., Goldberg, J., et al. (1998). Co-occurence of abuse of different drugs in men: The role of drug-specific and shared vulnerabilities. *Archives of General Psychiatry, 55,* 967–972.

Uhl, G. R., Persisco, A. M., & Smith, S. S. (1992). Current excitement with D2 dopamine receptor gene alleles in substance abuse. *Archives of General Psychiatry, 49,* 157–160.

U.S. Department of Health and Human Services. (1999). *1998 National Household Survey on Drug Abuse.* Washington, DC: Author.

Van Den Bres, M. B. M., Johnson, E. O., Neale, M. C., & Pickens, R. W. (1998). Genetic and environmental influences on drug use and abuse/dependence in male and female twins. *Drug and Alcohol Dependence, 52,* 231–241.

Wagner, F. A., & Anthony, J. C. (2001). Into the world of illegal drug use: Exposure opportunity and other mechanisms linking the use of alcohol, tobacco, marijuana, and cocaine. *American Journal of Epidemiology, 155*(10), 918–925.

Wagner, F. A., & Anthony, J. C. (2002). Into the world of illegal drug use: Exposure opportunity and other mechanisms linking the use of alcohol, tobacco, marijuana, and cocaine. *American Journal of Epidemiology, 15,* 918–925.

Wallace, J. M., Bachman, J. G., O'Malley, P. M., Schulenberg, J. E., Cooper, S. M., & Johnston, L. D. (2003). Gender and ethnic differences in smoking, drinking, and illicit drug use among American 8th, 10th, and 12th grade students, 1976–2000. *Addiction, 98*(2), 225–234.

Wallace, J. M., Jr., & Muroff, J. R. (2002). Preventing substance abuse among African American children and youth: Race differences in risk factor exposure and vulnerability. *Journal of Primary Prevention, 22,* 235–261.

Whitmore, E. A., Mikulich, S. K., Thompson, L. L., Riggs, P. D., Aarons, G. A., Crowley, T. J. et al. (1997). Influences on adolescent substance dependence, conduct disorders, depression, attention deficit hyperactivity disorder, and gender. *Drug and Alcohol Dependence, 47,* 87–97.

Wilcox, H. C., Wagner, F. A., & Anthony, J. C. (2002). Exposure opportunity as a mechanism linking youth marijuana use to hallucinogen use. *Drug and Alcohol Dependence, 66*(2), 127–135.

Wilens, T. E., Biederman, J., Millstein, R. B., Wozniak, J., Hahesy, A. L., & Spencer, T. J. (1999). Risk for substance use disorders in youth with child and adolescent onset bipolar disorder. *Journal of the American Academy of Child and Adolescent Psychiatry, 38,* 680–685.

Wilens, T. E., Biederman, J., & Spencer, T. (1996). Attention deficit hyperactivity disorder and psychoactive substance use disorders. *Child and Adolescent Clinics of North America, 5,* 73–91.

Wills, T. A., DuHummel, K., & Vaccaro, D. (1995). Activity and mood temperament as predictors of adolescent substance use. *Journal of Personality and Social Psychology, 68,* 901–916.

Wills, T. A., Gibbons, F. X., Gerard, M., & Brody, G. H. A. (2000). Protection and vulnerability processes relevant for early onset of substance abuse: A test among African American children. *Health Psychology, 19,* 253–263.

Wills, T. A., Sandy, J. M., Shinar, O., & Yaeger, A. (1999). Contributions of positive and negative affect to adolescent substance use: Test of a bidimensional model in a longitudinal study. *Psychology of Addictive Behaviors, 13,* 327–338.

Wills, T. A., Sandy, J. M., Yaeger, A. M., Cleary, S. D., & Shinar, O. (2001). Coping dimensions, life stress, and adolescent substance use: A latent growth analysis. *Journal of Abnormal Psychology, 110,* 309–323.

Wills, T. A., Vaccaro, D., & McNamara, G. (1992). The role of life events, family support, and competence in adolescent substance use: A test of vulnerability and protective factors. *American Journal of Community Psychology, 20,* 349–374.

Yamaguchi, K., & Kandel, D. B. (1984). Patterns of drug involvement from adolescence to young adulthood: III. Predictors of progress. *American Journal of Public Health, 74,* 673–681.

CHAPTER 17

Alcohol Use and the Alcohol Use Disorders: A Developmental-Biopsychosocial Systems Formulation Covering the Life Course

ROBERT A. ZUCKER

ALCOHOLISM AND THE ALCOHOL USE DISORDERS

In 1980, with the advent of the third edition of the *Diagnostic and Statistical Manual of Mental Disorders* (*DSM-III;* American Psychiatric Association, 1980), Alcohol Use Disorder (AUD) replaced the broader umbrella of alcoholism by distinguishing between recurring alcohol use concomitant with problems but lacking tolerance, dependence, and compulsive alcohol-seeking behavior (alcohol abuse) and recurring use with those three characteristics present (dependence). *DSM-IV* (American Psychiatric As-

sociation, 1994) continues that differentiation. I use the term AUD when I refer to the umbrella of both, and the differentiated terminology when issues relating to distinguishing features need to be addressed.

Preparation of this chapter was supported by grants from the National Institute on Alcohol Abuse and Alcoholism (R37 AA07065, R01 AA12217) and the National Institute on Drug Abuse (R01 DA15398 and U10 DA13710). I am also indebted to Stephanie Herzberg, Ru Knoedler, and Lisa McLaughlin for their considerable help in putting this chapter together.

HISTORICAL INTRODUCTION AND ISSUES
FOR THE FIELD

Evidence that alcoholism runs in families has been present in the literature for at least 200 years (Hogarth, 1751; Rush, 1790), but the definitive evidence that this assortment had a genetic basis has only gradually accumulated in the past 30 years (Cotton, 1979; R. L. Hall, Hesselbrock, & Stabenau, 1983a, 1983b; McGue, 1994). The landmark study of the modern era that firmly established a heritable basis for the disorder was the adoption study of Donald Goodwin and colleagues (Goodwin, Schulsinger, Knop, Mednick, & Guze, 1973), conducted in Denmark and involving children born to alcoholic and nonalcoholic parents who were adopted away in early life. Although subjected to strong challenges from staunch environmentalists (Searles, 1988), the Goodwin study and others to follow have repeatedly demonstrated that the disorder has a substantial heritable component (McGue, 1994; McGue, Pickens, & Svikis, 1992; Prescott et al., 2005).

Studies in the early 1980s, most notably that of Cloninger, Bohman, and Sigvardsson (1981) but supported by work from several other groups (Babor et al., 1992; Hesselbrock et al., 1984; Zucker, 1987), were critical in taking the discourse to another level by providing strong evidence for heterogeneity of the phenotype, with different patterns of heritability, psychiatric comorbidity, course, and severity found among them. Although this author in 1987 summarized evidence for at least four subtypes, the preponderance or work in the field until quite recently has focused on only two (Babor, 1996; Windle, & Scheidt, 2004). Type I, also called *milieu limited* by Cloninger (1987), was observed in both men and women and involved adult onset, relatively moderate symptomatology, a low or absent psychiatric comorbidity, and a shorter course. Heritability was mild, and the evidence suggested that development of the alcoholic phenotype was heavily influenced by risk factors in the social environment. Type II or *male-limited* alcoholism was marked by early onset (late adolescence through early adulthood), strong heritability (typically marked by a dense family history, positive pedigree, and passed through the father), severe symptomatology, and aggressive/antisocial comorbidity. Later work (Kendler, Heath, Neale, Kessler, & Eaves, 1992; McGue, Pickens, & Svikis, 1992; Pickens et al., 1991) challenged the male-limited nature of this subtype and demonstrated significant, albeit lower heritability among women, but continued to show lower transmission of drinking problems and conduct problems.

Although this more recent work conceptually paid tribute to the importance of environmental factors in shaping the eventual diagnostic outcome, the dominant perspective was that "alcoholism is a genetic disorder" (National Institute on Alcohol Abuse and Alcoholism, 1985), and the conceptualization of the epigenesis of the disorder was a heavily bottom-up model. In fact, one prominent genetic researcher of that era made the assertion as recently as 5 years ago that environmental factors would only be important *after* the "alcoholism" genes were discovered, at which time the manner in which the social environment moderated their expression would be of scientific and preventive interest. Social and psychological influences were viewed as risk factors for drinking behavior and drinking problems in adolescence, but their potential impact on developmentally later clinical-level phenomena was discounted (cf. Fillmore et al., 1991; Zucker & Gomberg, 1986).

In contrast, the dominant scientific paradigm for understanding the emergence and maintenance of drinking behavior (not alcoholism) has been sociological and social psychological. Some 40 years ago, the sociologists George Maddox and Bevode McCall (1964) made the point that the use of alcohol is a social act within a larger society whose dominant perspective is that alcohol use is "good." In that broader context, alcohol use is perceived by teenagers as one of the markers of entry into adult status, along with the initiation of sexual activity and obtaining the right to drive an automobile (Maddox & McCall, 1964). Explanations of the emergence of drinking behavior have sustained this social psychological emphasis ever since and have targeted peer influences as major instigators of the initiation of drinking on the one hand, and the transition into problem drinking on the other. Peers serve as role models as well as proximal sources of availability in a society where purchase before age 21 (until 1988, age 18) is illegal. Such explanations are suitable to handle the normative behavior of the general population, where median age of first use is 14 and where median age of first drunkenness is 17 (Johnston, O'Malley, & Bachman, 2003).

However, a normative explanation is not sufficient to handle the substantial individual differences known to occur in adolescence, and it likewise can only poorly handle the fact that not all adolescents move from drinking to drunkenness or to other problem use and that others start substantially earlier than adolescence. Approximately 20% of the population are still nondrinkers in 12th grade (Johnston, O'Malley, & Bachman, 2001), whereas 9% have started drinking by 11 to 12 years of age and 5% have started by ages 9 to 10 (Johnston, O'Malley, Bachman, &

Schulenberg, 2004a). To account for this variability, in the late 1960s and 1970s, Richard and Shirley Jessor (and later with the collaboration of John Donovan) developed a social-psychological conceptual framework called "problem behavior theory" (Jessor & Jessor, 1977) that incorporated this normative explanation for drinking behavior into a general model of adolescent development. In problem behavior theory, the acquisition of alcohol and other drug taking behavior, as well as its progression into problem use, is viewed as part of a broader developmental process that encompasses (1) the *social context* of neighborhood, church and other formal religious groups, social class, and family; (2) the *personality system,* including values and expectancies about alcohol and other drugs, but also about the broader social environment; and (3) the *behavior system.* Within the personality system are included values and expectancies about independence versus achievement, about feeling integrated versus alienated from others, about one's sense of internal versus external control, and about the extent of acceptance and tolerance of deviant behavior.

An extensive series of studies by these investigators and others since have shown that the transition to involvement in the problem behaviors of adolescence was predictable by this theoretical model. These studies also demonstrated that each of these "problem behavior" variables, including the earlier use of alcohol, the use of marijuana and other illicit drugs, involvement in problem alcohol use, and earlier sexual experience, had substantial variance in common and could all be subsumed within a "general deviance" factor (Donovan, Jessor, & Costa, 1988; McGee & Newcomb, 1992; Sadava, 1985). The advantages of the theory are that it connected a number of behaviors previously regarded as unconnected, it predicted who would transition into use as well as progress to more problematic alcohol or other drug involvement, and it tied these behavioral adaptations into a much broader matrix of both personality structure and the social environment. The strength of the theory was also demonstrated by its ability to predict decline in these activities as development proceeded from adolescence into early adulthood (Jessor, Donovan, & Costa, 1991).

Although not heavily emphasized by the Jessors, problem behavior theory is of special interest because it focuses on a core transition from socialization by parents, including acceptance of their values and guidance, to reliance on peers as a source of both norms and social reinforcement. Insofar as the adolescent peer culture emphasizes independence from parents and experimentation with deviant behavior, this becomes the normative choice of that age stage. With the move into adult status, a different set of values involving greater conformity come to the fore, and

problem drinking behavior decreases (Bachman et al., 2002). This has been a highly useful and powerful theory that integrates individual behavior with influences from the proximal social environment. The theory also implicitly specifies that behavior is developmentally responsive to the changes in role demands imposed by the larger society that occur with the transitions from childhood to adolescence and from adolescence to adulthood. To that degree, it was a harbinger of life course theory, articulated by Glen Elder (1998) a generation later.

These two literatures, one on the etiology of adult AUD and the other on the development of drinking and adolescent problem drinking, remained largely independent of each other until the late 1980s and early 1990s, when a number of studies were initiated on high risk for alcoholism and other drug use beginning in childhood and early adolescence (Brook, Whiteman, Cohen, & Tanaka, 1992; Chassin, Barrera, Bech, & Kossak-Fuller, 1993; Cohen, Cohen, & Brook, 1993; Tarter et al., 1999, 2003; Zucker, 1987). These studies incorporated a developmental psychopathological framework (Cicchetti & Cohen, 1995) and utilized epigenetic models to varying degrees. Even with this progress, and with explicit, theory-driven reviews on the issue periodically appearing (Tarter et al., 1999; Zucker, Boyd, & Howard, 1994; Zucker, Fitzgerald, & Moses, 1995), the field is still far from embracing this framework. Although it is gratifying to see that the lead institute for alcohol research, the National Institute on Alcohol Abuse and Alcoholism (NIAAA), now accepts that alcoholism is both a genetic and a developmental disorder (Li, 2004), the progression into AUD is described as taking place between adolescence and adulthood, and the manifest evidence that the process begins much earlier is still not appreciated. I return to this issue later in the chapter.

The multilevel causal structure coming out of these different disciplinary frameworks is a large one to integrate, and most scientists and working groups lack the multidisciplinary training and collaborative network to allow this to happen. Thus, the development of the field has to a degree remained split between the biomedical and the psychosocial, as evident even in the Program Committee structure of the Research Society on Alcoholism, the primary international scientific society focusing on these problems. Despite the large nature of the integrative task, in our chapter in the first edition of these volumes (Zucker, Fitzgerald, et al., 1995) we advanced a developmental systems perspective (Ford & Lerner, 1992) on the etiology of AUD. We also made that case that this was the only framework sufficient to effectively handle the multilayered etiology of these disorders. The present chapter continues to utilize this formulation. The reader will judge whether this effort has been successful.

In the remainder of the chapter, we review the epidemiology of both Alcohol Use Disorder and earlier alcohol involvement. We then articulate the developmental systems framework that guides the content of this review. We follow this scaffolding in laying out the risk structure, course, and heterogeneity of the disorder. The chapter concludes with a section on future directions for the field.

EPIDEMIOLOGY

Table 17.1 provides the 12-month and lifetime prevalence rates (in percentages) for *DSM-III-R* alcohol abuse and dependence, based on the National Comorbidity Study (NCS) of U.S. population estimates for the noninstitutionalized civilian population between the ages of 15 and 54 years (Kessler et al., 1994). To give a larger perspective on the problem, rates for other drug abuse and dependence are also presented.

A number of points about these rate variations are of importance:

1. Alcohol abuse and dependence are the most common of the substance use disorders.
2. Among men, 1 in 3 adults have at some point in their lives met either abuse or dependence criteria.
3. Gender differences are significant and are of the order of 2:1 for abuse and 3:1 for dependence.
4. Abuse without dependence represents 40% of the life course problem and 26% of the current (12-month prevalence) problem. Or, to put these figures in a slightly different perspective, 40% of the lifetime national problem is of subclinical proportions but involves socially and personally significant misbehavior (e.g., compromised driving, risky sex, date rape, job absenteeism, neglect of household responsibilities). These data also indicate that the diagnostic burden of abuse in any year will be a smaller proportion of the AUD burden than it will be for the nation over time. This is so because the abuse diagnosis is less likely to recur than the dependence diagnosis, but it will ultimately involve more people.

5. In addition, because of gender differences in abuse versus dependence, abuse is a relatively greater problem among women, accounting for 30% of the 12-month total problem, but accounting for only 24% among men.
6. Other drug disorders are substantially less of an issue than alcohol abuse/dependence, with a ratio of 12-month alcohol to drug disorder of 2.7.
7. Other drug disorders are to a large degree superimposed on alcohol use disorders, given that only 14% of 12-month drug disorders occur without a concomitant alcohol diagnosis.
8. The visibility of other drug disorders is likely because the disorders are more dramatic, hence socially compelling, because they appear to be more of a threat to the social order (e.g., because of their links with crime, as well as out of the belief that they may be less responsive to treatment) and because the social costs involved in interdiction and treatment are proportionately much larger. The lay view, as well, is that the disorders occur in isolation, which heightens the differentiation between the types of drug involvement.

Related to these points but not shown in the table, AUD is the nation's most prevalent disorder, with 23.5% of the adult population reporting symptomatology that qualifies for an abuse or dependence diagnosis at some point in their

TABLE 17.1   Lifetime and 12-Month Prevalence of UM-CIDI/*DSM-III-R* Substance Use Disorders (Percentages)

Disorder	Total		Male		Female	
	Lifetime	12 Months	Lifetime	12 Months	Lifetime	12 Months
Alcohol abuse without dependence	9.4	2.5	12.5	3.4	6.4	1.6
Alcohol dependence	14.1	7.2	20.1	10.7	8.2	3.7
Alcohol abuse/dependence combined	23.5	9.7	32.5	14.1	14.6	5.3
Other drug abuse without dependence	4.4	0.8	5.4	1.3	3.5	0.3
Other drug dependence	7.5	2.8	9.2	3.8	5.9	1.9
Other drug abuse/dependence combined	11.9	3.6	14.6	5.1	9.4	2.1
Any substance abuse/dependence	26.6	11.3	35.4	16.1	17.9	6.6

Source: Data are from Kessler et al.'s (1994) National Comorbidity Study utilizing the Comprehensive International Diagnostic Interview (CIDI) and are weighted for noninstitutionalized U.S. population percentage estimates for persons 15 to 54 years of age.

TABLE 17.2   Grade of First Alcohol Use and Drunkenness as Retrospectively Reported by 10th-Graders (Percentage of U.S. Population)

	Grade	Approximate Age	Use	Cumulative User Population	First Time Drunk	Cumulative Drunk Population
Grade school	4	10	5.2	5.2	0.9	0.9
	5	11	3.3	8.5	0.9	1.8
	6	12	6.2	14.7	2.4	4.2
Middle school	7	13	10.6	25.3	5.2	9.4
	8	14	16.3	41.6	9.7	19.1
High school	9	15	17.7	59.3	15.7	34.8
	10	16	6.7	66	7.6	42.4

Source: From *Monitoring the Future National Survey Results on Drug Use, 1975–2003: Vol. I. Secondary school students* (NIH Pub. No. 04-5507, Table 6.2, p. 243), by L. D. Johnston, P. M. O'Malley, J. G. Bachman, and J. E. Schulenberg, 2004b, Bethesda, MD: National Institute on Drug Abuse.

lives (Kessler et al., 1994). Thus, the set of problems encompassed by this disorder is an extraordinarily large one.[1]

A major point of this chapter is that the adult disorder does not emerge full blown in adulthood, but rather develops over time in a process for which childhood precursors are identifiable. To home in on the early harbingers of this process, Table 17.2 presents national data on first alcohol use and drunkenness onset, the latter selected as an indicator of early problem use. Data are 10th-grader retrospective reports from the Monitoring the Future (MTF) study (Johnston, O'Malley, Bachman, & Schulenberg, 2004b). The 10th-graders' data are utilized rather than those from another age group because, as Johnston et al. note, younger informants are likely to more literally interpret questions about first use and overreport on "first drink" experience. Conversely, to use 12th-grade informants is to lengthen the time interval for retrospection and also to increasingly lose heavier-using respondents because of their greater likelihood for school dropout. These data indicate that alcohol use has already begun for 1 out of 20 10-year-olds; by age 15, 60% of the population have had some drinking experience. The drunkenness data, taken as an indicator of incipient problem alcohol involvement, show that 1% of 10-year-olds have already crossed this threshold, and by age 15, the rate is about 33% of the population. Moreover, when these figures are broken down by gender, more than 50% of all boys meet this criterion at age 15.

Other MTF data make the case for early problem involvement even more compellingly. Thus, 11.9% of eighth-graders (ca. age 14) report they have had five or more

drinks in a row at least once in the past 2 weeks (Johnston et al., 2004b, p. 504), and a fifth of that group (2.3% of the population) report this consumption level 3 to 5 times or more during the 2-week interval[2] (Johnston et al., 2004b, p. 102). To recast these figures, given that drinking for adolescents is heavily confined to weekends, this high-end group of approximately 1 out of 8 14-year-olds is reporting drinking at adult heavy-drinking levels, and a fifth of that group, involving 5% of drinking 14-year-olds, is indicating that they are drinking at adult heavy-drinking rates at most available opportunities. Using *DSM-IV* criteria, and assuming any additional trouble related to the drinking (a not unreasonable assumption at this age), behavior sufficient to achieve a diagnosis of alcohol abuse has already been achieved by that group.

At the same time, it would be a mistake to presume that everyone with early signs of problem use will go on to develop an Alcohol Use Disorder. As already noted, the adolescent developmental literature has been clear that early alcohol use as well as alcohol problems need to be regarded as one component of a deviance syndrome. The syndrome emerges in adolescence and is adolescence-specific in the sense that the majority of individuals with such problems do not go on to develop adult disorder, al-

---

[1] Although these rates vary somewhat from survey to survey and when using different measurement criteria to establish a diagnosis (e.g., Grant, 1997; Narrow, Rae, Robins, & Regier, 2002), the basic story remains unchanged.

[2] The 5 drinks/occasion measure, sometimes called binge drinking, was originally used in MTF and other surveys as an index of heavy and potentially problematic drinking, hence the use of the term "binge" even though this consumption level is substantially less than what would occur in an alcoholic binge. A more recent referent for the measure, developed by NIAAA, suggests the measure is still a useful problem indicator. As pointed out by NIAAA (2004): If a typical 160-pound male drinks 5 standard drinks over a 2-hour period, he would reach a BAC of .08, making him legally intoxicated in all 50 states.

though some may reach diagnosable levels during their adolescent years (Blane, 1979; Donovan & Jessor, 1985; Jessor & Jessor, 1977). Conversely, the problem prevalence figures, especially for those still in grade school, suggest that some etiologic factors have already been in place by the time middle school is started. Despite the ready availability of these incidence data, which drive the point home, this is not yet a widely known fact. Here and there one can find accounts in the clinical literature of the previous generation (e.g., Mitchell, Hong, & Corman, 1979) and even as far back as a century ago (e.g., Madden, 1884), which call attention to these occurrences of very early and very severe child alcohol involvement. The effort to account for such beginnings leads us to cast an etiologic net considerably earlier than adolescence. I do so later in the chapter, when dealing with the evidence about variations in risk and course of the disorder. However, this issue of differences in course, and a related set of questions about how many different variations there may be, what their determinants are, how best to describe and understand them, has become a major set of questions for the field because it encompasses issues of phenotypic heterogeneity as well as definitional issues about what the "true" nature of alcoholic disorder might be. I also return to that set of questions later.

A MULTILEVEL NET FOR DEVELOPMENTAL VARIATION

Although it may seem a trivial point that one cannot have alcohol problems without the presence of alcohol, it is not trivial that such presence is regulated by societal norms about appropriate contexts of use and the availability of the drug in society. At the same time, alcohol is not just a social object; it is also a drug, and understanding the pharmacodynamic and neurodynamic matrix of its action on the human organism is essential to understanding how the symptomatology of AUD comes to be. To chart the manner in which these causal structures interact requires model building that will cross multiple levels of analysis and multiple disciplines, operating over social, individual, and biological time (Cacioppo, Berntson, Sheridan, & McClintock, 2000; Cicchetti & Dawson, 2002). This perspective is inherent to a developmental psychopathological framework, but it is not one regularly embraced by substance abuse researchers. To capture such a multilevel structure, a developmental systems framework (cf. Ford & Lerner, 1992; Sameroff, 1995) is essential as a means to organize these diverse levels of action.

This is simultaneously both a challenging and an intriguing interdisciplinary puzzle that sets the psychopathology of addictive disorders apart from their sister disorders. Although such macro- and microlevel influences may play *some* role in the anxiety disorders or Schizophrenia or depression, the macrostructure can to a much greater degree be ignored for the nonaddictive disorders, at least in the early levels of analysis. It cannot be for the substance use disorders, and for Alcohol Use Disorder in particular, given the central role that alcohol plays in civilized society (Pittman & White, 1991). The magnitude of the disorder's prevalence is also a testimony to the magnitude of the drug's social presence, as indexed by its availability and use.

AUD rates have been shown to vary with larger economic trends that impact the rate of employment and unemployment (Brenner, 1973) and the level of production of alcohol in the society (Edwards et al., 1994). Even population density, as it indexes living in an urban versus a rural environment, has become a useful explanatory mechanism for some of the variation in individual consumption patterns and ensuing problems (Edwards et al., 1994; Fitzgerald & Zucker, 1995). At the most distal level, the social regulatory structure influences manufacture and distribution of this beverage/drug, sets the rules that tax its sale, makes the drug legal or illegal to use at different ages, and also determines whether distribution can legally take place in the community. It is this social control structure that also sets the penalties for illegal or inappropriate use, which function as both threat and deterrent to those contemplating the illegal act. The evidence is clear that such controls affect individual behavior. Thus, a shift in the legal drinking age from 18 to 21 decreased drinking and driving accidents significantly during the age 18 to 21 period (Wagenaar & Toomey, 2002). A spread of effect beyond the age period within which the law had applicability has also been observed. Lower drinking rates were found in the subsequent 21- to 25-year age period as well (O'Malley & Wagenaar, 1991).

Etiologic models that currently dominate the field have either largely ignored this macrostructure or dealt with its effects at the neighborhood and local social environmental level. In only a few instances has work been done that examines interface phenomena such as the manner in which larger social forces influence individual alcohol-seeking behavior (Edwards et al., 1994). To provide but one example, the "wetness or dryness" of the society (Skog, 1985) changes the threshold within which microlevel phenomena such as alcoholism diagnostic subtypes will appear (Helzer & Canino, 1992; Reich, Cloninger, Van Eeerdewegh, Rice,

& Mullaney, 1988); a wetter society will increase the rate of AUD in its population, a drier one decrease it. Another longer-term effect of such influences is that a lower level of genetic susceptibility is more likely to be expressed in higher- as compared to lower-consumption societies because drinking rates will be higher in the higher-consumption environment. Under those circumstances, even persons with a higher genetic threshold of susceptibility will be more likely to move into diagnosis because they are more likely to drink heavily due to greater environmental cuing (for other examples of such interactions, see Kuh, Power, Blane, & Barley, 1997; Rose, Kaprio, Winter, Koskenvuo, & Viken, 1999).

Variable networks more proximal to the individual have also been shown to significantly predict level of alcohol involvement. These include variations in socialization practices, which create differential inculcation of values about the desirability of alcohol use. These values in turn foster the development of expectancies stimulating or dampening earlier use and stimulating or dampening expectancies about the effects the drug will have. A considerable amount of evidence exists that such learning plays a causal role in eventual alcohol involvement (Gaines, Brooks, Maisto, Dietrich, & Shagena, 1998; Goldman, Del Boca, & Darkes, 1999; Smith, Goldman, Greenbaum, & Christiansen, 1995), and some newer work indicates that it also plays a role thereafter in whether or not there is progression into problem use (i.e., drunkenness and binge drinking; Jester et al., 2005).

This multitiered influencing structure of sociocultural and relational systems is bounded at its lowest level by individual behavior that is only partially regulated by social influences. That boundary is also an upper-level limit on a second multidomain influencing structure, located within the individual, that plays a major role in determining life course variations in alcohol use and alcohol dependence. Patterns of use are known to be regulated by cognitive and motivational networks, determined by the user's subjective experience of the drug, the user's knowledge of the rule structure for appropriate use, and a subjective probability computation of whether it is more or less desirable to go about drinking at a given point in time (Dunn & Goldman, 1996). The immediate encouragement and availability offered by peers regulates onset and course not only through social reinforcement, but also through cuing. The timing of when initial use takes place and the development and maintenance of problem use are heavily influenced by the patterns of alcohol use occurring in the surrounding peer structure. The concomitant presence of individual behavioral repertoires that encourage such use (e.g., risk taking, antisocial

behavior) also heighten the likelihood that drinking problems will emerge and be sustained (Hawkins et al., 1997).

At the same time, alcohol-related disorders are brain disorders, involving the brain's structures for appetite, reward, planning and forethought, and affective and behavioral control. It is also essential to recognize that alcoholism is a complex genetic disorder, with a heterogeneous phenotype. It fits the genetic definition of a complex trait: It shows familial aggregation, its transmission patterns do not follow Mendel's laws, and it appears to result from more than one genetic locus and more than one aspect of the environment (Risch, 1990; Sing, Haviland, & Reilly, 1996).

The within- and across-domain interactive system presented so far has primarily been described in the vertical language of top-down and bottom-up relationships, to the neglect of the other major dimension of the system: time. As noted at the beginning of this section, multiple times influence these relationships. They range from cultural time (involving stability or change in patterns of alcohol availability, use, and diagnostic prevalence among different cohorts), to social time (involving variations in the character of relationships at different age stages, as a function of the social timetable and rule and role structure of the society), to individual time (involving developmental and maturational changes), to biological time (involving the turning on, turning off, tuning, development, and degradation of biological systems over the course of aging). These relationships are captured by the terse observation that alcoholism is a developmental disorder. They also are captured by the observation that substance abuse is a chronic, remitting disorder (McLellan, Lewis, O'Brien & Kleber, 2000). Both observations underscore the dynamic nature of top-down and bottom-up relationships as development proceeds. They also imply that the nature of the interactive relationships may not be constant across the life span, as social and biological climates shift with changing historical, social, and developmental time parameters. Figures 17.1 and 17.2 illustrate the nature of these relationships more concretely.

Figure 17.1 is my elaboration on Elder and Caspi's (1990) three-dimensional life course grid. It shows the multigenerational linkage of individual, family, and historical events across three generations. The x axis depicts cohort time for the twentieth century, showing major marker events throughout the interval that have shaped the course of the societies taking part in them. An individual born around 1915 has had a different experience of alcohol and other drug availability during an adolescence marked by Prohibition than did one born in the early 1950s, who experienced adolescence during the Vietnam era's advocacy of "turning on, tuning in, and dropping

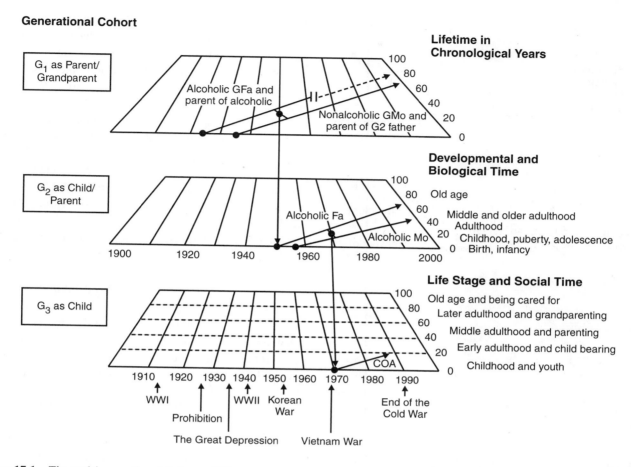

Figure 17.1 The multigenerational linkage of life course trajectories in individual/developmental time, life stage time, family time, and historical time.

out" (Holdcraft & Iacono, 2004). The y axis is simultaneously one of life stage/social time, developmental/maturational time, and biological time. Although these dimensions are obviously correlated with each other, the relationship is far from perfect. The example in the figure depicts a grandparental generation (G1 cohort) with an alcoholic grandfather born just before the advent of Prohibition, whose life ends in suicide at age 40. He is married to a nonalcoholic spouse who was born toward the end of the Great Depression. The two have a son born just after the end of World War II. The grandmother continues to live into her 70s. Her son (G2 cohort), who also becomes alcoholic, experiences his father's death at around age 10. He marries a woman who is also alcoholic, and the two bear a son (G3 cohort) in 1969, during the Vietnam era. The son has a low-normal IQ and is impulsive, and there are soft signs of the presence of fetal alcohol effects. This diagram illustrates how both historical and family events can have different impacts on trajectories of the next (or even the subsequent) generation, as their unique chronol-

ogy impacts a different life stage for the younger generation's members (Elder, 1998). The figure also shows how each parent's influencing structure projects downward onto the child's developmental trajectory, with influence both at the point of conception by way of genetic endowment, as well as developmentally thereafter.

Figure 17.2 provides a more detailed schematic of the nature of the bottom-up and top-down structure at the variable level. This heuristic diagram is derived from Charles Sing's (Sing et al., 1996) model of the genetic architecture of complex diseases, but the variable network has been modified to make it suitable for Alcohol Use Disorder; the diagram also depicts the contribution of top-down environmental variation in the process, an element not characterized in Sing's account. The figure shows the reaction surface of individual alcohol problem variation (or its proxy, alcohol problem risk, at ages where use does no yet occur) across the age span. This surface of individual symptomatology (number of problems) is shaped by both the top-down structure (abbreviated here from the

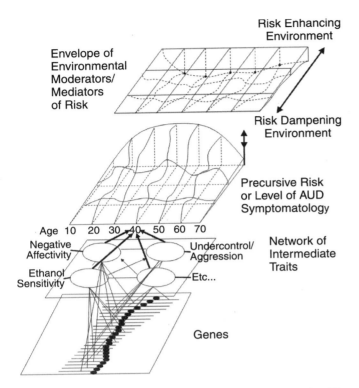

Figure 17.2 Probability of drug abuse (risk) over the life course: the envelope of risk expression as a function of genes, intermediate traits, environment, and life stage.

multigenerational structure depicted in Figure 17.1) into a single index of degree of risk enhancement versus risk dampening provided by the environment and by the bottom-up variable network.

In a chronologic sense, the causal structure of the end point phenotype begins with the polygenetic network at the gene level. This is a set of variables that remains unaltered from conception onward. Genes interact in combinations to produce a network of intermediate traits (alternatively termed "endophenotypes"; Gottesman & Gould, 2003), and these interactions in turn are influenced by the risk-dampening/risk-enhancement network, a network that is not constant as development proceeds. The unevenness of the reaction envelope of alcohol problem expression across levels of environmental risk, even at the same life stage, indicates that the impact of genetic risk may vary as a function of the environmental risk-dampening/risk-enhancement structure.

VARIATIONS IN RISK AND COURSE OF THE DISORDER

When does risk for alcohol involvement begin? It is extremely rare to see a 5-year-old consuming alcoholic

beverages; as already noted, the normative expectation among youth, as well as the modal behavior in American society, is for self-initiated drinking of alcoholic beverages to commence around age 14. The problem use figures also slowly move upward with age, with 22% of 10th graders, 28% of 12th graders, and 40% of 21- to 22-year-olds reporting binge use in the prior 2-week period (Johnston et al., 2004b, 2004c). At the same time, age progression is, of itself, not an explanation of process but rather a chronological marker of other events that lead to onset or problem use. Thus, individual differences in age of onset are attributable to differences in the rapidity of emergence of the underlying causal event structure. The developmental question then becomes one of specifying the events and circumstances in which they show up.

From this perspective, neither first drinking experience nor first bingeing experience is the beginning of the process of alcohol involvement, or even of the emergence of alcohol problems, abuse, and dependence. Alcohol has a place in the ritual practices of many religions and thus allows children to have some minor consumption experience well before they have made any conscious decision to drink (Glassner, 1991; D. B. Heath, 1991). Moreover, media exposure assures that some knowledge of alcoholic beverages is present even before peers offer the opportunity for drinking to take place (Atkin, 1995; Wylie, Casswell, & Stewart, 1989). More generally, for regular (volitional) drinking to take place, first, the potential user implicitly needs to be aware that there is a class of substances collectively known as alcoholic beverages; second, he or she must know that these substances have certain properties (effects) connected to their ingestion; and third, such effects need to be viewed as sufficiently desirable to mobilize the individual to engage in alcohol seeking (or at least alcohol accepting). These properties, collectively known as implicit cognitions (Stacy, 1997; Stacy, Ames, Sussman, & Dent, 1996) and outcome expectancies (e.g., Goldman, Brown, Christiansen, & Smith, 1991; Rather, Goldman, Roehrich, & Brannick, 1992), have been shown to predict subsequent adolescent drug use, as well as to be direct effect predictors of both alcohol and other drug use (Smith et al., 1995; Stacy et al., 1996). The theoretical base for this work has been the social cognition and memory process literatures (e.g., Ajzen & Fishbein, 1980; Tiffany, 1990), which have emphasized not only the representational but also the motivational attributes of internally constructed cognitive models (schemas). From the perspective of the observer, the actual "decision making" may appear too rapid for this to occur. But a now voluminous literature involving carefully controlled laboratory studies has shown how the underlying details that shape the decision making can be identified. A complex interplay of affective as well as rational elements is factored into the subjective equations that underlie ongoing drinking behavior, as well as the decision making about whether one should initiate drinking in specific situations or refrain (Fischhoff & Quadrel, 1995). The developmental question is, How and under what conditions are these elements learned?

Within this conceptual tradition, a series of developmentally earlier studies using methods that allow children to tell the experimenter about their knowledge of the rules that govern alcohol use have shown that preschoolers in the general population already know two of the core alcohol use schemas of the larger culture: The children, even at ages 3 to 5, already attribute alcoholic beverage consumption more to adults than to children and more to adult males than adult females (Noll, Zucker, & Greenberg, 1990). In addition, the ability to identify alcoholic beverages by smell (an indicator of personal exposure rather than simply media exposure) was both age-graded and based on experiences in the home. Older children were better at identifying these beverages than younger ones, and the ability to recognize alcoholic beverages was directly related to the amount of alcohol the parents consumed, as well as the degree to which their parents' reported use of alcohol for "escape" reasons.

A logical extension of this work is the examination of possible differences in schema structure in high-risk populations such as children of alcoholics (COAs), for it is here that exposure differences would be most likely expected and also where the early identification of "risky cognitions" would be anticipated to be of greatest long-term significance. Zucker, Kincaid, Fitzgerald, and Bingham (1995) explored this possibility by examining differences in alcohol use schemas in preschooler COAs and suitably age-matched children from nonalcoholic homes. They asked children to identify photographs of alcoholic beverages and examined the degree to which alcoholic beverage use was attributed to people depicted in common situations where beverages are consumed (e.g., at a meal, on a picnic, at an adult party). COAs were more likely to identify at least one alcoholic beverage and were better able to correctly identify specific alcoholic beverages. Differences in the children's attributions of alcoholic beverage use to adults were again predicted by their parents' reported level of alcohol consumption. In short, alcohol schemas relating to both knowledge and use were more common in the alcoholic families.

Empirical work has yet to demonstrate the manner in which such schemas relate to the emergence of actual drinking-onset behavior in later childhood, but other research on the cognitive organization of such schemas as observed in second- to fifth-graders has shown that the same evaluative and arousal-sedation dimensions used by adults are also detectable in 8- to 11-year-olds, and that the older of these children are more likely to expect positive and arousing outcomes from drinking (Dunn & Goldman, 1996). Following on these earlier studies, the Michigan group examined whether individual differences in positivity of middle childhood expectancies would predict differences in later drinking behavior. Given the developmentally earlier findings linking schema presence to heavier alcohol use in the child's home, we anticipated that children with more positive schemas would begin earlier and progress more quickly into problem use. Newly completed work found that although positive expectancies in middle childhood did not predict onset of drinking, they did predict to a variety of problem indicators, including earlier first binge drinking and earlier drunkenness in the higher positive expectancy group (Jester et al., 2005). Taken together, these early to middle childhood findings indicate that a developmental progression in expectancy structure is taking place substantially before the regular use of alcohol has begun, that this progression is age-graded, that it is to a degree reflective of differences in exposure to heavier versus lighter consumption environments, and that it is anticipatory of greater problem alcohol involvement.

Differences in Alcohol Nonspecific-Risk Structure for Later Disorder Are Present in Early Childhood

Not all of the causal structure for earlier alcohol use and alcohol problems is attributable to alcohol-specific processes. In fact, one of the historically most important findings of the past generation has been the repeated documentation of a link between delinquent and aggressive activity in adolescence and earlier onset of alcohol use, as well as more problematic use (Donovan & Jessor, 1985; Jessor & Jessor, 1977; D. B. Kandel, 1978). Earlier, I provided an overview of the work on problem behavior theory that emphasized the social psychological matrix for these differences. A parallel line of reasoning, driven strongly by a seminal paper by Tarter and colleagues (Tarter, Alterman, & Edwards, 1984), proposed that individual differences in temperament, ostensibly genetically mediated and relating to activity level, low attention span, and behavioral dysregulation are an essential early link in the chain of risk for alcohol use and problems in later childhood and adolescence. The temperamental substrate, coupled with an environmental structure that facilitates and even presses for the development of these initially neutral temperamental attributes, is hypothesized to culminate in a behavioral adaptation involving antisocial personality, on the one hand, and a deviant peer network as a facilitating context, on the other (Tarter et al., 1999; Zucker, Fitzgerald, et al., 1995). These attributes together are hypothesized to drive both initial alcohol use and the transition into early problem use.

Studies carried out in the early to mid-1990s confirmed these hypotheses cross-sectionally in adolescents (Blackson, 1997; Blackson & Tarter, 1994; Blackson, Tarter, Martin, & Moss, 1994) and in 3- to 5-year-olds from alcoholic and ecologically matched but not alcoholic families (Fitzgerald et al., 1993; Jansen, Fitzgerald, Ham, & Zucker, 1995). In the preschoolers, the outcome proxies were undercontrol measures of impulsivity and a broadband measure of behavior problems (Fitzgerald et al., 1993). Moreover, the highest behavior problem subgroup of children in this study scored higher on the difficult temperament dimensions described by the Tarter group. The difficult temperament children were also more likely to come from families where the alcoholic fathers were lower in socioeconomic status and higher in antisocial comorbidity and had alcohol problems of greater severity and of longer duration (Jansen et al., 1995; Zucker, Ellis, Bingham, & Fitzgerald, 1996).

Over the past decade, the prospective evidence has steadily amassed for these connections, to the point now that six longitudinal studies, two beginning as early as age 3 (Caspi, Moffitt, Newman, & Silva, 1996; Zucker,

Fitzgerald, et al., 2000), have shown a direct link between the early child manifestations of these attributes, specifically behavioral undercontrol and aggressiveness, and AUD and other alcohol problem outcomes in adolescence and early adulthood (Caspi et al., 1996; Masse & Tremblay, 1997; Mayzer, Puttler, Wong, Fitzgerald, & Zucker, 2002, 2003; Mayzer, Wong, Puttler, Fitzgerald, & Zucker, 2001; Zucker, Fitzgerald, et al., 2000). These studies join with two earlier reports of projects beginning in middle childhood (Cloninger, Sigvardsson, & Bohman, 1988; Eron, Huesmann, Dubow, Romanoff, & Yarmel, 1987) with similar childhood markers at baseline and with alcoholism and drunk driving outcomes in adulthood. Another study from the 1990s, the Seattle Social Development Project, replicated these findings into adolescence (Hawkins & Catalano, 1992; Hawkins, Catalano, Kosterman, Abbott, & Hill, 1999). Four of the studies, the Dunedin Health and Development Study (Caspi et al., 1996), the Columbia County Study (Eron et al., 1987), the Seattle Project (Hawkins & Catalano, 1992), and the Montreal Longitudinal Study (Masse & Tremblay, 1997), involved general population samples, and two involved COA samples and matched controls (Cloninger et al., 1988; Mayzer et al., 2001, 2002; Zucker, Fitzgerald, et al., 2000). Table 17.3 summarizes the ages at baseline and follow-up and the baseline behaviors and adolescent/adult outcomes of the study. The level of replication shown across this work must be taken as definitive evidence that a robust relationship exists between early childhood behavior and adult AUD. Combined with the adolescent studies noted earlier, findings indicate that a continuity

TABLE 17.3   Longitudinal Studies Connecting Early and Middle Childhood Behavior to AUD and Alcohol Problem Outcomes in Adolescence and Adulthood: I. Problems of Undercontrol and Aggressiveness

Study	Early Child Behavior	Baseline Age (Years)	Follow-up Age (Years)	Outcome Behavior
General Populations Studies				
Caspi et al. (1996)	Behavioral undercontrol	3	21	Alcohol dependence
Masse and Tremblay (1997)	Low fearfulness; hyperactivity	6 and 10	11–15	Earlier drunkenness onset
Eron et al. (1987)	Aggression	8	30	Driving while intoxicated
Hawkins et al. (1992, 1999)	Externalizing behavior; delinquency	10	21	Alcohol abuse and alcohol dependence
COA Studies				
Zucker, Chermack, et al. (2000), Mayzer et al. (2001, 2002)	Externalizing behavior	3–5	12–14	Early drinking onset
Cloninger et al. (1988)	High novelty seeking; low harm avoidance	11	27	Alcoholism

pathway exists from very early childhood to an alcoholism outcome in adulthood.

Equally important, both of the COA studies (Cloninger et al., 1988; Mayzer et al., 2002) as well as four general population studies (Caspi et al., 1996; Hawkins & Catalano, 1992; Hawkins et al., 1999; Kellam, Brown, Rubin, & Ensminger, 1983; Kellam, Ensminger, & Simon, 1980; Werner, 1986) found that a behavioral inhibition/shyness/social fearfulness cluster predicted alcoholism and alcohol problem outcomes in adolescence and early adulthood (Table 17.4). These latter characteristics have only sporadically been reported in the adolescent literature (Kaplan, Martin, & Robbins, 1982), but they are consistent with the known adult relationship between Social Phobia and AUD (Kushner, Sher, & Beitman, 1990), and they also have been reported in some historically earlier prospective studies begun in early childhood.

In all of this work, parallel findings are reported from both the COA and the general population studies, suggesting that it is the risk factor(s) rather than the COA status of the sample that is accounting for these relationships. At the same time, the socialization environment is virtually uncharacterized in most of these studies. Thus, it is not possible to determine the degree to which contextual factors may be moderating or mediating the relationship. Moreover, even in the non-COA samples, one cannot automatically assume a more benign environment. In fact, in three of the general population studies reviewed here, the Montreal Longitudinal Study (Masse & Tremblay, 1997), the

Seattle Project (Hawkins & Catalano, 1992), and the Woodlawn Study (Kellam et al., 1980), the study design was deliberately set up to provide a sample of families of low socioeconomic status and high social adversity. Thus, even in the non-COA studies, the level of environmental adversity may have been sufficiently damaging and sufficiently similar to what existed in the alcoholic homes to produce the parallel effects.

A recent report from the Michigan Longitudinal Study suggests that the multifactorial causal structure for AUD extends even more broadly than undercontrol and shyness/social inhibition. Wong, Brower, Fitzgerald, and Zucker (2004) observed a relationship between ratings of sleep problems at ages 3 to 5 and early onset of drug use (alcohol, cigarettes, marijuana, other hard drugs). The relationship remained even when a number of other plausible mediators, including family history of alcoholism and externalizing problems (specifically, attention problems and aggression) were added into the predictive model. In other words, sleep difficulties very early in life appear to be a marker of an independent contributor to early substance involvement. Given that early alcohol use has repeatedly been identified as a proxy for elevated later risk of alcohol dependence, as well as a host of adolescent problems, including injuries, violence, and drunk driving (Gruber, DiClemente, Anderson, & Lodico, 1996), these data support a third risk pathway. Although a self-medication hypothesis and a central dysregulatory deficit hypothesis are both plausible mechanistic explanations for the effect, the

TABLE 17.4 Longitudinal Studies Connecting Early and Middle Childhood Behavior to AUD and Alcohol Problem Outcomes in Adolescence and Adulthood: II. Internalizing Problems

Study	Early Child Behavior	Baseline Age (Years)	Follow-up Age (Years)	Outcome Behavior
General Populations Studies				
Caspi et al. (1996)	Behavioral inhibition	3	21	More alcohol problems
Hawkins et al. (1992, 1999)	Internalizing behavior (also poor school bonding)	10	21	Alcohol abuse and alcohol dependence
Kellam et al. (1980, 1983)	Shyness/social inhibition	6	16–17	More alcohol and drug use
Werner (1986)	Low sociability temperament	<1	18, 30+	Alcoholism
COA Studies				
Zucker, Fitzgerald, et al. (2000); Mayzer et al. (2001, 2002)	Internalizing behavior	3–5	12–14	Early drinking onset
Cloninger et al. (1988)	High harm avoidance; low novelty seeking	11	27	Alcoholism

mechanisms undergirding that relationship remain to be identified.

Heterogeneity in the Course of Risk and Heterogeneity of Nonspecific Risk

Although young children who are high in undercontrol present very differently from those with fearfulness and social inhibition, the studies reviewed in the previous section indicate that they have at least one common end point: a higher probability of developing an Alcohol Use Disorder. This seeming anomaly is a clear example of a well-known systems theory concept—equifinality—wherein multiple, sometimes linked and sometimes disparate processes engage in a way that produces a common phenotypic end point (Cicchetti & Rogosch, 1996). The core etiologic questions are, How did they get there, and to what degree will their longer-term developmental trajectories converge or diverge over time? The moderately high correlation observed between externalizing and internalizing problems in childhood (Achenbach & Edelbrock, 1991; Krueger, Capsi, Moffitt, & Silva, 1998) suggests that the pathway of risk is a converging one. Conversely, even a moderately high relationship indicates that in some instances the behavioral syndromes are linked and in some not. The existing comorbidity evidence from developmental studies in childhood suggests that developmental pathways are different when the two syndromes co-occur than when they do not. Thus, Ialongo and colleagues (Ialongo, Edelsohn, Werthamer-Larsson, Crockett, & Kellam, 1996) found that the stability of aggression among first graders strengthened rather than attenuated in the presence of comorbid anxiety, and Wong and colleagues (Wong, Zucker, Fitzgerald, & Puttler, 1999) observed that over the interval from preschool to early adolescence, children with a faster rate of increase in internalizing problems had a slower rate of decrease in externalizing problems.

The strength of these interactive relationships has not yet been evaluated vis-à-vis a substance abuse outcome, but what little comorbidity data there are suggest that the most efficacious model of risk from early childhood to adolescence is an additive one. When externalizing, undercontrolled behavior is present along with depression/anxiety, onset of use is earlier and a later problem outcome is more likely. A good deal of evidence, both direct (Tarter et al., 1999, 2003) and indirect (Sung, Erkanli, Angold, & Costello, 2004), is supportive of this position. Evidence from our own group is also largely confirmatory of this conclusion but indicates that the developmental manifestations of this process are not linear. Support for a continuity

model of process is present only at certain points in development. Furthermore, the process is significantly impacted by the level of adversity in the family, a level of influence that often is not measured.

I illustrate the developmental variation and complexity of the process by briefly summarizing recent work from the Michigan Longitudinal Study (Zucker, Fitzgerald, et al., 2000). This longitudinal family study is following alcoholic men, their spouse, their initially 3- to 5-year-old sons, other siblings, and a suitably matched but nonalcoholic set of contrast families drawn from the same high-risk neighborhoods where the alcoholic families live. N for these analyses involved 303 families. All family members were assessed at 3-year intervals beginning when the target boy was 3 to 5 years of age. A person-centered approach was used in examining the joint effects of family adversity and child risk vulnerability over the interval between 3 and 14 years of age.[3] The adversity index we used assessed level of family pathology. A summative family psychopathology measure was created that scaled both currency and severity of AUD in each of the parents, as well as the presence/absence of antisocial behavior in each, then added them together (cf. Wong, Zucker, Fitzgerald, & Puttler, 1999; Zucker, Wong, Puttler, & Fitzgerald, 2003). Highest family adversity involved having two parents with currently active alcoholism, or one parent with a comorbid Antisocial Personality Disorder diagnosis, or both. This index, although established by way of parental psychopathology, is an effective proxy for a number of other pertinent indicators of family adversity, including greater conflict, violence, economic difficulty, family crises, other psychiatric comorbidity, and trouble with the law (Zucker, Ellis, Fitzgerald, Bingham, & Sanford, 1996). In addition, on the basis of national Epidemiologic Catchment Area Study alcoholism comorbidity rates (Helzer, Burnam, & McEvoy, 1991) and national familial alcoholism figures (Grant, 2000; Huang, Cerbone, & Gfroerer, 1998), these cutoff criteria would yield a population encompassing slightly less than 1% of U.S. households but approximately 20% of alcoholic families (the severest subset).

The child's initial risk status at age 3 to 5 was described by a global sociobehavioral psychopathology measure that was nationally normed (the Total Behavior Problems scale of the Child Behavior Checklist; Achenbach, 1991). Low risk was defined as being within normal limits on this global index; high risk was defined as being at the 80th per-

---

[3] This section is based heavily on two unpublished working papers written by M. Burmeister and the author on the genetics of substance use disorders.

centile or higher on the measure (0.84 SDs above the norm). A 2-by-2 grid was created by crosscutting these dimensions. Initially, *resilient children* were defined as having normal to high adaptation (i.e., low "risk" scores) even though they were living in high-adversity families. The group having normal risk under conditions of low family adversity was labeled *nonchallenged* to emphasize that their behavior was unremarkable, in families with low parent psychopathology that exerted no pressure for deviance and that were more likely to be nurturant and encouraging. The group with high risk (high psychopathology) under conditions of high family adversity was labeled *vulnerable* to emphasize the continuing exposure to family difficulty that took place there (cf. Clark, Lesnick, & Hegedus, 1997), as well as the likely high genetic load for substance use disorder. Other evidence from the study shows that these children had been negatively impacted by this exposure (Wong, Zucker, Fitzgerald, & Puttler, 1999). Finally, those children with high risk (high psychopathology) under conditions of low family adversity were characterized as *troubled* to emphasize that, even without the familial adversity, they still showed a poor behavioral adaptation.

Figure 17.3a shows the trajectory of externalizing problems for each of the groups, and Figure 17.3b shows the trajectory of internalizing problems from preschool to early adolescence. Overall across-age group differences were significant for both externalizing and internalizing problem trajectories. The nonchallenged group sustained the lowest level of externalizing problems over the course of childhood and early adolescence, followed by the resilient group, the troubled group, and the vulnerable group. At all ages, the vulnerable group remained highest in externalizing problems. The figure also shows a consistent pattern of decline in externalizing behavior over childhood, a pattern that is normative for this age range (Loeber, 1982). In addition, there is increasing convergence in the level of externalizing difficulties through middle childhood. At the transition to adolescence, the normative pattern of a developmental shift involving increasing externalizing (aggressive/delinquent/impulsive) behavior (cf. Jessor & Jessor, 1977) is present. The individual-difference data indicate that whereas the resilient children were not distinguishable from their nonchallenged peers as preschoolers, they showed a small but reliably higher level of externalizing problems as they grew older. In other words, a small but detectable convergence with the initially more externalizing two groups starts to become manifest. At the same time, they still occupied an intermediate place, having a lower level of these behaviors than did their vulnerable peers. In addition, the divergence of slopes between ages 9 to 11 and

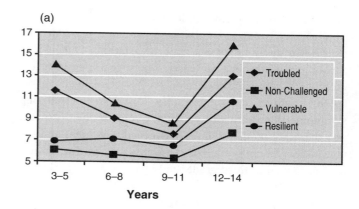

(a)

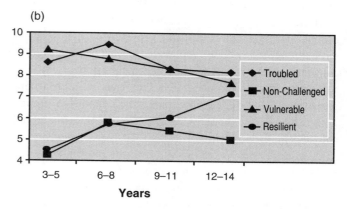

(b)

Figure 17.3 (a) Externalizing symptoms over time in groups differing on risk and adversity. (b) Internalizing symptoms over time in groups differing on risk and adversity. *Source:* "Resilience and Vulnerability among Sons of Alcoholics: Relationship to Developmental Outcomes between Early Childhood and Adolescence" (p. 88), by R. A. Zucker, M. M. Wong, L. I. Puttler, and H. E. Fitzgerald, 2003, in S. Luthar (Ed.), *Resilience and Vulnerability: Adaptation in the Context of Childhood Adversities,* New York: Cambridge University Press. Reprinted with permission.

12 to 14 involved a significant interaction between child individual differences in initial risk and level of family adversity exposure during a period of life when the overall norm is for increasingly deviant and impulsive activity. This interaction had previously been observed cross-sectionally among these children when they were 3 to 5 years of age (Wong, Zucker, Fitzgerald, & Puttler, 1999). The trajectory data indicate the pattern is sustained developmentally; they depict *continuity over time* in group positioning vis-à-vis level of undercontrolled behavior, and the positioning is sustained across the risk-adversity groups even though level of group differentiation varies, as does absolute level of undercontrolled activity.

Figure 17.3b shows the trajectories for internalizing problems; here also the nonchallenged group shows the lowest level of problems, followed by the resilient group. The troubled group is similar to the vulnerable group. The figure also shows important pattern variations. During preschool and up through the early school years, an identical individual-difference pattern exists. Nonchallenged and resilient children are significantly lower in internalizing symptoms than both the vulnerable and troubled groups, and there are no differences between the resilient and the nonchallenged children. The pattern begins to diverge following second to third grade, and by early adolescence the nonchallenged group is significantly lower than all others, and no differences exist between any of the other three groups. In other words, at this juncture, the resilient children have developed a level of internalizing symptoms that is similar to both the vulnerable and the troubled children's. Here also we tested this group by time interaction with a repeated measures analysis of variance. A significant interaction effect of time and adaptation group indicated that the developmental trajectories of internalizing problems varied differently among the adaptation groups, with three of the four showing a continuity pattern and one a discontinuity pattern.

At a more phenomenological level, the internalizing trajectory pattern of the resilient group implies that a weathering process has been taking place, wherein an initially happier adaptation gives way to the sustained exposure to an adverse, more conflictual environment involving more family stress and disruption. The result, by early adolescence, is that the level of internalizing behavior for this group is indistinguishable from that of the initially more troubled and vulnerable children. These data provide a poignant illustration of how the shift from normal to pathological adaptation may take place under circumstances of sustained adversity. Recall, however, that this shift occurs only in the more covert, internalizing behavior domain; the more obvious externalizing behavior differences remain, with the resilient children sustaining a pattern that differentiates them from their vulnerable and troubled peers.

These patterns of trajectory variation in both externalizing and internalizing problems also illustrate the nonlinearity of risk development over time. Moreover, other work by our group (Fuller et al., 2003) indicates that the salience of different aspects of the parental environment varies developmentally. Level of child externalizing behavior (aggressiveness) in the preschool years was predicted by marital aggression/conflict as well as parental alcoholism but not by direct punishment; in middle childhood, the child outcome was predicted only by direct punishment.

The trajectory variations reflect more than just differences in nonspecific risk over time. They also are proxies for

differences in probability of eventual problem drinking, other problem behavior, and alcohol dependence (Ellickson, Tucker, & Klein, 2003; Grant & Dawson, 1997; Pederson & Skrondal, 1998). In the Michigan study, Mayzer, Puttler, Wong, Fitzgerald, and Zucker (2002, 2003) have already confirmed the first step in this chain of effect by showing that higher levels of early externalizing and internalizing behavior are predictive of both early onset of drinking and higher levels of externalizing and internalizing behavior and delinquent activity in adolescence. On both these grounds, and given what is known about early onset of alcohol use as a precursive marker (Gruber et al., 1996), these results indicate that the children identified as vulnerable are at highest risk for a later AUD outcome, the nonchallenged group is at lowest risk, and the resilient group is at intermediary risk, in part because of the increasing experience of internalizing problems as they move into adolescence.

More generally, given what has already been established about the utility of the externalizing and internalizing behavior as proxy indicators of alcohol problems and elevated risk for later AUD, these findings emphasize the importance of characterizing both familial risk and individual risk in understanding the variability of pathways into problem alcohol use (also see Garnier & Stein, 2002). When individual vulnerability is present early, even a nonchallenging family environment is insufficient to moderate the child's vulnerability. Conversely, from the perspective of risk for externalizing problems, a subset of COAs moves through childhood relatively trouble-free and another subset, showing early risk, is the highest-risk vulnerable subgroup.

This pattern is tempered to a considerable degree for internalizing risk. For one subgroup of young COAs, the resilient children, their early behavior indicates that they are relatively free of sadness, anxiety, depression, and worry. Exposure to the adversity of an actively alcoholic home with its attendant strain and conflict (Loukas, Zucker, Fitzgerald, & Krull, 2003) leads to a gradual degradation of their affective status, such that by the time adolescence is reached, their level of internal trouble is equivalent to that of their more obviously less fortunate peers (the troubled and vulnerable children).

One caveat is needed to temper these conclusions: The evidence from both the Loukas et al. (2003) and Fuller et al. (2003) studies indicates that the family effects are partially attributable to an active environment, with level of parental conflict as well as type of conflict (marital aggression/conflict at preschool, direct punishment in middle school) influencing child risk. However, these studies cannot disentangle the nesting of high-child risk in high-biological-risk families. Vulnerable children are more likely to come from high-adversity families, and the correlation of family and child risk that is present leaves open the possibility that the exacerbation of behavioral problems that appears to be a socialization effect is actually the result of indirect genetic effects. The variable network we currently have at our disposal makes it impossible to evaluate these two plausible and not necessarily competing hypotheses about mechanism.

Heterogeneity of Alcohol-Specific Risk: Prolegomenon to Phenotypic Heterogeneity of Alcohol Use Disorder

The work presented so far has focused on precursive risk factors that are nonspecific to an alcohol problem or AUD outcome. However, parallel evidence for heterogeneity has been described by Schulenberg and colleagues for one of the core end points of this chapter, problem alcohol use. Drawing on national Monitoring the Future panel data on consumption, Schulenberg, O'Malley, Bachman, Wadsworth, and Johnston (1996) examined patterning of problem alcohol use over the age 18 to 24 interval, the period where peak rates of use and problems are present. The consumption measure they used was binge drinking (5 or more drinks in a row), the index already described earlier. The problem indicator was *frequent* bingeing, defined as two or more occasions in the past 2 weeks. Six distinct trajectories of binge drinking were identified that accounted for over 90% of the sample and that included stable patterns (never, rare, and chronic) as well as patterns of cross-temporal variation (decreased, increased, and fling; see Figure 17.4). Women were overrepresented in the never group and underrepresented in the chronic and increased groups. Binge trajectories differences were related to concomitant variation in problems with alcohol, attitudes about heavy drinking, time spent with heavy-drinking peers, and extent of illicit drug involvement. In other words, a pattern of behaviors was being indexed by the binge variation, but it encompassed a substantially larger set of characteristics that shifted (or remained stable) along with the drinking. Furthermore, being lower in conventionality and self-efficacy and drinking to get drunk were senior-year risk factors for membership in the increased trajectory group, and higher self-efficacy and lower motivation pertaining to drinking to get drunk were protective factors against involvement in the continued bingeing trajectory for initially frequent binge drinkers (Schulenberg, Wadsworth, O'Malley, Bachman, & Johnston, 1996). This study was the first in this age range to demonstrate the importance of distinguishing trajectory classes. When one looks at the population "trajectory" (the total group) in Figure 17.4, it is evident how misleading a characterization of developmental process is

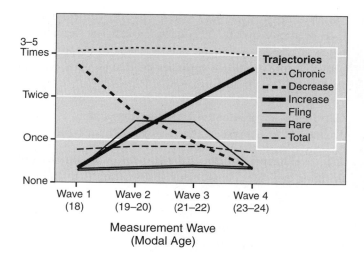

Figure 17.4 Mean binge drinking scores of 5 or more drinks in a row in the past 2 weeks by binge drinking trajectory. Reprinted with permission from "Getting Drunk and Growing up: Trajectories of Frequent Binge Drinking during the Transition to Early Adulthood," by J. Schulenberg, P. M. O'Malley, J. G. Bachman, K. N. Wadsworth, and L. D. Johnston, *Journal of Studies on Alcohol, 57,* pp. 289–304, 1996. Copyright by Alcohol Research Documentation, Inc., Rutgers Center of Alcohol Studies, Piscataway, NJ, 08854.

conveyed by using population means. At the same time, an essential empirical as well as prevention-related question still to be answered is: What characteristics prior to age 18 predict trajectory variation? The answer to this must remain equivocal because the MTF database provides information only on essentially contemporaneous factors in late adolescence that predict later patterning. This question is an essential one for future studies to address.

At this intermediary point in the chapter, a summary observation is in order about the level of discourse so far. From the vantage point of the developmental map outlined earlier, the variation we have so far addressed operates at the second surface, the envelope of behavioral risk and symptomatology, and to some degree the first surface (family and subcultural variation). Although such variation is at the microlevel from the standpoint of societal and environmental structure, it is at the macrolevel from the vantage point of variability assessed lower down in the network. As we address familial variation along with variation in undercontrol/aggression, internalizing behavior, and alcohol using behavior, it needs to be kept in mind that each of these sources of variation may in turn be disaggregated into component segments. Determination of what the active ingredients are in a complete model of the development of risk and disorder needs ultimately to identify what the most useful levels of specificity are, what the critical variables are at those levels, and what the critical across-level relationships are. This question is not yet capable of being answered, but it continually needs to be posed and plausible core candidate variables need to be put forth and evaluated.

Heterogeneity of Alcohol Use Disorder and Variations in Course of the Disorder/Phenotype

The developmental focus of the etiologic work on onset of drinking and drinking problems leads naturally to an interest in change, and increasingly has led investigators in this field to the utilization of newer statistical methods to analyze change and identify individuals with different patterns of growth over time (Collins & Horn, 1991; Muthén and Muthén, 2000). This focus has been on growth and trajectories of both nonspecific risk and alcohol problems/symptomatology. In the two studies we reviewed in the prior section, along with a host of others (cf. D. B. Kandel, 1978; Zucker, Fitzgerald, et al., 1995), one problem use trajectory emerges that is characterized by elevated child problems prior to adolescence, along with a damaged socialization environment. In the two studies just reviewed, both the vulnerable group trajectory and the MTF chronic group fit this pattern. The residual group (or groups) isolated in earlier work has typically been less well defined, and the more recent and more precise analytic work gives some clues about why this might be. If more developmental variability exists in those lower-risk, lower-symptomatology subgroups, as is the case for the resilient group in the Michigan study and for the increasing, decreasing, and fling groups in the MTF study, then less differentiating analyses will more often merge them, sometimes identifying them as one "other" group and sometimes identifying more than one.

In contrast to the work on youth and early adulthood, efforts to characterize course in adulthood started not from a developmental but from a clinical vantage point. Here the intent historically has been to find coherent symptomatic groupings that would parse the clinical symptomatology and history in a way that would allow the clinician to evaluate severity, anticipate/predict course, and, it was hoped, also suggest subtype-specific treatments that would be more effective than a one-size-fits-all classification scheme. Babor's (1996) historical review of the classification/typology literature has been able to identify type classifications as far back as 1850. He observed that the English physician

[William] Carpenter proposed three categories of oinomania [wine mania]: acute, periodic, and chronic. In the acute form

the desire to drink occurs suddenly, but the disease rarely progresses beyond irregular intoxication. The periodic form is characterized by a pattern of binge drinking that becomes progressively more severe and damaging. In the chronic form, the desire for alcohol stimulation becomes an overwhelming preoccupation that precipitates constant alcohol consumption. (p. 7)

Although mention of drinking consequences was missing from Carpenter's acute category, the acute form maps reasonably well onto the *DSM-IV* classification of alcohol abuse. Carpenter's periodic and chronic forms bear some resemblance to Cloninger, Bohman, and Sigvardsson (1981) milieu-limited and male-limited types, which have more recently been designated as Type I and Type II alcoholism, respectively (Cloninger, 1987).

Babor's (1996) review concluded that the major empirical classification studies repeatedly rediscover these two types, which he more generically labels as Apollonian and Dionysian. The former is characterized by later onset of alcohol dependence, a slower disease course, fewer social complications, less psychological impairment, and a better prognosis, and the latter is characterized by early onset, physical aggression, more severe symptomatology, a denser positive family history (suggesting a stronger genetic basis for the disorder), and more personality disturbance (p. 13). Newer studies using factor-analytic and cluster-analytic techniques continue to document the utility of this two-category scheme, but periodically other subtypes show up. Thus, Del Boca and Hesselbrock (1996) observed in a cluster analysis of a heterogeneous inpatient population that another nonantisocial subtype could be identified that was heavily comorbid with depression and anxiety and was twice as common in women as in men (also see Ball, 1996; Windle & Scheidt, 2004).

In coming to a conclusion about how much differentiated variation exists in the adult course of AUD, it is essential to keep in mind that the use of treatment samples to establish typologies is inherently a biased activity, given the restrictions in range of variation, severity, and comorbidity that are found in such subject populations. As far back as 1946, Berkson noted the bias in such samples. They are restricted to more severe and nonremitting cases and also may be socioeconomically biased, given who ends up in large public institutions. It is on these grounds that both the earlier Epidemiologic Catchment Area data set (Helzer et al., 1991; Regier et al., 1990) and the more recent National Comorbidity Study (Kessler et al., 1994, 1997) are so important in understanding the manner in which comorbidity and course are linked over time. Working from these databases, in a series of earlier papers (Zucker, 1987, 1994; Zucker, Chermack, & Curran, 2000) I have described six subtypes that account for the observed epidemiologic and comorbid variation. The types were established based on the epidemiologic evidence of major differences in developmental trajectory as well as differences in adult function, comorbidity, course, and prognosis for the different subtypes, and although several of them were proposed solely on the basis of a careful literature review rather than typological analysis, recent efforts to characterize this heterogeneity continue to support their validity (Hasin, Paykin, & Endicott, 2001; Windle & Scheidt, 2004).

Figure 17.5 provides graphic representations of the trajectories of the different types. Three are characterized by way of their association with specific forms of psychiatric comorbidity (Figure 17.5a); the other three, as a group, are differentiated by their *lack of significant comorbidity* (Figure 17.5b). One of the comorbid forms, the one most commonly described, is the *antisocial alcoholic* type. This subtype has already been described from the perspective of emerging adolescent problem behavior, but it has not been given a clinical label by adolescence researchers (Weber, Graham, Hansen, Flay, & Anderson, 1989). This is Babor's Dionysian type, also Cloninger's male-limited

(Type II) group, and involves a continuity pathway, a co-association of long standing between alcohol problems and antisocial behavior in its developmentally progressing forms (Zucker, Ellis, Bingham, et al., 1996). The antisocial behavior first shows as conduct problems, later emerges into delinquent activity, and ultimately shows as Antisocial Personality Disorder. The antisocial behavior is a central part of the emergence of the alcoholism, and the alcohol problems and alcoholism are an essential piece in the emergence of the antisocial adaptation (see Zucker, Ellis, Bingham, et al., 1996, for a fuller description of this type). A second type, *developmentally limited alcoholism,* likewise involves a comorbid antisocial connection, but the Conduct Disorder is stage-limited (i.e., this is the stage-specific delinquent and impulsive activity of the adolescent problem behavior syndrome that was described earlier; cf. Donovan & Jessor, 1985). The antisociality is coupled with the problem alcohol use endemic to adolescence. Howard Blane (1979) called attention to it more than a generation ago without giving it a formal "alcoholism" label. (He called it "frequent heavy drinking.") The third type involves the emergence in childhood and adolescence of internalizing symptomatology in high-risk populations (Colder & Chassin, 1993; Earls, Reich, Jung, & Cloninger, 1988; Rolf, Johnson, Israel, Baldwin, & Chandra, 1988; Sher, Walitzer, Wood, & Brent, 1991), but it is linked to a trajectory of severe and sustained alcohol-related difficulty only in adulthood. This third pattern, termed *negative affect alcoholism,* is more common among women (Del Boca & Hesselbrock, 1996; Turnbull & Gomberg, 1990) and has also been tied to the special role demands that women face (Wilsnack, Klassen, Schur, & Wilsnack, 1991), as well as to the influence of genetic factors common to both Major Depression and alcoholism (Kendler, Heath, Neale, Kessler, & Eaves, 1992; Merikangas, Leckman, Prusoff, Pauls, & Weissman, 1985).

In contrast to the comorbid subtypes, the trajectories schematically presented in Figure 17.5b depict a set of alcoholisms that have no clearly demarcated childhood antecedents. They involve sustained alcohol intake, which leads to severe alcohol-related symptomatology. No other behavioral covariation is known to have linkages to their onset, and they are identifiable more by their drinking-related consequences than their nondrinking etiology. This is the type that is most often viewed as the pure example of alcoholism as an addictive disorder. It is almost certainly driven by alcohol-specific vulnerabilities, including a lower sensitivity to ethanol's intoxicating effects (Schuckit et al., 2001; Schuckit, Smith, & Tipp, 1997) and a greater subjective experience of activation and

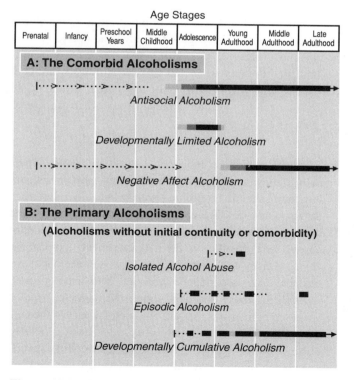

Figure 17.5 Course of the comorbid alcoholisms and the primary alcoholisms.

energy that makes consumption both more reinforcing and less aversive (Newlin & Thomson, 1990). In its more extreme form, a strongly addictive disorder emerges over time (Hill, 1992). A secondary hypothesis is that this trajectory and the other noncomorbid forms are driven by the presence of elevated environmental stress, occurring in a social context that provides a support and value structure for alcohol as the drug of choice for tension reduction. Under circumstances of nonsustained stress (e.g., immediately preceding or following the breakup of a marriage; cf. Cahalan, 1970), *isolated abuse* may occur. Under circumstances where the stress is recurring (e.g., times of heightened stress related to periodic job layoffs; cf. Brenner, 1973), or for those in intermittently high-stress occupations, the symptomatology becomes *episodic*. For those whose contextual and individual vulnerability match is greatest, the alcohol-seeking behavior eventually moves into a chronic adaptation. This latter trajectory has been termed *developmentally cumulative alcoholism*. There are obvious parallels between these latter three trajectories and the developmentally limited but antisocially comorbid pattern of adolescence. Although the form of all four of these types is similar, for the developmentally limited pattern, individual-level etiologic risk factors have already been identified, but the onset and termination of the disorder is driven by non-individual-level contextual factors to which the individual responds. Nonresponsivity (i.e., the perseverance of the high consumption level in the face of increasing social stigma and penalty) is what differentiates the developmentally cumulative pattern from both the developmentally limited and the episodic pattern. This may also be the case for the episodic and developmentally cumulative variants; in fact, both Schuckit and Moos and their colleagues (Moos, Brennan, & Schutte, 1998; Schuckit, 1988, 1994) have addressed this issue. But at the moment, their causal structure has been less well charted.

THE OTHER HALF OF THE STORY: ETIOLOGY FROM A NEUROBIOLOGICAL PERSPECTIVE

The review thus far has focused primarily on the environmental and behavioral segments of the risk matrix. In this and the following section, I review genetic and other neurobiological contributors to this matrix.[4]

---

[4] See note 3.

Alcoholism as a Genetic Disorder

Alcoholism is a complex phenotype; the previous two sections on heterogeneity of risk and disorder drive this point home. The fact that the phenotype's expression is dependent on the presence of an environmental object (ethanol) suggests that environmental factors play a significant role in etiology, but the evidence for a genetic contribution to alcoholism risk is also indisputable. Evidence from family, adoption, twin, and cross-fostering studies all support this conclusion. A summary report by McGue (1994) of seven twin studies concluded that heritability estimates range from 40% to 60% for males and from 0 to 58% for females. However, other work with larger samples indicates that heritability of female alcoholism is approximately the same as it is for men (Kendler, Neale, Heath, Kessler, & Eaves, 1994; Nurnberger et al., 2004).

It is important to note that the widely observed variability in heritability effects is not evidence indicating weakness of the effect. Rather, a characteristic of multifactorial phenotypes such as alcoholism is that the variability in estimation is both a function of the way the phenotype (such as diagnosis) is measured, as well as the variability in the population (Falconer & MacKay, 1996). In turn, the population variability is itself a function of environmental exposure (e.g., alcohol availability), age structure, and population genetic variations. The latter determine the allele frequency of a particular gene, which in turn determines the degree to which the active variant is or is not present; population-specific environmental variability interacts with that in determining whether a particular gene will or will not be expressed.

The heritability studies point up four other aspects of the genetic etiology of the disorder:

1. Alcohol dependence and alcohol abuse are not unequivocally the same phenotype; that is, they may be not just indicators that differentiate severity but rather differentiable phenotypes. Recent epidemiologic data supporting this view show that approximately a third of the alcohol dependence population do not also meet criteria for abuse (Hasin & Grant, 2004). That is, one may have physiological dependence without ever having gone through an abuse phase involving the adverse, usually social complications that are an essential part of the category. Differences in heritability rates have generally been found for the two categories, with alcohol dependence being the more heritable form (Kaij, 1960; Pickens et al., 1991). But the dialogue remains active both in the genetic and the epidemiologic literature (Grant, 1996;

Hasin & Grant, 2004; Nurnberger et al., 2004; Ridenour et al., 2003; Schuckit & Smith, 2001). This is an essential issue that needs clarification.

2. It is well-known from the epidemiologic literature that other substance use disorders assort in alcoholic families along with alcoholism, and the more severe Type II/Dionysian form commonly includes comorbid other drug use. This phenomenon is consistent with genetic studies indicating that a large portion of the heritable variance for substance use disorders is not drug-specific, but is shared across drugs of abuse (Kendler, Jacobson, Prescott, & Neale, 2003a; Kreek, Nielsen, & La Forge, 2004; Krueger et al., 2002; Tsuang et al., 1998).

3. The heritability studies also parse the non-drug-specific heritability pathway in another way. Alcoholism is frequently comorbid with other nondrug psychiatric disorders. This phenomenon has been observed in the epidemiologic literature (Helzer et al., 1991; Kessler et al., 1997) and in the trajectory/subtype literature,

and it has already been discussed in early portions of the chapter. What is less often articulated is that the comorbidity itself can be differentiated by content into two clusters, one involving externalizing disorders of undercontrol (Attention-Deficit/Hyperactivity Disorder and Antisocial Personality Disorder), the other involving internalizing/negative affectivity symptomatology (anxiety, depression). Recent family and twin studies indicate that *heritability of AUD is also primarily through these non-alcohol-specific externalizing and internalizing pathways* (Kendler, Prescott, Myers, & Neale, 2003b; Nurnberger et al., 2004). This work, not yet part of the mainstream etiologic literature, indicates significant convergence with the findings on early behavioral risk indicators of later AUD reviewed in an earlier part of this chapter.

Figure 17.6 provides a summary of the core Kendler et al. (2003b) findings. It shows that the strongest heritable pathway is through a common externalizing factor,

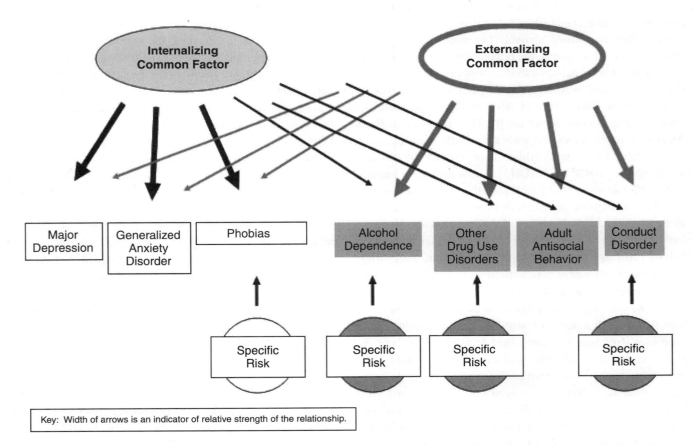

Figure 17.6 Structure of common and disorder-specific genetic risk for common psychiatric and substance use disorders. *Source:* Based on Figures 1 and 3 in "The Structure of Genetic and Environmental Risk Factors for Common Psychiatric and Substance Use Disorders in Men and Women," by K. S. Kendler, C. A. Prescott, J. Myers, and M. C. Neale, 2003, *Archives of General Psychiatry, 60,* pp. 929–937, and an earlier version of this model by J. Lappalainen.

with a secondary pathway through an internalizing common genetic factor (also see point 4). Each of these factors are almost certainly polygenic traits.

4. Also as shown in Figure 17.6, the Kendler et al. (2003b) analysis indicates that some of the genetic variance for alcohol dependence is disorder-specific. Although their study was not designed to identify the mechanisms and genes that account for this specific variance, a significant body of other work has identified a few of the component pieces that appear to be part of the process.

The most robust genetic markers are variants involved in the metabolism of alcohol—specifically involving aldehyde dehydrogenase (ADH) and aldehyde dehydrogenase (ALDH). The two candidate genes that protect against heavy drinking are the functional genetic variants of alcohol dehydrogenase that exhibit high alcohol oxidizing activity (ADH) and the genetic variant of aldehyde dehydrogenase (ALDH2) that exhibits low acetaldehyde oxidizing activity (Li, 2000). The ALDH2 variant is common in some Asian populations. Those who have it experience a flushing reaction, headache, palpitations, dizziness, and nausea after consuming alcohol. The aversive experience appears to be protective in the populations where that variant exists (Thomasson, Crabb, Eadenberg, & Li, 1993). However, the low prevalence of the ALDH2 deficiency in individuals of European and African ancestry results in very low explanatory power for the U.S. population. High ADH activity is associated with a similarly unpleasant set of symptoms following drinking; here the genetic variants involving the ADH2[2] and ADH3[1] alleles appear to be protective (Thomasson et al., 1993). At the same time, consistent with a complex genetic model, a cross-national study by Reich and Li (1994) observed that even though Koreans have a relatively high rate of ALDH2 deficiency, alcoholism rates are very high in this population, suggesting that cultural influences may sometimes override the impact of the biological feedback system.

Beyond the genetic variants involved in alcohol metabolism pathways, a number of plausible candidate genes have been identified that may contribute to etiology, but studies are not uniformly confirmatory of a link either to alcoholism or to some intermediary trait such as externalizing or internalizing behavior. Moreover, mechanisms of action are only partially understood at best. Of these, genes involved in regulation of the serotonergic system have received the largest amount of attention in the past generation. Serotonin (5HT) is generally considered to operate as a regulator, with increased 5HT function operating to inhibit behavior (Lucki, 1998). Thus, genes involved in the system's operation should

show some relationship to impulsivity and to the externalizing/undercontrol system. Genetic variants of tryptophan hydroxylase (TPH), the rate-limiting enzyme of the biosynthesis of 5HT, have been associated with anger-related traits (New et al., 1998) and suicide (Turecki et al., 2001). Genetic variants in monoamine oxidase A (the primary enzyme for 5HT catabolism), specifically involving the MAOA promoter, have been associated with impulsive aggression, as well as alcohol-related traits (Brunner, Nelen, Breakefield, Ropers, & van Oost, 1993; Manuck, Flory, Ferrell, Mann, Muldoon, 2000; Schmidt et al., 2000), antisocial alcoholism (Vanyukov, Moss, Yu, Tarter, & Deka, 1995), and impulsive antisocial behavior when in interaction with the presence of childhood maltreatment (Caspi et al., 2002). The 5HT1B receptor has been linked with antisocial alcoholism in humans (Lappalainen et al., 1998) and with increased impulsive aggression in mice (Saudou et al., 1994). Lesch et al. (1996) reported on another gene in the 5HT system that also has potential relevance, namely 5HTTLPR, the promoter for the serotonin transporter. They observed that two common allelic forms of the promoter were associated with variation in neuroticism score, a general index of negative affectivity and emotionality. Since that time, the literature of over a dozen replication attempts has been evenly divided between replications and nonreplications. More than 100 publications have since also reported association with aggression, suicidality, and depression (see Stoltenberg & Burmeister, 2000 for a detailed review). Again, however, none of these studies has been consistently replicated. Although this may be due to lack of power, it also is quite possible that the correct underlying phenotype has not yet been identified, in which case the targeted phenotype would at best be an imprecise indicator of the correct one. More generally, the uncertain relevance of this gene, illustrated by the equivocal findings, indicates the relative infancy of the field, although the burgeoning of genotyping technology, allowing fine-grained genome-wide scans at ever decreasing cost, suggests that this situation will become much more resolved in the next 5 to 10 years.

Other candidate genes beyond the serotonin system have also been put forward as plausible candidates because of a direct connection to alcoholism, because of a demonstrated relationship to intermediate traits subsumable under the externalizing/undercontrol or internalizing/negative affectivity, or because of a known relationship to an intermediate trait (e.g., P300) or behavioral phenotype (e.g., smoking) that has separately been etiologically linked to AUD. I provide a brief laundry list in Table 17.5.

The diversity of potential pathways to the AUD end point that is implied in this list underscores four points that are taken for granted by geneticists but that are less com-

TABLE 17. 5   Other Candidate Genes with a Potential Causal Relationship to Alcoholism

Locus Symbol	Variant	Gene Name and Description	Evidence in Literature	Citation
SLC6A3	rs27072; promoter repeat	DAT; dopamine transporter	Smoking; ADHD; alcohol withdrawal, Bipolar Disorder	Waldman et al. (1998)
DRD4	1–10 copies of 48 bp/16 aa-521 C/T	Dopamine receptor D4; exon 3 coding repeat in C-terminal domain; promoter SNP	ADHD, possibly novelty seeking	Faraone, Doyle, Mick, & Biederman (2001)
DAT1	G2319A SNP	Dopamine transporter in the 3′ untranslated region	Increased risk for alcoholism	Ueno et al. (1999)
BDNF	Val66Met	Brain-derived neurotrophic factor; Met lower BDNF activity	Bipolar Disorder, neuroticism	Sklar et al. (2002)
COMPT	Val158Met	Catechol-O-methyltransverase; enzyme activity variant	Differentiates late-onset alcoholism from early, although evidence mixed	Tiihonen et al. (1999); Wang et al. (2001)
GABRA2	3 SNPs	GABA alpha 2 subunit; haplotype association	Alcoholism, brain EEG (P300)	Sander et al. (1999)
GABRA6	3 locus haplotypes	$GABA_A$ receptor subunit genes	Alcoholism	Radel et al. (2005)
CYP2E1	1D	Regulatory (expression)	Alcohol, nicotine	Hayashi et al. (1991)

Note: See text for description of genes involved in alcohol metabolism and in regulation of the serotonergic system.

monly appreciated by the behavioral science community. One is that the final common pathway for AUD not only is multifactorial, but also probably includes variables that account for small amounts of variance that make their detection difficult. Thus, studies with low statistical power will be limited in their ability to uncover them, and the etiologic models they create will be underspecified.

Second, the pathway from genetic variation to phenotype is almost certainly indirect, involving a multistage process. The three-step case, from genetic variation to alcohol metabolism to alcoholism, is only the simplest case scenario, and it involves no motivational (reward), appetitive (drug sensitivity, craving), or cognitive (expectancy) mechanisms. Pathways through impulsivity and emotionality involve at least another step in this chain of effect and would suggest that several additional steps are also part of the sequence leading to the end point addictive disorder. Gene-environment interactions, especially those that are developmentally dependent, almost certainly ensure the multistage nature of these sequences (cf. Caspi et al., 2002).

The third point follows from the second point, namely, that intermediate processes are often not going to be visible and detectable at the behavioral level.

Fourth, genes have dual functions: One is a template function, which allows them to replicate with a very high degree of fidelity over time and across generations. They also have a transcriptional function that determines structure and function at the cellular level and at the level of

brain and ultimately also determines the phenotype. The transcriptional function is the one that is highly regulated, and this regulation is susceptible to environmental input (variation; E. R. Kandel, 1998). Environmental experiences such as stress, arousal, learning, and social interaction impact the brain either directly, through changes in the development of neural networks, or through the production of hormones that alter their development. Thus, the brain is the playing field on which gene-environment interactions ultimately take place. All of these observations are implicit in the schematic model presented in Figure 17.2 at the beginning of this chapter, but the details of the bottom-up flow-through process were only briefly touched on at that point.

Intermediate-Level Etiology in Brain

Given the interplay of these mechanisms in brain, two different lines of investigation have worked at delineating the structures and neural circuitry that are involved in the development of alcoholic etiology.[5] One, more than a century old with a history in both neuropathology and neuropsychology, has worked to identify those structures crucial to

---

[5] This section is based heavily on unpublished working papers and ongoing collaborations between Joel T. Nigg, Mary M. Heitzeg, Jon-Kar Zubieta, and the author.

the action of ethanol on the brain. Up until a generation ago, this work focused on brain impairments from high alcohol dosing over long periods of time, as found in chronic alcoholism (see the reviews by Ron, 1987; Victor, Adams, & Collins, 1971). This work has implicated the mesocorticolimbic dopamine system, including the nucleus accumbens, amygdala, hippocampus, and prefrontal cortex, as the system where the pharmacological actions of ethanol converge to produce their reinforcing effects (see review in Weiss & Porrino, 2002).

Using this as baseline evidence for site of action, a second line of investigation in more recent years has asked whether any of these sites has a predispositional vulnerability both to impairment and to alcohol-seeking behavior. At the neurocognitive level, a number of constructs have been identified as important to risk. Executive functioning entails the ability to regulate behavior to context and to maintain a goal set; it relies on multiple constituent functions (Miyake et al., 2000). This is a multicomponent construct, including such elements as response suppression/inhibition (the ability to strategically suppress a prepotent or prepared motor response), working memory (itself multicomponential), set shifting, and interference control (Pennington & Ozonoff, 1996). These capacities are represented to a large degree in parallel frontal-subcortical-thalamic neural loops; important structures include right inferior frontal cortex-to-basal-ganglia (response inhibition; Aron, Fletcher, Bullmore, Sahakian, & Robbins, 2003), dorsolateral prefrontal cortex and associated structures (working memory; Klingberg, Forssberg, & Westerberg, 2002; Marshuetz, Smith, Jonides, DeGutis, & Chenevert, 2000; Thomas et al., 1999), and anterior cingulate cortex. These networks are heavily subserved by catecholamine innervation. To the extent that they translate directly to behavioral differences, they have relevance to a spectrum of activities that elevate or dampen risk. They relate to wisdom in choice of peers, understanding of the importance of context to appropriate drinking behavior, ability to desist when encouraged to drink or encouraged to continue drinking under circumstances that indicate drinking consequences, such as increasing intoxication, and the ability to get to work or school the next day and adequately function—behaviors that may be costly in the long term.

Extensive theory as far back as a generation ago (Tarter, Alterman, & Edwards, 1985) would link aspects of executive control with alcoholism risk, although data to support that link are mixed (Finn, Mazas, Justus, & Steinmetz, 2002; Giancola & Moss, 1998; Peterson, Finn, & Pihl, 1992; Tarter et al., 1999). More recent work (Nigg, Wong, et al., 2005) suggests that the risk element here is primarily re-

lated to response inhibition. In addition, Finn and colleagues (Finn, Justus, Mazas, & Steinmetz, 1999) have theorized that auditory working memory moderates temperamental risk for alcoholism. Other neuropsychological theories of individual vulnerability to alcoholism are numerous, but a great many are at a level of low specificity (cf. Tarter et al., 2003), thus making it impossible, on the one hand, to link findings to activation of specific brain regions/functions and, on the other, to develop specific testable models that can be confirmed or disconfirmed and that will allow for the development of a systematic knowledge base. For these reasons, it is essential to develop (and test) models at a high level of specificity. In particular, in addition to response suppression and working memory from the executive domain, the role of right-lateralized visual-spatial functioning as a correlate of substance use risk (Schandler, Thomas, & Cohen, 1995) is of great current interest. Although this correlation is often observed, a process explanation of why spatial weakness would cause maladjustment may have to rely on appeal to related right hemisphere processes, most notably social information processing. Conceivably, a social information-processing weakness may mediate any observed visual-spatial deficit effects on drinking problems in early adulthood.

Closely intersecting with these processes is the domain of motivation, and reward responsivity in particular. Reward response involves dopaminergic pathways in the mesocortical and mesolimbic pathways that are closely related to those involved in executive control. The literature clearly indicates that executive and reward response mutually influence one another (Nigg, 2000; Rothbart & Bates, 1998) both in development and dynamically. Extensive data suggest that at both the behavioral and the neural level, substance use problems are associated with a dysregulation of reward responsivity, such that the subcortical, involuntary elements (subserved by limbic and striatal circuitry) are overresponding to salient drug-associated stimuli, and the normal cortical control (via frontal circuitry) over this response is impaired or inhibited, leading to excessive risk-taking behavior (Goldstein & Volkow, 2002; Jentsch & Taylor, 1999; Rosenkranz & Grace, 2001). Furthermore, there is preliminary evidence for a dysregulation of reward-related circuitry in at-risk populations before alcohol and illicit drug use occurs (Heitzeg, Zucker, & Zubieta, 2003).

Developmental Significance of Neural Models in Late Adolescence

At the same developmental time during which a major buildup of alcohol use and alcohol problem behavior is taking place, neural alterations in the frontal executive and reward systems involved in impulse and emotion regulation are occurring. The dorsolateral prefrontal cortex (important to executive functioning as well as motivation) is one of the last brain regions to mature, with myelogenesis continuing at least until early adolescence (Fuster, 1997) and potentially all the way into early adulthood (Benes, 2001; Gogtay et al., 2004). Progressive increases in the white matter of this region have been shown during childhood and adolescence (Reiss, Abrams, Singer, Ross, & Denckla, 1996). These developmental changes directly impact impulse and emotion regulation. It is known that throughout childhood, there are developmental gains in the ability to suppress or inhibit prepotent responses and the ability to suppress irrelevant information (Brainerd & Reyna, 1993; Casey, Tottenham, & Fossella, 2002; Diamond, 1990). Social and emotional skills, such as the ability to discriminate emotional facial expressions, also develop throughout childhood and early adolescence (Kolb, Wilson, & Taylor, 1992), with associated changes in amygdala responsivity (Thomas et al., 2001). Furthermore, during the interval from childhood through adolescence, the prefrontal cortex gains greater efficiency in its inhibitory control over the amygdala and other limbic structures involved in emotion and reward response (Damasio, 1998; Hariri, Bookheimer, & Mazziotta, 2000; Killgore, Oki, & Yurgelun-Todd, 2001). In addition to these structural brain changes, both human and animal studies indicate that there is an alteration in mesocorticolimbic dopamine systems in the adolescent brain (reviewed in Spear, 2002). Dopamine input to the prefrontal cortex peaks during adolescence in nonhuman primates (Rosenberg & Lewis, 1994) and rats (Kalsbeek, Voorn, Buijs, Pool, & Uylings, 1988), and dopamine binding, primarily in the striatum but also in the nucleus accumbens (important for reward responsivity), also peaks during adolescence (Seeman et al., 1987). Understanding, at the neural activation level, how these mechanisms operate is crucial to a full explanation of individual risk using neurocognitive and neurobehavioral models.

The developmental significance of these changes, when superimposed on a social structure that is encouraging the emergence of alcohol use, is major. Extensive neuroimaging evidence indicates that alcohol and other substances of abuse have acute and lasting effects on these frontolimbic and frontostriatal systems that are implicated in impulse control and reward responsivity (Moselhy, Georgiou, & Kahn, 2001; Pfefferbaum, Sullivan, Rosenbloom, Mathalon, & Lim, 1998; Tiihonen et al., 1994; Vogel-Sprott, Easdon, Fillmore, Finn, & Justus, 2001; Volkow et al., 1993; Volkow et al., 1988). Such effects are thus being superimposed on

this developing circuitry. Major issues not yet addressed concern the relative importance of amount and timing of alcohol (and other drug exposure) in bringing about such changes, the degree to which other environmental exposures (e.g., stress) also play a role, and the degree to which early neurocognitive vulnerabilities interact with the drug exposure in producing change. An understanding of these processes will require the kind of multilevel-multisystem explanatory structure advanced here. A full explanation will benefit from careful neurobehavioral/neurocognitive characterization that takes into account key aspects of executive functioning and motivation and selected associated systems such social information processing, along with a characterization of the social context in which they occur. At the same time, it is important to understand how these constructs are actually operating neurally by mapping changes in neural response patterns associated with both risk for alcohol problems and with actual use and its sequelae.

OTHER EPIGENETIC ISSUES

Epigenetic process is by definition interactive, but the degree to which this takes place as a multilevel, multi-system process has received relatively little attention in the literature. In this section, I consider two major factors that contribute to stability and change in risk and disorder over time.

The Nestedness of Environmental, Behavioral, and Neurobiological Risk

From an etiologic perspective, there is special interest in the degree to which risk aggregation is correlated, both at the individual and familial levels as well as at the neighborhood level. At the individual level, the literature has increasingly acknowledged the clustering of comorbid symptomatology, social dysfunction, and psychiatric severity among adults in both AUD (Kessler et al., 1997) and non-AUD populations (Babor, 1996). In fact, as noted earlier, such assortment has been one of the driving forces for the notion that subtypes of disorder need to be demarcated. The association of severe alcoholism with poverty also has a long and visible history (Brenner, 1973; Fitzgerald & Zucker, 1995), and analyses even at the microenvironmental level have documented a clear association between neighborhood disadvantage and alcoholism rates (Pallas, 1992). The most common explanation of this has been that poverty, and the neighborhood structure in which it is embedded, drive the alcoholism (i.e., a top-down explanation). Less clear is the degree to which niche seeking is also at work here, which would lead persons to seek out and assort in environments as well as in marriages (cf. Scarr & McCartney, 1983). Some evidence suggests that such a process is operative, at least for those with antisocial alcoholism. Thus, antisocial alcoholic men are more likely to marry/couple with antisocial and heavy-drinking/alcoholic women (Zucker, Ellis, Bingham, et al., 1996), and the families they create are more likely to be disadvantaged in their capacity to socialize offspring. Antisocial alcoholism is similarly associated with downward social mobility (Zucker, Ellis, Fitzgerald, et al., 1996), and offspring in these families, even early in life, appear to be developmentally more disadvantaged. They have more learning disabilities and intellectual deficits and show weaker delay of gratification than do offspring from alcoholic but not antisocial families (Nigg, Glass, et al., 2004; Poon, Ellis, Zucker, & Fitzgerald, 1998).

A risk cumulation model would predict that as these factors cumulate, they increasingly create a risk structure that moves the child into peer networks high in aggression, negative mood, and substance use, thus providing a familial, a neighborhood, and a peer structure, all of which act in concert in encouraging the development of (1) an expectancy structure that is positive toward use and abuse of alcohol and other drugs, (2) very early onset for such use, and (3) a stable repertoire of behaviors that are prototypic for the eventual emergence of abuse/dependence. Such environments are also likely to be high in stress, which would impact hypothalamic-pituitary-adrenal axis activity and the development of negative affectivity. Some portions of this emerging matrix have already been confirmed. That is, children from antisocial alcoholic families have earlier onset of alcohol use, and they move more quickly into alcohol problems. Further, their own conduct problems (i.e., their burgeoning antisociality) is a partial mediator of this relationship, above and beyond the effects of the parental alcoholism (Nigg, Glass, et al., 2004).

My colleagues and I have elsewhere described this risk aggregation in certain ecological and familial microenvironments as a "nesting structure" (Zucker, Fitzgerald, et al., 1995) that makes stability of psychopathological outcome much more likely and therefore encourages stability of risk over time. The trajectories of externalizing and internalizing behavior for high-risk youth shown in Figure 17.3 are consistent with this view, although, as noted earlier, the main effects of genetic variation have not been parsed out of that work. Also consistent with this view is the work of Loukas et al. (2003). Although the normal developmental course of child aggressiveness is one of decreasing aggression over the interval from early childhood

to late middle school, Loukas and colleagues found that initial level of child conduct problems as well as level of family conflict separately predicted dampening in the rate of decrease of the aggressiveness. That is, both operated to flatten the decrease in aggressiveness. These data are suggestive of an epigenetic process (Gottlieb, 1991) whereby the organism is shaped not only by "initial value" levels of temperament, by its interaction with a responding environment over time. The individual response changes the environmental response in return, and so on, in an iterative process that leads to developmental change.

I have elsewhere argued that the high-risk aggregation structure changes the process model of risk because the variable network determining the effective causal structure has become sufficiently different; it initially contains more variance pertaining to parental and child psychopathology, social deviance, and neurobiological vulnerability than is true of other nonaggregated structures, and the nested nature of these different risks is therefore more likely to produce coalescence and overlearning of the risky behavioral repertoire than would be true in a less densely risk-laden system (Zucker, Chermack, & Curran, 2000). In contrast, when the microenvironment has less collinearity, the developmental course should be more fluid, and also apparently more probabilistic. This line of reasoning is consistent with normative studies of adolescence that have shown the enhanced effects on drug use and timing of onset when family conflict, association with deviant peers, and poor academic performance are clustered (Duncan, Duncan, Biglan, & Ary, 1998). This is a major issue to understand, and design for, when prevention programming is being developed. Its relevance has been relatively ignored by the prevention community (although see Biglan et al., 2004).

Stability and Change in Alcohol Use Disorder Over Time: Factors Predicting Recovery, or Not

One of the diagnostic categories in *DSM-IV* is remission (early versus sustained, full versus partial). Despite the implicit acknowledgment of course variation that this category provides, the literature has paid surprisingly little attention to the understanding of changes in diagnostic status and adaptation over the adult life course and the critical related questions of what creates stability and change.[6] The empirical evidence from both epidemiologic and treatment studies is clear that course is not uniform for all alco-

---

[6] I am indebted to Mary J. McAweeney for her help in writing this section.

holics, whether in treatment or not. A review summarizing results from eight long-term follow-up studies of primarily treatment-recruited alcoholics published between 1982 and 1994 (Vaillant, 1995) noted that approximately 2% per year become abstinent, and that after age 40, approximately 2% die every year.

However, general population studies of alcoholic course suggest a more fluid process. Thus, Hasin, Grant, and Endicott's (1990) general population follow-up study of stability and change in indicators of *DSM-III-R* alcohol abuse and dependence among males over a 4-year interval found that changes away from dependence status involved 54% of the sample (i.e., about half remitted), with 73% of this group remitting entirely. (The parallel figures for the move away from *abuse* involved 46% moving into remission.) Conversely, 46% of those dependent at baseline remained so. Of the initial abuse group, 30% moved into dependence. These rates are quite close to those reported in two more recent and longer-term community prospective studies. Humphreys, Moos, and Cohen (1997), in a study of 395 (50% male) untreated alcoholics followed over 8 years, observed half of the sample to be free of alcohol-related problems at follow-up. Similarly, McAweeney, Zucker, Fitzgerald, Puttler, and Wong (2005) followed 134 community-recruited, initially coupled men meeting criteria for *DSM-IV* AUD diagnosis at baseline. Assessments at three later points over the 9-year interval allowed characterization of intervening course and functioning. They found 44% remitting at the 9-year end point, with approximately half moving out of diagnosis and staying out in during the first 3 years and the remainder experiencing remission at some later point in the interval. Forty-one percent of those meeting diagnosis at baseline continued to make AUD diagnosis over the following 3-, 6- and 9-year intervals, and a small subset of the original group (15%) fluctuated between meeting diagnosis and not meeting diagnosis over the 9 years, but recurring at the 9-year point. Another recent study involving initially untreated alcoholics who were recruited during their first contact with a treatment system observed similar rates of remission, with variation dependent on the level of risk at treatment entry (Moos & Moos, 2003). Subjects with over nine risk factors had a remission rate of 22% and those with two or fewer risk factors had a remission rate of 76% after 8 years.

The risk factors identified by the Mooses and others as contributing to better or worse outcome are of several types. Moos and Moos (2003) found that more participation in Alcoholics Anonymous (AA) or formal treatment over the 8-year follow-up period predicted remission. Also, alcoholics who at baseline consumed more alcohol were in-

toxicated more often, had a heavier drinking pattern, and had increased tolerance, were more likely to be nonremitted at 8-year follow-up. In contrast, in the Humphreys et al. (1997) nontreatment sample, addictive behavior factors such as alcohol consumption and alcohol dependence at baseline did not predict recovery. This was also true in the McAweeney et al. (2005) nontreatment sample. More generally, the existing literature indicates that recovery (movement out of diagnosis, and then staying out) is a dynamic behavior change process at the individual level, involving continued practice of lifestyle change, which reinforces and perpetuates a desire to maintain the change in a positive spiral (Kaskutas, Bond, & Humphreys, 2002; Prochaska, DiClemente, & Norcross, 1992; Vaillant, 1995). For instance, it has been shown in both natural and treatment settings that a pattern of decreased drinking or total abstinence from drinking produced a rise in self-esteem, lessening of depression, and greater confidence to resist drinking (Blomqvist, 1999; S. M. Hall, Wasserman, & Havassy, 1991; Humphreys, Moos, & Finney, 1994).

The across-study discrepancy in the utility of baseline symptom severity as a predictor of later outcome highlights another issue. The McAweeney et al. (2005) study found that social environmental factors played a role in recovery that overrode the effects of current alcoholic functioning. Thus, the study found that wives' baseline AUD status and the extensiveness of their social support network were robust predictors of recovery from diagnosis, above and beyond the alcoholic husband predictors of higher educational achievement, treatment involvement, and the help of a history of prior success (more intervening years of recovery). A parallel set of findings was observed in the Humphreys et al. (1997) study, where social/community resources were more predictive of recovery than individual demographic variables. The effective social/community resources included being an active member of a religious organization, number of outpatient treatment sessions, family relationships, and attendance at AA meetings. One possible reason for the across-study difference in predictive utility of drinking severity at baseline may lie with the difference in populations being studied. In community samples, greater levels of variation exist in social relationships. When the social environment is less fluid, more likely in treatment samples that tend to be older and involve more socially damaged alcoholics, then the severity indicator at baseline may be a more effective predictor.

Thus, recovery from diagnosis appears at least in part to be an interactive, epigenetic process that may not be entirely predictable on the basis of prior history. More than a generation ago, Moos, Finney, and Chan (1982) observed that spouses of relapsed alcoholics drank more alcohol and participated in fewer social activities. These findings suggest that the marital partner's ongoing functioning plays a role in stability or change of their husband's diagnosis. A parallel observation in the McAweeney et al. study suggests the same. Recovered men's partners decreased their AUD in the interim, but nonremitters' partners increased. The next step for research in this area clearly needs to move to the microanalytic, real-time level of social interaction to isolate the critical behavioral and interactional ingredients that create these macrolevel variables. Such factors might include the quality of microinteractions between partners (leading to divorce or not), the level of negativity associated with the drinking, the specific nature of peer relationships, and their social networks outside the marriage (Jacob, Leonard, & Haber, 2001; Leonard & Jacob, 1997; McCrady, Hayaki, Epstein, & Hirsch, 2002). At the same time, it is conceivable that the putative interactive effects are a product of marital assortment, which thereafter is responsible for the differences in marital interaction and social functioning of partners. This hypothesis will also need to be evaluated, although evidence to date is not consistent with this explanation (Floyd et al., in press).

FUTURE WORK AND CONCLUDING SUMMARY

In this section, I comment on three next-step problems that the field needs to address. They involve the need for (1) redefinitions of the phenotype, (2) a change in the core paradigm of the field, and (3) better articulation of gene-brain-behavior-environment relationships.

Redefining the Phenotype

A number of generalizations about the characteristics of AUD are derivative from this review:

- The etiology of AUD is emergent, and significant portions of the risk structure are identifiable in very early childhood.
- Variations in trajectory of risk in earlier life and symptomatology and course in adulthood provide clear evidence that AUD is a heterogeneous family of disorders, and the time has passed for it to any longer be regarded as a single phenotype. In its crudest form, the AUD category is differentiable into an early-onset, high-risk,

high-chronicity trajectory that emerges out of a nested matrix involving high individual undercontrol and high family, socioenvironmental, and genetic risk, and a number of shorter course trajectories that appear to be strongly driven by environmental, stage-dependent (late youth and young adulthood) influences or specific environmental stressors (divorce, death, trauma/abuse). A third group display as gradual-onset, primary addictions to ethanol that occur in high-use environments among those with a prior drug vulnerability (e.g., low sensitivity to ethanol) and that continue without significant co-occurring psychiatric comorbidity.

- The occurrence of externalizing or internalizing symptomatology, or both, or neither, in childhood and externalizing or internalizing disorder, or neither, in adulthood is critical to the classification of the phenotype.

- Because risk is emergent and takes place in a fairly well-defined risk matrix, cross-sectional classification of symptomatology in adulthood is not a sufficient marker of course. A new diagnostic framework is required that takes account of trajectory variation, onset characteristics (early versus later; within a high-adversity, nested risk environment or not), and offset characteristics (how long symptomatology has been absent; whether it has recurred or not, and if it has, its duration and severity) and that evaluates the degree of risk of the nesting structure within which the current symptomatology is embedded.

  The author and colleagues began such a formulation in the early 1990s by creating an index to scale the "mass" and "momentum" of the disorder (Zucker, 1991; Zucker, Davies, Kincaid, Fitzgerald, & Reider, 1997). The index, called the Lifetime Alcohol Problem Score (LAPS), is a developmentally based measure that conceptualized the disorder as a mass of greater or lesser breadth (indexed by variety of different symptoms) with properties of extensiveness in time and life course invasiveness (the index had an onset component, a "life-% with symptomatology" component, and a more recent version also has an offset component; Jester et al., 2001). It has proven to be an effective dimensional measure of life course diagnostic weight in a number of different studies (e.g., McAweeney et al., 2005; Wong et al., 1999), but it has not been widely used outside of our own group.

- Ethanol has been called a "dirty" drug, because there are so many sites of action in the brain that appear to have relevance in the development and maintenance of the addictive disorder. In parallel, this review clearly indicates that the etiology of this family of disorders is likewise dirty, involving a large matrix of causal systems that operate in concert to produce one or another of the AUD end points. Apropos point two, the different concerts need to be better differentiated and scored for the field to move to the next level of understanding of the family.

Is the Child Father to the Man, or Mother to the Woman? Problems in Embracing a Developmental Psychopathology Paradigm

As noted in point 1, and as articulated at some length earlier in this chapter, eight different longitudinal studies conducted in three countries have replicated the finding that early externalizing and internalizing problems are developmental precursors of AUD. The earliest of these studies was published almost a generation ago. Thus, it remains extraordinarily puzzling that this work has not been integrated into the common knowledge base and remains virtually unknown by the treatment community. Conversely, in the past several years, considerable attention has been given to a developmentally intermediary indicator of course and of AUD risk, namely, early onset of drinking. There are a host of studies that have observed this relationship in the past decade, and National Longitudinal Alcohol Epidemiologic Survey (NLAES) data have also documented it (Grant, 1998; Grant & Dawson, 1998). But from the perspective of a developmentalist, that marker, and those processes, are already well down the road of risk development.

There are a number of reasons this problem still exists. I have recently addressed some of the clinical and social policy reasons for this state of affairs (Zucker & Wong, 2005). But for this set of volumes, it is more appropriate to note that an epigenetic understanding of risk and disorder still remains outside the accepted framework of understanding for substance use disorders more broadly. I hope this chapter will contribute to rectifying this situation. It remains a major issue for the field to address.

(As a historical note, when this chapter was written in the summer and fall of 2004, this was the situation. But during that time, under the direction of NIAAA Director Ting-Kai Li, a major shift in the Institute's direction began, which reconceptualized alcoholism as a developmental disorder whose origins begin before adulthood. A number of new initiatives were started, foremost among which was NIAAA's Underage Drinking Initiative [http://www.niaaa.nih.gov/about/underage.htm#welcome], which, with the help of an outside team of experts, has

begun to explore the precursive elements in this process at levels ranging from the genetic to the systemic, and ranging back in developmental time from conception into early childhood, and thereafter. The initiative not only represents a major reframing of the core nature of the disorder, including nonspecific-to-alcohol as well as alcohol-specific components, but it also articulates a perspective on behavior disorder that represents a paradigm shift for a national policymaking body charged with understanding the causes, etiology, and treatment of a major psychopathological disorder. It is noteworthy that the two main professional organizations whose membership deal with these issues on a day-to-day basis, the American Psychiatric Association and the American Psychological Association, have not yet made that shift.)

Articulating Specific Gene-Brain-Behavior-Environment Relationships

Given current developments in molecular biology and statistical genetics, earlier questions about heritability and relative effects of genes and environment are no longer important for the field to consider. Alcoholism, in its varying forms, is both a genetic and an environmental disorder (A. Heath, 1995; Jacob et al., 2001; McGue, 1994), and next-step research needs to be focused on questions of mechanism: of which genes, acting in which combinations, affect which intermediary neurobiological systems in the development of risky traits, which, if emergent long enough, under exposure in critical risky environments, will lead to the clinical phenotypes of alcoholic disorder.

In this multilevel explanatory structure, it is equally important to understand the role of specific environmental influences in stimulating or dampening gene expression and, in parallel fashion, stimulating or dampening behavioral expression of the risky trait(s), and in allowing it (them) to remain in place long enough to become specialized. Time is also a significant part of this multifactorial structure, functioning as a proxy for development. A mounting body of evidence has demonstrated that these processes are dynamic, involving the creation of a chain of risk that varies developmentally and whose course appears not to be the same for individuals with different clusters of risk (Kuh et al., 1997; Zucker, 2000). Solving this puzzle requires a multidisciplinary team with expertise ranging from molecular genetics to life span developmental psychopathology. It also is an analytically very demanding puzzle, given the multilevel, multigene, across-time nature of the required models. At the same time, with the appropriate database, modeling of these interrelated domains would provide the first integrative descriptions of the development of the disorder.

Summary and Concluding Remarks

A multilevel-multidomain set of factors produces life course variation in alcohol use, abuse, and dependence. At the macro level, the rule, availability, and activity structure of the larger society plays a significant role in regulating drinking behavior. This larger social system restrains heavy consumption in some eras and in some community settings, and allows it to flourish in others, and level of dampening even has impact on population rates of AUD. Prohibition and wartime rationing are but two extremes of a phenomenon that continues to change as lawmakers and policymakers dampen down or open up the availability and penalty structure for use. In turn, social environmental availability makes alcohol-seeking behavior easier or more difficult, and the cuing it provides encourages use to the degree that it activates existing individual expectancy and motivational networks.

Thus, to a degree, alcohol-seeking and -using behavior is social behavior because it occurs in response to the social environment. However, it is considerably more than that. The use of ethanol is a self-dosing act, and the pharmacodynamics of the drug experience engage the brain's structures for appetite, sensitization, adaptation, reward, planning and forethought, and affective and behavioral control. This activity, and the network of risk factors connected to it, is characterizable at a number of levels of specificity, ranging from the behavioral to the neuroanatomical to the genetic.

Behavioral risk involves an expectancy network about the positive or negative effects of alcohol use, that has its beginnings in early childhood, and develops over time as a function of both observational learning and consumption. Two major traits nonspecific to alcohol use, undercontrol and negative affectivity, also are major predictors of early use, of problem use and ultimately of AUD. They also are predictive that adult disorder will be more severe and more socially problematic.

Brain circuitry related to these behaviors includes circuitry regulating stress and anxiety, response suppression, working memory, reward responsivity, and social information processing and involves both cortical and subcortical sites.

The heritable basis of behavioral risk has been firmly established over the past generation and accounts for 40% to 60% of the risk variance. Heritability of AUD is heavily non-drug-specific, and the risk pathway is primarily through the two intermediate behavioral phenotypes of undercontrol and negative affectivity. At the same time, several genes conveying specific risk for AUD on the one hand, and protection on the other, have also been identified. Promising candidate genes regulate aspects of the serotonin, dopamine, and GABAergic systems. More generally, the genetics of AUD is that of a complex trait, involving heterogeneity of phenotype, multiple genes, a significant environmental set of risks, and developmental variation in course.

This matrix is a multidisciplinary puzzle, and the problem from a science and a training standpoint is that most investigations are still single discipline activities, with each investigative group attempting to capture the explanatory variance from the vantage point of their own discipline. The current state of knowledge is at a point that such efforts are increasingly of limited value because the models they generate underspecify the risk matrix and are unable to evaluate the critical interactions that the current data suggest are in operation.

For the same reason, the resolution of this puzzle requires an interdisciplinary effort to resolve, and anything less is going to fall short. The same concern needs to be voiced about policy formulations that focus on only one level of the dilemma while ignoring the others. A sufficient knowledge base now exists to begin to address this family of problems at multiple levels of cause and at multiple places in their life history.

REFERENCES

Achenbach, T. M. (1991). *Manual for the Child Behavior Checklist/4–18 and 1991 profile.* Burlington: University of Vermont, Department of Psychiatry.

Achenbach, T. M., & Edelbrock, C. S. (1991). *Manual for the Child Behavior Checklist and Revised Child Behavior Profile.* Burlington, VT: University Associates in Psychiatry.

Ajzen, I., & Fishbein, M. (1980). *Understanding attitudes and predicting social behavior.* Englewood Cliffs, NJ: Prentice-Hall.

American Psychiatric Association. (1980). *Diagnostic and Statistical Manual of Mental Disorders* (3rd ed.). Washington, DC: Author.

American Psychiatric Association. (1994). *Diagnostic and Statistical Manual of Mental Disorders* (4th ed.). Washington, DC: Author.

Aron, A. R., Fletcher, P. C., Bullmore, E. T., Sahakian, B. J., & Robbins, T. W. (2003). Stop-signal inhibition disrupted by damage to right inferior frontal gyrus in humans. *Nature Neuroscience, 6,* 115–116.

Atkin, C. K. (1995). Survey and experimental research on effects of alcohol advertising. In S. E. Martin & P. Mail (Eds.), *The effects of the mass media on the use and abuse of alcohol* (NIAAA Research Monograph No. 28, pp. 39–68, NIH Pub. No. 95-3743). Bethesda, MD: National Institute on Alcohol Abuse and Alcoholism.

Babor, T. F. (1996). The classification of alcoholics: Typology theories from the 19th century to the present. *Alcohol Health and Research World, 20,* 6–17.

Babor, T. F., Hofmann, M., DelBoca, F. K., Hesselbrock, V., Meyer, R. E., Dolinsky, Z. S., et al. (1992). Type of alcoholics: I. Evidence for an empirically derived typology based on indicators of vulnerability and severity. *Archives of General Psychiatry, 49,* 599–608.

Bachman, J. G., O'Malley, P. M., Schulenberg, J. E., Johnston, L. D., Bryant, A. L., & Merline, A. C. (2002). *The decline of substance use in young adulthood: Changes in social activities, roles, and beliefs.* Mahwah, NJ: Erlbaum.

Ball, S. A. (1996). Type A and Type B alcoholism: Applicability across subpopulations and treatment settings. *Alcohol Health and Research World, 20*(1), 30–35.

Benes, F. M. (2001). The development of prefrontal cortex: The maturation of neurotransmitter systems and their interactions. In C. A. Nelson & M. Luciana (Eds.), *Handbook of developmental cognitive neuroscience* (pp. 79–92). Cambridge, MA: MIT Press.

Berkson, J. B. (1946). Limitations of the application of fourfold table analysis to hospital data. *Biometrics, 2,* 47–51.

Biglan, A., Brennan, P. A., Foster, S. L., Holder, H. D., Miller, T. L., Cunningham, P. B., et al. (2004). *Helping adolescents at risk: Prevention of multiple problem behaviors.* New York: Guilford Press.

Blackson, T. C. (1997). Temperament: A salient correlate of risk factors for alcohol and drug abuse. *Drug and Alcohol Dependence, 36,* 205–214.

Blackson, T. C., & Tarter, R. E. (1994). Individual, family, and peer affiliation factors predisposing to early-age onset of alcohol and drug use. *Alcoholism: Clinical and Experimental Research, 18,* 813–821.

Blackson, T. C., Tarter, R. E., Martin, R. E., & Moss, H. B. (1994). Temperament-induced father-son family dysfunction: Etiologic implications for child behavior problems and substance abuse. *American Journal of Orthopsychiatry, 64,* 280–292.

Blane, H. T. (1979). Middle-aged alcoholics and young drinkers. In H. T. Blane & M. E. Chafetz (Eds.), *Youth, alcohol and social policy* (pp. 5–38). New York: Plenum Press.

Blomqvist, J. (1999). Treated and untreated recovery from alcohol misuse: Environmental influences and perceived reasons for change. *Substance Use and Misuse, 34,* 1807–1852.

Brainerd, C. J., & Reyna, V. F. (1993). Memory independence and memory interference in cognitive development. *Psychological Review, 100,* 42–67.

Brenner, M. H. (1973). *Mental illness and the economy.* Cambridge, MA: Harvard University Press.

Brook, J. S., Whiteman, M., Cohen, P., & Tanaka, J. S. (1992). Childhood precursors of adolescent drug use: A longitudinal analysis. *Genetic, Social, and General Psychology Monographs, 118,* 195–213.

Brunner, H. G., Nelen, M., Breakefield, X. O., Ropers, H. H., & van Oost, B. A. (1993). Abnormal behavior associated with a point mutation in the structural gene for monoamine oxidase A. *Science, 262,* 578–580.

Cacioppo, J. T., Berntson, G. G., Sheridan, J. F., & McClintock, M. K. (2000). Multilevel integrative analyses of human behavior: Social neuroscience and the complementing nature of social and biological approaches. *Psychological Bulletin, 126,* 829–843.

Cahalan, D. (1970). *Problem Drinkers.* San Francisco: Jossey-Bass.

Casey, B. J., Tottenham, N., & Fossella, J. (2002). Clinical, imaging, lesion, and genetic approaches toward a model of cognitive control. *Developmental Psychobiology, 40,* 237–254.

Caspi, A., McClay, J., Moffitt, T. E., Mill, J., Martin, J., Craig, I. W., et al. (2002). Role of genotype in the cycle of violence in maltreated children. *Science, 297,* 851–854.

Caspi, A., Moffitt, T. E., Newman, D. L., & Silva, E. A. (1996). Behavioral observations at age 3 years predict adult psychiatric disorders: Longitudinal evidence from a birth cohort. *Archives of General Psychiatry, 53,* 1033–1039.

Chassin, L., Barrera, M., Bech, K., & Kossak-Fuller, J. (1993). Recruiting a community sample of alcoholic families: A comparison of three methods. *Journal of Studies on Alcohol, 53,* 316–320.

Cicchetti, D., & Cohen, D. J. (1995). Perspectives on developmental psychopathology. In D. Cicchetti & D. J. Cohen (Eds.), *Developmental psychopathology: Vol. 1. Theory and methods* (pp. 3–20). New York: Wiley.

Cicchetti, D., & Dawson, G. (2002). Editorial: Multiple levels of analysis. *Developmental Psychopathology, 14,* 417–420.

Cicchetti, D., & Rogosch, F. A. (1996). Equifinality and multifinality in developmental psychopathology. *Developmental Psychopathology, 8,* 597–600.

Cloninger, C. R. (1987). Neurogenetic adaptive mechanisms in alcoholism. *Science, 236,* 410–416.

Cloninger, C. R., Bohman, M., & Sigvardsson, S. (1981). Inheritance of alcohol abuse: Cross-fostering analysis of adopted men. *Archives of General Psychiatry, 38,* 861–868.

Cloninger, C. R., Sigvardsson, S., & Bohman, M. (1988). Childhood personality predicts alcohol abuse in young adults. *Alcoholism: Clinical and Experimental Research, 12,* 494–505.

Cohen, P., Cohen, J., & Brook, J. S. (1993). Persistence of disorders in children: Epidemiologic data. *Journal of Child Psychology and Psychiatry, 34,* 869–877.

Colder, C. R., & Chassin, L. (1993). The stress and negative affect model of adolescent alcohol use and the moderating effects of behavioral under control. *Journal of Studies on Alcohol, 54,* 326–334.

Collins, L. M., & Horn, J. L. (Eds.). (1991). *Best methods for the analysis of change.* Washington, DC: American Psychological Association.

Cotton, N. S. (1979). The familial incidence of alcoholism: A review. *Journal of Studies on Alcohol, 4,* 89–116.

Damasio, A. R. (1998). Emotion in the perspective of an integrated nervous system. *Brain Research Review, 26*(2/3), 83–86.

Diamond, A. (1990). Rate of maturation of the hippocampus and the developmental progression of children's performance on the delayed non-matching to sample and visual paired comparison tasks. *Annals of the New York Academy of Sciences, 608,* 394–433.

Donovan, J. E., & Jessor, R. (1985). Structure of problem behavior in adolescence and young adulthood. *Journal of Consulting and Clinical Psychology, 53,* 890–904.

Donovan, J. E., Jessor, R., & Costa, F. M. (1988). Syndrome of problem behavior in adolescence: A replication. *Journal of Consulting and Clinical Psychology, 56,* 762–765.

Duncan, S. C., Duncan, T. E., Biglan, A., & Ary, D. (1998). Contributions of the social context to the development of adolescent substance use: A multivariate latent growth modeling approach. *Drug and Alcohol Dependence, 50,* 57–71.

Dunn, M. E., & Goldman, M. S. (1996). Empirical modeling of an alcohol expectancy memory network in elementary school children as a function of grade. *Experimental and Clinical Psychopharmacology, 4,* 209–217.

Earls, F., Reich, W. W., Jung, K. G., & Cloninger, C. R. (1988). Psychopathology in children of alcoholic and antisocial parents. *Alcoholism: Clinical and Experimental Research, 12,* 481–487.

Edwards, G., Anderson, P., Babor, T. R., Casswell, S., Ferrence, R., Giesbrech, N., et al. (1994). *Alcohol policy and the public good.* New York: Oxford University Press.

Elder, G. H. (1998). The life course and human development. In R. M. Lerner (Ed.), *Handbook of child psychology: Vol. 1. Theoretical models of human development* (pp. 939–991). New York: Wiley.

Elder, G. H., & Caspi, A. (1990). Studying lives in a changing society: Sociological and personological explorations. In A. I. Rabin, R. A. Zucker, R. A. Emmons, & S. Frank (Eds.), *Studying persons and lives* (pp. 201–247). New York: Springer.

Ellickson, P. L., Tucker, J. S., & Klein, D. J. (2003). Ten-year prospective study of public health problems associated with early drinking. *Pediatrics, 111,* 949–955.

Eron, L. D., Huesmann, L. R., Dubow, E., Romanoff, R., & Yarmel, P. W. (1987). Aggression and its correlates over 22 years. In D. H. Crowell, I. M. Evans, & C. R. O'Donnell (Eds.), *Childhood aggression and violence* (pp. 249–262). New York: Plenum Press.

Falconer, D. S., & MacKay, T. F. C. (1996). *Introduction to quantitative genetics.* Boston, MA: Edinburgh Gate: Addison-Wesley Longman.

Faraone, S. V., Doyle, A. E., Mick, E., & Biederman, J. (2001). Meta-analysis of the association between the 7-repeat allele of the dopamine D(4) receptor gene and attention deficit hyperactivity disorder. *American Journal of Psychiatry, 158,* 1052–1057.

Fillmore, K. M., Hartka, E., Johnston, B., Leino, V., Motoyoshi, M., & Temple, M. T. (1991). Life course variation in drinking: A meta-analysis of multiple longitudinal studies from the collaborative alcohol-related longitudinal project. *British Journal of Addiction, 86,* 1221–1268.

Finn, P. R., Justus, A., Mazas, C., & Steinmetz, J. E. (1999). Working memory, executive processes and the effects of alcohol on go/no-go learning: Testing a model of behavioral regulation and impulsivity. *Psychopharmacology (Berl) 146,* 465–472.

Finn, P. R., Mazas, C. A., Justus, A. N., & Steinmetz, J. (2002). Early-onset alcoholism with conduct disorder: Go/no go learning deficits, working memory capacity, and personality. *Alcoholism: Clinical and Experimental Research, 26,* 186–206.

Fischhoff, B., & Quadrel, M. J. (1995). Adolescent alcohol decisions. In G. M. Boyd, J. Howard, & R. A. Zucker (Eds.), *Alcohol problems among adolescents: Current directions in prevention research* (pp. 59–84). Hillsdale, NJ: Erlbaum.

Fitzgerald, H. E., Sullivan, L. A., Ham, H. P., Zucker, R. A., Bruckel, S., & Schneider, A. M. (1993). Predictors of behavioral problems in three-year-old sons of alcoholics: Early evidence for onset of risk. *Child Development, 64,* 110–123.

Fitzgerald, H. E., & Zucker, R. A. (1995). Socioeconomic status and alcoholism: Structuring developmental pathways to addiction. In H. E. Fitzgerald, B. M. Lester, & B. Zuckerman (Eds.), *Children of poverty: Research, health, and policy issues* (pp. 125–148). New York: Garland Press.

Floyd, F. J., Cranford, J. A., Klotz Daugherty, M., Fitzgerald, H. E., & Zucker, R. A. (in press). Marital interaction in alcoholic and nonalcoholic couples: Alcoholic subtype variations and wives' alcoholism status. *Journal of Abnormal Psychology.*

Ford, D. H., & Lerner, R. M. (1992). *Developmental systems theory: An integrative approach.* Newbury Park, CA: Sage.

Fuller, B. E., Chermack, S. T., Cruise, K. A., Kirsch, E., Fitzgerald, H. E., & Zucker, R. A. (2003). Predictors of aggression across three generations among sons of alcoholics: Relationships involving grandparental and parental alcoholism, child aggression, marital aggression and parenting practices. *Journal of Studies on Alcohol, 64,* 472–483.

Fuster, J. M. (1997). *The prefrontal cortex: Anatomy, physiology, and neuropsychology of the frontal lobe* (3rd ed.). Philadelphia: Lippincott-Raven.

Gaines, L. S., Brooks, P. H., Maisto, S., Dietrich, M., & Shagena, M. (1998). The development of children's knowledge of alcohol and the role of drinking. *Journal of Applied Developmental Psychology, 9,* 441–457.

Garnier, H. E., & Stein, J. A. (2002). An 18-year model of family and peer effects on adolescent drug use and delinquency. *Journal of Youth and Adolescence, 31,* 45–56.

Giancola, P. R., & Moss, H. B. (1998). Executive cognitive functioning in alcohol use disorders. *Recent Developments in Alcoholism, 14,* 227–251.

Glassner, B. (1991). Jewish sobriety. In D. J. Pittman & H. R. White (Eds.), *Society, culture, and drinking patterns reexamined* (pp. 311–326). New Brunswick, NJ: Rutgers Center of Alcohol Studies.

Gogtay, N., Giedd, J. N., Lusk, L., Hayashi, K. M., Greenstein, D., Vaituzis, A. C., et al. (2004). Dynamic mapping of human cortical development during childhood through early adulthood. *Proceedings of the National Academy of Science USA, 101,* 8174–8179.

Goldman, M. S., Brown, S. A., Christiansen, B. A., & Smith, G. T. (1991). Alcoholism and memory: Broadening the scope of alcohol expectancy research. *Psychological Bulletin, 110,* 137–146.

Goldman, M. S., Del Boca, F. K., & Darkes, J. (1999). Alcohol expectancy theory: The application of cognitive neuroscience. In K. Leonard & H. Blane (Eds.), *Psychological theories of drinking and alcoholism* (2nd ed., pp. 203–246). New York: Guilford Press.

Goldstein, R. Z., & Volkow, N. D. (2002). Drug addiction and its underlying neurobiological basis: Neuroimaging evidence for the involvement of the frontal cortex. *American Journal of Psychiatry, 159,* 1642–1652.

Goodwin, D. W., Schulsinger, F., Knop, J., Mednick, S., & Guze, S. B. (1973). Alcohol problems in adoptees raised apart from alcoholic biological parents. *Archives of General Psychiatry, 28,* 238–243.

Gottesman, I. I., & Gould, T. D. (2003). The endophenotype concept in psychiatry: Etymology and strategic intentions. *American Journal of Psychiatry, 160,* 636–645.

Gottlieb, G. (1991). Epigenetic systems view of human development. *Developmental Psychology, 27,* 33–34.

Grant, B. F. (1996). DSM-IV, DSM-III-R and draft DSM-IV alcohol and drug abuse/harmful use and dependence, United States, 1992: A nosological comparison. *Alcoholism: Clinical and Experimental Research, 20,* 1481–1488.

Grant, B. F. (1997). Prevalence and correlates of alcohol use and DSM-IV alcohol dependence in the United States: Results of the national longitudinal alcohol epidemiologic survey. *Journal of Studies on Alcohol, 58,* 464–473.

Grant, B. F. (1998). The impact of a family history of alcoholism on the relationship between age at onset of alcohol use and DSM-IV alcohol dependence: Results from the National Longitudinal Alcohol Epidemiologic Survey. *Alcohol Health & Research World, 22,* 144–147.

Grant, B. F. (2000). Estimates of U.S. children exposed to alcohol abuse and dependence in the family. *American Journal of Public Health, 90,* 112–115.

Grant, B. F., & Dawson, D. A. (1997). Age at onset of alcohol use and its association with DSM-IV alcohol abuse dependence: Results from the national longitudinal alcohol epidemiologic survey. *Journal of Substance Abuse, 9,* 103–110.

Grant, B. F., & Dawson, D. A. (1998). Age at onset of drug use and its association with DSM-IV drug abuse and dependence: Results from the National Longitudinal Alcohol Epidemiologic Survey. *Journal of Substance Abuse, 10,* 163–173.

Gruber, E., DiClemente, R. J., Anderson, M. M., & Lodico, M. (1996). Early drinking onset and its association with alcohol use and problem behavior in late adolescence. *Preventive Medicine, 25(3),* 293–300.

Hall, R. L., Hesselbrock, V. M., & Stabenau, J. R. (1983a). Familial distribution of alcohol use: Pt. I. Assortative mating in the parents of alcoholics. *Behavior Genetics, 13,* 361–372.

Hall, R. L., Hesselbrock, V. M., & Stabenau, J. R. (1983b). Familial distribution of alcohol use: Pt. II. Assortative mating of alcoholic probands. *Behavior Genetics, 13,* 373–382.

Hall, S. M., Wasserman, D. A., & Havassy, B. E. (1991). Relapse prevention. *NIDA Research Monograph, 106,* 279–292.

Hariri, A. R., Bookheimer, S. Y., & Mazziotta, J. C. (2000). Modulating emotional responses: Effects of a neocortical network on the limbic system. *NeuroReport, 11,* 43–48.

Hasin, D., & Grant, B. F. (2004). The co-occurrence of DSM-IV alcohol abuse in DSM-IV alcohol dependence: Results of the national epidemiologic survey on alcohol and related conditions on heterogeneity that differ by population subgroup. *Archives of General Psychiatry, 61,* 891–896.

Hasin, D., Grant, B. F., & Endicott, J. (1990). The natural history of alcohol abuse: Implications for definitions of alcohol use disorders. *American Journal of Psychiatry, 147,* 1537–1541.

Hasin D., Paykin A., & Endicott J. (2001). Course of DSM-IV alcohol dependence in a community sample: Effects of parental history and binge drinking. *Alcoholism: Clinical and Experimental Research, 25,* 411–414.

Hawkins, J. D., & Catalano, R. F. (1992). *Communities that care: Action for drug abuse prevention.* San Francisco: Jossey-Bass.

Hawkins, J. D., Catalano, R. F., Kosterman, R., Abbott, R., & Hill, K. G. (1999). Preventing adolescent health-risk behaviors by strengthening protection during childhood. *Archives of Pediatrics and Adolescent Medicine, 153,* 226–234.

Hawkins, J. D., Catalano, R. F., & Miller, J. Y. (1992). Risk and protective factors for alcohol and other drug problems in adolescence and early adulthood: Implications for substance abuse prevention. *Psychological Bulletin, 112,* 64–105.

Hawkins, J. D., Graham, J. W., Maguin, E., Abbott, R., Hill, K. G., & Catalano, R. F. (1997). Exploring the effects of age of alcohol use initiation and psychosocial risk factors on subsequent alcohol misuse. *Journal of Studies on Alcohol, 58,* 280–290.

Hayashi, S., Watanabe, J., & Kawajiri, K. (1991). Genetic polymorphisms in the 5′-flanking region change transcriptional regulation of the human cytochrome P450IIE1 gene. *Journal of Biochemistry (Tokyo), 110,* 559–565.

Heath, A. (1995). Genetic influences on alcoholism risk? A review of adoption and twin studies. *Alcohol Health and Research World, 19,* 166–171.

Heath, D. B. (1991). Drinking patterns of the Bolivian Camba. In D. J. Pittman & H. R. White (Eds.), *Society, culture, and drinking patterns reexamined* (pp. 62–77). New Brunswick, NJ: Rutgers Center of Alcohol Studies.

Heitzeg, M. M., Zucker, R. A., & Zubieta, J.-K. (2003). An fMRI study of impulse and emotion modulation in children of alcoholics [Abstract]. *Alcoholism: Clinical and Experimental Research, 27,* 6A.

Helzer, J. E., Burnam, A., & McEvoy, L. T. (1991). Alcohol abuse and dependence. In L. Robins (Ed.), *Psychiatric disorders in America: The Epidemiologic Area Catchment studies* (pp. 81–115). New York: Free Press.

Helzer, J. E., & Canino, G. J. (Eds.). (1992). *Alcoholism in North America, Europe, and Asia.* New York: Oxford University Press.

Hesselbrock, M. N., Hesselbrock, V. M., Babor, T. F., Stabenau, J. R., Meyer, R. E., & Weidenman, M. (1984). Antisocial behavior, psychopathology, and problem drinking in the natural history of alcoholism. In D. W. Goodwin, K. T. Van Dusen, & S. A. Mednick (Eds.), *Longitudinal research in alcoholism* (pp. 197–214). Boston: Kluwer Academic.

Hill, S. Y. (1992). Absence of paternal sociopathy in the etiology of severe alcoholism: Is there a Type III alcoholism? *Journal of Studies on Alcohol, 53,* 161–169.

Hogarth, W. (1751). *Gin lane* [Engraving]. London: British Museum.

Holdcraft, L. C., & Iacono, W. G. (2004). Cross-generational effects on gender differences in psychoactive drug abuse and dependence. *Drug and Alcohol Dependence, 74,* 147–158.

Huang, L. X., Cerbone, F. G., & Gfroerer, J. C. (1998). Children at risk because of substance abuse. In Office of Applied Studies, Substance Abuse and Mental Health Services Administration (Eds.), *Analyses of substance abuse and treatment need issues* (DHHS Publication Document No. SMA 98-3227, pp. 5–18). Rockville, MD: US Department of Health and Human Services.

Humphreys, K., Moos, R. H., & Cohen, C. (1997). Social and community resources and long-term recovery from treated and untreated alcoholism. *Journal of Studies on Alcohol, 58,* 231–238.

Humphreys, K., Moos, R. H., & Finney, J. W. (1994). Two pathways out of drinking problems without professional treatment. *Addictive Behavior, 20,* 427–441.

Ialongo, N., Edelsohn, G., Werthamer-Larsson, L., Crockett, L., & Kellam, S. (1996). The course of aggression in first-grade children with and without comorbid anxious symptoms. *Journal of Abnormal Child Psychology, 24,* 445–456.

Jacob, T., Leonard, K. E., & Haber, J. R. (2001). Family interactions of alcoholics as related to alcoholism type and drinking condition. *Alcoholism, Clinical and Experimental Research, 25,* 835–843.

Jansen, R. E., Fitzgerald, H. E., Ham, H. P., & Zucker, R. A. (1995). Pathways into risk: Temperament and behavior problems in three- to five-year-old sons of alcoholics. *Alcoholism: Clinical and Experimental Research, 19,* 501–509.

Jentsch, J. D., & Taylor, J. R. (1999). Impulsivity resulting from frontostriatal dysfunction in drug abuse: Implications for the control of behavior by reward-related stimuli. *Psychopharmacology (Berl) 146,* 373–390.

Jessor, R., Donovan, J. E., & Costa, F. M. (1991). *Beyond adolescence: Problem behavior and young adult development.* New York: Cambridge University Press.

Jessor, R., & Jessor, S. L. (1977). *Problem behavior and psychosocial development: A longitudinal study of youth.* New York: Academic Press.

Jester, J. M., Zucker, R. A., Carello, P. D., Wong, M. M., Cranford, J. A., & Fitzgerald, H. E. (2005). *Alcohol expectancies in childhood: Changes with the onset of drinking and utility in predicting adolescent drunkenness and binge drinking.* Manuscript submitted for publication. Reprint requests to Ann Arbor, MI: University of Michigan Addiction Research Center. MLS Doc #134.

Jester, J. M., Zucker, R. A., Wong, M. M., Puttler, L. I., Twitchell, G. R., & Fitzgerald, H. E. (2001). Time since last alcoholic symptom predicts current social adaptation in men and women [Abstract]. *Alcoholism: Clinical and Experimental Research, 25*(Suppl.), 48A.

Johnston, L. D., O'Malley, P. M., & Bachman, J. G. (2001). *Monitoring the future national results on adolescent drug use: Overview of key findings, 2001.* Bethesda, MD: National Institute on Drug Abuse.

Johnston, L. D., O'Malley, P. M., & Bachman, J. G. (2003). *Monitoring the future national results on adolescent drug use: Overview of key findings, 2002.* Bethesda, MD: National Institute on Drug Abuse.

Johnston, L. D., O'Malley, P. M., Bachman, J. G., & Schulenberg, J. E. (2004a). *Monitoring the future national results on adolescent drug use: Overview of key findings, 2003.* Bethesda, MD: National Institute on Drug Abuse.

Johnston, L. D., O'Malley, P. M., Bachman, J. G., & Schulenberg, J. E. (2004b). *Monitoring the future national survey results on drug use,*

1975–2003: Vol. I. Secondary school students (NIH Pub. No. 04-5507). Bethesda, MD: National Institute on Drug Abuse.

Johnston, L. D., O'Malley, P. M., Bachman, J. G., & Schulenberg, J. E. (2004c). *Monitoring the future national survey results on drug use, 1975–2003: Vol. II. College students and adults ages 19–45* (NIH Pub. No. 04-5508). Bethesda, MD: National Institute on Drug Abuse.

Kaij, L. (1960). *Alcoholism in twins.* Stockholm: Almqvist and Wiksell.

Kalsbeek, A., Voorn, P., Buijs, R. M., Pool, C. W., & Uylings, H. B. (1988). Development of the dopaminergic innervation in the prefrontal cortex of the rat. *Journal of Comparative Neurology, 269,* 58–72.

Kandel, D. B. (1978). Convergences in prospective longitudinal surveys of drug use in normal populations. In D. B. Kandel (Ed.), *Longitudinal research on drug use* (pp. 3–38). Washington, DC: Hemisphere.

Kandel, E. R. (1998). A new intellectual framework for psychiatry. *American Journal of Psychiatry, 155*(4), 457–468.

Kaplan, H. B., Martin, S. S., & Robbins, C. (1982). Applications of a general theory of deviant behavior: Self-derogation and adolescent drug use. *Journal of Health and Social Behavior, 23,* 274–294.

Kaskutas, L. A., Bond, J., & Humphreys, K. (2002). Social networks as mediators of the effect of Alcoholics Anonymous. *Addiction, 97,* 891–900.

Kellam, S. G., Brown, C. H., Rubin, B. R., & Ensminger, M. E. (1983). Paths leading to teenage psychiatric symptoms and substance use: Developmental epidemiological studies in Woodlawn. In S. B. Guze, F. J. Earls, & J. E. Barrett (Eds.), *Childhood psychopathology and development* (pp. 17–47). New York: Plenum Press.

Kellam, S. G., Ensminger, M. E., & Simon, M. B. (1980). Mental health in first grade and teenage drug, alcohol, and cigarette use. *Drug and Alcohol Dependence, 5,* 273–304.

Kendler, K. S., Heath, A. C., Neale, M. C., Kessler, R. C., & Eaves, L. J. (1992). A population-based twin study of alcoholism in women. *Journal of the American Medical Association, 268,* 1877–1882.

Kendler, K. S., Jacobson, K. C., Prescott, C. A., & Neale, M. C. (2003a). Specificity of genetic and environmental risk factors for use and abuse/dependence of cannabis, cocaine, hallucinogens, sedatives, stimulants, and opiates in male twins. *American Journal of Psychiatry, 160,* 687–695.

Kendler, K. S., Neale, M. C., Heath, A. C., Kessler, R. C., & Eaves, L. J. (1994). A twin-family study of alcoholism in women. *American Journal of Psychiatry, 15,* 707–715.

Kendler, K. S., Prescott, C. A., Myers, J., & Neale, M. C. (2003b). The structure of genetic and environmental risk factors for common psychiatric and substance use disorders in men and women. *Archives of General Psychiatry, 60,* 929–937.

Kessler, R. C., Crum, R. M., Warner, L. A., Nelson, C. B., Schulenberg, J., & Anthony, J. C. (1997). Lifetime co-occurrence of DSM-III-R alcohol abuse and dependence with other psychiatric disorders in the National Comorbidity Survey. *Archives of General Psychiatry, 54,* 313–321.

Kessler, R. C., McGonagle, K. A., Zhao, S., Nelson, C. B., Hughes, M., Eshleman, S., et al. (1994). Lifetime and 12-month prevalence of DSM-III-R psychiatric disorders in the United States: Results from the National Comorbidity Survey. *Archives of General Psychiatry, 51,* 8–19.

Killgore, W. D., Oki, M., & Yurgelun-Todd, D. A. (2001). Sex-specific developmental changes in amygdala responses to affective faces. *NeuroReport, 12,* 427–433.

Klingberg, T., Forssberg, H., & Westerberg, H. (2002). Increased brain activity in frontal and parietal cortex underlies the development of visuospatial working memory capacity during childhood. *Journal of Cognitive Neuroscience, 14,* 1–10.

Kolb, B., Wilson, B., & Taylor, L. (1992). Developmental changes in the recognition and comprehension of facial expression: Implications for frontal lobe function. *Brain and Cognition, 20,* 74–84.

Kreek, M. J., Nielsen, D. A., & LaForge, K. S. (2004). Genes associated with addiction: Alcoholism, opiate, and cocaine addiction. *NeuroMolecular Medicine, 5,* 85–108.

Krueger, R. F., Caspi, A., Moffitt, T. E., & Silva, P. A. (1998). The structure and stability of common mental disorders (DSM-III-R): A longitudinal-epidemiological study. *Journal of Abnormal Psychology, 107,* 216–227.

Krueger, R. F., Hicks, B. M., Patrick, C. J., Carlson, S. R., Iacono, W. G., & McGue, M. (2002). Etiologic connections among substance dependence, antisocial behavior, and personality: Modeling the externalizing spectrum. *Journal of Abnormal Psychology, 111,* 411–424.

Kuh, D., Power, C., Blane, D., & Barley, M. (1997). Social pathways between childhood and adult health. In D. Ku & Y. Ben-Schlomo (Eds.), *A life course approach to chronic disease epidemiology* (pp. 169–198). Oxford: Oxford University Press.

Kushner, M. G., Sher, K. J., & Beitman, B. D. (1990). The relation between alcohol problems and the anxiety disorders. *American Journal of Psychiatry, 147,* 685–695.

Lappalainen, J., Long, J. C., Eggert, M., Ozaki, N., Brown, R. W., Brown, G. L., et al. (1998). Linkage of antisocial alcoholism to the serotonin 5-HT1B receptor gene in 2 populations. *Archives of General Psychiatry, 55* 989–994.

Leonard, K. E., & Jacob, T. T. (1997). Sequential interactions among episodic and steady alcoholics and their wives. *Psychiatric Addictive Behaviors, 11,* 18–25.

Lesch, K. P., Bengel, D., Heils, A., Sabol, S. Z., Greenberg, B. D., Petri, S., et al. (1996). Association of anxiety-related traits with a polymorphism in the serotonin transporter gene regulatory region. *Science, 274,* 1527–1531.

Li, T. K. (2000). Pharmacogenetics of responses to alcohol and genes that influence alcohol drinking. *Journal of Studies on Alcohol, 61,* 5–12.

Li, T. K. (2004, June 10). Alcohol abuse increases, dependence declines across decade. Young adult minorities emerge as high-risk subgroups. *NIH News.*

Loeber, R. (1982). The stability of antisocial and delinquent child behavior: A review. *Child Development, 53,* 1431–1446.

Loukas, A., Zucker, R. A., Fitzgerald, H. E., & Krull, J. L. (2003). Developmental trajectories of disruptive behavior problems among sons of alcoholics: Effects of parent psychopathology, family conflict, and child undercontrol. *Journal of Abnormal Psychology, 112,* 119–131.

Lucki, I. (1998). The spectrum of behaviors influenced by serotonin. *Biological Psychiatry, 44,* 151–162.

Madden, T. M. (1884). Alcoholism in childhood and youth: Proceedings of the 52nd annual meeting. *British Medical Journal,* 358–359.

Maddox, G. L., & McCall, B. C. (1964). *Drinking among teen-agers: A sociological interpretation of alcohol use by high-school students.* New Brunswick, NJ: Rutgers Center of Alcohol Studies College and University Press.

Manuck, S. B., Flory, J. D., Ferrell, R. E., Mann, J. J., & Muldoon, M. F. (2000). A regulatory polymorphism of the monoamine oxidase-A gene may be associated with variability in aggression, impulsivity, and central nervous system serotonergic responsivity. *Psychiatry Research, 95,* 9–23.

Marschuetz, C., Smith, E. E., Jonides, J., DeGutis, J., & Chenevert, T. L. (2000). Order information in working memory: FMRI evidence for parietal and prefrontal mechanisms. *Journal of Cognitive Neuroscience, 12,* 130–144.

Masse, L. C., & Tremblay, R. E. (1997). Behavior of boys in kindergarten and the onset of substance use during adolescence. *Archives of General Psychiatry, 54,* 62–68.

Mayzer, R., Puttler, L. I., Wong, M. M., Fitzgerald, H. E., & Zucker, R. A. (2002). Predicting early onset of first alcohol use from behavior problem indicators in early childhood. *Alcoholism: Clinical and Experimental Research, 26*(Suppl.), 124A.

Mayzer, R., Puttler, L. I., Wong, M. M., Fitzgerald, H. E., & Zucker, R. A. (2003). Development constancy of social misbehavior from early childhood to adolescence as a predictor of early onset of alcohol use [Abstract]. *Alcoholism: Clinical and Experimental Research, 27*(Suppl.), 65A.

Mayzer, R., Wong, M. M., Puttler, L. I., Fitzgerald, H. E., & Zucker, R. A. (2001, November). *Onset of alcohol use: Profiling adolescents characterized as "early drinkers"* [Abstract]. Annual meeting of the American Society of Criminology, Atlanta, GA.

McAweeney, M. J., Zucker, R. A., Fitzgerald, H. E., Puttler, L., & Wong, M. M. (2005). Individual and partner predictors of recovery from alcohol use disorder over a nine-year interval: Findings from a community sample of alcoholic married men. *Journal of Studies on Alcohol, 66,* 220–228.

McCrady, B. S., Hayaki, J., Epstein, E. E., & Hirsch, L. S. (2002). Testing hypothesized predictors of change in conjoint behavioral alcoholism treatment for men. *Alcoholism: Clinical and Experimental Research, 26,* 463–470.

McGee, L., & Newcomb, M. D. (1992). General deviance syndrome: Expanded hierarchical evaluations at four ages from early adolescence to adulthood. *Journal of Consulting and Clinical Psychology, 60,* 766–776.

McGue, M. (1994). Evidence for causal mechanisms from human genetics data bases. In R. A. Zucker, G. M. Boyd, & J. Howard (Eds.), *The development of alcohol problems: Exploring the biopsychosocial matrix of risk* (Research Monograph No. 26, pp. 1–40). Rockville, MD: National Institute on Alcohol Abuse and Alcoholism.

McGue, M., Pickens, R. W., & Svikis, D. S. (1992). Sex and age effects on the inheritance of alcohol problems: A twin study. *Journal of Abnormal Psychology, 101,* 3–17.

McLellan, A. T., Lewis, D. C., O'Brien, C. P., & Kleber, H. D. (2000). Drug dependence, a chronic medical illness: Implications for treatment, insurance, and outcomes evaluation. *Journal of the American Medical Association, 284,* 1689–1695.

Merikangas, K. R., Leckman, J. F., Prusoff, B. A., Pauls, D. L., & Weissman, M. M. (1985). Familial transmission of depression and alcoholism. *Archives of General Psychiatry, 42,* 367–372.

Mitchell, J. E., Hong, K. M., & Corman, C. (1979). Childhood onset of alcohol abuse. *American Journal of Orthopsychiatry, 49,* 511–513.

Miyake, A., Friedman, N. P., Emerson, M. J., Witzki, A. H., Howerter, A., & Wager, T. D. (2000). The unity and diversity of executive functions and their contributions to complex "frontal lobe" tasks: A latent variable analysis. *Cognitive Psychology, 41,* 49–100.

Moos, R., Brennan, P., & Schutte, K. (1998). Life context factors, treatment, and late-life drinking behavior. In E. S. L. Gomberg, A. M. Hegedus, & R. A. Zucker (Eds.), *Alcohol problems and aging* (NIAAA Research Monograph No. 33, chap. 17). Rockville, MD: U.S. Department of Health and Human Services.

Moos, R. H., Finney, J. W., & Chan, D. (1982). The process of recovery from alcoholism: Pt. II. Comparing spouses of alcoholic patients and matched community controls. *Journal of Studies on Alcohol, 43,* 888–909.

Moos, R. H., & Moos, B. S. (2003). Long-term influence of duration and intensity of treatment on previously untreated individuals with alcohol use disorders. *Addiction, 98,* 325–337.

Moselhy, H. F., Georgiou, G., & Kahn, A. (2001). Frontal lobe changes in alcoholism: A review of the literature. *Alcohol and Alcoholism, 36,* 357–368.

Muthén, B., & Muthén, L. (2000). Integrating person-centered and variable-centered analysis: Growth mixture modeling with latent trajectory classes. *Alcoholism: Clinical and Experimental Research, 24,* 882–891.

Narrow, W. E., Rae, D. S., Robins, L. N., & Regier, D. A. (2002). Revised prevalence estimates of mental disorders in the United States: Using a clinical significance criterion to reconcile 2 surveys' estimates. *Archives of General Psychiatry, 59*(2), 115–123.

National Institute on Alcohol Abuse and Alcoholism. (1985). *Alcoholism: An inherited disease* (DHHS Publication No. ADM 85–1426). Washington, DC: U.S. Government Printing Office.

National Institute on Alcohol Abuse and Alcoholism. (2004). *NIAAA Initiative on underage drinking.* Available from http://www.niaaa.nih .gov/about/underage.htm.

New, A. S., Gelernter, J., Yovell, Y., Trestman, R. L., Nielsen, D. A., Silverman, J., et al. (1998). Tryptophan dydroxylase genotype is associated with impulsive-aggression measures: A preliminary study. *American Journal of Medical Genetics, 81,* 13–17.

Newlin, D. B., & Thomson, J. B. (1990). Alcohol challenge with sons of alcoholics: A critical review and analysis. *Psychological Bulletin, 108,* 383–402.

Nigg, J. T. (2000). On inhibition/disinhibition in developmental psychopathology: Views from cognitive and personality psychology and a working inhibition taxonomy. *Psychological Bulletin, 126,* 220–246.

Nigg, J. T., Glass, J. M., Zucker, R. A., Poon, E., Wong, M. M., Fitzgerald, H. E., et al. (2004). Neuropsychological executive functioning in children at elevated risk for alcoholism: Findings in early adolescence. *Journal of Abnormal Psychology, 113,* 302–314.

Nigg, J. T., Wong, M. M., Martel, M. M., Jester, J. M., Puttler, L. I., Adams, K. M., et al. (2005). *Poor response inhibition as predictor of onset of problem drinking and illicit drug use in adolescents at risk of alcoholism and other substance use disorders.* Michigan Longitudinal Study manuscript submitted for publication. Ann Arbor: University of Michigan Addiction Research Center.

Noll, R. B., Zucker, R. A., & Greenberg, G. S. (1990). Identification of alcohol by smell among preschoolers: Evidence for early socialization about drugs occurring in the home. *Child Development, 61,* 1520–1527.

Nurnberger, J. I., Jr., Wiegand, R., Bucholz, K., O'Connor, S., Meyer, E. T., Reich, T., et al. (2004). A family study of alcohol dependence: Coaggregation of multiple disorders in relatives of alcohol-dependent probands. *Archives of General Psychiatry, 61,* 1246–1256.

O'Malley, P. M., & Wagenaar, A. C. (1991). Effects of minimum drinking age laws on alcohol use, related behaviors and traffic crash involvement among American youth. *Journal of Studies on Alcohol, 52,* 478–491.

Pallas, D. M. (1992). *The ecological distribution of alcoholic families: A community study in mid-Michigan.* Unpublished master's thesis, University of Wisconsin, Oshkosh.

Pederson, W., & Skrondal, A. (1998). Alcohol consumption debut: Predictors and consequences. *Journal of Studies on Alcohol, 59,* 32–42.

Pennington, B. F., & Ozonoff, S. (1996). Executive functions and developmental psychopathology. *Journal of Child Psychology and Psychiatry and Allied Disciplines, 37,* 51–87.

Peterson, J. B., Finn, P. R., & Pihl, R. O. (1992). Cognitive dysfunction and the inherited predisposition to alcoholism. *Journal of Studies on Alcohol, 53,* 154–160.

Pfefferbaum, A., Sullivan, E. V., Rosenbloom, M. J., Mathalon, D. H., & Lim, K. O. (1998). A controlled study of cortical gray matter and ventricular changes in alcoholic men over a 5-year interval. *Archives in General Psychiatry, 55,* 905–912.

Pickens, R. W., Svikis, D. S., McGue, M., Lykken, D. T., Heston, L. L., & Clayton, P. J. (1991). Heterogeneity in the inheritance of alcoholism: A study of male and female twins. *Archives of General Psychiatry, 48,* 19–28.

Pittman, D. J., & White, H. R. (Eds.). (1991). *Society, culture, and drinking patterns reexamined.* New Brunswick, NJ: Rutgers Center of Alcohol Studies.

Poon, E., Ellis, D. A., Zucker, R. A., & Fitzgerald, H. E. (1998). Academic under achievement in elementary school children of alcoholics as related to familial alcoholism subtype. *Alcoholism: Clinical and Experimental Research, 22,* 27A.

Prochaska, J. O., DiClemente, C. C., & Norcross, J. C. (1992). In search of how people change: Applications to addictive behaviors. *American Psychologist, 9,* 1102–1114.

Radel, M., Vallejo, R. L., Iwata, N., Aragon, R., Long, J. C., Virkkunen, M., et al. (2005). Halotype-based localization of an alcohol dependence gene to the 5q34 {gamma}-aminobutyric acid type A gene cluster. *Archives of General Psychiatry, 62,* 47–55.

Rather, B. C., Goldman, M. S., Roehrich, L., & Brannick, M. (1992). Empirical modeling of an alcohol expectancy memory network using multidimensional scaling. *Journal of Abnormal Psychology, 101,* 174–183.

Regier, D. A., Farmer, M. E., Rae, D. S., Locke, B. Z., Keith, S. J., Judd, L. L., et al. (1990). Comorbidity of mental disorders with alcohol and other drug use. *Journal of the American Medical Association, 264*(19), 2511–2518.

Reich, T., Cloninger, C. R., Van Eerdewegh, P., Rice, J. P., & Mullaney, J. (1988). Secular trends in the familial transmission of alcoholism. *Alcoholism: Clinical and Experimental Research, 12,* 458–464.

Reich, T., & Li, T. K. (1994). Is there a single locus contributing to alcohol vulnerability? In E. S. Gershon & C. R. Cloninger (Eds.), *Genetic approaches to mental disorders* (pp. 311–325). Washington, DC: American Psychopathological Association.

Reiss, A. L., Abrams, M. T., Singer, H. S., Ross, J. L., & Denckla, M. B. (1996). Brain development, gender and IQ in children: A volumetric imaging study. *Brain, 119*(Pt. 5), 1763–1774.

Ridenour, T. L., Cottler, L. B., Compton, W. M., Spitznagel, E. L., & Cunningham-Williams, R. M. (2003). Is there a progression from abuse disorders to dependence disorders? *Addiction, 98,* 635–644.

Risch, N. (1990). Linkage strategies for genetically complex traits: Pt. I. Multilocus models. *American Journal of Human Genetics, 46,* 222–228.

Rolf, J. E., Johnson, J. L., Israel, E., Baldwin, J., & Chandra, A. (1988). Depressive affect in school-aged children of alcoholics. *British Journal of Addiction, 83,* 841–848.

Ron, M. A. (1987). Brain damage in chronic alcoholism: A neuropathological, neuroradiological and psychological review. *Psychological Medicine, 7,* 103–112.

Rose, R. J., Kaprio, J., Winter, T., Koskenvuo, M., & Viken, R. J. (1999). Familial and socioregional environmental effects on abstinence from alcohol at age sixteen. *Journal of Studies on Alcohol, 13*(Suppl.), 63–74.

Rosenberg, D. R., & Lewis, D. A. (1994). Changes in the dopaminergic innervation of monkey prefrontal cortex during late postnatal development: A tyrosine hydroxylase immunohistochemical study. *Biological Psychiatry, 36,* 272–277.

Rosenkranz, J. A., & Grace, A. A. (2001). Dopamine attenuates prefrontal cortical suppression of sensory inputs to the basolateral amygdala of rats. *Journal of Neuroscience, 21,* 4090–4103.

Rothbart, M. K., & Bates, J. E. (1998). Temperament. In W. Damon & N. Eisenberg (Eds.), *Handbook of child psychology* (Vol. 3, pp. 105–176). New York: Wiley.

Rush, B. (1790). *An inquiry into the effects of spirituous liquors on the human body and mind.* Boston: Thomas and Andrews.

Sadava, S. W. (1985). Problem behavior theory and consumption and consequences of alcohol use. *Journal of Studies on Alcohol, 46,* 297–392.

Sameroff, A. J. (1995). General systems theories and developmental psychopathology. In D. Cicchetti & D. J. Cohen (Eds.), *Developmental psychopathology: Vol. 1. Theory and method* (pp. 659–695). New York: Wiley.

Sander, T., Samochowiec, J., Ladehoff, M., Smolka, M., Peters, C., Riess, O., et al. (1999). Association analysis of exonic variants of the gene encoding the GABAB receptor and alcohol dependence. *Psychiatric Genetics, 9,* 69–373.

Saudou, F., Amara, D. A., Dierich, A., LeMeur, M., Ramboz, S., Segu, L., et al. (1994). Enhanced aggressive behavior in mice lacking 5-HT1B receptor. *Science, 265,* 1875–1878.

Scarr, S., & McCartney, K. (1983). How people make their own environments: A theory of genotype-environment effects. *Child Development, 54,* 424–435.

Schandler, S. L., Thomas, C. S., & Cohen, M. J. (1995). Spatial learning deficits in preschool children of alcoholics. *Alcoholism: Clinical and Experimental Research, 19,* 1067–1072.

Schmidt, L. G., Sander, T., Kuhn, S., Smolka, M., Rommelspacher, H., Samochowiec, J., et al. (2000). Different allele distribution of a regulatory MAOA gene promoter polymorphism in antisocial and anxious-depressive alcoholics. *Journal of Neural Transmission, 107,* 681–689.

Schuckit, M. A. (1988). Reactions to alcohol in sons of alcoholics and controls. *Alcoholism: Clinical and Experimental Research, 12,* 465–470.

Schuckit, M. A. (1994). Low level of response to alcohol as a predictor of future alcoholism. *American Journal of Psychiatry, 151,* 184–189.

Schuckit, M. A., Edenberg, H. J., Kalmijin, J., Flury, L., Smith, T. L., Reich, T., et al. (2001). A genome-wide search for genes that relate to a low level of response to alcohol. *Alcoholism: Clinical and Experimental Research, 25,* 323–329.

Schuckit, M. A., & Smith, T. L. (2001). A comparison of correlates of DSM-IV alcohol abuse or dependence among more than 400 sons of alcoholics and controls. *Alcoholism: Clinical and Experimental Research, 25,* 1–8.

Schuckit, M. A., Smith, T. L., & Tipp, J. E. (1997). The self-rating of the effects of alcohol (SRE) form as a retrospective measure of the risk for alcoholism. *Addiction, 92,* 979–988.

Schulenberg, J., O'Malley, P. M., Bachman, J. G., Wadsworth, K. N., & Johnston, L. D. (1996). Getting drunk and growing up: Trajectories of frequent binge drinking during the transition to early adulthood. *Journal of Studies on Alcohol, 57,* 289–304.

Schulenberg, J., Wadsworth, K. N., O'Malley, P. M., Bachman, J. G., & Johnston, L. D. (1996). Adolescent risk factors for binge drinking during the transition to young adulthood: Variable- and pattern-centered approaches to change. *Developmental Psychology, 32,* 659–674.

Searles, J. S. (1988). The role of genetics in the pathogenesis of alcoholism. *Journal of Abnormal Psychology, 97,* 153–167.

Seeman, P., Bzowej, N. H., Guan, H. C., Bergeron, C., Becker, L. E., Reynolds, G. P., et al. (1987). Human brain dopamine receptors in children and aging adults. *Synapse, 1,* 399–404.

Sher, K. J., Walitzer, K. S., Wood, P. K., & Brent, E. E. (1991). Characteristics of children of alcoholics: Putative risk factors, substance use and abuse, and psychopathology. *Journal of Abnormal Psychology, 100,* 427–448.

Sing, C. F., Haviland, M. B., & Reilly, S. L. (1996). Genetic architecture of common multifactorial diseases. *Ciba Fund Symposium, 197,* 211–229.

Sklar, P., Gabriel, S. B., McInnis, M. G., Bennett, P., Lim, Y. M., Tsan, G., et al. (2002). Family-based association study of 76 candidate genes in bipolar disorder: BDNF is a potential risk locus. *Molecular Psychiatry, 7,* 579–593.

Skog, O.-J. (1985). The wetness of drinking cultures: A key variable in epidemiology of alcoholic liver cirrhosis. *Acta Medica Scandinavica, 703,* 157–184.

Smith, G. T., Goldman, M. S., Greenbaum, P. E., & Christiansen, B. A. (1995). Expectancy for social facilitation from drinking: The divergent paths of high-expectancy and low-expectancy adolescents. *Journal of Abnormal Psychology, 104,* 32–40.

Spear, L. P. (2002). The adolescent brain and the college drinker: Biological basis of propensity to use and misuse alcohol. *Journal of Studies on Alcohol (Suppl.), 6,* 71–81.

Stacy, A. W. (1997). Memory activation and expectancy as prospective predictors of alcohol and marijuana use. *Journal of Abnormal Psychology, 106,* 61–73.

Stacy, A. W., Ames, S. L., Sussman, S., & Dent, C. W. (1996). Implicit cognition in adolescent drug use. *Psychology of Addictive Behaviors, 10,* 190–203.

Stoltenberg, S. F., & Burmeister, M. (2000). Recent progress in psychiatric genetics: Some hope but no hype. *Human Molecular Genetics, 9,* 927–935.

Sung, M., Erkanli, A., Angold, A., & Costello, E. J. (2004). Effects of age at first substance use and psychiatric comorbidity on the development of substance use disorders. *Drug and Alcohol Dependence, 75,* 287–299.

Tarter, R. E., Alterman, A. I., & Edwards, K. L. (1984). Alcoholic denial: A biopsychological interpretation. *Journal of Studies on Alcohol, 45,* 214–218.

Tarter, R. E., Alterman, A. I., & Edwards, K. L. (1985). Vulnerability to alcoholism in men: A behavior-genetic perspective. *Journal of Studies on Alcohol, 46,* 329–356.

Tarter, R. E., Kirisci, L., Mezzich, A., Cornelius, J. R., Pajer, K., Vanyukov, M., et al. (2003). Neurobehavioral disinhibition in childhood predicts early age at onset of substance use disorder. *American Journal of Psychiatry, 160,* 1078–1085.

Tarter, R. E., Vanyukov, M., Giancola, P., Dawes, M., Blackson, T., Mezzich, A., et al. (1999). Etiology of early age onset substance use disorder: A maturational perspective. *Development and Psychopathology, 38,* 115–142.

Thomas, K. M., Drevets, W. C., Whalen, P. J., Eccard, C. H., Dahl, R. E., Ryan, N. D., et al. (2001). Amygdala response to facial expressions in children and adults. *Biological Psychiatry, 49,* 309–316.

Thomas, K. M., King, S. W., Franzen, P. L., Welsch, T. F., Berkowitz, A. L., Noll, D. C., et al. (1999). A developmental functional MRI study of spatial working memory. *Neuroimage, 10,* 327–338.

Thomasson, H. R., Crabb, D. W., Eadenberg, H. J., & Li, T.-K. (1993). Alcohol and aldehyde dehydrogenase polymorphisms and alcoholism. *Behavior Genetics, 23*(2), 131–136.

Tiffany, S. T. (1990). A cognitive model of drug urges and drug-use behavior: Role of automatic and nonautomatic processes. *Psychological Review, 97,* 147–168.

Tiihonen, J., Hallikainen, T., Lachman, H., Saito, T., Volavka, J., Kauhanen, J., et al. (1999). Association between the functional variant of the catechol-O-methyltransference (COMT) gene and Type 1 alcoholism. *Molecular Psychiatry, 4,* 286–289.

Tiihonen, J., Kuikka, J., Hakola, P., Paanila, J., Airaksinen, J., Eronen, M., et al. (1994). Acute ethanol-induced changes in cerebral blood flow. *American Journal of Psychiatry, 151,* 1505–1508.

Tsuang, M. T., Lyons, M. J., Meyer, J. M., Doyle, T., Eisen, S. A., Goldberg, J., et al. (1998). Co-occurrence of abuse of different drugs in men. *Archives of General Psychiatry, 55,* 967–972.

Turecki, G., Zhu, Z., Tzenova, J., Lesage, A., Seguin, M., Tousignant, M., et al. (2001). TPH and suicidal behavior: A study in suicide completers. *Molecular Psychiatry, 6,* 98–102.

Turnbull, J. E., & Gomberg, E. S. L. (1990). The structure of depression in alcoholic women. *Journal of Studies on Alcohol, 51,* 148–154.

Ueno, S., Nakamura, M., Mikami, M., Kondoh, K., Ishiguro, H., Arinami, T., et al. (1999). Identification of a novel polymorphism of the human dopamine transporter (DAT1) gene and the significant association with alcoholism. *Molecular Psychiatry, 4,* 552–557.

Vaillant, G. E. (1995). *The natural history of alcoholism revisited.* Cambridge, MA: Harvard University Press.

Vanyukov, M. M., Moss, H. B., Yu, L. M., Tarter, R. E., & Deka, R. (1995). Preliminary evidence for an association of a dinucleotide repeat polymorphism at the MAOA gene with early onset alcoholism/substance abuse. *American Journal of Medical Genetics: Part B. Neuropsychiatric Genetics, 60,* 122–126.

Victor, M., Adams, R. D., & Collins, G. H. (1971). *The Wenicke-Korsakoff syndrome.* Philadelphia: F. A. Davis.

Vogel-Sprott, M., Easdon, C., Fillmore, M., Finn, P., & Justus, A. (2001). Alcohol and behavioral control: Cognitive and neural mechanisms. *Alcoholism: Clinical and Experimental Research, 25,* 117–121.

Volkow, N. D., Fowler, J. S., Wang, G. J., Hitzemann, R., Logan, J., Schlyer, D. L., et al. (1993). Decreased dopamine D2 receptor availability is associated with reduced frontal metabolism in cocaine abusers. *Synapse, 14,* 169–177.

Volkow, N. D., Mullani, N., Gould, L., Adler, S. S., Guynn, R. W., Overall, J. E., et al. (1988). Effects of acute alcohol intoxication on cerebral blood flow measured with PET. *Psychiatry Research, 24,* 201–209.

Wagenaar, A., & Toomey, T. (2002). Effects of minimum drinking age laws: Review and analysis of the literature from 1960–2000. *Journal of Studies on Alcohol, 4*(Suppl. 14), 206–225.

Waldman, I. D., Rowe, D. C., Abramowitz, A., Kozel, S. T., Mohr, J. H., Sherman, S. L., et al. (1998). Association and linkage of the dopamine transporter gene (DAT1) and Attention Deficit Hyperactivity Disorder in children. *American Journal of Human Genetics, 63,* 1767–1776.

Wang, T., Franke, P., Neidt, H., Cichon, S., Knapp, M., Lichtermann, D., et al. (2001). Association study of the low-activity allele of catechol-O-methyltransferase and alcoholism using a family-based approach. *Molecular Psychiatry, 6,* 109–111.

Weber, M. D., Graham, J. W., Hansen, W. B., Flay, B. R., & Anderson, C. A. (1989). Evidence for two paths of alcohol use onset in adolescents. *Addictive Behaviors, 14,* 399–408.

Weiss, F., & Porrino, L. J. (2002). Behavioral neurobiology of alcohol addiction: Recent advances and challenges. *Journal of Neuroscience, 22,* 3332–3337.

Werner, E. E. (1986). Resilient offspring of alcoholics: A longitudinal study from birth to age 18. *Journal of Studies on Alcohol, 47,* 34–40.

Wilsnack, S. C., Klassen, A. D., Schur, B. E., & Wilsnack, R. W. (1991). Predicting onset and chronicity of women's problem drinking: A five-year longitudinal analysis. *American Journal of Public Health, 81,* 305–318.

Windle, M., & Scheidt, D. M. (2004). Alcoholic subtypes: Are two sufficient? *Addiction, 99,* 1508–1519.

Wong, M. M., Brower, K. J., Fitzgerald, H. E., & Zucker, R. A. (2004). Sleep problems in early childhood and early onset of alcohol and other drug use in adolescence. *Alcoholism: Clinical and Experimental Research, 28,* 578–587.

Wong, M. M., Zucker, R. A., Fitzgerald, H. E., & Puttler, L. I. (1999). Parent psychopathology, internalizing and externalizing symptomatology among children of alcoholics [Abstract]. *Alcoholism: Clinical and Experimental Research, 23,* 37A.

Wylie, A., Casswell, S., & Stewart, J. (1989). The response of New Zealand boys to corporate and sponsorship alcohol advertising on television. *British Journal of Addictions, 84,* 639–646.

Zucker, R. A. (1987). The four alcoholisms: A developmental account of the etiologic process. In P. C. Rivers (Ed.), *Nebraska Symposium on Motivation: Vol. 34. Alcohol and addictive behaviors* (pp. 27–83). Lincoln: University of Nebraska Press.

Zucker, R. A. (1991). Scaling the developmental momentum of alcoholic process via the Lifetime Alcohol Problems Scores. *Alcohol and Alcoholism* (Suppl. 1), 505–510.

Zucker, R. A. (1994). Pathways to alcohol problems and alcoholism: A developmental account of the evidence for multiple alcoholisms and for contextual contributions to risk. In R. A. Zucker, G. Boyd, & J. Howard (Eds.), *The development of alcohol problems: Exploring the biopsychosocial matrix of risk* (NIAAA Research Monograph No. 26, NIH Publication No. 94-3495, pp. 255–289). Rockville, MD: Department of Health and Human Services.

Zucker, R. A. (2000). Alcohol involvement over the life course. In NIAAA (ed.) *National Institute on Alcohol Abuse and Alcoholism tenth special report to the U.S. Congress on alcohol and health: Highlights from current research* (pp. 28–53). Bethesda, MD: U.S. Department of Health and Human Services.

Zucker, R. A., Boyd, G. M., & Howard, J. (Eds.). (1994). *The development of alcohol problems: Exploring the biopsychosocial matrix of risk* (NIAAA Research Monograph No. 26). Rockville, MD: Department of Health and Human Services.

Zucker, R. A., Chermack, S. T., & Curran, G. M. (2000). Alcoholism: A lifespan of etiology and course. In A. Sameroff, M. Lewis, & S. Miller (Eds.), *Handbook of developmental psychopathology* (2nd ed., pp. 569–587). New York: Plenum Press.

Zucker, R. A., Davies, W. H., Kincaid, S. B., Fitzgerald, H. E., & Reider, E. E. (1997). Conceptualizing and scaling the developmental structure of behavior disorder: The Lifetime Alcohol Problems Score as an example. *Developmental Psychopathology, 9,* 453–471.

Zucker, R. A., Ellis, D. A., Bingham, C. R., & Fitzgerald, H. E. (1996). The development of alcoholic subtypes: Risk variation among alcoholic families during early childhood. *Alcohol Health and Research World, 20,* 46–54.

Zucker, R. A., Ellis, D. A., Fitzgerald, H. E., Bingham, C. R., & Sanford, K. P. (1996). Other evidence for at least two alcoholisms: II. Life course variation in antisociality and heterogeneity of alcoholic outcome. *Development and Psychopathology, 8,* 831–848.

Zucker, R. A., Fitzgerald, H. E., & Moses, H. M. (1995). Emergence of alcohol problems and the several alcoholisms: A developmental perspective on etiologic theory and life course trajectory. In D. Cicchetti & D. J. Cohen (Eds.), *Developmental psychopathology: Vol. 2. Risk, disorder, and adaptation* (pp. 677–711). New York: Wiley.

Zucker, R. A., & Gomberg, E. S. L. (1986). Etiology of alcoholism reconsidered: The case for a biopsychosocial process. *American Psychologist, 41,* 783–793.

Zucker, R. A., Kincaid, S. B., Fitzgerald, H. E., & Bingham, C. R. (1995). Alcohol schema acquisition in preschoolers: Differences between children of alcoholics and children of nonalcoholics. *Alcoholism: Clinical and Experimental Research, 19,* 1011–1017.

Zucker, R. A., & Wong, M. M. (2005). Prevention for children of alcoholics and other high risk groups. In M. Galanter (Ed.), *Recent developments in alcoholism: Vol. 17. Alcohol problems in adolescents and young adults* (pp. 299–319). New York: Kluwer Academic/Plenum Press.

Zucker, R. A., Wong, M. M., Puttler, L. I., & Fitzgerald, H. E. (2003). Resilience and vulnerability among sons of alcoholics: Relationship to developmental outcomes between early childhood and adolescence. In S. Luthar (Ed.), *Resilience and vulnerability: Adaptation in the context of childhood adversities* (pp. 76–103). New York: Cambridge University Press.

CHAPTER 18

Dissociative Disorders

FRANK W. PUTNAM

WHY IS DISSOCIATION INTERESTING FROM A DEVELOPMENTAL PERSPECTIVE?

The concept of dissociation as a psychopathological process has long been controversial. For well over a century this controversy has raged, and it remains as acrimonious now as it has ever been (McHugh & Putnam, 1995). Yet, an increasing number of clinicians and researchers, especially those with a developmental orientation, are including measures of dissociation in their clinical practice and research studies. Dissociation is now considered by some researchers to be a major mediating factor for the development of certain types of psychopathology. The growing recognition of the impact of dissociation on long-term psychological health emerges both from clinical work with traumatized individuals and from research with normal

and clinical populations. Dissociation appears to account for a significant amount of the variance in specific psychopathological outcomes as well as for some important clinical phenomena.

In parallel with the growing recognition of the contribution of dissociation to psychopathology is an emerging awareness of dissociation as a fundamental developmental process, similar to emotional regulation, in that it more or less continuously shapes a child's interaction with his or her environment during sensitive periods. As a result, high levels of dissociation appear to profoundly influence the long-term development of identity and sense of self, cognitive functioning, and psychological and physiological responses to stressors in some individuals (Putnam, 1997).

Indeed, if the taxonic model of Dissociative Identity Disorder (DID) is correct, then high levels of dissociation acting over the course of early development produce a distinctly different type of psychological organization. In opposition to a unified sense of self, dissociative individuals experience themselves as a collection of independent or semi-independent agents, referred to as "personality systems," which are often at cross-purposes. Some researchers believe that understanding the effects of early dissociation on child development will provide crucial insights into the effects of early trauma and psychosocial adversity on long-term mental health.

GOALS OF THE CHAPTER

The overall goal of this chapter is to provide a comprehensive developmental, clinical, and research overview of dissociation, its history, phenomenology, the *Diagnostic and Statistical Manual of Mental Disorders* (*DSM*) taxonomy, developmental precursors, diagnosis, and treatment.

The history of dissociation is instructive in that it exemplifies both the enduring conceptual influence that early theorizing about the nature of a disorder can have on modern formulations and the troublesome baggage that such theorizing leaves in its wake. It has been said that much of what mental health professionals know about the dissociative disorders is based on the portrayal of Multiple Personality Disorder in the popular media. From their earliest clinical accounts in the eighteenth century onward, dissociative disorders have evoked public fascination. Many of the misleading stereotypes about these conditions originated in the popular media over a century ago and have been promulgated forward ever since. A goal of this chapter is to trace the early historical roots of dissociation theory and its subsequent revisions in the light of new and better data.

The history of dissociative disorders is interesting in that it is also, in many respects, the history of the emergence of psychodynamic psychiatry. Dissociative psychopathology, such as double personality, fugue, somnambulism, psychogenic amnesia, and depersonalization, was pivotal in the larger recognition of the existence and influence of unconscious processes on behavior. These dissociative conditions, in which an individual behaved in ways that were often antithetical to his or her normal behavior and interests, spurred the recognition of a hidden mental world that could erupt and take control of an individual's thoughts and actions in times of personal crisis. Most of the great figures of early nineteenth-century psychology and psychiatry described cases

and presented their theories of dissociation. The cumulative result was the "discovery of the unconscious" during the late nineteenth century and the subsequent articulation of therapeutic approaches that directly addressed unconscious processes in treatment (Ellenberger, 1970). Freudian psychoanalysis is the most notable of these treatments, but many other dynamic psychiatry treatment models exist and are still practiced.

Psychoanalysis, once the dominant psychiatric treatment model, has long since lost its cachet and been replaced by neurobiologically oriented approaches to treatment, primarily psychopharmacology. Dissociation, however, remains clinically and scientifically important to current theorizing, especially as related to the development of psychopathology, the nature of cognitive processes, and the linkage between mental processes and somatic symptoms. An awareness of the history of dissociation and the dissociative disorders will help the reader appreciate the critical role of dissociation in understanding mental illness and health as well as to sort the proverbial wheat from the chaff with regard to the claims and counterclaims raised by proponents and opponents of dissociation theory.

Another goal of this chapter is to articulate the essential features of dissociation and the corresponding dissociative diagnoses such that clinicians can recognize these conditions in their work and researchers can include dissociation in their clinical and laboratory investigations. In this regard, the chapter seeks to delineate the nature of dissociation through a convergence of data drawn from multiple sources.

Dissociative disorders have been formally defined in every version of the *DSM* published by the American Psychiatric Association since *DSM-I* in 1952. A number of the *DSM*-defined disorders are discussed in this chapter to provide detailed descriptions of dissociative psychopathology. These discussions include the essential features of the disorder, a table of the *DSM-IV-TR* diagnostic criteria, relevant epidemiology, and a brief description of currently accepted treatment. In addition to the *DSM* disorders, the chapter includes more general discussions of dissociative symptoms that commonly occur across most of the *DSM* disorders and thus can be considered core symptoms.

The best validated approaches to the measurement of dissociation are also discussed. Current dissociation scales and structured interviews for adults have been proven to be as reliable and valid as corresponding measures for depression and anxiety. Although fewer in number, dissociation measures for children and adolescents also exhibit good psychometric properties and are proving informative both clinically and in the laboratory setting. The inclusion of standard dissociation measures in clinical and experimental research has revolutionized our understanding of the dissociative process. A goal of this chapter is to review existing quantitative research using standard dissociation measures on etiological antecedents, the impact of dissociation on development, dissociative alterations of cognition, and the neurobiological markers and mechanisms of dissociation.

One of the major results of this process is the documentation of the role of trauma in the etiology of pathological levels of dissociation. Historically, dissociation has been linked to trauma since the nineteenth century by authorities such as Pierre Janet (van der Kolk, Brown, & van der Hart, 1989; van der Hart, Brown, & van der Kolk, 1989) the great French psychologist and psychiatrist. The advent of good measures of dissociation allows us to quantify this early observation for multiple different types of trauma in independent samples. The magnitude of the relationship of increased dissociation to traumatic antecedents is equivalent to that demonstrated for trauma and posttraumatic stress symptoms. Induced stressor studies, such as those conducted on military training of Special Forces troops, further strengthen our conviction that experiences of major stress and trauma play an etiological role in the production of pathological levels of dissociation.

A second process making an etiological contribution to dissociation appears to be a particular disorder of attachment, Type D or Disoriented/Disorganized Attachment. Type D attachment, most commonly found in maltreated children, appears to be an important antecedent process that predisposes individuals to dissociate in the context of stress or trauma as opposed to exhibiting some other symptomatic expression and/or coping response. Preliminary longitudinal data linking Type D attachment in infancy to subsequent increased dissociation in adolescence suggests that, together with early maltreatment/childhood stressors, fundamental parent-child difficulties contribute to the propensity to dissociate.

A final important goal of this chapter, in keeping with the theme of this book, is to describe the current data and thinking with respect to dissociation as a critical developmental process influencing cognition, behavior, and psychopathology. A growing body of research is strongly linking dissociation to a range of negative long-term sequelae. Sophisticated statistical studies confirm that dissociation plays a significant role in the mediation of traumatic experiences into these negative outcomes. An awareness of the powerful developmental role played by

increased dissociation in certain forms of psychopathology provides a clinical target for the next generation of treatments and interventions with maltreated and traumatized children.

BRIEF HISTORY OF DISSOCIATION AND THE DISSOCIATIVE DISORDERS

Eighteenth and Nineteenth Century

The study of dissociation began in the late eighteenth century with Eberhardt Gmelin's (Ellenberger, 1970) medical report of a German woman who alternatively "exchanged" her peasant personality for that of a French aristocratic lady, with each personality amnesic for the other. By the early nineteenth century, diagnoses of dual, double, and duplex personality/consciousness were being regularly reported in Europe and North America. Widely hailed as the father of American psychiatry, Benjamin Rush (Putnam, 1991) included examples in his medical school lectures. He proposed that the condition was caused by a disconnection between the two hemispheres of the brain—a theory that continues to attract modern interest. The case of Mary Reynolds, which was to become the American archetype of multiple personality for the remainder of the century, was first described shortly thereafter.

In France, Antoine Despine (Despine, 1840) a country doctor, compiled systematic case reports of several multiple personality patients, including child and adolescent cases. Many also suffered from classic conversion symptoms such as psychogenic blindness, deafness, and paralysis. It was then commonly believed that these patients, primarily women, suffered from sexual frustration. Hysteria became the preferred diagnosis for these patients. In a mid-nineteenth-century study involving nuns, prostitutes and maid servants, Paul Briquet (Ellenberger, 1970) disputed the notion that hysteria was an expression of forbidden impulses. He believed instead that these symptoms arose as a result of overwhelming trauma and loss, frequently in childhood.

Toward the end of the nineteenth century, Jean-Martin Charcot (Ellenberger, 1970), director of the great French psychiatric hospital La Salpêtrière, gave dramatic demonstrations with "hysterical" patients who were "magnetized" before crowds of physicians and the interested public. Among those attending were Sigmund Freud, Pierre Janet, and Joseph Babinski. Following Charcot's sudden death, Babinski (Babinski, 1901, 1909), who believed that the patients' symptoms were merely the effects of Charcot's "suggestion," assumed directorship of the Salpêtrière and halted further studies, thereby roundly discrediting dissociation and hysteria. The then considerable prestige of French psychiatry influenced the adoption of similar positions internationally, although American academic interest in dissociation continued into the early twentieth century under the influence of William James, Morton Prince, and others.

Pierre Janet (Ellenberger, 1970), though similarly critical of Charcot's performances as encouraging of hysterical symptoms, nonetheless recognized the existence of a legitimate underlying mental disturbance. Conducting carefully documented case studies (ultimately numbering in the thousands, which he ordered destroyed upon his death), Janet elucidated the psychological principles that he believed characterized dissociative psychopathology. As had Briquet a half-century before him, Janet attributed hysteria to overwhelming stress and actual trauma. He believed that the fundamental process in dissociation was the "narrowing of consciousness," which prevented the person from perceiving certain subjective phenomena, such as traumatic memories. These then became dissociated, quasi-independent aspects of the mind. He developed a cognitive psychotherapy, including hypnosis, which sought to identify and correct these "fixed ideas." The First World War interrupted Janet's writing and teaching, and in the immediate postwar years the rise of psychoanalysis, with its emphasis on repression of unacceptable ideas and impulses, eclipsed his earlier therapeutic approach of "psychological analysis."

Today, most authorities regard Janet as the father of modern theories of dissociation and note that many of Freud's early ideas were borrowed from him. Indeed, Freud cites Janet's work in his first book, *Studies on Hysteria,* coauthored with Josef Breuer, which is widely revered as the beginning of psychoanalysis (Breuer & Freud, 1957). In his review of their book, Janet somewhat sarcastically observes that these young Austrians have discovered some of his "already old ideas" (Ellenberger, 1970, p. 772). As time passed, however, many psychoanalysts severely criticized Janet, and his ideas were largely repudiated or forgotten in the post-World War I infatuation with Freud's theories about sexual drives. Psychoanalytic thinking posited the idea of a dynamic unconscious, which defended against unacceptable thoughts, wishes, and memories. Freud's subsequent retraction of his seduction theory further detracted from Janet's position that hysterical patients had experienced actual trauma.

Twentieth Century

World War II brought many "hysterical" battlefield casualties, called "shell shock" in WWI, who exhibited florid dissociative reactions, including amnesia for their own identity, fugues, conversion blindness, and paralysis. Treatment generally involved "narcosynthesis," induced by hypnosis or drugs such as sodium amytal, which created a twilight mental state in which the traumatic memories underlying the symptoms were recalled and defused in an often emotional abreaction. Although their long-term effects were never followed up, these battlefield treatments were regarded as hugely successful, returning the vast majority of soldiers to the front lines within days (Menninger, 1945). Despite initial optimism, the successes of military psychiatry with abreactive treatments for acute traumatic reactions could not be duplicated with peacetime mental patients. The majority of these patients suffered from chronic forms of mental illness such as Schizophrenia and Bipolar Disorder. As a consequence, abreactive forms of therapy were largely discarded in the 1950s, only to be rediscovered and used with Vietnam veterans and Dissociative Disorder patients in the 1970s and 1980s.

The publication of the *DSM-III* in 1980 brought new attention to the dissociative disorders as a distinct category of psychiatric conditions. This renewed recognition of dissociation, especially Multiple Personality Disorder, stimulated both clinical recognition and reporting and more formal research. Subsequently a large body of data has accrued for DID (as Multiple Personality Disorder was renamed in the *DSM-IV*), Depersonalization Disorder, and dissociation in general.

Modern Perspectives on Dissociation

From the 1980s on, clinicians and researchers have reported high rates of trauma, particularly child abuse, in Dissociative Disorder patient samples. These reports, together with sensationalized media portrayals, have contributed to a series of controversies that have affected the credibility of dissociation despite the overwhelming scientific data attesting to its validity as a pathological process. The core controversies are (1) whether Dissociative Disorders, particularly DID, are an iatrogenic creation induced by the therapist's fascination/credulity with a "suggestible" patient and (2) whether the traumatic memories recalled by many of these patients are based on actual experiences (McHugh & Putnam, 1995). These primary controversies, which are both predicated on a notion of increased "suggestibility," have become politicized around the implicit issue of true versus false claims of victimization. These controversies have overshadowed much of the research findings published in the past decade. Indeed, the two sides generally discount each other's data, although relevant research has been done by both camps.

DEFINITIONS OF DISSOCIATION

Definitions of dissociation emerge from a number of disciplines and research traditions, including hypnosis research, descriptive psychiatry, information-processing theory, and cognitive psychology. These definitions converge around the notion that dissociation is manifest by the failure to connect or associate mental information in the fashion that it would normally be expected to be linked. The *DSM-IV* states that "the essential feature of the dissociative disorders is a disruption in the usually integrative functions of consciousness, memory, identity, or perception of the environment. The disturbance may be sudden or gradual, transient or chronic" (American Psychiatric Association, 1994, p. 477).

This failure to integrate certain kinds of information operating over the course of development gives rise to a set of life experiences that shape both dissociative and compensatory behaviors. As a result, most measures of dissociation ask about the frequency with which certain "unusual" experiences occur. For example, the Dissociative Experiences Scale (Bernstein & Putnam, 1986) asks, "Some people have the experience of finding themselves in a place and having no idea how they got there. Circle a number to show what percentage of the time (0% to 100% in 11 steps) this happens to you." This question inquires about fugue episodes, a common experience for many people with DID but extremely rare for individuals who do not qualify as having a Dissociative Disorder.

Dissociative Symptoms

For the most part, clinically based measures of dissociation inquire about the same basic set of constructs: (1) amnesias and "lost" time; (2) alterations in sense of identity; (3) depersonalization and derealization; (4) experiences of intense absorption; and (5) passive influence experiences. Most dissociation measures do not include all of these constructs, leading to some variability across studies. However, there is very high convergent validity across the most widely accepted measures of dissociation. A meta-analysis yielded an overall combined correlation of $r = .67$ with a Cohen's $d = 1.81$ (a Cohen's $d \geq 0.80$ is considered evidence of a strong effect; van Ijzendoorn & Schuengel, 1996).

Each of these dissociative constructs is typically manifest both as a set of subjective experiences that the individual may report and as a set of distinct behaviors that may be observed, recorded, and to some extent quantified. The phenomenology of these dissociative signs and symptoms has shown good stability across culture and over time. Janet's nineteenth-century dissociative patients by and large resemble those seen on psychiatric wards today. Clinical dissociative case series have been reported for many different cultures, including non-Western, Latin, Asian, European, and Near Eastern (Boon & Draijer, 1993; Coons, Bowman, Kluft, & Milstein, 1991; Middleton & Butler, 1998; Sar, Yargic, & Tutkun, 1996). Comparisons of symptoms reveal many strong similarities across these different samples. This reliability in the clinical manifestations of dissociation across time and culture is one element of a larger proof of the validity of pathological dissociation as a meaningful construct and the dissociative disorders as a distinct manifestation of psychopathology. Nonetheless, it should be acknowledged that there are cultural variations in clinical dissociative presentations, so that different cultures may package the core set of dissociative constructs in unique ways.

The five *DSM* dissociative disorders, Dissociative Amnesia, Dissociative Fugue, Depersonalization Disorder, DID, and Dissociative Disorder Not Otherwise Specified (DDNOS), share overlapping dissociative symptoms. Each disorder is characterized by a primary dissociative symptom that dominates the clinical presentation, but careful inquiry will reveal the existence of other dissociative symptoms. To further confuse the reader, many dissociative symptoms share the name of the *DSM* disorder. For example, Dissociative Amnesia is both a symptom that may be found in several dissociative disorders and the name of a *DSM* disorder. To clarify for the reader whether a symptom or a *DSM* disorder is being discussed, all *DSM* disorders are capitalized in the text.

Amnesia and Memory Symptoms

Time loss, blackouts, and various amnesias in the absence of substance abuse or organic conditions are a hallmark of pathological dissociation. Specific disturbances in memory are core features of all of the dissociative disorders except perhaps Depersonalization Disorder. Patients generally report becoming aware of these gaps in the continuity of their memory in two ways. In the first instance, they "come to" in the midst of doing something, for example, finding themselves in a room talking with strangers or driving in a car. Often, they have little or no recall of how they got to be where they are or what they were doing there. The second way that large gaps in awareness of the continuity of time come to an individual's attention is when that person is continually confronted with evidence of having gone somewhere or done something that he or she cannot recall. Family and friends tell these individuals about events and behaviors that they cannot remember, they find purchases that they do not recall buying, or they find themselves married to people whom they do not know. One patient told me that she was tired of going to work and discovering that she had quit her job in a stormy scene the day before.

Family and friends often describe the patient as forgetful or as always changing his or her mind. There is a perplexing quality to this forgetfulness in that the individual often appears not to recognize people or possessions or forgets important information that he or she would be expected to remember without difficulty. At other times, a dissociative individual may show profound shifts in personal preferences, for example, taste in food or clothing, and refuse to acknowledge his or her prior favorite choice. Dissociative individuals often report significant gaps in the continuity of their autobiographical memory. For example, a patient reported that she had clear memories of fifth and sixth grade but no recall of seventh and eighth grade. These gaps in autobiographical recall do not fit the profile of "childhood amnesia," which typically manifests as a significantly decreased number of memories below age 5 to 6 years, with few memories before age 3 years. Rather, dissociative patients often report abrupt, age- or event-demarcated gaps in autobiographical recall that do not fit the memory decay curve associated with childhood amnesia.

Dissociative disturbances of memory wax and wane dynamically so that information that was unavailable in one context may be readily available in others. Generally the individual and his or her significant others find ways to rationalize these discrepancies in memory, preferences, skills, and knowledge until some event occurs that makes it overwhelmingly evident that this level of forgetfulness is seriously compromising the quality and effectiveness of the individual's performance. Nonetheless, high levels of dissociation operating over the course of development shape an individual's approach to situations and his or her responses to certain events.

Alterations in Identity

Alterations in identity are a critical feature of all dissociative disorders and a core component of pathological dissociation. These alterations take a number of forms. In Dissociative Amnesia, the individual loses awareness of his or her identity; these are the John and Jane Doe cases who show up in most large city hospital emergency rooms several times a year. In Dissociative Fugue, characterized by a sudden trip or wandering episode, the individual is largely amnesic for his or her principal identity but often elaborates a secondary identity during the journey. When the primary identity is reestablished, there is often a reciprocal amnesia for the events and experiences of the secondary identity. Memory for fugue experiences may, however, return gradually or in response to specific cues. In Depersonalization Disorder, the individual often feels either "unreal" or "dead." Dissociative Identity Disorder or Multiple Personality Disorder is characterized by individuals feeling as if they consist of a number of separate and distinct alter identities or personalities that exchange control over behavior, often in a rather contentious fashion. The *DSM* category of DDNOS is a heterogeneous collection of dissociative syndromes and trance state conditions, many unique to specific cultures or situations, which typically includes full or partial spirit possession experiences or episodes during which the individual is not fully cognizant of his or her identity and behavior.

Depersonalization and Derealization

Depersonalization is both a symptom and a *DSM* disorder. As a psychiatric symptom, depersonalization is remarkably common and is included among the symptom profiles of a wide span of disorders, ranging from epilepsy to Borderline Personality Disorder. The *DSM-IV-TR* identifies the essential feature of depersonalization as the persistent or recurrent feeling of detachment or estrangement from one's self. The individual may report feeling like an automaton or as if in a dream or watching himself or herself in a movie. There may be a sensation of being an outside observer of one's mental processes, one's body, or parts of one's body. There is often a sense of an absence of control over one's actions.

Described clinically since the 1870s, depersonalization was named in 1898 by L. Dugas (Dugas, 1898), who sought to convey "the feeling of loss of ego." Freud, Janet, Eugén Bleuler, and other nineteenth-century authorities reported patients with symptoms of depersonalization and derealization. A 1914 report by Schilder (1939) is regarded as a turning point in psychiatric interest. In 1954, Ackner (Ackner, 1954a, 1954b) enumerated the essential features of current diagnostic definitions. Symptoms of Depersonalization as a *DSM* disorder include

(1) the feeling of unreality or strangeness apropos the self; (2) the retention of insight and lack of "delusional elaboration"; (3) the lack of affective response ("numbness") except for the discomfort regarding depersonalization; and (4) an unpleasant property that inversely varies in intensity

with the subject's familiarity with the phenomenon. (Kaplan & Sadock, 1991, p. 51)

In the past decade, research by Eric Hollander, Daphne Simeon, and colleagues (Hollander et al., 1990, 1992, 1994; Simeon et al., 1997, 2000; Simeon, Guralnik, Knutelska, Yehuda, & Schmeidler, 2003; Simeon & Hollander, 1993) has significantly increased our understanding of Depersonalization Disorder through systematic case series, medication trials, brain imaging, and improved measurement.

Derealization is defined as a "sensation of changed reality or that one's surroundings have altered" (Kaplan & Sadock, 1991, p. 51). Derealization is quantified on dissociation scales by questions such as "Have you ever felt as if the world and/or people around you was unreal, or seemed as if in a dream (Bernstein & Putnam, 1986)?"

Transient experiences of depersonalization and derealization are the third most commonly reported psychiatric symptom after depression and anxiety. A random sampling of over 1,000 adults found a 1-year prevalence of 19% for depersonalization and 14% for derealization (Aderibigbe, Bloch, & Walker, 2001). Common in seizure patients and migraine sufferers, depersonalization also occurs with the use of marijuana, LSD, and mescaline, and less frequently as a side effect of certain medications, particularly anticholinergic agents. Albert Hoffman, the chemist who first synthesized LSD, reported on his first deliberate ingestion: "Occasionally I felt as if I were out of my body. . . . I thought I had died. My 'ego' was suspended somewhere in space and I saw my body lying dead on the sofa" (quoted in Lee & Shlain, 1992, p. xviii). Depersonalization has also been reported following meditation, hypnosis, mirror and crystal gazing, and sensory deprivation experiences. It is also common after mild to moderate head injury where there is little or no loss of consciousness; for some reason, it is much less likely if unconsciousness lasts for more than a half-hour. Depersonalization, derealization, or out-of-body experiences are also common following life-threatening experiences with or without serious bodily injury and may occur in up to 70% of individuals with a serious injury or near-death experience (Putnam, 1985).

Experiences of Intense Absorption and Deep Hypnosis

Experiences of intense absorption, deep hypnosis, or deep relaxation are considered dissociative by some, but by no means all, authorities. Their inclusion as dissociative comes out of the hypnosis research tradition, which has long equated hypnosis with dissociation. A number of lines of evidence, however, indicate that clinical phenomena that are often referred to as "pathological dissociation" are distinct from seemingly analogous phenomena that may be induced under hypnosis in highly hypnotizable individuals. More than a dozen studies that have administered measures of both hypnotizability and dissociation found virtually no correlation between these two constructs (Putnam & Carlson, 1998). Nor do measures of hypnotizability correlate with psychopathology in the same fashion as dissociation. As a consequence, many authorities are dropping absorption items from their scales and interviews, as these are not predictive of clinical consequences.

Passive Influence/Interference Symptoms

Passive influence or interference symptoms encompass many first-rank Schneiderian symptoms, such as audible thoughts, voices arguing with each other, divine or demonic powers controlling the body, thought withdrawal or insertion, and "made" feelings, impulses, and actions. Once considered to be pathognomonic for Schizophrenia, passive influence experiences are not uncommon in patients with affective, organic, and dissociative disorders. In fact, passive influence symptoms are more common in dissociative patients than in patients with psychotic disorders (Kluft, 1987). In dissociative patients, the agents of the passive influence symptoms are usually experienced as internal, as opposed to individuals with psychotic disorders, who typically feel controlled by external entities. In addition, dissociative patients may experience strong affects or impulses that feel as if they are imposed on them and are not their own feelings or desires.

Passive influence experiences are a central component of spirit possession, which is a core feature of a number of religious traditions. Possession typically takes either a divine or a demonic form. In the divine form in Western religions, the individual usually feels as if he or she is a passive vessel filled and moved by the Holy Spirit and he or she is serving as an instrument of divine will. There is typically a powerful affective memory of this experience, which may be life-changing. In African, Caribbean, and South American cultures, the individual may become a divine entity, with distinctive speech and demeanor. Often, this god issues commands and pronouncements or bargains with relatives and friends about its terms for relinquishing possession of the body. The individual is typically amnesic for the duration of the possession.

Demonic possession likewise occurs in both Western and non-Western cultures and typically takes the form of an evil entity either attempting to seize physical control or tormenting the individual into doing something against his or her will. In Western cultures, the individual is typically aware of this possession and feels as if he or she is in a physical struggle with the evil entity, "wrestling with demons." In non-Western cultures, the individual is often amnesic for these experiences. Possession experiences often occur in the context of a personal crisis and frequently serve in some fashion to alter the individual's life circumstances in ways that reduce stress. Although more common than generally appreciated, demonic possession is typically treated by religious rituals and thus rarely encountered in clinical settings.

CLINICAL AND RESEARCH MEASURES OF DISSOCIATION

Dissociation Scales and Diagnostic Interviews

Dissociation screening measures and scales have proliferated in the past decade. The best of these instruments equal the levels of reliability and validity established for measures of depression, anxiety, and Posttraumatic Stress Disorder (PTSD). Measurement of dissociation has proven particularly important to understanding the clinical contribution of dissociation to trauma-associated disorders as well as for laboratory studies. Many of these measures are in the public domain and available on the Internet. Establishing the provenance of a given measure downloaded from the Internet is critical to ensuring that a properly validated version is being used, as, unfortunately, some measures have been significantly modified and then reposted under their original name.

Symptom Screening Measures

A number of general dissociation screening scales exist. The Dissociative Experiences Scale (DES), developed by Bernstein and Putnam in the mid-1980s, is the most widely used and has been included in hundreds of studies (Bernstein & Putnam, 1986; E. B. Carlson & Putnam, 1993). The 28 items primarily focus on amnesias, identity alteration, depersonalization, derealization, and absorption. The overall DES score can range from 0 to 100. Using receiver operating characteristics methodology, multiple studies converge on DES scores of 30 or greater as a threshold for identifying pathological levels of dissociation (Waller, Putnam, & Carlson, 1996). An overall DES score of 30 or a score of 30 on the 8-item DES-T (taxon; see later discussion) is typically used by studies dividing a sample into high- and low-scoring subjects. Highly correlated with other dissociation measures, the DES has excellent coefficients of internal and test-retest reliability across multiple studies. A trifactorial solution with subscales for amnesia,

depersonalization, and absorption is typically found with clinical samples, whereas general population samples often yield a one-factor solution with absorption items loading most strongly. Within reason, gender, socioeconomic status, and IQ do not appear to have significant influence on DES scores. Translated into over 40 languages, DES studies across cultures reveal strong similarities for both Western and non-Western samples, attesting to the universality of the core constructs of dissociation.

Developed by Marmar, Weiss, and colleagues (1994), the Peritraumatic Dissociative Experiences Questionnaire (PDEQ) assesses dissociative experiences at the time of the traumatic event. A 10-item self-report version (PDEQ-10-SRV) is widely used for both research and clinical screening. A meta-analytic study established that peritraumatic dissociation is the single best predictive factor for the subsequent development of PTSD (Ozer, Best, Lipsey, & Weiss, 2003). Many of the somatosensory and conversion symptoms common in dissociative patients, which include motor inhibitions, loss of function, anesthesias and analgesias, pain, and problems with vision, hearing, and smell, are tapped by the Somatoform Dissociation Questionnaire (SDQ-20) developed by Nijenhuis (1999). Whereas the 20-item version (SDQ-20) has good reliability and validity for discriminating Dissociative Disorder patients, a 5-item version (SDQ-5) can serve as a quick screening measure. Administered by a trained rater, the Clinician Administered Dissociative States Scale (CADSS) by Bremner et al. (1998) has proven useful in laboratory studies of acute dissociative states for assessing symptoms of amnesia, depersonalization, and derealization.

For children and adolescents, three primary measures have been used most widely. A parent/caretaker/teacher 20-item report measure, the Child Dissociative Checklist (CDC), is a reliable and valid screen for dissociation in children 5 to 12 years of age. Rating each behavior on a 3-point scale, scores can range from 0 to 40, with scores of 12 or greater indicative of pathological levels of dissociation. Several investigators have identified items of the ever popular Child Behavior Checklist (CBCL) that load on a dissociative subscale. These CBCL dissociation subscales have proven useful in research studies, although the clinical utility has yet to be tested with dissociative patients (Becker-Blease et al., 2004). An adolescent version of the DES, the Adolescent Dissociative Experiences Scale (ADES), measures similar constructs of amnesia, identity alteration, depersonalization, and derealization using age-appropriate item content. A 30-item instrument, the ADES uses a 0 to 10 answer format and has good reliability and validity both as a research tool and as a clinical screening instrument (Armstrong, Putnam, Carlson, Libero, & Smith, 1997; Bonanno, Noll, Putnam, O'Neill, & Trickett, 2003; Brunner, Parzer, Schuld, & Resch, 2000; Fehon, Grilo, & Lipschitz, 2001; Friedrich et al., 2001; Kisiel & Lyons, 2001; Noll, Horowitz, Bonanno, Trickett, & Putnam, 2003).

Diagnostic Interviews

Two structured, *DSM*-based diagnostic interviews have been developed: the Structured Clinical Interview for *DSM-IV* Dissociative Disorders-Revised (SCID-D-R) and the Dissociative Disorders Interview Schedule (DDIS). Developed by Marlene Steinberg (1994), the SCID-D-R is widely regarded as the gold standard for research studies. A semistructured, clinician-administered interview, the SCID-D-R assesses the presence and severity of amnesias, identity confusion/alteration, depersonalization, and derealization and renders a *DSM-IV* diagnosis for all five dissociative disorders as well as for Acute Stress Disorder. Administration time for the 276 questions typically ranges from 1 to 2 hours for Dissociative Disorder patients. Interrater and test-retest reliability is good to excellent and validity is well established in numerous studies. Translated into at least a dozen languages, it yields largely similar results in different cultures.

Ross's (Ross, Heber, et al., 1989) DDIS is primarily a clinical diagnostic instrument but is sometimes used as a screening measure. Inquiring about a wide range of phenomena in addition to dissociative symptoms, the DDIS also includes questions about child abuse history, Major Depression, somatic complaints, substance abuse, and paranormal experiences. This instrument requires about 60 minutes to administer to DID patients. Interrater reliability is regarded as acceptable for all dissociative disorders except Depersonalization Disorder, and convergent validity includes strong correlations with the DES and with clinical diagnoses of dissociative disorders.

DSM DISSOCIATIVE DISORDERS

Dissociative Amnesia

History and Epidemiology

Researchers are increasingly looking at the prevalence of dissociative amnesia, originally studied in combat samples, in cases of sexual abuse, physical abuse, and emotional abuse. During World War II, prevalence rates for dissociative amnesia ranged from 5% to 14.4%, with only a small percentage reported to have suffered significant head injuries. In one study of 1,000 soldiers exposed to intense combat, 35% had amnesia. In soldiers with minimal battlefield exposure, past or family history of dissociation or "hysterical" symptoms was associated with dissociative amnesia.

Dissociative Amnesia was found in approximately 6% of a stratified, general population survey sample in Winnipeg, Canada (Waller & Ross, 1997). Onset typically begins in late adolescence and adulthood, with no apparent differences across gender. Dissociative Amnesia may be especially difficult to assess in preadolescent children, where it can be difficult to differentiate from daydreaming, inattention, anxiety, oppositional behavior, cognitive limitations, and psychotic disturbances. Adolescents are better able to verbalize their experiences of amnesia and may have personal names for the phenomenon. For example, one teenager said, "I skip time," and another called the experience "flickering." Most individuals describe more than one amnesia episode.

Over 70 studies have examined dissociative amnesia in child abuse samples using clinical, community, and forensic populations, including retrospective, prospective, and longitudinal study designs. In various studies of clinical populations and individuals who identified themselves as survivors of abuse, 16% to 90% reported amnesia for the abuse at some time in their lives, averaging about 20% across studies. In studies of college undergraduates and women in the community, prevalence of amnesia for abuse ranged from 13% to over 50%. A study by Goodman et al. (2003) using children whose cases were accepted for prosecution and who therefore were highly likely to recall their sexual abuse, having already repeatedly described it to police and district attorneys, found that 19% were unable to recall the target episode. Failure to recall the target episode was correlated significantly with dissociation scale scores. To date, every study that has investigated the existence of amnesia for sexual abuse has found a nontrivial percentage of subjects reporting that at some time in their lives they were not able to recall the sexual abuse or were not aware of having been sexually abused until they "remembered it" many years later.

Diagnosis

The essential feature of Dissociative Amnesia, according to the *DSM-IV-TR,* is the inability to recall important personal information, usually of a traumatic or stressful nature, that is too extensive to be explained by normal forgetfulness (American Psychiatric Association, 2000).

More broadly defined, Dissociative Amnesia is a reversible memory impairment in which groups of autobiographical memories that would ordinarily be available for recall cannot be retrieved or retained in a verbal form (or, if temporarily retrieved, cannot be wholly retained in consciousness). Although this amnesia may result from trauma-related changes in the brain, gross destruction of brain structures that subserve memory does not occur, and the disorder expresses itself as a potentially reversible form of psychological inhibition.

The diagnosis of Dissociative Amnesia generally connotes four factors: (1) Relatively large groups of memories and associated affects have become unavailable, not just single memories, feelings, or thoughts; (2) the unavailable memories usually relate to day-to-day information that would ordinarily be a more or less routine part of conscious awareness: who I am, what I did, where I went, what happened, whom I spoke with, what was said, what I thought and felt at the time, and so on; (3) the ability to remember new factual information, general cognitive functioning, and language capacity are intact; and (4) the dissociated memories often indirectly reveal their presence in more or less disguised forms such as intrusive visual images, flashbacks, somatoform symptoms, nightmares, conversion symptoms, and behavioral reenactments. Dissociative Amnesia is part of a larger spectrum of memory dysfunction related to traumatic stress.

Dissociative Amnesia presents in two basic forms. The first is a dramatic onset of amnesia for extensive and/or important personal information. These patients are often brought to emergency rooms by police and usually cannot recall their name, age, marital status, and other information central to one's identity. During the acute episode, their behavior may include disorientation, perplexity, alterations in consciousness, and aimless wandering. Despite being frequently portrayed in the popular media, this presentation is relatively rare.

An inability to recall significant aspects of one's personal history is a common form of Dissociative Amnesia. Most patients with Dissociative Amnesia do not complain about this, and it is often discovered only while taking a careful life history. Dissociative amnesic gaps are frequently clearly demarcated in the individual's mind so that he or she is aware of a significant discontinuity in memory. For example, although having clear memory for earlier and later school years, a patient reported that she did not "remember being in sixth grade." Such symptoms are usually associated with traumatic circumstances. It was reported that during the sixth grade, she was kidnapped for several months by her estranged father in a custody dispute and sexually abused by him. A few individuals may deny recall of their entire childhood or other major life epochs.

Treatment

Approaches to the treatment of Dissociative Amnesia have been swept up in the controversy about its existence. Crit-

ics have accused therapists of using "recovered memory therapy" in which they "implant false memories" of sexual abuse or other fictitious trauma. There is scientific evidence that pseudomemories can be created with therapeutic techniques such as hypnosis or narcosynthesis, so therapists should be well versed in appropriate nonsuggestive approaches to facilitating the therapeutic processing of traumatic material (Putnam, 1997). Nonetheless, all of the currently endorsed, evidence-based trauma therapies include a cognitive processing component in which traumatic memories are examined, distortions are corrected, and new and hopeful life meanings are constructed (Foa, Keane, & Friedman, 2000).

In individuals presenting clinically with Dissociative Amnesia or Dissociative Fugues, hypnosis can be a useful adjunct to recalling personal information such as name and life circumstance. Having been involved in over a dozen such acute cases, I have found that hypnosis can be very useful in helping persons recall who they are. The directly verifiable information obtained in this fashion has always been essentially correct, demonstrating that hypnosis may facilitate the accurate recall of dissociated identity and other pertinent information in such cases. Once an individual's identity has been established, arrangements can be made for an extended treatment, which may focus on the acute traumatic precipitant and/or the more extensive prior traumatic history that is strongly associated with a propensity to experience dissociative amnesia or fugue episodes. The second presentation of Dissociative Amnesia, the extended autobiographical gap in memory for often traumatic experiences, is best addressed in a psychotherapy setting using nonsuggestive approaches and generally does not require the use of hypnosis or narcosynthesis. If there is a possibility that the memories recalled during treatment may be used in a legal proceeding, every effort should be made to document that they were recalled in a nonsuggestive fashion, and hypnosis and other techniques should be avoided. In forensic cases, videotaping the interview is usually the best way to document how the interview was conducted, what questions were asked, and the specific responses elicited.

Dissociative Fugue

Dissociative Fugue is the least understood of the dissociative disorders. As defined by the *DSM-IV-TR*, the essential feature is a sudden, unexpected travel away from home or one's customary place of daily activities, with inability to recall some or all of one's past (Criterion A). This is accompanied by confusion about one's identity, sometimes with the assumption of a new identity (Criterion B). Dissociative Fugue may not occur exclusively during the course of DID or be due to the direct physiological effects of a substance or a general medical condition (Criterion C). Dissociative Fugue symptoms must cause significant distress or impairment in social, occupational, or other important areas of functioning (Criterion D).

History and Epidemiology

Charcot (Putnam, 1989) described a number of cases of dissociative fugue, which he divided into an epileptic, traumatic, or hysterical etiology. In the United States, William James (1890) described one of the classic cases of fugue, that of Ansel Bourne. Bourne was an itinerant preacher who disappeared from his home in Providence, Rhode Island. After withdrawing $500 from his bank account to pay some bills in January 1887, Bourne "awoke" 2 months later. He found himself in Norristown, Pennsylvania, where he had been living quietly under the name of A. J. Brown and working as a shopkeeper. Subsequently, he had no memory for the time between his disappearance and his awakening in the Bourne identity. Under hypnosis, he could describe his activities during the fugue but was not able to retain this information during normal consciousness. As is often the case during a fugue, Bourne apparently behaved normally and did not attract attention to his situation.

Janet (Janet, 1890) also described cases, hypothesizing that fugues involve the dissociation of more complex groups of mental functions than occurs in amnesia and that they are organized around a powerful emotion or feeling state that is linked to many mental associations, all of which are accompanied by a wish to run away. Military psychiatrists described many cases of Dissociative Fugue in both World Wars.

No cases of Dissociative Fugue were diagnosed in the single epidemiological study of dissociative disorders conducted to date. Fugues are thought to be more common during natural disasters, wartime, or times of major social dislocation and violence, although no systematic data exist on this point. Pre-*DSM-III* cases are often difficult to assess as prior diagnostic criteria were sometimes quite different. Most case reports describe males, primarily in military samples, but insufficient data exist to document a gender bias to this disorder. Fugue is usually described in adults, but adolescent cases have been reported.

Diagnosis

The underlying cause of most fugue episodes is thought to be overwhelming or traumatic circumstances, which pro-duce an altered state of consciousness dominated by a wish to flee and forget. Fugues have been linked to combat, rape, recurrent childhood sexual abuse, massive social dislocations, and natural disasters. In cases where there is not an immediate traumatic precipitant, there is often an antecedent history of serious trauma or social disruption. In these cases, individuals were usually struggling with extreme emotions or impulses such as overwhelming fear, guilt, shame, and/or intense incestuous, sexual, suicidal, or violent urges.

Dissociative fugues have been reported to last from minutes to months, with some individuals reporting multiple fugues. In some severe cases of PTSD, nightmares may terminate in a fugue in which the patient runs outside or elsewhere. Classically, three types of fugue have been described: (1) fugue with awareness of loss of personal identity; (2) fugue with change of personal identity; and (3) fugue with retrograde amnesia. During a fugue, individuals most often do not attract attention or exhibit overt psychopathology. Occasionally, some individuals display bizarre, disorganized, or dangerous behavior, such as a soldier who begins a fugue episode by standing up and walking away, exposing himself to intense enemy fire. Following termination of a fugue, the person may experience perplexity, confusion, trance-like behaviors, depersonalization, derealization, and conversion symptoms, in addition to amnesia for the events of the fugue. Some patients terminate a fugue with an episode of generalized Dissociative Amnesia. They may be brought to public attention in an attempt to discover who they are and from where they have come.

Dissociative Fugue can be differentiated from Dissociative Amnesia in that individuals with Dissociative Amnesia may engage in confused wandering during an amnesia episode. In Dissociative Fugue, there is *purposeful* travel away from the individual's home or customary place of daily activities, and usually the individual is preoccupied with a single idea accompanied by a wish to run away from some stressor. Patients with DID may have symptoms of dissociative fugue, usually recurring throughout their lives. Some complex-partial seizures patients wander or exhibit semipurposeful behavior during seizures or postictally, for which there is amnesia. In an epileptic fugue, however, individuals often exhibit abnormal behavior, including confusion, perseveration, and abnormal or stereotypic movements. A variety of general medical conditions, toxic and substance-related disorders, delirium, dementia, and organic amnestic syndromes may give rise to random wandering. In most cases, however, the somatic, toxic, neurological, or substance-related etiology can be identified by history or by physical and laboratory findings.

Treatment

An eclectic, psychodynamically informed psychotherapy focused on helping the patient recover memory for identity and recent experience is the recommended treatment for Dissociative Fugue. Adjunctive techniques such as hypnotherapy and pharmacologically facilitated interviews to assist with memory recovery are frequently necessary. Therapy should be carefully paced to avoid overwhelming the individual with traumatic material. Clinical stabilization, safety, and a therapeutic alliance using supportive and educative interventions constitute the initial phase. Once stabilization is achieved, subsequent therapy is focused on helping the patient regain memory for identity, life circumstances, and personal history. During this period, extreme emotions and/or severe psychological conflict related to trauma may emerge. A supportive and nonjudgmental stance, especially if the fugue has been precipitated by intense guilt or shame over an indiscretion, is an important therapeutic element. Simultaneously, it is important for the therapist to balance this stance with helping the patient take realistic responsibility for misbehavior that may have occurred.

Dissociative Disorder Not Otherwise Specified

All of the conditions characterized by a primary dissociative response that do not meet diagnostic criteria for one of the *DSM-IV-TR* dissociative disorders are covered under the catch-all diagnosis of DDNOS. Dissociative Disorder Not Otherwise Specified is a heterogeneous collection of dissociative reactions, some of which are common expressions of distress in other cultures but relatively rare in Western societies. Included in DDNOS are the many cultural variants of dissociative trance. Anthropologists have identified forms of dissociation in every culture that they have examined. In some instances, this takes the form of specific trance-state disorders; in others, it is manifest in religious rites and rituals; and in still others, in the form of traditional healing practices. All of these forms of dissociation are common in many non-Western societies. Increasingly, measures such as the DES and SCID-D are being adapted for these cultures and used to investigate these conditions.

The *DSM* also includes under DDNOS those dissociative reactions elicited by coercive persuasive practices such as torture, brainwashing, thought reform, mind control, and indoctrination intended to induce an individual to relinquish basic political, social, or religious beliefs in exchange for antithetical ideas and beliefs. Finally, Ganser's syndrome, a rare and poorly understood condition, characterized by the giving of approximate answers is also included in this category.

Dissociative Trance Disorder

Dissociative Trance Disorder is manifest by a temporary, marked alteration in the state of consciousness or by loss of the customary sense of personal identity without the replacement by an alternative sense of identity. There is often a narrowing of awareness of the immediate surroundings or a selective focus on stimuli within the environment and/or the manifestation of stereotypic behaviors or movements that the individual experiences as beyond his or her control. A variant of this, Possession Trance, involves single or episodic alternations in the state of consciousness characterized by the exchange of the person's customary identity with a new identity, usually attributed to a spirit, divine power, deity, or another person.

The best described example of the dissociative trance-state disorder form of DDNOS is Ataque de nervios (Lewis-Fernandez et al., 2002; Schechter et al., 2000). Ataque de nervios is characterized by somatic symptoms such as fainting, numbness and tingling, fading of vision, seizure-like convulsive movements, palpitations, and sensations of heat rising through the body. Individuals may moan, cry out, curse uncontrollably, attempt to harm themselves or others, or fall down and lie with death-like stillness. During an episode of Ataque de nervios, there is a narrowing of consciousness and lack of awareness of the larger environment. Following an episode, the individual typically has partial or full amnesia for the events and his or her actions. Attacks may occur only once, be episodic, or occasionally become chronically recurring with significant functional impairment. DES scores were correlated with frequency of episodes in one study (Lewis-Fernandez et al., 2002).

Family, marital, or other interpersonal conflicts or losses are the most common precipitants of Ataque de nervios. Alcohol, physical or sexual violence, financial loss, or stress and fear may also trigger an attack. Histories of physical and sexual abuse are commonly reported but are not strongly correlated with severity or frequency of episodes. A sense of being overwhelmed, hopeless, and helpless often evokes an episode. This is followed by an abrupt narrowing of consciousness and the appearance of more florid symptoms. Attacks are usually a few hours in duration but can last from minutes to days.

Brainwashing, Mind Control, Thought Reform

The concept of brainwashing, mind control, or thought reform emerged from the Korean conflict after some American prisoners of war made anti-American statements. A journalist, Edward Hunter (later identified as a CIA agent), proposed that the Chinese Communists had discovered techniques to modify mental attitudes and beliefs, a process he called brainwashing. Following the Armistice, a team of psychiatrists and psychologists interviewed the returning prisoners and concluded that they had not been subjected to a systematic thought reform program. Rather, the statements were the result of rewarding severely deprived prisoners with food and warm clothing, but their basic attitudes had not, in fact, been altered. However, the subsequent release of another group of prisoners (missionaries, businessmen, doctors, and students) caught in China at the beginning of the war did seem to suggest that some form of thought reform had occurred with these individuals, several of whom continued to falsely insist that they were spies.

In the late 1960s and 1970s, allegations of brainwashing or mind control resurfaced in the context of counterculture religious movements. Dr. Louis (Jolly) West (West & Singer, 1980), who consulted on the famous case of Patty Hearst, the heiress who was kidnapped, tortured, sexually abused, and held in prolonged solitary confinement, was largely responsible for the reintroduction of this concept. After prolonged isolation and mistreatment, Hearst developed another identity, the revolutionary Tania, who aided her captors in criminal acts, including bank robbery and murder. Margaret T. Singer (West & Singer, 1980), a psychologist associated with West, subsequently widely publicized her ideas about "conditioning techniques" that she believed were used by religious cults to render their members incapable of complex rational thought and unable to make decisions. In a series of lawsuits by ex-cult members, she testified that these techniques were capable of overpowering a person's free will and that the group's control over a member could be total. The notion that brainwashing was a common practice in religious cults was popularized by media coverage of these sensational trials.

A group of academics, primarily psychologists and sociologists, subsequently challenged Singer, pointing out that individuals who joined cults often came from dysfunctional families. Marc Galanter (Galanter, 1982), a psychiatrist involved in some of these cases, reframed the religious cult mind control debate by advocating the more neutral term "charismatic religious sects." He pointed out that an individual's behavior in such a social group may reflect psychological adaptation rather than psychopathology. The manner of leaving the group, voluntarily or by being kidnapped and involuntarily deprogrammed, was a significant predictor of an individual's report of whether he or she had been brainwashed, with the latter the most likely to express this belief. In the context of a particularly sensational case (Molko vs. Holy Spirit Association), the American Psycho-

logical Association and the American Sociological Association submitted amicus briefs refuting the concept of brainwashing as lacking scientific validity. This served to nullify its legal status as a legal defense. Although the academic community has largely avoided the subject, the notion of brainwashing continues to fascinate the public and to be invoked by a few psychotherapists and others as evidence of occult or government conspiracies.

Ganser's Syndrome

Ganser's syndrome is a poorly understood condition, reclassified from a factitious disorder to a dissociative disorder in the *DSM-III,* characterized by the giving of approximate answers (paralogia) together with a clouding of consciousness and frequently accompanied by psychogenic somatic or conversion symptoms (Andersen, Sestoft, & Lillebaek, 2001). The symptom of "passing over" (*vorbeigehen*) the correct answer for a related but incorrect one is the hallmark of Ganser's syndrome. The approximate answers often just miss the mark but bear an obvious relation to the question, indicating that it has been understood. For example, when asked how old she was, a 25-year-old woman answered, "I'm not 5." Another patient, when asked how many legs a horse had, replied, "Three." If asked to do simple calculations (e.g., $2 \times 2 = 5$) or for general information (capital of the United States is New York) or to identify simple objects (a pencil is a key) or to name colors (green is gray), these individuals give erroneous but comprehensible answers.

There is also a clouding of consciousness, usually manifest by disorientation, amnesias, loss of personal information, and some impairment of reality testing. Visual and auditory hallucinations occur in roughly half of the cases. Many of the case reports include histories of head injuries, dementia, or organic brain insults. Neurological examination may reveal what Ganser (Ganser, 1898) called "hysterical stigmata," for example, a nonneurologic analgesia or shifting hyperalgesia. Many authorities make a distinction between Ganser's symptoms of approximate answers, which may occur in a number of psychiatric and neurological conditions, and Ganser's syndrome, which must be accompanied by other dissociative symptoms such as amnesias, conversion symptoms, or trance-like behaviors.

Dissociative Identity Disorder

Diagnosis

Dissociative Identity Disorder, formerly Multiple Personality Disorder, is the best researched of all the dissociative disorders. In many respects, it is the paradigmatic dissociative disorder in that the symptoms of all the other dissociative disorders are common, including amnesias, fugues, depersonalization, derealization, and possession-like experiences.

The *DSM-IV-TR* defines DID as characterized by "the presence of two or more distinct identities or personality states" that "recurrently take control of the person's behavior," accompanied by an "inability to recall important personal information that is too extensive to be explained by ordinary forgetfulness" (American Psychiatric Association, 2000, p. 529). These identities or personality states—sometimes called "alters," "self states," "alter identities," or "parts"—differ from one another in that each presents as having "its own relatively enduring pattern of perceiving, relating to, and thinking about the environment and self."

History and Epidemiology

During the nineteenth century there was a lively academic interest in dual and multiple personality cases, which stimulated a larger public awareness that was shaped in large part by often inaccurate artistic and general media representations. Multiple personality became a common plot device in pulp thrillers as well as part of the larger public interest in mysticism, mediumship, and the occult that flourished at the end of the century. Although some nineteenth-century case reports include paranormal features, most are fairly straightforward clinical accounts, which typically resemble today's cases.

By the 2nd decade of the twentieth century, the study of DID had begun to wane. Authorities suggest a variety of factors contributing to this loss of interest, including the rising dominance of Freudian paradigms of hysteria, the disrepute into which hypnosis fell at this time, the rise of Bleuler's then newly coined diagnosis of Schizophrenia, which specifically included dissociative patients, and a loss of interest in the works of Janet, Prince, and others who had been so crucial in the development of models of dissociation. Morton Prince observed that their ideas were being drowned by the rising tide of psychoanalysis, which he regarded as antithetical to the concept of dissociation (cited in Hale, 1975).

Although scattered multiple personality cases continued to be reported in reputable journals in the 1930s to 1960s, most notably the famous "The Three Faces of Eve," (Thigpen & Cleckley, 1957) it was not until the 1970s that systematic research was again undertaken. The modern era begins with the work of Arnold Ludwig and colleagues (Larmore, Ludwig, & Cain, 1977; Ludwig, 1983; Ludwig, Brandsma, Wilbur, Bendfeldt, & Jameson, 1972) at the University of Kentucky during the 1970s. These studies in-cluded systematic comparisons of psychophysiological and neurocognitive measures across the alter personality states of individuals with Multiple Personality Disorder. Beginning in the 1980s, researchers in North America, Europe, Turkey, Japan, and elsewhere began systematic research studies on the phenomenology, epidemiology, psychobiology, and treatment of DID in adults, children, and adolescents. Despite the thousands of cases described in the world's literature and the hundreds of scientific papers on multiple personality and dissociation, controversy continues over the validity of the disorder, with a vocal minority of clinicians subscribing to an iatrogenic explanation for multiple personality.

The best epidemiological data available for multiple personality come from the Winnipeg stratified sample ($n = 1,055$) study by Ross, Joshi, and Currie (1989). This yielded a prevalence rate of 3.1%, although a more conservative reanalysis of these data suggests a prevalence of about 1.3% for DID. An independent analysis of the DES data collected on the same sample yielded a prevalence rate of 3.3% for "pathological dissociation," a construct including DES items for amnesia, depersonalization, derealization, identity confusion and alteration, and inner voices (pseudohallucinations), a symptom profile typical of clinical DID patients (Waller & Ross, 1997). A second epidemiological study of a community sample ($N = 1,007$) in Memphis, Tennessee, found that although dissociative symptoms were common, only 2% scored in the Taxon level on the DES-II (Seedat, Stein, & Forde, 2003). Higher dissociation levels were associated with male gender, minority status, and harmful alcohol consumption, all variables associated with higher incidence of risk for dissociative disorders and for traumatic experiences.

The prevalence rate of DID in general psychiatric patient samples has been investigated by several studies using the SCID-D or DDIS structured diagnostic interviews (Putnam, 1997). Across these studies, including samples from the United States, Canada, Turkey, and several western European countries, an average of 5% to 15% of adult psychiatric inpatients meet *DSM* criteria for DID. Higher rates were found in substance abuse treatment populations and inpatient adolescents.

Gender differences in the frequency of DID have long been noted. Clinical studies generally include 5 : 1 to 9 : 1 female to male ratios. Interestingly, research with measures such as the DES finds no evidence of gender differences in the propensity or capacity to dissociate. Developmental studies indicate that the ratio of female to male DID cases steadily increases from 1 : 1 in early childhood to about 8 : 1 by late adolescence (Putnam, Hornstein, & Peterson, 1996).

A number of reasons have been proposed for the increased numbers of female DID patients, including gender-related differences in the types, age of onset, and duration of maltreatment experienced by males and females; differences in clinical presentations such that male cases are more likely to be missed; and the possibility that more male DID cases end up in the criminal justice and/or alcohol and drug treatment systems rather than the mental health system.

Dissociative Identity Disorder is strongly linked to experiences of severe, early childhood trauma, usually maltreatment. All studies, in both Western and non-Western cultures, that have systematically examined this link have documented this relationship. Across a wide variety of studies, the reported rates of severe childhood trauma for both child and adult DID patients range from 85% to 97% of cases. The most frequently reported sources of childhood trauma in clinical research studies are physical and sexual abuse, usually in combination. Other kinds of trauma have also been reported, including painful medical and surgical procedures and wartime trauma. Critics have raised questions about the validity of DID patients' self-reports of childhood trauma. Recent studies, including large samples of maltreated children with dissociative disorders and intensively validated case studies, have provided rigorous independent corroboration of the patients' reports of maltreatment (Hornstein & Putnam, 1992; Lewis, Yeager, Swica, Pincus, & Lewis, 1997). These studies continue to strongly support a developmental link between childhood trauma and DID.

Evaluation of Memory and Amnesia Symptoms

Dissociative disturbances of memory are manifest in several basic ways and are frequently observable in clinical settings. Clinicians should routinely inquire about experiences of "losing time," blackout spells, and major gaps in the continuity of recall for personal information. These experiences are rarely spontaneously reported by patients, who often consider them to be evidence of "craziness." Thus, active inquiry by the interviewer is necessary to uncover amnesia. The clinician should ask for specific examples when the patient acknowledges a symptom such as time loss. Sometimes, patients describe "coming to" or "waking up" in the middle of an activity with little or no recall of how they came to be there. At other times, patients find evidence of having done or acquired things for which they have no memory. Family members and friends may tell them about significant things that they have said or done for which they have no recall. They may have traveled to some unexplained place (a fugue episode) or may not be able to remember what they did for days or even weeks.

Dissociative time loss experiences are too extensive to be explained by normal forgetting. Typically, they have clearly demarcated beginnings and endings. It is important to establish that such time loss experiences are not associated with drug or alcohol use. Unfortunately, the high comorbid rates of drug and alcohol abuse in dissociative patients complicates this determination.

Perplexing fluctuations in skills, habits, or well-learned abilities such as fluency in a foreign language or athletic abilities are common in patients with severe dissociative memory disturbances. Patients report the experience of "all of a sudden drawing a complete blank" for skills or knowledge, whereas at other times the skills are present and the information is easily and reliably recalled. This "perplexing forgetfulness" is thought to relate to the state-dependent disturbances of implicit memory functions noted in experiments with dissociative patients (Bremner, Krystal, Southwick, & Charney, 1995; DePrince & Freyd, 1999, 2001; Dorahy, 2001; Eich, Macaulay, Loewenstein, & Dihle, 1997).

Significant gaps in autobiographical memory, particularly for childhood events, are often reported for dissociative patients. The historical gaps are usually sharply defined and do not fit the normal, age-related decrease in memory for events of younger ages. In dissociative patients, recall of autobiographical memories may have a depersonalized quality such that recalled events are likened to recalling a dream or as if they had happened to someone else.

Dissociative Process Symptoms

Dissociative process symptoms include depersonalization and derealization, dissociative hallucinations, passive influence/interference experiences, and dissociative cognition. Some authorities also include dissociative alterations in identity. Depersonalization and derealization are commonly reported by DID patients, as well as out-of-body experiences. Patients frequently describe feeling "spaced out" or cut off from themselves and others. There is a distant or unreal, hazy or foggy quality to the world at large. Patients may liken it to being in a dream. Out-of-body experiences commonly take the form of watching oneself from a great distance. The observer's point of view may be experienced as either internal or external to the patient. That is, some patients report a sense of an internal distance, as if watching from "somewhere way back in my head." Experiences of watching oneself do something—often dangerous—but being unable to stop one's actions are also common.

Dissociative auditory hallucinations typically take the form of voices heard in one's head (sometimes called pseudohallucinations), as opposed to voices coming from the environment. Dissociative hallucinations typically have distinctive qualities of age, gender, and affect that mark them as individual. The voices may comment negatively about the patient, argue with each other, or command the patient to perform certain acts. They also have secondary process characteristics in that they may, at times, discuss neutral topics with the patient, provide useful information, or support and comfort during stressful experiences. Patients usually recognize the voices as hallucinations, but they may be reluctant to disclose their existence for fear of being considered psychotic. Unless they are stressed, many patients report some capacity to ignore or disregard hallucinations. Over the course of treatment, specific alter personality states often come to be identified with specific hallucinated voices. Visual hallucinations typically take the form of graphic images, usually having traumatic or frightening content. Tactile, somatic, and olfactory "hallucination-like" experiences can occur in DID patients, leading to misdiagnosis of other neurological disorders (Devinsky, Putnam, Grafman, Bromfield, & Theodore, 1989).

Cognitive Impairments

The recognition that dissociative patients frequently manifest subtle, but often clinically significant, cognitive impairments emerges from clinical research with psychological and cognitive test batteries. Research using projective testing finds distinctive cognitive process markers, including evidence of confusing and contradictory responses to the same stimulus. Distinctive responses to standardized projective testing can often be helpful in distinguishing dissociative patients from other diagnostic groups, such as patients with affective disorders, nondissociative forms of PTSD, personality disorders, psychotic disorders, and factitious disorders (Armstrong, 1996; Armstrong & Loewenstein, 1990; E. B. Carlson & Armstrong, 1994).

Silberg (1996b) has described specialized approaches to psychological and cognitive testing in children and adolescents. A number of behavioral features during testing were observed significantly more often in dissociative children compared with other children admitted to a psychiatric unit. These included forgetting, staring, unusual motor behaviors, dramatic fluctuations, fearful and angry reactions and physical complaints during the testing, and expressions of internal conflict. Test responses included increased images of multiplicity, malevolent religiosity, depersonalized imagery, extreme dichotomization, images of mutilation and torture, and

magical transformation. A discriminant analysis correctly classified 93% of the sample.

Dissociative Alterations in Identity

Odd first-person plural or third-person singular/plural self-references are typical early clinical manifestations of dissociative alterations in identity. Patients may refer to themselves by their own first name or make depersonalized self-references such as "the body" when referring to themselves. When describing traumatic events, they may take considerable referential distance, for example, "The father hurt the body, so she was upset. We tried to protect her, but it didn't work." Patients often report a profound sense of concretized internal division or personified internal conflicts between different "parts" of themselves. In many cases, these parts have proper names or are designated by a strong affect, behavior, or function, for example, "the angry one" or "the wife." Patients may suddenly change the way they refer to others in relation to themselves, for example, "the son" replaces "my son" at some point in the discussion.

"Switching behaviors" occur when DID patients change alter personality states. They may manifest during evaluation or therapy sessions. Intrainterview amnesias, in which the patient does not seem to recall or is very confused about the process and content of that session, are a common manifestation. Switching may be evidenced by abrupt shifts in the train of thought or sudden inexplicable changes in affect or in rapport. Physical signs of switching may be observed in conjunction with shifts in affect. These include pronounced upward eye rolls or bursts of rapid blinking and eyelid fluttering. There are often alterations in the patient's tone of voice and manner of speaking, posture, and demeanor. When possible indications of dissociation are noted, the clinician should ask nondirective, open-ended questions that seek to clarify what the patient is experiencing and recalling about what just happened. The clinician should try to establish whether the patient can give a coherent and continuous description of their immediately preceding interactions. Significant gaps or confusion should be identified and delineated as much as possible. This is a good moment to inquire whether the patient has experienced similar discontinuities in other contexts. If a patient acknowledges prior experiences, it is important to ask for specific examples, both to make certain that these experiences are sufficiently extensive and complex enough to qualify as dissociative and to get a sense of when such experiences are likely to occur.

The alter personalities of DID patients are best conceptualized as discrete behavioral states, each organized around a prevailing affect, a sense of self (often including a distinct body image), a set of state-dependent autobiographical memories, and a limited behavioral repertoire. Authorities have long cautioned that alter personalities should not be regarded as "separate people" (Putnam, 1997). Rather, the alter personalities should be conceptualized as relatively stable and enduring patterns of behavior that are largely unintegrated with each other and often in direct conflict. A common, and serious, clinical mistake made by novice therapists is to conceptualize and treat specific alter personalities as if they are distinct individuals with interests that are independent of the person as a whole. The basic therapeutic stance is that all of the alter personalities belong to a greater whole and share a basic set of interests.

This set of alter personality states, frequently referred to as the "personality system," constitutes the larger personality of the individual. Much of the therapeutic focus is directed toward this larger personality system and thus toward the individual as a whole. The psychological and physiological differences observed among the alter personality states of individuals with DID is a source of continuing fascination. Popular accounts in the media overemphasize the differences among alters. Laboratory studies do support the existence of significant differences; however, much general information and many functions and abilities are shared in common across alter personality states. These shared aspects of function, knowledge, and behavior indicate the fundamental unity of the mental processes of the dissociative individual. This common ground provides a foundation for therapeutic efforts focused on the development of a consciously integrated sense of self in the DID patient.

As a group, DID patients show considerable variability in the complexity and therapeutic tractability of their alter personality systems. For more than a century, clinicians have sought to classify DID patients by differences in the organization and dynamics of alter personality systems. However, the validity of these classifications remains to be proven. Alter personality types that are commonly reported include child alter personalities, internalized persecutory alters who inflict pain and may attempt to kill the individual, and depleted and depressed "host" personality states who function as the primary identity with respect to the world at large. Alter personality states often personify painful psychological issues and frequently occur as polarized pairs representing antithetical positions. Alter personality states representing neutral and conflict-free processes also occur. In many DID patients, almost every aspect of mental life is structured and personified in this form.

Dissociative Identity Disorder is conceptualized as a trauma-based disorder; therefore, it is not surprising that the majority of these patients also meet diagnostic criteria for PTSD either by clinical criteria or by using standardized measures and diagnostic inventories. Depending on the study, 70% to 100% of DID patients have been shown to meet diagnostic criteria for PTSD by *DSM-III-R/IV/IV-TR* criteria. In addition, DID patients commonly exhibit multiple types of psychophysiological, somatoform, and conversion symptoms. For example, across studies, 40% to 60% of DID patients also met diagnostic criteria for Somatization Disorder, and many others will meet diagnostic criteria for Somatoform Pain Disorder and/or Conversion Disorder (Ellason, Ross, & Fuchs, 1996; Sar, Akyuz, Kundakci, Kiziltan, & Dogan, 2004).

Treatment

Course and Prognosis. The natural history of untreated DID is largely unknown. A small number of single case studies of partially treated patients followed up many years later suggests that the disorder becomes less active over time, with a decrease in dramatic dissociative symptoms and diminishing conflicts among the alter personality states. The cases are too few, however, to risk generalization. A few small sample studies of DID cases diagnosed in middle age and in geriatric populations indicate that major dissociative symptoms can persist and/or appear in older patients. Clinical experience suggests that a life course of relapse and remission depending on life circumstances is likely in many untreated or partially treated cases. Patients may also be successful in masking or suppressing symptoms for periods of time, even in the face of considerable stress. This may be mistaken for spontaneous remission of the disorder. There is a great need for better longitudinal characterization of all of the dissociative disorders, but most especially the outcomes for treated and untreated DID.

Shared clinical experience with DID cases suggests to many that there are several distinct subgroups of DID patients. Dissociative Identity Disorder patients range from those who function at quite high levels for long periods of time to those who are severely impaired and whose dysfunctional life trajectories began early in childhood. Both clinical presentation and general prognosis vary to some extent across the life span. Children with diagnosable DID show many dissociative symptoms and behaviors but typically have fewer and less crystallized alter personality states. The alter personalities seen in children are typically less invested in their individuality. Thus, if diagnosed early, children often have an excellent prognosis. Indeed, many children appear to have essentially spontaneous resolution of their DID when they are removed from abusive and neglectful environments. However, in adolescence, alter personalities typically become more behaviorally and affectively distinct and more aggressively invested in their autonomy. Additional alter personalities, typically thematically associated with life stresses, such as academic, athletic, social, or sexual challenges, may appear; then the intrapersonality system dynamics become more complicated and polarized. Adolescents, as a group, have a poorer short-term prognosis than children or adults. This is, in part, because they are often not invested in their treatment and do not see their dissociative symptoms as a problem. Adolescents, particularly if not deeply engaged in school or work, do not experience the same kinds of negative consequences for the discontinuities in their behavior that adults seeking to keep jobs and raise families encounter. Better outcome with DID adolescents has been reported when the patient's family was successfully engaged in treatment. Young adults usually come to clinical attention in the midst of a crisis and may have significant comorbid affective, somatic, posttraumatic, and substance abuse issues in addition to their core dissociative pathology.

Current approaches to the treatment of DID have evolved considerably over the past 2 decades. A major factor has been the reconceptualization of DID as a complex developmental trauma disorder. In addition, the broad spectrum of functioning seen in DID patients has also been better appreciated. A phasic or stages-of-treatment model, similar to the current standard psychotherapeutic approach for PTSD, is now the standard approach to DID. The phases or stages of treatment include (1) symptom stabilization, (2) a period of focused in-depth attention to traumatic material (which is considered optional in some cases), and (3) a phase of "integration" or "reintegration" in which the DID patient practices new cognitive and emotional regulatory skills in place of dissociative defenses. Obviously, these stages are partly heuristic, and aspects of each may be part of the others.

Outcome Studies. Case reports of successful treatments for DID date back over a century. Systematic outcome studies, however, have only appeared within the past 2 decades. These studies remain largely descriptive, with many methodological confounds. The first such study followed up 20 DID patients an average of 3 years after intake following treatment (Coons, 1986). Many of these patients were in treatment with therapists new to DID. Nonetheless, two-thirds of the clinicians treating these patients reported moderate to great improvement. Severe retraumatization at some point during the course of treatment was associated with poorer outcomes. A chart review study of 101 Dutch Dissociative Disorder outpatients found that clinical improvement was related to the intensity of the treatment, with more comprehensive therapies having better outcomes (Boon & Draijer, 1993). Using the DES to track treatment progress of 21 DID inpatients, Ross (1989; Ross, Joshi, et al., 1989) found a significant drop in overall scores over a 4-week hospitalization. To date, the largest and best conducted treatment outcome study reevaluated 54 DID inpatients 2 years after discharge to outpatient treatment (Ellason & Ross, 1997). Overall, there were significant decreases in psychopathology, including the number of Axis I and Axis II disorders. The study also found decreased DES scores, decreased depression on the Beck and Hamilton scales, and decreased dissociative symptoms on all of the subscales of the DDIS. The most improved were patients who were reported to be "integrated" according to specific criteria.

The cost-effectiveness of DID treatment has been the subject of two studies (Loewenstein, 1994; Ross & Dua, 1993). Both found that outcome depends on clinical profile. The most responsive group showed significant remission of symptoms within 3 to 5 years after beginning appropriate treatment. A second DID subgroup, with more alter personalities and more Axis II features, had good outcomes but required more hospitalizations in addition to outpatient treatment. The third group, characterized by the longest period of treatment before DID diagnosis, largest number of alters, and most personality disorder problems, had a more lengthy, more expensive, and more problematic course (Ellason & Ross, 1997). When compared with prior treatment costs for these patients, however, treatment specifically targeting DID symptoms showed significant reductions in overall cost after the 1st year. A secondary finding is that more intensive treatment for DID patients has not only reduced overall psychiatric costs, but also decreased medical costs associated with somatoform symptoms. It should be noted that these are preliminary studies with significant limitations, including the diverse and nonstandardized nature of the therapy and lack of comparison groups. Nonetheless, they indicate that many DID patients do improve when treatment is focused on their dissociative symptoms. In the long run, overall treatment costs may be saved by adopting the phasic trauma treatment model for these patients. More and better treatment outcome research for DID is desperately needed, but so far has not attracted the necessary funding.

PSYCHOLOGICAL TRAUMA AND DISSOCIATION: SCIENTIFIC APPROACHES

Janet is credited by many as being the first to recognize the relationship between dissociation and trauma (van der Hart & Friedman, 1989). His insight remained largely unappreciated until almost a century later. In the past 2 decades, research has elucidated multiple lines of evidence linking dissociative disorders with antecedent trauma. In aggregate, these separate lines of evidence constitute a strong case for significant trauma as a necessary antecedent to the development of pathological dissociation.

Clinical Cases

The basic set of these lines of evidence involves quantification of Janet's early clinical observations. For each of the *DSM* dissociative disorders, multiple independent case series exist, including non-Western samples, documenting unusually high rates of trauma in Dissociative Disorder patients (although this linkage is weaker for Depersonalization Disorder). Critics often point out that these studies are retrospective, and thus the accuracy of the reports of trauma cannot be established. However, several case series exist in which the majority of subjects had one or more traumas verified (Coons, 1994; Putnam, Hornstein, et al., 1996). Lewis et al. (1997), for example, were able to independently verify childhood trauma in 12 convicted murderers with DID.

Peer-reviewed studies, now numbering in the hundreds, comparing traumatized and nontraumatized groups have found significantly higher levels of dissociation, as measured by well-validated instruments such as the DES, in the traumatized groups for a variety of types of trauma (van Ijzendoorn & Schuengel, 1996). This finding for many different forms of trauma (e.g., combat, rape, natural and man-made disasters, and child abuse) has been documented for many and varied cultures, indicating the universality of the association between trauma and dissociation. Measures of trauma severity, for example, rape and combat severity scales, are correlated about equally with PTSD and dissociation measures ($r \sim .25$ to $.40$), indicating a weak to moderate dose effect-like relationship. The lack of a stronger correlational relationship between trauma and PTSD and dissociation probably reflects the difficulties in quantifying the subjective elements of traumatic experiences. Although these findings clearly link dissociation with antecedent trauma, they are not sufficient to demonstrate that the trauma actually causes the dissociation.

Thus, numerous lines of independent evidence point toward a causal relationship between trauma and dissociation. Thus far, for all cultures in which it has been investigated, a significant relationship has been found between dissociation and many forms of trauma. In the immediate aftermath of a trauma, significant levels of dissociation appear to predispose an individual to develop PTSD and trauma-related psychopathology, although additional factors involving the psychological appraisal of past trauma appear to be involved. Thus, dissociation may serve as a major mediating process between traumatic experiences and subsequent psychopathology. As a mediating factor, dissociation could serve as an important target for prevention and early intervention efforts. In part, stress-resistant individuals are characterized by a lack of dissociative responses to significant stressors.

Military Stress Studies

Charles A. Morgan and colleagues (2001) have conducted a remarkable series of studies on military special operations units under extremely stressful conditions. These studies are as close as we can ethically come to an experimental model of trauma-induced dissociation (Morgan et al., 2001). Morgan examined the neurobiological and psychological effects of intense stress uniformly applied to drug-free, healthy, nonclinical subjects in units undergoing forms of simulated combat, such as survival school. Stressors included semistarvation, exhaustion, sleep deprivation, lack of control over hygiene and bodily functions, and lack of control over movement, social contact, and communication. In these soldiers, the neuroendocrine stress effects equaled or exceeded those measured in other individuals in life-threatening experiences. There were significant overall and scale item differences between pre- and posttest scores on the CADSS. The greatest effects were for depersonalization items such as looking at the world through a fog, feeling time slow down, and spacing out. Forty-one percent of the variance in health complaints following the stress experience was accounted for by dissociation scores.

The results of Morgan's military studies are congruent with clinical reports of the high frequency of dissociation, especially depersonalization symptoms, in normal individuals exposed to life-threatening stress. The ubiquity of dissociative experiences during extreme stress suggests that other factors, perhaps past traumatic experiences, are involved in the peritraumatic dissociation-PTSD linkage discussed earlier. In the military studies, both pre- and poststress dissociative symptoms were significantly correlated with perceived life threat from a prior trauma. Intense subjective appraisal of life threat from past trauma was associated with the highest dissociation scores. Interestingly, Special Forces soldiers, a highly traumatized subgroup, had low life-threat appraisals of their past trauma and the lowest pre- to poststress change in dissociation scores. These individuals, who often had horrendous histories of early trauma, nonetheless discounted its severity and impact. The existence of this "stress hardy" group underscores the importance of psychological adaptation to past trauma on responses to current trauma. A significant relationship ($r = .67$) was found between the pre-post change dissociation scores and somatic symptoms. This is compatible with clinical studies reporting significant correlations between somatization and dissociation.

Mediation of Trauma Outcomes

A number of studies now indicate that dissociation serves as a mediator of the relationship between antecedent trauma and subsequent psychopathology, including PTSD, aggression, and other externalizing symptoms (Kisiel & Lyons, 2001; Offen, Thomas, & Waller, 2003; Somer, 2002). Thus, if the level of dissociation is statistically controlled, the strength of the relationship between antecedent trauma and current psychopathology is significantly decreased or disappears. High levels of dissociation may also alter the psychophysiological responses of traumatized individuals to traumatic reminders. Dividing traumatized subjects into high and low dissociative subgroups based on standard scales reveals that high dissociators show lower psychophysiological arousal when confronted with stimuli that are reminiscent of their traumatic experiences (e.g., Griffin, Resick, & Mechanic, 1997). Nonetheless, the high dissociative subjects often report significantly more psychological distress than the low dissociative group, who typically show more classic patterns of hyperarousal for physiological indices such as heart rate and skin conductance. These findings should be considered preliminary and require further replication. These data do indicate that increased dissociation associated with trauma may serve as an important mediating process involved in the transformation of traumatic experiences into subsequent psychopathology.

Sophisticated statistical methods, physiological measures, and brain imaging technologies are now uncovering new lines of evidence indicating that increased dissociation is instrumental in shaping outcomes related to traumatic experience and psychophysiologic responses to future stress and trauma. Peritraumatic dissociation, sometimes measured proximal to the trauma and sometimes retrospectively about the trauma, has been found to predict the subsequent development of PTSD in many, but not all, studies (Ozer et al., 2003). Predictive power is both a form of validity and clinically important for identifying individuals at risk for developing PTSD following an acute trauma.

Dissociation in the Laboratory

The experiments of Morton Prince (Prince & Peterson, 1908) using a crude polygraph to measure galvanic skin resistance (GSR) across the alter personality states of a DID patient—a physiological measure that remains of interest today—initiated the scientific study of DID in 1908. Prince recorded differential GSR reactivity responses to words that were emotionally charged for one alter personality but not for another. Several dozen psychophysiological and cognitive performance studies were added to the literature over the next century (Alvarado, 1989). Most of these reported data indicating that DID alter personality states differ in responses to common stimuli. However, the small sample sizes—typically only a single case—and the lack of control subjects limit their credibility. The few better-controlled studies with larger samples generally support the earlier findings of differences across alter personality states. The heterogeneity of research methods and measures together with the often idiosyncratic differential responses elicited in DID subjects have limited opportunities for replication across studies. However, investigation of differential neurobiological responses and differences in cognitive performance across alter personality states of DID patients remain an important source of information about the nature of dissociation.

A new avenue of experimental investigation was opened up with the advent of reliable and valid measures of dissociation. The correlation of scale scores with a variety of physiological, neuroendocrine, cognitive, and brain imaging data facilitates examination of the biological underpinnings of dissociation and the impact of dissociation on physical and mental functioning. The division of subjects into high and low dissociative subgroups has led to the identification of significant differences in physiological and cognitive measures.

Studies with the CADSS document dissociative-like experiences pharmacologically induced in normal controls and in clinical populations such as PTSD patients (Bremner et al., 1998). These studies primarily focus on traumatized individuals who suffer from PTSD or trauma-associated psychopathology but who do not have a dissociative disorder. Laboratory studies using pulsed photo and audio stimulation have induced dissociative symptoms in normal individuals (Leonard, Telch, & Harrington, 1999). Subjects scoring higher on pretest dissociation measures show greater effects, although these are well below clinical thresholds. In aggregate, the large numbers of studies including measures of dissociation in their assessment have taught us much of what we have learned in the past decade.

Brain Imaging Studies of Dissociation

Case reports continue to describe EEG differences across DID alter personality states, but investigators are increasingly turning to the newer brain imaging technologies in their efforts to document dissociation. A functional magnetic resonance imaging (fMRI) study of 12 switches among three alter personality states in a single patient found changes in brain activity bilaterally in the hippocampus and in the right parahippocampal and medial temporal regions (Tsai, Condie, Wu, & Chang, 1999). Saxe, Vasile, Hill, Bloomingdale, and van der Kolk (1992) used single positron emission tomography (PET) to scan four alter personality states. The left temporal lobe was the brain region that showed the greatest variation across personality states. Using single PET imaging, Sar, Unal, Kiziltan, Kundakci, and Ozturk (2001) compared 15 DID patients with 8 controls. They reported that the DID patients showed significant hypoactivity bilaterally in the orbitofrontal region and increased left lateral temporal activity. In a PET study of 11 DID subjects who listened to traumatic and neutral scripts in a "traumatic" and "neutral" personality, Reinders et al. (2003) found correlates to two distinct activation states marked by different regional cerebral blood flow patterns. Thus, to date, multiple imaging studies of DID patients have found significant differences across alter personality states, although no signature differences have been identified.

Two studies have focused on the functional imaging of depersonalization. Mathew et al. (1999) infused THC, an active component in marijuana, into 59 normal subjects, who showed significantly increased overall cerebral blood flow with the largest changes in the right hemisphere. Increases in depersonalization were most significantly correlated with increased blood flow in the frontal lobes and anterior cingulated cortex. Using PET imaging with Depersonalization Disorder patients and controls, Simeon and colleagues (2000) found that the patients had lower activity in the right superior and middle temporal gyri and higher activity in the parietal and left occipital cortex. It is difficult to compare these two studies, as one uses healthy controls receiving a psychoactive drug producing mild to moderate feelings of depersonalization and the other uses chronic Depersonalization Disorder patients. They do,

however, suggest that feelings of depersonalization may be detectable with functional brain imaging methods.

In a series of well-conducted, well-controlled studies, Ruth Lanius and colleagues (Lanius, Bluhm, Lanius, & Pain, in press; Lanius, Hopper, & Menon, 2003; Lanius et al., 2002, 2004; Lanius, Williamson, et al., 2003) have conducted the most systematic fMRI investigations of both PTSD and dissociative symptoms in traumatized individuals. Using the script-driven traumatic imagery methodology developed with PTSD patients, they have compared patients exhibiting dissociative responses with those exhibiting hyperarousal responses (Lanius et al., 2002). Compared with the PTSD patients exhibiting hyperarousal, the dissociative subjects had higher brain activation in the superior and middle temporal gyri, inferior frontal gyrus, and occipital and parietal lobes. PTSD patients with hyperarousal responses showed increased heart rate during the traumatic imagery segment, but those with dissociative responses did not.

In a remarkable case study, Lanius and colleagues (Lanius, Hopper, et al., 2003) assessed the fMRI and heart rate responses of a couple who were trapped in their automobile during a massive highway wreck involving over 100 vehicles. The couple witnessed a child burn to death and feared that they would also die. Both met diagnostic criteria for PTSD 4 weeks after the accident, when they participated in a script-driven imagery study. The husband reported a vivid memory for the experience, including his desperate search for an escape route. His heart rate increased dramatically and he manifested increases in brain activity over baseline in the anterior, frontal, anterior cingulated, superior temporal, parietal, occipital, and left thalamic regions. In contrast, his wife reported feeling extremely numb and frozen during the traumatic script segment. Her fMRI showed only a tiny increase in activity in the occipital region and her heart rate did not change. Although their traumatic exposure was about as matched as possible, these two individuals had markedly different subjective responses to a standard traumatic reminder, which were paralleled by distinct differences in brain activation patterns.

In aggregate, imaging studies indicate that there are brain activation markers that distinguish dissociative phenomena from other conditions. In several of the studies, the brain regions showing increases or decreases in metabolic activity were largely overlapping. No definitive dissociative pattern has emerged, however, and much additional research will likely be required before we understand what we are really seeing in these imaging studies. Nonetheless, the fact that dissociative effects can be detected in brain imaging as well as in physiological and cognitive studies offers an opportunity to trace some of the neural circuitry underlying this powerful process.

Memory and Cognitive Studies

A central feature of the dissociative disorders is their dysfunctions of memory. Prince's original GSR experiment sought to capture the often reported directional amnesias between alter personality states (Prince & Peterson, 1908). Many of the case studies that followed also sought to document these amnesias. Until the 1985 NIMH study by Silberman, Putnam, Weingartner, Braun, and Post, several small case series published by Ludwig, Larmore, and colleagues during the 1970s were the most sophisticated investigations of DID (Larmore et al., 1977; Ludwig, 1983; Ludwig et al., 1972). Silberman et al. used 9 DID patients and 10 matched controls, who were tested as themselves and in a simulated alter personality state. Testing the separateness of memory between pairs of reportedly mutually amnesic alter personality states by measuring intrusions from categorically similar word lists learned by the other alter personality states, Silberman et al. found that "the DID patients were more likely to compartmentalize the stimuli learned, whereas those mimicking dissociation showed far less evidence of information partitioning" (quoted in Dorahy, 2001, p. 778). Preliminary studies suggesting that dissociation had differential impacts on the domains of implicit and explicit memory remain to be replicated (Dorahy, 2001).

Recent studies of memory in DID patients have, however, found that the most salient marker of which information is likely to be available or unavailable across alter personality states is the degree of cognitive processing required for stimulus comprehension and interpretation (Dorahy, 2001). The greater the mental effort required and the more the encoding of that information is biased in some fashion by the "personality" of a given alter personality state, the less likely that information is to transfer to another personality state. Studying the alter personalities of 9 DID subjects with a battery of explicit and implicit memory tests, Eich et al. (1997) concluded that the distinction between explicit and implicit memory was not the critical factor. Rather, it "appears that how much leakage occurs across alter personality states depends on the extent to which encoding and retrieval processes are susceptible to personality-specific factors" (p. 421). Similarly, Peters, Uyterlinde, Consemulder, and van der Hart (1998) substantiated the existence of directional or asymmetric amnesias across alter personality states but did not find performance differences between implicit and explicit memory tests.

The existence of differential and directional amnesias across DID alter personality states have been found in all but one study to date. The more rigorous studies, however, also document considerable leakage or transfer of information across alter personality states, which report being completely amnesic for one another. At the end of the nineteenth century, Ribot (1882) first articulated the most parsimonious neuropsychological explanation put forward thus far: that these amnesias are examples of state-dependent learning and retrieval. The degree of amnesia demonstrated in DID patients, however, exceeds that which is typically seen in experimental studies of state-dependent memory (Peters et al., 1998). The advent of fMRI studies of cognition and memory offers opportunities to take a new look at differences in encoding and retrieval of learned information across DID alter personality states.

Studies of individuals with high and low dissociative tendencies have revealed interesting differences in cognitive performance. Using DES scores, DePrince and Freyd (1999) divided undergraduates into high and low dissociative groups and administered selective and divided attention tasks using a version of the Stroop color naming test. This task requires the subject to name the color of ink that a word is printed in as rapidly as possible, but to ignore the word itself. Subjects were tested under two conditions. In the first, they named the color but ignored the words; in the second, they named the color and were told to memorize the words for later recall. The word list contained both neutral words and selected emotionally charged words. Following each condition, subjects were tested on their recall of words, although they had not been instructed to memorize the words in the first condition. Interference with the Stroop task was measured as the length of time required for the subject to accurately name the color of ink. High DES subjects showed more interference on the selective attention task (just naming the color) but performed better on the dual attention task (naming the color and memorizing the word). The researchers replicated these findings using a directed forgetting paradigm and new divided attention tasks. In the divided attention segment, the high DES subjects recalled fewer traumas but more neutral words than did the low DES subjects (DePrince & Freyd, 2001).

These studies, together with the Silberman et al. (1985) study, show that certain memory tasks can be constructed such that highly dissociative individuals perform better than control subjects. Memory tasks that involve division of attention or compartmentalization of highly similar information seem to favor highly dissociative individuals. Memory tasks that demand focused attention place them at a significant disadvantage. These attentional and memory differences, perhaps together with other, as yet unrecognized cognitive differences, operating during critical periods of development and over the life span of the individual could lead to considerable deviation from normal developmental trajectories, as described in the section on the developmental model.

Psychophysiology of Dissociation

Reports of differences in handedness, visual ability, differential responses to various visual, tactile, olfactory, and auditory stimuli, and marked variations in energy level date back to some of the earliest case descriptions and by the nineteenth century became a staple of most case reports (Alvarado, 1989). Prince's GSR study begins a tradition of efforts at documentation using the most advanced technology of the time. By the 1950s, EEG became a favored measure, with famous cases such as Thigpen and Cleckley's (1957) *The Three Faces of Eve* and Lugwig's (Ludwig et al., 1972) Jonas demonstrating reported differences in mean alpha frequency across alter personality states. Today, these studies would be challenged for their uncontrolled designs and simple methodology. Recent, better-controlled studies, however, continue to find interesting differences. Measuring a battery of autonomic nervous system indices, including GSR, Zahn and colleagues (Zahn, Moraga, & Ray, 1996) found that 8 of 9 DID patients consistently manifested physiologically distinct personality states over several weeks. Three of the five simulating controls could, by using either hypnosis or deep relaxation, also manifest distinct "personality states," although these were significantly physiologically different from those produced by the DID patients.

J. J. B. Allen and Movius (2000) compared event-related potentials elicited by words learned in either the same or a different alter personality state for 4 DID patients. By this measure, they found little support for the existence of amnesia between personality states when compared with controls from another study who had deliberately concealed knowledge of previously learned words. Hopper et al. (2002) compared EEG coherence, a statistical estimate of the correlation between pairs of electrodes as a function of frequency, across the alter personality states of 5 DID patients and 5 simulating controls. The patients showed significant differences between personality states for alpha coherence in six brain regions; there were no differences for the controls. On average, the alpha coherence was higher in the host personality states than in the designated alter personality. EEG coherence is thought to be less sensitive to movement and muscle artifacts, which are potential confounds for prior EEG studies (Putnam, 1997).

The strategy of dividing traumatized subjects into high and low dissociative subgroups has also yielded interesting results for psychophysiological measures. Griffin and colleagues (1997) measured heart rate and skin conductance in 85 rape victims within 2 weeks of their rape. When asked to describe the rape, the high dissociative group reported the greatest subjective sense of distress, yet they decreased their heart rate and GSR arousal level relative to a neutral baseline. Other investigators are reporting similar findings in both child and adult samples. Using an index that includes both heart rate change and subjective distress, Bonanno and colleagues (2003) found that increased dissociation predicted a drop in heart rate together with an increased sense of distress for both sexually abused and control girls talking about a self-selected "most traumatic" life experience. This combination of increased distress and decreased heart rate predicted more PTSD symptoms, blunted emotion, and poorer outcome. Similar correlations between increased dissociation and decreased heart rate to stressors have been found in other studies (Koopman et al., 2004).

An inverse relationship between dissociation scores and urinary catecholamines has been reported by two studies. In 59 motor vehicle accident victims, peritraumatic dissociation was correlated with epinephrine but not norepinephrine in males, whereas females showed a reversed pattern of significance (Delahanty, Royer, Raimonde, & Spoonster, 2003). Simeon et al. (2003) found strong negative correlations between urinary norepinephrine and depersonalization scores in subjects with a *DSM-IV* diagnosis of Depersonalization Disorder. These results are congruent with the heart rate data, suggesting that high levels of dissociation act to suppress arousal in the face of stressors but do little or nothing to dampen subjective distress.

Neurobiology of Dissociation

Two primary sources of information inform our understanding of the neurobiology of dissociation. First, a body of case reports describes dissociative reactions in the context of illicit drug use or as a side effect of medications. Drugs that can precipitate dissociative-like reactions include alcohol, barbiturates and related hypnotics, benzodiazepines, scopolamine, ß-adrenergic blockers, marijuana, other psychedelics, and anesthetics such as ketamine and its relatives. The number of different types of drugs producing dissociative-like reactions would suggest that many neurotransmitter systems could be involved in producing dissociative reactions.

A second source of information is the data from challenge studies using a range of "dissociative" drugs. Challenge studies with marijuana, infusions of lactate, yohimbine, mCPP, and ketamine elicit depersonalization in some subjects. These studies serve to narrow down the number of neurotransmitter systems likely to make significant contributions to dissociative states. The N-methyl-d-aspartate (NMDA) glutamate receptor, in particular, appears to play a central role in producing dissociative symptoms (Chambers et al., 1999).

Many of the drug challenge studies were conducted by John Krystal, Douglas Bremner, Steven Southwick, and colleagues (Bremner, Davis, Southwick, Krystal, & Charney, 1993; Bremner et al., 1995; Chambers et al., 1999; Charney, Deutch, Krystal, Southwich, & Davis, 1993; Krystal, Bennett, Bremner, Southwick, & Charney, 1995; Krystal et al., 1994) at the PTSD research center of the Yale-New Haven Veterans Administration Hospital. In a series of studies, they found that ketamine, an NMDA antagonist that increases glutamate release, produced dose-dependent increases in dissociation scores. In high doses, ketamine slows perception of time and produces tunnel vision, derealization, and depersonalization, similar to that described by trauma victims. Pretreatment with an anticonvulsant, either a benzodiazepine or lomotragine, which decreases glutamate release, reduces but does not entirely eliminate the dissociative effects of ketamine. Thus, dissociation, widely regarded as unresponsive to medication, may be susceptible to certain classes of drugs.

Krystal and colleagues (Chambers et al., 1999) propose the most comprehensive neurobiological theory of dissociation to date. This theory draws on preclinical data indicating that stress increases the release of glutamate and shows the similarity of the hyperglutamatergic effects of NMDA antagonists with stress- and trauma-induced dissociative symptoms. In summary, Krystal postulates that NMDA blockade decreases inhibitory tone, leading to increased glutamate release and consequently dissociative symptoms. This theory also accounts for the structural brain changes in the hippocampus found in MRI studies of PTSD subjects and controls. In two studies (DeBellis et al., 1999; Stein, Koverola, Hanna, Torchia, & McClarty, 1997), dissociation measures strongly correlated with volume loss in key brain regions implicated in PTSD.

Glutamate has a well-documented role in neuroplasticity, and increased glutamate release can lead to neurotoxic cellular events (De Bellis et al., 1999; Stein et al., 1997). Studies with marijuana and mCPP, however, implicate serotonin, and studies with yohimbine suggest that noradrenergic components may play roles in dissociation and PTSD symptoms, so additional systems beyond the NMDA receptor system may be involved. Morgan and colleagues (2002), for example, found an important role for neuropeptide peptide Y (NPY) in dissociative responses to extreme stress. In two studies of military subjects undergoing high-stress training, they found a strong negative relationship between NPY levels and dissociative symptoms (Morgan et al., 2002). Thus, a number of candidate neurotransmitter systems have been identified that may contribute to dissociative symptoms individually and interactively.

THE CONTINUUM VERSUS THE TAXON MODEL OF PATHOLOGICAL DISSOCIATION

A century-old debate about whether dissociation occurs along a continuum proceeding from normal to pathological or represents a wholly different type of psychological organization has been resurrected by recent interest in the taxon model of dissociation. Janet (Putnam, 1989) advocated for a dissociative type, set apart from normal individuals. He believed that constitutional factors, suggestibility, and powerful emotional events contributed to the creation of a group of individuals who were fundamentally different from normal individuals. On the other hand, William James and Morton Prince (Putnam, 1989) argued for a continuum model, ranging from "normal" dissociative phenomena, such as absorption, to pathology, such as amnesias, fugues, and multiple personalities. Until recently, the continuum theory carried the day, although a few authorities cautioned about the possibility of a discontinuity of dissociative or trance phenomena. However, as data accrued across clinical and normal samples, it became apparent that there existed a distinct group of individuals who score high on dissociation measures irrespective of their psychiatric diagnosis. Different diagnostic groups contained different percentages of these high scorers, yielding different diagnostic group mean scores. The greater the percentage of high scorers, the greater the elevation of the group's mean score relative to the group's modal score. On the DES, for example, high scorers cluster around a mean score of 45, with the rest of the sample clustering around 8 (Putnam, Carlson, et al., 1996).

Based on these observations, a statistical study directly investigating the possibility of a dissociative "type" of individual was undertaken. Using newly developed taxometric approaches, Waller et al. (1996) examined item-response data for manifestations of a latent class variable. Eight DES items, composing the DES-T subscale, could robustly differentiate Dissociative Disorder patients from other psychiatric patients and normal controls. Indeed, the normal controls almost never endorsed these eight items. Subsequent studies confirm that a taxonic approach is a clinically useful way to identify a distinct subgroup of dissociative patients within any given diagnosis. These high dissociative individuals will differ on important symptoms and features from the rest of the diagnostic group (J. G. Allen, Fultz, Huntoon, & Brethour, 2002; Seedat et al., 2003; Waller, Ohanian, Meyer, Everill, & Rouse, 2001). Dividing subjects into high and low scorers has proven fruitful for identifying distinctly different physiological and cognitive responses to stimuli that serve as traumatic reminders.

Implications of the Taxon Model

A taxonic model of dissociation would imply a significantly different developmental trajectory than the continuum model. It would also require a different approach to treatment, that is, changing a type rather than lowering an elevated level of dissociation. The typological differences between high dissociators and others either could be the result of a strong genetic predisposition or could arise from a fundamentally different early developmental trajectory. A convincing genetic difference remains to be demonstrated, but research linking dissociation with Type D attachment disturbances offers a potential mechanism for the latter.

The continuum model of dissociation conceptualizes a positive treatment response as moving the individual back toward the "normal" segment of the dissociation continuum. In a taxonic model, a positive treatment outcome implies shifting the individual's type from the dissociative to the nondissociative type. Treatment outcomes such as fusion or integration into a unified personality of the DID alter personalities suggests this possibility (Kluft, 1984b). Beyond these clinical accounts, however, no empirical data exist to confirm that integration clinically produces a taxonic change. To date, the few treatment outcome studies of DID patients including pre- and posttreatment dissociation measures show moderate (but significant) decreases in scale scores rather than a significant taxonic shift from the dissociative to nondissociative categories (Choe & Kluft, 1995; Coons, 1986; Kluft, 1988; Ross, 1989). The taxonic model has proven valuable in spurring researchers to compare high and low dissociators on a variety of measures. The clinical utility of the taxon as an index of therapeutic success remains to be tested.

CHILD AND ADOLESCENT DISSOCIATION

In the 1970s, pioneers with child cases such as Cornelia Wilbur and Richard Kluft sparked modern interest in dissociative disorders in children and adolescents (Kluft, 1984a; Putnam, 1997). In particular, Wilbur's recognition

of the role played by child abuse in DID was instrumental in focusing attention on the effects of early trauma on child development. Long forgotten case reports, in which nineteenth-century clinicians sometimes used Latin phrases to mask their suspicions of incest, were subsequently rediscovered. Small case series and reviews of childhood dissociative disorders began appearing by the mid-1980s, with ever more systematic studies appearing in the past decade. In modern cases, significant early trauma is a common feature.

Diagnosis

For the most part, the core phenomenology of child and adolescent dissociative disorders is similar to corresponding adult dissociative symptoms (Hornstein & Putnam, 1992). The day-to-day manifestation of the dissociative symptoms does vary with the child's age, as is the case for childhood manifestations of virtually all lifelong psychiatric disorders. Older children and adolescents, in general, are more overtly symptomatic than younger children. This may reflect, in part, the ability of older children to better report subjective distress as well as their greater opportunity to manifest their psychopathology in ways that bring attention to their problems.

Putnam, Hornstein, et al. (1996) found that amnesias, identity disturbances, and auditory hallucinations increased with age in a pooled sample of 177 child and adolescent dissociative disorder cases. Trance-like and spaced-out behavior, however, were ubiquitous across all age groups. Comorbid pathology such as suicidal ideation, self-mutilation, and somatization increased with age in parallel with dissociative symptoms. Children and adolescents with DID were the most symptomatic across all age groups. This is congruent with the belief that DID is the most severe of the dissociative disorders.

Males and females did not differ on dissociative symptoms, but females were significantly more symptomatic for anxiety and phobic symptoms, PTSD, sleep disturbances, sexual acting-out, and somatization. These findings closely parallel the gender differences in adult clinical profiles. The other significant finding was the steady increase in the ratio of female to male cases reported for each age group (Putnam, Hornstein, et al., 1996). By late adolescence, approximately 80% of the cases in the sample were female (Figure 18.1, "Age"), which duplicates the percentages of females reported in many adult samples (Putnam, 1997).

The most extensive examination of the clinical phenomenology of formally diagnosed child and adolescent dissociative disorders is a sample of 64 cases collected at two separate sites. Using a standard case collection protocol,

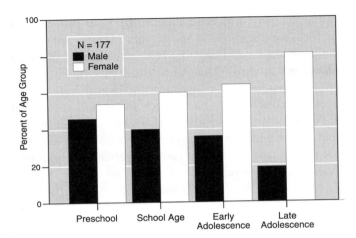

Figure 18.1   Increasing ratio of female to male dissociative disorder diagnoses by age. *Source:* From "Clinical Phenomenology of Child and Adolescent Dissociative Disorders: Gender and Age Effects," by F. W. Putnam, N. L. Hornstein, & G. Peterson, 1996, *Child and Adolescent Psychiatric Clinics of North America, 5*(2), pp. 351–360.

Hornstein and Putnam (1992) first compared the two case series on 16 clinical factors, abuse histories, and CDC scores. Finding no differences, they combined the two samples and enumerated the clinical profiles. There were significant differences between cases diagnosed as DID versus DDNOS. On every measure, the DID cases were more symptomatic, with most differences reaching Bonferroni-corrected levels of significance. Dissociative Identity Disorder patients were significantly older than DDNOS patients. The average child in the sample had received 2.7 (± 1.3) prior diagnoses, the most common being Major Depression (45.3%) and PTSD (29.6%). Affective and anxiety symptoms were prominent in many clinical presentations, and suicidal ideation was common in both groups, with DID cases making significantly more attempts. Rapid mood swings and marked irritability were almost universally reported for all cases.

The most common dissociative symptom was frequent episodes of amnesia reported by and observed in these children. Dissociative Identity Disorder cases had more total amnesias and more amnesias that could not be directly related to traumatic precipitants or reminders. Dissociative Identity Disorder patients had significantly more passive influence experiences (made thoughts and feelings, involuntary motor activity, automatic writing, etc.). Dissociative Identity Disorder cases also had more auditory hallucinations, particularly command hallucinations, urging the child to commit aggressive or self-harm acts. Both DID and DDNOS groups exhibited rapid age regression

phenomena and rapid shifts in demeanor or personality characteristics. Trance-like behavior was ubiquitous.

A comparison of child and adolescent presentations, irrespective of dissociative diagnosis, revealed that adolescents were more symptomatic across the board, although not all comparisons of symptoms reached Bonferroni-corrected statistical significance. Significantly more (>95%) adolescent cases met criteria for DID. It should be noted, however, that the determination of symptoms and the verification of a diagnosis of DID by meeting one or more alter personality states is easier in adolescents.

As is apparent from the Hornstein and Putnam (1992) study, DID is often not formally diagnosable until mid- to late adolescence, although pathological dissociative precursors may be apparent in younger children. Clinicians sometimes refer to such cases as "incipient multiple personality" or "multiple personality in evolution." Peterson and Putnam (1994) proposed an alternative diagnosis of Dissociative Disorder of Childhood (DDoC) to characterize children who were showing significant dissociative psychopathology but who did not have fully crystallized alter personalities. This diagnosis called attention to the pathological dissociation while seeking to avoid the stigma, controversy, and unwelcome attention often associated with a diagnosis of DID. They tested a set of diagnostic criteria by surveying therapists treating children and adolescents carrying a dissociative diagnosis. The four-part diagnostic criteria required (1) 6 months or more of a significant behavioral disturbance characterized by amnesia or trance-like states; (2) perplexing fluctuations in behavior or preferences; (3) at least three dissociative process symptoms (internal auditory hallucinations, vivid imaginary companionship, third-person self-references); and (4) that the patient did not meet criteria for DID. Cases meeting DDoC criteria were distinguishable on clinician report measures such as the Child Dissociative Checklist from patients meeting *DSM* criteria for DID and from a second group with few dissociative symptoms. Although this proposed diagnosis was not adopted in *DSM-IV*, efforts continue to refine diagnostic criteria for a more developmentally sensitive Dissociative Disorder.

Dissociation and the Development of Psychopathology

A second developmental look at the interactions of childhood trauma, family environment, dissociation, and psychopathology emerges from studies with dissociation scales. Validated child and/or adolescent dissociation measures have been administered to a variety of clinical and nonclinical samples (Brunner et al., 2000; Calamari & Pini,

2003; Carrion & Steiner, 2000; Farrington et al., 2002; Kisiel & Lyons, 2001; Macfie, Cicchetti, & Toth, 2001a; Prohl, Resch, Parzer, & Brunner, 2001). Scores were significantly higher for traumatized (typically physically abused) versus nontraumatized subjects across all age groups. Higher levels of dissociation were also significantly associated with more general psychopathology. Among maltreated preschoolers, Macfie, Cicchetti, and Toth (2001b) found robust correlations with externalizing and internalizing behavior problems for both boys and girls. A comparison of these maltreated preschoolers with demographically and family constellation-matched, nontraumatized preschoolers found that the maltreatment group had significantly increased levels of dissociation a year later, with the physically abused children accounting for the greatest increase in scores. The controls showed substantial decreases in their dissociation scores over the same period, in line with the often reported decrease in dissociation scores with age in normal children.

DEVELOPMENTAL PRECURSORS AND SUBSTRATES OF PATHOLOGICAL DISSOCIATION

Imaginary Companionship

Clinicians working with childhood DID initially focused on childhood imagination phenomena such as imaginary companionship as likely developmental precursors for dissociative disorders. Depending on the age of the child and the definition used, imaginary companions are reported in 20% to 60% of normal children (Taylor, 1999). Widely regarded as benign, normal imaginary companionship is commonly considered to be a sign of creativity in young children. It does become increasingly suspect, however, in older children and adolescents and is generally considered to be a sign of psychopathology in adults. The rates of imaginary companionship in child dissociative cases range from 42% to 84%, with the highest rates reported for children diagnosed with DID (Putnam, 1997). It should be noted, however, that the rates reported in DID case series overlap with the range reported in studies of normal children. Thus, although imaginary companionship may be a developmental substrate that is reshaped by early trauma for psychological defensive purposes, it is not pathognomic for pathological dissociation.

The best clinical study, by Trujillo, Lewis, Yeager, and Gidlow (1996), found imaginary companions in 57% of a residential treatment sample of maltreated boys compared to 30% of a normal comparison group of schoolchildren.

The imaginary companions in the clinical sample differed, however, in significant ways from the normal boys' imaginary companions. Maltreated boys averaged 6.4 entities compared with 2.5 imaginary companions in the normal boys. The imaginary companions of the normal boys were benign and benevolent, often with endearing names like "Thumper" and "Boom-Boom." They were typically voluntarily elicited, primarily as playmates. Most appeared between ages 2 and 4 years, and all had disappeared by age 8 years. In contrast, the imaginary companions described by the boys in residential treatment served other functions, including (1) helpers and comforters, (2) powerful protectors, and (3) family members. The imaginary companions of the residential boys were still present at a mean age of 10.6 years, well after they had disappeared in the normal boys. The imaginary companions of the maltreated boys often had names such as "God," "The Devil," and "Guardian Angel." Clinicians should be aware of the possibility that children who report talking with God or the Devil may actually be referring to their imaginary companion and not expressing more abstract religious beliefs. Clinicians experienced with DID cases theorize that at least some of the imaginary companions found in maltreated children eventually evolve into the alter personality states that characterize DID. As yet, no one has documented this transformation; however, autobiographical accounts of DID patients do sometimes report that this happened with them.

Type D Attachment

In the context of seeking to code attachment with disturbed mother-infant pairs, Main and Solomon (1986) identified a new pattern of attachment: insecure-disorganized/disoriented or Type D attachment (Hesse & Main, 2000; Main & Solomon, 1986). Type D attachment is defined by a characteristic set of behaviors in the standard Strange Situation (Ainsworth, Blehar, Waters, & Wall, 1978): (1) the complete absence of an apparent attachment strategy; (2) contradictory behaviors or affects occurring virtually simultaneously; (3) freezing, stilling, apparent dissociation; (4) abnormal movements; or (5) direct indices of apprehension of the parent (Green & Goldwyn, 2002). The wide range of behaviors included under this classification makes it apparent that Type D samples are behaviorally heterogeneous. The base rate for Type D attachments in low-risk families is approximately 15% but rises much higher in certain samples (van Ijzendoorn, Schuengel, & Bakermans-Kranenburg, 1999).

Main and Hesse (1990) theorized that Type D attachment arose as a result of the child simultaneously experiencing the parent as both frightening and necessary for survival. They characterized the caregiver behavior as being frightening and/or frightened (Main & Hesse, 1990). Research has now convincingly linked parental factors, especially unresolved parental loss or trauma, in the development of Type D attachment in children (Schuengel, Bakermans-Kranenburg, & van Ijzendoorn, 1999). Not surprisingly, the highest rates of Type D attachment occur in samples of maltreated infants and toddlers. For example, V. Carlson, Cicchetti, Barnett, and Braunwald (1989) found that 82% of a maltreated group of 12-month-olds were classified as Type D compared with 19% of a demographically matched, welfare-dependent sample. They also found that more maltreated boys than girls qualified as Type D. Following a maltreatment sample and matched controls for 1 year, Barnett, Ganiban, and Cicchetti (1999) found that Type D classifications were stable and predictive of negativity in the child.

Children classified as Type D or disorganized have poorer outcomes across many domains (Green & Goldwyn, 2002). These include lower academic attainment, lower self-esteem, poor peer interactions, unusual or bizarre classroom behaviors, cognitive immaturity, and externalizing behavior problems (Green & Goldwyn, 2002; Lyons-Ruth, Alpern, & Repacholi, 1993). Studies have also found that Type D children show significantly greater hypothalamic-pituitary-adrenal (HPA) axis reactivity to stressors (Hertsgaard, Gunnar, Erickson, & Nachmias, 1995; Schuengel et al., 1999). Salivary cortisol collected after a Strange Situation did not differ among infants classified as having A, B, or C attachment patterns but was significantly higher in Type D infants (Hertsgaard et al., 1995). Given that the Strange Situation is considered to be a mild stressor, it is likely that many of their life experiences evoke even stronger HPA axis responses.

Type D Attachment and Dissociation

In 1992, Giovanni Liotti extended a line of theory, first proposed by Peter Barach (1991), that dissociation is etiologically related to disturbances in parent-child attachment, specifically Type D attachment disorder (Liotti, 1992). He hypothesized that "the infant's disorganized/disoriented attachment behavior . . . correspond[s] to the construction of an internal working model of self and the attachment figure that is multiple and incoherent" (Liotti, 1992, p. 199). He further speculated that the severity of the dissociative outcome of Type D attachment patterns would depend on subsequent life experiences, especially on the degree of exposure to frightening and nonfrightening caretakers or traumatic experiences.

Indeed, subsequent research finds converging evidence for a linkage between pathological dissociation and Type D attachment patterns. Two separate analyses of data from the prospective, longitudinal Minnesota Mother-Child Project study found that attachment disorganization in infancy predicted increased dissociation in adolescence (E. A. Carlson, 1998; Ogawa, Sroufe, Weinfield, Carlson, & Egeland, 1997). In a sample of 168 young adults, Ogawa et al. found that three variables measured in infancy accounted for 30% of the variance in DES scores at age 18 to 19 years: (1) attention span subscale of the Carey (negative ß), (2) maternal psychological unavailability, and (3) a disorganized pattern in the Strange Situation. Using a structural equation modeling approach with an overlapping sample of 157 subjects, E. A. Carlson likewise found that early caregiving mediated disorganized attachment, which, in turn, mediated dissociation, accounting for 15% of the variance in DES-T scores at age 19.

In further support of this hypothesis, Main and Morgan (1996) found that a mother's DES score was a good predictor of her infant's disorganized behavior. Examining the nature of parent-child interactions with parents of Type D infants, Hesse and Main (2000) described many dissociative-like behaviors, including alternations among multiple discrete behavioral states that trigger disorganized behaviors in their infants. Thus, one can begin to posit a transgenerational dynamic in which increased maternal dissociation contributes to disorganized attachment, which, in turn, contributes to increased dissociation in adulthood, including parenting behaviors—and on through successive generations when other factors (e.g., trauma and adversity) co-occur.

Developmental Mediation of Psychopathology by Dissociation

Several studies have examined whether dissociation mediates the relationship between trauma and one or more types of psychopathology. The standard statistical approaches to determining mediation involve three variables: (1) the predictor variable: in this case, some form of trauma; (2) the putative mediating variable: dissociation; and (3) the outcome. All three variables must be intercorrelated. Mediating effects are tested by partialling out the contribution of the putative mediating variable, either through multiple regression or an analysis of covariance (Baron & Kenny, 1986). If there is a mediation effect, the strength of the relationship between the predictor variable and the outcome variable will be significantly reduced or eliminated.

In clinical samples of adult women with histories of abuse, dissociation mediated a range of symptoms, including anxiety, compulsions, depression, phobias, and ruminations (Becker-Lausen, Sanders, & Chinsky, 1995; Ross-Gower, Waller, Tyson, & Elliott, 1998). Kisiel and Lyons (2001) explored the possible mediating role of dissociation in the development of psychopathology in sexually abused children and adolescents. Measuring psychopathology with a variety of standard measures, they found that the main effect of sexual abuse on behavioral problems disappeared when they controlled for levels of dissociation as measured either by a self-report measure (A-ADES) or by observer report (CDC). This is a well-accepted statistical test of a putative mediating variable. These data are congruent with similar studies showing dissociation as mediating psychopathology in adults (Lyubomirsky, Casper, & Soursa, 2001; Offen et al., 2003; Ross-Gower et al., 1998; Somer, 2002). A path analysis study of 156 sexually abused children found three direct pathways to PTSD symptoms, of which dissociation was by far the strongest contributor (Kaplow, Dodge, Amaya-Jackson, & Saxe, 2005). The authors concluded that children who reported dissociative symptoms immediately after disclosure of abuse were at greatest risk for subsequent PTSD. They theorized that the dissociative symptoms may have interfered with the processing of traumatic effects and memories and increased reexperiencing symptoms.

Psychopathological Mechanisms

The possibility that dissociation is a critical mediating variable for subsequent psychopathology has significant implications for early intervention with maltreated and traumatized children. Assessment of dissociation should be a standard part of the evaluation of traumatized children and adolescents, and significant elevations should be addressed as part of the treatment plan. The mechanism(s) through which dissociation mediates the development of psychopathology remains to be established. It is theorized that dissociative effects on memory, coherence of self, and self-agency play a significant role in undermining the development of a healthy sense of self and appropriate socialization (Putnam, 1997). The negative effects of high levels of dissociation on child development are postulated to operate through impacts on elaboration of a sense of self, acquisition of emotional regulation, impulse control, impairments in information processing, and psychophysiological responses to stressors. Each of these developmental threads interacts with others to shape the child's emerging capacities in ways that may lead to profound differences in

psychological organization compared to individuals with low levels of dissociation.

Children elaborate, assemble, and seek to integrate a complex, multidimensional sense of self over the course of development. Dissociative symptoms such as autobiographical amnesias, depersonalization, and passive influence experiences interfere with the integration of self and the development of a unified sense of self-agency. In a study of outcomes of Israeli rape and domestic violence victims and controls, dissociation mediated much of the variance between trauma and emotional distress (Somer, 2002). Dissociation also indirectly mediated increased introspectiveness, which accounted for part of the trauma-emotional distress relationship. Introspectiveness has been associated with developmental discontinuities, which are theorized to stimulate intensive reappraisal of the self.

Dissociative amnesias that interrupt the continuity of experience disrupt a child's understanding of cause-and-effect sequences. Antecedent negative or risky behaviors do not seem to be connected to their subsequent consequences; thus, consequences of prior actions are experienced as coming from out of the blue. These "expectable" consequences, then, are not associated with the behaviors that caused them. As a result, dissociative children have a great deal of difficulty learning from experience (Putnam, 1997). Dissociative symptoms such as depersonalization disrupt the metacognitive function of self-monitoring behavior. In turn, this is believed to interfere with the integration of a sense of self across contexts, thus further complicating the child's ability to learn and practice self-control, particularly in the context of stressors. Dissociation is well-correlated in numerous studies with increased aggression, impulsivity, and poorer social skills (Brunner et al., 2000; Carrion & Steiner, 2000; Kisiel & Lyons, 2001; Macfie et al., 2001a, 2001b; Putnam, 1997; Walker, 2002; Zoroglu et al., 2003).

Chronic depersonalization, believed to be related to the emotional numbing seen in PTSD patients, is theorized to promote a sense of detachment from self that fosters risky and self-destructive behavior, including self-mutilation. Increased dissociation is highly correlated with increased self-mutilation in numerous studies (Paul, Schroeter, Dahme, & Nutzinger, 2002; Saxe, Chawla, & van der Kolk, 2002; Zoroglu et al., 2003). Self-inflicting pain is often described by dissociative patients as an attempt to break through profound states of depersonalization. At other times, however, they describe feeling no pain when they cut or burn themselves. This sense of alienation from self is also believed to contribute to the high rate of suicide attempts in dissociative patients. Dissociation has been implicated in predisposing an individual to revictimization (Noll et al., 2003); whether this represents a form of self-harm, a lack of investment in self, or a failure of vigilance remains to be determined. In total, these experiences increase an individual's risk for further traumatization, which takes a cumulative toll on the individual's life.

Studies with high and low dissociators have established significant cognitive differences for certain attentional tasks. The full range of these cognitive differences remains to be elucidated, but it is postulated that they alter the dissociative child's ability to process information in normative ways. Prospectively comparing sexually abused girls with carefully matched controls, Trickett, McBride-Chang, and Putnam (1994) found that dissociation was negatively associated with competent learning and overall classroom performance and strongly predictive of school avoidance. The combination of cognitive dysfunctions and negative school trajectories puts dissociative children at an academic disadvantage, which has profound implications for adult attainment. Other, longer-term social effects, such as cross-generational impact on the quality of parenting and thus attachment with one's own children, are also likely. For example, a cross-sectional study of college students found dissociation to be a mediator between child abuse histories and scores on a measure of child abuse potential (Narang & Contreras, 2000). Thus, as many have speculated clinically, increased dissociation may increase risk for poor parenting and thus perpetuation of child maltreatment into another generation.

Protective Factors

The military stress studies by Morgan and colleagues (2002) suggest that some factors must help to protect individuals against developing dissociation under severe stress. The major biological finding to date is that levels of neuropeptide-Y secreted during stress are inversely related to dissociative symptoms and positively related to superior performance (Morgan et al., 2002). The longitudinal Minnesota Mother-Child Project found that in high-risk children, dissociation at Time 5 was negatively correlated with Time 2 measures of self-esteem and ego resilience for children subsequently traumatized at Times 3 and 4. Thus, a more developed and healthier sense of self at an early age appeared to act as a protective factor against dissociation from later trauma (Ogawa et al., 1997). There are probably other protective factors operating that have yet to be elucidated.

The influence of genetic factors remains unclear. The two twin studies to date report contradictory findings, with one attributing a significant amount of the variance to genetic

factors and the other finding only a significant relationship with shared environment. Identification of environmental protective factors may help stimulate intervention models that prevent the development of significant dissociation in acutely traumatized children.

In summary, the developmental model of pathological dissociation postulates that childhood trauma-related dissociation may be mediated in part through its effects on attachment, especially Type D disturbances of attachment. Attachment is a basic social/biological process that fundamentally impacts the development of self and socialization. Much of the comorbid psychopathology common in Dissociative Disorder patients and in psychiatric patients with high levels of dissociation are believed to be associated with early disturbances of attachment with a primary caretaker. The developmental model of dissociation is consistent with the taxonic model of dissociation that postulates that individuals with dissociative disorders differ in a fundamental way from others, as opposed to simply being further along on a continuum of dissociation. The taxonic model implies that the dissociative individual must travel a very different developmental trajectory, particularly with respect to the integration of self, over childhood and adolescence than do nondissociative individuals. A fundamental disturbance of attachment, as represented by the Type D classification, could set the stage for the elaboration of dissociation, which, in turn, may mediate the development of the associated comorbidity commonly seen in such cases.

Treatment of Dissociation in Children and Adolescents

Dissociative Children

A discussion of the current state of the art of treatment for dissociative children and adolescents needs to differentiate between children with discernable dissociative symptoms and behaviors but without a diagnosable dissociative disorder and those who meet formal *DSM* criteria. The former are relatively common, but the latter are relatively rare. The inclusion of child and adolescent scales and measures in numerous studies has documented high levels of dissociation in clinical samples of children and adolescents with a number of disorders (Brunner et al., 2000; Calamari & Pini, 2003; Keck-Seeley, Perosa, & Perosa, 2004; Prohl et al., 2001; Sanders & Becker-Lausen, 1995; Sanders & Giolas, 1991; Yoshizumi, Murase, Honjo, Kaneko, & Murakami, 2004; Zoroglu, Sar, Tuzun, Tutkun, & Savas, 2002). Elevated dissociation is also common in adolescents in the juvenile justice system and among runaways (Brosky

& Lally, 2004; Friedrich et al., 2001; Koopman et al., 2004; Plattner et al., 2003; Tyler, Cauce, & Whitbeck, 2004).

Eating disorders have been among the best documented disorders associated with increased dissociation in adolescents (Farrington et al., 2002; Gleaves & Eberenz, 1995; Hartt & Waller, 2002; Rosen & Petty, 1994; Valdiserri & Kihlstrom, 1995). Although most reports link disordered eating with increased dissociation, there is no clear pattern differentiating anorectic from bulimic patients. Eating disorder patients scoring high on dissociation measures are, however, generally more symptomatic and more refractory to treatment than low-scoring patients. In some studies, the magnitude of the dissociation effect, though significant, does not account for much of the variance. Where childhood trauma, especially sexual abuse, has been concurrently assessed, it is more highly correlated with the dissociation than with measures of disordered eating. This suggests that dissociation is probably not a major mediator of disordered eating but is more likely related to the high incidence of sexual abuse reported by many eating disorder studies.

Self-mutilation and self-destructive behaviors seem to be more directly related to increased dissociation in a subset of troubled adolescents (Gratz, Conrad, & Roemer, 2002; Matsumoto, Azekawa, Yamaguchi, Asami, & Iseki, 2004; Noll et al., 2003; Turell & Armsworth, 2000; Yates, 2004; Zoroglu et al., 2003; Zweig-Frank, Paris, & Guzder, 1994). In some instances, the self-destructive behavior occurs during a dissociative state; in other instances, it seems to be an attempt by the individual to break out of a painful state of depersonalization/derealization. In a number of instances, individuals have committed murder while in a dissociative state (Ferracuti & DeMarco, 2004; Spinelli, 2001). Spinelli's investigation of multiple cases of neonaticide found a common pattern of a denial of the pregnancy, followed by depersonalization, dissociative hallucinations, and intermittent amnesia during delivery.

In aggregate, these reports indicate that dissociation should be routinely assessed in troubled children and adolescents, particularly if they have histories of self-destructive or assaultive behavior. Currently, there are no systematic data on responsiveness of dissociative symptoms and behaviors in children or adolescents who meet criteria for another disorder. Unpublished data indicate that dissociation, as measured by the CDC, declines in traumatized preschoolers treated in a therapeutic preschool program (J. Sites, personal communication, November 2004). This decline in dissociation scores over a 1-year period was accompanied by marked improvements across a broad range of social and academic measures, although a causal relationship was not demonstrated. Similar, and as

yet anecdotal, results among young children have been described by others but remain to be fully documented. The improvement in many of these cases was not associated with treatment directed at the dissociation, but rather the creation of safe, stable, supportive, and structured environments with clear expectations and contingencies. This is congruent with some recommendations for treatment of dissociative disorders in young children (Putnam, 1997).

Children with Dissociative Disorders

A set of guidelines for the treatment of dissociative disorders in children and adolescents has been published by a task force of the International Society for the Study of Dissociation (ISSD; Silberg, 2000b). These guidelines provide a general framework from which to approach the treatment of highly dissociative children and adolescents. The first step is an assessment, including a complete history of the child and the child's caretaking environment. The clinical interview should include questions about imaginary friends, auditory and visual hallucinations, perplexing forgetfulness, numbing, anxiety, nightmares, self-injury, flashbacks, somatic concerns, depersonalization and derealization, and identity alteration or confusion. In addition, measures such as the CDC or A-ADES are recommended. Formal psychological testing, including documentation of the signs and behaviors noted by Silberg (1996a), may be indicated if resources are available. Given the significant comorbidity that often accompanies pathological dissociation, the evaluation should also assess for Obsessive-Compulsive Disorder, PTSD, Reactive Attachment Disorder, Attention-Deficit/Hyperactivity Disorder, affective disorders, substance abuse, and developmental disorders. A thorough physical examination may well be indicated. Conditions such as epilepsy, narcolepsy, and other neurological disorders should be considered in the differential diagnosis (Putnam, 1997).

The creation of true safety for the child, both physical and psychological, is a necessary prerequisite to successful treatment (Putnam, 1997; Silberg, 2000b). Once safety has been ensured, the role of the therapist is to create a stable sense of continuity and structure for the dissociative child, both in terms of the therapist's interactions and in the child's larger milieu. Often, this requires working with caretakers, teachers, and others important in the child's daily life (Putnam, 1997). A team approach is best but, as always, requires active and ongoing efforts to coordinate care and to ensure the continuity of cause and effect, stimulus and response that is critical to cutting across the dissociative compartmentalization of knowledge and behavior that fragments the child's experience of the world. This must be balanced against the issues of confidentiality that become increasingly important with adolescents.

The ISSD guidelines list a series of therapeutic goals (Silberg, 2000b). Foremost among these is helping the child acquire a sense of cohesiveness and continuity of self and behavior. The effort is to help children become aware of their behavior and its relationship to prior experience, current stressors, and subsequent consequences. The therapist must help the child accept responsibility and exert control over his or her actions. As with PTSD, dissociative disorders sap motivation and the hope that things can improve. The therapist should help the child identify strengths and motivate the child to explore possibilities for change. Internal conflicts, often personified as pejorative auditory hallucinations or dueling alter personalities, need to be identified and articulated. Depending on the child's age, various therapeutic modalities can be used to work through these issues, including play therapy, art therapy, journaling, and video narratives.

The core of treatment for most dissociative disorders, as with PTSD, is the processing of traumatic memories. This is made more difficult by the amnesias for traumatic experiences and dissociative responses to threatening and anxiety-provoking material. Discussions of various approaches to therapeutic processing of traumatic material with children and adolescents are detailed in volumes devoted to treating dissociative children and adolescents (Putnam, 1997; Silberg, 1996a). Promotion of autonomy and the self-regulation of affective state are also important treatment goals. Helping dissociative children identify traumatic triggers and stimuli that elicit changes in emotional state should occur both in therapy and in the milieu. Cognitive-behavioral and anxiety-reduction techniques are tools to help children and adolescents gain mastery over their dissociative and traumatic reactions to stressors.

Finally, the promotion of healthy relationships is aimed at the disrupted attachments that these children experienced in the context of maltreatment and other traumas. Helping these children to express their feelings, fears, and compulsions rather than acting on them is an ongoing task for the therapist, caretakers, and important others in the child's environment. It often falls to the therapist to work with foster parents, teachers, residential treatment staff, and others to help them to maintain appropriate boundaries and the continuity of their relationships with the child in the face of acting-out behavior. The maintenance of stable, predictable, reasonable responses to provocative and dissociative behavior by the child helps to promote healthy relationships.

Treatment of children and adolescents with dissociative disorders generally occurs simultaneously in a series of arenas, including individual, family, and educational settings. Inpatient and/or residential treatment may also occur during the course of treatment. Beyond the clinical reports and anecdotal accounts, little is known about the outcomes of these interventions. Overall, the literature has been optimistic for children (Putnam, 1997; Silberg, 1996a, 2000a). There appears to be somewhat less success with adolescents (Dell & Eisenhower, 1990; Putnam, 1997). Randomized clinical trial studies now demonstrate the efficacy of cognitive-behavioral treatments for sexually abused children with PTSD symptoms in general (Cohen, Deblinger, Mannarino, & Steer, 2004). These approaches should be extended to research with children with high levels of dissociation and dissociative disorders.

SUMMARY AND FUTURE DIRECTIONS

This chapter provided a comprehensive and synthetic overview of the relevant features of dissociation and the dissociative disorders as they pertain to the development of psychopathology. Dissociation is a remarkably global process that appears to influence the expression of a wide range of critical psychological and biological capacities in ways that lead to fundamental differences in some individuals' subjective experience of self and others.

Historically, dissociative individuals have been clinical and public curiosities who generated fascination and skepticism in turn. Yet, the early study of these conditions was instrumental in the recognition of unconscious mental processes and the emergence of psychodynamic psychology and psychiatry. This fascination also led to the elaboration of misleading stereotypes, particularly for Multiple Personality Disorder, that continue to plague the field and obscure the importance of dissociation as a fundamental mental process capable of leaving a profound stamp on the development of an individual. Modern perspectives on dissociation, increasingly informed by experimental data, are gradually shedding this historical baggage and replacing prior fascination with a more calibrated understanding of the effects of dissociation on memory, cognition, biology, and behavior.

The measurement of dissociation by reliable and valid scales and diagnostic interviews has revolutionized our understanding of both the fundamental process and the disorders that arise from pathological levels of dissociation. Similar to the change in our understanding that occurred for depression and anxiety, the ability to simply and meaningfully quantify dissociation has resulted in hundreds of peer-reviewed publications including dissociation among the constructs measured for a wide range of clinical and population samples. The results have better elucidated the relationship of dissociation to etiological factors as well as its relationship to a range of comorbid psychopathology.

Increasingly sophisticated statistical approaches are extracting latent information embedded in the distributions of dissociation scores. The preliminary results suggest the possible existence of a latent dissociative type or taxon that may mark a different psychological organization with respect to the integration of self and behavior. Although this remains to be proven, the broader recognition that high levels of dissociation seem to lead to qualitatively different types of responses to standard stimuli has led to laboratory experiments in which subjects are divided into high and low dissociative groups. Cognitive experimental tasks can be devised such that high dissociative individuals perform significantly better than normal individuals. Likewise, experimental tasks can be constructed in which high dissociative individuals perform more poorly than normal controls. In these experiments, the critical difference between the two tasks is the subject's focus of attention, with dissociative subjects performing poorly on selective attention tasks but superiorly on dual attention tasks. A similar high-low division strategy with clinical samples such as rape victims has demonstrated that highly dissociative individuals manifest significantly different physiological responses to experimental stimuli that are reminiscent of the original trauma. In this case, they typically show a decrease in sympathetic arousal in the face of stressors, while nonetheless experiencing significant subjective distress. Future research should both expand our understanding of the range of cognitive and physiological differences associated with high levels of dissociation and further elucidate their underlying neurobiological mechanisms.

Dissociation scales such as the DES and PDEQ were central to the documentation that antecedent traumatic experiences are highly related to increased levels of dissociation, both acutely and chronically. The set of cognitive and psychophysiological responses to experimental stimuli exhibited by high dissociative patients can be profitably compared with low dissociative subjects with and without PTSD. These and other contrasts will be important in better characterizing the range of human responses to trauma of all kinds. Comparison of high and low dissociative subjects on various indices of trauma severity as well as age/developmental stage and other factors should help identify some of the missing variance in our understanding of what makes a given experience traumatic.

Incorporation of dissociation measures into longitudinal studies will permit us to follow its operation across development and identify susceptible periods that may also represent opportunities for intervention. Within a given diagnostic group, for example, Borderline Personality Disorder or Somatization Disorder, dividing subjects into high and low dissociative groups may yield critical evidence about responses to treatment and help to clarify why certain patients fail to improve with standard therapies. A baseline evaluation with follow-up monitoring of dissociation over the course of treatment may provide an important marker of clinical improvement or deterioration for clinicians. Experimental studies with dissociogenic drugs such as ketamine point to pharmacologically responsive neurobiological substrates that may ultimately prove to be targets for antidissociative medications. We have reached a stage in our understanding of dissociation when we can test more systematic approaches to treatment than the roughly staged psychodynamic psychotherapy that is the current mainstay.

Developmentally, the discovery that attachment disorders, especially Type D attachment, predict long-term dissociation levels has opened up a fertile area of scientific investigation. The strong relationship between Type D attachment and maltreatment, in turn, completes a loop linking the two factors that predict the most variance in long-term levels of dissociation. Much remains to be sorted out here in terms of developmental sequences and a myriad of interactions with other variables, but, unlike many other psychiatric conditions, in the case of dissociation there is a strong early developmental marker, Type D attachment, that can be traced forward. Current child and adolescent dissociation measures are sufficiently psychometrically sound and concordant to allow us to confidently follow dissociative trajectories in long-term longitudinal studies and assess their contribution to a range of psychopathology.

The preliminary results indicating that dissociation acts as an important mediating factor for the transduction of traumatic experience into maladaptive symptoms and behavior are congruent with a wide array of cross-sectional studies linking elevated levels of dissociation to broadly increased psychopathology in clinical and non-clinical samples. Dissociation is most strongly correlated with externalizing behavior problems, sexual behavioral problems, and somatization in children. Many studies demonstrate that increased externalizing behavioral problems are associated with deviant life trajectories and negative outcomes. By adolescence, revictimization and self-harmful behaviors become increasingly linked to dissociation, indicating its deleterious impact on the development of a stable and healthy sense of self. The developmental theory proposed for the DID/taxon model is predicated on the belief that pathological levels of dissociation beginning early in life and operating across sensitive developmental periods produce a distinctly different type of psychological organization of self compared to low dissociative individuals. This theoretical model remains to be proven, but it is sufficiently well supported to provide a solid basis for the formulation of testable hypotheses.

Pathological dissociation has been included in the enigmatic category of an "experiment of nature," in which scientific knowledge is gained through the suffering of individuals with a unique injury or illness that offers insight into the underlying workings of mind or body. Perhaps dissociation is more properly analogized to the Rosetta stone, which enabled the translation of silent hieroglyphics into a living language, thereby unlocking the latent information within the symbols. Dissociation is robustly connected to fundamental developmental antecedents and long-term psychopathological outcomes. Its developmental impact can be detected in cognition, memory, psychophysiology, neurobiology, and behavior. The relatively doable process of tracing these pathways in longitudinal studies offers enormous opportunities to understand fundamental mind-body-behavior questions across multiple levels of scientific inquiry. Few other psychological processes have been shown to exhibit such a profound range of correlations and effects on body and behavior. Our ability to identify markers of increased dissociation across methodological levels ranging from fMRI scans to cognition performance to psychophysiological reactivity to specific psychopathology offers an extraordinary opportunity to translate bodies of knowledge at one level of scientific inquiry to other levels. In doing so, much latent information should be revealed. It is this sense of possibility that is stimulating a growing interest in dissociation as a unique example of developmental psychopathology that offers to help reveal the causal linkages between early caretaking and environmental aversive experiences with adult psychopathology.

REFERENCES

Ackner, B. (1954a). Depersonalization: I. Aetiology and phenomenology. *Journal of Mental Science, 100,* 838–853.

Ackner, B. (1954b). Depersonalization: II. Clinical syndromes. *Journal of Mental Science, 100,* 854–872.

Aderibigbe, Y. A., Bloch, R. M., & Walker, W. R. (2001). Prevalence of depersonalization and derealization experiences in a rural population. *Social Psychiatry and Psychiatric Epidemiology, 36,* 63–69.

Ainsworth, M. D. S., Blehar, M. C., Waters, E., & Wall, S. (1978). *Patterns of attachment: A psychological study of the Strange Situation.* Hillsdale, NJ: Erlbaum.

Allen, J. G., Fultz, J., Huntoon, J., & Brethour, J. R. (2002). Pathological dissociative taxon membership, absorption and reported childhood trauma in women with trauma-related disorders. *Journal of Trauma and Dissociation, 3,* 89–110.

Allen, J. J. B., & Movius, H. L. (2000). The objective assessment of amnesia in dissociative identity disorder using event-related potentials. *International Journal of Psychophysiology, 38,* 21–41.

Alvarado, C. S. (1989). Dissociation and state-specific psychophysiology during the nineteenth century. *Dissociation, 2,* 160–168.

American Psychiatric Association. (1952). *Diagnostic and statistical manual of mental disorders.* Washington, DC: Author.

American Psychiatric Association. (1994). *Diagnostic and statistical manual of mental disorders* (4th ed.). Washington, DC: Author.

American Psychiatric Association. (2000). *Diagnostic and statistical manual of mental disorders* (4th ed., text rev.). Washington, DC: Author.

Andersen, H. S., Sestoft, D., & Lillebaek, T. (2001). Ganser syndrome after solitary confinement in prison: A short review and case report. *Nordic Journal of Psychiatry, 55,* 199–201.

Armstrong, J. G. (1996). Psychological assessment. In J. L. Spira (Ed.), *Treating dissociative identity disorder* (pp. 3–38). San Francisco: Jossey-Bass.

Armstrong, J. G., & Loewenstein, R. J. (1990). Characteristics of patients with multiple personality and dissociative disorders on psychological testing. *Journal of Nervous and Mental Diseases, 178,* 448–454.

Armstrong, J. G., Putnam, F. W., Carlson, E. B., Libero, D. Z., & Smith, S. R. (1997). Development and validation of a measure of adolescent dissociation: The Adolescent Dissociative Experiences Scale (A-DES). *Journal of Nervous and Mental Diseases, 185*(8), 491–497.

Babinski, J. (1901). Définition de l'hystérie. *Revue Neurologique, 9,* 1074–1080.

Babinski, J. (1909). Démembrement de l'hystérie traditionelle. *La Semaine Médicale, 59,* 3–8.

Barach, P. M. (1991). Multiple personality as an attachment disorder. *Dissociation, 4,* 117–123.

Barnett, D., Ganiban, J., & Cicchetti, D. (1999). Maltreatment, negative expressivity, and the development of Type D attachments from 12 to 24 months of age. *Monographs of the Society for Research in Child Development, 64,* 97–118.

Baron, R. M., & Kenny, D. A. (1986). The moderator-mediator variable distinction in social psychological research: Conceptual, strategic and statistical considerations. *Journal of Personality and Social Psychology, 51,* 1173–1182.

Becker-Blease, K., Deater-Deckard, K., Eley, T., Freyd, J. J., Stevenson, J., & Plomin, R. (2004). A genetic analysis of individual differences in dissociative behaviors in childhood and adolescence. *Journal of Child Psychology and Psychiatry, 45,* 522–532.

Becker-Lausen, E., Sanders, B., & Chinsky, J. M. (1995). Mediation of abusive childhood experiences: Depression, dissociation, and negative life outcomes. *American Journal of Orthopsychiatry, 65,* 560–573.

Bernstein, E., & Putnam, F. W. (1986). Development, reliability and validity of a dissociation scale. *Journal of Nervous and Mental Diseases, 174,* 727–735.

Bonanno, G., Noll, J. G., Putnam, F. W., O'Neill, M., & Trickett, P. K. (2003). Predicting the willingness to disclose childhood sexual abuse from measures of repressive coping and dissociative tendencies. *Child Maltreatment, 8*(4), 302–318.

Boon, S., & Draijer, N. (1993). Multiple personality disorder in the Netherlands: A clinical investigation of 71 patients. *American Journal of Psychiatry, 150,* 489–494.

Bremner, J. D., Davis, M., Southwick, S. M., Krystal, J. H., & Charney, D. S. (1993). Neurobiology of posttraumatic stress disorder. In J. M. Oldham, M. B. Riba, & A. Tasman (Eds.), *Review of psychiatry* (Vol. 12, pp. 183–205). Washington, DC: American Psychiatric Press.

Bremner, J. D., Krystal, J. H., Putnam, F. W., Southwick, S. M., Marmar, C., Charney, D. S., et al. (1998). Measurement of dissociative states with the Clinician-Administered Dissociative States Scale (CADSS). *Journal of Traumatic Stress, 11,* 125–136.

Bremner, J. D., Krystal, J. H., Southwick, S. M., & Charney, D. S. (1995). Functional neuroanatomical correlates of the effects of stress on memory. *Journal of Traumatic Stress, 8,* 527–553.

Breuer, J., & Freud, S. (1957). *Studies on hysteria.* New York: Basic Books.

Brosky, B., & Lally, S. (2004). Prevalence of trauma, PTSD, and dissociation in court-referred adolescents. *Journal of Interpersonal Violence, 19,* 801–814.

Brunner, R., Parzer, P., Schuld, V., & Resch, F. (2000). Dissociative symptomatology and traumatogenic factors in adolescent psychiatric patients. *Journal of Nervous and Mental Diseases, 188,* 71–77.

Calamari, E., & Pini, M. (2003). Dissociative experiences and anger proneness in late adolescent females with different attachment styles. *Adolescence, 38,* 287–303.

Carlson, E. A. (1998). A prospective longitudinal study of attachment disorganization/disorientation. *Child Development, 69,* 1107–1128.

Carlson, E. B., & Armstrong, J. G. (1994). The diagnosis and assessment of dissociative disorders. In S. J. Lynn & J. W. Rhue (Eds.), *Dissociation: Clinical and theoretical perspectives* (pp. 159–174). New York: Guilford Press.

Carlson, E. B., & Putnam, F. W. (1993). An update on the Dissociative Experiences Scale. *Dissociation, 6,* 16–27.

Carlson, V., Cicchetti, D., Barnett, D., & Braunwald, K. (1989). Disorganized/disoriented attachment relationships in maltreated infants. *Developmental Psychology, 25,* 525–531.

Carrion, V. G., & Steiner, H. (2000). Trauma and dissociation in delinquent adolescents. *Journal of the American Academy of Child and Adolescent Psychiatry, 39,* 353–359.

Chambers, R. A., Bremner, J. D., Moghaddam, B., Southwick, S. M., Charney, D. S., & Krystal, J. H. (1999). Glutamate and post-traumatic stress disorder: Toward a psychobiology of dissociation. *Seminars in Clinical Neuropsychiatry, 4,* 274–281.

Charney, D. S., Deutch, A. Y., Krystal, J. H., Southwick, S. M., & Davis, M. (1993). Psychobiological mechanisms of posttraumatic stress disorder. *Archives of General Psychiatry, 50,* 294–305.

Choe, B. M., & Kluft, R. P. (1995). The use of the DES in studying treatment outcome with dissociative identity disorder: A pilot study. *Dissociation, 8,* 160–164.

Cohen, J., Deblinger, E., Mannarino, A., & Steer, R. (2004). A multisite, randomized controlled trial for children with sexual abuse-related PTSD symptoms. *Journal of the American Academy of Child and Adolescent Psychiatry, 43,* 393–402.

Coons, P. M. (1986). Treatment progress in 20 patients with multiple personality disorder. *Journal of Nervous and Mental Diseases, 174*(12), 715–721.

Coons, P. M. (1994). Confirmation of childhood abuse in child and adolescent cases of multiple personality disorder and dissociative disorder not otherwise specified. *Journal of Nervous and Mental Diseases, 182*(8), 461–464.

Coons, P. M., Bowman, E. S., Kluft, R. P., & Milstein, V. (1991). The cross-cultural occurrence of MPD: Additional cases from a recent survey. *Dissociation, 4,* 124–128.

De Bellis, M. D., Keshavan, M. S., Clark, D. B., Casey, B. J., Giedd, J. N., Boring, A. M., et al. (1999). Developmental traumatology: Pt. II. Brain development. *Biological Psychiatry, 45,* 1271–1284.

Delahanty, D. L., Royer, D. K., Raimonde, A. J., & Spoonster, E. (2003). Peritraumatic dissociation is inversely related to catecholamine levels in initial urine samples of motor vehicle accident victims. *Journal of Trauma and Dissociation, 4,* 65–80.

Dell, P. F., & Eisenhower, J. W. (1990). Adolescent multiple personality disorder: A preliminary study of eleven cases. *Journal of the American Academy of Child and Adolescent Psychiatry, 29,* 359–366.

DePrince, A. P., & Freyd, J. J. (1999). Dissociative tendencies, attention, and memory. *Psychological Science, 10,* 449–452.

DePrince, A. P., & Freyd, J. J. (2001). Memory and dissociative tendencies: The roles of attentional context and word meaning in a directed forgetting task. *Journal of Trauma and Dissociation, 2,* 67–82.

Despine, A. (1840). *De l'emploi du magnétisme animal et des eaux minérales dans le traitment des maladies nervveuses, suivi d'une observation tres curieuse de nevropathie.* Paris: Baillière.

Devinsky, O., Putnam, F. W., Grafman, J., Bromfield, E., & Theodore, W. H. (1989). Dissociative states and epilepsy. *Neurology, 39,* 835–840.

Dorahy, M. J. (2001). Dissociative identity disorder and memory dysfunction: The current state of experimental research and its future directions. *Clinical Psychology Review, 5,* 771–795.

Dugas, L. (1898). Un cas de dépersonnalisation (M. Sierrs & G. E. Berrios, Trans. & Introduced, 1996). *History of psychiatry, 7,* 451–461.

Eich, E., Macaulay, D., Loewenstein, R. J., & Dihle, P. H. (1997). Memory, amnesia, and dissociative identity disorder. *Psychological Science, 8,* 417–422.

Ellason, J. W., & Ross, C. A. (1997). Two-year follow-up of inpatients with dissociative identity disorder. *American Journal of Psychiatry, 154,* 832–839.

Ellason, J. W., Ross, C. A., & Fuchs, D. (1996). Lifetime Axis I and II comorbidity and childhood trauma history in dissociative identity disorder. *Psychiatry, 59,* 255–266.

Ellenberger, H. F. (1970). *The discovery of the unconscious: The history and evolution of dynamic psychiatry.* New York: Basic Books.

Farrington, A., Waller, G., Neiderman, M., Sutton, V., Chopping, J., & Lask, B. (2002). Dissociation in adolescent girls with anorexia: Relationship to comorbid psychopathology. *Journal of Nervous and Mental Diseases, 190,* 746–751.

Fehon, D. C., Grilo, C. M., & Lipschitz, D. S. (2001). Correlates of community violence exposure in hospitalized adolescents. *Comprehensive Psychiatry, 42*(4), 283–290.

Ferracuti, S., & DeMarco, M. (2004). Ritual homicide during dissociative trance disorder. *International Journal of Offender Therapy and Comparative Criminology, 48,* 59–64.

Foa, E. B., Keane, T. M., & Friedman, M. J. (Eds.). (2000). *Effective treatments for PTSD.* New York: Guilford Press.

Friedrich, W., Gerber, P., Koplin, B., Davis, M., Giese, J., Mykelbust, C., et al. (2001). Multimodal assessment of dissociation in adolescents: Inpatients and juvenile sex offenders. *Sex Abuse, 13,* 167–177.

Galanter, M. (1982). Charismatic religious sects and psychiatry: An overview. *American Journal of Psychiatry, 139,* 1539–1548.

Ganser, S. J. M. (1898). Über einen eigenartigen hysterischen Dämmerzustand. *Archiv für Psychiatrie und Nervenkrankheiten, Berlin, 30.*

Gleaves, D., & Eberenz, K. (1995). Assessing dissociative symptoms in eating disordered patients: Construct validation of two self-report measures. *International Journal of Eating Disorders, 18,* 99–102.

Goodman, G. S., Ghetti, S., Quas, J. A., Edelstein, R. S., Alexander, K. W., Redlich, A. D., et al. (2003). A prospective study of memory for child sexual abuse: New findings relevant to the repressed-memory controversy. *Psychological Science, 14,* 113–118.

Gratz, K., Conrad, S., & Roemer, L. (2002). Risk factors for deliberate self-harm among college students. *American Journal of Orthopsychiatry, 72,* 128–140.

Green, J., & Goldwyn, R. (2002). Annotation: Attachment disorganisation and psychopathology: New findings in attachment research and their potential implications for developmental psychopathology in childhood. *Journal of Child Psychology and Psychiatry, 43,* 835–846.

Griffin, M. G., Resick, P. A., & Mechanic, M. B. (1997). Objective assessment of peritraumatic dissociation: Psychophysiological indicators. *American Journal of Psychiatry, 154,* 1081–1088.

Hale, N. G. (Ed.). (1975). *Morton Prince: Psychotherapy and multiple personality.* Cambridge, MA: Harvard University Press.

Hartt, J., & Waller, G. (2002). Child abuse, dissociation, and core beliefs in bulimic disorders. *Child Abuse and Neglect, 26,* 923–938.

Hertsgaard, L., Gunnar, M., Erickson, M. F., & Nachmias, M. (1995). Adrenocortical responses to the Strange Situation in infants with disorganized/disoriented attachment relationships. *Child Development, 66,* 1100–1106.

Hesse, E., & Main, M. (2000). Disorganized infant, child, and adult attachment: Collapse in behavioral and attentional strategies. *Journal of the American Psychoanalytic Association, 48,* 1097–1127.

Hollander, E., Carrasco, J. L., Mullen, L. S., Trungold, S., DeCaria, C. M., & Towey, J. (1992). Left hemispheric activation in depersonalization disorder: A case report. *Biological Psychiatry, 31*(11), 1157–1162.

Hollander, E., Liebowitz, M. R., DeCaria, C., Fairbanks, J., Fallon, B., & Klein, D. F. (1990). Treatment of depersonalization with serotonin reuptake blockers. *Journal of Clinical Psychopharmacology, 10,* 200–203.

Hollander, E., Stein, D. J., DeCaria, C. M., Cohen, L., Saoud, J. B., Skodol, A. E., et al. (1994). Serotonergic sensitivity in borderline personality disorder: Preliminary findings. *American Journal of Psychiatry, 151*(2), 277–280.

Hopper, A., Ciorciari, J., Johnson, G., Spensley, J., Sergejew, A., & Stough, C. (2002). EEG coherence and dissociative identity disorder: Comparing EEG coherence in DID hosts, alters, controls and acted alters. *Journal of Trauma and Dissociation, 3,* 75–88.

Hornstein, N., & Putnam, F. W. (1992). Clinical phenomenology of child and adolescent dissociative disorders. *Journal of the American Academy of Child and Adolescent Psychiatry, 31,* 1077–1085.

James, W. (1890). *Principles of psychology.* New York: Henry Holt.

Janet, P. (1890). *The Major Symptoms of Hysteria.* New York: Macmillan.

Kaplan, H. I., & Sadock, B. J. (1991). *Comprehensive glossary of psychiatry and psychology.* Baltimore: Williams & Wilkins.

Kaplow, J., Dodge, K., Amaya-Jackson, L., & Saxe, G. N. (2005). Pathways to PTSD: Pt. II. Sexually abused children. *American Journal of Psychiatry, 162,* 1305–1310.

Keck-Seeley, S., Perosa, S., & Perosa, L. (2004). A validation study of the Adolescent Dissociative Experiences Scale. *Child Abuse and Neglect, 28,* 755–769.

Kisiel, C. L., & Lyons, J. S. (2001). Dissociation as a mediator of psychopathology among sexually abused children and adolescents. *American Journal of Psychiatry, 158,* 1034–1039.

Kluft, R. P. (1984a). Multiple personality in childhood. *Psychiatric Clinics of North America, 7*(1), 121–134.

Kluft, R. P. (1984b). Treatment of multiple personality disorder: A study of 33 cases. *Psychiatric Clinics of North America, 7*(1), 9–29.

Kluft, R. P. (1987). First-rank symptoms as a diagnostic clue to multiple personality disorder. *American Journal of Psychiatry, 144,* 293–298.

Kluft, R. P. (1988). The postunification treatment of multiple personality disorder: First findings. *American Journal of Psychotherapy, 62,* 212–228.

Koopman, C., Carrion, V., Butler, L., Sudhaker, S., Palmer, L., & Steiner, H. (2004). Relationships of dissociation and childhood abuse and neglect with heart rate in delinquent adolescents. *Journal of Traumatic Stress, 17,* 47–54.

Krystal, J. H., Bennett, A. L., Bremner, D. J., Southwick, S. M., & Charney, D. S. (1995). Towards a cognitive neuroscience of dissociation and altered memory function in post-traumatic stress disorder. In M. J. Friedman, D. S. Charney, & A. Y. Deutch (Eds.), *Neurobiological and clinical consequences of stress: From normal adaptation to post-traumatic stress disorder* (pp. 239–269). Philadelphia: Lippincott-Raven.

Krystal, J. H., Karper, L. P., Seibyl, J. P., Freeman, G. K., Delaney, R., Bremner, J. D., et al. (1994). Subanesthetic effects of the noncompetitive NMDA antagonist, ketamine, in humans: Psychotomimetic, perceptual, cognitive, and neuroendocrine responses. *Archives of General Psychiatry, 51,* 199–214.

Lanius, R. A., Bluhm, R., Lanius, U., & Pain, C. (in press). Neuroimaging of hyperarousal and dissociation in PTSD: Heterogeneity of response to symptom provocation. *Psychopharmacology Bulletin.*

Lanius, R. A., Hopper, A., & Menon, R. S. (2003). Individual differences in a husband and wife who develop PTSD after a motor vehicle accident: A functional MRI case study. *American Journal of Psychiatry, 160,* 667–669.

Lanius, R. A., Williamson, P. C., Boksman, K., Densmore, M., Gupta, M., Neufeld, R. W. J., et al. (2002). Brain activation during script-driven imagery induced dissociative responses in PTSD: A functional magnetic resonance imaging investigation. *Biological Psychiatry, 52,* 305–311.

Lanius, R. A., Williamson, P. C., Densmore, M., Boksman, K., Neufeld, R. W. J., Gati, J. S., et al. (2004). The nature of traumatic memories: A 4-T fMRI functional connectivity analysis. *American Journal of Psychiatry, 161,* 36–44.

Lanius, R. A., Williamson, P. C., Hopper, J., Densmore, M., Boksman, K., Madhulika, A., et al. (2003). Recall of emotional states in post-traumatic stress disorder: An fMRI investigation. *Biological Psychiatry, 53,* 204–210.

Larmore, K., Ludwig, A. M., & Cain, R. L. (1977). Multiple personality: An objective case study. *British Journal of Psychiatry, 131,* 35–40.

Lee, M. A., & Shlain, B. (1992). *Acid dreams: The complete social history of LSD: The CIA, the sixties, and beyond.* New York: Grove Press.

Leonard, K., Telch, M., & Harrington, P. (1999). Dissociation in the laboratory: A comparison of strategies. *Behaviour Research and Therapy, 37,* 49–61.

Lewis, D. O., Yeager, C. A., Swica, Y., Pincus, J. H., & Lewis, M. (1997). Objective documentation of child abuse and dissociation in 12 murderers with dissociative identity disorder. *American Journal of Psychiatry, 154,* 1703–1710.

Lewis-Fernandez, R., Garrido-Castillo, P., Bennasar, M. C., Parrilla, E. M., Laria, A. J., Guoguang, M., et al. (2002). Dissociation, childhood trauma, and ataque de nervios among Puerto Rican psychiatric outpatients. *American Journal of Psychiatry, 159,* 1603–1605.

Liotti, G. (1992). Disorganization of attachment as a model for understanding dissociative pathology. *Dissociation, 5,* 196–204.

Loewenstein, R. J. (1994). Diagnosis, epidemiology, clinical course, treatment, and cost effectiveness of treatment for dissociative disorders and Multiple Personality Disorder: Report submitted to the Clinton administration task force on health care financing reform. *Dissociation, 7,* 3–11.

Ludwig, A. M. (1983). The psychobiological functions of dissociation. *American Journal of Clinical Hypnosis, 26,* 93–99.

Ludwig, A. M., Brandsma, J. M., Wilbur, C. B., Bendfeldt, F., & Jameson, D. H. (1972). The objective study of a multiple personality. *Archives of General Psychiatry, 26,* 298–310.

Lyons-Ruth, K., Alpern, L., & Repacholi, B. (1993). Disorganized infant attachment classification and maternal psychological problems as predictors of hostile-aggressive behavior in the preschool classroom. *Child Development, 64,* 572–585.

Lyubomirsky, S., Casper, R. C., & Soursa, L. U. (2001). What triggers abnormal eating in bulimic and nonbulimic women? The role of dissociative experiences, negative affect, and psychopathology. *Psychology of Women Quarterly, 25,* 223–232.

Macfie, J., Cicchetti, D., & Toth, S. L. (2001a). The development of dissociation in maltreated preschool-aged children. *Development and Psychopathology, 13,* 233–254.

Macfie, J., Cicchetti, D., & Toth, S. L. (2001b). Dissociation in maltreated versus nonmaltreated preschool-aged children. *Child Abuse and Neglect, 25,* 1253–1267.

Main, M., & Hesse, E. (1990). Parents' unresolved traumatic experiences are related to infant disorganized attachment status: Is frightened and/or frightening parental behavior the linking mechanism? In M. T. Greenberg, D. Cicchetti, & E. M. Cummings (Eds.), *Attachment in the preschool years* (pp. 161–182). Chicago: University of Chicago Press.

Main, M., & Morgan, H. (1996). Disorganization and disorientation in infant Strange Situation behavior: Phenotypic resemblance to dissociative states. In L. Michelson & W. Ray (Eds.), *Handbook of dissociation: Theoretical, empirical and clinical perspectives* (pp. 107–138). New York: Plenum Press.

Main, M., & Solomon, J. (1986). Discovery of an insecure-disorganized/disoriented attachment pattern. In T. Brazelton & M. Yogman (Eds.), *Affective development in infancy* (pp. 95–124). Westport, CT: Ablex.

Marmar, C. R., Weiss, D. S., Schlenger, W. E., Fairbank, J. A., Jordan, B. K., Kulka, R. A., et al. (1994). Peritraumatic dissociation and posttraumatic stress in male Vietnam theater veterans. *American Journal of Psychiatry, 151*(6), 902–907.

Mathew, R., Wilson, W., Chiu, N., Turkington, T., Degrado, T., & Coleman, R. (1999). Regional cerebral blood flow and depersonalization after tetrahydrocannabinol administration. *Acta Psychiatrica Scandinavica, 100,* 67–75.

Matsumoto, T., Azekawa, T., Yamaguchi, A., Asami, T., & Iseki, E. (2004). Habitual self-mutilation in Japan. *Psychiatry and Clinical Neurosciences, 58,* 191–198.

McHugh, P., & Putnam, F. (1995). Resolved: Multiple personality disorder is an individually and socially created artifact. *Journal of the American Academy of Child and Adolescent Psychiatry, 34,* 957–963.

Menninger, W. (1945). Psychiatry and the war. *Atlantic, 176,* 107–114.

Middleton, W., & Butler, J. (1998). Dissociative identity disorder: An Australian series. *Australian and New Zealand Journal of Psychiatry, 32,* 794–804.

Molko vs. Holy Spirit Association for the Unification of World Christianity, 224 Cal. Rptr. 817, 825 (Cal. Ct. App. 1st Dist., rev'd in part, 46 Cal. 3d 1092, 1988, cert. denied, 490 U.S. 1084, 1989).

Morgan, C. A., Hazlett, G., Wang, S., Richardson, E. G., Schnurr, P., & Southwick, S. M. (2001). Symptoms of dissociation in humans experiencing acute, uncontrollable stress: A prospective investigation. *American Journal of Psychiatry, 158,* 1239–1247.

Morgan, C. A., Rasmusson, A. M., Wang, S., Hoyt, G., Hauger, R. L., & Hazlett, G. (2002). Neuropeptide-Y, cortisol, and subjective distress in humans exposed to acute stress: Replication and extension of previous report. *Biological Psychiatry, 52,* 136–142.

Narang, D. S., & Contreras, J. M. (2000). Dissociation as a mediator between child abuse history and adult abuse potential. *Child Abuse and Neglect, 24,* 653–665.

Nijenhuis, E. R. S. (1999). *Somatoform dissociation: Phenomena, measurement, and theoretical issues.* Assen, The Netherlands: Van Gorcum.

Noll, J. G., Horowitz, L. A., Bonanno, G. A., Trickett, P. K., & Putnam, F. W. (2003). Revictimization and self-harm in females who experienced childhood sexual abuse. *Journal of Interpersonal Violence, 18*(12), 1452–1471.

Offen, L., Thomas, G., & Waller, G. (2003). Dissociation as a mediator of the relationship between recalled parenting and the clinical correlates of auditory hallucinations. *British Journal of Clinical Psychology, 42,* 231–241.

Ogawa, J. R., Sroufe, L. A., Weinfield, N. S., Carlson, E. A., & Egeland, B. (1997). Development and the fragmented self: Longitudinal study of dissociative symptomatology in a nonclinical sample. *Development and Psychopathology, 9,* 855–879.

Ozer, E. J., Best, S. R., Lipsey, T. L., & Weiss, D. S. (2003). Predictors of posttraumatic stress disorder and symptoms in adults: A meta-analysis. *Psychological Bulletin, 129,* 52–73.

Paul, T., Schroeter, K., Dahme, B., & Nutzinger, D. O. (2002). Self-injurious behavior in women with eating disorders. *American Journal of Psychiatry, 159,* 408–411.

Peters, M. L., Uyterlinde, S. A., Consemulder, J., & van der Hart, O. (1998). Apparent amnesia on experimental memory tests in dissociative identity disorder: An exploratory study. *Consciousness and Cognition, 7,* 27–41.

Peterson, G., & Putnam, F. W. (1994). Preliminary results of the field trial of proposed criteria for dissociative disorder of childhood. *Dissociation, 7,* 212–220.

Plattner, B., Silverman, M., Redlich, A. D., Carrion, V. G., Feucht, M., Friedrich, M., et al. (2003). Pathways to dissociation: Intrafamilial versus extrafamilial trauma in juvenile delinquents. *Journal of Nervous and Mental Diseases, 191,* 781–788.

Prince, M., & Peterson, F. (1908). Experiments in psychogalvanic reactions from co-conscious ideal in a case of multiple personality. *Journal of Abnormal Psychology, 3,* 114–131.

Prohl, J., Resch, F., Parzer, P., & Brunner, R. (2001). Relationship between dissociative symptomatology and declarative and procedural memory in adolescent psychiatric patients. *Journal of Nervous and Mental Diseases, 189,* 602–607.

Putnam, F. W. (1985). Dissociation as a response to extreme trauma. In R. P. Kluft (Ed.), *Childhood antecedents of multiple personality* (pp. 66–97). Washington, DC: American Psychiatric Press.

Putnam, F. W. (1989). Pierre Janet and modern views of dissociation. *Journal of Traumatic Stress, 2*(4), 413–429.

Putnam, F. W. (1991). Recent research on multiple personality disorder. *Psychiatric Clinics of North America, 14,* 489–502.

Putnam, F. W. (1997). *Dissociation in children and adolescents: A developmental perspective.* New York: Guilford Press.

Putnam, F. W., & Carlson, E. B. (1998). Hypnosis, dissociation and trauma: Myths, metaphors and mechanisms. In J. D. Bremner & C. Marmar (Eds.), *Trauma, memory, and dissociation* (pp. 29–60). Washington, DC: American Psychiatric Press.

Putnam, F. W., Carlson, E. B., Ross, C. A., Anderson, G., Clark, P., Torem, M., et al. (1996). Patterns of dissociation in clinical and nonclinical samples. *Journal of Nervous and Mental Diseases, 184,* 673–679.

Putnam, F. W., Hornstein, N. L., & Peterson, G. (1996). Clinical phenomenology of child and adolescent dissociative disorders: Gender and age effects. *Child and Adolescent Psychiatric Clinics of North America, 5*(2), 351–360.

Reinders, A., Nijenhuis, E., Paans, A., Korf, J., Willemsen, A., & den Boer, J. (2003). One brain, two selves. *Neuroimage, 20,* 2119–2125.

Ribot, T. (1882). *Diseases of memory.* London: Kegan, Paul, Trench, & Co.

Rosen, E., & Petty, L. (1994). Dissociative states and disordered eating. *American Journal of Clinical Hypnosis, 36,* 266–275.

Ross, C. A. (1989). *Multiple personality disorder: Diagnosis, clinical features and treatment.* New York: Wiley.

Ross, C. A., & Dua, V. (1993). Psychiatric health care costs of multiple personality disorder. *American Journal of Psychotherapy, 47*(1), 103–112.

Ross, C. A., & Ellason, J. W. (1998). Treatment outcome for dissociative identity disorder. *American Journal of Psychiatry, 155*(9), 1304–1305.

Ross, C. A., Heber, S., Norton, G. R., Anderson, D., Anderson, G., & Barchet, P. (1989). The Dissociative Disorders Interview Schedule: A structured interview. *Dissociation, 2,* 169–189.

Ross, C. A., Joshi, S., & Currie, R. (1989). Dissociative experiences in the general population. *American Journal of Psychiatry, 147,* 1547–1552.

Ross-Gower, J., Waller, G., Tyson, M., & Elliott, P. (1998). Reported sexual abuse and subsequent psychopathology among women attending psychology clinics: The mediating role of dissociation. *British Journal of Clinical Psychology, 37,* 313–326.

Sanders, B., & Becker-Lausen, E. (1995). The measurement of psychological maltreatment: Early data on the Child Abuse and Trauma Scale. *Child Abuse and Neglect, 19,* 315–323.

Sanders, B., & Giolas, M. (1991). Dissociation and childhood trauma in psychologically disturbed adolescents. *American Journal of Psychiatry, 148,* 50–54.

Sar, V., Akyuz, G., Kundakci, T., Kiziltan, E., & Dogan, O. (2004). Childhood trauma, dissociation, and psychiatric comorbidity in patients with conversion disorder. *American Journal of Psychiatry, 161,* 2271–2276.

Sar, V., Unal, S. N., Kiziltan, E., Kundakci, T., & Ozturk, E. (2001). HMPAO SPECT study of regional cerebral blood flow in dissociative identity disorder. *Journal of Trauma and Dissociation, 2,* 5–25.

Sar, V., Yargic, L. I., & Tutkun, H. (1996). Structured interview data on 35 cases of dissociative identity disorder in Turkey. *American Journal of Psychiatry, 153,* 1329–1333.

Saxe, G. N., Chawla, N., & van der Kolk, B. A. (2002). Self-destructive behavior in patients with dissociative disorders. *Suicide and Life-Threatening Behavior, 32,* 313–320.

Saxe, G. N., Vasile, R., Hill, T., Bloomingdale, K., & van der Kolk, B. A. (1992). SPECT imaging and multiple personality disorder. *Journal of Nervous and Mental Diseases, 180,* 662–663.

Schechter, D. S., Marshall, R., Salman, E., Goetz, D., Davies, S., & Liebowitz, M. R. (2000). Ataque de nervios and history of childhood trauma. *Journal of Traumatic Stress, 13,* 529–534.

Schilder, P. (1939). The treatment of depersonalization. *Bulletin of New York Academy of Medicine, 15,* 258–272.

Schuengel, C., Bakers-Kranenburg, M. J., & van Ijzendoorn, M. H. (1999). Frightening maternal behavior linking unresolved loss and disorganized infant attachment. *Journal of Consulting and Clinical Psychology, 67,* 54–63.

Seedat, S., Stein, M. B., & Forde, D. R. (2003). Prevalence of dissociative experiences in a community sample: Relationship to gender, ethnicity, and substance use. *Journal of Nervous and Mental Diseases, 191,* 115–120.

Silberg, J. (Ed.). (1996a). *The dissociative child: Diagnosis, treatment, and management.* Lutherville, MD: Sidran Press.

Silberg, J. (1996b). Psychological testing with dissociative children and adolescents. In J. Silberg (Ed.), *The dissociative child* (pp. 85–102). Lutherville, MD: Sidran Press.

Silberg, J. (2000a). Fifteen years of dissociation in maltreated children: Where do we go from here? *Child Maltreatment, 5,* 119–136.

Silberg, J. (2000b). Guidelines for the evaluation and treatment of dissociative symptoms in children and adolescents. *Journal of Trauma and Dissociation, 1,* 105–134.

Silberman, E. K., Putnam, F. W., Weingartner, H., Braun, B. G., & Post, R. M. (1985). Dissociative states in multiple personality disorder: A quantitative study. *Psychiatry Research, 15,* 253–260.

Simeon, D., Gross, S., Guralnik, O., Stein, D. J., Schmeidler, J., & Hollander, E. (1997). Feeling unreal: 30 cases of DSM-III-R depersonalization disorder. *American Journal of Psychiatry, 154,* 1107–1113.

Simeon, D., Guralnik, O., Hazlett, E. A., Spiegel-Cohen, J., Hollander, E., & Buchsbaum, M. S. (2000). Feeling unreal: A PET study of depersonalization disorder. *American Journal of Psychiatry, 157,* 1782–1788.

Simeon, D., Guralnik, O., Knutelska, M., Yehuda, R., & Schmeidler, J. (2003). Basal-norepinephrine in depersonalization disorder. *Psychiatry Research, 121*(1), 93–97.

Simeon, D., & Hollander, E. (1993). Depersonalization disorder. *Psychiatric Annals, 23,* 382–388.

Somer, E. (2002). Posttraumatic dissociation as a mediator of the effects of trauma on distressful introspectiveness. *Social Behavior and Personality, 30,* 671–682.

Spinelli, M. (2001). A systematic investigation of 16 cases of neonaticide. *American Journal of Psychiatry, 158,* 811–813.

Stein, M. B., Koverola, C., Hanna, C., Torchia, M. G., & McClarty, B. (1997). Hippocampal volume in women victimized by childhood sexual abuse. *Psychological Medicine, 27*(4), 951–959.

Steinberg, M. (1994). *Structured Clinical Interview for DSM-IV Dissociative Disorders-Revised (SCID-D-R).* Washington, DC: American Psychiatric Press.

Taylor, M. (1999). *Imaginary companions and the children who create them.* New York: Oxford University Press.

Thigpen, C. H., & Cleckley, H. (1954). A case of multiple personality. *Journal of Abnormal Psychology, 49,* 135–151.

Thigpen, C. H., & Cleckley, H. (1957). *The three faces of Eve.* New York: McGraw-Hill.

Trickett, P. K., McBride-Chang, C., & Putnam, F. W. (1994). The classroom performance and behavior of sexually abused females. *Development and Psychopathology, 6,* 183–194.

Trujillo, K., Lewis, D. O., Yeager, C. A., & Gidlow, B. (1996). Imaginary companions of school boys and boys with dissociative identity disorder/multiple personality disorder. *Child and Adolescent Psychiatric Clinics of North America, 5,* 375–391.

Tsai, G. E., Condie, D., Wu, M. T., & Chang, I. W. (1999). Functional magnetic resonance imaging of personality switches in a woman with dissociative identity disorder. *Harvard Review of Psychiatry, 7,* 119–122.

Turell, S., & Armsworth, M. (2000). Differentiating incest survivors who self-mutilate. *Child Abuse and Neglect, 24,* 237–249.

Tyler, K., Cauce, A., & Whitbeck, L. (2004). Family risk factors and prevalence of dissociative symptoms among homeless and runaway youth. *Child Abuse and Neglect, 28,* 355–366.

Valdiserri, S., & Kihlstrom, J. (1995). Abnormal eating and dissociative experiences. *International Journal of Eating Disorders, 17,* 373–380.

van der Hart, O., Brown, P., & van der Kolk, B. A. (1989). Pierre Janet's treatment of post-traumatic stress. *Journal of Traumatic Stress, 2*(4), 379–395.

van der Hart, O., & Friedman, B. (1989). A reader's guide to Pierre Janet on dissociation: A neglected intellectual heritage. *Dissociation, 2,* 3–16.

van der Kolk, B. A., Brown, P., & van der Hart, O. (1989). Pierre Janet on post-traumatic stress. *Journal of Traumatic Stress, 2*(4), 365–378.

van Ijzendoorn, M. H., & Schuengel, C. (1996). The measurement of dissociation in normal and clinical populations: Meta-analytic validation of the Dissociative Experiences Scale (DES). *Clinical Psychology Review, 16,* 365–382.

van Ijzendoorn, M. H., Schuengel, C., & Bakermans-Kranenburg, M. J. (1999). Disorganized attachment in early childhood: Meta-analysis of precursors, concomitants and sequelae. *Development and Psychopathology, 11,* 225–249.

Walker, A. (2002). Dissociation in incarcerated juvenile offenders: A pilot study in Australia. *Psychiatry, Psychology and the Law, 9,* 56–61.

Waller, N. G., Ohanian, V., Meyer, C., Everill, J., & Rouse, H. (2001). The utility of dimensional and categorical approaches to understanding dissociation in eating disorders. *British Journal of Clinical Psychology, 40,* 387–397.

Waller, N. G., Putnam, F. W., & Carlson, E. B. (1996). Types of dissociation and dissociative types: A taxometric analysis of dissociative experiences. *Psychological Methods, 1,* 300–321.

Waller, N. G., & Ross, C. A. (1997). The prevalence and biometric structure of pathological dissociation in the general population: Taxometric and behavior genetic findings. *Journal of Abnormal Psychology, 106*(4), 499–510.

West, J. L., & Singer, M. T. (1980). Cults, quack, and nonprofessional psychotherapies. In H. I. Kaplan, A. M. Freedman & B. J. Sadock (Eds.), *Comprehensive textbook of psychiatry* (3rd ed.). Baltimore, MD: Williams & Wilkins.

Yates, T. (2004). The developmental psychopathology of self-injurious behavior: Compensatory regulation in posttraumatic adaptation. *Clinical Psychology Review, 24,* 35–74.

Yoshizumi, T., Murase, S., Honjo, S., Kaneko, H., & Murakami, T. (2004). Hallucinatory experiences in a community sample of Japanese children. *Journal of the American Academy of Child and Adolescent Psychiatry, 43,* 1030–1036.

Zahn, T. P., Moraga, R., & Ray, W. J. (1996). Psychophysiological assessment of dissociative disorders. In L. Michelson & W. Ray (Eds.), *Handbook of dissociation: Theoretical, empirical, and clinical perspectives* (pp. 269–287). New York: Plenum Press.

Zoroglu, S. S., Sar, V., Tuzun, U., Tutkun, H., & Savas, H. A. (2002). Reliability and validity of the Turkish version of the Adolescent Dissociative Experiences Scale. *Psychiatry and Clinical Neurosciences, 56,* 551–556.

Zoroglu, S. S., Tuzun, U., Sar, V., Tutkun, H., Savas, H. A., Ozturk, M., et al. (2003). Suicide attempts and self-mutilation among Turkish high school students in relation with abuse, neglect, and dissociation. *Psychiatry and Clinical Neurosciences, 57,* 119–126.

Zweig-Frank, H., Paris, J., & Guzder, J. (1994). Psychological risk factors and self-mutilation in male patients with BPD. *Canadian Journal of Psychiatry, 39,* 266–268.

CHAPTER 19

Competence and Psychopathology in Development

ANN S. MASTEN, KEITH B. BURT, and J. DOUGLAS COATSWORTH

The concept of adaptation is fundamental to developmental psychopathology as a comprehensive and integrative approach to understanding behavior in the context and course of development. Moreover, it is a fundamental premise of developmental psychopathology that understanding paths toward and away from positive development as well as psychopathology is crucial to the twin goals of promoting children's mental health and reducing or averting the damage and burden of suffering attributable to psychopathology in individuals, families, and society. The focus on adaptation and its vicissitudes in development has characterized developmental psychopathology from its inception, as this integrative perspective emerged in the second half of the twentieth century (Cicchetti, 1984, 1990a; Cum-

mings, Davies, & Campbell, 2000; Masten, 1989; Sroufe & Rutter, 1984). It follows from the history and tenets of this integrative and comprehensive perspective on psychosocial problems that developmental psychopathology would encompass the study of competence and resilience, positive adjustment, protective processes, and prevention along with investigation of problems, mental illness, treatment, and vulnerability (Cicchetti, 1984, 1989; Cicchetti & Cohen, 1995; Masten, 1989, 2001; Masten & Braswell, 1991; Masten & Coatsworth, 1995; Luthar, Chapter 20, this *Handbook,* this volume; Sroufe & Rutter, 1984).

The focus of this chapter is *competence* as it relates to psychopathology in development. In the first edition of this volume, our chapter also included *resilience* (Masten &

Coatsworth, 1995), but the burgeoning attention to competence *and* resilience over the past decades dictated devoting two chapters to these interrelated topics in this edition, one focused on competence and the other on resilience in developmental psychopathology.

Resilience refers to processes and patterns of positive adaptation in development during or following severe threats to adaptation. In many cases, the quality of adaptation as studied by resilience investigators is judged on the basis of competence criteria (Garmezy, 1974, 1987; Luthar, Chapter 20, this *Handbook,* this volume; Masten, 1989, 2001). Thus, the study of competence and the study of resilience are inextricably linked, with resilience focused more sharply on adaptation under extenuating circumstances of deprivation, trauma, disaster, or other acute and chronic adversities. This chapter emphasizes the meaning and history of competence and its historical, theoretical, and empirical links with psychopathology. The chapter by Luthar is focused on resilience and adaptation in relation to adversity and the vulnerability and protective processes that explain individual differences and development in the context of adversity.

The first section of this chapter describes the historical roots of the two traditions of competence and psychopathology. Given that so many other chapters of these volumes are focused on psychopathology, this section emphasizes the history of concepts most pertinent to competence. Similarly, the section on the history of competence emphasizes constructs that are most important for developmental psychopathology, particularly in relation to the history and definitions of psychopathology, its diagnosis, and interventions to prevent or treat mental health problems. Early roots of prevention science are also briefly examined in relation to the conceptual history of adaptation in development in this first section.

The second section of the chapter is focused on defining competence. Key themes and issues from the literature on competence constructs are summarized. A working definition of competence is presented, and the contemporary work on developmental task theory is examined.

In the third section, psychopathology is defined in relation to competence, with a particular focus on the concepts of impairment, harmful dysfunction, and disability in the definition and classification of mental illness. Selected measures of impairment are reviewed and controversies pertinent to competence are considered.

The fourth section delineates several models depicting how competence and psychopathology might come to be related. Confounded concepts and measures are addressed first, to consider how spurious connections might arise in the literature. Then a sequence of causal models is presented and described, with examples. Common causal models include shared risk factors, common mediators, and a common underlying disorder influencing both competence and symptoms of psychopathology. Psychopathology and competence can also influence each other. The symptoms of psychopathology may cause competence problems, competence failures may contribute to psychopathology, and both of these can occur simultaneously or in sequence. Complex dynamic models are considered, with transactional, progressive, and cascade effects.

The fifth section of the chapter examines intervention efforts pertinent to competence, with an emphasis on prevention science, which is historically and conceptually related to both competence and psychopathology science. Examples of prevention research in which competence plays a major role are presented. The role of intervention designs is discussed as a strategy for experimentally testing models linking competence and psychopathology.

In the conclusion, we evaluate the progress made in developmental psychopathology toward integrating the study of positive and maladaptive development and discuss the implications for improving developmental science and its applications. We discuss the possibility of strategic developmental policy and prevention, built on a foundation of knowledge about competence and psychopathology in development. Finally, we describe exciting future directions and the potential benefit for stakeholders in the development of competence.

HISTORICAL ROOTS OF TWO TRADITIONS

The ideas and concepts encompassed by *competence* and *psychopathology* have old and somewhat overlapping origins. Ancient concepts pertinent to modern versions date back at least to classical Greek traditions in philosophy, government, and medicine (Masten & Curtis, 2000).

Origins of Psychopathology Concepts

Concepts of psychopathology have ancient roots in the history of medicine (Alexander & Selesnick, 1966; Menninger, 1963). In the school of thought associated with Hippocrates (460–377 B.C.), dysfunctions of body and behavior were attributed to imbalances in the four humors of the body (blood, phlegm, yellow bile, black bile), and one of the earliest known classification systems for mental illnesses was described. This system included categories for epilepsy, mania, melancholia, and "paranoia" or mental deterioration (Alexander & Selesnick, 1966). Already present in this school of thought was the idea that brain dysfunction was involved in mental and behavioral problems. Yet, it would be 2,000 years before the science of mental disease began to flourish.

Modern concepts of psychopathology took hold in the late eighteenth and nineteenth centuries, as modern science and medicine emerged from the Renaissance and the Enlightenment. Behavior that had been observed centuries earlier began to be systematically studied and organized into classification systems by pioneers like Pinel and Kraepelin (Alexander & Selesnick, 1966; Menninger, 1963). At this time, more attention was given to the notion that diseases of the mind and behavior could be differentiated by their *course,* and, implicitly, the *quality* of functioning and the *development* of symptoms over time was given more importance in classification. Age of onset and course were recognized as significant by several nineteenth-century psychiatrists, including Kahlbaum and Savage (Menninger, 1963).

Also during this period, childhood disorders were described systematically by clinicians, who noted major distinctions in types of cognitive, behavioral, and emotional problems observed in children (Alexander & Selesnick, 1966). Esquirol observed differences between children with primarily mental functioning disabilities and those with psychotic symptoms (though not in these terms). Emminghaus observed that some childhood diseases appeared to result from physical causes, whereas others resulted from poor rearing conditions or excessive fear. Emminghaus also viewed childhood disorders as distinctly different from adult disorders, but the prevailing view of his time in the nineteenth century—an idea enduring well into the next century—was that many conditions of adults could be found in basically the same form in children.

The perspective that came to be called the *medical model,* based on the premise that psychopathology is caused by brain disease, dominated psychiatry in the nineteenth and early twentieth centuries, though there were occasional dissenters. Griesinger (1817–1868) is quoted by Menninger (1963, pp. 26, 454) in his history of psychiatry as stating that "mental diseases are brain diseases." In contrast, Pierre Janet (1859–1947) would later take issue with the idea of organic dysfunction as the root of *all* mental health problems, noting that, whereas sometimes an automobile stops because it is broken, sometimes it stops because it is out of fuel (Menninger, 1963, p. 445).

Influences of Darwin and Freud

Two towering figures of the nineteenth century, Darwin and Freud, had profound influences on the concepts of psychopathology and competence; both of them, in different ways, spurred the study of behavior from the perspectives of adaptation and development (Alexander & Selesnick, 1966; Cairns, 1998; Masten & Coatsworth, 1995). Their influence is evident in the classification system of Adolf Meyer, who departed dramatically from the nineteenth-century disease model to promote a biosocial theory of psychopathology, conceptualizing psychopathology in terms of reactions of the whole organism to life experiences and stress (Kendell, 1975; Menninger, 1963). It is also evident in the classification system of Jellife and White, which included such disorders as shellshock as well as dementia praecox and manic-depressive disorder, which were described so vividly by pioneering psychiatrists (Menninger, 1963). By 1945, when Menninger (1963) synthesized the ideas of the time into a classification system for mental disorders, the system included neurotic and other reactive disorders that were not conceptualized strictly as brain diseases but also incorporated ideas about adaptation and trauma that stemmed from the theory of evolution and also psychoanalytic theory. This system, which was adopted with adaptations by the Veterans Administration in the United States, strongly influenced the first version of the *Diagnostic and Statistical Manual of Mental Disorders* (*DSM*), published by the American Psychiatric Association in 1952. Subsequently, in revisions and critiques of the *DSM* system, many controversies have arisen about the definition of psychopathology in relation to impairment, organic dysfunction, and competence, as examined in following sections.

Origins of Competence Concepts

Concepts of competence also have roots in classical Greek thought and share some of the same origins as ideas about psychopathology (Masten & Coatsworth, 1995; Masten & Curtis, 2000). Plato, for example, in *The Republic,* made recommendations about the individual characteristics that would make a good ruler many centuries before such qualities would be assessed and studied systematically in the behavioral and social sciences.

Competence in developmental psychopathology generally refers to a broad family of constructs related to the effectiveness of individual adaptation in developmental context (Masten & Coatsworth, 1995). The systematic study of variations in the quality of adaptation in children and adults dates to the nineteenth century and was heavily influenced by both Darwinian and Freudian theory (Borstelmann, 1983; Cairns, 1983; Masten & Coatsworth, 1995; Mayr, 1982). As Mayr noted, the idea of adaptation was transformed in the nineteenth century from a static concept (reflecting a perfect harmony in nature) to a dynamic concept. Natural selection of individuals who varied in heritable ways provided the mechanism for evolution. The ego in Freudian theory was assigned the task of coordinating internal and external adaptation, balancing the personal (and often unconscious) needs of the individual with the requirements for getting along in society. Anna Freud, Heinz Hartmann, Erik Erikson, John Bowlby, and others extended and elaborated classical psychoanalytic theory to describe the processes and developmental course of adaptive functioning in children and adolescents (and adults; see Masten & Coatsworth, 1995). These ideas had a profound influence on subsequent theories about adaptation and competence, particularly on the concepts of *ego resiliency, intelligent behavior, mastery motivation, self-efficacy,* and *developmental tasks.*

Intelligence Theory and Assessment in the History of Competence

In the study of individual differences and personality in psychology, two prominent conceptual clusters have focused on individual differences in the quality of psychological functioning pursuant to successful adaptation: concepts about *intelligence* and concepts about *ego.* Over the years, theories about intelligence explicitly or implicitly encompassed the capacity for adaptation to the environment and adaptive behavior (see Masten & Coatsworth, 1995). Alfred Binet (Binet & Simon, 1905/1916; Sattler, 1988) believed that intelligence was a collection of abilities that included judgment, common sense, initiative, and the ability to adapt to circumstances. Jean Piaget viewed intelligence in cognitive development variously as "a particular instance of biological adaptation" and as "the form of equilibrium toward which successive adaptations and exchanges between the organization and the environment are directed" (quoted in Ginsburg & Opper, 1988, p. 13). Piaget's concepts of assimilation and accommodation in cognitive development were fundamentally processes of adaptation (Flavell, 1963). David Wechsler (1958, p. 7) defined intelligence broadly as "the aggregate or global capacity of the individual to act purposefully, to think rationally and to deal effectively with his environment." Developmental ethologist William Charlesworth (1978,

1979) argued that we could infer intelligence (the internal disposition) from intelligent behavior, which referred to behaviors under cognitive control that were utilized to solve problems pertinent to an individual's survival. Robert Sternberg (1985, p. 45) described intelligence as "mental activity directed toward purposive adaptation to, and selection and shaping of, real-world environments relevant to one's life."

The importance of adaptive success for defining intelligence has been recognized most influentially through the diagnostic criteria and related assessment tools for identifying mental retardation. A diagnosis of mental retardation requires evidence not only that cognitive functioning is well below average but also that there is adaptive impairment (American Psychiatric Association, 2000). Edgar Doll (1935, 1953), creator of the Vineland Social Maturity Scale (an instrument still widely used to determine level of adaptive functioning), believed that the essential requirement for defining mental deficiency was not performance on a standardized test of intellectual functioning, but whether the individual could function independently in the world. Doll argued that adaptive behavior, what he termed "social competence," was evident only in manifest, typical performance in the environment. The view that mental retardation must include some degree of observable failure to adapt to specific environments gained wide acceptance, though debate continued about how to measure adaptive behavior (McGrew & Bruininks, 1989). At present, the influential American Association of Mental Retardation (see www.aamr.org) defines mental retardation as a disability originating by age 18, "characterized by significant limitations both in intellectual functioning and in adaptive behavior as expressed in conceptual, social, and practical adaptive skills" (http://www.aamr.org/Policies /faq_mental_retardation.shtml).

Ego and Self Psychology in the History of Competence

The concept of the *ego,* so prominent in psychoanalytic theory, has many permutations, but all concern adaptation. In Freudian theory, the concept of ego evolved and changed over time, although the function of the ego in psychoanalytic theory is always centered on adaptation. In *The Ego and the Id,* S. Freud (1923/1960) described his later conceptualization of the ego as a mental structure that served the purpose of both self-preservation and adaptation to the world. The ego functioned to resolve conflicts among needs or instincts, one's conscience, and the environment; if the ego did not succeed in this balancing act, unconscious conflict would produce the symptom of anxiety. A major goal of therapy in this regard was to strengthen the functioning of the ego. Freud's daughter, Anna Freud (1936/1966), elaborated the adaptive functions of the ego in terms of defense mechanisms, which were viewed as psychologically healthy. Heinz Hartmann's (1939/1958) landmark volume, *Ego Psychology and the Problem of Adaptation,* also elaborated the development and functions of the ego; he viewed adaptation and achievement in the external world as hallmarks of mental health. His contemporary, Ives Hendrick (1942), proposed that there must be an "instinct to master" the environment in addition to the pleasure-seeking instincts that psychoanalytic theory up to that time had emphasized.

These early psychoanalytic theorists set the stage for further advances in ego theory by Erik Erikson, Jane Loevinger, and Jeanne and Jack Block. Erikson (1963, 1968) focused on the adaptive nature of the ego and the processes of adaptation over the life span, describing sequential stages of psychosocial ego development that became the bedrock for developmental task theory (discussed later in the chapter). Erikson's well-known epigenetic theory outlined eight stages of development over the life course, each with a focal crisis or issue to address and resolve, such as trust in infancy and identity in adolescence. Each issue remained a task throughout life but rose to ascendancy during a particular epoch of development. Fundamental to his theory was the idea that adaptive responses to the issue of a developmental period would equip the individual well for the future. Like Erikson, Loevinger (1976) proposed sequential stages of ego development. In her theory, ego development encompassed the processes by which individuals organize and find coherence in their cognitions, affects, and behaviors, and she proposed a typology of personality based on individual differences in levels of ego development within an age cohort. Jack Block and Jeanne Block (1980) also proposed a personality theory based on ego functioning. The adaptive functions of the ego were differentiated in their theory in the concepts of *ego control* (referring to the modulation of impulses) and *ego resiliency* (referring to the modulation of one's behavior to meet contextual circumstances). Individuals could be maladaptive in terms of undercontrolling or overcontrolling impulses as well as due to low ego resiliency.

Self-Efficacy and Mastery Motivation in the History of Competence

The work of Hartmann and the other early psychoanalytic theorists also set the stage for the theories of Robert White, Susan Harter, and Albert Bandura, among others, on competence, mastery motivation, and self-efficacy (Masten & Coatsworth, 1995). In a seminal essay, "Motivation Reconsidered: The Concept of Competence," White (1959) argued that humans and animals were motivated to master the environment as part of their evolutionary heritage. In a brilliant integration of developmental and evolutionary theory and observations of animal and child behavior, White suggested that humans and animals are biologically predisposed to interact with the environment in ways that promote effective adaptation, exploring and learning even when they are not motivated by hunger, thirst, pain, anxiety, or sexual desires. White termed this motivation *effectance* and the feelings of satisfaction associated with this motivation *efficacy*. In other words, people are motivated to be effective in their interactions with the environment, and they are motivated by the feelings of pleasure that follow successful interactions (or their perception). Harter (1978) later elaborated on the role of self-perception, the types of competence, and the role of failure in her extensions of mastery motivation theory. Harter proposed a model for effectance motivation that differentiated three domains of competence (cognitive, social, physical) and that included processes by which success or failure influenced motivation. Harter attempted to fill in the broad strokes of White's theory, linking his ideas to psychological concepts of the self, self-perception, intrinsic and extrinsic motivation, locus of control, and perceived competence. Connell and Wellborn (Connell, 1990; Connell & Wellborn, 1991) extended these ideas further to argue that people have psychological needs for competence, autonomy, and relatedness, which motivate many interactions with the environment.

The self-efficacy theory of Albert Bandura (1977, 1982, 1989, 1997) has focused on the role of perceived effectiveness in adaptation and related processes in human development, describing how beliefs about such effectiveness, what he termed *self-efficacy,* arise from interactions with the environment and influence subsequent adaptive behavior. This is a theory about human agency and the role of the beliefs people hold about "their capabilities to produce desired effects by their actions" (Bandura, 1997, p. vii). Successful adaptation engenders confidence, and confidence engenders subsequent adaptive efforts, though beliefs can be influenced or altered in many ways. Cognitive, affective, and motivational processes are linked in this model, which has been supported by elegant experiments (Bandura, 1997). Robust self-efficacy arises from experiences of overcoming manageable setbacks and challenges in life, and people with a positive and sturdy sense of their own efficacy are more likely to persevere in the face of failure.

Beliefs about one's efficacy include beliefs about one's control over experience. In Bandura's theory, if people do not believe they have any influence on what happens, they will lose the motivation to try to make things happen. Attributions about the self and control and their influence have been central to several lines of work related to self-efficacy. A maladaptive cousin to self-efficacy in the history of competence-related concepts is the notion of "learned helplessness" (Abramson, Seligman, & Teasdale, 1978; Garber & Seligman, 1980; Seligman, 1975). In the later versions of the learned helplessness theory, attributing one's failure to stable, global, and internal causes is expected to produce depressive affect (Abramson et al., 1978). Other scholars have argued that perceived control of successes and failures in adaptation has important influences on the self, mood, and subsequent motivation (Connell & Wellborn, 1991; Harter, 1985; Skinner, 1991; Skinner, Chapman, & Baltes, 1988). Generally, in this cluster of theories about self and self-efficacy, attributions about one's failure can lead to negative moods and self-concepts as well as diminished motivation to adapt, and more favorable attributions can contribute to positive moods and self-concepts and increased motivation.

Developmental Issues and Tasks in the History of Competence

The evaluation of effective adaptation, whether by self or others, requires criteria. The concept of *developmental tasks* focused attention on the developmental nature of the standards by which success in adaptation is judged. The idea of developmental tasks was anticipated in Sigmund Freud's psychosexual theory and subsequently in Erikson's theory of psychosocial development and in various elaborations of ego development (see Masten & Coatsworth, 1995). However, it was Robert Havighurst who articulated the role of developmental tasks in expectations, education, and society in an influential series of lectures and publications. Havighurst (1972) introduced his ideas about developmental tasks in a 1948 pamphlet designed for a course he was teaching at the University of Chicago. He proposed that living in society imposed on individual members a series of tasks to learn and accomplish in order to gain approval and rewards. These expectations become the basis for both self and society to judge whether a person is reasonably successful. Havighurst was primarily interested in the educational implications of developmental tasks and the role of the educational system in helping children accomplish the tasks. Nonetheless, like Erikson, Havighurst outlined a series of tasks over the life course. In earlier pe-

riods of development, tasks included learning to walk, talk, read, and distinguish right from wrong. In later periods of development, tasks included starting a family, civic responsibility, and adjusting to retirement. His age-graded developmental tasks were grounded in middle-class, American values of his time (Oerter, 1986).

Following Havighurst and Erikson, a series of developmental theorists built on their ideas and generated developmentally sequential lists of tasks and issues over the life course. The salient developmental issues of infancy and early childhood, for example, were delineated by Greenspan (1981), Sander (1975), Sroufe (1979), and Hill (1980, 1983) described the developmental challenges and tasks of adolescence.

Around this time, Waters and Sroufe (1983), in a seminal paper, integrated the construct of competence into an organizational theory of development, conceptualizing competence as a broad developmental construct. In their view, competence referred to an individual's ability to coordinate psychological functioning (behavioral, affective, cognitive) and environmental resources to achieve developmental goals. Developmental tasks played a central organizational role in their thinking, in that mastering the challenges posed by these issues reflected the capacity to coordinate behavior in adaptive ways and also set the stage for future competence. They predicted that competence in developmental tasks would show coherence through time, even as the nature of developmental issues and challenges changed. They also argued that the best measures of competence, and those with the best predictive validity, would be broad in scope, tap success in regard to age-salient developmental issues, hence requiring coordinated behavior, and also reflect naturally occurring challenges. Subsequently, developmental task theory (discussed later in the chapter) would be expanded to encompass the contextual features of such tasks and to address the importance of task success for defining successful and unsuccessful adaptation, both for competence and psychopathology.

Key Intersections in the History of Competence and Psychopathology

The histories of competence and psychopathology did not unfold independently. There were important points of intersection early in their respective histories, both in relation to science and practice. Scientists and clinicians attending to the course of psychopathology noticed the significance of premorbid competence for the outcomes of their patients, whereas others concerned with preventing mental health problems in youth began to notice the effectiveness of early interventions to promote competence as a strategy for preventing mental illness.

Premorbid Competence in the History of Psychopathology

A key intersection in the history of ideas pertaining to competence and psychopathology was the notion of *premorbid competence* in studies of risk and psychopathology (Feffer & Phillips, 1953; Garmezy, 1970; Phillips, 1953, 1968; Phillips & Cowitz, 1953; Zigler & Glick, 1986). Clinicians had long noted that patients who had a better track record of success in expected adaptive functioning for people of their age and situation prior to the onset of mental illness had better prognosis. Experimental psychopathologists, conducting studies to document the role of what they termed premorbid competence, developed measures of individual success in age-appropriate adaptive tasks, such as the Phillips Premorbid Scale of Adjustment (Phillips, 1953) and its successor, the Zigler-Phillips Social Competence Scale, that demonstrated predictive validity (Zigler & Glick, 1986; Zigler & Phillips, 1961). These tools focused on adult tasks, such as success in marriage and work, long recognized as hallmarks of good adult adjustment, as evident in the famous answer by Sigmund Freud to a question about what a normal adult should be able to do well: "Lieben und arbeiten" (to love and to work; as recounted by Erik Erikson, 1968, p. 136).

Child Welfare, Mental Hygiene, and the Early History of Prevention

Another important intersection in the history of competence and psychopathology can be traced to late nineteenth- and early twentieth-century child guidance and mental hygiene movements, which gave rise to the first mental health prevention efforts and community psychology (Coie, Miller-Johnson, & Bagwell, 2000). Founded in part through the efforts of seminal figures Clifford Beers and Adolf Meyer, these dual movements were committed to promoting mental health and to the humane treatment of individuals with mental illness. Their efforts focused on changing the system, delivery, and practices in mental health services within the framework of a broad public health perspective. The methods behind these movements were founded mainly in public health and focused primarily on changing the broad environmental factors purportedly associated with problem behavior and on altering the systems of care for individuals with mental illness and early behavior problems. The child guidance movement extended such efforts to work with families to enhance child mental health and development, and research institutes were founded to study child development and to educate parents, often with the explicit goal of improving children and preventing future problems:

> There began a great interest in children and a belief that by starting early we could improve people greatly, and perhaps avoid some of the personality difficulties of adults. It seemed highly desirable to study children and to develop new patterns of child care and rearing, and preschool education. (L. K. Frank, 1962, p. 207)

The child guidance movement had as one of its stated goals the prevention of juvenile delinquency (Horn, 1989). Primary prevention became a focus of psychiatry and psychology significantly later than it did for public health (Caplan, 1964). During the emergence of community psychology directed at mental health during the 1950s and 1960s, aspects of a public health perspective were adopted, including the term *prevention* itself, along with concepts of primary, secondary, and tertiary prevention, which differentiated intervention efforts aimed before, during, or after the emergence of significant psychopathology (Coie et al., 2000). Subsequently, prevention efforts would be differentiated more often on the basis of target population, as suggested by Gordon (1983): *universal* (targeting general public), *selective* (targeting those at presumed risk for the problem of interest), and *indicated* (targeting those at high risk but not yet clinically disordered). The influential Institute of Medicine Report of 1994 recommended Gordon's approach to classifying preventive interventions, with some modifications (Mrazek & Haggerty, 1994).

Central to the early prevention models was the idea of facilitating capacity for social and interpersonal behavior that would help individuals maintain functioning despite life crises. Strategies included both *social engineering* and *competence enhancement* programs. Among the earliest social competence-promotion efforts on record (beyond public education itself) was a program developed by Ojemann and colleagues (Ojemann, Levitt, Lyne, & Whitesie, 1955) to help children develop causal thinking, a precursor to many of the social problem-solving approaches commonly used in today's prevention programs.

DEFINING COMPETENCE IN DEVELOPMENTAL PSYCHOPATHOLOGY

During the last two decades of the twentieth century, the concept of competence underwent a renaissance as developmental psychopathology emerged (Cicchetti, 1987; Cicchetti & Cohen, 1995; Cicchetti & Toth, 1995; D. H. Ford, 1987;

Garmezy, 1987; Garmezy & Masten, 1986; Garmezy, Masten, & Tellegen, 1984; Masten & Coatsworth, 1995; Masten & Curtis, 2000; Sroufe, 1979, 1997; Waters & Sroufe, 1983). As attention focused on theories of competence and how to judge success or failure in behavioral development, key themes and issues emerged (D. H. Ford, 1987; Masten & Coatsworth, 1995).

Key Themes among Competence Constructs

As noted in our chapter in the first edition of this handbook (Masten & Coatsworth, 1995), competence-related concepts encompass a diverse array of ideas and phenomena. Yet, there are common themes across these constructs, consistent with a meaningful family of ideas. Competence concepts share the following assumptions: (1) There are behaviors and related processes consistently related to the effectiveness of adaptation in the environment; (2) there are individual differences in effective behavior that can be evaluated; (3) there are developmental changes in the behaviors associated with effective adaptation; (4) adaptation requires coordination and integration of multiple functions in the organism to achieve purposive goals; (5) many processes are involved in facilitating effective functioning in the environment; and (6) some of these processes reflect intraindividual processes, whereas others reflect interactions of an individual with the many systems in which the individual organism develops, including relationships with other people.

We also noted differences among members of the broad family of competence constructs (see Masten & Coatsworth, 1995, p. 723). Concepts and theories about competence differ in several major ways. Though all competence family constructs focus on effective adaptation in the environment, some focus on internal adaptation or behavior, others focus on external behavior, and still others focus primarily on interactions or relationships. Considered from a systems perspective, such differences could be viewed as focusing attention on different aspects of system dynamics: Some focus on how a living system maintains its own equilibrium across development, some focus on the transactions of the individual organism with the other living systems in its milieu, and some focus on whether the system is adapting to its environment. Accordingly, ideas vary in terms of their focus on levels of analysis, with some competence concepts focused on individual functioning and others focused on competence in social interactions, family process, or the context of larger ecological systems. Competence constructs also vary in focus on processes versus attributes or outcomes. As a final

example, competence constructs also vary in scope from very broad to narrow domains of functioning.

Key Issues in Conceptualizing Competence

Key issues also emerged as scholars revisited competence concepts in developmental psychopathology (M. E. Ford, 1985; Masten & Coatsworth, 1995; Waters & Sroufe, 1983). One major set of issues concerns *who decides the criteria.* Evaluating the effectiveness of adaptation requires criteria that can be expected to vary by perspectives and context, including culture and period of history and who is doing the judging and for what purposes.

A second set of issues concerns *when to judge success.* Success can be judged by short-term criteria or by long-term adaptive success. It is conceivable that behavior appearing to be successful over the short term has negative long-term consequences. It is also conceivable that a person who fails now can turn around and succeed later. Waters and Sroufe (1983) argued that the criteria for evaluating competence from a developmental perspective must include both proximate and ultimate criteria of adaptation. If adaptations worked in the short term but compromised future development, a child would not be viewed as competent by their standards. Presumably, widely held developmental task expectations, particularly those held across cultures, have been recognized over time not only as markers of current effectiveness but also as important harbingers of future adaptation in society.

Another set of issues concerns *broad versus narrow criteria,* or *multidimensional versus one-dimensional success criteria.* Clearly, competence can be defined in broader and narrower ways (a competent child versus a child who is a competent mathematician). Broad definitions of competence typically require either integrated functioning or success in multiple domains. Even narrow-focused judgments about competence typically presume the coordinated functioning of many processes to achieve and execute the competent behavior, such as the processes involved in reading, spelling, and solving mathematical problems.

Level and consistency of achievement is another cluster of issues found in competence constructs and assessment. Does competence refer to high levels of effectiveness, or adequate levels? Does competence refer to relative achievement (better than others or better than average), or absolute standards? Does one need to be doing well in multiple domains all the time, or in only some domains most of the time? Investigators have taken different positions on these questions in their theoretical and operational definitions of competence.

Capacity versus performance issues are related to consistency and also to internal versus external criteria. The capacity for effective adaptation can be inferred from indicators such as intelligence and personality tests or from a track record of past effectiveness as observed or reported. There have been debates about whether competence refers to a personal aptitude (or trait), something a person *has,* or to a pattern of observably effective behavior, something a person *does,* over time in relation to (and often supported by) the context. In either case, however, competence always involves an inference about effectiveness, past or expected.

A Working Definition of Competence

With these themes and issues in mind, we define competence in developmental psychopathology broadly as follows:

> Competence refers to a family of constructs related to the capacity or motivation for, process of, or outcomes of effective adaptation in the environment, often inferred from a track record of effectiveness in age-salient developmental tasks and always embedded in developmental, cultural, and historical context.

This definition is closely related to definitions of competence articulated by us with other members of the Project Competence research team over the years (Masten & Coatsworth, 1995; Masten & Curtis, 2000; Masten et al., 1995, 1999) and it has been influenced by numerous mentors and colleagues (M. E. Ford, 1985; Garmezy, 1971, 1974; Garmezy & Nuechterlein, 1972; Hartmann, 1939/1958; Phillips, 1968; Sroufe, 1979; Waters & Sroufe, 1983; White, 1959; Zigler & Glick, 1986). By this definition, competence is inherently multidimensional, contextual, and developmentally dynamic. This definition requires criteria by which to judge the success of meeting standards for behavior related to adaptive functioning in society and also suggests that the appropriate criteria for general competence are "doing adequately well" in age-salient developmental tasks (described further, later in the chapter). It assumes that competence is a judgment about a behavioral pattern over time, based on generalizations about a track record, and allowing for instances of poor performance. It assumes that the expectations for individual behavior change with development and over historical time and may vary across cultures. An individual who shows such a pattern is presumed to have the capacity for future competence, though this capacity may reflect relationships and resources as well as individual aptitudes or

skills; hence, to call an individual "competent" means that he or she has manifested behavior that leads one to expect future competence.

This definition is broad, reflecting a global judgment that life for this individual is going okay in the expected ways necessary for positive adaptation in the individual's ecological and historical situation. Competence can also be used more narrowly to refer to more specific domains, as in academic competence, or even more narrow subdomains, such as reading competence. In addition, competence by this definition may be influenced by many ongoing processes within the organism, or between the organism and the environment, in relationships with other people or other kinds of transactional interactions with the environment. Therefore, general or specific competence could be undermined or destroyed by damage to the organism, problematic relationships or transactions with the environment, traumatic life experiences, and many other processes that affect the capacity for adaptation and achievement in relevant domains.

Developmental Tasks in the Definition of Competence

As noted, scholars of diverse persuasions have recognized the importance of broad, developmentally based standards for behavior and achievement in the concepts of developmental tasks or issues, following the lead of Havighurst (1972) and the organizational-developmental theorists (e.g., Sroufe, 1979). These tasks are akin to psychosocial milestones of development, broad indicators of how well adaptation and adjustment in development are proceeding from a societal point of view. Clearly, such standards would be expected to change as a function of major changes in culture and to vary across cultures and dramatically diverse contexts. Thus, the expectation that a child will learn to hunt for meat effectively might be a key task for a male youth in a hunter society and completely unimportant for a girl in the same society or any youth in an urban, technological society. At the same time, one would expect some developmental tasks to occur across cultures and time because they reflect the characteristic developmental course and adaptive attributes of the species. Examples include learning to talk, to control anger, and to attach to other people.

Various lists of developmental tasks have appeared over the years (see Erikson, 1963, 1968; Havighurst, 1972; Hill, 1980; Klaczynski, 1990; Masten & Braswell, 1991; Masten & Coatsworth, 1998; Sroufe, 1979; Waters & Sroufe, 1983). These lists show striking similarities, reflecting a general consensus on age-salient developmental tasks, at least in the developmental literature of contemporary industrial/technological societies. A list of broad developmental tasks is shown in Table 19.1.

In the Project Competence research program, we have argued that there are a small number of readily identifiable task domains of expected engagement and achievement for a given age cohort, time, and culture, and these wax and wane in salience across developmental periods and contexts (Masten & Coatsworth, 1995, 1998; Masten et al., 1999; Roisman, Masten, Coatsworth, & Tellegen, 2004). In line with the perspectives of the early developmental task theorists (Erikson, 1963, 1968; Sroufe, 1979; Waters & Sroufe, 1983), we believe that doing adequately well in core developmental domains of one developmental period is a harbin-

TABLE 19.1 Developmental Tasks of Early Life in Contemporary Industrial Societies

Infants, Toddlers, Nursery School-Age Children
Attachment to one or more specific adults.
Learning to sit, stand, walk, run, and jump.
Acquiring functional language.
Obedience to simple commands and instructions of adults.
Toilet training.
Self-control of proscribed physical aggression (e.g., not biting people).
Appropriate play with toys and other people.

Young School-Age Children
Learning to read and write a language.
Learning basic mathematics.
Attending and behaving appropriately at school.
Following rules for behavior at home, at school, and in public places.
Getting along with peers in school.
Making friends with peers.

Adolescents
Attending and behaving appropriately at school.
Learning to solve problems with numbers, algebra.
Learning required language, history, and other subjects.
Completing a course of secondary schooling.
Getting along with peers in school.
Making and maintaining close friendships.
Obeying the laws of the society.

Young Adults
Working or preparing for future in higher education (or caring for a family).
If working: behaving appropriately in the workplace.
If in school: meeting academic standards for courses or degrees.
If a parent: taking care of child or children.
Forming and maintaining romantic relationships.
Obeying the laws of the society.
Learning to maintain a household.

ger of future successful adaptation and development, even for domains that have not yet emerged as important (Roisman et al., 2004). This conclusion follows from observing that age-salient core expectations are being met, because this kind of success indicates that development is proceeding in the right direction with adequate adaptive capacity, resources, and support. In contrast, it is not as important how well one is doing in not yet salient, still-emerging domains. Thus, for example, in contemporary U.S. society, we would expect eventual success in work and romantic relationships (salient adult developmental tasks) to be forecast better by the quality of academic achievement and friendships in adolescence, which are core developmental task domains, than by the quality of work achievement and romantic relationships during adolescence, when these are emerging task domains (Roisman et al., 2004).

Many life experiences may influence the achievement of these tasks, ranging from dysfunctions of the organism to symptoms of disease or disorder, bad choices, and overwhelming negative life events. It is possible that many kinds of social interference by other people, ranging from discrimination to child abuse, could interfere with achieving these tasks. Anything that restricts the opportunities to engage these tasks or accomplish them can create difficulties, not only for present well-being but well into the future, if mastering these tasks reflects skills, knowledge, resources, or credentials that at some level are required for success in the future tasks.

Children who appear unable to accomplish or have great difficulty accomplishing age-salient developmental tasks or meeting associated expectations on time (normatively speaking) would be expected to generate concern in parents, teachers, and other people in the community; similarly, perceived failure in these tasks could be expected to generate distress or concern in the individual person as well. For example, an infant who does not show any signs of bonding with parents during the 1st year or a toddler who does not acquire any language would concern most parents everywhere. In many societies worldwide, there would also be concern about a school-age child who refused to go to school or is not able to read after years of instruction. Also in most societies, a young adult who does not do any kind of work, inside or outside the home (nor follow any alternative, approved life course), would also likely cause concern to parents and community members.

Not surprisingly, the quality of functioning in age-salient developmental tasks also constitutes the implicit or explicit criteria by which *impairment* is judged in the diagnosis of psychiatric disorders in major classification systems. The quality of functioning in these tasks is embedded in these systems in other ways as well. The following section addresses the role of competence in the definition and diagnosis of psychopathology.

DEFINING PSYCHOPATHOLOGY IN RELATION TO COMPETENCE: IMPAIRMENT AND DISABILITY

The theme of competence is connected to the *DSM* of the American Psychiatric Association through the manual's definition of mental disorder as well as through criteria sets for particular disorders, associated impairments and nondiagnostic codes, and Axis V of the multiaxial classification system. The most recent revision of the manual retains the basic definition of mental disorder adopted in the third edition (*DSM-III* and *DSM-III-R*), as follows:

> a clinically significant behavioral or psychological syndrome or pattern that occurs in an individual and that is associated with present distress (e.g., a painful symptom) or disability (i.e., impairment in one of more important areas of functioning) or with a significantly increased risk of suffering death, pain, disability, or an important loss of freedom. (American Psychiatric Association, 2000, p. xxxi)

The disorder must also not be an expectable or culturally sanctioned response to an event and must be considered as some sort of "behavioral, psychological, or biological dysfunction in the individual" (p. xxxi). However, the manual's introduction notes that there is no precise boundary to the construct of *mental disorder* and that disorders can be represented at various levels of analysis and abstraction.

Perhaps the most notable way competence concepts enter into the *DSM* classification system is in the requirement of significant distress or impairment and dysfunction in the individual (Masten & Curtis, 2000). During the *DSM-IV* revision process, variants of this so-called clinical significance criterion were added to criteria sets of approximately 70% of *DSM* disorders in an attempt to rectify what many felt was an abundance of false-positive cases (Wakefield & First, 2003). In addition, however, many disorder criteria require specific impairments that are connected to age-salient developmental tasks. For example, a diagnosis of a learning disorder requires significant interference with academic achievement; a diagnosis of Mental Retardation requires impairment in at least two of several competence-related areas, such as social skills, academic skills, and work; and diagnosis of Pervasive De-

velopmental Disorder often requires qualitative impairment in social interaction and/or language skills (Masten & Coatsworth, 1995; Masten & Curtis, 2000). Finally, as discussed in more detail later in the chapter, the use of a global assessment of functioning (GAF) scale (Axis V) represents an explicit acknowledgment of the interrelationship of competence and psychopathology by the authors of *DSM*.

There is widespread consensus that the construct of mental disorder has eluded precise delineation, at least to date, and debate over its definition and scope has continued over the recent past. Most discussions center on Wakefield's harmful dysfunction analysis (HDA; Wakefield, 1992a, 1992b, 1999, 2001, 2003), which proposes two necessary conditions for the presence of a mental disorder: (1) failure of a natural, evolutionarily selected function in the individual that (2) causes harm to the individual or to society. This analysis dovetails closely with the official definition included in the *DSM,* and calls have been made to incorporate the HDA explicitly into the definition of mental disorder in *DSM-V* (Spitzer, 1999; Wakefield & First, 2003). Critics of Wakefield's proposal have offered alternative conceptions of disorder as a fuzzy-bounded Roschian prototype (Lilienfeld & Marino, 1995, 1999) and as any condition that significantly interferes with an organism's deliberate action (Bergner, 1997). Others have focused on potential weaknesses in the HDA analysis or have argued against attempts to provide an absolute definition of mental disorder that consists of separate factual and evaluative components (Fulford, 1999; Kirmayer & Young, 1999).

However, most of the current debate around Wakefield's proposal and the definition of mental disorder has centered on the concept of *dysfunction* and the pitfalls inherent in basing it in evolutionary theory (e.g., Houts, 2001; Sadler, 1999). Indeed, the attempt to provide an operational definition of the term "dysfunction" is perhaps the most notable way in which the HDA extends the *DSM* definition. Less controversial in most debates is the idea that disorder requires some harm or distress for the individual, and that judgments of harm often require inclusion of value considerations. It is this conception of harm, and closely related ideas of impairment and disability, that seem closest to the definitions of competence outlined in the previous section.

The construct of *functional impairment* is central to the harm component of the *DSM* definition of mental disorder. In the psychiatric literature, symptoms and impairment have traditionally been seen as closely related but nonetheless independent constructs (Lehman, Alexopoulos, Goldman, Jeste, & Üstün, 2002). Lehman et al. note that in

DSM-III, raters of adaptive functioning were instructed to focus on three areas: social relations, occupational functioning, and use of leisure time. However, despite research emphasizing the measurement of functional impairment as a multidimensional construct, in *DSM-III-R* and more recent revisions adaptive functioning has been changed to the single GAF scale. In addition, users of the GAF are instructed to consider both symptom severity (i.e., psychological functioning) and level of social and occupational functioning and to assign the lower score if the two judgments are discrepant. Although such aggregation may improve prediction of service utilization, it does not provide conceptual clarity to relations between symptoms and competence. Historically, as noted earlier, part of the motivation for inclusion of impairment ratings in the diagnostic system was the belief that individuals tended to return to premorbid levels of functioning following a circumscribed disorder episode (Masten & Coatsworth, 1995).

Within the *DSM* framework, a common assumption is that psychiatric symptoms are the cause of functional impairment. For example, Lehman et al. (2002) take the example of an individual diagnosed with Schizophrenia to illustrate how basic dysfunctions (e.g., disorganized thought processes) can lead to functional impairment (e.g., impaired social relationships due to inability to speak in coherent sentences). Although this example captures one potential mechanism by which competence and symptoms might be connected, more ambiguous situations can easily be conceived, as demonstrated by Richters and Cicchetti (1993) in their discussion of the mental disorder status of Conduct Disorder. As they note in this penetrating and witty paper, it is not that easy to determine whether the misbehavior of the young Samuel Clemens (author Mark Twain) and friends, fictionalized in the adventures of Tom Sawyer and Huckleberry Finn, should be diagnosed as psychopathology.

In contrast to the American *DSM* system, the World Health Organization's (WHO; 1992) *International Classification of Diseases (ICD-10)* does not present a generic definition of mental disorder. In addition, the "clinical significance criterion" noted earlier is not included in *ICD-10* criteria sets. Instead, the WHO has commissioned work groups to create and research a separate system for the assessment of functional impairment and disability. This has resulted in the WHO's (2001) Disability Assessment Schedule, which attempts to classify the activities of a person across several categories: cognition, mobility, self-care, interpersonal interactions, leisure and work, and participation in community activities. Thus, the *ICD* sys-

tem explicitly and deliberately attempts to separate the question of impairment from disorder judgments.

Impairment and Adaptive Functioning

In providing a context for discussing relationships between competence and psychopathology, it is beneficial to examine more closely how functional impairment has been assessed and measured in psychological and psychiatric research. As Canino, Costello, and Angold (1999, p. 94) have pointed out in a review of impairment instruments, "The area under the label 'functional impairment' is wide and poorly bounded, shading off into areas that have their own armamentarium of measures." Canino et al. note the issue of impairment and competence potentially representing opposite ends of the same continuum in many areas and discuss the need for measures developed in particular contexts that capture cultural as well as developmental differences.

One closely related area of research not directly touched on by most reviews of functional impairment is quality of life (QL). In this area, researchers often distinguish between general QL and health-related QL (the latter exemplified by symptom- and disease-specific measures, such as those that have been developed for asthma, cancer, epilepsy, diabetes, and other physical conditions; Eiser & Morse, 2001). Although QL research has evolved largely independently of research on functional impairment, similarities exist between these systems of measurement that make cross-disciplinary links increasingly likely. Typically, however, general QL represents a broader conceptual space than either impairment or competence, incorporating those constructs but also including domains such as material well-being (e.g., physical safety, housing quality, availability of transportation) and emotional well-being (e.g., faith, fulfillment, self-esteem; Wallander, Schmitt, & Koot, 2001). Debates in the QL literature include whether QL can be represented as a holistic, universal concept versus one that is specific to particular groups of children (such as those with a particular health condition), which particular domains represent QL most definitively, and whether objective or subjective assessments (or both) should be given primacy (Wallander et al., 2001).

In the psychological research tradition on functional impairment, a useful way of grouping assessments is one-dimensional versus multidimensional scales. No doubt due in part to concerns over professional staff burden, the *DSM* system has employed one-dimensional scales under Axis V that are designed to be completed rapidly by a clinician familiar with the individual being rated. *DSM-IV* retains the GAF for Axis V but also includes two related one-dimensional scales under appendixes for further study: the Social and Occupational Functioning Scale (SOFAS) and the Global Assessment of Relational Functioning (GARF). The GARF assigns anchor points based on a continuum of functioning in a relational unit, instructing the clinician to consider domains of problem solving, organization, and emotional climate. The SOFAS is akin to the GAF with symptom content removed, and thus appears to be the closest approximation to a competence scale produced by the *DSM* system. It is of note that the original version of Axis V from *DSM-III* (American Psychiatric Association, 1980, pp. 28–30) required the clinician to rate the highest level of adaptive functioning in the past year (not symptoms), using a 7-point scale and taking into consideration social functioning, occupational functioning, and use of leisure time (listed in order of designated importance).

Despite its designation as worthy of further study, there is little recent research that specifically addresses the psychometric and predictive properties of the SOFAS. One recent study presents predictive validity information for the three unidimensional scales and supports the view that the SOFAS may have better predictive validity of future illness and impairment (correlations with future GAF and severity scales) than the GAF itself; the authors suggest that this is because the SOFAS measures a narrower construct (Hay, Katsikitis, Begg, Da Costa, & Blumenfeld, 2003). Hilsenroth et al. (2000) report that all three main Axis V scales show good interrater reliability and that the SOFAS predicts self-reported social adjustment and interpersonal problem scores. In the latter study, symptom distress (Global Severity Index of the Symptom Checklist-90-R) predicted both the GAF and the SOFAS, although distress was more strongly related to the GAF. Some have questioned the discriminant validity of the SOFAS, noting that a revised GAF that is nearly identical to the SOFAS correlated with symptoms as strongly as or stronger than a quality of life scale (Roy-Byrne, Dagadakis, Unutzer, & Ries, 1996). Although the overall evidence on SOFAS validity thus appears mixed, calls continue for Axis V to consist solely of adaptive functioning as a way of decoupling symptom distress and functional impairment (e.g., Gruenberg & Goldstein, 2003) or to split Axis V into several different areas of symptom distress and impairment (J. A. Kennedy & Foti, 2003).

Other unidimensional impairment scales, either derived from official *DSM* scales or developed independently, have been employed in clinical and epidemiological research. A version of the GAF specific to children and adolescents,

the Children's Global Assessment Scale (CGAS), has been published (Shaffer et al., 1983). The CGAS continues to base ratings on either symptoms or impairment but aims to provide anchor point descriptions that are more appropriate for children and adolescents. Bird et al. (1996) report positive validity evaluation for both a nonclinical version of the CGAS as well as the Columbia Impairment Scale (CIS), a 13-item Likert-format scale that uses items from several domains (interpersonal relations, broad psychopathological domains, functioning in work or school, and use of leisure time) but is scored unidimensionally.

Common multidimensional scales of functional impairment used in child clinical research include the Child and Adolescent Functional Assessment Scale (CAFAS), the Functional Impairment Scale for Children and Adolescents (FISCA), and the Social Adjustment Inventory for Children and Adolescents (SAICA). These are selected as representative measures, as many others exist and it is not the purpose of this discussion to provide an exhaustive review (see Canino et al., 1999, for more information on other scales). These scales often require specific information from the youth being rated as well as collaterals such as parents or teachers, in addition to including items more dependent of clinical judgment. The CAFAS consists of 165 behavioral descriptions selected by the rater that fall into five domains: role performance (including school/work, home, and community subscales), behavior toward others/self, moods/self-harm (including emotions and self-harmful behavior subscales), thinking, and substance use (Hodges & Wong, 1996). Commentators have noted that aside from those on the role performance scales, CAFAS items are closely related to psychiatric symptoms (Bird, 1999). Bates (2001) has questioned whether the validity database on the instrument is complete enough to support its widespread use in service eligibility contexts.

The FISCA is conceptually based on the CAFAS but is briefer (85 items) and is designed to have a somewhat streamlined response format. It has a hierarchical factor structure in which eight lower-order domains (aggression, thinking, home behavior, delinquency, alcohol and drugs, school behavior, self-harm, and feelings and moods) are grouped under three higher-order domains of undercontrolled aggression, social role violations, and self-focused impairment (S. J. Frank, Paul, Marks, & Van Egeren, 2000). Structural agreement has been noted between parent- and adolescent-report versions of the instrument (S. J. Frank, Van Egeren, Fortier, & Chase, 2000). The SAICA consists of 77 items designed to be administered in a semistructured interview by clinicians. Items are grouped under four broad domains: school, peer relations, home life, and spare-time activities (John, Davis, Prusoff, & Warner, 1987). Although the SAICA provides relatively rich item content and allows assessment of a variety of social roles in different contexts, it combines competence-related items with more symptomatic content (e.g., bullying, inattention) in the total score (Bird, 1999).

An additional strategy in the assessment of functional impairment is the use of symptom-specific judgments that are tied into the diagnostic interview itself, rather than separate axes, questionnaires, or interviews. The Child and Adolescent Psychiatric Assessment (CAPA; Angold & Costello, 1995, 2000) requires interviewers to revisit endorsed symptoms (whether or not formal diagnostic thresholds are met) and assess disability related to each area of psychopathology. Reporting on a factor analysis of such disability data, Ezpeleta, Keeler, Erkanli, Costello, and Angold (2001) show that the CAPA disability questions tend to group into three domains of family, peer, and school impairment. They also report several complex demographic and disorder type differences on manifestations of impairment. This research, taken along somewhat different lines than that of the impairment measures just reviewed, represents an interesting and informative epidemiological angle on the classification of psychiatric disability in children and adolescents. Ezpeleta et al. decry the relative lack of attention paid to the impairment side of mental disorders in youth and call for more systematic research on the nature and measurement of psychiatric disability.

Overall, these instruments and interviews include several domains that are commonly seen as areas of competence from a developmental tasks viewpoint; examples include academic success, avoiding trouble with the law, positive relationships with peers and romantic partners, and effective participation in the larger society. In addition, however, multidimensional impairment indices commonly include areas, such as emotional state and self-harm, conceptualized as outside certain definitions of competence. A salient omission from most, if not all, unidimensional and multidimensional impairment scales is the lack of an explicitly developmental framework. That is, though clinicians and other raters clearly take developmental considerations into account when completing these measures, there is little discussion of whether or how domains of impairment change across developmental time in importance, boundaries, or evaluative standards (Masten & Curtis, 2000).

Studies examining predictors to and from functional impairment measures have, not surprisingly, identified symptoms as one of the most consistent predictors; however, some recent work has also emphasized taking into account onset and duration of disturbance in regression models pre-

dicting impairment (Ezpeleta, Granero, de la Osa, & Guillamón, 2000). Childhood impairment ratings themselves have been found to be good predictors of disorder effects later in adolescence (Costello, Angold, & Keeler, 1999). Impairment adds unique predictive power (above psychiatric symptoms) for course and outcome of disturbance (Canino et al., 1999; Costello et al., 1999; Pine et al., 2002), which surely adds motivation under the *DSM* system for including impairment criteria to definition sets of mental disorders. In fact, Angold, Costello, Farmer, Burns, and Erkanli (1999) advocated that individuals with symptomatic impairment, but who do not meet official diagnostic criteria, should nonetheless be treated as if suffering from a psychiatric disorder. Pickles et al. (2001), analyzing CAPA data from the Virginia Twin Study of Adolescent Development, found that the additional predictive power of impairment ratings for later symptoms and diagnosis varied by disorder class (adding prediction above current symptoms for Conduct and Oppositional Defiant Disorders but not for Major Depression).

Controversies in the Role of Competence in the Classification of Psychopathology

Several ongoing controversies in the assessment and measurement of functional impairment and in the inclusion of competence-related criteria in the *DSM* system parallel debates noted earlier with respect to the definition and assessment of competence itself. One issue concerns *who decides;* that is, What standard is used to designate impairment and how is impairment information used to inform service delivery? Important issues here include informant agreement and cultural and contextual considerations. Regarding informant agreement, evidence that parents and children (or adolescents) will provide similar pictures of impairment is mixed, as is research on symptoms (e.g., Achenbach, McConaughy, & Howell, 1987). Using the FISCA measure, S. J. Frank, Van Egeren, et al. (2000) demonstrated strong structural and relative agreement between parent and adolescent inpatient report; however, not surprisingly, parents and adolescents tended to disagree on impairment ratings that concerned more private/intrapersonal domains of functioning. Using a measure based on the CIS, Kramer et al. (2004) showed evidence for generally poor agreement between parent- and adolescent-reported impairment. They also found that clinicians tended to rate problems reported only by parents as more serious than those reported only by adolescents.

Cultural factors in diagnosis are, of course, broader than even the question of where and how to set diagnostic boundaries. *DSM-IV-TR* (American Psychiatric Association, 2000) includes a glossary of so-called culture-bound syndromes that lists psychopathological conditions described as indigenous to particular cultures. In this respect, the manual recognizes in some fashion that distress and disorder presentation varies markedly across cultural boundaries. However, even this limited acknowledgment was reduced during the editorial process, and cultural variations in the manifestation of "core" *DSM* disorders are generally limited to a sentence or two in introductory text for each section that then preface the "universal" criteria sets. Alarcón et al. (2002) provide an extended discussion of several issues related to cultural variables and psychiatric diagnosis, including content of criteria sets, diagnostic thresholds, overall classification systems, and epidemiology.

A methodological issue in the impairment literature related to the Who decides? question is employing categories versus dimensions in the assessment of functioning. Although there appears to be a strong consensus that functional impairment measures should take a continuous/dimensional format, this ultimately requires setting cutoff points for entry into services. Bird (1999) comments on the varied methods that researchers have used for determining "caseness," noting that in practice, this tends to remain the province of clinical judgment. In addition, conceptions of caseness and need for intervention depend to a large extent on financial and practical considerations on what level interventions take place and whether or not to intervene at all. Of course, researchers and clinicians in areas of physical medicine have long struggled with similar debates, and conditions such as hypertension are often cited as continuous-risk illnesses in which intervention/prevention cutoffs are set in part by consensus and change based both on new findings and the larger medical context.

In addition, similar to the "internal versus external criteria" of competence issue, debate outside of impairment measurement research has raised the question of whether suffering and/or distress alone, without associated external disability, justifies a mental disorder diagnosis. In many ways, distress can be thought of as a psychiatric analogue to fever or physical pain, in that it is a signal of an adaptational threat but is also a sign of one's bodily response. Simply adding "clinical significance" to disorder criteria sets will not solve this controversy, due in part to problems with circularity of such a criterion (Wakefield & First, 2003). In addition, evidence that adding a clinical significance criterion reduces disorder rates differentially by category of disturbance (Romano, Tremblay, Vitaro, Zoccolillo, & Pagani, 2001) suggests that when one

takes away impairment, certain classes of distress (e.g., some anxiety symptoms) are virtually normative. Clinical significance as currently implemented in the *DSM* system is also problematic because it refers to distress *or* disability and thus adds another potential confound to the classification process (Lehman et al., 2002).

Similarly, debates continue over the potential inclusion or exclusion in *DSM* of subthreshold and "mild" disorders. On the one hand, there is considerable confusion over how to conceptualize these disorders, leading to difficulties in interpreting research results due to heterogeneity of conditions (Pincus, McQueen, & Elinson, 2003). However, Kessler et al. (2003) analyzed data from the National Comorbidity Survey and found evidence for a continuous and graded correlation between severity of illness and later outcomes, without a marked inflection point at the mild severity level; similarly, Pickles et al. (2001) have reported a continuous relationship in their adolescent sample between symptom counts and concurrent impairment without an inflection point at diagnostic thresholds. Kessler et al. recommend that service utilization decisions be made on the basis of cost-effectiveness, including the potential benefit of preventing future deterioration of functioning in subthreshold cases. This issue also exemplifies possible tensions between service organizations and researchers: The former may be concerned about lack of third-party reimbursement for "nondisorder" conditions, and the latter desire inclusion of those conditions to spark new studies and to investigate and evaluate preventive interventions.

Overall, it is clear that researchers in areas of competence and in psychopathology, though often following somewhat independent traditions, have wrestled with some of the same conceptual and methodological challenges. However, as already noted, there are some promising areas of research (such as the epidemiology of impairment) that aim, directly or indirectly, to bridge these traditions. The next section of this chapter examines these links more explicitly by discussing theoretical models and empirical evidence from the developmental and child clinical literature related to connections between competence and psychopathology.

MODELS AND PERTINENT EVIDENCE LINKING COMPETENCE AND PSYCHOPATHOLOGY

As already noted, competence and psychopathology have numerous connections in the theoretical, historical, and empirical literatures concerned with behavior. In this section, we examine the possible explanations for the observed co-occurrence of behaviors described in terms of competence and psychopathology in the lives of individuals, utilizing illustrative evidence supporting these explanations. The first set of explanations focuses on methodological issues that could produce spurious linkages, and the second set focuses on substantive causal explanations.

Confounded Meanings and Measures

Before examining the causal explanations for links between competence and psychopathology, it is important to consider the more mundane possibility that these types of behavior are related because the terms reflect overlapping concepts or overlapping methods rather than true causal processes. These possibilities could produce spurious associations in research linking psychopathology and competence.

Overlapping Concepts

As evident in the preceding sections on the history and definitions of these complex concepts, psychopathology and competence sometimes refer to the same behavior or opposite ends of the same dimension of behavior, or the same behavior is used as a marker for both types of judgment (positive or negative) about the quality of adaptive functioning. Thus, for example, routinely breaking the rules or laws of society is viewed as a symptom of psychopathology (externalizing symptoms or a criterion for Conduct Disorder) as well as an indicator of poor performance in the competence domain of socialized conduct. Similarly, academic achievement (and failure) is considered to be an age-salient developmental task for school-age children, a criterion by which impairment is judged in diagnostic manuals for psychopathology, and is a common criterion for mental disorders related to learning.

The pervasive criterion of impairment for most *DSM*-defined mental disorders presents a challenge for interpreting research on the linkage of competence to psychopathology because the diagnosis of disorder is inherently confounded with the level of competence, often on the most salient developmental tasks, and yet the criteria for impairment are not well-specified, so the degree of the confounding is unclear. Moreover, the severity of impairment is related to referral, and therefore the samples in clinical studies may be unrepresentative and restricted in range on competence (e.g., Costello & Janiszewski, 1990). For anxiety disorders, for example, impairment is often viewed as crucial for distinguishing between normative fears and disorder: "A useful rule of thumb is to judge the child's ability to participate in ex-

pected, age-appropriate social and academic activities" (Klein, 1994, p. 354).

Overlapping Measures

Measures utilized to assess both of these aspects of behavior may also have overlapping content, related in many cases to overlapping concepts. In other words, the operational definitions of competence and symptoms may overlap. Measures of externalizing symptoms, such as the Child Behavior Checklist (Achenbach, 1991), contain items that overlap with measures of social competence, such as "Gets in many fights" (Externalizing broadband scale, Aggressive Behavior narrow-band scale) or "Would rather be alone than with others" and "Shy or timid" (Internalizing broadband scale, Withdrawn narrow-band scale) or "Not liked by other kids" (Social Problems narrow-band scale). The Revised Class Play measure (Masten, Morison, & Pellegrini, 1985), often used to assess peer social competence, includes the item "Gets into a lot of fights" on the Aggressive/Disruptive scale, "Would rather play alone than with others" and "Very shy" on the Sensitive/Isolated scale, and "A person everyone likes to be with" on the Popular/Leader scale. Harter's (1982, 1998) perceived (self-rated) and observed (rated by teacher or parent) competence rating scales have items with wording such as "Always doing things with a lot of people their age" versus "Usually do things by themselves" and "Not well-liked by other kids" versus "Liked by most other teenagers."

Impairment measures used in diagnosing psychopathology contain many items found on competence measures. For example, one of the questions from the 14-item Columbia Impairment Scale asks the rater to judge, for children or adolescents who are in school, "how much of a problem the target has with her/his school work." In addition, longer impairment measures such as the CAFAS and FISCA have several items relating to poor school work and the consequences thereof. Yet, Harter's perceived competence measure also includes "Does very well at one's classwork" versus "Doesn't do very well at one's classwork" as a competence item.

When similar confounded measurement tools are used to diagnose psychopathology and measure competence in a particular study, it is not surprising to find significant correlations among measures or to find that children who meet diagnostic criteria have worse social or academic competence scores. Thus, some of the links found in research on competence and psychopathology stem from measurement artifacts and conceptual overlap. However, even when great care is taken to distinguish concepts and measure these concepts independently with nonoverlapping content, links continue to be found between competence and psychopathology, both within and across time. These findings offer strong support to causal theories about the connections between competence and psychopathology.

Causal Models

Causal models and related empirical findings fall into three broad categories: (1) Common causes or chains of causes contribute to problems in both aspects of adaptation (the linkage is therefore spurious); (2) the symptoms of psychopathology contribute to competence problems; or (3) competence problems contribute to the development or exacerbation of psychopathology. There are also more complex models that combine these effects within or across time. These include bidirectional (transactional), progressive and cascade models. Figure 19.1 provides abstract illustrations of these models in their simplest forms.

Common Cause Models

Common cause models (see Figure 19.1a–d) include diverse theories and levels of analysis. These models implicate shared vulnerabilities (e.g., genes, traits); common risk factors in many forms, including psychosocial disadvantage; shared mediators (such as parenting and physiological stress); and complex combinations (e.g., risk gradients, diathesis-stressor models). These models also include classical disease models, where one disease process produces two kinds of problems at the same time or sequentially (illustrated in Figure 19.1d). Some models focus on one or two levels of analysis (individual behavior and parenting; cognitive functioning and peer interactions); others focus on many levels (genes, neural function, personality, family functioning, school and neighborhood qualities).

Competence problems and symptoms of psychopathology can be caused by the same disease process manifesting in multiple ways. In some cases (discussed in the next section), this model is assumed to be true (e.g., for Autism and other mental illnesses viewed as neurodevelopmental disorders). In other cases, there may be an unknown disease process leading to what is currently viewed as two or more different disorders. For example, Pine, Cohen, and Cohen (2000) have reported evidence that respiratory regulation might play a role in the development and expression of both childhood anxiety disorders (specifically, Separation Anxiety Disorder and perhaps Generalized Anxiety Disorder of Childhood) and adult Panic Disorder. They have shown that childhood anxiety disorders, in a similar fashion to Panic

Disorder in adults, are associated with carbon dioxide hypersensitivity. In addition, work on comorbidity and relationships among Tourette's syndrome, Obsessive-Compulsive Disorder, and Attention-Deficit/Hyperactivity Disorder (ADHD) has suggested that related brain dysfunction in circuits involving basal-ganglia thalamocortical pathways might explain the high co-occurrence of these nonetheless distinct clinical conditions (Pennington, 2002; Sheppard, Bradshaw, Purcell, & Pantelis, 1999). Such work, though intriguing, remains somewhat speculative and awaits further delineation of relevant neural pathway models in nonclinic samples (Sheppard et al., 1999).

Vulnerability, common underlying disease, and diathesis-stressor models suggest that a common trait or dysfunction in the organism contributes to more than one form of adaptive problem. For example, a twin family study suggested that depressive symptoms and antisocial behavior might have a common genetic liability (O'Connor, McGuire, Reiss, Hetherington, & Plomin, 1998). As another example, individual differences in the capacity to regulate emotion, attention, or behavior could easily contribute to multiple domains of competence (such as peer relations and school performance) and are also found in diagnostic criteria for disorders such as ADHD and on measures of problem behavior. Attention problems, inhibition, impulsivity, and negative emotionality all have been associated with multiple problems and disorders. As a simple example, inhibition to the unfamiliar is a robust individual difference evident early in childhood that predicts anxiety disorder, internalizing symptoms, lower social competence, and delays in taking on new social roles (Caspi, 1998; Caspi & Shiner, in press; Fox, Henderson, Marshall, Nichols, & Ghera, 2005; Gest, 1997; Kagan, 1998). More broadly, Rothbart and Bates (1998) have delineated multiple ways that temperament and adjustment could be related. It is likely that multiple processes, direct and indirect, are involved in the explanation of how particular genes, temperaments, and other individual differences lead to both competence problems and psychopathology.

Other personality traits, such as levels of impulsivity and conscientiousness, predict multiple outcomes, including school success, drug use, conduct problems, some personality disorders, and work problems (Caspi, 1998; Caspi & Shiner, in press; Shiner, 2000). The processes by which a personality trait predicts diverse outcomes such as drug addiction and school failure in the same person may differ. These processes also could differ across individuals, depending on their circumstances: In one case, a child in a neglecting family, poor neighborhood, and bad school may encounter many stressors with few assets, getting into

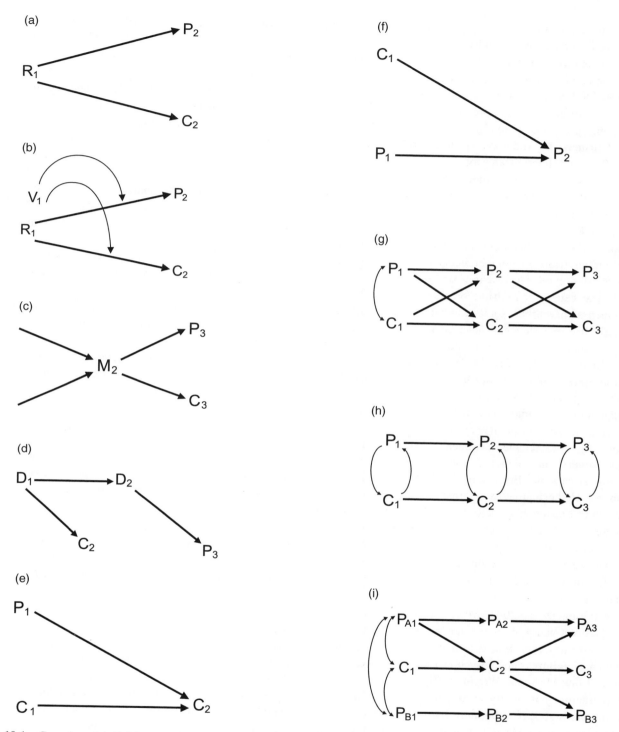

Figure 19.1 Causal models linking competence and psychopathology. (a) Common cause, with common risk factor; (b) Common risk factor and common vulnerability/moderator; (c) Common mediating cause; (d) Common underlying disease or disorder; (e) Psychopathology influences competence; (f) Competence influences psychopathology; (g) Transactional model, with lagged bidirectional effects; (h) Transactional model, with concurrent bidirectional effects; (i) Cascade or progressive chain of causes. *Notes:* Subscript numerals denote time point of assessment: C = Competence, D = Underlying disease process, M = Mediator, P = Psychopathology, R = Risk factor, V = Vulnerability.

every conceivable form of trouble; in another case, a child may have every advantage and be influenced by well-off, popular peers to try fashionable drugs, which leads to addiction and consequent academic problems.

Lower intellectual ability, as well as difficulties directing and sustaining attention, predict both academic and externalizing problems (Coie & Dodge, 1998; Hinshaw, 1992; Hinshaw & Anderson, 1996; Rothbart & Bates, 1998). Good intellectual and attentional skills have been associated with resilience among children at risk due to psychosocial adversity, as indexed by multiple criteria for adaptation, including competence and psychopathology (Masten & Reed, 2002).

Though there has been considerable interest in the role of individual traits in competence and symptoms, there also has been extensive research on shared contextual or experiential causes of multiple outcomes. Major risk factors—such as parenting, socioeconomic disadvantage, and traumatic life experiences—have been implicated as predictors of many aspects of competence as well as predictors of many disorders and symptom dimensions. Shared risk, therefore, could account for some of the observed co-occurrence of problems in competence and psychopathology, particularly if many risk factors or high cumulative risk has primarily nonspecific effects.

Parenting, for example, has been linked to many symptoms, disorders, and competence problems in normative and high-risk situations (Bornstein, 1995; Collins, Maccoby, Steinberg, Hetherington, & Bornstein, 2000; Cummings et al., 2000; Masten & Powell, 2003; Masten & Shaffer, in press; Repetti, Taylor, & Seeman, 2002). Parenting itself has many determinants (Belsky, 1984), and, as a result, parenting can serve as a final common pathway through which psychosocial disadvantage, adversity, or work problems of parents are mediated in the family, to the detriment of child rearing (Grant et al., 2003; Masten & Shaffer, in press). Child maltreatment, often but not always perpetrated by parents, also has been linked to many outcomes, including competence failures and psychopathology (Cicchetti & Carlson, 1989; Masten & Wright, 1998).

Risk factors commonly co-occur, and when they do, poor outcomes appear to be more likely in general, across multiple domains (Masten & Gewirtz, 2005; Masten, Morison, Pellegrini, & Tellegen, 1990; Sameroff, 2000a, 2000b, in press; Sameroff & Chandler, 1975; Sameroff, Gutman, & Peck, 2003; Wright & Masten, 2005). *Risk gradients* reflect the rising likelihood of problems as risk factors aggregate in the life of an individual. There has been considerable interest in identifying the underlying processes that account for these gradients (Keating &

Hertzman, 1999; Rutter, 1979; Sameroff, Seifer, & Bartko, 1997; Sameroff, in press). These may be very diverse, with different processes accounting for effects in different domains. Alternatively, these risks could operate through a common mediator, such as parenting or stress, with broad effects on behavior. It would not be surprising for major dysfunction in key adaptive systems to have broad effects across multiple domains.

The breadth of the domains related to high cumulative risk in many studies suggests that important adaptive systems for human development likely have been compromised, either by damage or by overload (Masten & Coatsworth, 1998; Masten & Curtis, 2000). When cumulative risk is very high, and nonetheless the children are doing well, then there is presumed to be either some kind of protection of these adaptive systems, more capacity available to the child, or resources not assessed by the gradient counteracting the risk. In effect, such children are "off-gradient" in doing better than one would predict based on risk factors alone. Similarly, when children known to be vulnerable encounter the key threat and do not develop the expected problems to which they are vulnerable, protective processes also are assumed to be operating.

Psychopathology Undermines Competence

In contrast to the common cause models, wherein the same underlying cause (whether a disease process, vulnerability, or experience) results independently in symptoms of disorder and also competence problems, the following categories of causal models implicate processes by which either psychopathology leads to competence problems (depicted in simple form in Figure 19.1e), or competence failures lead to psychopathology (depicted in Figure 19.1f), or both. When psychopathology is presumed to undermine competence, then in some way, the causal explanation involves features of the disorder interfering with the capacity or success of adaptive behavior. In the words of Ezpeleta et al. (2001, p. 901), "It is well established that psychiatric disorders result in many psychosocial problems, deviations, and limitations in addition to the 'symptoms' that are used to establish the nature of the disorder itself." In other words, the nature of the psychopathology under consideration produces impairment in key domains of adaptive function.

Adequate mastery of developmental tasks requires the coordinated use of multiple capabilities to direct behavior in context over time. Academic achievement in school-age children requires a child to be able to understand language, pay attention, sit still, concentrate, control the impulse to attack other people or laugh at the teacher, organize work, remember numbers, words, ideas, or pictures, get along reasonably well with the teacher and classmates, and many other skills and learning tools. Disorders characterized by profound difficulties in directing attention, thinking, learning, or relating to other people, including ADHD, Mental Retardation, Schizophrenia, and Autism, would be expected to interfere with academic progress, and they typically do. Not surprisingly, the *DSM* often describes academic difficulties as key related features of these disorders.

The Pervasive Developmental Disorders, including Autism, are defined by severe, chronic problems in basic cognitive and social dysfunctions that would be expected to interfere with most, if not all, major developmental task domains. Children with Autism have great difficulty making friends, learning in a regular school setting, and later managing all the social and cognitive tasks associated with living on one's own, working, and romantic relationships (Dawson et al., 2002; Travis & Sigman, 2000).

In other cases, where basic cognitive, emotional, or other neuropsychological functions are severely disturbed for a period of time, there may be a deterioration of functioning that tracks the development of the disorder or appears as a clear consequence of disturbed behavior (as noted earlier in the example from Lehman et al., 2002). Individuals experiencing delusional or disorganized thinking or severe disruptions of mood associated with psychosis, for example, may behave in ways that wreak havoc with relationships, make learning impossible, or require confinement, thereby impairing or even destroying the accomplishments and adaptive behavior expected by society.

More subtle disturbances of specific aspects of functioning are also associated with distinct profiles of impairment, although when dysfunction in the individual is less severe or less widespread in nature, it is more likely that the organism can compensate. Children with ADHD often have difficulties in their peer relations as well as their school work, because difficulties with directing attention and controlling impulses can interfere with play as well as learning (Campbell, 2000; Hinshaw, 2002b). Children with Tourette's syndrome or Obsessive-Compulsive Disorder have hallmark symptoms (such as tics or time-consuming rituals) that interfere with classroom performance and peer acceptance (Carter, Pauls, & Leckman, 1995; Peterson, Leckman, & Cohen, 1995). In the case of mood disorders, there may be complex transactional effects (described later in the chapter), but in some cases, the behavior associated with extremely depressed or elated mood clearly influences relationships. A depressed adolescent, for example, may withdraw from all social interactions with friends or become socially unappealing to peers, and a manic youth may become sexually promiscuous or engage in risky or dangerous behaviors that alienate peers or harm friendships and romantic relationships in other ways (Cicchetti & Toth, 1998; Geller et al., 2000; Puig-Antich et al., 1993).

Broadly defined antisocial behaviors have been clearly associated with changes in competence over time, most particularly academic performance. Antisocial behavior appears to have negative effects on academic achievement, even controlling for the initial links (Bardone, Moffitt, Caspi, Dickson, & Silva, 1996; Chen, Rubin, & Li, 1997; Hawkins, Smith, Hill, Kosterman, & Abbott, 2003; Masten et al., 1995; Risi, Gerhardstein, & Kistner, 2003; Williams & McGee, 1994).

Broadly defined internalizing behaviors are less clearly associated with changes in competence over time, though severe depression and anxiety (meeting diagnostic criteria for Major Depression or anxiety disorders) do forecast future competence problems. For example, adolescents with anxiety disorders or depression have more academic problems currently and in the future compared with nondisordered youth (Bardone et al., 1996; Bernstein & Borchardt, 1991; Kovacs & Devlin, 1998). Yet, there are not many consistent longitudinal data indicating predictive validity for internalizing symptoms in relation to undermining academic or social attainments (Cole, Martin, Powers, & Truglio, 1996; Roeser, Eccles, & Sameroff, 2000). One of the most intriguing linkages of psychopathology symptoms and competence in the literature actually works in the opposite direction.

There is reason to believe that internalizing symptoms may function to reduce the risk for subsequent competence failures among youth with some antisocial behavior, acting as a kind of braking system for the development of rule-breaking conduct problems and associated risky behaviors. Though limited, data suggest that internalizing symptoms have a negative predictive effect with respect to changes in externalizing symptoms, such that youth with more internalizing problems show less increase in externalizing problems over time (Farrington, 1995; Kellam, 1990; Loeber & Keenan, 1994; Mesman, Bongers, & Koot, 2001; Moffitt, Caspi, Harrington, & Milne, 2002; Verhulst, Eussen, Berden, Sanders-Woudstra, & Van Der Ende, 1993). This effect, if further substantiated, might be related to the role of inhibition in development or a protective effect of self-isolating behavior when peers are deviant (Gest, 1997; Kagan, 1998; Moffitt et al., 2002).

In other cases, the pathways by which psychopathology undermines competence may be less direct, with mediating processes. For example, a child with ADHD or conduct problems or both may be removed from a normal classroom and placed in a special education classroom for behaviorally disturbed children. If this classroom placement leads to either social stigma or association with more deviant peers who reinforce antisocial behavior or less adequate instruction, there may be unintended negative consequences for the child's academic and social competence. In a related fashion, Dishion, McCord, and Poulin (1999) have compellingly described the potential iatrogenic effects of aggregating deviant adolescents in peer-group-based intervention efforts, with evidence of increasing delinquent behavior through "deviancy training" and peer reinforcement of deviant talk, shown at both 1-year (Dishion, Andrews, & Crosby, 1995) and 3-year (Poulin, Dishion, & Burraston, 2001) follow-ups.

Competence Failures Contribute to Psychopathology

Causal models and empirical studies have also implicated the consequences of failures in adaptive achievements expected by self and society in the development of symptoms of psychopathology. There are several major ways that competence problems may contribute to psychopathology: (1) Perceived failure could lead directly to distress and related internalizing symptoms; (2) competence problems could increase the risk of negative experiences with peers, teachers, parents, or others that aggravate or increase symptoms; and (3) competence problems could lead to a change in context (e.g., special classroom placement or school dropout) that alters the nature of opportunities, results in stigmatization, or increases affiliation with negative associates.

Failure models in developmental psychopathology incorporate causal effects of competence failures on the development or exacerbation of symptoms, though some of these models involve complex transactions and cascades discussed further, later in the chapter. Patterson and Capaldi, with colleagues (Capaldi, 1992; Patterson & Capaldi, 1990; Patterson & Stoolmiller, 1991), have proposed one of the classic models of this kind, a "dual failure model" of depression, where failures in social and academic arenas were hypothesized to lead to dysphoric mood. In an influential longitudinal study of conduct problems and depressed mood in adolescence, this team found that conduct problems predicted increasing depressed affect over time, whereas depressed affect did not add significantly to the prediction of changes in conduct problems (Capaldi, 1992). Their developmental model posits that behavior problems arising early in development contribute to competence fail-

ures, which in turn contribute to worsening conduct problems and also worsening mood.

David Cole and colleagues (Cole, Martin, & Powers, 1997; Cole et al., 1996; Jacquez, Cole, & Searle, 2004) also proposed a failure model for depression, in which competence problems contributed to depressed mood. Through path analysis and structural equation modeling (SEM), this group found that social competence predicted changes in depressed affect over time, whereas the reverse was not found. Cole et al. (1997) have suggested that this effect is mediated by perceived competence. Additional work by this research team testing mediating versus moderating influence of self-perceived competence shows additional support for mediation (Jacquez et al., 2004; Tram & Cole, 2000).

With respect to academic achievement, there is evidence consistent with failure effects for both externalizing and internalizing domains of behavior. Though the evidence is more consistent with externalizing symptoms undermining academic attainment in the elementary school years, by secondary school academic achievement problems appear to have negative effects on subsequent conduct, which could result from association with deviant peers, greater exposure to violence, or other intermediary processes (Deater-Decker, 2001; Dishion, Patterson, Stoolmiller, & Skinner, 1991; Patterson, Forgatch, Yoerger, & Stoolmiller, 1998; Williams & McGee, 1994). It has also been observed that academic achievement during adolescence is associated with desistance from antisocial behavior (Maguin & Loeber, 1996; Thornberry, Lizotte, Krohn, Smith, & Porter, 2003). Academic failure also appears to relate to increases in internalizing symptoms, and achievement gains predict improvements in depressive symptoms, though this evidence is relatively sparse and somewhat less consistent than the evidence linking conduct and academic achievement over time (Chen, Rubin, & Li, 1995; Cole et al., 1997; Kellam, Rebok, Mayer, Ialongo, & Kalodner, 1994; Maughan, Rowe, Loeber, & Stouthamer-Loeber, 2003).

It is also interesting to consider the effects of conduct problems on internalizing behavior, given that conduct problems can be viewed as failure in a major competence domain. In this context, externalizing problems would be taken as evidence of failure in the developmental task of rule-governed behavior. There is some evidence implicating externalizing behavior problems as a predictor of changes in internalizing symptoms, congruent with a failure model (Capaldi, 1992; Garber, Quiggle, Panak, & Dodge, 1991; Kiesner, 2002; Lahey, Loeber, Burke, Rathouz, & McBurnett, 2002; Loeber & Keenan, 1994; McGee, Feehan, Williams, & Anderson, 1992; Robins, 1986).

Getting along with peers is widely viewed as a central developmental task by middle childhood; later in middle childhood and throughout adolescence, having a chum (Sullivan, 1953) or friends is also recognized as a hallmark of good development and a harbinger of future competence (Hartup, 1996; Masten, 2005; Masten & Coatsworth, 1998; Roisman et al., 2004). Peer rejection, which can occur for many reasons, some unrelated to already existing psychopathology in the rejected individual (such as discrimination), has been associated with increasing risk for externalizing and internalizing behavior (Deater-Deckard, 2001; Hartup, 1996; Masten, 2005; Parker, Rubin, Price, & DeRosier, 1995; Rubin, Bukowski, & Parker, 1998). Of course, symptoms in a child such as aggression (Ladd & Troop-Gordon, 2003) and anxiety (Gazelle & Ladd, 2003) may contribute to peer rejection, which in turn may contribute to subsequent internalizing and externalizing symptoms. Peer rejection can be viewed as a source of adversity in the form of "relational stressors" (e.g., victimization, exclusion) that contribute to psychological problems (Ladd & Troop-Gordon, 2003).

The practice of tracking children into lower-achieving classrooms due to academic performance or retaining them in grade may increase the risk for subsequent internalizing or externalizing problems (Pagani, Tremblay, Vitaro, Boulerice, & McDuff, 2001; Roeser & Eccles, 2000). Increases in behavior and emotional problems could result from the effects of concentrating deviant children together in a classroom, who may reinforce each other's negative behaviors (Dishion et al., 1999), or by lowering expectations for academic performance of children, teachers, and parents, or injuring self-esteem (Roeser & Eccles, 2000).

The most powerful tests of these competence failure models would consist of intervention studies to enhance competence in experimental designs and ascertain if preventing failure prevents psychopathology. This evidence is addressed in more detail in the subsequent section on prevention. However, an early example of this strategy is provided by the work of Kellam and colleagues (1994), who hypothesized that a reading intervention in the early primary grades would prevent internalizing symptoms; their results from a classic study in the Baltimore public schools supported this view. Similarly, the long-term effects of early intervention programs to promote academic and social competence in preschoolers on later antisocial behavior and other negative outcomes of interest have been interpreted as evidence that promoting social competence

early in development reduces the risk for antisocial behavior and psychopathology (Ramey & Ramey, 1998; Reynolds & Ou, 2003; Shonkoff & Meisels, 2000; Shonkoff & Phillips, 2000; Zigler, Taussig, & Black, 1992).

It is interesting to note that Model f in Figure 19.1 is usually discussed in terms of competence failure leading to symptoms, but it is also plausible that there is action at the high end of competence. In other words, competence achievement may be reducing psychopathology. In fact, many of the early theories about competence suggest that evolution and societies are selecting for competence, and, as a consequence, it is reasonable to assume that many aspects of competence may be linked to powerful motivation and reward systems and that self-righting systems would be in place to promote positive adaptation. If so, interventions that focus on improving competence may work in part by harnessing some of these powerful adaptive systems (Masten, 2001).

Complex Dynamic Models: Transactional, Progressive, and Cascade Effects

One of the most striking changes evident in developmental psychopathology over the past decade, since the publication of the first edition of this volume, has been the growth of models with a dynamic systems perspective (Cummings et al., 2000; Cicchetti & Davies, 2004; Masten, in press; Sameroff, 2000a, 2000b). Concomitantly, there are more conceptual and empirical models linking competence and psychopathology that include bidirectional influences and progressive effects across domains over time.

The complex, dynamic models owe much of their conceptual perspective to the developmental systems theorists (e.g., Bronfenbrenner, 1979; Cicchetti, 1990b; D. H. Ford & Lerner, 1992; Granic & Hollenstein, 2003; Gunnar & Thelen, 1989; Sameroff, 1983, 2000a, 2000b; Sroufe, 1979; Thelen & Smith, 1998). These models assume that many interactions of organisms and environments give rise to behavior, and that causal effects are often mutual or bidirectional. As a result, competence and psychopathology may be linked by more complex processes over time than implied earlier in the chapter, such that all of the effects described earlier could be occurring at the same time or sequentially. Effects within these more dynamic and complex models are described by terms such as *transactional, cascade, amplification, growth,* and *snowballing,* suggesting more dynamic, complex, and embedded effects in a context of interactions (Cicchetti & Cannon, 1999; Cicchetti & Tucker, 1994; Dodge & Pettit, 2003; Hinshaw

& Anderson, 1996; Masten et al., 2004, in press; Masten & Coatsworth, 1998; Patterson, Reid, & Dishion, 1992; Sameroff, 2000a, 2000b). These effects account for the long-observed diffusion of problems over time, particularly when there are antisocial or academic problems (Dodge & Pettit, 2003; Hinshaw, 1992; Kohlberg, LaCrosse, & Ricks, 1972; Maguin & Loeber, 1996; Masten et al., 2004, in press; Masten & Coatsworth, 1995).

In Figure 19.1, several of these complex models are illustrated. Figure 19.1g shows transactional, bidirectional effects over time between psychopathology and competence in a cross-lagged model that controls for the stability within each domain of behavior. Figure 19.1h also illustrates transactional effects but emphasizes that the transactions occur within the measurement window at each point in time and carry forward the effects of these interactions on each domain of behavior. In models of this type, popular among systems theorists, the association of competence and psychopathology would be expected to increase over time as a result of ongoing bidirectional influences (cf. Sameroff & Fiese, 2000). Figure 19.1i illustrates a cascade effect, where problems in one domain undermine competence, which in turn causes a worsening of symptoms in the original problem domain but also causes problems in a different psychopathology domain, thus affecting a third aspect of behavior. Cascade (or similar progressive) models conceptually require consideration of three or more domains of behavior across three or more points in time.

In the case of disorders characterized by conduct problems and linked with academic failure, evidence suggests that conduct problems and cognitive problems co-occur long before a disorder can be diagnosed and before children enter school (Hinshaw & Anderson, 1996). As noted, once children enter school, evidence suggests that antisocial behavior undermines achievement, and later, in secondary school, that academic failure is associated with worsening behavior. Clearly, this could be a progressive or cascade effect, though there are virtually no studies that directly test effects from one domain to another back to the first over time, controlling for all the initial covariance.

There also is evidence to suggest that internalizing symptoms show reciprocal linkages over time with peer social adjustment, though again, very few data with adequate controls for initial covariance exist (Harrington & Clark, 1998; Lewinsohn, Rohde, Klein, & Seeley, 1999; Masten & Coatsworth, 1995; Pine, Cohen, Gurley, Brook, & Ma, 1998; Rubin et al., 1998; Rubin, Chen, McDougall, Bowker, & McKinnon, 1995). However, studies using at least two

time points of data and controlling for initial levels of internalizing symptoms have shown peer status (Kiesner, 2002), sociability (Chen, Li, Li, Li, & Liu, 2000), popularity and friendship status (Nangle, Erdley, Newman, Mason, & Carpenter, 2003), and overall social competence (Cole et al., 1996) to predict later internalizing symptoms across diverse age ranges and sample contexts. There is more limited evidence in the opposite direction, that is, from internalizing symptoms to later social competence, controlling for initial levels of the latter construct. For example, Cole et al. found little evidence for such an effect using structural equation models over a 6-month interval, although the authors note that the very high stability of their social competence latent variable may have added to the difficulty of such a search.

It can be argued that a true cascading effect requires measurement of three constructs across three time points to account for concurrent and homotypic associations throughout the entire model. Although much of the empirical evidence reviewed here on links between competence and symptoms does not fall into such a category, there are intriguing examples of cross-domain links that seem best classified as developmental cascades. For example, a study by Mesman et al. (2001) used SEM to examine links among early preschool behavioral problems, social problems at school entry, and internalizing and externalizing problems in preadolescence. Using parent-reported behavioral checklist data, as part of their overall model for boys the authors found significant paths from time 1 aggression to time 2 social problems and also from time 2 social problems to time 3 internalizing problems. Time 1 anxious and withdrawn/depressed symptoms were included in the model. Although Mesman et al. were unable to include a full set of control variables, they establish compelling cross-domain links that are consistent with existing research on the development of internalizing problems (e.g., Panak & Garber, 1992; Rubin, Hymel, Mills, & Rose-Krasnor, 1991).

Cascade and progressive models resemble longitudinal mediation models, which also require (ideally) three variables and three time points and control for all the relevant continuity and concurrent correlations (Cole & Maxwell, 2003). The primary difference is in the goals of these models. Mediation models attempt to account for the association between two variables at two different points in time through a variable that represents an intervening process ($X_1 \rightarrow M_2 \rightarrow Y_3$). Cascade models attempt to account for the spread over time of success or failure in one domain to success/failure in multiple other domains over time ($X_1 \rightarrow Y_2 \rightarrow Z_3$); although the second variable in a sequence could be construed as a mediator (if a significant portion of the variance in Z explained by X is accounted for by Y), the focus of the cascade model is on explaining the effect of X on multiple later domains of behavior. In fact, in cascade models, there often is an interest in the mediators of each step in the progression (what processes mediate X effects on Y and also Y effects on Z).

INTERVENTIONS TO PROMOTE COMPETENCE AND REDUCE PSYCHOPATHOLOGY

Understanding how and why competence and psychopathology are connected in individual development has important implications for practice and policy, particularly given the twin societal goals of increasing competence and reducing the psychological, social, and economic suffering associated with psychopathology. If there is a common cause, then preventive intervention efforts that address the cause will serve both goals. If changing competence alters the subsequent risks for various problems and disorders, then prevention efforts to promote competence may be effective ways to prevent psychopathology or ameliorate its impact. If symptoms of psychopathology erode the achievement of developmental tasks, then early detection and treatment is important, not only for the relief of suffering related to the symptoms, but also to prevent further damage in the development of competence. Once the interference in competence is under way, it will be important to address the competence problems as well as treat the disorder; otherwise, there could be later consequences in competence or psychopathology domains. In the case of core developmental tasks, significant interference may have serious repercussions for future developmental tasks, as achieving some mastery of tasks in one period of development appears to serve as a foundation for attaining future competence. Thus, the developmental timing of interventions and also the nature of assessments pertinent to any kind of action or evaluation will be important.

Prevention and Competence

Over the past decade, three major trends are evident in the preventive intervention literature in regard to competence in developmental psychopathology. First, there has been a shift in how prevention scientists conceptualize interventions and what the primary goals and foci of interventions

are. Contemporary intervention design and evaluations tend to focus as much attention on changing proximal mediating developmental processes as they do on achieving distal outcomes of preventing psychopathology. This has illuminated more clearly and reinforced a general competence, or wellness-enhancement, model for preventing problem behaviors (Cowen, 1991, 1996; Masten & Coatsworth, 1998; Weissberg & Greenberg, 1998). Second, a resilience framework for prevention and intervention has been articulated for children at risk due to high adversity exposure and other negative circumstances (Cicchetti, Rappaport, Sandler, & Weissberg, 2000; Coie et al., 1993; Cowen, 2000; Kumpfer, 1999; Luthar & Cicchetti, 2000; Masten, 1994, 2001; Masten & Coatsworth, 1998; Masten & Garmezy, 1985; Masten & Powell, 2003; Masten & Reed, 2002; Rolf & Johnson, 1999; Sandler, Wolchik, Davis, Haine, & Ayers, 2003; Weissberg, Kumpfer, & Seligman, 2003; Wyman, 2003; Wyman, Sandler, Wolchik, & Nelson, 2000; Yates & Masten, 2004). Third, there is growing attention to developmental theory in the design of preventive interventions, with a particular eye toward developmentally strategic timing and approach (Cicchetti & Hinshaw, 2002; Cicchetti & Toth, 1992b, 1999: Coie, Lochman, Terry, & Hyman, 1992; Kellam & Rebok, 1992).

Preventive interventions have been criticized for having a deficit orientation and for emphasizing youth problems (Benson, 1997; Lerner & Benson, 2003; Pittman & Cahill, 1991), which purportedly leads to a focus on problems over health, competence, and well-being. Although this criticism is valid in some respects, mainly in that some early-generation programs designed to prevent mental health problems did focus too strongly on trying to prevent singular problem outcomes (drug use, Conduct Disorder/juvenile delinquency), a review of the history of prevention theory and research indicates that enhancing and promoting competence, well-being, and health have *always been a hallmark of this approach.*

As noted in the history section, prevention of mental illness and promotion of mental health began to emerge as a national priority in the late 1950s and early 1960s. President John F. Kennedy (1963), in his "Message on Mental Illness and Mental Retardation to the Congress of the United States" in 1963, described prevention as "far more desirable," "far more economical," and "far more likely to be successful" than treatment-focused approaches. The salience of prevention was further enhanced by the President's Commission on Mental Health during the Carter presidency. One important result of this commission was a report from the Task Panel on Prevention (1978), reviewing the extant literature, that outlined definitions of primary prevention of mental health and concluded that there was evidence indicating that some programs worked. Taking a broad public perspective, the report pointed to competence enhancement as a fundamental aspect of prevention, specifically noting that prevention was (1) proactive, meaning that it seeks to build adaptive strengths, coping resources, and health in people (e.g., *competence*) rather than containing already manifest deficits; (2) about total populations rather than individual cases; (3) relying on intervention strategies of education and social engineering rather than therapy and rehabilitation; and (4) founded on the premise that helping people develop the personal and environmental resources for coping is the best of all ways to ward off maladaptive problems. Another major outcome of this report was the establishment of a prevention office in the National Institute of Mental Health. Clearly, this report provided political impetus for promoting prevention; however, at the time, the strength of the scientific evidence supporting the claims for prevention was still weak.

Over the past few decades, primary prevention gained considerable scientific support through well-designed and carefully evaluated programs yielding empirical evidence that interventions can prevent occurrence of disorder. This early growth culminated in publication of *14 Ounces of Prevention* (Price, Cowen, Lorion, & Ramos-McKay, 1988), one of the first compendia of efficacious prevention programs. The project was conceived by the American Psychological Association's Board of Professional Affairs Task Force on Promotion, Prevention and Intervention Alternatives in Psychology. The task force selected the 14 model programs from 300 submissions. The programs were selected primarily on the basis of their outcomes but also to include diversity in targeted age and the settings in which the intervention was conducted. Of the 10 programs that represent interventions with children and adolescents, two are designed to alter broad systems that might influence youth adjustment (school, Juvenile Justice), and the remaining eight are programs that clearly are intended to enhance competence by building specific social, emotional, intellectual, or behavioral skills that are linked with successful adaptation. For example, Interpersonal Cognitive Problem Solving (Shure & Spivack, 1988) and Life Skills Training (Botvin & Tortu, 1988) are programs that teach generic cognitive problem-solving skills, personal, or social skills. Life Skills Training also teaches specific drug resistance and refusal skills, but these are embedded in a broader curriculum of social competence enhancement. Moreover, these programs emphasized building parenting competence as a method of influencing youth development.

Four of the programs contained some form of parental skill training. Empirical results were mounting that competence enhancement was an effective strategy for the promotion of adaptation, health, and the prevention of problem behavior.

Despite this accumulating data, conceptual confusion remained over whether a program should be defined as a prevention program or a competence enhancement program.

The premise that interventions should be founded on the dual goals of promoting competence and preventing problem behaviors (Cowen, 1986, 1994) was challenged by the influential Institute of Medicine (IOM; Mrazek & Haggerty, 1994) report *Reducing Risks for Mental Disorders: Frontiers for Preventive Intervention Research*. The authors of that report elected not to include mental health promotion efforts and distinguished them conceptually from prevention programs. They reasoned that the programs were not focused on "illness"; instead, the goals were to "enhance competence, self-esteem, and a sense of well-being, rather than to intervene to prevent psychological or social problems or mental disorders" (p. 27). Many prevention scientists criticized the decision to exclude health promotion and competence enhancement programs from a book intended to have profound scientific and political influence (Cowen, 1996; Durlak & Wells, 1997). Based on the results of a meta-analysis of 177 primary prevention programs, Durlak and Wells concluded that the IOM's decision to exclude health promotion may have been premature. Their results indicated that these primary prevention programs that were designed to strengthen children's affective, cognitive, and behavioral competencies showed effects for both problem reduction and competence enhancement that were comparable to other kinds of psychosocial interventions.

The distinctions made in the IOM report may have contributed to the competitive spirit between a positive youth development (PYD) frame and a prevention science frame. Fundamental to the PYD frame is the argument that "problem free is not fully prepared" (Pittman, 1991) and that a shift in focus is required for interventions with youth, de-emphasizing risk reduction and placing more importance on promoting youth development. Pittman, O'Brien, and Kimball (1993) contend that the required shift is more than semantic, because it has implications for program development, implementation, and evaluation. They acknowledge that "most of the strategies used to prevent substance abuse are, in fact, strategies that promote development—social skills, communication skills, self-awareness, family and community commitment" (p. 1). Other supporters of this approach have called for an exclusive focus on building assets, strengths, and protective factors (Benson, 1997).

PYD from a developmental systems view has been articulated in a series of books and papers written and edited by Lerner, Benson, Damon, and their colleagues (Damon & Gregory, 2003; Lerner, 2004; Lerner & Benson, 2003; Lerner, Dowling, & Anderson, 2003, 2005). This view emphasizes the multilevel and dynamic nature of adaptation and development (focusing on relations, regulation, and interactions of person with context), views youth as resources to be developed, and focuses on the processes by which valued, positive development and change occur: "The healthy and successful development of young people may be understood within the context of human evolution and of how adaptive regulation of person-context relations constitutes the basic process of ontogenetic change within the developmental systems" (Lerner et al., 2005, p. 861). They note that societies vary in expectations for what kind of behaviors will be judged as positive in development across the life span, much as we discussed earlier in terms of developmental tasks. At its best, successful youth development as conceptualized by these theorists results in *thriving* young people as well as thriving societies.

In prevention science, it appears that a shift has taken place so that the PYD and prevention science frameworks show a convergence of approaches (Catalano, Hawkins, Berglund, Pollard, & Arthur, 2002). This can be seen in publications resulting from the work of a task force appointed by Seligman when he was president of the American Psychological Association on Promoting Strength, Resilience and Health in Young People. This task force endorsed a broad model of intervention that encompassed the dual goals of promoting health and wellness and reducing problem behavior (Weissberg et al., 2003). In some respects, prevention research and competence enhancement have shifted back to a point at which they are seen less as competing frameworks and more as coordinated parts of integrated programming to improve the life conditions of youth (Catalano et al., 2002).

Promoting mental health (a goal of youth development programs) and preventing problems (a goal of prevention science) need not be competing endeavors (Catalano, Berglund, Ryan, Lonczak, & Hawkins, 2004). The primary tenets of these two approaches seem to derive from many common roots, they appear to have arrived at similar conclusions about the essentials for helping young people develop successfully, and both now reflect a developmental approach (Catalano et al., 2004). Currently, a substantial amount of work is being conducted on the measurement of the positive youth development constructs and other constructs from such perspectives as positive psychology, human strengths/virtues, and positive character traits.

Conceptual Evolution of Preventive Interventions

Over the past decade, prevention science gained considerable theoretical and empirical ground. Not too surprisingly, this progress has paralleled advancements in developmental psychopathology and the study of resilience (Cicchetti & Hinshaw, 2002; Cicchetti & Toth, 1999; Luthar, Chapter 20, this *Handbook,* this volume; Luthar & Cicchetti, 2000; Masten, 1999; Wright & Masten, 2005). Developmental psychopathology was described in the 1994 IOM report (Mrazek & Haggerty, 1994) as the "core integrative discipline for the knowledge base for prevention research" (p. 62). As basic research in developmental psychopathology has generated knowledge on the etiology, course, and plasticity of both adaptive and maladaptive development, prevention scientists have incorporated this knowledge in the design of their interventions. Consequently, many preventive interventions are better grounded in theory and research, with scientific justification for what they are doing.

Two kinds of theory-based approaches have emerged in prevention science, one focused on the problem and the other focused on the intervention. A "theory of the problem" is a developmental, explanatory theory of etiology, and a "theory of the intervention" specifies what needs to be changed and how it will be changed (Kellam, Koretz, & Moscicki, 1999). In both cases, clearly articulated developmental models are now more common (e.g., Conduct Problems Prevention Research Group, 1992, 2002; Lacourse et al., 2002; Toth, Maughan, Manly, Spagnola, & Cicchetti, 2002); researchers often think of their interventions as "interactions with development" (Coie et al., 1993; Kellam & Rebok, 1992; Tolan, 2002), as protective processes to promote resilience (Sandler et al., 2003), and as tests of developmental theory (Cicchetti & Hinshaw, 2002). This has meant more than simply developing a model of some risk and protective factors that precede a specified outcome in time; rather, it means that greater attention has been given to drawing from current understanding of complex etiological models with hypothesized causal and interactive and transactional processes and using them to inform a pragmatic model that can be used in intervention design and evaluation (Dishion & Patterson, 1999). Moreover, these models often address risk and protective *processes* rather than risk and protective factors, which had been the guiding model for prevention for so many years (Coie et al., 1993). Thus, interventions are designed to change interactive social or intrapersonal psychological processes that are hypothesized to be associated with subsequent occurrence of problem behavior.

Incorporating developmental models in prevention has also illustrated the importance of influencing proximal processes that will, in turn, influence distal outcomes. The emphasis in developmentally informed preventive interventions is placed as strongly on the hypothesized mediating factors and processes (e.g., promoting competence or skill acquisition) as on the ultimate outcomes (reduced future risk-taking behaviors or psychopathology). Initial efforts in prevention research were directed at understanding whether a program worked based on evidence that they changed the distal outcomes. Second-generation prevention programs have shifted to understanding the mechanisms by which a program works. Therefore, in intervention models that hypothesize building competence as a means of preventing psychopathology, competence often shares equal footing with psychopathology.

A second important influence on the design of preventive interventions has come through widespread adoption of broad ecological-contextual-systems models of development and change that have dominated the field of developmental psychopathology, as noted earlier. The implication of these kinds of systems models is that interventions can be designed to address risk and protection within and across systems. Intervention designers assume that it will be more effective to intervene on multiple levels or in multiple systems rather than within single domains of interaction (Nation et al., 2003). This approach also suggests that one can alter the environment or system that helps to maintain the behaviors. With respect to competence promotion programs, this might mean that changes to families (parent training, changing family functioning) or schools (structural and curriculum changes) might be important ways of reinforcing and maintaining cognitive, affective, and behavioral changes that are achieved through interventions directly with individuals.

Developmental psychopathology has also reinforced the need to examine competence and psychopathology, risks and assets, vulnerability and protection together to fully understand adaptation in development. For prevention, this means that exclusive focus on one or the other is likely to reduce the efficacy of an intervention or to overlook many possible targets for intervention or change leverage. The need to attend to both risk and protection has been a central tenet in prevention research (Coie et al., 1993), and recent evidence suggests that to maximize preventive effects, it would be strategically wise to focus on both positive and negative processes and outcomes (Pollard, Hawkins, & Arthur, 1999).

Model Prevention Programs with an Emphasis on Competence

The advancements made in prevention science over the past decade are reflected in the model programs that are promoted by federal agencies (see relevant Web sites of the agencies) such as the Center for Substance Abuse Prevention and the Substance Abuse and Mental Health Services Administration or Blueprints for Violence Prevention (Mihalic, Fagan, Irwin, Ballard, & Elliott, 2004), supported by the Office of Juvenile Justice and Delinquency Prevention. Careful examination of the theoretical underpinnings and intervention strategies of these programs does not reveal much support for the idea that prevention is primarily problem- and risk-oriented, as critics have sometimes suggested (noted earlier). Many of the programs are competence enhancement programs that emphasize building positive skills such as problem solving, self-awareness, effective communication, and conflict resolution as the proximal targets of the intervention. In the next section, several examples are provided to briefly illustrate the emphasis on competence characteristic of these model programs, which have demonstrated success in promoting development and reducing problems. Of course, these programs cannot possibly reflect the full extent of evidence-based competence promotion programs. However, these examples serve to highlight advancements occurring in competence promotion and prevention science over the past decade, in their theoretical clarity about the model of etiology and intervention underlying the program and their emphasis on development and context.

Life Skills Training Program

One of the most well-researched and -disseminated intervention programs with a focus on competence is the Life Skills Training program (Botvin & Griffin, 2004; Botvin & Tortu, 1988), a school-based competence promotion program that targets middle school and junior high school youth. The intervention is based on social learning theory (Bandura, 1986) and problem behavior theory (Jessor & Jessor, 1977), both of which posit that individuals who lack general interpersonal and coping skills show greater vulnerability to various influences that lead to substance use. Theoretically, building life skill and general competencies will protect youth from maladaptation. The program is delivered by classroom teachers who use traditional didactic teaching methods, group discussion, demonstration, and cognitive-behavioral skills training techniques to teach students personal self-management skills, social skills, and the consequences of drug use, accurate information about normative drug use, techniques used by media and advertisers to promote cigarette and alcohol use, and peer resistance skills. Extensive evaluation indicates generally strong effects with respect to alcohol, marijuana, and tobacco that have been replicated across sites and ethnically diverse samples (Botvin & Griffin, 2004; Botvin, Griffin, Diaz, & Ifill-Williams, 2001; Botvin, Mihalic, & Grotpeter, 1998). Studies have also supported (though not consistently) the effects of the intervention on hypothesized mediating variables (competence), including assertiveness, social skills, decision making, and problem solving (Botvin, 2000).

Promoting Alternative Thinking Strategies

The Promoting Alternative Thinking Strategies program is a comprehensive school-based program for promoting emotional and social competencies and reducing aggression and behavior problems in elementary-age children. The program is designed to be used by educators and counselors as a multiyear prevention model, applied universally to all students. It was developed specifically to promote social and emotional competence as a strategy for preventing or reducing future behavior problems (Greenberg, Kusche, & Mihalic, 1998). The program integrates five conceptual perspectives in a multilevel systems model of development and change to focus on building protective processes (e.g., emotional awareness and problem solving) that will decrease maladaptive behavior. Teachers are given extensive training to change the way they attend to children's behavior and reinforce and support effective socialization patterns. Results from clinical trials with groups of regular education and special education youth indicate that the program increases mediating competence factors and decreases distal outcomes of behavior problems. At 1 year postintervention, youth who received the intervention showed less internalizing and externalizing symptoms by teacher report and less sadness/depression and fewer conduct problems according to self-report (Greenberg & Kusche, 1998; Greenberg, Kusche, Cook, & Quamma, 1995).

The Incredible Years: Parent, Teacher, and Child Training Series

The Incredible Years series (Webster-Stratton et al., 2001) is a set of three comprehensive, developmentally based interventions that are designed to work together to promote emotional and social competence in children ages 2 to 8 who are at risk for (selective) or already presenting with (indicated) aggressive, defiant, oppositional, and impulsive behavior. The parent-training curriculum serves as the primary element of the Incredible Years series, with optional

teacher and child training. It is a flexible intervention program that has been implemented in a variety of settings (e.g., schools, Head Start classrooms, community centers). The parent program consists of three interrelated components, including the core component that consists of parent training for 12 to 14 weeks, founded on social learning and attachment models of development (Webster-Stratton, 2001). Based in the empirical literature reflecting parenting practices as critical components to the development of conduct problems in children and adolescents (e.g., Deater-Deckard, Dodge, Bates, & Pettit, 1996; Dishion & Loeber, 1985), the program uses videotapes, didactic presentations, and group discussion to enhance parenting skills, such as empathy and reinforcement skills, use of nonviolent disciplinary and child management practices, monitoring, problem-solving strategies, and responding in clear and predictable ways to child behavior. The other two components focus on teaching parents how to foster school readiness and skills of their own for dealing with depression and marital problems (Webster-Stratton et al., 2001). Teacher-training components include a 6-day workshop that trains teachers, counselors, and other school personnel in effective classroom management techniques aimed at reducing problem behavior in the classroom and also promoting positive relationships, strengthening child social skills, and encouraging effective interactions with parents. The child training program is intended to enhance children's appropriate behavior in the classroom (e.g., compliance, turn-taking), promote social skills and positive peer interactions, and develop age-appropriate conflict-resolution skills.

The core parent training program of the Incredible Years series has been evaluated extensively over the past 20 years, and results from six randomized clinical trials indicate significant improvements on parental management skills and reductions in child behavior problems (Webster-Stratton, 1985, 1990a; Webster-Stratton & Hammond, 1997) and lasting improvements for at least 3 years postintervention (Webster-Stratton, 1990b). The child-training component has also been evaluated in two clinical trials and found to be efficacious in improving social skills, conflict management strategies, and overall interactions with peers (Webster-Stratton & Reid, 1999). Evaluations of the separate components of the Incredible Years program have demonstrated effectiveness in changing child social competencies, parent competence, and teacher competence (management skills). A recently published study reported on additive effects across the three parent, teacher, and child programs demonstrating interesting main and interactive effects (Webster-Stratton, Reid, & Hammond, 2004). Results suggest that all intervention combinations had significant effects in lowering child behavior problems with parents, teachers, and peers as compared to controls. Conditions that included parent training had greatest effects on parenting skills, and conditions that included child training had significant effects on youth behavior at home, at school, and with peers. Findings also indicated that parent training decreased youth negative behaviors at home and school but did not enhance prosocial behaviors. Interestingly, parent- and child-training-only conditions also influenced teacher behaviors in the school. Purportedly, the changes in youth behavior resulting from child or parent training influenced the teachers to improve management practices. This finding suggests the critical nature of a systems perspective that encourages close examination of how intervention effects at one level of analysis or in one domain (e.g., individual) might influence behavior at other levels or other domains (e.g., school). Youth social competence can be influenced by direct intervention to improve parenting.

Skills, Opportunities, and Recognition

The Skills, Opportunities, and Recognition program, formerly known as the Seattle Social Development Project (Hawkins, Von Cleve, & Catalano, 1992), is a multicomponent program designed to enhance protection and reduce risk in the school and family environments. Based on the social development model (Hawkins & Weis, 1985), which is predicated on social control and social learning theories, the program hypothesizes that promoting positive social bonds to school and family (e.g., enhancing competence as attachments to parents and important others, such as teachers) will reduce the likelihood of problem behaviors. To create and strengthen those bonds, social development theory proposes that the contexts of family and school must help youth develop the skills needed to be successful (e.g., academic competence), provide ample opportunities for youth to practice and refine their skills, and consistently reinforce youth for behaving competently. Classroom teachers are trained in proactive classroom management skills, interactive teaching, and cooperative learning. In first grade, direct competence enhancement included having teachers provide classroom-based communication, conflict resolution, and decision-making and negotiation skills training. In sixth grade, teachers taught refusal skills. The intervention also targeted parental competence, with optional parent-training programs throughout the child's schooling. The parent-training component emphasized teaching child behavior management techniques (monitoring and consistent discipline) to parents in grades 1 and 2; academic support (establishing home learning environment, helping their child develop reading and math skills)

and family-school communication; and parent reinforcement of antidrug and antidelinquency messages in fifth and sixth grades. The study was conducted as a controlled trial in which eight urban and ethnically diverse schools in the Seattle area were assigned to receive the intervention or not (Hawkins, Catalano, et al., 1992). Youth began receiving the intervention in first grade. Results of ongoing evaluations have found that very early at grade 2, boys who were exposed to the intervention had lower levels of problem behaviors (aggression, externalizing behaviors) and girls had lower levels of destructive behaviors. By follow-up at grade 5, program effects demonstrated differences between program youth and controls on the purported mediators of family management practices, family bonding and commitment, and bonding to school. Intervention youth also showed lower levels of alcohol and delinquency initiation. By grade 11, program youth showed less violence, sexual activity, and fewer times drunk. Ongoing, long-term evaluations have demonstrated that the effects of changing early school bonding may persist well beyond the elementary school years (Hawkins, Guo, Hill, Battin-Pearson, & Abbott, 2001) and that competence-enhancing interventions in early childhood may have long-term promotive effects on positive adult functioning (Hawkins, Kosterman, Catalano, Hill, & Abbott, 2005).

Summary Comments on Model Programs That Promote Competence to Prevent Psychopathology

These successful competence promotion and psychopathology prevention programs provide examples of efforts to change competence in order to reduce future psychopathology, including internalizing and externalizing behavior, risky behavior, and substance use. Longitudinal data have suggested that there may well be more intermediate, mediating processes between specific skills or achievements and distal outcomes. For example, drug use may be mediated by psychological well-being (Epstein, Griffin, & Botvin, 2002; Griffin, Scheier, Botvin, & Diaz, 2001) and social expectancies (Griffin, Epstein, Botvin, & Spoth, 2001). Mediational analyses directed at delineating the intervening processes of change are now viewed as a hallmark of good prevention program evaluation (MacKinnon & Dwyer, 2003; MacKinnon, Taborga, & Morgan-Lopez, 2002) and provide the most complete test of the intervention's developmental model (Cicchetti & Hinshaw, 2002; Hinshaw, 2002a). At the same time, there remains very little long-term evidence documenting how the changes that result from an intervention lead to lasting improvements, often in multiple domains of both competence and symptoms. In many ways, this lack of evidence parallels the vast "black box" of data on long-term change in development, how developmental cascades occur, and the causal processes underlying the connections of competence and psychopathology over time.

A Note on Treatment and Competence

Prevention, broadly conceived, encompasses some elements of treatment that are designed to prevent recurrence, worsening of problems, or further complications of a disorder or problem. The literature linking competence and psychopathology, highlighted in this chapter and documented in many other chapters of this compendium, however, suggests both that psychopathology can have damaging effects on competence and that current competence as evidenced by impairment is often a strong indicator of prognosis, the level of risk for complications such as suicide or school failure, and even of the likely success of a given intervention. These observations suggest that attention to competence in the formulation of a treatment plan is essential, as has been noted by many clinicians and scholars in the treatment field.

Intervention Designs to Test Theories Linking Competence and Psychopathology in Development

Interventions to alter the quality of adaptation in development, whether conceptualized as positive youth development, prevention, or treatment, offer opportunities to test different models of how competence and psychopathology are related. Experimental studies, with random assignment to intervention or enhancement group, provide powerful designs for testing hypotheses about causal effects among competence and psychopathology domains of behavior, as well as potential common causes and mediators. The potential of experimental intervention research for illuminating the processes of adaptation in development and vice versa has been noted for some time (Cicchetti & Toth, 1992b; Masten, 1994). To date, however, the potential of experimental designs to illuminate how and why competence and psychopathology are associated in development has not been fully realized. Most research, perhaps understandably, has been focused on what works, for whom, and how to improve these effects, rather than the significance for developmental science and psychopathology.

An interesting case in point is provided by the longitudinal intervention study implemented in the 1980s by the Seattle Social Development Research Group (Hawkins, Catalano, Kosterman, Abott, & Hill, 1999; Hawkins et al., 2003). This important study, described earlier, was embedded in a large panel study of antisocial behavior, which it-

self has provided a remarkable look at naturally occurring growth patterns in behavior over time, particularly in regard to risky and antisocial behavior (Hawkins et al., 2003). The intervention was successful at its conclusion (end of elementary school) and on long-term follow-up (end of high school and beyond). Though the design was not a completely randomized experiment, the findings provided compelling evidence that the intervention beginning early and continuing through elementary school worked to reduce the risk of various negative outcomes, and did so, at least in part, by means of school bonding, which was the theory-driven target mediator of the intervention. This finding has been interpreted by the investigators and others as good evidence for the efficacy of their model of antisocial behavior and their model of intervention. However, it is also interesting to note (Masten, 2004) that the treatment effects were not apparent for a period of time during middle school, in the transition to adolescence, a time of biological, behavioral, social, and contextual change. The results of the study could be discussed in relation to their significance for developmental theories of adolescence (see Steinberg et al., Chapter 18, this *Handbook,* Volume 2). It is possible that treatment effects were obscured for a time by individual differences in growth and response to contextual changes of this period, much like relative height and strength are obscured by variations in pubertal change during the same period of time.

One of the best examples of an experimental intervention study that has made a significant contribution to developmental theory is provided by van den Boom (1994, 1995) in her studies of irritable infants. Mothers in the experimental group were trained to be more sensitive and attuned to their babies, in accordance with attachment theory (using strategies developed by van Ijzendoorn and colleagues; van Ijzendoorn, Juffer, & Duyvesteyn, 1995), and their babies were not only more securely attached but also more competent over time. These findings offer compelling evidence in support of key aspects of attachment theory concerning the causal role of sensitive care for secure attachment and secure attachment for later development (Sroufe, 1979).

CONCLUSIONS AND FUTURE DIRECTIONS

The theoretical and empirical literature on competence and psychopathology in development examined in this chapter is indicative of progress toward a more integrated understanding of adaptation in development. This progress underscores the potential of research linking competence and psychopathology to contribute to theories of normal development, as well as the classification, etiology, course, prevention, and treatment of psychopathology. In this section, we highlight this progress and the implications of the current literature on competence and psychopathology for classification, practice, and future research.

Signs of Progress for an Integrated Approach to Adaptation in Development

There are multiple signs of progress reflected in this chapter (and also in many other chapters of this volume) toward the goal of delineating how competence and psychopathology are linked. As evident across many of the chapters collected here, there have been improvements in theory, research design, and the simple volume of relevant work. Serious consideration is being given to the meaning and significance of impairment in relation to diagnosis and competence. More nuanced studies of developmental tasks are under way. Research on resilience has expanded so much that a separate chapter on resilience was required in this volume. There are many more longitudinal studies in the literature that take advantage of repeated measures, multiple informants and methods, and powerful statistical tools, such as growth curve modeling and structural equation modeling, to test causal models that control for within-time correlations and error and help sort out the direction and timing of cross-domain effects. Models are more dynamic. Person- and variable-focused approaches are combined for testing change over time within individuals. Mediating processes that may explain why competence influences symptoms or vice versa are being considered, both conceptually and empirically. Samples are larger in some cases, allowing for more comprehensive models to be tested. Prevention science that encompasses the constructs of competence, psychopathology, risk, resilience, and promotion is burgeoning. There is a growing group of investigators, practitioners, and policymakers focused on competence, strengths, positive youth development, the practice of positive psychology, and resilience.

It is striking to note the growing attention to positive aspects of psychology and youth development that have occurred over the past decade. Positive psychology gained enormous momentum under the leadership of Seligman (particularly when he was president of the American Psychological Association) and others who have published articles and books, sponsored meetings, formed task forces, founded centers, and in other ways promoted positive perspectives on human behavior (Linley & Joseph, 2004;

Lopez, 2002; Seligman, 2002; Seligman & Csikszentmihalyi, 2000). These scholars recognized the kinship of developmental research on competence and resilience, including chapters on competence and resilience in development in special issues and books on positive psychology (Masten, 2001; Masten & Reed, 2002; Yates & Masten, 2004).

The interest in positive youth development also expanded rapidly in recent years, underscoring the importance of society and communities investing in the development of competence in young people (Lerner et al., 2003, 2005; Smith, Steinman, Chorev, Hertzog, & Lerner, 2005). In light of the surge of interest in resilience and prevention already under way, the rise of positive psychology and positive youth development may signify a general renaissance in competence theory and research.

Improving Assessment, Diagnosis, and Classification

The salience of competence in research and practice related to resilience, prevention, positive psychology, and positive youth development appears to have had a considerable effect on the medically oriented tasks of assessing, diagnosing, and classifying psychopathology. Masten and colleagues (Masten & Gewirtz, 2005; Masten & Reed, 2002; Wright & Masten, 2005; Yates & Masten, 2004) have noted the transformational impact of resilience research in developmental psychopathology for the practice of psychology in terms of changing the way that the mission, models, measures, and methods are conceptualized and implemented. The goals of intervention are more often conceived in terms of positive goals and competence achievement; models include competence as well as symptoms, assets as well as risks, protective factors as well as vulnerabilities; measures (likewise) include strengths and resources as well as problems and risks; and strategies target risk prevention and competence promotion, bolstering protective systems and adding assets (in child, family, school, neighborhood, and other contexts), along with the many traditional methods of ameliorating and treating problems in the child and family. This transformation was forecast early in the history of developmental psychopathology (Garmezy, 1971), and its occurrence has been noted by many scholars (Cicchetti et al., 2000; Coie et al., 2000; Lerner et al., 2003; Luthar, 2003, Chapter 20, this *Handbook,* this volume; Masten & Gewirtz, 2005; Shonkoff & Meisels, 2000; Weissberg et al., 2003).

Much work has been done to develop tools for differentiating and assessing competence, symptoms, and various aspects of impairment. There have been serious efforts toward the development of distinct criteria for adaptive functioning and context to go along with diagnostic criteria for disorder.

Nonetheless, evidence strongly suggests that it would be very useful to develop better tools for tracking competence over time in relation to psychopathology symptoms and other important variables. There are some practical issues to keep in mind with such a goal, including the often difficult task of assigning co-occurring disability or impairment to particular symptoms and management of clinician workload. However, work by Costello, Angold, and others with the CAPA interview and impairment assessment has shown (albeit in an epidemiological research context) that such goals are attainable.

Evidence also suggests that further revision of the diagnostic and classification systems is needed in regard to the definition of mental disorder, specification of disorders, and parsing of axes on which to diagnose and classify individuals. We can see clear benefits in the WHO *ICD* system that explicitly decouples impairment from disorder, though noting that this framework poses more of a challenge for developing symptom criteria that accurately capture the targeted phenomena; perhaps advances in molecular genetics and neuroscience will contribute to this effort. In the *DSM* system, in the short term we are sympathetic to the calls of Gruenberg and Goldstein (2003), among others, for a revised Axis V that assesses functional impairment as distinct from level of symptomatology. Ideally, such a revised "impairment axis" for the diagnosis of adaptive functioning status could be segmented into multiple dimensions, building on our growing body of knowledge about competence and developmental tasks from the developmental sciences, as well as the research on psychosocial disability. Of course, such efforts need to consider practicality and clinician time; however, given the demonstrated importance of impairment in prognosis and treatment planning, work to develop better tools and ensure their proper use in the field should prove to be a good investment.

Strategic Developmental Policy and Prevention

The traditions of competence, psychopathology, and prevention science as described in this chapter appear to be converging through the integrative and explanatory power of a developmental perspective, and there appears to be benefit all around. Here too, however, there is clearly room for growth. There are still many gaps in knowledge of de-

velopmental pathways leading toward and away from specific problems and disorders that could inform intervention and policy. Yet, there is also evidence suggesting robust pathways that are not yet integrated into interventions design. Interventionists may not build their models on the most up-to-date theory or evidence, and developmental theorists and investigators not directly engaged in intervention may fail to keep up with state-of-the-art intervention findings that could refute or enrich their theories.

A more complete picture of developmental pathways encompassing both competence and psychopathology would provide a better foundation for strategic prevention and treatment. For example, the knowledge base about early starter pathways in antisocial behavior has led to prevention studies with very young children that focus on addressing early problems in self-regulation and seek to move children onto competence pathways (Shaw, Dishion, Supplee, Gardner, & Arnds, in press). Different strategies are employed with these preschoolers as compared to the school-age children in other developmentally designed interventions, such as FAST Track (Conduct Problems Prevention Research Group, 1992). Cascade models suggest that it may be important (when more is known about timing and sequencing of such progressions) to intervene early to treat one problem before it affects other critical domains of adaptation. If the cascade has already occurred, treating the starting problem (e.g., aggression), no matter how successfully, may not affect the long-term consequences of the progressions (academic or social difficulties) that have already been precipitated. Interventions would be most effective if the right domains are addressed with strategic timing and methods, and experimental tests of interventions based on cascade models would provide strong evidence pertinent to such etiological models.

It is also conceivable that competence promotion will work regardless of natural patterns of influence among dimensions of competence and psychopathology. Developmental task expectations and reinforcements are inherently powerful, and successes in these desirable domains of behavior could redirect development in positive directions, regardless of how young people got on the wrong road to begin with. Late bloomers in the resilience literature (Masten et al., 2004; Masten, Obradovic, & Burt, in press; see also Luthar, Chapter 20, this *Handbook,* this volume) and dramatic recovery in natural experiments (Cicchetti, 2003) suggest that recovery to good adaptation occurs among children who get off-track developmentally, particularly when major changes occur in the favorableness of their adaptive systems and context.

Dynamic, Multilevel, Multidisciplinary Approaches to Adaptation in Development

As evident throughout this second edition, advances in genomics, developmental neuroscience, statistics, and many other research areas and strategies, combined with advances in multidisciplinary collaboration and the growing availability of rich, longitudinal data sets, is revolutionizing the nature of research and theory in developmental psychopathology. These changes will benefit the process of integrating theories and applications of developmental adaptation studies and may shed new light on the undoubtedly complex processes that account for the striking patterns observed in competence in relation to psychopathology. We expect to see much more longitudinal research designed to test how and why success in developmental tasks is related to the etiology, symptoms, course, and recovery from psychopathology and also its prevention and treatment.

Research in developmental psychopathology is generally expanding to encompass more levels of analysis and interaction. Therefore, we expect that the study of competence in relation to psychopathology over the next decade will expand to include competence in systems beyond the individual and family, such as the competence of schools and systems of care for children (e.g., Masten, 2003). In the other direction, we expect there to be much more attention to the systems within the individual child as they relate to each other and to behavior and experience, such as gene expression, brain function, hormonal systems, and their development (e.g., Dahl & Spear, 2004; Steinberg et al., Chapter 18, this *Handbook,* Volume 2). These new frontiers may take the study of adaptation in surprising new directions.

Stakeholders in Competence

Parents, children, societies, and the global community all have a stake in the quality of adaptation achieved by individuals in development. There are unique developmental tasks across communities, cultures, and nations, but also many common expectations for children as they grow up. And the world grows smaller every day as a result of exploding technology for sharing knowledge and communication. Psychopathology, in many forms, under many names in different lands, interferes with the development of competence and the human and social capital that promotes competence. The psychopathology of adults may undermine the competence and functioning of caregivers and relationships that constitute critical protective systems for child development. Developmental task achieve-

ment sets the stage for successful individual development and also healthy societies. Negotiating and mastering such tasks requires an extraordinarily complex orchestration of processes, often codirected by children and people in their contexts, always changing over the course of development. Yet, competence as indexed by success in age-salient developmental tasks appears to be robust under many challenging circumstances and may function as the best general inoculation or preparation for the vicissitudes of life, akin to physical health and fitness. Understanding the development of competence and its role in normative and deviant development is a key task for developmental psychopathology and for prevention science; at the same time, it is a valuable investment for stakeholders in successful human development.

REFERENCES

Abramson, L. Y., Seligman, M. E. P., & Teasdale, J. D. (1978). Learned helplessness in humans: Critique and reformulation. *Journal of Abnormal Psychology, 87,* 49–74.

Achenbach, T. M. (1991). *Manual for the Child Behavior Checklist/4–18 and 1991 Profile.* Burlington: University of Vermont, Department of Psychiatry.

Achenbach, T. M., McConaughy, S. H., & Howell, C. T. (1987). Child/adolescent behavioral and emotional problems: Implications of cross-informant correlations for situational specificity. *Psychological Bulletin, 101*(2), 213–232.

Alarcón, R. D., Alegria, M., Bell, C. C., Boyce, C., Kirmayer, L. J., Lin, K.-M., et al. (2002). Beyond the funhouse mirrors. In D. J. Kupfer, M. B. First, & D. A. Regier (Eds.), *A research agenda for DSM-V* (pp. 219–281). Washington, DC: American Psychiatric Association.

Alexander, F. G., & Selesnick, S. T. (1966). *The history of psychiatry.* New York: New American Library.

American Psychiatric Association. (1952). *Diagnostic and statistical manual of mental disorders.* Washington, DC: Author.

American Psychiatric Association. (1980). *Diagnostic and statistical manual of mental disorders* (3rd ed.). Washington, DC: Author.

American Psychiatric Association. (2000). *Diagnostic and statistical manual of mental disorders* (4th ed., text rev.). Washington, DC: Author.

Angold, A., & Costello, E. J. (1995). A test-retest reliability study of child-reported psychiatric symptoms and diagnoses using the Child and Adolescent Psychiatric Assessment (CAPA-C). *Psychological Medicine, 25,* 755–762.

Angold, A., & Costello, E. J. (2000). The Child and Adolescent Psychiatric Assessment (CAPA). *Journal of the American Academy of Child and Adolescent Psychiatry, 39,* 39–48.

Angold, A., Costello, E. J., Farmer, E. M. Z., Burns, B. J., & Erkanli, A. (1999). Impaired but undiagnosed. *Journal of the American Academy of Child and Adolescent Psychiatry, 38,* 129–137.

Bandura, A. (1977). Self-efficacy: Toward a unifying theory of behavioral change. *Psychological Review, 84,* 191–215.

Bandura, A. (1982). Self-efficacy mechanism in human agency. *American Psychologist, 37,* 122–147.

Bandura, A. (1986). *Social foundations of thought and action: A social cognitive theory.* Englewood Cliffs, NJ: Prentice-Hall.

Bandura, A. (1989). Human agency in social cognitive theory. *American Psychologist, 44,* 1175–1184.

Bandura, A. (1997). *Self-efficacy: The exercise of control.* New York: Freeman.

Bardone, A. M., Moffit, T. E., Caspi, A., Dickson, N., & Silva, P. A. (1996). Adult mental health and social outcomes of adolescent girls with depression and conduct disorder. *Development and Psychopathology, 8,* 811–829.

Bates, M. P. (2001). The Child and Adolescent Functional Assessment Scale (CAFAS). Review and current status. *Clinical Child and Family Psychology Review, 4*(1), 63–84.

Belsky, J. (1984). The determinants of parenting: A process model. *Child Development, 55,* 83–96.

Benson, P. L. (1997). *All kids are our kids: What communities must do to raise caring and responsible children and adolescents.* San Francisco: Jossey-Bass.

Bergner, R. M. (1997). What is psychopathology? And so what? *Clinical Psychology: Science and Practice, 4,* 235–248.

Bernstein, G. A., & Borchardt, C. M. (1991). Anxiety disorders of childhood and adolescence: A critical review. *Journal of the American Academy of Child and Adolescent Psychiatry, 30,* 519–532.

Binet, A., & Simon, T. (1916). *The development of intelligence in children* (E. S. Kite, Trans.). Baltimore: Williams & Wilkins. (Original work published 1905)

Bird, H. R. (1999). The assessment of functional impairment. In D. Shaffer, C. P. Lucas, & J. E. Richters (Eds.), *Diagnostic assessment in child and adolescent psychopathology* (pp. 209–229). New York: Guilford Press.

Bird, H. R., Andrews, H., Schwab-Stone, M., Goodman, S., Dulcan, M., Richters, J., et al. (1996). Global measures of impairment for epidemiologic and clinical use with children and adolescents. *International Journal of Methods in Psychiatric Research, 6,* 295–307.

Block, J. H., & Block, J. (1980). The role of ego-control and ego-resilience in the organization of behavior. In W. A. Collins (Ed.), *Development of cognition, affect, and social relations* (pp. 39–101). Hillsdale, NJ: Erlbaum.

Bornstein, M. H. (Ed.). (1995). *Handbook of parenting.* Mahwah, NJ: Erlbaum.

Borstelmann, L. J. (1983). Children before psychology: Ideas about children from antiquity to the late 1800s. In W. Kessen (Ed.), *Handbook of child psychology: Vol. 1. History, theory, and methods* (pp. 1–40). New York: Wiley.

Botvin, G. J. (2000). Preventing drug abuse in schools: Social and competence enhancement approaches targeting individual-level etiological factors. *Addictive Behaviors, 25,* 887–897.

Botvin, G. J., & Griffin, K. W. (2004). Life skills training: Empirical findings and future directions. *Journal of Primary Prevention, 25,* 211–232.

Botvin, G. J., Griffin, K. W., Diaz, T., & Ifill-Williams, M. (2001). Drug abuse prevention among minority adolescents: Posttest and one-year follow-up of a school-based preventive intervention. *Prevention Science, 2,* 1–13.

Botvin, G. J., Mihalic, S., & Grotpeter, J. K. (1998). *Blueprints for violence prevention, Book 5: Life skills training.* Boulder, CO: Center for the Study and Prevention of Violence.

Botvin, G. J., & Tortu, S. (1988). Preventing adolescent substance abuse through life skills training. In R. H. Price, E. L. Cowen, R. P. Lorion, & J. Ramos-McKay (Eds.), *14 ounces of prevention: A casebook for practitioners* (pp. 98–110). Washington, DC: American Psychological Association.

Bronfenbrenner, U. (1979). *The ecology of human development: Experiments by nature and design.* Cambridge, MA: Harvard University Press.

Cairns, R. B. (1983). The emergence of developmental psychology: History, theory, and methods. In W. Kessen (Ed.), *Handbook of child psychology* (Vol. 1, pp. 41–102). New York: Wiley.

Cairns, R. B. (1998). The making of developmental psychology. In R. M. Lerner (Ed.), *Handbook of child psychology: Vol. 1. Theoretical models of human development* (5th ed., pp. 25–105). New York: Wiley.

Campbell, S. B. (2000). Attention-deficit/hyperactivity disorder: A developmental view. In A. J. Sameroff, M. Lewis, & S. M. Miller (Eds.), *Handbook of developmental psychopathology* (2nd ed., pp. 383–402). New York: Kluwer Press.

Canino, G., Costello, E. J., & Angold, A. (1999). Assessing functional impairment for child mental health services research: A review of measures. *Mental Health Services Research, 1,* 93–108.

Capaldi, D. M. (1992). Co-occurrence of conduct problems and depressive symptoms in early adolescent boys: Pt. II. A 2-year follow-up at grade 8. *Development and Psychopathology, 4,* 125–144.

Caplan, G. (1964). *Principles of preventive psychiatry.* New York: Basic Books.

Carter, A. S., Pauls, D. L., & Leckman, J. F. (1995). The development of obsessionality: Continuities and discontinuities. In D. Cicchetti & D. J. Cohen (Eds.), *Developmental psychopathology: Vol. 2. Risk, disorder, and adaptation* (pp. 609–632). New York: Wiley.

Caspi, A. (1998). Personality development across the life course. In N. Eisenberg (Ed.), *Handbook of child psychology: Vol. 3. Social, emotional, and personality development* (5th ed., pp. 311–388). New York: Wiley.

Caspi, A., & Shiner, R. L. (in press). Personality development. In N. Eisenberg (Ed.), *Handbook of child psychology: Vol. 3. Social, emotional, and personality development* (6th ed.). New York: Wiley.

Catalano, R. F., Berglund, M. L., Ryan, J. A. M., Lonczak, H. S., & Hawkins, J. D. (2004). Positive youth development in the United States: Research findings on evaluations of positive youth development programs. *Annals of the American Academy of Political and Social Science, 591,* 98–124.

Catalano, R. F., Hawkins, D. J., Berglund, M. L., Pollard, R. A., & Arthur, M. W. (2002). Prevention science and positive youth development: Competitive or cooperative frameworks? *Journal of Adolescent Health, 31*(Suppl.), 230–239.

Charlesworth, W. R. (1978). Ethology: Its relevance for observational studies of human adaptation. In G. Sackett (Ed.), *Observing behavior: Theory and applications in mental retardation* (Vol. 1, pp. 7–32). Baltimore: University Park Press.

Charlesworth, W. R. (1979). Ethology: Understanding the other half of intelligence. In M. V. Cranach, K. Foppa, W. Lepenies, & D. Ploog (Eds.), *Human ethology: Claims and limits of a new discipline* (pp. 491–519). Cambridge, England: Cambridge University Press.

Chen, X., Li, D., Li, Z.-Y., Li, B.-S., & Liu, M. (2000). Sociable and prosocial dimensions of social competence in Chinese children: Common and unique contributions to social, academic, and psychological adjustment. *Developmental Psychology, 36,* 302–314.

Chen, X., Rubin, K. H., & Li, B. (1995). Depressed mood in Chinese children: Relations with school performance and family environment. *Journal of Consulting and Clinical Psychology, 63,* 938–947.

Chen, X., Rubin, K. H., & Li, D. (1997). Relation between academic achievement and social adjustment: Evidence from Chinese children. *Developmental Psychology, 33,* 518–525.

Cicchetti, D. (1984). The emergence of developmental psychopathology. *Child Development, 55,* 1–7.

Cicchetti, D. (1987). Developmental psychopathology in infancy: Illustration from the study of maltreated youngsters. *Journal of Consulting and Clinical Psychology, 55,* 837–845.

Cicchetti, D. (1989). Developmental psychopathology: Past, present, and future. In D. Cicchetti (Ed.), *The emergence of a discipline* (pp. 1–12). Hillsdale, NJ: Erlbaum.

Cicchetti, D. (1990a). An historical perspective on the discipline of developmental psychopathology. In J. Rolf, A. S. Masten, D. Cicchetti, K. H. Nuechterlein, & S. Weintraub (Eds.), *Risk and protective factors in the development of psychopathology* (pp. 2–28). New York: Cambridge University Press.

Cicchetti, D. (1990b). The organization and coherence of socioemotional, cognitive, and representational development: Illustrations through a developmental psychopathology perspective on Down syndrome and child maltreatment. In R. Thompson (Ed.), *Nebraska Symposium on Motivation: Vol. 36. Socioemotional development* (pp. 259–366). Lincoln: University of Nebraska Press.

Cicchetti, D. (Ed.). (2003). Experiments of nature: Contributions to developmental theory [Special issue]. *Development and Psychopathology, 15*(4).

Cicchetti, D., & Cannon, T. D. (1999). Neurodevelopmental processes in the ontogenesis and epigenesis of psychopathology. *Development and Psychopathology, 11,* 375–393.

Cicchetti, D., & Carlson, V. (Eds.). (1989). *Child maltreatment.* New York: Cambridge University Press.

Cicchetti, D., & Cohen, D. J. (Eds.). (1995). *Developmental psychopathology: Vol. 1. Theory and methods.* New York: Wiley.

Cicchetti, D., & Davies, P. T. (Eds.). (2004). Family systems and developmental psychopathology [Special issue]. *Development and Psychopathology, 16*(3).

Cicchetti, D., & Hinshaw, S. P. (2002). Editorial: Prevention and intervention science: Contributions to developmental theory. *Development and Psychopathology, 14,* 667–671.

Cicchetti, D., Rappaport, J., Sandler, I., & Weissberg, R. P. (Eds.). (2000). *The promotion of wellness in children and adolescents.* Washington, DC: CWLA Press.

Cicchetti, D., & Toth, S. L. (Eds.). (1992a). *Rochester Symposium on Developmental Psychopathology: Vol. 4. Developmental perspectives on depression.* Rochester, NY: University of Rochester Press.

Cicchetti, D., & Toth, S. L. (1992b). The role of developmental theory in prevention and intervention. *Development and Psychopathology, 4,* 489–493.

Cicchetti, D., & Toth, S. L. (1995). Developmental psychopathology and disorders of affect. In D. Cicchetti & S. L. Toth (Eds.), *Developmental psychopathology: Vol. 2. Risk, disorder, and adaptation* (pp. 369–420). New York: Wiley.

Cicchetti, D., & Toth, S. L. (1998). The development of depression in children and adolescents. *American Psychologist, 53,* 221–241.

Cicchetti, D., & Toth, S. L. (Eds.). (1999). *Rochester Symposium on Developmental Psychopathology: Vol. 9. Developmental approaches to prevention and intervention.* Rochester, NY: University of Rochester Press.

Cicchetti, D., & Tucker, D. (1994). Development and self-regulatory structures of the mind. *Development and Psychopathology, 6,* 533–549.

Coie, J. D., & Dodge, K. A. (1998). Aggression and antisocial behavior. In N. Eisenberg (Ed.), *Handbook of child psychology: Vol. 3. Social, emotional, and personality development* (5th ed., pp. 779–862). New York: Wiley.

Coie, J. D., Lochman, J. E., Terry, R., & Hyman, C. (1992). Predicting early adolescent disorder from childhood aggression and peer rejection. *Journal of Consulting and Clinical Psychology, 60,* 783–792.

Coie, J. D., Miller-Johnson, S., & Bagwell, C. (2000). Prevention science. In A. Sameroff, M. Lewis, & M. Miller (Eds.), *Handbook of developmental psychopathology* (pp. 93–112). New York: Kluwer Press.

Coie, J. D., Watt, N. F., West, S. G., Hawkins, J. D., Asarnow, J. R., Markman, H. J., et al. (1993). The science of prevention: A conceptual framework and some directions for a national research program. *American Psychologist, 48,* 1013–1022.

Cole, D. A., Martin, J. M., & Powers, B. (1997). A competency-based model of child depression: A longitudinal study of peer, parent, teacher, and self-evaluations. *Journal of Child Psychology and Psychiatry, 38,* 505–514.

Cole, D. A., Martin, J. M., Powers, B., & Truglio, R. (1996). Modeling causal relations between academic and social competence and depression: A multitrait-multimethod longitudinal study of children. *Journal of Abnormal Psychology, 105,* 258–270.

Cole, D. A., & Maxwell, S. E. (2003). Testing mediational models with longitudinal data: Questions and tips in the use of structural equation modeling. *Journal of Abnormal Psychology, 112*(4), 558–577.

Collins, W. A., Maccoby, E. E., Steinberg, L., Hetherington, E. M., & Bornstein, M. H. (2000). Contemporary research on parenting: The case for nature and nurture. *American Psychologist, 55,* 218–232.

Conduct Problems Prevention Research Group. (1992). A developmental and clinical model for the prevention of conduct disorder: The FAST Track program. *Development and Psychopathology, 4,* 509–527.

Conduct Problems Prevention Research Group. (2002). Using the FAST Track randomized prevention trial to test the early-starter model of the development of serious conduct problems. *Development and Psychopathology, 14,* 925–943.

Connell, J. P. (1990). Context, self, and action: A motivational analysis of self-system processes across the life span. In D. Cicchetti & M. Beeghly (Eds.), *The self in transition: Infancy to childhood* (pp. 61–97). Chicago: University of Chicago Press.

Connell, J. P., & Wellborn, J. G. (1991). Competence, autonomy, and relatedness: A motivational analysis of self-system processes. In M. R. Gunnar & L. A. Sroufe (Eds.), *Minnesota Symposia on Child Development: Vol. 23. Self processes and development* (pp. 43–77). Hillsdale, NJ: Erlbaum.

Costello, E. J., Angold, A., & Keeler, G. (1999). Adolescent outcomes of childhood disorders: The consequences of severity and impairment. *Journal of the American Academy of Child and Adolescent Psychiatry, 38*(2), 121–128.

Costello, E. J., & Janiszewski, S. (1990). Who gets treated? Factors associated with referral in children with psychiatric disorders. *Acta Psychiatrica Scandinavica, 81,* 523–529.

Cowen, E. L. (1986). Primary prevention in mental health: Ten years of retrospect and ten years of prospect. In S. E. Goldston & M. Kessler (Eds.), *A decade of progress in primary prevention* (pp. 3–45). Hanover, NH: University Press of New England.

Cowen, E. L. (1991). In pursuit of wellness. *American Psychologist, 46,* 404–408.

Cowen, E. L. (1994). The enhancement of psychological wellness: Challenges and opportunities. *American Journal of Community Psychology, 24,* 239–245.

Cowen, E. L. (1996). The ontogenesis of primary prevention: Lengthy strides and stubbed toes. *American Journal of Community Psychology, 24,* 239–245.

Cowen, E. L. (2000). Psychological wellness: Some hopes for the future. In D. Cicchetti, J. Rappaport, I. Sandler, & R. P. Weissberg (Eds.), *The promotion of wellness in children and adolescents* (pp. 477–503). Thousand Oaks, CA: Sage.

Cummings, E. M., Davies, P. T., & Campbell, S. B. (2000). *Developmental psychopathology and family process.* New York: Guilford Press.

Dahl, R. E., & Spear, L. P. (Eds.). (2004). *Adolescent brain development: Vulnerabilities and opportunities* (Vol. 1021). New York: New York Academy of Sciences.

Damon, W., & Gregory, A. (2003). Bringing in a new era in the field of youth development. In R. M. Lerner & P. L. Benson (Eds.), *Developmental assets and asset-building communities: Implications for research, policy, and practice* (pp. 47–64). Norwell, MA: Kluwer Press.

Dawson, G. E., Webb, S., Schellenberg, G. D., Dager, S., Friedman, S., Aylward, E., et al. (2002). Defining the broader phenotype of Autism: Genetic, brain, and behavioral perspectives. *Development and Psychopathology, 14*(3), 581–611.

Deater-Deckard, K. (2001). Annotation: Recent research examining the role of peer relationships in the development of psychopathology. *Journal of Child Psychology and Psychiatry, 42,* 565–579.

Deater-Deckard, K., Dodge, K. A., Bates, J. E., & Pettit, G. S. (1996). Physical discipline among African-American and European-American mothers: Links to externalizing behaviors. *Developmental Psychology, 32,* 1065–1072.

Dishion, T. J., Andrews, D. W., & Crosby, L. (1995). Antisocial boys and their friends in early adolescence: Relationship characteristics, quality, and interactional process. *Child Development, 66,* 139–151.

Dishion, T. J., & Loeber, R. (1985). Adolescent marijuana and alcohol use: The role of parents and peers revisited. *American Journal of Drug and Alcohol Abuse, 11,* 11–25.

Dishion, T. J., McCord, J., & Poulin, F. (1999). When interventions harm: Peer groups and problem behavior. *American Psychologist, 54,* 755–764.

Dishion, T. J., & Patterson, G. R. (1999). Model building in developmental psychopathology: A pragmatic approach to understanding and intervention. *Journal of Clinical Child Psychology, 28,* 502–512.

Dishion, T. J., Patterson, G. R., Stoolmiller, M., & Skinner, M. L. (1991). Family, school, and behavioral antecedents to early adolescent involvement with antisocial peers. *Developmental Psychology, 27,* 172–180.

Dodge, K. A., & Pettit, G. S. (2003). A biopsychosocial model of the development of chronic conduct problems in adolescence. *Developmental Psychology, 39*(2), 349–371.

Doll, E. A. (1935). A genetic scale of social maturity. *American Journal of Orthopsychiatry, 5,* 180–188.

Doll, E. A. (1953). *The measurement of social competence: A manual for the Vineland Social Maturity Scale.* Minneapolis, MN: Educational Media.

Durlak, J. A., & Wells, A. M. (1997). Primary prevention mental health programs for children and adolescents: A meta-analytic review. *American Journal of Community Psychology, 25,* 115–151.

Eiser, C., & Morse, R. (2001). A review of measures of quality of life for children with chronic illness. *Archives of Diseases of Childhood, 84,* 205–211.

Epstein, J. A., Griffin, K. W., & Botvin, G. J. (2002). Positive impact of competence skills and psychological wellness in protecting inner-city adolescents from alcohol use. *Prevention Science, 3,* 95–104.

Erikson, E. H. (1963). *Childhood and society* (2nd ed.). New York: Norton.

Erikson, E. H. (1968). *Identity, youth and crisis.* New York: Norton.

Ezpeleta, L., Granero, R., de la Osa, N., & Guillamón, N. (2000). Predictors of functional impairment in children and adolescents. *Journal of Child Psychology and Psychiatry, 41*(6), 793–801.

Ezpeleta, L., Keeler, G., Erkanli, A., Costello, E. J., & Angold, A. (2001). Epidemiology of psychiatric disability in childhood and adolescence. *Journal of Child Psychology and Psychiatry, 42*(7), 901–914.

Farrington, D. P. (1995). The development of offending and antisocial behaviour from childhood: Key findings from the Cambridge study in delinquent development. *Journal of Child Psychology and Psychiatry, 36,* 929–964.

Feffer, M., & Phillips, L. (1953). Social attainment and performance under stress. *Journal of Personality, 22,* 284–297.

Flavell, J. H. (1963). *The developmental psychology of Jean Piaget.* New York: D. Van Nostrand.

Ford, D. H. (1987). *Humans as self-constructing living systems: A developmental perspective on behavior and personality.* Hillsdale, NJ: Erlbaum.

Ford, D. H., & Lerner, R. M. (1992). *Developmental systems theory: An integrative approach.* Newbury Park, CA: Sage.

Ford, M. E. (1985). The concept of competence: Themes and variations. In J. H. A. Marlowe & R. B. Weinberg (Eds.), *Competence development: Theory and practice in special populations* (pp. 3–49). Springfield, IL: Charles C. Thomas.

Fox, N. A., Henderson, H. A., Marshall, P. J., Nichols, K. E., & Ghera, M. M. (2005). Behavioral inhibition: Linking biology and behavior within a developmental framework. *Annual Review of Psychology, 56,* 235–262.

Frank, L. K. (1962). The beginnings of child development and family life education in the twentieth century. *Merrill-Palmer Quarterly, 8,* 207–208.

Frank, S. J., Paul, J. S., Marks, M., & Van Egeren, L. A. (2000). Initial validation of the Functional Impairment Scale for Children and Adolescents. *Journal of the American Academy of Child and Adolescent Psychiatry, 39*(10), 1300–1308.

Frank, S. J., Van Egeren, L. A., Fortier, J. L., & Chase, P. (2000). Structural, relative, and absolute agreement between parents' and adolescent inpatients' reports of adolescent functional impairment. *Journal of Abnormal Child Psychology, 28*(4), 395–402.

Freud, A. (1966). *The Ego and the mechanisms of defense.* New York: International Universities Press. (Original work published 1936)

Freud, S. (1960). *The ego and the id.* New York: Norton. (Original work published 1923)

Fulford, K. W. M. (1999). Nine variations and a coda on the theme of an evolutionary definition of dysfunction. *Journal of Abnormal Psychology, 108*(3), 412–420.

Garber, J., Quiggle, N. L., Panak, W., & Dodge, K. A. (1991). Aggression and depression in children: Comorbidity, specificity, and social cognitive processing. In D. Cicchetti & S. L. Toth (Eds.), *Rochester Symposium on Developmental Psychopathology: Vol. 2. Internalizing and externalizing expressions of dysfunction* (pp. 225–264). Rochester, NY: University of Rochester Press.

Garber, J., & Seligman, M. E. P. (Eds.). (1980). *Human helplessness: Theory and applications.* New York: Academic Press.

Garmezy, N. (1970). Process and reactive Schizophrenia: Some conceptions and issues. *Schizophrenia Bulletin, 2,* 30–74.

Garmezy, N. (1971). Vulnerability research and the issue of primary prevention. *American Journal of Orthopsychiatry, 41,* 101–116.

Garmezy, N. (1974). The study of competence in children at risk for severe psychopathology. In A. Koupernik (Ed.), *The child in his family: Children at psychiatric risk* (Vol. 3, pp. 77–97). New York: Wiley.

Garmezy, N. (1987). Stress, competence, and development: Continuities in the study of schizophrenic adults, children vulnerable to psychopathology, and the search for stress-resistant children. *American Journal of Orthopsychiatry, 57*(2), 159–174.

Garmezy, N., & Masten, A. S. (1986). Stress, competence, and resilience: Common frontiers for therapist and psychopathologist. *Behavior Therapy, 17,* 500–521.

Garmezy, N., Masten, A. S., & Tellegen, A. (1984). The study of stress and competence in children: A building block for developmental psychology. *Child Development, 55,* 97–111.

Garmezy, N., & Nuechterlein, K. (1972). Invulnerable children: The fact and fiction of competence and disadvantage. *American Journal of Orthopsychiatry, 42,* 328–329.

Gazelle, H., & Ladd, G. W. (2003). Anxious solitude and peer exclusion: A diathesis-stress model of internalizing trajectories in childhood. *Child Development, 74,* 257–278.

Geller, B., Bolhofner, K., Craney, J. L., Williams, M., Delbello, M. P., & Gundersen, K. (2000). Psychosocial functioning in a prepubertal and early adolescent bipolar disorder phenotype. *Journal of the American Academy of Child and Adolescent Psychiatry, 39,* 1543–1548.

Gest, S. D. (1997). Behavioral inhibition: Stability and associations with adaptation from childhood to adolescence. *Journal of Personality and Social Psychology, 72,* 467–475.

Ginsburg, H. P., & Opper, S. (1988). *Piaget's theory of intellectual development* (3rd ed.). Englewood Cliffs, NJ: Prentice-Hall.

Gordon, R. (1983). An operational classification of disease prevention. *Public Health Reports, 98,* 107–109.

Granic, I., & Hollenstein, T. (2003). Dynamic systems methods for models of developmental psychopathology. *Development and Psychopathology, 15,* 641–669.

Grant, K. E., Compas, B. E., Stuhlmacher, A. F., Thurm, A. E., McMahon, S. D., & Halpert, J. A. (2003). Stressors and child and adolescent psychopathology: Moving from markers to mechanisms of risk. *Psychological Bulletin, 129*(3), 447–466.

Greenberg, M. T., & Kusche, C. A. (1998). Preventive intervention for school-age deaf children: The PATHS curriculum. *Journal of Deaf Studies and Deaf Education, 3,* 49–63.

Greenberg, M. T., Kusche, C. A., Cook, E. T., & Quamma, J. P. (1995). Promoting emotional competence in school-aged children: The effects of the PATHS curriculum. *Development and Psychopathology, 7,* 117–136.

Greenberg, M. T., Kusche, C. A., & Mihalic, S. F. (1998). *Blueprints for violence prevention, Book 10: Promoting Alternative Thinking Strategies (PATHS).* Boulder, CO: Center for the Study and Prevention of Violence.

Greenspan, S. I. (1981). *Psychopathology and adaptation in infant and early childhood: Principles of clinical diagnosis and preventive intervention.* New York: International Universities Press.

Griffin, K. W., Epstein, J. A., Botvin, G. J., & Spoth, R. L. (2001). Social competence and substance use among rural youth: Mediating role of social benefit expectancies of use. *Journal of Youth and Adolescence, 30,* 485–498.

Griffin, K. W., Scheier, L. M., Botvin, G. J., & Diaz, T. (2001). The protective role of personal competence skills in adolescent substance use: Psychological well-being as a mediating factor. *Psychology of Addictive Behaviors, 15,* 194–203.

Gruenberg, A. M., & Goldstein, R. D. (2003). Multiaxial assessment in the twenty-first century. In K. A. Phillips, M. B. First, & H. A. Pincus (Eds.), *Advancing DSM: Dilemmas in psychiatric diagnosis* (pp. 145–152). Washington, DC: American Psychiatric Association.

Gunnar, M. R., & Thelen, E. (Eds.). (1989). *Minnesota Symposia on Child Psychology: Vol. 22. Systems and development.* Hillsdale, NJ: Erlbaum.

Harrington, R., & Clark, A. (1998). Prevention and early intervention for depression in adolescence and early adult life. *European Archives of Psychiatry and Clinical Neuroscience, 248,* 32–45.

Harter, S. (1978). Effectance motivation reconsidered: Toward a developmental model. *Human Development, 21,* 34–64.

Harter, S. (1982). The Perceived Competence Scale for Children. *Child Development, 53,* 87–97.

Harter, S. (1985). Competence as a dimension of self-evaluation: Toward a comprehensive model of self-worth. In R. L. Leahy (Ed.), *The development of the self* (pp. 55–121). New York: Academic Press.

Harter, S. (1998). The development of self-representations. In W. Damon & N. Eisenberg (Eds.), *Handbook of child psychology* (Vol. 3, pp. 553–618). New York: Wiley.

Hartmann, H. (1958). *Ego psychology and the problem of adaptation.* New York: International Universities Press. (Original work published 1939)

Hartup, W. (1996). The company they keep: Friendships and their developmental significance. *Child Development, 67,* 1–13.

Havighurst, R. J. (1972). *Developmental tasks and education* (3rd ed.). New York: David McKay.

Hawkins, J. D., Catalano, R. F., Kosterman, R., Abott, R. D., & Hill, K. G. (1999). Preventing adolescent health-risk behavior by strengthening protection during childhood. *Archives of Pediatrics and Adolescent Medicine, 153,* 226–234.

Hawkins, J. D., Catalano, R. F., Morrison, D. M., O'Donnell, J., Abbott, R. D., & Day, L. E. (1992). The Seattle Social Development Project: Effects of the first four years on protective factors and problem behavior. In J. McCord & R. E. Tremblay (Eds.), *Preventing antisocial behavior: Interventions from birth through adolescence* (pp. 139–161). New York: Guilford Press.

Hawkins, J. D., Guo, J., Hill, K. G., Battin-Pearson, S., & Abbott, R. D. (2001). Long-term effects of the Seattle social development intervention on school bonding trajectories. *Applied Developmental Science, 5,* 225–236.

Hawkins, J. D., Kosterman, R., Catalano, R. F., Hill, K. G., & Abbott, R. D. (2005). Promoting positive adult functioning through social development intervention in childhood: Long-term effects from the Seattle Social Development Project. *Archives of Pediatrics and Adolescent Medicine, 159,* 25–31.

Hawkins, J. D., Smith, B. H., Hill, K. G., Kosterman, R. F. C., & Abbott, R. D. (2003). Understanding and preventing crime and violence: Findings from the Seattle Social Development Project. In T. P. Thornberry & M. D. Krohn (Eds.), *Taking stock of delinquency: An overview of findings from contemporary longitudinal studies* (pp. 255–312). New York: Kluwer Academic/Plenum Press.

Hawkins, J. D., Von Cleve, E., & Catalano, R. F. (1992). Reducing early childhood aggression: Results of a primary prevention program. *Journal of the American Academy of Child and Adolescent Psychiatry, 30,* 208–217.

Hawkins, J. D., & Weiss, J. G. (1985). The social development model: An integrated approach to delinquency prevention. *Journal of Primary Prevention, 6*(73–79).

Hay, P., Katsikitis, M., Begg, J., Da Costa, J., & Blumenfeld, N. (2003). A two-year follow-up study and prospective evaluation of the DSM-IV Axis V. *Psychiatric Services, 54*(7), 1028–1030.

Hendrick, I. (1942). Instinct and the ego during infancy. *Psychoanalytic Quarterly, 11,* 33–58.

Hill, J. P. (1980). *Understanding early adolescence: A framework.* Carrboro, NC: Center for Early Adolescence.

Hill, J. P. (1983). Early adolescence: A research agenda. *Journal of Early Adolescence, 3,* 1–21.

Hilsenroth, M. J., Ackerman, S. J., Blagys, M. D., Baumann, B. D., Baity, M. R., Smith, S. R., et al. (2000). Reliability and validity of DSM-IV Axis V. *American Journal of Psychiatry, 157,* 1858–1863.

Hinshaw, S. P. (1992). Externalizing behavior problems and academic underachievement in childhood and adolescence: Causal relationships and underlying mechanisms. *Psychological Bulletin, 111,* 127–155.

Hinshaw, S. P. (2002a). Intervention research, theoretical mechanisms, and causal processes related to externalizing behavior patterns. *Development and Psychopathology, 14,* 789–818.

Hinshaw, S. P. (2002b). Is ADHD an impairing condition in childhood and adolescence? In P. S. Jensen & J. R. Cooper (Eds.), *Attention deficit hyperactivity disorder: State of the science, best practices* (pp. 1–21). Kingston, NJ: Civic Research Institute.

Hinshaw, S. P., & Anderson, C. A. (1996). Conduct and oppositional defiant disorders. In E. J. Mash & R. A. Barkley (Eds.), *Child psychopathology* (pp. 113–149). New York: Guilford Press.

Hodges, K., & Wong, M. M. (1996). Psychometric characteristics of a multidimensional measure to assess impairment: The Child and Adolescent Functional Assessment Scale. *Journal of Child and Family Studies, 5*(4), 445–467.

Horn, M. (1989). *Before it's too late: The child guidance movement in the United States, 1922–1945.* Philadelphia: Temple University Press.

Houts, A. C. (2001). The Diagnostic and Statistical Manual's new white coat and circularity of plausible dysfunctions: Response to Wakefield, Part 1. *Behaviour Research and Therapy, 39,* 315–345.

Jacquez, F., Cole, D. A., & Searle, B. (2004). Self-perceived competence as a mediator between maternal feedback and depressive symptoms in adolescents. *Journal of Abnormal Child Psychology, 32*(4), 355–367.

Jessor, R., & Jessor, S. L. (1977). *Problem behavior and psychosocial development.* New York: Academic Press.

John, K., Davis, G., Prusoff, B. A., & Warner, V. (1987). The Social Adjustment Inventory for Children and Adolescents (SAICA): Testing of a new semi-structured interview. *Journal of the American Academy of Child and Adolescent Psychiatry, 26,* 898–911.

Kagan, J. (1998). Biology and the child. In N. Eisenberg (Ed.), *Handbook of child psychology: Vol. 3. Social, emotional, and personality development* (5th ed., pp. 177–235). New York: Wiley.

Keating, D. P., & Hertzman, C. (1999). *Developmental health and the wealth of nations: Social, biological, and educational dynamics.* New York: Guilford Press.

Kellam, S. G. (1990). Developmental epidemiological framework for family research on depression and aggression. In G. R. Patterson (Ed.), *Depression and aggression in family interaction* (pp. 11–48). Hillsdale, NJ: Erlbaum.

Kellam, S. G., Koretz, D., & Moscicki, E. K. (1999). Core elements of developmental epidemiologically based prevention research. *American Journal of Community Psychology, 27*(4), 463–482.

Kellam, S. G., & Rebok, G. W. (1992). Building developmental and etiological theory through epidemiologically based preventive intervention trials. In J. McCord & R. E. Tremblay (Eds.), *Preventing antisocial behavior: Interventions from birth through adolescence* (pp. 162–194). New York: Guilford Press.

Kellam, S. G., Rebok, G. W., Mayer, L. S., Ialongo, N., & Kalodner, C. R. (1994). Depressive symptoms over first grade and their response to a developmental epidemiologically based preventive trial aimed at improving achievement. *Development and Psychopathology, 6,* 463–481.

Kendell, R. E. (1975). *The role of diagnosis in psychiatry.* Oxford: Blackwell Scientific.

Kennedy, J. A., & Foti, M. E. (2003). Axis V revisited. *Psychiatric Services, 54*(10), 1413.

Kennedy, J. F. (1963). *A message from the president of the United States relative to mental illness and mental retardation* (88th Congress, 1st Session, Doc. 58). Washington, DC: U.S. Government Printing Office.

Kessler, R. C., Merikangas, K. R., Berglund, P., Eaton, W. W., Koretz, D. S., & Walters, E. E. (2003). Mild disorders should not be eliminated from the DSM-V. *Archives of General Psychiatry, 60,* 1117–1121.

Kiesner, J. (2002). Depressive symptoms in early adolescence: Their relations with classroom problem behavior and peer status. *Journal of Research on Adolescence, 12,* 463–478.

Kirmayer, L. J., & Young, A. (1999). Culture and context in the evolutionary concept of mental disorder. *Journal of Abnormal Psychology, 108*(3), 446–452.

Klaczynski, P. A. (1990). Cultural-developmental tasks and adolescent development: Theoretical and methodological considerations. *Adolescence, 25,* 811–823.

Klein, R. G. (1994). Anxiety disorders. In M. Rutter, E. Taylor, & L. Hersov (Eds.), *Child and adolescent psychiatry: Modern approaches* (Vol. 3, pp. 351–374). Oxford: Blackwell Scientific.

Kohlberg, L., LaCrosse, J., & Ricks, D. (1972). The predictability of adult mental health from childhood behavior. In B. B. Wolman (Ed.), *Manual of child psychopathology* (pp. 1217–1284). New York: McGraw-Hill.

Kovacs, M., & Devlin, B. (1998). Internalizing disorders in childhood. *Journal of Child Psychology and Psychiatry, 39,* 47–63.

Kramer, T. L., Phillips, S. D., Hargis, M. B., Miller, T. L., Burns, B. J., & Robbins, J. M. (2004). Disagreement between parent and adolescent reports of functional impairment. *Journal of Child Psychology and Psychiatry, 45*(2), 248–259.

Kumpfer, K. L. (1999). Factors and processes contributing to resilience: The resilience framework. In M. D. Glantz & J. L. Johnson (Eds.), *Resilience and development: Positive life adaptations* (pp. 179–224). New York: Kluwer Academic/Plenum Press.

Lacourse, E., Cotes, S., Nagin, D. S., Vitaro, F., Brendgen, M., & Tremblay, R. E. (2002). A longitudinal-experimental approach to testing theories of antisocial behavior development. *Development and Psychopathology, 14,* 909–924.

Ladd, G. W., & Troop-Gordon, W. (2003). The role of chronic peer difficulties in the development of children's psychological adjustment problems. *Child Development, 74*(5), 1344–1367.

Lahey, B. B., Loeber, R., Burke, J., Rathouz, P. J., & McBurnett, K. (2002). Waxing and waning in concert: Dynamic comorbidity of conduct disorder with other disruptive and emotional problems over 7 years among clinic-referred boys. *Journal of Abnormal Psychology, 111,* 556–567.

Lehman, A. F., Alexopoulos, G. S., Goldman, H., Jeste, D., & Üstün, B. (2002). Mental disorders and disability: Time to re-evaluate the relationship. In D. J. Kupfer, M. B. First, & D. A. Regier (Eds.), *A research agenda for DSM-V* (pp. 201–218). Washington, DC: American Psychiatric Association.

Lerner, R. M. (2004). *Liberty: Thriving and civic engagement among America's youth.* Thousand Oaks, CA: Sage.

Lerner, R. M., & Benson, P. L. (Eds.). (2003). *Developmental assets and asset-building communities: Implications for research, policy, and practice.* New York: Kluwer Academic/Plenum Press.

Lerner, R. M., Dowling, E. M., & Anderson, P. M. (2003). Positive youth development: Thriving as a basis of personal and civil society. *Applied Developmental Science, 7*(3), 172–180.

Lerner, R. M., Dowling, E. M., & Anderson, P. M. (2005). Positive youth development: A developmental systems view. In C. B. Fisher & R. M. Lerner (Eds.), *Encyclopedia of applied developmental science* (Vol. 2, pp. 859–863). Thousand Oaks, CA: Sage.

Lewinsohn, P. M., Rohde, P., Klein, D. N., & Seeley, J. R. (1999). Natural course of adolescent major depressive disorder: I. Continuity into young adulthood. *Journal of the American Academy of Child and Adolescent Psychiatry, 38,* 56–63.

Lilienfeld, S. O., & Marino, L. (1995). Mental disorder as a Roschian concept: A critique of Wakefield's "harmful dysfunction" analysis. *Journal of Abnormal Psychology, 104,* 411–420.

Lilienfeld, S. O., & Marino, L. (1999). Essentialism revisited: Evolutionary theory and the concept of mental disorder. *Journal of Abnormal Psychology, 108*(3), 400–411.

Linley, P. A., & Jospeh, S. (Eds.). (2004). *Positive psychology in practice.* Hoboken, NJ: Wiley.

Loeber, R., & Keenan, K. (1994). Interaction between conduct disorder and its comorbid conditions: Effects of age and gender. *Clinical Psychology Review, 14,* 497–523.

Lopez, J. (Ed.). (2002). *Handbook of positive psychology.* New York: Oxford University Press.

Loevinger, J. (1976). *Ego development.* San Francisco: Jossey-Bass.

Luthar, S. S. (Ed.). (2003). *Resilience and vulnerability: Adaptation in the context of childhood adversities.* New York: Cambridge University Press.

Luthar, S. S., & Cicchetti, D. (2000). The construct of resilience: Implications for interventions and social policies. *Development and Psychopathology, 12,* 857–885.

MacKinnon, D. P., & Dwyer, J. H. (2003). Major data analysis issues in drug abuse prevention research. In Z. Sloboda & W. J. Bukowski (Eds.), *Handbook for drug abuse prevention: Theory, science, and practice* (pp. 541–556). New York: Kluwer Academic/Plenum Press.

MacKinnon, D. P., Taborga, M. P., & Morgan-Lopez, A. A. (2002). Mediation designs for tobacco prevention research. *Drug and Alcohol Dependence, 68*(Suppl. 1), 69–83.

Maguin, E., & Loeber, R. (1996). Academic performance and delinquency. *Crime and Justice: A Review of Research, 20,* 145–264.

Masten, A. S. (1989). Resilience in development: Implications of the study of successful adaptation for developmental psychopathology. In D. Cicchetti (Ed.), *Rochester Symposium on Developmental Psychopathology: Vol. 1. The emergence of a discipline* (pp. 261–294). Hillsdale, NJ: Erlbaum.

Masten, A. S. (1994). Resilience in individual development: Successful adaptation despite risk and adversity. In M. Wang & E. Gordon (Eds.), *Educational resilience in inner-city America: Challenges and prospects* (pp. 3–25). Hillsdale, NJ: Erlbaum.

Masten, A. S. (1999). Resilience comes of age: Reflections on the past and outlook for the next generation of research. In M. D. Glantz, J. Johnson, & L. Huffman (Eds.), *Resilience and development: Positive life adaptations* (pp. 289–296). New York: Plenum Press.

Masten, A. S. (2001). Ordinary magic: Resilience processes in development. *American Psychologist, 56*(3), 227–238.

Masten, A. S. (2003). Commentary: Developmental psychopathology as a unifying context for mental health and education models, research, and practice in schools. *School Psychology Review, 32*(2), 170–174.

Masten, A. S. (2004). Regulatory processes, risk and resilience in adolescent development. *Annals of the New York Academy of Sciences, 1021*(1/11), 1–25.

Masten, A. S. (2005). Peer relationships and psychopathology in developmental perspective: Reflections on progress and promise. *Journal of Clinical Child and Adolescent Psychology, 34,* 87–92.

Masten, A. S. (in press). Developmental psychopathology: Pathways to the future. *International Journal of Behavioral Development.*

Masten, A. S., & Braswell, L. (1991). Developmental psychopathology: An integrative framework. In P. R. Martin (Ed.), *Handbook of behavior therapy and psychological science: An integrative approach* (pp. 35–56). Elmsford, NY: Pergamon Press.

Masten, A. S., Burt, K., Roisman, G. I., Obradovic, J., Long, J. D., & Tellegen, A. (2004). Resources and resilience in the transition to adulthood: Continuity and change. *Development and Psychopathology, 16,* 1071–1094.

Masten, A. S., & Coatsworth, J. D. (1995). Competence, resilience, and psychopathology. In D. Cicchetti & D. J. Cohen (Eds.), *Developmental psychopathology: Vol. 2. Risk, disorder, and adaptation* (pp. 715–752). New York: Wiley.

Masten, A. S., & Coatsworth, J. D. (1998). The development of competence in favorable and unfavorable environments: Lessons from research on successful children. *American Psychologist, 53*(2), 205–220.

Masten, A. S., Coatsworth, J. D., Neemann, J., Gest, S. D., Tellegen, A., & Garmezy, N. (1995). The structure and coherence of competence from childhood through adolescence. *Child Development, 66*(6), 1635–1659.

Masten, A. S., & Curtis, W. J. (2000). Integrating competence and psychopathology: Pathways toward a comprehensive science of adaptation in development. *Development and Psychopathology, 12,* 529–550.

Masten, A. S., & Garmezy, N. (1985). Risk, vulnerability, and protective factors in developmental psychopathology. In B. B. Lahey & A. E. Kazdin (Eds.), *Advances in clinical child psychology* (Vol. 8, pp. 1–52). New York: Plenum Press.

Masten, A. S., & Gewirtz, A. H. (in press). Vulnerability and resilience in early child development. In K. McCartney & D. A. Phillips (Eds.), *Handbook of early childhood development* Oxford, UK: Blackwell's.

Masten, A. S., Hubbard, J. J., Gest, S. D., Tellegen, A., Garmezy, N., & Ramirez, M. L. (1999). Competence in the context of adversity: Pathways to resilience and maladaptation from childhood to late adolescence. *Development and Psychopathology, 11,* 143–169.

Masten, A. S., Morison, P., & Pellegrini, D. S. (1985). A revised class play method of peer assessment. *Developmental Psychology, 21*(3), 523–533.

Masten, A. S., Morison, P., Pellegrini, D., & Tellegen, A. (1990). Competence under stress: Risk and protective factors. In J. Rolf, A. S. Masten, D. Cicchetti, K. Nuechterlein, & S. Weintraub (Eds.), *Risk and protective factors in the development of psychopathology* (pp. 236–256). New York: Cambridge University Press.

Masten, A. S., Obradovic, J., & Burt, K. (in press). Resilience in emerging adulthood. In J. J. Arnett & J. Tanner (Eds.), *Growing into adulthood: The lives and contexts of emerging adults.* Washington, DC: American Psychological Association.

Masten, A. S., & Powell, J. L. (2003). A resilience framework for research, policy, and practice. In S. S. Luthar (Ed.), *Resilience and vulnerability: Adaptation in the context of childhood adversities* (pp. 1–25). New York: Cambridge University Press.

Masten, A. S., & Reed, M.-G. J. (2002). Resilience in development. In C. R. Snyder & S. J. Lopez (Eds.), *Handbook of positive psychology* (pp. 74–88). London: Oxford University Press.

Masten, A. S., Roisman, G. I., Long, J. D., Burt, K. B., Obradovic, J., Riley, J. R., et al. (in press). Developmental cascades: Linking academic achievement, externalizing and internalizing symptoms over 20 years. *Developmental Psychology, 41.*

Masten, A. S., & Shaffer, A. (in press). How families matter in child development: Reflections from research on risk and resilience. In A. Clarke-Stewart & J. Dunn (Eds.), *Families count: Effects on child and adolescent development.* Cambridge, England: Cambridge University Press.

Masten, A. S., & Wright, M. O. D. (1998). Cumulative risk and protection models of child maltreatment. *Journal of Aggression, Maltreatment, and Trauma, 2*(1), 7–30.

Maughan, B., Rowe, R., Loeber, R., & Stouthamer-Louber, M. (2003). Reading problems and depressed mood. *Journal of Abnormal Child Psychology, 31*(2), 219–229.

Mayr, E. (1982). *The growth of biological thought: Diversity, evolution, and inheritance.* Cambridge, MA: Harvard University Press.

McGee, R., Feehan, M., Williams, S., & Anderson, J. (1992). DSM-III disorders from age 11 to age 15 years. *Journal of the American Academy of Child and Adolescent Psychiatry, 31,* 50–59.

McGrew, K., & Bruininks, R. (1989). Factor structure of adaptive behavior. *School Psychology Review, 18,* 64–81.

Menninger, K. (1963). *The vital balance: The life process in mental health and illness.* New York: Viking Press.

Mesman, J., Bongers, I. L., & Koot, H. M. (2001). Preschool developmental pathways to preadolescent internalizing and externalizing problems. *Journal of Child Psychology and Psychiatry, 42,* 679–689.

Mihalic, S., Fagan, A., Irwin, K., Ballard, D., & Elliott, D. (2004). *Blueprints for violence prevention.* Washington, DC: U.S. Department of Justice, Office of Justice Programs, Office of Juvenile Justice and Delinquency Prevention.

Moffitt, T. E., Caspi, A., Harrington, H., & Milne, B. J. (2002). Males on the life-course-persistent and adolescence-limited antisocial pathways: Follow-up at age 26 years. *Development and Psychopathology, 14,* 179–207.

Mrazek, P. J., & Haggerty, R. J. (Eds.). (1994). *Reducing risks for mental disorders: Frontiers for prevention intervention research.* Washington, DC: National Academy Press.

Nangle, D. W., Erdley, C. A., Newman, J. E., Mason, C. A., & Carpenter, E. M. (2003). Popularity, friendship quantity, and friendship quality: Interactive influences on children's loneliness and depression. *Journal of Clinical Child and Adolescent Psychology, 32*(4), 546–555.

Nation, M., Crusto, C., Wandersman, A., Kumpfer, K. L., Seybolt, D., Morrissey-Kane, E., et al. (2003). What works in prevention: Principles of effective prevention programs. *American Psychologist, 58,* 449–456.

O'Connor, T. G., McGuire, S., Reiss, D., Hetherington, E. M., & Plomin, R. (1998). Co-occurrence of depressive symptoms and antisocial behavior in adolescence: A common genetic liability. *Journal of Abnormal Psychology, 107,* 27–37.

Oerter, R. (1986). Developmental tasks throughout the life span: A new approach to an old concept. In P. A. Baltes, D. L. Featherman, & R. M. Lerner (Eds.), *Life span development and behavior* (Vol. 7, pp. 233–269). Hillsdale, NJ: Erlbaum.

Ojemann, R. H., Levitt, E. E., Lyle, W. H., & Whitesie, M. F. (1955). The effects of a "causal" teacher-training program and certain curricular changes on grade school children. *Journal of Exceptional Education, 24,* 97–114.

Pagani, L., Tremblay, R. E., Vitaro, F., Boulerice, B., & McDuff, P. (2001). Effects of grade retention on academic performance and behavioral development. *Development and Psychopathology, 13,* 297–315.

Panak, W. F., & Garber, J. (1992). Role of aggression, rejection, and attributions in the prediction of depression in children. *Development and Psychopathology, 4,* 145–165.

Parker, J. G., Rubin, K. H., Price, J. M., & DeRosier, M. E. (1995). Peer relationships, child development and adjustment: A developmental psychopathology perspective. In D. Cicchetti & D. Cohen (Eds.), *Developmental psychopathology, Vol. 2: Risk, disorder, and adaptation* (pp. 96–161). New York: Wiley.

Patterson, G. R., & Capaldi, D. M. (1990). A mediational model for boys' depressed mood. In J. Rolf, A. S. Masten, D. Cicchetti, K. H. Nuechterlein, & S. Weintraub (Eds.), *Risk and protective factors in the development of psychopathology* (pp. 141–163). New York: Cambridge University Press.

Patterson, G. R., Forgatch, M. S., Yoerger, K. L., & Stoolmiller, M. (1998). Variables that initiate and maintain an early-onset trajectory for juvenile offending. *Development and Psychopathology, 10,* 531–547.

Patterson, G. R., Reid, J. B., & Dishion, T. J. (1992). *A social interactional approach: Vol. 4. Antisocial boys.* Eugene, OR: Castalia.

Patterson, G. R., & Stoolmiller, M. (1991). Replications of a dual failure model for boys' depressed mood. *Journal of Consulting and Clinical Psychology, 59,* 491–498.

Pennington, B. F. (2002). *The development of psychopathology.* New York: Guilford Press.

Peterson, B. S., Leckman, J. F., & Cohen, D. J. (1995). Tourette's syndrome: A genetically predisposed and an environmentally specified developmental psychopathology. In D. Cicchetti & D. J. Cohen (Eds.), *Developmental psychopathology: Vol. 2. Risk, disorder, and adaptation* (pp. 213–242). New York: Wiley.

Phillips, L. (1953). Case history data and prognosis in Schizophrenia. *Journal of Nervous and Mental Disease, 117,* 515–525.

Phillips, L. (1968). *Human adaptation and its failures.* New York: Academic Press.

Phillips, L., & Cowitz, B. (1953). Social attainment and reaction to stress. *Journal of Personality, 22,* 270–283.

Pickles, A., Rowe, R., Simonoff, E., Foley, D., Rutter, M., & Silberg, J. (2001). Child psychiatric symptoms and psychosocial impairment: Relationship and prognostic significance. *British Journal of Psychiatry, 179,* 230–235.

Pincus, H. A., McQueen, L. E., & Elinson, L. (2003). Subthreshold mental disorders: Nosological and research recommendations. In K. A. Phillips, M. B. First, & H. A. Pincus (Eds.), *Advancing DSM: Dilemmas in psychiatric diagnosis* (pp. 129–144). Washington, DC: American Psychiatric Association.

Pine, D. S., Alegria, M., Cook, E. H., Costello, E. J., Dahl, R. E., Koretz, D., et al. (2002). Advances in developmental science and DSM-V. In D. J. Kupfer, M. B. First, & D. A. Regier (Eds.), *A research agenda for DSM-V* (pp. 85–122). Washington, DC: American Psychiatric Association.

Pine, D. S., Cohen, E., & Cohen, P. (2000). Social phobia and the persistence of conduct problems. *Journal of Child Psychology and Psychiatry, 41*(5), 657–665.

Pine, D. S., Cohen, P., Gurley, D., Brook, J., & Ma, Y. (1998). The risk for early-adulthood anxiety and depressive disorders in adolescents with anxiety and depressive disorders. *Archives of General Psychiatry, 55,* 56–64.

Pittman, K. J. (1991). *Promoting youth development: Strengthening the role of youth-serving and community organizations.* Washington, DC: U.S. Department of Agriculture Extension Services.

Pittman, K. J., & Cahill, M. (1991). *A new vision: Promoting youth development.* Washington, DC: Academy for Educational Development, Center for Youth Development and Policy Research.

Pittman, K. J., O'Brien, R., & Kimball, M. (1993). *Youth development and resiliency research: Making connections to substance abuse prevention* (Report prepared for the Center for Substance Abuse Prevention). Washington, DC: Center for Youth Development and Policy Research.

Pollard, J. A., Hawkins, D. J., & Arthur, M. W. (1999). Risk and protection: Are both necessary to understand diverse behavioral outcomes in adolescence? *Social Work Research, 23,* 145–158.

Poulin, F., Dishion, T. J., & Burraston, B. (2001). 3-year iatrogenic effects associated with aggregating high-risk adolescents in cognitive-behavioral preventive interventions. *Applied Developmental Psychology, 5*(4), 214–224.

Price, R. H., Cowne, E. L., Lorion, R. P., & Ramos-McKay, J. (Eds.). (1988). *14 ounces of prevention: A casebook for practitioners.* Washington, DC: American Psychological Association.

Puig-Antich, J., Kaufman, J., Ryan, N. D., Williamson, D. E., Dahl, R. E., Lukens, E., et al. (1993). The psychosocial functioning and family environment of depressed adolescents. *Journal of the American Academy of Child and Adolescent Psychiatry, 32,* 244–253.

Ramey, C. T., & Ramey, S. L. (1998). Early intervention and early experience. *American Psychologist, 53,* 109–120.

Repetti, R. L., Taylor, S. E., & Seeman, T. E. (2002). Risky families: Family social environments and the mental and physical health of offspring. *Psychological Bulletin, 128,* 330–366.

Reynolds, A. J., & Ou, S.-R. (2003). Promoting resilience through early childhood intervention. In S. Luthar (Ed.), *Resilience and vulnerability: Adaptation in the context of childhood adversities* (pp. 436–459). New York: Cambridge University Press.

Richters, J. E., & Cicchetti, D. (1993). Mark Twain meets DSM-III-R: Conduct disorder, development, and the concept of harmful dysfunction. *Development and Psychopathology, 5,* 5–29.

Risi, S., Gerhardstein, R., & Kistner, J. (2003). Children's classroom peer relationships and subsequent educational outcomes. *Journal of Child and Adolescent Psychology, 32*(3), 351–361.

Robins, L. N. (1986). The consequences of conduct disorders in girls. In D. Olweus, J. Block, & M. Radke-Yarrow (Eds.), *Development of antisocial and prosocial behavior: Research, theories, and issues* (pp. 385–414). Orlando, FL: Harcourt Brace Jovanovich.

Roeser, R. W., & Eccles, J. S. (2000). Schooling and mental health. In A. J. Sameroff, M. Lewis, & S. M. Miller (Eds.), *Handbook of developmental psychopathology* (2nd ed., pp. 135–156). New York: Kluwer Academic/Plenum Press.

Roeser, R. W., Eccles, J. S., & Sameroff, A. J. (2000). School as a context of early adolescents' academic and social-emotional development: A summary of research findings. *Elementary School Journal, 100,* 443–471.

Roisman, G. I., Masten, A. S., Coatsworth, J. D., & Tellegen, A. (2004). Salient and emerging developmental tasks in the transition to adulthood. *Child Development, 75*(1), 1–11.

Rolf, J. E., & Johnson, J. L. (1999). Opening doors to resilience prevention for prevention research. In M. D. Glantz & J. L. Johnson (Eds.), *Resilience and development: Positive life adaptations* (pp. 229–249). New York: Kluwer Academic/Plenum Press.

Romano, E., Tremblay, R. E., Vitaro, F., Zoccolillo, M., & Pagani, L. (2001). Prevalence of psychiatric diagnoses and the role of perceived impairment: Findings from an adolescent community sample. *Journal of Child Psychology and Psychiatry, 42*(4), 451–461.

Rothbart, M. K., & Bates, J. E. (1998). Temperament. In N. Eisenberg (Ed.), *Handbook of child psychology: Vol. 4. Social, emotional, and personality development* (5th ed., pp. 105–176). New York: Wiley.

Roy-Byrne, P., Dagadakis, C., Unutzer, J., & Ries, R. (1996). Evidence for limited validity of the revised Global Assessment of Functioning Scale. *Psychiatric Services, 47*(9), 864–866.

Rubin, K. H., Bukowski, W., & Parker, J. G. (1998). Peer interactions, relationships, and groups. In N. Eisenberg (Ed.), *Handbook of child psychology: Vol. 3. Social, emotional, and personality development* (5th ed., pp. 619–700). New York: Wiley.

Rubin, K. H., Chen, X., McDougall, P., Bowker, A., & McKinnon, J. (1995). The Waterloo Longitudinal Project: Predicting internalizing and externalizing problems in adolescence. *Development and Psychopathology, 7,* 751–764.

Rubin, K. H., Hymel, S., Mills, R. S. L., & Rose-Krasnor, L. (1991). Conceptualizing different developmental pathways to and from social isolation in childhood. In D. Cicchetti & S. L. Toth (Eds.), *Rochester Symposium on Developmental Psychopathology* (Vol. 2, pp. 91–122). Hillsdale, NJ: Erlbaum.

Rutter, M. (1979). Protective factors in children's responses to stress and disadvantage. *Annals of the Academy of Medicine, Singapore, 8,* 324–338.

Sadler, J. Z. (1999). Horsefeathers: A commentary on "Evolutionary versus prototype analyses of the concept of disorder." *Journal of Abnormal Psychology, 108*(3), 433–437.

Sameroff, A. J. (1983). Developmental systems: Contexts and evolution. In W. Kessen (Ed.), P. H. Mussen (Series Ed.), *Handbook of child psychology, Vol. 1: History, theory and methods* (pp. 237–294). New York: Wiley.

Sameroff, A. J. (2000a). Developmental systems and psychopathology. *Development and Psychopathology, 12,* 297–312.

Sameroff, A. J. (2000b). Dialectical processes in developmental psychopathology. In A. J. Sameroff, M. Lewis, & S. M. Miller (Eds.), *Handbook of developmental psychopathology* (2nd ed., pp. 23–40). New York: Kluwer Academic/Plenum Press.

Sameroff, A. J. (in press). Identifying risk and protective factors for healthy child development. In A. Clark-Stewart & J. Dunn (Eds.), *Families count: Effects on child and adolescent development.* Cambridge, England: Cambridge University Press.

Sameroff, A. J., & Chandler, M. J. (1975). Reproductive risk and the continuum of caretaking casualty. *Review of Child Development Research, 4,* 187–244.

Sameroff, A. J., & Fiese, B. H. (2000). Transactional regulation: The developmental ecology of early intervention. In J. P. Shonkoff & S. J. Meisels (Eds.), *Handbook of early childhood intervention* (pp. 135–159). New York: Cambridge University Press.

Sameroff, A. J., Gutman, L. M., & Peck, S. C. (2003). Adaptation among youth facing multiple risks: Prospective research findings. In S. Luthar (Ed.), *Resilience and vulnerability: Adaptation in the context of childhood adversities* (pp. 364–391). New York: Cambridge University Press.

Sameroff, A. J., Seifer, R., & Bartko, W. T. (1997). Environmental perspectives on adaptation during childhood and adolescence. In S. S. Luthar, J. A. Burack, D. Cicchetti, & J. R. Weisz (Eds.), *Developmental psychopathology: Perspectives on adjustment, risk, and disorder* (pp. 507–526). New York: Cambridge University Press.

Sander, L. W. (1975). Infant and caretaking environment: Investigation and conceptualization of adaptive behavior in a system of increasing complexity. In E. J. Anthony (Ed.), *Explorations in child psychiatry* (pp. 129–166). New York: Plenum Press.

Sandler, I., Wolchik, S., Davis, C., Haine, R., & Ayers, T. (2003). Correlational and experimental study of resilience in children of divorce and parentally bereaved children. In S. Luthar (Ed.), *Resilience and vulnerability: Adaptation in the context of childhood adversities* (pp. 213–242). New York: Cambridge University Press.

Sattler, J. M. (1988). *Assessment of children* (3rd ed.). San Diego: Author.

Seligman, M. E. P. (1975). *Helplessness: On depression, development, and death.* San Francisco: Freeman.

Seligman, M. E. P. (2002). Positive psychology, positive prevention, and positive therapy. In S. J. Lopez (Ed.), *Handbook of positive psychology* (pp. 3–9). New York: Oxford University Press.

Seligman, M. E. P., & Csikszentmihalyi, M. (2000). Positive psychology: An introduction. *American Psychologist, 55,* 5–14.

Shaffer, D., Gould, M. S., Brasic, J., Ambrosini, P., Fisher, P., Bird, H., et al. (1983). A Children's Global Assessment Scale (CGAS). *Archives of General Psychiatry, 40,* 1228–1231.

Shaw, D. S., Dishion, T. J., Supplee, L. H., Gardner, F., & Arnds, K. (in press). A family-centered approach to the prevention of early-onset antisocial behavior. Two-year effects of the family check-up in early childhood. *Journal of Consulting and Clinical Psychology.*

Sheppard, D. M., Bradshaw, J. L., Purcell, R., & Pantelis, C. (1999). Tourette's and comorbid syndromes: Obsessive compulsive and attention deficit hyperactivity disorder. A common etiology? *Clinical Psychology Review, 19*(5), 531–552.

Shiner, R. L. (2000). Linking childhood personality with adaptation: Evidence for continuity and change across time into late adolescence. *Journal of Personality and Social Psychology, 78,* 310–325.

Shonkoff, J. P., & Meisels, S. J. (Eds.). (2000). *Handbook of early childhood intervention* (2nd ed.). New York: Cambridge University Press.

Shonkoff, J. P., & Phillips, D. A. (Eds.). (2000). *From neurons to neighborhoods: The science of early childhood development.* Washington, DC: National Academy Press.

Shure, M. B., & Spivak, G. (1988). Interpersonal cognitive problem solving. In R. H. Price, E. L. Cowen, R. P. Lorion, & J. Ramos-McKay (Eds.), *14 ounces of prevention: A casebook for practitioners* (Vol. 4, pp. 1822–1863). Washington, DC: U. S: Government Printing Office.

Skinner, E. A. (1991). Development and perceived control: A dynamic model of action in context. In M. R. Gunnar & L. A. Sroufe (Eds.), *Minnesota Symposia on Child Psychology: Vol. 23. Self processes and development* (pp. 167–216). Hillsdale, NJ: Erlbaum.

Skinner, E. A., Chapman, M., & Baltes, P. B. (1988). Control, means-ends, and agency beliefs: A new conceptualization and its measurement during childhood. *Journal of Personality and Social Psychology, 54,* 117–133.

Smith, M., Steinman, J., Chorev, M., Hertzog, S., & Lerner, R. (2005). Positive youth development: Service-learning versus community-collaborative models. In C. B. Fisher & R. M. Lerner (Eds.), *Encyclopedia of applied developmental science* (Vol. 2, pp. 863–867). Thousand Oaks, CA: Sage.

Spitzer, R. L. (1999). Harmful dysfunction and the DSM definition of mental disorder. *Journal of Abnormal Psychology, 108*(3), 430–432.

Sroufe, L. A. (1979). The coherence of individual development: Early care, attachment, and subsequent developmental issues. *American Psychologist, 34,* 834–841.

Sroufe, L. A. (1997). Psychopathology as an outcome of development. *Development and Psychopathology, 9,* 251–268.

Sroufe, L. A., & Rutter, M. (1984). The domain of developmental psychopathology. *Child Development, 55,* 17–29.

Sternberg, R. J. (1985). *Beyond IQ: A triarchic theory of human intelligence.* New York: Cambridge University Press.

Sullivan, H. S. (1953). *The interpersonal theory of psychiatry.* New York: Norton.

Task Panel on Prevention. (1978). *Task panel reports submitted to the President's Commission on Mental Health* (Vol. 4). Washington, DC: U.S. Government Printing Office.

Thelen, E., & Smith, L. (1998). Dynamic systems theories. In R. M. Lerner (Ed.), *Handbook of child psychology: Vol. 1. Theoretical models of human development* (5th ed., pp. 563–634). New York: Wiley.

Thornberry, T. P., Lizotte, A. J., Krohn, M. D., Smith, C. A., & Porter, P. K. (2003). Causes and consequences of delinquency: Findings from the Rochester Youth Development Study. In T. P. Thornberry & M. D. Krohn (Eds.), *Taking stock of delinquency: An overview of findings from contemporary longitudinal studies* (pp. 11–46). New York: Kluwer Academic/Plenum Press.

Tolan, P. H. (2002). Family-focused prevention research: "Tough but tender." In H. A. Liddle, D. A. Santisteban, R. L. Levant, & J. H. Bray (Eds.), *Family psychology intervention science* (pp. 197–213). Washington, DC: American Psychological Association Books.

Toth, S. L., Maughan, A., Manly, J. T., Spagnola, M., & Cicchetti, D. (2002). The relative efficacy of two interventions in altering maltreated preschool children's representational models: Implications for attachment theory. *Development and Psychopathology, 14,* 877–908.

Tram, J. M., & Cole, D. A. (2000). Self-perceived competence and the relation between life events and depressive symptoms in adolescence: Mediator or moderator? *Journal of Abnormal Psychology, 109,* 753–760.

Travis, L. L., & Sigman, M. D. (2000). A developmental approach to Autism. In A. J. Sameroff, M. Lewis, & S. M. Miller (Eds.), *Handbook of developmental psychopathology* (2nd ed., pp. 641–655). New York: Kluwer Press.

van den Boom, D. C. (1994). The influence of temperament and mothering on attachment and exploration: An experimental manipulation of sensitive responsiveness among lower-class mothers with irritable infants. *Child Development, 65,* 1457–1477.

van den Boom, D. C. (1995). Do first-year intervention effects endure? Follow-up during toddlerhood of a sample of Dutch irritable infants. *Child Development, 66,* 1798–1816.

van Ijzendoorn, M. H., Juffer, F., & Duyvesteyn, M. G. C. (1995). Breaking the intergenerational cycle of insecure attachment: A review of the effects of attachment-based interventions on maternal sensitivity and infant security. *Journal of Child Psychology and Psychiatry and Allied Disciplines, 36,* 225–248.

Verhulst, F. C., Eussen, M. L. J. M., Berden, G. F. M. G., Sanders-Woudstra, J., & Van Der Ende, J. (1993). Pathways of problem behaviors from childhood to adolescence. *Journal of the American Academy of Child and Adolescent Psychiatry, 32,* 388–396.

Wakefield, J. C. (1992a). The concept of mental disorder: On the boundary between biological facts and social values. *American Psychologist, 47,* 373–388.

Wakefield, J. C. (1992b). Disorder as harmful dysfunction: A conceptual critique of DSM-III-R's definition of mental disorder. *Psychological Review, 99,* 233–247.

Wakefield, J. C. (1999). Evolutionary versus prototype analyses of the concept of disorder. *Journal of Abnormal Psychology, 108*(3), 374–399.

Wakefield, J. C. (2001). Evolutionary history versus current causal role in the definition of disorder: Reply to McNally. *Behaviour Research and Therapy, 39,* 347–366.

Wakefield, J. C. (2003). Dysfunction as a factual component of disorder. *Behaviour Research and Therapy, 41,* 969–990.

Wakefield, J. C., & First, M. B. (2003). Clarifying the distinction between disorder and nondisorder: Confronting the overdiagnosis (false-positives) problem in DSM-V. In K. A. Phillips, M. B. First, & H. A. Pincus (Eds.), *Advancing DSM: Dilemmas in psychiatric diagnosis* (pp. 23–56). Washington, DC: American Psychiatric Association.

Wallander, J. L., Schmitt, M., & Koot, H. M. (2001). Quality of life measurement in children and adolescents: Issues, instruments, and applications. *Journal of Clinical Psychology, 57*(4), 571–585.

Waters, E., & Sroufe, L. A. (1983). Social competence as a developmental construct. *Developmental Review, 3,* 79–97.

Webster-Stratton, C. (1985). The effects of treatment outcome in parent training for conduct disordered children. *Behavior Therapy, 16,* 223–243.

Webster-Stratton, C. (1990a). Enhancing the effectiveness of self-administered videotape parent training for families with conduct-problem children. *Journal of Abnormal Child Psychology, 18,* 479–492.

Webster-Stratton, C. (1990b). Long-term followup of families with young conduct problem children: From preschool to grade school. *Journal of Clinical Child Psychology, 19,* 144–149.

Webster-Stratton, C. (2001). The Incredible Years: Parents, teachers, and children training series. *Residential Treatment for Children and Youth, 18,* 31–45.

Webster-Stratton, C., & Hammond, M. (1997). Treating children with early-onset conduct problems: A comparison of child and parent training interventions. *Journal of Consulting and Clinical Psychology, 65,* 93–109.

Webster-Stratton, C., Mihalic, S., Fagan, A., Arnold, D., Taylor, T., & Tingley, C. (2001). *Blueprints for violence prevention, Book 11: The Incredilbe Years: Parent, teacher, and child training series.* Boulder, CO: Center for the Study and Prevention of Violence.

Webster-Stratton, C., & Reid, M. J. (1999, November). *Treating children with early onset conduct problems: The importance of teacher training.* Paper presented at the Association for the Advancement of Behavior Therapy, Toronto, Canada.

Webster-Stratton, C., Reid, M. J., & Hammond, M. (2004). Treating children with early-onset conduct problems: Intervention outcomes for parent, child, and teacher training. *Journal of Clinical Child and Adolescent Psychology, 33,* 105–124.

Wechsler, D. (1958). *The measurement and appraisal of adult intelligence.* Baltimore: Williams & Wilkins.

Weissberg, R. P., & Greenberg, M. T. (1998). School and community competence-enhancement and prevention programs. In I. E. Sigel & K. A. Renninger (Eds.), *Handbook of child psychology: Vol. 4. Child psychology in practice* (5th ed., pp. 877–954). New York: Wiley.

Weissberg, R. P., Kumpfer, K. L., & Seligman, M. E. P. (2003). Prevention that works for children and youth. *American Psychologist, 58*(6/7), 425–432.

White, R. W. (1959). Motivation reconsidered: The concept of competence. *Psychological Review, 66,* 297–333.

Williams, S., & McGee, R. (1994). Reading attainment and juvenile delinquency. *Journal of Child Psychology and Psychiatry, 35,* 441–459.

World Health Organization. (1992). *The ICD-10 classification of mental and behavioral disorders: Clinical descriptions and diagnostic guidelines.* Geneva, Switzerland: Author.

World Health Organization. (2001). *International classification of functioning, disability, and health.* Geneva, Switzerland: Author.

Wright, M. O. D., & Masten, A. S. (2005). Resilience processes in development: Fostering positive adaptation in the context of adversity. In S. Goldstein & R. Brooks (Eds.), *Handbook of resilience in children* (pp. 17–37). New York: Kluwer Academic/Plenum Press.

Wyman, P. A. (2003). Emerging perspectives on context-specificity of children's adaptation and resilience: Evidence from a decade of research with urban children in adversity. In S. S. Luthar (Ed.), *Resilience and vulnerability: Adaptation in the context of childhood adversities* (pp. 293–317). New York: Cambridge University Press.

Wyman, P. A., Sandler, I., Wolchik, S., & Nelson, K. (2000). Resilience as cumulative competence promotion and stress protection: Theory and intervention. In D. Cicchetti, J. Rappaport, I. Sandler, & R. P. Weissberg (Eds.), *The promotion of wellness in children and adolescents* (pp. 133–184). Thousand Oaks, CA: Sage.

Yates, T. M., & Masten, A. S. (2004). Fostering the future: Resilience theory and the practice of positive psychology. In P. A. Linley & S. Joseph (Eds.), *Positive psychology in practice* (pp. 521–539). Hoboken, NJ: Wiley.

Zigler, E., & Glick, M. (1986). *A developmental approach to adult psychopathology.* New York: Wiley.

Zigler, E., & Phillips, L. (1961). Social competence and outcome in psychiatric disorder. *Journal of Abnormal and Social Psychology, 61,* 231–238.

Zigler, E., Taussig, C., & Black, K. (1992). Early childhood intervention: A promising preventative for juvenile delinquency. *American Psychologist, 47,* 997–1006.

CHAPTER 20

Resilience in Development: A Synthesis of Research across Five Decades

SUNIYA S. LUTHAR

In the field of developmental psychopathology, resilience, a construct representing positive adaptation despite adversity, has received increasing attention over the past several decades. Since its introduction in the scientific literature during the second half of the twentieth century, this construct has been increasingly recognized as one of considerable importance from a theoretical and an applied perspective. Theoretically, knowledge of all "deviant" or atypical processes has great potential to promote understanding of normative development (Cicchetti & Cohen, 1995). Resilience by definition encompasses atypical

processes, in that positive adaptation is manifested in life circumstances that usually lead to maladjustment. From an applied perspective, similarly, there is broad consensus that in working with at-risk groups, it is far more prudent to promote the development of resilient functioning early in the course of development rather than to implement treatments to repair disorders once they have already crystallized (Cowen, 1991, 1994; Knitzer, 2000a, 2000b; Luthar, Cicchetti, & Becker, 2000a; Rutter, 2000; Werner, 2000). Knowledge about resilient processes in specific at-risk circumstances can be critical in pointing to the particular issues that most urgently warrant attention in the context of particular types of adversity.

In this chapter, we describe the major developments in the field of resilience since its inception more than 40 years ago. The chapter is organized in four sections, the first one presenting a brief history of work on resilience. The second section is devoted to elucidating critical features of research on this construct, highlighting three sets of issues: definitions and operationalization of the two constructs at its core, protective and vulnerability factors; distinctions between the construct of resilience and related

Preparation of this chapter was funded in part by grants from the National Institutes of Health (RO1-DA10726 and RO1-DA11498, R01-DA14385) and the William T. Grant Foundation. For her considerable help with background research and editing, I am most grateful to Pamela Brown; many thanks as well to Elizabeth Ekeblad and Chris Sexton at Teachers College and to Erica Shirley and Karen Shoum of the Yale Child and Family Research Group.

This chapter is dedicated to Chanchal Wadhwa and Zena Vijay-Kumar, two teachers who so generously gave of themselves in fostering adolescent resilience.

constructs, such as competence and ego resiliency; and differences between resilience research and related fields, including risk research, prevention science, and positive psychology.

The third section of the chapter is focused on major findings on vulnerability and protective factors. These are discussed not only in terms of the specific factors found to modify risk within three broad categories—attributes of the family, community, and child—but also in terms of factors that exert strong effects across many risk conditions and those more idiosyncratic to specific risk contexts. The final section includes a summary of extant evidence in the field along with major considerations for future work on resilience across the life span.

HISTORICAL OVERVIEW OF CHILDHOOD RESILIENCE

The roots of resilience research can be traced back to pioneering research with children of schizophrenics during the 1960s and 1970s. In studies intending to capture the etiology and prognosis of severe psychopathology, Norman Garmezy (1974) found that among these children at high risk for psychopathology was a subset of children who had surprisingly healthy adaptive patterns. Whereas these youngsters had been dismissed by scientists as being atypical cases, Garmezy and colleagues sought to identify factors associated with their unusually high well-being. This approach reflected a notable departure from the symptom-based medical models of the time in its focus on positive outcomes and the factors that foster them in the context of life's adversity.

Along with Garmezy, two other prominent scientists who studied resilience among children of schizophrenics at the time were E. James Anthony and Michael Rutter. Anthony (1974) described a set of "invulnerable" children who resisted becoming engulfed by a parent's psychopathology while still maintaining compassion for the affected parent. Rutter (1979) also identified a distinct subgroup of resilient children in this population, reporting them to be characterized by traits such as high creativity, effectiveness, and competence.

In research with groups other than families of schizophrenics, Murphy and Moriarty (1976) examined vulnerability and coping patterns in children exposed to naturally occurring stressors such as deaths or injuries in the family. Based on rich clinical observations, these authors described resilient youth as having several attributes in common, including social charisma and the capacity to relate well to others, the ability to experience a range of emotions, and the ability to regulate the expression of these emotions.

Emmy Werner's (Werner & Smith, 1982, 1992, 2001) study of infants at risk on the Hawaiian island of Kauai is a landmark in the scientific study of resilience. The study was begun in 1954 with a cohort of all known pregnancies on the island, with several follow-up assessments that continue up to the present time. The earliest reports on this cohort showed that children manifested significant deficits when family poverty was accompanied by perinatal risk. Furthermore, effects of poverty status seemed to operate via disruptions in the quality of the caregiving environment, particularly instability and disorganization of the family. Major protective factors, distinguishing well-functioning at-risk children from those faring more poorly, included affectional ties with the family, informal support systems outside the home, and dispositional attributes such as sociability.

The 1980s saw the publication of several scholarly papers on resilience, two of which were particularly influential; one was a research report by Garmezy, Masten, and Tellegen (1984) at the University of Minnesota, and the other was an analysis of conceptual issues in the study of this construct by Michael Rutter (1987). The former reported on Project Competence, a study of competence among children who experienced life stressors (Garmezy et al., 1984). The conceptualization of major constructs, methods, and data analytic strategies in this article (described later in this chapter) came to serve as models for scores of subsequent research seeking to illuminate vulnerability and protective factors.

Rutter's (1987) article was seminal in clarifying major conceptual issues in the study of resilience. In this paper, he provided several examples of a particularly intriguing class of protective processes, those with interactive components (also examined by Garmezy et al., 1984). Boys, for example, reacted more severely to family discord than did girls such that being female was "protective," and having a supportive spouse was more strongly related to good parenting among ex-institutionalized women than comparison mothers. Rutter also provided one of the first discussions on the importance of identifying processes in resilience and delineated various ways via which risk effects can be reduced: by altering the *experience* of risk itself (e.g., preparing a child before hospitalization); by altering *exposure* to the risk (e.g., via strict parental supervision in high-risk environments); by averting *negative chain reactions* (which serve to perpetuate risk effects, as harsh discipline perpetuates oppositionality); by *raising self-esteem* (through secure relationships and tasks well done); and through *turning points* or opportunities (such as entry into army service).

During the 1980s and early 1990s, there were several changes in conceptual approaches to studying the construct, two of which were particularly salient. The first concerned perspectives on the "locus" of resilience. In early studies in this area, the effort had been to identify personal qualities of resilient children such as autonomy or belief in oneself. As work in the area evolved, however, researchers acknowledged that resilient adaptation may often derive from factors external to the child. Three sets of factors thus came to be commonly cited as implicated in the development of resilience: attributes of the children themselves, aspects of their families, and characteristics of their wider social environments (Garmezy, 1987; Rutter, 1987; Werner & Smith, 1982, 1992).

The second change involved conceptions of resilience as potentially fluctuating over time rather than fixed forever. In some early writings, those who did well despite multiple risks were labeled "invulnerable" (Anthony, 1974). Recognizing that this term implied that risk evasion was absolute and unchanging, researchers gradually began to use the more qualified term "resilience" instead. Implicit in this change of terminology was the recognition that positive adaptation despite adversity is never permanent; rather, there is a developmental progression, with new vulnerabilities and strengths emerging with changing life circumstances (Garmezy & Masten, 1986; Werner & Smith, 1982).

A related qualifier was that children can seem resilient in terms of their behaviors but still might struggle with inner distress in the form of problems such as depression and anxiety. First reported in work on maltreated children (Farber & Egeland, 1987) and subsequently among inner-city adolescents (Luthar, 1991), this finding has since been replicated in various at-risk groups. Among children of depressed mothers, for instance, there is a distinct adaptation pattern involving adoption of the caretaker role: a kind of false maturity, which may initially appear to be healthy but is likely to have negative consequences over time (see Hammen, 2003; Hetherington & Elmore, 2003). In work with children of alcoholics, Zucker and colleagues (Zucker, Wong, Puttler, & Fitzgerald, 2003) found that children who showed little outward disturbance as preschoolers generally continued to show low behavioral deviance several years later. On the other hand, these preschoolers, initially

identified as resilient, came to show internalizing symptoms as high as those of the initially most troubled group. Recognizing that (1) children can retain their manifest resilience but still experience inner distress, and (2) internalizing problems, if left unattended, can eventually derail apparently resilient trajectories (Luthar & Cicchetti, 2000; Raver, 2002), scholars now underscore the need to consider the unique profiles, and the associated intervention needs, of youth who are behaviorally stellar but at the same time psychologically vulnerable (D'Imperio, Dubow, & Ippolito, 2000; Luthar & Zelazo, 2003; Zucker et al., 2003).

Finally, it was recognized that even considering only domains of behavioral competence, resilience is never an across-the-board phenomenon, but inevitably shows some domain-specificity. Much as children in general do not manifest uniformly positive or negative adaptation across different areas of adjustment, researchers cautioned that at-risk children, too, can display remarkable strengths in some areas but, at the same time, show notable deficits in others (Luthar, Doernberger, & Zigler, 1993). In view of the accumulated evidence, therefore, scientists have—prudently—begun to use more circumspect terms that specify domains in which resilience is seen, referring, for example, to educational resilience (Wang & Gordon, 1994) or emotional resilience (Denny, Clark, Fleming, & Wall, 2004).

By the turn of the century, the burgeoning popularity of the resilience construct was reflected not only in the number of scientific publications on this topic but also the breadth of at-risk circumstances examined. Several scholarly articles were published about critical conceptual issues in studying resilience and summarizing the research findings until that time (e.g., Cohler, Stott, & Musick, 1995; Luthar, 1993; Luthar & Zigler, 1991; Masten, 2001; Masten, Best, & Garmezy, 1990; Masten & Coatsworth, 1998; Rutter, 1993, 2000). Resilience was the focus of a special issue of the journal *Development and Psychopathology* (Cicchetti & Garmezy, 1993) as well as several books encompassing diverse topics and scientific methods (e.g., Cicchetti, Rappaport, Sandler, & Weissberg, 2000; Glantz & Johnson, 1999; Haggerty, Sherrod, Garmezy, & Rutter, 1996; Hetherington, 1999; Luthar, 2003; McCubbin, Thompson, Thompson, & Futrell, 1999; Rolf, Masten, Cicchetti, Nuechterlein, & Weintraub, 1990; R. D. Taylor & Wang, 2000; Ungar, 2004; Wang & Gordon, 1994). In terms of diversity of risks examined, by the year 2000, resilience had been examined in the context of adversities ranging from parental mental illness (Masten & Coatsworth, 1998), maltreatment (Cicchetti & Rogosch, 1997), and chronic illness (Wells & Schwebel, 1987), to socioeconomic disadvantage and associated risks

(Garmezy, 1993; Luthar, 1999; Rutter, 1979; Werner & Smith, 1982, 1992), community violence (Richters & Martinez, 1993), and catastrophic life events (O'Dougherty-Wright, Masten, Northwood, & Hubbard, 1997).

Alongside the rapid proliferation of studies on resilience, however, were increasing concerns about the rigor of methods used in this body of work (e.g., Cicchetti & Garmezy, 1993; Glantz & Johnson, 1999; Luthar, 1993; Rutter, 2000). In particular, critics alleged (and with good reason) that the literature on resilience reflected considerable confusion around pivotal constructs and definitions, about criteria used to label people as resilient, and about the definition and measurement of protective and vulnerability processes (Luthar, Cicchetti, & Becker, 2000a). Given the centrality of these notions and the fact that there are still some uncertainties about them in the field, they are discussed at some length in the section that follows.

RESILIENCE RESEARCH: CENTRAL FEATURES

Resilience is defined as a phenomenon or process reflecting relatively *positive adaptation despite experiences of significant adversity or trauma.* Resilience is a superordinate construct subsuming two distinct dimensions—significant adversity and positive adaptation—and thus is never directly measured, but is indirectly inferred based on evidence of the two subsumed constructs.

Considering the two component constructs in turn, risk is defined in terms of statistical probabilities: A high-risk condition is one that carries high odds for measured maladjustment in critical domains (Masten, 2001). Exposure to community violence, for example, constitutes high risk given that children experiencing it reflect significantly greater maladjustment than those who do not (Margolin & Gordis, 2000). Similarly, maternal depression is a risk factor in that children of mothers with depressive diagnoses can be as much as 8 times as likely as others to develop depressive disorders themselves by adolescence (Wickramaratne & Weissman, 1998).

In addition to discrete risk dimensions such as community violence, poverty, and parent mental illness, researchers have examined composites of multiple risk indices such as parents' low income and education, their histories of mental illness, and disorganization in their neighborhoods. Seminal research by Rutter (1979) demonstrated that when risks such as these coexist (as they often do in the real world), effects tend to be synergistic, with children's outcomes being far poorer than when any of these risks existed in isolation. Use of this cumulative risk

approach is exemplified in work by Sameroff and his colleagues (e.g., Gutman, Sameroff, & Cole, 2003; Sameroff, Gutman, & Peck, 2003). These authors computed a total risk score across 10 different dimensions, assigning for each one a score of 1 (versus zero) if the child fell in the highest quartile of continuous risk dimensions and, for dichotomous dimensions such as single-parent family status, if they were present in that child's life. Masten and colleagues (Masten, Morison, Pellegrini, & Tellegen, 1990) used a somewhat different approach to deriving total risk based on continuous scores; these researchers standardized the values on different risk scales and added them to obtain a composite.

Decisions regarding the use of single or multiple risk indices in resilience research depend on the substantive research questions. The former is used, obviously, when applied researchers seek to identify factors that might modify the effects of *particular* environmental risks known to have strong adverse effects, so as to eventually derive specific directions for interventions. Examples are parental divorce and bereavement; knowledge of what ameliorates the ill effects of these particular adversities has been valuable in designing appropriate interventions (C. R. Martinez & Forgatch, 2001; Sandler, Wolchik, Davis, Haine, & Ayers, 2003). Additive approaches are more constrained in this respect, precluding identification, for example, of which of the indices subsumed in the composite are more influential than others. On the other hand, composite risk indices generally explain more variance in adjustment than do any of them considered alone, and as noted earlier, they may be more realistic in that many of these risks do co-occur in actuality (Luthar et al., 2000a; Masten, 2001).

Positive adaptation, the second component in the construct of resilience, is adaptation that is substantially better than what would be expected given exposure to the risk circumstance being studied. In many studies of resilience across diverse risk circumstances, this has been defined in terms of behaviorally manifested social competence, or success at meeting stage-salient developmental tasks (Luthar et al., 2000a; Masten, 2001; Masten & Coatsworth, 1998). Among young children, for example, competence was operationally defined in terms of the development of a secure attachment with primary caregivers (Yates, Egeland, & Sroufe, 2003), and among older children, in terms of aspects of school-based functioning such as good academic performance and positive relationships with classmates and teachers (Masten & Coatsworth, 1998; Wyman et al., 1999).

In addition to being developmentally appropriate, indicators used to define positive adaptation must be conceptually of high relevance to the risk examined in terms of domains assessed and stringency of criteria used (Luthar, 1993). When communities carry many risks for antisocial problems, for example, it makes sense to assess the degree to which children are able to maintain socially conforming behaviors (Seidman & Pedersen, 2003), whereas among children of depressed parents, the absence of depressive diagnoses would be of special significance (Beardslee, 2002; Hammen, 2003). With regard to stringency of criteria, similarly, decisions must depend on the seriousness of the risks under consideration. In studying children facing major traumas, it is entirely appropriate to define risk evasion simply in terms of the absence of serious psychopathology rather than superiority or excellence in everyday adaptation (Masten & Powell, 2003).

Whereas approaches to measuring risk can involve one or multiple negative circumstances, *competence* must necessarily be defined across multiple spheres, for overly narrow definitions can convey a misleading picture of success in the face of adversity. Adolescents, for example, might be viewed very positively by their peers but, at the same time, perform poorly academically or even demonstrate conduct disturbances (Luthar & Burack, 2000; O'Donnell, Schwab-Stone, & Muyeed, 2002). Statistical examination of different outcome domains can, again, be done via various strategies. In variable-based analyses such as regressions, some researchers have simply examined each one in separate analyses, for example, predicting to scores on school achievement, peer acceptance, and emotional well-being (Zucker et al., 2003). An alternative approach, parallel to that previously described for cumulative risk scores, is to standardize scores across different adjustment domains and then add these to gauge overall competence across multiple spheres (Bolger & Patterson, 2003).

An innovative approach to defining competence is seen in research by Kim-Cohen, Moffitt, Caspi, and Taylor (2004), who statistically computed competence scores that were better than what would be expected given the presence of risk. In their sample of largely low-income children, these authors assessed several dimensions of risk: socioeconomic disadvantages, housing problems, and mothers' perceptions of economic deprivation. Multiple regression analyses were used with the three scores of deprivation predicting to two outcomes—conduct problems and intelligence scores—and the residuals from these analyses were standardized and saved. These residual scores represented, for each child, the difference between what would be expected given the level of risk, and what was actually observed (see also Elder & Conger, 2000). The investigators therefore arrived at two scores, behavioral resilience

and cognitive resilience (residuals of low conduct and high intelligence scores, respectively), and these were used as outcome variables in statistical analyses.

It should be noted that in some situations, competence is most appropriately operationalized in terms of "better than expected" functioning of families or communities rather than of the children themselves. As Seifer (2003) has argued, infants and even toddlers are still too young to reliably be judged as manifesting resilience because their functioning is so integrally regulated by others. At these young ages, therefore, it may be more logical to operationalize positive adjustment in terms of the mother-child dyad or family unit. In a similar vein, the label resilience can be most appropriate for communities of well-functioning at-risk youth. Research on neighborhoods, for example, has demonstrated that some low-income urban neighborhoods reflect far higher levels of cohesiveness, organization, and social efficacy than others (Leventhal & Brooks-Gunn, 2000; Sampson, Raudenbush, & Earls, 1997), with the potential, therefore, to serve as important buffers against negative socializing influences.

Vulnerability and Protective Processes

The central objective of resilience researchers is to identify *vulnerability* and *protective factors* that might *modify* the negative effects of adverse life circumstances, and, having accomplished this, to identify *mechanisms* or *processes* that might underlie associations found (Luthar & Cicchetti, 2000; Masten, 2001; Rutter, 2000, 2003). Vulnerability factors or markers encompass those indices that exacerbate the negative effects of the risk condition. Among youth living in the ecology of urban poverty, for example, male gender can be a vulnerability marker, for boys are typically more reactive than girls to negative community influences (see Luthar, 1999; Spencer, 1999). For children experiencing severe and chronic life adversities, those with low intelligence are more vulnerable to adjustment difficulties over time than are those with higher intelligence (Masten, 2001). Protective factors are those that modify the effects of risk in a positive direction. Examples include an internal locus of control and having a positive relationship with at least one adult; in groups of youngsters exposed to significant adversities, those with such attributes frequently fare better than youth who lack them (Luthar & Zigler, 1991; Masten, 2001; Rutter, 1999; Werner & Smith, 1992).

In the literature on resilience, discussions on the notions of vulnerability and protection have reflected considerable confusion around definition, measurement, and interpretation of statistical findings. As these processes form the crux of what resilience researchers are interested in, salient issues in this regard are addressed individually in discussions that follow.

Identifying Protective and Vulnerability Factors: Variable-Based Approaches

In the resilience literature, there have been two major approaches to identifying protective or vulnerability factors, the first involving variable-based statistical analyses such as multivariate regressions. One of the first empirical efforts to use this approach was the previously mentioned groundbreaking paper by Garmezy et al. (1984). In this research, risk was considered on a continuous scale of cumulative life stress scores, and competence was defined in terms of three dimensions: good school grades and two dimensions of classroom behavior as rated by both classmates and teachers, engaged-disengaged and classroom disruptiveness. Hypothesized protective factors included the child's female sex, high intelligence, and high socioeconomic status (SES). These were examined not only in terms of direct links with competence outcomes (main effects) but also in interaction with stress (to determine if they might benefit children at high stress more than those at low stress). Hierarchical multiple regressions were performed, which showed significant main effect links for all hypothesized protective factors as well as a significant IQ × stress interaction effect (Garmezy et al., 1984). Thus, high SES, female sex, and high IQ were each advantageous for children with high life stress as well as those at low stress. The lone interaction effect showed that high IQ children maintained a generally high level of competence regardless of stress levels, whereas low IQ youth did far more poorly at high than low stress.

Garmezy and colleagues (1984) initially used the terms "compensatory" to describe their main effect findings and "protective" to describe the interaction effect they found, but other researchers have commonly used protective to refer to main effect links as well. In two other major programs of research, Werner's (Werner & Smith, 1982) study in Hawaii and Cowen, Wyman, and colleagues' Rochester Child Resilience Project (Cowen et al., 1996; Wyman et al., 1999), protective factors were simply those that distinguished between high-risk children who did well and those who did poorly (what this variable did or did not do for low-risk youth was not relevant). Given this differential use of the term, there were increasing exhortations for researchers to enhance specificity in how they referred to interactive effects (e.g., Luthar et al., 2000a; Luthar & Zelazo, 2003), with terms such as "protective-stabilizing" for trends such as those in the Garmezy et al. study and

"protective-enhancing," when at-risk children with the attribute performed much better than all others. Encouragingly, researchers are in fact using more differentiated terms in describing interactive effects (e.g., Brody, Dorsey, Forehand, & Armistead, 2002; Gerard & Buehlar, 2004; Hammack, Richards, Luo, Edlynn, & Roy, 2004); despite some continuing variations in the labels used, there is a growing convention of clearly specifying what exactly the terms resilience, risk, vulnerability, and protection signify as operationally defined in particular studies.

Person-Based Analyses

Person-based analyses in resilience research essentially involve comparisons between a group of children who experience high risk and show high competence—a manifestly resilient group—and others varying on these two dimensions. Of particular interest are comparisons with youth at high risk and low competence, as these can illuminate factors that might confer protection against adversity. Comparisons with low risk and high competence groups, conversely, are particularly useful in determining whether the high competence of manifestly resilient children is actually commensurate with the levels shown by youth with relatively benign life circumstances.

Demarcating groups of manifestly resilient children is a little more complicated when there are multiple aspects of competence involved, as is the preferred approach; two strategies have been used in such instances (see Luthar & Zelazo, 2003). One involves standardizing and adding the scores across the different dimensions to obtain an overall competence score, and then allotting children to groups based on distribution of these composites. An advantage of this approach is that it takes into account where exactly people fall on the continuum of scores across various outcomes, so that a person extremely high on multiple domains of everyday competence, for example, would fall well above the sample mean on the composite score, even if he or she had significant problems in one particular symptom domain. The alternative strategy is to stipulate cutoffs that represent positive and negative adjustment on each indicator and designate children into different groups depending on where they fall across all of these, that is, in terms of competence scores that are above the sample mean and symptom levels that are below clinically significant levels. The subgroup of children who meet these success criteria across all indices is identified, and these children—again, ostensibly resilient—are compared with others who do not meet these criteria.

In the recent past, researchers have begun to use both variable- and person-based approaches in their analyses of multiple competence domains. Buckner, Mezzacappa, and Beardslee (2003), for instance, conducted a study with 155 children from very low-income families and considered five different competence outcomes: a global rating of overall adaptive functioning and one of behavioral competence, and symptom levels on externalizing behaviors, depression, and anxiety. For their variable-based analyses, these authors derived a continuum of adaptation scores by converting into z-scores values on all five dimensions, adding these, and then computing an average. Hierarchical regressions were then conducted, with the hypothesized protective factors predicting to the continuous adaptation scores. In person-based analyses, the authors identified a subgroup of manifestly resilient children ($n = 45$) who had better than average adaptation and competence scores and symptom levels below clinically significant levels on all three domains. Nonresilient children ($n = 70$) were those who had at least one elevated symptom measure as well as global adjustment scores that fell below the very good range (40 children did not fit in either group). Again, the manifestly resilient youth were compared with others on the hypothesized protective factors.

Whereas person-based analyses have commonly been used to compare resilient and nonresilient groups, as in the preceding example, another useful application in resilience research, and one less often explored, is to ascertain conditional effects of influences as an alternative to using interaction terms. The latter strategy is exemplified in Seidman and Pedersen's (2003) work with low-income adolescents. These authors hypothesized that the benefits of adolescents' engagement in particular extracurricular domains—peer relations, academics, athletics, religion, employment, and culture—would depend on whether they were simultaneously invested in other activities as well. Cluster analyses yielded nine distinct groups of youth with varying profiles of activity involvement. Two clusters represented "pan-competence": high engagement and high quality across most domains. Others included children high in one domain but low in others, such as the "academically disengaged athletes" (high in athletics but very low in academics). Cluster comparisons showed that the benefits of engagement in any one domain did in fact depend on engagement in the others: Youth with positive experiences in two or more domains showed significantly better adjustment than those with high-quality engagement in only one domain. To have examined the conditional links via variable-based analyses would have necessitated an impossibly high number of interaction terms (i.e., different combinations of seven engagement domains). In future resilience research, person-based analyses such as these carry much

promise for exploring the implications of different combinations of vulnerability and protective influences in individuals' lives.

Longitudinal Analyses: Resilience as "Bouncing Back"

Much of resilience research has involved identification of factors that correlate with relatively positive outcomes among at-risk youth, but in some instances, the approach has been to see what determines who will "bounce back" from earlier dysfunction (e.g., Ackerman, Brown, & Izard, 2003; Sroufe, Egeland, & Kreutzer, 1990). Long-term prospective studies are critical in illuminating turning points not only in childhood but across the life span, and at this time, data are available from a growing number of studies. Exemplary in this regard is Emmy Werner's (Werner & Smith, 2001) study of children in Hawaii followed from infancy through their 40s. Also spanning multiple decades is Laub and Sampson's (2003) follow-up of the Glueck and Glueck (1950) sample of low-income delinquent boys, originally assessed when they were 10 to 17 years old and most recently in their 60s, as well as George Vaillant's (Vaillant & Davis, 2000) parallel follow-up of the nondelinquent (but also low-income) comparison group. Hauser and Allen (Allen & Hauser, 1996; Hauser, 1999), similarly, have followed a group of psychiatrically hospitalized adolescents well into their adult years. Outside of the United States, critical longitudinal studies, all still ongoing, include the Isle of Wight study in England, where a 2-year-old birth cohort was followed to the age of 44 to 45 years (Collinshaw, Maughan, Pickles, Messer, & Rutter, 2004), the Dunedin Multidisciplinary Health and Development Study in New Zealand, where a cohort of 1,037 children were assessed through age 26 years (Moffitt, Caspi, Rutter, & Silva, 2001), and the Christchurch Health and Development Study, also in New Zealand, involving an unselected birth cohort of 1,265 children followed until the age of 21 years (Fergusson & Horwood, 2003).

Increasingly used in prospective studies are newer analytic techniques such as hierarchical linear modeling (HLM; Bryk & Raudenbush, 1987, 1992). HLM has the advantage of being able to accommodate data with some missing data points in different assessments over time and uneven time gaps between assessment points. Traditional methods such as multivariate repeated measures of analyses of variance require complete data for all subjects across all points of assessment as well as equal intervals between all points. Guttman et al. (2003) demonstrate the effective use of HLM in resilience research, showing academic trajectories between grades 1 through 12 among youth who had been at high versus low levels of risk when they were assessed at the age of 4 years.

Another useful approach is that developed by Nagin and colleagues (Jones, Nagin, & Roeder, 2001; Nagin, 1999), which allows examination of different growth trajectories within a given group. Even when study samples consist of individuals who are similar on broad demographic indices, their growth trajectories over time can show some heterogeneity, and Nagin's procedure enables identification of disparate subgroups of individuals who each show the same distinct trajectories (e.g., those who increase, decrease, or remain stable on symptom or competence indices). Other advantages of this approach are that it can be used with both continuous and frequency data, and it allows for determination of links between different vulnerability or protective indices on the one hand, with diverse trajectories of maladjustment on the other (where harsh parenting, for example, is highly represented in trajectories of high stable or sharply increasing psychopathology, but not in others; see Latendresse & Luthar, 2005).

Interpretation of Findings on Risk Modifiers: Common Questions, Concerns, and Solutions

In variable-based analyses, a complication of interpretation has to do with whether significant main effect associations imply that low levels of the hypothesized asset imply unusually poor adjustment, or that high levels imply excellence in functioning, or both. There are, admittedly, a few "pure" vulnerability indices that can only create disorder when present but not excellence when absent, such as child maltreatment, whereas others can be beneficial when present without conferring vulnerability when absent, such as artistic or musical talents (Rutter, 2003). Many, if not most, indices, however, are bipolar in nature, with the potential for effects at both extremes (Masten, 2001). To illustrate, a significant main effect for extraversion among high-risk youth could imply either that high levels lead to exceptional competence (protection), or that low levels lead to unusual maladjustment (vulnerability).

Although researchers have often used these terms interchangeably, choosing somewhat arbitrarily between labels of vulnerability or protection for such bipolar variables, it can be useful to examine the distribution of scores to guide choices in this regard (Luthar & Zelazo, 2003). To continue with the same example, this could be done by demarcating, for interpretive purposes, a group high on extraversion (e.g., as defined by the top tertile) and one with low extraversion. Depending on the degree to which the mean competence scores of the low and high extraversion groups each deviate from the sample mean, this could illuminate

whether low extraversion connoted significant vulnerability (with competence scores much poorer than average), or whether high extraversion reflected protection (with competence well above the sample average). If both points deviated equally from the mean, the terms protection and vulnerability could in fact be used interchangeably. This type of scrutiny of mean competence scores—associated with high and low levels of the hypothesized risk modifier—can be useful not only in clarifying the nature of linear links, but also in detecting curvilinear links, where extraversion, for instance, is most adaptive at moderate levels with very high and low levels each being maladaptive. Use of this strategy is exemplified in Luthar and Latendresse's (2005b) study on the risk-modifying potential of different family processes (see also Stouthamer-Loeber et al., 1993).

Although there has been some confusion surrounding main effect findings, there has been a great deal more confusion around interaction effects; these have often been viewed as being at the crux of research on resilience, sometimes inappropriately emphasized as more important for inferring protection than direct, main effects (Luthar et al., 2000a, 2000b). It is certainly true that in the now classic papers of Garmezy et al. (1984) and Rutter (1987), protective effects were, in fact, defined in terms of interactions. On the other hand, neither of these scholars was dismissive of main effect findings. In point of fact, soon after publication of the 1984 Project Competence paper discussed earlier, Masten and Garmezy (1985, p. 14) defined protective factors as representing "a broader term. . . . [They are generally] associated with a lower than expected incidence of negative outcome, or, to take the more appropriate positive perspective, these factors are associated with better than expected outcomes." In another paper, Garmezy (1987, p. 170) characterized early main effect findings from Project Competence for both SES and IQ as being "protective factors against disruptive-aggressive responses to stress." None of these statements implies that factors cannot be "protective" unless they are in statistical interaction terms.

Over 2 decades ago, Rutter (1983) warned against an inappropriately high emphasis on statistical interactions because they are confused with interactions between the *person* and the environment. Discussing this problem in some depth, he noted that

> personal interactions are not synonymous with statistical interaction effects. Most of the (person-environment) interactions that I have considered would not be detectable in terms of the conventional testing for multiplicative interactions in multivariate analyses. . . . [Further,] because interactions can take many forms and cannot be examined satisfactorily

through any one overall multivariate analysis, there is a considerable danger that spurious interactions will be detected as a consequence of looking at the data in numerous alternative combinations and permutations. (p. 315)

Similarly, in discussing interactional models, Masten and Garmezy (1985, pp. 36–37)) underscored the importance of transactional perspectives, which involve "recognition that adaptation is an ongoing process of interactions between the systems of individual, family, social network, community, and society." At the same time, these authors warned against an overreliance on multiple interaction terms to detect meaningful ways in which individual attributes transact with aspects of the environment to affect adjustment outcomes.

Aside from the fact that they typically have small effect sizes and thus are hard to detect, another concern about using interaction terms is that considering them might constrain detection of important *main effect* links. In contemporary studies involving analyses like those of Garmezy et al. (1984), it is not uncommon to see five or more protective factors explored in a given sample. When these variables are all considered as main effects, along with each of them in interaction with risk (as well as controls for demographics such as age, ethnicity, or gender), the resultant loss of statistical power, due to use of a large number of variables, renders Type III errors quite likely, with the potential of failing to detect main effect links that do actually exist. Unless researchers have specific a priori hypotheses predicting particular patterns of links between hypothesized risk modifiers and outcomes, therefore, it may be more prudent to omit them.

This suggestion is resonant with increasingly heard suggestions (Garcia Coll, Akerman, & Cicchetti, 2000; García Coll et al., 1996; Hobfoll, Ritter, Lavin, Hulsizer, & Cameron, 1995; Luthar, 1999; Tucker & Herman, 2002) that in working with groups who have been little studied so far, as many at-risk groups are, it is best to focus intensively on how different processes operate *within* that sample, rather than seeking to document how they compare with patterns in other mainstream (or low-risk) groups. To be sure, many forces will show similar patterns—maltreatment hurts all children, as good parenting benefits all—but there are also several forces that are highly salient in some contexts but not others (Wyman, 2003). Experiences of discrimination, for example, are potent negative forces for minority children (García Coll et al., 1996; Szalacha et al., 2003) but do not apply to Caucasians. Optimism is related to life satisfaction and low depression among Caucasians but not among Asians (E. C. Chang, 2001). In other in-

stances, processes may actually reflect diametrically opposed patterns in different samples. Parental strictness is generally seen as detrimental for mainstream children but often benefits inner-city teens (Cauce, Stewart, Rodriguez, Cochran, & Ginzler, 2003; Sameroff et al., 2003). In cases such as these, it would likely be a mistake for researchers to explore main and interaction effects with high- and low-risk samples combined. Nonsignificant main effect associations may well be found—with opposing direction of links in the two samples canceling each other out—and interaction effects also statistically nonsignificant, given their instability and small effect sizes.

As resilience researchers consider using or not using interaction terms to assess samples including both high-risk and comparison groups, therefore, it is critical that they carefully consider the substantive questions of interest. What within-group multivariate analyses of at-risk samples illuminate is the *relative significance of particular protective process,* for example, school safety or neighborhood patrolling, vis-à-vis other influences in the same population. Knowledge such as this can be far more useful, conceptually and practically (in prioritizing intervention themes), than is evidence that a particular set of links is statistically stronger or weaker than parallel associations in a low-risk group. Even if a researcher's goals were to examine the generalizability of processes identified among youth facing high adversity, this could easily be accomplished with separate analyses of the comparison group (by contrasting of beta weights in regressions, if necessary, to determine whether links differ significantly in strength). In sum, within-group analyses are often the strategy of choice when seeking to learn about intervention priorities in subgroups of the population about whom we currently understand little. The conceptual appeal of interaction effects must not obscure the fact that including multiple interaction terms for "exploratory" purposes can sacrifice much in terms of statistical power, possibly reducing the likelihood of detecting main effects that do exist in reality.

A final cautionary note regarding the joint consideration of high- and low-risk groups is the potential for spurious findings on protection. In other words, statistically significant main effect terms might be erroneously labeled as compensatory or protective against risk even when the effects occur only in the *low-risk* group (Luthar & Goldstein, 2004). To illustrate, a series of studies on children varying in level of violence exposure showed significant overall links with competence for various positive family variables, such as high family support and high levels of monitoring (Hammack et al., 2004; Kliewer et al., 2004; Sullivan, Kung, & Farrell, 2004). More in-depth analyses, however, revealed that in many cases, the family assets were helpful only among children with low exposure to community violence. Among children whose scores were at the higher end of the violence exposure measures, the benefits of variables such as family support were essentially negligible (Luthar & Goldstein, 2004). For circumstances such as these, Sameroff and colleagues (Gutman et al., 2003; Sameroff et al., 2003) have argued that terms such as "promotive"—which do not imply that any benefits are conferred at high-risk levels—are more appropriate than is "protective." Other terms that avoid implying effects at high risk include "beneficial" and "salutary" (Luthar & Zelazo, 2003); researchers could also simply refer to the attributes as "assets" (Masten & Powell, 2003).

Understanding Underlying Processes

A hallmark of the current generation of resilience research is attention to process: If studies are truly to be informative to interventions, they must move beyond simply identifying variables linked with competence to explain the specific underlying processes (Cowen et al., 1996; Luthar & Cicchetti, 2000; Masten, 2001; Rutter, 2000, 2003; Werner & Johnson, 1999; Wyman et al., 1999). This need to "unravel" underlying mechanisms applies to the risk condition itself as well as to hypothesized protective and vulnerability indices. With regard to risk transmission, for example, maternal depression can affect children through various environmental processes, including conflict between parents, stressful events in the family, children's modeling of ineffective coping styles, and negative parenting behaviors (Hammen, 2003); biological processes such as diffuse reductions in cortical activation or generally lowered left frontal activation, may also be implicated (see Dawson et al., 2003). Similarly, the negative effects of maternal drug abuse on children may derive from various problems that tend to co-occur with women's addiction, such as depressive and anxiety disorders and high life stress, as much as or more than from the drug abuse per se (Luthar, D'Avanzo, & Hites, 2003). Disaggregating or unpacking the relative contributions of each of these family processes is critical not only for theory and research, but also for designing interventions.

Although many global sociodemographic and psychological constructs (such as family SES and parents' mental illness) are commonly thought of as connoting high versus low risk, attention to processes has sometimes led to findings belying commonplace assumptions. To consider family SES, for example, material wealth is generally viewed as connoting low risk. However, an accumulating body of literature indicates that (1) among adults, high preoccupation with wealth and status may often compromise well-being (see Kasser, 2002), and (2) children of the wealthy and well-educated can show elevated maladjustment in some domains, particularly substance use and internalizing symptoms, possibly as a result of high achievement pressures and isolation from parents (Luthar, 2003; Luthar & Latendresse, 2005a; Luthar & Sexton, 2004). Findings such as these support what elders in developmental psychology cautioned us about decades ago: Global indicators of children's "social addresses" are limited in what they can tell us about children's family lives (Bronfenbrenner, 1986; Zigler, Lamb, & Child, 1982). In trying to illuminate who is at risk and why, we need direct attention to the processes that actually exist within their families.

Turning to mechanisms underlying protective and vulnerability factors, examples of possibilities in this regard are seen in Criss and colleagues' (Criss, Pettit, Bates, Dodge, & Lapp, 2002) descriptions of various processes via which peer acceptance might confer advantages for children with disturbed family functioning. When parents are highly stressed, good peer relationships can provide alternative ways to meet needs for connectedness or concrete help. They may also serve to modify inappropriate child behaviors, such as aggression, that distressed parents cannot discipline adequately. Indirect effects on adults may also be involved; children's peer relationships may lead their parents to network with the other children's parents, which in turn may confer benefits such as illuminating new approaches to discipline. Finally, positive peer relations in the school context may promote bonding with school and teachers.

With regard to vulnerability factors, an example of diverse underlying mechanisms is seen in research on hostile, coercive family environments (e.g., Compton, Snyder, Schrepferman, Bank, & Shortt, 2003). These are likely to exacerbate further the vulnerability of children in high-risk groups via various conduits, including ineffective parenting, unresolved conflict and discord, insufficient child monitoring and supervision, and lack of close relationships with one or both parents (Rutter, 2000).

Moving beyond Psychological Processes: The Importance of Biology and Interdisciplinary Work

The preceding examples—like most of resilience research thus far—generally encompass psychological variables; there is a critical need for scientists to increase consideration also of biological indices, again, both as mediators of risk itself and as processes underlying vulnerability and protective factors (Cicchetti, 2003; Rutter, 2002b). In a seminal overview paper, Curtis and Cicchetti (2003) have explained the importance of diverse biological processes ranging from neuroendocrinology to capacities to regulate emotions. Modern neuroscience, for example, has established the phenomenon of neural plasticity, where there is structural and functional reorganization of the brain in response to environmental inputs. These physical changes in the brain, in turn, can have substantive implications in determining vulnerability and protective processes to future psychopathology (Curtis & Nelson, 2003). Evidence such as this points to several issues worthy of investigation by future resilience researchers, such as whether stressful or challenging tasks might evoke activation in different areas of the brain (e.g., as assessed by functional magnetic resonance imaging) among competent and noncompetent performers, or whether resilient and nonresilient children, matched on adversity type and level, might show differing patterns of brain structure and functioning.

In terms of protective processes, the capacity to regulate or modulate negative emotions in the face of threats is of obvious importance for managing well in the face of threat (e.g., Aspinwall & Taylor, 1997; Buckner et al., 2003; Eisenberg, Champion, & Ma, 2004), and here again, biological processes can be salient. Various environmental influences likely affect whether individuals become adept or inept at regulating their emotions, such as significant adults' responses to and tolerance of displays of negative affect in the early childhood years. However, at least three biological processes might also be implicated. The first is the capacity to recover relatively quickly from negative events experienced (Davidson, 2000). Such "rapid recovery" tendencies can be gauged by studying the startle reflex, which is an involuntary response (a fast twitch of facial and body muscles) to a sudden and intense visual, tactile, or acoustic stimulus. Studies have shown that adverse environmental influences affect not only the startle reflex, but also the neural network that underlies this response (Curtis & Cicchetti, 2003).

A second aspect of brain functioning that might affect emotion regulation, according to Curtis and Cicchetti (2003), is hemispheric electroencephalograph (EEG) activity. In general, the right hemisphere participates more heavily in negative affect and the left hemisphere more in positive emotion. Individuals who show relatively high activation of the left prefrontal cortex have been found to report more positive affect both when at rest and in response to positive stimuli, and also show less negative emotion in

responding to negative stimuli (Sutton & Davidson, 1997; Wheeler, Davidson, & Tomarken, 1993). Thus, asymmetry in brain functioning might be implicated in differing capacities to regulate emotions.

A third biological mechanism that might be implicated is neuroendocrinal in nature. Chronic exposure to stressful experiences tends to lead to excessive activation of the hypothalamic-pituitary-adrenal (HPA) axis and the resultant elevation of the stress hormone cortisol. Hypercortisolism in turn can cause damaging and sometimes pathogenic effects on neurons (McEwen & Sapolsky, 1995; Sapolsky, 2000) and can also affect the synthesis and reuptake of neurotransmitters as well as the density of sensitivity of receptors (McEwen, 1994; Watson & Gametchu, 1999). Again, these findings point to the possibility that resilient individuals are those who, in the face of various stressors, tend to return relatively quickly to baseline levels of neuroendocrine functioning and thus avoid the damage conferred by hypercortisolism.

Aside from the aforementioned categories, another important set of biological processes are those involving genetic influences. Noteworthy in this regard are works of Rutter, Caspi, and their colleagues (Caspi et al., 2003; Kim-Cohen et al., 2004; Rutter, 2003) on genetic factors potentially involved in resilience. Discussed at some length in the next section of this chapter (under "Family-Level Processes"), recent studies have identified G-E interactions—wherein both genes and child-specific environmental influences contribute to behavioral resilience—as well as specific gene markers that contribute to protection or vulnerability in the face of childhood adversities.

In the years ahead, it is imperative that resilience researchers begin to pay concerted attention to biological processes such as these, in addition to psychological ones. Thus far, the neglect of biology in this literature could be attributed to at least two factors: (1) The technology for assessing many of these processes is relatively new and complicated, and (2) most resilience researchers have little formal training in biological processes, and those who do have such training have not studied resilience (Curtis & Cicchetti, 2003). Admittedly, there are few who will develop skills and expertise across both of these realms, as is exemplified by Rutter (2002a, 2002b) and Cicchetti (2003), but interdisciplinary collaborations provide a viable route to bringing together both bodies of knowledge. Concerted movement toward such collaborations must be treated as an imperative for the continued vitality of the science of resilience in future years.

Another type of interdisciplinary collaboration that will be critical in moving the field of resilience forward is with qualitative researchers from fields such as anthropology. Ethnographic, qualitative research is critical, particularly in guiding our exploration of groups little studied thus far (Garcia Coll, 2005; Luthar, 1999). Being generative, inductive, and focused on *describing* salient processes in naturally occurring phenomena (LeCompte & Preissle, 1993), this type of research can provide critical directions for future quantitative studies (typically favored by psychologists) involving hypothesis testing of resilience processes. Put simply, meaningful hypothesis testing presupposes knowledge of the web of interrelated forces that can affect the phenomenon under study: "We must understand how persons within a culture or ethnic group symbolically construct concepts such as self and others before we can understand factors attributed to vulnerability and resilience" (Cohler et al., 1995, p. 781).

Ethnographic studies involving at-risk families have illuminated several potentially important processes that merit further scrutiny in verificative or predictive research on resilience (see Hauser, 1999). To illustrate, interviews with inner-city families led Burton and colleagues (Burton, Allison, & Obeidallah, 1995) to identify several aspects of adolescent adaptation, all rarely considered in psychological research, that might promote long-term resilience. These include contribution to cohesion at the family and the community level (e.g., helping elderly folk in the community) and development of creative talents in contextually relevant models (such as rapping or doing hair and nails well).

It should be noted, too, that qualitative research is particularly critical in trying to translate findings from basic research on vulnerability and protective processes into interventions. The importance of this is exemplified in work on benefit finding in the face of bereavement. In the aftermath of bereavement, it has been found that some individuals report some positive outcomes, such as feelings of having grown personally, developed new perspectives on life, and increased closeness in other relationships (Affleck, Tennen, & Rowe, 1991; Davis, Nolen-Hoeksema, & Larson, 1998). However, any intervention efforts to help people identify such benefits following bereavement can be counterproductive, perceived by the bereaved individuals as insensitive and personally offensive (Nolen-Hoeksema & Davis, 2002; Tennen & Affleck, 2002).

In addition to the biological and qualitative literatures, evidence on clinical interventions also subsumes potentially valuable lessons on processes in resilience. Examples are seen in studies of the companionship provided by pets as well as therapeutic properties of music and art. With re-

gard to the former, almost 2 decades ago, the National Institutes of Health (NIH; 1988) convened the NIH Technology Assessment Workshop on the Health Benefits of Pets, as research had demonstrated that pet owners experienced increased 1-year survival after discharge from a coronary care unit (Friedmann, Katcher, Lynch, & Thomas, 1980). A decade later, scientific papers reported that pet owners had slightly lower systolic blood pressure, plasma cholesterol, and triglyceride values than non-pet owners (Anderson, Reid, & Jennings, 1992) and that dog ownership was associated with an increased likelihood of 1-year survival after a myocardial infarction (Friedmann & Thomas, 1995). Findings on pet ownership were seen as operating through the reduction of psychosocial risk factors (Patronek & Glickman, 1993), and the final report of the NIH Technology Assessment Workshop proposed that future studies of human health should consider the nature of relationships with pets as significant variables (Beck & Glickman, 1987). A series of recent papers in the *American Behavioral Scientist* (e.g., Barker, Rogers, Turner, Karpf, & Suthers-Mccabe, 2003; Beck & Katcher, 2003; Meadows, 2003) underscore the value of pursuing such research.

In a similar vein, therapeutic interventions suggest that creative self-expression warrants some attention by resilience researchers. In a meta-analysis published in the *Journal of Child Psychology and Psychiatry and Allied Disciplines,* Gold, Voracek, and Wigram (2004) included 11 studies on music therapy that resulted in a total of 188 subjects for analyses. Effect sizes from these studies were combined, with weighting for sample size, and their distribution was examined. Results showed that music therapy has a medium to large positive effect ($ES = .61$) on clinically relevant outcomes. The finding was statistically significant at $p < .001$ and statistically homogeneous, and no evidence of a publication bias was identified.

Resilience and Related Constructs

Aside from confusion about aspects of research on resilience itself, there also have been questions about whether it is truly a unique scientific construct or redundant with others. The reality is that there are in fact similarities but also some important differences. Of the psychological constructs with which resilience has some overlap, social competence is perhaps the most salient. The roots of this dimension lie in Havighurst's theory of developmental tasks, where social competence is defined as a track record of effective performance in developmental tasks that are salient for people of a given age, society or context, and historical time (Masten & Coatsworth, 1998).

As Masten (2001, p. 716) has noted, competence and resilience may be described as closely related subconstructs within the broader construct of adaptation; both constructs represent "doing okay." Furthermore, both are relative terms, in that social competence is defined relative to what society expects of the average child, whereas resilience is defined relative to expectations of the average child given exposure to a particular risk (i.e., "better than expected functioning"). Finally, in themselves, the terms competence and resilience do not imply exceptional performance in any *specific* domain; rather, they allude to adjustment domains that are salient within a particular developmental and ecological context.

There are four major differences between the two concepts. First, resilience, but not competence, presupposes risk. Second, resilience encompasses both negative and positive adjustment indices (absence of disorder and presence of health), and competence chiefly the latter. Third, resilient outcomes are defined in terms of emotional and behavioral indices, whereas competence usually involves manifest, observable behaviors. Fourth, resilience is a superordinate construct that subsumes aspects of competence (along with high levels of risk).

A second overlapping construct—and one with which resilience is often confused—is *ego resiliency,* which is a trait reflecting general resourcefulness and sturdiness of character and flexibility of functioning in response to varying environmental circumstances (see Eisenberg, Spinrad, et al., 2004). Commonalities with resilience are that both involve strengths; illustrative descriptors of ego resiliency (Block, 1969) include "engaged with the world but not subservient to it" and "integrated performance under stress." Differences are that (1) only resilience presupposes conditions of risk, and (2) resilience is a phenomenon, not a personality trait. Finally, just as competence is subsumed within resilience, ego resiliency has been examined as a potential predictor, that is, a personality trait that may protect individuals against stressful experiences (Cicchetti & Rogosch, 1997).

Hardiness is a construct in the adult literature that shares some attributes with resilience—it, too, presupposes risk—but also with ego resiliency; it refers to a specific set of traits in the individual rather than the combination of risk plus competence, as does resilience. Proposed by Kobasa and colleagues (Kobasa, Maddi, & Kahn, 1982) to account for individual differences in responses to life stressors, hardiness is defined as the presence of three personality dispositions: commitment (feeling connected, having a purpose, being active, etc.), control (feelings of being able to control what happens in one's environment),

and challenge (welcoming change instead of perceiving it as disruptive).

Resilience and Related Disciplines

As the construct of resilience has some features overlapping with others, such as competence and hardiness, the scientific study of resilience has much in common with other disciplines in terms of central research questions and the constructs and samples assessed; similarities are most pronounced with risk research, prevention science, applied psychology, and positive psychology. Considering *risk research* to begin with, there are more similarities than differences, which is not surprising as resilience research grew out of the risk paradigm (Luthar & Zelazo, 2003). In both these traditions, researchers are concerned with children who face notable life adversities, seeking to understand the types of forces that might lead to variability in adjustment outcomes. A major point of difference, however, is that resilience researchers are explicitly concerned with positive forces as well as negative ones—assets as well as deficits in both socializing forces and child outcomes—whereas risk research is focused primarily on negative forces.

A second difference is that studies of resilience entail concerted attention to process. At the core of both risk and resilience research is the common goal of identifying correlates of adjustment among children at risk, but for resilience researchers, this represents but a fraction of the overall task. As noted earlier, once statistically significant associations are found, there must be an in-depth scrutiny of processes that might underlie statistical links with an eye toward informing future interventions.

Similar distinctions apply with *prevention science* as traditionally defined, although in current conceptualizations, differences are much smaller, pertaining less to substantive areas of interest than to the degree of attention to the development and implementation of programs. Prevention science has long been seen as having as its core objective the reduction of disorder or disease among individuals at risk and not the promotion of health or competence (see Munoz, Mrazek, & Haggerty, 1996). In resilience research, there is explicit consideration of maximization of positive outcomes as well as the minimization of pathology or disease (Luthar et al., 2000b). However, several senior scientists have sought to broaden the scope of the prevention discipline to include positive outcomes as well (Cowen & Durlak, 2000; Elias, 1995; Weissberg & Greenberg, 1998), arguing that efforts to reduce problems are most effective when coordinated with explicit attempts to also foster competence (Weissberg, Kumpfer, & Seligman, 2003). In point of fact, the terms prevention and resilience coexisted in a task force, Seligman's American Psychological Association Presidential Task Force on Prevention: Promoting Strength, Resilience, and Health in Young People (Weissberg et al., 2003). Thus, at this time, the only minor difference between the fields of resilience and prevention is that the former is focused equally on basic and applied research, whereas the latter is more strongly focused on applications of research findings in programs for youth and families.

Applied developmental science (ADS) is a relatively new discipline, which is defined as "scholarship that seeks to advance the integration of developmental research with actions—policies and programs—that promote positive development and/or enhance the life chances of vulnerable children and families" (Lerner, Fisher, & Weinberg, 2000). ADS and the study of resilience are, again, highly overlapping: Both involve a focus on children and families at risk, on positive outcomes and assets among them, on normative and atypical developmental processes as they emerge in different cultural settings, and on interventions and policies to promote positive development. In both instances, furthermore, there is a strong emphasis on collaborations between universities and communities to ensure the relevance of research activities and components of interventions and policies to the needs and values of people in that community (Luthar & Cicchetti, 2000). A minor point of difference is that ADS places somewhat more emphasis on outreach interventions conducted under real-world circumstances and constraints, whereas resilience research more equally emphasizes such efforts and the more traditional laboratory-based clinical trials, which allow for more stringent documentation and evaluation even though they are conducted under highly controlled, contrived conditions that cannot be replicated in the real world (Lerner et al., 2000; Weisz, Hawley, Pilkonis, Woody, & Follette, 2000).

Also closely related is the applied science of *early childhood intervention*. Major points of emphasis in this discipline are the interchange between biology and experience, on cultural variations in child-rearing beliefs and practices, on relationships as the building blocks of healthy development, on children's self-regulation as a critical capacity affecting all domains of behavior, and on the potential to shape human development by reducing risk and promoting protective influences. The construct of resilience is specifically mentioned among the core concepts guiding the science of early childhood intervention (Shon-

koff & Phillips, 2000). Again, the differences between this and the field of resilience are minor; early childhood interventions concern children up to 5 years of age and their families, whereas resilience research thus far has been focused as much on middle childhood and adolescence as on early childhood (if not more so). Furthermore, early childhood interventions have often been focused on cognition, intelligence, and language development and, in some instances, behavioral conformity; there is relatively little attention to mental health or psychiatric disturbances. Resilience research, by contrast, is concerned with psychological, emotional, social, and psychiatric outcomes among children and parents; cognition and language are not considered outcome domains.

Turning from developmentally based disciplines with a focus on children to one focused primarily on adults, resilience has features in common with *positive psychology,* also a relatively new field. Martin Seligman (2002, p. 3), who played a seminal role in the emergence of this discipline, defined it thus:

> The field of positive psychology at the subjective level is about positive subjective experience: well-being and satisfaction (past); flow, joy, the sensual pleasures, and happiness (present); and constructive cognitions about the future—optimism, hope, and faith. At the individual level it is about positive personal traits—the capacity for love and vocation, courage, interpersonal skill, aesthetic sensibility, perseverance, forgiveness, originality, future-mindedness, high talent, and wisdom. At the group level it is about the civic virtues and the institutions that move individuals toward better citizenship: responsibility, nurturance, altruism, civility, moderation, tolerance, and work ethic.

Unlike the minor differences with the three fields previously discussed, there are several factors that set the field of resilience apart from positive psychology, the first of which concerns the presence of life adversities. As noted earlier, resilience research presupposes exposure to significant adversity, whereas positive psychology concerns all individuals, not just those who have experienced major risks.

The second difference concerns the presence of developmental issues. Emerging as a part of the discipline of developmental psychopathology, resilience research has involved concerted attention to developmental themes (Luthar & Cicchetti, 2000; Masten, 2001), with a focus generally on childhood and adolescence, but recently, on processes among adults as well (e.g., Bonnano, 2004; Collinshaw et al., 2004; Staudinger, Freund, Linden, & Maas, 1999; Vaillant & Davis, 2000). In positive psychology research thus far, by contrast, developmental issues are not highlighted, and the focus is overwhelmingly on adults. In a chapter discussing children in the *Handbook of Positive Psychology* (Snyder & Lopez, 2002), the authors noted: "We strongly urge that positive psychology theorists and researchers consider a developmental perspective rather than focusing only on adults (and children as 'smaller humans') or giving minimal attention to development by considering childhood *only* as a period preceding adulthood" (Roberts, Brown, Johnson, & Reinke, 2002, p. 671).

The third difference pertains to operationalization of positive outcomes, and there are two issues relevant here. One is that, as its name suggests, positive psychology is concerned only with positive aspects of adjustment and health promotion and not with the evasion of mental illness. Resilience encompasses both poles. As noted earlier, positive adaptation is defined as the best possible outcomes that can be achieved given the risk experienced; in the face of severe trauma, risk evasion has—appropriately—been defined in terms of the avoidance of major psychiatric problems.

Another difference concerns the use of behavioral versus psychological dimensions to operationalize positive adaptation. Resilience researchers have strongly emphasized overt behavioral success as judged by others: "adaptive behaviors" as rated by teachers, classmates, friends, parents, or others. Whereas there is some effort to ascertain subjective feelings of unhappiness, there have been no attempts, to our knowledge, to ask children about their own subjective feelings of happiness (see also Roberts et al., 2002). And these are the constructs that form the very crux of positive psychology; interestingly, in this case, there do not seem to be efforts to ascertain *others'* opinions on whether the individual is "doing well," as a good spouse or parent, for example, or a colleague at work. In fact, even when there are constructs tapping into interpersonal themes, these largely involve the individual's own reports, with social acceptance defined in terms of *their* having positive attitudes toward others, and social integration as their feelings of being supported by their community (Keyes & Lopez, 2002).

The reasons for this differential emphasis are not entirely clear, although it could derive partly from the fact that much of the work on positive psychology has been done in Western countries, where individualism is highly emphasized. It is possible that in Eastern cultures with a strong emphasis on collectivism, positive psychology would be defined as much in terms of *others'* judgments of adults' doing right by significant others (as resilience is commonly described among children in contemporary research). This could be a direction usefully explored in future positive psychology research. By the same token, there is a need for childhood resilience researchers to consider not only the degree to which young people conform to adults' expectations and evade personal psychopathology, but also the degree to which they themselves subjectively experience feelings of happiness.

Despite these areas of difference, it should be emphasized again that resilience research has many similarities to all the other disciplines considered here, and researchers in each of these traditions have much to learn from those in the others. The excessive splintering of psychology as a field has increasingly been deplored (e.g., Catalano, Hawkins, Berglund, Pollard, & Arthur, 2002; Sternberg & Grigorenko, 2001); to remain insulated from others' research that clearly overlaps with one's own is ill-advised. Encouragingly, there have been increasing efforts to bring together the major themes and ideas from these fields. Two recent compendia of articles (Sheldon & King, 2001; Snyder & Lopez, 2002) included, along with several articles on positive psychology among adults, papers on resilience in childhood (see Masten, 2001; Masten & Reed, 2002). More recently, in a book on children facing familial and community adversities (Luthar, 2003), senior investigators in the risk, resilience, and prevention science traditions came together, allowing a distillation of major findings across all of these disciplines. In future efforts, the choice of terms that each of us chooses to characterize our respective research efforts is, in essence, not substantively important (i.e., whether we call ourselves resilience researchers, prevention scientists, or applied developmental scientists). What is much more important is that we remain aware of the body of knowledge, highly relevant to our own research efforts, subsumed in the other literatures mentioned (Garcia Coll, 2005). In the pithy words of Shonkoff and Phillips (2000, p. 339), we must guard against "narrow parochial interests that invest more energy in the protection of professional turf than in serving the best interests of children and families."

VULNERABILITY AND PROTECTIVE PROCESSES: SUMMARIZING EXTANT EVIDENCE

This section of the chapter encompasses major findings from almost half a decade of research on resilience. In describing the forces that might modify effects of high-risk life circumstances, discussions are focused largely on research with children, as there are still relatively few studies of resilience among adults. Additionally, the effort is toward prioritization of different categories of risk modifiers. Resilience researchers have been criticized for producing lists of sundry protective and vulnerability factors (see Gorman-Smith & Tolan, 2003; Luthar et al., 2000a); although possibly comprehensive, such lists are of limited practical use because all itemized indicators (ranging from parents' intelligence, to neighborhood safety, to children's social skills) can never be addressed in a given intervention. From an intervention standpoint, what is needed is some type of prioritization of domains in terms of overall likelihood of yielding substantial benefits (Luthar & Zelazo, 2003).

Accordingly, organization of this section is based on the following considerations. In general, primacy in discussions is given to the most *influential* vulnerability and protective factors, that is, those whose effects are relatively enduring, robust, or hard to overcome by others. Second, more emphasis is placed on *modifiable modifiers*. Whereas intrinsic characteristics like gender and race certainly can affect outcomes, these are afforded less prominence than are those that are more amenable to change, such as parental discipline and teacher support.

Third, discussions focus, in sequence, on vulnerability and protective forces in the domains of the family, the community, and the children themselves. The family is not only the most proximal of children's external environments but also the most enduring; it therefore makes sense to focus on this first in the triad of factors (Luthar & Zelazo, 2003). The community, in turn, affects children both directly and indirectly through their parents, so that modifying aspects of the wider environment can have benefits through both routes. With regard to children's own attributes, these obviously do play a major role in resilient adaptation, but many child attributes (such as self-efficacy and even intelligence) are themselves shaped by forces in the environment. Accordingly, these are discussed third in the sequence (cf. Luthar & Zelazo, 2003).

Rather than describing findings of individual studies in the research literature, the emphasis in this section is on summarizing major themes that have emerged regarding salient vulnerability and protective processes, with a few investigations briefly described for illustrative purposes. Along with empirical evidence on the three sets of risk modifiers, relevant evidence from intervention efforts is also considered. As Cicchetti and Hinshaw (2002) have noted, basic research must inform interventions; at the same time, data from interventions can provide valuable lessons for science by showing, for example, whether targeting hypothesized protective factors does in fact predicate resilient adaptation.

Family Relationships: Effects of Maltreatment

Of the many factors that affect the trajectories of at-risk individuals, among the most potent is maltreatment by primary caregivers. Maltreatment co-occurs with many high-risk circumstances, including parent mental illness, parental conflict, community violence, and poverty (Eckenrode et al., 2000; Lynch & Cicchetti, 1998), thus serving as a rampant vulnerability factor. Maltreated children show deficits spanning multiple domains; as Cicchetti (2002, p. 1416) has noted, "Child maltreatment exerts deleterious effects on cognitive, social, emotional, representational, and linguistic development, as well as disrupts the development of emotion regulation, secure attachment relationships, an autonomous and integrated self-system, effective peer relations, and the successful adaptation to school."

Even when positive profiles of adaptation are displayed among maltreated children, they tend to be unstable over time. In their longitudinal study of low-income children, Farber and Egeland (1987) found that, of 44 children identified as maltreated, *none* maintained competent functioning across the period from infancy to preschool. Cicchetti and Rogosch (1997) examined resilience in a sample of 213 maltreated and nonmaltreated low-income children. On a composite measure of adaptive functioning, only 9.8% of maltreated children were ever classified as high-functioning during any of the three annual assessments; fewer than 2% were classified as high-functioning across time. Similarly, Bolger and Patterson (2003) identified maltreated children who showed positive adjustment in at least one of four domains (peer acceptance, internalizing, externalizing, and academic achievement) without doing very poorly in any, and only 1 of the 107 maltreated children met these criteria across multiple assessments over time.

This degree of dysfunction is not surprising given that maltreatment connotes serious disturbances in the most proximal level of the child's ecology, with the caregiving environment failing to provide multiple expectable experiences essential for normal development (Cicchetti, 2002,). In maltreating families, parental care does not meet children's basic needs for physical sustenance and protection, emotional security, and social interaction. Parents interact with their children less than do others and display more negative affect to them. Anger and conflict are often pervasive, both between parents themselves and between the adults and the children, and the family system as a whole is characterized by chaos and instability. Thus, it is unsurprising that the "social, biological, and psychological conditions that are associated with maltreatment set in motion a probabilistic path of epigenesis for maltreated children characterized by an increased likelihood of failure and disruption in the successful resolution of major stage-salient tasks of development" (Cicchetti, 2002, p. 1416).

Despite evidence that resilience is rare among maltreated children, profiles of adjustment are obviously not homogeneous, and the degree of diversity that is observed might rest largely on the heterogeneity of maltreatment experiences in terms of severity, pervasiveness, age at onset, or chronicity (Cicchetti & Rogosch, 1997). To illustrate, studies have shown that children experiencing maltreatment early in life and continuing into the adolescent years tend to show early onset, persistent behavior problems (such as conduct problems, substance use, and early sexual activity), and difficulties in different aspects of peer relationships (Aguilar, Sroufe, Egeland, & Carlson, 2000; Bolger & Patterson, 2003; Eckenrode et al., 2001).

Other forces that can make a difference include positive relationships with others (see Reis & Collins, 2004). As will be discussed later in this section, quality parenting is the single most robust of protective factors for children exposed to various adversities (Luthar & Zelazo, 2003; Masten & Coatsworth, 1998), so that positive relationships with alternative caregivers could serve protective functions for maltreated youth (although this has not yet been systematically examined, to our knowledge). The potential of other relationships is seen in Bolger and Patterson's (2003) longitudinal data showing that friendship—though not a substitute for adult caregiving—may play a protective role. Among chronically maltreated children, having a positive, reciprocal friendship was associated with an increase over time in self-esteem, possibly due to a mediating process such as decreases in loneliness, increases in perceived acceptance, improved social skills, and changes in working models of attachment.

Personality factors may also make a difference. Cicchetti and Rogosch (1997) found that ego resiliency and ego control as well as positive self-esteem predicted relatively competent functioning in maltreated children, as Bolger and Patterson (2003) found that maltreated children with higher internal control had lower symptom levels than others. The mechanisms underlying such "protective child attributes" are discussed later in this section, but for the moment, a critical caveat bears explicit mention: The experience of maltreatment also compromises the very personal attributes that could serve protective functions (Bolger & Patterson, 2003). As Cicchetti (2002) notes, maltreated children as a group show many deficits in emotional regulation, either showing excessive amounts of negative affect or blunted affect with little positive or negative emotion. As a result of difficulty in effectively modulating physiological arousal, they also have trouble coping with emotionally stressful situations. In other words, the repeated developmental disruptions of a maltreating environment not only directly increase risk for maladjustment, but tend to work against positive personal attributes that could have served protective functions.

Protective Family Forces: Attachment, Nurturance, and Support

Whereas chronic maltreatment is pernicious, child abuse is obviously not inevitable among parents facing major life adversities, and positive family relationships can do much to promote resilience in children faced with challenging circumstances (Conger & Conger, 2002; Elder & Conger, 2000). The critical importance of strong family relationships has been emphasized by child development theorists from diverse perspectives. This theme is at the core of classic psychodynamic perspectives ranging from Bowlby's (1988) attachment theory and the Eriksonian emphasis on trust versus mistrust (Erikson, 1993), to Freud's (Freud & Gay, 1995) stages of psychosexual development and Mahler's (1986) notion of human symbiosis. Outside of psychodynamic viewpoints, Havighurst's (1948) earliest developmental tasks—learning to walk, talk, and distinguish right from wrong—presuppose the presence of an attentive adult to foster these, as learning theorists have long emphasized the role of parents' reinforcement patterns as well as modeling particular behaviors to powerfully shape the child's emerging personality (Bandura, 1977; B. F. Skinner, 1974).

Consistent with these theories of normative child development, strong family relationships have long been seen as critical in maintaining good adjustment in the face of adversities. The earliest studies of resilience indicated that the presence of a close relationship with at least one parent figure was highly protective across risks ranging from early institutionalization and serious parent mental illness, to chronic family poverty and multiple coexisting adversities (Anthony & Koupernik, 1974; Garmezy, 1974; Murphy & Moriarty, 1976; Rutter, 1979; Werner & Smith, 1977). Similarly, recent reviews of the existing literature continue to point to supportive and responsive parenting as being among the most robust predictors of resilient adaptation (Luthar & Zelazo, 2003; Masten, 2001; Rutter, 2000; Werner, 2000).

Particularly important in shaping long-term resilient trajectories are early family relationships. In their comprehensive review of the early childhood literature, Shonkoff and Phillips (2000, pp. 27–28) emphasized, "From the moment of conception to the finality of death, intimate and caring relationships are the fundamental mediators of successful human development. Those that are created in the earliest years . . . constitute a basic structure within which all meaningful development unfolds." The critical role of early relationships has been effectively established by Egeland, Sroufe, and their colleagues in their work with children of low-income mothers. Based in Bowlby's (1988) attachment theory, these scholars argue that individuals' adaptation is always a product of both their developmental histories and current life circumstances—never of just one of these. Early experience places people on probabilistic trajectories of relatively good or poor adaptation, shaping the lens through which subsequent relationships are viewed and the capacity to utilize support resources in the environment. Thus, if early attachments are insecure in nature, at-risk children tend to anticipate negative reactions from others and can eventually elicit these; these experiences of rejection further increase feelings of insecurity (Allen, Hauser, & Borman-Spurrell, 1996; Sroufe, 2002; Weinfield, Sroufe, & Egeland, 2000). Conversely, at-risk children with at least one good relationship are able to take more from nurturant others subsequently encountered in development (Conger, Cui, Bryant, & Elder, 2000; Shonkoff & Phillips, 2000; Sroufe, 2002; Yates et al., 2003).

Among young children, the benefits of secure attachment have been demonstrated in diverse research paradigms. Research by Gunnar and her colleagues has shown that strong, secure attachments to caregivers can buffer or prevent elevations of stress hormones in situations that usually elicit distress in infants. In contrast, children with insecure attachments to caregivers tend to react to potentially threatening situations with increased levels of the stress hormone, cortisol (see Gunnar, 2000). In a literature review on the ontogeny of the two arms of the stress system, the limbic-hypothalamic-pituitary- adrenocortical and brain stem norepinephrine/sympathetic-adrenomedullary systems, the authors concluded that individual differences in the reactivity and regulation of both these systems are related not only to temperamental characteristics but also to quality of caregiving (Gunnar & Davis, 2003).

Even among older children and adolescents, competent parenting plays a critical role in promoting competent child outcomes over and above the effects of contextual factors such as parents' socioeconomic status (Werner & Smith, 1982, 1992). To illustrate, among 6- to 12-year-old African American youth in poverty, supportive mother-child relationships were linked both concurrently and prospectively with children's depressive mood and disruptive behavior (Klein & Forehand, 2000). In two cohorts of low-income, urban youth (of 7- to 9-year-olds and 9- to 12-year-olds) in the Rochester Child Resilience Project, resilient status was significantly more likely among those dyads where parents were emotionally responsive and had relatively good mental health and high psychosocial resources (Wyman, Cowen, Work, & Parker, 1991; Wyman et al., 1999).

Even when risk factors stem from within the family, as when one parent has a mental illness, a strong relationship with the other parent can be substantially protective. Among children of alcoholics, Berlin and Davis (1989) found that the mother's support and nurturance were important in leading to nonalcoholic outcomes of offspring during adulthood. Similarly, McCord (1988) demonstrated the critical role of the nonalcoholic spouse as someone who could help the child to differentiate from the father's alcoholism, and Beardslee (2002) underscored the importance of strong, supportive relationships with at least one parent in families affected by parental depression.

The protective potential of strong relationships has been demonstrated not only for mothers but also for fathers and father figures, as seen in several studies of low-income, African American families. Fathers who were nurturant, satisfied with parenting, and employed had children with fewer behavior problems (Black, Dubowitz, & Starr, 1999). In addition, warm, close relationships with fathers (even those not living in the same house) benefited children in terms of lower levels of behavioral problems and higher self-esteem and less depression (Zimmerman, Salem, & Maton, 1995). In her review of the literature on low-income, unmarried, and minority fathers, Coley (2001) noted the widespread but insufficiently studied phenomenon of "social fathering," wherein men other than biological fathers fulfill the father-figure role. Among low-income, African American preschoolers, between a third to half had a father figure involved with them; among adolescents, 24% nominated a nonbiological father figure when asked to name a man who was "most like a father" to them (Coley, 2001).

Whereas several studies have shown that children benefit from close involvement with fathers, some also have indicated that father involvement can sometimes be related to negative outcomes (see Coley, 2001; Leadbeater, Way, & Raden, 1996). Such findings may reflect elevated conflict between highly involved fathers and mothers, deriving, for example, from disagreements about disciplinary practices for their young children (Shaw, Owens, Vondra, Keenan, &

Winslow, 1996). Additionally, some young children of highly involved fathers in poverty may be exposed to high levels of paternal problem behaviors, such as antisocial behaviors and substance abuse (Jaffee, Moffitt, Caspi, & Taylor, 2003; Leadbeater et al., 1996). As Coley has noted, we need more research to disentangle these findings, teasing apart, for example, the effects of different types of father involvement such as emotional and financial involvement, as well as the amount of time spent with the child.

Apart from primary caregivers, siblings can help modify the effects of high-risk circumstances. In their research with sibling pairs in rural African American families, Brody (2004) and his colleagues demonstrated that the older siblings' competent behaviors at school were linked with increases in younger siblings' competence over time, through the intervening variable of younger siblings' self-regulation. Conversely, siblings also can exacerbate vulnerability in at-risk families. In families with one child already at high risk for deviant behaviors, Bullock and Dishion (2002) found that the deviance of siblings was promoted by collusion in the presence of adult caregivers. Furthermore, sibling collusion was found to uniquely predict adolescent problem behavior over and above associations with deviant peer groups.

A potentially critical source of support to at-risk children lies in extended kin, with the beneficial effects occurring directly as well as indirectly via their parents' adjustment (Elder & Conger, 2000; McLoyd, 1997). Grandparents often provide substantial emotional and material support directly to their grandchildren; in fact, they may sometimes be more willing to offer support to grandchildren than to their own children, such as when the latter have problems of substance abuse (Apfel & Seitz, 1997). Indirect effects involving parents are evident in findings that kin support can bolster authoritative parenting behaviors, feelings of well-being, and involvement in children's schools, benefits that are reflected, in turn, in positive child adaptation (R. D. Taylor, 1996; R. D. Taylor, Casten, & Flickinger, 1993).

Correcting Lack of Parent Nurturance

Whereas early relationships are critical in shaping the lens through which people view their subsequent interactions, a faulty lens can be corrected to some degree. In general, developmental psychopathologists maintain that there is continuity and coherence in development so that positive adaptation in early years determines, in probabilistic rather than determinative fashion, the likely success at later stages (Carlson, Sroufe, & Egeland, 2004; Sroufe, Carlson, Levy, & Egeland, 1999; Yates et al.,

2003). At the same time, scholars acknowledge that lawful discontinuities often do occur, and in the context of attachment status these frequently derive from changes in the caregiving environment (Egeland & Sroufe, 1981; Sroufe et al., 1999; Thompson, 2000; Waters, Weinfield, & Hamilton, 2000).

Such lawful discontinuities are illustrated by findings that children show a shift from secure to insecure patterns if the availability of the primary caregiver becomes attenuated due to circumstances such as maternal depression or chronic illness or life events such as parental divorce (Waters, Merrick, Treboux, Crowell, & Albersheim, 2000; Waters, Weinfield, et al., 2000). In longitudinal research spanning infancy through adulthood, individuals' insecure attachment at the age of 18 years was not related to insecure status at 1 year, but it was significantly related to experiences of parental divorce in the intervening years (Lewis, Feiring, & Rosenthal, 2000).

Intervention studies also provide consistent evidence with regard to the possibility of shifting attachment status, as seen in work by Heinicke and his colleagues (Heinicke, Rineman, Ponce, & Guthrie, 2001). Among young children of low-income mothers, these investigators offered a relationship-based intervention aimed at fostering mother's encouragement of infants' autonomy and self-regulation, as well as development of a secure attachment. Children of intervention mothers were in fact more securely attached, more autonomous, and more task-oriented 2 years later. Similar evidence is seen in Cicchetti and colleagues' (Cicchetti, Toth, & Rogosh, 1999) intervention for young children of depressed mothers.

Parallel lawful discontinuities have been documented in terms of shifts from insecure to secure attachment status as a function of ameliorative relationship experiences. Dozier (Dozier, Albus, Fisher, & Sepulveda, 2002; Dozier, Stovall, Albus, & Bates, 2001) has shown that among children entering foster care, all of whom experienced significant disruptions in relationships with caregivers during the 1st year and a half, insecure early attachments were remediated to some degree by intervention services and foster caregivers' positive qualities of nurturance, responsiveness, and their own attachment state of mind. Similarly, among low-income children with insecure and avoidant patterns of early attachment, several came to show secure attachments by adulthood, manifesting good parenting behaviors themselves and close relationships with romantic partners (Roisman, Padron, Sroufe, & Egeland, 2002). Again, the shift in attachment status was seen as deriving from positive experiences with caregivers through the later childhood and adolescent years.

In other longitudinal research, the corrective power of good relationships is seen in Rutter's (1987) classic study of women who had been institutionalized as young children. When these women were grown, those who had good marital relationships—characterized by harmony and a warm, supportive spouse—showed good parenting behavior much more frequently than did ex-care women who lacked such marital support. More recently, among delinquent adolescent boys followed through the age of 70 years, Laub and Sampson (2003) found that changes in rates of crime over time were generally unrelated to childhood risk factors but were systematically linked with adult transitions to marriage, unemployment, and military service. The effects for marriage were the strongest, accounting for as much as a 40% reduction in the rate of criminal offending. The authors viewed the effects as involving nurturance as well as informal social control: "Men who desisted from crime were embedded in structured routines, socially bonded to wives, children, and significant others, drew on resources and social support from their relationships, and were virtually and directly supervised and monitored" (p. 279; see also Conger, Rueter, & Elder, 1999; Vaillant & Davis, 2000).

Research with adults also has yielded some biological evidence on the benefits of good relationships. In one study mapping quality of adults' relationships and their physical health, the researchers derived cumulative relationship pathways encompassing prior relationships with parents and current ones with spouses. Individuals were defined as being on the positive relationship pathway if they had had at least one parent who was affectionate and caring and, as adults, had at least one of two forms of intimacy with their spouse: sexual or intellectual/recreational. Those on the negative relationship trajectory had poor bonds with both parents and/or had a marriage low on both intimacy dimensions. The investigators then examined whether cumulative relationship profiles were related to levels of allostatic load (a measure of the cumulative wear and tear on multiple physiological systems, including metabolic, cardiovascular, HPA axis, and sympathetic nervous system). As predicted, people on the positive relationship pathways were significantly less likely than those on negative pathways to show high allostatic load. Furthermore, positive relationships were found to serve as buffers against persistent economic adversities: In the presence of economic risks, only 22% of those with positive relationship pathways showed high allostatic load, compared with 69% of those with negative relationship pathways. Although the authors conceded the relatively preliminary nature of their findings, the findings were seen as illustrating

a type of biopsychosocial pathway of resilience warranting further empirical attention (Ryff & Singer, 2002; see also Evans, 2003; Reis & Collins, 2004).

The reversibility of early insecure attachments depends on the duration and severity of early deprivation, as seen in research on children adopted into United Kingdom families following early severe deprivation in Romanian orphanages, and a comparison sample of nondeprived within-UK adoptees. In the sample of deprived adoptees, dose-response associations were found between duration of deprivation (as indexed by age at which children were adopted) and atypical patterns of attachment to adoptive parents (O'Connor & Rutter, 2000). Research by Gunnar and colleagues (Gunnar, Morison, Chisholm, & Schuder, 2001) showed similar dose-response effects with levels of the stress hormone cortisol as the outcome of interest. Six and a half years after adoption, children reared in Romanian orphanages for more than 8 months in their first years of life had higher cortisol levels over the daytime hours than did those adopted before 4 months of age. For the former group, furthermore, the longer the period of institutionalization beyond 8 months, the higher their cortisol levels.

Over a longer developmental period, dose-response associations are evident in findings on ramifications of family climate during early childhood, middle childhood, and early adolescence for intergenerational relationships between participants at age 26 years and their parents (Belsky, Jaffee, Hsieh, & Silva, 2001). Results showed that unsupportive child rearing during one of the three developmental periods could be offset if family relations in the other two periods were relatively supportive. Such amelioration was not found if two of the three periods reflected disruptions.

It is unclear, however, whether the quality of these "corrected" relationships is entirely comparable to that experienced by individuals who did not face early risks. In another study of the children in Romanian orphanages, Rutter and O'Connor (2004) showed that at the age of 6 years, most of these children showed social and cognitive functioning in the normal range after being adopted into British families. At the same time, a substantial minority manifested major persistent deficits. The pattern of findings was interpreted as suggesting some form of early biological programming or neural damage stemming from institutional deprivation and also, given the heterogeneity in outcome, that the effects are not deterministic (Rutter & O'Connor, 2004). Other research has shown that among ex-institutionalized children, a nontrivial group do fail to develop secure attachments with adoptive or foster parents and have difficulty forming intimate relationships later in development (Hodges & Tizard, 1989; O'Connor et al., 1999). Treboux, Crowell, and Waters (2004) found that when adults had insecure attachment representations based on early relationships but secure attachments in current relationships with partners, they were more reactive to stress than were those who had secure attachments in both early and current relationships. Finally, in Werner's (Werner & Smith, 1992) 30-year follow-up, children who had initially seemed resilient despite several life adversities came to show some difficulties in achieving intimacy in their adult relationships.

Protective Parenting: Discipline and Monitoring

In addition to dimensions of attachment, another broad parenting construct critical for resilient adaptation falls in the broad domain of discipline: limit setting and monitoring. Limit setting refers to the use of appropriate rules and expectations in shaping socially desirable behavior in the child. The degree to which parents clearly define limits and consistently enforce rules is critical in shaping the child's future compliance (Cavell, 2000; Schneider, Cavell, & Hughes, 2003). Conversely, inappropriately harsh discipline exacerbates vulnerability to maladaptive behaviors. As Patterson (1983) theorized, when parents respond to young children's annoying behaviors in ways that are coercive and based on power assertion, children tend to escalate their own aversive behaviors in attempts to control the parents. As the child's aversive behaviors increase in intensity and frequency, parents sometimes acquiesce, thereby reinforcing the maladaptive behaviors. Conversely, if parents resort again to power-assertive and harsh techniques, they come to serve as role models for hostile behavior patterns.

Patterson's (1983) coercion theory is at the core of Shaw and colleagues' research on the importance of appropriate limit setting for young children (for an overview, see Shaw, Bell, & Gilliom, in press). These researchers followed two cohorts of low-income mothers and their children, first assessed when the children were about 1 year of age. The authors postulated that when mother was unresponsive to infant's continued bids for attention, this tended to lead to later coercive exchanges between mother and child by age 2, which in turn would be linked with elevated risk for externalizing behavior problems by age 3. These postulates were supported in analyses based on both cohorts of mother-child dyads (Shaw et al., in press).

In another set of studies, the focus was not on maternal unresponsiveness but hostility. Noting toddlers' tendencies to evoke frustration from caregivers (e.g., because of their increase in mobility and assertion of independence), the re-

searchers noted that a critical developmental task for mothers is the capacity to maintain a nonhostile, relatively positive approach while shaping the child's behaviors. During a laboratory clean-up task, when mothers of 2-year-olds were observed to show rejecting behaviors, the children displayed a heightened risk for conduct problems at 3.5 years (Shaw et al., in press). When such rejecting, overcontrolling behaviors reflected a general parenting approach, children showed escalated risk for conduct problems not only at home but also at school, with such effects documented during the preteen years and adolescence (Shaw et al., in press; see also Dishion & Kavanagh, 2003).

Related to limit setting and also important for resilient adaptation is the construct of parental monitoring, which is defined as a "set of correlated parenting behaviors involving attention to and tracking of the child's whereabouts, activities, and adaptations" (Dishion & McMahon, 1998, p. 61). The salutary effects of consistent parental monitoring across various high-risk circumstances have been demonstrated from the elementary school years onward (Buckner et al., 2003). In a group of inner-city 8- to 10-year-olds, Chilcoat and Anthony (1996) found that those with high parental monitoring manifested a 2-year delay in the subsequent onset of drug use when compared with those in a low parental monitoring group. Other studies have shown links with positive indices of adjustment such as scholastic achievement and self-esteem (see Dishion & Kavanagh, 2003; Romer, 2003).

The benefits of consistent parental monitoring are particularly pronounced among preadolescents and adolescents, who have increasing independence from parents and thus growing exposure to a host of risks in the peer and community environments. Haapasalo and Tremblay (1994) reported that high parental supervision was a distinctive characteristic among low SES boys who consistently displayed low levels of physical aggression between the ages 6 and 12 years. More so than their aggressive counterparts, these nonfighters indicated that their parents were constantly aware of where and with whom they spent their free time through the period spanning the preadolescent years. Among low-income 8- to 17-year-olds, Buckner et al. (2003) found that of several variables external to the child, only parental monitoring significantly differentiated resilient from nonresilient youths, and a study of sixth graders with deviant peers showed that firm parental control inhibited the development of externalizing problems in later years (Galambos, Barker, & Almeida, 2003; see also Brody et al., 2002; Lloyd & Anthony, 2003). Studies have shown also that when their parents tend to know of their daily activities and associations, adolescents are less likely to engage in delinquent behavior, drug use, risky sexual activity, and association with gangs (Dishion & Kavanagh, 2003; Romer, 2003).

Links between parent monitoring and adolescent adjustment are not always simple linear ones, but can depend on coexisting risks in the environment or even be curvilinear. To illustrate, Mason, Cauce, Gonzales, and Hiraga (1996) showed that in terms of ramifications for children's problem behaviors, optimal levels of control exerted by African American parents varied according to negative influences in the community. When adolescents reported relatively high problem behaviors in their peer groups, for example, optimal levels of parental control tended to be higher than when children's peer problem behaviors were low.

In terms of underlying processes, ethnographers (Burton et al., 1995; Jarrett, 1999) have delineated several expeditious limit-setting strategies used by inner-city families. These include the avoidance of dangerous areas, temporal use of the neighborhood (e.g., avoiding being outside in the evening hours), and restriction of children's relationships with deviant peers. Other posited mechanisms include those resting on psychological processes: Continuity and structure in the adolescent's environment can promote the development of effective coping skills, and when parents impart a sense of interest and concern for the adolescent's well-being, this tends to enhance children's self-esteem (Buckner et al., 2003; Luthar, 1999).

Related to monitoring—in some ways, the converse of it—is autonomy granting, also important for resilient adaptation. Observational research involving mother-infant interactions suggests that maternal support of exploration and autonomy (versus maternal restriction and control) is associated with the child's mastery motivation, persistence at tasks, competence, self-regulation, and positive affect through subsequent years (see Bornstein, Davidson, Keyes, & Moore, 2003; Shonkoff & Phillips, 2000). Among older children, perceptions of their own autonomy are linked with various indices of adaptive development such as academic engagement and prosocial behavior (Bornstein et al., 2003).

Autonomy has high significance during the teen years as well. A major developmental task of adolescence is to negotiate the struggle between the development of autonomy on the one hand, and the maintenance of close bonds with parents on the other. Among youth at high risk by virtue of psychiatric hospitalization, observed autonomy and relatedness displayed by both parents and adolescents were related to high levels of adolescents' self-esteem as well as their ego development (Allen, Hauser, Bell, & O'Connor, 1994). In a subsequent study of this cohort 11 years later,

maternal behaviors promoting adolescent autonomy and relatedness were also associated with coherence/security of attachment during adulthood (Marsh, McFarland, Allen, McElhaney, & Land, 2003).

As was seen in relation to parental monitoring, the optimal level of autonomy granted to adolescents can vary as a function of sociodemographic disadvantage. This is seen in McElhaney and Allen's (2001) research with adolescents living in urban poverty. Among these youth, maternal behaviors undermining of children's autonomy (i.e., interrupting them to shut down discussions) was positively linked with mother-adolescent relationship quality, whereas among low-risk comparison youth, links were inverse in nature. The authors suggest that behaviors potentially seen as overprotective might be seen as expressions of care and concern among youth in high-risk contexts, although they tend to be seen as inappropriately inhibiting and even guilt producing by adolescents in low-risk settings. Finally, the possibility of curvilinear effects is seen in research on adolescents at risk because of problems at school (such as grade retention or school suspension). When mothers were low in autonomy granting, adolescents with insecure preoccupations were found to be vulnerable to high internalizing problems. Conversely, if mothers were excessively high on autonomy granting, vulnerability to externalizing behaviors was pronounced (Marsh et al., 2003).

Coexisting Warmth and Appropriate Control

Whereas high levels of warmth and appropriate control each have protective functions, the benefits of each depend to some degree on levels of the other: High warmth with lax discipline can be linked with poor adjustment, as can strict discipline without affection. The authoritative parenting style, characterized by the appropriate balance of parental warmth and control (Baumrind, 1989), is generally optimal; authoritative parents are defined as those who "are warm, supportive, communicative, and responsive to their children's needs, and who exert firm, consistent, and reasonable control and close supervision" (Hetherington & Elmore, 2003, p. 196).

Among low-income mothers, efforts to facilitate warm and responsive interactions with infants or toddlers enhanced the quality of future discipline techniques, in turn serving as a powerful force against externalizing disorders in childhood and adolescence (Shaw et al., 1996). In a related vein, among rural African American families, the development of adaptive self-regulatory behavior was significantly enhanced by mothers who provided support along with structure and clear behavioral expectations, even among children with difficult temperaments. Moreover, positive parenting promoted greater self-regulation than both individual child and community protective factors (Murry & Brody, 1999). Authoritative parenting also has repeatedly been found to promote resilience in children facing disruptions in family life due to divorce (Hetherington & Elmore, 2003).

Timothy Cavell (2000) has emphasized the importance of an appropriate balance of warmth and discipline in the notion of parental *containment,* which is "any behavior that fosters in children a sense of restraint while not threatening their relationship security" (p. 131). Recent studies have pointed to the protective potential of this construct. Building on Cavell's arguments on the significance of children's beliefs about the likelihood of being disciplined, Schneider et al. (2003) defined perceived containment as the child's beliefs concerning the parent's capacity to enforce firm limits and the likelihood that the parent will prevail in conflict. They found that children with a particularly strong sense of containment had a mother who applied effective discipline in the context of an emotionally positive relationship. Furthermore, high perceived containment was protective against externalizing behaviors as rated by parents and teachers (Schneider et al., 2003).

Intervention studies with at-risk youth further buttress the conclusions from basic research on the importance of firm, consistent discipline in the context of supportive parent-child relationships (see Biglan & Taylor, 2000; Webster-Stratton & Taylor, 2001). In a review of the literature, Kumpfer and Alvarado (2003, p. 457) note, "Effective parenting is the most powerful way to reduce adolescent problem behaviors"; they describe three approaches that have generally been successful. The first includes behavior training approaches that are highly structured and involve working only with parents; the second entails an integration of parent behavior training and children's social skills training, both administered in group format; and the third involves family therapy programs that are administered with individual families.

Underlying Processes and Other Potentially Important Dimensions: Future Research Needs

Whereas good relationships are clearly critical for resilience, there remain several questions about the active ingredients therein: What are the core processes that might explain this effect? The most obvious mechanism is that discussed earlier: that early attachments shape the lens through which later interactions are viewed. However, there are various other parenting constructs that probably

coexist with generally good parenting and warrant further study, one of which is children's trust that the parent will shield or protect them against danger (an interesting parallel to perceived containment, children's beliefs that the parents will be able to discipline effectively). In their research with children who experienced foster care, Dozier and colleagues (Dozier, Lindhiem, & Ackerman, in press) found that possibly even more than security of early attachment, foster parents' investment in their children was particularly powerful. When foster parents were highly invested in their children (as assessed through an interview), the children fared better not only in terms of neuroendocrine regulation but also, several years later, in self- and other representations. Among children who have experienced the considerable disruptions of early foster placement, therefore, the authors speculate that an important factor might be the child's confidence that the caregiver will stand between him or her and danger, rather than whether the caregiver will comfort the child when distressed. They suggest that this component of the attachment system is not assessed in the standard assessment of attachment among human young (the Strange Situation), but is a key component of attachment assessed among nonhuman primates.

Also warranting more attention is the role of simple family routines. In their study of rural, single-parent African American families, Brody, Flor, and Gibson (1999) defined effective parenting not only in terms of mother-child relationship quality and school involvement, but also family routines, as measured by variables such as "Family has a 'quiet time' each evening when everyone talks or plays quietly," and "Working parents come home from work at the same time every day." Among youth at the two extremes of family socioeconomic status, Luthar and Latendresse (2005b) showed that even after considering indices such as emotional closeness and parental supervision, a simple indicator of time spent together—eating dinner with at least one parent most evenings—was significantly related to several child outcomes (see also National Center on Addiction and Substance Abuse, 2002). In terms of underlying mechanisms, the findings could reflect either of two patterns: that parents are typically not at home late in the evenings, or that they are present but do not eat with their children. Both options could lead the average 12-year-old to feel psychologically adrift and to do things that parents would disallow had they been at home, including experimentation with substances and the blatant neglect of homework (Luthar & Latendresse, 2005b).

Beyond these specific parenting constructs, Rutter (1987) noted various possible mechanisms to explain why, in the context of family adversity, a good relationship with one parent can confer protection processes. There could, for example, be less overall disruption when one relationship in the family is harmonious; the "close" parent can ensure that the child is away from the home at times when things became particularly difficult; this parent can help the child understand the origins and nature of the family's problems; or the security of the good relationship can increase the child's self-esteem, and this in turn confers protection. Despite exhortations almost 2 decades ago that underlying processes need to be understood (Rutter, 1987), there has been relatively little headway in disentangling the relative importance of such processes in conferring protection not only during childhood but also beyond, extending into the adult years. Much more needs to be done on this front.

Parenting as a Dependent Variable

Another set of issues critically needing more empirical attention pertains to the ways children affect parents' mental health. By far most of child development research has been focused on the ways parents' behaviors influence children, but some have shown that children's behaviors might affect parents' behaviors and even their psychological functioning (e.g., Garcia Coll, Surrey, & Weingarten, 1998; Luthar, Doyle, Suchman, & Mayes, 2001). A study of more than 300 families showed that young children's difficult temperaments were associated with their mother's sense of parent competence and depressed affect, which in turn were related to their work outcomes—work role quality and rewards from combining work and family (Hyde, Else-Quest, Goldsmith, & Biesanz, 2004). In their study of sibling pairs in rural, African American families, Brody (2004) and his colleagues found that older siblings' competence levels significantly contributed to changes in mother's psychological well-being over time and that children's competence forecast mother's supportive and involved parenting a year later.

More broadly, we need more research focusing squarely on the parents' functioning, understanding what it is that allows some individuals to be effective parents in spite of serious stressors affecting their family. Juxtaposed with findings on the protective power of good parenting, unfortunately, is the inescapable fact that this very factor is substantially imperiled under the risk circumstances commonly considered in resilience research (Luthar & Zelazo, 2003). Adverse effects on parenting have been documented for risks ranging from chronic poverty (Owens & Shaw, 2003) to parental mental illness (Seifer, 2003) and family disruptions such as divorce (Hetherington & Elmore,

2003); child maltreatment by definition implies a disturbed parent-child relationship. Despite knowledge of these threats to parenting, it is curious that among at-risk families, good parenting is relatively rarely examined as an outcome domain, but far more often examined in terms of its associations with children's developmental outcomes.

Little is understood also about pathways or mechanisms to positive parenting; although families are commonly viewed as engines of change in early interventions, the mechanisms by which parenting improves remains largely opaque. Reviewing the early childhood intervention literature, Brooks-Gunn, Berlin, and Fuligni (2000) note that several programs have led to improvements in parenting dimensions, but most programs do not encompass explicit theories on pathways through which improvements actually occur. It is conceivable, for example, that change essentially occurs because mothers receive increased emotional support (which in turn can lead to reduced stress and improved mental health), or because mothers have learned new coping skills and parenting behaviors (which leads them to feel more efficacious and empowered), or some combination of these possibilities (e.g., Bishop & Leadbeater, 1999). Disentangling the relative salience of such mechanisms should be a priority in future research on resilience.

Processes Unique to Ethnic Minority Subgroups

Families' ethnic minority status often represents a salient vulnerability factor in today's world, yet there continues to be a troubling dearth of studies that explicitly address socializing influences and challenges specifically among minority families. There are clearly some universals in children's social-emotional development—the previously highlighted power of supportive caregiving is but one—but at the same time, one-model-fits-all perspectives are of limited value (García Coll et al., 1996; Luthar, 1999). Ethnic minority parents contend with several unique challenges in socializing their children.

In a seminal article on these issues, García Coll and colleagues (1996) provide a useful framework that can guide researchers in studying critical socializing influences in ethnic minority groups. Anchored in social stratification theory, the integrative model posits that there are eight major sets of constructs that affect the development of minority children: (1) social position variables (e.g., race or social class, gender); (2) racism and discrimination; (3) segregation; (4) promoting/inhibiting environments (school, neighborhoods, and health care); (5) adaptive culture (traditions and legacies); (6) child characteristics such as age and temperament; (7) family values and beliefs; and

(8) developmental competencies in the cognitive and social-emotional domains.

Of the various challenges they confront, perhaps the single greatest is poverty: Families of color are highly overrepresented in poverty groups. In 2002, 58% of all African American children and 62% of Hispanic children live below the national poverty level, as compared with 25% of White children (http://www.nccp.org/pub_cpf04.html). Furthermore, their low-income status accounts for much of the psychosocial maladjustment that has been documented. Studies show that once income is taken into account, African American youth can fare not just as well as but even better than their Caucasian peers in terms of mental health indices as well as competent behaviors (see Luthar, 1999). Similarly, Hashima and Amato (1994) showed that with income controlled, ethnic minority parents were no different from their White counterparts in terms of the frequency of harsh or punitive parenting behaviors.

Aside from poverty, racism and discrimination are powerful challenges in the daily lives of minority families, so much so that they are now considered to be essential ingredients in research on minority children's development (Bigler, Averhart, & Liben, 2003; Garcia Coll, Meyer, & Brillon, 1995; D. Hughes, 2003; Oyserman, Bybee, & Terry, 2003; Spencer, Fegley, & Harpalani, 2003; Spencer, Noll, Stoltzfus, & Harpalani, 2001). In a literature review, Szalacha and colleagues (2003) cite nationwide survey findings that 44.4% of non-Hispanic Whites reported that they had never experienced day-to-day discrimination, in contrast to only 8.8% of non-Hispanic Blacks; parallel frequencies for often experiencing discrimination were 3.4% and 24.8%, respectively. In a sample of African American adults, 98% reported personally having experienced a racist event in the prior year—such as being treated badly by various people or having one's intentions misunderstood because of being Black—and 100% had experienced such in their lifetime (Landrine & Klonoff, 1996). Research with Hispanics similarly showed that 94% reported that they experienced some racist event in the past year; over 70% reported being treated unfairly by people in service jobs; and 50% indicated that their lives would be different if they had not been treated in a racist manner during the past year (Szalacha et al., 2003).

Racial and ethnic discrimination experiences are demeaning and degrading, inducing stress as well as feelings of frustration, depression, and anxiety (Brown et al., 2000; Williams, Yu, Jackson, & Anderson, 1997). In survey research of teens from various ethnic backgrounds, all of the minority youth in the sample reported distress associated with perceived racial prejudice in educational contexts, and their self-esteem scores were negatively correlated with that distress (Fisher, Wallace, & Fenton, 2000). Similarly, Szalacha and colleagues (2003) report that among Puerto Rican children, perceived discrimination was related to high levels of depression, stress, and conduct problems, as well as low self-esteem. Furthermore, even worrying about discrimination (reported by nearly half the youth in this sample) was a risk factor for lower self-esteem. These findings resonate with Franklin's (1999) arguments that ethnic minority individuals' inner vigilance for racial slights can create a state of constant watchfulness, leading to chronic tension and feelings of stress.

Studies of adults also have shown that institutional racism has powerful effects on minority mental health (see Rollock & Gordon, 2000). In a nationwide study, Kessler, Mickelson, and Williams (1999) found that reports of day-to-day and lifetime discrimination were related to general psychological distress and depression. Landrine and Klonoff (1996) found that the individuals reporting racist events had relatively high depression and anxiety, as well as somatization and obsessive-compulsive symptoms. In a review of the public health literature, Krieger (1999) found recurrent links between perceived discrimination and levels of stress, psychological distress, and depression.

In terms of underlying mechanisms, vulnerability is likely to be conferred by two processes: (1) the internalization of negative feedback and the stress attributable to repeated exposure to discrimination, and (2) the associated anxiety that one will be a victim of discrimination (see Szalacha et al., 2003). Furthermore, bidirectional links are possible, wherein psychological factors—such as high depression and anxiety, or low intergroup competence—can predispose people to perceive discrimination (e.g., Phinney, Madden, & Santos, 1998).

The likelihood of perceiving discrimination can be suppressed somewhat by factors such as ethnic pride and biculturalism, as well as attributional ambiguity. Racial socialization, ethnic pride, competence in relating to others of different racial/ethnic groups, and biculturalism have all been documented as mitigating the negative effects of discrimination (García Coll et al., 1995; Phinney et al., 1998; Spencer et al., 2003; Szalacha et al., 2003). Experiments have shown that if people can attribute negativity to another's prejudice, this can render discrimination irrelevant to their self-views (Ruggiero & Taylor, 1997). But it should be emphasized that the likelihood of such attributions obviously diminishes as experiences of discrimination are continually encountered over time (Szalacha et al., 2003).

Other environmental forces involved in heightening risks for minority families are those at the neighborhood level. If they are poor, minority group children are more likely than Caucasians to live in neighborhoods where institutional supports are meager (Duncan, Brooks-Gunn, & Klebanov, 1994). Among African American children more than their Caucasian counterparts, male joblessness in the neighborhood is linked with increased risk for externalizing behavior problems (Chase-Lansdale & Gordon, 1996). Drawing on Wilson's (1991) writings on social isolation, authors of this study reasoned that in inner-city neighborhoods with high male joblessness—areas in which African Americans are disproportionately represented—the dearth of role models of disciplined behaviors, which accompany regular adult employment, can significantly exacerbate behavior problems among African American youth.

Similar suggestions involving social structures have been offered in explaining findings that academic failure can increase risk for subsequent delinquency among Black youth more than among Whites (e.g., Lynam, Moffitt, & Stouthamer-Loeber, 1993). Many of these youngsters are unconvinced that success at school will lead to success in later life due to their ongoing experiences with racism and marginalization and perceptions of job ceilings that deny them access to prestigious jobs (see Arroyo & Zigler, 1995; Ogbu, 1991; Spencer et al., 2001). Even among those minority students who do invest in school, exposure to negative stereotypes about their scholastic abilities tends to trigger high anxiety, which in turn can substantially jeopardize the level of academic success they are able to achieve (Steele, 1997). When African American boys become frustrated with school as a result of academic failure, they often remove themselves from its social control and thus become vulnerable to alternative social influences—often those of delinquents in the unstable, socially isolated neighborhoods in which Blacks are overrepresented (Wilson, 2003).

Immigrant families are among the most vulnerable at many levels. For example, Hispanic parents experience several unique stressors related to migration, acculturation, difficulties with language, and social isolation (Sanders-Phillips, Moisan, Wadlington, Morgan, & English, 1995). As Garcia Coll and Vasquez García (1995) noted, new Hispanic immigrants to the United States must acculturate not only to an alien culture and language but also, frequently, to urban poverty at the same time. In addition, aspects of cultural values can lead to problems. For example, Latino children can find it difficult to negotiate the value placed on individuation and separation in the mainstream White American world with the emphasis on obedience to and respect for elders of Latino culture (Sanders-Phillips et al.,

1995). Among Latino youth, the consistency of values between youth and their parents was the key predictor of low levels of risky sexual behavior (Liebowitz, Castellano, & Cuellar, 1999).

These very differences can also, however, confer protection; the value of family connectedness, for example, brings loyalty and support from kin. Research by Fuligni and his colleagues (Fuligni, Tseng, & Lam, 1999) showed that Asian and Latin American adolescents possessed stronger values about their duty to respect, support, and help their family than their peers of European backgrounds. Furthermore, emphasis on family obligations tended to be associated with more positive relationships with family and peers as well as higher academic motivation among mid- to late adolescents. In other research, educational resilience among Latino youth was strongly associated with supportive relationships in families (Arellano & Padilla, 1996). As Szalacha and colleagues (2003) noted, "la familia," a core cultural characteristic of Latino cultures, is appropriately beginning to be included in studies of resilience among Latino youth (Falicov, 1996; McNeill et al., 2001). Finally, several studies involving African American families have shown that extended kin support helps promote positive outcomes among both parents and children in poverty (Luthar, 1999). The benefits of social supports for parents are evident in increases in their greater well-being and positive parenting behaviors, benefits that are reflected, in turn, across several domains of child adaptation, including behavioral conformity and school achievement (Burchinal, Follmer, & Bryant, 1996; R. D. Taylor, 1996; R. D. Taylor et al., 1993).

As with strong family values, acculturation to mainstream America can have both positive and negative effects. Among Hispanic individuals, for example, higher level of acculturation is linked with relatively high English fluency and low depression but, at the same time, with higher risk behaviors such as delinquency and pregnancy among youth and substance use among both adolescents and adults (see McQueen, Getz, & Bray, 2003; Rogler, Cortes, & Malgady, 1991). In terms of underlying mechanisms, alienation from the family seems to be implicated to some degree. With increasing acculturation can come some attenuation of familial obligations and influence of families as referents, along with greater family conflict and children's emotional separation from parents (Hill, Bush, & Roosa, 2003; McQueen et al., 2003).

Gene-Environment Interactions

An exciting set of new developments in the field of resilience is inquiry into the role of genetic contributions to vulnerability and protective mechanisms in the family, as seen in the seminal research by Caspi and his colleagues. Two studies by this group identified specific genes implicated in protecting some maltreated children from developing psychopathology in adulthood. The first of these showed reduced likelihood of antisocial behavior in the presence of a genotype that confers high levels of the monoamine oxidase A enzyme (Caspi et al., 2002). In the second study, likelihood of developing depression was lower in the presence of a genotype conferring the efficient transport of serotonin (Caspi et al., 2003). Although the specific processes through which these gene markers exert their protective effects are unknown, it is possible that they operate by shaping aspects of children's social-cognitive reactions to life stressors, as in their propensity for attributional biases, for example, or capacities for emotion recognition (Kim-Cohen et al., 2004).

A subsequent study by Kim-Cohen and colleagues (2004) was the first to specifically examine both genetic and environmental processes in the resilience framework. The study involved an epidemiological cohort of 1,116 twin pairs from low SES families. Two aspects of resilience were examined—behavioral and cognitive—and results of quantitative genetic models showed that additive genetic effects accounted for approximately 70% of the variation in children's behavioral resilience and 40% of the variation in cognitive resilience.

Further analyses established protective effects of both maternal warmth and child's outgoing temperament, with each factor operating through both genetically and environmentally mediated effects. Specifically, 66% of the phenotypic correlation between maternal warmth and behavioral resilience was accounted for by genetic influences, and the remaining 34% by child-specific environmental influences. Similarly, 71% of the correlation between outgoing temperament and cognitive resilience was accounted for by genetic influences, 17% by environmental influences shared by the siblings, and 12% by environmental influences specific to the child. In addition, familywide environmental influences accounted for 22% of the population variation in cognitive resilience, and a significant contributor to this shared environmental factor was the degree of parents' provision of stimulating activities in the home.

The authors note several important inferences deriving from their findings. First, the additive genetic effects observed could each operate via either passive or active gene-environment correlations (Rutter, 2003; Rutter & Silberg, 2002). In the context of maternal warmth and behavioral resilience associations, for example, passive ge-

netic effects could result because parents who are warm and affectionate transmit genes to their children that promote good behavioral regulation; genes operate as a third variable, as it were, linking the other two. Active gene-environment correlations, by contrast, would derive if children had heritable characteristics that tended to elicit warmth from adults around them, and this in turn would help foster good behavioral regulation. Parallel explanations were provided for genetic contributions to links between outgoing temperament and cognitive resilience. In this case, passive correlations may derive because parents provided genes that affect both the child's disposition and his or her cognitive competence, whereas an active correlation could result if children's genetically inherited dispositions (e.g., sociability) led them to elicit more attention and learning experiences from adults. The disentangling of passive versus active components underlying such genetic effects constitutes an exciting new direction for future research.

A particularly critical conclusion drawn by these researchers, however, has to do with implications for interventions: *Heritability does not imply untreatability* (Plomin & Rutter, 1998; Rutter, 2002b). As Kim-Cohen et al. (2004, p. 14) note, their study entailed "a genetically sensitive design [demonstrating] that environmental effects can make a positive difference in the lives of poor children. . . . Even child temperament promoted resilience through environmental processes." Of vital importance is their conclusion that if families confronting the myriad stresses of poverty are helped to move toward warm, supportive parenting and providing stimulating learning materials, children can be helped to achieve greater behavioral and cognitive resilience.

At this stage, there are several important directions for future work involving gene-environment influences in resilience (Rutter, 2000, 2003). Twin and adoptee studies of at-risk children can be used to (1) examine the relative contributions of genetic versus environmental influences in the ways that different protective and vulnerability factors operate; (2) understand the mechanisms entailed in each of these (e.g., passive or active gene-environment mechanisms and critical influences underlying the environmental component); and (3) identify genetic markers that confer protection or vulnerability and describe processes underlying their effects. Also needed are sibling studies illuminating the relative contributions of shared versus nonshared extrafamilial environments on different outcomes. Finally, genetics research can contribute to new developments in the study of resilience through precise quantification of risk. As noted in the first section of this chapter, risk is generally inferred based on statistical links between aspects of the environment (e.g., maltreatment or poverty) and children's maladjustment, but this measure of risk is imprecise at best. With knowledge that some children have genes conferring liability to particular disorders, examining factors in the lives of those who do not succumb could contribute vastly to our understanding of processes in resilience.

Communities: Effects of Violence

As with chronic maltreatment in the family, chronic exposure to violence in the community can have overwhelming deleterious effects, difficult for other positive forces to override and affecting multiple domains. Exposure to violence substantially exacerbates risks for internalizing problems such as anxiety, depression, and Posttraumatic Stress Disorder, as well as impaired academic performance due to disruptions in concentration and memory (for reviews, see Cauce et al., 2003; Cooley-Quille, Boyd, Frantz, & Walsh, 2001; Garbarino, 1995; Margolin & Gordis, 2000; Osofksy, 1995). Also heightened is vulnerability to externalizing problems such as delinquent, antisocial behaviors, with prospective associations being significant even when controlling for previous levels of aggression (Gorman-Smith & Tolan, 1998; Miller, Wasserman, Neugebauer, Gorman-Smith, & Kamboukos, 1999; Schwab-Stone et al., 1995).

There also has been increasing attention to effects on children's neurobiology, with suggestions that violence exposure, particularly repeated exposure early in development, can fundamentally alter neurological system development (e.g., Perry, 1997; Pynoos, Steinberg, Ornitz, & Goenjian, 1997; Pynoos, Steinberg, & Piacentini, 1999). During the early years, the central nervous system is believed to be particularly responsive to traumatic organizing and structuring experiences (Weiss & Wagner, 1998); brain development is seen as particularly sensitive to overarousal affecting the organization and development of specific brain areas (Perry, 1997). Thus, children exposed to trauma may experience abnormal neurological development due to overstimulation of certain brain structures, with the degree of impact depending somewhat on the developmental timing of the event(s). In addition, exposure to violence may also affect children's arousal and ability to react appropriately to stress. To illustrate, children exposed to trauma have been found to have increased overall arousal, increased startle response, sleep disturbance, and abnormalities in cardiovascular regulation (Curtis & Cicchetti, 2003; Perry, 1997).

Several aspects of violence can affect a youth's reaction to it, including proximity and relation to the violence (Gorman-Smith & Tolan, 2003). To illustrate, in a 14-month follow-up of children attending a school where a sniper shot 14 students on the playground, Nader, Pynoos, Fairbanks, and Frederick (1990) found that children on the playground had the most severe symptoms, followed by those in the school building, and then those not at school on that day. Another important factor is the child's relationship to the individuals involved: Children are most affected when the victim is someone close to them. P. Martinez and Richters (1993) found that only those incidents involving people known, as both victims and perpetrators, were significantly related to distress, and Jenkins and Bell (1994) reported that victimization of family members (witnessed or not) was as strongly related to psychological distress as was personal victimization.

In terms of family functioning, there is some modest evidence for the role of parents' functioning as mediators and moderators of community violence effects. When mother can appear calm and effective in the face of danger, children tend to do better than when the parent is either absent or is overwhelmed by the situation (Pynoos, 1993). Linares and colleagues (2001) showed that links between community violence exposure and children's behavior problems were mediated by maternal distress (Posttraumatic Stress Disorder as well as global distress), suggesting, again, that if maternal distress were kept low, this could attenuate the association between violence exposure and child maladjustment.

In the face of community circumstances where people's very survival is continually under threat, however, families are obviously constrained in how much they can confer psychological protection to children. This is evident from results of a collection of studies on violence exposure, all considering whether good family functioning might show "protective-stabilizing" influences: helping children to retain good adaptation even as exposure escalated. Considered together, the findings provided modest support at best for such effects (Hammack et al., 2004; Kliewer et al., 2004; Sullivan et al., 2004; see also Furstenburg, Cook, Eccles, Elder, & Sameroff, 1999; Miller et al., 1999). A common theme across all these studies was that positive family functioning (as represented, for example, by closeness to parents, time spent with them, level of perceived support) were beneficial at low levels of violence exposure. On the other hand, when violence exposure was high, the benefits of these variables tended to diminish, suggesting effects that were promotive in general (Sameroff et al., 2003) but not necessarily protective against the effects of community violence.

By contrast, *poor* family function does clearly exacerbate the risks of community violence: When children experience significant dysfunction in their proximal and their distal environments, their risk for psychopathology becomes substantial. In a study by Gorman-Smith and Tolan (1998), family structure (level of organization and support within the family) and cohesion (emotional closeness and support) were inversely linked to changes in both aggression and anxiety and depression for those exposed to community violence. Overall, the results corroborate the view that lack of a dependable, supportive refuge, or dearth of emotional connectedness to family, tends to exacerbate the risk for maladjustment for children exposed to high levels of community violence.

In view of accumulated evidence, the most obvious intervention direction is to reduce levels of violence, with efforts at both national policy and community levels addressing issues such as gun control and safety in schools (e.g., Bloomberg, Daley, Hahn, & King, 2004; Henrich, Schwab-Stone, Fanti, Jones, & Ruchkin, 2004; Ozer & Weinstein, 2004). As such policy-level initiatives are pursued, it is also critical to mobilize forces within communities and families, and Gorman-Smith and Tolan (2003) have provided some useful directions in this regard. The first involves efforts to shield children from violence through broad-based community efforts, involving coalitions of community groups and agencies (such as police, faith-based organizations). Examples include Operation Ceasefire in Boston, which sought to lower youth homicide through a direct attack on the illegal gun trade and creating a strong deterrent to gang violence (Braga, Kennedy, Waring, & Piehl, 2001), and the Child Development-Community Policing Program in New Haven, Connecticut (http://info .med.yale.edu/chldstdy/CDCP/programs/overview.html). The second level entails preventive interventions with families, such as their family-focused preventive SAFE Children intervention, aimed at promoting positive parenting practices within the ecological setting of urban poverty (Tolan, Gorman-Smith, & Henry, 2004). The third level involves therapeutic interventions for those exposed to the violence: services directed to the individual child and to caregivers or systems that can continue to provide support for the child (e.g., Pynoos, 1993).

Protective Processes in Communities: Early Intervention and Schools

Whereas the power of chronic exposure to violence in the community is rarely superseded by other protective processes, there certainly are exosystemic forces that can attenuate the ill effects of other types of adversities. Stud-

ies have pointed to the potential of the broader community to shape outcomes by affecting children themselves not only directly but also indirectly, via their parents.

In the early childhood years, the quality of child care can serve vital ameliorative functions, particularly as the home circumstances of children reflect increasing levels of risk. Reports by the National Institute of Child Health and Development (NICHD) Early Child Care Research Network (1997, 2002) suggest that for families living in or near poverty, mothers whose children are in high-quality child care tend to show more positive interactions with their infants. Furthermore, children of mothers who were very low on maternal sensitivity were more likely to be securely attached to them if the children were in higher-quality child care.

Results of several early childhood interventions also have shown protective effects accruing when highly disadvantaged children are provided with quality care (see Reynolds, 2000; Shonkoff & Meisels, 2000; Shonkoff & Phillips, 2000). A review by Yoshikawa (1994) showed that early intervention programs with long-term effects on chronic delinquency had not only early childhood components but also comprehensive family support. While the early education component attenuated child risks, family support reduced family risks and was deemed a necessary component for inhibiting at-risk children's later delinquency levels.

Of course, obtaining high-quality care is generally the most difficult for the poorest and most needy families. Among the major features defining quality of care, primary are the characteristics of the child care providers (e.g., their education and training), the child-to-adult ratios (e.g., with three or fewer infants per caregiver being advisable; see Shonkoff & Phillips, 2000), and stability of child care providers. Not surprisingly, these aspects of quality are often in jeopardy given the poor working conditions of most child care workers: The average hourly wage of child care workers in the United States is $8.57 (the hourly wage of school bus drivers is $11.33 and of animal trainers, $12.48); turnover rates are among the highest of any profession that is tracked by the U.S. Department of Labor (U.S. Bureau of Labor Statistics, 2004). Improving the quality of child care available to all families, but particularly those at high risk, therefore must be treated as a critical social policy priority.

Exemplary in illustrating the effective use of existing resources for providing quality care for low-income preschoolers is Zigler's "school of the twenty-first century," a comprehensive program that is built into extant school systems (Finn-Stevenson & Zigler, 1999). In this program, public school buildings, which remain unoccupied for large portions of the day and the calendar year, are used not only to house child care programs for children 3 years and older, but also to host regular support group meetings for parents. Information and referral networks also are developed in schools to help families make better use of the various existing services scattered across their communities, such as those offering counseling, physical health care, or night care for children. In the years ahead, it is critical that preventionists and social policy scholars increase the creative use of existing community resources in mobilizing protective influences to benefit different at-risk groups (Barrera & Prelow, 2000; Knitzer, 2000a, 2000b; Luthar, 1999; Pianta & Walsh, 1998).

Researchers have expanded their definitions of quality need to go beyond indices such as the caregiver-to-child ratio, physical space, and materials to stimulate learning, to consider also the emotional quality of caregiving children receive. It will be important to explore systematically the protective effects of such variables in early child care as the caregiver's personality characteristics, the sensitivity, warmth, and consistency in caregiving, and the quality of the relationship developed (Vandell, Dadisman, & Gallagher, 2000).

With regard to the relative effects of child care versus family characteristics, Shonkoff and Phillips (2000, p. 309) indicated, based on their review of the literature, that "when child care effects are examined net of parental effects on child outcomes, parent's behaviors and beliefs show substantially larger associations with their children's development than do any other features of the child care arrangement." Exemplifying this statement is evidence from the NICHD Early Child Care Research Network (2003), where the most consistent predictor of positive outcomes during the early school years was the sensitivity of mothers' behaviors observed across the infant, toddler, and preschool years (see also Vandell et al., 2000).

Turning to older children: K–12 schools can also bring substantial salutary effects to youth in at-risk circumstances (B. J. Feldman, Conger, & Burzette, 2004). There are several studies corroborating the protective functions of supportive relationships with teachers (e.g., Hamre & Pianta, 2001; NICHD Early Child Care Research Network, 2003; Reddy, Rhodes, & Mulhall, 2003). Assessing more than 3,000 teacher-child relationships, Howes and Ritchie (1999) demonstrated that in a sample of toddlers and preschoolers with difficult life circumstances, the quality of attachment with teachers was significantly related to measures of behavior problems as well as social competence with peers. Meehan, Hughes, and Cavell (2003) found that among a group of aggressive second- and third-

graders, African American and Hispanic students benefited more than did Caucasian students from supportive relationships with their teachers. Noting that minority group students typically have lower access to positive relationships with teachers, the authors suggested that they could be more responsive than Caucasians to supportive teachers when such relationships are encountered (see also J. N. Hughes, Cavell, & Jackson, 1999). Similarly, among African American 7- to 15-year-olds from low-income, mother-headed households, Brody et al. (2002) demonstrated protective-stabilizing effects among children whose classrooms reflected organized, predictable environments in which students participated in procedures governing their behaviors. Furthermore, positive classrooms were beneficial even when parent-child relationships were compromised as well as vice versa, indicating unique, significant contributions from both contexts in which children and adolescents spend appreciable amounts of time (Brody et al., 2002; Way & Robinson, 2003).

These findings are entirely consistent with results of interventions targeting features of the school and classroom as well as the family. The Seattle Social Development Project is a case in point; this is a universal intervention designed to work with teachers, parents, and the children themselves to decrease children's problem behaviors. Evaluations have shown gains in several domains, including students' school performance, substance use, delinquency, and commitment to school and the quality of family management practices (Hawkins et al., 2003). Another large-scale, multifaceted school-based intervention is the FAST Track project (Conduct Problems Prevention Research Group, 2004), designed for children at risk for conduct disorders, designed to provide interventions at the levels of the family, child, classroom, peer group, and school setting. High-risk intervention children have shown some improvements in various social, emotional, and academic skills as rated by teachers as well as by parents (Conduct Problems Prevention Research Group, 2004).

Attachment-Based Interventions in Schools

There are many rigorously evaluated programs addressing structure and discipline in the classroom, but there are currently few programs built around the notion of strong attachments to teachers. This is surprising, given recurrent findings that a supportive relationship with adults is critical in resilience and that teachers can play a major socializing role (e.g., L. Chang, 2003; E. A. Skinner, Zimmer-Gembeck, & Connell, 1998; Wentzel, 2002). Writing from an attachment perspective, Robert Pianta (1999) has eloquently described the benefits that can derive from close child-teacher relationships developed and then sustained for as long a period of time as feasible. Commenting on the neglect of attachment-based interventions in schools, he notes the important possibility of broadening the pool of adults in schools who might contribute to such preventive efforts, to go beyond school psychologists or counselors. Pianta argues that there are often enough adults in a given school building to provide some support to children who need it; to some degree, what is needed is creative reassigning of responsibilities and continuity in relationships forged. Thus, in Felner and colleagues' (2001) School Transition Environment Program (STEP), and its successor, the Project on High Performance Learning Communities, the role of homeroom teachers was changed such that they accepted responsibility for counseling and advisory functions and served as a consistent link between students, families, and the school.

Going still further, some have suggested involving not only subject or homeroom teachers but also other adults to whom students are naturally drawn. As Noam and Hermann (2002) note, some at-risk students may actually be inhibited about seeking support from their own teachers, perceiving them primarily as disciplinarians and evaluators of academic progress. Similarly, Luthar and Zelazo (2003) note that students often seek out, as confidants or mentors, diverse school-based adults ranging from sports coaches and music instructors to administrative and support staff (see also Hetherington, 1993). To the degree that such interactions are already occurring in schools, it could be useful to formalize the process to some degree. Adults likely to be most effective as informal mentors could be identified via student nominations (Luthar & Zelazo, 2003). Systematizing their efforts in this regard could be fostered by (1) using student nominations to identify informal mentors (Lindsey & Kalafat, 1998), (2) some creative reassigning of responsibilities, and (3) provision of in-service training and supervision (again, using resources already existing in schools and through collaborative arrangements with applied psychology or social work programs in local universities; see Felner et al., 2001; Luthar & Zelazo, 2003; Pianta, 1999; Pianta & Walsh, 1998).

Although not necessarily tested by the same rigorous designs involving randomized assignments and multiple sites, two programs have in fact attempted to use attachment-based interventions in schools with some promising results. One is Cowen's (Cowen et al., 1996) Primary Mental Health Project, focused on preventing mental health problems among elementary school children, and the second is Noam and colleagues' (Noam & Hermann, 2002) Responsive Advocacy for Life and Learning in Youth (RALLY),

designed for middle school students in high-risk environments. At the core of both interventions are strong relationships. Discussing intervention gains, Cowen and colleagues noted, "The existence of a warm, trusting associate-child relationship is the foundation on which significant attitudinal and behavioral change in children rests" (p. 92). The RALLY intervention is grounded in the core premise that "resilience cannot develop without the personal, interpersonal, and emotional dimensions inherent in relationships" (Noam & Hermann, 2002, p. 874).

Schneider and colleagues (2003) have suggested that children with low perceived containment—who do not believe in adults' capacities to enforce firm limits—and are therefore at risk for Conduct Disorder might actually be better served by interventions focusing on sustained, positive relationships rather than short-term disciplinary techniques designed to counter misbehavior. Similarly, in their literature review of school-based programs effective in fostering resilient outcomes, Forman and Kalafat (1998) emphasized the protective potential of caring adults who hold high expectations and convey positive feedback, school structures that foster the development of relationships between students and adults, and fostering relationships between the school, parents, and community. Accentuating such informal school-based support systems could be particularly critical for the wellness of at-risk junior high and high school students because they face schools that are increasingly impersonal, with diminishing supports infused in daily curricula, and because adolescents can be particularly reluctant to seek professionals to help with even the most serious of adjustment problems (Doll & Lyon, 1998; Eccles et al., 1993; Forman & Kalafat, 1998; Short, 2003).

In considering the enhanced use of school-based interventions in future years, a number of potential impediments must be considered carefully, significant among which is schools' overarching emphasis on developing literacy skills. Although there are in fact ongoing opportunities to foster good problem-solving skills and social competence (Doll & Lyon, 1998), Adelman and Taylor (1999, p. 138) caution, "Schools are not in the mental health business. Their mandate is to educate." To foster more inclusive thinking, the authors underscore that scientists must systematically disseminate evidence that children's psychological problems can substantially impede achievement of literacy goals, and conversely, that mental health services can help in reaching them (Adelman & Taylor, 2003). All major stakeholders—parents, teachers, school administrators, and legislators—are likely to be more receptive of interventions if they clearly understand the evidence that children with social-emotional problems are at elevated risk for poor academic performance and eventually are at elevated risk for dropping out of school and subsequent problems in adulthood (National Institutes of Health, 2000; Noam & Hermann, 2002; Rones & Hoagwood, 2000; Short, 2003).

Another major impediment to the widespread use of schools to foster mental health has been interventionists' neglect of critical contextual factors. Ringeisen, Henderson, and Hoagwood (2003) argue that the children's mental health literature does encompass multiple evidence-based interventions (such as those previously cited here). In efforts to transfer interventions developed in laboratories to the school setting, however, there has been an unfortunate lack of attention to aspects of the school context that strongly affect intervention delivery (e.g., by involving teachers in the design and implementation of interventions). The third impediment is perhaps the most obvious one, that of burden: Resources are already stretched thin, particularly so in those schools that most need them. For example, it is estimated that the ratio of school psychologists or school social workers to students is about 1 : 2,500; for school counselors, the ratio is 1 : 1,000. Acknowledging these constraints, several authors have indicated that the most urgent task need of the day is not necessarily to provide more resources for mental health services in schools, but to use existing resources more prudently than they typically are used. We need movement away from individually based mental health service delivery to integrated models involving group- and classroom-based approaches, ongoing professional consultations for school personnel, and involvement of families and communities (Atkins, Graczyk, Frazier, & Abdul-Adil, 2003; Doll & Lyon, 1998; Felner et al., 2001; Hoagwood & Johnson, 2003).

Peers and Social Networks

Aside from adults at school, positive relationships with peers can also serve important ameliorative functions for at-risk children (Benard, 2004; Elder & Conger, 2000; Jackson & Warren, 2000). Among children of divorce, for example, a supportive relationship with a single friend may help to buffer children from the deleterious effects of marital disruption (Hetherington & Elmore, 2003; see also Bolger & Patterson, 2003). Other longitudinal research has shown that peer acceptance and friendships attenuated the association between aspects of family adversity and subsequent externalizing behaviors at the time of entry into elementary school and between fifth and seventh grades (Criss et al., 2002; Lansford, Criss, Pettit, Dodge, & Bates,

2003; Schwartz, Dodge, Pettit, & Bates, 2000). Findings such as these are viewed as reflecting three potential mechanisms: (1) the provision of "remedial" socializing contexts for skills not acquired in dysfunctional homes; (2) modification of parents' and children's negative behaviors by the more well-functioning peers and their parents; and (3) enhanced bonds with the social institution of the school (Lansford et al., 2003).

Intervention studies have also shown that peer-assisted learning can result in significant increases in achievement (Rohrbeck, Ginsburg-Block, Fantuzzo, & Miller, 2003), although there have been relatively few large-scale, randomized trials involving use of peers to promote outcomes. The potential in this regard is seen in Fantuzzo and colleagues' (1996) resilient peer treatment program, a peer-mediated classroom intervention involving pairing of socially withdrawn children with manifestly resilient peers in the classroom. In addition, several elementary and middle schools throughout the country tend to use peer mediation to reduce conflict and promoting positive behaviors (e.g., Johnson & Johnson, 2001; Smith & Daunic, 2002), but again, there is a need for more rigorous evaluations of their effectiveness. Underscoring the socializing potential of peer environments, Kupersmidt, Coie, and Howell (2004) advocate enhanced exploration of programs to prevent the spiraling of problems of aggressive children by promoting contacts between them and their more conventional peers.

Just as positive peer relationships can ameliorate effects of adversity, problems in this domain can exacerbate vulnerability: Children who have been rejected by their peers show relatively poor outcomes across multiple domains in later life, including internalizing problems, school dropout, and delinquency (Kupersmidt & Dodge, 2004). In a series of studies with longitudinal designs, social rejection was a consistent predictor of adolescent and adult criminality, sexual promiscuity, suicide, Schizophrenia, and substance use (McFadyen-Ketchum & Dodge, 1998). The combination of aggression and rejection spells particularly high risk for long-term adjustment outcomes (see Kupersmidt & Dodge, 2004).

Affiliation with deviant peers is a factor well known to exacerbate vulnerability among at-risk youth, particularly in relation to conduct problems and substance use. Among preadolescent children of substance-abusing fathers, affiliation with deviant peers was a robust predictor of child psychopathology (Moss, Lynch, Hardie, & Baron, 2002), as it is among adolescents experiencing stressful life experiences both within and outside the family (e.g., Barrera et al., 2002; Scaramella, Conger, Spoth, & Simons, 2002;

Tyler, Hoyt, Whitbeck, & Cauce, 2001). In the Great Smoky Mountains Study, data on 9- to 15-year-olds interviewed during the first three waves of this project showed that association with deviant peers, along with increasing levels of circulating testosterone, contributed to increases in conduct disorders with age. Furthermore, these associations were mediated primarily by increases in non-physically aggressive behaviors (Rowe, Maughan, Worthman, Costello, & Angold, 2004).

Dishion, McCord, and Poulin (1999) provided powerful evidence on the potentially iatrogenic effects of peer aggregation during early adolescence. These authors reviewed longitudinal research data showing that adolescent friendships can involve "deviancy training," which in turn predicts increases in delinquency, substance use, violence, and adult maladjustment. In addition, they presented findings from two experimentally controlled intervention studies showing that (1) as compared to control conditions, peer-group interventions actually increased adolescent problem behaviors and negative life outcomes in adulthood, and (2) high-risk youth were particularly vulnerable to such peer aggregations (i.e., more so than low-risk youth). Two developmental processes were discussed as possibly accounting for the powerful iatrogenic effects; the first involved active reinforcement for deviant behavior through laughter and social attention, and the second entailed the derivation of meaning and values that provided the cognitive basis for motivation to commit delinquent acts in the future.

The potential for such iatrogenic effects has often been discussed in relation to the ecology of urban poverty. In inner-city neighborhoods and schools, the peer culture tends to reflect the larger community, so that youth growing up in high-crime neighborhoods can be exposed to more delinquent peers than are youth in other environments (Cauce et al., 2003; Leventhal & Brooks-Gunn, 2000; Richters & Cicchetti, 1993). In turn, affiliation with delinquent peers exacerbates the risk for the development of adolescent behavior problems. Furthermore, the personal characteristics valued by peers in inner-city settings are often at odds with those endorsed more conventionally (Jarrett, 1999). For example, high peer popularity can be associated with disruptive, aggressive behaviors at school as well as low academic effort (Fordham & Ogbu, 1986; Luthar, 1995; Luthar & McMahon, 1996), ostensibly reflecting the lack of conviction in poor urban communities that conformity and application at school will actually result in long-term life successes.

Adding still further to the complexities of peer group effects, some have shown that influences of the inner-city

adolescent peer group can be beneficial in some spheres of adjustment, even as they are counterproductive in others. Seidman and Pedersen (2003), for example, reported that inner-city adolescents who were antisocial and highly engaged with friends were in fact at risk for delinquency. At the same time, they were notably less depressed than were comparison youth from the same background. There are also probably varying effects of high status in the wider peer group as opposed to support from close friends. Gutman, Sameroff, and Eccles (2002) found that levels of support from peers, as opposed to popularity with the wider peer group in previously discussed studies, was associated with higher math achievement test scores for high-risk adolescents, but not their lower-risk counterparts. The authors argued that peer support for academic success may in fact be limited for African American adolescents (Steinberg, Dornbusch, & Brown, 1992), but that among African American teens exposed to multiple risks, those who feel that they can depend on peers for help with problems fare better academically than their counterparts with low perceived peer supportiveness.

Aside from members of the peer group, relationships with informal mentors can serve critical protective functions. Evidence in this regard is seen in the Big Brothers Big Sisters of America (BBBSA) movement, a program that typically targets youth ages 6 to 18 years from single-parent homes. Service delivery is by volunteers who interact regularly with a youth in a one-to-one relationship, and supervision is provided on a monthly basis for the 1st year and on a quarterly basis subsequently. An evaluation of the program has shown that as compared to their non-participating peers, BBBSA youth were 46% less likely to initiate illegal drug use, 27% less likely to initiate alcohol use, and 52% less likely to skip school. They also fared substantially better on academic behavior and attitudes and had higher-quality relationships with their parents or guardians as well as their peers (Tierney, Grossman, & Resch, 1995).

With regard to mediators and moderators, Rhodes, Grossman, and Resch (2000) tested a conceptual model in which the effects of mentoring were mediated through improvements in parental relationships. The study included almost 1,000 youth, randomly assigned to BBBSA or a control group, and questions were administered at baseline and 18 months later. Results indicated that improved family relations did in fact mediate mentoring effects. In another study, Grossman and Rhodes (2002) found that duration of the relationship was a significant moderator variable. Adolescents in relationships lasting a year or longer reported the largest number of improvements, with progressively fewer gains (and sometimes even decrements) seen with reductions in relationship length.

Salutary socialization experiences can derive from religious affiliation as well (Elder & Conger, 2000; Pearce, Jones, Schwab-Stone, & Ruchkin, 2003). Studies by Miller and her colleagues have demonstrated that religious adolescents have relatively lower risk for problems such as depression and substance use (e.g., Miller, Davies, & Greenwald, 2000; Miller & Gur, 2002). Mechanisms posited include indirect effects of primary socialization (in that religion shapes the primary socialization sources, comprising parents, peers, and school) as well as direct ones (aiding in the adolescent's search for meaning, purpose, and identity in life).

The benefits of community supports to at-risk children are paralleled by those to their parents: Parents with informal social support networks show better psychological well-being and positive parenting and fewer negative parenting practices (Belsky, 1980; Burchinal et al., 1996; R. D. Taylor et al., 1993). Among inner-city mothers, those with high levels of perceived support displayed relatively few depressive symptoms, experienced less negativity about the parental role, and used less punishment (McLoyd, Jayaratne, Ceballo, & Borquez, 1994). By the same token, feelings of social isolation and loneliness tend to characterize low-SES parents who are neglectful of their children more than those who are not (Luthar, 1999).

Perceptions of social support may be more critical for disadvantaged individuals than support actually used (Berman, Kurtines, Silverman, & Serafini, 1996). Actual receipt of help from others—for example, with child care—benefited parents from different economic backgrounds, but expectations of adequate support in crises were more advantageous for low-income families than for others (Hashima & Amato, 1994). Given the paucity of resources and the multiplicity of life stressors among parents who contend with conditions of serious economic disadvantage, convictions that help will be forthcoming when needed may be particularly comforting to them.

Indirect benefits to children via support received by parents are also evident in research on interventions (e.g., Luthar & Suchman, 2000). In the Chicago Parent-Child Project, for example, many of the benefits deriving from this program were mediated by parents' involvement in children's education and school (Reynolds, 2000; Reynolds & Ou, 2003), probably reflecting improvements in parenting practices and attitudes, as well as enhanced family support. As noted earlier, in Yoshikawa's (1994) review of early intervention programs successful in reducing long-

term delinquency, comprehensive support to parents constituted a key ingredient.

Support to parents via religious communities can also be beneficial. Brody, Stoneman, and Flor (1996) showed that among rural African American families, relatively high formal religiosity was linked to more cohesive and less conflictual family relationships. Associations such as these might reflect, in part, the connectedness and social supports experienced by those who attend church regularly, as church attendance provides a place for families to gather and socialize (Brody et al., 1996). In addition, intrapersonal processes might be implicated, such as reliance on relatively effective coping strategies. Kendler, Gardner, and Prescott (1997) reported, based on twin study data, that adults with high personal religiosity reflected comparatively low susceptibility to the depressogenic levels of stressful life events; they also reported lower levels of alcohol and nicotine use compared to others. Among parents who had lost an infant to Sudden Infant Death Syndrome, those high on religious participation and importance showed less distress than others, and these effects were mediated by two dimensions of coping: cognitive processing of the loss and finding meaning in the death (McIntosh, Silver, & Wortman, 1993). Similarly, among elderly women who had suffered hip fractures, those who were more religious had better physical and psychological coping than did others (Pressman, Lyons, Larson, & Strain, 1990).

The connotations of religiousness are not invariably positive, however; in fact, it can sometimes exacerbate vulnerability. Among women (but not men) who had been depressed as children, personal religiousness was found to pose as much as a twofold increase in risk for depression in adulthood (Miller, Weissman, Gur, & Greenwald, 2002). The authors suggest that childhood depressive symptoms such as guilt, low self-worth, and excessive self-blame (all common features of female depression) can sometimes distort religious messages emphasizing altruism, empathy, and other-centeredness, leading some women to become excessively submissive, self-depriving, and lacking in self-expression. Furthermore, Garcia Coll and Vasquez García (1995) have argued that strong beliefs in the supernatural may sometimes take the form of fatalism, and if at-risk youth and families come to believe that nothing can be done to improve one's lot in life, this can create formidable barriers in improving the overall quality of their lives.

Neighborhoods

Moving on from the relatively proximal extrafamilial contexts of school, peers, and interpersonal supports to those more distal, aspects of the community may also play an important role in buffering risk for children (Garbarino, Hammond, Mercy, & Yung, 2004; Gorman-Smith & Tolan, 2003; Sampson, 2001). Particularly important are social organization processes in the neighborhood (Sampson et al., 1997; Wilson, 2003), which involve features such as high levels of cohesion, a sense of belonging to the community, supervision of youth by community adults, and high participation in local organizations. Such neighborhood social processes can help buffer the impact of structural characteristics of the community (e.g., poverty, violence) either by affecting parents' behaviors or directly benefiting children themselves (Furstenberg et al., 1999; Leventhal & Brooks-Gunn, 2000; Sampson, 2001). To illustrate the former, Mahoney and Magnusson (2001) found that among at-risk youth, fathers' involvement in community activities in late childhood was associated with significantly lower risk for persistent criminal involvement over time. These findings were seen as possibly reflecting the effects of more conventional values of fathers who were involved in community activities, their relatively greater personal resources, or their generally higher levels of involvement in their sons' lives. Direct benefits to children are seen in Gorman-Smith and Tolan's (2003) findings that when inner-city families are lacking in warmth and closeness, children's vulnerability can be reduced somewhat if they feel a sense of belonging and support in the neighborhood.

Whereas extracurricular activity involvement is widely believed to confer protective functions, the type of benefit depends, to some extent, on the degree of structure of the activities. Research by Mahoney (2000) showed that among pre- and early adolescent children manifesting multiple adjustment problems, involvement in school extracurricular activities was linked with reduced rates of early dropout and criminal arrest over time. Results of another study, however, indicated that it was only participation in structured leisure activities that reduced risk for antisocial behavior; when structure was low (as in youth recreation centers), risks for deviant peer relations and antisocial behaviors were actually heightened (Mahoney & Stattin, 2000).

Youth-serving community organizations can directly provide protective functions to low-income youth, but the number that actually deliver this in contemporary society is woefully inadequate. Just as quality day care is rarely obtainable by those who need it the most, so are quality youth organizations rare in those neighborhoods that most need them, where economic and political resources are low and social disorganization is high (Cauce et al., 2003). This dearth of institutional services, along with low resources in schools, results in a lack of attractive, organized, and positive afterschool activities for youth, leaving them open to the allure of illegal activities with peers and adults in the community (Luthar & Burack, 2000; Seidman & Pedersen, 2003).

There have been few neighborhood-level interventions thus far that have been focused on children's well-being (Leventhal & Brooks-Gunn, 2000), yet promising efforts are seen in Tolan and colleagues' (2004) Schools and Families Educating Children (SAFE Children) intervention. This preventive program is focused on promoting strong family relationships and developing support networks in the neighborhood, with attention also to children's academic functioning. Intervention families have shown improvements in parents' functioning and in children's academic performance, with gains most pronounced among those who, at the outset, manifested the highest levels of disturbance (Tolan et al., 2004).

Based on their own experiences, Gorman-Smith and Tolan (2003) note that in designing future interventions based at the neighborhood level, two interrelated considerations are critical. The first is that they should involve constituent groups as far as possible, and the second is that (as with families), they should strive to promote benefits that can be sustained by recipients over time. Gorman-Smith and Tolan also point to the promise of community efforts involving coalitions of local groups and agencies (such as police and faith-based organizations) in addressing risks specifically associated with urban poverty (e.g., initiatives to inhibit illegal gun trade).

Finally, among adults, relocation out of at-risk communities can be beneficial by providing major changes in life opportunities or in people's cognitive set and self-views (Werner & Smith, 1992). Movement toward relatively positive trajectories has been shown, for example, with respect to army experiences for low-income youth prone to delinquency (Laub & Sampson, 2003; Sampson & Laub, 1996). Among low-income children who had poor grades and self-inadequacy, those who entered military service relatively early showed more positive outcomes in terms of completing their education, getting married, and having their first child later than did nonveterans (Elder, 1986).

Individual Attributes: Malleability in Contexts

In overviewing the triad of vulnerability and protective processes in resilience, it has been argued that children's own attributes should be considered after aspects of their family and community for three critical reasons (see Luthar & Zelazo, 2003). From a basic research perspective, numerous studies, described in some detail in discussions that follow, have shown that many positive child attributes are themselves often dependent on processes in the proximal and distal environments. From an applied perspective, it is logical that interventions to foster resilience should focus less on what young children are able to do for themselves and more on what adults must do to bolster the children's own efforts. From a policy perspective, to place primary emphasis on child attributes could carry the risk that public debate will shift away from the major environmental risks that affect children, leading to decreased allocation of resources to ameliorate these risks (see Luthar et al., 2000a; Luthar & Zelazo, 2003). It is these due to considerations, rather than any devaluing of children's own strengths, that the emphasis is placed on families and communities in transaction with the children rather than the other way around.[1]

To underscore the perils of overemphasizing children's own attributes, we begin this section by presenting evidence on the malleability of some of the most commonly cited *protective child attributes,* starting with intelligence (probably the single most often mentioned asset). Studies on diverse risk groups show that individuals with high IQ tend to fare better than others (Luthar, 2003; Masten, 2001). At the same time, evidence of environmental influence is seen in Sameroff and colleagues' (Sameroff, Seifer, Zax, & Barocas, 1987) findings almost 2 decades ago that children facing no environmental risks scored more than 30 points higher than children with eight or nine risk factors. No preschoolers in the zero-risk group had an IQ below 85, whereas 26% of those in the high-risk group did.

Since then, others have shown that disturbances in parents' functioning can affect child intelligence. A twin study by Koenen, Moffitt, Caspi, Taylor, and Purcell (2003) showed that among 5-year-old children, those exposed to high amounts of domestic violence had an IQ that was 8 points lower, on average, than the IQ of children not exposed to domestic violence. Furthermore, domestic violence accounted for significant variation in IQs even after considering possible genetic effects and externalizing and internalizing problems that could impair performance on

standardized tests. Similarly, maternal depression has been associated with relatively low child cognitive functioning both in the postpartum period (Murray, 1992; Sharp et al., 1995) and in the preschool years (NICHD, 1999; see also Cicchetti et al., 2000).

Powerful testimony on this issue lies in work by Rutter, O'Connor, and their colleagues, on adoptees from Romanian orphanages. Caregiving conditions in these orphanages ranged from poor to appalling: Infants were typically confined to cots, there was no personalized caregiving and few toys, feeding often occurred via propped-up bottles, and washing was done by hosing the babies down (Rutter & the English and Romanian Adoptees Study Team, 1998). When these children entered into adoptive families in the United Kingdom, they had mean cognitive functioning scores in the mentally retarded range. However, longitudinal evaluations showed catch-up effects, in that babies who were adopted by 2 years of age by families in the United Kingdom lost their profound early deficits, and by the age of 4 came to show near-average developmental status.

In terms of underlying mechanisms, environmental deprivation may lead to cognitive deficits because of lack of appropriate stimulation and even adverse effects on brain development. Depressed and psychologically withdrawn caregivers, for example, can provide limited stimulation for the development of cognitive skills and expressive language, and deficits in the mother-child relationship can constrain the child's developing sense of self-efficacy and agency, in turn inhibiting her active exploration of the environment (Cicchetti et al., 2000). Biologically, studies have shown that stress generates high levels of catecholamines and cortisol, and chronic activation of the stress response can result in the death of neurons in specific brain regions, with these effects most profound during early childhood, when neuroplasticity is high (Cicchetti & Walker, 2003; DeBellis, 2001; DeBellis et al., 1999; Sanchez, Ladd, & Plotsky, 2001). Results of animal studies clearly establish that early enriched versus deprived environments connote substantial differences in animals' neurochemical, physiological, and neuroanatomical functioning, with the last including variations in the weight of the brain and structural modifications of the cerebellar cortex (Curtis & Nelson, 2003).

Discussions on intelligence thus far have been focused on periods early in development, and one might argue that high IQ would be more powerful in resilience later in development; though probably true, the evidence is not unequivocal even at older ages. Up through middle childhood, it does seem that bright children tend to show stability in everyday competence despite increasing levels

---

[1] A parallel approach is evident in the Search Institute's listing of 40 developmental assets. The list begins with the *external assets,* and noted first are dimensions of support, including the categories of family support, positive family communication, other adult relationships, caring neighborhoods, and caring school climates. *Internal assets* are the second 20 items on the list, subsumed in categories such as commitment to learning, positive values, and positive identity.

of life stress (e.g., Garmezy et al., 1984; Masten, 2001). On the other hand, among three different samples of low-income adolescents, intelligence was not found to be protective; to the contrary, there were suggestions that bright youth may be more sensitive than others to negative environmental forces (Gutman et al., 2003; Luthar, 1991; Luthar & Ripple, 1994). In other words, intelligent adolescents fared far better at school than did less intelligent ones when life stress levels were low, but when stress was high, they lost much of this advantage and showed competence levels similar to those of their less intelligent counterparts. More striking, Fiedler (1995) found that high IQ adults showed leadership success under conditions of low stress, but that when stress was high, IQ was *inversely* correlated with leadership success.

Findings such as these have been viewed as suggesting that the manifest benefits of innate intelligence vary depending on aspects of the proximal environment. In areas of concentrated poverty, where conventional means of achieving self-worth (e.g., good grades, productive employment) are generally scarce, for example, intelligent and creative teenagers may use their talents in ways that bring more immediate gains, such as illegal entrepreneurship, rather than through striving for excellence at school (Gutman et al., 2003; Luthar, 1991; Richters & Cicchetti, 1993). Freitas and Downey (1998) cite research showing such patterns among adult women who were incarcerated; among recidivists, many personal attributes commonly seen as protective in nature were identified as actually aiding them in their criminal activities.

The previously described evidence on intelligence is paralleled by similar evidence on temperament, also shown to confer protection against stress (e.g., Mendez, Fantuzzo, & Cicchetti, 2002; Murry, Bynum, Brody, Willert, & Stephens, 2001). Benefits have been found in relation to not only psychological and behavioral but also biological outcomes. To illustrate, children low on behavioral inhibition may react less to stress than others, as suggested by evidence of resting right frontal EEG activation among inhibited children (Calkins & Fox, 2002); as noted earlier, this pattern is linked with tendencies to respond to stressful events with negative affect or depressive symptoms (Curtis & Cicchetti, 2003).

Whereas temperamental differences can be seen as early as 4 months of age and show continuity over early childhood (e.g., Kagan, Snidman, & Arcus, 1998), both the manifestation and ramifications of temperament can be modified by environmental features. During the preschool years, for example, children show differences in terms of

shyness versus extraversion, as well as the tendency to feel negative emotions more or less deeply (Rothbart & Jones, 1998), and the external manifestations of both these dimensions can be modulated by effortful control. As Rutter (2000) has noted, scientists long ago moved past the point of misleading assumptions that "constitutional" factors are unalterable; whereas some children do have a tendency to be more impulsive or oppositional than others, their interactions with the world contribute to determining the behavioral conformity they display. In a similar vein, some children are temperamentally more exuberant than others, and some feel negative emotions more intensely than do others, but the external manifestation of these emotions and whether they lead to rejection by peers depends on the degree to which they can modulate their emotions (Fabes et al., 1999; Rubin, Coplan, Fox, & Calkins, 1995). And children's abilities to modulate or inhibit the expression of emotions depend, as described in the paragraphs that follow, on the nature of their interpersonal relationships, particularly those early in life.

Several studies have established the protective effects of self-regulation from early childhood onward (see Shonkoff & Philips, 2000). Among low-income children, emotion regulation at the age of 3½ was related to self-control on entry into first grade (Gilliom, Shaw, Beck, Schonberg, & Lukon, 2002), and those with low emotional knowledge at first grade showed significant increases in internalizing symptoms over the next 4 years (Fine, Izard, Mostow, Trentacosta, & Ackerman, 2003). These findings suggest that among children just entering school, those who find it difficult to interpret others' emotions may get into a cycle where dysfunctional social exchanges lead to isolation and thus sadness, and these emotions in turn jeopardize future interactions with others. Among adolescents in low-income families, Buckner et al. (2003) found that good self-regulation contributed to resilience—good mental health and emotional well-being—even after considering self-esteem and nonverbal intelligence. Even perceived self-efficacy to regulate positive and negative affect is related to adolescents' beliefs that they can manage academic, transgressive, and empathic aspects of their lives, with these forms of perceived self-efficacy, in turn, related to later levels of depression, delinquency, and prosocial behaviors (Bandura, Caprara, Barbaranelli, Gerbino, & Pastorelli, 2003).

As suggested earlier, self-regulation itself depends squarely on relationships; in point of fact, children's compliance within the mother-child dyad is the first sign of internalizing adults' rules (R. Feldman, Greenbaum, &

Yirmiya, 1999; Kochanska, 1997; Kochanska, Coy, & Murray, 2001; Stifter, Spinrad, & Braungart-Rieker, 1999). As Shonkoff and Phillips (2000, p. 121) emphasize:

> It is clear at this point that the various components of active, internally guided regulation of attention, behavior, and emotion emerge . . . in the context of caregiving relationships that explicitly guide the child from her dependence on adults to regulate virtually every aspect of functioning to gradually taking over and self-regulating her own behaviors and feelings in one aspect of her life after another.

In their study of 90 toddlers, R. Feldman and Klein (2003) showed that compliance to parents in child care centers was associated with parents' sensitivity and philosophy. Among young boys in low-income families, secure attachment to mother and positive maternal control at the age of 1½ years predicted effectiveness of emotion regulation at the age of 3½, and this in turn was related to capacities for self-control on entry into first grade (Gilliom et al., 2002). Finding that self-regulation distinguished manifestly resilient low-income adolescents from others, Buckner and colleagues (2003) noted that this capacity is itself shaped by teenagers' relationships in the family.

Aside from self-regulation, individuals' propensities to cope effectively with challenges also rests on "meaning making"—phenomenological interpretations of events in their lives (e.g., Beardslee, 2002; Hauser, 1999; Noam & Hermann, 2002)—and this, too, is shaped by the environment as demonstrated in Spencer's (1999; Spencer et al., 2003) phenomenological variant of ecological systems theory (PVEST). At the core of PVEST lie identity processes, which define how adolescents view themselves within and between their various contexts of development. Emerging identities, however, are themselves conceptualized as emerging within the framework of contextual forces that potentially confer vulnerability (e.g., poverty or racial subordination) and net stress engagement, which is the individual's actual experiences of both risks experienced and support systems drawn on. Depending on the nature and balance of these risks and supports, the individual develops reactive coping methods, which in turn shape emergent identities and, eventually, long-term life stage-specific coping outcomes. A particularly attractive feature of Spencer's PVEST theory is the careful articulation of policy implications. She specifically underscores the need for policymakers to recognize that "problem behaviors" cannot be conceptualized as stemming simply from a child's own faulty coping processes or aberrant meaning making, for these often are products of uncontrollable contextual forces. Accordingly, interventions should address multiple levels of the environment rather than focusing primarily on the child labeled as being at risk.

There is similar evidence showing that many other child attributes commonly labeled as protective factors can themselves be shaped substantially by the environment. Self-efficacy, as Maddux (2002) notes, is strongly influenced by the degree to which adults encourage or hinder the child's attempts at manipulation and control (Bandura, 1997). Self-esteem can be protective for at-risk children but is itself affected by parental warmth (Sandler et al., 2003). Internal locus of control is commonly cited as being protective (e.g., Capella & Weinstein, 2001), and Bolger and Patterson (2003) showed that early onset of maltreatment reduces the chances that children are able to maintain internality of control. Other research has shown that when teachers are perceived as cold and inconsistent, this progressively erodes students' convictions that they can produce their own successes and avoid failures (E. A. Skinner et al., 1998).

The preceding examples resonate with recommendations from resilience researchers for caution against inordinately emphasizing the importance of protective child attributes that are themselves malleable by the environment (see Luthar et al., 2000a; Yates et al., 2003); at the same time, there are several other caveats that warrant attention. First, as we noted at the outset, prior discussions are not intended to detract in any way from children's own strengths. Rather, the effort is (1) to circumvent any misguided blaming of the victim that might stem from an emphasis on child traits, and (2) concomitantly, to underscore the need for policies alleviating the contextual risks facing many youth. Second, there is no suggestion that personal attributes do little for resilience in any absolute sense. In fact, bright children likely fare better than others in many ways; the point here is simply that even these youth may not realize their full potential if they continually contend with environmental assaults. Third, the relative salience of personal versus others' attributes obviously shifts over time, with young children's well-being being more dependant on the emotional sustenance they receive than is the well-being of adults. Fourth, our arguments are not intended to minimize the possibility that children's attributes can themselves exert effects on the environment, for example, by eliciting different reactions from adults (e.g., Laird, Pettit, Bates, & Dodge, 2003; MacKinnon-Lewis, Lamb, Hattie, & Baradaran, 2001). From an intervention standpoint, however, applied scientists are less likely to "change" a young child to evoke positive feelings in parents and teachers than to help adults behave in ways that evoke positive reactions in the child. In the words of Shonkoff and Miesels (2000, p. 123):

For children whose problems do not fall within the clinical range, early interventions to address regulatory behavior focused on "fixing" the environment . . . warrant serious attention to balance the current focus on "fixing" the child. It is also clear that focusing on young children's relationships with adults and peers is a promising and complementary, yet poorly exploited approach.

In a related vein, we do not imply in any way that programs addressing children's own competencies do not work, merely that the successful ones focus not only on the child, but also on the environment, by working, for example, with teachers and parents (Shonkoff & Phillips, 2000; Zigler & Styfco, 2001). This is true even among children well past the infancy and preschool years, as is exemplified in research by Sandler and colleagues. Working with school-age children of divorce, these investigators designed an intervention with separate programs for mothers and for children. Experimentally induced change in maternal warmth did in fact lead to a reduction in children's mental health problems, whereas working with children's coping alone did not (Sandler et al., 2003; see also Maton, Schellenbach, Leadbeater, & Solarz, 2004).

Other Individual Assets: Future Research Needs

The personal characteristics already discussed—intelligence, easygoing temperament, self-regulation, self-esteem, self-efficacy, and internal locus of control—are commonly cited in the resilience literature (see Masten, 2001), but there are many others that warrant further empirical attention. Among these are practical and emotional intelligence. Sternberg and Grigorenko (2000, p. 215) have defined practical intelligence as "intelligence as it applies in everyday life in adaptation to, shaping of, and selection of environments"; it is complementary to but distinct from crystallized intelligence as measured by IQ tests. The importance of this construct is evident in studies of children and adults. In a village in Kenya, Sternberg and his colleagues (2001) found that children who had learned how to use natural herbal medicines to cure their various ailments were viewed by the community as both intelligent and adaptive. However, this aspect of practical intelligence was negatively correlated with conventional tests of crystallized abilities. Similarly, among adults, assemblers in milk-processing plants use complex strategies for combining partially filled cases of milk to minimize the number of moves needed to fill an order (e.g., Scribner, 1984). The order-filling performance of the assemblers was unrelated to intelligence test scores or arithmetic test scores and grades (Sternberg et al., 2001). In future research, greater

attention is clearly needed to practical intelligence as a protective factor across different risk conditions and in relation to different outcomes.

Emotional intelligence, as conceptualized by Mayer, Salovey, and their colleagues (Mayer, Salovey, Caruso, & Sitarenios, 2003; Salovey, Mayer, Caruso, & Lopes, 2003), is the ability to perceive and express emotions, to understand and use them, and to manage them to foster personal growth. The construct has four dimensions: (1) perceiving emotion, (2) using emotion to facilitate thought, (3) understanding emotion, and (4) managing emotion. In terms of its potential association with resilience, emotional intelligence is in fact a central construct in school-based initiatives aimed at promoting social-emotional learning in children (see Elias, Arnold, & Hussey, 2003; Greenberg et al., 2003). Among adolescents, furthermore, researchers have shown that this construct is linked with relatively low likelihood of smoking cigarettes and drinking alcohol (Trinidad & Johnson, 2002) and, following the major life transition to beginning college, with greater likelihood of attaining high academic grades (Parker, Summerfeldt, Hogan, & Majeski, 2004). In adulthood, emotional intelligence has been associated with relatively positive health outcomes, possibly reflecting psychophysiological responses to stress (e.g., relatively low cortisol and blood pressure responses to acute laboratory stressors; Salovey, Stroud, Woolery, & Epel, 2002).

In future research on intelligence and resilience, it is important not only to disentangle the contributions of practical, emotional, and crystallized intelligence, but also to move from focusing on discrete skills or particular milestones to the *underlying processes and functional capacities* that underlie skills that span multiple domains (Cicchetti & Wagner, 1990). Rather than relying on standardized IQ or achievement tests, for example, it will be most useful to assess the underlying capacities that make it possible for children to learn, such as the development of different problem-solving strategies, the ability to generalize learning across situations, and the unfolding of high motivation to explore and master new challenges (Shonkoff & Phillips, 2000).

Aside from dimensions of intelligence, studies with adults have shown the importance to resilient adaptation of developmental maturity, as reflected in the types of defense mechanisms typically used. Vaillant (2000) has noted that the more mature defenses—such as altruism, suppression, humor, anticipation, and sublimation—tend to be linked with relatively positive outcomes among individuals at risk and, at the same time, are relatively independent of social class, education, and IQ. In a long-term follow-up study of 73 14-year-old inner-city boys with low IQ and a socioeconomically matched group with an average IQ of 115, Vaillant and Davis (2000) found that at the age of 65, half of the low-IQ men were comparable to the high-IQ group in terms of their own income and their children's level of education. These resilient low-IQ men were far more likely than their low-IQ, poor-outcome counterparts to use predominantly adaptive defenses, with the latter group more often using maladaptive defenses such as turning against the self, projection, and fantasy.

Potentially counterintuitive findings on the role of defenses in resilience stem from research on bereavement. Whereas repressive coping is generally viewed as maladaptive, research by Bonanno and colleagues suggests that it can foster resilience in the face of bereavement, as defined by the maintenance of relatively stable, healthy levels of psychological and physical functioning following the loss (see Bonanno, 2004). Studies by this group have shown that among bereaved individuals, repressors manifested relatively little grief or distress at any point across 5 years of bereavement. Among victims of childhood sexual abuse, similarly, repressors were less likely to voluntarily disclose their abuse when provided the opportunity to do so, but they also showed better adjustment than others (Bonanno, Noll, Putnam, O'Neill, & Trickett, 2003). Counter to psychodynamic emphases on the importance of working through negative emotions, therefore, Bonanno's literature review indicates that interventions emphasizing grief work can be not just ineffective but sometimes even deleterious.

Of particular importance, the effects of talking about grief might vary with developmental status; unlike bereaved adults, children may benefit significantly from being encouraged to talk about their loss. In research by Sandler and his colleagues (2003), bereaved children who talked about their feelings with family members had lower rates of mental health problems, whereas inhibition of emotional expression was associated with higher rates of internalizing and externalizing problems both cross-sectionally and prospectively. Differences in findings between children and adults may partly reflect children's more limited cognitive understanding of death (i.e., in terms of comprehending its finality), so that speaking about this could be generally helpful for them. On the other hand, for adults, continuing to talk about the loss could approach Nolen-Hoeksema's (2001) notion of rumination, which can compromise mental health. Another factor underlying the differences between studies might be variations in definitions of repression or inhibition of emotions. Sandler and colleagues note that they assessed children's

efforts to actively hide or inhibit their grief, whereas in many adult bereavement studies, repression was defined not in terms of deliberate efforts to inhibit affect, but in terms of discrepancies between autonomic arousal and verbal expression of distress.

Complex associations involving developmental maturity are also evident in findings on ego development, in that it is generally associated with positive adjustment but can also signal relatively keen sensitivity to distress. As conceptualized by Loevinger (1976), ego development refers to a "master" trait reflecting character development, which is related to various aspects of cognitive and interpersonal development, but that represents more than any of them considered individually. High levels of ego development attenuate risk for psychopathology in general and also among at-risk individuals (see Westenberg, Blasi, & Cohn, 1998). To illustrate, high ego development was linked with better coping strategies and fewer symptoms among psychiatrically hospitalized 12- to 16-year-olds (Recklitis & Noam, 1999) and with apparently lower reactivity to negative life events among inner-city youth (Luthar, 1991). Among substance-abusing mothers, those at high developmental levels were observed to have relatively positive interactions with their 1-month-old infant (Fineman, Beckwith, Howard, & Espinosa, 1997); among elderly women (75 to 103 years) living in long-term care facilities, higher versus lower levels of ego development showed links with affirming, negating, and despairing styles of reminiscence, in that order (Beaton, 1991).

As with intelligence, however, high levels of ego development are not necessarily an unmitigated blessing; as Noam (1998) has argued, higher developmental levels imply not just greater maturity but also greater complexity, so that individuals at high levels may manifest more complex problems. In a similar vein, Luthar and colleagues (2001) argued that among mothers who admitted to having "socially unacceptable" adjustment problems, such as uncontrolled displays of anger, those at high levels of ego development (being more introspective and self-critical) would suffer greater setbacks than others. Results were consistent with this reasoning, suggesting that the complexity and introspection characteristic of high developmental levels may be advantageous in general, but once disturbing problems have set in, introspection may come to take the form of counterproductive rumination or guilt.

Wolin and Wolin's (1993) definition of resilience encompasses a collection of several protective personal attributes. Their definition refers to the capacity to bounce back, to withstand hardship and to repair oneself, and is based on the following elements: (1) insight, or asking difficult questions and giving honest answers; (2) independence, or distancing emotionally and physically from the sources of trouble in one's life; (3) relationships, or making fulfilling connections to others; (4) initiative, or taking charge of problems; (5) creativity, or using imagination and expressing oneself; (6) humor, or finding the humor even in difficult circumstances; and (7) morality, or acting on the basis of a conscience.

The protective potential of such constellations of attributes also has been demonstrated by Hauser, Allen, and their colleagues in narrative analyses in their long-term study of individuals psychiatrically hospitalized as adolescents (e.g., Allen et al., 1994, 1996). Hauser (1999) reported on a subgroup of these youth who seemed resilient as individuals; they had relatively high scores on multiple competence dimensions (e.g., relationship closeness and ego development) and low scores on several domains of psychopathology (crime and hard drug use). In-depth interviews revealed five major protective attributes: (1) self-reflection or high awareness of their feelings and thoughts; (2) self-efficacy, or agency in making conscious choices about their lives; (3) self-complexity in recognizing multiple facets to different situations; (4) persistence and ambition in education and careers; and (5) self-esteem that, on balance, was tipped more toward positive than negative self-views.

Beardslee (2002) has reported similar protective effects in his work with adolescent children of depressed parents. Resilient youth were aware of what they were facing—they recognized the parents' illness, knew that they were not responsible for it, and saw themselves as separate from their parents. In addition, they were able to put this experience in words and could articulate some strategies to offset the effects of the illness on them, for example, by forging nurturing relationships with adults outside the family. Among inner-city youth, Noam and Hermann (2002) noted the protective potential of both insight and the capacity to use symptoms and problems to motivate themselves toward positive change.

Of the various social-cognitive constructs linked with resilience, an intriguing one identified in the adult literature is benefit finding: the ability to see benefits in traumatic events. Among bereaved individuals, for example, Davis and colleagues (1998) found that 6 months after they had lost a loved one, as many as 73% of participants reported that they had experienced something positive, such as strengthened relationships with others, personal growth, and a new perspective on life. Furthermore, this capacity

for benefit finding uniquely predicted distress several months later. Similar trends were cited in a study of mothers whose infants were in neonatal intensive care units; again, three quarters of the participants indicated at least one benefit from the child's hospitalization experience (Affleck et al., 1991). Obviously, such benefit finding has greater potential to help with single or discrete traumatic events than with stressors that are ongoing, over time, from the external environment; they are also likely to be more useful for individuals capable of formal operational thought than children who think more concretely.

Empathy and altruism are two other attributes that can confer benefits to individuals facing adversities; both have been highlighted in the emerging positive psychology movement (e.g., Masten & Reed, 2002; Zhou, Valiente, & Eisenberg, 2003). In families with a depressed parent, Beardslee (2002) found that resilient youth had a well-developed capacity to see things from others' point of view and to think about their needs. Feeling useful and important to someone can also be critically important for one's own sense of well-being (Elder & Conger, 2000; Werner & Smith, 1992); the Search Institute (2004) lists several related positive values, such as caring for others, standing up for social justice, and involvement in service to others, among their 40 assets for healthy development.

High self-esteem can be protective, as feeling positive about ones' capabilities provides strength in coping with adversities, but frequently, there are complexities in associations involving self-views. As Bandura et al. (2003) showed, high perceived empathic self-efficacy among adolescents was related to high prosocial behavior and less delinquency among both males and females, but among the latter, was also related to depressive problems, possibly reflecting girls' greater tendencies to vicariously experience the distress of others and their relatively low sense of efficacy to manage their own negative affect. Similarly, unrealistic, overly positive views of oneself—self-enhancement—are often maladaptive, for example, in terms of evoking dislike from others (Paulhus, 1998). At the same time, self-enhancers can fare better than others in the face of serious trauma, when threats to the self are most salient. Among bereaved adults, self-enhancers showed better adjustment than others in terms of ratings by themselves, their close friends, and mental health professionals (Bonanno, 2004).

Harter's (2002) recent work suggests the value of another interesting construct that warrants attention: personal authenticity. This construct involves owning one's personal thoughts and emotions and acting in accord with these (captured, respectively, by the injunctions "Know thyself" and "To thine own self be true"). Encompassing as it does integration across multiple selves, this construct may be particularly prominent, for example, in the adjustment of immigrant youth, who often face differing expectations at home and in the mainstream culture of public schools. Along with forces such as discrimination, language barriers, and conflicts between subcultural and mainstream value systems, this may affect their psychological adjustment.

Tendencies to use positive emotions can also help offset the effects of loss by quieting or undoing negative emotion and by increasing support from important people in the environment. Among bereaved individuals, for example, those who exhibited genuine laughs and smiles when speaking about a loved one recently lost manifested better adjustment, as rated by different respondents (Bonanno, 2004). The field of positive psychology has pointed to several other personal attributes that warrant further examination as potential correlates of resilience in the face of not only bereavement but other risks. Among people in general, positive outcomes have been found among people with high levels of hope, optimism, and "flow" (Snyder & Lopez, 2002; S. E. Taylor, Kemeny, Reed, Bower, & Gruenewald, 2000); all of these attributes also may be beneficial for individuals who contend with adverse life conditions across the developmental span.

SUMMARY OF EVIDENCE AND FUTURE DIRECTIONS: RECONCEPTUALIZING RESILIENCE

In concluding this chapter, the evidence reviewed from almost half a century of work on resilience is briefly summarized. Along with major findings from the literature, directions for future research and interventions are delineated.

The first major take-home message is this: Resilience rests, fundamentally, on relationships. The desire to belong is a basic human need, and positive connections with others lie at the very core of psychological development; strong, supportive relationships are critical for achieving and sustaining resilient adaptation. During the childhood years, early relationships with primary caregivers affect several emerging psychological attributes and influence the negotiation of major developmental tasks; resolution of these tasks, in turn, affects the likelihood of success at future tasks. Accordingly, serious disruptions in the early re-

lationships with caregivers—in the form of physical, sexual, or emotional abuse—strongly impair the chances of resilient adaptation later in life. Whereas some maltreated children will obviously do better in life than others, the likelihood of sustained competence, without corrective, ameliorative relationship experiences, remains compromised at best. On the positive side, strong relationships with those in one's proximal circle serve vital protective processes, for children as well as adults.

Two broad ingredients are well known to be important in good relationships: warmth and support, and appropriate control or discipline. These dimensions have been at the core of childhood socialization research for decades. Moreover, recent research shows that later in life, strong intimate relationships, such as those in marriage, provide both the support and the informal social control needed to negotiate ongoing challenges in life.

There are several aspects of protective family processes that warrant further attention in future research, such as dimensions of containment and investment (children's beliefs that parents will prevail in disciplining them and protecting them from harm, respectively) and the role of consistency in simple family routines such as regularly eating dinner together. Also needed is much more work on parenting as a dependent variable. Good parenting is beneficial to all children and, to this extent, is ordinary (Masten, 2001). On the other hand, it is clearly extraordinary among at-risk families because it is so difficult to sustain in the face of major life risks such as chronic poverty and major mental illnesses. A central task for the future, therefore, is to identify the specific protective processes that make for positive parenting patterns among parents in high-risk circumstances, as well as the processes via which intervention programs eventuate in improved parenting behaviors.

Additionally, more needs to be learned about the specific relationship ingredients that are particularly influential or important in the context of particular types of risk; in neighborhoods rife with community violence, for instance, strategies to ensure physical safety are clearly of unique importance. Similarly, there must be more research on developmental processes in ethnic minority families. These individuals experience several stressors, including overrepresentation in poverty and experiences of discrimination, and there should be greater inquiry into factors that (in addition to the universals, such as warmth and discipline) are especially salient in particular ethnic minority groups. Examples of such factors include notions of family responsibility, support, and obligations both in the immediate and the extended family, as well as racial socialization and ethnic pride.

Aside from these dimensions of psychological processes, a critical priority must be to explore the role of genes in relation to familial influences on resilience. We know that both genes and the environment affect outcomes, and resilience researchers must increase their attention to the former. Studies are needed that illuminate gene × environment interactions in resilient adaptation and genetic markers conferring vulnerability or resilience, with attention to the mechanisms that might underlie their effects.

In the community domain, a major message from extant research is that ongoing exposure to community violence is highly inimical not only for children but also for their parents and other adults. Among those who fear for their very lives, it is unrealistic to expect psychological robustness: When physical survival threatens, all developmental tasks and processes are jeopardized. In the case of such risks, therefore, our first order of business should be to focus on eradicating these experiences in whatever way possible. This is not to say that we should cease attempts to attend to factors allowing some exposed individuals to fare better than others. Rather, the suggestion is that even as we attempt to identify such protective processes, any reports of research findings must be accompanied by unequivocal statements that these experiences are highly noxious and fundamentally undermine children's abilities to do well over time. In the interest of averting research-based impressions that some do indeed rise above such potent risks, we must caution, as we present our findings, that all regularly traumatized children are damaged in some integral way.

The community can be an important source of alternative support and care when the child's own parents are unable to provide these. High-quality child care is particularly helpful for children in the most at-risk families, as strong, supportive relationships with teachers can be highly beneficial for school-age children and adolescents. There is also great potential to use K–12 schools as a venue to foster resilient adaptation. Thus far, several school-based interventions based in social control and social learning theories, involving teachers as well as parents, have shown some success in randomized trials. What remains insufficiently explored is the effectiveness of attachment-based interventions in schools, where the emphasis is on developing close, supportive bonds with teachers that are sustained for as long as is feasible. Paralleling future work with parents, scientists need to learn more about resilience-inducing teachers by illuminating the factors that enable some teachers to bring out the best in their at-risk students. In addition, interventions using positive peer relationships to foster resilience warrant further exploration. In considering the enhanced use of schools to foster re-

silience, it will be critical to (1) disseminate evidence that psychological problems impair achievement, (2) carefully consider contextual factors (characteristics of the school and the wider community), and (3) maximize use of existing resources rather than necessarily seeking new ones.

Support provided by informal mentors (as in Big Brothers Big Sisters) can also serve important protective functions, especially when the relationships are of relatively long duration. Similarly, involvement in religion, can confer benefits via the availability of a stable support network in addition to promoting relatively positive coping strategies. At the neighborhood level, cohesion and shared supervision of children are important positive influences, as is high participation in local and voluntary organizations. Children benefit from participation in structured extracurricular activities, but unstructured settings (as in youth recreation centers) can exacerbate risks. In the years ahead, it will be useful to explore more interventions that involve families in the context of their communities, with emphasis, on developing strong networks among parents, school personnel, and neighborhood groups and agencies.

People's personal characteristics obviously affect resilience, but many personal attributes are themselves shaped by aspects of the external environment, especially among children. This is powerfully demonstrated in evidence on changes in cognitive ability as a function of the quality of the early environment in orphanages versus adoptive families. Other protective traits, such as good self-regulation, high self-efficacy, and internal locus of control, are also highly affected by the quality of proximal interpersonal relationships.

Studies with adults have suggested the importance of several personal attributes relatively rarely examined thus far in the context of childhood resilience, including practical and emotional intelligence and the capacities for insight, empathy, and altruism. The ramifications of developmental maturity are complex: Whereas developmentally mature defense mechanisms are often beneficial, there can be times when repressive coping can be helpful (e.g., among bereaved adults). Similarly, high ego developmental level is generally an asset but can be linked with heightened tendencies to self-recrimination and rumination. In future research, there is value in studies not only on the changing developmental significance of these various psychological attributes, but also on the functional capacities that might lie at their roots.

As with family factors, of critical importance in the realm of personal characteristics are more studies on biological attributes, with attention to dimensions outlined in the first section of this paper: hemispheric EEG activity, the startle reflex, stress hormones, and neurotransmitters such as serotonin. Just as the environment sets confidence limits within which biology determines functioning, biology sets limits within which the environment determines adaptation levels. If there is a chemical imbalance in the brain that predisposes a person to depression, then the threshold of tolerance to environmental stressors becomes considerably lower, so that even stressors of moderate severity could precipitate a debilitating depression. In many instances, discovery of the biology involved in psychiatric disorders can pave the way for appropriate pharmacological interventions.

Research Designs: Optimizing Selection of Risk Modifiers for Study

Aside from these suggestions about specific research questions and topics, there are some broader guidelines that are critical from an applied research perspective, and these have to do with prioritizing domains targeted for inquiry. The evidence presented in this chapter reflects enormous progress in the field but at the same time has the potential to be somewhat overwhelming. Knowing that resilience is affected by multiple processes at the social, psychological, and biological levels, often interlinked bidirectionally, how does the resilience researcher best design future research? How should one prioritize in terms of the types of constructs and questions most usefully examined in the years ahead?

A major consideration in designing research that will truly move this field forward will be to ensure *concerted attention to context* in selecting risk modifiers for empirical study. We know that there are certainly some processes that are beneficial across contexts and others that are harmful. Beyond such universals (such as closeness and discipline in families), there are risk modifiers that can be highly influential in some risk settings but not others, and we need more within-group studies that consider these processes simultaneously, disentangling their relative significance in particular contexts. Exemplifying this are the following two illustrative questions. Beyond warmth and discipline, among children of depressed parents, what is the relative significance of the following as protective family attributes: support from the nondepressed parent, open discussions on the causes of depression, maintenance of regular family schedules, and low genetic loading for affective disorders in the other parent? Among children in highly affluent, achievement-oriented communities (and again, beyond warmth and discipline), what is the relative influence of the amount of down time spent as a family, a

large number of weekly extracurricular activities for children, and parents' high standards for performance and their tendency to be overtly critical of children's failures?

A useful rule of thumb, particularly for scientists with a largely applied focus, will be to focus most intensively on risk modifiers with high *promotive potential,* as defined by five major characteristics: forces that are:

1. Conceptually highly *salient* in the context of that particular high-risk setting;
2. Relatively *malleable,* or responsive to environmental interventions;
3. *proximal* to the individual rather than distal;
4. *enduring* for long periods in the individual's life; and
5. *generative* of other assets, catalyzing or setting into motion other strengths and mitigating vulnerabilities.

Early family relationships meet all of these five criteria, being salient across risk settings, modifiable via interventions, directly affecting the child, exerting this effect for several years, and catalyzing other assets such as high self-esteem and positive views of relationships. Another example is the receipt of high-quality early childhood education. This is particularly important in low-income communities, can be provided by external interventions, directly affects the child and over several years, and, again, produces functional capacities that, in turn, promote the acquisition of diverse cognitive as well as psychological and social skills.

Of parallel importance would be reduction of influences with high *vulnerability potential,* those that are contextually salient, modifiable via interventions, proximal, relatively enduring in the absence of interventions, and generative of other vulnerabilities. An example is youth's involvement in deviant peer networks. Biological vulnerabilities also could fall in this category, as deficits in serotonin can be salient among individuals in families with high genetic loading for depression; these deficits can be modified pharmacologically; they directly affect the individual's everyday functioning; they tend to be stable in the absence of interventions; and in inducing depressive affect, they lead to other problems that further compromise adjustment, such as loss of relationships or jobs.

In conclusion, the field of resilience has grown enormously, and in exciting ways, in the half-century or so since its inception. At this stage, scientists must broaden the lens through which the phenomenon is viewed, drawing on not only quantitative developmental psychology research but also biological, genetic, anthropological, sociological, and clinical evidence. It would also be beneficial to move beyond conceptualizing the search for processes simply in terms of the triad of family, community, and individual factors. To best inform future interventions, researchers must consider the resilience-enhancing quotients of the specific risk modifiers chosen for study—in terms of their contextual salience, malleability, proximity, stability, and generativity of other processes—as well as the degree to which the constructs and questions might illuminate our understanding of psychological, biological, and social processes implicated in resilience. Concerted efforts in these new directions are critical if we are, in fact, to borrow from Curtis and Cicchetti (2003, p. 773), to "move research on resilience into the twenty-first century."

REFERENCES

Ackerman, B. P., Brown, E., & Izard, C. E. (2003). Continuity and change in levels of externalizing behavior in school of children from economically disadvantaged families. *Child Development, 74*, 694–709.

Adelman, H. S., & Taylor, L. (1999). Mental health in schools and system restructuring. *Clinical Psychology Review, 19*, 137–163.

Adelman, H. S., & Taylor, L. (2003). Rethinking school psychology: Commentary on public health framework series. *Journal of School Psychology, 41*, 83–90.

Affleck, G., Tennen, H., & Rowe, J. (1991). *Infants in crises: How parents cope with newborn intensive care and its aftermath.* New York: Springer-Verlag.

Aguilar, B., Sroufe, L. A., Egeland, B., & Carlson, E. (2000). Distinguishing the early-onset/persistent and adolescent-onset antisocial behavior types: From birth to 16 years. *Development and Psychopathology, 12*, 109–132.

Allen, J. P., & Hauser, S. T. (1996). Autonomy and relatedness in adolescent-family interactions as predictors of young adults' states of mind regarding attachment. *Development and Psychopathology, 3*, 793–809.

Allen, J. P., Hauser, S. T., Bell, K. L., & O'Connor, T. G. (1994). Longitudinal assessment of autonomy and relatedness in adolescent-family interactions as predictors of adolescent ego development and self-esteem. *Child Development, 65*, 179–194.

Allen, J. P., Hauser, S. T., & Borman-Spurrell, E. (1996). Attachment theory as a framework for understanding sequelae of severe adolescent psychopathology: An 11-year follow-up study. *Journal of Consulting and Clinical Psychology, 64*, 254–263.

Anderson, W. P., Reid, C. M., & Jennings, G. L. (1992). Pet ownership and risk factors for cardiovascular disease. *Medical Journal of Australia, 157*, 298–301.

Anthony, E. J. (1974). The syndrome of the psychologically invulnerable child. In E. J. Anthony & C. Koupernik (Eds.), *The child in his family: Children at psychiatric risk* (Vol. 3, pp. 3–10). New York: Wiley.

Anthony, E. J., & Koupernik, C. (Eds.). (1974). *The child in his family: Children at psychiatric risk* (Vol. 3). New York: Wiley.

Apfel, N., & Seitz, V. (1997). The firstborn sons of African-American teenage mothers: Perspectives on risk and resilience. In S. S. Luthar, J. A. Burack, D. Cicchetti, & J. R. Weisz (Eds.), *Developmental psychopathology: Perspectives on adjustment, risk, and disorder* (pp. 486–506). New York: Cambridge University Press.

Arellano, A., & Padilla, A. (1996). Academic invulnerability among a selected group of Latino university students. *Hispanic Journal of Behavioral Sciences, 18*, 485–507.

Arroyo, C. G., & Zigler, E. (1995). Racial identity, academic achievement, and the psychological well-being of economically disadvantaged adolescents. *Journal of Personality and Social Psychology, 69*, 903–914.

Aspinwall, L. G., & Taylor, S. E. (1997). A stitch in time: Self-regulation and proactive coping. *Psychological Bulletin, 121*, 417–436.

Atkins, M. S., Graczyk, P. A., Frazier, S. L., & Abdul-Adil, J. (2003). Toward a new model for promoting urban children's mental health: Accessible, effective, and sustainable school-based mental health services. *School Psychology Review, 32*, 503–514.

Bandura, A. (1977). *Social learning theory.* Englewood Cliffs, NJ: Prentice-Hall.

Bandura, A. (1997). *Self-efficacy: The exercise of control.* New York: Freeman.

Bandura, A., Caprara, G. V., Barbaranelli, C., Gerbino, M., & Pastorelli, C. (2003). Role of affective self-regulatory efficacy in diverse spheres of psychosocial functioning. *Child Development, 74*, 3.

Barker, S. B., Rogers, C. S., Turner, J. W., Karpf, A. S., & Suthers-Mc-cabe, H. M. (2003). Benefits of interacting with companion animals: A bibliography of articles published in referred journals during the past 5 years. *American Behavioral Scientist, 47*, 94–99.

Barrera, M. J. R., & Prelow, H. M. (2000). Interventions to promote social support in children and adolescents. In D. Cicchetti, J. Rappaport, I. Sandler, & R. Weissberg (Eds.), *The promotion of wellness in children and adolescents* (pp. 309–339). Washington, DC: Child Welfare League of America Press.

Barrera, M. J. R., Prelow, H. M., Dumka, L. E., Gonzales, N. A., Knight, G. P., Michaels, M. L., et al. (2002). Pathways from family economic conditions to adolescents' distress: Supportive parenting, stressors outside the family and deviant peers. *Journal of Community Psychology, 30*, 135–152.

Baumrind, D. (1989). Rearing competent children. In W. Damon (Ed.), *Child development today and tomorrow* (pp. 349–378). San Francisco: Jossey-Bass.

Beardslee, W. R. (2002). *Out of the darkened room. When a parent is depressed: Protecting the children and strengthening the family.* New York: Little, Brown.

Beaton, S. R. (1991). Styles of reminiscence and ego development of older women residing in long-term care settings. *International Journal of Aging and Human Development, 32*, 53–63.

Beck, A. M., & Glickman, L. T. (1987, September). *Future research on therapy: A plea for comprehension before intervention.* Paper presented at Assessment Workshop: Health Benefits of Pets, Washington, DC.

Beck, A. M., & Katcher, A. H. (2003). Future directions in human-animal bond research. *American Behavioral Scientist, 47*, 79–93.

Belsky, J. (1980). Child maltreatment: An ecological integration. *American Psychologist, 35*, 320–335.

Belsky, J., Jaffee, S., Hsieh, K., & Silva, P. A. (2001). Childrearing antecedents of intergenerational relations in young adulthood: A prospective study. *Developmental Psychology, 37*, 801–814.

Benard, B. (2004). *Resiliency: What we have learned.* San Francisco: WestEd.

Berlin, R., & Davis, R. B. (1989). Children from alcoholic families: Vulnerability and resilience. In T. F. Dugan & R. Coles (Eds.), *The child in our times* (pp. 81–105). New York: Brunner/Mazel.

Berman, S. L., Kurtines, W. M., Silverman, W. K., & Serafini, L. T. (1996). The impact of exposure to crime and violence on urban youth. *American Journal of Orthopsychiatry, 66*, 329–336.

Biglan, A., & Taylor, T. K. (2000). Increasing the use of science to improve child-rearing. *Journal of Primary Prevention, 21,* 207–226.

Bigler, R. S., Averhart, C. J., & Liben, L. S. (2003). Race and the workforce: Occupational status, aspirations, and stereotyping among African American children. *Developmental Psychology, 39,* 572–580.

Bishop, S. J., & Leadbeater, B. J. (1999). Maternal social support patterns and child maltreatment: Comparison of maltreating and nonmaltreating mothers. *American Journal of Orthopsychiatry, 69,* 172–181.

Black, M. M., Dubowitz, H., & Starr, R. H., Jr. (1999). African American fathers in low income, urban families: Development, behavior, and home environment of their three-year-old children. *Child Development, 70,* 967–978.

Block, J. (1969). Parents of schizophrenic, neurotic, asthmatic, and congenitally ill children. *Archives of General Psychiatry, 20,* 659–674.

Bloomberg, M. R., Daley, R. M., Hahn, J. K., & King, S. L. (2004, February 25). Lawyers, guns and mayors: Doesn't Congress want to help make our cities safer? *New York Times,* p. A25.

Bolger, K. E., & Patterson, C. J. (2003). Sequelae of child maltreatment: Vulnerability and resilience. In S. S. Luthar (Ed.), *Resilience and vulnerability: Adaptation in the context of childhood adversities* (pp. 156–181). New York: Cambridge University Press.

Bonanno, G. A. (2004). Loss, trauma, and human resilience: Have we underestimated the human capacity to thrive after extremely aversive events? *American Psychologist, 59,* 20–28.

Bonanno, G. A., Noll, J. G., Putnam, F. W., O'Neill, M., & Trickett, P. (2003). Predicting the willingness to disclose childhood sexual abuse from measures of repressive coping and dissociative experiences. *Child Maltreatment, 8,* 1–17.

Bornstein, M. H., Davidson, L., Keyes, C. L. M., & Moore, K. A. (Eds.). (2003). *Well-being: Positive development across the life course.* Mahwah, NJ: Erlbaum.

Bowlby, J. (1988). *A secure base: Parent-child attachment and healthy human development.* New York: Basic Books.

Braga, A. A., Kennedy, D. M., Waring, E. J., & Piehl, A. M. (2001). Problem-oriented policing, deterrence, and youth violence: An evaluation of Boston's Operation Ceasefire. *Journal of Research in Crime and Delinquency, 38,* 195–225.

Brody, G. H. (2004). Siblings' direct and indirect contributions to child development. *Current Directions in Psychological Science, 13,* 124–126.

Brody, G. H., Dorsey, S., Forehand, R., & Armistead, L. (2002). Unique and protective contributions of parenting and classroom processes to the adjustment of African American children living in single-parent families. *Child Development, 73,* 274–286.

Brody, G. H., Flor, D. L., & Gibson, N. M. (1999). Linking maternal efficacy beliefs, developmental goals, parenting practices, and child competence in rural single-parent African American families. *Child Development, 70,* 1197–1208.

Brody, G. H., Stoneman, Z., & Flor, D. (1996). Parental religiosity, family processes, and youth competence in rural, two-parent African American families. *Developmental Psychology, 32,* 696–706.

Bronfenbrenner, U. (1986). Ecology of the family as a context for human development: Research perspectives. *Developmental Psychology, 22,* 723–742.

Brooks-Gunn, J., Berlin, L. J., & Fuligni, A. S. (2000). Early childhood intervention programs: What about the family? In J. P. Shonkoff & S. J Meisels (Eds.), *Handbook of early childhood intervention* (2nd ed., pp. 549–588). New York: Cambridge University Press.

Brown, T. N., Williams, D. R., Jackson, J. S., Neighbors, H. W., Torres, M., Sellers, S. L., et al. (2000). Being Black and feeling blue: The mental health consequences of racial discrimination. *Race and Society, 2,* 117–131.

Bryk, A. S., & Raudenbush, S. W. (1987). Applications of hierarchical linear models to assessing change. *Psychological Bulletin, 101,* 147–158.

Bryk, A. S., & Raudenbush, S. W. (1992). *Hierarchical linear models: Applications and data analysis methods.* Thousand Oaks, CA: Sage.

Buckner, J. C., Mezzacappa, E., & Beardslee, W. R. (2003). Characteristics of resilient youths living in poverty: The role of self-regulatory processes. *Development and Psychopathology, 15,* 139–162.

Bullock, B. M., & Dishion, T. J. (2002). Sibling collusion and problem behavior in early adolescence: Toward a process model for family mutuality. *Journal of Abnormal Child Psychology, 30,* 143–153.

Burchinal, M. R., Follmer, A., & Bryant, D. M. (1996). The relations of maternal social support and family structure with maternal responsiveness and child outcomes among African-American families. *Developmental Psychology, 32,* 1073–1083.

Burton, L. M., Allison, K. W., & Obeidallah, D. (1995). Social context and adolescence: Perspectives on development among inner-city African-American teens. In L. J. Crockett & A. C. Crouter (Eds.), *Pathways through adolescence: Individual development in relation to social contexts* (pp. 119–138). New York: Erlbaum.

Calkins, S. D., & Fox, N. A. (2002). Self-regulatory processes in early personality development: A multilevel approach to the study of childhood social withdrawal and aggression. *Development and Psychopathology, 14,* 477–498.

Capella, E., & Weinstein, T. S. (2001). Turning around reading achievement: Predictors of high schools' academic resilience. *Journal of Educational Psychology, 93,* 758–771.

Carlson, E. A., Sroufe, L. A., & Egeland, B. (2004). The construction of experience: A longitudinal study of representation and behavior. *Child Development, 75,* 66–83.

Caspi, A., McClay, J., Moffitt, T., Mill, J., Martin, J., Craig, I. W., et al. (2002). Role of genotype in the cycle of violence in maltreated children. *Science, 297,* 851–854.

Caspi, A., Sugden, K., Moffitt, T. E., Taylor, A., Craig, I. W., Harrington, H., et al. (2003). Influence of life stress on depression: Moderation by a polymorphism in the 5-HTT gene. *Science, 301,* 386–389.

Catalano, R. F., Hawkins, J. D., Berglund, L., Pollard, J. A., & Arthur, M. W. (2002). Prevention science and positive youth development: Competitive or cooperative frameworks? *Journal of Adolescent Health, 31*(Suppl. 6), 230–239.

Cauce, A. M., Stewart, A., Rodriguez, M. D., Cochran, B., & Ginzler, J. (2003). Overcoming the odds? Adolescent development in the context of urban poverty. In S. S. Luthar (Ed.), *Resilience and vulnerability: Adaptation in the context of childhood adversities* (pp. 343–363). New York: Cambridge University Press.

Cavell, Timothy A. (2000). *Working with parents of aggressive children: A practitioner's guide.* Washington, DC: American Psychological Association.

Chang, E. C. (2001). Cultural influences on optimism and pessimism: Differences in Western and Eastern conceptualizations of the self. In E. C. Chang (Ed.), *Optimism and pessimism: Theory, research, and practice* (pp. 257–280). Washington, DC: American Psychological Association.

Chang, L. (2003). Variable effects of children's aggression, social withdrawal, and prosocial leadership as functions of teacher beliefs and behaviors. *Child Development, 74,* 535–548.

Chase-Lansdale, P. L., & Gordon, R. A. (1996). Economic hardship and the development of five- and six-year olds: Neighborhood and regional perspectives. *Child Development, 67,* 3338–3367.

Chilcoat, H. D., & Anthony, J. C. (1996). Impact of parent monitoring on initiation of drug use through late childhood. *Journal of the American Academy of Child and Adolescent Psychiatry, 35,* 91–100.

Cicchetti, D. (2002). The impact of social experience on neurobiological systems: Illustration from a constructivist view of child maltreatment. *Cognitive Development, 17,* 1407–1428.

Cicchetti, D. (2003). Foreword. In S. S. Luthar (Ed.), *Resilience and vulnerability: Adaptation in the context of childhood adversities* (pp. xix–xxvii). New York: Cambridge University Press.

Cicchetti, D., & Cohen, D. J. (1995). Perspectives on developmental psychopathology. In D. Cicchetti & D. J. Cohen (Eds.),*Developmental psychopathology: Theory and methods* (pp. 3–20). New York: Wiley.

Cicchetti, D., & Garmezy, N. (Eds.). (1993). Milestones in the development of resilience [Special issue]. *Development and Psychopathology, 5*(4), 497–774.

Cicchetti, D., & Hinshaw, S. P. (2002). Development and Psychopathology: Editorial: Prevention and intervention science: Contributions to developmental theory. *Development and Psychopathology, 14,* 667–671.

Cicchetti, D., Rappaport, J., Sandler, I., & Weissberg, R. (Eds.). (2000). *The promotion of wellness in children and adolescents.* Washington, DC: Child Welfare League of America.

Cicchetti, D., & Rogosch, F. A. (1997). The role of self-organization in the promotion of resilience in maltreated children. *Development and Psychopathology, 9,* 799–817.

Cicchetti, D., Toth, S. L., & Rogosch, F. A. (1999). The efficacy of toddler-parent psychotherapy to increase attachment security in offspring of depressed mothers. *Attachment and Human Development, 1,* 34–66.

Cicchetti, D., & Wagner, S. (1990). Alternative assessment strategies for the evaluation of infants and toddlers: An organizational perspective. In S. J. Meisels & J. P. Shonkoff (Eds.), *Handbook of early childhood intervention* (pp. 247–277). New York: Cambridge University Press.

Cicchetti, D., & Walker, E. (Eds.). (2003). *Neurodevelopmental mechanisms in psychopathology.* New York: Cambridge University Press.

Cohler, B. J., Stott, F. M., & Musick, J. S. (1995). Adversity, vulnerability, and resilience: Cultural and developmental perspectives. In D. Cicchetti & D. J. Cohen (Eds.), *Developmental psychopathology: Vol. 2. Risk, disorder, and adaptation* (pp. 753–800). New York: Wiley.

Coley, R. L. (2001). (In)visible men: Emerging research on low-income, unmarried, and minority fathers. *American Psychologist, 56,* 743–753.

Collinshaw, S., Maughan, B., Pickles, A., Messer, J., & Rutter, M. (2004, August). *Resilience to psychopathology following childhood maltreatment: Evidence from a community sample.* Paper presented at the 16th World Congress of the International Association for Child and Adolescent Psychiatry and Allied Professions, Berlin.

Compton, K., Snyder, J., Schrepferman, L., Bank, L., & Shortt, J. W. (2003). The contribution of parents and siblings to antisocial and depressive behavior in adolescents: A double jeopardy coercion model. *Development and Psychopathology, 15,* 163–182.

Conduct Problems Prevention Research Group. (2004). The FAST Track experiment: Translating the developmental model into a prevention design. In J. B. Kupersmidt & K. A. Dodge (Eds.), *Children's peer relations: From development to intervention* (pp. 181–208). Washington, DC: American Psychological Association.

Conger, R. D., & Conger, K. J. (2002). Resilience in Midwestern families: Selected findings from the first decade of a prospective, longitudinal study. *Journal of Marriage and the Family, 64,* 361–373.

Conger, R. D., Cui, M., Bryant, M., & Elder, G. H. (2000). Competence in early adult romantic relationships: A developmental perspective on family influences. *Journal of Personality and Social Psychology, 79,* 224–237.

Conger, R. D., Rueter, M. A., & Elder, G. H. (1999). Couple resilience to economic pressure. *Journal of Personality and Social Psychology, 76,* 54–71.

Cooley-Quille, M., Boyd, R. C., Frantz, E., & Walsh, J. (2001). Emotional and behavioral impact of exposure to community violence in inner-city adolescents. *Journal of Clinical Child Psychology, 30,* 199–206.

Cowen, E. L. (1991). In pursuit of wellness. *American Psychologist, 46,* 404–408.

Cowen, E. L. (1994). The enhancement of psychological wellness: Challenges and opportunities. *American Journal of Community Psychology, 22,* 149–179.

Cowen, E. L., & Durlak, J. A. (2000). Social policy and prevention in mental health. *Development and Psychopathology, 12,* 815–834.

Cowen, E. L., Hightower, A. D., Pedro-Carroll, J. L., Work, W. C., Wyman, P. A., & Haffey, W. G. (1996). *School based prevention for children at risk: The Primary Mental Health Project.* Washington, DC: American Psychological Association.

Criss, M. M., Pettit, G. S., Bates, J. E., Dodge, K. A., & Lapp, A. L. (2002). Family adversity, positive peer relationships, and children's externalizing behavior: A longitudinal perspective on risk and resilience. *Child Development, 73,* 1220–1237.

Curtis, W. J., & Cicchetti, D. (2003). Moving research on resilience into the 21st century: Theoretical and methodological considerations in examining the biological contributors to resilience. *Development and Psychopathology, 15,* 773–810.

Curtis, W. J., & Nelson, C. A. (2003). Toward building a better brain: Neurobehavioral outcomes, mechanisms, and processes of environmental enrichment. In S. S. Luthar (Ed.), *Resilience and vulnerability: Adaptation in the context of childhood adversities* (pp. 463–488). New York: Cambridge University Press.

Davidson, R. J. (2000). Affective style, psychopathology, and resilience: Brain mechanisms and plasticity. *American Psychologist, 55,* 1196–1214.

Davis, C. G., Nolen-Hoeksema, S., & Larson, J. (1998). Making sense of loss and benefiting from the experience: Two construals of meaning. *Journal of Personality and Social Psychology, 75,* 561–574.

Dawson, G., Ashman, S. B., Panagiotides, H., Hessl, D., Self, J., Yamada, E., et al. (2003). Preschool outcomes of children of depressed mothers: Role of maternal behavior, contextual risk, and children's brain activity. *Child Development, 74,* 1158–1175.

DeBellis, M. D. (2001). Developmental traumatology: The psychobiological development of maltreated children and its implications for research, treatment, and policy. *Development and Psychopathology, 13,* 539–564.

DeBellis, M. D., Keshavan, M. S., Casey, B. J., Clark, D. B., Giedd, J., Boring, A. M., et al. (1999). Developmental traumatology: Biological stress systems and brain development in maltreated children with PTSD: Pt. II. *Biological Psychiatry, 45,* 1271–1284.

Denny, S., Clark, T. C., Fleming, T., & Wall, M. (2004). Emotional resilience: Risk and protective factors for depression among alternative education students in New Zealand. *American Journal of Orthopsychiatry, 74,* 137–149.

D'Imperio, R. L., Dubow, E. F., & Ippolito, M. F. (2000). Resilient and stress-affected adolescents in an urban setting. *Journal of Clinical Child Psychology, 29,* 129–142.

Dishion, T. J., & Kavanagh, K. (2003). *Intervening in adolescent problem behavior: A family-centered approach.* New York: Guilford Press.

Dishion, T. J., McCord, J., & Poulin, F. (1999). When interventions harm: Peer groups and problem behavior. *American Psychologist, 54,* 755–764.

Dishion, T. J., & McMahon, R. J. (1998). Parental monitoring and the prevention of child and adolescent problem behavior: A conceptual and empirical formulation. *Clinical Child and Family Psychology Review, 1,* 61–75.

Doll, B., & Lyon, M. A. (1998). Risk and resilience: Implications for the delivery of educational and mental health services in schools. *School Psychology Review, 27,* 348–363.

Dozier, M., Albus, K., Fisher, P., & Sepulveda, S. (2002). Interventions for foster parents: Implications for developmental theory. *Development and Psychopathology, 14,* 843–860.

Dozier, M., Lindhiem, O., & Ackerman, J. (in press). Attachment and biobehavioral catch-up: An intervention targeting specific needs of young foster children. In L. Berlin, M. Greenberg, & Y. Zaiv (Eds.), *Enhancing early attachments: Theory, research, intervention, and policy.* New York: Guilford Press.

Dozier, M., Stovall, K. C., Albus, K. E., & Bates, B. (2001). Attachment for infants in foster care: The role of caregiver state of mind. *Child Development, 72,* 1467–1477.

Duncan, G. J., Brooks-Gunn, J., & Klebanov, P. K. (1994). Economic deprivation and early childhood development. *Child Development, 65,* 296–318.

Eccles, J., Midgley, C., Wigfield, A., Buchanan, C. M., Reuman, D., Flanagan, C., et al. (1993). Development during adolescence: The impact of stage-environment fit on young adolescents' experiences in schools and in families. *American Psychologist, 48,* 90–101.

Eckenrode, J., Ganzel, B., Henderson, C. R., Jr., Smith, E., Olds, D. L., Powers, J., et al. (2000). Preventing child abuse and neglect with a program of nurse home visitation: The limiting effects of domestic violence. *Journal of the American Medical Association, 284,* 1385–1391.

Eckenrode, J., Zielinski, D., Smith, E., Marcynyszyn, L. A., Henderson, C. R., Jr., Kitzman, H., et al. (2001). Child maltreatment and the early onset of problem behaviors: Can a program of nurse home visitation break the link? *Development and Psychopathology, 13,* 873–890.

Egeland, B., & Sroufe, L. A. (1981). Attachment and early maltreatment. *Child Development, 52,* 44–52.

Eisenberg, N., Champion, C., & Ma, Y. (2004). Emotion-related regulation: An emerging construct. *Merrill-Palmer Quarterly, 50,* 236–259.

Eisenberg, N., Spinrad, T. L., Fabes, R. A., Reiser, M., Cumberland, A., Shepard, S. A., et al. (2004). The relations of effortful control and impulsivity to children's resiliency and adjustment. *Child Development, 75,* 25–46.

Elder, G. H. (1986). Military times and turning points in men's lives. *Developmental Psychology, 22,* 233–245.

Elder, G. H., & Conger, R. D. (2000). *Children of the land: Adversity and success in rural America.* Chicago: University of Chicago Press.

Elias, M. J. (1995). Primary prevention as health and social competence promotion. *Journal of Primary Prevention, 16,* 5–24.

Elias, M. J., Arnold, H., & Hussey, C. S. (Eds.). (2003). *EQ + IQ = best leadership practices for caring and successful schools.* Thousand Oaks, CA: Corwin Press.

Erikson, E. H. (1993). *Childhood and society.* New York: Norton.

Evans, G. W. (2003). A multimethodological analysis of cumulative risk and allostatic load among rural children. *Developmental Psychology, 39,* 924–933.

Fabes, R. A., Eisenberg, N., Jones, S., Smith, M., Guthrie, I., Poulin, R., et al. (1999). Regulation, emotionality, and preschoolers' socially competent peer interactions. *Child Development, 70,* 432–442.

Falicov, C. J. (1996). Mexican families. In M. McGoldrick, J. Giordano, & J. K. Pearce (Eds.), *Ethnicity and family therapy* (2nd ed., pp. 169–182). New York: Guilford Press.

Fantuzzo, J., Sutton-Smith, B., Atkins, M., Meyers, R., Stevenson, H., Coolahan, K., et al. (1996). Community-based resilient peer treatment of withdrawn maltreated preschool children. *Journal of Consulting and Clinical Psychology, 64,* 1377–1386.

Farber, E. A., & Egeland, B. (1987). Invulnerability in abused and neglected children. In E. J. Anthony & B. J. Cohler (Eds.), *The invulnerable child* (pp. 253–288). New York: Guilford Press.

Feldman, B. J., Conger, R. D., & Burzette, R. G. (2004). Traumatic events, psychiatric disorders, and pathways of risk and resilience during the transition to adulthood. *Research in Human Development, 1,* 259–290.

Feldman, R., Greenbaum, C. W., & Yirmiya, N. (1999). Mother-infant affect synchrony as an antecedent of the emergence of self-control. *Developmental Psychology, 35,* 223–231.

Feldman, R., & Klein, P. S. (2003). Toddlers' self-regulated compliance to mothers, caregivers, and fathers: Implications for theories of socialization. *Developmental Psychology, 39,* 680–692.

Felner, R. D., Favazza, A., Shim, M., Brand, S., Gu, K., & Noonan, N. (2001). Whole school improvement and restructuring as prevention and promotion: Lessons from STEP and the project on high performance learning communities. *Journal of School Psychology, 39,* 177–202.

Fergusson, D. M., & Horwood, L. J. (2003). Resilience to childhood adversity: Results of a 21 year study. In S. S. Luthar (Ed.), *Resilience and vulnerability: Adaptation in the context of childhood adversities* (pp. 130–155). New York: Cambridge University Press.

Fiedler, F. E. (1995). Cognitive resources and leadership performance. *Applied Psychology: An International Review, 44,* 5–28.

Fine, S. E., Izard, C. E., Mostow, A. J., Trentacosta, C. J., & Ackerman, B. P. (2003). First grade emotion knowledge as a predictor of fifth grade self-reported internalizing behaviors in children from economically disadvantaged families. *Development and Psychopathology, 15,* 331–342.

Fineman, N. R., Beckwith, L., Howard, J., & Espinosa, M. (1997). Maternal ego development and mother-infant interaction in drug-abusing women. *Journal of Substance Abuse Treatment, 14,* 307–317.

Finn-Stevenson, M., & Zigler, E. (1999). *School of 21st century: Linking child care and education.* Boulder, CO: Westview Press.

Fisher, C. B., Wallace, S. A., & Fenton, R. E. (2000). Discrimination distress during adolescence. *Journal of Youth and Adolescence, 29,* 679–695.

Fordham, S., & Ogbu, J. U. (1986). Black students' school success: "Coping with the burden of 'acting White.' " *Urban Review, 18,* 176–206.

Forman, S. G., & Kalafat, J. (1998). Substance abuse and suicide: Promoting resilience against self-destructive behavior in youth. *School Psychology Review, 27,* 398–406.

Franklin, A. J. (1999). Invisibility syndrome and racial identity development in psychotherapy and counseling African American men. *Counseling Psychologist, 27,* 761–793.

Freitas, A. L., & Downey, G. (1998). Resilience: A dynamic perspective. *International Journal of Behavioral Development, 22,* 263–285.

Freud, S., & Gay, P. (1995). *The Freud reader.* New York: Norton.

Friedmann, E., Katcher, A. H., Lynch, J. J., & Thomas, S. A. (1980). Animal companions and one year survival of patients after discharge from a coronary care unit. *Public Health Reports, 95,* 307–312.

Friedmann, E., & Thomas, S. A. (1995). Pet ownership, social support, and one-year survival after acute myocardial infarction in the Cardiac Arrhythmia Suppression Trial (CAST). *American Journal of Cardiology, 76,* 1213–1217.

Fuligni, A. J., Tseng, V., & Lam, M. (1999). Attitudes toward family obligations among American adolescents with Asian, Latin American, and European backgrounds. *Child Development, 70,* 1030–1044.

Furstenberg, F. F., Cook, T. D., Eccles, J., Elder, G. H., & Sameroff, A. (1999). *Managing to make it: Urban families and adolescent success.* Chicago: University of Chicago Press.

Galambos, N. L., Barker, E. T., & Almeida, D. M. (2003). Parents do matter: Trajectories of change in externalizing and internalizing problems in early adolescence. *Child Development, 74,* 578–594.

Garbarino, J. (1995). The American war zone: What children can tell us about living with violence. *Developmental and Behavioral Pediatrics, 16*(6), 431–434.

Garbarino, J., Hammond, W. R., Mercy, J., & Yung, B. R. (2004). Community violence and children: Preventing exposure and reducing harm. In K. Maton, C. J. Schellenbach, B. J. Leadbeater, & A. L. Solarz (Eds.), *Investing in children, youth, families, and communities: Strengths-based research and policy* (pp. 303–320). Washington, DC: American Psychological Association.

García Coll, C. (2005). Editorial. *Developmental Psychology, 41*, 299–300.

García Coll, C., Akerman, A., & Cicchetti, D. (2000). Cultural influences on developmental processes and outcomes: Implications for the study of development and psychopathology. *Development and Psychopathology, 12*, 333–356.

García Coll, C., Lamberty, G., Jenkins, R., McAdoo, H. P., Crnic, K., Wasik, B. H., et al. (1996). An integrative model for the study of developmental competencies in minority children. *Child Development, 67*, 1891–1914.

García Coll, C., Meyer, E. C., & Brillon, L. (1995). Ethnic and minority parenting. In M. H. Bornstein (Ed.), *Handbook of parenting* (Vol. 2, pp. 189–210). Mahwah, NJ: Erlbaum.

García Coll, C., Surrey, J. L., & Weingarten, K. (Eds.). (1998). *Mothering against the odds: Diverse voices of contemporary mothers.* New York: Guilford Press.

Garcia Coll, C., & Vasquez García, H. A. (1995). Hispanic children and their families: On a different track from the very beginning. In H. E. Fitzgerald, B. M. Lester, & B. Zuckerman (Eds.), *Children of poverty: Research, health, and policy issues* (pp. 57–83). New York: Garland.

Garmezy, N. (1974). The study of competence in children at risk for severe psychopathology. In E. J. Anthony & C. Koupernik (Eds.), *The child in his family: Children at psychiatric risk: III* (p. 547). New York: Wiley.

Garmezy, N. (1987). Stress, competence, and development: Continuities in the study of schizophrenic adults, children vulnerable to psychopathology, and the search for stress-resistant children. *American Journal of Orthopsychiatry, 57*, 159–174.

Garmezy, N. (1993). Children in poverty: Resilience despite risk. *Psychiatry: Interpersonal and Biological Processes, 56*, 127–136.

Garmezy, N., & Masten, A. S. (1986). Stress, competence, and resilience: Common frontiers for therapist and psychopathologist. *Behavior Therapy, 17*, 500–521.

Garmezy, N., Masten, A. S., & Tellegen, A. (1984). The study of stress and competence in children: A building block for developmental psychopathology. *Child Development, 55*, 97–111.

Gerard, J. M., & Buehler, C. (2004). Cumulative environmental risk and youth maladjustment: The role of youth attributes. *Child Development, 75*, 1832–1849.

Gilliom, M., Shaw, D. S., Beck, J. E., Schonberg, M. A., & Lukon, J. L. (2002). Anger regulation in disadvantaged preschool boys: Strategies, antecedents, and the development of self-control. *Developmental Psychology, 38*, 222–235.

Glantz, M., & Johnson, J. (Eds.). (1999). *Resilience and development: Positive life adaptations.* New York: Plenum Press.

Glueck, S., & Glueck, E. (1950). *Unraveling juvenile delinquency.* New York: Commonwealth Fund.

Gold, C., Voracek, M., & Wigram, T. (2004). Effects of music therapy for children and adolescents with psychopathology: A meta-analysis. *Journal of Child Psychology and Psychiatry, 45*, 1054–1063.

Gorman-Smith, D., & Tolan, P. (1998). The role of exposure to community violence and developmental problems in inner-city youth. *Development and Psychopathology, 10*, 101–116.

Gorman-Smith, D., &. Tolan, P. H. (2003). Positive adaptation among youth exposed to community violence. In S. S. Luthar (Ed.), *Resilience and vulnerability: Adaptation in the context of childhood adversities* (pp. 392–413). New York: Cambridge University Press.

Greenberg, M. T., Weissberg, R. P., O'Brien, M. U., Zins, J. E., Fredericks, L., Resnik, H., et al. (2003). Enhancing school-based prevention and youth development through coordinated social, emotional, and academic learning. *American Psychologist, 58*, 466–474.

Grossman, J. B., & Rhodes, J. E. (2002). The test of time: Predictors and effects of duration in youth mentoring relationships. *American Journal of Community Psychology, 30*, 199–219.

Gunnar, M. R. (2000). Early adversity and the development of stress reactivity and regulation. In C. A. Nelson (Ed.), *Minnesota Symposia on Child Psychology: Vol. 31. The effects of adversity on neurobehavioral development* (pp. 163–200). Mahwah, NJ: Erlbaum.

Gunnar, M. R., & Davis, E. P. (2003). Stress and emotion in early childhood. In R. M. Lerner, M. A. Easterbrooks, & J. Mistry (Eds.), *Handbook of psychology: Vol. 6. Developmental psychology* (pp. 113–134). Hoboken, NJ: Wiley.

Gunnar, M. R., Morison, S. J., Chisholm, K., & Schuder, M. (2001). Salivary cortisol levels in children adopted from Romanian orphanages. *Development and Psychopathology, 13*, 611–628.

Gutman, L. M., Sameroff, A. J., & Cole, R. (2003). Academic growth curve trajectories from 1st grade to 12th grade: Effects of multiple social risk factors and preschool child factors. *Developmental Psychology, 39*, 777–790.

Gutman, L. M., Sameroff, A. J., & Eccles, J. S. (2002). The academic achievement of African-American students during early adolescence: An examination of multiple risk, promotive, and protective factors. *American Journal of Community Psychology, 30*, 367–400.

Haapasalo, J., & Tremblay, R. E. (1994). Physically aggressive boys from ages 6 to 12: Family background, parenting behavior and prediction of delinquency. *Journal of Consulting and Clinical Psychology, 62*, 1044–1050.

Haggerty, R. J., Sherrod, L. R., Garmezy, N., & Rutter, M. (Eds.). (1996). *Stress, risk, and resilience in children and adolescents: Processes, mechanisms, and interventions.* New York: Cambridge University Press.

Hammack, P. L., Richards, M. H., Luo, Z. P., Edlynn, E. S., & Roy, K. (2004). Social support factors as moderators of community violence exposure among inner-city African American young adolescents. *Journal of Clinical Child and Adolescent Psychology, 33*, 450–462.

Hammen, C. (2003). Risk and protective factors for children of depressed parents. In S. S. Luthar (Ed.), *Resilience and vulnerability: Adaptation in the context of childhood adversities* (pp. 50–75). New York: Cambridge University Press.

Hamre, B. K., & Pianta, R. C. (2001). Early teacher-child relationships and the trajectory of children's school outcomes through eighth grade. *Child Development, 72*, 625–638.

Harter, S. (2002). Authenticity. In C. R. Snyder & S. J. Lopez (Eds.), *Handbook of positive psychology* (pp. 382–394). London: Oxford University Press.

Hashima, P. Y., & Amato, P. R. (1994). Poverty, social support, and parental behavior. *Child Development, 65*, 394–403.

Hauser, S. T. (1999). Understanding resilient outcomes: Adolescent lives across time and generations. *Journal of Research on Adolescence, 9*, 1–24.

Havighurst, R. J. (1948). *Developmental tasks and education.* Chicago: University of Chicago Press.

Hawkins, J. D., Smith, B. H., Hill, K. G., Kosterman, R., Catalano, R. F., & Abbott, R. D. (2003). Understanding and preventing crime and violence: Findings from the Seattle Social Development Project. In T. P. Thornberry & M. D. Krohn (Eds.), *Taking stock of delinquency: An overview of findings from contemporary longitudinal studies* (pp. 255–312). New York: Kluwer Academic/Plenum Press.

Heinicke, C. M., Rineman, N. R., Ponce, V. A., & Guthrie, D. (2001). Relation-based intervention with at-risk mothers: Outcome in the second year of life. *Infant Mental Health Journal, 22,* 431–462.

Henrich, C. C., Schwab-Stone, M., Fanti, K., Jones, S. M., & Ruchkin, V. (2004). The association of community violence exposure with middle-school achievement: A prospective study. *Journal of Applied Developmental Psychology, 25,* 327–348.

Hetherington, E. M. (1993). An overview of the Virginia Longitudinal Study of Divorce and Remarriage with a focus on early adolescence. *Journal of Family Psychology, 7,* 39–56.

Hetherington, E. M. (1999). *Coping with divorce, single parenting, and remarriage: A risk and resiliency perspective.* Mahwah, NJ: Erlbaum.

Hetherington, E. M., & Elmore, A. M. (2003). Risk and resilience in children coping with their parents' divorce and remarriage. In S. S. Luthar (Ed.), *Resilience and vulnerability: Adaptation in the context of childhood adversities* (pp. 182–212). New York: Cambridge University Press.

Hill, N. E., Bush, K. R., & Roosa, M. W. (2003). Parenting and family socialization strategies and children's mental health: Low-income, Mexican-American and Euro-American mothers and children. *Child Development, 74,* 189–204.

Hoagwood, K., & Johnson, J. (2003). School psychology: A public health framework I: From evidence-based practices to evidence-based policies. *Journal of School Psychology, 41,* 3–21.

Hobfoll, S. E., Ritter, C., Lavin, J., Hulsizer, M. R., & Cameron, R. P. (1995). Depression prevalence and incidence among inner-city pregnant and postpartum women. *Journal of Consulting and Clinical Psychology, 63,* 445–453.

Hodges, J., & Tizard, B. (1989). IQ and behavioural adjustment of ex-institutional adolescents. *Journal of Child Psychology and Psychiatry and Allied Disciplines, 30,* 53–75.

Howes, C., & Ritchie, S. (1999). Attachment organizations in children with difficult life circumstances. *Development and Psychopathology, 11,* 251–268.

Hughes, D. (2003). Correlates of African American and Latino parents' messages to children about ethnicity and race: A comparative study of racial socialization. *American Journal of Community Psychology, 31,* 15–33.

Hughes, J. N., Cavell, T. A., & Jackson, T. (1999). Influence of the teacher-student relationship on childhood conduct problems: A prospective study. *Journal of Clinical Child Psychology, 28,* 173–184.

Hyde, J. S., Else-Quest, N. M., Goldsmith, H. H., & Biesanz, J. C. (2004). Children's temperament and behavior problems predict their employed mothers' work functioning. *Child Development, 75,* 580–594.

Jackson, Y., & Warren, J. S. (2000). Appraisal, social support, and life events: Predicting outcome behavior in school-age children. *Child Development, 71,* 1441–1457.

Jaffee, S. R., Moffitt, T. E., Caspi, A., & Taylor, A. (2003). Life with (or without) father: The benefits of living with two biological parents depend on the father's antisocial behavior. *Child Development, 74,* 109–126.

Jarrett, R. L. (1999). Successful parenting in high-risk neighborhoods. *Future of Children, 9,* 45–50.

Jenkins, E. J., & Bell, C. C. (1994). Violence exposure, psychological distress, and high risk behaviors among inner-city high school students. In S. Friedman (Ed.), *Anxiety disorders in African-Americans* (pp. 76–88). New York: Springer.

Johnson, D. W., & Johnson, R. (2001). Peer mediation in an inner-city elementary school. *Urban Education, 36,* 165–178.

Jones, B. L., Nagin, D. S., & Roeder, K. (2001). A SAS procedure based on mixture models for estimating developmental trajectories. *Sociological Methods and Research, 29,* 374–393.

Kagan, J., Snidman, N., & Arcus, D. (1998). Childhood derivatives of high and low reactivity in infancy. *Child Development, 69,* 1483–1493.

Kasser, T. (2002). *The high price of materialism.* Cambridge, MA: MIT Press.

Kendler, K. S., Gardner, C. O., & Prescott, C. A. (1997). Religion, psychopathology, and substance use and abuse: A multimeasure, genetic-epidemiologic study. *American Journal of Psychiatry, 154,* 322–329.

Kessler, R. C., Mickelson, K. D., & Williams, D. R. (1999). The prevalence, distribution, and mental health correlates of perceived discrimination in the United States. *Journal of Health and Social Behavior, 40,* 208–230.

Keyes, C. L. M., & Lopez, S. J. (2002). Toward a science of mental health: Positive directions in diagnosis and interventions. In C. R. Snyder & S. J. Lopez (Eds.), *Handbook of positive psychology* (pp. 45–59). London: Oxford University Press.

Kim-Cohen, J., Moffitt, T. E., Caspi, A., & Taylor, A. (2004). Genetic and environmental processes in young children's resilience and vulnerability to socioeconomic deprivation. *Child Development, 75,* 651–668.

Klein, K., & Forehand, R. (2000). Family processes as resources for African American children exposed to a constellation of sociodemographic risk factors. *Journal of Clinical Child Psychology, 29,* 53–65.

Kliewer, W., Cunningham, J. N., Diehl, R., Parrish, K. A., Walker, J. M., Ativeh, C., et al. (2004). Violence exposure and adjustment in inner-city youth: Child and caregiver emotion regulation skill, caregiver-child relationship quality, and neighborhood cohesion as protective factors. *Journal of Clinical Child and Adolescent Psychology, 33,* 477–487.

Knitzer, J. (2000a). Early childhood mental health services: A policy and systems development perspective. In J. P. Shonkoff & S. J. Meisels (Eds.), *Handbook of early childhood intervention* (2nd ed., pp. 416–438). New York: Cambridge University Press.

Knitzer, J. (2000b). Promoting resilience: Helping young children and families affected by substance abuse, domestic violence, and depression in the context of welfare reform. *Children and Welfare Reform Issue Brief # 8.* New York: National Center for Children in Poverty.

Kobasa, S. C., Maddi, S. R., & Kahn, S. (1982). Hardiness and health: A prospective study. *Journal of Personality and Social Psychology, 42,* 168–177.

Kochanska, G. (1997). Mutually responsive orientation between mothers and their young children: Implications for early socialization. *Child Development, 68,* 94–112.

Kochanska, G., Coy, K. C., & Murray, K. T. (2001). The development of self-regulation in the first four years of life. *Child Development, 72,* 1091–1111.

Koenen, K. C., Moffitt, T. E., Caspi, A., Taylor, A., & Purcell, S. (2003). Domestic violence is associated with environmental suppression of IQ in young children. *Development and Psychopathology, 15,* 297–311.

Krieger, N. (1999). Embodying inequality: A review of concepts, measures, and methods for studying health consequences of discrimination. *International Journal of Health Services, 29,* 295–352.

Kumpfer, K. L., & Alvarado, R. (2003). Family-strengthening approaches for the prevention of youth problem behaviors. *American Psychologist, 58,* 457–465.

Kupersmidt, J. B., Coie, J. D., & Howell, J. C. (2004). Resilience in children exposed to negative peer influences. In K. Maton, C. J. Schellenbach, B. J. Leadbeater, & A. L. Solarz (Eds.), *Investing in children, youth, families, and communities: Strengths-based research and policy* (pp. 251–268). Washington, DC: American Psychological Association.

Kupersmidt, J. B., & Dodge, K. A. (Eds.). (2004). *Children's peer relations: From development to intervention.* Washington, DC: American Psychological Association.

Laird, R. D., Pettit, G. S., Bates, J. E., & Dodge, K. A. (2003). Parents' monitoring-relevant knowledge and adolescents' delinquent behavior: Evidence of correlated developmental changes and reciprocal influences. *Child Development, 74,* 752–768.

Landrine, H., & Klonoff, E. A. (1996). The schedule of racist events: A measure of racial discrimination and a study of its negative physical and mental health consequences. *Journal of Black Psychology, 22,* 144–168.

Lansford, J. E., Criss, M. M., Pettit, G. S., Dodge, K. A., & Bates, J. E. (2003). Friendship quality, peer group affiliation, and peer antisocial behavior as moderators of the link between negative parenting and adolescent externalizing behavior. *Journal of Research on Adolescence, 13,* 161–184.

Latendresse, S. J., & Luthar, S. S. (2005). *Perceptions of parenting among affluent youth: Antecedents of middle school adjustment trajectories.* Manuscript submitted for publication.

Laub, J. H., & Sampson, R. J. (2003). *Shared beginnings, divergent lives: Delinquent boys to age 70.* Cambridge, MA: Harvard University Press.

Leadbeater, B. J., Way, N., & Raden, A. (1996). Why not marry your baby's father? Answers from African-American and Hispanic adolescent mothers. In B. J. Leadbeater & N. Way (Eds.), *Urban girls: Resisting stereotypes, creating identities* (pp. 193–212). New York: New York University Press.

LeCompte, M. D., & Preissle, J. (1993). *Ethnography and qualitative design in educational research.* New York: Academic Press.

Lerner, R. M., Fisher, C. B., & Weinberg, R. A. (2000). Toward a science for and of the people: Promoting civil society through the application of developmental science. *Child Development, 71,* 11–20.

Leventhal, T., & Brooks-Gunn, J. (2000). The neighborhoods they live in: The effects of neighborhood residence on child and adolescent outcomes. *Psychological Bulletin, 126,* 309–337.

Lewis, M., Feiring, C., & Rosenthal, S. (2000). Attachment over time. *Child Development, 71,* 707–720.

Liebowitz, S. W., Castellano, D. C., & Cuellar, I. (1999). Factors that predict sexual behaviour among young Mexican American adolescents: An exploratory study. *Hispanic Journal of Behavioural Sciences, 21,* 470–479.

Linares, L., Heeren, T., Bronfman, E., Zuckerman, B., Augustyn, M., & Tronick, E. (2001). A mediational model for the impact of exposure to community violence on early child behavior problems. *Child Development, 72,* 639–652.

Lindsey, C. R., & Kalafat, J. (1998). Adolescents' views of preferred helper characteristics and barriers to seeking help from school-based adults. *Journal of Educational and Psychological Consultation, 9,* 171–193.

Lloyd, J. J., & Anthony, J. C. (2003). Hanging out with the wrong crowd: How much difference can parents make in an urban environment? *Journal of Urban Health: Bulletin of the New York Academy of Medicine, 80,* 383–390.

Loevinger, J. (1976). *Ego development: Conceptions and theories.* San Francisco: Jossey-Bass.

Luthar, S. S. (1991). Vulnerability and resilience: A study of high-risk adolescents. *Child Development, 62,* 600–616.

Luthar, S. S. (1993). Annotation: Methodological and conceptual issues in the study of resilience. *Journal of Child Psychology and Psychiatry, 34,* 441–453.

Luthar, S. S. (1995). Social competence in the school setting: Prospective cross-domain associations among inner-city teens. *Child Development, 66,* 416–429.

Luthar, S. S. (1999). *Poverty and children's adjustment.* Thousand Oaks, CA: Sage.

Luthar, S. S. (Ed.). (2003). *Resilience and vulnerability: Adaptation in the context of childhood adversities.* New York: Cambridge University Press.

Luthar, S. S., & Burack, J. A. (2000). Adolescent wellness: In the eye of the beholder. In D. Cicchetti, J. Rappaport, I. Sandler, & R. Weissberg (Eds.), *The promotion of wellness in children and adolescents* (pp. 29–57). Washington, DC: Child Welfare League of America.

Luthar, S. S., & Cicchetti, D. (2000). The construct of resilience: Implications for interventions and social policies. *Development and Psychopathology, 12,* 857–885.

Luthar, S. S., Cicchetti, D., & Becker, B. (2000a). The construct of resilience: A critical evaluation and guidelines for future work. *Child Development, 71,* 543–562.

Luthar, S. S., Cicchetti, D., & Becker, B. (2000b). Research on resilience: Reply to commentaries. *Child Development, 71,* 573–575.

Luthar, S. S., D'Avanzo, K., & Hites, S. (2003). Parental substance abuse: Risks and resilience. In S. S. Luthar (Ed.), *Resilience and vulnerability: Adaptation in the context of childhood adversities* (pp. 104–129). New York: Cambridge University Press.

Luthar, S. S., Doernberger, C. H., & Zigler, E. (1993). Resilience is not a unidimensional construct: Insights from a prospective study of inner-city adolescents. [Special issue: Milestones in the development of resilience]. *Development and Psychopathology, 5,* 703–717.

Luthar, S. S., Doyle, K., Suchman, N. E., & Mayes, L. (2001). Developmental themes in women's emotional experiences of motherhood. *Development and Psychopathology, 13,* 165–182.

Luthar, S. S., & Goldstein, A. (2004). Children's exposure to community violence: Implications for understanding risk and resilience. *Journal of Clinical Child and Adolescent Psychology, 33,* 499–505.

Luthar, S. S., & Latendresse, S. J. (2005a). Children of the affluent: Challenges to well-being. *Current Directions in Psychological Science, 14,* 49–53.

Luthar, S. S., & Latendresse, S. J. (2005b). Comparable "risks" at the SES extremes: Pre-adolescents' perceptions of parenting. *Development and Psychopathology, 17,* 207–230.

Luthar, S. S., & McMahon, T. J. (1996). Peer reputation among inner-city adolescents: Structure and correlates. *Journal of Research on Adolescence, 6,* 581–603.

Luthar, S. S., & Ripple, C. H. (1994). Sensitivity to emotional distress among intelligent adolescents: A short-term prospective study. *Development and Psychopathology, 6,* 343–357.

Luthar, S. S., & Sexton, C. (2004). The high price of affluence. In R. V. Kail (Ed.), *Advances in Child Development, 32,* 126–162. San Diego, CA: Academic Press.

Luthar, S. S., & Suchman, N. E. (2000). Relational Psychotherapy Mothers' Group: A developmentally informed intervention for at-risk mothers. *Development and Psychopathology, 12,* 235–253.

Luthar, S. S., & Zelazo, L. B. (2003). Research on resilience: An integrative review. In S. S. Luthar (Ed.), *Resilience and vulnerability: Adaptation in the context of childhood adversities* (pp. 510–549). New York: Cambridge University Press.

Luthar, S. S., & Zigler, E. (1991). Vulnerability and competence: A review of research on resilience in childhood. *American Journal of Orthopsychiatry, 61,* 6–22.

Lynam, D., Moffitt, T., & Stouthamer-Loeber, M. (1993). Explaining the relation between IQ and delinquency: Class, race, test motivation, school failure, or self-control? *Journal of Abnormal Psychology, 102,* 187–196.

Lynch, M., & Cicchetti, D. (1998). An ecological-transactional analysis of children and contexts: The longitudinal interplay among child maltreatment, community violence, and children's symptomatology. *Development and Psychopathology, 10,* 235–257.

MacKinnon-Lewis, C., Lamb, M. E., Hattie, J., & Baradaran, L. P. (2001). A longitudinal examination of the associations between mothers' and sons' attributions and their aggression. *Development and Psychopathology, 13,* 69–81.

Maddux, J. E. (2002). Self-efficacy: The power of believing you can. In C. R. Snyder & S. J. Lopez (Eds.), *Handbook of positive psychology* (pp. 277–287). London: Oxford University Press.

Mahler, M. S. (1986). On human symbiosis and the vicissitudes of individuation. In P. Buckley (Ed.), *Essential papers on object relations: Essential papers in psychoanalysis* (pp. 200–221). New York: New York University Press.

Mahoney, J. L. (2000). School extracurricular activity participation as a moderator in the development of antisocial patterns. *Child Development, 71,* 502–551.

Mahoney, J. L., & Magnusson, D. (2001). Parent participation in community activities and the persistence of criminality. *Development and Psychopathology, 13,* 125–141.

Mahoney, J. L., & Stattin, H. (2000). Leisure activities and adolescent antisocial behavior: The role of structure and social context. *Journal of Adolescence, 23,* 113–127.

Margolin, G., & Gordis, E. B. (2000). The effects of family and community violence on children. *Annual Review of Psychology, 51,* 445–479.

Marsh, P., McFarland, F. C., Allen, J. P., McElhaney, K. B., & Land, D. (2003). Attachment, autonomy, and multifinality in adolescent internalizing and risky behavioral symptoms. *Development and Psychopathology, 15,* 451–467.

Martinez, C. R., Jr., & Forgatch, M. S. (2001). Preventing problems with boys' noncompliance: Effects of a parent training intervention for divorcing mothers. *Journal of Consulting and Clinical Psychology, 69,* 416–428.

Martinez, P., & Richters, J. E. (1993). The NIMH Community Violence Project: II. Children's distress symptoms associated with violence exposure. *Psychiatry, 56,* 22–35.

Mason, C. A., Cauce, A. M., Gonzales, N., & Hiraga, Y. (1996). Neither too sweet nor too sour: Problem peers, maternal control, and problem behavior in African American adolescents. *Child Development, 67,* 2115–2130.

Masten, A. (2001). Ordinary magic: Resilience processes in development. *American Psychologist, 56,* 227–238.

Masten, A., Best, K., & Garmezy, N. (1990). Resilience and development: Contributions from the study of children who overcome adversity. *Development and Psychopathology, 2,* 425–444.

Masten, A., & Coatsworth, J. D. (1998). The development of competence in favorable and unfavorable environments: Lessons from research on successful children. *American Psychologist, 53,* 205–220.

Masten, A., & Garmezy, N. (1985). Risk, vulnerability, and protective factors in developmental psychopathology. In B. Lahey & A. Kazdin (Eds.), *Advances in clinical child psychology* (Vol. 8, pp. 1–52). New York: Plenum Press.

Masten, A. S., Morison, P., Pellegrini, D., & Tellegen, A. (1990). Competence under stress: Risk and protective factors. In J. Rolf, A. Masten, D. Cicchetti, K. Neuchterlein, & S. Weintraub (Eds.), *Risk and protective factors in development of psychopathology* (pp. 236–256). New York: Cambridge University Press.

Masten, A. S., & Powell, J. L. (2003). A resilience framework for research, policy, and practice: Contributions from Project Competence. In S. S. Luthar (Ed.), *Resilience and vulnerability: Adaptation in the context of childhood adversities* (pp. 1–25). New York: Cambridge University Press.

Masten, A. S., & Reed, M. J. (2002). Resilience in development. In C. R. Snyder & S. J. Lopez (Eds.), *Handbook of positive psychology* (pp. 74–88). London: Oxford University Press.

Maton, K., Schellenbach, C. J., Leadbeater, B. J., & Solarz, A. L. (Eds.). (2004). *Investing in children, youth, families, and communities: Strengths-based research and policy.* Washington, DC: American Psychological Association.

Mayer, J. D., Salovey, P., Caruso, D. R., & Sitarenios, G. (2003). Measuring emotional intelligence with the MSCEIT V2.0. *Emotion, 3,* 97–105.

McCord, J. (1988). Identifying developmental paradigms leading to alcoholism. *Journal of Studies on Alcohol, 49,* 357–362.

McCubbin, H. I., Thompson, E. A., Thompson, A. I., & Futrell, J. A. (Eds.). (1999). *The dynamics of resilient families.* Thousand Oaks, CA: Sage.

McElhaney, K. B., & Allen, J. P. (2001). Autonomy and adolescent social functioning: The moderating effect of risk. *Child Development, 72,* 220–235.

McEwen, B. S. (1994). Steroid hormone actions on the brain: When is the genome involved? *Hormones and Behavior, 28,* 396–405.

McEwen, B. S., & Sapolsky, M. M. (1995). Stress and cognitive function. *Current Opinion in Neurobiology, 5,* 205–216.

McFadyen-Ketchum, S. A., & Dodge, K. A. (1998). Problems in social relationships. In E. J. Mash & R. A. Barkley (Eds.), *Treatment of childhood disorders* (2nd ed., pp. 338–365). New York: Guilford Press.

McIntosh, D. N., Silver, R. R., & Wortman, C. B. (1993). Religion's role in adjustment to a negative life event: Coping with the loss of a child. *Journal of Personality and Social Psychology, 65,* 812–821.

McLoyd, V. C. (1997). Children in poverty: Development, public policy, and practice. In W. Damon, I. E. Siegel, & K. A. Renninger (Eds.), *Handbook of child psychology: Child psychology in practice* (5th ed., pp. 135–208). New York: Wiley.

McLoyd, V. C., Jayaratne, T. E., Ceballo, R., & Borquez, J. (1994). Unemployment and work interruption among African-American single mothers: Effects on parenting and adolescent socioemotional functioning. *Child Development, 65,* 562–589.

McNeill, B. W., Prieto, L. R., Niemann, Y. F., Pizarro, M., Vera, E. M., & Gomez, S. P. (2001). Current directions in Chicana/o psychology. *Counseling Psychologist, 29,* 5–17.

McQueen, A., Getz, J. G., & Bray, J. H. (2003). Acculturation, substance use, and deviant behavior: Examining separation and family conflict as mediators. *Child Development, 74,* 1737–1750.

Meadows, R. L. (2003). Commentary. *American Behavioral Scientist, 47,* 100–102.

Meehan, B. T., Hughes, J. N., & Cavell, T. A. (2003). Teacher-student relationships as compensatory resources for aggressive children. *Child Development, 74,* 1145–1157.

Mendez, J. L., Fantuzzo, J., & Cicchetti, D. (2002). Profiles of social competences among low-income African-American preschool children. *Child Development, 73,* 1085–1100.

Miller, L., Davies, M., & Greenwald, S. (2000). Religiosity and substance use and abuse among adolescents in the national comorbidity survey. *Journal of the American Academy of Child and Adolescent Psychiatry, 39,* 1190–1197.

Miller, L., & Gur, M. (2002). Religiosity, depression and physical maturation in adolescent girls. *Journal of the American Academy of Child and Adolescent Psychiatry, 41,* 206–214.

Miller, L., Wasserman, G. A., Neugebauer, R., Gorman-Smith, D., & Kamboukos, D. (1999). Witnessed community violence and antisocial behavior in high-risk, urban boys. *Journal of Clinical Child Psychology, 28,* 2–11.

Miller, L., Weissman, M., Gur, M., & Greenwald, S. (2002). Adult religiousness and history of childhood depression: Eleven-year follow-up study. *Journal of Nervous and Mental Diseases, 190,* 86–93.

Moffitt, T. E., Caspi, A., Rutter, M., & Silva, P. A. (2001). *Sex differences in antisocial behavior: Conduct disorder, delinquency, and violence in the Dunedin longitudinal study.* Cambridge, England: Cambridge University Press.

Moss, H. B., Lynch, K. G., Hardie, T. L., & Baron, D. A. (2002). Family functioning and peer affiliation in children of fathers with antisocial personality disorder and substance dependence: Associations with problem behaviors. *American Journal of Psychiatry, 159,* 607–614.

Munoz, R. F., Mrazek, P. J., & Haggerty, R. J. (1996). Institute of Medicine report on prevention of mental disorder: Summary and commentary. *American Psychologist, 51,* 1116–1122.

Murphy, L. B., & Moriarty, A. (1976). *Vulnerability, coping, and growth: From infancy to adolescence.* New Haven, CT: Yale University Press.

Murray, L. (1992). The impact of postnatal depression on infant development. *Journal of Child Psychology and Psychiatry, 33,* 543–561.

Murry, V. M., & Brody, G. H. (1999). Self-regulation and self-worth of Black children reared in economically stressed, rural, single mother-headed families: The contribution of risk and protective factors. *Journal of Family Issues, 20,* 458–484.

Murry, V. M., Bynum, M. S., Brody, G. H., Willert, A., & Stephens, D. (2001). African American single mothers and children in context: A review of studies on risk and resilience. *Clinical Child and Family Psychology Review, 4,* 133–155.

Nader, K., Pynoos, R., Fairbanks, L., & Frederick, C. (1990). Children's PTSD reactions one year after a sniper attack at their school. *American Journal of Psychiatry, 147,* 1526–1530.

Nagin, D. S. (1999). Analyzing developmental trajectories: A semiparametric group-based approach. *Psychological Methods, 4,* 139–157.

National Center on Addiction and Substance Abuse at Columbia University. (2002). *CASA Annual Report.* New York: Author.

National Institute of Child Health and Development Early Child Care Research Network. (1997). The effects of infant child care on infant-mother attachment security: Results of the NICHD Study of Early Child Care. *Child Development, 68,* 860–879.

National Institute of Child Health and Development Early Child Care Research Network. (1999). Chronicity of maternal depressive symptoms, maternal sensitivity, and child functioning at 36 months. *Developmental Psychology, 35,* 1297–1310.

National Institute of Child Health and Development Early Child Care Research Network. (2002). Parenting and family influences when children are in child care: Results from the NICHD Study of Early Child Care. In J. G. Borkowski, S. L. Ramey, & M. Bristol-Power (Eds.), *Parenting and the child's world: Influences on academic, in-* *tellectual, and social-emotional development—Monographs in parenting* (pp. 99–123). Mahwah, NJ: Erlbaum.

National Institute of Child Health and Development Early Child Care Research Network. (2003). Social functioning in the first grade: Associations with earlier home and child care predictors and with current classroom experiences. *Child Development, 74,* 1639–1662.

National Institutes of Health. (1988). *Health benefits of pets: Summary of working group.* Washington, DC: U.S. Department of Health and Human Services.

National Institutes of Health, National Institute of Mental Health. (2000). *A good beginning: Sending America's children to school with the social and emotional competence they need to succeed* (A report sponsored by the Child Mental Health Foundations and Agencies Network). Available from http://www.nimh.nih.gov/childhp/fdnconsb.htm.

Noam, G. G. (1998). Solving the ego development–mental health riddle. In P. M. Westenberg, A. Blasi, & L. D. Cohn (Eds.), *Personality development: Theoretical, empirical, and clinical investigations of Loevinger's conception of ego development* (pp. 271–295). Mahwah, NJ: Erlbaum.

Noam, G. G., & Hermann, C. A. (2002). Where education and mental health meet: Developmental prevention and early intervention in schools. *Development and Psychopathology, 14,* 861–875.

Nolen-Hoeksema, S. (2001). Ruminative coping and adjustment to bereavement. In M. S. Stroebe, R. O. Hansson, W. Stroebe, & H. Schut (Eds.), *Handbook of bereavement research: Consequences, coping, and care* (pp. 545–562). Washington, DC: American Psychological Association.

Nolen-Hoeksema, S., & Davis, C. G. (2002). Positive responses to loss: Perceiving benefits and growth. In C. R. Snyder & S. J. Lopez (Eds.), *Handbook of positive psychology* (pp. 598–607). New York: Oxford University Press.

O'Connor, T. G., Bredenkamp, D., Rutter, M., & the English and Romanian Adoptees Study Team. (1999). Attachment disturbances and disorders in children exposed to early severe deprivation. *Infant Mental Health Journal, 20,* 10–29.

O'Connor, T. G., & Rutter, M. (2000). Attachment disorder behavior following early severe deprivation: Extension and longitudinal follow-up. *Journal of the American Academy of Child and Adolescent Psychiatry, 39,* 703–712.

O'Donnell, D. A., Schwab-Stone, M. E., & Muyeed, A. Z. (2002). Multidimensional resilience in urban children exposed to community violence. *Child Development, 73,* 1265–1282.

O'Dougherty-Wright, M., Masten, A. S., Northwood, A., & Hubbard, J. J. (1997). Long-term effects of massive trauma: Developmental and psychobiological perspectives. In D. Cicchetti & S. L. Toth (Eds.), *Rochester Symposium on Developmental Psychopathology: Vol. 8. Developmental perspectives on trauma* (pp. 181–225). Rochester, NY: University of Rochester Press.

Ogbu, J. U. (1991). Minority coping responses and school experience. *Journal of Psychohistory, 18,* 433–456.

Osofsky, J. D. (1995). The effects of exposure to violence on young children. *American Psychologist, 50*(9), 782–788.

Owens, E. B., &. Shaw, D. S. (2003). Poverty and early childhood adjustment. In S. S. Luthar (Ed.), *Resilience and vulnerability: Adaptation in the context of childhood adversities* (pp. 267–292). New York: Cambridge University Press.

Oyserman, D., Bybee, D., & Terry, K. (2003). Gendered racial identity and involvement with school. *Self and Identity, 2,* 1–18.

Ozer, E. J., & Weinstein, R. S. (2004). Urban adolescents' exposure to community violence: The role of support, school safety, and social constraints in a school-based sample of boys and girls. *Journal of Clinical Child and Adolescent Psychology, 33,* 463–476.

Parker, J. D. A., Summerfeldt, L. J., Hogan, M. J., & Majeski, S. A. (2004). Emotional intelligence and academic success: Examining the transition from high school to university. *Personality and Individual Differences, 36,* 163–172.

Patronek, G. J., & Glickman, L. T. (1993). Pet ownership protects the risks and consequences of coronary heart disease. *Medical Hypotheses, 40,* 245–249.

Patterson, G. R. (1983). Stress: A change agent for family process. In N. Garmezy & M. Rutter (Eds.), *Stress, coping, and development in children* (pp. 235–264). New York: McGraw-Hill.

Paulhus, D. L. (1998). Interpersonal and intrapsychic adaptiveness of trait self-enhancement: A mixed blessing? *Journal of Personality and Social Psychology, 74,* 1197–1208.

Pearce, M. J., Jones, S. M., Schwab-Stone, M. E., & Ruchkin, V. (2003). The protective effects of religiousness and parent involvement on the development of conduct problems among youth exposed to violence. *Child Development, 74,* 1682–1696.

Perry, B. D. (1997). Incubated in terror: Neurodevelopmental factors in the "cycle of violence." In J. D. Osofsky (Ed.), *Children in a violent society* (pp. 124–149). New York: Guilford Press.

Phinney, J. S., Madden, T., & Santos, L. J. (1998). Psychological variables as predictors of perceived ethnic discrimination among minority and immigrant adolescents. *Journal of Applied Social Psychology, 28,* 937–953.

Pianta, R. C. (1999). *Enhancing relationships between children and teachers.* Washington, DC: American Psychological Association.

Pianta, R. C., & Walsh, D. J. (1998). *High-risk children in schools: Constructing sustaining relationships.* New York: Routledge.

Plomin, R., & Rutter, M. (1998). Child development, molecular genetics, and what to do with genes once they are found. *Child Development, 69,* 1223–1242.

Pressman, P., Lyons, J. S., Larson, D. B., & Strain, J. J. (1990). Religious belief, depression, and ambulation status in elderly women with broken hips. *American Journal of Psychiatry, 147,* 758–760.

Pynoos, R. S. (1993). Traumatic stress and developmental psychopathology in children and adolescents. In J. M. Oldham, M. B. Riba, & A. Tasman (Eds.), *Review of psychiatry* (Vol. 12, pp. 205–238). Washington, DC: American Psychiatric Press.

Pynoos, R. S., Steinberg, A. M., Ornitz, E. M., & Goenjian, A. K. (1997). Issues in the developmental neurobiology of traumatic stress. *Annals of the New York Academy of Sciences, 821,* 176–193.

Pynoos, R. S., Steinberg, A. M., & Piacentini, J. C. (1999). A developmental psychopathology model of childhood traumatic stress and intersection with anxiety disorders. *Biological Psychiatry, 46,* 1542–1554.

Raver, C. (2002). Emotions matter: Making the case for the role of young children's emotional development for early school readiness. *Social Policy Report, 16*(3), 3–18.

Recklitis, C. J., & Noam, G. G. (1999). Clinical and developmental perspectives on adolescent coping. *Child Psychiatry and Human Development, 30,* 87–101.

Reddy, R., Rhodes, J. E., & Mulhall, P. (2003). The influence of teacher support on student adjustment in the middle school years: A latent growth curve study. *Development and Psychopathology, 15,* 119–138.

Reis, H. T., & Collins, W. A. (2004). Relationships, human behavior, and psychological science. *Current Directions in Psychological Science, 13,* 233–237.

Reynolds, A. J. (2000). *Success in early intervention: The Chicago child-parent centers.* Lincoln: University of Nebraska Press.

Reynolds, A. J., & Ou, S. (2003). Promoting resilience through early childhood intervention. In S. S. Luthar (Ed.), *Resilience and vulnerability: Adaptation in the context of childhood adversities* (pp. 436–459). New York: Cambridge University Press.

Rhodes, J. E., Grossman, J. B., & Resch, N. L. (2000). Agents of change: Pathways through which mentoring relationships influence adolescents' academic adjustment. *Child Development, 71,* 1662–1671.

Richters, J. E., & Cicchetti, D. (1993). Mark Twain meets DSM-III-R: Conduct disorders, development, and the concept of harmful dysfunction. *Development and Psychopathology, 5,* 5–29.

Richters, J. E., & Martinez, P. E. (1993). Violent communities, family choices, and children's chances: An algorithm for improving the odds. *Development and Psychopathology, 5,* 609–627.

Ringeisen, H., Henderson, K., & Hoagwood, K. (2003). Context matters: Schools and the "research to practice gap" in children's mental health. *School Psychology Review, 32,* 153–168.

Roberts, M. C., Brown, K. J., Johnson, R. J., & Reinke, J. (2002). Positive psychology for children: Development, prevention, and promotion. In C. R. Snyder & S. J. Lopez (Eds.), *Handbook of positive psychology* (pp. 663–675). London: Oxford University Press.

Rogler, L. H., Cortes, D. E., & Malgady, R. G. (1991). Acculturation and mental health status among Hispanics: Convergence and new directions for research. *American Psychologist, 46,* 585–597.

Rohrbeck, C. A., Ginsburg-Block, M. D., Fantuzzo, J. W., & Miller, T. R. (2003). Peer-assisted learning interventions with elementary school students: A meta-analytic review. *Journal of Educational Psychology, 95,* 240–257.

Roisman, G. I., Padron, E., Sroufe, L. A., & Egeland, B. (2002). Learned-secure attachment status in retrospect and prospect. *Child Development, 73,* 1204–1219.

Rolf, J., Masten, A., Cicchetti, D., Nuechterlein, K., & Weintraub, S. (Eds.). (1990). *Risk and protective factors in the development of psychopathology.* New York: Cambridge University Press.

Rollock, D., & Gordon, E. W. (2000). Racism and mental health into the 21st century: Perspectives and parameters. *American Journal of Orthopsychiatry, 70,* 5–13.

Romer, D. (Ed.). (2003). *Reducing adolescent risk: Toward an integrated approach.* Thousand Oaks, CA: Sage.

Rones, M., & Hoagwood, K. (2000). School-based mental health services: A research review. *Clinical Child and Family Psychology Review, 3,* 223–241.

Rothbart, M. K., & Jones, L. B. (1998). Temperament, self-regulation and education. *School Psychology Review, 27,* 479–491.

Rowe, R., Maughan, B., Worthman, C. M., Costello, E. J., & Angold, A. (2004). Testosterone, antisocial behavior, and social dominance in boys: Pubertal development and biosocial interaction. *Biological Psychiatry, 55,* 546–552.

Rubin, K. H., Coplan, R. J., Fox, N. A., & Calkins, S. D. (1995). Emotionality, emotion regulation, and preschoolers' social adaptation. *Development and Psychopathology, 7,* 49–62.

Ruggiero, K. M., & Taylor, D. M. (1997). Why minority group members perceive or do not perceive the discrimination that confronts them: The role of self-esteem and perceived control. *Journal of Personality and Social Psychology, 22,* 373–389.

Rutter, M. (1979). Protective factors in children's responses to stress and disadvantage. In M. W. Kent & J. E. Rolf (Eds.), *Primary prevention in psychopathology: Vol. 8. Social competence in children* (pp. 49–74). Hanover, NH: University Press of New England.

Rutter, M. (1983). Statistical and personal interactions, facets and perspectives. In D. Magnusson & V. Allen (Eds.), *Human development: An interactional perspective* (pp. 295–319). New York: Academic Press.

Rutter, M. (1987). Psychosocial resilience and protective mechanisms. *American Journal of Orthopsychiatry, 57,* 316–331.

Rutter, M. (1993). Resilience: Some conceptual considerations. *Journal of Adolescent Health, 14,* 626–631.

Rutter, M. (1999). Psychosocial adversity and child psychopathology. *British Journal of Psychiatry, 174,* 480–449.

Rutter, M. (2000). Resilience reconsidered: Conceptual considerations, empirical findings, and policy implications. In J. P. Shonkoff & S. J. Meisels (Eds.), *Handbook of early childhood intervention* (2nd ed., pp. 651–682). New York: Cambridge University Press.

Rutter, M. (2002a). The interplay of nature, nurture, and developmental influences: The challenge ahead for mental health. *Archives of General Psychiatry, 59,* 996–1000.

Rutter, M. (2002b). Nature, nurture, and development: From evangelism through science toward policy and practice. *Child Development, 73,* 1–21.

Rutter, M. (2003). Genetic influences on risk and protection: Implications for understanding resilience. In S. S. Luthar (Ed.), *Resilience and vulnerability: Adaptation in the context of childhood adversities* (pp. 489–509). New York: Cambridge University Press.

Rutter, M., & the English and Romanian Adoptees Study Team. (1998). Developmental catch-up, and deficit, following adoption after severe global early privation. *Journal of Child Psychology and Psychiatry and Allied Disciplines, 39,* 465–476.

Rutter, M., & O'Connor, T. G. (2004). Are there biological programming effects for psychological development? Findings from a study of Romanian adoptees. *Developmental Psychology, 40,* 81–94.

Rutter, M., & Silberg, J. (2002). Gene-environment interplay in relation to emotional and behavioral disturbance. *Annual Review of Psychology, 53,* 463–490.

Ryff, C. D., & Singer, B. (2002). From social structure to biology: Integrative science in pursuit of human health and well-being. In C. R. Snyder & S. J. Lopez (Eds.), *Positive psychological assessment: A handbook of models and measures* (pp. 541–554). Washington, DC: American Psychological Association.

Salovey, P., Mayer, J. D., Caruso, D., & Lopes, P. N. (2003). Measuring emotional intelligence as a set of abilities with the Mayer-Salovey-Caruso Emotional Intelligence Test. In S. J. Lopez & C. R. Snyder (Eds.), *Positive psychological assessment: A handbook of models and measures* (pp. 251–265). Washington, DC: American Psychological Association.

Salovey, P., Stroud, L. R., Woolery, A., & Epel, E. S. (2002). Perceived emotional intelligence, stress reactivity, and symptom reports: Further explorations using the trait meta-mood scale. *Psychology and Health, 17,* 611–627.

Sameroff, A. J., Gutman, L., & Peck, S. C. (2003). Adaptation among youth facing multiple risks: Prospective research findings. In S. S. Luthar (Ed.), *Resilience and vulnerability: Adaptation in the context of childhood adversities* (pp. 364–391). New York: Cambridge University Press.

Sameroff, A. J., Seifer, R., Zax, M., & Barocas, R. (1987). Early indicators of developmental risk: The Rochester Longitudinal Study. *Schizophrenia Bulletin, 13,* 383–393.

Sampson, R. J. (2001). How do communities undergird or undermine human development? Relevant contexts and social mechanisms. In A. Booth & A. C. Crouter (Eds.), *Does it take a village? Community effects on children, adolescents, and families* (pp. 3–30). Mahwah, NJ: Erlbaum.

Sampson, R. J., & Laub, J. H. (1996). Socioeconomic achievement in the life course of disadvantaged: Military service as a turning point, circa 1940–1965. *American Sociological Review, 61,* 347–367.

Sampson, R. J., Raudenbush, S. W., & Earls, F. (1997). Neighborhoods and violent crime: A multilevel study of collective efficacy. *Science, 277,* 918–924.

Sanchez, M. M., Ladd, C. O., & Plotsky, P. M. (2001). Early adverse experience as a developmental risk factor for later psychopathology: Evidence from rodent and primate models. *Development and Psychopathology, 13,* 419–450.

Sanders-Phillips, K., Moisan, P. A., Wadlington, S., Morgan, S., & English, K. (1995). Ethnic difference in psychological functioning among Black and Latino sexually abused girls. *Child Abuse and Neglect, 19,* 691–706.

Sandler, I., Wolchik, S., Davis, C., Haine, R., & Ayers, T. (2003). Correlational and experimental study of resilience for children of divorce and parentally bereaved children. In S. S. Luthar (Ed.), *Resilience and vulnerability: Adaptation in the context of childhood adversities* (pp. 213–240). New York: Cambridge University Press.

Sapolsky, R. M. (2000). Glucocorticoids and hippocampal atrophy in neuropsychiatric disorders. *Archives of General Psychiatry, 57,* 925–935.

Scaramella, L. V., Conger, R. D., Spoth, R., & Simons, R. L. (2002). Evaluation of a social contextual model of delinquency: A cross-study replication. *Child Development, 73,* 175–195.

Schneider, W. J., Cavell, T. A., & Hughes, J. N. (2003). A sense of containment: Potential moderator of the relation between parenting practices and children's externalizing behaviors. *Development and Psychopathology, 15,* 95–117.

Schwab-Stone, M. E., Ayers, T. S., Kasprow, W., Voyce, C., Barone, C., Shriver, T., et al. (1995). No safe haven: A study of violence exposure in an urban community. *Journal of the American Academy of Child and Adolescent Psychiatry, 34,* 1343–1352.

Schwartz, D., Dodge, K. A., Pettit, G. S., & Bates, J. E. (2000). Friendship as a moderating factor in the pathway between early harsh home environment and later victimization in the peer group. *Developmental Psychology, 36,* 646–662.

Scribner, S. (1984). Studying working intelligence. In B. Rogoff & J. Lave (Eds.), *Everyday cognition: Its development in social context* (pp. 9–40). Cambridge, MA: Harvard University Press.

Search Institute. (2004). *Asset categories.* http://www.search-institute .org/assets/assetcategories.html.

Seidman, E., & Pedersen, S. (2003). Holistic, contextual perspectives on risk, protection, and competence among low-income urban adolescents. In S. S. Luthar (Ed.), *Resilience and vulnerability: Adaptation in the context of childhood adversities* (pp. 318–342). New York: Cambridge University Press.

Seifer, S. (2003). Young children with mentally ill parents: Resilient developmental systems. In S. S. Luthar (Ed.), *Resilience and vulnerability: Adaptation in the context of childhood adversities* (pp. 29–49). New York: Cambridge University Press.

Seligman, M. E. P. (2002). Positive psychology, positive prevention, and positive therapy. In C. R. Snyder & S. J. Lopez (Eds.), *Handbook of positive psychology* (pp. 3–9). New York: Oxford University Press.

Sharp, D., Hay, D., Pawlby, S., Schmucker, G., Allen, H., & Kumar, R. (1995). The impact of postnatal depression on boys' intellectual development. *Journal of Child Psychology and Psychiatry, 36,* 1315–1336.

Shaw, D. S., Bell, R. Q., & Gilliom, M. (in press). A truly early starter model of antisocial behavior revisited. *Clinical Child and Family Psychology Review.*

Shaw, D. S., Owens, E. B., Vondra, J. I., Keenan, K., & Winslow, E. B. (1996). Early risk factors and pathways in the development of early disruptive behavior problems. *Development and Psychopathology, 8,* 679–699.

Sheldon, K. M., & King, L. (2001). Why positive psychology is necessary. *American Psychologist, 56,* 216–217.

Shonkoff, J. P., & Meisels, S. J. (Eds.). (2000). *Handbook of early childhood intervention* (2nd ed.). New York: Cambridge University Press.

Shonkoff, J. P., & Phillips, D. A. (Eds.). (2000). *From neurons to neighborhoods: The science of early childhood development.* Washington, DC: National Academy Press.

Short, R. J. (2003). Commentary: School psychology, context, and population-based practice. *School Psychology Review, 32,* 181–184.

Skinner, B. F. (1974). *About behaviorism.* Oxford: Knopf.

Skinner, E. A., Zimmer-Gembeck, M. J., & Connell, J. P. (1998). Individual differences and the development of perceived control. *Monographs of the Society for Research in Child Development, 63*(2–3), 1–220.

Smith, S. W., & Daunic, A. P. (2002). Using conflict resolution and peer mediation to support positive behavior. In B. Algozzine & P. Kay (Eds.), *Preventing problem behaviors: A handbook of successful prevention strategies* (pp. 142–161). Thousand Oaks, CA: Corwin Press.

Snyder, C. R., & Lopez, S. J. (Eds.). (2002). *Handbook of positive psychology.* London: Oxford University Press.

Spencer, M. B. (1999). Social and cultural influences on school adjustment: The application of an identity-focused cultural ecological perspective. *Educational Psychologist, 34,* 43–57.

Spencer, M. B., Fegley, S. G., & Harpalani, V. (2003). A theoretical and empirical examination of identity as coping: Linking coping resources to the self processes of African American youth. *Applied Developmental Science, 7,* 181–188.

Spencer, M. B., Noll, E., Stoltzfus, J., & Harpalani, V. (2001). Identity and school adjustment: Revisiting the "acting White" assumption. *Educational Psychologist, 36,* 21–30.

Sroufe, L. A. (2002). From infant attachment to promotion of adolescent autonomy: Prospective, longitudinal data on the role of parents in development. In J. G. Borkowski & S. L. Ramey (Eds.), *Parenting and the child's world: Influences on academic, intellectual, and social-emotional development—Monographs in parenting* (pp. 187–202). Mahwah, NJ: Erlbaum.

Sroufe, L. A., Carlson, E. A., Levy, A. K., & Egeland, B. (1999). Implications of attachment theory for developmental psychopathology. *Development and Psychopathology, 11,* 1–13.

Sroufe, L. A., Egeland, B., & Kreutzer, T. (1990). The fate of early experience following developmental change: Longitudinal approaches to individual adaptation in childhood. *Child Development, 61,* 1363–1373.

Staudinger, U. M., Freund, A. M., Linden, M., & Maas, I. (1999). Self, personality, and life regulation: Facets of psychological resilience in old age. In P. B. Baltes & K. U. Mayer (Eds.), *The Berlin Aging Study: Aging from 70 to 100* (pp. 302–328). New York: Cambridge University Press.

Steele, C. M. (1997). A threat in the air: How stereotypes shape intellectual identity and performance. *American Psychologist, 52,* 613–629.

Steinberg, L., Dornbusch, S. M., & Brown, B. B. (1992). Ethnic differences in adolescent achievement: An ecological perspective. *American Psychologist, 47,* 723–729.

Sternberg, R. J., & Grigorenko, E. L. (2000). Practical intelligence and its development. In R. Bar-On & J. D. A. Parker (Eds.), *The handbook of emotional intelligence: Theory, development, assessment, and application at home, school, and in the workplace* (pp. 215–243). San Francisco: Jossey-Bass.

Sternberg, R. J., & Grigorenko, E. L. (2001). Unified psychology. *American Psychologist, 56,* 1069–1079.

Sternberg, R. J., Nokes, C., Geissler, P. W., Prince, R., Okatcha, F., Bundy, D. A., et al. (2001). The relationship between academic and practical intelligence: A case study in Kenya. *Intelligence, 29,* 401–418.

Stifter, C. A., Spinrad, T., & Braungart-Rieker, J. M. (1999). Toward a developmental model of child compliance: The role of emotion regulation in infancy. *Child Development, 70,* 21–32.

Stouthamer-Loeber, M., Loeber, R., Farrington, D. P., Zhang, Q., van Kammen, W., & Maguin, E. (1993). The double edge of protective and risk factors for delinquency: Interrelations and developmental patterns. *Development and Psychopathology, 5,* 683–701.

Sullivan, T. N., Kung, E. M., & Farrell, A. D. (2004). Relation between witnessing violence and drug use initiation among rural adolescents: Parental monitoring and family support as protective factors. *Journal of Clinical Child and Adolescent Psychology, 33,* 488–498.

Sutton, S. K., & Davidson, R. J. (1997). Prefrontal brain asymmetry: A biological substrate of the behavioral approach and inhibition systems. *Psychological Science, 8,* 204–210.

Szalacha, L. A., Erkut, S., García Coll, C., Fields, J. P., Alarcón, O., & Ceder, I. (2003). Perceived discrimination and resilience. In S. S. Luthar (Ed.), *Resilience and vulnerability: Adaptation in the context of childhood adversities* (pp. 414–435). New York: Cambridge University Press.

Taylor, R. D. (1996). Adolescents' perceptions of kinship support and family management practices: Associations with adolescent adjustment in African-American families. *Developmental Psychology, 32,* 687–695.

Taylor, R. D., Casten, R., & Flickinger, S. (1993). The influence of kinship social support on the parenting experiences and psychosocial adjustment of African American adolescents. *Developmental Psychology, 29,* 382–388.

Taylor, R. D., & Wang, M. C. (Eds.). (2000). *Resilience across contexts: Family, work, culture, and community.* Mahwah, NJ: Erlbaum.

Taylor, S. E., Kemeny, M. E., Reed, G. M., Bower, J. E., & Gruenewald, T. L. (2000). Psychological resources, positive illusions, and health. *American Psychologist, 55,* 99–109.

Tennen, H., & Affleck, G. (2002). Benefit-finding and benefit-reminding. In C. R. Snyder & S. J. Lopez (Eds.), *Handbook of positive psychology* (pp. 584–597). New York: Oxford University Press.

Thompson, R. A. (2000). The legacy of early attachments. *Child Development, 71,* 145–152.

Tierney, J. P., Grossman, J. B., & Resch, N. L. (1995). *Making a difference: An impact study of Big Brothers Big Sisters.* Philadelphia: Public/Private Ventures.

Tolan, P., Gorman-Smith, D., & Henry, D. (2004). Supporting families in a high-risk setting: Proximal effects of the SAFE children prevention program. *Journal of Consulting and Clinical Psychology, 72,* 855–869.

Treboux, D., Crowell, J. A., & Waters, E. (2004). When "new" meets "old": Configurations of adult attachment representations and their implications for marital functioning. *Developmental Psychology, 40,* 295–314.

Trinidad, D. R., & Johnson, C. A. (2002). The association between emotional intelligence and early adolescent tobacco and alcohol use. *Personality and Individual Differences, 32,* 95–105.

Tucker, C. M., & Herman, K. C. (2002). Using culturally sensitive theories and research to meet the academic needs of low-income African American children. *American Psychologist, 57,* 762–773.

Tyler, K. A., Hoyt, D. R., Whitbeck, L. B., & Cauce, A. M. (2001). The impact of childhood sexual abuse on later sexual victimization among runaway youth. *Journal of Research on Adolescence, 11,* 151–176.

Ungar, M. (2004). *Nurturing hidden resilience in troubled youth.* Toronto, Ontario, Canada: University of Toronto Press.

U.S. Bureau of Labor Statistics. (2004). *May 2004 National Occupational Employment and Wage Estimates.* http://www.bls.gov/oes/current/oes_nat.htm.

Vaillant, G. E. (2000). Adaptive mental mechanisms: Their role in a positive psychology. *American Psychologist, 55,* 89–98.

Vaillant, G. E., & Davis, J. T. (2000). Social/emotional intelligence and midlife resilience in schoolboys with low tested intelligence. *American Journal of Orthopsychiatry, 70,* 215–222.

Vandell, D. L., Dadisman, K., & Gallagher, K. (2000). Another look at the elephant: Child care in the nineties. In R. D. Taylor & M. C. Wang (Eds.), *Resilience across contexts: Family, work, culture, and community* (pp. 91–120). Mahwah, NJ: Erlbaum.

Wang, M. C., & Gordon, E. W. (Eds.). (1994). *Educational resilience in inner-city America: Challenges and prospects.* Hillsdale, NJ: Erlbaum.

Waters, E., Merrick, S., Treboux, D., Crowell, J., & Albersheim, L. (2000). Attachment security in infancy and early adulthood: A twenty-year longitudinal study. *Child Development, 71,* 684–689.

Waters, E., Weinfield, N. S., & Hamilton, C. E. (2000). The stability of attachment security from infancy to adolescence and early adulthood: General discussion. *Child Development, 71,* 703–706.

Watson, C., & Gametchu, B. (1999). Membrane-initiated steroid actions and the proteins that mediate them. *Proceedings of the Society for Experimental Biology and Medicine, 220,* 9–19.

Way, N., & Robinson, M. G. (2003). A longitudinal study of the effects of family, friends, and school experiences on the psychological adjustment of ethnic minority, low-SES adolescents. *Journal of Adolescent Research, 18,* 324–346.

Webster-Stratton, C., & Taylor, T. (2001). Nipping early risk factors in the bud: Preventing substance abuse, delinquency, and violence in adolescence through interventions targeted at young children (0–8 years). *Prevention Science, 2,* 165–192.

Weinfield, N. S., Sroufe, L. A., & Egeland, B. (2000). Attachment from infancy to early adulthood in a high-risk sample: Continuity, discontinuity, and their correlates. *Child Development, 71,* 695–702.

Weiss, M. J. S., & Wagner, S. H. (1998). What explains the negative consequences of adverse childhood experiences on adult health? Insights from cognitive and neuroscience research. *American Journal of Preventive Medicine, 14,* 356–360.

Weissberg, R. P., & Greenberg, M. T. (1998). School and community competence-enhancement and prevention programs. In I. E. Siegel & K. A. Renninger (Eds.), *Handbook of child psychology* (5th ed., pp. 877–954). New York: Wiley.

Weissberg, R. P., Kumpfer, K. L., & Seligman, M. E. P. (2003). Prevention that works for children and youth: An introduction. *American Psychologist, 58,* 425–432.

Weisz, J. R., Hawley, K. M., Pilkonis, P. A., Woody, S. R., & Follette, W. C. (2000). Stressing the (other) three Rs in the search for empirically supported treatments: Review procedures, research quality, relevance to practice and the public interest. *Clinical Psychology: Science and Practice, 7,* 243–258.

Wells, R. D., & Schwebel, A. I. (1987). Chronically ill children and their mothers: Predictors of resilience and vulnerability to hospitalization and surgical stress. *Journal of Developmental and Behavioral Pediatrics, 18,* 83–89.

Wentzel, K. R. (2002). Are effective teachers like good parents? Interpersonal predictors of school adjustment in early adolescence. *Child Development, 73,* 287–301.

Werner, E. E. (2000). Protective factors and individual resilience. In R. Meisells & J. Shonkoff (Eds.), *Handbook of early intervention* (pp. 115–132). Cambridge, England: Cambridge University Press.

Werner, E. E., & Johnson, J. L. (1999). Can we apply resilience? In M. Glantz & J. L. Johnson (Eds.), *Resilience and development: Positive life adaptations* (pp. 259–268). New York: Plenum Press.

Werner, E. E., & Smith, R. (1977). *Kauai's children come of age.* Honolulu: University of Hawaii Press.

Werner, E. E., & Smith, R. (1982). *Vulnerable but invincible: A study of resilient children.* New York: McGraw-Hill.

Werner, E. E., & Smith, R. S. (1992). *Overcoming the odds: High risk children from birth to adulthood.* Ithaca, NY: Cornell University Press.

Werner, E. E., & Smith, R. S. (2001). *Journeys from childhood to midlife: Risk, resilience, and recovery.* Ithaca, NY: Cornell University Press.

Westenberg, P. M., Blasi, A., & Cohn, L. D. (Eds.). (1998). *Personality development: Theoretical, empirical, and clinical investigations of Loevinger's conception of ego development.* Mahwah, NJ: Erlbaum.

Wheeler, R. E., Davidson, R. J., & Tomarken, A. J. (1993). Frontal brain asymmetry and emotional reactivity: A biological substrate of affective style. *Psychophysiology, 30,* 82–89.

Wickramaratne, P. J., & Weissman, M. M. (1998). Onset of psychopathology in offspring by developmental phase and parental depression. *Journal of the American Academy of Child and Adolescent Psychiatry, 37,* 933–942.

Williams, D. R., Yu, Y., Jackson, J. S., & Anderson, N. B. (1997). Racial differences in physical and mental health: Socio-economic status, stress and discrimination. *Journal of Health Psychology, 2,* 335–351.

Wilson, W. J. (1991). Studying inner-city social dislocations: The challenge of public agenda research. *American Sociological Review, 56,* 1–14.

Wilson, W. J. (2003). Race, class and urban poverty: A rejoinder. *Ethnic and Racial Studies, 26,* 1096–1114.

Wolin, S. J., & Wolin, S. (1993). *The resilient self.* New York: Villard.

Wyman, P. A. (2003). Emerging perspectives on context-specificity of children's adaptation and resilience: Evidence from a decade of research with urban children in adversity. In S. S. Luthar (Ed.), *Resilience and vulnerability: Adaptation in the context of childhood adversities* (pp. 293–317). New York: Cambridge University Press.

Wyman, P. A., Cowen, E. L., Work, W. C., Hoyt-Meyers, L., Magnus, K. B., & Fagen, D. B. (1999). Caregiving and developmental factors differentiating young at-risk urban children showing resilient versus stress-affected outcomes: A replication and extension. *Child Development, 70,* 645–659.

Wyman, P. A., Cowen, E. L., Work, W. C., & Parker, G. R. (1991). Developmental and family milieu correlates of resilience in urban children who have experienced major life stress. *American Journal of Community Psychology, 19,* 405–426.

Yates, T. M., Egeland, B., & Sroufe, L. A. (2003). Rethinking resilience: A developmental process perspective. In S. S. Luthar (Ed.), *Resilience and vulnerability: Adaptation in the context of childhood adversities* (pp. 243–266). New York: Cambridge University Press.

Yoshikawa, H. (1994). Prevention as cumulative protection: Effects of early family support and education on chronic delinquency and its risks. *Psychological Bulletin, 115,* 28–54.

Zhou, Q., Valiente, C., & Eisenberg, N. (2003). Empathy and its measurement. In S. J. Lopez & C. R. Snyder (Eds.), *Positive psychological assessment: A handbook of models and measures* (pp. 269–284). Washington, DC: American Psychological Association.

Zigler, E. F., Lamb, M. E., & Child, I. L. (1982). *Socialization and personality development (2nd ed.).* New York: Oxford University Press.

Zigler, E., & Styfco, S. J. (2001). Extended childhood intervention prepares children for school and beyond. *Journal of the American Medical Association, 85,* 2378–2380.

Zimmerman, M. A., Salem, D. A., & Maton, K. I. (1995). Family structure and psychosocial correlates among urban African-American adolescent males. *Child Development, 66,* 1598–1613.

Zucker, R. A., Wong, M. W., Puttler, L. I., & Fitzgerald, H. E. (2003). Resilience and vulnerability among sons of alcoholics: Relationship to developmental outcomes between early childhood and adolescence. In S. S. Luthar (Ed.), *Resilience and vulnerability: Adaptation in the context of childhood adversities* (pp. 76–103). New York: Cambridge University Press.

CHAPTER 21

Resilience in Later Adulthood and Old Age: Resources and Potentials for Successful Aging

WERNER GREVE and URSULA M. STAUDINGER

From its very beginning, human development is dependent on the physical and social context for support. Some of this support is very basic and is required equally by all people (air, water, food); other support is more complex (social care, language training) and is necessary to varying degrees (culture-specific competencies, multilingualism). Individual demand profiles vary widely: People may have hereditary and acquired vulnerabilities or deficits that require support and

fostering, including specific kinds of intervention and preventive measures (e.g., special diets in the case of inherited metabolic disorders such as phenylketonuria). But in all cases, development can take place only given an appropriate fit between individual and environment. Within the range of possibilities that meet this requirement, human development can unfold in a wide variety of ways. Even if all the necessary preconditions have been fulfilled, development, if it occurs at all, by no means follows a predetermined path. The dispositions and characteristics inherent in each individual and in human beings in general are confronted by an incalculably vast array of environmental influences (education and socialization, learning environments and experiences, biographical characteristics and influences, critical and nonnormative life events, historical influences, etc.). These factors, furthermore, extend their influence throughout the entire process of ontogenesis (P. B. Baltes, 1987; P. B. Baltes, Lindenberger, & Staudinger, 1998).

A large body of empirical and theoretical research, however, supports the idea that negative changes increase in

---

This text is in many ways a follow-up to the chapter "Resilience and Reserve Capacity in Later Adulthood: Potentials and Limits of Development across the Life Span" (Staudinger et al., 1995), which appeared in the first edition of this book. The present chapter expands on the considerations and theories presented there, offering modifications of some details but taking fundamentally the same approach. Therefore, we do not mention each of the parallels and shared lines of argumentation in an explicit citation. One of the authors of this chapter, Werner Greve, would like to thank the colleagues who authored the earlier chapter for their many useful comments and suggestions.

later adulthood and old age, as everyday experiences and stereotypes might indeed lead us to expect (P. B. Baltes, 1997). At the same time, many studies show that for the large majority of older people, subjective well-being does not decrease in later adulthood (Brandtstädter, Wentura, & Greve, 1993; Staudinger, 2000b), at least into the early phases of old age (P. B. Baltes, 1997). This implies the existence of different mechanisms at work, which buffer or completely absorb the impact of increasingly negative development influences.

This aspect of aging has never been more important than it is today, at the beginning of the twenty-first century: Society is graying (Williamson, 2002), and historically speaking, this is a "young" phenomenon (P. B. Baltes & Baltes, 1990). Nevertheless, despite the growing population of elderly people—both because more people are living to reach old age and because on average they are living longer (Maier & Vaupel, 2003)—there is much evidence that elderly people in *this* aging society will do better socially, physically, and psychologically than any older generation before them. In the last decade of the twentieth century, for example, extensive evidence was published indicating that older people do not develop symptoms of clinical depression more frequently, but in fact less frequently than younger people. Furthermore, they often remain fully capable of social interactions after cognitive deficiencies arise (for a summary, see Carstensen & Charles, 2003). Although these findings contradict many of our expectations (which are probably derived in part from textbooks on developmental psychology and gerontology), they may be more than just the exception to the rule. Kegan (1998, p. 198) reports what a friend told him when she reached her 50th birthday: She experienced none of the symptoms of "empty nest syndrome" (which she had expected), but realized that "the true meaning of liberation is when the last child goes off to college and the dog dies." This does not challenge the idea that aging is associated with losses, but suggests that these losses can be compensated for in manifold ways. Furthermore, it emphasizes that consequences of these losses are less severe than widely feared and that their onset occurs at an increasingly later stage in the life course.

Aside from the fact that this is good news to most of us, *why* is it the case? An initial answer is: because of the progress in medicine and in social and medical care—in short, the high living standards that prevail in the Western world. But we argue that this answer falls short. Above all, providing for people's physical and material needs is not everything. Even when these needs are met, age-correlated losses frequently still occur, for example, the end of work-

ing life, children leaving home, the deaths of loved ones, or diminishing fluid cognitive competence (mechanics). Why does the "paradox of well-being" (Staudinger, 2000b) still prevail? Why do the majority of older and elderly people not get sick or show any significant decline in their well-being or mental health? To help answer these questions, this chapter seeks to better understand and explain the phenomenon of *resilience*.

The importance of resilient adaptation in the face of adversity, in particular in childhood and adolescence, has been stressed in several papers and books (e.g., Cicchetti, Rappaport, Sandler, & Weissberg, 2000; Glantz & Johnson, 1999). Only recently has this concept been expanded and applied to later stages of life, in particular to late adulthood and old age (Brandtstädter, 1999b; Staudinger, Marsiske, & Baltes, 1993, 1995). In the present chapter, we argue that resilience—beyond childhood and adolescence, but also beyond old age—is a central concept for both the life span perspective on human development and for developmental psychopathology. It conveys the idea that individuals can avoid negative outcomes or decreasing trajectories of development despite the presence of significant risk factors in their environment or potentially harmful experiences during their lives. It also includes the proposition that individuals can return to a normal, or their initial, level of functioning following developmental setbacks or crises, either with or without external support (e.g., Garmezy, 1991; Masten & Coatsworth, 1998; Rutter, 1987). By explaining the processes and mechanisms that stabilize, protect, or help in the recovery of the psychological functions affected in each particular case, it will not only become more evident how development actually works, but also that negative developments and maladaptation cannot only be explained by the *presence* of specific risk factors, but also by the *absence* of protective factors. Obviously, this implies that risk and protective factors are defined independently.

As mentioned, both scientific conceptions and widespread stereotypes traditionally associate age and aging with loss, decline, and negative changes. In the following, we argue that such negative stereotypes and conceptions of aging are in part wrong, but for most one-sided (despite their usefulness for stabilizing processes in downward comparisons, e.g., Heckhausen, 1999; Pinquart, 2002; Rothermund, 2005). We pursue the thesis that the majority of aging individuals are able to maintain a satisfying level of functioning and social networks and to stabilize their subjective well-being, life satisfaction, and sense of identity and self-esteem. We argue that this ability to preserve the quality of life throughout long phases of middle and late adulthood and into early phases of old age is both an expression and a result of resilience-related processes and resources. This claim has two implications. First, resilience is not the exception but the rule: Resilience is a much more common and ordinary phenomenon than was thought in early stages of investigation (Masten, 2001). Second, it follows from this that processes of resilience substantially contribute to the explanation of development in later adulthood and old age in general. Thus, the perspective on resilience presented in this chapter also contributes to our understanding of what adult development and aging actually is.

In this chapter, resilience in later adulthood and old age is investigated from the perspective of life span development. According to this view, human development is characterized by multidirectionality, multifunctionality, plasticity, and permanent change of the individual's experiences of gains and losses (P. B. Baltes, 1997; P. B. Baltes, Lindenberger, et al., 1998; P. B. Baltes, Staudinger, & Lindenberger, 1999; Staudinger & Lindenberger, 2003a). Human development is embedded in historical, cultural, and social contexts. Thus, an individual's course of life cannot be understood or explained without referring to the historical circumstances, the cultural influences, and the social interactions that frame and form it. Although age-graded and nonnormative individual experiences and events determine the individual's development throughout the life span, development is necessarily *development in context*. Socializing agents (parents, peers, partners, and teachers) actively influence and shape our biographies, and their efforts and actions depend to a large degree on the cultural framework within which they act.

Moreover, human development is, to a large degree, actively and intentionally steered and regulated by the developing individual (Brandtstädter, 1998; Brandtstädter & Lerner, 1999). To some extent, we are and become who and what we want to be (Greve, Rothermund, & Wentura, 2005). Yet, the implied intentionality contained in this phrase, even if it is accepted, carries a variety of connotations. Some approaches argue that humans intentionally coproduce their development (Brandtstädter, 1998; Brandtstädter & Lerner, 1999; Greve, 2005; Lerner, Dowling, & Roth, 2003); others take a constructivist stance and interpret "producing" as semantic reconstruction (Straub, Zielke, & Werbik, 2005). Within this range of perspectives, one central aspect of resilience includes the adaptive processes and the dynamic interplay between the pursuit of personal (developmental) goals and the (developmental) adjustment of these goals to constraints, losses, or changes

in action and developmental resources (Ryff, Singer, Love, & Essex, 1998; Staudinger et al., 1995).

Hence, resilience is one of the key features of psychological aging. We are interested here not only in studying the "normal" occurrence of resilience, but also in showing how it can be fostered and enhanced both by the social environment and by intentional intervention. In research on resilience during childhood and adolescence, modes of supporting resilience have long been recognized (Cicchetti, 1993; Masten, 2001; Masten & Coatsworth, 1998; Werner, 1995). With respect to late adulthood and old age, however, options and opportunities for actively supporting resilience have only recently gained attention (with the exception of cognitive training; Ryff et al., 1998; Staudinger et al., 1993, 1995). The activation of resilience constitutes a central interface between life span development and developmental psychopathology, two domains that we aim to connect more closely in this chapter.

A LIFE SPAN PERSPECTIVE ON DEVELOPMENT IN LATER ADULTHOOD AND OLD AGE

Resilience, as we conceptualize it in this chapter, entails plasticity (cf. Staudinger et al., 1995). Plasticity, in turn, is a central concept of the life span approach to development. Thus, we start our discussion by presenting an overview of the central assumptions and concepts of life span psychology.

The life span approach to human development is characterized by six central propositions (e.g., P. B. Baltes, 1987): (1) Human development actually continues throughout the whole life span, (2) it proceeds multidirectionally, (3) it can be described as a gain:loss ratio, (4) it reveals great plasticity, (5) it is comprehensible only with reference to its historical embeddedness, and (6) a scientific explanation of development has to include contextualism as a paradigm (see also P. B. Baltes, 1987; P. B. Baltes, Reese, & Lipsitt, 1980; Lerner, 1984).

At the beginning of this debate, developmental psychologists extended their perspective beyond youth and adolescence to also include later phases of life, focusing their investigations mainly on late adulthood and old age. In these early days, the life span perspective on human development was sometimes difficult to distinguish from gerontopsychology. However, more recent approaches (e.g., P. B. Baltes, 1997; P. B. Baltes, Lindenberger, et al., 1998; Brandtstädter, 1998; Roberts & Caspi, 2003; Staudinger & Bluck, 2001; Staudinger et al., 1995) are finally linking with earlier longitudinal studies on childhood and adolescence that have "grown older" over the years (e.g., Eichorn, Clausen, Hann, Honzik, & Mussen, 1981; Hetherington, Lerner, & Perlmutter, 1988; Pulkinnen & Kokko, 2000; Reese, 1993; Sorensen, Weinert, & Sherrod, 1986). This link is carried by the idea that the life span perspective on human development offers a unique and integrative perspective on development that goes far beyond the simplistic claim that developmental changes can be observed in every stage of life. This approach is incompatible with reducing development to stages or with portraying the second half of life as largely a period of decline and despair. Understanding development throughout the life span as multidirectional (i.e., encompassing gains and losses at the same time) and modifiable implies a view on aging that acknowledges the losses but also focuses on stability and gain. Thus, this view challenges models of aging that are oriented *exclusively* toward decrements (P. B. Baltes, 1993; Riley & Riley, 1989; Rowe & Kahn, 1987). Rather, it conceptualizes development over the individual's entire lifetime as a dynamic ratio of gains and losses. This applies not only to later life, but also to childhood, a period that is often viewed as characterized exclusively by progression and increase. As early as 1965, Piaget described some visual illusions that increase with age and others that decrease. Even on a neurological level of description, when looking at brain development between the ages of 8 and 12 months, we can observe the phenomenon of neural pruning, that is, the disappearance of neural connections that were established in earlier flourishing phases but are no longer useful or necessary (e.g., Huttenlocher, 2002). At the same time, there are domains of cognitive functioning that show stability through old age. For instance, work on wisdom has repeatedly demonstrated the considerable progression and advantages of older adults with respect to life experience and advice (e.g., P. B. Baltes & Staudinger, 1993, 2000; Staudinger, 1999a; Staudinger & Baltes, 1996). Even in the development of memory, an area prototypically connected with decline in old age, there is evidence that implicit memory shows stability or even increases across the life span (Graf, 1990; Howard, 1991). Moreover, what constitutes a developmental gain or loss is a complex question and changes with age, both subjectively and theoretically (we return to this issue later).

These propositions delineate a research program that aims to identify the processes and potential of individual development—within the specific cultural and historical context (the present chapter aims to contribute to this). Please note, however, that the propositions of the life span perspective on human development (P. B. Baltes, 1987) refer to different conceptual levels. They lend themselves more or less directly to empirical testing. The proposition that human development is a lifelong process is not so much a directly testable hypothesis as it is a conceptual perspective that does not equate development with increase or gain. Even in the first half of the twentieth century, the debate was not about whether or not in part severe changes occurred during old age, but about whether they should be conceptualized as *development*. The life span approach (and this chapter as well) proceeds from the understanding that development at all ages (including old age) is a ratio of gains and losses. Similarly, the commitment to contextualism as a research paradigm is foremost a methodological demand and, as such, not empirically falsifiable; it highlights the crucial forms of interaction that are missed by focusing on the individual. This is also true of the demand that historical embeddedness be taken into account. Although this proposition reflects primarily a methodological and theoretical requirement, the ignorance of cultural and historical contexts would certainly lead to false inferences about development.

The theory of the plasticity of organisms or their attributes, and thus of their development (Lerner, 1984), poses a number of empirical challenges. In this context, it is crucial to underscore that the two concepts of development and plasticity in principle are not logically interdependent (they are, of course, interdependent in a life span perspective of development). Basically, the claim of plasticity of organisms and their courses of development would also be compatible with a concept of development that is limited to specific phases of an organism's evolving complexity. In this respect, there are indications that in the first few months of life, brain structures pass through sensitive developmental phases that are almost impossible to be compensated later. Simultaneously, it was demonstrated that the brain remains plastic even into advanced old age (Li, 2003). When the idea of plasticity and thus the context sensitivity of development is taken seriously, a narrow concept of development as a sequence of qualitatively separable stages of development that ends when "maturity" is reached in adolescence appears highly implausible. However, claiming development as a gain:loss ratio (Smith, 2003) makes it crucial to demonstrate significant gains and losses across the whole life span (a few examples have already been cited).

How do gains and losses come about? Life span psychology claims that gains and losses do not simply follow an age-graded biological program. Rather, we need to take into account age-graded cultural influences such as norms that regulate behavior at different phases in our life (Heckhausen, 1999; Kim & Moen, 2001a, 2001b;

Neugarten, Moore, & Lowe, 1965). Those norms not only operate as a constraint for the age-related behavior in question, but also determine the self-image of the aging person and thus influence which competencies are used or trained and thus maintained over time (e.g., individuals who do not walk or jog on a regular basis can be expected to experience a tendency toward reduced mobility). Besides, biology and culture, the two big sources of development, themselves change depending on historical time. Due to medical and nutritional progress, we seemingly have become biologically "younger" at higher ages. And clearly, historical influences, such as a war, change development across ages. Finally, we need not forget the importance of idiosyncratic constellations and events on development.

Development as Lifelong Transactional Adaptation

The central claim of the life span development approach is, obviously, that developmental changes occur from birth until death. The developmental processes that occur throughout the life span are not simply the mechanical unfolding of predetermined maturational programs, or the cumulative expression of the reactions of the developing organism to environmental conditions or stimuli. Rather, development can be characterized as "transactional adaptation" (e.g., Lerner, 1984, 1986) or continuous "person-environment interaction" (e.g., Magnusson, 1990). In short, development is adaptation. Human development in context can be viewed as a system of structures that must integrate through a transactional process of adaptation (Ford & Lerner, 1992; Lerner et al., 2003; Masten & Coatsworth, 1995; Thelen & Smith, 1998). The phenotypic appearance of development is the present outcome of the individual's interactions with changing contextual circumstances (influences, stimuli, stable conditions) under the prevailing genotypic and sociohistorical constraints or facilitators. Moreover, some of these circumstances and conditions are not only actively selected by the individual, but also actively shaped and modified (Caspi, 1998; Roberts & Caspi, 2003; Scarr & McCartney, 1983). This person-environment interaction is thus not a one-way street, but a real *trans*action, in which both person and environment experience (developmental) changes. Individuals transform their contexts and are transformed by their contexts, sometimes simultaneously. As a consequence, the investigation of (human) development has to take into account several levels of observation, and hence levels of explanation. Not only psychological functions change with age, but so do contexts, and the risks, resources, and functional consequences asso-

ciated with them. To give one example, our speech competence (vocabulary, fluency, etc.) develops with age, but so do the contexts and conditions in which language changes are acquired and used. One major consequence of an interactional perspective on human development is that the environment becomes pivotally important for a proper understanding of developmental processes. Far beyond being a mere cue or motor for these processes, context has to be viewed as a constitutive part of it. Accordingly, Ford and Lerner (1992), following several earlier propositions (e.g., Oyama, 1985), talk about "developmental systems" (see also Lerner et al., 2003).

Continuity and Discontinuity

Developmental processes may appear continuous or discontinuous. For instance, in both the intellectual domain and the personality domain, different authors have reported mean level and interindividual retest stability on repeated occasions (Costa & McCrae, 1988; Hertzog & Schaie, 1988; Schaie, 1994; Siegler, George, & Okun, 1979), indicating a high level of individual stability for each respective aspect. At the same time, however, Nesselroade (1991) has argued empirically and theoretically that there are several indicators of remarkable intraindividual variability. Thus, individual continuity and group-level stability have to be reconciled with individual variability. As will become increasingly clear in later sections, it is one of the theoretical aims of this chapter to demonstrate that the concept of resilience can be understood as the crucial theoretical link between continuity and change.

However, development can also be characterized by phenotypic discontinuity, that is, by disruption or innovation. Innovation is perhaps the classic constitutive concept of development. From Piaget to Erikson and Havighurst, when the individual is confronted with a new challenge, "crisis," or "developmental task" (Erikson, Erikson, & Kivnick, 1986; Havighurst, 1973; Labouvie-Vief, 1982; Levinson, 1978; Oerter, 1986) that disturbs its "equilibrium," he or she has to assimilate the disturbing information or accommodate the disturbed part of the system. By doing so, the individual develops toward a new level (often characterized as a higher level) of intellectual or personal functioning. It is the crisis that promotes development. For instance, the transfer from school to an employment context in late adolescence presents the individual with an array of new tasks and challenges, as well as opportunities that have to be dealt with, that require adaptation of concepts and competencies, and that, in short, force development. Retirement or children leaving home are further examples of life changes with developmental consequences.

In this context, the term "continuity" bears potential for misunderstanding. Besides connoting constancy and stability (as opposed to change), it can also signify *continuous change*. For example, the decrease of mobility and sensory functions in later adulthood (P. B. Baltes, Lindenberger, et al., 1998; Lindenberger & Baltes, 1994) occurs, under normal conditions at least, not suddenly, from one moment to the next, but as a *continuous* process. As such, it requires—and at the same time facilitates—*permanent* adaptation of the developmental system (i.e., the organism itself, the internal self-representation, physical and social support systems). Thus, continuity can also be interpreted as a process of change without reversals or gaps. Because this is probably the most typical form of developmental process (we usually do not even recognize that we are "currently developing"), continuity can in a certain sense be considered an essential part of development, even if the concept of development should entail qualitative changes. As will become clearer in later sections, this is one of the reasons resilience is not a phenomenon separate from development, but is itself a developmental concept.

Finally, continuity, stability, and change depend on the level of observation. Whereas a certain process can be viewed as continuous from one perspective, is can appear as changing from another (Brandtstädter & Greve, 1994b; Lerner, 1984). For instance, although a tightrope walker's progress along the high wire appears to be completely continuous (stable), at the level of neuronal and muscular phenomena almost everything is in motion (unstable). In short, development as a phenomenon does not depend on the immediate visibility of dramatic changes. Rather, phenotypic stability (say, of personality) can be, and often is, precisely the result of developmental processes that enable and maintain this stable aspect of the person (P. B. Baltes, Staudinger, & Lindenberger, 1999; Greve, 2005). In turn, phenotypic continuity and stability as well as discontinuities can result from interactive processes that combine—that is, integrate—both stable and variable components. Thus, one central tenet of the life span developmental perspective is that we can never infer stable causes from stable outcomes or variable causes from observable changes.

Multidirectionality and Multidimensionality of Life Span Development

If lifelong development always entails gains and losses, then every conception that claims that development is confined to gains and to one universal goal, that is, a higher state of functioning, is rendered untenable. Numerous concepts from developmental psychology do, however, contain precisely this implication, such as the concept of

"maturing out" (Vaillant, 1993). One consequence of the life span approach is that such concepts can be applied only to specifically defined domains, for example, to the maturation of specific organs or the development of basic competencies (e.g., walking, digestive control, sexual maturation). When various domains of functioning are considered together, however, one must assume that development is multidirectional at one point in time, which is obviously true within individual domains of functioning as well. Thus, the differentiation between fluid and crystallized intelligence (P.B. Baltes, Staudinger, & Lindenberger, 1999) shows that in the domain of cognitive abilities, different developmental trajectories exist for different aspects. Similar differentiations have been suggested for the area of personality development (Cloninger, 2003; Staudinger & Pasupathi, 2000).

The concept of multidirectionality is inextricably linked to conceiving development as multidimensional. Not only does a one-sided focus on individual domains of functioning (e.g., intellectual capacities) ignore the multifacetedness and heterogeneity of developmental processes, it also causes salient interactions between different domains of functioning to be missed entirely. The close interaction between cognition and sensory functioning or between cognition and motor performance are two illustrations of this. Development is based on three major influences: biology, culture, and the developing individual. These three forces vary in their importance between domains of functioning and depending on chronological age. For instance, the pragmatic component of cognitive functioning is more strongly based on cultural than on biological influences, whereas for the mechanic component, the opposite is the case (e.g., P. B. Baltes, 1987). Only through this multidimensionality can multidirectionality, as discussed previously, ultimately be understood. Thus, during adolescence, for example, an increase in some abilities (e.g., physical strength, sexual maturing) is accompanied by a decrease in others (e.g., ease of language acquisition)—a further example of the permanently fluid gain : loss ratio.

Numerous findings do, however, favor the idea that this individual gain : loss ratio worsens steadily over the life course; as we age, we register this as well (Heckhausen, Dixon, & Baltes, 1989). One should not jump to hasty conclusions here, however: Individuals register their particular losses in a *domain-specific* manner. If we add up all of these individually registered losses (see Brandtstädter et al., 1993), we see that with increasing age, the losses outweigh the gains—objectively, as it were. But in assessing these losses, the individual weights them individually (and metaphorically speaking, the weight of some losses may even be 0), such that the *individual* balance may differ significantly from the objective balance. In addition, individuals tend not to assess all domains in a balanced manner. Instead, as a rule, we focus on one specific domain (which explains why one's current self-image within the "working self" can vary so widely from situation to situation; Hannover & Kühnen, 2005). It all depends, in other words, on one's internal, subjective evaluation and perspective. We return to this in greater detail later, as this aspect already hints at a process that is central to resilience (with regard to specific domains). For the purposes of our argument at this stage, however, it is important to note that the respective domain-specific losses are not in general denied or refuted: Defensive coping strategies (e.g., Haan, 1977; Vaillant, 1993) may sometimes be useful for practical purposes (e.g., Lazarus & Golden, 1981) but are not the major force underlying resilience.

Inter- and Intraindividual Variability of Life Span Development

This leads to a further point of pivotal importance for the study of resilience at an advanced age from the life span perspective. Human beings differ among themselves, in some cases considerably, and not just at particular points in time but also with regard to entire developmental trajectories. There are significant interindividual differences in the magnitude, timing, sequencing, and even directionality of change throughout the life span. Interindividual differences tend to increase as we age. Whereas some people are able to preserve their intellectual acuity and mental abilities up to an extremely advanced age, others already begin to show decreased mental faculties at a very early age. Even if one can generalize that negative changes are to be expected and are therefore normal in some cognitive domains (memory, speed of information processing, concentration) in the 7th and 8th decades of life (Salthouse, 1991), some people experience these changes earlier than others, and others experience them to a lesser degree or not at all (Nelson & Dannefer, 1992; Schaie, 1996).

In addition, there is a significant level of *intraindividual variability* in these changes *between* different domains (Nesselroade, 1989). The domain- and age-specific intraindividual variability of development is important as it demonstrates the plasticity of development, a central precondition for resilience to occur. An individual's intellectual performance on an achievement test can vary dramatically depending on the prevailing personal and situational conditions (e.g., distraction, fear, fatigue, preparation, practice, disturbances). Furthermore, this domain-specific intraindividual variability helps to prevent stark generalizations from becoming established stereotypes. It is not necessarily given

that a person experiencing deterioration processes in one functional domain will also show functional losses in all others as well. A person who is physically frail, for example, can still remain intellectually alert, creative, and productive (e.g., Smith & Baltes, 1993).

In summary, the concepts of multidimensionality, multidirectionality, and, in particular, interindividual and intraindividual variability indicate that an almost infinite variety of developmental constellations can emerge. The degree of phenotypically recognizable individuality tends to increase over the life course (at least up to age 85), first because the individualizing (nonnormative) influences of the biography cumulatively increase, and second because the canalizing effect of preformed biological dispositions decreases (P. B. Baltes, 1993, 1997; Staudinger & Lindenberger, 2003b).

Development as Dynamic Change of Individual- and Domain-Specific Gain : Loss Ratios

What may be the central hypothesis of the life span perspective on human development is that the numerous changes people experience in the course of their lives do not have any a priori fixed directionality. Even in particular domains or phases of development that appear very uniform (e.g., learning to walk in the first 12 months of life), there is actually a high degree of individual variability: Strongly divergent trajectories can always emerge (e.g., with hereditary physical disabilities), and changes beyond midlife show that physical mobility does not demonstrate generally "upward" development over the entire life span. Each area can show gains, stability, or losses in each phase of development, both objectively and subjectively. From the perspective of the approach taken here, development consists of a highly interlinked system of changes in different directions that can have different consequences—either positive or negative—from case to case (P. B. Baltes, 1987, 1997; Staudinger & Lindenberger, 2003a; Weinert, 1994). As will become clear in this chapter, although processes of resilience ensure in many ways that the individual achieves a tolerable or even satisfactory final result overall, these diverse mechanisms naturally also contain the potential for maladaptive and dysfunctional processes. Developmental psychopathology thus seeks to identify the risk factors and developmental constellations that render individuals vulnerable and can lead to pathological development trajectories (Cicchetti, 1993; Cicchetti & Garmezy, 1993; Jessor, 1993; Rutter, 1987). This is precisely the point where developmental psychopathology and life span developmental psychology meet.

The perspective discussed here—that development should be conceptualized as a dynamic system of gain : loss ratios (Smith, 2003)—goes far beyond merely establishing the existence of multidirectionality within and between different domains of development. It aspires to the idea that the processes of human development can be understood only when the organism and the environment with which it interacts are understood as a complex developmental system (e.g., Ford & Lerner, 1992; Lerner et al., 2003). The different developmental domains discussed earlier interact with the environmental resources that are affected or involved in each particular case, and this creates the dynamic system of gains and losses. In addition, the individual's resources (energy, time, material resources, etc.) are always limited (P. B. Baltes & Baltes, 1990; Staudinger et al., 1995), and thus each investment decision for a task in one domain at least implies opportunity costs that usually also result in losses in other domains (e.g., Brandtstädter & Wentura, 1995; for an economic perspective on human development, see Berman, 2003). As it is not possible to do everything, it is necessary to make choices that will in turn result in other decisions and thus canalize development (cf. Edelman, 1987; Waddington, 1975) and possibly have ripple effects far beyond the development domain originally considered. Thus, even these kinds of investments, which bring about gains (e.g., practicing the piano, which leads to an improvement of playing skills and possibly increased overall musicality and pleasure from music), also imply losses (during the same period of time, one has played less sports, cultivated fewer social contacts, read or danced less). In the extreme case, this can lead to a one-sided and premature draining of resources: Someone who "gives everything" to reach a goal pays a high price in the end, even if the goal is ultimately achieved (e.g., the father who neglects his wife and children, not to mention his own health, to meet his career objectives), and may realize too late that the goal was not worth the price. If this individual does not achieve the goals for which he has made so many sacrifices, he or she may lose everything. Furthermore, many resources diminish with age (Baltes, 1997; Staudinger et al., 1995): physical resources in particular, as we will see later, but social resources as well. This process increases the probability of risk constellations and in turn alters the conditions for resilience and recovery under threatening and burdening circumstances.

Influences on Individual Development: The Interaction between Biological Disposition, Sociocultural Context, and Volitional Action

Developmental contextualism (Lerner & Kauffman, 1985; Reese & Overton, 1970; Riegel, 1976) and other approaches share the central assumption that development is always the product of a complex interaction between nature and nurture, genes and environment, individual and social influences. The evaluation of a given behavior or behavioral change has always to refer to a certain context; this is true particularly when categorizing a given behavior or pattern of adaptation as psychopathological (Cicchetti & Aber, 1998). A certain attribute or competence may be considered helpful and adaptive in one environment or situation, but maladaptive or a burden in another. For instance, the goal to overcome obstacles and to stick tenaciously to one's purposes may help in finally reaching one's goals in situations that do not exceed one's resources (e.g., in a complicated professional task), but the very same goal will lead to a fruitless exhaustion of resources in unconquerable situations (e.g., if a professional boxer who has grown older attempts to regain his former championship). The context dependency of development has often been discussed from an evolutionary point of view. Here, it is rather clear that a certain adaptation produced by evolutionary changes (e.g., attributes of a large predator among the dinosaurs) can become useless or even an obstacle for survival if the environment changes dramatically (e.g., Gould, 1989). For the psychological perspective on development pursued throughout this chapter, context should not be viewed as monolithic and deterministic, but as a complex, closely interlinked system; as a concept, it embraces physical, biological, and sociocultural aspects (Bronfenbrenner, 1979; Lawton & Nahemow, 1973).

More than half a century ago, Havighurst (1953) differentiated among three types of developmental tasks that structure the human life course (Heckhausen & Lang, 1994). The concrete list of tasks, which he assigned to different phases of development following the developmental psychology Zeitgeist and in particular the work of Erikson (1959), must be seen not only as anachronistic but also as irredeemable in view of its ambition to posit a completely self-contained system of universally valid truths. Nevertheless, the fundamental idea that development is guided by tasks or challenges (Erikson used the term "crises") retains its validity to this day. Havighurst differentiated among biologically conditioned, socially conditioned, and individually set tasks. A slightly expanded version of this notion can be found in modern approaches that differentiate among different internal and external influences on human development (P. B. Baltes, Cornelius, & Nesselroade, 1979; P. B. Baltes, Lindenberger, et al., 1998; P. B. Baltes et al., 1980). In general, one can distinguish among age-graded, history-graded, and nonnormative influences that can either concern biological or cultural aspects of development (Brandtstädter, 1990, 1998). Although scientists, despite our long-standing interest in this perspective, are only just now beginning to understand the biological, that is, in particular, the genetic preconditions for development (e.g., Gottlieb, 1998; McClearn, 2003; Plomin, DeFries, McClearn, & McGuffin, 2001), there is a long tradition of studying the social conditions and contextual factors of development. The third category of developmental task (autonomous or self-defined tasks), however, has long been neglected and was not systematically taken into account. Only very recently has an action-oriented perspective on human development been articulated in more detail (Brandtstädter, 1998; Brandtstädter & Lerner, 1999).

Biology and Development: The Interaction between Predisposition and Environment

Obviously, human development occurs in a complex context. Even genetically predetermined developmental trajectories are fundamentally dependent on the right contextual conditions in order to unfold (cf. Anastasi, 1958). This applies not only to the extreme state of biological immaturity in which people are born, making them dependent on supportive conditions (and especially on other people) much longer than other animals in order to reach maturity (P. B. Baltes, 1997; Staudinger & Lindenberger, 2003a); this is also true of the immediate preconditions required for the genetic code to unfold. Without the right conditions in the cellular environment (cytoplasm, ribosomes), the DNA sequence that leaves the cell's nucleus cannot be translated into RNA sequences (which in turn code for the particular amino acids only under specific conditions) and thus does not transmit its information (McClearn, 2003). Thus, genes need specific environmental conditions to develop their potentials. The extreme heterogeneity of the environment, especially on the level of the individual organism, is the basis for the emergence of the impressive heterogeneity of the human phenotype and its developmental trajectories. Conversely, the high level of human variability and plasticity is the adaptive response to the fact that environments are not only heterogeneous but also changeable.

When it comes to determining the strength of influences, be it biological or cultural, the field of behavior genetics is called for (e.g., Plomin & Caspi, 1999). Several studies suggest that interindividual variance of personality traits (i.e., among those who have been investigated) can be explained by genetic variance to an amount of 40% to 50% (Plomin & Caspi, 1999), and this share stays stable or even slightly decreases across the life span (Pedersen & Reynolds, 1998). To put such a result into perspective, however, it must be emphasized that the relationship between genetic factors and the environment is one of complex interaction (which takes place at many different intermediate

levels; Asendorpf, 1999; McClearn, 2003). Among the numerous assumptions on which arguments for heritability are typically based, the assumption of the *additive* effects of genotype and environment in particular is either false or at least drastically simplified and thus misleading (Plomin & Caspi, 1999). Even the activation of genes depends on the environment, including the presence and activation of other genes (Caspi, 1998; Scarr & McCartney, 1983). An illustrative example of the interplay between genetic disposition and environment is the metabolic disorder phenylketonuria (PKU; cf. McClearn, 2003; Plomin & Caspi, 1999; Plomin & Crabbe, 2000; Plomin, DeFries, et al., 2001). Due to the lack of a specific enzyme, the body is unable to adequately break down the substance phenylalanine, which is found in many foods. The unduly high concentration of this substance in turn damages the developing brain to an irreparable degree (according to current knowledge) and leads to a severe impairment and reduction of cognitive abilities. There is no disagreement that PKU is genetically determined, but by maintaining a diet low in phenylalanine, its effects on cognitive development can practically be neutralized (Weglage, 2000). To formulate this in abstract terms, the development of the phenotype (in this case, important cognitive functions) can follow a completely normal development (i.e., no different than for individuals without this disposition) despite an unfavorable genetic disposition if the environment (in this case, nutrition) fits in a differentially adaptive manner. This shows that the question of whether genetic disposition or environment is responsible for the development of intelligence is formulated in misleading terms: It is the interaction (in a technical metaphor, the multiplication rather than the addition) of the two factors that brings forth the phenotype. Precisely because of the defect, the emergence of the phenotype—that is, cognitive development—is *crucially* dependent here on environmental conditions (normally, the type of nutrition has a less severe impact on cognitive development). This example is not intended to contest the significance of genetic determinants (vulnerabilities). Rather, it demonstrates how and to what degree they are relevant (Plomin, DeFries, et al., 2001).

Of course, it is also important not to overlook the fact that environments are, by and large, fairly stable (at least when compared to the average human life expectancy). Independent of the arguments presented earlier, this alone can explain much of why adult personality configurations are so stable: There are few reasons to change, and certainly not to change drastically, and these reasons to change become fewer and fewer as we grow older (Roberts & Caspi, 2003). Ultimately, and not least of all, individuals *choose* their environments; they *seek them out* systematically, *influence,* and *change* them (Caspi, 1998; Rowe, 1997; Scarr & McCartney, 1983). The person-environment interactions discussed here can be grouped into at least three categories (Roberts & Caspi, 2003): reactive interactions (people react to the environment as they perceive it), evocative interactions (the social environment reacts to individuals specifically, i.e., in different ways to different people), and proactive interactions (people seek out and create environments, e.g., partnerships). This is particularly true, as the example of PKU vividly demonstrates, when understanding of the mechanisms through which genetic dispositions function informs decisions or intentional changes in environmental conditions (e.g., nutrition in this example; Plomin & Caspi, 1999). To date, empirical study of the interactions (among genes, among environments, and particularly between genes and environments) has barely been attempted, and the majority of studies are still based on an oversimplified and misleading additive model (Gottlieb, 1998).

Social Context Matters: The Interdependence of Individual and Social Developmental Norms

In line with the interactive point of view outlined in the previous section, genetic conditions at best merely demarcate the framework for the individual's processes of change and development (the so-called norm of reaction). Influences of the physical and social environment determine how the individual phenotype is actually shaped and changed. This highlights the influence of social context on individual development. Biological and sociocultural influences can be subdivided according to the earlier mentioned categories, that is, age-graded, history-graded, and nonnormative.

Age-graded biological influences are, for instance, puberty and menopause. *History-graded* biological influences include, for instance, secular trends in physical development such as changes in the average age when menses begins and the dramatic secular trend toward increased life expectancy in the twentieth century (Maier & Vaupel, 2003). Similarly, the availability of food can vary dramatically according to time and region (Elder & O'Rand, 1995) and, either as a result of this availability or completely independent thereof, can differ according to cultural customs of food distribution, preparation, and preferences (Garner, Garfinkel, Schwartz, & Thompson, 1980). Of course, here as well, social influences ultimately explain these trends in development, but in individual development, these aspects appear as biological influences (or developmental tasks). *Nonnormative* biological influences include the results of climate change on development, demanding not only cul-

tural adaptation in the regions affected (e.g., modified hunting practices among the inhabitants of the northern Arctic Circle, storm-proof homes in areas with a higher probability of severe storms) but also individual efforts at adjustment. It is thus important to always keep in mind the embeddedness of development in its particular historical context (P. B. Baltes, 1997). This is true both on the general and the individual level: Both social and biological influences always operate against the background of the particular influences that preceded them. A sudden dramatic change in nutrition has entirely different effects on the development of an individual whose physical development and maturation has already progressed relatively far under relatively good conditions than it does on a newborn baby. Similarly, the outbreak of an epidemic will obviously have completely different consequences depending on whether an antidote or treatment has already been found for the disease.

Let's now turn to sociocultural influences. *Age-graded* social influences are, first of all, explicit social age norms such as the legal regulations governing retirement age (for employees in public service jobs, but in many cases also for standard contractual employment relations), which force active working life to end even if the individual in question feels fully capable and productive and is also motivated to continue working. Implicit social age norms are socially agreed-upon guidelines that define which ways of behaving in late adulthood and old age are deemed appropriate and socially acceptable.

History-graded social influences are events of overarching importance (wars, economic crises, major political changes such as the fall of the Berlin Wall in 1989). The influence of such events depends not only on particular preconditions at the personal level (especially previous experiences and currently available resources) but also on the particular point in the individual's biography at which this experience occurs. A severe economic crisis, for example, could bring about nutritional difficulties and result in specific shortages (e.g., a vitamin deficiency). Adults may experience some limitations due to such events, but usually they are not severely debilitated, whereas newborn babies and especially unborn children in an exceptionally vulnerable phase of physical development may suffer irreparable damage (e.g., in brain or organ development). The same is true for phases of economic decline that create a lack of job training opportunities for young people, in some cases robbing an entire age cohort of their long-term opportunities, whereas previous and following cohorts are affected little if at all. *Nonnormative* social influences, such as an escalating social conflict or the meeting of a person (e.g., a future life partner or mentor) who will dramatically influence the individual's further development, do not occur on a regular basis and thus can neither be predicted nor planned for.

According to Glen Elder (1994, p. 5), "Overall the life course can be viewed as a multilevel phenomenon, ranging from structured pathways through social institutions and organizations to the social trajectories of individuals and their developmental pathways." Although this is uncontroversial today, it remains unclear how these various levels interact. How do changing societies impact individual development, and conversely, how do individual life courses impact society? One of the most promising hypotheses relating to this question claims that social norms shape individual developmental pathways. The individual life course follows a timetable or calendar that is segmented and geared to follow individual and social (developmental) norms, that is, normative guidelines as to what is and is not appropriate or necessary at a particular time and for a particular person (e.g., Heckhausen, 1999; Neugarten, 1979; Neugarten et al., 1965; Settersten & Mayer, 1997). However, it is useful to differentiate here among several aspects. Social norms and their accompanying sanctions influence individual norms. Individual norms regulate individual intentions and thus individual actions. These, in turn, influence or produce life course events that shape the individual's development.[1]

Many developmental norms are merely descriptive norms: It is "normal" to go through puberty at the age of 14, but this normality varies according to time and context. Descriptive norms shape the course of human development, not by implementing prescriptions, but simply as a matter of fact. These norms should therefore be investigated; they may ultimately be proven false, or true only within certain specific historical and cultural contexts. Social tasks constitute a second type of developmental norm: They are prescriptive norms and impose a schedule on individual development by setting times for certain life transitions, for example, school age, voting age, and retirement age. These norms can be violated but not falsified. Some prescriptive social tasks, although nevertheless obligatory, are much less explicit. They involve the subjective experience and evaluation of social prescriptions regarding what is appropriate or necessary at which particular age, and so

on. Four groups of developmental norms can be identified in particular:

1. *Age norms:* "Act your age!" Age norms are prescriptions or proscriptions about behavior to keep people on track or on time in the normative life course or to bring them back into line (Settersten & Mayer, 1997). It may prove useful to differentiate between appropriate or even optimal ages and age margins, that is, upper and lower limits of when it is acceptable to engage in a certain behavior or to decide on taking a certain step. Settersten and Hägestad (1996) define these margins as "cultural age deadlines"; when considering social norms as well as biological realities, such deadlines may be called "developmental deadlines" (Heckhausen, 1999; Wrosch & Heckhausen, 1999).

2. *Sequencing norms:* "Who follows whom?" Some sequences in human development follow a logically or naturally fixed order. For example, one cannot learn to read a clock before having learned to count to 12, understand the concept of hours, minutes, and seconds, and tell the difference between the long and short hands on analog clocks. Reversing this sequence is logically impossible. To cite a further example, a woman must possess certain physical features in order to give birth, and in this case, the reverse sequence is impossible due not to logical but to biological reasons. Other sequences may vary from one individual to another; for example, it is largely a matter of personal choice whether an individual first finishes higher education or first gets married or has children. However, social norms determine the sequence of these life course transitions and thus their respective presuppositions ("You cannot marry before first finishing college and finding a job!").

3. *Quantum norms:* "How much is enough?" One of the most important quantum norms is the socially shared belief about the optimal, minimal, and maximal number of children a family should have. A norm that has been changing rapidly over the past century applies to the number of successive marital partners. Up to the beginning of the twentieth century, the specific number—both minimum and maximum—was one (with notable exceptions, such as Henry VIII in England in the sixteenth century). It seems that, during the past century, two or three is becoming more and more common and thus "normal"; even six or seven successive marriages have become acceptable (at least among film celebrities).

4. *Perceived* chronological age is, along with gender, one of the first categories that can be used to categorize a person at first glance (Neugarten, 1968; Settersten, 1997;

---

[1] However, it is important to look at the reverse direction as well. The actual course of the individual development influences how the individual evaluates his or her development, and this in turn shapes the individual's developmental norms (Kalicki, 1996).

Settersten & Mayer, 1997). Chronological age is in almost all societies segmented into phases of social age (Neugarten & Hagestad, 1976; Neugarten, Moore, & Lowe, 1965). The transitions between social age phases are often marked by rites of initiation (e.g., to manhood).

The notion of social time is based on the meanings of age, and refers to the ordering of events and social roles by age-linked expectations, sanctions and options. The variable meanings of age represent social constructs, which take the form of age norms and sanctions, and social timetables for the occurrence and arrangements of events. (Elder, 1978, pp. 25–26)

Thus, the concept of social time implies the addition of content to chronological time. Its function is, of course, to segment and structure the individual's life course and, at the same time, to coordinate social functions, roles, tasks, and duties among individuals of different ages.

The resulting age-status systems, in their simplest form, apply a sequence of specific roles to the process of aging and attaches to them specific norms and expectations. An adult is expected to be financially independent, and an older person is expected not to go out dancing to a discotheque at night. These age-related roles are partly explicit (e.g., voting age), partly implicit (e.g., age of first pregnancy). This structure is not deterministic, however, particularly in modern societies. "Social differentiation in complex societies takes the form of plural age structures and timetables, across institutional spheres, and underscores the utility of a multidimensional concept of the life course, a concept of interdependent life paths, which vary in synchronization" (Elder, 1975, p. 173).

Social developmental norms affect the individual's development in various ways. First, they will show indirect effects. Cultural and political policy decisions based (at least partially) on social norms as perceived by decision makers influence the actual developmental courses of individuals throughout society (e.g., retirement age; Jacobs, Kohli, & Rein, 1991). Second, "social institutional constraints provide time-ordered opportunity structures for certain life-course events and thus form part of the 'sociostructural scaffolding' of life-course development" (Heckhausen & Schulz, 1999, p. 81).

Bernice Neugarten (1979; Neugarten & Hagestad, 1976) has aptly termed this structuralizing power of social age norms for individual behavior and development the "social clock." There exists what might be called a "prescriptive timetable for the time ordering of major life events: A time in the life span when men and women are expected to marry, a time to raise children, a time to retire" (Neu-

garten, Moore, & Lowe, 1965, p. 711). The core assumption of the social clock approach focuses on deviations from the social timetable. Individuals who are too early or too late experiencing a certain event or transition suffer consequences. These range from explicit negative social sanctions (e.g., punishment, social exclusion, stigmatization) to intrapersonal problems (e.g., low self-esteem because of negative social comparisons: "I'm still not married!") and reduced interpersonal resources (e.g., reduced social support). This leads to a second argument. If a person is off with respect to the timing of certain life events or transitions, social comparison processes highlight a significant difference between this individual and most of the people around him or her (Brandtstädter & Greve, 1994a; Heckhausen, 1990; Heckhausen & Schulz, 1999; Neugarten & Hagestad, 1976). These social comparisons force attributional processes in order to explain the difference registered by the individual and his or her social environment.

However, modern societies are characterized by a steadily increasing de-institutionalization (Held, 1986; Settersten & Mayer, 1997). One result is a separation between cycles of family development and of work development that is leading to an increased differentiation of life courses. The "normalization" of the individual life course (Held, 1986) through age norms is thus becoming less effective, and perhaps overall less important. Neugarten and Hagestad (1976) speak about an "age-irrelevant society" (see also Neugarten, 1979), in which social developmental norms have decreased in obligation or increased in variance over the past 100 years or so: "Over the last century, everyday ideas about what constitutes the 'normal' biography have become less clear" (Settersten & Mayer, 1997, p. 234). Sociocultural age-related developmental norms vary among cultures and societies to a large degree. To refer to a well-known example, a 14-year-old girl in our culture is a schoolgirl, whereas in other countries, perhaps in India, she may already be married and the mother of her first child. These age norms vary as well *within* particular societies between historical periods and social conditions. For example, the concept of childhood was largely unknown up to the seventeenth century; prior to that, children were perceived—and treated—simply as little adults (Neugarten, 1979).

Action and Development: Intentional Self-Regulation

The very idea that social norms influence individual developmental patterns implies an action-oriented approach to human development. Prescriptive norms are *reasons for actions,* not only causes for behavior (Brandtstädter, 1998;

Elder, 1994; Greve, 2001). There is now broad consensus that human development is not a uniformly operating, irreversible sequence of stages and phases, but a process that individuals themselves actively influence in substantial ways (Ford & Lerner, 1992). This may be termed the "action perspective" on human development (Brandtstädter, 1998, 2002; Brandtstädter & Lerner, 1999). In this view, individuals can be regarded as "co-producers of their development" (Featherman & Lerner, 1985), shaping and altering their scope of action within the framework set by their actual and perceived opportunities and thus substantially steering their own paths through life. Accordingly, not only does the objective framework play an important role in the individual's development (the opportunities and constraints created by his or her environment and by his or her own competences and deficiencies); personal developmental goals are decisive as well. In terms of both timing and content, individuals structure their own development by recognizing and assigning themselves developmental tasks.

From an action perspective on human development (Brandtstädter, 1998, 2001; Brandtstädter & Lerner, 1999; Greve, 2005), adulthood is characterized by an exceptionally high importance of self-defined and actively pursued developmental goals and tasks. What people do often has far-reaching consequences for them. For example, the decision to quit a job or to move to a new city can impact further development, sometimes substantially altering the individual's entire future life. The interesting point goes beyond the mere interactional quality of human behavior and human development. In some cases, individuals not only foresee but actually intend the regulatory effects of their actions on their development: These outcomes are the precise aim of the action. I make the decision to study a specific subject and act on this decision to bring me closer to my developmental goal, that is, to become an expert in my chosen field. In other words, action volitionally changes, influences, and contributes to my development.

On the one hand, intervening action can be motivated not only by perceived but also by anticipated developmental problems, for example in a preventive action mode. Furthermore, behavior-initiating discrepancies are not simply passively experienced as "deviations." In fact, they can be purposefully generated and self-defined, as, for instance, when the orientation toward ideals forms the basis for targeted "upward comparisons" and similar behavioral and developmental incentives (see also Bandura, 1989). Self-defined discrepancies are typically coupled with the individual's conviction of being able to develop in the direction

of a positive contrasting image; that is, they stimulate individuals to posit corresponding *learning goals* (Dweck & Legget, 1988). Experienced actual/ought discrepancies can admittedly be redressed in different ways. They can be approached through an active problem-oriented altering of an actual situation or, conversely, through the changing of goals and aspirations (Brandtstädter, 1998; Brandtstädter & Rothermund, 2002). This latter mode is, in many cases, overlooked in behavior theory models because the dissolution or reevaluation of goals, the adjustment of demands—although fundamental for behavior regulation—in itself cannot be regarded as intentional behavior (we address this point in detail later).

On the other hand, enabling people to *act* is not only the outcome but the central function of development. All the changes that people pass through between birth and early adulthood that show and constitute their growth can be understood as integral components of the basis, evolution, and expansion of their ability to act (Bandura, 1999). In middle adulthood, it becomes increasingly necessary to stabilize and secure this ability. Although it is possible to progressively differentiate and expand the preconditions and competencies for action and thus to continue developing into later adulthood and old age, the importance of defending the status quo and compensating for the onset of subjective and objective decline in capacities and competences increases at the same time, to safeguard a sense of personal continuity and identity and thus to ensure personal well-being (Brandtstädter, 1999a; Greve et al., 2005; Staudinger et al., 1995).

Intentional behavior is thus of interest to developmental psychology research and theory, not only because of the inherent value in understanding the genesis of intentional behavior and changes in behavior-guiding orientations (goals, value orientations, convictions) throughout the life span, but also to answer the question of what role intentional behavior plays in shaping personal development. Behavior theory concepts such as "personal projects" (Little, 1999), "self-guides" (E. T. Higgins, 1996), and personal life instruments (Staudinger, 1999c) provide promising access to the developmental psychology of adulthood. Here it is fundamental to assume not only that ontogenesis operates automatically, so to speak, on and within individuals, but also that individuals actively shape the course of their own development (see Brandtstädter, 1998, 2001; Brandtstädter & Lerner, 1999). The theoretical focus of an action perspective on human development takes the idea of a transactional influence on one's own development (for a detailed account, see Roberts & Caspi, 2003; Staudinger & Pasupathi, 2000) one step further. Development and individual action are related to one another in a causal and at the same time in an intentional way: Through our behavior, we not only actuate factual causal effects, which then partially determine our future lives and behavioral histories; our activities also explicitly aim to shape our development (and indeed, to actively shape the self) in a specific way (Brandtstädter, 1998, 2001). This intentional aspect of developmentally relevant action assumes that individuals have formed conceptual representations of themselves and their lives, that is, notions as to what their lives could and should be. Furthermore, this intentional self-development also means that these feedback processes are not merely registered by the developing person but are subject to systematic considerations and intention formation and thus in a stricter sense are the results of development-related actions (Greve et al., 2005).

At first glance, this seems to contradict the frequently replicated findings regarding the high stability (and thus predictability) of adult identity and personality (Pervin & John, 1999). The available evidence indicates that adults behave so consistently over longer periods of time and also exhibit comparatively robust and increasing stability with age, regardless of these methodological and empirical restrictions. This evidence should not be completely rejected (see Roberts & Caspi, 2003; Staudinger & Pasupathi, 2000). The question is whether it entails that there is *therefore* no development of the adult personality (P. B. Baltes, Lindenberger, et al., 1998). The trait approach, and in particular, the five-factor model, pursues the idea that no ontogenetic development of these basic factors worth mentioning *can* take place at all (after the individual's phenotype unfolds over the course of childhood and into early adulthood). McCrae and Costa (1996, p. 76) consistently argue that the question of personality development is a completely irrelevant research issue.

Several arguments suggest that this cannot be the final word on the subject. To begin with, it must once again be underscored that even optimistic estimates of diachronic stability are accompanied by a considerable amount of unresolved (and thus not stable) variance (a diachronic correlation of $r = .60$ implies a nonpredictable variation of 64%). As we argued previously, an additive (components of variance) model of development probably falls short precisely because it underestimates the interactional quality of the underlying processes. Thus, the stability of manifest behavior is not evidence for the stability of these explanatory variables, and certainly not for the stability of these causal traits (Greve, 2005). Human behavior can, as should become clear in this chapter, appear consistent even for dynamic reasons.

Many experiences and influences within the individual biography shape development in adulthood, not in the sense that they become unalterable at some point, but rather in that the interaction of the accumulated consequences of earlier effects and influences render a radical change increasingly less likely (this is another aspect of the historicity of development mentioned earlier: Development always takes place against the background of its *own* history). In this sense, Roberts and Caspi (2003; see also Caspi & Roberts, 1999) aptly speak of a "cumulative continuity." This cumulative continuity can, however, certainly be intended and deliberately brought about. The allocation of personal resources and efforts changes throughout the life course from a growth-oriented to an increasingly maintenance- and recovery-oriented strategy of personal resource investment (P. B. Baltes & Graf, 1996; P. B. Baltes, Lindenberger, et al., 1998; Staudinger et al., 1995). Development-related actions thus become a decisive factor in explaining the stable and consistent behavior of adults.

Precisely when development-related intentions are oriented toward attaining comprehensive goals that require long-term planning and action (such as career goals), or in a certain sense constitute "insatiable" (Gollwitzer, 1987) intentions (e.g., moral qualities such as faithfulness and honesty, which must constantly be proven), stability of behavior is explainable without having to refer back to a stable *trait* (e.g., honesty). Rather, the observed behavioral stability and high predictability would be explainable by the constant *motive* ("Be honest!"). Kant (1787/1998) employed this argument to point out that stability and predictability are not sufficient to demonstrate the fundamental unchangeability of the cause.

A central research issue, then, from the perspective of the concept of resilience is the relative stability of our comprehensive developmental goals and conceptions—of our self-concepts, life plans, and ideas of who we are and who we want to be—during adulthood. These self-perceptions, self-constructs, and self-plans obviously not only constitute the basis for how we present ourselves as individuals in the social context and therefore convey our personality in professional and everyday life, but also offer the central explanation for the essential consistency of personal behavior in different life contexts and phases. The literature on personality development in adulthood and old age (e.g., Bertrand & Lachman, 2003) has shifted from a documentation of greater stability (McCrae & Costa, 1987; Roberts & DelVecchio, 2000) to an investigation of developmental processes that ensure stability (P. B. Baltes, Lindenberger, et al., 1998; Greve, 2005).

Plasticity of Development: Ranges, Limits, Reserve Capacities

Resilience implies adaptability. A prerequisite for adaptation is the plasticity of human development; that is, it is changeable according to the challenges and opportunities of developmental contexts (P. B. Baltes, 1987; P. B. Baltes, Lindenberger, et al., 1998; Lerner, 1984; Staudinger et al., 1995). Lerner discussed the concept of plasticity extensively some 20 years ago. He referred to Gottlieb's (1998) concept of "probabilistic epigenesis," which describes the fact that the development of each individual within a species is not compelled to follow a single course that is predetermined and identical for all species members, but rather can follow different paths within a "norm of reaction." The more complex the species' structure and the greater the organism's flexibility (e.g., the ability of individual elements of the system to learn, but also variability of interaction between system elements), the broader is the resulting variability of developmental trajectories. Of course, plasticity is evident at multiple levels of analysis. Plasticity has been demonstrated for highly complex phenomena, such as the self. But plasticity has empirically also been demonstrated at very basic levels of functioning. Curtis and Cicchetti (2003) have recently argued that phenomena of neural plasticity can—and have to—be integrated into any future theory of resilience with considerable scope.

The mark of this flexibility and plasticity is the ability to adapt to changed contextual circumstances, that is, to change with regard to specific aspects of the organism (traits, attributes, behavioral tendencies) in order to preserve (stabilize) central characteristics (criteria) of the organism, for example, environment-controlling capacities, general well-being, or health. In this regard, Cicchetti and Aber (1998) have aptly argued that individual flexibility and adaptability is challenged but, at the same time, supported by the fact that changing and varying contexts may demand and thus allow for various ways of adaptation.

Plasticity refers to the latent possibilities of individual development, to a range of possibilities and reserve capacities (Staudinger et al., 1995). As a neutral concept, plasticity comprises processes of falling below as well as of exceeding the normal developmental trajectories, and thus calls attention to processes of developmental optimization as well as developmental psychopathology. The concept of reserve capacity designates the retrievable, maximal individual range of possibilities under optimal developmental conditions (including the best possible support), which is, in a certain sense the positive half of plasticity. Note that the concept of plasticity also includes the notion of its own limits; its latitude is not infinite, not all changes are possi-

ble, and reserve capacity is not inexhaustible. In behavioral genetics (Plomin, De Fries, et al., 2001), this idea is defined through the concept of the "norm of reaction" (Lerner, 1984), which indicates the ontogenetic range of variability that is limited by the genetic makeup of the individual organism, or within which individual biographical conditions produce the interindividual variability and heterogeneity of developmental trajectories referred to earlier.

The concept of resilience focuses specifically on those conditions that ensure that "normal" development is maintained or recovered (we will return to issues of definition in the following section). Based on the understanding of plasticity just introduced, resilience covers those aspects of plasticity that are concerned with maintenance and recovery rather than surpassing natural development. Resilience is a crucial expression and result of plasticity. Resilience-based maintenance and recovery require a lot of adaptation and change. Normal reaction patterns must frequently be replaced by alternative (adaptive) forms of reaction to secure the original "desired" developmental state or course on a higher level. It is this "stabilization through change" that constitutes the salient feature of the phenomenon of resilience.

CONSTELLATIONS OF RESILIENCE: RESILIENCE AS A PRODUCT OF PERSON-CONTEXT INTERACTION

"Resilience is defined as a [person's] achievement of positive developmental outcomes and avoidance of negative outcomes, under significantly adverse conditions" (Wyman, Sandler, Wolchik, & Nelson, 2001, p. 133). Simply stated, resilience describes normal development under non-normal circumstances (compare also Olsson, Bond, Burns, Vella-Brodrock, & Sawyer, 2003). In a summary work, Luthar, Cicchetti, and Becker formulate this concept as follows: "a dynamic process encompassing positive adaptation within the context of significant adversity" (Luthar, Cicchetti, & Becker, 2000, p. 543). Although at first glance the basic idea seems clear, the literature, according to Luthar, Cicchetti, et al. (2000), has failed to reach consensus either on a unified conceptualization or (as a result) on a unified understanding of the central constructs (Lösel, Bliesener, & Köferl, 1989; Ryff et al., 1998). Perhaps because the viewpoint is relatively new, a process-oriented notion of resilience has been primarily studied indirectly on the basis of general patterns in empirical findings, rather than measured directly. As will become clear, this is problematic. In any case, it is crucial to first of all examine the concept of resilience more closely.

Remarks on Resilience: Outlining the Contours of the Concept

When discussing resilience as a basic concept for empirical research, we are confronted with a serious problem: the risk of circular logic. Why does one person survive a particular stressful developmental situation so undamaged while another does not? Because she is "resilient." How do I know and how can I decide that a particular person is resilient? By the fact that she survived this stressful developmental situation unscathed—if she had not been resilient, she would have been (more seriously) damaged by it. Actually, traces of this danger of circular logic can sometimes be identified in definitions of the concept ("protective factors are correlates of resilience"; Masten & Coatsworth, 1995, p. 737). It is possible to steer clear of this danger only by emphasizing that the concept of resilience initially just *designates* a complex process of resistance against stressful developmental conditions. The concept of resilience does not answer the question *why* specific conditions did not produce a negative effect; rather, it formulates this very question.

A more precise *description* of the *phenomenon* of resilience is not easy. To the contrary: resilience is at first glance an issue without an object, even without indicators. Its main theme is (to explain) the *lack* of something: the lack of negative consequences of a developmental experience or constellation that (for other individuals) is stressful, threatening, burdensome, or harmful. If some individuals suffer from the consequences of a certain experience and others do not, it is not clear whether the suffering persons possess or *do not possess* certain attributes, that is, vulnerabilities in the case of the former and protective resources in the latter. Any *difference* between the two (groups of) individuals can be interpreted either way, or so it seems.

Moreover, there are various broader and narrower conceptualizations of the concept of resilience. The terms used to formulate it range from "better-than-expected" development to descriptions of "well-recovered" individuals and "positive adaptation despite adversity" (Arrington & Wilson, 2002; Masten, 2002). Bonanno (2004) explicitly differentiates between recovery and resilience, while other authors even subsume growth processes under the concept of resilience (e.g., Ryff et al., 1998). Growth phenomena, however, even under adverse conditions, may *possibly* refer to resistance capacity, but may also indicate completely different processes, for example, growth stimulation by provoking discrepancies. To subsume these phenomena under the concept of resilience may therefore be misleading. Thus, it is conceptually safer to demarcate the two concepts from each other (Staudinger et al., 1995). Carver

(1998) has proposed applying the concept of "thriving" rather than "resilience" to those growth phenomena that occur under conditions of adversity.

As mentioned above, most conceptions resilience differentiate between the recovery of normal functioning ability subsequent to the suffering of a trauma, and the retention of the ability to function despite the presence of adverse circumstances. It seems to make sense, with regard to old age, to add a third form to these two: loss management (Staudinger et al., 1995). With increasing age, there are further adverse occurrences which bring with them irreversible losses, whether the loss of friends and relatives or of bodily, mental, and/or social functions. Success in dealing with such situations, that is, adapting at a lower level of functioning (but higher as one could have predicted given the adversity the individual has to cope with), which are indeed typical for this age, we would also subsume under constellations of resilience.

Nevertheless, even if the exact conceptual definitions and accordingly the methods of measurement diverge (for a summary, cf. Luthar et al., 2000), it does not mean that resilience is used here merely as an umbrella term encompassing completely disparate phenomena. In fact, there is probably little disagreement about the core meaning (in the sense of the definition outlined at the beginning of this section) of this phenomenon. If there exists basic agreement over the central conceptualization of this phenomenon, but various ways of measuring it for the purposes of scientific study, this can only help to further clarify the concept (regardless of whether the findings correspond entirely or not). On the contrary: the validity of one type of measurement can only be checked through others. As Luthar, Cicchetti, et al. (2000) have pointed out, this does not preclude that the members of the resilience research community should attempt to reach an agreement over a working definition.

The Object of Study: What Actually Is Resilience?

Even more confusion around the concept of resilience is generated through different accents in its content than through differences in its scope. In an overview, Kaplan (1999) describes two basic understandings of the concept. The first views "resilience as outcome," and here the criterion for the existence of resilience is a (sufficiently positive) result, for example in self-esteem, well-being, health, and so on. From this point of view, resilience is to be explained through various processes. The second understanding sees "resilience as the cause of an outcome," and here resilience is the concept that helps to explain an independently defined positive outcome. This source of misunderstanding is important to bear in mind (the concept of adaptation also has a similar double connotation).

With regard to the more frequently pursued second understanding, which we also adopt in this chapter, two general research approaches can be distinguished. The first, a *variable-* or *process-centered* research approach, investigates how aspects of the person (e.g., traits or abilities) and environment (e.g., social support) are connected with developmental consequences of certain adversities and risks (summarized in Aspinwall, 2001; Masten, 2001). Here we can draw a distinction between additive (cumulative) and interactive (especially mediator or moderator) models (Masten, 2001; Masten & Reed, 2002). There can be little doubt that interactive models are the "heart and soul of resilience" (Roosa, 2000, p. 567) much more than main effect or additive effect models. Each concrete domain can be further differentiated in detail (e.g., by distinguishing compensatory and neutralizing effects). Generally these approaches always consider the interrelationships among different aspects of a person, different people, and between people and the meso- and macro-aspects of their social and physical environments (Arrington & Wilson, 2000).

In contrast, the second, *person-centered* research approach looks at resilient individuals and attempts to determine what sets them apart from non-resilient individuals ("maladaptive personality functioning"; Widinger & Seidlitz, 2002). A classic example of this investigative paradigm is the Kauai longitudinal study (Werner, 1995; Werner & Smith, 1982, 1992, 2001). For this line of research, understanding resilience as a trait is thus logical. This conception is often referred to as "resiliency" (see Masten, 1994; Luthar et al., 2000), a term we therefore do not employ here.

One classic application of this latter approach is the concept of ego resilience (Block & Block, 1980; for an overview cf. also Luthar et al., 2000), which has also been taken up in various ways in the recent literature (e.g., Cicchetti & Rogosch, 1997; Fredrickson, Tugade, Waugh, & Larkin, 2003; Klohnen, 1996; Tugade & Fredrickson, 2004). This personality characteristic is often used with the connotation of a strong orientation toward action concepts like "ego control" and "self-regulation." Klohnen (1996) summarized this as follows: "resilient individuals have a sense of active and meaningful engagement with the world. Their positive and energetic approach to life is grounded in confident, autonomous, and competent functioning and a sense of mastery within a wide range of life-domains" (p. 1075). Kobasa (1979) has proposed a similar construct (also summarized by Aspinwall, 2001) with the

personality trait "hardiness." These individuals believe in their own potential to exercise influence and control, are committed to their activities and view change as a challenge (cf. Beasley, Thompson, & Davidson, 2003). Sharply and Yardley (1999) found, for example, that in older people, cognitive hardiness is a good predictor of happiness.

Within this research paradigm, empirical investigation of this phenomenon starts with epidemiological study of these resilience constellations and their empirical characteristics (e.g., Jessor, 1993; Rutter & Rutter, 1993). However, the four conceivable configurations of the two dimensions (high versus low risk, positive versus negative developmental outcome; cf. also von Eye & Schuster, 2000) designed to identify "resilient" individuals are seldom subjected to thorough examination, and particularly not longitudinally. For this reason, interactive or even merely cumulative effects will be harder to identify (and indeed impossible without longitudinal designs) than dominant (practically significant) protective "assets" or risk factors. It should also be taken into consideration that in the investigation of extreme groups, interaction effects could appear masked as main effects (Roosa, 2000).

Asendorpf and van Aken (1999) and Robins, John, Caspi, Moffitt, and Stouthamer-Loeber (1996) are current examples of investigations into personality-oriented resilience (in children as well as youth). However, these studies do not focus on a trait, which would offer a possible bridge to a variable-centered approach (as in the concept of ego-resilience; cf., e.g., also Cicchetti & Rogosch, 1997), but rather on a personality structure. Our argument is that this approach goes only part of the way conceptually: a situational and social constellation must be added to the intrapsychic constellation (cf. in this regard Masten & Garmezy, 1985; cf. also Luthar et al., 2000). Above all, however, developmental potential must be taken into consideration as well: What develops out of a stressful situation (Bonanno, 2004)? These potentials barely become apparent in longitudinal studies such as those by Asendorpf and van Aken (1999), precisely because resilience potential and resources (at least in part) only develop in situations of stress.

In fact, this separation of the research on resilience into person-oriented versus process-oriented approaches (Luthar et al., 2000) is unfortunate since a strictly person-oriented perspective that does not take processes into consideration cannot adequately conceptualize even the very idea of personality (Greve, 2005). Accordingly, numerous conceptions see personality less as a configuration of (stable) traits and more as a dynamic agentic system (e.g., Caprara & Cervone, 2003). A combination of both approaches on resilience therefore seems to be the most sensible (Masten, 2001; Masten & Reed, 2002), also because high-risk groups are few in numbers and thus seldomly encountered. Therefore, without targeted sampling, a process-centered approach would be unable to tap the full potential range of variance precisely in the areas of interest here: stressful and dangerous developmental conditions, and highly "successful" or "unsuccessful" developmental trajectories.

In fact, the differentiation between resilience as outcome, resilience as process, and protective factors can be fairly arbitrary (Staudinger, Marsiske, et al., 1993). Our understanding connects these approaches: here resilience is used as a designation for a developmental process, more precisely as a collective designation for the multitude of processes and the individual and social constellations affecting them, all of which share this characterization because they show a (relatively) positive developmental result despite the presence of unfavorable (adverse) conditions. Resilience is clearly not a simple one-dimensional construction (Luthar, Doernberger, & Zigler, 1993; Olsson et al., 2003; Rutter, 2000). It is obvious that "resilient children" who have developed adaptively in some domains sometimes show completely maladaptive patterns in others (Arrington & Wilson, 2000; Luthar et al., 2000; Tiét & Huizinga, 2002). This alone should clearly demonstrate not only the futility of attempting a comprehensive overall statement about what resilience is, but also and above all, the likelihood that such an enterprise would bear little fruit theoretically. Any given developmental outcome is always conditioned by multiple factors (Rutter, 2000); since it is always the case that more than one developmental path could have led to a given (intermediary) outcome, "the" resilience constellation is pure fiction.

However, the process-oriented definition of resilience (cf., e.g., Olsson et al., 2003) as proposed here brings with it one further problem: from this point of view, resilience "exists" in a strict sense only *if* stressful conditions occur (which are then successfully overcome). Thus, it appears that *potentials* for resilience are by definition impossible (a person- or a trait-oriented approach does not have this problem; Luthar et al., 2000). Once again the answer is that resilience is only the term used to designate a complex occurrence, which we strive to explain through the combination (i.e., interaction) of individual factors (perhaps including certain traits; Roosa, 2000). Provided that these types of factors are identified, their effects can be investigated separately and in combination or interaction (preferably in prospective designs). Frequently the concept of adaptation is contained in the definition as well (e.g., Arrington & Wilson, 2000, p. 225; Luthar et al.,

2000, p. 543; Masten, 2001, p. 228; Masten & Reed, 2002, p. 75), making a circular logic in the explanation almost unavoidable. Especially if "adaptive" is used only as a synonym for "positive outcome" (e.g., Affleck & Tennen, 1996), the potential explanatory value of the concept is lost. This explanatory value consists precisely in the fact that a certain type of adaptation (e.g., a change of semantic associations) of certain structures (such as the availability of self-defining attributes) in a certain way (e.g., through change in the probability of an affective priming of certain information) is causally responsible for a certain positive outcome (e.g., subjective well-being; e.g., Greve & Wentura, 2003). The scientific challenge for psychology is then to more precisely explain this developmental process with reference to concrete self-regulatory mechanisms and processes, that is, to uncover what exactly is concealed behind the macro-phenomenon of resilience. This implies among other things that "resilience" does not denote a real, ascertainable, or measurable entity or anything similar (Tarter & Vanyukov, 1999), and thus not a trait.

From our point of view (and in opposition to sharp critique: Glantz & Sloboda, 1999; Kaplan, 1999), resilience is an unusually useful concept. This is not because it designates a construct with special explanatory power; as we just argued, resilience designates an *explanandum,* not an *explanans.* Resilience is important, first of all, because it can describe a particularly interesting group of developmental phenomena (i.e., developmental trajectories), the identification and explanation of whose common features poses a challenge—but a potentially fruitful one—for developmental psychology. These phenomena could be a central reason for the impressive career of this concept in current debates, since it highlights developmental trajectories that are not only unpredictable but also even tend to run counter to theoretical prediction.

Second, the concept of resilience is especially useful and fruitful because it marks and can further stimulate a change in perspective in developmental psychology as well as in developmental psychopathology. According to the view entailed in the concept of resilience, development may frequently occur even when at first glance no substantial changes are observed. This may be able to tell us more about the processes that produce the changes than a perspective focused exclusively on observable changes. Stability and stabilization as developmental phenomena are closely linked with resilience. It thus follows that not only can resilience validly be applied to individuals (perhaps not even primarily to them); it also can (and should; Glantz & Sloboda, 1999) be applied to constellations, that is, the relation between risk factors, processes, and positive outcomes (Staudinger & Greve, 2001).

Third, in order to understand and explain phenomena of developmental psychopathology, the concept of resilience may support—and even shape—this endeavor in several respects. It reminds us that sometimes potentially harmful effects can be overseen or underestimated because the individuals "show" resilience. This may shift the focus when trying to explain certain maladaptive reactions from the harmful impact to the lack of resources. A proper understanding of processes and constellations of resilience can also support our search for effective interventive and preventive measures. One aim of research should, for instance, be the development of environments that support resilience. And finally, the life span concept of resilience pursued in this chapter also highlights that individual and social possibilities to overcome developmental adversities—that is, the danger of developmental pathologies—are richer than obvious at first sight and that they are present throughout the life span.

Successful Development: The Problem of Universal Evaluation Criteria

A particularly prominent and at the same time serious problem with the concept of resilience is that it requires two value judgments to be made before the phenomenon can be identified at all (Luthar et al., 2000, p. 549ff.; Masten, 2001; Masten & Reed, 2002, p. 75; Rutter, 2000; Tiét & Huizinga, 2002). On the one hand, the developmental situation must be judged to be adverse, stressful, and potentially dangerous.[2] At first glance, one might assume that this is statistically possible (e.g., when "the majority of the affected persons developed negatively under such conditions").[3] However, this would by definition exclude the possibility that a majority of the population possesses resources of resilience which is completely plausible in the case of specific types of adversity (e.g., burdens or dangers for development that have existed for a longer period);

the adaptation by groups or populations to relatively stable risk factors is, briefly stated, the principle of evolutionary development and thus the concept of evolutionary adaptation (Barkow, Cosmides, & Tooby, 1992). Accordingly, Tiét and Huizinga (2002) apply the concepts resilience and adaptation largely interchangeably. This is also the principle of biological immunization against a virus: the virus remains dangerous—it has not been rendered harmless or even become extinct—even if the majority of (surviving) persons in whom it is still detectable are now immune. Actually, several studies are now arriving at the conclusion that resilience is a normal phenomenon (Masten, 2001). Therefore the possibility of calling widespread immunization "resilience" (simply because the majority of people are immune at a given time) cannot by definition be ruled out. This means that one would have to define risk factors as well as assets in other than statistically descriptive ways. Referring to prototypical examples, however, is also problematic. There may be indisputable cases (a serious accident on the one hand, a loving grandmother on the other; Masten, 2001), but these may not be indisputable under all circumstances (the grandmother's loving care may be perceived by the grandchild as incomprehension, while the accident, even if it was the cause of injury, may have prevented a much larger catastrophe, such as the boarding of an airplane, which then crashed). On the other hand, most cases are not even indisputable at first glance (under normal circumstances), but rather part of a continuum of favorable and less favorable events that must be classified individually (Masten, 2001). However, this is only possible within the framework of a developmental theory that specifies normal development against which negative deviations can be identified.

This implies that it is impossible to avoid making a value judgment when determining "resilience" and that the very concept of resilience is based on a developmental theory that includes a theory of "good" and "optimal" development. This leads us to the second value judgment: it is necessary to evaluate the resilience of individuals affected by these adverse, unfavorable, or even hostile conditions as "good," "successful," and so on. Analogously, the approach of developmental psychopathology (summarized in Cicchetti & Rogosch, 2002) also needs to be able to make recourse to a developmental theory based on (evaluative) definitions of criteria for normal, successful development. One can also distinguish between internal (e.g., health, cognitive, emotional) and external (e.g., behavioral or social) aspects (Staudinger & Greve, 2001; Tiét & Huizinga, 2002). The present (outcome-oriented) literature has put forward a considerable variety of criteria on which to base

---

[2] For example, Arrington and Wilson (2000, p. 223) suggest applying the concept of risk to groups and vulnerability to individuals. Although this appears to be helpful, it would be practically inconsistent, as individuals also face risks, that is, external constellations of conditions, which can lead, in the absence of individual protective factors, to maladaptive development and developmental disruptions.

[3] The second value problem (see later discussion) is implied by the first in this case as well.

this value judgment (for an overview, cf. also Olsson et al., 2003).[4] Apart from this lack of uniformity it is conceptually unclear what a generally agreed upon definition of "developmental success" could look like. Making use of this statistically is particularly problematic, since again here the possibility cannot be excluded that the majority of the persons observed at any given time responded maladaptively. Both value judgments thus point toward a theory of *successful* development (Greve, 2001). The idea of positive psychology (Aspinwall & Staudinger, 2003; Seligman & Csikszentmihalyi, 2000; Snyder & Lopez, 2002) implies from the developmental psychological perspective the conception of "optimal" or at least "successful" development (P. B. Baltes & Baltes, 1990; Brandtstädter & Schneewind, 1977; Greve, 2001).

Many authors, in sketching the contours for their definition of successful development, make reference to the successful accomplishment of developmental tasks, according to specifically defined criteria for each task (e.g., Masten & Coatsworth, 1995; Masten & Reed, 2002; Wyman et al., 2001). The central idea here is to formulate age-specific tasks that define normative standards, which in turn form the basis for judging the success of individual development in relatively differentiated terms. This nevertheless probably only constitutes a temporary solution, for three reasons. First, these types of lists must always remain unfinished (due to cultural and historical changes, but also to the self-designated developmental). Second, the normative specifications of the goals contained in such lists can always be subjected to critique. (Is, for example, marriage a *criterion*, that is, a necessary condition for successful development? Obviously not always and everywhere.) Third and above all, these developmental goals in many cases implicitly or explicitly contain the acquisition or construction of aspects that must be at the center of any theory of resilience (e.g., as resources or assets)—identity, self-worth, self-efficacy, stable social relations, and so on. More explicitly normative models such as Erikson's well-known theory of psychosocial development (1959, 1984) are either empirically untenable (why should there be exactly eight stages, everywhere, at all times, for everyone?) or—precisely because of the normative claims—in principle untestable, and thus unsuitable as a measure of successful development. The classic

functionality criteria, moreover, are possibly not applicable to all age groups alike (Widinger & Seidlitz, 2002). Here again as with other aspects, it can be argued that in the case of older people, other measurement standards should be applied. This is clear not only for personality characteristics (Widinger & Seidlitz, 2002), but also for other criteria. For example, the classic criteria of depression (changes in sleep or sexual behavior, also possibly without the presence of depressive trajectories) may be age-correlated, which raises the demand for development of age-sensitive instruments of measurement. This again calls attention to the exigency of a theory of successful development that explicitly addresses this need.

In contrast, however, many scholars in the field of developmental psychology take the view that (for the reasons indicated above) the articulation of concrete, content-based criteria—as they were referred to in numerous classic psychological approaches (cf., e.g., Kohlberg, 1971; Maslow, 1970; for a summary, see, e.g., Ryff & Singer, 2002), and still often continue to be called uncritically (e.g., authenticity; Harter, 2002)—can no longer be defended (e.g., P. B. Baltes, Glück, & Kunzmann, 2002; M. Baltes & Carstensen, 2003; Staudinger et al., 1995). This is especially true when referring to middle-class norms and to white, male standards (M. Baltes & Carstensen, 2003). Concepts that impose substantive value judgments cannot, according to the objections, be postulated as essential to a positive psychology without additional (value or normative) premises. It is necessary to provide at least a functionally or otherwise empirically (scientifically) grounded argument, which in turn must relate back to a criterion of developmental success. Thus, a life span perspective on developmental psychology is focused less on concrete indicators (e.g., happiness, social integration, authenticity) and more on a balance between internal needs and aspirations on the one hand, and the demands of the environment on the other (Freund & Riedinger, 2003). According to this view—at least in our increasingly fast, increasingly changing, increasingly complex world—the (hopeless) search for generally agreed, concrete criteria is less important than the "delineation of a behavioral system that promotes as a 'whole' the continued adaptation to and mastery of new life circumstances" (P. B. Baltes & Freund, 2003, p. 25).

In fact, the relationship between empirical description and explanation on the one hand and positions based on value judgments or normative demands on the other is more complex. Even if empirical facts do not constitute a *sufficient* condition for passing judgment, they are nevertheless usually *necessary* conditions (Brandtstädter & Schneewind, 1977). Whenever practical decisions are

---

[4] It is perhaps worth mentioning that the problem is often not even recognized as a *problem*. Thus, Widinger and Seidlitz (2002) gather examples of positive (e.g., conscientious, efficient) and negative (e.g., anxious, negligent) traits of people without even discussing that the two groups are "positive" or "negative" depending on the context and valuation measures used.

made, empirical assertions of fact (typically in the form of expectations) are entailed. The demand to encourage active mobility and autonomy among older people presupposes that this actually serves to maintain their mobility and autonomy and thereby promote their general well-being; this assumption is empirically testable. Science thus plays a key role in answering the question of successful development, even when the criterion for this "success" must be defined pre-scientifically.

The search for *universally applicable* criteria—regardless of people's particular individual, cultural, and historical circumstances—appears unpromising, however, if only because people's "success" from the action perspective on human development depends not least of all on what they judge to be successful *themselves*. Brandtstädter and Schneewind (1977) pointed out that objective definitions of the meaning of "optimal development" and the recourse to purely subjective evaluation criteria are equally inadequate (partly because both cases always lead to a relativization of current [perceived] social standards and benchmarks; Brandtstädter, 2002, p. 383).

These considerations point toward a solution to the criteria question. Beyond the fulfillment of basic vital conditions, the preconditions for successful development are evidently meta-competencies and meta-resources which ensure that individuals use opportunities and support to compensate for deficits and vulnerabilities and are able to actively influence their development within the framework of the options currently and theoretically available to them (Baltes & Carstensen, 2003; Brandtstädter & Schneewind, 1977; Greve, 2001; Staudinger, 1999b). Human ontogeny is characterized by the fact that it is shaped over long stretches by *us*, by our goals in life, and by our self-concepts. The individual biography, which constitutes our lives, is admittedly also the result of the constraints and conditions we encounter and the preconditions we start off with (and only sometimes are able to influence). Since we navigate through life with equal measures of intention and accident, a convincing model of successful development must take two separate aspects into account: the possibilities (and limits) of individual and social control over our own development, as well as the resources for managing and coping with coincidental and unpredictable events, be they positive or challenging (Brandtstädter, 2002). If this observation is correct, two aspects of human development in particular hold a key function in explaining the aforementioned meta-competencies. The option of seizing opportunities and actively influencing and controlling our own development is centrally dependent on self-regulatory competencies.

Autonomy: Preconditions and Processes of Self-Development

If human development is essentially a product of culture and a result of actions (P. B. Baltes, 1997; Brandtstädter, 1998; Staudinger, Marsiske, & Baltes, 1995), then the ability to take action—that is, to select developmental goals, make decisions, form intentions, put them into action, and if necessary also overcome obstacles and revise strategies—is an essential precondition for successful development (Brandtstädter & Lerner, 1999). Heckhausen (2003; Heckhausen & Schulz, 1995) has therefore passionately argued in favor of regarding primary control as an actual universal developmental goal—and thus as a criterion of successful development. We do not support this strong position ("ultimate criterion," p. 387) above all because primary control depends just as much on subjective attributions of relevancy and significance as on individual standards of evaluation. Which areas I want to control and what degree of "personal control" I am satisfied with (or consider adequate) will depend not least of all on my individual evaluations, which constantly change over the course of development, also in dependence on my development trajectories (Brandtstädter, 1998). However, it is without doubt accurate to say that striving to influence the environment (relevant to life) is a primary motive for the action of human and living beings in general. Successful action requires not only the specific competencies necessary to carry out the selected action, but also that these competencies are adequately represented in the individual's self-image. Any given action, including development-regulative action, can only succeed if the person taking it has a sufficiently realistic image of him or herself. This applies not only to the present real self, but also to an adequate representation of the possible self (Markus & Nurius, 1986), that is, of the options and possibilities the individual envisions for him or herself. At the same time, this is also a precondition for making a suitable choice from among the possible developmental options (Ryan, 1993). The self thus has an integrating, "orchestrating" function for human development (Staudinger, Marsiske, et al., 1995). This bestows particular significance on processes that ensure the integration, continuity, stability and (sufficient) reality orientation, and simultaneously sufficiently positive (optimistic) shading of the self (Greve et al., 2005).

Coping

This brings us to the second point. In many cases, personal coping resources are a precondition for allowing development to take a successful course, as outlined above. Coping in general is, today, conceived as a process (in contrast to a personal disposition or current state) by which individuals manage the challenging, threatening, or harmful demands placed upon them (Lazarus & Folkman, 1984; Montada, Filipp, & M. Lerner, 1992). Thus, the concept is a neutral one that includes active, "problem-focused" efforts as well as re-active ("emotion-focused") adaptations (Lazarus, 1991). Going one step further, human development in general may be regarded as a hierarchical, interactive sequence of micro- and macroscopic coping processes. Skinner and Edge (1998) have argued that coping and development are inherently interconnected. No account of development is complete without a consideration of how individuals adapt to adversity and master challenges. Developmental tasks are challenging discrepancies between the (perceived) current reality and a normative standard (e.g., ideal self, personal goal or value, social norms, and so on; Brandtstädter, Wentura, & Greve, 1993). Coping brings into focus the question of how the individual deals with a particular set of demands. Moreover, while current coping processes and resources are shaped by developmental conditions, coping reactions can also act as forces in creating future development. The distinction between short-term or current adaptive processes ("coping") and long-term or diachronic adaptation ("development") appears all the more arbitrary and fuzzy the more closely a specific change is observed.

Development essentially consists in upholding and implementing the individual's capacity to adapt to discrepancies in new situations and developmental tasks, while seeking (via assimilation or accommodation) to solve—or dissolve—the discrepancies that generate crises or create burdens and seem unavoidable in the long run (Brandtstädter & Rothermund, 2002). Thus, successful development implies a progressive adaptation that simultaneously maintains or indeed expands this plasticity and adaptivity. As far as we know today, this is possible—and usual—even into the late years of very old age (P. B. Baltes, 1997). This leads to the seemingly tautological statement that successful development essentially means ensuring that development, that is, progressive adaptation, will always be possible and really will occur.

Resilience and Coping: Two Sides of the Same Coin?

The theoretical and empirical relation between resilience and coping seems to need some further consideration. There appears to be a considerable overlap between the two concepts, both at first glance and upon closer inspection. Sometimes, the terms are even used synonymously. We suggest to avoid such an all encompassing notion of "coping," but rather suggest that coping is an important facet of a re-

silience constellation but not the same as resilience (see also Ryff et al., 1998). Coping comes into play when investigating the process component of resilience and there it constitutes an important part (Beasley et al., 2003). Coping, usually structural, lacks the constellation aspect of resilience that includes risks and protective factors on the one and developmental outcomes on the other hand. The coping literature has a much clearer focus on the process component and does also not include resources such as intellectual capacity or financial resources (e.g., Lazarus, 1993). In other words, coping is an important process resource of a resilience constellation (see also, Staudinger & Greve, 2001).

Furthermore, coping in the strict sense describes the management of stress factors (at least in the classic use of the term which characterizes, e.g., Lazarus' approach) that overtax an individual's own immediately available resources. The term resilience, however, evidently implies successful management.

Of course, resilience may comprise processes that can be also described as coping. In particular, two basic ways of dealing with stressful experiences have been distinguished that are also of particular importance for theoretical and empirical work on resilience. First, there are the *active efforts* undertaken to master critical events. Here, coping means reducing the actual/ought discrepancy through problem-oriented action that aims to end the adverse situation. Second, coping is understood as the *adaptive adjustment* to a course of development experienced as irrevocably negative, an adaptation, which eventually leads to regaining well-being and life satisfaction. The subjective perception of the critical situation's controllability is thus decisive for the "selection" of the coping tendency. The question of what is adaptive has to be answered with regard to the particular situation. For instance, so called "regressive" coping activities such as "giving up responsibility" have been found to be of adaptive value if the situation does not allow for change but rather asks for accepting the loss (cf. Staudinger, Freund, Linden, & Maas, 1999). The same may be true for "defensive" strategies such as denial.

The subject of "coping in old age" can be discussed from two perspectives. First, it is a question of specific events to be managed in old age: *coping with old age*. As referred to above, common stereotypes and a series of findings indicate that adverse problem situations begin to accumulate in later adulthood. Physical and mental performance tend to decline, serious illness and disabilities occur (with a higher probability than in younger years), the remaining years of life decrease, career goals disappear due to retirement, important friends and relatives die. The fact that these problems are increasingly characterized by leads us to the second aspect. With increasing age and the changing problems that accompany it, the means of *coping in old age* change as well. Adaptive reactions and processes that do not actively solve but "dissolve" the problem, that is, remove it, become increasingly promising and probable (Brandtstädter & Renner, 1990; Brandtstädter & Rothermund, 2002). It is interesting to note that the overwhelming majority of individuals in late adulthood and old age are apparently successful in "managing" crises (including the negative aspects of aging) in this way (Brandtstädter & Greve, 1994; Brandtstädter & Wentura, 1995; Staudinger, 2000; Staudinger et al., 1995).

In cases where individuals face losses and deficits, they actively confront them in a variety of ways. The model "selective optimization with compensation" (P. B. Baltes & Baltes, 1990; Freund, Li, & Baltes, 1999; Staudinger & Lindenberger, 2003) examines these strategic responses to losses that threaten to occur or already have. Active forms of coping are characterized by adherence to the standards and the value and goal orientations under threat. However, not every actual/ought discrepancy can be reduced through active, and in particular proactive problem solving. Nor can definitive failure or irreversible losses be compensated for by delegation. The possible emotional consequences, which may—depending on the subjective importance of the life domain affected—be dramatic and range from desperation and grief through hopelessness to depression, can, however, be regulated or possibly even avoided entirely through adaptive coping reactions. One characteristic aspect is that the threatened "ought" values are changed to such that the discrepancy is reduced or entirely resolved. Adaptations of the system of personal values and preferences, reinterpretations of stressful problem situations, changes in perspective and deliberate (downwards) comparisons are typical examples of processes that contribute to resolving the actual/ought discrepancy, thereby reducing the adverse effect of this discrepancy on well-being and life satisfaction (Brandtstädter & Renner, 1990). The end point of these "accommodative" processes (Brandtstädter & Greve, 1994a; Brandtstädter & Wentura, 1995) is that the individual's self-image, and the image of his or her goals and situation in life is altered and no longer contains the negative actual/ought discrepancy.

Coping episodes can be typically reconstructed as an interlocking combination of complementary active-strategic *and* accommodative processes, as the two modes of coping may be used to achieve different goals. Not least, modifying personal goal structures and preferences can also make it possible again to exercise control over highly valued

goals, thereby also (subjectively) enabling active efforts that previously appeared pointless and would have taken up valuable resources unnecessarily (Brandtstädter & Rothermund, 1995). This is a central function of the aforementioned selection processes (P. B. Baltes & Baltes, 1990). For instance, in old age and under circumstances of physical constraints, it may be highly adaptive to give up independence, that is, move into assisted living quarters or have permanent help come in. By choosing dependence in old age we may gain powers that we can use for keeping up friendships or for pursuing other interest (M. Baltes, 1996). The reduction of aspiration levels can be similarly classified. Being irreversibly unable to fulfill a specific criterion of physical fitness—for example, climbing several flights of stairs with ease—due to aging stimulates accommodative coping. This may, however, result in a more age-appropriate definition of physical fitness, which individuals then indeed actively pursue. Equally, compensation processes also call for active *and* accommodative regulations. If otherwise effective repertoires of action fail to achieve goals or maintain standards, the individual seeks alternative paths of action, possibly involving compensatory aids (for instance, a hearing aid). The precondition for this step, however, is an acceptance of irreversible losses on a subordinate goal level: only individuals who can cope with a self-definition as hard of hearing, and thus accept a hearing aid, can continue to communicate (relatively) effortlessly.

Coping in old age does, of course, have its limits. Health problems are often neither curable nor can they be looked at in relative terms. Permanent eyesight restrictions o the loss of a long-term partner, for example, can only be compensated for to a certain extent and only partially emotionally alleviated. Not least in very old age, there is an increasing probability of deficits and losses that no longer appear "manageable." The perspective of coping and regulation dynamics must not seduce scholars to assess negative emotional reactions as "failure." Quite the opposite: Only a more comprehensive concept of coping opens up the possibility of recognizing grief and desperation reactions as facets of a regulation process that enables individuals to live with even difficult situations and crises.

The observations described here illustrate that the coping theories relating to late adulthood and old age clearly include functions and regulative processes that can help to explain the phenomenon of resilience. We will therefore go into somewhat more detail on the models of development regulation mentioned here in a later section. For the purpose of our argument in this section, it is initially only important to recognize that coping processes are clearly a constitutive element of resilience, particularly in cases where they include adaptive processes that are characteristic of later adulthood.

Resilience as an Issue of Empirical Research

Having more clearly outlined the concept of resilience that we intend to use here through the discussion up to this point, it is easier to survey and evaluate the research landscape. Early studies (starting with the work of Rutter, Garmezy, and Werner in the 1970s; for an overview, cf., e.g., Kaplan, 1999; Luthar et al., 2000; Masten, 2001; Masten & Coatsworth, 1998; Masten & Reed, 2002; Rutter, 2000; Ryff et al., 1998; Tiét & Huizinga, 2002) focused in particular on psychopathological conditions in childhood (including biological risk factors, e.g., parents diagnosed with Schizophrenia, or perinatal stress), social risks (e.g., poverty or other social disadvantages) and traumatic biographical stress during childhood (e.g., sexual abuse, physical maltreatment). The phenomenon has also been examined in very extreme cases of stress, such as among Holocaust survivors (Greene, 2002) and among parents of children with disabilities (Heiman, 2002). In general, two types of studies can be distinguished. One kind of studies is based on very low sample sizes but with highly nuanced observations or qualitative data (e.g., Felten, 2000). The other kind of studies is rather large scale studies using quantitative assessment and pursuing almost an epidemiological approach (e.g., Jessor, 1993; Masten, 2001; Rutter & Rutter, 1993).

Broad-based research activities as early as the 1980s indicate increasing attention on the phenomenon of sound development in the context of multiple life stressors and adversities (for a summary, cf., e.g., Masten & Reed, 2002; e.g., Wyman et al., 2001). These studies were initially concerned with identifying resources available to children under such conditions (for a summary, cf., e.g., Kumpfer, 1999), and primarily with developing and testing theoretical models specifying the relation of these resources to the processes of adaptation. Research on the development of family dynamics also demonstrates a clear trend toward a resilience-oriented perspective (cf., e.g., the meta-analysis of Allen, Blieszner, & Roberto, 2000). One example of prototypical resilience research is the study of various prototypical development courses (cf. Masten & Reed, 2002 on the basic approach) regarding antisocial behavior (e.g., Loeber & Stouthamer-Loeber, 1998).

Studies of resilience highlight above all the considerable differences between individuals in their responses to adverse circumstances. Although extreme situations (e.g., severe abuse) exceed the resources and reserves of almost all those affected, there is a considerable breadth of variation in the forms of reaction, and thus of development, that negative circumstances induce. The existence of a large number of protective resources or assets has been proven empirically, although many of the combinations thereof (cf. regarding children, e.g., Masten & Reed, 2002, p. 83) have not been subjected to theoretical systematization (Masten, 2001). However, the most important problem is that quite often aspects that are psychologically directly or indirectly influential (e.g., self-efficacy, intellectual capacities) are combined with variables that merely point to underlying mechanisms rather than being of explanatory value themselves (e.g., socio-economic status). Often it is unclear whether a given variable belongs to the former or the latter. For example, gender is in most cases a variable of the second category, while parenting behavior may be assigned to either category depending on how it is defined and measured. Consequently, risk factors are usually risk *markers*. As Rutter has aptly noted, it is of crucial importance to differentiate between risk indicators and risk mechanisms (2000, p. 653). The empirical detection of risk markers (indicators, at best) is based on group data; thus, a risk in this perspective is an estimated probability that a member of a certain group (or population) will exhibit a maladaptive developmental outcome. Risk markers thus make it possible to predict (with a certain probability) the specific (maladaptive) developmental course. Correspondingly, meta-studies (e.g., Norris et al., 2002) also indicate little more than a very heterogeneous combination of risk and protective factors on very differing theoretical levels.

Further, there are a number of variables that empirically demonstrate differences with regard to their protective value depending on given contextual circumstances. An interesting example of this phenomenon is the connection of resilience to self-enhancement (for a summary, cf. Bonanno, 2004), and thus to self-esteem (cf. Masten & Garmezy, 1985). On the one hand, self-esteem (at least of a moderate kind) appears to be a resource (moderator variable) for coping with threats and stress (e.g., Cicchetti, 1997; cf. also Aspinwall, 2001). On the other hand, reduced self-esteem is frequently a consequence of stress and threats (e.g., in victims of school violence; Greve & Wilmers, 2003). Simultaneously, however, self-esteem is likely to be a positive precondition for mobilizing or even simply accepting social support (and thus a mediator variable for problem management). Yet other studies indicate that high self-esteem is not always positive per se (cf.

Baumeister, 1993; Crocker & Park, 2004). Two aspects may be important when trying to integrate those seemingly contradictory findings. First, the functionality of self-esteem does not follow a linear function, that is, if self-esteem surpasses a certain level, it turns into being dysfunctional (which by the way is also true for optimism; cf. Baltes et al., 1998). Second, it is important to consider the process dynamics of self-esteem regulations that is, for instance, how robust or vulnerable is a given level of self-esteem (e.g., Greve & Enzmann, 2003). The protective significance of self-esteem can therefore presumably only be clearly formulated when clarifying which structural and procedural bases for self-esteem can be protective, and which can be dangerous, under what specific (individual and situational) conditions. Moreover, empirical evidence that positive self-esteem co-varies with successful development presents theoretical problems simply because an adequate level of self-esteem will always be a central *criterion* of successful development (no matter how it is defined). In any case, significantly low self-esteem cannot, for conceptual reasons, occur in conjunction with "successful" development, let alone be considered a defining characteristic thereof. Some studies therefore also construct their examination of resilience around the factor of self-esteem (e.g., Lösel, Bliesener, & Köferl, 1989; Tiét & Huizinga, 2002). Nevertheless, it is also conceivable that other aspects of successful development, such as social integration, competence in pro-social behavior, empathy, might themselves be explained by self-esteem. The complex role of self-esteem thus appears to be an empirical issue; a differentiated study of state and trait components is likely to play a key role in this context.

When we turn to older people in particular, we face the problem that diachronic reflexive interactions are characteristic of the phenomenon of resilience. Thus, the question of whether disengagement or continued activity indicates successful aging is wrongly phrased, not only because (under certain circumstances) *both* can obviously be defined as "successful" (Freund & Riediger, 2003); it is also misleading because social engagement as well as social withdrawal, seen diachronically, can be both products and producers of well-being (or dissatisfaction and suffering). For example, if sickness forces me to reduce my social contacts (e.g., because I am less mobile, hard of hearing) and I am unable to compensate for this in other ways (e.g., through closer relationships with family members, e.g., grandchildren, or through pursuing a hobby at home), this may then (and *only* then) trigger a progressive downwards spiral into increasing social isolation. Conversely, the de-liberate continuation of social activities that consume all available energy and resources can indicate unsuccessful regulation of development, rigid intractability, and reality avoidance, and can also prompt high medium-term costs in terms of satisfaction (and health).

Although there have been repeated calls for theoretically guided research dealing with precisely *these* issues (e.g., Luthar et al., 2000; Masten & Reed, 2002), this may well constitute the most important desideratum of resilience studies at present. One important path that has been pursued rather seldom to date, particularly in the context of later adulthood and old age, is to design experimental, or quasi-experimental, scientific models to accompany systematically planned intervention studies (cf. Masten & Reed, 2002).

Resilience Is Ordinary and Universal

In general, all the evidence currently indicates that even extraordinary resilience results from "ordinary" processes. There is no reason to assume at present that psychological resistance and the ability to overcome or cope with stress, difficulties, and adversities require special individual skills or conditions only attainable or available in exceptional cases. In fact, in any given case, just one of a multitude of possible configurations or combinations (and not any specific combination) of protective factors appears to suffice to overcome even extreme stress and adversities (Masten, 2001). Bonanno (2004) argues that resilience is far more widespread than assumed, even in cases of extreme loss and traumata. An indication of this is apparently that, roughly estimated, at least 50% to 60% of all adults have been exposed to an instance of stress which can be described as traumatic at least once in their lives, but only one-tenth are reported to have developed PTSD symptoms (Ozer, Best, Lipsey, & Weiss, 2003). The figure is less than 20% even for victims of serious violence (for a summary, cf. Bonanno, 2004). Bonanno, Papa, and O'Neill (2002) also argue that resilience occurs much more frequently than is often assumed. They give the example that grief (e.g., after the death of friends or relatives) does not occur frequently, which—in contrast to numerous myths from certain schools of therapy—can also be seen as a positive indicator (Wortman & Silver, 2001). Furthermore, the psychology of the self has provided firm evidence of a multiple self-system that adapts to current demands, not only over the course of life but also from situation to situation, without losing its continuity (and thus identity), again confirming that phenomena of resilience are an everyday occurrence. Structurally similar phenomena also ensure personal continuity in cases of (what initially appear to be) serious losses or stress. We have to realize that resilience indeed is a normatively occurring phenomenon. It is not confined to (but does not exclude) spectacular circumstances. For instance, in the realm of cognitive development across the life span resilience occurs normatively; that is, the rather strong decline of fluid abilities during adulthood and into old age does not undermine overall cognitive functioning (Baltes, Lindenberger, & Staudinger, 1998). It is through the acquisition of a great number of bodies of knowledge that the decline in speed of processing and in coordinating information is compensated.

The question is, which mechanisms—aside from the coping processes discussed above—can give rise to resilience? For example, adults have been shown not only to increasingly focus on positive affects, but also to use cognitive-affective complexity as a possible buffer (Labouvie-Vief & Medler, 2002). Self-complexity (Linville, 1985, 1987) could be one protective resource (cf., e.g., Affleck & Tennen, 1996). The basic idea is that, if one aspect is under threat, a differentiated self in which various domains (semantic or affective) are not too closely networked, protects many other areas from being affected by this threat. In a meta-analysis, however, Rafaeli-Mor and Steinberg (2002) come to the cautious conclusion that this buffer hypothesis is not very well supported, but the extreme heterogeneity of the findings (and of the quality of the studies involved) does not permit a firm conclusion. It seems clear, however, that complexity by itself does not do the trick but needs to be complemented by integration at the same time and the various self-aspects need to be evaluated positively (cf. Staudinger & Pasupathi, 2000).

Resilience appears to consist not least in flexibly coping with that which subjectively presents itself to us as "reality." Even if we have the strong impression in everyday life that reality is outside of us and thus always undoubtedly present (and that it can be influenced by active behavior at most in the medium term—and then only to a limited extent), there is nevertheless no doubt that different individuals experience the same "reality" differently, in some cases *very* differently. This means there is a certain possible scope for "reality negotiation" (e.g., R. L. Higgins, 2002) for example, with regard to causal attributions or emotional evaluations, and which can be—and is—utilized functionally. This does not necessarily contradict the goal of authenticity (Harter, 2002; in as far as one regards this goal as indisputable; cf. above), it merely requires a person to not knowingly deceive others or put on an act (even though at times this can be a tough distinction).

Not least of all, it is important to find positive aspects even in negative developments (reframing). There are many indications that "benefit-finding" (Affleck & Tennen, 1996; Tennen & Affleck, 2002) or "meaning-making" (Nolen-Hoeksema & Davis, 2002; cf. also Baumeister & Vohs, 2002) are valuable resources against the negative consequences of stressful experiences or losses. However, it is by no means certain that these are mere constructions of the individual with a self-deceptive character (in the sense of "positive illusion"; Taylor & Brown, 1994). Rather, recognizing the often hidden but in fact real benefit of a challenging situation is actually an indication—almost a criterion—of self-related wisdom (Staudinger, Dörner, & Mickler, in press). Forms of reaction that reduce or even entirely avoid negative consequences by means of reevaluations and new perspectives on initially negative experiences (reframing) can be attributed to the "accommodative mode" (Brandtstädter & Renner, 1990, 1992) in Brandtstädter's dual process model of development regulation (Brandtstädter & Rothermund, 2002).

If one regards development from a life span perspective, that is, as a permanent, dynamically changing subjective gain-loss ratio (e.g., P. B. Baltes, Staudinger, & Lindenberger, 1999; Staudinger & Bluck, 2001), it is clear that phenomena of resilience are by no means concentrated within certain life stages. Staudinger and Bluck (2001) have pointed out that traditional developmental psychology initially prioritized the study of childhood and (somewhat later) of adolescence, later supplementing this with an examination of old age from the mid-twentieth century onwards, but still largely ignored the long phase of middle adulthood. The argument developed there is that indeed midlife had not "caused any trouble" and therefore there was less need for investigating this life period. However, it is also argued that this lack of trouble is actually linked to the adaptive capacity of midlife rather than to a lack of stressors and crises (Staudinger & Bluck, 2001). And indeed middle adulthood is characterized by numerous crises. When parents die, children leave home, and the years left to work and live are steadily decreasing (Kim & Moen, 2001), this generates more acute awareness of one's own finitude (cf. also Carstensen, Isaacowitz, & Charles, 1999), as well as the insight that many life goals may well remain unfulfilled forever and that "developmental deadlines" (Heckhausen, Wrosch, & Fleeson, 2001) may already have passed. Nevertheless on average no "midlife crisis" has been deserved. Thus, most likely the stressors are buffered by a rich set of resources and a resilience constellation occurs (Staudinger & Bluck, 2001).

Interestingly, also discussions of developmental psychopathology have traditionally (and, to a large degree, until recently) centered on childhood and adolescence. From the arguments presented up to this point follows, however, that successful ("healthy") as well as maladaptive ("pathological") development can and will occur throughout the life span. Thus, developmental psychopathology must not stay restricted to certain (early) stages of life, but rather broaden its perspective to also encompass middle and later adulthood. By doing so, additional options for interventions can be explored and potential structural equivalencies among developmental processes in childhood and old age may be discovered.

If our argument is correct that resilience designates a complex developmental dynamic whose effectiveness consists in avoiding clear phenotypic changes (Brandtstädter & Greve, 1994b; Greve, 2005), then middle to late adulthood would be the exact prototype for virulent, dynamic, and highly complex development, taking place to a certain extent "behind the scenes." We may only notice these developmental resilient processes as such again in later adulthood because we tend to expect developmental losses, processes of disintegration and decline, and seek explanations for why these fail to occur (e.g., in the case of the "well-being paradox"; Staudinger, 2000).

With the action-related concept of development in mind, we must point out that resilience not only is reaction but frequently "proaction," before the negative event or the degenerative development actually takes place. Findings on older people's allegedly "paradoxical" fear of crime provide an interesting example of this phenomenon (Greve, 1998, 2000b). The common stereotype that older people are considerably more afraid of crime than younger age groups, although objectively the justification for this fear decreases with age, makes it clear that many discussions must be revised in the light of the conception of resilience. A closer look shows that this pattern of findings—frequently interpreted as an indication of "irrationality of old age"—is based on a simultaneously adaptive and highly functional behavioral tendency, which can be interpreted, in the light of the considerations presented in this chapter, as an expression of a proactive resilience. According to replicated findings, older people are *not* more frequently or more intensely afraid of criminality than younger age groups, nor do they consider themselves more likely to fall victim to criminal actions. Old people behave more cautiously than younger people, with the desired—and from this point of view not at all "paradoxical"—effect of a decreasing probability of victimization (Greve, 1998). The explanation as to *why* caution increases with age is complex

(Greve, 2004). One important aspect may well be the increasing—and also subjectively registered—biological vulnerability of older people, along with the consideration that *intentionally* cautious behavior in particular is determined by expectation-value calculations, which weigh the expected gain from risk behavior ("walking alone outside at night") against the possible costs (falling and physical injuries in the event of attack) and make cautious behavior appear the more appropriate ("rational") choice. A decreasing victim rate among older people over a period of several years can be described as an expression and consequence of a resilience constellation.

In the wider context of the arguments outlined here, it becomes particularly clear that it is inappropriate from our point of view to understand resilience as a state or even just a process (and certainly not as a trait). It is probably more appropriate to conceptualize the term resilience as a constellation of risk factors on the one and developmental outcomes on the other hand that is held together by resources encompassing regulatory processes as well as structural characteristics (Figure 21.1). We will return to two theoretical conceptions that describe the orchestrated interaction of this constellation through intrapersonal processes in more detail at a later point.

The phenomenon of resilience in late adulthood and old age can be examined and demonstrated in very varied psychosocial domains of functioning. For example, Staudinger, Marsiske, et al. (1995) have examined the domain of cognitive functions, and social relations and interactions in particular, in greater detail (cf. also P. B. Baltes, Lindenberger, & Staudinger, 1998; P. B. Baltes, Staudinger, & Lindenberger, 1999; Staudinger & Greve, 2001). However, the domain of self and personality is of crucial and indeed exceptional importance for the study of resilience in adulthood in two main respects. First, the plasticity and adaptivity observed in this domain offers a vivid and prototypical example for the resilience of adult individuals. Second, the adult self has an "orchestrating" function for human development in general and for resilient processes in particular (P. B. Baltes, 1997; see also Staudinger et al., 1995). We therefore focus on examples from the domain of self and personality in the following discussion, particularly because the theoretical approaches to be examined here have been studied extensively in this context.

The Resilient Self: Stabilization, Defense, and Adaptation of the Aging Self

A large number of national and international studies show that the functionality and overall positive status of self

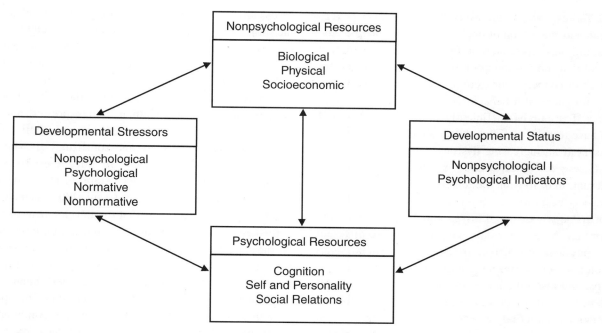

Figure 21.1   A model of resilience as a constellation of personal and contextual resources.

and personality generally diminish little if at all in old age (e.g., Greve, 2005; Roberts & Caspi, 2003; Smith & Baltes, 1996; Staudinger, 2000a; Staudinger, Freund, Linden, & Maas, 1999). Indicators for state of mind such as self-esteem (Bengtson, Reedy, & Gordon, 1985; Brandstädter et al., 1993), general well-being (Ryff, 1995), contentment with one's own age (Staudinger et al., 1999), and the conviction of being able to directly or indirectly control one's own life (M. M. Baltes, 1995; Brandtstädter & Rothermund, 1994) show little to no change with age. This has made an essential contribution to rejecting, as too partial and incomplete, the stereotype of aging characterized by deficits and losses. This picture has been replaced by the more multifaceted image of "productive" aging, which emphasizes the opportunities and options of "successful aging" alongside the undisputed crises and losses (M. M. Baltes & Montada, 1996; P. B. Baltes & Baltes, 1990; Bond, Cutler, & Grams, 1995).

The aforementioned (cumulative) stability of the adult personality has, however, only at first glance been demonstrated clearly; as discussed earlier, genetic explanations in particular by no means suffice. Moreover, various approaches closely connect the concept of personality with that of the self ("personality as integrated self-system"; Bandura, 1999, p. 187; see summary in Greve, 2005).

However, if self and personality are not an endogenous component of the human psyche, their stability requires far more explanation than their variability, particularly in view of the plasticity repeatedly referred to earlier.

This finding of plasticity seems particularly astonishing in light of the well-documented fact that development-related processes of decline and functional setbacks emerge in many life and functional domains beginning in midlife. In fact, not only common stereotypes but also a large number of findings suggest that adverse situations begin to accumulate in later adulthood: Physical and mental performance declines, as demonstrated earlier, serious illness and disabilities are more likely to occur than in younger years, number of remaining years to live decreases, career orientations are lost due to retirement, close friends and relatives die. In relation to cognitive development (e.g., Reischies & Lindenberger, 1996), changes in sensory functions (Tesch-Römer & Wahl, 1996), and morbidity (e.g., Steinhagen-Thiessen & Borchelt, 1996), old age is characterized by an increase in factual losses and setbacks (for a summary, see, e.g., P. B. Baltes, Lindenberger, et al., 1998; P. B. Baltes, Mittelstraß, & Staudinger, 1994; P. B. Baltes, Staudinger, et al., 1999; Bond et al., 1995). This continually deteriorating balance of developmental gains and losses is apparently also perceived as such by the aging individuals themselves (Heckhausen,

Dixon, & Baltes, 1989). Moreover, the very subjective representation and evaluation of one's own person, that is, "the self,"[5] would lose its function for behavioral regulation and control if it did not integrate the individual's objective developmental changes. For example, it is a necessary precondition for successful behavior to assess one's own competences and resources sufficiently realistically. The self does not have to be as veridical as possible, but as adequate as necessary if an increasing dysfunction with age is to be avoided (Greve & Wentura, 2003; see also the concept of "optimal margin of illusion"; Baumeister, 1989).

Old age is certainly a very rough indicator of the increase of risks, stresses, and losses (Staudinger & Fleeson, 1996). In fact, here one should not only separate different aspects (physical, cognitive, psychological, social, etc.) that develop in very different (sometimes even complementary) ways, but also take into account marked interindividual and situational differences that lead to an increasing heterogeneity of actual and chronic stresses in and throughout old age. In this respect, the success of coping is always relative; that is, it depends on the dimension under examination and the success criterion chosen (e.g., Filipp & Klauer, 1991).

Nevertheless, it is precisely the seeming contradiction between stresses and losses that increase with age, on the one hand, and the phenotypic stability of self and well-being of the aging person, on the other hand, that makes the processes and conditions of this constellation of resilience in old age such a fascinating research issue (Brandtstädter, 1999b; Brandtstädter & Greve, 1994a). The "discovery" of this apparent paradox is also due, however, to a negatively biased view of aging that also expects a failure in coping. In other words, it is the late effect of a deficit-oriented image of development in later life (Ryff et al., 1998).

The experience of the "coherence of personality" (Cervone & Shoda, 1999a) is due to a number of phenomena such as the observable convergence of human behavior even across different contexts, but not least it is also due to the subjective (phenomenal) constancy referred to in the experience of the self that makes my biography *my* biography (Brandtstädter & Greve, 1994a; Cervone & Shoda, 1999b). Indeed, personality can really be understood as an integrated self-system (Bandura, 1999): the unity of behavior and personal identity. Human beings present and shape themselves and their environment through their behavior. Continuity is thus actively and sometimes also intentionally produced (Bandura, 1999; Brandtstädter, 1998, 2001; Greve et al., 2005). We produce stability by observing and checking ourselves (Roberts & Caspi, 2002). Hence, on the one hand, it becomes clear that the development of the self is the key to the question of development of the personality. At the same time, this also makes it clear that the combination of the themes "self and personality" is more than just two facets of the same domain that complement and supplement each other. Instead, this combination of perspectives may in fact be regarded as specifying the combination of genotypic and phenotypic perspectives on lasting behavioral tendencies; the *visible* stability and continuity of the behavior ("phenotypic personality") may be explained by the structural and motivational process continuity of the self in the interaction with variable situations and correspondingly specific cognitions and evaluations. Hence, our argument is that the apparent paradox of stability of the self-image and well-being in the event of permanent internal and external changes disappears if the personal constellation of resilience is moved into the focal point of the theoretical perspective (Brandtstädter, 1999b; Brandtstädter & Greve, 1994a; Staudinger, in press). Surprisingly, the application of the concept of resilience to explain the stability of self and personality in later life was attempted only relatively late (Ryff et al., 1998, p. 71; see also Staudinger et al., 1995). This is all the more astonishing as resilience apparently seems to be the rule rather than the exception (e.g., Brandtstädter & Wentura, 1995; Staudinger, 2000b).

Personality Traits as Elements of Constellations of Resilience

One aspect of resilience in the domain of self and personality is the search for personality factors that contribute to constellations of resilience, that is, that promote adaptive processes. (We have already pointed out that we do not follow approaches that view resilience itself as a personality attribute.) Thus, for example, findings from the Berlin Aging Study show that emotional instability, that is, neuroticism, moderates the correlation between physical risks and well-being (Staudinger et al., 1999). The authors argue

---

[5] In the context of this discussion, we have chosen not to go into more detail on the various conceptualizations of the self (see Leary & Tangney, 2003). In relation to the *contents* of the self, scholars generally distinguish between a cognitive-descriptive and an evaluative-judgmental (emotional) perspective. Both are highly multilayered and differentiated (e.g., in relation to affective, cognitive, and conative components). The *processes* of the self can be roughly divided into two functional categories: First, it processes self-relevant information in such a way that the individual capacity for life and action is retained or improved; second, it attempts at the same time to maintain as high a level of self-evaluation as possible (Greve, 2000a).

that it is precisely the intense experience of—also negative—feelings in the face of intense stressors that can have an adaptive effect, especially under conditions of lack of control. This is consistent with the discovery that under conditions of socioeconomic stress, the experience of negative emotions is more protective than a "surplus" of positive emotions (Staudinger et al., 1999). Other lasting aspects of personality (see Staudinger & Pasupathi, 2000, for an overview) that have proven to be at work in constellations of resilience are conscientiousness, openness to new experiences (Costa & McCrae, 1985), and self-efficacy (Bandura, 1986).

Self-Regulatory Processes as Part of Constellations of Resilience

It is no coincidence that the research on coping has paid so little attention to the concept of resilience for so long. Individual reactions to sources of stress and crises are typically made a topic of research only when they become apparent, or at least when sufficient cause arises to expect such reactions. The concept of "critical life events" (Filipp, 1995) illustrates this perspective aptly. The obvious link to clinical questions (Posttraumatic Stress Disorder or issues from the theory of depression) has lent additional support to the tendency to concentrate on phenotypic processes of change. This largely loses sight of the fact that, in many constellations of resilience, "active," observable "coping" with "objective" sources of stress does not appear to occur at all.

When dealing with the subject of coping processes, one must keep several potential misunderstandings in mind. First, it should be pointed out that we are proceeding from a neutral conception of coping that includes both problem-oriented and emotion-centered coping forms (Lazarus & Folkman, 1984) in reaction to sources of stress and crises that, from a subjective perspective, exceed the individual's currently and potentially available personal and social resources (Lazarus, 1991). This also includes what is known as "regressive" behavior (e.g., "relinquishing responsibility"; Haan, 1977). Both problem-oriented and emotion-centered forms of reaction presuppose an awareness or anticipation of a relevant cause, challenge, stress, threat, loss, or crisis: only perceived stresses must (and can) be coped with. Second, as mentioned earlier, in this sense, coping processes are not to be understood as antecedents or causes of resilience, but as elements of a constellation of resilience (see Figure 21.1). We argue, as explained earlier, in favor of a conception that identifies constellations of resilience—precisely in old age—as ways of dealing successfully with threatening and stressful life events and cir-

cumstances such that the former status and/or functionality of the relevant domains is restored or maintained. These conceptions raise the question as to what specific forms of reaction (under which personal and situational conditions) allow, for example, subjective well-being to be maintained or increase the probability of survival and thus contribute to a constellation of resilience.

In principle, as already addressed, it is possible to distinguish here between reactions in two different directions. First, losses and deficits that are impending or have already occurred may be confronted in a wide variety of active or assimilative ways (Brandtstädter & Greve, 1994a). Here, in other words, an attempt is made to change something about the menacing or critical situation, which is also possible even when the individual no longer has full control over this domain of reality. The active delegation of control may be another promising coping option: By delegating to others high-effort tasks that can no longer be carried out by oneself, while still maintaining control of localization, scope, and quality in the process, older people exercise a form of "proxy control" (M. M. Baltes, 1995). Proxy control can solve the problem without necessitating specific individual adjustments. However, in all the earlier mentioned cases, these active forms of coping are characterized by adherence to the threatened standards, value, and goal orientations.

However, not every problem can be reduced by active problem solving. Nor can eventual failure or irreversible losses be compensated through delegation. As the studies mentioned at the beginning of this section show, even in these cases, potential emotional and psychological effects (e.g., despair, grief, hopelessness, or depression) can apparently be regulated or completely avoided in the majority of cases. It is characteristic of the forms of reaction discussed here that changes in the threatened life and functional domains are evaluated in such a way that the stress is reduced or completely resolved. Adjustments of the personal value and preference systems, reinterpretations of stressful problem situations, changes in perspective, and downward comparisons are typical examples of self-regulatory processes that contribute, to a certain extent, to a resolution of the stressful problem situation and thus reduce its adverse effect on well-being and life satisfaction. The end point of these "accommodative" processes (Brandtstädter & Renner, 1990, 1992; Brandtstädter & Rothermund, 1995, 2002; see also P. B. Baltes & Freund, 2003) is that the individual has an altered view of his or her own person, goals, and situation in life. This, in contrast to defensive problem-avoidance reactions involving denial, actually makes the problem go away permanently; denying the existence of a sickness does not cure it, but looking at it in relative terms makes it bearable. This is why we should not interpret denial and suppression as processes of resilience.

Assimilative and accommodative forms of coping are to be considered opposites to a certain degree. It appears that accommodative adaptation is primarily used if assimilative attempts to cope seem pointless. Conversely, premature adaptations of personal goals may unnecessarily hinder active attempts at problem solving. However, subjective goals are always integrated into a complex structure of value and goal hierarchies (Brandtstädter & Greve, 1994a). Goals defined at a lower level are simultaneously a means to achieve higher goals and values in the hierarchy. Thus, for instance, unrestricted physical mobility usually serves goals that, according to one's own personal definition of a good life and a life worth living, must be achieved or at least be achievable: traveling, walking, meeting friends, taking care of home and garden, and so on. In addition, physical mobility may (at least implicitly) be part of a positive self-image, a central component of which is not being dependent on the help of others. However, different goals and objectives are frequently incompatible simply because limited resources prevent them from being realized or maintained simultaneously (Brandtstädter & Wentura, 1995).

Self-Resilience: Content and Process

Bearing these findings in mind, the resilience of self and personality in old age, the starting point for our discussion in this section, now appears less paradoxical and more conclusive theoretically and empirically (see Staudinger, in press). Apparently, the (phenotypic) stability of the self in adulthood and old age is an indicator of resilience if the arguments in favor of change occurring throughout all of adulthood are taken seriously. This stability, however, may still seem surprising from a different point of view. Throughout a period of more than 50 years, experimental studies focusing on the processes of the self have frequently demonstrated a relatively high situational changeability of the self (e.g., Hannover, 1997; for a recent overview, see Leary & Tangney, 2003). Assuming that defensive processing of self-relevant information usually is not resilient, and that age-related decrements are recognized by the aging individual (Heckhausen, Dixon, & Baltes, 1989), how can the stability of the aging self be explained at all, let alone be conceptualized as a constitutive part of resilience in adulthood and age? The decisive point of our argument is that dealing with adversities (such as experienced losses or deficits) requires both a sufficiently realistic and, at the same time, a sufficiently stabilizing way

of processing. Several recent studies have successfully demonstrated that this task of reconciliation can be solved.

For instance, processes of "self-immunization" (Greve & Wentura, 2003) offer one way to continue maintaining aspects of the self-concept that constitute identity despite the admission of concrete individual changes and losses. Gutmann (1998) also uses the metaphor that the adult self is an immune system whose function is to safeguard integrity, identity, and well-being (self-esteem). Ryff et al. (1998, p. 77) use the term "immune competence." Self-immunization is achieved, for example, when a certain ability (e.g., remembering names or telephone numbers) has been acknowledged by the aging individual as lost or impaired, and the diagnostic value attributed to this ability with respect to the relevant higher domain (here, memory) is reduced and a comparatively higher value is attributed to other memory-relevant abilities (e.g., memorizing poems), which the person still believes he or she possesses. This is a further reason a multifaceted self-concept is advantageous. If the "good memory" aspect of the self-image is resting solely on memorizing telephone numbers, it is difficult to compensate by moving emphasis to other characteristics of a good memory (e.g., Freund & Smith, 1997). In addition to multifacetedness, research on the self-concept has demonstrated that the different facets need to be integrated and positively evaluated (Staudinger & Pasupathi, 2000).

A person's theory about himself or herself can also be immunized by restricting its range: The conviction "I have a good memory" is thus reinterpreted as "I have a better memory than other people my age," or even as "better than everyone else in my retirement home." This, too, is a peripheral concept adaptation that leaves the self-concept intact without disputing realities, such as that younger people do have a better memory than oneself (Greve & Wentura, 2003). Such processes explain how, through adulthood, people can apparently act in a very realistic and reality-oriented way and maintain a continuous and coherent self-concept despite even considerable change and development. Ryff (Ryff et al., 1998) refers in a similar context to the concept of (optimal) "allostasis," that is, of "stability through change" (Sterling & Eyer, 1988, p. 638; see also Staudinger & Pasupathi, 2000), which was originally conceptualized with regard to physiological stability (e.g., with regard to cardiovascular stresses and/or changes).

Analogous accommodative adaptations also manifest themselves with regard to the evaluative perspective of the self. Numerous studies have shown that a lower subjective significance is attributed to domains of functioning where losses have been experienced, and to compensate, aspects of the self that appear to continue to be possible or available to a greater extent are given a higher value (e.g., Brandtstädter & Greve, 1994a; Kling, Ryff, & Essex, 1997). It is important to note that these adjustments do not deny realities (e.g., losses of abilities). Rather, they evaluate or interpret these (acknowledged) losses in a palliative or even neutralizing fashion. Precisely these accommodative dynamics of selection and compensation are the focus of the two models of developmental regulation in old age (P. B. Baltes & Baltes, 1990; Brandtstädter & Renner, 1990).

SUCCESSFUL AGING: A THEORETICAL FRAMEWORK

We have repeatedly pointed out that the stability of self and personality increases cumulatively over the life span (Caspi & Roberts, 1999; Roberts & Caspi, 2003). It is a widely held belief that in childhood and youth and up to early adulthood, change and transformation are not just normal, but indeed, are to be expected (the *absence* of observable short-term changes in children triggers astonishment and questions), whereas with adults, it tends instead to be dramatic change that requires explanation. The central thesis of this chapter is, however, that it is indeed the increasing stability and continuity in adulthood that is an expression of underlying change. The phenomenon of ordinary resilience in middle and later adulthood turns such changes into stability (Roberts & Caspi, 2003; Staudinger, in press). In particular, structures and processes of the self play a dual key role here (Greve et al., 2005). On the one hand, they actively contribute to the stabilization of behavior (the reaction of the person to his or her environment) by means of various mechanisms. On the other hand, as we mentioned, a central function of many processes of the self is to stabilize the self-perception precisely when objective conditions (of the environment as well as of one's own person) change; this in turn not only stabilizes self-presentation (in everyday behavior and also in questionnaires) but also produces the subjective continuity that makes it possible to be certain that one has remained the same person as before. In this sense, the self acts as the interface between the subjective and objective sides of the person and, at the same time, as the stabilizer of both sides. The development of the self in middle and later adulthood produces the internal and external impression of stability that has long been established through empirical research (Greve, 2000a).

Surprisingly, research in developmental psychology has only very recently focused attention on the resilience of the self in adulthood and later life and thus still lacks dif-

ferentiation in many respects. There are three main reasons for this late development. First, only recently has developmental psychology extended its perspective on the self and personality to encompass periods beyond childhood and adolescence, the latter of which was formerly a particularly strong focus. Although the dynamics of identity development throughout the entire life span were highlighted as early as Bühler (1933) and, from another perspective, Erikson (1959), research in developmental psychology on the self-concept has remained narrowly confined to those aspects of self-development in which processes of change are prominent or dominant, or at least easily recognizable. This applies in particular to the development of the self during youth and adolescence, when establishment of a differentiated and integrated, autonomous and socially competent identity may be seen as the central developmental task (for a summary, see Harter, 1998, 1999). The high stability of the self beyond adolescence has apparently been widely viewed as an indicator of the *lack* of developmental processes (for an exception see Freund & Smith, 1997).

Second, with regard to the period of later adulthood and old age, which is characterized by visible changes, gerontopsychology has long directed attention to other functional domains through a deficit-oriented model of age and aging. These domains include, at the individual level, primarily cognitive developmental processes and regressive processes of sensory and motor functioning, along with the social dynamics of "disengagement" (see Cummings & Henry, 1961). This point of view has defined psychological and physical health and/or stability as the absence of illness or stress (Ryff et al., 1998) rather than as a positive phenomenon (see also Aspinwall & Staudinger, 2003).

Third and above all, however, research on the self-concept and on coping, conducted to date primarily in social psychology, has investigated mainly *visible* changes or at least reactions to *obvious* causes for changes—insofar as *changes* in the self beyond childhood and youth were dealt with at all. From this perspective, the high diachronic intraindividual stability of the self in middle and later adulthood up to old age (see Pinquart, 1998) has been taken to indicate, if anything, the fact that coping resources are being utilized well. This in turn produced the conclusion that the self does not develop in later adulthood or old age (Greve, 2000a).

A Theoretical Framework for Research on Resilience in Middle and Late Adulthood

In this chapter, we have referred at various points to the model of selective optimization with compensation (P. B.

Baltes & Baltes, 1990; P. B. Baltes & Freund, 2003; Freund, Li, & Baltes, 1999; Freund & Riedinger, 2003) and to the dual process model of development regulation (Brandtstädter & Rothermund, 2002). It is evident that both take the phenomenon of resilience in adulthood and later life as a starting point (this term is also used in P. B. Baltes, 1997; Brandtstädter, 1999b; Staudinger et al., 1995). We argue in favor of the idea that not only do these two models deal with the same phenomena, but they can also be directly connected.

As already indicated, in the face of irreversible setbacks and losses (e.g., partner's death, chronic illness, progressive processes of decline), accommodative reactions that do not attempt to actively solve the problem but to counteract the resultant stress become increasingly promising and probable with advancing age (Brandtstädter & Renner, 1990), and assimilative strategies decrease in importance (Brandtstädter, 1992). For both assimilative and accommodative reactions, it is possible to differentiate among selective, optimizing, and compensatory processes. As far as selection is concerned, it is a question of choosing between alternatives and setting limits. However, selection alone is not sufficient; what is also required is a commitment to achieve the desired condition—in other words, optimization. This may be done by improving the means available or by finding other, more optimal contexts. Finally, if the endeavors are met with obstacles, the option of switching to other paths to achieve the goal is required—in other words, compensation. Compensation becomes necessary if the means originally used are no longer available or have lost their effectiveness. The following example aims to illustrate how the two development regulation models can be combined.

Assume that I am no longer able to climb the stairs to the fourth floor. I can, for example, rent an apartment on the first floor (assimilative selection). If I place a lower value on my physical abilities and a higher value on my education (accommodative selection) in my own self-evaluation, I do not feel any worse about myself as a result. If I would like to stay in the fourth-floor apartment, I could have a chair lift installed (assimilative compensation). Furthermore, I can maintain my self-concept—the idea that I possess good physical abilities—by changing the person or group I compare myself with in self-evaluation in order to appear more competent by comparison (accommodative compensation). Finally, I can engage in assimilative optimization by buying myself the best chair lift available and practicing how to use it. Alternatively, I can engage in accommodative optimiza-

tion by having a wide choice of reference groups available that produce the same result.

Even with an increase of irreversible losses and deficits, coping episodes in later adulthood and old age can usually be reconstructed as interlocking combinations of complementary assimilative and accommodative processes, as the two directions of coping can point toward different goals. Not least, modifying personal goal structures and preferences can also recreate the ability to control highly valued goals and thereby also (subjectively) enable active efforts that previously appeared to be pointless and would have taken up valuable resources unnecessarily (Brandtstädter & Rothermund, 1994). And indeed this is what we find when studying the distribution of psychological energy across central life domains, that is, personal life investment (e.g., Staudinger et al., 1999), across different ages. Developmental tasks of different ages are reflected in the respective investment profiles. The domain's friends receive highest investment priority in adolescence, profession and friends rank high in young adulthood, profession and family rank high in middle adulthood, and health and family rank high in old age.

These phenomena are a central function of the aforementioned selection processes (P. B. Baltes & Baltes, 1990). The reduction of aspiration levels can be similarly classified. Being permanently unable to fulfill a specific criterion of physical fitness—for example, climbing several flights of stairs with ease—due to aging motivates accommodative coping. This may, however, lead to a more age-appropriate definition of physical fitness that can then be actively pursued. Equally, compensation processes call for active *and* accommodative regulations. If otherwise effective repertoires of action fail to achieve goals or maintain standards, the individual seeks alternative paths of action, possibly involving compensatory aids (e.g., a hearing aid). The precondition for this step, however, is an acceptance of irreversible losses on a subordinate goal level: Only individuals who can cope with a self-definition of being hard of hearing, and thus accept a hearing aid, can maintain (relatively) effortless communication (Tesch-Römer, 1997).

Coping may also be preventive, that is, take place before the stressful event or the degenerative development occurs (compare the concept of anticipatory coping in Aspinwall & Taylor, 1997). One interesting example of this phenomenon is provided by the aforementioned findings on older people's allegedly paradoxical fear of crime interpreted in the light of our conception of resilience. The fact that our knowledge compensates for losses in the mechanics of our mind (P. B. Baltes, Lindenberger, et al., 1998) may also be viewed as anticipatory coping. However, in this case, coping is not an intentional but an automatic process.

A Life Span View on Resilience as a Helpful Framework for the Study of Developmental Psychopathology

Throughout this chapter, we have argued in favor of a life span perspective on development in general and on processes of resilience in particular. If these arguments hold, the study of developmental psychopathology also has to be viewed as a life span science. Without doubt, it is important to further investigate processes of resilience (and vulnerability) among children and adolescents (Luthar, 2003), particularly to learn as much as possible about means of early prevention and intervention. However, it might be not only too narrow, but even misleading to restrict research in developmental psychopathology to these earlier phases of the life span. The acknowledgment of processes of maladaptation and pathology throughout the life span surely will help to properly understand the basic nature and dynamic of these processes. The study of psychopathology and resilience shares a number of characteristics—one may even argue that they are two sides of one coin—that support this proposal.

First, the identification of developmental psychopathology as well as of resilience asks for an evaluative judgment. Moreover, both concepts refer to the very same normative points, namely, the "normality" (or even successfulness) of a certain course of development (which is maintained in cases of resilience and lost in cases of maladaptation or pathology). As a consequence, both developmental psychopathology and research programs focusing on resilience share the common need for a normative theory of development.

Second, the research on resilience has demonstrated that development occurs even in cases in which stability or at least no dramatic changes are observed. This refocuses attention on the dynamics going on behind the scenes, a perspective that may also prove useful (or even necessary) for research on developmental pathology. Irrespective of whether a certain developmental state (say, a certain degree of grief) is labeled maladaptive, the crucial question may be not to declare an arbitrary cutoff value for a phenotypic phenomenon (be it stable or varying), but rather to identify the adaptivity or maladaptivity of the processes producing this developmental phenotype. This refocusing may further help to identify more general patterns and processes of (successful or maladaptive) development.

Third, please recall that the life span notion of resilience suggested in this chapter encompasses maintenance and recovery as well as loss management as three important facets. To make loss management a part of resilience calls attention to the relativity of what is called resilient and what is called pathological. A resilience constellation in the sense of loss management may actually result in levels of functioning that are below normal. But given the stressors and threats under which the individual is operating, this level of functioning is still to be called resilient rather than pathological. By the same token, sometimes maintaining "only" normal levels of functioning may not be called resilient because extant stressors could be dealt with more successfully. In other words, the focus on resilience in old age can help to identify cases of developmental pathology that, at first glance, seemed to be cases of stability (and, at the same time, declare other cases as nonpathological that seemed to be maladaptive).

Finally, taking a life span perspective on developmental psychopathology asks for taking into consideration a diachronous as well as a synchronous effect of a given constellation. That is, a certain developmental path in early childhood may be the root of a successful course of later development even if, at a first synchronous glance, it seems to be a maladaptive constellation or vice versa. For example, the mother of a blind child who refuses to allow the child to move through the house may be the cause of synchronous desperation on behalf of the child, but also of assimilative efforts of the child to use other senses to gain orientation. In turn, a concurrently successful developmental constellation, such as the big success of a child in sports, may in the long run have dysfunctional effects, such as a heart condition or hurting joints.

RESILIENCE IN LATER ADULTHOOD AND OLD AGE: PERSPECTIVES FOR RESEARCH AND INTERVENTION

Resilience, like vulnerability and adaptivity, entails a normative facet as a constitutive part. It means more than simply stability (or continuity or unchangeability), but rather the capability to resist (potentially) harmful influences, circumstances, or experiences. Whether or not a given event is harmful (etc.) cannot be decided without referring to a normative standard. With respect to subjective well-being, this observation often seems trivial: If a person feels sad or depressed, if he or she suffers from the symptoms or consequences of a disease or decrease of capacities (e.g., deterioration of hearing and sight) or has experienced serious losses (e.g., death of partner), it seems obvious that a reduction of well-being is the result by default. However, even in these cases, it is less obvious what period of grief or sadness, what amount or degree of depression or pain is normal or appropriate, and at what point it might be described as "too much." Moreover, in many other cases, and with respect to most other possible indicators of a critical event, it is often just the reaction itself that indicates that an event has been "critical." Only if a person shows depressive symptoms over a long period after a separation is it called a critical life event. Otherwise, it may be viewed as a relief or a challenge.

Human development is characterized by a considerable plasticity (e.g., P. B. Baltes, Staudinger, et al., 1999; Lerner, 1984), which not only forms the central prerequisite for the resilience processes mentioned, but is generally a precondition for lifelong development. Processes of self-regulation are not only a central criterion of this adaptation process, but also steer it to a large extent. Subjective well-being and psychological health can be preserved or improved only if resilient constellations of resources protect the person against unfavorable conditions, if personal and social coping resources help to offset and compensate the—inevitable—occurrence of crises and losses, and if individual competence is preserved in large part, whether by stabilizing the respective prerequisites or reorienting efforts toward attainable goals. Development consists, if these arguments hold, essentially in the maintenance and implementation of the individual's ability to adapt to discrepant situations (developmental tasks) by seeking, either through assimilation or accommodation, to (dis)solve the critical and stressful discrepancy in cases where the situation cannot be avoided permanently. Optimal, successful development implies *progressive* adaptation, which preserves or increases this plasticity and adaptivity as much as possible. This leads to the apparently paradoxical statement that development can be described as *successful* when it (i.e., progressive adaptation) can take place at any given time, and in fact does.

Successes and failures are constitutive for actions and histories of action and make up the dramaturgy of life; essential aspects of our activities in life consist in coming to terms with unanticipated and undesired effects of earlier actions and decisions. This also has consequences for theoretical questions of optimal development and successful aging. The unfortunate choice of either electing specific values and goals (authenticity, control) as criteria for successful development or forgoing judgments of success or failure altogether, can be avoided if metacompetencies are

included as criteria that enable the person's further development and adaptation (P. B. Baltes & Baltes, 1990; Brandtstädter & Schneewind, 1977; Greve, 2001; Staudinger, 1999b). Beyond merely demanding that vital basic needs are met, successful development and successful aging call for competencies and resources that can compensate for deficits and vulnerabilities and help us successfully achieve personal goals, while taking into consideration basic conditions for sensible coexistence. From this perspective, the abilities to select developmental goals, make competent decisions, actually realize them and thus overcome resistance, as well as to review goals and strategies in the light of new experiences are all essential aspects of successful development (see Bandura, 1989; Brandtstädter & Lerner, 1999). The basis for successful development appears to be that competencies are built up and perfected, and thus that opportunities for further development are sustained and expanded.

In this context, the Janus-faced function of goals should not be overlooked. On the one hand, goals give life meaning and coherence. Having goals is indeed itself an indicator of life satisfaction (see Brunstein, 1993). On the other hand, goals become sources of dissatisfaction and frustration if they are not—or no longer—attainable. Goal importance and goal commitment moderate the relevant effects; a strong *commitment* intensifies positive feelings in the event of success but also intensifies negative feelings in the event of failure. Precisely for this reason, the attempt to theoretically define optimal development and successful aging in terms of the successful pursuit of goals is inadequate. As explained earlier, individual action takes place in life situations and developmental contexts that are sometimes nontransparent and controllable only to a certain extent. A more comprehensive theoretical explanation of optimal development and successful aging hence also requires taking into consideration the processes and resources that make it possible for a person to cope with irreversible losses, to detach himself or herself from unattainable goals or life projects, and to flexibly balance personal goals with available options of action (Brandtstädter, 1998).

Despite the relatively short period in which the concept of resilience has been dealt with in the context of later adulthood and old age, the research has produced substantive and differentiated results (i.e., the phenomenon has been investigated thoroughly, although the term resilience itself is not always used, or in any case, not in the sense described here). The surprisingly high (in view of widespread aging stereotypes) psychosocial robustness and plasticity of the aging person and of his or her personality and identity, which can also be found in many different domains of functioning, have come to the fore of research interest. The life span perspective additionally calls attention to the limits of resilience and plasticity and the increasing dependence on external resources in later life.

What is crucially needed at this stage, apart from the replication and differentiation of many findings referred to here, is a comprehensive theoretical framework for psychogerontological resilience research. This framework would not only overcome the conceptual heterogeneity mentioned earlier and lamented repeatedly in the literature (Luthar et al., 2000; Masten, 2001), but would in particular integrate the various approaches—from life span developmental psychology, gerontopsychology, and research on self-concept and coping—that all help to explain the phenomenon of resilience. In addition to the models of selective optimization with compensation (P. B. Baltes & Baltes, 1990; P. B. Baltes & Freund, 2003; Freund et al., 1999) and the dual process model of developmental regulation (Brandtstädter, 1998; Brandtstädter & Rothermund, 2002), other approaches worth mentioning here are the model of primary and secondary (development) control (Heckhausen & Schulz, 1995; Rothbaum, Weisz, & Snyder, 1982), the distinction between problem-centered and emotion-centered coping (Lazarus, 1991), and social-psychological research into the "dynamic" self (Leary & Tangney, 2003; Markus & Wurf, 1987). The theoretical framework to be established should, at the same time, be theoretically and empirically linked with the subpersonal level (e.g., cognitive psychology) and the transpersonal level of macrosocial approaches (e.g., social risk factors). In particular with respect to the former aspect, it is crucial to focus more on the "biological contributors to resilience" (Curtis & Cicchetti, 2003). In a recent review, Curtis and Cicchetti have convincingly argued that research on resilience in the past 30 years or so has mainly focused on psychosocial correlates and conditions of resilience processes. They argue in favor of an expansion of the scope of the concept of resilience to include the biological level. At the same time, however, Curtis and Cicchetti demonstrate that a reduction of resilient processes to this level must be avoided for several reasons. Beside aspects of resilience such as equifinality and multifinality that are mentioned in their plea, we would add that the inherently normative basis of resilience makes it impossible to reduce this concept to a mere physiological (e.g., neural) level. Obviously, however, the proper explanation of processes of resilience entails basic physiological processes as well. Neural plasticity (Huttenlocher, 2002) is one of the central fundaments for the mere possibility of resilience to occur.

Research on resilience will develop productively in the future only if unnecessarily confrontational stances (e.g., person-centered versus variable-centered approaches, nature versus nurture of resources of resilience) are set aside in favor of integrative approaches. It is increasingly important to better understand processes of resilience in their relational character. Gaining knowledge about the mediating processes, including their diachronic logic, is also of central significance, among other things because diverse research on self-regulation has shown that the adaptivity of self-regulation resources depends largely on when during the regulation process it is implemented (e.g., Staudinger, 1997). For instance, there is indication that realism promotes adaptation in the phase of setting a goal, but optimism promotes adaptation more in the phase of implementing a goal (Taylor & Gollwitzer, 1995). Similarly, research on coping shows that spending time in deep thought after a bereavement is functional in the first 6 months, but dysfunctional if it continues longer (e.g., Filipp & Klauer, 1991; Wortman & Silver, 2001). Therefore, whether something is a resource or a hindrance also depends on when the behavior or trait is implemented.

We have singled out in particular two theoretical approaches that appear most promising in this context and that have, in the past decade in particular, been responsible for great strides with regard to overall theoretical integration. However, more far-reaching efforts toward integration are both desirable and urgently needed. The conceptual differentiation outlined here among plasticity, resilience, and loss management is only one example in this context (e.g., Staudinger et al., 1995). A further pressing task would be to examine functional equivalents between the dynamics and processes discussed and adaptive aspects of psychomotor functioning and cognitive development in later adulthood and old age. The structural parallel between phylogenetic and ontogenetic development dynamics has also been widely ignored in the current theoretical discussion, and thus concepts of evolutionary biology have been used very little to develop theories of psychogerontology (see, however, P. B. Baltes, 1997).

This suggests that it would be most promising to extend empirical research on the concept of resilience in old age in the psychosocial domain beyond this domain as well. Scholars are already discussing physiological and particularly psychoneuroimmunological processes, particularly in the context of stress reactions and their consequences for mental and physical health (for a summary, see Curtis & Cicchetti, 2003; Ryff et al., 1998). However, countless other areas are conceivable and logical, precisely concerning the issue of predictors of optimal aging, for instance, questions of motoric resilience (e.g., under which personal conditions do, for example, falls cause no harm?), communicative resilience (e.g., who seeks and finds a constructive way out, even in "unsuccessful" discussions, social "dead ends" and conflicts?), resilience in partner relationships (e.g., who maintains a positive and balanced relationship, even under stressful conditions, for example, in a caring context—"wife cares for husband"?), economic resilience (e.g., who can keep the components of a certain standard of living—healthy eating, leisure activities, social commitment—stable even under varying, particularly increasingly tight economic restrictions?).

Two further directions of research previously neglected in connection with resilience, but forming one focus of the life span perspective, appear very promising. The first is support of constellations of resilience. Particularly in old age, when external resources take on increasingly important functions, this form of resilience comes to the fore. At this point, we must emphasize once again that the domain of self and personality represents only one sector of the relevant components of constellations of resilience. For instance, the nonsocial, that is, physical and material, characteristics of the environment form a component of resilience in old age that cannot be overestimated (e.g., Lawton, 1989). We are only beginning to explore the intervention potential in the physical and material characteristics of the environment.

A second main desideratum is to conduct prospective longitudinal studies, which should also include data recorded before the onset of stress, if possible (e.g., Wortman & Silver, 2001). This could take the form of studies covering the entire life span (e.g., Robins et al., 1996) or of targeted samplings from risk groups (e.g., Bonanno, 2004; Fredrickson et al., 2003). These studies are extremely important because the interaction between stress factors and the protective resources that constitute the phenomenon of resilience has not yet been researched sufficiently (Masten & Coatsworth, 1995). Thus, adverse conditions on the one hand could (under certain conditions) erode the existing resources (and thus intensify the negative effect of stress on well-being and further development), but on the other hand also have a strengthening effect on the individual (Pellegrini, 1990; Rutter, 1985; see also Kobasa, 1979): They could challenge the individual to build and develop resources that at some point could diminish or completely neutralize the effect of this stressor.

A central objective for further research will have to be better understanding of the processes of adaptation. Since Barkow et al. (1992) established the discipline of evolutionary psychology with the publication of their pioneering work *The Adapted Mind* (for a summary, see Buss, 2004; Gaulin & McBurney, 2004), it has become impermissible to use the concept in a purely metaphorical or summary sense. Indeed, research on resilience (and also on coping) might well benefit from a study of the functional equivalents between an evolutionary concept of adaptation and the intrapsychological adjustment to adverse conditions.

To put it another way, the goal of future research must be to bring together psychological and biological perspectives, not only combining the variables observed in each case (e.g., cognitions and emotions on the one hand and brain activity and hormones on the other), but also integrating them in a theoretical sense (Curtis & Cicchetti, 2003). On this point, Ryff and Singer (2002) refer to E. O. Wilson's (1998) call to again begin striving for a unity of science, which he calls "consilience." As we have seen here, resilience could help pave the way toward achieving this goal.

REFERENCES

Affleck, G., & Tennen, H. (1996). Construing benefits from adversity: Adaptional significance and dispositional underpinnings. *Journal of Personality, 64,* 899–922.

Allen, K. R., Blieszner, R., & Roberto, K. A. (2000). Families in the middle and later years: A review and critique of research in the 1990s. *Journal of Marriage and the Family, 62,* 911–926.

Anastasi, A. (1958). Heredity, environment, and the question "how." *Psychological Review, 65,* 197–208.

Arrington, E. G., & Wilson, M. N. (2000). A re-examination of risk and resilience during adolescence: Incorporating culture and diversity. *Journal of Child and Family Studies, 9,* 221–230.

Asendorpf, J. B. (1999). *Psychologie der Persönlichkeit* [Psychology of personality]. Berlin, Germany: Springer.

Asendorpf, J. B., & van Aken, M. A. G. (1999). Resilient, overcontrolled, and undercontrolled personality prototypes in childhood: Replicability, predictive power, and the trait-type issue. *Journal of Personality and Social Psychology, 77,* 815–832.

Aspinwall, L. G. (2001). Dealing with adversity: Self-regulation, coping, adaptation, and health. In A. Tesser & N. Schwarz (Eds.), *Blackwell handbook of social psychology: Intraindividual processes* (pp. 591–614). Malden, MA: Blackwell.

Aspinwall, L. G., & Staudinger, U. M. (Eds.). (2003). *A psychology of human strengths.* Washington, DC: American Psychological Association.

Aspinwall, L. G., & Taylor, S. E. (1997). A stitch in time: Self-regulation and proactive coping. *Psychological Bulletin, 121,* 417–436.

Baltes, M. M. (1995). Verlust der Selbständigkeit im Alter: Theoretische Überlegungen und empirische Befunde [Loss of autonomy in old age: Theoretical considerations and empirical results]. *Psychologische Rundschau, 46,* 159–170.

Baltes, M. M., & Carstensen, L. L. (2003). The process of successful aging: Selection, optimization, and compensation. In U. M. Staudinger & U. Lindenberger (Eds.), *Understanding human development: Dialogues with lifespan psychology* (pp. 81–104). Dordrecht, The Netherlands: Kluwer Press.

Baltes, M. M., & Montada, L. (Eds.). (1996). *Produktives leben im alter [Productive life in old age].* Frankfurt, Germany: Campus.

Baltes, P. B. (1987). Theoretical propositions of life-span developmental psychology: On the dynamics between growth and decline. *Developmental Psychology, 23,* 611–626.

Baltes, P. B. (1993). The aging mind: Potential and limits. *Gerontologist, 33,* 580–594.

Baltes, P. B. (1997). On the incomplete architecture of human ontogeny. *American Psychologist, 52,* 366–380.

Baltes, P. B., & Baltes, M. M. (1990). Psychological perspectives on successful aging: The model of selective optimization with compensation. In P. B. Baltes & M. M. Baltes (Eds.), *Successful aging: Perspectives from the behavioral sciences* (pp. 1–34). New York: Cambridge University Press.

Baltes, P. B., Cornelius, S. W., & Nesselroade, J. R. (1979). Cohort effects in developmental psychology. In J. R. Nesselroade & P. B. Baltes (Eds.), *Longitudinal research in the study of behavior and development* (pp. 61–87). New York: Academic Press.

Baltes, P. B., & Freund, A. M. (2003). Human strengths as the orchestration of wisdom and selective optimization with compensation. In L. G. Aspinwall & U. M. Staudinger (Eds.), *A psychology of human strengths* (pp. 23–35). Washington, DC: American Psychological Association.

Baltes, P. B., Glück, J., & Kunzmann, U. (2002). Wisdom: Its structure and function in regulating successful life span development. In C. R. Snyder & S. J. Lopez (Eds.), *Handbook of positive psychology* (pp. 327–347). Oxford: Oxford University Press.

Baltes, P. B., & Graf, P. (1996). Psychological aspects of aging: Facts and frontiers. In D. Magnusson (Ed.), *The life-span development of individuals: Behavioural, neurobiological and psychosocial perspectives* (pp. 427–459). Cambridge, England: Cambridge University Press.

Baltes, P. B., Lindenberger, U., & Staudinger, U. M. (1998). Life-span theory in developmental psychology. In R. M. Lerner (Ed.), *Handbook of child psychology: Vol. 1. Theoretical models of human development* (5th ed., pp. 1029–1143). New York: Wiley.

Baltes, P. B., Mittelstraß, J., & Staudinger, U. M. (Eds.). (1994). *Alter und altern* [Age and aging]. Berlin, Germany: de Gruyter.

Baltes, P. B., Reese, H. W., & Lipsitt, L. P. (1980). Life-span developmental psychology. *Annual Review of Psychology, 31,* 65–110.

Baltes, P. B., & Staudinger, U. M. (1993). The search for a psychology of wisdom. *Current Directions in Psychological Science, 2,* 75–80.

Baltes, P. B., & Staudinger, U. M. (2000). Wisdom: A metaheuristic (pragmatic) to orchestrate mind and virtue toward excellence. *American Psychologist, 55*(1), 122–136.

Baltes, P. B., Staudinger, U. M., & Lindenberger, U. (1999). Life-span developmental psychology. *Annual Review of Psychology, 50,* 471–507.

Bandura, A. (1986). *Social foundations of thought and action: A social cognitive theory.* Englewood Cliffs, NJ: Prentice-Hall.

Bandura, A. (1989). Human agency in social cognitive theory. *American Psychologist, 44,* 1175–1184.

Bandura, A. (1999). Social cognitive theory of personality. In L. Pervin & O. John (Eds.), *Handbook of personality* (2nd ed., pp. 154–196). New York: Guilford Press.

Barkow, J. H., Cosmides, L., & Tooby, J. (Eds.). (1992). *The adapted mind: Evolutionary psychology and the generation of culture.* New York: Oxford University Press.

Baumeister, R. F. (1989). The optimal margin of illusion. *Journal of Social and Clinical Psychology, 8,* 176–189.

Baumeister, R. F. (Ed.). (1993). *Self-esteem: The puzzle of low self-regard.* New York: Plenum Press.

Baumeister, R. F., & Vohs, K. D. (2002). The pursuit of meaningfulness in life. In C. R. Snyder & S. J. Lopez (Eds.), *Handbook of positive psychology* (pp. 608–618). Oxford: Oxford University Press.

Beasley, M., Thompson, T., & Davidson, J. (2003). Resilience in response to life stress: The effects of coping style and cognitive hardiness. *Personality and Individual Differences, 34,* 77–95.

Bengtson, V. L., Reedy, M. N., & Gordon, C. (1985). Aging and self-conceptions: Personality processes and social contexts. In J. E. Birren & K. W. Schaie (Eds.), *Handbook of the psychology of aging* (2nd ed., pp. 544–593). New York: Van Nostrand Reinhold.

Berman, J. R. (2003). An economic perspective on selection, optimization, and compensation (SOC). In U. M. Staudinger & U. Lindenberger (Eds.), *Understanding human development: Dialogues with lifespan psychology* (pp. 125–155). Dordrecht, The Netherlands: Kluwer Press.

Bertrand, R. M., & Lachman, M. E. (2003). Personality development in adulthood and old age. In I. B. Weiner (Editor-in-Chief), R. M. Lerner, M. A. Easterbrooks, & J. Mistry (Eds.), *Handbook of psychology: Vol. 6. Developmental psychology* (pp. 463–483). Hoboken, NJ: Wiley.

Block, J. H., & Block, J. (1980). The role of ego-control and ego-resiliency in the organization of behavior. In W. A. Collins (Ed.), *Development of cognition, affect, and social relations* (pp. 39–101). Hillsdale, NJ: Erlbaum.

Bonanno, G. A. (2004). Loss, trauma, and human resilience: Have we underestimated the human capacity to thrive after extremely aversive events? *American Psychologist, 59,* 20–28.

Bond, L. A., Cutler, S. J., & Grams, A. (Eds.). (1995). *Promoting successful and productive aging.* Thousand Oaks, CA: Sage.

Brandtstädter, J. (1990). Entwicklung im lebensablauf: Ansätze und probleme einer lebensspannen-enwticklungspsychologie [Development in the life-course. Approaches and problems of a life-span developmental psychology]. In K.-U. Mayer (Ed.), *Lebensläufe und sozialer Wandel: Kölner Zeitschrift für Soziologie und Sozialpsychologie, 31*(Sonderheft), 351–373.

Brandtstädter, J. (1992). Personal control over development: Some developmental implications of self-efficacy. In R. Schwarzer (Ed.), *Self-efficacy: Thought control of action* (pp. 127–145). Washington, DC: Hemisphere.

Brandtstädter, J. (1998). Action perspectives on human development. In R. M. Lerner (Ed.), *Handbook of child psychology: Vol. I. Theoretical models of human development* (5th ed., pp. 807–863). New York: Wiley.

Brandtstädter, J. (1999a). The self in action and development. In J. Brandtstädter & R. M. Lerner (Eds.), *Action and self-development: Theory and research through the life-span* (pp. 37–65). Thousand Oaks, CA: Sage.

Brandtstädter, J. (1999b). Sources of resilience in the aging self. In F. Blanchard-Fields & T. Hess (Eds.), *Social cognition and aging* (pp. 123–141). New York: Academic Press.

Brandtstädter, J. (2001). *Entwicklung—Intention—Handeln* [Development—intention—action]. Stuttgart, Germany: Kohlhammer.

Brandtstädter, J. (2002). Searching for paths to successful development and aging: Integrating developmental and action-theoretic perspectives. In L. Pulkkinen & A. Caspi (Eds.), *Paths to successful development: Personality in the life course* (pp. 380–408). Cambridge, England: Cambridge University Press.

Brandtstädter, J., & Greve, W. (1994a). The aging self: Stabilizing and protective processes. *Developmental Review, 14,* 52–80.

Brandtstädter, J., & Greve, W. (1994b). Entwicklung im lebenslauf als kulturprodukt und handlungsergebnis: Aspekte der konstruktion und kritik [Development through the life course as cultural product and action result: Aspects of construction and critique]. In K. A.

Schneewind (Ed.), *Psychologie der erziehung und sozialisation: Pädagogische psychologie* [Psychology of education and socializatio] (*Enzyklopädie der Psychologie*, Bd.1, S41–S71). Göttingen, Germany: Hogrefe.

Brandtstädter, J., & Lerner, R. M. (Eds.). (1999). *Action and self-development.* Thousand Oaks, CA: Sage.

Brandtstädter, J., & Renner, G. (1990). Tenacious goal pursuit and flexible goal adjustment: Explication and age-related analysis of assimilative and accommodative strategies of coping. *Psychology and Aging, 5,* 58–67.

Brandtstädter, J., & Renner, G. (1992). Coping with discrepancies between aspirations and achievments in adult development: A dual process model. In L. Montada, S.-H. Filipp, & M. Lerner (Eds.), *Life crises and life experiences of loss in adulthood* (pp. 301–319). Hillsdale, NJ: Erlbaum.

Brandtstädter, J., & Rothermund, K. (1994). Self-perceptions of control in middle and later adulthood: Buffering losses by rescaling goals. *Psychology and Aging, 9,* 265–273.

Brandtstädter, J., & Rothermund, K. (1995). Self-percepts of control in middle and later adulthood: Buffering losses by rescaling goals. *Psychology and Aging, 9,* 265–273.

Brandtstädter, J., & Rothermund, K. (2002). The life course dynamics of goal pursuit and goal adjustment: A two-process framework. *Developmental Review, 22,* 117–150.

Brandtstädter J., & Schneewind, K. A. (1977). Optimal human development: Some implications for psychology. *Human Development, 20,* 1–30.

Brandtstädter, J., & Wentura, D. (1995). Adjustment to shifting possibility frontiers in later life: Complementary adaptive modes. In R. A. Dixon & L. Bäckman (Eds.), *Compensating for psychological deficits and declines: Managing losses and promoting gains* (pp. 83–106). Mahwah, NJ: Erlbaum.

Brandtstädter, J., Wentura, D., & Greve, W. (1993). Adaptive resources of the aging self: Outlines of an emergent perspective. *International Journal of Behavioral Development, 16,* 323–349.

Bronfenbrenner, U. (1979). *The ecology of human development.* Cambridge, MA: Harvard University Press.

Brunstein, J. C. (1993). Personal goals and subjective well-being: A longitudinal study. *Journal of Personality and Social Psychology, 65,* 1061–1070.

Bühler, C. (1933). *Der menschliche Lebenslauf als psychologisches problem* [The human life course as problem]. Leipzig, Germany: Hirzel.

Buss, D. M. (2004). *Evolutionary psychology* (2nd ed.). Boston: Pearson.

Caprara, G. V., & Cervone, D. (2003). A conception of personality for a psychology of human strengths: Personality as an agentic, self-regulating system. In L. G. Aspinwall & U. M. Staudinger (Eds.), *A psychology of human strengths* (pp. 61–74). Washington, DC: American Psychological Association.

Carstensen, L. L., & Charles, S. T. (2003). Human aging: Why is even good news taken as bad? In L. G. Aspinwall & U. M. Staudinger (Eds.), *A psychology of human strengths* (pp. 75–86). Washington, DC: American Psychological Association.

Carstensen, L. L., Isaacowitz, D., & Charles, S. T. (1999). Taking time seriously in life span development. *American Psychologist, 54,* 165–181.

Carver, C. S. (1998). Resilience and thriving: Issues, models, and linkages. *Journal of Social Issues, 54,* 245–266.

Caspi, A. (1998). Personality development across the life course. In N. Eisenberg (Ed.), *Handbook of child psychology: Vol. 3. Social, emotional, and personality development* (5th ed., pp. 311–387). New York: Wiley.

Caspi, A., & Roberts, B. W. (1999). Personality continuity and change over the life course. In L. A. Pervin & O. P. John (Eds.), *Handbook of*

personality: Theory and research* (2nd ed., pp. 300–326). New York: Guilford Press.

Cervone, D., & Shoda, Y. (Eds.). (1999a). *The coherence of personality.* New York: Guilford Press.

Cervone, D., & Shoda, Y. (1999b). Social-cognitive theories and the coherence of. personality. In D. Cervone & Y. Shoda (Eds.), *The coherence of personality* (pp. 3–33). New York: Guilford Press.

Cicchetti, D. (1993). Developmental psychopathology: Reactions, reflections, projections [Special issue: Setting a path for the coming decade—Some goals and challenges]. *Developmental Review, 13,* 471–502.

Cicchetti, D., & Aber, J. L. (1998). Contextualism and developmental psychopathology. *Development and Psychopathology, 10,* 137–141.

Cicchetti, D., & Garmezy, N. (1993). Prospects and promises in the study of resilience. *Development and Psychopathology, 5,* 497–502.

Cicchetti, D., Rappaport, J., Sandler, I., & Weissberg, R. P. (Eds.). (2000). *The promotion of wellness in children and adolescents.* Washington, DC: Child Welfare League of America Press.

Cicchetti, D., & Rogosch, F. A. (1997). The role of self-organization in the promotion of resilience in maltreated children. *Development and Psychopathology, 9,* 797–815.

Cicchetti, D., & Rogosch, F. A. (2002). A developmental psychopathology perspective on adolescence. *Journal of Consulting and Clinical Psychology, 70,* 6–20.

Cloninger, C. R. (2003). Completing the architecture of human personality development: Temperament, character, and coherence. In U. M. Staudinger & U. Lindenberger (Eds.), *Understandung human development: Dialogues with lifespan psychology* (pp. 159–181). Dordrecht, The Netherlands: Kluwer Press.

Costa, P. T., & McCrae, R. R. (1985). *The NEO Personality Inventory manual from S and from R.* Odessa, FL: Psychological Assessment Resources.

Costa, P. T., Jr., & McCrae, R. R. (1988). Personality in adulthood: A six-year longitudinal study of self reports and spouse ratings on the NEO Personality Inventory. *Journal of Personality and Social Psychology, 54,* 853–863.

Crocker, J., & Park, L. (2004). The costly pursuit of self-esteem. *Psychological Bulletin, 130*(3), 392–414.

Cummings, E., & Henry, W. C. (1961). *Growing old: The process of disengagement.* New York: Basic Books.

Curtis, W. J., & Cicchetti, D. (2003). Moving research on resilience into the 21st century: Theoretical and methodological considerations in examining the biological contributors to resilience. *Development and Psychopathology, 15,* 773–810.

Dweck, C. S., & Leggett, E. L. (1988). A social-cognitive approach to motivation and personality. *Psychological Review, 95,* 256–273.

Edelman, G. M. (1987). *Neural Darwinism: The theory of neuronal group selection.* New York: Basic Books.

Eichorn, D. H., Clausen, J. A., Hann, N., Honzik, M. P., & Mussen, P. H. (Eds.). (1981). *Present and past in middle life.* New York: Academic Press.

Elder, G. H., Jr. (1975). Age differentiation and the life course. *Annual Review of Sociology, 1,* 165–190.

Elder, G. H., Jr. (1978). Family history and the life course. In T. K. Hareven (Ed.), *Transitions: The family and the life course in historical perspective* (pp. 17–64). New York: Academic Press.

Elder, G. H. (1994). Time, human agency, and social change: Perspectives on the life course. *Social Psychology Quarterly, 57,* 4–15.

Elder, G. H., Jr., & O'Rand, A. M. (1995). Adult lives in a changing society. In K. Cook, J. S. House, & G. Fine (Eds.), *Sociological perspec-*

tives on social psychology (pp. 452–475). Needham Heights, MA: Allyn & Bacon.

Erikson, E. H. (1959). *Identity and the life cycle.* New York: International University Press.

Erikson, E. H. (1984). *The life-cycle completed.* New York: Norton.

Erikson, E. H., Erikson, J. M., & Kivnick, H. (1986). *Vital involvement in old age: The experience of old age in our time.* London: Norton.

Featherman, D. L., & Lerner, R. M. (1985). Ontogenesis and sociogenesis: Problematics for theory and research about development and socialization across the life span. *American Sociological Review, 50,* 659–676.

Felten, B. S. (2000). Resilience in a multicultural sample of community-dwelling women older than age 85. *Clinical Nursing Research, 9,* 102–123.

Filipp, S.-H. (Ed.). (1995). *Kritische lebensereignisse [Critical life events]* (3rd ed.). Weinheim, Germany: Psychologie Verlags Union.

Filipp, S.-H., & Klauer, T. (1991). Subjective well-being in the face of critical life events: The case of successful coping. In F. Strack, M. Argyle, & N. Schwarz (Eds.), *The social psychology of subjective well-being* (Vol. 21, pp. 213–234). Oxford: Pergamon Press.

Ford, D. H., & Lerner, R. M. (1992). *Developmental systems theory: An integrative approach.* Newbury Park, CA: Sage.

Fredrickson, B., Tugade, M., Waugh, C., & Larkin, G. (2003). What good are positive emotions in crisis? A prospective study of resilience and emotions following the terrorist attacks on the United States on September 11th, 2001. *Journal of Personality and Social Psychology, 84*(2), 365–376.

Freund, A., Li, K., & Baltes, P. B. (1999). The role of selection, optimization, and compensation in successful aging. In J. Brandtstädter & R. M. Lerner (Eds.), *Action and self-development: Theory and research through the life-span* (pp. 401–434). Thousand Oaks, CA: Sage.

Freund, A., & Riedinger, M. (2003). Successful aging. In I. B. Weiner (Editor-in-Chief), R. M. Lerner, M. A. Easterbrooks, & J. Mistry (Eds.), *Handbook of psychology: Vol. 6. Developmental psychology* (pp. 601–628). Hoboken, NJ: Wiley.

Freund, A., & Smith, J. (1997). Das Selbstdefinition in hohen alter [Self-definition in old age]. *Zeitschrift Für Sozialpsychologie, 28*(1/2), 44–59.

Garmezy, N. (1991). Resilience in children's adaptation to negative life events and stressed environments. *Pediatric Annals, 20,* 459–466.

Garner, D. M., Garfinkel, P. E., Schwartz, D., & Thompson, M. (1980). Cultural expectations of thinness in women. *Psychological Reports, 47,* 483–491.

Gaulin, S. J. C., & McBurney, D. H. (2004). *Evolutionary psychology* (2nd ed.). Upper Saddle River, NJ: Pearson.

Glantz, M. D., & Johnson, J. L. (1999). *Resilience and development: Positive life adaptations.* New York: Kluwer Academic/Plenum Press.

Glantz, M. D., & Sloboda, Z. (1999). Analysis and reconceptualization of resilience. In M. D. Glantz & J. L. Johnson (Eds.), *Resilience and development: Positive life adaptations* (pp. 109–126). New York: Kluwer Academic/Plenum Press.

Gollwitzer, P. M. (1987). Suchen, finden und festigen der eigenen identität: Unstillbare zielintentionen [Searching, finding and stabilizing of one's identity]. In H. Heckhausen, P. M. Gollwitzer, & F. E. Weinert (Eds.), *Jenseits des Rubikon: Der wille in den sozialwissenschaften [Beyond the Rubicon: The will in the social sciences]* (S176–S189). Berlin, Germany: Springer.

Gottlieb, G. (1998). Normally occurring environmental and behavioral influences on gene activity: From central dogma to probabilistic epigenesis. *Psychological Review, 105,* 792–802.

Gould, S. J. (1989). *Wonderful life: The Burgess shale and the nature of history.* New York: Norton.

Graf, P. (1990). Life-span change in implicit and explicit memory. *Bulletin of the Psychonomic Society, 28,* 353–358.

Greene, R. R. (2002). Holocaust survivors: A study of resilience. *Journal of Gerontological Social Work, 37,* 3–18.

Greve, W. (1998). Fear of crime among the elderly: Foresight, not fright. *International Review of Victimology, 5,* 277–309.

Greve, W. (2000a). Das erwachsene selbst [The adult self]. In W. Greve (Ed.), *Psychologie des selbst [Psychology of the self]* (pp. 96–114). Weinheim, Germany: Psychologie Verlags Union.

Greve, W. (2000b). Furcht vor kriminalität im alter: Befunde und überlegungen zu einer schnittstelle zwischen gerontopsychologie und viktimologie [Fear of crime in old age: Results and arguments on an interface between gerontopsychology and victimology]. *Zeitschrift für entwicklungspsychologie und pädagogische psychologie, 32,* 123–133.

Greve, W. (2001). Successful human development: Psychological conceptions. In N. J. Smelser & P. B. Baltes (Eds.-in-Chief), *International encyclopedia of the social and behavioral sciences* (Vol. 10, pp. 6970–6974). Oxford: Elsevier Science.

Greve, W. (2004). Fear of crime among older and younger adults: Paradoxes and other misconceptions. In H.-J. Albrecht, T. Serassis, & H. Kania (Eds.), *Images of crime II* (pp. 167–186). Freiburg, Germany: Max-Planck-Institut für Internationales und vergleichendes Strafrecht.

Greve, W. (2005). Maintaining personality: The active and adaptive self as core of individuality and personhood. In W. Greve, K. Rothermund, & D. Wentura (Eds.), *The adaptive self: Personal continuity and intentional self-development* (pp. 49–70). New York: Hogrefe/Huber.

Greve, W., & Enzmann, D. (2003). Self-esteem maintenance among incarcerated young males. *International Journal of Behavioral Development, 27,* 12–20.

Greve, W., Rothermund, K., & Wentura, D. (Eds.). (2005). *The adaptive self: Personal continuity and intentional self-development.* New York: Hogrefe/Huber.

Greve, W., & Wentura, D. (2003). Immunizing the self: Self-concept stabilization through reality-adaptive self-definitions. *Personality and Social Psychology Bulletin, 29,* 39–50.

Greve, W., & Wilmers, N. (2003). Schulgewalt und selbstwertempfinden: Zum moderierenden einfluss von bewältigungsressourcen bei tätern und opfern [School violence and self-esteem: Moderating influences of coping resources among offenders and victims]. *Psychologie in Erziehung und Unterricht, 50,* 353–368.

Gutmann, D. (1998). The psychoimmune system in later life. In J. Lomranz (Ed.), *Handbook of aging and mental health: An integrative approach* (pp. 281–295). New York: Plenum Press.

Haan, N. (1977). *Coping and defending.* New York: Academic Press.

Hannover, B. (1997). *Das dynamische selbst [The dynamic self].* Bern, Switzerland: Huber.

Hannover, B., & Kühnen, U. (2005). Culture, context, and cognition: The semantic-procedural interface model of the self. *European Review of Social Psychology.* Manuscript submitted for publication.

Harter, S. (1998). The development of self-representations. In W. Damon & N. Eisenberg (Eds.), *Handbook of child psychology: Vol. 3. Social, emotional, and personality development* (5th ed., pp. 553–617). New York: Wiley.

Harter, S. (1999). *The construction of self: A developmental perspective.* New York: Guilford Press.

Harter, S. (2002). Authenticity. In C. R. Snyder & S. J. Lopez (Eds.), *Handbook of positive psychology* (pp. 382–394). Oxford: Oxford University Press.

Havighurst, R. J. (1953). *Human development and education.* New York: Longmans & Green.

Havighurst, R. J. (1973). History of developmental psychology: Socialization and personality development through the life-span. In P. B. Baltes & K. W. Schaie (Eds.), *Life-span developmental psychology: Personality and socialization* (pp. 3–24). New York: Academic Press.

Heckhausen, J. (1990). Erwerb und funktion normativer vorstellungen über den lebenslauf [Development and function of normative ideas about the life-course]. *Kölner Zeitschrift für Soziologie und Sozialpsychologie, 31*(Sonderheft), 351–373.

Heckhausen, J. (1999). *Developmental regulation in adulthood: Age-normative and sociostructural constraints as adaptive challenges.* New York: Cambridge University Press.

Heckhausen, J. (2003). The future of lifespan developmental psychology: Perspectives from control theory. In U. M. Staudinger & U. Lindenberger (Eds.), *Understandung human development: Dialogues with lifespan psychology* (pp. 383–400). Dordrecht, The Netherlands: Kluwer Press.

Heckhausen, J., Dixon, R. A., & Baltes, P. B. (1989). Gains and losses in development throughout adulthood as perceived by different adult age groups. *Developmental Psychology, 25,* 109–121.

Heckhausen, J., & Lang, F. R. (1994). Social construction and old age: Normative conceptions and interpersonal processes. In G. R. Semin & K. Fiedler (Eds.), *Applied social psychology* (pp. 374–398). London: Sage.

Heckhausen, J., & Schulz, R. (1995). A life-span theory of control. *Psychological Review, 102,* 284–304.

Heckhausen, J., & Schulz, R. (1999). Selectivity in life-span development. In J. Brandtstädter & R. M. Lerner (Eds.), *Action and self-development: Theory and research through the life-span* (pp. 67–103). Thousand Oaks, CA: Sage.

Heckhausen, J., Wrosch, C., & Fleeson, W. (2001). Developmental regulation before and after a developmental deadline: The sample case of "biological clock" for childbearing. *Psychology and Aging, 16,* 400–413.

Heiman, T. (2002). Parents of children with disabilities: Resilience, coping, and future expectations. *Journal of Developmental and Physical Disabilities, 14,* 159–171.

Held, T. (1986). Institutionalization and deinstitutionalization of the life course. *Human Development, 29,* 157–162.

Hertzog, C., & Schaie, K. W. (1988). Stability and change in adult intelligence: 2. Simultaneous analysis of longitudinal means and covariance structures. *Psychology and Aging, 3,* 122–130.

Hetherington, E. M., Lerner, R. M., & Perlmutter, M. (Eds.). (1988). *Child development in life-span perspective.* Hillsdale, NJ: Erlbaum.

Higgins, E. T. (1996). The "self digest": Self-knowledge serving self-regulatory functions. *Journal of Personality and Social Psychology, 71,* 1062–1083.

Higgins, R. L. (2002). Reality negotiation. In C. R. Snyder & S. J. Lopez (Eds.), *Handbook of positive psychology* (pp. 351–365). Oxford: Oxford University Press.

Howard, D. V. (1991). Implicit memory: An expanding picture of cognitive aging. *Annual Review of Gerontology and Geriatrics, 11,* 1–22.

Huttenlocher, P. R. (2002). *Neural plasticity: The effects of experience on the development of the cerebral cortex.* Cambridge, MA. Harvard University Press.

Jacobs, K., Kohli, M., & Rein, M. (1991). Germany: The diversity of pathways. In M. Kohli, M. Rein, A.-M. Guillard, & H. V. Gunsteren (Eds.), *Time for retirement: Comparative studies of early exit from the labor force* (pp. 181–221). Cambridge, England: Cambridge University Press.

Jessor, R. (1993). Successful adolescent development among youth in high-risk settings. *American Psychologist, 48,* 117–126.

Kalicki, B. (1996). *Lebensverläufe und selbstbilder: Die normalbiografie als psychologisches regulativ* [Life courses and self images]. Opladen, Germany: Leske & Budrich.

Kant, I. (1998). *Critique of pure reason* (P. Guyer & A. W. Wood, Trans. & Ed.). Cambridge, England: Cambridge University Press. (Original work published 1787)

Kaplan, H. B. (1999). Toward an understanding of resilience: A critical review of definitions and models. In M. D. Glantz & J. L. Johnson (Eds.), *Resilience and development: Positive life adaptations* (pp. 17–83). New York: Kluwer Academic/Plenum Press.

Kegan, R. (1998). Epistemology, expectation, and aging. A developmental analysis of the gerontological curriculum. In J. Lomranz (Ed.), *Handbook of aging and mental health: An integrative approach* (pp. 197–216). New York: Plenum Press.

Kim, J., & Moen, P. (2001a). Is retirement good or bad for subjective well-being? *Current Directions in Psychological Science, 10*(3), 83–86.

Kim, J., & Moen, P. (2001b). Moving into retirement: Preparation and transitions in late midlife. In M. E. Lachman (Ed.), *Handbook of midlife development* (pp. 487–527). New York: Wiley.

Kling, K. C., Ryff, C. D., & Essex, M. J. (1997). Adaptive changes in the self-concept during a life transition. *Personality and Social Psychology Bulletin, 23,* 981–990.

Klohnen, E. C. (1996). Conceptual analysis and measurement of the construct of ego-resiliency. *Journal of Personality and Social Psychology, 70,* 1067–1079.

Kobasa, S. C. (1979). Stressful life events, personality and health: An inquiry into hardiness. *Journal of Personality and Social Psychology, 37,* 1–11.

Kohlberg, L. (1971). From is to ought: How to commit the naturalistic fallacy and get away with it in the study of moral development. In T. Mischel (Ed.), *Psychology and genetic epistemology* (pp. 151–235). New York: Academic Press.

Kumpfer, K. L. (1999). Factors and processes contributing to resilience: The resilience framework. In M. D. Glantz & J. L. Johnson (Eds.), *Resilience and development: Positive life adaptations* (pp. 179–224). New York: Kluwer Academic/Plenum Press.

Labouvie-Vief, G., & Medler, M. (2002). Affect optimization and affect complexity: Modes and styles of regulation in adulthood. *Psychology and Aging, 17,* 571–588.

Lawton, M. P. (1989). Environmental proactivity in older people. In V. L. Bengston & K. W. Schaie (Eds.), *The course of later life: Research and reflections* (pp. 15–23). New York: Springer.

Lawton, M. P., & Nahemow, L. (1973). Ecology and the aging process. In C. Eisdorfer & M. P. Lawton (Eds.), *Psychology of adult development and aging* (pp. 619–674). Washington, DC: American Psychological Association.

Lazarus, R. S. (1991). *Emotion and adaptation.* New York: Oxford University Press.

Lazarus, R. S. (1993). From psychological stress to the emotions: A history of changing outlooks. *Annual Review of Psychology, 44,* 1–21.

Lazarus, R. S., & Folkman, S. (1984). *Stress, appraisal, and coping.* New York: Springer.

Lazarus, R. S., & Golden, G. Y. (1981). The function of denial in stress, coping, and aging. In J. L. McGaugh & S. B. Kiesler (Eds.), *Aging: Biology and behavior* (pp. 283–307). New York: Academic Press.

Leary, M. R., & Tangney, J. P. (Eds.). (2003). *Handbook of self and identity.* New York: Guilford.

Lerner, R. M. (1984). *On the nature of human plasticity.* Cambridge, England: Cambridge University Press.

Lerner, R. M. (1986). *Concepts and theories of human development* (2nd ed.). New York: Random House.

Lerner, R. M., Dowling, E., & Roth, S. L. (2003). Contributions of lifespan psychology to the future elaboration of developmental systems theory. In U. M. Staudinger & U. Lindenberger (Eds.), *Understandung human development: Dialogues with lifespan psychology* (pp. 413–422). Dordrecht, The Netherlands: Kluwer Press.

Lerner, R. M., & Kauffman, M. B. (1985). The concept of development in contextualism. *Developmental Review, 5,* 309–333.

Levinson, D. J. (1978). *The seasons of a man's life.* New York: Ballantine Books.

Li, S.-C. (2003). Biocultural orchestration of developmental plasticity across levels: The interplay of biology and culture in shaping the mind and behavior across the life span. *Psychological Bulletin, 129*(2), 171–194.

Lindenberger, U., & Baltes, P. B. (1994). Sensory functioning and intelligence in old age: A powerful connection. *Psychology and Aging, 9,* 339–355.

Linville, P. W. (1985). Self-complexity and affective extremity: Don't put all your eggs in one cognitive basket. *Social Cognition, 3,* 94–120.

Linville, P. W. (1987). Self-complexity as a cognitive buffer against stress-related illness and depression. *Journal of Personality and Social Psychology, 52,* 663–676.

Little, B. R. (1999). Personal projects and social ecology: Themes and variations across the life-span. In J. Brandtstädter & R. M. Lerner (Eds.), *Action and self-development: Theory and research through the life-span* (pp. 197–221). Thousand Oaks, CA: Sage.

Loeber, R., & Stouthamer-Loeber, M. (1998). Development of juvenile aggression and violence: Some common misconceptions and controversies. *American Psychologist, 53,* 242–459.

Lösel, F., Bliesener, T., & Köferl, P. (1989). On the concept of "invulnerability": Evaluation and first results of the Bielefeld project. In M. Brambring, F. Lösel, & H. Skowronek (Eds.), *Children at risk: Assessment, longitudinal research and intervention.* Berlin, Germany: de Gruyter.

Luthar, S. S. (Ed.). (2003). *Resilience and vulnerability.* New York: Cambridge University Press.

Luthar, S. S., Cicchetti, D., & Becker, B. (2000). The construct of resilience: A critical evaluation and guidelines for future work. *Child Development, 71,* 543–562.

Luthar, S. S., Doernberger, C. H., & Zigler, E. (1993). Resilience is not a unidimensional construct: Insights from a prospective study of innercity adolescents. *Child Development, 71,* 543–562.

Magnusson, D. (1990). Personality development from an interactional perspective. In L. A. Pervin (Ed.), *Handbook of personality: Theory and research* (pp. 193–222). New York: Guilford Press.

Maier, H., & Vaupel, J. W. (2003). Age differences in cultural efficiency: Secular trends in longevity. In U. M. Staudinger & U. Lindenberger (Eds.), *Understanding human development: Dialogues with lifespan psychology* (pp. 59–78). Dordrecht, The Netherlands: Kluwer Press.

Markus, H. R., & Nurius, P. (1986). Possible selves. *American Psychologist, 41,* 954–969.

Markus, H. R., & Wurf, E. (1987). The dynamic self-concept: A social psychological perspective. *Annual Review of Psychology, 38,* 299–337.

Maslow, A. H. (1970). *Motivation and personality.* New York: Harper & Row.

Masten, A. (1994). Resilience in individual development: Successful adaptation despite risk and adversity. In M. Wang & E. Gordon (Eds.), *Risk and resilience in inner city America: Challenges and prospects* (pp. 3–25). Hillsdale, NJ: Erlbaum.

Masten, A. (2001). Ordinary magic: Resilience processes in development. *American Psychologist, 56,* 227–238.

Masten, A., & Coatsworth, J. D. (1995). Competence, resilience, and psychopathology. In D. Cicchetti & D. Cohen (Eds.), *Developmental psychopathology* (Vol. 2, pp. 715–752). New York: Wiley.

Masten, A., & Coatsworth, J. D. (1998). The development of competence in favorable and unfavorable environments: Lessons from research on successful children. *American Psychologist, 53,* 205–220.

Masten A., & Garmezy, N. (1985). Risk, vulnerability, and protective factors in developmental psychopathology. In B. Lahey & A. Kazdin (Eds.), *Advances in clinical child psychology* (Vol. 8, pp. 1–52). New York: Plenum Press.

Masten, A., & Reed, M.-G. J. (2002). Resilience in development. In C. R. Snyder & S. J. Lopez (Eds.), *Handbook of positive psychology* (pp. 74–88). Oxford: Oxford University Press.

McClearn, G. E. (2003). Combining molecular and quantitative genetics: Decomposing the architecture of lifespan development. In U. M. Staudinger & U. Lindenberger (Eds.), *Understanding human development: Dialogues with lifespan psychology* (pp. 361–379). Dordrecht, The Netherlands: Kluwer Press.

McCrae, R. R., & Costa, P. T. J. (1987). Validation of the five-factor model of personality across instruments and observers. *Journal of Personality and Social Psychology, 52*(1), 81–90.

McCrae, R. R., & Costa, P. T. J. (1996). Toward a new generation of personality theories: Theoretical contexts for the five factor model. In J. S. Wiggins (Ed.), *The five-factor model of personality: Theoretical perspectives* (pp. 51–87). New York: Guilford Press.

Montada, L., Filipp, S.-H., & Lerner, M. J. (Eds.). (1992). *Life-crises and experiences of loss in adulthood.* Hillsdale, NJ: Erlbaum.

Nelson, A. E., & Dannefer, D. (1992). Aged heterogeneity: Fact or fiction? The fate of diversity in gerontological research. *Gerontologist, 32,* 17–23.

Nesselroade, J. R. (1989). Adult personality development: Issues in addressing constancy and change. In A. I. Rabin, R. A. Zucker, R. A. Emmons, & S. Frank (Eds.), *Studying persons and lives* (pp. 41–85). New York: Springer.

Nesselroade, J. R. (1991). Interindividual differences in intraindividual change. In L. M. Collins & J. L. Horn (Eds.), *Best methods for the analysis of change* (pp. 92–105). Washington, DC: American Psychological Association.

Neugarten, B. L. (1968). *Adult personality: Toward a psychology of the life cycle.* Chicago: University of Chicago Press.

Neugarten, B. L. (1979). Time, age, and the life cycle. *American Journal of Psychiatry, 136,* 887–894.

Neugarten, B. L., & Hagestad, G. O. (1976). Age and the life course. In R. H. Binstock & E. Shanas (Eds.), *Handbook of aging and the social sciences* (pp. 35–55). New York: Van Nostrand Reinhold.

Neugarten, B. L., Moore, J. W., & Lowe, J. C. (1965). Age norms, age constraints, and adult socialization. *American Journal of Sociology, 70,* 710–717.

Nolen-Hoeksema, S., & Davis, C. G. (2002). Positive responses to loss: Perceiving benefits and growth. In C. R. Snyder & S. J. Lopez (Eds.), *Handbook of positive psychology* (pp. 598–607). Oxford: Oxford University Press.

Norris, F. H., Friedman, M. J., Watson, P. J., Byrne, C. M., Diaz, E., & Kaniasty, K. (2002). 60,000 disaster victims speak, Pt. I: An empirical review of the empirical literature, 1981–2001. *Psychiatry, 65,* 207–239.

Oerter, R. (1986). Developmental task through the life span: A new approach to an old concept. In P. B. Baltes, D. L. Featherman, & R. M. Lerner (Eds.), *Life-span development and behavior* (Vol. 7, pp. 233–269). Hillsdale, NJ: Erlbaum.

Olsson, C. A., Bond, L., Burns, J. M., Vella-Brodrock, D. A., & Sawyer, S. M. (2003). Adolescent resilience: A concept analysis. *Journal of Adolescence, 26,* 1–11.

Oyama, S. (1985). *The ontogeny of information: Developmental systems and evolution.* Cambridge, England: Cambridge University Press.

Ozer, E. J., Best, S. R., Lipsey, T. L., & Weiss, D. S. (2003). Predictors of posttraumatic stress disorder and symptoms in adults: A meta-analysis. *Psychological Bulletin, 129,* 52–71.

Pedersen, N. L., & Reynolds, C. A. (1998). Stability and change in adult personality: Genetic and environmental components. *European Journal of Personality, 12*(5), 365–386.

Pellegrini, D. S. (1990). Psychosocial risk and protective factors in childhood. *Developmental and Behavioral Pediatrics, 11,* 201–209.

Pervin, L., & John, O. (Eds.). (1999). *Handbook of personality: Theory and research* (2nd ed.). New Brunswick, NJ: Rutgers University Press.

Piaget, J. (1965). *The moral judgment of the child.* New York: Free Press.

Pinquart, M. (1998). *Das selbstkonzept im seniorenalter* [The self-concept in old age]. Weinheim, Germany: Psychologie Verlags Union.

Pinquart, M. (2002). Good news about the effect of bad old-age stereotypes. *Experimental Aging Research, 28,* 317–336.

Plomin, R., & Caspi, A. (1999). Behavioral genetics and personality. In L. A. Pervin & O. P. John (Eds.), *Handbook of personality theory and research* (Vol. 2, pp. 251–276). New York: Guilford Press.

Plomin, R., & Crabbe, J. (2000). DNA. *Psychological Bulletin, 126,* 806–828.

Plomin, R., DeFries, J. C., McClearn, G. E., & McGuffin, P. (Eds.). (2001). *Behavioral genetics* (4th ed.). New York: Worth Publishers.

Pulkkinen, L., & Kokko, K. (2000). Identity development in adulthood: A longitudinal study. *Journal of Research in Personality, 34,* 445–470.

Rafaeli-Mor, E., & Steinberg, J. (2002). Self-complexity and well-being: A review and research synthesis. *Personality and Social Psychology Review, 6,* 31–58.

Reese, H. W. (1993). Developments in child psychology from the 1960s to the 1990s. *Developmental Review, 13,* 503–524.

Reese, H. W., & Overton, W. F. (1970). Models of development and theories of development. In L. R. Goulet & P. B. Baltes (Eds.), *Life-span developmental psychology: Research and theory* (pp. 115–145). New York: Academic Press.

Reischies, F. M., & Lindenberger, U. (1996). Grenzen und potentiale kognitiver leistungsfähigkeit im alter [Limits and potentials of cognitive abilities in old age]. In K. U. Mayer & P. B. Baltes (Eds.), *Die berliner altersstudie* [The Berlin aging study] (pp. 351–377). Berlin, Germany: Akademie Verlag.

Riegel, K. F. (1976). The dialectics of human development. *American Psychologist, 31,* 689–700.

Riley, M. W., & Riley, J. W. (1989). The lives of older people and changing social roles. *Annals of the American Academy of Political and Social Science, 503,* 14–28.

Roberts, B. W., & Caspi, A. (2003). The cumulative continuity model of personality development: Striking a balance between continuity and change in personality traits across the life course. In U. M.

Staudinger & U. Lindenberger (Eds.), *Understanding human development: Dialogues with lifespan psychology* (pp. 183–214). Dordrecht, The Netherlands: Kluwer Press.

Roberts, B. W., & DelVecchio, W. F. (2000). The rank-order consistency of personality traits from childhood to old age: A quantitative review of longitudinal studies. *Psychological Bulletin, 126,* 3–25.

Robins, R. W., John, O. P., Caspi, A., Moffitt, T. E., & Stouthamer-Loeber, M. (1996). Resilient, overcontrolled, and undercontrolled boys: Three replicable personality types. *Journal of Personality and Social Psychology, 70,* 157–171.

Roosa, M. W. (2000). Some thoughts about resilience versus positive development, main effects versus interactions, and the value of resilience. *Child Development, 71,* 567–569.

Rothbaum, F., Weisz, J. R., & Snyder, S. S. (1982). Changing the world versus changing the self: A two-process model of perceived control. *Journal of Personality and Social Psychology, 42,* 5–37.

Rothermund, K. (2005). Effects of age stereotypes on self-views and adaptation. In W. Greve, K. Rothermund, & D. Wentura (Eds.), *The adaptive self: Personal continuity and intentional self-development* (pp. 223–242). New York: Hogrefe/Huber.

Rowe, J. W. (1997). Editorial: The new gerontology. *Science, 278,* 367.

Rowe, J. W., & Kahn, R. L. (1987). Human aging: Usual and successful. *Science, 237,* 143–149.

Rutter, M. (1985). Resilience in the face of adversity: Protective factors and resistance to psychiatric disorder. *British Journal of Psychiatry, 147,* 598–611.

Rutter, M. (1987). Psychosocial resilience and protective mechanisms. *American Journal of Orthopsychiatry, 57,* 316–331.

Rutter, M. (2000). Resilience reconsidered: Conceptual considerations, empirical findings, and policy implications. In J. P. Shonkoff & S. J. Meisels (Eds.), *Handbook of early childhood intervention* (2nd ed., pp. 651–682). Cambridge, England: Cambridge University Press.

Rutter, M., & Rutter, M. (1993). *Developing minds: Challenge and continuity across the life span.* New York: Basic Books.

Ryan, R. M. (1993). Agency and organization: Intrinsic motivation, autonomy, and the self in psychological development. In J. E. Jacobs (Ed.), *Nebraska Symposium on Motivation* (Vol. 40, pp. 1–56). Lincoln: University of Nebraska Press.

Ryff, C. D. (1995). Psychological well-being in adult life. *Current Directions in Psychological Science, 4,* 99–104.

Ryff, C. D., & Singer, B. (2002). From social structure to biology: Integrative science in pursuit of human health and well-being. In C. R. Snyder & S. J. Lopez (Eds.), *Handbook of positive psychology* (pp. 541–555). Oxford: Oxford University Press.

Ryff, C. D., Singer, B., Love, G. D., & Essex, M. J. (1998). Resilience in adulthood and later life: Defining features and dynamic processes. In J. Lomranz (Ed.), *Handbook of aging and mental health: An integrative approach* (pp. 69–96). New York: Plenum Press.

Salthouse, T. A. (1991). *Theoretical perspectives on cognitive aging.* Hillsdale, NJ: Erlbaum.

Scarr, S., & McCartney, K. (1983). How people make their own environment: A theory of genotype environment effects. *Child Development, 54,* 424–435.

Schaie, K. W. (1994). The course of adult intellectual development. *American Psychologist, 49,* 304–313.

Schaie, K. W. (1996). *Adult intellectual development: The Seattle Longitudinal Study.* New York: Cambridge University Press.

Seligman, M. E. P., & Csikszentmihalyi, M. (2000). Positive psychology: An introduction. *American Psychologist, 55,* 5–14.

Settersten, R. A. (1997). The salience of age in the life course. *Human Development, 40,* 257–281.

Settersten, R. A., Jr., & Hägestad, G. O. (1996). What's the latest? Cultural age deadlines for family transitions. *Gerontologist, 36*(2), 178–188.

Settersten, R. A., & Mayer, K. U. (1997). The measurement of age, age structuring, and the life course. *Annual Review of Sociology, 23,* 233–261.

Sharpley, C. F., & Yardley, P. (1999). The relationship between cognitive hardiness, explanatory style, and depression-happiness in post-retirement men and women. *Australian Psychologist, 34*(3), 198–203.

Siegler, I. C., George, L. K., & Okun, M. A. (1979). Cross-sequential analysis of adult personality. *Developmental Psychology, 15*(3), 350–351.

Skinner, E., & Edge, K. (1998). Reflections on coping and development across the lifespan. *International Journal of Behavioral Development, 22,* 357–366.

Smith, J. (2003). The gain-loss dynamic in lifespan development: Implications for change in self and personality during old and very old age. In U. M. Staudinger & U. Lindenberger (Eds.), *Understanding human development: Dialogues with lifespan psychology* (pp. 215–241). Dordrecht, The Netherlands: Kluwer Press.

Smith, J., & Baltes, P. B. (1993). Differential psychological aging: Profiles of the old and very old. *Ageing and Society, 13,* 551–587.

Smith, J., & Baltes, P. B. (1996). Altern aus psychologischer perspektive: Trends und profile im hohen alter [Aging from a psychological perspective: Trends and profiles in advanced age]. In K. U. Mayer & P. B. Baltes (Eds.), *Die berliner altersstudie* [The Berlin aging study] (pp. 221–250). Berlin, Germany: Akademie Verlag.

Snyder, C. R., & Lopez, S. J. (Eds.). (2002). *Handbook of positive psychology.* Oxford: Oxford University Press.

Sorensen, A. B., Weinert, F. E., & Sherrod, L. (1986). *Human development and the life course: Multidisciplinary perspectives.* Hillsdale, NJ: Erlbaum.

Staudinger, U. M. (1997). Grenzen der Bewältigung und ihre überschreitung: Vom entweder-oder zum sowohl-als-auch und weiter. [Limits of Coping and their transgression]. In C. T. Tesch-Römer, C. Salewski, & G. Schwarz (Eds.), *Psychologie der bewältigung* [Psychology of coping] (pp. 247–260). Weinheim, Germany: Psychologie Verlags Union.

Staudinger, U. M. (1999a). Older and wiser? Integrating results from a psychological approach to a study of wisdom. *International Journal of Behavioral Development, 23,* 641–664.

Staudinger, U. M. (1999b). Perspektiven der resilienzforschung aus der sicht der lebensspannen-psychologie [Perspectives of resilience research as viewed from the life-span perspective]. In G. Opp, M. Fingerle, & A. Freytag (Eds.), *Was kinder stärkt: Erziehung zwischen risiko und resilienz* [What strengthens children: Education between risk and resilience]. München, Germany: Reinhardt.

Staudinger, U. M. (1999c). Social cognition and a psychological approach to an art of life. In F. Blanchard-Fields & T. Hess (Eds.), *Social cognition and aging* (pp. 340–376). New York: Academic Press.

Staudinger, U. M. (2000a). Selbst und persönlichkeit aus der sicht der lebenspannen-psychologie [Self and personality from a life-span psychology perspective]. In W. Greve (Ed.), *Psychologie des selbst* [Psychology of the self] (pp. 133–148). Weinheim, Germany: PVU.

Staudinger, U. M. (2000b). Viele gründe sprechen dagegen und trotzdem fühlen viele menschen sich wohl: Das paradox des subjektiven wohlbefindens [Although many reasons speak against it, many elder persons feel fine: The paradox of subjective well-being]. *Psychologische Rundschau, 51,* 185–197.

Staudinger, U. M. (in press). Personality and aging. In M. Johnson, V. L. Bengtson, P. G. Coleman, & T. Kirkwood (Eds.), *Cambridge: Handbook of age and ageing.* Cambridge, England: Cambridge University Press.

Staudinger, U. M., & Baltes, P. B. (1996). Interactive minds: A facultative setting for wisdom-related performance? *Journal of Personality and Social Psychology, 71,* 746–762.

Staudinger, U. M., & Bluck, S. (2001). A view on midlife development from life-span theory. In M. E. Lachman (Ed.), *Handbook of midlife development* (pp. 3–39). New York: Wiley.

Staudinger, U. M., Dörner, J., & Mickler, C. (in press). Wisdom and personality. In R. Sternberg & J. Jordan (Eds.), *Handbook of wisdom.* New York: Cambridge University Press.

Staudinger, U. M., & Fleeson, W. (1996). Self and personality in old and very old age: A sample case of resilience? *Development and Psychopathology, 8,* 867–885.

Staudinger, U. M., Freund, A. M., Linden, M., & Maas, I. (1999). Self, personality, and life management: Psychological resilience and vulnerability. In P. B. Baltes & K. U. Mayer (Eds.), *The Berlin Aging Study: Aging from 70 to 100* (pp. 302–328). New York: Cambridge University Press.

Staudinger, U. M., & Greve, W. (2001). Resilienz im alter [Resilience in old age]. In Deutsches Zentrum für Altersfragen (Hrsg.), *Expertisen zum Dritten Altenbericht der bundesregierung* [Third Report on Aging of the Federal Gouvernment] (S. 95–144). Opladen: Leske & Budrich.

Staudinger, U. M., & Lindenberger, U. (Eds.). (2003a). *Understanding human development: Lifespan psychology in exchange with other disciplines.* Amsterdam: Kluwer Academic.

Staudinger, U. M., & Lindenberger, U. (2003b). Why read another book on human development? Understanding human development takes a meta-theory and multiple disciplines. In U. M. Staudinger & U. Lindenberger (Eds.), *Understanding human development: Dialogues with lifespan psychology* (pp. 1–13). New York: Kluwer Academic/Plenum Press.

Staudinger, U. M., Marsiske, M., & Baltes, P. B. (1993). Resilience and levels of reserve capacity in later adulthood: Perspectives from life-span theory. *Development and Psychopathology, 5,* 541–566.

Staudinger, U. M., Marsiske, M., & Baltes, P. B. (1995). Resilience and reserve capacity in later adulthood: Potentials and limits of development across the life span. In D. Cicchetti & D. Cohen (Eds.), *Developmental psychopathology* (Vol. 2, pp. 801–847). New York: Wiley.

Staudinger, U. M., & Pasupathi, M. (2000). Life-span perspectives on self, personality and social cognition. In T. Salthouse & F. Craik (Eds.), *Handbook of cognition and aging* (pp. 633–688). Hillsdale, NJ: Erlbaum.

Steinhagen-Thiessen, E., & Borchelt, M. (1996). Körperliche gesundheit und medizinische versorgung im alter [Physical health and medical care in old age]. In K. U. Mayer & P. B. Baltes (Eds.), *Die berliner altersstudie.* Berlin, Germany: Akademie Verlag.

Sterling, P., & Eyer, J. (1988). Allostasis: A new paradigm to explain arousal pathology. In S. Fisher & J. Reason (Eds.), *Handbook of life stress, cognition, and health* (pp. 629–649). Chichester, England: Wiley.

Straub, J., Zielke, B., & Werbik, H. (2005). Autonomy, narrative identity, and their critics: A reply to some provocations of postmodern accounts in psychology. In W. Greve, K. Rothermund, & D. Wentura (Eds.), *The adaptive self: Personal continuity and intentional self-development* (pp. 323–350). New York: Hogrefe/Huber.

Tarter, R. E., & Vanyukov, M. (1999). Re-visiting the validity of the construct of resilience. In M. D. Glantz & J. C. Johnson (Eds.), *Resilience and development: Positive life adaptations* (pp. 85–100). Dordrecht, Netherlands: Kluwer.

Taylor, S. E., & Brown, J. D. (1994). Positive illusions and well-being revisited: Separating fact from fiction. *Psychological Bulletin, 116,* 21–27.

Taylor, S. E., & Gollwitzer, P. M. (1995). Effects of mindset on positive illusions. *Journal of Personality and Social Psychology, 69,* 213–226.

Tennen, H., & Affleck, G. (2002). Benefit-finding and benefit-remeding. In C. R. Snyder & S. J. Lopez (Eds.), *Handbook of positive psychology* (pp. 584–597). Oxford: Oxford University Press.

Tesch-Römer, C. (1997). Psychological effects of hearing aid use in older adults. *Journal of Gerontology, 52B,* 127–138.

Tesch-Römer, C., & Wahl, H.-W. (Eds.). (1996). *Seh- und höreinbußen älterer menschen* [Declines in seeing and hearing among elder persons]. Darmstadt, Germany: Steinkopff.

Thelen, E., & Smith, L. B. (1998). Dynamic systems theories. In R. M. Lerner (Ed.), *Handbook of child psychology: Vol. I. Theoretical models of human development* (5th ed., pp. 563–634). New York: Wiley.

Tiét, Q. Q., & Huizinga, D. (2002). Dimensions of the construct of resilience and adaptation among inner-city youth. *Journal of Adolescent Research, 17,* 260–276.

Tugade, M., & Fredrickson, B. (2004). Resilient individuals use positive emotions to bounce back from negative emotional experiences. *Journal of Personality and Social Psychology, 86*(2), 320–333.

Vaillant, G. E. (1993). *The wisdom of the ego.* Cambridge, MA: Harvard University Press.

Von Eye, A., & Schuster, C. (2000). The odds of resilience. *Child Development, 71,* 563–566.

Waddington, C. H. (1975). *The evolution of an evolutionist.* Edinburgh, Scotland: Edinburgh University Press.

Weglage, J. (2000). *Diätbehandlung bei phenylketonurie* [Dietical treatment of phenylcetnouria]. Göttingen, Germany: Hogrefe.

Weinert, F. E. (1994). *Altern in psychologischer perspektive* [Aging from a psychological perspective]. In P. B. Baltes, J. Mittelstrass, & U. M. Staudinger (Eds.), *Alter und altern* [Age and aging] (pp. 180–203). Berlin, Germany: de Gruyter.

Werner, E. E. (1995). Resilience in development. *Current Directions in Psychological Science, 4,* 81–85.

Werner, E. E., & Smith, R. S. (1982). *Vulnerable but invincible: A study of resilient children.* New York: McGraw-Hill.

Werner, E. E., & Smith, R. S. (1992). *Overcoming the odds: High risk children from birth to adulthood.* Ithaca, NY: Cornell University Press.

Werner, E. E., & Smith, R. S. (2001). *Journey from childhood to midlife: Risk, resilience and recovery.* Ithaca, NY: Cornell University Press.

Widinger, T. A., & Seidlitz, L. (2002). Personality, psychopathology, and aging. *Journal of Research in Personality, 36,* 335–362.

Williamson, G. M. (2002). Aging well: Outlook for the 21st century. In C. R. Snyder & S. J. Lopez (Eds.), *Handbook of positive psychology* (pp. 676–686). Oxford: Oxford University Press.

Wilson, E. O. (1998). *Consilience: The unity of knowledge.* New York: Knopf.

Wortman, C. B., & Silver, R. C. (1990). Successful mastery of bereavement and widow-hood: A life-course perspective. In P. B. Baltes & M. M. Baltes (Eds.), *Successful aging: Perspectives from the behavioral sciences* (pp. 225–264). New York: Cambridge University Press.

Wortman, C. B., & Silver, R. C. (2001). The myths of coping with loss revisited. In M. S. Stroebe & R. O. Hansson (Eds.), *Handbook of bereavement research: Consequences, coping, and care* (pp. 405–429). Washington, DC: American Psychological Association.

Wrosch, C., & Heckhausen, J. (1999). Control processes before and after passing a developmental deadline: Activation and deactivation of intimate relationship goals. *Journal of Personality and Social Psychology, 77,* 415–427.

Wyman, P. A., Sandler, I., Wolchik, S., & Nelson, K. (2001). Resilience as cumulative competence promotion and stress protection: Theory and intervention. In D. Cicchetti, J. Rappaport, I. Sandler, & R. P. Weissberg (Eds.), *The promotion of wellness in children and adolescents* (pp. 133–184). Washington, DC: Child Welfare League of America Press.

CHAPTER 22

Stigma and Mental Illness: Developmental Issues and Future Prospects

STEPHEN P. HINSHAW

In the past decade, consensus has emerged that the stigma incurred by mental illness represents the most important issue facing the entire mental health field (Corrigan, 2004; Crisp, 2000; U.S. Department of Health and Human Services, 1999). Specifically, whereas the symptoms of mental disorders produce considerable impairment and suffering and often limit the attainment of developmental competencies, the extreme social disapproval of persons with mental illness greatly compounds these problems. For one thing, stigmatization precludes opportunities for treatment. Indeed, current estimates are that over three-fourths of children and adolescents with mental disorders in the United States never receive evaluation or treatment (New Freedom Commission on Mental Health, 2003), reflecting (1) ignorance that many behavioral and emotional prob-

lems reflect mental disorders, (2) shame on the part of families with respect to admitting that their offspring have a mental illness, and (3) a lack of adequate funding for treatment, even if it is sought (Hinshaw, 2005). In addition, stigma limits the potential for independent functioning; it also stands in the way of the kinds of research funding needed for advances in the struggle to overcome mental disorders (Sartorius, 1998). Thus, as highlighted by Link and Phelan (2001), stigma occurs at structural levels in society (laws, cultural norms, policies) and within individuals and families (stereotypes, beliefs, prejudicial attitudes). Self-stigmatization is also salient, to the extent that persons with mental disorders internalize the negative messages they receive (Corrigan, 2004). Overall, the devaluation of mental illness has effects that emanate across individual and family lives, the well-being of communities, and the nature of the very enterprises of research and treatment efforts that could help to overcome the impairments related to mental disorder. Given the increasing recognition that mental illnesses are now among the most debilitating and impairing diseases that exist worldwide (Murray & Lopez, 1996), understanding the reasons for the shunning, exclusion, and punishment of persons with mental illness across history is an essential goal.

Developmental factors are crucial to the discussion. Indeed, because of the continuity and predictability of development across the life span (Rutter & Sroufe, 2000), stigma at a given phase of development is likely to have profound implications for future functioning. Furthermore, when parents suffer from mental illness, their own propensity to be stigmatized can have major effects on their children's development (Hinshaw, 2005). In short, the stigma related to mental disorder is ripe for developmental theorizing and developmentally oriented research efforts.

The outline of this chapter is as follows: I first define stigma and then discuss psychological, social, and evolutionary models and mechanisms related to stigmatization. I next consider historical themes related to stigma, particularly with respect to children with mental disorders, and weigh various types of evidence for stigma regarding mental disorder, including both empirical research and broader kinds of data from general cultural practices. After evaluating developmental issues and concerns, I present a model of stigmatization as it pertains to mental disorder across the life span. Finally, I review key research questions remaining to be addressed by future generations of investigators. Although overcoming stigma is a topic of vast importance, space limitations allow only a brief conclusion regarding the types of intervention strategies that may be most effective in reducing stigma (for more extensive coverage of such ideas and procedures, see Corrigan, 2005; Corrigan & Penn, 1999; Hinshaw, 2006).

DEFINING STIGMA AND STIGMATIZATION

Stigma is a term originating from ancient Greece signifying an actual mark or brand placed on or burned into the skin of members of castigated groups, such as slaves and traitors. The mark graphically signaled the devalued nature of its carrier (Goffman, 1963). In present usage, the mark is typically symbolic, referring to the social judgment placed on members of groups considered deviant or im-

moral, the discrimination they receive at the hands of the majority, and the psychological sense of shame and degradation likely to develop in those who are stigmatized.

Several key points are central to current notions of stigma. First, stigmatization exists as part of a series of interchanges, with a group carrying social power denigrating and castigating a group lower in power (Link & Phelan, 2001). Thus, what is stigmatized cannot be dissociated from social hierarchies and social orders. Note that because there is malleability in terms of what is considered proper and good in various cultures, this point gives some hope, in that if persons with mental illness become less disenfranchised, stigmatizing practices may diminish.

Second, stigma carries particularly stressful consequences if the stigmatized condition is potentially concealable—as is the case for many persons with histories of mental illness—because of ramifications that emanate from decisions about disclosing versus hiding the stigmatized attribute (Goffman, 1963; Jones et al., 1984). Unlike the overt nature of racial characteristics, the covert experience of mental disorder presents a host of choices that may yield considerable anxiety for both individuals and family members.

Third, stigmatization can be viewed as a set of social processes (comparison, castigation, "marking") that lead to continuing denigration. One such process involves the nearly automatic social cognitions that are invoked when members of a society confront a member of the outgroup (Myers, 1998). Another is the tendency for global attribution of negative traits to the individual's "mark." Still another includes the potential for self-fulfilling prophecies, whereby the expectation of deeply dysfunctional behavior and interaction may color and shape subsequent encounters with the individual. That is, with any imperfections automatically attributed to the flawed character of the entire person, the degraded individual's behavior may begin to conform to the initial stereotype (Jussim, Palumbo, Chatman, Madon, & Smith, 2000).

Fourth, although stigma shares elements with stereotyping (a cognitive process of viewing a subgroup in global terms), prejudice (an affective, negative prejudgment of members of a castigated group), and discrimination (the behavioral curtailing of rights of such a group), it transcends these constructs because of the strong tendency for perceivers to view all aspects of stigmatized individuals in terms of the fundamental flaw or deviance involved and for the castigated individual to internalize the aspersions that are made (Hinshaw, 2006). Thus, stigma processes are at once fascinating, complex, and pernicious.

At first glance, it would be logical to assume that stereotypes, prejudices, and discrimination are linked in expectable and predictable ways, such that stereotypes lead inevitably and automatically to prejudicial attitudes, which in turn predict and promote discriminatory practices and lead to stigmatization (for discussion of the fluid boundaries among cognitive, affective, and behavioral components of stigmatization, see Dovidio, Major, & Crocker, 2000). Yet, it is quite possible for an individual to voice stereotyped beliefs ("People with mental disorders are unpredictable") or prejudicial attitudes ("Such people are despicable and filthy") but also to maintain contact with certain persons with mental illnesses. Complicating matters further are the forces in modern society that tend to inhibit overt expression of prejudicial attitudes, so that many biases may exist at covert, implicit levels (Greenwald & Banaji, 1995). Finally, although the usual assumption is that stereotypes and prejudices predate and cause discriminatory practices, the causal arrow may be reversed: A history of discrimination against an outgroup can foster stereotyping and prejudice, with the prejudicial attitudes serving as "system justification" for the inequities that are the core of the problem (Biernat & Dovidio, 2000; Crocker, Major, & Steele, 1998). In other words, given the ubiquity of hierarchical divisions of power and resources in all societies, those at or near the top rung will engage in denigration and derogation of less enfranchised members of the hierarchy to fuel the perspective that their higher status is justified and fair. Such "legitimating myths" (e.g., the belief in a merit-based society or in a world that is fundamentally impartial and fair) serve to bolster the status quo and ease the minds of high-status perceivers, such that their privileged status appears to be the result of effort and sacrifice rather than emanating from an enforced, discriminatory system (Pratto, Sidanius, Stalworth, & Malle, 1994). This point exemplifies a theme that runs through the entire chapter, namely, that stigmatization is located simultaneously in psychological processes, such as social cognitions; social interchanges, including those at dyadic and large-group levels; and cultural practices and policies, involving structural inequalities and legislative mandates.

A key underpinning of stigmatization was perceptively noted by Goffman (1963): The globalized, negative nature of stigma means that perceivers often come to believe that the marked person is less than human. When such an ascription is made, harsh punishment, exploitation, and even annihilation are not far behind (Sternberg, 2004). Later in the chapter I address the crucial issue, in terms of mental illness, of the kinds of causal theories that may lead to perceptions of the fundamental humanity versus subhumanity of individuals with extremes of behavioral deviance.

Does stigma always portend negative self-image for members of stigmatized groups? Although this was formerly held to be the case (Allport, 1954), it is now well-known that many stigmatized individuals, particularly those in ethnic or racial minorities, have self-esteem that is quite high (e.g., Crocker & Major, 1989). Hence, although stigmatization is likely to lead to shame in many instances, lowered self-image is not inevitable. In the case of mental illness, however, the symptoms of many disorders include dysphoria and low self-esteem; when these are coupled with the moral outrage and blame often voiced by social perceivers, decreases in self-worth would be quite predictable. The reality is that individual differences in response to stigma are vast, and understanding these varied reactions and coping strategies is a major goal for future research efforts (Corrigan & Watson, 2002).

Finally, is stigma universal or culturally specific? Increasing attention is being paid to the universal aspects of stigmatization, which may betray an evolutionary basis for at least some aspects of social exclusion (Kurzban & Leary, 2001). Indeed, mental illness has received consistent castigation and stigmatization across history, leading to speculation as to the ingrained roots of fundamental social tendencies to exclude persons with extreme behavioral deviance—with the clear implication that efforts to overcome the stigma of mental illness will need to be hard-fought. On the other hand, traits or conditions that are stigmatized in one culture or one historical era may come to be valued in others; for example, note the fluctuating ideals of women's body size in different nations and periods. Thus, there is hope that increased tolerance for diversity of behavior will help to erode the stigmatization received by persons with mental illness in the future.

THEORETICAL PERSPECTIVES ON STIGMA

Stigma is a vibrant topic in current research on social psychology, intergroup relations, and evolutionary psychology. Although most research on stigma has focused on racial and ethnic minority groups, a host of conditions are stigmatized in current society: gay/lesbian status, adoption, receipt of welfare, old age, and left-handedness, to name just several among a long list. As I discuss subsequently, mental illness is one of the most stigmatized attributes or traits that a person can have (Hinshaw, 2006; Tringo,

1970). My purpose in this section is to lay out some of the core themes from social and evolutionary psychology perspectives on stigma and comment on their applicability to mental disorder. The research on stigma in recent years has been voluminous; see other sources for a more comprehensive account (e.g., Crocker et al., 1998; Gaertner & Dovidio, 2000; Heatherton, Kleck, Hebl, & Hull, 2000; Hinshaw, 2006; Major & O'Brien, 2005).

Social Psychology and Stigma

Fifty years ago, most accounts from a psychological perspective were based on the proposition that prejudice and stigma stem from deep-seated, individual-difference proclivities (such as authoritarian personality styles) that predispose an individual to bias and hatred (e.g., Adorno, Frankel-Brunswik, Levinson, & Sanford, 1950). Currently, the social psychological view has shifted to emphasize the universality of social comparisons, the ubiquity of stigmatization processes, and the embeddedness of stigma in normal psychological functions and processes (e.g., Dovidio et al., 2000). In other words, social comparisons, even those that are sufficiently negative and harsh to earn the name "stigmatization," emanate from common and pervasive social and developmental mechanisms.

Specifically, the formation of social groups was—and still is—necessary for survival. Accordingly, there is a fundamental tendency to identify with ingroups, those social groupings of which one is a member by birth or community, and to distinguish fellow ingroup members from those in outgroups, those foreign social groupings, tribes, or communities posing a threat to survival, particularly when resources are scarce. The deeply rooted nature of ingroup identification is revealed by so-called minimal group research, which reveals that even the color of clothing or the flip of a coin can invoke strong tendencies to align with like members and castigate those in the outgroup (Brewer, 1979; Tajfel, 1982).

When an outgroup member poses actual or symbolic threat to the ingroup perceiver, the likelihood of prejudice and stigmatization is increased considerably (Stangor & Crandall, 2000). In the case of serious, psychotic-proportion mental illness, the threat value of out-of-control, irrational symptoms may be palpable, even at the level of physical harm. In the case of other forms of mental disorder, however, which are not as overtly threatening, the very term mental illness conveys connotations of loss of reason, despair, weakness, and dependency, indicating symbolic threat. In fascinating research, Solomon, Greenberg, and Pyszczynski (1991) showed that harsh judgments against outgroup members are strongly intensified when thoughts of death or mortality are primed in perceivers. This tendency may be particularly strong when the outgroup suffers from physical deformities or extremes of behavior, which may remind perceivers directly of the fragile and transitory nature of health and of life. This provocative idea incorporates existential, meaning-based perspectives on the types of situations and interpersonal interactions that are likely to elicit harsh, brittle reactions against marked individuals.

Dimensions of Stigmatization

Several features of castigated traits and conditions have major implications for their propensity to be stigmatized (see the seminal exposition by Jones et al., 1984). As noted earlier, the *concealability* of a stigmatized attribute raises anxiety regarding decision making with respect to openness versus disclosure (Goffman, 1963). Furthermore, the *threat* or *peril* induced by the mark has strong implications for stigmatization. Indeed, when pervasive cultural stereotypes emphasize the dangerousness and potential for violence of persons with mental disorders (see section on cultural indicators of stigma), the perception of threat, and of the potential for *disruptiveness* in social interchange, is magnified. Another core dimension is *aesthetics;* conditions that lead to bodily disfigurements have often received great stigmatization (see subsequent section on evolutionary psychological perspectives).

The final two dimensions from the taxonomy of Jones et al. (1984) are of particular relevance for mental disorder. First, the *course,* or longitudinal stability, of the mark in question is typically related to the propensity for stigmatization, in that conditions viewed as long-lasting or chronic are far more likely to be castigated than transitory states. In the case of mental disorder, the predominant view in the field—and in the minds of the general public—is that most variants of mental illness are chronic, lifelong conditions, fueling high levels of stigmatization. The actual evidence, however, is complex. For example, whereas mood disorders are highly likely to be recurrent, great numbers of individuals with such conditions have protracted periods that are relatively symptom-free (Goodwin & Jamison, in press). And Schizophrenia, long held to be a persistent condition marked by progressive, inevitable deterioration (see Neale & Oltmanns, 1980, for historical perspective), is now known to yield at least partial resolution in a significant proportion of individuals (Davison, Neale, & Kring, 2004). As for disorders of childhood onset, Attention-Deficit/Hyperactivity Disorder (ADHD) usually persists into adolescence, but adult outcomes are hugely varied (Mannuzza & Klein, 1999). Conduct disturbances are chronic in a small subset of youth who tend to have multiple, interacting risk factors spanning biological, psychological, and environmental domains, but most youth with aggression and conduct problems show a course that is largely limited to adolescence (Moffitt, 1993). Autistic Disorder, on the other hand, has a more uniformly negative prognosis, although early intervention may make a real difference in some cases (Klinger, Dawson, & Renner, 2003). In short, the view that all types of mental illness yield inevitable, chronic maladaptation is a distortion; promotion of the malleability and treatability of mental disorders is an important goal.

Second, a particularly crucial dimension is related to the *origin* or cause of stigmatized conditions, as well as the closely linked feature of their perceived *controllability*. Attribution theory is clear in this regard: Negative behavioral traits or features that are believed to arise for reasons outside the individual's personal control should elicit sympathy and concern, whereas those that are directly controllable will engender resentment and castigation. Weiner, Perry, and Magnusson (1988) present clear experimental evidence in this regard: Disabling conditions viewed as out of the individual's control (i.e., physical deformities) are likely to be met with compassion, whereas those linked to personal blame (i.e., behavioral or mental problems) generate rejection and hostility (see Corrigan et al., 2000, for further extrapolation to mental disorder).

Along with the considerable advances in neuroscience and genetics, this attributional perspective is clearly a reason for the promotion of efforts, in recent decades, to portray mental illness in medical model terms, as set of conditions analogous to physical illnesses or as "brain diseases" (Johnson, 1989). Indeed, such views are strongly supported by advocacy groups. I hasten to point out, however, that an unthinking rush to recast all mental disorder in reductionistic, biogenetic terms is no panacea for reducing stigma. For one thing, certain traits—most saliently, racial characteristics—that are clearly outside personal control have been among the most castigated and disparaged conditions in the history of our species. For another, it may be an uphill battle to convince the general public that constellations of behavior and affect are actually the products of genes and temperament, given the predominant cultural view that personal effort and volition are the sources of most behavioral displays. And even if a large segment of the populace is convinced that strongly heritable, biologically based proclivities underlie much of mental disturbance, there is no guarantee that benign attitudes will follow.

First, at its extremes, such a causal model is reductionistic, failing to account for the transactional nature of the development of nearly all forms of psychopathology (Cicchetti & Cohen, this *Handbook,* Volume 1). Second, for reasons that should become clearer upon reading the forthcoming section on evolutionary perspectives on stigma, ascriptions to genetic etiologies and exclusively neural loci for mental illness may actually fuel a backlash, such that interpersonal responses will be harshly punitive (e.g., Mehta & Farina, 1997). The headline version of the reasoning behind this seemingly paradoxical state of affairs is that an exclusively biological perspective appears to promote the views that mental disorder is chronic, unremitting, and hopeless (Phelan, Cruz-Rojas, & Reiff, 2002) and that mental illnesses are linked with genetic flaws, rendering the individual somehow less than fully human. Thus, although it would appear to be preferable to ascribe the causal locus of mental illness to biological proclivities rather than personal weakness, that is, to uncontrollable rather than controllable factors (Weiner et al., 1988), an exclusive attribution to deviant genetic makeup may be far from a panacea. Much more research needs to be done on the complex nature of control attributions and stigma related to mental illness.

Key Aspects of Stigma

Abridged from the discussion in Hinshaw (2006), I present information on several additional mechanisms and processes related to stigmatization, particularly as related to mental illness.

Pervasiveness and Implicit Stigma. The most marked and castigated conditions in a given society are likely to yield to widespread agreement from members of the culture as to their devalued status (Crocker et al., 1998). In other words, stereotypes about devalued groups are extremely *pervasive*. Especially given the access to print and visual media in modern societies, but also through storytelling, literature, and folklore in less Westernized cultures, there is typically widespread consensus on the racial, religious, and behavioral subtypes that are devalued and shunned. As a result, nearly all members of a society are confronted with images of the stereotyped group, children learn of these images at young ages, and the views of such negative characteristics become overlearned.

An upshot of this pervasiveness is that stereotypes and negative attitudes come to be automatically induced when an outgroup member is identified or recognized (Crocker et al., 1998). Such automatic induction is likely to yield strongly conditioned emotional and behavioral responses, experienced unconsciously (Fiske, 1998). Furthermore, conscious efforts to suppress the automatic stereotypes in question may backfire when the perceiver has limited or overtaxed cognitive resources, fueling a paradoxical over-accessibility of the negative stereotype (see Wegner, 1997). Indeed, what are now termed *implicit* stereotypes and prejudices are those that are unconscious and over-learned as opposed to consciously and overtly expressed (Greenwald & Banaji, 1995). A wealth of current research in social psychology relates to implicit stereotyping and prejudice, particularly with respect to racial/ethnic perceptions. Measures of implicit attitudes comprise reaction-time tests that capture associations made without conscious introspection (e.g., Dasgupta & Greenwald, 2001; Greenwald, McGhee, & Schwartz, 1998; Greenwald, Nosek, & Banaji, 2003). Understudied, however, are the presence and pervasiveness of implicit attitudes toward individuals with mental disorder.

Ambivalence. A second key feature of stigmatizing reactions is the *ambivalence* inherent in their display (Hebl, Tickle, & Heatherton, 2000; Katz, 1981). The argument is as follows: Social valuations of outgroups are inherently complex, balancing compassion on the one hand and harsh judgment on the other. Many, if not most, members of modern society hold two often conflicting values: (1) egalitarianism, the belief in the equal worth of all humans and the equal opportunities that should be available to all members of society, versus (2) individualism, the belief that individual efforts are essential to personal advancement and are rewarded by monetary and social gains. Egalitarian views should yield sympathy, identification with victims, and efforts to correct social injustices that led to discrimination, whereas individualistic views will turn this perception on its head, such that members of stigmatized groups will receive blame for insufficient efforts on their own behalf.

Thus, confrontation with a member of a stigmatized group will tend to elicit ambivalence: the co-occurring display of sympathy and castigation. Reactions to stigmatized persons will be unstable (shifting between empathy and revulsion), extreme, and variable across time. It may take only a small stimulus (e.g., witnessing one additional member of a stigmatized group) to shift an initially positive response to a castigating one, or vice versa. Through a series of experimental manipulations, investigators have shown that responses to stigmatized persons are fluctuating and volatile, reflecting an underlying ambivalence toward the

castigated individual (Katz, 1981). This complexity makes for clear difficulties in investigating, much less reducing, stigma. Yet the presence of at least some initial compassion for stigmatized individuals gives hope, as it provides a starting place for intervention efforts.

With respect to racial and ethnic bias as well as discrimination against women, social changes in recent years have fostered a different set of social standards for what is acceptable in terms of publicly displayed attitudes. Thus, expressed racism or sexism may be far more masked than the overt, bigoted expressions that were formerly commonplace. Proponents of the concept of "modern" or "symbolic" prejudice or racism hold that such attitudes are expressed via conservative political views emphasizing individual responsibility or meritocratic beliefs rather than direct sentiments of antipathy toward the ethnic outgroup. Gaertner and Dovidio (2000) describe an important variant termed "aversive" prejudice or racism, in which an individual consciously committed to nonstigmatizing views still holds overlearned, unconscious, negative attitudes that emanate from cultural exposure to negative stereotypes, which may "leak" when there is no clear set of cues to show egalitarian expression. Such expressions reflect the deep, even unconscious ambivalence in members of modern society regarding prejudicial attitudes and emotions. Although it is still largely permissible to stereotype and castigate persons with aberrant behavior patterns or mental disorders, implicit attitudes may become the predominant means of castigating such individuals as social mores change in the future, as such attitudes may predict discrimination more than does their overt expression, which tends to be colored by social desirability and secular trends. Thus as noted, implicit as well as explicit attitudes and biases need to be emphasized in the next generation of research investigations.

Motivations for Stigma: Cognitive Schema, Self-Esteem Enhancement, and Institutional Supports. Why do members of ingroups castigate and stigmatize those in outgroups? As postulated by Allport (1954), ingroup identification does not require outgroup derogation. Yet several psychological and social proclivities often dictate that the two processes become intertwined:

1. *Social cognitions:* There is an overwhelming amount of social information in our everyday social worlds, and humans have highly developed cognitive structures and processes for dealing with the barrage of social information surrounding them (see Myers, 1998). These include strong tendencies to categorize the world through templates, which are termed, in relation to fellow humans, social *schemas*. People therefore make quick judgments about individuals from different towns, those with different hair color, or those who are of higher or lower social status on the basis of the schemas formed about such groups.

Such ways of perceiving the world, which can quickly become stereotypes, preserve cognitive resources when perceivers are tired, pressed for time, or cognitively or emotionally engaged with other stimuli or decisions. This kind of categorizing leads people to see those from foreign social groups as "all the same," exemplifying the *outgroup homogeneity* effect, whereas ingroup members are perceived as distinct and individualized (Ryan, Park, & Judd, 1996). Another cognitive tendency is to make linkages between rare, negative events (e.g., violence, aggression) and other infrequent categories (e.g., minority groups, perhaps including those with mental disorder), because of the distinctiveness of both (Haghighat, 2001; Stoessner & Mackie, 1993). Such processes are activated quickly and unconsciously; the resultant cognitive processing, which is schema-driven and automatic, serves to preserve cognitive resources.

In short, some roots of prejudice and stigma do not require grossly unequal social conditions or discriminatory practices but stem from normal patterns of social cognition, particularly those linked to schema-driven processing. Note, however, that the presence of these tendencies does not mean that resultant stigmatization is inevitable or unchangeable. Indeed, people can and do invest the cognitive and emotional energy necessary for effortful social processing, whereby complex information about individuals is integrated into balanced, thoughtful judgments rather than quick stereotypes (Devine, 1989).

2. *Self-esteem enhancement:* Evidence exists that derogation of outgroup members serves to bolster not only social identity with the ingroup but also one's self-esteem. In an intriguing series of studies, Fein and Spencer (1997) showed that individuals who had received information damaging to their own self-esteem made disparaging characterizations of members of stereotyped outgroups, and such negative evaluations served, reciprocally, to bolster and restore their own self-image. Thus, stereotypes may provide a viable tool through which self-esteem maintenance and enhancement can occur when a person has suffered a blow to his or her own self-worth. Furthermore, this tool does not engender much remorse, because the stereotype is accepted and reinforced throughout the culture. Interestingly, this phenomenon may be most prominent for those whose self-esteem is initially high rather than low (Baumeister, Smart, & Boden, 1996).

Note, however, that self-esteem enhancement is not a sufficient criterion on which to base a model of the functions of stigma and stigmatization. For instance, it does not explain the strong consensus that tends to develop in most cultures about the recipients of denigration and stigmatization; other social processes must be at work to shape the consistency of targets of stigma. Also, it does not deal well with the tendencies for outgroup members to believe the stereotypes foisted on them and, at times, to display lowered self-worth in terms of the denigration they experience. In short, enhancement of self-esteem may well be a motivator for at least some ingroup members to participate in derogation and denigration of the outgroup, but research on the applicability of this phenomenon to mental disorder is sparse.

3. *Institutional supports:* I noted earlier that prejudice and stigmatization may follow from structural inequities in society, serving as system-justification mechanisms. In addition, cultures typically reveal institutional supports for discrimination. If segregation (or, indeed, slavery) is the law of the land, then castigating, system-justifying processes related to derogation of the disenfranchised group in question are likely, in order to rationalize the legally mandated unequal treatment. Consider other kinds of supports that are simply part of cultural life. For example, the crayons labeled flesh-colored in young children's coloring supplies are light tan/pink in hue, consistent with the coloring of European Americans but not other ethnic groups. Dolls have also typically been "White" in color. During the middle of the twentieth century, African American children were noted to select skin colors for drawings that were closer to the White norm than their own skin color (Clark & Clark, 1950). Media portrayals provide another source of cultural modeling and strong institutional support for pervasive stereotypes. In this regard, the overwhelming portrayal of persons with mental disorders in the print and visual media is one of violence, unpredictability, dangerousness, and irrationality (Wahl, 1995). Clearly, societal and institutional factors motivate stigma.

Another macro variable pertains to *economics*. In brief, it is likely that there are harsher reactions to deviance during periods of difficult economic circumstances than during affluent times (see Jones et al., 1984). In what is termed "realistic group conflict theory," competition for scarce resources motivates high levels of outgroup derogation (Sherif & Sherif, 1953; Stangor & Crandall, 2000). In fact, Hovland and Sears (1940) found evidence for a statistical association between economic indicators such as the price of cotton in the southern United States and the number of lynchings of African Americans during corresponding periods, whereby lower prices were associated with a rise in such murders. Subsequently, Hepworth and West (1988) reanalyzed the same data with more sophisticated statistical techniques, concluding that although the original findings may have exaggerated the magnitude of the associations, the core conclusions withstood stringent statistical controls. With respect to mental disorder, society provides sizable amounts of money and resources for individuals with serious mental illness as well as mental retardation, although not to the extent of parallel expenditures regarding physical illness. During times of economic hardship, the willingness to provide such support may well wane. This is clearly an empirically testable question.

Evolutionary Psychology and Stigma

Is there a deeper, more fundamental way in which humans are predisposed or programmed to detect, identify, and shun fellow humans with deviant behavior patterns? In recent years, interest has surged in accounts of human behavior that emphasize its naturally selected roots (see deWaal, 2002, for promises and cautions regarding this perspective). Indeed, evolutionary psychology has entered the debate about stigma (Fishbein, 2002; Kurzban & Leary, 2001; Neuberg, Smith, & Asher, 2000), and the implications are provocative. The near universality of the stigmatization of mental illness provides clear impetus to consider evolutionary processes as roots for such social exclusion.

From an evolutionary point of view, humans have been selected over their history not only for prosocial tendencies but also for certain limitations on social interchange, as indiscriminate affiliations may pose a survival threat. That is, members of our species have always needed others for procreation, investment in parenting, and cooperation to achieve mutual goals, but there are real costs to some social interactions, including (1) competition over shelter, economic resources, and mating partners; (2) the potential for aggression and violence; and (3) the contraction of parasites or contagious diseases. According to Kurzban and Leary (2001, p. 188):

> There exists a collection of discrete, domain-specific psychological mechanisms that have evolved to solve adaptive problems associated with sociality. . . . Together, the behavioral manifestations of these exclusionary mechanisms generate the phenomena that have fallen under the rubric of stigmatization. . . . Furthermore, because humans everywhere are endowed with the same psychological systems, we should expect

cross-cultural similarities in behavior driven by the similarities in underlying psychological architecture.

Underlying this perspective are two core premises: Humans require brakes on unbridled sociality, as indiscriminate social contacts may compromise survival, and many other animal species have been observed to display exclusionary strategies against conspecifics displaying certain forms of deviant behavioral patterns (Neuberg et al., 2000).

The attributes most likely to engender naturally selected exclusionary mechanisms are those that presumably posed clear threats to early human societies: (1) fellow humans who foster parasitic infestation (revealing themselves through unsightly appearance or display of atypical behaviors), (2) those who provide low social capital or direct exploitation of social partners, and (3) members of rival nationalities or cultures. Intriguingly, these three hypothesized types of social exclusion modules are nearly identical to the three kinds of stigmatized attributes posited by Goffman (1963): abominations of the body, character flaws, and "tribal" characteristics related to differences in skin color or place of origin. Thus, whereas social psychological accounts of stigma have largely ignored the typology of Goffman, the evolutionary model has resurrected them.

Kurzban and Leary (2001) postulate that the characteristics of mental disorder foster the first two types of exclusion tendencies. Specifically, behavioral and physical dishevelment, or even overly compulsive behavioral patterns, associated with serious mental disorders may trigger primitive fears of infestation or contagion (indeed, birds and primates signal parasites by excessive grooming). Furthermore, behavioral excesses, erratic and unpredictable behavior, and poor inhibition—all linked with some forms of mental illness—suggest both low social status and the potential for exploitation of others, putatively spawning the fear of being cheated. On the other hand, the kinds of features related to tribal or nationalistic differences are not, on the face of it, related to mental illness exclusion modules.

The specificity of predictions from evolutionary models is compelling. First, *emotional responses* are postulated to differ across the three detection mechanisms. Those suspected of spreading parasites or disease will elicit disgust, violators of dyadic exchange (i.e., cheaters) are predicted to evoke anger (related to the violation of the implicit or explicit social contract), and members of tribal outgroups will tend to elicit fear and hatred as a function of their threat to the home group or nation. Second, with respect to *behavioral responses*, the clear expectation is that those believed to be contagious will be avoided or shunned, those with character flaws will be punished for their social violations, and those in outgroup tribes will be retaliated against and exploited (Kurzban & Leary, 2001). In terms of mental disorder, which is linked to both social contract violations and some types of parasitic infection avoidance—but not, by and large, to national or tribal status—the expected social responses would range from avoidance to punishment but would not entail the types of exploitation reserved for national or ethnic groups who are in conflict with the ingroup or home tribe.

Consider, however, the scenario in which mental illness is attributed to reductionistic, biogenetic medical models, that is, when it is viewed as the product of flawed genes or biochemistry. Some evidence exists from attitude surveys that those individuals who ascribe mental afflictions to biological/genetic causal factors are less likely to blame or desire social distance from individuals with mental illness, as might be expected from attribution theory (see Martin, Pescosolido, & Tuch, 2000). On the other hand, if such biogenetic attributions are made in extreme, reductionistic fashion, afflicted individuals may come to be viewed not only as chronically diseased and therefore beyond intervention but also as a separate, inferior, and even subhuman group. Thus, despite the supposed attributional advantages of making medical model ascriptions for deviant behavior, it may be the case that overzealous ascriptions to medical/genetic causes fuel a harsh and exploitive set of behavioral responses, at the level of tribal stigmas. Recent empirical investigations show that exclusively genetic/biomedical attributions for mental disorder fuel social distance and extremely punitive responses (Dietrich et al., 2004; Mehta & Farina, 1997; Read & Harre, 2001; see also Phelan et al., 2002). Furthermore, the harshly punitive and even genocidal tendencies of the eugenics movement in the early decades of the twentieth century, which originated in Britain (spreading quickly to the United States) and which then expanded horribly in Germany, stemmed directly from views of mental illness that emphasized their hereditary, immutable origins (Black, 2003; Kevles, 1985).

Overall, the evolutionary perspective is a bold attempt to account for the universality of many forms of stigmatization, particularly those related to mental illness. As currently proposed, it is not particularly developmental; understanding how children and adolescents come to perceive attributes that may be stigmatizing in terms of behavioral deviance is an important research topic. Although this viewpoint is pessimistic to the extent that it posits inherent human tendencies to exclude, shun, and even punish other

persons with certain forms of behavioral deviance, even advocates of evolutionary models agree that such proclivities do not inevitably portend that humans will act on these exclusionary modules. Indeed, as discussed by Neuberg et al. (2000), stigmatization modules that may have been adaptive in the environment of evolutionary adaptation are often extremely maladaptive in the present era. Their presence does not imply that they are correct or right in current times. Humans need to learn how to overcome such ingrained proclivities if stigmatization is to be reduced.

Summary

Stigma is multifaceted, complex, and overdetermined. Major theoretical advances in social psychology have propelled the understanding of stigma processes, which have roots in social cognition, intergroup processes, and social hierarchies. In addition, natural selection may have shaped fundamental exclusion tendencies in humans, some of which appear directly related to the propensity for stigmatization of mental illness. Whereas the roots of stigma appear to lie deep within (1) typical modes of social cognitive processing, (2) rules of social interchange between ingroups and outgroups, and (3) the social and political structures that have been created in all human cultures, the degrading, humiliating, and terrorizing aspects of prejudice and stigma are not predestined. Because stigma typically involves deep ambivalence, involving a mixture of empathy and concern with fear and hostility, promoting identification and sympathy is a key goal.

HISTORICAL PERSPECTIVES ON STIGMA

Too often, historical accounts portray the past in sweeping terms. For instance, the naturalistic, medical models of ancient Greece and Rome are juxtaposed with the chaos and ignorance of the Dark Ages; moralistic crusades against deviance in the middle of the previous millennium (including witch hunting) are contrasted with the humane treatment of the late Enlightenment or the current era. In fact, such global trends contain many distortions, as does the perspective that history moves inexorably toward progress and rationality. Cycles of reform and retrenchment lie closer to the truth, in which themes of biological versus environmental causation, personal control versus lack of control, and punitive treatment versus humane care wax and wane over time (Allderidge, 1979; Hinshaw, 2006).

One of the challenges of the present is to plan for realistic reform that can yield lasting change rather than counterreactions, retrenchment, and despair.

Despite the clear presence of cycles of human response to mental illness, the predominant theme across recorded history regarding the treatment of persons with mental disorder includes a depressing tendency toward exclusion and punishment, as would be suggested strongly by evolutionary psychological accounts. Indeed, once people began to write down narratives of their cultural practices, descriptions of individuals with atypical behavior patterns soon followed. Ancient texts, such as the Bible, provide richly detailed accounts of mentally disordered behavior, which portend modern classification systems with great accuracy.

It may be the case that a good deal of unofficial history has been marked by attempts at custodial care of persons with mental illness at home, but official accounts are filled with cruelty and banishment as primary modes of response (Zilboorg, 1941). I can present only a brief summation of key historical trends to illuminate both the core tendencies toward maltreatment and the reforms that have emerged from time to time. One of the core themes from a careful reading of history is that views of and treatments for mental illness have lagged considerably behind mainstream scientific and humanistic advances throughout history; the stigma surrounding the entire topic has greatly limited the spread of human knowledge to this subject matter (Hinshaw, 2006). During the Renaissance, for instance, the explosion of scientific and artistic advances was not matched by parallel improvements in the understanding or care of those with mental illness, who continued to be viewed with a blend of moralistic, superstitious, and primitive biological perspectives (Zilboorg, 1941). I also emphasize the important point that children and adolescents with behavioral aberrations have been at risk for a double stigma, in that fear and castigation of mental illness have been compounded by the generally low status of children throughout history.

Adults with Mental Disorder

Across nearly all historical periods, a core perspective on disturbed behavior has been that it emanates from possession by evil spirits or the devil. Given their moralistic framework, such demonologic views have been associated with harshly punitive social responses. Yet, in some instances, religious and moral perspectives have been linked to hopeful, humane care. For example, monasteries were sometimes refuges during the Middle Ages, and the theory and practice of "moral treatment" in the early nineteenth century had both humanitarian and religious overtones (Grob, 1994).

In terms of biological perspectives, one of the first recorded naturalistic views of mental disorder occurred in classical Athens, when Hippocrates posited that mental illnesses originated from imbalances in one or more of the four major bodily humors. This theory was accompanied by the view that afflicted persons required careful diagnosis, compassion, and humane care emphasizing restoration of bodily balances. On the other hand, the lack of sophistication of biological theorizing meant that such practices as bloodletting and purging (through emetics) were primary treatments for the next 2,000 years. In addition, exclusively biological views have also been associated with the perspective that mental illness is hopeless and chronic, fostering the belief that isolated custodial care in institutions is the primary treatment option.

Thus, there is no simple, one-to-one association between etiologic views of mental illness and humane versus cruel social responses. What appears necessary in the future is the promotion of multifaceted views of mental disorder that emphasize biological vulnerabilities as causal factors, plus environmental risks as precipitants and personal and family responsibility necessary for ultimate outcome (Hinshaw, 2006).

History is replete with instances of cruelty and maltreatment toward persons with mental disorder. One of the predominant views of so-called insanity and lunacy in Western cultures has been that the afflicted individual had lost his or her fundamental abilities to reason, thereby spurring the belief that he or she was less than fully human. Hence, many treatments involved terror and fright to spur the individual back to full mental faculties. At the level of physical sensation and pain, it was believed that beatings or subjugation to extremes of cold in unprotected winter quarters did not affect the mentally disordered in the same ways as they would affect normal individuals (Zilboorg, 1941).

Institutional care, first in special wards of general hospitals and then in asylums created for the insane, spurred excursions by citizens of the nearby cities to observe, for an admission fee, the raving, psychotic, and "amusing" behavior of the inmates. Given the clear parallels with tours of zoos, the underlying belief was that the persons in the institutions were less than human. Even some of the great liberators of the mentally ill—Pinel in France, Tuke in England, Rush in the New World—held harshly authoritarian views of the childlike nature of persons with mental illness (Hinshaw, 2006). It is important to note that more progressive and humane perspectives on the care of mental illness often emerged from non-Western cultures, particularly Middle Eastern nations.

A strong custom in many cultures was to force persons with mental illness outside of cities, towns, and villages to wander the countryside, begging for subsistence. Hence, shunning and exclusion were strong undercurrents of response to mental disorder (Zilboorg, 1941). As with institutional care in distant asylums, such banishment served to place the issue of mental disorder outside of the everyday awareness of most citizens, constituting another legacy of stigmatization.

The twentieth century was marked by the rise of increasingly secular, and increasingly scientific, views of mental illness, as evidenced by the expansive growth of the fields of psychology and psychiatry. One core trend was the eugenics movement, which originated in the United Kingdom but which quickly spread to the United States (Black, 2003). The underlying belief in the genetic locus of mental retardation and mental illness led to the passage of mandatory sterilization laws in a majority of states and set the stage for even more stringent measures in Nazi Germany, where hundreds of thousands of persons with mental illnesses were not only sterilized but annihilated (Kevles, 1985). Once again, reductionistic perspectives on biological loci of mental disorder have been associated with extremes of cruelty.

At the same time, psychological perspectives were emerging, most notably the psychoanalytic views of Freud and his followers. Although these perspectives, like the biological perspectives just discussed, tended to rid mental illness of demonologic overtones, for much of the century they directly implicated poor parenting as responsible for most forms of mental disturbance. In fact, conditions such as Autism and Schizophrenia were held to result directly from faulty, cold, and unresponsive parenting, fueling decades of direct parental stigmatization regarding the mental disorders of their offspring (e.g., Bettelheim, 1967). Other theoretical models, such as behaviorism, were also extreme in their positing of environmental determinants of mental illness. Note too that the very term "mental illness," including its dualistic separation from physical conditions, often implies that the underlying conditions are "in the mind" and not real illnesses.

By the later decades of the twentieth century, biomedical/genetic frameworks regained ascendancy, fostered by major advances in neuroscience, neuroimaging, biological psychiatry, and molecular genetics. Such views have prompted the perspective that mental illnesses are "diseases like any other," beyond volitional control, with the hope of a resultant reduction in personal and family blame (see Johnson, 1989, for promotion of the view of mental disorders as brain diseases). As highlighted earlier, however, unidimensional, reductionistic biomedical views are often paradoxically associated with extremely punitive responses, probably because they cast persons with mental illnesses as chronically flawed, deviant, and even subhuman and invoke the kinds of tribal stigmas usually reserved for racial and ethnic minorities. As noted later in the chapter, developmental models of mental illness have the potential to promote more accurate perspectives.

Finally, I note the deinstitutionalization movement of the past 40 years. The advent of psychotropic medications, plus the emergence of a community mental health model, led to the curtailing or closing of public hospital settings for children and adults with mental disorder from the 1960s through the present day (Grob, 1994). Whereas few would argue against the core tenets of this movement, including its goal of ending the dehumanizing, isolating conditions of mass institutionalization, the reality is that governments have often viewed deinstitutionalization as a primary means of cost saving (e.g., Appelbaum, 2002). The resultant absence of needed community-based services has allowed severely mentally ill adults, adolescents, and children to exist in the kinds of underfunded community residences—or even on the streets—that are the legacy of cost-cutting measures. Thus, the great hopes for the deinstitutionalization movement of the second half of the twentieth century have too often been met with retrenchment and despair. Note a parallel with the extreme promise of the campaign of Dorthea Dix in the 1800s to replace almshouses and prisons with specially designed mental hospitals: The very institutions she initiated came to be distant, fortress-like, total institutions that often promoted cruel treatment and hopelessness. Stigma has doubtless been increased by community care models that emphasize cost savings over integrated, well-funded programs and that have allowed countless persons with severe mental illnesses to be left to city streets or suboptimal and even subhuman community residential care.

Children with Mental Illness

What has been the plight of children—and, in particular, children with mental disturbances—across history? One sobering perspective is that relatively few children have survived childbirth, infancy, and childhood across most cultures and historical periods, limiting parental attachment to and investment in young children. Even as late as seventeenth- and eighteenth-century America and Europe, the clear majority of children did not survive until age 4 or 5 years (Donohue, Hersen, & Ammerman, 1995). Children have also been viewed as miniature adults in many cultures, with childhood viewed as a brief period of time before youngsters were, of necessity, brought into the labor force (Aries, 1962). As a result, children's rights have been virtually nonexistent, with extremely high rates of harsh treatment, including exploitation, neglect, abandonment, and abuse (Phares, 2003). Indeed, a common practice throughout multiple cultures has been the practice of infanticide, the intentional killing of babies and young children, when family size became too large and when providing for yet another mouth to feed was not possible. This practice was much more likely to occur when the child possessed physical or behavioral deviance. Short of the killing of deviant or disabled children, evidence is strong that such youth were treated with scorn and derision (Donohue et al., 1995).

Only in the past several hundred years has childhood been viewed as a distinct developmental phase, and only in the past century and a half have movements to curtail child labor and mandate education been in place. Indeed, no recordings of children's games or children's literature are evident from the Dark and Middle Ages, suggesting strongly that children were viewed primarily as adults of small stature, with no special accommodations made to their developmental status and with a high premium placed on their ability to provide labor as soon as possible. Youth were commonly put to full-time work by the age of 6 years, and marriages were arranged before adolescence to assure economic well-being for families. Children were often sold into slavery, and beatings were routinely accepted as discipline. In agrarian societies, as soon as children could provide labor, they typically did (Donohue et al., 1995). With the advent of industry in the past several hundred years, children provided a cheap source of labor until restrictions on such practices were recently instituted.

Furthermore, until only the past few decades, parents have had the right to physically and emotionally devastate children, largely because of the view that disciplinary matters within a family are inherently private (see Helfer & Kempe, 1968). The brutalization of children has been such a part of many cultures that intergenerational patterns of maltreatment of children have been nearly endemic (Rhodes, 1999). Note that, in the late nineteenth century, the Society for Prevention of Cruelty to Children was founded *after* the establishment of the Society for Prevention of Cruelty to Animals, demonstrating again the strongly held notion that family business was subject to privacy and that the rights of parents to perform nearly any

act of cruelty on children was unchallenged. Indeed, it has only been in the past 125 years that social institutions have been created to deal with the emotional and behavioral problems of children (Levine & Levine, 1992). Many special protections for children that are taken for granted today have been put in place only during the past century, including child labor laws, universal compulsory education, and child guidance centers and specialized facilities for dealing with child mental health.

In fact, throughout history, when children, typically lacking any protected status, have displayed mental illness, the combination has led to extremes of castigation and cruelty. Even during the modern era, as noted earlier, the growth of child psychology and child psychiatry served to harshly stigmatize parents for causing the mental disturbances of children. Revealing the dual stigmatization of both children and mental illness, basic and applied research on children's mental disorders has lagged well behind parallel efforts for adults.

In recent years, the biological Zeitgeist has replaced environmental views of etiology, tempering a great deal of family and parental blame for mental disorders of youth. Yet, the stigma and shame encountered by far too many families coping with a child suffering from mental disturbance have not abated (Lefley, 1992), and service utilization rates have been extremely low for children and families (New Freedom Commission on Mental Health, 2003). Thus, the legacy of the joint stigmatization of children and mental illness continues. In short, whereas mental disorder has incurred banishment and harsh treatment throughout history, the plight of children and adolescents has been even worse, given the low status and utter lack of power afforded to youth. Stigma of child and adolescent mental disorders must contend with a compound struggle: the general effort for children's rights and the specific attempt to guarantee rights to persons with mental illness.

EMPIRICAL AND CULTURAL EVIDENCE FOR STIGMA

With this historical information in mind, what do empirical research investigations reveal regarding the actual presence of stigma during our current, modern era? And what does a broader examination of cultural, linguistic, and institutional practices uncover? I begin with attitudes of the general public, then highlight families and mental health professionals, and conclude with examination of less empirically based but nonetheless essential evidence that stems from general practices in the culture.

Empirical Research

Empirical investigations have focused on the responses of several groups: the general public, individuals experiencing mental illness, family members, and mental health professionals.

General Public

A long tradition of research on stigma began to emerge in the 1940s and 1950s. Early investigators often utilized the methodology of presenting written case history vignettes to probe respondents' abilities to identify whether mental illness was present as well as their attitudes toward mental disorder. Outcome measures typically included (1) social distance scales, whereby respondents appraised the degree of desired contact with or distance from an individual so depicted; (2) informational and attitudinal measures; and (3) semantic differentials, for which respondents would choose between opposite pairs of adjectives, such as "dirty" versus "clean," to describe the vignette (see, e.g., Nunnally, 1961). The overarching conclusion from the early era of research on public attitudes was the devastating nature of the stigmatization experienced by individuals with mental illness. That is, once members of the public could identify a certain pattern of behavior as representing mental disorder, negative and rejecting responses were highly likely. The clearest explanations for such stigmatizing attitudes were the unpredictability and threat value of the behavior patterns in question (Rabkin, 1972, 1974). Ignorance and intolerance of mental illness were found to be associated with lower levels of respondent education, although negative attitudes were certainly not restricted to those members of society with poor educational backgrounds. Furthermore, empirical studies revealed the presence of stigmatization even in mental health professionals and staff members, who had apparently internalized the general cultural messages of fear, distancing, and prejudice (see subsequent section). As stated by Rabkin (1972, p. 154), "In a very real sense, mental patients have taken the place of lepers as targets of public disgust, dislike, and rejection."

By the 1960s and 1970s, however, some investigators were finding that public attitudes, as revealed by questionnaire responses, were beginning to shift toward a more empathic and altruistic stance toward individuals with mental illness (see Crocetti, Spiro, & Siassi, 1971; Gove, 1982). Yet, a closer look at the empirical literature reveals that such conclusions were premature. First, research in which direct comparisons were made between persons with mental illness and other stigmatized groups (e.g., those with

physical diseases; ex-convicts) consistently showed that mental disorder was ranked at the bottom in terms of social acceptance (e.g., Albrecht, Walker, & Levy, 1982; Tringo, 1970). More recent studies reveal that only substance abuse and homelessness rival mental disorder in terms of stigmatization. Second, questionnaire responses may be greatly influenced by social desirability. Careful work by Link and colleagues (e.g., Link & Cullen, 1983; Link, Cullen, Frank, & Wozniak, 1987) revealed that the wording of typical questionnaires predisposes respondents to overrate their tolerance of mental illness. Furthermore, when participants hold the core belief that mental disorder is linked to violence, attitudes are highly denigrating. Thus, attitude scales may well underplay the actual extent of stigmatization. Third, and crucially, research on the behavioral (as opposed to attitudinal) responses of the public to mental illness has been strongly consistent in revealing tendencies toward shunning, devaluation, and discrimination. For example, the work of Farina and colleagues (Farina, Allen, & Saul, 1968; Farina, Gliha, Boudreau, Allen, & Sherman, 1971; Farina & Ring, 1965) revealed that even a participant's *belief* that interaction partners knew of his or her mental illness negatively influenced a subsequent encounter, exemplifying a self-fulfilling prophecy effect. A classic example of behavioral, as opposed to attitudinal, research is the experimental work of Page (1995), who, across 3 decades, found that landlords were far more likely to deny housing opportunities to potential renters who disclosed a history of mental hospitalization than to those who did not present such a history. In commenting on this work, Page decried the "naïve acceptance of interviews, surveys, or questionnaire-based data" (p. 67).

More recent research, both attitudinal and behavioral, has confirmed that although the general public appears to have gained basic knowledge about mental illness over the past decades, attitudes and behavioral responses are still highly prejudicial and stigmatizing (e.g., Crisp, Gelder, Rix, Meltzer, & Rowlands, 2000; Link, Phelan, Bresnahan, Stueve, & Pescosolido, 1999; A. H. Thompson et al., 2002; Wahl, 1999). Specifically, based on a large, representative sample of the U.S. population (sampled in the General Social Survey), the work of Link et al. (1999) reveals that depictions of substance abuse incur more social distance than do vignettes of Schizophrenia or depression—although all are associated with strong desire for social distance—and that stigma emanates from perceptions of violence linked with such conditions. Indeed, compared to the 1950s, the general populace of the United States is now more likely to link mental illness (particularly its most severe, psychotic variants, such as Schizophrenia) with tendencies toward violence—and it is just such beliefs that fuel stigma and fear (Phelan, Link, & Pescosolido, 2000). This general pattern of stigmatization appears to be the case worldwide (e.g., Angermeyer & Matschinger, 1997; Guimon, Fischer, & Sartorius, 1999).

In terms of the basic question as to whether the behavioral display characteristic of mental illness or the label itself is more likely to be stigmatized, the answer is complex: When behaviors and the label are pitted against each other, the behaviors characterizing mental disorder receive more castigation and social distance. Yet, when the label occurs alone or in the presence of minimal behavioral disruption, stigmatization is strong, and, as just noted, the effects of the label are magnified greatly when respondents associate mental disorder with risk for dangerousness and violence (Link et al., 1987; Phelan et al., 2000).

With respect to children, the bulk of research on stigma has focused on the effects of diagnostic labels on the attitudes of social perceivers, both adults and youth. A number of investigations reveal negative effects of labeling on stigma-related processes. For example, Farrington (1977) showed that the label "delinquency" for youth displaying antisocial behavior had negative effects on eventual outcome (see Adams, Robertson, Gray-Ray, & Ray, 2003). Holguin and Hansen (2003) demonstrated the negative consequences of the label "sexual abuser" for individuals so termed. In fascinating experimental research, Harris, Milich, Corbitt, Hoover, and Brady (1992) had children in third through sixth grades interact dyadically with a peer. Experimentally manipulated were both the actual diagnostic status of the peer, who either did or did not have ADHD, and the child's expectation for the peer interaction partner in the form of the label "behavior problem" or no label. Both factors (interacting with a peer with ADHD and holding the expectancy that the partner would have a behavior problem) negatively influenced the subsequent interaction, with the labeling effect indicative of stigmatization related to the expectancy of problem behavior. Thus, not only are children with behavioral and emotional disorders highly likely to receive peer rejection in response to the symptoms of their conditions (e.g., Erhardt & Hinshaw, 1994), but age-mates' perceptions of labels related to mental illness fuel denigration and castigation (see also Milich, McAninch, & Harris, 1992).

Note that negative effects of labeling extend downward in age to infancy: Labeling videotaped infants as "cocaine exposed" yielded more negative adult ratings of the behaviors displayed than did no label (Woods, Eyler, Conlon, Behnke, & Webie, 1998). Similarly, labeling infants "de-pressed" increased negative ratings, particularly if parents (fathers, in this case) showed symptoms of depression themselves (Hart, Field, Stern, & Jones, 1997).

Other investigations, however, suggest that labeling of child behavior problems is not always pejorative and may even have positive effects. MacDonald and MacIntyre (1999) showed that altering labels of mental disability and attention-disordered behavior did not influence participants' evaluations of the behavior patterns that were depicted. In addition, Klasen (2000) found that for parents of children with ADHD, the diagnosis of the child was actually empowering, as it reduced parental blame and increased the likelihood of obtaining treatment. Indeed, appropriate diagnosis and responsive treatment can be liberating, particularly if they facilitate the opening of opportunities for future independence and life satisfaction (Hinshaw, 2002). Efforts to educate the populace about the realities of mental disorder and to promote egalitarian contact between persons with mental illness and the rest of society will be crucial for enhancing such receptivity, particularly for family members (see Hinshaw, 2006).

Developmentally, when do children recognize the concept of mental illness, and does their knowledge of or attitudes toward peers or adults with either behavioral deviance or the label of mental illness vary with age? Wahl (2002) has reviewed the rather sparse literature on this important topic. In brief, results are difficult to discern with precision because of varied instrumentation across investigations as well as a lack of reporting of psychometric properties of many of the attitudinal and social distance measures utilized. Generally speaking, young children do not have clear conceptions of the mental illness term, often confusing it with physical illnesses or mental retardation. Indeed, children in the early elementary grades often do not know the term mental illness at all, so that some investigators use the term "crazy person" (or variants thereof) as the independent variable. By the later elementary grades, more differentiated knowledge structures are beginning to emerge, such that mental disorders can be distinguished from other forms of deviance or illness. Yet stigmatizing attitudes and desire for social distance are clearly present from early ages. As stated by Wahl, "Even if young children do not know the precise definitions or characteristics of people with mental illnesses, they seem to know that they are undesirable and to be avoided" (p. 147). Intriguingly, some research indicates that the mental illness concept can be applied more readily by youth to adults than to children per se; it is therefore unclear how children attribute the deviant behaviors of peers with mental conditions. Overall, the pervasive influence of public media on the early display of children's negative attitudes toward mental disorder is difficult to avoid as an explanatory factor (see Wahl, 2002; Wilson, Nairn, Coverdale, & Panapa, 2000).

Individuals with Mental Illness

Distressingly, adults with mental illness are highly likely to have internalized many of the negative stereotypes and prejudicial attitudes related to mental disorder that are part of the general culture. They frequently report being the victims of overt or covert discrimination as well as harshly stigmatizing attitudes and general cultural practices related to prejudice (Read & Baker, 1996; Wahl, 1999). Furthermore, stigma and social rejection predict subsequent life adjustment problems for patients with mental illness, over and above initial symptom levels (e.g., Wright, Gronfein, & Owens, 2000). Of particular importance, the expectation of stigmatization predicts premature termination from therapy (Sirey et al., 2001). Secrecy about mental illness and withdrawal from social contact are two of the key coping mechanisms employed by persons with mental disorders in response to stigma; note that such reaction tendencies are likely to perpetuate, rather than overcome, stigmatization (Wahl, 1999). This kind of self-stigmatization may have far-reaching impact on the lives of persons with mental illness (Corrigan, 2004).

Largely unexplored are the various coping styles and strategies deployed by persons with mental illness in response to the stigmatization they receive (Corrigan & Watson, 2002; for a thorough review of identity threat theory in relation to other stigmatized conditions, see Major & O'Brien, 2005). Indeed, almost entirely unknown are the processes by which some persons internalize prejudice and stigma to a large degree, others apparently ignore such castigation, and still others view it as a call to social action. And, as noted by Wahl (2002), there is an utter dearth of research on the self-perceptions and coping strategies of children who have experienced mental disorder. Developmental factors are bound to be essential to such self-perceptions and coping strategies, constituting a major area for future research.

Families and Relatives

There is a growing database on family experiences of mental illness (e.g., Lefley, 1989, 1992; Tessler & Gamache, 2000; Wahl & Harman, 1989). Systematic research on this topic emerged in the 1950s (see Clausen & Yarrow, 1955). Stages of recognition of symptoms were noted, analogous to those in reaction to the development of physical illnesses, with initial anxiety and denial giving way to adoption of a

"sick" role and eventual rehabilitation. As reviewed by Kreisman and Joy (1974), the early years of work in the field focused on a variety of negative responses to relatives with mental disturbance, including fear and dislike, and a host of reactions in the relatives themselves, such as sensitivity to criticism by others, a perception of marginality (with few resources available to help their plight), and self-dislike. Concealment and secrecy were cited as extremely prevalent coping responses. In all, the ramifications of having a relative with mental illness were found to be considerable, encompassing Goffman's (1963) notion of "courtesy stigma," signifying the devaluation that attends to persons who are associated with a stigmatized group.

Investigators have distinguished two types of consequences to families of having a relative with mental illness: *objective burden,* comprising the financial costs, seeking of housing, and logistic negotiations needed to manage a relative with mental illness, and *subjective burden,* constituting the psychological pain, embarrassment, and mental anguish related to caring for the family member. Families report that subjective burden is the stronger of the two (Lefley, 1989; Tessler & Gamache, 2000; E. H. Thompson & Doll, 1982; for a cogent review of the impact of stigma on familes, see Corrigan & Miller, 2004). This finding provides distressing evidence for the pervasive nature of stigmatization. Indeed, in the words of Lefley (1992, pp. 128–129):

> In many cases mental illness in the family jeopardizes relationships with friends and neighbors; in extreme situations it may lead to an almost total social isolation of the family unit. . . . Emotional reactions to major mental illness in a family member frequently include bewilderment, fear, denial, self-blame, sorrow, grieving, and empathic suffering. . . . The added perception of stigma may elicit rage and resentment or intensify depression and social withdrawal. Normative ambivalence toward mentally ill loved ones—the typical swing between exasperation provoked by the patient's behavior, guilt at the reaction, and sorrow evoked by the patient's suffering—may be exacerbated by social stigmatization of families.

What is extent of family burden? In a telling comparison, Struening and colleagues (1995) documented that the subjective burden of those caring for seriously mentally disordered relatives was as strong as that related to a homeless relative and even more salient that associated with multiple sclerosis. Concealment is still a prevalent response among family members, with greater levels of stigmatization perceived by families with higher educational levels than those from lower socioeconomic strata (Phelan, Bromet, & Link, 1998), probably because of the greater shame involved in having a relative with a low-status condition like mental illness in upper socioeconomic brackets. Siblings of adults who suffer from serious forms of mental disorder also carry a great deal of subjective burden, comparable to levels experienced by parents (Greenberg, Kim, & Greenley, 1997). Recent evidence indicates that courtesy stigma applies, at least to some extent, to parents of children with ADHD (Norvitilis, Scime, & Lee, 2002). The overwhelming majority of caregivers believe that most members of society devalue persons with mental illness, with nearly half contending that society also devalues the family members of such individuals (Struening et al., 2001; Wahl & Harman, 1989).

Family burden and perceived stigma are not restricted to the United States. In Sweden, the majority of relatives of persons with mental disorder feel "stigma by association," with 18% admitting that they thought, at times, that the mentally disordered relative would be better off dead (Oestman & Kjellin, 2002). In China, 60% of family members of adults with Schizophrenia stated that stigma had moderate to severe effects on the afflicted person's life, with 26% claiming the same level of effect on the lives of family members (Phillips, Pearson, Li, Xu, & Yang, 2002). Not surprisingly, such effects were perceived to be stronger for patients with more severe levels of pathology and in families with higher levels of negative emotion regarding the member with Schizophrenia; as noted earlier with respect to the United States, they were also stronger in families with higher, rather than lower, levels of education. In recent investigations, stigma was also strongly perceived by caregivers in the African nations of Ethiopia and Nigeria (Ohaeri & Abdullahi, 2001; Shibre et al., 2001), as well as in India (Thara & Srinivasan, 2000; for an overview of mental illness and its stigmatization in Islamic countries, see Al-Issa, 2000).

Another perspective on family stigmatization emerges from turning the generational issues in the other direction. That is, what are the effects on children when a parent has a mental illness, particularly when the parent himself or herself is stigmatized? First, having a parent with a major mental illness is a key risk factor for disorder and impairment in offspring (e.g., Beardslee, Versage, & Gladstone, 1998). The mechanisms underlying this association are varied; they include the potential for genetic mediation, marital disharmony, lack of parental responsiveness, and modeling of emotional dysregulation (Hinshaw, 2004). Second, one key variable underlying the risk may include the difficulties parents have in communicating directly and clearly with their children about the nature of their own mental disorder. Indeed, in the presence of stigma, the predominant parental tendency is concealment and silence (Lefley, 1992; Wahl &

Harman, 1989). Yet, when no information is forthcoming about parental absence or disruption, children will tend to blame themselves, compounding other sources of risk for disorder and dysfunction (Hinshaw, 2005). Thus, a key antidote to stigma is the promotion of family communication to children and adolescents about the mental disorders of parents or close relatives (Beardslee, 2002; Hinshaw, 2004). Such communication not only demystifies the puzzling behaviors but also models openness on the part of parents and opens the door for more adaptive coping.

In sum, with the closure of most institutional facilities in the past half-century, family members have increasingly dealt with both the actual care of relatives with serious mental disorder and the emotional and psychological costs of such care in a stigmatizing society. Findings include a wide and distressing pattern of perceived stigmatization, evident cross-culturally. Lacking from such research, however, are (1) considerations of families dealing with forms of mental disorder beyond the most serious, psychotic variants; (2) a more complete perspective on children who live with mentally disordered parents; and (3) developmental factors in the life of a family that predict adaptive versus maladaptive coping and adjustment.

Mental Health Professionals

It might be assumed that those who work directly with persons with mental disorders would be immune to stigmatizing attitudes and practices, but data reveal otherwise. Such evidence began to be accumulated by pioneers in stigma research (see Nunnally, 1961). Many investigations were performed with attitude scales completed by staff of psychiatric facilities during the 1950s and 1960s; note that nearly all relevant research pertains to staff and professional attitudes regarding adult forms of mental disturbance. Findings included the general result that mental health personnel were somewhat more accepting of mental disorder than members of the general community but that different attitudes of mental health workers, such as authoritarianism and benevolence—the latter signifying a belief in the childlike qualities of "mental patients"—were associated with worse patient outcomes (see Cohen & Struening, 1962; reviewed in Rabkin, 1974). Even as funding and models of care have shifted to community-based rather than institutional settings, a continuing pattern of stereotypic beliefs and stigmatizing attitudes has been noted (see Keane, 1990, 1991; Scott & Philip, 1985). In addition, large surveys reveal that mental health staff of many varieties have continued to perceive a lack of integrated services available for their clientele (Mirabi, Weinman, Magnetti, & Keppler, 1985). Also, Fryer and Cohen (1988) found that staff of a Veterans Administration facility ascribed a host of negative traits, including apathy, hostility, immaturity, selfishness, and aloofness, to persons branded as psychiatric patients as opposed to general medical patients. As recently as 2002, Mukherjee, Fialho, Wijetunge, Checinski, and Surgenor provided evidence that, in London, half of medical students and physicians surveyed had beliefs in the dangerousness and unpredictability of individuals with Schizophrenia and drug/alcohol problems. The general pattern therefore appears to be one of continuing stigmatization of persons with mental disorder, emanating from some of the very professionals entrusted with their care.

Tellingly, a systematic survey in the United States (Wahl & Harman, 1989) revealed that one of the primary sources of stigmatization perceived by persons with mental illness—and their family members—emanated from demeaning attitudes and low expectations for improvement from professionals providing care. Indeed, among a list of eight potential coping resources for combating stigma, the respondents ranked the act of talking with mental health professionals as the least helpful alternative.

Whereas a great number of those in the mental health professions are genuinely committed to improving their clients' clinical status and helping foster autonomy, the models of training in psychology, psychiatry, and other helping professions often convey a superior attitude, promoting an "us versus them" mentality (Hinshaw & Cicchetti, 2000). In addition, the mental health professions have low status in comparison with other medical subdisciplines—again providing evidence for courtesy stigmatization—and medical professionals have often voiced disparaging attitudes toward clientele with mental disorders (for historical information, see Nunnally, 1961; see also Wahl, 1999). Working with patients who have serious mental disorders can be stressful, particularly with relatively low pay and low status. As a result, staff burnout, use of inappropriate humor, and scapegoating of particularly difficult clients and diagnostic categories occur (Wahl, 1999). In short, mental health professionals may inadvertently foster stigmatization through attitudes of superiority, paternalism, and separation from persons with mental illnesses and through theoretical modes that fundamentally blame parents and family members for mental disorders of children and adolescents.

Summary

The present review has barely scratched the surface of the voluminous research on stigmatization related to mental disorder. Although the general public is more knowledgeable than before about mental illness, fundamentally negative attitudes still abound; these have apparently increased over the last 50 years. Behavioral research indicates that persons with mental illness are highly prone to receive discrimination. When persons with mental disorders receive stigma, negative influences on future outcomes are likely, even with initial mental symptoms taken into account. Family shame and stigma regarding mental disorder are major issues, with parental blame emanating from professional and scientific perspectives that attribute the etiology of mental illness exclusively to poor parenting. In addition, when parents have mental disorders, the risk of transmission to offspring is compounded by the presence of stigmatization and silence. Finally, at least some mental health professionals themselves are prone to display stigmatizing, patronizing, and sometimes hopeless attitudes regarding the very persons they are serving.

Overall, has stigmatization toward persons with mental illness increased or decreased in recent years? Although some improvements in knowledge and overtly expressed attitudes are apparent, no research has been performed on perceivers' implicit, unconscious biases, which remains a major priority for future investigations. Furthermore, Sartorius (1999) claims that stigma has actually increased in recent times, related to three key factors: (1) increased urbanization, making displays of deviance salient to more of the population; (2) increased educational levels and increased skill demands for technological jobs, rendering educational failure and unemployment related to mental disorder more noticeable; and (3) extensive growth of a middle class in many societies, yielding a tendency toward standardization and conformity of behavioral displays that make nonconforming behavior more visible and disturbing. Together with the increased tendency for the populace to link mental illness with violence and danger (Phelan et al., 2000), this analysis provides caution for those who posit linear reductions in stigmatization with the continued advent of modernization and Westernization.

Beyond the empirical evidence just reviewed, less formal indicators of stigmatization are even more revealing. I therefore expand my coverage to include broader types of evidence for stigma, including indicators in the general culture and language of everyday life; depictions in the public media; discrimination with respect to such areas as housing, employment, and health care coverage; and personal, narrative accounts from individuals with mental illness and their family members.

Broader Evidence in the General Culture for Stigma

The task of searching for general indicators of stigma in relation to mental illness is more difficult than might be thought. The reason is that widely held attitudes and stances in a given culture are often so pervasive and grounded in everyday life that specific mention of them is hard to find. Goldhagen (1996) noted a parallel problem in his search for anti-Semitic attitudes in Germany during the 1930s, in that the very pervasiveness of such beliefs masked their presence. He quoted an unnamed scholar: "To be an anti-Semite in Hitler's Germany was so commonplace as to go practically unnoticed" (p. 32). Similarly, the stigmatization of mental illness is so deeply embedded in our culture's words, pictures, and practices as to escape easy detection unless a concerted effort is made to uncover such images and to realize that many cultural epithets are, in fact, directed against those with mental illness.

Everyday Language

The very words in common use convey stereotyping and stigmatization about mental illness. If, during the course of an argument about even trivial matters, a person makes a statement that appears out of line with the flow and logic of the discussion, a common response from his or her interaction partner may well be "Are you insane?" Unpopular ideas are commonly dismissed as "crazy" or "nuts"; outlandish plans are branded as "madness." When individuals say or do things that fail to show foresight or forethought, they are all too commonly called "idiots," "imbeciles," or "morons," the formal terms to indicate mental retardation during much of the past century. It is revealing to recognize the extent to which a host of disparaging terms relate to mental disorder: Ideas are "deranged," persons who behave outside the norms are "lunatics," strange behavior is branded as "psycho," and an individual whom one would not want to meet is often a "mental case." The frequency of use of such terms reveals a veritable preoccupation with the rationality and conformity of social partners.

Other linguistic practices are even more graphic. Murderers are "psycho killers," even in popular rock songs. Those who promote strange ideas are "wacked," and facilities for those with mental illness are "loony bins" or "nut houses." This kind of language reveals fear as well as fascination: fear that the affliction could befall the perceiver and fascination with the illicit, perhaps dangerous or bizarre behavior patterns underlying the terms and labels. Children come to use such terms at early ages, signaling the pervasiveness of the cultural disparagement of persons with mental disorders. Indeed, pejorative labels linked to mental illness or mental retardation ("crazy," "retard") are among the initial terms used to castigate socially rejected peers.

Media Depictions

Perhaps the most telling evidence in modern culture related to the stereotyping and stigmatization of mental disturbance is found through analyses of media portrayals of those with mental disorders (Wahl, 1995). Although there are a few recent signs that depictions in public media are beginning to be less disparaging than has been the case for many decades (Wahl, Ward, & Richards, 2002), the pervasiveness of distorted media images is a major issue for anyone concerned with stigma. Nunnally (1961) presented disheartening accounts of media practices in the 1950s, concluding that images from visual media were grossly negative, unflattering, stereotyped, and sensationalistic. Commercials, soap operas, prime-time dramas, advertisements, and newspaper/magazine accounts continue to portray persons with mental illness as deranged, violent, and unpredictable with alarming frequency (Coverdale, Nairn, & Claasen, 2002; Diefenbach, 1997). Most accounts of mental disorder focus on the most extreme variants of mental illness, such as Schizophrenia; descriptions of violence have been almost omnipresent (Shain & Phillips, 1981). Tellingly, television cartoons are quite likely to depict mental illness in characters, and such portrayals are typically stereotyped and pejorative (Wilson et al., 2000). Even when media portrayals do not include stereotyped depictions of violence and utter irrationality, they still often depict incompetence, unemployment, and grossly disturbed affect (Hinshaw, 2006; Nunnally, 1961). The firsthand accounts of persons with mental illness, and their family members, are hardly ever reported. Overall, pervasive and negative media images—replete with ridicule, violence, and disrespect—are a primary vehicle for promoting stigma in the current era.

Discriminatory Policies

A host of discriminatory policies are still in place. Several levels of discrimination can be differentiated: (1) direct discrimination, where, for example, housing is denied based on knowledge of an applicant's mental disorder; (2) structural discrimination, entailing the curtailing of rights of those with mental illness because of policies and the formation of societal barriers; and (3) discrimination via self-stigmatization, a subtle but pernicious form through which an individual's internalized stigma prevents his or her utilizing life opportunities (Angermeyer & Schulze, 2001).

Of great significance is the lack of full parity of insurance coverage for mental, as opposed to physical, illnesses. For one thing, many individuals often do not recognize that behavioral and emotional problems emanate from mental disorders; this process may be related to general ignorance as well as stigmatization. Yet, even if such recognition exists, stigma may limit help seeking, even among military personnel who are experiencing posttraumatic responses (Hoge et al., 2004). Indeed, this phenomenon is an example of self-stigmatization. Crucially, however, imagine the scenario when recognition and willingness to seek treatment are in place, which itself is a major victory, yet inadequate funding for treatment may still preclude the receipt of treatment. That is, an individual wishing for treatment, or a family seeking intervention for their child, may be able to receive full reimbursement for "physical" illnesses but lower levels of care, often inadequate to the task, for a disabling mental disorder. It is hard to imagine a more blatant form of stigmatization than this, which is clearly a factor in spurring the low service utilization rates for persons and families with mental illnesses (New Freedom Commission, 2003; Wang, Demler, & Kessler, 2002).

As I write this chapter, partial parity legislation is the law of the land, with more stringent bills (e.g., the Senator Paul Wellstone Mental Health Equitable Treatment Act) undergoing congressional debate. Although there would certainly be some cost increases related to such legislation—on the order of 1% a year for premiums—the overall cost of lost productivity related to mental disorder approaches $100 billion per year, so that parity legislation would almost certainly effect overall savings.

Several other legal issues are salient. Independent housing for persons with mental illness is extremely difficult to find, related in part to the fact that public assistance benefits in several U.S. states are not enough to cover the cost of a monthly rental, much less food and other necessities (Cooper & O'Hara, 2003). In addition, as highlighted earlier, the disclosure of a history of mental disorder greatly limits the availability of even being shown an apartment that has been advertised (Page, 1995). Because housing is a key variable related to self-esteem and productivity (Carling, 1990), this issue remains a major priority.

In terms of employment, although the Americans with Disabilities Act supposedly eliminated discrimination in public and work settings, persons with a history of mental illness know that disclosure of their past can nearly automatically exclude their consideration for various jobs and can lead to loss of status—or even of work itself (Wahl, 1999). Furthermore, the rigorous economic analyses of Marcotte and Wilcox-Goek (2001) showed that each year in the United States, between 5 million and 6 million individuals with mental disorders lose, fail to seek, or cannot find employment as a consequence of their mental illness. As a result, poverty is a common consequence of mental

disorder. Finally, persons with a history of mental illness even have difficulties obtaining a driver's license, securing voting rights, maintaining child custody, or performing jury service (Corrigan, Markowitz, & Watson, 2004; Wahl, 1999). All of these indicators of discrimination constitute prima facie evidence of continuing stigmatization.

Personal and Family Narratives

Powerful accounts of stigma emanate from personal stories of individuals who have been affected by mental disorder and its castigation. Such accounts, however, have typically been discounted and ignored. From a scientific perspective, there are well-documented limitations to case studies, whether written by clinicians or those persons directly affected. How is it known, for example, that the individual described is representative of the population of interest? What about the variables that are not controlled? Second, because persons with mental disorders have been devalued, with their very rationality questioned, a common rejoinder is that no one would be tempted to believe their personal narrative accounts. Indeed, wouldn't their personal stories be tainted by distorted thinking?

I contend, however, that studying narratives can give a sense of the teller's personal interpretation of key events, of the variables important to the narrator's self-definition, and of the relation of events and perceptions to cultural context of the account. Most important, narrative may effectively humanize crucial social issues. Indeed, as noted earlier, when individuals with mental disorders are perceived as subhuman, the most vehement stigmatization is likely to occur. To the extent that narratives can portray the real person behind symptoms, treatments, discrimination, struggles, and triumphs, empathy may be greatly enhanced. Although there are certainly instances in which severe mental disorder may lead to highly irrational thinking and writing, accounts from lucid periods may be highly revealing of both symptoms and social practices.

Until recent years, there have been only sporadic examples of personal accounts and narratives capturing the public imagination sufficiently to motivate change in the mental health system (e.g., Beers, 1945). More recently, however, a number of compelling personal accounts have appeared, and these have opened up the topic of mental illness to large segments of the general populace (e.g., Jamison, 1995; see also the Academy Award-winning film *A Beautiful Mind*).

The increasing numbers of disclosures from individuals with mental illness, as well as their family members, provide poignant testimony to not only the vicissitudes and ravages of mental disorder but also to the pernicious effects of stigma and the resilience and strength that can emerge from mental illness (e.g., Hinshaw, 2002; Jamison, 1998; Neugeboren, 1997). Recently, Beard and Gillespie (2002) have provided testimonials from many families in which a child has been diagnosed with a mental disorder, revealing considerable stigma. To the extent that such narratives become more accessible, more complete and compelling evidence for stigmatization, as well as strength and courage, can emerge. Personal and family narratives provide rich, firsthand views of the experience of mental disorder and the stigma that frequently accompanies it. They can portray the realities of mental illness as both human and real, supplanting both statistical accounts and stereotypic depictions. Narrative can thus provide the message that stigma is a topic worth discussion and that individuals with mental illness are first and foremost human (for more complete reviews, see Angell, Cooke, & Kovac, 2005; Hinshaw, 2006).

Summary

In short, a host of "everyday" evidence reveals pervasive and often devastating effects of stigmatization on the lives of persons with mental disorders and their family members. Coupled with the empirical research cited, this evidence leaves little doubt that stigma related to mental illness is still a central issue for the research and clinical fields as well as society at large. I next consider the specific ways in which prejudice, discrimination, and stigmatization may reveal themselves across the life span, as well as how key developmental principles can benefit the future investigation of stigma processes.

DEVELOPMENTAL THEMES

Much of the current social psychological and evolutionary psychological work on stigma is developmental, dealing with adult manifestations of stigma processes but failing to take into account either mechanisms related to stigmatization across the life span or key principles from developmental psychopathology that could enrich understanding of the causes and effects of stigma. In this section, I provide coverage of both of these essential points. For elaboration, see Hinshaw (2005), Hinshaw and Cicchetti (2000), and Hinshaw (2006).

Stigma across the Life Span

Here I consider various life stages, in chronological order, and the potential for stigmatization to play a key role in each.

Infancy and Toddlerhood

At first glance, stigma pertaining to disorders of infancy and toddlerhood might not appear to be a major concern. Indeed, infants and toddlers have limited language skills and self-reflective abilities. But stigma processes can be quite intense—and quite important developmentally—when there is the possibility of mental illness in a very young child. Indeed, when the topic is expanded to include the entire family, the potential for diagnosis of mental dysfunction in a child of this age almost always incorporates implicit, if not explicit, blaming of parents. Indeed, as noted earlier, faulty parental socialization practices constituted the key etiologic models for mental illness throughout much of the past century. With ascription for the locus of such problems made explicitly to poor attachment or unresponsive parenting, it is little wonder that parents would be reluctant to seek assessments and diagnoses. Alternatively, the attribution may be made to genetic flaws (e.g., Rutter, 2000), which may convey substantial stigma as well, as the previous discussion has illuminated.

The point is all the more important because of the utter need for accurate screening, diagnosis, and treatment of the earliest child mental disorders, such as Autistic Disorder, other pervasive developmental disorders, very early onset depression, and ADHD. But the general ignorance of the possibility that serious mental disturbances can exist at this age, coupled with the stigma attached to having a young child with mental illness, often serve to delimit early assessment and detection.

Preschool and School-Age Children

During the preschool and school-age years, similar issues are salient, in that ignorance of the existence of mental disorders, shame at admitting their presence, and a lack of treatment options (and funding) all conspire to delimit needed prevention and intervention. Indeed, as noted throughout this chapter, rates of treatment seeking for children with mental disorder are abysmally low in the United States and are undoubtedly even lower elsewhere (e.g., New Freedom Commission on Mental Health, 2003). Compounding the problem is the importance of academic achievement during childhood. The presence of a mental disorder may hamper the child's ability to focus on school curricula and master educational material (see Hinshaw, 1992, for information on the complex associations among ADHD, aggressive behavior, and underachievement). Under federal law, parents are guaranteed the right to a school-based assessment and, if special needs are documented, appropriate accommodations under the concept of the "least restrictive alternative" (i.e., that the youngster is placed in settings that are as close as possible to mainstream classrooms). If, however, stigmatization leads to the family's reluctance to acknowledge a child's emotional and behavioral difficulties, neither assessments nor accommodations can be implemented. Stigma may therefore limit important life opportunities during years that are crucial for gaining academic skills.

Therapeutic efforts with children nearly always require collateral work with parents, even if systemic intervention with the family is not the treatment of choice. Such work requires careful attention to stigma processes. Crucially, clinicians must become familiar with current scientific literature that has largely debunked prior conceptions of psychogenic, particularly child discipline-related, causation of most childhood mental disorders (e.g., Mash & Barkley, 2003; Phares, 2003). Psychoeducation about the complex array of biological predispositions and life stresses that produce psychopathology may go a long way in limiting blame, recrimination, and self-doubt among parents and family members.

At the same time, it is essential that clinicians do not head to the other extreme and posit reductionistic, biological causal factors as the sole determinants of child mental health issues. Recent research has made it clear that child and family influence in child behavior disorders is reciprocal and transactional in nature (e.g., Hinshaw & Lee, 2003). Even for conditions with substantial heritability, psychosocial influences such as parenting and stressful life events are highly related to outcome in certain subgroups (e.g., Caspi et al., 2002, 2003; Hinshaw et al., 2000; Tully, Arsenault, Caspi, Moffitt, & Morgan, 2004).

The findings from Hinshaw et al. (2000) are noteworthy because they reflect mediator processes in a randomized controlled trial of long-term medication, behavioral, and combination treatments for 579 children with carefully diagnosed ADHD, known as the Multimodal Treatment Study of Children with ADHD (MTA; MTA Cooperative Group, 1999a, 1999b). The important backdrop for this discussion is that behavioral genetic investigations reveal substantial heritability for ADHD, on the order of .7 to .8 (Swanson & Castellanos, 2002). In fact, with such strong genetic liability, it might be believed that parenting cannot be related to outcome. The MTA findings, however, revealed that in the combination treatment, incorporating the multimodal approach of well-delivered medication plus intensive school- and home-based behavioral consultation, the children whose parents showed the strongest improvements in their negative/ineffective discipline styles ended treatment with not just improved but fully normalized rates of disruptive

behavior in their school settings. That is, changes in parental discipline were linked with the superiority of the combination treatment in *normalizing* teacher-reported aggressive and hyperactive behavior; they also served as a mediator variable for comparable improvements in the children's social skills (Hinshaw et al., 2000). Thus, even for a condition as psychobiologically based as ADHD, socialization processes appear quite related to maintaining and even improving clinical symptomatology and impairment over time (see Cicchetti & Hinshaw, 2002, for detailed accounts of the ability of clinical and prevention trials to yield conceptually rich information on processes and mechanisms of psychopathology). The message for stigma reduction is clear: Although parents do not appear to *cause* ADHD in terms of parenting styles, their socialization practices are essential for determining *outcome and course*.

In other words, clinicians can simultaneously reduce parental blame and foster parental responsibility for children's mental health. Stigma reduction can be facilitated when families are no longer blamed as the causes of Autistic Disorder, ADHD, learning disorders, and other key childhood conditions. Yet, along with the message that parents are not the causal agents for such disorders, the counterpart communication is equally crucial, namely, that parents and other socialization forces are clearly and centrally responsible for shaping outcome (see also Campbell, 2002). In addition, with respect to other conditions for which parental negativity and dysfunctional parenting practices are more causally linked to symptomatology (e.g., conduct problems), stigma may delimit parental treatment seeking; hence, responsive clinicians must simultaneously work to improve family discipline and communication and to reduce the self-blame that parents may be experiencing.

Adolescence

Adolescence is noted as a period in which identity consolidation and the gradual gaining of autonomy occur (see Feldman & Elliott, 1990). Mental illnesses with onset, or continued presence, during adolescence may be particularly devastating for the solidification of identity, independence, and the sense of fitting in with peers or "belonging" in the regular world (Hinshaw, 2005). Indeed, the devastating impact of a mood disorder, the disorganization and fragmentation that characterize psychosis, and the paralysis of psychological and even physical development that can accompany Obsessive-Compulsive Disorder and severe eating disorders are all highly likely to emerge during the adolescent years; they may shape self-perceptions and the potential for independent functioning for years to come. When self-stigmatization is added to the mix—that is, when the adolescent is ashamed to admit that he or she suffers from a mental disorder—the chances for intact self-esteem and for maintaining a sense of personal agency are further compromised.

Furthermore, if the illness is severe and hospitalization is required, the kinds of institutional practices of past years, which featured dehumanizing settings, punitive procedures, and major restrictions on autonomy, may have far-reaching effects on an individual's self-image (Hinshaw, 2002). Indeed, essential for destigmatization is that mental health staff and therapists show respect for the integrity and autonomy of their clientele, particularly those who are adolescents (see earlier section on mental health professionals). Improved personnel selection, training, and pay scales can all play important roles in this effort.

I point out that social policies currently in place in the United States convey both stigmatizing and fragmenting messages for families of adolescents. In fact, parents of adolescents with serious behavioral or mood disturbances are sometimes able to procure needed day treatment or residential services only if they give up custody of their offspring (see Hinshaw, 2006). This practice reflects both the critical shortage of needed facilities for children and adolescents with severe problem behavior and the inherently stigmatizing messages regarding family unity embedded in current policy. Essential federal legislation, such as the Keeping Families Together Act under consideration by the U.S. Congress, could help to stop this forced practice of family dissolution to obtain needed services.

Adulthood

During adulthood, many persons with mental disorders utilize a core strategy of secrecy and concealment (see Link, 1987). Shame, fear of losing employment or housing, and the potential reality of curtailed health insurance if a history of mental disorder is divulged are all potential motivators for such a stance. This strategy may compound the loneliness, isolation, and lack of social support that are frequent accompaniments to many forms of mental disorder, perpetuating a vicious cycle of despair, silence, and impairment. I am not advocating that individuals with a history of mental illness disclose their personal narratives indiscriminately. Indeed, given the climate of stigma, such a strategy could well be counterproductive. Rather, because of the potential consequences of a life filled with silence, shame, and isolation, opportunities for disclosure and support should be utilized to the greatest extent possible (Hinshaw, 2002).

When adults with mental disorders are also parents, the impact of stigma can be particularly devastating for the family. Specifically, children are highly likely to internalize blame for their parents' conditions if they do not understand the absences, erratic behavior, and deprivations they may experience in terms that they can understand. To the extent that youngsters begin to comprehend that such experiences are outside their personal control, they can be freed from potentially devastating guilt and self-blame. Parental mental illness is clearly a risk factor for disordered functioning in children, as argued earlier, but stigmatization may compound the problems exponentially, to the extent that the family is engulfed in shame and silence and offspring do not receive assurance and needed information (Hinshaw, 2004). Finding ways to encourage productive discussion among family members is a needed step, requiring a form of family intervention that demands honesty, frank disclosure, and a willingness to receive input from multiple sources of support (Beardslee, 2002).

Another relevant issue is a pervasive social attitude toward mental illness, namely, that it permeates all aspects of the person's being. This perspective may foster the individual's becoming identified with the disorder. In other words, because having a mental disorder is associated with the person's entire being, the individual may begin to view himself or herself as "a schizophrenic," "a manic depressive," or "an obsessive-compulsive." This practice is all too often perpetuated by professionals who link the individual with his or her disorder. The underlying humanity of the person in question is likely to be buried beneath the diagnostic label, which connotes weakness, deviance, permanence, and a sense of fundamental flaw. Individuals with mental illnesses are first and foremost human, a view that may get lost unless the diagnostic label is applied to the condition rather than the entire person (American Psychiatric Association, 2000; Hinshaw & Cicchetti, 2000). Because stigma processes are by definition pervasive and globalizing, the struggle to retain the individual's identity and humanity in the face of a mental illness may be a difficult one.

Finally, I note in passing that elderly persons with mental illnesses must fight the dual stigma of being old (and often disenfranchised financially as well as isolated from their family) and mentally disordered. Differential diagnostic issues related to cognitive decline versus mental disorder, or their comorbidity, are paramount. Yet the isolation and stigma that pertain to decrements in psychological and mental functioning for elderly persons often curtail any efforts to obtain diagnostic clarity.

Summary

Across the life span, stigma has important implications for the attainment of competence, the development of a sense of self, the ability to gain independence and a sense of personal agency, the ability to receive social support and acceptance, and the struggle for families to maintain services for their offspring with mental disorders. The pain and impairments that emanate from mental disorders are often quite severe; when stigma and discrimination are included, chances for life success are markedly diminished (Hinshaw, 2006; U.S. Department of Health and Human Services, 1999). A life span perspective is essential to understand the pervasiveness of the consequences of stigma for multiple aspects of individual and family functioning.

Developmental Psychopathology Issues Related to Stigma

The enterprise of developmental psychopathology, the field that explicitly links normal and atypical development and that comprises the overarching topic of this entire volume (see also Rutter & Sroufe, 2000), embraces a number of core principles. I note several of the most salient of these and integrate them with the many considerations already raised regarding stigma in relation to mental disorder.

Continuities and Boundaries between Normal and Atypical

A core tenet of developmental psychopathology is that atypical, pathological behavior patterns represent aberrations in pathways that otherwise lead to normative development. That is, mental disorders are not fixed, static entities but rather the end points of developmental processes marked by flux and change (Cicchetti, 1993; Hinshaw, 1994). Indeed, they represent fluid states that typically alternate with periods of more normative functioning, best understood as disruptions in developmental processes that typically yield adaptation. Thus, persons with mental disorders are not fundamentally different, in type, from other humans, even though they may have genetic propensities for emotional and behavioral disturbances that render them susceptible to the influence of stressful environments ranging from prenatal and familial settings to wider cultural socialization contexts.

Although it is possible that certain mental disorders are best understood as taxa—that is, as categorical entities discrete from the norm—most mental illnesses appear to be far more continuous in nature, presenting as extremes of distributions of underlying behavioral, cognitive, and emotional statues. (In actuality, categories of mental disturbance can be simultaneously continuous and categorical, depending on which criteria are used to examine their fea-

tures, in the same way that light can represent both waves and photons; for a lucid discussion, see Pickles & Angold, 2003.) It is therefore mistaken to view mental illness as qualitatively distinct from normative processes. The upshot for stigmatization is that views of mental disorder as constituting qualitatively different, flawed, and inferior kinds of functioning are misguided (see Haslam & Ernst, 2002, for a critique of essentialist ideas about mental illness). The fundamental humanity of individuals with mental illnesses must be emphasized, potentially leading to increases in compassion and hope for amelioration of their course.

Ecological Models

Developmental psychopathology emphasizes the linkages between individuals and their environments, such that pathology and coping are hypothesized to reside in the interface between persons and settings (Bronfenbrenner, 1977). Thus, pathology does not reside in the individual per se or in the environment per se but rather in the "fit" between them. Psychopathology constitutes an imbalance between personal resources and environmental supports.

Intriguingly, stigma itself is also a relational construct, constituting a mark of degradation made by society related to membership in a group believed to be evil, flawed, or contagious. For children and adolescents, stigma processes occur in families, schools, and communities; thus, the concept of fit between individual and setting is crucial to the diagnosis of the child as mentally disturbed. Adults, as well, are judged by societal standards of appropriate deportment in decisions regarding mental illness. Although the impairments related to serious mental disorder are undoubted, it is also important to understand that changing environmental standards may render certain behavioral tendencies more or less adaptive. Deviancies and flaws in one cultural context may well be adaptive in others. Again, with the adoption of essentialist beliefs that mental illness is a fixed, discrete type of behavior rather than a product of fit between person and environment (Haslam & Ernst, 2002), stigma may be intensified. Fostering tolerance and acceptance of deviant behavior patterns, so long as they are not threatening to others, will require adapting contexts and environments (i.e., school, home, workplace) to maximize the potential for productive behavior.

Reciprocal Determinism and Transaction

In developmental psychopathology models, mental disorder results from interactive linkages between individual-level constructs (such as genotypes and temperament), relational variables (including attachment and parenting styles), and wider systems influences (school or neighborhood settings) in shaping typical as well as atypical development. Such interactive influences unfold over time and across development, reflecting the construct of *transaction* (Sameroff & MacKenzie, 2003). The upshot of such transactional perspectives for stigma is that preconditions for psychopathology are modifiable by environmental circumstances. For example, in groundbreaking work, Caspi and colleagues have recently found that both genotypes and crucial environmental circumstances work interactively to yield risk for psychopathology. Specifically, polymorphisms of the monoamine oxidase gene are shaped differentially by abusive encounters in childhood to yield risk for antisocial behavior (Caspi et al., 2002), and different alleles of the serotonin transporter gene are affected in different ways by negative life events to produce clinical-range depression (Caspi et al., 2003). Once again, psychopathology is not a fixed product of biology or environment but a product of interactive processes.

With such dynamic models in mind, it is difficult to make reductionistic arguments that mental disorder is a sole product of genes or of dysfunctional environments. Implications for stigma are important. That is, stigmatization of families is likely to occur when parenting is viewed as the primary cause of mental illness, and derogation and punishment of the individual are strong possibilities when deviant genetic makeup is indicated as the primary determinant of mental disorder (e.g., Mehta & Farina, 1997). On the other hand, understanding the inherently transactional nature of mental disorder should help to take blame away from both parenting styles and flawed individual constitutions as the exclusive loci of mental disturbance. Transactional models are not intuitively obvious, especially in a culture that continues to value simplistic sound bites as the predominant mode of communicating complex biological, social, cultural, and even political messages. Yet promoting the notions of vulnerability, life stress, interaction, and transaction may help to reduce the stigmatization associated with extremes of exclusively environmental or exclusively biological perspectives. Such promotion may help to shape lay views of psychopathology as reflecting combinations of internal preconditions and external stressors, working together across time.

Resilience

The pain and impairment related to mental disorder are undoubted, but it is also the case that the symptoms of many mental disorders wax and wane over time, that periods of relatively normal functioning are prevalent in many persons with mental disturbances, and that many such individuals can make unexpectedly good life adjustments. In other words, resilience is a real possibility for individuals with mental illness (Hinshaw, 2002). Resilience is defined as the attainment of positive outcomes in the presence of risk for maladjustment (Luthar, Cicchetti, & Becker, 2000; Masten & Coatsworth, 1998) and provides a needed antidote to views of mental disorder based solely on pathology. Involving both individual characteristics (humor, intelligence, persistence, certain temperamental traits) and familial and community supports (presence of mentors or extrafamilial supports in childhood, healthy partners in adulthood), it is a concept that is important to consider with respect to mental disturbance. That is, when the general public comes to understand that mental illness is not inevitably associated with despair and degradation and that a range of healthy outcomes is possible in persons who have experienced mental disorder, stigmatizing attitudes may change. Indeed, views of mental disturbance that show its malleability rather than chronicity should facilitate stigma reduction (see Jones et al., 1984).

It would be a mistake, however, to apply "Pollyanna" approaches to depictions of mental illness. Indeed, many reform efforts have foundered on the shores of unrealistic, overly optimistic views of the amenability of serious mental illness to community treatments (see Grob, 1994). The promotion of realistic, rather than oversimplified or sensationalistic, portrayals of mental disorder is urgently needed at the level of public media. There are signs that more positive images of mental disorder have made their way into cultural consciousness (e.g., see Wahl et al., 2002). Extending these images to children and adolescents with Autism, ADHD, learning disorders, conduct problems, depression, and other developmental disorders, as well as adults with a variety of mental illnesses, is a needed step to overcome stigma. When it is realized that individuals with serious forms of mental illness can attend school and learn as children, can be sensitive and loving parents as adults, and can maintain their integrity and retain a strong sense of meaning in life (see Hinshaw, 2002), then stigma reduction will have begun in earnest. The more human and realistic the portrayals, the stronger the likelihood of stigma reduction.

INTEGRATIVE MODEL OF THE STIGMATIZATION OF MENTAL ILLNESS

I now attempt a brief synthesis of the many concepts reviewed above about the stigma of mental illness. This model features principles from social, evolutionary, and developmental psychology as well as sociology and developmental psychopathology, with particular emphasis on concepts linked to threat (Stangor & Crandall, 2000; see also Blasovich, Mendes, Hunter, & Lickel, 2000). (I do not have space to consider another variant of such models, namely identity threat theory, with regard to responses of those stigmatized; see Major & O'Brien, 2005.) Note that any accurate portrayal of stigma must acknowledge its overdetermined nature, with stigma processes operating at the levels of individuals, families, communities, and broader social and political contexts (e.g., Hinshaw, 2006; Link & Phelan, 2001). Attempting to find which level of analysis is primary is destined to be futile, as all levels interact and transact. In other words, stigma is a joint function of individual psychology (and even naturally selected proclivities), forces related to dyadic and larger group social interactions, and cultural and economic forces at work in a given society. All too little is known about its emergence across development, constituting a key research question for the future.

First, symptoms of the most severe forms of mental illness are threatening to social perceivers. Some of this threat may not require much in the way of cognitive mediation on the part of perceivers; for instance, psychotic behavior, with its inherently irrational and unpredictable nature, may yield threat to personal space or physical integrity. It may also give the perceiver a sense of the fragility of control over his or her own mental life. Some of the symptoms may, at a primitive level, convey a sense of potential contagion (see Kurzban & Leary, 2001); they may also disrupt the perceiver's fundamental foundation of a stable, predictable world and thus stir fears of mortality. Thus, the threat value of such symptoms is multifaceted.

Despite real variations across history and across cultures regarding response to such symptoms (see Littlewood, 1998), these patterns of behavior have tended to evoke, fairly consistently and even automatically, emotional responses of anger (over the violations of social contracts and reciprocation) and revulsion (over the fear of contamination related to grossly disordered behavior and disheveled appearance). Such responses are expectable from an evolutionary perspective on the development of automatic exclusion modules (Fishbein, 2002; Kurzban & Leary, 2001). In addition, the very label of "mental illness" has taken on a variety of meanings (as have many other poorly understood diseases throughout history; see Sontag, 1978/1989), including depravity, weakness, filth, and loss of control. Thus, even mental disorders that are not as inherently threatening as psychotic-level variants carry a

large amount of baggage to social perceivers. Finally, although mental illness does not usually invoke the type of social reactions reserved for nationalistic, racial, or "tribal" differences—involving punitive, exploitive responses (Kurzban & Leary, 2001)—when persons with mental disorder are specifically highlighted as threats to the survival of a nation's viability (as in the case of the heightened eugenics movements in the United Kingdom and United States early in the past century and of Hitler's pointing to persons with mental illness and mental retardation as threats to the Aryan race), then sterilization and even genocide are expectable results.

Persons with mental disorder therefore invoke both real threats to perceivers' expectations of social reciprocity or worries about health status and symbolic threats to their sense of rationality and order in the world. Perceptions of the unpredictability, peril, and chronicity of the disturbance serve to fuel such threat (Jones et al., 1984). Symbolic threat is particularly salient, as the irrational, out-of-control nature of the symptom patterns may elicit fears in perceivers with respect to their own abilities to maintain behavioral and emotional control. Such threats to self-integrity, combined with anxiety raised about stability and even mortality, play an important role in the extremity of avoidance, shunning, and castigation of persons with mental disorder. Note that it is unclear precisely when these responses emerge during individual development; work on this topic should be a priority.

Stangor and Crandall (2000) posit three stages to threat reactions: (1) the initial phase of real or symbolic threat; (2) the subsequent deployment of cognitive distortions and stereotypes to exaggerate differences with the outgroup, serving as a breeding ground for prejudice; and (3) the amplification of such distorted perceptions through societal communication (e.g., mass media) and the invocation of system justification (i.e., blaming the victim) to promote the view that it is not social inequity but rather weakness or deviance on the part of the stigmatized individual that is to blame. In the second and third stages, when the individual in question comes to be viewed as less than human—perhaps because of perceivers' fears of losing their own rationality and reason—then the most harsh, extreme, and even lethal responses will be justified.

One of the hopes of recent decades has been that when mental illness is finally seen from a naturalistic, medical model perspective rather than as a volitional, morally depraved set of behaviors, stigmatization would markedly decrease. As I have highlighted, however, despite some value in viewing mental illness as biologically based rather than denoting personal culpability (Martin et al., 2000), an exclusive focus on genetic, biological models of the locus of mental illness may actually increase punitive social responses (Dietrich et al., 2004; Mehta & Farina, 1997; Read & Harre, 2001). Factors other than attributions are clearly at play in this regard. Indeed, the threat value of disturbed behavior, its media-promoted association with violence and danger, and general cultural norms regarding the assumption of personal responsibility for behavior and emotion all predispose perceivers to shun and stigmatize those with mental disturbance well before attributions to biological loci are even invoked (Haslam, 2005). Even more, an exclusively biomedical ascription may foster a view of the individual as tainted and flawed, leading to dehumanization and even elimination.

What of the effects of stigmatization on those experiencing mental disorder themselves, termed self-stigmatization by Corrigan and Watson (2002)? Crucially, and unlike ethnic characteristics or physical disabilities, a history of experiencing mental disorder usually exemplifies a concealable mark (unless the individual is floridly symptomatic), meaning that the individual faces the dilemma of whether to reveal such a history to social partners. Considerable anxiety, related to the potential for rejection, is likely with such a concealable stigma. Furthermore, as elaborated by Smart and Wegner (2000), attempts to suppress symptoms and relevant history require great mental effort and are thus likely to be peppered with intrusive thoughts about the concealed attribute in question, in addition to high levels of cognitive and physiological activation. Thus, stigmatization of mental disorder yields intense consequences for those who must contend with its effects on a day-to-day basis. Far greater understanding is required of the kinds of coping strategies utilized by persons with mental disorder in contending with prejudice and stigma, particularly in children and adolescents. Indeed, as emphasized by Wahl (2002), almost nothing is known about the personal experiences of youth with mental disorders.

In closing, I note two key points. First, stigma exists only when social and political power backs the views of the majority over those of the stigmatized outgroup (Link & Phelan, 2001). In other words, individual differences alone do not fuel stigma; only when the traits or attributes in question are officially devalued do prejudice and stigmatization occur. Thus, full consideration of stigma must include structural aspects of social power and the predominant culture's view of what is acceptable in terms of behavioral display (see also Corrigan, 2004). Second, despite the automatic nature of many forms of stereotyping and stigmatization, individuals can and do have the ability

to overcome unconscious, automatic processing of social information through effortful control (Devine, 1989). Thus, the translation of automatic schema and stereotyping into prejudicial attitudes and discrimination is not inevitable, particularly if active, conscious efforts are fostered and reinforced. Thus, despite the perniciousness and pervasiveness of the stigmatization of mental disorder, the situation can change, at both individual and structural levels.

KEY RESEARCH DIRECTIONS

Despite the great volume of research on stigma and stigma processes in recent decades, the vast majority of such work has concerned racial and ethnic prejudice. A host of key questions remain to be addressed regarding the applicability of such models and views to the stigmatization of mental illness. I highlight several of the most salient of these in the current section.

Measurement and Appraisal of Stigma

This is a huge research area, dealing with such issues as basic definitions of stigma (and the related constructs of stereotyping, prejudice, and discrimination) in relation to mental disorder, attitude-behavior distinctions, and the explicit versus implicit nature of stigmatizing attitudes. For a recent, authoritative review, see Link, Yang, Phelan, and Collins (2004).

Defining Stereotyping, Prejudice, Discrimination, and Stigmatization in Relation to Mental Disorder

Too often, investigators do not make clear distinctions among these terms and processes. For example, much of the research reportedly dealing with the stigmatization of mental disorder utilizes surveys of cognitions or attitudes as the chief, or only, measurement tool. Other investigators infer the presence of stigma from a behavioral indicator of discrimination alone. As highlighted earlier, stigmatization should incorporate more than the invocation of stereotypes, the harboring of negative attitudes, or a single act of discrimination. That is, when individuals are stigmatized, they often carry the degradation of the group to which they belong; subsequent interactions are typically strained. A propensity for self-fulfilling prophecies exists, along with the crystallization of castigating attitudes and a propensity for internalization of the devalued mark on the part of those who are so castigated.

Although no single investigation can incorporate all such aspects of stigmatization, inclusion of a few items signifying negative attitudes on a questionnaire is not sufficient to constitute evidence for stigmatization. Optimal research should include, when possible, at least some of the key dimensions of Jones and colleagues (1984)—concealability, course/chronicity, disruptiveness, aesthetics, peril/danger, and origin—in terms of defining stigmatized attributes. It should also consider examination of the potential impact of devaluation on the victim himself or herself, over and above the documentation of negative attitudes and behaviors on the part of perceivers. Documenting reciprocal processes of influence, both attitudinal and behavioral, is also a priority in order to elucidate the cyclic nature of stigmatization and its effects across time. When stigma is characterized solely in terms of isolated negative attitudes or a single act of behavioral exclusion, essential components of this crucial construct may get overlooked. If the database in the field comprises such a thin line of evidence, the contention that mental disorders are stigmatized may come to be perceived as based on trivial evidence, potentially leading to counterreactions (e.g., "Stigma doesn't really exist"). The burden is on the next generation of investigators to ensure that documentation of stigmatization is as complete as possible.

Linking Attitudes and Behaviors in Relation to Stigmatization

Attitudes and beliefs on the part of perceivers do not translate automatically or directly into behavioral responses (see, e.g., Azjen, & Fishbein, 1980). In other words, negative attitudes may not always yield behavioral rejection, and supposedly positive attitudes may be followed by harsh behavioral responses. Several points are salient with respect to this distinction.

First, to make an obvious point but one that is underappreciated in actual practice, attitude measures may be subject to social desirability as a key determinant of responses. That is, research participants may express kind or benevolent attitudes toward those with mental disorder on their questionnaire responses chiefly because they do not want to appear callous or prejudiced on paper and because social norms have tended, over time, to proscribe derogation of disadvantaged individuals. The work of Link and Cullen (1983) was instrumental in showing that, when primed by a stimulus indicating that a person had a history of mental hospitalization, respondents displayed social desirability in their response tendencies. Specifically, when asked to provide "their own" opinions, respondents provided a more lenient view than when asked to indicate what "most people" would say. Investigators would do well to consider strongly the types of response biases, particularly social desirability, that may taint overt attitude surveys.

Second, measures of attitudes of the general public need to utilize the types of large and representative samples evident in many early studies (see reviews of Rabkin, 1972, 1974). Convenience samples of undergraduates are usually less than ideal in terms of representing the age, educational, and social class levels of the population. The external validity, or generalizability, of both attitude and behavioral research is dependent on the collection of data from broadly representative samples of participants.

Third, in the domain of racial attitudes, it has been found that placing good-bad evaluative adjectives on the same, bipolar, semantic-differential scales tends to yield evidence of no differences in evaluation of Blacks versus Whites. For example, respondents tend to rate Blacks and Whites at the same point of the "lazy-ambitious" continuum. When items endorsing positive adjectives are separated from those pertaining to negative adjectives, however, an interesting pattern emerges: Respondents tend to rate Blacks and Whites equally negatively (e.g., equally "lazy") but rate Whites more positively (e.g., more "ambitious"). Thus, a variety of positive versus negative qualities and attributes should be included in attitude scales. Furthermore, in the area of mental disorder, Brockman, D'Arcy, and Edmonds (1979) found that questionnaires with fixed, objective response formats tended to yield weaker evidence for derogation and stigmatization than did those requesting open-ended responses, with the latter presumably allowing for freer answers that were not suggested by multiple-choice items or other preselected formats. Investigators in the area of stigma and mental disorder would do well to include narrative response formats, in which respondents are asked to provide open-ended descriptions of their attitudes and beliefs.

Fourth, a major problem in reviewing research on public conceptions of mental disorder is that attitude measures across different investigations and across time are quite difficult to compare. Indeed, on what basis can one assert with confidence that public attitudes have either improved or worsened across a given time period? Investigations in which respondents directly compare individuals with mental disorder to those with other forms of disability or outgroup status are often far more informative. In fact, studies forcing such explicit contrasts have shown that mental disorder is typically one of the least preferred and most rejected among all categories under consideration (e.g., Albrecht et al., 1982; Tringo, 1970). Thus, forced comparisons may be a valuable research strategy, in that they afford appraisal of the castigation of mental disorder relative to other conditions at a given point in time.

Fifth, I highlighted earlier that behavioral research reveals high levels of rejection and discrimination against persons with mental disorder (e.g., Page, 1995). A basic disconnection, however, still exists between most investigations of attitudes and those focused on appraising behavioral indicators. For example, it is nearly impossible to come up with an example of a study in which respondents in behavioral, interactional research—that is, those in which participants interact directly with a person labeled mentally disordered—have also been asked to provide responses on general attitudinal measures toward mental disorder. Admittedly, giving attitude or social distance measures related to mental illness to respondents who are about to interact with persons suspected of having mental disorders could taint or prime the experimental manipulations, if done without forethought. Yet, it would be a significant advance in knowledge to see just what behavioral tendencies and responses emerged from those research participants whose attitudinal responses had also been recorded.

Implicit versus Explicit Expression of Prejudice and Stigma

Many investigators who study ethnic and racial prejudice have come to the conclusion that overt measures of attitude and acceptance fail to tap underlying, implicit attitudes and biases, those that are the most likely to be exhibited in current times, when it is no longer socially acceptable to express overtly prejudicial attitudes. As discussed earlier, the concepts of symbolic racism and aversive racism have come to the fore, signifying forms of racist belief systems that are not commonly expressed on overt questionnaires but that may be revealed through such substitute means as favoring of the Protestant work ethic or strong belief in meritocracy. Needed, therefore, are measurement tools that transcend the overt expression of prejudice.

A key advance in research on prejudice and bias is found in the development of instruments designed to tap covert, or implicit, attitudes, defined as those that exist without the conscious knowledge of the respondent. A major example of such a measure is the Implicit Association Test (see Greenwald et al., 2003). Here, the outcome measure is response latency, or reaction time, as participants associate pairs of concepts with the stimulus of interest. For example, to appraise implicit attitudes toward old versus young people, investigators have respondents view a picture of an old and a young face on a computer screen. From a pair of adjectives (e.g., "old" versus "young," "good" versus "bad"), respondents indicate the one that best describes the picture. Two sets of adjective pairs are subsequently presented, each of which crosses the age-related and valence-related descriptors. Unconscious or implicit bias toward elderly faces would be revealed by a quicker latency to the pair "old or bad" than to "old or good"; similarly, bias in favor of younger faces would be signaled by faster latencies to "young or good" than to "young or bad." In fact, many individuals who profess no age-related bias on explicit response measures show just such implicit biases. Measuring implicit attitudes provides a unique window on the types of responses biases that exist below individuals' usual levels of awareness.

A key question is whether such a paradigm can be applied to the area of mental disorder. Initial forays are occurring in relation to certain behavioral characteristics. For example, the careful work of Teachman, Gaspinski, Brownell, Rawlins, and Jeyeran (2003) reveals that antifat bias exists at implicit but not explicit levels (for examples of the use of implicit associations in clinical treatment research related to reductions of fears and anxieties, see Teachman, Gregg, & Woody, 2001; Teachman & Woody, 2003). The objective is to circumvent the common problems embedded in explicit means of appraising prejudice: social desirability and a lack of self-awareness of deeply conditioned, underlying response proclivities. Although it is unclear whether such implicit measures actually tap underlying bias versus the salience of cultural stereotypes in the perceiver's mind, knowing of individual preferences below the level of conscious awareness is important in a full account of stigmatization.

What if mental disorders are the objects of implicit bias? Although troubling, I note that such findings would not imply that such automatic forms of prejudice are immutable. In fact, in the field of racial and ethnic prejudice, it has been shown that individuals who evidence unconscious, implicit antipathy can still make strides—via intentional, planned, effortful means or through repeated exposure to counterstereotypic images—to overcome such biases (e.g., Dasgupta & Greenwald, 2001; Devine, 1989). Indeed, as just noted, it may be the case that some measures of implicit bias detect the amount of exposure one has to certain stimuli in positive or negative contexts but that they do not inevitably portend discriminatory practices. Overall, a key priority for research is to link explicit attitudes, implicit attitudes, and actual behavioral responses toward individuals with mental illness.

Issues Regarding the Independent Variable of Mental Disorder

What is actually stigmatized in the realm of mental illness: the symptoms themselves, particular diagnostic entities, the general labels of "mental illness" or "ex-mental patient," or the associations commonly made to such terms? Whereas evidence exists that all of these may be the focus of stereotypes, prejudice, discrimination, and stigmatization, the lesson for researchers is that the independent variable—that is, the construct that is the potential subject of such castigation—must be specified with precision.

Much early research on stigma of mental disorder dealt with the presentation of vignettes of various forms of mental disturbance to participants from the general public to determine whether such descriptions would be recognized as mental disorders and how much social distance would be desired in relation to an individual displaying such symptoms (see Rabkin, 1972). Although evidence now exists that greater segments of the general public recognize several different forms of symptomatology as falling under the rubric of mental disorder than was the case some decades ago, such recognition is far from universal. Furthermore, a key question remains as to whether such "accuracy" in recognition is associated with more favorable attitudes, including deceased social distance (see Link et al., 1999).

A key point from such research is that behavioral depictions of symptoms are more salient triggers of negative attitudes and stigmatization than is the label of mental illness (or "ex-mental patient") per se, when both types of stimuli are presented to research participants (see Link et al., 1987). Yet, recall that there are key exceptions to this general conclusion. That is, when *normal* levels of behavior are branded as related to mental illness, prejudice and stigmatization are now quite likely to occur, as is the case when labels are presented without any accompanying behavioral symptoms. Furthermore, when a given respondent carries in mind a general association between mental disorder and risk for *dangerousness or violence,* the label propels a strong trigger for stigmatizing attitudes, even when the behaviors associated with mental illness are presented simultaneously (Link et al., 1987). (The flip side of this finding is that if individuals do not hold in mind an association between the label of mental disorder and violence, presentation of the label actually leads to benign attitudes. Hence, the linkage of mental disorder with violence is a key aspect of prejudice and stigma.) Thus, labels *do* matter, and investigations of the effects of diagnoses or labels are still extremely viable as independent variables for future research efforts (see Link, Cullen, Struening, Shrout, & Dohrenwend, 1989, for expert presentation of a modified labeling theory in relation to mental illness).

A great diversity of mental aberrations exist (see American Psychiatric Association, 2000), belying the conception of an overall construct or label of mental illness that is

homogeneous or uniform. Indeed, considering mental disorder to be undifferentiated is not only ill-informed but also potentially stereotypic and stigmatizing in and of itself, given its implicit assumption that people with mental illnesses are all the same. Recognition of the great differences in symptomatology and impairment across the many forms of mental disturbance has led investigators of recent large-scale surveys of public attitudes, both in the United States and abroad, to make careful distinctions among various forms of mental disorder. Findings of such research clearly reveal that the different categories of mental illness are associated with unique profiles of misinformation and stigmatization, even though all forms continue to receive at least some degree of pejorative beliefs and attitudes (e.g., Crisp et al., 2000; Link et al., 1999; A. H. Thompson et al., 2002). Overall, investigators should prioritize the distinction between different types of mental illnesses as the independent variable for most studies that they plan, unless, of course, the generic label of mental disorder or mental illness is the explicit research focus.

Three corollary issues emanate from this general point. First, the chronicity or permanence of a stigmatizing condition is quite likely to be related to negative perceptions of that condition (see Jones et al., 1984). Thus, to the extent that mental disorder is believed to be a chronic pattern of behavioral dysregulation, with little or no chance of cure or rehabilitation, harshly stigmatizing responses are expectable. I point out that such stereotypes continue to exist even among scientists and clinicians. For example, official accounts of mental disorders such as Schizophrenia have repeatedly emphasized its extreme likelihood of being a permanent condition (see Neale & Oltmanns, 1980). Yet, increasing evidence attests to the fact that Schizophrenia is not chronically deteriorating in all, or even a majority of cases. It is essential that such information be explicitly imparted to the general public. Indeed, the term Schizophrenia continues to retain a metaphoric linkage with despair, hopelessness, and devaluation (Finzen & Hoffman-Richter, 1999), and its serious impairments are often associated in the mind of the public as representing all forms of mental disturbance. In short, the specificity of depictions of mental disorder should be emphasized, along with accurate information that may break down common stereotypes.

Second, viewing mental disorder in its specific, variegated forms rather than as a global, amorphous entity prompts consideration of the crucial point that many forms of mental disturbance are less severe, and less inherently threatening at a behavioral level, than the typically investigated conditions of Schizophrenia and other psychotic-level disorders. Yet, far too little is known about the responses of the general public, family members, mental health professionals, and patients themselves with respect to these more common but less severe forms of mental disturbance. A research priority is to extend work on prejudice, discrimination, and stigmatization to the full range of mental disorders.

Third, when considering the depictions of mental disorder in typical research investigations, mental illness is almost always presented in terms of written vignettes that describe various symptom patterns. Alternatively, the manipulation may relate to the presence or absence of the label of mental illness or ex-mental patient. Yet, direct confrontation of the behavioral and emotional patterns would be far more powerful stimuli than written accounts or verbal labels. It would be extremely worthwhile for investigators to consider research paradigms in which symptoms of mental disorder are presented in videotaped formats, or even, in the near future, via virtual reality simulations. Such depictions may be far more likely to incur real, rather than artificial, encounters with the manifestations of mental disorder, opening the door for more generalizable and viable research. Indeed, virtual reality simulations might yield the side benefit of enhancing empathy for the difficult experiences associated with mental disorder, if presented with appropriate framing and contextualization.

Overall, investigators need to exert care and thought when depicting the independent variable of mental disorder in research on stigma. The presentation of overly inclusive, global, and vague accounts will serve to cloud interpretations of stigmatizing responses and may fuel stereotypes of the notion that all mental disorder is chronic and irremediable. Furthermore, the types of paper-and-pencil accounts of mental disorder in many forms of attitude research may fail to engender the kinds of castigating, stigmatizing responses that are essential to document.

Attributional Analysis of Stigmatizing Responses to Mental Disorder

Attribution research has been an important tool for understanding behavioral and emotional responses of individuals to unexpected and unpredictable events, particularly those that are negative in nature (e.g., Heider, 1958; Weiner, 1985). A key tenet of this work regarding the stigmatization of mental disorder is that attributions of personal control and responsibility for devalued conditions should increase the blame, punishment, and castigation they receive, whereas ascriptions to noncontrollable causes should foster sympathy. Thus, to the extent that mental illness is

believed to be volitional and under the personal control of the individual in question, harsh reactions and stigmatizing responses would be expectable responses. Along this line, the general public tends to believe that mental disorders are personally controllable and that individuals with mental illnesses are more responsible for their conditions than are those with physical disorders (Weiner et al., 1988). It is not surprising, then, that mental disorders are highly stigmatized.

As I have emphasized repeatedly, however, although tendencies to ascribe mental illness to biological roots rather than personal flaws or other controllable circumstances may help to reduce blame and social distance (Martin et al., 2000), attributing mental disorder exclusively to noncontrollable biomedical or genetic causal factors does not appear to reduce punitive responses on the part of respondents and may, in fact, increase such reactions (see Mehta & Farina, 1997). Attributional accounts of mental disorder, in particular the controllable versus noncontrollable origins of mental illness, therefore remain a puzzling, fascinating, and important research topic.

There may be plausible explanations for the attributional paradox under discussion. First, the symptoms of many forms of mental disturbance are sufficiently threatening to observers that they may precede and override attributional accounts. Thus, the unpredictability and irrationality of such symptoms—along with the symbolic threat they bring to the perceiver's notion of a rational world and to his or her own sense of personal behavioral and emotional control—may engender fear, castigation, and distancing prior to any mitigating effect of a causal explanation, even one that attempts to diminish personal blame and control for the symptom display. The common association, in the public mind, between violence and mental disorder would only fuel such tendencies (Link et al., 1987; Martin et al., 2000).

Second, when respondents are told that mentally disturbed behavior should be attributed to noncontrollable factors that involve aberrant genes or biochemistry, initial resistance would be likely, given the pervasive belief systems in our culture that behavior and emotion are under volitional control. Attempts to foster a medical model of mental illness may thus be viewed as "excuse making" or coddling, engendering reactance. For many, the response might be that medical model ascriptions are part of an overly disease-oriented culture that is attempting to absolve persons with reprehensible behavior from personal control.

Third, however, what if such medical, genetic ascriptions are ultimately accepted, particularly in relation to deeply disturbing behavior patterns that pose realistic or symbolic threat to perceivers? Again, intriguing evidence suggests that harshly punitive reactions may ensue. This tendency may relate to the linkage of exclusively biomedical/genetic ascriptions to a deep sense of chronicity and hopelessness regarding the sufferer's mental disorder. In addition, if mental disorder is believed to emanate from faulty genes or deficient brain chemistry, essentialist views of its underlying nature as a separately caused, qualitatively distinct entity may be likely to take hold, potentially invoking the forms of tribal stigmas usually reserved for racial or national minorities (Kurzban & Leary, 2001). Paradoxically, then, the medical model attribution may incur an additional source of stigmatization, one that yields exploitation and harsh punishment related to the perception of mental illness as linked with subhumanity.

These ideas are provocative but remain speculative. To gain understanding of their veracity, investigators will need to take social psychological and attributional accounts of mental disorder to more sophisticated levels. That is, we still do not fully know *how* persons in current society view mental disorder and its biomedical attributions. They may, in fact, fundamentally discount reattributions of mental disturbance to biological and genetic causes, continuing to believe that the individual in question really could have controlled his or her behavior and that the biomedical ascription is a kind of modern-day excuse for aberrant behavior. Alternatively, some respondents may undergo a radical attributional shift, coming to the belief that the behaviors in question are the result of a deep, underlying, inborn flaw. Still other respondents may take a perspective that is parallel to demonological accounts of mental disorder in former eras. In such views, a supposedly uncontrollable causal factor, namely, possession by evil spirits or the devil, was actually linked to the belief that the afflicted person was responsible for his or her vulnerability to the possession, perhaps through a moral weakness or lack of faith (Hinshaw, 2004, 2006; Zilboorg, 1941). Reductionistic medical model/genetic views may similarly convey the notion that the individual displaying aberrant behavior is still responsible for being vulnerable to the biological flaw.

In terms of empirical investigations, more open-ended, narrative responses than those encountered in traditional multiple-choice studies of attribution may help to illuminate how members of society comprehend various explanations of mental illness. More complex blends of attribution may be apparent than can be found from forced-choice questions. It may take the exploration of intensive personal narratives, content analyses of advertisements and media

portrayals, and examination of cultural practices and language structures (e.g., jokes, common stories told in various cultures) to uncover the contents of such personal representations of and attributions for mental disorder. It will be particularly important to understand the cultural and linguistic representations of genetic ascriptions for mental disturbance. Indeed, in the coming years, when genetic selection will become far more intentionally directed than has ever been the case in human history, having "deviant genes" may be viewed as an entirely controllable facet of one's makeup. It will be important to know the content of future societal messages regarding individuals who show the behavioral manifestations of a presumed genetic inferiority—and one that could have potentially been controlled or prevented through prenatal selection or genetic manipulation. Overall, it is incumbent on investigators to decode the content of current societal messages regarding the ascriptions for mental disorder and to anticipate the nature of future messages, particularly in relation to genetic loci and their attributional consequences, in terms of their implications for stigma.

Responses of Individuals with Mental Disorder to Stigma

Although research on the responses of the general public to mental disorder has been plentiful for almost 60 years, far less is known about how persons with mental disorder comprehend, internalize, and/or cope with the devaluation and stigmatization they experience. Furthermore, there is an almost complete absence of such information related to children and adolescents with the experience of mental illness. As noted earlier, it was originally assumed that victims of stigmatization would inevitably respond by internalizing the castigation foisted upon them (Allport, 1954). Current social psychological perspectives, however, emphasize that lowered self-esteem and shame are not universal responses to being stigmatized (Crocker et al., 1998). Indeed, many individuals in minority groups display self-esteem and self-concepts fully as positive as those in the majority group. Still, individuals with mental disorders may be particularly likely to evidence shame and reduced self-esteem—related to the very symptoms of many forms of mental illness and to the lack of social cohesion compared to other stigmatized minorities (such as racial groups). Indeed, self-advocacy and political solidarity have been a relatively recent occurrence with respect to mental disorder. For such reasons, internalization of blame may well be expected.

Recall the subdivision of personal coping responses posited by Corrigan and Watson (2002). For one subgroup of persons with mental illness, shame and loss of self-esteem appear to be quite salient, over and above the symptoms of mental disorder. Such individuals display self-stigma. A second group displays active coping responses, including activism; this strategy appears to dissipate shame and self-blame. A third subgroup seems to ignore stigmatizing messages for the most part, going on with their daily lives. Unknown, however, are the proportions of such coping types among individuals with mental disorder, whether these three tendencies constitute the universe of coping responses, the relevant cognitive and emotional processes utilized by individuals in such groups to aid and abet their coping strategies, and the extent to which such a typology applies to youth.

Two additional themes should be investigated. First, research has revealed that some persons in the general population are particularly sensitive to interpersonal rejection and that such *rejection sensitivity* incurs negative consequences for subsequent relationships and the individual's sense of self-worth (Downey & Feldman, 1996). It is quite possible that individual differences in coping with interpersonal rejection may predict adaptive versus maladaptive responses to stigmatization in persons with mental disorder. A degree of imperviousness to rejection could fuel persistence and patience as individuals struggle to complete education, find jobs and housing, and establish meaningful relationships in a stigmatizing and discriminatory society. Others, however, may deeply internalize castigation and attribute it to inner flaws, showing exquisite sensitivity to rejection. The core point is that research on such individual differences in coping styles is almost entirely absent with regard to mental illness.

I do not aim to promote blaming the victim through a call for study of coping responses to stigma. Indeed, it would be a grave mistake to portray the discrimination of mental disorder as a problem related to internal characteristics of the group that is castigated and to blame the consequences of stigmatization on inadequate coping. Still, because systems-level determinants of stigma are not likely to disappear overnight, it is crucial to search for processes that can facilitate adaptive coping.

Second, *stereotype threat* is a phenomenon that has received considerable attention in recent years regarding ethnic and racial minorities. In brief, when a particular societal stereotype is invoked (e.g., "African American individuals are inferior in terms of academic achievement" or "Women are poor at math"), performance on relevant tests suffers accordingly for members of the group in question, once baseline differences in performance are controlled (McKown & Weinstein, 2003; Steele, 1997). Yet, when tests are portrayed in ways that do not invoke the stereotype threat—for example, the test items are stated to be interesting puzzles rather than tests of innate ability—the performance of the stigmatized group does *not* suffer. A salient question is whether stereotype threat exists for at least some individuals with mental disorder. Although this is an interesting possibility, investigators will have to contend with the crucial issue of just what the relevant stereotypes are and in what performance domains they might matter. For example, does the stereotype that persons with mental disorder are unpredictable and unable to hold jobs weaken the performance of at least some persons with mental illness during job interviews? More ominous, does the stereotype that mental disorders are associated with violence (Phelan et al., 2000; Wahl, 1995) serve to instigate a self-fulfilling prophecy, whereby internal mechanisms in the castigated individual as well as expectancies in social partners come to fuel aggressive or acting-out tendencies? These are tantalizing questions that require creative and rigorous research efforts to put them to the empirical test.

In all, the responses of persons with mental disorder to stigma and discrimination is a crucial topic for future research. The most noteworthy social psychological approach, at present, regarding the responses of castigated individuals is identity threat theory, a comprehensive model that integrates multiple levels of social influence and personal appraisal to understanding the potential for stigma to incur negative consequences (Major & O'Brien, 2005). Unfortunately, almost no work related to such models has been applied to the stigmatization of mental disorder.

Although I have argued that self-stigmatization is likely to be particularly salient for individuals with mental disorder, there are few data indeed on which to base such a supposition. Needed are (1) instruments that effectively tap self-blame, shame, and internalization of castigating messages; (2) research paradigms that can separate such features of self-stigmatization from the symptoms of mental disorder; and (3) any viable research on this topic related to children and adolescents. Developing a taxonomy of such coping options would be an important first step. Whether certain individuals with mental disorder are particularly sensitive to rejection is, as yet, unexplored; whether stereotypes related to mental disorder invoke threat and performance decrements on relevant life tasks is unknown.

Families and Mental Health Professionals

Even more than objective types of burden, such as financial costs, finding housing, and providing care, family members of persons with serious mental illness incur a great deal of subjective burden, a term that entails embarrassment, shame, and a host of related negative emotions related to the difficulties associated with caring for their afflicted relatives (Lefley, 1989, 1992). Beyond descriptive information about such burden, there is an important need to understand the following: Which types of families tend to stay silent about a relative's mental disorder, and which types exhibit openness? Do certain forms of mental illness predict one or the other stance with any specificity? What are the kinds of extrafamilial supports that successful families utilize? At which points in the life cycle of the relative's mental illness do families show the greatest chance of engaging in open dialogue with one another and with relevant professionals? How have changing views of the etiology of mental illness shaped family shame and guilt? Such questions will not be simple to address, but they are crucial for millions of individuals and families worldwide.

I point out, as well, that nearly all of the literature on this topic has emphasized the negative impact of family burden. Hardly investigated, however, is the important question of whether some families' experiences with mental illness in a relative can increase sensitivity, humanity, or ability to cope. In other words, just as individual resilience may emerge from the experience of mental illness, family resilience and strength may be real possibilities as well. But unless family views are solicited and heard in their actual, complex configurations, this possibility cannot be considered to have viability.

The subjective experiences of family members are inextricably linked with professional and scientific views on mental illness. As discussed earlier, some professionals in the field convey stereotypic views of and stigmatizing attitudes toward individuals with mental illness. Yet, nearly all information about attitudes emanates from explicit attitude measures or from selected personal accounts (see Wahl, 1999). Obtaining information on the actual behavioral responses of professionals to persons with mental disorder is a key objective, as are data on the types of *implicit* associations and biases of mental health workers and professionals toward both the constituent behaviors of mental illness and the label itself. Again, research in this area will not be simple to perform, but the dearth of knowledge of this crucial topic needs to be redressed. Finally, it may well be that the majority of current and newly trained mental health professionals hold positive, nonstigmatizing attitudes toward persons with mental disorder—and that such positive outlooks can greatly facilitate strength and coping in individuals and their family

members. Relevant research that could shed light on this topic has simply been lacking.

Developmental Issues Regarding Stigma

Recent research on racial and ethnic bias has taken a decidedly developmental perspective in an attempt to ascertain the ages at which children become aware of prejudice and bias toward people of color (e.g., McKown & Weinstein, 2003). Almost nothing, however, is known about the parallel topic of bias and stigma regarding mental disorder (see Wahl, 2002). In fact, developmental considerations have been sorely lacking from nearly all research on this topic.

Space limitations preclude a full exploration of this critical issue, but I propose several key questions that require elucidation. First, how do stigmatizing attitudes in society (and from mental health professionals) account for the kinds of parental rejection versus acceptance of a diagnosis of mental illness diagnosis in their child? And how does the age of the child relate to such family response? In other words, what are the distinct issues for families of infants/toddlers, preschoolers, grade schoolers, and adolescents in contending with an offspring's mental disorder?

Second, what are children's own reactions, at different ages, to receiving a mental disorder diagnosis? Can such a label be empowering, in that one can begin to attribute negative experiences to an outside entity (an illness) rather than to one's flawed self? Or does the stigma still attached to mental disorder make the receipt of a diagnosis a trigger for even lower self-esteem? Even more basically, how do children of various ages understand what mental illness signifies, both in general and for themselves?

Third, as noted in an earlier section, at what ages and developmental stages do children in the general population begin to understand the concept of behavioral deviance as related to a mental illness? Furthermore, what are the models of mental disorder held by children? Are such perspectives inherently moralistic? Do they pertain to social deviance? Can children understand biological conceptions of mental disturbance? Are youth more or less likely than adults to split their ascriptions to moral versus biomedical causation?

Fourth, at a broader level, how do cultural messages about mental disorder—from the media, from school-based lessons, from peer networks—influence the thoughts and attitudes of children and adolescents in relation to mental disorder? Even children's television cartoons contain frequent, and disparaging, images of mental illness (Wilson et al., 2000), and some of the first words young children use to denigrate disliked peers are slang terms for mental disorder. A host of research questions emerge from consideration of the ways visual and verbal images regarding mental illness are communicated to and processed by children.

In short, the field is ripe for developmentally oriented investigators to probe both basic and applied questions about the origins and manifestations of stigma in children and adolescents. Such work would enhance knowledge of social cognitive processes across development and facilitate interventions designed to attenuate stigma in its earliest manifestations.

Current Social Issues in Relation to Stigma and Mental Disorder

A number of political and social events and issues in recent years would appear to have important implications for the stigmatization of mental disorder. I list these briefly, in the hope of stimulating relevant inquiries. First, nearly all state budgets across the United States have become awash in red ink during the early years of the twenty-first century. Funds for education, welfare, and mental health are often the first victims of the budget slashing. Will stigmatization of persons with mental disorder increase in such times of economic downturn, as might be predicted from past evidence linking lynchings of African Americans in the South to the price of cotton (Hovland & Sears, 1940; see also Hepworth & West, 1988)? Or will other social and political currents outweigh such economically driven trends? Linking public attitudes temporally with economic and political trends is not a simple undertaking; it typically requires longitudinal data across large time spans, along with a large number of control variables. Yet, investigations of this topic could shed light on important macrolevel variables in relation to stigmatization.

An immediate concern is the potential for parity legislation to be stalled or abandoned because of fears of rising insurance premiums and mental health care costs. Indeed, at the time of the final writing of this chapter (2005), whether more stringent legislation will be passed is an open question. A priority for research on economic-level influences on stigmatization will be to ascertain changes in treatment rates for those with mental disorders as a function of parity laws and other mental health legislation that may become enacted in coming years.

Second, since the terrorist attacks on the United States in September 2001, a surge of ethnic and cultural hatred, often directed against persons of Middle Eastern descent and those of the Islamic faith, has surfaced in this country. It is unknown whether such intolerance has spread, or will spread, to persons with mental disorder. Two reasons make

such an occurrence likely. For one thing, the huge, media-driven stereotype that persons with mental illness are prone to violence would clearly tend to fuel such beliefs. That is, fears of violence have realistically increased in the wake of the terrorist attacks, and those whose behavior patterns are stereotypically linked with danger and aggression—that is, persons with mental disorders—would be expected to increase in salience during such fearful times. For another, recall the fascinating linkage noted between fears of mortality and intolerance of those who are deviant (e.g., Solomon et al., 1991). It has been posited that anxiety over death or annihilation may raise the perceiver's consciousness of the transitory nature of life, spurring stereotyping and castigation of those individuals who threaten community norms as well as personal or societal security and safety. Given the fears raised by the terrorist attack, the blaming of scapegoated individuals, such as those with mental illness, may be expected. Research on such possibilities could reveal systems-level processes, and their interplay with psychological mechanisms, related to prejudice, discrimination, and stigma.

Summary

A host of research questions emerge from analysis of the literature on stigmatization. Indeed, the vast majority of empirical work on stigma pertains to racial and ethnic prejudice, but the applicability of a great deal of such research to mental illness is largely unknown. Important issues pertain to the specification of the dependent variable of stigma (in particular, ensuring that it is more than a few items related to negative attitudes), parallel specification of the independent variable of mental illness (in terms of its inherent variability and specificity), attributional analyses related to personal control versus biogenetic ascriptions and their impact on stigma, the effects of stigma on the self-perceptions of individuals with mental disorders (particularly children and adolescents, on whom relevant research is nearly nonexistent), questions related to parental and family stigma, critical work on developmental factors related to stigmatization, and the impact of current social issues on stigma regarding mental disorder. The importance of the entire topic, and the lack of systematic research to date, make this a potentially exciting and fruitful venture for both basic and applied investigators.

STRATEGIES FOR OVERCOMING STIGMA

Given that stigmatization of mental disorders has been prevalent throughout history, and given the likelihood of naturally selected roots for at least some aspects of stigmatization, finding strategies to overcome stigma will not be a simple task. Indeed, as noted earlier, increased knowledge of mental illness does not always translate into improved attitudes. Hence, believing that public education about core facts related to mental illness will be sufficient to solve the problem of stigmatization is naïve. A core principle is that stigma processes operate in individual perceivers, whose social cognitions, stereotypes, and implicit biases are relevant; in families, who may internalize messages to conceal and deny mental disorder in a relative; in communities, where ingroup and outgroup processes occur; in cultures, in which stereotyped media portrayals of and other messages about mental illness are promoted; and in broad social policies (e.g., through legislation that does not mandate parity of insurance coverage for mental disorders). Thus, strategies to eliminate stigma that operate at only one level are bound to be shortsighted and ultimately counterproductive (Link & Phelan, 2001). Viable procedures to overcome stigma must occur at multiple, interacting levels. I can address only the most salient procedures in the space remaining (for a recent compendium of multiple views, see Corrigan, 2005).

Social Policy and Culture-Wide Levels

Beginning with broad levels of intervention in the realm of policy, changes in laws can help to limit the discrimination that too often attends mental disorder. For instance, parity of insurance coverage is a major goal; without it, physical illnesses will be treated to a far greater extent than devastating mental illnesses. General health care reform is a priority as well, given the large numbers of uninsured in the United States (note that parity laws pertain only to those individuals and families who already have insurance coverage). Enforcing existing legislation mandating nondiscrimination in employment and housing is also essential. Beyond such enforcement, new initiatives will be required to help promote job skills (and, hence, income levels) in persons with mental disorders.

Regarding children and adolescents, strengthening the provisions of the Individuals with Disabilities Education Act (IDEA) will help to ensure adequate academic attainment for youth with mental disorders. Included here is the guarantee of funding for IDEA; at present, providing assessments and accommodations is mandated under this law, but no federal funds are set aside to assure compliance. An additional suggestion with potentially far-reaching implications is to include behavioral and emotional functioning as part of the medical checkup that children receive each

year from health care providers. Such a preventive approach could bring discussion of children's social and behavioral functioning into the everyday language of doctors and families, helping to deal with the precursors of mental disorders before they become entrenched (Hinshaw, 2006). Although critics attack such screenings as a front for use of psychotropic medications early in a child's life, there is no automatic correspondence between emotional and behavioral checkups and mandatory medication for youngsters at risk. Also important is passage of legislation to end the need for family dissolution or the ceding of child custody to obtain services for troubled youth.

In terms of public media, a far different kind of message about mental illness needs to be transmitted. Information about mental disorder in the print and visual media continues to pertain largely to danger, violence, and utter irrationality, and all too little information about strength, courage, resilience, and positive accomplishments is given. Protest by consumer groups may lead to consciousness raising among writers and producers, although protest movements could lead, in some instances, to a counterproductive rebound of the very messages that are being targeted (Corrigan & Penn, 1999; Wahl, 1995). Furthermore, promotion of poignant disclosures by individuals and families who deal with mental illness on a daily basis provide a different set of images (see Jamison, 1995; Leete, 1992; Styron, 1990; for family accounts, see Hinshaw, 2002; Lachenmeyer, 2000; Neugeboren, 1997). Portrayals of the realities of such conditions as child Autism and ADHD and adolescent mood disorders and eating disorders can set the stage for openness and discussion, rather than silence and shame, about mental illness during childhood and adolescence (Beard & Gillespie, 2002).

Communities

At a community level, the predominant empirically based strategy for overcoming discrimination and stigma has been the "contact hypothesis" (Allport, 1954). From this perspective, changes in attitudes and behaviors are most likely to occur through direct behavioral contact with members of outgroups. In fact, the review of Kolodziej and Johnson (1996) revealed that contact between mental health personnel or students and persons with mental disorder generally facilitated better attitudes.

Overall, it is the *conditions* of contact that are crucial for success. Specifically, contact is most likely to lead to improved attitudes when ingroup and outgroup members have regular, informal contact on an egalitarian basis rather than contrived, artificial contact in which the status differentials are great. Thus, visiting patients in a mental hospital is not nearly as likely to facilitate enhanced attitudes as is regular interchange in stores, communities, and the workplace. Clearly, improvements in mental health care and enhanced employment opportunities are needed for contact to be more egalitarian than it often is today. Another prerequisite is locating persons with mental disorders in communities, rather than institutions or inner-city board-and-care residences isolated from the mainstream of society. Adequate treatment and social supports are essential aspects of such community intervention. Finally, stigma is likely to diminish when ingroup and outgroup members work toward common, superordinate goals and foster expanded ingroup identity (Gaertner & Dovidio, 2000; Sherif & Sherif, 1953). Advocacy and support groups in which persons with mental disorders, their family members, and the general public interact provide a clear example of such collaboration.

Families

For families, a number of procedures and interventions may serve to lessen subjective burden and bolster coping resources. For example, education about the causes and realities of mental illness, social support from other families grappling with similar issues, and engagement in family-based therapies that provide strategies for dealing with the difficult life issues presented by mental illness are all essential. Furthermore, when a parent has a mental illness, families need to engage children in treatment in such a way as to help them understand that they themselves are not to blame and that their parent is getting help (Beardslee, 2002). Self-help and advocacy groups can reduce isolation, provide needed information, and aid in family coping. In addition, theoretical models in the field that reduce parental blame for the mental illnesses of their offspring, yet simultaneously promote family responsibility for enhancing the course of the disorder, are paramount.

Persons with Mental Illness

Finally, for individuals with mental disorder, including children and adolescents, engagement in empirically supported treatments that can reduce symptoms and facilitate competent academic, social, and vocational performance is an important means of stigma reduction. That is, to the extent that interventions can lessen threatening and maladaptive symptoms, perceivers in society will have less reason to stigmatize those with mental disorders. Note that there are potential dangers in this line of reasoning. Indeed, I do not contend that all responsibility for stigma reduction should fall on persons with mental illness eliminating all signs of disturbance. This kind of blaming-the-victim mentality is tantamount to positing that the solution for racial prejudice is to have members of minority groups change their skin color. Mental disorder is unlike ethnicity and race in that it is indeed a form of illness: Its signs and symptoms are maladaptive, and treatment may clearly enhance independence and personal growth. Thus, successful treatment is one part of stigma reduction, but clearly not the only component.

Beyond engagement in intervention, finding means of bolstering the coping resources of persons with mental illness is needed. For example, when individuals encounter prejudice, it would seem optimal that they learn to attribute such stigma to the limitations and biases of society rather than to flaws inherent in themselves. Such attributional changes should occur across all family members if the message is to have lasting value. However, given that many forms of mental illness serve to erode self-confidence and a sense of personal value and agency, teaching such coping strategies is a formidable objective.

Summary

The ultimate goal is to find means of promoting change strategies that span individual, family, community, media-related, and social policy levels. Again, there is a danger that ameliorating stigma processes at any one level will leave untouched the pernicious problems at other levels, leading to fragmented, unsustainable change (Link & Phelan, 2001). Yet systematic efforts must begin in earnest (see Hinshaw, 2006, for a more systematic review).

Thus, a great academic, clinical, and policy-related challenge is to apply the basic principles related to stigmatization—across the multiple levels of influence that are operative—to create, implement, and evaluate stigma reduction practices for children, adolescents, adults, and their families and communities. The pervasive shame and silence that surround mental illness, the cyclic nature of reform and retrenchment throughout history, and the deep, automatic, and even naturally selected levels of stigmatizing tendencies toward severe behavioral deviance present major challenges for those who would attempt such intervention. All human societies, however, require diversity, so long as the diverse behavioral manifestations are not threatening to fellow humans. Thus, at the broadest level, successful stigma reduction will require promoting tolerance for a variety of behavioral and emotional styles and allowing all individuals to reach their full potential. Although severe forms of mental disorder may always receive some degree of social distance and castigation, when compassion and empathy can replace silence, shunning, and blame, and when funding and support for validated treatments allow them to be widely utilized by those who require them, individuals with mental disorder and society at large will benefit. Neither mental illness nor stigma is a static process; understanding the dynamic, developmental nature of both constructs is essential to promote needed change.

REFERENCES

Adams, M. S., Robertson, C. T., Gray-Ray, P., & Ray, M. C. (2003). Labeling and delinquency. *Adolescence, 38,* 171–186.

Adorno, T., Frankel-Brunswik, E., Levinson, D., & Sanford, R. N. (1950). *The authoritarian personality.* New York: Harper.

Albrecht, G., Walker, V., & Levy, J. (1982). Social distance from the stigmatized: A test of two theories. *Social Science and Medicine, 16,* 1319–1327.

Al-Issa, I. (Ed.). (2000). *Al-Junun: Mental illness in the Islamic world.* Madison, CT: International Universities Press.

Allderidge, P. (1979). Hospitals, madhouses, and asylums: Cycles in the care of the insane. *British Journal of Psychiatry, 134,* 321–334.

Allport, G. (1954). *The nature of prejudice.* New York: Addison-Wesley.

American Psychiatric Association. (2000). *Diagnostic and statistical manual of mental disorders* (4th ed., text rev.). Washington, DC: Author.

Angell, B., Cooke, A., & Kovac, K. (2005). First-person accounts of stigma. In P. W. Corrigan (Ed.), *On the stigma of mental illness: Practical strategies for research and social change* (pp. 69–98). Washington, DC: American Psychological Association.

Angermeyer, M. C., & Matschinger, D. (1997). Social distance towards the mentally ill: Results of representative surveys in the Federal Republic of Germany. *Psychological Medicine, 27,* 131–141.

Angermeyer, M. C., & Schulze, B. (2001). Reducing the stigma of Schizophrenia: Understanding the process and options for intervention. *Epidemiologia e Psichiatria Sociale, 10,* 1–7.

Appelbaum, P. S. (2002). Response to the presidential address: The systematic defunding of psychiatric care—A crisis at our doorstep. *American Journal of Psychiatry, 159,* 1638–1640.

Aries, P. (1962). *Centuries of childhood: A social history of family life.* New York: Knopf.

Azjen, I., & Fishbein, M. (1980). *Understanding attitudes and predicting social behavior.* Englewood Cliffs, NJ: Prentice-Hall.

Baumeister, R. F., Smart, L., & Boden, J. N. (1996). Relation of threatened egotism to violence and aggression: The dark side of high self-esteem. *Psychological Review, 103,* 5–33.

Beard, J. J., & Gillespie, P. (2002). *Nothing to hide: Mental illness in the family.* New York: New Press.

Beardslee, W. R. (2002). *Out of the darkened room: When a parent is depressed: Protecting the children and strengthening the family.* Boston: Little, Brown.

Beardslee, W. R., Versage, E. M., & Gladstone, T. R. G. (1998). Children of affectively ill parents: A review of the last 10 years. *Journal of the American Academy of Child and Adolescent Psychiatry, 37,* 1134–1141.

Beers, C. (1945). *A mind that found itself.* Garden City, NY: Doubleday. (Original work published 1908)

Bettelheim, B. (1967). *The empty fortress: Infantile Autism and the birth of the self.* Oxford: Free Press of Glencoe.

Biernat, M., & Dovidio, J. F. (2000). Stigma and stereotypes. In T. F. Heatherton, R. E. Kleck, M. R. Hebl, & J. G. Hull (Eds.), *The social psychology of stigma* (pp. 88–125). New York: Guilford Press.

Black, E. (2003). *War against the weak: Eugenics and America's campaign to create a master race.* New York: Four Walls Eight Windows.

Blasovich, J., Mendes, W. B., Hunter, S., & Lickel, B. (2000). Stigma, threat, and social interactions. In T. F. Heatherton, R. E. Kleck, M. R. Hebl, & J. G. Hull (Eds.), *The social psychology of stigma* (pp. 337–333). New York: Guilford Press.

Brewer, M. B. (1979). Ingroup bias in the minimal intergroup situation: A cognitive-motivational analysis. *Psychological Bulletin, 86,* 307–324.

Brockman, J., D'Arcy, C., & Edmonds, L. (1979). Facts or artifacts? Changing public attitudes toward the mentally ill. *Social Science and Medicine, 13A,* 673–682.

Bronfenbrenner, U. (1977). Toward an experimental ecology of human development. *American Psychologist, 32,* 513–531.

Campbell, S. B. (2002). *Behavior problems in preschool children* (2nd ed.). New York: Guilford Press.

Carling, P. J. (1990). Major mental illness, housing, and supports: The promise of community integration. *American Psychologist, 45,* 969–975.

Caspi, A., McClay, J., Moffitt, T., Mill, J., Martin, J., Craig, I. W., et al. (2002). Role of genotype in the cycle of violence in maltreated children. *Science, 297,* 851–854.

Caspi, A., Sugden, K., Moffitt, T. E., Taylor, A., Craig, I. W., Harrington, H., et al. (2003). Influence of life stress on depression: Moderation by a polymorphism in the 5-HTT gene. *Science, 301,* 386–389.

Cicchetti, D. (1993). Developmental psychopathology: Reactions, reflections, projections. *Developmental Review, 13,* 471–502.

Cicchetti, D., & Hinshaw, S. P. (Eds.). (2002). Prevention and intervention science: Contributions to developmental theory [Special issue]. *Development and Psychopathology, 13.*

Clark, K. B., & Clark, M. P. (1950). Emotional factors in racial identification and preference in Negro children. *Journal of Negro Education, 19,* 341–350.

Clausen, J., & Yarrow, M. R. (Eds.). (1955). The impact of mental illness on the family. *Journal of Social Issues, 11*(4).

Cohen, J., & Struening, E. L. (1962). Opinions about mental illness in the personnel of two large mental hospitals. *Journal of Abnormal Social Psychology, 64,* 349–360.

Cooper, E., & O'Hara, A. (2003, May). Priced out in 2002: Housing crisis worsens for people with disabilities. *Open Doors* (21).

Corrigan, P. W. (2004). How stigma interferes with mental health care. *American Psychologist, 59,* 614–625.

Corrigan, P. W. (Ed.). (2005). *On the stigma of mental illness: Practical strategies for research and social change.* Washington, DC: American Psychological Association.

Corrigan, P. W., Markowitz, F. E., & Watson, A. C. (2004). Structural levels of mental illness stigma and discrimination. *Schizophrenia Bulletin, 30,* 481–491.

Corrigan, P. W., & Miller, F. E. (2004). Shame, blame, and contamination: A review of the impact of mental illness stigma on family members. *Journal of Mental Health, 13,* 537–548.

Corrigan, P. W., & Penn, D. L. (1999). Lessons from social psychology on discrediting psychiatric stigma. *American Psychologist, 54,* 765–776.

Corrigan, P. W., River, L. P., Lundin, R. K., Wasowski, K. U., Campion, J., Mathieson, J., et al. (2000). Stigmatizing attributions about mental illness. *Journal of Community Psychology, 28,* 91–102.

Corrigan, P. W., & Watson, A. C. (2002). The paradox of self-stigma and mental illness. *Clinical Psychology: Science and Practice, 9,* 35–53.

Coverdale, J., Nairn, R., & Claasen, D. (2002). Depiction of mental illness in print media: A prospective national sample. *Australian and New Zealand Journal of Psychiatry, 36,* 697–700.

Crisp, A. H. (2000). Changing minds: Every family in the land: An update on the college's campaign. *Psychiatric Bulletin, 24,* 267–268.

Crisp, A. H., Gelder, M. G., Rix, S., Meltzer, H. I., & Rowlands, G. J. (2000). Stigmatisation of people with mental illnesses. *British Journal of Psychiatry, 177,* 4–7.

Crocetti, G., Spiro, H., & Siassi, I. (1971). Are the ranks closed? Attitudinal social distance and mental illness. *American Journal of Psychiatry, 127,* 1121–1127.

Crocker, J., & Major, B. (1989). Social stigma and self-esteem: The self-protective properties of stigma. *Psychological Review, 96,* 608–630.

Crocker, J., Major, B., & Steele, C. (1998). Social stigma. In D. T. Gilbert, S. T. Fiske, & G. Lindzey (Eds.), *Handbook of social psychology* (4th ed., Vol. 2, pp. 504–553). Boston: McGraw-Hill.

Dasgupta, N., & Greenwald, A. G. (2001). On the malleability of automatic attitudes: Combating automatic prejudice with images of admired and disliked individuals. *Journal of Personality and Social Psychology, 81,* 800–814.

Davison, G. C., Neale, J. M., & Kring, A. M. (2004). *Abnormal psychology* (9th ed.). Hoboken, NJ: Wiley.

Devine, P. G. (1989). Stereotypes and prejudice: Their automatic and controlled components. *Journal of Personality and Social Psychology, 56,* 5–18.

deWaal, F. B. M. (2002). Evolutionary psychology: The wheat and the chaff. *Current Directions in Psychological Science, 11,* 187–191.

Diefenbach, D. L. (1997). The portrayal of mental illness on prime time television. *Journal of Community Psychology, 25,* 289–302.

Dietrich, S., Beck, M., Bujantugs, B., Kenzine, D., Matschinger, H., & Angermeyer, M. C. (2004). The relationship between public causal beliefs and social distance toward mentally ill people. *Australian and New Zealand Journal of Psychiatry, 38,* 348–354.

Donohue, B., Hersen, M., & Ammerman, R. T. (1995). Historical overview. In M. Hersen & R. T. Ammerman (Eds.), *Advanced abnormal child psychology* (pp. 3–19). Mahwah, NJ: Erlbaum.

Dovidio, J. F., Major, B., & Crocker, J. (2000). Stigma: Introduction and overview. In T. F. Hetherton, R. E. Kleck, M. R. Hebl, & J. G. Hull (Eds.), *The social psychology of stigma* (pp. 1–28). New York: Guilford Press.

Downey, G., & Feldman, S. (1996). Implications of rejection sensitivity for intimate relationships. *Journal of Personality and Social Psychology, 70,* 1327–1343.

Erhardt, D., & Hinshaw, S. P. (1994). Initial sociometric impressions of ADHD and comparison boys: Predictions from social behaviors and from nonbehavioral variables. *Journal of Consulting and Clinical Psychology, 62,* 833–842.

Farina, A., Allen, J. G., & Saul, B. B. (1968). The role of the stigmatized in affecting social relationships. *Journal of Personality, 36,* 169–182.

Farina, A., Gliha, D., Boudreau, L. A., Allen, J. G., & Sherman, M. (1971). Mental illness and the impact of believing others know about it. *Journal of Abnormal Psychology, 77,* 1–5.

Farina, A., & Ring, K. (1965). The influence of perceived mental illness on interpersonal relations. *Journal of Abnormal Psychology, 70,* 47–51.

Farrington, D. P. (1977). The effects of public labeling. *British Journal of Criminology, 17,* 112–125.

Fein, S., & Spencer, S. J. (1997). Prejudice as self-image maintenance: Affirming the self through derogating others. *Journal of Personality and Social Psychology, 73,* 31–44.

Feldman, S. S., & Elliott, G. R. (Eds.). (1990). *At the threshold: The developing adolescent.* Cambridge, MA: Harvard University Press.

Finzen, A., & Hoffman-Richter, U. (1999). Mental illness as metaphor. In J. Guimon, W. Fischer, & N. Sartorius (Eds.), *The image of madness: The public facing mental illness and psychiatric treatment* (pp. 13–19). Basel, Switzerland: Karger.

Fishbein, H. D. (2002). *Peer prejudice and discrimination: The origins of prejudice* (2nd ed.). Mahwah, NJ: Erlbaum.

Fiske, S. T. (1998). Stereotyping, prejudice, and discrimination. In D. T. Gilbert, S. T. Fiske, & G. Lindzey (Eds.), *Handbook of social psychology* (4th ed., Vol. 2, pp. 357–411). Boston: McGraw-Hill.

Fryer, J. H., & Cohen, L. (1988). Effects of labeling patients "psychiatric" or "medical": Favorability of traits ascribed by hospital staff. *Psychological Reports, 62,* 779–793.

Gaertner, S. L., & Dovidio, J. F. (2000). *Reducing intergroup bias: The common ingroup identity model.* Philadelphia: Psychology Press.

Goffman, E. (1963). *Stigma: Notes on the management of spoiled identity.* Englewood Cliffs, NJ: Prentice Hall.

Goldhagen, D. J. (1996). *Hitler's willing executioners: Ordinary Germans and the Holocaust.* New York: Vintage Books.

Goodwin, F. K., & Jamison, K. R. (in press). *Manic-depressive illness* (2nd ed.). Hoboken, NJ: Wiley.

Gove, W. (1982). The current status of the labeling theory of mental illness. In W. Gove (Ed.), *Deviance and mental illness: A critique* (pp. 273–300). Beverly Hills, CA: Sage.

Greenberg, E., Kim, H. W., & Greenley, J. R. (1997). Factors associated with subjective burden in siblings of adults with severe mental illness. *American Journal of Orthopsychiatry, 67,* 231–241.

Greenwald, A. G., & Banaji, M. (1995). Implicit social cognition: Attitudes, self-esteem, and stereotypes. *Psychological Review, 105,* 4–27.

Greenwald, A. G., McGhee, D. E., & Schwartz, J. L. K. (1998). Measuring individual differences in implicit cognition: The Implicit Association Test. *Journal of Personality and Social Psychology, 74,* 1464–1480.

Greenwald, A. G., Nosek, B. A., & Banaji, M. R. (2003). Understanding and using the Implicit Association Test: An improved scoring algorithm. *Journal of Personality and Social Psychology, 85,* 197–216.

Grob, G. N. (1994). *The mad among us: A history of care of America's mentally ill.* New York: Free Press.

Guimon, J., Fischer, W., & Sartorius, N. (Eds.). (1999). *The image of madness: The public facing mental illness and psychiatric treatment.* Basel, Switzerland: Karger.

Haghighat, R. (2001). A unitary theory of stigmatisation. *British Journal of Psychiatry, 178,* 207–215.

Harris, M. J., Milich, R., Corbitt, D. W., Hoover, D. W., & Brady, M. (1992). Self-fulfilling effects of stigmatizing information on children's social interactions. *Journal of Personality and Social Psychology, 63,* 41–50.

Hart, S., Field, T., Stern, M., & Jones, N. (1997). Depressed fathers' stereotyping of infants labeled "depressed." *Infant Mental Health Journal, 18,* 436–445.

Haslam, N. (2005). Dimensions of folk psychiatry. *Review of General Psychology, 9,* 35–47.

Haslam, N., & Ernst, D. (2002). Essentialist beliefs about mental disorders. *Journal of Social and Clinical Psychology, 21,* 628–644.

Heatherton, T. F., Kleck, R. E., Hebl, M. R., & Hull, J. G. (Eds.). (2000). *The social psychology of stigma.* New York: Guilford Press.

Hebl, M. R., Tickle, J., & Heatherton, T. F. (2000). Awkward moments in interactions between nonstigmatized and stigmatized individuals. In T. F. Heatherton, R. E. Kleck, M. R. Hebl, & J. G. Hull (Eds.), *The social psychology of stigma* (pp. 275–306). New York: Guilford Press.

Heider, F. (1958). *The social psychology of interpersonal relations.* New York: Wiley.

Helfer, R. E., & Kempe, C. H. (1968). *The battered child.* Chicago: University of Chicago Press.

Hepworth, J., & West, S. G. (1988). Lynchings and the economy: A time-series reanalysis of Hovland and Sears (1940). *Journal of Personality and Social Psychology, 55,* 239–247.

Hinshaw, S. P. (1992). Externalizing behavior problems and academic underachievement in childhood and adolescence: Causal relationships and underlying mechanisms. *Psychological Bulletin, 111,* 127–155.

Hinshaw, S. P. (1994). *Attention deficits and hyperactivity in children.* Thousand Oaks, CA: Sage.

Hinshaw, S. P. (2002). *The years of silence are past: My father's life with bipolar disorder.* New York: Cambridge University Press.

Hinshaw, S. P. (2004). Parental mental disorder and children's functioning: Silence and communication, stigma, and resilience. *Journal of Clinical Child and Adolescent Psychology, 33,* 400–411.

Hinshaw, S. P. (2005). Stigma of mental disorders in children and parents: Developmental issues, family concerns, and research needs. *Journal of Child Psychology and Psychiatry, 36,* 714–734.

Hinshaw, S. P. (2006). *The mark of shame: Stigma of mental illness and an agenda for change.* New York: Oxford University Press.

Hinshaw, S. P., & Cicchetti, D. (2000). Stigma and mental disorder: Conceptions of illness, public attitudes, personal disclosure, and social policy. *Development and Psychopathology, 12,* 555–598.

Hinshaw, S. P., & Lee, S. S. (2003). Oppositional defiant and conduct disorder. In E. J. Mash & R. A. Barkley (Eds.), *Child psychopathology* (2nd ed., pp. 144–198). New York: Guilford Press.

Hinshaw, S. P., Owens, E. B., Wells, K. C., Kraemer, H. C., Abikoff, H. B., Arnold, L. E., et al. (2000). Family processes and treatment outcome in the MTA: Negative/ineffective parenting practices in relation to multimodal treatment. *Journal of Abnormal Child Psychology, 28,* 555–568.

Hoge, C. W., Castro, C. A., Messer, S. C., McGurk, D., Cotting, D. I., & Koffman, R. L. (2004). Combat duty in Iraq and Afghanistan, mental health problems, and barriers to care. *New England Journal of Medicine, 351,* 13–22.

Holguin, G., & Hansen, D. J. (2003). The "sexually abused" child: Potential mechanisms of adverse influences of such a label. *Aggressive and Violent Behavior, 8,* 645–670.

Hovland, C., & Sears, R. R. (1940). Minor studies in aggression: Pt. VI. Correlation of lynchings with economic indices. *Journal of Psychology, 9,* 301–310.

Jamison, K. R. (1995). *An unquiet mind: A memoir of moods and madness.* New York: Knopf.

Jamison, K. R. (1998). Stigma of manic depression: A psychologist's experience. *Lancet, 352,* 1053.

Johnson, D. L. (1989). Schizophrenia as a brain disease: Implications for psychologists and families. *American Psychologist, 44,* 553–555.

Jones, E. E., Farina, A., Hastorf, A. H., Markus, H., Miller, D. T., & Scott, R. A. (1984). *Social stigma: The psychology of marked relationships.* New York: Freeman.

Jussim, L., Palumbo, P., Chatman, C., Madon, S., & Smith, A. (2000). Stigma and self-fulfilling prophecies. In T. F. Heatherton, R. E. Kleck, M. R. Hebl, & J. G. Hull (Eds.), *The social psychology of stigma* (pp. 374–418). New York: Guilford Press.

Katz, I. (1981). *Stigma: A social psychological analysis.* Mahwah, NJ: Erlbaum.

Keane, M. (1990). Contemporary beliefs about mental illness among medical students. *Academic Psychiatry, 14,* 172–177.

Keane, M. (1991). Acceptance vs. rejection: Nursing students' attitudes about mental illness. *Perspectives in Psychiatric Care, 27,* 13–18.

Kevles, D. J. (1985). *In the name of eugenics: Genetics and the uses of human heredity.* New York: Knopf.

Klasen, H. (2000). A name, what's in a name? The medicalization of hyperactivity, revisited. *Harvard Review of Psychiatry, 7,* 339–344.

Klinger, L. G., Dawson, G., & Renner, P. (2003). Autistic disorder. In E. J. Mash & R. A. Barkley (Eds.), *Child psychopathology* (2nd ed., pp. 409–454). New York: Guilford Press.

Kolodziej, R., & Johnson, B. T. (1996). Interpersonal contact and acceptance of persons with psychiatric disorders: A research synthesis. *Journal of Consulting and Clinical Psychology, 64,* 1387–1396.

Kreisman, D. E., & Joy, V. D. (1974). Family response to the mental illness of a relative. A review of the literature. *Schizophrenia Bulletin, 1*(10), 34–57.

Kurzban, R., & Leary, M. R. (2001). Evolutionary origins of stigmatization: The functions of social exclusion. *Psychological Bulletin, 127,* 187–208.

Lachenmeyer, N. (2000). *The outsider: A journey into my father's struggle with madness.* New York: Broadway Books.

Leete, E. (1992). The stigmatized patient. In P. J. Fink & A. Tasman (Eds.), *Stigma and mental illness* (pp. 17–25). Washington, DC: American Psychiatric Press.

Lefley, H. P. (1989). Family burden and family stigma in major mental illness. *American Psychologist, 44,* 556–560.

Lefley, H. P. (1992). The stigmatized family. In P. J. Fink & A. Tasman (Eds.), *Stigma and mental illness* (pp. 127–138). Washington, DC: American Psychiatric Press.

Levine, M., & Levine, A. (1992). *Helping children: A social history.* New York: Oxford University Press.

Link, B. G. (1987). Understanding labeling effects in the area of mental disorders: An assessment of the effects of expectations of rejection. *American Sociological Review, 52,* 96–112.

Link, B. G., & Cullen, F. T. (1983). Reconsidering the rejection of ex-mental patients: Levels of attitudinal response. *American Journal of Community Psychology, 11,* 261–273.

Link, B. G., Cullen, F. T., Frank, J., & Wozniak, J. (1987). The social rejection of ex-mental patients: Understanding why labels matter. *American Journal of Sociology, 92,* 1461–1500.

Link, B. G., Cullen, F. T., Struening, E. L., Shrout, P. E., & Dohrenwend, B. P. (1989). A modified labeling theory approach in the area of mental disorders: An empirical assessment. *American Sociological Review, 54,* 100–123.

Link, B. G., & Phelan, J. C. (2001). Conceptualizing stigma. *Annual Review of Sociology, 27,* 363–385.

Link, B. G., Phelan, J. C., Bresnahan, M., Stueve, A., & Pescosolido, B. A. (1999). Public conceptions of mental illness: Labels, causes, dangerousness, and social distance. *American Journal of Public Health, 89,* 1328–1333.

Link, B. B., Yang, L. H., Phelan, J. C., & Collins, P. Y. (2004). Measuring mental illness stigma. *Schizophrenia Bulletin, 30,* 511–541.

Littlewood, R. (1998). Cultural variation in the stigmatisation of mental illness. *Lancet, 352,* 1056–1057.

Luthar, S., Cicchetti, D., & Becker, B. (2000). The construct of resilience: A critical evaluation and guide for future work. *Child Development, 71,* 543–562.

MacDonald, J. D., & MacIntyre, P. D. (1999). A rose is a rose: Effects of label change, education, and sex on attitudes toward mental disabilities. *Journal of Developmental Disabilities, 6,* 15–31.

Major, B., & O'Brien, L. T. (2005). The social psychology of stigma. *Annual Review of Psychology, 56,* 393–421.

Mannuzza, S., & Klein, R. G. (1999). Adolescent and adult outcomes in attention-deficit/hyperactivity disorder. In H. C. Quay & A. E. Hogan (Eds.), *Handbook of disruptive behavior disorders* (pp. 279–294). New York: Kluwer Academic/Plenum Press.

Marcotte, D. E., & Wilcox-Goek, V. (2001). Estimating the employment and earnings costs of mental illness: Recent developments in the U.S. *Social Science and Medicine, 53,* 21–27.

Martin, J. K., Pescosolido, B. A., & Tuch, S. A. (2000). Of fear and loathing: The role of "disturbing behavior," labels, and causal attributions in shaping public attitudes toward people with mental illness. *Journal of Health and Social Behavior, 41,* 208–223.

Mash, E. J., & Barkley, R. A. (Eds.). (2003). *Child psychopathology* (2nd ed.). New York: Guilford Press.

Masten, A., & Coatsworth, J. D. (1998). The development of competence in favorable and unfavorable environments: Lessons from research on successful children. *American Psychologist, 53,* 205–220.

McKown, C., & Weinstein, R. S. (2003). The development and consequences of stereotype consciousness in middle childhood. *Child Development, 74,* 498–515.

Mehta, S., & Farina, A. (1997). Is being "sick" really better? Effect of the disease view of mental disorder on stigma. *Journal of Social and Clinical Psychology, 16,* 405–419.

Milich, R., McAninch, C. B., & Harris, M. (1992). Effects of stigmatizing information on children's peer relationships: Believing is seeing. *School Psychology Review, 21,* 400–409.

Mirabi, M., Weinman, M. L., Magnetti, S. M., & Keppler, K. N. (1985). Professional attitudes toward the chronically mentally ill. *Hospital and Community Psychology, 36,* 404–405.

Moffitt, T. E. (1993). Adolescence-limited and life-course-persistent antisocial behavior: A developmental taxonomy. *Psychological Review, 100,* 674–701.

MTA Cooperative Group. (1999a). Fourteen-month randomized clinical trial of treatment strategies for attention-deficit hyperactivity disorder. *Archives of General Psychiatry, 56,* 1073–1086.

MTA Cooperative Group. (1999b). Moderators and mediators of treatment response for children with ADHD: The MTA Study. *Archives of General Psychiatry, 56,* 1088–1096.

Mukherjee, R., Fialho, A., Wijetunge, A., Checinski, T., & Surgenor, T. (2002). The stigmatisation of psychiatric illness: The attitudes of medical students and doctors in a London teaching hospital. *Psychiatric Bulletin, 26,* 178–181.

Murray, C. J., & Lopez, A. D. (Eds.). (1996). *The global burden of disease: A comprehensive assessment of mortality and disability from diseases, injuries, and risk factors in 1990 and projected to 2020.* Cambridge, MA: Harvard University School of Public Health.

Myers, D. G. (1998). *Social psychology* (5th ed.). New York: McGraw-Hill.

Neale, J. M., & Oltmanns, T. (1980). *Schizophrenia.* New York: Wiley.

Neuberg, S. L., Smith, D. M., & Asher, T. (2000). Why people stigmatize: Toward a biocultural framework. In T. F. Heatherton, R. E. Kleck, M. R. Hebl, & J. G. Hull (Eds.), *The social psychology of stigma* (pp. 31–61). New York: Guilford Press.

Neugeboren, J. (1997). *Imagining Robert: My brother, madness, and survival.* New York: Henry Holt.

New Freedom Commission on Mental Health. (2003). *Achieving the promise: Transforming mental health care in America.* Available from www.mentalhealthcommission.gov.

Norvitilis, J. M., Scime, M., & Lee, J. S. (2002). Courtesy stigma in mothers of children with attention deficit/hyperactivity disorder: A preliminary investigation. *Journal of Attention Disorders, 6,* 61–68.

Nunnally, J. C. (1961). *Popular conceptions of mental health: Their development and change.* New York: Holt, Rinehart and Winston.

Oestman, M., & Kjellin, L. (2002). Stigma by association: Psychological factors in relatives of people with mental illness. *British Journal of Psychiatry, 181,* 494–498.

Ohaeri, J. U., & Abdullahi, A. (2001). The opinion of caregivers on aspects of Schizophrenia and major affective disorders in a Nigerian setting. *Social Psychiatry and Psychiatric Epidemiology, 36,* 403–409.

Page, S. (1995). Effects of the mental illness label in 1993: Acceptance and rejection in the community. *Journal of Health and Social Policy, 7,* 61–68.

Phares, V. (2003). *Understanding abnormal child psychology.* Hoboken, NJ: Wiley.

Phelan, J. C., Bromet, E., & Link, B. (1998). Psychiatric illness and family stigma. *Schizophrenia Bulletin, 24,* 115–126.

Phelan, J. C., Cruz-Rojas, R., & Reiff, M. (2002). Genes and stigma: The connection between perceived genetic etiology and attitudes and beliefs about mental illness. *Psychiatric Rehabilitation Skills, 6,* 159–185.

Phelan, J. C., Link, B. G., & Pescosolido, B. A. (2000). Public conceptions of mental illness in the 1950's and 1960's: What is mental illness and is it to be feared? *Journal of Health and Social Behavior, 41,* 188–207.

Phillips, M. R., Pearson, V., Li, F., Xu, M., & Yang, L. (2002). Stigma and expressed emotion: A study of people with Schizophrenia and their relatives in China. *British Journal of Psychiatry, 181,* 488–493.

Pickles, A., & Angold, A. (2003). Natural categories or fundamental dimensions: On carving nature at its joints and the rearticulation of psychopathology. *Development and Psychopathology, 15,* 529–555.

Pratto, F., Sidanius, J., Stalworth, L., & Malle, B. F. (1994). Social dominance orientation: A personality variable prediction of social and political attitudes. *Journal of Personality and Social Psychology, 67,* 741–763.

Rabkin, J. G. (1972). Opinions about mental illness: A review of the literature. *Psychological Bulletin, 77,* 153–171.

Rabkin, J. G. (1974). Public attitudes toward mental illness: A review of the literature. *Schizophrenia Bulletin, 1*(10), 9–33.

Read, J., & Baker, S. (1996). *Not just sticks and stones: A survey of stigma, taboo, and discrimination experiences by people with mental health problems.* London: Mind.

Read, J., & Harre, N. (2001). The role of biological and genetic causal beliefs in the stigmatization of "mental patients." *Journal of Mental Health, 10,* 223–235.

Rhodes, R. (1999). *Why they kill: The discoveries of a maverick criminologist.* New York: Vintage Books.

Rutter, M. (2000). Genetic studies of Autism: From the 1970's into the millennium. *Journal of Abnormal Child Psychology, 28,* 3–14.

Rutter, M., & Sroufe, L. A. (2000). Developmental psychopathology: Concepts and challenges. *Development and Psychopathology, 12,* 265–296.

Ryan, C. S., Park, B., & Judd, C. M. (1996). Assessing stereotype accuracy: Implications for understanding the stereotyping process. In C. N. Macrae, C. Stangor, & M. Hewstone (Eds.), *Stereotypes and stereotyping* (pp. 121–157). New York: Guilford Press.

Sameroff, A., & MacKenzie, M. J. (2003). Research strategies for capturing transactional models of development: The limits of the possible. *Development and Psychopathology, 15,* 613–640.

Sartorius, N. (1998). Stigma: What can psychiatrists do about it? *Lancet, 352,* 1058–1059.

Sartorius, N. (1999). One of the last obstacles to better mental health care: The stigma of mental illness. In J. Guimon, W. Fischer, & N. Sartorius (Eds.), *The image of madness: The public facing mental illness and psychiatric treatment* (pp. 138–142). Basel, Switzerland: Karger.

Scott, D. J., & Philip, A. E. (1985). Attitudes of psychiatric nurses to treatment and patients. *British Journal of Medical Psychology, 58,* 169–173.

Shain, R., & Phillips, J. (1991). The stigma of mental illness: Labeling and stereotyping in the news. In L. Wilkins & P. Patterson (Eds.), *Risky business: Communicating issues of science, risk, and public policy* (pp. 61–74). Westport, CT: Greenwood Press.

Sherif, M., & Sherif, C. W. (1953). *Groups in harmony and tension.* New York: Harper & Row.

Shibre, T., Negash, A., Kullgren, G., Kebede, D., Alem, A., Fekadu, A., et al. (2001). Perceptions of stigma among family members of individuals with Schizophrenia and major affective disorders in Ethiopia. *Social Psychiatry and Psychiatric Epidemiology, 36,* 299–303.

Sirey, J., Bruce, M. L., Alexopoulos, G. S., Perlick, D. A., Friedman, S. J., & Meyers, B. S. (2001). Perceived stigma as a predictor of treatment discontinuation in young and older outpatients with depression. *American Journal of Psychiatry, 158,* 479–481.

Smart, L., & Wegner, D. M. (2000). The hidden costs of hidden stigma. In T. F. Heatherton, R. E. Kleck, M. R. Hebl, & J. G. Hull (Eds.), *The social psychology of stigma* (pp. 220–242). New York: Guilford Press.

Solomon, S., Greenberg, J., & Pyszczynski, T. (1991). A terror management theory of social behavior: The psychological functions of self-esteem and cultural worldviews. In M. P. Zanna (Ed.), *Advances in experimental social psychology* (Vol. 24, pp. 93–159). San Diego: Academic Press.

Sontag, S. (1989). *Illness as metaphor and AIDS and its metaphors.* New York: Doubleday. (Original work published 1978)

Stangor, C., & Crandall, C. S. (2000). Threat and the social construction of stigma. In T. F. Heatherton, R. E. Kleck, M. R. Hebl, & J. G. Hull (Eds.), *The social psychology of stigma* (pp. 62–87). New York: Guilford Press.

Steele, C. M. (1997). A threat in the air: How stereotypes shape intellectual identity and performance. *American Psychologist, 52,* 613–629.

Sternberg, R. J. (2004). A duplex theory of hate: Development and application to terrorism, massacres, and genocide. *Review of General Psychology, 7,* 299–328.

Stoessner, S. J., & Mackie, D. M. (1993). Affect and perceived group variability: Implications for stereotyping and prejudice. In D. M. Mackie & D. L. Hamilton (Eds.), *Affect, cognition, and stereotyping: Interactive processes in group perception* (pp. 63–86). San Diego: Academic Press.

Struening, E. L., Perlick, D. A., Link, B. G., Hellman, F. G., Herman, D., & Sirey, J. A. (2001). Stigma as a barrier to recovery: The extent to which caregivers believe most people devalue consumers and their families. *Psychiatric Services, 52,* 1633–1638.

Struening, E. L., Stueve, A., Vine, P., Kreisman, D. E., Link, B. G., & Herman, D. B. (1995). Factors associated with grief and depressive symptoms in caregivers of people with serious mental illness. In J. R. Greenley (Ed.), *Research in community and mental health* (Vol. 8, pp. 91–124). Greenwich, CT: JAI Press.

Styron, W. (1990). *Darkness visible: A memoir of madness.* New York: Harper & Row.

Swanson, J. M., & Castellanos, F. X. (2002). Biological bases of ADHD: Neuroanatomy, genetics, and pathophysiology. In P. S. Jensen & J. R. Cooper (Eds.), *Attention deficit hyperactivity disorder: State of the science, best practices* (pp. 7-1–7-20). Kingston, NJ: Civic Research Institute.

Tajfel, H. (1982). Social psychology of intergroup relations. *Annual Review of Psychology, 33,* 1–39.

Teachman, B. A., Gaspinski, K. D., Brownell, K. D., Rawlins, M., & Jeyeran, S. (2003). Demonstrations of implicit anti-fat bias: The impact of providing causal information and evoking empathy. *Health Psychology, 22,* 68–78.

Teachman, B. A., Gregg, A. P., & Woody, S. R. (2001). Implicit associations for fear-related stimuli among individuals with snake and spider fears. *Journal of Abnormal Psychology, 110,* 226–235.

Teachman, B. A., & Woody, S. R. (2003). Automatic processing in spider phobia: Implicit fear associations over the course of treatment. *Journal of Abnormal Psychology, 112,* 100–109.

Tessler, R., & Gamache, G. (2000). *Family experiences with mental illness.* Westport, CT: Auburn House.

Thara, R., & Srinivasan, T. N. (2000). How stigmatising is Schizophrenia in India? *International Journal of Social Psychiatry, 46,* 135–141.

Thompson, A. H., Stuart, H., Bland, R. C., Arbodele-Florez, J., Warner, R., & Dickson, R. A. (2002). Attitudes about Schizophrenia from the pilot site of the WPA worldwide campaign against the stigma of Schizophrenia. *Social Psychiatry and Psychiatric Epidemiology, 37,* 475–482.

Thompson, E. H., & Doll, W. (1982). The burden of families coping with the mentally ill: An invisible crisis. *Family Relations, 31,* 379–388.

Tringo, J. L. (1970). The hierarchy of preference toward disability groups. *Journal of Special Education, 4,* 295–306.

Tully, L. A., Arsenault, L., Caspi, A., Moffitt, T. E., & Morgan, J. (2004). Does maternal warmth moderate the effects of birth weight on attention-deficit/hyperactivity disorder symptoms and low IQ? *Journal of Consulting and Clinical Psychology, 72,* 218–226.

U.S. Department of Health and Human Services. (1999). *Mental health: A report of the surgeon general.* Rockville, MD: Author.

Wahl, O. F. (1995). *Media madness: Public images of mental illness.* New Brunswick, NJ: Rutgers University Press.

Wahl, O. F. (1999). *Telling is risky business: Mental health consumers confront stigma.* New Brunswick, NJ: Rutgers University Press.

Wahl, O. F. (2002). Children's views of mental illness: A review of the literature. *Psychiatric Rehabilitation Services, 6,* 134–158.

Wahl, O. F., & Harman, C. R. (1989). Family views of stigma. *Schizophrenia Bulletin, 15,* 131–139.

Wahl, O. F., Ward, A., & Richards, R. (2002). Newspaper coverage of mental illness: Is it changing? *Psychiatric Rehabilitation Skills, 6,* 9–31.

Wang, P. S., Demler, O., & Kessler, R. C. (2002). Adequacy of treatment for serious mental illness in the United States. *American Journal of Public Health, 92,* 92–98.

Wegner, D. M. (1997). When the antidote is worse than the poison: Ironic mental control processes. *Psychological Science, 8,* 148–150.

Weiner, B. (1985). An attributional theory of achievement motivation and emotion. *Psychological Review, 92,* 548–573.

Weiner, B., Perry, R. P., & Magnusson, J. (1988). An attributional analysis of reactions to stigmas. *Journal of Personality and Social Psychology, 55,* 738–748.

Wilson, C., Nairn, R., Coverdale, J., & Panapa, A. (2000). How mental illness is portrayed in children's television: A prospective study. *British Journal of Psychiatry, 176,* 440–443.

Woods, N. S., Eyler, F. D., Conlon, M., Behnke, M., & Webie, K. (1998). Pygmalion in the cradle: Observer bias against cocaine-exposed infants. *Journal of Developmental and Behavioral Pediatrics, 19,* 283–285.

Wright, E. R., Gronfein, W. P., & Owens, T. J. (2000). Deinstitutionalization, social rejection, and the self-esteem of former mental patients. *Journal of Health and Social Behavior, 44,* 68–90.

Zilboorg, G. (1941). *A history of medical psychology.* New York: Norton.

Author Index

Beck, J., 332, 775, 776
Beck, M., 849, 866
Becker, B., 98, 117, 165, 739, 742, 744, 746, 751, 754, 774, 776, 810, 811, 812, 813, 814, 819, 820, 831, 864
Becker, D., 606
Becker, L. E., 643
Becker, R. E., 485
Becker-Blease, K., 664
Becker-Lausen, E., 685, 686
Beckett, C., 212, 219, 385, 388
Beckman, P., 252
Beckmann, D., 44, 45
Beckmann, H., 544
Beckner, C., 605
Beckwith, L., 574, 778
Bedard, A. C., 371, 385
Bedi, G., 300
Beebe, B., 208
Beecher, R., 455
Beeghly, M., 143, 148, 149, 150, 151, 152, 153, 244, 326
Beeman, S. K., 17
Beers, C., 859
Beers, S. R., 558, 559
Beezley, P., 41
Begg, J., 708
Begley, S., 423
Behan, P., 297
Behan, W. M., 297
Behar, D., 417
Behen, M., 220, 337
Behnke, M., 854
Behr, J., 439
Behr, S. K., 252
Behrman, R. E., 28, 29
Beidel, D. C., 473, 479, 485, 486
Beitchman, J. H., 268, 269, 274, 276
Beitman, B. D., 631
Belfer, M., 215
Belfiore, P. J., 341
Belin, P., 303
Belitz, S., 301
Bell, C. C., 710, 766
Bell, K. L., 760, 779
Bell, R. M., 610
Bell, R. Q., 42, 248, 250, 259, 388, 518, 519, 759
Belle, D., 3, 7, 11, 13
Belleville, S., 334
Bellgrove, M. A., 380
Bellino, S., 441
Bellodi, L., 415, 417, 440
Bellugi, U., 242, 255
Belmaker, R. H., 485
Belmont, B., 53, 55
Belsky, J., 38, 39, 40, 41, 42, 44, 45, 46, 47, 49, 50, 52, 59, 61, 62, 63, 64, 65, 66, 67, 68, 69, 70, 71, 74, 105, 106, 110, 117, 134, 138, 146, 152, 178, 714, 758, 772
Belzer, A., 70, 71
Bem, D. J., 115, 516
Bemis, B. G., 599
Bemis, B. W., 599
Benard, B., 770
Benasich, A. A., 269, 271, 273, 274, 276, 293, 297, 298, 299, 302, 304, 332, 336
Bench, C. J., 419
Bendahhou, E., 446
Bendall, D., 53
Bender, M., 268, 274
Bendfeldt, F., 670, 678, 679
Benedek, G., 456

Benedict, R. H., 455
Benes, F. M., 367, 369, 385, 558, 643
Bengel, D., 177, 640
Bengtson, V. L., 823
Benitez, J. G., 57
Benjamin, J., 485
Benkelfat, C., 419
Bennasar, M. C., 668
Benner, A., 333
Bennett, A. L., 680
Bennett, B., 162
Bennett, E. L., 559
Bennett, E. M., 603
Bennett, F. C., 224
Bennett, K. S., 387, 393
Bennett, M., 481
Bennett, P., 333, 641
Bennetto, L., 153
Ben-Pazi, H., 382
Ben-Shlomo, Y., 216
Benson, M., 448, 449
Benson, P. J., 336
Benson, P. L., 719, 720, 721
Bentler, E. M., 607, 609
Bentler, P. M., 604
Benton, A. L., 271
Bentovim, A., 139
Benz, B., 442, 443
Berardi, N., 204, 212
Berden, G. F. M. G., 715
Berenbaum, S. A., 217
Beresford, S. A. A., 483
Berg, C., 417
Berg, C. A., 412, 414
Berg, C. J., 406, 414
Berg, E. A., 54
Berg, P., 290
Bergen, D., 453
Berger, A., 360, 373, 375, 376, 378, 393
Berger, D. F., 375
Berger, G. E., 553
Berger, L. M., 137, 138
Berger, M., 439, 455
Berger, Y., 453
Bergeron, C., 643
Berglund, L., 753
Berglund, M. L., 721
Berglund, P., 479, 710
Bergman, A., 140, 148, 547
Bergman, C. S., 39, 40
Bergman, E., 291, 292, 301
Bergman, H., 382
Bergman, K. S., 419
Bergman, L. R., 182
Bergman, R. L., 470, 476
Bergner, R. M., 706
Bergson, C. M., 608, 609
Berk, L. E., 383, 386
Berkowitz, A. L., 642
Berkson, J. B., 440, 444, 636
Berlin, L. J., 762
Berlin, R., 271, 756
Berman, J. R., 803
Berman, K. F., 544
Berman, S. L., 772
Berman, T., 372
Bernal, G., 19
Bernard, S. M., 392
Bernbaum, J. C., 224
Bernheimer, L. P., 252
Bernier, R., 332
Berninger, V., 286, 287

Bernstein, D. P., 134, 164, 165
Bernstein, E., 661, 663, 664
Bernstein, G. A., 715
Bernstein, G. G., 209
Bernstein, L. E., 268, 274
Berntson, G. G., 625
Berrettini, W., 420, 561, 609
Berrios, G. E., 421, 422
Berry-Kravis, E. M., 337
Berscheid, R., 3
Berti, F. B., 272
Bertolino, A., 335, 544, 545, 553
Bertrand, J., 242, 245, 246, 255, 256, 324
Bertrand, R. M., 809
Berument, S. K., 331
Besharov, D., 132
Bessler, A., 449
Best, K., 98, 529, 741
Best, M., 287
Best, S. R., 664, 676, 820
Bettelheim, B., 851
Bettes, B., 547
Bettinardi, V., 336
Bevan, R., 336
Beveridge, M., 211, 216
Bhavnagri, N. P., 6
Biagini, G., 215
Biederman, J., 20, 321, 364, 379, 390, 414, 439, 440, 441, 456, 475, 485, 599, 605, 606, 641
Bieling, P., xii
Bienvenu, O. J., 414, 416, 473
Bienvenu, O., III, 416, 418
Bierer, L. M., 474
Bierman, K. L., 521
Biernat, M., 843
Biesanz, J. C., 762
Bifulco, A., 14, 139
Bigbee, M. A., 506
Bigelow, L. B., 549
Biglan, A., 53, 54, 603, 644, 761
Bigler, R. S., 763
Bihrle, S., 573
Bilbe, G., 204
Bilder, R. M., 493, 494, 544
Bilker, W., 543, 550, 551
Billard, C., 288
Billett, E. A., 415
Billings, A. G., 54
Binder, M., 406
Binet, A., 699
Bingham, C. R., 571, 629, 630, 632, 637, 644
Bingham Mira, C., 26
Birbaumer, N., 485
Birch, H. G., 43, 46
Bird, G., 261
Bird, H., 487, 599, 604, 708, 709, 710
Bird, J., 278
Biringen, Z., 50
Birkle, D. L., 215
Birmaher, B., 172, 173, 174, 338, 417, 494, 599, 605
Birnbrauer, J. S., 339
Bishop, D., 274, 275, 276, 277, 278, 279, 282, 283, 293, 294, 295, 296, 302, 303, 319, 326
Bishop, S. J., 282, 283, 293, 295, 762
Bisson, E., 332
Bittel, D. C., 236, 257
Bittencourt Kiss, M. H., 448
Bjorklund, D. F., 144
Bjorson, B. H., 283
Blacher, J., 249, 252

Subject Index